RAND McNALLY

GOODE'S
W O R L D   A T L A S

19TH EDITION

Edward B. Espenshade, Jr.	John C. Hudson	Joel L. Morrison
EDITOR	ASSOCIATE EDITOR	SENIOR CONSULTANT

RAND McNALLY

CONTENTS

Goode's World Atlas
Copyright © 1995 by Rand McNally & Company
Copyright © 1922, 1923, 1932, 1933, 1937, 1939, 1943, 1946, 1949, 1954, 1957, 1960, 1964, 1970, 1974, 1978, 1982, 1986, 1990 by Rand McNally & Company
Formerly Goode's School Atlas
Made in U.S.A.

Library of Congress Catalog Card Number 94–68645

CONTENTS, *continued*

Major Cities Maps   *Scale 1:300,000* [226–244]

Geographical Tables and Indexes [245–372]

ACKNOWLEDGMENTS

This is the nineteenth edition of the Rand McNally *Goode's World Atlas*, which was first published more than seventy years ago. The name of Dr. J. Paul Goode, the original editor and distinguished cartographer who designed the early editions, has been retained to affirm the high standards that all those who have participated in the preparation of the atlas during these years have sought to attain.

Through the years, general-reference map coverage has been expanded; the number of thematic maps has been increased and their subject range broadened; and systematic improvements in symbolism, cartographic presentation, and map production and printing have been incorporated.

The nineteenth edition continues this tradition, and includes five new thematic maps. World maps have been added on ecoregions, conflicts, refugees and tectonics. A new map of the United States and Southern Canada depicts federal lands and the interstate highway system. New reference maps for the Caucasus and parts of central Asia have been added. Finally, a new design for the maps of the Indian and Atlantic Oceans replaces the former ones.

Thematic maps, statistics, graphs and various tables have been revised to incorporate the latest available data. The list of source materials and an index to thematic topics (subject index) have been revised. These additions and other revisions reflect the editors' and publisher's commitment to increasing the usefulness and quality of each edition of the Rand McNally *Goode's World Atlas*, thus maintaining it as a standard among world atlases.

Sources

Every effort was made to assemble the latest and most authentic source materials to use in this edition. In the general physical-political maps, data from national and state surveys, recent military maps, and hydrographic charts were utilized. Source materials for the specialized maps were even more varied (see the partial list of sources at the end of the atlas). They included both published and unpublished items in the form of maps, descriptions in articles and books, statistics, and correspondence with geographers and others. To the various agencies and organizations, official and unofficial, that cooperated, appreciation and thanks are expressed. Noteworthy among these organizations and agencies were: The United Nations (for demographic and trade statistics); the Food and Agriculture Organization of The United Nations (for production statistics on livestock, crops, and forest products and for statistics on world trade); the Population Reference Bureau (for population data); the Office of the Geographer, Department of State (for the map "Surface Transport Facilities" and other items); the office of Foreign Agricultural Relations, Department of Agriculture (for information on crop and livestock production and distribution); the Bureau of Mines, Department of the Interior (for information on mineral production); various branches of the national military establishment and the Weather Bureau, Department of Commerce (for information on temperature, wind, pressure, and ocean currents); the Maritime Commission and the Department of Commerce (for statistics on ocean trade); the American Geographical Society (for use of its library and permission to use the Miller cylindrical projection); the University of Chicago Press, (for permission to use Goode's Homolosine equal-area projection); the McGraw-Hill Book Company (for cooperation in permitting the use of Glenn Trewartha's map of climatic regions and Petterssen's diagram of zones of precipitation); the Association of American Geographers (for permission to use Richard Murphy's map of landforms); and publications of the World Bank (for nutrition, health, and economic information).

Some additional sources of specific data and information are as follows: World Oil (for oil and gas data); International Labor Organization (for labor statistics); and the International Road Federation (for transportation data). The United Nations High Commissioner for refugees (UNHCR) and the Bureau for Refugee Programs, U.S. Department of State provided data for the refugees map.

Other Acknowledgments

The variety and complexity of the problems involved in the preparation of a world atlas make the participation of specialists highly desirable. In preparation of this new edition, the editors have been ably assisted by several such experts. They express their deep appreciation and thanks to each of them.

They are particularly indebted to the following experts who have cooperated over the years. A. W. Kuchler, Department of Geography, University of Kansas; Richard E. Murphy, late professor of geography, University of New Mexico; Erwin Raisz, late cartographer, Cambridge, Massachusetts; Glenn T. Trewartha, late professor of geography, University of Wisconsin; Derwent Whittlesey, late professor of geography, Harvard University; and Bogdan Zaborski, professor emeritus of geography, University of Ottawa.

The editors thank the entire Cartographic and Design staff of Rand McNally & Company for their continued outstanding contributions. We particularly appreciate the help and dedication of the following staff members: Pat Healy and Jon Leverenz for many years of valuable input, along with Jill M. Stift, Susan Hudson, Winifred Farbman, Dara Thompson, Patty Porter and Audrey Curry. Joel L. Morrison has continued to act as a consultant.

Edward B. Espenshade, Jr.
John C. Hudson

INTRODUCTION

Geography and Maps

The study of geography is the study of the location, description, and interrelations of the earth's features—its people, landforms, climate, and natural resources. In fact, anything on the earth is fair game for geographic inquiry, and mapping. Helping to answer the questions of *where* something is, and *why* it is there, is fundamental to any geographic study.

Maps, photographs, and images based on radar and the electromagnetic spectrum increase one's ability to study the earth. They enable geographers and other earth scientists to record information about the earth through time and to examine and study areas of the earth's surface far too large to view firsthand.

Geographic Education

There are five fundamental themes of geography that help people organize and understand information about the earth. The maps in *Goode's World Atlas* present information that is essential for applying these themes. The themes are as follows:

Theme 1. **Location: Absolute and Relative.** Maps show where places are located in absolute terms, such as latitude and longitude, and where they are in relation to other places—their relative location. By locating and graphically portraying places and things, maps reveal the patterns of the earth's diverse landscape.

Theme 2. **Place: Physical and Human Characteristics.**
Maps provide useful information about the physical and human characteristics of places. Landform maps show the surface features of the earth. Climate and natural vegetation maps may be compared to reveal how vegetation responds to climate conditions. Human characteristics include those effects people have on places. Population maps show the density and distribution of people, while maps of language and religion provide information about cultural characteristics.

Theme 3. **Human/Environment Interaction.** People interact with the natural environment, and the extent to which they alter the environment can be studied by viewing maps. The maps in the atlas provide information about current and past conditions of the environment and are useful in making informed decisions about the future effects of people on the land.

Theme 4. **Movement: Interactions Between Places.** The movement of people and products between places results in networks that span the earth. The dynamics of global interdependence are illustrated by maps that show the movement of commodities from places of production to places of consumption. Maps in the atlas depict highways, air traffic corridors, and shipping lanes that use the world's rivers, lakes, and oceans.

Theme 5. **Regions: How They Form and Change.** A *region* is a part of the earth's surface that displays similar characteristics in terms of selected criteria. Climates, nations, economies, languages, religions, diets, and urban areas are only a few of the topics that can be shown regionally on maps. The region is the basic unit of geographic study. It makes the complex world more readily understandable by organizing the earth according to selected criteria, allowing the similarities and differences from place to place to be studied and understood more fully.

Organization of the Atlas

The maps in *Goode's World Atlas* are grouped into four parts, beginning with *World Thematic Maps*, portraying the distribution of climatic regions, raw materials, landforms, and other major worldwide features. The second part is the *Regional Maps* section and main body of the atlas. It provides detailed reference maps for all inhabited land areas on a continent-by-continent basis. Thematic maps of the continents are also contained in this part. The third part is devoted to *Ocean Maps*. In the fourth part, *Major Cities Maps*, the focus is on individual cities and their environs, all mapped at a consistent scale.

Geographical tables, an index of places, a subject index, and a list of sources complete the atlas. The tables provide comparative data, a glossary of foreign geographical terms, and the index of places—a universal place-name pronouncing index for use with the reference maps.

Cartographic Communication

To communicate information through a map, cartographers must assemble the geographic data, use their personal perception of the world to select the relevant information, and apply graphic techniques to produce the map. Readers must then be able to interpret the mapped data and relate it to their own experience and need for information. Thus, the success of any map depends on both the cartographer's and the map reader's knowledge and perception of the world and on their common understanding of a map's purpose and limitations.

The ability to understand maps and related imagery depends first on the reader's skill at recognizing how a curved, three-dimensional world is symbolized on a flat, two-dimensional map. Normally, we view the world horizontally (that is, our line of vision parallels the horizon), at the eye level about five and one-half to six feet above ground. Images appear directly in front and to either side of us, with our eyes encompassing all details as nonselectively as a camera. Less frequently, when we are atop a high platform or in an airplane, we view the world obliquely, as shown in *Figure 1*, in which both vertical and horizontal facets of objects can be seen. And only those persons at very high altitudes will view the world at a vertical angle (*Figure 2*). Yet maps are based on our ability to visualize the world from an overhead, or vertical, perspective.

A map differs from a purely vertical photograph in two important respects. First, in contrast to the single focal point of a photograph, a map is created as if the viewer were directly overhead at all points (See *Figure 3*). Second, just as our brains select from the myriad items in our field of vision those objects of interest or importance to us, so each map presents only those details necessary for a particular purpose—a map is not an inventory of all that is visible. Selectivity is one of a map's most important and useful characteristics.

Skill in reading maps is basically a matter of practice, but a fundamental grasp of cartographic principles and the symbols, scales, and projections commonly employed in creating maps is essential to comprehensive map use.

Map Data

When creating a map, the cartographer must select the objects to be shown, evaluate their relative importance, and find some way to simplify their form. The combined process is called *cartographic generalization*. In attempting to generalize data, the cartographer is limited by the purpose of the map, its scale, the methods used to produce it, and the accuracy of the data.

Figure 1. Oblique aerial photograph of New York City.

Figure 2. High-altitude vertical photograph of New York City area.

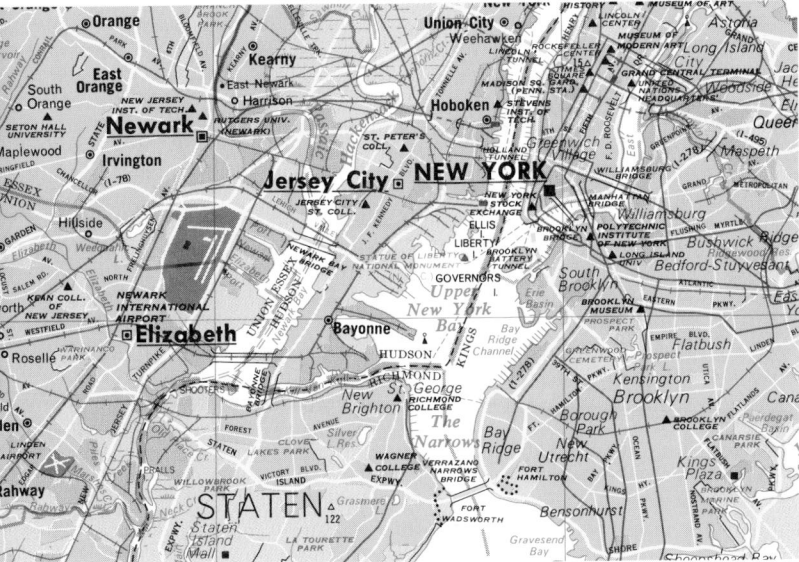

Figure 3. Map of New York City and environs.

Cartographic generalization consists of simplification, classification, symbolization, and induction.

Simplification involves omitting details that will clutter the map and confuse the reader. The degree of simplification depends on the purpose and scale of the map. If the cartographer is creating a detailed map of Canada and merely wants to show the location of the United States, he or she can draw a simplified outline of the country. However, if the map requires a precise identification of the states in New England and the Great Lakes region, the mapmaker will have to draw a more detailed outline, still being careful not to distract the reader from the main features of the Canadian map.

Classification of data is a way of reducing the information to a form that can be easily presented on a map. For example, portraying precise urban populations in the United States would require using as many different symbols as there are cities. Instead, the cartographer groups cities into population categories and assigns a distinct symbol to each one. With the help of a legend, the reader can easily decode the classifications.

Symbolization of information depends largely on the nature of the original data. Information can be *nominal* (showing differences in kind, such as land versus water, grassland versus forest); or *ordinal* (showing relative differences in quantities as well as kind, such as *major* versus *minor* ore deposits); or *interval* (degrees of temperature, inches of rainfall) or *ratio* (population densities), both expressing quantitative details about the data being mapped.

Cartographers use various shapes, colors, or patterns to symbolize these categories of data, and the particular nature of the information being communicated often determines how it is symbolized. Population density, for example, can be shown by the use of small dots or different intensities of color. However, if nominal data is being portrayed—for instance, the desert and fertile areas of Egypt—the mapmaker may want to use a different method of symbolizing the data, perhaps pattern symbols. The color, size, and style of type used for the different elements on a map are also important to symbolization.

Induction is the term cartographers use to describe the process whereby more information is represented on a map than is actually supplied by the original data. For instance, in creating a rainfall map, a cartographer may start with precise rainfall records for relatively few points on the map. After deciding the interval categories into which the data will be divided (e.g., thirty inches or more, fifteen to thirty inches, under fifteen inches), the mapmaker infers from the particular data points that nearby places receive the same or nearly the same amount of rainfall and draws the lines that distinguish the various rainfall regions accordingly. Obviously, generalizations arrived at through induction can never be as precise as the real-world patterns they represent. The map will only tell the reader that all the cities in a given area received about the same amount of rainfall; it will not tell exactly how much rain fell in any particular city in any particular time period.

Cartographers must also be aware of the map reader's perceptual limitations and preferences. During the past two decades, numerous experiments have helped determine how much information readers actually glean from a map and how symbols, colors, and shapes are recognized and interpreted. As a result, cartographers now have a better idea of what kind of rectangle to use; what type of layout or lettering suggests qualities such as power, stability, movement; and what colors are most appropriate.

Map Scale

Since part or all of the earth's surface may be portrayed on a single page of an atlas, the reader's first question should be: What is the relation of map size to the area represented? This proportional relationship is known as the *scale* of a map.

Scale is expressed as a ratio between the distance or area on the map and the same distance or area on the earth. The map scale is commonly represented in three ways: (1) as a simple fraction or ratio called the representative fraction, or RF; (2) as a written statement of map distance in relation to earth distance; and (3) as a graphic representation or a bar scale. All three forms of scale for distances are expressed on Maps A–D.

The RF is usually written as 1:62,500 (as in Map A), where 1 always refers to a unit of distance on the map. The ratio means that 1 centimeter or 1 millimeter or 1 foot on the map represents 62,500 centimeters or millimeters or feet on the earth's surface. The units of measure on both sides of the ratio must always be the same.

Maps may also include a *written statement* expressing distances in terms more familiar to the reader. In Map A the scale 1:62,500 is expressed as being (approximately) 1 inch to 1 mile; that is, 1 inch on the map represents roughly 1 mile on the earth's surface.

The *graphic scale* for distances is usually a bar scale, as shown in Maps A–D. A bar scale is normally subdivided, enabling the reader to measure distance directly on the map.

An *area scale* can also be used, in which one unit of area (square inches, square centimeters) is proportional to the same square units on the earth. The scale may be expressed as either $1:62,500^2$ or 1 to the square of 62,500. Area scales are used when the transformation of the globe to the flat map has been made so that areas are represented in true relation to their respective area on the earth.

When comparing map scales, it is helpful to remember that the *larger* the scale (see Map A) the smaller the area represented and the greater the amount of detail that a map can include. The *smaller* the scale (see Maps B, C, D) the larger the area covered and the less detail that can be presented.

Large-scale maps are useful when readers need such detailed information as the location of roadways, major buildings, city plans, and the like. On a smaller scale, the reader is able to place cities in relation to one another and recognize other prominent features of the region. At the smallest scale, the reader can get a broad view of several states and an idea of the total area. Finer details cannot be shown.

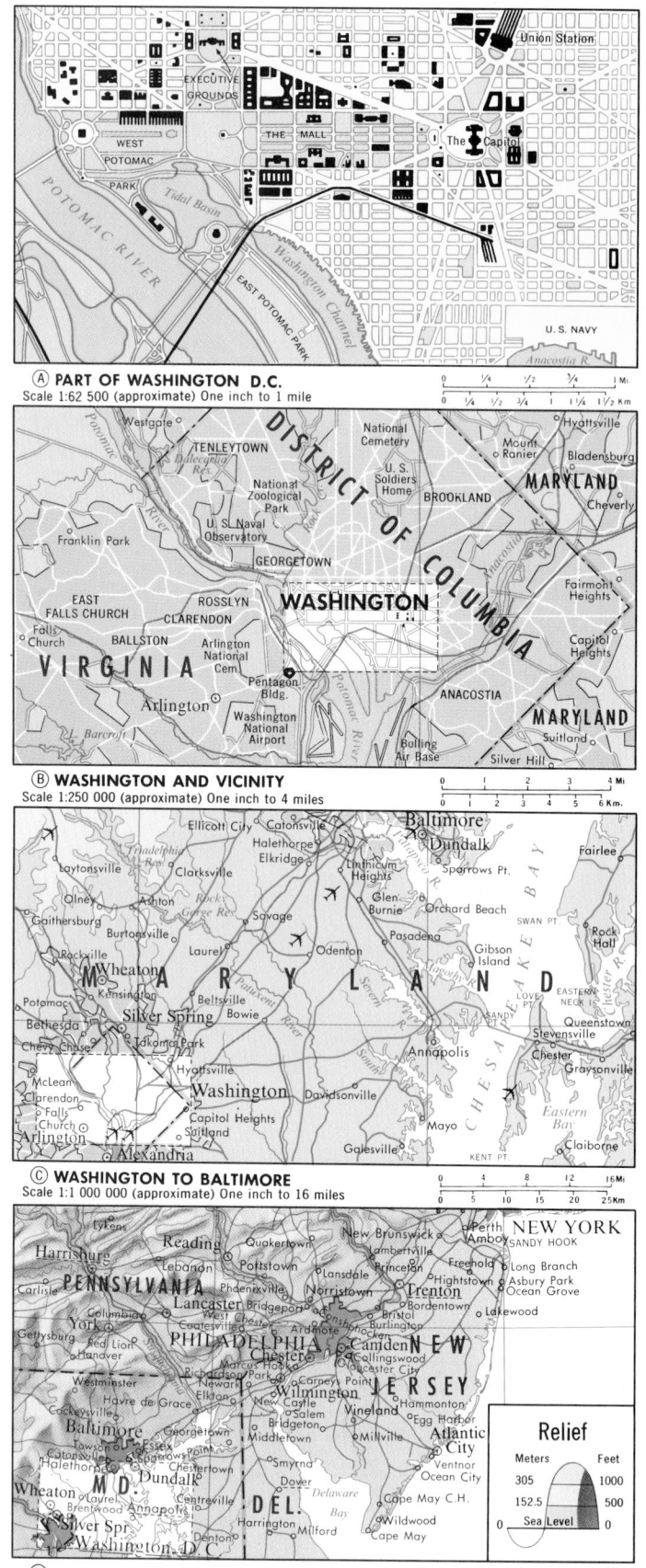

Ⓐ PART OF WASHINGTON D.C.
Scale 1:62 500 (approximate) One inch to 1 mile

Ⓑ WASHINGTON AND VICINITY
Scale 1:250 000 (approximate) One inch to 4 miles

Ⓒ WASHINGTON TO BALTIMORE
Scale 1:1 000 000 (approximate) One inch to 16 miles

Ⓓ WASHINGTON TO NEW YORK
Scale 1:4 000 000 one inch to 64 miles. Conic Projection

Map Projections

Every cartographer is faced with the problem of transforming the curved surface of the earth onto a flat plane with a minimum of distortion. The systematic transformation of locations on the earth (spherical surface) to locations on a map (flat surface) is called projection.

It is not possible to represent on a flat map the spatial relationships of angle, distance, direction, and area that only a globe can show faithfully. As a result, projection systems inevitably involve some distortion. On large-scale maps representing a few square miles, the distortion is generally negligible. But on maps depicting large countries, continents, or the entire world, the amount of distortion can be significant. Some maps of the Western Hemisphere, because of their projection, incorrectly portray Canada and Alaska as larger than the United States and Mexico, while South America looks considerably smaller than its northern neighbors.

One of the more practical ways map readers can become aware of projection distortions and learn how to make allowances for them is to compare the projection grid of a flat map with the grid of a globe. Some important characteristics of the globe grid are found listed on page xi.

There are an infinite number of possible map projections, all of which distort one or more of the characteristics of the globe in varying degrees. The projection system that a cartographer chooses depends on the size and location of the area being projected and the purpose of the map. In this atlas, most of the maps are drawn on projections that give a consistent area scale; good land and ocean shape; parallels that are parallel; and as consistent a linear scale as possible throughout the projection.

The transformation process is actually a mathematical one, but to aid in visualizing this process, it is helpful to consider the earth reduced to the scale of the intended map and then projected onto a simple geometric shape—a cylinder, cone, or plane. These geometric forms are then flattened to two dimensions to produce cylindrical, conic, and plane projections (see Figures 4, 5, and 6). Some of the projection systems used in this atlas are described on the following pages. By comparing these systems with the characteristics of a globe grid, readers can gain a clearer understanding of map distortion.

Mercator: This transformation—bearing the name of a famous sixteenth century cartographer—is conformal; that is, land masses are represented in their true shapes. Thus, for every point on the map, the angles shown are correct in every direction within a limited area. To achieve this, the projection increases latitudinal and longitudinal distances away from the equator. As a result, land *shapes* are correct, but their *areas* are distorted. The farther away from the equator, the greater the area distortion. For example, on a Mercator map, Alaska appears far larger than Mexico, whereas in fact Mexico's land area is greater. The Mercator projection is used in nautical navigation, because a line connecting any two points gives the compass direction between them. (See Figure 4.)

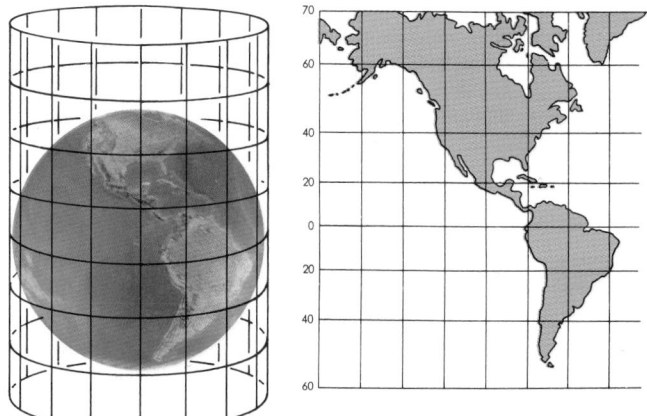

Figure 4. Mercator Projection (right), based upon the projection of the globe onto a cylinder.

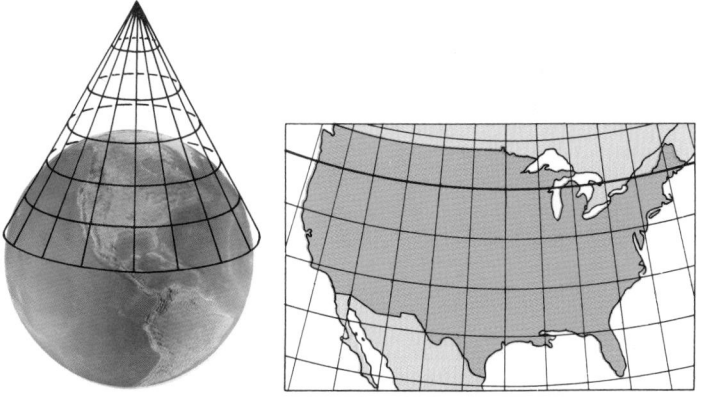

Figure 5. Projection of the globe onto a cone and a resultant Conic Projection.

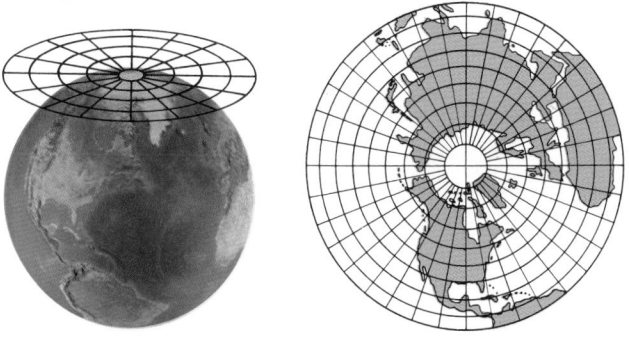

Figure 6. Lambert Equal-Area Projection (right), which assumes the projection of the globe onto a plane surface.

Conic: In this transformation—a globe projected onto a tangent cone—meridians of longitude appear as straight lines, and lines of latitude appear as parallel arcs. The parallel of tangency (that is, where the cone is presumed to touch the globe) is called a standard parallel. In this projection, distortion increases in bands away from the standard parallel. Conic projections are helpful in depicting middle-latitude areas of east-west extension. (See Figure 5.)

Lambert Equal Area *(polar case):* This projection assumes a plane touching the globe at a single point. It shows true distances close to the center (the tangent point) but increasingly distorted ones away from it. The equal-area quality (showing land areas in their correct proportion) is maintained throughout; but in regions away from the center, distortion of shape increases. (See Figure 6.)

Miller Cylindrical: O. M. Miller suggested a modification to the Mercator projection to lessen the severe area distortion in the higher latitudes. The Miller projection is neither conformal nor equal-area. Thus, while shapes are less accurate than on the Mercator, the exaggeration of *size* of areas has been somewhat decreased. The Miller cylindrical is useful for showing the entire world in a rectangular format. (See Figure 7.)

Mollweide Homolographic: The Mollweide is an equal-area projection; the least distorted areas are ovals centered just above and below the center of the projection. Distance distortions increase toward the edges of the map. The Mollweide is used for world-distribution maps where a pleasing oval look is desired along with the equal-area quality. It is one of the bases used in the Goode's Interrupted Homolosine projection. (See Figure 8.)

Sinusoidal, or Sanson-Flamsteed: In this equal-area projection the scale is the same along all parallels and the central meridian. Distortion of shapes is less along the two main axes of the projection but increases markedly toward the edges. Maps depicting areas such as South America or Africa can make good use of the Sinusoidal's favorable characteristics by situating the land masses along the central meridian, where the shapes will be virtually undistorted. The Sinusoidal is also one of the bases used in the Goode's Interrupted Homolosine. (See Figure 9.)

Goode's Interrupted Homolosine: An equal-area projection, Goode's is composed of the Sinusoidal grid from the equator to about 40° N and 40° S latitudes; beyond these latitudes, the Mollweide is used. This grid is interrupted so that land masses can be projected with a minimum of shape distortion by positioning each section on a separate central meridian. Thus, the shapes as well as the sizes of land masses are represented with a high degree of fidelity. Oceans can also be positioned in this manner. (See Figure 10.)

Robinson: This projection was designed for Rand McNally to present an uninterrupted and visually correct map of the earth. It maintains overall shape and area relationships without extreme distortion and is widely used in classrooms and textbooks. (See Figure 11.)

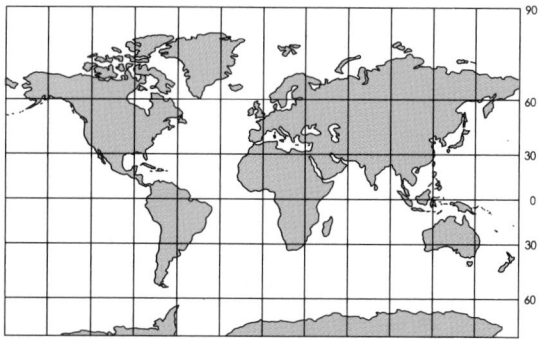

Figure 7. Miller Cylindrical Projection.

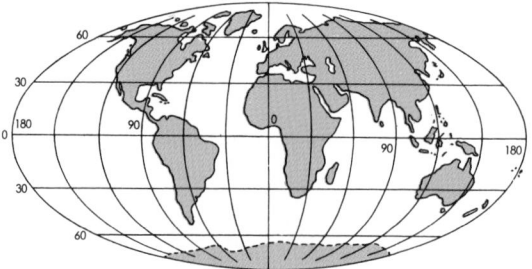

Figure 8. Mollweide Homolographic Projection.

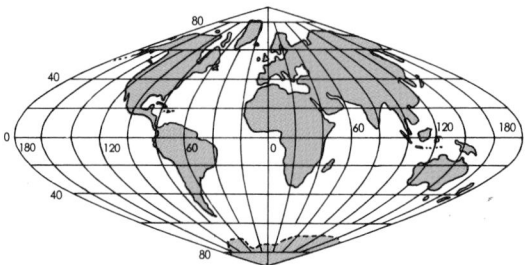

Figure 9. Sinusoidal Projection.

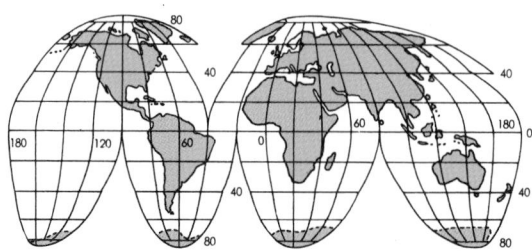

Figure 10. Goode's Interrupted Homolosine Projection.

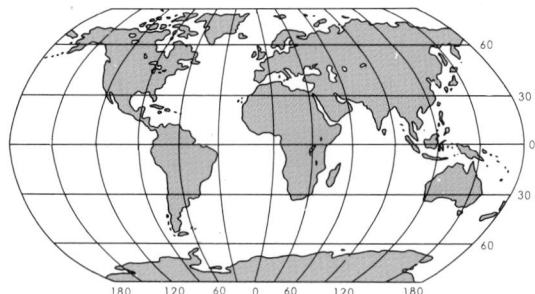

Figure 11. Robinson Projection.

Bonne: This equal-area transformation is mathematically related to the Sinusoidal. Distances are true along all parallels and the central meridian. Farther out from the central meridian, however, the increasing obliqueness of the grid's angles distorts shape and distance. This limits the area that can be usefully projected. Bonne projections, like conics, are best employed for relatively small areas in middle latitudes. (See Figure 12.)

Conic with Two Standard Parallels: The linear scale of this projection is consistent along two standard parallels instead of only one as in the simple conic. Since the spacing of the other parallels is reduced somewhat between the standard parallels and progressively enlarged beyond them, the projection does not exhibit the equal-area property. Careful selection of the standard parallels, however, provides good representation of limited areas. Like the Bonne projection, this system is widely used for areas in middle latitudes. (See Figure 13.)

Polyconic: In this system, the globe is projected onto a series of strips taken from tangent cones. Parallels are nonconcentric circles, and each is divided equally by the meridians, as on the globe. While distances along the straight central meridian are true, they are increasingly exaggerated along the curving meridians. Likewise, general representation of areas and shapes is good near the central meridian but progressively distorted away from it. Polyconic projections are used for middle-latitude areas to minimize all distortions and were employed for large-scale topographic maps. (See Figure 14.)

Lambert Conformal Conic: This conformal transformation system usually employs two standard parallels. Distortion increases away from the standard parallels, being greatest at the edges of the map. It is useful for projecting elongated east-west areas in the middle latitudes and is ideal for depicting the forty-eight contiguous states. It is also widely used for aeronautical and meteorological charts. (See Figure 15.)

Lambert Equal Area *(oblique and polar cases):* This equal-area projection can be centered at any point on the earth's surface, perpendicular to a line drawn through the globe. It maintains correct angles to all points on the map from its center (point of tangency), but distances become progressively distorted toward the edges. It is most useful for roughly circular areas or areas whose dimensions are nearly equal in two perpendicular directions.

The two most common forms of the Lambert projection are the oblique and the polar, shown in Figures 6 and 16. Although the meridians and parallels for the forms are different, the distortion characteristics are the same.

Important characteristics of the globe grid

1. All meridians of longitude are equal in length and meet at the Poles.
2. All lines of latitude are parallel and equally spaced on meridians.
3. The length, or circumference, of the parallels of latitude decreases as one moves from the equator to the Poles. For instance, the circumference of the parallel at 60° latitude is one-half the circumference of the equator.
4. Meridians of longitude are equally spaced on each parallel, but the distance between them decreases toward the Poles.
5. All parallels and meridians meet at right angles.

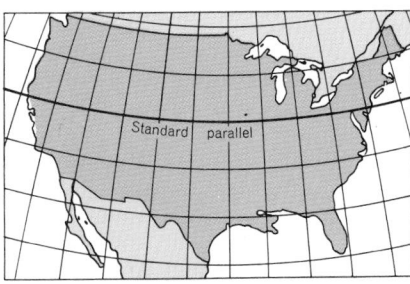

Figure 12.
Bonne Projection.

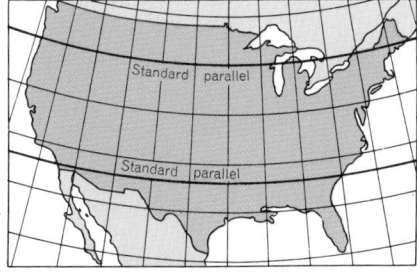

Figure 13.
Conic Projection with Two Standard Parallels.

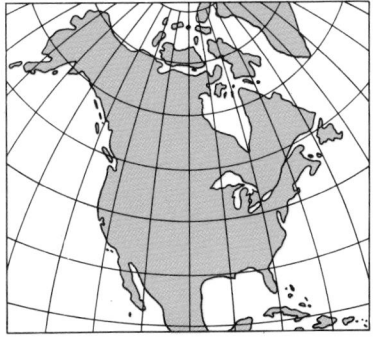

Figure 14.
Polyconic Projection.

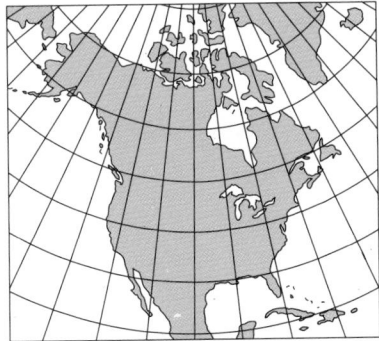

Figure 15.
Lambert Conformal Conic Projection.

Figure 16.
Lambert Equal-Area Projection (oblique case).

Edward B. Espenshade, Jr.
John C. Hudson

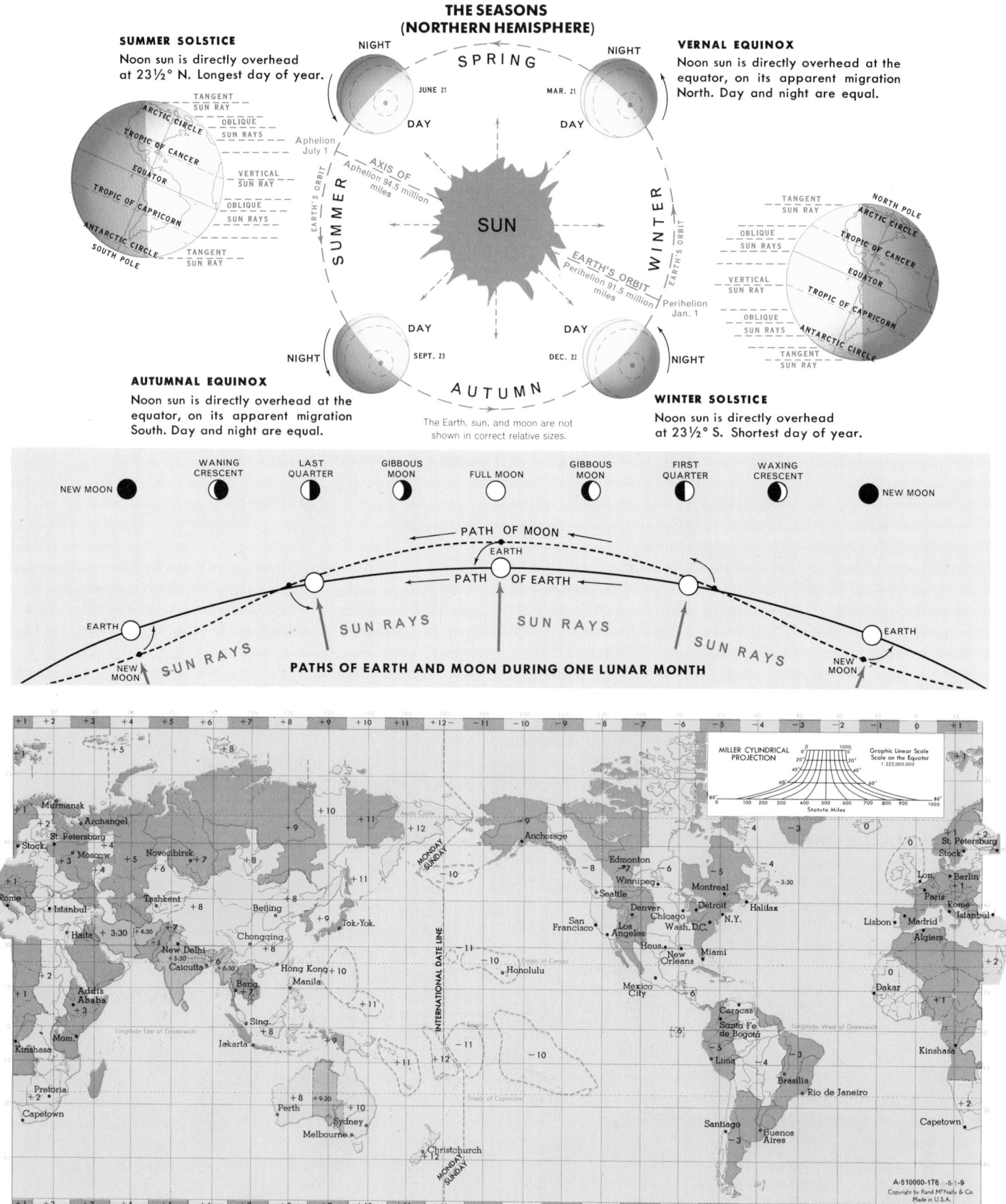

THE SEASONS
(NORTHERN HEMISPHERE)

SUMMER SOLSTICE
Noon sun is directly overhead at 23½° N. Longest day of year.

SPRING

NIGHT

JUNE 21

DAY

VERNAL EQUINOX
Noon sun is directly overhead at the equator, on its apparent migration North. Day and night are equal.

NIGHT

MAR. 21

DAY

TANGENT SUN RAY
ARCTIC CIRCLE
OBLIQUE SUN RAYS
TROPIC OF CANCER
EQUATOR
VERTICAL SUN RAY
TROPIC OF CAPRICORN
OBLIQUE SUN RAYS
ANTARCTIC CIRCLE
SOUTH POLE
TANGENT SUN RAY

Aphelion July 1
AXIS OF Aphelion 94.5 million miles
EARTH'S ORBIT
SUMMER

SUN

WINTER
EARTH'S ORBIT
EARTH'S ORBIT Perihelion 91.5 million miles
Perihelion Jan. 1

TANGENT SUN RAY
NORTH POLE
ARCTIC CIRCLE
OBLIQUE SUN RAYS
TROPIC OF CANCER
EQUATOR
VERTICAL SUN RAY
TROPIC OF CAPRICORN
OBLIQUE SUN RAYS
ANTARCTIC CIRCLE
TANGENT SUN RAY

DAY

SEPT. 23

NIGHT

DAY

DEC. 22

NIGHT

AUTUMN

AUTUMNAL EQUINOX
Noon sun is directly overhead at the equator, on its apparent migration South. Day and night are equal.

The Earth, sun, and moon are not shown in correct relative sizes.

WINTER SOLSTICE
Noon sun is directly overhead at 23½° S. Shortest day of year.

NEW MOON · WANING CRESCENT · LAST QUARTER · GIBBOUS MOON · FULL MOON · GIBBOUS MOON · FIRST QUARTER · WAXING CRESCENT · NEW MOON

PATH OF MOON
EARTH
PATH OF EARTH
EARTH
EARTH
SUN RAYS
NEW MOON
SUN RAYS
SUN RAYS
SUN RAYS
NEW MOON

PATHS OF EARTH AND MOON DURING ONE LUNAR MONTH

MILLER CYLINDRICAL PROJECTION
Graphic Linear Scale on the Equator
1:222,000,000
Statute Miles

Time Zones

The surface of the earth is divided into 24 time zones. Each zone represents 15° of longitude or one hour of time. The time of the initial, or zero, zone is based on the central meridian of Greenwich and is adopted eastward and westward for a distance of 7½° of longitude. Each of the zones in turn is designated by a number representing the hours (+ or −) by which its standard time differs from Greenwich mean time. These standard time zones are indicated by bands of orange and yellow. Areas which have a fractional deviation from standard time are shown in an intermediate color. The irregularities in the zones and the fractional deviations are due to political and economic factors.

(After U.S. Defense Mapping Agency)

WORLD THEMATIC MAPS

This section of the atlas consists of more than sixty thematic maps presenting world patterns and distributions. Together with accompanying graphs, these maps communicate basic information on mineral resources, agricultural products, trade, transportation, and other selected aspects of the natural and cultural geographical environment.

A thematic map uses symbols to show certain characteristics of, generally, one class of geographical information. This "theme" of a thematic map is presented upon a background of basic locational information—coastline, country boundaries, major drainage, etc. The map's primary concern is to communicate visually basic impressions of the distribution of the theme. For instance, on page 43 the distribution of cattle shown by point symbols impresses the reader with relative densities—the distribution of cattle is much more uniform throughout the United States than it is in China, and cattle are more numerous in the United States than in China.

Although it is possible to use a thematic map to obtain exact values of a quantity or commodity, it is not the purpose intended, any more than a thematic map is intended to be used to give precise distances from New York to Moscow. If one seeks precise statistics for each country, he may consult the bar graph on the map or a statistical table.

The map on this page is an example of a special class of thematic maps called cartograms. The cartogram assigns to a named earth region an area based on some value other than land surface area. In the cartogram below the areas assigned are proportional to their countries' populations and tinted according to their rate of natural increase. The result of mapping on this base is a meaningful way of portraying this distribution since natural increase is causally related to existing size of population. On the other hand, natural increase is not causally related to earth area. In the other thematic maps in this atlas, relative earth sizes have been considered when presenting the distributions.

Real and hypothetical geographical distributions of interest to man are practically limitless but can be classed into point, line, area, or volume information relative to a specific location or area in the world. The thematic map, in communicating these fundamental classes of information, utilizes point, line, and area symbols. The symbols may be employed to show *qualitative* differences (differences in *kind*) of a certain category of information and may also show *quantitative* differences in the information (differences in *amount*). For example, the natural-vegetation map (page 18) was based upon information gathered by many observations over a period of time. It utilizes area symbols (color and pattern) to show the difference in the *kind* of vegetation as well as the extent. Quantitative factual information was shown on the annual-precipitation map, page 16, by means of isohyets (lines connecting points of equal rainfall). Also, area symbols were employed to show the intervals between the lines. In each of these thematic maps, there is one primary theme, or subject; the map communicates the information far better than volumes of words and tables could.

One of the most important aspects of the thematic-map section is use of the different maps to show comparisons and relationships among the distributions of various types of geographical information. For example, the relationship of dense population (page 24) to areas of intensive subsistence agriculture (page 34) and to manufacturing and commerce (page 32) is an important geographic concept.

The statistics communicated by the maps and graphs in this section are intended to give an idea of the relative importance of countries in the distributions mapped. The maps are not intended to take the place of statistical reference works. No single year affords a realistic base for production, trade, and certain economic and demographic statistics. Therefore, averages of data for three or four years have been used. Together with the maps, the averages and percentages provide the student with a realistic idea of the importance of specific areas.

POPULATION

Note: Size of each country is proportional to population.

Tints indicate rate of natural increase.

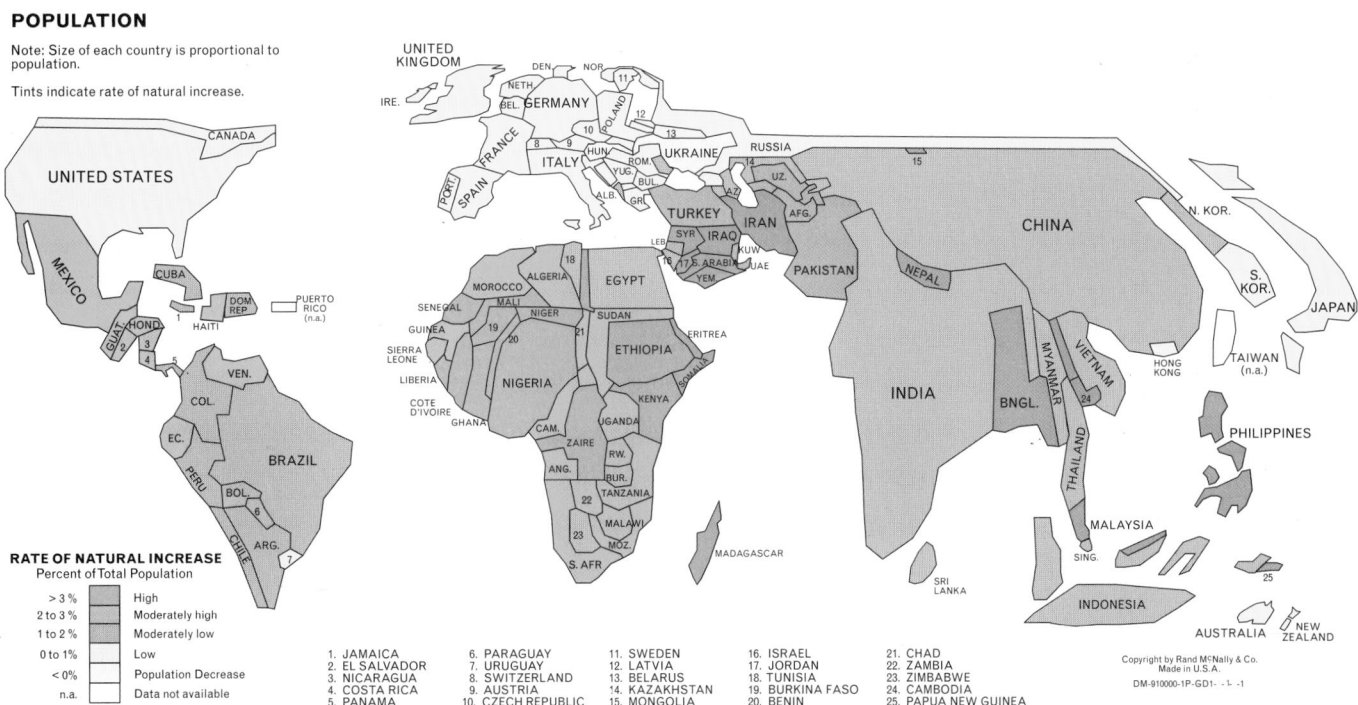

RATE OF NATURAL INCREASE
Percent of Total Population

> 3 %	High
2 to 3 %	Moderately high
1 to 2 %	Moderately low
0 to 1%	Low
< 0%	Population Decrease
n.a.	Data not available

1. JAMAICA
2. EL SALVADOR
3. NICARAGUA
4. COSTA RICA
5. PANAMA
6. PARAGUAY
7. URUGUAY
8. SWITZERLAND
9. AUSTRIA
10. CZECH REPUBLIC
11. SWEDEN
12. LATVIA
13. BELARUS
14. KAZAKHSTAN
15. MONGOLIA
16. ISRAEL
17. JORDAN
18. TUNISIA
19. BURKINA FASO
20. BENIN
21. CHAD
22. ZAMBIA
23. ZIMBABWE
24. CAMBODIA
25. PAPUA NEW GUINEA

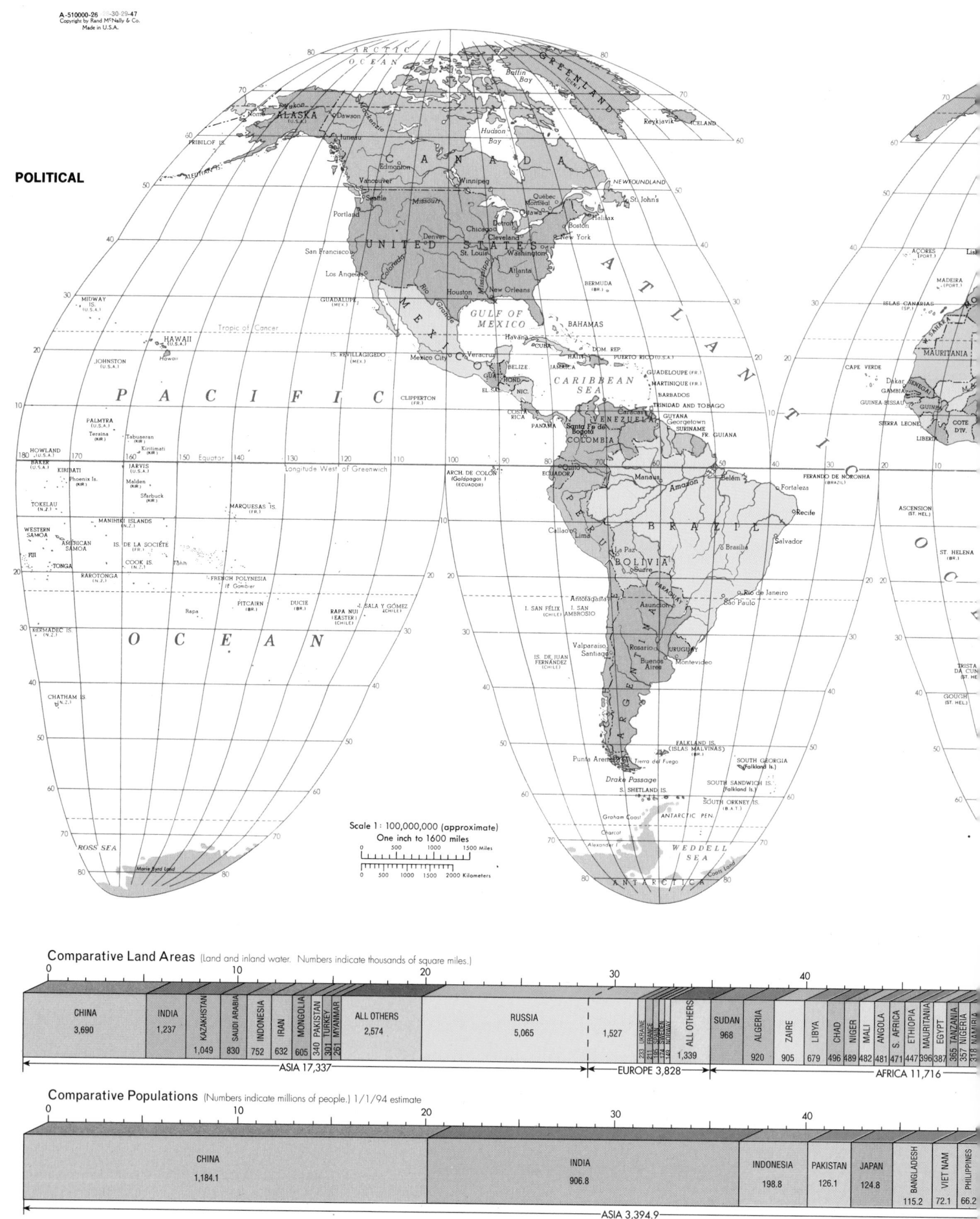

POLITICAL

Scale 1 : 100,000,000 (approximate)
One inch to 1600 miles

0   500   1000   1500 Miles

0   500 1000 1500 2000 Kilometers

Comparative Land Areas (Land and inland water. Numbers indicate thousands of square miles.)

0							10							20							30							40							
CHINA 3,690	INDIA 1,237	KAZAKHSTAN 1,049	SAUDI ARABIA 830	INDONESIA 752	IRAN 632	MONGOLIA 605	PAKISTAN 340	TURKEY 301	MYANMAR 261	ALL OTHERS 2,574	RUSSIA 5,065		1,527	UKRAINE 233	FRANCE 211	SPAIN 195	SWEDEN 174	NORWAY 125	ALL OTHERS 1,339	SUDAN 968	ALGERIA 920	ZAIRE 905	LIBYA 679	CHAD 496	NIGER 489	MALI 482	ANGOLA 481	S. AFRICA 471	ETHIOPIA 447	MAURITANIA 396	EGYPT 387	TANZANIA 365	NIGERIA 357	NAMIBIA 318

ASIA 17,337 ——— EUROPE 3,828 ——— AFRICA 11,716 ———

Comparative Populations (Numbers indicate millions of people.) 1/1/94 estimate

0										10										20									30									40						
CHINA 1,184.1										INDIA 906.8									INDONESIA 198.8				PAKISTAN 126.1			JAPAN 124.8			BANGLADESH 115.2		VIET NAM 72.1	PHILIPPINES 66.2

ASIA 3,394.9 ———

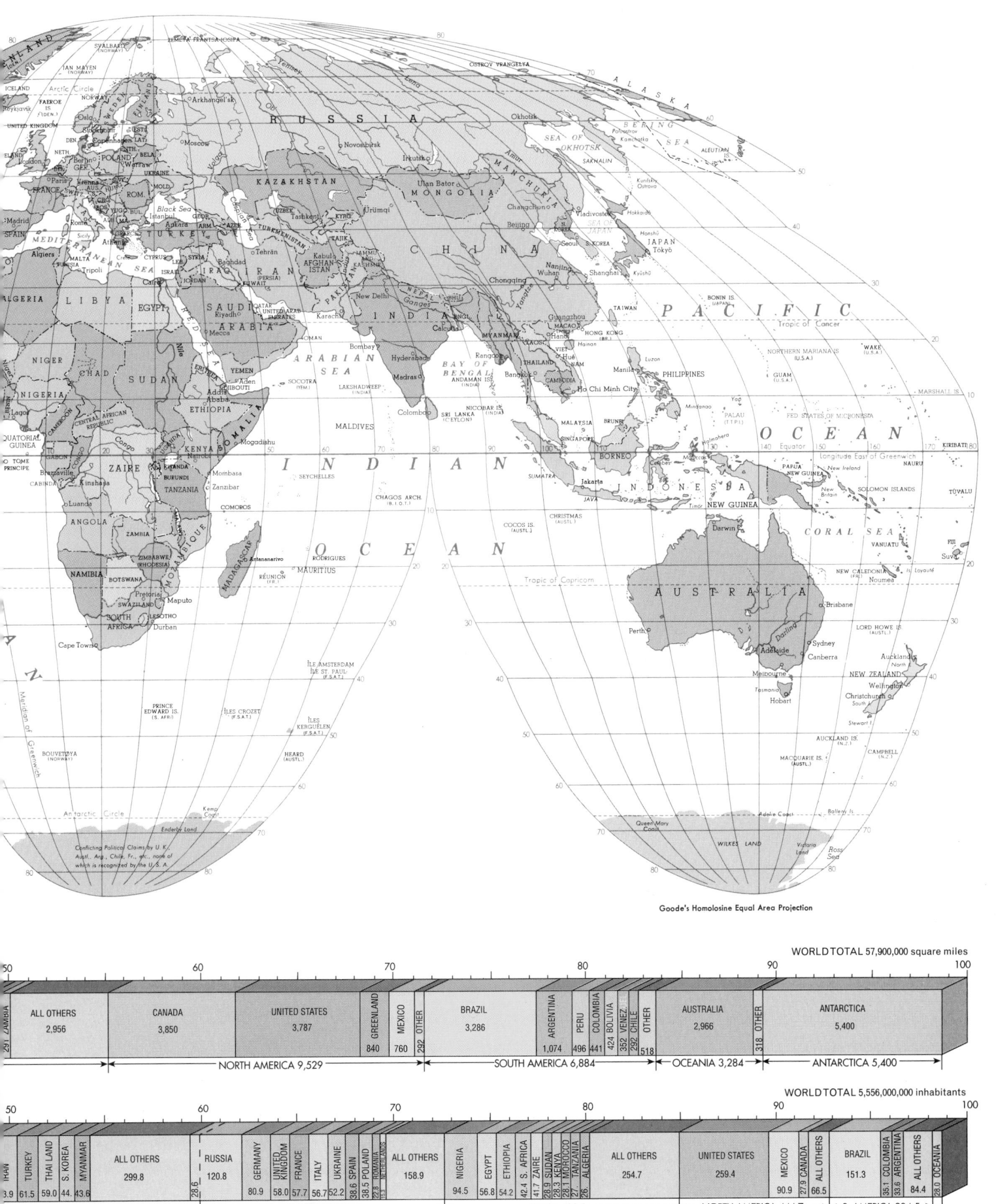

Goode's Homolosine Equal Area Projection

WORLD TOTAL 57,900,000 square miles

50		60		70			80							90		100
ALL OTHERS 2,956	CANADA 3,850		UNITED STATES 3,787	GREENLAND 840	MEXICO 760	OTHER 292	BRAZIL 3,286	ARGENTINA 1,074	PERU 496	COLOMBIA 441	BOLIVIA 424	VENEZ. 352	CHILE 292	OTHER 518	AUSTRALIA 2,966	OTHER 318	ANTARCTICA 5,400

ZAMBIA 291

NORTH AMERICA 9,529 — SOUTH AMERICA 6,884 — OCEANIA 3,284 — ANTARCTICA 5,400

WORLD TOTAL 5,556,000,000 inhabitants

50					60										70								80									90					100
IRAN 3.9	TURKEY 61.5	THAILAND 59.0	S. KOREA 44.	MYANMAR 43.6	ALL OTHERS 299.8	RUSSIA 120.8	28.6	GERMANY 80.9	UNITED KINGDOM 58.0	FRANCE 57.7	ITALY 56.7	UKRAINE 52.2	SPAIN 38.5	POLAND 38.5	ROMANIA 22.7	NETHERLANDS 15.3	ALL OTHERS 158.9	NIGERIA 94.5	EGYPT 56.8	ETHIOPIA 54.2	S. AFRICA 42.4	ZAIRE 41.7	KENYA 28.3	MOROCCO 28.1	TANZANIA 27.	ALGERIA 26.	ALL OTHERS 254.7	UNITED STATES 259.4	MEXICO 90.9	CANADA 27.9	ALL OTHERS 66.5	BRAZIL 151.3	COLOMBIA 35.1	ARGENTINA 33.6	ALL OTHERS 84.4	OCEANIA 28.0

EUROPE 700.5 — AFRICA 683.8 — NORTH AMERICA 444.7 — S. AMERICA 304.5

A-510000-76 -4 14-26
Copyright by Rand McNally & Co.
Made in U.S.A.

PHYSICAL

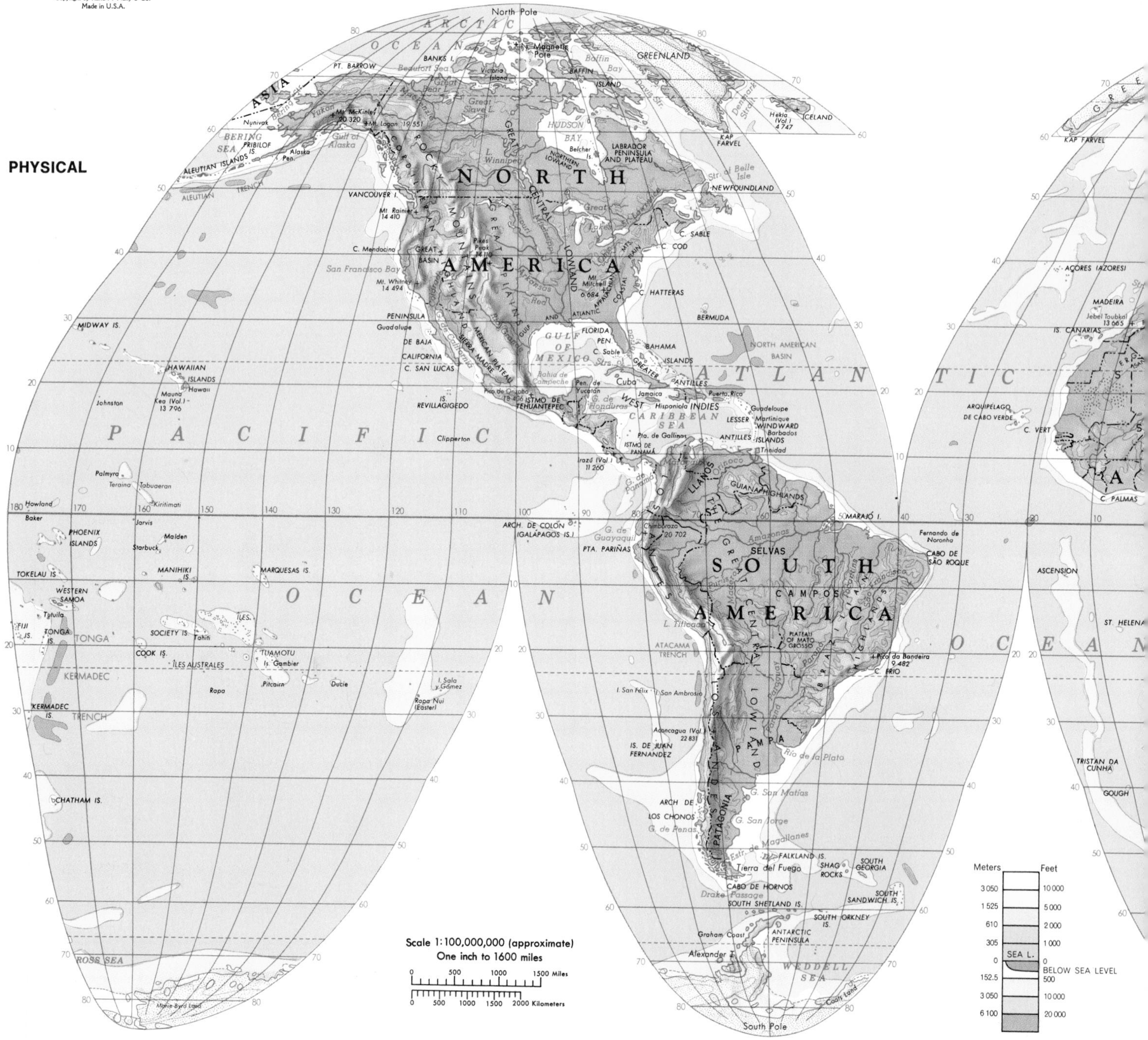

North Pole

ARCTIC OCEAN

ASIA

NORTH AMERICA

SOUTH AMERICA

ATLANTIC OCEAN

PACIFIC OCEAN

Scale 1:100,000,000 (approximate)
One inch to 1600 miles

0   500   1000   1500 Miles

0   500   1000   1500   2000 Kilometers

Meters	Feet
3 050	10 000
1 525	5 000
610	2 000
305	1 000
SEA L.	0
	BELOW SEA LEVEL
152.5	500
3 050	10 000
6 100	20 000

Land Elevations in Profile

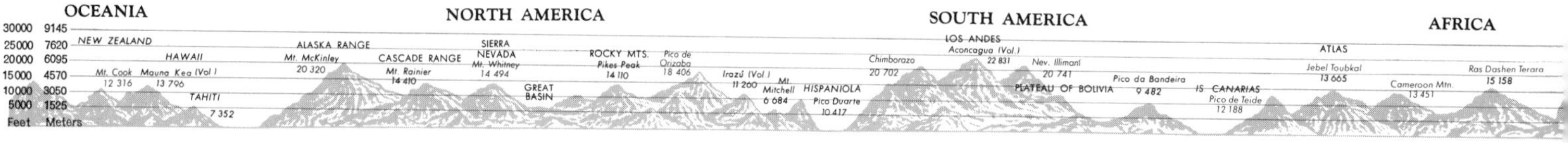

Ocean Depths in Profile

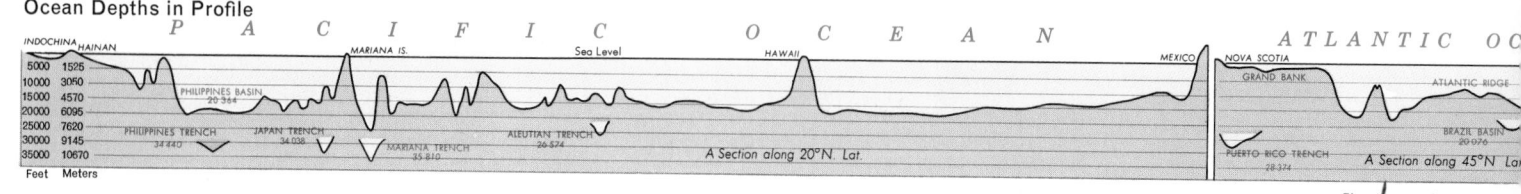

Elevations and depressions

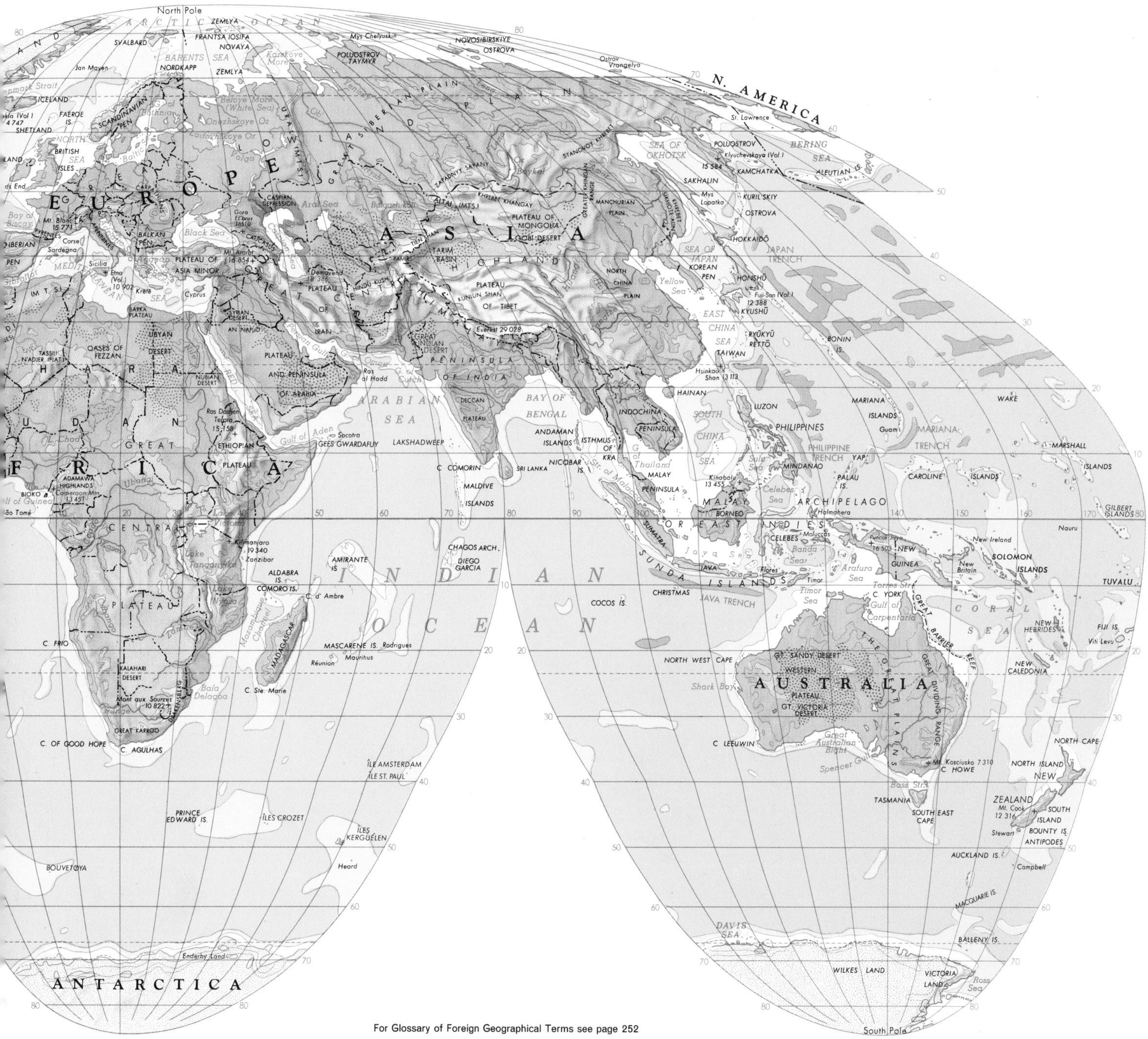

North Pole

ARCTIC OCEAN

NORTH ZEMLYA
SVALBARD
NOVAYA ZEMLYA
Jan Mayen
NORDKAPP
BARENTS SEA
Myt Chelyuskin
NOVOSIBIRSKIYE OSTROVA
Ostrov Vrangelya
N. AMERICA

ICELAND
FAEROE IS.
SHETLAND
BRITISH ISLES
NORTH SEA
SCANDINAVIAN PEN.
Onezhskoye Oz.
Tenoye More (White Sea)
WEST SIBERIAN PLAIN
CENTRAL SIBERIAN PLATEAU
St. Lawrence
SEA OF OKHOTSK
BERING SEA
POLUOSTROV Klyuchevskaya (Vol.) IS 584
KAMCHATKA
ALEUTIAN IS.

EUROPE
ASIA
Mt. Blanc 15 771
BALKAN PEN.
Black Sea
CASPIAN DEPRESSION
Aral Sea
URAL MTS.
Baykal, Kul.
ALTAI (MTS.)
PLATEAU OF MONGOLIA
GOBI DESERT
MANCHURIAN PLAIN
SAKHALIN
Mys Lopatka
KURIL'SKIY OSTROVA
HOKKAIDŌ
JAPAN
JAPAN TRENCH

MEDITERRANEAN
Sicilia
Sardegna
Corse
Etna (Vol.) 10 902
Crete
Cyprus
PLATEAU OF ASIA MINOR
Mt. Ararat
CAUCASUS
Gora El'brus 18 510
Demavend
HINDU KUSH
Plateau of 14 854
TARIM BASIN
HIGHLAND
PLATEAU OF TIBET
KUNLUN SHAN
Everest 29 028
HONSHŪ
KOREAN PEN.
Fuji-San (Vol.) 12 388
KYŪSHŪ
YELLOW SEA
NORTH CHINA PLAIN
EAST CHINA SEA
RYŪKYŪ RETTŌ
TAIWAN
BONIN IS.

IRAN
AN NAFŪD
PLATEAU
GREAT INDIAN DESERT
HIMALAYAS
PENINSULA AND PLATEAU OF INDIA
DECCAN PLATEAU
BAY OF BENGAL
INDOCHINA PENINSULA
HAINAN
SOUTH CHINA SEA
LUZON
PHILIPPINES
Guam
MARIANA ISLANDS
WAKE
MARIANA TRENCH
PHILIPPINE TRENCH
YAP
MARSHALL ISLANDS

LIBYAN DESERT
OASES OF FEZZAN
SAHARA
NUBIAN DESERT
PLATEAU AND PENINSULA OF ARABIA
Ras al Hadd
Gulf of Aden
ARABIAN SEA
C. COMORIN
SRI LANKA
NICOBAR IS.
ANDAMAN ISLANDS
ISTHMUS OF KRA
G. of Thailand
MALAY PENINSULA
MINDANAO
Kinabalu 13 455
Celebes Sea
PALAU IS.
CAROLINE ISLANDS

TASSILI N'ADJER (PLAT.)
GREAT AFRICAN PLATEAU
ETHIOPIAN PLATEAU
Ras Dashan Terara 15 158
Socotra
GEES GWARDAFUY
LAKSHADWEEP
MALDIVE ISLANDS
CHAGOS ARCH.
DIEGO GARCIA
BORNEO
MALAY ARCHIPELAGO
EAST INDIES
CELEBES
MOLUCCAS
Banda Sea
NEW GUINEA
Puncak Jaya 16 503
NEW IRELAND
New Britain
SOLOMON ISLANDS
Nauru
GILBERT ISLANDS

BIOKO
CAMEROON MTN. 13 451
ADAMAWA HIGHLANDS
São Tomé
Gulf of Guinea
CENTRAL AFRICA
Kilimanjaro 19 340
Zanzibar
Lake Tanganyika
AMIRANTE IS.
SUMATRA
Java Sea
JAVA
Flores
Timor
Arafura Sea
NEW HEBRIDES
CORAL SEA
FIJI IS.
Viti Levu
TUVALU

PLATEAU
ALDABRA IS.
COMORO IS.
C. d'Ambre
MADAGASCAR
Maromokotro
COCOS IS.
CHRISTMAS
SUNDA ISLANDS
JAVA TRENCH
Timor Sea
C. YORK
Gulf of Carpentaria
GT. SANDY DESERT
GREAT BARRIER REEF
NEW CALEDONIA

C. FRIO
INDIAN OCEAN
MASCARENE IS.
Rodrigues
Réunion
Mauritius
NORTH WEST CAPE
Shark Bay
WESTERN PLATEAU
GT. VICTORIA DESERT
AUSTRALIA
GREAT DIVIDING RANGE
THE GREAT PLAINS

KALAHARI DESERT
Mont aux Sources 10 822
GREAT KARROO
C. OF GOOD HOPE
C. Agulhas
C. Ste. Marie
Delagoa
ÎLE AMSTERDAM
ÎLE ST. PAUL
C. LEEUWIN
Great Australian Bight
Spencer Gulf
Mt. Kosciusko 7310
C. HOWE
NORTH CAPE
NEW ZEALAND
NORTH ISLAND

PRINCE EDWARD IS.
ÎLES CROZET
ÎLES KERGUÉLEN
Heard
BASS STR.
TASMANIA
SOUTH EAST CAPE
Mt. Cook 12 316
SOUTH ISLAND
Stewart
BOUNTY IS.
ANTIPODES

BOUVETOYA
AUCKLAND IS.
Campbell

Enderby Land
MACQUARIE IS.
BALLENY IS.
DAVIS SEA

ANTARCTICA
WILKES LAND
VICTORIA LAND
Ross Sea
South Pole

For Glossary of Foreign Geographical Terms see page 252

Goode's Homolosine Equal Area Projection

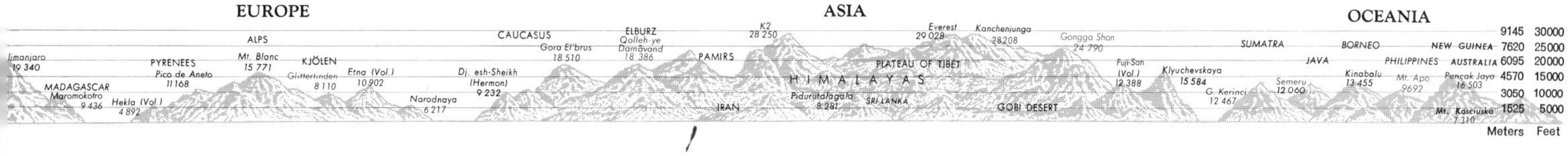

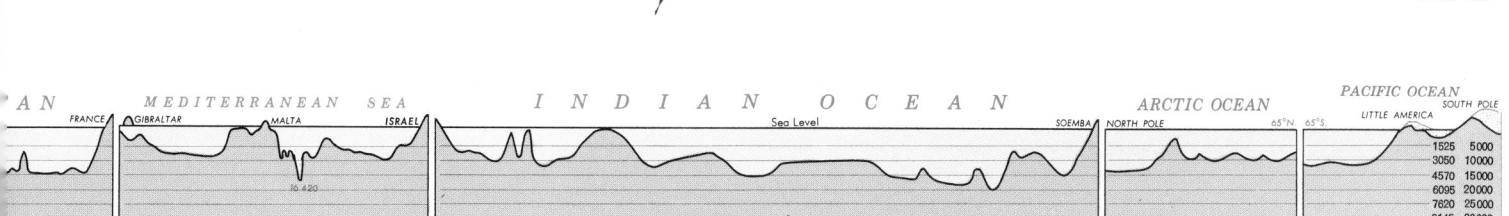

EUROPE — ASIA — OCEANIA cross-section profiles

ALPS — Mt. Blanc 15 771 — CAUCASUS — Gora El'brus — ELBURZ — Qolleh-ye Damāvand 18 386 — PAMIRS — K2 28 250 — Everest 29 028 — Kancheniunga 28 208 — Gongga Shan 24 790 — SUMATRA — BORNEO — NEW GUINEA 9145 30000

PYRENEES — Pico de Aneto 11 168 — KJÖLEN — Glittertinden 8 110 — Etna (Vol.) 10 902 — Dj. esh-Sheikh (Hermon) 9 232 — IRAN — PLATEAU OF TIBET — HIMALAYAS — GOBI DESERT — Fuji-San (Vol.) 12 388 — Klyuchevskaya 15 584 — JAVA — Kinabalu 13 455 — G. Kerinci — Semeru 12 060 — PHILIPPINES — Mt. Apo 9692 — Pencak Jaya 16 503 — AUSTRALIA 6095 20000

Imanjaro 19 340 — MADAGASCAR — Maromokotro 9 436 — Hekla (Vol.) 4 892 — Narodnaya 6 217 — Piduruталаgala 8 291 — SRI LANKA — Mt. Kosciusko 7 310 — 3050 10000

1525 5000

Meters Feet

MEDITERRANEAN SEA — INDIAN OCEAN — ARCTIC OCEAN — PACIFIC OCEAN

FRANCE — GIBRALTAR — MALTA — ISRAEL — Sea Level — SOEMBA — NORTH POLE — 65°N. 65°S. — LITTLE AMERICA — SOUTH POLE

A Section along 10°S. Lat.

are given in feet

1525 5000
3050 10000
4570 15000
6095 20000
7620 25000
9145 30000
10670 35000

Meters Feet

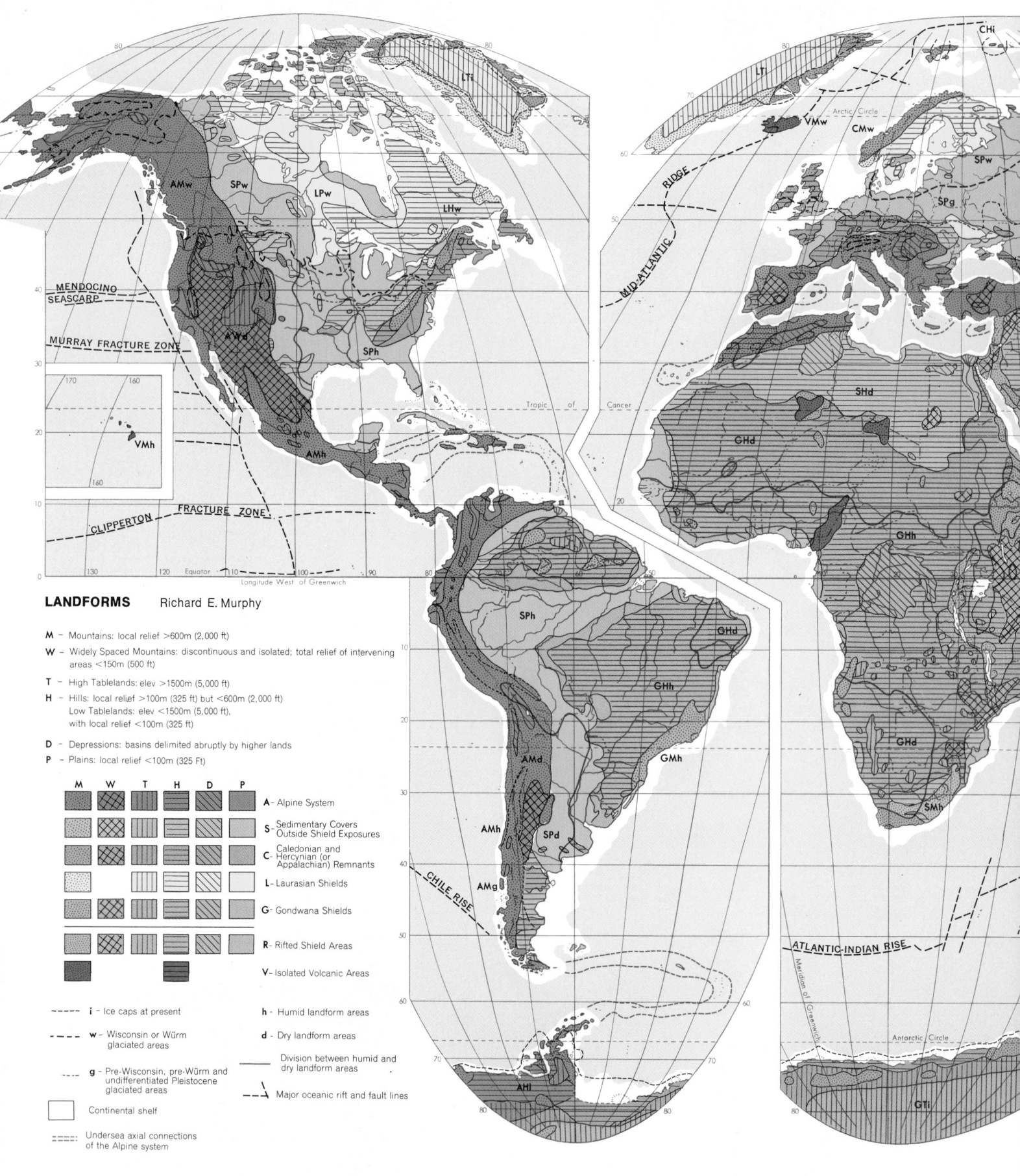

LANDFORMS   Richard E. Murphy

M – Mountains: local relief >600m (2,000 ft)

W – Widely Spaced Mountains: discontinuous and isolated; total relief of intervening areas <150m (500 ft)

T – High Tablelands: elev >1500m (5,000 ft)

H – Hills: local relief >100m (325 ft) but <600m (2,000 ft)
Low Tablelands: elev <1500m (5,000 ft), with local relief <100m (325 ft)

D – Depressions: basins delimited abruptly by higher lands

P – Plains: local relief <100m (325 Ft)

M   W   T   H   D   P

A - Alpine System

S - Sedimentary Covers Outside Shield Exposures

C - Caledonian and Hercynian (or Appalachian) Remnants

L - Laurasian Shields

G - Gondwana Shields

R - Rifted Shield Areas

V - Isolated Volcanic Areas

- - - - **i** - Ice caps at present

— — **w** - Wisconsin or Würm glaciated areas

·—·— **g** - Pre-Wisconsin, pre-Würm and undifferentiated Pleistocene glaciated areas

Continental shelf

— — — Undersea axial connections of the Alpine system

h - Humid landform areas

d - Dry landform areas

——— Division between humid and dry landform areas

—·—· Major oceanic rift and fault lines

Map labels

MENDOCINO SEASCARP
MURRAY FRACTURE ZONE
CLIPPERTON FRACTURE ZONE
Longitude West of Greenwich
Tropic of Cancer
Equator

AMw   SPw   LPw   LHw
AWd   SPh   AMh
VMh

MID-ATLANTIC RIDGE
CHi   LTi   VMw   CMw   SPw   SPg
SHd   GHd   GHh   GHd   SMh

SPh   GHd   GHh   GMh   AMd   AMh   SPd   AMg
CHILE RISE
ATLANTIC-INDIAN RISE
AHI   GTi
Arctic Circle   Antarctic Circle   Meridian of Greenwich

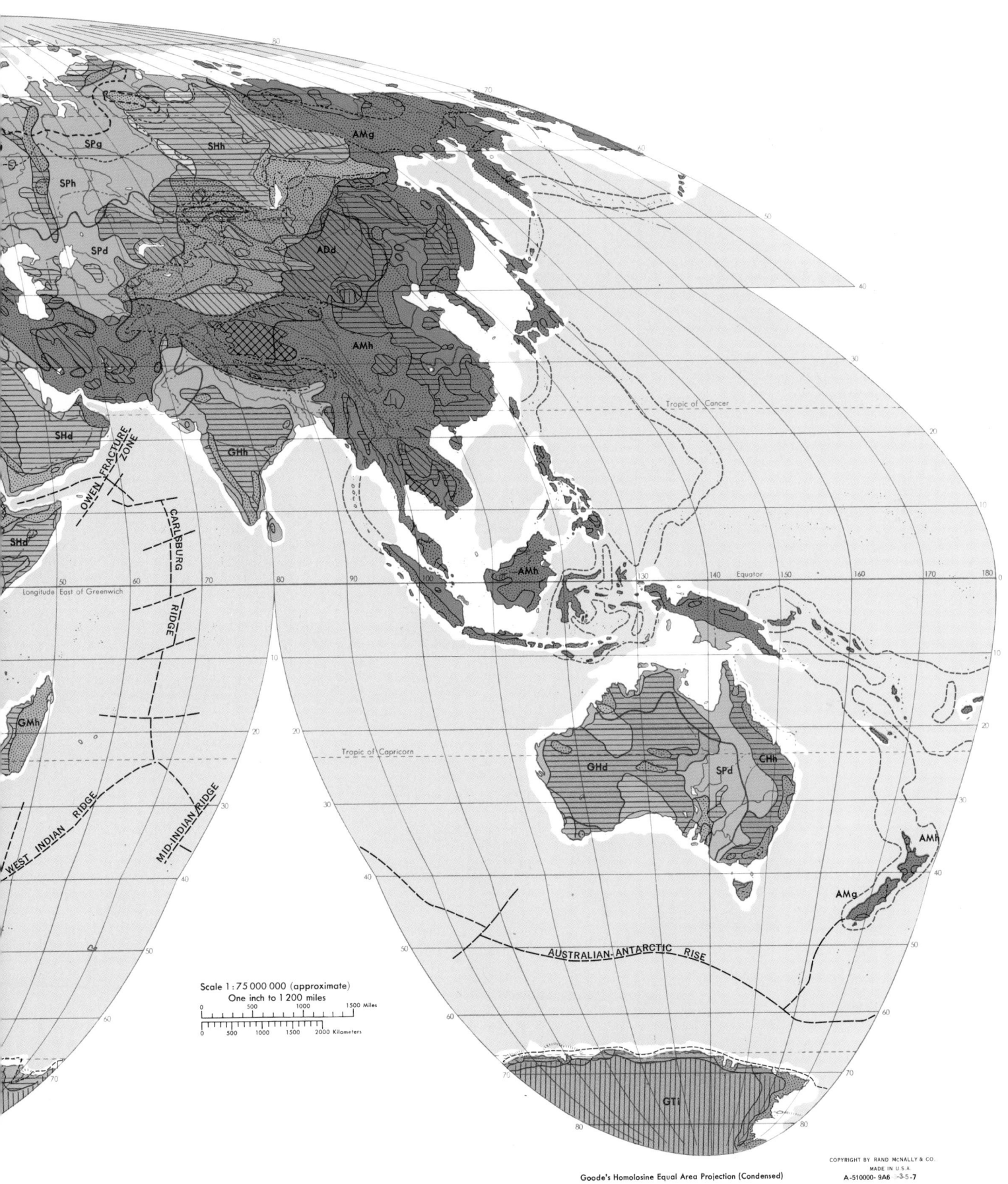

SPg

SHh

AMg

SPh

SPd

ADd

AMh

SHd

GHh

Tropic of Cancer

OWEN FRACTURE ZONE

CARLSBURG RIDGE

SHd

Longitude East of Greenwich

50 60 70 80 90 100 130 140 Equator 150 160 170 180 0

AMh

GMh

WEST INDIAN RIDGE

MID-INDIAN RIDGE

Tropic of Capricorn

GHd

SPd

CHh

AMh

AMg

AUSTRALIAN-ANTARCTIC RISE

Scale 1 : 75 000 000 (approximate)
One inch to 1 200 miles

0   500   1000   1500 Miles

0 500 1000 1500 2000 Kilometers

GTi

Goode's Homolosine Equal Area Projection (Condensed)

CONTINENTAL DRIFT

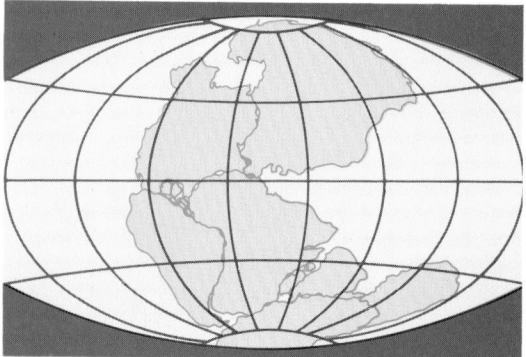

225 million years ago the supercontinent of Pangaea exists and Panthalassa forms the ancestral ocean. Tethys Sea separates Eurasia and Africa.

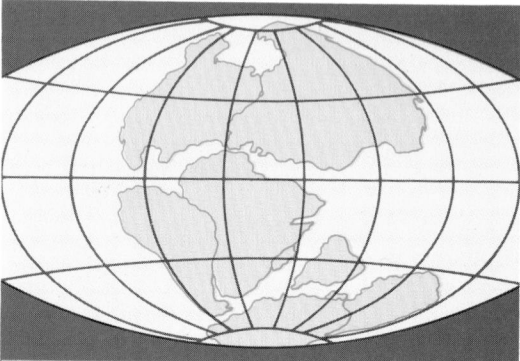

180 million years ago Pangaea splits, Laurasia drifts north. Gondwanaland breaks into South America/Africa, India, and Australia/Antarctica.

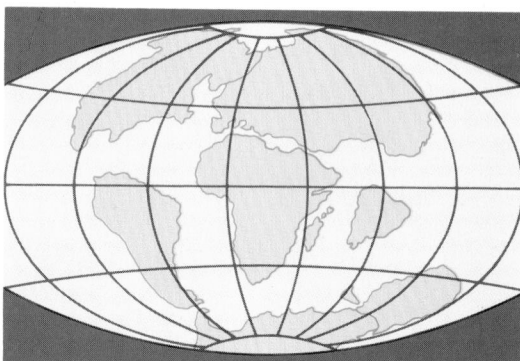

65 million years ago ocean basins take shape as South America and India move from Africa and the Tethys Sea closes to form the Mediterranean Sea.

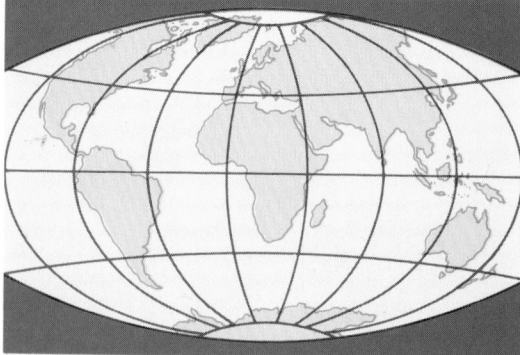

The present day: India has merged with Asia, Australia is free of Antarctica, and North America is free of Eurasia.

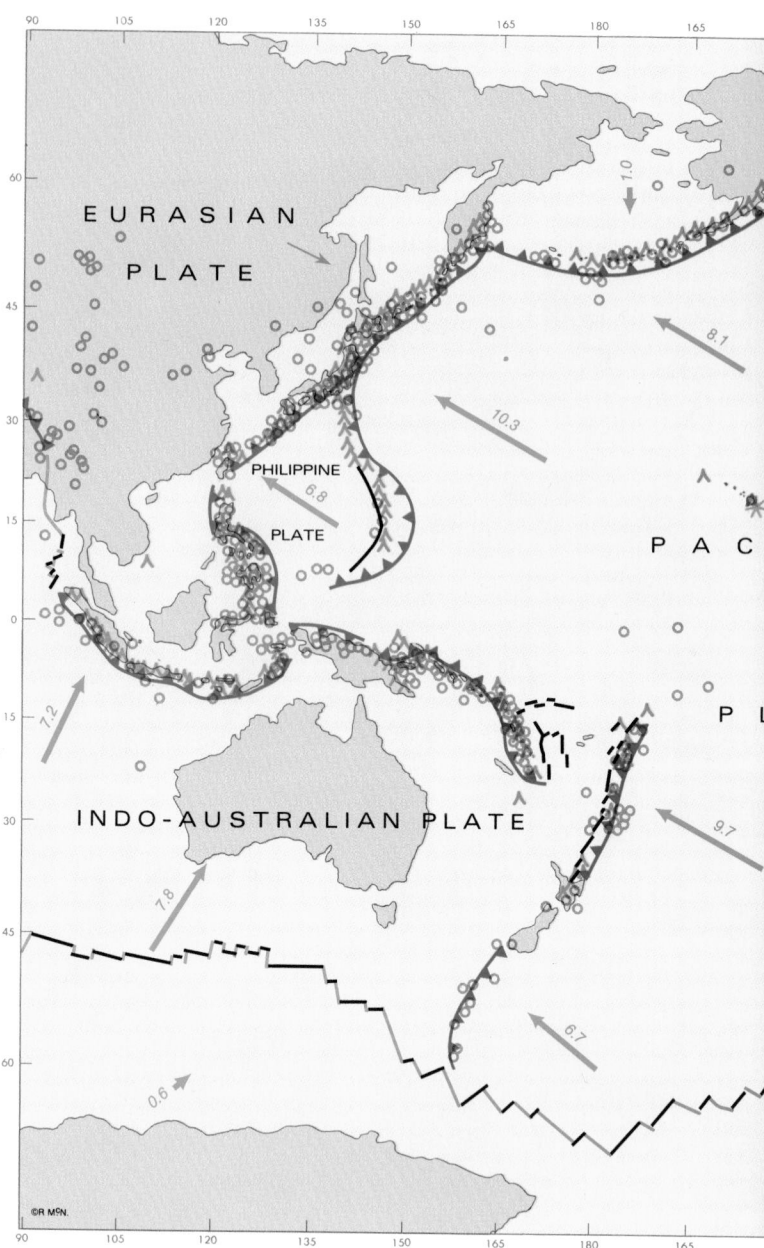

PLATE TECTONICS

Types of plate boundaries

Divergent: magma emerges from the earth's mantle at the mid-ocean ridges forming new crust and forcing the plates to spread apart at the ridges.

Convergent: plates collide at subduction zones where the denser plate is forced back into the earth's mantle forming deep ocean trenches.

Transform: plates slide past one another producing faults and fracture zones.

Other map symbols

→ Direction of plate movement

6.7 Length of arrow is proportional to the amount of plate movement (number indicates centimeters of movement per year)

○ Earthquake of magnitude 7.5 and above (from 10 A.D. to the present)

∧ Volcano (eruption since 1900)

✳ Selected hot spots

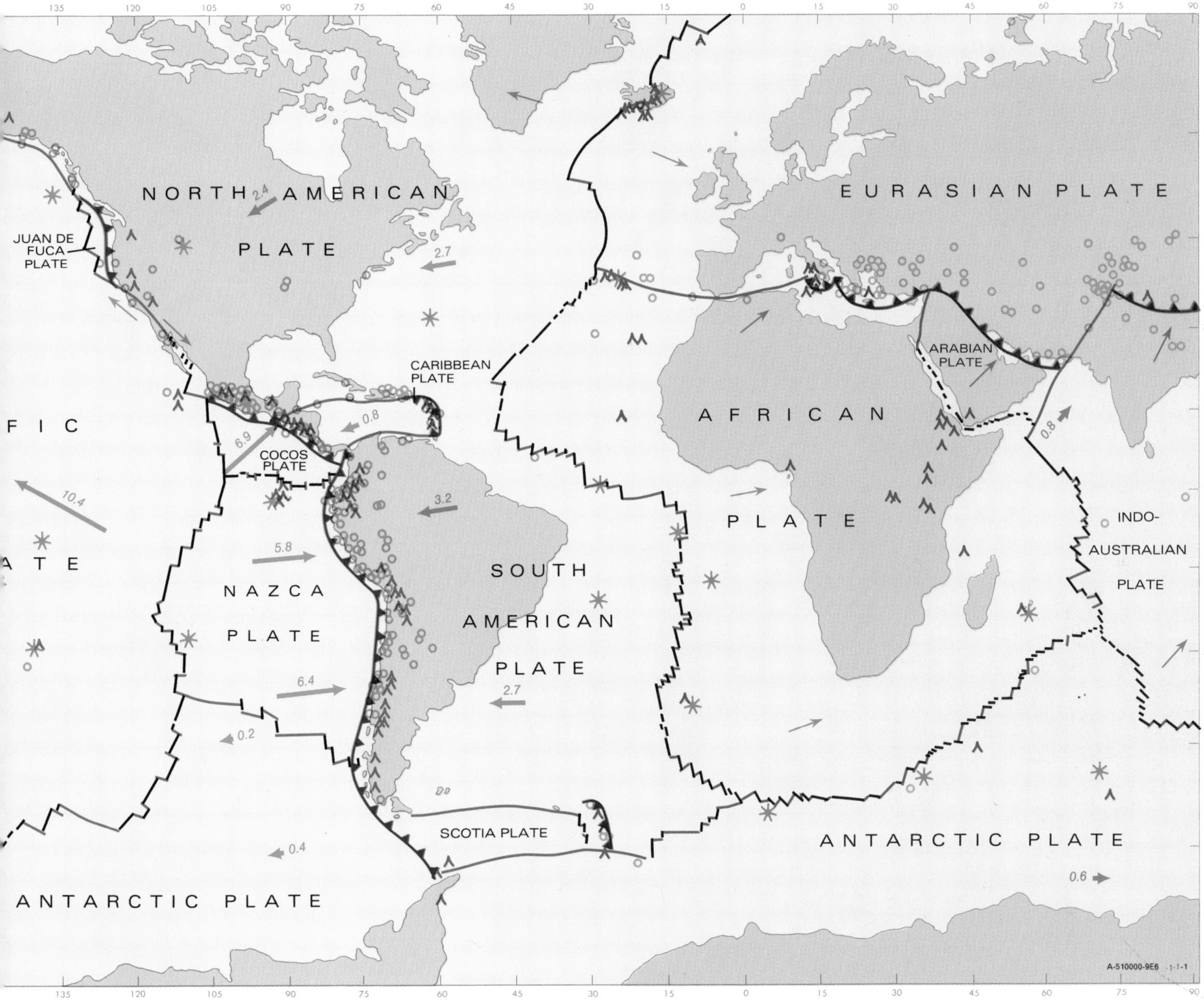

NORTH AMERICAN PLATE

JUAN DE FUCA PLATE

2.4

2.7

CARIBBEAN PLATE

COCOS PLATE

6.9

0.8

FIC

10.4

5.8

3.2

NAZCA PLATE

SOUTH AMERICAN PLATE

6.4

2.7

0.2

0.4

SCOTIA PLATE

ANTARCTIC PLATE

EURASIAN PLATE

ARABIAN PLATE

AFRICAN PLATE

0.8

INDO-AUSTRALIAN PLATE

ANTARCTIC PLATE

0.6

A-510000-9E6 -1-1-1

The plate tectonic theory describes the movement of the earth's surface and subsurface and explains why surface features are where they are.

Stated concisely, the theory presumes the lithosphere - the outside crust and uppermost mantle of the earth - is divided into about a dozen major rigid plates and several smaller platelets that move relative to one another. The position and names of the plates are shown on the map above.

The motor that drives the plates is found deep in the mantle. The theory states that because of temperature differences in the mantle, slow convection currents circulate there. Where two molten currents converge and move upward, they separate, causing the crustal plates to bulge and move apart in mid-ocean regions. Transverse fractures disrupt these broad regions. Lava wells up at these points to cause volcanic activity and to form ridges. The plates grow larger by accretion along these mid-ocean ridges, cause vast regions of the crust to move apart, and force the plates to collide with one another. As the plates do so, they are destroyed at subduction zones, where the plates are consumed downward, back into the earth's mantle, forming deep ocean trenches. The diagrams to the right illustrate the processes.

Most of the earth's volcanic and seismic activities occur where plates slide past each other at transform boundaries or collide along subduction zones. The friction and heat caused by the grinding motion of the subducted plates causes rock to liquify and rise to the surface as volcanoes and eventually form vast mountain ranges. Strong and deep earthquakes are common here.

Volcanoes and earthquakes also occur at random locations around the earth known as "hot spots". Hot rock from deep in the mantle rises to the surface creating some of the earth's tallest mountains. As the lithospheric plates move slowly over these stationary plumes of magma, island chains (such as the Hawaiian Islands) are formed.

The overall result of tectonic movement is that the crustal plates move slowly and inexorably as relatively rigid entities, carrying the continents along with them. The history of this continental drifting is illustrated in the four maps to the left. It began with a single landmass called the supercontinent of Pangaea and the ancestral sea, the Panthalassa Ocean. Pangaea first split into a northern landmass called Laurasia and a southern block called Gondwanaland and subsequently into the continents we map today. The map of the future will be significantly different as the continents continue to drift.

Subduction Zone

Ocean Ridge Zone

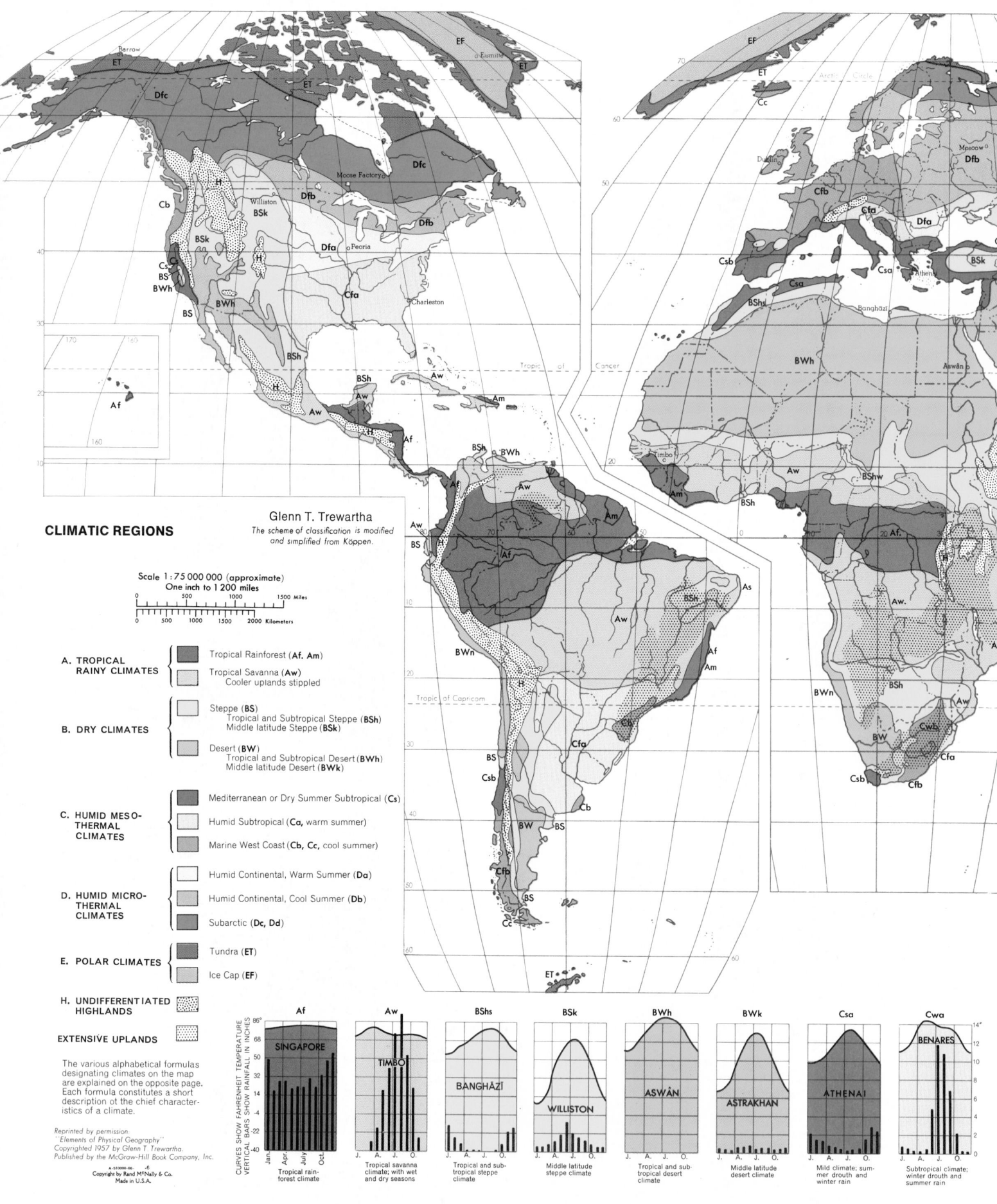

CLIMATIC REGIONS

Glenn T. Trewartha

*The scheme of classification is modified
and simplified from Köppen.*

Scale 1:75 000 000 (approximate)
One inch to 1 200 miles

0   500   1000   1500 Miles

0   500   1000   1500   2000 Kilometers

A. TROPICAL RAINY CLIMATES
Tropical Rainforest (**Af. Am**)
Tropical Savanna (**Aw**)
Cooler uplands stippled

B. DRY CLIMATES
Steppe (**BS**)
Tropical and Subtropical Steppe (**BSh**)
Middle latitude Steppe (**BSk**)
Desert (**BW**)
Tropical and Subtropical Desert (**BWh**)
Middle latitude Desert (**BWk**)

C. HUMID MESO-THERMAL CLIMATES
Mediterranean or Dry Summer Subtropical (**Cs**)
Humid Subtropical (**Ca**, warm summer)
Marine West Coast (**Cb, Cc**, cool summer)

D. HUMID MICRO-THERMAL CLIMATES
Humid Continental, Warm Summer (**Da**)
Humid Continental, Cool Summer (**Db**)
Subarctic (**Dc, Dd**)

E. POLAR CLIMATES
Tundra (**ET**)
Ice Cap (**EF**)

H. UNDIFFERENTIATED HIGHLANDS

EXTENSIVE UPLANDS

The various alphabetical formulas
designating climates on the map
are explained on the opposite page.
Each formula constitutes a short
description ot the chief characteristics of a climate.

Reprinted by permission
''Elements of Physical Geography''
Copyrighted 1957 by Glenn T. Trewartha.
Published by the McGraw-Hill Book Company, Inc.

CURVES SHOW FAHRENHEIT TEMPERATURE
VERTICAL BARS SHOW RAINFALL IN INCHES

Af	Aw	BShs	BSk	BWh	BWk	Csa	Cwa
SINGAPORE	TIMBO	BANGHĀZĪ	WILLISTON	ASWÂN	ASTRAKHAN	ATHENAI	BENARES
Tropical rain-forest climate	Tropical savanna climate; with wet and dry seasons	Tropical and sub-tropical steppe climate	Middle latitude steppe climate	Tropical and sub-tropical desert climate	Middle latitude desert climate	Mild climate; sum-mer drouth and winter rain	Subtropical climate; winter drouth and summer rain

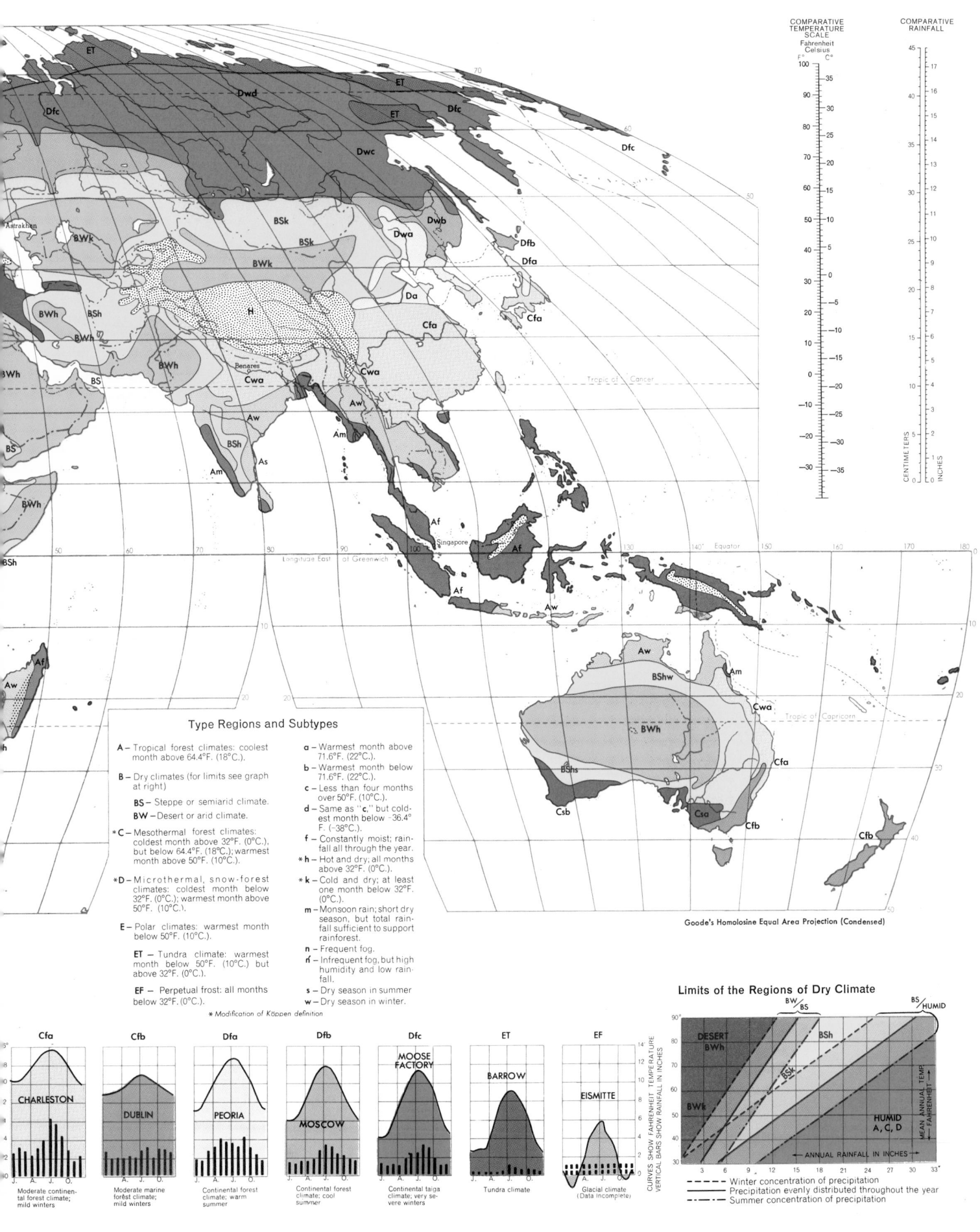

COMPARATIVE
TEMPERATURE
SCALE
Fahrenheit
Celsius

COMPARATIVE
RAINFALL

Goode's Homolosine Equal Area Projection (Condensed)

Type Regions and Subtypes

A – Tropical forest climates: coolest month above 64.4°F. (18°C.).

B – Dry climates (for limits see graph at right)

BS – Steppe or semiarid climate.

BW – Desert or arid climate.

*__**C**__ – Mesothermal forest climates: coldest month above 32°F. (0°C.), but below 64.4°F. (18°C.); warmest month above 50°F. (10°C.).

*__**D**__ – Microthermal, snow-forest climates: coldest month below 32°F. (0°C.); warmest month above 50°F. (10°C.).

E – Polar climates: warmest month below 50°F. (10°C.).

ET – Tundra climate: warmest month below 50°F. (10°C.) but above 32°F. (0°C.).

EF – Perpetual frost: all months below 32°F. (0°C.).

a – Warmest month above 71.6°F. (22°C.).

b – Warmest month below 71.6°F. (22°C.).

c – Less than four months over 50°F. (10°C.).

d – Same as "c," but coldest month below -36.4° F. (-38°C.).

f – Constantly moist; rainfall all through the year.

*__**h**__ – Hot and dry; all months above 32°F. (0°C.).

*__**k**__ – Cold and dry; at least one month below 32°F. (0°C.).

m – Monsoon rain; short dry season, but total rainfall sufficient to support rainforest.

n – Frequent fog.

n′ – Infrequent fog, but high humidity and low rainfall.

s – Dry season in summer.

w – Dry season in winter.

*Modification of Köppen definition

Limits of the Regions of Dry Climate

DESERT
BWh

BWk

BShk

BSk

BSh

HUMID
A, C, D

MEAN ANNUAL TEMPERATURE FAHRENHEIT

ANNUAL RAINFALL IN INCHES

BW/BS

BS/HUMID

- - - - Winter concentration of precipitation
———— Precipitation evenly distributed throughout the year
—·—·— Summer concentration of precipitation

Cfa

CHARLESTON

Moderate continental forest climate; mild winters

Cfb

DUBLIN

Moderate marine forest climate; mild winters

Dfa

PEORIA

Continental forest climate; warm summer

Dfb

MOSCOW

Continental forest climate; cool summer

Dfc

MOOSE FACTORY

Continental taiga climate; very severe winters

ET

BARROW

Tundra climate

EF

EISMITTE

Glacial climate (Data incomplete)

CURVES SHOW FAHRENHEIT TEMPERATURE
VERTICAL BARS SHOW RAINFALL IN INCHES

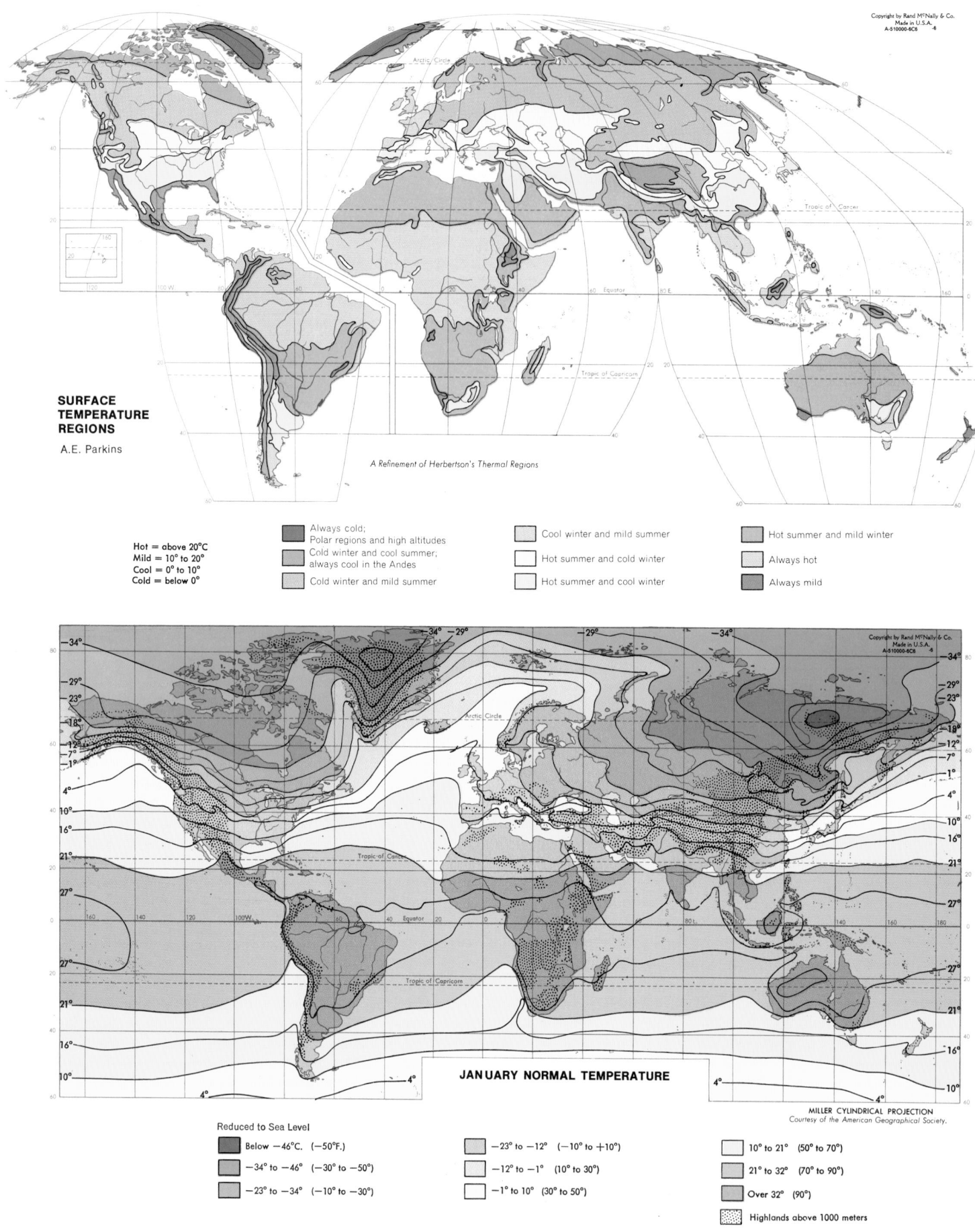

SURFACE
TEMPERATURE
REGIONS

A.E. Parkins

A Refinement of Herbertson's Thermal Regions

Hot = above 20°C
Mild = 10° to 20°
Cool = 0° to 10°
Cold = below 0°

Always cold;
Polar regions and high altitudes

Cold winter and cool summer;
always cool in the Andes

Cold winter and mild summer

Cool winter and mild summer

Hot summer and cold winter

Hot summer and cool winter

Hot summer and mild winter

Always hot

Always mild

JANUARY NORMAL TEMPERATURE

MILLER CYLINDRICAL PROJECTION
Courtesy of the American Geographical Society.

Reduced to Sea Level

Below −46°C. (−50°F.)

−34° to −46° (−30° to −50°)

−23° to −34° (−10° to −30°)

−23° to −12° (−10° to +10°)

−12° to −1° (10° to 30°)

−1° to 10° (30° to 50°)

10° to 21° (50° to 70°)

21° to 32° (70° to 90°)

Over 32° (90°)

Highlands above 1000 meters

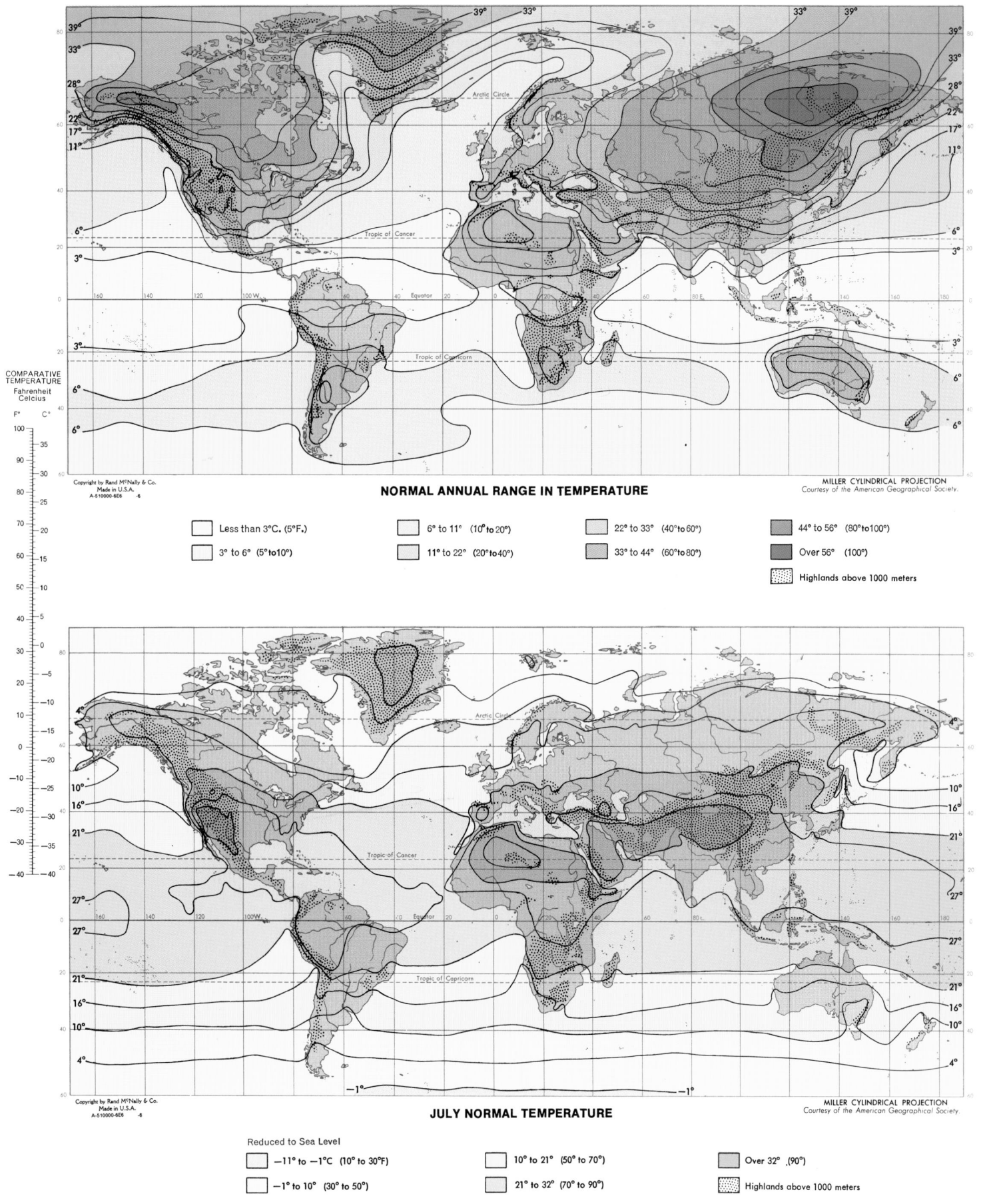

NORMAL ANNUAL RANGE IN TEMPERATURE

MILLER CYLINDRICAL PROJECTION
Courtesy of the American Geographical Society.

Copyright by Rand McNally & Co.
Made in U.S.A.
A-510000-6E6   -6

| | Less than 3°C. (5°F.) | | 6° to 11° (10° to 20°) | | 22° to 33° (40° to 60°) | | 44° to 56° (80° to 100°) |
| | 3° to 6° (5° to 10°) | | 11° to 22° (20° to 40°) | | 33° to 44° (60° to 80°) | | Over 56° (100°) |

Highlands above 1000 meters

COMPARATIVE
TEMPERATURE
Fahrenheit
Celcius

JULY NORMAL TEMPERATURE

MILLER CYLINDRICAL PROJECTION
Courtesy of the American Geographical Society.

Copyright by Rand McNally & Co.
Made in U.S.A.
A-510000-6E6   -6

Reduced to Sea Level

| | −11° to −1°C (10° to 30°F) | | 10° to 21° (50° to 70°) | | Over 32° (90°) |
| | −1° to 10° (30° to 50°) | | 21° to 32° (70° to 90°) | | Highlands above 1000 meters |

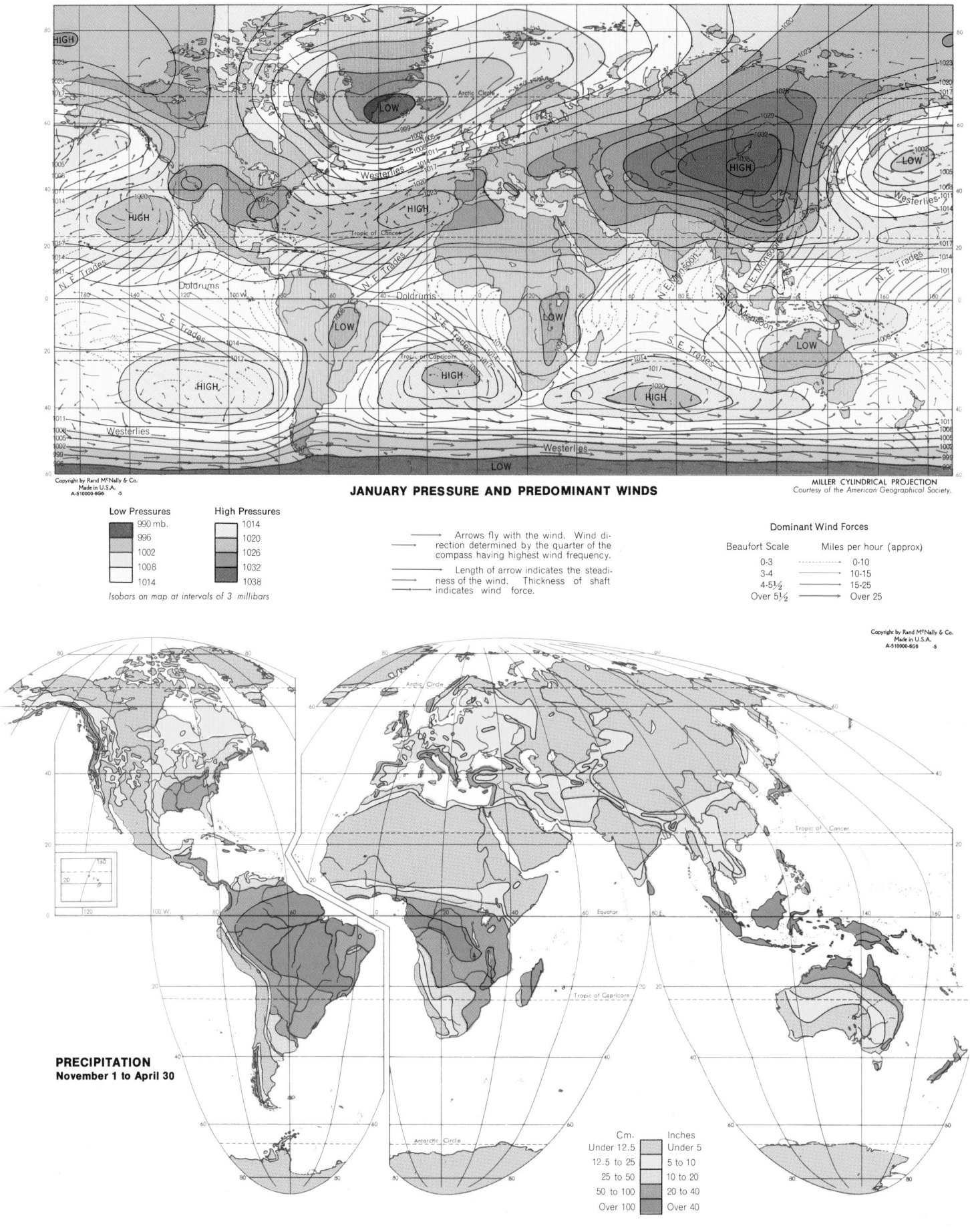

JANUARY PRESSURE AND PREDOMINANT WINDS

MILLER CYLINDRICAL PROJECTION
Courtesy of the American Geographical Society.

Copyright by Rand McNally & Co.
Made in U.S.A.
A-510000-6G6   -5

Low Pressures
990 mb.
996
1002
1008
1014

High Pressures
1014
1020
1026
1032
1038

Isobars on map at intervals of 3 millibars

Arrows fly with the wind. Wind direction determined by the quarter of the compass having highest wind frequency.

Length of arrow indicates the steadiness of the wind. Thickness of shaft indicates wind force.

Dominant Wind Forces

Beaufort Scale	Miles per hour (approx)
0-3	0-10
3-4	10-15
4-5½	15-25
Over 5½	Over 25

Copyright by Rand McNally & Co.
Made in U.S.A.
A-510000-6G6   -5

PRECIPITATION
November 1 to April 30

Cm.	Inches
Under 12.5	Under 5
12.5 to 25	5 to 10
25 to 50	10 to 20
50 to 100	20 to 40
Over 100	Over 40

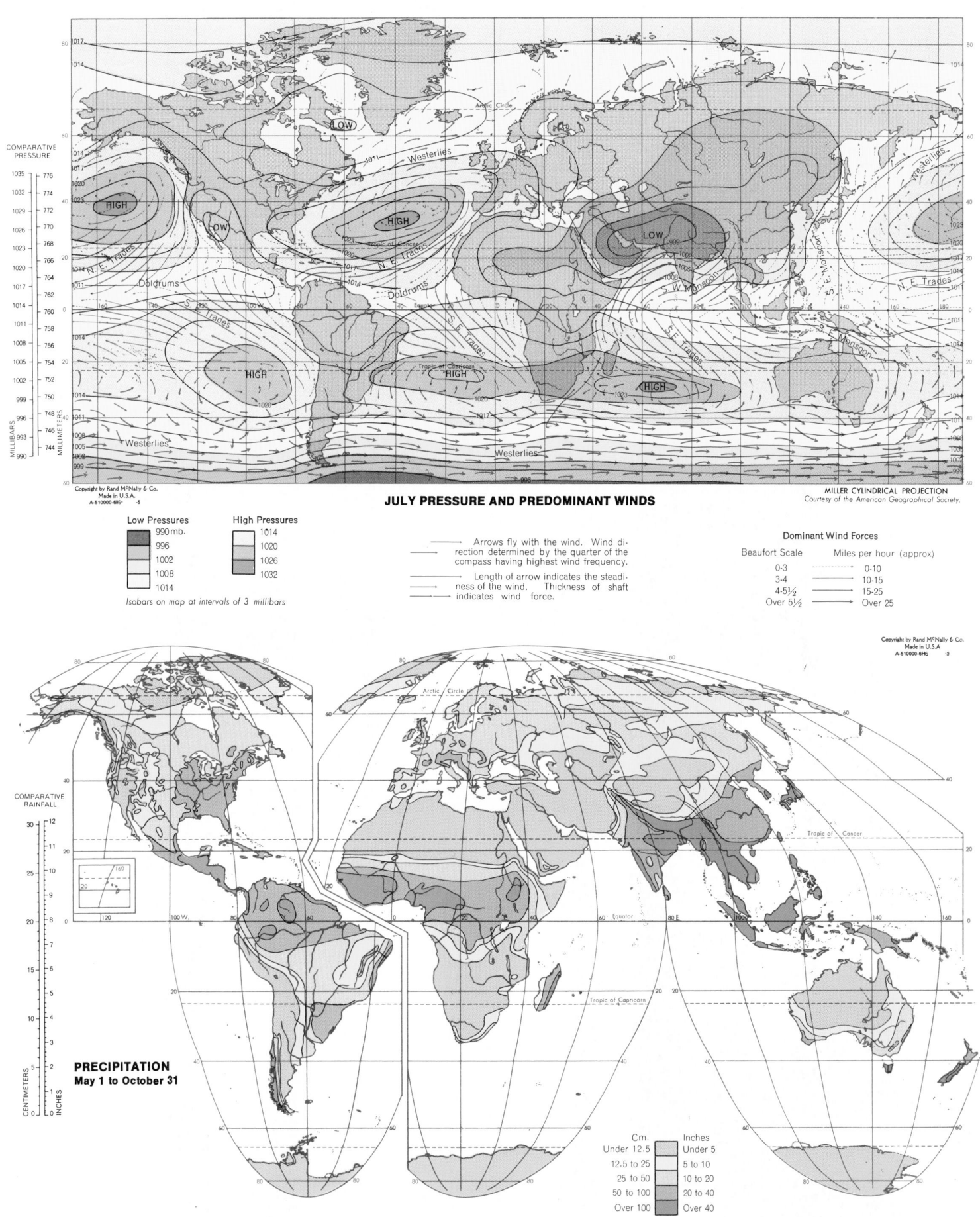

JULY PRESSURE AND PREDOMINANT WINDS

MILLER CYLINDRICAL PROJECTION
Courtesy of the American Geographical Society.

Copyright by Rand McNally & Co.
Made in U.S.A.
A-510000-6HI-   -5

COMPARATIVE PRESSURE

Low Pressures
990 mb.
996
1002
1008
1014

High Pressures
1014
1020
1026
1032

Isobars on map at intervals of 3 millibars

Arrows fly with the wind. Wind direction determined by the quarter of the compass having highest wind frequency.

Length of arrow indicates the steadiness of the wind. Thickness of shaft indicates wind force.

Dominant Wind Forces

Beaufort Scale	Miles per hour (approx)
0-3	0-10
3-4	10-15
4-5½	15-25
Over 5½	Over 25

COMPARATIVE RAINFALL

PRECIPITATION
May 1 to October 31

Copyright by Rand McNally & Co.
Made in U.S.A
A-510000-6H6   -5

Cm.	Inches
Under 12.5	Under 5
12.5 to 25	5 to 10
25 to 50	10 to 20
50 to 100	20 to 40
Over 100	Over 40

ANNUAL PRECIPITATION AND OCEAN CURRENTS

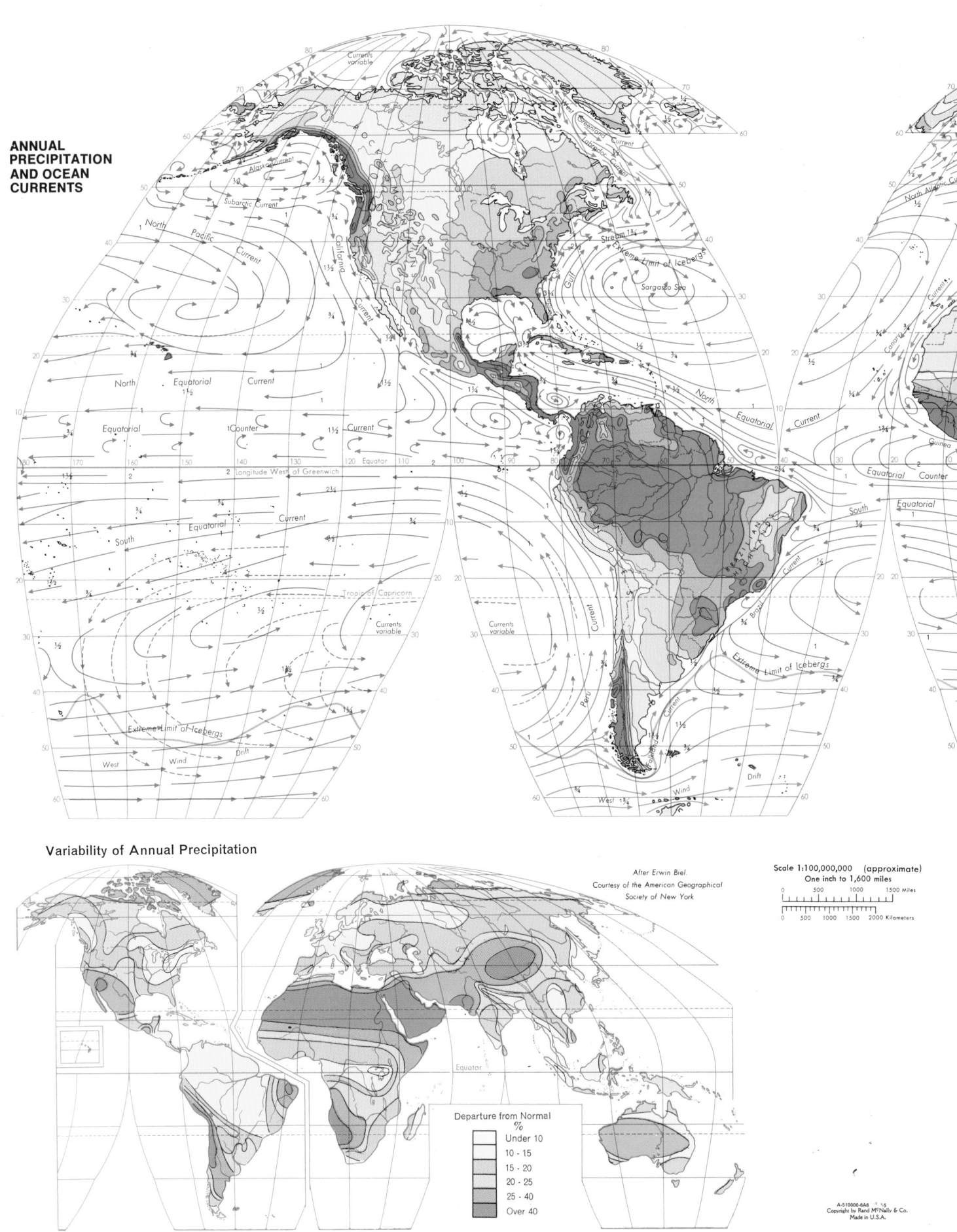

Currents variable

Greenland Current

Labrador Current

Alaska Current

Subarctic Current

North Pacific Current

California Current

Gulf Stream

Extreme Limit of Icebergs

Sargasso Sea

North Atlantic Current

Canaries Current

North Equatorial Current

North Equatorial Current

Equatorial Counter Current

Equatorial Counter Current

Guinea Current

Longitude West of Greenwich

South Equatorial Current

Equatorial Current

Tropic of Capricorn

South Equatorial Current

Brazil Current

Currents variable

Currents variable

Peru Current

Falkland Current

Extreme Limit of Icebergs

Extreme Limit of Icebergs

West Wind Drift

West Wind Drift

Variability of Annual Precipitation

After Erwin Biel.
Courtesy of the American Geographical
Society of New York

Scale 1:100,000,000 (approximate)
One inch to 1,600 miles

0   500   1000   1500 Miles

0   500   1000   1500   2000 Kilometers

Equator

Departure from Normal %	
	Under 10
	10 - 15
	15 - 20
	20 - 25
	25 - 40
	Over 40

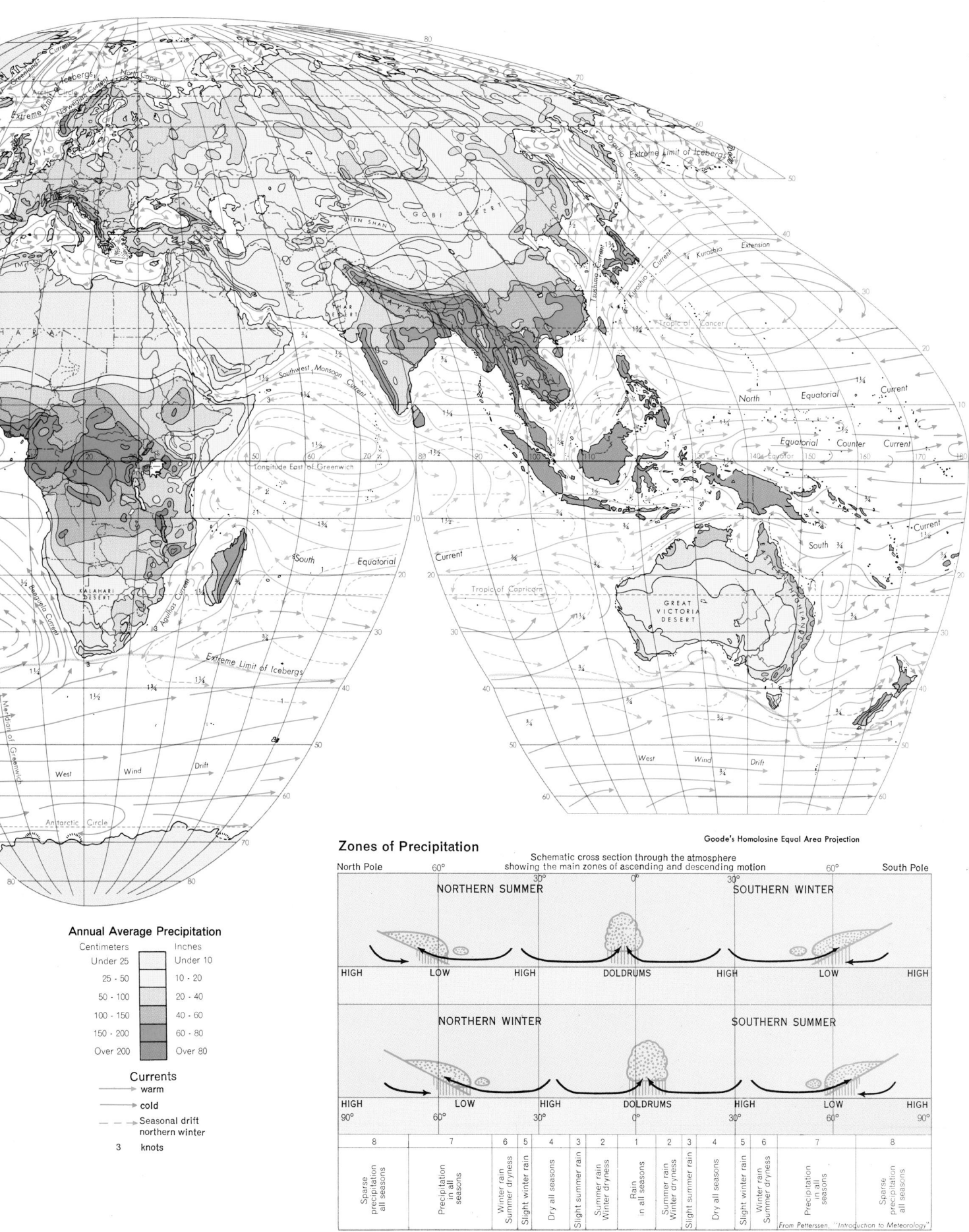

Goode's Homolosine Equal Area Projection

Zones of Precipitation

Schematic cross section through the atmosphere
showing the main zones of ascending and descending motion

Annual Average Precipitation

Centimeters	Inches
Under 25	Under 10
25 - 50	10 - 20
50 - 100	20 - 40
100 - 150	40 - 60
150 - 200	60 - 80
Over 200	Over 80

Currents

warm
cold
Seasonal drift
northern winter

3   knots

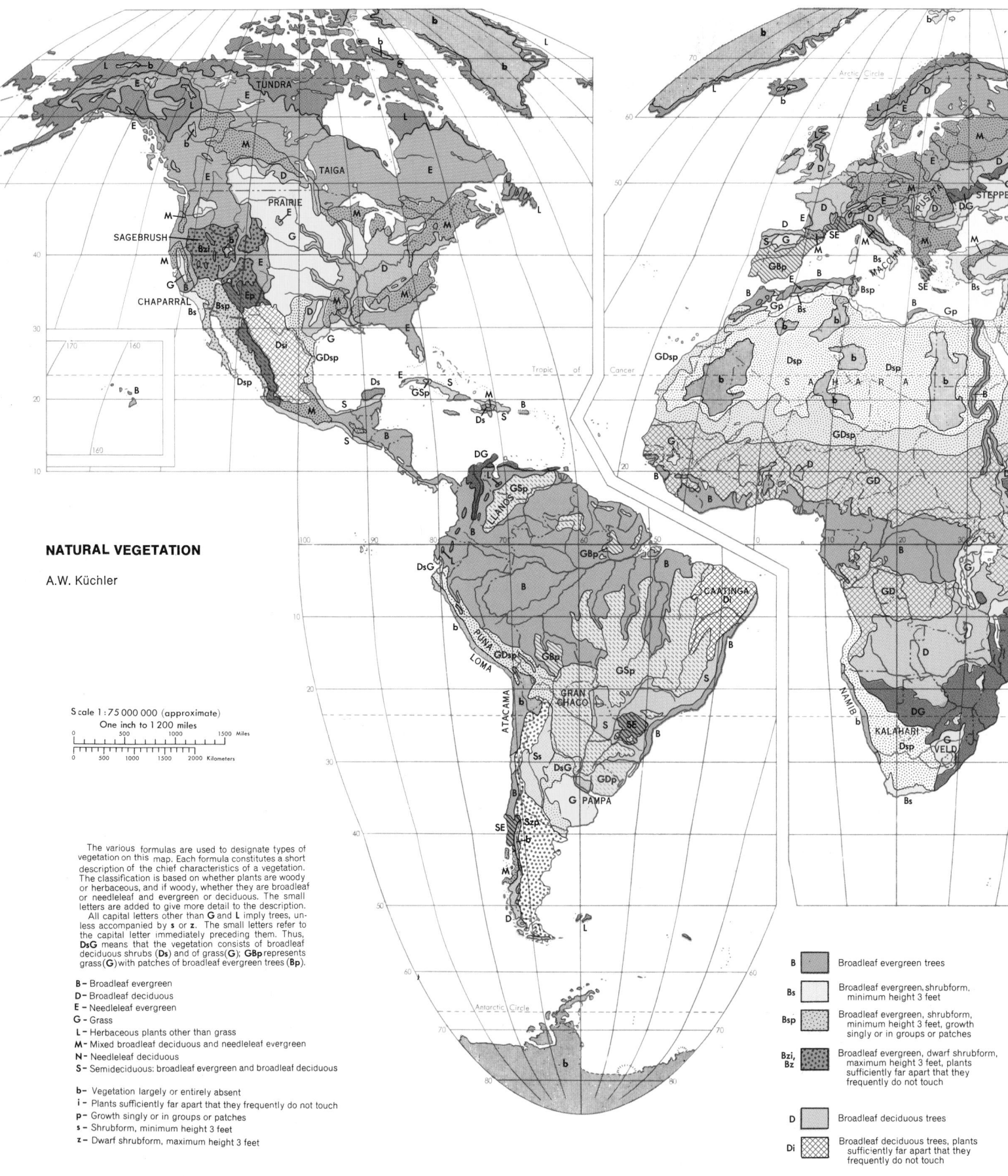

18

NATURAL VEGETATION

A.W. Küchler

Scale 1:75 000 000 (approximate)
One inch to 1 200 miles

The various formulas are used to designate types of
vegetation on this map. Each formula constitutes a short
description of the chief characteristics of a vegetation.
The classification is based on whether plants are woody
or herbaceous, and if woody, whether they are broadleaf
or needleleaf and evergreen or deciduous. The small
letters are added to give more detail to the description.
All capital letters other than **G** and **L** imply trees, un-
less accompanied by **s** or **z**. The small letters refer to
the capital letter immediately preceding them. Thus,
DsG means that the vegetation consists of broadleaf
deciduous shrubs (**Ds**) and of grass (**G**); **GBp** represents
grass (**G**) with patches of broadleaf evergreen trees (**Bp**).

B – Broadleaf evergreen
D – Broadleaf deciduous
E – Needleleaf evergreen
G – Grass
L – Herbaceous plants other than grass
M – Mixed broadleaf deciduous and needleleaf evergreen
N – Needleleaf deciduous
S – Semideciduous: broadleaf evergreen and broadleaf deciduous

b – Vegetation largely or entirely absent
i – Plants sufficiently far apart that they frequently do not touch
p – Growth singly or in groups or patches
s – Shrubform, minimum height 3 feet
z – Dwarf shrubform, maximum height 3 feet

B	Broadleaf evergreen trees
Bs	Broadleaf evergreen, shrubform, minimum height 3 feet
Bsp	Broadleaf evergreen, shrubform, minimum height 3 feet, growth singly or in groups or patches
Bzi, Bz	Broadleaf evergreen, dwarf shrubform, maximum height 3 feet, plants sufficiently far apart that they frequently do not touch
D	Broadleaf deciduous trees
Di	Broadleaf deciduous trees, plants sufficiently far apart that they frequently do not touch

Goode's Homolosine
Equal Area Projection
(Condensed)

Ds	Broadleaf deciduous, shrubform, minimum height 3 feet	
ssi	Broadleaf deciduous, shrubform, minimum height 3 feet, plants sufficiently far apart that they frequently do not touch	
sp	Broadleaf deciduous, shrubform, minimum height 3 feet, growth singly or in groups or patches	
Kp	Broadleaf deciduous, dwarf shrubform, maximum height 3 feet, growth singly or in groups or patches	
G	Broadleaf deciduous, shrubform, minimum height 3 feet Grass and other herbaceous plants	
G	Broadleaf deciduous trees Grass and other herbaceous plants	
Bs	Broadleaf deciduous trees Broadleaf evergreen, shrubform, minimum height 3 feet	

E	Needleleaf evergreen trees	
Ep	Needleleaf evergreen trees, growth singly or in groups or patches	
G	Grass and other herbaceous plants	
Gp	Grass and other herbaceous plants, growth singly or in groups or patches	
GBp	Grass and other herbaceous plants Broadleaf evergreen trees, growth singly or in groups or patches	
GD	Grass and other herbaceous plants Broadleaf deciduous trees	
GDp	Grass and other herbaceous plants Broadleaf deciduous trees, growth singly or in groups or patches	

GDsp	Grass and other herbaceous plants Broadleaf deciduous, shrubform, minimum height 3 feet, growth singly or in groups or patches	
GSp	Grass and other herbaceous plants Semideciduous: broadleaf evergreen and broadleaf deciduous trees, growth singly or in groups or patches	
L	Herbaceous plants other than grass	
M	Mixed: broadleaf deciduous and needleleaf evergreen trees	
N	Needleleaf deciduous trees	
ND	Needleleaf deciduous trees Broadleaf deciduous trees	

S	Semideciduous: broadleaf evergreen and broadleaf deciduous trees	
Ss	Semideciduous: broadleaf evergreen and broadleaf deciduous, shrubform, minimum height 3 feet	
SsG	Semideciduous: broadleaf evergreen and broadleaf deciduous, shrubform, minimum height 3 feet Grass and other herbaceous plants	
Szp	Semideciduous: broadleaf evergreen and broadleaf deciduous, dwarf shrubform, maximum height 3 feet, growth singly or in groups or patches	
SE	Semideciduous: broadleaf evergreen and broadleaf deciduous trees Needleleaf evergreen trees	
b	Vegetation largely or entirely absent	

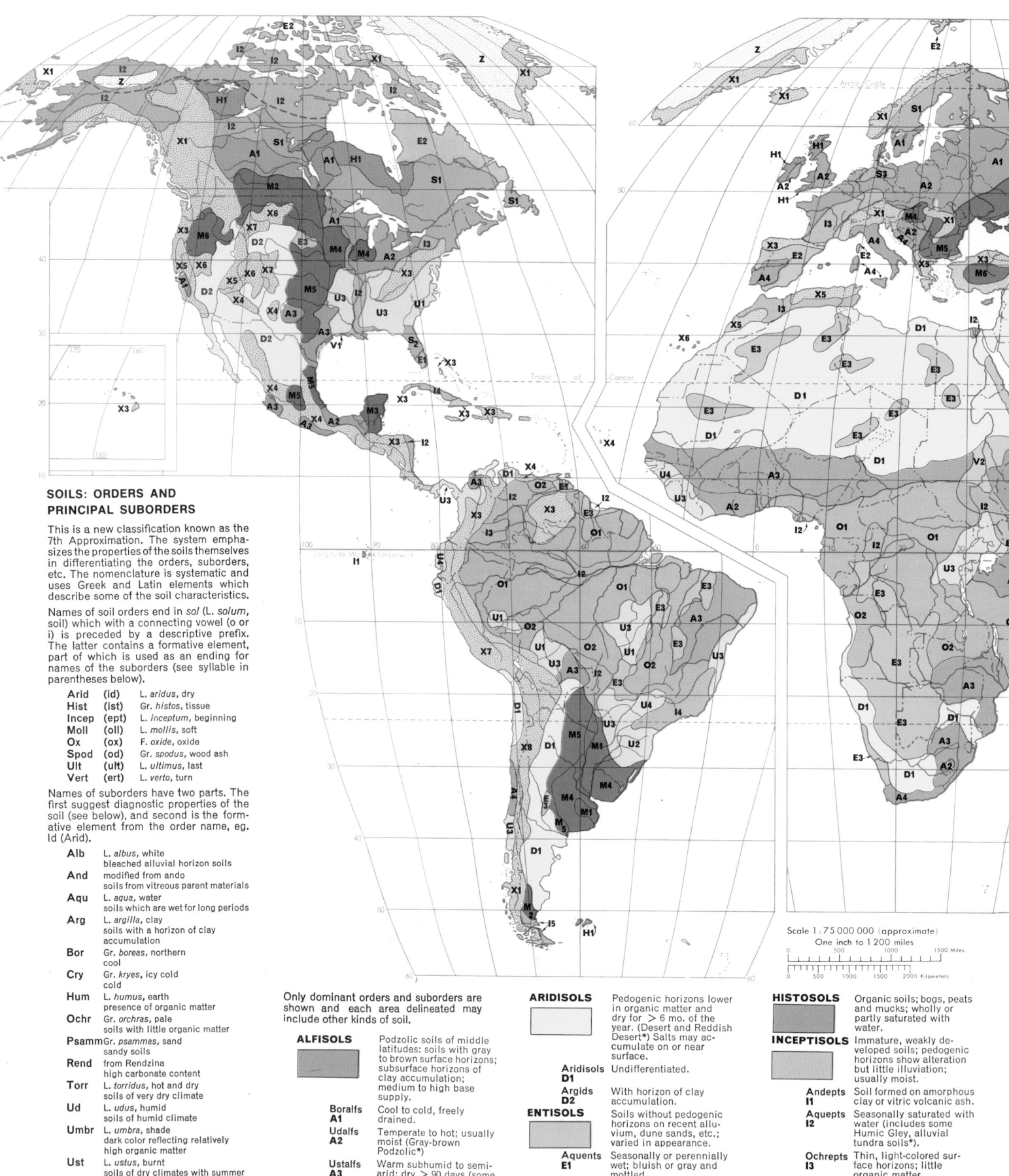

20

SOILS: ORDERS AND PRINCIPAL SUBORDERS

This is a new classification known as the 7th Approximation. The system emphasizes the properties of the soils themselves in differentiating the orders, suborders, etc. The nomenclature is systematic and uses Greek and Latin elements which describe some of the soil characteristics.

Names of soil orders end in *sol* (L. *solum*, soil) which with a connecting vowel (o or i) is preceded by a descriptive prefix. The latter contains a formative element, part of which is used as an ending for names of the suborders (see syllable in parentheses below).

Arid	(id)	L. *aridus*, dry
Hist	(ist)	Gr. *histos*, tissue
Incep	(ept)	L. *inceptum*, beginning
Moll	(oll)	L. *mollis*, soft
Ox	(ox)	F. *oxide*, oxide
Spod	(od)	Gr. *spodus*, wood ash
Ult	(ult)	L. *ultimus*, last
Vert	(ert)	L. *verto*, turn

Names of suborders have two parts. The first suggest diagnostic properties of the soil (see below), and second is the formative element from the order name, eg. Id (Arid).

Alb	L. *albus*, white bleached alluvial horizon soils
And	modified from ando soils from vitreous parent materials
Aqu	L. *aqua*, water soils which are wet for long periods
Arg	L. *argilla*, clay soils with a horizon of clay accumulation
Bor	Gr. *boreas*, northern cool
Cry	Gr. *kryes*, icy cold cold
Hum	L. *humus*, earth presence of organic matter
Ochr	Gr. *orchras*, pale soils with little organic matter
Psamm	Gr. *psammas*, sand sandy soils
Rend	from Rendzina high carbonate content
Torr	L. *torridus*, hot and dry soils of very dry climate
Ud	L. *udus*, humid soils of humid climate
Umbr	L. *umbra*, shade dark color reflecting relatively high organic matter
Ust	L. *ustus*, burnt soils of dry climates with summer rains
Xer	Gr. *xeros*, dry soils of dry climates with winter rains

Only dominant orders and suborders are shown and each area delineated may include other kinds of soil.

ALFISOLS

Podzolic soils of middle latitudes: soils with gray to brown surface horizons; subsurface horizons of clay accumulation; medium to high base supply.

Boralfs A1	Cool to cold, freely drained.
Udalfs A2	Temperate to hot; usually moist (Gray-brown Podzolic*)
Ustalfs A3	Warm subhumid to semi-arid; dry > 90 days (some Reddish Chestnut and Red & Yellow Podzolic soils*)
Xeralfs A4	Warm, dry in summer; moist in winter.

ARIDISOLS

Pedogenic horizons lower in organic matter and dry for > 6 mo. of the year. (Desert and Reddish Desert*) Salts may accumulate on or near surface.

Aridisols D1	Undifferentiated.
Argids D2	With horizon of clay accumulation.

ENTISOLS

Soils without pedogenic horizons on recent alluvium, dune sands, etc.; varied in appearance.

Aquents E1	Seasonally or perennially wet; bluish or gray and mottled.
Orthents E2	Shallow; or recent erosional surfaces (Lithosols*). A few on recent loams.
Psamments E3	Sandy soils on shifting and stabilized sands.

HISTOSOLS

Organic soils; bogs, peats and mucks; wholly or partly saturated with water.

INCEPTISOLS

Immature, weakly developed soils; pedogenic horizons show alteration but little illuviation; usually moist.

Andepts I1	Soil formed on amorphous clay or vitric volcanic ash.
Aquepts I2	Seasonally saturated with water (includes some Humic Gley, alluvial tundra soils*).
Ochrepts I3	Thin, light-colored surface horizons; little organic matter.
Tropepts I4	Continuously warm to hot; brownish to reddish.
Umbrepts I5	Dark colored surface horizons; rich in organic matter; medium to low base supply.

Scale 1:75 000 000 (approximate)
One inch to 1 200 miles

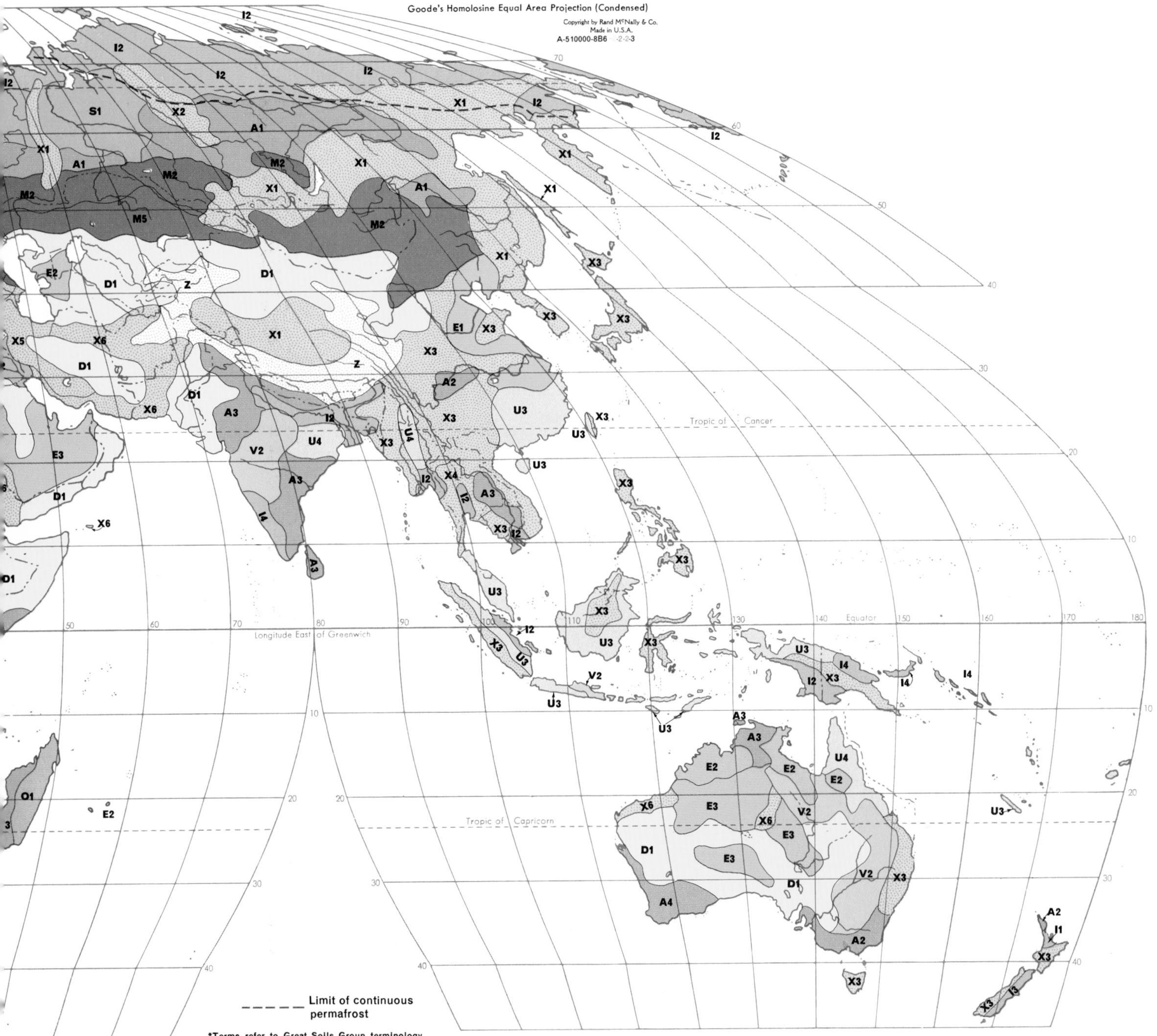

Goode's Homolosine Equal Area Projection (Condensed)

Copyright by Rand McNally & Co.
Made in U.S.A.
A-510000-8B6   -2-2-3

— — — — Limit of continuous
permafrost

*Terms refer to Great Soils Group terminology.

Longitude East of Greenwich

Tropic of Cancer

Tropic of Capricorn

Equator

MOLLISOLS	Soils of the steppe (incl. Chernozem and Chestnut soils*). Thick, black organic rich surface horizons and high base supply.	**OXISOLS**	Deeply weathered tropical and subtropical soils (Laterites*); rich in sesquioxides of iron and aluminum; low in nutrients; limited productivity without fertilizer.	**ULTISOLS**

MOLLISOLS — Soils of the steppe (incl. Chernozem and Chestnut soils*). Thick, black organic rich surface horizons and high base supply.

Albolls M1 — Seasonally saturated with water; light gray subsurface horizon.

Borolls M2 — Cool or cold (incl. some Chernozem, Chestnut and Brown soils*).

Rendolls M3 — Formed on highly calcareous parent materials (Rendzina*).

Udolls M4 — Temperate to warm; usually moist (Prairie soils*).

Ustolls M5 — Temperate to hot; dry for > 90 days (incl. some Chestnut and Brown soils*).

Xerolls M6 — Cool to warm; dry in summer; moist in winter.

OXISOLS — Deeply weathered tropical and subtropical soils (Laterites*); rich in sesquioxides of iron and aluminum; low in nutrients; limited productivity without fertilizer.

Orthox O1 — Hot and nearly always moist.

Ustox O2 — Warm or hot; dry for long periods but moist > 90 consecutive days.

SPODOSOLS — Soils with a subsurface accumulation of amorphous materials overlaid by a light colored, leached sandy horizon.

Spodosols S1 — Undifferentiated (mostly high latitudes).

Aquods S2 — Seasonally saturated with water; sandy parent materials.

Humods S3 — Considerable accumulations of organic matter in subsurface horizon.

Orthods S4 — With subsurface accumulations of iron, aluminum and organic matter (Podzols*).

ULTISOLS — Soils with some subsurface clay accumulation; low base supply; usually moist and low inorganic matter; usually moist and low in organic matter; can be productive with fertilization.

Aquults U1 — Seasonally saturated with water; subsurface gray or mottled horizon.

Humults U2 — High in organic matter; dark colored; moist, warm to temperate all year.

Udults U3 — Low in organic matter; moist, temperate to hot (Red-Yellow Podzolic; some Reddish-Brown Lateritic soils*).

Ustults U4 — Warm to hot; dry > 90 days.

VERTISOLS — Soils with high content of swelling clays; deep, wide cracks in dry periods dark colored.

Uderts V1 — Usually moist; cracks open < 90 days.

Usterts V2 — Cracks open > 90 days; difficult to till (Black tropical soils*).

MOUNTAIN SOILS — Soils with various moisture and temperature regimes; steep slopes and variable relief and elevation; soils vary greatly within short distance.

X1 Cryic great groups of Entisols, Inceptisols and Spodosols.

X2 Boralfs and Cryic great groups of Entisols and Inceptisols.

X3 Udic great groups of Alfisols, Entisols and Ultisols; Inceptisols.

X4 Ustic great groups of Alfisols, Entisols, Inceptisols, Mollisols and Ultisols.

X5 Xeric great groups of Alfisols, Entisols, Inceptisols, Mollisols and Ultisols.

X6 Torric great groups of Entisols; Aridisols.

X7 Ustic and cryic great groups of Alfisols, Entisols; Inceptisols and Mollisols; ustic great groups of Ultisols; cryic great groups of Spodosols.

X8 Aridisols; torric and cryic great groups of Entisols, and cryic great groups of Spodosols and Inceptisols.

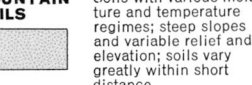

z Areas with little or no soil; icefields, and rugged mountain.

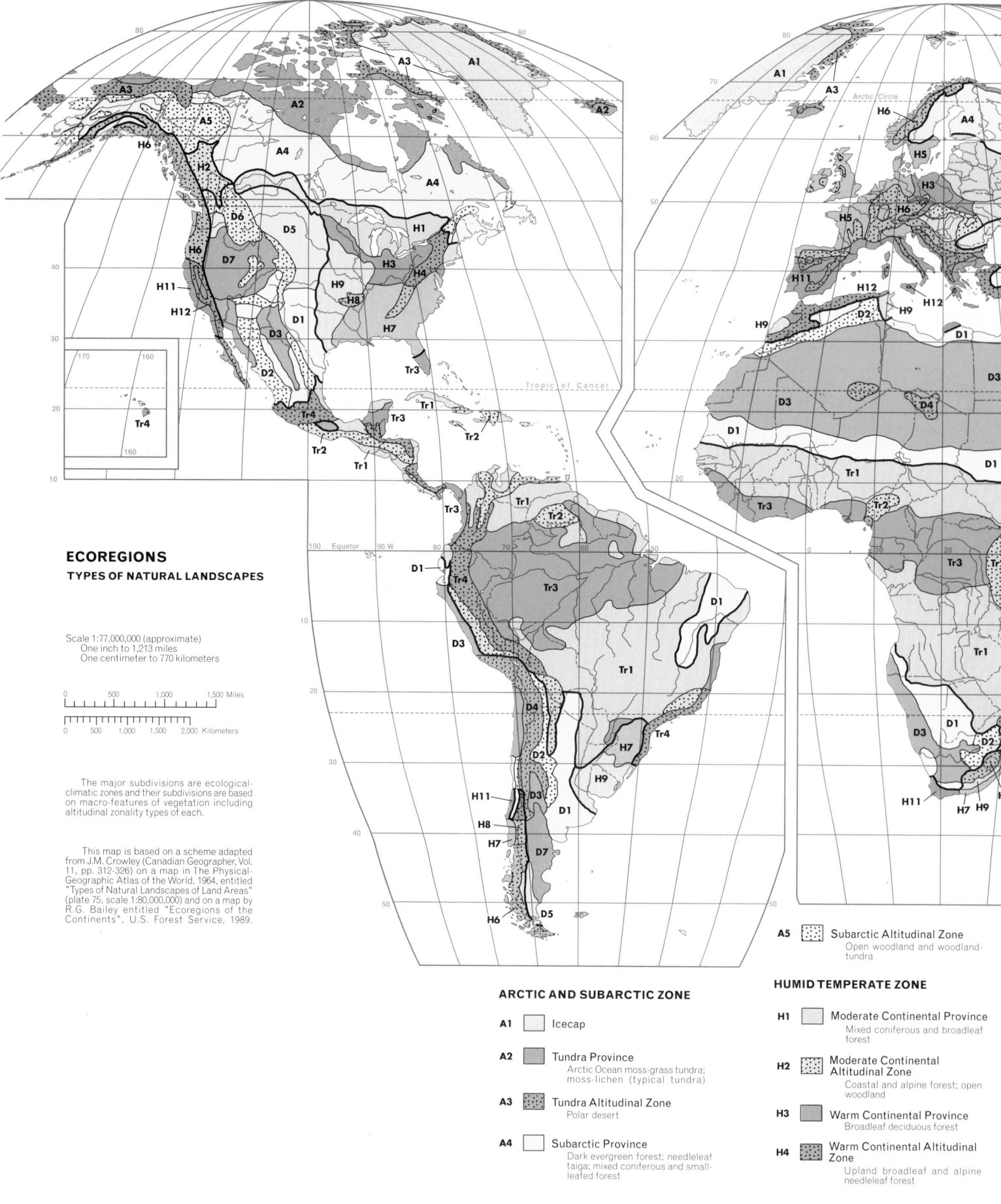

ECOREGIONS

TYPES OF NATURAL LANDSCAPES

Scale 1:77,000,000 (approximate)
One inch to 1,213 miles
One centimeter to 770 kilometers

0   500   1,000   1,500 Miles

0   500   1,000   1,500   2,000 Kilometers

The major subdivisions are ecological-
climatic zones and their subdivisions are based
on macro-features of vegetation including
altitudinal zonality types of each.

This map is based on a scheme adapted
from J.M. Crowley (Canadian Geographer, Vol.
11, pp. 312-326) on a map in The Physical-
Geographic Atlas of the World, 1964, entitled
"Types of Natural Landscapes of Land Areas"
(plate 75, scale 1:80,000,000) and on a map by
R.G. Bailey entitled "Ecoregions of the
Continents", U.S. Forest Service, 1989.

A5 ⬚ Subarctic Altitudinal Zone
Open woodland and woodland-
tundra

ARCTIC AND SUBARCTIC ZONE

A1 ☐ Icecap

A2 ▨ Tundra Province
Arctic Ocean moss-grass tundra;
moss-lichen (typical tundra)

A3 ⬚ Tundra Altitudinal Zone
Polar desert

A4 ☐ Subarctic Province
Dark evergreen forest; needleleaf
taiga; mixed coniferous and small-
leafed forest

HUMID TEMPERATE ZONE

H1 ☐ Moderate Continental Province
Mixed coniferous and broadleaf
forest

H2 ⬚ Moderate Continental
Altitudinal Zone
Coastal and alpine forest; open
woodland

H3 ▨ Warm Continental Province
Broadleaf deciduous forest

H4 ▨ Warm Continental Altitudinal
Zone
Upland broadleaf and alpine
needleleaf forest

H5 Marine Province
Lowland, west-coastal humid forest

H6 Marine Altitudinal Zone
Humid coastal and alpine coniferous forest

H7 Humid Subtropical Province
Broadleaf evergreen and broadleaf deciduous forest

H8 Humid Subtropical Altitudinal Zone
Upland, subtropical broadleaf forest

H9 Prairie Province

H10 Prairie Altitudinal Zone
Upland mixed prairie and woodland

H11 Mediterranean Province
Sclerophyll woodland, shrub, and steppe

H12 Mediterranean Altitudinal Zone
Upland shrub and steppe

DRY AND DESERT ZONE

D1 Tropical/Subtropical Steppe Province
Dry steppe, desert shrub, semi-desert savanna

D2 Tropical/Subtropical Steppe Altitudinal Zone
Upland steppe and desert shrub

D3 Tropical/Subtropical Desert Province
Hot, lowland desert at subtropical and coastal locations

D4 Tropical/Subtropical Desert Altitudinal Zone
Desert shrub

D5 Temperate Steppe Province
Medium to short steppe grassland

D6 Temperate Steppe Altitudinal Zone
Alpine meadow and coniferous woodland

D7 Temperate Desert Province
Midlatitude rainshadow desert

D8 Temperate Desert Altitudinal Zone
Extreme continental desert-steppe

HUMID TROPICAL ZONE

Tr1 Savanna Province
Seasonally dry forest, open woodland, tall grass

Tr2 Savanna Altitudinal Zone
Open woodland-steppe

Tr3 Rainforest Province
Constantly humid, broadleaf evergreen forest

Tr4 Rainforest Altitudinal Zone
Broadleaf evergreen and subtropical deciduous forest

24

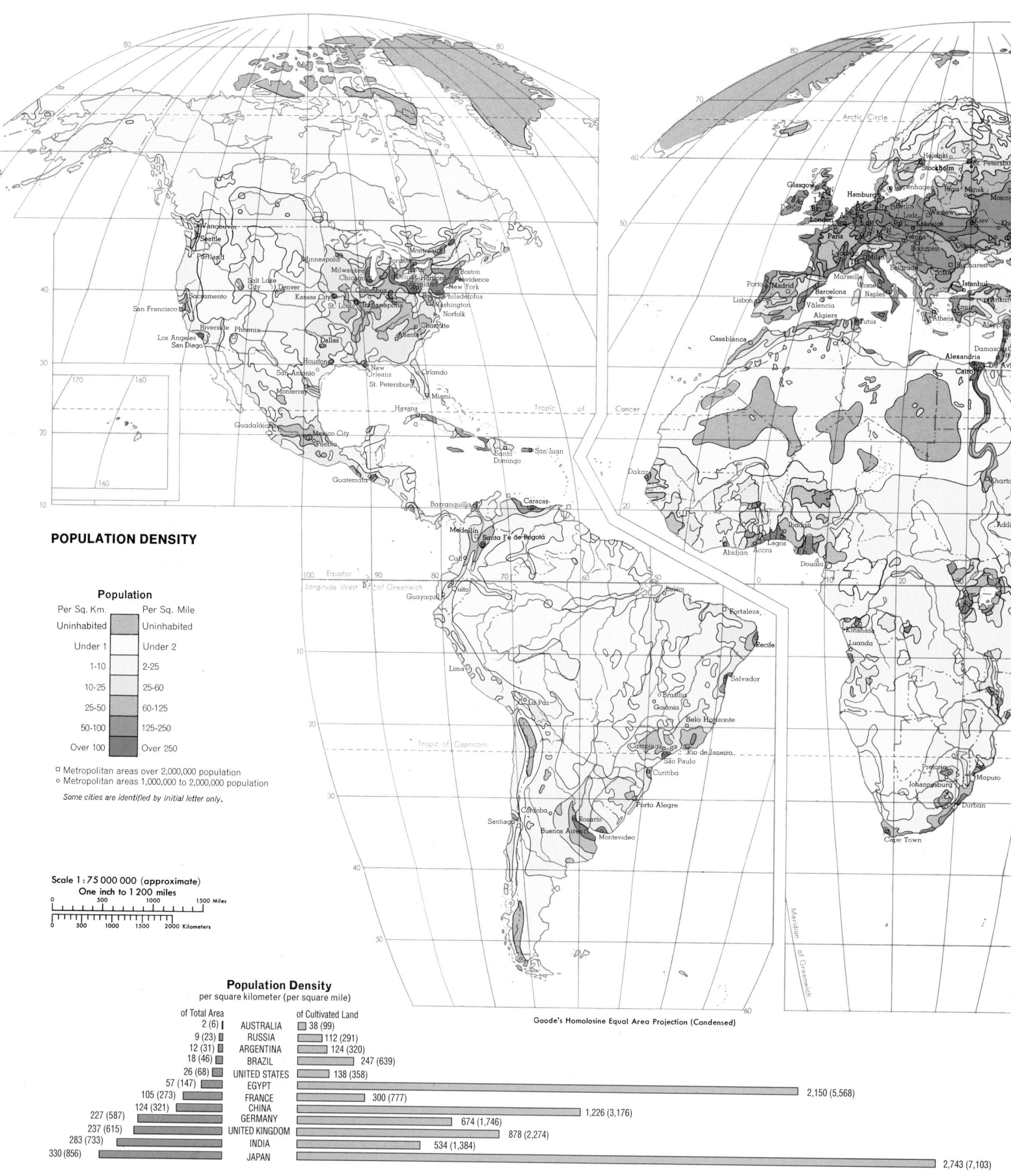

POPULATION DENSITY

Population

Per Sq. Km.	Per Sq. Mile
Uninhabited	Uninhabited
Under 1	Under 2
1-10	2-25
10-25	25-60
25-50	60-125
50-100	125-250
Over 100	Over 250

□ Metropolitan areas over 2,000,000 population
○ Metropolitan areas 1,000,000 to 2,000,000 population

Some cities are identified by initial letter only.

Scale 1:75 000 000 (approximate)
One inch to 1 200 miles

Goode's Homolosine Equal Area Projection (Condensed)

Population Density
per square kilometer (per square mile)

of Total Area		of Cultivated Land
2 (6)	AUSTRALIA	38 (99)
9 (23)	RUSSIA	112 (291)
12 (31)	ARGENTINA	124 (320)
18 (46)	BRAZIL	247 (639)
26 (68)	UNITED STATES	138 (358)
57 (147)	EGYPT	2,150 (5,568)
105 (273)	FRANCE	300 (777)
124 (321)	CHINA	1,226 (3,176)
227 (587)	GERMANY	674 (1,746)
237 (615)	UNITED KINGDOM	878 (2,274)
283 (733)	INDIA	534 (1,384)
330 (856)	JAPAN	2,743 (7,103)

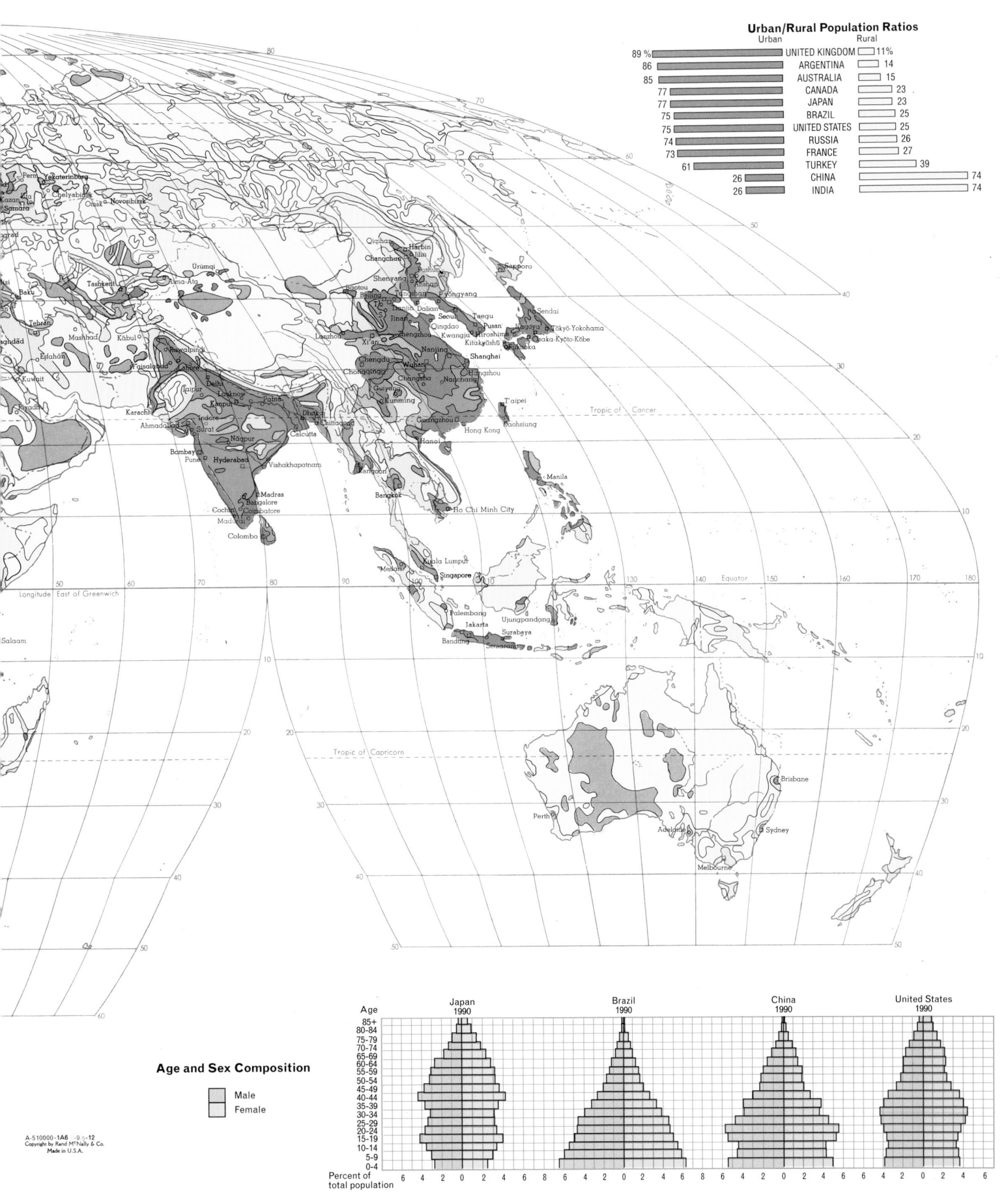

A-510000-1A6 -9.5-12
Copyright by Rand McNally & Co.
Made in U.S.A.

Urban/Rural Population Ratios

	Urban		Rural
89 %	UNITED KINGDOM	11%	
86	ARGENTINA	14	
85	AUSTRALIA	15	
77	CANADA	23	
77	JAPAN	23	
75	BRAZIL	25	
75	UNITED STATES	25	
74	RUSSIA	26	
73	FRANCE	27	
61	TURKEY	39	
26	CHINA	74	
26	INDIA	74	

Age and Sex Composition

Male
Female

Japan 1990   Brazil 1990   China 1990   United States 1990

Age
85+
80-84
75-79
70-74
65-69
60-64
55-59
50-54
45-49
40-44
35-39
30-34
25-29
20-24
15-19
10-14
5-9
0-4

Percent of total population
6 4 2 0 2 4 6   8 6 4 2 0 2 4 6 8   6 4 2 0 2 4 6   6 4 2 0 2 4 6

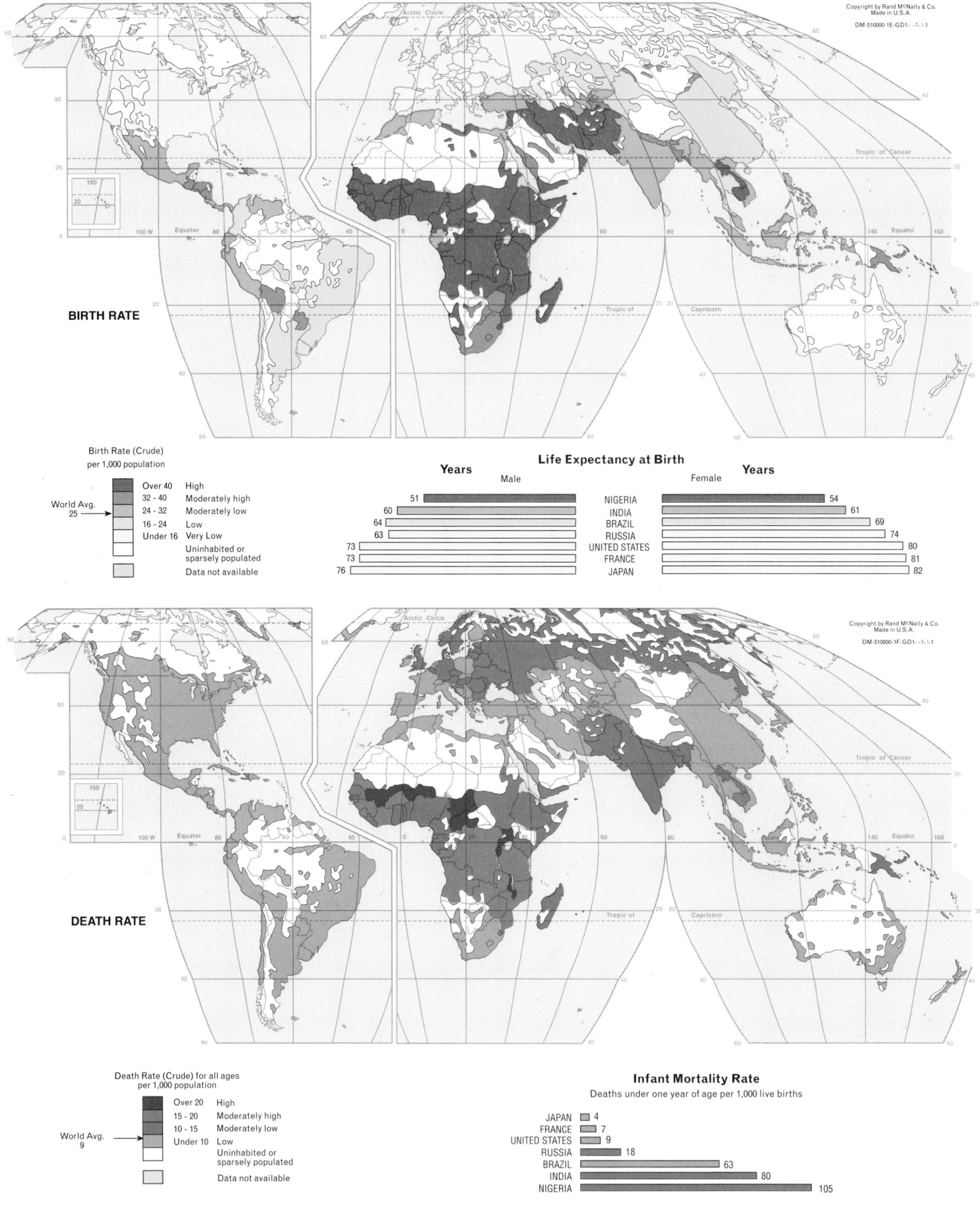

Copyright by Rand McNally & Co.
Made in U.S.A.
DM-510000-1E-GD1- -1-1-1

BIRTH RATE

Birth Rate (Crude)
per 1,000 population

	Over 40	High
	32 - 40	Moderately high
	24 - 32	Moderately low
World Avg.	16 - 24	Low
25 →	Under 16	Very Low
	Uninhabited or sparsely populated
	Data not available

Life Expectancy at Birth

Years
Male

Years
Female

	Male		Female
NIGERIA	51		54
INDIA	60		61
BRAZIL	64		69
RUSSIA	63		74
UNITED STATES	73		80
FRANCE	73		81
JAPAN	76		82

Copyright by Rand McNally & Co.
Made in U.S.A.
DM-510000-1F-GD1- -1-1-1

DEATH RATE

Death Rate (Crude) for all ages
per 1,000 population

	Over 20	High
	15 - 20	Moderately high
	10 - 15	Moderately low
World Avg. →	Under 10	Low
9		Uninhabited or sparsely populated
	Data not available

Infant Mortality Rate
Deaths under one year of age per 1,000 live births

JAPAN	4
FRANCE	7
UNITED STATES	9
RUSSIA	18
BRAZIL	63
INDIA	80
NIGERIA	105

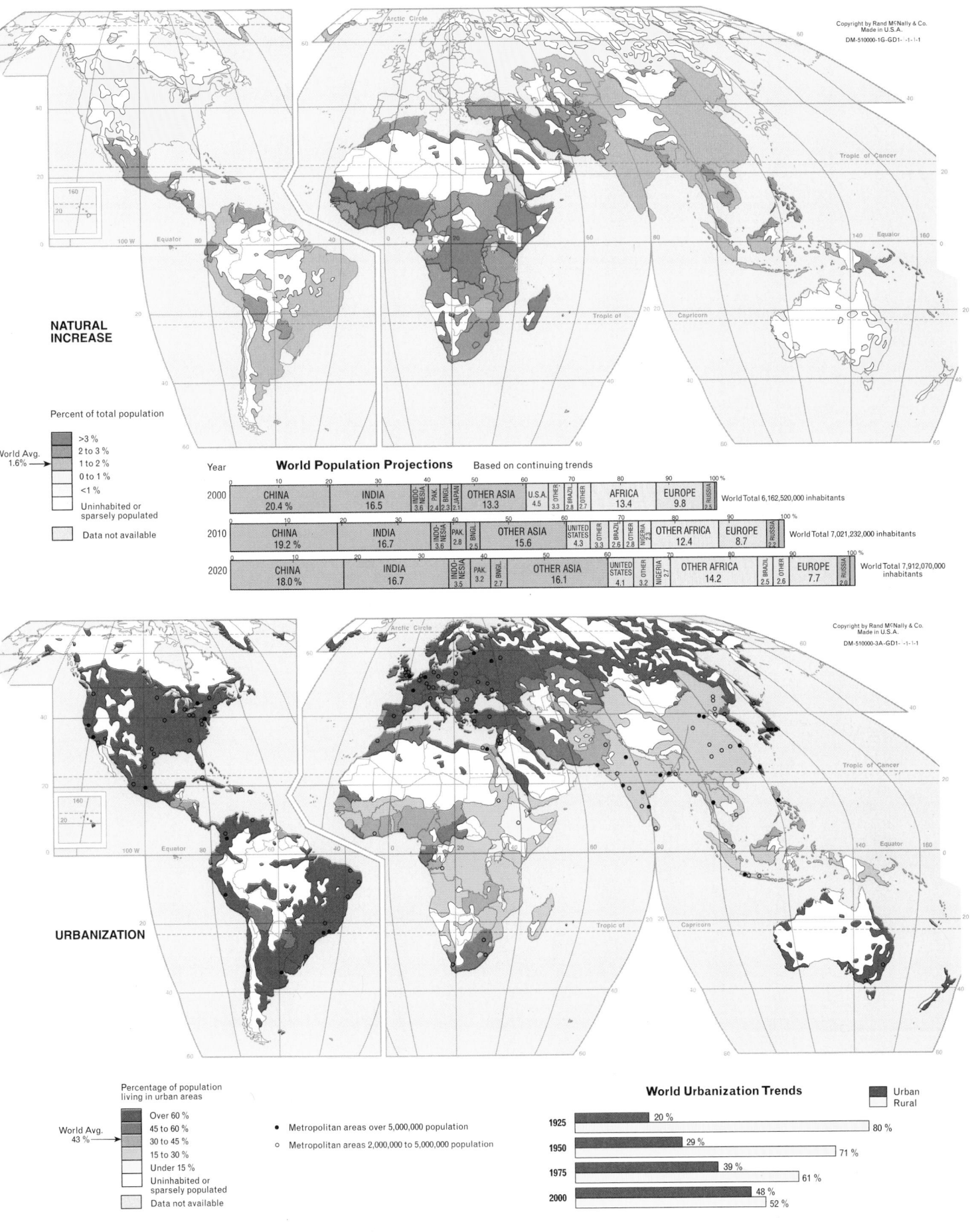

NATURAL INCREASE

Percent of total population

- >3 %
- 2 to 3 %
- World Avg. 1.6% → 1 to 2 %
- 0 to 1 %
- <1 %
- Uninhabited or sparsely populated
- Data not available

World Population Projections   Based on continuing trends

Year		
2000	CHINA 20.4 % · INDIA 16.5 · INDO-NESIA 3.6 · PAK. 2.4 · BNGL. 2.3 · JAPAN 2.1 · OTHER ASIA 13.3 · U.S.A. 4.5 · OTHER 3.3 · BRAZIL 2.8 · OTHER 2.7 · AFRICA 13.4 · EUROPE 9.8 · RUSSIA 2.2	World Total 6,162,520,000 inhabitants
2010	CHINA 19.2 % · INDIA 16.7 · INDO-NESIA 3.6 · PAK. 2.8 · BNGL. 2.5 · OTHER ASIA 15.6 · UNITED STATES 4.3 · OTHER 3.3 · BRAZIL 2.6 · NIGERIA 2.3 · OTHER 2.8 · OTHER AFRICA 12.4 · EUROPE 8.7 · RUSSIA 2.2	World Total 7,021,232,000 inhabitants
2020	CHINA 18.0 % · INDIA 16.7 · INDO-NESIA 3.5 · PAK. 3.2 · BNGL. 2.7 · OTHER ASIA 16.1 · UNITED STATES 4.1 · OTHER 3.2 · NIGERIA 2.7 · OTHER AFRICA 14.2 · BRAZIL 2.5 · OTHER 2.6 · EUROPE 7.7 · RUSSIA 2.0	World Total 7,912,070,000 inhabitants

URBANIZATION

Percentage of population living in urban areas

- Over 60 %
- 45 to 60 %
- 30 to 45 %
- World Avg. 43 % → 15 to 30 %
- Under 15 %
- Uninhabited or sparsely populated
- Data not available

● Metropolitan areas over 5,000,000 population

○ Metropolitan areas 2,000,000 to 5,000,000 population

World Urbanization Trends

■ Urban   □ Rural

Year	Urban	Rural
1925	20 %	80 %
1950	29 %	71 %
1975	39 %	61 %
2000	48 %	52 %

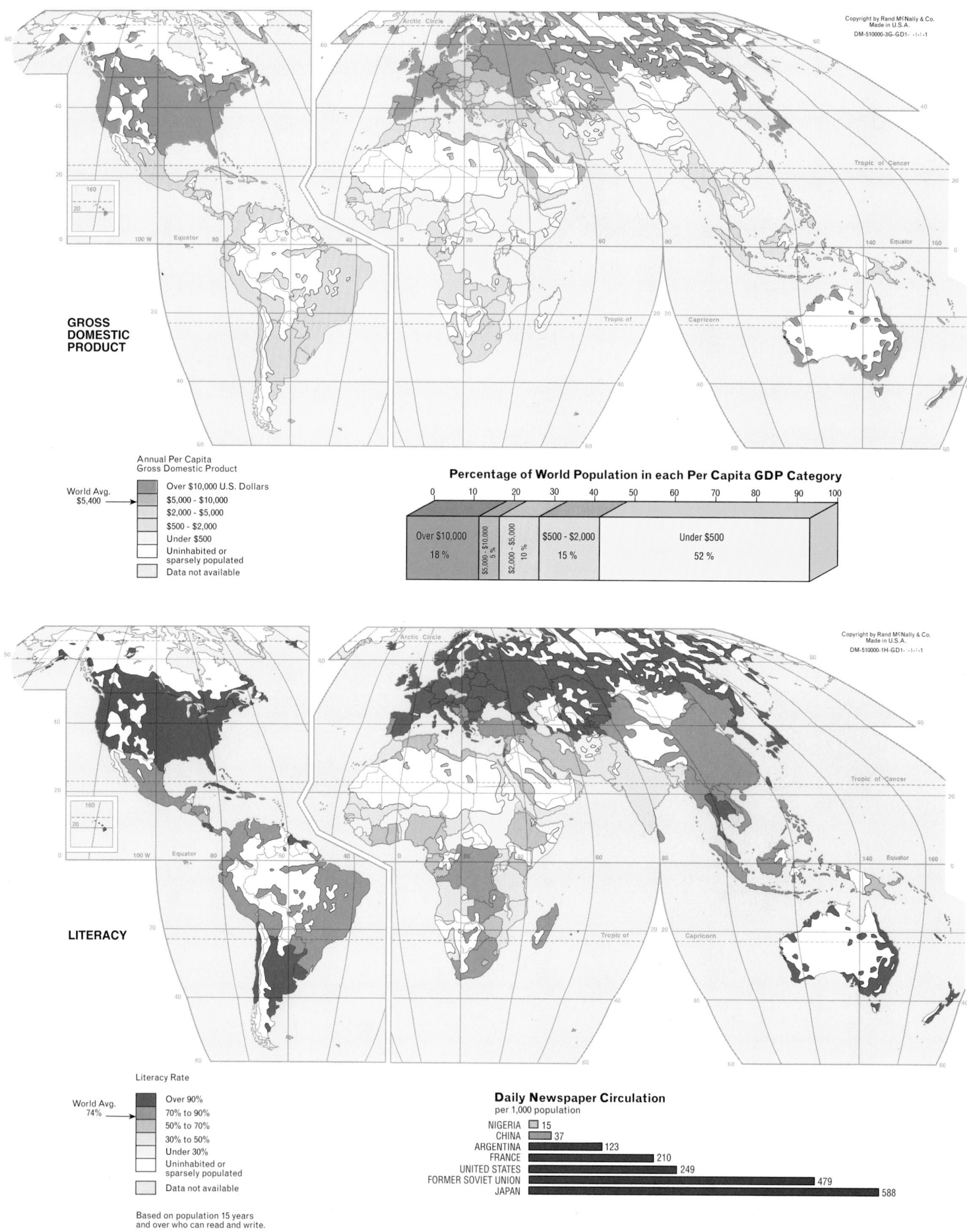

GROSS DOMESTIC PRODUCT

Annual Per Capita
Gross Domestic Product

World Avg. $5,400

- Over $10,000 U.S. Dollars
- $5,000 - $10,000
- $2,000 - $5,000
- $500 - $2,000
- Under $500
- Uninhabited or sparsely populated
- Data not available

Percentage of World Population in each Per Capita GDP Category

Over $10,000	$5,000 - $10,000	$2,000 - $5,000	$500 - $2,000	Under $500
18 %	5 %	10 %	15 %	52 %

LITERACY

Literacy Rate

World Avg. 74%

- Over 90%
- 70% to 90%
- 50% to 70%
- 30% to 50%
- Under 30%
- Uninhabited or sparsely populated
- Data not available

Based on population 15 years and over who can read and write.

Daily Newspaper Circulation
per 1,000 population

NIGERIA	15
CHINA	37
ARGENTINA	123
FRANCE	210
UNITED STATES	249
FORMER SOVIET UNION	479
JAPAN	588

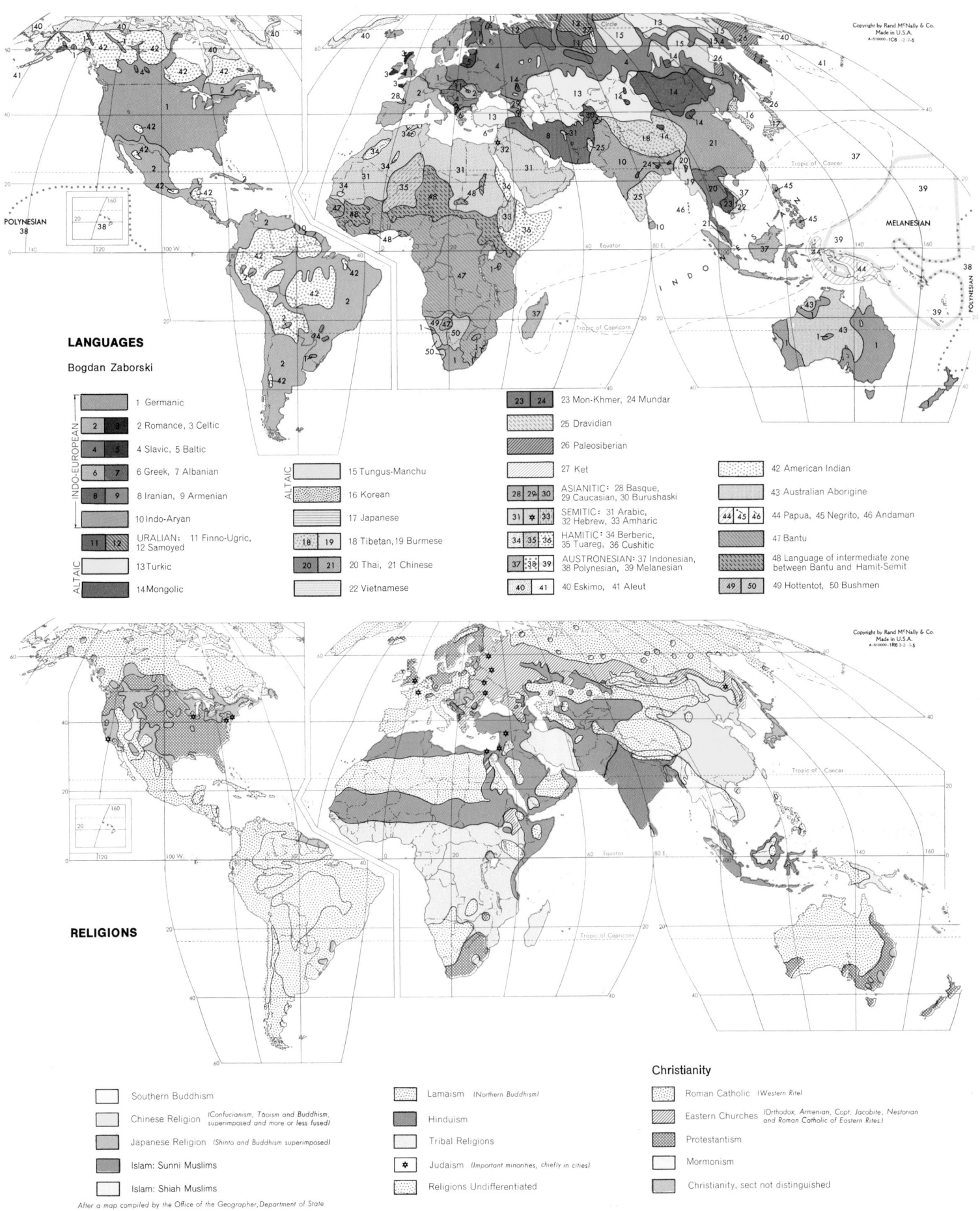

Copyright by Rand McNally & Co.
Made in U.S.A.

LANGUAGES

Bogdan Zaborski

INDO-EUROPEAN:
1 Germanic
2 Romance, 3 Celtic
4 Slavic, 5 Baltic
6 Greek, 7 Albanian
8 Iranian, 9 Armenian
10 Indo-Aryan
URALIAN: 11 Finno-Ugric, 12 Samoyed

ALTAIC:
13 Turkic
14 Mongolic
15 Tungus-Manchu
16 Korean
17 Japanese

18 Tibetan, 19 Burmese
20 Thai, 21 Chinese
22 Vietnamese
23 Mon-Khmer, 24 Mundar
25 Dravidian
26 Paleosiberian
27 Ket
ASIANITIC: 28 Basque, 29 Caucasian, 30 Burushaski
SEMITIC: 31 Arabic, 32 Hebrew, 33 Amharic
HAMITIC: 34 Berberic, 35 Tuareg, 36 Cushitic
AUSTRONESIAN: 37 Indonesian, 38 Polynesian, 39 Melanesian
40 Eskimo, 41 Aleut

42 American Indian
43 Australian Aborigine
44 Papua, 45 Negrito, 46 Andaman
47 Bantu
48 Language of intermediate zone between Bantu and Hamit-Semit
49 Hottentot, 50 Bushmen

POLYNESIAN 38
MELANESIAN

Copyright by Rand McNally & Co.
Made in U.S.A.

RELIGIONS

Southern Buddhism

Chinese Religion (Confucianism, Taoism and Buddhism, superimposed and more or less fused)

Japanese Religion (Shinto and Buddhism superimposed)

Islam: Sunni Muslims

Islam: Shiah Muslims

Lamaism (Northern Buddhism)

Hinduism

Tribal Religions

✿ Judaism (Important minorities, chiefly in cities)

Religions Undifferentiated

Christianity

Roman Catholic (Western Rite)

Eastern Churches (Orthodox, Armenian, Copt, Jacobite, Nestorian and Roman Catholic of Eastern Rites.)

Protestantism

Mormonism

Christianity, sect not distinguished

After a map compiled by the Office of the Geographer, Department of State

CALORIE SUPPLY

Note: Size of each country is proportional to population.

Calorie supply per capita
(percentage of requirements*)

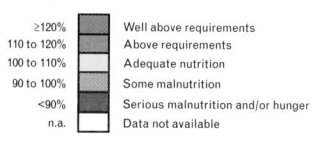

≥120%	Well above requirements
110 to 120%	Above requirements
100 to 110%	Adequate nutrition
90 to 100%	Some malnutrition
<90%	Serious malnutrition and/or hunger
n.a.	Data not available

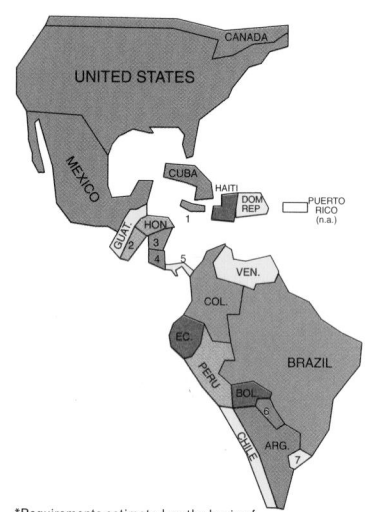
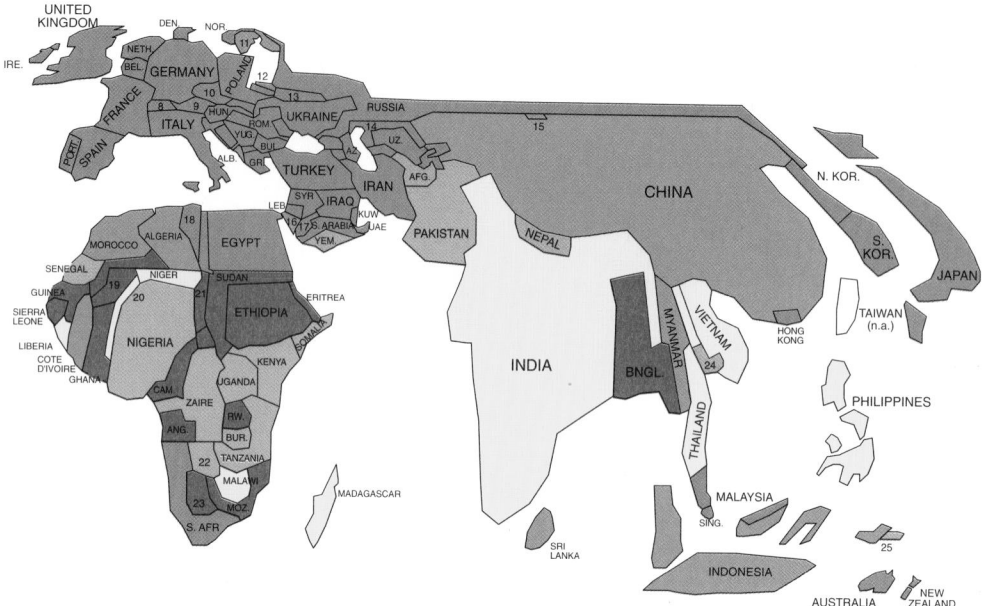

*Requirements estimated on the basis of physiological needs for normal activity with consideration of environmental temperature, body weight, and age and sex distribution of the population in various countries. Estimates are for 1990.

Copyright by Rand McNally & Co.
Made in U.S.A.
DM-910000-1V-GD1- -¦-¦-1

1. JAMAICA
2. EL SALVADOR
3. NICARAGUA
4. COSTA RICA
5. PANAMA
6. PARAGUAY
7. URUGUAY
8. SWITZERLAND
9. AUSTRIA
10. CZECH REPUBLIC
11. SWEDEN
12. LATVIA
13. BELARUS
14. KAZAKHSTAN
15. MONGOLIA
16. ISRAEL
17. JORDAN
18. TUNISIA
19. BURKINA FASO
20. BENIN
21. CHAD
22. ZAMBIA
23. ZIMBABWE
24. CAMBODIA
25. PAPUA NEW GUINEA

PROTEIN CONSUMPTION

Note: Size of each country is proportional to population.

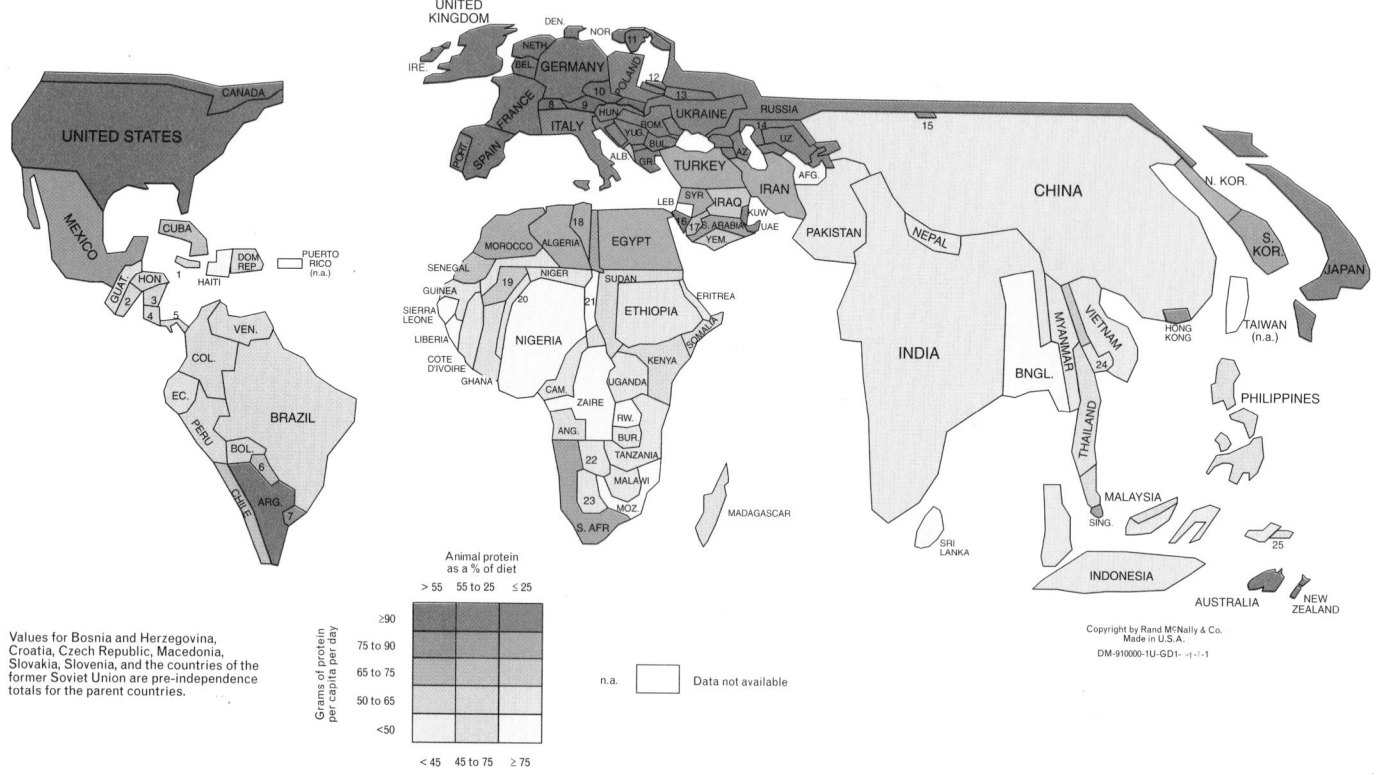

Values for Bosnia and Herzegovina, Croatia, Czech Republic, Macedonia, Slovakia, Slovenia, and the countries of the former Soviet Union are pre-independence totals for the parent countries.

Animal protein as a % of diet

Grams of protein per capita per day	> 55	55 to 25	≤ 25
≥90			
75 to 90			
65 to 75			
50 to 65			
<50			

< 45 | 45 to 75 | ≥ 75
Vegetable protein as a % of diet

n.a. Data not available

Copyright by Rand McNally & Co.
Made in U.S.A.
DM-910000-1U-GD1- -¦-¦-1

PHYSICIANS

Note: Size of each country is proportional to population.

Population per Physician

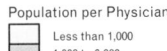

Less than 1,000
1,000 to 6,000
6,000 to 18,000
Greater than 18,000

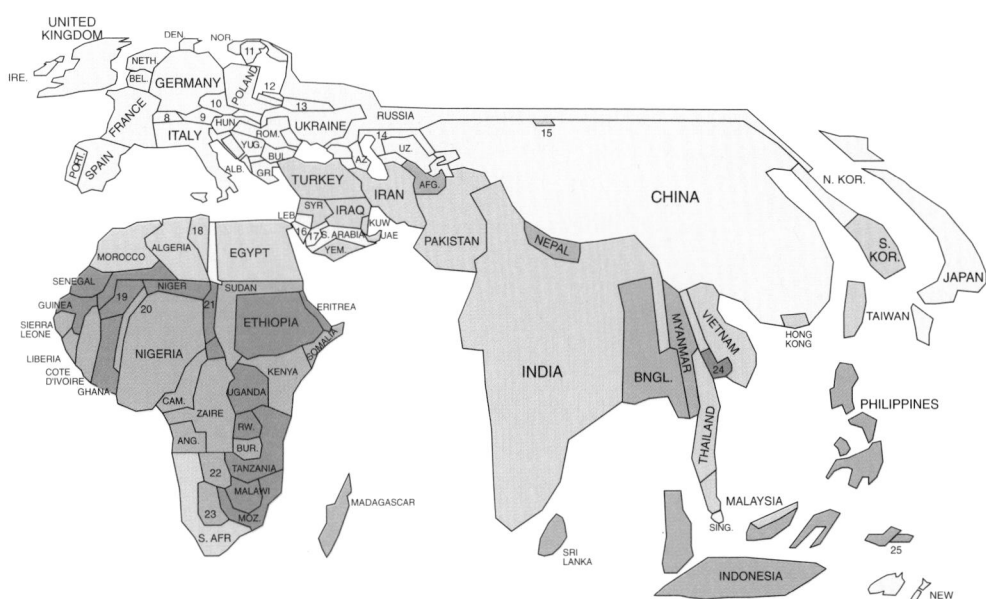

1. JAMAICA	6. PARAGUAY	11. SWEDEN	16. ISRAEL	21. CHAD
2. EL SALVADOR	7. URUGUAY	12. LATVIA	17. JORDAN	22. ZAMBIA
3. NICARAGUA	8. SWITZERLAND	13. BELARUS	18. TUNISIA	23. ZIMBABWE
4. COSTA RICA	9. AUSTRIA	14. KAZAKHSTAN	19. BURKINA FASO	24. CAMBODIA
5. PANAMA	10. CZECH REPUBLIC	15. MONGOLIA	20. BENIN	25. PAPUA NEW GUINEA

LIFE EXPECTANCY

Note: Size of each country is proportional to population.

Life Expectancy at Birth

Greater than 70 years
60 to 70
50 to 60
Less than 50
Data not available

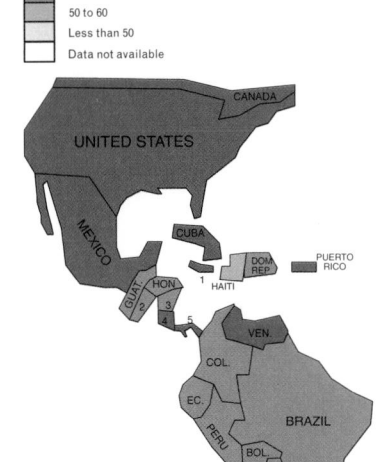
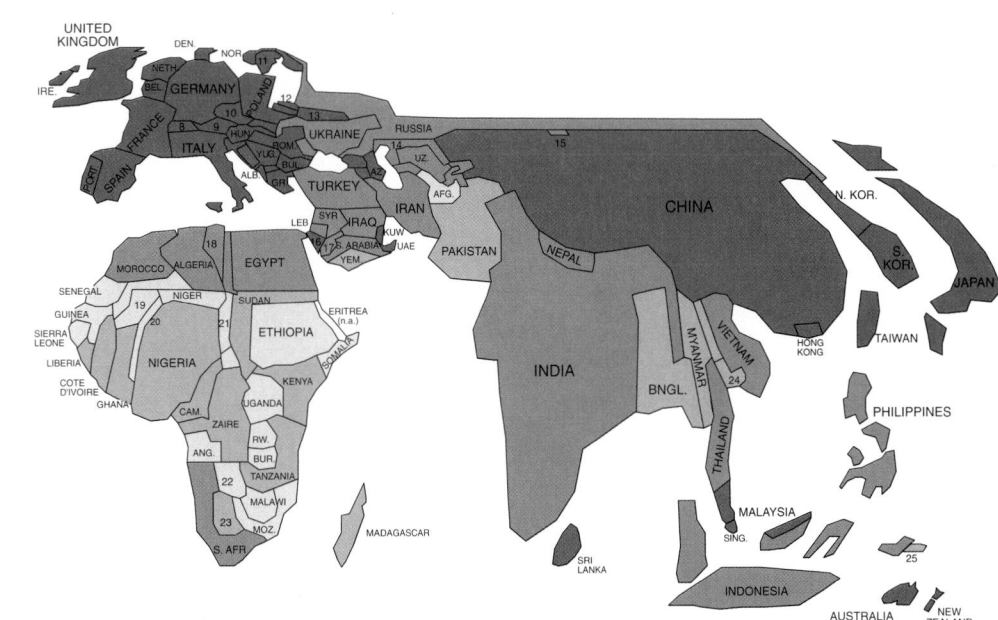

Deaths by Age Group as a Percent of Total Deaths

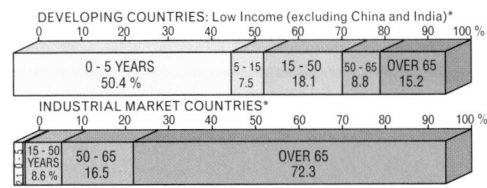

DEVELOPING COUNTRIES: Low Income (excluding China and India)*

| 0 - 5 YEARS 50.4 % | 5 - 15 7.5 | 15 - 50 18.1 | 50 - 65 8.8 | OVER 65 15.2 |

INDUSTRIAL MARKET COUNTRIES*

| 15 - 50 YEARS 8.6 % | 50 - 65 16.5 | OVER 65 72.3 |

Life Expectancy at Birth

LOW INCOME* — 62 years
LOWER-MIDDLE INCOME* — 67
UPPER-MIDDLE INCOME* — 69
HIGH INCOME* — 77

*as defined by the World Bank

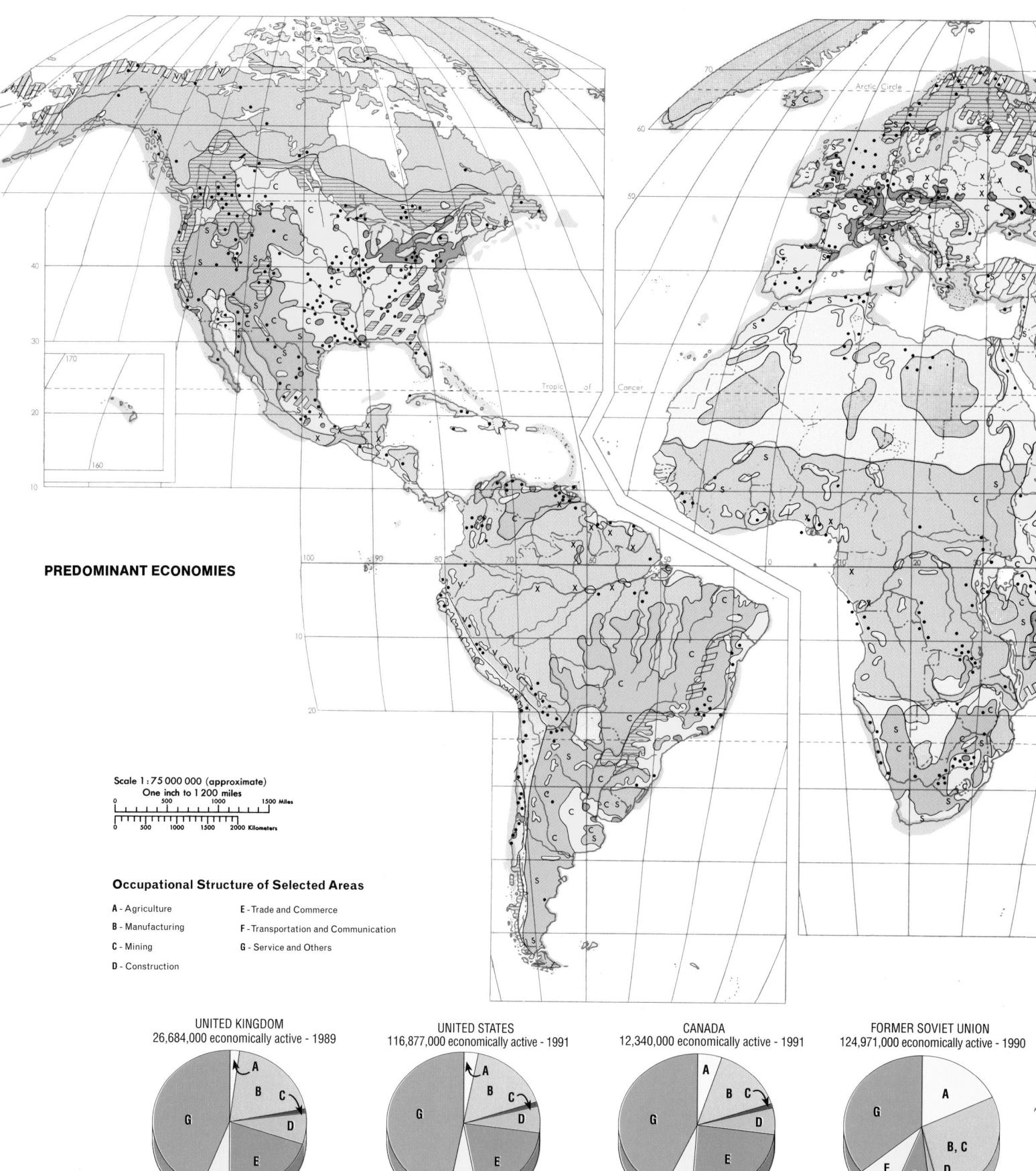

PREDOMINANT ECONOMIES

Scale 1 : 75 000 000 (approximate)
One inch to 1 200 miles

0   500   1000   1500 Miles

0   500   1000   1500   2000 Kilometers

Occupational Structure of Selected Areas

A - Agriculture   E - Trade and Commerce

B - Manufacturing   F - Transportation and Communication

C - Mining   G - Service and Others

D - Construction

UNITED KINGDOM
26,684,000 economically active - 1989

UNITED STATES
116,877,000 economically active - 1991

CANADA
12,340,000 economically active - 1991

FORMER SOVIET UNION
124,971,000 economically active - 1990

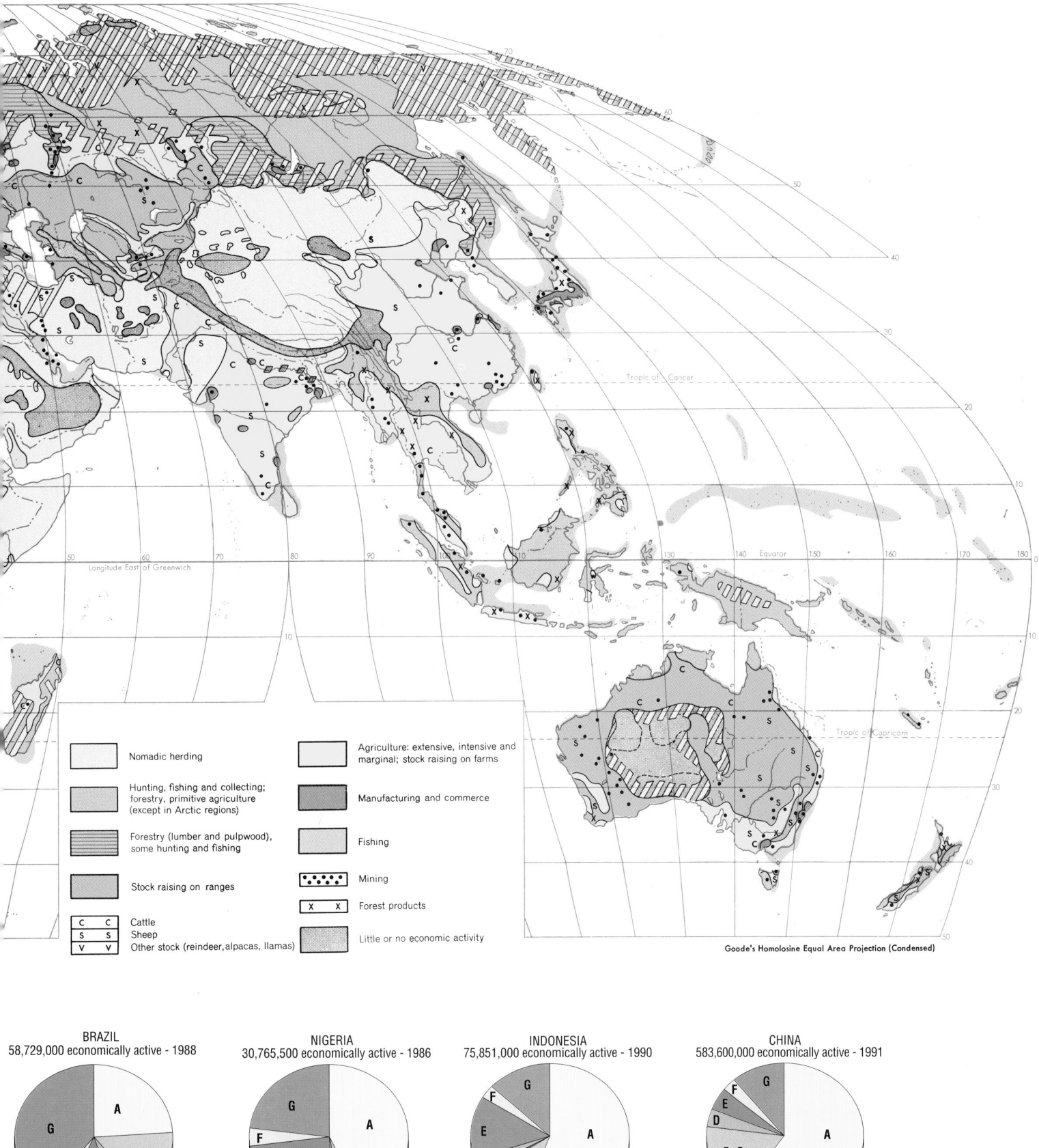

Goode's Homolosine Equal Area Projection (Condensed)

Legend:

Nomadic herding

Hunting, fishing and collecting; forestry, primitive agriculture (except in Arctic regions)

Forestry (lumber and pulpwood), some hunting and fishing

Stock raising on ranges

C   C   Cattle
S   S   Sheep
V   V   Other stock (reindeer, alpacas, llamas)

Agriculture: extensive, intensive and marginal; stock raising on farms

Manufacturing and commerce

Fishing

Mining

X   X   Forest products

Little or no economic activity

BRAZIL
58,729,000 economically active - 1988

NIGERIA
30,765,500 economically active - 1986

INDONESIA
75,851,000 economically active - 1990

CHINA
583,600,000 economically active - 1991

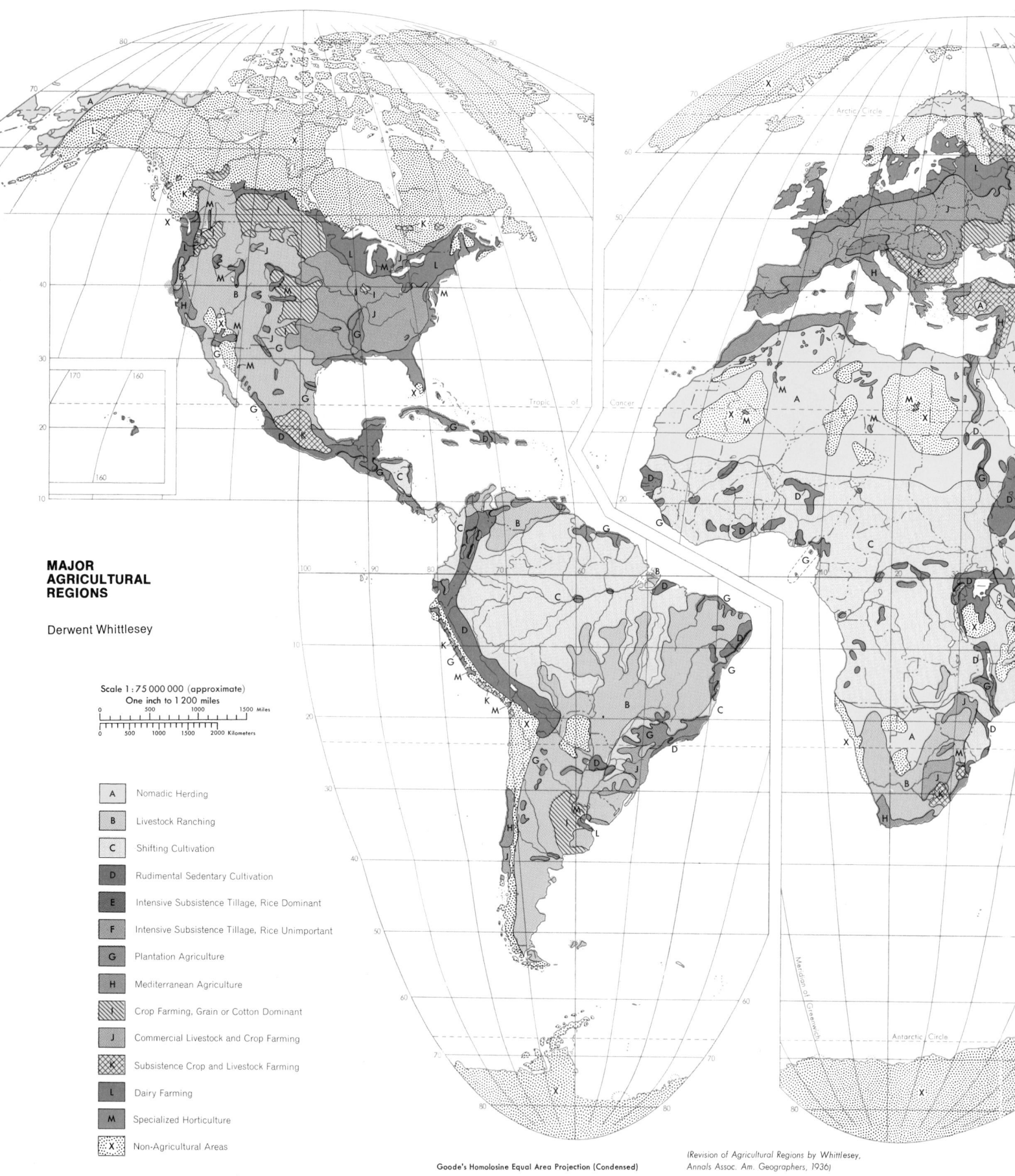

MAJOR AGRICULTURAL REGIONS

Derwent Whittlesey

Scale 1 : 75 000 000 (approximate)
One inch to 1 200 miles

0   500   1000   1500 Miles

0   500   1000   1500   2000 Kilometers

A	Nomadic Herding
B	Livestock Ranching
C	Shifting Cultivation
D	Rudimental Sedentary Cultivation
E	Intensive Subsistence Tillage, Rice Dominant
F	Intensive Subsistence Tillage, Rice Unimportant
G	Plantation Agriculture
H	Mediterranean Agriculture
I	Crop Farming, Grain or Cotton Dominant
J	Commercial Livestock and Crop Farming
K	Subsistence Crop and Livestock Farming
L	Dairy Farming
M	Specialized Horticulture
X	Non-Agricultural Areas

Goode's Homolosine Equal Area Projection (Condensed)

(Revision of Agricultural Regions by Whittlesey,
Annals Assoc. Am. Geographers, 1936)

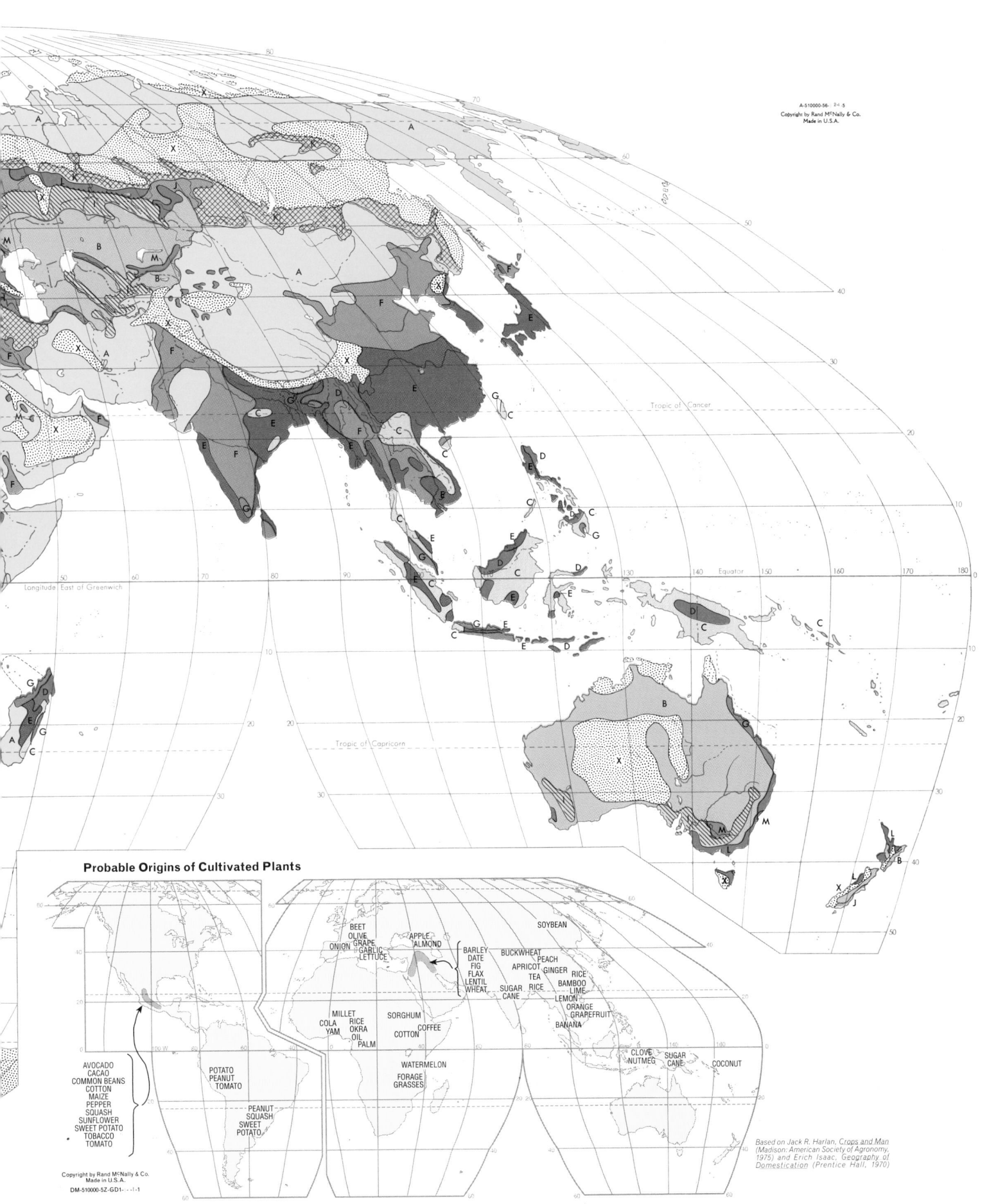

A-510000-56- ᵇᵃ-5
Copyright by Rand McNally & Co.
Made in U.S.A.

Tropic of Cancer

Equator

Longitude East of Greenwich

Tropic of Capricorn

Probable Origins of Cultivated Plants

SOYBEAN

BEET
OLIVE
GRAPE
ONION GARLIC
LETTUCE

APPLE
ALMOND

BARLEY
DATE
FIG
FLAX
LENTIL
WHEAT

BUCKWHEAT
APRICOT PEACH
TEA GINGER
RICE
BAMBOO
SUGAR LIME
CANE RICE LEMON
ORANGE
GRAPEFRUIT
BANANA

MILLET
COLA RICE
YAM OKRA
OIL
PALM

SORGHUM

COFFEE
COTTON

CLOVE SUGAR
NUTMEG CANE COCONUT

AVOCADO
CACAO
COMMON BEANS
COTTON
MAIZE
PEPPER
SQUASH
SUNFLOWER
SWEET POTATO
TOBACCO
TOMATO

POTATO
PEANUT
TOMATO

WATERMELON

FORAGE
GRASSES

PEANUT
SQUASH
SWEET
POTATO

Copyright by Rand McNally & Co.
Made in U.S.A.

DM-510000-5Z-GD1- - -:-1

*Based on Jack R. Harlan, Crops and Man
(Madison: American Society of Agronomy,
1975) and Erich Isaac, Geography of
Domestication (Prentice Hall, 1970)*

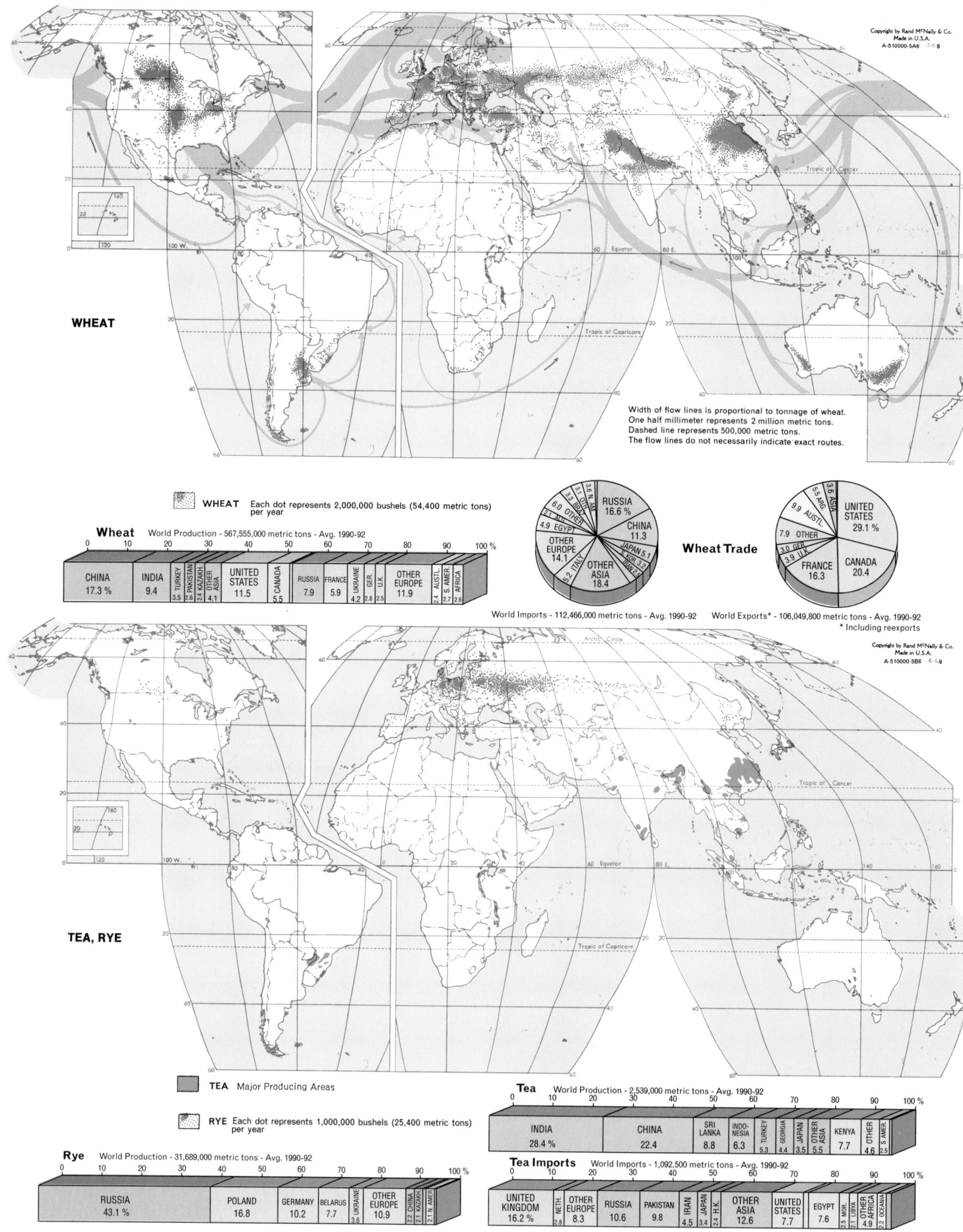

WHEAT

Copyright by Rand McNally & Co.
Made in U.S.A.
A-510000-5A6

Width of flow lines is proportional to tonnage of wheat.
One half millimeter represents 2 million metric tons.
Dashed line represents 500,000 metric tons.
The flow lines do not necessarily indicate exact routes.

WHEAT Each dot represents 2,000,000 bushels (54,400 metric tons) per year

Wheat World Production - 567,555,000 metric tons - Avg. 1990-92

| CHINA 17.3 % | INDIA 9.4 | TURKEY 3.5 | PAKISTAN 2.4 | KAZAKH. | OTHER ASIA 4.1 | UNITED STATES 11.5 | CANADA 5.5 | RUSSIA 7.9 | FRANCE 5.9 | UKRAINE 4.2 | GER. 2.8 | U.K. 2.5 | OTHER EUROPE 11.9 | AUSTL. 2.4 | S. AMER. 2.7 | AFRICA 2.6 |

Wheat Trade

World Imports - 112,466,000 metric tons - Avg. 1990-92

RUSSIA 16.6 %
CHINA 11.3
JAPAN 5.1
KOR. 3.2
IRAN 2.
OTHER ASIA 18.4
ITALY 5.2
OTHER EUROPE 14.1
EGYPT 4.9
BRZ. 6.0
3.6 N.
3.1

World Exports* - 106,049,800 metric tons - Avg. 1990-92
* Including reexports

UNITED STATES 29.1 %
CANADA 20.4
FRANCE 16.3
3.9 U.K.
3.0 GER.
7.9 OTHER
9.9 AUSTL.
5.5 ARG.
3.6 ASIA

TEA, RYE

Copyright by Rand McNally & Co.
Made in U.S.A.
A-510000-5B6

TEA Major Producing Areas

RYE Each dot represents 1,000,000 bushels (25,400 metric tons) per year

Tea World Production - 2,539,000 metric tons - Avg. 1990-92

| INDIA 28.4 % | CHINA 22.4 | SRI LANKA 8.8 | INDO-NESIA 6.3 | TURKEY 5.3 | GEORGIA 4.4 | JAPAN 3.5 | OTHER ASIA 5.5 | KENYA 7.7 | OTHER 4.6 | S. AMER. 2.5 |

Rye World Production - 31,689,000 metric tons - Avg. 1990-92

| RUSSIA 43.1 % | POLAND 16.8 | GERMANY 10.2 | BELARUS 7.7 | UKRAINE 3.6 | OTHER EUROPE 10.9 | CHINA 2.2 | N. AMER. 2.1 |

Tea Imports World Imports - 1,092,500 metric tons - Avg. 1990-92

| UNITED KINGDOM 16.2 % | NETH. 2.8 | OTHER EUROPE 8.3 | RUSSIA 10.6 | PAKISTAN 9.8 | IRAN 4.5 | JAPAN 3.4 | OTHER ASIA 12.6 | UNITED STATES 7.7 | EGYPT 7.6 | MOR. 2.1 | LIBYA | OTHER AFRICA 4.9 | OCEANIA 2.2 |

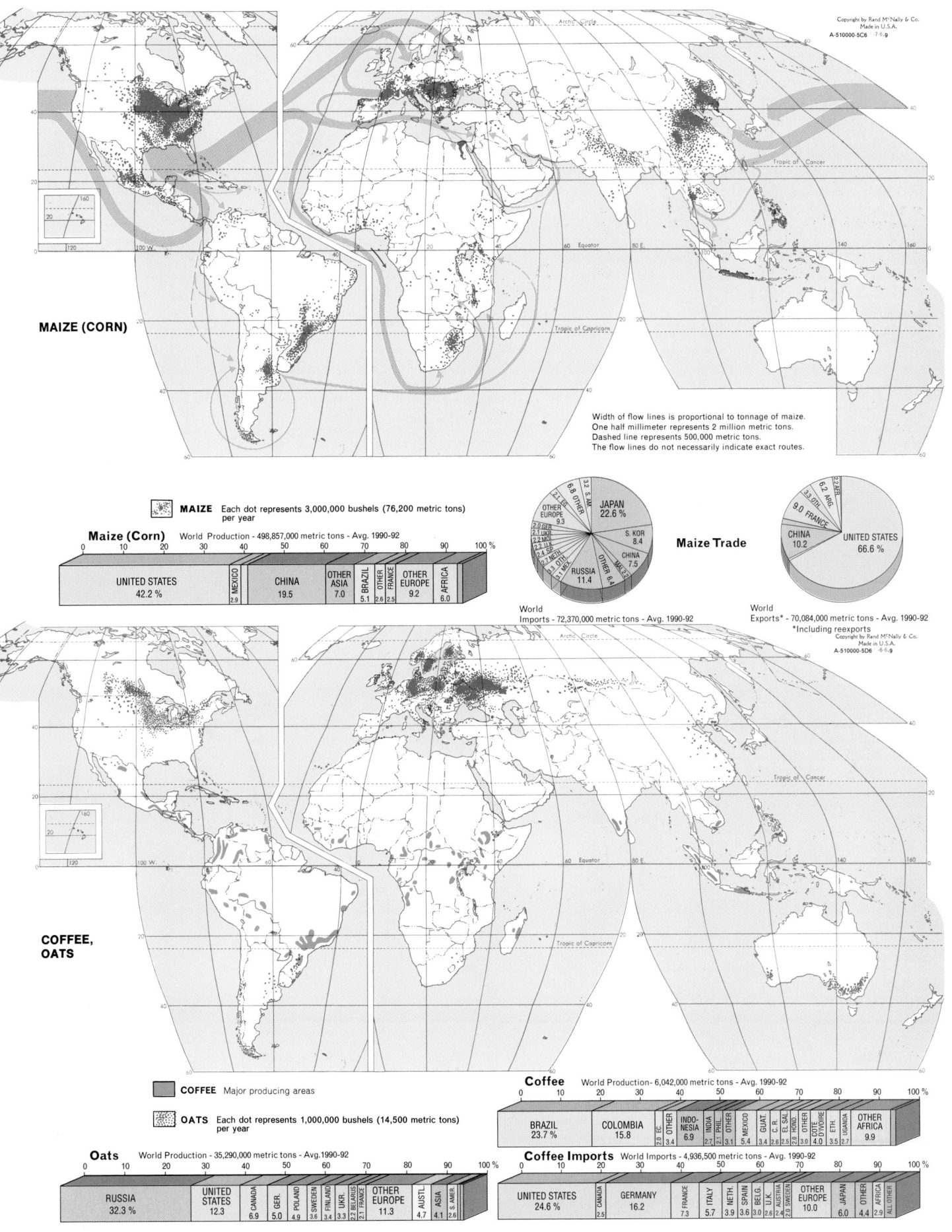

MAIZE (CORN)

Width of flow lines is proportional to tonnage of maize.
One half millimeter represents 2 million metric tons.
Dashed line represents 500,000 metric tons.
The flow lines do not necessarily indicate exact routes.

MAIZE Each dot represents 3,000,000 bushels (76,200 metric tons) per year

Maize (Corn) World Production - 498,857,000 metric tons - Avg. 1990-92

0	10	20	30	40	50	60	70	80	90	100 %

| UNITED STATES 42.2 % | MEXICO 2.9 | CHINA 19.5 | OTHER ASIA 7.0 | BRAZIL 5.1 | OTHER 2.6 | FRANCE 2.5 | OTHER EUROPE 9.2 | AFRICA 6.0 |

Maize Trade

World Imports - 72,370,000 metric tons - Avg. 1990-92

JAPAN 22.6 %
S. KOR 8.4
CHINA 7.5
ITAL 2.2
OTHER 6.4
RUSSIA 11.4
3.1 MEX
3.3 OTH
2.4 SP
2.2 MOL
2.2 MOL
2.1 UKR.
2.0 GER.
OTHER EUROPE 9.3
6.8 OTHER
3.2 S. AM.

World Exports* - 70,084,000 metric tons - Avg. 1990-92
*Including reexports

UNITED STATES 66.6 %
CHINA 10.2
9.0 FRANCE
3.3 OTH.
6.2 ARG.
2.2 AFR.

COFFEE, OATS

COFFEE Major producing areas

OATS Each dot represents 1,000,000 bushels (14,500 metric tons) per year

Coffee World Production- 6,042,000 metric tons - Avg. 1990-92

0	10	20	30	40	50	60	70	80	90	100 %

| BRAZIL 23.7 % | COLOMBIA 15.8 | 2.9 EC. | OTHER | INDO-NESIA 6.9 | 2.7 INDIA | 3.1 PHIL. | OTHER | MEXICO 5.4 | GUAT. 3.4 | C. R. 2.6 | EL SAL 2.5 | HOND. 2.9 | CÔTE D'IVOIRE 4.0 | 3.5 ETH. | UGANDA 2.7 | OTHER AFRICA 9.9 |

Oats World Production - 35,290,000 metric tons - Avg.1990-92

0	10	20	30	40	50	60	70	80	90	100 %

| RUSSIA 32.3 % | UNITED STATES 12.3 | CANADA 6.9 | GER. 5.0 | POLAND 4.9 | SWEDEN 3.6 | FINLAND 3.4 | UKR. 2.2 | BELARUS | FRANCE 2.1 | OTHER EUROPE 11.3 | AUSTL. 4.7 | ASIA 4.1 | S. AMER. 2.6 |

Coffee Imports World Imports - 4,936,500 metric tons - Avg. 1990-92

0	10	20	30	40	50	60	70	80	90	100 %

| UNITED STATES 24.6 % | CANADA 2.5 | GERMANY 16.2 | FRANCE 7.3 | ITALY 5.7 | NETH. 3.9 | SPAIN 3.6 | BELG. | U.K. | AUSTRIA 2.0 | SWEDEN | OTHER EUROPE 10.0 | JAPAN 6.0 | OTHER 4.4 | AFRICA 2.9 | ALL OTHER |

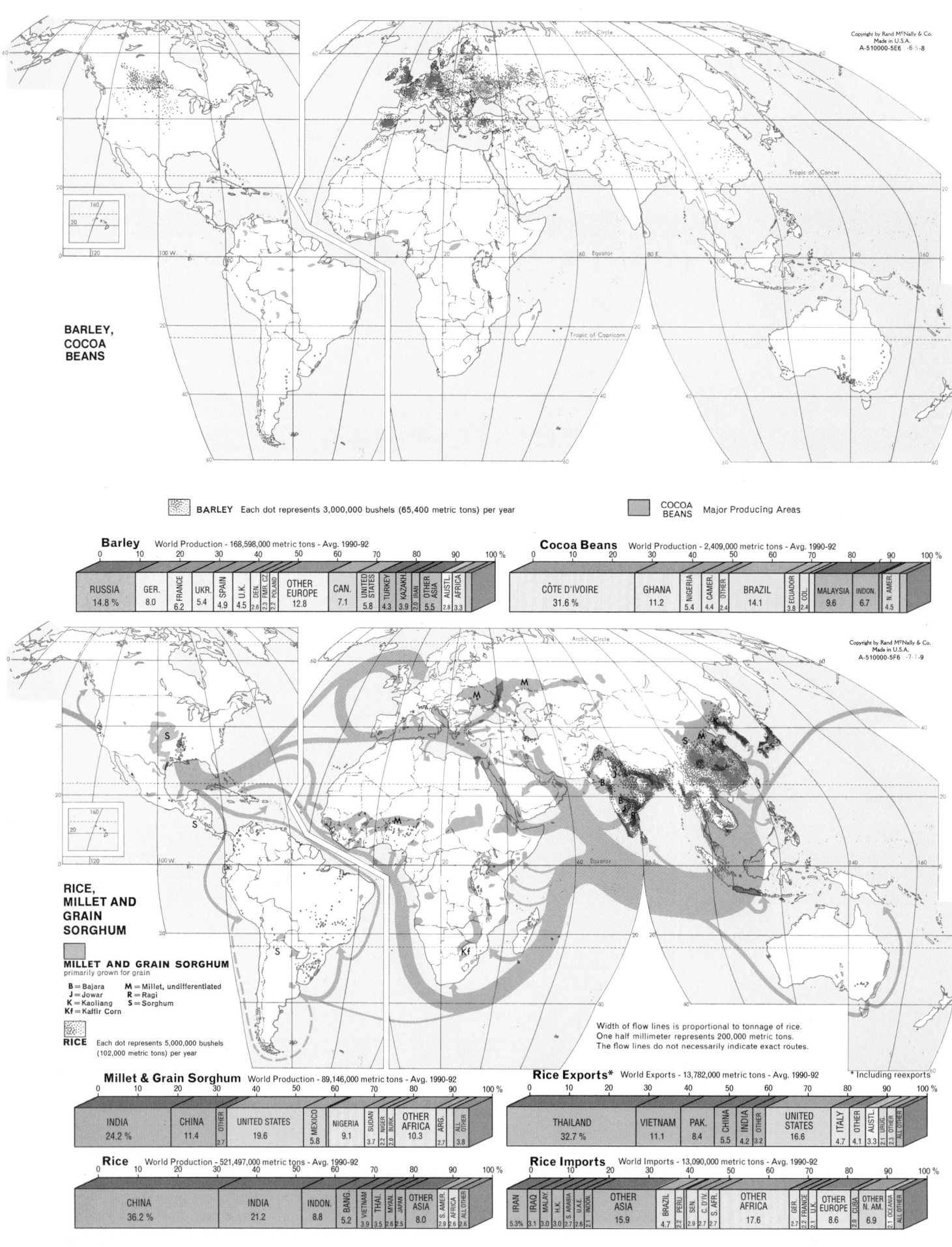

Copyright by Rand McNally & Co.
Made in U.S.A.
A-510000-5E6 -6-5-8

**BARLEY,
COCOA
BEANS**

BARLEY Each dot represents 3,000,000 bushels (65,400 metric tons) per year

COCOA BEANS Major Producing Areas

Barley
World Production - 168,598,000 metric tons - Avg. 1990-92

| 0 | 10 | 20 | 30 | 40 | 50 | 60 | 70 | 80 | 90 | 100 % |

| RUSSIA 14.8 % | GER. 8.0 | FRANCE 6.2 | UKR. 5.4 | SPAIN 4.9 | U.K. 4.5 | DEN. 2.6 | FMR. CZ. 2.3 | POLAND 2.2 | OTHER EUROPE 12.8 | CAN. 7.1 | UNITED STATES 5.8 | TURKEY 4.3 | KAZAKH. 3.9 | IRAN 2.0 | OTHER ASIA 5.5 | AUSTL. 2.8 | AFRICA 3.3 |

Cocoa Beans
World Production - 2,409,000 metric tons - Avg. 1990-92

| 0 | 10 | 20 | 30 | 40 | 50 | 60 | 70 | 80 | 90 | 100 % |

| CÔTE D'IVOIRE 31.6 % | GHANA 11.2 | NIGERIA 5.4 | CAMER. 4.4 | OTHER 2.4 | BRAZIL 14.1 | ECUADOR 3.8 | COL. 2.4 | MALAYSIA 9.6 | INDON. 6.7 | N. AMER. 4.5 |

Copyright by Rand McNally & Co.
Made in U.S.A.
A-510000-5F6 -7-7-9

**RICE,
MILLET AND
GRAIN
SORGHUM**

MILLET AND GRAIN SORGHUM
primarily grown for grain

B = Bajara
J = Jowar
K = Kaoliang
Kf = Kaffir Corn

M = Millet, undifferentiated
R = Ragi
S = Sorghum

RICE Each dot represents 5,000,000 bushels (102,000 metric tons) per year

Width of flow lines is proportional to tonnage of rice.
One half millimeter represents 200,000 metric tons.
The flow lines do not necessarily indicate exact routes.

Millet & Grain Sorghum
World Production - 89,146,000 metric tons - Avg. 1990-92

| 0 | 10 | 20 | 30 | 40 | 50 | 60 | 70 | 80 | 90 | 100 % |

| INDIA 24.2 % | CHINA 11.4 | OTHER 2.7 | UNITED STATES 19.6 | MEXICO 5.8 | NIGERIA 9.1 | SUDAN 3.7 | NIGER 2.2 | BURK. 2.0 | OTHER AFRICA 10.3 | ARG. 2.7 | ALL OTHER 3.8 |

Rice Exports*
World Exports - 13,782,000 metric tons - Avg. 1990-92   * Including reexports

| 0 | 10 | 20 | 30 | 40 | 50 | 60 | 70 | 80 | 90 | 100 % |

| THAILAND 32.7 % | VIETNAM 11.1 | PAK. 8.4 | CHINA 5.5 | INDIA 4.2 | OTHER 3.2 | UNITED STATES 16.6 | ITALY 4.7 | OTHER 4.1 | AUSTL. 3.3 | URUG. 2.3 | OTHER | ALL OTHER |

Rice
World Production - 521,497,000 metric tons - Avg. 1990-92

| 0 | 10 | 20 | 30 | 40 | 50 | 60 | 70 | 80 | 90 | 100 % |

| CHINA 36.2 % | INDIA 21.2 | INDON. 8.8 | BANG. 5.2 | VIETNAM 3.9 | THAI. 3.5 | MYAN. 2.6 | JAPAN 2.5 | OTHER ASIA 8.0 | S. AMER. 2.9 | AFRICA 2.6 | ALL OTHER |

Rice Imports
World Imports - 13,090,000 metric tons - Avg. 1990-92

| 0 | 10 | 20 | 30 | 40 | 50 | 60 | 70 | 80 | 90 | 100 % |

| IRAN 5.3% | IRAQ 3.1 | MALAY. 3.0 | H.K. 2.7 | S. ARABIA 2.6 | U.A.E. 2.5 | INDON. 2.1 | OTHER ASIA 15.9 | BRAZIL 4.7 | PERU 2.2 | SEN. 2.9 | C.DIV. 2.7 | S. AFR. 2.7 | OTHER AFRICA 17.6 | GER. 2.2 | FRANCE 2.2 | U.K. 2.1 | OTHER EUROPE 8.6 | CUBA 2.0 | OTHER N. AM. 6.9 | OCEANIA 2.1 | ALL OTHER |

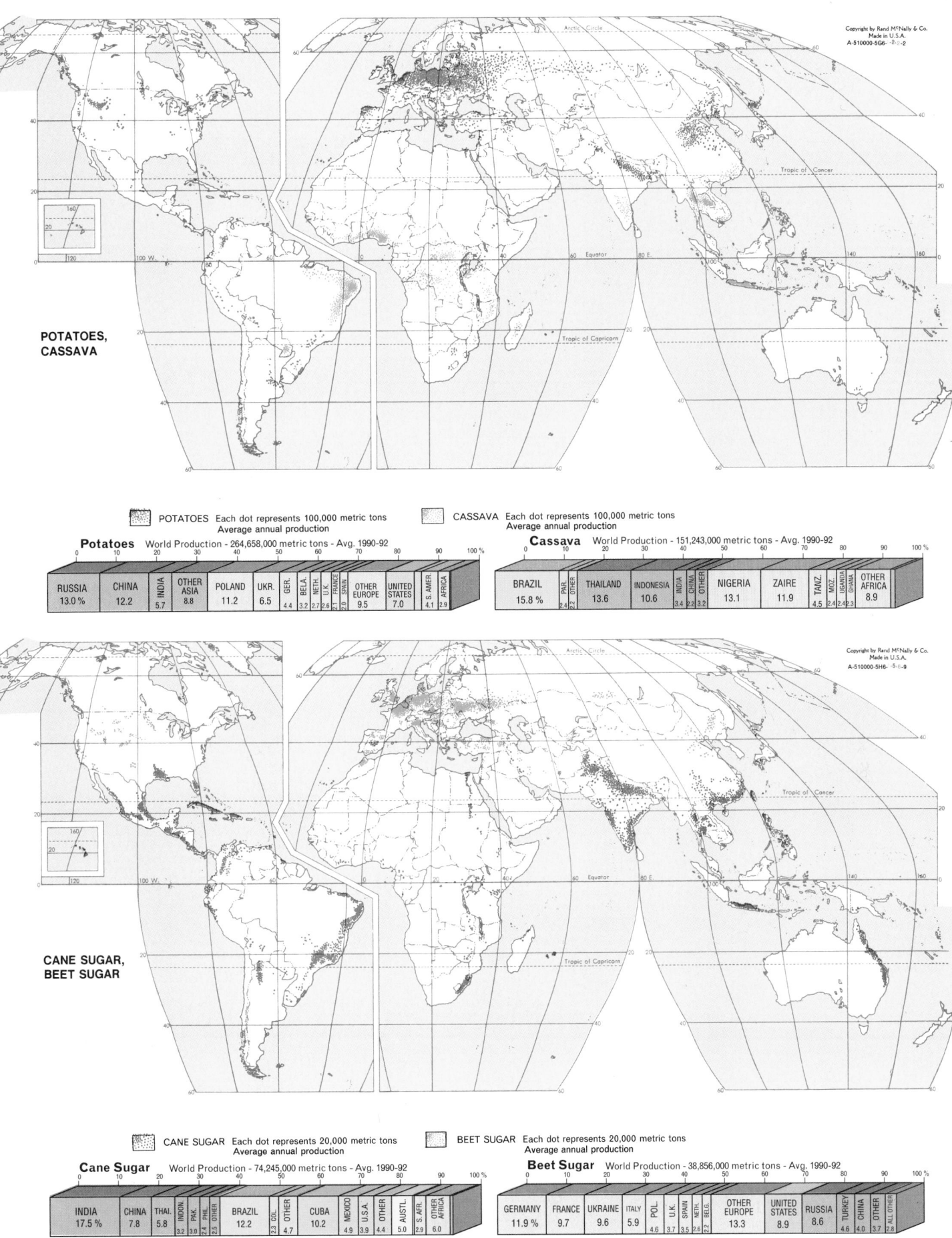

POTATOES,
CASSAVA

POTATOES Each dot represents 100,000 metric tons
Average annual production

CASSAVA Each dot represents 100,000 metric tons
Average annual production

Potatoes World Production - 264,658,000 metric tons - Avg. 1990-92

0	10	20	30	40	50	60	70	80	90	100 %

| RUSSIA 13.0 % | CHINA 12.2 | INDIA 5.7 | OTHER ASIA 8.8 | POLAND 11.2 | UKR. 6.5 | GER. 4.4 | BELA. 3.2 | NETH. 2.7 | U.K. 2.6 | FRANCE 2.1 | SPAIN 2.0 | OTHER EUROPE 9.5 | UNITED STATES 7.0 | S. AMER. 4.1 | AFRICA 2.9 |

Cassava World Production - 151,243,000 metric tons - Avg. 1990-92

0	10	20	30	40	50	60	70	80	90	100 %

| BRAZIL 15.8 % | PAR. 2.4 | OTHER 2.2 | THAILAND 13.6 | INDONESIA 10.6 | INDIA 3.4 | CHINA 2.2 | OTHER 3.2 | NIGERIA 13.1 | ZAIRE 11.9 | TANZ. 4.5 | MOZ. 2.4 | UGANDA 2.4 | GHANA 2.3 | OTHER AFRICA 8.9 |

CANE SUGAR,
BEET SUGAR

CANE SUGAR Each dot represents 20,000 metric tons
Average annual production

BEET SUGAR Each dot represents 20,000 metric tons
Average annual production

Cane Sugar World Production - 74,245,000 metric tons - Avg. 1990-92

0	10	20	30	40	50	60	70	80	90	100 %

| INDIA 17.5 % | CHINA 7.8 | THAI. 5.8 | INDON. 3.2 | PAK. 3.0 | PHIL. 2.5 | OTHER | BRAZIL 12.2 | COL. 2.3 | OTHER 4.7 | CUBA 10.2 | MEXICO 4.9 | U.S.A. 3.9 | OTHER 4.4 | AUSTL. 5.0 | S. AFR. 2.9 | OTHER AFRICA 6.0 |

Beet Sugar World Production - 38,856,000 metric tons - Avg. 1990-92

0	10	20	30	40	50	60	70	80	90	100 %

| GERMANY 11.9 % | FRANCE 9.7 | UKRAINE 9.6 | ITALY 5.9 | POL. 4.6 | U.K. 3.7 | SPAIN 3.5 | NETH. 2.2 | BELG. | OTHER EUROPE 13.3 | UNITED STATES 8.9 | RUSSIA 8.6 | TURKEY 4.6 | CHINA 4.0 | OTHER 3.7 | ALL OTHER 2.8 |

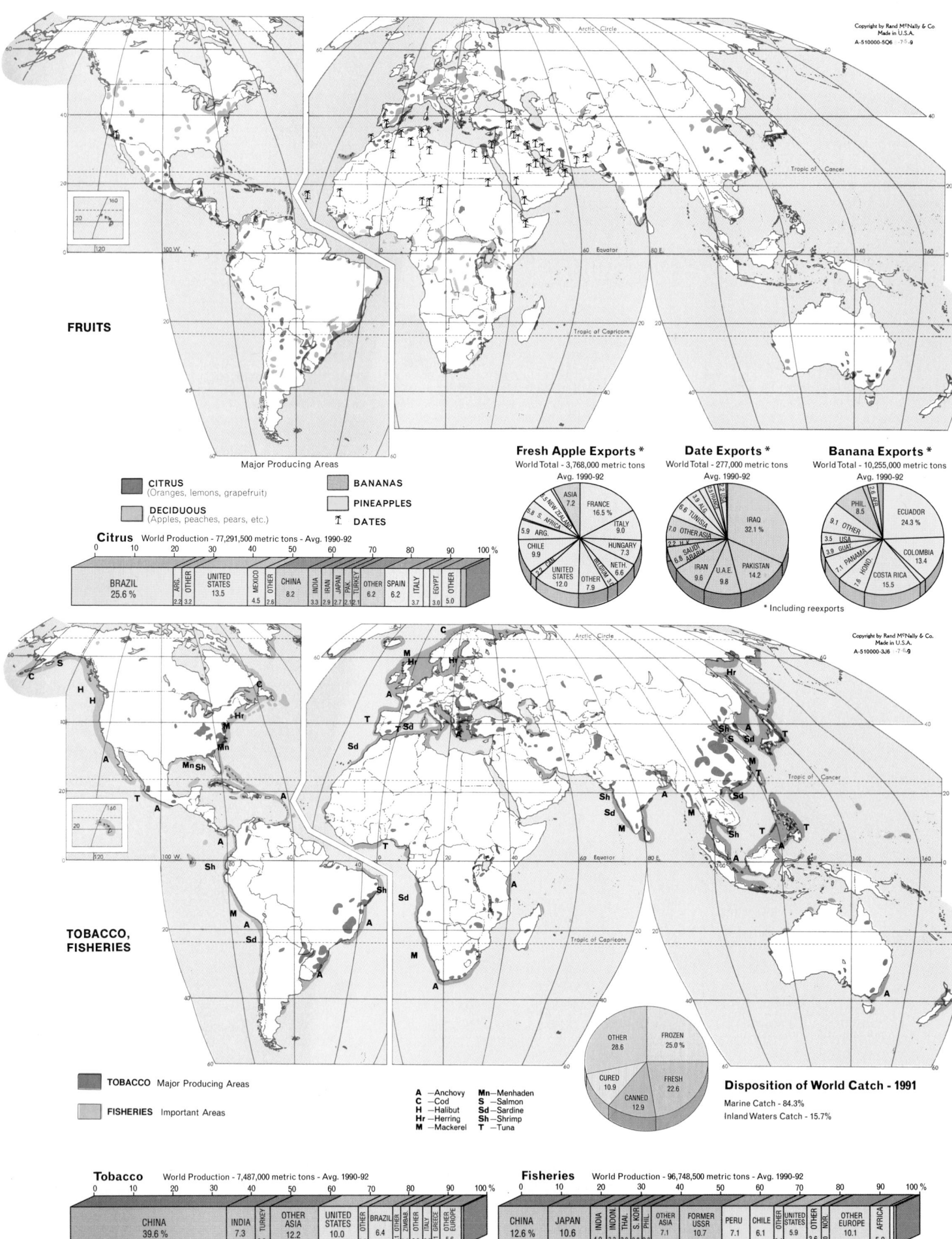

FRUITS

Major Producing Areas

Copyright by Rand McNally & Co.
Made in U.S.A.
A-510000-5Q6 -7 0 -9

CITRUS
(Oranges, lemons, grapefruit)

DECIDUOUS
(Apples, peaches, pears, etc.)

BANANAS

PINEAPPLES

DATES

Citrus World Production - 77,291,500 metric tons - Avg. 1990-92

| BRAZIL 25.6 % | ARG. 2.2 | OTHER 3.2 | UNITED STATES 13.5 | MEXICO 4.5 | OTHER 2.6 | CHINA 8.2 | INDIA 3.3 | IRAN 2.9 | JAPAN 2.7 | PAK. 2.1 | TURKEY | OTHER 6.2 | SPAIN 6.2 | ITALY 3.7 | EGYPT 3.0 | OTHER 5.0 |

Fresh Apple Exports *
World Total - 3,768,000 metric tons
Avg. 1990-92

- ASIA 7.2
- S NEW ZEALAND
- S. AFRICA 5.8
- ARG. 5.9
- CHILE 9.9
- FRANCE 16.5 %
- ITALY 9.0
- HUNGARY 7.3
- NETH. 6.6
- BELGIUM 2.2
- OTHER 7.9
- UNITED STATES 12.0

Date Exports *
World Total - 277,000 metric tons
Avg. 1990-92

- ALG. 3.8
- TUNISIA 6.6
- OTHER ASIA 7.0
- SAUDI ARABIA 2.2
- IRAN 9.6
- U.A.E. 9.8
- PAKISTAN 14.2
- IRAQ 32.1 %

Banana Exports *
World Total - 10,255,000 metric tons
Avg. 1990-92

- PHIL. 8.5
- OTHER 9.1
- GUAT. 3.5
- USA 3.9
- PANAMA 7.1
- HOND. 7.6
- COSTA RICA 15.5
- COLOMBIA 13.4
- ECUADOR 24.3 %

* Including reexports

TOBACCO, FISHERIES

Copyright by Rand McNally & Co.
Made in U.S.A.
A-510000-3J6 -7 0 -9

TOBACCO Major Producing Areas

FISHERIES Important Areas

A —Anchovy
C —Cod
H —Halibut
Hr —Herring
M —Mackerel

Mn—Menhaden
S —Salmon
Sd —Sardine
Sh —Shrimp
T —Tuna

Disposition of World Catch - 1991

- FROZEN 25.0 %
- FRESH 22.6
- CANNED 12.9
- CURED 10.9
- OTHER 28.6

Marine Catch - 84.3%
Inland Waters Catch - 15.7%

Tobacco World Production - 7,487,000 metric tons - Avg. 1990-92

| CHINA 39.6 % | INDIA 7.3 | TURKEY 3.8 | OTHER ASIA 12.2 | UNITED STATES 10.0 | OTHER | BRAZIL 6.4 | ZIMBABWE 2.1 | ITALY 3.3 | GREECE 2.1 | OTHER EUROPE 3.6 |

Fisheries World Production - 96,748,500 metric tons - Avg. 1990-92

| CHINA 12.6 % | JAPAN 10.6 | INDIA 4.0 | INDON. 3.2 | THAI. 2.9 | S. KOR 2.8 | PHIL. | OTHER ASIA 7.1 | FORMER USSR 10.7 | PERU 7.1 | CHILE 6.1 | OTHER | UNITED STATES 5.9 | OTHER 3.6 | NOR. 2.0 | OTHER EUROPE 10.1 | AFRICA 5.0 |

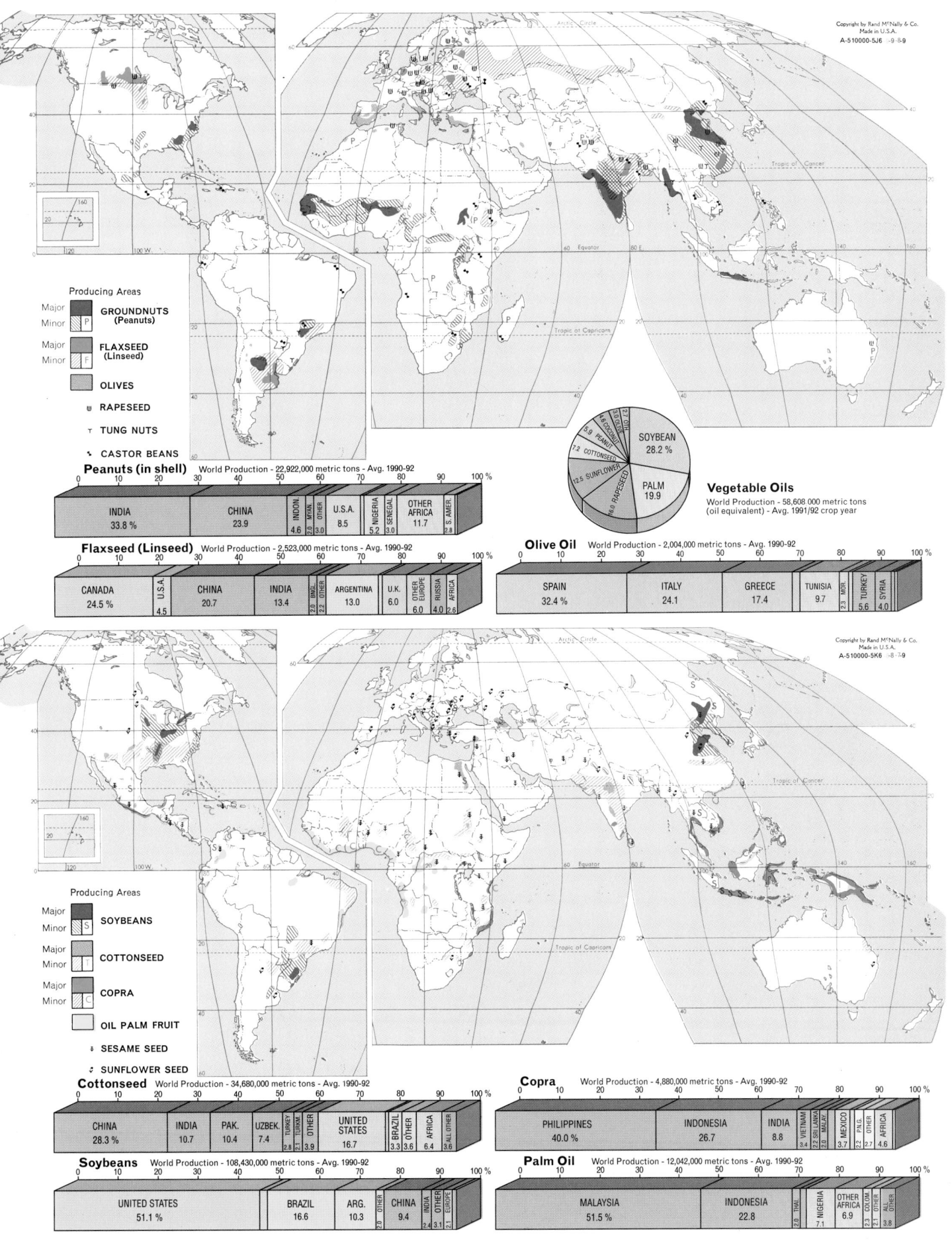

Copyright by Rand McNally & Co.
Made in U.S.A.
A-510000-5J6 -9-8-9

Producing Areas

Major / Minor — GROUNDNUTS (Peanuts) — P

Major / Minor — FLAXSEED (Linseed) — F

OLIVES

ய RAPESEED

T TUNG NUTS

✕ CASTOR BEANS

Peanuts (in shell) World Production - 22,922,000 metric tons - Avg. 1990-92

	INDIA 33.8 %	CHINA 23.9	INDON. 4.6	MYAN. 2.0	OTHER 3.0	U.S.A. 8.5	NIGERIA 5.2	SENEGAL 3.0	OTHER AFRICA 11.7	S. AMER. 2.8

Flaxseed (Linseed) World Production - 2,523,000 metric tons - Avg. 1990-92

CANADA 24.5 %	U.S.A. 4.5	CHINA 20.7	INDIA 13.4	BNGL. 2.0	OTHER 2.2	ARGENTINA 13.0	U.K. 6.0	OTHER EUROPE 6.0	RUSSIA 4.0	AFRICA 2.6

Vegetable Oils

World Production - 58,608,000 metric tons (oil equivalent) - Avg. 1991/92 crop year

Pie chart:
SOYBEAN 28.2 %
PALM 19.9
RAPESEED 16.0
SUNFLOWER 12.5
COTTONSEED 7.2
PEANUT 5.9
COCONUT 4.6
OLIVE 3.0
OTHER 2.7

Olive Oil World Production - 2,004,000 metric tons - Avg. 1990-92

SPAIN 32.4 %	ITALY 24.1	GREECE 17.4	TUNISIA 9.7	MDR. 2.3	TURKEY 5.6	SYRIA 4.0

Copyright by Rand McNally & Co.
Made in U.S.A.
A-510000-5K6 -8-7-9

Producing Areas

Major / Minor — SOYBEANS — S

Major / Minor — COTTONSEED — T

Major / Minor — COPRA — C

OIL PALM FRUIT

⚘ SESAME SEED

☙ SUNFLOWER SEED

Cottonseed World Production - 34,680,000 metric tons - Avg. 1990-92

CHINA 28.3 %	INDIA 10.7	PAK. 10.4	UZBEK. 7.4	TURKEY 2.8	TURKM. 2.1	OTHER 3.9	UNITED STATES 16.7	BRAZIL 3.3	OTHER 3.6	AFRICA 6.4	ALL OTHER 3.6

Copra World Production - 4,880,000 metric tons - Avg. 1990-92

PHILIPPINES 40.0 %	INDONESIA 26.7	INDIA 8.8	VIETNAM 3.4	SRI LANKA 2.2	MALAY. 2.0	MEXICO 3.7	P.N.G. 2.2	OTHER 2.7	AFRICA 4.6

Soybeans World Production - 108,430,000 metric tons - Avg. 1990-92

UNITED STATES 51.1 %	BRAZIL 16.6	ARG. 10.3	OTHER 2.0	CHINA 9.4	INDIA 2.4	OTHER EUROPE 3.1	2.1

Palm Oil World Production - 12,042,000 metric tons - Avg. 1990-92

MALAYSIA 51.5 %	INDONESIA 22.8	THAI. 2.0	NIGERIA 7.1	OTHER AFRICA 6.9	COLOM. 2.3	OTHER 2.1	ALL OTHER 3.8

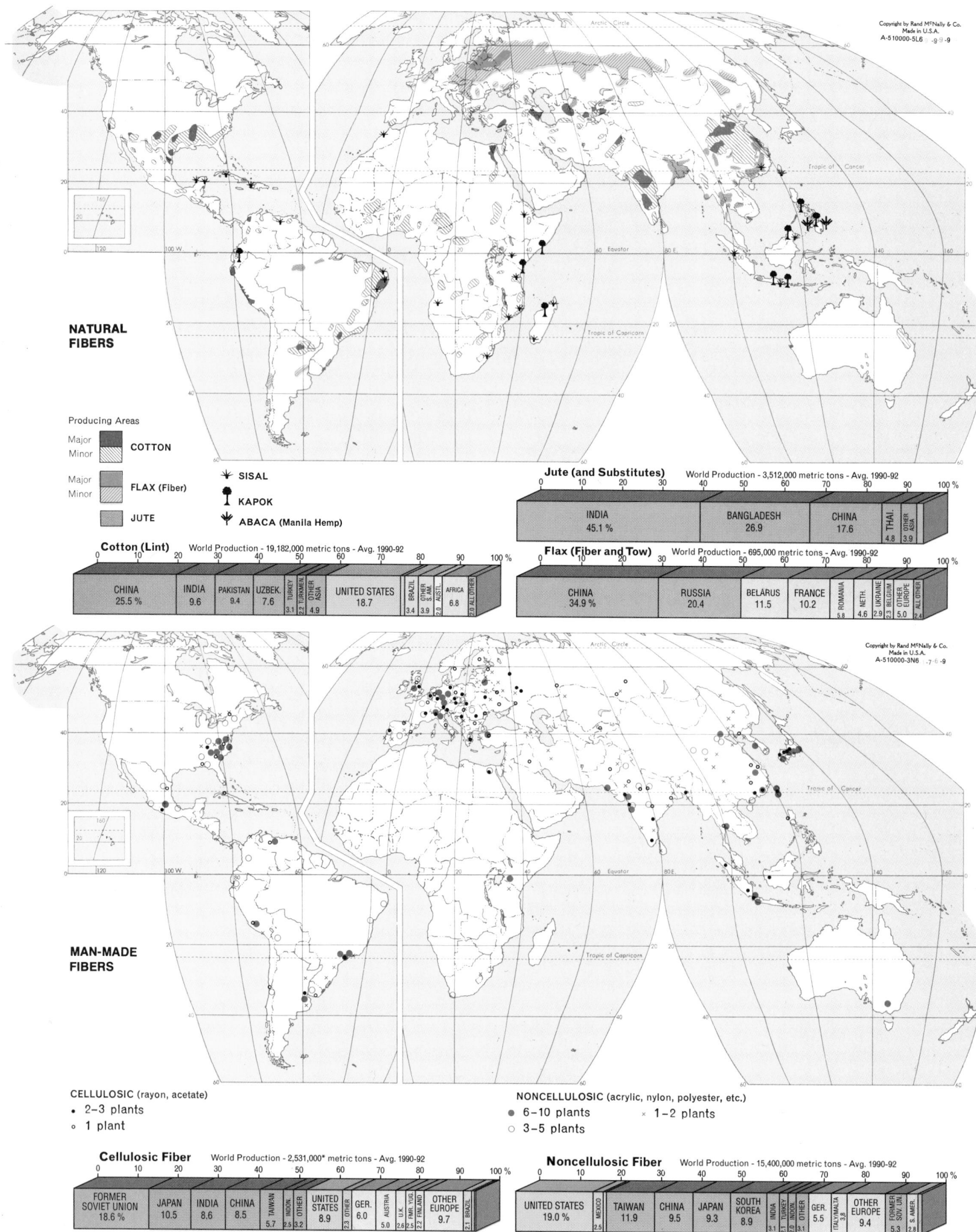

Copyright by Rand McNally & Co.
Made in U.S.A.
A-510000-5L6

**NATURAL
FIBERS**

Producing Areas

Major	
Minor	**COTTON**
Major	
Minor	**FLAX (Fiber)**
	JUTE

SISAL

KAPOK

ABACA (Manila Hemp)

Cotton (Lint)   World Production - 19,182,000 metric tons - Avg. 1990-92

CHINA 25.5 %	INDIA 9.6	PAKISTAN 9.4	UZBEK. 7.6	TURKEY 3.1	TURKMEN 2.2	OTHER ASIA 4.9	UNITED STATES 18.7	BRAZIL 3.4	OTHER S. AM. 3.9	AUSTL. 2.0	AFRICA 6.8	ALL OTHER 2.0

Jute (and Substitutes)   World Production - 3,512,000 metric tons - Avg. 1990-92

INDIA 45.1 %	BANGLADESH 26.9	CHINA 17.6	THAI. 4.8	OTHER ASIA 3.9

Flax (Fiber and Tow)   World Production - 695,000 metric tons - Avg. 1990-92

CHINA 34.9 %	RUSSIA 20.4	BELARUS 11.5	FRANCE 10.2	ROMANIA 5.8	NETH. 4.6	UKRAINE 2.9	BELGIUM OTHER EUROPE 5.0	ALL OTHER 2.4

Copyright by Rand McNally & Co.
Made in U.S.A.
A-510000-3N6

**MAN-MADE
FIBERS**

CELLULOSIC (rayon, acetate)

• 2-3 plants

○ 1 plant

NONCELLULOSIC (acrylic, nylon, polyester, etc.)

● 6-10 plants   × 1-2 plants

○ 3-5 plants

Cellulosic Fiber   World Production - 2,531,000* metric tons - Avg. 1990-92

FORMER SOVIET UNION 18.6 %	JAPAN 10.5	INDIA 8.6	CHINA 8.5	TAIWAN 5.7	INDON. 3.2	OTHER	UNITED STATES 8.9	OTHER 2.3	GER. 6.0	AUSTRIA 5.0	U.K. 2.6	FMR. YUG. 2.2	FINLAND 2.1	OTHER EUROPE 9.7	BRAZIL

*Excluding production in Indonesia and North Korea

Noncellulosic Fiber   World Production - 15,400,000 metric tons - Avg. 1990-92

UNITED STATES 19.0 %	MEXICO 2.5	TAIWAN 11.9	CHINA 9.5	JAPAN 9.3	SOUTH KOREA 8.9	INDIA 3.1	TURKEY 2.0	INDON. 3.1	OTHER	GER. 5.5	ITALY/MALTA 3.3	OTHER EUROPE 9.4	FORMER SOV. UN. 5.3	S. AMER. 2.8

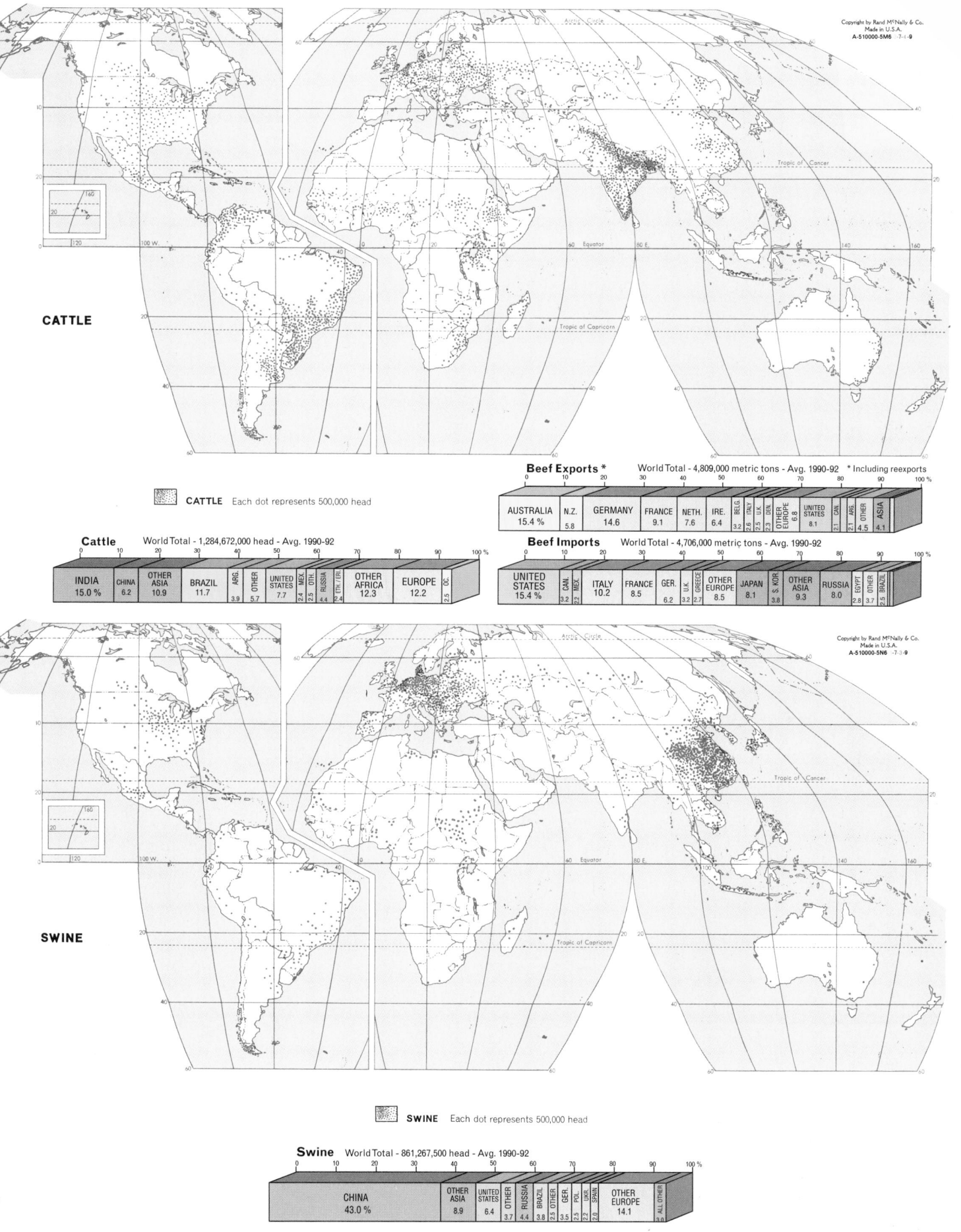

CATTLE

CATTLE Each dot represents 500,000 head

Cattle World Total - 1,284,672,000 head - Avg. 1990-92

| INDIA 15.0 % | CHINA 6.2 | OTHER ASIA 10.9 | BRAZIL 11.7 | ARG. 3.9 | OTHER 5.7 | UNITED STATES 7.7 | MEX. 2.4 | OTH 2.5 | RUSSIA 4.4 | ETH./ERI. 2.4 | OTHER AFRICA 12.3 | EUROPE 12.2 | OC. 2.5 |

Beef Exports * World Total - 4,809,000 metric tons - Avg. 1990-92 * Including reexports

| AUSTRALIA 15.4 % | N.Z. 5.8 | GERMANY 14.6 | FRANCE 9.1 | NETH. 7.6 | IRE. 6.4 | BELG. 3.2 | ITALY 2.6 | U.K. 2.5 | DEN. 2.3 | OTHER EUROPE 8.1 | UNITED STATES 6.8 | CAN. 2.1 | ARG. 2.1 | OTHER 4.5 | ASIA 4.1 |

Beef Imports World Total - 4,706,000 metric tons - Avg. 1990-92

| UNITED STATES 15.4 % | CAN. 3.2 | MEX. 2.2 | ITALY 10.2 | FRANCE 8.5 | GER. 6.2 | U.K. 3.2 | GREECE 2.7 | OTHER EUROPE 8.5 | JAPAN 8.1 | S. KOR. 3.8 | OTHER ASIA 9.3 | RUSSIA 8.0 | EGYPT 2.8 | OTHER 2.5 | BRAZIL |

SWINE

SWINE Each dot represents 500,000 head

Swine World Total - 861,267,500 head - Avg. 1990-92

| CHINA 43.0 % | OTHER ASIA 8.9 | UNITED STATES 6.4 | OTHER 3.7 | RUSSIA 4.4 | BRAZIL 3.8 | GER. 3.5 | POL. 2.5 | UKR. 2.2 | SPAIN 2.0 | OTHER EUROPE 14.1 | ALL OTHER |

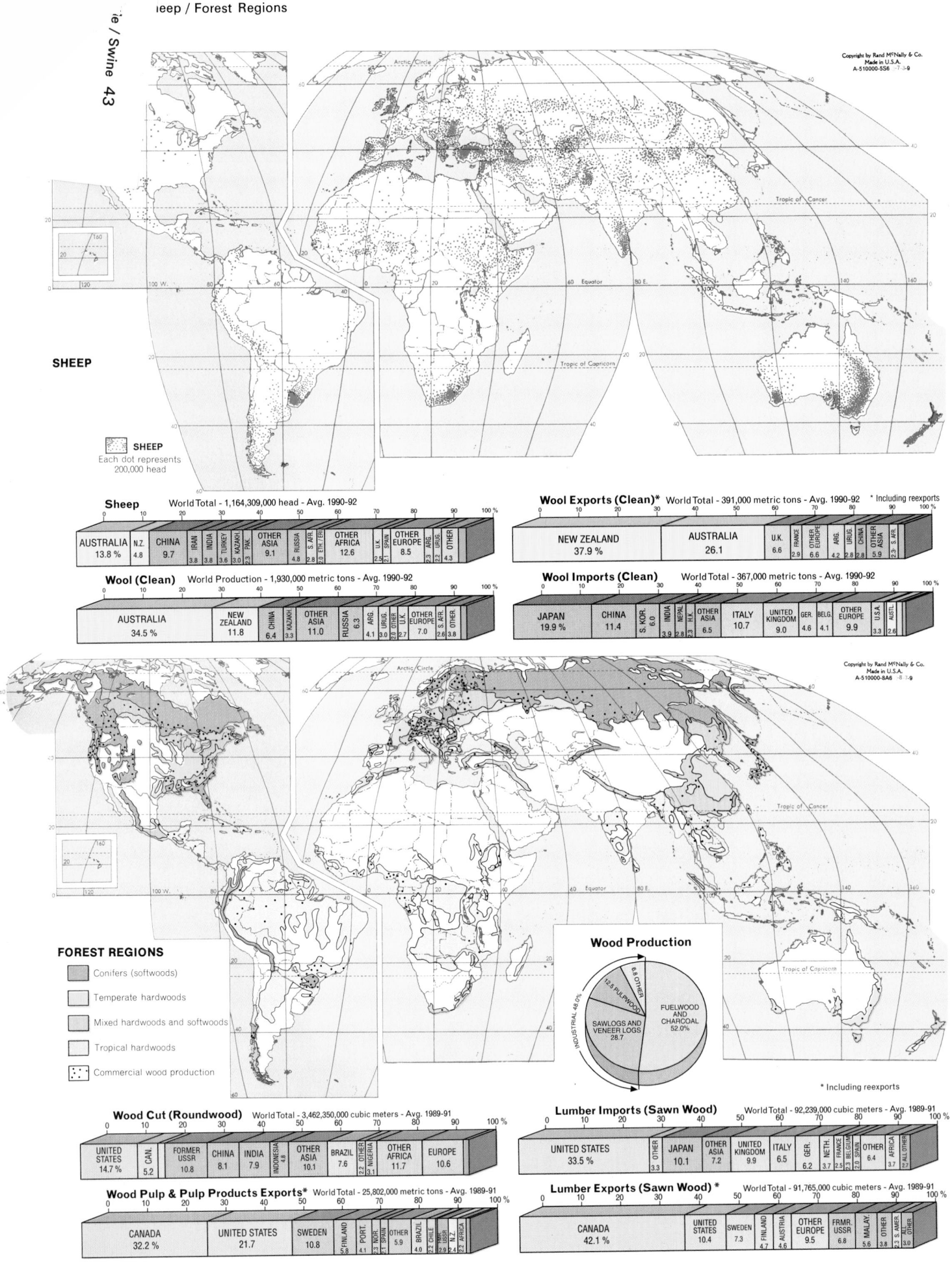

Copyright by Rand McNally & Co.
Made in U.S.A.
A-510000-5S6

SHEEP

SHEEP
Each dot represents
200,000 head

Sheep World Total - 1,164,309,000 head - Avg. 1990-92

AUSTRALIA 13.8 %	N.Z. 4.8	CHINA 9.7	IRAN 3.8	INDIA 3.8	TURKEY 3.6	KAZAKH. 3.0	PAK. 2.3	OTHER ASIA 9.1	RUSSIA 4.8	S. AFR. 2.8	ETH. ERI. 2.0	OTHER AFRICA 12.6	U.K. 2.5	SPAIN 2.1	OTHER EUROPE 8.5	ARG. 2.3	URUG.	OTHER 4.3

Wool (Clean) World Production - 1,930,000 metric tons - Avg. 1990-92

AUSTRALIA 34.5 %	NEW ZEALAND 11.8	CHINA 6.4	KAZAKH. 3.3	OTHER ASIA 11.0	RUSSIA 6.3	ARG. 4.1	URUG. 3.0	U.K. 2.7	OTHER EUROPE 7.0	S. AFR. 2.6	OTHER 3.8

Wool Exports (Clean)* World Total - 391,000 metric tons - Avg. 1990-92 *Including reexports

NEW ZEALAND 37.9 %	AUSTRALIA 26.1	U.K. 6.6	FRANCE 2.9	OTHER EUROPE 6.6	ARG. 4.2	URUG. 2.8	CHINA 2.9	OTHER ASIA 5.9	S. AFR. 2.3

Wool Imports (Clean) World Total - 367,000 metric tons - Avg. 1990-92

JAPAN 19.9 %	CHINA 11.4	S. KOR. 6.0	INDIA 3.9	NEPAL 2.8	H.K. 2.3	OTHER ASIA 6.5	ITALY 10.7	UNITED KINGDOM 9.0	GER. 4.6	BELG. 4.1	OTHER EUROPE 9.9	U.S.A. 3.3	AUSTL. 2.6

Copyright by Rand McNally & Co.
Made in U.S.A.
A-510000-8A6

FOREST REGIONS

- Conifers (softwoods)
- Temperate hardwoods
- Mixed hardwoods and softwoods
- Tropical hardwoods
- Commercial wood production

Wood Production

INDUSTRIAL 48.0%
12.5 PULPWOOD
6.8 OTHER
SAWLOGS AND VENEER LOGS 28.7
FUELWOOD AND CHARCOAL 52.0%

* Including reexports

Wood Cut (Roundwood) World Total - 3,462,350,000 cubic meters - Avg. 1989-91

UNITED STATES 14.7%	CAN. 5.2	FORMER USSR 10.8	CHINA 8.1	INDIA 7.9	INDONESIA 4.8	OTHER ASIA 10.1	BRAZIL 7.6	OTHER 2.2	NIGERIA 3.1	OTHER AFRICA 11.7	EUROPE 10.6

Wood Pulp & Pulp Products Exports* World Total - 25,802,000 metric tons - Avg. 1989-91

CANADA 32.2 %	UNITED STATES 21.7	SWEDEN 10.8	FINLAND 5.8	PORT. 4.1	NOR. 2.3	OTHER 5.9	BRAZIL 4.0	CHILE 2.2	FMR. USSR 2.9	S. AFRICA 2.4	OTHER 2.2

Lumber Imports (Sawn Wood) World Total - 92,239,000 cubic meters - Avg. 1989-91

UNITED STATES 33.5 %	OTHER 3.3	JAPAN 10.1	OTHER ASIA 7.2	UNITED KINGDOM 9.9	ITALY 6.5	GER. 6.2	NETH. 3.7	FRANCE 2.2	BELGIUM 2.0	OTHER 6.4	AFRICA 3.7	ALL OTHER

Lumber Exports (Sawn Wood)* World Total - 91,765,000 cubic meters - Avg. 1989-91

CANADA 42.1 %	UNITED STATES 10.4	SWEDEN 7.3	FINLAND 4.7	AUSTRIA 4.6	OTHER EUROPE 9.5	FRMR. USSR 6.8	MALAY. 5.6	OTHER 3.8	S. AMER. 3.7	OTHER 3.0

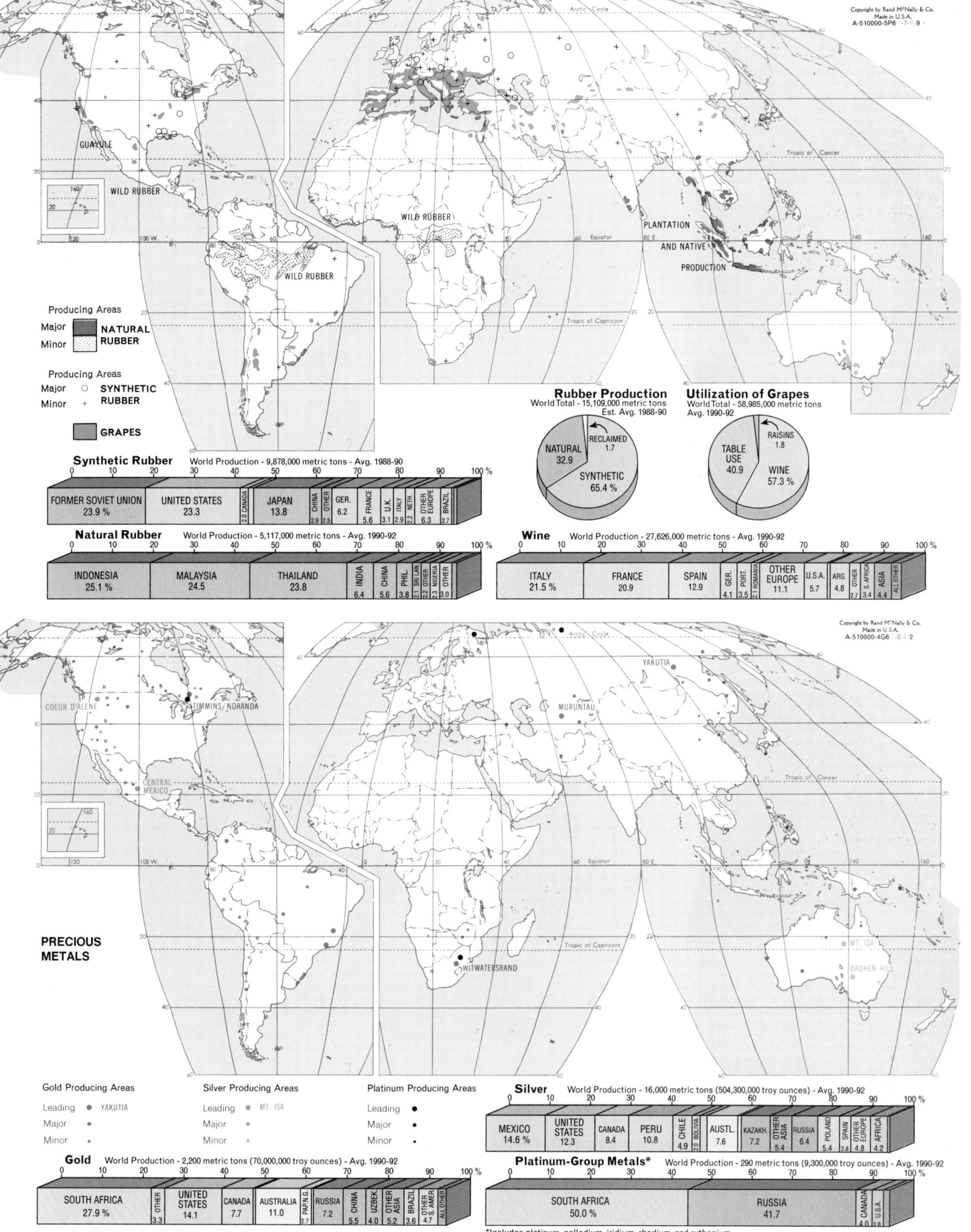

Copyright by Rand McNally & Co.
Made in U.S.A.
A-510000-5P6 -7-8-9

GUAYULE

WILD RUBBER

WILD RUBBER

WILD RUBBER

PLANTATION

AND NATIVE

PRODUCTION

Equator

Arctic Circle

Tropic of Cancer

Tropic of Capricorn

80 E.

Producing Areas

Major ▨ **NATURAL**

Minor ⣿ **RUBBER**

Producing Areas

Major ○ **SYNTHETIC**

Minor + **RUBBER**

▨ **GRAPES**

Rubber Production
World Total - 15,109,000 metric tons
Est. Avg. 1988-90

NATURAL 32.9
RECLAIMED 1.7
SYNTHETIC 65.4%

Utilization of Grapes
World Total - 58,985,000 metric tons
Avg. 1990-92

TABLE USE 40.9
RAISINS 1.8
WINE 57.3%

Synthetic Rubber   World Production - 9,878,000 metric tons - Avg. 1988-90

0	10	20	30	40	50	60	70	80	90	100 %

| FORMER SOVIET UNION 23.9 % | UNITED STATES 23.3 | JAPAN 13.8 | CANADA 2.0 | CHINA 2.9 | OTHER 6.2 | GER. 5.6 | FRANCE 5.6 | U.K. 3.1 | ITALY 2.9 | NETH. 2.2 | OTHER EUROPE 6.3 | BRAZIL 2.7 |

Natural Rubber   World Production - 5,117,000 metric tons - Avg. 1990-92

0	10	20	30	40	50	60	70	80	90	100 %

| INDONESIA 25.1 % | MALAYSIA 24.5 | THAILAND 23.8 | INDIA 6.4 | CHINA 5.6 | PHIL. 3.8 | SRI LAN. 2.1 | OTHER 2.3 | NIGERIA 2.3 | OTHER 9.0 |

Wine   World Production - 27,626,000 metric tons - Avg. 1990-92

0	10	20	30	40	50	60	70	80	90	100 %

| ITALY 21.5 % | FRANCE 20.9 | SPAIN 12.9 | GER. 4.1 | PORT. 3.5 | ROMANIA 2.7 | OTHER EUROPE 11.1 | U.S.A. 5.7 | ARG. 4.8 | OTHER 4.8 | S. AFRICA 3.4 | ASIA 4.4 | ALL OTHER |

Copyright by Rand McNally & Co.
Made in U.S.A.
A-510000-4G6 -2-2-2

COEUR D'ALENE

TIMMINS/NORANDA

CENTRAL MEXICO

YAKUTIA

MURUNTAU

MT. ISA

BROKEN HILL

WITWATERSRAND

PRECIOUS METALS

Arctic Circle
Tropic of Cancer
Equator
80 E.
Tropic of Capricorn

Gold Producing Areas

Leading ● YAKUTIA

Major ●

Minor ·

Silver Producing Areas

Leading ● MT. ISA

Major ·

Minor ·

Platinum Producing Areas

Leading ●

Major ●

Minor ●

Silver   World Production - 16,000 metric tons (504,300,000 troy ounces) - Avg. 1990-92

0	10	20	30	40	50	60	70	80	90	100 %

| MEXICO 14.6 % | UNITED STATES 12.3 | CANADA 8.4 | PERU 10.8 | CHILE 4.9 | BOLIVIA 2.6 | AUSTL. 7.6 | KAZAKH. 7.2 | OTHER ASIA | RUSSIA 6.4 | POLAND 5.4 | SPAIN 2.8 | OTHER EUROPE 4.8 | AFRICA 4.2 |

Gold   World Production - 2,200 metric tons (70,000,000 troy ounces) - Avg. 1990-92

0	10	20	30	40	50	60	70	80	90	100 %

| SOUTH AFRICA 27.9 % | OTHER 3.3 | UNITED STATES 14.1 | CANADA 7.7 | AUSTRALIA 11.0 | PAPU. G. 2.7 | RUSSIA 7.2 | CHINA 5.5 | UZBEK. 4.0 | OTHER ASIA 5.2 | BRAZIL 3.6 | OTHER S. AMER. 4.7 | ALL OTHER |

Platinum-Group Metals*   World Production - 290 metric tons (9,300,000 troy ounces) - Avg. 1990-92

0	10	20	30	40	50	60	70	80	90	100 %

| SOUTH AFRICA 50.0 % | RUSSIA 41.7 | CANADA 4.0 | U.S.A. 2.8 |

*Includes platinum, palladium, iridium, rhodium, and ruthenium

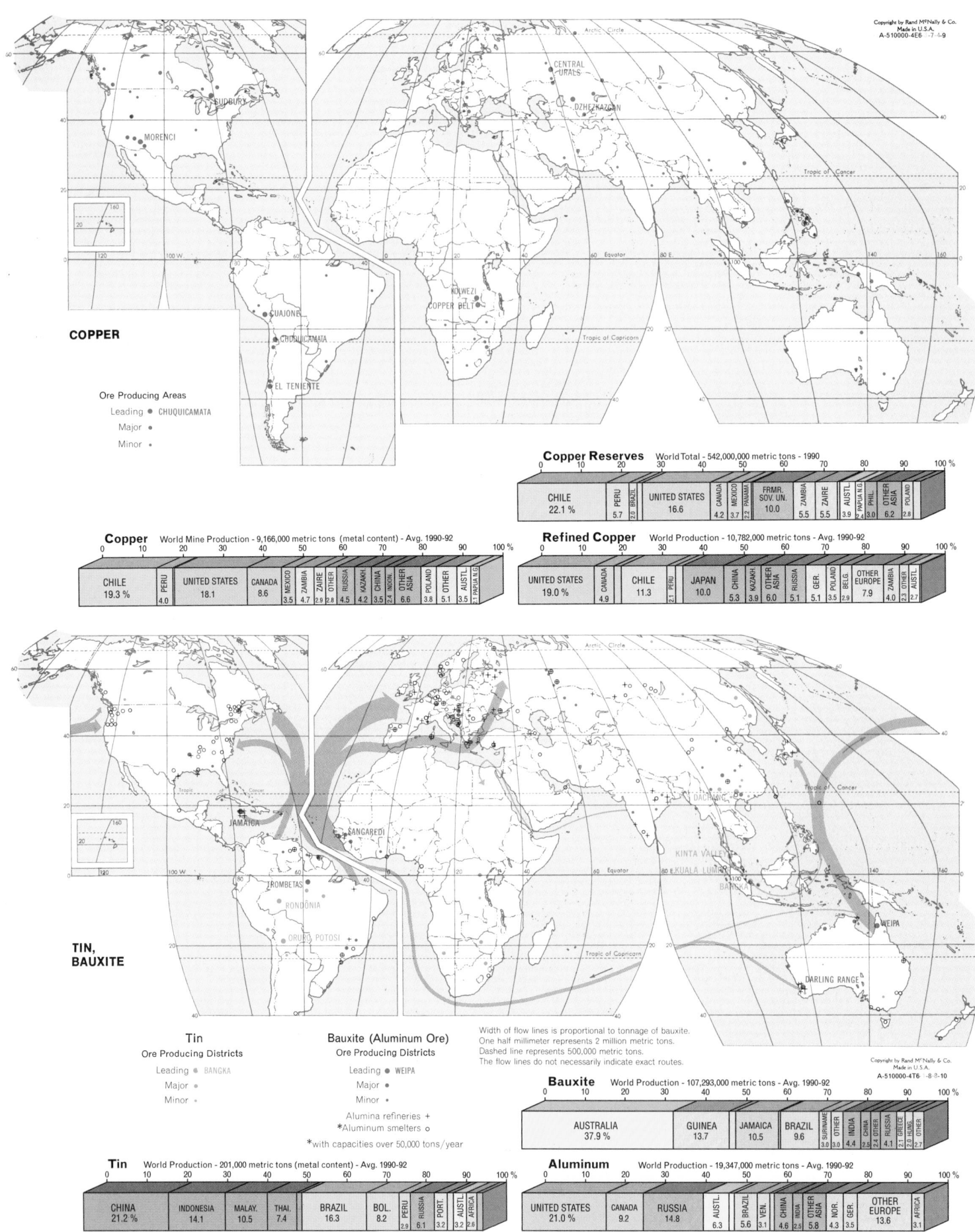

COPPER

Ore Producing Areas

Leading ● CHUQUICAMATA

Major ●

Minor ·

Copper Reserves World Total - 542,000,000 metric tons - 1990

		0	10	20	30	40	50	60	70	80	90	100 %

| CHILE 22.1 % | PERU 5.7 | BRAZIL 2.0 | UNITED STATES 16.6 | CANADA 4.2 | MEXICO 3.7 | PANAMA 2.2 | FRMR. SOV. UN. 10.0 | ZAMBIA 5.5 | ZAIRE 5.5 | AUSTL. 3.9 | PAPUA N.G. 2.4 | PHIL. 3.0 | OTHER ASIA 6.2 | POLAND 2.8 |

Copper World Mine Production - 9,166,000 metric tons (metal content) - Avg. 1990-92

0	10	20	30	40	50	60	70	80	90	100 %

| CHILE 19.3 % | PERU 4.0 | UNITED STATES 18.1 | CANADA 8.6 | MEXICO 3.5 | ZAMBIA 4.7 | ZAIRE 2.9 | OTHER 4.5 | RUSSIA 4.2 | KAZAKH. 3.5 | CHINA 2.4 | INDON. 6.6 | OTHER ASIA 3.8 | POLAND 5.1 | OTHER AUSTL. 3.5 | PAPUA N.G. 2.1 |

Refined Copper World Production - 10,782,000 metric tons - Avg. 1990-92

0	10	20	30	40	50	60	70	80	90	100 %

| UNITED STATES 19.0 % | CANADA 4.9 | CHILE 11.3 | PERU 2.1 | JAPAN 10.0 | CHINA 5.3 | KAZAKH. 3.9 | OTHER ASIA 6.0 | RUSSIA 5.1 | GER. 5.1 | POLAND 2.9 | BELG. 5.1 | OTHER EUROPE 7.9 | ZAMBIA 2.3 | OTHER 2.7 | AUSTL. |

TIN, BAUXITE

Width of flow lines is proportional to tonnage of bauxite.
One half millimeter represents 2 million metric tons.
Dashed line represents 500,000 metric tons.
The flow lines do not necessarily indicate exact routes.

Tin

Ore Producing Districts

Leading ● BANGKA

Major ●

Minor ·

Bauxite (Aluminum Ore)

Ore Producing Districts

Leading ● WEIPA

Major ●

Minor ·

Alumina refineries +

*Aluminum smelters o

*with capacities over 50,000 tons/year

Bauxite World Production - 107,293,000 metric tons - Avg. 1990-92

0	10	20	30	40	50	60	70	80	90	100 %

| AUSTRALIA 37.9 % | GUINEA 13.7 | JAMAICA 10.5 | BRAZIL 9.6 | SURINAME 3.0 | OTHER 3.0 | INDIA 4.4 | CHINA 2.4 | OTHER 2.4 | RUSSIA 4.1 | GREECE 2.0 | HUNG. 2.1 | OTHER 2.7 |

Tin World Production - 201,000 metric tons (metal content) - Avg. 1990-92

0	10	20	30	40	50	60	70	80	90	100 %

| CHINA 21.2 % | INDONESIA 14.1 | MALAY. 10.5 | THAI. 7.4 | BRAZIL 16.3 | BOL. 8.2 | PERU 2.9 | RUSSIA 6.1 | PORT. 3.2 | AUSTL. 3.2 | AFRICA 2.6 |

Aluminum World Production - 19,347,000 metric tons - Avg. 1990-92

0	10	20	30	40	50	60	70	80	90	100 %

| UNITED STATES 21.0 % | CANADA 9.2 | RUSSIA 14.8 | AUSTL. 6.3 | BRAZIL 5.6 | VEN. 3.1 | CHINA 4.6 | INDIA 2.5 | OTHER ASIA 5.8 | NOR. 4.3 | GER. 3.5 | OTHER EUROPE 13.6 | AFRICA 3.1 |

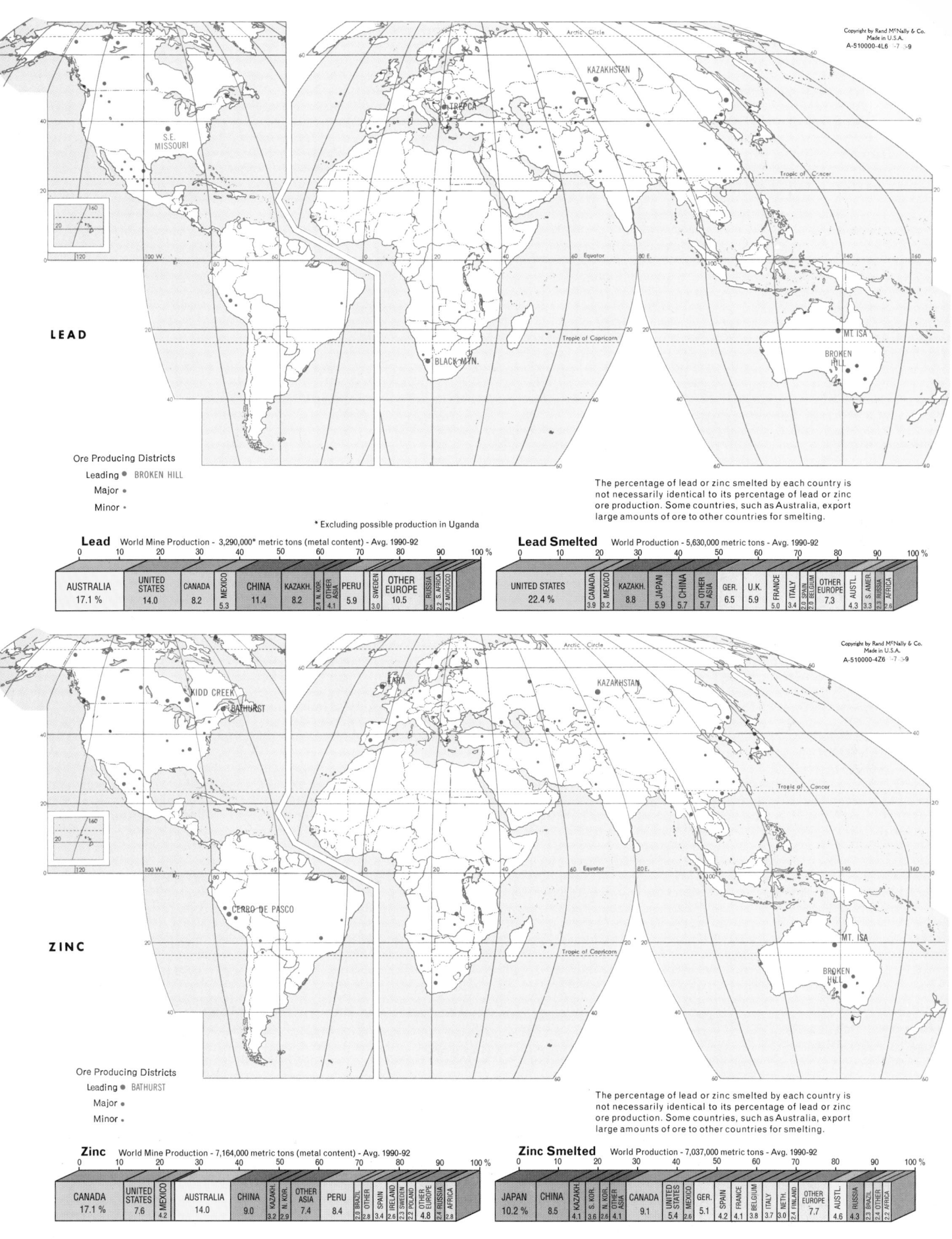

KAZAKHSTAN

TREPCA

S.E.
MISSOURI

LEAD

BLACK MTN.

MT. ISA

BROKEN
HILL

Ore Producing Districts

Leading ● BROKEN HILL

Major ●

Minor ·

* Excluding possible production in Uganda

The percentage of lead or zinc smelted by each country is
not necessarily identical to its percentage of lead or zinc
ore production. Some countries, such as Australia, export
large amounts of ore to other countries for smelting.

Lead World Mine Production - 3,290,000* metric tons (metal content) - Avg. 1990-92

| AUSTRALIA 17.1 % | UNITED STATES 14.0 | CANADA 8.2 | MEXICO 5.3 | CHINA 11.4 | KAZAKH. 8.2 | N. KOR. 2.4 | OTHER ASIA 4.1 | PERU 5.9 | SWEDEN 3.0 | OTHER EUROPE 10.5 | RUSSIA 2.6 | S. AFRICA 2.2 | MOROCCO 2.2 |

Lead Smelted World Production - 5,630,000 metric tons - Avg. 1990-92

| UNITED STATES 22.4 % | CANADA 3.9 | MEXICO 3.2 | KAZAKH. 8.8 | JAPAN 5.9 | CHINA 5.7 | OTHER ASIA 5.7 | GER. 6.5 | U.K. 5.9 | FRANCE 5.0 | ITALY 3.4 | SPAIN 2.0 | BELGIUM 2.0 | OTHER EUROPE 7.3 | AUSTL. 4.3 | S. AMER. 3.3 | RUSSIA 2.3 | AFRICA 2.6 |

LARA

KAZAKHSTAN

KIDD CREEK
BATHURST

CERRO DE PASCO

ZINC

MT. ISA

BROKEN
HILL

Ore Producing Districts

Leading ● BATHURST

Major ●

Minor ·

The percentage of lead or zinc smelted by each country is
not necessarily identical to its percentage of lead or zinc
ore production. Some countries, such as Australia, export
large amounts of ore to other countries for smelting.

Zinc World Mine Production - 7,164,000 metric tons (metal content) - Avg. 1990-92

| CANADA 17.1 % | UNITED STATES 7.6 | MEXICO 4.2 | AUSTRALIA 14.0 | CHINA 9.0 | KAZAKH. 3.2 | N. KOR. 2.9 | OTHER ASIA 7.4 | PERU 8.4 | BRAZIL 2.0 | OTHER 2.8 | SPAIN 3.4 | IRELAND 2.3 | SWEDEN 2.2 | OTHER EUROPE 4.8 | RUSSIA 2.4 | AFRICA |

Zinc Smelted World Production - 7,037,000 metric tons - Avg. 1990-92

| JAPAN 10.2 % | CHINA 8.5 | KAZAKH. 4.1 | S. KOR. 3.6 | N. KOR. 4.1 | OTHER ASIA 4.1 | CANADA 9.1 | UNITED STATES 5.4 | MEXICO 2.6 | GER. 5.1 | SPAIN 4.2 | FRANCE 4.1 | BELGIUM 3.8 | ITALY 3.7 | NETH. 3.0 | FINLAND 2.4 | OTHER EUROPE 7.7 | AUSTL. 4.6 | RUSSIA 4.3 | OTHER 2.2 | AFRICA 2.2 |

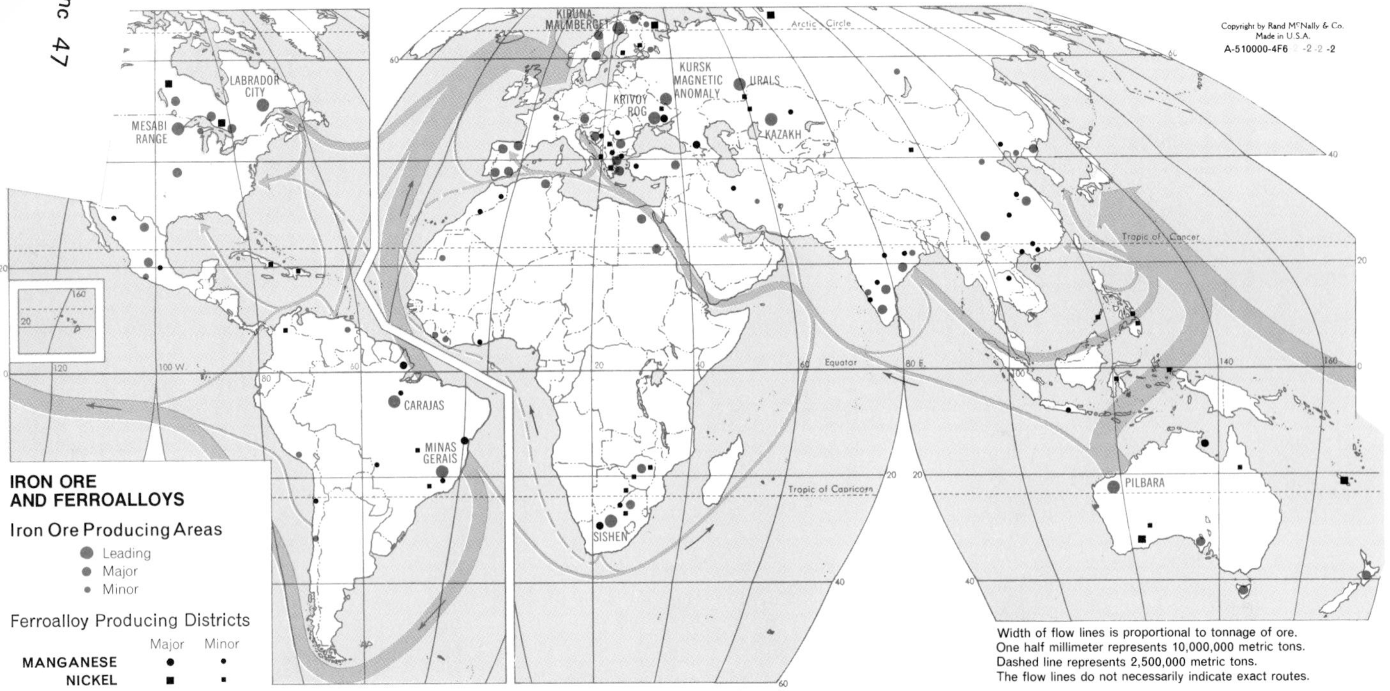

Zinc 47

Copyright by Rand McNally & Co.
Made in U.S.A.
A-510000-4F6 -2 -2 -2

KIRUNA
MALMBERGET

Arctic Circle

KURSK
MAGNETIC
ANOMALY

URALS

LABRADOR
CITY

KRIVOY
ROG

KAZAKH

MESABI
RANGE

Tropic of Cancer

100 W

Equator

80 E

CARAJAS

MINAS
GERAIS

Tropic of Capricorn

PILBARA

SISHEN

IRON ORE AND FERROALLOYS

Iron Ore Producing Areas

- Leading
- Major
- Minor

Ferroalloy Producing Districts

	Major	Minor
MANGANESE	●	●
NICKEL	■	■

Width of flow lines is proportional to tonnage of ore.
One half millimeter represents 10,000,000 metric tons.
Dashed line represents 2,500,000 metric tons.
The flow lines do not necessarily indicate exact routes.

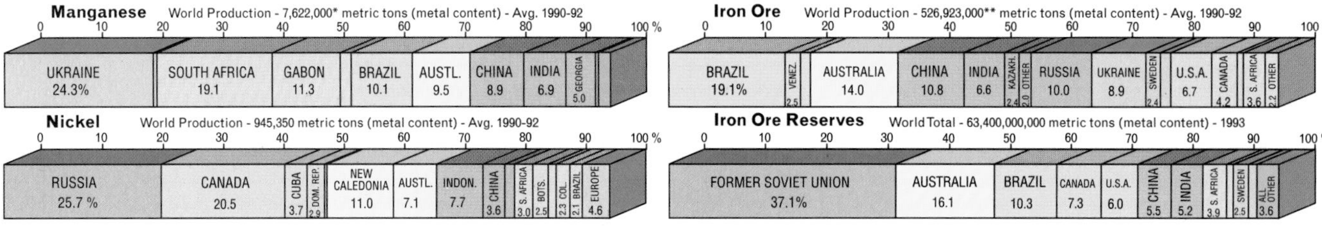

Manganese
World Production - 7,622,000* metric tons (metal content) - Avg. 1990-92

UKRAINE 24.3%	SOUTH AFRICA 19.1	GABON 11.3	BRAZIL 10.1	AUSTL. 9.5	CHINA 8.9	INDIA 6.9	GEORGIA 5.0

Iron Ore
World Production - 526,923,000** metric tons (metal content) - Avg. 1990-92

BRAZIL 19.1%	VENEZ. 2.5	AUSTRALIA 14.0	CHINA 10.8	INDIA 6.6	KAZAKH. 2.0	OTHER	RUSSIA 10.0	UKRAINE 8.9	SWEDEN 2.4	U.S.A. 6.7	CANADA 4.2	S. AFRICA 3.6	OTHER 2.2

Nickel
World Production - 945,350 metric tons (metal content) - Avg. 1990-92

RUSSIA 25.7%	CANADA 20.5	CUBA 3.7	DOM. REP. 2.9	NEW CALEDONIA 11.0	AUSTL. 7.1	INDON. 7.7	CHINA 3.6	S. AFRICA 3.0	BOTS. 2.5	COL. 2.3	BRAZIL 2.1	EUROPE 4.6

Iron Ore Reserves
World Total - 63,400,000,000 metric tons (metal content) - 1993

FORMER SOVIET UNION 37.1%	AUSTRALIA 16.1	BRAZIL 10.3	CANADA 7.3	U.S.A. 6.0	CHINA 5.5	INDIA 5.2	S. AFRICA 3.9	SWEDEN 2.5	ALL OTHER 3.6

*Excluding possible production in Colombia, Cuba, Panama, Peru, Sudan, and Vietnam

**Excluding possible production in Cuba and Vietnam

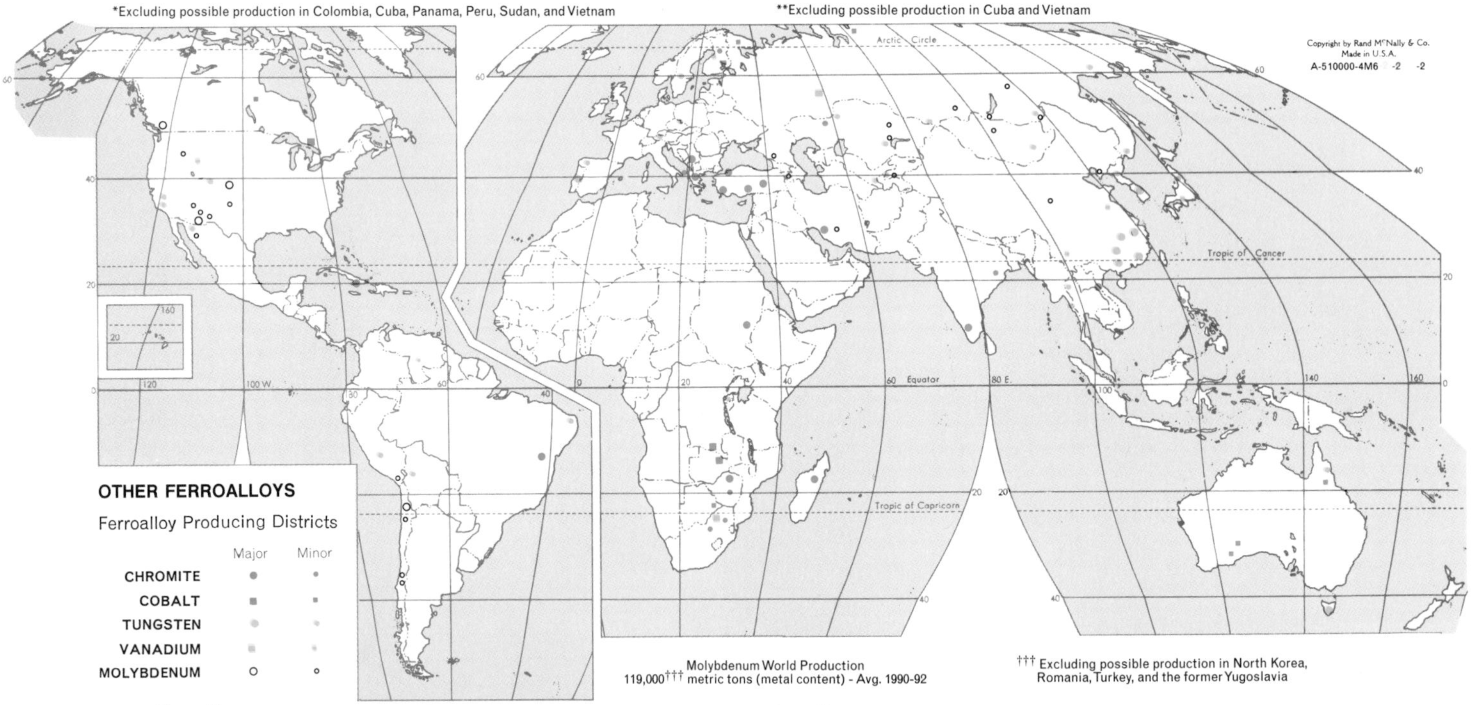

Copyright by Rand McNally & Co.
Made in U.S.A.
A-510000-4M6 -2 -2

Arctic Circle

Tropic of Cancer

100 W

Equator

80 E

Tropic of Capricorn

OTHER FERROALLOYS

Ferroalloy Producing Districts

	Major	Minor
CHROMITE	●	●
COBALT	■	■
TUNGSTEN	●	●
VANADIUM	●	●
MOLYBDENUM	○	○

Molybdenum World Production
119,000††† metric tons (metal content) - Avg. 1990-92

††† Excluding possible production in North Korea, Romania, Turkey, and the former Yugoslavia

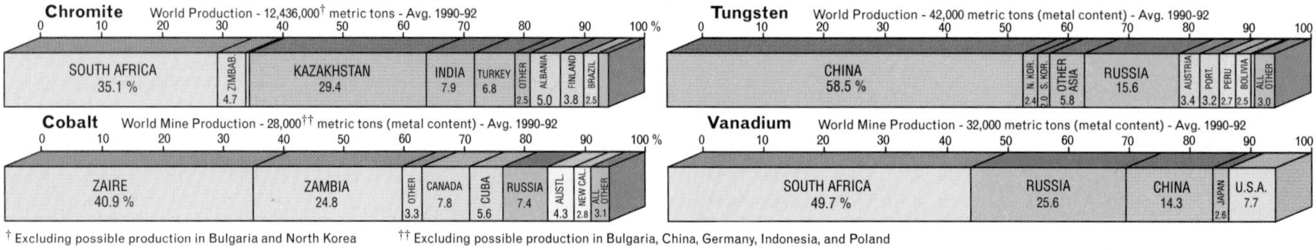

Chromite
World Production - 12,436,000† metric tons - Avg. 1990-92

SOUTH AFRICA 35.1%	ZIMBAB. 4.7	KAZAKHSTAN 29.4	INDIA 7.9	TURKEY 6.8	OTHER 2.5	ALBANIA 5.0	FINLAND 3.8	BRAZIL 2.5

Tungsten
World Production - 42,000 metric tons (metal content) - Avg. 1990-92

CHINA 58.5%	N. KOR. 2.0	S. KOR.	OTHER ASIA 5.8	RUSSIA 15.6	AUSTRIA 3.4	PORT. 3.2	PERU 2.7	BOLIVIA 2.5	ALL OTHER 3.0

Cobalt
World Mine Production - 28,000†† metric tons (metal content) - Avg. 1990-92

ZAIRE 40.9%	ZAMBIA 24.8	OTHER 3.3	CANADA 7.8	CUBA 5.6	RUSSIA 7.4	AUSTL. 4.3	NEW CAL. 2.8	ALL OTHER 3.1

Vanadium
World Mine Production - 32,000 metric tons (metal content) - Avg. 1990-92

SOUTH AFRICA 49.7%	RUSSIA 25.6	CHINA 14.3	JAPAN	U.S.A. 7.7

† Excluding possible production in Bulgaria and North Korea   †† Excluding possible production in Bulgaria, China, Germany, Indonesia, and Poland

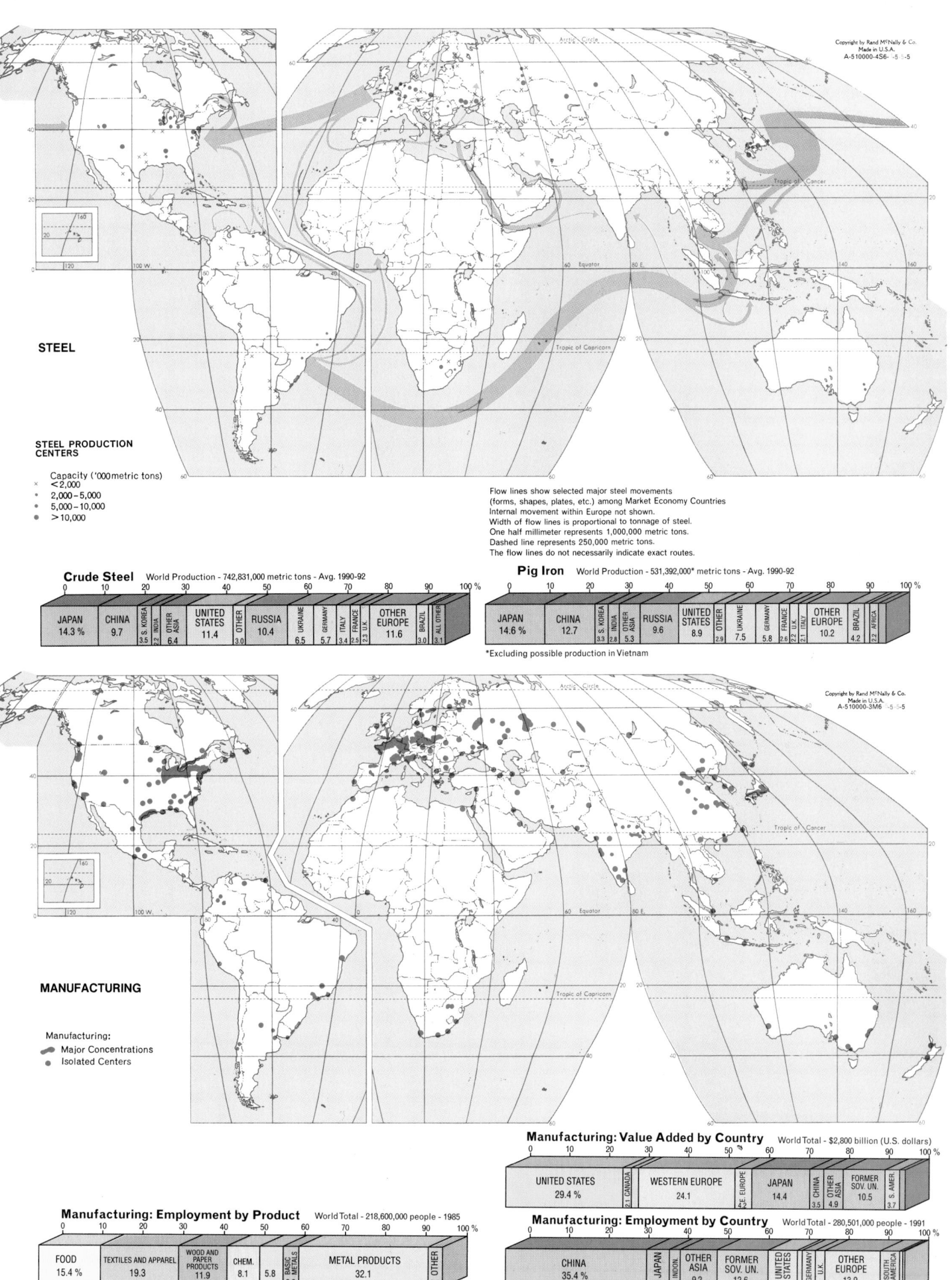

STEEL

STEEL PRODUCTION CENTERS

Capacity ('000 metric tons)
- × <2,000
- • 2,000–5,000
- • 5,000–10,000
- ● >10,000

Flow lines show selected major steel movements
(forms, shapes, plates, etc.) among Market Economy Countries
Internal movement within Europe not shown.
Width of flow lines is proportional to tonnage of steel.
One half millimeter represents 1,000,000 metric tons.
Dashed line represents 250,000 metric tons.
The flow lines do not necessarily indicate exact routes.

Crude Steel World Production - 742,831,000 metric tons - Avg. 1990-92

JAPAN 14.3 %	CHINA 9.7	S. KOREA 3.5	INDIA 2.2	OTHER ASIA 6.4	UNITED STATES 11.4	OTHER 3.0	RUSSIA 10.4	UKRAINE 6.5	GERMANY 5.7	ITALY 3.4	FRANCE 2.5	U.K. 2.3	OTHER EUROPE 11.6	BRAZIL 3.0	ALL OTHER 3.1

Pig Iron World Production - 531,392,000* metric tons - Avg. 1990-92

JAPAN 14.6 %	CHINA 12.7	S. KOREA 3.3	INDIA 2.8	OTHER ASIA 5.3	RUSSIA 9.6	UNITED STATES 8.9	OTHER 2.9	UKRAINE 7.5	GERMANY 5.8	FRANCE 2.6	U.K. 2.2	ITALY 2.1	OTHER EUROPE 10.2	BRAZIL 4.2	AFRICA 2.2

*Excluding possible production in Vietnam

MANUFACTURING

Manufacturing:
- ⌇ Major Concentrations
- • Isolated Centers

Manufacturing: Value Added by Country World Total - $2,800 billion (U.S. dollars)

UNITED STATES 29.4 %	CANADA 2.1	WESTERN EUROPE 24.1	E. EUROPE	JAPAN 14.4	CHINA 3.5	OTHER ASIA 4.9	FORMER SOV. UN. 10.5	S. AMER. 3.7

Manufacturing: Employment by Product World Total - 218,600,000 people - 1985

FOOD 15.4 %	TEXTILES AND APPAREL 19.3	WOOD AND PAPER PRODUCTS 11.9	CHEM. 8.1	5.8	BASIC METALS 3.9	METAL PRODUCTS 32.1	OTHER 3.5

NON-METAL MINERAL PRODUCTS

Manufacturing: Employment by Country World Total - 280,501,000 people - 1991

CHINA 35.4 %	JAPAN 5.7	INDON. 2.8	OTHER ASIA 9.2	FORMER SOV. UN. 12.6	UNITED STATES 7.3	GERMANY 3.3	U.K. 2.4	OTHER EUROPE 13.9	SOUTH AMERICA 4.9

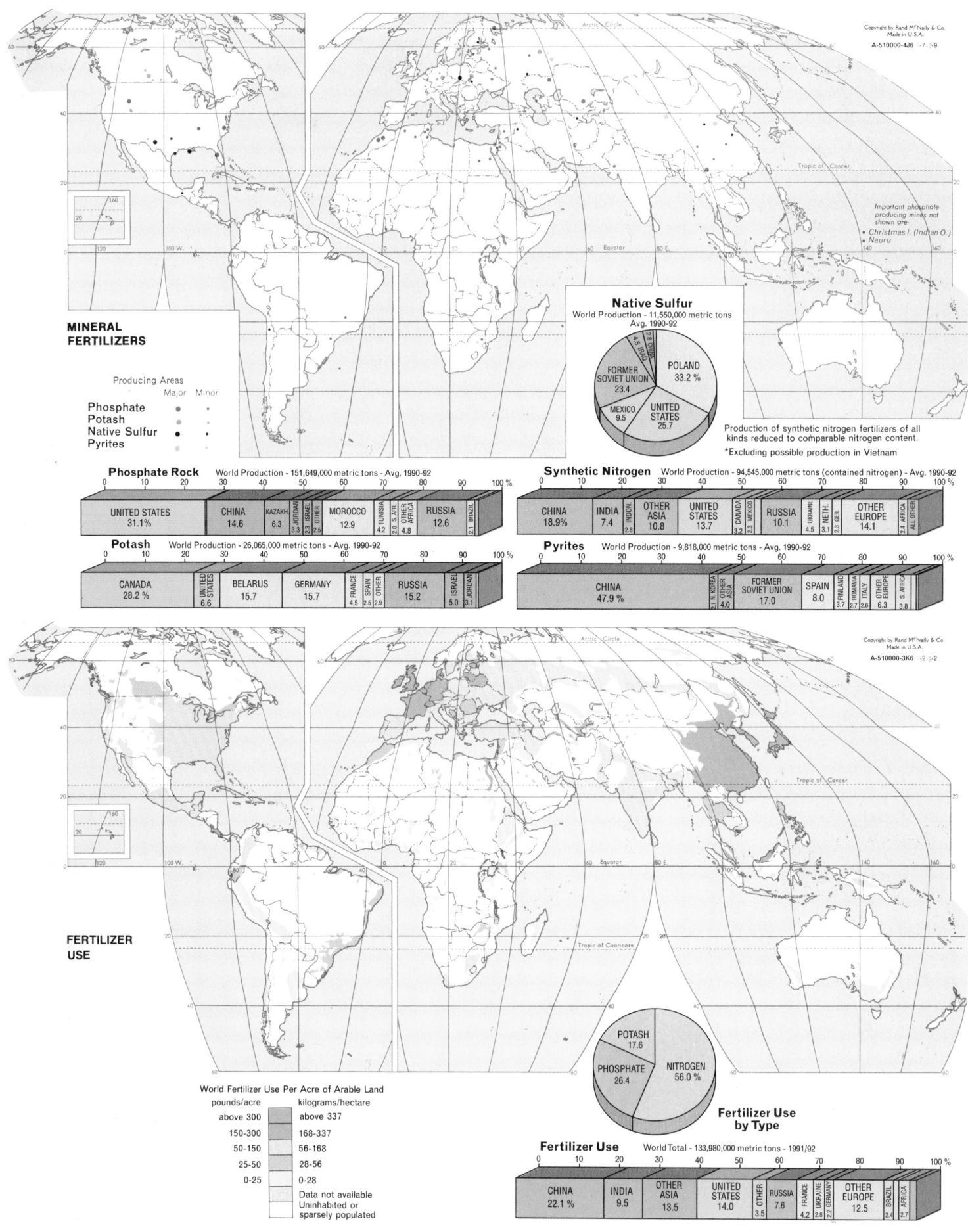

Important phosphate producing mines not shown are:
• *Christmas I. (Indian O.)*
• *Nauru*

MINERAL FERTILIZERS

Producing Areas

	Major	Minor
Phosphate	•	•
Potash	•	•
Native Sulfur	•	•
Pyrites	•	•

Native Sulfur

World Production - 11,550,000 metric tons
Avg. 1990-92

- POLAND 33.2%
- UNITED STATES 25.7
- FORMER SOVIET UNION 23.4
- MEXICO 9.5
- IRAN 4.5
- CHINA 2.8

Production of synthetic nitrogen fertilizers of all kinds reduced to comparable nitrogen content.

*Excluding possible production in Vietnam

Phosphate Rock
World Production - 151,649,000 metric tons - Avg. 1990-92

| UNITED STATES 31.1% | CHINA 14.6 | KAZAKH. 6.3 | JORDAN 3.3 | ISRAEL 2.3 | OTHER 2.5 | MOROCCO 12.9 | TUNISIA 4.2 | S. AFR. 2.0 | OTHER AFRICA 4.8 | RUSSIA 12.6 | BRAZIL 2.1 |

Potash
World Production - 26,065,000 metric tons - Avg. 1990-92

| CANADA 28.2% | UNITED STATES 6.6 | BELARUS 15.7 | GERMANY 15.7 | FRANCE 4.5 | SPAIN 2.5 | OTHER 2.9 | RUSSIA 15.2 | ISRAEL 5.0 | JORDAN 3.1 |

Synthetic Nitrogen
World Production - 94,545,000 metric tons (contained nitrogen) - Avg. 1990-92

| CHINA 18.9% | INDIA 7.4 | INDON. 2.8 | OTHER ASIA 10.8 | UNITED STATES 13.7 | CANADA 3.2 | MEXICO 2.3 | RUSSIA 10.1 | UKRAINE 4.5 | NETH. 3.1 | GER. 2.3 | OTHER EUROPE 14.1 | AFRICA 2.4 | ALL OTHER |

Pyrites
World Production - 9,818,000 metric tons - Avg. 1990-92

| CHINA 47.9% | N. KOREA 2.1 | OTHER ASIA 4.0 | FORMER SOVIET UNION 17.0 | SPAIN 8.0 | FINLAND 3.7 | ROMANIA 2.7 | ITALY 2.6 | OTHER EUROPE 6.3 | S. AFRICA 3.8 |

FERTILIZER USE

World Fertilizer Use Per Acre of Arable Land

pounds/acre	kilograms/hectare
above 300	above 337
150-300	168-337
50-150	56-168
25-50	28-56
0-25	0-28
Data not available	
Uninhabited or sparsely populated	

Fertilizer Use by Type

- NITROGEN 56.0%
- PHOSPHATE 26.4
- POTASH 17.6

Fertilizer Use
World Total - 133,980,000 metric tons - 1991/92

| CHINA 22.1% | INDIA 9.5 | OTHER ASIA 13.5 | UNITED STATES 14.0 | OTHER 3.5 | RUSSIA 7.6 | FRANCE 4.2 | UKRAINE 2.8 | GERMANY 2.2 | OTHER EUROPE 12.5 | BRAZIL 2.4 | AFRICA 2.7 |

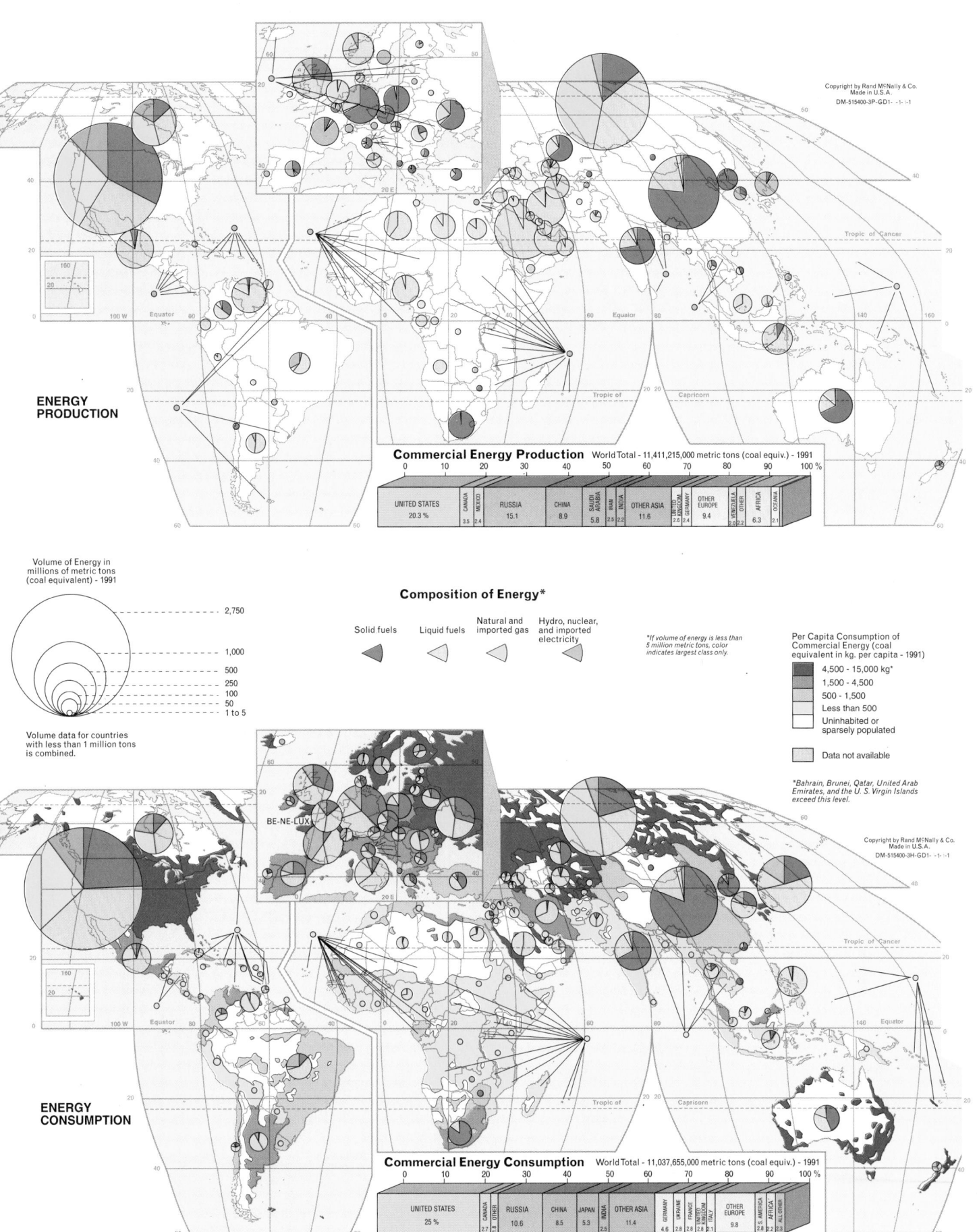

ENERGY
PRODUCTION

Copyright by Rand McNally & Co.
Made in U.S.A.
DM-515400-3P-GD1- -1- -1

Commercial Energy Production World Total - 11,411,215,000 metric tons (coal equiv.) - 1991

| 0 | 10 | 20 | 30 | 40 | 50 | 60 | 70 | 80 | 90 | 100 % |

| UNITED STATES 20.3 % | CANADA 3.5 | MEXICO 2.4 | RUSSIA 15.1 | CHINA 8.9 | SAUDI ARABIA 5.8 | IRAN 2.5 | INDIA 2.2 | OTHER ASIA 11.6 | UNITED KINGDOM 2.6 | GERMANY 2.4 | OTHER EUROPE 9.4 | VENEZUELA 2.0 | OTHER 2.2 | AFRICA 6.3 | OCEANIA 2.1 |

Volume of Energy in
millions of metric tons
(coal equivalent) - 1991

- - - - - 2,750
- - - - - 1,000
- - - - - 500
- - - - - 250
- - - - - 100
- - - - - 50
- - - - - 1 to 5

Volume data for countries
with less than 1 million tons
is combined.

Composition of Energy*

Solid fuels Liquid fuels Natural and imported gas Hydro, nuclear, and imported electricity

*If volume of energy is less than
5 million metric tons, color
indicates largest class only.

Per Capita Consumption of
Commercial Energy (coal
equivalent in kg. per capita - 1991)

4,500 - 15,000 kg*
1,500 - 4,500
500 - 1,500
Less than 500
Uninhabited or
sparsely populated

Data not available

*Bahrain, Brunei, Qatar, United Arab
Emirates, and the U. S. Virgin Islands
exceed this level.

Copyright by Rand McNally & Co.
Made in U.S.A.
DM-515400-3H-GD1- -1- -1

BE-NE-LUX

ENERGY
CONSUMPTION

Commercial Energy Consumption World Total - 11,037,655,000 metric tons (coal equiv.) - 1991

| 0 | 10 | 20 | 30 | 40 | 50 | 60 | 70 | 80 | 90 | 100 % |

| UNITED STATES 25 % | CANADA 2.7 | OTHER 1.8 | RUSSIA 10.6 | CHINA 8.5 | JAPAN 5.3 | INDIA 2.5 | OTHER ASIA 11.4 | GERMANY 4.6 | UKRAINE 2.8 | FRANCE 2.8 | UNITED KINGDOM 2.8 | ITALY 2.1 | OTHER EUROPE 9.8 | S. AMERICA 2.8 | AFRICA 2.2 | ALL OTHER 2.3 |

MINERAL FUELS

BEAUFORT BASIN
INTERIOR
APPALACHIAN
PERMIAN BASIN
GULF OF CAMPECHE
MARACAIBO
NORTH SEA
SILESIA
Arctic Circle
Tropic of Cancer
Coal and Lignite
Major bituminous coal deposit
Minor bituminous coal deposit
Lignite deposit
Major anthracite deposit
Minor anthracite deposit
Petroleum
Major Producing field
Minor Producing field
Movement of Petroleum
Width of flow lines is proportional to tonnage of oil.
One half millimeter represents 40 million metric tons.
Dashed line represents 10 million metric tons.
The flow lines do not necessarily indicate exact routes.
Natural Gas
Natural Gas Major Field
Uranium
Major deposits
Minor deposits
Scale 1:75 000 000 (approximate)
One inch to 1 200 miles
0 500 1000 1500 Miles
0 500 1000 1500 2000 Kilometers

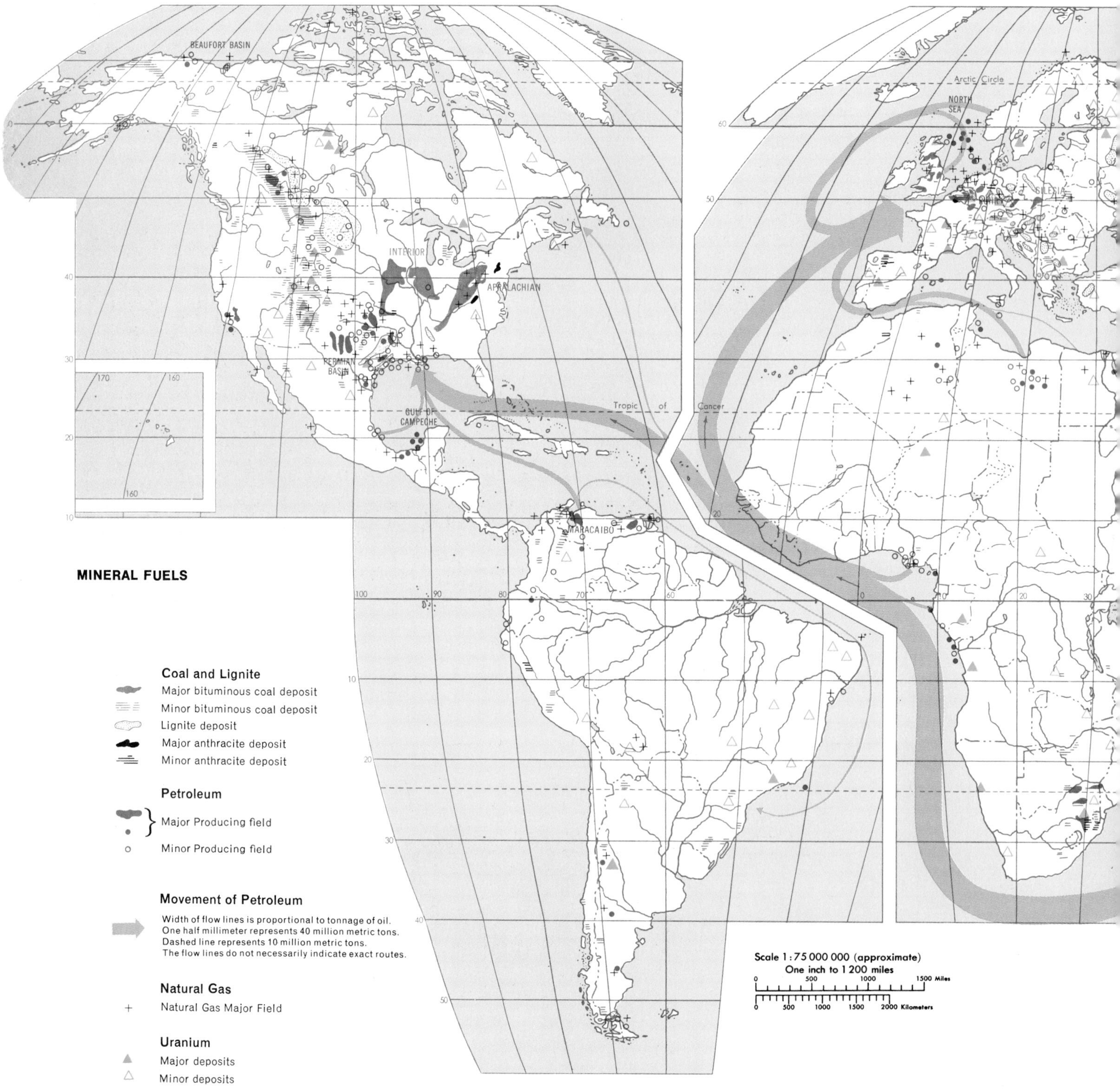

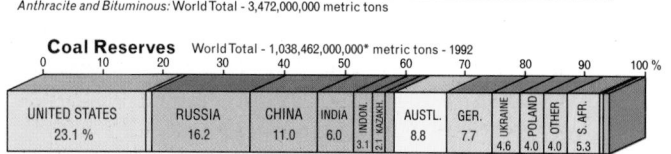

Coal World Production - 4,568,000,000* metric tons - Avg. 1990-92

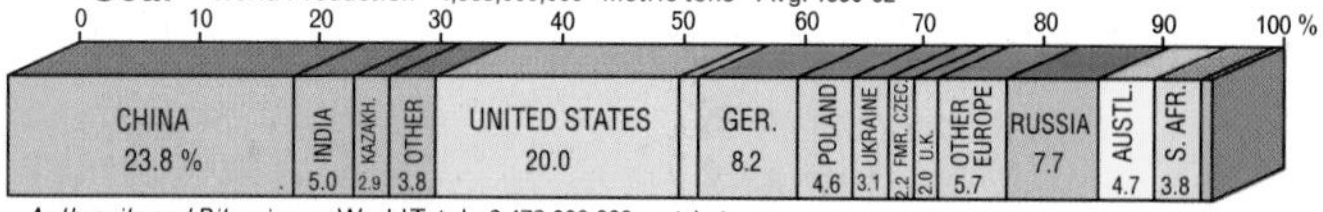

0 10 20 30 40 50 60 70 80 90 100 %
CHINA 23.8 %
INDIA 5.0
KAZAKH. 2.9
OTHER 3.8
UNITED STATES 20.0
GER. 8.2
POLAND 4.6
UKRAINE 3.1
FMR. CZEC. 2.2
U.K. 2.0
OTHER EUROPE 5.7
RUSSIA 7.7
AUSTL. 4.7
S. AFR. 3.8

Anthracite and Bituminous: World Total - 3,472,000,000 metric tons

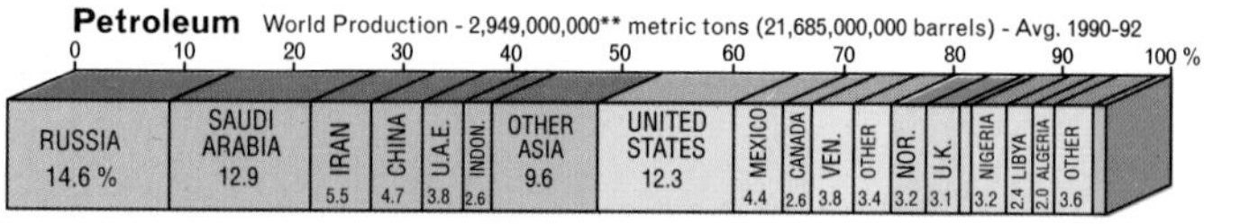

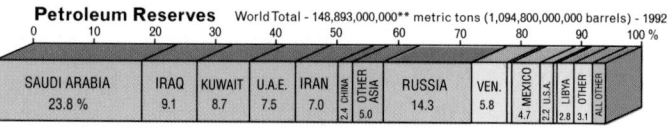

Petroleum World Production - 2,949,000,000** metric tons (21,685,000,000 barrels) - Avg. 1990-92

0 10 20 30 40 50 60 70 80 90 100 %
RUSSIA 14.6 %
SAUDI ARABIA 12.9
IRAN 5.5
CHINA 4.7
U.A.E. 3.8
INDON. 2.6
OTHER ASIA 9.6
UNITED STATES 12.3
MEXICO 4.4
CANADA 2.6
VEN. 3.8
OTHER 3.4
NOR. 3.2
U.K. 3.1
NIGERIA 3.2
2.4 LIBYA
2.0 ALGERIA
OTHER 3.6

Coal Reserves World Total - 1,038,462,000,000* metric tons - 1992

0 10 20 30 40 50 60 70 80 90 100 %
UNITED STATES 23.1 %
RUSSIA 16.2
CHINA 11.0
INDIA 6.0
INDON. 3.1
2.1 KAZAKH.
AUSTL. 8.8
GER. 7.7
UKRAINE 4.6
POLAND 4.0
OTHER 4.0
S. AFR. 5.3

Anthracite and Bituminous: World Total - 519,231,000,000 metric tons

* Includes anthracite, subanthracite, bituminous, subbituminous, lignite, and brown coal

Petroleum Reserves World Total - 148,893,000,000** metric tons (1,094,800,000,000 barrels) - 1992

0 10 20 30 40 50 60 70 80 90 100 %
SAUDI ARABIA 23.8 %
IRAQ 9.1
KUWAIT 8.7
U.A.E. 7.5
IRAN 7.0
2.4 CHINA
OTHER ASIA 5.0
RUSSIA 14.3
VEN. 5.8
MEXICO 4.7
2.2 U.S.A.
LIBYA 2.8
OTHER 3.1
ALL OTHER

** Crude Petroleum

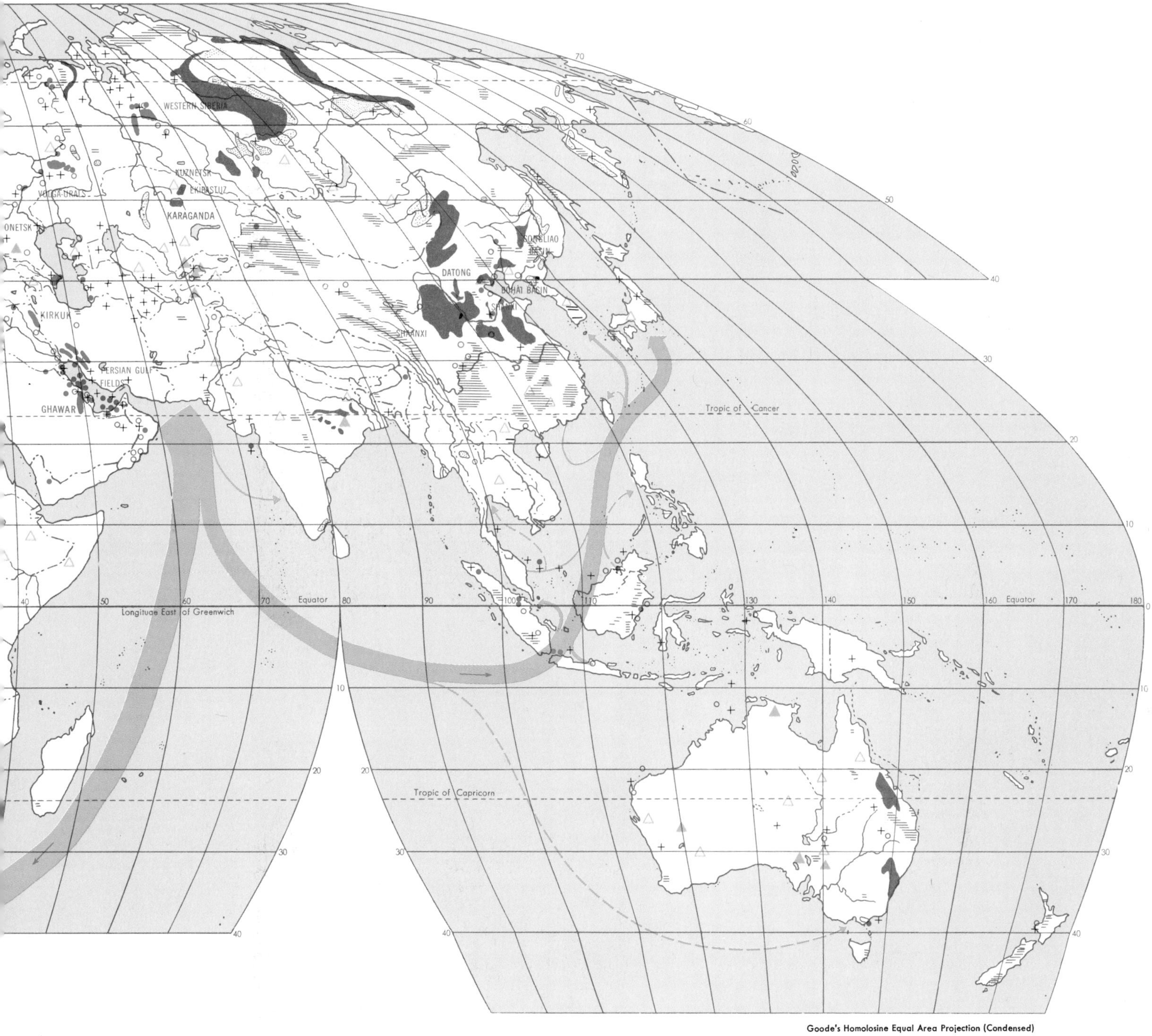

Goode's Homolosine Equal Area Projection (Condensed)

Natural Gas

World Production - 2,076,000,000,000 cubic meters - Avg. 1990-92

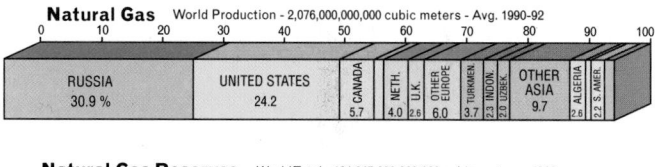

| RUSSIA 30.9 % | UNITED STATES 24.2 | CANADA 5.7 | NETH. 4.0 | U.K. 2.6 | OTHER EUROPE 6.0 | TURKMEN. 3.7 | INDON. 2.3 | OTHER ASIA 9.7 | ALGERIA 2.2 | S. AMER. 2.5 |

Uranium

World Production - 43,500 metric tons - Avg. 1990-92

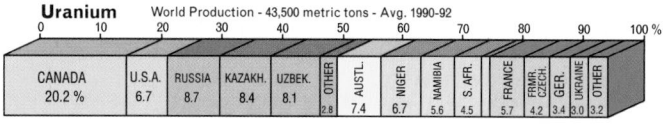

| CANADA 20.2 % | U.S.A. 6.7 | RUSSIA 8.7 | KAZAKH. 8.4 | UZBEK. 8.1 | OTHER 2.8 | AUSTL. 7.4 | NIGER 6.7 | NAMIBIA 5.6 | S. AFR. 4.5 | FRANCE 5.7 | FRMR CZECH 4.2 | GER. 3.4 | UKRAINE 3.0 | OTHER 3.2 |

Natural Gas Reserves

World Total - 134,947,000,000,000 cubic meters - 1992

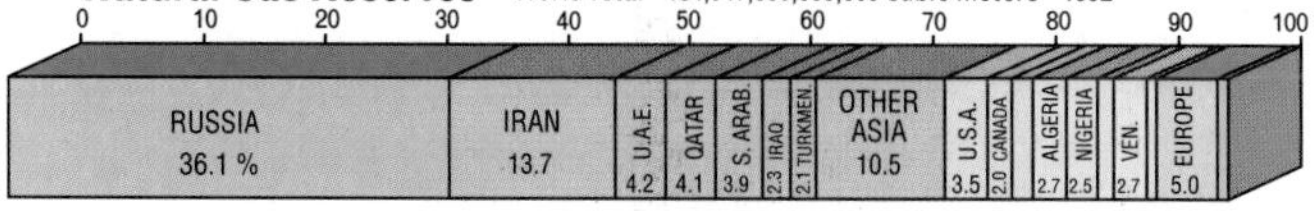

| RUSSIA 36.1 % | IRAN 13.7 | U.A.E. 4.2 | QATAR 4.1 | S. ARAB 3.9 | IRAQ 2.3 | TURKMEN. 2.1 | OTHER ASIA 10.5 | U.S.A. 3.5 | ALGERIA 2.0 | NIGERIA 2.7 | VEN 2.5 | EUROPE 5.0 |

Uranium Reserves

World Total - 2,512,000 metric tons † - 1990/91

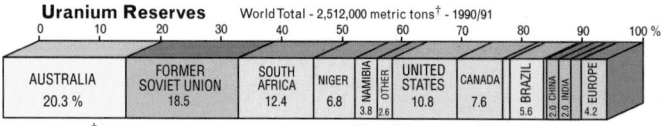

| AUSTRALIA 20.3 % | FORMER SOVIET UNION 18.5 | SOUTH AFRICA 12.4 | NIGER 6.8 | NAMIBIA 3.8 | OTHER | UNITED STATES 10.8 | CANADA 7.6 | BRAZIL 5.6 | CHINA 2.0 | INDIA | EUROPE 4.2 |

† Excluding possible reserves in Cuba, North Korea, Mongolia, and Vietnam

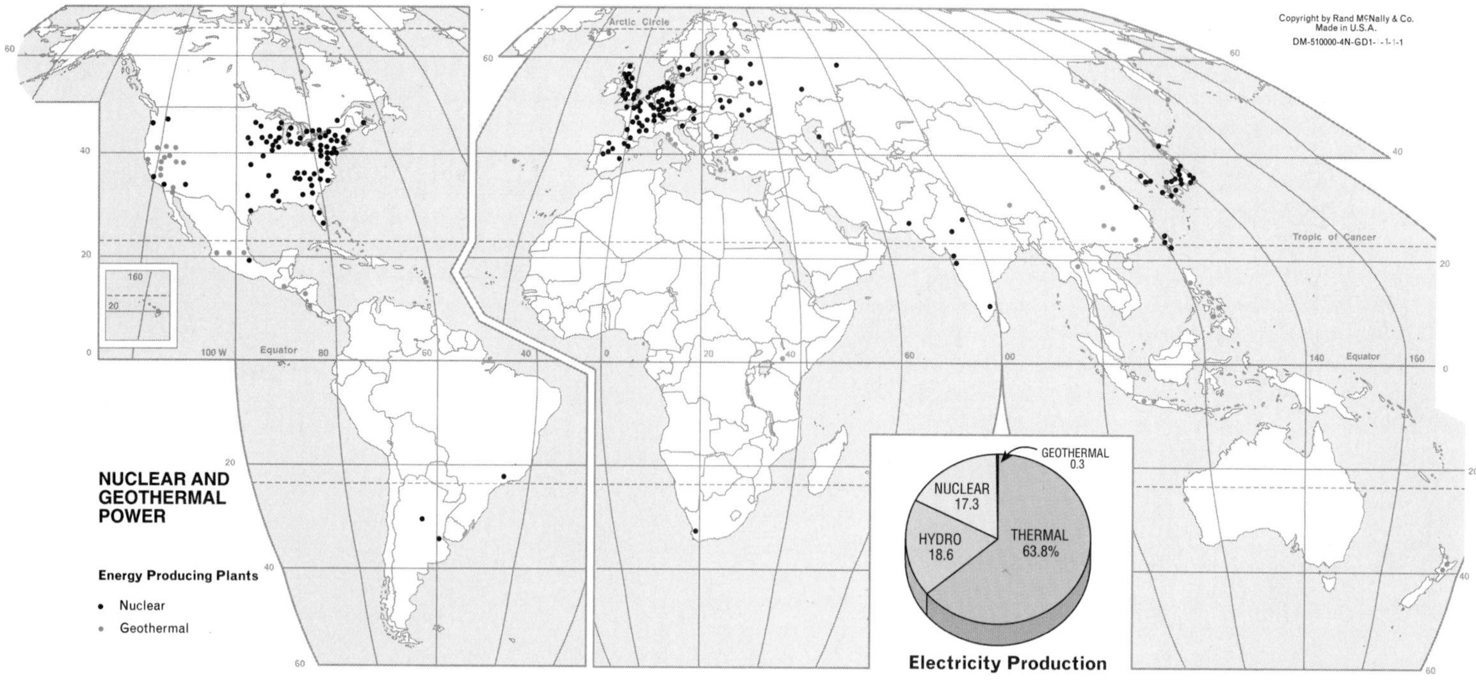

Copyright by Rand McNally & Co.
Made in U.S.A.
DM-510000-4N-GD1-
Arctic Circle
Tropic of Cancer
Equator
NUCLEAR AND GEOTHERMAL POWER
Energy Producing Plants
Nuclear
Geothermal
GEOTHERMAL 0.3
NUCLEAR 17.3
HYDRO 18.6
THERMAL 63.8%
Electricity Production

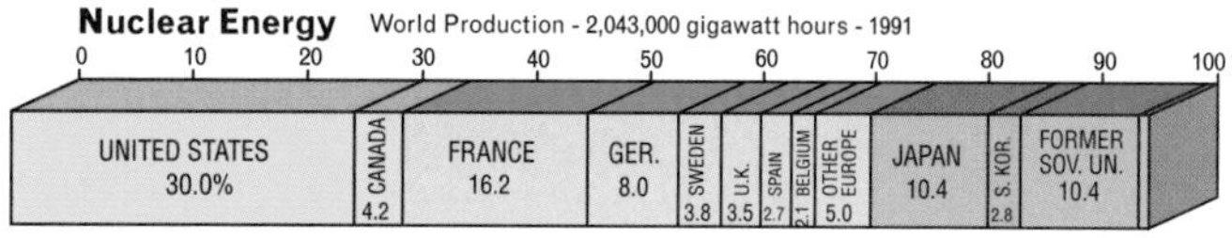

Nuclear Energy
World Production - 2,043,000 gigawatt hours - 1991
UNITED STATES 30.0%
CANADA 4.2
FRANCE 16.2
GER. 8.0
SWEDEN 3.8
U.K. 3.5
SPAIN 2.7
BELGIUM 2.1
OTHER EUROPE 5.0
JAPAN 10.4
S. KOR. 2.8
FORMER SOV. UN. 10.4

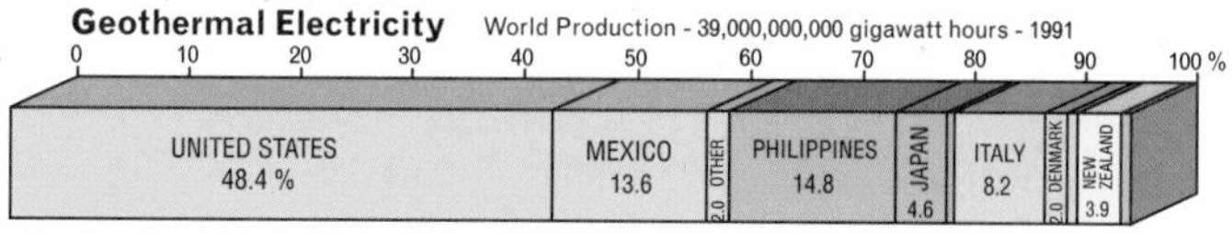

Geothermal Electricity
World Production - 39,000,000,000 gigawatt hours - 1991
UNITED STATES 48.4 %
MEXICO 13.6
OTHER 2.0
PHILIPPINES 14.8
JAPAN 4.6
ITALY 8.2
DENMARK 2.0
NEW ZEALAND 3.9

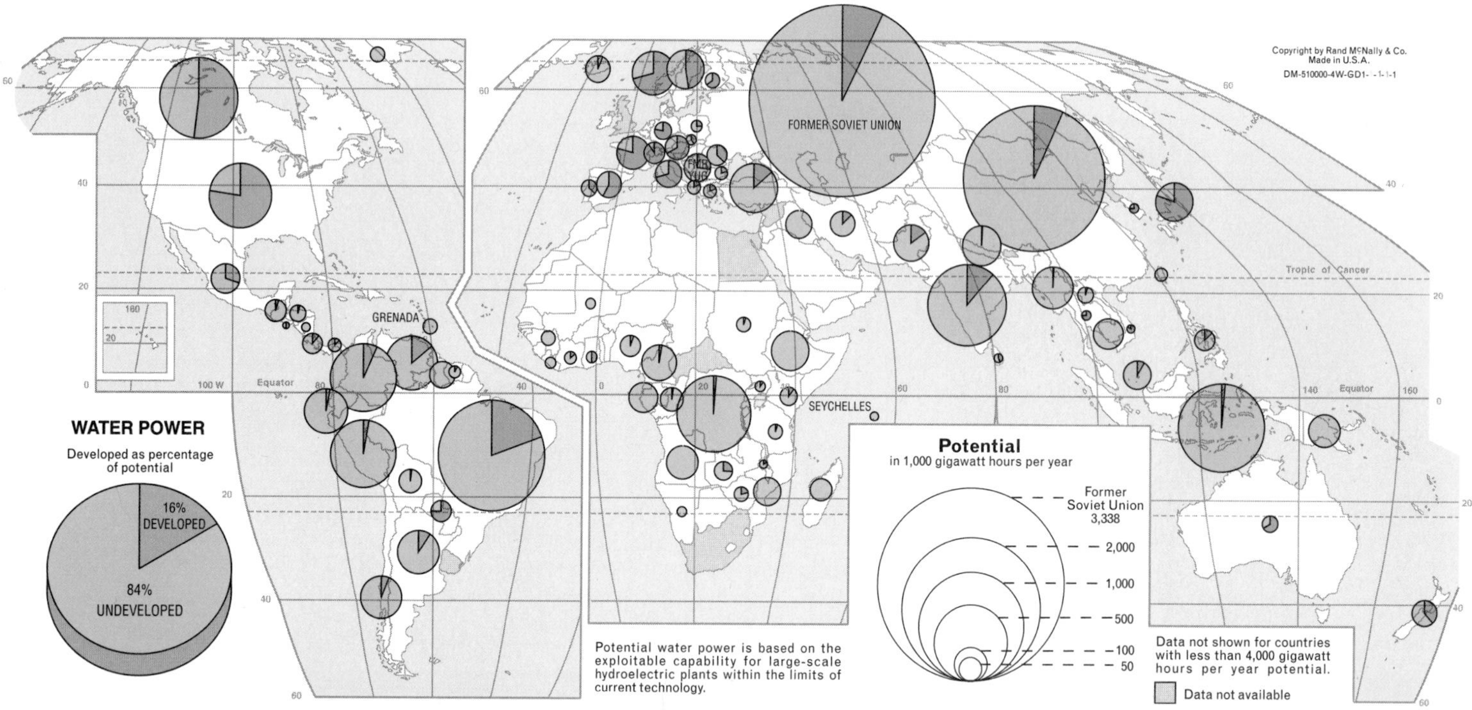

Copyright by Rand McNally & Co.
Made in U.S.A.
DM-510000-4W-GD1-
FORMER SOVIET UNION
GRENADA
SEYCHELLES
Tropic of Cancer
Equator
WATER POWER
Developed as percentage of potential
16% DEVELOPED
84% UNDEVELOPED
Potential
in 1,000 gigawatt hours per year
Former Soviet Union 3,338
2,000
1,000
500
100
50
Potential water power is based on the exploitable capability for large-scale hydroelectric plants within the limits of current technology.
Data not shown for countries with less than 4,000 gigawatt hours per year potential.
Data not available

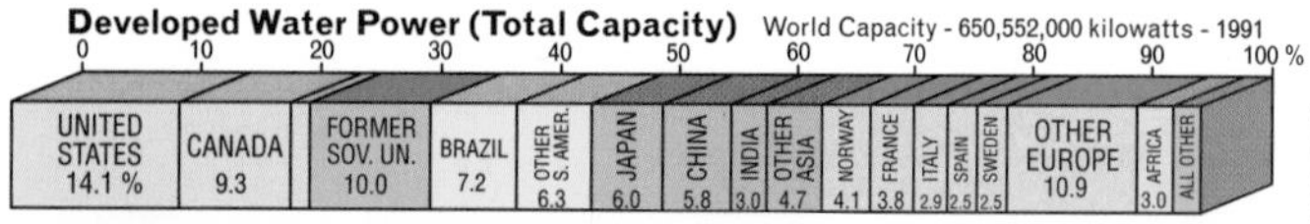

Developed Water Power (Total Capacity)
World Capacity - 650,552,000 kilowatts - 1991
UNITED STATES 14.1 %
CANADA 9.3
FORMER SOV. UN. 10.0
BRAZIL 7.2
OTHER S. AMER. 6.3
JAPAN 6.0
CHINA 5.8
INDIA 3.0
OTHER ASIA 4.7
NORWAY 4.1
FRANCE 3.8
ITALY 2.9
SPAIN 2.5
SWEDEN 2.5
OTHER EUROPE 10.9
AFRICA 3.0
ALL OTHER

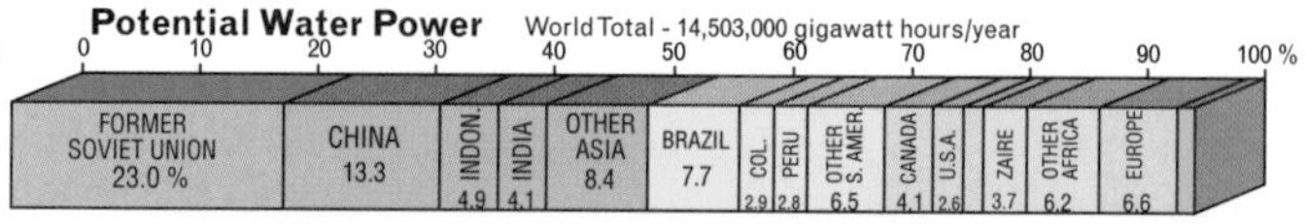

Potential Water Power
World Total - 14,503,000 gigawatt hours/year
FORMER SOVIET UNION 23.0 %
CHINA 13.3
INDON. 4.9
INDIA 4.1
OTHER ASIA 8.4
BRAZIL 7.7
COL. 2.9
PERU 2.8
OTHER S. AMER. 6.5
CANADA 4.1
U.S.A. 2.6
ZAIRE 3.7
OTHER AFRICA 6.2
EUROPE 6.6

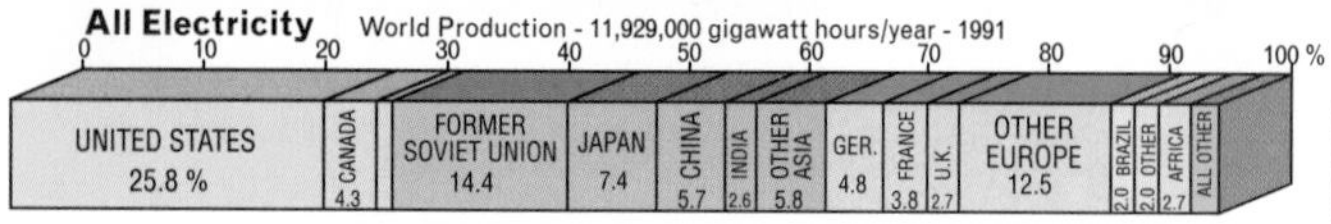

All Electricity
World Production - 11,929,000 gigawatt hours/year - 1991
UNITED STATES 25.8 %
CANADA 4.3
FORMER SOVIET UNION 14.4
JAPAN 7.4
CHINA 5.7
INDIA 2.6
OTHER ASIA 5.8
GER. 4.8
FRANCE 3.8
U.K. 2.7
OTHER EUROPE 12.5
BRAZIL 2.0
OTHER 2.0
OTHER 2.7
ALL OTHER

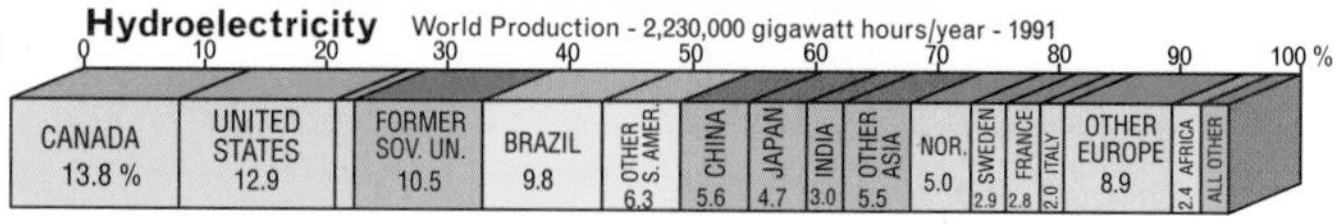

Hydroelectricity
World Production - 2,230,000 gigawatt hours/year - 1991
CANADA 13.8 %
UNITED STATES 12.9
FORMER SOV. UN. 10.5
BRAZIL 9.8
OTHER S. AMER. 6.3
CHINA 5.6
JAPAN 4.7
INDIA 3.0
OTHER ASIA 5.5
NOR. 5.0
SWEDEN 2.9
FRANCE 2.8
ITALY 2.0
OTHER EUROPE 8.9
AFRICA 2.4
ALL OTHER

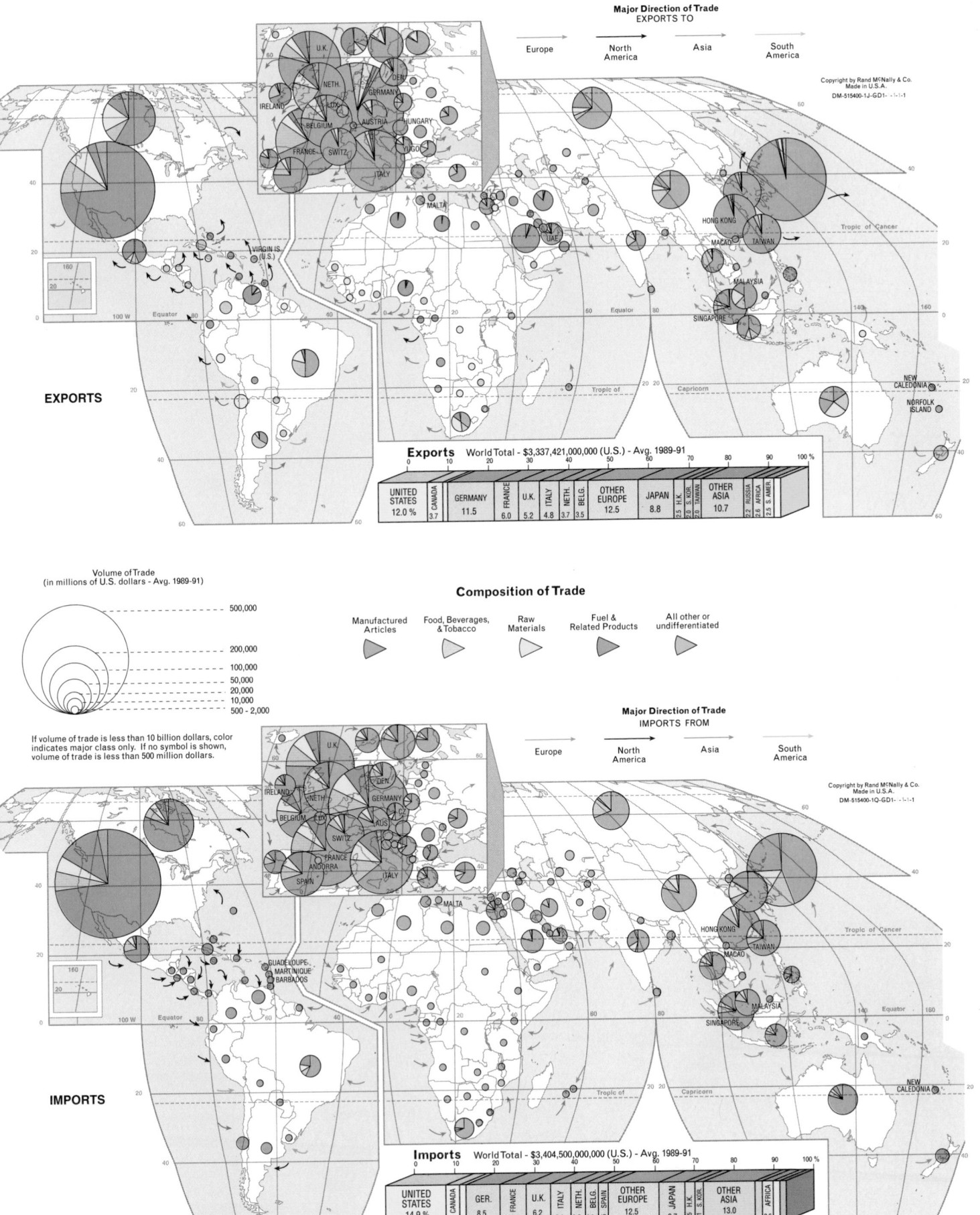

Major Direction of Trade
EXPORTS TO

Europe → North America → Asia → South America

EXPORTS

Exports   World Total - $3,337,421,000,000 (U.S.) - Avg. 1989-91

| UNITED STATES 12.0 % | CANADA 3.7 | GERMANY 11.5 | FRANCE 6.0 | U.K. 5.2 | ITALY 4.8 | NETH. 3.7 | BELG. 3.5 | OTHER EUROPE 12.5 | JAPAN 8.8 | H.K. 2.5 | S. KOR. 2.0 | TAIWAN | OTHER ASIA 10.7 | RUSSIA 2.2 | AFRICA 2.6 | S. AMER. 2.5 |

Volume of Trade
(in millions of U.S. dollars - Avg. 1989-91)

- - - - - - 500,000
- - - - - - 200,000
- - - - - - 100,000
- - - - - - 50,000
- - - - - - 20,000
- - - - - - 10,000
- - - - - - 500 - 2,000

If volume of trade is less than 10 billion dollars, color indicates major class only. If no symbol is shown, volume of trade is less than 500 million dollars.

Composition of Trade

Manufactured Articles   Food, Beverages, & Tobacco   Raw Materials   Fuel & Related Products   All other or undifferentiated

Major Direction of Trade
IMPORTS FROM

Europe → North America → Asia → South America

IMPORTS

Imports   World Total - $3,404,500,000,000 (U.S.) - Avg. 1989-91

| UNITED STATES 14.9 % | CANADA 3.4 | GER. 8.5 | FRANCE 6.4 | U.K. 6.2 | ITALY 5.1 | NETH. 3.5 | BELG. | SPAIN 2.5 | OTHER EUROPE 12.5 | JAPAN 6.7 | H.K. 2.5 | S. KOR. 2.1 | OTHER ASIA 13.0 | AFRICA 2.6 |

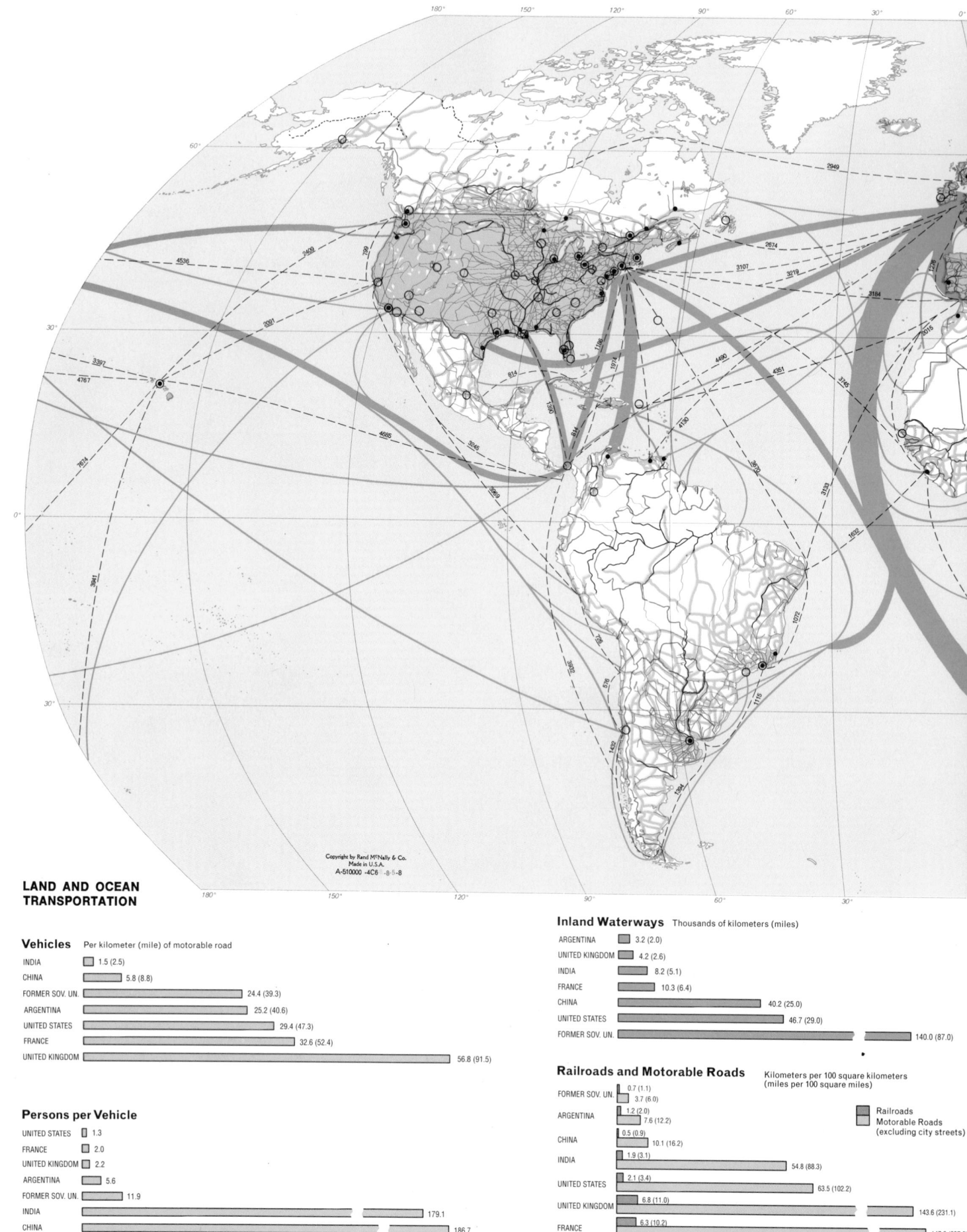

56

LAND AND OCEAN TRANSPORTATION

Vehicles Per kilometer (mile) of motorable road

INDIA	1.5 (2.5)
CHINA	5.8 (8.8)
FORMER SOV. UN.	24.4 (39.3)
ARGENTINA	25.2 (40.6)
UNITED STATES	29.4 (47.3)
FRANCE	32.6 (52.4)
UNITED KINGDOM	56.8 (91.5)

Persons per Vehicle

UNITED STATES	1.3
FRANCE	2.0
UNITED KINGDOM	2.2
ARGENTINA	5.6
FORMER SOV. UN.	11.9
INDIA	179.1
CHINA	186.7

Inland Waterways Thousands of kilometers (miles)

ARGENTINA	3.2 (2.0)
UNITED KINGDOM	4.2 (2.6)
INDIA	8.2 (5.1)
FRANCE	10.3 (6.4)
CHINA	40.2 (25.0)
UNITED STATES	46.7 (29.0)
FORMER SOV. UN.	140.0 (87.0)

Railroads and Motorable Roads Kilometers per 100 square kilometers (miles per 100 square miles)

Railroads
Motorable Roads (excluding city streets)

	Railroads	Motorable Roads
FORMER SOV. UN.	0.7 (1.1)	3.7 (6.0)
ARGENTINA	1.2 (2.0)	7.6 (12.2)
CHINA	0.5 (0.9)	10.1 (16.2)
INDIA	1.9 (3.1)	54.8 (88.3)
UNITED STATES	2.1 (3.4)	63.5 (102.2)
UNITED KINGDOM	6.8 (11.0)	143.6 (231.1)
FRANCE	6.3 (10.2)	147.6 (237.6)

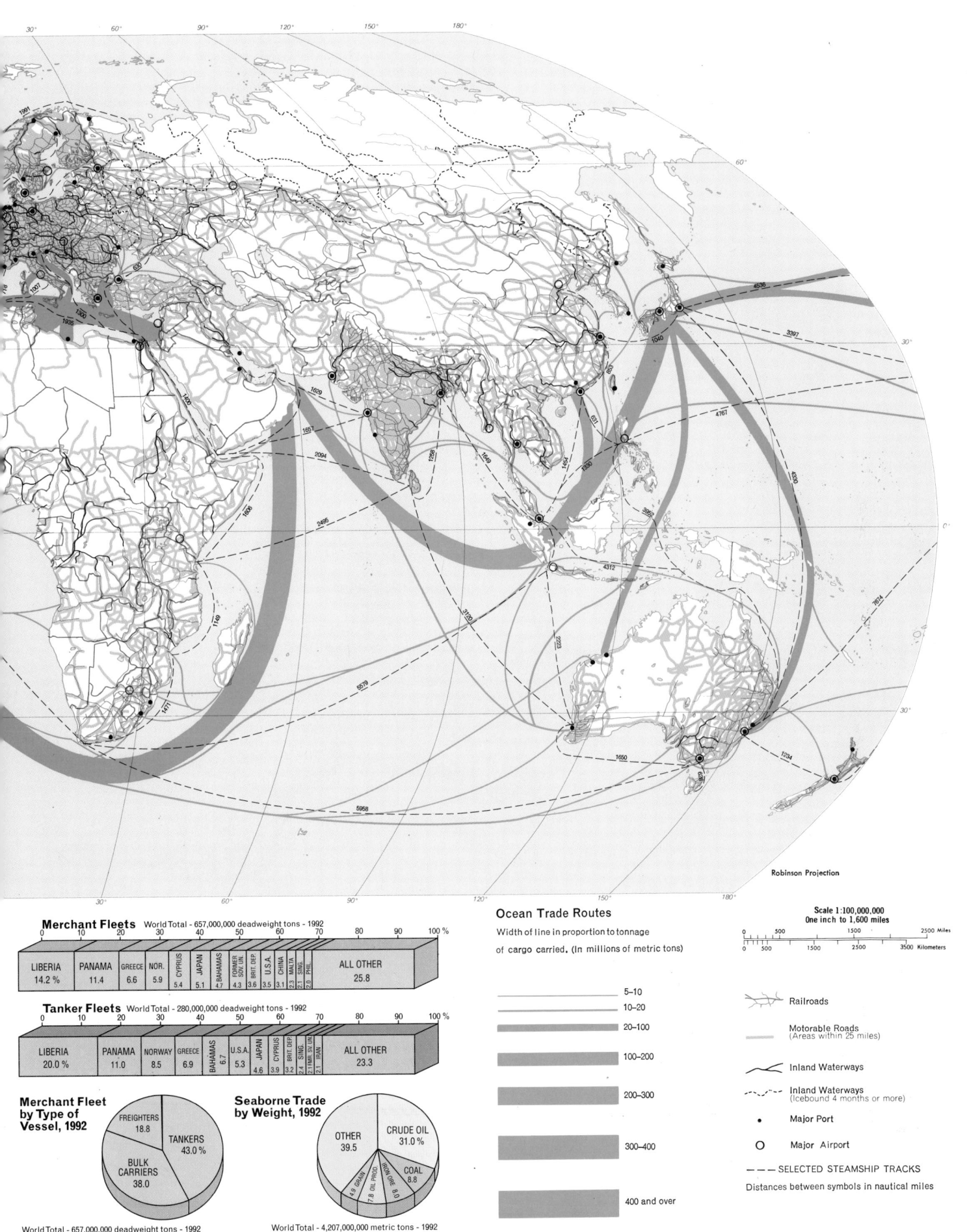

Robinson Projection

Merchant Fleets World Total - 657,000,000 deadweight tons - 1992

0	10	20	30	40	50	60	70	80	90	100 %

| LIBERIA 14.2 % | PANAMA 11.4 | GREECE 6.6 | NOR. 5.9 | CYPRUS 5.4 | JAPAN 5.1 | BAHAMAS 4.7 | FORMER SOV. UN. 4.3 | BRIT. DEP. 3.6 | U.S.A. 3.5 | CHINA 3.1 | MALTA 2.3 | SING. 2.2 | PHIL. 2.0 | ALL OTHER 25.8 |

Tanker Fleets World Total - 280,000,000 deadweight tons - 1992

0	10	20	30	40	50	60	70	80	90	100 %

| LIBERIA 20.0 % | PANAMA 11.0 | NORWAY 8.5 | GREECE 6.9 | BAHAMAS 6.7 | U.S.A. 5.3 | JAPAN 4.6 | CYPRUS 3.9 | BRIT. DEP. 3.2 | SING. 2.4 | FMR. SV. UN. 2.1 | IRAN 2.1 | ALL OTHER 23.3 |

Merchant Fleet by Type of Vessel, 1992

- FREIGHTERS 18.8
- TANKERS 43.0 %
- BULK CARRIERS 38.0

World Total - 657,000,000 deadweight tons - 1992

Seaborne Trade by Weight, 1992

- OTHER 39.5
- CRUDE OIL 31.0 %
- COAL 8.8
- IRON ORE 8.0
- OIL PROD. 7.8
- GRAIN 4.9

World Total - 4,207,000,000 metric tons - 1992

Ocean Trade Routes

Width of line in proportion to tonnage of cargo carried. (In millions of metric tons)

———	5–10
———	10–20
———	20–100
———	100–200
———	200–300
———	300–400
———	400 and over

Scale 1:100,000,000
One inch to 1,600 miles

0   500   1500   2500 Miles
0   500   1500   2500   3500 Kilometers

- Railroads
- Motorable Roads (Areas within 25 miles)
- Inland Waterways
- Inland Waterways (Icebound 4 months or more)
- • Major Port
- ○ Major Airport
- – – – SELECTED STEAMSHIP TRACKS

Distances between symbols in nautical miles

Copyright by Rand McNally & Co.
Made in U.S.A.
A-510000-9G6 -3-4-4

**POLITICAL
AND
MILITARY
ALLIANCES**

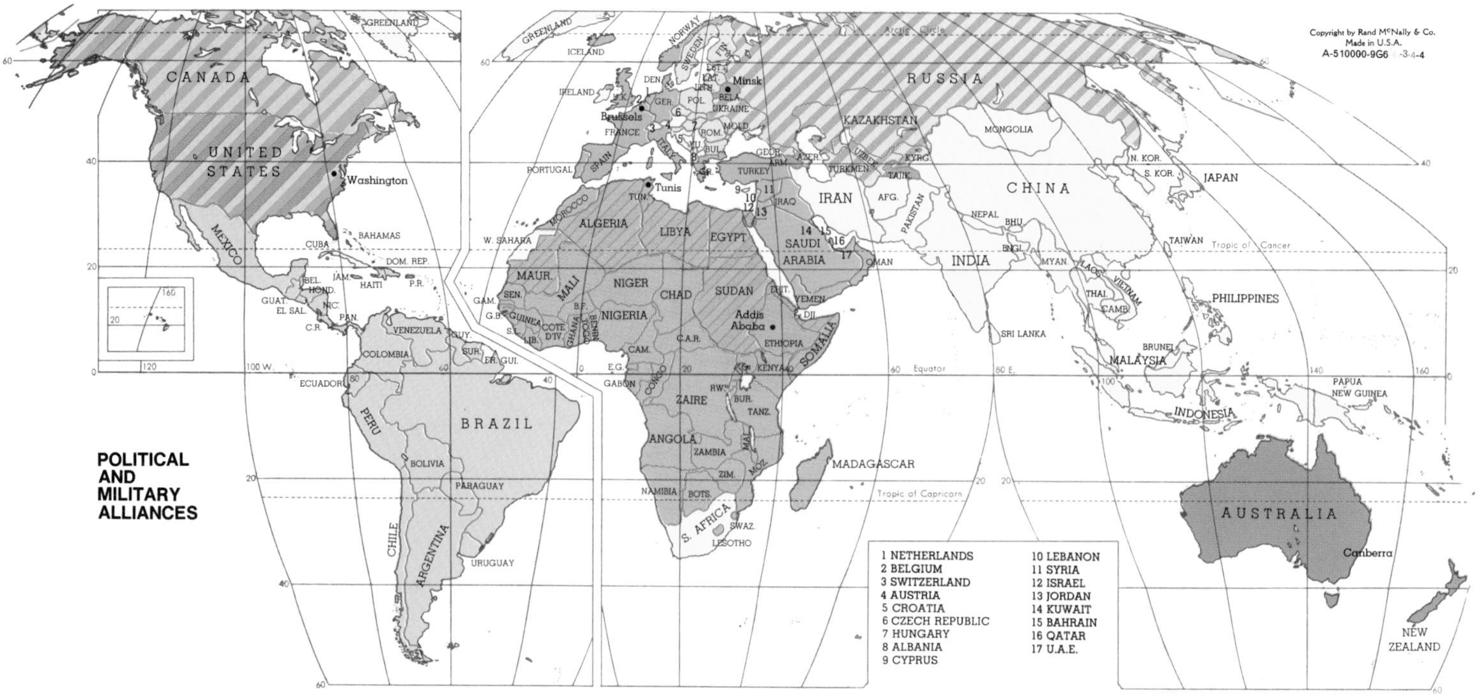

1 NETHERLANDS	10 LEBANON
2 BELGIUM	11 SYRIA
3 SWITZERLAND	12 ISRAEL
4 AUSTRIA	13 JORDAN
5 CROATIA	14 KUWAIT
6 CZECH REPUBLIC	15 BAHRAIN
7 HUNGARY	16 QATAR
8 ALBANIA	17 U.A.E.
9 CYPRUS	

NATO-North Atlantic Treaty Organization, founded 1949. Headquarters in Brussels, Belgium.

NATO-Partnership for Peace Program

ANZUS-Australia-New Zealand-U.S. Security Treaty, founded 1952. Headquarters in Canberra, Australia.

OAS-Organization of American States, founded 1948. Headquarters in Washington, D.C., United States.

CIS-Commonwealth of Independent States, founded 1991. Headquarters in Minsk, Belarus.

AL-Arab League (League of Arab States), founded 1945. Headquarters in Tunis, Tunisia.

OAU-Organization of African Unity, founded 1963. Headquarters in Addis Ababa, Ethiopia.

Not affiliated with above organizatons.

Copyright by Rand McNally & Co.
Made in U.S.A.
A-510000-9H6 -3-3-4

**ECONOMIC
ALLIANCES**

1 NETHERLANDS	10 LEBANON
2 BELGIUM	11 SYRIA
3 SWITZERLAND	12 ISRAEL
4 AUSTRIA	13 JORDAN
5 CROATIA	14 KUWAIT
6 CZECH REPUBLIC	15 BAHRAIN
7 HUNGARY	16 QATAR
8 ALBANIA	17 U.A.E.
9 CYPRUS	

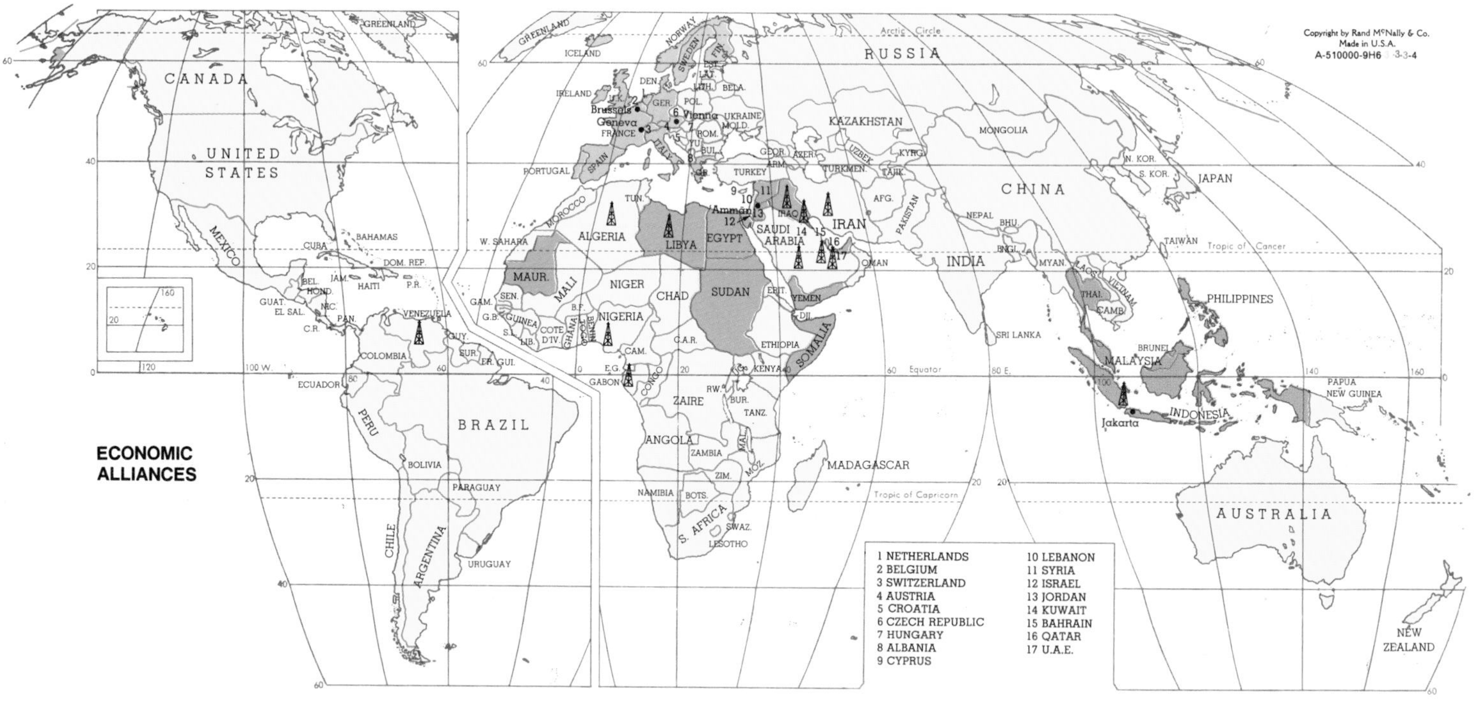

EU (Common Market)-European Union, founded 1957. Headquarters in Brussels, Belgium.

EFTA-European Free Trade Association, founded 1960. Headquarters in Geneva, Switzerland.

OPEC-Organization of Petroleum Exporting Countries, founded 1960. Headquarters in Vienna, Austria.

ASEAN-Association of Southeast Asian Nations, founded 1967. Headquarters in Jakarta, Indonesia.

CAEU-Council of Arab Economic Unity, founded 1964. Headquarters in 'Ammān, Jordan. Includes Arab Common Market countries.

Not affiliated with above organizations.

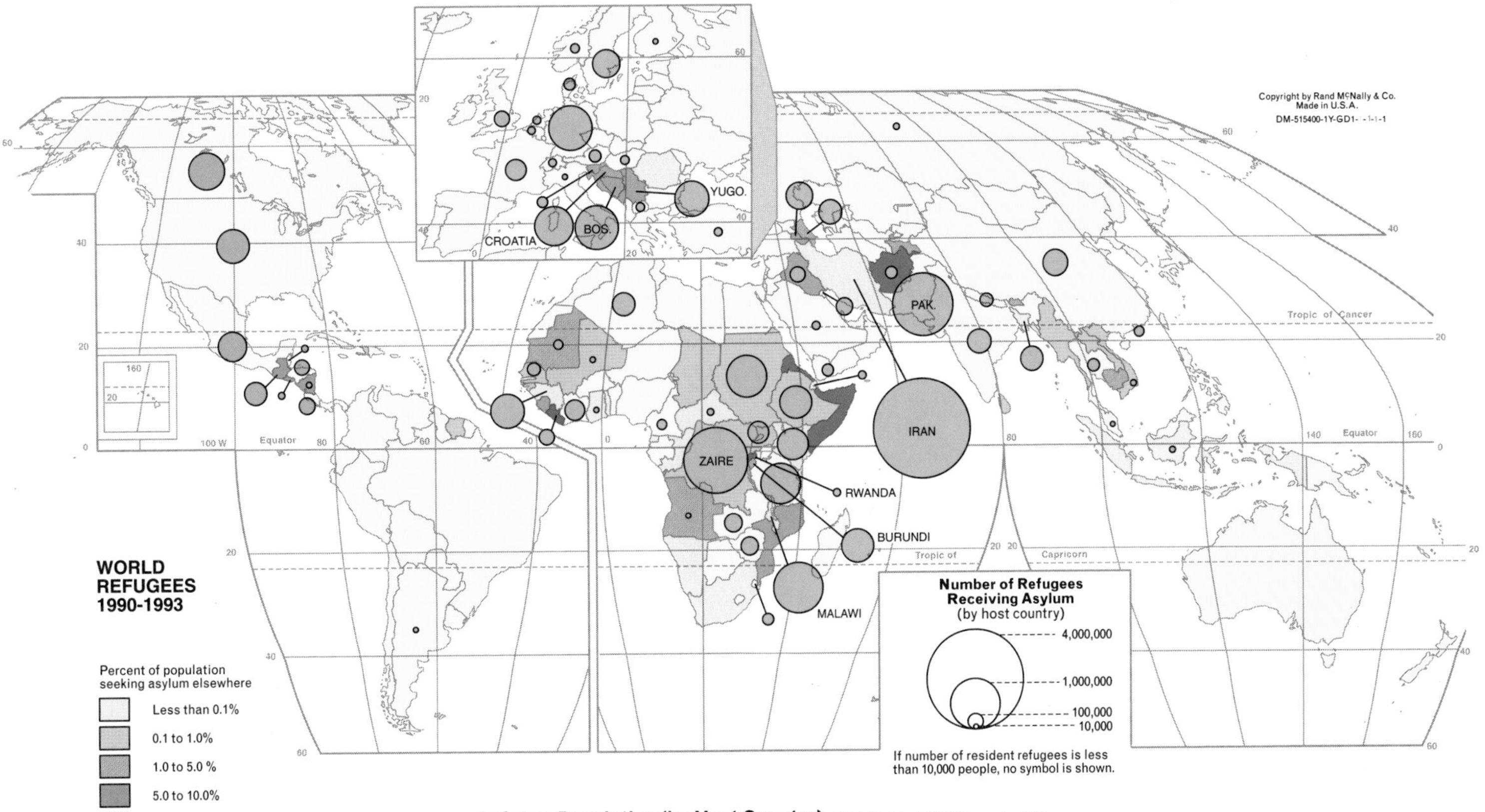

**WORLD
REFUGEES
1990-1993**

YUGO.

CROATIA

BOS.

PAK.

IRAN

ZAIRE

RWANDA

BURUNDI

MALAWI

Tropic of Cancer

Equator

Tropic of

Capricorn

Percent of population
seeking asylum elsewhere

Less than 0.1%

0.1 to 1.0%

1.0 to 5.0 %

5.0 to 10.0%

Greater than 10.0%

Map data for Rwanda,
Tanzania, and Zaire revised
07/20/94

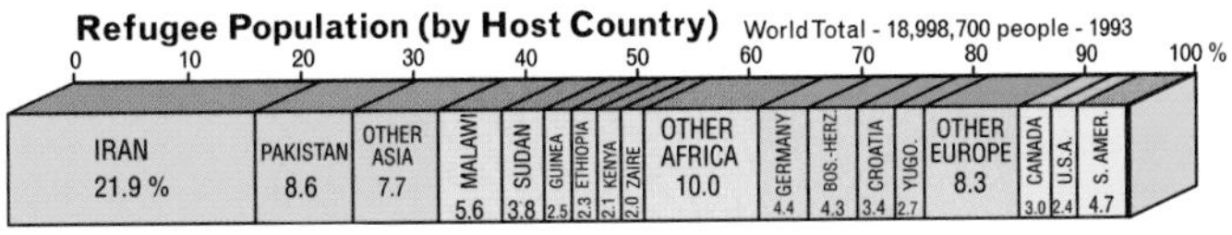

**Number of Refugees
Receiving Asylum**
(by host country)

---- 4,000,000

---- 1,000,000

---- 100,000

---- 10,000

If number of resident refugees is less
than 10,000 people, no symbol is shown.

Refugee Population (by Host Country) World Total - 18,998,700 people - 1993

0	10	20	30	40	50	60	70	80	90	100 %

| IRAN 21.9 % | PAKISTAN 8.6 | OTHER ASIA 7.7 | MALAWI 5.6 | SUDAN 3.8 | GUINEA 2.5 | ETHIOPIA 2.3 | KENYA 2.1 | ZAIRE 2.0 | OTHER AFRICA 10.0 | GERMANY 4.4 | BOS.-HERZ. 4.3 | CROATIA 3.4 | YUGO. 2.7 | OTHER EUROPE 8.3 | CANADA 3.0 | U.S.A. 2.4 | S. AMER. 4.7 |

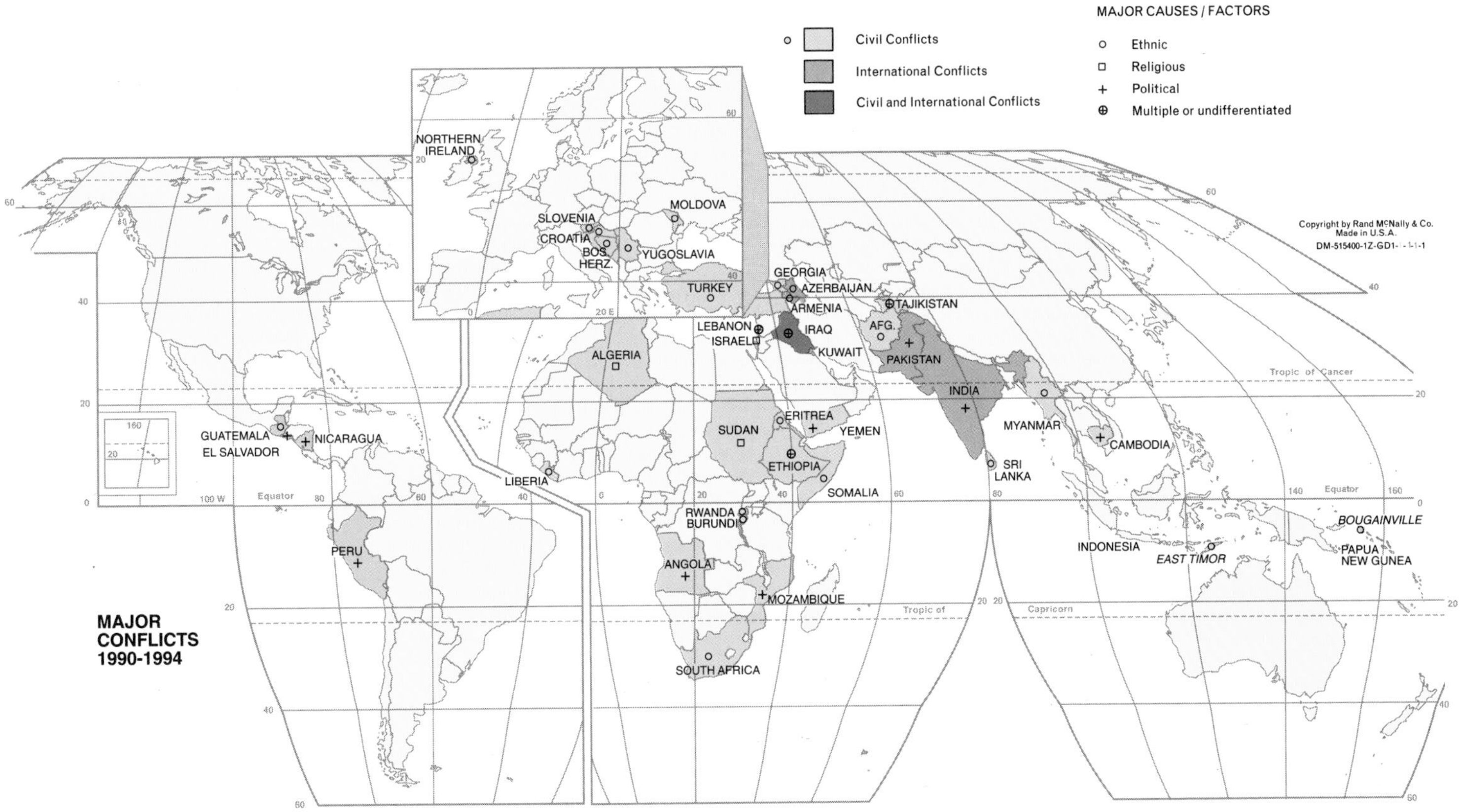

Civil Conflicts

International Conflicts

Civil and International Conflicts

MAJOR CAUSES / FACTORS

o   Ethnic

□   Religious

+   Political

⊕   Multiple or undifferentiated

NORTHERN
IRELAND

MOLDOVA

SLOVENIA

CROATIA

BOS.
HERZ.

YUGOSLAVIA

TURKEY

GEORGIA

AZERBAIJAN

ARMENIA

TAJIKISTAN

LEBANON

ISRAEL

IRAQ

KUWAIT

AFG.

PAKISTAN

ALGERIA

INDIA

GUATEMALA

EL SALVADOR

NICARAGUA

SUDAN

ERITREA

YEMEN

MYANMAR

CAMBODIA

ETHIOPIA

SRI
LANKA

LIBERIA

SOMALIA

RWANDA

BURUNDI

BOUGAINVILLE

PERU

INDONESIA

PAPUA
NEW GUINEA

EAST TIMOR

ANGOLA

MOZAMBIQUE

**MAJOR
CONFLICTS
1990-1994**

SOUTH AFRICA

Tropic of Cancer

Equator

Tropic of

Capricorn

REGIONAL MAPS

Basic continental and regional coverage of the world's land areas is provided by the following section of physical-political reference maps. The section falls into a continental arrangement: North America, South America, Europe, Asia, Australia, and Africa. (Introducing each regional reference-map section are basic thematic maps and the environment maps.)

To aid the student in acquiring concepts of the relative sizes of continents and of some of the countries and regions, uniform scales for comparable areas were used so far as possible. Continental maps are at a uniform scale of 1:40,000,000. In addition, most of the world is covered by a series of regional maps at scales of 1:16,000,000 and 1:12,000,000.

Maps at 1:10,000,000 provide even greater detail for parts of Europe, Africa, and Southeast Asia. The United States, parts of Canada, and much of Europe are mapped at 1:4,000,000. Seventy-six urbanized areas are shown at 1:1,000,000. The new, separate metropolitan-area section contains larger-scale maps of selected urban areas.

Many of the symbols used are self-explanatory. A complete legend below provides a key to the symbols on the reference maps in this atlas.

General elevation above sea level is shown by layer tints for altitudinal zones, each of which has a different hue and is defined by a generalized contour line. A legend is given on each map, reflecting this color gradation.

The surface configuration is represented by hill-shading, which gives the three-dimensional impression of landforms. This terrain representation is superimposed on the layer tints to convey a realistic and readily visualized impression of the surface. The combination of altitudinal tints and hill-shading best shows elevation, relief, steepness of slope, and ruggedness of terrain.

If the world used one alphabet and one language, no particular difficulty would arise in understanding place-names. However, some of the people of the world, the Chinese and the Japanese, for example, use nonalphabetic languages. Their symbols are transliterated into the Roman alphabet. In this atlas a "local-name" policy generally was used for naming cities and towns and all local topographic and water features. However, for a few major cities the Anglicized name was preferred and the local name given in parentheses, for instance, Moscow *(Moskva),* Vienna *(Wien),* Cologne *(Köln).* In countries where more than one official language is used, a name is in the dominant local language. The generic parts of local names for topographic and water features are self-explanatory in many cases because of the associated map symbols or type styles. A complete list of foreign generic names is given in the Glossary.

Place-names on the reference maps are listed in the Pronouncing Index, which is a distinctive feature of *Goode's World Atlas.*

Physical-Political Reference Map Legend

Cultural Features

Political Boundaries

▬▬▬ ‑‑‑ (over water)	International (Demarcated, Undemarcated, and Administrative)
▬·▬·▬·	Disputed de facto
‑ · ‑ · ‑ ·	Claim Boundary
▬ ▬ ▬ ▬	Indefinite or Undefined
▬▬‑‑‑ (over water)	Secondary, State, Provincial, etc.

⌐‑ ¬	Parks, Indian Reservations
⌐‑ ¬	City Limits 🐾 Urbanized Areas
▫	Neighborhoods, Sections of City

Populated Places

⊙	1,000,000 and over
◎	250,000 to 1,000,000
☉	100,000 to 250,000
•	25,000 to 100,000
○	0 to 25,000
TŌKYŌ	National Capitals
Boise	Secondary Capitals

Note: On maps at 1:20,000,000 and smaller the town symbols do not follow the specific population classification shown above. On all maps, type size indicates the relative importance of the city.

Transportation

────	Railroads
────	Railroads On 1:1,000,000 scale maps
‑‑‑‑‑	Railroad Ferries

Roads

Major	On 1:1,000,000 scale maps
Other	
Major	On 1:4,000,000 scale maps
Other	
────	On other scale maps
········	Caravan Routes
✈	Airports

Other Cultural Features

⌐↘	Dams
·•·•·•·	Pipelines
▲	Points of Interest
∴	Ruins

Land Features

△	Peaks, Spot Heights
=	Passes
	Sand
	Contours

Water Features

Lakes and Reservoirs

⬭	Fresh Water
⬭	Fresh Water: Intermittent
⬭	Salt Water
⬭	Salt Water: Intermittent

Other Water Features

	Salt Basins, Flats
	Swamps
	Ice Caps and Glaciers
	Rivers
	Intermittent Rivers
	Aqueducts and Canals
	Ship Channels
	Falls
	Rapids
	Springs
△	Water Depths
	Fishing Banks
	Sand Bars
	Reefs

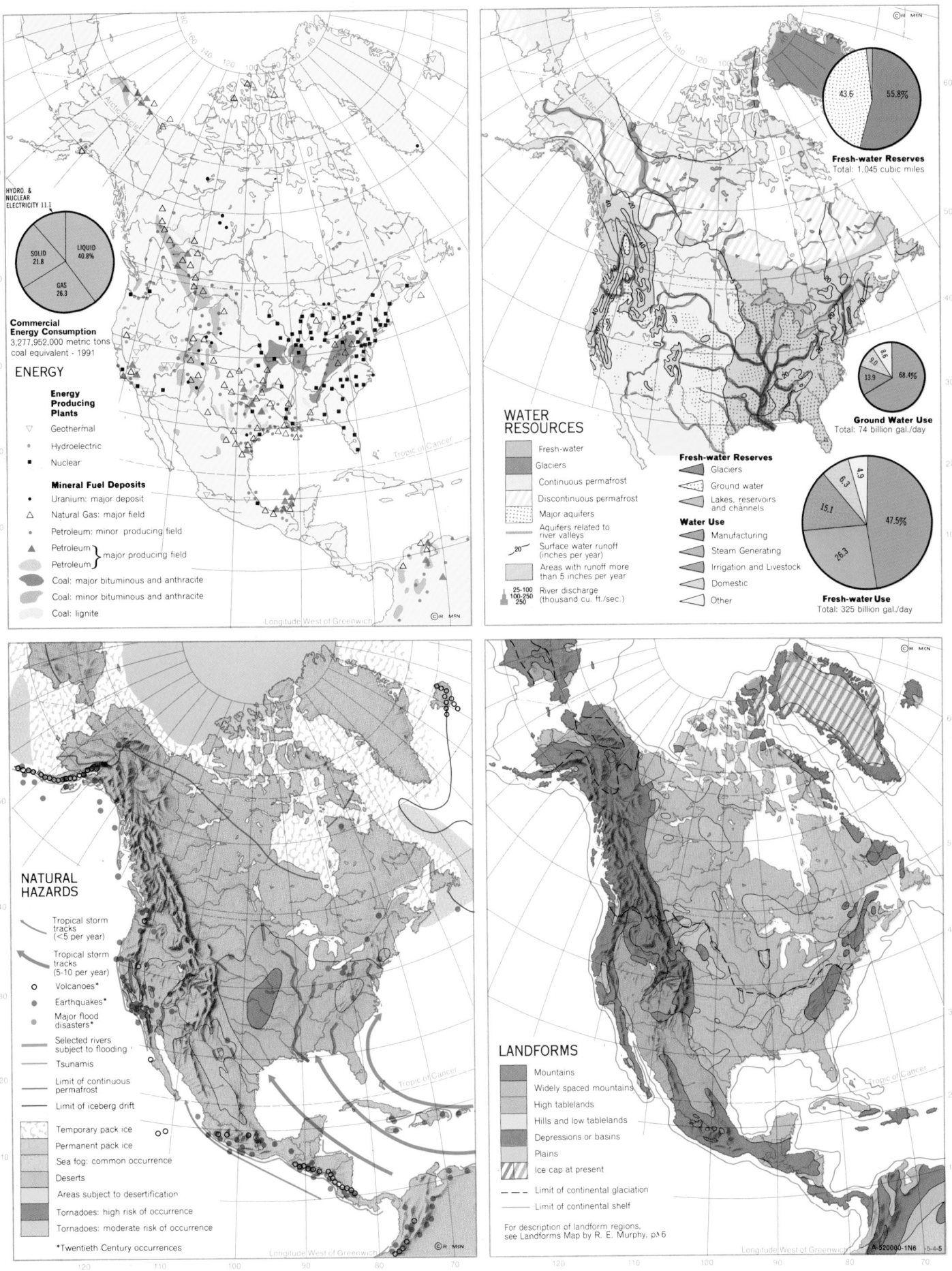

ENERGY

HYDRO. & NUCLEAR ELECTRICITY 11.1

SOLID 21.8
LIQUID 40.8%
GAS 26.3

Commercial Energy Consumption
3,277,952,000 metric tons coal equivalent - 1991

Energy Producing Plants
▽ Geothermal
• Hydroelectric
■ Nuclear

Mineral Fuel Deposits
• Uranium: major deposit
△ Natural Gas: major field
· Petroleum: minor producing field
▲ Petroleum } major producing field
Petroleum }
Coal: major bituminous and anthracite
Coal: minor bituminous and anthracite
Coal: lignite

WATER RESOURCES

Fresh-water Reserves
Total: 1,045 cubic miles
43.5   55.8%

Ground Water Use
Total: 74 billion gal./day
8.6 9.0 13.9 68.4%

Fresh-water Use
Total: 325 billion gal./day
4.9 6.3 15.1 26.3 47.5%

Fresh-water
Glaciers
Continuous permafrost
Discontinuous permafrost
Major aquifers
Aquifers related to river valleys
—20— Surface water runoff (inches per year)
Areas with runoff more than 5 inches per year
River discharge (thousand cu. ft./sec.)
25-100
100-250
250

Fresh-water Reserves
◣ Glaciers
◹ Ground water
◣ Lakes, reservoirs and channels

Water Use
◣ Manufacturing
◣ Steam Generating
◣ Irrigation and Livestock
◣ Domestic
◹ Other

NATURAL HAZARDS

↝ Tropical storm tracks (<5 per year)
⟶ Tropical storm tracks (5-10 per year)
○ Volcanoes*
● Earthquakes*
● Major flood disasters*
━ Selected rivers subject to flooding
━ Tsunamis
━ Limit of continuous permafrost
━ Limit of iceberg drift
Temporary pack ice
Permanent pack ice
Sea fog: common occurrence
Deserts
Areas subject to desertification
Tornadoes: high risk of occurrence
Tornadoes: moderate risk of occurrence

*Twentieth Century occurrences

LANDFORMS

Mountains
Widely spaced mountains
High tablelands
Hills and low tablelands
Depressions or basins
Plains
Ice cap at present
━ ━ Limit of continental glaciation
━ Limit of continental shelf

For description of landform regions, see Landforms Map by R. E. Murphy, p. 6

A-520000-1N6

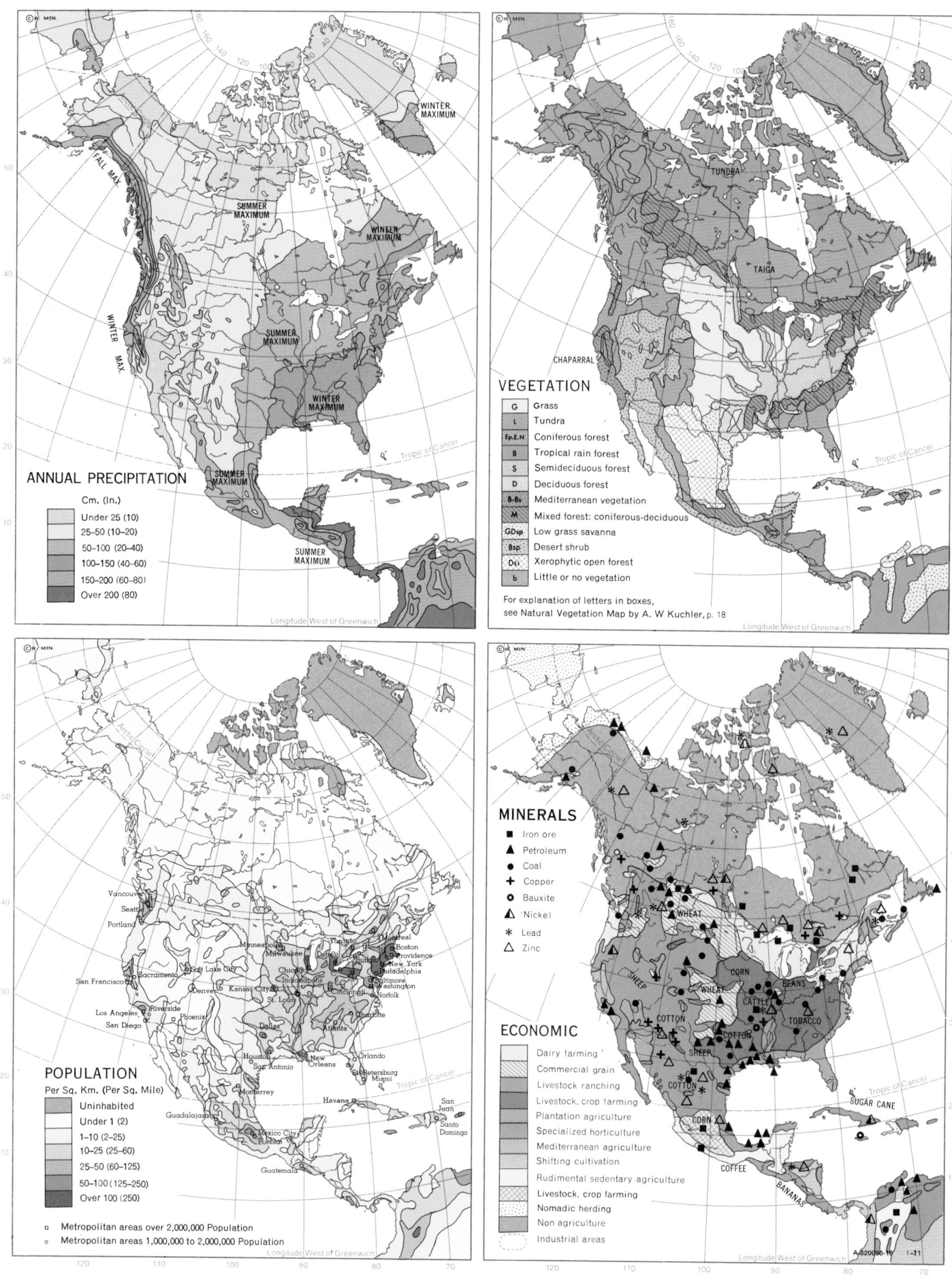

ANNUAL PRECIPITATION

Cm. (In.)

- Under 25 (10)
- 25–50 (10–20)
- 50–100 (20–40)
- 100–150 (40–60)
- 150–200 (60–80)
- Over 200 (80)

FALL MAX.

WINTER MAX.

WINTER MAX.

WINTER MAXIMUM

SUMMER MAXIMUM

SUMMER MAXIMUM

WINTER MAXIMUM

SUMMER MAXIMUM

SUMMER MAXIMUM

VEGETATION

G	Grass
L	Tundra
Ep.E.N	Coniferous forest
B	Tropical rain forest
S	Semideciduous forest
D	Deciduous forest
B-Bs	Mediterranean vegetation
M	Mixed forest: coniferous-deciduous
GDsp	Low grass savanna
Bsp	Desert shrub
Dsi	Xerophytic open forest
b	Little or no vegetation

For explanation of letters in boxes,
see Natural Vegetation Map by A. W Kuchler, p. 18

TUNDRA

TAIGA

CHAPARRAL

POPULATION

Per Sq. Km. (Per Sq. Mile)

- Uninhabited
- Under 1 (2)
- 1–10 (2–25)
- 10–25 (25–60)
- 25–50 (60–125)
- 50–100 (125–250)
- Over 100 (250)

□ Metropolitan areas over 2,000,000 Population

○ Metropolitan areas 1,000,000 to 2,000,000 Population

MINERALS

- ■ Iron ore
- ▲ Petroleum
- ● Coal
- + Copper
- ◉ Bauxite
- ▲ Nickel
- ✳ Lead
- △ Zinc

ECONOMIC

- Dairy farming
- Commercial grain
- Livestock ranching
- Livestock, crop farming
- Plantation agriculture
- Specialized horticulture
- Mediterranean agriculture
- Shifting cultivation
- Rudimental sedentary agriculture
- Livestock, crop farming
- Nomadic herding
- Non agriculture
- Industrial areas

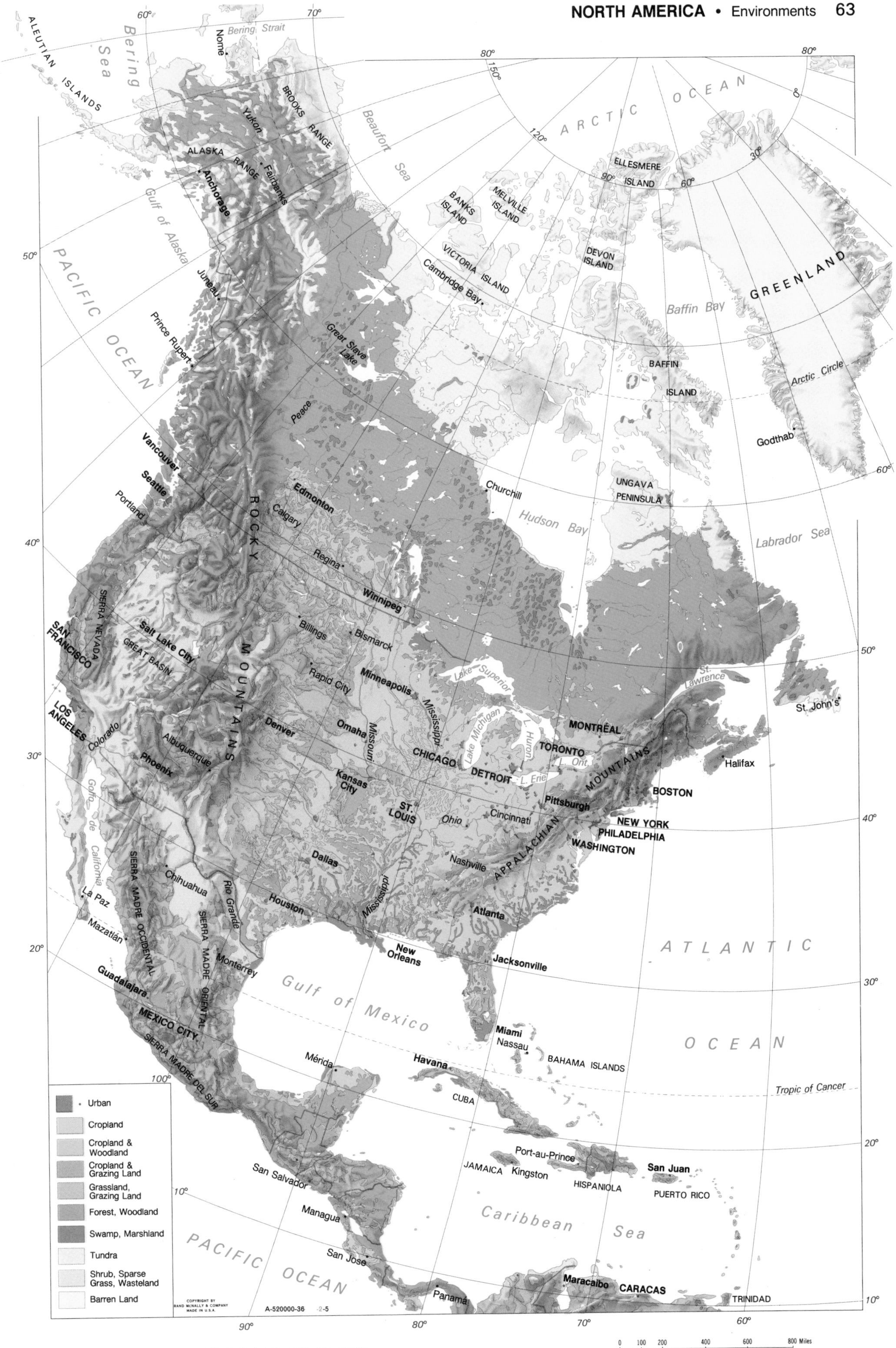

ALEUTIAN ISLANDS
Bering Sea
Bering Strait
Nome
BROOKS RANGE
Yukon
Fairbanks
ALASKA RANGE
Anchorage
Beaufort Sea
ARCTIC OCEAN
BANKS ISLAND
MELVILLE ISLAND
ELLESMERE ISLAND
DEVON ISLAND
VICTORIA ISLAND
Cambridge Bay
GREENLAND
Baffin Bay
Arctic Circle
Godthab
BAFFIN ISLAND
UNGAVA PENINSULA
Hudson Bay
Labrador Sea
Churchill
Great Slave Lake
PACIFIC OCEAN
Gulf of Alaska
Juneau
Prince Rupert
Vancouver
Seattle
Portland
Peace
Edmonton
Calgary
Regina
Winnipeg
Billings
Bismarck
Rapid City
St. Lawrence
St. John's
Halifax
MONTRÉAL
TORONTO
L. Ont.
BOSTON
SAN FRANCISCO
SIERRA NEVADA
Salt Lake City
GREAT BASIN
ROCKY MOUNTAINS
Minneapolis
Lake Superior
Lake Michigan
Huron
CHICAGO
DETROIT
L. Erie
Pittsburgh
NEW YORK
PHILADELPHIA
LOS ANGELES
Colorado
Denver
Omaha
Missouri
Mississippi
Kansas City
ST. LOUIS
Ohio
Cincinnati
WASHINGTON
APPALACHIAN MOUNTAINS
Phoenix
Albuquerque
Dallas
Nashville
Atlanta
Golfo de California
SIERRA MADRE OCCIDENTAL
Chihuahua
Rio Grande
Houston
Mississippi
New Orleans
Jacksonville
ATLANTIC OCEAN
La Paz
Mazatlán
Monterrey
SIERRA MADRE ORIENTAL
Gulf of Mexico
Miami
Nassau
BAHAMA ISLANDS
Guadalajara
MEXICO CITY
SIERRA MADRE DEL SUR
Mérida
Havana
CUBA
Tropic of Cancer
San Salvador
Port-au-Prince
JAMAICA
Kingston
HISPANIOLA
San Juan
PUERTO RICO
Managua
Caribbean Sea
PACIFIC OCEAN
San Jose
Panamá
Maracaibo
CARACAS
TRINIDAD

Legend:

- • Urban
- Cropland
- Cropland & Woodland
- Cropland & Grazing Land
- Grassland, Grazing Land
- Forest, Woodland
- Swamp, Marshland
- Tundra
- Shrub, Sparse Grass, Wasteland
- Barren Land

COPYRIGHT BY
RAND McNALLY & COMPANY
MADE IN U.S.A.

A-520000-36   -2-5

Scale 1:36,000,000; one inch to 570 miles. Lambert Azimuthal Equal-Area Projection

0 100 200 400 600 800 Miles
0 150 300 600 900 1200 Kilometers

PACIFIC

OCEAN

Vancouver

Seattle

Spokane

ROCKY

Calgary

Regina

W

Portland

Columbia

CASCADE RANGE

Bismarck

Billings

Medford

Boise

Rapid City

Missouri

125°

ROCKY

Casper

Great Salt Lake

Great Salt Lake

Salt Lake City

Reno

GREAT BASIN

SAN FRANCISCO

SIERRA NEVADA

Fresno

Denver

Oma

MOUNTAINS

Wichita

Las Vegas

LOS ANGELES

Albuquerque

Oklahoma City

Colorado

San Diego

Phoenix

Amarillo

Red

El Paso

Odessa

PACIFIC

OCEAN

Hermosillo

Gulf of California

SIERRA

Chihuahua

Rio Grande

San Antonio

SIERRA MADRE ORIENTAL

SIERRA MADRE OCCIDENTAL

Torreón

Rio Grande

Monterrey

PACIFIC OCEAN

Lake Winnipeg

50°

45°

40°

35°

30°

25°

125°

120°

115°

110°

105°

100°

Urban

Cropland

Cropland & Woodland

Cropland & Grazing Land

Grassland, Grazing Land

Forest, Woodland

Swamp, Marshland

Shrub, Sparse Grass; Wasteland

Barren Land

Scale 1:12,000,000; one inch to 190 miles.
Albers Conical Equal Area Projection

0   50   100   200   300   400 Miles

0   75   150   300   450   600 Kilometers

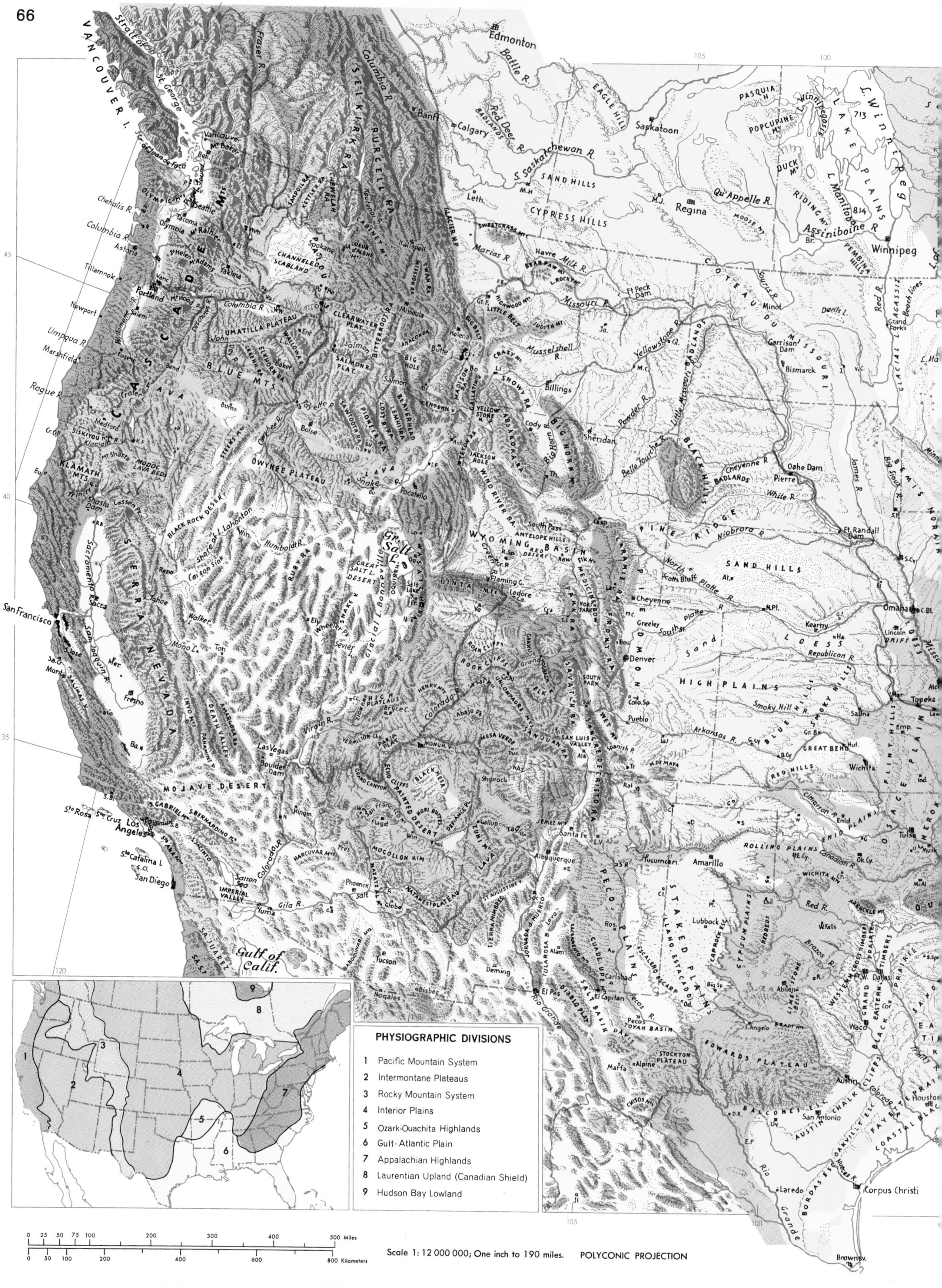

PHYSIOGRAPHIC DIVISIONS

1 Pacific Mountain System
2 Intermontane Plateaus
3 Rocky Mountain System
4 Interior Plains
5 Ozark-Ouachita Highlands
6 Gulf-Atlantic Plain
7 Appalachian Highlands
8 Laurentian Upland (Canadian Shield)
9 Hudson Bay Lowland

Scale 1: 12 000 000; One inch to 190 miles.   POLYCONIC PROJECTION

0 25 50 75 100   200   300   400   500 Miles
0   50   100   200   400   600   800 Kilometers

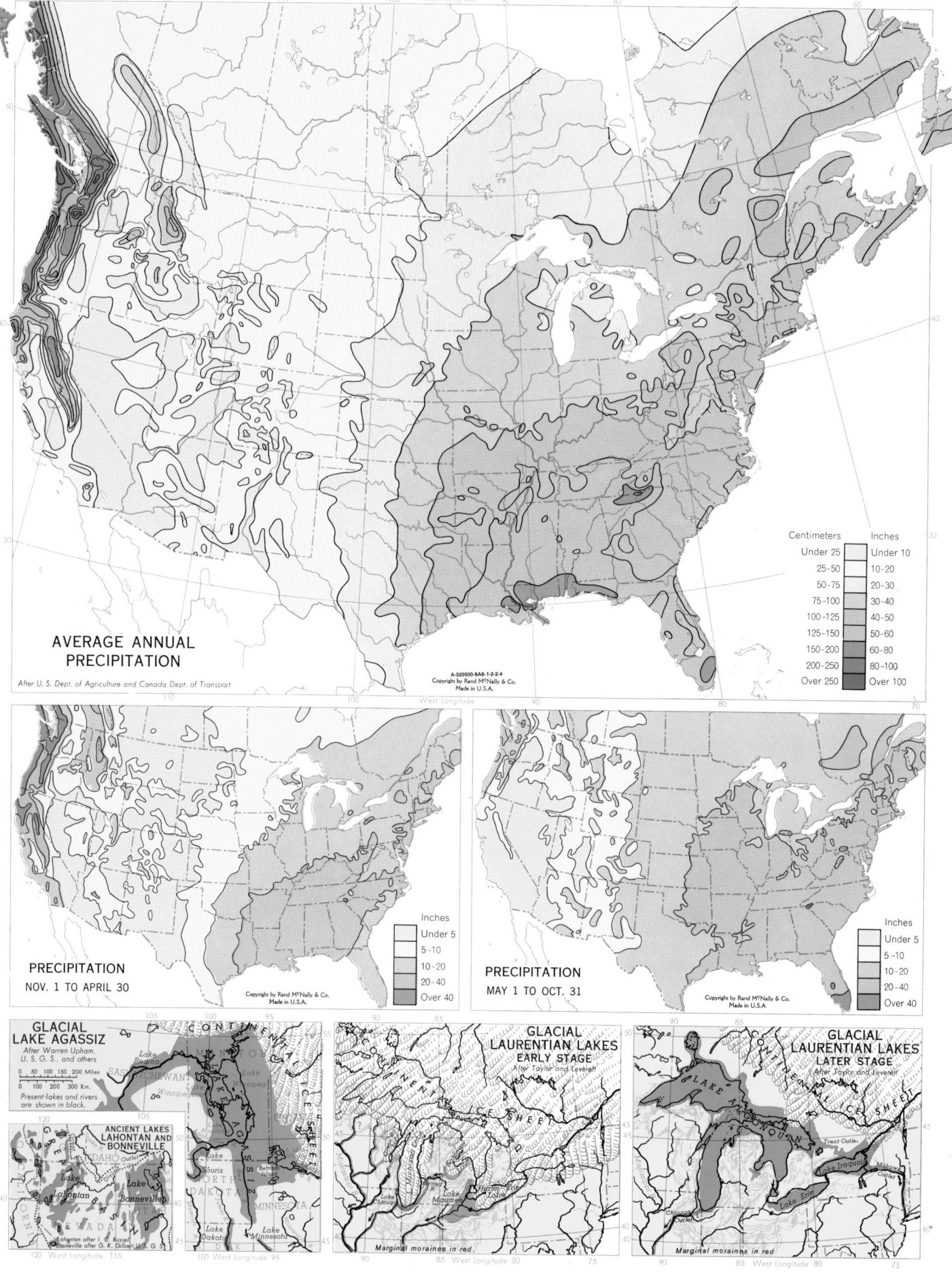

AVERAGE ANNUAL PRECIPITATION

After U. S. Dept. of Agriculture and Canada Dept. of Transport

A-520500-6A6-1-2-2-4
Copyright by Rand McNally & Co.
Made in U.S.A.

Centimeters	Inches
Under 25	Under 10
25–50	10–20
50–75	20–30
75–100	30–40
100–125	40–50
125–150	50–60
150–200	60–80
200–250	80–100
Over 250	Over 100

PRECIPITATION
NOV. 1 TO APRIL 30

Copyright by Rand McNally & Co.
Made in U.S.A.

Inches
Under 5
5–10
10–20
20–40
Over 40

PRECIPITATION
MAY 1 TO OCT. 31

Copyright by Rand McNally & Co.
Made in U.S.A.

Inches
Under 5
5–10
10–20
20–40
Over 40

GLACIAL LAKE AGASSIZ

After Warren Upham,
U. S. G. S., and others

0 50 100 150 200 Miles
0 100 200 300 Km.

Present lakes and rivers
are shown in black.

ANCIENT LAKES LAHONTAN AND BONNEVILLE

Lahontan after I. C. Russell
Bonneville after G. K. Gilbert, U. S. G. S.

GLACIAL LAURENTIAN LAKES EARLY STAGE

After Taylor and Leverett

Marginal moraines in red.

GLACIAL LAURENTIAN LAKES LATER STAGE

After Taylor and Leverett

Marginal moraines in red.

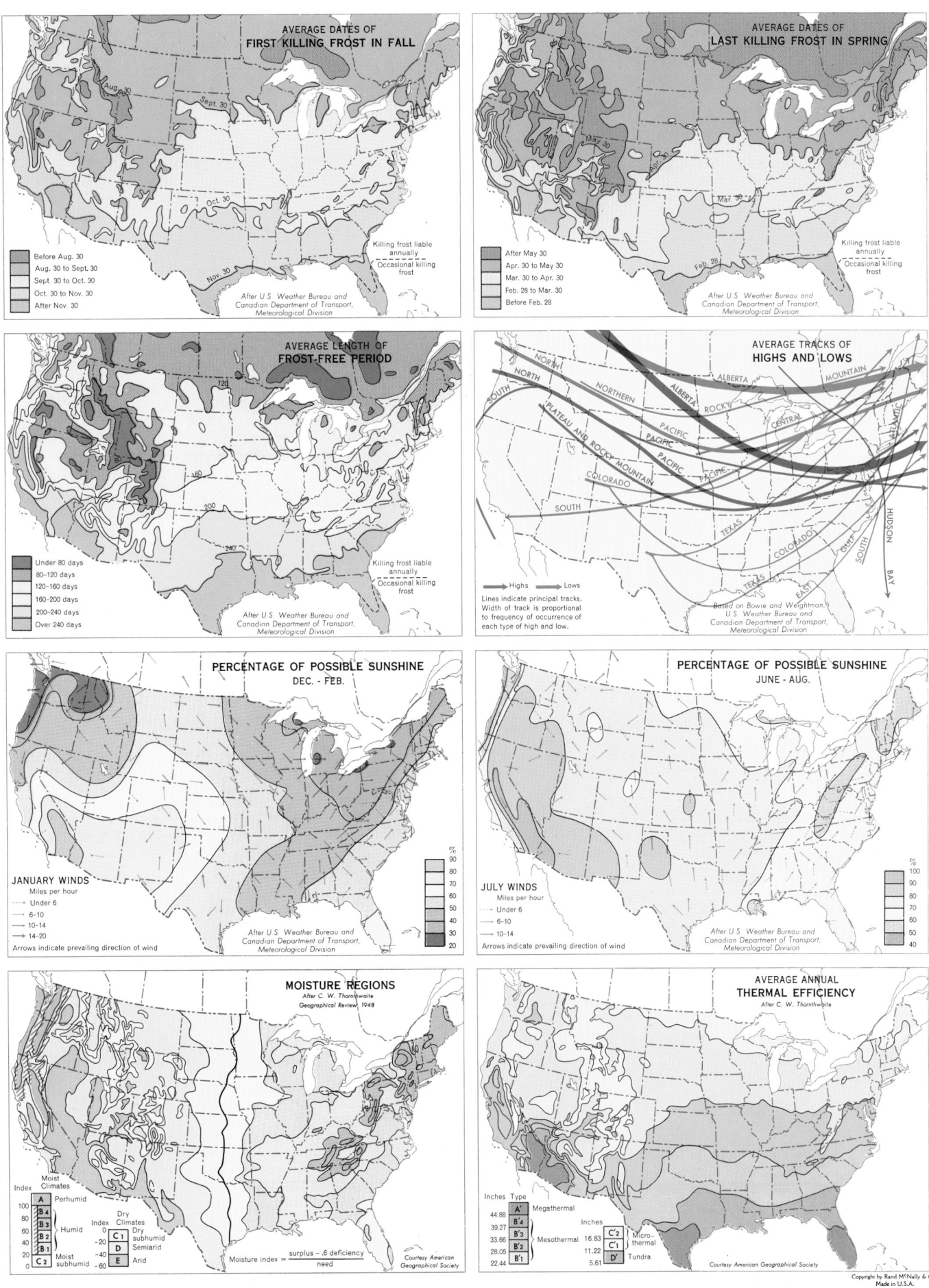

AVERAGE DATES OF FIRST KILLING FROST IN FALL

Before Aug. 30
Aug. 30 to Sept. 30
Sept. 30 to Oct. 30
Oct. 30 to Nov. 30
After Nov. 30

Killing frost liable annually
Occasional killing frost

After U.S. Weather Bureau and Canadian Department of Transport, Meteorological Division

AVERAGE DATES OF LAST KILLING FROST IN SPRING

After May 30
Apr. 30 to May 30
Mar. 30 to Apr. 30
Feb. 28 to Mar. 30
Before Feb. 28

Killing frost liable annually
Occasional killing frost

After U.S. Weather Bureau and Canadian Department of Transport, Meteorological Division

AVERAGE LENGTH OF FROST-FREE PERIOD

Under 80 days
80–120 days
120–160 days
160–200 days
200–240 days
Over 240 days

Killing frost liable annually
Occasional killing frost

After U.S. Weather Bureau and Canadian Department of Transport, Meteorological Division

AVERAGE TRACKS OF HIGHS AND LOWS

Highs   Lows

Lines indicate principal tracks. Width of track is proportional to frequency of occurrence of each type of high and low.

Based on Bowie and Weightman, U.S. Weather Bureau and Canadian Department of Transport, Meteorological Division

PERCENTAGE OF POSSIBLE SUNSHINE DEC. - FEB.

JANUARY WINDS
Miles per hour
Under 6
6–10
10–14
14–20
Arrows indicate prevailing direction of wind

%
90
80
70
60
50
40
30
20

After U.S. Weather Bureau and Canadian Department of Transport, Meteorological Division

PERCENTAGE OF POSSIBLE SUNSHINE JUNE - AUG.

JULY WINDS
Miles per hour
Under 6
6–10
10–14
Arrows indicate prevailing direction of wind

%
100
90
80
70
60
50
40

After U.S. Weather Bureau and Canadian Department of Transport, Meteorological Division

MOISTURE REGIONS
After C. W. Thornthwaite
Geographical Review, 1948

Index | Moist Climates
100 | A Perhumid
80 | B4
60 | B3 Humid
40 | B2
20 | B1
0 | C2 Moist subhumid

Index | Dry Climates
0 | C1 Dry subhumid
-20 | D Semiarid
-40 | E Arid
-60 |

Moisture index = surplus − .6 deficiency / need

Courtesy American Geographical Society

AVERAGE ANNUAL THERMAL EFFICIENCY
After C. W. Thornthwaite

Inches | Type
44.88 | A' Megathermal
39.27 | B'4
33.66 | B'3 Mesothermal
28.05 | B'2
22.44 | B'1

Inches
16.83 | C'2 Micro-
11.22 | C'1 thermal
5.61 | D' Tundra

Courtesy American Geographical Society

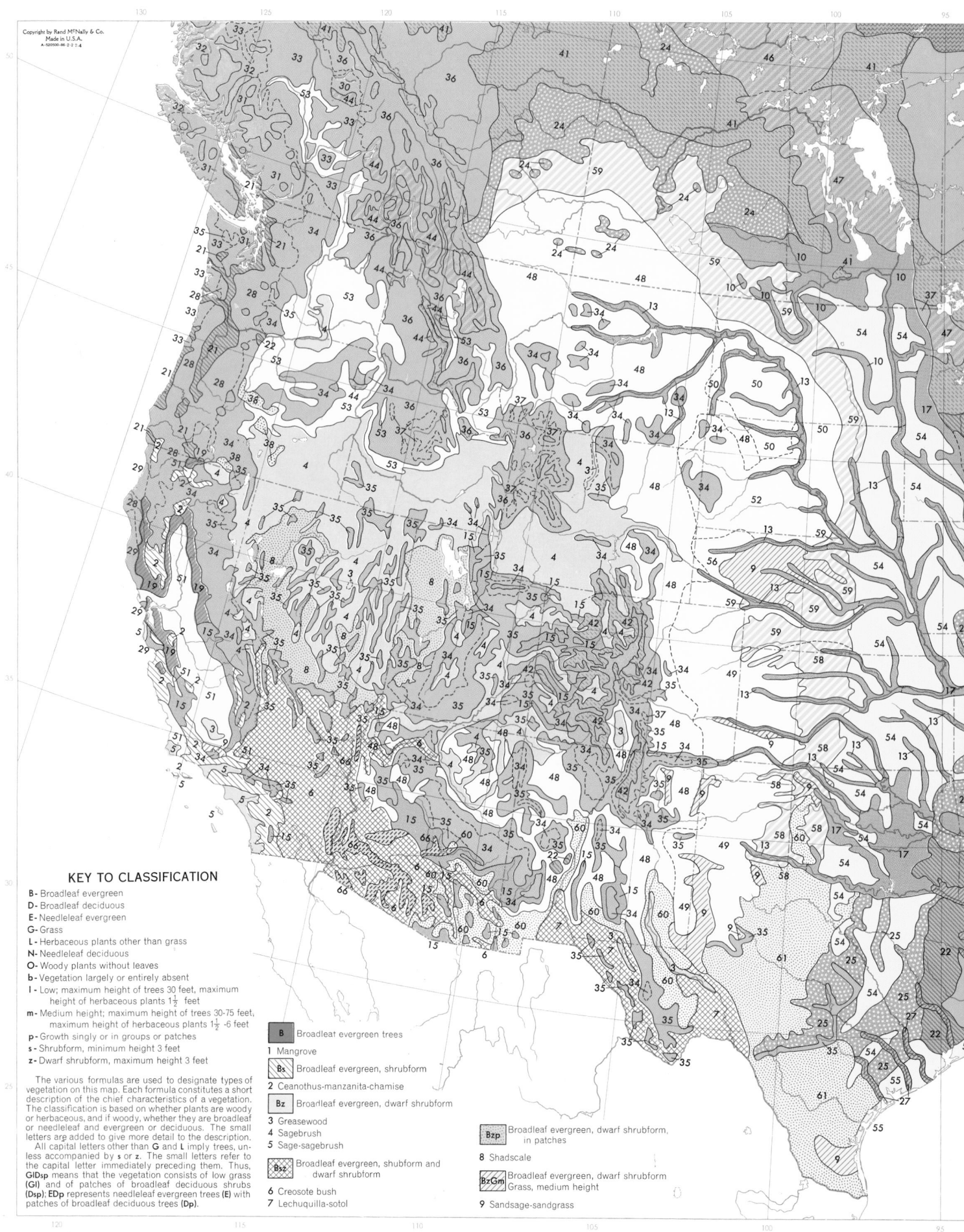

Copyright by Rand McNally & Co.
Made in U.S.A.
A-520500-96-2-2 2 4

KEY TO CLASSIFICATION

B- Broadleaf evergreen
D- Broadleaf deciduous
E- Needleleaf evergreen
G- Grass
L- Herbaceous plants other than grass
N- Needleleaf deciduous
O- Woody plants without leaves
b- Vegetation largely or entirely absent
l- Low; maximum height of trees 30 feet, maximum
   height of herbaceous plants 1½ feet
m- Medium height; maximum height of trees 30-75 feet,
   maximum height of herbaceous plants 1½ -6 feet
p- Growth singly or in groups or patches
s- Shrubform, minimum height 3 feet
z- Dwarf shrubform, maximum height 3 feet

The various formulas are used to designate types of
vegetation on this map. Each formula constitutes a short
description of the chief characteristics of a vegetation.
The classification is based on whether plants are woody
or herbaceous, and if woody, whether they are broadleaf
or needleleaf and evergreen or deciduous. The small
letters are added to give more detail to the description.
All capital letters other than G and L imply trees, un-
less accompanied by s or z. The small letters refer to
the capital letter immediately preceding them. Thus,
GlDsp means that the vegetation consists of low grass
(Gl) and of patches of broadleaf deciduous shrubs
(Dsp); EDp represents needleleaf evergreen trees (E) with
patches of broadleaf deciduous trees (Dp).

B	Broadleaf evergreen trees
	1 Mangrove
Bs	Broadleaf evergreen, shrubform
	2 Ceanothus-manzanita-chamise
Bz	Broadleaf evergreen, dwarf shrubform
	3 Greasewood
	4 Sagebrush
	5 Sage-sagebrush
Bsz	Broadleaf evergreen, shubform and dwarf shrubform
	6 Creosote bush
	7 Lechuquilla-sotol

Bzp	Broadleaf evergreen, dwarf shrubform, in patches
	8 Shadscale
BzGm	Broadleaf evergreen, dwarf shrubform Grass, medium height
	9 Sandsage-sandgrass

0 25 50 75 100   200   300   400   500 Miles
0 50 100   200   400   600   800 Kilometers

Scale 1 : 14 000 000; One inch to 220 mil

NATURAL VEGETATION
BY A. W. KÜCHLER

Based on "A Physiognomic Classification of Vegetation"
Annals of the Assoc. of American Geographers, Vol. 39, September, 1949

D Broadleaf deciduous trees

10 Aspen-oak
11 Beech-maple
12 Beech-tulip tree-maple-basswood
13 Cottonwood-willow
14 Maple-basswood
15 Oak
16 Oak-ash-maple
17 Oak-hickory
18 Oak-tulip tree

DB Broadleaf deciduous trees
Broadleaf evergreen trees

19 Oak-madrone

DE Broadleaf deciduous trees
Needleleaf evergreen trees

20 Maple-yellow birch-hemlock-pine
21 Oak-Douglas fir
22 Oak-pine
23 Maple-beech-hemlock

D / Gmp Broadleaf deciduous trees
Grass, medium height, in patches

24 Aspen-needle grass-wheat grass
25 Oak-hickory-bluestem

DN Broadleaf deciduous trees
Needleleaf deciduous trees

26 Bay trees-bald cypress
27 Tupelo-gum-bald cypress

E Needleleaf evergreen trees

28 Douglas fir
29 Douglas fir-redwood
30 Hemlock-arbor vitae
31 Hemlock-arbor vitae-Douglas fir
32 Hemlock-arbor vitae-fir
33 Hemlock-spruce
34 Pine
35 Pine-juniper
36 Pine-spruce
37 Spruce-fir

Esp Needleleaf evergreen, shrubform, in patches

38 Juniper

EDp Needleleaf evergreen trees
Broadleaf deciduous trees, in patches

39 Douglas fir-pine-aspen
40 Pine-spruce-birch
41 Spruce-aspen
42 Spruce-fir-aspen
43 Spruce-poplar-birch

EN Needleleaf evergreen trees
Needleleaf deciduous trees

44 Hemlock-arbor vitae-Douglas fir-larch
45 Pine-bald cypress
46 Pine-spruce-larch
47 Spruce-larch

Gl Grass, low

48 Grama grass
49 Grama grass-buffalo grass
50 Grama grass-needle grass
51 Needle grass-blue grass
52 Wheat grass
53 Wheat grass-blue grass

Gm Grass, medium height

54 Bluestem
55 Broom grass-water grass
56 Marsh grass
57 Saw grass

Gml Grass, medium and low height

58 Bluestem-bunch grass
59 Needle grass-wheat grass

Gl / Dsp Grass, low
Broadleaf deciduous, shrubform, in patches

60 Bunch grass-oak

Gm / Dsp Grass, medium height
Broadleaf deciduous, shrubform, in patches

61 Mesquite grass-mesquite

L Herbaceous plants other than grass

62 Lichens, etc.

LEp Herbaceous plants other than grass
Needleleaf evergreen trees, in patches

63 Lichens-spruce

LEp / Np Herbaceous plants other than grass
Needleleaf evergreen trees, in patches
Needleleaf deciduous trees, in patches

64 Lichens-spruce-larch

N Needleleaf deciduous trees

65 Bald cypress

Op Woody plants without leaves, in patches

66 Palo verde-cacti-ocotillo

b Vegetation largely or entirely absent

LAMBERT CONFORMAL CONIC PROJECTION

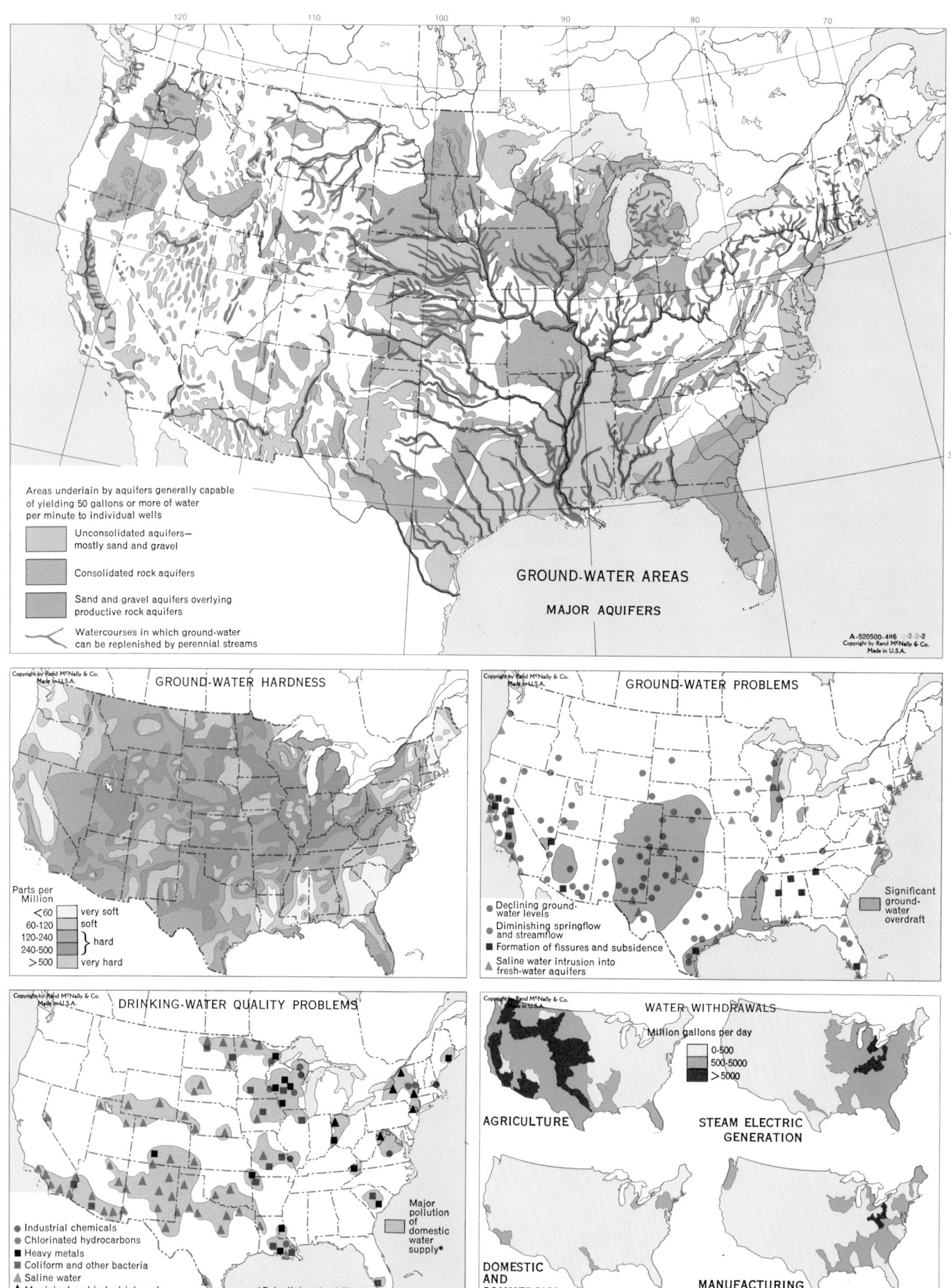

GROUND-WATER AREAS

MAJOR AQUIFERS

Areas underlain by aquifers generally capable of yielding 50 gallons or more of water per minute to individual wells

Unconsolidated aquifers— mostly sand and gravel

Consolidated rock aquifers

Sand and gravel aquifers overlying productive rock aquifers

Watercourses in which ground-water can be replenished by perennial streams

A-520500-4H6
Copyright by Rand McNally & Co.
Made in U.S.A.

GROUND-WATER HARDNESS

Parts per Million
<60   very soft
60-120   soft
120-240 } hard
240-500
>500   very hard

GROUND-WATER PROBLEMS

Declining ground-water levels
Diminishing springflow and streamflow
Formation of fissures and subsidence
Saline water intrusion into fresh-water aquifers

Significant ground-water overdraft

DRINKING-WATER QUALITY PROBLEMS

Industrial chemicals
Chlorinated hydrocarbons
Heavy metals
Coliform and other bacteria
Saline water
Municipal and industrial wastes

Major pollution of domestic water supply*

*Potential and existing

WATER WITHDRAWALS

Million gallons per day
0-500
500-5000
>5000

AGRICULTURE

STEAM ELECTRIC GENERATION

DOMESTIC AND COMMERCIAL

MANUFACTURING

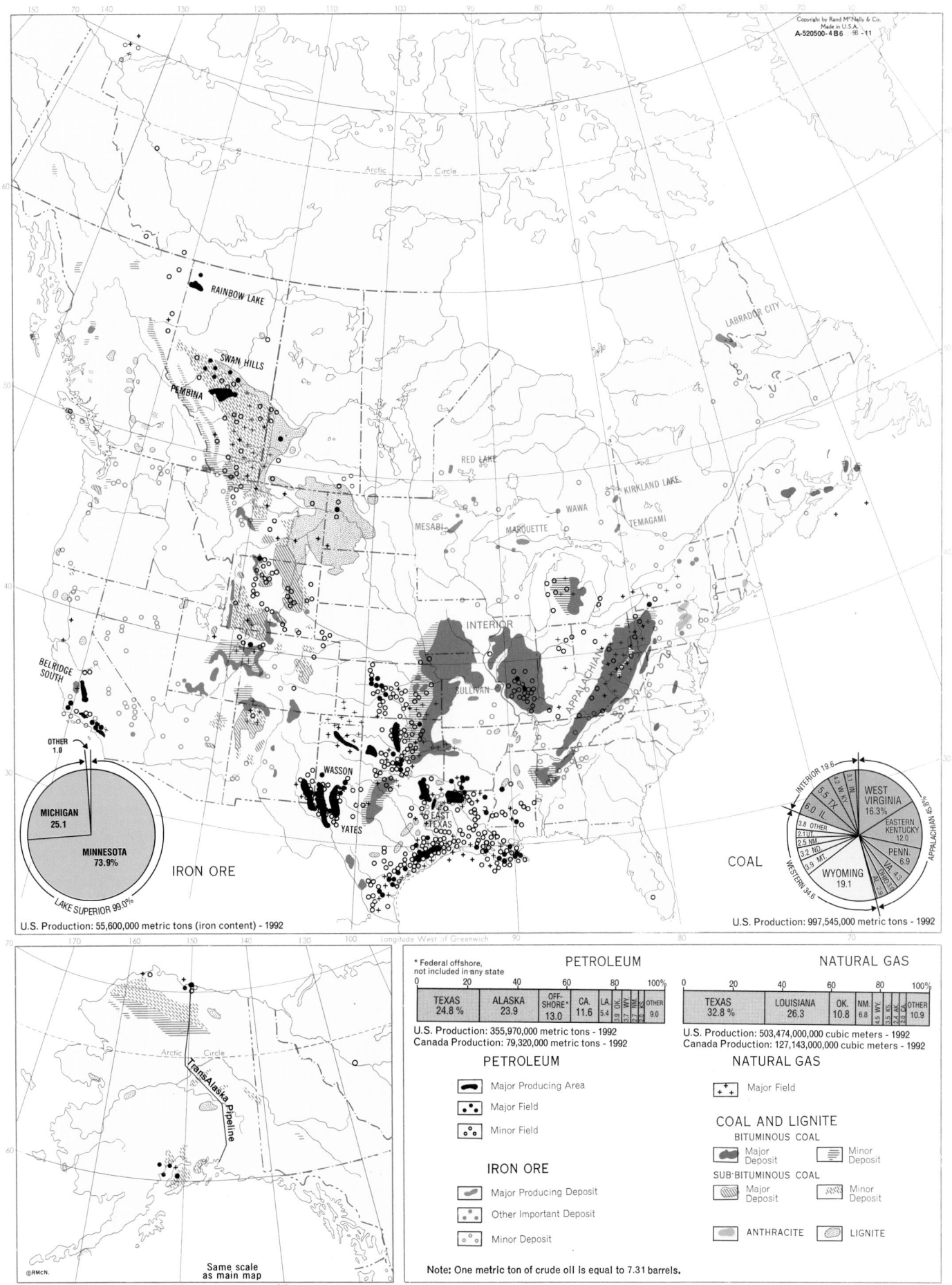

Copyright by Rand M°Nally & Co.
Made in U.S.A.
A-520500-4 B 6 · 98 - 11

RAINBOW LAKE

SWAN HILLS

PEMBINA

LABRADOR CITY

Arctic Circle

RED LAKE

KIRKLAND LAKE

WAWA

MESABI

MARQUETTE

TEMAGAMI

INTERIOR

BELRIDGE
SOUTH

SULLIVAN

APPALACHIAN

OTHER
1.0

**MICHIGAN
25.1**

**MINNESOTA
73.9%**

WASSON

EAST
TEXAS

YATES

IRON ORE

LAKE SUPERIOR 99.0%

U.S. Production: 55,600,000 metric tons (iron content) - 1992

COAL

INTERIOR 19.6
3.1 IN.
4.2 W. KY.
5.5 TX.
6.0 IL.
3.8 OTHER
2.1 UT.
2.5 NM.
3.2 ND.
3.9 MT.
WESTERN 34.6
WYOMING
19.1

WEST
VIRGINIA
16.3%

EASTERN
KENTUCKY
12.0

PENN.
6.9

VA. 4.3
OHIO 2.6
APPALACHIAN 45.6%

U.S. Production: 997,545,000 metric tons - 1992

Longitude West of Greenwich

TransAlaska Pipeline

Arctic Circle

Same scale
as main map

©RMcN.

PETROLEUM

* Federal offshore,
not included in any state

0	20	40	60	80	100%

TEXAS 24.8 %	ALASKA 23.9	OFF-SHORE* 13.0	CA. 11.6	LA. 5.4	OK.	WY.	NM.	KS.	OTHER 9.0

U.S. Production: 355,970,000 metric tons - 1992
Canada Production: 79,320,000 metric tons - 1992

NATURAL GAS

0	20	40	60	80	100%

TEXAS 32.8 %	LOUISIANA 26.3	OK. 10.8	NM. 6.8	WY.	KS.	LA.	OTHER 10.9

U.S. Production: 503,474,000 cubic meters - 1992
Canada Production: 127,143,000,000 cubic meters - 1992

PETROLEUM

- ⬛ Major Producing Area
- ⬤⬤ Major Field
- ◯◯ Minor Field

IRON ORE

- Major Producing Deposit
- Other Important Deposit
- Minor Deposit

NATURAL GAS

- +++ Major Field

COAL AND LIGNITE

BITUMINOUS COAL

- Major Deposit
- Minor Deposit

SUB-BITUMINOUS COAL

- Major Deposit
- Minor Deposit

- ANTHRACITE
- LIGNITE

Note: One metric ton of crude oil is equal to 7.31 barrels.

Scale 1: 32 000 000; One inch to 500 miles.   LAMBERT CONFORMAL CONIC PROJECTION

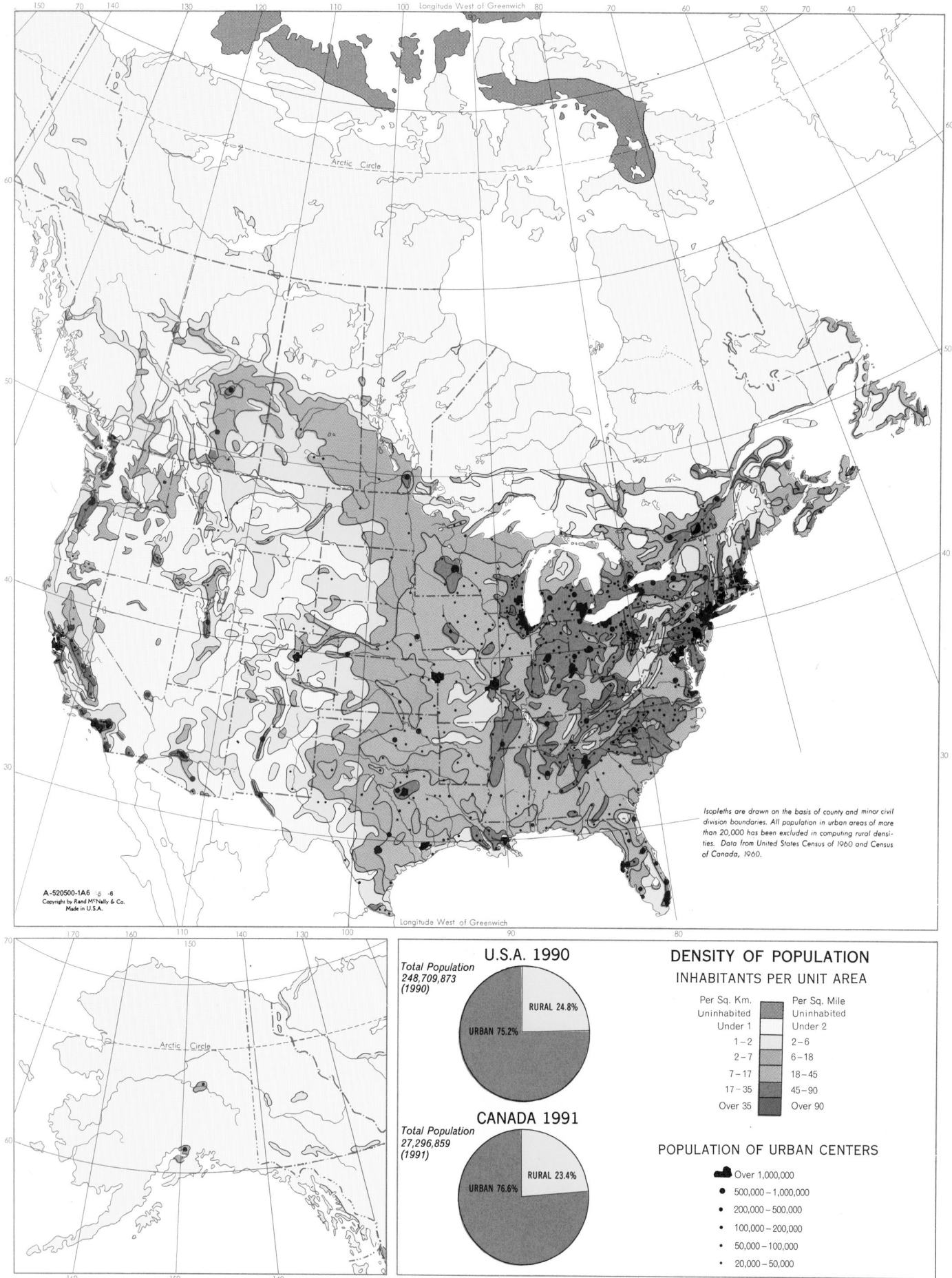

Isopleths are drawn on the basis of county and minor civil division boundaries. All population in urban areas of more than 20,000 has been excluded in computing rural densities. Data from United States Census of 1960 and Census of Canada, 1960.

A-520500-1A6 -5 -6
Copyright by Rand McNally & Co.
Made in U.S.A.

U.S.A. 1990

Total Population 248,709,873 (1990)

RURAL 24.8%

URBAN 75.2%

CANADA 1991

Total Population 27,296,859 (1991)

RURAL 23.4%

URBAN 76.6%

DENSITY OF POPULATION
INHABITANTS PER UNIT AREA

Per Sq. Km.	Per Sq. Mile
Uninhabited	Uninhabited
Under 1	Under 2
1 – 2	2 – 6
2 – 7	6 – 18
7 – 17	18 – 45
17 – 35	45 – 90
Over 35	Over 90

POPULATION OF URBAN CENTERS

Over 1,000,000
500,000 – 1,000,000
200,000 – 500,000
100,000 – 200,000
50,000 – 100,000
20,000 – 50,000

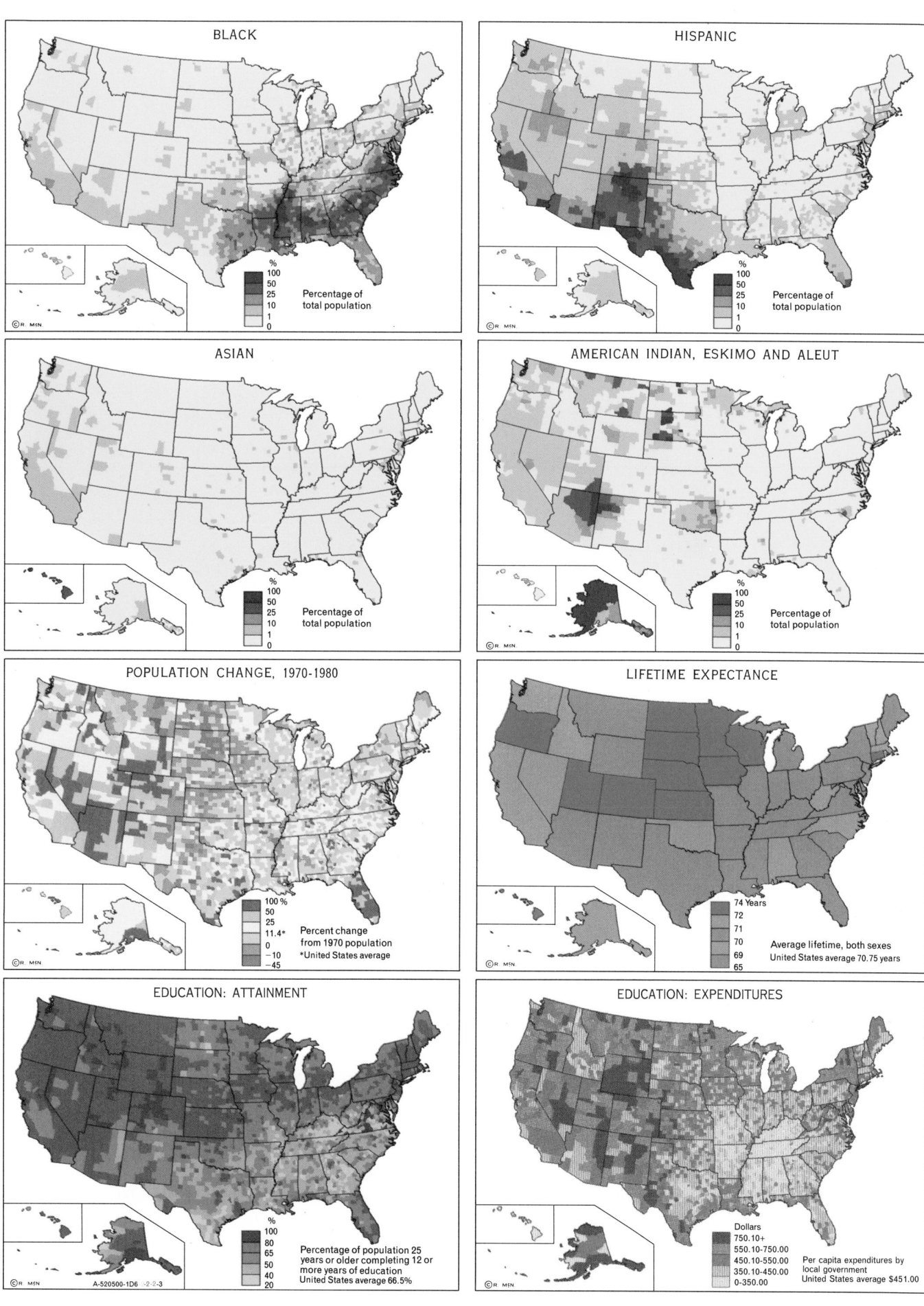

BLACK

HISPANIC

%
100
50
25
10
1
0
Percentage of
total population

ASIAN

AMERICAN INDIAN, ESKIMO AND ALEUT

%
100
50
25
10
1
0
Percentage of
total population

POPULATION CHANGE, 1970-1980

100 %
50
25
11.4*
0
–10
–45
Percent change
from 1970 population
*United States average

LIFETIME EXPECTANCE

74 Years
72
71
70
69
65
Average lifetime, both sexes
United States average 70.75 years

EDUCATION: ATTAINMENT

%
100
80
65
50
40
20
Percentage of population 25
years or older completing 12 or
more years of education
United States average 66.5%

A-520500-1D6   -2-2-3

EDUCATION: EXPENDITURES

Dollars
750.10+
550.10-750.00
450.10-550.00
350.10-450.00
0-350.00
Per capita expenditures by
local government
United States average $451.00

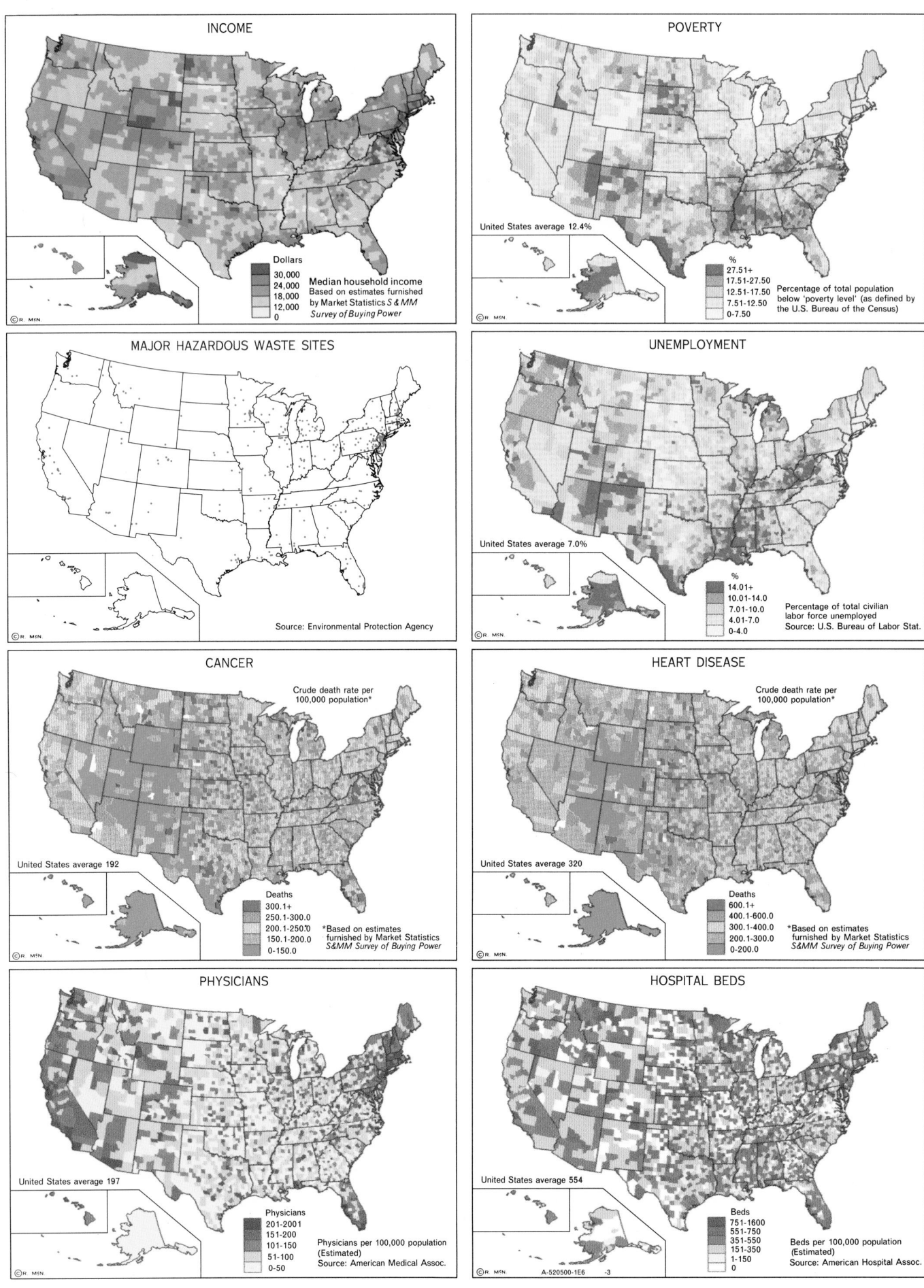

INCOME

Dollars
30,000
24,000
18,000
12,000
0

Median household income
Based on estimates furnished
by Market Statistics *S & MM*
Survey of Buying Power

POVERTY

United States average 12.4%

%
27.51+
17.51-27.50
12.51-17.50
7.51-12.50
0-7.50

Percentage of total population
below 'poverty level' (as defined by
the U.S. Bureau of the Census)

MAJOR HAZARDOUS WASTE SITES

Source: Environmental Protection Agency

UNEMPLOYMENT

United States average 7.0%

%
14.01+
10.01-14.0
7.01-10.0
4.01-7.0
0-4.0

Percentage of total civilian
labor force unemployed
Source: U.S. Bureau of Labor Stat.

CANCER

Crude death rate per
100,000 population*

United States average 192

Deaths
300.1+
250.1-300.0
200.1-250.0
150.1-200.0
0-150.0

*Based on estimates
furnished by Market Statistics
S&MM Survey of Buying Power

HEART DISEASE

Crude death rate per
100,000 population*

United States average 320

Deaths
600.1+
400.1-600.0
300.1-400.0
200.1-300.0
0-200.0

*Based on estimates
furnished by Market Statistics
S&MM Survey of Buying Power

PHYSICIANS

United States average 197

Physicians
201-2001
151-200
101-150
51-100
0-50

Physicians per 100,000 population
(Estimated)
Source: American Medical Assoc.

HOSPITAL BEDS

United States average 554

Beds
751-1600
551-750
351-550
151-350
1-150
0

Beds per 100,000 population
(Estimated)
Source: American Hospital Assoc.

A-520500-1E6   -3

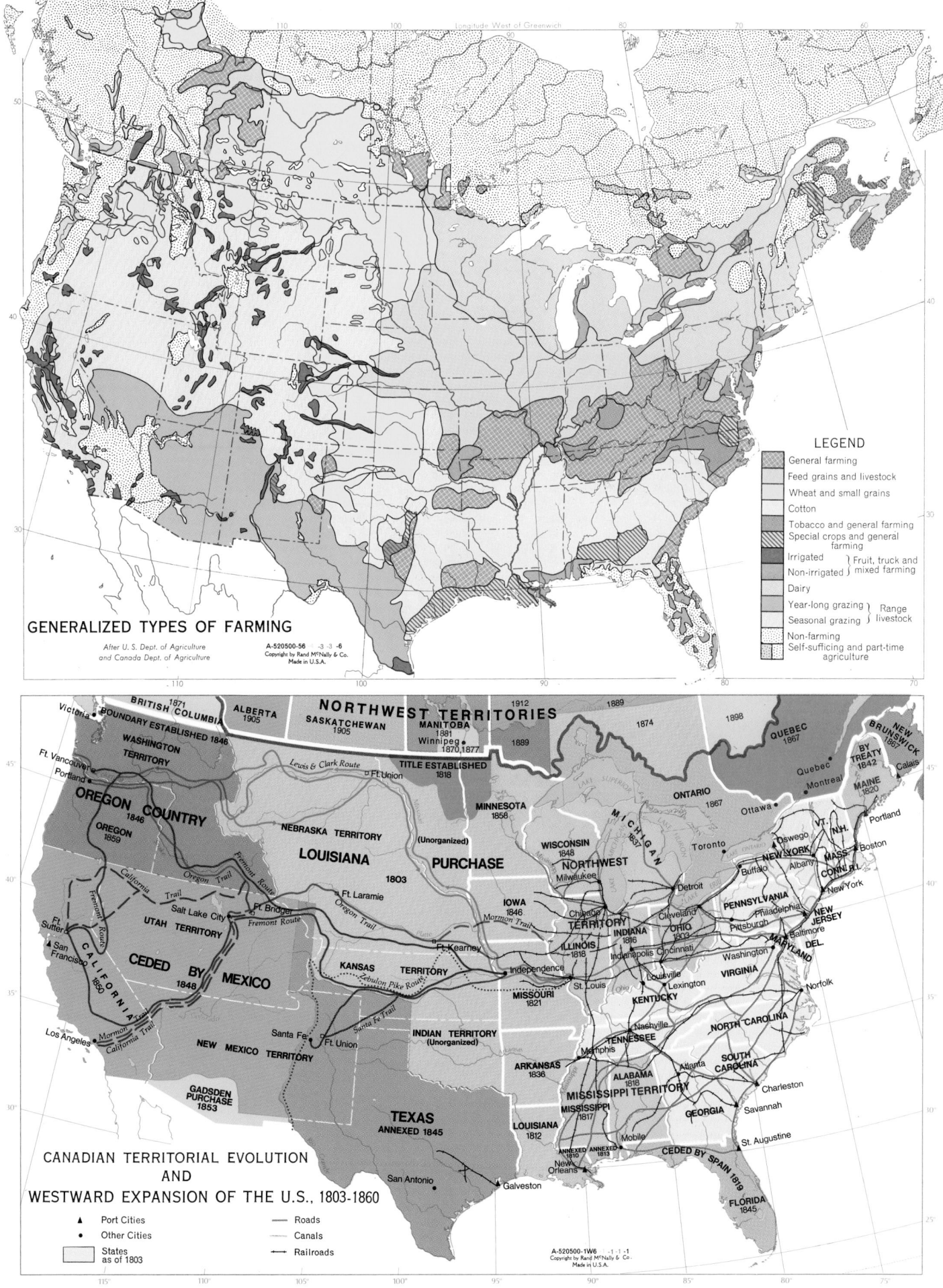

GENERALIZED TYPES OF FARMING

After U. S. Dept. of Agriculture
and Canada Dept. of Agriculture

A-520500-56 -3 -3 -6
Copyright by Rand McNally & Co.
Made in U.S.A.

LEGEND

General farming
Feed grains and livestock
Wheat and small grains
Cotton
Tobacco and general farming
Special crops and general farming
Irrigated } Fruit, truck and
Non-irrigated } mixed farming
Dairy
Year-long grazing } Range
Seasonal grazing } livestock
Non-farming
Self-sufficing and part-time agriculture

CANADIAN TERRITORIAL EVOLUTION
AND
WESTWARD EXPANSION OF THE U.S., 1803-1860

▲ Port Cities
● Other Cities
▨ States as of 1803

— Roads
--- Canals
→ Railroads

A-520500-1W6 -1 -1 -1
Copyright by Rand McNally & Co.
Made in U.S.A.

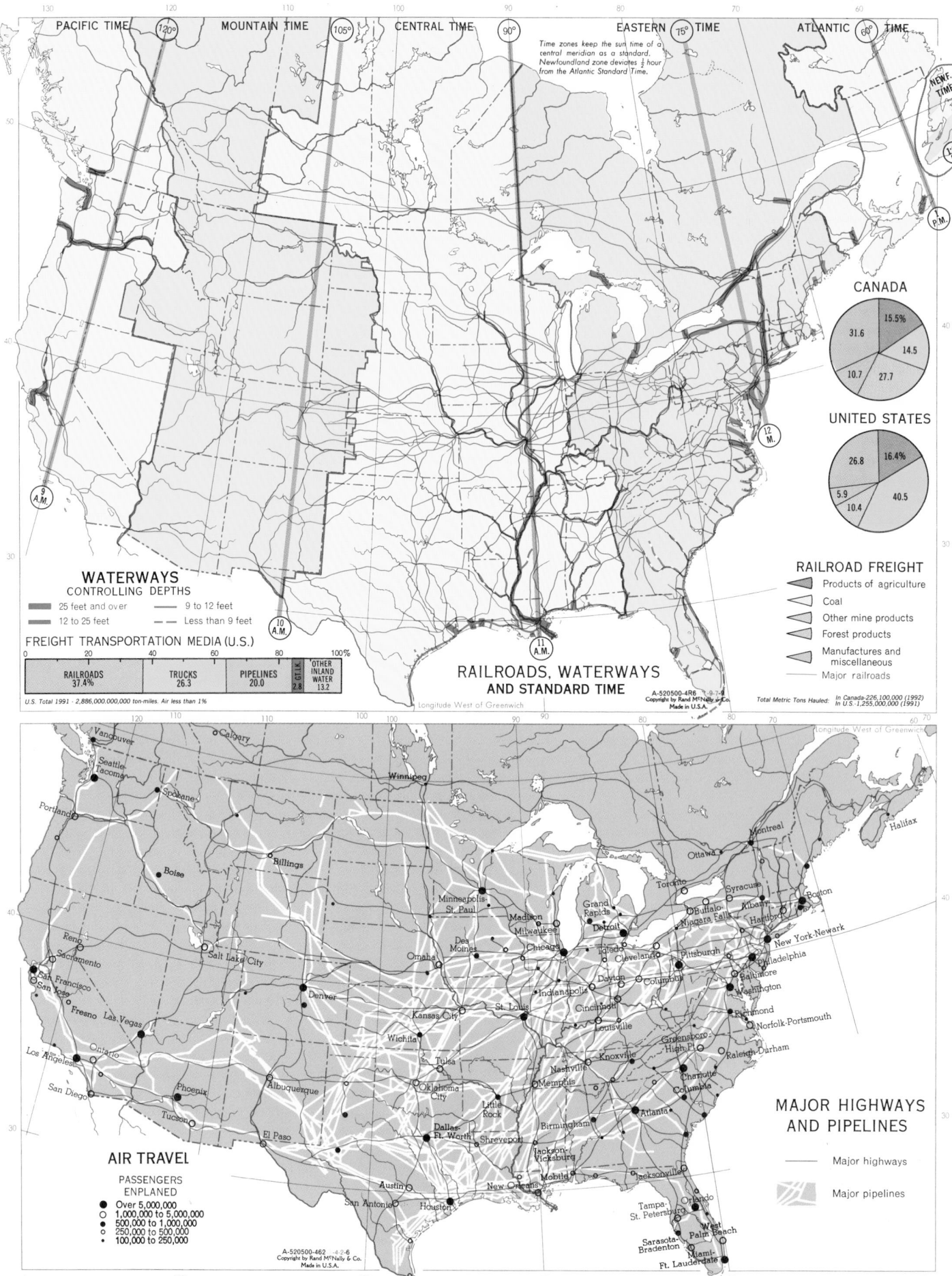

PACIFIC TIME · MOUNTAIN TIME · CENTRAL TIME · EASTERN TIME · ATLANTIC TIME

Time zones keep the sun time of a central meridian as a standard. Newfoundland zone deviates ½ hour from the Atlantic Standard Time.

NEWF. TIME

WATERWAYS
CONTROLLING DEPTHS

▬ 25 feet and over	▬ 9 to 12 feet
▬ 12 to 25 feet	- - - Less than 9 feet

FREIGHT TRANSPORTATION MEDIA (U.S.)

0   20   40   60   80   100%

| RAILROADS 37.4% | TRUCKS 26.3 | PIPELINES 20.0 | G.T.L.K. 2.8 | OTHER INLAND WATER 13.2 |

U.S. Total 1991 - 2,886,000,000,000 ton-miles. Air less than 1%

RAILROADS, WATERWAYS
AND STANDARD TIME

Longitude West of Greenwich

A-520500-4R6 7-9-7-8
Copyright by Rand McNally & Co.
Made in U.S.A.

CANADA

15.5%
14.5
27.7
10.7
31.6

UNITED STATES

16.4%
40.5
10.4
5.9
26.8

RAILROAD FREIGHT

- ◤ Products of agriculture
- ◁ Coal
- ◁ Other mine products
- ◀ Forest products
- ◀ Manufactures and miscellaneous
- ── Major railroads

Total Metric Tons Hauled: In Canada-226,100,000 (1992)
In U.S.-1,255,000,000 (1991)

MAJOR HIGHWAYS
AND PIPELINES

── Major highways

▨ Major pipelines

AIR TRAVEL

PASSENGERS ENPLANED

- ● Over 5,000,000
- ○ 1,000,000 to 5,000,000
- ● 500,000 to 1,000,000
- ○ 250,000 to 500,000
- · 100,000 to 250,000

A-520500-462   4-2-6
Copyright by Rand McNally & Co.
Made in U.S.A.

Scale 1: 28 000 000; One inch to 440 miles.   LAMBERT CONFORMAL CONIC PROJECTION

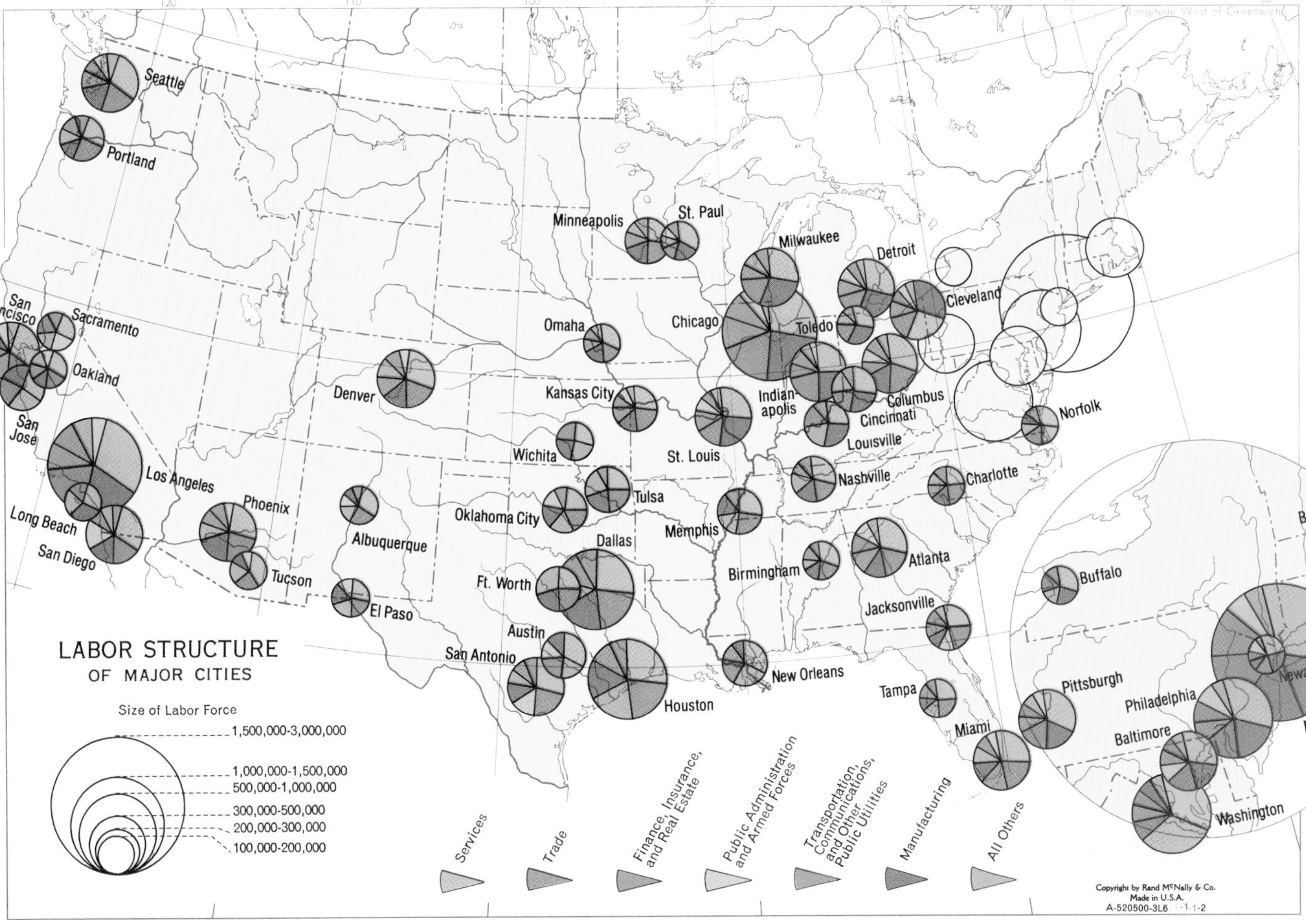

LABOR STRUCTURE
OF MAJOR CITIES

Size of Labor Force

- 1,500,000-3,000,000
- 1,000,000-1,500,000
- 500,000-1,000,000
- 300,000-500,000
- 200,000-300,000
- 100,000-200,000

Services

Trade

Finance, Insurance, and Real Estate

Public Administration and Armed Forces

Transportation, Communications, and Other Public Utilities

Manufacturing

All Others

Seattle
Portland
San Francisco
Sacramento
Oakland
San Jose
Los Angeles
Long Beach
San Diego
Phoenix
Tucson
El Paso
Albuquerque
Denver
Minneapolis
St. Paul
Omaha
Kansas City
Wichita
Oklahoma City
Ft. Worth
Dallas
Austin
San Antonio
Houston
St. Louis
Milwaukee
Chicago
Indianapolis
Memphis
Tulsa
Nashville
Birmingham
New Orleans
Detroit
Toledo
Cleveland
Columbus
Cincinnati
Louisville
Charlotte
Atlanta
Jacksonville
Tampa
Miami
Norfolk
Buffalo
Pittsburgh
Philadelphia
Baltimore
Washington
Newark
New York
Boston

Copyright by Rand McNally & Co.
Made in U.S.A.
A-520500-3L6 -1-1-2

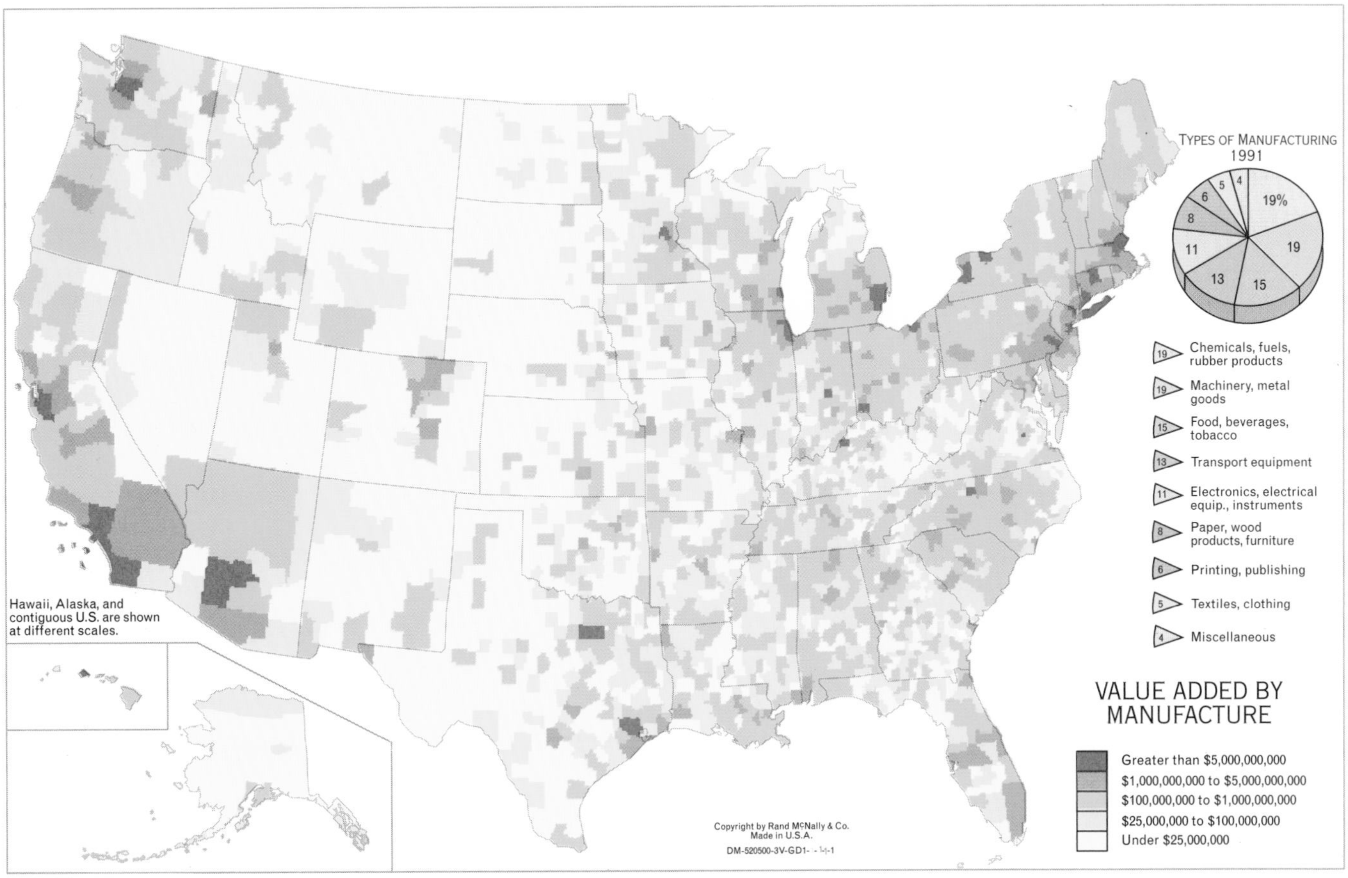

TYPES OF MANUFACTURING
1991

19%
19
15
13
11
8
6
5
4

19	Chemicals, fuels, rubber products
19	Machinery, metal goods
15	Food, beverages, tobacco
13	Transport equipment
11	Electronics, electrical equip., instruments
8	Paper, wood products, furniture
6	Printing, publishing
5	Textiles, clothing
4	Miscellaneous

VALUE ADDED BY MANUFACTURE

- Greater than $5,000,000,000
- $1,000,000,000 to $5,000,000,000
- $100,000,000 to $1,000,000,000
- $25,000,000 to $100,000,000
- Under $25,000,000

Hawaii, Alaska, and contiguous U.S. are shown at different scales.

Copyright by Rand McNally & Co.
Made in U.S.A.
DM-520500-3V-GD1- -4-1

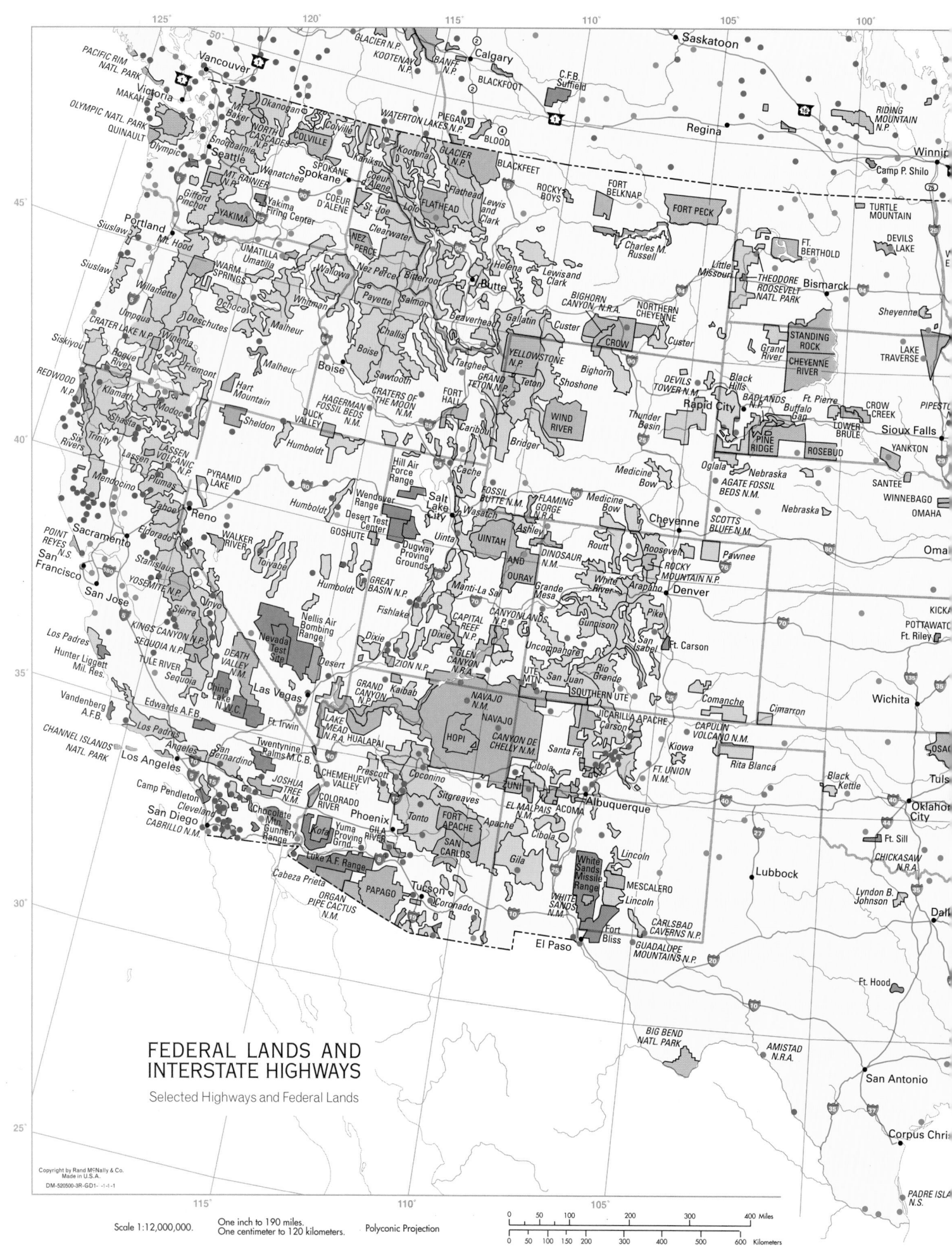

FEDERAL LANDS AND
INTERSTATE HIGHWAYS

Selected Highways and Federal Lands

Scale 1:12,000,000.

One inch to 190 miles.
One centimeter to 120 kilometers.

Polyconic Projection

0	50	100	200	300	400 Miles

0	50	100	150	200	300	400	500	600 Kilometers

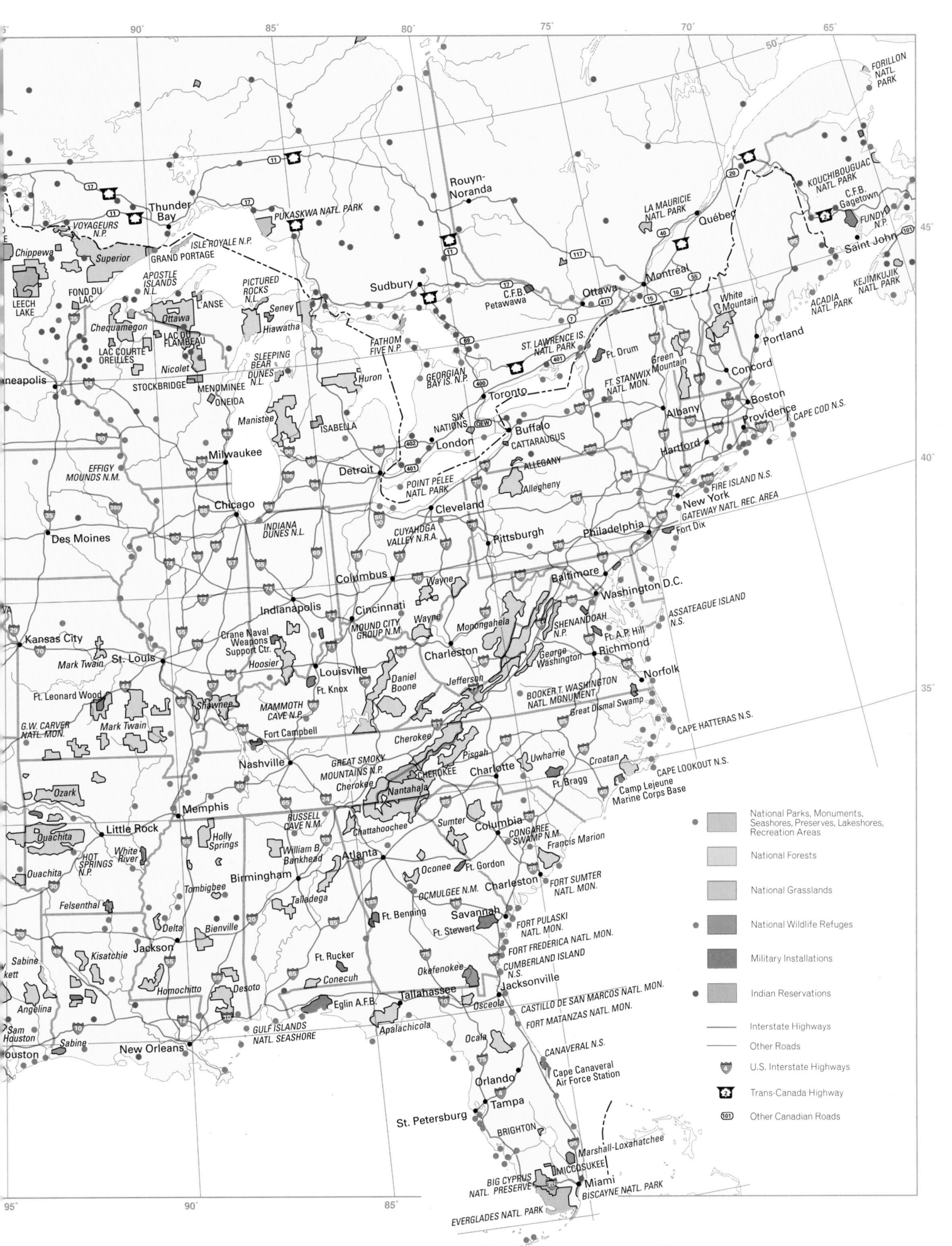

FORILLON NATL. PARK

KOUCHIBOUGUAC NATL. PARK
C.F.B. Gagetown
FUNDY N.P.
Saint John
KEJIMKUJIK NATL. PARK

LA MAURICIE NATL. PARK
Québec
Montréal
Ottawa
C.F.B. Petawawa
ST. LAWRENCE IS. NATL. PARK
Ft. Drum
FT. STANWIX NATL. MON.
Green Mountain
White Mountain
Portland
ACADIA NATL. PARK
Concord
Albany
Boston
Providence
CAPE COD N.S.
Hartford

Rouyn-Noranda
Sudbury
Toronto
Buffalo
CATTARAUGUS
ALLEGANY
Allegheny
New York
GATEWAY NATL. REC. AREA
Philadelphia
Fort Dix
FIRE ISLAND N.S.

PUKASKWA NATL. PARK
ISLE ROYALE N.P.
GRAND PORTAGE
Thunder Bay
VOYAGEURS N.P.
Chippewa
Superior
APOSTLE ISLANDS N.L.
PICTURED ROCKS N.L.
Seney
Hiawatha
L'ANSE
FOND DU LAC
LEECH LAKE
Chequamegon
LAC COURTE OREILLES
LAC DU FLAMBEAU
Ottawa
Nicolet
STOCKBRIDGE
MENOMINEE
ONEIDA
neapolis

FATHOM FIVE N.P.
GEORGIAN BAY IS. N.P.
SIX NATIONS
London
POINT PELEE NATL. PARK
Detroit
Cleveland
Pittsburgh
Baltimore
Washington D.C.
ASSATEAGUE ISLAND N.S.
Richmond
Norfolk
Great Dismal Swamp

SLEEPING BEAR DUNES N.L.
Manistee
Huron
ISABELLA
Milwaukee
Chicago
INDIANA DUNES N.L.
CUYAHOGA VALLEY N.R.A.
Columbus
Wayne
Cincinnati
Wayne
Monongahela
SHENANDOAH N.P.
George Washington
Ft. A.P. Hill
BOOKER T. WASHINGTON NATL. MONUMENT
CAPE HATTERAS N.S.

EFFIGY MOUNDS N.M.
Des Moines
Indianapolis
MOUND CITY GROUP N.M.
Charleston
Jefferson
CAPE LOOKOUT N.S.

Kansas City
Crane Naval Weapons Support Ctr.
Hoosier
Louisville
Ft. Knox
Daniel Boone
Cherokee
Pisgah
Uwharrie
Croatan
Camp Lejeune Marine Corps Base

Mark Twain
St. Louis
Ft. Leonard Wood
G.W. CARVER NATL. MON.
Mark Twain
Shawnee
MAMMOTH CAVE N.P.
Fort Campbell
Nashville
GREAT SMOKY MOUNTAINS N.P.
Cherokee
Cherokee
Nantahala
Charlotte
Ft. Bragg

Ozark
Little Rock
Ouachita
HOT SPRINGS N.P.
White River
Holly Springs
RUSSELL CAVE N.M.
Chattahoochee
Sumter
Columbia
CONGAREE SWAMP N.M.
Francis Marion

Ouachita
Memphis
WILLIAM B. Bankhead
Talladega
Atlanta
Oconee
Ft. Gordon
Charleston
FORT SUMTER NATL. MON.
Felsenthal
Birmingham
OCMULGEE N.M.
Savannah
FORT PULASKI NATL. MON.

G.W. CARVER NATL. MON.
Tombigbee
Ft. Benning
Ft. Stewart
FORT FREDERICA NATL. MON.
CUMBERLAND ISLAND N.S.

Delta
Bienville
Jackson
Ft. Rucker
OCMULGEE N.M.
Conecuh
Okefenokee
CASTILLO DE SAN MARCOS NATL. MON.
Jacksonville
Sabine
Kisatchie
Homochitto
Desoto
Eglin A.F.B.
Tallahassee
Osceola
FORT MATANZAS NATL. MON.
Ocala

Sabine
kett
Angelina
Felsenthal
Sam Houston
Sabine
New Orleans
ouston
GULF ISLANDS NATL. SEASHORE
Apalachicola
CANAVERAL N.S.
Orlando
Cape Canaveral Air Force Station

St. Petersburg
Tampa
BRIGHTON
Marshall-Loxahatchee
MICCOSUKEE
Miami
BISCAYNE NATL. PARK
BIG CYPRESS NATL. PRESERVE
EVERGLADES NATL. PARK

National Parks, Monuments, Seashores, Preserves, Lakeshores, Recreation Areas

National Forests

National Grasslands

National Wildlife Refuges

Military Installations

Indian Reservations

——— Interstate Highways

——— Other Roads

U.S. Interstate Highways

Trans-Canada Highway

Other Canadian Roads

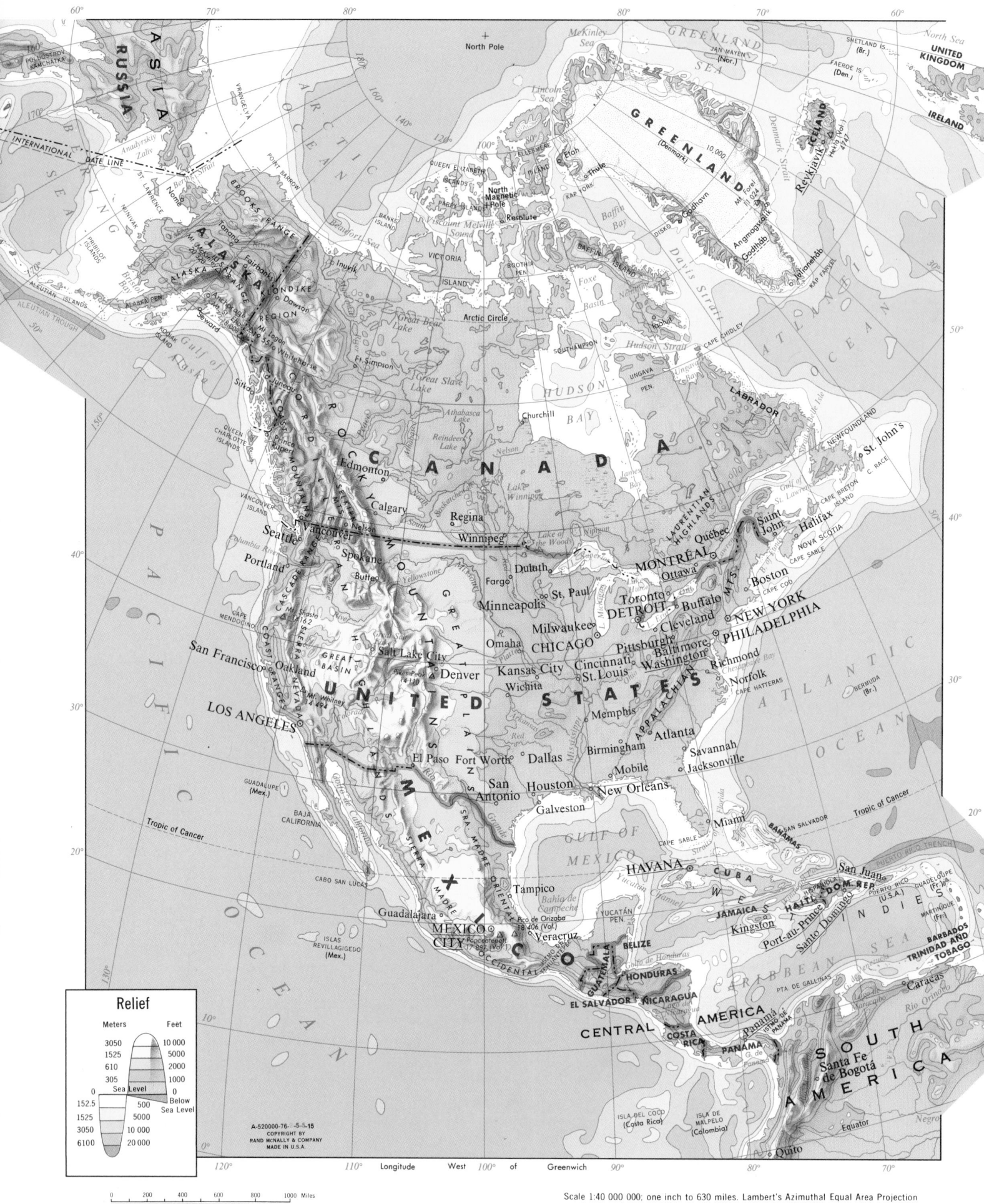

Relief

Meters	Feet
3050	10 000
1525	5000
610	2000
305	1000
0 Sea Level	0
152.5	500 Below Sea Level
1525	5000
3050	10 000
6100	20 000

A-520000-76- -5-5-15
COPYRIGHT BY
RAND McNALLY & COMPANY
MADE IN U.S.A.

0 200 400 600 800 1000 Miles
0 400 800 1200 1600 Kilometers

Scale 1:40 000 000; one inch to 630 miles. Lambert's Azimuthal Equal Area Projection
Elevations and depressions are given in feet

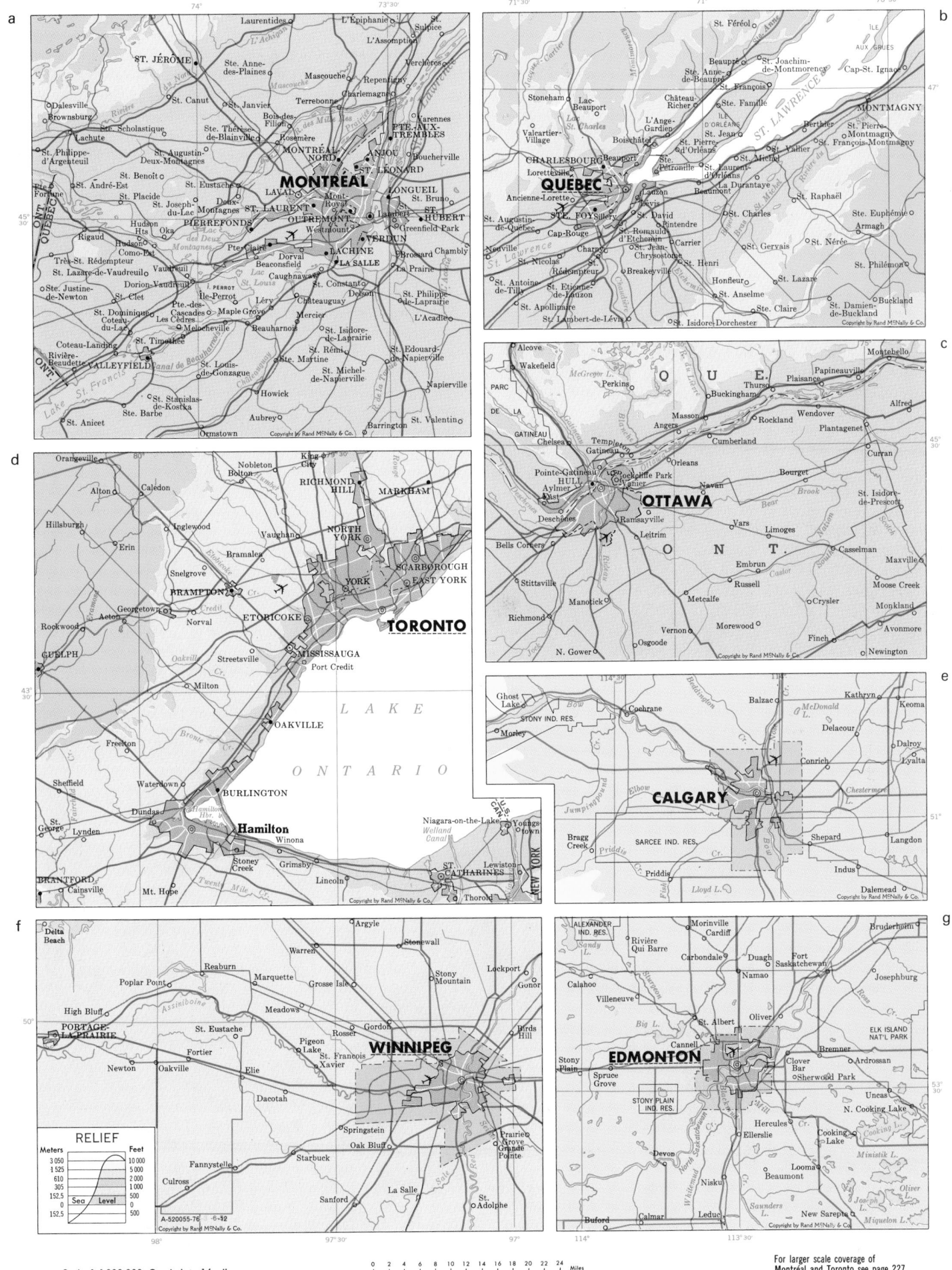

a MONTREAL

St. Jérôme, Laurentides, L'Épiphanie, St. Sulpice, Ste. Anne-des-Plaines, L'Assomption, Verchères, Mascouche, Repentigny, Terrebonne, Charlemagne, Bois-des-Filion, Varennes, PTE.-AUX-TREMBLES, Rosemère, MONTRÉAL NORD, ANJOU, Boucherville, ST. LÉONARD, MONTREAL, LONGUEIL, St. Bruno, St. Hubert, LAVAL, Mont-Royal, OUTREMONT, St. Lambert, Greenfield Park, PIERREFONDS, Westmount, VERDUN, Brossard, Chambly, Pte-Claire, Dorval, LACHINE, Beaconsfield, LA SALLE, La Prairie, Caughnawaga, St. Constant, Delson, Léry, Châteauguay, St. Philippe-de-Laprairie, Mercier, L'Acadie, Beauharnois, St. Isidore-de-Laprairie, St. Rémi, St. Édouard-de-Napierville, Ste. Martine, St. Michel-de-Napierville, Napierville, Howick, Aubrey, St. Valentin, Barrington

b QUEBEC

St. Féréol, ST. LAWRENCE, MONTMAGNY, Stoneham, Lac-Beauport, Château-Richer, Beaupré, St. Joachim-de-Montmorency, Cap-St. Ignace, Valcartier-Village, Ste. Famille, St. Pierre-Montmagny, St. François-Montmagny, CHARLESBOURG, Beauport, Ancienne-Lorette, Loretteville, L'Ange-Gardien, St. Jean, St. Michel, Berthier, Lauzon, Lévis, Beaumont, La Durantaye, Ste. Euphémie, St. Raphaël, STE. FOY, Sillery, St. David, St. Augustin-de-Québec, Cap-Rouge, St. Romuald-d'Etchemin, Carrier, Armagh, Neuville, Charny, St. Jean-Chrysostome, St. Gervais, St. Nérée, St. Nicolas, Breakeyville, St. Henri, St. Antoine-de-Tilly, St. Étienne-de-Lauzon, Honfleur, St. Lazare, St. Philémon, St. Apollinaire, St. Anselme, Ste. Claire, St. Damien-de-Buckland, St. Lambert-de-Lévis, St. Isidore-Dorcheste, Buckland

c OTTAWA

Alcove, Montebello, Wakefield, Papineauville, Perkins, QUE., Plaisance, PARC, Thurso, DE, LA, Buckingham, GATINEAU, Chelsea, Masson, Rockland, Wendover, Plantagenet, Alfred, Angers, Templeton, Cumberland, Curran, Gatineau, Orleans, Bourget, St. Isidore-de-Prescott, Pointe-Gatineau, Rockcliffe Park, HULL, Vanier, Navan, Aylmer East, OTTAWA, Deschênes, Ramsayville, ONT., Bells Corners, Leitrim, Vars, Limoges, Casselman, Maxville, Stittsville, Embrun, Moose Creek, Russell, Manotick, Metcalfe, Crysler, Monkland, Richmond, Vernon, Morewood, Finch, Avonmore, Osgoode, N. Gower, Newington

d TORONTO

Orangeville, Nobleton, King City, RICHMOND HILL, MARKHAM, Alton, Caledon, Bolton, Hillsburgh, Inglewood, Vaughan, NORTH YORK, Erin, Bramalea, Snelgrove, BRAMPTON, YORK, SCARBOROUGH, EAST YORK, Georgetown, Acton, Norval, ETOBICOKE, TORONTO, Rockwood, GUELPH, Streetsville, MISSISSAUGA, Port Credit, Milton, LAKE ONTARIO, OAKVILLE, Freelton, Bronte, Sheffield, Waterdown, BURLINGTON, Dundas, Hamilton Hbr., Niagara-on-the-Lake, Welland Canal, Youngstown, St. George, Lynden, HAMILTON, Winona, Lewiston, Cainsville, Stoney Creek, Grimsby, St. CATHARINES, NEW YORK, BRANTFORD, Mt. Hope, Lincoln, Thorold

e CALGARY

Ghost Lake, Bow, Balzac, Kathryn, Keoma, STONY IND. RES., Cochrane, McDonald L., Morley, Delacour, Dalroy, Conrich, Lyalta, CALGARY, Chestermere, Bragg Creek, SARCEE IND. RES., Shepard, Langdon, Priddis, Lloyd L., Indus, Dalemead

f WINNIPEG

Delta Beach, Argyle, Stonewall, Warren, Reaburn, Marquette, Grosse Isle, Lockport, Gonor, Poplar Point, Stony Mountain, High Bluff, Meadows, Birds Hill, PORTAGE LA PRAIRIE, St. Eustache, Pigeon Lake, Rosser, Gordon, Newton, Oakville, Fortier, St. François Xavier, WINNIPEG, Elie, Dacotah, Springstein, Prairie Grove, Grande Pointe, Oak Bluff, Fannystelle, Starbuck, Culross, Sanford, La Salle, St. Adolphe

g EDMONTON

ALEXANDER IND. RES., Morinville, Cardiff, Bruderheim, Rivière Qui Barre, Carbondale, Duagh, Fort Saskatchewan, Josephburg, Calahoo, Villeneuve, Namao, St. Albert, Oliver, Cannell, ELK ISLAND NAT'L PARK, Stony Plain, Clover Bar, Bremner, Ardrossan, EDMONTON, Sherwood Park, Spruce Grove, STONY PLAIN IND. RES., Devon, Hercules, Uncas, N. Cooking Lake, Ellerslie, Cooking Lake, Nisku, Beaumont, Looma, Buford, Calmar, Leduc, New Sarepta, Saunders

RELIEF

Meters	Feet
3 050	10 000
1 525	5 000
610	2 000
305	1 000
152.5	500
0 Sea Level	0
152.5	500

A-520055-76 -6-12

Scale 1:1 000 000; One inch to 16 miles.
Elevations and depressions are given in feet.

Miles / Kilometers scale bar

For larger scale coverage of Montréal and Toronto see page 227.

84

Continued on pages 96-97

Scale 1: 12 000 000; one inch to 190 miles. Conic Projection

Elevations and depressions are given in feet

Longitude West of Greenwich

QUEBEC

Gulf of

St. Lawrence

GROS MORNE
NAT'L PARK

Corner Brook
Stephenville
St.
George's

Deer Lake

Grand Falls

Windsor

Gander

Botwood

Twillingate

Bonavista

NEWFOUNDLAND Trinity

TERRA NOVA
NAT'L PARK

Same scale as
main map

CAPE BAULD

C. ST. JOHN

Grand Bank

Burin

St. John's

Channel-Port-aux-Basques

CAPE RAY
CAPE NORTH
CAPE BRETON
ISLAND

ST. PIERRE AND MIQUELON (Fr.)

ATLANTIC OCEAN

MELVILLE
PENINSULA

Foxe
Basin

BAFFIN
ISLAND NAT'L PARK

BAFFIN

ISLAND

Arctic Circle

PRINCE
CHARLES
ISLAND

Iqaluit

Lake Harbour

HALL
PEN.

Frobisher Bay

Foxe
Channel

SOUTHAMPTON
ISLAND

FOXE
PEN.

NOTTINGHAM
ISLAND

SALISBURY

Hudson

Strait

EVERETT
MTS.

RESOLUTION

C. LOW

MANSEL

COATS

PENINSULE

D'UNGAVA

Ungava
Bay

TORNGAT
MTS.

Hebron

HUDSON

BAY

Povungnituk

Kuujjuaq

Nain

Hopedale

Makkovik

Rigolet

OTTAWA
ISLANDS

All islands within bays and straits
lie within Northwest Territories.

Payne

Happy
Valley

Goose Bay

MEALY MTS.

Cartwright

Battle Harbour

BELCHER
ISLANDS

Lac
Bienville

Schefferville

LABRADOR

ST. ANTHONY

Ft. Severn

C. HENRIETTA MARIA

PTE. LOUIS XIV

Natashquan

Corner Brook
Stephenville
St. George

QUEBEC

James
Bay

Chisasibi

MTS.
OTISH

Clarke City

Sept-Iles

Mingan

ILE D'ANTICOSTI

Gulf of

St. Lawrence

Channel-
Port-aux-Basques

CAPE BRETON
HIGHLANDS
NAT'L PARK

Ft. Albany

Moosonee

Chibougamau

Mistassini

Cap-Chat
MTS.
CHIC-CHOCS

Gaspé

PEN. DE GASPÉ

New Carlisle

St. Joseph

Coral
Rapids

Fraserdale

La Sarre

Amos
Senneterre

St. Félicien
Roberval
Chambord

Alma

Kenogami
Jonquière

Chicoutimi

Kénogami

Grande

Riviere-du-Loup

Edmundston

Rimouski

Matane

Mont-Joli

Campbellton

Bathurst

Chatham

Newcastle

NEW

BRUNSWICK

Caraquet

Richibucto

Moncton

P.E.I.
PRINCE EDWARD
ISLAND
NAT'L PARK

Summerside
Charlottetown

Amherst

New
Glasgow
Stellarton

Sydney Mines
Sydney

New Waterford

Armstrong Sta.

Hearst

Makina

Cochrane

Rouyn

Malartic
Val-d'Or

La Tuque

Grand
Mère

Shawinigan
Trois-
Rivières

Victoriaville

Drummondville

MAINE

FUNDY
NAT'L PARK

Fredericton

Woodstock

Saint John

**NOVA
SCOTIA**

Springhill
Truro

Kentville

Dartmouth

Halifax

Geraldton

Longlac

Nakina

Kapuskasing

Oba

Iroquois Falls

Timmins

Kirkland Lake

Ville-Marie
Témiscaming

Cobalt

Joliette

Sorel
St.
Hyacinthe

Granby
Sherbrooke

St.
Jean

Sherbrooke

St. Andrews
St. Stephen

Lunenburg
Bridgewater
Liverpool

Shelburne

CAPE SABLE

Yarmouth

Digby

VERMONT

NEW HAMPSHIRE

Dryden

Nipigon

Marathon

PUKASKWA
NAT'L PARK

MICHIPICOTEN

Chapleau

ONTARIO

Sudbury

Sturgeon Falls
Mattawa

North
Bay

Ottawa

Pembroke
Renfrew

Hull

MONTRÉAL

Laval

St.
Jean

Valleyfield

Montpelier

Concord

Portland

Augusta

BOSTON

**ATLANTIC

OCEAN**

Thunder Bay

Lake Superior

Sault Ste. Marie

Thessalon

Blind River

Espanola

MANITOULIN

Georgian
Bay

Parry
Sound

Huntsville

Bancroft

Smiths Falls

Brockville

Kingston

Alexandria
Bay

Ogdensburg

**NEW

YORK**

MASS.

Hartford

Providence

CONN.

R.I.

CAPE COD

Duluth

Superior

Marquette

Escanaba

MICHIGAN

Wiarton

Owen Sound

Midland

Orillia

Barrie

Lindsay

Peterborough

Cobourg

Trenton

Oshawa

Whitby

Lake Ontario

Rochester

Albany

Scranton

PENNSYLVANIA

St. Paul

Green Bay

WISCONSIN

Lake Michigan

Kincardine

Goderich

London

St.
Thomas

TORONTO

Kitchener

Hamilton

St.
Catharines

Niagara
Falls

BUFFALO

NEW YORK

N.J.

Newark

Minneapolis

Madison

MILWAUKEE

CHICAGO

Saginaw

Flint

Lansing

DETROIT

Windsor

Leamington

Sarnia

Chatham

Port
Huron

Lake Erie

Toledo

OHIO

ILL.

INDIANA

A-520200-76   9-J-20

COPYRIGHT BY

RAND McNALLY & COMPANY

MADE IN U.S.A.

Relief

Meters	Feet
3050	10 000
1525	5000
610	2000
305	1000
152.5	500
0 Sea Level	0
152.5	500
1525	5000
3050	10 000

0 25 50 100   200   300   400   500 Miles

0   100   200   400   600   800 Kilometers

134° 132° 130° 128° 126° 124°

PRINCE
OF
WALES
ISLAND

Klawock

Hydaburg
△ Copper Mtn.
3216

Mt. Reid
4592 △ REVILLAGIGEDO
ISLAND

Ketchikan

Metlakatla

ANNETTE
ISLAND

DALL
ISLAND

CLARENCE
STRAIT

Clarence

Portland

Alice Arm

SKEENA
MOUNTAINS

Spedin Pk.
8750 △

Mt. Thomlinson
△ 8050

OMINECA

MOUNTAINS

Williston
Lake

UNITED STATES
CANADA

Dixon Entrance

DUNDAS
ISLAND

Chatham
Sound

Nass

HAZELTON

Hazelton

Terrace

Smithers

BUTKLEY
RANGES

Tchentlo
Lake

McLeod La

54°

CAPE KNOX

Masset

Masset
Inlet

QUEEN

QUEEN

CHARLOTTE

GRAHAM ISLAND

Skidegate Inlet

MORESBY ISLAND

Mount Kermode
3550 △

CHARLOTTE

ISLANDS

RANGES

Prince Rupert

PORCHER
ISLAND

Hecate

Strait

BANKS
ISLAND

Kitimat

Hartley Bay

GIL
ISLAND

PITT
ISLAND

ESTEVAN
GROUP

PRINCESS
ROYAL
ISLAND

Mt. Parry △
3450

ARISTAZABAL
ISLAND

ROTHBAY
ISLAND

SWINDLE
ISLAND

KITIMAT

COAST

Hawson Pk.
9050

Morice Lake

B R I T I S H

RANGES

Burns Lake

Michel Pk.
△ 7396

Whitesail
Lake

Oosa
Lake

Nechako

Eutsuk Lake

Tetachuck
Lake

PLATEAU

KENNEY DAM

NECHAKO
RANGE

Babine
Lake

Stuart
Lake

Fort
St. James

NECHAKO

Vanderhoof

West R

West Road

West Road River

Babine

52°

CAPE ST. JAMES

Queen

Charlotte

Sound

CALVERT ISLAND

Ocean Falls

Bella Bella

Namu

Rivers Inlet

Bella Coola

Monarch Mtn.
△ 11590

Silverthrone Mtn.
△ 8700

Razorback Mtn.
10432 △

C O L U M

Charlotte
Lake

Redstone

FRASER

PLATE

Chilko

Chilcotin

50°

PACIFIC

OCEAN

CAPE SCOTT

Bull Harbour

CAPE
CAUTION

Queen Charlotte Strait

Port Hardy

Quatsino Sound

Port Alice

CAPE COOK

Mt. Waddington
△ 13163

Mt. Queen Bess
△ 10791

Good Hope Mtn.
△ 10157

PACIFIC

RANGES

Simoom
Sound

Kelsey Bay

Victoria Pk.
7095 △

Bloedel

Campbell
River

VANCOUVER

NOOTKA
ISLAND

Nootka
Sound

VANCOUVER

ISLAND

Golden Hinde
△ 7291

Courtenay

Comox

Mt. Tatlow
△ 10058

Monmouth Mtn.
△ 10480

Mt. Gilbert
△ 9100

RANGES

Powell River

Mt. Garibaldi
8787 △

Bralo

Wedge

Squamish

ISLAND

Tofino

Port Alberni

PACIFIC RIM
NATIONAL PARK

Barkley
Sound

CAPE BEALE

RANGES

Mt. Whymper
5056 △

North Vancouver M
Vancouver
BURNABY
New Westmin

Nanaimo

Ladysmith
Duncan

Lake Cowichan

Sidney

Strait of Juan de Fuca

CAPE FLATTERY

OLYMPIC
NATIONAL
PARK

OLYMPIC
NATIONAL
PARK

Esquimalt

Victoria

Port
Angeles

48°

PACIFIC

Longitude West of Greenwich

Continued on pages 104-105

130° 128° 126° 124°

Scale 1:4 000 000; one inch to 64 miles. Conic Projection

Elevations and depressions are given in feet.

Relief

Meters		Feet
3050		10 000
1525		5000
610		2000
305		1000
152.5		500
0	Sea Level	0
152.5		500
1525		5000

A-520220-76 6-68
COPYRIGHT BY
RAND McNALLY & COMPANY
MADE IN U.S.A.

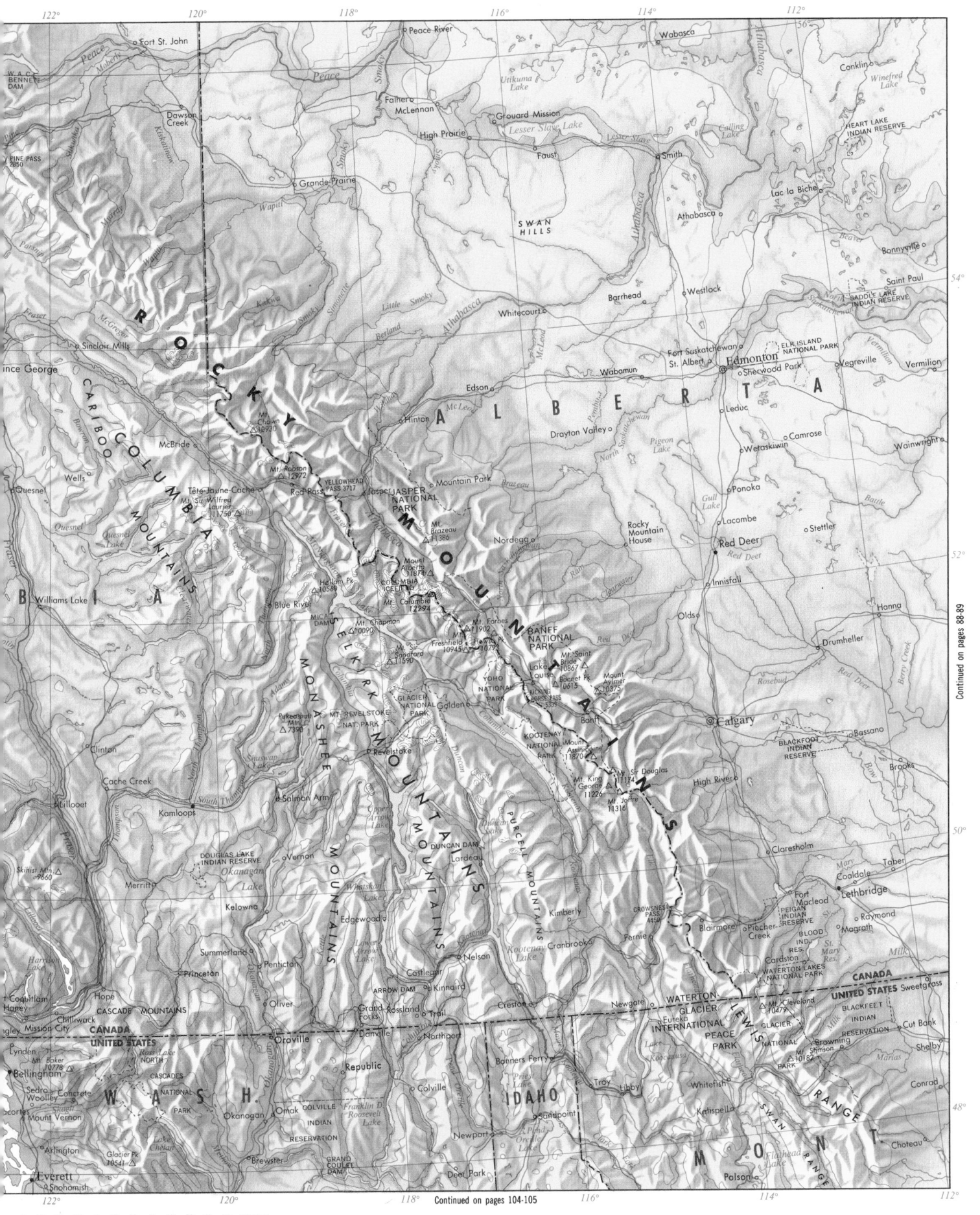

Continued on pages 88-89

Continued on pages 104-105

0 10 20 30 40 50 60 70 80 90 100 110 120 Miles

0   20   40   60   80   100   120   140   160   180   200 Kilometers

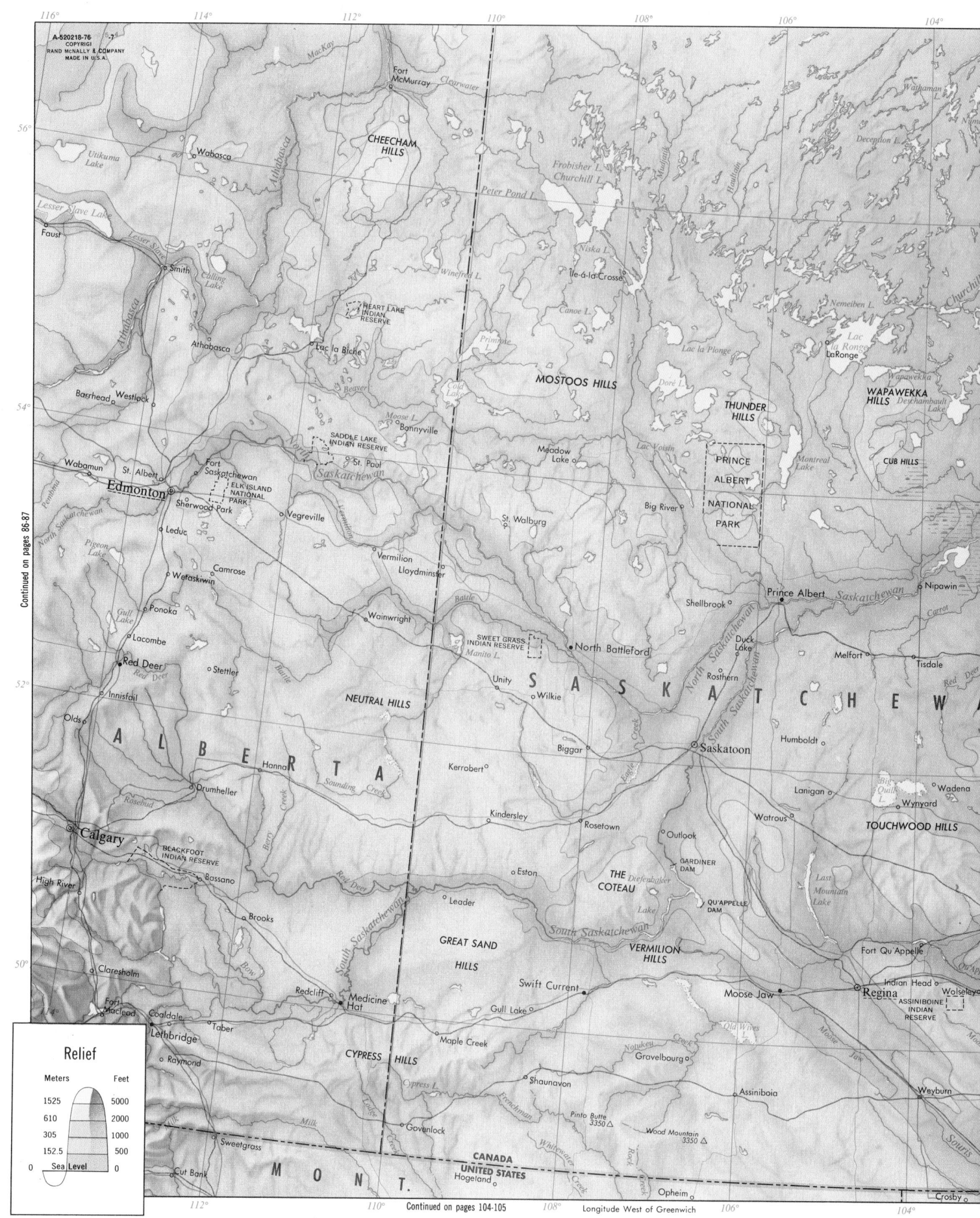

Continued on pages 86-87

Continued on pages 104-105

A-520218-76
COPYRIGHT
RAND McNALLY & COMPANY
MADE IN U.S.A.

Relief

Meters		Feet
1525		5000
610		2000
305		1000
152.5		500
0	Sea Level	0

Longitude West of Greenwich

Scale 1:4 000 000; one inch to 64 miles. Conic Projection

Elevations and depressions are given in feet.

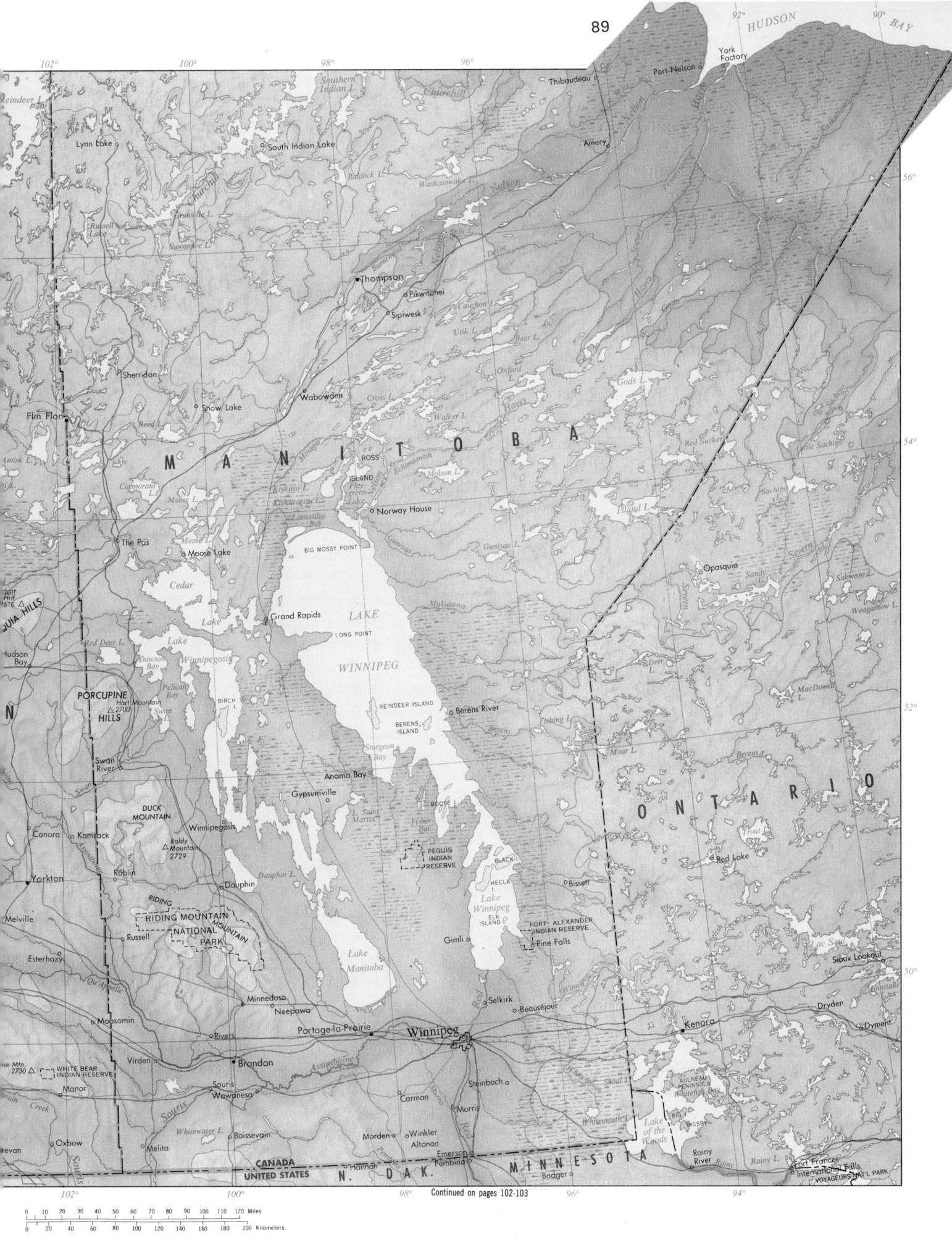

HUDSON BAY

York Factory

Port Nelson

Thibaudeau

Amery

Reindeer L.

Lynn Lake

South Indian Lake

Southern Indian L.

Baldock L.

Waskaiowaka L.

Churchill

Nelson

Russell Lake

Granville L.

Suwannee L.

Thompson

Pikwitonei

Sipiwesk

Split L.

Burntwood

Sherridon

Snow Lake

Wabowden

Cross L.

Oxford

Gods L.

M A N I T O B A

Flin Flon

Reed L.

Walker L.

Hayes

Red Sucker L.

Little Sachigo L.

Amisk L.

Cormorant L.

ROSS

Echimamish

Island L.

Sachigo

Sachigo

Salewaso L.

PORCUPINE

Moose L.

Kiskittogisu L.

Kiskitto L.

ISLAND

Playgreen Lake

Limestone Bay

Norway House

Gunisao

Mukutawa

Opasquia

Sandy

Weagamow L.

The Pas

Moose Lake

Cedar

BIG MOSSY POINT

Lake

LAKE

Grand Rapids

LONG POINT

WINNIPEG

Deer L.

MacDowell L.

Hudson Bay

Red Deer L.

Lake

Winnipegosis

Dawson Bay

REINDEER ISLAND

BERENS ISLAND

Berens River

Fishing L.

Berens

O N T A R I O

Hart Mountain

PORCUPINE

HILLS

Pelican Bay

Swan

BIRCH

Sturgeon Bay

Moar L.

Berens R.

N

Swan River

Anama Bay

Gypsumville

L. Saint Martin

MOOSE I.

Fisher Bay

Trout L.

Red Lake

Canora

Kamsack

Winnipegosis

Baldy Mountain 2729

Dauphin L.

PEGUIS INDIAN RESERVE

BLACK I.

Bissett

Yorkton

Roblin

Dauphin

HECLA I.

Lac Seul

RIDING

Melville

RIDING MOUNTAIN

NATIONAL

Lake

Winnipeg

ELK ISLAND

FORT ALEXANDER INDIAN RESERVE

Sioux Lookout

Russell

PARK

Manitoba

Esterhazy

Gimli

Pine Falls

Dryden

Qu'Appelle

Minnedosa

Neepawa

Lake

Manitoba

Selkirk

Beauséjour

Kenora

Dymeht

Moosomin

Rivers

Portage-la-Prairie

Winnipeg

se Mtn. 2730

WHITE BEAR INDIAN RESERVE

Virden

Brandon

Assiniboine

Steinbach

AULNEAU PENINSULA

Whitefish Bay

Manor

Souris

Wawanesa

Carman

Morris

Lake of the Woods

Oxbow

Melita

Whitewater L.

Boissevain

Morden

Winkler

Altonao

Emerson

Pembina

Rainy River

Fort Frances

International Falls

VOYAGEURS NAT'L PARK

CANADA
UNITED STATES

N. DAK. MINNESOTA

Hannah

Badger

Continued on pages 102-103

0 10 20 30 40 50 60 70 80 90 100 110 120 Miles

0   20   40   60   80   100   120   140   160   180   200 Kilometers

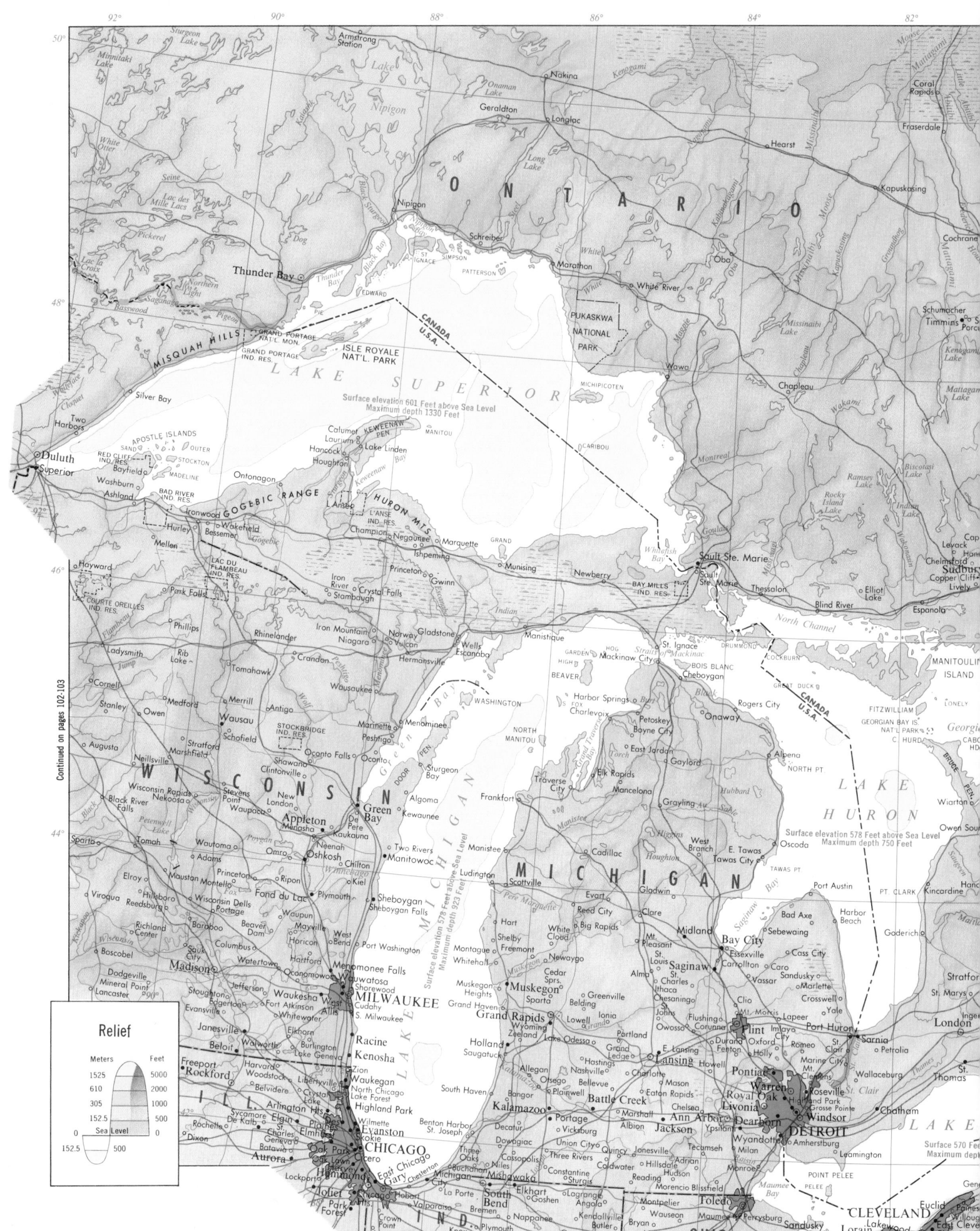

Continued on pages 102-103

Relief

Meters	Feet
1525	5000
610	2000
305	1000
152.5	500
0	Sea Level 0
152.5	500

LAKE SUPERIOR
Surface elevation 601 Feet above Sea Level
Maximum depth 1330 Feet

LAKE HURON
Surface elevation 578 Feet above Sea Level
Maximum depth 750 Feet

Surface elevation 578 Feet above Sea Level
Maximum depth 923 Feet

ONTARIO

WISCONSIN

MICHIGAN

ILL.

IND.

OHIO

Continued on pages 92-93

Continued on pages 98-99

Scale 1:4 000 000; one inch to 64 miles. Conic Projection
Elevations and depressions are given in feet

Longitude West of Greenwich

| 0 | 10 | 20 | 30 | 40 | 50 | 60 | 70 | 80 | 90 | 100 | 110 | 120 Miles |

| 0 | 20 | 40 | 60 | 80 | 100 | 120 | 140 | 160 | 180 | 200 Kilometers |

Continued on pages 90-91

Continued on pages 98-99

Scale 1:4 000 000; one inch to 64 miles. Conic Projection

Elevations and depressions are given in feet.

Longitude West of Greenwich

Relief

Meters		Feet
1525		5000
610		2000
305		1000
152.5		500
0	Sea Level	0
152.5		500
1525		5000

Scale 1:1 000 000

For larger scale coverage
of Boston see page 227.

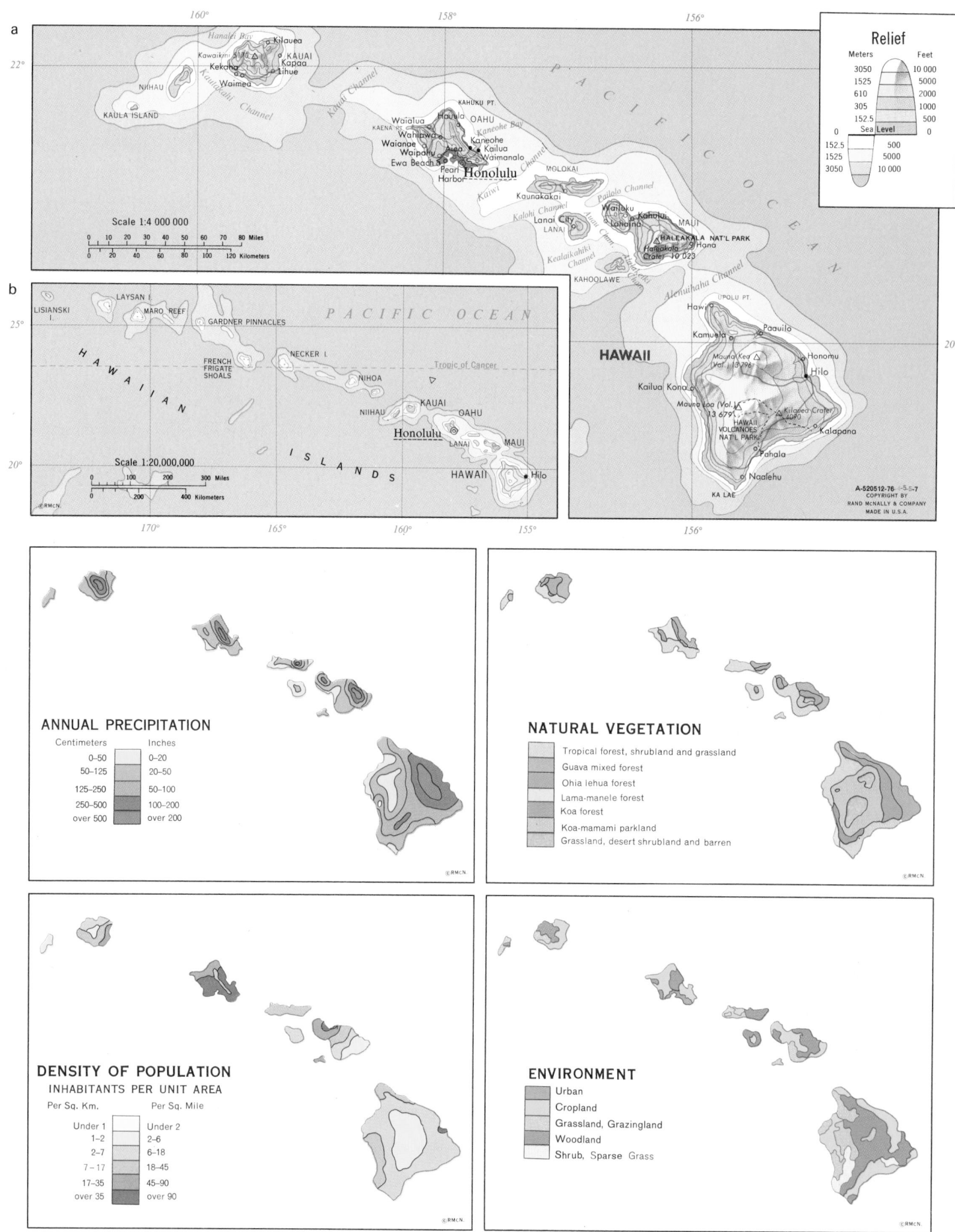

a

b

Relief

Meters		Feet
3050		10 000
1525		5000
610		2000
305		1000
152.5		500
0	Sea Level	0
152.5		500
1525		5000
3050		10 000

Scale 1:4 000 000

Scale 1:20,000,000

HAWAII

A-520512-76
COPYRIGHT BY
RAND MCNALLY & COMPANY
MADE IN U.S.A.

ANNUAL PRECIPITATION

Centimeters	Inches
0–50	0–20
50–125	20–50
125–250	50–100
250–500	100–200
over 500	over 200

NATURAL VEGETATION

Tropical forest, shrubland and grassland
Guava mixed forest
Ohia lehua forest
Lama-manele forest
Koa forest
Koa-mamami parkland
Grassland, desert shrubland and barren

DENSITY OF POPULATION
INHABITANTS PER UNIT AREA

Per Sq. Km.	Per Sq. Mile
Under 1	Under 2
1–2	2–6
2–7	6–18
7–17	18–45
17–35	45–90
over 35	over 90

ENVIRONMENT

Urban
Cropland
Grassland, Grazingland
Woodland
Shrub, Sparse Grass

Relief

Meters		Feet
3050		10 000
1525		5000
610		2000
305		1000
152.5		500
0	Sea Level	0
152.5		500
1525		5000
3050		10 000
6100		20 000

A-520502-76 -5- -11
COPYRIGHT BY
RAND McNALLY & COMPANY
MADE IN U.S.A.

Longitude West of Greenwich

a

Longitude East of Greenwich   Longitude West of Greenwich

Same scale as main map

Scale 1: 12 000 000; one inch to 190 miles.   Conic Projection
Elevations and depressions are given in feet

Continued on pages 84-85

Scale 1:12 000 000; one inch to 190 miles. Polyconic Projection
Elevations and depressions are given in feet

CANADA

ONTARIO — QUEBEC — NEW BRUNSWICK — PRINCE EDWARD ISLAND — NOVA SCOTIA — MAINE

MINNESOTA · WISCONSIN · MICHIGAN · IOWA · ILLINOIS · INDIANA · OHIO · MISSOURI · KENTUCKY · TENNESSEE · ARKANSAS · MISSISSIPPI · ALABAMA · GEORGIA · FLORIDA · LOUISIANA · SOUTH CAROLINA · NORTH CAROLINA · VIRGINIA · WEST VIRGINIA · PENNSYLVANIA · NEW YORK · NEW JERSEY · MD. · DEL. · CONN. · R.I. · MASS. · VT. · N.H.

Lake of the Woods, Rainy, Thunder Bay, QUETICO PROV. PARK, International Falls, ISLE ROYALE NAT'L PARK, LAKE SUPERIOR, Marquette, Sault Ste. Marie, Sudbury, North Bay, Cochrane, Roberval, Chicoutimi, Campbellton, Chatham

Kenora, Hibbing, Virginia, Duluth, Superior, Ashland, Hancock, Escanaba, Marinette, Alpena, Owen Sound, Parry Sound, Nipissing, Pembroke, ALGONQUIN PROVINCIAL PARK, Ottawa, Brockville, Ogdensburg, Québec, Trois-Rivières, St. Jean, Sherbrooke, Montpelier, Mt. Washington 6288, Augusta, Lewiston, Auburn, Bangor, Saint John, Calais, Fredericton, Moncton, Charlottetown, Truro, Windsor, Halifax, Yarmouth, C. SABLE

St. Cloud, St. Paul, MINNEAPOLIS, Mankata, Winona, Rochester, Mason City, Fort Dodge, Sioux City, Des Moines, Council Bluffs, Omaha, Waterloo, Dubuque, Cedar Rapids, Davenport, Rock Island, Burlington, Galesburg, Peoria, Bloomington, Ottumwa, Keokuk, Kirksville, IOWA

Eau Claire, Wausau, Appleton, Oshkosh, Fond du Lac, Madison, La Crosse, MILWAUKEE, Racine, Kenosha, Beloit, Rockford, Freeport, Elgin, Aurora, CHICAGO, Waukegan, Evanston, Gary, Hammond, South Bend, Fort Wayne, Green Bay, Sheboygan, Muskegon, Grand Rapids, Battle Creek, Kalamazoo, Lansing, Flint, Saginaw, Bay City, Pontiac, DETROIT, Ann Arbor, Jackson, Toledo, Sandusky, Lima, Marion, Logansport, Lafayette, INDIANAPOLIS, Muncie, Terre Haute, Vincennes, Evansville, Springfield, Decatur, Champaign, Danville, Hamilton, CINCINNATI, Dayton, Columbus, Portsmouth, Huntington, Charleston, Parkersburg, Covington, Frankfort, Lexington, Louisville, Owensboro, Paducah, Bowling Green, Hopkinsville, Cairo, Cape Girardeau, ST. LOUIS, East St. Louis, Jefferson City, Sedalia, Columbia, Hannibal, Quincy, Jacksonville, Mattoon, Alton, KANSAS CITY, St. Joseph, Atchison, Leavenworth, Topeka, Lawrence, Emporia, Chanute, Pittsburg, Parsons, Coffeyville, Joplin, Springfield, MISSOURI, OZARK PLATEAU, Table Rock Res., Bull Shoals Res., BOSTON MTS., Tulsa, Muskogee, Fort Smith, McAlester, Paris, Texarkana, El Dorado, Hot Springs, OUACHITA MTS., HOT SPRINGS NAT'L PARK, Little Rock, Pine Bluff, ARKANSAS, Helena, Jonesboro, Memphis, Nashville, Clarksville, Knoxville, Asheville, Chattanooga, MAMMOTH CAVE NAT'L PARK, GREAT SMOKY MTS. NAT'L PARK, Johnson City, Bristol, Winston-Salem, Durham, Raleigh, Greensboro, NORTH CAROLINA, New Bern, C. HATTERAS, Charlotte, Rock Hill, Greenville, Spartanburg, Anderson, Athens, Columbia, SOUTH CAROLINA, Wilmington

BUFFALO, Niagara Falls, Rochester, Syracuse, Utica, Oswego, Watertown, ADIRONDACK MTS., Albany, Troy, Schenectady, Binghamton, Elmira, Ithaca, Jamestown, Olean, NEW YORK, Scranton, Wilkes-Barre, Allentown, Reading, Harrisburg, York, Lancaster, Altoona, Johnstown, PITTSBURGH, Youngstown, Akron, Canton, CLEVELAND, Erie, Ashtabula, Lakewood, WASHINGTON D.C., Alexandria, Frederick, Hagerstown, Cumberland, BALTIMORE, Annapolis, Dover, Camden, PHILADELPHIA, Trenton, NEW YORK, Newark, Jersey City, Bridgeport, New Haven, Hartford, Springfield, Worcester, BOSTON, Providence, Fall River, New Bedford, NANTUCKET, C. COD, Lynn, Lowell, Nashua, Manchester, Concord, Portland, Portsmouth, Poughkeepsie, Kingston, CATSKILL MTS., GREEN MTS., Richmond, Petersburg, Lynchburg, Roanoke, Charlottesville, SHENANDOAH NAT'L PARK, WEST VIRGINIA, VIRGINIA, APPALACHIAN, Newport News, Norfolk, Portsmouth, Danville

ATLANTA, GEORGIA, Rome, Gadsden, Anniston, Birmingham, Tuscaloosa, La Grange, Macon, Augusta, Columbus, Americus, Albany, Waycross, Savannah, Brunswick, ALABAMA, Montgomery, Selma, Meridian, MISSISSIPPI, Jackson, Vicksburg, Greenville, Monroe, Shreveport, LOUISIANA, Natchez, Hattiesburg, Laurel, Mobile, Biloxi, Pensacola, Dothan, Tallahassee, Valdosta, Gainesville, Jacksonville, St. Augustine, Daytona Beach, Sanford, Orlando, FLORIDA, Tampa, St. Petersburg, Lakeland, Okeechobee, W. Palm Beach, CAPE CANAVERAL, EVERGLADES NAT'L PARK, MIAMI, C. SABLE, Key West, FLORIDA KEYS

Baton Rouge, New Orleans, Lake Charles, Lafayette, Port Arthur, Beaumont, HOUSTON, Galveston, Tyler, Marshall, Palestine, Alexandria

GULF OF MEXICO, ATLANTIC OCEAN, BAHAMAS, GT. ABACO, ANDROS

Relief		
Meters		Feet
3050		10 000
1525		5000
610		2000
305		1000
152.5		500
0	Sea Level	0
152.5	Below Sea Level	500
1525		5 000
3050		10 000
6100		20 000

Scale: 0 25 50 75 100 200 300 400 500 Miles
0 100 200 400 600 800 Kilometers

Cities and Towns: 0 to 50,000 · 50,000 to 500,000 · 500,000 to 1,000,000 · 1,000,000 and over

Cities and Towns

0 to 50,000	°	500,000 to 1,000,000
50,000 to 500,000	⊙	1,000,000 and over

Longitude West of Greenwich

Continued on pages 102-103

Continued on pages 114-115

Scale 1:4 000 000; one inch to 64 miles. Conic Projection
Elevations and depressions are given in feet

Continued on pages 90-91

Relief

Meters	Feet
1525	5000
610	2000
305	1000
152.5	500
0	Sea Level
152.5	500
1525	5000
3050	10 000

A-520596-76
COPYRIGHT BY
RAND McNALLY & COMPANY
MADE IN U.S.A.

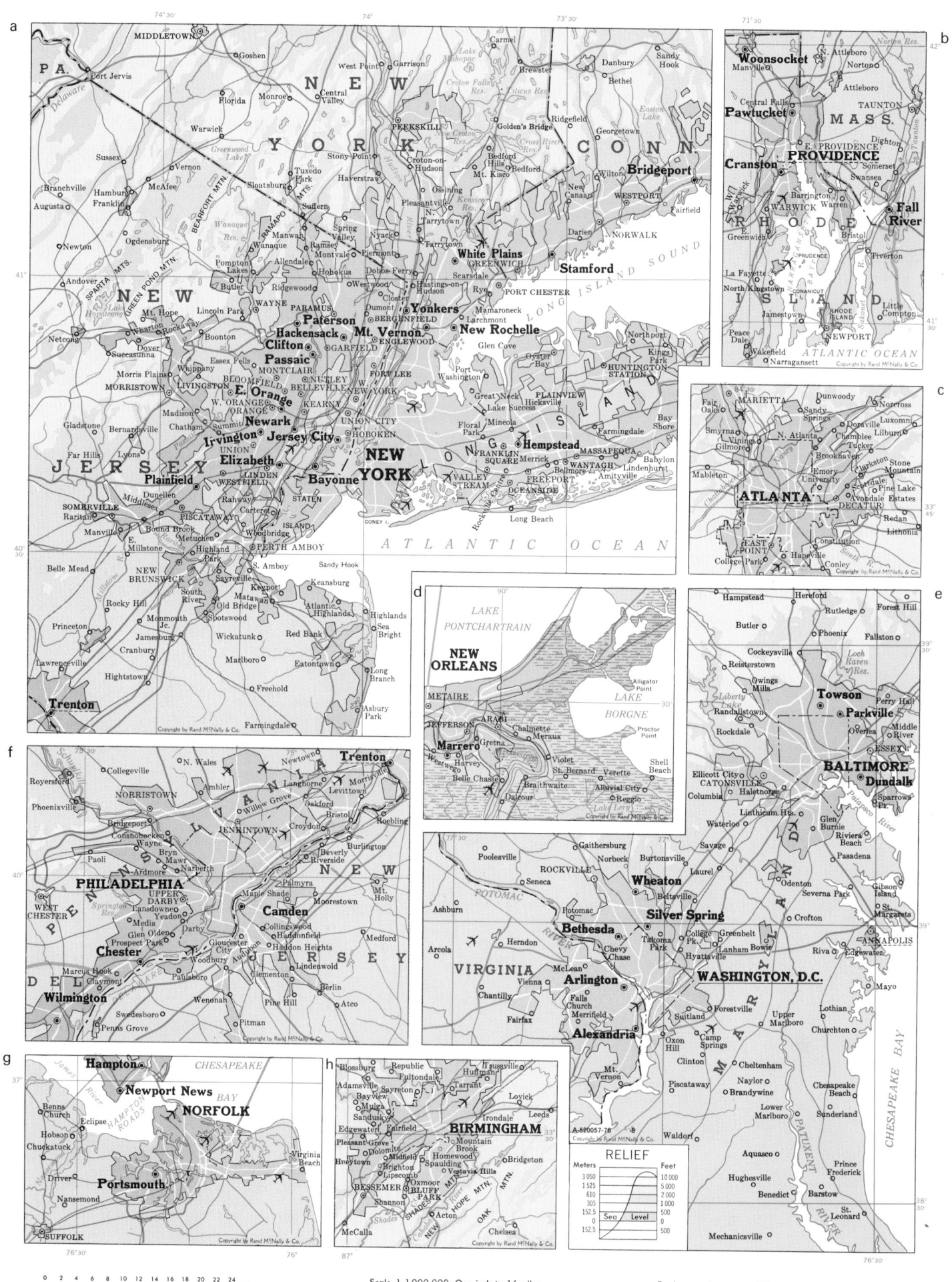

Scale 1:1 000 000; One inch to 16 miles.
Elevations and depressions are given in feet.

For larger scale coverage of New York, Baltimore,
Washington, D.C. and Philadelphia see pages 228 and 229.

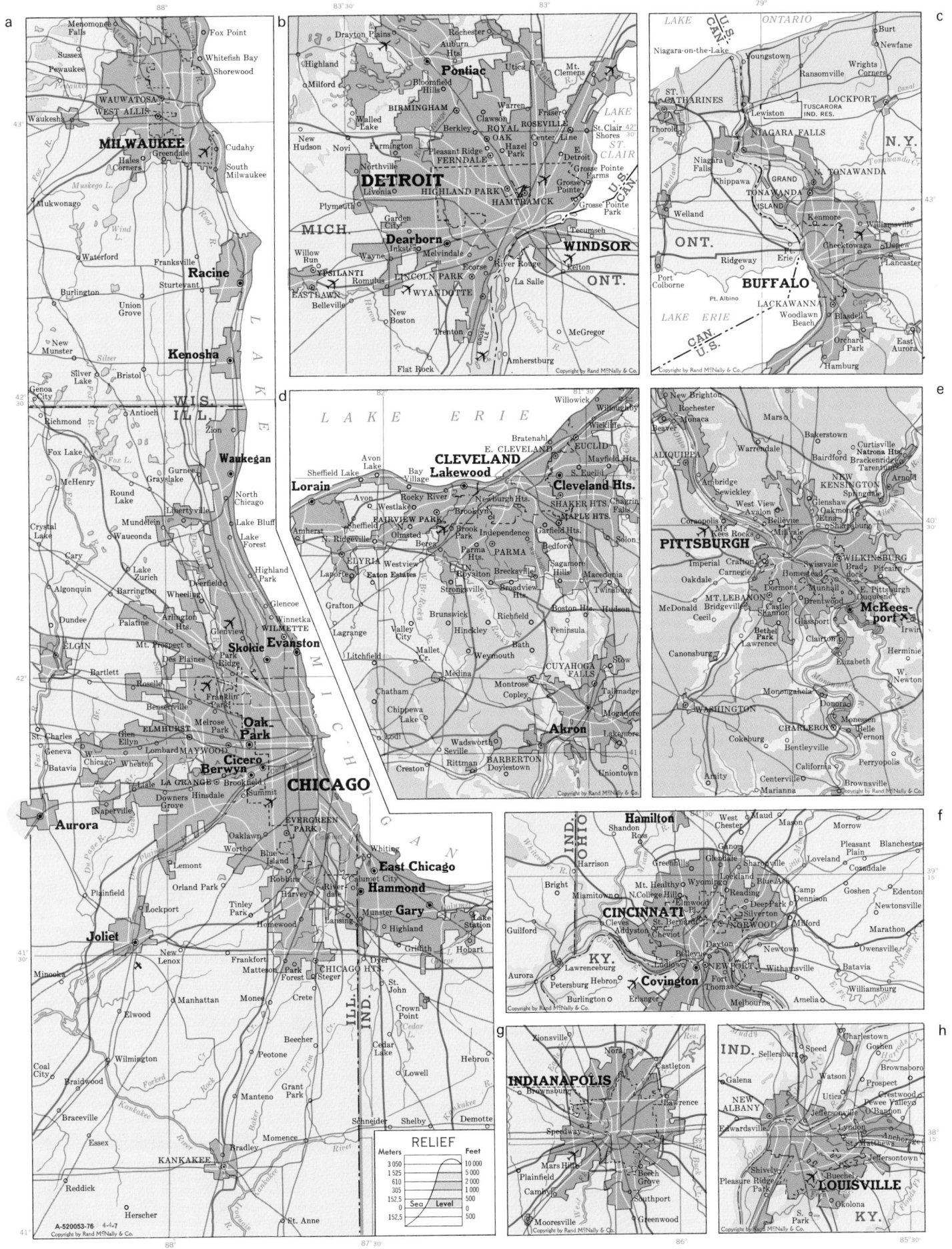

Scale 1:1 000 000; One inch to 16 miles.
Elevations and depressions are given in feet.

For larger scale coverage of Cleveland, Buffalo, Pittsburgh, Detroit and Chicago see pages 229-231.

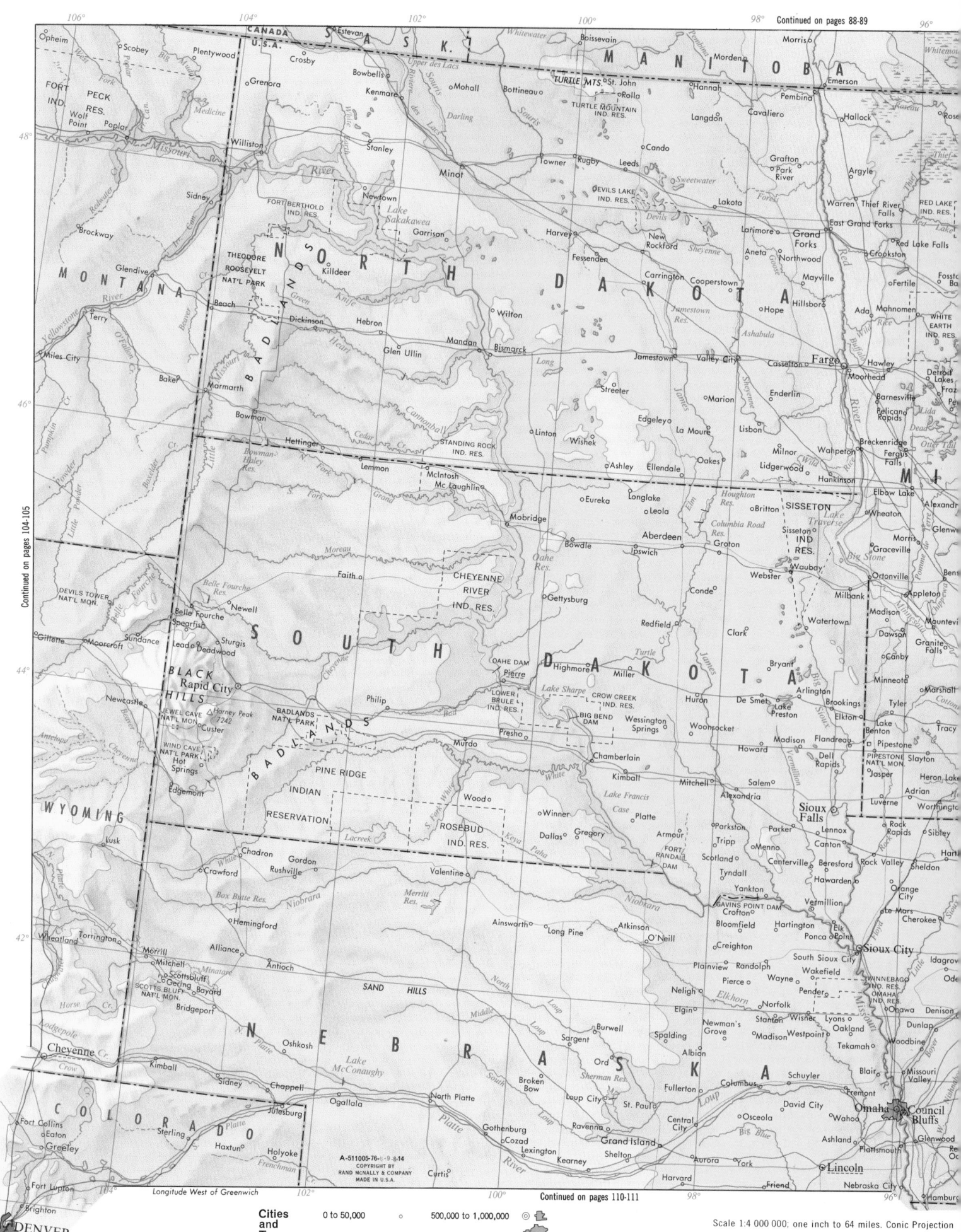

Continued on pages 88-89

Continued on pages 104-105

Continued on pages 110-111

Longitude West of Greenwich

A-511005-76-6-9-8-14
COPYRIGHT BY
RAND MCNALLY & COMPANY
MADE IN U.S.A.

Cities
and
Towns

| 0 to 50,000 | ○ | 500,000 to 1,000,000 | ◉ |
| 50,000 to 500,000 | ⊙ | 1,000,000 and over | |

Scale 1:4 000 000; one inch to 64 miles. Conic Projection
Elevations and depressions are given in feet

DENVER

Continued on pages 98-99

Continued on pages 110-111

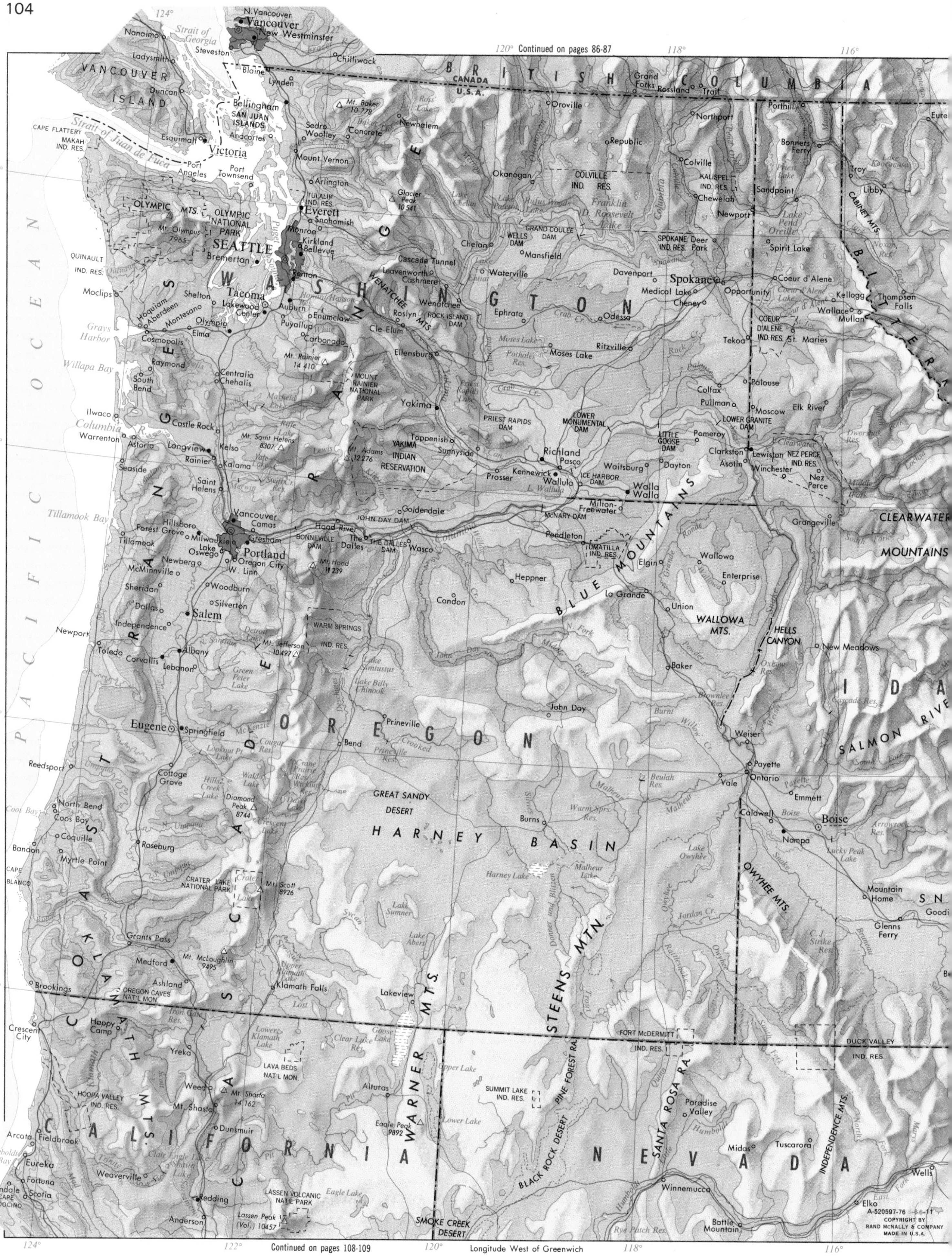

124°   120° Continued on pages 86-87   118°   116°

Strait of Georgia

N. Vancouver
Vancouver
New Westminster
Nanaimo
Steveston
Chilliwack
BRITISH COLUMBIA
CANADA
U.S.A.
Ladysmith
Blaine
Lynden
Grand Forks Rossland Trail
VANCOUVER
Duncan
Bellingham
Oroville
Northport
Porthill
ISLAND
SAN JUAN
ISLANDS
Sedro
Woolley
Mt. Baker
10,778
Newhalem
Republic
Colville
Bonners
Ferry
CAPE FLATTERY
Esquimalt Anacortes
Concrete
KALISPEL
IND. RES.
Libby
MAKAH
IND. RES.
Victoria
Port
Angeles
Port
Townsend
Mount Vernon
Okanogan
COLVILLE
IND. RES.
Colville
Sandpoint
Troy
CABINET MTS.
Strait of Juan de Fuca
Arlington
TULALIP
IND. RES.
Glacier
Peak
10,541
Chelan
Franklin
D. Roosevelt
Lake
Chewelah
Newport
Lake
Pend
Oreille
48°
OLYMPIC
MTS.
OLYMPIC
NATIONAL
PARK
Everett
Snohomish
WELLS
DAM
GRAND COULEE
DAM
SPOKANE
IND. RES.
Deer
Park
Spirit Lake
Wilson
Res.
Moclips
Mt. Olympus
7965
Monroe
Kirkland
Bellevue
SEATTLE
Cascade Tunnel
Leavenworth
Cashmere
Chelan
Mansfield
Davenport
Spokane
Medical Lake
Coeur d'Alene
Opportunity
Coeur d'Alene
Kellogg
Thompson
Falls
QUINAULT
IND. RES.
Bremerton
Renton
WENATCHEE
Wenatchee
Waterville
Cheney
COEUR
D'ALENE
IND. RES.
Wallace
Mullan
Shelton
Tacoma
Lakewood
Center
Auburn
Roslyn
MTS.
ROCK ISLAND
DAM
Ephrata
Odessa
Tekoa
St. Maries
Hoquiam
Aberdeen
Montesano
Olympia
Puyallup
Enumclaw
Cle Elum
Ellensburg
Moses Lake
Moses Lake
Ritzville
Colfax
Grays
Harbor
Cosmopolis
Elma
Carbonado
POTHOLES
RES.
Palouse
Pullman
Moscow
Elk River
Cosmopolis
Centralia
Chehalis
Mt. Rainier
14,410
MOUNT
RAINIER
NATIONAL
PARK
Yakima
PRIEST RAPIDS
DAM
LOWER
MONUMENTAL
DAM
Pomeroy
Dworshak
Res.
Raymond
South
Bend
Toppenish
Sunnyside
YAKIMA
INDIAN
RESERVATION
Richland
Pasco
LITTLE
GOOSE
DAM
LOWER GRANITE
DAM
Clarkston
Lewiston
Clearwater
NEZ PERCE
IND. RES.
46°
Ilwaco
Willapa Bay
Columbia R.
Warrenton
Astoria
Longview
Kelso
Mt. Saint Helens
8307
Mt. Adams
12,276
Kennewick
Wallula
L. Wallula
ICE HARBOR
DAM
Dayton
Waitsburg
Asotin
Winchester
Nez
Perce
Seaside
Rainier
Kalama
Prosser
Walla
Walla
MILTON-
FREEWATER
CLEARWATER
Cannon Beach
Saint
Helens
Goldendale
JOHN DAY DAM
McNARY DAM
Pendleton
Elgin
Grangeville
MOUNTAINS
Vancouver
Camas
Hood River
The
Dalles
THE DALLES
DAM
Wasco
UMATILLA
IND. RES.
BLUE
Wallowa
Tillamook
Hillsboro
Forest Grove
Gresham
BONNEVILLE
DAM
Mt. Hood
11,239
Heppner
MOUNTAINS
Enterprise
Tillamook Bay
Lake
Oswego
Milwaukie
Portland
Oregon City
W. Linn
La Grande
WALLOWA
MTS.
HELLS
CANYON
New Meadows
Newberg
McMinnville
Woodburn
Condon
Union
Sheridan
Silverton
WARM SPRINGS
IND. RES.
Baker
Dallas
Salem
Mt. Jefferson
10,497
Powder
44°
Independence
Albany
Detroit
Lake
Lake
Simtustus
Newport
Corvallis
Lebanon
Green
Peter
Lake
Lake Billy
Chinook
John Day
Burnt
Brownlee
Res.
Toledo
Eugene
Springfield
McKenzie
Prineville
PRINEVILLE
RES.
John Day
Weiser
SALMON RIVER
Reedsport
Cougar
Res.
Bend
Payette
LOOKOUT PT.
LAKE
HILLS
CREEK
LAKE
Crooked
Ontario
Emmett
Cottage
Grove
Diamond
Peak
8744
GREAT SANDY
DESERT
Beulah
Res.
Vale
Caldwell
Boise
North Bend
Coos Bay
Coos Bay
Crescent
Lake
HARNEY
Warm Sprs.
Res.
Nampa
Coquille
Roseburg
Burns
Malheur
Lake
Mountain
Home
Bandon
Myrtle Point
BASIN
Lake
Owyhee
Glenns
Ferry
CAPE
BLANCO
CRATER LAKE
NATIONAL PARK
Mt. Scott
8926
Harney Lake
Jordan Cr.
C. J.
Strike
Res.
Lake
Sumner
Malheur
Lake
OWYHEE
MTS.
42°
Grants Pass
Crater
Lake
Lake
Abert
STEENS MTN.
Medford
Mt. McLoughlin
9495
Upper
Klamath
Lake
Sycan
Ashland
OREGON CAVES
NAT'L MON.
Klamath Falls
Lakeview
FORT McDERMITT
IND. RES.
DUCK VALLEY
IND. RES.
Brookings
Lost
WARNER MTS.
Crescent
City
Happy
Camp
Yreka
Lower
Klamath
Lake
Clear Lake
Res.
Goose
Lake
PINE FOREST RA.
LAVA BEDS
NAT'L MON.
Alturas
Upper Lake
SUMMIT LAKE
IND. RES.
SANTA ROSA MTS.
INDEPENDENCE MTS.
Fieldbrook
Mt. Shasta
14,162
Eagle Peak
9892
Lower Lake
Paradise
Valley
Midas
Tuscarora
Arcata
Weed
Mt. Shasta
Pit
CALIFORNIA
NEVADA
Humboldt
Bay
Eureka
Fortuna
Dunsmuir
HOOPA VALLEY
IND. RES.
Eagle Lake
BLACK ROCK DESERT
Winnemucca
Wells
Ferndale
Scotia
Weaverville
LASSEN VOLCANIC
NAT'L PARK
Lassen Peak
(Vol.) 10,457
SMOKE CREEK
DESERT
Elko
CAPE
MENDOCINO
Redding
Anderson
Battle
Mountain
124°   122°   Continued on pages 108-109   120°   Longitude West of Greenwich   118°   116°

A-520597-76 8-6-11
COPYRIGHT BY
RAND McNALLY & COMPANY
MADE IN U.S.A.

Scale 1: 4,000 000; one inch to 64 miles. Conic Projection
Elevations and depressions are given in feet

Continued on pages 88-89

Continued on pages 102-103

Continued on pages 108-109

SASKATCHEWAN
ALBERTA
CANADA
U.S.A.
MONTANA
WYOMING
UTAH
N. DAK.
COLO.

Relief

Meters		Feet
3050		10000
1525		5000
610		2000
305		1000
152.5		500
0	Sea Level	0
1525		500

0   20   40   60   80   100   120 Miles
0   20   40   60   80   100   120   140   160   180   200 Kilometers

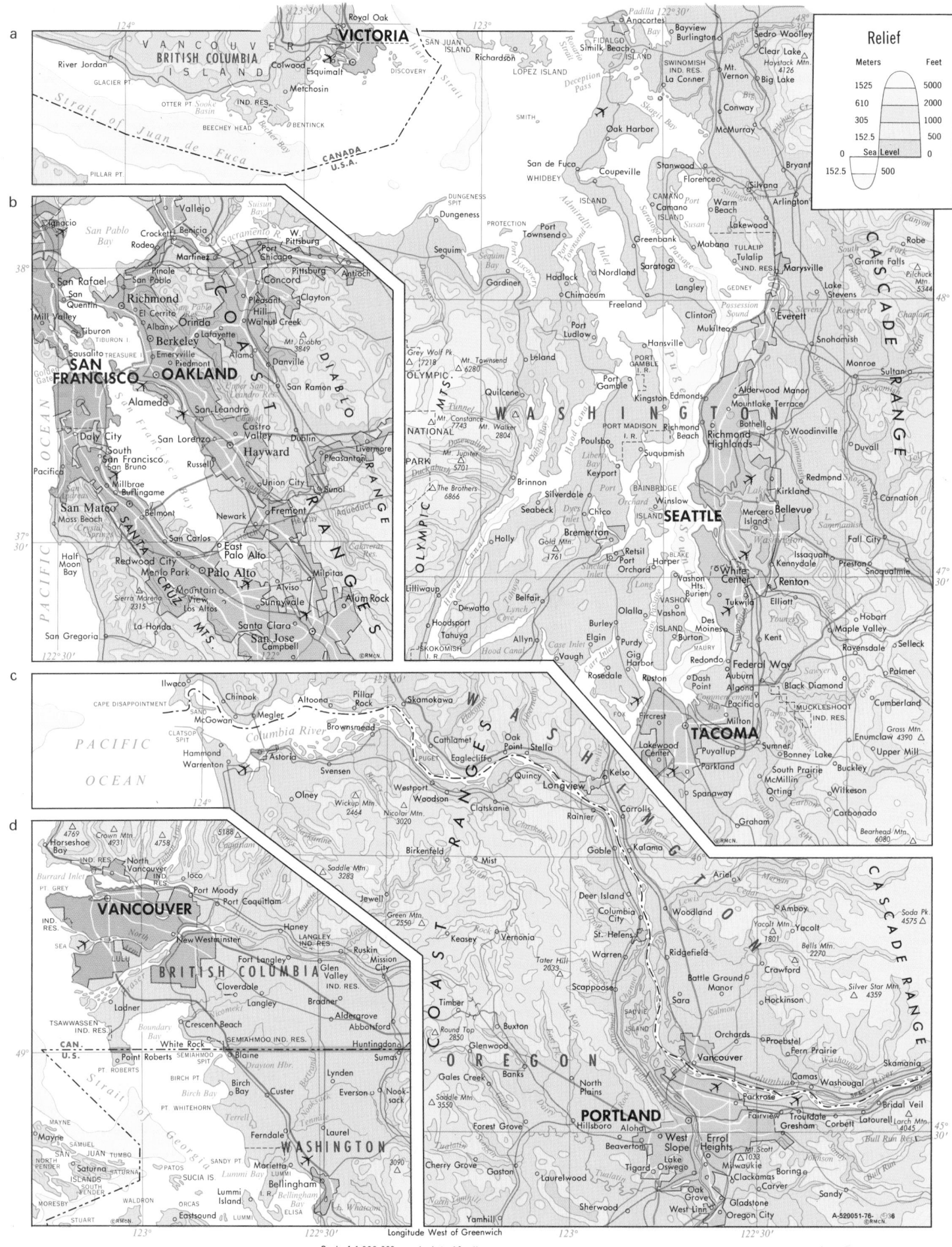

Relief

Meters		Feet
1525		5000
610		2000
305		1000
152.5		500
0	Sea Level	0
152.5		500

Scale 1:1 000 000; one inch to 16 miles.
Elevations and depressions are given in feet.

Longitude West of Greenwich

For larger scale coverage of San Francisco see page 231.

0 5 10 15 20 Miles
0 4 8 12 16 20 24 28 32 Kilometers

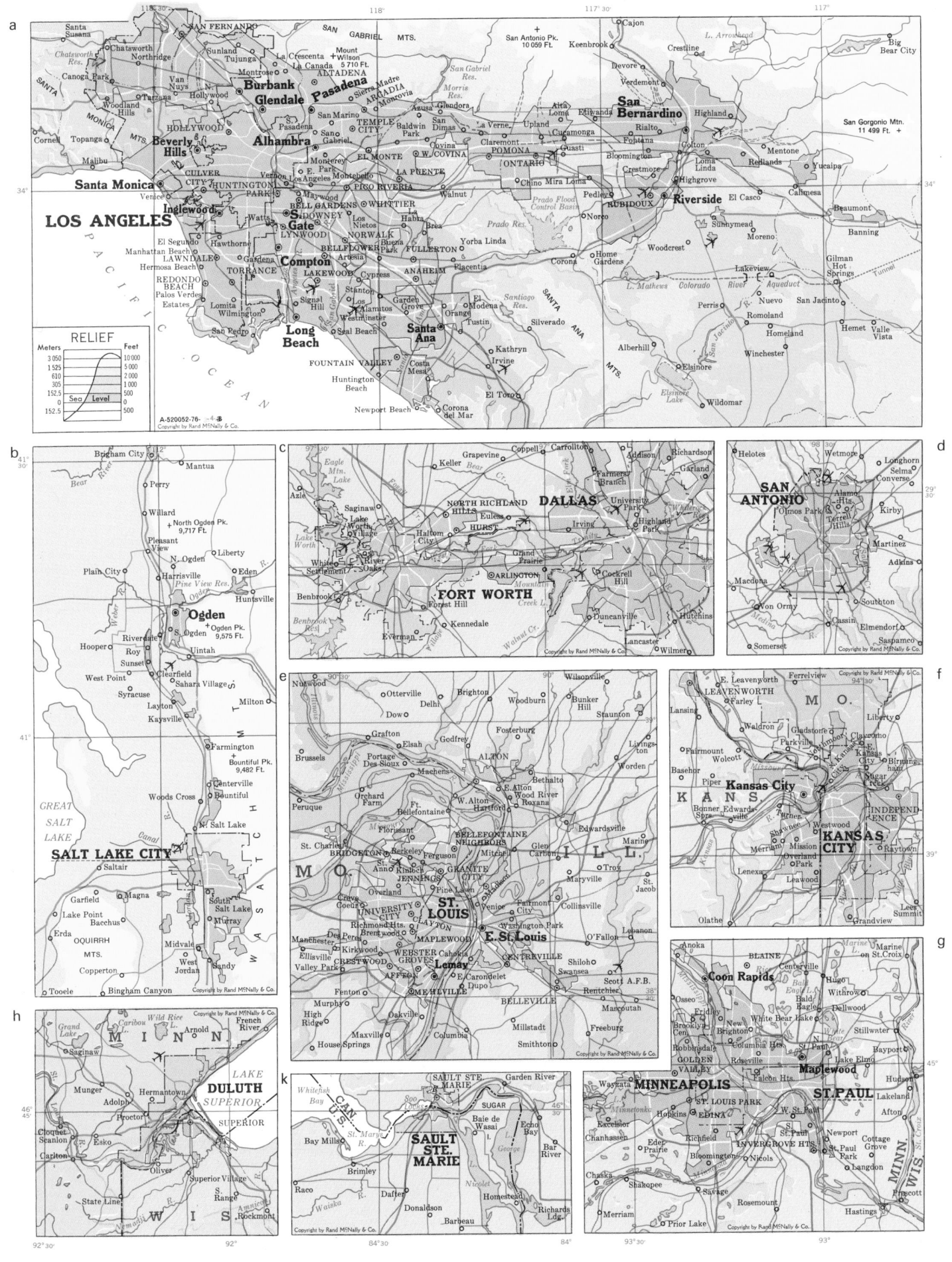

a
Santa Susana
Chatsworth Res.
Santa Susana
Chatsworth Northridge
Canoga Park
SANTA
MONICA
MTS.
Cornell Topanga
Malibu
Woodland Hills
Tarzana
Van Nuys
Hollywood
N.
Sunland Tujunga
La Crescenta
La Canada
Montrose
Sierra Madre
SAN FERNANDO
SAN GABRIEL MTS.
San Antonio Pk. 10 059 Ft.
Mount Wilson 5 710 Ft.
San Gabriel Res.
Morris Res.
Cajon
L. Arrowhead
Keenbrook
Crestline
Big Bear City
Devore
Verdemont
Burbank
Glendale
Pasadena
ALTADENA
ARCADIA
Monrovia
Azusa
Glendora
Alta Loma
Etiwanda
San Bernardino
Highland
San Gorgonio Mtn. 11 499 Ft.
HOLLYWOOD
Pasadena
San Marino
TEMPLE CITY
Baldwin Park
San Dimas
La Verne
Upland
Cucamonga
Rialto
Fontana
Beverly Hills
Alhambra
San Gabriel
E. Monterey Park
EL MONTE
W. COVINA
POMONA
Claremont
ONTARIO
Guasti
Bloomington
Colton
Loma Linda
Redlands
Mentone
Santa Monica
CULVER CITY
Vernon
Los Angeles
Montebello
PICO RIVERA
Covina
Chino Mira Loma
Crestmore
Highgrove
Yucaipa
34°
Los Angeles
Inglewood
HUNTINGTON PARK
Maywood
BELL GARDENS
Downey
WHITTIER
La Habra
Brea
Prado Flood Control Basin
RUBIDOUX
Riverside
El Casco
Calimesa
34°
Venice
S. Gate
LYNWOOD
NORWALK
Buena Park
FULLERTON
Yorba Linda
Prado Res.
Noreo
Sunnymead
Moreno
Beaumont
Manhattan Beach
El Segundo
LAWNDALE
Hermosa Beach
Gardena
Hawthorne
Watts
Compton
BELLFLOWER
Artesia
Cypress
ANAHEIM
Placentia
Corona
Home Gardens
Woodcrest
Banning
Gilman Hot Springs
REDONDO BEACH
Palos Verdes Estates
TORRANCE
LAKEWOOD
Stanton
Garden Grove
Orange
Santiago Res.
Silverado
Lakeview
Perris
Nuevo
San Jacinto
Lomita
Wilmington
Signal Hill
Los Alamitos
El Modena
Tustin
Alberhill
Romoland
Homeland
Hemet
Valle Vista
San Pedro
Long Beach
Seal Beach
Westminster
Santa Ana
Kathryn
Irvine
L. Mathews
Colorado River
Aqueduct
San Jacinto
Winchester
FOUNTAIN VALLEY
Costa Mesa
Huntington Beach
Newport Beach
Corona del Mar
El Toro
Elsinore
Wildomar
Elsinore Lake

RELIEF
Meters Feet
3 050 10 000
1 525 5 000
610 2 000
305 1 000
152.5 500
0 Sea Level 0
152.5 500
A-520052-76- -4-B
Copyright by Rand McNally & Co.

b
Brigham City
Mantua
Perry
Willard
North Ogden Pk. 9,717 Ft.
Pleasant View
N. Ogden
Liberty
Plain City
Harrisville
Eden
Pine View Res.
Ogden
S. Ogden
Ogden Pk. 9,575 Ft.
Hooper
Riverdale
Uintah
Roy
Sunset
Clearfield
Sahara Village
West Point
Layton
Milton
Syracuse
Kaysville
41°
Farmington
Bountiful Pk. 9,482 Ft.
Centerville
Bountiful
Woods Cross
GREAT SALT LAKE
N. Salt Lake
Salt Lake City
Saltair
Garfield
Magna
Lake Point
Bacchus
South Salt Lake
Murray
Erda
OQUIRRH MTS.
Midvale
Copperton
West Jordan
Sandy
Tooele
Bingham Canyon

c
Eagle Mtn. Lake
Keller
Grapevine
Coppell
Carrollton
Addison
Richardson
Garland
Helotes
Wetmore
Longhorn
Azle
Saginaw
NORTH RICHLAND HILLS
Euless
DALLAS
University Park
Highland Park
Whiterock
Lake Worth
Lake Worth Village
Haltom City
HURST
Irving
Fort Worth
White Settlement
River Oaks
Grand Prairie
ARLINGTON
Cockrell Hill
Benbrook
Mountain Creek L.
Duncanville
Hutchins
Benbrook Res.
Forest Hill
Everman
Kennedale
Duncanville
Lancaster
Wilmer
Copyright by Rand McNally & Co.

d
San Antonio
Alamo Hts.
Olmos Park
Terrell Hills
Kirby
Macdona
Von Ormy
Southton
Elmendorf
Somerset
Cassin
Saspamco
Copyright by Rand McNally & Co.

e
Nutwood
Otterville
Delhi
Brighton
Wilsonville
Grafton
Elsah
Godfrey
Woodburn
Bunker Hill
Staunton
Brussels
Portage Des Sioux
ALTON
Bethalto
Wood River
Roxana
Livingston
St. Charles
Ft. Bellefontaine
W. Alton
Hartford
Edwardsville
Florissant
BELLEFONTAINE NEIGHBORS
Glen Carbon
Marine
Bridgeton
Berkeley
Ferguson
Mitchell
MO.
Granite City
ILL.
Troy
Overland
JENNINGS
Pine Lawn
Venice
Maryville
St. Jacob
UNIVERSITY CITY
Clayton
St. Louis
E. St. Louis
Collinsville
O'Fallon
Lebanon
Manchester
Brentwood
MAPLEWOOD
Washington Park
Scott A.F.B.
Kirkwood
WEBSTER GROVES
Cahokia
CENTREVILLE
Shiloh
Swansea
CRESTWOOD
AFFTON
Lemay
E. Carondelet
Dupo
BELLEVILLE
Fenton
MEHLVILLE
Rentchler
Mascoutah
Oakville
Dupo
Freeburg
High Ridge
Maxville
Columbia
Millstadt
House Springs
Smithton

f
Ferrelview
E. Leavenworth
LEAVENWORTH
Farley
MO.
Lansing
Waldron
Gladstone
Liberty
Claycomo
Fairmount
Wolcott
Parkville
Basehor
Piper
Kansas City
KANS.
Bonner Springs
Edwardsville
Turner
INDEPENDENCE
Sugar Cr.
Birmingham
Shawnee
Westwood
Kansas City
Merriam
Mission
Raytown
Lenexa
Overland Park
Leawood
Lees Summit
Olathe
Grandview

g
Anoka
BLAINE
Centerville
Marine on St. Croix
Coon Rapids
Hugo
Withrow
Osseo
Fridley
New Brighton
White Bear Lake
Dellwood
Brooklyn Center
Columbia Hts.
Stillwater
Robbinsdale
Roseville
St. Paul
Bayport
GOLDEN VALLEY
Falcon Hts.
Maplewood
Hudson
45°
MINNEAPOLIS
St. Louis Park
EDINA
ST. PAUL
Lakeland
Wayzata
Minnetonka
Hopkins
W. St. Paul
Afton
Excelsior
Eden Prairie
Richfield
INVERGROVE HTS.
Newport
St. Paul Park
Cottage Grove
Chanhassen
Bloomington
Nicols
Langdon
Chaska
Shakopee
Savage
Rosemount
MINN.
WIS.
Merriam
Prior Lake
Hastings

h
Grand Lake
Caribou
Wild Rice
Arnold
French River
MINN.
Saginaw
Hermantown
LAKE SUPERIOR
Munger
Adolph
Proctor
Duluth
Cloquet
Scanlon
Esko
Oliver
SUPERIOR
Carlton
Superior Village
S. Range
WIS.
State Line
Rockmont

k
Whitefish Bay
SAULT STE. MARIE
Garden River
CAN.
U.S.
Soo Locks
Sugar
St. Mary
Bay Mills
Baie de Wasai
Echo Bay
SAULT STE. MARIE
Brimley
L. George
Bar River
Raco
Dafter
Donaldson
Homestead
Richards Ldg.
Waiska
Barbeau

Scale 1:1 000 000; One inch to 16 miles.
Elevations and depressions are given in feet.

For larger scale coverage of Los Angeles see page 232.

Miles
0 2 4 6 8 10 12 14 16 18 20 22 24
0 4 8 12 16 20 24 28 32 36 40
Kilometers

Continued on pages 104-105

Scale 1:4 000 000; one inch to 64 miles. Conic Projection
Elevations and depressions are given in feet

Longitude West of Greenwich

A-520599-76

COPYRIGHT BY
RAND McNALLY & COMPANY
MADE IN U.S.A.

Scale 1:1 000 000

0   5   10 Miles

0 4 8 12 16 Kilometers

Relief

Meters		Feet
3050		10000
1525		5000
610		2000
305		1000
152.5		500
0	Sea Level	Sea Level
152.5		500 Below Sea Level
1525		5000
3050		10000

114° 110° 108°

GREAT SALT LAKE DESERT

Great Salt Lake

Salt Lake City
Tooele Murray
West Jordan Midvale Heber City
Lehi Park City
American Fork TIMPANOGOS CAVE N.M.
Orem Provo
Springville
Spanish Fork
Payson

GOSHUTE IND. RES.

Vernal
Roosevelt
UINTAH AND OURAY IND. RES.
Duchesne

Oak Creek
Meeker
Bond

ROCKY
Rifle Glenwood Springs
Leadville Mt. Massive 14 421
Aspen Mt. Elbert 14 433

U T A H

U T A H P L A T E A U

Nephi
Fairview
Moroni Mount Pleasant
Ephraim Price Sunnyside
Manti Hiawatha
Castle Dale

WEST TAVAPUTS PLATEAU
EAST TAVAPUTS PLATEAU

Delta
Fillmore
Gunnison
Salina
Richfield
Monroe

Fruita Grand Junction
Delta
Paonia Crested Butte
Montrose
Castle Pk 14 265 Mt. Elbert 14 361
Mt. Harvard 14 420 Buena Vista Cripple Creek

C O L O R A D O

Canon City

Milford
Beaver
Delano Pk 12 169

Green River
ARCHES NATL. PARK
Moab Mt. Peale 12 721

COLORADO NATL. MON.

CAPITOL REEF NATL. PARK
Mt. Ellen 11 522
HENRY MTS.

CANYONLANDS NATL. PARK
La Sal

Mt. Sneffels 14 150
Ouray Uncompahgre Pk. 14 309
Telluride Silverton

SAN JUAN MTS.

GREAT SAND DUNES N.M.
Saguache
Del Norte Blanca Pk 14 345
Monte Vista
Alamosa

SANGRE DE CRISTO MTS.

Parowan
Panguitch
Cedar City
CEDAR BREAKS NATL. MON.
BRYCE CANYON NATL. PARK
Escalante
GLEN CANYON NATL. RECR. AREA

Abajo Pk. 11 360
Monticello
Blanding

HOVENWEEP NATL. MON.
Cortez MESA VERDE NATL. PARK
NATURAL BRIDGES NATL. MON.
Durango Pagosa Springs

Antonito

ZION NATL. PARK
Hurricane
Saint George
Kanab

Mexican Hat
Bluff

SOUTHERN UTE INDIAN RES.

UTE MTN. IND. RES.
AZTEC RUINS NATL. MON.
JICARILLA APACHE
Wheeler Pk. 13 161
Taos

KAIBAB IND. RES.
PIPE SPRING NATL. MON.
Mt. Bangs 8012

GLEN CANYON DAM
Page INSCRIPTION HOUSE RUIN KEET SEEL RUIN
BETATAKIN RUIN
NAVAJO NATL. MON.

INDIAN

Farmington
Aztec

INDIAN
RESERVATION

Santa Clara IND. RES.
Truchas Pk. 13 101

NAVAJO INDIAN RES.

BLACK MESA
NAVAJO HOPI JOINT USE AREA
CANYON DE CHELLY NATL. MON.

Los Alamos
BANDELIER NATL. MON.
JEMEZ IND. RES.
Santa Fe

SHIVWITS PLATEAU
MEAD RECR. AREA
HUALAPAI
KANAB PLATEAU
KAIBAB PLATEAU
GRAND CANYON NATIONAL PARK
Grand Canyon
HAVASUPAI IND. RES.

Moenkopi
HOPI
INDIAN
RESERVATION

R E S E R V A T I O N

CHACO CANYON NATL. MON.
CHACO CULTURE NATL. HIST. PARK

ZIA IND. RES.
SANTO DOMINGO
SAN FELIPE IND. RES.
Bernalillo SANDIA IND. RES.
Galisteo

Chloride
Kingman
Oatman
Tapock

COCONINO PLATEAU

COLORADO DESERT

WUPATKI NATL. MON.
Humphreys Pk 12 633
SUNSET CRATER N.M.
Ash Fork Williams Flagstaff
WALNUT CANYON NATL. MON.
Winslow
Holbrook

Gallup
Mt. Taylor 11 301

C O L O R A D O P L A T E A U S

ZUNI
ZUNI MTS.
EL MORRO NATL. MON.
ACOMA IND. RES.
LAGUNA IND. RES.
CANONCITO IND. RES.
Albuquerque
Isleta
Belen

N E W M E X I C O

Lake Havasu City
HUALAPAI MTS.
PARKER DAM
Bill Williams

PETRIFIED FOREST NATL. PARK

Clarkdale TUZIGOOT N.M.
Jerome MONTEZUMA CASTLE NATL. MON.
Prescott

MOGOLLON RIM

Saint Johns
McNary
Springerville

ALAMO IND. RES.

Magdalena
Socorro

SALINAS NATL. MON.

COLORADO RIVER IND. RES.
Quartzsite
Wickenburg

THEODORE ROOSEVELT LAKE
THEODORE ROOSEVELT DAM
TONTO NATL. MON.

FORT APACHE INDIAN RESERVATION
Mt. Ord 11 357 Baldy Peak 11 403
Maverick

San Marcial
Carrizozo
Sierra Blanca Peak 11 973
MESCALERO APACHE IND. RES.
Tularosa
Alamogordo
WHITE SANDS NATL. MON.

A R I Z O N A

SALT RIVER IND. RES.
Glendale
Phoenix Mesa
Tempe
GILA RIVER IND. RES.

Miami Globe
Superior
SAN CARLOS INDIAN RESERVATION
San Carlos Lake
Hayden

Glenwood
GILA CLIFF DWELLINGS NATL. MON.
Morenci Clifton
Silver City
Bayard
Truth or Consequences
Caballo Res.

BLACK RANGE

SAN ANDRES MTS.

Painted Rock Res.
Florence
Gila Bend
CASA GRANDE N.M.
Casa Grande

Safford

San Manuel

Las Cruces
Mesilla

PAPAGO INDIAN RESERVATION
Ajo
ORGAN PIPE CACTUS N.M.

San Xavier IND. RES.
Tucson
SAGUARO N.M.

Willcox
Willcox Playa Lake
CHIRICAHUA NATL. MON.

Lordsburg
Deming

FLORIDA MTS.

N. Franklin Mtn. 7192
T E X A S
El Paso Ysleta
Ciudad Juárez

Benson
Tombstone
Columbus
Playas Lake

TUMACACORI NATL. MON.
Fort Huachuca
Bisbee Lowell Pirtleville
Nogales
Douglas

S O N O R A

C H I H U A H U A

USA MEXICO

Continued on pages 110-111
Continued on pages 112-113

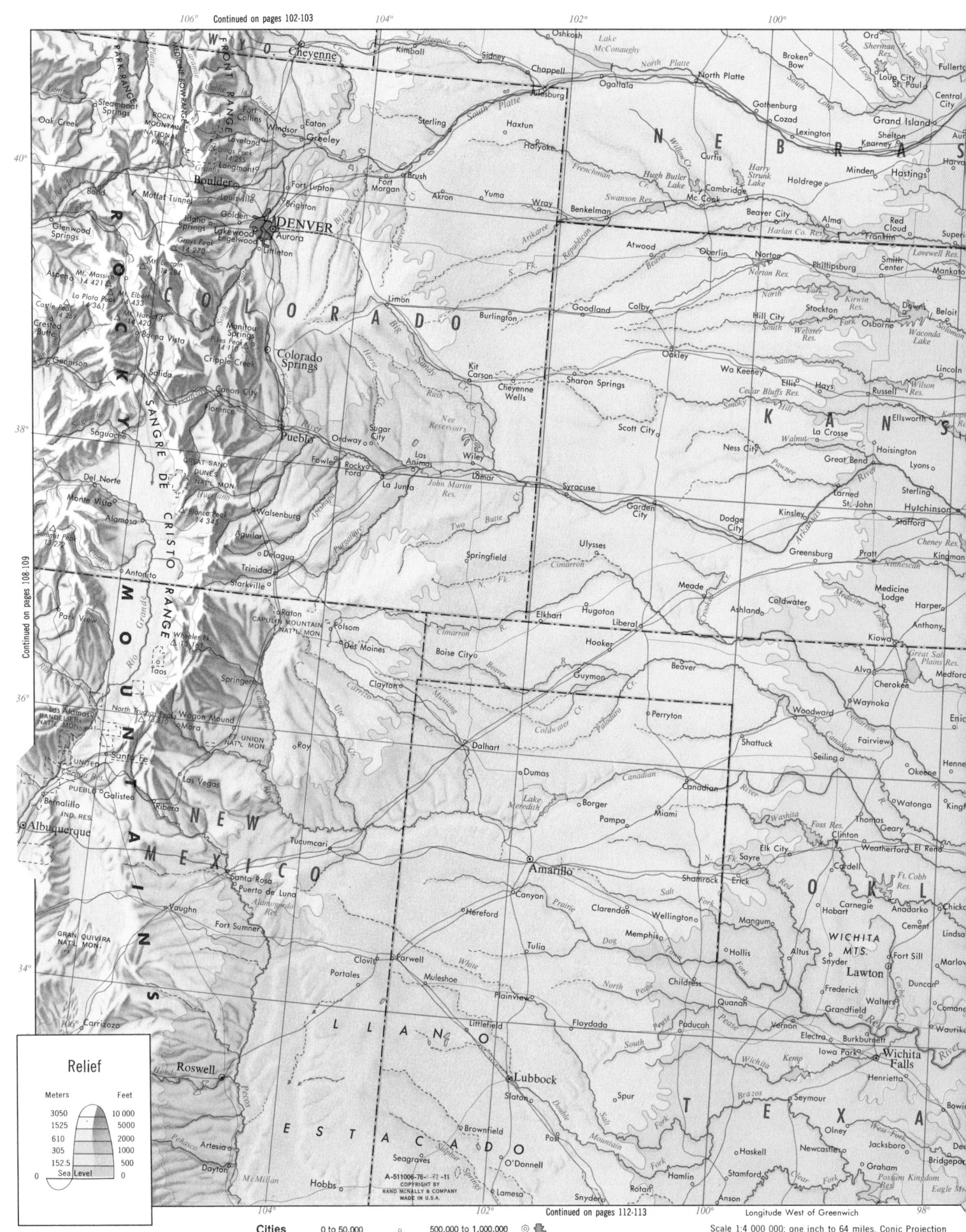

Continued on pages 102-103

106°   104°   102°   100°

W Y O.   Cheyenne

Kimball   Oshkosh   Lake McConaughy   Ord   Sherman   Fullert
Lodgepole   Sidney   North Platte   Broken Bow   Loup City   Sh. Paul   Central
                                                          North Platte   Gothenburg   Grand Island   City
Chappell   Ogallala   Cozad   Lexington   Shelton   Kearney
N E B R A S   Minden   Hastings   Harva

FRONT RANGE   Fort Collins   Windsor   Greeley   Sterling   Haxtun   Holyoke   Frenchman   Hugh Butler Lake   Curtis   Harry Strunk Lake   Cambridge   Mc Cook   Holdrege   Superi
PARK RANGE   Loveland   Eaton   Swanson Res.   Beaver City   Alma   Red Cloud   Franklin
MEDICINE BOW RANGE   Longmont   Fort Lupton   Brush   Akron   Yuma   Wray   Benkelman   Harlan Co. Res.   Lovewell Res.

Steamboat Springs   Fort Morgan   Atwood   Beaver   Oberlin   Norton   Phillipsburg   Smith Center   Mankato
Oak Creek   ROCKY MOUNTAIN NATIONAL PARK   Longs Peak 14 255   Louisville   Brighton   Bijou   Republican   Norton Res.

Glenwood Springs   Bond   Moffat Tunnel   Golden   DENVER   Aurora   Limon   Burlington   Goodland   Colby   Hill City   Stockton   Osborne   Downs   Beloit
Idaho Springs   Lakewood   Engelwood   Littleton   Oakley   Wa Keeney   Ellis   Hays   Russell   Waconda Lake   Lincoln
R O C K Y   Grays Peak 14 270   C O L O R A D O   Kit Carson   Sharon Springs   Scott City   Ness City   La Crosse   Ellsworth   Kanop

Aspen   Mt. Massive 14 421   Mt. Lincoln 14 284   Manitou Springs   Cheyenne Wells   Smoky Hill   Great Bend   Lyons
La Plata Peak 14 433   Mt. Elbert 14 433   Pikes Peak 4 111   Colorado Springs   Horse   Big Sandy   Walnut   Hoisington
Castle Peak 14 265   Mt. Harvard 14 420   Buena Vista   Cripple Creek   Ness City   La Crosse
Crested Butte   La Plata Peak 14 361   Canon City   Pueblo   Ordway   Sugar City   Rush   Nee Reservoirs   Scott City   Dodge City   Kinsley   St. John   Hutchinson
Gunnison   SANGRE DE CRISTO RANGE   Florence   Fowler   Rocky Ford   Las Animas   Wiley   John Martin Res.   Syracuse   Garden City   Greensburg   Pratt   Stafford   Cheney Res.

Saguache   Salida   GREAT SAND DUNES NAT'L MON.   Walsenburg   La Junta   Lamar   Two Butte   Garden City   Dodge City   Larned   Sterling   Kingman
Del Norte   Blanca Peak 14 345   Aguilar   Springfield   Cimarron   Meade   Ulysses   Coldwater   Ashland   Medicine Lodge   Harper
Monte Vista   Alamosa   Delagua   Trinidad   Purgatoire   Cimarron   Elkhart   Hugoton   Liberal   Anthony
Summit Peak 13 272   Antonito   Starkville   N. Fk.   Boise City   Hooker   Guymon   Beaver   Kiowa   Great Salt Plains Res.

Park View   Raton   CAPULIN MOUNTAIN NAT'L MON.   Folsom   Cimarron   Clayton   Beaver   Woodward   Waynoka   Medford
Wheeler Pk.   Des Moines   Carrizo   Perryton   Fairview   Cherokee   Alva
Taos   Springer   Mustang   Coldwater   Palo Duro   Canadian   Seiling   Okeene   Enic
NORTH TRUCHAS PEAK   Wagon Mound   Dalhart   Shattuck   Henne
BANDELIER NAT'L MON.   LOS ALAMOS   Mora   UNION NAT'L MON.   Roy   Dumas   Lake Meredith   Canadian   Canadian River   Woodward   Fairview   Watonga   King
Santa Fe   Las Vegas   Borger   Miami   Foss Res.   Thomas
Bernalillo IND. RES.   Ribera   Pampa   Washita   Geary   Elk City   Clinton   Weatherford   El Reno
ALBUQUERQUE   Galisteo   Tucumcari   Amarillo   Shamrock   Erick   Sayre   Cordell   Ft. Cobb Res.
N E W   Santa Rosa   Canyon   Prairie   Clarendon   Wellington   Mangum   Hobart   Anadarko   Cement   Lindsa
Puerto de Luna   Hereford   Memphis   Elk City   Carnegie   WICHITA MTS.
Vaughn   Alamogordo Res.   Tulia   Dog   Hollis   Altus   Fort Sill   Marlow
Fort Sumner   M E X I C O   Clovis   Farwell   White   Quanah   Snyder   Lawton   Duncan
GRAN QUIVIRA NAT'L MON.   Portales   Muleshoe   Plainview   Childress   Frederick   Walters   Comanc
Carrizozo   Floydada   Paducah   Vernon   Grandfield   Waurika
Roswell   L L A N O   Littlefield   Floydada   Electra   Burkburnett   Iowa Park   Wichita Falls
Honda   Spur   Pease   Kemp   Seymour   Henrietta
ESTACADO   Lubbock   Slaton   Brazos   Olney   Bowie
Penasco   Brownfield   Post   Double   Stamford   Jacksboro   Bridgeport
Artesia   Seagraves   O'Donnell   Haskell   Newcastle   Graham   Possum Kingdom Res.
Dayton   McMillan   Hobbs   Lamesa   Snyder   Hamlin   Anson   Eagle Mt.
                                                          T E X A S   Rotan   Clear   Fk.

O K L.   WICHITA

106°   104°   102°   100°   98°

A-511006-76-   -71-11
COPYRIGHT BY
RAND McNALLY & COMPANY
MADE IN U.S.A.

Continued on pages 112-113

Longitude West of Greenwich

Relief

Meters		Feet
3050		10 000
1525		5000
610		2000
305		1000
152.5		500
0	Sea Level	0

Cities and Towns

0 to 50,000 ○   500,000 to 1,000,000 ⊙
50,000 to 500,000 ⊙   1,000,000 and over

Scale 1:4 000 000; one inch to 64 miles. Conic Projection
Elevations and depressions are given in feet.

Continued on pages 102-103

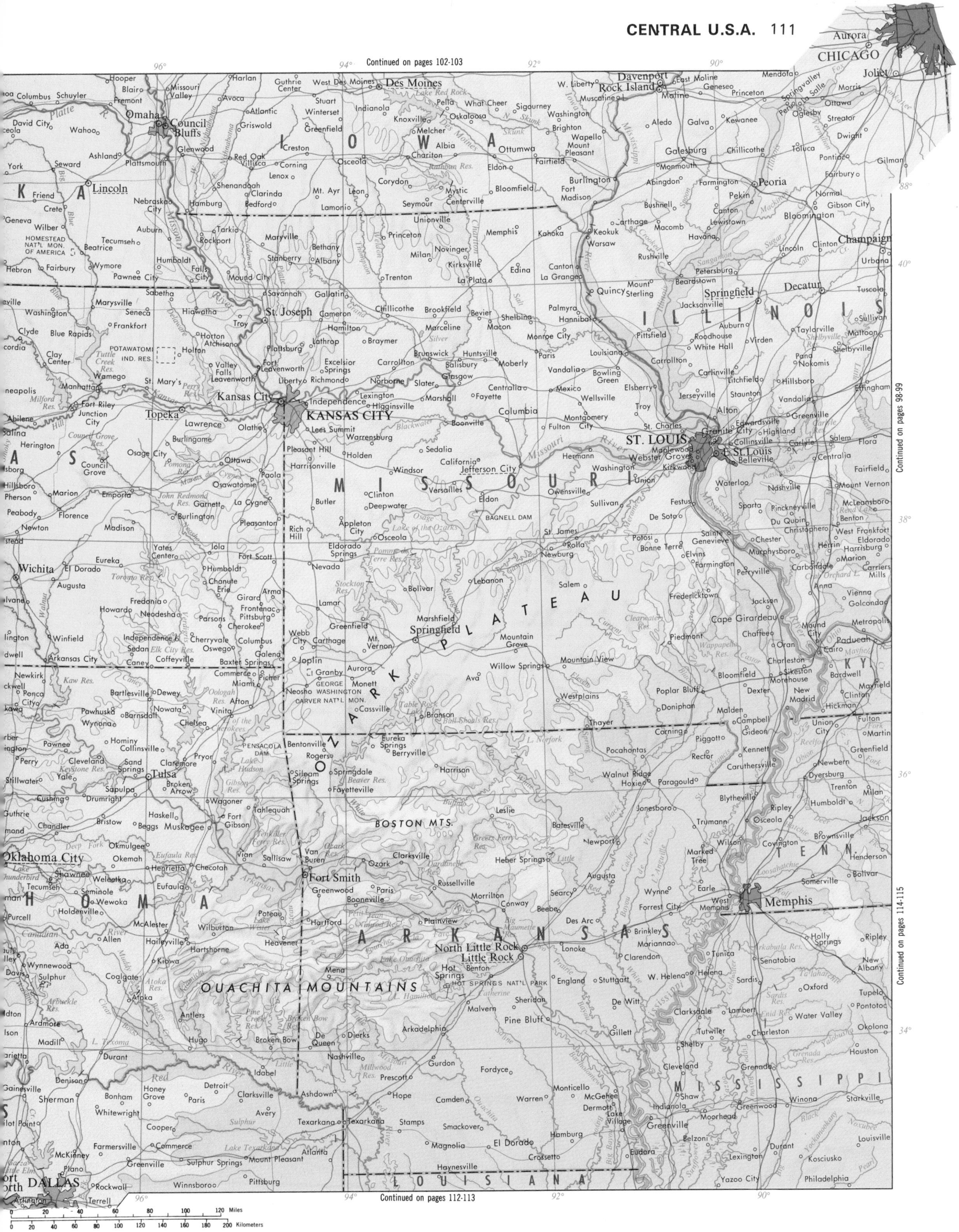

Continued on pages 98-99

Continued on pages 114-115

Continued on pages 112-113

CHICAGO

Aurora · Joliet

IOWA

ILLINOIS

KANSAS

MISSOURI

OKLAHOMA

ARKANSAS

TENN.

MISSISSIPPI

LOUISIANA

KY

OZARK PLATEAU

BOSTON MTS.

OUACHITA MOUNTAINS

Omaha · Council Bluffs

Lincoln

Des Moines

Davenport · Rock Island

Peoria

Springfield

Decatur

Champaign

Kansas City

KANSAS CITY

Topeka

St. Joseph

St. Louis

ST. LOUIS · E. St. Louis

Wichita

Tulsa

Oklahoma City

Fort Smith

North Little Rock · Little Rock

Hot Springs

Memphis · West Memphis

Dallas

HOMESTEAD NAT'L MON. OF AMERICA

GEORGE WASHINGTON CARVER NAT'L MON.

HOT SPRINGS NAT'L PARK

Lake of the Ozarks

BAGNELL DAM

PENSACOLA DAM

Red River

20 40 60 80 100 120 Miles

20 40 60 80 100 120 140 160 180 200 Kilometers

96°   94°   92°   90°   88°

40°   38°   36°   34°

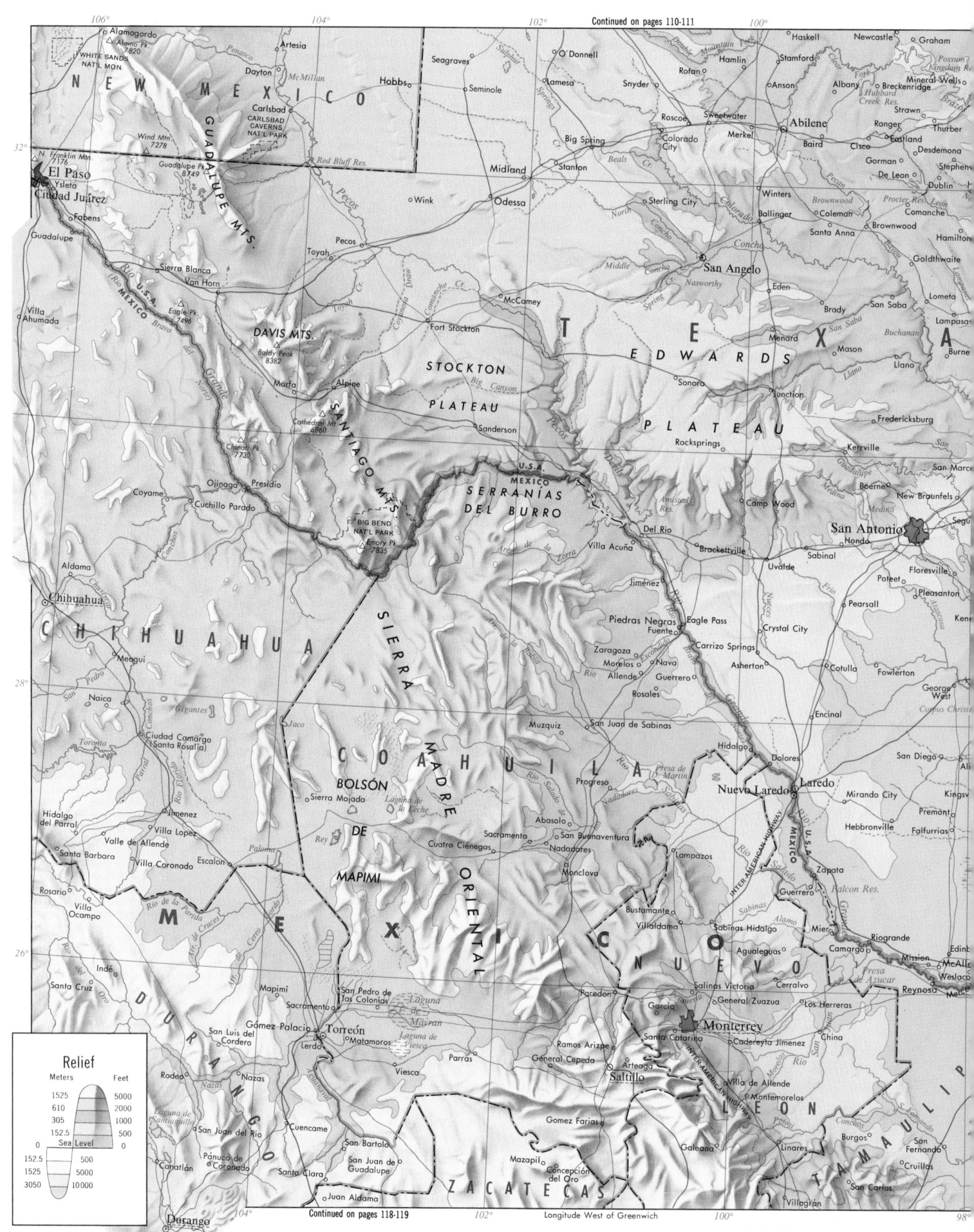

Continued on pages 110-111

NEW MEXICO

Alamogordo
Alamo Pk.
7820
WHITE SANDS
NAT'L MON.
N. Franklin Mtn.
7176
El Paso
Ysleta
Ciudad Juárez
Fabens
Guadalupe
Villa
Ahumada

Penasco
Artesia
Dayton
McMillan
Carlsbad
CARLSBAD
CAVERNS
NAT'L PARK
Wind Mtn.
7278
Red Bluff Res.
GUADALUPE MTS.
Guadalupe Pk.
8749

Seagraves
Seminole
Hobbs

O'Donnell
Lamesa
Snyder

Haskell
Newcastle
Graham
Rotan
Hamlin
Stamford
Kingdom Pk.
Anson
Albany
Breckenridge
Strawn
Thurber
Ranger
Eastland
Cisco
Gorman
De Leon
Stephenv
Dublin

Midland
Odessa
Wink

Big Spring
Stanton

Roscoe
Colorado
City
Sweetwater
Merkel
Abilene
Baird

Pecos
MEXICO U.S.A.
Rio Grande

Toyah
Pecos

Sierra Blanca
Van Horn
Eagle Pk.
7496

DAVIS MTS.
Baldy Peak
8382
Marfa
Alpine

Sterling City
Ballinger
Coleman
Santa Anna
Brownwood
Comanche
Brownwood
Hamilton
Winters

San Angelo
Middle Concho
Nasworthy
Spring

TEXAS

EDWARDS

PLATEAU

McCamey
Fort Stockton

STOCKTON

PLATEAU
Sanderson

Eden
Menard
Brady
San Saba
Mason
Llano
Lometa
Burne
Lampasas
Buchanan
Sonora
Junction

Rocksprings

Fredericksburg

Kerrville

San Marc
Boerne
New Braunfels

Cathedral Mt.
8860
Chinati Pk.
7730
SANTIAGO MTS.
Ojinaga
Presidio
Coyame
Cuchillo Parado
BIG BEND
NAT'L PARK
Emory Pk.
7835

Big Canyon

U.S.A.
MEXICO
SERRANÍAS
DEL BURRO

Camp Wood

San Antonio

CHIHUAHUA

Chihuahua

Aldama

Meaqui

Del Rio
Villa Acuña
Jiménez

Piedras Negras
Fuente
Zaragoza
Morelos
Nova
Allende
Guerrero
Rosales

Amistad
Res.
Brackettville
Uvalde
Hondo

Eagle Pass
Carrizo Springs
Asherton

Sabinal
Floresville
Poteet
Pleasanton
Pearsall
Crystal City
Cotulla
Fowlerton
Encinal
George
West
Corpus Christi

Naica
Gigantes
SIERRA

COAHUILA

Muzquiz
San Juan de Sabinas

Ciudad Camargo
(Santa Rosalía)

Jaco
MADRE
BOLSÓN
Sierra Mojada
Laguna de
la Leche
DE
Rey
MAPIMI
ORIENTAL

Progreso
Abasolo
Sacramento
San Buenaventura
Nadadores
Monclova

Hidalgo
del Parral
Jimenez
Villa Lopez
Valle de Allende
Santa Barbara
Villa Coronado
Escalon

Cuatro Ciénegas

Presa de
D. Martin

Hidalgo
Dolores
San Diego
Ali

Nuevo Laredo
Laredo
Mirando City
Kingsv
Premont
Falfurrias
Hebbronville

Rosario
Villa
Ocampo
Indé
Santa Cruz

Paloma
Rio de la Parrida
Cerro

MEXICO

DURANGO

Santa Barbara
Escalon

Lampazos
Bustamante
Villaldama
Sabinas Hidalgo
Aguileguas
Zapata
Guerrero
Camargo
Mier
Riogrande
Mission
McAlle
Edinb

Falcon Res.

Sabinas
Alamo

Presa
de Azucar
Reynosa
Wesloco

Rodeo
Nazas
Gómez Palacio
Lerdo
San Luis
del Cordero
Torreón
Matamoros
San Pedro de
las Colonias
Sacramento
Mapimi
Laguna de
Mayran

Laguna de
Viesca
Parras
Viesca

Cerralvo
Los Herreras
General Zuazua
Salinas Victoria
Garcia
Paredon
Ramos Arizpe
General Cepeda
Monterrey
Santa Catarina

China
Cadereyta Jimenez

NUEVO

Laguna de
Santiaguillo
San Juan del Rio
Cuencame
Rodeo
Nazas
San Luis
del Cordero
Gómez Palacio
San Juan de
Guadalupe
San Bartolo
Mazapil
Concepción
del Oro

Gomez Farias
General Cepeda
Saltillo
Arteaga
Villa de Allende
Montemorelos
Galeana
Linares

LEON

Burgos
San Fernando

Durango

Pánuco de
Coronado
Canatlán
Santa Clara
Juan Aldama

ZACATECAS

Villagrán
San Carlos

TAMAULIP

Longitude West of Greenwich

Relief

Meters	Feet
1525	5000
610	2000
305	1000
152.5	500
0 Sea Level	0
152.5	500
1525	5000
3050	10000

Scale 1:4 000 000; one inch to 64 miles. Conic Projection
Elevations and depressions are given in feet

Continued on pages 110-111

Continued on pages 114-115

ARK.

MISSISSIPPI

LOUISIANA

GULF OF MEXICO

a

HOUSTON

GALVESTON BAY

EAST BAY

BOLIVAR PENINSULA

GULF OF MEXICO

GALVESTON ISLAND

Scale 1:1 000 000

0   5   10 Miles

0   4   8   12   16 Kilometers

®RMcN.

Cities	0 to 50,000 ○	500,000 to 1,000,000 ◎
and Towns	50,000 to 500,000 ⊙	1,000,000 and over

0   20   40   60   80   100   120 Miles

0   20   40   60   80   100   120   140   160   180   200 Kilometers

Continued on pages 98-99

Continued on pages 110-111

Continued on pages 112-113

GULF OF MEXICO

A-520598-76- -:-7-11
COPYRIGHT BY
RAND McNALLY & COMPANY
MADE IN U.S.A.

Longitude West of Greenwich

Scale 1:4 000 000; one inch to 64 miles. Conic Projection
Elevations and depressions are given in feet

Relief

Meters		Feet
1525		5000
610		2000
305		1000
152.5		500
0	Sea Level	0
152.5		500
1525		5000

Same scale as main map

a

a

Scale 1:16 000 000; one inch to 250 miles. Polyconic Projection
Elevations and depressions are given in feet

A-530000-76-9 8-25
COPYRIGHT BY
RAND McNALLY & COMPANY
MADE IN U.S.A.

b

ATLANTIC OCEAN

Arecibo • • San Juan
• Aguadilla • Bayamón   CABEZAS DE   St. Thomas   TORTOLA
PTA. HIGUERO   Utuado   SAN JUAN   (U.S.A.)   (Br.)
PUERTO RICO   Fajardo   CULEBRA   Charlotte   ST. JOHN
• Mayagüez   (U.S.A.) • Caguas   Vieques   Amalie   (U.S.A.)
            • Caamo • Cayey   Humacao   VIEQUES
CABO ROJO   • Ponce   • Salinas   • Guayama
                                        Christiansted
CARIBBEAN   SEA   SAINT CROIX
                                        (U.S.A.)

Scale 1:4 000 000
0   10   20   30   40 Miles
0 10 20 30 40 50 60 Kilometers
©RMcN

c

OUTER BRASS   LITTLE   64°50'
                HANS LOLLICK
INNER BRASS   PICARA PT   HANS LOLLICK
STORMY PT   THATCH CAY   GRASS
                                    CAY
        ST. △ THOMAS   18°
        Crown Mt. (U.S.A.)   Charlotte Amalie
        1558   (St. Thomas)
WATER   Nadir   20'
FLAMINGO PT   St. Thomas
©RMcN   Harbor   Scale 1:500 000

Continued on pages 130-131

Relief
Meters   Feet
3050   10 000
1525   5000
610   2000
305   1000
152.5   500
0   Sea Level
152.5   500
1525   5000
3050   10 000
6100   20 000

Cities
and
Towns
0 to 50,000   o   500,000 to 1,000,000
50,000 to 500,000   ⊙   1,000,000 and over

0   50   100   200   300   400   500 Miles
0   100   200   400   600   800 Kilometers

Longitude West of Greenwich

Continued on pages 112-113

106°   104°   102°   100°

24°

San Dimas

Durango

Miguel Auza   Juan Aldama

Nieves

Gruñidora

N U E V O
Ascensión
Aramberri   Hidalgo   Jiménez

S   Padilla   Absol

El Salto   Nombre de Dios   L E Ó N
Zaragoza

Vanegas   Cedral
Doctor Arroyo   Ciudad Victoria

Miquihuana   TAMAULIPA

Pánuco   Río Grande
Mezquital   La Paz

Siqueros   Concordia   Pueblo   Chalchihuites   Sain Alto   Cañitas   Matehuala
Nuevo   10 100   Sombrerete   S A N   L U I S   A   Jaumave
Z A C A T E C A S   Llera   Xicotencatl

22°   Villa Unión   Rosario   11 700   Charcas   Venado   Ocampo   Magiscatzin   Gonzale
Escuinapa   Fresnillo   Moctezuma   Ciudad Mante

Santa María   Calera   Ramos   Guadalcázar   P O T O S Í   El Ebano
de Ocotán   Víctor Rosales   Peotillos   Cerritos   Ciudad del Maíz   Tamuín   Panuc
San Felipe   C. Pimal   Valparaíso   Morelos   Troncoso   Bocas   Ciudad Valles

Rosamorada   San Juan   Huejuquilla el Alto   Ciudad   Zacatecas   Ojocaliente   11 000   Soledad Díez Gutiérrez   Pastora   Alaquines   General Pedro   Xilitla
Capistrano   García   Luis Moya   San Luis   Pozos   Antonio Santos
Ruiz   Mezquitic   Huejúcar   Asientos   Potosí   Zaragoza   Rayón   Lagunillas   San Martín   Chalchicuau
N A Y A R I T   Monte   Villanueva   Tepezala   A G U A S C A L I E N T E S   Gogorrón   Ojo Caliente   Ríoverde   Arroyo Seco   Tanto
Escobedo   Sta. María de   Villa García   San Felipe   Villa Pedro   Xilitla   Platón
Tuxpan   Sta. María   los Ángeles   Rincón   Sta. María del Río   Montoya   Calnalí   Chicdin
San Blas   de Oro   Colotlán   de Romoso   San Luis   Dolores Hidalgo   10 469   Jacala   Huautla

a

MEXICO

MÉXICO
Morelos
Cuautitlán
Tecamac
Teotihuacán
Otumba
Apan
HIDALGO
Nicolás Romero
Tutitlán
Acolman
Chiconautla
Pyramids of Teotihuacán
Calpulalpan
Cahuacán
Coacalco
Tepexpan
San Bartolo
Atizapán
Tulpetlac
Tepetlaoxtoc
TLAXCALA
Ixtlahuaca
Cerro La Catedral 13 000
Mazatla
Tlalnepantla
Texcoco
San Jerónimo
Nanacamilpa
Jiquipilco
Atzcapotzalco
Gustavo A. Madero
Lago de Texcoco (Dry Lake)
Coatlinchán
Temoaya
Naucalpan de Juárez
MEXICO CITY
Chicoloapan
Mimiapan
Chimalpa
Nezahualcóyotl
PUEBLA
Huixquilucan
Cuajimalpa
Iztacalco
Ixtapalapa
Los Reyes
Río Frío
HY
Toluca
Lerma
Villa Obregón Contreras
Coyoacán
Ayotla
INTER-AMERICAN
Ixtapaluca
Texmelucan
Capultitlán
Tlálpan
Xochimilco
Tláhuac
Metepec
San Andrés
Cerro Muneco 12 655
Ajusco
DISTRITO
Tecómitl
Tlalmanalco
Mexicalcingo
Chalco
Almoloya
Cerro Ajusco 12 850
FEDERAL
Milpa Alta
Tenango
Iztaccíhuatl 17 343
Nevado de Toluca 14 409
Coatepec
Oxtotepec
Amecameca
Tenango
Tres Cumbres
Ozumba
Volcán Popocatépetl 17 887
Huitzilac
Tepoztlán
Tlalnepantla
MORELOS
Tlayacapan
Cuernavaca
Scale 1:1 000 000
©RMCN.

GULF OF MEXICO

Tropic of Cancer

Laguna Almagre
PTA. JEREZ
Laguna de San Andrés
amira
iudad Madero
Tampico
Villa Cuauhtémoc
Tampico Alto
Laguna Tamiahua
luama
Tancoco
Tamiahua
CABO ROJO
ARRECIFE BLANQUILLA
ISLA DE LOBOS
Alamo
Túxpan
ARRECIFE TANQUIJO
ARRECIFE TÚXPAN
palapa
Poza Rica
Tecolutla
Gutiérrez Zamora
Coyutla
Furbero
Nautla
Tihuatlán
Tecolutla
Vega de Alatorre
tlapan
Cuetzalan del Progreso
Misantla
atlán
Atempan
Jalacingo
Altotonga
poaxtla
Teziutlán
Naolinco
BAHÍA DE CAMPECHE
Las Vigas
PUNTA ZEMPOALA
Libres
Perote
14 048
Xalapa
nantla
Nauchampatepetl
Coatepec
Antigua Veracruz
Teocelo
Punta Zempoala
 an Juan
xtenco
18 406
Huatusco
◎**Veracruz**
Ciudad Serdán
Pico de Orizaba (Vol.)
Cascomatepec
ARRECIFE CABEZA
aca
Acatzingo de Hidalgo
Orizaba
Córdoba
Tlalixcoyan
oyatempan
Heroica Nogales
Omealca
Alvarado
CAMPECHE
acotepec
Maltrata
Medellín
ISLA DEL CARMEN
Laguna de Términos
Chicbul
Tehuacan
Ajalpan
Tierra Blanca
San Martín (Vol.) 6000
PTA. ZAPOTITLÁN
San Pedro
Mamantel
San Gabriel Chilac
Zoquitlán
Santiago Tuxtla
San Andrés Tuxtla
Catemaco
Pajápan
Ciudad del Carmen
Chazumba
Zinacatepec
Cosamaloápan
Chacaltianguis
Coatzacoalcos (Puerto México)
PUNTA FONTERA
Frontera
Palizada
tlalcingo
Miguel
Huatla de Jiménez
Ojitlán (S. Lucas)
Tésecheacan
Soteapan
Paraíso
Allende
Teotitlán del Camino
Jalapa de Díaz (San Felipe)
Tuxtepec
Jaltipan
Coatzacoalco
Comalcalco
Jalpa B
Teapa
Tepelmeme
San Juan Evangelista
Acayucan
Minatitlán
Cunduacán
Jonuta
MEXICO
Huajuapan de León
Cuicatlán
Playa Vicente
Sayula
Texistepec
Cárdenas
Villahermosa
San Carlos
Tacotalpa
Balancán
GUATEMALA
azulapan Progreso
Coixtlahuaca
Tejúpan (Santiago)
Huimanguillo
Emiliano Zapata
Teposcolula
Nochixtlán (Asunción)
Talea de Castro (San Miguel)
Jesús Carranza
Pueblo Viejo
Teapa
Pichucalco
Patenque
Tenosique
Pedro y San Pablo
Tlaxiaco
Sta. María Asunción
Ixtlán de Juárez
Villa Alta (San Ildefonso)
ISTMO
Chapultenango
Yajalón
Hidalgo Yalalag
Zempoaltepetl 11 142
Zacatepec (Santiago)
DE
Tecpatán
Pantepec
Simojovel
Bachajón
Ocosingo
San Mateo (Etlatongo)
Tlacolula de Matamoros
Mazatlán (San Juan)
Guichicovi (San Juan)
Compainalá
Jitotol
Oaxaca
Zaachila
Tlaxiaco
TEHUANTEPEC
CHIAPAS
MESETA DE AGUA ESCONDIDA
Zimatlán de Álvarez
Ocotlán de Morelos
Tuxtla Gutiérrez 9400
Bohom
Cancuc
Oxchuc
San Cristóbal de las Casas
Sola de Vega (S. Miguel)
Táviche (San Miguel)
INTER-AMERICAN HY
Berriozábal
Ozocoautla
Chiapa de Corzo
Acala
Amatenango
Ejutla de Crespo
Jalapa del Marqués
Ixtepec
Ixtaltepec (Asunción)
Zanatepec (Sto. Domingo)
Unión Hidalgo
Cintalapa
Las Cruces
Suchiapa
Teopisca
Las Rosas
Comitán
Miahuatlán
Juchitán de Zaragoza
Tapanatepec
Venustiano Carranza
Socoltenango
Las Vacas
Tehuantepec Sta. Domingo
Ixhuatán (San Francisco) 8202
Villa Flores
La Concordia
Trinitaria
Loxicha (Sta. Catarina)
Arriaga
Tonalá
SA. CUCHUMATANES
SIERRA DE OAXACA
Salina Cruz
CORD. DE CHIAPAS
SIERRA MADRE
GUATEMALA
Pluma Hidalgo
Golfo de Tehuantepec
Cuauhtémoc
Jacatango
Pochutla (San Pedro)
Puerto Ángel
Pijilipan
Mapastepec
San Miguel

YUCATÁN
Sisal
Hunucmá
Maxcanú
Halachó
Calkiní
Dzitbalché
Hecelchakán
Lerma
Campeche
Seybaplaya
Champotón
Pustunich
Sabancuy

Continued on pages 120-121

For larger scale coverage of Mexico City see page 233.

0 20 40 60 80 100 120 Miles
0 20 40 60 80 100 120 140 160 180 200 Kilometers

Continued on pages 118-119

Continued in inset below

MEXICO

BELIZE

GUATEMALA

HONDURAS

EL SALVADOR

NICARAGUA

Gulf of Honduras

PACIFIC OCEAN

SA. DE LOS CUCHUMATANES

SA. DE CHAMA

SA. DE LAS MINAS

SA. DE MERENDÓN

CORDILLERA DE AGALTA

CORDILLERA ISABELLA

Tegucigalpa

San Salvador

Guatemala

Quezaltenango

Managua

Comitán
Trinitaria (Zapaluta)
Cuauhtemoc
Jacaltenango
La Libertad
Santa Cruz Barillas
Huehuetenango
Cobán
S. Cristóbal
Panzós
Izabal
Livingston
Puerto Barrios
Puerto Cortés
Omoa
San Pedro Sula
Villanueva
Macuelizo
Monkey River
Punta Gorda
Barranco
ROATÁN
Roatan
UTILA
Puerto Castilla
Limón
Iriona
Trujillo
Tocoa
La Ceiba
Tela
Salado
Balfate
Nueva Armenia
Progreso
Olanchito
Yoro
San Esteban
Catacamas
Juticalpa
Minas de Oro
Salamá
Cedros
Comayagua
La Paz
Talanga
Danlí
El Paraíso
Yuscarán
Sabanagrande
Ocotal
Somoto
Condega
Estelí
Jinotega
Matagalpa
Ciudad Darío
Sébaco
Boaco
Santo Domingo
Juigalpa
León
Chinandega
Corinto
Nagarote
Masaya
Granada
Diriamba
Jinotepe
Rivas
San Juan del Sur
La Cruz
Liberia
Cañas
Filadelfia
Santa Cruz
Nicoya
Tacaná (Vol.) 13341
Tajumulco (Vol.) 13 845
S. Marcos
Tapachula
Ayutla
Coatepeque
Retalhuleu
Ocós
Champerico
Concepción del Mar
San José
Acajutla
La Libertad
La Unión
Amapala
El Triunfo
Cosigüina (Vol.) 2 776
El Viejo (Vol.) 5839
Telica (Vol.) 3409
Las Pilas (Vol.) 3515
Momotombo
Concepción (Vol.) 5106
Madera (Vol.) 4960
ISLA ZAPATERA
ISLA DE OMOTEPE

Golfo de Fonseca

Lago de Managua

Lago de Nicaragua

Golfo del Papagayo

Bahía de Salinas

PEN. DE NICOYA

CORD. DE DARIÉN

Inset map (a)

GULF OF MEXICO

YUCATAN

YUCATAN PENINSULA

QUINTANA ROO

MEXICO

CAMPECHE

BELIZE

GUATEMALA

CARIBBEAN SEA

Mérida
Progreso
Sisal
Celestún
Hunucmá
Umán
Maxcanú
Halachó
Becal
Calkiní
Nunkiní
Hecelchakán
Dzitbalché
Pomuch
Tenabó
Campeche
Hool
Hopelchén
Iturbide
Dzibalchén
Bolonchenticul
Chicxulub
Dzidzantún
Dzilam González
Cansahcab
Motul
Temax
Tizimín
Panabá
El Cuyo
Holbox
ISLA HOLBOX
Isla Mujeres
Cancún
Kantunilkín
Espita
Calotmul
Valladolid
Chichimilá
Cozumel
ISLA DE COZUMEL
Coba (Ruins)
Tulum (Ruins)
Chichen Itzá (Ruins)
Izamal
Hoctún
Seyé
Acanceh
Kanasín
Tecoh
Tekit
Muna
Ticul
Uxmal (Ruins)
Oxkutzcab
Tekax de Álvaro Obregón
Tzucacab
Peto
Felipe Carrillo Puerto
Pedro Antonio Santos (Sta. Cruz Chico)
Ciudad Chetumal (Payo Obispo)
Corozal
Xcalak
Orange Walk
Belize City
Belmopan
San Ignacio
Benque Viejo
Mullins River
Stann Creek
All Pines
Tikal (Ruins)
Flores
La Libertad
Victoria Peak 3681
MONTAÑAS MAYAS
Monkey River
AMBERGRIS CAY
TURNEFFE
BANCO CHINCHORRO
Laguna de Bacalar
L. Ocom

PUNTA NICCHEHABIN
PUNTA HERRERO
Bahía de la Ascención
Bahía del Espíritu Santo

Same scale as main map

©RMcN.

A-539200-76 7-518
COPYRIGHT BY
RAND McNALLY & COMPANY
MADE IN U.S.A.

Longitude West of Greenwich

Scale 1:4 000 000; one inch to 64 miles. Sinusoidal Projection

Elevations and depressions are given in feet

Cities and Towns

0 to 50,000 ○	500,000 to 1,000,000 ◎	
50,000 to 500,000 ⊙	1,000,000 and over	

Longitude West of Greenwich

Relief

Meters	Feet
3050	10 000
1525	5000
610	2000
305	1000
152.5	500
Sea Level	
152.5	500
1525	5000
3050	10 000

b

ANGUILLA (Br.)
ST. MARTIN (Neth. and Fr.)
ST BARTHÉLEMY (Fr.)
SABA (Neth.)
Codrington BARBUDA
ST. EUSTATIUS (Neth.)
Mt. Misery 3792 ST KITTS
Basseterre
ST. KITTS AND NEVIS
Charlestown Nevis Peak 3596 St Johns
NEVIS Boggy Peak 1319 **ANTIGUA AND BARBUDA**
REDONDA
MONTSERRAT (Br.)
Plymouth Chances Pk. 3000

L E E W A R D

Guadeloupe Passage

POINTE DE LA GRANDE VIGIE
GRANDE TERRE
Ste. Rose Le Moule
DESIRADE (Fr.)
Pointe-à-Pitre Ste. Anne PETITE TERRE (Fr.)
BASSE TERRE Soufrière 4813 Capesterre (Fr.) **GUADELOUPE**
Basse Terre MARIE GALANTE
LES SAINTES IS. Grand Bourg

I S.

Portsmouth Morne Diablotins 4747
St. Joseph **DOMINICA**
Roseau

Dominica Channel

Mt. Pelée (Vol.) 4583 Trinité
St. Pierre Pitons du Carbet 3960
Fort-de-France Le François **MARTINIQUE** (Fr.)
Le Marin
POINTE D'ENFER

St. Lucia Channel

Castries
Morne Gimie 3117 **ST. LUCIA**
Soufrière

St. Vincent Passage

Soufrière 4048
ST. VINCENT AND THE GRENADINES
Kingstown
BEQUIA
MUSTIQUE
CANOUAN

CARRIACOU

Mt. St. Catherine 2757 Grenville
St. George's **GRENADA**

NORTH POIN
BARBADOS Mt. Hillaby 1115 Bathsheba
Bridgetown
SOUTH POINT

W I N D W A R D

C A R I B B E A N   S E A

THE GRENADINES

©RMcN

Same scale as main map

A T L A N T I C   O C E A N

PUNTA PATUCA
COLÓN
Cabo Gracias a Dios
CAYOS MISKITO

C A R I B B E A N

M O S Q U I T O S

Laguna Caratasca
Puerto Cabezas
Lone Star Laguna Carata
Huaunta Laguna Huaunta
Prinzapolca Prinzapolca

D E

C O S T A

Rama
Bluefields
ISLA DE LA CIERVO
PUNTA MICO

Laguna las Perlas

ISLA DE PROVIDENCIA (Colombia)

SAN ANDRÉS (Colombia)
CAYOS DE ESE

LITTLE CORN
GREAT CORN (Nicaragua)
CAYOS DE ALBUQUERQUE (Colombia)

S E A

Bahía de San Juan del Norte
San Juan del Norte (Greytown)
San Carlos

San Ramón Guápiles Cairo Matina
Alajuela Heredia Turrialba Limón
San José Irazú Vol.
Cartago Paraíso
Parrita

C O S T A   R I C A

Cordillera de Talamanca
Cerro Chirripó 12 530
Quepos Cerro Kámuk 11 696
San Isidro
Buenos Aires Cerro Echandi 10 394
PUNTA QUEPOS Guabito
Bahía de Coronada Volcán Barú 11 401
Puerto Cortés Boquete
Golfito Concepción
ISLA DE CAÑO David
PENÍNSULA DE OSA
Puerto Jiménez
La Cuesta
CABO MATAPALO Morsancitos
Puerto Armuelles Remedios
Bahía Charco de Azul Las Palmas
PUNTA BURICA Soná

PUNTA CAHUITA

PUNTA MANZANILLO Nombre de Dios El Porvenir PUNTA SAN BLAS
Portobelo Mandinga Golfo de San Blas
Colón C. Brewster 3018 CORD. DE SAN BLAS
Gatún Silver City Chepo
Lago Gatún North Gamboa
Balboa Heights
Balboa **Panamá**
Chorrea Bahía de Panamá
PUNTA CHAME
Bejuco
Penonomé
Antón
Nata Río Hato
ARCHIPIÉLAGO DE LAS PERLAS
San Miguel ISLA DEL REY
ISLA DE SAN JOSÉ
La Palma

P A N A M Á

SERRANÍA DEL DARIÉN

Bocas del Toro Golfo de los Mosquitos
Bahía de Almirante
Almirante
Chiriquí Grande PUNTA CHIRIQUÍ
ESCUDO DE VERAGUAS
Laguna de Chiriquí

SERRANÍA DE TABASARA
C. de Santa Catalina 5249
C. Negro 4429
Aguadulce
Santiago
Río de Jesús Golfo de Parita
Chitré Los Santos
PENÍNSULA Las Tablas
DE AZUERO
PUNTA MALA
ISLA COIBA ISLA CEBACO
Bahía Montijo
PUNTA MARIATO
ISLA JICARÓN
Golfo de Chiriquí
Golfo de Panamá

CABO TIBURÓN

El Real
Garachiné
PUNTA GARACHINE

COLOMBIA

0 20 40 60 80 100 120 Miles
0 20 40 60 80 100 120 140 160 180 200 Kilometers

FLORIDA

Naples
Delray Beach
Fort Lauderdale
Dania
Miami Beach
MIAMI
Homestead
Everglades
EVERGLADES
NATIONAL PARK

GULF

OF

MEXICO

Dry Tortugas
Marquesas Keys
Key West
Pine Is.
KEY LARGO
Cape Sable
Florida Bay
Cape Romano
Ten Thousand Islands
Sanibel
Seminole Ind. Res.
The Everglades
Big Cypress Swamp

FLORIDA KEYS

Straits of Florida

Tropic of Cancer

LITTLE BAHAMA BANK
GREAT SALE CAY
LITTLE ABACO
GREAT ABACO
Marsh Harbour
Elbow Cay
Cherokee Cha
Settlement Pt.
West End
Freeport
GRAND BAHAMA
Pinder Point
Northwest Providence Channel
Great Isaac
Brothers
Little Isaac
North Bimini
South Bimini
N. Cat Cay
Barnett Harbor
Riding Rocks
Dollar Harbor
Orange Cay
Great Stirrup Cay
Great Harbour Cay
Berry Islands
Bonds Cay
Whale Cay
Frazers Hog Cay
Cornwall
Southwest Pt.
Royal
Joulter's Cays
Nicolls Town
Simms Pt.
Nassau
Paradise
New Providence
Ship Channel Cay
Highborne Cay
Staniard Creek
Williams
Andros Island
Salvador Pt.
North Bight
Middle Bight
South Bight
Shroud Ca
Turner Sound
Green Cay
Booby Ro
Tongue of the Ocean
Snap Pt.
Curly Cut Cays
Hurricane Flats
Nicholas Channel
Santaren Channel
Cay Sal Bank
North Elbow Cays
Damas Cays
Cay Sal
Anguilla Cays
Dog Rocks
Cayo Blancos
Archipiélago de Sabana
Cayo Santa María
Cayo Coco
Old Bahama Channel
Cayo Lobos
Cayo Cruz
Cayo Romano
Cayo Guajaba
Cayo Sabinal
Nuevitas

CUBA

Havana
Ciudad de la Habana
Marianao
Regla
Guanabacoa
Guanajay
San Antonio de los Baños
Artemisa
Bejucal
Güines
Güira de Melena
Batabanó
Union de Reyes
Alacranes
Matanzas
Cárdenas
Corralillo
Martí
Jovellanos
Quemado de Güines
Sagua la Grande
Colón
Pedro Betancourt
Jagüey Grande
Navajas
Bolondrón
Santo Domingo
Cruces
Rodas
Aguada Lajas
Esperanza
Santa Clara
Remedios
Caibarién
Camajuaní
Zulueta
Yaguajay
Palmira
Cienfuegos
Placetas
Florida
Sancti Spíritus
Jatibonico
Morón
Trinidad
Casilda
Sánct. Spíritus
Ciego de Ávila
Júcaro
Jatibonico
Tunas de Zaza
Fomento
Camagüey
Minas
Santa Lucía
Puerto Padr
Las Tunas
Victoria de las Tunas
Guayabal
Santa Cruz del Sur
Manzanillo
Campechuela
Granma
Sierra
Niquero
Pico Ojo del Toro 1748
Cabo Cruz

PINAR DEL RIO
Pan de Guajaibón 2532
Consolación del Sur
Candelaria
Los Palacios
Pinar del Río
San Juan Martínez
Mantua
Guane
Pta. Frances
Cabo Frances
Cabo Corrientes
Cabo Pepe
Archipiélago de los Colorados
Sierra de los Órganos
Vueltabajo
Bahía Honda
Santa Lucía
Bahía Guadiana
Ensenada de Cortés
Pen. de Guanahacabibes
Nueva Gerona
Santa Fé
Isla de la Juventud
Cayos de Juan Luis
Cayos de los Indios
Cayos de San Felipe
Archipiélago de los Canarreos
Cayo de Dios
Islas de Mangles
Cayo Largo
Cayo Rosario
Cayo Cantiles
Golfo de Batabanó
Punta Gorda
Península de Zapata
Ensenada de la Broa
Golfo de Cazones
Bahía de Cochinos
Banco Jardines
Banco Xagua
Cayos de las Doce Leguas
Laberinto de las Doce Leguas
Canal de Caballones
Cayos Cinco Balas
Cayos Ana María
Golfo de Guacanayabo
Bahía de Perros
Bahía Buena Vista
Turiguano
Laguna de Leche
Santaren Channel

Pico San Juan 1156
Sierra de Trinidad
Pico Turquino 2045

GOLFO DE

CARIBBEAN

SEA

CAYMAN ISLANDS
Little Cayman
Cayman Brac (Br.)
George Town
Grand Cayman

JAMAICA
Montego Bay
Lucea
Falmouth
St. Ann's Bay
Galina
Port Ma
South Negril Pt.
Savanna la Mar
Mt. Denham 2256
Annotto Bay
Black River
Bull Head 2728
May Pen
Spanish To
Kingston
Gt. Pedro Bluff
Portland Bight
Portland Pt.

Longitude West of Greenwich

Relief

Meters	Feet
3050	10 000
1525	5000
610	2000
305	1000
152.5	500
0	Sea Level 0
152.5	500
1525	5000
3050	10 000
6100	20 000

Cities and Towns

0 to 50,000
50,000 to 500,000
500,000 to 1,000,000
1,000,000 and over

Scale 1:4 000 000; one inch to 64 miles. Conic Projection
Elevations and depressions are given in feet.

Scale 1:1 000 000

HAVANA
(La Habana)

GULF OF MEXICO

Playa de Guanabo

Cojimar

Guanabacoa

Regla

Campo Florido

San Francisco de Paula

Playa de Santa Fé

Marianao

Baracoa

Cotorro

Arroya Arena

Calabazar

Rancho Boyeros

Cuatro Caminos

Bauta

Managua

San José de las Lajas

Caimito del Guayabal

Santiago de las Vegas

Bejucal

La Sabina

Ceiba del Agua

San Antonio de los Baños

Buenaventura

San Antonio de las Vegas

©RMcN. △ 950

JAMES PT.

Governor's Harbour

PALMETTO PT.

ELEUTHERA

Rock Sound

A T L A N T I C

Arthur's Town

NORTHEAST PT.

EUTHERA PT.

LITTLE SAN SALVADOR

CAT

Old Bight

O C E A N

HAWKS NEST PT.

COLUMBUS PT.

SAN SALVADOR
(WATLING)
(Columbus, Oct. 12, 1492)

GREAT GUANA CAY

CONCEPTIÓN

SOUTHWEST PT.

LEE STOCKING

CAPE STA. MARIA

RUM CAY

GREAT EXUMA

Rolleville

George Town

Tropic of Cancer

LITTLE EXUMA

HOG CAY

LONG

24°

JUMENTO CAYS

Clarence Town

SAMANA OR ATWOOD CAY

WATER CAY

FLAMINGO CAY

CAP VERDE

BIRD ROCK

CROOKED

NORTHEAST PT.

JAMAICA CAY

FORTUNE

PLANA OR FLAT CAYS

Man of War Channel

SEAL CAYS

DIANA BANK

FISH CAY

ACKLINS

The Bight of Acklins

Abraham's Bay

MAYAGUANA

NURSE CAY

SALINA PT.

RACCOON CAY

CASTLE

OCHINOS BANKS

GREAT RAGGED

MIRA POR VOS ISLETS

CAY VERDE

22°

COLUMBUS BANK

NORTH CAICOS

CAY STA. DOMINGO

PROVIDENCIALES

GRAND CAICOS

CAPE COMETE

EAST CAICOS

HOGSTY REEF

CAICOS IS.
(Br.)

WEST CAICOS

GRAND TURK

LITTLE INAGUA

SOUTH CAICOS

Grand Turk

CAICOS BANK

TURKS IS. (Br.)

BROWN BANK

WEST SAND SPIT

AMBERGRIS CAYS

SALT CAY

NORTHEAST PT.

PALMETTO PT.

Ocean Bight

SEAL CAYS

MOUCHOIR BANK

Tucks I. Passage

Mouchoir Passage

Gibara

CABO LUCRECIA

Holguin

Banes

Antilla

Bahía de Nipe

The Lake

GREAT INAGUA

Man of War Bay

Matthew Town

Silver Bank Passage

SILVER BANK

OLGUÍN

Mayari

a Sagua de Tánamo

CUCHILLAS DE TOAR

20°

Cauto

SA. DE NIPE

3100

Baracoa

NAVIDAD BANK

ESTRA

SA. DEL PURIAL

PUNTA MAISÍ

GUANTANAMO

ILE DE LA TORTUE

CABO ISABELA

DE CUBA

Alto Songo

Bahía de Ovando

Canal de la Tortue

Monte Cristi

Puerto Plata

na Soriano

Canex

401

Gran Piedra

Port de Paix

Le Borgne

Cap-Haïtien

CORDILLERA SEPTENTRIONAL

Pico Diego de Ocampo

San Luis

Caimanera

Yateras

Le Môle

Limbé

Fort Liberté

Guayubin

Dajabón

4009

Mao

Gaspar Hernández

CABO FRANCÉS VIEJO

Santiago de Cuba

Naval Station (U.S.A.)

CAP ST. NICOLAS

Grande Rivière du Nord

Santiago Rodríguez

Moca

San Francisco de Macorís

Nagua

Bahía de Samaná

Bahía de Gnanana

PTE. PLATEFORME

Gonaïves

Ouanaminthe

Valliere

Santiago de los Caballeros

VEGA

La Vega

CABO SAMANÁ

GOLFE DES GONAÏVES

St. Michel de l'Atalaye

Hinche

DOMINICAN

Jarabacoa

Cotuí

Rivá

Sánchez

Samaná

CABO SAN RAFAEL

Pic Bonhomme

5883

Pico Duarte

10417

Cotuí

Sabana de la Mar

Miches

HAITI

St. Marc

CORDILLERA CENTRAL

Jérémie

POINT OUEST

ILE DE LA GONÂVE

2548

Mirebalais

Lascahobas

Bánica

San Juan

Mte. Tina

9285

Yamasá

Hato Mayor

Bayaguana

Seibo

CABO DAME MARIE

ILE GRANDE CAYEMITE

Canal de Saint-Marc

Péonville

Port-au-Prince

Léogane

REPUBLIC

Los Llanos

Higüey

Anse d'Hainault

CAP DES JROIS

Baie des Baradères

Anse à Veau

SIERRA DE NEIBA

Neiba

Azua

San Cristóbal

La Romana

NAVASSA (U.S.A.)

Pico de Macaya

7920

MASSIF DE LA HOTTE

Miragoâne

Petit Goave

Bani

Santo Domingo

S. Pedro de Macorís

CATALINA

Tiburon

Aquin

MASSIF DE LA SELLE

8773

Duverge

Barahona

PTA. PALENQUE

Les Cayes

Roche à Bateau

Jacmel

Belle-Anse

SIERRA DE BAHORUCO

SAONA

POINTE À GRAVOIS

ILE À VACHE

H

I

S

P

A

N

I

O

L

A

Port Antonio

MORANT PT.

Enriquillo

Oviedo

Trujin

CABO FALSO

CABO BEATA

BEATA

ALTO VELO

70°

For larger scale coverage
of Havana see page 233.

0 10 20 30 40 50 60 70 80 90 100 110 120 Miles

0 20 40 60 80 100 120 140 160 180 200 Kilometers

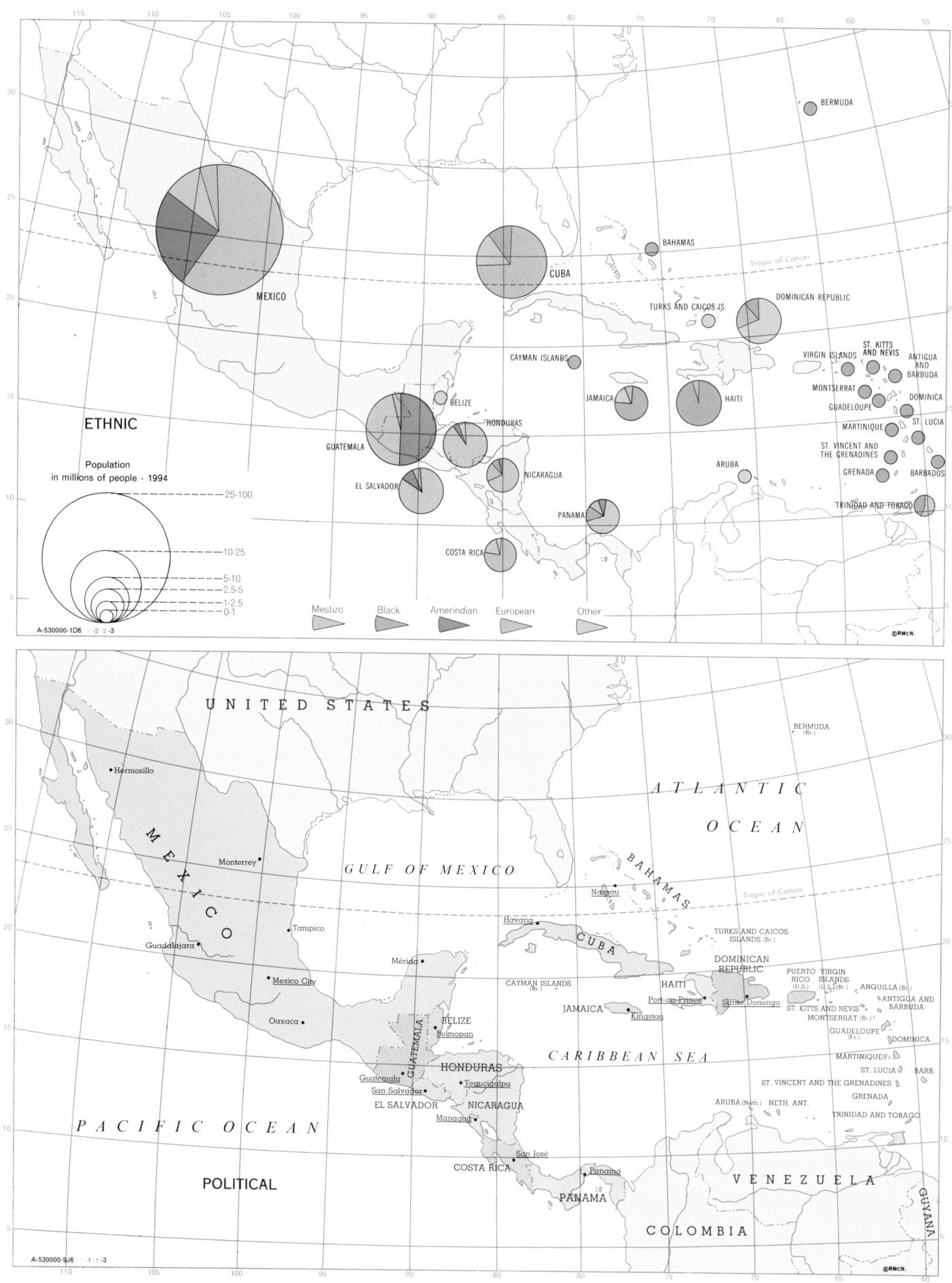

ETHNIC

Population
in millions of people - 1994

25-100
10-25
5-10
2.5-5
1-2.5
0-1

A-530000-1D6

Mestizo   Black   Amerindian   European   Other

MEXICO

BERMUDA

BAHAMAS

CUBA

TURKS AND CAICOS IS.

DOMINICAN REPUBLIC

CAYMAN ISLANDS

ST. KITTS AND NEVIS

VIRGIN ISLANDS

ANTIGUA AND BARBUDA

MONTSERRAT

BELIZE

JAMAICA

HAITI

DOMINICA

GUADELOUPE

HONDURAS

GUATEMALA

MARTINIQUE

ST. LUCIA

EL SALVADOR

NICARAGUA

ST. VINCENT AND THE GRENADINES

ARUBA

GRENADA

BARBADOS

PANAMA

TRINIDAD AND TOBAGO

COSTA RICA

©RMCN.

UNITED STATES

BERMUDA
(Br.)

ATLANTIC

OCEAN

Hermosillo

M E X I C O

Monterrey

GULF OF MEXICO

BAHAMAS

Tropic of Cancer

Tampico

Nassau

Guadalajara

Mérida

Havana

CUBA

TURKS AND CAICOS
ISLANDS (Br.)

Mexico City

CAYMAN ISLANDS
(Br.)

DOMINICAN
REPUBLIC

PUERTO VIRGIN
RICO ISLANDS
(U.S.) (U.S.) (Br.)

ANGUILLA (Br.)

Oaxaca

HAITI

Port-au-Prince

Santo Domingo

ANTIGUA AND
BARBUDA

ST. KITTS AND NEVIS

JAMAICA

Kingston

MONTSERRAT (Br.)

BELIZE

GUATEMALA

Belmopan

GUADELOUPE
(Fr.)

HONDURAS

CARIBBEAN SEA

DOMINICA

Guatemala

Tegucigalpa

MARTINIQUE (Fr.)

San Salvador

ST. LUCIA

BARB.

EL SALVADOR

NICARAGUA

ST. VINCENT AND THE GRENADINES

Managua

ARUBA (Neth.)

NETH. ANT.

GRENADA

PACIFIC OCEAN

San José

TRINIDAD AND TOBAGO

COSTA RICA

Panamá

VENEZUELA

POLITICAL

PANAMA

GUYANA

COLOMBIA

A-530000-6J6

©RMCN.

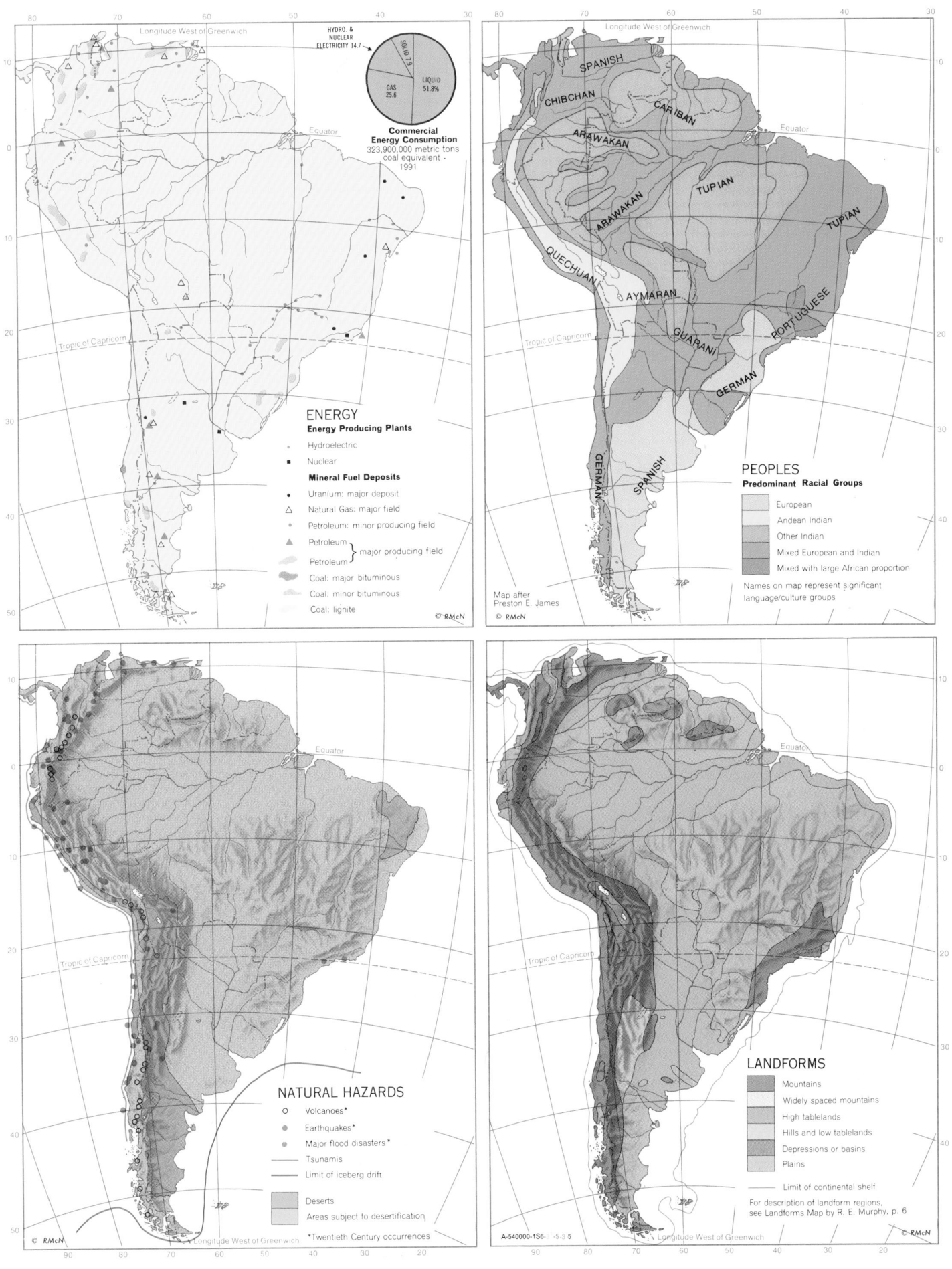

ENERGY

Energy Producing Plants
- Hydroelectric
- Nuclear

Mineral Fuel Deposits
- Uranium: major deposit
- Natural Gas: major field
- Petroleum: minor producing field
- Petroleum } major producing field
- Petroleum
- Coal: major bituminous
- Coal: minor bituminous
- Coal: lignite

HYDRO. & NUCLEAR ELECTRICITY 14.7

SOLID 7.9
LIQUID 51.8%
GAS 25.6

Commercial Energy Consumption
323,900,000 metric tons coal equivalent - 1991

© RMcN

PEOPLES
Predominant Racial Groups
- European
- Andean Indian
- Other Indian
- Mixed European and Indian
- Mixed with large African proportion

Names on map represent significant language/culture groups

Map after Preston E. James
© RMcN

SPANISH
CHIBCHAN
ARAWAKAN
ARAWAKAN
QUECHUAN
AYMARAN
CARIBAN
TUPIAN
TUPIAN
GUARANI
PORTUGUESE
GERMAN
GERMAN
SPANISH

NATURAL HAZARDS
- Volcanoes*
- Earthquakes*
- Major flood disasters*
- Tsunamis
- Limit of iceberg drift
- Deserts
- Areas subject to desertification

*Twentieth Century occurrences

© RMcN
A-540000-1S6-   -5-3 5

LANDFORMS
- Mountains
- Widely spaced mountains
- High tablelands
- Hills and low tablelands
- Depressions or basins
- Plains
- Limit of continental shelf

For description of landform regions, see Landforms Map by R. E. Murphy, p. 6

© RMcN

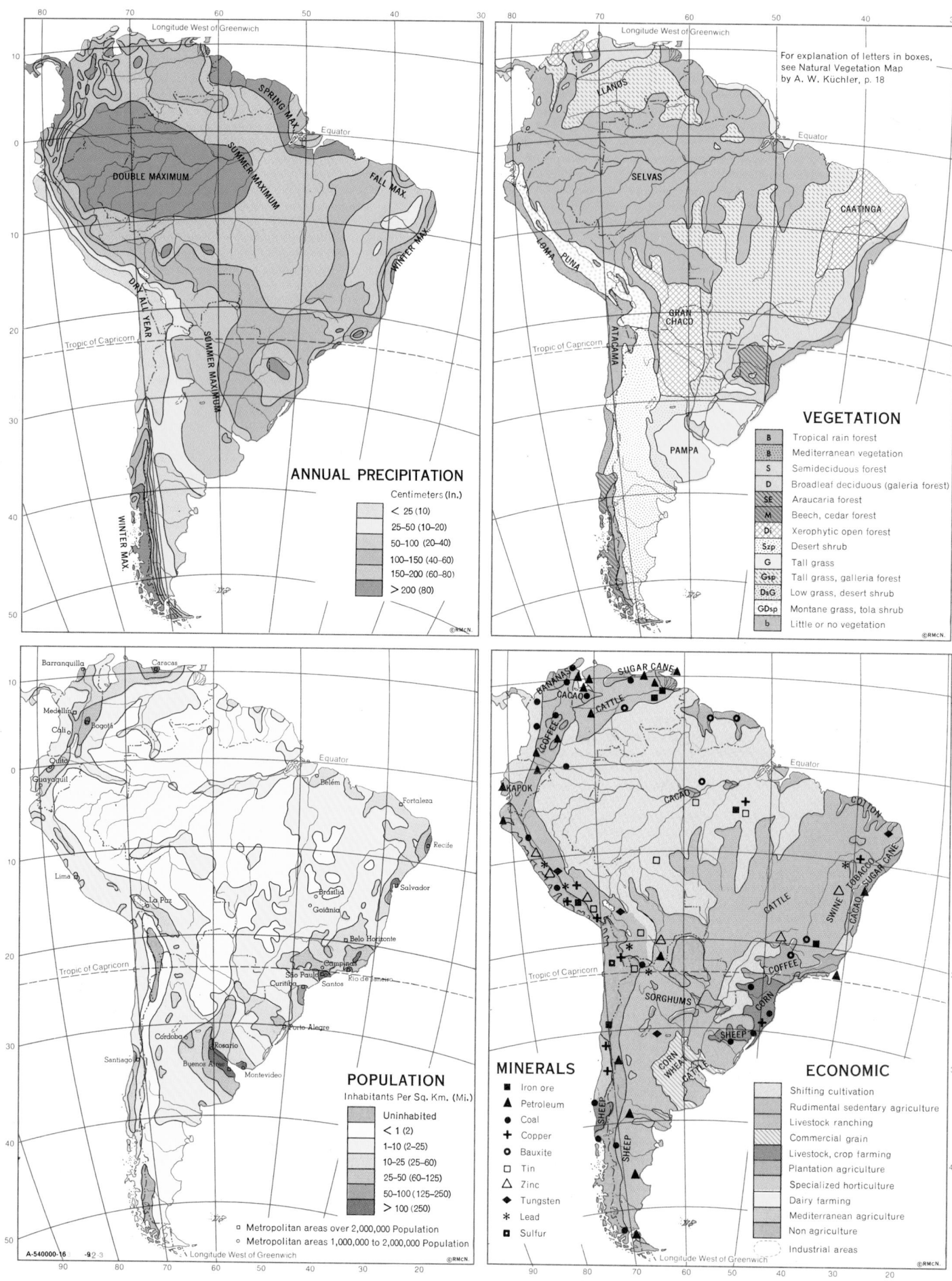

ANNUAL PRECIPITATION

Centimeters (In.)

- < 25 (10)
- 25–50 (10–20)
- 50–100 (20–40)
- 100–150 (40–60)
- 150–200 (60–80)
- > 200 (80)

VEGETATION

For explanation of letters in boxes, see Natural Vegetation Map by A. W. Küchler, p. 18

B	Tropical rain forest
B	Mediterranean vegetation
S	Semideciduous forest
D	Broadleaf deciduous (galeria forest)
SE	Araucaria forest
M	Beech, cedar forest
Di	Xerophytic open forest
Szp	Desert shrub
G	Tall grass
Gsp	Tall grass, galleria forest
DsG	Low grass, desert shrub
GDsp	Montane grass, tola shrub
b	Little or no vegetation

POPULATION

Inhabitants Per Sq. Km. (Mi.)

- Uninhabited
- < 1 (2)
- 1–10 (2–25)
- 10–25 (25–60)
- 25–50 (60–125)
- 50–100 (125–250)
- > 100 (250)

□ Metropolitan areas over 2,000,000 Population
○ Metropolitan areas 1,000,000 to 2,000,000 Population

A-540000-16   -9 2 -3

MINERALS

- ■ Iron ore
- ▲ Petroleum
- ● Coal
- + Copper
- ○ Bauxite
- □ Tin
- △ Zinc
- ◆ Tungsten
- ✳ Lead
- ⊡ Sulfur

ECONOMIC

- Shifting cultivation
- Rudimental sedentary agriculture
- Livestock ranching
- Commercial grain
- Livestock, crop farming
- Plantation agriculture
- Specialized horticulture
- Dairy farming
- Mediterranean agriculture
- Non agriculture
- Industrial areas

CUBA
JAMAICA
Kingston HISPANIOLA
San Juan
PUERTO
RICO

Caribbean Sea

A T L A N T I C

O C E A N

Barranquilla Maracaibo CARACAS
Port of Spain
TRINIDAD

Panamá

L L A N O S
Orinoco

Georgetown

SANTA FE
DE BOGOTÁ

Quito

Negro

Equator

Belém

Manaus

Fortaleza

Iquitos

Amazon

S E L V A S

Rio Branco

Recife

A N D E S

São
Francisco

LIMA

Salvador

La Paz

Cuiabá
M A T O
G R O S S O

Brasília

Belo Horizonte

Iquique

G R A N   C H A C O

Paraná

SÃO
PAULO

RIO DE JANEIRO

Tropic of Capricorn

Asunción

San Miguel
de Tucumán

Porto Alegre

Córdoba

SANTIAGO

BUENOS AIRES

Montevideo

PACIFIC

P A M P A

A T L A N T I C

Bahía Blanca

OCEAN

OCEAN

P A T A G O N I A

Puerto Montt

FALKLAND
ISLANDS

Punta Arenas

TIERRA
DEL FUEGO

SOUTH
GEORGIA

Drake   Passage

A-540000-36 2-6

	Urban
	Cropland
	Cropland & Woodland
	Cropland & Grazing Land
	Grassland, Grazing Land
	Forest, Woodland
	Swamp, Marshland
	Shrub, Sparse Grass, Wasteland
	Barren Land

Scale 1:36,000,000; one inch to 570 miles Lambert Azimuthal Equal-Area Projection

0 100 200   400   600   800 Miles

0 150 300   600   900   1200 Kilometers

Relief

Meters		Feet
3050		10 000
1525		5000
610		2000
305		1000
0	Sea Level	0
152.5		500
1525		5000
3050		10 000
6100		20 000

A-540000-76-3-5--14
COPYRIGHT BY
RAND McNALLY & COMPANY
MADE IN U.S.A.

Longitude West of Greenwich

0   200   400   600   800   1000 Miles
0   400   800   1200   1600 Kilometers

Scale 1:40 000 000; one inch to 630 miles. Lambert's Azimuthal, Equal Area Projection
Elevations and depressions are given in feet

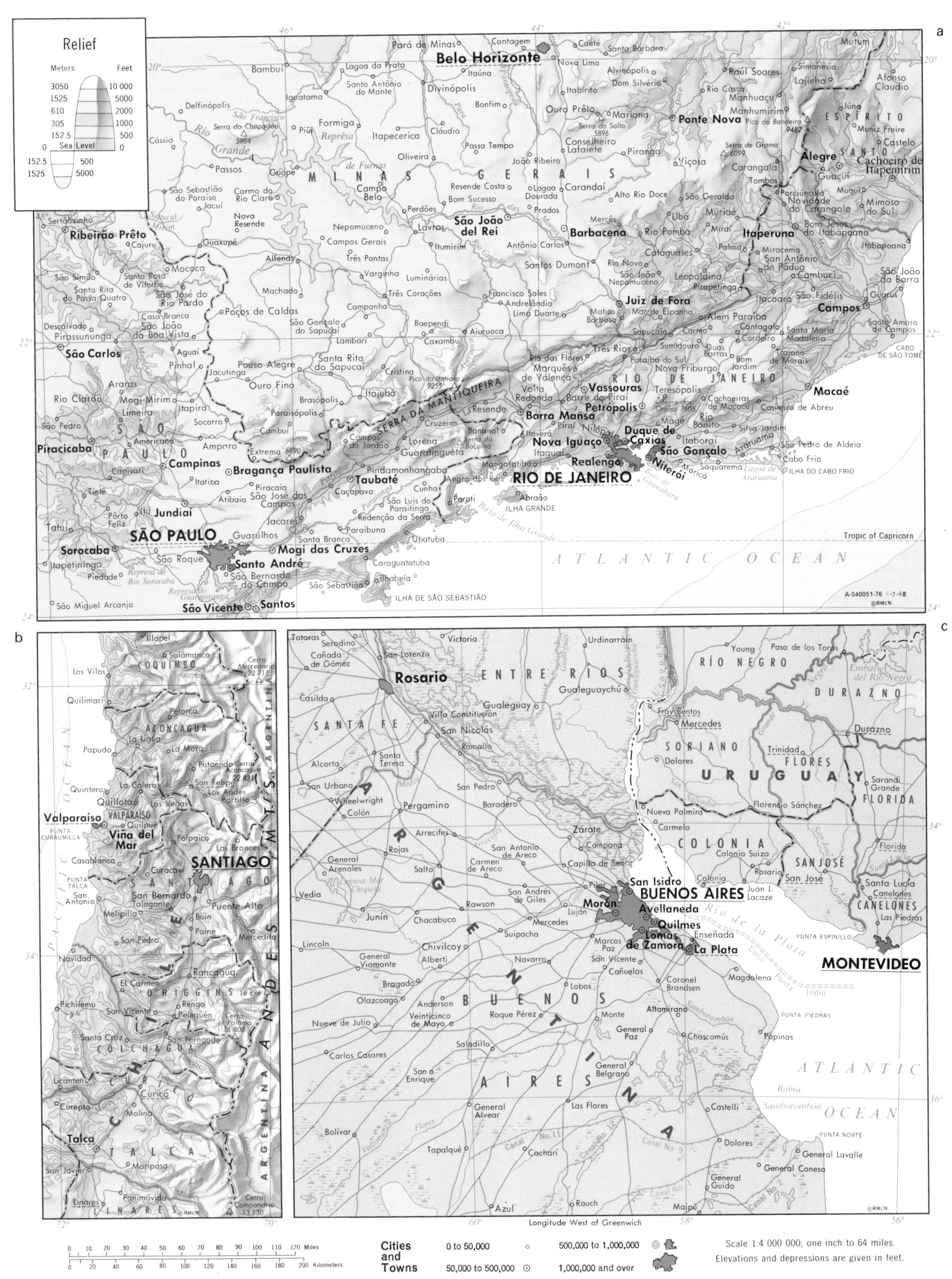

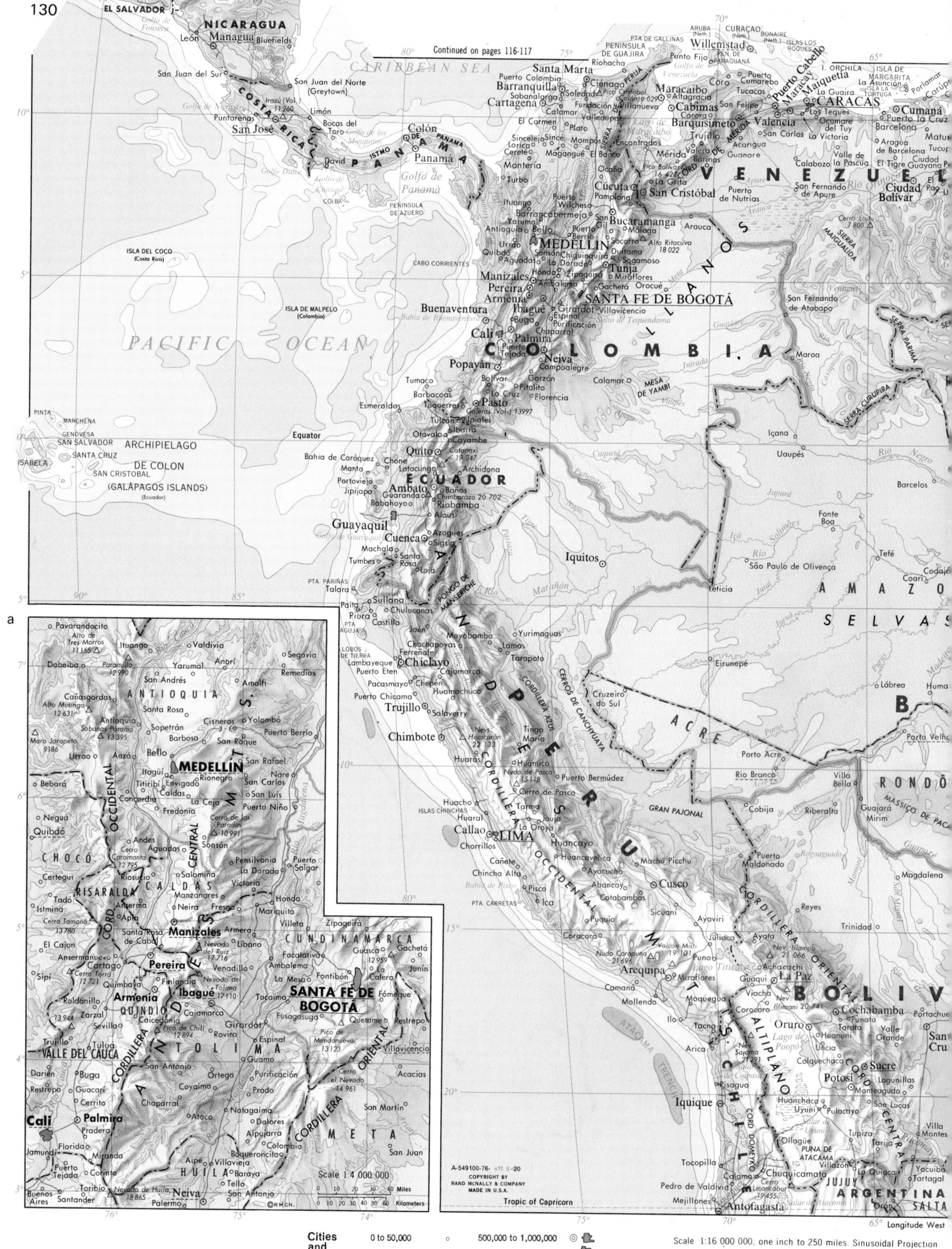

EL SALVADOR
NICARAGUA
Managua Bluefields
León

CARIBBEAN SEA

Continued on pages 116-117

PTA DE GALLINAS
ARUBA (Neth.) CURAÇAO (Neth.) BONAIRE (Neth.) ISLAS LOS ROQUES
PENÍNSULA DE GUAJIRA
PEN. DE PARAGUANÁ
Willemstad I. ORCHILA ISLA DE TORTUGA ISLA DE MARGARITA
La Asunción Porlamar

Santa Marta
Ríohacha
Puerto Colombia
Barranquilla
Cartagena

Golfo de Venezuela
Maracaibo
Coro Cumarebo Puerto Cabello
La Guaira Maiquetía
CARACAS Cumaná

San Juan del Sur
San Juan del Norte (Greytown)

Costa Rica
Irazú (Vol.) 11 260
Limón
San José
Puntarenas

Bocas del Toro
Golfo de los Mosquitos
Colón
PANAMÁ
Panamá
Golfo de Panamá
Istmo

PACIFIC OCEAN

ISLA DEL COCO (Costa Rica)

ISLA DE MALPELO (Colombia)

Buenaventura
Bahía de Buenaventura
Cali Palmira

COLOMBIA

MEDELLÍN
Manizales
Pereira
Armena
Ibagué

SANTA FE DE BOGOTÁ
Villavicencio

Popayán
Tumaco
Barbacoas
Túquerres
Esmeraldas
Pasto
Galeras (Vol.) 13 997

Equator

ARCHIPIELAGO
PINTA MARCHENA GENOVESA
SAN SALVADOR SANTA CRUZ
ISABELA SAN CRISTÓBAL
DE COLON
(GALÁPAGOS ISLANDS)
(Ecuador)

Quito Cotopaxi 19 347
ECUADOR
Ambato Chimborazo 20 702
Guayaquil
Cuenca

Iquitos

PERU

Chiclayo

Trujillo

Chimbote

Lima
Callao

Cusco

La Paz
BOLIVIA

Sucre
Potosí

Oruro

Arequipa

ARGENTINA

Tropic of Capricorn

Scale 1:4 000 000

Cities and Towns   0 to 50,000   500,000 to 1,000,000
                    50,000 to 500,000   1,000,000 and over

Scale 1:16 000 000, one inch to 250 miles. Sinusoidal Projection
Elevations and depressions are given in feet

b

CARIBBEAN SEA

ISLA DE MARGARITA

Boca del Pozo △2303
PUNTA ARENAS
Punta de Piedras
NUEVA ESPARTA
ISLA CUBAGUA

ISLA
LA TORTUGA

PUNTA DE ARAYA

FALCÓN

Tocuyo de la Costa
Chichiriviche
CAYO SOMBRERO
Tucacas
Golfo Triste

Maiquetía
Puerto
Cabello
CARACAS
Petare
Maracay

YARACUY

Morón
El Cambur
San Joaquín
Montalbán Guacara
Miranda

La Guaira Naiguatá La Sabana
Carayaca
DISTRITO FEDERAL
Guatire
Santa Lucía
Los Teques
Santa Teresa

CABO CODERA

Higuerote
Río Chico

CARABOBO

Valencia
Güigüe
Tinaquillo
Villa de Cura
San Sebastián

Cagua
La Victoria
MIRANDA

Ocumare
del Tuy
Cúa
San
Casimira

Boca de Uchire
El Guapo
Sabana de
Uchire

San Francisco
de Macaira
Altagracia
de Orituco

Cumaná
Las Vegas
SUCRE

Cumanacoa
Puerto La Cruz
Guanta
El Hatillo
Puerto Píritu
Clarines
Barcelona
Bergantín

Manicuare
San Miguel
El Pilar
Santa Inés

COJEDES
GUÁRICO
San Juan
de los Morros
Parapara
Camatagua
San José
de Gauribe

Soublette
San Antonio
de Tamanaco

Valle de
Guanape
San
Pablo

San Mateo

Dos Caminos
GUÁRICO
Barbacoas
Libertad
de Orituco

Onoto
Aragua de
Barcelona

Santa Rosa
Anaco
ANZOÁTEGUI

Scale 1:4 000 000

0 10 20 30 40 Miles
0 10 20 30 40 50 60 Kilometers

©RMcN.

Port of Spain
TRINIDAD AND TOBAGO
TRINIDAD

TOBAGO

Boca Grande

Morawhanna

Georgetown

Bartica Rosignol New
Wismar Amsterdam
Rockstone Skeldon Nieuw
Nickerie
Paranam

Paramaribo
Moengo
St.
Laurent
Albina
Sinnamary
ILE DU DIABLE (DEVILS I.)

Cayenne

MERUME MTS.
432

GUYANA

SURINAME
WILHELMINA GEB.

FRENCH
GUIANA

Saint-Georges

ACARAÍ MTS.
TUMUC-HUMAC MTS.

Amapá

Vista do
Branco

BRAZIL

AMAPÁ

Macapá
Mazagão

CABO
ORANGE

ILHA CAVIANA

ATLANTIC OCEAN

Equator

0°

Moura

Manaus
(Manáos)

Óbidos
Faro
Alenquer
Parintins
Itacoatiara
ILHA
TUPINAMBARANAS
Maués
Borba
Itaituba
Brasília Legal
(Fordlândia)

Santarém

Amazonas

ILHA
DE
MARAJÓ

Breves
Gurupá
Cametá

Belém (Pará)
Abaetetuba

Marapanim
Bragança

Cururupu
Alcântara

São Luís
(Maranhão)

Tutóia
Camocim
Acaraú

Manicoré

PARÁ

Altamira
Tucuruí

Rosário
Viana
Itapecuru-
Mirim
Brejo

Parnaíba
FORTALEZA (Ceará)

Maranguape

Codó
Pedreiras
Caxias

Mação

Barras
Pedro II
Crateús
Quixadá
Russas
Areia Branca
Baturité
Ipu
Sobral
SERRA DA IBIAPABA

Macau

CEARÁ

Mossoró
RIO GRANDE
DO NORTE

Ceará-Mirim
Natal

São João
do Araguaia

MARANHÃO
Teresina

Grajaú

Barra do Corda

Mirador

Senador
Pompeu
Iguatu
Icó
Crateús
Campo
Maior

PIAUÍ

Quixadá

Currais Novos
Nova
Cruz

Caruaru

Campina
Grande

Guarabira
Cabedelo
João Pessoa
(Paraíba)
Nazaré da Mata

SERRA DO GURUPI

Araguatins
Tocantinópolis

Loreto
Riachão
Carolina

Balsas

Floriano

Oeiras

Picos

Paulistana

Juazeiro
do Norte
Crato
Flores
Granito
PLANALTO
DA BORBOREMA
PARAÍBA
PERNAMBUCO

Jaboatão
Olinda
RECIFE
(Pernambuco)

Santa
Filomena

São Raimundo
Nonato

Cabrobó
Sertânia
Garanhuns
Palmeira
dos Índios

Palmares
Pôrto de Pedras
Maceió
ALAGOAS

Miracema
do Tocantins
Palmas

Porto
Nacional

SERRA DO ESTRONDO
SERRA DO RONCADOR

Natividade

TOCANTINS

Parnaguá

Barra

SERRA DO PIAUÍ

Juazeiro
Petrolina

Jeremoabo
Propriá
Penedo
Córipe
SERGIPE
Aracaju

Morro do Chapéu
Jacobina
Senhor do Bonfim
Itabaiana
São Cristóvão
Estância
Serrinha
Inhambupe

BAHIA

Feira de Santana
Lençóis

Alagoinhas
Catu
Santo Amaro
Cachoeira
Nazaré
SALVADOR (Bahia)

CHAPADA DE MATO
GROSSO

MATO
GROSSO

Diamantino

Rosário Oeste

Cuiabá

SERRA DOS PARECIS

SERRA DO NORTE
SERRA DO TOMBADOR

SERRA FORMOSA

Barreiras

Correntina

Carinhanha

Caetité

Condeúba

Mucugê

Jequié
Vitória da
Conquista
Valença

Ilhéus
Itabuna
Canavieiras
Belmonte

Pilar de
Goiás

Cavalcante

SERRA GERAL DE GOIÁS

GOIÁS

Pirenópolis

Goiás
Anápolis

Goiânia
Silvânia

Bela Vista de Goiás

Formosa
D.F.
Brasília

São Francisco

Januária

Rio Pardo de Minas
Grão
Mogol

Pedra Azul

Porto Seguro

ARQUIPÉLAGO
DOS ABROLHOS

Caravelas

São Mateus

Aracruz

MINAS
GERAIS

Paracatu
Luziânia
Ipameri

Morrinhos
Rio
Verde
Catalão

Coxim

SERRA DO CAIAPÓ

Araguari
Ituiutaba
Uberlândia
Uberaba

MATO GROSSO
DO SUL

Campo
Grande
Paranaíba

Bahia Negra

Aquidauana

Corumbá
Miranda

Cáceres
Barão de Melgaço

La Gaiba

El Roboré

Puerto
Suárez

San José

Mato Grosso

PARAGUAY

Fuerte Olimpo

Porto Murtinho

Mariscal Estigarribia

Puerto Casado
Puerto Pinasco

Pedro Juan
Caballero
Bella
Vista

Ponta Porã

Concepción
Belén
Horqueta

Três
Lagoas

Presidente Epitácio
Assis

Londrina

Maringá

Jacarèzinho

PARANÁ

Tibagi

Castro

Ponta Grossa
Guarapuava

Curitiba

São José
do Rio Prêto
Araçatuba
Tupã
Marília
Bauru
Araraquara
São Carlos
Piracicaba
SÃO PAULO
Assis
Ourinhos
Botucatu
Sorocaba
Itapetininga
Itararé
Itapira
Franca
Ribeirão Prêto
Poços de Caldas
Pouso Alegre
Jundiaí
Campinas
Mogi das Cruzes
SÃO PAULO
São
Vicente
Santos

GRÃN CHACO

Concepción

SERRA DA CANASTRA

Araxá
Pará de Minas
Divinópolis
Formiga
Lafaiete
Conselheiro
Barbacena
Dom
Bom
Pico da Bandeira
△2890

BELO
HORIZONTE
Sete
Lagoas
Santa Bárbara
Ponte Nova
Diamantina

Curvelo
Pirapora
Montes
Claros

Minas
Novas
Araçuaí
Teófilo
Otoni
Pecanha

Gov.
Valadares
Colatina

Aimorés

Vitória
Espírito Santo
ESPÍRITO SANTO

Cachoeiro do Itapemirim

Campos

Itaperuna
Nova Friburgo
Niterói
RIO DE JANEIRO

Juiz
de Fora
Taubaté
Petrópolis
Barra
Mansa
Volta
Redonda
RIO DE JANEIRO

Tropic of Capricorn

Continued on page 132

0 50 100 200 300 400 500 Miles
0 100 200 400 600 800 Kilometers

Relief

Meters	Feet
3050	10 000
1525	5000
610	2000
305	1000
152.5	500
Sea Level	0

152.5	500
1525	5000
3050	10 000
6100	20 000

Continued on pages 130-131

BOLIVIA

PARAGUAY

GRAN CHACO

CHACO

BRAZIL

PARANÁ

SANTA CATARINA

RIO GRANDE DO SUL

URUGUAY

PORTO ALEGRE

BUENOS AIRES

MONTEVIDEO

CHILE

ARGENTINA

LA PAMPA

RIO NEGRO

CHUBUT

SANTA CRUZ

TIERRA DEL FUEGO

PACIFIC OCEAN

ATLANTIC OCEAN

FALKLAND IS.
(ISLAS MALVINAS)
(Br.)
(Claimed by Argentina)
Stanley

Relief

Meters	Feet
3050	10 000
1525	5000
610	2000
305	1000
152.5	500
Sea Level	0
152.5	500
1525	5000
3050	10 000
6100	20 000

Sea Level
Below Sea Level

A-549200-76 -11-1-13
COPYRIGHT BY
RAND McNALLY & COMPANY
MADE IN U.S.A.

Scale 1:16 000 000; one inch to 250 miles. Sinusoidal Projection
Elevations and depressions are given in feet

0   50   100   200   300   400   500 Miles
0   100   200   400   600   800 Kilometers

a

Scale 1:1 000 000

BUENOS AIRES

RIO DE LA PLATA

0   5   10 Miles
0   4   8   12   16 Kilometers

©RMcN.

b

SERRA DAS ARARAS

SERRA DO COULTO

RIO   DE   JANEIRO

RIO DE JANEIRO

Baía de Guanabara

ATLANTIC OCEAN

Scale 1:1 000 000

0   5   10 Miles
0   4   8   12   16 Kilometers

©RMcN.

For larger scale coverage of Buenos Aires,
Rio de Janeiro, and São Paulo see pages 233 and 234.

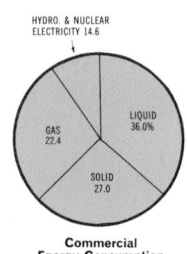

HYDRO. & NUCLEAR
ELECTRICITY 14.6

LIQUID
36.0%

GAS
22.4

SOLID
27.0

**Commercial
Energy Consumption**
2,768,953,000 metric tons
coal equivalent - 1991

ENERGY

Energy Producing Plants

▽   Geothermal

·   Hydroelectric

■   Nuclear

Mineral Fuel Deposits

·   Uranium: major deposit

△   Natural Gas: major field

·   Petroleum: minor producing field

▲   Petroleum }

Petroleum } major producing field

Coal: major bituminous and anthracite

Coal: minor bituminous and anthracite

Coal: lignite

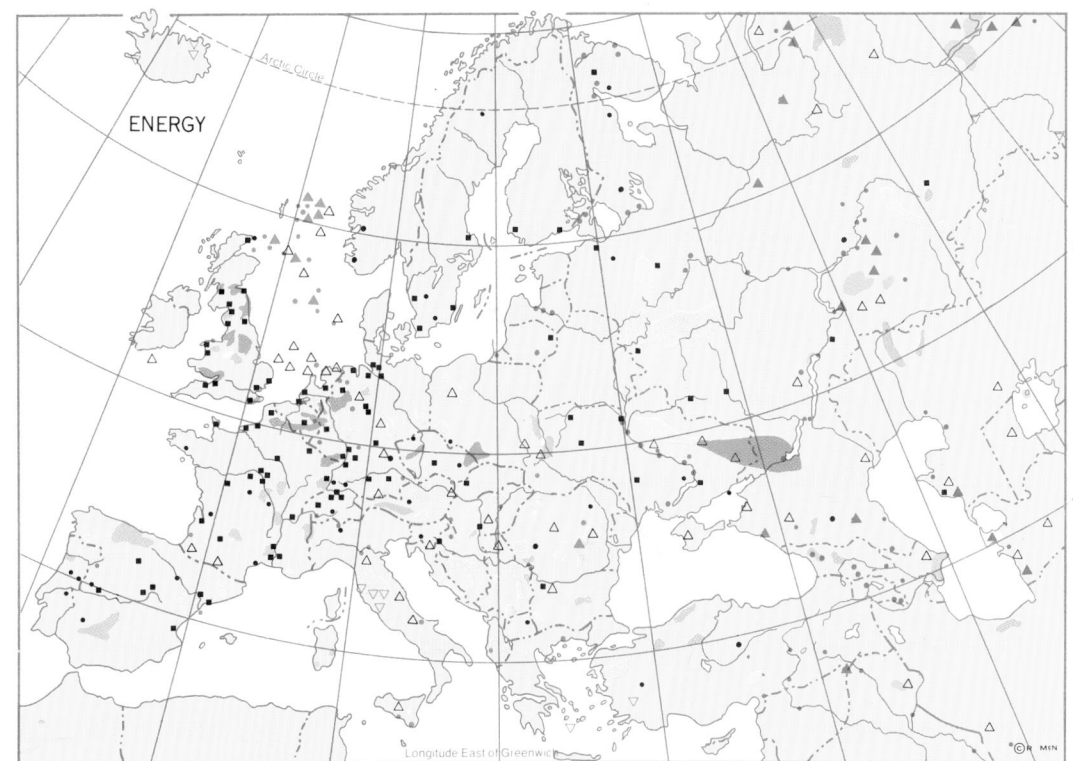

NATURAL HAZARDS

○   Volcanoes*

●   Earthquakes*

●   Major flood disasters*

——   Tsunamis

——   Limit of iceberg drift

Temporary pack ice

Areas subject to desertification

*Twentieth Century occurrences

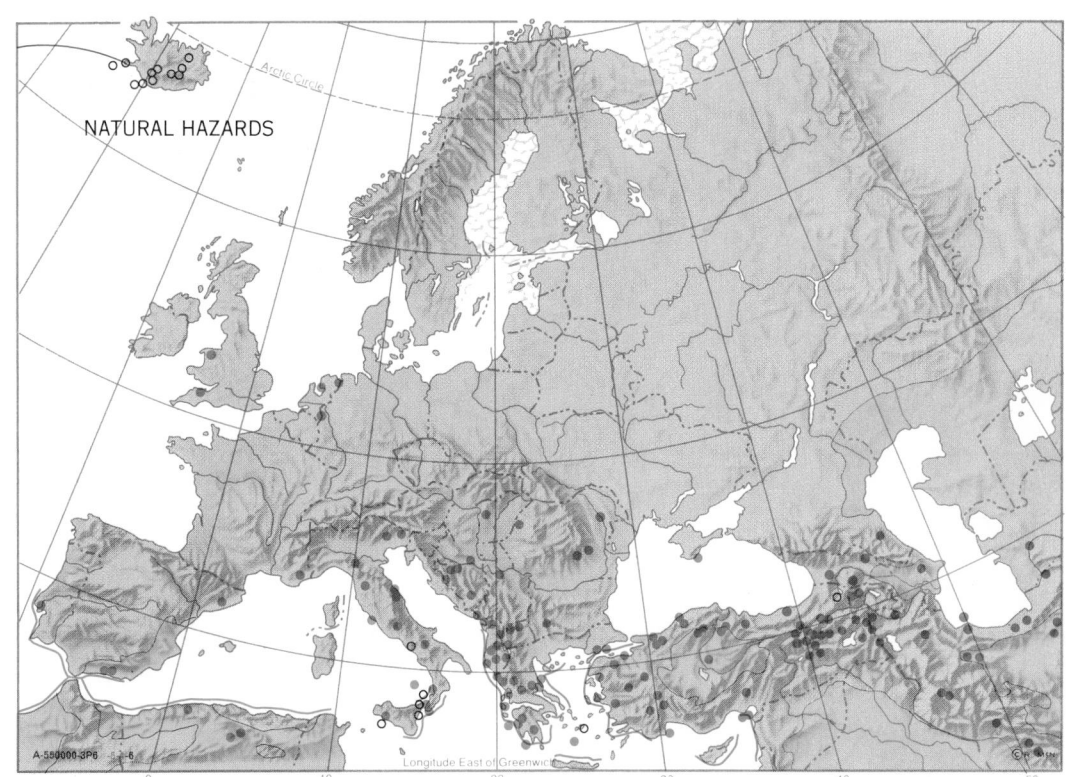

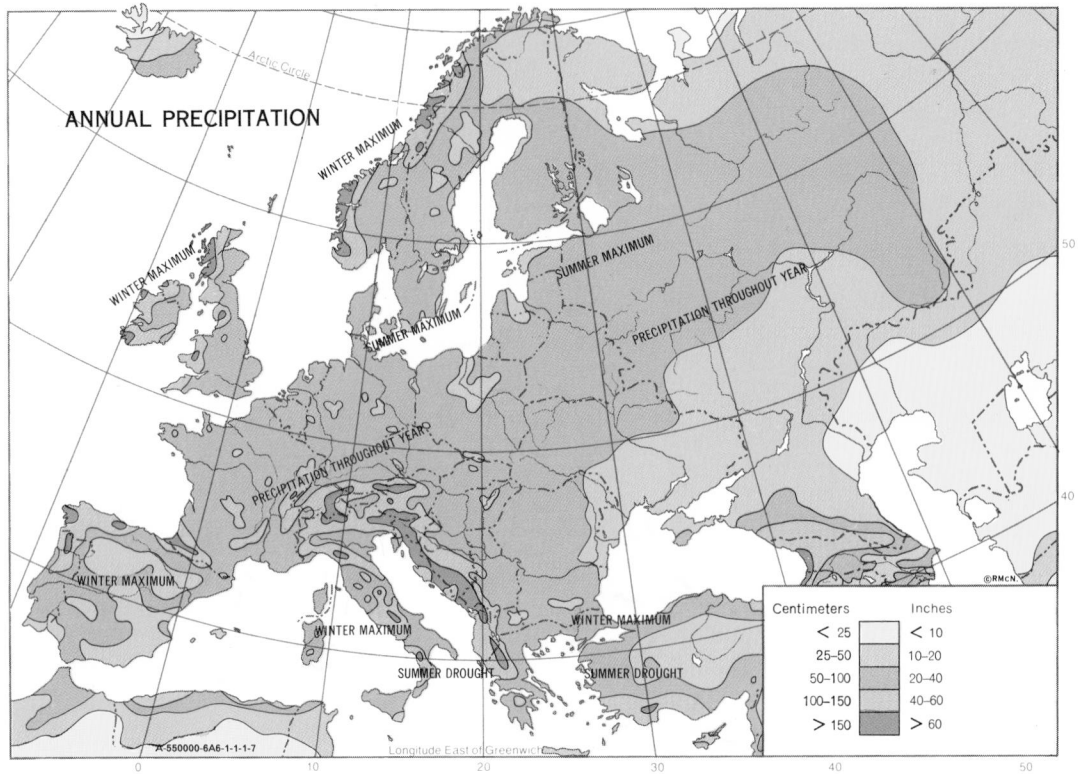

ANNUAL PRECIPITATION

WINTER MAXIMUM

WINTER MAXIMUM

WINTER MAXIMUM

SUMMER MAXIMUM

SUMMER MAXIMUM

SUMMER MAXIMUM

PRECIPITATION THROUGHOUT YEAR

PRECIPITATION THROUGHOUT YEAR

WINTER MAXIMUM

WINTER MAXIMUM

WINTER MAXIMUM

SUMMER DROUGHT

SUMMER DROUGHT

Longitude East of Greenwich

A-550000-6A6-1-1-1-7

Centimeters	Inches
< 25	< 10
25–50	10–20
50–100	20–40
100–150	40–60
> 150	> 60

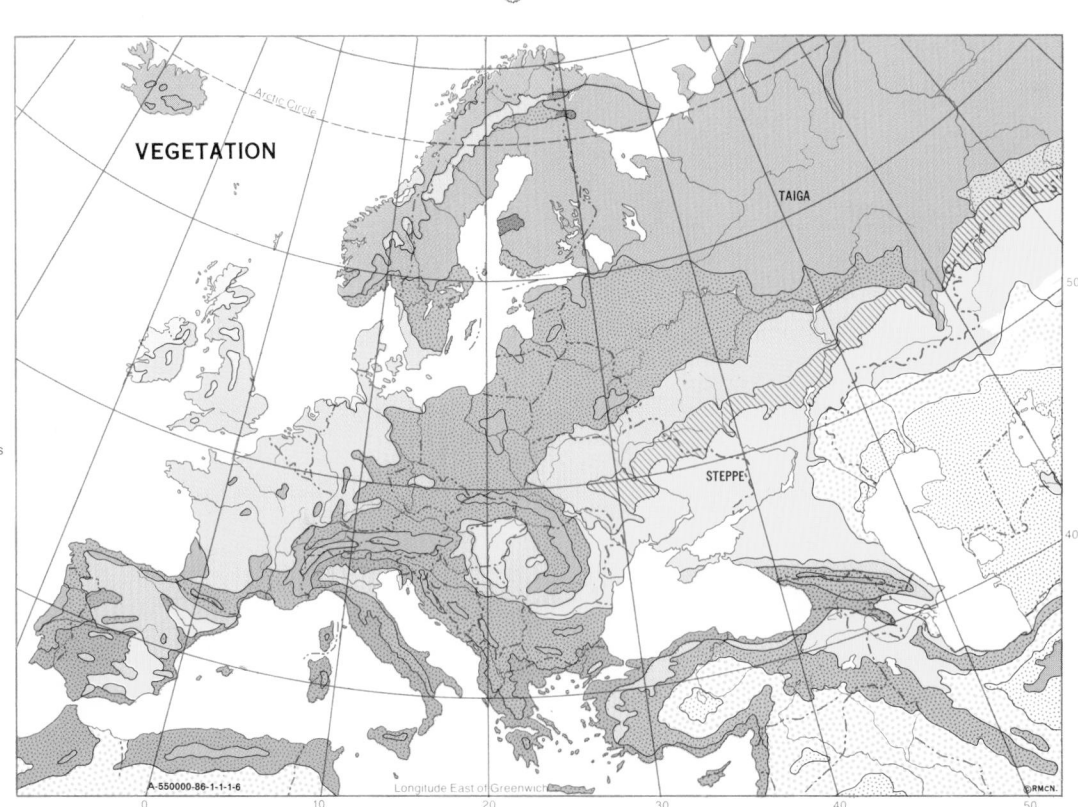

VEGETATION

TAIGA

STEPPE

Longitude East of Greenwich

A-550000-86-1-1-1-6

VEGETATION

E	Coniferous forest
B,Bs	Mediterranean vegetation
M	Mixed forest: coniferous-deciduous
S	Semi-deciduous forest
D	Deciduous forest
DG	Wooded steppe
G	Grass (steppe)
Gp	Short grass
Dsp	Desert shrub
L	Heath and moor
L	Alpine vegetation, tundra
b	Little or no vegetation

For explanation of letters in boxes,
see Natural Vegetation Map
by A. W. Kuchler, p. 18

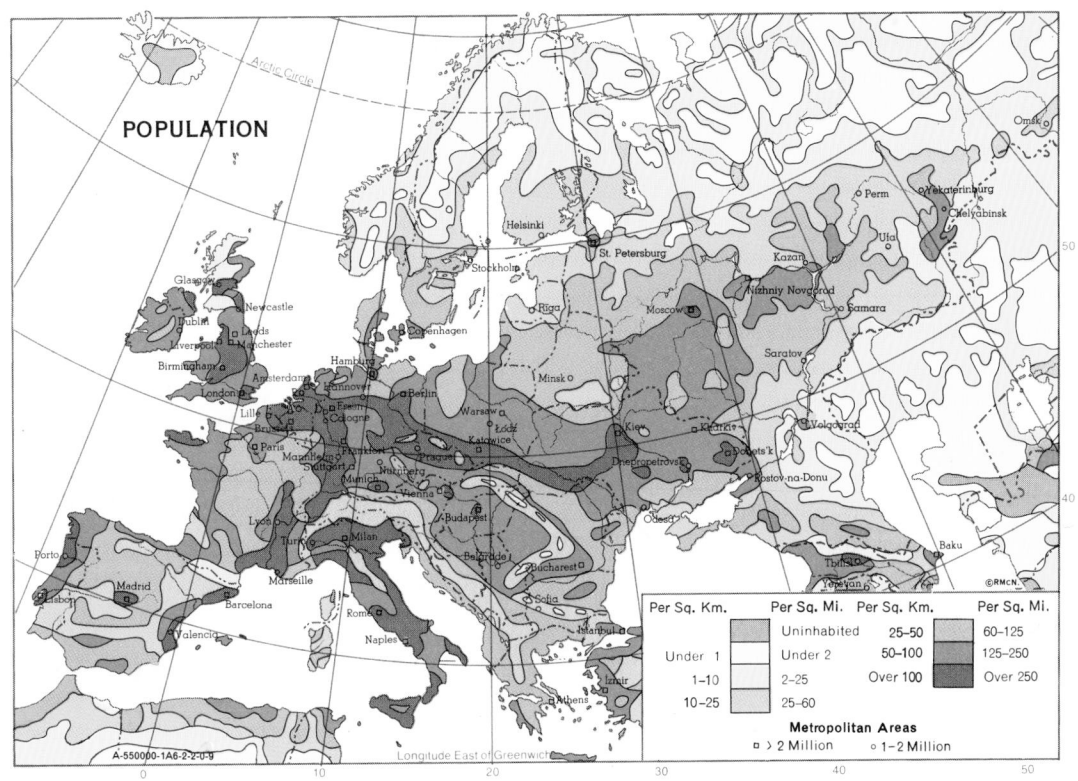

POPULATION

Per Sq. Km.	Per Sq. Mi.	Per Sq. Km.	Per Sq. Mi.
	Uninhabited	25–50	60–125
Under 1	Under 2	50–100	125–250
1–10	2–25	Over 100	Over 250
10–25	25–60		

Metropolitan Areas

□ > 2 Million   ○ 1–2 Million

A-550000-1A6-2-2-0-9   Longitude East of Greenwich

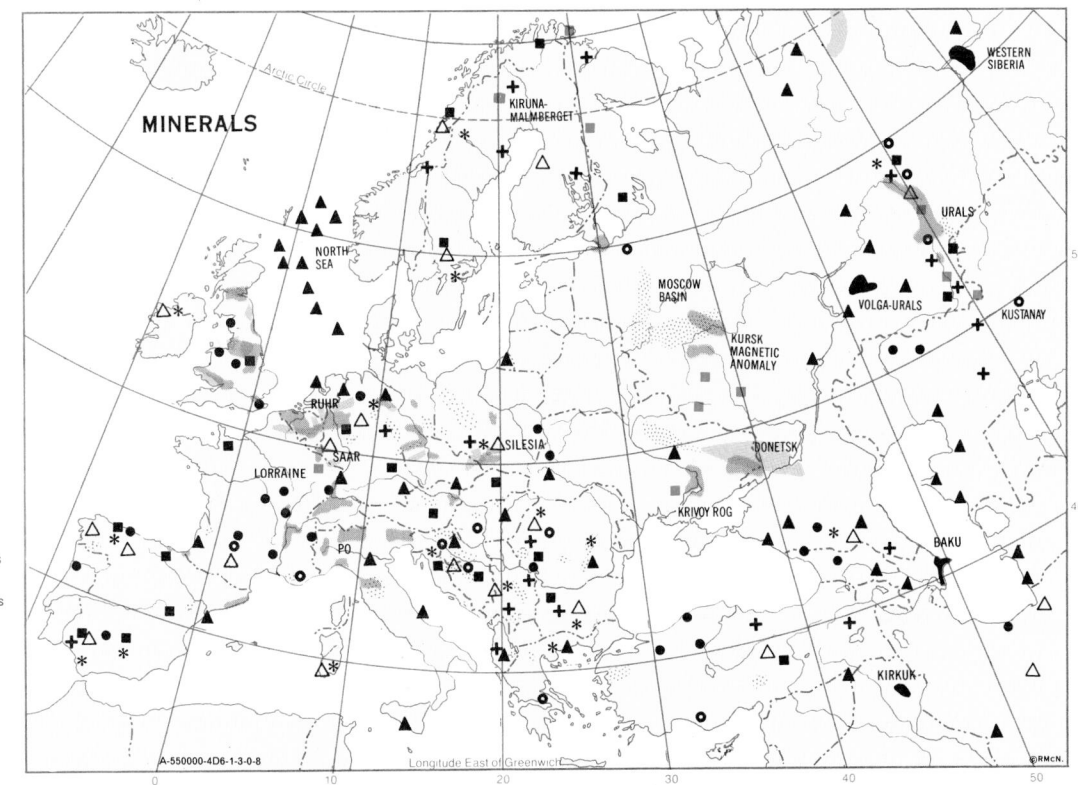

MINERALS

MINERALS

- Industrial areas
- Major coal deposits
- Major petroleum deposits
- Lignite deposits
▲ Minor petroleum deposits
● Minor coal deposits
■ Major iron ore
■ Minor iron ore
✱ Lead
◉ Bauxite
△ Zinc
✛ Copper

A-550000-4D6-1-3-0-8   Longitude East of Greenwich

Urban

Cropland

Cropland & Woodland

Cropland & Grazing Land

Grassland, Grazing Land

Forest, Woodland

Swamp, Marshland

Tundra

Shrub, Sparse Grass,
Wasteland (pattern)

Barren Land

Oasis

Longitude West of Greenwich   0°   Longitude East of Greenwich

Scale 1: 16,000,000; one inch to 250 miles. Conic Projection

0 50 100   200   300   400   500 Miles

0   100   200   400   600   800 Kilometers

Reykjavik

ATLANTIC

OCEAN

North
Sea

Narvik

Murmar

Trondheim

Une

Gulf of Bothnia

Bergen

Oslo

Helsinki ST.
PETERSBURG

Tallinn

Stockholm

Göteborg

Rīga

Copenhagen

Baltic Sea

Kaliningrad

Vilnius

Minsk

Glasgow

Belfast

MANCHESTER

Dublin

LONDON

Amsterdam

Hamburg

Elbe

BERLIN

Oder

Warsaw

Pripyat

Antwerp

Essen

Leipzig

Brest

Frankfurt

Kraków

L'viv

PARIS

Seine

Strasbourg

Prague

C
A
R
P
A
T
H
I
A
N
S

Loire

Rhine

Munich

Danube

VIENNA

Dnies

La Coruña

Bay of Biscay

Bordeaux

Garonne

Zürich

Tisza

Lyon

A L P S

BUDAPEST

Rhône

MILAN

Venice

Zagreb

Sava

Belgrade

Bilbao

PYRENEES

Ebro

Genoa

Bucharest

Douro

MADRID

Marseille

Danube

Lisbon

BARCELONA

CORSICA

ROME

Sofia

Sevilla

ISLAS BALEARES

SARDINIA

Adriatic
Sea

Tirane

Naples

Tanger

Mediterranean

Tyrrhenian Sea

Aegean
Sea

Algiers

Oran

Palermo

Athens

Casablanca

ATLAS   MOUNTAINS

Tunis

SICILY

MALTA

Sea

CRETE

White Sea

Nar'yan-Mar

Archangelsk

Pechora

Ob'

Irtysh

Novosibirsk

Ob'

Omsk

Qaraghandy

URALS

YEKATERINBURG

Perm'

Kirov

Vologda

Kama

Ufa

Balqash

Volga

Kazan'

Nizhniy
Novgorod

Magnitogorsk

MOSCOW

Samara

Orsk

Qyzylorda

Tula

Volga

Syr Darya

Saratov

Ural

PESKI
KYZYLKUM

Kiev

Kharkiv

Don

VOLGOGRAD

CASPIAN

DEPRESSION

Aral
Sea

Amu Dar'ya

Dnipropetrovs'k

Donets'k

Volga

Astrakhan'

MANYCH
DEPRESSION

PESKI KARAKUMY

Dnieper

Krasnodar

Odesa

CAUCASUS

Caspian Sea

Ashkhabad

Black   Sea

TBILISI

BAKU

Yerevan

İSTANBUL

ELBURZ   MTS.

DASHT-E-KAVIR

Ankara

TEHRAN

TOROS

AĞRI

Tigris

ZAGROS

Kerman

Nicosia

CYPRUS

Euphrates

Baghdad

MOUNTAINS

Beirut

Abâdân

A-550000-36   2GE-2GE—12
COPYRIGHT BY
RAND MCNALLY & COMPANY
MADE IN U.S.A.

138

Scale 1:16 000 000; one inch to 250 miles. Conic Projection
Elevations and depressions are given in feet.

PHYSIOGRAPHIC PROVINCES

0 _____ 400
Miles

Western Uplands (Mostly old rocks) | Great European Plain | Central Uplands | Alpine System

EUROPE DURING THE ICE AGE

Tundra | Forest | Steppe

PHYSIOGRAPHY
BY
ERWIN RAISZ

LITHOLOGY AND STRUCTURE

Unconsolidated deposits: alluvium, sands, bottom lands.

Essentially horizontal sediments, also uplands and terraces in the plains.

Moderately folded sedimentary rocks.

Strongly folded and faulted rocks. The "Younger Series" in Norway.

Metamorphic and intrusive igneous rocks.

volcanics, lava flows, basalts, etc.

LANDFORMS

PLATEAUS   CUESTAS   SAND

HILLS   FOLDED MOUNTAINS   SINKS

MOUNTAINS   BASIN RANGES   MORAINES

MESAS   VOLCANO AND LAVA   DRUMLINS

0 50 100   200   300   400   500 Miles
0 100 200   400   600   800 Kilometers

EUROPE LANGUAGES
BY
BOGDAN ZABORSKI

Scale 1:16,500,000; one inch to 260 miles Conic Projection

B-550000-1C6-1-1-1-3
COPYRIGHT BY
RAND McNALLY & COMPANY
MADE IN U.S.A.

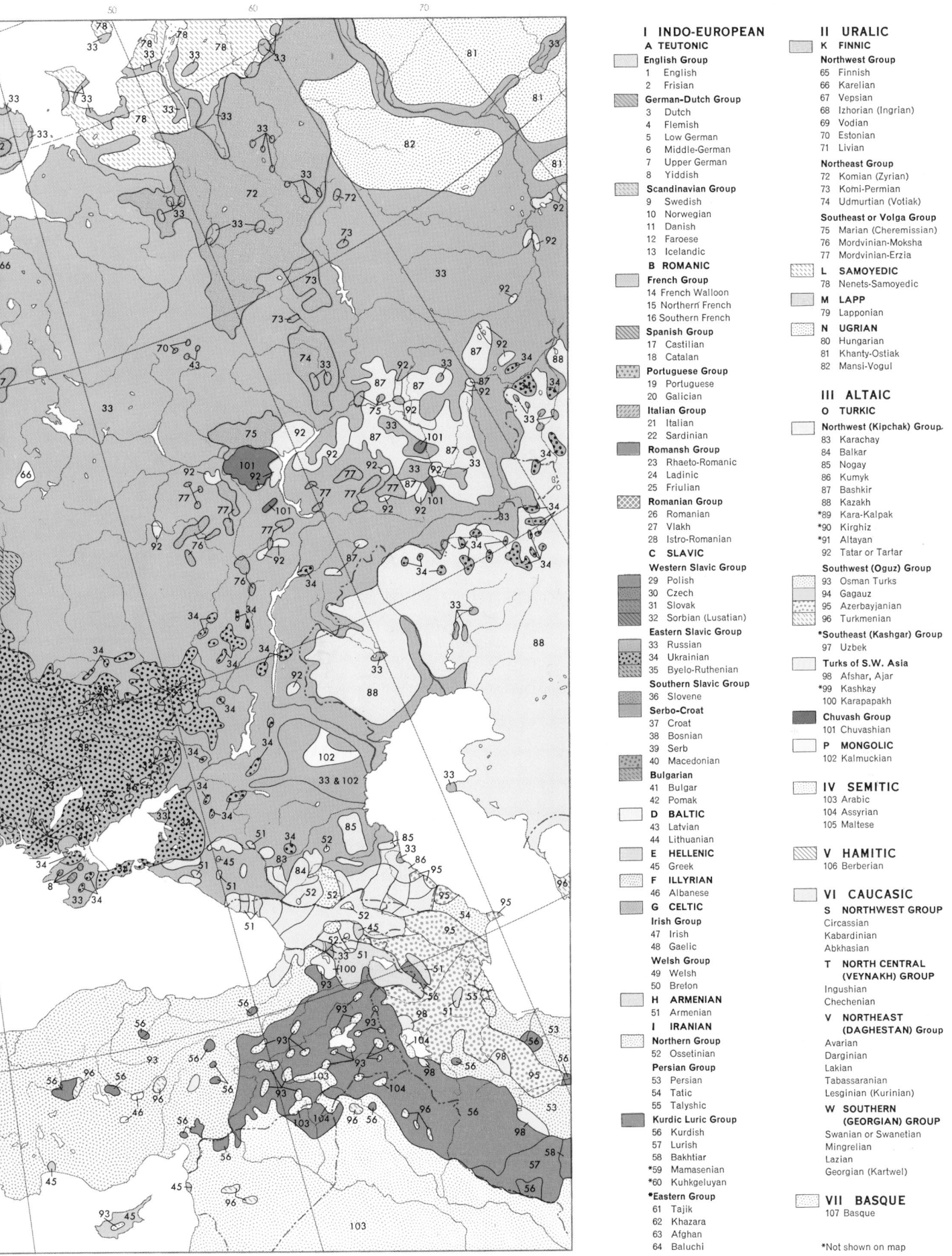

I INDO-EUROPEAN
A TEUTONIC
English Group
1 English
2 Frisian
German–Dutch Group
3 Dutch
4 Flemish
5 Low German
6 Middle-German
7 Upper German
8 Yiddish
Scandinavian Group
9 Swedish
10 Norwegian
11 Danish
12 Faroese
13 Icelandic
B ROMANIC
French Group
14 French Walloon
15 Northern French
16 Southern French
Spanish Group
17 Castilian
18 Catalan
Portuguese Group
19 Portuguese
20 Galician
Italian Group
21 Italian
22 Sardinian
Romansh Group
23 Rhaeto-Romanic
24 Ladinic
25 Friulian
Romanian Group
26 Romanian
27 Vlakh
28 Istro-Romanian
C SLAVIC
Western Slavic Group
29 Polish
30 Czech
31 Slovak
32 Sorbian (Lusatian)
Eastern Slavic Group
33 Russian
34 Ukrainian
35 Byelo-Ruthenian
Southern Slavic Group
36 Slovene
Serbo-Croat
37 Croat
38 Bosnian
39 Serb
40 Macedonian
Bulgarian
41 Bulgar
42 Pomak
D BALTIC
43 Latvian
44 Lithuanian
E HELLENIC
45 Greek
F ILLYRIAN
46 Albanese
G CELTIC
Irish Group
47 Irish
48 Gaelic
Welsh Group
49 Welsh
50 Breton
H ARMENIAN
51 Armenian
I IRANIAN
Northern Group
52 Ossetinian
Persian Group
53 Persian
54 Tatic
55 Talyshic
Kurdic Luric Group
56 Kurdish
57 Lurish
58 Bakhtiar
*59 Mamasenian
*60 Kuhkgeluyan
***Eastern Group**
61 Tajik
62 Khazara
63 Afghan
64 Baluchi

II URALIC
K FINNIC
Northwest Group
65 Finnish
66 Karelian
67 Vepsian
68 Izhorian (Ingrian)
69 Vodian
70 Estonian
71 Livian
Northeast Group
72 Komian (Zyrian)
73 Komi-Permian
74 Udmurtian (Votiak)
Southeast or Volga Group
75 Marian (Cheremissian)
76 Mordvinian-Moksha
77 Mordvinian-Erzia
L SAMOYEDIC
78 Nenets-Samoyedic
M LAPP
79 Lapponian
N UGRIAN
80 Hungarian
81 Khanty-Ostiak
82 Mansi-Vogul

III ALTAIC
O TURKIC
Northwest (Kipchak) Group
83 Karachay
84 Balkar
85 Nogay
86 Kumyk
87 Bashkir
88 Kazakh
*89 Kara-Kalpak
*90 Kirghiz
*91 Altayan
92 Tatar or Tartar
Southwest (Oguz) Group
93 Osman Turks
94 Gagauz
95 Azerbayjanian
96 Turkmenian
***Southeast (Kashgar) Group**
97 Uzbek
Turks of S.W. Asia
98 Afshar, Ajar
*99 Kashkay
100 Karapapakh
Chuvash Group
101 Chuvashian
P MONGOLIC
102 Kalmuckian

IV SEMITIC
103 Arabic
104 Assyrian
105 Maltese

V HAMITIC
106 Berberian

VI CAUCASIC
S NORTHWEST GROUP
Circassian
Kabardinian
Abkhasian
T NORTH CENTRAL (VEYNAKH) GROUP
Ingushian
Chechenian
V NORTHEAST (DAGHESTAN) Group
Avarian
Darginian
Lakian
Tabassaranian
Lesginian (Kurinian)
W SOUTHERN (GEORGIAN) GROUP
Swanian or Swanetian
Mingrelian
Lazian
Georgian (Kartwel)

VII BASQUE
107 Basque

*Not shown on map

Relief

Meters	Feet
3050	10 000
1525	5000
610	2000
305	1000
152.5	500
0 Sea Level	0
152.5	500 Below Sea Level
1525	5000
3050	10 000

Continued on pages 210-211

Scale 1: 16 000 000; one inch to 250 miles. Conic Projection
Elevations and depressions are given in feet

Longitude West of Greenwich   Longitude East of Greenwich

0 50 100   200   300   400   500 Miles
0 100 200   400   600   800 Kilometers

Continued on pages 170-171

Continued on pages 182-183

A-519697-76 1-30
COPYRIGHT BY
RAND M?NALLY & COMPANY
MADE IN U.S.A.

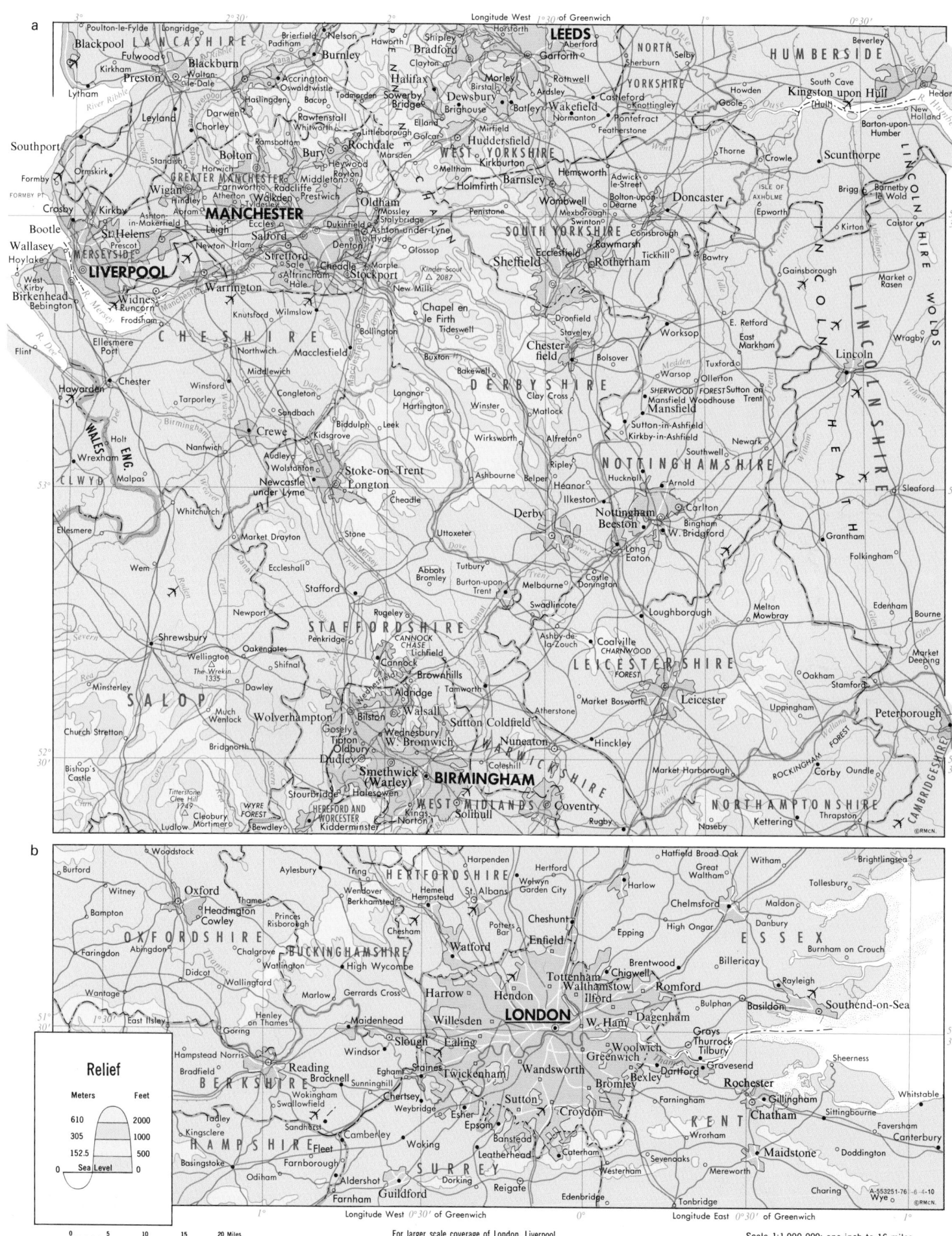

For larger scale coverage of London, Liverpool
and Manchester see pages 235 and 237.

Scale 1:1 000 000; one inch to 16 miles.

Elevations and depressions are given in feet.

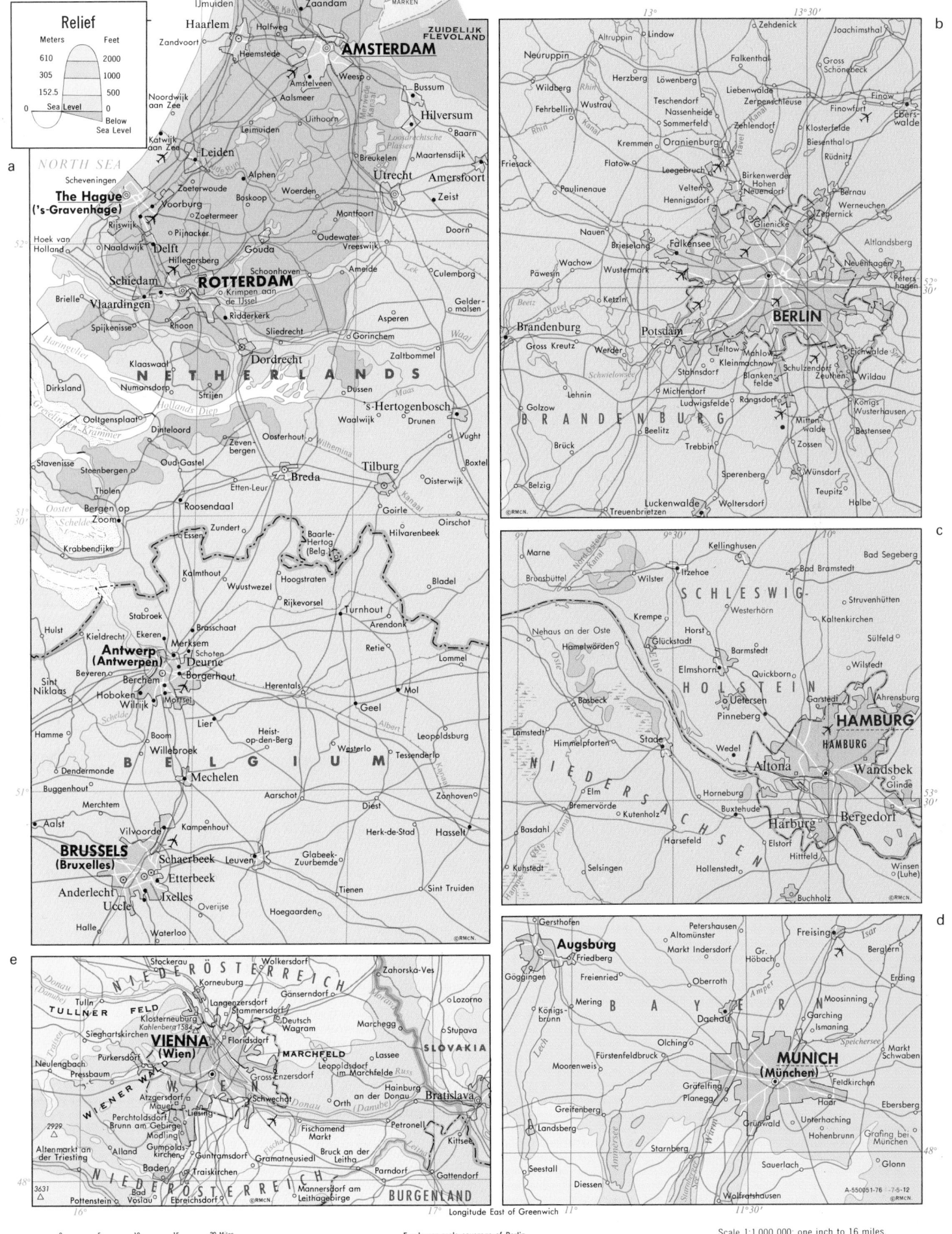

Relief

Meters	Feet
610	2000
305	1000
152.5	500
0 Sea Level	0
	Below Sea Level

a

NORTH SEA

IJmuiden
Zaandam
MARKEN
IJsselmeer
Noordzee Kan
Haarlem
Halfweg
Heemstede
Zandvoort
Amstelveen
AMSTERDAM
Weesp
Bussum
ZUIDELIJK FLEVOLAND
Aalsmeer
Noordwijk aan Zee
Uithoorn
Hilversum
Leimuiden
Baarn
Katwijk aan Zee
Loosdrechtse Plassen
Leiden
Alphen
Maartensdijk
Breukelen
Boskoop
Woerden
Utrecht
Amersfoort
Scheveningen
Zoeterwoude
Montfoort
Zeist
The Hague (’s-Gravenhage)
Voorburg
Zoetermeer
Oudewater
Doorn
Rijswijk
Pijnacker
Vreeswijk
Hoek van Holland
Naaldwijk
Delft
Hillegersberg
Gouda
Schoonhoven
Ameide
Culemborg
Gelder-malsen
Schiedam
ROTTERDAM
Krimpen aan de IJssel
Lek
Brielle
Vlaardingen
Ridderkerk
Asperen
Gorinchem
Spijkenisse
Rhoon
Sliedrecht
Waal
Zaltbommel
Klaaswaal
Dordrecht
NETHERLANDS
Dirksland
Numansdorp
Strijen
Dussen
Maas
Ooltgensplaat
Dinteloord
Zeven-bergen
Oosterhout
Waalwijk
Drunen
s-Hertogenbosch
Vught
Stavenisse
Steenbergen
Oud-Gastel
Breda
Tilburg
Boxtel
Tholen
Etten-Leur
Oisterwijk
Bergen op Zoom
Roosendaal
Goirle
Oirschot
Krabbendijke
Essen
Zundert
Baarle-Hertog (Belg)
Hilvarenbeek
Bladel
Kalmthout
Hoogstraten
Kieldrecht
Wuustwezel
Rijkevorsel
Turnhout
Arendonk
Retie
Lommel
Stabroek
Brasschaat
Antwerp (Antwerpen)
Merksem
Schoten
Deurne
Herentals
Mol
Beveren
Berchem
Borgerhout
Geel
Sint Niklaas
Hoboken
Mortsel
Wilrijk
Lier
Heist-op-den-Berg
Leopoldsburg
Hamme
Boom
Westerlo
Tessenderlo
Dendermonde
Willebroek
BELGIUM
Mechelen
Aarschot
Diest
Zonhoven
Buggenhout
Merchtem
Herk-de-Stad
Hasselt
Aalst
Vilvoorde
Kampenhout
Glabbeek-Zuurbemde
Sint Truiden
BRUSSELS (Bruxelles)
Schaerbeek
Leuven
Anderlecht
Etterbeek
Tienen
Uccle
Ixelles
Overijse
Halle
Hoegaarden
Waterloo

b

Neuruppin
Altruppin
Lindow
Zehdenick
Joachimsthal
Herzberg
Löwenberg
Falkenthal
Gross Schönebeck
Wildberg
Wustrau
Teschendorf
Liebenwalde
Finow
Fehrbellin
Nassenheide
Zerpenschleuse
Finowfurt
Eberswalde
Sommerfeld
Zehlendorf
Klosterfelde
Friesack
Flatow
Kremmen
Oranienburg
Biesenthal
Rüdnitz
Leegebruch
Birkenwerder
Paulinenaue
Velten
Hohen Neuendorf
Bernau
Werneuchen
Hennigsdorf
Glienicke
Zepernick
Nauen
Brieselang
Falkensee
Altlandsberg
Wachow
Neuenhagen
Päwesin
Wustermark
BERLIN
Petershagen
Beetz
Havel
Ketzlin
Brandenburg
Potsdam
Teltow
Mahlow
Eichwalde
Gross Kreutz
Werder
Stahnsdorf
Kleinmachnow
Schulzendorf
Zeuthen
Wildau
Lehnin
Michendorf
Blankenfelde
Golzow
Ludwigsfelde
Rangsdorf
Königs Wusterhausen
BRANDENBURG
Beelitz
Mittenwalde
Bestensee
Brück
Trebbin
Zossen
Belzig
Sperenberg
Wünsdorf
Teupitz
Luckenwalde
Woltersdorf
Halbe
Treuenbrietzen

c

Marne
Kellinghusen
Bad Segeberg
Brunsbüttel
Wilster
Itzehoe
Bad Bramstedt
Nord-Ostsee Kanal
Struvenhütten
Nehaus an der Oste
Krempe
Horst
Westerhörn
Kaltenkirchen
SCHLESWIG-HOLSTEIN
Sülfeld
Glückstadt
Barmstedt
Hamelwörden
Elmshorn
Quickborn
Wilstedt
Basbeck
Uetersen
Pinneberg
Garstedt
Ahrensburg
Lamstedt
Himmelpforten
Stade
Wedel
HAMBURG
Elm
Horneburg
Altona
HAMBURG
Wandsbek
Bremervörde
Buxtehude
Glinde
Bergedorf
Basdahl
Kutenholz
Harburg
Elstorf
Hittfeld
Kuhstedt
Harsefeld
Selsingen
Hollenstedt
Winsen (Luhe)
Buchholz
NIEDERSACHSEN

d

Gersthofen
Petershausen
Freising
Augsburg
Altomünster
Markt Indersdorf
Gr. Höbach
Berglern
Friedberg
Freienried
Oberroth
Erding
Göggingen
Königs-brunn
Mering
Moosinning
Garching
Ismaning
Dachau
BAYERN
Olching
Fürstenfeldbruck
MUNICH (München)
Moorenweis
Markt Schwaben
Lech
Amper
Gräfelfing
Haar
Feldkirchen
Greifenberg
Planegg
Ebersberg
Landsberg
Grünwald
Unterhaching
Grafing bei München
Starnberg
Hohenbrunn
Seestall
Sauerlach
Glonn
Diessen
Wolfratshausen

e

Stockerau
Wolkersdorf
Zahorska-Ves
Donau (Danube)
NIEDERÖSTERREICH
Tulln
Korneuburg
Gänserndorf
Lozorno
TULLNER FELD
Langenzersdorf
Stammersdorf
Deutsch Wagram
Marchegg
Stupava
Klosterneuburg
Kahlenberg 1584
Floridsdorf
Sieghartskirchen
Lassee
Morava
VIENNA (Wien)
MARCHFELD
SLOVAKIA
Neulengbach
Pressbaum
Purkersdorf
Leopoldsdorf im Marchfelde
WIEN
Gross-Enzersdorf
Atzgersdorf
Mauer
Schwechat
Orth an der Donau
Bratislava
WIENER WALD
Liesing
Donau (Danube)
2929
Perchtoldsdorf
Brunn am Gebirge
Mödling
Fischamend Markt
Petronell
Altenmarkt an der Triesting
Gumpolds-kirchen
Bruck an der Leitha
Kittsee
Alland
Baden
Guntramsdorf
Gramatneusiedl
Parndorf
Neustift
Vöslau
Traiskirchen
Mannersdorf am Leithagebirge
Gattendorf
3631
Pottenstein
Bad Vöslau
Ebreichsdorf
BURGENLAND
NIEDERÖSTERREICH

0 5 10 15 20 Miles
0 4 8 12 16 20 24 28 32 Kilometers

Longitude East of Greenwich

Scale 1:1 000 000; one inch to 16 miles.
Elevations and depressions are given in feet.

A-550951-76 7-5-12

Continued on pages 166-167

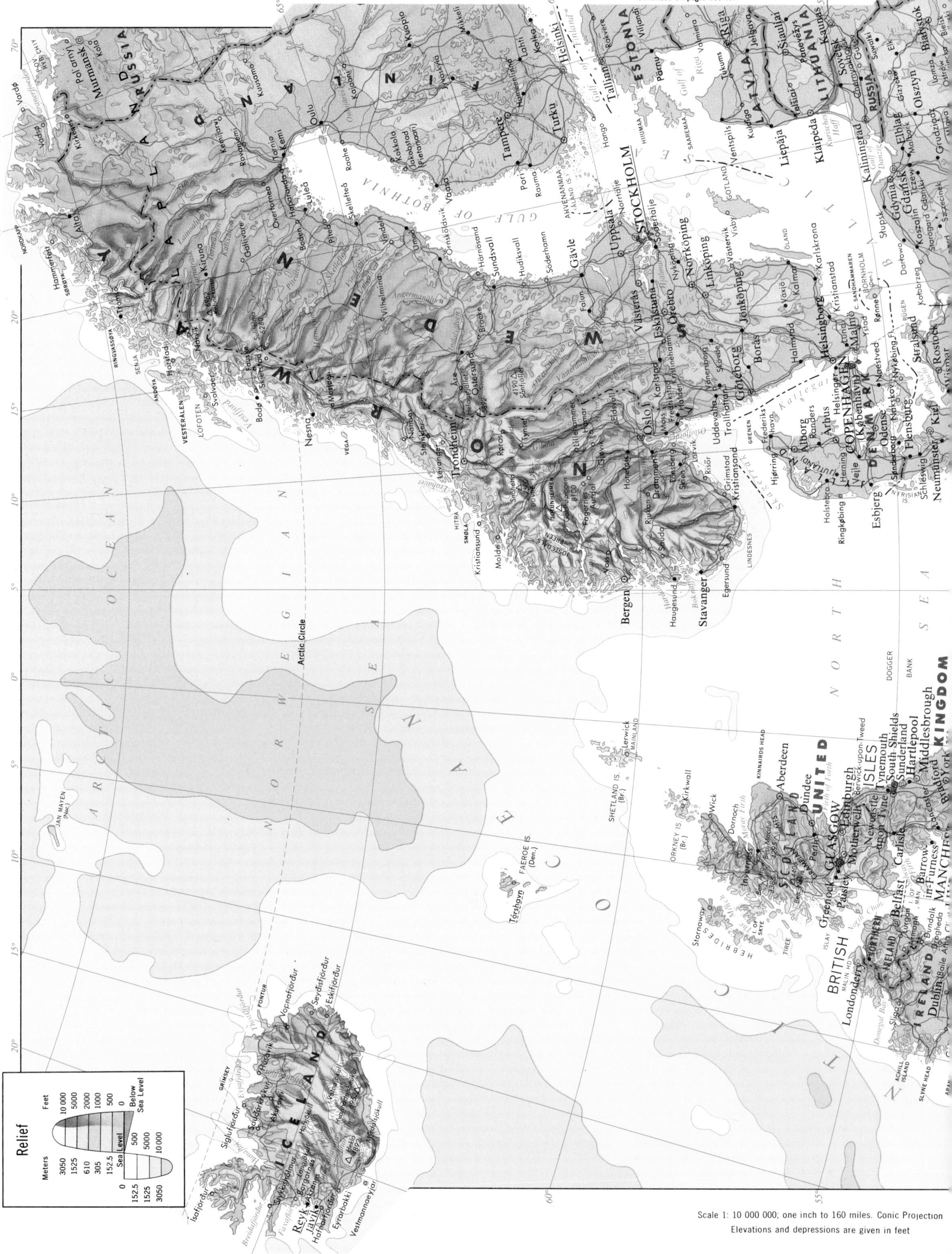

BELARUS

RUSSIA

LAPLAND

FINLAND

ESTONIA

LATVIA

LITHUANIA

RUSSIA

S W E D E N

N O R W A Y

DENMARK

GULF OF BOTHNIA

Gulf of Finland

B A L T I C   S E A

Kattegat

Skagerrak

N O R T H   S E A

A R C T I C   O C E A N

N O R W E G I A N   S E A

UNITED KINGDOM

SCOTLAND

BRITISH ISLES

NORTHERN IRELAND

IRELAND

ICELAND

Arctic Circle

Murmansk

Helsinki

Tampere

Turku

STOCKHOLM

Uppsala

Göteborg

Oslo

Bergen

Stavanger

Trondheim

COPENHAGEN

DENMARK

Riga

Kaliningrad

Gdańsk

Gdynia

Glasgow

Edinburgh

Aberdeen

Dundee

Belfast

Dublin

Londonderry

MANCHESTER

Reykjavík

SHETLAND IS. (Br.)

ORKNEY IS. (Br.)

FAEROE IS. (Den.)

JAN MAYEN (Nor.)

DOGGER BANK

HEBRIDES

VESTERÅLEN

LOFOTEN

GOTLAND

ÖLAND

BORNHOLM

Relief

Meters	Feet
3050	10 000
1525	5000
610	2000
305	1000
152.5	500
0	0

Below Sea Level

Sea Level

152.5	500
1525	5000
3050	10 000

Scale 1: 10 000 000; one inch to 160 miles. Conic Projection

Elevations and depressions are given in feet

Continued on pages 146-147

Relief

Meters	Feet
3050	10000
1525	5000
610	2000
305	1000
152.5	500
0 Sea Level	Sea Level
	0 Below
152.5	500 Sea Level
1525	5000
3050	10000

A-558300-76 -18-12-33
COPYRIGHT BY
RAND MCNALLY & COMPANY
MADE IN U.S.A.

Longitude West of Greenwich 0° Longitude East of Greenwich

Scale 1:10 000 000; one inch to 160 miles. Bonne's Projection
Elevations and depressions are given in feet

Continued on pages 166-167

The Turkish Republic of Northern Cyprus
unilaterally declared its independence
on Nov. 15, 1983.

Areas occupied by Israel since 1967.

50 100 150 200 250 300 Miles
100   200   300   400   500 Kilometers

a

Same scale as main map

ATLANTIC

SHETLAND

St. Magnus Bay

ISLANDS
(Br.)

Lerwick

YELL

MAINLAND

FOULA

SUMBURGH HD.

OCEAN

FAIR
ISLAND

WESTRAY

N. RONALDSAY

SANDAY

ROUSAY

STRONSAY

ORKNEY

Kirkwall

MAINLAND

ISLANDS
(Br.)

HOY

S. RONALDSAY

Pentland
Firth

Thurso

DUNCANSBY HD.

SCOTLAND

©RMCN.

ATLANTIC

OCEAN

MALIN HD.

Carndonagh

ARAN
ISLAND

Errigal
2466

Dunfanaghy

Coleraine

ROSSAN POINT

Donegal Bay

Strabane

Londonderry

Danegal

NORTHERN

Omagh

ULSTER

Lough
Neagh

Belfast

IRELAND

Lisburn

Killala

Ballina

Sligo

Enniskillen

Armagh

Lurgan

Newtownards

ACHILL
ISLAND

Castlebar

Boyle

Lough
Allen

Monaghan

MOURNE
MTS.

CLARE ISLAND

Clew B.

CONNACHT

Cavan

Dundalk

Westport

Dundalk
Bay

Claremorris

Longford

Drogheda

Clifden

Lough
Mask

Athlone

Mullingar

Royal Canal

SLYNE HEAD

Galway Bay

Ballinasloe

Lough
Ree

ARAN IS.

Galway

Tullamore

Grand Canal

Dublin
(Baile Átha Cliath)

Kildare

Dún Laoghaire

LOOP HEAD

Ennis

Lough
Derg

Athy

Bray

Carlow

Lugnaquillia Mts.
3038

Wicklow

Kilrush

Nenagh

Thurles

Kilkenny

WICKLOW MTS.

Brandon Mtn.
3127

Limerick

Tipperary

LEINSTER

Arklow

Dingle

MUNSTER

GALTY MTS.

Clonmel

Enniscorthy

GREAT BLASKET
ISLAND

Tralee

Carrick-on-Sur

New Ross

Wexford

Dingle Bay

Mallow

Fermoy

Waterford

VALENCIA ISLAND

Killarney

Blackwater

Dungarvan

CARNSORE PT.

Carrauntohill
3400

Bantry

Youghal

Cork

Youghal Bay

Cóbh

Bantry Bay

Skibbereen

Clonakilty Bay

OLD HEAD OF KINSALE

Cork Harbour

CAPE WRATH

HOY

RONALDSAY

Pentland

Firth

DUNCANSBY HD.

BUTT OF LEWIS

Thurso

NORTH

Wick

Ben Hope
3041

ISLE OF
LEWIS

Stornoway

HEBRIDES

Ben More
3274

Loch
Shin

Dornoch

Dornoch Firth

Dingwall

Moray Firth

KINNAIRDS HD.

Ben Dearg
3547

ST KILDA

OUTER

NORTH
UIST

HARRIS

Nairn

Elgin

Buckie

Banff

Fraserburgh

Peterhead

ISLAND
OF SKYE

SOUTH
UIST

INNER

Inverness

S C O T L A N D

Ben Macdui
4295

Ballater

Aberdeen

Sea of
RHUM
The Hebrides

Mallaig

Ben Attow
3386

G R A M P I A N   M T S.

Dee

Stonehaven

HEBRIDES

RHUM

Fort William

Ben Nevis
4406

Forfar

Montrose

COLL

ISLAND
OF MULL

Oban

Loch
Tay

Perth

Dundee

Arbroath

TIREE

Buckhaven

St. Andrews

FIFE NESS

COLONSAY

Firth of Lorn

Helensburgh

Edmond

Kirkcaldy

Dunfermline

Stirling

ISLAY

Sound of Jura

Rothesay

Greenock

Dumbarton

Falkirk

Firth of Forth

Berwick-upon-Tweed

GLASGOW

Edinburgh

Paisley

Motherwell

HOLY ISLAND

Campbeltown

RATHLIN
ISLAND

ISLAND
OF ARRAN

Firth of Clyde

Kilmarnock

Lanark

Peebles

Galashiels

Tweed

FARNE IS.

Irvine

Ayr

Hawick

U   N   I   T   E   D

North Channel

Girvan

Dumfries

NEWCASTLE UPON
TYNE

Blyth

Tynemouth

South Shields

Belfast
Lough

Stranraer

Luce
Bay

Solway Firth

Carlisle

Gateshead

Sunderland

Strangford
Lough

ST BEES HD.

Workington

Whitehaven

Durham

Hartlepool

Dundrum
Bay

ISLE OF
MAN
(Br.)

Ramsey

LAKE
DISTRICT

Windermere

Kendal

Stockton

Middlesbrough

Darlington

Barrow-in-
Furness

Northallerton

NORTH YORK
MOORS

Scarbo

Douglas

Lancaster

IRISH

Blackpool

Burnley

Halifax

Bradford

York

YORKSHIRE
WOLDS

Beverley

Kings
upo

Bridl

SEA

Preston

Blackburn

LEEDS

Southport

Rochdale

Wakefield

Doncaster

Hull

Bolton

Wigan

Oldham

Huddersfield

Holyhead

ANGLESEY

LIVERPOOL

MANCHESTER

Sheffield

Lincoln

HOLY ISLAND

Birkenhead

Stockport

Lindum

Llandudno

Denbigh

Chester

Crewe

Chesterfield

Bangor

Caernarfon

Wrexham

Stoke-
on-Trent

Nottingham

Ffestiniog

Snowdon
3560

Stafford

Burton

Derby

Grantham

Caernarfon
Bay

Welshpool

Shrewsbury

Leicester

BARDSEY
ISLAND

Wolverhampton

Walsall

Nuneaton

Peterb

Cardigan
Bay

Aberystwyth

Dudley

Smethwick

BIRMINGHAM

Coventry

C A M B R I A N

Dudley

Leamington

Northampton

Camb

Worcester

Warwick

Stratford-upon-
Avon

Bedford

Cardigan

Hereford

K   I   N   G   D   O   M

Merthyr
Tydfil

Gloucester

Cheltenham

Aylesbury

Luto

ST DAVID'S
HD.

Carmarthen

Llanelli

Abergavenny

Oxford

St. Albans

Hertford

Pembroke

Neath

Aberdare

Newport

High
Wycombe

Watfo

COTSWOLD HILLS

Swansea

Rhondda

Cardiff

Bristol

Swindon

Reading

Windso

LONDON

Guildfo

Weston-
super-Mare

Bath

Newbury

Ilfracombe

Bristol Channel

Aldershot

Reigate

LUNDY

Barnstaple

SALISBURY
PLAIN

Tunbridge

HARTLAND PT.

EXMOOR

Taunton

Salisbury

Winchester

SOUTH DOWNS

Chichester

Hove

BLACK DOWN
HILLS

Yeovil

Southampton

Honiton

Cowes

Ryde

Worthing

Exeter

DARTMOOR

Dorchester

Poole

Portsmouth

BODMIN
MOOR

Launceston

Exmouth

Weymouth

Bournemouth

ISLE
OF WIGHT

Newport

Camborne

Bodmin

Plymouth

Torquay
(Torbay)

Truro

Dartmouth

START PT.

Penzance

LAND'S END

Falmouth

ISLES OF SCILLY

LIZARD PT.

E N G L I S H

IRELAND

Relief

Meters   Feet

610   2000

305   1000

152.5   500

0   Sea Level
     Sea Level

152.5   500
              Below
1525   5000   Sea Level

A-559700-76 -9-.15

COPYRIGHT BY
RAND McNALLY & COMPANY
MADE IN U.S.A

Longitude West of Greenwich

Scale 1: 4 000 000; one inch to 64 miles. Conic Projection

Elevations and depressions are given in feet

Continued on pages 152-153

Continued on pages 154-155

Continued on pages 156-157

Longitude East of Greenwich

0 10 20 30 40 50 60 70 80 90 100 110 120 Miles
0 20 40 60 80 100 120 140 160 180 200 Kilometers

NORWEGIAN SEA

SMØLA
Kristiansund
Trondheim
Orkanger
Stjørdalshalsen
Selbusjøen
Averøya
Molde
Støren
Østersund
Ragunda
Sollefteå
TROLLHEIMEN
Storsjön
Bräcke
Kramfors
HEMSÖN
Ålesund
Åndalsnes
Oppdal
Røros
Sylarna 5781
Helagsfjället 5892
Storsjö
Ange
Fränsta
Stöde
Härnösand
Sundsvall
ALNÖN
Njurunda
BREMANGERLANDET
Snøhetta 7500
Tynset
Fermunden
Sånfjället 4190
(NATIONAL PARK)
TÖFSINGDALENS (NATIONAL PARK)
Sveg
Ramsjö

Floro
DOVRE FJELL
Nordfjord
Savalen
JOSTEDALSBREEN
JOTUNHEIMEN
Galdøpiggen 8100
Glittertinden 8084
Bøverdal
Lillehammer
Rena
Ljusdal
Hudiksvall
Leikanger
Viksøyri
Lærdalsøyri
Fagernes
Aurdal
Elverum
Ålvdalen
Orsa
Mora
Enånger
Söderhamn
Gudvangen
Flåm
Gjøvik
Mæl
Hamar
Lima
Dale
Voss
Gol
Raufoss
Skreia
Mjøsa
Falun
Rättvik
Ockelbo
Gävle
Gävlebukten
Eidfjord
Hønefoss
Eidsvoll
Filsa
Äppelbo
Siljan
Leksand
Borlänge
Storvik
GRÅSÖ
Odda
Vickersund
Kongsvinger
Torsby
Ludvika
Säter
Hedemora
Tierp
Öreg
BØMLO
Rjukan
Tinnoset
Oslo
Lillestrøm
Øyeren
Charlottenberg
Sunne
Filipstad
Smedjebacken
Avesta
Krylbo
Vattholma
Östhar
STORD
Sauda
Notodden
Kongsberg
Svelvik
Drammen
Dröbak
Holmsbu
Arvika
Kil
Forshaga
Nora
Kopparberg
Sala
Heby
Uppsala
Norr
Haugesund
Kopervik
Holmestrand
Horten
Moss
Mysen
Karlstad
Kristinehamn
Karlskoga
Arboga
Enköping
Rimbo
Sigtuna
Västerås
KARMØY
Skien
Porsgrunn
Tønsberg
Sarpsborg
Fredrikstad
Åmål
Säffle
Köping
Lindesberg
Örebro
Eskilstuna
Strängnäs
Sundbyberg
STO
Skudeneshavn
Sandefjord
Larvik
Halden
Kristineham
Hallsberg
Hjälmaren
Malmköping
Mariefred
Södertälje
Stavanger
Tau
Brevik
Langesund
Strömstad
Kragerø
Askersund
Katrineholm
Trosa
Nynäshamn
Sandnes
Byglandsfjord
Risør
Tvedestrand
Grebbestad
Mellerud
Mariestad
Töreboda
Motala
Norrköping
Nyköping
Egersund
Arendal
Fjällbacka
Lidköping
Vänersborg
Skara
Skövde
Vadstena
Söderköping
Bråviken
Flekkefjord
Grimstad
Lillesand
Lysekil
Vara
Trollhättan
Falköping
Tidaholm
Hjo
Linköping
Farsund
Mandal
Kristiansand
LINDESNES
Uddevalla
Mjölby
Åtvidaberg
Valdemarsvik
Marstrand
Ålingsås
Ulricehamn
Gränna
Tranås
Gamleby
Västervik
GRENEN
Kungälv
Borås
Jönköping
Huskvarna
Nässjö
Eksjö
Vimmerby
Visby
GOTLAND
Skagen
Göteborg
Mölndal
Eksjö
Lär
Hjørring
Frederikshavn
Kungsbacka
Varberg
Vetlanda
Virserum
Figeholm
Klintehamn
Brønderslev
Sæby
LÆSØ
Falkenberg
Oskarström
Värnamo
Oskarshamn
Monsterås
ÖLAND
Thisted
Ålborg
Nørresundby
Nibe
Løgstør
Halmstad
Ljungby
Alvesta
Växjö
Nybro
Kalmar
Borgholm
Burg
MORS
Nykøbing
Hobro
Mariager
Randers
ANHOLT
Laholm
Bastad
Markaryd
Almhult
Tingsryd
Mörbylånga
Lemvig
Struer
Skive
Viborg
Grenå
Båstad
Ängelholm
Ronneby
Holstebro
Silkeborg
Herning
Århus
Skanderborg
Ebeltoft
Klippan
Hässleholm
Karlshamn
Karlskrona
Ringkøbing
Nykøbing Sj
Helsingør
Helsingborg
Kristianstad
Sölvesborg
Åhus
Hanöbukten
JYLLAND
Ringkøbing Fjord
Varde
Horsens
SAMSØ
Frederikssund
Hillerød
Landskrona
Esbjerg
Kolding
Fredericia
Middelfart
Bogense
Kalundborg
Holbæk
København
COPENHAGEN
Eslöv
Hörby
Simrishamn
FANØ
Ribe
Vejle
FYN
Odense
Slagelse
Ringsted
Roskilde
Svedala
Lund
Malmö
ALS
Assens
Nyborg
SJÆLLAND
Köge
Køge Bugt
Skurup
Tomelilla
Haderslev
Åbenrå
Fåborg
Korsør
Næstved
Skanör
Falsterborg
Trelleborg
Ystad
SANDHAMMAREN
Tønder
Sønderborg
Svendborg
Rudkøbing
LANGE LAND
Nakskov
Vordingborg
MØN
Allinge
BORNHOLM (Den.)
Rønne
Svaneke
SYLT
AERØ
Maribo
Nykøbing
FALSTER
Nexø
FØHR
Flensburg
SCHLESWIG
Schleswig
LOLLAND
FEHMARN
Gedser
RÜGEN
KAP ARKONA
Łeba
Ustka
Lebork
Wejherowo
Gdynia
Sopot
Husum
Eckernförde
Kiel Bay
Bergen
Sassnitz
Darłowo
Słupsk
HOLSTEIN
Tønning
Heide
Rendsburg
Kiel
Neustadt in Holstein
Warnemünde
Barth
Stralsund
Greifswald
Kołobrzeg
POLAND
Gda
Cuxhaven
Neumünster
Rostock
Wismar
Pomeranian Bay
Wolgast
Świnoujście
Kamień Pomorski
Lübeck
Elbe
Trave
GERMANY

NORTH SEA

SKAGERRAK
KATTEGAT
NORTH FRISIAN ISLANDS
Jammerbugten
Nissum Fjord
Limfjorden
Thyborøn
Nissum Fjord
Ringkøbing Fjord
Kiel Bay
Lübecker Bucht
Pomeranian Bay

A-559195-76 12-8-17
COPYRIGHT BY
RAND McNALLY & COMPANY
MADE IN U.S.A.

Relief

Meters		Feet
1525		5000
610		2000
305		1000
152.5		500
0	Sea Level	0
152.5		500 Below Sea Level

Longitude East of Greenwich

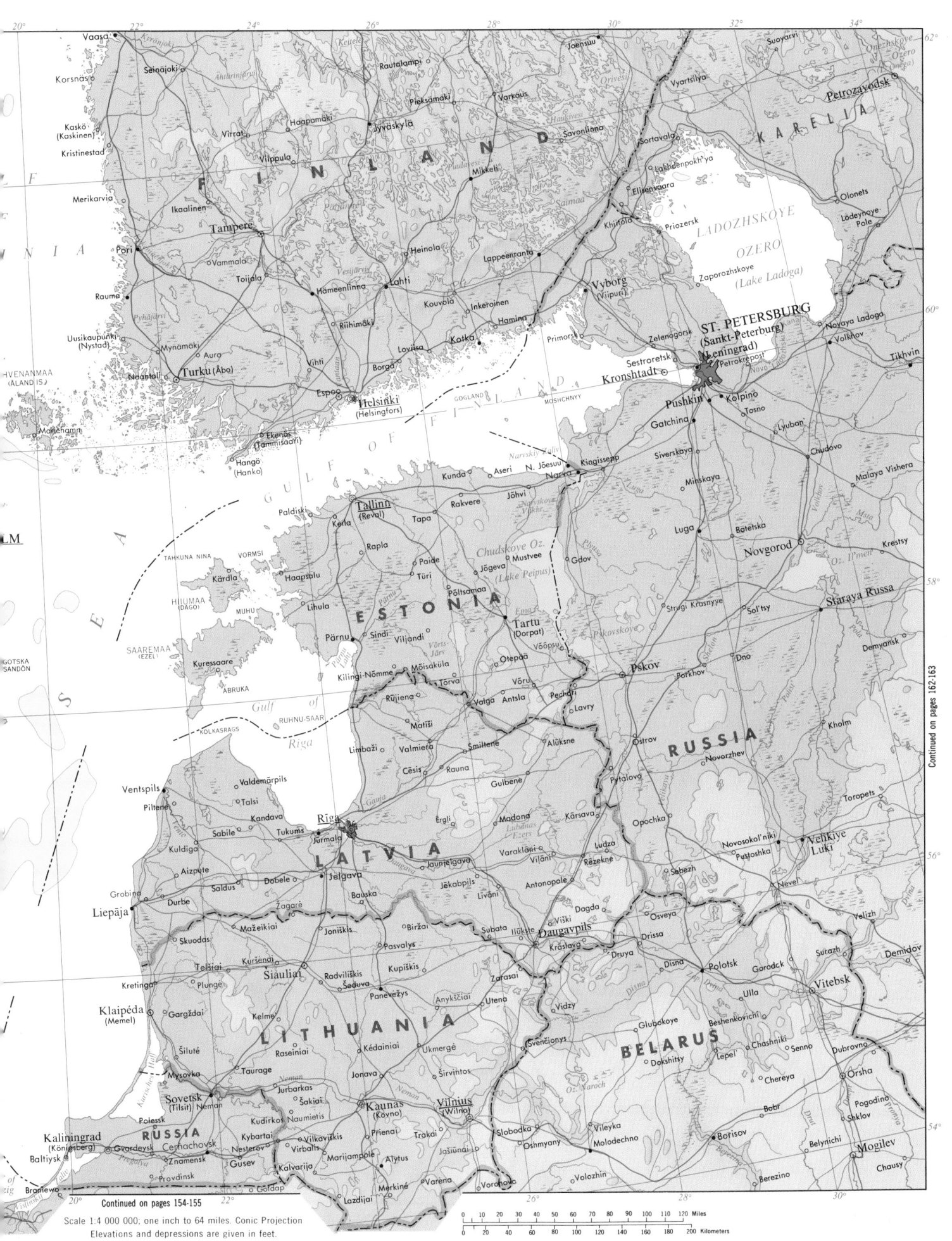

Continued on pages 162-163

Continued on pages 154-155

Scale 1:4 000 000; one inch to 64 miles. Conic Projection
Elevations and depressions are given in feet.

0 10 20 30 40 50 60 70 80 90 100 110 120 Miles

0 20 40 60 80 100 120 140 160 180 200 Kilometers

Continued on pages 152-153

DENMARK

NORTH SEA

BALTIC

FRISIAN ISLANDS

NETHERLANDS

AMSTERDAM

SCHLESWIG-HOLSTEIN

Flensburg Sønderborg Rudkøbing Nakskov MØN

Kiel Kiel Bay Nykøbing FALSTER Gedser

RÜGEN Stralsund Sassnitz Bergen

Rostock Wismar Greifswald Wolgast Anklam

MECKLENBURG Güstrow Schwerin Neubrandenburg Pasewalk

POMERANIA Kolobrzeg Koszalin

Neumünster Lübeck

HAMBURG Bremerhaven Bremen

NIEDERSACHSEN LÜNEBURGER HEIDE

Leeuwarden Groningen Oldenburg Delmenhorst

Wilhelmshaven Emden

Szczecin (Stettin) Stargard Szczeciński

Potsdam BERLIN Frankfurt an der Oder

BRANDENBURG Magdeburg

Gorzów Wlkp. Zielona Góra

Hannover Braunschweig Wolfsburg Hildesheim

Münster Bielefeld Herford Paderborn Hameln

DÜSSELDORF ESSEN Dortmund Duisburg Bochum

Wuppertal Solingen

COLOGNE (Köln) Bonn Aachen

G E R M A N Y

Kassel Göttingen Halle Leipzig Dresden Görlitz

THÜRINGEN Weimar Jena Erfurt Gotha Eisenach

Chemnitz Zwickau Plauen Hof

FRANKFURT AM MAIN Wiesbaden Mainz Offenbach Darmstadt

HESSEN Giessen Koblenz

LUXEMBOURG Trier Saarbrücken SAARLAND

MANNHEIM Heidelberg Ludwigshafen Speyer

Karlsruhe Pforzheim STUTTGART Esslingen Reutlingen Tübingen Ulm

Würzburg Bamberg Bayreuth Nürnberg Fürth Erlangen

BAYERN (BAVARIA) Regensburg Ingolstadt Augsburg

CZECH REPUBLIC PRAGUE (Praha) Plzeň Hradec Králové Pardubice Brno

BÖHMEN BOHEMIA

FRANCE Nancy Metz Strasbourg Colmar Mulhouse Belfort Basel

SCHWARZWALD Freiburg Offenburg

MUNICH (München) Dachau Freising Landshut Passau Linz

OBERÖSTERREICH Salzburg Wels Steyr

VIENNA (Wien) Wiener Neustadt

SWITZERLAND Zürich Winterthur Sankt Gallen Bern Luzern

LIECHTENSTEIN VORARLBERG Innsbruck Kitzbühel

A L P S HOHE TAUERN NIEDERE TAUERN Graz

KÄRNTEN Klagenfurt Villach KARAWANKEN

SLOVENIA Maribor CROATIA

Continued on pages 156-157

Continued on pages 160-161

Longitude East of Greenwich

Scale 1:4 000 000; one inch to 64 miles. Conic Projection
Elevations and depressions are given in feet.

Continued on pages 152-153

Continued on pages 162-163

Relief

Meters		Feet
3050		10 000
1525		5000
610		2000
305		1000
152.5		500
0	Sea Level	0
		Below Sea Level

LITHUANIA

RUSSIA

Kaliningrad (Königsberg)

BELARUS

Minsk

Gdynia
Sopot
Gdańsk (Danzig)
Gulf of Danzig

MASURIA

Białystok

Grodno

WARSAW (Warszawa)

POLAND

Łódź

Brest

UKRAINE

Luts'k
Rivne

Lublin

Kraków
KATOWICE

GALICIA

L'viv

Ternopil'

Rzeszów

Przemyśl

Ivano-Frankivs'k

CARPATHIAN

RUTHENIA

Uzhhorod
Mukacheve

Chernivtsi

MOLDOVA

SLOVAKIA

Košice

Bălţi

HIGH TATRA MTS.
NÍZKE TATRY

Bratislava

MOUNTAINS

BUKOVINA

Iaşi

Miskolc

Nyíregyháza

Satu Mare

Baia Mare

HUNGARY

BUDAPEST

Debrecen

Oradea

Cluj-Napoca
Târgu Mureş

ROMANIA

TRANSYLVANIA

Szeged

Arad

Timişoara

YUGO.

Sibiu

Braşov

MUNTII RODNEI
MUNTII HARGHITA

Wrocław
Opole

Częstochowa

Kielce

Radom

Zamość

Chełm

Bydgoszcz
Toruń

Olsztyn

Elbląg

Kalisz

Piotrków Trybunalski
Tomaszów Mazowiecki

Ostrava
Olomouc

Žilina

Vilnius

156

Continued on pages 150-151

Relief

Meters		Feet
3050		10 000
1525		5000
610		2000
305		1000
152.5		500
0	Sea Level	0
152.5		500
1525		5000

UNITED KINGDOM

Exeter Honiton Dorchester Southampton Worthing Hove Lewes Folkstone Dover Dunkerque
Poole Portsmouth Chichester Brighton Hastings Str. of Dover Calais Roeselare Ieper Gent Aalst Mechelen
Launceston Exmouth Cowes Ryde Newport Bexhill Eastbourne Boulogne-sur-Mer St. Omer Armentières Kortrijk Anderlecht BRUSSELS
Torquay (Torbay) Weymouth Bournemouth ISLE OF WIGHT Lille Tourcoing Roubaix BELGIU
Plymouth Dartmouth START POINT Béthune Bruay-en-Artois Valenciennes Mons Namur
Étaples Douai Denain Charleroi
Berck Arras Crécy-en-Ponthieu Cambrai Hautmont Maubeuge Dinant

ENGLISH CHANNEL

C. DE LA HAGUE St. Valéry-sur-Somme Abbeville Albert PICARDIE Amiens Corbie St. Quentin Charleville-Mézières Revin Nouzonville RDE
ALDERNEY Le Tréport Bohain-en-Vermandois Péronne Roye Guise Hirson Givet
GUERNSEY PTE. DE BARFLEUR Dieppe Neufchâtel-en-Bray Montdidier Chauny Laon Rethel Sedan Verd
St. Peter Port SARK Cherbourg Fécamp Bolbec Yvetot Montdidier Compiègne Oise Soissons Aisne Reims ARGONNE
CHANNEL ISLANDS Valognes Baie de la Seine Le Havre Honfleur Pont-Audemer Rouen Beauvais Méru Creil Châlons-sur-Marne
(Br.) Carentan Bayeux Trouville Lisieux Elbeuf Louviers Gisors Pontoise Château-Thierry Marne Épernay Bar-le-Duc
JERSEY St. Helier Saint-Lô Caen Conde Flers Argentan Évreux Vernon Mantes-la-Jolie St. Germain-en-Laye St. Denis Meaux Vitry-le-François Joinville
I. D'OUESSANT St. Pol-de-Léon Golfe de St. Malo Granville Avranches COLLINES DE NORMANDIE L'Aigle Dreux Rambouillet Versailles Clichy PARIS Melun Corbeil-Essonnes Romilly-sur-Seine Arcis-sur-Aube Troyes
Morlaix Guingamp St. Brieuc Dinard Fougères L'Aigle Chartres Boulogne Billancourt Étampes Fontainebleau Montereau-faut-Yonne Chaumont
Landerneau MTS. D'ARRÉE St. Malo Dinan Vitré Nogent-le-Rotrou Versailles Nemours Sens
Brest Carhaix-Plouguer Lamballe Alençon Châteaudun Pithiviers Joigny Auxerre Lang
PTE. DU RAZ Douarnenez Quimper BRETAGNE Ploërmel Rennes Laval Le Mans Orléans Montargis Clamecy Avallon PLATE
Audierne Pont-l'Abbé Concarneau Pontivy Redon Châteaubriant Château-Gontier Sablé-sur-Sarthe Vendôme Gien Briare Cosne-sur-Loire Montbard MORVAN Dijon CÔTE D'OR
ÎLES DE GLÉNAN Lorient Hennebont Vannes Angers Trélazé Tours Amboise Romorantin-Lanthenay Autun Beaun
ÎLE DE GROIX Quiberon St. Nazaire Nantes Saumur Chinon Loches Vierzon Bourges Nevers Le Creusot Chalon-sur-Saône
BELLE-ÎLE Pornic Cholet Chemillé Loudun Descartes Issoudun St. Florent-sur-Cher St. Amand-Mont Rond Digoin Montceau Paray-le-Monial Cluny Mâc
ÎLE DE NOIRMOUTIER L. de Grand Lieu Thouars Vienne Châteauroux Moulins Commentry Autun Bour-en-Bre
ÎLE D'YEU La Roche-sur-Yon Bressuire Châtellerault Creuse Argenton-sur-Creuse Montluçon Vichy Roanne Villefranche
Les Sables-d'Olonne Fontenay-le-Comte Parthenay Poitiers Le Blanc Guéret Thiers MTS. DU FOREZ Tarare Lyo
Luçon HAUTEURS DE GÂTINE Montmorillon Aubusson Riom St. Chamond Villeurbanne
Pertuis Breton ÎLE DE RÉ Ruffec Confolens St. Junien Limoges Ussel Clermont-Ferrand Oullins Givo
ÎLE D'OLÉRON La Rochelle Surgères Rochefort St. Jean-d'Angély PLATEAUX DU LIMOUSIN Ambert Puy de Sancy Montbrison Rive-de-Gier St. Étienne Vie
BAY OF BISCAY Marennes Saintes Charente St. Yrieix-la-Perche Bort-les-Orgues Issoire Brioude Annonay Issingeaux
La Tremblade Royan Cognac Angoulême Tulle AUVERGNE Le Puy Valence
Barbezieux Jonzac Périgueux Brive-la-Gaillarde MASSIF Murat Plomb du Cantal 6076 St. Flour Mt-Mézenc 5751 Romans-sur-
Blaye-et-Ste. Luce Cautras Argentat Aurillac CENTRAL Langogne Aubenas Privas
Étang de Lacanau Blanquefort Libourne Dordogne Satat-la-Caneda Entraygues Le Teil
Bassin d'Arcachon Mérignac Pessac Bordeaux Bergerac Figeac Decazeville Mende Mantéli
Arcachon Bègles La Réole Cahors Aubin Rodez Millau CÉVENNES Bagnols-sur-Ceze Oran
La Teste-de-Buch Langon Marmande Tonneins Villeneuve-sur-Lot Villefranche-de-Rouergue La Grand Combe Alès Carpentras
Étang de Biscarosse Labouheyre Nérac Agen Moissac Carmaux Albi St. Affrique Vigan Nîmes Beaucaire Avignon
LANDE Castelsarrasin Montauban Gaillac Lodève Montpellier Lunel Tarasc
Mont-de-Marsan Verdun GASCOGNE Auch Toulouse Castres Bédarieux Pézenos Béziers Miramas
Dax Aire-sur-l'Adour Condom Muret Bazièye Castelnaudary Limoux Agde Sète Martigu
Biarritz Bayonne Orthez Pau Tarbes St. Gaudens Carcassonne Sigean Narbonne Golfe du Lio
Irún Salies-de-Béarn Bagnères-de-Bigorre St. Girons Foix Quillan Rivesaltes ME
St. Jean-de-Luz Oloron-Ste. Marie Lourdes Bagnères-de-Luchon Tarascon Perpignan
Pamplona Roncesvalles Laruns PYRÉNÉES Ax-les-Thermes Prades Céret Port Vendres
Jaca Mt. Perdido 11007 Pico de Aneta 11168 ANDORRA C. DE CREUS
SPAIN Boltaña Andorra
Tafalla

FRANCE

SOLOGNE

Bay of Biscay

a

Miramas St. Chamas Équilles Aix-en-Provence
Istres Rognac Gardanne Simiane
Berre-l'Étang Étang de Berre Marignane Victoret St. Simiane Allauch
Port-de-Bouc Martigues L'Estaque La Penne-sur-Huveaune
Lavéra Châteauneuf Carry-le-Rouet Marseille
La Couronne Sausset-les-Pins Mazargues
Carro La Madrague CÔTE DE LA GINESTE 1073
Golfe du Lion

MEDITERRANEAN SEA

Scale 1:1 000 000

©RMCN.

Longitude West of Greenwich Longitude East of Greenwich

Continued on pages 158-159

Scale 1:4 000 000; one inch to 64 miles. Conic Projection
Elevations and depressions are given in feet

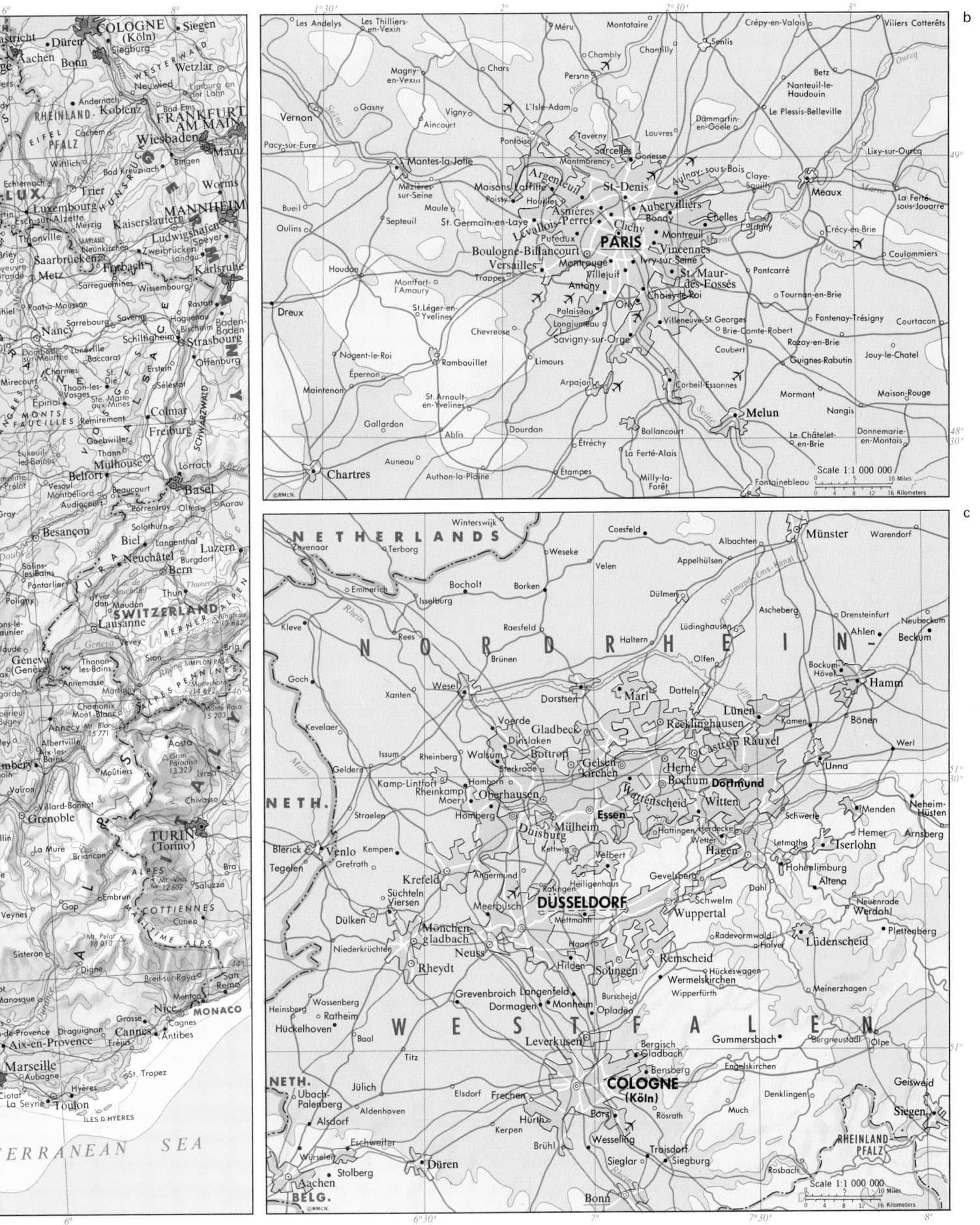

Scale 1:1 000 000

For larger scale coverage of Dusseldorf and Paris see pages 236 and 237.

BAY OF BISCAY

ATLANTIC OCEAN

CORDILLERA CANTABRICA

SISTEMA

GALICIA

ASTURIAS

VASCONGADAS

NAVARRA

IBÉRICO

LEÓN

CASTILLA LA VIEJA

TRAS-OS-MONTES

BEIRA

PORTUGAL

ESTREMADURA

ALENTEJO

ALGARVE

ANDALUCIA

SIERRA MORENA

CASTILLA LA NUEVA

MURCIA

MADRID

LISBON (Lisboa)

SIERRA DE GREDOS

SIERRA NEVADA

Mulhacén 11.424

Strait of Gibraltar

Gibraltar (Br.)

Ceuta (Sp.)

MOROCCO

MEDI

Relief

Meters	Feet
3050	10000
1525	5000
610	2000
305	1000
152.5	500
0 Sea Level	0
152.5	500
1525	5000
3050	10000

A-552900-76
COPYRIGHT BY
RAND McNALLY & COMPANY
MADE IN U.S.A.

Scale 1:4 000 000, one inch to 64 miles. Conic Projection
Elevations and depressions are given in feet

Longitude West of Greenwich

Continued on pages 156-157

a

MADRID

S. DEL HOYO
4606
S. Lorenzo de El Escorial   Colmenar Viejo   Fuente el Saz
El Escorial   Galapagar   Algete
El Pardo   S. Sebastián de los Reyes   Alcobendas
Valdemorillo   Las Rozas de Madrid   Fuencarral   Barajas de Madrid   Torrejón de Ardoz   Alcalá de Henares
Pozuelo de Alarcón   Vicálvaro   S. Fernando de Henares
Brunete   Alcorcón   Vallecas   Loeches
Villaviciosa de Odón   Leganés   Getafe   Arganda   Campo Real
Navalcarnero   Móstoles   Valdilecha
Parla   Pinto   Tielmes
S. Martín de la Vega   Morata de Tajuña   Carabaña
Peraies de Tajuña

Scale 1:1 000 000
0   5   10 Miles
0   4   8   12   16 Kilometers
©RMcN.

b

LISBON (Lisboa)

Mafra   Alhandra   Samora Correia
São João das Lampas   Cheleiros   Alverca
Montelavar   Almargem do Bispo
Colares   Sintra   Loures   Sacavém   Moscavide
CABO DA ROCA   Odivelas   Alcochete
Queluz   Barcarena   Amadora
Alcabideche   Carnaxide
Cascais   Estoril   Oeiras   Almada   Montijo
ATLANTIC OCEAN   Costa de Caparica   Barreiro   Moita
Seixal   Altos Vedras   Pinhal Novo
Coina   Palmela
Setúbal
Sesimbra   Ba. de Setúbal
CABO ESPICHEL   Rio Sado
Comporta

Scale 1:1 000 000
0   5   10 Miles
0   4   8   12   16 Kilometers
©RMcN.

c

NAPLES (Napoli)

Frattamaggiore   Acerra   Nola
Afragola   Pomigliano d'Arco   Monteforte Irpino   Avellino
Marano di Napoli   Somma Vesuviana
Vesuvio   S. Giuseppe Vesuviano   3710
Pozzuoli   4190   Sarno   Mercato Severino
Bacòli   Portici   Torre del Greco   Nocera Inf.
Brocida   Torre Annunziata   Pompeii Ruins   Angri   Cava de' Tirreni
I. DI PROCIDA   C. MISENO   Castellammare di Stabia   Gragnano   Salerno
Forìo   Golfo di Napoli   4734
2585   Ischia   Amalfi
I. D'ISCHIA   Sorrento   Golfo di Salerno
TYRRHENIAN SEA   PUNTA CAMPANELLA
1932
I. DI CAPRI   Capri

Scale 1:1 000 000
0   5   10 Miles
0   4   8   12   16 Kilometers
©RMcN.

d

ROME (Roma)

Monterotondo
Pyrgi   Caere   Veio   Mentana
Cerveteri   Guidonia
ROME (Roma)   Tivoli
Ladispoli   VATICAN CITY   Villa Adriana
Zagarolo
Fregene   Frascati
Fiumicino   Marino   COLLI ALBANI   3114
Ostia Antica   Albano Laziale   Lago Albano   Genzano di Roma
Lido di Roma   Laurentum   Velletri
Pomezia   Lanuvio
AGRO PONTINO   Cisterna di Latina
TYRRHENIAN SEA   Aprilia
Anzio   Nettuno

Scale 1:1 000 000
0   5   10 Miles
0   4   8   12   16 Kilometers
©RMcN.

For larger scale coverage of Lisbon, Madrid and Rome see pages 238 and 239.

Longitude East of Greenwich

0   20   40   60   80   100   120 Miles
0   20   40   60   80   100   120   140   160   180   200 Kilometers

Continued on pages 154-155

Continued on pages 156-157

SWITZERLAND   AUSTRIA

SLOVENIA   CROATIA   BOSNIA

Brenner Pass   Merano   Bressanone   Lienz   Villach   Klagenfurt   Maribor   Čakovec

CARNIC ALPS   KARAWANKEN   Ptuj   Koprivnica

Bolzano   Pieve di Cadore   Tolmezzo   FRIULI   VENEZIA GIULIA   Kranj   Škofja Loka   Celje   Brežice   Zagreb   Bjelovar

TRENTINO-ALTO ADIGE   Trento   Belluno   Udine   Gorizia   Ljubljana   Novo Mesto   Daruvar

St. Moritz   Sondrio   Tirano   Feltre   Pordenone   San Vito al Tagliamento   Postojna   Cerknica   Sisak

ALPI OROBIE   Rovereto   Vittorio   Conegliano   Monfalcone   Trieste   Rijeka (Fiume)   Karlovac   Petrinja

Como   Lecco   Lago di Garda   Schio   Cittadella   Treviso   San Donà di Piave   Piran   ISTRA   Ogulin   Kostajnica

Varese   Bergamo   Brescia   Vicenza   Verona   Padova (Padua)   Mestre   Venice (Venezia)   Gulf of Venice   Poreč   Pazin   Rovinj   VELIKA KAPELA

Busto Arsizio   Monza   LOMBARDIA   Cremona   Mantova (Mantua)   Rovigo   Adria   Chioggia   Pula   Gospić

MILAN (Milano)   Novara   Pavia   Piacenza   Parma   Reggio nell'Emilia   Modena   Ferrara   Comacchio

TURIN (Torino)   PIEMONTE   Asti   Alessandria   EMILIA   Bologna   Ravenna

Cuneo   MARITIME ALPS   FRANCE   LIGURIA   Genoa (Genova)   ROMAGNA   Forlì   Cesena   Rimini   Pesaro   Fano

Nice   S. Remo   Ventimiglia   MONACO   Savona   Rapallo   La Spezia   Carrara   Massa   SAN MARINO   Ancona   Senigallia

LIGURIAN SEA   Viareggio   Lucca   Pisa   Livorno (Leghorn)   Florence (Firenze)   Prato   Arezzo   MARCHE   Recanati

ISOLA DI GORGONA   CAPRAIA   TOSCANA   Siena   Perugia   Fabriano   Macerata   Fermo

C. CORSE   Piombino   Portoferraio   ISOLA D'ELBA   Grosseto   UMBRIA   Assisi   Foligno   Ascoli Piceno   San Benedetto del Tronto

Bastia   Calvi   PIANOSA   I. DI MONTECRISTO   Orvieto   Spoleto   Teramo

CORSICA (Fr.)   Corte   Orbetello   Viterbo   Terni   Rieti   L'Aquila   Penne   Pescara   Ortona   Chieti

Ajaccio   Sartène   Porto-Vecchio   Civitavecchia   C. LINARO   ABRUZZI E MOLISE   Vasto   Termoli   Vieste   TESTA DEL GARGANO

Bonifacio   Strait of Bonifacio   ROME (Roma)   VATICAN CITY   Tivoli   Avezzano   Sulmona   Isernia   Campobasso   San Severo   Manfredonia

CAPRERA   ASINARA   Albano Laziale   Frosinone   Cassino   Benevento   Foggia   Barletta   Andria   Trani   Molfetta   Bari

Porto Torres   Sassari   Aprilia   Velletri   Sezze   Gaeta   Caserta   Avellino   Cerignola   APULIA   Bitonto

Alghero   Ozieri   Anzio   Terracina   CAMPANIA   NAPLES (Napoli)   Salerno   Potenza   BASILICATA   Matera

SARDINIA   Nuoro   ISOLE PONZIANE   ISOLA D'ISCHIA   Torre del Greco   Vesuvio   Sorrento   I. DI CAPRI   Golfo di Salerno   Eboli

TYRRHENIAN SEA

Oristano   Arborea   Lanusei   Golfo di Orosei   Dorgali

Villacidro   Iglesias   Cagliari   Quartu Sant'Elena   Golfo di Cagliari

I. DI S. PIETRO   Carloforte   I. DI S. ANTIOCO   C. CARBONARA   C. SPARTIVENTO

CALABRIA   Cosenza   San Giovanni in Fiore   Nicastro   Catanzaro   Golfo di Sant'Eufemia   Vibo Valentia   Golfo di Squillace

ISOLE EOLIE   STROMBOLI (VOL.)   PANAREA   LIPARI   SALINA   FILICUDI   ALICUDI   VULCANO   Messina   Reggio di Calabria   Palmi   Bagnara

I. DI USTICA   Palermo   Bagheria   Cefalù   Milazzo   Barcellona   Taormina   Acireale

Trapani   ISOLE EGADI   Alcamo   Partinico   Termini   SICILY   Mistretta   Mt. Etna 10,902   Adrano   Paternò   Catania

Marsala   Mazara del Vallo   Castelvetrano   Salemi   Corleone   Caltanissetta   Piazza Armerina   Enna   Augusta

Sciacca   Agrigento   Canicattì   Caltagirone   Gela

ADRIATIC   Zadar   DALMATIA   Šibenik   Split   DUGI OTOK   KORNAT   HVAR   KORČULA   LASTOVO   PALAGRUŽA (Cro.)   Golfo di Manfredonia

Banja Luka   Bihać   Knin   Sinj   Livno   DINARA

a   AEGEAN SEA   Same scale as main map

AKRA SPATHA   Kissamos   Khania   Kólpos Khaníon   Kólpos Almirou   DIA   Iráklion (Candia)   AKRA SIDHEROS

Khóra Sfakion   Réthimnon   CRETE (Greece)   Neápolis   Sitia

AKRA LITHINON   Áno Viánnos   Ierápetra

MEDITERRANEAN SEA   GÁVDHOS

Scale 1:4 000 000; one inch to 64 miles. Conic Projection
Elevations and depressions are given in feet

Relief

Feet	Meters
5000	1525
2000	610
1000	305
500	152.5
Sea Level 0	0
500	152.5

Cities and Towns

0 to 50,000 · o
50,000 to 500,000 · ⊙
500,000 to 1,000,000 · ◉
1,000,000 and over

Scale 1:4 000 000; one inch to 64 miles. Conic Projection
Elevations and depressions are given in feet

Scale 1:20 000 000; one inch to 315 miles.
Lambert's Azimuthal, Equal Area Projection
Elevations and depressions are given in feet

Continued on pages 146-147

Scale 1:10 000 000; one inch to 160 miles. Conic Projection
Elevations and depressions are given in feet.

Continued on pages 148-149

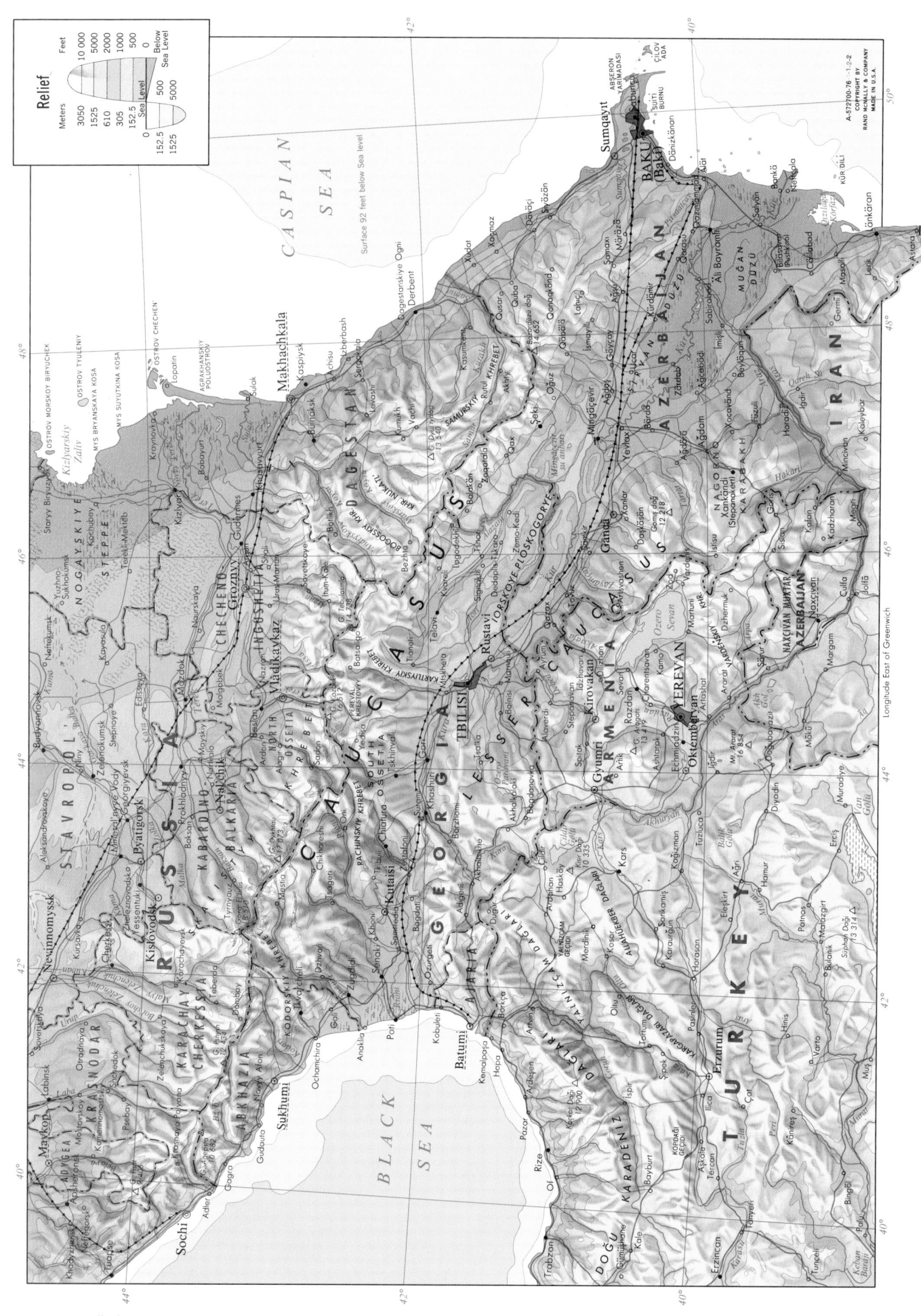

Relief

Meters	Feet	
3050	10 000	
1525	5000	
610	2000	
305	1000	
152.5	500	
	Sea Level	0 Below Sea Level
152.5	500	
1525	5000	

Scale 1:4 000 000; one inch to 64 miles. Conic Projection
Elevations and depressions are given in feet

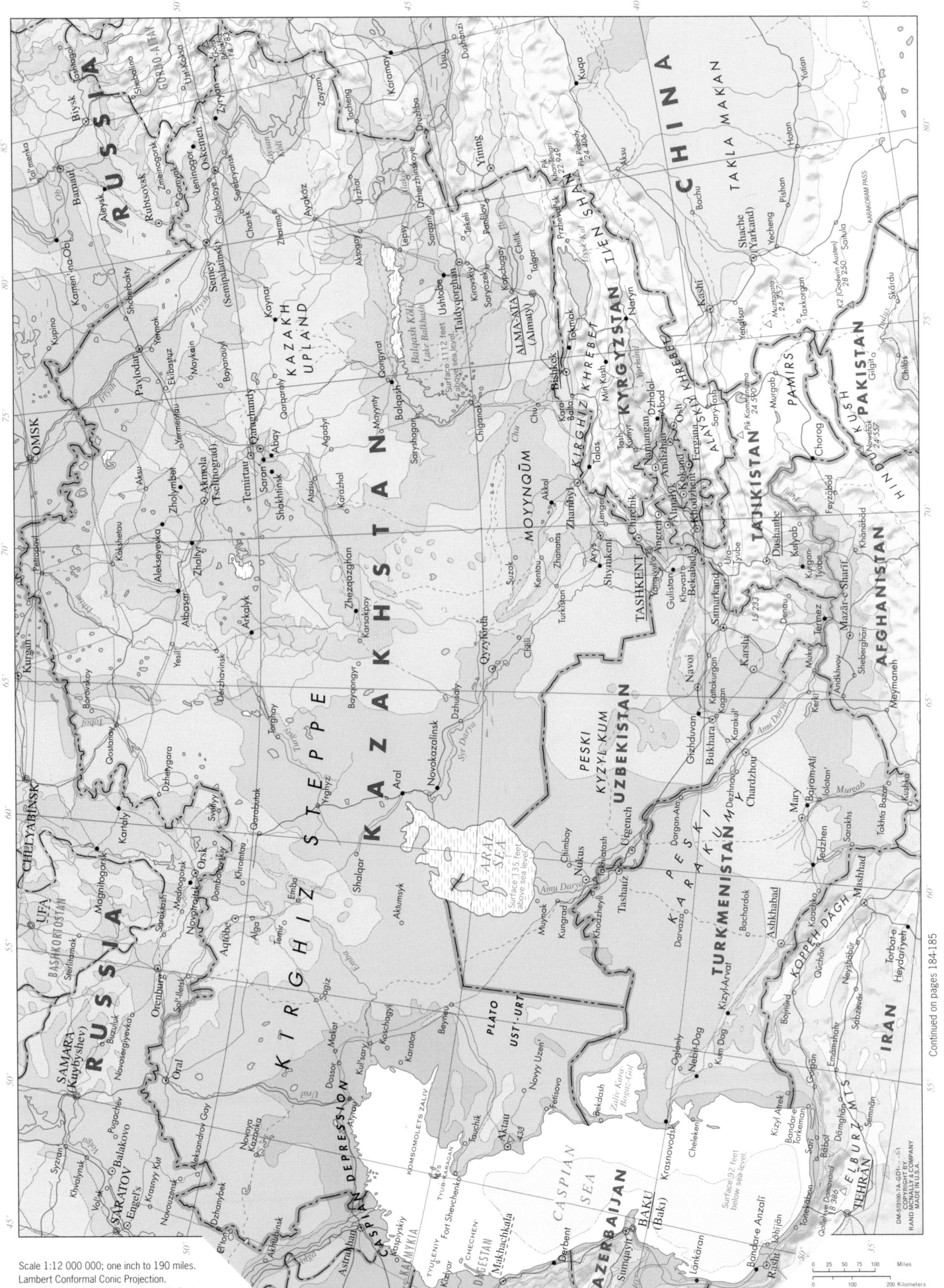

Continued on pages 184-185

Scale 1:12 000 000; one inch to 190 miles.
Lambert Conformal Conic Projection.
Elevations and depressions are given in feet.

DM-573100-7A-GDT--551
COPYRIGHT
RAND M9NALLY & COMPANY
MADE IN U.S.A.

Miles
0 25 50 75 100

0   100   200 Kilometers

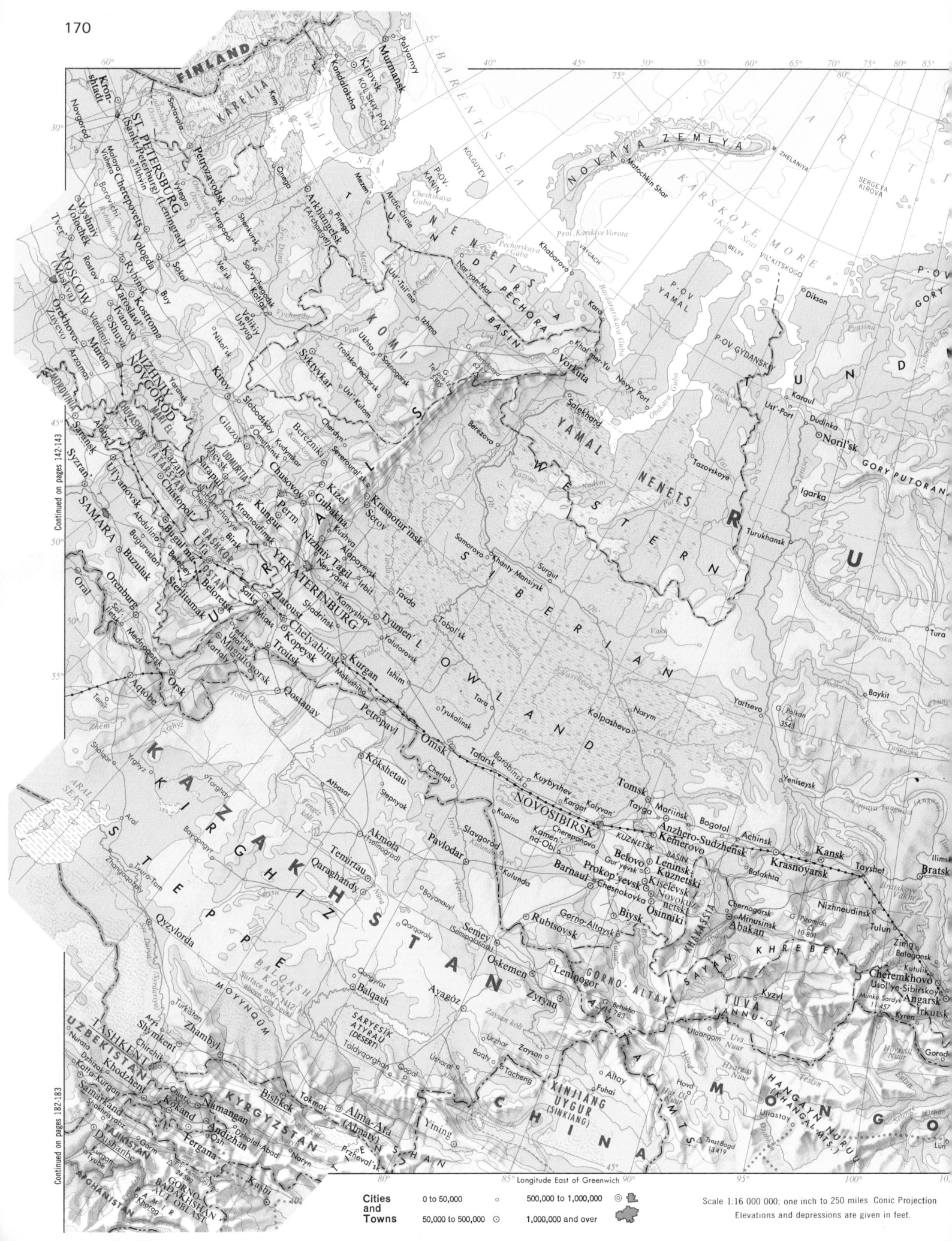

FINLAND

KARELIA

Kronshtadt
Novgorod
ST. PETERSBURG
(Sankt Peterburg) (Leningrad)
Vyshniy Volochek
Tver'
MOSCOW
(Moskva)
Orekhovo-Zuyevo
MORDVINIA
Saransk
Syzran'
SAMARA
Oral
Orenburg
Orsk
Aqtöbe

Murmansk
Polyarnny
Kirovsk
KOL'SKY POV
Kandalaksha
Kem
Kol
Onega

BARENTS SEA

NOVAYA ZEMLYA
M. ZHELANIYA

ARCTIC

SERGEYA
KIROVA

KARSKOYE MORE
(Kara Sea)

BELY
VIL'KITSKOGO

Dikson

P-OV
GORY

Petrozavodsk
Vytegra
Cherepovets
Rybinsk
Vologda
Yaroslavl'
Kostroma
Ivanovo
Shuya
Vladimir
Murom
Arzamas
NIZHNIY NOVGOROD
CHUVASHIA
MARI EL
Kazan
TATARSTAN
Ulyanovsk
BASHKOR
Ufa
Sterlitamak

Arkhangelsk
KOMI
Syktyvkar
Ust'-Kulom
Perm
YEKATERINBURG
Nizhniy Tagil
Chelyabinsk
Magnitogorsk

Vorkuta
Salekhard
YAMAL
NENETS

WESTERN

R U

Noril'sk
GORY PUTORANA

Igarka

SIBERIAN

Khanty-Mansiysk
Surgut

Turukhansk

Tura

LOWLAND

Tyumen'
Tobol'sk
Kurgan
Petropavl
Omsk
Ishim

Narym

Kolpashevo

Yartsevo
G. Pakan
3549

Qostanay

KAZAKHSTAN

KIRGIZ
TEPPE

Aral
ARAL
SEA

Qyzylorda

MOYYNQUM

BALQASH
KÖLI

UZBEKISTAN
TASHKENT
Shymkent
Chirchik
Khodzhent
Samarkand
TAJIKISTAN
Dushanbe

KYRGYZSTAN
Bishkek
Tokmak

AFGHANISTAN

GORNO-
BADAKHSHAN
AUT. OBLAST

Kashi

Kökshetau
Atbasar
Stepnyak
Akmola
(Tselinograd)
Temirtau
Qaraghandy

Pavlodar

Tomsk
NOVOSIBIRSK
Kuybyshev
Tayga
Mariinsk
Bogotol
Achinsk
Kemerovo
KUZNETSK
Anzhero-Sudzhensk
Kansk
BASIN
Belovo
Leninsk
Kuznetski
Barnaul
Prokop'yevsk
Biysk
Novokuznetsk
Osinniki
Rubtsovsk
Gorno-Altaysk
Leninogor
Zyryan
Semey
(Semipalatinsk)
Oskemen

Krasnoyarsk
Tayshet
Bratsk
Nizhneudinsk
Tulun
Zima
Balagansk
Chernogorsk
Minusinsk
Abakan
KHAKASSIA
G. Piramida
10 801
SAYAN
KHREBET
Cheremkhovo
Usol'ye-Sibirskoye
Angarsk
Irkutsk
Kyzyl
TUVA
TANNU-OLA

GORNO-
ALTAY

ALTAI

MTS

XINJIANG
UYGUR
(SINKIANG)

CHINA

HANGAYN
(KHANGAI MTS.)
NURUU

MONGO

TIAN SHAN
Alma-Ata
(Almaty)
Yining

SARYESIK
ATYRAU
(DESERT)

Balgash

Ayagöz

Zaysan
köli

Tsast Bogd
13 419

Continued on pages 142-143

Continued on pages 182-183

Cities
and
Towns

0 to 50,000
50,000 to 500,000

500,000 to 1,000,000
1,000,000 and over

Scale 1:16 000 000; one inch to 250 miles Conic Projection
Elevations and depressions are given in feet.

Longitude East of Greenwich

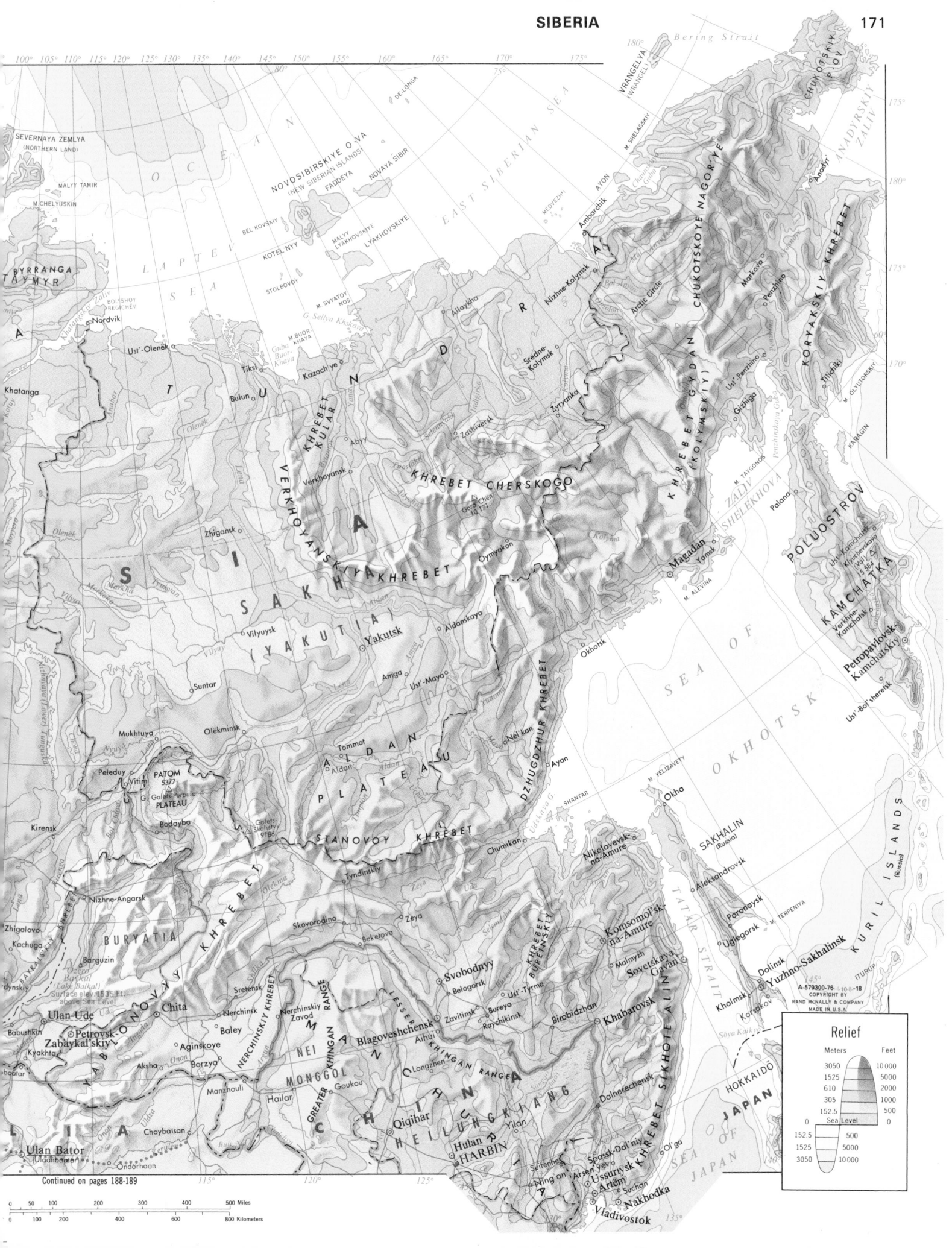

Bering Strait

SEVERNAYA ZEMLYA
(NORTHERN LAND)

MALYY TAYMYR

M. CHELYUSKIN

NOVOSIBIRSKIYE O VA
(NEW SIBERIAN ISLANDS)

FADDEYA

NOVAYA SIBIR

DE LONGA

BEL'KOVSKIY

KOTEL'NYY

MALYY
LYAKHOVSKIYE

LYAKHOVSKIYE

STOLBOVOY

EAST SIBERIAN SEA

WRANGELYA
(WRANGEL)

CHUKOTSKIY POV

ANADYRSKIY ZALIV

Anadyr'

BYRRANGA
TAYMYR

O C E A N

L A P T E V   S E A

M. SVYATOY
NOS

M SHELAGSKIY

AYON

Ambarchik

Arctic Circle

CHUKOTSKOYE NAGOR'YE

Markovo

Penzhino

Khatanga

Nordvik

Ust'-Olenëk

Tiksi

Bulun

Kazach'ye

Sredne-
Kolymsk

Nizhne-Kolymsk

Zyryanka

KHREBET GYDAN
(KOLYMSKIY)

Ust' Penzhino

Gizhiga

Tilichiki

KORYAKSKIY KHREBET

KARAGIN

Khatanga

Olenëk

Zhigansk

VERKHOYANSKIY KHREBET

KHREBET
KULAR

Verkhoyansk

Abyy

Zashiversk

KHREBET CHERSKOGO

Gora Chen
10,171

Oymyakon

Kolyma

Yamsk

Magadan

ZALIV SHELEKHOVA

Palana

POLUOSTROV

KAMCHATKA

S I B

S A K H A

(Y A K U T I A)

Vilyuysk

Yakutsk

Aldanskaya

M. ALEVINA

Klyuchevskaya
15,584

Verkhne-
Kamchatsk

Suntar

Amga

Okhotsk

SEA OF
OKHOTSK

Petropavlovsk-
Kamchatskiy

Mukhtuya

Olëkminsk

ALDAN

Tommot

Aldan

Ust'-Maya

Nel'kan

DZHUGDZHUR KHREBET

Ayan

Ust' Bol'sheretsk

PLATEAU

PATOM
5327

Peleduy

Vitim

G. Golets Purpula
PLATEAU

Bodaybo

G. Golets Skalistyy
9186

P L A T E A U

Kirensk

STANOVOY KHREBET

Chumikan

SHANTAR

Okha

M. YELIZAVETY

SAKHALIN
(Russia)

M. TERPENIYA

Zhigalovo

Kachuga

Nizhne-Angarsk

Olëkma

Tyndinskiy

Nikolayevsk-
na-Amure

Aleksandrovsk

Poronaysk

Uglegorsk

TATAR STRAIT

KURIL ISLANDS

BURYATIA

Barguzin

YABLONOVYY KHREBET

Zeya

Komsomol'sk-
na-Amure

Malmyzh

Dolinsk

Yuzhno-Sakhalinsk

ITURUP

Ozero
Baykal
(Lake Baikal)
Surface elev. 1535 Ft.
above Sea Level

Ulan-Ude

Petrovsk-
Zabaykal'skiy

Chita

Nerchinsk

NERCHINSKIY KHREBET

Nerchinskiy
Zavod

Sretensk

Baley

Skovorodino

Bekelova

Svobodnyy

Belogorsk

Ust'-Tyrma

KHREBET
BUREINSKIY

Bureya

Raychikinsk

Soyetskaya
Gavan'

Kholmsk

Korsakov

Kyakhta

Babushkin

Aginskoye

Aksha

Borzya

NEI

MONGGOL

GREATER KHINGAN RANGE

Blagoveshchensk

Aihun

LESSER KHINGAN RANGE

Birobidzhan

Khabarovsk

SIKHOTE ALIN'

Dalnerechensk

HOKKAIDO

JAPAN

SEA OF JAPAN

Manzhouli

Hailar

Goukou

Longzhen

Qiqihar

Yilan

C H I N A

H E I L U N G K I A N G

Hulan

HARBIN

Suifenho

Ning'an

Arsen'yevo

Spassk-Dal'niy

Ussuriysk

Artëm

Ol'ga

Suchan

Nakhodka

Vladivostok

Ulan Bator
(Ulaanbaatar)

Choybalsan

Ondorhaan

Continued on pages 188-189

0   50   100   200   300   400   500 Miles
0   100   200   300   400   500   600   800 Kilometers

Relief

Meters	Feet
3050	10000
1525	5000
610	2000
305	1000
152.5	500
0 Sea Level	0
152.5	500
1525	5000
3050	10000

A-579300-76
COPYRIGHT BY
RAND McNALLY & COMPANY
MADE IN U.S.A.

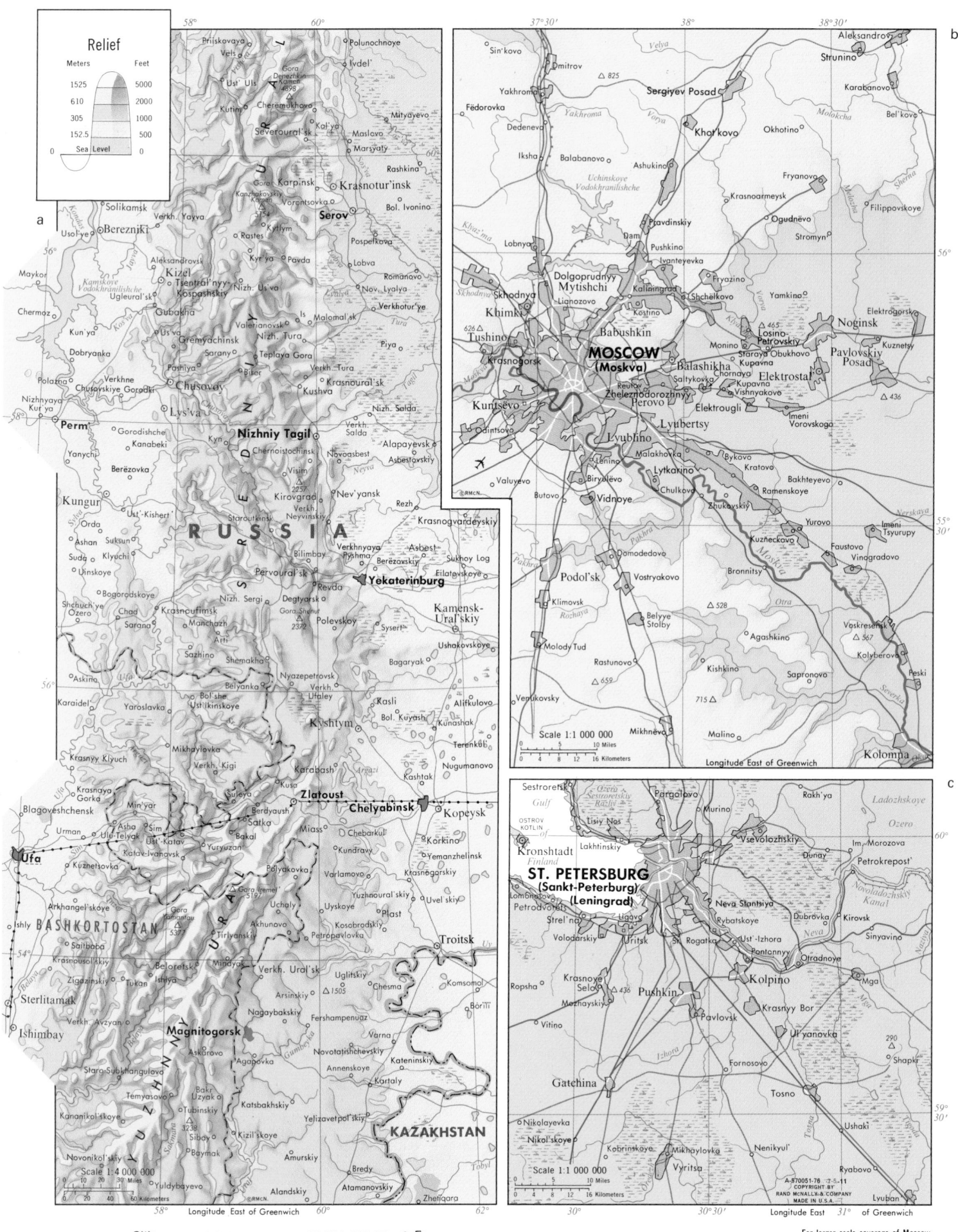

Relief

Meters	Feet
1525	5000
610	2000
305	1000
152.5	500
0	Sea Level	0

Scale 1:4 000 000

Scale 1:1 000 000

Longitude East of Greenwich

A-S70051-76 -7-5-11
COPYRIGHT BY
RAND MCNALLY & COMPANY
MADE IN U.S.A.

Cities and Towns

| | 0 to 50,000 | ○ | 500,000 to 1,000,000 | ◎ |
| | 50,000 to 500,000 | ⊙ | 1,000,000 and over | |

For larger scale coverage of Moscow and St. Petersburg see page 239.

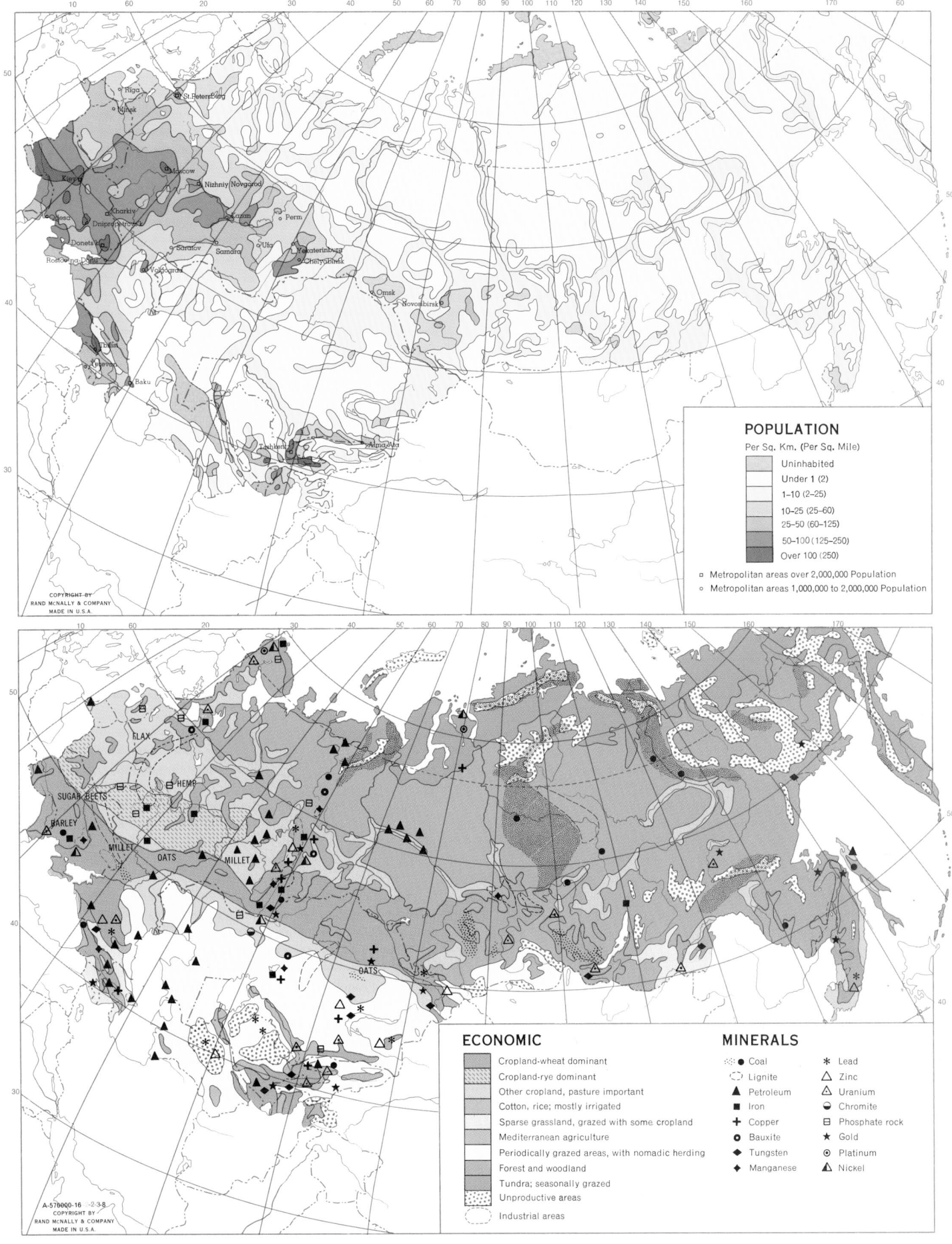

POPULATION

Per Sq. Km. (Per Sq. Mile)

Uninhabited
Under 1 (2)
1–10 (2–25)
10–25 (25–60)
25–50 (60–125)
50–100 (125–250)
Over 100 (250)

▫ Metropolitan areas over 2,000,000 Population
◦ Metropolitan areas 1,000,000 to 2,000,000 Population

ECONOMIC

Cropland-wheat dominant
Cropland-rye dominant
Other cropland, pasture important
Cotton, rice; mostly irrigated
Sparse grassland, grazed with some cropland
Mediterranean agriculture
Periodically grazed areas, with nomadic herding
Forest and woodland
Tundra; seasonally grazed
Unproductive areas

Industrial areas

MINERALS

● Coal	✳ Lead	
◌ Lignite	△ Zinc	
▲ Petroleum	△ Uranium	
■ Iron	◒ Chromite	
✚ Copper	⊟ Phosphate rock	
◎ Bauxite	★ Gold	
◆ Tungsten	◉ Platinum	
◆ Manganese	◭ Nickel	

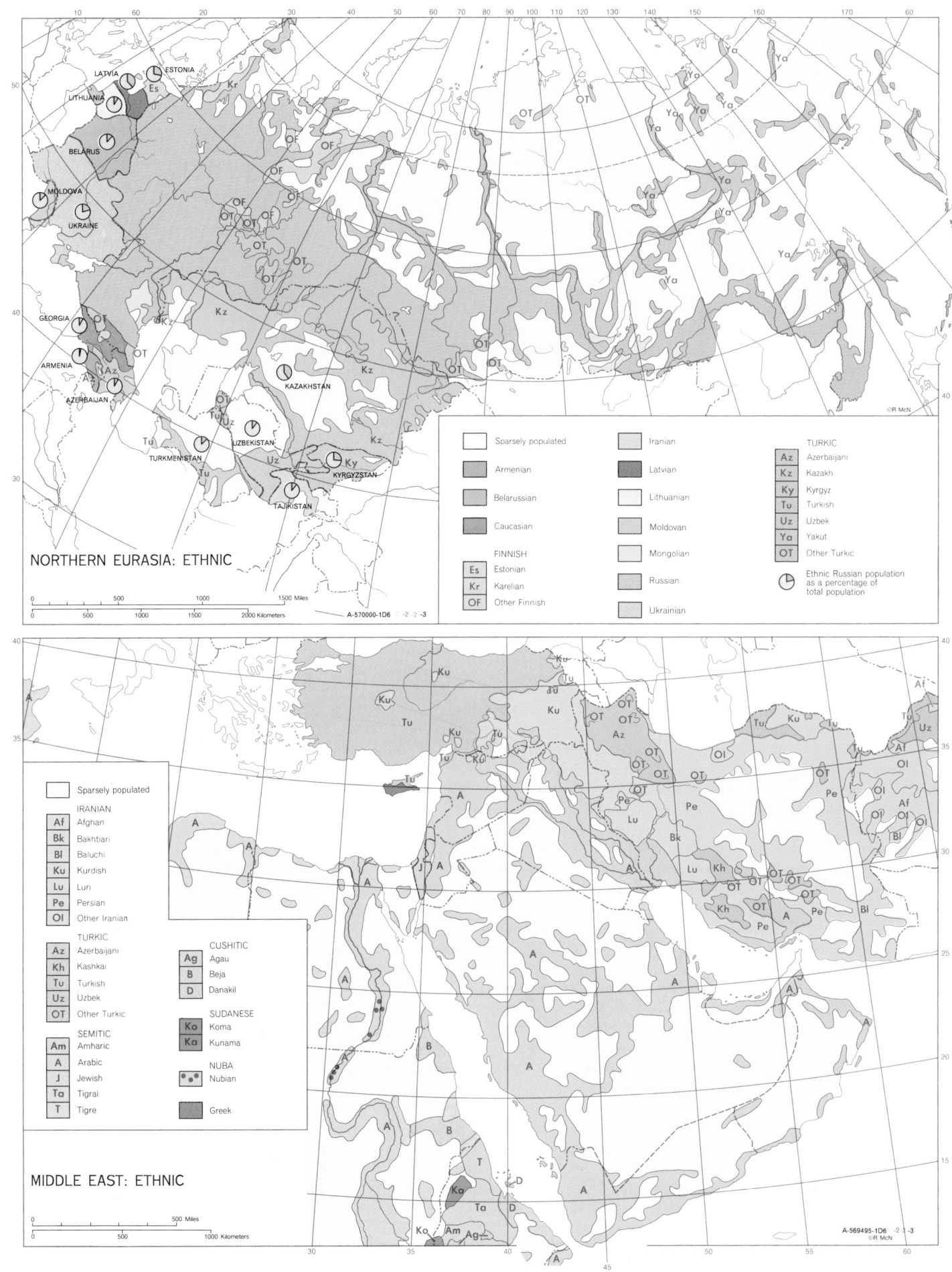

NORTHERN EURASIA: ETHNIC

					TURKIC	
	Sparsely populated		Iranian		Az	Azerbaijani
	Armenian		Latvian		Kz	Kazakh
	Belarussian		Lithuanian		Ky	Kyrgyz
	Caucasian		Moldovan		Tu	Turkish
FINNISH			Mongolian		Uz	Uzbek
Es	Estonian		Russian		Ya	Yakut
Kr	Karelian		Ukrainian		OT	Other Turkic
OF	Other Finnish					

Ethnic Russian population as a percentage of total population

MIDDLE EAST: ETHNIC

	Sparsely populated
IRANIAN	
Af	Afghan
Bk	Bakhtiari
Bl	Baluchi
Ku	Kurdish
Lu	Luri
Pe	Persian
Ol	Other Iranian

TURKIC			**CUSHITIC**	
Az	Azerbaijani		Ag	Agau
Kh	Kashkai		B	Beja
Tu	Turkish		D	Danakil
Uz	Uzbek			
OT	Other Turkic		**SUDANESE**	
			Ko	Koma
SEMITIC			Ka	Kunama
Am	Amharic			
A	Arabic		**NUBA**	
J	Jewish			Nubian
Ta	Tigrai			
T	Tigre			Greek

A-570000-1D6
©R McN

A-569495-1D6
©R McN

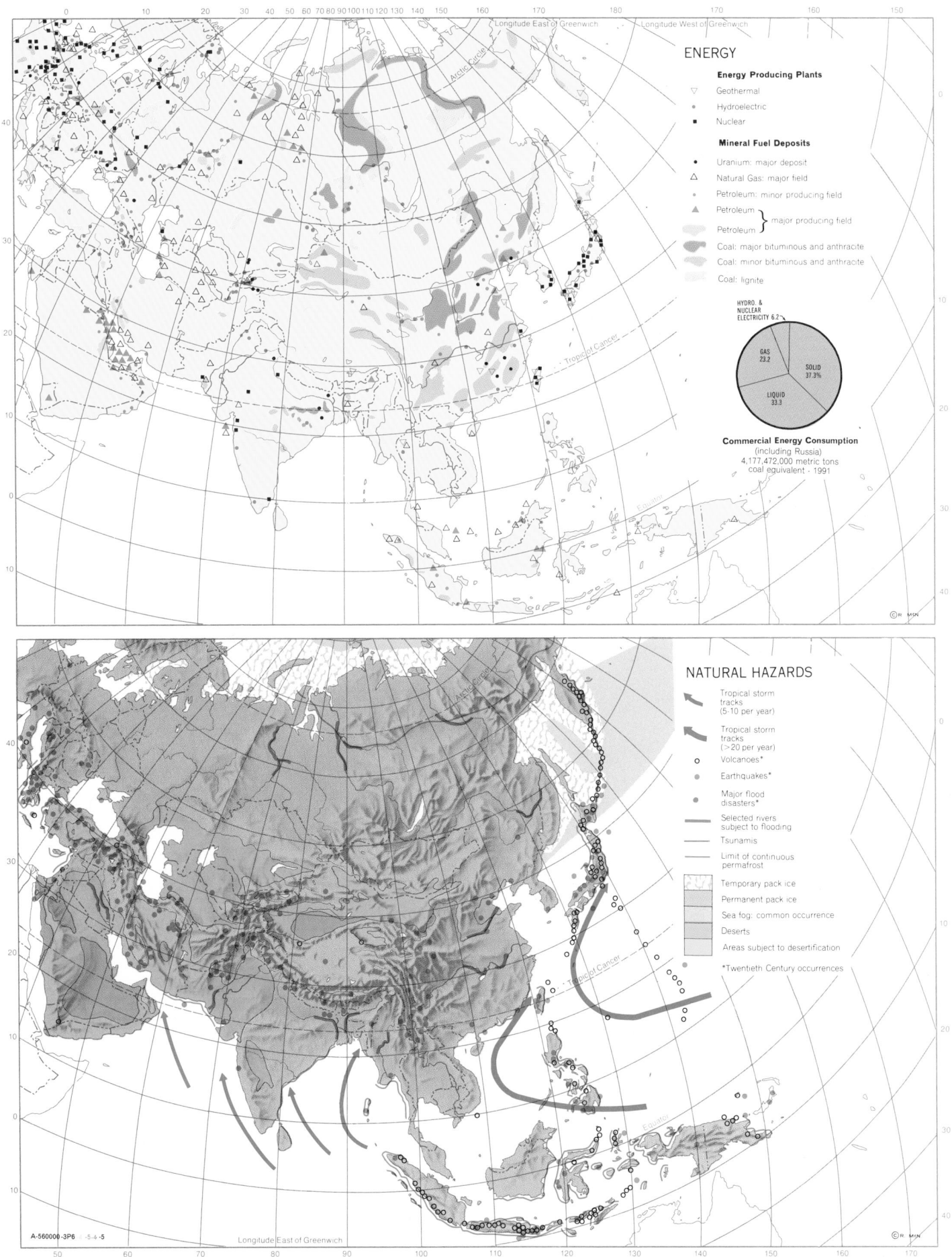

ENERGY

Energy Producing Plants

▽ Geothermal

• Hydroelectric

■ Nuclear

Mineral Fuel Deposits

● Uranium: major deposit

△ Natural Gas: major field

• Petroleum: minor producing field

▲ Petroleum } major producing field

Petroleum }

Coal: major bituminous and anthracite

Coal: minor bituminous and anthracite

Coal: lignite

HYDRO. & NUCLEAR ELECTRICITY 6.2

GAS 23.2

SOLID 37.3%

LIQUID 33.3

Commercial Energy Consumption
(including Russia)
4,177,472,000 metric tons
coal equivalent · 1991

NATURAL HAZARDS

← Tropical storm tracks (5-10 per year)

← Tropical storm tracks (>20 per year)

○ Volcanoes*

● Earthquakes*

● Major flood disasters*

━ Selected rivers subject to flooding

━ Tsunamis

━ Limit of continuous permafrost

Temporary pack ice

Permanent pack ice

Sea fog: common occurrence

Deserts

Areas subject to desertification

*Twentieth Century occurrences

A-560000-3P6 -5-4 -5

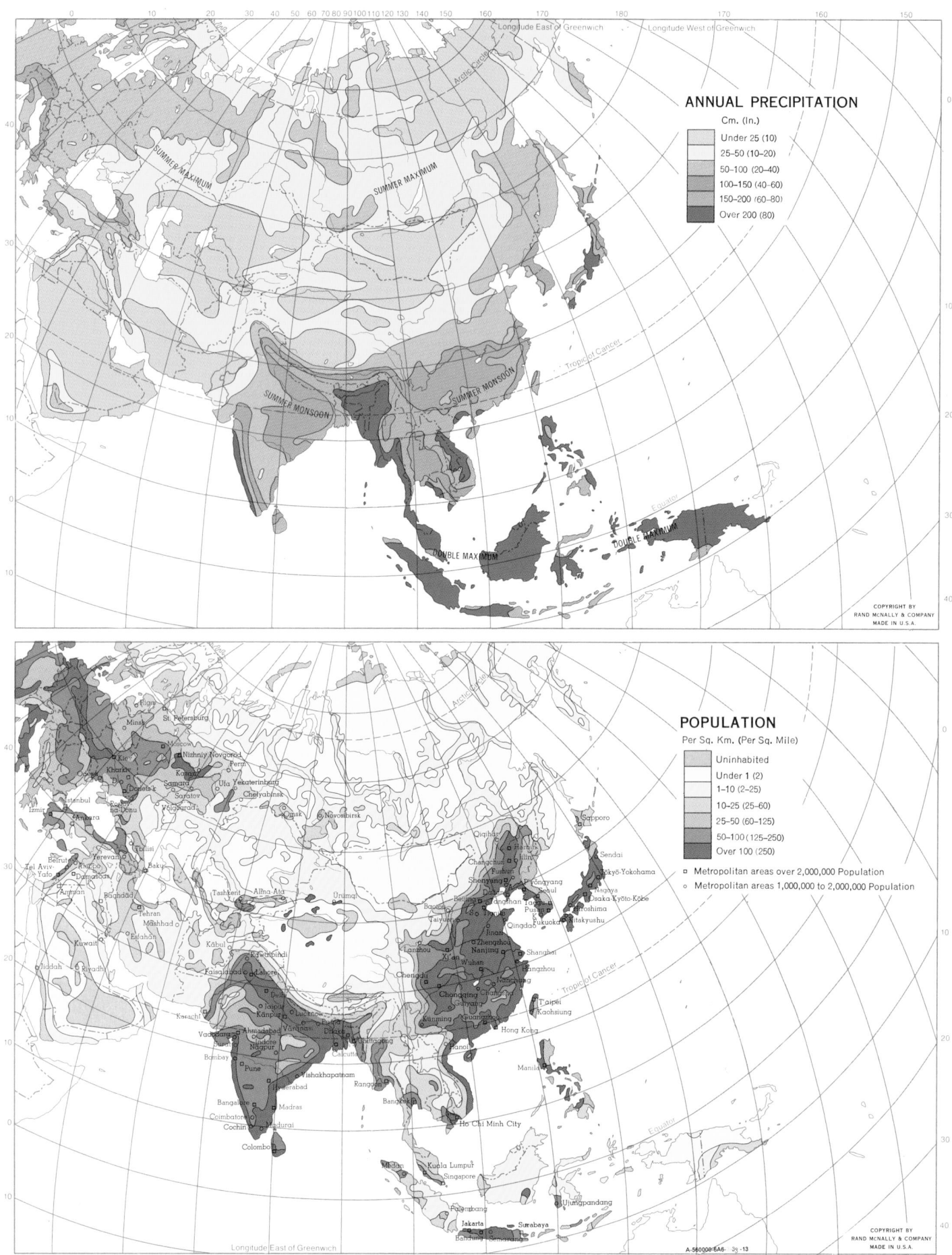

ANNUAL PRECIPITATION

Cm. (In.)

- Under 25 (10)
- 25–50 (10–20)
- 50–100 (20–40)
- 100–150 (40–60)
- 150–200 (60–80)
- Over 200 (80)

POPULATION

Per Sq. Km. (Per Sq. Mile)

- Uninhabited
- Under 1 (2)
- 1–10 (2–25)
- 10–25 (25–60)
- 25–50 (60–125)
- 50–100 (125–250)
- Over 100 (250)

□ Metropolitan areas over 2,000,000 Population

○ Metropolitan areas 1,000,000 to 2,000,000 Population

A-560000-5A6- 3g-13

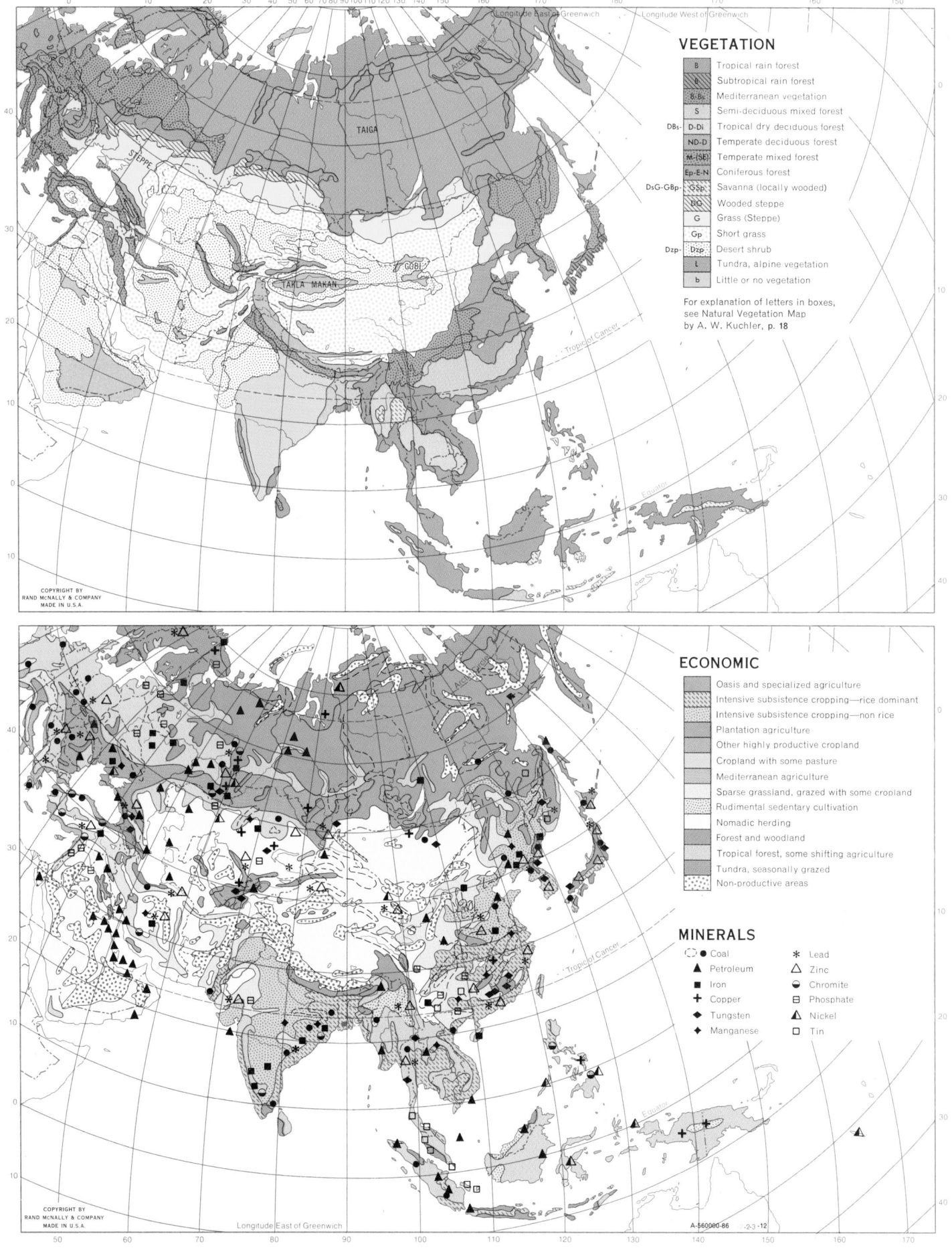

VEGETATION

B	Tropical rain forest
B	Subtropical rain forest
B-Bs	Mediterranean vegetation
S	Semi-deciduous mixed forest
DBs- D-Di	Tropical dry deciduous forest
ND-D	Temperate deciduous forest
M-(SE)	Temperate mixed forest
Ep-E-N	Coniferous forest
DsG-GBp- GSp	Savanna (locally wooded)
DG	Wooded steppe
G	Grass (Steppe)
Gp	Short grass
Dzp- Dzp	Desert shrub
L	Tundra, alpine vegetation
b	Little or no vegetation

For explanation of letters in boxes,
see Natural Vegetation Map
by A. W. Kuchler, p. 18

TAIGA
STEPPE
GOBI
TAKLA MAKAN

ECONOMIC

	Oasis and specialized agriculture
	Intensive subsistence cropping—rice dominant
	Intensive subsistence cropping—non rice
	Plantation agriculture
	Other highly productive cropland
	Cropland with some pasture
	Mediterranean agriculture
	Sparse grassland, grazed with some cropland
	Rudimental sedentary cultivation
	Nomadic herding
	Forest and woodland
	Tropical forest, some shifting agriculture
	Tundra, seasonally grazed
	Non-productive areas

MINERALS

●	Coal	✳	Lead
▲	Petroleum	△	Zinc
■	Iron	◖	Chromite
✚	Copper	⊟	Phosphate
◆	Tungsten	▲	Nickel
✦	Manganese	□	Tin

Longitude East of Greenwich

A-560000-86   -2-3 -12

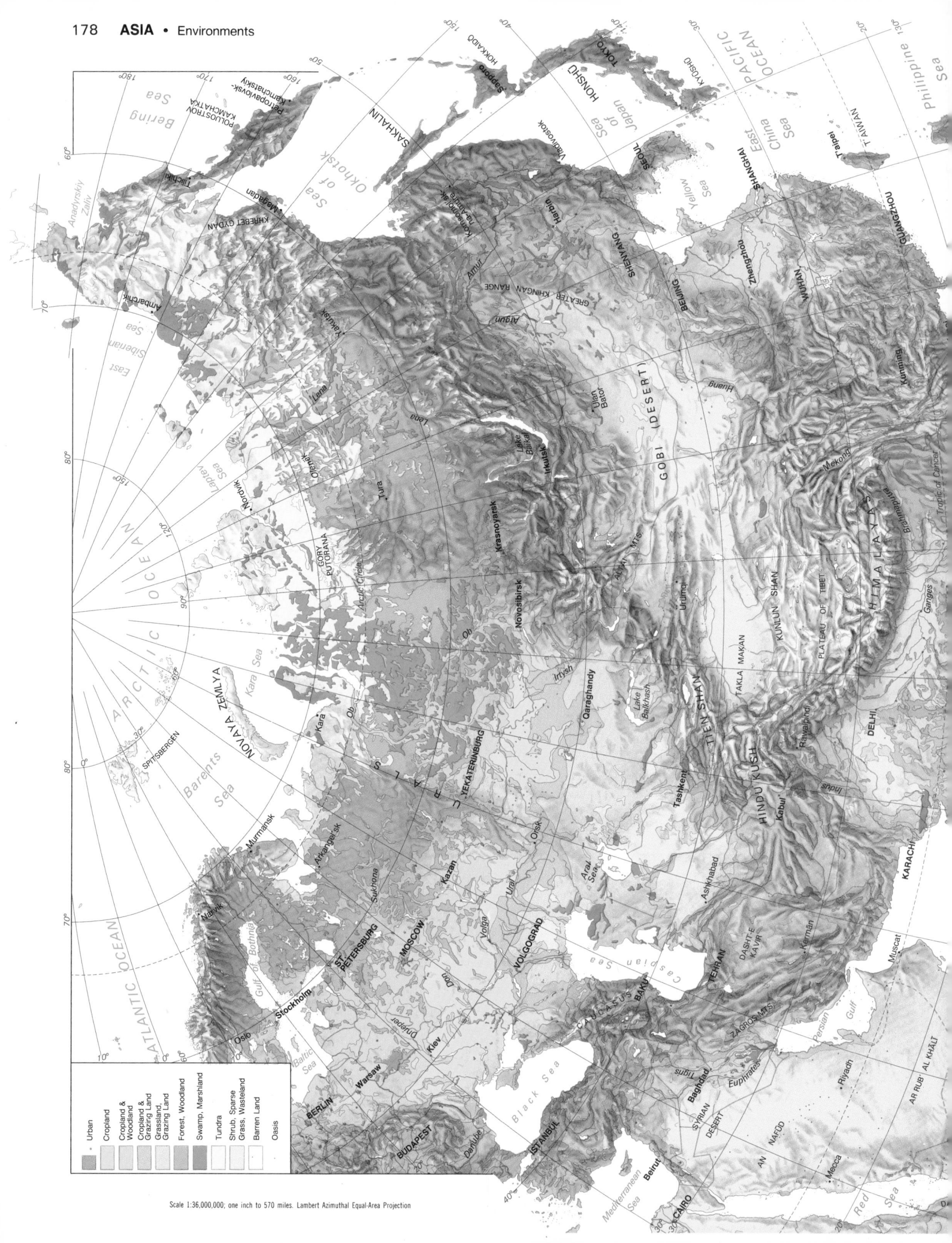

Scale 1:36,000,000; one inch to 570 miles. Lambert Azimuthal Equal-Area Projection

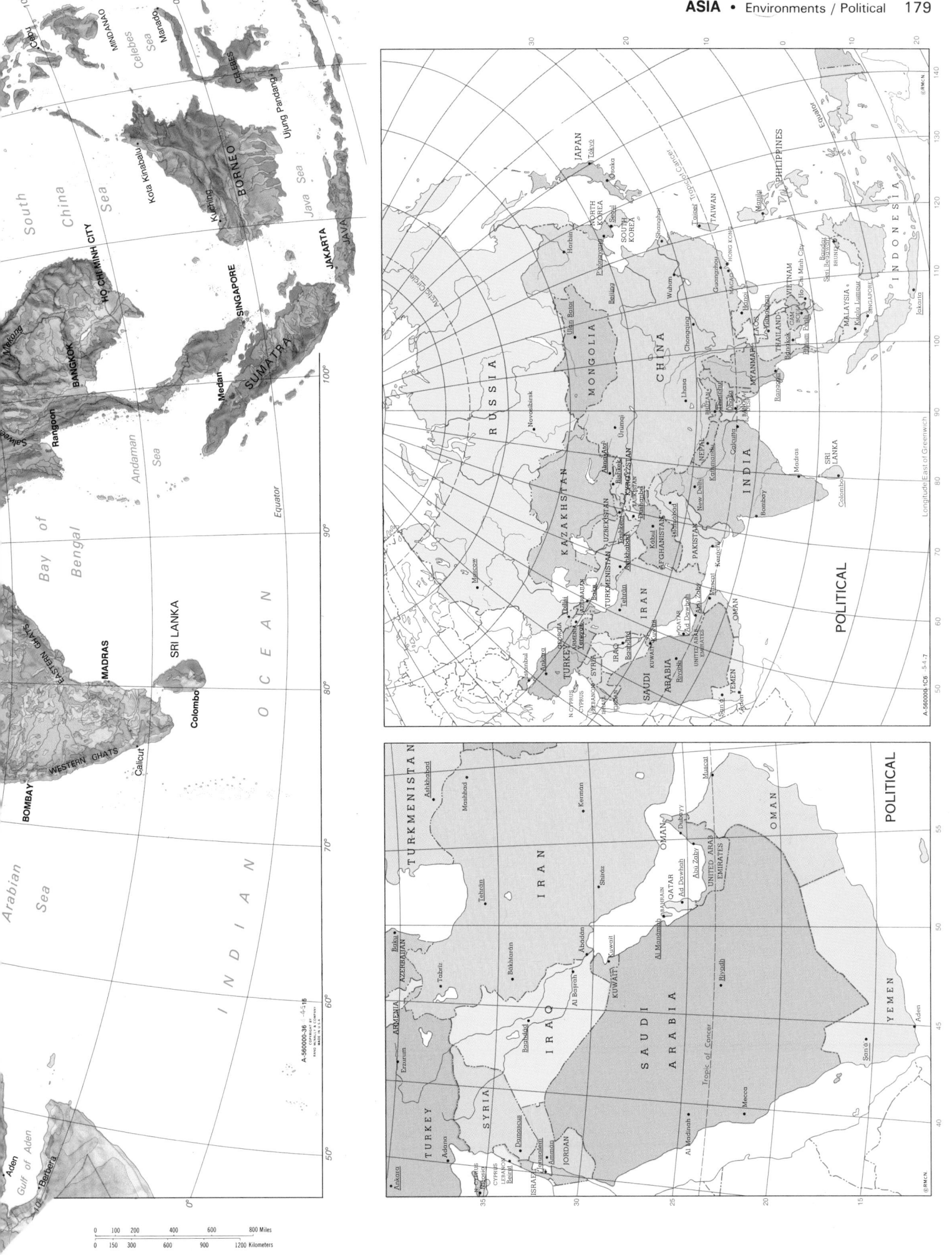

POLITICAL

POLITICAL

Continued on page 209

Relief

Meters		Feet
3050		10 000
1525		5000
610		2000
305		1000
0	Sea Level	0
		Below Sea Level
152.5		500
1525		5000
3050		10 000
6100		20 000

A-519695-76   -1918-37
COPYRIGHT BY
RAND McNALLY & COMPANY
MADE IN U.S.A.

Scale 1:40 000 000; one inch to 630 miles. Lambert's Azimuthal, Equal Area Projection
Elevations and depressions are given in feet

a

NORTH AMERICA

Bering Str.
M. DEZHNEVA
(EAST CAPE)

WRANGELYA
S. VRANGELYA

Arctic Circle

Anadырskiy Zaliv

M. LOPATKA

PRIBILOF IS. (USA)

ALEUTIAN ISLANDS (USA)

ALEUTIAN TRENCH

West Longitude

East Longitude

SIBERIAN

KHREBET GYDAN

KORYAKSKIY KHREBET

KOMANDORSKIYE OSTROVA (Sov. Union)

Petropavlovsk-Kamchatskiy

P-ov KAMCHATKA

M. Kronotskiy

Yakutsk

HOYANSKIY KHREBET

DZHUGDZHUR KHREBET

Okhotsk

SEA OF OKHOTSK

KURIL ISLANDS (Sov. Union)

Hakodate

HOKKAIDO

JAPAN

PACIFIC OCEAN

Nerchinsk

STANOVOY KHREBET

Blagoveshchensk
Sovetskaya Gavan
Svobodny
Khabarovsk

Komsomolsk

SAKHALIN

Tatar Strait

SIKHOTE ALIN

Vladivostok

SEA OF JAPAN

HONSHU

Sendai

TOKYO
YOKOHAMA

A

GREATER KHINGAN RANGE

HARBIN

MANCHURIA

CHANGCHUN

Jilin

Pyongyang

KYOTO
KOBE OSAKA

SHENYANG

NORTH KOREA

SEOUL

SOUTH KOREA

KITAKYUSHU
Nagasaki

KYUSHU

NANSEI SHOTO

Zhangjiakou

BEIJING

TIANJIN
Jinan

Dalian

Bo Hai

QINGDAO

NANJING

SHANGHAI

EAST CHINA SEA

Tropic of Cancer

TAIYUAN

XI'AN

WUHAN

Changsha

NAN LING

Fuzhou

Xiamen

Shantou

GUANGZHOU

HONG KONG

Macao (Port.)

Wuzhou

HAINAN DAO

PHILIPPINES

Quezon City

MANILA

LUZON

SAMAR

MINDORO

PANAY

LEYTE

NEGROS

PALAWAN

MINDANAO

PHILIPPINE SEA

BABUYAN IS.

TAIWAN (FORMOSA)

T'AIPEI

Taiwan Strait

Hue

Phnom Penh

HO CHI MINH CITY (Saigon)

MUI BAI BUNG

SOUTH CHINA SEA

Kota Kinabalu

Sandakan

SULU SEA

SULU IS.

CELEBES SEA

HALMAHERA

NEW GUINEA

CELEBES

BRUNEI

MALAYSIA

Kuching

BORNEO

INDONESIA

SINGAPORE

Equator

CYPRUS

Néa Pátos

Ólimbos 1953
6401

Lárnax

Kólpos Lárnakos

PIDÁLION

Longitude 35° East of Greenwich 36°

Episkopi

Lemesós

AKR. GÁTAS

Ţarābulus (Tripoli)

Al Qusayr

Halba

Al Hirmil

Al Batrūn

Zgharta

Amyūn 10,731

Jubayl (Byblos)

2625

Beirut (Bayrūt)

Jūniyah

Ba'labakk

Zaḥlah

Az Zabdānī

Ad Dāmūr

MEDITERRANEAN

Şaydā (Sidon)

Jazzīn

Damascus (Dimashq)

Dūmā

Rāshayyā

Şūr (Tyre)

Marj 'Uyūn

Al Kiswah

SYRIA

Qiryat Shemona

Al Qunayṭirah

Tibnīn

SEA

Nahariyya

Zefat

Sanamayn

Hare Meron 3963

Teverya

'Akko

Dar'ā

Haifa (Hefa)

Nazerat

Irbid

'Afula

Bet She'an

Hadera

Jenin

Tülkarm

Netanya

Shechem (Ruins)

Jarash

Herzliyya

Nabulus

Al Mafraq

Petaḥ Tiqwa

As Salt

Az Zarqā'

Tel Aviv-Yafo

B

Rishon leZiyyon

Artha

Ammān

Rehovot

Lod

Jericho

Ma'daba

Jerusalem

Bayt Lahm (Bethlehem)

Zuwayẓā

Ashdod

Qiryat Gat

Dhibān

Ashqelon

Al Khalīl (Hebron)

Al Mazra'ah

Mahattat al Qaṭrānah

Gaza (Ghazzah)

Be'er Sheva

Arad

Al Karak

Port Said (Būr Sa'īd)

Khan Yūnus

Rafah

C

Al Mazār

Khalīj aṭ Tīnah

Sabkhat al Bardawil

Dimona
Sedom

Ras al Naqb

At Ṭafīlah

Al 'Arīsh

Horvot Shiva (Ruins)

Qezi'ot

5383

Jabal al Mil'itah

Mahattat Jurf ad Darāwīsh

Rummānah

Daphnae (Ruins)

Al Qantarah

NEGEV

Ash Shawbak

Ismailia (Al Isma'īlīyah)

Al Qusaymah

Petra (Ruins)

Wādī Mūsā

Ras Abū Qurūn

JABAL YU'ALLIQ
3578

Fā'id

Great Bitter Lake

Ma'ān

QA' AL JAFR

Suez (As Suways)

MITLA PASS

EGYPT

An Nakhl

Al Kuntillah

Ra's an Naqb

Mahattat 'Aqabat al Hijāzīyah

Jabal Ramm 5755

Mahattata ar Ramlah

Ath Thamad 3513

Elat

Al 'Aqabah

Al Mudawwarah

JABAL AT TĪH

3789

Haql

SAUDI ARABIA

4138
JABAL JALĀLAH AL BAHRĪYAH

JABAL AL 'AJMAH

Ra's al Junaynah

Nuwaybi' al Muzayyinah

JABAL MAZHAFAH

Scale 1:4 000 000

Bi'r Za'farānah

4833
JABAL AL JALĀLAT AL QIBLĪYAH

Abū Zanimah

5335

SINAI PEN (SHIBH JAZĪRAT SĪNĀ)

6232

RMCN

Golan Heights area. Occupied by Israel since 1967. Unilaterally annexed by Israel, 1981.

West Bank area. Unilaterally annexed by Jordan, 1950. Occupied by Israel since 1967. Status to be determined.

Gaza Strip. Occupied by Israel since 1967. Status to be determined.

b

Scale 1:4 000 000

Kuala Lumpur

Kelang

PAHANG

Merchong

3°

Kajang

Kuala Klawang

Gunung Telapa 3915
Burok

Bahau

TIOMAN

SELANGOR

Telok Datok

Padang Endau

Gunung Kajang 3444

NEGERI SEMBILAN

Sepang

Rantau

Seremban

Rompin

Gemas

PEMANGGIL

Port Dickson

Rembau

Tampin

Segamat

Mersing

AUR

CAPE RACHADO

Alor Gajah

Jasin

Mt. Ophir 4187

Labis

2002

SOUTH

Melaka (Malacca)

MELAKA

Panchor

MALAYSIA

Paloh

TINGGI

MALAY

Bandar Maharani

JOHOR

Keluang

3312

CHINA

Batu Pahat

Ayer Hitam

Gunung Blumut

Rengam

PENINSULA

Jumrah

RUPAT

Teluklecak

Pontian Kechil

Layang Layang

Kota Tinggi

Jason Bay

SEA

Dumai

Batupanjang

TANJONG TOHOR

Johor Bahru

Bengkalis

BENGKALIS

SINGAPORE

Ketamputih

TANJONG PIAI

SINGAPORE

TANJUNG RAMUNIA

TANJONG BERAKIT

SUMATRA

Kudap

1837

KARIMUN BESAR

BATAM

Singapore Strait

Pinggir

PADANG

Telesung

KEPULAUAN RIAU

BINTAN

INDONESIA

RIAU

341

Buatan

Siaksriinderapura

KUNDUR

RANGSANG

Baranpauh

REMPANG

Tanjungbatu

Tanjungpinang

Serangung

TEBINGTINGGI

Minas

Baranpauh

RMCN

0 200 400 600 800 1000 Miles

0 400 800 1200 1600 Kilometers

BLACK SEA

İstanbul Boğazı (Bosporus)
ISTANBUL
Marmara Denizi
Truva (Ruins)
Mitilini
Bergama
İzmir
Aydın
Büyük Menderes
Muğla
RÓDHOS

Zonguldak
Kastamonu
Sinop
Kütahya
Eskişehir
Çankırı
Bursa
Sakarya
Afyon
Eğridir Gölü
Isparta
Antalya
TOROS DAĞLARI
İçel

Kutaisi
Merzifon
Çorum
Yozgat
Tokat
Sivas
Samsun
Giresun
Trabzon

Ankara
Kırıkkale
Kırşehir
Kayseri
Konya
Kahramanmaraş
Adana
Tarsus
İskenderun
Hatay
Gaziantep

TURKEY

Batumi
Poti
Vladikavkaz
Grozny
Makhachkala
Derbent

GEORGIA
Tbilisi
Gyumri
Kars
ARMENIA
Yerevan
Erzurum
Erzincan
Malatya
Elâzığ
Diyarbakır
Şanlıurfa
Siverek
Mardin
Cizre

RUSSIA
CAUCASUS
Gäncä
AZERBAIJAN
BAKU (Bakı)
Tabrīz
Ardabīl
Lānkāran

Fort Shevchenko
Aqtaū
ARAL SEA
PLATO UST-URT
KAZA
Kungrad
Chimbay
Nukus
UZBEKISTAN
PESKI KYZYLK (DESERT)
Khiva
Turtkul

CASPIAN SEA
Surface 92 feet below Sea Level
Krasnovodsk
Nebit-Dag
Chikishlyar
Bandar-e Anzali
Rasht
Bandar-e Torkeman
Gorgan
Emāmshahr
TURKMENISTAN
Ashkhabad
Chardzhou
Mary
KOPPEH DAGH
Kushka

MEDITERRANEAN SEA

CYPRUS
NORTH CYPRUS
Nicosia
Tarābulus (Tripoli)
LEBANON
Beirut
Şaydā (Sidon)
Haifa
ISRAEL
Tel Aviv-Yafo
Jerusalem
Gaza
Areas occupied by Israel since 1967
Rashīd
Damietta
Port Saïd
ALEXANDRIA (Al Iskandarīyah)
CAIRO (Al Qāhirah)
Suez (As Suways)
SINAI
GULF OF SUEZ

Al Lādhiqīyah (Latakia)
Ḥalab (Aleppo)
Ḥimṣ
Ḥamāh
Dayr az Zawr
SYRIA
Palmyra (Ruins)
Damascus (Dimashq)
As Suwaydā'
Amman
JORDAN
Ma'ān
Al 'Aqabah

Al Mawṣil
Irbil
As Sulaymānīyah
Kirkūk
Ar Ramādī
BAGHDAD
Karbalā'
An Najaf
Babylon (Ruins)
IRAQ
Tikrīt
Abū Kamāl
An Nāṣirīyah
Al Baṣrah
Khorramshahr
Ābādān

Khvoy
Orūmīyeh
Mīāneh
Zanjān
Qazvīn
Sanandaj
Bakhtarān
Hamadān
Arāk
Bojūrd
Kāshān
Qom
TEHRĀN
ELBURZ MTS.
Qolleh-ye Damāvand
Dāmghān
Neyshābūr
Mashhad
DASHT-E KAVIR DESERT
Ferdows
Bajestān
Qāyen
Bīrjand
Herāt
AFGHA

Dezfūl
Shūshtar
Masjed-e Soleymān
Ahvāz
Esfahān
Qomsheh
Yazd
Bāfq
PLATEAU OF IRAN
Farāh

I R A N

Bandar-e Būshehr
Shīrāz
Persepolis (Ruins)
Kāzerūn
Borāzjān
Jahrom
Kermān
Rafsanjān
Zāhedān
CHAGAI H

Kuwait (Al Kuwayt)
KUWAIT
Al Jubayl
RA'S AT TANNŪRAH
Ad Dammām
Al Qaṭīf
Az Zahrān (Dhahran)
Al Hufūf
BAHRAIN
Al Manāmah
QATAR
Ad Dawḥah
Abū Ẓaby
UNITED ARAB EMIRATES
Dubayy
PERSIAN GULF
Bandar-e Lengeh
Qeshm
Bandar-e 'Abbās
Jāsk
STR. OF HORMUZ
GULF OF OMAN
Bandar Beheshtī
Gwādar

AN NAFŪD
Taymā'
JABAL SHAMMAR
Ḥā'il
Al Qayṣūmah
Al Wajh
Khaybar
Burayḍah
'Unayzah
Sudayr
Ash Shaqrā'
Riyadh (Ar Riyāḍ)
AL HASĀ
ADDAHNĀ
SAUDI NAJD

RA'S BANAS
Būr Safājah
Al Quṣayr
EGYPT
Jabal Radwah
Yanbu'
Al Madīnah (Medina)
AL HIJAZ
Jiddah
Mecca (Makkah)
Aṭ Ṭā'if
Al Khurmah
Wādī ad Dawāsir
Al Lidām
ARABIA

JABAL AL TUWAYQ
AL AFLAJ
Ad Dilam
AD DAHNĀ
NAFŪD
Mubarraz

Al Khābūrah
Matraḥ
Muscat
JABAL AL AKHDAR
Jabal ash Shām
Ṣūr
RA'S AL HADD
RA'S AL MADRAKAH
AR RUB' AL KHĀLĪ
OMAN
Al Buraymī
Al Maṣīrah
KHŪRYĀN-MŪRYĀN (Oman)
Mirbāt
Ṣayḥūt

Tropic of Cancer

SUDAN
Būr Sūdān
Sawākin
ADMINISTR. BDY.
Tawkar
Al Qunfudhah
Abhā
ERITREA
Kassalā
Sebderat
Keren
Miṭwa (Massawa)
Akordat
Asmera
Adi Ugri
ETHIOPIA

JĀZA'IR FARASAN
Qīzān
Abū 'Arīsh
Ṣa'dah
Al Luḥayyah
KAMARAN
Al Ḥudaydah
Al Mukhā (Mocha)
Madīnat ash Sha'b
Aden ('Adan)
Bāb el Mandeb
DJIBOUTI
Djibouti
Tadjoura
Aysha
Dese
Seylac

NAJRAN
RAMLAT AS SAB'ATAYN
Shibām
Tarīm
Say'ūn
Al Ḥawṭah
Ḥadūr Shu'ayb
San'ā'
YEMEN
HADRAMAWT
Ash Shiḥr
Al Mukallā
Shuqrah
GULF OF ADEN
Caluula
GEES GWARDAFUY
SUQUTRA (SOCOTRA) (Yemen)
Ḥadībū
Lass Qoray
Berbera
SOMALIA

RED SEA

Continued on pages 210-211

Relief

Meters		Feet
3050		10 000
1525		5000
610		2000
305		1000
152.5		500
0	Sea Level	0
152.5		500 Below Sea Level
1525		5000
3050		10 000

A-569400-76 -21 -37
COPYRIGHT BY
RAND-MCNALLY & COMPANY
MADE IN U.S.A.

40°   45°   50°   55°   60°   Longitude East of Greenwich

Scale 1:16 000 000; one inch to 250 miles. Polyconic Projection
Elevations and depressions are given in feet

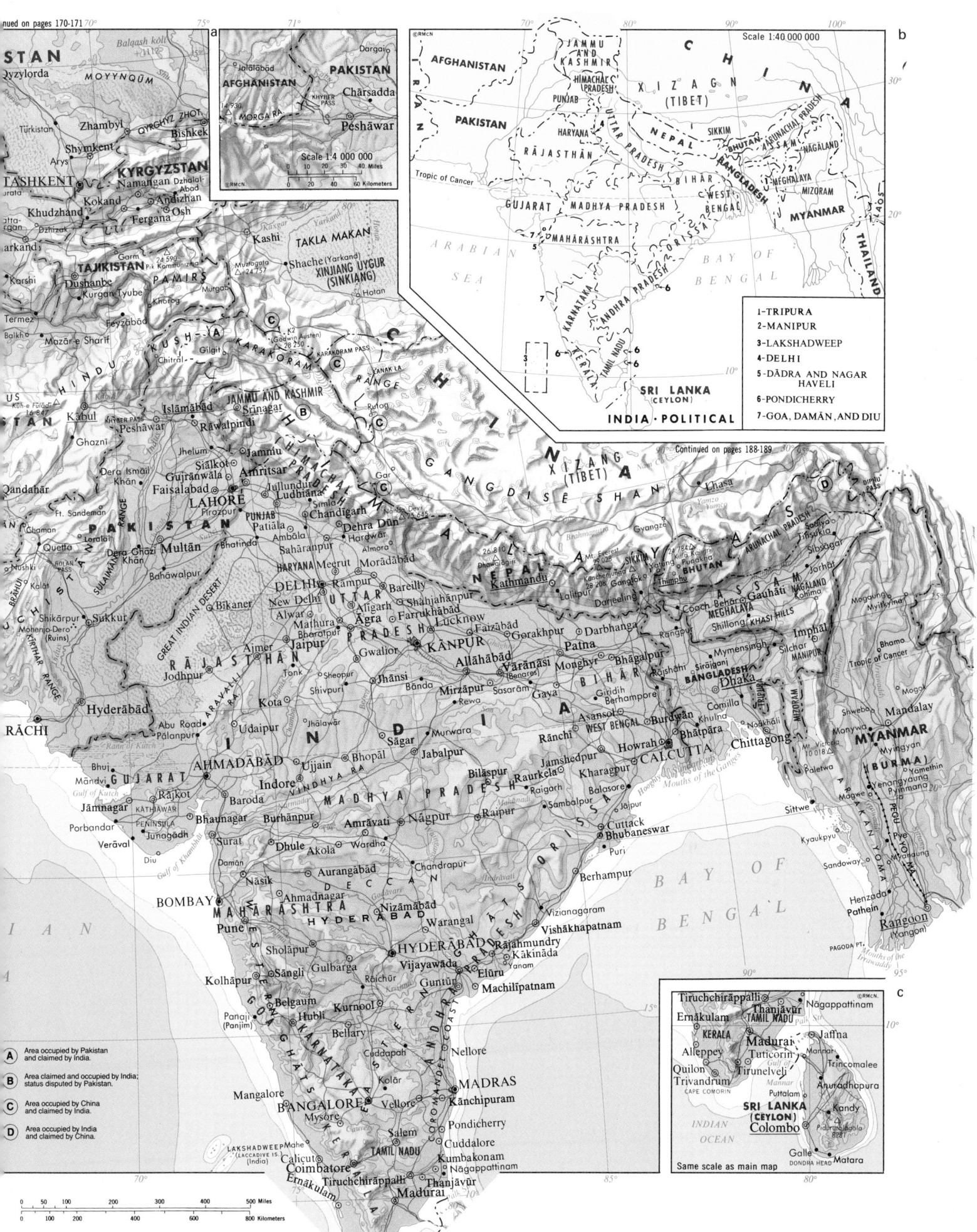

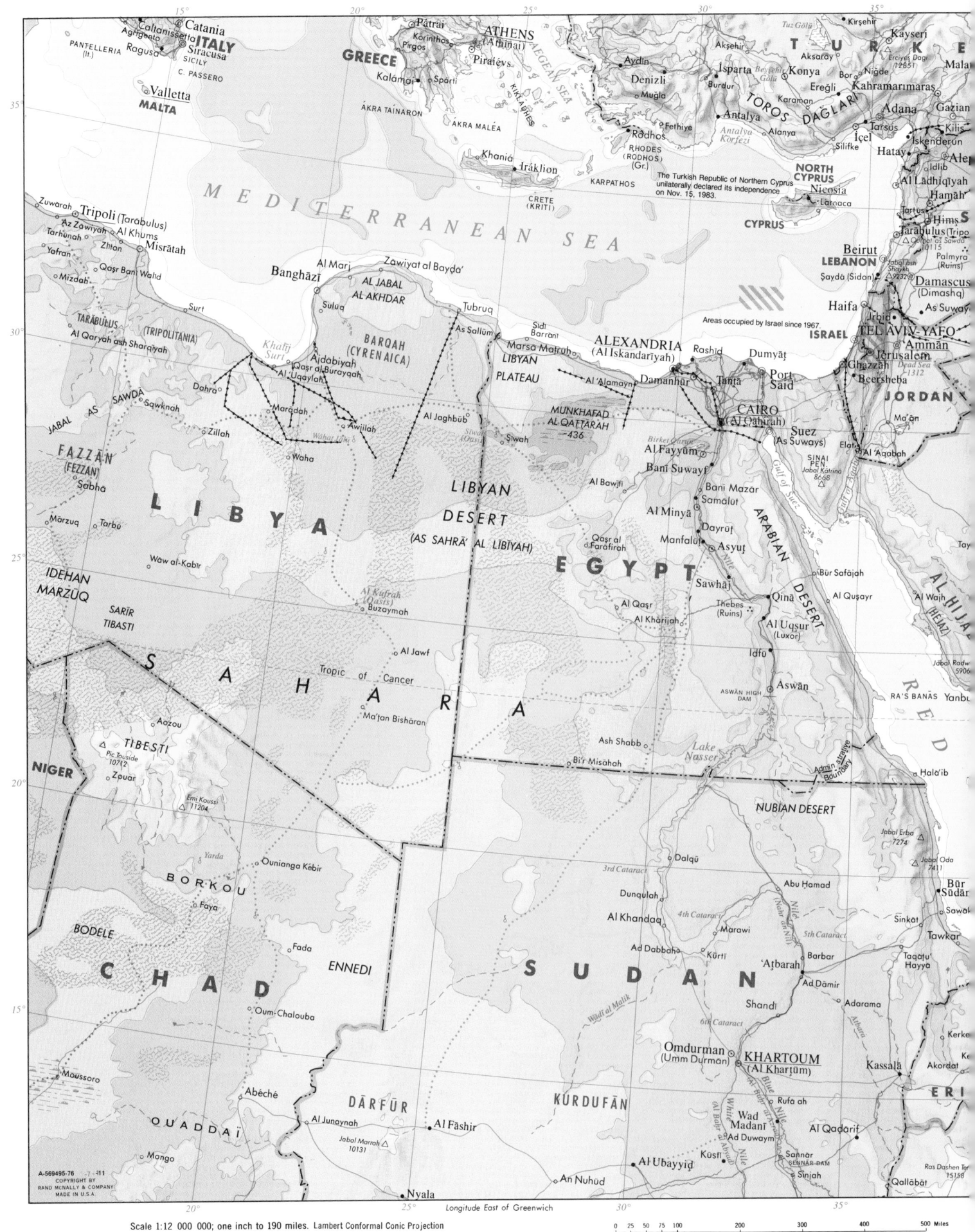

Scale 1:12 000 000; one inch to 190 miles. Lambert Conformal Conic Projection

Elevations and depressions are given in feet

Longitude East of Greenwich

Scale bar: 0 25 50 75 100 200 300 400 500 Miles
0 100 200 400 600 800 Kilometers

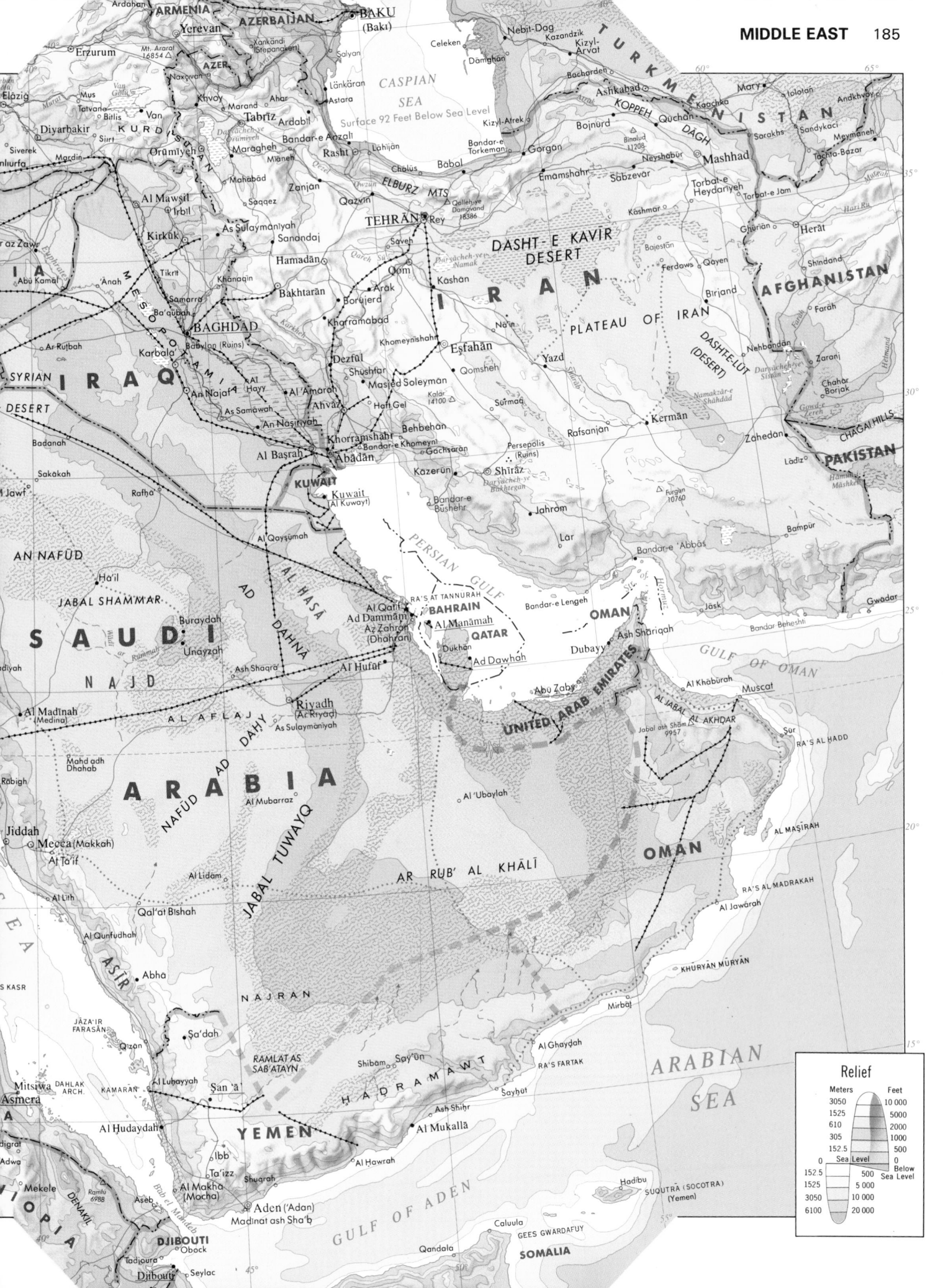

a

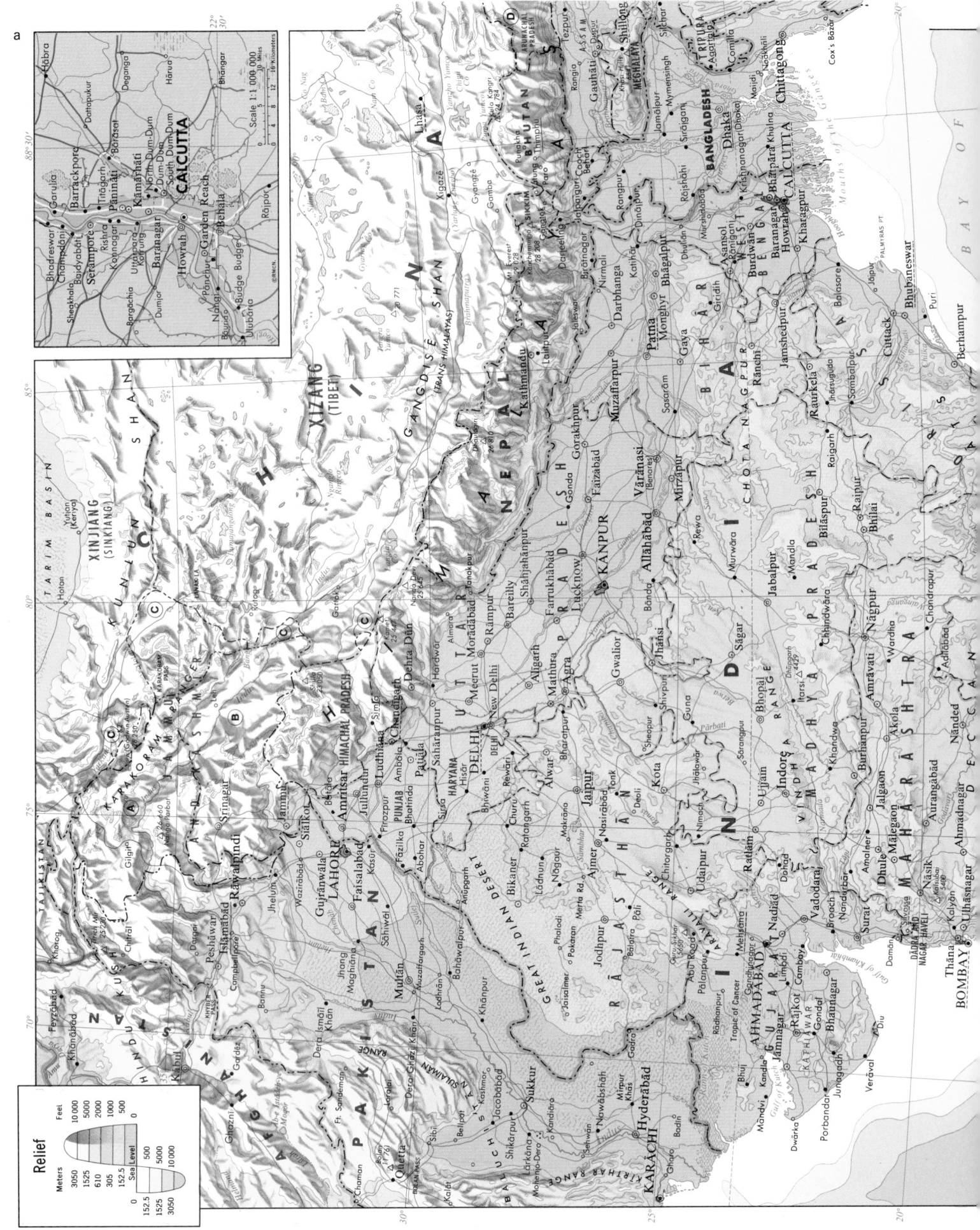

Scale 1:10 000 000; one inch to 160 miles. Lambert Conformal Conic Projection
Elevations and depressions are given in feet

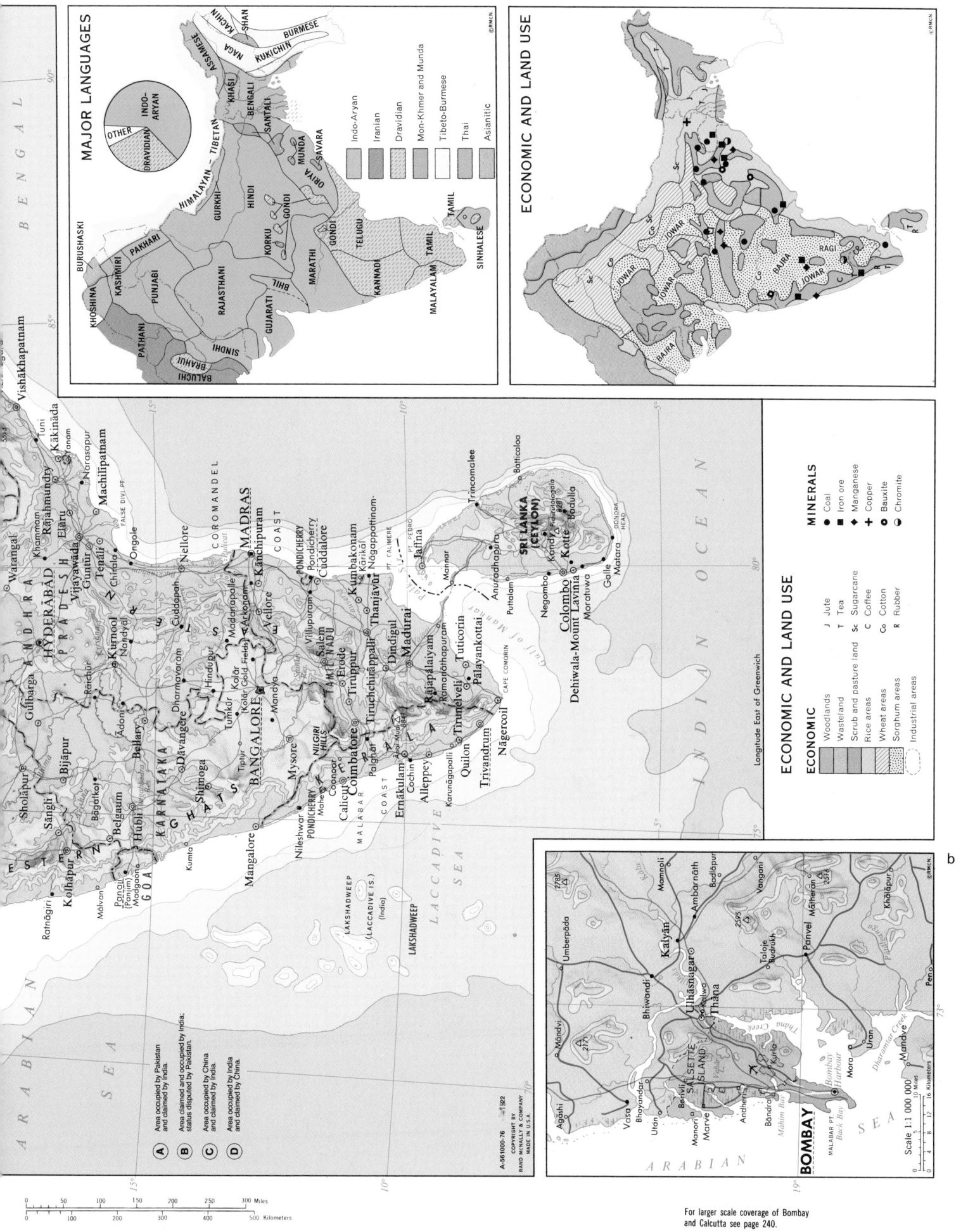

For larger scale coverage of Bombay and Calcutta see page 240.

Continued on pages 170-171

Continued on pages 182-183

Scale 1:16 000 000; one inch to 250 miles. Polyconic Projection
Elevations and depressions are given in feet

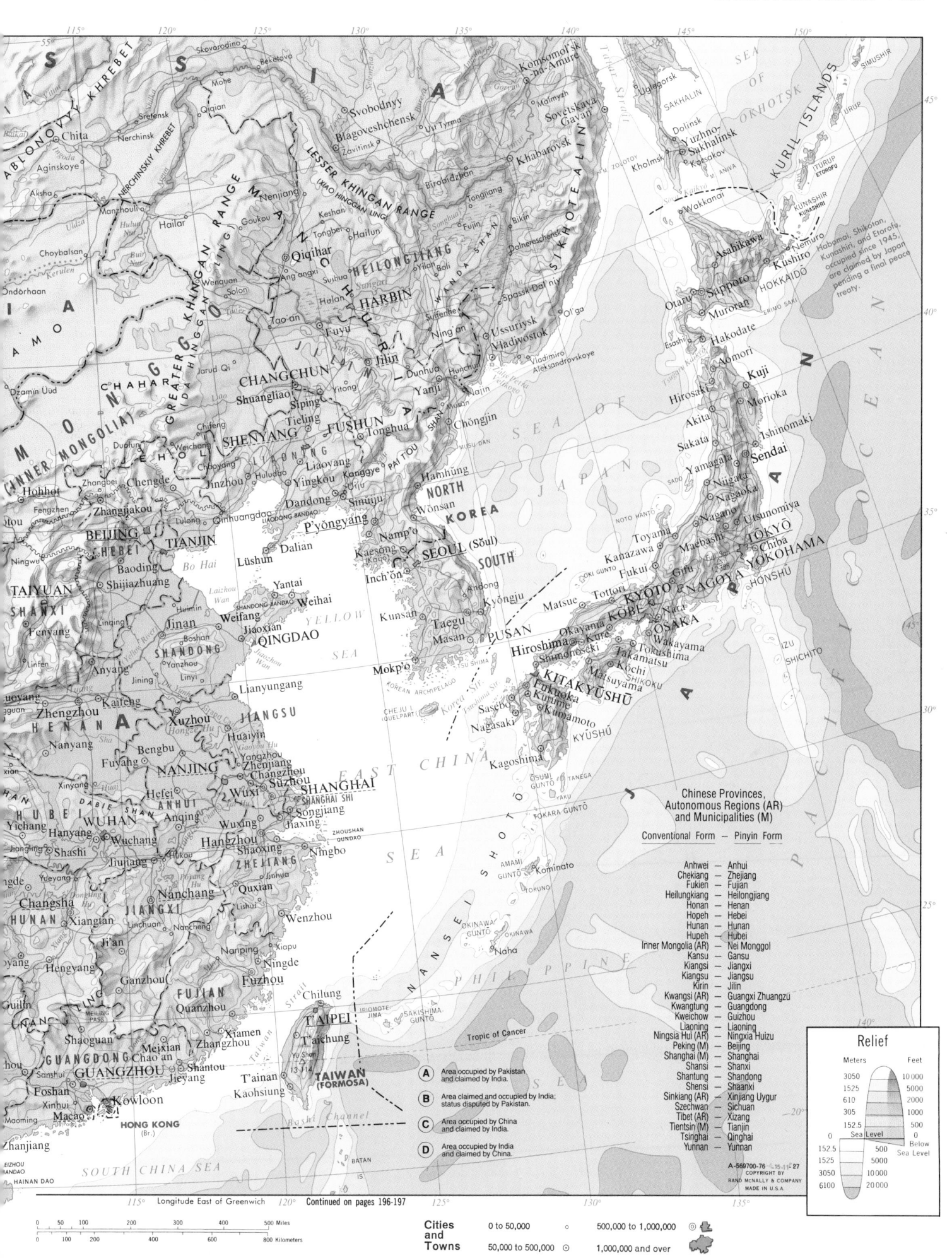

Relief

Meters		Feet
3050		10 000
1525		5000
610		2000
305		1000
152.5		500
0	Sea Level	0
152.5		500
1525		Below Sea Level
1525		5000
3050		10 000
6100		20 000

Chinese Provinces, Autonomous Regions (AR) and Municipalities (M)

Conventional Form — Pinyin Form

Conventional	Pinyin
Anhwei	Anhui
Chekiang	Zhejiang
Fukien	Fujian
Heilungkiang	Heilongjiang
Honan	Henan
Hopeh	Hebei
Hunan	Hunan
Hupeh	Hubei
Inner Mongolia (AR)	Nei Monggol
Kansu	Gansu
Kiangsi	Jiangxi
Kiangsu	Jiangsu
Kirin	Jilin
Kwangsi (AR)	Guangxi Zhuangzu
Kwangtung	Guangdong
Kweichow	Guizhou
Liaoning	Liaoning
Ningsia Hui (AR)	Ningxia Huizu
Peking (M)	Beijing
Shanghai (M)	Shanghai
Shansi	Shanxi
Shantung	Shandong
Shensi	Shaanxi
Sinkiang (AR)	Xinjiang Uygur
Szechwan	Sichuan
Tibet (AR)	Xizang
Tientsin (M)	Tianjin
Tsinghai	Qinghai
Yunnan	Yunnan

(A) Area occupied by Pakistan and claimed by India.

(B) Area claimed and occupied by India; status disputed by Pakistan.

(C) Area occupied by China and claimed by India.

(D) Area occupied by India and claimed by China.

Habomai, Shikotan, Kunashiri, and Etorofu, occupied since 1945, are claimed by Japan pending a final peace treaty.

A-569700-76 15-11-27
COPYRIGHT BY
RAND McNALLY & COMPANY
MADE IN U.S.A.

Continued on pages 196-197

Longitude East of Greenwich

	0	50	100	200	300	400	500 Miles
0	100	200	400	600		800 Kilometers	

Cities and Towns

0 to 50,000	○	500,000 to 1,000,000
50,000 to 500,000	⊙	1,000,000 and over

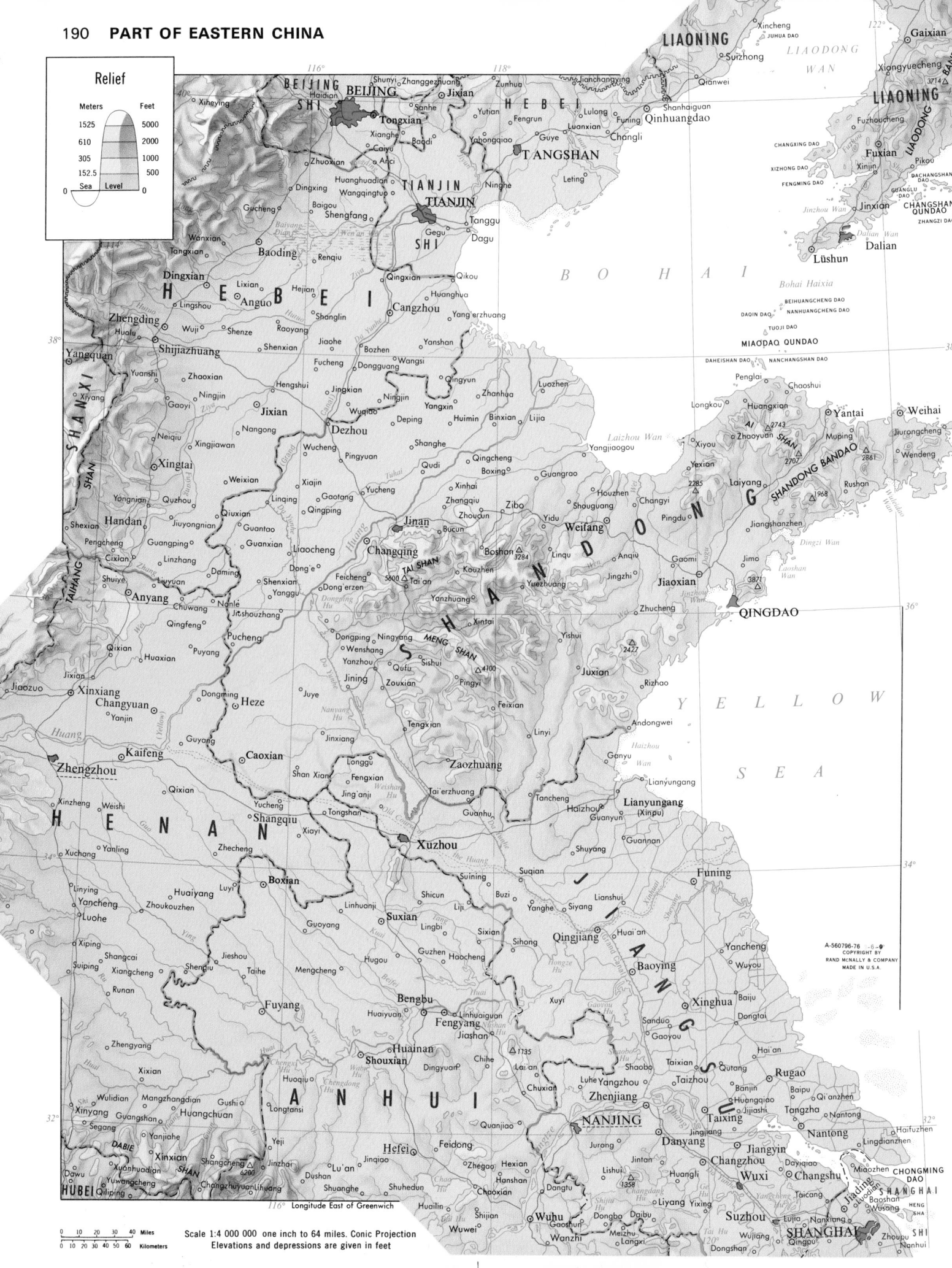

Relief

Meters	Feet
1525	5000
610	2000
305	1000
152.5	500
0 Sea Level	0

Scale 1:4 000 000 one inch to 64 miles. Conic Projection
Elevations and depressions are given in feet

0 10 20 30 40 Miles
0 10 20 30 40 50 60 Kilometers

116° Longitude East of Greenwich

A-560796-76
COPYRIGHT BY
RAND McNALLY & COMPANY
MADE IN U.S.A.

LIAONING

LIAODONG WAN

LIAONING

BOHAI

Bohai Haixia

LIAODONG BANDAO

BEIJING SHI

BEIJING

HEBEI

TIANJIN SHI

TIANJIN

TANGSHAN

SHANDONG BANDAO

SHANDONG

HEBEI

SHANXI

TAIHANG SHAN

Laizhou Wan

YELLOW SEA

HENAN

JIANGSU

ANHUI

DABIE SHAN

HUBEI

MENG SHAN

TAI SHAN

QINGDAO

Dalian

Lüshun

Yantai

Weihai

Qinhuangdao

Baoding

Shijiazhuang

Jinan

Weifang

Xuzhou

Zhengzhou

Kaifeng

Nanjing

Hefei

Shanghai

Suzhou

Wuxi

Changzhou

Zhenjiang

Yangzhou

Lianyungang (Xinpu)

SHANGHAI SHI

CHONGMING DAO

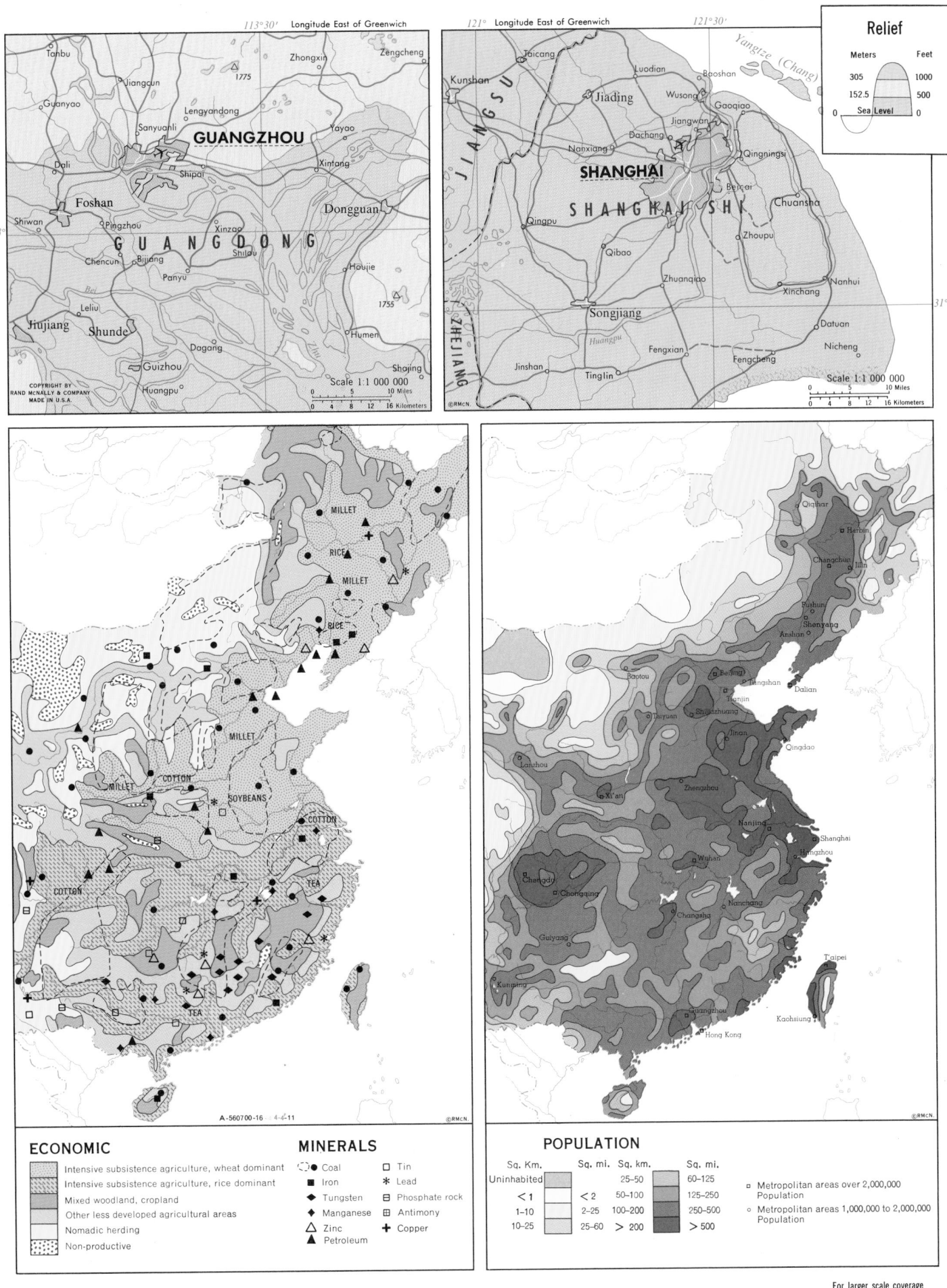

Relief

Meters	Feet
305	1000
152.5	500
0 Sea Level	0

113°30' Longitude East of Greenwich

Tanbu
Jiangcun
Guanyao
Lengyandong
Sanyuanli
GUANGZHOU
Yayao
Dali
Shipai
Xintang
Foshan
Pingzhou
Xinzao
Dongguan
Shiwan
Chencun
Bijiang
Shilou
Houjie
Leliu
Panyu
Hujiang
Shunde
Humen
Guizhou
Dagang
Shojing
Huangpu

G U A N G D O N G

Bei

1775

Zhongxin
Zengcheng

1755

COPYRIGHT BY
RAND McNALLY & COMPANY
MADE IN U.S.A.

Scale 1:1 000 000
0 5 10 Miles
0 4 8 12 16 Kilometers

121° Longitude East of Greenwich · 121°30'

Yangtze (Chang)

Kunshan
Taicang
Luodian
Baoshan
Jiading
Wusong
Gaoqiao
Nanxiang
Dachang
Jiangwan
SHANGHAI
Qingningsi
S H A N G H A I   S H I
Chuansha
Qingpu
Zhoupu
Qibao
Beicai
Zhuanqiao
Xinchang
Nanhui
Songjiang
Huangpu
Datuan
Fengxian
Nicheng
Jinshan
Tinglin
Fengcheng

J I A N G S U
Z H E J I A N G

Scale 1:1 000 000
0 5 10 Miles
0 4 8 12 16 Kilometers

31°

A-560700-16   4-4-11

©RMCN.

ECONOMIC

- Intensive subsistence agriculture, wheat dominant
- Intensive subsistence agriculture, rice dominant
- Mixed woodland, cropland
- Other less developed agricultural areas
- Nomadic herding
- Non-productive

MINERALS

- ● Coal
- ■ Iron
- ◆ Tungsten
- ◆ Manganese
- △ Zinc
- ▲ Petroleum
- □ Tin
- ✳ Lead
- ⊟ Phosphate rock
- ⊞ Antimony
- ✛ Copper

POPULATION

Sq. Km.	Sq. mi.	Sq. km.	Sq. mi.
Uninhabited		25–50	60–125
<1	<2	50–100	125–250
1–10	2–25	100–200	250–500
10–25	25–60	> 200	>500

- □ Metropolitan areas over 2,000,000 Population
- ○ Metropolitan areas 1,000,000 to 2,000,000 Population

©RMCN.

For larger scale coverage of Shanghai see page 241.

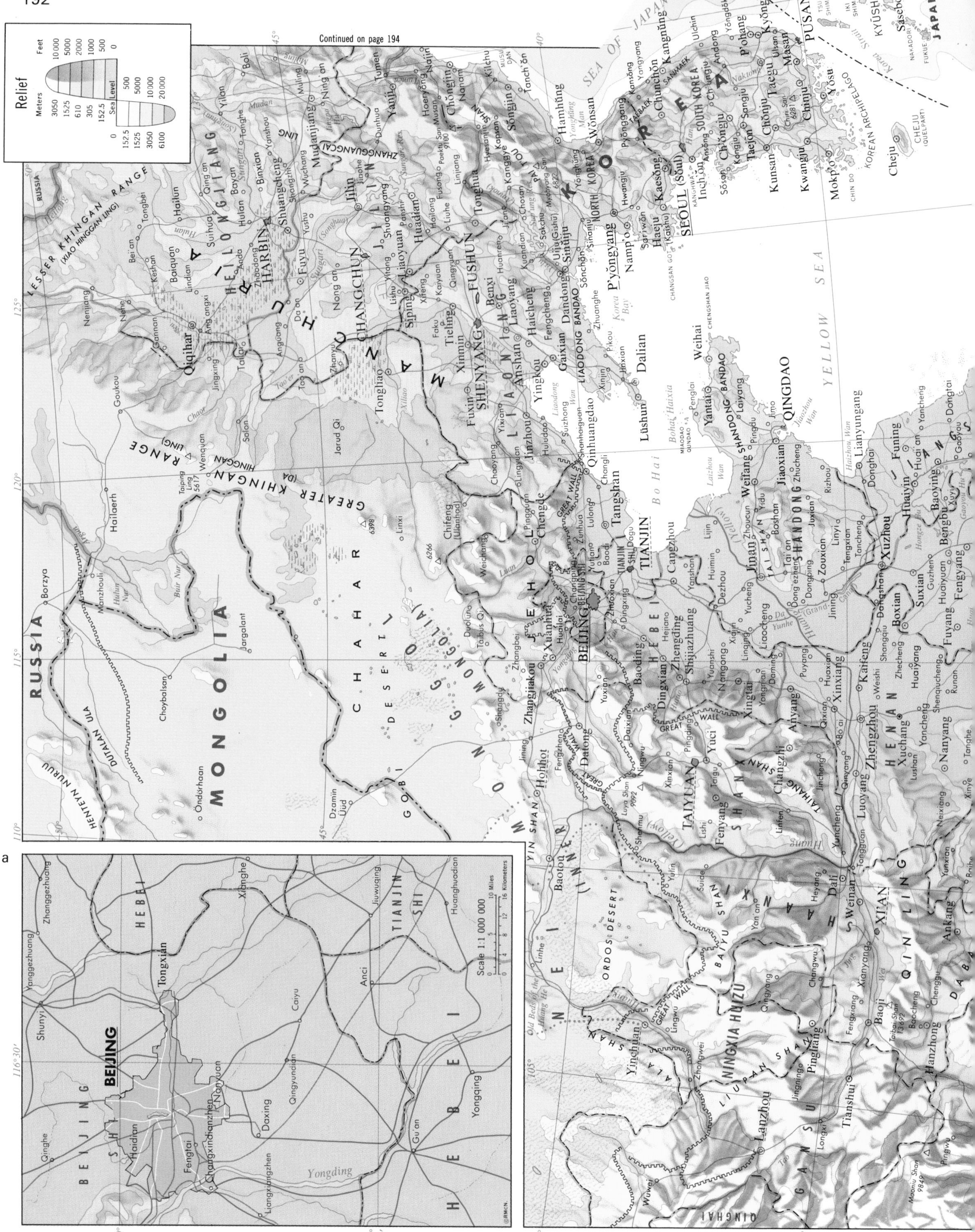

Continued on page 194

Relief

Meters	Feet
3050	10000
1525	5000
610	2000
305	1000
152.5	500
Sea Level	0

0	500
152.5	5000
1525	10000
3050	20000
6100	

RUSSIA

MONGOLIA

GOBI DESERT

LESSER KHINGAN RANGE (XIAO HINGGAN LING)

GREATER KHINGAN (DA HINGGAN LING) RANGE

HENTIYN NURUU

DUTAYAN ULA

CHAHAR

HEILONGJIANG

Harbin

Qiqihar

Hailaer

Manzhouli

Borzya

Choybalsan

Öndörhaan

Dzamin Üüd

Hailun

Bei'an

Nenjiang

Nehe

Keshan

Gannan

Tailai

Angangxi

Zhaodong

Anda

Hulan

Binxian

Shuangcheng

Wuchang

Shangzhi

Boli

Yilan

Jiamusi

Hegang

Tongjiang

Fujin

Baoqing

Mudanjiang

Jixi

Mishan

Muling

Dunhua

Yanji

Tumen

Hunchun

JILIN

Jilin

Changchun

Siping

Liaoyuan

Tonghua

Baicheng

Tongliao

Jarud Qi

Chifeng (Ulanhad)

Linxi

NEI MONGOL (INNER MONGOLIA)

ORDOS DESERT

YIN SHAN

Hohhot

Baotou

Linhe

Yinchuan

NINGXIA HUIZU

LIAONING

Shenyang

Fushun

Benxi

Anshan

Liaoyang

Haicheng

Yingkou

Jinzhou

Fuxin

Chaoyang

Huludao

LIAODONG BANDAO

Dandong

Dalian

Lüshun

Lüda

REHOL

Chengde

Zhangjiakou

Datong

HEBEI

BEIJING SHI

BEIJING

TIANJIN SHI

Tianjin

Tangshan

Qinhuangdao

Baoding

Shijiazhuang

Handan

GREAT WALL

SHANXI

Taiyuan

Yuci

Linfen

Yuncheng

Datong

SHAANXI

Xi'an

Baoji

Hanzhong

Ankang

QIN LING

DABA SHAN

Tianshui

Lanzhou

Wuwei

GANSU

QINGHAI

SHANDONG

Jinan

Qingdao

Yantai

Weihai

Zibo

Weifang

SHANDONG BANDAO

Linyi

Jining

HENAN

Zhengzhou

Luoyang

Kaifeng

Xuchang

Anyang

Nanyang

JIANGSU

Xuzhou

Lianyungang

ANHUI

Bengbu

Fuyang

HUANG HE (Yellow River)

Bo Hai

YELLOW SEA

SEA OF JAPAN

Bohai Haixia

Korea Bay

KOREA

NORTH KOREA

SOUTH KOREA

Pyongyang

SEOUL (Soul)

Inch'on

Hamhung

Wonsan

Kaesong

Nampo

Sinuiju

Taegu

Taejon

Pusan

Kwangju

Mokp'o

Ulsan

Masan

Cheju

CHEJU (QUELPART)

KOREA STRAIT

JAPAN

KYUSHU

Sasebo

Nagasaki

TSUSHIMA

RUSSIA

Inset map a (Beijing):

HEBEI

BEIJING SHI

TIANJIN SHI

BEIJING

Tongxian

Shunyi

Haidian

Fengtai

Daxing

Anci

Gu'an

Yongqing

Yongding

Zhangjiawan

Huangcun

Scale 1:11 000 000

Cities and Towns

| 0 to 50,000 | o | 500,000 to 1,000,000 | ◎ |
| 50,000 to 500,000 | ⊙ | 1,000,000 and over | |

For larger scale coverage of Beijing see page 240.

Scale 1:10 000 000; one inch to 160 miles. Lambert Conformal Conic Projection
Elevations and depressions are given in feet

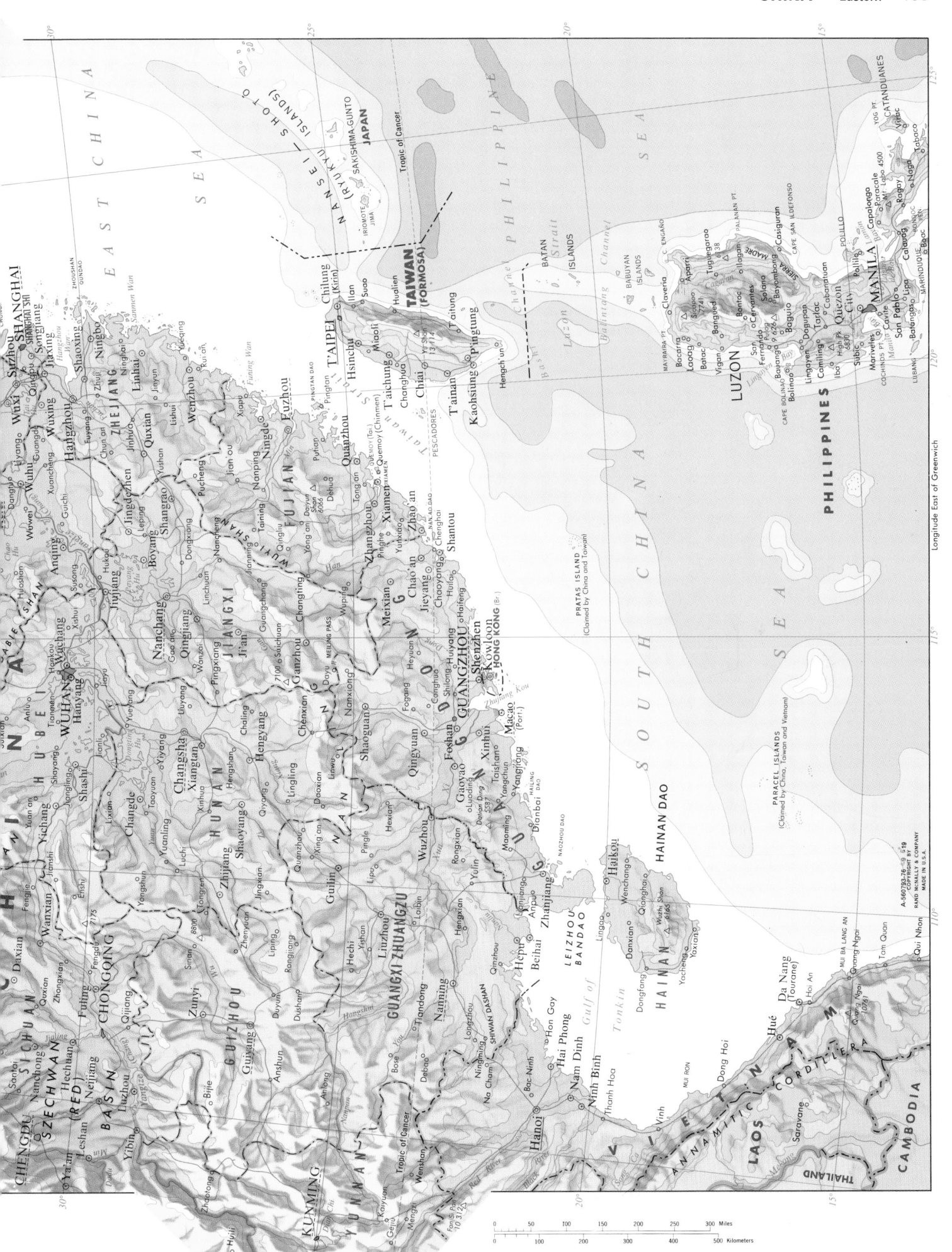

Continued on pages 192-193

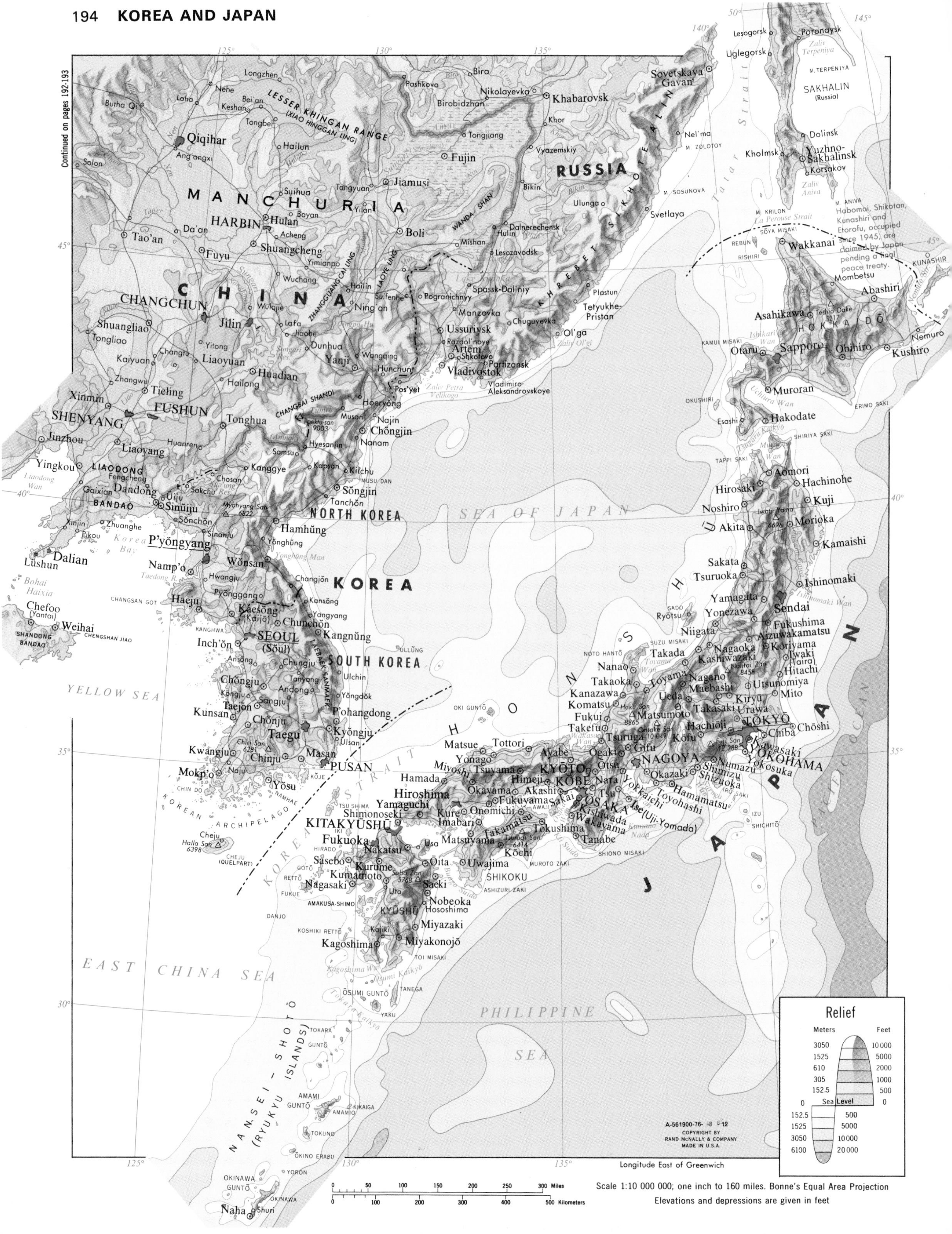

RUSSIA

SAKHALIN (Russia)

MANCHURIA

CHINA

HARBIN

CHANGCHUN

SHENYANG

FUSHUN

HOKKAIDŌ

Sapporo

NORTH KOREA

KOREA

P'yŏngyang

SEA OF JAPAN

SEOUL (Sŏul)

SOUTH KOREA

PUSAN

YELLOW SEA

KOREA STRAIT

KOREAN ARCHIPELAGO

HONSHU

KYŌTO

OSAKA

KŌBE

NAGOYA

TŌKYŌ

YOKOHAMA

JAPAN

PACIFIC OCEAN

KITAKYŪSHŪ

Fukuoka

Nagasaki

KYŪSHŪ

Kagoshima

SHIKOKU

EAST CHINA SEA

NANSEI-SHOTŌ (RYUKYU ISLANDS)

PHILIPPINE SEA

Naha

Habomai, Shikotan, Kunashiri and Etorofu, occupied since 1945, are claimed by Japan pending a final peace treaty.

Relief

Meters		Feet
3050		10 000
1525		5000
610		2000
305		1000
152.5		500
0	Sea Level	0
152.5		500
1525		5000
3050		10 000
6100		20 000

A-561900-76- -8 ⊙12
COPYRIGHT BY
RAND McNALLY & COMPANY
MADE IN U.S.A.

Longitude East of Greenwich

Scale 1:10 000 000; one inch to 160 miles. Bonne's Equal Area Projection
Elevations and depressions are given in feet

0 50 100 150 200 250 300 Miles
0 100 200 300 400 500 Kilometers

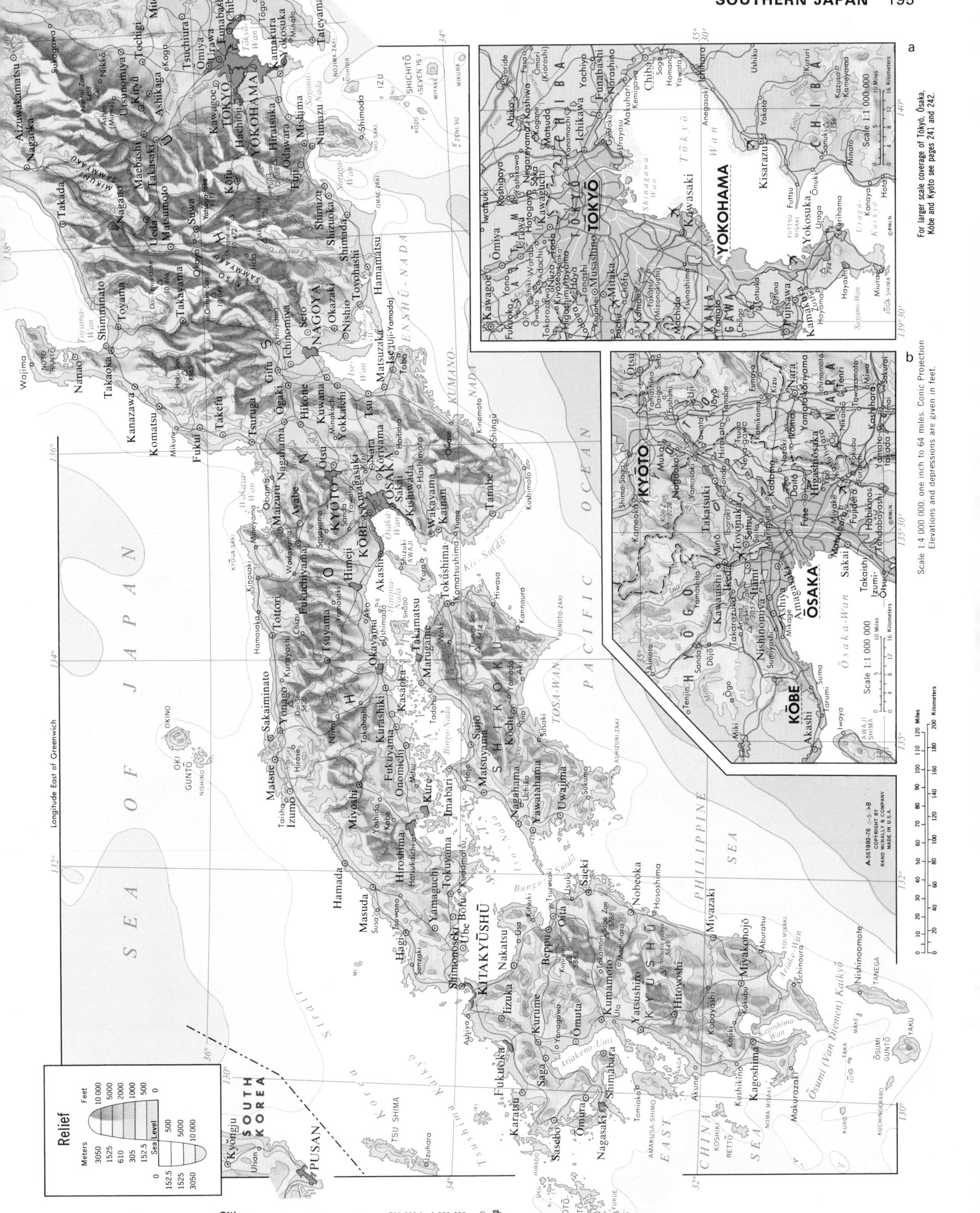

a

b

For larger scale coverage of Tōkyō, Ōsaka, Kōbe and Kyōto see pages 241 and 242.

Scale 1:4 000 000: one inch to 64 miles. Conic Projection
Elevations and depressions are given in feet.

Scale 1:1 000 000

Relief

Meters	Feet
3050	10 000
1525	5000
610	2000
305	1000
152.5	500
0	Sea Level
152.5	500
1525	5000
3050	10 000

Cities and Towns

| 0 to 50,000 | ○ | 500,000 to 1,000,000 | ◎ |
| 50,000 to 500,000 | ⊙ | 1,000,000 and over | |

A-561992-76 -5--5--8
COPYRIGHT BY
RAND McNALLY & COMPANY
MADE IN U.S.A.

SEA OF JAPAN

PACIFIC OCEAN

PHILIPPINE SEA

EAST CHINA SEA

SHIKOKU

KYŪSHŪ

SOUTH KOREA

TŌKYŌ

YOKOHAMA

KYŌTO

ŌSAKA

KŌBE

NAGOYA

Longitude East of Greenwich

Scale 1:1 000 000

Miles
0 10 20 30 40 50 60 70 80 90 100 110 120

Kilometers
0 40 80 120 160 200

Scale 1:16 000 000; one inch to 250 miles. Polyconic Projection
Elevations and depressions are given in feet

Continued on pages 188-189

PHILIPPINES

PHILIPPINE

SEA

PHILIPPINES

PHILIPPINE

SEA

LUZON

Cabugao
Iguig
Tuguegarao
Bangued
Vigan
Bontoc
Narvacan
Lubuagan
Cabagan
Cauayan
Candon
Ilagan
Divilacan Bay
Palaman Bay
PALANAN PT.
Luna
Cervantes
Mt. Amuyao 8799
Santiago
Echague
Jones
San Fernando
S. Juan
Bagabag
Solana
Bayombong
Dijohan Pt.
Bauang
Baguio
Bambang
Aringay
Dupax
Casiguran
Bolinao
CORDILLERA CENTRAL
Mt. Pulog 9626
Santiago
Bani
Alaminos
S. Nicolas
Tayug
Agno
Dagupan
S. Quintin
Burgos
Lingayen
Urdaneta
Rosales
Baler Bay
San Carlos
Bayambang
Baler CAPE ENCANTO
Infanta
San Jose
Santa Cruz
Mangatarem
Gerona
Candelaria
Camiling
Muñoz
Dingalan Bay
High Pk. 6683
Tarlac
Victoria
Cabanatuan
Palauig
Concepcion
Gapan
Iba
S. Miguel
POLILLO IS.
Pinatubo 5771
Angeles
Arayat
S. Fernando
POLILLO
S. Narciso
Guagua
Infanta
Patnanongan
S. Antonio
Subic
Malolos
Polillo
JOMALIG
Olongapo
Orani
Malabon
Sta. Maria
Balanga
Quezon City
Lamon Bay
Orion
MANILA
Pasig
BALESIN
Sampaloc PT.
Cavite
Pasig
CALAGUAS ISLAND
Mariveles
Bay
Naic
Laguna
Capalonga
Paracale
CORREGIDOR ISLAND
Sta. Cruz
TALIM
Labo
Talisay
Silang
Calamba
Mauban
Nagcarlan
Mt. Labo 5066
Daet
CABRA ISLAND
Lubang
Lemery
Lipa
S. Pablo
Atimonan
Gumaca
Ragay
San Miguel Bay
Balayan
Rosario
Lucena
Macalelon
Mt. Isarog 4450
LUBANG IS.
GOLD ISLAND
Lobo
Batangas
Unisan
S. Narciso
Naga
Baao
AMBIL ISLAND
Balayan Bay
Tayabas Bay
Catanauan
S. Cruz
Pili
Bula
MARICABAN
Verde I. Passage
Mt. Banghao
Macalelon
Moyano
Tabaco
CAPE CALAVITE
VERDE
Calapan
Boac
S. Cruz Pers
Polangui Volcano 8077
Paluan
Naujan
Gasan
Torrijos
Ligao
Mamburao
Mt. Halcon 8471
MARINDUQUE ISLAND
San Pascual
Legazpi

MINDORO

DUMALI PT.
Pinamalayan
BANTON
BURIAS
Mt. Baco 8163
Jones
SIBUYAN
Sablayan
DONGON PT.
Knob Pk. 3031
ROMBLON ISLAND
TICAO ISLAND
S. Jacinto
Odiongan
Romblon
Aroroy
S. Jose
TABLAS
Masbate
BUSUANGA
Bulalacao
Looc
MASBATE
TARA
ILIN ISLAND
SIBUYAN SEA

Scale 1:4 000 000
0 10 20 30 40 Miles
0 10 20 30 40 50 60 Kilometers
©RMCN

Left side labels

Legazpi
Sorsogon
CATANDUANES ISLAND
Catbalogan
SAMAR
Tacloban
Cebu
LEYTE
DINAGAT ISLAND
PHILIPPINE
BOHOL
34 578
TRENCH
Mindanao Sea
Butuan
Cagayan
MINDANAO
Mt. Apo 9692
Davao
Cotabato
Davao Gulf
PULAU MIANGAS
PALAU IS.
(T.T.P.I.)
SONSOROL ISLANDS
KEPULAUAN TALAUD
PULAU SANGIHE
PULAU SIAU
MOROTAI
Manado
Tondano
Ternate
HALMAHERA
KEPULAUAN MAPIA

Indonesia / Papua New Guinea section

Equator

Laut Maluku
(Molucca Sea)
Laut Halmahera
(Halmahera Sea)
PULAU WAIGEO
Selat Dampier
NINIGO GROUP
HERMIT IS.
ADMIRALTY ISLANDS
MUSSAU ISLAND
EMIRA ISLAND
KEPULAUAN BANGGAI
PULAU TALIBU
PULAU MANGOLE
KEPULAUAN OBI
SALAWATI
Sorong
Manokwari
JAZIRAH DOBERAI
BIAK
PULAU NUMFOOR
PULAU YAPEN
TG. PERKAM
MANUS ISLAND
NEW HANOVER
Kavieng
KEPULAUAN SULA
PULAU MISOOL
Teluk Berau
Teluk Cenderawasih
Jayapura (Sukarnapura)
PEGUNUNGAN VAN REES
BISMARCK
CERAM (SERAM)
Piru
Fakfak
PEGUNUNGAN MAOKE
Aitape
Wewak
NEW IRELAND
A S I A
Bula
Namatanai
Rabaul
BURU
Ambon
PULAU AMBON
Kaimana
Puncak Jaya 16 503
Puncak Trikora 15 584
Sepik
WITU ISLANDS
ARCH.
Kakopo
WOWONI
PULAU ADI
The Father 7546
KEPULAUAN BANDA
PULAU BANDA
Dobo
Karkar Island
LONG ISLAND
Talasea
KEPULAUAN TUKANGBESI
KEPULAUAN LUCIPARA
KEPULAUAN KAI
KAI KECIL
KEPULAUAN ARU
Mt. Giluwe 14 330
Madang
NEW GUINEA
Mt. Wilhelm 14 793
NEW BRITAIN
Laut Banda
(Banda Sea)
PULAU DAMAR
PULAU TRANGAN
NEW GUINEA
Mt. Bangeta 13 529
Lae
BISMARCK
NEW BRITAIN TRENCH
PULAU WETAR
YAMDENA
KEPULAUAN TANIMBAR
PAPUA
Huon Gulf
PULAU ALOR
PULAU BABAR
PULAU SELARU
NEW GUINEA
Morobe
DE ATAURO
PULAU MOA
PULAU YOS SUDARSA
Mt. Albert Edward 13 090
Dili
TIMOR
Kupang
TANJUNG VALS
Merauke
Daru
TROBRIAND IS.
ARAFURA SEA
Buna
WOODLARK ISLAND
TIMOR SEA
Port Moresby
OWEN STANLEY RA.
D'ENTRECASTEAUX IS.
MELVILLE ISLAND
COBOURG PEN.
CROKER ISLAND
Torres Strait
Mt. Victoria 13 238
WESSEL IS
C. YORK
GREAT BARRIER REEF
BATHURST ISLAND
Van Diemen Gulf
CAPE YORK PEN.
Samarai
Darwin
C. ARNHEM
CORAL SEA

AUSTRALIA

Gulf of Papua
Gulf of Carpentaria

Continued on pages 202-203

0 50 100 200 300 400 500 Miles
0 100 200 400 600 800 Kilometers

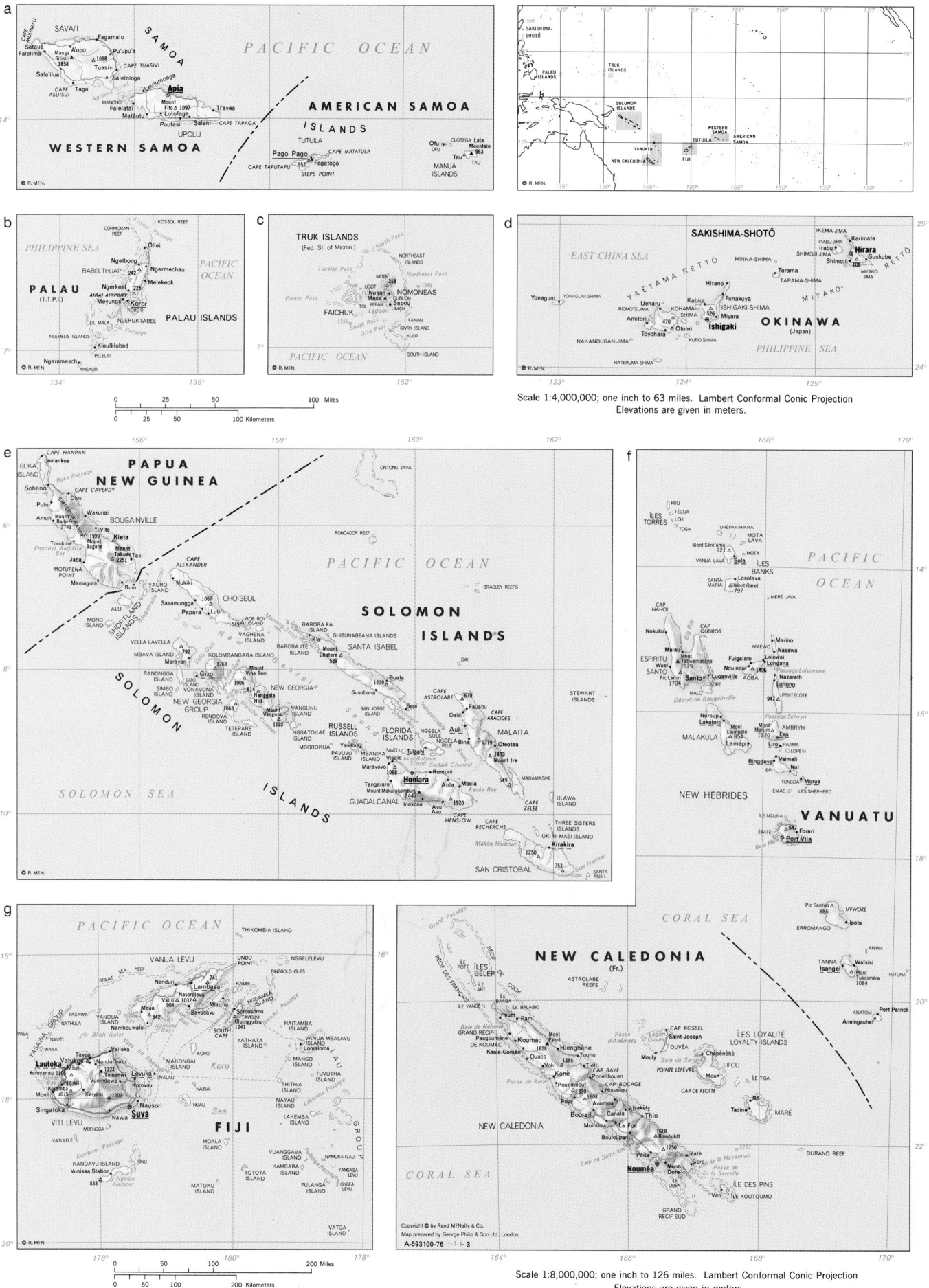

Scale 1:4,000,000; one inch to 63 miles. Lambert Conformal Conic Projection
Elevations are given in meters.

Scale 1:8,000,000; one inch to 126 miles. Lambert Conformal Conic Projection
Elevations are given in meters.

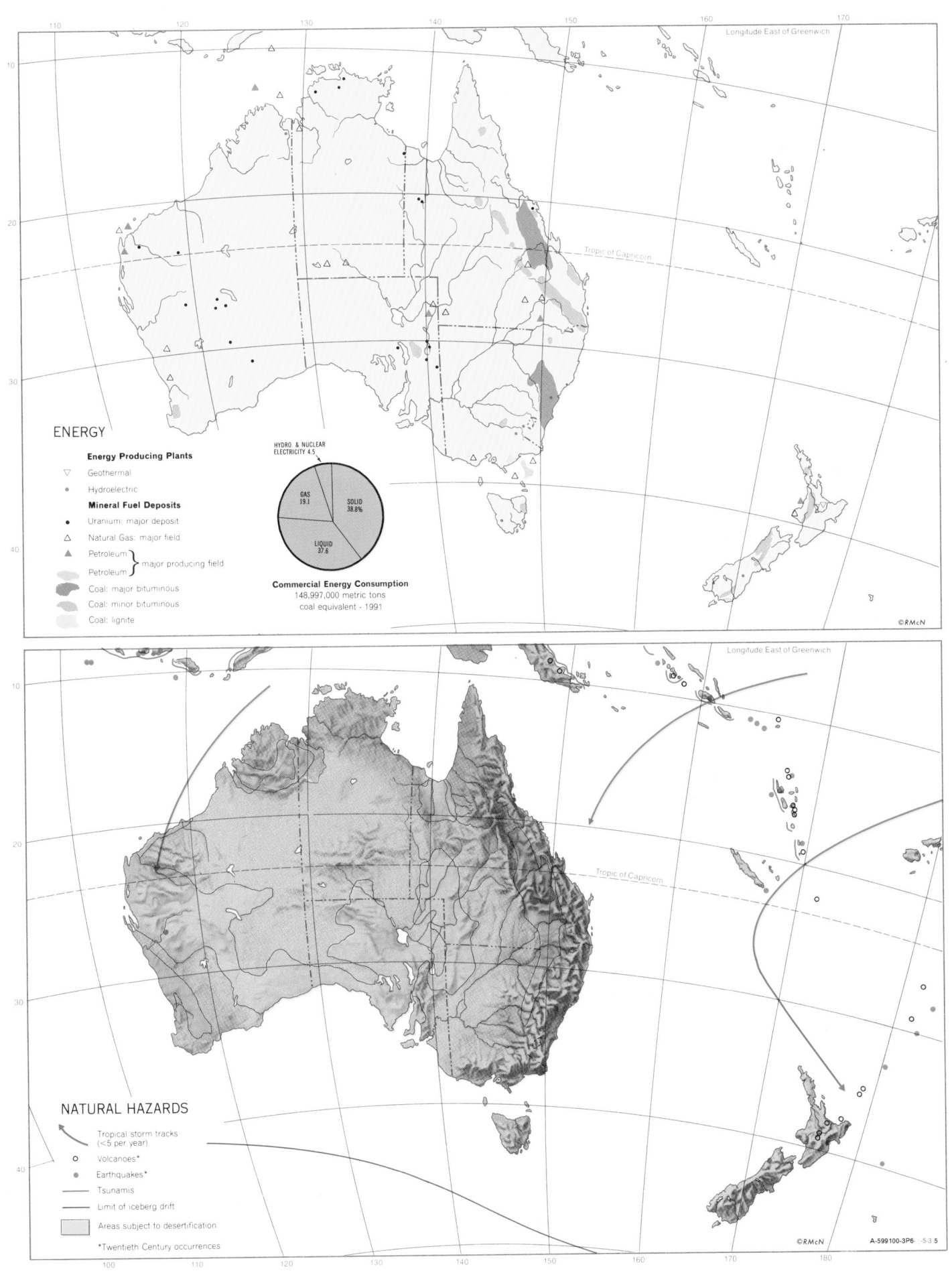

ENERGY

Energy Producing Plants

▽   Geothermal

●   Hydroelectric

Mineral Fuel Deposits

●   Uranium: major deposit

△   Natural Gas: major field

▲   Petroleum

              } major producing field

   Petroleum

   Coal: major bituminous

   Coal: minor bituminous

   Coal: lignite

HYDRO. & NUCLEAR
ELECTRICITY 4.5

GAS
19.1

SOLID
38.8%

LIQUID
37.6

Commercial Energy Consumption
148,997,000 metric tons
coal equivalent - 1991

©RMcN

NATURAL HAZARDS

↗   Tropical storm tracks
(<5 per year)

○   Volcanoes*

●   Earthquakes*

——   Tsunamis

——   Limit of iceberg drift

   Areas subject to desertification

*Twentieth Century occurrences

©RMcN   A-599100-3P6- -5-3 5

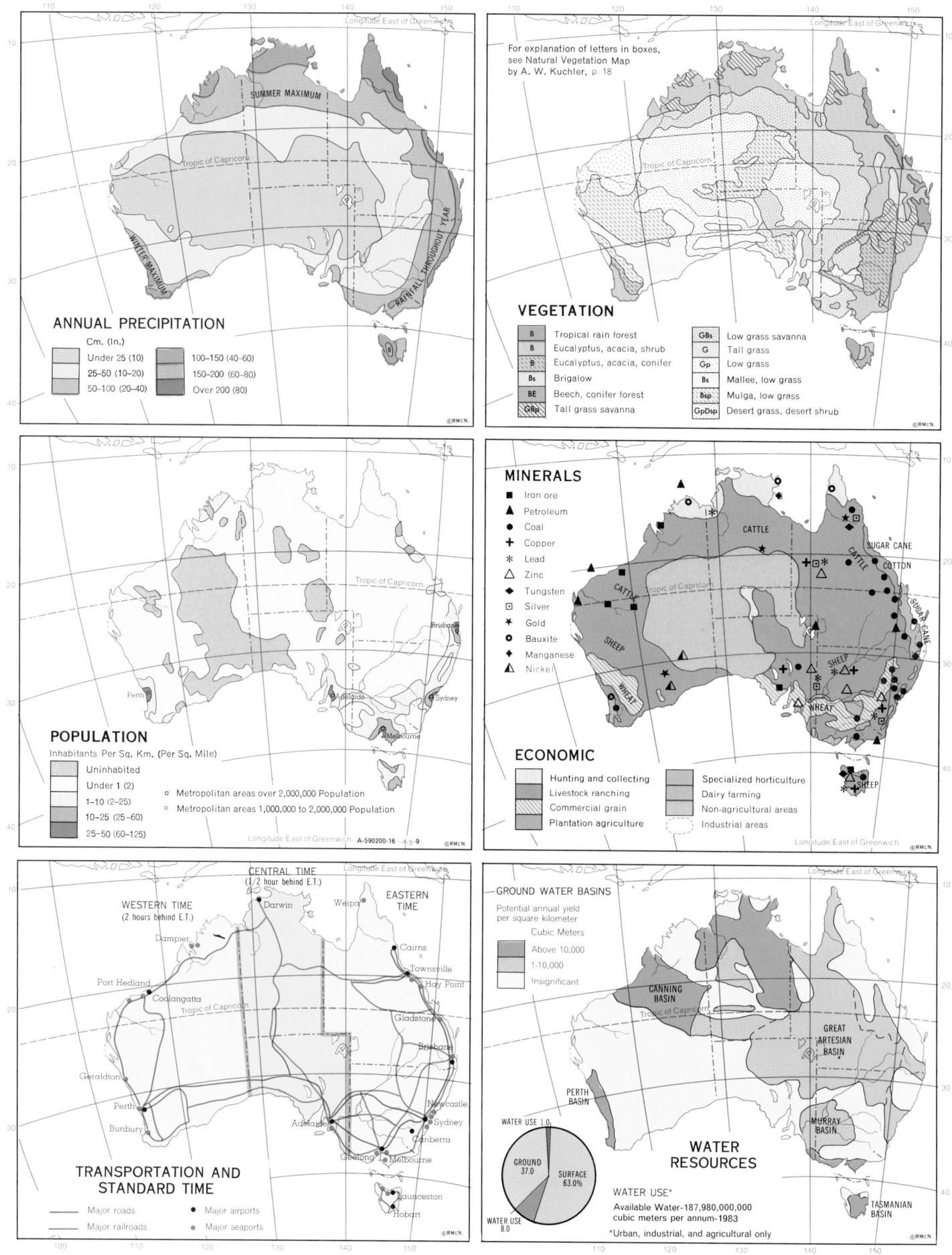

ANNUAL PRECIPITATION

Cm. (In.)

Under 25 (10)
25–50 (10–20)
50–100 (20–40)
100–150 (40–60)
150–200 (60–80)
Over 200 (80)

VEGETATION

For explanation of letters in boxes,
see Natural Vegetation Map
by A. W. Kuchler, p. 18

B	Tropical rain forest	GBs	Low grass savanna
B	Eucalyptus, acacia, shrub	G	Tall grass
B	Eucalyptus, acacia, conifer	Gp	Low grass
Bs	Brigalow	Bs	Mallee, low grass
BE	Beech, conifer forest	Bsp	Mulga, low grass
GBp	Tall grass savanna	GpDsp	Desert grass, desert shrub

POPULATION

Inhabitants Per Sq. Km. (Per Sq. Mile)

Uninhabited
Under 1 (2)
1–10 (2–25)
10–25 (25–60)
25–50 (60–125)

□ Metropolitan areas over 2,000,000 Population
○ Metropolitan areas 1,000,000 to 2,000,000 Population

A-590200-16 4-5-9

MINERALS

■ Iron ore
▲ Petroleum
● Coal
+ Copper
✳ Lead
△ Zinc
◆ Tungsten
⊡ Silver
✱ Gold
◉ Bauxite
◆ Manganese
▲ Nickel

ECONOMIC

Hunting and collecting
Livestock ranching
Commercial grain
Plantation agriculture
Specialized horticulture
Dairy farming
Non-agricultural areas
Industrial areas

TRANSPORTATION AND STANDARD TIME

WESTERN TIME
(2 hours behind E.T.)

CENTRAL TIME
(1/2 hour behind E.T.)

EASTERN TIME

—— Major roads
—— Major railroads
● Major airports
● Major seaports

WATER RESOURCES

GROUND WATER BASINS

Potential annual yield
per square kilometer
Cubic Meters

Above 10,000
1–10,000
Insignificant

CANNING BASIN
GREAT ARTESIAN BASIN
PERTH BASIN
MURRAY BASIN
TASMANIAN BASIN

WATER USE 1.0
GROUND 37.0
SURFACE 63.0%
WATER USE 8.0

WATER USE*

Available Water-187,980,000,000
cubic meters per annum-1983

*Urban, industrial, and agricultural only

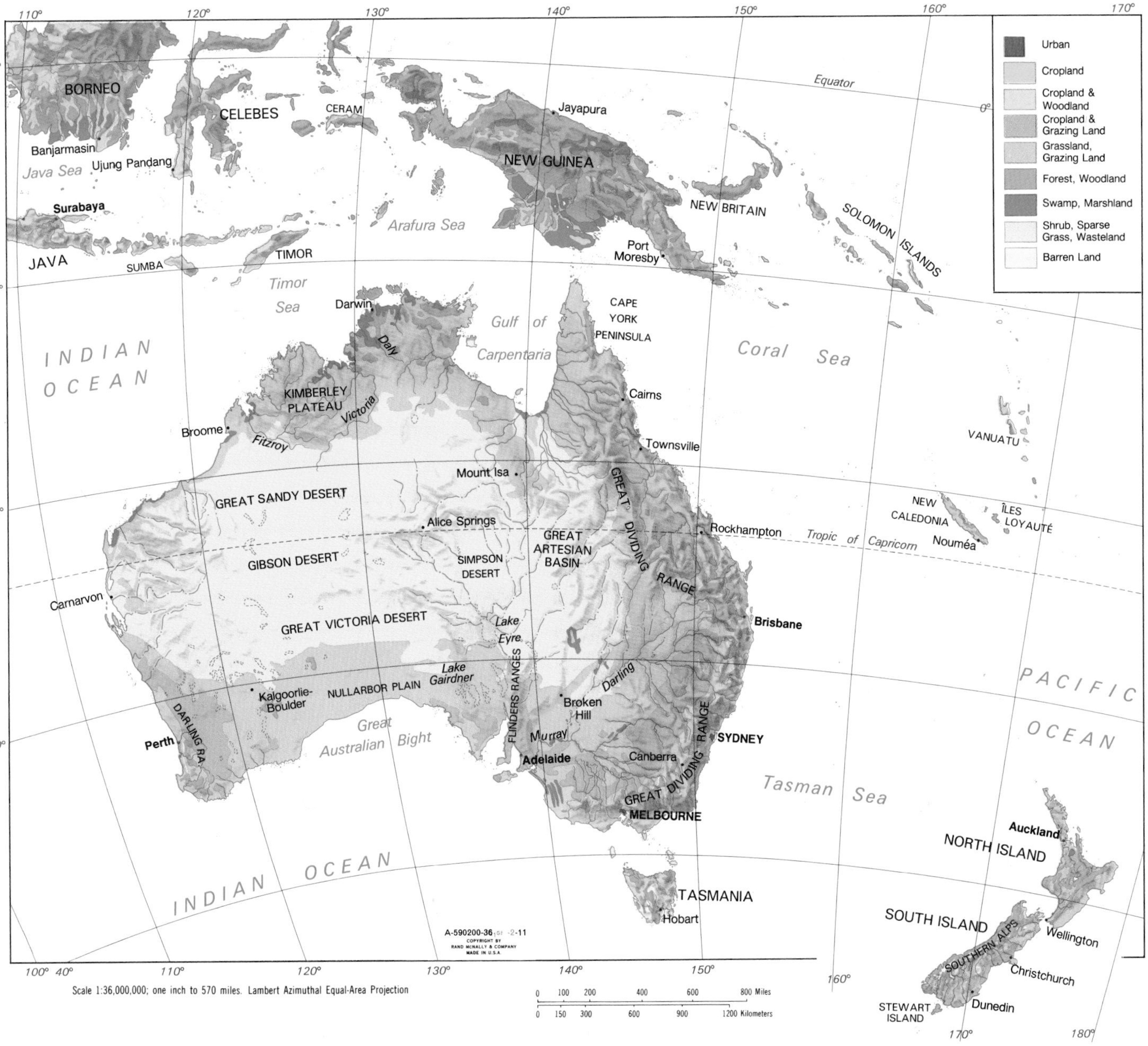

110°   120°   130°   140°   150°   160°   170°

	Urban
	Cropland
	Cropland & Woodland
	Cropland & Grazing Land
	Grassland, Grazing Land
	Forest, Woodland
	Swamp, Marshland
	Shrub, Sparse Grass, Wasteland
	Barren Land

Equator

0°

BORNEO

CELEBES

CERAM

Jayapura

Banjarmasin

Ujung Pandang

Java Sea

NEW GUINEA

NEW BRITAIN

SOLOMON ISLANDS

Surabaya

JAVA

SUMBA

TIMOR

Arafura Sea

Port Moresby

0°

10°

Timor Sea

Darwin

Daly

Gulf of Carpentaria

CAPE YORK PENINSULA

Coral Sea

VANUATU

ÎLES LOYAUTÉ

10°

INDIAN OCEAN

KIMBERLEY PLATEAU

Victoria

Cairns

Broome

Fitzroy

Townsville

NEW CALEDONIA

Nouméa

20°

GREAT SANDY DESERT

Mount Isa

GREAT DIVING RANGE

Rockhampton

Tropic of Capricorn

20°

Alice Springs

GIBSON DESERT

SIMPSON DESERT

GREAT ARTESIAN BASIN

Carnarvon

GREAT VICTORIA DESERT

Lake Eyre

Brisbane

PACIFIC OCEAN

Lake Gairdner

Darling

DARLING RA.

Kalgoorlie-Boulder

NULLARBOR PLAIN

FLINDERS RANGES

Broken Hill

30°

Perth

Great Australian Bight

Murray

Adelaide

Canberra

SYDNEY

30°

Tasman Sea

GREAT DIVIDING RANGE

MELBOURNE

Auckland

NORTH ISLAND

INDIAN OCEAN

TASMANIA

Hobart

SOUTH ISLAND

SOUTHERN ALPS

Wellington

40°

A-590200-36
COPYRIGHT BY
RAND McNALLY & COMPANY
MADE IN U.S.A.

STEWART ISLAND

Christchurch

Dunedin

Scale 1:36,000,000; one inch to 570 miles. Lambert Azimuthal Equal-Area Projection

0 100 200   400   600   800 Miles

0 150 300   600   900   1200 Kilometers

100° 40°   110°   120°   130°   140°   150°   160°   170°   180°

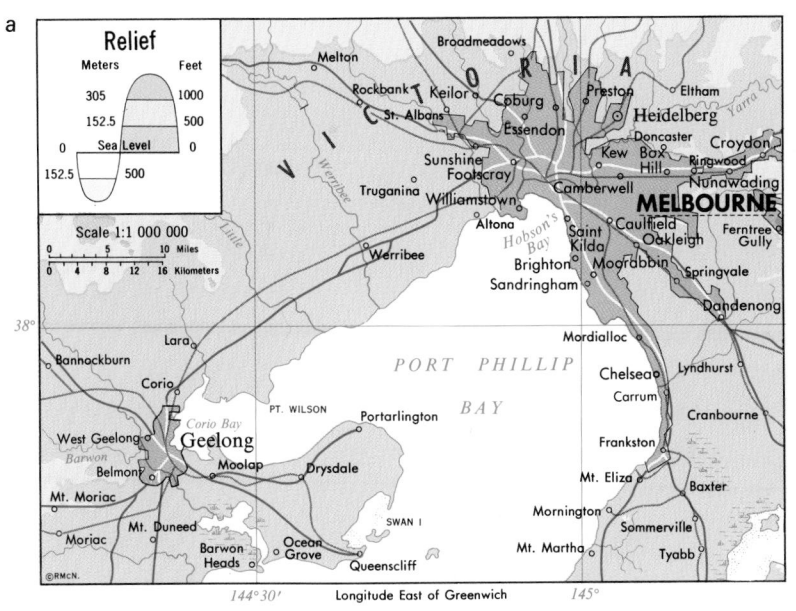

a

Relief

Meters		Feet
305		1000
152.5		500
0	Sea Level	0
152.5		500

Scale 1:1 000 000

0   5   10 Miles

0 4 8 12 16 Kilometers

Melton

Broadmeadows

VICTORIA

Rockbank

Keilor

Preston

Eltham

St. Albans

Coburg

Heidelberg

Yarra

Essendon

Doncaster

Croydon

Sunshine

Kew

Box Hill

Ringwood

Footscray

Nunawading

Truganina

Williamstown

Camberwell

MELBOURNE

Altona

Saint Kilda

Caulfield

Ferntree Gully

Hobson's Bay

Oakleigh

Werribee

Brighton

Moorabbin

Springvale

Sandringham

Dandenong

Lara

Mordialloc

Bannockburn

Corio

Lyndhurst

PORT PHILLIP

Chelsea

West Geelong

Corio Bay

Portarlington

Carrum

Belmont

Moolap

BAY

Cranbourne

Mt. Moriac

Drysdale

Frankston

Moriac

Mt. Duneed

Mt. Eliza

Baxter

SWAN I.

Sommerville

Barwon Heads

Ocean Grove

Queenscliff

Mornington

Mt. Martha

Tyabb

©RMCN

144°30'   Longitude East of Greenwich   145°

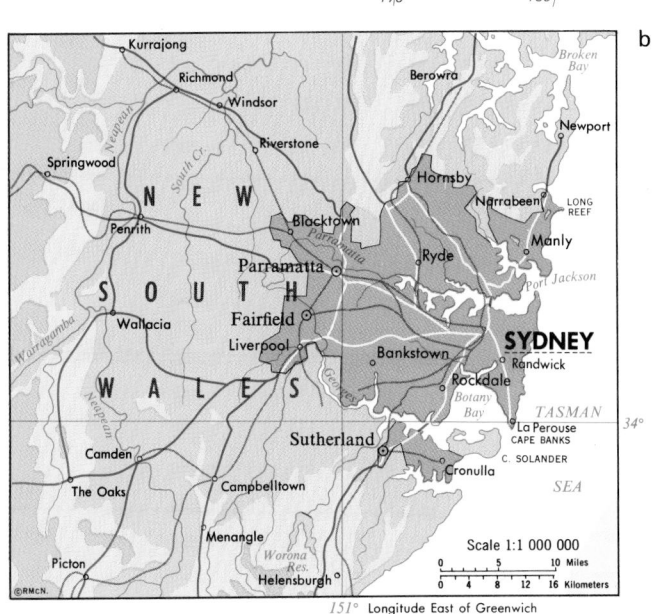

b

Kurrajong

Broken Bay

Richmond

Windsor

Berowra

Newport

Springwood

Riverstone

Hornsby

Narrabeen

LONG REEF

Penrith

Blacktown

Manly

NEW

Wallacia

Parramatta

Ryde

Port Jackson

SOUTH

Fairfield

SYDNEY

Liverpool

Bankstown

Randwick

WALES

Rockdale

Camden

Sutherland

Botany Bay

La Perouse
CAPE BANKS

TASMAN

Cronulla

C. SOLANDER

The Oaks

Campbelltown

Menangle

SEA

Picton

Helensburgh

34°

Scale 1:1 000 000

0   5   10 Miles

0 4 8 12 16 Kilometers

©RMCN

151° Longitude East of Greenwich

For larger scale coverage of Melbourne and Sydney see page 243.

Continued on pages 196-197

Relief

Meters	Feet
3050	10 000
1525	5000
610	2000
305	1000
152.5	500
0 Sea Level	0
152.5	500 Below
1525	5000 Sea Level
3050	10 000
6100	20 000

Longitude 115° East of Greenwich

Scale 1:16 000 000; one inch to 250 miles. Lambert's Azimuthal, Equal Area Projection
Elevations and depressions are given in feet

NEW GUINEA
PAPUA NEW GUINEA
Mt. Albert Edward 13,100
Mt. Victoria 13,363
Buna
Port Moresby
OWEN STANLEY RA.
TROBRIAND IS.
WOODLARK
D'ENTRECASTEAUX ISLANDS
Samarai
SOUTH CAPE
LOUISIADE ARCHIPELAGO
TAGULA
ROSSEL

CHOISEUL
VELLA LAVELLA
NEW GEORGIA
RENDOVA
SANTA ISABEL
FLORIDA
MALAITA
RUSSELL IS.
TULAGI
Honiara
GUADALCANAL
SOLOMON ISLANDS
SAN CRISTÓBAL
RENNELL

SANTA CRUZ ISLANDS

Torres Strait
BANKS
THURSDAY
HORN
NCE OF WALES
CAPE YORK

TORRES IS.
BANKS ISLANDS

ESPÍRITU SANTO
MAEWO
NEW
PENTECOST
MALEKULA
AMBRIM
EPI
HEBRIDES
AMBRYM
VANUATU
EFATE
Port Vila

CORAL   SEA

P A C I F I C   O C E A N

ÎLES CHESTERFIELD (Fr.)
ÎLES BÉLEP
OUVÉA
LIFOU
ÎLES LOYAUTÉ (French)
MARÉ
NEW CALEDONIA (Fr.)
Nouméa
ÎLE DES PINS
EROMANGA
TANA
ANEITYUM

Tropic of Capricorn

CAPE YORK PENINSULA
CAPE MELVILLE
OSPREY REEF
Cooktown
Laura
Palmerville
ATHERTON
Cairns
HOLMES REEFS
WILLIS IS.
Mungana
Mt. Bartle Frere 5322
PLATEAU
Ingham
HINCHINBROOK I.
FLINDERS REEFS
LIHOU REEF
Forsayth
Halifax Bay
Townsville
TREGROSSE IS.
Charters Towers
Bowen
WHITSUNDAY
CUMBERLAND IS.
MARION REEF
Mt. Dalrymple 4190
Mackay
NORTHUMBERLAND IS.
SWAIN REEFS
CONNORS RANGE
WRECK REEFS
Clermont
Emerald
Rockhampton
Mount Morgan
CURTIS
Gladstone
SANDY CAPE
Bundaberg
Hervey Bay
FRASER I.
Maryborough
Gympie

Croydon
GREAT
GREGORY RANGE
G R E A T   D I V I D I N G   R A N G E
Hughenden
Winton
Galilee
Barcaldine
Jericho
QUEENSLAND
Longreach
Blackall
BUCKLAND TABLELAND
Tambo
Yaraka
Windorah
Quilpie
Charleville
Roma
Dalby
Toowoomba
DARLING DOWNS
Ipswich
BRISBANE
N. STRADBROKE I.
Southport
Warwick
Lismore
Tenterfield
Roberts

T E S I   R A N G E
Thargomindah
Hungerford
Cunnamulla
St. George
Disranbandi
Mungindi
Moree
NEW ENGLAND RANGE
Glen Innes
Inverell
Grafton
Armidale
The Round Mountain 5300
Tamworth
Kempsey
Port Macquarie

MAIN BARRIER RANGE
Broken Hill
Wilcannia
Cobar
Nyngan
Coonamble
Narrabri
WARRUMBUNGLE RA.
Gilgandra
LIVERPOOL RA.
Dubbo
Maitland
Newcastle
Bourke
Brewarrina
Walgett
Nymagee

NEW   SOUTH   WALES
MURRAY
West Wyalong
Forbes
Bathurst
Orange
Lithgow
BLUE MTS.
SYDNEY
Botany Bay
Wollongong

RIVERINA REGION
Hay
Narrandera
Wagga Wagga
Goulburn
Canberra
AUST. CAP. TER.
JERVIS BAY
Swan Hill
Kerang
Deniliquin
Albury
SNOWY MTS.
Mt. Kosciusko 7316
Cooma
Bega
Bombala

Wentworth
Mildura
Echuca
Bendigo
VICTORIA
Ararat
Maryborough
Bendigo
Ballarat
MELBOURNE
Geelong
Bairnsdale
CAPE HOWE
NINETY MILE BEACH

Hamilton
Warrnambool
CAPE OTWAY
Wonthaggi
WILSON'S PROMONTORY
T A S M A N   S E A

KING I.
BASS STRAIT
FLINDERS
FURNEAUX GROUP
CAPE BARREN
HUNTER IS.
TASMANIA
Burnie
Ulverstone
Devonport
Launceston
Mt. Ossa 5305
Strahan
New Norfolk
Hobart
Risdon
BRUNY
SOUTH EAST CAPE

| 0 | 50 | 100 | 200 | 300 | 400 | 500 Miles |
| 0 | 100 | 200 | 400 | 600 | 800 Kilometers |

a

NEW ZEALAND (inset)
NORTH CAPE
Kaitaia
Russell
HAURAKI GULF
GREAT BARRIER
Devonport
Auckland
NORTH ISLAND
Hamilton
Bay of Plenty
EAST CAPE
P A C I F I C   O C E A N
North Taranaki Bight
New Plymouth
C. Egmont
Mt. Egmont (Vol.)
South Taranaki Bight
Mt. Ruapehu (Vol.)
Wanganui
Gisborne
Napier
Hastings
Palmerston North
CAPE FAREWELL
Tasman Bay
Nelson
Karamea Bight
CAPE FOULWIND
CAPE
Lower Hutt
Wellington
Cook Strait
Greymouth
Hokitika
SOUTHERN ALPS
SOUTH ISLAND
CASCADE PT.
Mt. Cook 12,316
Pegasus Bay
Christchurch
T A S M A N   S E A
Canterbury Bight
Timaru
RESOLUTION ISLAND
Dunedin
CAPE SAUNDERS
P A C I F I C   O C E A N
Foveaux Strait
Invercargill
STEWART ISLAND
SOUTHWEST CAPE
Same scale as main map

| **Cities and Towns** | 0 to 50,000 | ○ | 500,000 to 1,000,000 | ◎ |
| | 50,000 to 500,000 | ⊙ | 1,000,000 and over | |

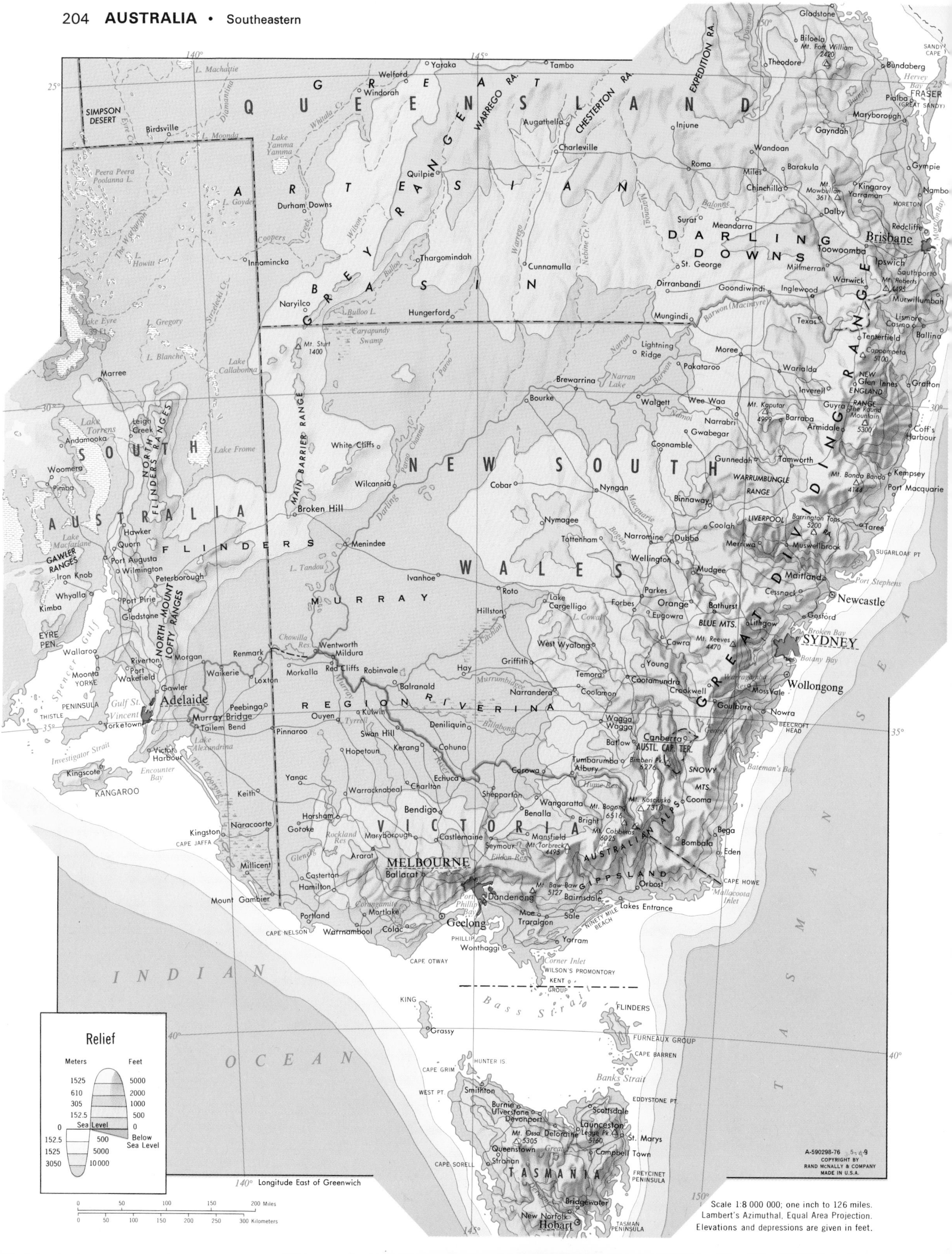

QUEENSLAND

GREAT DIVIDING RANGE

GREAT ARTESIAN BASIN

SIMPSON DESERT

NEW SOUTH WALES

SOUTH AUSTRALIA

FLINDERS RANGES

NORTH MOUNT LOFTY RANGES

GAWLER RANGES

EYRE PEN.

MAIN BARRIER RANGE

MURRAY

RIVERINA REGION

VICTORIA

AUSTL. CAP. TER.

SNOWY MTS.

AUSTRALIAN ALPS

GIPPSLAND

WARRUMBUNGLE RANGE

NEW ENGLAND RANGE

BLUE MTS.

DARLING DOWNS

Brisbane
Ipswich
Southport
Toowoomba
Warwick
Gympie
Maryborough
Gladstone
Bundaberg
Bioela
Theodore

Birdsville
Marree
Innamincka
Durham Downs
Thargomindah
Quilpie
Windorah
Welford
Yaraka
Tambo
Augathella
Charleville
Injune
Roma
Miles
Chinchilla
Dalby
Surat
Meandarra
St. George
Dirranbandi
Goondiwindi
Inglewood
Mungindi
Moree
Narrabri
Walgett
Bourke
Brewarrina
Lightning Ridge
Pakataroo
Wee Waa
Coonabarabran
Gunnedah
Tamworth
Armidale
Guyra
Glen Innes
Tenterfield
Casino
Lismore
Ballina
Grafton
Coff's Harbour
Kempsey
Port Macquarie
Taree
Muswellbrook
Maitland
Cessnock
Newcastle
Gosford
SYDNEY
Botany Bay
Wollongong
Nowra
Goulburn
Canberra
Bega
Eden
Cooma
Orbost
Bairnsdale
Lakes Entrance
Sale
Traralgon
Moe
Yarram
Wonthaggi
Geelong
MELBOURNE
Ballarat
Dandenong
Warrnambool
Colac
Portland
Mount Gambier
Millicent
Kingston
Naracoorte
Hamilton
Casterton
Horsham
Ararat
Maryborough
Castlemaine
Bendigo
Seymour
Mansfield
Benalla
Wangaratta
Albury
Wagga Wagga
Tumbarumba
Cootamundra
Temora
Young
Cowra
Bathurst
Orange
Forbes
Parkes
Dubbo
Wellington
Mudgee
Lithgow
West Wyalong
Griffith
Narrandera
Hay
Deniliquin
Echuca
Shepparton
Cohuna
Swan Hill
Kerang
Hopetoun
Pinnaroo
Murray Bridge
Tailem Bend
Adelaide
Gawler
Port Wakefield
Port Pirie
Port Augusta
Whyalla
Iron Knob
Wilmington
Quorn
Hawker
Leigh Creek
Woomera
Pimba
Andamooka

Lake Eyre
Lake Torrens
Lake Frome
Lake Gairdner
Lake Blanche
Lake Gregory
Lake Callabonna
Spencer Gulf
Gulf St. Vincent
Encounter Bay
Kangaroo I.
Yorke Peninsula
Flinders I.
Furneaux Group
Cape Barren
Bass Strait
King I.
Cape Otway
Wilson's Promontory
Kent Group

TASMANIA
Hobart
Launceston
Devonport
Burnie
Smithton
Queenstown
Strahan
Scottsdale
St. Marys
Campbell Town
Deloraine
New Norfolk
Bridgewater
Cape Grim
West Pt.
Cape Sorell
Freycinet Peninsula

INDIAN OCEAN
TASMAN SEA

Relief

Meters	Feet
1525	5000
610	2000
305	1000
152.5	500
0 Sea Level	0
152.5	500 Below
1525	5000 Sea Level
3050	10 000

0 50 100 150 200 Miles
0 50 100 150 200 250 300 Kilometers

Scale 1:8 000 000; one inch to 126 miles.
Lambert's Azimuthal, Equal Area Projection.
Elevations and depressions are given in feet.

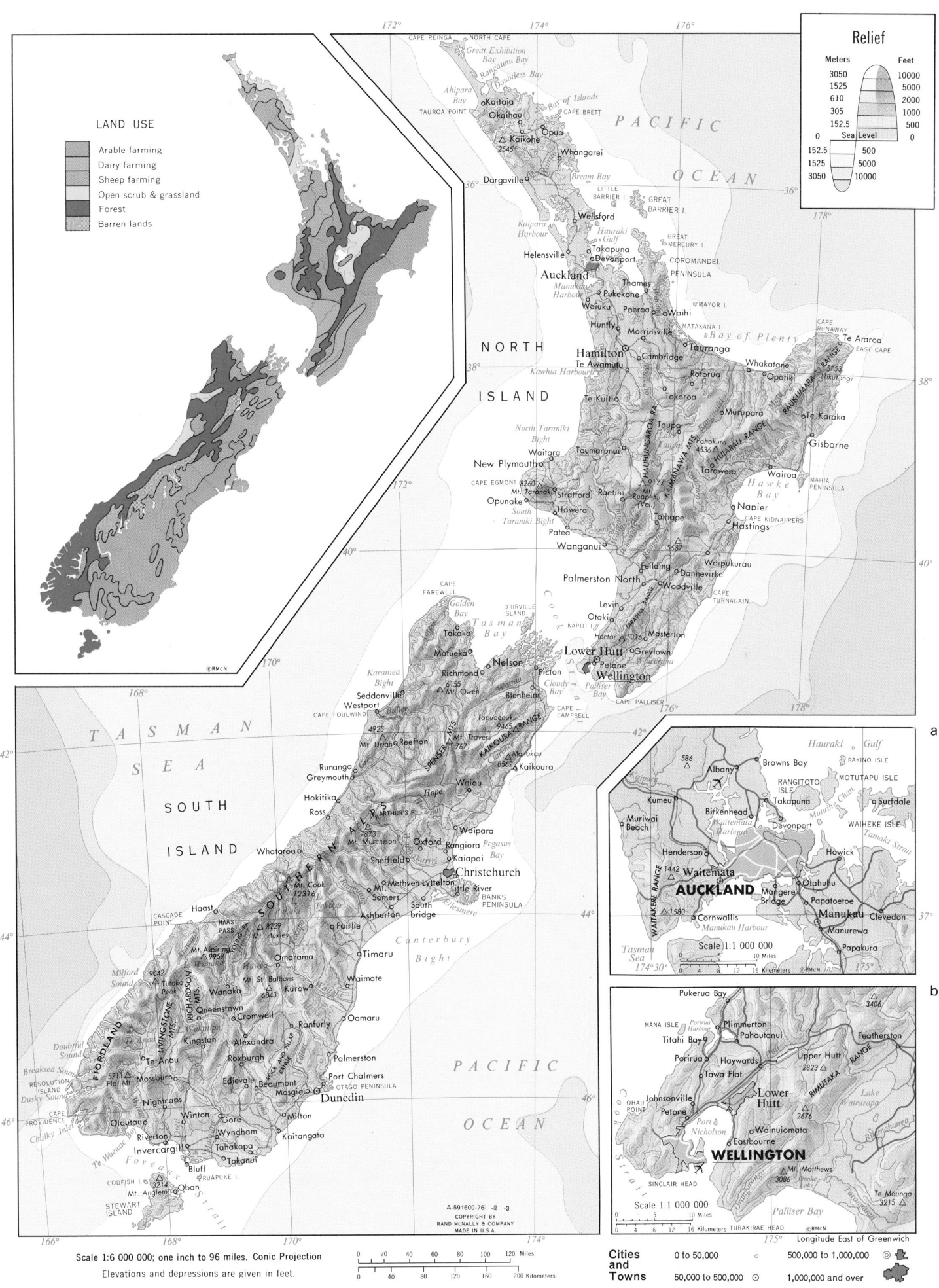

Relief

Meters		Feet
3050		10000
1525		5000
610		2000
305		1000
152.5		500
0	Sea Level	
152.5		500
1525		5000
3050		10000

LAND USE

- Arable farming
- Dairy farming
- Sheep farming
- Open scrub & grassland
- Forest
- Barren lands

©RMCN.

a

Scale 1:1 000 000

b

Scale 1:1 000 000

Longitude East of Greenwich

Cities
and
Towns

0 to 50,000
50,000 to 500,000
500,000 to 1,000,000
1,000,000 and over

Scale 1:6 000 000; one inch to 96 miles. Conic Projection
Elevations and depressions are given in feet.

A-591600-76 -2 -3
COPYRIGHT BY
RAND McNALLY & COMPANY
MADE IN U.S.A.

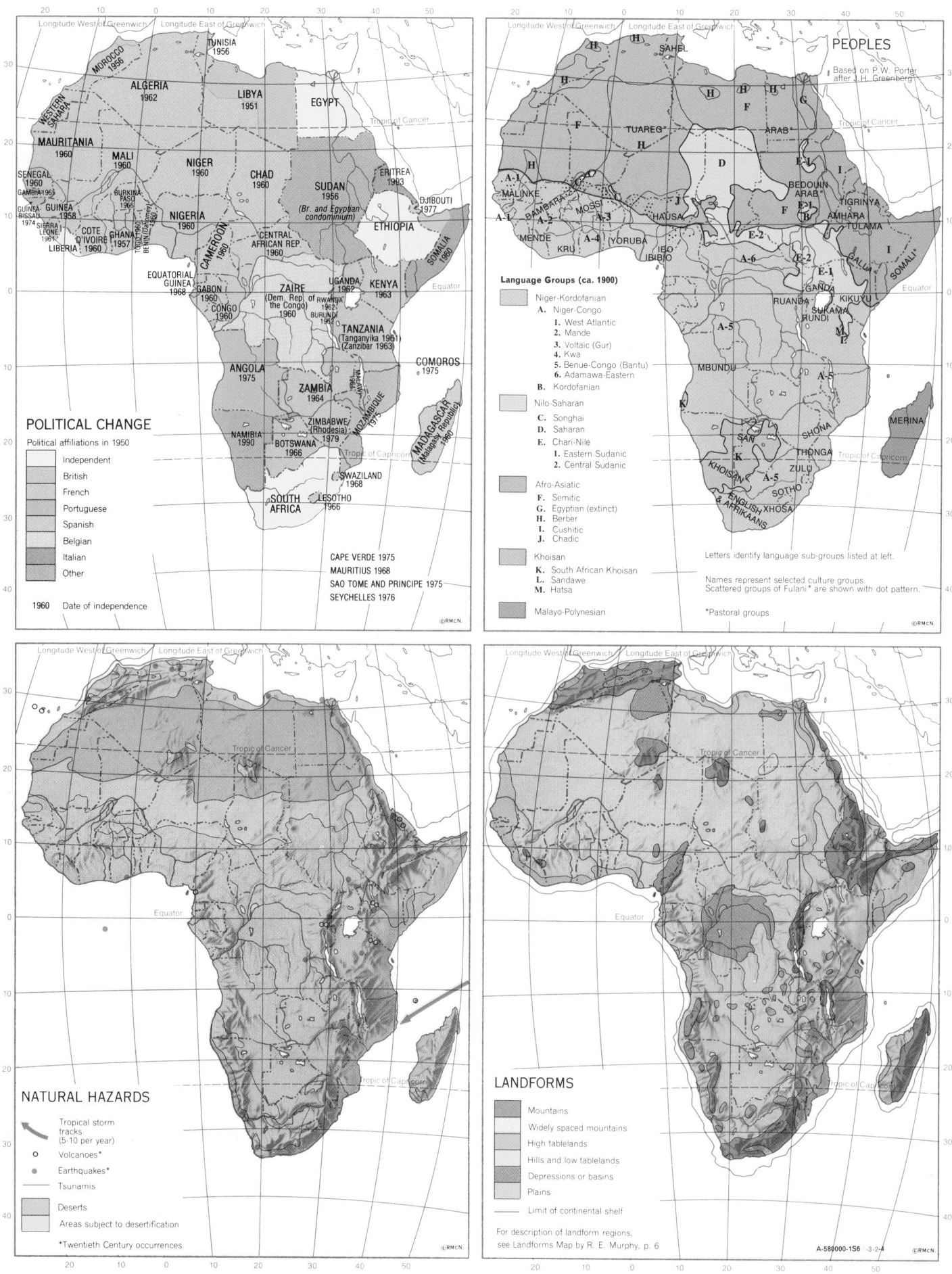

POLITICAL CHANGE (top-left map)

TUNISIA 1956
MOROCCO 1956
ALGERIA 1962
LIBYA 1951
EGYPT
WESTERN SAHARA
MAURITANIA 1960
MALI 1960
NIGER 1960
CHAD 1960
SUDAN 1956 (Br. and Egyptian condominium)
ERITREA 1993
DJIBOUTI 1977
SENEGAL 1960
GAMBIA 1965
GUINEA 1958
GUINEA-BISSAU 1974
SIERRA LEONE 1961
LIBERIA 1960
BURKINA FASO 1960
COTE D'IVOIRE 1960
GHANA 1957
TOGO 1960
BENIN (Dahomey) 1960
NIGERIA 1960
CAMEROON 1960
CENTRAL AFRICAN REP. 1960
ETHIOPIA
SOMALIA 1960
EQUATORIAL GUINEA 1968
GABON 1960
CONGO 1960
ZAIRE (Dem. Rep. of the Congo) 1960
RWANDA 1962
BURUNDI 1962
UGANDA 1962
KENYA 1963
TANZANIA (Tanganyika 1961) (Zanzibar 1963)
ANGOLA 1975
ZAMBIA 1964
MALAWI 1964
MOZAMBIQUE 1975
COMOROS 1975
NAMIBIA 1990
ZIMBABWE (Rhodesia) 1979
BOTSWANA 1966
MADAGASCAR (Malagasy Republic) 1960
MERINA
SWAZILAND 1968
SOUTH AFRICA
LESOTHO 1966

POLITICAL CHANGE

Political affiliations in 1950
- Independent
- British
- French
- Portuguese
- Spanish
- Belgian
- Italian
- Other

1960 Date of independence

CAPE VERDE 1975
MAURITIUS 1968
SAO TOME AND PRINCIPE 1975
SEYCHELLES 1976

©RMcN

PEOPLES (top-right map)

Based on P. W. Porter after J. H. Greenberg

SAHEL
TUAREG
ARAB
MALINKE
BAMBARA
MOSSI
HAUSA
BEDOUIN ARAB
TIGRINYA
MENDE
KRU
YORUBA
IBO IBIBIO
AMHARA
TULAMA
GALLA
SOMALI
MBUNDU
GANDA
KIKUYU
RUANDA
RUNDI
SUKUMA
SAN
SHONA
THONGA
ZULU
KHOISAN
SOTHO
ENGLISH XHOSA & AFRIKAANS
MERINA

Language Groups (ca. 1900)

Niger-Kordofanian
A. Niger-Congo
1. West Atlantic
2. Mande
3. Voltaic (Gur)
4. Kwa
5. Benue-Congo (Bantu)
6. Adamawa-Eastern
B. Kordofanian

Nilo-Saharan
C. Songhai
D. Saharan
E. Chari-Nile
1. Eastern Sudanic
2. Central Sudanic

Afro-Asiatic
F. Semitic
G. Egyptian (extinct)
H. Berber
I. Cushitic
J. Chadic

Khoisan
K. South African Khoisan
L. Sandawe
M. Hatsa

Malayo-Polynesian

Letters identify language sub-groups listed at left.

Names represent selected culture groups.
Scattered groups of Fulani* are shown with dot pattern.

*Pastoral groups

©RMcN

NATURAL HAZARDS (bottom-left map)

→ Tropical storm tracks (5-10 per year)
○ Volcanoes*
● Earthquakes*
— Tsunamis
Deserts
Areas subject to desertification

*Twentieth Century occurrences

©RMcN

LANDFORMS (bottom-right map)

- Mountains
- Widely spaced mountains
- High tablelands
- Hills and low tablelands
- Depressions or basins
- Plains
— Limit of continental shelf

For description of landform regions, see Landforms Map by R. E. Murphy, p. 6

A-580000-1S6 -3-2-4

©RMcN

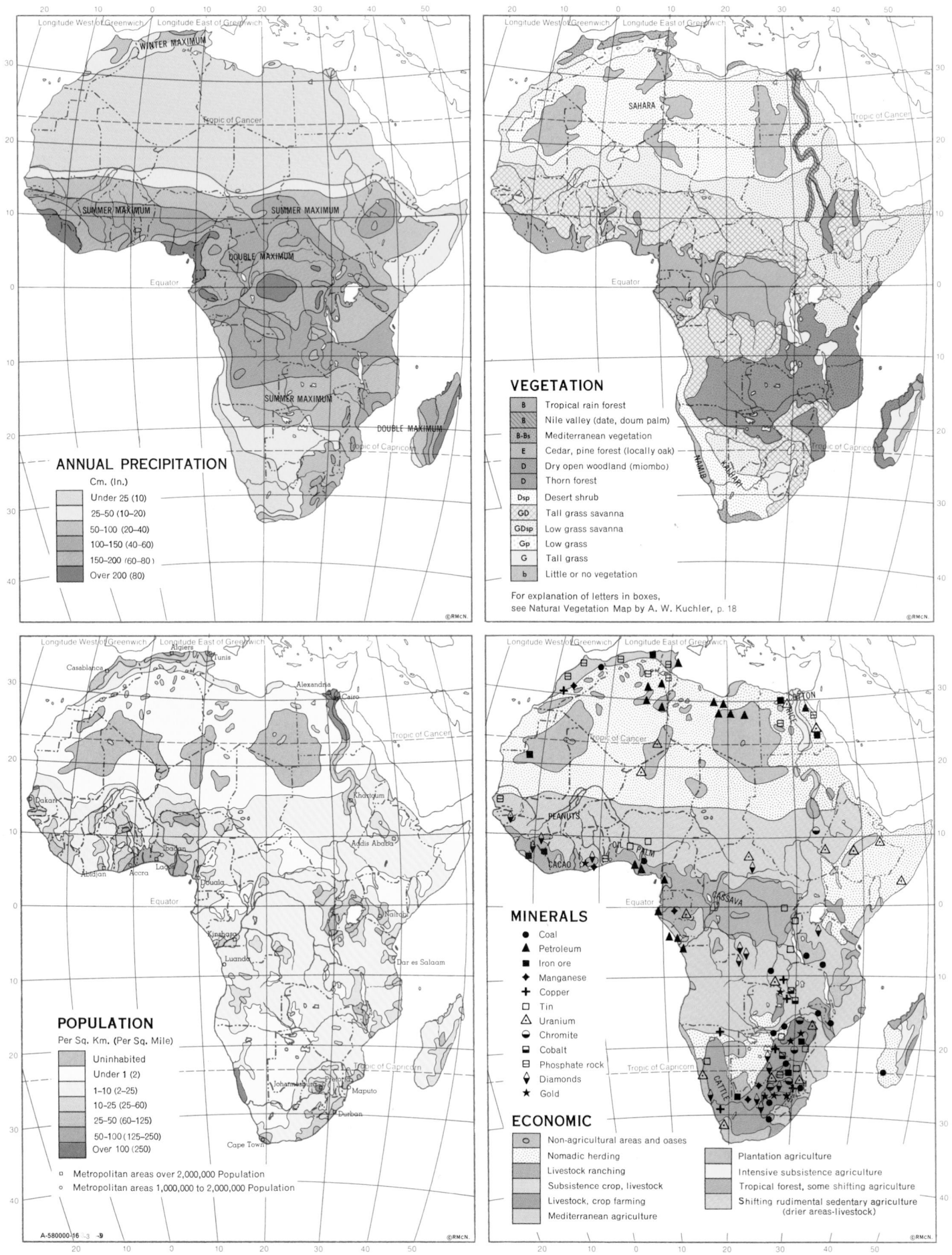

ANNUAL PRECIPITATION

Cm. (In.)

Under 25 (10)
25–50 (10–20)
50–100 (20–40)
100–150 (40–60)
150–200 (60–80)
Over 200 (80)

VEGETATION

B	Tropical rain forest
B	Nile valley (date, doum palm)
B–Bs	Mediterranean vegetation
E	Cedar, pine forest (locally oak)
D	Dry open woodland (miombo)
D	Thorn forest
Dsp	Desert shrub
GD	Tall grass savanna
GDsp	Low grass savanna
Gp	Low grass
G	Tall grass
b	Little or no vegetation

For explanation of letters in boxes,
see Natural Vegetation Map by A. W. Kuchler, p. 18

POPULATION

Per Sq. Km. (Per Sq. Mile)

Uninhabited
Under 1 (2)
1–10 (2–25)
10–25 (25–60)
25–50 (60–125)
50–100 (125–250)
Over 100 (250)

□ Metropolitan areas over 2,000,000 Population
○ Metropolitan areas 1,000,000 to 2,000,000 Population

MINERALS

● Coal
▲ Petroleum
■ Iron ore
◆ Manganese
+ Copper
□ Tin
△ Uranium
◖ Chromite
▭ Cobalt
⊟ Phosphate rock
◈ Diamonds
★ Gold

ECONOMIC

Non-agricultural areas and oases
Nomadic herding
Livestock ranching
Subsistence crop, livestock
Livestock, crop farming
Mediterranean agriculture

Plantation agriculture
Intensive subsistence agriculture
Tropical forest, some shifting agriculture
Shifting rudimental sedentary agriculture
(drier areas-livestock)

ATLANTIC
OCEAN

MADRID
CORSICA
ROME
SARDINIA
Algiers
Tunis
Casablanca
ATLAS
MOUNTAINS
Tripoli
Banghāzī
CANARY ISLANDS
El Aaíun
GRAND ERG OCCIDENTAL
GRAND ERG ORIENTAL
Tropic of Cancer
AHAGGAR
Tarenghest
S A H A R A
EL DJOUF
TIBESTI
Tombouctou
ADRAR
DES IFÔGHAS
ENNEDI
S U D A N
Dakar
Niger
Bamako
Lake Chad
N'Djamena
Al-Fāshir
Freetown
Niger
Kano
Lake Volta
Lagos
Abidjan
Gulf of Guinea
Yaoundé
Bangui
Uele
Equator
Congo (Zaire)
Kisangani
Ubangi
ATLANTIC OCEAN
Congo (Zaire)
Kasai
Kinshasa
Luanda
Lubumbashi
Lusaka
Zambezi
Harare
NAMIB
DESERT
Windhoek
KALAHARI
DESERT
Limpopo
Tropic of Capricorn
Johannesburg
Orange
Orange
Durban
Cape
Town

SICILY
MALTA
ISTANBUL
Athens
CRETE
CYPRUS
Beirut
Alexandria
CAIRO
Nile
ARABIAN DESERT
LIBYAN
DESERT
Lake Nasser
Nile
NUBIAN DESERT
Khartoum
Asmera
White Nile
DANAKIL
Blue Nile
Addis Ababa
Mountain Nile
Lake
Victoria
Nairobi
Lake
Tanganyika
Dar es Salaam
Lake Nyasa
Blantyre
Moçambique
COMORO ISLANDS
Mozambique Channel
MADAGASCAR
Antananarivo
INDIAN
OCEAN
INDIAN OCEAN

Black Sea
BAKU
Caspian Sea
TEHRĀN
Tigris
Baghdad
SYRIAN
DESERT
Euphrates
AN NAFŪD
Riyadh
Red Sea
Mecca
Aden
Gulf of Aden
Berbera
Mogadishu

Mediterranean Sea

Legend

- Urban
- Cropland
- Cropland & Woodland
- Cropland & Grazing Land
- Grassland, Grazing Land
- Forest, Woodland
- Swamp, Marshland
- Shrub, Sparse Grass, Wasteland
- Barren Land
- Oasis

A-580000-36-1-2 3-9
COPYRIGHT BY
RAND MCNALLY & COMPANY
MADE IN U.S.A.

Scale 1:36,000,000; one inch to 570 miles.   Lambert Azimuthal Equal-Area Projection

0   100   200   400   600   800 Miles
0   150 300   600   900   1200 Kilometers

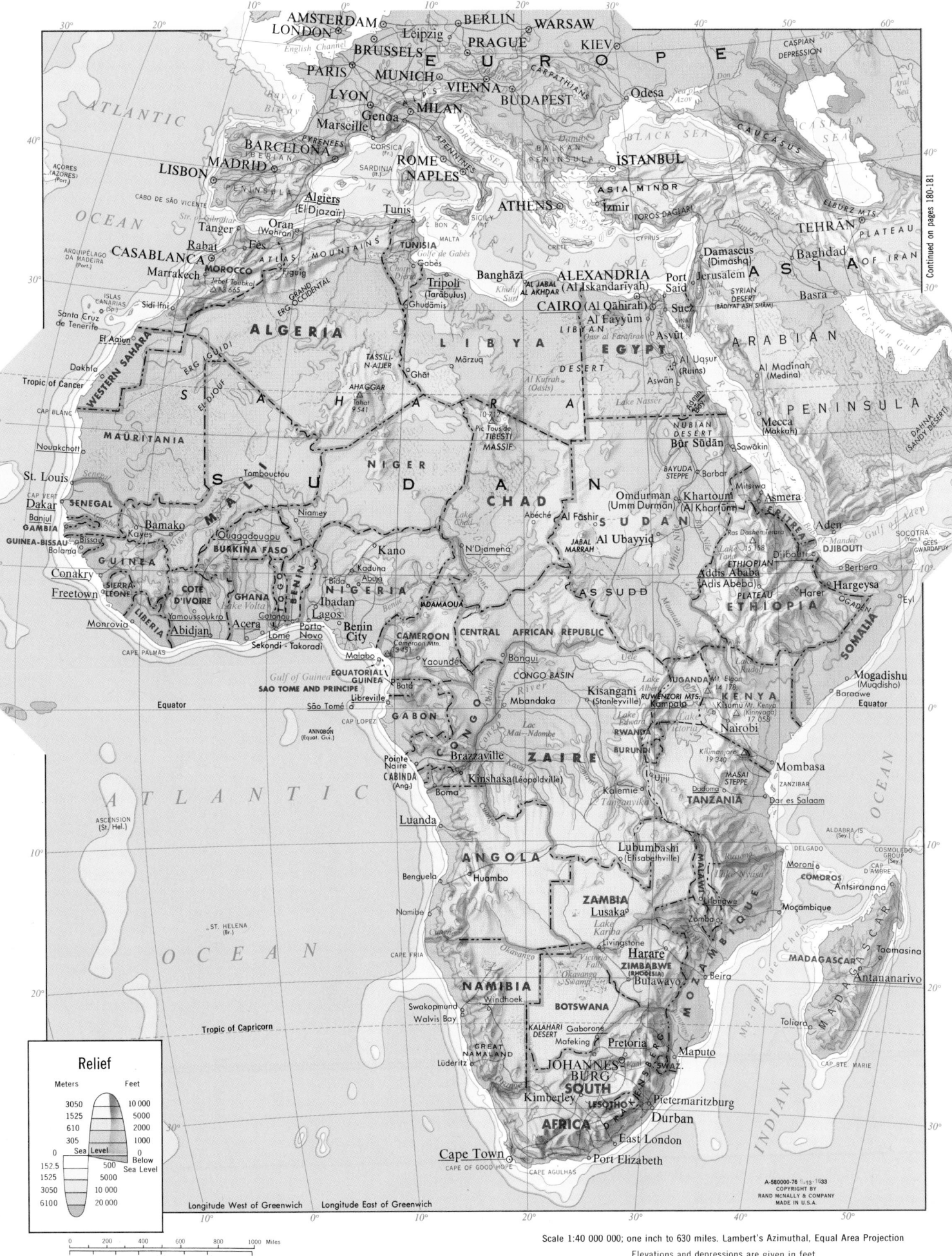

Continued on pages 180-181

Relief

Meters		Feet
3050		10 000
1525		5000
610		2000
305		1000
0	Sea Level	0
152.5		500 Below
1525		Sea Level
3050		5000
		10 000
6100		20 000

Longitude West of Greenwich   Longitude East of Greenwich

0   200   400   600   800   1000 Miles
0   400   800   1200   1600 Kilometers

A-580000-76 9-15-1933
COPYRIGHT BY
RAND McNALLY & COMPANY
MADE IN U.S.A.

Scale 1:40 000 000; one inch to 630 miles. Lambert's Azimuthal, Equal Area Projection
Elevations and depressions are given in feet.

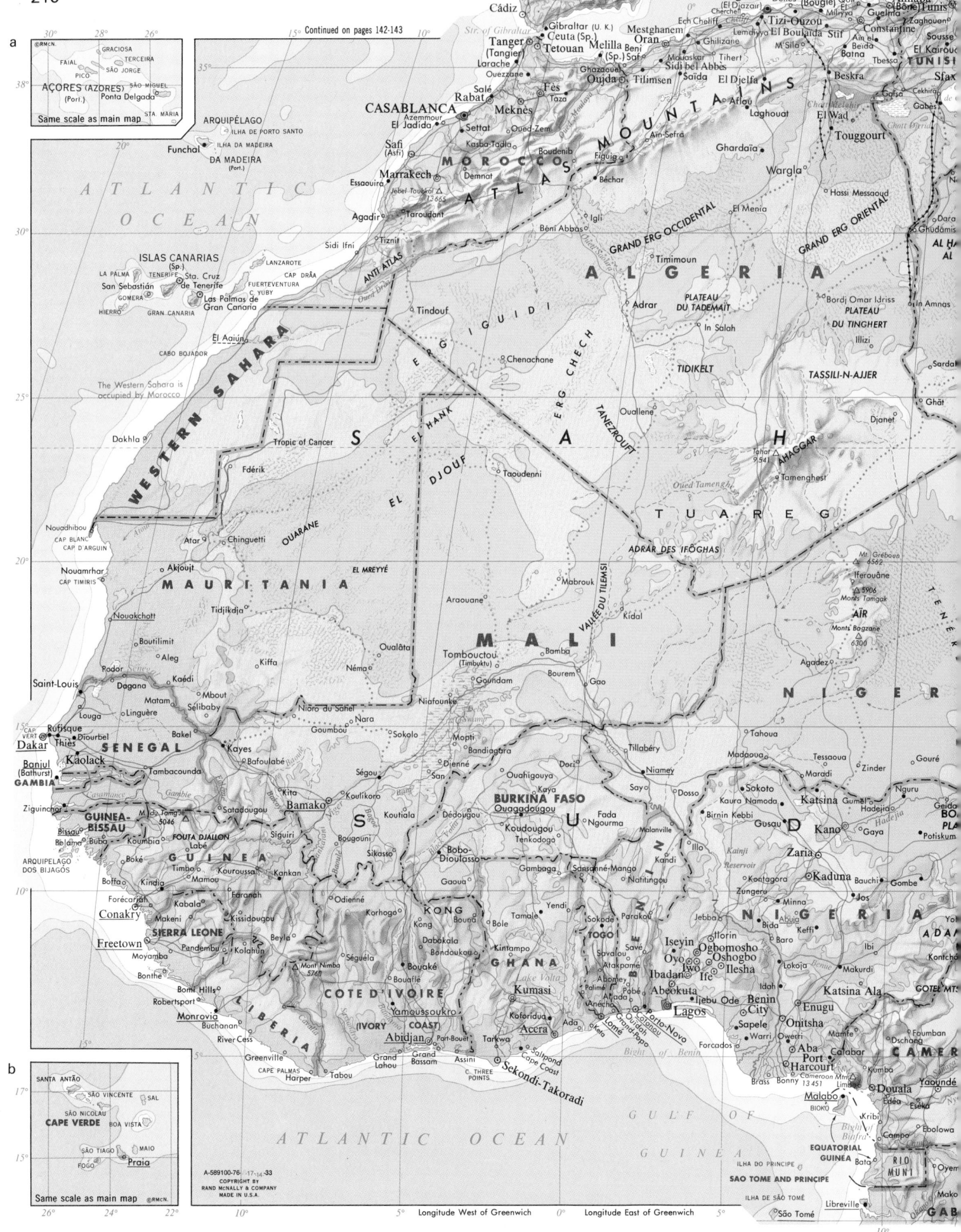

a

ⓇRMCN.

30°   28°   26°

FAIAL   PICO   GRACIOSA   TERCEIRA
SÃO JORGE

AÇORES (AZORES)   SÃO MIGUEL
(Port.)   Ponta Delgada

STA. MARIA

Same scale as main map

38°

35°

Continued on pages 142-143

15°   10°

SPAIN

Cádiz

Bizerte

Algiers   Delles   Bejaïa   Skikda   Annaba   Tunis
(El Djazaïr)   Cherchell   (Bougie)   Djidjelli   (Bône)   Guelma
Gibraltar (U. K.)   Ech Cheliff   Tizi-Ouzou   Miliya   Constantine
Tanger   Ceuta (Sp.)   Mestghanem   El Boulaïda   Sétif   Aïn-el-Beïda   TUNISIA
(Tangier)   Tetouan   Melilla   Oran   Ghilizane   M'Sila   Batna   Tbessa   Sousse
Larache   (Sp.)   Saïda   Sidi bel Abbès   Beskra   El Kairouan
Ouezzane   Oujda   Tilimsen   El Djelfa   Gafsa   Sfax

Salé   Fès   Taza
Rabat   Meknès

CASABLANCA   Laghouat   El Oued   Gabès

El Jadida   Oued-Zem   Aïn-Sefra   Touggourt   Djerba
Azemmour   Settat   Kasba-Tadla   Boudenib   Figuig   Ghardaïa   Wargla   Dara
Safi   Demnat   Béchar   Hassi Messaoud
(Asfi)

Marrakech   Igli   El Menia   Ghûdamis
Jebel Toubkal   Béni Abbès   AL HA
13665   GRAND ERG OCCIDENTAL   GRAND ERG ORIENTAL   AL

Essaouira   Agadir   Taroudant

Sidi Ifni   Tiznit   Timimoun   Bordj Omar Idriss   In Amnas

Adrar   PLATEAU   In Salah   PLATEAU
DU TADEMAIT   DU TINGHERT

Tindouf   ALGERIA   Illizi

PLATEAU
Chenachane   TIDIKELT   TASSILI-N-AJJER

Ouallene   Ghât   Sarda
Djanet

Taoudenni   AHAGGAR
Tahat
9541

Tamanghest

20°   10°

Funchal   ILHA DE PORTO SANTO   20°
ARQUIPÉLAGO   ILHA DA MADEIRA
DA MADEIRA
(Port.)

A T L A N T I C

O C E A N

ISLAS CANARIAS   LANZAROTE
(Sp.)   CAP DRÂA
La Palma   TENERIFE   Sta. Cruz   ANTI ATLAS
de Tenerife   FUERTEVENTURA
San Sebastián   C. YUBY
GOMERA   Las Palmas de
HIERRO   GRAN CANARIA   Gran Canaria

El Aaiún   WESTERN SAHARA

CABO BOJADOR

The Western Sahara is
occupied by Morocco   Tropic of Cancer   S   El Hank   A   H   A   R

Dakhla   Fdérik   EL   DJOUF   TUAREG

Nouâdhibou   OUARANE   ADRAR DES IFÔGHAS
CAP BLANC
CAP D'ARGUIN   Atar   Chinguetti   Mt. Gréboun
6562

Nouamrhar   EL MREYYÉ   Iferouâne   AÏR
CAP TIMIRIS   Akjoujt   5906
Monts Tamgak   6300

MAURITANIA   Araouane   Kidal   Monts Bagzane

Nouakchott   Tidjikdja   Mabrouk   VALLÉE DU TILEMSI   Agadez

Boutilimit   MALI   NIGER

Saint-Louis   Aleg   Kiffa   Néma   Tombouctou   Bamba   Gao
Podor   (Timbuktu)   Goundam   Bourem
Dagana   Kaédi   Oualâta   Tahoua
Louga   Matam   Nioro du Sahel   Niafounké   Tessaoua
Linguère   Nara   Goumbou   Gouré
Rufisque   Bakel   Sokoto   Madaoua
CAP   Thiès   Diourbel   Kayes   Sokolo   Mopti   Tillabéry   Zinder
VERT   SENEGAL   Bandiagara   Dori   Niamey   Maradi   Nguru

Dakar   Kaolack   Bafoulabé   Dienné   San   Ouahigouya   Say   Dosso   Kaura Namoda   Katsina   Gumel   BO
GAMBIA   Tambacounda   Ségou   BURKINA FASO   Birnin Kebbi   Gusau   Hadejia   PLA
Banjul   Kita   Koulikoro   Ouagadougou   Malanville   Kano
(Bathurst)   Koutiala   Dédougou   Fada   Illo   Gaya   Potiskum
Ziguinchor   Bamako   Ngourma   Kontagora   Zaria
GUINEA-   M. du Tamgè   Sikasso   Koudougou   Zungeru   Kaduna
BISSAU   5046   Bobo-   Tenkodogo   Gambaga   Sansanné-Mango   Bauchi   Gombe
Bissau   FOUTA DJALLON   Siguiri   Dioulasso   Natitingou   Minna   Jos
Bolama   Labé   Gaoua   Kandi   NIGERIA
Buba   GUINEA   Timbo   Kankan   Odienné   KONG   Bouna   Yendi   Abuja
ARQUIPÉLAGO   Boké   Mamou   Korhogo   Kong   Tamale   Sokodé   Parakou   Keffi
DOS BIJAGÓS   Kindia   Dabakala   Bole   Ibi
Forécariah   Kabala   Faranah   Bondoukou   Kintampo   TOGO   Iseyin   Ilorin   Bida   Baro
Conakry   Makeni   Kissidougou   Beyla   Séguéla   Bouaké   Savalou   Saki   Ogbomosho   Oshogbo   Lokoja   Idah   Katsina Ala
SIERRA LEONE   Mont Nimba   Bouaflé   Atakpamé   Oyo   Iwo   Ife   Ilesha   ADA
Freetown   5760   GHANA   Palimé   Abomey   Ibadan   Ijebu Ode   Makurdi   GOTEL MTS.
Moyamba   Pandembu   Kolahun   COTE D'IVOIRE   Kumasi   Pobé   Abeokuta   Benin   Enugu
Bonthe   Bomi Hills   Koforidua   Ada   Anecho   Porto-Novo   City   Onitsha   Foumban
Robertsport   LIBERIA   (IVORY COAST)   Tarkwa   Lagos   Sapele   Aba   Dschang
Monrovia   Yamoussoukro   Accra   Cape Coast   Warri   Calabar   CAMER
Buchanan   Abidjan   Port-Bouet   Forcados   Port
Harcourt   Kumba   Yaoundé
River Cess   Grand   Grand   Sekondi-Takoradi   Cameroon Mtn.   Douala
Greenville   Lahou   Bassam   Assini   13451   Edéa
CAPE PALMAS   Harper   Tabou   C. THREE   Bonny   Kribi
POINTS   Brass   Malabo   BIOKO

GULF OF   EQUATORIAL   Eséka
GUINEA   Bata   Ebolowa
A T L A N T I C   O C E A N   SÃO TOMÉ AND PRINCIPE   GUINEA   Campo
ILHA DO PRINCIPE   RIO   Oyem
MUNI   GAB
ILHA DE SÃO TOMÉ   São Tomé   Libreville

b

SANTA ANTÃO

SÃO VICENTE   SAL

SÃO NICOLAU   BOA VISTA

CAPE VERDE

SÃO TIAGO   MAIO

FOGO   Praia

Same scale as main map   ⓇRMCN.

A-589100-76   17-14-33
COPYRIGHT BY
RAND MCNALLY & COMPANY
MADE IN U.S.A.

10°   5°   Longitude West of Greenwich   Longitude East of Greenwich   5°   10°

Scale 1:16 000 000; one inch to 250 miles. Sinusoidal Projection
Elevations and depressions are given in feet

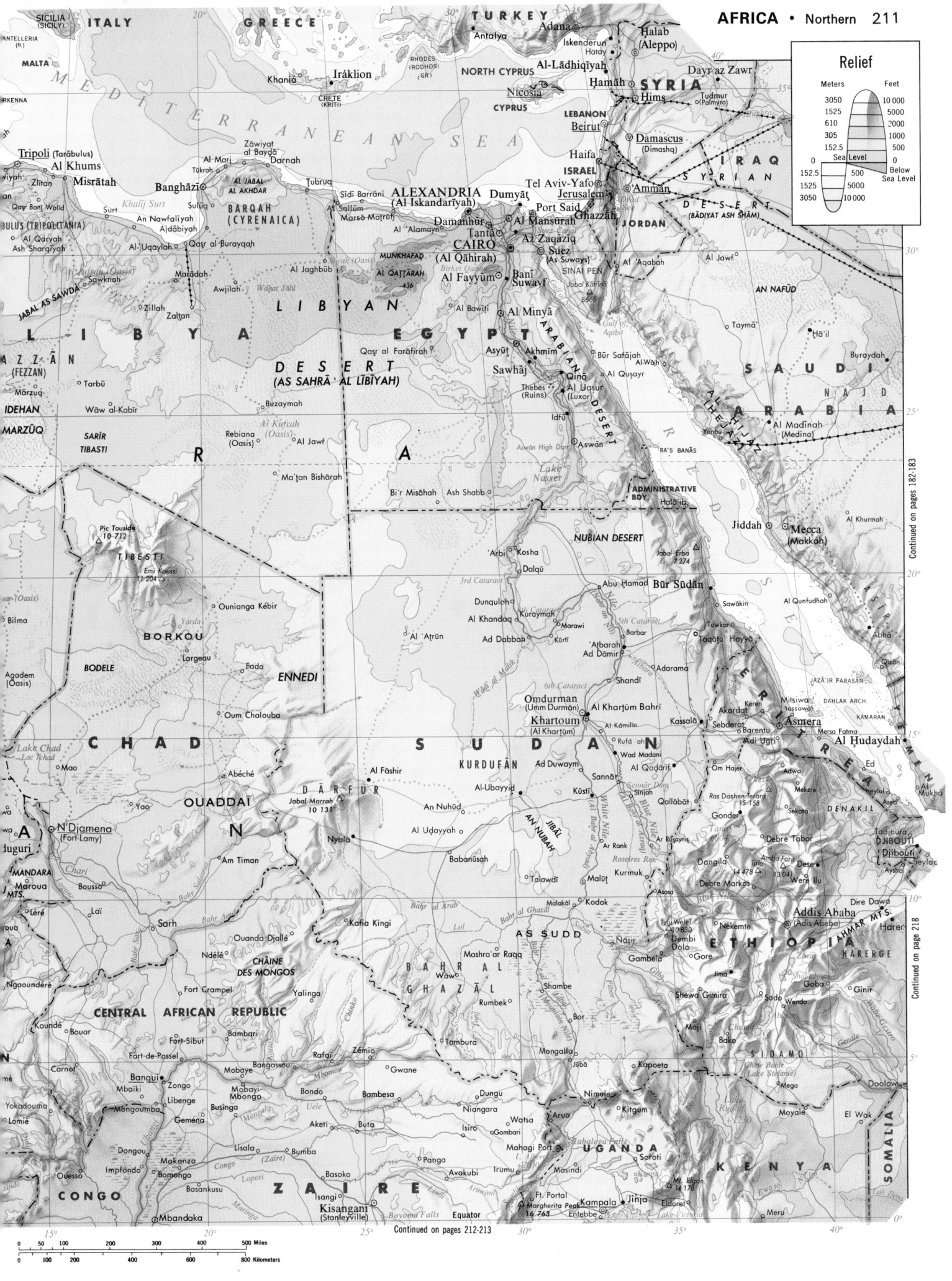

Relief

Meters	Feet
3050	10 000
1525	5000
610	2000
305	1000
152.5	500
0 Sea Level	Sea Level
152.5	500
1525	5000
3050	10 000
	Below Sea Level

ITALY
SICILIA (SICILY)
PANTELLERIA (It.)
MALTA
GREECE
Khaniá
Iráklion
CRETE (KRITI)
RHODES (RODHOS) (GR)
NORTH CYPRUS
Nicosia
CYPRUS
TURKEY
Antalya
Adana
Iskenderun
Hatay
Halab (Aleppo)
Al-Lādhiqīyah
Ḥamāh
Ḥimṣ
Dayr az Zawr
Tudmur (Palmyra)
SYRIA
LEBANON
Beirut
Damascus (Dimashq)
Haifa
Tel Aviv-Yafo
Jerusalem
Amman
ISRAEL
JORDAN
IRAQ
SYRIAN DESERT (BĀDIYAT ASH SHĀM)
Al Jawf
AN NAFŪD
Taymā
Ḥā'il
Buraydah
SAUDI ARABIA
NAJD
AL HIJAZ
Al Madīnah (Medina)
Yanbu
RA'S BĀNĀS
Al Khurmah
Jiddah
Mecca (Makkah)
Al Qunfudhah
Abhā
Qīzān
JAZĀ'IR FARASAN
DAHLAK ARCH.
KAMARAN
Al Ḥudaydah
Al Mukhā
YEMEN

MEDITERRANEAN SEA
Tripoli (Ṭarābulus)
Al Khums
Miṣrātah
Zlītan
Zāwiyat al Bayḍā
Al Marj
Ṭūkrah
Darnah
Banghāzī
Tūbruq
Sīdī Barrānī
Marsā Maṭrūḥ
Sallūm
ALEXANDRIA (Al Iskandarīyah)
Damanhūr
Ṭanṭā
Dumyāṭ
Port Said
Al Manṣūrah
Az Zaqāzīq
CAIRO (Al Qāhirah)
Suez (As Suways)
Ghazzāh
SINAI PEN.
Al 'Aqabah
MUNKHAFAD AL QAṬṬĀRAH -436
Siwah (Oasis)
Birket Qarūn
Al Jaghbūb
Banī Suwayf
Al Fayyūm
Al 'Alamayn
Al Bawītī
Jabal Kātrīnā 8668
Gulf of Suez
Gulf of Aqaba

LIBYA
BARQAH (CYRENAICA)
AL JABAL AL AKHḌAR
Khalīj Surt
An Nawfalīyah
Ajdābiyah
Al 'Uqaylah
Qaṣr al Burayqah
Suluq
Surt
JABAL AS SAWDĀ
Marādah
Sawknah
Awjilah
Wāḥat Jālū
LIBYAN DESERT (AS SAHRĀ AL LĪBĪYAH)
EGYPT
Al Minyā
Asyūṭ
Akhmīm
Qaṣr al Farāfirah
Sawhāj
Thebes (Ruins)
Al Uqṣur (Luxor)
Qinā
Al Quṣayr
Idfū
Būr Safājah
Al-Wajh
ARABIAN DESERT
RED SEA
Aswān High Dam
Aswān
Lake Nasser

FEZZĀN (FEZZAN)
MARZŪQ
Mārzūq
Tarbū
Wāw al-Kabīr
IDEHAN MARZŪQ
SARĪR TIBASTI
Zillah
Zaltan
Buzaymah
Rebiana (Oasis)
Al Kufrah (Oasis)
Al Jawf
Ma'tan Bishārah
Bi'r Misāḥah
Ash Shabb
ADMINISTRATIVE BDY.
Halā'ib

Pic Touside 10 712
Emi Koussi 11 204
TIBESTI
Bilma
Agadem (Oasis)
'Ar (Oasis)
Ounianga Kébir
Largeau
BORKOU
BODELE
Fada
ENNEDI
Oum Chalouba
Yarda
Jabal Erba 7 274
NUBIAN DESERT
'Arbi
Kosha
Dalqū
3rd Cataract
Dunqulah
Al Khandaq
Kuraymah
Marawi
Kūrtī
Ad Dabbah
4th Cataract
5th Cataract
Abu Ḥamad
Bārbar
Atbarah
'Aṭbarah
Ad Dāmir
Adarama
Tawkar
Taqāṭū Ḥayyā
Sawākin
Būr Sūdān

CHAD
Lake Chad Lac Tchad
Mao
N'Djamena (Fort-Lamy)
Abéché
Yao
DĀRFŪR
Al Fāshir
Jabal Marrah 10 131
Nyala
Al Uḍayyah
An Nuhūd
Al-Ubayyid
KURDUFĀN
Ad Duwaym
SUDAN
Al Quḍārif
Wad Madanī
Sannār
Kūstī
Sinjah
Sennar Dam
Roseires Res.
Ar Rank
Malūṭ
Kurmuk
Kodok
Malakāl
Nāṣir
AS SUDD
Shandī
6th Cataract
Omdurman (Umm Durmān)
Al Khartūm Bahrī
Khartoum (Al Khartūm)
Al Kāmilīn
Rufā'a
ERITREA
Akordat
Keren
Mitsiwa (Massawa)
Kassalā
Sebderat
Barentu
Adi Ugri
Asmera
Adīgrāt
ADWA
Ras Dashen Terara 15 158
Gonder
Mekele
Sekota
Lake Tana
Om Hajer
DENAKIL
Tala
Amba Farit 13 041
Dangila
Debre Tabor
Debre Markos
Wera Ilu
Desē
Ed
Beylul
Aseb
Tadjoura
DJIBOUTI
Djibouti
Aysha
Seylac

OUADDAÏ
Am Timan
MANDARA MTS.
Maroua
Léré
Boussõ
Chari
Bousso
Baba Nūsah
Talawdī
Malūṭ
AN NUBAH
JIBĀL
Ar Rank
White Nile
Bahr al 'Arab
Blue Nile
Bahr al Azraq
Qallābāt
Debre Markos
ETHIOPIA
Addis Ababa (Adis Abeba)
Harer
HARERGE
Dire Dawa
Tulu Welel 10 830
Nekemte
Dembi Dolo
Gambela
Gore
Jima
AHMAR MTS.
Goba
Ginir
SIDAMO
Baka
Bako
Maji
Shewa Gimira
Soddo Wenda
Chaw Bahr Lake Stefanie
Mega
Moyale
El Wak

CENTRAL AFRICAN REPUBLIC
Koundé
Bouar
Fort-Sibut
Fort-de-Possel
Bambari
Bangui
Mbaïki
Zongo
Mobaye
Bangassou
Zémio
Rafaï
CHAÎNE DES MONGOS
Yalinga
Ndélé
Ouanda Djallé
Fort Crampel
BAHR AL GHAZĀL
Kafia Kingi
Wāw
Rumbek
Tambura
Bor
Mashra'ar Raqq
Shambe
Mongalla
Jūbā
Kapoeta
Lake Rudolf
KENYA

CONGO
Ouesso
Impfondo
Bomongo
Mbandaka
ZAIRE
Basankusu
Isangi
Kisangani (Stanleyville)
Boyoma Falls
Basoko
Bumba
Lisala
Makanza
Dongou
Aketi
Buta
Niangara
Isiro
Gombari
Watsa
Avakubi
Irumu
Mahagi Port
Panga
Arua
Kitgum
Gulu
Soroti
UGANDA
Masindi
Ft. Portal
Margherita Peak 16 763
Mt. Elgon 14 178
Kampala
Jinja
Entebbe
Eldoret
Lake Victoria
Meru
Equator
SOMALIA
Doolow

Continued on pages 182-183
Continued on page 218
Continued on pages 212-213

0 50 100 200 300 400 500 Miles
0 100 200 400 600 800 Kilometers

Continued on pages 210-211

GABON
CONGO
ZAIRE
UGANDA
RWANDA
BURUNDI
TANZANIA
Brazzaville
CABINDA (Angola)
Kinshasa (Léopoldville)
Pointe-Noire
Luanda
ANGOLA
KATANGA
Kananga (Luluabourg)
Lubumbashi (Elisabethville)
ZAMBIA
Lusaka
BAROTSELAND
CAPRIVI STRIP
OWAMBO
NAMIB DESERT
NAMIBIA
DAMARALAND
Windhoek
ZIMBABWE (RHODESIA)
Harare (Salisbury)
Bulawayo
MOZAMBIQUE
Beira
BOTSWANA
KALAHARI DESERT
GREAT NAMALAND
Tropic of Capricorn
BUSHMANLAND
SOUTH AFRICA
JOHANNESBURG
Pretoria
Maputo (Lourenço Marques)
SWAZILAND
KWAZULU
LESOTHO
DRAKENSBERG
Bloemfontein
Kimberley
Durban
Pietermaritzburg
East London
GREAT KARROO
LITTLE KARROO
Cape Town
Port Elizabeth
CAPE OF GOOD HOPE
Cape Agulhas

15° Longitude East of Greenwich

A-589200-76 14-1-80
COPYRIGHT BY
RAND McNALLY & COMPANY
MADE IN U.S.A.

Scale 1:16 000 000; one inch to 250 miles. Sinusoidal Projection
Elevations and depressions are given in feet

0 50 100 200 300 400 500 Miles
0 100 200 400 600 800 Kilometers

Inset: Cape Town

a

ROBBENEILAND
Bloubergstrand
Kanonkop 1502
Durbanville
CAPE TOWN
MOUILLE PT
Table Bay
Milnerton
Parow
Bellville
Goodwood
Camps Bay
Table Mt. 3567
Pinelands
Kuilsrivier
Nuweland
Wynberg
Ottery
CAPE FLATS
Houtbaai 3048
Chapman's Bay
Muizenberg
Vishoek
Kommetjie
Grootkop 1286
Simonstad
Swartkop 2229
SMITSWINKEL VLAKTE
Valsbaai (False Bay)
SEAL ISLAND
KAAPPUNT
CAPE OF GOOD HOPE

ATLANTIC OCEAN

Scale 1:1 000 000
0 1 5 10 Miles
0 4 8 12 16 Kilometers
©RMcN
18°30'

b

INDIAN

SOMALIA

Nairobi

Mt. Kenya
(Kirinyaga)
17,058
Ft. Hall

Kismaayo

Buur Gaabo

Equator

Witu
Lamu

Malindi
Takaungu

Mombasa

Vanga

PEMBA ISLAND

Tango
Pangani

ZANZIBAR
Zanzibar

Bagamoyo

Dar es Salaam

Morogoro

Kisaki

Utete

MAFIA

Kilwa Kivinje

Lindi

Mikindani

Masasi

CABO DELGADO

Moçímboa
da Praia

Ibo

Pemba

Lúrio

Memba

Nacala

Moçambique

ALDABRA IS.
(Sey.)

COSMOLEDO GROUP
(Sey.)

ÎLES GLORIEUSES
(Fr.)

CAP D'AMBRE

Antsiranana

Moroni

COMOROS

NJAZIDJA
MWALI
NZWANI

Dzaoudzi

MAYOTTE
(Fr.)

NOSY BE

Iharana

Maromokotro
9436

Mahajanga

Mandritsara

Maroantsetra

NOSY BORAHA

Helodrano
Antongila

Fenoarivo
Atsinanana

Ambatondrazaka

Toamasina

Angoche

ILHA Angoche

CAP SAINT-
ANDRÉ

Besalampy

ÎLE JUAN DE NOVA
(Fr.)

NOSY BARREN

MADAGASCAR

Maintirano

Pebane

Antananarivo

Moramanga

Vatomandry

Tsiafajavona
8671

Antsirabe

Mahanoro

BASSAS DA INDIA
(Fr.)

EUROPA
(Fr.)

Morondava

Fianarantsoa

Mananjary

Ambositra

Ivohibe

Manakara

Morombe

Farafangana

Mahaly

Trafonomby
5417

Faradofay

CAP STE. MARIE

Toliara

Betroka

BANKBERG
6606

Cradock

Pearston

Somerset East

Bedford

SUURBERGE

Alicedale

Kirkwood

Addo

Uitenhage

SAINT CROIX
ISLAND

BIRD ISLAND

Port Elizabeth

KAAP RECIFE

Whittlesea

Tylden

Seymour

Adelaide

Keiskammahoek

Fort Alice
Beaufort

Bisho

King William's
Town

Breidbach

Riebeek-Oos

Grahamstown

Salem

Bathurst

Port Alfred (Kowie)

Alexandria

Peddie

Hamburg

Kidd's Beach

Gonubie

East London

Komga

Kei Mouth

Morgan's Bay

Macleantown

Berlin

Kentani

Butterworth

Willowvale

Idutywa

Ngamakwe

Tsomo

Cofimvaba

Tsolo

Qumbu

Elliotdale

Mqanduli

Umtata

Libode

Port St. Johns

RAME HEAD

Waterloo

Arlington

Paul Roux

Senekal

Bethlehem

Harrismith

Dannhauser

Glencoe

Dundee

Wasbank

Nqutu

Mahlabatini

Babanango

Fouriesburg

Ficksburg

Clocolan

Teyateyaneng

Clarens

Butha Buthe
Leribe

Pitseng

Mokhotlong

ORANGE FREE STATE

ROYAL NATAL
NAT'L. PK.

Bergville
Winterton

Cathedral Pk.
9856

Mt. aux
Sources
10,822

MALOTI MTS.

Machache
9464

Roma

Thabana
Ntlenyana
11425

LESOTHO

Ladysmith

Colenso

Estcourt

Weenen

Mooirivier

Tugela Ferry

Greytown

Kranskop

Mt. Gilboa
5803

New
Hanover

Howick

Dalton

Wartburg

Stanger

Verulam

Pietermaritzburg

Camperdown

Pinetown

Isipingo

Durban

Nkandla

Melmoth

Eshowe

Mapumulo

Nthoni
5851

Impendle

Bulwer

Underberg

Richmond

Donnybrook

Mid Illovo

Creighton

Ixopo

Umkomaas

Scottburgh

Park Rynie

Sezela

Umzinto

Umtentweni

Port Shepstone

Uvongo Beach

Margate

Port Edward

Qacha's Nek
8820

Franklin

EASTERN

CAP E

Swartberg
7619

8326

The Twins

Mohale's
Hoek

Matatiele

Cedarville

Mt. Currie
7297

Kokstad

Harding

Bizana

Flagstaff

Lusikisiki

Tabankulu

Mount Ayliff

Mount Frere

Maclear

Qumbu

Ngqeleni

Ugie

Zastron

Quthing

9684

Herschel

Witberg
2853

Ben Macdhui
9846

Rhodes

Mount
Fletcher
7426

Barkly East

Lady Grey

Jamestown

Rossouw

8430

Molteno

Dordrecht

Elliot

Cala

Engcobo

Indwe

STORMBERG

Sterkstroom

Lady Frere

Queenstown

Tarkastad

Cathcart

SOUTH

WINTERBERG
7778

Frankfort

Stutterheim

INDIAN

OCEAN

Scale 1:4 000 000

0 10 20 30 40 Miles
0 10 20 30 40 50 60 Kilometers

Longitude East of Greenwich

For larger scale coverage of
Johannesburg see page 244.

MOZAMBIQUE CHANNEL

Tsiribihina

Mangoky

Onilahy

Mania

Menarandra

Fish

Sundays

Tarka

Great Fish

Kei

Mbashe

Mzimvubu

Umtata

Mzimkulu

Umkomaas

Drakensberg

Orange

Falls

Sehlabathebe

10159

Thukela

White Umfolozi

Mhlatuze

Wilge

Sand

Tugela

40°

45°

45°

Equator

10°

15°

20°

25°

30°

35°

40°

50°

c

Pretoria

Wolhuterskop

Jacksonstuin

Kosmos

Hartbeespoort

Swartspruit

Skeerpoort

Magaliesberg

4549

Hennopsrivier

Olievenhoutpoort

Foothills

Tarlton

JOHANNESBURG

Krugersdorp

Roodepoort

Randfontein

5725

Florida
Maraisburg

Orlando

Pimville

Discovery

Turffontein

Rosetten-
ville

WITWATERSRAND

Pretoria
North

Cullinan

Silverton

Rayton

4426

Voortrekkerhoogte

Valhalla

Lyttelton

Irene

Tierpoort

Halfway
House

Kaaltontein

Bapsfontein

Moddetfontein

Kempton Park

Putfontein

Alexandra

Edenvale

Primrose

5557

Boksburg

Benoni

Germiston

Alberton

Brakpan

Springs

Scale 1:1 000 000

0   5   10 Miles
0 4 8 12 16 Kilometers

WITWATERSBERG

Magaliesberg

Krokodil

Hennops

Sesmyl

Pienaar

28°

28°30'

26°

Relief

Meters   Feet

3050   10 000
1525   5000
610   2000
305   1000
152.5   500
0   Sea Level   0
152.5   500
1525   5000
3050   10 000

PUNTILLA
NEGRA
CABO
BARBAS
ADRAR SOTUF
WESTERN SAHARA
Fdérik
Kediet Ijill
Tichla
Nouadhibou
CAP BLANC

MAKTEÏR
OUARANE

TAOUDENNI
EL DJOUF

S A H A
TANEZROU
N-AHNET
Bordj le Prieat

ÎLE TIDRA
20°
CAP TIMIRIS
Nouamrhar
Akjoujt
MAURITANIA
ADÂFER EL ABIOD
EL MREYYE

Timetrine
Monts
Aguelhok

Araouane
A Z A O U A D
VALLÉE DU TILEMSI

Sebkha de
Ndrhamcha
Nouakchott
T R A R Z A
Tidjikdja
A O U K Â R

Tombouctou
(Timbuktu)
Niger
Taoussa
Gao
Ansongo

Rosso
Dagana
Aleg
Moudjéria
Kiffa
Ayoun el Atrous
Néma
I R I G U I
Lac Foguibine
Lac Do

M A L I

Saint-Louis
Louga
Linguère
Ranérou
Kaédi
Matam
Nioro du Sahel
Ballé
Lac Débo
Léré
Deventza
Hombori
A
Ayo

15°
CAP VERT
Thiès
Rufisque
Touba
SENEGAL
F E R L O
Naye
Kayes
S U D A N
Goumbou
Kogoni
Macina
Kona
 Deventza

Dakar
Diourbel
Salourn
Diéma
Didiéni
Ségou
San
Mopti
Koro
Aribinda
Djiba
Téra

Kaolack
Sokone
CAPE SAINT MARY
Tambacounda
Bafoulabé
Koulouguidi
PARC NATIONAL
DE LA BOUCLE
DU BAOULÉ
Banamba
Bla
Djibasso
Ouahigouya
Kaya
Doni

GAMBIA
Banjul
(Bathurst)
Médina Gonasse
PARC
NATIONAL
DU NIOKOLO
KOBA
Goumbati
1 368
Kita
Koulikoro
Tougan
Nyou
BURKINA
FASO
Kantcha

Kolda
Bignona
CAP ROXO
Ziguinchor
Casamance
Gamble
Koundara
Satadougou
Bamako
Niger
Bani
Dédougou
Koudougou
Ouagadougou
Fada Ngour
Taécé
Tenkodogo
Madjori

GUINEA-BISSAU
Bissau
ARQUIPÉLAGO
DOS
BIJAGÓS
Eticoga
Massif Du
Tamgué
5 046
Danea
Tambadonkéa
Dinguiraye
Siguiri
Badogo
Kouyalé
Zangasso
Ouarkoye
Boromo
Léo
Po
Pô
PARC NATIO
DE LA BENDA
Dápánga
Sansanné-
Mango
Natitingou

Kabot
Fria
Labé
GUINEA
Mamou
Kankan
Sikasso
Banfora
Bobo Dioulasso
Lawra
Bolgatanga
Wa
Walewale
Gushiago

10°
Conakry
Forécariah
Kindia
Faranah
Kouroussa
Niélé
Tingréla
Lokosse
White
Volta
Tamale
Niamtougou
Yendi
Bassari

SIERRA
Makeni
Bintimani
Tingi
6 080
Sankanbiriwa
Kissidougou
Kérouané
Pic De Tio
4 934
Odienné
Korhogo
Boundiali
Ferkessédougou
PARK
NATIONAL
DE BOUNA
Bouna
Bole
Bio
Gorge
Forêt
Classée
Du Fazao
Djebobo
873
Blitta
Sol

Freetown
Pôrsar
LEONE
Bo
Pendembu
Beyla
Touba
COTE D'IVOIRE
Séguéla
Katiola
Niakaramandougou
Bondoukou
Wenchi
GHANA
Techiman
Kintampo
TOGO
Atakpamé
Hohoé
Pahme

Moyamba
Bonthe
Njarekoré
Tomou
NAT PARK
Biankouma
Man
Danané
(IVORY COAST)
Bouaké
Ouellé
Sunyani
Mampong
Ejura
Agogo
Lome

SHERBRO ISLAND
TURNERS
PENINSULA
CAPE MOUNT
Robertsport
Brewerville
Gbarnga
Mount
Kahous
3 658
Daloa
Bouafle
Yamoussoukro
Dimbokro
Abengourou
Bibiani
Obuasi
Kumasi
Kwahu
Plateau
Nkawkaw
Akwatia
Begoro
CAP
SAINT

LIBERIA
Monrovia
Buchanan
Tchien
Duabo
Mont
Niénokoué
2 044
Guiglo
Duékoué
Gagnoa
Divo
Adzopé
Agboville
Abidjan
Dunkwa
Oda
Nyakrom
Nsawam
Koforidua
Accra
Winneba
Tema
Anloga

Greenville
Sassandra
Lagune
Tadio
Grand-Bassam
Lagune
Ebrié
Aboisso
Prestea
Tarkwa
Esiama
Accra
Sekondi-Takoradi

Harper
Tabou
CAPE
PALMAS
CAPE THREE
POINTS

G U L F   O F   G

A T L A N T I C   O C E A N

Relief

Meters	Feet
3050	10 000
1525	5000
610	2000
305	1000
152.5	500
Sea Level	0
152.5	500
1525	5000
3050	10 000

Copyright by Rand McNally & Co.
Made in U.S.A.
A-589400-76   2-1-11

Scale 1:10,000,000; one inch to 160 miles. Lambert Azimuthal Equal Area Projection
Elevations and depressions are given in feet.

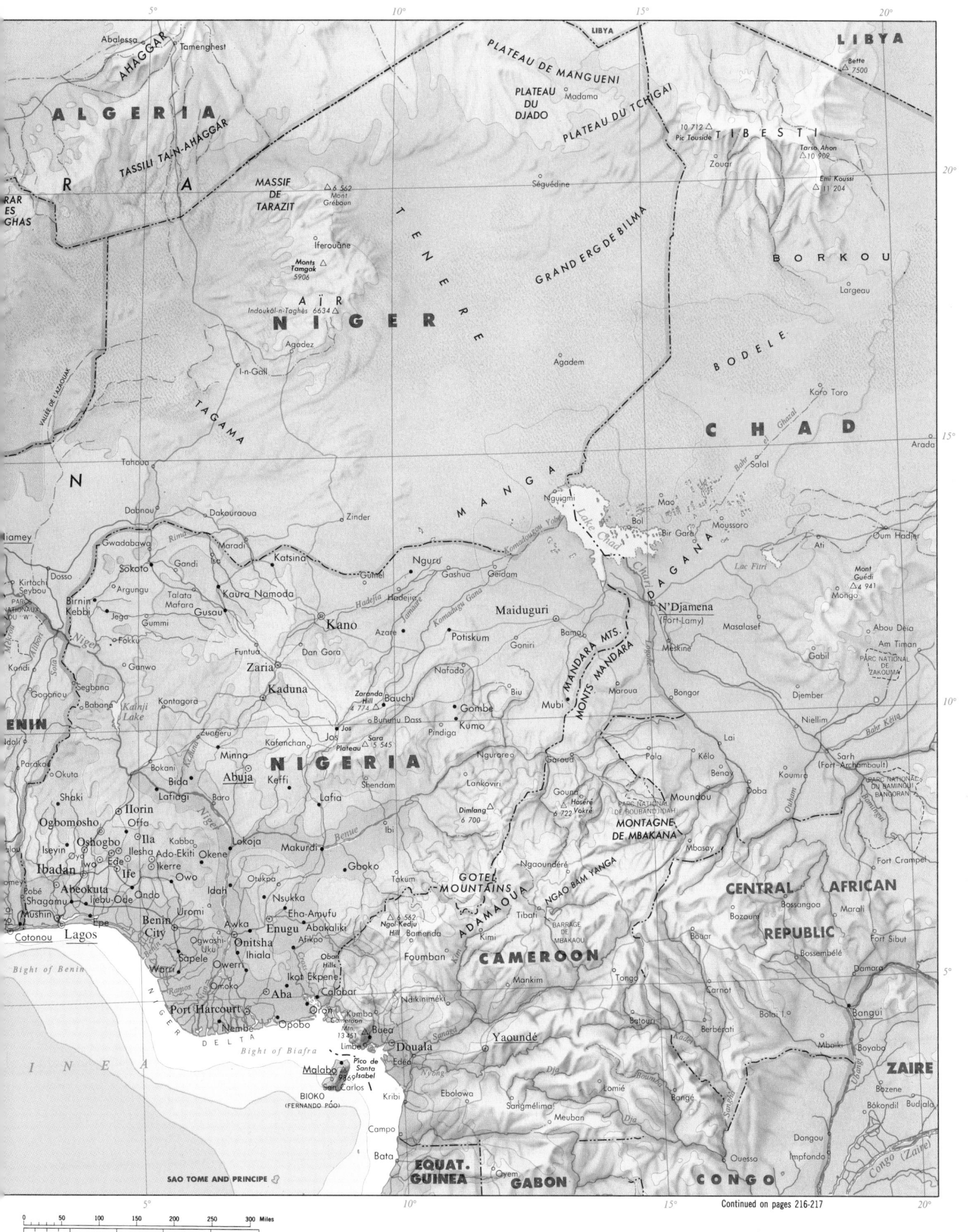

ALGERIA

AHAGGAR

Abalessa   Tamenghest

TASSILI TA-N-AHAGGAR

RAR ES GHAS

RA

LIBYA

PLATEAU DE MANGUENI

PLATEAU DU DJADO

Madama

PLATEAU DU TCHIGAI

LIBYA

Bette △ 7500

10 712 △   TIBESTI

Pic Tousside

Tarso Ahon △ 10 902

Zouar

Séguédine

Emi Koussi △ 11 204

MASSIF DE TARAZIT

△ 6 562 Mont Grébaun

Iferouâne

T E N E R E

GRAND ERG DE BILMA

BORKOU

Largeau

Monts Tamgak 5906 △

AÏR

Indoukâl-n-Taghès 6634 △

N I G E R

Agadez

Agadem

BODELE

Koro Toro

I-n-Gall

TAGAMA

CHAD

Arada

N   Tahoua

M A N G A

Bahr el Ghazal   Salal

15°

Dabnou   Dakouraoua   Zinder   Nguigmi   Mao   Moussoro   Ati   Oum Hadjer

iamey   Gwadabawa   Maradi   Rima   Gumel   Nguru   Gashua   Geidam   Lake Chad   Bol   Bir Gara   Mont Guédi △ 4 941

Sokoto   Gandi   Isa   Katsina   Komadougou Yobé   Bongor   Lac Fitri   Mongo

Kirtachi Seybou   Argungu   Talata Mafara   Gusau   Kaura Namoda   Hadejia   Hadejia   Komadugu Gana   Maiduguri   Bama   N'Djamena (Fort-Lamy)   Masalasef   Abou Deïa

PARC NATIONAL DU "W"   Birnin Kebbi   Jega   Gummi   Kano   Azare   Potiskum   Goniri   Meskine   Am Timan

Dosso   Fokku   Funtua   Dan Gora   Nafada   Biu   Maroua   Djember   Gabil   PARC NATIONAL DE ZAKOUMA

Kondi   Ganwo   Zaria   Kaduna   Zaranda Hill 4 774 △   Bauchi   Gombe   Mubi   MANDARA MTS.   Niellim

Gogonou   Segbana   Babana   Kainji Lake   Kontagora   Jos   Bunu Dass   Kumo   Pindiga   MONTS MANDARA   Lai   Sarh (Fort-Archambault)

BENIN   Zungeru   Jos Plateau   Sara △ 5 545   Nguroreo   Garoua   Pala   Kélo   Koumra   PARC NATIONAL DU BAMINGUI BANGORAN

Idal   Minna   Kafanchan   NIGERIA   Lankoviri   Gouna   Moundou

Parakou   Bokani   Bida   Keffi   Shendam   Dimlang △ 6 700   Hoséré △ 6 722 Vokré   PARC NATIONAL DE BOUBANDJIDAH   Benoy

Okuta   Lafiagi   Baro   Lafia   MONTAGNE DE MBAKANA   CENTRAL   AFRICAN

Shaki   Ilorin   Offa   Ibi   Mbasay   Bossangoa   Marali

Ogbomosho   Oshogbo   Ila   Kabba   Lokoja   Makurdi   Benue   GOTEL   Ngaoundéré   NGAO BAM YANGA   Bouar   REPUBLIC   Fort Sibut

Iseyin   Ilesha   Ado-Ekiti   Okene   MOUNTAINS   ADAMAOUA   Tibati   BARRAGE DE MBAKAOU   Bozoum   Bossembélé

Ibadan   Iwo   Ife   Ikerre   Owo   Otukpa   Gboko   Takum   △ 6 562   Bamenda   Kimi   Damara

Pobé   Ondo   Idah   Nsukka   Ngol-Kedju Hill   Foumban   CAMEROON   Tongo   Carnot   Fort Crampel

Abeokuta   Jebu-Ode   Uromi   Eha-Amufu   Afikpo   Mankim   Bangui

Shagamu   Awka   Enugu   Abakaliki   Oban Hills   Yaoundé   Bétaré   Berbérati   Bozoum

Cotonou   Lagos   Benin City   Onitsha   Ihiala   Ikot Ekpene   Kumba   Botai I.

Bight of Benin   Ogwashi-Uku   Owerri   Calabar   Cameroon Mtsn. 13 451 △ Buea   CENTRAL   Mbaiki   ZAIRE

Sapele   Warri   Aba   Oron   Douala   Yaoundé   Mbomo   Boyabo

Port Harcourt   Opobo   Edéa   Bozene

Nembe   DELTA   Bight of Biafra   Pico de Santa Isabel △ 9369   Kribi   Ebolowa   Sangmélima   Budjala

GUINEA   Malabo   San Carlos   Campo   Meuban   Dja   Dongou

BIOKO (FERNANDO PÓO)   Bata   EQUAT. GUINEA   GABON   Oyem   Ouesso   CONGO   Congo (Zaire)

SAO TOME AND PRINCIPE

Continued on pages 216-217

0   50   100   150   200   250   300 Miles

0   100   200   300   400   500 Kilometers

Continued on pages 214-215

NIGERIA
Opobo
Bight of Biafra
Cameroon Mtn. 13 451 △
Buea
Douala
Edéa
Yaoundé
Malabo
San Carlos
BIOKO
(FERNANDO PÓO)
Kribi
Campo
Ebolowa
Sangmélima
Yokadouma
Doumé
Batouri
Berbérati
Bolai
Bangui
CENTRAL AFRICAN REPUBLIC
Fort de Possel
Boali
Kongbo
Bangassou
Rafaï
Zémio
Gitam
Mbaiki
Mbandi
Boyabo
Mobaye
Zakoma
Bondo
Ndongou
Bosobolo
Gemena
Businga
Bodalang
Aketi
Buta

EQUATORIAL GUINEA
Bata
Benito
Oyem
Djoua
Souanké
Ouesso
Moloundou
Bangé
Mongoumba
Bozene
Budjala
Yandongi
Bumba
Lisala
Itumbari
Bana
Basoko

PRÍNCIPE
CABO SAN JUAN
ISLA DE CORISCO
SAO TOME AND PRINCIPE
Acalayong
MONTS DE CRISTAL
Makokou
Mekambo
Lebango
Djokoumatombi
Loka
Lokofa
Boende
Bokungu
Ekoli
Litoko
Bengamisa
Kisangani
(Stanleyville)
Isangi
Simba
Lifanga

SÃO TOMÉ
SÃO TOMÉ
Libreville
Kango
Booué
GABON
St. François de Boundji
Owando
CONGO
Mbandaka
(Coquilhatville)
Bikoro
Lac Tumba
Mange
Lomela
Yayama
ZAIRE
Katopa

CAP LOPEZ
Port-Gentil
Bifoum
Lambaréné
3360 △
Koula-Moutou
Franceville
Gamboma
Djambala
Tongo
Monkoto
Lokolama
Ekanga

Omboué
Mouila
Mbinda
2965 △
Kindanba
Bandundu
Lac Mai-Ndombe
Fimi
Makaw
Lukenie
Dekese
Sankuru
Esambo

Petit Loango
Tchibanga
Massendjo
Sibiti
Kindanba
Brazzaville
Stanley Pool
Kwilu
Tiebo (Port-Francqui)
Domiongo
Lusambo

Mayumba
Madingo
Madingou
Loubomo
Stanley Pool
Kinshasa
(Léopoldville)
Masi-Manimba
Kikwit
Kilembe
Damba
Tsh
Mbuji-May
(Bakwanga)

Pointe-Noire
CABINDA
(Ang.)
Cabinda
Tshela
Boma
Matadi
Kisantu
Mbanza-Ngungu
Popokabaka
Djokupunda
Bulunga
Tshikapa
Chitata
Kanda-Kanda
Kananga
(Luluabourg)
Kab

PONTA DO PADRÃO
Soyo
Náqui
Kimvula
Kitenda
Kwango
Kapanga
Kamin

SERRA DO CONGO
M'banza Congo
Quimbele
Damba
Kahemba
Chicapa
Kibenga

N'zeto
Mabaia
Uíge
Marimba
Quimbonge
Caluango
Sambungo
Kangowa
KATANGA
Kind

Ambriz
Caxito
Kalandula
Quela
Cuilo
Luo
KASHIJI
PLAIN
Kand

Luanda
PONTA DAS PALMEIRINHAS
Catete
N'dalatando
Dondo
Malanje
Cambundi-Catembo
Cacólo
Luena
PARQUE NACIONAL DA CAMEIA
Calunda
Lomwa

PARQUE NACIONAL DE QUICAMA
Mussende
Saútar
Curunga
Malanga
Nasondo

CABO DAS TRÊS PONTAS
Porto Amboim
Sumbe
Gabela
Waku Kundo
Calucinga
ANGOLA
Coemba
Cangamba
KASHIJI
PLAIN
Chitokoloki

Covelo
SERRA CAMBONDA
Wama
Serra do Moco
△ 8596
Kuito
Chitembo
Chá Pungana
LIUWA
PLAIN
Ninda

Lobito
Benguela
Catumbela
Huambo
(Nova Lisboa)
Caconda
Caluquembe
Menongue
Lunga
BAROTSE
PLAIN
Mongu

SERRA DA NEVE
SERRE DO CHILENGUE
Cacula
Caiundo
Mavinga
Nangweshi

CABO DE SANTA MARTA
Bentiaba
Lubango
Folgares
Cassinga
SILOANA
PLAINS
Luiana

Namibe
PARQUE NACIONAL DO BIKUAR
Chiange
Caiundo
Catula
Cuangar
Kazur

PONTA ALBINA
Tombua
Cahama
Oncocua
Cuamato
Melunga
NAMIBIA
Shakawe
Kasink
BOTS.
CHOBE NAT'L PARK

PONTA DA MARCA
Baia dos Tigres
PARQUE NACIONAL DO IONA
Foz do Cunene
Ruacana Falls
CAPRIVI STRIP

ATLANTIC OCEAN

Relief

Meters		Feet
3050		10 000
1525		5000
610		2000
305		1000
152.5		500
0	Sea Level	0
152.5		500
1525		5000
3050		10 000

Scale 1:10,000,000; one inch to 160 miles. Lambert Azimuthal Equal Area Projection
Elevations and depressions are given in feet.

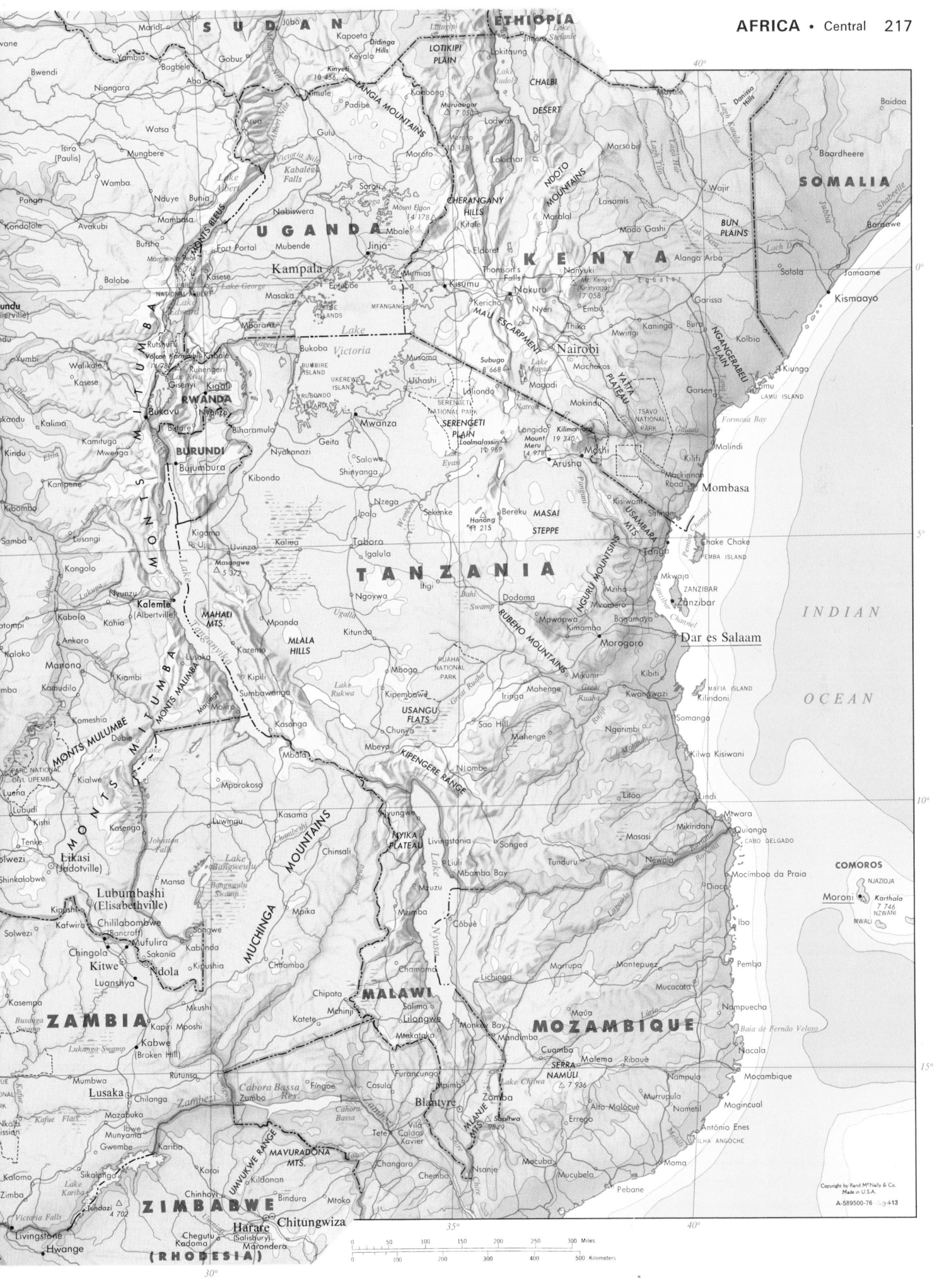

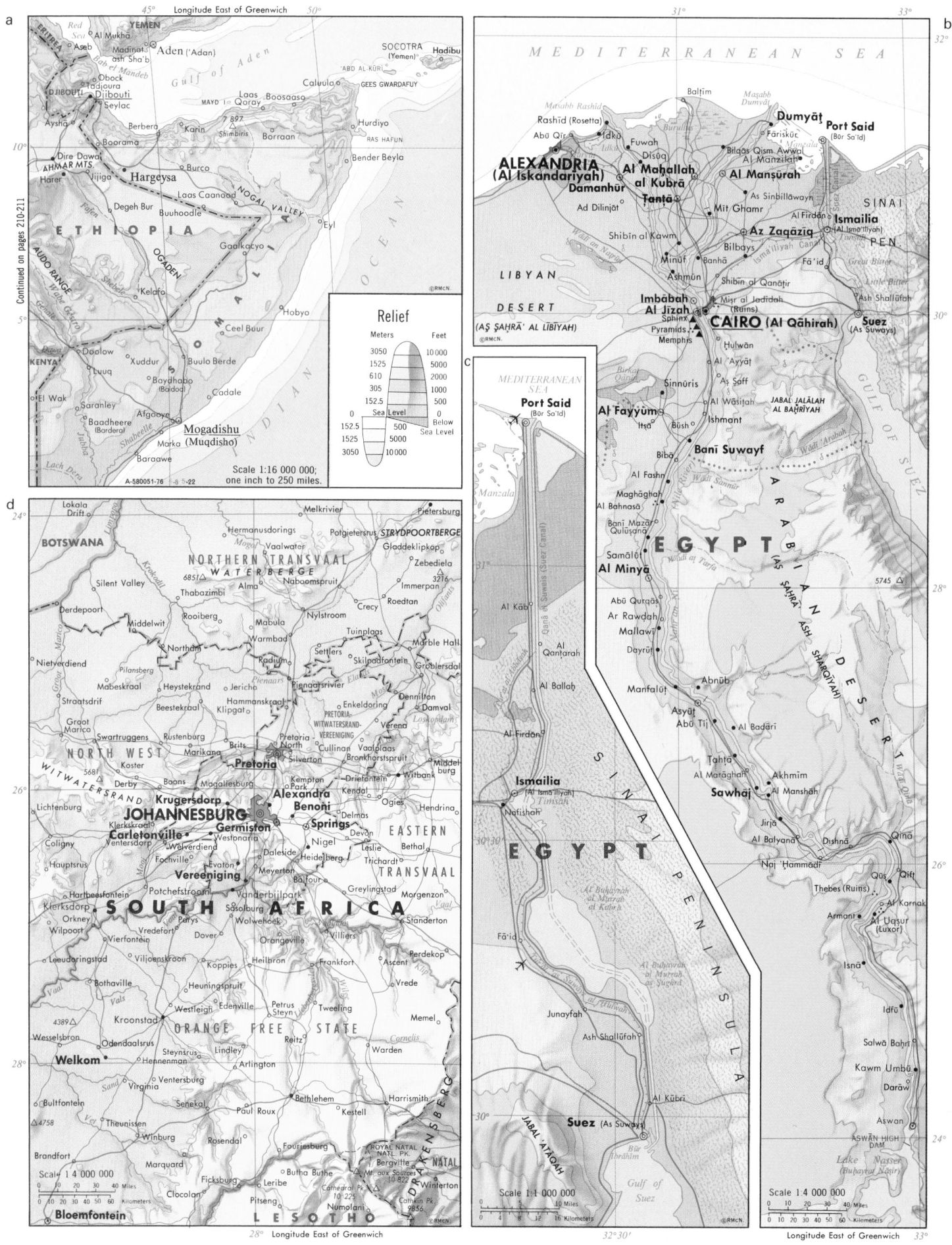

a

Longitude East of Greenwich

45°   50°

YEMEN

Al Mukhā

Madīnat
ash Sha'b   Aden ('Adan)

SOCOTRA
(Yemen)   Hadibu
ABD AL-KŪRĪ

GEES GWARDAFUY

Gulf of Aden

Calulula

Boosaaso

Laas Qoray

Hurdiyo

RAS HAFUN

Bender Beyla

ERITREA

Aseb

Red
Sea

DJIBOUTI
Tadjoura   Obock
Djibouti
Seylac

Aysha

Berbera

Karin

Shimbiris
7 897

Borraan

MAYD I

Dire Dawa

AHMAR MTS

Harer   Jijiga

Burco

Hargeysa

Degeh Bur

Buuhoodle

Laas Caanood

NOGAL VALLEY

Eyl

E T H I O P I A

Gaalkacyo

Kelafo

Hobyo

AUDO RANGE

OGADEN

Doolow

Luuq

KENYA

Xuddur

Baydhabo
(Baidoa)

Buulo Berde

Cadale

El Wak

Saranley

Afgooye

Baadheere
(Bardera)

Mogadishu
(Muqdisho)

Marka (Merca)

Baraawe

Relief

Meters   Feet

3050   10 000
1525   5000
610   2000
305   1000
152.5   500

0   Sea Level   0
Sea Level   Below
152.5   500   Sea Level
1525   5000
3050   10 000

Scale 1:16 000 000;
one inch to 250 miles.

A-580051-76   -8 5-22

---

b

31°   33°

32°

M E D I T E R R A N E A N   S E A

Baltīm

Maşabb
Dumyāt

Dumyāt   **Port Said**
(Būr Sa'īd)

Maşabb Rashīd

Rashīd (Rosetta)   Idkū

Abū Qīr   Fuwah

Fāriskūr

Bilqās Qism Awwal
Al Manzilah

Disūq

ALEXANDRIA
(Al Iskandariyah)   **Al Maḥallah
al Kubrā**   **Al Manşūrah**

Damanhūr

Ad Dilinjāt   **Tanţā**

Mīt Ghamr

As Sinbillāwayn

SINAI
PEN.

Al Firdān   **Ismailia**
(Al Ismā'īliyah)

Shibīn al Kawm

Az Zaqāziq

Fā'id

Great Bitter

LIBYAN   Minūf   Bilbays

Banhā

Ashmūn   Shibīn al Qanāţir

Little Bitter

DESERT   **Imbābah**
Al Jīzah   Mişr al Jadīdah
(Ruins)   Ash Shallūfah

(AŞ ŞAḤRĀ' AL LĪBĪYAH)   Pyramids   **CAIRO** (Al Qāhirah)   **Suez**
(As Suways)

Sphinx

Memphis   Ḥulwān

30°

Al 'Ayyāţ

Birkat
Qārūn

Sinnūris   As Şaff

Al Fayyūm   Al Wāsiţah

Itsā   Ishmant

JABAL JALĀLAH
AL BAḤRĪYAH

GULF OF SUEZ

Banī Suwayf

Bibā

Al Fashn   Wādī Araba

Maghāghah

Al Bahnasā

Banī Mazār
Qulūşana

E G Y P T

Samālūţ   Wādī aţ Ţarfa

Al Minyā   Abū Qurqāş

Ar Rawdah

Mallawī

Dayrūţ

28°

5745 △

Manfalūţ

Abnūb

Asyūţ   Al Badārī

Abū Tīj

Ţahţā

Al Marāghah   Akhmīm

Sawhāj   Al Manshāh

Jirjā

Al Balyanā   Dishnā

Naj' Ḥammādī   Qinā

26°

Thebes (Ruins)

Qūş   Qifţ

Armant   Al Karnak

Al Uqşur
(Luxor)

Isnā

Idfū

Salwā Baḥrī

Kawm Umbū

Darāw

ASWĀN HIGH
DAM   Aswān

Lake
Nasser
(Buḥayrat Nāşir)

24°

---

c

MEDITERRANEAN
SEA

Port Said
(Būr Sa'īd)

Manzala

Al Kāb

Qanā el Suweis (Suez Canal)

Al
Qanţarah

Al Ballaḥ

SINAI

Al-Firdān

Ismailia
(Al Ismā'īlīyah)

Nafīshah

Timsāḥ

E G Y P T

Al Bukayrah
al Murrah
al Kubrā

Fā'id

Al Buḥayrah
al Murrah
aş Şughrá

Junayfah

Ash Shallūfah

Al Kūbrī

JABAL
ATĀQAH

Suez (As Suways)

Būr
Ibrāhīm

Gulf of
Suez

Scale 1:1 000 000

0 2 4 8 10 Miles

0 4 8 16 Kilometers

31°

30°30'

30°

S I N A I   P E N I N S U L A

32°30'   Longitude East of Greenwich   33°

Scale 1:4 000 000

0 10 20 30 40 Miles

0 10 20 30 40 50 60 Kilometers

Longitude East of Greenwich

ARABIAN

(AŞ ŞAḤRĀ' ASH SHARQĪYAH)

DESERT

---

d

24°

BOTSWANA

Lokala
Drift   Melkrivier

Pietersburg

Hermanusdorings

Potgietersrus   *STRYDPOORTBERGE*

Vaalwater   Gladdeklipkop

NORTHERN TRANSVAAL

Mogol   *WATERBERGE*   Zebediela

6851 △   Naboomspruit

Thabazimbi   Alma   Immerpan

Silent Valley

Derdepoort   Rooiberg   3216 △   Roedtan

Mabula   Crecy

Nietverdiend   Pilansberg   Warmbad   Nylstroom

Oliphants

Middelwit   Tuinplaas

Northam   Settlers   Marble Hall

Mabeskraal   Heystekrand   Radium   Skilpadfontein   Groblersdal

Straatsdrif   Jericho   Klipgat

Groot   Beestekraal   Pienaarsrivier   Elands   Denmilton

Marico   Swartruggens   Rustenburg   *PRETORIA-*   Damval

Brits   *WITWATERSRAND-*   Verena

NORTH WEST   Marikana   Pretoria   *VEREENIGING*   Loskopdam

5681 △   Koster   North   Cullinan   Bronkhorstspruit

Boons   **Pretoria**   Silverton   Middelburg

Lichtenburg   Magaliesburg   Kempton   Witbank

WITWATERSRAND   **Krugersdorp**   Park   Kendal

Alexandra   Ogies   EASTERN

Coligny   Derby   **JOHANNESBURG**   **Benoni**   Hendrina

Hauptrus   **Carletonville**   **Germiston**   **Springs**   TRANSVAAL

Vereeniging   Devon   Bethal

Klerkskraal   Westonaria   Delmas

Fochville   Nigel   Leslie

Ventersdorp   Daleside   Trichardt

SOUTH AFRICA   Evaton   Meyerton   Heidelberg   Morgenzon

Hartbeesfontein   Potchefstroom   Balfour

Vanderbijlpark   Greylingstad   Standerton

Klerksdorp   Sasolburg   Wolwehoek   Villiers

Orkney   Vredefort   Orangeville   Vaal

Wilpoort   Vierfontein   Dover   Perdekop

Leeudoringstad   Viljoenskroon   Koppies   Frankfort   Ascent

Bothaville   Heilbron   Vrede   Memel

Heuningspruit   Warden

4389 △   Petrus
Steyn   *Cornelis*

Wesselsbron   Kroonstad   Reitz

ORANGE   FREE   STATE

Odendaalsrus   Steynsrus   Lindley   Arlington

Virginia   Hennenman   Tweeling

Welkom   Ventersburg   Winburg   Harrismith

Bultfontein   Senekal   *DRAKENSBERG*

△4758   Theunissen   Paul Roux   Bethlehem   Kestell

Brandfort   Winburg   ROYAL NATAL
NATL. PK.   NATAL

Marquard   Rosendal   Bergville   Sources
10-822   Winterton

Fouriesburg   Cathedral Pk.
10-225

Scale 1:4 000 000   Ficksburg   Leribe   Clocolan   Cathkin Pk.
9856

0 10 20 30 40 Miles   Butha Buthe   Pitseng

0 10 20 30 40 50 60
Kilometers   **Bloemfontein**   **LESOTHO**

28°   Longitude East of Greenwich

Continued on pages 210-211

INDIAN   OCEAN

10°

5°

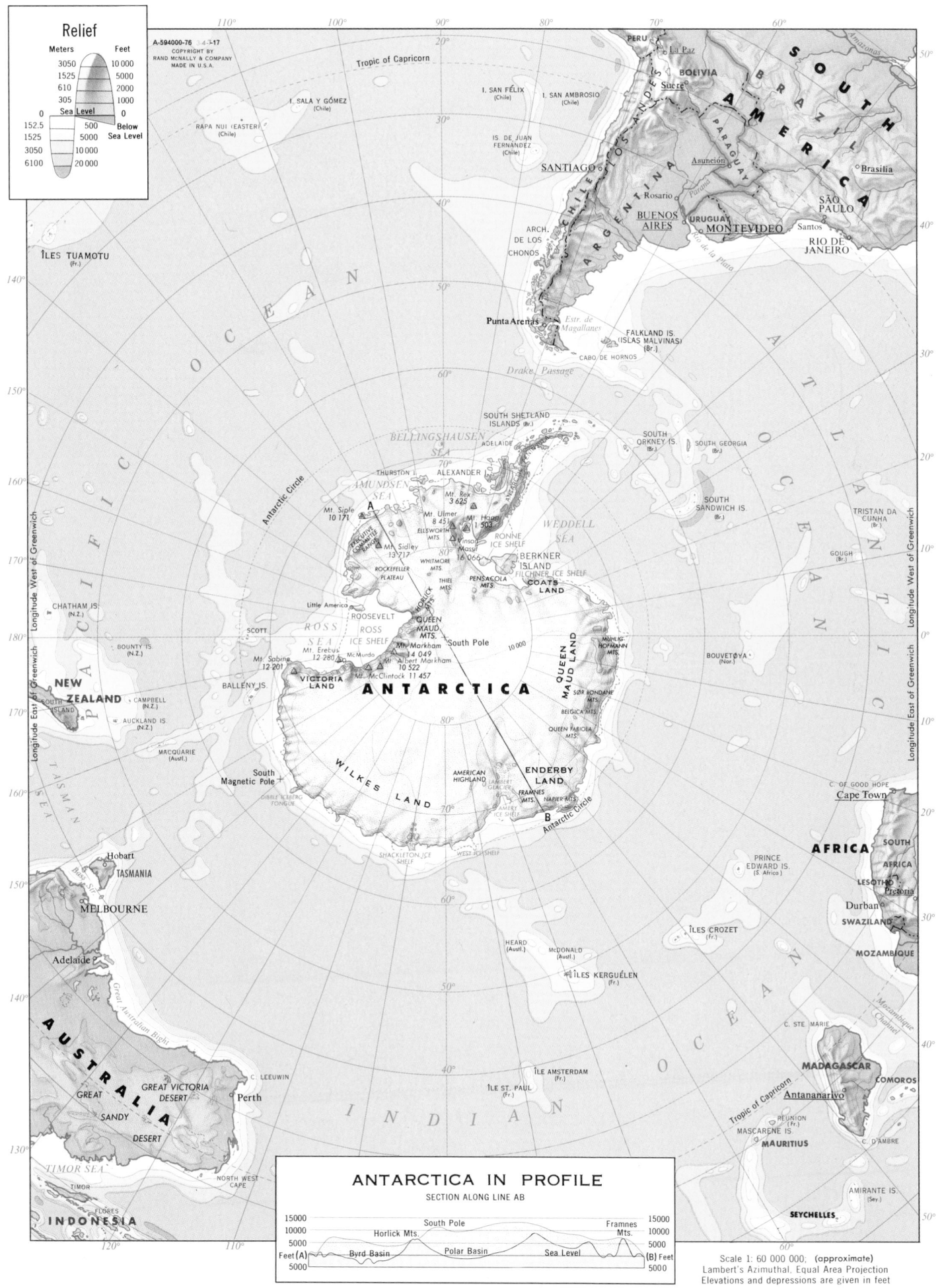

Relief

Meters		Feet
3050		10 000
1525		5000
610		2000
305		1000
0	Sea Level	0
152.5		500 Below
1525		5000 Sea Level
3050		10 000
6100		20 000

ANTARCTICA IN PROFILE
SECTION ALONG LINE AB

Scale 1: 60 000 000; (approximate)
Lambert's Azimuthal, Equal Area Projection
Elevations and depressions are given in feet

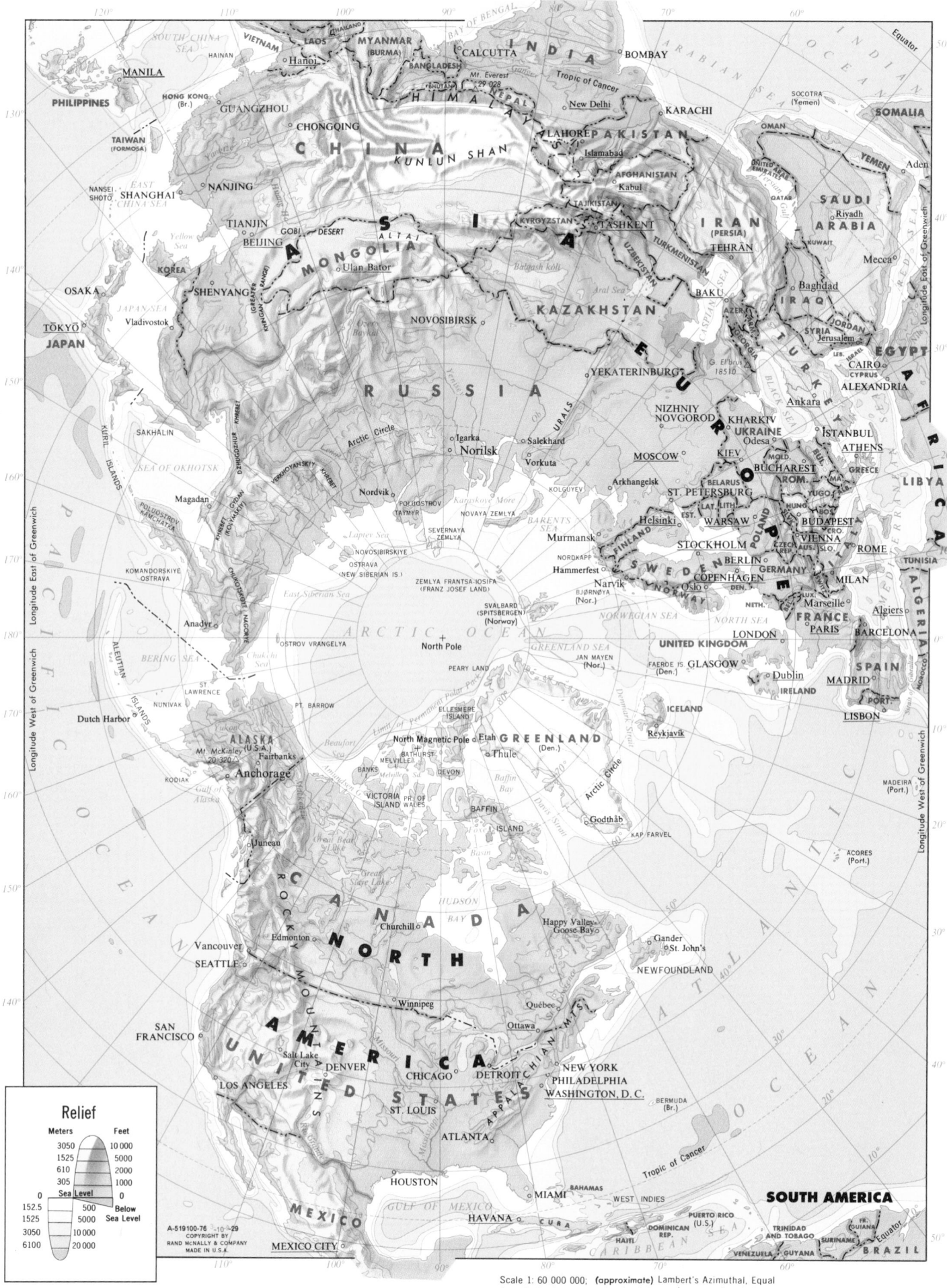

Relief

Meters		Feet
3050		10 000
1525		5000
610		2000
305		1000
	Sea Level	0
0	Sea Level	
152.5		500 Below
1525		5000 Sea Level
3050		10 000
6100		20 000

A-519100-76 -10-29
COPYRIGHT BY
RAND MCNALLY & COMPANY
MADE IN U.S.A.

Scale 1: 60 000 000; (approximate) Lambert's Azimuthal, Equal
Area Projection   Elevations and depressions are given in feet

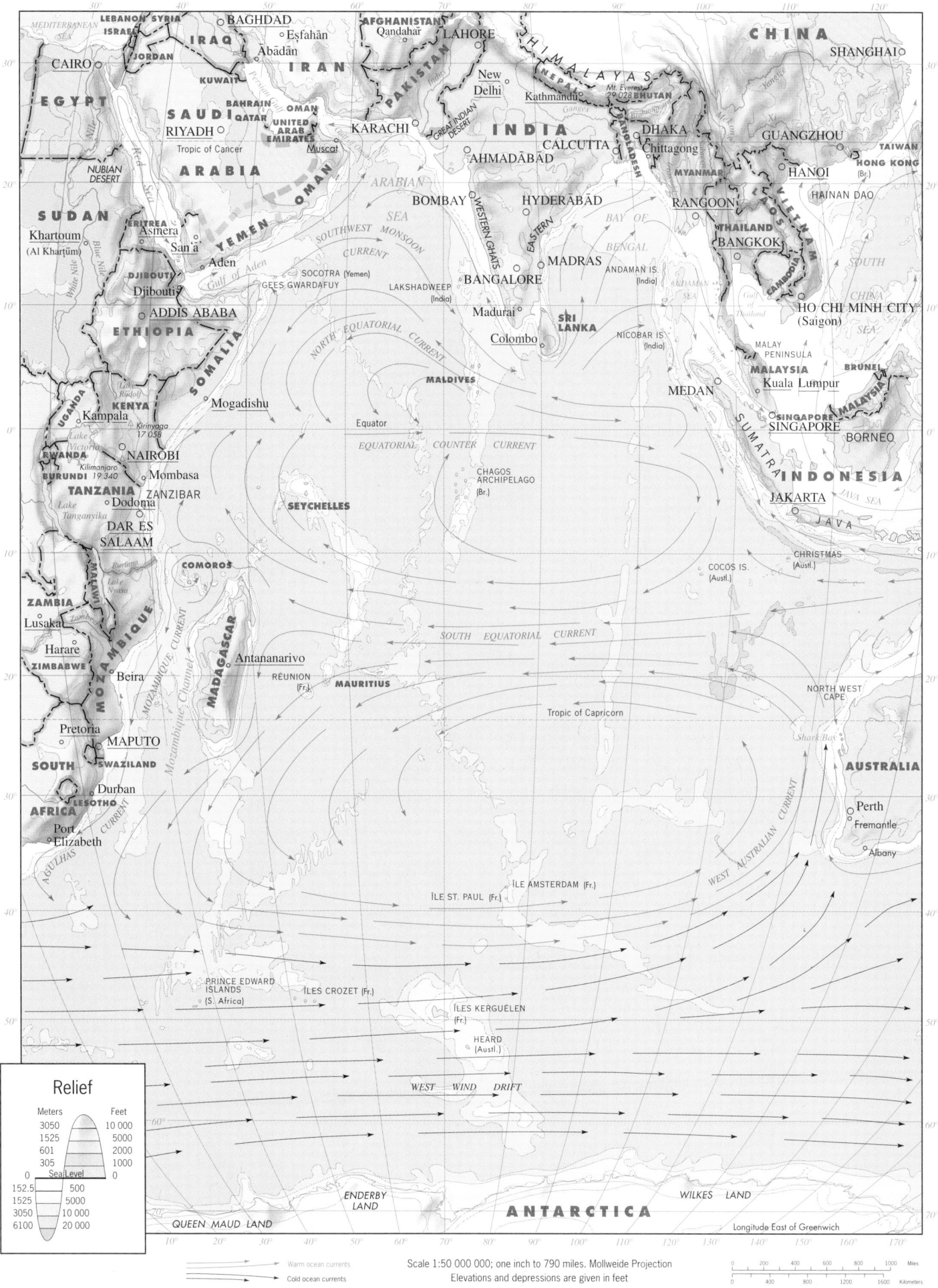

MEDITERRANEAN SEA
LEBANON SYRIA
ISRAEL
JORDAN
BAGHDAD
IRAQ
Eşfahān
Ābādān
AFGHANISTAN
Qandahār
LAHORE
New Delhi
HIMALAYAS
Kathmandu
Mt. Everest 29 028
BHUTAN
CHINA
SHANGHAI
CAIRO
EGYPT
KUWAIT
IRAN
PAKISTAN
Indus
Ganges
BANGLADESH
DHAKA
Chittagong
GUANGZHOU
HANOI
TAIWAN
HONG KONG (Br.)
SAUDI
RIYADH
BAHRAIN QATAR
UNITED ARAB EMIRATES
OMAN
Muscat
KARACHI
New Delhi
INDIA
CALCUTTA
AHMADĀBĀD
MYANMAR
RANGOON
LAOS
VIETNAM
HAINAN DAO
Tropic of Cancer
ARABIA
NUBIAN DESERT
Red Sea
YEMEN
OMAN
ARABIAN SEA
BOMBAY
WESTERN GHATS
HYDERĀBĀD
EASTERN GHATS
BAY OF BENGAL
THAILAND
BANGKOK
SOUTH CHINA SEA
SUDAN
Khartoum (Al Kharţūm)
ERITREA
Asmera
San'a
Aden
Gulf of Aden
SOCOTRA (Yemen)
GEES GWARDAFUY
SOUTHWEST MONSOON CURRENT
MADRAS
ANDAMAN IS. (India)
ANDAMAN SEA
Gulf of Thailand
CAMBODIA
HO CHI MINH CITY (Saïgon)
White Nile
Blue Nile
DJIBOUTI
Djibouti
ADDIS ABABA
ETHIOPIA
Lake Rudolf
LAKSHADWEEP (India)
BANGALORE
Madurai
SRI LANKA
Colombo
NICOBAR IS. (India)
MALAY PENINSULA
MALAYSIA
Kuala Lumpur
BRUNEI
UGANDA
Kampala
SOMALIA
Mogadishu
NORTH EQUATORIAL CURRENT
MALDIVES
MEDAN
SINGAPORE
SINGAPORE
BORNEO
KENYA
Kirinyaga 17 058
NAIROBI
Lake Victoria
Equator
EQUATORIAL COUNTER CURRENT
CHAGOS ARCHIPELAGO (Br.)
SUMATRA
JAKARTA
INDONESIA
RWANDA
BURUNDI
Kilimanjaro 19 340
Mombasa
ZANZIBAR
TANZANIA
Dodoma
DAR ES SALAAM
Lake Tanganyika
SEYCHELLES
JAVA SEA
JAVA
MALAWI
Lake Nyasa
ZAMBIA
Lusaka
COMOROS
CHRISTMAS (Austl.)
COCOS IS. (Austl.)
Harare
ZIMBABWE
Beira
MOZAMBIQUE
MOZAMBIQUE CURRENT
MADAGASCAR
Antananarivo
RÉUNION (Fr.)
MAURITIUS
SOUTH EQUATORIAL CURRENT
Tropic of Capricorn
NORTH WEST CAPE
Shark Bay
AUSTRALIA
Pretoria
MAPUTO
SOUTH
SWAZILAND
LESOTHO
Durban
Port Elizabeth
AFRICA
AGULHAS CURRENT
WEST AUSTRALIAN CURRENT
Perth
Fremantle
Albany
ÎLE AMSTERDAM (Fr.)
ÎLE ST. PAUL (Fr.)
WEST AUSTRALIAN CURRENT
PRINCE EDWARD ISLANDS (S. Africa)
ÎLES CROZET (Fr.)
ÎLES KERGUELEN (Fr.)
HEARD (Austl.)
WEST WIND DRIFT
ENDERBY LAND
QUEEN MAUD LAND
ANTARCTICA
WILKES LAND
Longitude East of Greenwich

Relief

Meters	Feet
3050	10 000
1525	5000
601	2000
305	1000
0 Sea Level	0
152.5	500
1525	5000
3050	10 000
6100	20 000

Warm ocean currents
Cold ocean currents

Scale 1:50 000 000; one inch to 790 miles. Mollweide Projection
Elevations and depressions are given in feet

0 200 400 600 800 1000 Miles
0 400 800 1200 1600 Kilometers

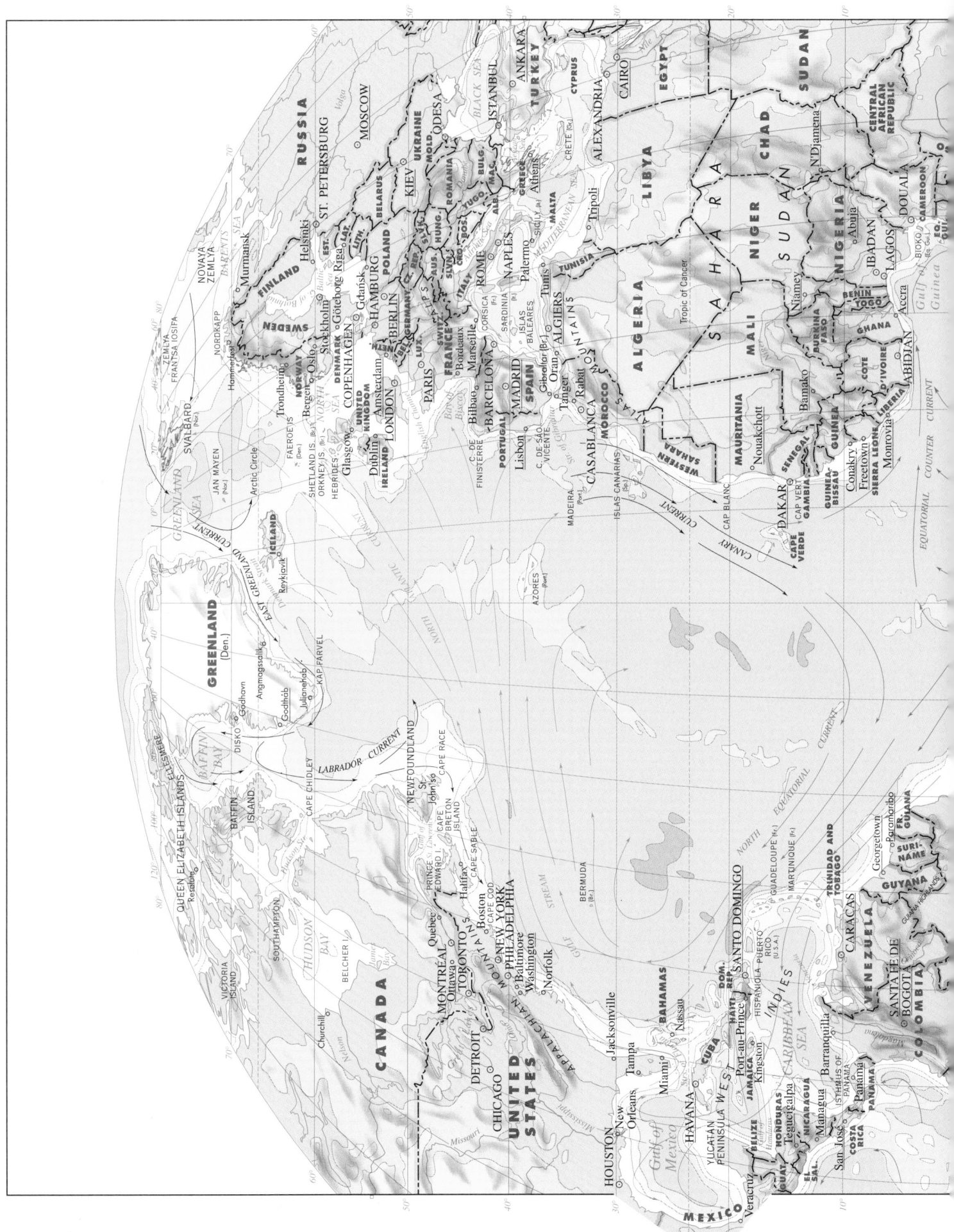

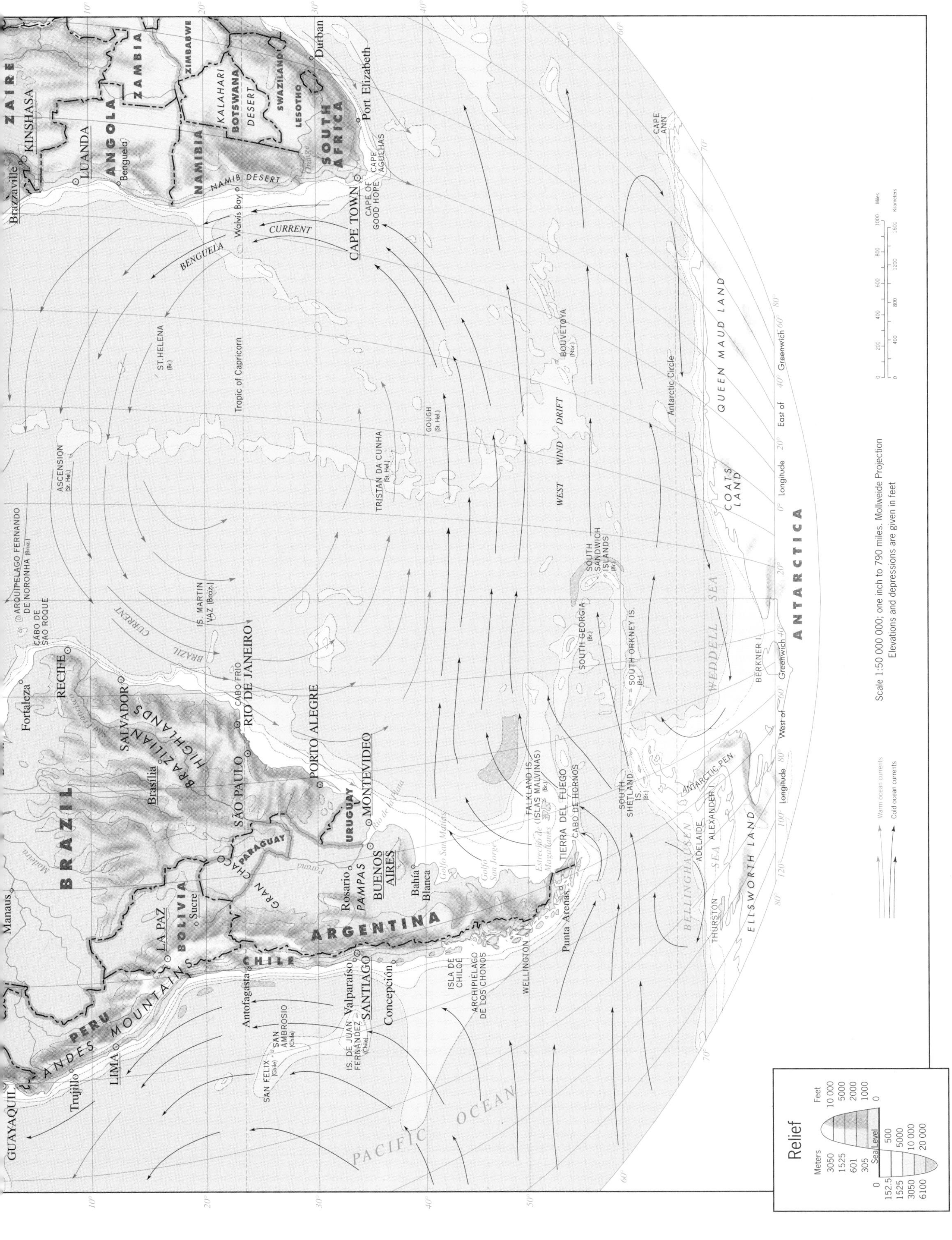

ZAIRE
KINSHASA
Brazzaville
LUANDA
ANGOLA
Benguela
ZAMBIA
ZIMBABWE
NAMIBIA
BOTSWANA
KALAHARI DESERT
SWAZILAND
LESOTHO
SOUTH AFRICA
Durban
Port Elizabeth
CAPE OF GOOD HOPE
CAPE AGULHAS
CAPE TOWN
Walvis Bay
NAMIB DESERT
Orange
BENGUELA
CURRENT

CAPE ANN
QUEEN MAUD LAND
Antarctic Circle
COATS LAND
BOUVETØYA (Nor.)
WEST WIND DRIFT
GOUGH (St. Hel.)
Tropic of Capricorn
ST. HELENA (Br.)
ASCENSION (St. Hel.)

ANTARCTICA

East of Greenwich
0° Longitude
West of Greenwich
0° Greenwich

TRISTAN DA CUNHA (St. Hel.)

ARQUIPELAGO FERNANDO DE NORONHA (Braz.)
CABO DE SÃO ROQUE
Fortaleza
RECIFE
BRAZIL
Manaus
SALVADOR
BRAZILIAN HIGHLANDS
Brasília
SÃO PAULO
BOLIVIA
LA PAZ
Sucre
PARAGUAY
GRAN CHACO
PERU
LIMA
Trujillo
GUAYAQUIL
ANDES MOUNTAINS
CHILE
Antofagasta
SAN FELIX (Chile)
SAN AMBROSIO (Chile)
IS. DE JUAN FERNÁNDEZ (Chile)
Valparaíso
SANTIAGO
Concepción
ARCHIPIELAGO DE LOS CHONOS
ISLA DE CHILOE
WELLINGTON
Punta Arenas
Estrecho de Magallanes
TIERRA DEL FUEGO
CABO DE HORNOS
ARGENTINA
PAMPAS
Rosario
BUENOS AIRES
Bahía Blanca
MONTEVIDEO
URUGUAY
PORTO ALEGRE
RIO DE JANEIRO
CABO FRIO
BRAZIL CURRENT
IS. MARTIN VAZ (Braz.)
Paraná
Golfo San Matías
Golfo San Jorge

FALKLAND IS. (ISLAS MALVINAS)
SOUTH GEORGIA (Br.)
SOUTH SANDWICH ISLANDS (Br.)
SOUTH ORKNEY IS. (Br.)
SOUTH SHETLAND IS. (Br.)
WEDDELL SEA
BERKNER I.
ANTARCTIC PEN.
ADELAIDE
ALEXANDER I.
BELLINGHAUSEN SEA
THURSTON
ELLSWORTH LAND

PACIFIC OCEAN

Scale 1:50 000 000; one inch to 790 miles. Mollweide Projection
Elevations and depressions are given in feet

Miles
Kilometers
0   200   400   600   800   1000
0   400   800   1200   1600

Warm ocean currents
Cold ocean currents

Relief

Meters	Feet
3050	10 000
1525	5000
601	2000
305	1000
0 Sea Level	0
152.5	500
1525	5000
3050	10 000
6100	20 000

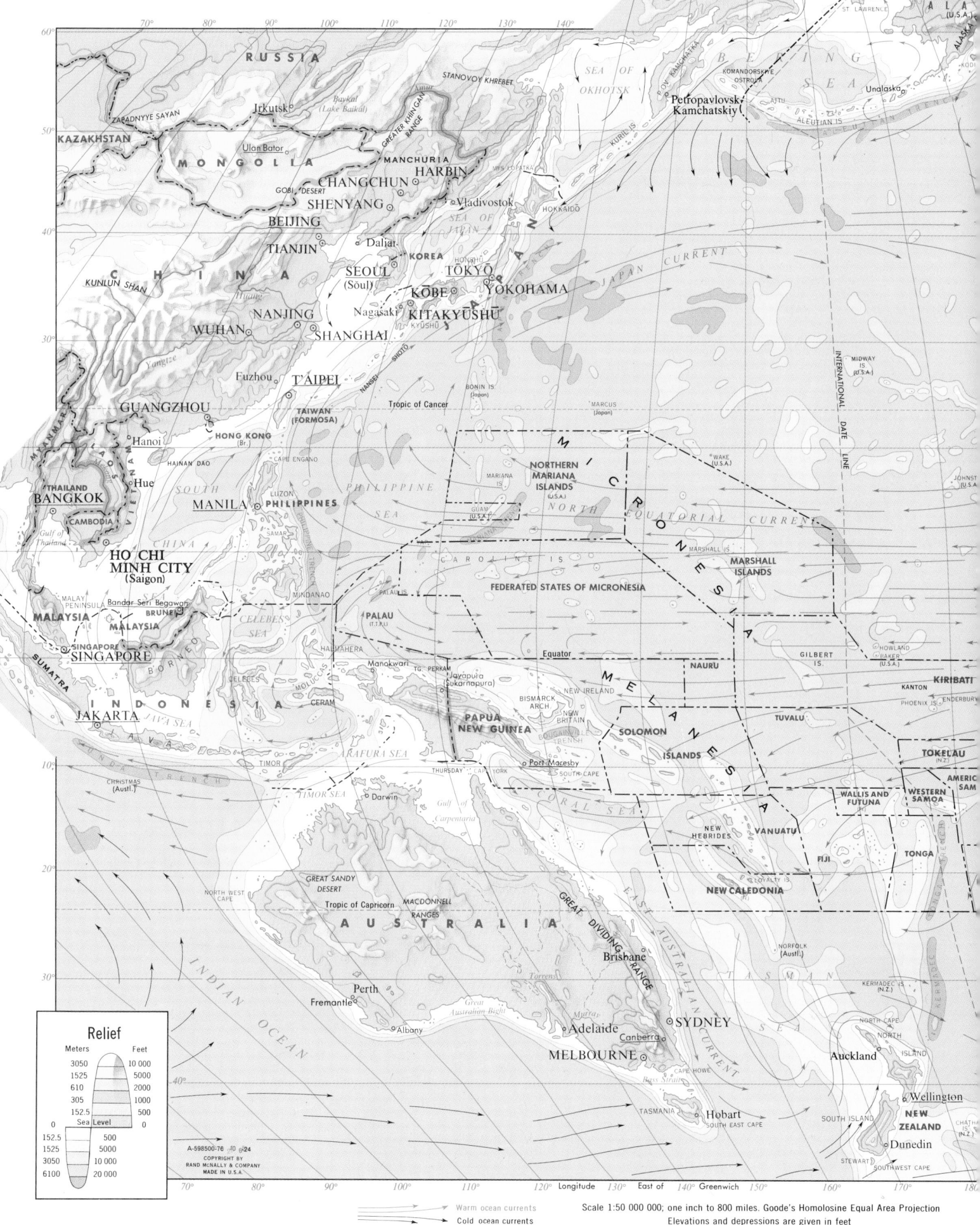

Relief

Meters		Feet
3050		10 000
1525		5000
610		2000
305		1000
152.5		500
0	Sea Level	0
152.5		500
1525		5000
3050		10 000
6100		20 000

→ Warm ocean currents
→ Cold ocean currents

Scale 1:50 000 000; one inch to 800 miles. Goode's Homolosine Equal Area Projection
Elevations and depressions are given in feet

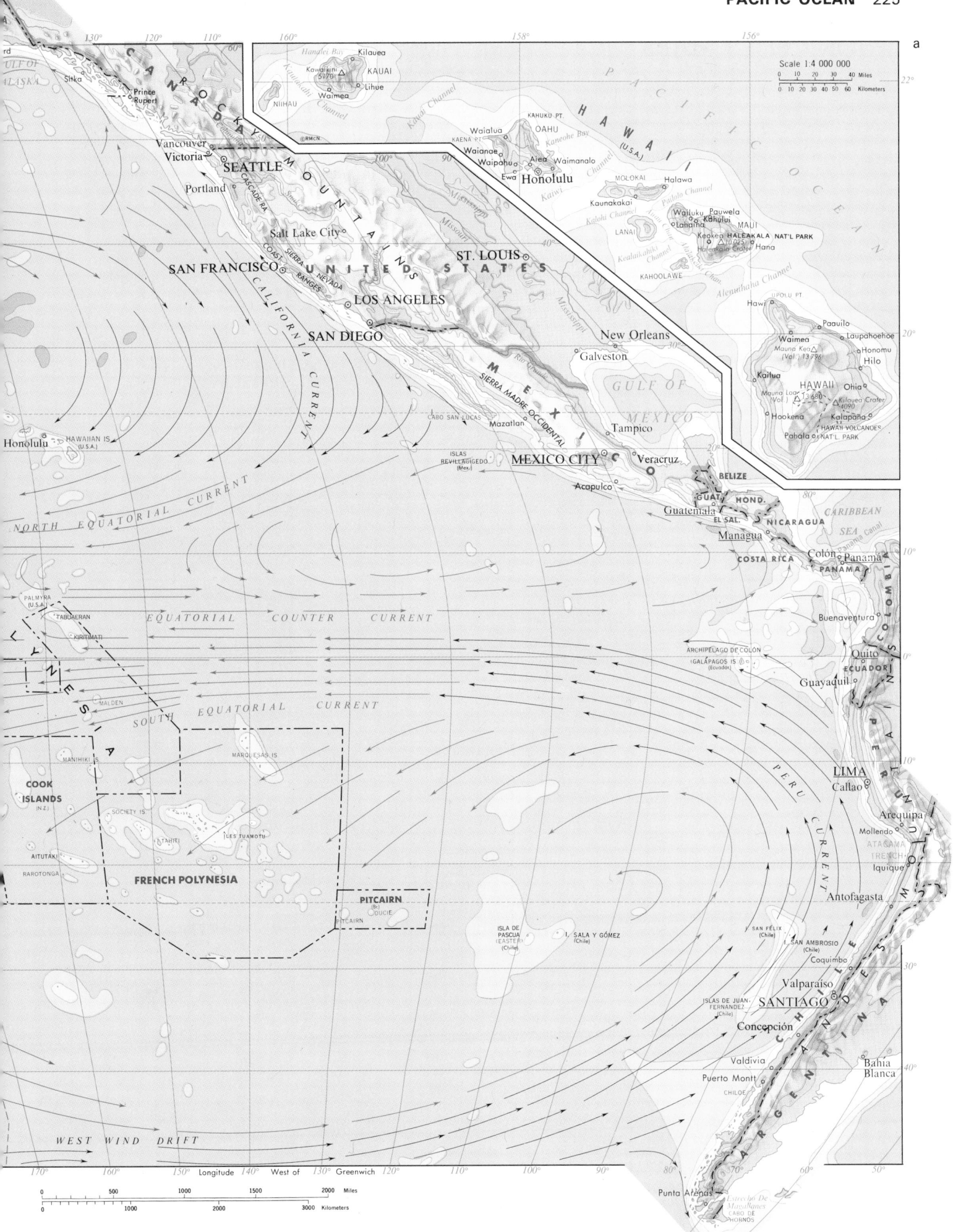

a

Scale 1:4 000 000
0 10 20 30 40 Miles
0 10 20 30 40 50 60 Kilometers

GULF OF ALASKA

Sitka

Prince Rupert

CANADA

ROCKY MOUNTAINS

Vancouver
Victoria
SEATTLE
Portland

CASCADE RA.

Salt Lake City

COAST RANGES
SIERRA NEVADA
CALIFORNIA CURRENT

SAN FRANCISCO

UNITED STATES

ST. LOUIS

LOS ANGELES

SAN DIEGO

MEXICO

SIERRA MADRE OCCIDENTAL

CABO SAN LUCAS

Mazatlan

ISLAS REVILLAGIGEDO (Mex.)

MEXICO CITY

Acapulco

Rio Grande

New Orleans

Galveston

GULF OF MEXICO

Tampico

Veracruz

BELIZE
GUAT. HOND.
Guatemala
EL SAL. NICARAGUA
Managua
COSTA RICA
Colón Panamá
PANAMA

CARIBBEAN SEA

Panama Canal

Honolulu
HAWAIIAN IS. (U.S.A.)

NORTH EQUATORIAL CURRENT

PALMYRA (U.S.A.)
TABUAERAN
KIRITIMATI

POLYNESIA

MALDEN

MANIHIKI IS.

COOK ISLANDS (N.Z.)

AITUTAKI
RAROTONGA

EQUATORIAL COUNTER CURRENT

SOUTH EQUATORIAL CURRENT

MARQUESAS IS.

SOCIETY IS.
TAHITI
ÎLES TUAMOTU

FRENCH POLYNESIA

PITCAIRN (Br.)
DUCIE
PITCAIRN

ISLA DE PASCUA (EASTER) (Chile)

I. SALA Y GÓMEZ (Chile)

SAN FÉLIX (Chile)
I. SAN AMBROSIO (Chile)

ARCHIPIÉLAGO DE COLÓN (GALÁPAGOS IS.) (Ecuador)

Buenaventura

Quito
ECUADOR
Guayaquil

COLOMBIA

PERU CURRENT

LIMA
Callao

Arequipa
Mollendo
ATACAMA TRENCH
Iquique

Antofagasta

Coquimbo

Valparaíso
ISLAS DE JUAN FERNÁNDEZ (Chile)
SANTIAGO
Concepción
Valdivia
Puerto Montt
CHILOE

Bahía Blanca

CHILE
ARGENTINA
ANDES

WEST WIND DRIFT

Punta Arenas
Estrecho De Magallanes
CABO DE HORNOS

HAWAII

PACIFIC OCEAN

Hanalei Bay
Kilauea
Kawaikini 5170
KAUAI
Lihue
Waimea
NIIHAU
Kaulakahi Channel
Kauai Channel

Waialua
KAHUKU PT.
KAENA PT.
OAHU
Kaneohe Bay
Waianae
Waipahu
Aiea Waimanalo
Ewa
Honolulu
Kaiwi Channel

MOLOKAI
Kaunakakai Halawa

Kalohi Channel
LANAI
Wailuku Pauwela
Lahaina Kahului
MAUI
Keokea HALEAKALA NAT'L PARK
Haleakala Crater 10025 Hana
KAHOOLAWE

Kealaikahiki Channel
Auau Chan.
Pailolo Channel

Alenuihaha Channel

UPOLU PT.
Hawi
Paauilo
Laupahoehoe
Waimea
Mauna Kea (Vol.) 13,796
Honomu
Hilo
Kailua
Ohia
Mauna Loa (Vol.) 13,680
Kilauea Crater 4090
Hookena
Kalapana
HAWAII VOLCANOES NAT'L PARK
Pahala

Scale (bottom):
0 500 1000 1500 2000 Miles
0 1000 2000 3000 Kilometers

Longitude West of Greenwich

MAJOR CITIES MAPS

This section consists of 62 maps of the world's most populous metropolitan areas. In order to make comparison easier, all the metropolitan areas are shown at the same scale, 1:300,000.

Detailed urban maps are an important reference requirement for a world atlas. The names of many large settlements, towns, suburbs, and neighborhoods can be located on these large-scale maps. From a thematic standpoint the maps show generalized land-use patterns. Included were the total urban extent, major industrial areas, parks, public land, wooded areas, airports, shopping centers, streets, and railroads. A special effort was made to portray the various metropolitan areas in a manner as standard and comparable as possible. (For the symbols used, see the legend below.)

Notable differences occur in the forms of cities. In most of North America these forms were conditioned by a rectangular pattern of streets; land-use zones (residential, commercial, industrial) are well defined. The basic structure of most European cities is noticeably different and more complex; street patterns are irregular and zones are less well defined. In Asia, Africa, and South America the form tends to be even more irregular and complex. Widespread dispersion of craft and trade activities has lessened zonation, there may be cities with no identifiable city centers, and sometimes there may be dual centers (old and modern). Higher population densities result in more limited, compact urban places in these areas of the world.

Inhabited Localities

The symbol represents the number of inhabitants within the locality

- · 0—10,000
- ○ 10,000—25,000
- ⊙ 25,000—100,000
- ⊡ 100,000—250,000
- ▣ 250,000—1,000,000
- ■ >1,000,000

The size of type indicates the relative economic and political importance of the locality

Écommoy	
Trouville	St.-Denis
Lisieux	PARIS

Hollywood	■ Section of a City,
Westminster	Neighborhood
Northland ■	
Center	■ Major Shopping Center

 Urban Area (area of continuous industrial, commercial, and residential development)

 Major Industrial Area

Wooded Area

Political Boundaries

International (First-order political unit)
- ▬·▬·▬ Demarcated, Undemarcated, and Administrative
- ▬ ▬ ▬ Demarcation Line

Internal
- State, Province, etc. (Second-order political unit)
- County, Oblast, etc. (Third-order political unit)
- — — — Okrug, Kreis, etc. (Fourth-order political unit)
- - - - - - - City or Municipality (may appear in combination with another boundary symbol)

Capitals of Political Units

BUDAPEST	Independent Nation
Recife	State, Province, etc.
White Plains	County, Oblast, etc.
Iserlohn	Okrug, Kreis, etc.

Transportation

Road

PASSAIC EXPWY. (1-80)
BERLINER RING

- Primary
- Secondary
- Tertiary

Railway

- ┼┼┼ CANADIAN NATIONAL — Primary
- ┼—┼— Secondary
- ▬▬▬ Rapid Transit

Airport

▨ LONDON (HEATHROW) AIRPORT

Rail or Air Terminal

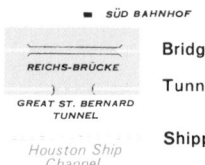

■ SÜD BAHNHOF

REICHS-BRÜCKE — Bridge

GREAT ST. BERNARD TUNNEL — Tunnel

Houston Ship Channel — Shipping Channel

Canal du Midi — Navigable Canal

TO MALMÖ — Ferry

Hydrographic Features

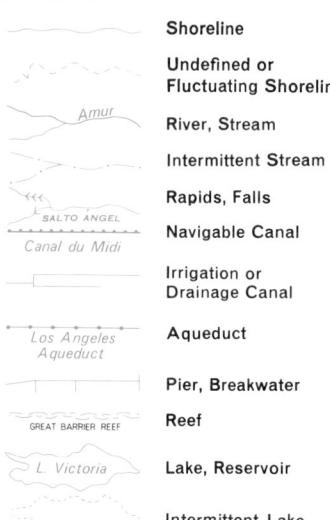

- Shoreline
- Undefined or Fluctuating Shoreline
- Amur — River, Stream
- Intermittent Stream
- Rapids, Falls
- SALTO ANGEL — Navigable Canal
- Canal du Midi
- Irrigation or Drainage Canal
- Los Angeles Aqueduct — Aqueduct
- Pier, Breakwater
- GREAT BARRIER REEF — Reef
- L. Victoria — Lake, Reservoir
- Intermittent Lake
- The Everglades — Swamp

Miscellaneous Cultural Features

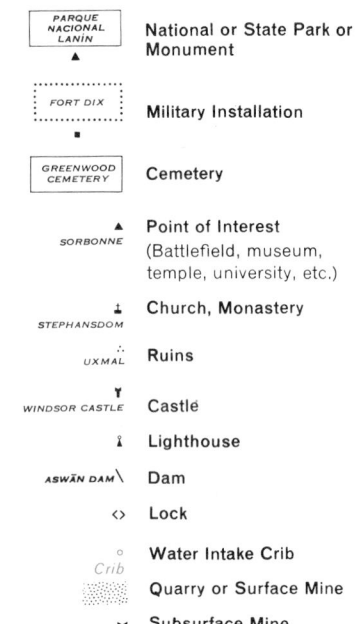

PARQUE NACIONAL LANÍN ▲	National or State Park or Monument
FORT DIX ▪	Military Installation
GREENWOOD CEMETERY	Cemetery
▲ SORBONNE	Point of Interest (Battlefield, museum, temple, university, etc.)
⊥ STEPHANSDOM	Church, Monastery
∴ UXMAL	Ruins
Υ WINDSOR CASTLE	Castle
Ⓘ	Lighthouse
ASWĀN DAM \	Dam
<>	Lock
○ Crib	Water Intake Crib
░	Quarry or Surface Mine
⋈	Subsurface Mine

Topographic Features

Mt. Kenya 5199 △ Elevation Above Sea Level

Elevations are given in meters

⋆ Rock

A N D E S Mountain Range, Plateau,
KUNLUNSHANMAI Valley, etc.

BAFFIN ISLAND Island

POLUOSTROV KAMČATKA Peninsula, Cape, Point, etc.
CABO DE HORNOS

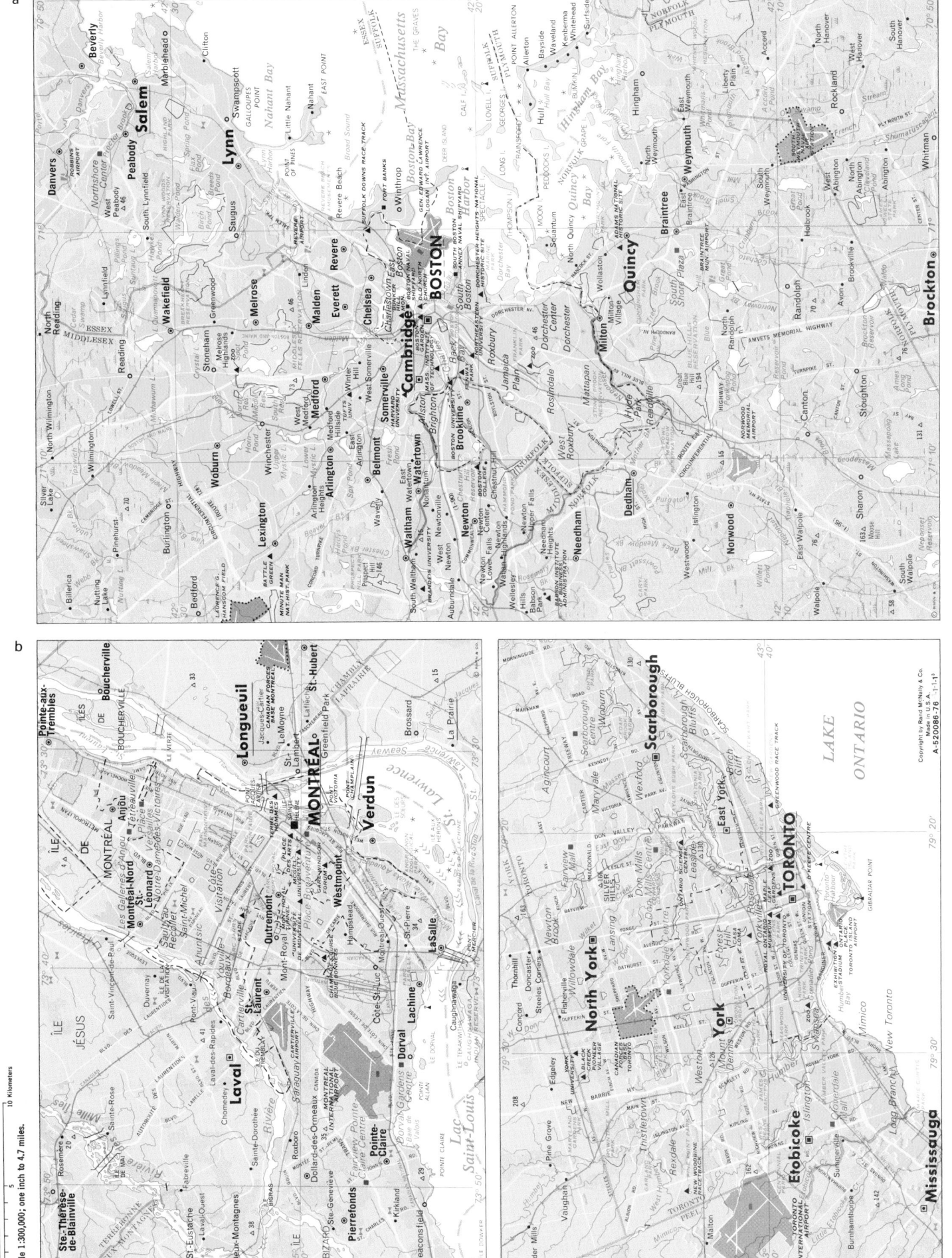

a

b

c

Scale 1:300,000; one inch to 4.7 miles.

10 Miles

10 Kilometers

Copyright by Rand McNally & Co.
Made in U.S.A.
A-520086-76 -1-1-1³

LONG ISLAND

NEW YORK

NEW JERSEY

ATLANTIC OCEAN

Long Island Sound

CONN.
NEW YORK

Oyster Bay

Hicksville

Bethpage

Levittown

Massapequa

Merrick

Hempstead

East Meadow

Garden City

Freeport

Baldwin

Oceanside

Rockville Centre

Long Beach

Lynbrook

Valley Stream

Franklin Square

West Hempstead

New Hyde Park

Floral Park

Elmont

Mineola

Glen Cove

New Rochelle

Mount Vernon

Yonkers

Scarsdale

Paramus

Hackensack

Paterson

Passaic

Clifton

Wayne

Ridgewood

Fair Lawn

Bloomfield

Nutley

Belleville

Kearny

Newark

East Orange

Orange

West Orange

Elizabeth

Jersey City

NEW YORK

Hoboken

Union City

North Bergen

Bayonne

STATEN ISLAND

The Bronx

Queens

Brooklyn

Manhattan

John F. Kennedy International Airport

La Guardia Airport

Newark International Airport

Flushing

Jamaica

Forest Hills

Rahway

Linden

Perth Amboy

Woodbridge

Westfield

Cranford

Plainview

Syosset

Jericho

Westbury

Uniondale

Rockville

Scale 1:300,000; one inch to 4.7 miles.

10 Miles

10 Kilometers

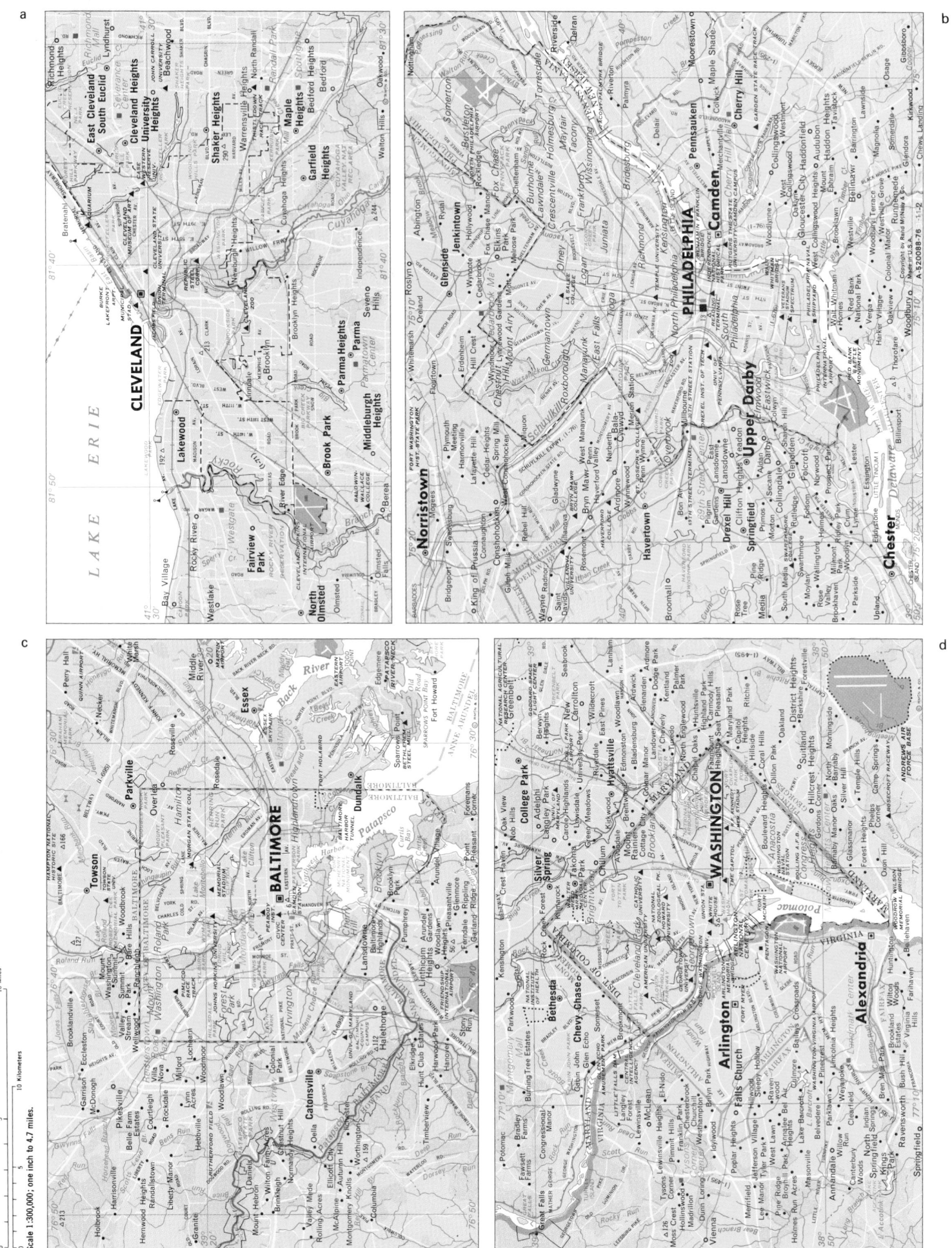

Scale 1:300,000; one inch to 4.7 miles.

a

b

Scale 1:300,000; one inch to 4.7 miles.

10 Miles

10 Kilometers

Copyright by Rand McNally & Co.
Made in U.S.A.
A-520064-76

Scale 1:300,000; one inch to 4.7 miles.

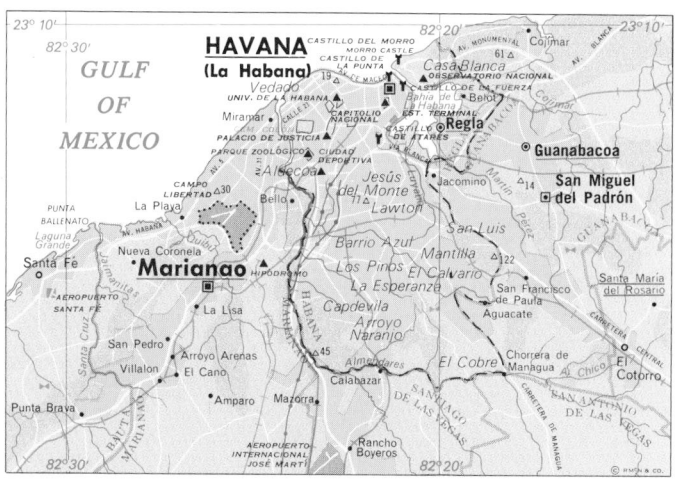

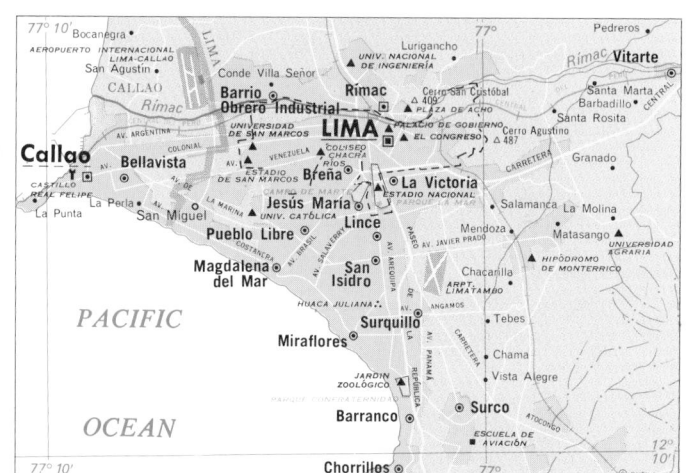

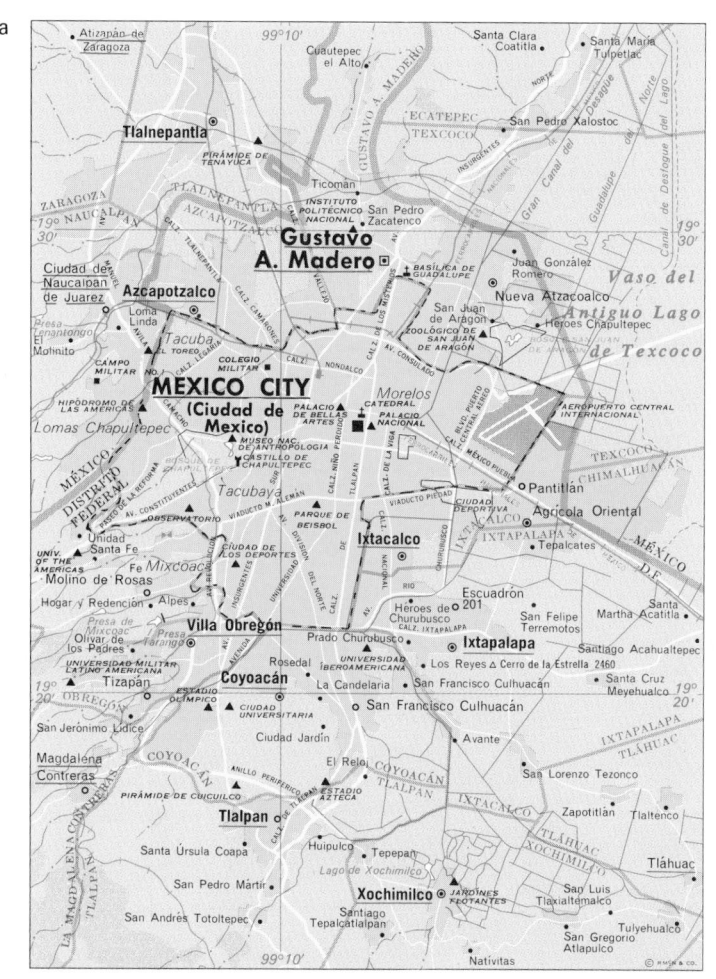

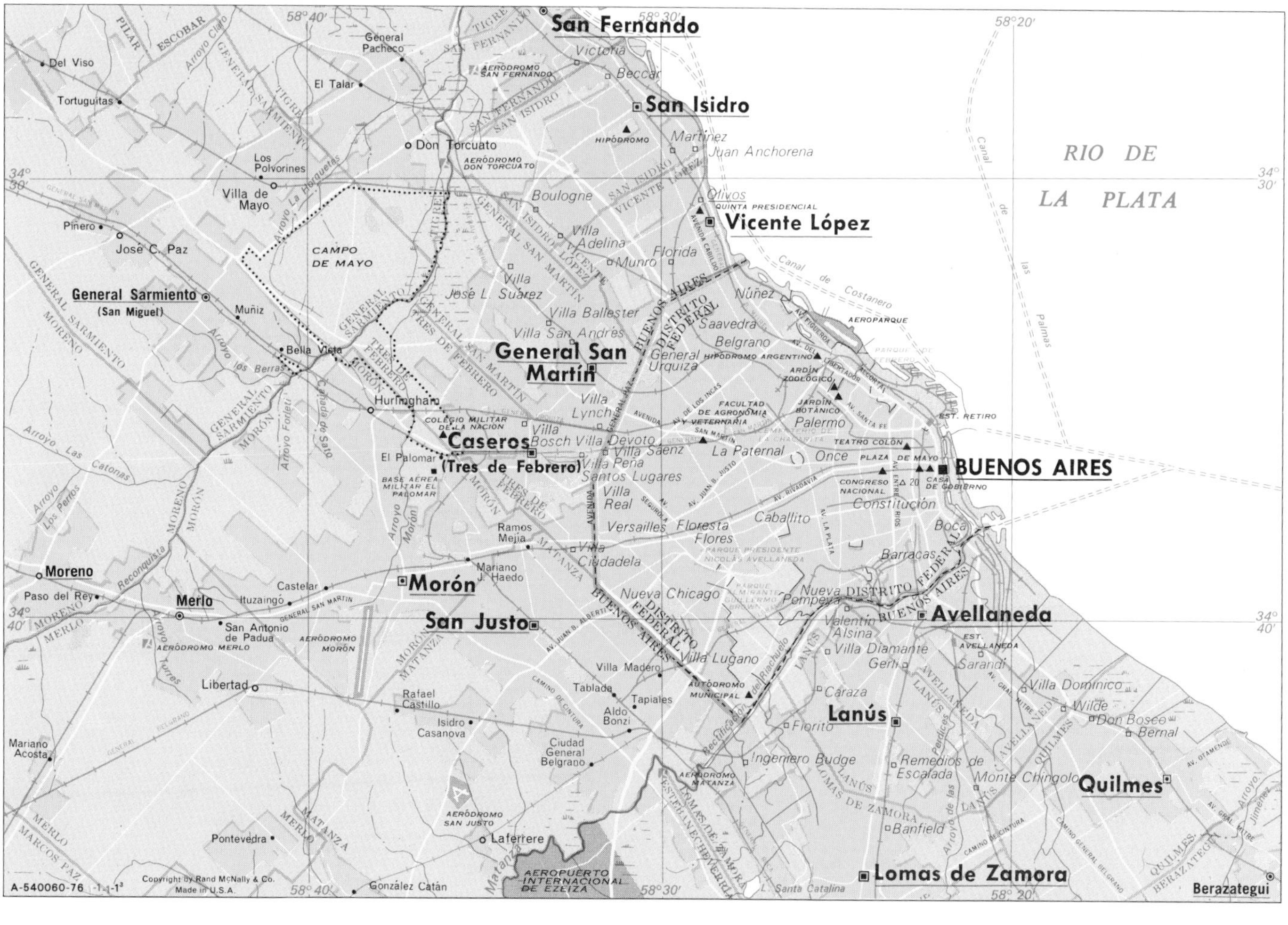

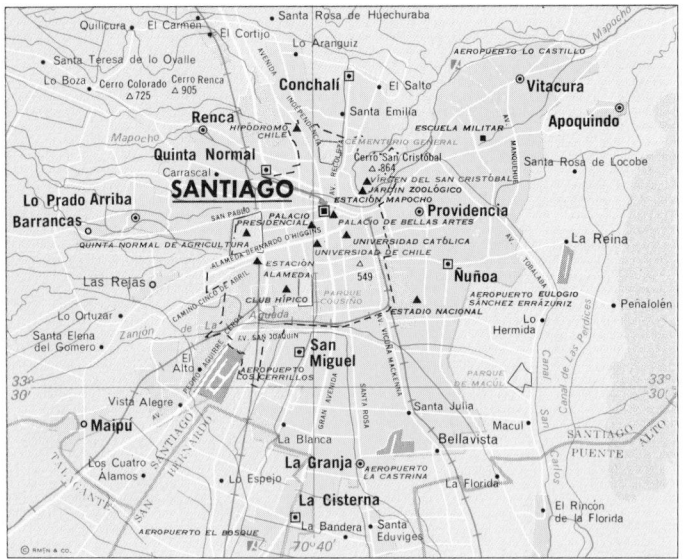

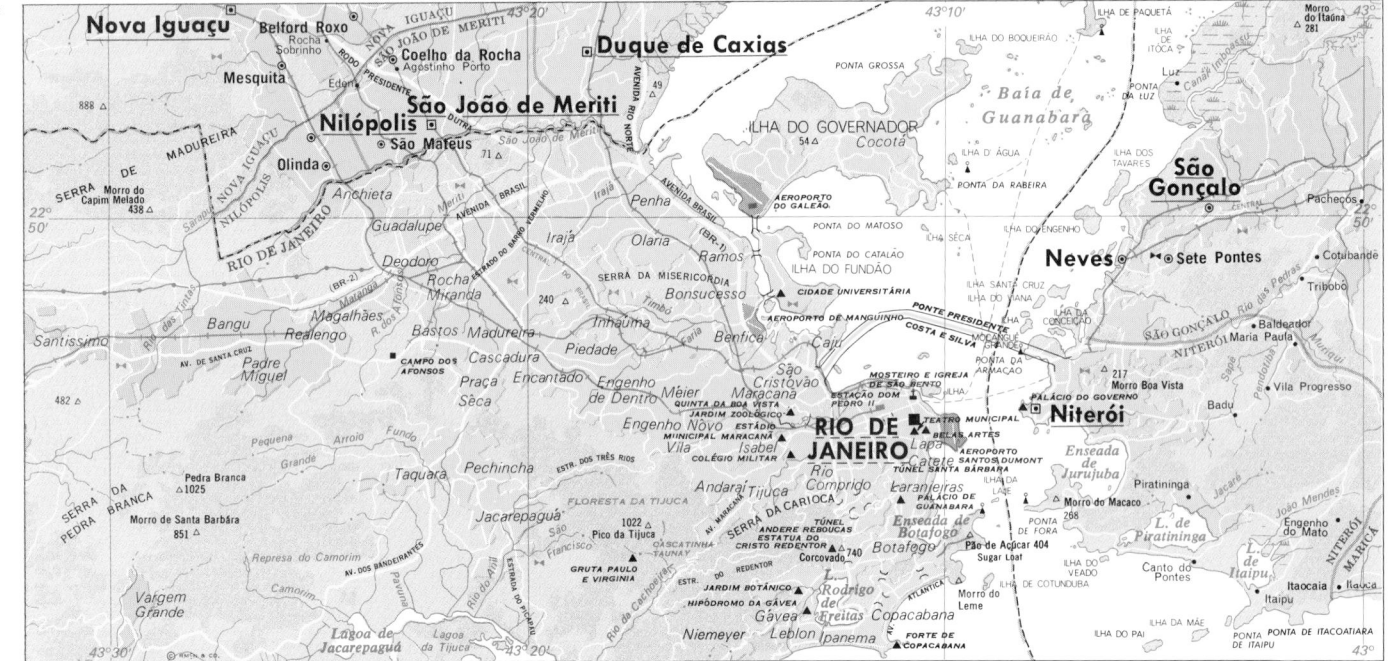

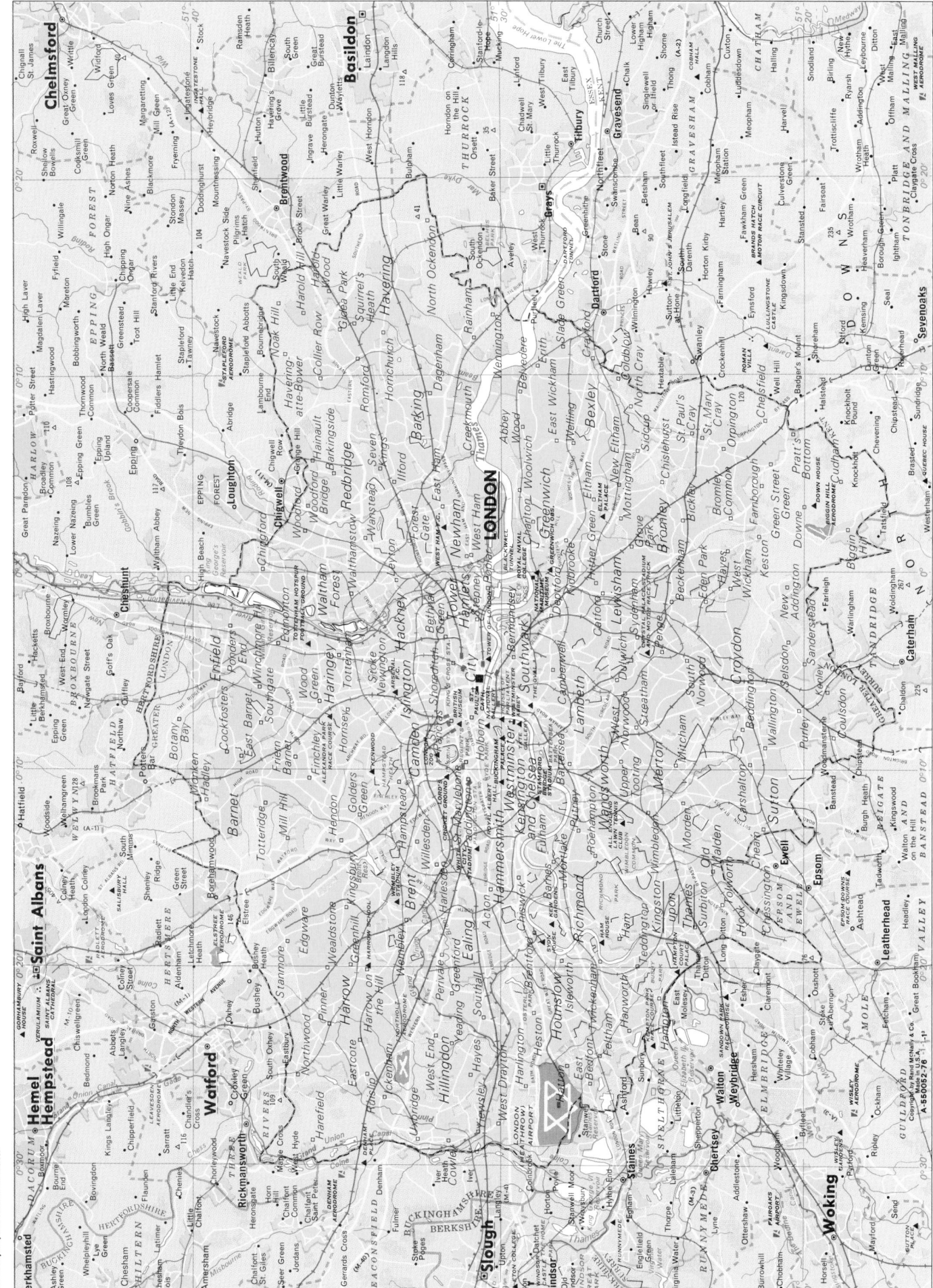

Scale 1:300,000; one inch to 4.7 miles.

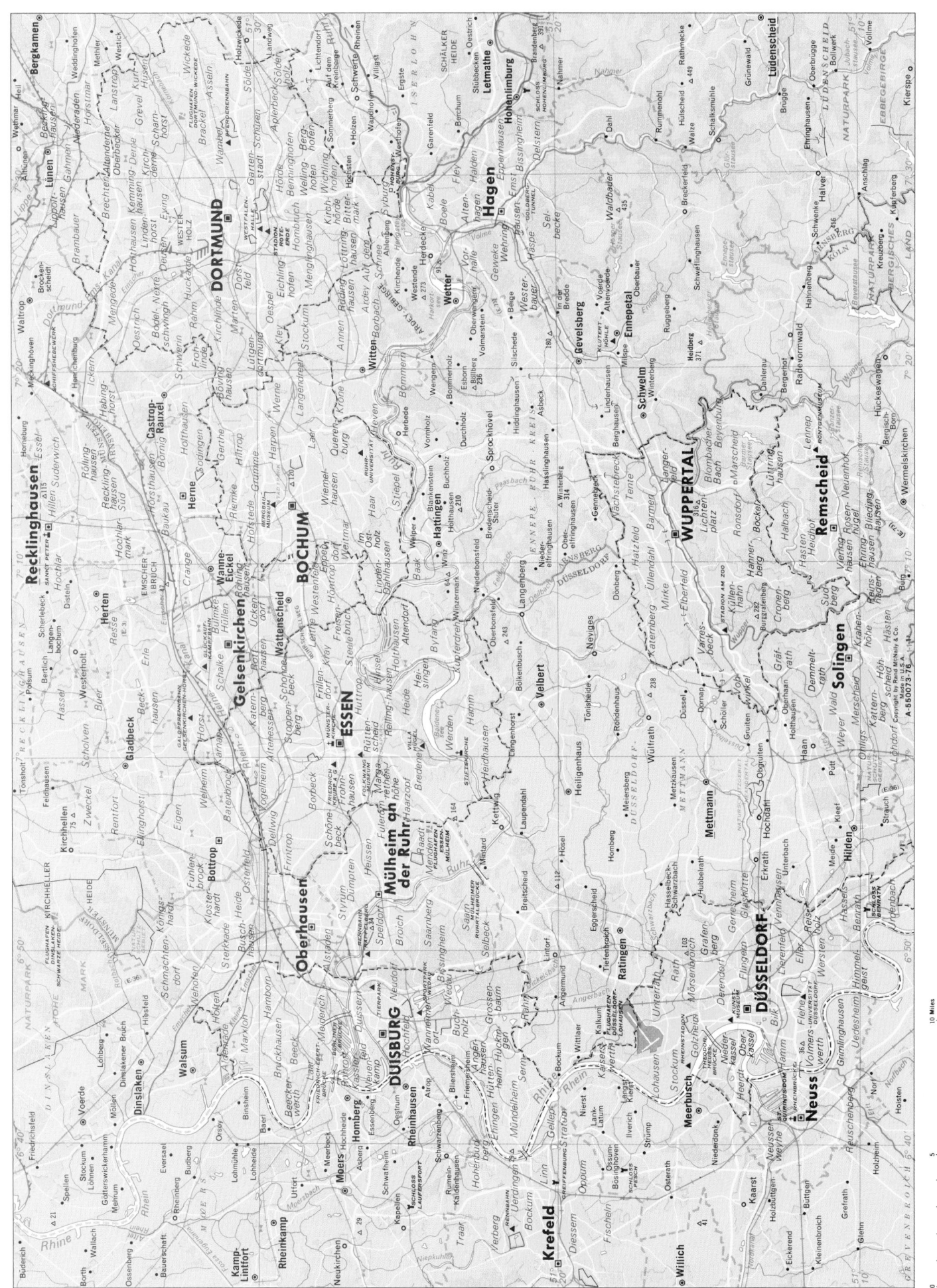

Scale 1:300,000; one inch to 4.7 miles.

a

Liverpool (panel a)

WOODVALE AIRFIELD · WEST LANCASHIRE · Freshfield · **Ormskirk** · Westhead · Dalton · Ashurst's Beacon 170 · FORMBY HILLS · Haskayne · Aughton Park · Scarth Hill · Skelmersdale · **Formby** · Great Altcar · Aughton · Digmoor · Up Holland · FORMBY POINT · Hightown · Lydiate · Bickerstaffe · SEFTON · Ince Blundell · Maghull · MERSEYSIDE · Rainford · Lunt · Kirkby · Crank · Thornton · Netherton · Melling · SIMMONSWOOD MOSS · Moss Bank · **Crosby** · Great Crosby · Sefton · LANCASHIRE ROAD · Waterloo · Litherland · Aintree · AINTREE RACE COURSE · Knowsley · **Saint Helens** · Seaforth · Bootle · Knowsley Park · Eccleston · Thatto Heath · Liverpool · Bay · **Bootle** · EVERTON FOOTBALL GROUND · KNOWSLEY HALL · West Derby · Prescot · New Brighton · Kirkdale · LIVERPOOL FOOTBALL GROUND · Whiston · Rainhill · **LIVERPOOL** · Wallasey · EXCHANGE STATION · Everton · Newsham · UNIV. OF LIVERPOOL · Roby · **Huyton** · Rainhill Stoops · Seacombe · LIME STREET STATION · Edge Hill · Olive Mount · Tarbock Green · (M-62) · **Birkenhead** · MERSEY TUNNEL · Dingle · Mossley Hill · Gateacre · Cronton · Farnworth · Moreton · Upton · BIRKENHEAD PARK · Rock Ferry · Aigburth · Grassendale · Woolton · Hough Green · Ditton · Greasby · Allerton · Frankby · WIRRAL · New Ferry · Hunt's Cross · **Widnes** · Irby · Prenton · Port Sunlight · Garston · Pensby · Bebington · Speke · Hale · Runcorn · Heswall · Storeton · Bromborough · LIVERPOOL (SPEKE) AIRPORT · SPEKE HALL · HALTON · Gayton · Thornton Hough · Hale Head · Weston · Parkgate · Raby · Eastham · HALE HEAD · ENGLAND · Neston · Hooton · Childer Thornton · Ince · Helsby · Helsby Hill 141 · WALES · Ness · MERSEYSIDE · CHESHIRE · Willaston · Stanlow · Manchester Canal (M-56) · Frodsham · Dee · Ledsham · Whitby · Thornton-le-Moors · Elton · Alvanley · FLINT CASTLE · Great Sutton · Hapsford · **Flint** · Burton · Little Sutton · **Ellesmere Port** · CLWYD · Puddington · Capenhurst · Little Stanney

Manchester (panel b)

b

Edgworth · Wayoh Reservoir · Ramsbottom · Wardle · Chapeltown · LANCASHIRE · Summerseat · Ashworth Moor Res. · Norden · GREATER MANCHESTER · Greenbooth Reservoir · Smallbridge · Littleborough · Hollingworth Lake · Astley Bridge · Bradshaw · Greenmount · Walmersley · **Rochdale** · Milnrow · HALL-I'-TH'-WOOD · Tottington · Limefield · Firgrove · **Bolton** · Harwood · **Bury** · Heywood · Castleton · Lower Place · New Hey · Denshaw · Ainsworth · Fishpool · Hollins · Top of Hebers · Royton · Shaw · Moorside · Little Lever · Radcliffe · Birch · Chadderton · Lees · Mossley · Farnworth · Kearsley · (M-62) · Whitefield · Middleton · HEATON HALL · Rhodes · **Oldham** · Failsworth · Little Hulton · Walkden · Prestwich · Cheetham Hill · Blackley · Harpurhey · TAMESIDE · Swinton · (A-580) · Pendlebury · MANCHESTER RACE COURSE · Higher Broughton · Lower Broughton · **Ashton-under-Lyne** · Boothstown · Leigh · Worsley · Ellesmere Park · Eccles · VICTORIA STATION · MANCHESTER CATHEDRAL · PICCADILLY STATION · Droylsden · Audenshaw · Dukinfield · Irlam · Davyhulme · Urmston · BARTON AERODROME · BARTON WATER SWING BRIDGE · TRAFFORD PARK · **Salford** · OLD TRAFFORD CRICKET GROUND · VICTORIA UNIV. OF MANCHESTER · BELLE VUE ZOOLOGICAL GARDENS · Gorton · Denton · Hyde · **MANCHESTER** · **Stretford** · MANCHESTER CITY FOOTBALL GROUND · Rusholme · Levenshulme · Haughton Green · Gee Cross · Cadishead · Ashton upon Mersey · Chorlton-cum-Hardy · PLATT HALL · Withington · Burnage · Reddish · Partington · Carrington · Sale · FLETCHER MOSS MUSEUM · Heaton Moor · Romiley · CARRINGTON MOSS · TRAFFORD · Didsbury · Bredbury · Broadheath · WYTHENSHAWE HALL · Timperley · Gatley · Cheadle · **Stockport** · Dunham Town · DUNHAM PARK · Altrincham · Wythenshawe · Heaviley · Marple · Bowdon · Hale · Halebarns · Cheadle Hulme · Heald Green · BRAMALL HALL · Hazel Grove · Bollington · Rostherne · MANCHESTER (RINGWAY) AIRPORT · Handforth · Woodford · DISLEY TUNNEL · GREATER MANCHESTER · CHESHIRE · Styal · PEAK DISTRICT NATIONAL PARK · Mere · ROSTHERNE MERE · TATTON PARK · WOODFORD AERODROME · Morley Green · Dean Row · ADLINGTON HALL · TATTON HALL · MACCLESFIELD · **Wilmslow** · Poynton · LYME PARK

Paris (panel c)

c

Jouy-le-Moutier · Neuville-sur-Oise · Chennevières · Saint-Prix · Ecouen · Goussainville · Le Mesnil-Amelot · Juilly · L'Hautil · Maurecourt · Beauchamp · Montlignon · Villiers-le-Bel · Le Thillay · AÉROPORT CHARLES DE GAULLE · Thieux · Conflans-Sainte-Honorine · Andrésy · Chanteloup-les-Vignes · Triel-sur-Seine · Herblay · Le Plessis-Bouchard · Eaubonne · Montigny-les-Cormeilles · Ermont · Saint-Brice-sous-Forêt · Roissy-en-France · Vaudherland · Nagtouillet · Compans · Denouval · Achères · FORÊT · La Frette-sur-Seine · Franconville · Cormeilles-en-Parisis · Sannois · Soisy-sous-Montmorency · Groslay · Montmagny · AÉROPORT DE PARIS LE BOURGET · Tremblay-les-Gonesse · Mitry-Mory · Saint-Mesmes · Médan · Carrières-sous-Poissy · Les Gressillons · **Maisons-Laffitte** · CHÂTEAU · Montmorency · Deuil-la-Barre · Gonesse · Villepinte · Mitry-Neuf · Messy · Carrières-sous-Bois · Saint-Gratien · Enghien-les-Bains · **Épinay-sur-Seine** · Pierrefitte-sur-Seine · Garges-les-Gonesse · Gressy · **Poissy** · SAINT-GERMAIN · **Argenteuil** · **Sarcelles** · Le Bourget · Sevran · Villeparisis · Claye-Souilly · Tessancourt · **Sartrouville** · Le Mesnil-le-Roi · Houilles · Villeneuve-la-Garenne · **Saint-Denis** · **Le Blanc-Mesnil** · **Aulnay-sous-Bois** · Annet-sur-Marne · TERRASSE · BASILIQUE SAINT-DENIS · La Courneuve · **Drancy** · **Livry-Gargan** · Villevaudé · Montjay-la-Tour · Chambourcy · CHÂTEAU DE SAINT-GERMAIN-EN-LAYE · Montesson · Bezons · **Gennevilliers** · **Colombes** · Bois-Colombes · **Asnières** · **Aubervilliers** · **Bobigny** · Coubron · Le Pin · **Saint-Germain-en-Laye** · Carrières-sur-Seine · La Garenne-Colombes · **Saint-Ouen** · CIMETIÈRE PARISIEN · **Bondy** · Les Pavillons-sous-Bois · Clichy-sous-Bois · FORÊT DE BONDY · AÉRODROME DE CHELLES-LE-PIN · Carnetin · Le Pecq · Chatou · FACULTÉ DE LETTRES · **Courbevoie** · **Clichy** · Le Pré-Saint-Gervais · **Romainville** · **Villemomble** · Montfermeil · Brou-sur-Chantereine · Pomponne · Fourqueux · **Nanterre** · **Levallois-Perret** · Les Lilas · Rosny-sous-Bois · **Gagny** · **Chelles** · Mareil-Marly · Croissy-sur-Seine · **Puteaux** · LA DÉFENSE · Montmartre · MONTMARTRE SACRÉ-CŒUR · **Bagnolet** · Le Raincy · Gournay-sur-Marne · Vaires-sur-Marne · Saint-Nom-la-Bretèche · Le Vésinet · **Neuilly-sur-Seine** · SAINT-LAZARE · GARE DE L'EST · Feucherolles · L'Étang-la-Ville · **Suresnes** · ARC DE TRIOMPHE · NORD EST · **Montreuil** · Neuilly-sur-Marne · Noisiel · Germantes · Chavenay · RUEIL-MALMAISON · 162 · HIPPODROME DE LONGCHAMP · LOUVRE · **PARIS** · CIMETIÈRE DU PÈRE-LACHAISE · Champs-sur-Marne · Lagny · Noisy-le-Roi · Marly-le-Roi · LA MALMAISON · Passy · TOUR EIFFEL · NOTRE DAME · **Vincennes** · CHÂTEAU DE VINCENNES · Le Perreux-sur-Marne · Noisy-le-Grand · Guermantes · Villepreux · Garches · BOIS DE BOULOGNE · Saint-Cloud · **Fontenay-sous-Bois** · Neuilly-sur-Marne · Torcy · Rocquencourt · HAUTS-DE-SEINE · JARDIN DU LUXEMBOURG · SORBONNE · AUSTERLITZ · GARE DE LYON · Saint-Mandé · BOIS DE VINCENNES · Lognes · Collégien · Villed'Avray · 176 · **Issy-les-Moulineaux** · Malakoff · CITÉ UNIVERSITAIRE · Charenton-le-Pont · Saint-Maurice · Croissy-Beaubourg · Ferrières · Les Clayes-sous-Bois · **Sèvres** · **Boulogne-Billancourt** · Vanves · Gentilly · Le Kremlin-Bicêtre · Joinville-le-Pont · Le Plessis-Trévise · AÉRODROME DE LOGNES-EMERAINVILLE · Fontenay-le-Fleury · AÉRODROME DE SAINT-CYR · **Meudon** · **Montrouge** · Arcueil · Ivry-sur-Seine · Alfortville · **Champigny-sur-Marne** · Émerainville · Bois-d'Arcy · L'ÉCOLE MILITAIRE · Chaville · Clamart · Cachan · **Villejuif** · **Maisons-Alfort** · **Saint-Maur-des-Fossés** · **Versailles** · Viroflay · Bourg-la-Reine · **Vitry-sur-Seine** · **Créteil** · La Queue-en-Brie · Combault · CAMP DE SATORY · Guyancourt · Buc · Jouy-en-Josas · Bièvres · Bagneux · Chevilly-Larue · Bonneuil-sur-Marne · Noiseau · Pontcarré · Trappes · 166 · ARPT. DE BUC-LOUIS-BLÉRIOT · Les Loges-en-Josas · Fontenay-aux-Roses · Châtenay-Malabry · **Sceaux** · CHÂTEAU DE SCEAUX · Thiais · MARCHÉ DE RUNGIS-HALLES · 123 · Sucy-en-Brie · BOIS NOTRE-DAME · Ozoir-la-Ferrière · Montigny-Bretonneux · AÉROPORT DE GUYANCOURT · Voisins-le-Bretonneux · Magny-les-Hameaux · Saint-Lambert · Val d'Albian · Igny · Verrières-le-Buisson · Fresnes · **Antony** · Rungis · CARREFOUR PARIGNY · (E-11-12) · Boissy-Saint-Léger · Chevry-Cossigny · ABBAYE DE PORT-ROYAL-DES-CHAMPS · CHÂTEAU DE DAMPIERRE · Chateaufort · Saclay · 116 · AÉROPORT DE PARIS-ORLY · Valenton · Santeny · Saint-Rémy-lès-Chevreuse · Milon-la-Chapelle · Saint-Remy-lès-Chevreuse · Bures-sur-Yvette · UNIVERSITÉ · **Palaiseau** · Massy · Champlan · Wissous · **Villeneuve-Saint-Georges** · Crosne · Brunoy · Brie-Comte-Robert · Choisel · 2° · Cressely · Villiers-le-Bâcle · Gif-sur-Yvette · Orsay · Longjumeau · Juvisy-sur-Orge · Athis-Mons · Montgeron · Yerres · Mandres-les-Roses · Servon · Rhodon · Courcelle · Le Val-d'Albian · Vauhallan · Morangis · Épinay-sous-Sénart · Périgny · **Choisy-le-Roi** · **Orly** · Chilly-Mazarin · Draveil · Vigneux-sur-Seine

Scale 1:300,000; one inch to 4.7 miles.

0 · 5 · 10 Miles · 0 · 5 · 10 Kilometers

Copyright by Rand McNally & Co. Made in U.S.A. A-550078-76 · -1-1-1

© RMcN & Co.

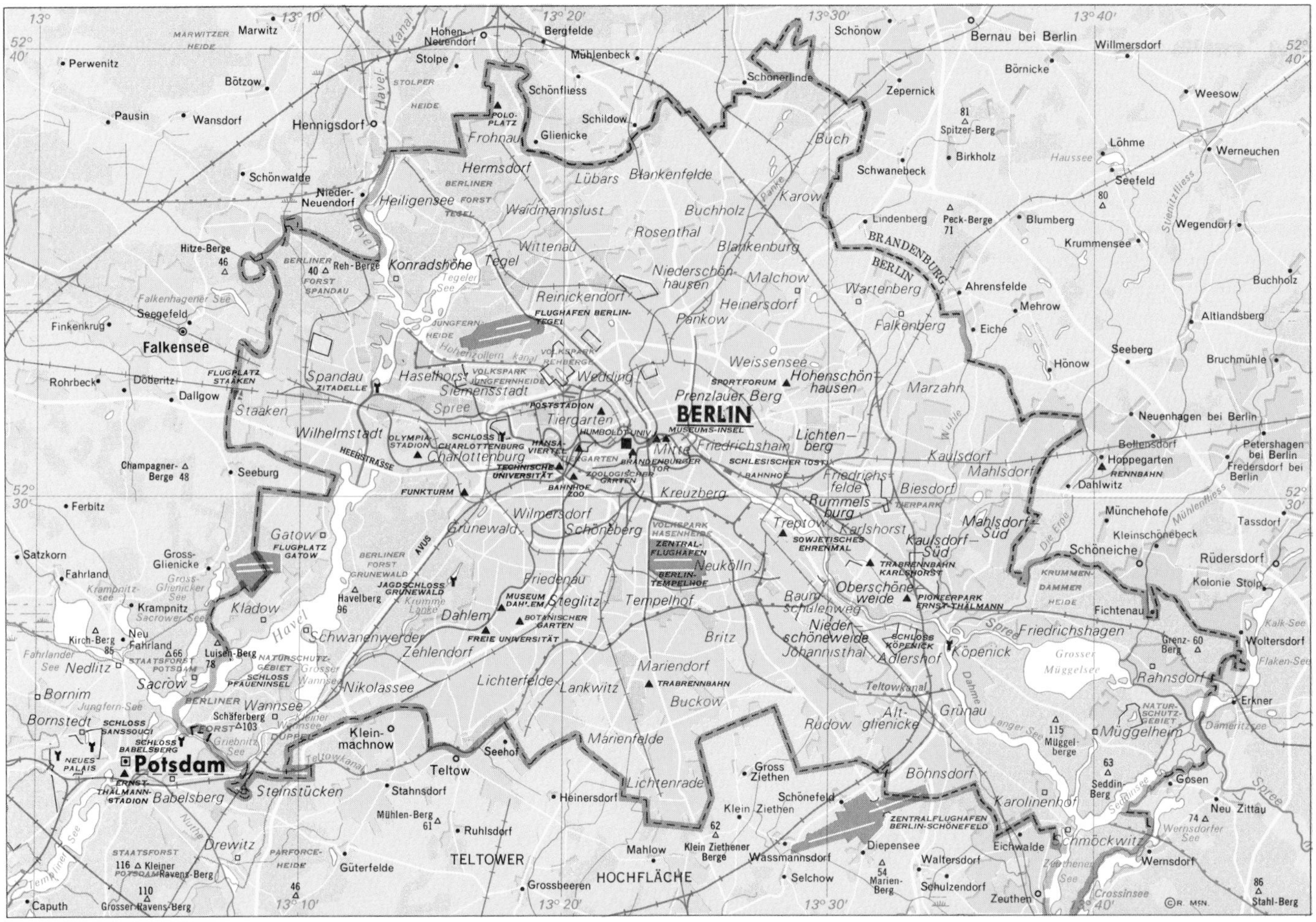

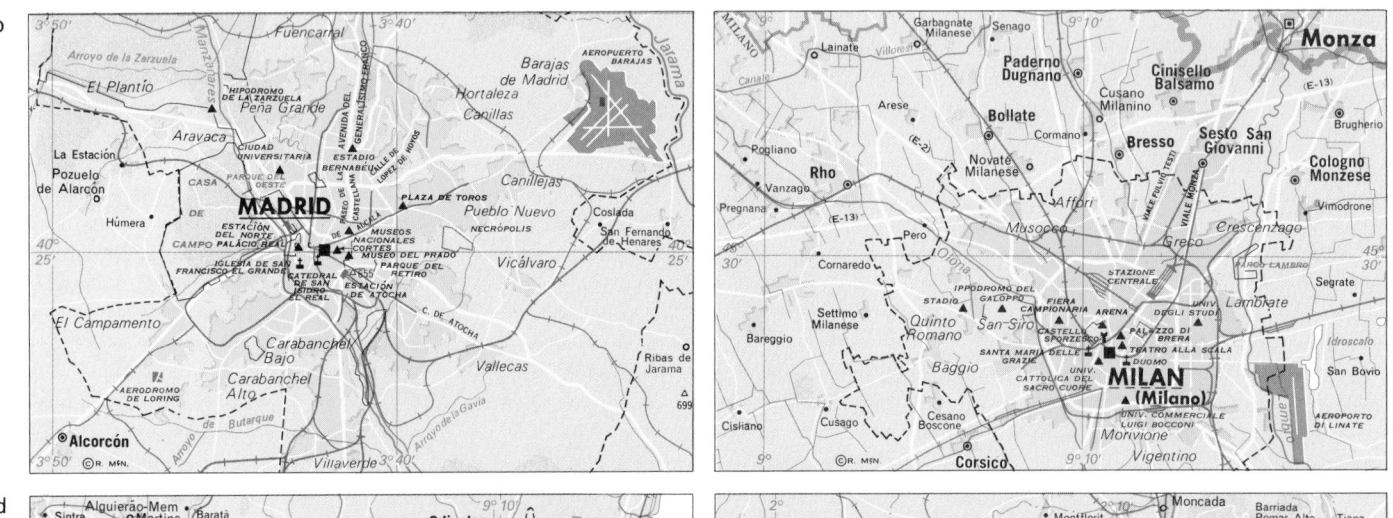

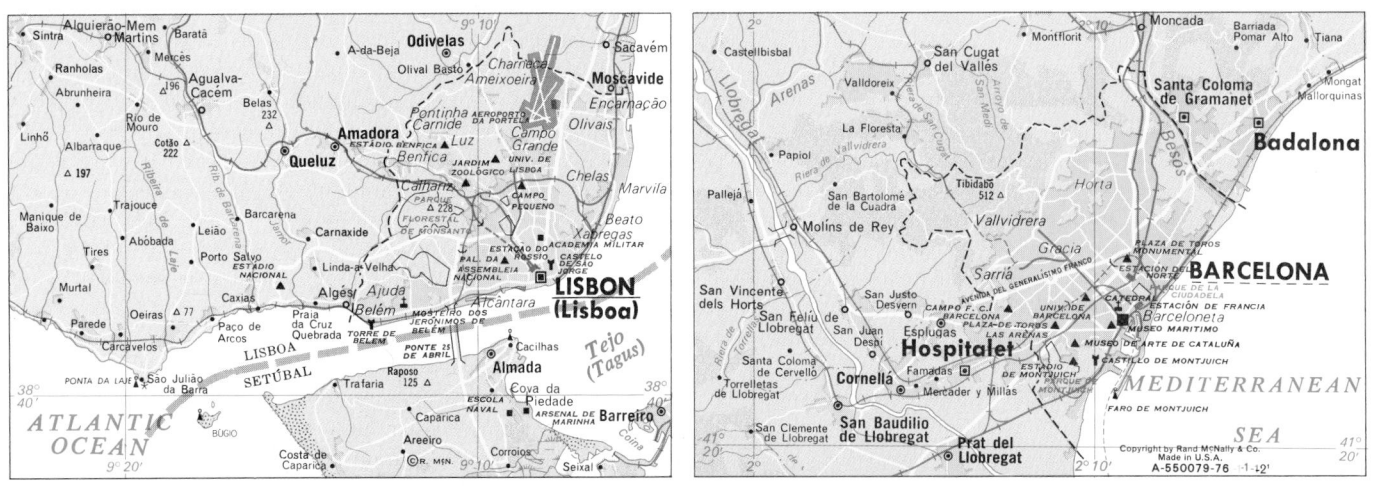

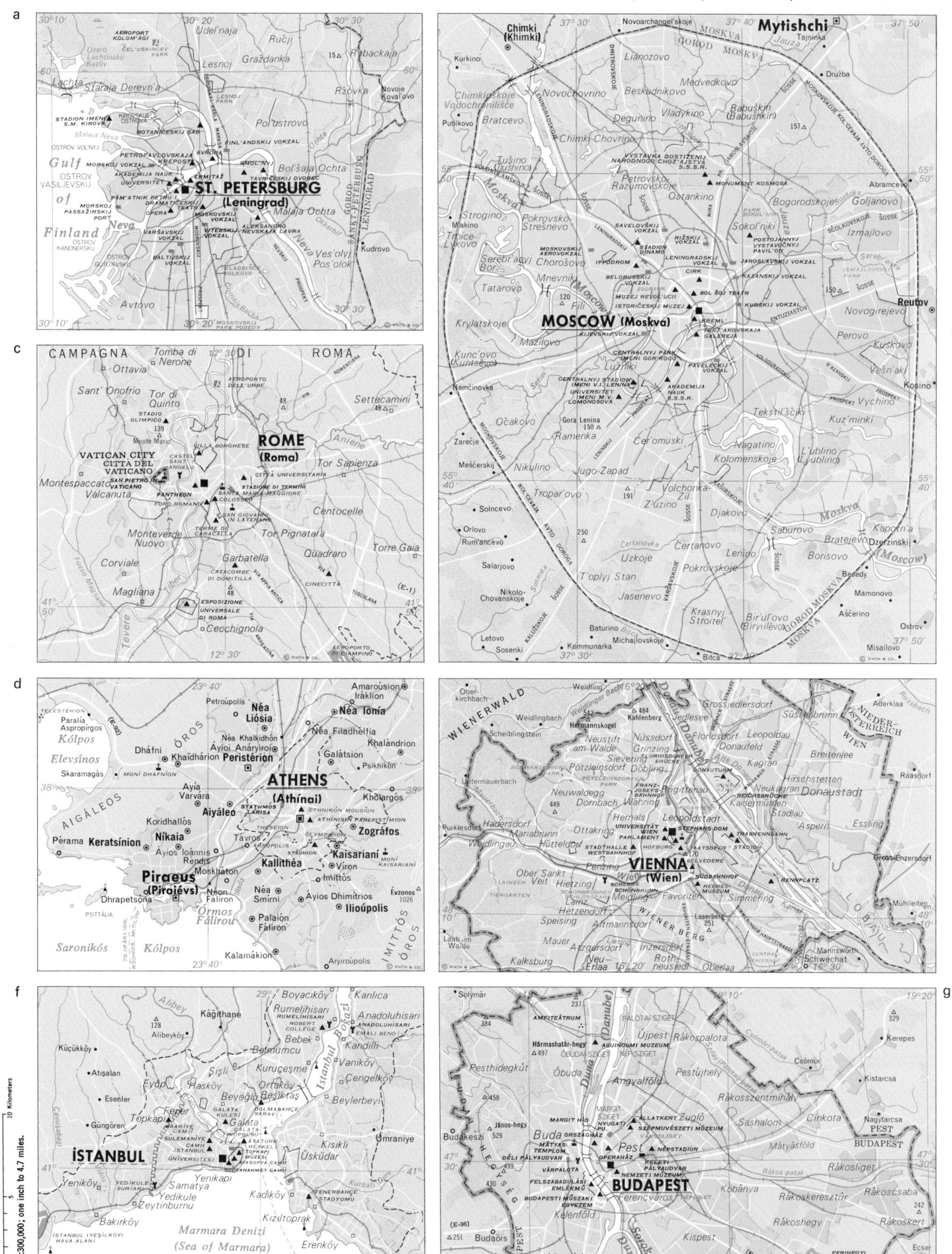

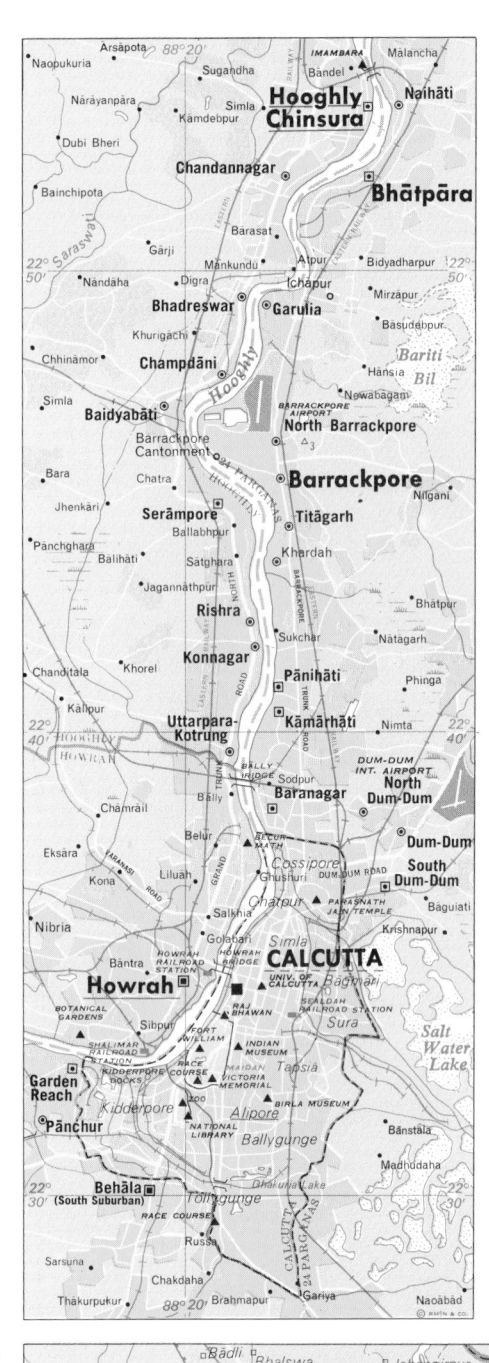

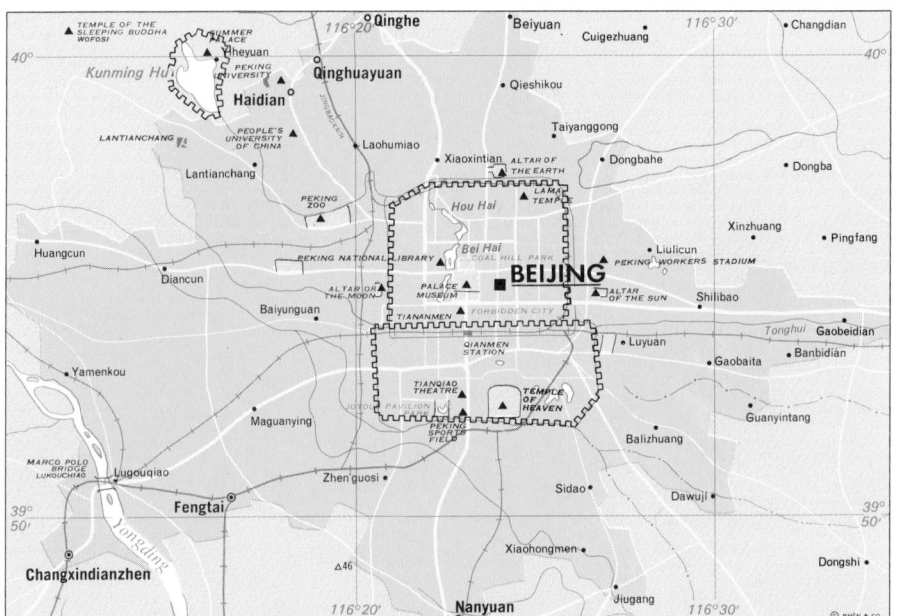

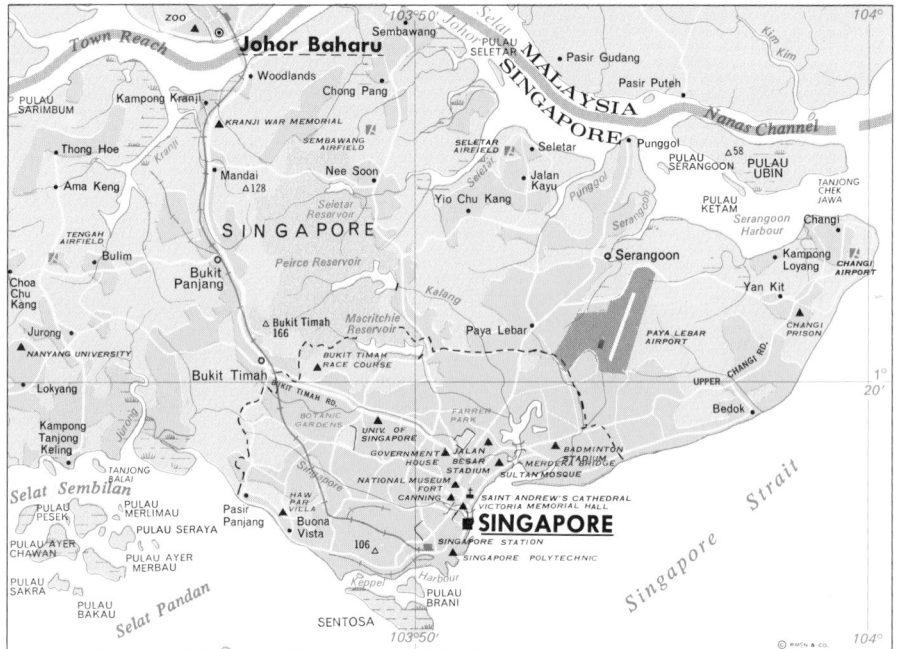

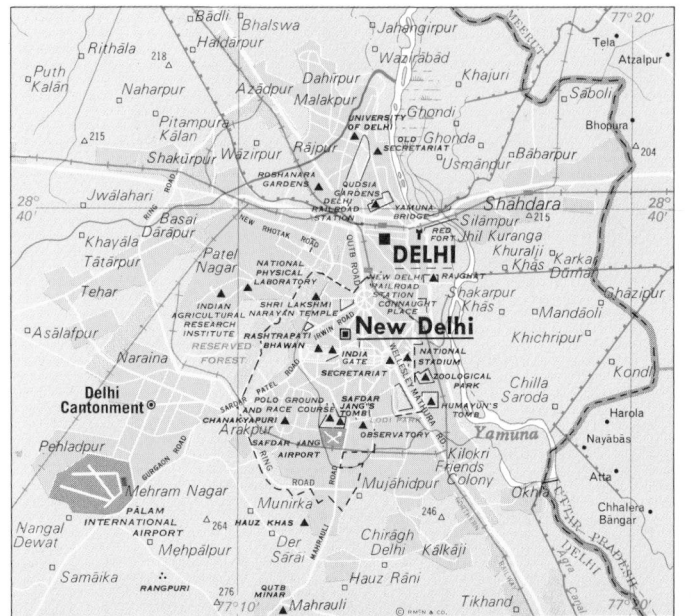

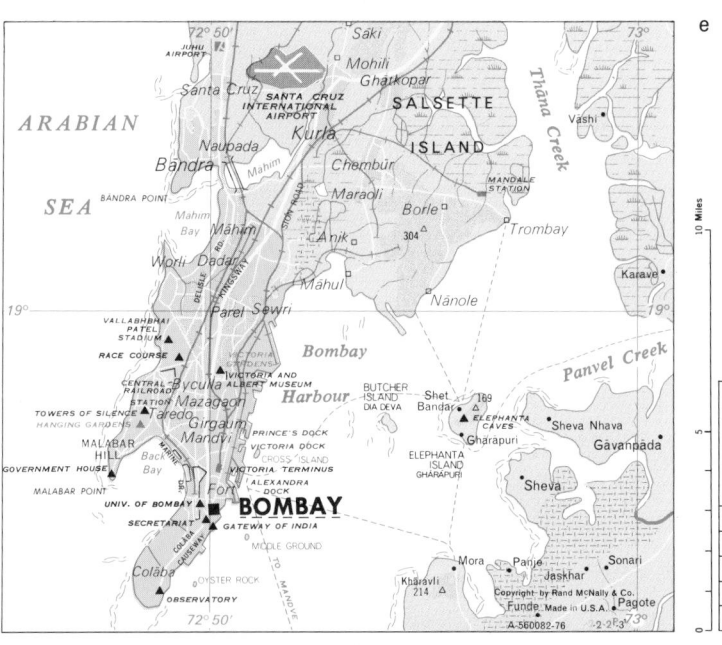

Scale 1:300,000; one inch to 4.7 miles.

Copyright by Rand McNally & Co.
Made in U.S.A.
A-560082-76

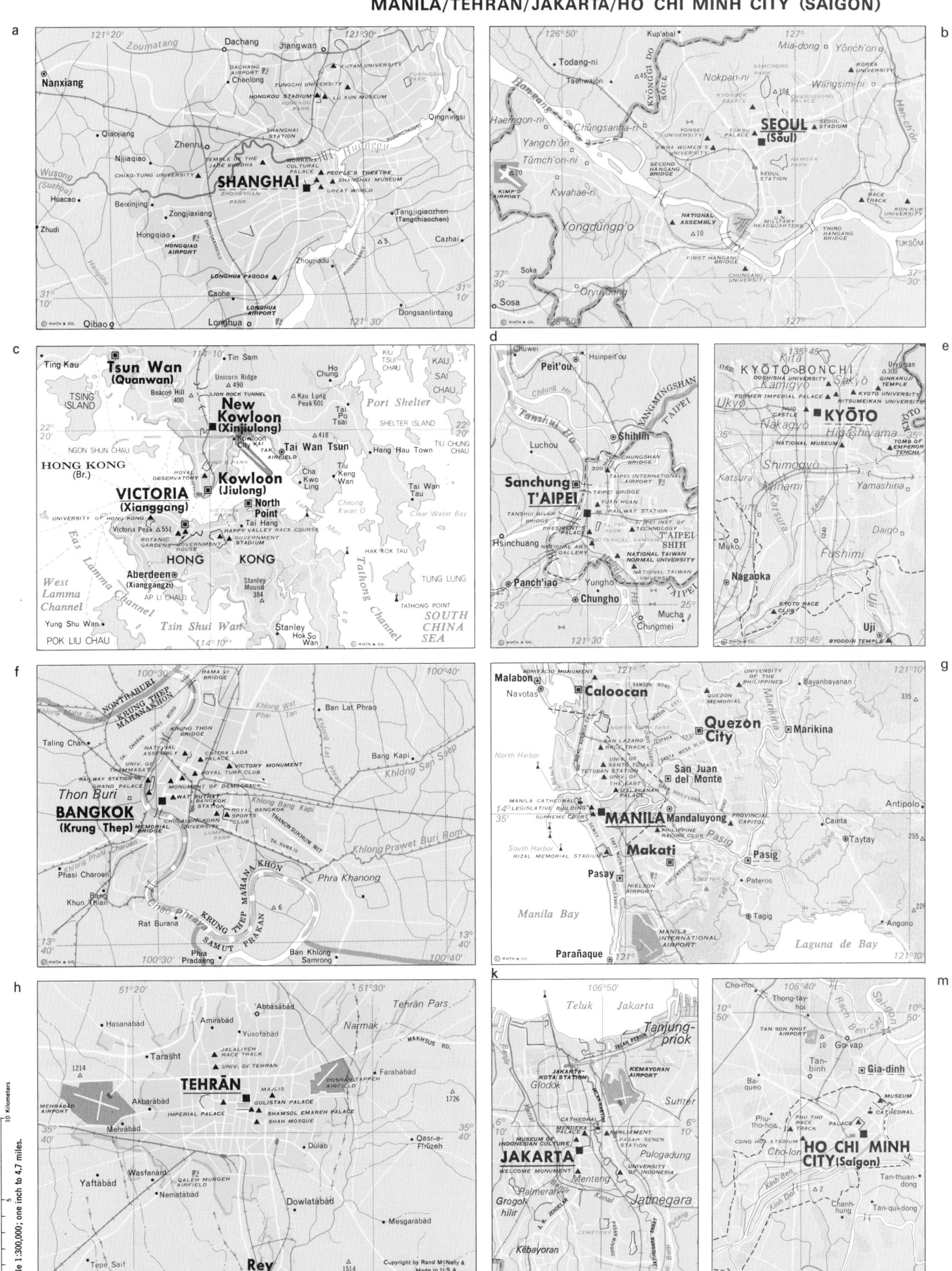

a

139°30' 139°40' 139°50'

SAYAMA-KYŪRYŌ Kitano Yamaguchi-chosuichi Mizonuma **Tokorozawa** Niiza **Asaka** SAITAMA Toda TŌKYŌ **Kawaguchi** CHIBA Mabashi △27 MATSUDO RACE TRACK **Matsudo**

• Mizuho YOKOTA AIR BASE (U.S.) Nakato • Kiyose CAMP ASAKA (U.S.) Yamato Shimonikura Kamiakatsuka Shimura Takenotsuka Nishiarai Gotanno Kanamachi Kamiari

Murayama **Higashimurayama** MUSASHINO-DAICHI Katayama CAMP ASAKA (U.S.) Kitamachi Inatsuke Maeno **Kita** Sumida Adachi Katsushika Sugano **Ichikawa**

YAMATO AIR STATION (U.S.) **Yamato** Kurume Shimohōya Higashiōizumi Shimoshakujii Nerima CAMP NERIMA Itabashi Komagome Arakawa Toshima Minamisenju Edogawa

• Haijima TACHIKAWA AIR BASE (U.S.) **Kodaira** Hōya Tanashi Shimoigusa Asagaya KAMIIGUSA STADIUM Hongo OCHANOMIZU WOMEN'S UNIV. Asakusa Taito Tokagi

△116 **Akishima** Jōgawara Kokubunji **Musashino** Kichijōji Suginami Nakano **Shinjuku** HOSEI UNIV. MEIJI UNIV. Nihonbashi Kōtō Mizue Hongyotoku

Hino HITOTSUBASHI UNIVERSITY Koganei INOKASHIRA PARK **Mitaka** Horinouchi Takaido Akatsutsumi Shibuya TOKYO STATION Ginza Fukagawa Ukita Kasai

Tachikawa △116 Kunitachi Yaho FUCHŪ AIR ARPT. CHOFU ARPT. Kamikitazawa Soshigaya **Minato** TOKYO TOWER IMPERIAL PALACE NATIONAL DIET SUPREME COURT Urayasu

Hachiōji Toyoda Manganji Bubai **Fuchū** Kamiishihara Setagaya Yoga KEIO UNIVERSITY Meguro Kamata

Shimoyugi Higashinakano Tama **Chōfu** Shibasaki Inagi Komae Noborito Tamagawa Okusawa Nakanobu Shimagawa Ōta

△214 Kamiyugi Kaidori Ikuta △121 Mizonokuchi Denenchōfu Magome Ōmori TŌKYŌ

Seibeeshiden Oyama Nozuta Kamiasao Eda Nakayama Hiyoshi Kizuki Rokugo TOKYO INTERNATIONAL AIRPORT

△131 Kamioyamada Kanai **Sagamihara** Kamimizo Kiso Haramachida △246 Maginu Tsunashima Yako Kamata

Onuma CAMP OCHINOBE (U.S.) **Machida** Kanamori Nagatsuta Kawawa Kōhoku Nakayama **Kawasaki** KAWASAKI STADIUM

Shimomizo Kamitsuruma CAMP ZAMA (U.S.) Tsurumi SOJIJI TEMPLE

△129 Sanda Kaneda **Zama** Shimotsuruma △75 **Yamato** Seya Imajuku Kanagawa Namamugi **Tōkyō-wan**

Kawasaki-ko MITSUSAWA PARK RACE TRACK Kawashima Futatsubashi Putamatagawa **YOKOHAMA** Yokohama-ko

Ebina ATSUGI N.A.S. (U.S.) HODOGAYA BASEBALL GROUND Hodogaya Nishi YOKOHAMA PARK BASEBALL GROUND

Atsugi SAGAMIHARA-DAICHI Ayase Nakajima

© RMcN & CO. 139°30' 139°40' 139°50'

35°40' 35°30'

---

b

135°10' 135°20' 135°30' 135°40'

34°50' MEIHIN-MORI-MINO-KOKUTEI-KŌEN Fukui Syukunosho Shodai Uyama Nagao

Yamaguchi Najio Kawanishi **Minō** Hancho (171) Tonda **Takatsuki**

Nose Tsukumono Arino Maitani **Ikeda** Kamishinden **Ibaraki** Tsuda Katano **Hirakata**

Taishaku-zan Funasaka SETO-NAIKAI- Arima **Takarazuka** CAMP SENZO OSAKA INTERNATIONAL AIRPORT **Toyonaka** Senriyama KANSAI UNIVERSITY Yamada **Neyagawa** Kisaichi

△586 Shikami-yama △550 △932 Rokkō-zan CAMP ITAMI Hirota **Suita** Hattori **Moriguchi** Shijonawate

Hyōgo Yamada Tanigami ROKKŌ-SANCHI △309 **Itami** Iwazono Higashiyodogawa **Kadoma** Kitatawara KONGŌ-IKOMA-KOKUTEI-KŌEN

Obu Maya-san △699 KOKURITSU-KŌEN Asuya SAN-YŌ HONSEN Jūsō **ŌSAKA-HEIYA** Asahi **Daitō** Ikoma △642 Ishikiri

Obu-tōge △365 KWANSEI GAKUIN UNIVERSITY Okamoto Narutaki Shin-yodo Miyakojima Jōtō Konoike IKOMA TUNNEL

Futatabi-yama △468 KOBE UNIVERSITY **Nishinomiya** KOSHIEN STADIUM Kanzaki Kita Nishiyodogawa ŌSAKA CASTLE **Higashiōsaka** Yamamoto

Shirakawa-tōge △190 Nada Fukiai **Ashiya** **Higashinada** OSAKA UNIVERSITY Umeda **Higashi** ŌSAKA Kizuri NARA

Ikuta **Amagasaki** Konohana **ŌSAKA** Higashinari Kyūhōji Heguri

KŌBE Kobe-ko Nishi **Minami** Shinsai-bashi Minatogawa Namba Ikuho Abeno Yamamoto Onchi

Nagata Shimomoto Namwa Moto-machi Tennōji △1700 Kyūhōji **Yao** Sango Ōji

Suma WADA-MISAKI Taishō Nishinari Higashisumiyoshi Tajnaka

SUMA BEACH **Ōsaka-Wan** Yamato Sumiyoshi Kyūhōji ŌSAKA AIRPORT **Kashiwara**

Osaka-ko Matsubara Fujiidera **Sakai**

34°40' 135°10' 135°20' 135°30'

Copyright by Rand McNally & Co. Made in U.S.A. A-560080-76 -1 -1-1³

Scale 1:300,000; one inch to 4.7 miles. 10 Miles 10 Kilometers

a

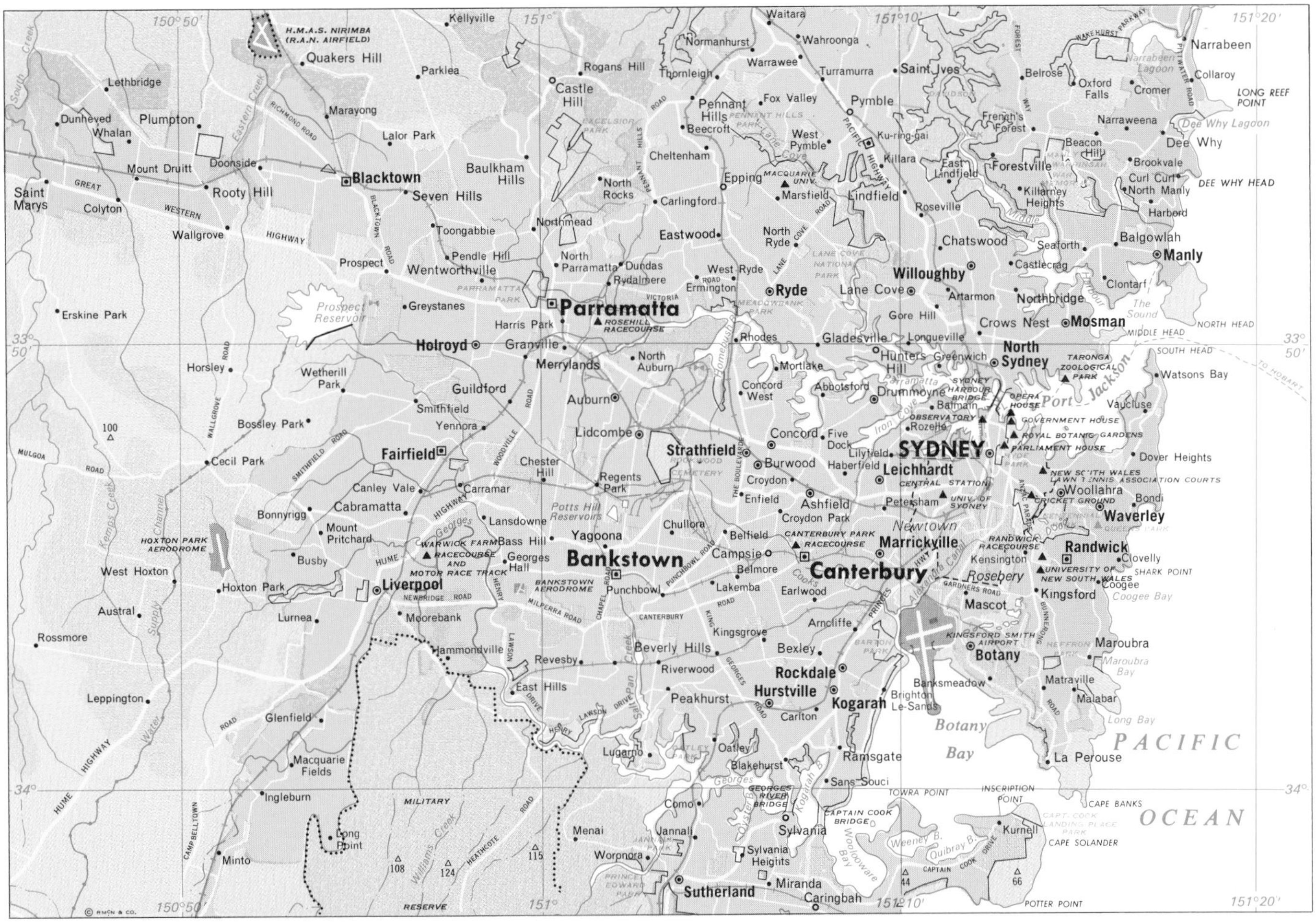

Kellyville · Waitara · Normanhurst · Wahroonga · Narrabeen · Collaroy
H.M.A.S. NIRIMBA (R.A.N. AIRFIELD) · Quakers Hill · Parklea · Rogans Hill · Thornleigh · Turramurra · Saint Ives · Belrose · Oxford Falls · Cromer · LONG REEF POINT
Lethbridge · Castle Hill · Pennant Hills · Beecroft · Warrawee · French's Forest · Narraweena · Dee Why Lagoon
Dunheved · Plumpton · Marayong · Lalor Park · Fox Valley · West Pymble · Ku-ring-gai · Killara · Beacon Hill · Dee Why
Whalan · Mount Druitt · Doonside · Cheltenham · Epping · MACQUARIE UNIV. · Marsfield · Lindfield · Roseville · Killarney Heights · North Manly · Brookvale · Curl Curl · DEE WHY HEAD
Saint Marys · Colyton · Rooty Hill · **Blacktown** · Baulkham Hills · North Rocks · Eastwood · North Ryde · Lane Cove · Chatswood · Seaforth · Balgowlah
Wallgrove · Seven Hills · Toongabbie · Northmead · Carlingford · West Ryde · LANE COVE NATIONAL PARK · Artarmon · Northbridge · Castlecrag · Clontarf · **Manly**
Erskine Park · Prospect · Pendle Hill · North Parramatta · Dundas · Rydalmere · Ermington · Gore Hill · Crows Nest · **Mosman**
Wentworthville · Harris Park · **Parramatta** · Rhodes · Hunters Hill · Greenwich · Longueville · **North Sydney** · TARONGA ZOOLOGICAL PARK · NORTH HEAD
Prospect Reservoir · **Holroyd** · Granville · Merrylands · North Auburn · Concord West · Gladesville · Mortlake · Drummoyne · Balmain · Rozelle · GOVERNMENT HOUSE · Watsons Bay
Horsley · Wetherill Park · Guildford · Smithfield · Yennora · Auburn · Lidcombe · Five Dock · OBSERVATORY · ROYAL BOTANIC GARDENS · PARLIAMENT HOUSE · Dover Heights
Bossley Park · **Fairfield** · Chester Hill · Regents Park · Concord · **Strathfield** · Burwood · Croydon · **SYDNEY** · Haberfield · **Leichhardt** · CENTRAL STATION · NEW S'TH WALES N'N'L LAWN TENNIS ASSOCIATION COURTS
Cecil Park · Canley Vale · Carramar · Lansdowne · Enfield · Ashfield · Petersham · UNIV. OF SYDNEY · Newtown · **Woollahra** · Bondi
Cabramatta · Bonnyrigg · Mount Pritchard · Bass Hill · WARWICK FARM RACECOURSE AND MOTOR RACE TRACK · Georges Hall · Yagoona · Chullora · Belfield · CANTERBURY PARK RACECOURSE · Campsie · **Marrickville** · RANDWICK RACECOURSE · **Randwick** · Clovelly
West Hoxton · Busby · HOXTON PARK AERODROME · Hoxton Park · **Liverpool** · NEWBRIDGE ROAD · **Bankstown** · BANKSTOWN AERODROME · Punchbowl · Belmore · Lakemba · Earlwood · **Canterbury** · UNIVERSITY OF NEW SOUTH WALES · Kingsford · Coogee · Coogee Bay · SHARK POINT
Austral · Lurnea · Moorebank · Hammondville · Revesby · Canterbury · Kingsgrove · Arncliffe · Mascot · Rosebery · Maroubra
Rossmore · Leppington · Glenfield · East Hills · Beverly Hills · Riverwood · Bexley · **Rockdale** · **Botany** · Matraville · Malabar · Maroubra Bay
Macquarie Fields · Peakhurst · **Hurstville** · Carlton · **Kogarah** · Banksmeadow · Brighton Le-Sands · Long Bay
Ingleburn · MILITARY RESERVE · Oatley · Blakehurst · Ramsgate · Sans Souci · PACIFIC OCEAN
Minto · Como · Jannali · GEORGES RIVER BRIDGE · Sylvania · CAPTAIN COOK BRIDGE · Kurnell · CAPE BANKS · CAPE SOLANDER
Menai · Worpnora · Sylvania Heights · Miranda · Caringbah · **Sutherland** · Botany Bay · Kurnell · TOWRA POINT · INSCRIPTION POINT · POTTER POINT · Quibray B.

b

Broadmeadows · Thomastown · Diamond Creek · Little Sugarloaf
TULLAMARINE INTERNATIONAL AIRPORT · Tullamarine · Campbellfield · Kangaroo Ground
Sydenham · Jacana · Glenroy · Keon Park · Bundoora · Greensborough · Research · Mount Lofty
Keilor · Oak Park · Hadfield · Fawkner · Reservoir · Watsonia · Montmorency · **Eltham** · Wonga Park
Airport West · Merlynston · Pascoe Vale · Regent · West Heidelberg · Lower Plenty · Warrandyte
Saint Albans · North Essendon · ESSENDON AIRPORT · **Coburg** · **Preston** · Macleod · Rosanna · Warrandyte South · Black Springs
Avondale Heights · **Essendon** · **Brunswick** · Thornbury · **Heidelberg** · **Templestowe** · Black Springs Hill · Lilydale
Maribyrnong · Braybrook · MOONEE VALLEY RACECOURSE · North Fitzroy · **Northcote** · Ivanhoe · VICTORIA STATE CAR CLUB RACE CIRCUIT · Mooroolbark
Deer Park · Albion · Maidstone · FLEMINGTON RACECOURSE · UNIV. OF MELBOURNE · **Fitzroy** · **Collingwood** · North Balwyn · Park Orchards · Doncaster · **Croydon** · Kilsyth
Sunshine · **Footscray** · CARLTON GARDENS · **Kew** · Balwyn · North Box Hill · Ringwood North · Montrose
Kingsville · Yarraville · **MELBOURNE** · STATE PARLIAMENT HOUSE · **Richmond** · **Hawthorn** · Blackburn · Mitcham · **Ringwood** · Mount Dandenong
Spotswood · Yarra · GOVERNMENT HOUSE · CRICKET GROUND · **Camberwell** · **Box Hill** · **Nunawading** · Forest Hill · Vermont · Bayswater North
Altona North · Newport · Paisley · Port Melbourne · ROYAL BOTANIC GARDENS · VICTORIAN LAWN TENNIS ASSOCIATION COURTS · Burwood · Bennettswood · Wantirna · Bayswater · The Basin · Olinda
Laverton · Galvin · Seaholme · South Melbourne · **Prahran** · Kooyong · Toorak · East Burwood · Wantirna South · Boronia · One Tree Hill · Sassafras
Altona · **Williamstown** · Hobsons Bay · **Malvern** · Ashburton · Tally Ho · Scoresby · Knox · Upper Ferntree Gully · Upwey
POINT GELLIBRAND · **Saint Kilda** · Elwood · **Caulfield** · Mount Waverley · Holmesglen · Syndal · Wheelers Hill · Ferny Creek · Belgrave
POINT COOK · **Brighton** · Glenhuntly · Chadstone · **Glen Waverley** · MONASH UNIVERSITY · Mulgrave · **Rowville** · Lysterfield · Mount Morton
POINT COOK ROYAL AUSTRALIAN AIR FORCE STATION · Bentleigh · **Oakleigh** · Notting Hill · FERNTREE GULLY ROAD · Scoresby · Lysterfield Hills · Sugarloaf Hill
Moorabbin · Hampton · Highett · Oakleigh South · Clayton · SANDOWN PARK RACECOURSE · Harrisfield · CHURCHILL NATIONAL PARK · Lysterfield Reservoir
Sandringham · CAULFIELD RACE COURSE · Cheltenham · Heatherton · **Springvale** · Noble Park · Springvale South · **Dandenong** · Narre Warren North
Port Phillip Bay · Half Moon Bay · MOORABBIN AIRPORT · Dingley · Keysborough · Hallam · Harkaway
Black Rock · Beaumaris · Mentone · Braeside · Doveton
RICKETTS POINT · Beaumaris Bay · **Mordialloc**

10 Miles · 10 Kilometers · 11

a — CAIRO (Al-Qāhirah)

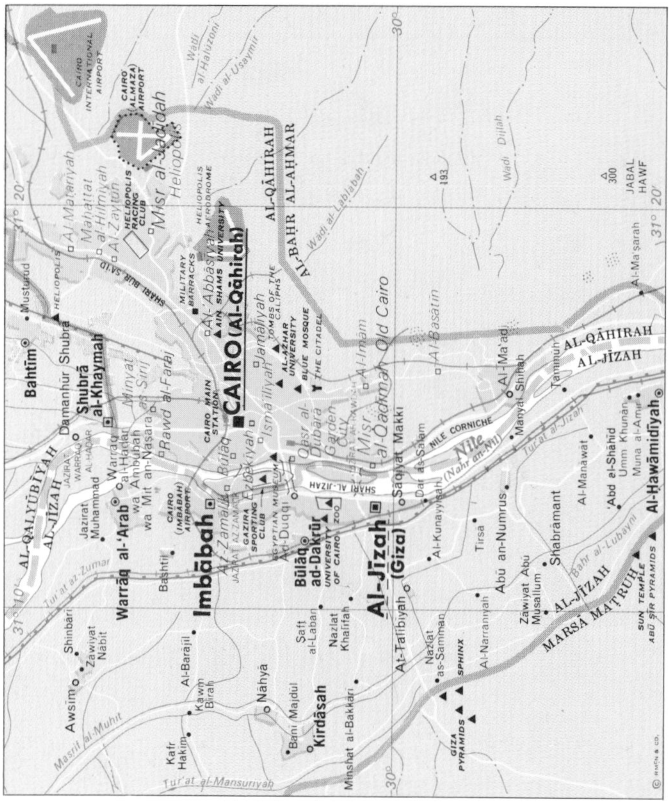

Al-Qāhirah · Al-Jīzah (Giza) · Imbābah · Shubrā al-Khaymah · Bahtim · Al-Ḥawāmidīyah · Kirdāsah · Warrāq al-'Arab · Bulāq ad-Dakrūr · NILE · Nile Corniche · MARSĀ MAṬRŪḤ · GIZA PYRAMIDS · SUN TEMPLE · SPHINX · CAIRO INTERNATIONAL AIRPORT · HELIOPOLIS · JABAL HAWF

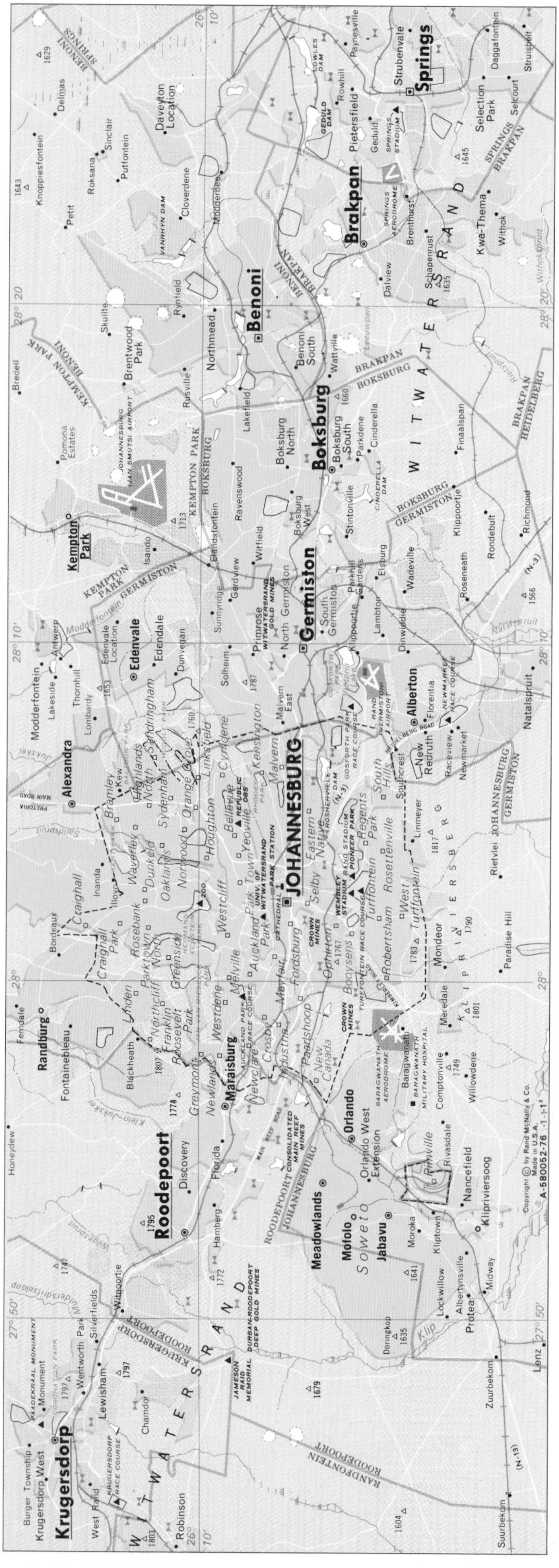

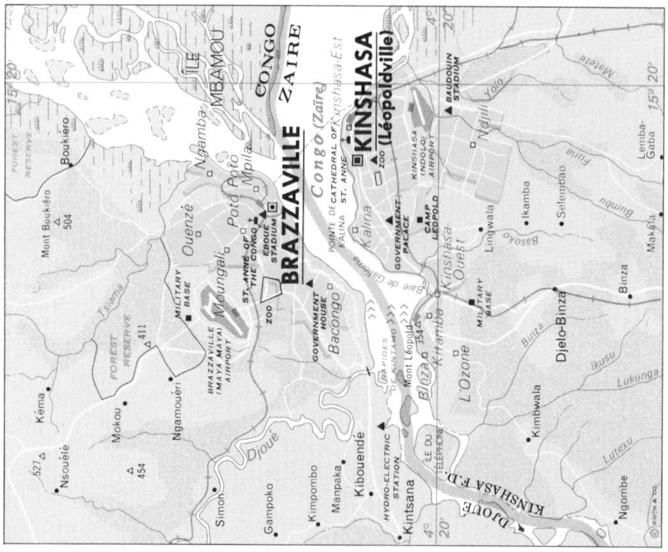

b — JOHANNESBURG

JOHANNESBURG · Springs · Brakpan · Benoni · Boksburg · Germiston · Alberton · Roodepoort · Krugersdorp · Randburg · Maraisburg · Soweto · Orlando · Meadowlands · Kempton Park · Edenvale · Alexandra · Mofolo · Jabavu · WITWATERSRAND · RAND · WITWATERSRAND

c — BRAZZAVILLE / KINSHASA

BRAZZAVILLE (Zaïre) · KINSHASA (Léopoldville) · CONGO · ZAIRE · Congo (Zaïre) · MBAMOU ILE · KINSHASA F.D. · DJOUE

d — LAGOS

LAGOS · Ikeja · Mushin · Shomolu · Agege · IKOYI ISLAND · LAGOS ISLAND · ATLANTIC OCEAN · Lagos Lagoon · IKEJA FEDERAL TERRITORY · LAGOS (IKEJA) AIRPORT · OGUN FOREST RESERVE

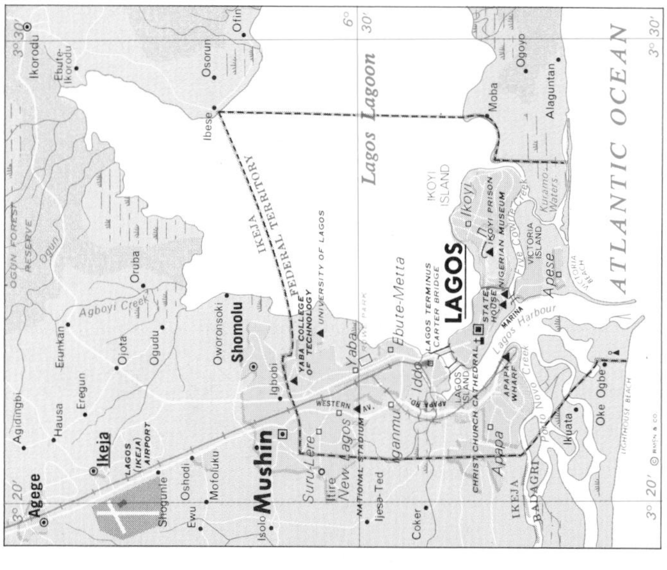

Scale 1:300,000; one inch to 4.7 miles.

10 Miles · 10 Kilometers

Copyright © by Rand McNally & Co. Made in U.S.A.
A-580052-76-1-1-1

WORLD POLITICAL INFORMATION TABLE

This table gives the area, population, population density, political status, capital, and predominant languages for every country in the world. The political units listed are categorized by political status in the form of government column of the table, as follows: A—independent countries; B—internally independent political entities which are under the protection of another country in matters of defense and foreign affairs; C—colonies and other dependent political units; and D—the major administrative subdivisions of Australia, Canada, China, the United

Kingdom, and the United States. For comparison, the table also includes the continents and the world. A key to abbreviations of country names appears on page 249. All footnotes to this table appear on page 245.

The populations are estimates for January 1, 1994, made by Rand McNally on the basis of official data, United Nations estimates, and other available information. Area figures include inland water.

REGION OR POLITICAL DIVISION	Area Sq. Mi.	Est. Pop. 1/1/94	Pop. Per. Sq. Mi.	Form of Government and Ruling Power		Capital	Predominant Languages
Afars and Issas see Djibouti							
† Afghanistan	251,826	16,595,000	66	Islamic republic	A	Kābul	Dari, Pashto, Uzbek, Turkmen
Africa	11,700,000	683,700,000	58				
Alabama	52,423	4,202,000	80	State (U.S.)	D	Montgomery	English
Alaska	656,424	597,000	0.9	State (U.S.)	D	Juneau	English, indigenous
† Albania	11,100	3,424,000	308	Republic	A	Tiranë	Albanian, Greek
Alberta	255,287	2,599,000	10	Province (Canada)	D	Edmonton	English
† Algeria	919,595	26,780,000	29	Provisional military government	A	Algiers (El Djazaïr)	Arabic, Berber dialects, French
American Samoa	77	53,000	688	Unincorporated territory (U.S.)	C	Pago Pago	Samoan, English
† Andorra	175	58,000	331	Parliamentary co-principality (Spanish and French)	B	Andorra	Catalan, Spanish (Castilian), French
† Angola	481,354	11,040,000	23	Republic	A	Luanda	Portuguese, indigenous
Anguilla	35	7,000	200	Dependent territory (U.K. protection)	B	The Valley	English
Anhui	53,668	58,850,000	1,097	Province (China)	D	Hefei	Chinese (Mandarin)
Antarctica	5,400,000	(1)					
† Antigua and Barbuda	171	64,000	374	Parliamentary state	A	St. John's	English, local dialects
† Argentina	1,073,519	33,635,000	31	Republic	A	Buenos Aires and Viedma (4)	Spanish, English, Italian, German, French
Arizona	114,006	3,943,000	35	State (U.S.)	D	Phoenix	English
Arkansas	53,182	2,438,000	46	State (U.S.)	D	Little Rock	English
† Armenia	11,506	3,743,000	325	Republic	A	Yerevan	Armenian, Russian
Aruba	75	68,000	907	Self-governing territory (Netherlands protection)	B	Oranjestad	Dutch, Papiamento, English, Spanish
Ascension	34	1,000	29	Dependency (St. Helena)	C	Georgetown	English
Asia	17,300,000	3,385,900,000	196				
† Australia	2,966,155	17,950,000	6.1	Federal parliamentary state	A	Canberra	English, indigenous
Australian Capital Territory	927	303,000	327	Territory (Australia)	D	Canberra	English
† Austria	32,377	7,913,000	244	Federal republic	A	Vienna (Wien)	German
† Azerbaijan	33,436	7,481,000	224	Republic	A	Baku (Bakı)	Azeri, Russian, Armenian
† Bahamas	5,382	270,000	50	Parliamentary state	A	Nassau	English, Creole
† Bahrain	267	572,000	2,142	Monarchy	A	Al Manāmah	Arabic, English, Farsi, Urdu
† Bangladesh	55,598	115,240,000	2,073	Republic	A	Dhaka	Bangla, English
† Barbados	166	260,000	1,566	Parliamentary state	A	Bridgetown	English
Beijing (Peking)	6,487	11,365,000	1,752	Autonomous city (China)	D	Beijing (Peking)	Chinese (Mandarin)
† Belarus	80,155	10,380,000	129	Republic	A	Minsk	Belarussian, Russian
Belau see Palau							
† Belgium	11,783	10,050,000	853	Constitutional monarchy	A	Brussels (Bruxelles)	Dutch (Flemish), French, German
† Belize	8,866	205,000	23	Parliamentary state	A	Belmopan	English, Spanish, Mayan, Garifuna
† Benin	43,475	5,292,000	122	Republic	A	Porto-Novo and Cotonou	French, Fon, Yoruba, indigenous
Bermuda	21	76,000	3,619	Dependent territory (U.K.)	C	Hamilton	English
† Bhutan	17,954	1,707,000	95	Monarchy (Indian protection)	B	Thimphu	Dzongkha, Tibetan and Nepalese dialects
† Bolivia	424,165	7,582,000	18	Republic	A	La Paz and Sucre	Aymara, Quechua, Spanish
† Bosnia and Herzegovina	19,741	4,442,000	225	Republic	A	Sarajevo	Serbo-Croatian
† Botswana	224,711	1,424,000	6.3	Republic	A	Gaborone	English, Tswana
† Brazil	3,286,500	151,310,000	46	Federal republic	A	Brasília	Portuguese, Spanish, English, French
British Columbia	365,948	3,354,000	9.2	Province (Canada)	D	Victoria	English
British Indian Ocean Territory	23	(1)		Dependent territory (U.K.)	C		English
British Virgin Islands	59	13,000	220	Dependent territory (U.K.)	C	Road Town	English
† Brunei	2,226	279,000	125	Monarchy	A	Bandar Seri Begawan	Malay, English, Chinese
† Bulgaria	42,855	8,813,000	206	Republic	A	Sofia (Sofiya)	Bulgarian, Turkish
† Burkina Faso	105,869	9,922,000	94	Republic	A	Ouagadougou	French, indigenous
Burma see Myanmar							
† Burundi	10,745	6,015,000	560	Republic	A	Bujumbura	French, Kirundi, Swahili
California	163,707	31,905,000	195	State (U.S.)	D	Sacramento	English
† Cambodia	69,898	10,010,000	143	Transitional government	A	Phnom Pénh (Phnom Penh)	Khmer, French
† Cameroon	183,568	12,845,000	70	Republic	A	Yaoundé	English, French, indigenous
† Canada	3,849,674	27,950,000	7.3	Federal parliamentary state	A	Ottawa	English, French
† Cape Verde	1,557	414,000	266	Republic	A	Praia	Portuguese, Crioulo
Cayman Islands	100	32,000	320	Dependent territory (U.K.)	C	George Town	English
† Central African Republic	240,535	3,089,000	13	Republic	A	Bangui	French, Sango, Arabic, indigenous
Ceylon see Sri Lanka							
† Chad	495,755	6,149,000	12	Republic	A	N'Djamena	Arabic, French, indigenous
Channel Islands	75	149,000	1,987	Dependent territory (U.K.)	B		English, French
† Chile	292,135	13,795,000	47	Republic	A	Santiago	Spanish
† China (excl. Taiwan)	3,689,631	1,184,060,000	321	Socialist republic	A	Beijing (Peking)	Chinese dialects
Christmas Island	52	1,300	25	External territory (Australia)	C	The Settlement	English, Chinese, Malay
Cocos (Keeling) Islands	5.4	600	111	Territory (Australia)	C	West Island	English, Cocos-Malay, Malay
† Colombia	440,831	35,085,000	80	Republic	A	Santa Fe de Bogotá	Spanish
Colorado	104,100	3,528,000	34	State (U.S.)	D	Denver	English
† Comoros (excl. Mayotte)	863	508,000	589	Federal Islamic republic	A	Moroni	Arabic, French, Comoran
† Congo	132,047	2,403,000	18	Republic	A	Brazzaville	French, Lingala, Kikongo, indigenous
Connecticut	5,544	3,272,000	590	State (U.S.)	D	Hartford	English
Cook Islands	91	19,000	209	Self-governing territory (New Zealand protection)	B	Avarua	English, Maori
† Costa Rica	19,730	3,285,000	166	Republic	A	San José	Spanish
† Cote d'Ivoire	124,518	13,930,000	112	Republic	A	Abidjan and Yamoussoukro (4)	French, Dioula and other indigenous
† Croatia	21,829	4,796,000	220	Republic	A	Zagreb	Sebo-Croatian
† Cuba	42,804	11,015,000	257	Socialist republic	A	Havana (La Habana)	Spanish
† Cyprus	2,276	574,000	252	Republic	A	Nicosia (Levkosía)	Greek, English

REGION OR POLITICAL DIVISION	Area Sq. Mi.	Est. Pop. 1/1/94	Pop. Per. Sq. Mi.	Form of Government and Ruling Power		Capital	Predominant Languages
Cyprus, North (2)	1,295	193,000	149	Republic	A	Nicosia (Lefkoşa)	Turkish
† Czech Republic	30,450	10,400,000	342	Republic	A	Prague (Praha)	Czech, Slovak
Delaware	2,489	700,000	281	State (U.S.)	D	Dover	English
† Denmark	16,639	5,181,000	311	Constitutional monarchy	A	Copenhagen (København)	Danish
District of Columbia	68	576,000	8,471	Federal district (U.S.)	D	Washington	English
† Djibouti	8,958	579,000	65	Republic	A	Djibouti	French, Arabic, Somali, Afar
† Dominica	305	87,000	285	Republic	A	Roseau	English, French
† Dominican Republic	18,704	7,715,000	412	Republic	A	Santo Domingo	Spanish
† Ecuador	105,037	10,515,000	100	Republic	A	Quito	Spanish, Quechua, indigenous
† Egypt	386,662	56,820,000	147	Socialist republic	A	Cairo (Al Qāhirah)	Arabic
Ellice Islands see Tuvalu							
† El Salvador	8,124	5,179,000	637	Republic	A	San Salvador	Spanish, Nahua
England	50,352	48,320,000	960	Administrative division (U.K.)	D	London	English
† Equatorial Guinea	10,831	379,000	35	Republic	A	Malabo	Spanish, indigenous, English
† Eritrea	36,170	3,540,000	98	Republic	A	Asmera	Tigre, Kunama, Cushitic dialects, Nora Bana, Arabic
† Estonia	17,413	1,608,000	92	Republic	A	Tallinn	Estonian, Latvian, Lithuanian, Russian
† Ethiopia	446,953	54,170,000	121	Provisional military government	A	Addis Ababa	Amharic, Tigrinya, Orominga, Guaraginga, Somali, Arabic
Europe	3,800,000	709,300,000	187				
Faeroe Islands	540	48,000	89	Self-governing territory (Danish protection)	B	Tórshavn	Danish, Faroese
Falkland Islands (3)	4,700	2,200	0.5	Dependent territory (U.K.)	C	Stanley	English
† Fiji	7,056	759,000	108	Republic	A	Suva	English, Fijian, Hindustani
† Finland	130,559	5,056,000	39	Republic	A	Helsinki (Helsingfors)	Finnish, Swedish, Lapp, Russian
Florida	65,758	13,855,000	211	State (U.S.)	D	Tallahassee	English
† France (excl. Overseas Departments)	211,208	57,680,000	273	Republic	A	Paris	French
French Guiana	35,135	134,000	3.8	Overseas department (France)	C	Cayenne	French
French Polynesia	1,359	211,000	155	Overseas territory (France)	C	Papeete	French, Tahitian
Fujian	46,332	31,375,000	677	Province (China)	D	Fuzhou	Chinese dialects
† Gabon	103,347	1,127,000	11	Republic	A	Libreville	French, Fang, indigenous
† Gambia	4,127	919,000	223	Republic	A	Banjul	English, Malinke, Wolof, Fula, indigenous
Gansu	173,746	23,445,000	135	Province (China)	D	Lanzhou	Chinese (Mandarin), Mongolian, Tibetan dialects
Gaza Strip	146	745,000	5,103	Israeli territory with limited self-government			Arabic
Georgia	59,441	6,875,000	116	State (U.S.)	D	Atlanta	English
† Georgia	26,911	5,646,000	210	Republic	A	Tbilisi	Georgian, Russian, Armenian, Azeri
† Germany	137,822	80,930,000	587	Federal republic	A	Berlin and Bonn	German
† Ghana	92,098	16,595,000	180	Republic	A	Accra	English, Akan and other indigenous
Gibraltar	2.3	32,000	13,913	Dependent territory (U.K.)	C	Gibraltar	English, Spanish, Italian, Portuguese, Russian
Gilbert Islands see Kiribati							
Golan Heights	454	29,000	64	Occupied by Israel			Arabic, Hebrew
Great Britain see United Kingdom							
† Greece	50,949	10,500,000	206	Republic	A	Athens (Athínai)	Greek, English, French
Greenland	840,004	57,000	0.1	Self-governing territory (Danish protection)	B	Godthåb	Danish, Greenlandic, Inuit dialects
† Grenada	133	91,000	684	Parliamentary state	A	St. George's	English, French
Guadeloupe (incl. Dependencies)	687	424,000	617	Overseas department (France)	C	Basse-Terre	French, Creole
Guam	209	147,000	703	Unincorporated territory (U.S.)	C	Agana	English, Chamorro, Japanese
Guangdong	68,726	65,830,000	958	Province (China)	D	Guangzhou (Canton)	Chinese dialects, Miao-Yao
Guangxi Zhuangzu	91,236	44,285,000	485	Autonomous region (China)	D	Nanning	Chinese dialects, Thai, Miao-Yao
† Guatemala	42,042	10,510,000	250	Republic	A	Guatemala	Spanish, Amerindian
Guernsey (incl. Dependencies)	30	63,000	2,100	Crown dependency (U.K. protection)	B	St. Peter Port	English, French
† Guinea	94,926	6,274,000	66	Provisional military government	A	Conakry	French, indigenous
† Guinea-Bissau	13,948	1,078,000	77	Republic	A	Bissau	Portuguese, Crioulo, indigenous
Guizhou	65,637	33,985,000	518	Province (China)	D	Guiyang	Chinese (Mandarin), Thai, Miao-Yao
† Guyana	83,000	732,000	8.8	Republic	A	Georgetown	English, indigenous ,
Hainan	13,127	6,867,000	523	Province (China)	D	Haikou	Chinese, Min, Tai
† Haiti	10,714	6,411,000	598	Provisional military government	A	Port-au-Prince	Creole, French
Hawaii	10,932	1,167,000	107	State (U.S.)	D	Honolulu	English, Hawaiian, Japanese
Hebei	73,359	63,940,000	872	Province (China)	D	Shijiazhuang	Chinese (Mandarin)
Heilongjiang	181,082	36,945,000	204	Province (China)	D	Harbin	Chinese dialects, Mongolian, Tungus
Henan	64,479	89,520,000	1,388	Province (China)	D	Zhengzhou	Chinese (Mandarin)
Holland see Netherlands							
† Honduras	43,277	5,206,000	120	Republic	A	Tegucigalpa	Spanish, indigenous
Hong Kong	414	5,890,000	14,227	Chinese territory under British administration	C	Victoria (Hong Kong)	Chinese (Cantonese), English, Putonghua
Hubei	72,356	56,480,000	781	Province (China)	D	Wuhan	Chinese dialects
Hunan	81,081	63,580,000	784	Province (China)	D	Changsha	Chinese dialects, Miao-Yao
† Hungary	35,919	10,295,000	287	Republic	A	Budapest	Hungarian
† Iceland	39,769	262,000	6.6	Republic	A	Reykjavík	Icelandic
Idaho	83,574	1,089,000	13	State (U.S.)	D	Boise	English
Illinois	57,918	11,750,000	203	State (U.S.)	D	Springfield	English
† India (incl. part of Jammu and Kashmir)	1,237,062	906,770,000	733	Federal republic	A	New Delhi	English, Hindi, Telugu, Bengali, indigenous
Indiana	36,420	5,733,000	157	State (U.S.)	D	Indianapolis	English
† Indonesia	752,410	198,810,000	264	Republic	A	Jakarta	Bahasa Indonesia (Malay), English, Dutch, indigenous
Iowa	56,276	2,827,000	50	State (U.S.)	D	Des Moines	English
† Iran	632,457	63,940,000	101	Islamic republic	A	Tehrān	Farsi, Turkish dialects, Kurdish
† Iraq	169,235	19,335,000	114	Republic	A	Baghdād	Arabic, Kurdish, Assyrian, Armenian
† Ireland	27,137	3,563,000	131	Republic	A	Dublin (Baile Átha Cliath)	English, Irish Gaelic
Isle of Man	221	72,000	326	Crown dependency (U.K. protection)	B	Douglas	English, Manx Gaelic
† Israel (excl. Occupied Areas)	8,019	4,950,000	617	Republic	A	Jerusalem (Yerushalayim)	Hebrew, Arabic
† Italy	116,324	56,670,000	487	Republic	A	Rome (Roma)	Italian, German, French, Slovene
Ivory Coast see Cote d'Ivoire							
† Jamaica	4,244	2,538,000	598	Parliamentary state	A	Kingston	English, Creole
† Japan	145,870	124,840,000	856	Constitutional monarchy	A	Tōkyō	Japanese
Jersey	45	86,000	1,911	Crown dependency (U.K. protection)	B	St. Helier	English, French
Jiangsu	39,614	70,210,000	1,772	Province (China)	D	Nanjing (Nanking)	Chinese dialects
Jiangxi	64,325	39,550,000	615	Province (China)	D	Nanchang	Chinese dialects
Jilin	72,201	25,815,000	358	Province (China)	D	Changchun	Chinese (Mandarin), Mongolian, Korean
† Jordan	35,135	3,858,000	110	Constitutional monarchy	A	'Ammān	Arabic
Kansas	82,282	2,568,000	31	State (U.S.)	D	Topeka	English
† Kazakhstan	1,049,156	17,190,000	16	Republic	A	Alma-Ata (Almaty) and Akmola (4)	Kazakh, Russian
Kentucky	40,411	3,813,000	94	State (U.S.)	D	Frankfort	English
† Kenya	224,961	28,280,000	126	Republic	A	Nairobi	English, Swahili, indigenous

REGION OR POLITICAL DIVISION	Area Sq. Mi.	Est. Pop. 1/1/94	Pop. Per. Sq. Mi.	Form of Government and Ruling Power		Capital	Predominant Languages
Kiribati	313	77,000	246	Republic	A	Bairiki	English, Gilbertese
† Korea, North	46,540	22,735,000	489	Socialist republic	A	P'yŏngyang	Korean
† Korea, South	38,230	44,250,000	1,157	Republic	A	Seoul (Sŏul)	Korean
† Kuwait	6,880	1,734,000	252	Constitutional monarchy	A	Kuwait	Arabic, English
† Kyrgyzstan	76,641	4,645,000	61	Republic	A	Bishkek	Kirghiz, Russian
† Laos	91,429	4,601,000	50	Socialist republic	A	Viangchan (Vientiane)	Lao, French, English
† Latvia	24,595	2,556,000	104	Republic	A	Rīga	Latvian, Russian, Lithuanian
† Lebanon	4,015	3,566,000	888	Republic	A	Beirut (Bayrūt)	Arabic, French, Armenian, English
† Lesotho	11,720	1,907,000	163	Constitutional monarchy under military rule	A	Maseru	English, Sesotho, Zulu, Xhosa
Liaoning	56,255	41,325,000	735	Province (China)	D	Shenyang	Chinese (Mandarin), Mongolian
† Liberia	38,250	2,901,000	76	Republic	A	Monrovia	English, indigenous
† Libya	679,362	4,917,000	7.2	Socialist republic	A	Tripoli (Ţarābulus)	Arabic
† Liechtenstein	62	30,000	484	Constitutional monarchy	A	Vaduz	German
† Lithuania	25,212	3,777,000	150	Republic	A	Vilnius	Lithuanian, Polish, Russian
Louisiana	51,843	4,332,000	84	State (U.S.)	D	Baton Rouge	English
† Luxembourg	998	401,000	402	Constitutional monarchy	A	Luxembourg	French, Luxembourgish, German
Macao	6.6	380,000	57,576	Chinese territory under Portuguese administration	C	Macao	Portuguese, Chinese (Cantonese)
† Macedonia	9,928	2,198,000	221	Republic	A	Skopje	Macedonian, Albanian
† Madagascar	226,658	13,110,000	58	Republic	A	Antananarivo	Malagasy, French
Maine	35,387	1,245,000	35	State (U.S.)	D	Augusta	English
† Malawi	45,747	8,942,000	195	Republic	A	Lilongwe	Chichewa, English
† Malaysia	127,320	19,060,000	150	Federal constitutional monarchy	A	Kuala Lumpur	Malay, Chinese dialects, English, Tamil
† Maldives	115	246,000	2,139	Republic	A	Male	Divehi
† Mali	482,077	8,922,000	19	Republic	A	Bamako	French, Bambara, indigenous
† Malta	122	365,000	2,992	Republic	A	Valletta	English, Maltese
Manitoba	250,947	1,118,000	4.5	Province (Canada)	D	Winnipeg	English
† Marshall Islands	70	52,000	743	Republic (U.S. protection)	A	Majuro (island)	English, indigenous, Japanese
Martinique	425	377,000	887	Overseas department (France)	C	Fort-de-France	French, Creole
Maryland	12,407	5,006,000	403	State (U.S.)	D	Annapolis	English
Massachusetts	10,555	6,106,000	578	State (U.S.)	D	Boston	English
† Mauritania	395,956	2,142,000	5.4	Republic	A	Nouakchott	Arabic, Pular, Soninke, Wolof
† Mauritius (incl. Dependencies)	788	1,110,000	1,409	Republic	A	Port Louis	English, Creole, Bhojpuri, French, Hindi, Tamil, others
Mayotte (5)	144	91,000	632	Territorial collectivity (France)	C	Dzaoudzi and Mamoudzou (4)	French, Swahili (Mahorian)
† Mexico	759,534	90,870,000	120	Federal republic	A	Mexico City (Ciudad de México)	Spanish, indigenous
Michigan	96,810	9,550,000	99	State (U.S.)	D	Lansing	English
† Micronesia, Federated States of	271	119,000	439	Republic (U.S. protection)	A	Kolonia and Paliker (4)	English, indigenous
Midway Islands	2.0	500	250	Unincorporated territory (U.S.)	C	....	English
Minnesota	86,943	4,539,000	52	State (U.S.)	D	St. Paul	English
Mississippi	48,434	2,646,000	55	State (U.S.)	D	Jackson	English
Missouri	69,709	5,266,000	76	State (U.S.)	D	Jefferson City	English
† Moldova	13,012	4,425,000	340	Republic	A	Chişinău (Kishinev)	Romanian (Moldovan), Russian
† Monaco	0.7	31,000	44,286	Constitutional monarchy	A	Monaco	French, English, Italian, Monegasque
† Mongolia	604,829	2,314,000	3.8	Republic	A	Ulan Bator (Ulaanbaatar)	Khalkha Mongol, Turkish dialects, Russian, Chinese
Montana	147,046	830,000	5.6	State (U.S.)	D	Helena	English
Montserrat	39	13,000	333	Dependent territory (U.K.)	C	Plymouth	English
† Morocco (excl. Western Sahara)	172,414	28,095,000	163	Constitutional monarchy	A	Rabat	Arabic, Berber dialects, French
† Mozambique	308,642	16,585,000	54	Republic	A	Maputo	Portuguese, indigenous
† Myanmar (Burma)	261,228	43,630,000	167	Provisional military government	A	Rangoon (Yangon)	Burmese, indigenous
† Namibia	318,253	1,555,000	4.9	Republic	A	Windhoek	English, Afrikaans, German, indigenous
Nauru	8.1	10,000	1,235	Republic	A	Yaren District	Nauruan, English
Nebraska	77,358	1,635,000	21	State (U.S.)	D	Lincoln	English
Nei Monggol (Inner Mongolia)	456,759	22,495,000	49	Autonomous region (China)	D	Hohhot	Mongolian
† Nepal	56,827	20,660,000	364	Constitutional monarchy	A	Kathmandu	Nepali, Maithali, Bhojpuri, other indigenous
† Netherlands	16,164	15,320,000	948	Constitutional monarchy	A	Amsterdam and The Hague ('s-Gravenhage)	Dutch
Netherlands Antilles	309	192,000	621	Self-governing territory (Netherlands protection)	B	Willemstad	Dutch, Papiamento, English
Nevada	110,567	1,375,000	12	State (U.S.)	D	Carson City	English
New Brunswick	28,355	755,000	27	Province (Canada)	D	Fredericton	English, French
New Caledonia	7,358	179,000	24	Overseas territory (France)	C	Nouméa	French, indigenous
Newfoundland	156,649	587,000	3.7	Province (Canada)	D	St. John's	English
New Hampshire	9,351	1,167,000	125	State (U.S.)	D	Concord	English
New Hebrides see Vanuatu	....	....	....				
New Jersey	8,722	7,915,000	907	State (U.S.)	D	Trenton	English
New Mexico	121,598	1,608,000	13	State (U.S.)	D	Santa Fe	English, Spanish
New South Wales	309,500	6,117,000	20	State (Australia)	D	Sydney	English
New York	54,475	18,375,000	337	State (U.S.)	D	Albany	English
† New Zealand	104,454	3,486,000	33	Parliamentary state	A	Wellington	English, Maori
† Nicaragua	50,054	4,267,000	85	Republic	A	Managua	Spanish, English, indigenous
† Niger	489,191	8,754,000	18	Provisional military government	A	Niamey	French, Hausa, Djerma, indigenous
† Nigeria	356,669	94,550,000	265	Provisional military government	A	Lagos and Abuja	English, Hausa, Fulani, Yorbua, Ibo, indigenous
Ningxia Huizu	25,637	4,855,000	189	Autonomous region (China)	D	Yinchuan	Chinese (Mandarin)
Niue	100	1,900	19	Self-governing territory (New Zealand protection)	B	Alofi	English, indigenous
Norfolk Island	14	2,700	193	External territory (Australia)	C	Kingston	English, Norfolk
North America	9,500,000	444,600,000	47			....	....
North Carolina	53,821	6,955,000	129	State (U.S.)	D	Raleigh	English
North Dakota	70,704	632,000	8.9	State (U.S.)	D	Bismarck	English
Northern Ireland	5,461	1,605,000	294	Administrative division (U.K.)	D	Belfast	English
Northern Mariana Islands	184	49,000	266	Commonwealth (U.S. protection)	B	Saipan (island)	English, Chamorro, Carolinian
Northern Territory	519,771	172,000	0.3	Territory (Australia)	D	Darwin	English, indigenous
Northwest Territories	1,322,910	56,000	0.1	Territory (Canada)	D	Yellowknife	English, indigenous
† Norway (incl. Svalbard and Jan Mayen)	149,412	4,301,000	29	Constitutional monarchy	A	Oslo	Norwegian, Lapp, Finnish
Nova Scotia	21,425	922,000	43	Province (Canada)	D	Halifax	English
Oceania (incl. Australia)	3,300,000	28,000,000	8.5			....	....
Ohio	44,828	11,155,000	249	State (U.S.)	D	Columbus	English
Oklahoma	69,903	3,242,000	46	State (U.S.)	D	Oklahoma City	English
† Oman	82,030	1,659,000	20	Monarchy	A	Muscat	Arabic, English, Baluchi, Urdu, Indian dialects
Ontario	412,581	10,315,000	25	Province (Canada)	D	Toronto	English
Oregon	98,386	3,009,000	31	State (U.S.)	D	Salem	English

REGION OR POLITICAL DIVISION	Area Sq. Mi.	Est. Pop. 1/1/94	Pop. Per. Sq. Mi.	Form of Government and Ruling Power	Capital	Predominant Languages
† Pakistan (incl. part of Jammu and Kashmir)	339,732	126,090,000	371	Federal Islamic republic A	Islāmābād	English, Urdu, Punjabi, Sindhi, Pashto
Palau (Belau)	196	16,000	82	Republic A	Koror and Melekeok [4]	Angaur, English, Japanese, Palauan, Sonsorolese, Tobi
† Panama	29,157	2,592,000	89	Republic A	Panamá	Spanish, English
† Papua New Guinea	178,704	3,989,000	22	Parliamentary state A	Port Moresby	English, Motu, Pidgin, indigenous
† Paraguay	157,048	4,297,000	27	Republic A	Asunción	Spanish, Guarani
Pennsylvania	46,058	12,145,000	264	State (U.S.) D	Harrisburg	English
† Peru	496,225	23,305,000	47	Republic A	Lima	Quechua, Spanish, Aymara
† Philippines	115,831	66,190,000	571	Republic A	Manila	English, Pilipino, Tagalog
Pitcairn (incl. Dependencies)	19	100	5.3	Dependent territory (U.K.) C	Adamstown	English, Tahitian
† Poland	121,196	38,540,000	318	Republic A	Warsaw (Warszawa)	Polish
† Portugal	35,516	9,961,000	280	Republic A	Lisbon (Lisboa)	Portuguese
Prince Edward Island	2,185	140,000	64	Province (Canada) D	Charlottetown	English
Puerto Rico	3,515	3,801,000	1,081	Commonwealth (U.S. protection) B	San Juan	Spanish, English
† Qatar	4,412	502,000	114	Monarchy A	Doha	Arabic, English
Qinghai	277,994	4,618,000	17	Province (China) D	Xining	Tibetan dialects, Mongolian, Turkish dialects, Chinese (Mandarin)
Quebec	594,860	7,070,000	12	Province (Canada) D	Québec	French, English
Queensland	666,876	3,111,000	4.7	State (Australia) D	Brisbane	English
Reunion	969	643,000	664	Overseas department (France) C	Saint-Denis	French, Creole
Rhode Island	1,545	1,012,000	655	State (U.S.) D	Providence	English
Rhodesia see Zimbabwe	....	....	....	....	....	....
† Romania	91,699	22,770,000	248	Republic A	Bucharest (București)	Romanian, Hungarian, German
† Russia	6,592,849	150,500,000	23	Federal republic A	Moscow (Moskva)	Russian, Tatar, Ukrainian
† Rwanda	10,169	8,196,000	806	Republic A	Kigali	French, Kinyarwanda, Kiswahili
St. Helena (incl. Dependencies)	121	7,000	58	Dependent territory (U.K.) C	Jamestown	English
† St. Kitts and Nevis	104	45,000	433	Parliamentary state A	Basseterre	English
† St. Lucia	238	151,000	634	Parliamentary state A	Castries	English, French
St. Pierre and Miquelon	93	7,000	75	Territorial collectivity (France) C	Saint-Pierre	French
† St. Vincent and the Grenadines	150	115,000	767	Parliamentary state A	Kingstown	English, French
† San Marino	24	24,000	1,000	Republic A	San Marino	Italian
† Sao Tome and Principe	372	125,000	336	Republic A	São Tomé	Portuguese, Fang
Saskatchewan	251,866	1,006,000	4.0	Province (Canada) D	Regina	English
† Saudi Arabia	830,000	16,585,000	20	Monarchy A	Riyadh (Ar Riyāḍ)	Arabic
Scotland	30,421	5,130,000	169	Administrative division (U.K.) D	Edinburgh	English, Scots Gaelic
† Senegal	75,951	8,522,000	112	Republic A	Dakar	French, Wolof, Fulani, Serer, indigenous
† Seychelles	175	72,000	411	Republic A	Victoria	English, French, Creole
Shaanxi	79,151	34,455,000	435	Province (China) D	Xi'an (Sian)	Chinese (Mandarin)
Shandong	59,074	88,450,000	1,497	Province (China) D	Jinan	Chinese (Mandarin)
Shanghai	2,394	13,970,000	5,835	Autonomous city (China) D	Shanghai	Chinese (Wu)
Shanxi	60,232	30,075,000	499	Province (China) D	Taiyuan	Chinese (Mandarin)
Sichuan	220,078	112,250,000	510	Province (China) D	Chengdu	Chinese (Mandarin), Tibetan dialects, Miao-Yao
† Sierra Leone	27,925	4,538,000	163	Transitional military government A	Freetown	English, Krio, Mende, Temne, indigenous
† Singapore	246	2,834,000	11,520	Republic A	Singapore	Chinese (Mandarin), English, Malay, Tamil
† Slovakia	18,933	5,342,000	282	Republic A	Bratislava	Slovak, Hungarian
† Slovenia	7,820	1,986,000	254	Republic A	Ljubljana	Slovenian, Serbo-Croatian
† Solomon Islands	10,954	376,000	34	Parliamentary state A	Honiara	English, indigenous
† Somalia	246,201	6,541,000	27	None A	Mogadishu (Muqdisho)	Arabic, Somali, English, Italian
† South Africa	471,010	42,320,000	90	Republic A	Pretoria, Cape Town, and Bloemfontein	Afrikaans, English, Xhosa, Zulu, other indigenous
South America	6,900,000	304,500,000	44	....	....	....
South Australia	379,925	1,495,000	3.9	State (Australia) D	Adelaide	English
South Carolina	32,007	3,657,000	114	State (U.S.) D	Columbia	English
South Dakota	77,121	726,000	9.4	State (U.S.) D	Pierre	English
South Georgia (incl. Dependencies)	1,450	[1]	....	Dependent territory (U.K.) C	Grytviken Harbour	English
South West Africa see Namibia	....	....	....	....	....	....
† Spain	194,885	38,640,000	198	Constitutional monarchy A	Madrid	Spanish (Castilian), Catalan, Galician, Basque
Spanish North Africa [6]	12	142,000	11,833	Five possessions (Spain) C	....	Spanish, Arabic, Berber dialects
Spanish Sahara see Western Sahara	....	....	....	....	....	....
† Sri Lanka	24,962	17,970,000	720	Socialist republic A	Colombo and Sri Jayawardenapura	English, Sinhala, Tamil
† Sudan	967,500	28,900,000	30	Provisional military government A	Khartoum (Al Kharṭūm)	Arabic, Nubian and other indigenous, English
† Suriname	63,251	418,000	6.6	Republic A	Paramaribo	Dutch, Sranan Tongo, English, Hindustani, Javanese
† Swaziland	6,704	854,000	127	Monarchy A	Mbabane and Lobamba	English, siSwati
† Sweden	173,732	8,747,000	50	Constitutional monarchy A	Stockholm	Swedish, Lapp, Finnish
Switzerland	15,943	7,001,000	439	Federal republic A	Bern (Berne)	German, French, Italian, Romansch
† Syria	71,498	13,695,000	192	Socialist republic A	Damascus (Dimashq)	Arabic, Kurdish, Armenian, Aramaic, Circassian
Taiwan	13,900	20,945,000	1,507	Republic A	T'aipei	Chinese (Mandarin), Taiwanese (Min), Hakka
† Tajikistan	55,251	5,720,000	104	Republic A	Dushanbe	Tajik, Uzbek, Russian
† Tanzania	364,900	27,450,000	75	Republic A	Dar es Salaam and Dodoma	English, Swahili, indigenous
Tasmania	26,178	483,000	18	State (Australia) D	Hobart	English
Tennessee	42,146	5,058,000	120	State (U.S.) D	Nashville	English
Texas	268,601	17,925,000	67	State (U.S.) D	Austin	English, Spanish
† Thailand	198,115	58,960,000	298	Constitutional monarchy A	Bangkok (Krung Thep)	Thai, indigenous
Tianjin (Tientsin)	4,363	9,235,000	2,117	Autonomous city (China) D	Tianjin (Tientsin)	Chinese (Mandarin)
† Togo	21,925	4,142,000	189	Provisional military government A	Lomé	French, Ewe, Mina, Kabye, Dagomba
Tokelau	4.6	1,500	326	Island territory (New Zealand) C	....	English, Tokelauan
Tonga	288	104,000	361	Constitutional monarchy A	Nuku'alofa	Tongan, English
† Trinidad and Tobago	1,980	1,288,000	651	Republic A	Port of Spain	English, Hindi, French, Spanish
Tristan da Cunha	40	300	7.5	Dependency (St. Helena) C	Edinburgh	English
† Tunisia	63,170	8,605,000	136	Republic A	Tunis	Arabic, French
† Turkey	300,948	61,540,000	204	Republic A	Ankara	Turkish, Kurdish, Arabic
† Turkmenistan	188,456	3,935,000	21	Republic A	Ashkhabad	Turkmen, Russian, Uzbek
Turks and Caicos Islands	193	13,000	67	Dependent territory (U.K.) C	Grand Turk	English
Tuvalu	10	10,000	1,000	Parliamentary state A	Funafuti	Tuvaluan, English
† Uganda	93,104	18,425,000	198	Republic A	Kampala	English, Luganda, Swahili, indigenous
† Ukraine	233,090	52,240,000	224	Republic A	Kiev (Kyyiv)	Ukrainian, Russian, Romanian, Polish
† United Arab Emirates	32,278	2,692,000	83	Federation of monarchs A	Abū Ẓaby (Abu Dhabi)	Arabic, Farsi, English, Hindi, Urdu
† United Kingdom	94,249	57,960,000	615	Parliamentary monarchy A	London	English, Welsh, Scots Gaelic

REGION OR POLITICAL DIVISION	Area Sq. Mi.	Est. Pop. 1/1/94	Pop. Per. Sq. Mi.	Form of Government and Ruling Power		Capital	Predominant Languages
† United States	3,787,425	259,390,000	68	Federal republic	A	Washington	English, Spanish
Upper Volta see Burkina Faso							
† Uruguay	68,500	3,181,000	46	Republic	A	Montevideo	Spanish
Utah	84,904	1,842,000	22	State (U.S.)	D	Salt Lake City	English
† Uzbekistan	172,742	22,240,000	129	Republic	A	Tashkent	Uzbek, Russian
† Vanuatu	4,707	160,000	34	Republic	A	Port-Vila	Bislama, English, French
Vatican City	0.2	900	4,500	Monarchical-sacerdotal state	A	Vatican City	Italian, Latin, other
† Venezuela	352,145	20,460,000	58	Federal republic	A	Caracas	Spanish, Amerindian
Vermont	9,615	585,000	61	State (U.S.)	D	Montpelier	English
Victoria	87,877	4,566,000	52	State (Australia)	D	Melbourne	English
† Vietnam	127,428	72,080,000	566	Socialist republic	A	Hanoi	Vietnamese, French, Chinese, English, Khmer, indigenous
Virginia	42,769	6,485,000	152	State (U.S.)	D	Richmond	English
Virgin Islands (U.S.)	133	97,000	729	Unincorporated territory (U.S.)	C	Charlotte Amalie	English, Spanish, Creole
Wake Island	3.0	300	100	Unincorporated territory (U.S.)	C		English
Wales	8,015	2,905,000	362	Administrative division (U.K.)	D	Cardiff	English, Welsh Gaelic
Wallis and Futuna	98	14,000	143	Overseas territory (France)	C	Mata-Utu	French, Wallisian
Washington	71,303	5,188,000	73	State (U.S.)	D	Olympia	English
West Bank (incl. Jericho and East Jerusalem)	2,347	1,460,000	622	Israeli territory with limited self-government			Arabic, Hebrew
Western Australia	975,101	1,703,000	1.7	State (Australia)	D	Perth	English
Western Sahara	102,703	208,000	2.0	Occupied by Morocco	C		Arabic
† Western Samoa	1,093	168,000	154	Constitutional monarchy	A	Apia	English, Samoan
West Virginia	24,231	1,816,000	75	State (U.S.)	D	Charleston	English
Wisconsin	65,503	5,058,000	77	State (U.S.)	D	Madison	English
Wyoming	97,818	467,000	4.8	State (U.S.)	D	Cheyenne	English
Xinjiang Uygur (Sinkiang)	617,764	15,865,000	26	Autonomous region (China)	D	Ürümqi	Turkish dialects, Mongolian, Tungus, English
Xizang (Tibet)	471,045	2,250,000	4.8	Autonomous region (China)	D	Lhasa	Tibetan dialects
† Yemen	203,850	10,840,000	53	Republic	A	San'ā'	Arabic
Yugoslavia	39,449	10,730,000	272	Republic	A	Belgrade (Beograd)	Serbo-Croatian 95%, Albanian 5%
Yukon Territory	186,661	28,000	0.2	Territory (Canada)	D	Whitehorse	English, Inuktitut, indigenous
Yunnan	152,124	38,720,000	255	Province (China)	D	Kunming	Chinese (Mandarin), Tibetan dialects, Khmer, Miao-Yao
† Zaire	905,446	41,675,000	46	Republic	A	Kinshasa	French, Kikongo, Lingala, Swahili, Tshiluba, Kingwana
† Zambia	290,586	8,625,000	30	Republic	A	Lusaka	English, Tonga, Lozi, other indigenous
Zhejiang	39,305	43,455,000	1,106	Province (China)	D	Hangzhou	Chinese dialects
† Zimbabwe	150,873	10,605,000	70	Republic	A	Harare (Salisbury)	English, Shona, Sindebele
WORLD	57,900,000	5,556,000,000	96				

† Member of the United Nations (1994).
. . . None, or not applicable.
(1) No permanent population.
(2) North Cyprus unilaterally declared its independence from Cyprus in 1983.
(3) Claimed by Argentina.
(4) Future capital.
(5) Claimed by Comoros.
(6) Comprises Ceuta, Melilla, and several small islands.

WORLD COMPARISONS

General Information

Equatorial diameter of the earth, 7,926.38 miles.
Polar diameter of the earth, 7,899.80 miles.
Mean diameter of the earth, 7,917.52 miles.
Equatorial circumference of the earth, 24,901.46 miles.
Polar circumference of the earth, 24,855.34 miles.
Mean distance from the earth to the sun, 93,020,000 miles.
Mean distance from the earth to the moon, 238,857 miles.
Total area of the earth, 197,000,000 square miles.

Highest elevation on the earth's surface, Mt. Everest, Asia, 29,028 feet.
Lowest elevation on the earth's land surface, shores of the Dead Sea, Asia, 1,312 feet below sea level.
Greatest known depth of the ocean, southwest of Guam, Pacific Ocean, 35,810 feet.
Total land area of the earth (incl. inland water and Antarctica), 57,900,000 square miles.

Area of Africa, 11,700,000 square miles.
Area of Antarctica, 5,400,000 square miles.
Area of Asia, 17,300,000 square miles.
Area of Europe, 3,800,000 square miles.
Area of North America, 9,500,000 square miles.
Area of Oceania (incl. Australia) 3,300,000 square miles.
Area of South America, 6,900,000 square miles.
Population of the earth (est. 1/1/94), 5,556,000,000.

Principal Islands and Their Areas

ISLAND	Area (Sq. Mi.)
Baffin I., Canada	195,928
Banks I., Canada	27,038
Borneo (Kalimantan), Asia	287,300
Bougainville, Papua New Guinea	3,600
Cape Breton I., Canada	3,981
Celebes (Sulawesi), Indonesia	73,057
Ceram (Seram), Indonesia	7,191
Corsica, France	3,367
Crete, Greece	3,190
Cuba, N. America	42,804
Cyprus, Asia	3,572
Devon I., Canada	21,331
Ellesmere I., Canada	75,767
Flores, Indonesia	5,502
Great Britain, U.K.	88,816
Greenland, N. America	840,004
Guadalcanal, Solomon Is.	2,060
Hainan Dao, China	13,200
Hawaii, U.S.	4,021
Hispaniola, N. America	29,300
Hokkaidō, Japan	32,245
Honshū, Japan	89,176
Iceland, Europe	39,769
Ireland, Europe	32,600
Jamaica, N. America	4,244
Java (Jawa), Indonesia	51,038
Kodiak I., U.S.	3,670
Kyūshū, Japan	17,129
Leyte, Philippines	2,785
Long Island, U.S.	1,401
Luzon, Philippines	40,420
Madagascar, Africa	226,658
Melville I., Canada	16,274
Mindanao, Philippines	36,537
Mindoro, Philippines	3,759
Negros, Philippines	4,907
New Britain, Papua New Guinea	14,093
New Caledonia, Oceania	6,467
Newfoundland, Canada	42,031
New Guinea, Asia-Oceania	309,000
New Ireland, Papua New Guinea	3,500
North East Land, Norway	6,350
North I., New Zealand	44,702
Novaya Zemlya, Russia	31,892
Palawan, Philippines	4,550
Panay, Philippines	4,446
Prince of Wales I., Canada	12,872
Puerto Rico, N. America	3,500
Sakhalin, Russia	29,498
Samar, Philippines	5,100
Sardinia, Italy	9,301
Shikoku, Japan	7,258
Sicily, Italy	9,927
Somerset I., Canada	9,570
Southampton I., Canada	15,913
South I., New Zealand	58,384
Spitsbergen, Norway	15,260
Sri Lanka, Asia	24,962
Sumatra (Sumatera), Indonesia	182,860
Taiwan, Asia	13,900
Tasmania, Australia	26,200
Tierra del Fuego, S. America	18,600
Timor, Indonesia	5,743
Vancouver I., Canada	12,079
Victoria I., Canada	83,897
Vrangelya (Wrangel), Russia	2,819

Principal Lakes, Oceans, Seas, and Their Areas

LAKE Country	Area (Sq. Mi.)
Arabian Sea	1,492,000
Aral Sea, Kazakhstan-Uzbekistan	14,900
Arctic Ocean	5,400,000
Athabasca, L., Canada	3,064
Atlantic Ocean	31,800,000
Balqash köl', (L. Balkhash) Kazakhstan	7,066
Baltic Sea, Europe	163,000
Baykal, Ozero, (L. Baikal) Russia	12,162
Bering Sea, Asia-N.A.	876,000
Black Sea, Europe-Asia	178,000
Caribbean Sea, N.A.-S.A.	1,063,000
Caspian Sea, Asia-Europe	143,244
Chad, L., Cameroon-Chad-Nigeria	6,300
Erie, L., Canada-U.S.	9,910
Eyre, L., Australia	3,700
Gairdner, L., Australia	1,660
Great Bear Lake, Canada	12,096
Great Salt Lake, U.S.	1,680
Great Slave Lake, Canada	11,030
Hudson Bay, Canada	475,000
Huron, L., Canada-U.S.	23,000
Indian Ocean	28,900,000
Japan, Sea of, Asia	389,000
Koko Nor, (Qinghai Hu) China	1,770
Ladozhskoye Ozero, (L. Ladoga) Russia	6,834
Manitoba, L., Canada	1,785
Mediterranean Sea, Europe-Africa-Asia	967,000
Mexico, Gulf of, N. America	596,000
Michigan, L., U.S.	22,300
Nicaragua, Lago de, Nicaragua	3,150
North Sea, Europe	222,000
Nyasa, L., Malawi-Mozambique-Tanzania	11,150
Onezhskoye Ozero, (L. Onega) Russia	3,753
Ontario, L., Canada-U.S.	7,540
Pacific Ocean	63,800,000
Red Sea, Africa-Asia	169,000
Rudolf, L., Ethiopia-Kenya	2,473
Superior, L., Canada-U.S.	31,700
Tanganyika, L., Africa	12,350
Titicaca, Lago, Bolivia-Peru	3,200
Torrens, L., Australia	2,280
Vänern, (L.) Sweden	2,156
Van Gölü, (L.) Turkey	1,434
Victoria, L., Kenya-Tanzania-Uganda	26,820
Winnipeg, L., Canada	9,416
Winnipegosis, L., Canada	2,075
Yellow Sea, China-Korea	480,000

Principal Mountains and Their Heights

MOUNTAIN Country	Elev. (Ft.)
Aconcagua, Cerro, Argentina	22,831
Annapurna, Nepal	26,504
Api, Nepal	23,399
Apo, Philippines	9,692
Ararat, Mt., Turkey	16,854
Ayers Rock, Australia	2,844
Barú, Volcán, Panama	11,491
Bangueta, Mt., Papua New Guinea	13,520
Belukha, Gora, Kazakhstan-Russia	14,783
Bia, Phu, Laos	9,249
Blanc, Mont, (Monte Bianco) France-Italy	15,771
Blanca Pk., Colorado, U.S.	14,345
Bolívar, Venezuela	16,427
Bonete, Cerro, Argentina	22,546
Borah Pk., Idaho, U.S.	12,662
Boundary Pk., Nevada, U.S.	13,140
Cameroon Mtn., Cameroon	13,451
Carrauntoohil, Ireland	3,406
Chaltel, Cerro, (Monte Fitzroy) Argentina-Chile	10,958
Chimborazo, Ecuador	20,702
Chirripó, Cerro, Costa Rica	12,530
Colima, Nevado de, Mexico	13,911
Cook, Mt., New Zealand	12,316
Cotopaxi, Ecuador	19,347
Cristóbal Colón, Pico, Colombia	19,029
Damāvand, Qolleh-ye, Iran	18,386
Dhawalāgiri, Nepal	26,810
Duarte, Pico, Dominican Rep.	10,417
Dufourspitze, (Monte Rosa) Italy-Switzerland	15,203
Elbert, Mt., Colorado, U.S.	14,433
El'brus, Gora, Russia	18,510
Elgon, Mt., Kenya-Uganda	14,178
Erciyeş Dağı, Turkey	12,848
Etna, Mt., Italy	10,902
Everest, Mt., China-Nepal	29,028
Fairweather, Mt., Alaska-Canada	15,300
Foraker, Mt., Alaska, U.S.	17,400
Fuji-san, Japan	12,388
Fūlādī, Kūh-e, Afghanistan	16,872
Galdhøpiggen, Norway	8,100
Gannett Pk., Wyoming, U.S.	13,785
Gasherbrum, China-Pakistan	26,470
Gerlachovský Stit, Slovakia	8,710
Giluwe, Mt., Papua New Guinea	14,331
Gongga Shan, China	24,790
Grand Teton Mtn., Wyoming, U.S.	13,770
Grossglockner, Austria	12,461
Hadūr Shu'ayb, Yemen	12,336
Haleakala Crater, Hawaii, U.S.	10,023
Hekla, Iceland	4,892
Hood, Mt., Oregon, U.S.	11,239
Hsinkao Shan, Taiwan	13,113
Huascarán, Nevado, Peru	22,205
Huila, Nevado de, Colombia	18,865
Hvannadalshnúkur, Iceland	6,952
Illampu, Nevado, Bolivia	21,066
Illimani, Nevado, Bolivia	20,741
Iztaccíhuatl, Mexico	17,930
Jaya, Puncak, Indonesia	16,503
Jungfrau, Switzerland	13,642
K2, (Godwin Austen) China-Pakistan	28,250
Kāmet, China-India	25,447
Kānchenjunga, India- Nepal	28,208
Kātrīnā, Jabal, Egypt	8,668
Kebnekaise, Sweden	6,962
Kenya, Mt., (Kirinyaga) Kenya	17,058
Kerinci, Gunung, Indonesia	12,467
Kilimanjaro, Tanzania	19,340
Kinabalu, Gunong, Malaysia	13,455
Klyuchevskaya, Russia	15,584
Kommunizma, Pik, Tajikistan	24,590
Kosciusko, Mt., Australia	7,310
Koussi, Emi, Chad	11,204
Kula Kangri, Bhutan	24,784
La Selle, Massif de, Haiti	8,793
Lassen Pk., California, U.S.	10,457
Llullaillaco, Volcán, Argentina-Chile	22,110
Logan, Mt., Canada	19,551
Longs Pk., Colorado, U.S.	14,255
Makālu, China-Nepal	27,825
Margherita Peak, Zaire-Uganda	16,763
Markham, Mt., Antarctica	14,049
Maromokotro, Madagascar	9,436
Massive, Mt., Colorado, U.S.	14,421
Matterhorn, Italy-Switzerland	14,692
Mauna Kea, Hawaii, U.S.	13,796
Mauna Loa, Hawaii, U.S.	13,679
Mayon Volcano, Philippines	7,943
McKinley, Mt., Alaska, U.S.	20,320
Meron, Hare, Israel	3,693
Meru, Mt., Tanzania	14,978
Misti, Volcán, Peru	19,101
Mitchell, Mt., North Carolina, U.S.	6,684
Môco, Serra do, Angola	8,596
Moldoveanu, Romania	8,343
Mulhacén, Spain (continental)	11,424
Musala, Bulgaria	9,596
Muztag, China	25,338
Muztagata, China	24,757
Namjagbarwa Feng, China	25,446
Nanda Devi, India	25,645
Nanga Parbat, Pakistan	26,650
Narodnaya, Gora, Russia	6,217
Nevis, Ben, United Kingdom	4,406
Ojos del Salado, Nevado, Argentina-Chile	22,615
Ólimbos, Cyprus	6,401
Ólimbos, Greece	9,570
Olympus, Mt., Washington, U.S.	7,965
Orizaba, Pico de, Mexico	18,406
Paektu San, North Korea-China	9,003
Paricutín, Mexico	9,186
Parnassós, Greece	8,061
Pelée, Montagne, Martinique	4,800
Pidurutalagala, Sri Lanka	8,281
Pikes Pk., Colorado, U.S.	14,110
Pobedy, pik, China-Kyrgyzstan	24,406
Popocatépetl, Volcán, Mexico	17,930
Pulog, Mt., Philippines	9,606
Rainier, Mt., Washington, U.S.	14,410
Ramm, Jabal, Jordan	5,755
Ras Dashen Terara, Ethiopia	15,158
Rinjani, Gunung, Indonesia	12,224
Robson, Mt., Canada	12,972
Roraima, Mt., Brazil-Guyana-Venezuela	9,452
Ruapehu, Mt., New Zealand	9,177
St. Elias, Mt., Alaska, U.S.-Canada	18,008
Sajama, Nevado, Bolivia	21,391
Semeru, Gunung, Indonesia	12,060
Shām, Jabal ash, Oman	9,957
Shasta, Mt., California, U.S.	14,162
Snowdon, Wales, U.K.	3,560
Tahat, Algeria	9,541
Tajumulco (Vol.), Guatemala	13,845
Taranaki, Mt., New Zealand	8,260
Tirich Mīr, Pakistan	25,230
Tomanivi (Victoria), (Victoria) Fiji	4,341
Toubkal, Jebel, Morocco	13,665
Triglav, Slovenia	9,396
Trikora, Puncak, Indonesia	15,584
Tupungato, Cerro, Argentina-Chile	21,555
Turquino, Pico, Cuba	6,470
Uncompahgre Pk., Colorado, U.S.	14,301
Vesuvio, (Vesuvius) Italy	4,190
Victoria, Mt., Papua New Guinea	13,238
Vinson Massif, Antarctica	16,066
Waddington, Mt., Canada	13,163
Washington, Mt., New Hampshire, U.S.	6,288
Whitney, Mt., California, U.S.	14,494
Wilhelm, Mt., Papua New Guinea	14,793
Wrangell, Mt., Alaska, U.S.	14,163
Xixabangma Feng (Gosainthan), (Gosainthan) China	26,286
Zugspitze, Austria-Germany	9,721

Principal Rivers and Their Lengths

RIVER Continent	Length (Mi.)
Albany, N. America	610
Aldan, Asia	1,412
Amazonas-Ucayali, S. America	4,000
Amu Darya, Asia	1,578
Amur, Asia	2,744
Amur-Argun, Asia	2,761
Araguaia, S. America	1,400
Arkansas, N. America	1,459
Athabasca, N. America	765
Brahmaputra, Asia	1,770
Branco, S. America	580
Brazos, N. America	870
Canadian, N. America	906
Churchill, N. America	1,000
Colorado, N. America (U.S.-Mexico)	1,450
Columbia, N. America	1,243
Congo, (Zaïre) Africa	2,880
Cumberland, N. America	720
Danube, Europe	1,776
Darling, Australia	864
Dnepr, (Dnieper) Europe	1,367
Dniester, Europe	840
Don, Europe	1,162
Elbe, Europe	724
Euphrates, Asia	1,510
Fraser, N. America	851
Ganges, Asia	1,560
Gila, N. America	630
Godāvari, Asia	930
Green, N. America	730
Huang, (Yellow) Asia	3,395
Indus, Asia	1,800
Irrawaddy, Asia	1,300
Juruá, S. America	1,250
Kama, Europe	1,122
Kasai, Africa	1,338
Kolyma, Asia	1,323
Lena, Asia	2,734
Limpopo, Africa	1,100
Loire, Europe	634
Mackenzie, N. America	2,635
Madeira, S. America	2,013
Magdalena, S. America	950
Marañón, S. America	1,000
Mekong, Asia	2,600
Meuse, Europe	590
Mississippi, N. America	2,348
Mississippi-Missouri, N. America	3,740
Missouri, N. America	2,315
Murray, Australia	1,566
Negro, S. America	1,300
Neman, Europe	582
Niger, Africa	2,600
Nile, Africa	4,145
North Platte, N. America	618
Ob'-Irtysh, Asia	3,362
Oder, Europe	567
Ohio, N. America	981
Oka, Europe	900
Orange, Africa	1,398
Orinoco, S. America	1,600
Ottawa, N. America	790
Paraguay, S. America	1,610
Paraná, S. America	2,800
Parnaíba, S. America	850
Peace, N. America	1,195
Pechora, Europe	1,124
Pecos, N. America	735
Pilcomayo, S. America	1,550
Plata-Paraná, S. America	3,030
Purús, S. America	1,860
Red, N. America	1,270
Rhine, Europe	820
Rhône, Europe	505
Rio Grande, N. America	1,885
Roosevelt, S. America	950
St. Lawrence, N. America	800
Salado, S. America	900
Salween, (Nu) Asia	1,750
São Francisco, S. America	1,988
Saskatchewan-Bow, N. America	1,205
Sava, Europe	584
Snake, N. America	1,038
Sungari, (Songhua) Asia	1,140
Syr Darya, Asia	1,370
Tagus, Europe	625
Tarim, Asia	1,328
Tennessee, N. America	652
Tigris, Asia	1,180
Tisa, Europe	607
Tobol, Asia	989
Tocantins, S. America	1,640
Ucayali, S. America	1,220
Ural, Asia	1,509
Uruguay, S. America	1,025
Verkhnyaya Tunguska, (Angara) Asia	1,105
Vilyuy, Asia	1,647
Volga, Europe	2,194
White, N. America (Ark.-Mo.)	720
Wisła (Vistula), Europe	651
Xiang, Asia	930
Xingu, S. America	1,230
Yangtze, (Chang) Asia	3,915
Yellowstone, N. America	671
Yenisey, Asia	2,543
Yukon, N. America	1,979
Zambezi, Africa	1,700

PRINCIPAL CITIES OF THE WORLD

Abidjan, Cote d'Ivoire	1,929,079
Accra, Ghana (1,390,000)	949,113
Addis Ababa, Ethiopia (1,990,000)	1,912,500
Adelaide, Australia (1,023,597)	14,843
Ahmadābād, India (3,312,216)	2,876,710
Aleppo (Halab), Syria (1,335,000)	1,261,000
Alexandria (Al Iskandarīyah), Egypt (3,350,000)	2,926,859
Algiers (El Djazaïr), Algeria (2,547,983)	1,507,241
Alma-Ata (Almaty), Kazakhstan (1,190,000)	1,156,200
'Ammān, Jordan (1,625,000)	936,300
Amsterdam, Netherlands (1,875,000)	713,407
Ankara (Angora), Turkey (2,650,000)	2,559,471
Antananarivo, Madagascar	1,250,000
Antwerp (Antwerpen), Belgium (1,100,000)	479,748
Asmera, Eritrea	358,100
Asunción, Paraguay (700,000)	502,426
Athens (Athínai), Greece (3,096,775)	748,110
Atlanta, Georgia, U.S. (2,833,511)	394,017
Auckland, New Zealand (855,571)	315,668
Baghdād, Iraq	3,841,268
Baku (Bakı), Azerbaijan (2,020,000)	1,080,500
Baltimore, Maryland, U.S. (2,382,172)	736,014
Bamako, Mali	658,275
Bandung, Indonesia (2,220,000)	2,058,122
Bangalore, India (4,130,288)	2,660,088
Bangkok (Krung Thep), Thailand (7,060,000)	5,620,591
Barcelona, Spain (4,040,000)	1,714,355
Beijing (Peking), China (7,320,000)	6,710,000
Beirut, Lebanon (1,675,000)	509,000
Belém, Brazil (1,355,000)	765,476
Belfast, N. Ireland, U.K. (685,000)	295,100
Belgrade (Beograd), Yugoslavia (1,554,826)	1,136,786
Belo Horizonte, Brazil (3,340,000)	1,529,566
Berlin, Germany (4,150,000)	3,433,695
Birmingham, England, U.K. (2,675,000)	1,013,995
Bishkek, Kyrgyzstan	631,300
Bombay, India (12,596,243)	9,925,891
Bonn, Germany (575,000)	292,234
Boston, Massachusetts, U.S. (4,171,643)	574,283
Brasília, Brazil	1,513,470
Bratislava, Slovakia	441,453
Brazzaville, Congo	693,712
Bremen, Germany (790,000)	551,219
Brisbane, Australia (1,334,017)	751,115
Brussels (Bruxelles), Belgium (2,385,000)	136,920
Bucharest (București), Romania (2,300,000)	2,064,474
Budapest, Hungary (2,515,000)	2,016,774
Buenos Aires, Argentina (11,000,000)	2,960,976
Cairo (Al Qāhirah), Egypt (9,300,000)	6,068,695
Calcutta, India (11,021,918)	4,399,819
Cali, Colombia (1,400,000)	1,350,565
Canberra, Australia (303,846)	276,162
Cape Town, South Africa (1,900,000)	854,616
Caracas, Venezuela (4,000,000)	1,822,465
Casablanca, Morocco (2,475,000)	2,139,204
Changchun, China (2,000,000†)	1,822,000
Chelyabinsk, Russia (1,325,000)	1,148,300
Chengdu, China (2,960,000†)	1,884,000
Chicago, Illinois, U.S. (8,065,633)	2,783,726
Chișinău (Kishinev), Moldova	676,700
Chittagong, Bangladesh (2,342,662)	1,566,070
Chongqing (Chungking), China (2,890,000†)	2,502,000
Cincinnati, Ohio, U.S. (1,744,124)	364,040
Cleveland, Ohio, U.S. (2,759,823)	505,616
Cologne (Köln), Germany (1,810,000)	953,551
Colombo, Sri Lanka (2,050,000)	612,000
Columbus, Ohio, U.S. (1,377,419)	632,910
Conakry, Guinea	800,000
Copenhagen (København), Denmark (1,670,000)	464,566
Cordoba, Argentina (1,260,000)	1,148,305
Curitiba, Brazil (1,815,000)	841,882
Dakar, Senegal	1,490,450
Dalian (Lüda), China	2,280,000
Dallas, Texas, U.S. (3,885,415)	1,006,877
Damascus (Dimashq), Syria (2,000,000)	1,326,000
Dar es Salaam, Tanzania	1,096,000
Delhi, India (8,419,084)	7,206,704
Denver, Colorado, U.S. (1,848,319)	467,610
Detroit, Michigan, U.S. (4,665,236)	1,027,974
Dhaka (Dacca), Bangladesh (6,537,308)	3,637,892
Dnipropetrovs'k, Ukraine (1,600,000)	1,189,300
Donets'k, Ukraine (2,125,000)	1,121,300
Dresden, Germany (870,000)	490,571
Dublin (Baile Átha Cliath), Ireland (1,140,000)	502,749
Durban, South Africa (1,740,000)	715,669
Düsseldorf, Germany (1,225,000)	575,794
Edinburgh, Scotland, U.K. (630,000)	434,520
Essen, Germany (5,050,000)	626,973
Faisalabad, Pakistan	1,104,209
Florence (Firenze), Italy (640,000)	402,316
Fortaleza, Brazil (2,040,000)	743,335
Frankfurt am Main, Germany (1,935,000)	644,865
Fukuoka, Japan (1,750,000)	1,237,067
Gdańsk (Danzig), Poland (909,000)	465,100
Geneva (Génève), Switzerland (470,000)	171,042
Genoa (Genova), Italy (805,000)	675,639
Glasgow, Scotland, U.K. (1,800,000)	689,210
Goiânia, Brazil (1,130,000)	912,136
Guadalajara, Mexico (2,430,000)	1,650,042
Guangzhou (Canton), China (3,420,000†)	3,100,000
Guatemala, Guatemala (1,400,000)	1,057,210
Guayaquil, Ecuador	1,508,444
Hamburg, Germany (2,385,000)	1,652,363
Hannover, Germany (1,000,000)	513,010
Hanoi, Vietnam (1,275,000)	905,939
Harare, Zimbabwe (890,000)	681,000
Harbin, China	2,710,000
Havana (La Habana), Cuba (2,210,000)	2,119,059
Helsinki, Finland (1,040,000)	497,542
Hiroshima, Japan (1,575,000)	1,085,705
Ho Chi Minh City (Saigon), Vietnam (3,300,000)	2,796,229
Hong Kong, Hong Kong (4,770,000)	1,250,993
Honolulu, Hawaii, U.S. (836,231)	365,272
Houston, Texas, U.S. (3,711,043)	1,630,553
Hyderābād, India (4,344,437)	3,058,093
Ibadan, Nigeria	1,144,000
Indianapolis, Indiana, U.S. (1,249,822)	731,327
İstanbul, Turkey (7,550,000)	6,620,241
İzmir, Turkey (1,900,000)	1,757,414
Jakarta, Indonesia (10,200,000)	8,227,746
Jerusalem, Israel (560,000)	524,500
Jiddah, Saudi Arabia	1,300,000
Jinan, China (2,140,000†)	1,546,000
Johannesburg, South Africa (4,000,000)	712,507
Kābul, Afghanistan	1,424,400
Kampala, Uganda	773,463
Kānpur, India (2,029,889)	1,874,409
Kansas City, Missouri, U.S. (1,566,280)	435,146
Kaohsiung, Taiwan (1,900,000)	1,401,239
Karāchi, Pakistan (5,300,000)	4,901,627
Katowice, Poland (2,778,000)	366,800
Kazan', Russia (1,165,000)	1,107,300
Kharkiv, Ukraine (2,050,000)	1,622,800
Khartoum (Al Kharṭūm), Sudan (1,450,000)	473,597
Kiev (Kyyiv), Ukraine (3,250,000)	2,635,000
Kingston, Jamaica (820,000)	661,600
Kinshasa, Zaire	3,000,000
Kitakyūshū, Japan (1,525,000)	1,026,455
Kōbe, Japan (*Ōsaka)	1,477,410
Kuala Lumpur, Malaysia (1,475,000)	919,610
Kunming, China (1,550,000†)	1,310,000
Kuwait (Al Kuwayt), Kuwait (1,375,000)	44,335
Kyōto, Japan (*Ōsaka)	1,461,103
Lagos, Nigeria (3,800,000)	1,213,000
Lahore, Pakistan (3,025,000)	2,707,215
La Paz, Bolivia	1,125,600
Leeds, England, U.K. (1,540,000)	445,242
Liège, Belgium (750,000)	200,891
Lille, France (1,050,000)	172,142
Lima, Peru (4,608,010)	371,122
Lisbon (Lisboa), Portugal (2,250,000)	807,167
Liverpool, England, U.K. (1,525,000)	538,809
London, England, U.K. (11,100,000)	6,574,009
Los Angeles, California, U.S. (14,531,529)	3,485,398
Luanda, Angola	1,459,900
Lucknow, India (1,669,204)	1,619,115
Lusaka, Zambia	982,362
Lyon, France (1,335,000)	415,487
Madras, India (5,421,985)	3,841,396
Madrid, Spain (4,650,000)	3,102,846
Managua, Nicaragua	682,000
Manaus, Brazil	1,005,634
Manchester, England, U.K. (2,775,000)	437,612
Manila, Philippines (9,650,000)	1,598,918
Mannheim, Germany (1,525,000)	310,411
Maputo, Mozambique	1,069,727
Maracaibo, Venezuela	1,249,670
Marseille, France (1,225,000)	800,550
Mashhad, Iran	1,463,508
Mecca (Makkah), Saudi Arabia	550,000
Medan, Indonesia	1,730,052
Medellín, Colombia (2,095,000)	1,468,089
Melbourne, Australia (3,022,439)	60,475
Memphis, Tennessee, U.S. (981,747)	610,337
Mexico City, Mexico (14,100,000)	8,235,744
Miami, Florida, U.S. (3,192,582)	358,548
Milan (Milano), Italy (3,750,000)	1,371,008
Milwaukee, Wisconsin, U.S. (1,607,183)	628,088
Minneapolis, Minnesota, U.S. (2,464,124)	368,383
Minsk, Belarus (1,694,000)	1,633,600
Mogadishu, Somalia	600,000
Monterrey, Mexico (2,015,000)	1,068,996
Montevideo, Uruguay (1,550,000)	1,251,647
Montréal, Canada (3,127,242)	1,017,666
Moscow (Moskva), Russia (13,150,000)	8,801,500
Munich (München), Germany (1,900,000)	1,229,026
Nagoya, Japan (4,800,000)	2,154,793
Nāgpur, India (1,664,006)	1,624,752
Nairobi, Kenya	1,505,000
Nanjing, China	2,390,000
Naples (Napoli), Italy (2,875,000)	1,204,601
Nashville, Tennessee, U.S. (985,026)	487,969
New Delhi, India (*Delhi)	301,297
New Kowloon, Hong Kong (*Hong Kong)	1,526,910
New Orleans, Louisiana, U.S. (1,238,816)	496,938
New York, New York, U.S. (18,087,251)	7,322,564
Nizhniy Novgorod, Russia (2,025,000)	1,445,000
Novosibirsk, Russia (1,600,000)	1,446,300
Nürnberg, Germany (1,065,000)	493,692
Odesa, Ukraine (1,185,000)	1,100,700
Oklahoma City, Oklahoma, U.S. (958,839)	444,719
Omsk, Russia (1,190,000)	1,166,800
Ōsaka, Japan (16,900,000)	2,623,801
Oslo, Norway (720,000)	452,415
Ottawa, Canada (920,857)	313,987
Panamá, Panama (770,000)	411,549
Paris, France (10,275,000)	2,152,423
Perm', Russia (1,180,000)	1,110,400
Perth, Australia (1,143,249)	80,517
Philadelphia, Pennsylvania, U.S. (5,899,345)	1,585,577
Phnum Pénh (Phnom Penh), Cambodia	620,000
Phoenix, Arizona, U.S. (2,122,101)	983,403
Pittsburgh, Pennsylvania, U.S. (2,242,798)	369,879
Port-au-Prince, Haiti (880,000)	797,000
Portland, Oregon, U.S. (1,477,895)	437,319
Porto Alegre, Brazil (2,850,000)	1,247,352
Prague (Praha), Czech Republic (1,328,000)	1,212,010
Pretoria, South Africa (1,100,000)	525,583
Providence, Rhode Island, U.S. (1,141,510)	160,728
Puebla, Mexico (1,200,000)	1,007,170
Pune, India (2,493,987)	1,566,651
Pusan, South Korea (3,800,000)	3,797,566
P'yŏngyang, North Korea	2,355,000
Qingdao, China	1,300,000
Québec, Canada (645,550)	167,517
Quezon City, Philippines (*Manila)	1,666,766
Quito, Ecuador (1,300,000)	1,100,847
Rabat, Morocco (980,000)	518,616
Rangoon (Yangon), Myanmar (2,800,000)	2,705,039
Recife, Brazil (2,880,000)	1,296,995
Rīga, Latvia (1,005,000)	910,200
Rio de Janerio, Brazil (11,050,000)	5,473,909
Riyadh, Saudi Arabia	1,250,000
Rome (Roma), Italy (3,175,000)	2,693,383
Rosario, Argentina (1,190,000)	894,645
Rostov-na-Donu, Russia (1,165,000)	1,027,600
Rotterdam, Netherlands (1,120,000)	589,707
St. Louis, Missouri, U.S. (2,444,099)	396,685
St. Petersburg (Leningrad), Russia (5,525,000)	4,466,800
Salt Lake City, Utah, U.S. (1,072,227)	159,936
Salvador, Brazil (2,340,000)	2,070,296
Samara, Russia (1,505,000)	1,257,300
San Antonio, Texas, U.S. (1,302,099)	935,933
San Diego, California, U.S. (2,949,000)	1,110,549
San Francisco, California, U.S. (6,253,311)	723,959
San José, Costa Rica (1,355,000)	278,600
San Juan, Puerto Rico (1,877,000)	426,832
San Salvador, El Salvador (920,000)	462,652
Santa Fe de Bogotá, Colombia (4,260,000)	3,982,941
Santiago, Chile (4,100,000)	232,667
Santo Domingo, Dominican Rep.	2,411,900
Santos, Brazil (1,165,000)	415,554
São Paulo, Brazil (16,925,000)	9,393,753
Sapporo, Japan (1,900,000)	1,671,742
Sarajevo, Bosnia and Herzegovina (479,688†)	341,200
Saratov, Russia (1,155,000)	911,100
Seattle, Washington, U.S. (2,559,164)	516,259
Seoul (Sŏul), South Korea (15,850,000)	10,627,790
Shanghai, China (9,300,000)	7,220,000
Shenyang (Mukden), China (4,370,000†)	3,910,000
Singapore, Singapore (3,025,000)	2,690,100
Skopje, Macedonia (547,214†)	444,900
Sofia (Sofiya), Bulgaria (1,205,000)	1,136,875
Stockholm, Sweden (1,491,726)	674,452
Stuttgart, Germany (2,005,000)	579,988
Surabaya, Indonesia	2,473,272
Sydney, Australia (3,538,749)	13,501
Taegu, South Korea	2,228,834
T'aipei, Taiwan (6,200,000)	2,706,453
Taiyuan, China (1,980,000†)	1,700,000
Tampa, Florida, U.S. (2,067,959)	280,015
Tashkent, Uzbekistan (2,325,000)	2,113,300
Tbilisi, Georgia (1,460,000)	1,279,000
Tegucigalpa, Honduras	576,661
Tehrān, Iran (7,500,000)	6,042,584
Tel Aviv-Yafo, Israel (1,735,000)	339,400
The Hague ('s-Gravenhage), Netherlands (773,000)	445,287
Tianjin (Tientsin), China (5,540,000†)	4,950,000
Tiranë, Albania	238,100
Tōkyō, Japan (30,300,000)	8,163,573
Toronto, Canada (3,893,046)	635,395
Tripoli (Tarābulus), Libya	591,062
Tunis, Tunisia (1,225,000)	596,654
Turin (Torino), Italy (1,550,000)	961,916
Ufa, Russia (1,118,000)	1,097,000
Ulan Bator, Mongolia	548,400
Valencia, Spain (1,270,000)	743,933
Vancouver, Canada (1,602,502)	471,844
Venice (Venezia), Italy (420,000)	85,100
Vienna (Wien), Austria (1,900,000)	1,539,848
Vilnius, Lithuania	596,900
Vladivostok, Russia	648,000
Volgograd (Stalingrad), Russia (1,360,000)	1,007,300
Warsaw (Warszawa), Poland (2,323,000)	1,655,700
Washington, D.C., U.S. (3,923,574)	606,900
Wellington, New Zealand (375,000)	150,301
Winnipeg, Canada (652,354)	616,790
Wuhan, China	3,570,000
Xi'an, China (2,580,000†)	2,210,000
Yekaterinburg, Russia (1,620,000)	1,375,400
Yerevan, Armenia (1,315,000)	1,199,000
Yokohama, Japan (*Tōkyō)	3,220,331
Zagreb, Croatia	697,925
Zurich, Switzerland (870,000)	365,043

Metropolitan area populations are shown in parentheses.
*City is located within the metropolitan area of another city; for example, Kyōto, Japan is located in the Ōsaka metropolitan area.
†Population of entire municipality or district, including rural area.

GLOSSARY OF FOREIGN GEOGRAPHICAL TERMS

- Annam ... Annamese
- Arab ... Arabic
- Bantu ... Bantu
- Bur ... Burmese
- Camb ... Cambodian
- Celt ... Celtic
- Chn ... Chinese
- Czech ... Czech
- Dan ... Danish
- Du ... Dutch
- Fin ... Finnish
- Fr ... French
- Ger ... German
- Gr ... Greek
- Hung ... Hungarian
- Ice ... Icelandic
- India ... India
- Indian ... American Indian
- Indon ... Indonesian
- It ... Italian
- Jap ... Japanese
- Kor ... Korean
- Mal ... Malayan
- Mong ... Mongolian
- Nor ... Norwegian
- Per ... Persian
- Pol ... Polish
- Port ... Portuguese
- Rom ... Romanian
- Rus ... Russian
- Siam ... Siamese
- So. Slav ... Southern Slavonic
- Sp ... Spanish
- Swe ... Swedish
- Tib ... Tibetan
- Tur ... Turkish
- Yugo ... Yugoslav

- å, Nor., Swe ... brook, river
- aa, Dan., Nor ... brook
- aas, Dan., Nor ... ridge
- āb, Per ... water, river
- abad, India, Per ... town, city
- ada, Tur ... island
- adrar, Berber ... mountain
- air, Indon ... stream
- akrotírion, Gr ... cape
- älf, Swe ... river
- alp, Ger ... mountain
- altipiano, It ... plateau
- alto, Sp ... height
- archipel, Fr ... archipelago
- archipiélago, Sp ... archipelago
- arquipélago, Port ... archipelago
- arroyo, Sp ... brook, stream
- ås, Nor., Swe ... ridge
- austral, Sp ... southern
- baai, Du ... bay
- bab, Arab ... gate, port
- bach, Ger ... brook, stream
- backe, Swe ... hill
- bad, Ger ... bath, spa
- bahía, Sp ... bay, gulf
- bahr, Arab ... river, sea, lake
- baia, It ... bay, gulf
- baía, Port ... bay
- baie, Fr ... bay, gulf
- bajo, Sp ... depression
- bak, Indon ... stream
- bakke, Dan., Nor ... hill
- balkan, Tur ... mountain range
- bana, Jap ... point, cape
- banco, Sp ... bank
- bandar, Mal., Per. ... town, port, harbor
- bang, Siam ... village
- bassin, Fr ... basin
- batang, Indon., Mal ... river
- ben, Celt ... mountain, summit
- bender, Arab ... harbor, port
- bereg, Rus ... coast, shore
- berg, Du., Ger., Nor., Swe. ... mountain, hill
- bir, Arab ... well
- birkat, Arab ... lake, pond, pool
- bit, Arab ... house
- bjaerg, Dan., Nor ... mountain
- bocche, It ... mouth
- boğazı, Tur ... strait
- bois, Fr ... forest, wood
- boloto, Rus ... marsh
- bolsón, Sp. ... flat-floored desert valley
- boreal, Sp ... northern
- borg, Dan., Nor., Swe ... castle, town
- borgo, It ... town, suburb
- bosch, Du ... forest, wood
- bouche, Fr ... river mouth
- bourg, Fr ... town, borough
- bro, Dan., Nor., Swe ... bridge
- brücke, Ger ... bridge
- bucht, Ger ... bay, bight
- bugt, Dan., Nor., Swe ... bay, gulf
- bulu, Indon ... mountain
- burg, Du., Ger ... castle, town
- buri, Siam ... town
- burun, burnu, Tur ... cape
- by, Dan., Nor., Swe ... village
- caatinga, Port. (Brazil) ... open brushland
- cabezo, Sp ... summit
- cabo, Port., Sp ... cape
- campo, It., Port., Sp ... plain, field
- campos, Port. (Brazil) ... plains
- cañón, Sp ... canyon
- cap, Fr ... cape
- capo, It ... cape
- casa, It., Port., Sp ... house
- castello, It., Port ... castle, fort
- castillo, Sp ... castle
- càte, Fr ... hill
- çay, Tur ... stream, river
- cayo, Sp ... rock, shoal, islet
- cerro, Sp ... mountain, hill
- champ, Fr ... field
- chang, Chn ... village, middle
- château, Fr ... castle
- chen, Chn ... market town
- chiang, Chn ... river
- chott, Arab ... salt lake
- chou, Chn. ... capital of district; island
- chu, Tib ... water, stream
- cidade, Port ... town, city
- cima, Sp ... summit, peak
- città, It ... town, city
- ciudad, Sp ... town, city
- cochilha, Port ... ridge
- col, Fr ... pass
- colina, Sp ... hill
- cordillera, Sp ... mountain chain
- costa, It., Port., Sp ... coast
- côte, Fr ... coast
- cuchilla, Sp ... mountain ridge
- dağ, Tur ... mountain(s)
- dake, Jap ... peak, summit
- dal, Dan., Du., Nor., Swe ... valley
- dan, Kor ... point, cape
- danau, Indon ... lake
- dar, Arab ... house, abode, country
- darya, Per ... river, sea
- dasht, Per ... plain, desert
- deniz, Tur ... sea
- désert, Fr ... desert
- deserto, It ... desert
- desierto, Sp ... desert
- détroit, Fr ... strait
- dijk, Du ... dam, dike
- djebel, Arab ... mountain
- do, Kor ... island
- dorf, Ger ... village
- dorp, Du ... village
- duin, Du ... dune
- dzong, Tib. ... fort, administrative capital
- eau, Fr ... water
- ecuador, Sp ... equator
- eiland, Du ... island
- elv, Dan., Nor ... river, stream
- embalse, Sp ... reservoir
- erg, Arab ... dune, sandy desert
- est, Fr., It ... east
- estado, Sp ... state
- este, Port., Sp ... east
- estrecho, Sp ... strait
- étang, Fr ... pond, lake
- état, Fr ... state
- eyjar, Ice ... islands
- feld, Ger ... field, plain
- festung, Ger ... fortress
- fiume, It ... river
- fjäll, Swe ... mountain
- fjärd, Swe ... bay, inlet
- fjeld, Nor ... mountain, hill
- fjord, Dan., Nor ... fiord, inlet
- fjördur, Ice ... fiord, inlet
- fleuve, Fr ... river
- flod, Dan., Swe ... river
- flói, Ice ... bay, marshland
- fluss, Ger ... river
- foce, It ... river mouth
- fontein, Du ... a spring
- forêt, Fr ... forest
- fors, Swe ... waterfall
- forst, Ger ... forest
- fos, Dan., Nor ... waterfall
- fu, Chn ... town, residence
- fuente, Sp ... spring, fountain
- fuerte, Sp ... fort
- furt, Ger ... ford
- gang, Kor ... stream, river
- gangri, Tib ... mountain
- gat, Dan., Nor ... channel
- gàve, Fr ... stream
- gawa, Jap ... river
- gebergte, Du ... mountain range
- gebiet, Ger ... district, territory
- gebirge, Ger ... mountains
- ghat, India ... pass, mountain range
- gobi, Mong ... desert
- gol, Mong ... river
- göl, gölü, Tur ... lake
- golf, Du., Ger ... gulf, bay
- golfe, Fr ... gulf, bay
- golfo, It., Port., Sp ... gulf, bay
- gomba, gompa, Tib ... monastery
- gora, Rus., So. Slav ... mountain
- góra, Pol ... mountain
- gorod, Rus ... town
- grad, Rus., So. Slav ... town
- guba, Rus ... bay, gulf
- gundung, Indon ... mountain
- guntō, Jap ... archipelago
- gunung, Mal ... mountain
- haf, Swe ... sea, ocean
- hafen, Ger ... port, harbor
- haff, Ger ... gulf, inland sea
- hai, Chn ... sea, lake
- hama, Jap ... beach, shore
- hamada, Arab ... rocky plateau
- hamn, Swe ... harbor
- hāmūn, Per ... swampy lake, plain
- hantō, Jap ... peninsula
- hassi, Arab ... well, spring
- haus, Ger ... house
- haut, Fr ... summit, top
- hav, Dan., Nor ... sea, ocean
- havn, Dan., Nor ... harbor, port
- havre, Fr ... harbor, port
- háza, Hung ... house, dwelling of
- heim, Ger ... hamlet, home
- hem, Swe ... hamlet, home
- higashi, Jap ... east
- hisar, Tur ... fortress
- hissar, Arab ... fort
- ho, Chn ... river
- hoek, Du ... cape
- hof, Ger ... court, farmhouse
- höfn, Ice ... harbor
- hoku, Jap ... north
- holm, Dan., Nor., Swe ... island
- hora, Czech ... mountain
- horn, Ger ... peak
- hoved, Dan., Nor ... cape
- hsien, Chn ... district, district capital
- hu, Chn ... lake
- hügel, Ger ... hill
- huk, Dan., Swe ... point
- hus, Dan., Nor., Swe ... house
- île, Fr ... island
- ilha, Port ... island
- indsö, Dan., Nor ... lake
- insel, Ger ... island
- insjö, Swe ... lake
- irmak, irmagi, Tur ... river
- isla, Sp ... island
- isola, It ... island
- istmo, It., Sp ... isthmus
- järvi, jaur, Fin ... lake
- jebel, Arab ... mountain
- jima, Jap ... island
- jökel, Nor ... glacier
- joki, Fin ... river
- jökull, Ice ... glacier
- kaap, Du ... cape
- kai, Jap ... bay, gulf, sea
- kaikyō, Jap ... channel, strait
- kalat, Per ... castle, fortress
- kale, Tur ... fort
- kali, Mal ... creek, river
- kand, Per ... village
- kang, Chn ... mountain ridge; village
- kap, Dan., Ger ... cape
- kapp, Nor., Swe ... cape
- kasr, Arab ... fort, castle
- kawa, Jap ... river
- kefr, Arab ... village
- kei, Jap ... creek, river
- ken, Jap ... prefecture
- khor, Arab ... bay, inlet
- khrebet, Rus ... mountain range
- kiang, Chn ... large river
- king, Chn ... capital city, town
- kita, Jap ... north
- ko, Jap ... lake
- köbstad, Dan ... market-town
- kol, Mong ... lake
- kólpos, Gr ... gulf
- kong, Chn ... river
- kopf, Ger ... head, summit, peak
- köpstad, Swe ... market-town
- körfezi, Tur ... gulf
- kosa, Rus ... spit
- kou, Chn ... river mouth
- köy, Tur ... village
- kraal, Du. (Africa) ... native village
- ksar, Arab ... fortified village
- kuala, Mal ... bay, river mouth
- kuh, Per ... mountain
- kum, Tur ... sand
- kuppe, Ger ... summit
- küste, Ger ... coast
- kyo, Jap ... town, capital
- la, Tib ... mountain pass
- labuan, Mal ... anchorage, port
- lac, Fr ... lake
- lago, It., Port., Sp ... lake
- lagoa, Port ... lake, marsh
- laguna, It., Port., Sp ... lagoon, lake
- lahti, Fin ... bay, gulf
- län, Swe ... county
- landsby, Dan., Nor ... village
- liehtao, Chn ... archipelago
- liman, Tur ... bay, port
- ling, Chn ... pass, ridge, mountain
- llanos, Sp ... plains
- loch, Celt. (Scotland) ... lake, bay
- loma, Sp ... long, low hill
- lough, Celt. (Ireland) ... lake, bay
- machi, Jap ... town
- man, Kor ... bay
- mar, Port., Sp ... sea
- mare, It., Rom ... sea
- marisma, Sp ... marsh, swamp
- mark, Ger ... boundary, limit
- massif, Fr ... block of mountains
- mato, Port ... forest, thicket
- me, Siam ... river
- meer, Du., Ger ... lake, sea
- mer, Fr ... sea
- mesa, Sp ... flat-topped mountain
- meseta, Sp ... plateau
- mina, Port., Sp ... mine
- minami, Jap ... south
- minato, Jap ... harbor, haven
- misaki, Jap ... cape, headland
- mont, Fr ... mount, mountain
- montagna, It ... mountain
- montagne, Fr ... mountain
- montaña, Sp ... mountain
- monte, It., Port., Sp. ... mount, mountain
- more, Rus., So. Slav ... sea
- morro, Port., Sp ... hill, bluff
- mühle, Ger ... mill
- mund, Ger ... mouth, opening
- mündung, Ger ... river mouth
- mura, Jap ... township
- myit, Bur ... river
- mys, Rus ... cape
- nada, Jap ... sea
- nadi, India ... river, creek
- naes, Dan., Nor ... cape
- nafud, Arab ... desert of sand dunes
- nagar, India ... town, city
- nahr, Arab ... river
- nam, Siam ... river, water
- nan, Chn., Jap ... south
- näs, Nor., Swe ... cape
- nez, Fr ... point, cape
- nishi, nisi, Jap ... west
- njarga, Fin ... peninsula
- nong, Siam ... marsh
- noord, Du ... north
- nor, Mong ... lake
- nord, Dan., Fr., Ger., It., Nor., Swe ... north
- norte, Port., Sp ... north
- nos, Rus ... cape
- nyasa, Bantu ... lake
- ö, Dan., Nor., Swe ... island
- occidental, Sp ... western
- ocna, Rom ... salt mine
- odde, Dan., Nor ... point, cape
- oeste, Port., Sp ... west
- oka, Jap ... hill
- oost, Du ... east
- oriental, Sp ... eastern
- óros, Gr ... mountain
- ost, Ger., Swe ... east
- öster, Dan., Nor., Swe ... eastern
- ostrov, Rus ... island
- oued, Arab ... river, stream
- ouest, Fr ... west
- ozero, Rus ... lake
- pää, Fin ... mountain
- padang, Mal ... plain, field
- pampas, Sp. (Argentina) ... grassy plains
- pará, Indian (Brazil) ... river
- pas, Fr ... channel, passage
- paso, Sp ... mountain pass, passage
- passo, It., Port. ... mountain pass, passage, strait
- patam, India ... city, town
- pei, Chn ... north
- pélagos, Gr ... open sea
- pegunungan, Indon ... mountains
- peña, Sp ... rock
- peresheyek, Rus ... isthmus
- pertuis, Fr ... strait
- peski, Rus ... desert
- pic, Fr ... mountain peak
- pico, Port., Sp ... mountain peak
- piedra, Sp ... stone, rock
- ping, Chn ... plain, flat
- planalto, Port ... plateau
- planina, Yugo ... mountains
- playa, Sp ... shore, beach
- pnom, Camb ... mountain
- pointe, Fr ... point
- polder, Du., Ger ... reclaimed marsh
- polje, So. Slav ... plain, field
- poluostrov, Rus ... peninsula
- pont, Fr ... bridge
- ponta, Port ... point, headland
- ponte, It., Port ... bridge
- pore, India ... city, town
- porthmós, Gr ... strait
- porto, It., Port ... port, harbor
- potamós, Gr ... river
- p'ov, Rus ... peninsula
- prado, Sp ... field, meadow
- presqu'île, Fr ... peninsula
- proliv, Rus ... strait
- pu, Chn ... commercial village
- pueblo, Sp ... town, village
- puerto, Sp ... port, harbor
- pulau, Indon ... island
- punkt, Ger ... point
- punt, Du ... point
- punta, It., Sp ... point
- pur, India ... city, town
- puy, Fr ... peak
- qal'a, qal'at, Arab ... fort, village
- qasr, Arab ... fort, castle
- rann, India ... wasteland
- ra's, Arab ... cape, head
- reka, Rus., So. Slav ... river
- represa, Port ... reservoir
- rettō, Jap ... island chain
- ría, Sp ... estuary
- ribeira, Port ... stream
- riberão, Port ... river
- rio, It., Port ... stream, river
- río, Sp ... river
- rivière, Fr ... river
- roca, Sp ... rock
- rt, Yugo ... cape
- rūd, Per ... river
- saari, Fin ... island
- sable, Fr ... sand
- sahara, Arab ... desert, plain
- saki, Jap ... cape
- sal, Sp ... salt
- salar, Sp ... salt flat, salt lake
- salto, Sp ... waterfall
- san, Jap., Kor ... mountain, hill
- sat, satul, Rom ... village
- schloss, Ger ... castle
- sebkha, Arab ... salt marsh
- see, Ger ... lake, sea
- şehir, Tur ... town, city
- selat, Indon ... stream
- selvas, Port. (Brazil) ... tropical rain forests
- seno, Sp ... bay
- serra, Port ... mountain chain
- serranía, Sp ... mountain ridge
- seto, Jap ... strait
- severnaya, Rus ... northern
- shahr, Per ... town, city
- shan, Chn ... mountain, hill, island
- shatt, Arab ... river
- shi, Jap ... city
- shima, Jap ... island
- shōtō, Jap ... archipelago
- si, Chn ... west, western
- sierra, Sp ... mountain range
- sjö, Nor., Swe ... lake, sea
- sö, Dan., Nor ... lake, sea
- söder, södra, Swe ... south
- song, Annam ... river
- sopka, Rus ... peak, volcano
- source, Fr ... a spring
- spitze, Ger ... summit, point
- staat, Ger ... state
- stad, Dan., Du., Nor., Swe. ... city, town
- stadt, Ger ... city, town
- stato, It ... state
- step', Rus ... treeless plain, steppe
- straat, Du ... strait
- strand, Dan., Du., Ger., Nor., Swe ... shore, beach
- stretto, It ... strait
- strom, Ger ... river, stream
- ström, Dan., Nor., Swe. ... stream, river
- stroom, Du ... stream, river
- su, suyu, Tur ... water, river
- sud, Fr., Sp ... south
- süd, Ger ... south
- suidō, Jap ... channel
- sul, Port ... south
- sund, Dan., Nor., Swe ... sound
- sungai, sungei, Indon., Mal ... river
- sur, Sp ... south
- syd, Dan., Nor., Swe ... south
- tafelland, Ger ... plateau
- take, Jap ... peak, summit
- tal, Ger ... valley
- tanjung, tanjong, Mal ... cape
- tao, Chn ... island
- târg, târgul, Rom ... market, town
- tell, Arab ... hill
- teluk, Indon ... bay, gulf
- terra, It ... land
- terre, Fr ... earth, land
- thal, Ger ... valley
- tierra, Sp ... earth, land
- tō, Jap ... east; island
- tonle, Camb ... river, lake
- top, Du ... peak
- torp, Swe ... hamlet, cottage
- tsangpo, Tib ... river
- tsi, Chn ... village, borough
- tso, Tib ... lake
- tsu, Jap ... harbor, port
- tundra, Rus ... treeless arctic plains
- tung, Chn ... east
- tuz, Tur ... salt
- udde, Swe ... cape
- ufer, Ger ... shore, riverbank
- ujung, Indon ... point, cape
- umi, Jap ... sea, gulf
- ura, Jap ... bay, coast, creek
- ust'ye, Rus ... river mouth
- valle, It., Port., Sp ... valley
- vallée, Fr ... valley
- valli, It ... lake
- vár, Hung ... fortress
- város, Hung ... town
- varoš, So. Slav ... town
- veld, Du ... open plain, field
- verkh, Rus ... top, summit
- ves, Czech ... village
- vest, Dan., Nor., Swe ... west
- vik, Swe ... cove, bay
- vila, Port ... town
- villa, Sp ... town
- villar, Sp ... village, hamlet
- ville, Fr ... town, city
- vostok, Rus ... east
- wad, wādī, Arab. ... intermittent stream
- wald, Ger ... forest, woodland
- wan, Chn., Jap ... bay, gulf
- weiler, Ger ... hamlet, village
- westersch, Du ... western
- wüste, Ger ... desert
- yama, Jap ... mountain
- yarimada, Tur ... peninsula
- yug, Rus ... south
- zaki, Jap ... cape
- zaliv, Rus ... bay, gulf
- zapad, Rus ... west
- zee, Du ... sea
- zemlya, Rus ... land
- zuid, Du ... south

Afg.	Afghanistan
Afr.	Africa
Ak., U.S.	Alaska, U.S.
Al., U.S.	Alabama, U.S.
Alb.	Albania
Alg.	Algeria
Am. Sam.	American Samoa
And.	Andorra
Ang.	Angola
Ant.	Antarctica
Antig.	Antigua and Barbuda
aq.	Aqueduct
Ar., U.S.	Arkansas, U.S.
Arg.	Argentina
Arm.	Armenia
arpt.	Airport
Aus.	Austria
Austl.	Australia
Az., U.S.	Arizona, U.S.
Azer.	Azerbaijan
b.	Bay, Gulf, Inlet, Lagoon
Bah.	Bahamas
Bahr.	Bahrain
Barb.	Barbados
B.A.T.	British Antarctic Territory
Bdi.	Burundi
Bel.	Belgium
Bela.	Belarus
Bhu.	Bhutan
bk.	Undersea Bank
bldg.	Building
Bngl.	Bangladesh
Bol.	Bolivia
Boph.	Bophuthatswana
Bos.	Bosnia and Hercegovina
Bots.	Botswana
Braz.	Brazil
Bru.	Brunei
bt.	Bight
Bul.	Bulgaria
Burkina	Burkina Faso
c.	Cape, Point
Ca., U.S.	California, U.S.
Cam.	Cameroon
Camb.	Cambodia
can.	Canal
Can.	Canada
Cay. Is.	Cayman Islands
Cen. Afr. Rep.	Central African Republic
C. Iv.	Cote d'Ivoire
clf.	Cliff, Escarpment
co.	County, Parish
Co., U.S.	Colorado, U.S.
Col.	Colombia
Com.	Comoros
cont.	Continent
Cook Is.	Cook Islands
C.R.	Costa Rica
Cro.	Croatia
cst.	Coast, Beach
Ct., U.S.	Connecticut, U.S.
C.V.	Cape Verde
Cyp.	Cyprus
Czech Rep.	Czech Republic
d.	Delta
D.C., U.S.	District of Columbia, U.S.
De., U.S.	Delaware, U.S.
Den.	Denmark
dep.	Dependency, Colony
depr.	Depression
dept.	Department, District
des.	Desert
Dji.	Djibouti
Dom.	Dominica
Dom. Rep.	Dominican Republic
Ec.	Ecuador
educ.	Educational Facility
El Sal.	El Salvador
Eng., U.K.	England, U.K.
Eq. Gui.	Equatorial Guinea
Erit.	Eritrea
Est.	Estonia
est.	Estuary
Eth.	Ethiopia
Eur.	Europe
Faer. Is.	Faeroe Islands
Falk. Is.	Falkland Islands
Fin.	Finland
fj.	Fjord
Fl., U.S.	Florida, U.S.
for.	Forest, Moor
Fr.	France
Fr. Gu.	French Guiana
Fr. Poly.	French Polynesia
F.S.A.T.	French Southern and Antarctic Territory
Ga., U.S.	Georgia, U.S.
Gam.	Gambia
Geor.	Georgia
Ger.	Germany
Grc.	Greece
Gren.	Grenada
Grnld.	Greenland
Guad.	Guadeloupe
Guat.	Guatemala
Gui.	Guinea
Gui.-B.	Guinea-Bissau

Guy.	Guyana
Hi., U.S.	Hawaii, U.S.
hist.	Historic Site, Ruins
hist. reg.	Historic Region
H.K.	Hong Kong
Hond.	Honduras
Hung.	Hungary
i.	Island
Ia., U.S.	Iowa, U.S.
ice	Ice Feature, Glacier
Ice.	Iceland
Id., U.S.	Idaho, U.S.
Il., U.S.	Illinois, U.S.
In., U.S.	Indiana, U.S.
Indon.	Indonesia
I. of Man	Isle of Man
I.R.	Indian Reservation
Ire.	Ireland
is.	Islands
Isr.	Israel
Isr. Occ.	Israeli Occupied Areas
isth.	Isthmus
Jam.	Jamaica
Jord.	Jordan
Kaz.	Kazakhstan
Kir.	Kiribati
Ks., U.S.	Kansas, U.S.
Kuw.	Kuwait
Ky., U.S.	Kentucky, U.S.
Kyrg.	Kyrgyzstan
l.	Lake, Pond
La., U.S.	Louisiana, U.S.
Lat.	Latvia
Leb.	Lebanon
Leso.	Lesotho
Lib.	Liberia
Liech.	Liechtenstein
Lith.	Lithuania
Lux.	Luxembourg
Ma., U.S.	Massachusetts, U.S.
Mac.	Macedonia
Madag.	Madagascar
Malay.	Malaysia
Marsh. Is.	Marshall Islands
Mart.	Martinique
Maur.	Mauritania
May.	Mayotte
Md., U.S.	Maryland, U.S.
Me., U.S.	Maine, U.S.
Mex.	Mexico
Mi., U.S.	Michigan, U.S.
Micron.	Micronesia, Federated States of
Mn., U.S.	Minnesota, U.S.
Mo., U.S.	Missouri, U.S.
Mol.	Moldova
Mong.	Mongolia
Monts.	Montserrat
Mor.	Morocco
Moz.	Mozambique
Ms., U.S.	Mississippi, U.S.
Mt., U.S.	Montana, U.S.
mth.	River Mouth or Channel
mtn.	Mountain
mts.	Mountains
Mwi.	Malawi
N.A.	North America
N.C., U.S.	North Carolina, U.S.
N. Cal.	New Caledonia
N. Cyp.	North Cyprus
N.D., U.S.	North Dakota, U.S.
Ne., U.S.	Nebraska, U.S.
neigh.	Neighborhood
Neth.	Netherlands
Neth. Ant.	Netherlands Antilles
N.H., U.S.	New Hampshire, U.S.
Nic.	Nicaragua
Nig.	Nigeria
N. Ire., U.K.	Northern Ireland, U.K.
N.J., U.S.	New Jersey, U.S.
N. Kor.	North Korea
N.M., U.S.	New Mexico, U.S.
N. Mar. Is.	Northern Mariana Islands
Nmb.	Namibia
Nor.	Norway
Nv., U.S.	Nevada, U.S.
N.Y., U.S.	New York, U.S.
N.Z.	New Zealand
o.	Ocean
Oc.	Oceania
Oh., U.S.	Ohio, U.S.
Ok., U.S.	Oklahoma, U.S.
Or., U.S.	Oregon, U.S.
p.	Pass
Pa., U.S.	Pennsylvania, U.S.
Pac. Is.	Pacific Islands, Trust Territory of the
Pak.	Pakistan
Pan.	Panama
Pap. N. Gui.	Papua New Guinea
Para.	Paraguay
pen.	Peninsula
Phil.	Philippines
Pit.	Pitcairn

pl.	Plain, Flat
plat.	Plateau, Highland
Pol.	Poland
Port.	Portugal
P.R.	Puerto Rico
prov.	Province, Region
pt. of i.	Point of Interest
r.	River, Creek
Reu.	Reunion
rec.	Recreational Site, Park
reg.	Physical Region
rel.	Religious Institution
res.	Reservoir
rf.	Reef, Shoal
R.I., U.S.	Rhode Island, U.S.
Rom.	Romania
Rw.	Rwanda
S.A.	South America
S. Afr.	South Africa
Sau. Ar.	Saudi Arabia
S.C., U.S.	South Carolina, U.S.
sci.	Scientific Station
Scot., U.K.	Scotland, U.K.
S.D., U.S.	South Dakota, U.S.
Sen.	Senegal
sea feat.	Undersea Feature
Sey.	Seychelles
S. Ga.	South Georgia
Sing.	Singapore
S. Kor.	South Korea
S.L.	Sierra Leone
Slvk.	Slovakia
Slvn.	Slovenia
S. Mar.	San Marino
Sol. Is.	Solomon Islands
Som.	Somalia
Sp. N. Afr.	Spanish North Africa
Sri L.	Sri Lanka
St. Hel.	St. Helena
St. K./N.	St. Kitts and Nevis
St. Luc.	St. Lucia
St. P./M.	St. Pierre and Miquelon
strt.	Strait, Channel, Sound
S. Tom./P.	Sao Tome and Principe
St. Vin.	St. Vincent and the Grenadines
Sur.	Suriname
Sval.	Svalbard
sw.	Swamp, Marsh
Swaz.	Swaziland
Swe.	Sweden
Switz.	Switzerland
Tai.	Taiwan
Taj.	Tajikistan
Tan.	Tanzania
T./C. Is.	Turks and Caicos Islands
ter.	Territory
Thai.	Thailand
Tn., U.S.	Tennessee, U.S.
trans.	Transportation Facility
Trin.	Trinidad and Tobago
Tun.	Tunisia
Tur.	Turkey
Turk.	Turkmenistan
Tx., U.S.	Texas, U.S.
U.A.E.	United Arab Emirates
Ug.	Uganda
U.K.	United Kingdom
Ukr.	Ukraine
Ur.	Uruguay
U.S.	United States
Ut., U.S.	Utah, U.S.
Uzb.	Uzbekistan
Va., U.S.	Virginia, U.S.
val.	Valley, Watercourse
Vat.	Vatican City
Ven.	Venezuela
V.I., Br.	Virgin Islands, British
Viet.	Vietnam
V.I.U.S.	Virgin Islands (U.S.)
vol.	Volcano
Vt., U.S.	Vermont, U.S.
Wa., U.S.	Washington, U.S.
Wi., U.S.	Wisconsin, U.S.
W. Sah.	Western Sahara
W. Sam.	Western Samoa
wtfl.	Waterfall
W.V., U.S.	West Virginia, U.S.
Wy., U.S.	Wyoming, U.S.
Yugo.	Yugoslavia
Zam.	Zambia
Zimb.	Zimbabwe
Zam.	Zambia

Key to the Sound Values of Letters and Symbols Used in the Index to Indicate Pronunciation

ă-ăt; băttle
ă-fĭnăl; ăppeal
ā-rāte; elāte
à-senāte; inanimàte
ä-ärm; cälm
à-àsk; bàth
a-sofà; màrine (short neutral or indeterminate sound)
â-fâre; prepâre
ch-choose; church
dh-as th in other; either
ē-bē; ēve
ĕ-ĕvent; crēate
ĕ-bĕt; ĕnd
ĕ-recĕnt (short neutral or indeterminate sound)
ẽ-cratẽr; cindẽr
g-gō; gāme
gh-guttural g
ĭ-bĭt; wĭll
ĭ-(short neutral or indeterminate sound)
ī-rīde; bīte
κ-guttural k as ch in German ich
ng-sing
ŋ-baŋk; liŋger
N-indicates nasalized
ŏ-nŏd; ŏdd
ŏ-cŏmmit; cŏnnect
ō-ōld; bōld
ô-òbey; hôtel
ô-ôrder; nôrth
oi-boil
o͞o-fo͞od; ro͞ot
ò-as oo in foot; wood
ou-out; thou
s-soft; so; sane
sh-dish; finish
th-thin; thick
ū-pūre; cūre
ù-ùnite; ùsùrp
û-ûrn; fûr
ŭ-stŭd; ŭp
ŭ-circŭs; sŭbmit
ü-as in French tu
zh-as z in azure
'-indeterminate vowel sound

In many cases the spelling of foreign geographic names does not even remotely indicate the pronunciation to an American, i.e., Słupsk in Poland is pronounced swόpsk; Jujuy in Argentina is pronounced ho͞oͪwē′; La Spezia in Italy is lä-spē′zyä.

This condition is hardly surprising, however, when we consider that in our own language Worcester, Massachusetts, is pronounced wòs′tẽr; Sioux City, Iowa, so͞o sī′ti; Schuylkill Haven, Pennsylvania, sko͞ol′kĭl hā-vĕn; Poughkeepsie, New York, pŏ-kĭp′sẽ.

The indication of pronunciation of geographic names presents several peculiar problems:

1. Many foreign tongues use sounds that are not present in the English language and which an American cannot normally articulate. Thus, though the nearest English equivalent sound has been indicated, only approximate results are possible.

2. There are several dialects in each foreign tongue which cause variation in the local pronunciation of names. This also occurs in identical names in the various divisions of a great language group, as the Slavic or the Latin.

3. Within the United States there are marked differences in pronunciation, not only of local geographic names, but also of common words, indicating that the sound and tone values for letters as well as the placing of the emphasis vary considerably from one part of the country to another.

4. A number of different letters and diacritical combinations could be used to indicate essentially the same or approximate pronunciations.

Some variation in pronunciation other than that indicated in this index may be encountered, but such a difference does not necessarily indicate that either is in error, and in many cases it is a matter of individual choice as to which is preferred. In fact, an exact indication of pronunciation of many foreign names using English letters and diacritical marks is extremely difficult and sometimes impossible.

PRONOUNCING INDEX

This universal index includes in a single alphabetical list approximately 34,000 names of features that appear on the reference maps. Each name is followed by a page reference and geographical coordinates.

Abbreviation and Capitalization Abbreviations of names on the maps have been standardized as much as possible. Names that are abbreviated on the maps are generally spelled out in full in the index. Periods are used after all abbreviations regardless of local practice. The abbreviation "St." is used only for "Saint". "Sankt" and other forms of this term are spelled out.

Most initial letters of names are capitalized, except for a few Dutch names, such as "'s-Gravenhage". Capitalization of noninitial words in a name generally follows local practice.

Alphabetization Names are alphabetized in the order of the letters of the English alphabet. Spanish *ll* and *ch,* for example, are not treated as distinct letters. Furthermore, diacritical marks are disregarded in alphabetization — German or Scandinavian *ä* or *ö* are treated as *a* or *o*.

The names of physical features may appear inverted, since they are always alphabetized under the proper, not the generic, part of the name, thus: "Gibraltar, Strait of". Otherwise every entry, whether consisting of one word or more, is alphabetized as a single continuous entity. "Lakeland," for example, appears after "La Crosse" and before "La Salle." Names beginning with articles (Le Havre, Den Helder, Al Manāmah, Ad Dawhah) are not inverted. Names beginning "St.", "Ste." and "Sainte" are alphabetized as though spelled "Saint."

In the case of identical names, towns are listed first, then political divisions, then physical features.

Generic Terms Except for cities, the names of all features are followed by terms that represent broad classes of features, for example, Mississippi, r. or Alabama, state. A list of all abbreviations used in the index is on page 249.

Country names and names of features that extend beyond the boundaries of one country are followed by the name of the continent in which each is located. Country designations follow the names of all other places in the index. The locations of places in the United States and the United Kingdom are further defined by abbreviations that indicate the state or political division in which each is located.

Pronunciations Pronunciations are included for most names listed. An explanation of the pronunciation system used appears on page 249.

Page References and Geographical Coordinates The geographical coordinates and page references are found in the last columns of each entry.

If a page contains several maps or insets, a lowercase letter identifies the specific map or inset.

Latitude and longitude coordinates for point features, such as cities and mountain peaks, indicate the locations of the symbols. For extensive areal features, such as countries or mountain ranges, or linear features, such as canals and rivers, locations are given for the position of the type as it appears on the map.

PLACE (Pronunciation)	PAGE	Lat. ° '	Long. ° '
A			
Aachen, Ger. (ä′kĕn)	147	50.46N	6.07 E
Aalen, Ger. (ä′lĕn)	154	48.49N	10.08 E
Aalsmeer, Neth.	145a	52.16N	4.44 E
Aalst, Bel.	151	50.58N	4.00 E
Aarau, Switz. (äróu)	147	47.22N	8.03 E
Aarschot, Bel.	145a	50.59N	4.51 E
Aba, Nig.	210	5.06N	7.21 E
Aba, Zaire	217	3.52N	30.14 E
Ābādān, Iran (ä-bŭ-dän′)	182	30.15N	48.30 E
Abaetetuba, Braz. (ä′bä̇-tĕ-tōō′bȧ)	131	1.44S	48.45W
Abajo Peak, mtn., Ut., U.S. (ä-bä′hŏ)	109	37.51N	109.28W
Abakaliki, Nig.	215	6.21N	8.06 E
Abakan, Russia (ŭ-bá̇-kän′)	165	53.43N	91.28 E
Abakan, r., Russia (u-bá̇-kän′)	170	53.00N	91.06 E
Abancay, Peru (ä-bän-kä′è)	130	13.44S	72.46W
Abashiri, Japan (ä-bä-shē′rê)	194	44.00N	144.13 E
Abasolo, Mex.	112	27.13N	101.25W
Abasolo, Mex. (ä-bä-sō′lô)	118	24.05N	98.24W
Abaya, Lake, l., Eth. (ä-bä′yä)	211	6.24N	38.22 E
'Abbāsābād, Iran	241h	35.44N	51.25 E
'Abbāsah, Tur′at al, can., Egypt	218c	30.45N	32.15 E
Abbeville, Fr. (àb-vēl′)	147	50.08N	1.49 E
Abbeville, Al., U.S. (ăb′ê-vĭl)	114	31.35N	85.15W
Abbeville, Ga., U.S. (ăb′ê-vĭl)	114	31.53N	83.23W
Abbeville, La., U.S.	113	29.59N	92.07W
Abbeville, S.C., U.S.	115	34.09N	82.25W
Abbey Wood, neigh., Eng., U.K.	235	51.29N	0.08 E
Abbiategrasso, Italy (äb-byä′tȧ-gräs′sô)	160	45.23N	8.52 E
Abbots Bromley, Eng., U.K. (ăb′ŭts brŭm′lê)	144a	52.49N	1.52W
Abbotsford, Can.	106d	49.03N	122.17W
Abbots Langley, Eng., U.K.	235	51.43N	0.25W
'Abd al Kūrī, i., Yemen (äbd-ĕl-kó′rê)	218a	12.12N	51.00 E
'Abd al-Shāhīd, Egypt	244a	29.55N	31.13 E
Abdulino, Russia (äb-dō-lê′nô)	166	53.42N	53.40 E
Abengourou, C. Iv.	214	6.44N	3.29W
Abeokuta, Nig. (ä-bå-ô-kōō′tä)	210	7.10N	3.26 E
Abercorn see Mbala, Zam.	212	8.50S	31.22 E
Aberdare, Wales, U.K. (ăb-ĕr-dâr′)	150	51.45N	3.35W
Aberdeen, Scot., U.K. (ăb-ĕr-dēn′)	142	57.10N	2.05W
Aberdeen, Ms., U.S.	114	33.49N	88.33W
Aberdeen, S.D., U.S. (ăb-ĕr-dēn′)	96	45.28N	98.29W
Aberdeen, Wa., U.S. (ăb-ĕr-dēn′)	96	47.00N	123.48W
Aberford, Eng., U.K. (ăb′ĕr-fĕrd)	144a	53.49N	1.21W
Abergavenny, Wales, U.K. (ăb′ĕr-gȧ-vĕn′ĭ)	150	51.45N	3.05W
Abert, Lake, l., Or., U.S. (ā′bĕrt)	104	42.39N	120.24W
Aberystwyth, Wales, U.K. (ä-bĕr-ĭst′wĭth)	150	52.25N	4.04W
Abidjan, C. Iv. (ä-bēd-zhän′)	210	5.19N	4.02W
Abiko, Japan (ä-bē-kō)	195a	35.53N	140.01 E
Abilene, Ks., U.S. (ăb′ĭ-lĕn)	111	38.54N	97.12W
Abilene, Tx., U.S.	96	32.25N	99.45W
Abingdon, Eng., U.K.	144b	51.38N	1.17W
Abingdon, Il., U.S. (ăb′ĭng-dŭn)	103	40.48N	90.21W
Abingdon, Va., U.S.	115	36.42N	81.57W
Abington, Ma., U.S. (ăb′ĭng-tŭn)	93a	42.07N	70.57W
Abington, Pa., U.S.	229b	40.07N	75.08W
Abiquiu Reservoir, res., N.M., U.S.	109	36.26N	106.42W
Abitibi, l., Can. (ăb-ĭ-tĭb′ĭ)	85	48.27N	80.20W
Abitibi, r., Can.	85	49.30N	81.10W
Abkhazia, , Geor.	167	43.10N	40.45 E
Ablis, Fr. (ȧ-blē′)	157b	48.31N	1.50 E
Ablon-sur-Seine, Fr.	237c	48.43N	2.25 E
Abnūb, Egypt (äb-nōōb′)	218b	27.18N	31.11 E
Åbo see Turku, Fin.	142	60.28N	22.12 E
Abóbada, Port.	238d	38.43N	9.20W
Abohar, India	186	30.12N	74.13 E
Aboisso, C. Iv.	214	5.28N	3.12W
Abomey, Benin (ăb-ô-mā′)	210	7.11N	1.59 E
Abony, Hung. (ô′bô-ny′)	155	47.12N	20.00 E
Abou Deïa, Chad	215	11.27N	19.17 E
Abra, r., Phil. (ä′brä)	197a	17.16N	120.38 E
Abraão, Braz. (äbrä-ouɴ′)	129a	23.10S	44.10W
Abraham's Bay, b., Bah.	123	22.20N	73.50W
Abram, Eng., U.K. (ā′brăm)	144a	53.31N	2.36W
Abramcevo, Russia	239b	55.50N	37.50 E
Abrantes, Port. (ä-brän′tĕs)	158	39.28N	8.13W
Abridge, Eng., U.K.	235	51.39N	0.07 E
Abrolhos, Arquipélago dos, is., Braz.	131	17.58S	38.40W
Abruka, i., Est. (ä-brò′kä)	153	58.09N	22.30 E
Abrunheira, Port.	238d	38.46N	9.21W
Abruzzi e Molise, hist. reg., Italy	160	42.10N	13.55 E
Absaroka Range, mts., U.S. (äb-să-rō-kä)	96	44.50N	109.47W
Abşeron Yarımadası, pen., Azer.	167	40.20N	50.30 E
Abū an-Numrus, Egypt	244a	29.57N	31.12 E
Abū Arīsh, Sau. Ar. (ä-bōō ä-rēsh′)	182	16.48N	43.00 E
Abu Dhabi see Abū Ẓaby, U.A.E.	182	24.15N	54.28 E
Abū Ḥamad, Sudan (ä′bōō hä′-mĕd)	211	19.37N	33.21 E
Abuja, Nig.	210	9.12N	7.11 E
Abū Kamāl, Syria	182	34.45N	40.46 E
Abunã, r., S.A.	130	10.25S	67.00W
Abū Qīr, Egypt (ä′bōō kēr′)	218b	31.18N	30.06 E
Abū Qurūn, Ra's, mtn., Egypt	181a	30.22N	33.32 E
Aburatsu, Japan (ä′bò-rät′sōō)	195	31.33N	131.20 E
Abu Road, India (ä′bōō)	183	24.38N	72.45 E
Abū Şīr Pyramids, hist., Egypt	244a	29.54N	31.12 E
Abū Tīj, Egypt	218b	27.03N	31.19 E
Abū Ẓaby, U.A.E.	182	24.15N	54.28 E
Abū Ẕanīmah, Egypt	181a	29.03N	33.08 E
Abyy, Russia	165	68.24N	134.00 E
Acacias, Col. (ä-kä′sēäs)	130a	3.59N	73.44W
Acadia National Park, rec., Me., U.S. (ȧ-kā′dĭ-ȧ)	97	44.19N	68.01W
Acajutla, El Sal. (ä-kä-hōōt′lä)	120	13.37N	89.50W
Acala, Mex. (ä-kä′lä)	119	16.38N	92.49W
Acalayong, Eq. Gui.	216	1.05N	9.40 E
Acámbaro, Mex. (ä-käm′bä-rō)	118	20.03N	100.42W
Acancéh, Mex. (ä-kän-sě′)	120a	20.50N	89.27W
Acapetlahuaya, Mex. (ä-kä-pĕt′lä-hwä′yä)	118	18.24N	100.04W
Acaponeta, Mex. (ä-kä-pô-nä′tä)	118	22.31N	105.25W
Acaponeta, r., Mex. (ä-kä-pô-nä′tä)	118	22.47N	105.23W
Acapulco, Mex. (ä-kä-pōōl′kō)	116	16.49N	99.57W
Acaraí Mountains, mts., S.A.	131	1.30N	57.40W
Acarigua, Ven. (äkä-rē′gwä)	130	9.29N	69.11W
Acatlán de Osorio, Mex. (ä-kät-län′dä ô-sō′rē-ō)	118	18.11N	98.04W
Acatzingo de Hidalgo, Mex.	119	18.58N	97.47W
Acayucan, Mex. (ä-kä-yōō′kän)	119	17.56N	94.55W
Accord, Ma., U.S.	227a	42.10N	70.53W
Accoville, W.V., U.S. (äk′kô-vǐl)	98	37.45N	81.50W
Accra, Ghana (ä′krä)	210	5.33N	0.13W
Accrington, Eng., U.K. (ăk′rĭng-tŭn)	144a	53.45N	2.22W
Acerra, Italy (ä-chě′r-rä)	159c	40.42N	14.22 E
Achacachi, Bol. (ä-chä-kä′chě)	130	16.11S	68.32W
Achill Island, i., Ire. (ä-chǐl′)	146	53.55N	10.05W
Achinsk, Russia (ä-chěnsk′)	170	56.13N	90.32 E
Acireale, Italy (ä-chē-rä-ä′lä)	160	37.37N	15.12 E
Acklins, i., Bah.	117	22.30N	73.55W
Acklins, The Bight of, bt., Bah. (ăk′lĭns)	123	22.35N	74.20W
Acolman, Mex.	119a	19.38N	98.56W
Acoma Indian Reservation, I.R., N.M., U.S.	109	34.52N	107.40W
Aconcagua, prov., Chile (ä-kön-kä′gwä)	129b	32.20S	71.00W
Aconcagua, r., Chile (ä-kön-kä′gwä)	129b	32.43S	70.53W
Aconcagua, Cerro, mtn., Arg. (ä-kön-kä′gwä)	132	32.38S	70.00W
Açores (Azores), is., Port.	209	37.44N	29.25W
Acoyapa, Nic. (ä-kô-yä′pä)	120	11.54N	85.11W
Acqui, Italy (äk′kwě)	160	44.41N	8.22 E
Acre, state, Braz. (ä′krä)	130	8.40S	70.45W
Acre, r., S.A.	130	10.33S	69.00W
Acton, Can. (äk′tŭn)	83d	43.38N	80.02W
Acton, Al., U.S. (äk′tŭn)	100h	33.21N	86.49W
Acton, Ma., U.S. (äk′tŭn)	93a	42.29N	71.26W
Acton, neigh., Eng., U.K. (äk′tŭn)	235	51.30N	0.16W
Actopan, Mex. (äk-tô-pän′)	118	20.16N	98.57W
Actópan, r., Mex. (äk-tô′pän)	119	19.25N	96.31W

ăt; finăl; rāte; senăte; ärm; ȧsk; sofȧ; fâre; ch-choose; dh-as th in other; bē; ĕvent; bĕt; recĕnt; cratĕr; g-gō; gh-guttural g; bĭt; ĭ-short neutral; rīde; ĸ-guttural k as ch in German ich;

PRONOUNCING INDEX

Acuitzio del Canje–Alaska 255

PLACE (Pronunciation)	PAGE	Lat. °′	Long. °′
Acuitzio del Canje, Mex. (ä-kwēt′zė-ō dĕl kän′hȧ)	118	19.28N	101.21W
Acul, Baie de l', b., Haiti (ä-ko͞ol′)	123	19.55N	72.20W
Ada, Mn., U.S. (ā′dŭ)	102	47.17N	96.32W
Ada, Oh., U.S. (ā′dŭ)	98	40.45N	83.45W
Ada, Ok., U.S. (ā′dŭ)	111	34.45N	96.43W
Ada, Yugo. (ä′dä)	161	45.48N	20.06E
Adachi, Japan	195a	35.50N	39.36E
Adachi, neigh., Japan	242a	35.45N	139.48E
Adak, Ak., U.S. (ă-dăk′)	95a	56.50N	176.48W
Adak, i., Ak., U.S. (ă-dăk′)	95a	51.40N	176.28W
Adak Strait, strt., Ak., U.S. (ă-dăk′)	95a	51.42N	177.16W
Adamaoua, mts., Afr.	210	6.30N	11.50E
Adams, Ma., U.S. (ăd′ămz)	99	42.35N	73.10W
Adams, Wi., U.S. (ăd′ămz)	103	43.55N	89.48W
Adams, r., Can. (ăd′ămz)	87	51.30N	119.20W
Adams, Mount, mtn., Wa., U.S. (ăd′ămz)	96	46.15N	121.19W
Adamsville, Al., U.S. (ăd′ămz-vĭl)	100h	33.36N	86.57W
Adana, Tur. (ä′dä-nä)	182	37.05N	35.20E
Adapazari, Tur. (ä-dä-pä-zä′rė)	149	40.45N	30.20E
Adarama, Sudan (ä-dä-rä′mä)	211	17.11N	34.56E
Adda, r., Italy (äd′dä)	160	45.43N	9.31E
Ad Dabbah, Sudan	211	18.04N	30.58E
Ad Dahnā, des., Sau. Ar.	182	26.05N	47.15E
Ad-Dāmir, Sudan (ad-dä′mĕr)	211	17.38N	33.57E
Ad Dammām, Sau. Ar.	182	26.27N	49.59E
Ad Dāmūr, Leb.	181a	33.44N	35.27E
Ad Dawhah, Qatar	182	25.02N	51.28E
Ad Dilam, Sau. Ar.	182	23.47N	47.03E
Ad Dilinjāt, Egypt	218b	30.48N	30.32E
Addington, Eng., U.K.	235	51.18N	0.23E
Addis Ababa, Eth.	211	9.00N	38.44E
Addison, Tx., U.S. (ă′dĭ-sŭn)	107c	32.58N	96.50W
Addlestone, Eng., U.K.	235	51.22N	0.30W
Addo, S. Afr. (ădō)	213c	33.33S	25.43E
Ad Duwaym, Sudan (ad-dȯ-ām′)	211	13.56N	32.22E
Addyston, Oh., U.S. (ăd′ė-stŭn)	101f	39.09N	84.42W
Adel, Ga., U.S. (ā-dĕl′)	114	31.08N	83.55W
Adelaide, Austl. (ăd′ė-lād)	202	34.46S	139.08E
Adelaide, S. Afr. (ăd-ĕl′ād)	213c	32.41S	26.07E
Adelaide Island, i., Ant. (ăd′ė-lād)	219	67.15S	68.40W
Adelphi, Md., U.S.	229d	39.00N	76.58W
Aden ('Adan), Yemen (ä′dĕn)	182	12.48N	45.00E
Aden, Gulf of, b.	182	11.45N	45.45E
Aderklaa, Aus.	239e	48.17N	16.32E
Adi, Pulau, i., Indon. (ä′dē)	197	4.25S	133.52E
Adige, r., Italy (ä′dė-jā)	148	46.38N	10.43E
Adigrat, Eth.	185	14.17N	39.28E
Adilābād, India (ŭ-dĭl-ä-bäd′)	186	19.47N	78.30E
Adirondack Mountains, mts., N.Y., U.S. (ăd-ĭ-rŏn′dăk)	97	43.45N	74.40W
Adis Abeba *see* Addis Ababa, Eth.	211	9.00N	38.44E
Adi Ugri, Erit. (ä-dē o͞o′grē)	211	14.54N	38.52E
Adjud, Rom. (äd′zhȯd)	155	46.05N	27.12E
Adkins, Tx., U.S.	107d	29.22N	98.18W
Adlershof, neigh., Ger.	238a	52.26N	13.33E
Admiralty, i., Ak., U.S. (ăd′mĭr*a*l-tė)	95	57.50N	133.50W
Admiralty Inlet, Wa., U.S. (ăd′mĭr*ȧ*l-tė)	106a	48.10N	122.45W
Admiralty Island National Monument, rec., Ak., U.S. (ăd′mĭr*a*l-tė)	95	57.50N	137.30W
Admiralty Islands, is., Pap. N. Gui. (ăd′mĭr*a*l-tė)	197	1.40S	146.45E
Ado-Ekiti, Nig.	215	7.38N	5.12E
Adolph, Mn., U.S. (ā′dolf)	107h	46.47N	92.17W
Ādoni, India	187	15.42N	77.18E
Adour, r., Fr. (ȧ-do͞or′)	147	43.43N	0.38W
Adra, Spain (ä′drä)	158	36.45N	3.02W
Adrano, Italy (ä-drä′nō)	160	37.42N	14.52E
Adrar, Alg.	210	27.53N	0.15W
Adria, Italy (ä′drė-ä)	160	45.03N	12.01E
Adrian, Mi., U.S. (ā′drĭ-*ă*n)	98	41.55N	84.00W
Adrian, Mn., U.S. (ā′drĭ-*ă*n)	102	43.39N	95.56W
Adrianople *see* Edirne, Tur.	142	41.41N	26.35E
Adriatic Sea, sea, Eur.	142	43.30N	14.27E
Adwa, Eth.	211	14.02N	38.58E
Adwick-le-Street, Eng., U.K. (ăd′wĭk-lė-strēt′)	144a	53.35N	1.11W
Adycha, r., Russia (ä′dĭ-chȧ)	171	66.11N	136.45E
Adygea, state, Russia	166	45.00N	40.00E
Adzhamka, Ukr. (ȧd-zhäm′kȧ)	163	48.33N	32.28E
Adz'va, r., Russia (ädz′vȧ)	166	67.00N	59.20E
Aegean Sea, sea (ė-jē′*ă*n)	142	39.04N	24.56E
Affton, Mo., U.S.	107e	38.33N	90.20W
Afghanistan, nation, Asia (ăf-găn-ĭ-stăn′)	182	33.00N	63.00E
Afgooye, Som. (äf-gô′ĭ)	218a	2.08N	45.08E
Afikpo, Nig.	215	5.53N	7.56E
Aflou, Alg. (ä-flo͞o′)	210	33.59N	2.04E
Afognak, i., Ak., U.S. (ä-fŏg-nȧk′)	95	58.28N	151.35W
Afonso Claudio, Braz. (äl-fōn′sȯ-klou′dēȯ)	129a	20.05S	41.05W
Afragola, Italy (ä-frȧ′gō-lä)	159c	40.40N	14.19E
Africa, cont.	209	10.00N	22.00E
Afton, Mn., U.S. (ăf′t*ŭ*n)	107g	44.54N	92.47W
Afton, Ok., U.S. (ăf′t*ŭ*n)	111	36.42N	94.56W
Afton, Wy., U.S. (ăf′t*ŭ*n)	105	42.42N	110.52W
'Afula, Isr. (ä-fò′lȧ)	181a	32.36N	35.17E
Afyon, Tur. (ä-fė-ōn)	182	38.45N	30.20E
Agadem, Niger (ä′gȧ-dĕm)	211	16.50N	13.17E
Agadez, Niger (ä′g*ȧ*-dĕs)	210	16.58N	7.59E
Agadir, Mor. (ä-g*ȧ*-dēr)	210	30.30N	9.37W
Agalta, Cordillera de, mts., Hond. (kȯr-dēl-yĕ′rä-dĕ-ä-gä′l-tä)	120	15.15N	85.42W
Agapovka, Russia (ä-gä-pôv′kä)	172a	53.18N	59.10E
Agartala, India	186	23.53N	91.22E
Agāshi, India	187b	19.28N	72.46E
Agashkino, Russia (ȧ-gäsh′kĭ-nô)	172b	55.18N	38.13E

PLACE (Pronunciation)	PAGE	Lat. °′	Long. °′
Agattu, i., Ak., U.S. (ȧ′gä-to͞o)	95a	52.14N	173.40E
Agboville, C. Iv.	214	5.56N	4.13W
Ağdam, Azer. (äg′dām)	167	40.00N	47.00E
Agde, Fr. (ägd)	156	43.19N	3.30E
Agege, Nig.	244d	6.37N	3.20E
Agen, Fr. (ȧ-zhäN′)	147	44.13N	0.31E
Agincourt, neigh., Can.	227c	43.48N	79.17W
Aginskoye, Russia (ä-hĭn′skȯ-yĕ)	165	51.15N	113.15E
Agno, Phil. (äg′nō)	197a	16.07N	119.49E
Agno, r., Phil.	197a	15.42N	120.28E
Agnone, Italy (än-yō′nā)	160	41.49N	14.23E
Agogo, Ghana	214	6.47N	1.04W
Agostinho Pôrto, Braz.	234c	22.47S	43.23W
Agra, India (ä′grä)	183	27.18N	78.00E
Ağri, Tur.	167	39.50N	43.10E
Agri, r., Italy (ä′grē)	160	40.15N	16.21E
Agrícola Oriental, Mex.	233a	19.24N	99.05W
Agrínion, Grc. (ȧ-grē′nyȯn)	149	38.38N	21.06E
Agua, vol., Guat. (ä′gwä)	120	14.28N	90.43W
Agua Blanca, Río, r., Mex. (rė′ō-ä-gwä-blä′n-kä)	118	21.46N	102.54W
Agua Brava, Laguna de, l., Mex.	118	22.04N	105.40W
Agua Caliente Indian Reservation, I.R., Ca., U.S. (ä′gwä kal-yĕn′tä)	108	33.50N	116.24W
Aguada, Cuba (ä-gwä′d*ȧ*)	122	22.25N	80.50W
Aguada, l., Mex. (ä-gwä′d*ȧ*)	120a	18.46N	89.40W
Aguadas, Col. (ä-gwä′dȧs)	130	5.37N	75.27W
Aguadilla, P.R. (ä-gwä-dēl′yä)	117b	18.27N	67.10W
Aguadulce, Pan. (ä-gwä-do͞ol′sä)	121	8.15N	80.33W
Agua Escondida, Meseta de, plat., Mex.	119	16.54N	91.35W
Agua Fria, r., Az., U.S. (ä′gwä frė-ä)	109	33.43N	112.22W
Aguai, Braz. (ägwä-ē′)	129a	22.04S	46.57W
Agualeguas, Mex. (ä-gwä-lä′gwäs)	112	26.19N	99.33W
Agualva-Cacém, Port.	238d	38.46N	9.18W
Aguán, r., Hond. (ä-gwȧ′n)	120	15.22N	87.00W
Aguanaval, r., Mex. (ȧ-guä-nä-väl′)	112	25.12N	103.28W
Aguanus, r., Can. (ȧ-gwā′n*ŭ*s)	93	50.45N	62.03W
Aguascalientes, Mex. (ä′gwäs-käl-yĕn′tās)	116	21.52N	102.17W
Aguascalientes, state, Mex. (ä′gwäs-käl-yĕn′tās)	118	22.00N	102.18W
Águeda, Port. (ä-gwā′d*ȧ*)	158	40.36N	8.26W
Agueda, r., Eur. (ä-gĕ-dä)	158	40.50N	6.44W
Aguelhok, Mali	214	19.28N	0.52E
Aguilar, Spain	158	37.32N	4.39W
Aguilar, Co., U.S. (ä-gė-lär′)	110	37.24N	104.38W
Aguilas, Spain (ä-gė-läs)	148	37.26N	1.35W
Aguililla, Mex. (ä-gē-lēl-yä)	118	18.44N	102.44W
Aguililla, r., Mex. (ä-gē-lēl-yä)	118	18.30N	102.48W
Aguja, Punta, c., Peru (pŭn′tȧ ȧ-go͞o′ hä)	130	6.00S	81.15W
Agulhas, Cape, c., S. Afr. (ä-go͞ol′yäs)	212	34.47S	20.00E
Agusan, r., Phil. (ä-go͞o′sän)	197	8.12N	126.07E
Ahaggar, mts., Alg. (ȧ-hȧ-gär′)	210	23.14N	6.00E
Ahar, Iran	185	38.28N	47.04E
Ahlen, Ger. (ä′lĕn)	154	51.45N	7.52E
Ahlenberg, Ger.	236	51.25N	7.28E
Ahmadābād, India (ŭ-mĕd-ā-bād′)	183	23.04N	72.38E
Ahmadnagar, India (ä′mûd-nû-gûr)	183	19.09N	74.45E
Ahmar Mountains, mts., Eth.	211	9.22N	42.00E
Ahoskie, N.C., U.S. (ā-hŏs′kē)	115	36.15N	77.00W
Ahrensburg, Ger. (ä′rĕns-bȯrg)	145c	53.40N	10.14E
Ahrensfelde, Ger.	238a	52.35N	13.35E
Ahrweiler, Ger. (är′vī-lĕr)	154	50.34N	7.05E
Ähtärinjärvi, l., Fin.	153	62.46N	24.25E
Ahuacatlán, Mex. (ä-wä-kät-län′)	118	21.05N	104.28W
Ahuachapán, El Sal. (ä-wä-chä-pän′)	120	13.57N	89.53W
Ahualulco, Mex. (ä-wä-lo͞ol′kō)	118	20.43N	103.57W
Ahuatempan, Mex. (ä-wä-tĕm-pän)	118	18.11N	98.02W
Ahuntsic, neigh., Can.	227b	45.33N	73.39W
Åhus, Swe. (ȯ′hȯs)	152	55.56N	14.19E
Ahvāz, Iran	182	31.15N	48.54E
Ahvenanmaa (Åland), is., Fin. (ä′vĕ-nȧn-mô) (ȯ′länd)	146	60.36N	19.55E
Aiea, Hi., U.S.	94a	21.18N	157.52W
Aigburth, neigh., Eng., U.K.	237a	53.22N	2.55W
Aiken, S.C., U.S. (ā′kĕn)	115	33.32N	81.43W
Aimorès, Serra dos, mts., Braz. (sĕ′r-rä-dȯs-ī-mō-rĕ′s)	131	17.40S	42.38W
Aimoto, Japan (ī-mȯ-tō)	195b	34.59N	135.09E
Aincourt, Fr. (âN-ko͞o′r)	157b	49.04N	1.47E
Aïn el Beïda, Alg.	210	35.57N	7.25E
Ainsworth, Eng., U.K.	237b	53.35N	2.22W
Ainsworth, Ne., U.S. (ānz′wûrth)	102	42.32N	99.51W
Aïn Témouchent, Alg. (ä′ėntĕ-mo͞o-shaN′)	148	35.20N	1.23W
Aintree, Eng., U.K.	237a	53.29N	2.56W
Aïn Wessara, Alg. (ĕn o͞o-sā-rȧ)	159	35.25N	2.50E
Aipe, Col. (ī′pĕ)	130a	3.13N	75.15W
Aïr, mts., Niger	210	18.00N	8.30E
Aire, r., Eng., U.K.	144a	53.42N	1.00W
Aire-sur-l'Adour, Fr. (âr)	156	43.42N	0.17W
Airhitam, Selat, strt., Indon.	181b	0.58N	102.38E
Airport West, Austl.	243b	37.44S	144.53E
Ai Shan, mts., China (ăī′shän)	190	37.27N	120.35E
Aisne, r., Fr. (ĕn)	147	49.28N	3.32E
Aitape, Pap. N. Gui. (ä-ė-tä′pȧ)	197	3.00S	142.10E
Aitkin, Mn., U.S. (āt′kĭn)	103	46.32N	93.43W
Aitolikón, Grc. (ȧ-tō′lĭ-kȯn)	161	38.27N	21.21E
Aitos, Bul. (ä-ē′tōs)	161	42.42N	27.17E
Aitutaki, i., Cook Is. (ī-to͞o-tä′kē)	225	19.00S	162.00W
Aiud, Rom. (ä′ė-ȯd)	149	46.19N	23.40E
Aiuruoca, Braz. (äē′o͞o-ro͞oȯ′-kȧ)	129a	21.57S	44.36W
Aiuruoca, r., Braz.	129a	22.11S	44.35W
Aix-en-Provence, Fr. (ĕks-prȯ-v*ȧ*Ns)	147	43.32N	5.27E
Aix-les-Bains, Fr. (ĕks′-lā-baN′)	157	45.42N	5.56E
Aiyáleo, Grc.	239d	37.59N	23.41E
Aíyina, Grc.	161	37.43N	23.35E
Aíyina, i., Grc.	161	37.43N	23.35E

PLACE (Pronunciation)	PAGE	Lat. °′	Long. °′
Aíyion, Grc.	161	38.13N	22.04E
Aizpute, Lat. (ä′ėz-po͞o-tĕ)	153	56.44N	21.37E
Aizuwakamatsu, Japan	194	37.27N	139.51E
Ajaccio, Fr. (ä-yät′chō)	142	41.55N	8.42E
Ajalpan, Mex. (ä-häl′pän)	119	18.21N	97.14W
Ajana, Austl. (āj-än′ĕr)	202	28.00S	114.45E
Ajaria, state, Geor.	168	41.40N	42.00E
Ajdābiyah, Libya	211	30.56N	20.16E
Ajjer, Tassili-n-, plat., Alg.	210	25.40N	6.57E
Ajmah, Jabal al, mts., Egypt	181a	29.12N	34.03E
Ajman, U.A.E.	182	25.15N	54.30E
Ajmer, India (ŭj-mēr′)	183	26.26N	74.42E
Ajo, Az., U.S. (ä′hȯ)	109	32.20N	112.55W
Ajuchitlán del Progreso, Mex. (ä-ho͞o-chet-lȧn)	118	18.11N	100.32W
Ajuda, neigh., Port.	238d	38.43N	9.12W
Ajusco, Mex. (ä-ho͞o′s-kō)	119a	19.13N	99.12W
Ajusco, Cerro, mtn., Mex. (sĕ′r-rȯ-ä-ho͞o′s-kō)	119a	19.12N	99.16W
Akaishi-dake, mtn., Japan (ä-kī-shē dä′kä)	195	35.30N	138.00E
Akashi, Japan (ä′kä-shē)	194	34.38N	134.59E
Akbarābād, Iran	241h	35.41N	51.21E
Aketi, Zaire (ä-kȧ-tē)	211	2.44N	23.46E
Akhaltsikhe, Geor. (äkȧ′l-tsĭ-kĕ)	167	41.40N	42.50E
Akhdar, Al Jabal al, mts., Libya	211	32.00N	22.00E
Akhḑar, Al Jabal al, mts., Oman	182	23.30N	56.43W
Akhelóös, r., Grc. (ä-hĕ′lȯ-ōs)	161	38.45N	21.26E
Akhisar, Tur. (äk-hĭs-sär′)	149	38.58N	27.58E
Akhtarskaya, Bukhta, b., Russia (bo͞ok′tä ȧK-tär′skȧ-yȧ)	163	45.53N	38.22E
Akhtopol, Bul. (äK′tȯ-pōl)	161	42.08N	27.54E
Akhunovo, Russia (ä-kû′nô-vô)	172a	54.13N	59.36E
Aki, Japan (ä′kė)	195	33.31N	133.51E
Akiak, Ak., U.S. (äk′yȧk)	95	61.00N	161.02W
Akimiski, i., Can. (ä-kĭ-mĭ′skĭ)	85	52.54N	80.22W
Akishima, Japan	242a	35.41N	139.22E
Akita, Japan (ä′kė-tä)	189	39.40N	140.12E
Akjoujt, Maur.	210	19.45N	14.23W
'Akko, Isr.	181a	32.56N	35.05E
Aklavik, Can. (äk′lä-vĭk)	84	68.28N	135.26W
'Aklé'Âouâna, dunes, Afr.	214	18.07N	6.00W
Akmola (Tselinograd), Kaz.	169	51.10N	71.43E
Ako, Japan (ä′kȯ)	195	34.44N	134.22E
Akola, India (ȧ-kȯ′lä)	183	20.47N	77.00E
Akordat, Erit.	211	15.34N	37.54E
Akpatok, i., Can. (ȧk′pȧ-tŏk)	85	60.30N	67.10W
Akranes, Ice.	146	64.18N	21.40W
Akron, Co., U.S. (ăk′r*ŭ*n)	110	40.09N	103.14W
Akron, Oh., U.S. (ăk′r*ŭ*n)	97	41.05N	81.30W
Akropolis, pt. of i., Grc.	239d	37.58N	23.43E
Aksaray, Tur. (äk-sȧ-rī′)	149	38.30N	34.05E
Akşehır, Tur. (äk′shȧ-hēr)	149	38.20N	31.20E
Akşehır Gölü, l., Tur. (ăk′shȧ-hēr)	182	38.40N	31.30E
Aksha, Russia (äk′shȧ)	165	50.28N	113.00E
Aksu, China (ä-kŭ-so͞o)	188	41.29N	80.15E
Akune, Japan (ä′kȯ-nȧ)	195	32.03N	130.16E
Akureyri, Ice. (ä-kȯ-rȧ′rė)	146	65.39N	18.01W
Akutan, i., Ak., U.S. (ä-ko͞o-tän′)	95a	53.58N	169.54W
Akwatia, Ghana	214	6.04N	0.49W
Alabama, state, U.S. (ăl-*ȧ*-băm′*ȧ*)	97	32.50N	87.30W
Alabama, r., Al., U.S. (ăl-*ȧ*-băm′*ȧ*)	97	31.20N	87.39W
Alabat, i., Phil. (ä-lä-bät′)	197a	14.14N	122.05E
Alacam, Tur. (ä-lä-chäm′)	167	41.30N	35.40E
Alacranes, Cuba (ä-lä-krä′nȧs)	122	22.45N	81.35W
Al Aflaj, des., Sau. Ar.	182	24.00N	44.47E
Alagôas, state, Braz. (ä-lä-gō′äzh)	131	9.50S	36.33W
Alagoinhas, Braz. (ä-lä-gō-ēn′yäzh)	131	12.13S	38.12W
Alagón, Spain (ä-lä-gōn′)	158	41.46N	1.07W
Alagón, r., Spain (ä-lä-gōn′)	158	39.53N	6.42W
Alaguntan, Nig.	244d	6.26N	3.30E
Alahuatán, r., Mex. (ä-lä-wä-tȧ′n)	118	18.30N	100.00W
Alajuela, C.R. (ä-lä-hwa′lä)	121	10.01N	84.14W
Alajuela, Lago, l., Pan. (ä-lä-hwa′lä)	116a	9.15N	79.34W
Alakȯl, l., Kaz.	169	45.45N	81.13E
Alalakeiki Channel, strt., Hi., U.S. (ä-lä-lä-kā′kė)	94a	20.40N	156.30W
Al 'Alamayn, Egypt	211	30.53N	28.52E
Al 'Amārah, Iraq	185	31.50N	47.09E
Alameda, Ca., U.S. (ăl-*ȧ*-mā′d*ȧ*)	96	37.46N	122.15W
Alameda, r., Ca., U.S. (ăl-*ȧ*-mā′d*ȧ*)	106b	37.36N	122.02W
Alaminos, Phil. (ä-lä-mē′nȯs)	197a	16.09N	119.58E
Al 'Amirīyah, Egypt	149	31.01N	29.52E
Alamo, Mex. (ä′lä-mȯ)	119	20.55N	97.41W
Alamo, Ca., U.S. (ă′l*ȧ*-mō)	106b	37.51N	122.02W
Alamo, Nv., U.S. (ă′lȧ-mō)	108	37.22N	115.10W
Alamo, r., Mex. (ä′lä-mȯ)	112	26.33N	99.35W
Alamogordo, N.M., U.S. (ăl-*ȧ*-mō-gôr′dō)	109	32.55N	106.00W
Alamo Heights, Tx., U.S. (ă′lȧ-mō)	107d	29.28N	98.27W
Alamo Indian Reservation, I.R., N.M., U.S.	109	34.30N	107.30W
Alamo Peak, mtn., N.M., U.S. (ă′l*ȧ*-mō pēk)	112	32.50N	105.55W
Ąlamosa, Co., U.S. (ăl-*ȧ*-mō′s*ȧ*)	109	37.25N	105.50W
Åland *see* Ahvenanmaa, is., Fin.	146	60.36N	19.55E
Alandskiy, Russia (ä-länt′skĭ)	172a	52.14N	59.48E
Alanga Arba, Kenya	217	0.07N	40.25E
Alanya, Tur.	149	36.40N	32.10E
Alaotra, l., Madag. (ä-lä-ō′tr*ȧ*)	213	17.15S	48.17E
Alapayevsk, Russia (ä-lä-pä′yĕfsk)	164	57.50N	61.35E
Al 'Aqabah, Jord.	182	29.32N	35.00E
Alaquines, Mex. (ā-lȧ-kē′nȧs)	118	22.07N	99.35W
Al 'Arīsh, Egypt (äl-a-rēsh′)	181a	31.08N	33.48E
Alaska, state, U.S. (ȧ-lăs′k*ȧ*)	96a	64.00N	150.00W
Alaska, Gulf of, b., Ak., U.S. (ȧ-lăs′k*ȧ*)	95	57.42N	147.40W

ng-sing; ŋ-baŋk; N-nasalized n; nŏd; cŏmmit; ōld; ôbey; ôrder; oi-boil; fo͞od; ȯ-as oo in foot; ou-out; s-soft; sh-dish; th-thin; pūre; ůnite; ûrn; stŭd; circ*ŭ*s; ü-as in French tu; ’-indeterminate vowel.

ăt; finăl; rāte; senâte; ärm; ȧsk; sofȧ; fâre; ch-choose; dh-as th in other; bē; ĕvent; bĕt; recĕnt; cratẽr; g-gō; gh-guttural g; bĭt; ĭ-short neutral; rīde; ᴋ-guttural k as ch in German ich;

PRONOUNCING INDEX Almanor–Andaman Sea 257

PLACE (Pronunciation)	PAGE	Lat. °'	Long. °'
Almanor, Lake, l., Ca., U.S. (ăl-măn'ôr)	108	40.11N	121.20W
Almansa, Spain (äl-män'sä)	158	38.52N	1.09W
Al Manshāh, Egypt	218b	26.31N	31.46E
Almansor, r., Port. (äl-män-sôr)	158	38.41N	8.27W
Al Manṣūrah, Egypt	211	31.02N	31.25E
Al Manzilah, Egypt (män'za-la)	218b	31.09N	32.05E
Almanzora, r., Spain (äl-män-thō'rä)	158	37.20N	2.25W
Al Marāghah, Egypt	218b	26.41N	31.35E
Almargem do Bispo, Port. (äl-mär-zhěN)	159b	38.51N	9.16W
Al-Marj, Libya	211	32.44N	21.08E
Al Maṣīrah, i., Oman	182	20.43N	58.58E
Al Mawṣil, Iraq	182	36.00N	42.53E
Almazán, Spain (äl-mä-thän')	158	41.30N	2.33W
Al Mazār, Jord.	181a	31.04N	35.41E
Al Mazra'ah, Jord.	181a	31.17N	35.33E
Almeirim, Port. (äl-māī-rěN')	158	39.13N	8.31W
Almelo, Neth. (äl'mě-lō)	151	52.20N	6.42E
Almendra, Embalse de, res., Spain	158	41.15N	6.10W
Almendralejo, Spain (äl-män-drä-lā'hō)	158	38.43N	6.24W
Almería, Spain (äl-mā-rē'ä)	142	36.52N	2.28W
Almería, Golfo de, b., Spain (gôl-fô-dě-äl-māī-reN')	158	36.45N	2.26W
Älmhult, Swe. (älm'hoolt)	152	56.35N	14.08E
Almina, Punta, c., Mor. (äl-mē'nä)	158	35.58N	5.17W
Al Minyā, Egypt	211	28.06N	30.45E
Almirante, Pan. (äl-mē-rän'tā)	121	9.18N	82.24W
Almirante, Bahía de, b., Pan.	121	9.22N	82.07W
Almirós, Grc.	161	39.13N	22.47E
Almodóvar del Campo, Spain (äl-mō-dhō'vär)	158	38.43N	4.10W
Almoloya, Mex. (äl-mō-lō'yä)	118	19.32N	99.44W
Almoloya, Mex. (äl-mō-lō'yä)	119a	19.11N	99.28W
Almonte, Can. (ăl-mŏn'tē)	91	45.15N	76.15W
Almonte, Spain (äl-mōn'tā)	158	37.16N	6.32W
Almonte, r., Spain (äl-mōn'tā)	158	39.35N	5.50W
Almora, India	183	29.20N	79.40E
Al Mubarraz, Sau. Ar.	182	22.31N	46.27E
Al Mudawwarah, Jord.	181a	29.20N	36.01E
Al Mukhā (Mocha), Yemen	182	13.11N	43.20E
Almuñécar, Spain (äl-moon-yā'kär)	158	36.44N	3.43W
Alnön, i., Swe.	152	62.20N	17.39E
Aloha, Or., U.S. (ä'lō-hä)	106c	45.29N	122.52W
Alondra, Ca., U.S.	232	33.54N	118.19W
Alor, Pulau, i., Indon. (ä'lôr)	197	8.07S	125.00E
Álora, Spain (ä'lô-rä)	158	36.49N	4.42W
Alor Gajah, Malay.	181b	2.23N	102.13E
Alor Setar, Malay. (ä'lôr stär)	196	6.10N	100.16E
Alouette, r., Can. (ä-loo-ět')	106d	49.16N	122.32W
Alpena, Mi., U.S. (ăl-pē'nȧ)	97	45.05N	83.30W
Alpes Cotiennes, mts., Eur.	157	44.46N	7.02E
Alphen, Neth.	145a	52.07N	4.38E
Alpiarça, Port. (äl-pyär'sȧ)	158	39.38N	8.37W
Alpine, N.J., U.S. (ăl'pīn)	228	40.56N	73.56W
Alpine, Tx., U.S. (ăl'pīn)	112	30.21N	103.41W
Alps, mts., Eur. (ălps)	142	46.18N	8.42E
Alpujarra, Col. (äl-poo-ká'rá)	130a	3.23N	74.56W
Al Qaḍārif, Sudan	211	14.03N	35.11E
Al Qāhirah see Cairo, Egypt	211	30.00N	31.17E
Al Qanṭarah, Egypt	218c	30.51N	32.20E
Al Qaryah Ash Sharqīyah, Libya	211	30.36N	13.13E
Al Qaṣr, Egypt	184	25.42N	28.53E
Al Qaṭīf, Sau. Ar.	182	26.30N	50.00E
Al Qayṣūmah, Sau. Ar.	182	28.15N	46.20E
Al Qunaytirah, Syria	181a	33.09N	35.49E
Al Qunfudhah, Sau. Ar.	182	19.08N	41.05E
Al Quṣaymah, Egypt	181a	30.40N	34.23E
Al Quṣayr, Egypt	211	26.14N	34.11E
Al Qusayr, Syria	181a	34.32N	36.33E
Als, i., Den. (äls)	152	55.06N	9.40E
Alsace, hist. reg., Fr. (äl-sá's)	157	48.25N	7.24E
Alsip, Il., U.S.	231a	41.40N	87.44W
Altadena, Ca., U.S. (ăl-tă-dē'nă)	107a	34.12N	118.08W
Alta Gracia, Arg. (äl'tä grä'sē-a)	132	31.41S	64.19W
Altagracia, Ven.	130	10.42N	71.34W
Altagracia de Orituco, Ven.	131b	9.53N	66.22W
Altai Mountains, mts., Asia (äl'tī')	188	49.11N	87.15E
Alta Loma, Ca., U.S. (ăl'tă lō'mä)	107a	34.07N	117.35W
Alta Loma, Tx., U.S. (ăl'tȧ lō-mȧ)	113a	29.22N	95.05W
Altamaha, r., Ga., U.S. (ôl-tȧ-mȧ-hô')	115	31.50N	82.00W
Altamira, Braz. (äl-tä-mē'rä)	131	3.13S	52.14W
Altamira, Mex.	119	22.25N	97.55W
Altamirano, Arg. (äl-tä-mē-rä'nō)	132	35.26S	58.12W
Altamura, Italy (äl-tä-moo'rä)	149	40.40N	16.35E
Altar of Heaven, pt. of i., China	240b	39.53N	116.25E
Altar of the Earth, rel., China	240b	39.57N	116.24E
Altar of the Moon, rel., China	240b	39.55N	116.20E
Altar of the Sun, rel., China	240b	39.54N	116.27E
Altavista, Va., U.S. (äl-tä-vĭs'tȧ)	115	37.08N	79.14W
Altay, China (äl-tā)	188	47.52N	86.50E
Altenburg, Ger. (äl-těn-boorgh)	154	50.59N	12.27E
Altenderne Oberbecker, neigh., Ger.	236	51.35N	7.33E
Altenessen, neigh., Ger.	236	51.29N	7.00E
Altenhagen, neigh., Ger.	236	51.22N	7.28E
Altenmarkt an der Triesting, Aus.	145e	48.02N	16.00E
Altenvoerde, Ger.	236	51.18N	7.22E
Alter do Chão, Port. (äl-těr'dò shäN'ôN)	158	39.13N	7.38W
Altiplano, pl., Bol. (äl-tē-plá'nō)	130	18.38S	68.20W
Altlandsberg, Ger. (ält länts'běrgh)	145b	52.34N	13.44E
Altlünen, Ger.	236	51.38N	7.31E
Altmannsdorf, neigh., Aus.	239e	48.10N	16.20E
Alto, La., U.S. (ăl'tō)	113	32.21N	91.52W
Alto da Moóca, neigh., Braz.	234d	23.34S	46.35W
Alto Marañón, Río, r., Peru (rē'ō-ȧl'tô-mä-rän-yō'n)	130	8.18S	77.13W
Altomünster, Ger. (äl'tō-mün'stěr)	145d	48.24N	11.16E
Alton, Can. (ôl'tŭn)	83d	43.52N	80.05W
Alton, Il., U.S. (ôl'tŭn)	97	38.53N	90.11W
Altona, Austl.	201a	37.52S	144.50E
Altona, Can.	89	49.06N	97.33W
Altona, Ger. (äl'tō-nȧ)	145c	53.33N	9.54E
Altona North, Austl.	243b	37.50S	144.51E
Altoona, Al., U.S. (ăl-too'nȧ)	114	34.01N	86.15W
Altoona, Pa., U.S. (ăl-too'nȧ)	97	40.25N	78.25W
Altoona, Wa., U.S. (ăl-too'nȧ)	106c	46.16N	123.39W
Alto Rio Doce, Braz. (äl'tô-rē'ô-dō'sě)	129a	21.02S	43.23W
Alto Songo, Cuba (äl-fō-sôŋ'gō)	123	20.10N	75.45W
Altotonga, Mex. (äl-tō-tôŋ'gä)	119	19.44N	97.13W
Alto Velo, i., Dom. Rep. (äl-tô-vě'lō)	123	17.30N	71.35W
Altrincham, Eng., U.K. (ôl'trĭng-ăm)	144a	53.18N	2.21W
Altruppin, Ger. (ält roo'ppēn)	145b	52.56N	12.50E
Altun Shan, mts., China (äl-tòn shän)	188	36.58N	85.09E
Alturas, Ca., U.S. (ăl-too'rȧs)	104	41.29N	120.33W
Altus, Ok., U.S. (ăl'tŭs)	110	34.38N	99.20W
Al 'Ubaylah, Sau. Ar.	185	21.59N	50.57E
Al-Uḍayyah, Sudan	211	12.06N	28.16E
Alūksne, Lat. (ä'lòks-ně)	166	57.24N	27.04E
Alumette Island, i., Can. (ȧ-lü-mět')	91	45.50N	77.00W
Alum Rock, Ca., U.S.	106b	37.23N	121.50W
Al 'Uqaylah, Libya	211	30.15N	19.07E
Al Uqṣur, Egypt	211	25.38N	32.59E
Alushta, Ukr. (äl'shò-tȧ)	163	44.39N	34.23E
Alva, Ok., U.S. (ăl'vȧ)	110	36.46N	98.41W
Alvanley, Eng., U.K.	237a	53.16N	2.45W
Alvarado, Mex. (äl-vä-rä'dhō)	119	18.48N	95.45W
Alvarado, Luguna de, l., Mex. (lä-gò'nä-dě-äl-vä-rá'dô)	119	18.44N	95.45W
Älvdalen, Swe. (ělv'dä-lěn)	152	61.14N	14.04E
Alverca, Port. (al-věr'kȧ)	159b	38.53N	9.02W
Alvesta, Swe. (äl-věs'tä)	152	56.55N	14.29E
Alvin, Tx., U.S. (ăl'vĭn)	113a	29.25N	95.14W
Alvinópolis, Braz. (äl-vēnō'pō-lēs)	129a	20.07S	43.03W
Alviso, Ca., U.S. (ăl-vī'sō)	106b	37.26N	121.59W
Al Wajh, Sau. Ar.	182	26.15N	36.32E
Alwar, India (ŭl'wŭr)	183	27.39N	76.39E
Al Wāsiṭah, Egypt	218b	29.21N	31.15E
Alytus, Lith. (ä'lē-tòs)	153	54.25N	24.05E
Amacuzac, r., Mex. (ä-mä-koo-zák)	118	18.00N	99.03W
Amadeus, l., Austl. (ăm-ȧ-dē'ŭs)	202	24.30S	131.25E
Amadjuak, l., Can. (ä-mädj'wăk)	85	64.50N	69.20W
Amadora, Port.	159b	38.45N	9.14W
Amagasaki, Japan (ä'mä-gä-sä'kē)	195	34.43N	135.25E
Ama Keng, Sing.	240c	1.24N	103.42E
Amakusa-Shimo, i., Japan (ämä-koo'sä shē-mō)	194	32.24N	129.35E
Åmål, Swe. (ô'môl)	152	59.05N	12.40E
Amalfi, Col. (ä'mä'l-fē)	130a	6.55N	75.04W
Amalfi, Italy (ä-mä'l-fē)	159c	40.23N	14.36E
Amaliás, Grc. (ȧ-măl'yȧs)	161	37.48N	21.23E
Amalner, India	186	21.07N	75.06E
Amambai, Serra de, mts., S.A.	131	20.06S	57.08W
Amami, i., Japan	189	28.10N	129.55E
Amapala, Hond. (ä-mä-pä'lä)	120	13.16N	87.39W
Amarante, Braz. (ä-mä-rän'tä)	131	6.17S	42.43W
Amargosa, r., Ca., U.S. (ȧ'mär-gō'sȧ)	108	35.55N	116.45W
Amarillo, Tx., U.S. (ăm-ȧ-rĭl'ō)	96	35.14N	101.49W
Amaro, Mount, mtn., Italy (ä-mä'rō)	148	42.07N	14.07E
Amaroúsion, Grc.	239d	38.03N	23.49E
Amasya, Tur. (ä-mä'sē-ȧ)	149	40.40N	35.50E
Amatenango, Mex. (ä-mä-tä-naŋ'gō)	119	16.30N	92.29W
Amatignak, i., Ak., U.S. (ä-mȧ'tē-năk)	95a	51.12N	178.30W
Amatique, Bahía de, b., N.A. (bä-ē'ä-dě-ä-mä-tē'kä)	120	15.58N	88.50W
Amatitlán, Guat. (ä-mä-tē-tlän')	120	14.27N	90.39W
Amatlán de Cañas, Mex. (ä-mät-län'dā kän-yäs)	118	20.50N	104.22W
Amazonas, state, Braz. (ä-mä-thō'näs)	130	4.15S	64.30W
Amazonas, Rio (Amazon), r., S.A. (rē'ō-ä-mä-thō'näs)	131	2.03S	53.18W
Ambāla, India (ŭm-bä'lŭ)	183	30.31N	76.48E
Ambalema, Col. (äm-bä-lā'mä)	130	4.47N	74.45W
Ambarchik, Russia (ŭm-bär'chĭk)	165	69.39N	162.18E
Ambarnāth, India	187b	19.12N	73.10E
Ambato, Ec. (äm-bä'tō)	130	1.15S	78.30W
Ambatondrazaka, Madag.	213	17.58S	48.43E
Amberg, Ger. (äm'běrgh)	154	49.26N	11.51E
Ambergris Cay, i., Belize (ăm'bēr-grēs kāz)	120a	18.04N	87.43W
Ambergris Cays, is., T./C. Is.	123	21.20N	71.40W
Ambérieu-en-Bugey, Fr. (äN-bā-rē-u')	157	45.57N	5.21E
Ambert, Fr. (äN-běr')	156	45.32N	3.41E
Ambil Island, i., Phil. (ăm'bēl)	197a	13.51N	120.25E
Ambler, Pa., U.S. (ăm'blěr)	100f	40.09N	75.13W
Amboise, Fr. (äN-bwăz')	156	47.25N	0.56E
Ambon, Indon.	197	3.45S	128.17E
Ambon, Pulau, i., Indon.	197	4.50S	128.45E
Ambositra, Madag. (äN-bō-sē'trä)	213	20.31S	47.28E
Amboy, Il., U.S. (ăm'boi)	98	41.41N	89.15W
Amboy, Wa., U.S. (ăm'boi)	106c	45.55N	122.27W
Ambre, Cap d', c., Madag.	213	12.06S	49.15E
Ambridge, Pa., U.S. (ăm'brĭdj)	101e	40.36N	80.13W
Ambrim, i., Vanuatu	203	16.25S	168.15E
Ambriz, Ang.	212	7.50S	13.06E
Amchitka, i., Ak., U.S. (ăm-chĭt'kȧ)	95a	51.25N	178.10E
Amchitka Passage, strt., Ak., U.S. (ăm-chĭt'kȧ)	95a	51.30N	179.36W
Amealco, Mex. (ä-mä-äl'kō)	118	20.12N	100.08W
Ameca, Mex. (ä-mě'kä)	116	20.34N	104.02W
Amecameca, Mex. (ä-mȧ-kä-mä'kä)	118	19.06N	98.46W
Ameide, Neth.	145a	51.57N	4.57E
Ameixoera, neigh., Port.	238d	38.47N	9.10W
Ameland, i., Neth.	151	53.29N	5.54E
Amelia, Oh., U.S. (ȧ-měl'yȧ)	101f	39.01N	84.12W
American, South Fork, r., Ca., U.S. (ȧ-měr'ĭ-kăn)	108	38.43N	120.45W
Americana, Braz. (ä-mě-rē-kȧ'nȧ)	129a	22.46S	47.19W
American Falls, Id., U.S. (ȧ-měr'ĭ-kăn-fôls')	105	42.45N	112.53W
American Falls Reservoir, res., Id., U.S. (ȧ-měr'ĭ-kăn-fôls')	96	42.56N	113.18W
American Fork, Ut., U.S.	109	40.20N	111.50W
American Highland, plat., Ant.	219	72.00S	79.00E
American Samoa, dep., Oc.	2	14.20S	170.00W
Americus, Ga., U.S. (ȧ-měr'ĭ-kŭs)	97	32.04N	84.15W
Amersfoort, Neth. (ä'měrz-fōrt)	145a	52.08N	5.23E
Amersham, Eng., U.K.	235	51.40N	0.38W
Amery, Can. (ā'mēr-ē)	85	56.34N	94.03W
Amery, Wi., U.S.	103	45.19N	92.24W
Ames, Ia., U.S. (āmz)	103	42.00N	93.36W
Amesbury, Ma., U.S. (āmz'běr-ē)	93a	42.51N	70.56W
Amfissa, Grc. (ȧm-fĭ'sȧ)	161	38.32N	22.26E
Amga, Russia (ŭm-gä')	165	61.08N	132.09E
Amga, r., Russia	171	61.41N	133.11E
Amgun', r., Russia	171	52.30N	138.00E
Amherst, Can. (ăm'hērst)	85	45.49N	64.14W
Amherst, N.Y., U.S.	230a	42.58N	78.48W
Amherst, Oh., U.S.	101d	41.24N	82.13W
Amherst, i., Can. (ăm'hērst)	91	44.08N	76.45W
Amiens, Fr. (ä-myăN')	147	49.54N	2.18E
Amirante Islands, is., Sey.	5	6.02S	52.30E
Amisk Lake, l., Can.	89	54.35N	102.13W
Amistad Reservoir, res., N.A.	112	29.20N	101.00W
Amite, La., U.S. (ä-mēt')	113	30.43N	90.32W
Amite, r., La., U.S.	113	30.45N	90.48W
Amity, Pa., U.S. (ăm'ĭ-tĭ)	101e	40.02N	80.11W
Amityville, N.Y., U.S. (ăm'ĭ-tĭ-vĭl)	100a	40.41N	73.24W
Amlia, i., Ak., U.S. (ȧ'mlēä)	95a	52.00N	173.28W
'Ammān, Jord. (äm'mȧn)	182	31.57N	35.57E
Ammersee, l., Ger. (äm'měr)	145d	48.00N	11.08E
Amnicon, r., Wi., U.S. (ăm'nė-kŏn)	107h	46.35N	91.56W
Amorgós, i., Grc. (ä-môr'gōs)	149	36.47N	25.47E
Amory, Ms., U.S. (ām'ô-rē)	114	33.58N	88.27W
Amos, Can. (ā'mŭs)	85	48.31N	78.04W
Amoy see Xiamen, China	189	24.30N	118.10E
Amparo, Braz. (äm-pá'-rô)	129a	22.43S	46.44W
Amper, r., Ger. (äm'pěr)	145d	48.18N	11.32E
Amposta, Spain (äm-pōs'tä)	159	40.42N	0.34E
Amqui, Can.	92	48.28N	67.28W
Amrāvati, India	183	20.58N	77.47E
Amritsar, India (ŭm-rĭt'sŭr)	183	31.43N	74.52E
Amstelveen, Neth.	145a	52.18N	4.51E
Amsterdam, Neth. (äm-stěr-däm')	142	52.21N	4.52E
Amsterdam, N.Y., U.S. (ăm'stēr-dăm)	99	42.55N	74.10W
Amsterdam, Île, i., Afr.	219	37.52S	77.32E
Amstetten, Aus. (äm'stět-ěn)	154	48.09N	14.53E
Am Timan, Chad (äm'tē-män')	211	11.18N	20.30E
Amu Darya, r., Asia (ä-mò-dä'rēä)	164	38.30N	64.00E
Amukta Passage, strt., Ak., U.S. (ä-mook'tȧ)	95a	52.30N	172.00W
Amundsen Gulf, b., Can. (ä'mŭn-sěn-gŭlf')	84	70.17N	123.28W
Amundsen Sea, sea, Ant. (ä'mŭn-sěn-sē')	219	72.00S	110.00W
Amungen, l., Swe.	152	61.07N	16.00E
Amur, r., Asia	165	49.00N	136.00E
Amurskiy, Russia (ä-mûr'skĭ)	172a	52.35N	59.36E
Amurskiy, Zaliv, b., Russia (zä'lĭf ä-môr'skĭ)	194	43.20N	131.40E
Amusgos, Mex.	118	16.39N	98.09W
Amuyao, Mount, mtn., Phil. (ä-moo-yä'ō)	197a	17.04N	121.09E
Amvrakikos Kólpos, b., Grc.	161	39.00N	21.00E
Amyun, Leb.	181a	34.18N	35.48E
Anabar, r., Russia (ăn-ȧ-bär')	171	71.15N	113.00E
Anaco, Ven. (ä-nä'kô)	131b	9.29N	64.27W
Anaconda, Mt., U.S. (ăn-ȧ-kŏn'dȧ)	96	46.07N	112.55W
Anacortes, Wa., U.S. (ăn-ȧ-kôr'těz)	106a	48.30N	122.37W
Anacostia, neigh., D.C., U.S.	229d	38.52N	76.59W
Anadarko, Ok., U.S. (ăn-ȧ-där'kō)	110	35.05N	98.14W
Anadyr', Russia (ŭ-nȧ-dĭr')	165	64.47N	177.01E
Anadyr, r., Russia	171	65.30N	172.45E
Anadyrskiy Zaliv, b., Russia	164	64.10N	178.00W
'Ānah, Iraq	185	34.28N	41.56E
Anaheim, Ca., U.S. (ăn'ȧ-hīm)	107a	33.50N	117.55W
Anahuac, Tx., U.S. (ä-nä'wăk)	113a	29.46N	94.41W
Ānai Mudi, mtn., India	187	10.10N	77.00E
Anama Bay, Can.	89	51.56N	98.05W
Ana María, Cayos, is., Cuba	122	21.25N	78.50W
Anambas, Kepulauan, is., Indon. (ä-näm-bäs)	196	2.41N	106.38E
Anamosa, Ia., U.S. (ăn-ȧ-mō'sȧ)	103	42.06N	91.18W
Anan'yiv, Ukr.	167	47.43N	29.59E
Anapa, Russia (ȧ-nä'pä)	167	44.54N	37.19E
Anápolis, Braz. (ä-nȧ'pō-lēs)	131	16.17S	48.47W
Añatuya, Arg. (ȧ-nyä-too'yȧ)	132	28.22S	62.45W
Anchieta, Braz. (ȧn-chyě'tȧ)	132b	22.49S	43.24W
Ancholme, r., Eng., U.K. (ăn'chŭm)	144a	53.28N	0.27W
Anchorage, Ak., U.S. (ăŋ'kēr-āj)	96a	61.12N	149.48W
Anchorage, Ky., U.S.	101h	38.16N	85.32W
Anci, China (än-tsŭ)	190	39.31N	116.41E
Ancienne-Lorette, Can. (äN-syěn' lō-rět')	83b	46.48N	71.21W
Ancon, Pan. (ăŋ-kōn')	116a	8.55N	79.32W
Ancona, Italy (än-kō'nä)	142	43.37N	13.32E
Ancud, Chile (äŋ-koodh')	132	41.52S	73.45W
Ancud, Golfo de, b., Chile (gôl-fô-dě-äŋ-koodh')	132	41.15S	73.00W
Anda, China	192	46.20N	125.20E
Åndalsnes, Nor.	152	62.33N	7.46E
Andalucia, hist. reg., Spain (än-dä-loo-sē'ä)	158	37.35N	5.40W
Andalusia, Al., U.S. (ăn-dȧ-loo'zhĭȧ)	114	31.19N	86.19W
Andaman Islands, is., India (ăn-dȧ-măn')	196	11.38N	92.17E
Andaman Sea, sea, Asia	196	12.44N	95.45E

PRONOUNCING INDEX Araya–Assiniboine 259

PLACE (Pronunciation)	PAGE	Lat. °'	Long. °'
Araya, Punta de, c., Ven. (pün'tä-dě-ä-rä'yä)	131b	10.40N	64.15W
Arayat, Phil. (ä-rä'yät)	197a	15.10N	120.44E
'Arbi, Sudan	211	20.36N	29.57E
Arboga, Swe. (är-bō'gä)	152	59.26N	15.50E
Arborea, Italy (är-bō-rē'ä)	160	39.50N	8.36E
Arbroath, Scot., U.K. (är-brōth')	150	56.36N	2.25W
Arcachon, Fr. (är-kä-shôn')	147	44.39N	1.12W
Arcachon, Bassin d', Fr. (bä-sěn' där-kä-shôn')	156	44.42N	1.50W
Arcadia, Ca., U.S. (är-kā'dĭ-ȧ)	107a	34.08N	118.02W
Arcadia, Fl., U.S.	115a	27.12N	81.51W
Arcadia, La., U.S.	113	32.33N	92.56W
Arcadia, Wi., U.S.	103	44.15N	91.30W
Arcata, Ca., U.S. (är-kå'tȧ)	104	40.54N	124.05W
Arc de Triomphe, pt. of i., Fr.	237c	48.53N	2.17E
Arc Dome Mountain, mtn., Nv., U.S. (ärk dōm)	108	38.51N	117.21W
Arcelia, Mex. (är-sā'lē-ä)	118	18.19N	100.14W
Archbald, Pa., U.S. (ärch'bôld)	99	41.30N	75.35W
Arches National Park, Ut., U.S. (är'ches)	109	38.45N	109.35W
Archidona, Ec. (är-chē-do'nä)	130	1.01S	77.49W
Archidona, Spain (är-chē-dô'nä)	158	37.08N	4.24W
Arcis-sur-Aube, Fr. (är-sēs'sûr-ōb')	156	48.31N	4.04E
Arco, Id., U.S. (är'kō)	105	43.39N	113.15W
Arcola, Tx., U.S.	113a	29.30N	95.28W
Arcola, Va., U.S. (ăr'cōlă)	100e	38.57N	77.32W
Arcos de la Frontera, Spain (är'kōs-dě-lä-frôn-tě'rä)	158	36.44N	5.48W
Arctic Ocean, o.	220	85.00N	170.00E
Arcueil, Fr. (ärk'tĭk)	237c	48.48N	2.20E
Arda, r., Bul. (är'dä)	161	41.36N	25.18E
Ardabīl, Iran	182	38.15N	48.00E
Ardahan, Tur. (är-dȧ-hän')	167	41.10N	42.40E
Ardatov, Russia (är-dȧ-tôf')	166	54.58N	46.10E
Ardennes, mts., Eur. (ȧr-děn')	147	50.01N	5.12E
Ardey, neigh., Ger.	236	51.26N	7.23E
Ardila, r., Eur. (är-dē'lȧ)	158	38.10N	7.15W
Ardmore, Md., U.S.	229d	38.56N	76.52W
Ardmore, Ok., U.S. (ärd'mōr)	96	34.10N	97.08W
Ardmore, Pa., U.S.	100f	40.01N	75.18W
Ardrossan, Can. (är-dros'ăn)	83g	53.33N	113.08W
Ardsley, Eng., U.K. (ärdz'lē)	144a	53.43N	1.33W
Åre, Swe.	146	63.12N	13.12E
Arecibo, P.R. (ä-rå-sē'bō)	117b	18.28N	66.45W
Areeiro, Port.	238d	38.39N	9.12W
Areia Branca, Braz. (ä-rě'yä-brä'n-kä)	131	4.58S	37.02W
Arena, Point, c., Ca., U.S. (ä-rā'nȧ)	108	38.57N	123.40W
Arenas, Punta, c., Ven. (pòn'tä-rě'näs)	131b	10.57N	64.24W
Arenas de San Pedro, Spain	158	40.12N	5.04W
Arendal, Nor. (ä'rěn-däl)	152	58.29N	8.44E
Arendonk, Bel.	145a	51.19N	5.07E
Arequipa, Peru (ä-rå-kē'pä)	130	16.27S	71.30W
Arezzo, Italy (ä-rět'sō)	148	43.28N	11.54E
Arga, r., Spain (är'gä)	158	42.35N	1.55W
Arganda, Spain (är-gän'dä)	159a	40.18N	3.27W
Argazi, l., Russia (är'gä-zĭ)	172a	55.24N	60.37E
Argazi, r., Russia	172a	55.33N	57.30E
Argentan, Fr. (ȧr-zhän-tän')	156	48.45N	0.01W
Argentat, Fr. (ȧr-zhän-tä')	156	45.07N	1.57E
Argenteuil, Fr. (är-zhän-tû'y')	156	48.56N	2.15E
Argentina, nation, S.A. (är-jěn-tē'nȧ)	132	35.30S	67.00W
Argentino, l., Arg. (är-kěn-tē'nō)	132	50.15S	72.45W
Argenton-sur-Creuse, Fr. (är-zhän'tôn-sür-krôs)	156	46.34N	1.28E
Argolikos Kólpos, b., Grc.	161	37.20N	23.00E
Argonne, mts., Fr. (ä'r-gôn)	157	49.21N	5.54E
Argos, Grc. (är'gŏs)	161	37.38N	22.45E
Argostólion, Grc. (är-gŏs-tô'lē-ōn)	161	38.10N	20.30E
Arguello, Point, c., Ca., U.S. (är-gwāl'yō)	108	34.35N	120.40W
Arguin, Cap d', c., Maur.	210	20.28N	17.46W
Argun', r., Asia (ȧr-gōōn')	165	50.00N	119.00E
Argungu, Nig.	215	12.45N	4.31E
Argyle, Can. (är'gīl)	83f	50.11N	97.27W
Argyle, Mn., U.S.	102	48.21N	96.48W
Århus, Den. (ôr'hōōs)	146	56.09N	10.10E
Ariakeno-Umi, b., Japan (ä-rē'ä-kä'nō ōō'nē)	195	33.03N	130.18E
Ariake-Wan, b., Japan (ä'rē-ä'kå wän)	195	31.19N	131.15E
Ariano, Italy (ä-rē-ä'nō)	160	41.09N	15.11E
Ariari, r., Col. (ä-ryà'rē)	130a	3.34N	73.42W
Aribinda, Burkina	214	14.14N	0.52W
Arica, Chile (ä-rē'kä)	130	18.34S	70.14W
Arichat, Can. (ä-rĭ-shät')	93	45.31N	61.01W
Ariège, r., Fr. (ȧ-rē-ězh')	156	43.26N	1.29E
Ariel, Wa., U.S. (ā'rĭ-ěl)	106c	45.57N	122.34W
Arieș, r., Rom.	155	46.25N	23.15E
Ariguanabo, Lago de, l., Cuba (lä'gô-dě-ä-rē-gwä-nä'bô)	123a	22.52N	82.33W
Arikaree, r., Co., U.S. (ä-rĭ-kȧ-rē')	110	39.51N	102.18W
Arima, Japan (ä'rē-mä')	195b	34.48N	135.16E
Aringay, Phil. (ä-rĭŋ-gä'ē)	197a	16.25N	120.20E
Arino, neigh., Japan	242b	34.50N	135.14E
Arinos, r., Braz. (ä-rē'nòzsh)	131	12.09S	56.49W
Aripuanã, r., Braz. (ȧ-rē-pwän'yȧ)	131	7.06S	60.29W
'Arīsh, Wādī al, r., Egypt (ȧ-rēsh')	181a	30.36N	34.07E
Aristazabal Island, i., Can.	86	52.30N	129.20W
Arizona, state, U.S. (ăr-ĭ-zō'nȧ)	96	34.00N	113.00W
Arjona, Spain (är-hō'nä)	158	37.58N	4.03W
Arka, r., Russia	171	60.45N	142.30E
Arkabutla Lake, res., Ms., U.S. (är-kȧ-bŭt'lă)	114	34.48N	90.00W
Arkadelphia, Ar., U.S. (är-kȧ-děl'fĭ-ȧ)	111	34.06N	93.05W
Arkansas, state, U.S. (är'kăn-sô) (är-kăn'sȧs)	97	34.50N	93.40W
Arkansas, r., U.S.	96	37.30N	97.00W
Arkansas City, Ks., U.S.	111	37.04N	97.02W

PLACE (Pronunciation)	PAGE	Lat. °'	Long. °'
Arkhangelsk (Archangel), Russia (ár-kän'gělsk)	164	64.30N	40.25E
Arkhangel'skiy, Kaz. (är-kän-gěl'skĭ)	169	52.52N	61.53E
Arkhangel'skoye, Russia (är-kän-gěl'skô-yě)	172a	54.25N	56.48E
Arklow, Ire. (ärk'lō)	150	52.47N	6.10W
Arkonam, India (ăr-kō-năm')	187	13.05N	79.43E
Arlanza, r., Spain (är-län-thä')	158	42.08N	3.45W
Arlanzón, r., Spain (är-län-thōn')	158	42.12N	3.58W
Arlberg Tunnel, trans., Aus. (ärl'běrgh)	154	47.05N	10.15E
Arles, Fr. (ärl)	156	43.42N	4.38E
Arlington, S. Afr.	218d	28.02S	27.52E
Arlington, Ga., U.S. (är'lĭng-tun')	114	31.25N	84.42W
Arlington, Ma., U.S.	93a	42.26N	71.13W
Arlington, S.D., U.S. (är'lèng-tŭn)	102	44.23N	97.09W
Arlington, Tx., U.S. (ár'lĭng-tŭn)	107c	32.44N	97.07W
Arlington, Vt., U.S.	99	43.05N	73.05W
Arlington, Va., U.S.	100e	38.55N	77.10W
Arlington, Wa., U.S.	106a	48.11N	122.08W
Arlington Heights, Il., U.S. (är'lēng-tŭn-hī'ts)	101a	42.05N	87.59W
Arlington National Cemetery, pt. of i., Va., U.S.	229d	38.53N	77.04W
Arltunga, Austl. (ärl-tòŋ'gȧ)	202	23.19S	134.45E
Arma, Ks., U.S. (är'mȧ)	111	37.34N	94.43W
Armagh, Can. (är-mä') (är-mäk')	83b	46.45N	70.36W
Armagh, N. Ire., U.K.	146	54.21N	6.25W
Armant, Egypt (är-mänt')	218b	25.37N	32.32E
Armaro, Col. (är-má'rō)	130a	4.58N	74.54W
Armavir, Russia (ár-mȧ-vĭr')	164	45.00N	41.00E
Armenia, Col. (är-mē'nė-ȧ)	130	4.33N	75.40W
Armenia, El Sal. (är-mā'nē-ä)	120	13.44N	89.31W
Armenia, nation, Asia	164	41.00N	44.39E
Armentières, Fr. (är-män-tyâr')	156	50.43N	2.53E
Armeria, Río de, r., Mex. (rē'ō-dě-är-mȧ-rē'ä)	118	19.36N	104.10W
Armherstburg, Can. (ärm'hěrst-bōōrgh)	90	42.06N	83.06W
Armidale, Austl. (är'mĭ-dāl)	203	30.27S	151.50E
Armour, S.D., U.S. (är'mēr)	102	43.18N	98.21W
Armstrong Station, Can. (ärm'strŏng)	85	50.21N	89.00W
Armyans'k, Ukr.	163	46.06N	33.42E
Arnedo, Spain (är-nā'dō)	158	42.12N	2.03W
Arnhem, Neth. (ärn'hěm)	147	51.58N	5.56E
Arnhem, Cape, c., Austl.	202	12.15S	137.00E
Arnhem Land, reg., Austl. (ärn'hěm-lănd)	202	13.15S	133.00E
Arno, r., Italy (ä'r-nò)	148	43.30N	11.00E
Arnold, Eng., U.K. (är'nŭld)	144a	53.00N	1.08W
Arnold, Mn., U.S. (är'nŭld)	107h	46.53N	92.06W
Arnold, Pa., U.S.	101e	40.35N	79.45W
Arnprior, Can. (ärn-prī'ēr)	91	45.25N	76.20W
Arnsberg, Ger. (ärns'běrgh)	157c	51.25N	8.02E
Arnstadt, Ger. (ärn'shtät)	154	50.51N	10.57E
Aroab, Nmb. (är'ō-åb)	212	25.40S	19.45E
Aroostook, r., Me., U.S. (ȧ-rōs'tòk)	92	46.44N	68.15W
Aroroy, Phil. (ä-rō-rō'ē)	197a	12.30N	123.24E
Arpajon, Fr. (är-pä-jō'n)	157b	48.35N	2.15E
Arpoador, Ponta do, c., Braz. (pô'n-tä-dō-är'pôä-dō'r)	132b	22.59S	43.11W
Arraiolos, Port. (är-rī-ō'lōzh)	158	38.47N	7.59W
Arran, Island of, Scot., U.K. (ă'răn)	150	55.25N	5.25W
Ar Rank, Sudan	211	11.45N	32.53E
Arras, Fr. (ȧ-räs')	147	50.21N	2.40E
Ar Rawḑah, Egypt	218b	27.47N	30.52E
Arrecifes, Arg. (är-rȧ-sē'fās)	129c	34.03S	60.05W
Arrecifes, r., Arg.	129c	34.07S	59.50W
Arrée, Monts d', mts., Fr. (är-rā')	156	48.27N	4.00W
Arriaga, Mex. (är-rē-ä'gä)	119	16.15N	93.54W
Arrone, r., Italy	159d	41.57N	12.17E
Arrow Creek, r., Mt., U.S. (ăr'ō)	105	47.29N	109.53W
Arrowhead, Lake, l., Ca., U.S. (lăk ăr'ōhěd)	107a	34.17N	117.13W
Arrowrock Reservoir, res., Id., U.S. (ăr'ō-rŏk)	104	43.40N	115.30W
Arroya Arena, Cuba (är-rō'yä-rě'nä)	123a	23.01N	82.30W
Arroyo de la Luz, Spain (är-rō'yō-dě-lä-lōō'z)	158	39.39N	6.46W
Arroyo Seco, Mex. (är-rō'yō sā'kō)	118	21.31N	99.44W
Ar Rub' al Khālī, des., Asia	182	20.00N	51.00E
Ar Rutbah, Iraq	185	33.02N	40.17E
Arsen'yev, Russia	165	44.13N	133.32E
Arsinskiy, Russia (är-sĭn'skĭ)	172a	53.46N	59.54E
Árta, Grc. (är'tä)	149	39.08N	21.02E
Artarmon, Austl.	243a	33.49S	151.11E
Arteaga, Mex. (är-tä-ä'gä)	112	25.28N	100.50W
Artëm, Russia (ȧr-tyôm')	165	43.28N	132.29E
Artemisa, Cuba (är-tȧ-mē'sä)	122	22.50N	82.45W
Artemivs'k, Ukr.	167	48.37N	38.00E
Arteria, Ca., U.S.	232	33.52N	118.05W
Artesia, N.M., U.S. (är-tē'sĭ-ȧ)	110	32.44N	104.23W
Arthabaska, Can.	91	46.03N	71.54W
Arthur's Town, Bah.	123	24.40N	75.40W
Arti, Russia (är'tĭ)	172a	56.20N	58.38E
Artibonite, r., N.A. (är-tē-bō-nē'tā)	123	19.00N	72.25W
Artigas, neigh., Ven.	234a	10.30N	66.56W
Aru, Kepulauan, is., Indon.	197	6.20S	133.00E
Arua, Ug. (ä'rōō-ä)	211	3.01N	30.55E
Aruba, i., Aruba (ä-rōō'bȧ)	117	12.29N	70.00W
Arunachal Pradesh, state, India	183	27.35N	92.56E
Arundel Gardens, Md., U.S.	229c	39.13N	76.37W
Arundel Village, Md., U.S.	229c	39.13N	76.36W
Arusha, Tan. (ȧ-rōō'shä)	212	3.22S	36.41E
Arvida, Can.	85	48.26N	71.11W
Arvika, Swe. (är-vē'kȧ)	152	59.41N	12.35E
Arzamas, Russia (är-zä-mäs')	166	55.20N	43.52E
Arziw, Alg.	148	35.50N	0.20W
Arzua, Spain (är-thōō'ä)	158	42.54N	8.19W

PLACE (Pronunciation)	PAGE	Lat. °'	Long. °'
Aš, Czech Rep. (äsh')	154	50.12N	12.13E
Asahi-Gawa, r., Japan (ȧ-sä'hē-gä'wä)	195	35.01N	133.40E
Asahikawa, Japan	189	43.50N	142.09E
Asaka, Japan (ä-sä'kä)	195a	35.47N	139.36E
Asālafpur, neigh., India	240d	28.38N	77.05E
Asansol, India	183	23.45N	86.58E
Asbest, Russia (äs-běst')	166	57.02N	61.28E
Asbestos, Can. (ăs-běs'tōs)	91	45.49N	71.52W
Asbestovskiy, Russia	172a	57.46N	61.23E
Asbury Park, N.J., U.S. (ăz'bēr-ĭ)	100a	40.13N	74.01W
Ascención, Bahía de la, b., Mex.	120a	19.39N	87.30W
Ascensión, Mex. (äs-sěn-sė-ōn')	118	24.21N	99.54W
Ascension, i., St. Hel. (ȧ-sěn'shŭn)	209	8.00S	13.00W
Ascent, S. Afr. (ăs-ěnt')	218d	27.14S	29.06E
Aschaffenburg, Ger. (ä-shäf'ěn-bòrgh)	154	49.58N	9.12E
Ascheberg, Ger. (ä'shě-běrg)	157c	51.47N	7.38E
Aschersleben, Ger. (äsh'ěrs-lā-běn)	154	51.46N	11.28E
Ascoli Piceno, Italy (äs'kō-lēpē-chä'nō)	160	42.50N	13.55E
Aseb, Erit.	211	12.52N	43.39E
Asenovgrad, Bul.	161	42.00N	24.49E
Aseri, Est. (ȧ'sě-rĭ)	153	59.26N	26.58E
Asha, Russia (ä'shä)	172a	55.01N	57.17E
Ashabula, l., N.D., U.S. (ăsh'ȧ-bū-lă)	102	47.07N	97.51W
Ashan, Russia (ä'shän)	172a	57.08N	56.25E
Ashbourne, Eng., U.K. (ăsh'bŭrn)	144a	53.01N	1.44W
Ashburn, Ga., U.S. (ăsh'bŭrn)	114	31.42N	83.42W
Ashburn, Va., U.S.	100e	39.02N	77.30W
Ashburton, r., Austl. (ăsh'bûr-tŭn)	202	22.30S	115.30E
Ashby-de-la-Zouch, Eng., U.K. (ăsh'bĭ-dě-lȧ zōōsh')	144a	52.44N	1.23W
Ashdod, Isr.	181a	31.46N	34.39E
Ashdown, Ar., U.S. (ăsh'doun)	111	33.41N	94.07W
Asheboro, N.C., U.S. (ăsh'bŭr-ō)	115	35.41N	79.50W
Asherton, Tx., U.S. (ăsh'ēr-tŭn)	112	28.26N	99.45W
Asheville, N.C., U.S. (ăsh'vĭl)	97	35.35N	82.35W
Ashfield, Austl.	243a	33.53S	151.08E
Ashford, Eng., U.K.	235	51.26N	0.27W
Ash Fork, Az., U.S.	109	35.13N	112.29W
Ashikaga, Japan (ä'shė-kä'gȧ)	195	36.22N	139.26E
Ashiya, Japan (ä'shė-yä')	195	33.54N	130.40E
Ashiya, Japan	195b	34.44N	135.18E
Ashizuri-Zaki, c., Japan (ä-shē-zō-rē zä-kē)	194	32.43N	133.04E
Ashkhabad, Turk. (ŭsh-kä-bät')	169	37.57N	58.23E
Ashland, Al., U.S. (ăsh'lȧnd)	114	33.15N	85.50W
Ashland, Ks., U.S.	110	37.11N	99.46W
Ashland, Ky., U.S.	98	38.25N	82.40W
Ashland, Me., U.S.	92	46.37N	68.26W
Ashland, Ma., U.S.	93a	42.16N	71.28W
Ashland, Ne., U.S.	102	41.02N	96.23W
Ashland, Oh., U.S.	98	40.50N	82.15W
Ashland, Or., U.S.	104	42.12N	122.42W
Ashland, Pa., U.S.	99	40.45N	76.20W
Ashland, Wi., U.S.	97	46.34N	90.55W
Ashley, N.D., U.S. (ăsh'lē)	102	46.03N	99.23W
Ashley, Pa., U.S.	99	41.15N	75.55W
Ashley Green, Eng., U.K.	235	51.44N	0.35W
Ashmūn, Egypt (äsh-mōōn')	218b	30.19N	30.57E
Ashqelon, Isr. (äsh'kě-lōn)	181a	31.40N	34.36E
Ash Shabb, Egypt (shěb)	211	22.34N	29.52E
Ash Shallūfah, Egypt (shäl'lò-fä)	218b	30.09N	32.33E
Ash Shaqrā', Sau. Ar.	182	25.10N	45.08E
Ash Shāriqah, U.A.E.	185	25.22N	55.23E
Ash Shawbak, Jord.	181a	30.31N	35.35E
Ash Shiḩr, Yemen	182	14.45N	49.32E
Ashtabula, Oh., U.S. (ăsh-tȧ-bū'lȧ)	97	41.55N	80.50W
Ashtead, Eng., U.K.	235	51.19N	0.18W
Ashton, Id., U.S. (ăsh'tŭn)	105	44.04N	111.28W
Ashton-in-Makerfield, Eng., U.K. (ăsh'tŭn-ĭn-māk'ēr-fēld)	144a	53.29N	2.39W
Ashton-under-Lyne, Eng., U.K. (ăsh'tŭn-ŭn-dēr-līn')	144a	53.29N	2.04W
Ashuanipi, l., Can. (ăsh-wȧ-nĭp'ĭ)	85	52.40N	67.42W
Ashukino, Russia (ȧ-shōō'kĭnô)	172b	56.10N	37.57E
Asia, cont.	180	50.00N	100.00E
Asia Minor, reg., Tur. (ā'zhȧ)	143	38.18N	31.18E
Asientos, Mex. (ä-sē-ěn'tōs)	118	22.13N	102.05W
Asilah, Mor.	158	35.30N	6.05W
Asinara, i., Italy	160	41.02N	8.22E
Asinara, Golfo dell', b., Italy (gôl'fō-děl-ä-sē-nä'rä)	160	40.58N	8.28E
Asīr, reg., Sau. Ar. (ä-sēr')	182	19.30N	42.00E
Askarovo, Russia (äs-kä-rô'vô)	172a	53.21N	58.32E
Askersund, Swe. (äs'kěr-sònd)	152	58.43N	14.53E
Askino, Russia (äs'kĭ-nô)	172a	56.06N	56.29E
Asmara *see* Asmera, Erit.	210	15.17N	38.56E
Asmera, Erit. (äs-mä'rä)	211	15.17N	38.56E
Asnieres, Fr. (ä-nyâr')	157b	48.55N	2.18E
Asosa, Eth.	211	10.13N	34.28E
Asotin, Wa., U.S. (ȧ-sō'tĭn)	104	46.19N	117.01W
Aspen, Co., U.S. (ăs'pěn)	109	39.15N	106.55W
Asperen, Neth.	145a	51.52N	5.07E
Aspern, neigh., Aus.	239e	48.13N	16.29E
Aspinwall, Pa., U.S.	230b	40.30N	79.55W
Aspy Bay, b., Can. (ăs'pē)	93	46.55N	60.25W
Aş Şaff, Egypt	218b	29.33N	31.23E
As Şallūm, Egypt	211	31.35N	25.05E
As Salt, Jord.	181a	32.02N	35.44E
Assam, state, India (ăs-săm')	183	26.00N	91.00E
As Samāwah, Iraq	185	31.18N	45.17E
Asseln, neigh., Ger.	236	51.32N	7.35E
Assens, Den. (ä'sěns)	152	55.16N	9.54E
As Sinbillāwayn, Egypt	218b	30.53N	31.37E
Assini, C. Iv. (ȧ-sē-nē')	210	4.52N	3.16W
Assiniboia, Can.	84	49.38N	105.59W
Assiniboine, r., Can. (ă-sĭn'ĭ-boin)	89	50.03N	97.57W
Assiniboine, Mount, mtn., Can.	87	50.52N	115.39W

ng-sing; ŋ-baŋk; N-nasalized n; nŏd; cŏmmit; ōld; ôbey; ôrder; oi-boil; fōōd; ò-as oo in foot; ou-out; s-soft; sh-dish; th-thin; pūre; ůnite; ûrn; stŭd; circŭs; ü-as in French tu; '-indeterminate vowel.

260 Assis–Aẓ Ẓahrān (Dhahran)

PLACE (Pronunciation)	PAGE	Lat. °′	Long. °′
Assis, Braz. (ä-sē's)	131	22.39S	50.21W
Assisi, Italy	148	43.04N	12.37E
As-Sudd, reg., Sudan	211	8.45N	30.45E
As Sulaymānīyah, Iraq	182	35.47N	45.23E
As Sulaymānīyah, Sau. Ar.	185	24.09N	46.19E
As Suwaydā', Syria	182	32.41N	36.41E
Astakós, Grc. (äs'tä-kôs)	161	38.42N	21.00E
Astara, Azer.	167	38.30N	48.50E
Asti, Italy (äs'tē)	148	44.54N	8.12E
Astipálaia, i., Grc.	149	36.31N	26.19E
Astley Bridge, Eng., U.K.	237b	53.36N	2.26W
Astorga, Spain (äs-tôr'gä)	158	42.28N	6.03W
Astoria, Or., U.S. (äs-tō'rĭ-ȧ)	96	46.11N	123.51W
Astoria, neigh., N.Y., U.S.	228	40.46N	73.55W
Astrakhan', Russia (äs-trȧ-kän')	164	46.15N	48.00E
Astrida, Rw. (äs-trē'dȧ)	212	2.37S	29.48E
Asturias, hist. reg., Spain (äs-tōō'ryäs)	158	43.21N	6.00W
Asunción *see* Nochistlán, Mex.	118	21.23N	102.52W
Asunción *see* Ixtaltepec, Mex.	119	16.33N	95.04W
Asunción, Para. (ä-sōōn-syōn')	132	25.25S	57.30W
Asunción Mita, Guat. (ä-sōōn-syō'n-mē'tä)	120	14.19N	89.43W
Aswān, Egypt (ä-swän')	211	24.05N	32.57E
Aswān High Dam, dam, Egypt	211	23.58N	32.53E
Atacama, Desierto de, des., Chile (dĕ-syĕ'r-tô-dĕ-ä-tä-kȧ'mä)	128	23.50S	69.00W
Atacama, Puna de, plat., Bol. (pōō'nä-dĕ-ä-tä-kȧ'mä)	130	21.35S	66.58W
Atacama, Puna de, reg., Chile (pōō'nä-dĕ-ȧtä-kȧ'mä)	132	23.15S	68.45W
Atacama, Salar de, l., Chile (sȧ-lȧr'dĕ-ȧtä-kȧ'mä)	132	23.38S	68.15W
Atacama Trench, deep	128	25.00S	71.30W
Ataco, Col. (ä-tȧ'kō)	130a	3.36N	75.22W
Atacora, Chaîne de l', mts., Benin	214	10.15N	1.15E
Atā 'itah, Jabal al, mtn., Jord.	181a	30.48N	35.19E
Atamanovskiy, Russia (ä-tä-mä'nôv-skĭ)	172a	52.15N	60.47E
'Atāqah, Jabal, mts., Egypt	218c	29.59N	32.20E
Atar, Maur. (ä-tär')	210	20.45N	13.16W
Atascadero, Ca., U.S. (ăt-ăs-kȧ-dâ'rō)	108	35.29N	120.40W
Atascosa, r., Tx., U.S. (ăt-ăs-kō'sȧ)	112	28.50N	98.17W
Atauro, Ilha de, i., Indon. (dĕ-ä-tä'ōō-rō)	197	8.20S	126.15E
Atbara, r., Afr.	211	17.14N	34.27E
'Aṭbarah, Sudan (ät'bȧ-rä)	211	17.45N	33.15E
Atbasar, Kaz. (ät'bä-sär')	169	51.42N	68.28E
Atchafalaya, r., La., U.S.	113	30.53N	91.51W
Atchafalaya Bay, b., La., U.S. (ăch-ȧ-fȧ-lī'ȧ)	113	29.25N	91.30W
Atchison, Ks., U.S. (ăch'ĭ-sŭn)	97	39.33N	95.08W
Atco, N.J., U.S. (ăt'kō)	100f	39.46N	74.53W
Atempan, Mex. (ä-tĕm-pá'n)	119	19.49N	97.25W
Atenguillo, r., Mex. (ä-tĕn-gē'l-yô)	118	20.18N	104.35W
Athabasca, Can. (ăth-ȧ-băs'kȧ)	84	54.43N	113.17W
Athabasca, l., Can.	84	59.04N	109.10W
Athabasca, r., Can.	84	57.30N	112.00W
Athens (Athínai), Grc.	161	38.00N	23.38E
Athens, Al., U.S. (ăth'ĕnz)	114	34.47N	86.58W
Athens, Ga., U.S.	97	33.55N	83.24W
Athens, Oh., U.S.	98	39.20N	82.10W
Athens, Pa., U.S.	99	42.00N	76.30W
Athens, Tn., U.S.	114	35.26N	84.36W
Athens, Tx., U.S.	113	32.13N	95.51W
Atherstone, Eng., U.K. (ăth'ĕr-stŭn)	144a	52.34N	1.33W
Atherton, Eng., U.K. (ăth'ĕr-tŭn)	144a	53.32N	2.29W
Atherton Plateau, plat., Austl. (ădh-ĕr-tŏn)	203	17.00S	144.30E
Athi, r., Kenya (ä'tē)	213	2.43S	38.30E
Athínai *see* Athens, Grc.	142	38.00N	23.38E
Athis-Mons, Fr.	237c	48.43N	2.24E
Athlone, Ire. (ăth-lōn')	146	53.24N	7.30W
Athos, mtn., Grc. (ăth'ŏs)	161	40.10N	24.15E
Ath Thamad, Egypt	181a	29.41N	34.17E
Athy, Ire. (ȧ-thī)	150	52.59N	7.08W
Ati, Chad	215	13.13N	18.20E
Atibaia, Braz. (ä-tē-bà'yȧ)	129a	23.08S	46.32W
Atikonak, l., Can.	85	52.34N	63.49W
Atimonan, Phil. (ä-tē-mō'nän)	197a	13.59N	121.56E
Atiquizaya, El Sal. (ä'tē-kē-zä'yä)	120	14.00N	89.42W
Atitlan, vol., Guat. (ä-tē-tlän')	120	14.35N	91.11W
Atitlan, Lago, l., Guat. (ä-tē-tlän')	120	14.38N	91.23W
Atizapán, Mex. (ä'tē-zà-pän')	119a	19.33N	99.16W
Atka, Ak., U.S. (ăt'kȧ)	95a	52.18N	174.18W
Atka, i., Ak., U.S.	96b	51.58N	174.30W
Atkarsk, Russia (ȧt-kärsk')	167	51.50N	45.00E
Atkinson, Ne., U.S. (ăt'kĭn-sŭn)	102	42.32N	98.58W
Atlanta, Ga., U.S. (ăt-lăn'tȧ)	97	33.45N	84.23W
Atlanta, Tx., U.S.	111	33.09N	94.09W
Atlantic, Ia., U.S. (ăt-lăn'tĭk)	103	41.23N	94.58W
Atlantic, N.C., U.S.	115	34.54N	76.20W
Atlantic Beach, N.Y., U.S.	228	40.35N	73.44W
Atlantic City, N.J., U.S.	97	39.20N	74.30W
Atlantic Highlands, N.J., U.S.	100a	40.25N	74.04W
Atlantic Ocean, o.	4	5.00S	25.00W
Atlas Mountains, mts., Afr. (ăt'lăs)	210	31.22N	4.57W
Atliaca, Mex. (ät-lē-ä'kä)	118	17.38N	99.24W
Atlin, l., Can. (ăt'lĭn)	84	59.34N	133.20W
Atlixco, Mex. (ät-lēz'kō)	118	18.52N	98.27W
Atmore, Al., U.S. (ăt'mōr)	114	31.01N	87.31W
Atoka, Ok., U.S. (ȧ-tō'kȧ)	111	34.23N	96.07W
Atoka Reservoir, res., Ok., U.S.	111	34.30N	96.05W
Atotonilco el Alto, Mex.	118	20.35N	102.32W
Atotonilco el Grande, Mex.	118	20.17N	98.41W
Atoui, r., Afr. (ȧ-tōō-ē')	210	21.00N	15.32W
Atoyac, Mex. (ä-tô-yäk')	118	20.01N	103.28W
Atoyac, r., Mex.	118	18.35N	98.16W
Atoyac, r., Mex.	119	16.27N	97.28W
Atoyac de Alvarez, Mex. (ä-tô-yäk'dā äl'vä-räz)	118	17.13N	100.29W
Atoyatempan, Mex. (ä-tō'yá-tĕm-pän')	119	18.47N	97.54W
Atrak, r., Asia	182	37.45N	56.30E
Åtran, r., Swe.	152	57.02N	12.43E
Atrato, Río, r., Col. (rē'ō-ä-trä'tō)	130	7.15N	77.18W
Atsugi, Japan	242a	35.27N	139.22E
Atta, India	240d	28.34N	77.20E
Aṭ Ṭafīlah, Jord. (tä-fē'la)	181a	30.50N	35.36E
Aṭ Ṭā'if, Sau. Ar.	182	21.03N	41.00E
At-Ṭalibīyah, Egypt	244a	30.00N	31.11E
Attalla, Al., U.S. (ȧ-tăl'yȧ)	114	34.01N	86.05W
Attawapiskat, r., Can. (ăt'ȧ-wȧ-pĭs'kăt)	85	52.31N	86.22W
Attersee, l., Aus.	154	47.57N	13.25E
Attica, N.Y., U.S. (ăt'ĭ-kȧ)	99	42.55N	78.15W
Attleboro, Ma., U.S. (ăt''l-bŭr-ô)	100b	41.56N	71.15W
Attow, Ben, mtn., Scot., U.K. (bĕn ăt'tō)	150	57.15N	5.25W
Attoyac Bay, Tx., U.S. (ă-toi'yăk)	113	31.45N	94.23W
Attu, i., Ak., U.S. (ät-tōō')	96b	53.08N	173.18E
Aṭ Ṭūr, Egypt	149	28.09N	33.47E
Aṭ Ṭurayf, Sau. Ar.	182	31.32N	38.30E
Åtvidaberg, Swe. (ôt-vē'dȧ-bĕrgh)	152	58.12N	15.55E
Atwood, Ks., U.S. (ăt'wŏod)	110	39.48N	101.06W
Atyraū, Kaz.	169	47.10N	51.50E
Atzalpur, India	240d	28.43N	77.21E
Atzcapotzalco, Mex. (ät'zkä-pô-tzäl'kō)	118	19.29N	99.11W
Atzgersdorf, Aus.	145e	48.10N	16.17E
Auau Channel, strt., Hi., U.S. (ä'ò-ä'ò)	94a	20.55N	156.50W
Aubagne, Fr. (ō-bän'y')	157	43.18N	5.34E
Aube, r., Fr. (ōb)	156	48.42N	3.49E
Aubenas, Fr. (ōb-nä')	156	44.37N	4.22E
Aubervilliers, Fr. (ō-bĕr-vē-yā')	157b	48.54N	2.23E
Aubin, Fr. (ō-băN')	156	44.29N	2.12E
Aubrey, Can. (ô-brē')	83a	45.08N	73.47W
Auburn, Austl.	243a	33.51S	151.02E
Auburn, Al., U.S. (ô'bŭrn)	114	32.35N	85.26W
Auburn, Ca., U.S.	108	38.52N	121.05W
Auburn, Il., U.S.	111	39.36N	89.46W
Auburn, In., U.S.	98	41.20N	85.05W
Auburn, Me., U.S.	97	44.04N	70.24W
Auburn, Ma., U.S.	93a	42.11N	71.51W
Auburn, Ne., U.S.	111	40.23N	95.50W
Auburn, N.Y., U.S.	99	42.55N	76.35W
Auburn, Wa., U.S.	106a	47.18N	122.14W
Auburndale, Ma., U.S.	227a	42.21N	71.22W
Auburn Heights, Mi., U.S.	101b	42.37N	83.13W
Aubusson, Fr. (ō-bü-sôN')	156	45.57N	2.10E
Auch, Fr. (ōsh)	147	43.38N	0.35E
Aucilla, r., Fl., U.S. (ô-sĭl'ȧ)	114	30.15N	83.55W
Auckland, N.Z. (ôk'lănd)	203a	36.53S	174.45E
Auckland Islands, is., N.Z.	3	50.30S	166.30E
Auckland Park, neigh., S. Afr.	244b	26.11S	28.00E
Aude, r., Fr. (ōd)	156	42.55N	2.08E
Audenshaw, Eng., U.K.	237b	53.28N	2.08W
Audierne, Fr. (ō-dyĕrn')	156	48.02N	4.31W
Audincourt, Fr. (ō-dăN-kōōr')	157	47.30N	6.49E
Audley, Eng., U.K. (ôd'lĭ)	144a	53.03N	2.18W
Audo Range, mts., Eth.	218a	6.58N	41.18E
Audubon, Ia., U.S. (ô'dŏ-bŏn)	103	41.43N	94.57W
Audubon, N.J., U.S.	100f	39.54N	75.04W
Aue, Ger. (ou'ĕ)	154	50.35N	12.44E
Auf dem Schnee, neigh., Ger.	236	51.26N	7.25E
Augathella, Austl. (ôr'gȧ'thĕ-lȧ)	204	25.49S	146.40E
Aughton, Eng., U.K.	237a	53.32N	2.56W
Augrabiesvalle, wtfl., S. Afr.	212	28.30S	20.00E
Augsburg, Ger. (ouks'bŏorgh)	147	48.23N	10.55E
Augusta, Ar., U.S. (ô-gŭs'tȧ)	111	35.16N	91.21W
Augusta, Ga., U.S.	97	33.26N	82.00W
Augusta, Ks., U.S.	111	37.41N	96.58W
Augusta, Ky., U.S.	98	38.45N	84.00W
Augusta, Me., U.S.	97	44.19N	69.42W
Augusta, N.J., U.S.	100a	41.07N	74.44W
Augusta, Wi., U.S.	103	44.40N	91.09W
Augustow, Pol. (ou-gŏs'tŏf)	155	53.52N	23.00E
Auki, Sol.Is.	198e	8.46S	160.42E
Aulnay-sous-Bois, Fr. (ō-nĕ'sōō-bwä')	157b	48.56N	2.30E
Aulne, r., Fr. (ōn)	156	48.08N	3.53W
Auneau, Fr. (ō-nëü)	157b	48.28N	1.45E
Auob, r., Afr. (ä'wŏb)	212	25.00S	19.00E
Aur, i., Malay.	181b	2.27N	104.51E
Aura, Fin.	153	60.38N	22.32E
Aurangābād, India (ou-rŭŋ-gä-bäd')	183	19.56N	75.19E
Aurdal, Nor. (äûr-däl)	146	60.54N	9.24E
Aurès, Massif de l', mts., Alg.	148	35.16N	5.53E
Aurillac, Fr. (ō-rē-yȧk')	147	44.57N	2.27E
Aurora, Can.	91	43.59N	79.25W
Aurora, Co., U.S.	110	39.44N	104.50W
Aurora, Il., U.S. (ô-rō'rȧ)	97	41.45N	88.18W
Aurora, In., U.S.	101f	39.04N	84.55W
Aurora, Mn., U.S.	103	47.31N	92.17W
Aurora, Mo., U.S.	111	36.58N	93.42W
Aurora, Ne., U.S.	110	40.54N	98.01W
Aursunden, l., Nor. (äûr-sûndĕn)	152	62.42N	11.10E
Au Sable, r., Mi., U.S. (ô-sä'b'l)	98	44.40N	84.25W
Ausable, r., N.Y., U.S.	99	44.25N	73.50W
Austerlitz, trans., Fr.	237c	48.50N	2.22E
Austin, Mn., U.S. (ôs'tĭn)	103	43.40N	92.58W
Austin, Nv., U.S.	108	39.30N	117.05W
Austin, Tx., U.S.	96	30.15N	97.42W
Austin, neigh., Il., U.S.	231a	41.54N	87.45W
Austin, l., Austl.	202	27.45S	117.30E
Austin Bayou, Tx., U.S. (ôs'tĭn bī-ōō')	113a	29.17N	95.21W
Austral, Austl.	243a	33.56S	150.48E
Australia, nation, Oc.	202	25.00S	135.00E
Australian Alps, mts., Austl.	204	37.10S	147.55E
Australian Capital Territory, , Austl. (ôs-trā'lĭ-ăn)	203	35.30S	148.40E
Austria, nation, Eur. (ôs'trĭ-ȧ)	142	47.15N	11.53E
Authon-la-Plaine, Fr. (ō-tô'N-lä-plĕ'n)	157b	48.27N	1.58E
Autlán, Mex. (ä-ōōt-län')	116	19.47N	104.24W
Autun, Fr. (ō-tûN')	156	46.58N	4.14E
Auvergne, mts., Fr. (ō-vĕrn'y')	156	45.12N	2.31E
Auxerre, Fr. (ō-sâr')	147	47.48N	3.32E
Ava, Mo., U.S. (ā'vȧ)	111	36.56N	92.40W
Avakubi, Zaire (ä-vȧ-kōō'bē)	211	1.20N	27.34E
Avallon, Fr. (ȧ-vȧ-lôN')	156	47.30N	3.58E
Avalon, Ca., U.S.	108	33.21N	118.22W
Avalon, Pa., U.S. (ăv'ȧ-lŏn)	101e	40.31N	80.05W
Aveiro, Port. (ä-vā'rō)	148	40.38N	8.38W
Avelar, Braz. (ä'vĕ-lȧ'r)	132b	22.20S	43.25W
Aveley, Eng., U.K.	235	51.30N	0.16E
Avellaneda, Arg. (ä-vĕl-yä-nā'dhä)	132	34.40S	58.23W
Avellino, Italy (ä-vĕl-lē'nō)	160	40.40N	14.46E
Avenel, N.J., U.S.	228	40.35N	74.17W
Averøya, i., Nor. (ävĕr-ûĕ)	152	63.40N	7.16E
Aversa, Italy (ä-vĕr'sä)	160	40.58N	14.13E
Avery, Tx., U.S. (ā'vĕr-ĭ)	111	33.34N	94.46W
Avesta, Swe. (ä-vĕs'tä)	152	60.16N	16.09E
Aveyron, r., Fr. (ä-vâ-rôN)	156	44.07N	1.45E
Avezzano, Italy (ä-vät-sä'nō)	160	42.03N	13.27E
Avigliano, Italy (ä-vēl-yä'nō)	160	40.45N	15.44E
Avignon, Fr. (ȧ-vē-nyôN')	147	43.55N	4.50E
Ávila, Spain (ä-vē-lä)	158	40.39N	4.42W
Avilés, Spain (ä-vē-lās')	148	43.33N	5.55W
Avoca, Ia., U.S. (ȧ-vō'kȧ)	111	41.29N	95.16W
Avocado Heights, Ca., U.S.	232	34.03N	118.00W
Avon, Ct., U.S. (ā'vŏn)	99	41.40N	72.50W
Avon, Ma., U.S. (ā'vŏn)	93a	42.08N	71.03W
Avon, Oh., U.S.	101d	41.27N	82.02W
Avon, r., Eng., U.K. (ā'vŭn)	150	52.05N	1.55W
Avondale, Ga., U.S.	100c	33.47N	84.16W
Avondale Heights, Austl.	243b	37.46S	144.51E
Avon Lake, Oh., U.S.	101d	41.31N	82.01W
Avonmore, Can. (ă'vŏN-mōr)	83c	45.11N	74.58W
Avon Park, Fl., U.S. (ā'vŏn pärk')	115a	27.35N	81.29W
Avranches, Fr. (ȧ-vräNsh')	156	48.43N	1.34W
Awaji-Shima, i., Japan	194	34.32N	135.02E
Awe, Loch, l., Scot., U.K. (lŏK ôr)	150	56.22N	5.04W
Awjilah, Libya	211	29.07N	21.21E
Awsīm, Egypt	244a	30.07N	31.08E
Ax-les-Thermes, Fr. (äks'lä tĕrm')	156	42.43N	1.50E
Axochiapan, Mex. (äks-ō-chyä'pän)	118	18.29N	98.49W
Ay, r., Russia	166	55.55N	57.55E
Ayabe, Japan (ä'yä-bē)	194	35.16N	135.17E
Ayachi, Arin', mtn., Mor.	148	32.29N	4.57W
Ayacucho, Arg. (ä-yä-kōō'chō)	132	37.05S	58.30W
Ayacucho, Peru	130	13.12S	74.03W
Ayakōz, Kaz.	169	48.00N	80.12E
Ayamonte, Spain (ä-yä-mô'n-tĕ)	148	37.14N	7.28W
Ayan, Russia (ȧ-yän')	165	56.26N	138.18E
Ayase, Japan	242a	35.26N	139.26E
Ayata, Bol. (ä-yä'tä)	130	15.17S	68.43W
Ayaviri, Peru (ä-yä-vē'rē)	130	14.46S	70.38W
Aydar, r., Eur. (ī-där')	163	49.15N	38.48E
Ayden, N.C., U.S. (ā'dĕn)	115	35.27N	77.25W
Aydın, Tur. (āīy-dĕn)	182	37.40N	27.40E
Ayer, Ma., U.S. (âr)	93a	42.33N	71.36W
Ayer Hitam, Malay.	181b	1.55N	103.11E
Ayers Rock, mtn., Austl.	202	25.23S	131.05E
Ayiassos, Grc.	161	39.06N	26.25E
Ayía Varvára, Grc.	239d	37.59N	23.39E
Áyion Óros (Mount Athos), hist. reg., Grc.	161	40.20N	24.15E
Ayíos Evstrátios, i., Grc.	149	39.30N	24.58E
Ayíou Orous, Kólpos, b., Grc.	161	40.15N	24.00E
Aylesbury, Eng., U.K. (ālz'bĕr-ĭ)	150	51.47N	0.49W
Aylmer, l., Can. (āl'mĕr)	84	64.27N	108.22W
Aylmer, Mount, mtn., Can.	87	51.19N	115.26W
Aylmer East, Can. (āl'mĕr)	91	45.24N	75.50W
Ayo el Chico, Mex. (ä'yō el chē'kō)	118	20.31N	102.21W
Ayon, i., Russia (ī-ôn')	165	69.50N	168.40E
Ayorou, Niger	214	14.44N	0.55E
Ayotla, Mex. (ä-yōt'lä)	119a	19.18N	98.55W
Ayoun el Atrous, Maur.	214	16.40N	9.37W
Ayr, Scot., U.K. (âr)	150	55.27N	4.40W
Aysha, Eth.	211	10.48N	42.32E
Ayutla, Guat. (ȧ-yōōt'lä)	120	14.44N	92.11W
Ayutla, Mex.	118	16.50N	99.16W
Ayutla, Mex.	118	20.09N	104.20W
Ayvalik, Tur. (āīy-wä-lĭk)	149	39.19N	26.40E
Azādpur, neigh., India	240d	28.43N	77.11E
Azaouad, reg., Mali	214	18.00N	3.20W
Azaouak, Vallée de l', val., Afr.	215	15.50N	3.10E
Azare, Nig.	215	11.40N	10.11E
Azemmour, Mor. (ȧ-zē-mōōr')	210	33.20N	8.21W
Azerbaijan, nation, Asia	164	40.30N	47.30E
Azle, Tx., U.S. (ăz'lē)	107c	35.54N	97.33W
Azogues, Ec. (ä-sō'gās)	130	2.47S	78.45W
Azores *see* Açores, is., Port.	209	37.44N	29.25W
Azov, Russia (ȧ-zôf') (ä-zôf)	167	47.07N	39.19E
Azov, Sea of, sea, Eur.	164	46.00N	36.20E
Aztec, N.M., U.S. (ăz'tĕk)	109	36.40N	108.00W
Aztec Ruins National Monument, rec., N.M., U.S.	109	36.50N	108.00W
Azua, Dom. Rep. (ä'swä)	123	18.30N	70.45W
Azuaga, Spain (ä-thwä'gä)	158	38.15N	5.42W
Azucar, Presa de, res., Mex.	112	26.06N	98.44W
Azuero, Península de, pen., Pan.	117	7.30N	80.34W
Azufre, Cerro (Copiapó), mtn., Chile	132	27.10S	69.00W
Azul, Arg. (ä-sōōl')	132	36.46S	59.51W
Azul, Cordillera, mts., Peru	130	7.15S	75.30W
Azul, Sierra, mts., Mex.	118	23.20N	98.28W
Azusa, Ca., U.S. (ȧ-zōō'sȧ)	107a	34.08N	117.55W
Aẓ Ẓahrān (Dhahran), Sau. Ar.	182	26.13N	50.00E

PRONOUNCING INDEX

Az-Zamālik–Banās 261

PLACE (Pronunciation)	PAGE	Lat. °′	Long. °′
Az-Zamālik, neigh., Egypt	244a	30.04N	31.13E
Az Zaqāzīq, Egypt	211	30.36N	31.36E
Az Zarqā', Jord.	181a	32.03N	36.07E
Az Zāwiyah, Libya	210	32.28N	11.55E

B

PLACE (Pronunciation)	PAGE	Lat. °′	Long. °′
Baadheere (Bardera), Som.	218a	2.13N	42.24E
Baak, Ger.	236	51.25N	7.10E
Baal, Ger. (bäl)	157c	51.02N	6.17E
Baao, Phil. (bä'ō)	197a	13.27N	123.22E
Baarle-Hertog, Bel.	145a	51.26N	4.57E
Baarn, Neth.	145a	52.12N	5.18E
Babaeski, Tur. (bä'bä-ĕs'kĭ)	161	41.25N	27.05E
Babahoyo, Ec. (bä-bä-ō'yō)	130	1.56S	79.24W
Babana, Nig.	215	10.36N	3.50E
Babanango, S. Afr.	213c	28.24S	31.11E
Babanūsah, Sudan	211	11.30N	27.55E
Babar, Pulau, i., Indon. (bä'bär)	197	7.50S	129.15E
Bābarpur, neigh., India	240d	28.41N	77.17E
Bab-el-Mandeb *see* Mandeb, Bab-el-, strt.	182	13.17N	42.49E
Babelsberg, neigh., Ger.	238a	52.24N	13.05E
Babelthuap, i., Palau	198b	7.30N	134.36E
Babia, Arroyo de la, r., Mex.	112	28.26N	101.50W
Babine, r., Can.	86	55.10N	127.00W
Babine Lake, l., Can. (băb'ēn)	84	54.45N	126.00W
Bābol, Iran	182	36.30N	52.48E
Babson Park, Ma., U.S.	227a	42.18N	71.23W
Babushkin, Russia	162	55.52N	37.42E
Babushkin, Russia (bä'bŏosh-kĭn)	170	51.47N	106.08W
Babuyan Islands, is., Phil. (bä-bōō-yän')	196	19.30N	122.38E
Babyak, Bul. (bäb'zhak)	161	41.59N	23.42E
Babylon, N.Y., U.S. (băb'ĭ-lŏn)	100a	40.42N	73.19W
Babylon, hist., Iraq	182	32.15N	45.23E
Bacalar, Laguna de, l., Mex. (lä-gōō-nä-dĕ-bä-kä-lär')	120a	18.50N	88.31W
Bacan, Pulau, i., Indon.	197	0.30S	127.00E
Bacarra, Phil. (bä-kär'rä)	193	18.22N	120.40E
Bacău, Rom.	149	46.34N	27.00E
Baccarat, Fr. (bȧ-kȧ-rȧ')	157	48.29N	6.42E
Bacchus, Ut., U.S. (băk'ŭs)	107b	40.40N	112.06W
Bachajón, Mex. (bä-chä-hōn')	119	17.08N	92.18W
Bachu, China (bä-chōō)	188	39.50N	78.23E
Back, r., Can.	84	65.30N	104.15W
Bačka Palanka, Yugo. (bäch'kä pälän-kä)	161	45.14N	19.24E
Bačka Topola, Yugo. (bäch'kä tô'pô-lä')	161	45.48N	19.38E
Back Bay, India (băk)	187b	18.55N	72.45E
Back Bay, neigh., Ma., U.S.	227a	42.21N	71.05W
Backstairs Passage, strt., Austl. (băk-stârs')	202	35.50S	138.15E
Bac Lieu, Viet.	196	9.45N	105.50E
Bac Ninh, Viet. (bäk'nēn'')	193	21.10N	106.02E
Baco, Mount, mtn., Phil. (bä'kō)	197a	12.50N	121.11E
Bacoli, Italy (bä-kō-lē')	159c	40.33N	14.05E
Bacolod, Phil. (bä-kō'lŏd)	197	10.42N	123.03E
Bacongo, neigh., Congo	244c	4.18S	15.16E
Bácsalmás, Hung. (bäch'ôl-mäs)	155	46.07N	19.18E
Bacup, Eng., U.K. (băk'ŭp)	144a	53.42N	2.12W
Bad, r., S.D., U.S. (băd)	102	44.04N	100.58W
Badajoz, Spain (bä-dhä-hōth')	148	38.52N	6.56W
Badalona, Spain (bä-dhä-lō'nä)	159	41.27N	2.15E
Badanah, Sau. Ar.	182	30.49N	40.45E
Bad Axe, Mi., U.S. (băd' ăks)	98	43.50N	82.55W
Bad Bramstedt, Ger. (bät bräm'shtĕt)	145c	53.55N	9.53E
Baden, Aus. (bä'dĕn)	154	48.00N	16.14E
Baden, Switz.	154	47.28N	8.17E
Baden-Baden, Ger. (bä'dĕn-bä'dĕn)	147	48.46N	8.11E
Baden-Württemberg, hist. reg., Ger. (bä'dĕn vür'tĕm-bĕrgh)	154	48.38N	9.00E
Bad Freienwalde, Ger. (bät frī'ĕn-väl'dĕ)	154	52.47N	14.00E
Badger's Mount, Eng., U.K.	235	51.20N	0.09E
Bad Hersfeld, Ger. (bät hĕrsh'fĕlt)	154	50.53N	9.43E
Badīn, Pak.	186	24.47N	69.51E
Bad Ischl, Aus. (bät ĭsh''l)	154	47.46N	13.37E
Bad Kissingen, Ger. (bät kĭs'ĭng-ĕn)	154	50.12N	10.05E
Bad Kreuznach, Ger. (bät kroits'näk)	154	49.52N	7.53E
Badlands, reg., N.D., U.S. (băd' lănds)	102	46.43N	103.22W
Badlands, reg., S.D., U.S.	102	43.43N	102.36W
Badlands National Park, S.D., U.S.	102	43.56N	102.37W
Badlāpur, India	187b	19.12N	73.12E
Bādli, India	240d	28.45N	77.09E
Badogo, Mali	214	11.02N	8.13W
Bad Oldesloe, Ger. (bät ōl'dĕs-lōē)	154	53.48N	10.21E
Bad Reichenhall, Ger. (bät rī'κĕn-häl)	154	47.43N	12.53E
Bad River Indian Reservation, I.R., Wi., U.S. (băd)	103	46.41N	90.36W
Bad Segeberg, Ger. (bät sē'gē-bōōrgh)	145c	53.56N	10.18E
Bad Tölz, Ger. (bät tûltz)	154	47.46N	11.35E
Badulla, Sri L.	187	6.55N	81.07E
Bad Vöslau, Aus.	145e	47.58N	16.13E
Badwater Creek, r., Wy., U.S. (băd'wô-tĕr)	105	43.13N	107.55W
Baena, Spain (bä-ā'nä)	148	37.38N	4.20W
Baependi, Braz. (bä-å-pĕn'dĭ)	129a	21.57S	44.51W
Baerl, Ger.	236	51.29N	6.41E
Baffin Bay, b., N.A. (băf'ĭn)	82	72.00N	65.00W
Baffin Bay, b., Tx., U.S.	113	27.11N	97.35W
Baffin Island, i., Can.	82	67.20N	71.00W
Bāfq, Iran (bäfk)	182	31.48N	55.23E
Bafra, Tur. (bäf'rä)	149	41.30N	35.50E
Bagabag, Phil. (bä-gä-bäg')	197a	16.38N	121.16E
Bāgalkot, India	187	16.14N	75.40E
Bagamoyo, Tan. (bä-gä-mō'yō)	213	6.26S	38.54E
Bagaryak, Russia (bȧ-gär-yäk')	172a	56.13N	61.32E
Bagbele, Zaire	217	4.21N	29.17E
Bagdad *see* Baghdād, Iraq	182	33.14N	44.22E
Baghdād, Iraq (bȧgh-dȧd') (băg'dăd)	182	33.14N	44.22E
Bagheria, Italy (bä-gȧ-rē'ä)	160	38.03N	13.32E
Bagley, Mn., U.S. (băg'lē)	102	47.31N	95.24W
Bagnara, Italy (bän-yä'rä)	160	38.17N	15.52E
Bagnell Dam, Mo., U.S. (băg'nĕl)	111	38.13N	92.40W
Bagnères-de-Luchon, Fr. (bän-yâr' dē-lu chôɴ')	156	42.46N	0.36E
Bagneux, Fr.	237c	48.48N	2.18E
Bagnolet, Fr.	237c	48.52N	2.25E
Bagnols-sur-Ceze, Fr. (bä-nyōl')	156	44.09N	4.37E
Bago, Myanmar	196	17.17N	96.29E
Bagoé, r., Mali (bȧ-gō'å)	210	12.22N	6.34W
Baguio, Phil. (bä-gē-ō')	196	16.24N	120.36E
Bagzane, Monts, mtn., Niger	210	18.40N	8.40E
Bahamas, nation, N.A. (bȧ-hä'mȧs)	117	26.15N	76.00W
Bahau, Malay.	181b	2.48N	102.25E
Bahāwalpur, Pak. (bŭ-hä'wŭl-pōōr)	183	29.29N	71.41E
Bahia, state, Braz.	131	11.05S	43.00W
Bahía, Islas de la, i., Hond. (ē's-läs-dĕ-lä-bä-ē'ä)	116	16.15N	86.30W
Bahia Blanca, Arg. (bä-ē'ä bläŋ'kä)	132	38.45S	62.07W
Bahía de Caráquez, Ec. (bä-ē'ä dä kä-rä'kĕz)	130	0.45S	80.29W
Bahía Negra, Para. (bä-ē'ä nā'grä)	131	20.11S	58.05W
Bahi Swamp, sw., Tan.	217	6.05S	35.10E
Bahoruco, Sierra de, mts., Dom. Rep. (sē-ĕ'r-rä-dĕ-bä-ō-rōō'kō)	123	18.10N	71.25W
Bahrain, nation, Asia (bä-rān')	182	26.15N	51.17E
Bahr al Ghazāl, hist. reg., Sudan (bär ĕl ghä-zäl')	211	7.56N	27.15E
Bahrīyah, oasis, Egypt (bȧ-hȧ-rē'yä)	149	28.34N	29.01E
Bahtīm, Egypt	244a	30.08N	31.17E
Baía dos Tigres, Ang.	216	16.36S	11.43E
Baia Mare, Rom. (bä'yä mä'rä)	149	47.40N	23.35E
Baidyabāti, India	186a	22.47N	88.21E
Baie-Comeau, Can.	92	49.13N	68.10W
Baie de Wasai, Mi., U.S. (bā dē wä-sä'ē)	107k	46.27N	84.15W
Baie-Saint Paul, Can. (bā'sănt-pôl')	85	47.27N	70.30W
Baigou, China (bī-gō)	190	39.08N	116.02E
Baihe, China (bī-hŭ)	192	32.30N	110.15E
Bai Hu, l., China (bī-hōō)	190	31.22N	117.38E
Baiju, China (bī-jyōō)	190	33.04N	120.17E
Baikal, Lake *see* Baykal, Lake, l., Russia	165	53.00N	109.28E
Bailén, Spain (bä-ē-lān')	158	38.05N	3.48W
Băileşti, Rom. (bă-ĭ-lĕsh'tē)	161	44.01N	23.21E
Baileys Crossroads, Va., U.S.	229d	38.51N	77.08W
Bainbridge, Ga., U.S. (bān'brĭj)	114	30.52N	84.35W
Bainbridge Island, i., Wa., U.S.	106a	47.39N	122.32W
Bainchipota, India	240a	22.52N	88.16E
Baipu, China (bī-pōō)	190	32.15N	120.47E
Baiquan, China (bī-chyuäŋ)	192	47.22N	126.00E
Baird, Tx., U.S. (bârd)	112	32.22N	99.28W
Bairdford, Pa., U.S. (bârd'fōrd)	101e	40.37N	79.53W
Baird Mountains, mts., Ak., U.S.	95	67.35N	160.10W
Bairnsdale, Austl. (bârnz'dāl)	203	37.50S	147.39E
Baïse, r., Fr. (bä-ēz')	156	43.52N	0.23E
Baiyang Dian, l., China (bī-yäŋ-dĭĕn)	190	39.00N	115.45E
Baiyunguan, China	240b	39.54N	116.19E
Baiyu Shan, mts., China (bī-yōō shän)	192	37.02N	108.30E
Baja, Hung. (bŏ'yō)	155	46.11N	18.55E
Baja California, state, Mex. (bä-hä)	116	30.15N	117.25W
Baja California, pen., Mex.	82	28.00N	113.30E
Baja California Sur, state, Mex.	116	26.00N	113.30W
Bajo, Canal, can., Spain	159a	40.36N	3.41W
Bakal, Russia (bä'kȧl)	172a	54.57N	58.50E
Baker, Mt., U.S. (bā'kẽr)	105	46.21N	104.12W
Baker, Or., U.S.	96	44.46N	117.52W
Baker, i., Oc.	2	1.00N	176.00W
Baker, l., Can.	84	63.51N	96.10W
Baker, Mount, mtn., Wa., U.S.	96	48.46N	121.52W
Baker Creek, r., Il., U.S.	101a	41.13N	87.47W
Bakersfield, Ca., U.S. (bā'kẽrz-fēld)	96	35.23N	119.00W
Bakerstown, Pa., U.S. (bā'kerz-toun)	101e	40.39N	79.56W
Baker Street, Eng., U.K.	235	51.30N	0.21E
Bakewell, Eng., U.K. (băk'wĕl)	144a	53.12N	1.40W
Bakhchysaray, Ukr.	163	44.46N	33.54E
Bakhmach, Ukr. (bȧκ-mäch')	163	51.09N	32.47E
Bakhtarān, Iran	182	34.01N	47.00E
Bakhtegan, Daryācheh-ye, l., Iran	182	29.29N	54.31E
Bakhteyevo, Russia	172b	55.35N	38.32E
Bakırköy, neigh., Tur.	239f	40.59N	28.52E
Bako, Eth. (bä'kō)	211	5.47N	36.39E
Bakony, mts., Hung. (bȧ-kōn'y')	155	46.57N	17.30E
Bakoye, r., Afr. (bȧ-kō'ē)	210	12.47N	9.35W
Bakr Uzyak, Russia (bȧkr ōō'yȧk)	172a	52.59N	58.43E
Baku (Bakı), Azer. (bȧ-kōō')	164	40.28N	49.45E
Bakwanga *see* Mbuji-Mayi, Zaire	216	6.09S	23.28E
Balabac Island, i., Phil. (bä'lä-bäk)	196	8.00N	116.28E
Balabac Strait, strt., Asia	196	7.23N	116.30E
Ba'labakk, Leb.	181a	34.00N	36.13E
Balabanovo, Russia (bȧ-lä-bä'nô-vô)	172b	56.10N	37.44E
Bala-Cynwyd, Pa., U.S.	229b	40.00N	75.14W
Balagansk, Russia (bä-lä-gänsk')	170	53.58N	103.09E
Balaguer, Spain (bä-lä-gĕr')	159	41.48N	0.50E
Balakhta, Russia (bȧ'lȧk-tȧ')	165	55.22N	91.43E
Balakliya, Ukr.	163	49.28N	36.51E
Balakovo, Russia (bȧ'lȧ-kô'vô)	167	52.00N	47.40E
Balancán, Mex. (bä-läŋ-kän')	119	17.47N	91.32W
Balanga, Phil. (bä-läŋ'gä)	197a	14.41N	120.31E
Ba Lang An, Mui, c., Viet.	193	15.18N	109.10E
Balashikha, Russia (bȧ-lä'shĭ-kȧ)	172b	55.48N	37.58E
Balashov, Russia (bȧ'lȧ-shôf)	167	51.30N	43.00E
Balasore, India (bä-lȧ-sōr')	183	21.38N	86.59E
Balassagyarmat, Hung. (bô'lôsh-shô-dyôr'môt)	155	48.04N	19.19E
Balaton Lake, l., Hung. (bô'lô-tôn)	149	46.47N	17.55E
Balayan, Phil. (bä-lä-yän')	197a	13.56N	120.44E
Balayan Bay, b., Phil.	197a	13.46N	120.46E
Balboa Heights, Pan. (bäl-bô'ä)	121	8.59N	79.33W
Balboa Mountain, mtn., Pan.	116a	9.05N	79.44W
Balcarce, Arg. (bäl-kär'sä)	132	37.49S	58.17W
Balchik, Bul.	161	43.24N	28.13E
Bald Eagle, Mn., U.S. (bôld ē'g'l)	107g	45.06N	93.01W
Bald Eagle Lake, l., Mn., U.S.	107g	45.08N	93.03W
Baldock Lake, l., Can.	89	56.33N	97.57W
Baldwin, N.Y., U.S.	228	40.39N	73.37W
Baldwin, Pa., U.S.	230b	40.23N	79.58W
Baldwin Park, Ca., U.S. (bôld'wĭn)	107a	34.05N	117.58W
Baldwinsville, N.Y., U.S. (bôld'wĭns-vĭl)	99	43.10N	76.20W
Baldy Mountain, mtn., Can.	89	51.28N	100.44W
Baldy Peak, mtn., Az., U.S. (bôl'dē)	96	33.55N	109.35W
Baldy Peak, mtn., Tx., U.S. (bôl'dē pēk)	112	30.38N	104.11W
Baleares, Islas, is., Spain (ē's-läs bä-lē-ä'rĕs)	142	39.25N	1.28E
Balearic Islands *see* Baleares, Islas, is., Spain	142	39.25N	1.28E
Balearic Sea, sea, Spain (băl-ē-ăr'ĭk)	159	39.40N	1.05E
Baleine, Grande Rivière de la, r., Can.	85	55.00N	75.30W
Baler, Phil. (bä-lar')	197a	15.46N	121.33E
Baler Bay, b., Phil.	197a	15.51N	121.40E
Balesin, i., Phil.	197a	14.28N	122.10E
Baley, Russia (bȧl-yä')	171	51.29N	116.12E
Balfate, Hond. (bäl-fä'tē)	120	15.48N	86.24W
Balfour, S. Afr. (băl'fōr)	218d	26.41S	28.37E
Balgowlah, Austl.	243a	33.48S	151.16E
Bali, i., Indon. (bä'lē)	196	8.00S	115.22E
Bālihāti, India	240a	22.44N	88.19E
Balıkeşir, Tur. (balĭk'īysĭr)	167	39.40N	27.50E
Balikpapan, Indon. (bä'lēk-pä'pän)	196	1.13S	116.52E
Balintang Channel, strt., Phil. (bä-lĭn-täng')	196	19.50N	121.08E
Balizhuang, China	240b	39.52N	116.28E
Balkan Mountains *see* Stara Planina, mts., Bul.	142	42.50N	24.45E
Balkh, Afg. (bälk)	183	36.48N	66.50E
Balkhash, Lake *see* Balqash kölí	169	45.58N	72.15E
Ballabhpur, India	240a	22.44N	88.21E
Ballancourt, Fr. (bä-äɴ-kōr')	157b	48.31N	2.23E
Ballarat, Austl. (băl'ȧ-răt)	203	37.37S	144.00E
Ballard, l., Austl. (băl'ȧrd)	202	29.15S	120.45E
Ballater, Scot., U.K. (bäl'ȧ-tẽr)	150	57.05N	3.06W
Ballenato, Punta, c., Cuba	233b	23.06N	82.30W
Balleny Islands, is., Ant. (băl'ĕ nē)	219	67.00S	164.00E
Ballina, Austl. (băl-ĭ-nä')	204	28.50S	153.35E
Ballina, Ire.	150	54.06N	9.05W
Ballinasloe, Ire. (băl'ĭ-nȧ-slō')	150	53.20N	8.09W
Ballinger, Tx., U.S. (băl'ĭn-jẽr)	112	31.45N	99.58W
Ballston Spa, N.Y., U.S. (bôls'tŭn spä')	99	43.05N	73.50W
Ballygunge, neigh., India	240a	22.31N	88.21E
Balmain, Austl.	243a	33.51S	151.11E
Balmazújváros, Hung. (bôl'mŏz-ōō'y'vä'rŏsh)	155	47.35N	21.23E
Balobe, Zaire	217	0.05N	28.00E
Balonne, r., Austl. (băl-ōn')	203	27.00S	149.10E
Bālotra, India	186	25.56N	72.12E
Balqash, Kaz.	169	46.58N	75.00E
Balqash kölí, l., Kaz.	169	45.58N	72.15E
Balranald, Austl. (băl'-rȧn-ăld)	204	34.42S	143.30E
Balsam, l., Can. (bôl'sȧm)	91	44.30N	78.50W
Balsas, Braz. (bäl'säs)	131	7.09S	46.04W
Balsas, r., Mex.	116	18.00N	101.00W
Balta, Ukr. (bäl'tȧ)	167	47.57N	29.38E
Bălţi, Mol.	167	47.47N	27.57E
Baltic Sea, sea, Eur. (bôl'tĭk)	142	55.20N	16.50E
Baltīm, Egypt (bäl-tēm')	218b	31.33N	31.04E
Baltimore, Md., U.S. (bôl'tĭ-môr)	97	39.20N	76.38W
Baltiysk, Russia (bäl-tēysk')	153	54.40N	19.55E
Baluarte, Río del, r., Mex. (rē'ō-dĕl-bä-lōō'r-tē)	118	23.09N	105.42W
Baluchistān, hist. reg., Asia (bȧ-lō-chĭ-stän')	183	27.30N	65.30E
Balwyn, Austl.	243b	37.49S	145.05E
Balzac, Can. (bôl'zăk)	83e	51.10N	114.01W
Bama, Nig.	215	11.30N	13.41E
Bamako, Mali (bä-mä-kō')	210	12.39N	8.00W
Bambang, Phil. (bäm-bäng')	197a	16.24N	121.08E
Bambari, Cen. Afr. Rep. (bäm-bȧ-rē)	211	5.44N	20.40E
Bamberg, Ger. (bäm'bĕrgh)	147	49.53N	10.52E
Bamberg, S.C., U.S. (băm'bûrg)	115	33.17N	81.04W
Bamenda, Cam.	215	5.56N	10.10E
Bamingui, r., Cen. Afr. Rep.	215	7.35N	19.45E
Bampton, Eng., U.K. (băm'tŭn)	144b	51.42N	1.33W
Bampūr, Iran (bŭm-pōōr')	182	27.15N	60.22E
Bam Yanga, Ngao, mts., Cam.	215	8.20N	14.40E
Banahao, Mount, mtn., Phil. (bä-nä-hä'ō)	197a	14.04N	121.45E
Banalia, Zaire	217	1.33N	25.20E
Banamba, Mali	214	13.33N	7.27W
Bananal, Braz. (bä-nä-näl')	129a	22.42S	44.17W
Bananal, Ilha do, i., Braz. (ē'lä-dô-bä-nä-näl')	131	12.09S	50.27W
Banās, r., India (bän-äs')	183	25.20N	75.20E
Banās, Ra's, c., Egypt	211	23.48N	36.39E

ng-sing; ŋ-baŋk; ɴ-nasalized n; nŏd; cŏmmit; ōld; ōbey; ôrder; oi-boil; fōōd; ŏ-as oo in foot; ou-out; s-soft; sh-dish; th-thin; pūre; ûnite; ûrn; stŭd; circŭs; ü-as in French tu; '-indeterminate vowel.

PLACE (Pronunciation)	PAGE	Lat. °′	Long. °′
Banat, reg., Rom. (bä-nät′)	161	45.35N	21.05E
Banbidian, China	240b	39.54N	116.32E
Bancroft, Can. (băn′krŏft)	85	45.05N	77.55W
Bancroft *see* Chililabombwe, Zam.	217	12.18S	27.43E
Bānda, India (bän′dă)	183	25.36N	80.21E
Banda, Kepulauan, is., Indon.	197	4.40S	129.56E
Banda, Laut (Banda Sea), sea, Indon.	197	6.05S	127.28E
Banda Aceh, Indon.	196	5.10N	95.10E
Banda Banda, Mount, mtn., Austl. (băn′dȧ băn′dȧ)	204	31.09S	152.15E
Bandama Blanc, r., C. Iv. (bän-dä′mä)	214	6.15N	5.00W
Bandar Beheshtī, Iran	182	25.18N	60.45E
Bandar-e ʿAbbās, Iran (bän-där′ ȧb-bäs′)	182	27.04N	56.22E
Bandar-e Būshehr, Iran	182	28.48N	50.53E
Bandar-e Lengeh, Iran	182	26.44N	54.47E
Bandar-e Torkeman, Iran	182	37.05N	54.08E
Bandar Maharani, Malay. (bän-där′ mä-hä-rä′nē)	181b	2.02N	102.34E
Bandar Seri Begawan, Bru.	196	5.00N	114.59E
Bande, Spain	158	42.02N	7.58W
Bandeira, Pico da, mtn., Braz. (pē′kō dä bän dā′rä)	131	20.27S	41.47W
Bāndel, India	240a	22.56N	88.22E
Bandelier National Monument, rec., N.M., U.S. (băn-dĕ-lēr′)	109	35.50N	106.45W
Banderas, Bahía de, b., Mex. (bä-ē′ä dē bän-dĕ′räs)	118	20.38N	105.35W
Bandirma, Tur. (bän-dĭr′mȧ)	149	40.25N	27.50E
Bandon, Or., U.S. (băn′dŭn)	104	43.06N	124.25W
Bāndra, India	187b	19.04N	72.49E
Bandundu, Zaire	212	3.18S	17.20E
Bandung, Indon.	196	7.00S	107.22E
Banes, Cuba (bä′nās)	123	21.00N	75.45W
Banff, Can. (bănf)	84	51.10N	115.34W
Banff, Scot., U.K.	150	57.39N	2.37W
Banff National Park, rec., Can.	84	51.38N	116.22W
Bánfield, Arg. (bȧ′n-fyĕ′ld)	132a	34.44S	58.24W
Banfora, Burkina	214	10.38N	4.46W
Bangalore, India (băŋ′gȧ′lôr)	183	13.03N	77.39E
Bangassou, Cen. Afr. Rep. (bäŋ-gȧ-sōō′)	211	4.47N	22.49E
Bangeta, Mount, mtn., Pap. N. Gui.	197	6.20S	147.00E
Banggai, Kepulauan, is., Indon. (bäng-gī′)	197	1.05S	123.45E
Banggi, Pulau, i., Malay.	196	7.12N	117.10E
Banghāzī, Libya	211	32.07N	20.04E
Bangka, i., Indon. (bäŋ′kȧ)	196	2.24S	106.55E
Bangkalan, Indon. (bäng-kȧ-län′)	196	6.07S	112.50E
Bang Khun Thian, Thai.	241f	13.42N	100.28E
Bangkok, Thai.	196	13.50N	100.29E
Bangladesh, nation, Asia	183	24.15N	90.00E
Bangong Co, l., Asia (băŋ-gôŋ tswo)	186	33.40N	79.30E
Bangor, Wales, U.K. (băŋ′ŏr)	150	53.13N	4.05W
Bangor, Me., U.S. (băn′gĕr)	97	44.47N	68.47W
Bangor, Mi., U.S.	98	42.20N	86.05W
Bangor, Pa., U.S.	99	40.55N	75.10W
Bangs, Mount, mtn., Az., U.S. (băngs)	109	36.45N	113.50W
Bangu, neigh., Braz.	234c	22.52S	43.27W
Bangued, Phil. (bän-gād′)	197a	17.36N	120.38E
Bangui, Cen. Afr. Rep. (bäɴ-gē′)	211	4.22N	18.35E
Bangweulu, Lake, l., Zam. (băng-wē-ōō′lōō)	212	10.55S	30.10E
Bangweulu Swamp, sw., Zam.	217	11.25S	30.10E
Bani, Dom. Rep. (bä′-nē)	123	18.15N	70.25W
Bani, Phil. (bä′nē)	197a	16.11N	119.51E
Bani, r., Mali	210	13.00N	5.30W
Bánica, Dom. Rep. (bä′-nē-kä)	123	19.00N	71.35W
Banī Majdūl, Egypt	244a	30.02N	31.07E
Banī Mazār, Egypt	184	28.29N	30.48E
Banister, r., Va., U.S. (băn′ĭs-tẽr)	115	36.45N	79.17W
Banī Suwayf, Egypt	211	29.05N	31.06E
Banja Luka, Bos. (bän-yä-lōō′kȧ)	149	44.45N	17.11E
Banjarmasin, Indon. (bän-jẽr-mä′sēn)	196	3.18S	114.32E
Banjin, China (bän-jyĭn)	190	32.23N	120.14E
Banjul, Gam.	210	13.28N	16.39W
Bankberg, mts., S. Afr. (bȧŋk′bûrg)	213c	32.18S	25.15E
Banks, Or., U.S. (bănks)	106c	45.37N	123.07W
Banks, i., Austl.	203	10.10S	143.08E
Banks, Cape, c., Austl.	201b	34.01S	151.17E
Banks Island, i., Can.	82	73.00N	123.00W
Banks Island, i., Can.	86	53.25N	130.10W
Banks Islands, is., Vanuatu	203	13.38S	168.23E
Banksmeadow, Austl.	243a	33.58S	151.13E
Banks Peninsula, pen., N.Z.	205	43.45S	172.20E
Banks Strait, strt., Austl.	204	40.45S	148.00E
Bankstown, Austl.	201b	33.55S	151.02E
Ban Lat Phrao, Thai.	241f	13.47N	100.36E
Bann, r., N. Ire., U.K. (băn)	150	54.50N	6.29W
Banning, Ca., U.S. (băn′ĭng)	107a	33.56N	116.53W
Bannockburn, Austl.	201a	38.03S	144.11E
Bannu, Pak.	186	33.03N	70.39E
Baños, Ec. (bä′-nyōs)	130	1.30S	78.22W
Banská Bystrica, Slvk. (bän′skä bē′strē-tzä)	147	48.46N	19.10E
Bansko, Bul. (bän′skō)	161	41.51N	23.33E
Banstala, India	240a	22.32N	88.25E
Banstead, Eng., U.K. (băn′stĕd)	144b	51.18N	0.09W
Banton, i., Phil. (bän-tōn′)	197a	12.54N	121.55E
Bantry, Ire. (băn′trĭ)	150	51.39N	9.30W
Bantry Bay, b., Ire.	150	51.25N	10.09W
Banyak, Kepulauan, is., Indon.	196	2.08N	97.15E
Banyuwangi, Indon. (bän-jō-wäŋ′gē)	196	8.15S	114.15E
Baocheng, China (bou-chŭŋ)	192	33.15N	106.58E
Baodi, China (bou-dē)	192	39.44N	117.19E
Baoding, China (bou-dĭŋ)	189	38.52N	115.31E
Baoji, China (bou-jyē)	192	34.10N	106.58E
Baoshan, China (bou-shän)	188	25.14N	99.03E
Baoshan, China	190	31.25N	121.29E
Baotou, China (bou-tō)	189	40.28N	110.10E
Baoying, China (bou-yĭŋ)	192	33.14N	119.20E
Bapsfontein, S. Afr. (băps-fŏn-tān′)	213b	26.01S	28.26E
Ba ʿqūbah, Iraq	185	33.45N	44.38E
Ba-queo, Viet.	241j	10.48N	106.38E
Baqueroncito, Col. (bä-kĕ-rô′n-sē-tô)	130a	3.18N	74.40W
Bara, India	240a	22.46N	88.17E
Baraawe, Som.	218a	1.20N	44.00E
Barabinsk, Russia (bȧ′rȧ-bĭnsk)	170	55.18N	78.00E
Baraboo, Wi., U.S. (bâr′ȧ-bōō)	103	43.29N	89.44W
Baracoa, Cuba (bä-rä-kō′ä)	123	20.20N	74.25W
Baracoa, Cuba	123a	23.03N	82.34W
Baradères, Baie des, b., Haiti (bä-rä-dâr′)	123	18.35N	73.35W
Baradero, Arg. (bä-rä-dĕ′ō)	129c	33.50S	59.30W
Baragwanath, S. Afr.	244b	26.16S	27.59E
Barahona, Dom. Rep. (bä-rä-ô′nä)	123	18.15N	71.10W
Barajas de Madrid, Spain (bä-rȧ′häs dā mä-drēdh′)	159a	40.28N	3.35W
Baranagar, India	186	22.38N	88.25E
Baranco, Belize (bä-räŋ′kō)	120	16.01N	88.55W
Baranof, i., Ak., U.S. (bä-rä′nôf)	95	56.48N	136.08W
Baranovichi, Bela. (bä′rä-nō-vē′chē)	164	53.08N	25.59E
Baranpauh, Indon.	181b	0.40N	103.28E
Barão de Melgaço, Braz. (bä-rouɴ-dĕ-mĕl-gä′sō)	131	16.12S	55.48W
Bārāsat, India	186a	22.42N	88.29E
Bārāsat, India	240a	22.51N	88.22E
Barataria Bay, b., La., U.S.	113	29.13N	89.50W
Baraya, Col. (bä-rȧ′yä)	130a	3.10N	75.04W
Barbacena, Braz. (bär-bä-sā′nȧ)	131	21.15S	43.46W
Barbacoas, Col. (bär-bä-kō′äs)	130	1.39N	78.12W
Barbacoas, Ven. (bä-bä-kô′ás)	131b	9.30N	66.58W
Barbados, nation, N.A. (bär-bā′dōz)	117	13.30N	59.00W
Barbar, Sudan	211	18.11N	34.00E
Barbastro, Spain (bär-bäs′trō)	159	42.05N	0.05E
Barbeau, Mi., U.S. (bȧr-bō′)	107k	46.17N	84.16W
Barberton, S. Afr.	212	25.48S	31.04E
Barberton, Oh., U.S. (bär′bẽr-tŭn)	101d	41.01N	81.37W
Barbezieux, Fr. (bärb′zyû′)	156	45.30N	0.11W
Barbosa, Col. (bär-bō′-sȧ)	130a	6.26N	75.19W
Barboursville, W.V., U.S. (bär′bẽrs-vĭl)	98	38.20N	82.20W
Barbourville, Ky., U.S.	114	36.52N	83.58W
Barbuda, i., Antig. (bär-bōō′dȧ)	117	17.45N	61.15W
Barcaldine, Austl. (bär′kôl-dīn)	203	23.33S	145.17E
Barcarrota, Spain (bär-kär-rō′tä)	158	38.31N	6.50W
Barcellona, Italy (bä-chĕl-lō′nä)	160	38.07N	15.15E
Barcelona, Spain (bär-thȧ-lō′nä)	142	41.25N	2.08E
Barcelona, Ven. (bär-sȧ-lō′nä)	130	10.09N	64.41W
Barcelos, Braz. (bär-sĕ′lōs)	130	1.04S	63.00W
Barcelos, Port. (bär-thȧ′lōs)	158	41.34N	8.39W
Barcroft, Lake, res., Va., U.S.	229d	38.51N	77.09W
Bardawīl, Sabkhat al, b., Egypt	181a	31.20N	33.24E
Bardejov, Czech Rep. (bär′dyĕ-yôf)	155	49.18N	21.18E
Bardsey Island, i., Wales, U.K. (bärd′sė)	150	52.45N	4.50W
Bardstown, Ky., U.S. (bärds′toun)	98	37.50N	85.30W
Bardwell, Ky., U.S. (bärd′wĕl)	114	36.51N	88.57W
Bare Hills, Md., U.S.	229c	39.23N	76.40W
Bareilly, India	183	28.21N	79.25E
Barents Sea, sea, Eur. (bä′rĕnts)	164	72.14N	37.28E
Barentu, Erit. (bä-rĕn′tōō)	211	15.06N	37.39E
Barfleur, Pointe de, c., Fr. (bȧr-flûr′)	156	49.43N	1.17W
Barguzin, Russia (bär′gōō-zĭn)	165	53.44N	109.28E
Bar Harbor, Me., U.S. (bär här′bẽr)	92	44.22N	68.13W
Bari, Italy (bä′rē)	142	41.08N	16.53E
Barinas, Ven. (bä-rē′näs)	130	8.36N	70.14W
Baring, Cape, c., Can. (bâr′ĭng)	84	70.07N	119.48W
Barisan, Pegunungan, mts., Indon. (bä-rē-sän′)	196	2.38S	101.45E
Bariti Bil, l., India	240a	22.48N	88.26E
Barito, r., Indon. (bä-rē′tō)	196	2.10S	114.38E
Barka, r., Afr.	211	16.44N	37.34E
Barking, neigh., Eng., U.K.	235	51.33N	0.06E
Barkingside, neigh., Eng., U.K.	235	51.36N	0.05E
Barkley Sound, strt., Can.	86	48.53N	125.20W
Barkly East, S. Afr. (bärk′lē ēst)	213c	30.58S	27.37E
Barkly Tableland, plat., Austl. (bär′klė)	202	18.15S	137.05E
Barkol, China (bär-kůl)	188	43.43N	92.50E
Bârlad, Rom.	149	46.15N	27.43E
Bar-le-Duc, Fr. (bär-lē-dük′)	157	48.47N	5.05E
Barlee, l., Austl. (bär-lē′)	202	29.45S	119.00E
Barletta, Italy (bär-lĕt′tä)	149	41.19N	16.20E
Barmen, neigh., Ger.	236	51.17N	7.13E
Barmstedt, Ger. (bärm′shtĕt)	145c	53.47N	9.46E
Barnaul, Russia (bär-nä-ōl′)	164	53.18N	83.23E
Barnes, neigh., Eng., U.K.	235	51.28N	0.15W
Barnesboro, Pa., U.S. (bärnz′bẽr-ō)	99	40.45N	78.50W
Barnesville, Ga., U.S. (bärnz′vĭl)	114	33.03N	84.10W
Barnesville, Mn., U.S.	102	46.38N	96.25W
Barnesville, Oh., U.S.	98	39.55N	81.10W
Barnet, Vt., U.S. (bär′nĕt)	99	44.20N	72.00W
Barnetby le Wold, Eng., U.K. (bär′nĕt-bī)	144a	53.34N	0.26W
Barnett Harbor, b., Bah.	122	25.40N	79.20W
Barnsdall, Ok., U.S. (bärnz′dôl)	111	36.38N	96.14W
Barnsley, Eng., U.K. (bärnz′lĭ)	144a	53.33N	1.29W
Barnstaple, Eng., U.K. (bärn′stā-p′l)	150	51.06N	4.05W
Barnston, Eng., U.K.	237a	53.21N	3.05W
Barnum Island, N.Y., U.S.	228	40.36N	73.39W
Barnwell, S.C., U.S. (bärn′wĕl)	115	33.14N	81.23W
Baro, Nig. (bä′rō)	210	8.37N	6.25E
Baroda, India (bär-rō′dä)	183	22.21N	73.12E
Barotse Plain, pl., Zam.	216	15.50S	22.55E
Barqah (Cyrenaica), hist. reg., Libya	211	31.09N	21.45E
Barquisimeto, Ven. (bär-kē-sē-mä′tō)	130	10.04N	69.16W
Barra, Braz. (bär′rä)	131	11.04S	43.11W
Barraba, Austl.	204	30.22S	150.36E
Barracas, neigh., Arg.	233d	34.38S	58.22W
Barrackpore, India	186a	22.46N	88.21E
Barra do Corda, Braz. (bär′rä dō cōr-dä)	131	5.33S	45.13W
Barra Funda, neigh., Braz.	234d	23.31S	46.39W
Barra Mansa, Braz. (bär′rä män′sä)	129a	22.35S	44.09W
Barrancabermeja, Col. (bär-räŋ′kä-bĕr-mā′hä)	130	7.06N	73.49W
Barrancas, Chile	234b	33.27S	70.46W
Barranco, Peru	233c	12.09S	77.02W
Barranquilla, Col. (bär-rän-kēl′yä)	130	10.57N	75.00W
Barras, Braz. (bȧ′r-räs)	131	4.13S	42.14W
Barre, Vt., U.S. (băr′ė)	99	44.15N	72.30W
Barreiras, Braz. (bär-rā′räs)	131	12.13S	44.59W
Barreiro, Port. (bär-rĕ′ē-rō)	148	38.39N	9.05W
Barren, r., Ky., U.S.	114	37.00N	86.20W
Barren, Cape, c., Austl. (băr′ĕn)	203	40.20S	149.00E
Barren, Nosy, is., Madag.	213	18.18S	43.57E
Barren River Lake, res., Ky., U.S.	114	36.45N	86.02W
Barretos, Braz. (bär-rā′tōs)	131	20.40S	48.36W
Barrhead, Can. (băr′ĭd)	84	54.08N	114.24W
Barriada Pomar Alto, Spain	238e	41.29N	2.14E
Barrie, Can. (băr′ĭ)	85	44.25N	79.45W
Barrington, Can. (bă-rĕng-tŏn)	83a	45.07N	73.35W
Barrington, Il., U.S.	101a	42.09N	88.08W
Barrington, N.J., U.S.	229b	39.52N	75.04W
Barrington, R.I., U.S.	100b	41.44N	71.16W
Barrington Tops, mtn., Austl.	204	32.00S	151.25E
Barrio Obrero Industrial, prov., Peru	233c	12.04S	77.04W
Bar River, Can. (bär)	107k	46.27N	84.02W
Barron, Wi., U.S. (băr′ŭn)	103	45.24N	91.51W
Barrow, Ak., U.S. (băr′ō)	96a	71.20N	156.00W
Barrow, i., Austl.	202	20.50S	115.00E
Barrow, r., Ire. (bȧ-rō)	150	52.35N	7.05W
Barrow, Point, c., Ak., U.S.	95	71.20N	156.00W
Barrow Creek, Austl.	202	21.23S	133.55E
Barrow-in-Furness, Eng., U.K.	146	54.10N	3.15W
Barstow, Ca., U.S. (bär′stō)	108	34.53N	117.03W
Barstow, Md., U.S.	100e	38.32N	76.37W
Barth, Ger. (bärt)	154	54.20N	12.43E
Bartholomew Bayou, r., U.S. (bär-thŏl′ō-mū bī-ōō′)	111	33.53N	91.45W
Barthurst, Can. (bär-thŭrst′)	85	47.38N	65.40W
Bartica, Guy. (bär′tĭ-kȧ)	131	6.23N	58.32W
Bartin, Tur. (bär′tĭn)	149	41.35N	32.12E
Bartle Frere, Mount, mtn., Austl. (bärt′′l frēr′)	203	17.30S	145.46E
Bartlesville, Ok., U.S. (bär′tlz-vĭl)	111	36.44N	95.58W
Bartlett, Il., U.S. (bärt′lĕt)	101a	41.59N	88.11W
Bartlett, Tx., U.S.	113	30.48N	97.25W
Barton, Vt., U.S. (bär′tŭn)	99	44.45N	72.05W
Barton-upon-Humber, Eng., U.K. (bär′tŭn-ŭp′ŏn-hŭm′bẽr)	144a	53.41N	0.26W
Bartoszyce, Pol. (bär-tō-shĭ′tsȧ)	155	54.15N	20.50E
Bartow, Fl., U.S. (bär′tō)	115a	27.51N	81.50W
Baruta, Ven.	234a	10.26N	66.53W
Barvinkove, Ukr.	163	48.55N	36.59E
Barwon, r., Austl. (bär′wŭn)	203	30.00S	147.30E
Barwon Heads, Austl.	201a	38.17S	144.29E
Barycz, r., Pol. (bä′rĭch)	154	51.30N	16.38E
Basai Dārāpur, neigh., India	240d	28.40N	77.08E
Basankusu, Zaire (bä-sän-kōō′sōō)	211	1.14N	19.45E
Basbeck, Ger. (bäs′bĕk)	145c	53.40N	9.11E
Basdahl, Ger. (bäs′däl)	145c	53.27N	9.00E
Basehor, Ks., U.S. (bās′hôr)	107f	39.08N	94.55W
Basel, Switz. (bä′z′l)	147	47.32N	7.35E
Bashee, r., S. Afr. (bă-shē′)	213c	31.47S	28.25E
Bashi Channel, strt., Asia (bäsh′ē)	189	21.20N	120.22E
Bashkortostan, state, Russia	166	54.12N	57.15E
Bashtanka, Ukr. (bȧsh-tän′kȧ)	163	47.32N	32.31E
Bashtīl, Egypt	244a	30.05N	31.11E
Basilan Island, i., Phil.	196	6.37N	122.07E
Basildon, Eng., U.K.	151	51.35N	0.25E
Basilicata, hist. reg., Italy (bä-zē-lē-kä′tä)	160	40.30N	15.55E
Basin, Wy., U.S. (bā′sĭn)	105	44.22N	108.02W
Basingstoke, Eng., U.K. (bă′zĭng-stōk)	144b	51.14N	1.06W
Baška, Cro. (bäsh′kȧ)	160	44.58N	14.44E
Baskale, Tur. (bäsh-kä′lĕ)	167	38.10N	44.00E
Baskatong, Réservoir, res., Can.	91	46.50N	75.50W
Baskunchak, l., Russia	167	48.20N	46.40E
Basoko, Zaire (bȧ-sō′kō)	211	0.52N	23.50E
Basque Lands *see* Vascongadas, hist. reg., Spain	158	43.00N	2.46W
Basra *see* Al Başrah, Iraq	182	30.35N	47.59E
Bassano, Can. (bäs-sän′ō)	84	50.47N	112.28W
Bassano del Grappa, Italy	160	45.46N	11.44E
Bassari, Togo	214	9.15N	0.47E
Bassas da India, i., Reu. (bäs′säs dä ēn′dē-ä)	213	21.23S	39.42E
Basse Terre, Guad. (bȧs′ târ′)	117	16.00N	61.43W
Basseterre, St. K./N.	121b	17.20N	62.42W
Basse Terre, i., Guad.	121b	16.10N	62.14W
Bassett, Va., U.S. (băs′sĕt)	115	36.45N	81.58W
Bass Hill, Austl.	243a	33.54S	151.00E
Bass Islands, is., Oh., U.S. (băs)	98	41.40N	82.50W
Bass Strait, strt., Austl.	203	39.40S	145.40E
Basswood, l., N.A. (băs′wŏŏd)	103	48.10N	91.36W
Båstad, Swe. (bô′stät)	152	56.26N	12.46E
Bastia, Fr. (bäs′tē-ä)	147	42.43N	9.27E
Bastogne, Bel. (bäs-tôn′y′)	151	50.02N	5.45E
Bastrop, La., U.S. (băs′trŭp)	113	32.47N	91.55W
Bastrop, Tx., U.S.	113	30.08N	97.18W
Bastrop Bayou, Tx., U.S.	113a	29.07N	95.22W
Bāsudebpur, India	240a	22.49N	88.25E
Bata, Eq. Gui. (bä′tä)	210	1.51N	9.45E
Batabano, Golfo de, b., Cuba (gôl-fō-dĕ-bä-tä-bä′nō)	122	22.10N	83.05W
Batāla, India	186	31.54N	75.18E
Bataly, Kaz. (bȧ-tä′lĭ)	169	52.51N	62.03E

PRONOUNCING INDEX

Batam–Bellary 263

PLACE (Pronunciation)	PAGE	Lat. °′	Long. °′
Batam, i., Indon. (bä-täm′)	181b	1.03N	104.00E
Batang, China (bä-täŋ)	188	30.08N	99.00E
Batangas, Phil. (bä-tän′gäs)	196	13.45N	121.04E
Batan Islands, is., Phil. (bä-tän′)	196	20.58N	122.20E
Bátaszék, Hung. (bä′tȧ-sěk)	155	46.07N	18.40E
Batavia, Il., U.S. (bȧ-tā′vĭ-ȧ)	101a	41.51N	88.18W
Batavia, N.Y., U.S.	99	43.00N	78.15W
Batavia, Oh., U.S.	101f	39.05N	84.10W
Bataysk, Russia (bȧ-tīsk′)	167	47.08N	39.44E
Bătdâmbâng, Camb. (bȧt-tȧm-bāng′)	196	13.14N	103.15E
Batenbrock, neigh., Ger.	236	51.31N	6.57E
Batesburg, S.C., U.S. (bāts′bûrg)	115	33.53N	81.34W
Batesville, Ar., U.S. (bāts′vĭl)	111	35.46N	91.39W
Batesville, In., U.S.	98	39.15N	85.15W
Batesville, Ms., U.S.	114	34.17N	89.55W
Batetska, Russia (bȧ-tě′tskȧ)	162	58.36N	30.21E
Bath, Can. (bȧth)	92	46.31N	67.36W
Bath, Eng., U.K.	147	51.24N	2.20W
Bath, Me., U.S.	92	43.54N	69.50W
Bath, N.Y., U.S.	99	42.25N	77.20W
Bath, Oh., U.S.	101d	41.11N	81.38W
Bathsheba, Barb.	121b	13.13N	60.30W
Bathurst, Austl. (bȧth′ŭrst)	203	33.28S	149.30E
Bathurst *see* Banjul, Gam.	210	13.28N	16.39W
Bathurst, S. Afr. (băt-hûrst)	213c	33.26S	26.53E
Bathurst, i., Austl.	202	11.19S	130.13E
Bathurst, Cape, c., Can. (bath′-ûrst)	84	70.33N	127.55W
Bathurst Inlet, b., Can.	84	68.10N	108.00W
Batia, Benin	214	10.54N	1.29E
Batley, Eng., U.K. (băt′lĭ)	144a	53.43N	1.37W
Batna, Alg. (bät′nä)	210	35.41N	6.12E
Baton Rouge, La., U.S. (băt′ŭn ro͞ozh′)	97	30.28N	91.10W
Battersea, neigh., Eng., U.K.	235	51.28N	0.10W
Batticaloa, Sri L.	187	7.40N	81.10E
Battle, r., Can.	88	52.20N	111.59W
Battle Creek, Mi., U.S. (băt′′l krēk′)	97	42.20N	85.15W
Battle Ground, Wa., U.S. (băt′′l ground)	106c	45.47N	122.32W
Battle Harbour, Can. (băt′′l här′bẽr)	85	52.17N	55.33W
Battle Mountain, Nv., U.S.	104	40.40N	116.56W
Battonya, Hung. (bät-tô′nyä)	155	46.17N	21.00E
Batu, Kepulauan, is., Indon. (bä′to͞o)	196	0.10S	98.00E
Batumi, Geor. (bŭ-to͞o′mē)	164	41.40N	41.30E
Batu Pahat, Malay.	196	1.51N	102.56E
Batupanjang, Indon.	181b	1.42N	101.35E
Bauang, Phil. (bä′wäng)	197a	16.31N	120.19E
Bauchi, Nig. (bȧ-o͞o′chė)	210	10.19N	9.50E
Bauerschaft, Ger.	236	51.34N	6.33E
Bauerstown, Pa., U.S.	230b	40.30N	79.59W
Baukau, neigh., Ger.	236	51.33N	7.12E
Bauld, Cape, c., Can.	85a	51.38N	55.25W
Baulkham Hills, Austl.	243a	33.46S	151.00E
Baumschulenweg, neigh., Ger.	238a	52.28N	13.29E
Bāuria, India	186a	22.29N	88.08E
Bauru, Braz. (bou-ro͞o′)	131	22.21S	48.57W
Bauska, Lat. (bou′skȧ)	153	56.24N	24.12E
Bauta, Cuba (bȧ′o͞o-tä)	123a	22.59N	82.33W
Bautzen, Ger. (bout′sĕn)	147	51.11N	14.27E
Bavaria *see* Bayern, state, Ger.	154	49.00N	11.16E
Baw Baw, Mount, mtn., Austl.	204	37.50S	146.17E
Bawean, Pulau, i., Indon. (bȧ′vē-än)	196	5.50S	112.40E
Bawtry, Eng., U.K. (bôtrĭ)	144a	53.26N	1.01W
Baxley, Ga., U.S. (băks′lĭ)	115	31.47N	82.22W
Baxter, Austl.	201a	38.12S	145.10E
Baxter Springs, Ks., U.S. (băks′tẽr sprĭngs′)	111	37.01N	94.44W
Bay, Laguna de, l., Phil. (lä-go͞o′nä dȧ bä′ė)	197a	14.24N	121.13E
Bayaguana, Dom. Rep. (bä-yä-gwä′nä)	123	18.45N	69.40W
Bay al Kabīr, Wadi, val., Libya	148	29.52N	14.28E
Bayambang, Phil. (bä-yäm-bäng′)	197a	15.50N	120.26E
Bayamo, Cuba (bä-yä′mō)	122	20.25N	76.35W
Bayamón, P.R.	117b	18.27N	66.13W
Bayan, China (bä-yän)	192	46.00N	127.20E
Bayanauyl, Kaz.	169	50.43N	75.37E
Bayard, Ne., U.S. (bā′ẽrd)	102	41.45N	103.20W
Bayard, N.M., U.S.	109	32.45N	108.07W
Bayard, W.V., U.S.	99	39.15N	79.20W
Bayburt, Tur. (bä′ĭ-bo̤rt)	167	40.15N	40.10E
Bay City, Mi., U.S. (bā)	97	43.35N	83.55W
Bay City, Tx., U.S.	113	28.59N	95.58W
Baydaratskaya Guba, b., Russia	166	69.20N	66.10E
Bay de Verde, Can.	93	48.05N	52.54W
Baydhabo (Baidoa), Som.	218a	3.19N	44.20E
Baydrag, r., Mong.	188	46.09N	98.52E
Bayern (Bavaria), hist. reg., Ger. (bī′ẽrn) (bȧ-vâ-rĭ-ȧ)	154	49.00N	11.16E
Bayeux, Fr. (bȧ-yû′)	147	49.19N	0.41W
Bayfield, Wi., U.S. (bā′fėld)	103	46.48N	90.51W
Bayford, Eng., U.K.	235	51.46N	0.06W
Baykal, Ozero (Lake Baikal), l., Russia	165	53.00N	109.28E
Baykal'skiy Khrebet, mts., Russia	165	53.30N	107.30E
Baykit, Russia (bī-kēt′)	165	61.43N	96.39E
Baymak, Russia (bȧy′mäk)	172a	52.35N	58.21E
Bay Mills, Mi., U.S. (bā mĭlls)	107k	46.27N	84.36W
Bay Mills Indian Reservation, I.R., Mi., U.S.	103	46.19N	85.03W
Bay Minette, Al., U.S. (bā′mĭn-ĕt′)	114	30.52N	87.44W
Bayombong, Phil. (bä-yȯm-bŏng′)	197a	16.28N	121.09E
Bayonne, Fr. (bȧ-yȯn′)	142	43.28N	1.30W
Bayonne, N.J., U.S. (bā-yōn′)	100a	40.40N	74.07W
Bayou Bodcau Reservoir, res., La., U.S. (bī′yo͞o bŏd′kō)	97	32.49N	93.22W
Bay Park, N.Y., U.S.	228	40.38N	73.40W
Bayport, Mn., U.S. (bā′pōrt)	107g	45.02N	92.46W
Bayqongyr, Kaz.	169	47.46N	66.11E
Bayramiç, Tur.	161	39.48N	26.35E
Bayreuth, Ger. (bī-roit′)	154	49.56N	11.35E
Bay Ridge, neigh., N.Y., U.S.	228	40.37N	74.02W
Bay Roberts, Can. (bā rŏb′ẽrts)	93	47.36N	53.16W
Bays, Lake of, l., Can. (bās)	91	45.15N	79.00W
Bay Saint Louis, Ms., U.S. (bā′ sånt lo͞o′ĭs)	114	30.19N	89.20W
Bay Shore, N.Y., U.S. (bā′ shôr)	100a	40.44N	73.15W
Bayside, Ma., U.S.	227a	42.18N	70.53W
Bayside, neigh., N.Y., U.S.	228	40.46N	73.46W
Bayswater, Austl.	243b	37.51S	145.16E
Bayswater North, Austl.	243b	37.49S	145.17E
Bayt Lahm, W. Bank (běth′lė-hěm)	181a	31.42N	35.13E
Baytown, Tx., U.S. (bā′town)	113a	29.44N	95.01W
Bayview, Al., U.S. (bā′vū)	100h	33.34N	86.59W
Bayview, Wa., U.S.	106a	48.29N	122.28W
Bayview, neigh., Ca., U.S.	231b	37.44N	122.23W
Bay Village, Oh., U.S. (bā)	101d	41.29N	81.56W
Bayville, N.Y., U.S.	228	40.54N	73.33W
Baza, Spain (bä′thä)	148	37.29N	2.46W
Baza, Sierra de, mts., Spain	158	37.19N	2.48W
Bazar-Dyuzi, mtn., Azer. (bä′zȧr-dyo͞oz′ĕ)	167	41.20N	47.40E
Bazaruto, Ilha do, i., Moz. (bȧ-zȧ-ro̤′tō)	212	21.42S	36.10E
Baziège, Fr.	156	43.25N	1.41E
Be, Nosy, i., Madag.	213	13.14S	47.28E
Beach, N.D., U.S. (bēch)	102	46.55N	104.00W
Beachwood, Oh., U.S.	229a	41.29N	81.30W
Beachy Head, c., Eng., U.K. (bēchē hĕd)	151	50.40N	0.25E
Beacon, N.Y., U.S. (bē′kŭn)	99	41.30N	73.55W
Beacon Hill, Austl.	243a	33.45S	151.15E
Beacon Hill, hill, China	241c	22.21N	114.09E
Beaconsfield, Can. (bē′kŭnz-fēld)	83a	45.26N	73.51W
Beals Creek, r., Tx., U.S. (bēls)	112	32.10N	101.14W
Bean, Eng., U.K.	235	51.25N	0.17E
Bear, r., U.S.	105	42.17N	111.42W
Bear, r., Ut., U.S.	107b	41.28N	112.10W
Bear Brook, r., Can.	83c	45.24N	75.15W
Bear Creek, Mt., U.S. (bâr krēk)	105	45.11N	109.07W
Bear Creek, r., Al., U.S. (bâr)	114	34.27N	88.00W
Bear Creek, r., Tx., U.S.	107c	32.56N	97.09W
Beardstown, Il., U.S. (bērds′toun)	111	40.01N	90.26W
Bearfort Mountain, mtn., N.J., U.S. (bē′fōrt)	100a	41.08N	74.23W
Bearhead Mountain, mtn., Wa., U.S. (bâr′hēd)	106a	47.01N	121.49W
Bear Lake, l., Can.	89	55.08N	96.00W
Bear Lake, l., Id., U.S.	105	41.56N	111.10W
Bear River Range, mts., U.S.	105	41.50N	111.30W
Beas de Segura, Spain (bā′äs dā sä-go͞o′rä)	158	38.16N	2.53W
Beata, i., Dom. Rep. (bĕ-ä′tä)	123	17.40N	71.40W
Beata, Cabo, c., Dom. Rep. (kȧ′bȯ-bĕ-ä′tä)	123	17.40N	71.20W
Beato, neigh., Port.	238d	38.44N	9.06W
Beatrice, Ne., U.S. (bē′ȧ-trĭs)	96	40.16N	96.45W
Beatty, Nv., U.S. (bēt′ė)	108	36.58N	116.48W
Beattyville, Ky., U.S. (bēt′ė-vĭl)	98	37.35N	83.40W
Beaucaire, Fr. (bō-kâr′)	156	43.49N	4.37E
Beaucourt, Fr. (bō-ko͞or′)	157	47.30N	6.54E
Beaufort, N.C., U.S. (bō′frt)	115	34.43N	76.40W
Beaufort, S.C., U.S.	115	32.25N	80.40W
Beaufort Sea, sea, N.A.	95	70.30N	138.40W
Beaufort West, S. Afr.	212	32.20S	22.45E
Beauharnois, Can. (bō-är-nwä′)	91	45.23N	73.52W
Beaumont, Can.	83b	46.50N	71.01W
Beaumont, Can.	83g	53.22N	113.18W
Beaumont, Ca., U.S. (bō′mŏnt)	107a	33.57N	116.57W
Beaumont, Tx., U.S.	97	30.05N	94.06W
Beaune, Fr. (bōn)	156	47.02N	4.49E
Beauport, Can. (bō-pôr′)	83b	46.52N	71.11W
Beauséjour, Can.	84	50.04N	96.33W
Beauvais, Fr. (bō-vĕ′)	156	49.25N	2.05E
Beaver, Ok., U.S. (bē′vẽr)	110	36.46N	100.31W
Beaver, Pa., U.S.	101e	40.42N	80.18W
Beaver, Ut., U.S.	109	38.15N	112.40W
Beaver, i., Mi., U.S.	98	45.40N	85.30W
Beaver, r., Can.	84	54.20N	111.10W
Beaver City, Ne., U.S.	110	40.08N	99.52W
Beaver Creek, r., Co., U.S.	110	39.42N	103.37W
Beaver Creek, r., Ks., U.S.	110	39.44N	101.05W
Beaver Creek, r., Mt., U.S.	102	46.45N	104.18W
Beaver Creek, r., Wy., U.S.	102	43.46N	104.25W
Beaver Dam, Wi., U.S.	103	43.29N	88.50W
Beaverhead, r., Mt., U.S.	105	45.25N	112.35W
Beaverhead Mountains, mts., Mt., U.S. (bē′vẽr-hĕd)	105	44.33N	112.59W
Beaver Indian Reservation, I.R., Mi., U.S.	98	45.40N	85.30W
Beaverton, Or., U.S. (bē′vẽr-tŭn)	106c	45.29N	122.49W
Bebek, neigh., Tur.	239f	41.04N	29.02E
Bebington, Eng., U.K. (bē′bĭng-tŭn)	144a	53.20N	2.59W
Beccar, neigh., Arg.	233d	34.28S	58.31W
Bečej, Yugo. (bč′chā)	161	45.36N	20.03E
Béchar, Alg.	210	31.39N	2.14W
Becharof, l., Ak., U.S. (bĕk-ȧ-rôf)	95	57.58N	156.58W
Becher Bay, b., Can. (bēch′ẽr)	106a	48.18N	123.37W
Beckenham, neigh., Eng., U.K.	235	51.24N	0.02W
Beckley, W.V., U.S. (bĕk′lĭ)	98	37.40N	81.15W
Bédarieux, Fr. (bā-dȧ-ryû′)	156	43.36N	3.11E
Beddington, neigh., Eng., U.K.	235	51.22N	0.08W
Beddington Creek, r., Can. (bĕd′ĕng tŭn)	83e	51.14N	114.13W
Bedford, Can. (bĕd′fẽrd)	91	45.10N	73.00W
Bedford, S. Afr.	213c	32.43S	26.19E
Bedford, Eng., U.K.	147	52.10N	0.25W
Bedford, In., U.S.	98	38.50N	86.30W
Bedford, Ia., U.S.	103	40.40N	94.41W
Bedford, Ma., U.S.	93a	42.30N	71.17W
Bedford, N.Y., U.S.	100a	41.12N	73.38W
Bedford, Oh., U.S.	101d	41.23N	81.32W
Bedford, Pa., U.S.	99	40.05N	78.20W
Bedford, Va., U.S.	115	37.19N	79.27W
Bedford Heights, Oh., U.S.	229a	41.22N	81.30W
Bedford Hills, N.Y., U.S.	100a	41.14N	73.41W
Bedford Park, Il., U.S.	231a	41.46N	87.49W
Bedford Park, neigh., N.Y., U.S.	228	40.52N	73.53W
Bedford-Stuyvesant, neigh., N.Y., U.S.	228	40.41N	73.55W
Bedmond, Eng., U.K.	235	51.43N	0.25W
Bedok, Sing.	240c	1.19N	103.57E
Beebe, Ar., U.S. (bē′bė)	111	35.04N	91.54W
Beecher, Il., U.S. (bē′chŭr)	101a	41.20N	87.38W
Beechey Head, c., Can. (bē′chĭ hĕd)	106a	48.19N	123.40W
Beech Grove, In., U.S. (bēch grōv)	101g	39.43N	86.05W
Beechview, neigh., Pa., U.S.	230b	40.25N	80.02W
Beeck, neigh., Ger.	236	51.29N	6.44E
Beeckerwerth, neigh., Ger.	236	51.29N	6.41E
Beecroft Head, c., Austl. (bē′krûft)	204	35.03S	151.15E
Beelitz, Ger. (bĕ′lētz)	145b	52.14N	12.59E
Be'er Sheva', Isr. (bēr-shē′bȧ)	181a	31.15N	34.48E
Be'er Sheva', r., Isr.	181a	31.23N	34.30E
Beestekraal, S. Afr.	218d	25.22S	27.34E
Beeston, Eng., U.K. (bēs′t'n)	144a	52.55N	1.11W
Beetz, r., Ger. (bĕtz)	145b	52.28N	12.37E
Beeville, Tx., U.S. (bē′vĭl)	113	28.24N	97.44W
Bega, Austl. (bā′gaă)	203	36.50S	149.49E
Beggs, Ok., U.S. (bĕgz)	111	35.46N	96.06W
Bégles, Fr. (bĕ′gl')	156	44.47N	0.34W
Begoro, Ghana	214	6.23N	0.23W
Behala, India	186a	22.31N	88.19E
Behbehān, Iran	185	30.35N	50.14E
Behm Canal, can., Ak., U.S.	86	55.41N	131.35W
Bei, r., China (bā)	191a	22.54N	113.08E
Bei'an, China (bā-än)	192	48.05N	126.26E
Beicai, China (bā-tsī)	191b	31.12N	121.33E
Beifei, r., China (bā-fā)	190	33.14N	117.03E
Beihai, China (bā-hī)	188	21.30N	109.10E
Beihuangcheng Dao, i., China (bā-hůäŋ-chŭŋ dou)	190	38.23N	120.55E
Beijing, China	189	39.55N	116.23E
Beijing Shi, China (bā-jyĭŋ shr)	192	40.07N	116.00E
Beira, Moz. (bā′rȧ)	212	19.45N	34.58E
Beira, hist. reg., Port. (bĕ′y-rä)	158	40.38N	8.00W
Beirut, Leb. (bā-ro͞ot′)	182	33.53N	35.30E
Beiyuan, China	240b	40.01N	116.24E
Beja, Port. (bā′zhä)	148	38.03N	7.53W
Béja, Tun.	148	36.52N	9.20E
Bejaïa (Bougie), Alg.	210	36.46N	5.00E
Bejar, Spain	158	40.25N	5.43W
Bejestān, Iran	182	34.30N	58.22E
Bejucal, Cuba (bā-ho͞o-käl′)	122	22.56N	82.23W
Bejuco, Pan. (bĕ-ko͞o′kŏ)	121	8.37N	79.54W
Békés, Hung. (bā′kāsh)	155	46.45N	21.08E
Békéscsaba, Hung. (bā′kāsh-chô′bô)	149	46.39N	21.06E
Beketova, Russia (bĕkė-to′vȧ)	171	53.23N	125.21E
Bela Crkva, Yugo. (bĕ′lä tsĕrk′vä)	161	44.53N	21.25E
Bel Air, Va., U.S.	229d	38.52N	77.10W
Bel Air, neigh., Ca., U.S.	232	34.05N	118.27W
Belalcázar, Spain (bāl-ȧ-kä′thär)	158	38.35N	5.12W
Belarus, nation, Eur.	164	53.30N	25.33E
Belas, Port.	238d	38.47N	9.16W
Belau *see* Palau, dep., Oc.	2	7.15N	134.30W
Bela Vista, neigh., Braz.	234d	23.33S	46.38W
Bela Vista de Goiás, Braz.	131	16.57S	48.47W
Belawan, Indon. (bȧ-lä′wȧn)	196	3.43N	98.43E
Belaya, r., Russia (byĕ′lĭ-yȧ)	167	52.30N	56.15E
Belcher Islands, is., Can. (bĕl′chẽr)	85	56.20N	80.40W
Belding, Mi., U.S. (bĕl′dĭng)	98	43.05N	85.25W
Belebey, Russia (byĕ′lĕ-bȧ′ĭ)	166	54.00N	54.10E
Belém, Braz. (bȧ-lĕN′)	131	1.18S	48.27W
Belém, neigh., Port.	238d	38.42N	9.12W
Belén, Para. (bā-lān′)	132	23.30S	57.09W
Belen, N.M., U.S. (bĕ-lȧn′)	109	34.40N	106.45W
Belènzinho, neigh., Braz.	234d	23.32S	46.35W
Bélep, Îles, is., N. Cal.	203	19.30S	164.00E
Belëv, Russia (byĕl′yĕf)	166	53.49N	36.06E
Belfair, Wa., U.S. (bĕl′far)	106a	47.27N	122.50W
Belfast, N. Ire., U.K.	142	54.36N	5.45W
Belfast, Me., U.S. (bĕl′fȧst)	92	44.25N	69.01W
Belfast, Lough, b., N. Ire., U.K. (lŏk bĕl′fȧst)	150	54.45N	6.00W
Belford Roxo, Braz.	132b	22.46S	43.24W
Belfort, Fr. (bā-fôr′)	147	47.40N	7.50E
Belgaum, India	183	15.57N	74.32E
Belgium, nation, Eur. (bĕl′jĭ-ŭm)	142	51.00N	2.52E
Belgorod, Russia (byĕl′gŭ-rut)	167	50.36N	36.32E
Belgorod, prov., Russia	163	50.40N	36.42E
Belgrade (Beograd), Yugo.	142	44.48N	20.32E
Belgrano, neigh., Arg.	233d	34.34S	58.28W
Belgrave, Austl.	243b	37.55S	145.21E
Belhaven, N.C., U.S. (bĕl′hā-vĕn)	115	35.33N	76.37W
Belington, W.V., U.S. (bĕl′ĭng-tŭn)	99	39.00N	79.55W
Belitung, i., Indon.	196	3.30S	107.30E
Belize, nation, N.A.	116	17.00N	88.40W
Belize, r., Belize	120a	17.16N	88.56W
Belize City, Belize (bĕ-lēz′)	116	17.31N	88.10W
Bel'kovo, Russia (byĕl′kô-vô)	172b	56.15N	38.49E
Bel'kovskiy, i., Russia (byĕl-kôf′skĭ)	171	75.45N	137.00E
Bell, Ca., U.S.	232	33.58N	118.11W
Bell, i., Can. (bĕl)	93	50.45N	55.35W
Bell, r., Can.	91	49.25N	77.15W
Bella Bella, Can.	86	52.10N	128.07W
Bella Coola, Can.	86	52.22N	126.46W
Bellaire, Oh., U.S. (bĕl-âr′)	98	40.00N	80.45W
Bellaire, Tx., U.S.	113a	29.43N	95.28W
Bellary, India (bĕl-lä′rė)	183	15.15N	76.56E

ng-sing; ŋ-baŋk; N-nasalized n; nŏd; cŏmmit; ōld; ôbey; ôrder; oi-boil; fo͞od; ȯ-as oo in foot; ou-out; s-soft; sh-dish; th-thin; pūre; ůnite; ûrn; stŭd; circŭs; ü-as in French tu; '-indeterminate vowel.

264 Bella Union–Betsiamites

PLACE (Pronunciation)	PAGE	Lat. °′	Long. °′
Bella Union, Ur. (bĕ'l-yä-ōō-nyô'n)	132	30.18S	57.26W
Bella Vista, Arg.	132	28.35S	58.53W
Bella Vista, Arg. (bä'lyä vēs'tä)	132	27.07S	65.14W
Bella Vista, Arg.	132a	34.35S	58.41W
Bellavista, Chile	234b	33.31S	70.37W
Bella Vista, Para.	131	22.16S	56.14W
Bellavista, Peru	233c	12.04S	77.08W
Belle-Anse, Haiti	123	18.15N	72.00W
Belle Bay, b., Can. (bĕl)	93	47.35N	55.15W
Belle Chasse, La., U.S. (bĕl shäs')	100d	29.52N	90.00W
Belle Farm Estates, Md., U.S.	229c	39.23N	76.45W
Bellefontaine, Oh., U.S. (bel-fŏn'tăn)	98	40.25N	83.50W
Bellefontaine Neighbors, Mo., U.S.	107e	38.46N	90.13W
Belle Fourche, S.D., U.S. (bĕl' fōōrsh')	102	44.28N	103.50W
Belle Fourche, r., Wy., U.S.	102	44.29N	104.40W
Belle Fourche Reservoir, res., S.D., U.S.	102	44.51N	103.44W
Bellegarde, Fr. (bĕl-gärd')	157	46.06N	5.50E
Belle Glade, Fl., U.S. (bĕl glād)	115a	26.39N	80.37W
Bellehaven, Va., U.S.	229d	38.47N	77.04W
Belle-Île, i., Fr. (bĕlēl')	147	47.15N	3.30W
Belle Isle, Strait of, strt., Can.	85	51.35N	56.30W
Belle Mead, N.J., U.S. (bĕl mēd)	100a	40.28N	74.40W
Belleoram, Can.	93	47.31N	55.25W
Belle Plaine, Ia., U.S. (bĕl plān')	103	41.52N	92.19W
Bellerose, N.Y., U.S.	228	40.44N	73.43W
Belle Vernon, Pa., U.S. (bĕl vûr'nŭn)	101e	40.08N	79.52W
Belleville, Can. (bĕl'vĭl)	91	44.15N	77.25W
Belleville, Il., U.S.	107e	38.31N	89.59W
Belleville, Ks., U.S.	111	39.49N	97.37W
Belleville, Mi., U.S.	101b	42.12N	83.29W
Belleville, N.J., U.S.	100a	40.47N	74.09W
Bellevue, Ia., U.S. (bĕl'vū)	103	42.14N	90.26W
Bellevue, Ky., U.S.	101f	39.06N	84.29W
Bellevue, Mi., U.S.	98	42.30N	85.00W
Bellevue, Oh., U.S.	98	41.15N	82.45W
Bellevue, Pa., U.S.	101e	40.30N	80.04W
Bellevue, Wa., U.S.	106a	47.37N	122.12W
Belley, Fr. (bĕ-lē')	157	45.46N	5.41E
Bellflower, Ca., U.S. (bĕl-flou'ẽr)	107a	33.53N	118.08W
Bell Gardens, Ca., U.S.	107a	33.59N	118.11W
Bellingham, Ma., U.S. (bĕl'ĭng-hăm)	93a	42.05N	71.28W
Bellingham, Wa., U.S.	96	48.46N	122.29W
Bellingham Bay, b., Wa., U.S.	106d	48.44N	122.34W
Bellingshausen Sea, sea, Ant. (bĕl'ĭngz houz'n)	219	72.00S	80.30W
Bellinzona, Switz. (bĕl-ĭn-tsō'nä)	154	46.10N	9.09E
Bellmawr, N.J., U.S.	229b	39.51N	75.06W
Bellmore, N.Y., U.S. (bĕl-mōr)	100a	40.40N	73.31W
Bello, Col. (bĕ'l-yō)	130	6.20N	75.33W
Bello, Cuba	233b	23.07N	82.24W
Bellow Falls, Vt., U.S. (bĕl'ōz fôls)	99	43.10N	72.30W
Bellpat, Pak.	186	29.08N	68.00E
Bell Peninsula, pen., Can.	85	63.50N	81.16W
Bells Corners, Can.	83c	45.20N	75.49W
Bells Mountain, mtn., Wa., U.S. (bĕls)	106c	45.50N	122.21W
Belluno, Italy (bĕl-lōō'nō)	160	46.08N	12.14E
Bell Ville, Arg. (bĕl vēl')	132	32.33S	62.36W
Bellville, S. Afr.	212a	33.54S	18.38E
Bellville, Tx., U.S. (bĕl'vĭl)	113	29.57N	96.15W
Bellwood, Il., U.S.	231a	41.53N	87.52W
Bélmez, Spain (bĕl'mĕth)	158	38.17N	5.17W
Belmond, Ia., U.S. (bĕl'mŏnd)	103	42.49N	93.37W
Belmont, Ca., U.S.	106b	37.34N	122.18W
Belmont, Ma., U.S.	227a	42.24N	71.10W
Belmonte, Braz. (bĕl-mōn'tä)	131	15.58S	38.47W
Belmopan, Belize	116	17.15N	88.47W
Belmore, Austl.	243a	33.55S	151.05E
Belogorsk, Russia	165	51.09N	128.32E
Belo Horizonte, Braz. (bĕ'lôre-sŏ'n-tĕ)	131	19.54S	43.56W
Beloit, Ks., U.S. (bē-loit')	110	39.26N	98.06W
Beloit, Wi., U.S.	97	42.31N	89.04W
Belomorsk, Russia (byĕl-ŏ-môrsk')	166	64.30N	34.42E
Beloretsk, Russia (byĕ'lŏ-rĕtsk)	166	53.58N	58.25E
Belosarayskaya, Kosa, c., Ukr.	163	46.43N	37.18E
Belot, Cuba	233b	23.08N	82.19W
Belovo, Russia (byĕ'lŭ-vû)	170	54.25N	86.18E
Beloye, l., Russia	166	60.10N	38.05E
Belozersk, Russia (byĕ-lŭ-zyôrsk')	166	60.00N	38.00E
Belper, Eng., U.K. (bĕl'pẽr)	144a	53.01N	1.28W
Belt, Mt., U.S. (bĕlt)	105	47.11N	110.58W
Belt Creek, r., Mt., U.S.	105	47.19N	110.58W
Belton, Tx., U.S. (bĕl'tŭn)	113	31.04N	97.27W
Belton Lake, l., Tx., U.S.	113	31.15N	97.35W
Beltsville, Md., U.S. (belts-vĭl)	100e	39.03N	76.56W
Belukha, Gora, mtn., Asia	164	49.47N	86.23E
Belvedere, Ca., U.S.	231b	37.52N	122.28W
Belvedere, Va., U.S.	229d	38.50N	77.10W
Belvedere, neigh., Eng., U.K.	235	51.29N	0.09E
Belvedere, pt. of i., Aus.	239e	48.11N	16.23E
Belvidere, Il., U.S. (bĕl-vĕ-dēr')	103	42.14N	88.52W
Belvidere, N.J., U.S.	99	40.50N	75.05W
Belyando, r., Austl. (bĕl-yän'dō)	203	22.09S	146.48E
Belyanka, Russia (byĕl'yán-ká)	172a	56.04N	59.16E
Belynichi, Bela. (byĕl-ĭ-nĭ'chĭ)	162	54.02N	29.42E
Belyy, Russia (byĕ'lē)	166	55.52N	32.58E
Belyy, i., Russia	164	73.19N	72.00E
Belyye Stolby, Russia (byĕ'lĭ-ye stôl'bĭ)	172b	55.20N	37.52E
Belzig, Ger. (bĕl'tsēg)	145b	52.08N	12.35E
Belzoni, Ms., U.S. (bĕl-zō'nē)	114	33.09N	90.30W
Bembe, Ang. (bĕn'bĕ)	212	7.00S	14.20E
Bembézar, r., Spain (bĕm-bā-thär')	158	38.00N	5.18W
Bemidji, Mn., U.S. (bē-mĭj'ĭ)	103	47.28N	94.54W
Bena Dibele, Zaire (bĕn'á dē-bĕ'lē)	212	4.00S	22.49E
Benalla, Austl. (bĕn-ăl'á)	203	36.30S	146.00E
Benares *see* Vārānasi, India	183	25.25N	83.00E
Benavente, Spain (bä-nä-vĕn'tä)	148	42.01N	5.43W
Ben Avon, Pa., U.S.	230b	40.31N	80.05W
Benbrook, Tx., U.S. (bĕn'brŏŏk)	107c	32.41N	97.27W
Benbrook Reservoir, res., Tx., U.S.	107c	32.35N	97.30W
Bend, Or., U.S. (bĕnd)	96	44.04N	121.17W
Bendeleben, Mount, mtn., Ak., U.S. (bĕn-dĕl-bĕn)	95	65.18N	163.45W
Bender Beyla, Som.	218a	9.40N	50.45E
Bendigo, Austl. (bĕn'dĭ-gō)	203	36.39S	144.20E
Benedict, Md., U.S. (bĕnĕ'dĭct)	100e	38.31N	76.41W
Benešov, Czech Rep. (bĕn'ĕ-shôf)	154	49.48N	14.40E
Benevento, Italy (bā-nā-vĕn'tō)	148	41.08N	14.46E
Benfica, neigh., Braz.	234c	22.53S	43.15W
Benfica, neigh., Port.	238d	38.45N	9.12W
Bengal, Bay of, b., Asia (bĕn-gôl')	180	17.30N	87.00E
Bengamisa, Zaire	217	0.57N	25.10E
Bengbu, China (bŭŋ-bōō)	189	32.52N	117.22E
Benghazi *see* Banghāzī, Libya	210	32.07N	20.04E
Bengkalis, Indon. (bĕng-kä'lĭs)	196	1.29N	102.06E
Bengkulu, Indon.	196	3.46S	102.18E
Benguela, Ang. (bĕn-gĕl'á)	212	12.35S	13.25E
Beni, r., Bol. (bā'nē)	130	13.41S	67.30W
Béni-Abbas, Alg. (bā'nē ä-bĕs')	210	30.11N	2.13W
Benicia, Ca., U.S. (bē-nĭsh'ĭ-á)	106b	38.03N	122.09W
Benin, nation, Afr.	210	8.00N	2.00E
Benin, r., Nig. (bĕn-ēn')	215	5.55N	5.15E
Benin, Bight of, bt., Afr.	210	5.30N	3.00E
Benin City, Nig.	210	6.19N	5.41E
Beni Saf, Alg. (bā'nē säf')	210	35.23N	1.20W
Benito, r., Eq. Gui.	216	1.35N	10.45E
Benkelman, Ne., U.S. (bĕn-kĕl-măn)	110	40.05N	101.35W
Benkovac, Cro. (bĕn'kō-väts)	160	44.02N	15.41E
Bennettsville, S.C., U.S. (bĕn'ĕts vĭl)	115	34.35N	79.41W
Bennettswood, Austl.	243b	37.51S	145.07E
Benninghofen, neigh., Ger.	236	51.29N	7.31E
Bennington, Vt., U.S. (bĕn'ĭng-tŭn)	99	42.55N	73.15W
Benns Church, Va., U.S. (bĕnz' chûrch')	100g	36.47N	76.35W
Benoni, S. Afr. (bĕ-nō'nĭ)	212	26.11S	28.19E
Benoni South, S. Afr.	244b	26.13S	28.18E
Benoy, Chad	215	8.59N	16.19E
Benque Viejo, Belize (bĕn-kĕ bĭē'hō)	120a	17.07N	89.07W
Benrath, neigh., Ger.	236	51.10N	6.52E
Bensberg, Ger.	157c	50.58N	7.09E
Bensenville, Il., U.S. (bĕn'sĕn-vĭl)	101a	41.57N	87.56W
Bensheim, Ger. (bĕns-hīm)	154	49.42N	8.38E
Benson, Az., U.S. (bĕn-sŭn)	109	32.00N	110.20W
Benson, Mn., U.S.	102	45.18N	95.36W
Bentiaba, Ang.	216	14.15S	12.21E
Bentleigh, Austl.	243b	37.55S	145.02E
Bentleyville, Pa., U.S. (bent'lē vĭl)	101e	40.07N	80.01W
Benton, Can.	92	45.59N	67.36W
Benton, Ar., U.S. (bĕn'tŭn)	111	34.34N	92.34W
Benton, Ca., U.S.	108	37.44N	118.22W
Benton, Il., U.S.	98	38.00N	88.55W
Benton Harbor, Mi., U.S. (bĕn'tŭn här'bẽr)	98	42.05N	86.30W
Bentonville, Ar., U.S. (bĕn'tŭn-vĭl)	111	36.22N	94.11W
Benue, r., Afr. (bā'nōō-â)	210	8.00N	8.00E
Benut, r., Malay.	181b	1.43N	103.20E
Benwood, W.V., U.S. (bĕn-wŏd)	98	39.55N	80.45W
Benxi, China (bŭn-shyē)	192	41.25N	123.50E
Beograd *see* Belgrade, Yugo.	142	44.48N	20.32E
Beppu, Japan (bĕ'pōō)	195	33.16N	131.30E
Bequia Island, i., St. Vin. (bĕk-ē'ä)	121b	13.00N	61.08W
Berakit, Tanjung, c., Indon.	181b	1.16N	104.44E
Berat, Alb. (bĕ-rät')	161	40.43N	19.59E
Berau, Teluk, b., Indon.	197	2.22S	131.40E
Berazategui, Arg. (bĕ-rä-zá'tĕ-gē)	132a	34.46S	58.14W
Berbera, Som. (bûr'bûr-á)	218a	10.25N	45.05E
Berbérati, Cen. Afr. Rep.	215	4.16N	15.47E
Berchum, Ger.	236	51.23N	7.32E
Berck, Fr. (bĕrk)	156	50.26N	1.36E
Berdyans'k, Ukr.	167	46.45N	36.47E
Berdyans'ka kosa, c., Ukr.	163	46.38N	36.42E
Berdyaush, Russia (bĕr'dyáûsh)	172a	55.10N	59.12E
Berdychiv, Ukr.	164	49.53N	28.32E
Berea, Ky., U.S. (bē-rē'á)	114	37.30N	84.19W
Berea, Oh., U.S.	101d	41.22N	81.51W
Berehove, Ukr.	155	48.13N	22.40E
Bereku, Tan.	217	4.27S	35.44E
Berens, r., Can. (bĕr'ĕnz)	89	52.15N	96.30W
Berens Island, i., Can.	89	52.18N	97.40W
Berens River, Can.	84	52.22N	97.02W
Beresford, S.D., U.S. (bĕr'ĕs-fẽrd)	102	43.05N	96.46W
Berettyóújfalu, Hung. (bĕ'rĕt-tyō-ōō'y'fō-lōō)	155	47.14N	21.33E
Berëza, Bela. (bĕ-rā'zá)	155	52.29N	24.59E
Berezhany, Ukr. (bĕr-yĕ'zhá-nĕ)	155	49.25N	24.58E
Berezina, r., Bela. (bĕr-yĕ'zē-ná)	162	53.20N	29.05E
Berezino, Bela. (bĕr-yä'zē-nô)	162	53.51N	28.54E
Berezivka, Ukr.	163	47.12N	30.56E
Berezna, Ukr. (bĕr-yôz'ná)	163	51.32N	31.47E
Bereznehuvate, Ukr.	163	47.19N	32.58E
Berezniki, Russia (bĕr-yôz'nyē-kē)	166	59.25N	56.46E
Berëzovka, Russia	172a	57.35N	57.19E
Berëzovo, Russia (bĭr-yô'zē-vû)	164	64.10N	65.10E
Berëzovskiy, Russia (bĕr-yô'zôf-skĭ)	172a	56.54N	60.47E
Berga, Spain (bĕr'gä)	159	42.05N	1.52E
Bergama, Tur. (bĕr'gä-mä)	182	39.08N	27.09E
Bergamo, Italy (bĕr'gä-mō)	148	45.43N	9.41E
Bergantin, Ven. (bĕr-gän-tē'n)	131b	10.04N	64.23W
Bergedorf, Ger. (bĕr'gĕ-dôrf)	145c	53.29N	10.12E
Bergen, Ger. (bĕr'gĕn)	154	54.26N	13.26E
Bergen, Nor.	142	60.24N	5.20E
Bergenfield, N.J., U.S.	100a	40.55N	73.59W
Bergen op Zoom, Neth.	151	51.29N	4.16E
Bergerac, Fr. (bĕr-zhĕ-räk')	147	44.49N	0.28E
Bergfelde, Ger.	238a	52.40N	13.19E
Berghausen, Ger.	236	51.18N	7.17E
Bergholtz, N.Y., U.S.	230a	43.06N	78.53W
Bergisch-Born, Ger.	236	51.09N	7.15E
Bergisch Gladbach, Ger. (bĕrg'ĭsh-glät'bäk)	157c	50.59N	7.08E
Bergkamen, Ger.	236	51.38N	7.38E
Berglern, Ger. (bĕrgh'lĕrn)	145d	48.24N	11.55E
Bergneustadt, Ger.	157c	51.01N	7.39E
Bergville, S. Afr. (bĕrg'vĭl)	213c	28.46S	29.22E
Berhampur, India	183	19.19N	84.48E
Bering Sea, sea (bē'rĭng)	224	58.00N	175.00W
Bering Strait, strt.	96a	64.50N	169.50W
Berja, Spain (bĕr'hä)	158	36.50N	2.56W
Berkeley, Ca., U.S. (bûrk'lĭ)	96	37.52N	122.17W
Berkeley, Il., U.S.	231a	41.53N	87.55W
Berkeley, Mo., U.S.	107e	38.45N	90.20W
Berkeley Hills, Pa., U.S.	230b	40.32N	80.00W
Berkeley Springs, W.V., U.S. (bûrk'lĭ springz)	99	39.40N	78.10W
Berkhamsted, Eng., U.K. (bĕk'hăm'stĕd)	144b	51.44N	0.34W
Berkhamsted, Eng., U.K.	235	51.46N	0.35W
Berkley, Mi., U.S. (bûrk'lĭ)	101b	42.30N	83.10W
Berkovitsa, Bul. (bĕ-kō'vē-tsá)	161	43.14N	23.08E
Berkshire, co., Eng., U.K.	144b	51.23N	1.07W
Berland, r., Can.	87	54.00N	117.10W
Berlenga, is., Port. (bĕr-lĕn'gäzh)	158	39.25N	9.33W
Berlin, Ger. (bĕr-lēn')	142	52.31N	13.28E
Berlin, S. Afr. (bĕr-lĭn)	213c	32.53S	27.36E
Berlin, N.H., U.S. (bûr-lĭn)	99	44.25N	71.10W
Berlin, N.J., U.S.	100f	39.47N	74.56W
Berlin, Wi., U.S. (bûr-lĭn')	103	43.58N	88.58W
Berlin-Tempelhof, Zentral Flughafen, arpt., Ger.	238a	52.29N	13.25E
Bermejo, r., S.A. (bĕr-mā'hō)	132	25.05S	61.00W
Bermeo, Spain (bĕr-mā'yō)	158	43.23N	2.43W
Bermuda, dep., N.A.	117	32.20N	65.45W
Bern, Switz. (bĕrn)	142	46.55N	7.25E
Bernal, Arg. (bĕr-näl')	132a	34.43S	58.17W
Bernalillo, N.M., U.S. (bĕr-nä-lē'yō)	109	35.20N	106.30W
Bernard, l., Can. (bẽr-närd')	99	45.45N	79.25W
Bernardsville, N.J., U.S. (bûr nårds'vĭl)	100a	40.43N	74.34W
Bernau, Ger. (bĕr'nou)	154	52.40N	13.35E
Bernburg, Ger. (bĕrn'bŏrgh)	154	51.48N	11.43E
Berndorf, Aus. (bĕrn'dôrf)	154	47.57N	16.05E
Berne, In., U.S. (bûrn)	98	40.40N	84.55W
Berner Alpen, mts., Switz.	154	46.29N	7.30E
Bernier, i., Austl. (bẽr-nēr')	202	24.58S	113.15E
Bernina, Pizzo, mtn., Eur.	154	46.23N	9.58E
Bero, r., Ang.	216	15.10S	12.20E
Beroun, Czech Rep. (bā'rōn)	154	49.57N	14.03E
Berounka, r., Czech Rep. (bĕ-rōn'ká)	154	49.53N	13.40E
Berowra, Austl.	201b	33.36S	151.10E
Berre, Étang de, l., Fr. (ā-tôn' dĕ bâr')	156a	43.27N	5.07E
Berre-l'Étang, Fr. (bâr'lā-tôn')	156a	43.28N	5.11E
Berriozabal, Mex. (bā'rēō-zä-bäl')	119	16.47N	93.16W
Berriyyane, Alg.	148	32.50N	3.49E
Berry Creek, r., Can.	88	51.15N	111.40W
Berryessa, r., Ca., U.S. (bĕ'rĭ ĕs'á)	108	38.35N	122.33W
Berry Islands, is., Bah.	122	25.40N	77.50W
Berryville, Ar., U.S. (bĕr'ē-vĭl)	111	36.21N	93.34W
Bershad', Ukr. (byĕr'shät)	163	48.22N	29.31E
Berthier, Can.	83b	46.56N	70.44W
Bertlich, Ger.	236	51.37N	7.04E
Bertrand, r., Wa., U.S. (bûr'tránd)	106d	48.58N	122.31W
Berwick, Pa., U.S. (bûr'wĭk)	99	41.05N	76.10W
Berwick-upon-Tweed, Eng., U.K. (bûr'ĭk)	146	55.45N	2.01W
Berwyn, Il., U.S. (bûr'wĭn)	101a	41.49N	87.47W
Berwyn Heights, Md., U.S.	229d	38.59N	76.54W
Beryslav, Ukr.	163	46.49N	33.24E
Besalampy, Madag. (bĕz-á-läm-pē')	213	16.48S	44.40E
Besançon, Fr. (bĕ-sän-sôn)	147	47.14N	6.02E
Besar, Gunong, mtn., Malay.	181b	2.31N	103.09E
Besed', r., Eur. (byĕ'syĕt)	162	52.58N	31.36E
Besedy, Russia	239b	55.37N	37.47E
Beshenkovichi, Bela. (byĕ'shĕn-kōvē'chĭ)	162	55.04N	29.29E
Beskid Mountains, mts., Eur.	155	49.23N	19.00E
Beskra, Alg.	210	34.52N	5.39E
Beskudnikovo, neigh., Russia	239b	55.52N	37.34E
Beslan, Russia	168	43.12N	44.33E
Besós, r., Spain	238e	41.25N	2.12E
Bessarabia, hist. reg., Mol.	163	47.00N	28.30E
Bességes, Fr. (bĕ-sĕzh')	156	44.20N	4.07E
Bessemer, Al., U.S. (bĕs'ē-mẽr)	100h	33.24N	86.58W
Bessemer, Mi., U.S.	103	46.29N	90.04W
Bessemer City, N.C., U.S.	115	35.16N	81.17W
Bestensee, Ger. (bĕs'tĕn-zā)	145b	52.15N	13.39E
Betanzos, Spain (bĕ-tän'thōs)	158	43.18N	8.14W
Betatakin Ruin, Az., U.S. (bĕt-á-tăk'ĭn)	109	36.40N	110.29W
Bethal, S. Afr. (bĕth'ăl)	218d	26.27S	29.28E
Bethalto, Il., U.S. (bá-thál'tō)	107e	38.54N	90.03W
Bethanien, Nmb.	212	26.20S	16.10E
Bethany, Mo., U.S.	111	40.15N	94.04W
Bethel, Ak., U.S. (bĕth'ĕl)	96a	60.50N	161.50W
Bethel, Ct., U.S.	100a	41.22N	73.24W
Bethel, Vt., U.S.	99	43.50N	72.40W
Bethel Park, Pa., U.S.	101e	40.19N	80.02W
Bethesda, Md., U.S. (bĕ-thĕs'dá)	100e	39.00N	77.10W
Bethlehem, S. Afr.	212	28.14S	28.18E
Bethlehem, Pa., U.S. (bĕth'lē-hĕm)	99	40.40N	75.25W
Bethlehem *see* Bayt Lahm, W. Bank	181a	31.42N	35.13E
Bethnal Green, neigh., Eng., U.K.	235	51.32N	0.03W
Bethpage, N.Y., U.S.	228	40.45N	73.29W
Béthune, Fr. (bā-tün')	156	50.32N	2.37E
Betroka, Madag. (bĕ-trōk'á)	213	23.13S	46.17E
Betsham, Eng., U.K.	235	51.25N	0.19E
Bet She'an, Isr.	181a	32.30N	35.30E
Betsiamites, Can.	85	48.57N	68.36W
Betsiamites, r., Can.	92	49.11N	69.20W

PRONOUNCING INDEX
Betsiboka–Black Volta (Volta Noire) 265

PLACE (Pronunciation)	PAGE	Lat. °′	Long. °′
Betsiboka, r., Madag. (bĕt-sĭ-bō'kȧ)	213	16.47S	46.45E
Bettles Field, Ak., U.S. (bĕt'tŭls)	95	66.58N	151.48W
Betwa, r., India (bĕt'wȧ)	183	25.00N	78.00E
Betz, Fr. (bĕ)	157b	49.09N	2.58E
Beveren, Bel.	145a	51.13N	4.14E
B. Everett Jordan Lake, res., N.C., U.S.	115	35.45N	79.00W
Beverly, Ma., U.S.	93a	42.34N	70.53W
Beverly, N.J., U.S.	100f	40.03N	74.56W
Beverly Hills, Austl.	243a	33.57S	151.05E
Beverly Hills, Ca., U.S.	107a	34.05N	118.24W
Beverly Hills, Mi., U.S.	230c	42.32N	83.15W
Bevier, Mo., U.S. (bē-vēr')	111	39.44N	92.36W
Bewdley, Eng., U.K. (būd'lĭ)	144a	52.22N	2.19W
Bexhill, Eng., U.K. (bĕks'hĭl)	151	50.49N	0.25E
Bexley, Austl.	243a	33.57S	151.08E
Bexley, Eng., U.K. (bĕks'ly)	144b	51.26N	0.09E
Beyenburg, neigh., Ger.	236	51.15N	7.18E
Beyla, Gui. (bā'lȧ)	210	8.41N	8.37W
Beylerbeyi, neigh., Tur.	239f	41.03N	29.03E
Beylul, Erit.	211	13.15N	42.21E
Beyoğlu, neigh., Tur.	239f	41.02N	28.59E
Beypazari, Tur. (bā-pȧ-zä'rĭ)	149	40.10N	31.40E
Beyşehir, Tur.	167	38.00N	31.45E
Beysugskiy, Liman, b., Russia (lĭ-măn' bĕy-sōōg'skĭ)	163	46.07N	38.35E
Bezhetsk, Russia (byĕ-zhĕtsk')	166	57.46N	36.40E
Bezhitsa, Russia (byĕ-zhĭ'tsȧ)	166	53.19N	34.18E
Béziers, Fr. (bā-zyā')	147	43.21N	3.12E
Bezons, Fr.	237c	48.56N	2.13E
Bhadreswar, India	186a	22.49N	88.22E
Bhāgalpur, India (bä'gŭl-pór)	183	25.15N	86.59E
Bhalswa, neigh., India	240d	28.44N	77.10E
Bhamo, Myanmar (bŭ-mō')	183	24.00N	96.15E
Bhāngar, India	186a	22.30N	88.36E
Bharatpur, India (bērt'pór)	183	27.21N	77.33E
Bhatinda, India (bŭ-tĭn-dȧ)	183	30.19N	74.56E
Bhātpāra, India	183	22.52N	88.24E
Bhaunagar, India (bäv-nŭg'ŭr)	183	21.45N	72.58E
Bhayandar, India	187b	19.20N	72.50E
Bhilai, India	186	21.14N	81.23E
Bhīma, r., India (bē'mȧ)	183	18.00N	74.45E
Bhiwandi, India	187b	19.18N	73.03E
Bhiwāni, India	186	28.53N	76.08E
Bhopāl, India (bó-päl)	183	23.20N	77.25E
Bhopura, India	240d	28.42N	77.20E
Bhubaneswar, India (bó-bŭ-näsh'vŭr)	183	20.21N	85.53E
Bhuj, India (bōōj)	183	23.22N	69.39E
Bhutan, nation, Asia (bōō-tän')	183	27.15N	90.30E
Biafra, Bight of, bt., Afr.	210	4.05N	7.10E
Biak, i., Indon. (bē'äk)	197	1.00S	136.00E
Biała Podlaska, Pol. (byä'wä pōd-läs'kä)	155	52.01N	23.08E
Białogard, Pol.	154	54.00N	16.01E
Bialystok, Pol. (byä-wĭs'tōk)	142	53.08N	23.12E
Biankouma, C. Iv.	214	7.44N	7.37W
Biarritz, Fr. (byä-rēts')	147	43.27N	1.39W
Bibb City, Ga., U.S. (bĭb' sĭ'tē)	114	32.31N	84.56W
Biberach, Ger. (bē'bĕräk)	154	48.06N	9.49E
Bibiani, Ghana	214	6.28N	2.20W
Bic, Can. (bĭk)	92	48.22N	68.42W
Bickerstaffe, Eng., U.K.	237a	53.32N	2.50W
Bickley, neigh., Eng., U.K.	235	51.24N	0.03E
Bicknell, In., U.S. (bĭk'nĕl)	98	38.45N	87.20W
Bicske, Hung. (bĭsh'kĕ)	155	47.29N	18.38E
Bida, Nig. (bē'dä)	210	9.05N	6.01E
Biddeford, Me., U.S. (bĭd'ē-fērd)	92	43.29N	70.29W
Biddulph, Eng., U.K. (bĭd'ŭlf)	144a	53.07N	2.10W
Bidston, Eng., U.K.	237a	53.24N	3.05W
Biebrza, r., Pol. (byĕb'zhȧ)	155	53.18N	22.25E
Biel, Switz. (bēl)	154	47.09N	7.12E
Bielefeld, Ger. (bē'lē-fĕlt)	147	52.01N	8.35E
Biella, Italy (byĕl'lä)	160	45.34N	8.05E
Bielsk Podlaski, Pol. (byĕlsk pŭd-lä'skĭ)	147	52.47N	23.14E
Bien Hoa, Viet.	196	10.59N	106.49E
Bienville, Lac, l., Can.	85	55.32N	72.45W
Biesenthal, Ger. (bē'sĕn-täl)	145b	52.46N	13.38E
Bièvres, Fr.	237c	48.45N	2.13E
Biferno, r., Italy (bē-fĕr'nō)	160	41.49N	14.46E
Bifoum, Gabon	216	0.22S	10.23E
Biga, Tur. (bē'ghȧ)	161	40.13N	27.14E
Big Bay de Noc, Mi., U.S. (bĭg bā dē nok')	103	45.48N	86.41W
Big Bayou, Ar., U.S. (bĭg'bī'yōō)	111	33.04N	91.28W
Big Bear City, Ca., U.S. (bĭg bâr)	107a	34.16N	116.51W
Big Belt Mountains, mts., Mt., U.S. (bĭg bĕlt)	96	46.53N	111.43W
Big Bend Dam, S.D., U.S. (bĭg bĕnd)	102	44.11N	99.33W
Big Bend National Park, rec., Tx., U.S.	96	29.15N	103.15W
Big Black, r., Ms., U.S. (bĭg blăk)	114	32.05N	90.49W
Big Blue, r., Ne., U.S. (bĭg blōō)	111	40.53N	97.00W
Big Canyon, Tx., U.S. (bĭg kăn'yŭn)	112	30.27N	102.19W
Big Creek, r., Oh., U.S.	229a	41.27N	81.41W
Big Cypress Indian Reservation, I.R., Fl., U.S.	115a	26.19N	81.11W
Big Cypress Swamp, sw., Fl., U.S. (bĭg sī'prĕs)	115a	26.02N	81.20W
Big Delta, Ak., U.S. (bĭg dĕl'tȧ)	95	64.08N	145.48W
Big Fork, r., Mn., U.S. (bĭg fôrk)	103	48.08N	93.47W
Biggar, Can.	84	52.04N	108.00W
Biggin Hill, neigh., Eng., U.K.	235	51.18N	0.04E
Big Hole, r., Mt., U.S. (bĭg hōl)	105	45.53N	113.15W
Big Hole National Battlefield, Mt., U.S. (bĭg hōl băt''l-fēld)	105	45.44N	113.35W
Bighorn, r., U.S.	96	45.30N	108.00W
Bighorn Lake, res., Mt., U.S.	105	45.00N	108.10W
Bighorn Mountains, mts., U.S. (bĭg hôrn)	96	44.47N	107.40W
Big Island, i., Can.	89	49.10N	94.40W
Big Lake, Wa., U.S. (bĭg lāk)	106a	48.24N	122.14W
Big Lake, l., Can.	83g	53.35N	113.47W
Big Lake, l., Wa., U.S.	106a	48.24N	122.14W
Big Lost, r., Id., U.S. (lôst)	105	43.56N	113.38W
Big Mossy Point, c., Can.	89	53.45N	97.50W
Big Muddy, r., Il., U.S.	98	37.50N	89.00W
Big Muddy Creek, r., Mt., U.S. (bĭg mud'ĭ)	105	48.53N	105.02W
Bignona, Sen.	214	12.49N	16.14W
Big Porcupine Creek, r., Mt., U.S. (pôr'kū-pīn)	105	46.38N	107.04W
Big Quill Lake, l., Can.	84	51.55N	104.22W
Big Rapids, Mi., U.S. (bĭg răp'ĭdz)	98	43.40N	85.30W
Big River, Can.	84	53.50N	107.01W
Big Sandy, r., Az., U.S. (bĭg sănd'ē)	109	34.59N	113.36W
Big Sandy, r., Ky., U.S.	98	38.15N	82.35W
Big Sandy, r., Wy., U.S.	105	42.08N	109.35W
Big Sandy Creek, r., Co., U.S.	110	39.08N	103.36W
Big Sandy Creek, r., Mt., U.S.	105	48.20N	110.08W
Bigsby Island, i., Can.	89	49.04N	94.35W
Big Sioux, r., U.S. (bĭg sōō)	102	44.34N	97.00W
Big Spring, Tx., U.S. (bĭg sprĭng)	112	32.15N	101.28W
Big Stone, l., Mn., U.S. (bĭg stōn)	102	45.29N	96.40W
Big Stone Gap, Va., U.S.	115	36.50N	82.50W
Big Sunflower, r., Ms., U.S. (sŭn-flou'ēr)	114	32.57N	90.40W
Big Timber, Mt., U.S. (bĭg'tĭm-bēr)	105	45.50N	109.57W
Big Wood, r., Id., U.S. (bĭg wód)	105	43.02N	114.30W
Bihār, state, India (bē-här')	186	23.48N	84.57E
Biharamulo, Tan. (bē-hä-rä-mōō'lō)	212	2.38S	31.20E
Bihorului, Munţii, mts., Rom.	155	46.37N	22.37E
Bijagós, Arquipélago dos, is., Gui.-B.	210	11.20N	17.10W
Bijāpur, India	187	16.53N	75.42E
Bijeljina, Bos.	161	44.44N	19.15E
Bijelo Polje, Yugo. (bē'yē-lō pō'lyĕ)	161	43.02N	19.48E
Bijiang, China (bē-jyän)	191a	22.57N	113.15E
Bijie, China (bē-jyĕ)	193	27.20N	105.18E
Bijou Creek, r., Co., U.S. (bē'zhōō)	110	39.41N	104.13W
Bīkaner, India (bĭ-kă'nûr)	183	28.07N	73.19E
Bikin, Russia (bē-kēn')	194	46.41N	134.29E
Bikin, r., Russia	194	46.37N	135.55E
Bikoro, Zaire (bē-kō'rō)	212	0.45S	18.07E
Bikuar, Parque Nacional do, rec., Ang.	216	15.07S	14.40E
Bilāspur, India (bē-läs'pōōr)	183	22.08N	82.12E
Bila Tserkva, Ukr.	167	49.48N	30.09E
Bilauktaung, mts., Asia	196	14.40N	98.50E
Bilbao, Spain (bĭl-bä'ō)	142	43.12N	2.48W
Bilbays, Egypt	218b	30.26N	31.37E
Bileća, Bos. (bē'lĕ-chä)	161	42.52N	18.26E
Bilecik, Tur. (bē-lĕd-zhĕk')	149	40.10N	29.58E
Bílé Karpaty, mts., Eur.	155	48.53N	17.35E
Biłgoraj, Pol. (bēw-gō'rī)	155	50.31N	22.43E
Bilhorod-Dnistrovs'kyy, Ukr.	167	46.09N	30.19E
Bilimbay, Russia (bē'lĭm-bày)	172a	56.59N	59.53E
Billabong, r., Austl. (bĭl'ȧ-bŏng)	203	35.15S	145.20E
Billerica, Ma., U.S. (bĭl'rĭk-ȧ)	93a	42.33N	71.16W
Billericay, Eng., U.K.	144b	51.38N	0.25E
Billings, Mt., U.S. (bĭl'ĭngz)	96	45.47N	108.29W
Billingsport, N.J., U.S.	229b	39.51N	75.14W
Bill Williams, r., Az., U.S. (bĭl-wĭl'yumz)	109	34.10N	113.50W
Bilma, Niger (bēl'mä)	211	18.41N	13.20E
Bilopillya, Ukr.	167	51.10N	34.19E
Bilovods'k, Ukr.	163	49.12N	39.36E
Biloxi, Ms., U.S. (bĭ-lŏk'sĭ)	97	30.24N	88.50W
Bilqās Qism Awwal, Egypt	218b	31.14N	31.25E
Bimberi Peak, mtn., Austl. (bĭm'bĕrĭ)	204	35.45S	148.50E
Binalonan, Phil. (bē-nä-lō'nän)	197a	16.03N	120.35E
Bingen, Ger. (bĭn'gĕn)	154	49.57N	7.54E
Bingham, Eng., U.K. (bĭng'ăm)	144a	52.57N	0.57W
Bingham, Me., U.S.	92	45.03N	69.51W
Bingham Canyon, Ut., U.S.	107b	40.33N	112.09W
Bingham Farms, Mi., U.S.	230c	42.32N	83.16W
Binghamton, N.Y., U.S. (bĭng'ăm-tŭn)	97	42.05N	75.55W
Bingo-Nada, b., Japan (bĭn'gō nä-dä)	195	34.06N	133.14E
Binjai, Indon.	196	3.59N	108.00E
Binnaway, Austl. (bĭn'ȧ-wā)	204	31.42S	149.22E
Binsheim, Ger.	236	51.31N	6.42E
Bintan, i., Indon. (bĭn'tän)	181b	1.09N	104.43E
Bintimani, mtn., S.L.	214	9.13N	11.07W
Bintulu, Malay. (bēn'tōō-lōō)	196	3.07N	113.06E
Binxian, China (bĭn-shyän)	190	37.27N	117.58E
Binxian, China	192	45.40N	127.20E
Bio Gorge, val., Ghana	214	8.30N	2.05W
Bioko (Fernando Póo), i., Eq. Gui.	210	3.35N	7.45E
Bira, Russia (bē'rȧ)	194	49.00N	133.18E
Bira, r., Russia	194	48.55N	132.25E
Birātnagar, Nepal (bĭ-răt'nŭ-gŭr)	186	26.35N	87.18E
Birbka, Ukr.	155	49.36N	24.18E
Birch, Eng., U.K.	237b	53.34N	2.13W
Birch Bay, Wa., U.S. (bûrch)	106d	48.55N	122.45W
Birch Bay, b., Wa., U.S.	106d	48.55N	122.52W
Birch Island, i., Can.	89	52.25N	99.55W
Birch Mountains, mts., Can.	84	57.36N	113.10W
Birch Point, c., Wa., U.S.	106d	48.57N	122.50W
Bird Island, i., S. Afr. (bērd)	213c	33.51S	26.21E
Bird Rock, i., Bah. (bûrd)	123	22.50N	74.20W
Birds Hill, Can. (bûrds)	83f	49.58N	97.00W
Birdsville, Austl. (bûrdz'vĭl)	202	25.50S	139.31E
Birdum, Austl. (bûrd'ŭm)	202	15.45S	133.25E
Birecik, Tur. (bē-rĕd-zhĕk')	149	37.10N	37.50E
Bir Gara, Chad	215	13.11N	15.58E
Bīrjand, Iran (bēr'jänd)	182	33.07N	59.16E
Birkenfeld, Or., U.S.	106c	45.59N	123.20W
Birkenhead, Eng., U.K. (bûr'kĕn-hĕd)	150	53.23N	3.02W
Birkenwerder, Ger. (bēr'kĕn-vĕr-dĕr)	145b	52.41N	13.22E
Birkholz, Ger.	238a	52.38N	13.34E
Birling, Eng., U.K.	235	51.19N	0.25E
Birmingham, Eng., U.K.	142	52.29N	1.53W
Birmingham, Al., U.S. (bûr'mĭng-häm)	97	33.31N	86.49W
Birmingham, Mi., U.S.	101b	42.32N	83.13W
Birmingham, Mo., U.S.	107f	39.10N	94.22W
Birmingham Canal, can., Eng., U.K.	144a	53.07N	2.40W
Bi'r Misāhah, Egypt	211	22.16N	28.04E
Birnin Kebbi, Nig.	210	12.32N	4.12E
Birobidzhan, Russia (bē'rō-bē-jän')	165	48.42N	133.28E
Birsk, Russia (bĭrsk)	164	55.25N	55.30E
Birstall, Eng., U.K. (bûr'stôl)	144a	53.44N	1.39W
Biryulëvo, Russia (bēr-yōōl'yô-vô)	172b	55.35N	37.39E
Biryusa, r., Russia (bēr-yōō'sä)	170	56.43N	97.30E
Bi'r Za'farānah, Egypt	181a	29.07N	32.38E
Biržai, Lith. (bēr-zhä'ē)	153	56.11N	24.45E
Bisbee, Az., U.S. (bĭz'bē)	96	31.30N	109.55W
Biscay, Bay of, b., Eur. (bĭs'kā')	142	45.19N	3.51W
Biscayne Bay, b., Fl., U.S. (bĭs-kān')	115a	25.22N	80.15W
Bischeim, Fr. (bĭsh'hĭm)	157	48.40N	7.48E
Biscotasi Lake, l., Can.	90	47.20N	81.55W
Biser, Russia (bē'sēr)	172a	58.24N	58.54E
Biševo, is., Yugo. (bē'shĕ-vō)	160	42.58N	15.50E
Bishkek, Kyrg.	169	42.49N	74.42E
Bisho, S. Afr.	212	32.50S	27.20E
Bishop, Ca., U.S. (bĭsh'ŭp)	108	37.22N	118.25W
Bishop, Tx., U.S.	113	27.35N	97.46W
Bishop's Castle, Eng., U.K. (bĭsh'ŏps käs''l)	144a	52.29N	2.57W
Bishopville, S.C., U.S. (bĭsh'ŭp-vĭl)	115	34.11N	80.13W
Bismarck, N.D., U.S. (bĭz'märk)	96	46.48N	100.46W
Bismarck Archipelago, is., Pap. N. Gui.	197	3.15S	150.45E
Bismarck Range, mts., Pap. N. Gui.	197	5.15S	144.15E
Bissau, Gui.-B. (bē-sä'ōō)	214	11.51N	15.35W
Bissett, Can.	89	51.01N	95.45W
Bissingheim, neigh., Ger.	236	51.24N	6.49E
Bistineau, l., La., U.S. (bĭs-tĭ-nō')	113	32.19N	93.45W
Bistrita, Rom. (bĭs-trĭt-sȧ)	149	47.09N	24.29E
Bistrita, r., Rom.	155	47.08N	25.47E
Bitlis, Tur. (bĭt-lēs')	182	38.30N	42.00E
Bitola, Mac. (bē'tô-lä) (mō'nä-stēr)	160	41.02N	21.22E
Bitonto, Italy (bē-tôn'tō)	160	41.08N	16.42E
Bitter Creek, r., Wy., U.S. (bĭt'ēr)	105	41.36N	108.29W
Bitterfeld, Ger. (bĭt'ēr-fĕlt)	154	51.39N	12.19E
Bittermark, neigh., Ger.	236	51.27N	7.28E
Bitterroot, r., Mt., U.S.	105	46.28N	114.10W
Bitterroot Range, mts., U.S. (bĭt'ēr-ōōt)	96	47.15N	115.13W
Bityug, r., Russia (bĭt'yōōg)	163	51.23N	40.33E
Biu, Nig.	215	10.35N	12.13E
Biwabik, Mn., U.S. (bē-wä'bĭk)	103	47.32N	92.24W
Biwa-ko, l., Japan (bē-wä'kō)	195	35.03N	135.51E
Biya, r., Russia (bĭ'yȧ)	170	52.22N	87.28E
Biysk, Russia (bēsk)	164	52.32N	85.28E
Bizana, S. Afr. (bĭz-änä)	213c	30.51S	29.54E
Bizerte, Tun. (bē-zĕrt')	210	37.23N	9.52E
Bjelovar, Cro. (byĕ-lō'vär)	160	45.54N	16.53E
Bjørnafjorden, fj., Nor.	152	60.11N	5.26E
Bla, Mali	214	12.57N	5.46W
Black, l., Mi., U.S. (blăk)	98	45.25N	84.15W
Black, l., N.Y., U.S.	99	44.30N	75.35W
Black, r., Asia	196	21.00N	103.30E
Black, r., Can.	90	49.20N	81.15W
Black, r., U.S.	111	35.47N	91.22W
Black, r., Az., U.S.	109	33.35N	109.35W
Black, r., N.Y., U.S.	99	43.45N	75.20W
Black, r., S.C., U.S.	115	33.55N	80.10W
Black, r., Wi., U.S.	103	44.07N	90.56W
Blackall, Austl. (blăk'ŭl)	203	24.23S	145.37E
Black Bay, b., Can. (blăk)	90	48.36N	88.32W
Blackburn, Austl.	243b	37.49S	145.09E
Blackburn, Eng., U.K. (blăk'bûrn)	150	53.45N	2.28W
Blackburn Mount, mtn., Ak., U.S.	95	61.50N	143.12W
Black Butte Lake, res., Ca., U.S.	108	39.45N	122.20W
Black Creek Pioneer Village, bldg., Can.	227c	43.47N	79.32W
Black Diamond, Wa., U.S. (dī'mŭnd)	106a	47.19N	122.00W
Black Down Hills, hills, Eng., U.K. (blăk'doun)	150	50.58N	3.19W
Blackduck, Mn., U.S. (blăk'dŭk)	103	47.41N	94.33W
Blackfeet Indian Reservation, I.R., Mt., U.S.	105	48.40N	113.00W
Blackfoot, Id., U.S. (blăk'fót)	105	43.11N	112.23W
Blackfoot, r., Mt., U.S.	105	46.53N	113.33W
Blackfoot Indian Reservation, I.R., Mt., U.S.	105	48.49N	112.53W
Blackfoot Indian Reserve, I.R., Can.	87	50.45N	113.00W
Blackfoot Reservoir, res., Id., U.S.	105	42.53N	111.23W
Black Forest *see* Schwarzwald, for., Ger.	154	47.54N	7.57E
Black Hills, mts., U.S.	96	44.08N	103.47W
Black Island, i., Can.	89	51.10N	96.30W
Black Lake, Can.	91	46.02N	71.24W
Blackley, neigh., Eng., U.K.	237b	53.31N	2.13W
Black Mesa, Az., U.S. (blăk māsȧ)	109	36.33N	110.40W
Blackmore, Eng., U.K.	235	51.41N	0.19E
Blackmud Creek, r., Can. (blăk'mŭd)	83g	53.28N	113.34W
Blackpool, Eng., U.K. (blăk'pōōl)	150	53.49N	3.02W
Black Range, mts., N.M., U.S.	96	33.15N	107.55W
Black River, Jam. (blăk')	122	18.00N	77.50W
Black River Falls, Wi., U.S.	103	44.18N	90.51W
Black Rock, Austl.	243b	37.59S	145.01E
Black Rock Desert, des., Nv., U.S. (rŏk)	104	40.55N	119.00W
Blacksburg, S.C., U.S. (blăks'bûrg)	115	35.09N	81.30W
Black Sea, sea	143	43.01N	32.16E
Blackshear, Ga., U.S. (blăk'shĭr)	115	31.20N	82.15W
Black Springs, Austl.	243b	37.46S	145.19E
Blackstone, Va., U.S. (blăk'stōn)	115	37.04N	78.00W
Black Sturgeon, r., Can. (stû'jŭn)	90	49.12N	88.41W
Blacktown, Austl. (blăk'toun)	201b	33.47S	150.55E
Blackville, Can. (blăk'vĭl)	92	46.44N	65.50W
Blackville, S.C., U.S.	115	33.21N	81.19W
Black Volta (Volta Noire), r., Afr.	210	11.30N	4.00W

ng-sing; ŋ-baŋk; N-nasalized n; nŏd; cŏmmit; ōld; ôbey; ôrder; oi-boil; fōōd; ó-as oo in foot; ou-out; s-soft; sh-dish; th-thin; pūre; ûnite; ûrn; stŭd; circŭs; ü-as in French tu; '-indeterminate vowel.

PLACE (Pronunciation)	PAGE	Lat. °'	Long. °'
Black Warrior, r., Al., U.S. (blăk wŏr'ĭ-ẽr)	114	32.37N	87.42W
Blackwater, r., Ire. (blăk-wô'tẽr)	150	52.05N	9.02W
Blackwater, r., Mo., U.S.	111	38.53N	93.22W
Blackwater, r., Va., U.S.	115	37.07N	77.10W
Blackwell, Ok., U.S. (blăk'wĕl)	111	36.47N	97.19W
Bladel, Neth.	145a	51.22N	5.15E
Bladensburg, Md., U.S.	229d	38.56N	76.55W
Blagodarnoye, Russia (blä'gô-där-nō'yĕ)	167	45.00N	43.30E
Blagoevgrad, Bul.	161	42.01N	23.06E
Blagoveshchensk, Russia (blä'gŏ-vyĕsh'chĕnsk)	165	50.16N	127.47E
Blagoveshchensk, Russia	172a	55.03N	56.00E
Blaine, Mn., U.S. (blān)	107g	45.11N	93.14W
Blaine, Wa., U.S.	106d	48.59N	122.49W
Blaine, W.V., U.S.	99	39.25N	79.10W
Blaine Hill, Pa., U.S.	230b	40.16N	79.53W
Blair, Ne., U.S. (blâr)	102	41.33N	96.09W
Blairmore, Can.	87	49.38N	114.25W
Blairsville, Pa., U.S. (blârs'vĭl)	99	40.30N	79.40W
Blake, i., Wa., U.S. (blāk)	106a	47.37N	122.28W
Blakehurst, Austl.	243a	33.59S	151.07E
Blakely, Ga., U.S. (blāk'lē)	114	31.22N	84.55W
Blanc, Cap, c., Afr.	210	20.39N	18.08W
Blanc, Mont, mtn., Eur. (môn blän)	142	45.50N	6.53E
Blanca, Bahía, b., Arg. (bä-ē'ä-blän'kä)	132	39.30S	61.00W
Blanca Peak, mtn., Co., U.S. (blăŋ'kà)	96	37.36N	105.22W
Blanche, r., Can.	83c	45.34N	75.38W
Blanche, Lake, l., Austl. (blănch)	204	29.20S	139.12E
Blanchester, Oh., U.S. (blăn'chĕs-tẽr)	101f	39.18N	83.58W
Blanco, r., Mex.	118	24.05N	99.21W
Blanco, r., Mex.	119	18.42N	96.03W
Blanco, Cabo, c., Arg. (blăŋ'kô)	132	47.08S	65.47W
Blanco, Cabo, c., C.R. (ká'bô-blăŋ'kō)	120	9.29N	85.15W
Blanco, Cape, c., Or., U.S. (blăn'kō)	104	42.53N	124.38W
Blancos, Cayo, i., Cuba (kä'yō-blăŋ'kōs)	122	23.15N	80.55W
Blanding, Ut., U.S.	109	37.40N	109.31W
Blankenburg, neigh., Ger.	238a	52.35N	13.28E
Blankenfelde, Ger. (blän'kĕn-fĕl-dĕ)	145b	52.20N	13.24E
Blankenfelde, neigh., Ger.	238a	52.37N	13.23E
Blankenstein, Ger.	236	51.24N	7.14E
Blanquefort, Fr.	156	44.53N	0.38W
Blanquilla, Arrecife, i., Mex. (är-rĕ-sē'fē-blän-kē'l-yä)	119	21.32N	97.14W
Blantyre, Mwi. (blăn-tīyr)	212	15.47S	35.00E
Blasdell, N.Y., U.S. (blăz'dĕl)	101c	42.48N	78.51W
Blato, Cro. (blä'tō)	160	42.55N	16.47E
Blawnox, Pa., U.S.	230b	40.29N	79.52W
Blaye-et-Sainte Luce, Fr. (blā'ā-sănt-lüs')	156	45.08N	0.40W
Blażowa, Pol. (bwä-zhō'vȧ)	155	49.51N	22.05E
Bleus, Monts, mts., Zaire	217	1.10N	30.10E
Bliersheim, Ger.	236	51.23N	6.43E
Blind River, Can. (blīnd)	85	46.10N	83.09W
Blissfield, Mi., U.S. (blĭs-fēld)	98	41.50N	83.50W
Blithe, r., Eng., U.K. (blĭth)	144a	52.22N	1.49W
Blitta, Togo	214	8.19N	0.59E
Block, i., R.I., U.S. (blŏk)	99	41.05N	71.35W
Bloedel, Can.	86	50.07N	125.23W
Bloemfontein, S. Afr. (blōōm'fŏn-tān)	212	29.09S	26.16E
Blois, Fr. (blwä)	147	47.36N	1.21E
Blombacher Bach, neigh., Ger.	236	51.15N	7.14E
Blood Indian Reserve, I.R., Can.	87	49.30N	113.10W
Bloomer, Wi., U.S. (blōōm'ẽr)	103	45.07N	91.30W
Bloomfield, In., U.S. (blōōm'fēld)	98	39.00N	86.55W
Bloomfield, Ia., U.S.	103	40.44N	92.21W
Bloomfield, Mo., U.S.	111	36.54N	89.55W
Bloomfield, Ne., U.S.	102	42.36N	97.40W
Bloomfield, N.J., U.S.	100a	40.48N	74.12W
Bloomfield Hills, Mi., U.S.	101b	42.35N	83.15W
Bloomfield Village, Mi., U.S.	230c	42.33N	83.15W
Blooming Prairie, Mn., U.S. (blōōm'ĭng prā'rĭ)	103	43.52N	93.04W
Bloomington, Ca., U.S. (blōōm'ĭng-tŭn)	107a	34.04N	117.24W
Bloomington, Il., U.S.	97	40.30N	89.00W
Bloomington, In., U.S.	98	39.10N	86.35W
Bloomington, Mn., U.S.	107g	44.50N	93.18W
Bloomsburg, Pa., U.S. (blōōmz'bûrg)	99	41.00N	76.25W
Blossburg, Al., U.S. (blŏs'bûrg)	100h	33.38N	86.57W
Blossburg, Pa., U.S.	99	41.45N	77.00W
Bloubergstrand, S. Afr.	212a	33.48S	18.28E
Blountstown, Fl., U.S. (blŭnts'tun)	114	30.24N	85.02W
Bludenz, Aus. (blōō-dĕnts')	154	47.09N	9.50E
Blue Ash, Oh., U.S. (blōō ăsh)	101f	39.14N	84.23W
Blue Earth, Mn., U.S. (blōō ûrth)	103	43.38N	94.05W
Blue Earth, r., Mn., U.S.	103	43.55N	94.16W
Bluefield, W.V., U.S. (blōō'fēld)	115	37.15N	81.11W
Bluefields, Nic. (blōō'fēldz)	117	12.03N	83.45W
Blue Island, Il., U.S.	101a	41.39N	87.41W
Blue Mesa Reservoir, res., Co., U.S.	109	38.25N	107.00W
Blue Mosque, rel., Egypt	244a	30.02N	31.15E
Blue Mountain, mtn., Can.	93	50.28N	57.11W
Blue Mountains, mts., Austl.	203	33.35S	149.00E
Blue Mountains, mts., Jam.	122	18.05N	76.35W
Blue Mountains, mts., U.S.	96	45.15N	118.50W
Blue Mud Bay, b., Austl. (bōō mŭd)	202	13.20S	136.45E
Blue Nile, r., Afr.	211	12.30N	34.00E
Blue Rapids, Ks., U.S. (blōō răp'ĭdz)	111	39.40N	96.41W
Blue Ridge, mtn., U.S. (blōō rĭj)	97	35.30N	82.50W
Blue River, Can.	84	52.05N	119.17W
Blue River, r., Mo., U.S.	107f	38.55N	94.33W
Bluff, Ut., U.S.	109	37.18N	109.34W
Bluff Park, Al., U.S.	100h	33.24N	86.52W
Bluffton, In., U.S. (blŭf-tŭn)	98	40.40N	85.15W
Bluffton, Oh., U.S.	98	40.50N	83.55W
Blumenau, Braz. (blōō'mĕn-ou)	132	26.53S	48.58W
Blumut, Gunong, mtn., Malay.	181b	2.03N	103.34E
Blyth, Eng., U.K. (blĭth)	150	55.03N	1.34W
Blythe, Ca., U.S.	109	33.37N	114.37W
Blytheville, Ar., U.S. (blĭth'vĭl)	111	35.55N	89.51W
Bo, S.L.	214	7.56N	11.21W
Boac, Phil.	197a	13.26N	121.50E
Boaco, Nic. (bô-ä'kō)	120	12.24N	85.41W
Bo'ai, China (bwo-ī)	192	35.10N	113.08E
Boa Vista, i., C.V. (bō-ä-vēsh'tȧ)	210b	16.01N	23.52W
Boa Vista do Rio Branco, Braz.	131	2.46N	60.45W
Bobbingworth, Eng., U.K.	235	51.44N	0.13E
Bobigny, Fr.	237c	48.54N	2.27E
Bobo Dioulasso, Burkina (bō'bō-dyōō-làs-sō')	210	11.12N	4.18W
Bobr, Bela. (bô'b'r)	162	54.19N	29.11E
Bóbr, r., Pol. (bŭ'br)	154	51.44N	15.13E
Bobrov, Russia (bŭb-rôf')	167	51.07N	40.01E
Bobrovytsya, Ukr. (bŭb-rô'vē-tsȧ)	163	50.43N	31.27E
Bobruysk, Bela. (bô-brōō'ĭsk)	166	53.07N	29.13E
Bobrynets', Ukr.	163	48.04N	32.10E
Boca, neigh., Arg.	233d	34.38S	58.21W
Boca del Pozo, Ven. (bô-kä-dĕl-pô'zō)	131b	11.00N	64.21W
Boca de Uchire, Ven. (bô-kä-dē-ōō-chē'rĕ)	131b	10.09N	65.27W
Bocaina, Serra da, mtn., Braz. (sĕ'r-rä-dà-bô-kä'ē-nä)	129a	22.47S	44.39W
Bocanegra, Peru	233c	12.01S	77.07W
Bocas, Mex. (bō'käs)	118	22.29N	101.03W
Bocas del Toro, Pan. (bō'käs dĕl tō'rō)	121	9.24N	82.15W
Bochnia, Pol. (bōĸ'nyä)	155	49.58N	20.28E
Bocholt, Ger. (bō'ĸōlt)	157c	51.50N	6.37E
Bochum, Ger.	154	51.29N	7.13E
Böckel, neigh., Ger.	236	51.13N	7.12E
Bockum, Ger.	236	51.20N	6.44E
Bockum, neigh., Ger.	236	51.21N	6.38E
Bockum-Hövel, Ger. (bō'kōm-hû'fĕl)	157c	51.41N	7.45E
Bodalang, Zaire	216	3.14N	22.14E
Bodaybo, Russia (bō-dī'bō)	165	57.12N	114.46E
Bodele, depr., Chad (bō-dȧ-lā')	211	16.45N	17.05E
Bodelschwingh, neigh., Ger.	236	51.33N	7.22E
Boden, Swe.	146	65.51N	21.29E
Bodensee, l., Eur. (bō'dĕn zā)	142	47.48N	9.22E
Bodmin, Eng., U.K. (bŏd'mĭn)	150	50.29N	4.45W
Bodmin Moor, Eng., U.K. (bŏd'mĭn mōr)	150	50.36N	4.43W
Bodrum, Tur.	167	37.10N	27.07E
Boende, Zaire (bô-ĕn'dȧ)	212	0.13S	20.52E
Boerne, Tx., U.S. (bō'ẽrn)	112	29.49N	98.44W
Boesmans, r., S. Afr.	213c	33.29S	26.09E
Boeuf, r., U.S. (bĕf)	113	32.23N	91.57W
Boffa, Gui. (bôf'ȧ)	210	10.10N	14.02W
Bōfu, Japan (bō'fōō)	195	34.03N	131.35E
Bogalusa, La., U.S. (bō-gȧ-lōō'sȧ)	113	30.48N	89.52W
Bogan, r., Austl. (bō'gĕn)	204	32.10S	147.40E
Bogense, Den. (bô'gĕn-sĕ)	152	55.34N	10.09E
Boggy Peak, mtn., Antig. (bŏg'ĭ-pēk)	121b	17.03N	61.50W
Bogong, Mount, mtn., Austl.	204	36.50S	147.15E
Bogor, Indon.	196	6.45S	106.45E
Bogoroditsk, Russia (bō-gō'rô-dĭtsk)	162	53.48N	38.06E
Bogorodsk, Russia	166	56.02N	43.40E
Bogorodskoje, neigh., Russia	239b	55.49N	37.44E
Bogorodskoye, Russia (bô-gô-rôd'skô-yĕ)	172a	56.43N	56.53E
Bogotá *see* Santa Fe de Bogotá, Col.	130	4.36N	74.05W
Bogota, N.J., U.S.	228	40.53N	74.02W
Bogotol, Russia (bŏ'gô-tŏl)	165	56.15N	89.45E
Boguchar, Russia (bŏ'gô-chär)	167	49.40N	41.00E
Bogue Chitto, Ms., U.S. (nôr'fēld)	114	31.26N	90.25W
Boguete, Pan. (bô-gĕ'tĕ)	121	8.54N	82.29W
Bo Hai, b., China	189	38.30N	120.00E
Bohai Haixia, strt., China (bwo-hī hī-shyä)	192	38.05N	121.40E
Bohain-en-Vermandois, Fr. (bô-ăn-ŏn-vâr-män-dwä')	156	49.58N	3.22E
Bohemia *see* Čechy, hist. reg., Czech Rep.	154	49.51N	13.55E
Bohemian Forest, mts., Eur. (bô-hē'mĭ-ăn)	142	49.35N	12.27E
Böhnsdorf, neigh., Ger.	238a	52.24N	13.33E
Bohodukhiv, Ukr.	167	50.10N	35.31E
Bohol, i., Phil. (bô-hŏl')	197	9.28N	124.35E
Bohom, Mex. (bō-ō'm)	119	16.47N	92.42W
Bohuslav, Ukr.	163	49.34N	30.51E
Boiestown, Can. (boiz'toun)	92	46.27N	66.25W
Bois Blanc, i., Mi., U.S. (boi' blăŋk)	98	45.45N	84.30W
Boischâtel, Can. (bwä-shä-tĕl')	83b	46.54N	71.08W
Bois-Colombes, Fr.	237c	48.55N	2.16E
Bois-des-Filion, Can. (bōō-ä'dĕ-fē-yōɴ')	83a	45.40N	73.46W
Boise, Id., U.S. (boi'zē)	96	43.38N	116.12W
Boise, r., Id., U.S.	104	43.43N	116.30W
Boise City, Ok., U.S.	110	36.42N	102.30W
Boissevain, Can. (bois'vān)	84	49.14N	100.03W
Boissy-Saint-Léger, Fr.	237c	48.45N	2.31E
Bojador, Cabo, c., W. Sah.	210	26.21N	16.08W
Bojnūrd, Iran	182	37.29N	57.13E
Bokani, Nig.	215	9.26N	5.13E
Boknafjorden, fj., Nor.	146	59.12N	5.37E
Boksburg, S. Afr. (bōks'bûrgh)	213b	26.13S	28.15E
Boksburg North, S. Afr.	244b	26.12S	28.15E
Boksburg South, S. Afr.	244b	26.14S	28.15E
Boksburg West, S. Afr.	244b	26.13S	28.14E
Bokungu, Zaire	216	0.41S	22.19E
Bol, Chad	215	13.28N	14.43E
Bolai I, Cen. Afr. Rep.	215	4.20N	17.21E
Bolama, Gui.-B. (bō-lä'mä)	210	11.34S	15.41W
Bolan, mtn., Pak. (bō-län')	186	30.13N	67.09E
Bolaños, Mex. (bō-län'yōs)	118	21.40N	103.48W
Bolaños, r., Mex.	118	21.26N	103.54W
Bolan Pass, p., Pak.	183	29.50N	67.10E
Bolbec, Fr. (bôl-bĕk')	156	49.37N	0.26E
Bole, Ghana (bō'lā)	210	9.02N	2.29W
Bolesławiec, Pol. (bō-lĕ-slä'vyĕts)	154	51.15N	15.35E
Bolgatanga, Ghana	214	10.46N	0.52W
Bolhrad, Ukr.	167	45.41N	28.38E
Boli, China (bwo-lē)	189	45.40N	130.38E
Bolinao, Phil. (bō-lē-nä'ô)	197a	16.24N	119.53E
Bolívar, Arg. (bō-lē'vär)	132	36.15S	61.05W
Bolívar, Col.	130	1.46N	76.58W
Bolivar, Mo., U.S. (bŏl'ĭ-vȧr)	111	37.37N	93.22W
Bolivar, Tn., U.S.	114	35.14N	88.56W
Bolívar, Pico, mtn., Ven.	130	8.44N	70.54W
Bolivar Peninsula, pen., Tx., U.S. (bŏl'ĭ-vȧr)	113a	29.25N	94.40W
Bolivia, nation, S.A. (bō-lĭv'ĭ-ȧ)	130	17.00S	64.00W
Bölkenbusch, Ger.	236	51.21N	7.06E
Bolkhov, Russia (bŏl-ĸôf')	166	53.27N	35.59E
Bollate, Italy	238c	45.33N	9.07E
Bollensdorf, Ger.	238a	52.31N	13.43E
Bollin, r., Eng., U.K. (bŏl'ĭn)	144a	53.18N	2.11W
Bollington, Eng., U.K. (bôl'ĭng-tŭn)	144a	53.18N	2.06W
Bollington, Eng., U.K.	237b	53.22N	2.25W
Bollnäs, Swe. (bôl'nĕs)	152	61.22N	16.20E
Bollwerk, Ger.	236	51.10N	7.35E
Bolmen, l., Swe. (bôl'mĕn)	152	56.58N	13.25E
Bolobo, Zaire (bō'lô-bô)	212	2.14S	16.18E
Bologna, Italy (bô-lōn'yä)	142	44.30N	11.18E
Bologoye, Russia (bô-lô-gô'yĕ)	166	57.52N	34.02E
Bolonchenticul, Mex. (bô-lôn-chĕn-tē-kōō'l)	120a	20.03N	89.47W
Bolondrón, Cuba (bô-lôn-drōn')	122	22.45N	81.25W
Bol'šaja Ochta, neigh., Russia	239a	59.57N	30.25E
Bolseno, Lago di, l., Italy (lä'gō-dē-bôl-sā'nô)	160	42.35N	11.40E
Bol'shaya Anyuy, r., Russia	171	67.58N	161.15E
Bol'shaya Chuya, r., Russia	171	58.15N	111.40E
Bol'shaya Kinel', r., Russia	166	53.20N	52.40E
Bol'she Ust'ikinskoye, Russia (bôl'she ôs-tyĭ-kĕn'skô-yĕ)	172a	55.58N	58.18E
Bol'shoy Begichëv, i., Russia	165	74.30N	114.40E
Bol'shoye Ivonino, Russia (ĭ-vô'nĭ-nô)	172a	59.41N	61.12E
Bol'shoy Kuyash, Russia (bôl'-shôy kōō'yàsh)	172a	55.52N	61.07E
Bol'šoj Teatr, bldg., Russia	239b	55.46N	37.37E
Bolsover, Eng., U.K. (bōl'zō-vẽr)	144a	53.14N	1.17W
Boltaña, Spain (bôl-tä'nä)	159	42.28N	0.03E
Bolton, Can. (bōl'tŭn)	83d	43.53N	79.44W
Bolton, Eng., U.K.	150	53.35N	2.26W
Bolton-upon-Dearne, Eng., U.K. (bōl'tŭn-ŭp'ŏn-dûrn)	144a	53.31N	1.19W
Bolu, Tur. (bō'lô)	149	40.45N	31.45E
Bolva, r., Russia (bôl'vä)	162	53.30N	34.30E
Bolvadin, Tur. (bôl-vä-dēn')	149	38.50N	30.50E
Bolzano, Italy (bôl-tsä'nō)	148	46.31N	11.22E
Boma, Zaire (bō'mä)	212	5.51S	13.03E
Bombala, Austl. (bŭm-bă'lă)	203	36.55S	149.07E
Bombay, India (bŏm-bā')	183	18.58N	72.50E
Bombay Harbour, b., India	187b	18.55N	72.52E
Bomi Hills, Lib.	210	7.00N	11.00W
Bom Jardim, Braz. (bôn zhär-dēɴ')	129a	22.10S	42.25W
Bom Jesus do Itabapoana, Braz.	129a	21.08S	41.51W
Bømlo, i., Nor. (bûmlô)	152	59.47N	4.57E
Bommerholz, Ger.	236	51.23N	7.18E
Bommern, neigh., Ger.	236	51.25N	7.20E
Bomongo, Zaire	211	1.22N	18.21E
Bom Retiro, neigh., Braz.	234d	23.32S	46.38W
Bom Sucesso, Braz. (bôn-sōō-sĕ'sō)	129a	21.02S	44.44W
Bomu *see* Mbomou, r., Afr.	211	4.50N	24.00E
Bon, Cap, c., Tun. (bôɴ)	148	37.04N	11.13E
Bon Air, Pa., U.S.	229b	39.58N	75.19W
Bonaire, i., Neth. Ant. (bô-nâr')	130	12.10N	68.15W
Bonavista, Can. (bŏ-nȧ-vĭs'tȧ)	85a	48.39N	53.07W
Bonavista Bay, b., Can.	85a	48.45N	53.20W
Bond, Co., U.S. (bŏnd)	110	39.53N	106.40W
Bondi, Austl.	243a	33.53S	151.17E
Bondo, Zaire (bôn'dô)	170	3.49N	23.40E
Bondoc Peninsula, pen., Phil. (bôn-dŏk')	197a	13.24N	122.30E
Bondoukou, C. Iv. (bŏn-dōō'kōō)	210	8.02N	2.48W
Bonds Cay, i., Bah. (bŏnds kē)	122	25.30N	77.45W
Bondy, Fr.	157b	48.54N	2.28E
Bône *see* Annaba, Alg.	210	36.57N	7.39E
Bone, Teluk, b., Indon.	196	4.09S	121.00E
Bonete, Cerro, mtn., Arg. (bô'nĕtĕh çĕrrô)	132	27.50S	68.35W
Bonfim, Braz. (bôɴ-fē'ɴ)	129a	20.20S	44.15W
Bongor, Chad	215	10.17N	15.22E
Bonham, Tx., U.S. (bŏn'ăm)	111	33.35N	96.09W
Bonhomme, Pic, mtn., Haiti	123	19.10N	72.20W
Bonifacio, Fr. (bō-nē-fä'chō)	160	41.23N	9.10E
Bonifacio, Strait of, strt., Eur.	148	41.14N	9.02E
Bonifay, Fl., U.S. (bŏn-ĭ-fā')	114	30.46N	85.40W
Bonin Islands, is., Japan (bō'nĭn)	225	26.30N	141.00E
Bonn, Ger. (bôn)	142	50.44N	7.06E
Bonne Bay, b., Can. (bŏn)	93	49.33N	57.55W
Bonners Ferry, Id., U.S. (bonẽrz fĕr'ĭ)	104	48.41N	116.19W
Bonner Springs, Ks., U.S. (bŏn'ẽr sprĭngz)	107f	39.04N	94.52W
Bonne Terre, Mo., U.S. (bŏn târ')	111	37.55N	90.32W
Bonnet Peak, mtn., Can. (bŏn'ĭt)	87	51.26N	115.53W
Bonneuil-sur-Marne, Fr.	237c	48.46N	2.29E
Bonneville Dam, dam, U.S. (bŏn'ē-vĭl)	104	45.37N	121.57W
Bonny, Nig. (bŏn'ē)	210	4.29N	7.13E
Bonny Lake, Wa., U.S. (bŏn'ē lăk)	106a	47.11N	122.11W
Bonnyrigg, Austl.	243a	33.54S	150.54E
Bonnyville, Can. (bŏnē-vĭl)	87	54.16N	110.44W
Bonorva, Italy (bô-nôr'vä)	160	40.26N	8.46E
Bonsúcesso, neigh., Braz.	234c	22.52S	43.15W
Bonthain, Indon. (bôn-tīn')	196	5.30S	119.52E

ăt; fĭnăl; rāte; senāte; ärm; åsk; sofȧ; fâre; ch-choose; dh-as th in other; bē; ēvent; bĕt; recĕnt; cratẽr; g-gō; gh-guttural g; bĭt; ĭ-short neutral; rīde; ĸ-guttural k as ch in German ich;

PLACE (Pronunciation)	PAGE	Lat. °′	Long. °′
Bonthe, S.L.	210	7.32N	12.30W
Bontoc, Phil. (bŏn-tŏk′)	197a	17.10N	121.01E
Booby Rocks, is., Bah. (bōō′bĭ rŏks)	122	23.55N	77.00W
Booker T. Washington National Monument, rec., Va., U.S. (bŏŏk′ẽr tē wŏsh′ĭng-tŭn)	115	37.07N	79.45W
Boom, Bel.	145a	51.05N	4.22E
Boone, Ia., U.S. (bōōn)	103	42.04N	93.51W
Booneville, Ar., U.S. (bōōn′vĭl)	111	35.09N	93.54W
Booneville, Ky., U.S.	98	37.25N	83.40W
Booneville, Ms., U.S.	114	34.37N	88.35W
Boons, S. Afr.	218d	25.59S	27.15E
Boonton, N.J., U.S. (bōōn′tŭn)	100a	40.54N	74.24W
Boonville, In., U.S.	98	38.00N	87.15W
Boonville, Mo., U.S.	111	38.57N	92.44W
Boorama, Som.	218a	10.05N	43.08E
Boosaaso, Som.	218a	11.19N	49.10E
Boothbay Harbor, Me., U.S. (bōōth′bā här′bẽr)	92	43.51N	69.39W
Boothia, Gulf of, b., Can. (bōō′thĭ-ȧ)	85	69.04N	86.04W
Boothia Peninsula, pen., Can.	82	73.30N	95.00W
Boothstown, Eng., U.K.	237b	53.30N	2.25W
Bootle, Eng., U.K. (bōō′t'l)	144a	53.29N	3.02W
Booysens, neigh., S. Afr.	244b	26.14S	28.01E
Bor, Sudan (bôr)	211	6.13N	31.35E
Bor, Tur. (bōr)	167	37.50N	34.40E
Boraha, Nosy, i., Madag.	213	16.58S	50.15E
Borah Peak, mtn., Id., U.S. (bō′rä)	105	44.12N	113.47W
Borås, Swe. (bō′rōs)	146	57.43N	12.55E
Borāzjān, Iran (bō-räz-jän′)	182	29.13N	51.13E
Borba, Braz. (bôr′bä)	131	4.23S	59.31W
Borbeck, neigh., Ger.	236	51.29N	6.57E
Borborema, Planalto da, plat., Braz. (plä-nàl′tō-dä-bôr-bō-rĕ′mä)	131	7.35S	36.40W
Bordeaux, Fr. (bôr-dō′)	142	44.50N	0.37W
Bordeaux, S. Afr.	244b	26.06S	28.01E
Bordentown, N.J., U.S. (bôr′dĕn-toun)	99	40.05N	74.40W
Bordj-bou-Arréridj, Alg. (bôrj-bōō-à-rā-rēj′)	148	36.03N	4.48E
Bordj Omar Idriss, Alg.	210	28.06N	6.34E
Borehamwood, Eng., U.K.	235	51.40N	0.16W
Borgarnes, Ice.	146	64.31N	21.40W
Borger, Tx., U.S. (bôr′gẽr)	110	35.40N	101.23W
Borgholm, Swe. (bôrg-hŏlm′)	152	56.52N	16.40E
Borgne, l., La., U.S. (bôrn′y′)	113	30.03N	89.36W
Borgomanero, Italy (bôr′gō-mä-nâ′rō)	160	45.40N	8.28E
Borgo Val di Taro, Italy (bô′r-zhō-väl-dē-tä′rō)	160	44.29N	9.44E
Borili, Kaz.	169	53.36N	61.55E
Boring, Or., U.S. (bōring)	106c	45.26N	122.22W
Borisoglebsk, Russia (bŏ-rē sô-glyĕpsk′)	164	51.20N	42.00E
Borisov, Bela. (bŏ-rē′sôf)	166	54.16N	28.33E
Borisovka, Russia (bŏ-rē-sôf′kȧ)	167	50.38N	36.00E
Borivli, India	187b	19.15N	72.48E
Borja, Spain (bôr′hä)	158	41.50N	1.33W
Borjas Blancas, Spain (bô′r-ĸäs-blä′n-käs)	159	41.29N	0.53E
Borken, Ger. (bōr′kĕn)	157c	51.50N	6.51E
Borkou, reg., Chad (bôr-kōō′)	211	18.11N	18.28E
Borkum, i., Ger. (bōr′kōōm)	154	53.31N	6.50E
Borlänge, Swe. (bôr-lĕŋ′gĕ)	152	60.30N	15.24E
Borle, neigh., India	240e	19.02N	72.55E
Borneo, i., Asia	196	0.25N	112.39E
Bornholm, i., Den. (bôrn-hôlm)	142	55.16N	15.15E
Bornim, neigh., Ger.	238a	52.26N	13.00E
Bornstedt, neigh., Ger.	238a	52.25N	13.02E
Borodayivka, Ukr.	163	48.44N	34.09E
Boromlya, Ukr. (bŏ-rôm′'l-yä)	163	50.36N	34.58E
Boromo, Burkina	214	11.45N	2.56W
Borough Green, Eng., U.K.	235	51.17N	0.19E
Borough Park, neigh., N.Y., U.S.	228	40.38N	74.00W
Borovan, Bul. (bō-rō-vän′)	161	43.24N	23.47E
Borovichi, Russia (bŏ-rô-vē′chė)	164	58.22N	33.56E
Borovsk, Russia (bô′rŏvsk)	162	55.13N	36.26E
Borraan, Som.	218a	10.38N	48.30E
Borracha, Isla la, i., Ven. (ē′s-lä-lȧ-bôr-rȧ′chä)	131b	10.18N	64.44W
Borroloola, Austl. (bŏr-rō-lōō′lȧ)	202	16.15S	136.19E
Borshchiv, Ukr.	155	48.47N	26.04E
Borth, Ger.	236	51.36N	6.33E
Bort-les-Orgues, Fr. (bôr-lā-zôrg)	156	45.26N	2.26E
Borūjerd, Iran	182	33.45N	48.53E
Boryslav, Ukr.	155	49.17N	23.24E
Boryspil', Ukr.	163	50.17N	30.54E
Borzna, Ukr. (bôrz′nȧ)	167	51.15N	32.26E
Borzya, Russia (bôrz′yȧ)	165	50.37N	116.53E
Bosa, Italy (bō′sä)	160	40.18N	8.34E
Bosanska Dubica, Bos. (bō′sän-skä dōō′bĭt-sä)	160	45.10N	16.49E
Bosanska Gradiška, Bos. (bō′sän-skä grä-dĭsh′kä)	161	45.08N	17.15E
Bosanski Novi, Bos. (bō′s sän-skĭ nō′vē)	160	45.00N	16.22E
Bosanski Petrovac, Bos. (bō′sän-skĭ pĕt′rō-väts)	160	44.33N	16.23E
Bosanski Šamac, Bos. (bō′sän-skĭ shä′màts)	161	45.03N	18.30E
Boscobel, Wi., U.S. (bŏs′kō-bĕl)	103	43.08N	90.44W
Bose, China (bwo-sŭ)	193	24.00N	106.38E
Boshan, China (bwo-shan)	189	36.32N	117.51E
Boskol', Kaz. (bȧs-kôl′)	169	53.45N	61.17E
Boskoop, Neth.	145a	52.04N	4.39E
Boskovice, Czech Rep. (bŏs′kō-vē-tsĕ)	154	49.26N	16.37E
Bosna, r., Yugo.	161	44.19N	17.54E
Bosnia and Herzegovina, nation, Eur.	161	44.15N	17.30E
Bosobolo, Zaire	216	4.11N	19.54E
Bosporus *see* İstanbul Boğazi, strt., Tur.	182	41.10N	29.10E
Bossangoa, Cen. Afr. Rep.	215	6.29N	17.27E
Bossier City, La., U.S. (bŏsh′ẽr)	113	32.31N	93.42W
Bossley Park, Austl.	243a	33.52S	150.54E
Bostanci, neigh., Tur.	239f	40.57N	29.05E
Bosten Hu, l., China (bwo-stŭn hōō)	188	42.06N	88.01E
Boston, Ga., U.S. (bôs′tŭn)	114	30.47N	83.47W
Boston, Ma., U.S.	97	42.15N	71.07W
Boston, Pa., U.S.	230b	40.18N	79.49W
Boston Bay, b., Ma., U.S.	227a	42.22N	70.54W
Boston Garden, pt. of i., Ma., U.S.	227a	42.22N	71.04W
Boston Harbor, b., Ma., U.S.	227a	42.20N	70.58W
Boston Heights, Oh., U.S.	101d	41.15N	81.30W
Boston Mountains, mts., Ar., U.S.	97	35.46N	93.32W
Botafogo, neigh., Braz.	234c	22.57S	43.11W
Botafogo, Enseada de, b., Braz.	234c	22.57S	43.10W
Botany, Austl.	243a	33.57S	151.12E
Botany Bay, neigh., Eng., U.K.	235	51.41N	0.07W
Botany Bay, b., Austl. (bŏt′ȧ-nĭ)	203	33.58S	151.11E
Botevgrad, Bul.	161	42.54N	23.41E
Bothaville, S. Afr. (bō′tä-vĭl)	218d	27.24S	26.38E
Bothell, Wa., U.S. (bŏth′ĕl)	106a	47.46N	122.12W
Bothnia, Gulf of, b., Eur. (bŏth′nĭ-ȧ)	142	63.40N	21.30E
Botoşani, Rom. (bō-tō-shàn′ĭ)	155	47.46N	26.40E
Botswana, nation, Afr. (bŏtswănȧ)	212	22.10S	23.13E
Bottineau, N.D., U.S. (bŏt-ĭ-nō′)	102	48.48N	100.28W
Bottrop, Ger. (bŏt′trōp)	154	51.31N	6.56E
Botwood, Can. (bŏt′wŏŏd)	85a	49.08N	55.21W
Bötzow, Ger.	238a	52.39N	13.08E
Bouafle, C. Iv. (bō-ȧ-flā′)	210	6.59N	5.45W
Bouar, Cen. Afr. Rep. (bōō-är)	211	5.57N	15.36E
Bou Areg, Sebkha, Mor.	158	35.09N	3.02W
Boubandjidah, Parc National de, rec., Cam.	215	8.20N	14.40E
Boucherville, Can. (bōō-shä-vĕl′)	83a	45.37N	73.27W
Boucherville, Îles de, is., Can.	227b	45.37N	73.28W
Boudenib, Mor. (bōō-dĕ-nĕb′)	210	32.14N	3.04W
Boudette, Mn., U.S. (bōō-dĕt)	103	48.42N	94.34W
Boudouaou, Alg.	159	36.44N	3.25E
Boufarik, Alg. (bōō-fȧ-rēk′)	159	36.35N	2.55E
Bougainville, i., Pap. N. Gui.	198e	6.00S	155.00E
Bougainville Trench, deep (bōō-găɴ-vēl′)	225	7.00S	152.00E
Bougie *see* Bejaïa, Alg.	210	36.46N	5.00E
Bougouni, Mali (bōō-gōō-nē′)	210	11.27N	7.30W
Bouïra, Alg. (boo-ē′rȧ)	148	36.25N	3.55E
Bouïra-Sahary, Alg. (bwē-rȧ sȧ′ä-rē)	159	35.16N	3.23E
Bouka, r., Gui.	214	11.05N	10.40W
Boukiéro, Congo	244c	4.12S	15.18E
Boulder, Co., U.S.	96	40.02N	105.19W
Boulder, r., Mt., U.S.	105	46.10N	112.07W
Boulder City, Nv., U.S.	96	35.57N	114.50W
Boulder Peak, mtn., Id., U.S.	105	43.53N	114.33W
Boulogne, neigh., Arg.	233d	34.31S	58.34W
Boulogne-Billancourt, Fr. (bōō-lôn′y′-bē-yän-kōōr′)	156	48.50N	2.14E
Boulogne-sur-Mer, Fr. (bōō-lôn′y′-sür-mâr′)	147	50.44N	1.37E
Boumba, r., Cam.	215	3.20N	14.40E
Bouna, C. Iv. (bōō-nä′)	210	9.16N	3.00W
Bouna, Parc National de, rec., C. Iv.	214	9.20N	3.35W
Boundary Bay, b., N.A. (boun′dȧ-rĭ)	106d	49.03N	122.59W
Boundary Peak, mtn., Nv., U.S.	108	37.52N	118.20W
Bound Brook, N.J., U.S. (bound brŏŏk)	100a	40.34N	74.32W
Bountiful, Ut., U.S. (boun′tĭ-fŏŏl)	107b	40.55N	111.53W
Bountiful Peak, mtn., Ut., U.S. (boun′tĭ-fŏŏl)	107b	40.58N	111.49W
Bounty Islands, is., N.Z.	5	47.42S	179.05E
Bourail, N. Cal.	198f	21.34S	165.30E
Bourem, Mali (bōō-rĕm′)	210	16.43N	0.15W
Bourg-en-Bresse, Fr. (bōōr-gĕɴ-brĕs′)	147	46.12N	5.13E
Bourges, Fr. (bōōrzh)	147	47.06N	2.22E
Bourget, Can. (bōōr-zhĕ′)	83c	45.26N	75.09W
Bourg-la-Reine, Fr.	237c	48.47N	2.19E
Bourgoin, Fr. (bōōr-gwăɴ′)	157	45.46N	5.17E
Bourke, Austl. (bŭrk)	203	30.10S	146.00E
Bourne, Eng., U.K. (bōrn)	144a	52.46N	0.22W
Bournebridge, Eng., U.K.	235	51.38N	0.11E
Bourne End, Eng., U.K.	235	51.45N	0.32W
Bournemouth, Eng., U.K. (bôrn′mŭth)	150	50.44N	1.55W
Bou Saâda, Alg. (bōō-sä′dä)	148	35.13N	4.17E
Bousso, Chad (bōō-sō′)	211	10.33N	16.45E
Boutilimit, Maur.	210	17.30N	14.54W
Bouvetøya, i., Ant.	3	55.00S	3.00E
Bövinghausen, neigh., Ger.	236	51.31N	7.19E
Bow, r., Can. (bō)	84	50.35N	112.15W
Bowbells, N.D., U.S. (bō′bĕls)	102	48.50N	102.16W
Bowdle, S.D., U.S. (bōd′'l)	102	45.28N	99.42W
Bowdon, Eng., U.K.	237b	53.23N	2.22W
Bowen, Austl. (bō′ĕn)	203	20.02S	148.14E
Bowie, Md., U.S. (bōō′ĭ) (bō′ė)	100e	38.59N	76.47W
Bowie, Tx., U.S.	111	33.34N	97.50W
Bowling Green, Ky., U.S. (bōlĭng grēn)	97	37.00N	86.26W
Bowling Green, Mo., U.S.	111	39.19N	91.09W
Bowling Green, Oh., U.S.	98	41.25N	83.40W
Bowman, N.D., U.S. (bō′măn)	102	46.11N	103.23W
Bowron, r., Can. (bō′rŭn)	87	53.20N	121.10W
Boxelder Creek, r., Mt., U.S. (bŏks′ĕl-dẽr)	102	45.35N	104.28W
Box Elder Creek, r., Mt., U.S.	105	47.17N	108.37W
Box Hill, Austl.	201a	37.49S	145.08E
Boxian, China (bwo shyĕn)	192	33.52N	115.47E
Boxing, China (bwo-shyĭŋ)	190	37.09N	118.08E
Boxmoor, Eng., U.K.	235	51.45N	0.29W
Boxtel, Neth.	145a	51.40N	5.21E
Boyabo, Zaire	216	3.43N	18.46E
Boyacıköy, neigh., Tur.	239f	41.06N	29.02E
Boyang, China (bwo-yäŋ)	193	29.00N	116.42E
Boyer, r., Can. (boi′ẽr)	83b	46.45N	70.56W
Boyer, r., Ia., U.S.	102	41.45N	95.36W
Boyle, Ire. (boil)	150	53.59N	8.15W
Boyne, r., Ire. (boin)	150	53.40N	6.40W
Boyne City, Mi., U.S.	98	45.15N	85.05W
Boyoma Falls, wtfl., Zaire	211	0.30N	25.12E
Boysen Reservoir, res., Wy., U.S.	105	43.19N	108.11W
Bozcaada, Tur. (bōz-cä′dä)	161	39.50N	26.05E
Bozca Ada, i., Tur.	161	39.50N	26.00E
Bozeman, Mt., U.S. (bōz′măn)	96	45.41N	111.00W
Bozene, Zaire	216	2.56N	19.12E
Bozhen, China (bwo-jŭn)	190	38.05N	116.35E
Bozoum, Cen. Afr. Rep.	215	6.19N	16.23E
Bra, Italy (brä)	160	44.41N	7.52E
Bracciano, Lago di, l., Italy (lä′gō-dē-brä-chä′nō)	160	42.05N	12.00E
Bracebridge, Can. (brās′brĭj)	91	45.05N	79.20W
Braceville, Il., U.S. (brās′vĭl)	101a	41.13N	88.16W
Bräcke, Swe. (brĕk′kĕ)	146	62.44N	15.28E
Brackenridge, Pa., U.S. (brăk′ĕn-rĭj)	101e	40.37N	79.44W
Brackettville, Tx., U.S. (brăk′ĕt-vĭl)	112	29.19N	100.24W
Braço Maior, mth., Braz.	131	11.00S	51.00W
Braço Menor, mth., Braz. (brä′zō-mē-nō′r)	131	11.38S	50.00W
Bradano, r., Italy (brä-dä′nō)	160	40.43N	16.22E
Braddock, Pa., U.S. (brăd′ŭk)	101e	40.24N	79.52W
Braddock Hills, Pa., U.S.	230b	40.25N	79.51W
Bradenburger Tor, pt. of i., Ger.	238a	52.31N	13.23E
Bradenton, Fl., U.S. (brā′dĕn-tŭn)	115a	27.28N	82.35W
Bradfield, Eng., U.K. (brăd′fēld)	144b	51.25N	1.08W
Bradford, Eng., U.K. (brăd′fẽrd)	146	53.47N	1.44W
Bradford, Oh., U.S.	98	40.10N	84.30W
Bradford, Pa., U.S.	99	42.00N	78.40W
Bradley, Il., U.S. (brăd′lĭ)	101a	41.09N	87.52W
Bradner, Can. (brăd′nẽr)	106d	49.05N	122.26W
Bradshaw, Eng., U.K.	237b	53.36N	2.24W
Brady, Tx., U.S. (brā′dĭ)	112	31.09N	99.21W
Braga, Port. (brä′gä)	148	41.20N	8.25W
Bragado, Arg. (brä-gä′dō)	132	35.07S	60.28W
Bragança, Braz. (brä-gän′sä)	131	1.02S	46.50W
Bragança, Port.	158	41.48N	6.46W
Bragança Paulista, Braz. (brä-gän′sä-pä′ōō-lē′s-tȧ)	132	22.58S	46.31W
Bragg Creek, Can. (brăg)	83e	50.57N	114.35W
Brahmaputra, r., Asia (brä′mȧ-pōō′trȧ)	183	26.45N	92.45E
Brāhui, mts., Pak.	183	28.32N	66.15E
Braidwood, Il., U.S. (brād′wŏŏd)	101a	41.16N	88.13W
Brăila, Rom. (brē′ēlȧ)	142	45.15N	27.58E
Brainerd, Mn., U.S. (brān′ẽrd)	103	46.20N	94.09W
Braintree, Ma., U.S. (brān′trē)	93a	42.14N	71.00W
Braithwaite, La., U.S. (brīth′wīt)	100d	29.52N	89.57W
Brakpan, S. Afr. (brăk′păn)	213b	26.15S	28.22E
Bralorne, Can. (brā′lôrn)	87	50.47N	122.49W
Bramalea, Can.	83d	43.48N	79.41W
Bramhall, Eng., U.K.	237b	53.22N	2.10W
Brampton, Can. (brămp′tŭn)	91	43.41N	79.46W
Branca, Pedra, mtn., Braz. (pĕ′drä-brä′ɴ-kä)	132b	22.55S	43.28W
Branchville, N.J., U.S. (branch′vĭl)	100a	41.09N	74.44W
Branchville, S.C., U.S.	115	33.17N	80.48W
Branco, r., Braz. (bräŋ′kō)	131	2.21N	60.38W
Brandberg, mtn., Nmb.	212	21.15S	14.15E
Brandenburg, Ger. (brän′dĕn-bŏŏrgh)	147	52.25N	12.33E
Brandenburg, hist. reg., Ger.	154	52.12N	13.31E
Brandfort, S. Afr. (brăn′d-fôrt)	218d	28.42S	26.29E
Brandon, Can. (brăn′dŭn)	84	49.50N	99.57W
Brandon, Vt., U.S.	99	43.45N	73.05W
Brandon Mountain, mtn., Ire. (brăn-dŏn)	150	52.15N	10.12W
Brandywine, Md., U.S. (brăndĭ′wīn)	100e	38.42N	76.51W
Branford, Ct., U.S. (brăn′fẽrd)	99	41.15N	72.50W
Braniewo, Pol. (brä-nyĕ′vō)	155	54.23N	19.50E
Brańsk, Pol. (brän′ sk)	155	52.44N	22.51E
Branson, Mo., U.S.	111	36.39N	93.13W
Brantford, Can. (brănt′fẽrd)	91	43.09N	80.17W
Bras d'Or Lake, l., Can. (brä-dôr′)	93	45.52N	60.50W
Brasília, Braz. (brä-sē′lvä)	131	15.49S	47.39W
Brasilia Legal, Braz.	131	3.45S	55.46W
Brasópolis, Braz. (brä-sô′pō-lēs)	129a	22.30S	45.36W
Braşov, Rom.	149	45.39N	25.35E
Brass, Nig. (brăs)	210	4.28N	6.28E
Brasschaat, Bel. (bräs′ĸät)	145a	51.19N	4.30E
Bratcevo, neigh., Russia	239b	55.51N	37.24E
Bratenahl, Oh., U.S. (bră′tĕn-ôl)	101d	41.34N	81.36W
Bratislava, Slvk. (brä′tĭs-lä-vä)	142	48.09N	17.07E
Bratsk, Russia (brätsk)	165	56.10N	102.04E
Bratskoye Vodokhranilishche, res., Russia	165	56.10N	102.05E
Bratslav, Ukr. (brät′släf)	163	48.48N	28.59E
Brattleboro, Vt., U.S. (brăt′'l-bŭr-ō)	99	42.50N	72.35W
Braunau, Aus. (brou′nou)	154	48.15N	13.05E
Braunschweig, Ger. (broun′shvīgh)	147	52.16N	10.32E
Bråviken, r., Swe.	152	58.40N	16.40E
Brawley, Ca., U.S. (brô′lĭ)	96	32.59N	115.32W
Bray, Ire. (brā)	150	53.10N	6.05W
Braybrook, Austl.	243b	37.47S	144.51E
Braymer, Mo., U.S. (brā′mẽr)	111	39.34N	93.47W
Brays Bay, Tx., U.S. (brās′bĭ′yōō)	113a	29.41N	95.33W
Brazeau, r., Can.	87	52.55N	116.10W
Brazeau, Mount, mtn., Can. (brȧ-zō′)	87	52.33N	117.21W
Brazil, In., U.S. (brȧ-zĭl′)	98	39.30N	87.00W
Brazil, nation, S.A.	131	9.00S	53.00W
Brazilian Highlands, mts., Braz. (brȧ zĭl yȧn hī-lȧndz)	128	14.00S	48.00W
Brazos, r., Tx., U.S. (brä′zōs)	96	33.10N	98.50W
Brazos, Clear Fork, r., Tx., U.S.	112	32.56N	99.14W
Brazos, Double Mountain Fork, r., Tx., U.S.	110	33.23N	101.21W

ng-sing; ŋ-baŋk; ɴ-nasalized n; nŏd; cŏmmit; ōld; ôbey; ôrder; oi-boil; fōōd; ŏŏ-as oo in foot; ou-out; s-soft; sh-dish; th-thin; pūre; ůnite; ûrn; stŭd; circŭs; ü-as in French tu; '-indeterminate vowel.

268 Brazos–Buckhorn Island State Park

PLACE (Pronunciation)	PAGE	Lat. °′	Long. °′
Brazos, Salt Fork, r., Tx., U.S. (sôlt fôrk)	110	33.20N	101.57W
Brazzaville, Congo (brá-zá-vēl′)	212	4.16S	15.17E
Brčko, Bos. (bērch′kô)	161	44.54N	18.46E
Brda, r., Pol. (bĕr-dä)	155	53.18N	17.55E
Brea, Ca., U.S. (brē′ȧ)	107a	33.55N	117.54W
Breakeyville, Can.	83b	46.40N	71.13W
Brechten, neigh., Ger.	236	51.35N	7.28E
Breckenridge, Mn., U.S. (brĕk′ĕn-rĭj)	102	46.17N	96.35W
Breckenridge, Tx., U.S.	112	32.46N	98.53W
Breckerfeld, Ger.	236	51.16N	7.28E
Brecksville, Oh., U.S. (brĕks′vĭl)	101d	41.19N	81.38W
Břeclav, Czech Rep. (brzhĕl′láf)	154	48.46N	16.54E
Breda, Neth. (brā-dä′)	151	51.35N	4.47E
Bredasdorp, S. Afr. (brā′das-dôrp)	212	34.15S	20.00E
Bredbury, Eng., U.K.	237b	53.25N	2.06W
Bredell, S. Afr.	244b	26.05S	28.17E
Bredeney, neigh., Ger.	236	51.24N	6.59E
Bredenscheid-Stüter, Ger.	236	51.22N	7.11E
Bredy, Russia (brĕ′dĭ)	172a	52.25N	60.23E
Breezewood, Pa., U.S.	230b	40.34N	80.03W
Bregenz, Aus. (brā′gĕnts)	154	47.30N	9.46E
Bregovo, Bul. (brĕ′gô-vô)	161	44.07N	22.45E
Breidafjördur, b., Ice.	146	65.15N	22.50W
Breidbach, S. Afr. (brĕd′băk)	213c	32.54S	27.26E
Breil-sur-Roya, Fr. (brĕ′y′)	157	43.57N	7.36E
Breitscheid, Ger.	236	51.22N	6.52E
Brejo, Braz. (brå′zhô)	131	3.33S	42.46W
Bremangerlandet, i., Nor.	152	61.51N	4.25E
Bremen, Ger. (brā-mĕn)	142	53.05N	8.50E
Bremen, In., U.S. (brē′mĕn)	98	41.25N	86.05W
Bremerhaven, Ger. (brām-ĕr-hä′fĕn)	146	53.33N	8.38E
Bremerton, Wa., U.S. (brĕm′ĕr-tŭn)	104	47.34N	122.38W
Bremervörde, Ger. (brĕ′mĕr-fûr-dĕ)	145c	53.29N	9.09E
Bremner, Can. (brĕm′nĕr)	83g	53.34N	113.14W
Bremond, Tx., U.S. (brĕm′ŭnd)	113	31.11N	96.40W
Breña, Peru	233c	12.04S	77.04W
Brenham, Tx., U.S. (brĕn′ăm)	113	30.10N	96.24W
Bren Mar Park, Md., U.S.	229d	38.48N	77.09W
Brenner Pass, p., Eur. (brĕn′ĕr)	147	47.00N	11.30E
Brentford, neigh., Eng., U.K.	235	51.29N	0.18W
Brenthurst, S. Afr.	244b	26.16S	28.23E
Brentwood, Eng., U.K. (brĕnt′wŏod)	151	51.37N	0.18E
Brentwood, Md., U.S.	99	39.00N	76.55W
Brentwood, Mo., U.S.	107e	38.37N	90.21W
Brentwood, Pa., U.S.	101e	40.22N	79.59W
Brentwood Heights, neigh., Ca., U.S.	232	34.04N	118.30W
Brentwood Park, S. Afr.	244b	26.08S	28.18E
Brescia, Italy (brā′shä)	148	45.33N	10.15E
Bressanone, Italy (brĕs-sä-nō′nā)	160	46.42N	11.40E
Bresso, Italy	238c	45.32N	9.11E
Bressuire, Fr. (grĕ-swēr′)	156	46.49N	0.14W
Brest, Bela.	164	52.06N	23.43E
Brest, Fr. (brĕst)	142	48.24N	4.30W
Brest, prov., Bela.	162	52.30N	26.50E
Bretagne, hist. reg., Fr. (brĕ-tän′yĕ)	156	48.00N	3.00W
Breton, Pertuis, strt., Fr. (pâr-twĕ′brĕ-tôn′)	156	46.18N	1.43W
Breton Sound, strt., La., U.S. (brĕt′ŭn)	114	29.38N	89.15W
Breukelen, Neth.	145a	52.09N	5.00E
Brevard, N.C., U.S. (brê-värd′)	115	35.14N	82.45W
Breves, Braz. (brā′vĕzh)	131	1.32S	50.13W
Brevik, Nor. (brĕ′vêk)	152	59.04N	9.39E
Brewarrina, Austl. (brōō-ēr-rē′nȧ)	203	29.54S	146.50E
Brewer, Me., U.S. (brōō′ēr)	92	44.46N	68.46W
Brewerville, Lib.	214	6.26N	10.47W
Brewster, N.Y., U.S. (brōō′stẽr)	100a	41.23N	73.38W
Brewster, Cerro, mtn., Pan. (sĕ′r-rô-brōō′stẽr)	121	9.19N	79.15W
Brewton, Al., U.S. (brōō′tŭn)	114	31.06N	87.04W
Brežice, Slvn. (brĕ′zhē-tsĕ)	160	45.55N	15.37E
Breznik, Bul. (brĕs′nĕk)	161	42.44N	22.55E
Briancon, Fr. (brē-än-sôn′)	157	44.54N	6.39E
Briare, Fr. (brē-är′)	156	47.40N	2.46E
Bridal Veil, Or., U.S. (brīd′ăl vāl)	106c	45.33N	122.10W
Bridge Point, c., Bah. (brĭj)	122	25.35N	76.40W
Bridgeport, Al., U.S. (brĭj′pôrt)	114	34.55N	85.42W
Bridgeport, Ct., U.S.	97	41.12N	73.12W
Bridgeport, Il., U.S.	98	38.40N	87.45W
Bridgeport, Ne., U.S.	102	41.40N	103.06W
Bridgeport, Oh., U.S.	98	40.00N	80.45W
Bridgeport, Pa., U.S.	100f	40.06N	75.21W
Bridgeport, Tx., U.S.	111	33.13N	97.46W
Bridgeport, neigh., Il., U.S.	231a	41.51N	87.39W
Bridgeton, Al., U.S. (brĭj′tŭn)	100h	33.27N	86.39W
Bridgeton, Mo., U.S.	107e	38.45N	90.23W
Bridgeton, N.J., U.S.	99	39.30N	75.15W
Bridgetown, Barb. (brĭj′ toun)	117	13.08N	59.37W
Bridgetown, Can.	92	44.51N	65.18W
Bridgeview, Il., U.S.	231a	41.45N	87.48W
Bridgeville, Pa., U.S. (brĭj′vĭl)	101e	40.22N	80.07W
Bridgewater, Austl. (brĭj′wô-tẽr)	204	42.50S	147.28E
Bridgewater, Can.	85	44.23N	64.31W
Bridgnorth, Eng., U.K. (brĭj′nôrth)	144a	52.32N	2.25W
Bridgton, Me., U.S. (brĭj′tŭn)	92	44.04N	70.45W
Bridlington, Eng., U.K. (brĭd′lĭng-tŭn)	150	54.06N	0.10W
Brie-Comte-Robert, Fr. (brē-kônt-ē-rō-bâr′)	157b	48.42N	2.37E
Brielle, Neth.	145a	51.54N	4.08E
Brierfield, Eng., U.K. (brī′ẽr fēld)	144a	53.49N	2.14W
Brierfield, Al., U.S. (brī′ẽr-fēld)	114	33.01N	86.55W
Brier Island, i., Can. (brī′ẽr)	92	44.16N	66.24W
Brieselang, Ger. (brē′zĕ-läng)	145b	52.36N	12.59E
Briey, Fr. (brē-ĕ′)	157	49.15N	5.57E
Brig, Switz. (brēg)	147	46.17N	7.59E
Brigg, Eng., U.K. (brĭg)	144a	53.33N	0.29W
Brigham City, Ut., U.S. (brĭg′ăm)	107b	41.31N	112.01W
Brighouse, Eng., U.K. (brĭg′hous)	144a	53.42N	1.47W
Bright, Austl. (brīt)	204	36.43S	147.00E
Bright, In., U.S. (brīt)	101f	39.13N	84.51W
Brightlingsea, Eng., U.K. (brī′t-lĭng-sē)	144b	51.50N	1.00E
Brightmoor, neigh., Mi., U.S.	230c	42.24N	83.14W
Brighton, Austl.	201a	37.55S	145.00E
Brighton, Eng., U.K.	147	50.47N	0.07W
Brighton, Al., U.S. (brī′tŭn)	100h	33.27N	86.56W
Brighton, Co., U.S.	110	39.58N	104.49W
Brighton, Il., U.S.	107e	39.03N	90.08W
Brighton, Ia., U.S.	103	41.11N	91.47W
Brighton, neigh., Ma., U.S.	227a	42.21N	71.08W
Brighton Indian Reservation, I.R., Fl., U.S.	115a	27.05N	81.25W
Brighton Le-Sands, Austl.	243a	33.58S	151.09E
Brightwood, neigh., D.C., U.S.	229d	38.58N	77.02W
Brigittenau, neigh., Aus.	239e	48.14N	16.22E
Brihuega, Spain (brê-wā′gä)	158	40.32N	2.52W
Brilyn Park, Va., U.S.	229d	38.54N	77.10W
Brimley, Mi., U.S. (brĭm′lē)	107k	46.24N	84.34W
Brindisi, Italy (brēn′dē-zē)	142	40.38N	17.57E
Brinje, Cro. (brēn′yĕ)	160	45.00N	15.08E
Brinkleigh, Md., U.S.	229c	39.18N	76.50W
Brinkley, Ar., U.S. (brĭŋk′lĭ)	111	34.52N	91.12W
Brinnon, Wa., U.S. (brĭn′ŭn)	106a	47.41N	122.54W
Brion, i., Can. (brē-ôn′)	93	47.47N	61.29W
Brioude, Fr. (brē-ōōd′)	156	45.18N	3.22E
Brisbane, Austl. (brĭz′bån)	204	27.30S	153.10E
Brisbane, Ca., U.S.	231b	37.41N	122.24W
Bristol, Eng., U.K.	147	51.29N	2.39W
Bristol, Ct., U.S. (brĭs′tŭl)	99	41.40N	72.55W
Bristol, Pa., U.S.	100f	40.06N	74.51W
Bristol, R.I., U.S.	100b	41.41N	71.14W
Bristol, Tn., U.S.	97	36.35N	82.10W
Bristol, Vt., U.S.	99	44.10N	73.00W
Bristol, Va., U.S.	97	36.36N	82.00W
Bristol, Wi., U.S.	101a	42.32N	88.04W
Bristol Bay, b., Ak., U.S.	95	58.05N	158.54W
Bristol Channel, strt., Eng., U.K.	147	51.20N	3.47W
Bristow, Ok., U.S. (brĭs′tō)	111	35.50N	96.25W
British Columbia, prov., Can. (brĭt′ĭsh kŏl′ŭm-bĭ-ȧ)	84	56.00N	124.53W
British Indian Ocean Territory, dep., Afr.	2	7.00S	72.00E
British Isles, is., Eur.	142	54.00N	4.00W
Brits, S. Afr.	218d	25.39S	27.47E
Britstown, S. Afr. (brĭts′toun)	212	30.30S	23.40E
Britt, Ia., U.S. (brĭt)	103	43.05N	93.47W
Brittany *see* Bretagne, hist. reg., Fr.	156	48.00N	3.00W
Britton, S.D., U.S. (brĭt′ŭn)	102	45.47N	97.44W
Brive-la-Gaillarde, Fr. (brēv-lä-gī-yärd′ĕ)	147	45.10N	1.31E
Briviesca, Spain (brê-vyās′kȧ)	158	42.34N	3.21W
Brno, Czech Rep. (b′r′nô)	142	49.18N	16.37E
Broa, Ensenada de la, b., Cuba	122	22.30N	82.00W
Broach, India	186	21.47N	72.58E
Broad, r., Ga., U.S. (brôd)	114	34.15N	83.14W
Broad, r., N.C., U.S.	115	35.38N	82.40W
Broadheath, Eng., U.K.	237b	53.24N	2.21W
Broadley Common, Eng., U.K.	235	51.45N	0.04E
Broadmeadows, Austl. (brôd′mĕd-ōz)	201a	37.40S	144.53E
Broadmeadows, Austl.	243b	37.40S	144.54E
Broadmoor, Ca., U.S.	231b	37.41N	122.29W
Broadview Heights, Oh., U.S. (brôd′vū)	101d	41.18N	81.41W
Brockenscheidt, Ger.	236	51.38N	7.25E
Brockport, N.Y., U.S. (brŏk′pōrt)	99	43.15N	77.55W
Brockton, Ma., U.S. (brŏk′tŭn)	93a	42.04N	71.01W
Brockville, Can. (brŏk′vĭl)	85	44.35N	75.40W
Brockway, Mt., U.S. (brŏk′wā)	105	47.24N	105.41W
Brodnica, Pol. (brôd′nĭt-så)	155	53.16N	19.26E
Brody, Ukr. (brô′dĭ)	167	50.05N	25.10E
Broich, neigh., Ger.	236	51.25N	6.51E
Broken Arrow, Ok., U.S. (brō′kĕn ăr′ō)	111	36.03N	95.48W
Broken Bay, b., Austl.	204	33.34S	151.20E
Broken Bow, Ne., U.S. (brō′kĕn bō)	102	41.24N	99.37W
Broken Bow, Ok., U.S.	111	34.02N	94.43W
Broken Hill, Austl. (brōk′ĕn)	203	31.55S	141.35E
Broken Hill *see* Kabwe, Zam.	212	14.27S	28.27E
Bromall, Pa., U.S.	229b	39.59N	75.22W
Bromborough, Eng., U.K.	237a	53.19N	2.59W
Bromley, Eng., U.K. (brŭm′lĭ)	144b	51.23N	0.01E
Bromley Common, neigh., Eng., U.K.	235	51.22N	0.03E
Bromptonville, Can. (brŭmp′tŭn-vĭl)	91	45.30N	72.00W
Brønderslev, Den. (brûn′dẽr-slĕv)	152	57.15N	9.56E
Bronkhorstspruit, S. Afr.	218d	25.50S	28.48E
Bronnitsy, Russia (brô-nyĭ′tsĭ)	162	55.26N	38.16E
Bronson, Mi., U.S. (brŏn′sŭn)	98	41.55N	85.15W
Bronte Creek, r., Can.	83d	43.25N	79.53W
Bronx, neigh., N.Y., U.S.	228	40.49N	73.56W
Bronxville, N.Y., U.S.	228	40.56N	73.50W
Brood, r., S.C., U.S. (brōōd)	115	34.46N	81.25W
Brookfield, Il., U.S. (brŏok′fēld)	101a	41.49N	87.51W
Brookfield, Mo., U.S.	111	39.45N	93.04W
Brookhaven, Ga., U.S. (brŏok′hāv′n)	100c	33.52N	84.21W
Brookhaven, Ms., U.S.	114	31.35N	90.26W
Brookhaven, Pa., U.S.	229b	39.52N	75.23W
Brookings, Or., U.S. (brŏok′ĭngs)	104	42.04N	124.16W
Brookings, S.D., U.S.	102	44.18N	96.47W
Brookland, neigh., D.C., U.S.	229d	38.56N	76.59W
Brooklandville, Md., U.S.	229c	39.26N	76.41W
Brooklawn, N.J., U.S.	229b	39.53N	75.08W
Brookline, Ma., U.S. (brŏok′lĭn)	93a	42.20N	71.08W
Brookline, N.H., U.S.	93a	42.44N	71.37W
Brooklyn, Oh., U.S. (brŏok′lĭn)	101d	41.26N	81.44W
Brooklyn, neigh., Md., U.S.	229c	39.14N	76.36W
Brooklyn Center, Mn., U.S.	107g	45.05N	93.21W
Brooklyn Heights, Oh., U.S.	229a	41.24N	81.40W
Brooklyn Park, Md., U.S.	229c	39.14N	76.36W
Brookmans Park, Eng., U.K.	235	51.43N	0.12W
Brookmont, Md., U.S.	229d	38.57N	77.07W
Brook Park, Oh., U.S. (brŏok)	101d	41.24N	81.50W
Brooks, Can.	87	50.35N	111.53W
Brooks Range, mts., Ak., U.S. (brŏoks)	96a	68.20N	159.00W
Brook Street, Eng., U.K.	235	51.37N	0.17E
Brooksville, Fl., U.S. (brŏoks′vĭl)	115a	28.32N	82.28W
Brookvale, Austl.	243a	33.46S	151.17E
Brookville, In., U.S. (brŏok′vĭl)	98	39.20N	85.00W
Brookville, Ma., U.S.	227a	42.08N	71.01W
Brookville, N.Y., U.S.	228	40.49N	73.35W
Brookville, Pa., U.S.	99	41.10N	79.00W
Brookwood, Al., U.S. (brŏok′wŏod)	114	33.15N	87.17W
Broome, Austl. (brōōm)	202	18.00S	122.15E
Brossard, Can.	83a	45.26N	73.28W
Brothers, is., Bah. (brŭd′hērs)	122	26.05N	79.00W
Broughton, Pa., U.S.	230b	40.21N	79.59W
Broumov, Czech Rep. (brōō′môf)	154	50.33N	15.55E
Brou-sur-Chantereine, Fr.	237c	48.53N	2.38E
Brown Bank, bk.	123	21.30N	74.35W
Brownfield, Tx., U.S. (broun′fēld)	110	33.11N	102.16W
Browning, Mt., U.S. (broun′ĭng)	105	48.37N	113.05W
Brownsboro, Ky., U.S. (brounz′bô-rô)	101h	38.22N	85.30W
Brownsburg, Can. (brouns′bûrg)	83a	45.40N	74.24W
Brownsburg, In., U.S.	101g	39.51N	86.23W
Brownsmead, Or., U.S. (brounz′-mĕd)	106c	46.13N	123.33W
Brownstown, In., U.S. (brounz′toun)	98	38.50N	86.00W
Brownsville, Pa., U.S. (brounz′vĭl)	101e	40.01N	79.53W
Brownsville, Tn., U.S.	114	35.35N	89.15W
Brownsville, Tx., U.S.	96	25.55N	97.30W
Brownville Junction, Me., U.S. (broun′vĭl)	92	45.20N	69.04W
Brownwood, Tx., U.S. (broun′wŏod)	96	31.44N	98.58W
Brownwood, l., Tx., U.S.	112	31.55N	99.15W
Broxbourne, Eng., U.K.	235	51.45N	0.01W
Brozas, Spain (brō′thäs)	158	39.37N	6.44W
Bruce, Mount, mtn., Austl. (brōōs)	202	22.35S	118.15E
Bruce Peninsula, pen., Can.	90	44.50N	81.20W
Bruceton, Tn., U.S. (brōōs′tŭn)	114	36.02N	88.14W
Bruchmühle, Ger.	238a	52.33N	13.47E
Bruchsal, Ger. (brŏok′zäl)	154	49.08N	8.34E
Bruck, Aus. (brŏok)	154	47.25N	15.14E
Bruck, Aus.	154	48.01N	16.47E
Brück, Ger. (brük)	145b	52.12N	12.45E
Bruckhausen, neigh., Ger.	236	51.29N	6.44E
Bruderheim, Can. (brōō′dẽr-hīm)	83g	53.47N	112.56W
Brugge, Bel.	147	51.13N	3.05E
Brügge, Ger.	236	51.13N	7.34E
Brugherio, Italy	238c	45.33N	9.18E
Brühl, Ger. (brül)	157c	50.49N	6.54E
Bruneau, r., Id., U.S. (brōō-nō′)	104	42.47N	115.43W
Brunei, nation, Asia (brŏ-nī′)	196	4.52N	113.38E
Brünen, Ger. (brü′nĕn)	157c	51.43N	6.41E
Brunete, Spain (brōō-nā′tå)	159a	40.24N	4.00W
Brunette, i., Can. (brŏ-nĕt′)	93	47.16N	55.54W
Brunn am Gebirge, Aus. (brōōn′äm gĕ-bĭr′gĕ)	145e	48.07N	16.18E
Brunoy, Fr.	237c	48.42N	2.30E
Brunsbüttel, Ger. (brŏns′büt-tĕl)	145c	53.58N	9.10E
Brunswick, Austl.	243b	37.46S	144.58E
Brunswick, Ga., U.S. (brŭnz′wĭk)	97	31.08N	81.30W
Brunswick, Me., U.S.	92	43.54N	69.57W
Brunswick, Md., U.S.	99	39.20N	77.35W
Brunswick, Mo., U.S.	111	39.25N	93.07W
Brunswick, Oh., U.S.	101d	41.14N	81.50W
Brunswick, Península de, pen., Chile	132	53.25S	71.15W
Bruny, i., Austl. (brōō′nē)	203	43.30S	147.50E
Brush, Co., U.S. (brŭsh)	110	40.14N	103.40W
Brusque, Braz. (brōō′s-kōō′ĕ)	132	27.15S	48.45W
Brussels, Bel.	142	50.51N	4.21E
Brussels, Il., U.S. (brŭs′ĕls)	107e	38.57N	90.36W
Bruxelles *see* Brussels, Bel.	142	50.51N	4.21E
Bryan, Oh., U.S. (brī′ăn)	98	41.25N	84.30W
Bryan, Tx., U.S.	113	30.40N	96.22W
Bryansk, Russia	164	53.15N	34.22E
Bryansk, prov., Russia	162	52.43N	32.25E
Bryant, S.D., U.S. (brī′ănt)	102	44.35N	97.29W
Bryant, Wa., U.S.	106a	48.14N	122.10W
Bryce Canyon National Park, rec., Ut., U.S. (brīs)	96	37.35N	112.15W
Bryn Mawr, Pa., U.S. (brĭn mär′)	100f	40.02N	75.20W
Bryson City, N.C., U.S. (brīs′ŭn)	114	35.25N	83.25W
Bryukhovetskaya, Russia (b′ryŭk′ô-vyĕt-skä′yä)	163	45.56N	38.58E
Buala, Sol.Is.	198e	8.08S	159.35E
Buatan, Indon.	181b	0.45N	101.49E
Buba, Gui.-B. (bōō′bȧ)	210	11.39N	14.58W
Buc, Fr.	237c	48.46N	2.08E
Bucaramanga, Col. (bōō-kä′rä-mäŋ′gä)	130	7.12N	73.14W
Buccaneer Archipelago, is., Austl. (bŭk-ȧ-nēr′)	202	16.05S	122.00E
Buch, neigh., Ger.	238a	52.38N	13.30E
Buchach, Ukr. (bŏ′chȧch)	155	49.04N	25.25E
Buchanan, Lib. (bŏ-kăn′ăn)	210	5.57N	10.02W
Buchanan, Mi., U.S.	98	41.50N	86.25W
Buchanan, l., Austl. (bû-kân′nŏn)	203	21.40S	145.00E
Buchanan, l., Tx., U.S. (bû-kăn′ăn)	112	30.55N	98.40W
Buchans, Can.	93	48.49N	56.52W
Bucharest, Rom.	142	44.23N	26.10E
Buchholz, Ger. (bōōk′hōltz)	145c	53.19N	9.53E
Buchholz, Ger.	238a	52.35N	13.47E
Buchholz, neigh., Ger.	236	51.23N	6.46E
Buchholz, neigh., Ger.	238a	52.36N	13.26E
Buck Creek, r., In., U.S. (bŭk)	101g	39.43N	85.58W
Buckhannon, W.V., U.S. (bŭk-hăn′ŭn)	98	39.00N	80.10W
Buckhaven, Scot., U.K. (bŭk-hā′v′n)	150	56.10N	3.10W
Buckhorn Island State Park, pt. of i., N.Y., U.S.	230a	43.03N	78.59W

ăt; finăl; rāte; senăte; ärm; åsk; sofȧ; fâre; ch-choose; dh-as th in other; bē; ēvent; bĕt; recĕnt; cratẽr; g-gō; gh-guttural g; bĭt; ĭ-short neutral; rīde; ĸ-guttural k as ch in German ich;

PLACE (Pronunciation)	PAGE	Lat. °′	Long. °′
Buckie, Scot., U.K. (bŭk′ĭ)	150	57.40N	2.50W
Buckingham, Can. (bŭk′ĭng-ăm)	83c	45.35N	75.25W
Buckingham, can., India (bŭk′ĭng-*ă*m)	187	15.18N	79.50E
Buckingham Palace, pt. of i., Eng., U.K.	235	51.30N	0.08W
Buckinghamshire, co., Eng., U.K.	144b	51.45N	0.48W
Buckland, Can. (bŭk′lănd)	83b	46.37N	70.33W
Buckland Tableland, reg., Austl.	203	24.31S	148.00E
Buckley, Wa., U.S. (buk′lē)	106a	47.10N	122.02W
Buckow, neigh., Ger.	238a	52.25N	13.26E
Bucksport, Me., U.S. (bŭks′pôrt)	92	44.35N	68.47W
Buctouche, Can. (bük-to͞osh′)	92	46.28N	64.43W
Bucun, China (bo͞o-tsȯn)	190	36.38N	117.26E
Bucureşti *see* Bucharest, Rom.	142	44.23N	26.10E
Bucyrus, Oh., U.S. (bů-sī′r*ŭ*s)	98	40.50N	82.55W
Buda, neigh., Hung.	239g	47.30N	19.02E
Budakeszi, Hung.	239g	47.31N	18.56E
Budaörs, Hung.	239g	47.27N	18.58E
Budapest, Hung. (bo͞o′dȧ-pĕsht′)	142	47.30N	19.05E
Budberg, Ger.	236	51.32N	6.38E
Büderich, Ger.	236	51.37N	6.34E
Budge Budge, India	186a	22.28N	88.08E
Budjala, Zaire	216	2.39N	19.42E
Budyonnovsk, Russia	168	44.46N	44.09E
Buea, Cam.	215	4.09N	9.14E
Buechel, Ky., U.S. (bĕ-chûl′)	101h	38.12N	85.38W
Bueil, Fr. (bwā′)	157b	48.55N	1.27E
Buena Park, Ca., U.S. (bwā′nȧ pärk)	107a	33.52N	118.00W
Buenaventura, Col. (bwā′nä-vĕn-to͞o′rȧ)	130	3.46N	77.09W
Buenaventura, Cuba	123a	22.53N	82.22W
Buenaventura, Bahía de, b., Col.	130	3.45N	79.23W
Buena Vista, Co., U.S. (bū′n*ȧ* vĭs′t*ȧ*)	110	38.51N	106.07W
Buena Vista, Ga., U.S.	114	32.15N	84.30W
Buena Vista, Va., U.S.	99	37.45N	79.20W
Buena Vista, Bahía, b., Cuba (bä-ē′ä-bwĕ-nä-vē′s-tä)	122	22.30N	79.10W
Buena Vista Lake Bed, l., Ca., U.S. (bū′n*ȧ* vĭs′t*ȧ*)	108	35.14N	119.17W
Buendia, Embalse de, res., Spain	158	40.30N	2.45W
Buenos Aires, Arg. (bwā′nōs ī′rās)	132	34.20S	58.30W
Buenos Aires, Col.	130a	3.01N	76.34W
Buenos Aires, C.R.	121	9.10N	83.21W
Buenos Aires, prov., Arg.	132	36.15S	61.45W
Buenos Aires, l., S.A.	132	46.30S	72.15W
Buer, neigh., Ger.	236	51.36N	7.03E
Buffalo, Mn., U.S. (buf′*ȧ* lō)	103	45.10N	93.50W
Buffalo, N.Y., U.S.	97	42.54N	78.51W
Buffalo, Tx., U.S.	113	31.28N	96.04W
Buffalo, Wy., U.S.	105	44.19N	106.42W
Buffalo, r., S. Afr.	213c	28.35S	30.27E
Buffalo, r., Ar., U.S.	111	35.56N	92.58W
Buffalo, r., Tn., U.S.	114	35.24N	87.10W
Buffalo Bayou, Tx., U.S.	113a	29.46N	95.32W
Buffalo Creek, r., Mn., U.S.	103	44.46N	94.28W
Buffalo Harbor, b., N.Y., U.S.	230a	42.51N	78.52W
Buffalo Head Hills, hills, Can.	84	57.16N	116.18W
Buford, Can. (bū′fûrd)	83g	53.15N	113.55W
Buford, Ga., U.S. (bū′fērd)	114	34.05N	84.00W
Bug (Zakhidnyy Buh), r., Eur.	155	52.29N	21.20E
Buga, Col. (bo͞o′gä)	130	3.54N	76.17W
Buggenhout, Bel.	145a	51.01N	4.10E
Buglandsfjorden, l., Nor.	152	58.53N	7.55E
Bugojno, Bos. (bȯ-gō ĭ nȯ)	161	44.03N	17.28E
Bugul′ma, Russia (bȯ-gȯl′mȧ)	164	54.40N	52.40E
Buguruslan, Russia (bȯ-gȯ-rȯs-lȧn′)	164	53.30N	52.32E
Buhi, Phil. (bo͞o′ė)	197a	13.26N	123.31E
Buhl, Id., U.S. (būl)	105	42.36N	114.45W
Buhl, Mn., U.S.	103	47.28N	92.49W
Buin, Chile (bȯ-ēn′)	129b	33.44S	70.44W
Buinaksk, Russia (bȯ′ē-näksk)	167	42.40N	47.20E
Buir Nur, l., Asia (bo͞o-ēr no͞or)	189	47.50N	117.00E
Bujalance, Spain (bo͞o-hä-län′thā)	158	37.54N	4.22W
Bujumbura, Bdi.	217	3.23S	29.22E
Buka Island, i., Pap. N. Gui.	198e	5.15S	154.35E
Bukama, Zaire (bo͞o-kä′mä)	212	9.08S	26.00E
Bukavu, Zaire	212	2.30S	28.52E
Bukhara, Uzb. (bȯ-kä′rä)	169	39.31N	64.22E
Bukitbatu, Indon.	181b	1.25N	101.58E
Bukit Panjang, Sing.	240c	1.23N	103.46E
Bukit Timah, Sing.	240c	1.20N	103.47E
Bukittinggi, Indon.	196	0.25S	100.28E
Bukoba, Tan.	212	1.20S	31.49E
Bukovina, hist. reg., Eur. (bȯ-kô′vĭ-nȧ)	155	48.06N	25.20E
Bula, Indon. (bo͞o′lä)	197	3.00S	130.30E
Bulalacao, Phil. (bo͞o-lȧ-lä′kä-ȯ)	197a	12.30N	121.20E
Bulawayo, Zimb. (bo͞o-lȧ-wă′yō)	212	20.12S	28.43E
Buldir, i., Ak., U.S. (bŭl dĭr)	95a	52.22N	175.50E
Bulgaria, nation, Eur. (bȯl-gā′rĭ-ă)	142	42.12N	24.13E
Bulim, Sing.	240c	1.23N	103.43E
Bulkley Ranges, mts., Can. (bŭlk′lė)	86	54.30N	127.30W
Bullaque, r., Spain (bȯ-lä′kå)	158	39.15N	4.13W
Bullas, Spain (bo͞ol′yäs)	158	38.07N	1.48W
Bullfrog Creek, r., Ut., U.S.	109	37.45N	110.55W
Bull Harbour, Can. (hăr′bẽr)	86	50.45N	127.55W
Bull Head, mtn., Jam.	122	18.10N	77.15W
Bull Run, r., Or., U.S. (bȯl)	106c	45.26N	122.11W
Bull Run Reservoir, res., Or., U.S.	106c	45.29N	122.11W
Bull Shoals Reservoir, res., U.S. (bȯl shōlz)	97	36.35N	92.57W
Bulmke-Hüllen, neigh., Ger.	236	51.31N	7.06E
Bulpham, Eng., U.K. (bo͞ol′făn)	144b	51.33N	0.21E
Bultfontein, S. Afr. (bȯlt′fŏn-tān′)	218d	28.18S	26.10E
Bulun, Russia (bo͞o-lȯn′)	165	70.48N	127.27E
Bulungu, Zaire (bo͞o-lȯŋ′go͞o)	216	6.04S	21.54E
Bulwer, S. Afr. (bȯl-wẽr)	213c	29.49S	29.48E
Bumba, Zaire (bȯm′bȧ)	211	2.11N	22.28E
Bumbire Island, i., Tan.	217	1.40S	32.05E
Bumbles Green, Eng., U.K.	235	51.44N	0.02E
Buna, Pap. N. Gui. (bo͞o′nȧ)	197	8.58S	148.38E
Bunbury, Austl. (bŭn′b*ŭ*rĭ)	202	33.25S	115.45E
Bundaberg, Austl. (bŭn′d*ȧ*-bûrg)	203	24.45S	152.18E
Bundoora, Austl. (Chan.)	243b	37.42S	145.04E
Bunguran Utara, Kepulauan, is., Indon.	196	3.22N	108.00E
Bunia, Zaire	217	1.34N	30.15E
Bunker Hill, Il., U.S. (bŭnk′ẽr hĭl)	107e	39.03N	89.57W
Bunker Hill Monument, pt. of i., Ma., U.S.	227a	42.22N	71.04W
Bunkie, La., U.S. (bŭŋ′kĭ)	113	30.55N	92.10W
Bun Plains, pl., Kenya	217	0.55N	40.35E
Bununu Dass, Nig.	215	10.00N	9.31E
Buona Vista, Sing.	240c	1.16N	103.47E
Buor-Khaya, Guba, b., Russia	171	71.45N	131.00E
Buor Khaya, Mys, c., Russia	165	71.47N	133.22E
Bura, Kenya	217	1.06S	39.57E
Buraydah, Sau. Ar.	182	26.23N	44.14E
Burbank, Ca., U.S. (bûr′bănk)	107a	34.11N	118.19W
Burco, Som.	218a	9.20N	45.45E
Burdekin, r., Austl. (bûr′dė-kĭn)	203	19.22S	145.07E
Burdur, Tur. (bo͞or-dȯr′)	149	37.50N	30.15E
Burdwān, India (bȯd-wän′)	183	23.29N	87.53E
Bureinskiy, Khrebet, mts., Russia	165	51.15N	133.30E
Bures-sur-Yvette, Fr.	237c	48.42N	2.10E
Bureya, Russia (bȯrā′*ȧ*)	165	49.55N	130.00E
Bureya, r., Russia (bȯ-rā′yä)	171	51.00N	131.15E
Burford, Eng., U.K. (bûr-fẽrd)	144b	51.46N	1.38W
Burg, Ger.	236	51.08N	7.09E
Burgas, Bul. (bȯr-gäs′)	149	42.29N	27.30E
Burgas, Gulf of, b., Bul.	149	42.30N	27.40E
Burgaw, N.C., U.S. (bûr′gô)	115	34.31N	77.56W
Burgdorf, Switz. (bȯrg′dôrf)	154	47.04N	7.37E
Burgenland, prov., Aus.	145e	47.58N	16.57E
Burgeo, Can.	93	47.36N	57.34W
Burger Township, S. Afr.	244b	26.05S	27.46E
Burgess, Va., U.S.	99	37.53N	76.21W
Burgh Heath, Eng., U.K.	235	51.18N	0.13W
Burgos, Mex. (bȯr′gōs)	112	24.57N	98.47W
Burgos, Phil.	197a	16.03N	119.52E
Burgos, Spain (bo͞o′r-gȯs)	148	42.20N	3.44W
Burgsvik, Swe. (bȯrgs′vĭk)	152	57.04N	18.18E
Burhānpur, India (bȯr′hȧn-po͞or)	183	21.26N	76.08E
Burholme, neigh., Pa., U.S.	229b	40.03N	75.05W
Burias Island, i., Phil. (bo͞o′rė-äs)	197a	12.56N	122.56E
Burias Pass, strt., Phil. (bo͞o′rė-äs)	197a	13.04N	123.11E
Burica, Punta, c., N.A. (po͞o′n-tä-bo͞o′rē-kä)	121	8.02N	83.12W
Burien, Wa., U.S. (bū′rĭ-ĕn)	106a	47.28N	122.20W
Burin, Can. (bûr′ĭn)	85a	47.02N	55.10W
Burin Peninsula, pen., Can.	93	47.00N	55.40W
Burkburnett, Tx., U.S. (bûrk-bûr′nĕt)	110	34.04N	98.35W
Burke, Vt., U.S. (bûrk)	99	44.40N	72.00W
Burke Channel, strt., Can.	86	52.07N	127.38W
Burketown, Austl. (bûrk′toun)	202	17.50S	139.30E
Burkina Faso, nation, Afr.	210	13.00N	2.00W
Burley, Id., U.S. (bûr′lĭ)	105	42.31N	113.48W
Burley, Wa., U.S.	106a	47.25N	122.38W
Burlingame, Ca., U.S. (bûr′lĭn-gām)	106b	37.35N	122.22W
Burlingame, Ks., U.S.	111	38.45N	95.49W
Burlington, Can. (bûr′lĭng-t*ŭ*n)	91	43.19N	79.48W
Burlington, Co., U.S.	110	39.17N	102.26W
Burlington, Ia., U.S.	97	40.48N	91.05W
Burlington, Ks., U.S.	111	38.10N	95.46W
Burlington, Ky., U.S.	101f	39.01N	84.44W
Burlington, Ma., U.S.	93a	42.31N	71.13W
Burlington, N.J., U.S.	100f	40.04N	74.52W
Burlington, N.C., U.S.	115	36.05N	79.26W
Burlington, Vt., U.S.	97	44.30N	73.15W
Burlington, Wa., U.S.	106a	48.28N	122.20W
Burlington, Wi., U.S.	101a	42.41N	88.16W
Burma *see* Myanmar, nation, Asia	180	21.00N	95.15E
Burnaby, Can.	84	49.14N	122.58W
Burnage, Eng., U.K.	237b	53.26N	2.12W
Burnet, Tx., U.S. (bûrn′ĕt)	112	30.46N	98.14W
Burnham, Il., U.S.	231a	41.39N	87.34W
Burnham on Crouch, Eng., U.K. (bûrn′*ă*m-ŏn-krouch)	144b	51.38N	0.48E
Burnhamthorpe, Can.	227c	43.37N	79.36W
Burnie, Austl. (bûr′nė)	203	41.15S	146.05E
Burning Tree Estates, Md., U.S.	229d	39.01N	77.12W
Burnley, Eng., U.K. (bûrn′lĕ)	150	53.47N	2.19W
Burns, Or., U.S. (bûrnz)	104	43.35N	119.05W
Burnside, Ky., U.S. (bûrn′sīd)	114	36.57N	84.33W
Burns Lake, Can. (bûrnz lăk)	84	54.14N	125.46W
Burnsville, Can. (bûrnz′vĭl)	92	47.44N	65.07W
Burnt, r., Or., U.S. (bûrnt)	104	44.26N	117.53W
Burntwood, r., Can.	89	55.53N	97.30W
Burrard Inlet, b., Can. (bûr′*ȧ*rd)	106d	49.19N	123.15W
Burr Gaabo, Som.	213	1.14N	51.47E
Burriana, Spain (bo͞or-rė-ȧ′nä)	148	39.53N	0.05W
Burro, Serranías del, mts., Mex. (sĕr-rä-nē′äs dĕl bo͞o′r-rô)	112	29.39N	102.07W
Burrowhill, Eng., U.K.	235	51.21N	0.36W
Burr Ridge, Il., U.S.	231a	41.46N	87.55W
Bursa, Tur. (bo͞or′sȧ)	182	40.10N	28.10E
Būr Safājah, Egypt	211	26.57N	33.56E
Burscheid, Ger. (bo͞or′shīd)	157c	51.05N	7.07E
Būr Sūdān, Sudan (so͞o-dȧn′)	211	19.30N	37.10E
Burt, N.Y., U.S. (bŭrt)	101c	43.19N	78.45W
Burt, l., Mi., U.S. (bŭrt)	98	45.25N	84.45W
Burton, Eng., U.K.	237a	53.16N	3.01W
Burton, Wa., U.S. (bûr′t*ŭ*n)	106a	47.24N	122.28W
Burton, Lake, res., Ga., U.S.	114	34.46N	83.40W
Burtonsville, Md., U.S. (bûrtŏns-vil)	100e	39.07N	76.57W
Burton-upon-Trent, Eng., U.K. (bŭr′t*ŭ*n-ŭp′-ŏn-trĕnt)	150	52.48N	1.37W
Buru, i., Indon.	197	3.30S	126.30E
Burullus, l., Egypt	218b	31.20N	30.58E
Burundi, nation, Afr.	212	3.00S	29.30E
Burwell, Ne., U.S. (bûr′w*ĕ*l)	102	41.46N	99.08W
Burwood, Austl.	243b	37.51S	145.06E
Bury, Eng., U.K. (bĕr′ĭ)	144a	53.36N	2.17W
Buryatia, state, Russia	171	55.15N	112.00E
Bury Saint Edmunds, Eng., U.K. (bĕr′ĭ-sānt ĕd′m*ŭ*ndz)	151	52.14N	0.44E
Burzaco, Arg. (bo͞or-zȧ′kȯ)	132a	34.50S	58.23W
Busanga Swamp, sw., Zam.	217	14.10S	25.50E
Busby, Austl.	243a	33.54S	150.53E
Buschhausen, neigh., Ger.	236	51.30N	6.51E
Būsh, Egypt (bo͞osh)	218b	29.13N	31.08E
Bushey, Eng., U.K.	235	51.39N	0.22W
Bushey Heath, Eng., U.K.	235	51.38N	0.20W
Bush Hill, Va., U.S.	229d	38.48N	77.07W
Bushmanland, hist. reg., S. Afr. (bȯsh-m*ă*n lănd)	212	29.15S	18.45E
Bushnell, Il., U.S. (bȯsh′nĕl)	111	40.33N	90.28W
Bushwick, neigh., N.Y., U.S.	228	40.42N	73.55W
Businga, Zaire (bȯ-siŋ′gȧ)	211	3.20N	20.53E
Busira, r., Zaire	216	0.05S	19.20E
Bus′k, Ukr.	155	49.58N	24.39E
Busselton, Austl. (bûs′l-t*ŭ*n)	202	33.40S	115.30E
Bussum, Neth.	145a	52.16N	5.10E
Bustamante, Mex. (bo͞os-tȧ-män′tȧ)	112	26.34N	100.30W
Bustleton, neigh., Pa., U.S.	229b	40.05N	75.02W
Busto Arsizio, Italy (bo͞os′tō är-sēd′zė-ō)	160	45.47N	8.51E
Busuanga, i., Phil. (bo͞o-swäŋ′gä)	197a	12.20N	119.43E
Buta, Zaire (bo͞o′tȧ)	211	2.48N	24.44E
Butha Buthe, Leso. (bo͞o-thȧ-bo͞o′thȧ)	213c	28.49S	28.16E
Butler, Al., U.S. (bŭt′lẽr)	114	32.05N	88.10W
Butler, In., U.S.	98	41.25N	84.50W
Butler, Md., U.S.	100e	39.32N	76.46W
Butler, N.J., U.S.	100a	41.00N	74.20W
Butler, Pa., U.S.	99	40.50N	79.55W
Butovo, Russia (bȯ-tô′vô)	172b	55.33N	37.36E
Butsha, Zaire	217	0.57N	29.13E
Buttahatchee, r., Al., U.S. (bŭt-ȧ-hăch′ė)	114	34.02N	88.05W
Butte, Mt., U.S. (būt)	96	46.00N	112.31W
Butterworth, S. Afr. (bŭ tẽr′wûrth)	213c	32.20S	28.09E
Büttgen, Ger.	236	51.12N	6.36E
Butt of Lewis, c., Scot., U.K. (bŭt ŏv lū′ĭs)	150	58.34N	6.15W
Butuan, Phil. (bo͞o-to͞o′än)	197	8.40N	125.33E
Buturlinovka, Russia (bo͞o-to͞o′lė-nôf′ka)	167	50.47N	40.35E
Buuhoodle, Som.	218a	8.15N	46.20E
Buulo Berde, Som.	218a	3.53N	45.30E
Buxtehude, Ger.	145c	53.29N	9.42E
Buxton, Eng., U.K. (bŭks′t′n)	144a	53.15N	1.55W
Buxton, Or., U.S.	106c	45.41N	123.11W
Buy, Russia (bwē)	164	58.30N	41.48E
Büyükmenderes, r., Tur.	182	37.50N	28.20E
Buzău, Rom. (bo͞o-z*ĕ*′ȯ)	161	45.09N	26.51E
Buzâu, r., Rom.	163	45.17N	27.22E
Buzaymah, Libya	211	25.14N	22.13E
Buzi, China (bo͞o-dz)	190	33.48N	118.13E
Buzuluk, Russia (bȯ-zȯ-lȯk′)	164	52.50N	52.10E
Bwendi, Zaire	217	4.01N	26.41E
Byala, Bul.	161	43.26N	25.44E
Byala Slatina, Bul. (byä′la slä′tēnä)	161	43.26N	23.56E
Byblos *see* Jubayl, Leb.	181a	34.07N	35.38E
Byčulla, neigh., India	240e	18.58N	72.49E
Bydgoszcz, Pol. (bĭd′gŏshch)	146	53.07N	18.00E
Byelorussia *see* Belarus, nation, Eur.	164	53.30N	25.33E
Byesville, Oh., U.S. (bīz-vĭl)	98	39.55N	81.35W
Byfang, neigh., Ger.	236	51.24N	7.06E
Byfleet, Eng., U.K.	235	51.20N	0.29W
Bygdin, l., Nor. (bügh-dėn′)	152	61.24N	8.31E
Byglandsfjord, Nor. (bügh′länds-fyȯr)	152	58.40N	7.49E
Bykhovo, Bela.	162	53.32N	30.15E
Bykovo, Russia (bĭ-kô′vô)	172b	55.38N	38.05E
Byrranga, Gory, mts., Russia	170	74.15N	94.28E
Bytantay, r., Russia (byän′täy)	171	68.15N	132.15E
Bytom, Pol. (bĭ′tŭm)	147	50.21N	18.55E
Bytosh′, Russia (bī-tôsh′)	162	53.48N	34.06E
Bytow, Pol. (bĭ′tŭf)	155	54.10N	17.30E

C

PLACE (Pronunciation)	PAGE	Lat. °′	Long. °′
Cabagan, Phil. (kä-bä-gän′)	197a	17.27N	121.50E
Cabalete, i., Phil. (kä-bä-lā′tå)	197a	14.19N	122.00E
Caballito, neigh., Arg.	233d	34.37S	58.27W
Caballones, Canal de, strt., Cuba (kä-nä′l-dĕ-kä-bäl-yô′nĕs)	122	20.45N	79.20W
Caballo Reservoir, res., N.M., U.S. (kä-bä-lyō′)	109	33.00N	107.20W
Cabanatuan, Phil. (kä-bä-nä-twän′)	197a	15.30N	120.56E
Cabano, Can. (kä-bä-nō′)	92	47.41N	68.54W
Cabarruyan, i., Phil. (kä-bä-ro͞o′yän)	197a	16.21N	120.10E
Cabedelo, Braz. (kä-bē-dā′lȯ)	131	6.58S	34.49W
Cabeza, Arrecife, i., Mex.	119	19.07N	95.52W
Cabeza del Buey, Spain (kȧ-bā′thä dĕl bwā′)	158	38.43N	5.18W
Cabimas, Ven. (kä-bė′mäs)	130	10.21N	71.27W
Cabinda, Ang.	212	5.33S	12.12E
Cabinda, hist. reg., Ang. (kä-bĭn′dȧ)	212	5.10S	10.00E

270 Cabinet Mountains-Canadian

PLACE (Pronunciation)	PAGE	Lat. °′	Long. °′
Cabinet Mountains, mts., Mt., U.S. (kăb′ĭ-nĕt)	104	48.13N	115.52W
Cabin John, Md., U.S.	229d	38.58N	77.09W
Cabo Frio, Braz. (kä′bô-frē′ô)	129a	22.53S	42.02W
Cabo Frio, Ilha do, Braz. (ē′lä-dô-kä′bô frē′ô)	129a	23.01S	42.00W
Cabo Gracias a Dios, Hond. (kà′bô-grä-syäs-ä-dyô′s)	121	15.00N	83.13W
Cabonga, Réservoir, res., Can.	91	47.25N	76.35W
Cabora Bassa Reservoir, res., Moz.	212	15.45S	32.00E
Cabot Head, c., Can. (kăb′ŭt)	90	45.15N	81.20W
Cabot Strait, strt., Can. (kăb′ŭt)	85a	47.35N	60.00W
Cabra, Spain (käb′rä)	158	37.28N	4.29W
Cabra, i., Phil.	197a	13.55N	119.55E
Cabramatta, Austl.	243a	33.54S	150.56E
Cabrera, i., Spain (kä-brā′rä)	159	39.08N	2.57E
Cabrera, Sierra de la, mts., Spain	158	42.15N	6.45W
Cabriel, r., Spain (kä-brē-ĕl′)	158	39.25N	1.20W
Cabrillo National Monument, rec., Ca., U.S. (kä-brēl′yō)	108a	32.41N	117.03W
Cabuçu, r., Braz. (kä-bo͞o′-so͞o)	132b	22.57S	43.36W
Cabugao, Phil. (kä-bo͞o′gä-ô)	197a	17.48N	120.28E
Čačak, Yugo. (chä′chák)	161	43.51N	20.22E
Caçapava, Braz. (kä′sä-pá′vä)	129a	23.05S	45.52W
Cáceres, Braz. (ká′sĕ-rēs)	131	16.11S	57.32W
Cáceres, Spain (ká′thå-rās)	148	39.28N	6.20W
Cachan, Fr.	237c	48.48N	2.20E
Cachapoal, r., Chile (kä-chä-pô-á′l)	129b	34.23S	70.19W
Cache, r., Ar., U.S. (kásh)	111	35.24N	91.12W
Cache Creek, Can.	87	50.48N	121.19W
Cache Creek, r., Ca., U.S. (kăsh)	108	38.53N	122.24W
Cache la Poudre, r., Co., U.S. (kásh lá po͝od′r′)	110	40.43N	105.39W
Cachi, Nevados de, mtn., Arg. (nĕ-vá′dôs-dĕ-ká′chē)	132	25.05S	66.40W
Cachinal, Chile (kä-chē-näl′)	132	24.57S	69.33W
Cachoeira, Braz. (kä-shô-ā′rä)	131	12.32S	38.47W
Cachoeirá do Sul, Braz. (kä-shô-ā′rä-dô-so͞o′l)	132	30.02S	52.49W
Cachoeiras de Macacu, Braz. (kä-shô-ā′räs-dĕ-mä-ká′ko͞o)	129a	22.28S	42.39W
Cachoeiro de Itapemirim, Braz.	131	20.51S	41.06W
Cacilhas, Port.	238d	38.41N	9.09W
Cacólo, Ang.	216	10.07S	19.17E
Caconda, Ang. (kä-kōn′dä)	212	13.43S	15.06E
Cacouna, Can.	92	47.54N	69.31W
Cacula, Ang.	216	14.29S	14.10E
Cadale, Som.	218a	2.45N	46.15E
Caddo, l., La., U.S. (kăd′ō)	113	32.37N	94.15W
Cadereyta, Mex. (kä-dā-rā′tä)	118	20.42N	99.47W
Cadereyta Jimenez, Mex. (kä-dā-rā′tä hē-mā′nāz)	112	25.36N	99.59W
Cadi, Sierra de, mts., Spain (sē-ĕ′r-rä-dĕ-kä′dē)	159	42.17N	1.34E
Cadillac, Mi., U.S. (kăd′ĭ-lăk)	98	44.15N	85.25W
Cadishead, Eng., U.K.	237b	53.25N	2.26W
Cádiz, Spain (ká′dēz)	142	36.34N	6.20W
Cadiz, Ca., U.S. (kā′dĭz)	108	34.33N	115.30W
Cadiz, Oh., U.S.	98	40.15N	81.00W
Cádiz, Golfo de, b., Spain (gôl-fô-dĕ-ká′dēz)	148	36.50N	7.00W
Caen, Fr. (käN)	147	49.13N	0.22W
Caernarfon, Wales, U.K.	146	53.08N	4.17W
Caernarfon Bay, b., Wales, U.K.	150	53.09N	4.56W
Cagayan, Phil. (kä-gä-yän′)	197	8.13N	124.30E
Cagayan, r., Phil.	196	16.45N	121.55E
Cagayan Islands, is., Phil.	196	9.40N	120.30E
Cagayan Sulu, i., Phil. (kä-gä-yän so͞o′lo͞o)	196	7.00N	118.30E
Cagli, Italy (käl′yē)	160	43.35N	12.40E
Cagliari, Italy (käl′yä-rē)	142	39.16N	9.08E
Cagliari, Golfo di, b., Italy (gôl-fô-dē-käl′yä-rē)	148	39.08N	9.12E
Cagnes, Fr. (kän′y′)	157	43.40N	7.14E
Cagua, Ven. (kä′gwä)	131b	10.12N	67.27W
Caguas, P.R. (kä′gwäs)	117b	18.12N	66.01W
Cahaba, r., Al., U.S. (ká hä-bä)	114	32.50N	87.15W
Cahama, Ang. (kä-á′mä)	212	16.17S	14.19E
Cahokia, Il., U.S. (kȧ-hō′kĭ-ȧ)	107e	38.34N	90.11W
Cahora-Bassa, wtfl., Moz.	217	15.40S	32.50E
Cahors, Fr. (kȧ-ôr′)	147	44.27N	1.27E
Cahuacán, Mex. (kä-wä-kä′n)	119a	19.38N	99.25W
Cahuita, Punta, c., C.R. (po͞o′n-tä-kä-wē′tȧ)	121	9.47N	82.41W
Cahul, Mol.	163	45.49N	28.17E
Caibarién, Cuba (kī-bä-rē-ĕn′)	122	22.35N	79.30W
Caicedonia, Col. (kī-sē-dô-nēä)	130a	4.21N	75.48W
Caicos Bank, bk. (kī′kōs)	123	21.35N	72.00W
Caicos Islands, is., T./C. Is.	117	21.45N	71.50W
Caicos Passage, strt., N.A.	123	21.55N	72.45W
Caillou Bay, b., La., U.S. (kȧ-yo͞o′)	113	29.07N	91.00W
Caimanera, Cuba (kī-mä-nā′rä)	123	20.00N	75.10W
Caiman Point, c., Phil. (kī′mán)	197a	15.56N	119.33E
Caimito, r., Pan. (kä-ē-mē′tô)	116a	8.50N	79.45W
Caimito del Guayabal, Cuba (kä-ē-mē′tō-dĕl-gwä-yä-bä′l)	123a	22.57N	82.36W
Cairns, Austl. (kârnz)	203	17.02S	145.49E
Cairo, C.R. (kī′rô)	121	10.06N	83.47W
Cairo, Egypt	211	30.00N	31.17E
Cairo, Ga., U.S. (kā′rō)	114	30.48N	84.12W
Cairo, Il., U.S.	97	36.59N	89.11W
Caistor, Eng., U.K. (kás′tĕr)	144a	53.30N	0.20W
Caiundo, Ang.	216	15.46S	17.28E
Caiyu, China (tsī-yo͞o)	190	39.39N	116.36E
Cajamarca, Col. (kä-ĸä-mä′r-kä)	130a	4.25N	75.25W
Cajamarca, Peru (kä-hä-mär′kä)	130	7.16S	78.30W
Čajniče, Bos. (chī′nĭ-chĕ)	161	43.32N	19.04E
Cajon, Ca., U.S. (kȧ-hōn′)	107a	34.18N	117.28W
Cajuru, Braz. (kȧ-zho͞o′ro͞o)	129a	21.17S	47.17W
Čakovec, Cro. (chá′kō-vĕts)	160	46.23N	16.27E
Cala, S. Afr. (cä-lȧ)	213c	31.33S	27.41E
Calabar, Nig. (kăl-ȧ-bär′)	210	4.57N	8.19E
Calabazar, Cuba (kä-lä-bä-zä′r)	123a	23.02N	82.25W
Calabozo, Ven. (kä-lä-bō′zō)	130	8.48N	67.27W
Calabria, hist. reg., Italy (kä-lä′brē-ä)	160	39.26N	16.23E
Calafat, Rom. (kȧ-lȧ-făt′)	161	43.59N	22.56E
Calaguas Islands, is., Phil. (kä-läg′wäs)	197a	14.30N	123.06E
Calahoo, Can. (kă-lȧ-ho͞o′)	83g	53.42N	113.58W
Calahorra, Spain (kä-lä-ôr′rä)	148	42.18N	1.58W
Calais, Fr. (kȧ-lĕ′)	142	50.56N	1.51E
Calais, Me., U.S.	97	45.11N	67.15W
Calama, Chile (kä-lä′mä)	132	22.17S	68.58W
Calamar, Col. (kä-lä-mär′)	130	10.24N	75.00W
Calamar, Col.	130	1.55N	72.33W
Calamba, Phil. (kä-läm′bä)	197a	14.12N	121.10E
Calamian Group, is., Phil. (kä-lä-myän′)	196	12.14N	118.38E
Calañas, Spain (kä-län′yäs)	158	37.41N	6.52W
Calanda, Spain	159	40.53N	0.20W
Calapan, Phil. (kä-lä-pän′)	197a	13.25N	121.11E
Călăraşi, Rom. (kŭ-lŭ-rásh′ĭ)	149	44.09N	27.20E
Calatayud, Spain (kä-lä-tä-yo͞odh′)	148	41.23N	1.37W
Calauag Bay, b., Phil.	197a	14.07N	122.10E
Calaveras Reservoir, res., Ca., U.S. (kăl-ȧ-vĕr′ăs)	106b	37.29N	121.47W
Calavite, Cape, c., Phil. (kä-lä-vē′tä)	197a	13.29N	120.00E
Calcasieu, r., La., U.S. (kăl′kȧ-shū)	113	30.22N	93.08W
Calcasieu Lake, l., La., U.S.	113	29.58N	93.08W
Calcutta, India (kăl-kŭt′ȧ)	183	22.32N	88.22E
Caldas, Col. (kà′l-däs)	130a	6.06N	75.38W
Caldas, dept., Col.	130a	5.20N	75.38W
Caldas da Rainha, Port. (käl′däs dä rīn′yȧ)	158	39.25N	9.08W
Calder, r., Eng., U.K. (kôl′dĕr)	144a	53.39N	1.30W
Caldera, Chile (käl-dá′rä)	132	27.02S	70.53W
Calder Canal, can., Eng., U.K.	144a	53.48N	2.25W
Caldwell, Id., U.S. (kôld′wĕl)	104	43.40N	116.43W
Caldwell, Ks., U.S.	111	37.04N	97.36W
Caldwell, N.J., U.S.	228	40.51N	74.17W
Caldwell, Oh., U.S.	98	39.40N	81.30W
Caldwell, Tx., U.S.	113	30.30N	96.40W
Caledon, Can. (kăl′ē-dŏn)	83d	43.52N	79.59W
Caledonia, Mn., U.S. (kăl-ē-dō′nĭ-ȧ)	103	43.38N	91.31W
Calella, Spain (kä-lĕl′yä)	159	41.37N	2.39E
Calera Victor Rosales, Mex. (kä-lā′rä-vē′k-tôr-rô-sá′lĕs)	118	22.57N	102.42W
Calexico, Ca., U.S. (kȧ-lĕk′sĭ-kō)	96	32.41N	115.30W
Calgary, Can. (kăl′gȧ-rĭ)	84	51.03N	114.05W
Calhariz, neigh., Port.	238d	38.44N	9.12W
Calhoun, Ga., U.S. (kăl-ho͞on′)	114	34.30N	84.56W
Cali, Col. (kä′lē)	130	3.26N	76.30W
Calicut, India (kăl′ĭ-kŭt)	183	11.19N	75.49E
Caliente, Nv., U.S. (kăl-yĕn′tȧ)	109	37.38N	114.30W
California, Mo., U.S. (kăl-ĭ-fôr′nĭ-ȧ)	111	38.38N	92.38W
California, Pa., U.S.	101e	40.03N	79.53W
California, state, U.S.	96	38.10N	121.20W
California, Golfo de, b., Mex. (gôl-fô-dĕ-kä-lē-fôr-nyä)	116	30.30N	113.45W
California Aqueduct, aq., Ca., U.S.	108	37.10N	121.10W
California-Los Angeles, University of (U.C.L.A.), educ., Ca., U.S.	232	34.04N	118.26W
Călimani, Munţii, mts., Rom.	155	47.05N	24.47E
Calimere, Point, c., India	187	10.20N	80.20E
Calimesa, Ca., U.S. (kă-lĭ-mā′sȧ)	107a	34.00N	117.04W
Calipatria, Ca., U.S. (kăl-ĭ-pát′rĭ-ȧ)	108	33.03N	115.30W
Calkini, Mex. (käl-kē-nē′)	119	20.21N	90.06W
Callabonna, Lake, l., Austl. (călă′bŏn ȧ)	204	29.35S	140.28E
Callao, Peru (käl-yä′ô)	130	12.02S	77.07W
Calling, l., Can. (kôl′ĭng)	87	55.15N	113.12W
Calmar, Can. (kăl′mär)	83g	53.16N	113.49W
Calmar, Ia., U.S.	103	43.12N	91.54W
Caloocan, Phil.	241g	14.39N	120.59E
Caloosahatchee, r., Fl., U.S. (kȧ-loo-sȧ-hăch′ē)	115a	26.45N	81.41W
Calotmul, Mex. (kä-lôt-mo͞ol)	120a	20.58N	88.11W
Calpulalpan, Mex. (käl-po͞o-läl′pän)	118	19.35N	98.33W
Caltagirone, Italy (käl-tä-jē-rō′nā)	148	37.14N	14.32E
Caltanissetta, Italy (käl-tä-nē-sĕt′tä)	148	37.30N	14.02E
Caluango, Ang.	216	8.21S	19.40E
Calucinga, Ang.	216	11.18S	16.12E
Calumet, Mi., U.S. (kă-lū-mĕt′)	103	47.15N	88.29W
Calumet, Lake, l., Il., U.S.	101a	41.43N	87.36W
Calumet City, Il., U.S.	101a	41.37N	87.33W
Calumet Park, Il., U.S.	231a	41.44N	87.33W
Calumet Sag Channel, can., Il., U.S.	231a	41.42N	87.57W
Calunda, Ang.	216	12.06S	23.23E
Caluquembe, Ang.	216	13.47S	14.44E
Caluula, Som.	218a	11.53N	50.40E
Calvert, Tx., U.S. (kăl′vērt)	113	30.59N	96.41W
Calvert Island, i., Can.	84	51.35N	128.00W
Calvi, Fr. (käl′vē)	160	42.33N	8.35E
Calvillo, Mex. (käl-vēl′yō)	119	21.51N	102.44E
Calvinia, S. Afr. (kăl-vĭn′ĭ-ȧ)	212	31.20S	19.50E
Cam, r., Eng., U.K. (kăm)	151	52.15N	0.05E
Camagüey, Cuba (kä-mä-gwā′)	117	21.25N	78.00W
Camagüey, prov., Cuba	122	21.30N	78.10W
Camajuani, Cuba (kä-mä-hwä′nē)	122	22.25N	79.50W
Camano, Wa., U.S. (kä-mä′no)	106a	48.10N	122.32W
Camano Island, i., Wa., U.S.	106a	48.11N	122.29W
Camargo, Mex. (kä-mär gō)	112	26.19N	98.49W
Camarón, Cabo, c., Hond. (ká′bô-kä-mä-rōn′)	120	16.06N	85.05W
Camas, Wa., U.S. (kăm′ȧs)	106c	45.36N	122.24W
Camas Creek, r., Id., U.S.	105	44.10N	112.09W
Camatagua, Ven. (kä-mä-tá′gwä)	131b	9.49N	66.55W
Ca Mau, Mui, c., Viet.	196	8.36N	104.43E
Cambay, India (kăm-bā′)	186	22.22N	72.39E
Camberwell, Austl.	243b	37.50S	145.04E
Cambodia, nation, Asia	196	12.15N	104.00E
Cambonda, Serra, mts., Ang.	216	12.10S	14.15E
Camborne, Eng., U.K. (kăm′bôrn)	150	50.15N	5.28W
Cambrai, Fr. (käN-brĕ′)	147	50.10N	3.15E
Cambrian Mountains, mts., Wales, U.K. (kăm′brĭ-ăn)	150	52.05N	4.05W
Cambridge, Can.	91	43.22N	80.19W
Cambridge, Eng., U.K. (kām′brĭj)	147	52.12N	0.11E
Cambridge, Md., U.S.	99	38.35N	76.10W
Cambridge, Ma., U.S.	93a	42.23N	71.07W
Cambridge, Mn., U.S.	103	45.35N	93.14W
Cambridge, Ne., U.S.	110	40.17N	100.10W
Cambridge, Oh., U.S.	98	40.00N	81.35W
Cambridge Bay, Can.	84	69.15N	105.00W
Cambridge City, In., U.S.	98	39.45N	85.15W
Cambridgeshire, co., Eng., U.K.	144a	52.26N	0.19W
Cambuci, Braz. (käm-bo͞o′sē)	129a	21.35S	41.54W
Cambuci, neigh., Braz.	234d	23.34S	46.37W
Cambundi-Catembo, Ang.	216	10.09S	17.31E
Camby, In., U.S. (kăm′bē)	101g	39.40N	86.19W
Camden, Austl.	201b	34.03S	150.42E
Camden, Al., U.S. (kăm′dĕn)	114	31.58N	87.15W
Camden, Ar., U.S.	111	33.36N	92.49W
Camden, Me., U.S.	92	44.11N	69.05W
Camden, N.J., U.S.	97	39.56N	75.06W
Camden, S.C., U.S.	115	34.14N	80.37W
Camden, neigh., Eng., U.K.	235	51.33N	0.10W
Cameia, Parque Nacional da, rec., Ang.	216	11.40S	21.20E
Camenca, Mol.	163	48.02N	28.43E
Cameron, Mo., U.S. (kăm′ēr-ŭn)	111	39.44N	94.14W
Cameron, Tx., U.S.	113	30.52N	96.57W
Cameron, W.V., U.S.	98	39.40N	80.35W
Cameron Hills, hills, Can.	84	60.13N	120.20W
Cameroon, nation, Afr.	210	5.48N	11.00E
Cameroon Mountain, mtn., Cam.	210	4.12N	9.11E
Camiling, Phil. (kä-mē-lĭng′)	197a	15.42N	120.24E
Camilla, Ga., U.S. (kȧ-mĭl′ȧ)	114	31.13N	84.12W
Caminha, Port. (kä-mĭn′yȧ)	158	41.52N	8.44W
Camoçim, Braz. (kä-mô-sĕN′)	131	2.56S	40.55W
Camooweal, Austl.	202	20.00S	138.13E
Campana, Arg. (käm-pä′nä)	129c	34.10S	58.58W
Campana, i., Chile (käm-pän′yä)	132	48.20S	75.15W
Campanario, Spain (käm-pä-nä′rē-ō)	158	38.51N	5.36W
Campanella, Punta, c., Italy (pô′n-tä-käm-pä-nĕ′lä)	159c	40.20N	14.21E
Campanha, Braz. (käm-pän-yän′)	129a	21.51S	45.24W
Campania, hist. reg., Italy (käm-pän′yä)	160	41.00N	14.40E
Campbell, Ca., U.S. (kăm′bĕl)	106b	37.17N	121.57W
Campbell, Mo., U.S.	111	36.29N	90.04W
Campbell, is., N.Z.	3	52.30S	169.00E
Campbellfield, Austl.	243b	37.41S	144.57E
Campbellpore, Pak.	186	33.49N	72.24E
Campbell River, Can.	84	50.01N	125.15W
Campbellsville, Ky., U.S. (kăm′bĕlz-vĭl)	114	37.19N	85.20W
Campbellton, Can. (kăm′bĕl-tŭn)	85	48.00N	66.40W
Campbelltown, Austl. (kăm′bĕl-toun)	201b	34.04S	150.49E
Campbeltown, Scot., U.K. (kăm′b′l-toun)	150	55.25N	5.50W
Camp Dennison, Oh., U.S. (dĕ′nĭ-sŏn)	101f	39.12N	84.17W
Campeche, Mex. (käm-pā′chå)	116	19.51N	90.32W
Campeche, state, Mex.	116	18.55N	90.20W
Campeche, Bahía de, b., Mex. (bä-ē′ä-dĕ-käm-pā′chå)	116	19.30N	93.40W
Campechuela, Cuba (käm-pâ-chwā′lä)	122	20.15N	77.15W
Camperdown, S. Afr. (kăm′pĕr-doun)	213c	29.44S	30.33E
Câmpina, Rom.	161	45.08N	25.47E
Campina Grande, Braz. (käm-pē′nä grän′dĕ)	131	7.15S	35.49W
Campinas, Braz. (käm-pē′názh)	131	22.53S	47.03W
Camp Indian Reservation, I.R., Ca., U.S. (kămp)	108	32.39N	116.26W
Campo, Cam. (käm′pō)	210	2.22N	9.49E
Campoalegre, Col. (kä′m-pô-ȧlē′grē)	130	2.34N	75.20W
Campobasso, Italy (käm′pô-bäs′sō)	160	41.35N	14.39E
Campo Belo, Braz.	129a	20.52S	45.15W
Campo de Criptana, Spain (käm′pō dä krēp-tä′nä)	158	39.24N	3.09W
Campo Florido, Cuba (kä′m-pō flô-rē′dō)	123a	23.07N	82.07W
Campo Grande, Braz. (käm-pô grän′dĕ)	131	20.28S	54.32W
Campo Grande, Braz.	132b	22.54S	43.33W
Campo Grande, neigh., Port.	238d	38.45N	9.09W
Campo Maior, Braz. (käm-pô mä-yôr′)	131	4.48S	42.12W
Campo Maior, Port.	158	39.03N	7.06W
Campo Real, Spain (käm′pô rå-äl′)	159a	40.21N	3.23W
Campos, Braz. (kä′m-pôs)	131	21.46S	41.19W
Campos do Jordão, Braz. (kä′m-pôs-dô-zhôr-dou′N)	129a	22.45S	45.35W
Campos Gerais, Braz. (kä′m-pôs-zhĕ-ráēs)	129a	21.17S	45.43W
Camps Bay, S. Afr. (kămps)	212a	33.57S	18.22E
Campsie, Austl.	243a	33.55S	151.06E
Camp Springs, Md., U.S. (cămp sprĭngz)	100e	38.48N	76.55W
Camp Springs, Md., U.S.	229d	38.48N	76.55W
Câmpulung, Rom.	149	45.15N	25.03E
Câmpulung Moldovenesc, Rom.	155	47.31N	25.36E
Camp Wood, Tx., U.S. (kămp wŏod)	112	29.39N	100.02W
Camrose, Can. (kăm-rōz)	84	53.01N	112.50W
Camu, r., Dom. Rep. (kä′mo͞o)	123	19.05N	70.15W
Canada, nation, N.A. (kăn′ȧ-dȧ)	84	50.00N	100.00W
Canada Bay, b., Can.	93	50.43N	56.10W
Cañada de Gómez, Arg. (kä-nyä′dä-dĕ-gô′mĕz)	132	32.49S	61.24W
Canadian, Tx., U.S. (kȧ-nā′dĭ-ăn)	110	35.54N	100.24W

ăt; finȧl; rāte; senåte; ärm; ȧsk; sofȧ; fâre; ch-choose; dh-as th in other; bē; ēvent; bĕt; recĕnt; cratĕr; g-gō; gh-guttural g; bĭt; ĭ-short neutral; rīde; ĸ-guttural k as ch in German ich;

PRONOUNCING INDEX Canadian-Carrington 271

PLACE (Pronunciation)	PAGE	Lat. °′	Long. °′
Canadian, r., U.S.	96	35.30N	102.30W
Canajoharie, N.Y., U.S. (kăn-ȧ-jō-hăr'ē)	99	42.55N	74.35W
Çanakkale, Tur. (chä-näk-kä'lĕ)	149	40.10N	26.26E
Çanakkale Boğazi (Dardanelles), strt., Tur.	149	40.05N	25.50E
Canandaigua, N.Y., U.S. (kăn-ăn-dā'gwȧ)	99	42.55N	77.20W
Canandaigua, l., N.Y., U.S.	99	42.45N	77.20W
Cananea, Mex. (kä-nä-nĕ'ä)	116	31.00N	110.20W
Canarias, Islas (Canary Is.), is., Spain (ê's-läs-kä-nä'ryäs)	209	29.15N	16.30W
Canarreos, Archipiélago de los, is., Cuba	122	21.35N	82.20W
Canarsie, neigh., N.Y., U.S.	228	40.38N	73.53W
Canary Islands *see* Canarias, Islas, is., Spain	209	29.15N	16.30W
Cañas, C.R. (kä'-nyäs)	120	10.26N	85.06W
Cañas, r., C.R.	120	10.20N	85.21W
Cañasgordas, Col. (kä'nyäs-gô'r-däs)	130a	6.44N	76.01W
Canastota, N.Y., U.S. (kăn-ăs-tō'tȧ)	99	43.05N	75.45W
Canastra, Serra de, mts., Braz. (sĕ'r-rä-dĕ-kä-nä's-trä)	131	19.53S	46.57W
Canatlán, Mex. (kä-nät-län')	112	24.30N	104.45W
Canaveral, Cape, c., Fl., U.S.	97	28.30N	80.23W
Canavieiras, Braz. (kä-nȧ-vē-ā'räs)	131	15.40S	38.49W
Canberra, Austl. (kăn'bĕr-ȧ)	203	35.21S	149.10E
Canby, Mn., U.S. (kăn'bĭ)	102	44.43N	96.15W
Canchyuaya, Cerros de, mts., Peru (sĕ'r-rôs-dĕ-kän-chōō-á'īä)	130	7.30S	74.30W
Cancuc, Mex. (kän-kōōk)	119	16.58N	92.17W
Cancún, Mex.	120a	21.25N	86.50W
Candelaria, Cuba (kän-dĕ-lä'ryä)	122	22.45N	82.55W
Candelaria, Phil. (kän-dȧ-lä'rē-ä)	197a	15.39N	119.55E
Candelaria, r., Mex. (kän-dĕ-lä-ryä)	119	18.25N	91.21W
Candeleda, Spain (kän-dhȧ-lā'dhä)	158	40.09N	5.18W
Candia *see* Iráklion, Grc.	142	35.20N	25.10E
Candle, Ak., U.S. (kăn'd'l)	95	65.00N	162.04W
Cando, N.D., U.S. (kăn'dō)	102	48.27N	99.13W
Candon, Phil. (kän-dōn')	197a	17.13N	120.26E
Canelones, Ur. (kä-nĕ-lô-nĕs)	129c	34.32S	56.19W
Canelones, dept., Ur.	129c	34.34S	56.15W
Cañete, Peru (kän-yā'tȧ)	130	13.06S	76.17W
Caney, Cuba (kä-nā') (kā'nĭ)	123	20.05N	75.45W
Caney, Ks., U.S. (kā'nĭ)	111	37.00N	95.57W
Caney Fork, r., Tn., U.S.	114	36.10N	85.50W
Cangamba, Ang.	212	13.40S	19.54E
Cangas, Spain (kän'gäs)	158	42.15N	8.43W
Cangas de Narcea, Spain (kä'n-gäs-dĕ-när-sĕ-ä)	158	43.08N	6.36W
Cangzhou, China (tsäŋ-jō)	192	38.21N	116.53E
Caniapiscau, l., Can.	85	54.10N	71.13E
Caniapiscau, r., Can.	85	57.00N	68.45W
Canicatti, Italy (kä-nē-kät'tē)	160	37.18N	13.58E
Canillas, neigh., Spain	238b	40.28N	3.38W
Canillejas, neigh., Spain	238b	40.27N	3.37W
Cañitas, Mex. (kän-yē'täs)	118	23.38N	102.44W
Cannell, Can.	83g	53.35N	113.38W
Cannelton, In., U.S. (kăn'ĕl-tŭn)	98	37.55N	86.45W
Cannes, Fr. (kȧn)	147	43.34N	7.05E
Canning, Can. (kăn'ĭng)	92	45.09N	64.25W
Cannock, Eng., U.K. (kăn'ŭk)	144a	52.41N	2.02W
Cannock Chase, reg., Eng., U.K. (kăn'ŭk chās)	144a	52.43N	1.54W
Cannon, r., Mn., U.S. (kăn'ŭn)	103	44.18N	93.24W
Cannonball, r., N.D., U.S. (kăn'ŭn-bäl)	102	46.17N	101.35W
Caño, Isla de, i., C.R. (ê's-lä-dĕ-kä'nō)	121	8.38N	84.00W
Canoga Park, Ca., U.S. (kä-nō'gȧ)	107a	34.07N	118.36W
Canoncito Indian Reservation, I.R., N.M., U.S.	109	35.00N	107.05W
Canon City, Co., U.S. (kăn'yŭn)	110	38.27N	105.16W
Canonsburg, Pa., U.S. (kăn'ŭnz-bûrg)	101e	40.16N	80.11W
Canoochee, r., Ga., U.S. (kȧ-nōō'chē)	115	32.25N	82.11W
Canora, Can. (kȧ-nōrȧ)	84	51.37N	102.26W
Canosa, Italy (kä-nō'sä)	160	41.14N	16.03E
Canouan, i., St. Vin.	121b	12.44N	61.10W
Cansahcab, Mex.	120a	21.11N	89.05W
Canso, Can. (kăn'sō)	93	45.20N	61.00W
Canso, Cape, c., Can.	93	45.21N	60.46W
Canso, Strait of, strt., Can.	93	45.37N	61.25W
Cantabrica, Cordillera, mts., Spain	142	43.05N	6.05W
Cantagalo, Braz. (kän-tä-gá'lo)	129a	21.59S	42.22W
Cantanhede, Port. (kän-tän-yā'dȧ)	158	40.22N	8.35W
Canterbury, Austl.	243a	33.55S	151.07E
Canterbury, Austl.	243b	37.49S	145.05E
Canterbury, Eng., U.K. (kăn'tĕr-bĕr-ē)	151	51.17N	1.06E
Canterbury Bight, bt., N.Z.	203a	44.15S	172.08E
Canterbury Woods, Va., U.S.	229d	38.49N	77.15W
Cantiles, Cayo, i., Cuba (ky-ō-kän-tē'lås)	122	21.40N	82.00W
Canto do Pontes, Braz.	234c	22.58S	43.04W
Canton *see* Guangzhou, China	189	23.07N	113.15E
Canton, Ga., U.S.	114	34.13N	84.29W
Canton, Il., U.S.	111	40.34N	90.02W
Canton, Ma., U.S.	93a	42.09N	71.09W
Canton, Ms., U.S.	114	32.36N	90.01W
Canton, Mo., U.S.	111	40.08N	91.33W
Canton, N.C., U.S.	115	35.32N	82.50W
Canton, Oh., U.S.	97	40.50N	81.25W
Canton, Pa., U.S.	99	41.50N	76.45W
Canton, S.D., U.S.	102	43.17N	96.37W
Cantu, Italy (kän-tōō')	160	45.43N	9.09E
Cañuelas, Arg. (kä-nyōĕ'-läs)	129c	35.03S	58.45W
Canyon, Ca., U.S.	231b	37.49N	122.09W
Canyon, Tx., U.S. (kăn'yŭn)	110	34.59N	101.57W
Canyon, r., Wa., U.S.	106a	48.09N	121.48W
Canyon de Chelly National Monument, rec., Az., U.S.	109	36.14N	110.00W
Canyon Ferry Lake, res., Mt., U.S.	105	46.33N	111.37W
Canyonlands National Park, Ut., U.S.	109	38.10N	110.00W
Caoxian, China (tsou shyĕn)	190	34.48N	115.33E
Capalonga, Phil. (kä-pä-lôŋ'gä)	197a	14.20N	122.30E
Capannori, Italy (kä-pän'nō-rē)	160	43.50N	10.30E
Capão Redondo, neigh., Braz.	234d	23.40S	46.46W
Caparica, Port.	238d	38.40N	9.12W
Capaya, r., Ven. (kä-pä-īä)	131b	10.28N	66.15W
Cap-Chat, Can. (kȧp-shä')	85	48.02N	65.20W
Cap-de-la-Madeleine, Can. (kȧp dē lȧ mȧ-d'lĕn')	91	46.23N	72.30W
Cape Breton, i., Can. (kāp brĕt'ŭn)	93	45.48N	59.50W
Cape Breton Highlands National Park, Can.	85	46.45N	60.45W
Cape Charles, Va., U.S. (kāp chärlz)	115	37.13N	76.02W
Cape Coast, Ghana	210	5.05N	1.15W
Cape Fear, r., N.C., U.S. (kāp fēr)	97	35.00N	79.00W
Cape Flats, pl., S. Afr. (kāp flăts)	212a	34.01S	18.37E
Cape Girardeau, Mo., U.S. (jē-rär-dō')	97	37.17N	89.32W
Cape Krusenstern National Monument, rec., Ak., U.S.	95	67.30N	163.40W
Cape May, N.J., U.S. (kāp mā)	99	38.55N	74.50W
Cape May Court House, N.J., U.S.	99	39.05N	75.00W
Capenhurst, Eng., U.K.	237a	53.15N	2.57W
Cape Romanzof, Ak., U.S. (rō' män zôf)	95	61.50N	165.45W
Capesterre, Guad.	121b	16.02N	61.37W
Cape Tormentine, Can.	92	46.08N	63.47W
Cape Town, S. Afr. (kāp toun)	212	33.48S	18.28E
Cape Verde, nation, Afr.	210b	15.48N	26.02W
Cape York Peninsula, pen., Austl. (kāp yôrk)	203	12.30S	142.35E
Cap-Haïtien, Haiti (kȧp ȧ-ē-syăn')	117	19.45N	72.15W
Capilla de Señor, Arg. (kä-pēl'yä dā sān-yôr')	129c	34.18S	59.07W
Capitachouane, r., Can.	91	47.50N	76.45W
Capitol Heights, Md., U.S.	229d	38.53N	76.55W
Capitol Reef National Park, Ut., U.S. (kăp'ĭ-tŏl)	109	38.15N	111.10W
Capitol View, Md., U.S.	229d	39.01N	77.04W
Capivari, Braz. (kä-pē-vá'rē)	129a	22.59S	47.29W
Capivari, r., Braz.	132b	22.39S	43.19W
Capoompeta, mtn., Austl. (kȧ-pōōm-pē'tȧ)	203	29.15S	152.12E
Capraia, i., Italy (kä-prä'yä)	148	43.02N	9.51E
Caprara Point, c., Italy (kä-prä'rä)	160	41.08N	8.20E
Capreol, Can.	91	46.43N	80.56W
Caprera, i., Italy (kä-prā'rä)	160	41.12N	9.28E
Capri, Italy	159c	40.18N	14.16E
Capri, Isola di, i., Italy (ê'-sō-lä-dē-kä'prē)	159c	40.19N	14.10E
Capricorn Channel, strt., Austl. (kăp'rĭ-kôrn)	203	22.27S	151.24E
Caprivi Strip, hist. reg., Nmb.	212	18.00S	22.00E
Cap-Rouge, Can. (kȧp rōōzh')	83b	46.45N	71.21W
Cap-Saint Ignace, Can. (kĭp săn-tē-nyȧs')	83b	47.02N	70.27W
Captain Cook Bridge, pt. of i., Austl.	243a	34.00S	151.08E
Capua, Italy (kä'pwä)	148	41.07N	14.14E
Capuáva, Braz.	234d	23.39S	46.29W
Capulhuac, Mex. (kä-pōl-hwäk')	118	19.33N	99.43W
Capulin Mountain National Monument, rec., N.M., U.S. (kä-pū'lĭn)	110	36.15N	103.58W
Capultitlán, Mex. (kä-pòl'l-tē-tlá'n)	119a	19.15N	99.40W
Caputh, Ger.	238a	52.21N	13.00E
Caquetá (Japurá), r., S.A.	130	0.20S	73.00W
Caraballeda, Ven.	234a	10.37N	66.50W
Carabaña, Spain (kä-rä-bän'yä)	159a	40.16N	3.15W
Carabanchel Alto, neigh., Spain	238b	40.22N	3.45W
Carabanchel Bajo, neigh., Spain	238b	40.23N	3.47W
Carabelle, Fl., U.S. (kăr'ȧ-bĕl)	114	29.50N	84.40W
Carabobo, dept., Ven. (kä-rä-bô'-bô)	131b	10.07N	68.06W
Caracal, Rom. (kȧ-rȧ-käl')	161	44.06N	24.22E
Caracas, Ven. (kä-rä'käs)	130	10.30N	66.58W
Carácuaro de Morelos, Mex. (kä-rä'kwä-rō-dĕ-mō-rĕ-lôs)	118	18.44N	101.04W
Caraguatatuba, Braz. (kä-rä-gwä-tȧ-tōō'bä)	129a	23.37S	45.26W
Carajás, Serra dos, mts., Braz. (sĕ'r-rä-dôs-kä-rä-zhà's)	131	5.58S	51.45W
Caramanta, Cerro, mtn., Col. (sĕ'r-rô-kä-rä-mà'n-tä)	130a	5.29N	76.01W
Carangola, Braz. (kä-rán'gō'lä)	129a	20.46S	42.02W
Carapicuíba, Braz.	234d	23.31S	46.50W
Caraquet, Can. (kȧ-rȧ-kĕt')	85	47.48N	64.57W
Carata, Laguna, l., Nic. (lä-gò'nä-kä-rä'tä)	121	13.59N	83.41W
Caratasca, Laguna, l., Hond. (lä-gò'nä-kä-rä-täs'kä)	121	15.20N	83.45W
Caravaca, Spain (kä-rä-vä'kä)	158	38.05N	1.51W
Caravelas, Braz. (kȧ-rä-vĕl'äzh)	131	17.46S	39.06W
Carayaca, Ven. (kȧ-rä-īá'kä)	131b	10.32N	67.07W
Caràzinho, Braz. (kä-rá'zē-nyŏ)	132	28.22S	52.33W
Carballino, Spain (kär-bäl-yē'nō)	148	42.26N	8.04W
Carballo, Spain (kär-bäl'yō)	158	43.13N	8.40W
Carbet, Pitons du, mtn., Mart.	121b	14.40N	61.05W
Carbon, r., Wa., U.S. (kär'bŏn)	106a	47.06N	122.08W
Carbonado, Wa., U.S. (kär-bō-nä'dō)	106a	47.05N	122.03W
Carbonara, Cape, c., Italy (kär-bō-nä'rä)	148	39.08N	9.33E
Carbondale, Can. (kär'bŏn-dāl)	83g	53.45N	113.32W
Carbondale, Il., U.S.	98	37.42N	89.12W
Carbondale, Pa., U.S.	99	41.35N	75.30W
Carbonear, Can. (kär-bō-nēr')	93	47.45N	53.14W
Carbon Hill, Al., U.S. (kär'bŏn hĭl)	114	33.53N	87.34W
Carcagente, Spain (kär-kä-hĕn'tā)	159	39.09N	0.29W
Carcans, Étang de, l., Fr. (ā-tan-dĕ-kär-kän)	156	45.12N	1.00W
Carcassonne, Fr. (kȧr-kȧ-sôn')	147	43.12N	2.23E
Carcross, Can. (kär'krôs)	84	60.18N	134.54W
Cárdenas, Cuba (kär'dȧ-näs)	117	23.00N	81.10W
Cárdenas, Mex.	118	22.01N	99.38W
Cárdenas, Mex. (ká'r-dĕ-näs)	119	17.59N	93.23W
Cárdenas, Bahía de, b., Cuba (bä-ē'ä-dĕ-kär'dȧ-näs)	122	23.10N	81.10W
Cardiff, Can. (kär'dĭf)	83g	53.46N	113.36W
Cardiff, Wales, U.K.	147	51.30N	3.18W
Cardigan, Wales, U.K. (kär'dĭ-găn)	147	52.05N	4.40W
Cardigan Bay, b., Wales, U.K.	147	52.35N	4.40W
Cardston, Can. (kärds'tŭn)	84	49.12N	113.18W
Carei, Rom. (kä-rĕ')	155	47.42N	22.28E
Carentan, Fr. (kä-rôn-tän')	156	49.19N	1.14W
Carey, Oh., U.S. (kā'rē)	98	40.55N	83.25W
Carey, l., Austl. (kâr'ē)	202	29.20S	123.35E
Carhaix-Plouguer, Fr. (kär-ĕ')	156	48.17N	3.37W
Caribbean Sea, sea (kăr-ĭ-bē'ăn)	117	14.30N	75.30W
Caribe, Arroyo, r., Mex. (är-ro'ī-kä-rē'bĕ)	119	18.18N	90.38W
Cariboo Mountains, mts., Can. (kă'rĭ-bōō)	84	53.00N	121.00W
Caribou, Me., U.S.	92	46.51N	68.01W
Caribou, i., Can.	90	47.22N	85.42W
Caribou Lake, l., Mn., U.S.	107h	46.54N	92.16W
Caribou Mountains, mts., Can.	84	59.20N	115.30W
Caringbah, Austl.	243a	34.03S	151.08E
Carinhanha, Braz. (kä-rĭ-nyän'yä)	131	14.14S	43.44W
Carini, Italy (kä-rē'nē)	160	38.09N	13.10E
Carinthia *see* Kärnten, prov., Aus.	154	46.55N	13.42E
Carleton Place, Can. (kärl'tŭn)	91	45.15N	76.10W
Carletonville, S. Afr.	218d	26.20S	27.23E
Carlingford, Austl.	243a	33.47S	151.03E
Carlinville, Il., U.S. (kär'lĭn-vĭl)	111	39.16N	89.52W
Carlisle, Eng., U.K. (kär-līl')	142	54.54N	3.03W
Carlisle, Ky., U.S.	98	38.20N	84.00W
Carlisle, Pa., U.S.	99	40.10N	77.15W
Carloforte, Italy (kär'lō-fôr-tȧ)	160	39.11N	8.28E
Carlos Casares, Arg. (kär-lôs-kä-sá'rĕs)	132	35.38S	61.17W
Carlow, Ire. (kär'lō)	150	52.50N	7.00W
Carlsbad, N.M., U.S. (kärlz'băd)	112	32.24N	104.12W
Carlsbad Caverns National Park, rec., N.M., U.S.	112	32.08N	104.30W
Carlstadt, N.J., U.S.	228	40.50N	74.06W
Carlton, Eng., U.K. (kärl'tŭn)	144a	52.58N	1.05W
Carlton, Mn., U.S.	107h	46.40N	92.26W
Carlton Center, Mi., U.S. (kärl'tŭn sĕn'tĕr)	98	42.45N	85.20W
Carlyle, Il., U.S. (kär-līl')	111	38.37N	89.23W
Carmagnolo, Italy (kär-mä-nyô'lä)	160	44.52N	7.48E
Carman, Can. (kär'mȧn)	84	49.32N	98.00W
Carmarthen, Wales, U.K. (kär-mär'thĕn)	150	51.50N	4.20W
Carmaux, Fr. (kȧr-mō')	156	44.05N	2.09E
Carmel, N.Y., U.S. (kär'mĕl)	100a	41.25N	73.42W
Carmelo, Ur. (kär-mĕ'lo)	129c	33.59S	58.15W
Carmen, Isla del, i., Mex. (ê's-lä-dĕl-kȧ'r-mĕn)	119	18.43N	91.40W
Carmen, Laguna del, l., Mex. (lä-gò'nä-dĕl-kȧ'r-mĕn)	119	18.15N	93.26W
Carmen de Areco, Arg. (kär'mĕn' dā ä-rā'kō)	129c	34.21S	59.50W
Carmen de Patagones, Arg. (kȧ'r-mĕn-dĕ-pä-tä-gô'nĕs)	132	41.00S	63.00W
Carmi, Il., U.S. (kär'mī)	98	38.05N	88.10W
Carmo, Braz. (kȧ'r-mô)	129a	21.57S	42.45W
Carmo do Rio Clara, Braz. (kȧ'r-mô-dô-rē'ô-klȧ'rä)	129a	20.57S	46.04W
Carmona, Spain	158	37.28N	5.38W
Carnarvon, Austl. (kär-när'vŭn)	202	24.45S	113.45E
Carnarvon, S. Afr.	212	31.00S	22.15E
Carnation, Wa., U.S. (kär-nā'shŭn)	106a	47.39N	121.55W
Carnaxide, Port. (kär-nä-shē'dĕ)	159b	38.44N	9.15W
Carndonagh, Ire. (kärn-dō-nä')	150	55.15N	7.15W
Carnegie, Ok., U.S. (kär-nĕg'ĭ)	110	35.06N	98.38W
Carnegie, Pa., U.S.	101e	40.24N	80.06W
Carnegie Institute, pt. of i., Pa., U.S.	230b	40.27N	79.57W
Carnetin, Fr.	237c	48.54N	2.42E
Carneys Point, N.J., U.S. (kär'nĕs)	99	39.45N	75.25W
Carnic Alps, mts., Eur.	147	46.43N	12.38E
Carnide, neigh., Port.	238d	38.46N	9.11W
Carnot, Alg. (kär nō')	159	36.15N	1.40E
Carnot, Cen. Afr. Rep.	211	5.00N	15.52E
Carnsore Point, c., Ire. (kärn'sôr)	150	52.10N	6.16W
Caro, Mi., U.S. (kȧ'rō)	98	43.30N	83.25W
Carolina, Braz. (kä-rô-lē'nä)	131	7.26S	47.16W
Carolina, S. Afr. (kär-ô-lī'nȧ)	212	26.07S	30.09E
Carolina, l., Mex. (kä-rō-lē'nä)	120a	18.41N	89.40W
Caroline Islands, is., Oc.	5	8.00N	140.00E
Caroni, r., Ven. (kä-rō'nē)	130	5.49N	62.57W
Carora, Ven. (kä-rō'rä)	130	10.09N	70.12W
Carpathians, mts., Eur. (kär-pā'thĭ-ăn)	142	49.23N	20.14E
Carpaţii Meridionali (Transylvanian Alps), mts., Rom.	142	45.30N	23.30E
Carpentaria, Gulf of, b., Austl. (kär-pĕn-târ'ĭȧ)	202	14.45S	138.50E
Carpentras, Fr. (kär-pän-träs')	157	44.04N	5.01E
Carpi, Italy	160	44.48N	10.54E
Carrara, Italy (kä-rä'rä)	148	44.05N	10.05E
Carrauntoohil, Ire. (kă-răn-tōō'ĭl)	150	52.01N	9.48W
Carretas, Punta, c., Peru (pōō'n-tä-kär-rĕ'tĕ'rȧs)	130	14.15S	76.25W
Carriacou, i., Gren.	121b	12.28N	61.20W
Carrick-on-Sur, Ire. (kăr'-ĭk)	150	52.20N	7.35W
Carrier, Can. (kăr'ĭ-ĕr)	83b	46.43N	71.05W
Carriere, Ms., U.S. (kȧ-rēr')	114	30.37N	89.37W
Carrières-sous-Bois, Fr.	237c	48.57N	2.07E
Carrières-sous-Poissy, Fr.	237c	48.57N	2.03E
Carrières-sur-Seine, Fr.	237c	48.55N	2.11E
Carriers Mills, Il., U.S. (kăr'ĭ-ērs)	98	37.40N	88.40W
Carrington, Eng., U.K.	237b	53.26N	2.24W

ng-sing; ŋ-baŋk; N-nasalized n; nŏd; cŏmmit; ōld; ôbey; ôrder; oi-boil; fōōd; ŏ-as oo in foot; ou-out; s-soft; sh-dish; th-thin; pūre; ûnite; ûrn; stŭd; circŭs; ü-as in French tu; '-indeterminate vowel.

272 Carrington–Central America

PLACE (Pronunciation)	PAGE	Lat. °′	Long. °′
Carrington, N.D., U.S. (kăr'ĭng-tŭn)	102	47.26N	99.06W
Carr Inlet, Wa., U.S. (kăr ĭn'lĕt)	106a	47.20N	122.42W
Carrion Crow Harbor, b., Bah. (kăr'ĭŭn krō)	122	26.35N	77.55W
Carrión de los Condes, Spain (kär-rê-ōn' dā los kōn'dås)	158	42.20N	4.35W
Carrizo Creek, r., N.M., U.S. (kär-rē'zō)	110	36.22N	103.39W
Carrizo Springs, Tx., U.S.	112	28.32N	99.51W
Carrizozo, N.M., U.S. (kär-rê-zō'zō)	109	33.40N	105.55W
Carroll, Ia., U.S. (kăr'ŭl)	103	42.03N	94.51W
Carrollton, Ga., U.S. (kăr-ŭl-tŭn)	114	33.35N	85.05W
Carrollton, Il., U.S.	111	39.18N	90.22W
Carrollton, Ky., U.S.	98	38.45N	85.15W
Carrollton, Mi., U.S.	98	43.30N	83.55W
Carrollton, Mo., U.S.	111	39.21N	93.29W
Carrollton, Oh., U.S.	98	40.35N	81.10W
Carrollton, Tx., U.S.	107c	32.58N	96.53W
Carrols, Wa., U.S. (kăr'ŭlz)	106c	46.05N	122.51W
Carrot, r., Can.	88	53.12N	103.50W
Carry-le-Rouet, Fr. (kä-rē'lĕ-rò-ā')	156a	43.20N	5.10E
Carsamba, Tur. (chär-shäm'bä)	149	41.05N	36.40E
Carshalton, neigh., Eng., U.K.	235	51.22N	0.10W
Carson, Ca., U.S.	232	33.50N	118.16W
Carson, r., Nv., U.S. (kär'sŭn)	108	39.15N	119.25W
Carson City, Nv., U.S.	96	39.10N	119.45W
Carsondale, Md., U.S.	229d	38.57N	76.50W
Carson Sink, Nv., U.S.	108	39.51N	118.25W
Cartagena, Col. (kär-tä-hā'nä)	130	10.30N	75.40W
Cartagena, Spain (kär-tä-κĕ'nä)	142	37.46N	1.00W
Cartago, Col. (kär-tä'gō)	130a	4.44N	75.54W
Cartago, C.R.	117	9.52N	83.56W
Cartaxo, Port. (kär-tä'shō)	158	39.10N	8.48W
Carteret, N.J., U.S. (kär'tē-ret)	100a	40.35N	74.13W
Cartersville, Ga., U.S. (kär'tērs-vĭl)	114	34.09N	84.47W
Carthage, Tun.	210	37.04N	10.18E
Carthage, Il., U.S. (kär'thåj)	111	40.27N	91.09W
Carthage, Mo., U.S.	111	37.10N	94.18W
Carthage, N.Y., U.S.	99	44.00N	75.45W
Carthage, N.C., U.S.	115	35.22N	79.25W
Carthage, Tx., U.S.	113	32.09N	94.20W
Carthcart, S. Afr. (cärth-cȧ't)	213c	32.18S	27.11E
Cartwright, Can. (kärt'rīt)	85	53.36N	57.00W
Caruaru, Braz. (kä-rò-ä-rōō')	131	8.19S	35.52W
Carúpano, Ven. (kä-rōō'pä-nō)	130	10.45N	63.21W
Caruthersville, Mo., U.S. (kȧ-rŭdh'ērz-vĭl)	111	36.09N	89.41W
Carver, Or., U.S. (kärv'ēr)	106c	45.24N	122.30W
Carvoeiro, Cabo, c., Port. (kå'bō-kär-vò-ĕ'y-rō)	158	39.22N	9.24W
Cary, Il., U.S. (kā'rė)	101a	42.13N	88.14W
Casablanca, Chile (kä-sä-bläŋ'kä)	129b	33.19S	71.24W
Casablanca, Mor.	210	33.32N	7.41W
Casa Branca, Braz. (kä'sä-brå'ν-kä)	129a	21.47S	47.04W
Casa Grande, Az., U.S. (kä'sä grän'dā)	109	32.50N	111.45W
Casa Grande National Monument, rec., Az., U.S.	109	33.00N	111.33W
Casale Monferrato, Italy (kä-sä'lā)	160	45.08N	8.26E
Casalmaggiore, Italy (kä-säl-mäd-jō'rā)	160	45.00N	10.24E
Casa Loma, pt. of i., Can.	227c	43.41N	79.25W
Casamance, r., Sen. (kä-sä-mäνs')	210	12.30N	15.00W
Cascade Mountains, mts., N.A.	87	49.10N	121.00W
Cascade Point, c., N.Z. (kăs-kād')	203a	43.59S	168.23E
Cascade Range, mts., N.A.	96	42.50N	122.20W
Cascade Tunnel, trans., Wa., U.S.	104	47.41N	120.53W
Cascais, Port. (käs-kȧ-ēzh)	158	38.42N	9.25W
Case Inlet, Wa., U.S. (kās)	106a	47.22N	122.47W
Caseros, Arg. (kä-sā'rōs)	132a	34.35S	58.34W
Caserta, Italy (kä-zĕr'tä)	160	41.04N	14.21E
Casey, Il., U.S. (kā'sĭ)	98	39.20N	88.00W
Cashmere, Wa., U.S. (kăsh'mĭr)	104	47.30N	120.28W
Casiguran, Phil. (käs-sē-gōō'rän)	197a	16.15N	122.10E
Casiguran Sound, strt., Phil.	197a	16.02N	121.51E
Casilda, Arg. (kä-sē'l-dä)	132	33.02S	61.11W
Casilda, Cuba	122	21.50N	80.00W
Casimiro de Abreu, Braz. (kä'sē-mē'ro-dĕ-ȧ-brĕ'ōō)	129a	22.30S	42.11W
Casino, Austl. (kȧ-sē'nō)	204	28.35S	153.10E
Casiquiare, r., Ven. (kä-sê-kyä'rā)	130	2.11N	66.15W
Caspe, Spain (käs'på)	159	41.18N	0.02W
Casper, Wy., U.S. (kăs'pēr)	96	42.51N	106.18W
Caspian Depression, depr. (kăs'pĭ-ȧn)	164	47.40N	52.35E
Caspian Sea, sea	164	40.00N	52.00E
Cass, W.V., U.S. (kăs)	99	38.25N	79.55W
Cass, l., Mn., U.S.	103	47.23N	94.28W
Cassai (Kasai), r., Afr. (kä-sä'ē)	212	11.30S	21.00E
Cass City, Mi., U.S. (kăs)	98	43.35N	83.10W
Casselman, Can. (kăs''l-mȧn)	83c	45.18N	75.05W
Casselton, N.D., U.S. (kăs''l-tŭn)	102	46.53N	97.14W
Cássia, Braz. (ká'syä)	129a	20.36S	46.53W
Cassin, Tx., U.S. (kăs'ĭn)	107d	29.16N	98.29W
Cassinga, Ang.	212	15.05S	16.15E
Cassino, Italy (käs-sē'nō)	148	41.30N	13.50E
Cass Lake, Mn., U.S. (kăs)	103	47.23N	94.37W
Cassopolis, Mi., U.S. (kăs-ŏ'pō-lĭs)	98	41.55N	86.00W
Cassville, Mo., U.S. (kăs'vĭl)	111	36.41N	93.52W
Castanheira de Pêra, Port. (käs-tän-yä'rä-dĕ-pĕ'rä)	158	40.00N	8.07W
Castellammare di Stabia, Italy	159c	40.26N	14.29E
Castellbisbal, Spain	238e	41.29N	1.59E
Castelli, Arg. (kȧs-tĕ'zhē)	129c	36.07S	57.48W
Castellón de la Plana, Spain (käs-tĕl-yō'n-dĕ-lä-plä'nä)	148	39.59N	0.05W
Castelnaudary, Fr. (kås'tĕl-nō-då-rē')	156	43.20N	1.57E
Castelo, Braz. (käs-tĕ'lô)	129a	20.37S	41.13W
Castelo Branco, Port. (käs-tä'lò bräŋ'kò)	148	39.48N	7.37W
Castelo de Vide, Port. (käs-tä'lò dĭ vē'dĭ)	158	39.25N	7.25W
Castelsarrasin, Fr. (kȧs'tĕl-sȧ-rȧ-zăν')	156	44.03N	1.05E
Castelvetrano, Italy (käs'tĕl-vê-trä'nō)	160	37.43N	12.50E
Castilla, Peru (kás-tē'l-yä)	130	5.18S	80.40W
Castilla La Nueva, hist. reg., Spain (käs-tē'lyä lä nwā'vä)	158	39.15N	3.55W
Castilla La Vieja, hist. reg., Spain (käs-tēl'yä lä vyā'hä)	158	40.48N	4.24W
Castillo de San Marcos National Monument, rec., Fl., U.S. (käs-tē'lyä de-sän mär-kōs)	115	29.55N	81.25W
Castle, i., Bah. (kås''l)	123	22.05N	74.20W
Castlebar, Ire. (kás''l-bär)	150	53.55N	9.15W
Castlecrag, Austl.	243a	33.48S	151.13E
Castle Dale, Ut., U.S. (kås'l dāl)	109	39.15N	111.00W
Castle Donington, Eng., U.K. (dŏn'ĭng-tŭn)	144a	52.50N	1.21W
Castleford, Eng., U.K. (kås'l-fērd)	144a	53.43N	1.21W
Castlegar, Can. (kås''l-gär)	87	49.19N	117.40W
Castle Hill, Austl.	243a	33.44S	151.00E
Castlemaine, Austl. (kăs''l-mān)	204	37.05S	144.10E
Castle Peak, mtn., Co., U.S.	109	39.00N	106.50W
Castle Rock, Wa., U.S. (kås''l-rŏk)	104	46.17N	122.53W
Castle Rock Flowage, res., Wi., U.S.	103	44.03N	89.48W
Castle Shannon, Pa., U.S. (shăn'ŭn)	101e	40.22N	80.02W
Castleton, Eng., U.K.	237b	53.35N	2.11W
Castleton, In., U.S. (kås''l-tŏn)	101g	39.54N	86.03W
Castor, r., Can. (kăs'tôr)	83c	45.16N	75.14W
Castor, r., Mo., U.S.	111	36.59N	89.53W
Castres, Fr. (käs'tr')	156	43.36N	2.13E
Castries, St. Luc. (kås-trē')	121b	14.01N	61.00W
Castro, Braz. (käs'trò)	131	24.56S	50.00W
Castro, Chile (käs'tro)	132	42.27S	73.48W
Castro Daire, Port. (käs'trò dīr'ĭ)	158	40.56N	7.57W
Castro del Río, Spain (käs-trô-dĕl rē'ō)	158	37.42N	4.28W
Castrop Rauxel, Ger. (käs'trōp rou'ksĕl)	157c	51.33N	7.19E
Castro Urdiales, Spain (käs'trō ōr-dyä'lås)	148	43.23N	3.11W
Castro Valley, Ca., U.S.	106b	37.42N	122.05W
Castro Verde, Port. (käs-trō vĕr'dĕ)	158	37.43N	8.05W
Castrovillari, Italy (käs'trō-vēl-lyä'rē)	160	39.48N	16.11E
Castuera, Spain (käs-tò-ā'rä)	158	38.43N	5.33W
Casula, Moz.	217	15.25S	33.40E
Cat, i., Bah.	123	24.30N	75.30W
Catacamas, Hond. (kä-tä-kä'mås)	120	14.52N	85.55W
Cataguases, Braz. (kä-tä-gwá'sĕs)	129a	21.23S	42.42W
Catahoula, l., La., U.S. (kăt-ȧ-hò'lȧ)	113	31.35N	92.20W
Catalão, Braz. (kä-tä-louν')	131	18.09S	47.42W
Catalina, i., Dom. Rep. (kä-tä-lē'nä)	123	18.20N	69.00W
Cataluña, hist. reg., Spain	159	41.23N	0.50E
Cataluña, Museo de Arte de, bldg., Spain	238e	41.23N	2.09E
Catamarca, Arg. (kä-tä-mä'r-kä)	132	28.29S	65.45W
Catamarca, prov., Arg. (kä-tä-mär'kä)	132	27.15S	67.15W
Catanaun, Phil. (kä-tä-nä'wän)	197a	13.36N	122.20E
Catanduanes Island, i., Phil. (kä-tän-dwä'nĕs)	197	13.55N	125.00E
Catanduva, Braz. (kä-tån-dōō'vä)	131	21.12S	48.47W
Catania, Italy (kä-tä'nyä)	142	37.30N	15.09E
Catania, Golfo di, b., Italy (gôl-fô-dē-kȧ-tä'nyä)	160	37.24N	15.28E
Catanzaro, Italy (kä-tän-dzä'rō)	149	38.53N	16.34E
Catarroja, Spain (kä-tär-rō'hä)	159	39.24N	0.25W
Catawba, r., N.C., U.S. (kȧ-tô'bȧ)	115	35.25N	80.55W
Catbalogan, Phil. (kät-bä-lō'gän)	197	11.45N	124.52E
Catemaco, Mex. (kä-tä-mä'kō)	119	18.26N	95.06W
Catemaco, Lago, l., Mex. (lä'gô-kä-tä-mä'kō)	119	18.23N	95.04W
Caterham, Eng., U.K. (kā'tēr-ŭm)	144b	51.16N	0.04W
Catete, Ang. (kä-tē'tē)	212	9.06S	13.43E
Catete, neigh., Braz.	234c	22.55S	43.10W
Catford, neigh., Eng., U.K.	235	51.27N	0.01W
Cathedral Mountain, mtn., Tx., U.S. (kȧ-thē'drȧl)	112	30.09N	103.46W
Cathedral Peak, mtn., Afr. (kă-thē'drȧl)	213c	28.53S	29.04E
Catherine, Lake, l., Ar., U.S. (kă-thēr-ĭn)	111	34.26N	92.47W
Cathkin Peak, mtn., Afr. (kăth'kĭn)	212	29.08S	29.22E
Cathlamet, Wa., U.S. (kăth-lăm'ĕt)	106c	46.12N	123.22W
Catia, neigh., Ven.	234a	10.31N	66.57W
Catlettsburg, Ky., U.S. (kăt'lĕts-bûrg)	98	38.20N	82.35W
Catoche, Cabo, c., Mex. (kä-tō'chĕ)	116	21.30N	87.15W
Catonsville, Md., U.S. (kā'tŭnz-vĭl)	100e	39.16N	76.45W
Catorce, Mex. (kä-tōr'sá)	118	23.41N	100.51W
Catskill, N.Y., U.S. (käts'kĭl)	99	42.15N	73.50W
Catskill Mountains, mts., N.Y., U.S.	97	42.20N	74.35W
Cattaraugus Indian Reservation, I.R., N.Y., U.S. (kăt'tȧ-rȧ-gŭs)	99	42.30N	79.05W
Catu, Braz. (kȧ-tōō)	131	12.26S	38.12W
Catuala, Ang.	216	16.29S	19.03E
Catumbela, r., Ang. (kä'tŏm-bĕl'ȧ)	216	12.40S	14.10E
Cauayan, Phil. (kou-ä'yän)	197a	16.56N	121.46E
Cauca, r., Col. (kou'kä)	130	7.30N	75.26W
Caucagua, Ven. (käò-kå'gwä)	131b	10.17N	66.22W
Caucasus, mts.	164	43.20N	42.00E
Cauchon Lake, l., Can. (kô-shŏn')	89	55.25N	96.30W
Caughnawaga, Can.	83a	45.24N	73.41W
Caulfield, Austl.	201a	37.53S	145.03E
Caulonia, Italy (kou-lō'nyä)	160	38.24N	16.22E
Cauquenes, Chile (kou-kā'nās)	132	35.54S	72.14W
Caura, r., Ven. (kou'rä)	130	6.48N	64.40W
Causapscal, Can.	92	48.22N	67.14W
Caution, Cape, c., Can. (kô'shŭn)	86	51.10N	127.47W
Cauto, r., Cuba (kou'tō)	122	20.33N	76.20W
Cauvery, r., India	183	12.00N	77.00E
Cava, Braz. (kå'vä)	132b	22.41S	43.26W
Cava de' Tirreni, Italy (kä'vä-dĕ-tēr-rĕ'nē)	159c	40.27N	14.43E
Cávado, r., Port. (kä-vä'dō)	158	41.43N	8.08W
Cavalcante, Braz. (kä-väl-kän'tā)	131	13.45S	47.33W
Cavalier, N.D., U.S. (kăv-ȧ-lēr')	102	48.45N	97.39W
Cavally, r., Afr.	214	4.40N	7.30W
Cavan, Ire. (kăv'ăn)	150	54.01N	7.00W
Cavarzere, Italy (kä-vär'dzå-rā)	160	45.08N	12.06E
Cavendish, Vt., U.S. (kăv'ĕn-dĭsh)	99	43.25N	72.35W
Caviana, Ilha, i., Braz. (kä-vyä'nä)	131	0.45N	49.33W
Cavite, Phil. (kä-vē'tä)	197a	14.30N	120.54E
Caxambu, Braz. (kä-shá'm-bōō)	131	22.00S	44.45W
Caxias, Braz. (kä'shê-äzh)	131	4.48S	43.16W
Caxias, Port.	238d	38.42N	9.16W
Caxias do Sul, Braz. (kä'shê-äzh-dò-sōō'l)	132	29.13S	51.03W
Caxito, Ang. (kä-shē'tò)	212	8.33S	13.36E
Cayambe, Ec. (kȧ-īä'm-bĕ)	130	0.03N	79.09W
Cayenne, Fr. Gu. (kā-ĕn')	131	4.56N	52.18W
Cayetano Rubio, Mex. (kä-yĕ-tà-nô-rōō'byô)	118	20.37N	100.21W
Cayey, P.R.	117b	18.05N	66.12W
Cayman Brac, i., Cay. Is. (kī-măn' bråk)	122	19.45N	79.50W
Cayman Islands, dep., N.A.	122	19.30N	80.30W
Cay Sal Bank, bk. (kē-säl)	122	23.55N	80.20W
Cayuga, l., N.Y., U.S. (kā-yōō'gȧ)	99	42.35N	76.35W
Cazalla de la Sierra, Spain	158	37.55N	5.48W
Cazaux, Étang de, l., Fr. (ā-tăν' dĕ kä-zō')	156	44.32N	0.59W
Cazenovia, N.Y., U.S. (kăz-ê-nō'vĭ-ȧ)	99	42.55N	75.50W
Cazenovia Creek, r., N.Y., U.S.	101c	42.49N	78.45W
Čazma, Cro. (chäz'mä)	160	45.44N	16.39E
Cazombo, Ang. (kä-zô'm-bō)	212	11.54S	22.52E
Cazones, r., Mex. (kä-zô'nĕs)	119	20.37N	97.28W
Cazones, Ensenada de, b., Cuba (ĕn-sĕ-nä-dä-dĕ-kä-zō'nås)	122	22.05N	81.30W
Cazones, Golfo de, b., Cuba (gôl-fô-dĕ-kä-zō'nås)	122	21.55N	81.15W
Cazorla, Spain (kä-thôr'lå)	158	37.55N	2.58W
Cea, r., Spain (thā'ä)	158	42.18N	5.10W
Ceará-Mirim, Braz. (sā-ä-rä'mē-rē'ν)	131	6.00S	35.13W
Cebaco, Isla, i., Pan. (ē's-lä-sä-bä'kō)	121	7.27N	81.08W
Cebolla Creek, r., Co., U.S. (sē-bōl'yä)	109	38.15N	107.10W
Cebreros, Spain (sē-brē'rôs)	158	40.28N	4.28W
Cebu, Phil. (sā-bōō')	197	10.22N	123.49E
Cecchignola, neigh., Italy	239c	41.49N	12.29E
Čechy (Bohemia), hist. reg., Czech Rep.	154	49.51N	13.55E
Cecil, Pa., U.S. (sē'sĭl)	101e	40.20N	80.10W
Cecil Park, Austl.	243a	33.52S	150.51E
Cedar, r., Ia., U.S.	103	42.23N	92.07W
Cedar, r., Wa., U.S.	106c	45.56N	122.32W
Cedar, West Fork, r., Ia., U.S.	103	42.49N	93.10W
Cedar Bayou, Tx., U.S.	113a	29.54N	94.58W
Cedar Breaks National Monument, rec., Ut., U.S.	109	37.35N	112.55W
Cedarbrook, Pa., U.S.	229b	40.05N	75.10W
Cedarburg, Wi., U.S. (sē'dēr bûrg)	103	43.23N	88.00W
Cedar City, Ut., U.S.	109	37.40N	113.10W
Cedar Creek, r., N.D., U.S.	102	46.05N	102.10W
Cedar Falls, Ia., U.S.	103	42.31N	92.29W
Cedar Grove, N.J., U.S.	228	40.51N	74.14W
Cedar Heights, Pa., U.S.	229b	40.05N	75.17W
Cedarhurst, N.Y., U.S.	228	40.38N	73.44W
Cedar Keys, Fl., U.S.	114	29.06N	83.03W
Cedar Lake, In., U.S.	101a	41.22N	87.27W
Cedar Lake, l., In., U.S.	101a	41.23N	87.25W
Cedar Lake, res., Can.	84	53.10N	100.00W
Cedar Rapids, Ia., U.S.	97	42.00N	91.43W
Cedar Springs, Mi., U.S.	98	43.15N	85.40W
Cedartown, Ga., U.S. (sē'dēr-toun)	114	34.00N	85.15W
Cedarville, S. Afr. (cēdȧr'vĭl)	213c	30.23S	29.04E
Cedral, Mex. (sā-dräl')	118	23.47N	100.42W
Cedros, Hond. (sā'drōs)	120	14.36N	87.07W
Cedros, i., Mex.	116	28.10N	115.10W
Ceduna, Austl. (sê-dò'nȧ)	202	32.15S	133.55E
Ceel Buur, Som.	218a	4.35N	46.40E
Cega, r., Spain (thā'gä)	158	41.25N	4.27W
Cegléd, Hung. (tsā'glād)	155	47.10N	19.49E
Ceglie, Italy (chĕ'lyĕ)	161	40.39N	17.32E
Cehegín, Spain (thā-å-hēn')	158	38.05N	1.48W
Ceiba del Agua, Cuba (sā'bä-dĕl-ȧ'gwä)	123a	22.53N	82.38W
Cekhira, Tun.	210	34.17N	10.00E
Celaya, Mex. (sā-lä'yä)	116	20.33N	100.49W
Celebes (Sulawesi), i., Indon.	196	2.15S	120.30E
Celebes Sea, sea, Asia	196	3.45N	121.52E
Celestún, Mex. (sĕ-lĕs-tōō'n)	120a	20.57N	90.18W
Celina, Oh., U.S. (sêlī'na)	98	40.30N	84.35W
Celje, Slvn. (tsĕl'yĕ)	160	46.13N	15.17E
Celle, Ger. (tsĕl'ē)	147	52.37N	10.05E
Cement, Ok., U.S. (sê-mĕnt')	110	34.56N	98.07W
Cenderawasih, Teluk, b., Indon.	197	2.20S	135.30E
Ceniza, Pico, mtn., Ven. (pē'kô-sĕ-nē'zä)	131b	10.24N	67.26W
Center, Tx., U.S. (sĕn'tēr)	113	31.50N	94.10W
Center Hill Lake, res., Tn., U.S. (sĕn'tēr-hĭl)	114	36.02N	86.00W
Center Line, Mi., U.S. (sĕn'tēr līn)	101b	42.29N	83.01W
Centerville, Ia., U.S. (sĕn'tēr-vĭl)	103	40.44N	92.48W
Centerville, Mn., U.S.	107g	45.10N	93.03W
Centerville, Pa., U.S.	101e	40.02N	79.58W
Centerville, S.D., U.S.	102	43.07N	96.56W
Centerville, Ut., U.S.	107b	40.55N	111.53W
Centocelle, neigh., Italy	239c	41.53N	12.34E
Central, Cordillera, mts., Bol. (kôr-dĕl-yĕ'rä-sĕn-trä'l)	130	19.18S	65.29W
Central, Cordillera, mts., Col.	130a	3.58N	75.55W
Central, Cordillera, mts., Dom. Rep.	123	19.05N	71.30W
Central, Cordillera, mts., Phil. (kôr-dĕl-yĕ'rä-sĕn-trä'l)	197a	17.05N	120.55E
Central African Republic, nation, Afr.	211	7.50N	21.00E
Central America, reg., N.A. (ä-mĕr'ĭ-kȧ)	116	10.45N	87.15W

ăt; finȧl; rāte; senåte; ärm; åsk; sofȧ; fâre; ch-choose; dh-as th in other; bē; ėvent; bĕt; recĕnt; cratēr; g-gō; gh-guttural g; bĭt; ĭ-short neutral; rīde; κ-guttural k as ch in German ich;

PRONOUNCING INDEX

Central City-Chaville 273

PLACE (Pronunciation)	PAGE	Lat. °'	Long. °'
Central City, Ky., U.S. (sĕn'trăl)	114	37.15N	87.09W
Central City, Ne., U.S. (sĕn'trăl sĭ'tĭ)	102	41.07N	98.00W
Central Falls, R.I., U.S. (sĕn'trăl fôlz)	100b	41.54N	71.23W
Central Highlands, Pa., U.S.	230b	40.16N	79.50W
Centralia, Il., U.S. (sĕn-trā'lĭ-à)	98	38.35N	89.05W
Centralia, Mo., U.S.	111	39.11N	92.07W
Centralia, Wa., U.S.	104	46.42N	122.58W
Central Intelligence Agency, pt. of i., Va., U.S.	229d	38.57N	77.09W
Central Park, pt. of i., N.Y., U.S.	228	40.47N	73.58W
Central Plateau, plat., Russia	166	55.00N	33.30E
Central Valley, N.Y., U.S.	100a	41.19N	74.07W
Centre Island, N.Y., U.S.	228	40.54N	73.32W
Centreville, Il., U.S. (sĕn'tĕr-vĭl)	107e	38.33N	90.06W
Centreville, Md., U.S.	99	39.05N	76.05W
Centro Simón Bolívar, pt. of i., Ven.	234a	10.30N	66.55W
Century, Fl., U.S. (sĕn'tů-rĭ)	114	30.57N	87.15W
Century City, neigh., Ca., U.S.	232	34.03N	118.26W
Ceram (Seram), i., Indon.	197	2.45S	129.30E
Céret, Fr.	156	42.29N	2.47E
Cerignola, Italy (chā-rē-nyô'lä)	160	41.16N	15.55E
Cerknica, Slvn. (tsĕr'knē-tsá)	160	45.48N	14.21E
Čern'achovsk, Russia (chĕr-nyä'kôfsk)	166	54.38N	21.49E
Čer'omuski, neigh., Russia	239b	55.41N	37.35E
Cerralvo, Mex. (sĕr-räl'vō)	112	26.05N	99.37W
Cerralvo, i., Mex.	116	24.00N	109.59W
Cerrito, Col. (sĕr-rē'-tô)	130a	3.41N	76.17W
Cerritos, Mex. (sĕr-rē'tôs)	118	22.26N	100.16W
Cerro de Pasco, Peru (sĕr'rō dā päs'kō)	130	10.45S	76.14W
Cerro Gordo, Arroyo de, r., Mex. (är-rô-yō-dĕ-sĕ'r-rô-gôr-dŏ)	112	26.12N	104.06W
Čertanovo, neigh., Russia	239b	55.38N	37.37E
Certegui, Col. (sĕr-tĕ'gē)	130a	5.21N	76.35W
Cervantes, Phil. (sĕr-vän'tās)	197a	16.59N	120.42E
Cervera del Río Alhama, Spain	158	42.02N	1.55W
Cerveteri, Italy (chĕr-vĕ'tĕ-rē)	159d	42.00N	12.06E
Cesano Boscone, Italy	238c	45.27N	9.06E
Cesena, Italy (chĕ'sĕ-nä)	160	44.08N	12.16E
Cēsis, Lat. (sā'sĭs)	153	57.19N	25.17E
Česká Lípa, Czech Rep. (chĕs'kä lē'pa)	154	50.41N	14.31E
České Budějovice, Czech Rep. (chĕs'kä bōō'dyĕ-yô-vēt-sĕ)	147	49.00N	14.30E
Českomoravská Vysočina, hills, Czech Rep.	154	49.21N	15.40E
Český Těšín, Czech Rep.	155	49.43N	18.22E
Çeşme, Tur. (chĕsh'mĕ)	161	38.20N	26.20E
Cessnock, Austl.	203	32.58S	151.15E
Cestos, r., Lib.	214	5.40N	9.25W
Cetinje, Yugo. (tsĕt'in-yĕ)	142	42.23N	18.55E
Ceuta, Sp. N. Afr. (thā-ōō'tä)	210	36.04N	5.36W
Cévennes, reg., Fr. (sā-vĕn')	147	44.20N	3.48E
Ceylon see Sri Lanka, nation, Asia	183b	8.45N	82.30E
Chabot, Lake, l., Ca., U.S. (sha'bŏt)	106b	37.44N	122.06W
Chacabuco, Arg. (chä-kä-bōō'kō)	129c	34.37S	60.27W
Chacaltianguis, Mex. (chä-käl-tē-äŋ'gwēs)	119	18.18N	95.50W
Chacao, Ven.	234a	10.30N	66.51W
Chachapoyas, Peru (chä-chä-poi'yäs)	130	6.16S	77.48W
Chaco, prov., Arg. (chä'kō)	132	26.00S	60.45W
Chaco Culture National Historic Park, rec., N.M., U.S. (chä'kô)	109	36.05N	108.00W
Chad, Russia (chäd)	172a	56.33N	57.11E
Chad, nation, Afr.	211	17.48N	19.00E
Chad, Lake, l., Afr.	211	13.55N	13.40E
Chadbourn, N.C., U.S. (chăd'bŭrn)	115	34.19N	78.55W
Chadderton, Eng., U.K.	237b	53.33N	2.08W
Chadron, Ne., U.S. (chăd'rŭn)	96	42.50N	103.10W
Chadstone, Austl.	243b	37.53S	145.05E
Chadwell Saint Mary, Eng., U.K.	235	51.29N	0.22E
Chafarinas, Islas, is., Sp. N. Afr.	158	35.08N	2.20W
Chaffee, Mo., U.S. (chăf'ē)	111	37.10N	89.39W
Chāgal Hills, hills, Afg.	182	29.15N	63.28E
Chagodoshcha, r., Russia (chä-gō-dôsh-chä)	162	59.08N	35.13E
Chagres, r., Pan. (chä'grĕs)	121	9.18N	79.22W
Chagrin, r., Oh., U.S. (shà'grĭn)	101d	41.34N	81.24W
Chagrin Falls, Oh., U.S. (shà'grĭn fôls)	101d	41.26N	81.23W
Chahar, hist. reg., China (chä-här)	189	44.25N	115.00E
Chahār Borjak, Afg.	185	30.17N	62.03E
Chakdaha, India	240a	22.28N	88.20E
Chake Chake, Tan.	217	5.15S	39.46E
Chalatenango, El Sal. (chäl-ä-tĕ-näŋ'gō)	120	14.04N	88.54W
Chalbi Desert, des., Kenya	217	3.40N	36.50E
Chalcatongo, Mex. (chäl-kä-tōŋ'gō)	119	17.04N	97.41W
Chalchihuites, Mex. (chäl-chē-wē'tās)	118	23.28N	103.57W
Chalchuapa, El Sal. (chäl-chwä'pä)	120	14.01N	89.39W
Chalco, Mex. (chäl-kō)	119a	19.15N	98.54W
Chaldon, Eng., U.K.	235	51.17N	0.07W
Chaleur Bay, b., Can. (shà-lûr')	85	47.58N	65.33W
Chalfant, Pa., U.S.	230b	40.25N	79.52W
Chalfont Common, Eng., U.K.	235	51.38N	0.33W
Chalfont Saint Giles, Eng., U.K.	235	51.38N	0.34W
Chalfont Saint Peter, Eng., U.K.	235	51.37N	0.33W
Chalgrove, Eng., U.K. (chăl'grôv)	144b	51.38N	1.05W
Chaling, China (chä'lĭng)	193	27.00N	113.31E
Chalk, Eng., U.K.	235	51.26N	0.25E
Chalmette, La., U.S. (shăl-mĕt')	100d	29.57N	89.57W
Châlons-sur-Marne, Fr. (shà-lôN'sür-märn)	147	48.57N	4.23E
Chalon-sur-Saône, Fr.	147	46.47N	4.54E
Chaltel, Cerro (Monte Fitzroy), mtn., S.A. (sĕ'r-rô-chäl'tĕl)	132	48.10S	73.18W
Chālūs, Iran	185	36.38N	51.26E
Chama, Rio, r., N.M., U.S. (chä'mä)	109	36.19N	106.31W
Chama, Sierra de, mts., Guat. (sē-ĕ'r-rä-dĕ-chä-mä)	120	15.48N	90.20W
Chamama, Mwi.	217	12.55S	33.43E
Chaman, Pak. (chŭm-än')	183	30.58N	66.21E
Chambal, r., India (chŭm-bäl')	183	24.30N	75.30E
Chamberlain, S.D., U.S. (chām'bĕr-lĭn)	102	43.48N	99.21W
Chamberlain, l., Me., U.S.	92	46.15N	69.10W
Chambersburg, Pa., U.S. (chām'bĕrz-bûrg)	99	40.00N	77.40W
Chambéry, Fr. (shäm-bā-rē')	147	45.35N	5.54E
Chambeshi, r., Zam.	217	10.35S	31.20E
Chamblee, Ga., U.S. (chăm-blē')	100c	33.55N	84.18W
Chambly, Can. (shäN-blē')	83a	45.27N	73.17W
Chambly, Fr.	157b	49.11N	2.14E
Chambord, Can.	85	48.22N	72.01W
Chambourcy, Fr.	237c	48.54N	2.03E
Chame, Punta, c., Pan. (pŏ'n-tä-chä'mà)	121	8.41N	79.27W
Chamelecón, r., Hond. (chä-mĕ-lĕ-kô'n)	120	15.09N	88.42W
Chamo, l., Eth.	211	5.58N	37.00E
Chamonix-Mont-Blanc, Fr. (shà-mō-nē')	157	45.55N	6.50E
Champagne, reg., Fr. (shäm-pän'yĕ)	156	48.53N	4.48E
Champaign, Il., U.S. (shăm-pān')	97	40.10N	88.15W
Champdāni, India	186a	22.48N	88.21E
Champerico, Guat. (chäm-pā-rē'kō)	120	14.18N	91.55W
Champigny-sur-Marne, Fr.	237c	48.49N	2.31E
Champion, Mi., U.S. (chăm'pĭ-ŭn)	103	46.30N	87.59W
Champlain, Lake, l., N.A. (shăm-plān')	97	44.45N	73.20W
Champlan, Fr.	237c	48.43N	2.16E
Champlitte-et-le-Prálot, Fr. (shäN-plēt')	157	47.38N	5.28E
Champotón, Mex. (chäm-pō-tōn')	119	19.21N	90.43W
Champotón, r., Mex.	119	19.19N	90.15W
Champs-sur-Marne, Fr.	237c	48.51N	2.36E
Chāmrāil, India	240a	22.38N	88.18E
Chañaral, Chile (chän-yä-räl')	132	26.20S	70.46W
Chances Peak, vol., Monts.	121b	16.43N	62.10W
Chandannagar, India	240a	22.51N	88.21E
Chandeleur Islands, is., La., U.S. (shăn-dĕ-lōōr')	114	29.53N	88.35W
Chandeleur Sound, strt., La., U.S.	114	29.47N	89.08W
Chandīgarh, India	183	30.51N	77.13E
Chandler, Can. (chăn'dlĕr)	85	48.21N	64.41W
Chandler, Ok., U.S.	111	35.42N	96.52W
Chandler's Cross, Eng., U.K.	235	51.40N	0.27W
Chandrapur, India	183	19.58N	79.21E
Chang see Yangtze, r., China	189	30.30N	117.25E
Changane, r., Moz.	212	22.42S	32.46E
Changara, Moz.	217	16.54S	33.14E
Changchun, China (chäŋ-chòn)	189	43.55N	125.25E
Changdang Hu, l., China (chäŋ-däŋ hōō)	190	31.37N	119.29E
Changde, China (chäŋ-dŭ)	189	29.00N	111.38E
Changdian, China	240b	40.01N	116.32E
Changhua, Tai. (chäng'hwä')	193	24.02N	120.32E
Changi, Sing.	240c	1.23N	103.59E
Changjŏn, N. Kor. (chäng'jŭn')	194	38.40N	128.05E
Changli, China (chäŋ-lē)	192	39.46N	119.10E
Changning, China (chäŋ-nĭŋ)	188	24.34N	99.49E
Changping, China (chäŋ-pĭŋ)	192	40.12N	116.10E
Changqing, China (chäŋ-chyĭŋ)	190	36.33N	116.42E
Changsan Got, c., N. Kor.	194	38.06N	124.50E
Changsha, China (chäŋ-shä)	189	28.20N	113.00E
Changshan Qundao, is., China (chäŋ-shän chyòn-dou)	190	39.08N	122.26E
Changshu, China (chäŋ-shōō)	190	31.40N	120.45E
Changting, China	193	25.50N	116.18E
Changwu, China (chäng'wōō')	192	35.12N	107.45E
Changxindianzhen, China (chäŋ-shyĭn-dĭĕn-jŭn)	192a	39.49N	116.12E
Changxing Dao, i., China (chäŋ-shyĭŋ dou)	190	39.38N	121.10E
Changyi, China (chäŋ-yē)	190	36.51N	119.23E
Changyuan, China (chyäŋ-yuän)	190	35.10N	114.41E
Changzhi, China (chäŋ-jr)	192	35.58N	112.58E
Changzhou, China (chäŋ-jō)	189	31.47N	119.56E
Changzhuyuan, China (chäŋ-jōō-yuän)	190	31.33N	115.17E
Chanhassen, Mn., U.S. (shăn'hăs-sĕn)	107g	44.52N	93.32W
Chanh-hung, Viet.	241j	10.43N	106.41E
Channel Islands, is., Eur. (chăn'ĕl)	142	49.15N	3.30W
Channel Islands, is., Ca., U.S.	108	33.30N	119.15W
Channel-Port-aux-Basques, Can.	85	47.35N	59.11W
Channelview, Tx., U.S. (chănĕlvū)	113a	29.46N	95.07W
Chantada, Spain (chän-tä'dä)	158	42.38N	7.36W
Chanteloup-les-Vignes, Fr.	237c	48.59N	2.02E
Chanthaburi, Thai.	196	12.37N	102.04E
Chantilly, Fr. (shäN-tē-yē')	157b	49.12N	2.30E
Chantilly, Va., U.S. (shăn'tĭlē)	100e	38.53N	77.26W
Chantrey Inlet, b., Can. (chăn-trē)	84	67.49N	95.00W
Chanute, Ks., U.S. (shà-nōōt')	97	37.41N	95.27W
Chany, l., Russia (chä'nē)	164	54.15N	77.31E
Chao'an, China (chou-än)	189	23.48N	116.35E
Chao Hu, l., China	193	31.45N	116.59E
Chao Phraya, r., Thai.	196	16.13N	99.33E
Chaor, r., China (chou-r)	192	47.20N	121.40E
Chaoshui, China (chou-shwā)	190	37.43N	120.56E
Chaoxian, China (chou shyĕn)	190	31.37N	117.50E
Chaoyang, China	189	41.32N	120.20E
Chaoyang, China (chou-yäŋ)	193	23.18N	116.32E
Chapada, Serra da, mts., Braz. (sĕ'r-rä-dä-shä-pä'dä)	131	14.57S	54.34W
Chapadão, Serra do, mtn., Braz. (sĕ'r-rä-dô-shä-pà-dou'N)	129a	20.31S	46.20W
Chapala, Mex. (chä-pä'lä)	118	20.18N	103.10W
Chapala, Lago de, l., Mex. (lä'gô-dĕ-chä-pä'lä)	116	20.14N	103.02W
Chapalagana, r., Mex. (chä-pä-lä-gà'nä)	118	22.11N	104.09W
Chaparral, Col. (chä-pär-rá'l)	130	3.44N	75.28W
Chapayevsk, Russia (châ-pī'ĕfsk)	166	53.00N	49.30E
Chapel Hill, N.C., U.S. (chăp''l hĭl)	115	35.55N	79.05W
Chapel Oaks, Md., U.S.	229d	38.54N	76.55W
Chapeltown, Eng., U.K.	237b	53.38N	2.24W
Chaplain, l., Wa., U.S. (chăp'lĭn)	106a	47.58N	121.50W
Chapleau, Can. (chăp-lō')	85	47.43N	83.28W
Chapman, Mount, mtn., Can. (chăp'măn)	87	51.50N	118.20W
Chapman's Bay, b., S. Afr. (chăp'măns bā)	212a	34.06S	18.17E
Chapman Woods, Ca., U.S.	232	34.08N	118.05W
Chappell, Ne., U.S. (chă-pĕl')	102	41.06N	102.29W
Chapultenango, Mex. (chä-pòl-tĕ-näŋ'gō)	119	17.19N	93.08W
Chapultepec, Castillo de, hist., Mex.	233a	19.25N	99.11W
Chá Pungana, Ang.	216	13.44S	18.39E
Charcas, Mex. (chär'käs)	118	23.09N	101.09W
Charco de Azul, Bahía, b., Pan.	121	8.14N	82.45W
Chardzhou, Turk. (chĕr-jô'ò)	169	38.52N	63.37E
Charente, r., Fr. (shà-räNt')	156	45.48N	0.28W
Charenton-le-Pont, Fr.	237c	48.49N	2.25E
Chari, r., Afr. (shä-rē')	215	12.45N	14.55E
Charing, Eng., U.K. (chă'rĭng)	144b	51.13N	0.49E
Chariton, Ia., U.S. (châr'ĭ-tŭn)	103	41.02N	93.16W
Chariton, r., Mo., U.S.	111	40.24N	92.38W
Charlemagne, Can. (shärl-mäny')	83a	45.43N	73.29W
Charleroi, Bel. (shàr-lĕ-rwä')	147	50.25N	4.35E
Charleroi, Pa., U.S. (shär'lĕ-roi)	101e	40.08N	79.54W
Charles, Cape, c., Va., U.S. (chärlz)	99	37.05N	75.48W
Charlesbourg, Can. (shàrl-bōōr')	83b	46.51N	71.16W
Charles City, Ia., U.S. (chärlz)	103	43.03N	92.40W
Charles de Gaulle, Aéroport, arpt., Fr.	237c	49.00N	2.34E
Charleston, Il., U.S. (chärlz'tŭn)	98	39.30N	88.10W
Charleston, Ms., U.S.	114	34.00N	90.02W
Charleston, Mo., U.S.	111	36.53N	89.20W
Charleston, S.C., U.S.	97	32.47N	79.56W
Charleston, W.V., U.S.	97	38.20N	81.35W
Charlestown, St. K./N.	121b	17.10N	62.32W
Charlestown, In., U.S. (chärlz'toun)	101h	38.46N	85.39W
Charleville, Austl. (chär'lē-vĭl)	203	26.16S	146.28E
Charleville Mézières, Fr. (shärl-vēl')	156	49.48N	4.41E
Charlevoix, Mi., U.S. (shär'lĕ-voi)	98	45.20N	85.15W
Charlevoix, Lake, l., Mi., U.S.	103	45.17N	85.43W
Charlotte, Mi., U.S. (shär'lŏt)	98	42.35N	84.50W
Charlotte, N.C., U.S.	97	35.15N	80.50W
Charlotte Amalie, V.I.U.S. (shär-lŏt'ĕ ä-mä'lĭ-à)	117	18.21N	64.54W
Charlotte Harbor, b., Fl., U.S.	115a	26.49N	82.00W
Charlotte Lake, l., Can.	86	52.07N	125.30W
Charlottenberg, Swe. (shär-lŭt'ĕn-bĕrg)	152	59.53N	12.17E
Charlottenburg, neigh., Ger.	238a	52.31N	13.16E
Charlottenburg, Schloss, hist., Ger.	238a	52.31N	13.14E
Charlottesville, Va., U.S. (shär'lŏtz-vĭl)	97	38.00N	78.25W
Charlottetown, Can. (shär'lŏt-toun)	85	46.14N	63.08W
Charlotte Waters, Austl. (shär'lŏt)	202	26.00S	134.50E
Charlton, neigh., Eng., U.K.	235	51.29N	0.02E
Charmes, Fr. (shärm)	157	48.23N	6.19E
Charneca, neigh., Port.	238d	38.47N	9.08W
Charnwood Forest, for., Eng., U.K. (chärn'wŏd)	144a	52.42N	1.15W
Charny, Can. (shär-nē')	83b	46.43N	71.16W
Chars, Fr. (shär)	157b	49.09N	1.57E
Chārsadda, Pak. (chŭr-sä'dä)	183a	34.17N	71.43E
Charters Towers, Austl. (chär'tĕrz)	203	20.03S	146.20E
Charterwood, Pa., U.S.	230b	40.33N	80.00W
Chartres, Fr. (shärt'r')	147	48.26N	1.29E
Chascomús, Arg. (chäs-kō-mōōs')	132	35.32S	58.01W
Chase City, Va., U.S. (chās)	115	36.45N	78.27W
Chashniki, Bela. (chăsh'nyĕ-kē)	162	54.51N	29.08E
Chaska, Mn., U.S. (chăs'kà)	107g	44.48N	93.36W
Châteaudun, Fr. (shä-tō-dăN')	156	48.04N	1.23E
Châteaufort, Fr.	237c	48.44N	2.06E
Château-Gontier, Fr. (chà-tō'gôN'tyā')	156	47.48N	0.43W
Châteauguay, Can. (chà-tō-gā)	83a	45.22N	73.45W
Châteauguay, r., N.A.	83a	45.13N	73.51W
Châteauneaut, Fr.	156a	43.23N	5.11E
Château-Renault, Fr. (shà-tō-rĕ-nō')	156	47.36N	0.57E
Château-Richer, Can. (shà-tō'rā-shā')	83b	47.00N	71.01W
Châteauroux, Fr. (shà-tō-rōō')	147	46.47N	1.39E
Château-Thierry, Fr. (shà-tō'ty-ĕr-rē')	156	49.03N	3.22E
Châtellerault, Fr. (shä-tĕl-rō')	147	46.48N	0.31E
Châtenay-Malabry, Fr.	237c	48.46N	2.17E
Chatfield, Mn., U.S. (chăt'fēld)	103	43.50N	92.10W
Chatham, Can.	85	47.02N	65.28W
Chatham, Can. (chăt'ăm)	85	42.25N	82.10W
Chatham, Eng., U.K. (chăt'ŭm)	151	51.23N	0.32E
Chatham, N.J., U.S. (chăt'ăm)	100a	40.44N	74.23W
Chatham, Oh., U.S.	101d	41.06N	82.01W
Chatham Islands, is., N.Z.	2	44.00S	178.00W
Chatham Sound, strt., Can.	86	54.32N	130.35W
Chatham Strait, strt., Ak., U.S.	95	57.00N	134.40W
Châtillon, Fr.	237c	48.48N	2.17E
Chatou, Fr.	237c	48.54N	2.09E
Chatpur, neigh., India	240a	22.36N	88.23E
Chatswood, Austl.	243a	33.48S	151.12E
Chatsworth, Ca., U.S. (chătz'wûrth)	107a	34.16N	118.36W
Chatsworth Reservoir, res., Ca., U.S.	107a	34.15N	118.41W
Chattahoochee, Fl., U.S. (chăt-tà-hōō' chē)	114	30.42N	84.47W
Chattahoochee, r., U.S.	97	32.00N	85.10W
Chattanooga, Tn., U.S. (chăt-à-nōō'gà)	97	35.01N	85.15W
Chattooga, r., Ga., U.S. (chă-tōō'gà)	114	34.47N	83.13W
Chaudière, r., Can. (shō-dyĕr')	91	46.26N	71.10W
Chaumont, Fr. (shō-mōN')	147	48.08N	5.07E
Chaunskaya Guba, b., Russia	171	69.15N	170.00E
Chauny, Fr. (shō-nē')	156	49.40N	3.09E
Chau-phu, Viet.	196	10.49N	104.57E
Chausy, Bela. (chou'sĭ)	162	53.57N	30.58E
Chautauqua, l., N.Y., U.S. (shà-tô'kwà)	99	42.10N	79.25W
Chavaniga, Russia	166	66.02N	37.50E
Chavenay, Fr.	237c	48.51N	1.59E
Chaves, Port. (chä'vĕzh)	158	41.44N	7.30W
Chaville, Fr.	237c	48.48N	2.10E

ng-sing; ŋ-baŋk; N-nasalized n; nŏd; cŏmmit; ōld; ōbey; ôrder; oi-boil; fōōd; ò-as oo in foot; ou-out; s-soft; sh-dish; th-thin; pūre; ûnite; ûrn; stŭd; circŭs; ü-as in French tu; '-indeterminate vowel.

PLACE (Pronunciation)	PAGE	Lat. °'	Long. °'
Chavinda, Mex. (chä-vē'n-dä)	118	20.01N	102.27W
Chazumba, Mex. (chä-zòm'bä)	119	18.11N	97.41W
Cheadle, Eng., U.K. (chē'd'l)	144a	52.59N	1.59W
Cheadle Hulme, Eng., U.K.	237b	53.22N	2.12W
Cheam, neigh., Eng., U.K.	235	51.21N	0.13W
Cheat, W.V., U.S. (chēt)	99	39.35N	79.40W
Cheb, Czech Rep. (κĕb)	154	50.05N	12.23E
Chebarkul', Russia (chĕ-bár-kûl')	172a	54.59N	60.22E
Cheboksary, Russia (chyĕ-bôk-sä'rè)	166	56.00N	47.20E
Cheboygan, Mi., U.S. (shė-boi'găn)	98	45.40N	84.30W
Chech, Erg, des., Alg.	210	24.45N	2.07W
Chechen', i., Russia (chyĕch'ĕn)	167	44.00N	48.10E
Checheno-Ingushetia, state, Russia	168	43.15N	45.40E
Checotah, Ok., U.S. (chė-kō'tá)	111	35.27N	95.32W
Chedabucto Bay, b., Can. (chĕd-á-bŭk-tō)	93	45.23N	61.10W
Cheduba Island, i., Myanmar	196	18.45N	93.01E
Cheecham Hills, hills, Can. (chēē'hăm)	88	56.20N	111.10W
Cheektowaga, N.Y., U.S. (chēk-tō-wä'gá)	101c	42.54N	78.46W
Cheetham Hill, neigh., Eng., U.K.	237b	53.31N	2.15W
Chefoo *see* Yantai, China	189	37.32N	121.22E
Chegutu, Zimb.	212	18.18S	30.10E
Chehalis, Wa., U.S. (chė-hā'lĭs)	104	46.39N	122.58W
Chehalis, r., Wa., U.S.	104	46.47N	123.17W
Cheju, S. Kor. (chĕ'jōō')	194	33.29N	126.40E
Cheju (Quelpart), i., S. Kor.	194	33.20N	126.25E
Chekalin, Russia (chĕ-kä'lĭn)	162	54.05N	36.13E
Chela, Serra da, mts., Ang. (sĕr'rá dä shā'lá)	212	15.30S	13.30E
Chelan, Wa., U.S. (chė-lăn')	104	47.51N	119.59W
Chelan, Lake, l., Wa., U.S.	104	48.09N	120.20W
Chelas, neigh., Port.	238d	38.45N	9.07W
Cheleiros, Port. (shĕ-la'rōzh)	159b	38.54N	9.19W
Chéliff, r., Alg. (shā-lēf)	210	36.00N	2.00E
Chelles, Fr.	157b	48.53N	2.36E
Chełm, Pol. (κĕlm)	147	51.08N	23.30E
Chełmno, Pol. (κĕlm'nō)	155	53.20N	18.25E
Chelmsford, Can.	90	46.35N	81.12W
Chelmsford, Eng., U.K. (chĕlm's-fĕrd)	151	51.44N	0.28E
Chelmsford, Ma., U.S.	93a	42.36N	71.21W
Chelsea, Austl.	201a	38.05S	145.08E
Chelsea, Can.	83c	45.30N	75.46W
Chelsea, Al., U.S. (chĕl'sė)	100h	33.20N	86.38W
Chelsea, Ma., U.S.	93a	42.23N	71.02W
Chelsea, Mi., U.S.	98	42.20N	84.00W
Chelsea, Ok., U.S.	111	36.32N	95.23W
Cheltenham, Eng., U.K. (chĕlt'nŭm)	150	51.57N	2.06W
Cheltenham, Md., U.S. (chĕltĕn-hăm)	100e	38.45N	76.50W
Chelva, Spain (chĕl'vä)	158	39.43N	1.00W
Chelyabinsk, Russia (chĕl-yä-bėnsk')	164	55.10N	61.25E
Chelyuskin, Mys, c., Russia (chĕl-yòs'-kĭn)	165	77.45N	104.45E
Chemba, Moz.	217	17.08S	34.52E
Chembūr, neigh., India	240e	19.04N	72.54E
Chemnitz, Ger.	147	50.48N	12.53E
Chemung, r., N.Y., U.S. (shė-mŭng)	99	42.20N	77.25W
Chĕn, Gora, mtn., Russia	165	65.13N	142.12E
Chenāb, r., Asia (chė-năb)	183	30.30N	71.30E
Chenachane, Alg. (shĕ-ná-shän')	210	26.14N	4.14W
Chencun, China (chŭn-tsòn)	191a	22.58N	113.14E
Cheney, Wa., U.S. (chē'nå)	104	47.29N	117.34W
Chengde, China (chŭŋ-dŭ)	189	40.50N	117.50E
Chengdong Hu, l., China (chŭŋ-dòŋ hōō)	190	32.22N	116.32E
Chengdu, China (chŭŋ-dōō)	188	30.30N	104.10E
Chenggu, China (chŭŋ-gōō)	192	33.05N	107.25E
Chenghai, China (chŭŋ-hī)	193	23.22N	116.40E
Chengshan Jiao, c., China (jyou chŭŋ-shän)	192	37.28N	122.40E
Chengxi Hu, l., China (chŭŋ-shyē hōō)	190	32.31N	116.04E
Chenies, Eng., U.K.	235	51.41N	0.32W
Chennevières, Fr.	237c	49.00N	2.07E
Chenxian, China (chŭn-shyĕn)	193	25.40N	113.00E
Chepén, Peru (chĕ-pĕ'n)	130	7.17S	79.24W
Chepo, Pan. (chā'pō)	121	9.12N	79.06W
Chepo, r., Pan.	121	9.10N	78.36W
Cher, r., Fr. (shâr)	147	47.14N	1.34E
Cherán, Mex. (chā-rän')	118	19.41N	101.54W
Cherangany Hills, hills, Kenya	217	1.25N	35.20E
Cheraw, S.C., U.S. (chē'rô)	115	34.40N	79.52W
Cherbourg, Fr. (shär-bòr')	142	49.39N	1.43W
Cherdyn', Russia (chĕr-dyĕn')	164	60.25N	56.32E
Cheremkhovo, Russia (chĕr'yĕm-kō-vō)	165	52.58N	103.18E
Cherëmukhovo, Russia (chĕr-yĕ-mû-kô-vô)	172a	60.20N	60.00E
Cherepanovo, Russia (chĕr'yĕ pä-nô'vō)	164	54.13N	83.22E
Cherepovets, Russia (chĕr-yĕ-pô'vyĕtz)	164	59.08N	37.59E
Chereya, Bela. (chĕr-ā'yä)	162	54.38N	29.16E
Chergui, i., Tun.	148	34.50N	11.40E
Chergui, Chott ech, l., Alg. (chĕr gē)	148	34.12N	0.10W
Cherikov, Bela. (chĕ'rē-kôf)	162	53.34N	31.22E
Cherkasy, Ukr.	163	49.26N	32.03E
Cherkasy, prov., Ukr.	163	48.58N	30.55E
Cherkessk, Russia	168	44.14N	42.04E
Cherlak, Russia (chĭr-läk')	164	54.04N	74.28E
Chermoz, Russia (chĕr-môz')	166	58.47N	56.08E
Chern', Russia (chĕrn)	162	53.28N	36.49E
Chërnaya Kalitva, r., Russia (chôr'ná yá ká-lēt'vá)	163	50.15N	39.16E
Chernihiv, Ukr.	167	51.23N	31.15E
Chernihiv, prov., Ukr.	163	51.28N	31.18E
Chernihivka, Ukr.	163	47.08N	36.20E
Chernivtsi, Ukr.	164	48.18N	25.56E
Chernobyl' (Chornobyl'), Ukr. (chĕr-nō-bĭl')	163	51.17N	30.14E
Chernogorsk, Russia (chĕr-nŏ-gôrsk')	170	54.01N	91.07E

PLACE (Pronunciation)	PAGE	Lat. °'	Long. °'
Chernoistochinsk, Russia (chĕr-nôy-stô'chĭnsk)	172a	57.44N	59.55E
Chernyanka, Russia (chĕrn-yäŋ'kä)	163	50.56N	37.48E
Cherokee, Ia., U.S. (chĕr-ô-kē')	102	42.43N	95.33W
Cherokee, Ks., U.S.	111	37.21N	94.50W
Cherokee, Ok., U.S.	110	36.44N	98.22W
Cherokee Lake, res., Tn., U.S.	114	36.22N	83.22W
Cherokees, Lake of the, res., Ok., U.S. (chĕr-ô-kēz')	97	36.32N	95.14W
Cherokee Sound, Bah.	122	26.15N	76.55W
Cherry City, Pa., U.S.	230b	40.29N	79.58W
Cherryfield, Me., U.S. (chĕr'ĭ-fēld)	92	44.37N	67.56W
Cherry Grove, Or., U.S.	106c	45.27N	123.15W
Cherry Hill, N.J., U.S.	229b	39.55N	75.01W
Cherry Hill, neigh., Md., U.S.	229c	39.15N	76.38W
Cherryvale, Ks., U.S.	111	37.16N	95.33W
Cherryville, N.C., U.S. (chĕr'ĭ-vĭl)	115	35.32N	81.22W
Cherskogo, Khrebet, mts., Russia	165	67.15N	140.00E
Chertsey, Eng., U.K.	144b	51.24N	0.30W
Cherven', Bela. (chĕr'vyĕn)	162	53.43N	28.26E
Chervonoye, l., Bela. (chĕr-vô'nô-yĕ)	162	52.24N	28.12E
Chesaning, Mi., U.S. (chĕs'á-nĭng)	98	43.10N	84.10W
Chesapeake, Va., U.S. (chĕs'á-pēk)	100g	36.48N	76.16W
Chesapeake Bay, b., U.S.	97	38.20N	76.15W
Chesapeake Beach, Md., U.S.	100e	38.42N	76.33W
Chesham, Eng., U.K. (chĕsh'ŭm)	144b	51.41N	0.37W
Chesham Bois, Eng., U.K.	235	51.41N	0.37W
Cheshire, Mi., U.S. (chĕsh'ĭr)	98	42.25N	86.00W
Cheshire, co., Eng., U.K.	144a	53.16N	2.30W
Chëshskaya Guba, b., Russia	164	67.25N	46.00E
Cheshunt, Eng., U.K.	144b	51.43N	0.02W
Chesma, Russia (chĕs'má)	172a	53.50N	60.42E
Chesnokovka, Russia (chĕs-nŏ-kôf'ká)	164	53.28N	83.41E
Chessington, neigh., Eng., U.K.	235	51.21N	0.18W
Chester, Eng., U.K. (chĕs'tēr)	150	53.12N	2.53W
Chester, Il., U.S.	111	37.54N	89.48W
Chester, Pa., U.S.	100f	39.51N	75.22W
Chester, Pa., U.S.	229b	39.51N	75.21W
Chester, S.C., U.S.	115	34.42N	81.11W
Chester, Va., U.S.	115	37.20N	77.24W
Chester, W.V., U.S.	98	40.35N	80.30W
Chesterbrook, Va., U.S.	229d	38.55N	77.09W
Chesterfield, Eng., U.K. (chĕs'tēr-fēld)	150	53.14N	1.26W
Chesterfield, Îles, is., N. Cal.	203	19.38S	160.08E
Chesterfield Inlet, Can.	85	63.19N	91.11W
Chesterfield Inlet, b., Can.	85	63.59N	92.09W
Chestermere Lake, l., Can. (chĕs'tē-mēr)	83e	51.03N	113.45W
Chesterton, In., U.S. (chĕs'tēr-tŭn)	98	41.35N	87.05W
Chestertown, Md., U.S. (chĕs'tēr-toun)	99	39.15N	76.05W
Chestnut Hill, Md., U.S.	229c	39.17N	76.47W
Chestnut Hill, Ma., U.S.	227a	42.20N	71.10W
Chesuncook, l., Me., U.S. (chĕs'ŭn-kòk)	92	46.03N	69.40W
Cheswick, Pa., U.S.	230b	40.32N	79.47W
Chetek, Wi., U.S. (chĕ'tĕk)	103	45.18N	91.41W
Chetumal, Bahía de, b., N.A. (bä-ē-ä dĕ chĕt-ōō-mäl')	116	18.07N	88.05W
Chevelon Creek, r., Az., U.S. (shĕv'á-lŏn)	109	34.35N	111.00W
Chevening, Eng., U.K.	235	51.18N	0.08E
Cheverly, Md., U.S.	229d	38.55N	76.55W
Chevilly-Larue, Fr.	237c	48.46N	2.21E
Cheviot, Oh., U.S. (shĕv'ĭ-ŭt)	101f	39.10N	84.37W
Chevreuse, Fr. (shĕ-vrûz')	157b	48.42N	2.02E
Chevy Chase, Md., U.S. (shĕvĭ chās)	100e	38.58N	77.06W
Chevy Chase View, Md., U.S.	229d	39.01N	77.05W
Chew Bahir, Afr. (stĕf-a-nē)	211	4.46N	37.31E
Chewelah, Wa., U.S. (chē-wē'lä)	104	48.17N	117.42W
Cheyenne, Wy., U.S. (shī-ĕn')	96	41.10N	104.49W
Cheyenne, r., U.S.	96	44.20N	102.15W
Cheyenne River Indian Reservation, I.R., S.D., U.S.	102	45.07N	100.46W
Cheyenne Wells, Co., U.S.	110	38.46N	102.21W
Chhalera Bāngar, India	240d	28.33N	77.20E
Chhināmor, India	240a	22.48N	88.18E
Chhindwāra, India	186	22.08N	78.57E
Chiai, Tai. (chī'ī')	193	23.28N	120.28E
Chiange, Ang.	216	15.45S	13.48E
Chiang Mai, Thai.	196	18.38N	98.44E
Chiang Rai, Thai.	196	19.53N	99.48E
Chiapa, Río de, r., Mex.	120	16.00N	92.20W
Chiapa de Corzo, Mex. (chė-ä'pä dā kôr'zō)	119	16.44N	93.01W
Chiapas, state, Mex. (chė-ä'päs)	116	17.10N	93.00W
Chiapas, Cordilla de, mts., Mex. (kôr-dēl-yĕ'rä-dĕ-chyä'räs)	119	15.55N	93.15W
Chiari, Italy (kyä'rē)	160	45.31N	9.57E
Chiasso, Switz.	154	45.50N	8.57E
Chiatura, Geor.	168	42.17N	43.17E
Chiautla, Mex. (chyä-ōōt'lá)	118	18.16N	98.37W
Chiavari, Italy (kyä-vä'rē)	160	44.18N	9.21E
Chiba, Japan (chē'bá)	189	35.37N	140.08E
Chiba, dept., Japan	195a	35.47N	140.02E
Chibougamau, Can. (chė-bōō'gă-mou)	85	49.57N	74.23W
Chibougamau, l., Can.	91	49.53N	74.21W
Chicago, Il., U.S. (shĭ-kô-gō) (chĭ-kä'gō)	97	41.49N	87.37W
Chicago, North Branch, r., Il., U.S.	231a	41.53N	87.38W
Chicago Heights, Il., U.S.	101a	41.30N	87.38W
Chicago Lawn, neigh., Il., U.S.	231a	41.47N	87.41W
Chicago-O'Hare International Airport, arpt., Il., U.S.	231a	41.59N	87.54W
Chicago Ridge, Il., U.S.	231a	41.42N	87.47W
Chicago Sanitary and Ship Canal, can., Il., U.S.	231a	41.42N	87.58W
Chicapa, r., Afr. (chė-kä'pä)	212	7.45S	20.25E
Chicbul, Mex. (chēk-bōō'l)	119	18.45N	90.56W
Chic-Chocs, Monts, mts., Can.	85	48.38N	66.37W
Chichagof, i., Ak., U.S. (chė-chä'gôf)	95	57.50N	137.00W

PLACE (Pronunciation)	PAGE	Lat. °'	Long. °'
Chichancanab, Lago de, l., Mex. (lä'gô-dĕ-chē-chän-kä-nä'b)	120a	19.50N	88.28W
Chichén Itzá, hist., Mex.	120a	20.40N	88.35W
Chichester, Eng., U.K. (chĭch'ĕs-tēr)	150	50.50N	0.55W
Chichimilá, Mex. (chē-chē-mė'lä)	120a	20.36N	88.14W
Chichiriviche, Ven. (chē-chē-rē-vē-chĕ)	131b	10.56N	68.17W
Chickamauga, Ga., U.S. (chĭk-á-mô'gá)	114	34.50N	85.15W
Chickamauga Lake, res., Tn., U.S.	114	35.18N	85.22W
Chickasawhay, r., Ms., U.S. (chĭk-á-sô'wā)	114	31.45N	88.45W
Chickasha, Ok., U.S. (chĭk'á-shā)	96	35.04N	97.56W
Chiclana de la Frontera, Spain (chė-klä'nä)	158	36.25N	6.09W
Chiclayo, Peru (chė-klä'yō)	130	6.46S	79.50W
Chico, Ca., U.S. (chē'kō)	108	39.43N	121.51W
Chico, Wa., U.S.	106a	47.37N	122.43W
Chico, r., Arg.	132	44.30S	66.00W
Chico, r., Arg.	132	49.15S	69.30W
Chico, r., Phil.	197a	17.33N	121.24E
Chicoloapan, Mex. (chė-kō-lwä'pän)	119a	19.24N	98.54W
Chiconautla, Mex.	119a	19.39N	99.01W
Chicontepec, Mex. (chė-kōn'tĕ-pĕk')	118	20.58N	98.08W
Chicopee, Ma., U.S. (chĭk'ô-pē)	99	42.10N	72.35W
Chicoutimi, Can. (shė-kōō'tė-mė')	85	48.26N	71.04W
Chicxulub, Mex. (chēk-sōō-lōō'b)	120a	21.10N	89.30W
Chiefland, Fl., U.S. (chēf'lánd)	115	29.30N	82.50W
Chiemsee, l., Ger. (κēm zā)	154	47.58N	12.20E
Chieri, Italy (kyâ'rē)	160	45.03N	7.48E
Chieti, Italy (kyĕ'tē)	148	42.22N	14.22E
Chifeng, China (chr-fŭŋ)	189	42.18N	118.52E
Chignall Saint James, Eng., U.K.	235	51.46N	0.25E
Chignanuapan, Mex. (chē'g-nä-nwä-pá'n)	118	19.49N	98.02W
Chignecto Bay, b., Can. (shĭg-nĕk'tō)	92	45.33N	64.50W
Chignik, Ak., U.S. (chĭg'nĭk)	95	56.14N	158.12W
Chignik Bay, b., Ak., U.S.	95	56.18N	157.22W
Chigu Co, l., China (chr-gōō tswo)	186	28.55N	91.47E
Chigwell, Eng., U.K.	144b	51.38N	0.05E
Chigwell Row, Eng., U.K.	235	51.37N	0.07E
Chihe, China (chr-hŭ)	190	32.32N	117.57E
Chihuahua, Mex. (chė-wä'wä)	116	28.37N	106.06W
Chihuahua, state, Mex.	116	29.00N	107.30W
Chikishlyar, Turk. (chė-kėsh-lyär')	170	37.40N	53.50E
Chilanga, Zam.	217	15.34S	28.17E
Chilapa, Mex. (chė-lä'pä)	118	17.34N	99.14W
Chilchota, Mex. (chėl-chō'tä)	118	19.40N	102.04W
Chilcotin, r., Can. (chĭl-kō'tĭn)	86	52.20N	124.15W
Childer Thornton, Eng., U.K.	237a	53.17N	2.57W
Childress, Tx., U.S. (chīld'rĕs)	110	34.26N	100.11W
Chile, nation, S.A. (chē'lā)	132	35.00S	72.00W
Chilecito, Arg. (chė-lå-sē'tō)	132	29.06S	67.25W
Chilengue, Serra do, mts., Ang.	216	13.20S	15.00E
Chilibre, Pan. (chē-lė'brĕ)	116a	9.09N	79.37W
Chililabombwe, Zam.	217	12.18S	27.43E
Chilka, l., India	186	19.26N	85.42E
Chilko, r., Can. (chĭl'kō)	86	51.53N	123.53W
Chilko Lake, l., Can.	86	51.20N	124.05W
Chillán, Chile (chēl-yän')	132	36.44S	72.06W
Chillicothe, Il., U.S. (chĭl-ĭ-kŏth'ė)	98	41.55N	89.30W
Chillicothe, Mo., U.S.	111	39.46N	93.32W
Chillicothe, Oh., U.S.	98	39.20N	83.00W
Chilliwack, Can. (chĭl'ĭ-wăk)	84	49.10N	121.57W
Chillum, Md., U.S.	229d	38.58N	76.59W
Chilly-Mazarin, Fr.	237c	48.42N	2.19E
Chiloé, Isla de, i., Chile	132	42.30S	73.55W
Chilpancingo de los Bravo, Mex.	116	17.32N	99.30W
Chilton, Wi., U.S. (chĭl'tŭn)	103	44.00N	88.12W
Chilung, Tai. (chī'lung)	189	25.02N	121.48E
Chilwa, Lake, l., Afr.	212	15.12S	36.30E
Chimacum, Wa., U.S. (chĭm'ä-kŭm)	106a	48.01N	122.47W
Chimalpa, Mex. (chē-mäl'pä)	119a	19.26N	99.22W
Chimaltenango, Guat. (chė-mäl-tå-näŋ'gō)	120	14.39N	90.48W
Chimaltitan, Mex. (chėmäl-tē-tän')	118	21.36N	103.50W
Chimbay, Uzb. (chĭm-bī')	169	43.00N	59.44E
Chimborazo, mtn., Ec. (chėm-bô-rä'zō)	130	1.35S	78.45W
Chimbote, Peru (chėm-bō'tå)	130	9.02S	78.33W
Chimki-Chovrino, neigh., Russia	239b	55.51N	37.30E
China, Mex. (chē'nä)	112	25.43N	99.13W
China, nation, Asia (chī'ná)	188	36.45N	93.00E
Chinameca, El Sal. (Chē-nä-mā'kä)	120	13.31N	88.18W
Chinandega, Nic. (chē-nän-dä'gä)	120	12.38N	87.08W
Chinati Peak, mtn., Tx., U.S. (chĭ-nä'tė)	112	29.56N	104.29W
Chinatown, neigh., Ca., U.S.	231b	37.48N	122.26W
Chincha Alta, Peru (chĭn'chä äl'tä)	130	13.24S	76.04W
Chinchas, Islas, is., Peru (ē's-läs-chē'n-chäs)	130	11.27S	79.05W
Chinchilla, Austl. (chĭn-chĭl'á)	204	26.44S	150.36E
Chinchorro, Banco, bk., Mex. (bä'n-kô-chĕn-chō'r-rō)	120a	18.43N	87.25W
Chincilla de Monte Aragon, Spain	158	38.54N	1.43W
Chinde, Moz. (shĕn'dĕ)	212	17.39S	36.34E
Chin Do, i., S. Kor.	194	34.30N	125.43E
Chindwin, r., Myanmar (chĭn-dwĭn)	183	23.30N	94.34E
Chingford, neigh., Eng., U.K.	235	51.38N	0.01E
Chingmei, Tai.	241d	24.59N	121.32E
Chingola, Zam. (chĭng-gōlä)	212	12.32S	27.52E
Chinguar, Ang. (chĭng-gär)	212	12.35S	16.15E
Chinguetti, Maur. (chėŋ-gĕt'ė)	210	20.34N	12.34W
Chinhoyi, Zimb.	212	17.22S	30.12E
Chinju, S. Kor. (chĭn'jōō)	194	35.13N	128.10E
Chinko, r., Cen. Afr. Rep. (shĭn'kô)	211	6.37N	24.31E
Chinmen *see* Quemoy, Tai.	193	24.30N	118.20E
Chino, Ca., U.S. (chē'nō)	107a	34.01N	117.42W
Chinon, Fr. (shē-nôN')	156	47.09N	0.13E
Chinook, Mt., U.S. (shĭn-ŏk')	105	48.35N	109.15W
Chinsali, Zam.	217	10.34S	32.03E
Chinteche, Mwi. (chĭn-tĕ'chĕ)	212	11.48S	34.14E

ăt; finăl; rāte; senåte; ärm; åsk; sofá; fâre; ch-choose; dh-as th in other; bē; ėvent; bĕt; recĕnt; cratĕr; g-gō; gh-guttural g; bĭt; ĭ-short neutral; rīde; κ-guttural k as ch in German ich;

PLACE (Pronunciation)	PAGE	Lat. °'	Long. °'
Chioggia, Italy (kyôd'jä)	160	45.12N	12.17E
Chipata, Zam.	212	13.39S	32.40E
Chipera, Moz. (zhě-pě'rä)	212	15.16S	32.30E
Chipley, Fl., U.S. (chĭp'lĭ)	114	30.45N	85.33W
Chipman, Can. (chĭp'mǎn)	92	46.11N	65.53W
Chipola, r., Fl., U.S. (chĭ-pō'lǎ)	114	30.40N	85.14W
Chippawa, Can. (chĭp'ê-wä)	101c	43.03N	79.03W
Chipperfield, Eng., U.K.	235	51.42N	0.29W
Chippewa, r., Mn., U.S. (chĭp'ê-wä)	102	45.07N	95.41W
Chippewa, r., Wi., U.S.	103	45.07N	91.19W
Chippewa Falls, Wi., U.S.	103	44.55N	91.26W
Chippewa Lake, Oh., U.S.	101d	41.04N	81.54W
Chipping Ongar, Eng., U.K.	235	51.43N	0.15E
Chipstead, Eng., U.K.	235	51.17N	0.09E
Chipstead, Eng., U.K.	235	51.18N	0.10W
Chiputneticook Lakes, l., N.A. (chĭ-pōt-nět'ĭ-kōk)	92	45.47N	67.45W
Chiquimula, Guat. (chē-kê-mōō'lä)	120	14.47N	89.31W
Chiquimulilla, Guat. (chē-kē-mōō-lê'l-yä)	120	14.08N	90.23W
Chiquinquira, Col. (chê-kēŋ'kê-rä')	130	5.33N	73.49W
Chirāgh Delhi, neigh., India	240d	28.32N	77.14E
Chirala, India	187	15.52N	80.22E
Chirchik, Uzb. (chĭr-chěk')	169	41.28N	69.18E
Chire (Shire), r., Afr.	217	17.15S	35.25E
Chiricahua National Monument, rec., Az., U.S. (chĭ-rä-cä'hwä)	109	32.02N	109.18W
Chirikof, i., Ak., U.S. (chĭ'rĭ-kôf)	95	55.50N	155.35W
Chiriquí, Punta, c., Pan. (pò'n-tä-chē-rê-kē')	121	9.13N	81.39W
Chiriquí Grande, Pan. (chē-rê-kē' grän'dā)	121	8.57N	82.08W
Chiri San, mtn., S. Kor. (chĭ'rĭ-sän')	194	35.20N	127.39E
Chiromo, Mwi.	212	16.34S	35.13E
Chirpan, Bul.	149	42.12N	25.19E
Chirripó, Río, r., C.R.	121	9.50N	83.20W
Chisasibi, Can.	85	53.40N	78.58W
Chisholm, Mn., U.S. (chĭz'ŭm)	103	47.28N	92.53W
Chişinău, Mol.	164	47.02N	28.52E
Chislehurst, neigh., Eng., U.K.	235	51.25N	0.04E
Chistopol', Russia (chĭs-tô'pôl-y')	164	55.21N	50.37E
Chiswellgreen, Eng., U.K.	235	51.44N	0.22W
Chiswick, neigh., Eng., U.K.	235	51.29N	0.16W
Chita, Russia (chê-tá')	165	52.09N	113.39E
Chitambo, Zam.	217	12.55S	30.39E
Chitato, Ang.	216	7.20S	20.47E
Chitembo, Ang.	216	13.34S	16.40E
Chitina, Ak., U.S. (chĭ-tē'ná)	95	61.28N	144.35W
Chitokoloki, Zam.	216	13.50S	23.13E
Chitorgarh, India	186	24.59N	74.42E
Chitrāl, Pak. (chē-träl')	183	35.58N	71.48E
Chittagong, Bngl. (chĭt-á-gông')	183	22.26N	90.51E
Chitungwiza, Zimb.	212	17.51S	31.05E
Chiumbe, r., Afr. (chê-ôm'bå)	212	9.45S	21.00E
Chivasso, Italy (kê-väs'sō)	160	45.13N	7.52E
Chivhu, Zimb.	212	18.59S	30.58E
Chivilcoy, Arg. (chē-vêl-koi')	132	34.51S	60.03W
Chixoy, r., Guat. (chē-ĸoi')	120	15.40N	90.35W
Chizu, Japan (chê-zōō')	195	35.16N	134.15E
Chloride, Az., U.S. (klō'rīd)	109	35.25N	114.15W
Chmielnik, Pol. (ĸmyěl'nêĸ)	155	50.36N	20.46E
Choa Chu Kang, Sing.	240c	1.22N	103.41E
Choapa, r., Chile (chô-á'pä)	129b	31.56S	70.48W
Chobham, Eng., U.K.	235	51.21N	0.36W
Choctawhatchee, r., Fl., U.S.	114	30.37N	85.56W
Choctawhatchee Bay, b., Fl., U.S. (chôk-tô-hăch'ê)	114	30.15N	86.32W
Chodziez, Pol. (ĸōj'yēsh)	154	52.59N	16.55E
Choele Choel, Arg. (chô-ĕ'lĕ-chô-ĕ'l)	132	39.14S	65.46W
Chōfu, Japan (chō'fōō')	195a	35.39N	139.33E
Chōgo, Japan (chō-gō)	195a	35.25N	139.28E
Choisel, Fr.	237c	48.41N	2.01E
Choiseul, i., Sol.Is. (shwä-zûl')	203	7.30S	157.30E
Choisy-le-Roi, Fr.	157b	48.46N	2.25E
Chojnice, Pol. (ĸoĭ-nē-tsĕ)	155	53.41N	17.34E
Cholet, Fr. (shō-lĕ')	147	47.06N	0.54W
Cho-lon, neigh., Viet.	241j	10.46N	106.40E
Cholula, Mex. (chō-lōō'lä)	118	19.04N	98.19W
Choluteca, Hond. (chō-lōō-tā'kä)	120	13.18N	87.12W
Choluteco, r., Hond.	120	13.34N	86.59W
Cho-moi, Viet.	241j	10.51N	106.38E
Chomutov, Czech Rep. (kō'mò-tôf)	154	50.27N	13.23E
Chona, r., Russia (chō'nä)	171	60.45N	109.15E
Chone, Ec. (chô'ně)	130	0.48S	80.06W
Chŏngjin, N. Kor. (chŭng-jĭn')	189	41.48N	129.46E
Chŏngju, S. Kor. (chŭng-jōō')	194	36.35N	127.30E
Chongming Dao, i., China (chôŋ-mĭŋ dou)	193	31.40N	122.30E
Chong Pang, Sing.	240c	1.26N	103.50E
Chongqing, China (chôŋ-chyĭŋ)	188	29.38N	107.30E
Chŏnju, S. Kor. (chŭn-jōō')	194	35.48N	127.08E
Chonos, Archipiélago de los, is., Chile	132	44.35N	76.15W
Chorley, Eng., U.K. (chôr'lĭ)	144a	53.40N	2.38W
Chorleywood, Eng., U.K.	235	51.39N	0.31W
Chorlton-cum-Hardy, Eng., U.K.	237b	53.27N	2.17W
Chornaya, neigh., Russia	172b	55.45N	38.04E
Chornobay, Ukr. (chěr-nō-bī')	163	49.41N	32.24E
Chornomors'ke, Ukr.	167	45.29N	32.43E
Chorošovo, neigh., Russia	239b	55.47N	37.28E
Chorrera de Managua, Cuba	233b	23.02N	82.19E
Chorrillos, Peru (chôr-rē'l-yōs)	130	12.17S	76.55W
Chortkiv, Ukr.	155	49.01N	25.48E
Chosan, N. Kor. (chō-sän')	194	40.44N	125.48E
Chosen, Fl., U.S. (chō'z'n)	115a	26.41N	80.41W
Chōshi, Japan (chō'shē)	194	35.40N	140.55E
Choszczno, Pol. (chôsh'chnô)	154	53.10N	15.25E
Chota Nagpur, plat., India	186	23.40N	82.50E
Choteau, Mt., U.S. (shō'tō)	105	47.51N	112.10W

PLACE (Pronunciation)	PAGE	Lat. °'	Long. °'
Chowan, r., N.C., U.S. (chô-wän')	115	36.13N	76.46W
Chowilla Reservoir, res., Austl.	204	34.05S	141.20E
Chown, Mount, mtn., Can. (choun)	87	53.24N	119.22W
Choybalsan, Mong.	189	47.50N	114.15E
Christchurch, N.Z. (krīst'chûrch)	203a	43.30S	172.38E
Christian, i., Can. (krĭs'chǎn)	91	44.50N	80.00W
Christiansburg, Va., U.S. (krĭs'chǎnz-bûrg)	115	37.08N	80.25W
Christiansted, V.I.U.S.	117b	17.45N	64.44W
Christmas Island, dep., Oc.	196	10.35S	105.40E
Christopher, Il., U.S. (krĭs'tô-fēr)	111	37.58N	89.04W
Chrudim, Czech Rep. (ĸrōō'dyĕm)	154	49.57N	15.46E
Chrzanów, Pol. (ĸzhä'nòf)	155	50.08N	19.24E
Chuansha, China (chůän-shä)	191b	31.12N	121.41E
Chubut, prov., Arg. (chò-bōōt')	132	44.00S	69.15W
Chubut, r., Arg. (chò-bōōt')	132	43.05S	69.00W
Chuckatuck, Va., U.S. (chŭck á-tŭck)	100g	36.51N	76.35W
Chucunaque, r., Pan. (chōō-kōō-nä'kā)	121	8.36N	77.48W
Chudovo, Russia (chò'dô-vô)	162	59.03N	31.56E
Chudskoye Ozero, l., Eur. (chòt'skô-yě)	166	58.43N	26.45E
Chuguchak, hist. reg., China (chōō'gōō-chäk')	188	46.09N	83.58E
Chuguyevka, Russia (chò-gōō'yěf-kå)	194	43.58N	133.49E
Chugwater Creek, r., Wy., U.S. (chŭg'wô-tēr)	102	41.43N	104.54W
Chuhuyiv, Ukr.	167	49.52N	36.40E
Chukot National Okrug, , Russia	171	68.15N	170.00E
Chukotskiy Poluostrov, pen., Russia	164	66.12N	175.00W
Chukotskoye Nagor'ye, mts., Russia	165	66.00N	166.00E
Chula Vista, Ca., U.S. (chōō'lá vĭs'tá)	108a	32.38N	117.05W
Chulkovo, Russia (chōōl-kô vô)	172b	55.33N	38.04E
Chulucanas, Peru	130	5.13S	80.13W
Chulum, r., Russia	170	57.52N	84.45E
Chumikan, Russia (chōō-mē-kän')	165	54.47N	135.09E
Chun'an, China (chòn-än)	193	29.38N	119.00E
Chunchŏn, S. Kor. (chòn-chŭn')	194	37.51N	127.46E
Chungju, S. Kor. (chŭng'jōō')	194	37.00N	128.19E
Chungking *see* Chongqing, China	188	29.38N	107.30E
Chŭngsanha-ri, neigh., S. Kor.	241b	37.35N	126.54E
Chunya, Tan.	217	8.32S	33.25E
Chunya, r., Russia (chòn'yä')	170	61.45N	101.28E
Chuquicamata, Chile (chōō-kê-kä-mä'tä)	132	22.08S	68.57W
Chur, Switz. (kōōr)	147	46.51N	9.32E
Churchill, Can. (chûrch'ĭl)	85	58.50N	94.10W
Churchill, Pa., U.S.	230b	40.27N	79.51W
Churchill, Va., U.S.	229d	38.54N	77.10W
Churchill, r., Can.	84	58.00N	95.00W
Churchill, Cape, c., Can.	85	59.07N	93.50W
Churchill Falls, wtfl., Can.	85	53.35N	64.27W
Churchill Lake, l., Can.	88	56.12N	108.40W
Churchill Peak, mtn., Can.	84	58.10N	125.14W
Church Street, Eng., U.K.	235	51.26N	0.28E
Church Stretton, Eng., U.K. (chûrch strĕt'ŭn)	144a	52.32N	2.49W
Churchton, Md., U.S.	100e	38.49N	76.33W
Churu, India	186	28.22N	75.00E
Churumuco, Mex. (chōō-rōō-mōō'kō)	118	18.39N	101.40W
Chuska Mountains, mts., Az., U.S. (chŭs-kǎ)	109	36.21N	109.11W
Chusovaya, r., Russia (chōō-sô-vä'yá)	166	58.08N	58.35E
Chusovoy, Russia (chōō-sô-vôy')	164	58.18N	57.50E
Chust, Uzb. (chòst)	169	41.05N	71.28E
Chuvashia, state, Russia	166	55.45N	46.00E
Chuviscar, r., Mex. (chōō-vês-kär')	112	28.34N	105.36W
Chuwang, China (chōō-wäŋ)	190	36.08N	114.53E
Chuxian, China (chōō shyěn)	192	32.19N	118.19E
Chuxiong, China (chōō-shyôŋ)	188	25.19N	101.34E
Chyhyryn, Ukr.	163	49.02N	32.39E
Cicero, Il., U.S. (sĭs'ēr-ō)	101a	41.50N	87.46W
Cide, Tur. (jē'dě)	149	41.50N	33.00E
Ciechanów, Pol. (tsyě-kä'nòf)	155	52.52N	20.39E
Ciego de Avila, Cuba (syā'gō dā ä'vê-lä)	117	21.50N	78.45W
Ciego de Avila, prov., Cuba	122	22.00N	78.40W
Ciempozuelos, Spain (thyěm-pô-thwā'lōs)	158	40.09N	3.36W
Ciénaga, Col. (syā'nä-gä)	130	11.01N	74.15W
Cienfuegos, Cuba (syěn-fwā'gōs)	117	22.10N	80.30W
Cienfuegos, prov., Cuba	122	22.15N	80.40W
Cienfuegos, Bahía, b., Cuba (bä-ē'ä-syěn-fwā'gōs)	122	22.00N	80.35W
Ciervo, Isla de la, i., Nic. (ē's-lä-dě-lä-syě'r-vô)	121	11.56N	83.20W
Cieszyn, Pol. (tsyě'shên)	155	49.47N	18.45E
Cieza, Spain (thyā'thä)	158	38.13N	1.25W
Cigüela, r., Spain	158	39.53N	2.54W
Cihuatlán, Mex. (sē-wä-tlä'n)	118	19.13N	104.36W
Cihuatlán, r., Mex.	118	19.11N	104.30W
Cijara, Embalse de, res., Spain	158	39.25N	5.00W
Cilician Gates, p., Tur.	167	37.30N	35.30E
Cimarron, r., U.S. (sĭm-ǎ-rōn')	96	36.26N	98.27W
Cimarron, r., Co., U.S.	110	37.13N	102.30W
Cinca, r., Spain (thēŋ'kä)	159	42.09N	0.08E
Cincinnati, Oh., U.S. (sĭn-sĭ-nát'ĭ)	97	39.08N	84.30W
Cinco Balas, Cayos, is., Cuba (kä'yōs-thēŋ'kō bä'läs)	122	21.05N	79.25W
Cinderella, S. Afr.	244b	26.15S	28.16E
Cinisello Balsamo, Italy	238c	45.33N	9.13E
Cinkota, neigh., Hung.	239g	47.31N	19.14E
Cintalapa, Mex. (sên-tä-lä'pä)	119	16.41N	93.44W
Cinto, Monte, mtn., Fr. (chēn'tō)	147	42.24N	8.54E
Circle, Ak., U.S. (sûr'k'l)	96a	65.49N	144.22W
Circleville, Oh., U.S. (sûr'k'lvĭl)	98	39.35N	83.00W
Cirebon, Indon.	196	6.50S	108.33E
Ciri Grande, r., Pan. (sē'rē-grá'n'dě)	116a	8.55N	80.04W
Cisco, Tx., U.S. (sĭs'kō)	112	32.23N	98.57W
Cisliano, Italy	238c	45.27N	8.59E
Cisneros, Col. (sēs-nĕ'rôs)	130a	6.33N	75.05W

PLACE (Pronunciation)	PAGE	Lat. °'	Long. °'
Cisterna di Latina, Italy (chēs-tě'r-nä-dē-lä-tē'nä)	159d	41.36N	12.53E
Cistierna, Spain (thês-tyěr'nä)	158	42.48N	5.08W
Citronelle, Al., U.S. (cĭt-rô'nĕl)	114	31.05N	88.15W
Cittadella, Italy (chēt-tä-děl'lä)	160	45.39N	11.51E
Città di Castello, Italy (chět-tä'dē käs-tĕl'lō)	160	43.27N	12.17E
City College of New York, pt. of i., N.Y., U.S.	228	40.49N	73.57W
City Island, neigh., N.Y., U.S.	228	40.51N	73.47W
City of Baltimore, Md., U.S.	229d	39.18N	76.37W
City of Commerce, Ca., U.S.	232	33.59N	118.08W
City of Industry, Ca., U.S.	232	34.01N	117.57W
City of London, neigh., Eng., U.K.	235	51.31N	0.05W
City of Westminster, neigh., Eng., U.K.	235	51.30N	0.09W
Ciudad Altamirano, Mex. (syōō-dä'd-äl-tä-mē-rä'nô)	118	18.24N	100.38W
Ciudad Bolívar, Ven. (syōō-dhädh' bô-lē'vär)	130	8.07N	63.41W
Ciudad Camargo, Mex.	116	27.42N	105.10W
Ciudad Chetumal, Mex.	116	18.30N	88.17W
Ciudad Darío, Nic. (syōō-dhädh'dä'rê-ō)	120	12.44N	86.08W
Ciudad de la Habana, prov., Cuba	122	23.20N	82.10W
Ciudad del Carmen, Mex. (syōō-dä'd-děl-kä'r-měn)	116	18.39N	91.49W
Ciudad del Maíz, Mex. (syōō-dhädh'del mä-ēz')	118	22.24N	99.37W
Ciudad Deportive, rec., Mex.	233a	19.24N	99.06W
Ciudadela, Spain (thyōō-dhä-dhä'lä)	159	40.00N	3.52E
Ciudad Fernández, Mex. (syōō-dhädh'fěr-nän'děz)	118	21.56N	100.03W
Ciudad García, Mex. (syōō-dhädh'gär-sē'ä)	116	22.39N	103.02W
Ciudad General Belgrano, Arg.	233d	34.44S	58.32W
Ciudad Guayana, Ven.	130	8.30N	62.45W
Ciudad Guzmán, Mex. (syōō-dhädh'gòz-män)	116	19.40N	103.29W
Ciudad Hidalgo, Mex. (syōō-dä'd-ê-dä'l-gô)	118	19.41N	100.35W
Ciudad Juárez, Mex. (syōō-dhädh hwä'räz)	116	31.44N	106.28W
Ciudad Madero, Mex. (syōō-dä'd-mä-dě'rô)	119	22.16N	97.52W
Ciudad Mante, Mex. (syōō-dä'd-mán'tě)	116	22.34N	98.58W
Ciudad Manual Doblado, Mex. (syōō-dä'd-män-wäl'dō-blä'dō)	118	20.43N	101.57W
Ciudad Obregón, Mex. (syōō-dhädh-ô-brě-gô'n)	116	27.40N	109.58W
Ciudad Real, Spain (thyōō-dhädh'rā-äl')	158	38.59N	3.55W
Ciudad Rodrigo, Spain (thyōō-dhädh'rô-drē'gō)	148	40.38N	6.34W
Ciudad Serdán, Mex. (syōō-dä'd-sěr-dá'n)	119	18.58N	97.26W
Ciudad Universitaria, educ., Spain	238b	40.27N	3.44W
Ciudad Victoria, Mex. (syōō-dhädh'vêk-tō'rê-ä)	116	23.43N	99.09W
Civitavecchia, Italy (chē'vê-tä-věk'kyä)	160	42.06N	11.49E
Cixian, China (tsē shyěn)	190	36.22N	114.23E
Clackamas, Or., U.S. (klăc-kǎ'măs)	106c	45.25N	122.34W
Claire, l., Can. (klâr)	84	58.33N	113.16W
Clair Engle Lake, l., Ca., U.S.	104	40.51N	122.41W
Clairton, Pa., U.S. (klârtŭn)	101e	40.17N	79.53W
Clamart, Fr.	237c	48.48N	2.16E
Clanton, Al., U.S. (klăn'tŭn)	114	32.50N	86.38W
Clare, Mi., U.S. (klâr)	98	43.50N	84.45W
Clare Island, i., Ire.	150	53.46N	10.00W
Claremont, Eng., U.K.	235	51.21N	0.22W
Claremont, Ca., U.S. (klâr'mŏnt)	107a	34.06N	117.43W
Claremont, N.H., U.S. (klâr'mŏnt)	99	43.20N	72.20W
Claremont, W.V., U.S.	98	37.55N	81.00W
Claremore, Ok., U.S. (klâr'mōr)	111	36.16N	95.37W
Claremorris, Ire. (klâr-mŏr'ĭs)	150	53.46N	9.05W
Clarence Strait, strt., Austl. (klăr'ěns)	202	12.15S	130.05E
Clarence Strait, strt., Ak., U.S.	86	55.25N	132.00W
Clarence Town, Bah.	123	23.05N	75.00W
Clarendon, Ar., U.S. (klâr'ěn-dŭn)	111	34.42N	91.17W
Clarendon, Tx., U.S.	110	34.55N	100.52W
Clarens, S. Afr. (clâ-rēns)	213c	28.34S	28.26E
Claresholm, Can. (klâr'ěs-hōlm)	84	50.02N	113.35W
Clarinda, Ia., U.S. (klå-rĭn'dǎ)	102	40.42N	95.00W
Clarines, Ven. (klä-rē'něs)	131b	9.57N	65.10W
Clarion, Ia., U.S. (klăr'ĭ-ŭn)	103	42.43N	93.45W
Clarion, Pa., U.S.	99	41.10N	79.25W
Clark, N.J., U.S.	228	40.38N	74.19W
Clark, S.D., U.S. (klärk)	102	44.52N	97.45W
Clark, Point, c., Can.	90	44.05N	81.50W
Clarkdale, Az., U.S. (klärk-dāl)	109	34.45N	112.05W
Clarke City, Can.	85	50.12N	66.38W
Clarke Range, mts., Austl.	203	20.30S	148.00E
Clark Fork, r., Mt., U.S.	104	47.50N	115.35W
Clarksburg, W.V., U.S. (klärkz'bûrg)	97	39.15N	80.20W
Clarksdale, Ms., U.S. (klärks-dāl)	114	34.10N	90.31W
Clark's Harbour, Can. (klärks)	92	43.26N	65.38W
Clarks Hill Lake, res., U.S. (klärk-hĭl)	97	33.50N	82.35W
Clarkston, Ga., U.S. (klärks'tŭn)	100c	33.49N	84.15W
Clarkston, Wa., U.S.	104	46.24N	117.01W
Clarksville, Ar., U.S. (klärks-vĭl)	111	35.28N	93.26W
Clarksville, Tn., U.S.	114	36.30N	87.23W
Clarksville, Tx., U.S.	111	33.37N	95.02W
Clatskanie, Or., U.S.	106c	46.04N	123.11W
Clatskanie, r., Or., U.S. (klăt-skā'nê)	106c	46.06N	123.11W
Clatsop Spit, Or., U.S. (klăt-sŏp)	106c	46.13N	124.04W
Cláudio, Braz. (klou'-dĕō)	129a	20.26S	44.44W
Claveria, Phil. (klä-vå-rē'ä)	193	18.38N	121.08E
Clawson, Mi., U.S. (klô's'n)	101b	42.32N	83.09W
Claxton, Ga., U.S. (kläks'tŭn)	115	32.07N	81.54W
Clay, Ky., U.S. (klā)	114	37.28N	87.50W

ng-sing; ŋ-baŋk; ɴ-nasalized n; nŏd; cŏmmit; ōld; ôbey; ôrder; oi-boil; fōōd; ò-as oo in foot; ou-out; s-soft; sh-dish; th-thin; pūre; ûnite; ûrn; stŭd; circŭs; ü-as in French tu; '-indeterminate vowel.

PLACE (Pronunciation)	PAGE	Lat. °′	Long. °′
Clay Center, Ks., U.S. (klā sĕn′tẽr)	111	39.23N	97.08W
Clay City, Ky., U.S. (klā sĭ′tĭ)	98	37.50N	83.55W
Claycomo, Mo., U.S. (kla-kō′mo)	107f	39.12N	94.30W
Clay Cross, Eng., U.K. (klā krŏs)	144a	53.10N	1.25W
Claye-Souilly, Fr. (klĕ-sōō-yē′)	157b	48.56N	2.43E
Claygate, Eng., U.K.	235	51.22N	0.20W
Claygate Cross, Eng., U.K.	235	51.16N	0.19E
Claymont, De., U.S. (klā-mōnt)	100f	39.48N	75.28W
Clayton, Eng., U.K.	144a	53.47N	1.49W
Clayton, Al., U.S. (klā′tŭn)	114	31.52N	85.25W
Clayton, Ca., U.S.	106b	37.56N	121.56W
Clayton, Mo., U.S.	107e	38.39N	90.20W
Clayton, N.M., U.S.	110	36.26N	103.12W
Clayton, N.C., U.S.	115	35.40N	78.27W
Clear, l., Ca., U.S.	108	39.05N	122.50W
Clear Boggy Creek, r., Ok., U.S. (klẽr bŏg′ĭ krēk)	111	34.21N	96.22W
Clear Creek, r., Az., U.S.	109	34.40N	111.05W
Clear Creek, r., Tx., U.S.	113a	29.34N	95.13W
Clear Creek, r., Wy., U.S.	105	44.35N	106.20W
Clearfield, Pa., U.S. (klẽr-fēld)	99	41.00N	78.25W
Clearfield, Ut., U.S.	107b	41.07N	112.01W
Clear Hills, Can.	84	57.11N	119.20W
Clearing, neigh., Il., U.S.	231a	41.47N	87.47W
Clear Lake, Ia., U.S.	103	43.09N	93.23W
Clear Lake, Wa., U.S.	106a	48.27N	122.14W
Clear Lake Reservoir, res., Ca., U.S.	104	41.53N	121.00W
Clearwater, Fl., U.S. (klẽr-wô′tẽr)	115a	27.43N	82.45W
Clearwater, r., Can.	87	52.00N	114.50W
Clearwater, r., Can.	87	52.00N	120.10W
Clearwater, r., Can.	88	56.10N	110.40W
Clearwater, r., Id., U.S.	104	46.27N	116.33W
Clearwater, Middle Fork, r., Id., U.S.	104	46.10N	115.48W
Clearwater, North Fork, r., Id., U.S.	104	46.34N	116.08W
Clearwater, South Fork, r., Id., U.S.	104	45.46N	115.53W
Clearwater Mountains, mts., Id., U.S.	104	45.56N	115.15W
Cleburne, Tx., U.S. (klē′bŭrn)	96	32.21N	97.23W
Cle Elum, Wa., U.S. (klē ĕl′ŭm)	104	47.12N	120.55W
Clementon, N.J., U.S. (klē′mĕn-tŭn)	100f	39.49N	75.00W
Cleobury Mortimer, Eng., U.K. (klĕō-bĕr′ĭ môr′tĭ-mẽr)	144a	52.22N	2.29W
Clermont, Austl. (klẽr′mŏnt)	203	23.02S	147.46E
Clermont, Can.	91	47.45N	70.20W
Clermont-Ferrand, Fr. (klĕr-mŏɴ′fĕr-räɴ′)	142	45.47N	3.03E
Cleveland, Ms., U.S. (klēv′lănd)	114	33.45N	90.42W
Cleveland, Oh., U.S.	97	41.30N	81.42W
Cleveland, Ok., U.S.	111	36.18N	96.28W
Cleveland, Tn., U.S.	114	35.09N	84.52W
Cleveland, Tx., U.S.	113	30.18N	95.05W
Cleveland Heights, Oh., U.S.	101d	41.30N	81.35W
Cleveland Museum of Art, pt. of i., Oh., U.S.	229a	41.31N	81.37W
Cleveland Park, neigh., D.C., U.S.	229d	38.56N	77.04W
Cleveland Peninsula, pen., Ak., U.S.	86	55.45N	132.00W
Cleves, Oh., U.S. (klē′vĕs)	101f	39.10N	84.45W
Clew Bay, b., Ire. (klōō)	150	53.47N	9.45W
Clewiston, Fl., U.S. (klē′wis-tŭn)	115a	26.44N	80.55W
Clichy, Fr. (klē-shē)	156	48.54N	2.18E
Clichy-sous-Bois, Fr.	237c	48.55N	2.33E
Clifden, Ire. (klĭf′dĕn)	150	53.31N	10.04W
Cliffside Park, N.J., U.S.	228	40.49N	73.59W
Clifton, Az., U.S. (klĭf′tŭn)	109	33.05N	109.20W
Clifton, Ma., U.S.	227a	42.29N	70.53W
Clifton, N.J., U.S.	100a	40.52N	74.09W
Clifton, S.C., U.S.	115	35.00N	81.47W
Clifton, Tx., U.S.	113	31.45N	97.31W
Clifton Forge, Va., U.S.	99	37.50N	79.50W
Clifton Heights, Pa., U.S.	229b	39.56N	75.18W
Clinch, r., Tn., U.S. (klĭnch)	114	36.30N	83.19W
Clingmans Dome, mtn., U.S. (klĭng′măns dōm)	114	35.37N	83.26W
Clinton, Can. (klĭn-′tŭn)	84	51.05N	121.35W
Clinton, Il., U.S.	98	40.10N	88.55W
Clinton, In., U.S.	98	39.40N	87.25W
Clinton, Ia., U.S.	103	41.50N	90.13W
Clinton, Ky., U.S.	114	36.39N	88.56W
Clinton, Md., U.S.	100e	38.46N	76.54W
Clinton, Ma., U.S.	93a	42.25N	71.41W
Clinton, Mo., U.S.	111	38.23N	93.46W
Clinton, N.C., U.S.	115	34.58N	78.20W
Clinton, Ok., U.S.	110	35.31N	98.56W
Clinton, S.C., U.S.	115	34.27N	81.53W
Clinton, Tn., U.S.	114	36.05N	84.08W
Clinton, Wa., U.S.	106a	47.59N	122.22W
Clinton, r., Mi., U.S.	101b	42.36N	83.00W
Clinton-Colden, l., Can.	84	63.58N	106.34W
Clintonville, Wi., U.S. (klĭn′tŭn-vĭl)	103	44.37N	88.46W
Clio, Mi., U.S. (klē′ō)	98	43.10N	83.45W
Cloates, Point, c., Austl. (klōts)	202	22.47S	113.45E
Clocolan, S. Afr.	218d	28.56S	27.35E
Clonakilty Bay, b., Ire. (klŏn-ȧ-kĭltē)	150	51.30N	8.50W
Cloncurry, Austl. (klŏn-kŭr′ē)	202	20.58S	140.42E
Clonmel, Ire. (klŏn-mĕl)	150	52.21N	7.45W
Clontarf, Austl.	243a	33.48S	151.16E
Cloquet, Mn., U.S. (klô-kā′)	107h	46.42N	92.28W
Closter, N.J., U.S. (klōs′tẽr)	100a	40.58N	73.57W
Cloud Peak, mtn., Wy., U.S. (kloud)	96	44.23N	107.11W
Clover, S.C., U.S. (klō′vẽr)	115	35.08N	81.08W
Clover Bar, Can. (klō′vẽr bär)	83g	53.34N	113.20W
Cloverdale, Can.	106d	49.06N	122.44W
Cloverdale, Ca., U.S. (klō′vẽr-dāl)	108	38.47N	123.03W
Cloverdene, S. Afr.	244b	26.09S	28.22E
Cloverport, Ky., U.S. (klō′vẽr pōrt)	98	37.50N	86.35W
Clovis, N.M., U.S. (klō′vĭs)	96	34.24N	103.11W
Cluj-Napoca, Rom.	142	46.46N	23.34E
Clun, r., Eng., U.K. (klŭn)	144a	52.25N	2.56W
Cluny, Fr. (klü-nē′)	156	46.27N	4.40E
Clutha, r., N.Z. (klōō′thȧ)	203a	45.52S	169.30E
Clwyd, co., Wales, U.K.	144a	53.01N	2.59W
Clyde, Ks., U.S.	111	39.34N	97.23W
Clyde, Oh., U.S.	98	41.15N	83.00W
Clyde, r., Scot., U.K.	150	55.35N	3.50W
Clyde, Firth of, b., Scot., U.K. (fûrth ŏv klīd)	150	55.28N	5.01W
Côa, r., Port. (kô′ä)	158	40.28N	6.55W
Coacalco, Mex. (kō-ä-käl′kō)	119a	19.37N	99.06W
Coachella, Canal, can., Ca., U.S. (kō′chĕl-lȧ)	108	33.15N	115.25W
Coahuayana, Río de, r., Mex. (rē′ō-dĕ-kō-ä-wä-yä′nä)	118	19.00N	103.33W
Coahuayutla, Mex. (kō′ä-wī-yōōt′lä)	118	18.19N	101.44W
Coahuila, state, Mex. (kō-ä-wē′lä)	116	27.30N	103.00W
Coal City, Il., U.S. (kōl sĭ′tĭ)	101a	41.17N	88.17W
Coalcomán, Río de, r., Mex. (rē′ō-dĕ-kō-äl-kō-män′)	118	18.45N	103.15W
Coalcomán, Sierra de, mts., Mex.	118	18.30N	102.45W
Coalcomán de Matamoros, Mex.	118	18.46N	103.10W
Coaldale, Can. (kōl′dāl)	87	49.43N	112.37W
Coalgate, Ok., U.S. (kōl′gāt)	111	34.44N	96.13W
Coal Grove, Oh., U.S. (kōl grōv)	98	38.20N	82.40W
Coal Hill Park, rec., China	240b	39.56N	116.23E
Coalinga, Ca., U.S. (kō-ȧ-lĭŋ′gȧ)	108	36.09N	120.23W
Coalville, Eng., U.K. (kōl′vĭl)	144a	52.43N	1.21W
Coamo, P.R. (kō-ä′mō)	117b	18.05N	66.21W
Coari, Braz. (kō-är′ē)	130	4.06S	63.10W
Coast Mountains, mts., N.A. (kōst)	84	54.10N	128.00W
Coast Ranges, mts., U.S.	96	41.28N	123.30W
Coatepec, Mex. (kō-ä-tā-pĕk)	118	19.23N	98.44W
Coatepec, Mex.	119	19.26N	96.56W
Coatepec, Mex.	119a	19.08N	99.25W
Coatepeque, El Sal.	120	13.56N	89.30W
Coatepeque, Guat. (kō-ä-tā-pā′kā)	120	14.40N	91.52W
Coatesville, Pa., U.S. (kōts′vĭl)	99	40.00N	75.50W
Coatetelco, Mex. (kō-ä-tā-tĕl′kō)	118	18.43N	99.17W
Coaticook, Can. (kō′tĭ-kŏŏk)	91	45.10N	71.55W
Coatlinchán, Mex. (kô-ä-tlē′n-chä′n)	119a	19.26N	98.52W
Coats, i., Can. (kōts)	85	62.23N	82.11W
Coats Land, reg., Ant.	219	74.00S	30.00W
Coatzacoalcos, Mex.	116	18.09N	94.26W
Coatzacoalcos, r., Mex.	119	17.40N	94.41W
Coba, hist., Mex. (kô′bä)	120a	20.23N	87.23W
Cobalt, Can. (kō′bôlt)	85	47.21N	79.40W
Cobán, Guat. (kō-bän′)	116	15.28N	90.19W
Cobar, Austl.	203	31.28S	145.50E
Cobberas, Mount, mtn., Austl. (cŏ-bẽr-ăs)	204	36.45S	148.15E
Cobequid Mountains, mts., Can.	92	45.35N	64.10W
Cobh, Ire. (kôv)	142	51.52N	8.09W
Cobham, Eng., U.K.	235	51.23N	0.24E
Cobija, Bol. (kô-bē′hä)	130	11.12S	68.49W
Cobourg, Can. (kō′bŏorgh)	85	43.55N	78.05W
Cobre, r., Jam. (kō′brā)	122	18.05N	77.00W
Coburg, Austl.	201a	37.45S	144.58E
Coburg, Ger. (kō′bōōrg)	154	50.16N	10.57E
Cocentaina, Spain (kō-thän-tä-ē′nȧ)	159	38.44N	0.27W
Cochabamba, Bol.	130	17.24S	66.09W
Cochin, India (kō-chĭn′)	187	9.58N	76.19E
Cochinos, Bahía, b., Cuba (bä-ē′ä-kô-chē′nōs)	122	22.05N	81.10W
Cochinos Banks, bk.	122	22.20N	76.15W
Cochiti Indian Reservation, I.R., N.M., U.S.	109	35.37N	106.20W
Cochran, Ga., U.S. (kŏk′răn)	114	32.23N	83.23W
Cochrane, Can.	83e	51.11N	114.28W
Cochrane, Can. (kŏk′rän)	85	49.01N	81.06W
Cockburn, i., Can. (kŏk-bûrn)	90	45.55N	83.25W
Cockeysville, Md., U.S. (kŏk′ĭz-vĭl)	100e	39.30N	76.40W
Cockfosters, neigh., Eng., U.K.	235	51.39N	0.09W
Cockrell Hill, Tx., U.S. (kŏk′rĕl)	107c	32.44N	96.53W
Coco, r., N.A.	117	14.55N	83.45W
Coco, Cayo, i., Cuba (kä′-yō-kô′kô)	122	22.30S	78.30W
Coco, Isla del, i., C.R. (ē′s-lä-dĕl-kô-kô)	116	5.33N	87.02W
Cocoa, Fl., U.S. (kō′kō)	115a	28.21N	80.44W
Cocoa Beach, Fl., U.S.	115a	28.20N	80.35W
Cocolí, Pan. (kō-kō′lē)	116a	8.58N	79.36W
Coconino, Plateau, plat., Az., U.S. (kō kō nē′nō)	109	35.45N	112.28W
Cocos (Keeling) Islands, is., Oc. (kō′kôs) (kē′lĭng)	3	11.50S	90.50E
Coco Solito, Pan. (kô-kô-sŏ-lē′tô)	116a	9.21N	79.53W
Cocotá, neigh., Braz.	234c	22.49S	43.11W
Cocula, Mex. (kō-kōō′lä)	118	20.23N	103.47W
Cocula, r., Mex.	118	18.17N	99.45W
Cod, Cape, pen., Ma., U.S.	97	41.42N	70.15W
Codajás, Braz. (kō-dä-häzh′)	130	3.44S	62.09W
Codera, Cabo, c., Ven. (kä′bô-kō-dĕ′rä)	131b	10.35N	66.06W
Codogno, Italy (kô-dō′nyō)	160	45.08N	9.43E
Codrington, Antig. (kŏd′rĭng-tŭn)	121b	17.39N	61.49W
Cody, Wy., U.S. (kō′dĭ)	105	44.31N	109.02W
Coelho da Rocha, Braz.	132b	22.47S	43.23W
Coemba, Ang.	216	12.08S	18.05E
Coesfeld, Ger. (kûs′fĕld)	157c	51.56N	7.10E
Coeur d'Alene, Id., U.S. (kûr dȧ-lān′)	96	47.43N	116.35W
Coeur d'Alene, r., Id., U.S.	104	47.26N	116.35W
Coeur d'Alene Indian Reservation, I.R., Id., U.S.	104	47.18N	116.45W
Coeur d'Alene Lake, l., Id., U.S.	104	47.32N	116.39W
Coffeyville, Ks., U.S. (kŏf′ĭ-vĭl)	97	37.01N	95.38W
Coff's Harbour, Austl.	204	30.20S	153.10E
Cofimvaba, S. Afr. (cäfĭm′vä-bȧ)	213c	32.01S	27.37E
Coghinas, r., Italy (kŏ′gē-näs)	160	40.31N	9.00E
Cognac, Fr. (kôn-yak′)	147	45.41N	0.22W
Cohasset, Ma., U.S. (kō-hăs′ĕt)	93a	42.14N	70.48W
Cohoes, N.Y., U.S. (kō-hōz′)	99	42.50N	73.40W
Coig, r., Arg. (kô′ēk)	132	51.15N	71.00W
Coimbatore, India (kō-ēm-bȧ-tôr′)	183	11.03N	76.56E
Coimbra, Port. (kō-ēm′brä)	142	40.14N	8.23W
Coín, Spain (kō-ēn′)	158	36.40N	4.45W
Coina, Port. (kō-ē′nȧ)	159b	38.35N	9.03W
Coina, r., Port. (kô′y-nä)	159b	38.35N	9.02W
Coipasa, Salar de, pl., Bol. (sä-lä′r-dĕ-koi-pä′-sä)	130	19.12S	69.13W
Coixtlahuaca, Mex. (kō-ēks′tlä-wä′kä)	119	17.42N	97.17W
Cojedes, dept., Ven. (kō-kĕ′dĕs)	131b	9.50N	68.21W
Cojimar, Cuba (kō-hē-mär′)	123a	23.10N	82.19W
Cojutepeque, El Sal. (kō-hō-tĕ-pā′kā)	120	13.45N	88.50W
Cokato, Mn., U.S. (kō-kā′tō)	103	45.03N	94.11W
Cokeburg, Pa., U.S. (kōk bŭgh)	101e	40.06N	80.03W
Coker, Nig.	244d	6.29N	3.20E
Colāba, neigh., India	240e	18.54N	72.48E
Colac, Austl. (kŏ′lăc)	204	38.25S	143.40E
Colares, Port. (kō-lä′rĕs)	159b	38.47N	9.27W
Colatina, Braz. (kō-lä-tē′nä)	131	19.33S	40.42W
Colby, Ks., U.S. (kōl′bĭ)	110	39.23N	101.04W
Colchagua, prov., Chile (kōl-chá′gwä)	129b	34.42S	71.24W
Colchester, Eng., U.K. (kōl′chĕs-tẽr)	151	51.52N	0.50E
Coldblow, neigh., Eng., U.K.	235	51.26N	0.10E
Cold Lake, l., Can. (kōld)	88	54.33N	110.05W
Coldwater, Ks., U.S. (kōld′wô-tẽr)	110	37.14N	99.21W
Coldwater, Mi., U.S.	98	41.55N	85.00W
Coldwater, r., Ms., U.S.	114	34.25N	90.12W
Coldwater Creek, r., Tx., U.S.	110	36.10N	101.45W
Coleman, Tx., U.S. (kōl′mȧn)	112	31.50N	99.25W
Colenso, S. Afr. (kō-lĕnz′ō)	213c	28.48S	29.49E
Coleraine, N. Ire., U.K.	150	55.08N	6.40W
Coleraine, Mn., U.S. (kōl-rān′)	103	47.16N	93.29W
Coleshill, Eng., U.K. (kōlz′hĭl)	144a	52.30N	1.42W
Colfax, Ia., U.S. (kōl′făks)	103	41.40N	93.13W
Colfax, La., U.S.	113	31.31N	92.42W
Colfax, Wa., U.S.	104	46.53N	117.21W
Colhué Huapi, l., Arg. (kôl-wā′ōä′pē)	132	45.30S	68.45W
Coligny, S. Afr.	218d	26.20S	26.18E
Colima, Mex. (kōlē′mä)	116	19.13N	103.45W
Colima, state, Mex.	118	19.10N	104.00W
Colima, Nevado de, mtn., Mex. (nĕ-vä′dō-dĕ-kō-lē′mä)	116	19.30N	103.38W
Coll, i., Scot., U.K. (kŏl)	150	56.42N	6.23W
College, Ak., U.S.	95	64.43N	147.50W
College Park, Ga., U.S. (kŏl′ĕj)	100c	33.39N	84.27W
College Park, Md., U.S.	100e	38.59N	76.58W
College Point, neigh., N.Y., U.S.	228	40.47N	73.51W
Collegeville, Pa., U.S. (kŏl′ĕj-vĭl)	100f	40.11N	75.27W
Collie, Austl. (kŏl′ē)	202	33.20S	116.20E
Collier Bay, b., Austl. (kŏl-yẽr)	202	15.30S	123.30E
Collier Row, neigh., Eng., U.K.	235	51.36N	0.10E
Collingdale, Pa., U.S.	229b	39.55N	75.17W
Collingswood, N.J., U.S. (kŏl′ĭngz-wŏŏd)	100f	39.54N	75.04W
Collingwood, Austl.	243b	37.48S	145.00E
Collingwood, Can.	91	44.30N	80.20W
Collins, Ms., U.S. (kŏl′ĭns)	114	31.40N	89.34W
Collinsville, Il., U.S. (kŏl′ĭnz-vĭl)	107e	38.41N	89.59W
Collinsville, Ok., U.S.	111	36.21N	95.50W
Colmar, Fr. (kôl′mär)	147	48.03N	7.25E
Colmenar de Oreja, Spain (kôl-mā-när′dāō rä′hä)	158	40.06N	3.25W
Colmenar Viejo, Spain (kôl-mā-när′vyā′hō)	158	40.40N	3.46W
Colnbrook, Eng., U.K.	235	51.29N	0.31W
Colney Heath, Eng., U.K.	235	51.44N	0.15W
Colney Street, Eng., U.K.	235	51.42N	0.20W
Cologne, Ger.	142	50.56N	6.57E
Cologno Monzese, Italy	238c	45.32N	9.17E
Colombes, Fr.	237c	48.55N	2.15E
Colombia, Col. (kō-lôm′bē-ä)	130a	3.23N	74.48W
Colombia, nation, S.A.	130	3.30N	72.30W
Colombo, Sri L. (kō-lôm′bō)	183b	6.58N	79.52E
Colón, Arg. (kō-lōn′)	129c	33.55S	61.08W
Colón, Cuba (kō-lō′n)	122	22.45N	80.55W
Colón, Mex. (kō-lōn′)	118	20.46N	100.02W
Colón, Pan. (kō-lō′n)	117	9.22N	79.54W
Colón, Archipiélago de, is., Ec.	130	0.10S	87.45W
Colón, Montañas de, mts., Hond. (môn-tä′n-yäs-dĕ-kō-lō′n)	121	14.58N	84.39W
Colonail Park, Md., U.S.	229c	39.19N	76.45W
Colonia, N.J., U.S.	228	40.35N	74.18W
Colonia, Ur. (kō-lō′nē-ä)	132	34.27S	57.50W
Colonia, dept., Ur.	129c	34.08S	57.50W
Colonial Manor, N.J., U.S.	229b	39.51N	75.09W
Colonia Suiza, Ur. (kō-lō′nēä-sōē′zä)	129c	34.17S	57.15W
Colonna, Capo, c., Italy	161	39.02N	17.15E
Colonsay, i., Scot., U.K. (kŏl-ôn-sā′)	151	56.08N	6.08E
Coloradas, Lomas, Arg. (lō′mäs-kō-lō-rä′däs)	132	43.30S	68.00W
Colorado, state, U.S.	96	39.30N	106.55W
Colorado, r., N.A.	96	36.00N	113.30W
Colorado, r., Tx., U.S.	96	30.08N	97.33W
Colorado, Río, r., Arg.	132	38.30S	66.00W
Colorado City, Tx., U.S. (kŏl-ô-rä′dō sĭ′tĭ)	112	32.24N	100.50W
Colorado National Monument, rec., Co., U.S.	109	39.00N	108.40W
Colorado Plateau, plat., U.S.	96	36.20N	109.25W
Colorado River Aqueduct, aq., Ca., U.S.	108	33.38N	115.43W
Colorado River Indian Reservation, I.R., Az., U.S.	109	34.03N	114.02W
Colorados, Archipiélago de los, is., Cuba	122	22.25N	84.25W
Colorado Springs, Co., U.S. (kŏl-ô-rä′dō)	96	38.49N	104.48W
Colosseo, hist., Italy	239c	41.54N	12.29E
Colotepec, r., Mex. (kô-lô′tĕ-pĕk)	119	15.56N	96.57W

ăt; finăl; rāte; senāte; ärm; àsk; sofȧ; fâre; ch-choose; dh-as th in other; bē; ėvent; bĕt; recĕnt; cratẽr; g-gō; gh-guttural g; bĭt; ĭ-short neutral; rīde; ĸ-guttural k as ch in German ich;

PRONOUNCING INDEX

Colotlán – Coronel Oviedo 277

PLACE (Pronunciation)	PAGE	Lat. °′	Long. °′
Colotlán, Mex. (kô-lô-tlän′)	118	22.06N	103.14W
Colotlán, r., Mex.	118	22.09N	103.17W
Colquechaca, Bol. (kôl-kā-chä′kä)	130	18.47S	66.02W
Colstrip, Mt., U.S. (kōl′strip)	105	45.54N	106.38W
Colton, Ca., U.S. (kōl′tŭn)	107a	34.04N	117.20W
Columbia, Il., U.S. (kô-lŭm′bĭ-*a*)	107e	38.26N	90.12W
Columbia, Ky., U.S.	114	37.06N	85.15W
Columbia, Md., U.S.	100e	39.15N	76.51W
Columbia, Ms., U.S.	114	31.15N	89.49W
Columbia, Mo., U.S.	97	38.55N	92.19W
Columbia, Pa., U.S.	99	40.00N	76.25W
Columbia, S.C., U.S.	97	34.00N	81.00W
Columbia, Tn., U.S.	114	35.36N	87.02W
Columbia, r., N.A.	84	46.00N	120.00W
Columbia, Mount, mtn., Can.	87	52.09N	117.25W
Columbia City, In., U.S.	98	41.10N	85.30W
Columbia City, Or., U.S.	106c	45.53N	112.49W
Columbia Heights, Mn., U.S.	107g	45.03N	93.15W
Columbia Icefield, ice., Can.	87	52.08N	117.26W
Columbia Mountains, mts., N.A.	87	51.30N	118.30W
Columbiana, Al., U.S. (kô-ŭm-bĭ-ă′n*ă*)	114	33.10N	86.35W
Columbia University, pt. of i., N.Y., U.S.	228	40.48N	73.58W
Columbretes, is., Spain (kô-lo͞om-brĕ′tĕs)	159	39.54N	0.54E
Columbus, Ga., U.S. (kô-lŭm′b*ŭ*s)	97	32.29N	84.56W
Columbus, In., U.S.	98	39.15N	85.55W
Columbus, Ks., U.S.	111	37.10N	94.50W
Columbus, Ms., U.S.	114	33.30N	88.25W
Columbus, Mt., U.S.	105	45.39N	109.15W
Columbus, Ne., U.S.	102	41.25N	97.25W
Columbus, N.M., U.S.	109	31.50N	107.40W
Columbus, Oh., U.S.	97	40.00N	83.00W
Columbus, Tx., U.S.	113	29.44N	96.34W
Columbus, Wi., U.S.	103	43.20N	89.01W
Columbus Bank, bk. (kô-lŭm′bŭs)	123	22.05N	75.30W
Columbus Grove, Oh., U.S.	98	40.55N	84.05W
Columbus Point, c., Bah.	123	24.10N	75.15W
Colusa, Ca., U.S. (kô-lū′s*ă*)	108	39.12N	122.01W
Colville, Wa., U.S. (kōl′vĭl)	104	48.33N	117.53W
Colville, r., Ak., U.S.	95	69.00N	156.25W
Colville Indian Reservation, I.R., Wa., U.S.	104	48.15N	119.00W
Colville R, Wa., U.S.	104	48.25N	117.58W
Colvos Passage, strt., Wa., U.S. (kōl′vōs)	106a	47.24N	122.32W
Colwood, Can. (kŏl′wŏŏd)	106a	48.26N	123.30W
Colwyn, Pa., U.S.	229b	39.55N	75.15W
Comacchio, Italy (kô-mäk′kyō)	160	44.42N	12.12E
Comala, Mex. (kō-mä-lä′)	118	19.22N	103.47W
Comalapa, Guat. (kō-mä-lä′-pä)	120	14.43N	90.56W
Comalcalco, Mex. (kō-mäl-käl′kō)	119	18.16N	93.13W
Comanche, Ok., U.S. (kô-măn′chê)	111	34.20N	97.58W
Comanche, Tx., U.S.	112	31.54N	98.37W
Comanche Creek, r., Tx., U.S.	112	31.02N	102.47W
Comayagua, Hond. (kō-mä-yä′gwä)	116	14.24N	87.36W
Combahee, r., S.C., U.S. (kŏm-b*ă*-hē′)	115	32.42N	80.40W
Comer, Ga., U.S. (kŭm′ẽr)	114	34.02N	83.07W
Comete, Cape, c., T./C. Is. (kô-mā′tå)	123	21.45N	71.25W
Comilla, Bngl. (kô-mĭl′ä)	183	23.33N	91.17E
Comino, Cape, c., Italy (kô-mē′nō)	160	40.30N	9.48E
Comitán, Mex. (kô-mē-tän′)	116	16.16N	92.09W
Commencement Bay, b., Wa., U.S. (k*ŏ*-mĕns′m*ĕ*nt bā)	106a	47.17N	122.21W
Commentry, Fr. (kô-mäN-trē′)	156	46.16N	2.44E
Commerce, Ga., U.S. (kŏm′ẽrs)	114	34.10N	83.27W
Commerce, Ok., U.S.	111	36.57N	94.54W
Commerce, Tx., U.S.	111	33.15N	95.52W
Como, Austl.	243a	34.00S	151.04E
Como, Italy (kō′mō)	148	45.48N	9.03E
Como, Lago di, l., Italy (lä′gō-dē-kō′mō)	148	46.00N	9.30E
Comodoro Rivadavia, Arg.	132	45.47S	67.31W
Como-Est, Can.	83a	45.27N	74.08W
Comonfort, Mex. (kô-mōn-fô′rt)	118	20.43N	100.47W
Comorin, Cape, c., India (kŏ′mô-rĭn)	183b	8.05N	78.05E
Comoros, nation, Afr.	213	12.30S	42.45E
Comox, Can. (kō′mŏks)	86	49.40N	124.55W
Companario, Cerro, mtn., S.A. (sĕ′r-rô-kôm-pä-nä′ryô)	129b	35.54S	70.23W
Compans, Fr.	237c	49.00N	2.40E
Compiègne, Fr. (kôN-pyĕn′y′)	147	49.25N	2.49E
Comporta, Port. (kôm-pôr′t*ă*)	159b	38.24N	8.48W
Compostela, Mex. (kōm-pô-stā′lä)	118	21.14N	104.54W
Compton, Ca., U.S. (kŏmpt′t*ŭ*n)	107a	33.54N	118.14W
Comrat, Mol. (kôm-rät′)	167	46.17N	28.38E
Conakry, Gui. (kô-nà-krē′)	210	9.31N	13.43W
Conanicut, i., R.I., U.S. (kŏn′*ă*-nĭ-kŭt)	100b	41.34N	71.20W
Conasauga, r., Ga., U.S. (kô-nà)	114	34.40N	84.51W
Concarneau, Fr. (kôN-kär-nō′)	156	47.54N	3.52W
Concepción, Bol. (kôn-sĕp′syōn′)	131	15.47S	61.08W
Concepción, Chile	132	36.51S	72.59W
Concepción, Pan.	121	8.31N	82.38W
Concepción, Para.	132	23.29S	57.18W
Concepcion, Phil.	197a	15.19N	120.40E
Concepción, vol., Nic.	120	11.36N	85.43W
Concepción, r., Mex.	116	30.25N	112.20W
Concepción del Mar, Guat. (kôn-sĕp-syōn′dĕl mär′)	120	14.07N	91.23W
Concepción del Oro, Mex. (kôn-sĕp-syōn′ dĕl ō′rō)	116	24.39N	101.24W
Concepción del Uruguay, Arg. (kôn-sĕp-syô′n-dĕl-o͞o-ro͞o-gwī′)	132	32.31S	58.10W
Conception, i., Bah.	123	23.50N	75.05W
Conception, Point, c., Ca., U.S.	96	34.27N	120.28W
Conception Bay, b., Can. (kŏn-sĕp′sh*ŭ*n)	93	47.50N	52.50W
Conchalí, Chile	234b	33.24S	70.39W
Concho, r., Tx., U.S. (kŏn′chō)	112	31.34N	100.00W
Conchos, r., Mex. (kōn′chōs)	112	25.03N	99.00W
Conchos, r., Mex.	116	29.30N	105.00W
Concord, Austl.	243a	33.52S	151.06E
Concord, Can.	227c	43.48N	79.29W
Concord, Ca., U.S. (kŏŋ′k*ŏ*rd)	106b	37.58N	122.02W
Concord, Ma., U.S.	93a	42.28N	71.21W
Concord, N.H., U.S.	97	43.10N	71.30W
Concord, N.C., U.S.	115	35.23N	80.11W
Concordia, Arg. (kōn-kôr′dĭ-à)	132	31.18S	57.59W
Concordia, Col.	130a	6.04N	75.54W
Concordia, Mex. (kôn-kô′r-dyä)	118	23.17N	106.06W
Concordia, Ks., U.S.	111	39.32N	97.39W
Concord West, Austl.	243a	33.51S	151.05E
Concrete, Wa., U.S. (kŏn-′krēt)	104	48.33N	121.44W
Conde, Fr.	156	48.50N	0.36W
Conde, S.D., U.S. (kŏn-dē′)	102	45.10N	98.06W
Condega, Nic. (kŏn-dĕ′gä)	120	13.20N	86.27W
Condeúba, Braz. (kōn-dā-o͞o′bä)	131	14.47S	41.44W
Condom, Fr.	156	43.58N	0.22E
Condon, Or., U.S. (kŏn′d*ŭ*n)	104	45.14N	120.10W
Conecun, r., Al., U.S. (kô-nē′kū)	114	31.05N	86.52W
Conegliano, Italy (kō-nāl-yä′nō)	160	45.59N	12.17E
Conejos, r., Co., U.S. (kô-nā′hōs)	109	37.07N	106.19W
Conemaugh, Pa., U.S. (kŏn′ê-mô)	99	40.25N	78.50W
Coney Island, neigh., N.Y., U.S.	228	40.34N	74.00W
Coney Island, i., N.Y., U.S. (kō′nĭ)	100a	40.34N	73.27W
Conflans-Sainte-Honorine, Fr.	237c	48.59N	2.06E
Confolens, Fr. (kôN-fä-läN′)	156	46.01N	0.41E
Congaree, r., S.C., U.S. (kŏŋ-g*ă*-rē′)	115	33.53N	80.55W
Conghua, China (tsôŋ-hwä)	193	23.30N	113.40E
Congleton, Eng., U.K. (kŏŋ′g′l-t*ŭ*n)	144a	53.10N	2.13W
Congo, nation, Afr. (kŏn′gō)	212	3.00S	13.48E
Congo (Zaire), r., Afr. (kŏn′gō)	209	2.00S	17.00E
Congo, Serra do, mts., Ang.	216	6.25S	13.30E
Congo, The *see* Zaire, nation, Afr.	212	1.00S	22.15E
Congo Basin, basin, Zaire	209	2.47N	20.58E
Congress Heights, neigh., D.C., U.S.	229d	38.51N	77.00W
Conisbrough, Eng., U.K. (kŏn′ĭs-b*ŭ*r-ô)	144a	53.29N	1.13W
Coniston, Can.	91	46.29N	80.51W
Conklin, Can. (kŏŋk′lĭn)	87	55.38N	111.05W
Conley, Ga., U.S. (kŏn′lĭ)	100c	33.38N	84.19W
Conn, Lough, l., Ire. (lŏk kŏn)	150	53.56N	9.25W
Connacht, hist. reg., Ire. (cŏn′ât)	150	53.50N	8.45W
Connaughton, Pa., U.S.	229b	40.05N	75.19W
Conneaut, Oh., U.S. (kŏn-ê-ôt′)	98	41.55N	80.35W
Connecticut, state, U.S. (kŏ-nĕt′ĭ-k*ŭ*t)	97	41.40N	73.10W
Connecticut, r., U.S.	97	43.55N	72.15W
Connellsville, Pa., U.S. (kŏn′nĕlz-vĭl)	99	40.00N	79.40W
Connemara, mts., Ire. (kŏn-nê-má′rá)	150	53.30N	9.54W
Connersville, In., U.S. (kŏn′ẽrz-vĭl)	98	39.35N	85.10W
Connors Range, mts., Austl. (kŏn′n*ŏ*rs)	203	22.15S	149.00E
Conrad, Mt., U.S. (kŏn′răd)	105	48.11N	111.56W
Conrich, Can. (kŏn′rĭch)	83e	51.06N	113.51W
Conroe, Tx., U.S. (kŏn′rō)	113	30.18N	95.23W
Conselheiro Lafaiete, Braz.	131	20.40S	43.46W
Conshohocken, Pa., U.S. (kŏn-shô-hŏk′*ĕ*n)	100f	40.04N	75.18W
Consolação, neigh., Braz.	234d	23.33S	46.39W
Consolación del Sur, Cuba (kōn-sô-lä-syōn′)	122	22.30N	83.55W
Consolidated Main Reef Mines, quarry, S. Afr.	244b	26.11S	27.56E
Con Son, is., Viet.	196	8.30N	106.28E
Constance, Mount, mtn., Wa., U.S. (kŏn′st*ă*ns)	106a	47.46N	123.08W
Constanța, Rom. (kōn-stån′tsá)	142	44.12N	28.36E
Constantina, Spain (kōn-stän-tē′nä)	158	37.52N	5.39W
Constantine, Alg. (kôN-stäN′tēn′)	210	36.28N	6.38E
Constantine, Mi., U.S. (kŏn′st*ă*n-tēn)	98	41.50N	85.40W
Constitución, Chile (kōn′stĭ-to͞o-syōn′)	132	35.24S	72.25W
Constitución, neigh., Arg.	233d	34.37S	58.23W
Constitution, Ga., U.S. (kŏn-stĭ-tū′sh*ŭ*n)	100c	33.41N	84.20W
Contagem, Braz. (kōn-tá′zhĕm)	129a	19.54S	44.05W
Contepec, Mex. (kōn-tĕ-pĕk′)	118	20.04N	100.07W
Contreras, Mex. (kôn-trĕ′räs)	119a	19.18N	99.14W
Contwoyto, l., Can.	84	65.42N	110.50W
Converse, Tx., U.S. (kŏn′vẽrs)	107d	29.31N	98.17W
Conway, Ar., U.S. (kŏn′wā)	111	35.06N	92.27W
Conway, N.H., U.S.	99	44.00N	71.10W
Conway, S.C., U.S.	115	33.49N	79.01W
Conway, Wa., U.S.	106a	48.20N	122.20W
Conyers, Ga., U.S. (kŏn′yŏrz)	114	33.41N	84.01W
Cooch Behār, India (kōoch bê-här′)	183	26.25N	89.34E
Coogee, Austl.	243a	33.55S	151.16E
Cook, Cape, c., Can. (kŏŏk)	86	50.08N	127.55W
Cook, Mount, mtn., N.Z.	203a	43.27S	170.13E
Cook, Point, c., Austl.	243b	37.55S	144.48E
Cookeville, Tn., U.S. (kŏŏk′vĭl)	114	36.07N	85.30W
Cooking Lake, Can. (ko͝ok′ĭng)	83g	53.25N	113.08W
Cooking Lake, l., Can.	83g	53.25N	113.02W
Cook Inlet, b., Ak., U.S.	95	60.50N	151.38W
Cook Islands, dep., Oc.	2	20.00S	158.00W
Cooksmill Green, Eng., U.K.	235	51.44N	0.22E
Cook Strait, strt., N.Z.	203a	40.37S	174.15E
Cooktown, Austl. (kŏŏk′toun)	203	15.40S	145.20E
Cooleemee, N.C., U.S. (ko͞o-lē′mē)	115	35.50N	80.32W
Coolgardie, Austl. (ko͞ol-gär′dê)	202	31.00S	121.25E
Cooma, Austl. (ko͞o′mà)	203	36.22S	149.10E
Coonamble, Austl. (ko͞o-năm′b′l)	203	31.00S	148.30E
Coonoor, India	187	10.22N	76.15E
Coon Rapids, Mn., U.S. (kōōn)	107g	45.09N	93.17W
Cooper, Tx., U.S. (ko͞op′ẽr)	111	33.23N	95.40W
Cooper Center, Ak., U.S.	95	61.54N	15.30W
Coopersale Common, Eng., U.K.	235	51.42N	0.08E
Coopers Creek, r., Austl. (ko͞o′pẽrz)	203	27.32N	141.19E
Cooperstown, N.Y., U.S. (ko͞op′ẽrs-toun)	99	42.45N	74.55W
Cooperstown, N.D., U.S.	102	47.26N	98.07W
Coosa, Al., U.S. (ko͞o′s*ă*)	114	32.43N	86.25W
Coosa, r., U.S.	97	34.00N	86.00W
Coosawattee, r., Ga., U.S.	114	34.37N	84.45W
Coos Bay, Or., U.S. (ko͞os)	104	43.21N	124.12W
Coos Bay, b., Or., U.S.	104	43.19N	124.40W
Cootamundra, Austl. (kŏt*ă*-m*ŭ*nd′r*ă*)	204	34.25S	148.00E
Copacabana, Braz. (kô′pä-kà-bá′nä)	132b	22.57S	43.11W
Copalita, r., Mex. (kô-pä-lē′tä)	119	15.55N	96.06W
Copán, hist., Hond. (kō-pän′)	120	14.50N	89.10W
Copano Bay, b., Tx., U.S. (kō-pän′ō)	113	28.08N	97.25W
Copenhagen (København), Den.	142	55.43N	12.27E
Copiapó, Chile (kō-pyä-pō′)	132	27.16S	70.28W
Copley, Oh., U.S. (kŏp′lê)	101d	41.06N	81.38W
Copparo, Italy (kôp-pä′rō)	160	44.53N	11.50E
Coppell, Tx., U.S. (kŏp′pĕl)	107c	32.57N	97.00W
Copper, r., Ak., U.S. (kŏp′ẽr)	95	62.38N	145.00W
Copper Cliff, Can.	90	46.28N	81.04W
Copper Harbor, Mi., U.S.	103	47.27N	87.53W
Copperhill, Tn., U.S. (kŏp′ẽr hĭl)	114	35.00N	84.22W
Coppermine, Can. (kŏp′ẽr-mīn)	84	67.46N	115.19W
Coppermine, r., Can.	84	66.48N	114.59W
Copper Mountain, mtn., Ak., U.S.	86	55.14N	132.36W
Copperton, Ut., U.S. (kŏp′ẽr-t*ŭ*n)	107b	40.34N	112.06W
Coquilee, Or., U.S. (kô-kēl′)	104	43.11N	124.11W
Coquilhatville *see* Mbandaka, Zaire	212	0.04N	18.16E
Coquimbo, Chile (kô-kēm′bō)	132	29.58S	71.31W
Coquimbo, prov., Chile	129b	31.50S	71.05W
Coquitlam Lake, l., Can. (kō-kwĭt-l*ă*m)	106d	49.23N	122.44W
Corabia, Rom. (kô-rä′bĭ-*ă*)	149	43.45N	24.29E
Coracora, Peru (kō′rä-kō′rä)	130	15.12S	73.42W
Coral Gables, Fl., U.S.	115a	25.43N	80.14W
Coral Rapids, Can. (kŏr′ăl)	85	50.18N	81.49W
Coral Sea, sea, Oc. (kŏr′ăl)	203	13.30S	150.00E
Coralville Reservoir, res., Ia., U.S.	103	41.45N	91.50W
Corangamite, Lake, l., Austl. (cŏr-ăŋg′á-mīt)	204	38.05S	142.55E
Coraopolis, Pa., U.S. (kō-rä-ŏp′ô-lĭs)	101e	40.30N	80.09W
Corato, Italy (kō′rä-tô)	160	41.08N	16.28E
Corbeil-Essonnes, Fr. (kôr-bă′yĕ-sŏn′)	156	48.31N	2.29E
Corbett, Or., U.S. (kôr′bĕt)	106c	45.31N	122.17W
Corbie, Fr. (kôr-bē′)	156	49.55N	2.27E
Corbin, Ky., U.S. (kôr′bĭn)	114	36.55N	84.06W
Corby, Eng., U.K. (kôr′bĭ)	144a	52.29N	0.38W
Corcovado, mtn., Braz. (kôr-kô-vä′dô)	132b	22.57S	43.13W
Corcovado, Golfo, b., Chile (kôr-kô-vä′dhō)	132	43.40S	75.00W
Cordeiro, Braz. (kôr-dā′rō)	129a	22.03S	42.22W
Cordele, Ga., U.S. (kôr-dēl′)	114	31.55N	83.50W
Cordell, Ok., U.S. (kôr-dĕl′)	110	35.19N	98.58W
Córdoba, Arg. (kôr′dô-vä)	132	30.20S	64.03W
Córdoba, Mex. (kô′r-dô-bä)	116	18.53N	96.54W
Córdoba, Spain (kô′r-dô-bä)	158	37.55N	4.45W
Córdoba, prov., Arg. (kôr′dô-vä)	132	32.00S	64.00W
Córdoba, Sierra de, mts., Arg.	132	31.15S	64.30W
Cordova, Al., U.S. (kôr′dô-*ă*)	114	33.45N	86.22W
Cordova, Ak., U.S. (kôr′dô-vä)	96a	60.34N	145.38W
Cordova Bay, b., Ak., U.S.	86	54.55N	132.35W
Corfu *see* Kérkira, i., Grc.	142	39.33N	19.36E
Corigliano, Italy (kō-rê-lyä′nō)	160	39.35N	16.30E
Corinth *see* Kórinthos, Grc.	142	37.56N	22.54E
Corinth, Ms., U.S. (kŏr′ĭnth)	114	34.55N	88.30W
Corinto, Braz. (kô-rē′n-tō)	131	18.20S	44.16W
Corinto, Col.	130a	3.09N	76.12W
Corinto, Nic. (kōr-ĭn′to)	120	12.30N	87.12W
Corio, Austl.	201a	38.05S	144.22E
Corio Bay, b., Austl.	201a	38.07S	144.25E
Corisco, Isla de, i., Eq. Gui.	216	0.50N	8.40E
Cork, Ire. (kôrk)	142	51.54N	8.25W
Cork Harbour, b., Ire.	150	51.44N	8.15W
Corleone, Italy (kôr-lå-ō′nā)	160	37.48N	13.18E
Cormano, Italy	238c	45.33N	9.10E
Cormeilles-en-Parisis, Fr.	237c	48.59N	2.12E
Cormorant Lake, l., Can.	89	54.13N	100.47W
Cornelia, Ga., U.S. (kôr-nē′ly*ă*)	114	34.31N	83.30W
Cornelis, r., S. Afr. (kôr-nē′lĭs)	218d	27.48S	29.15E
Cornell, Ca., U.S. (kôr-nĕl′)	107a	34.06N	118.46W
Cornell, Wi., U.S.	103	45.10N	91.10W
Cornellá, Spain	238e	41.21N	2.05E
Corner Brook, Can. (kôr′nẽr)	85	48.57N	57.57W
Corner Inlet, b., Austl.	204	38.55S	146.45E
Corning, Ar., U.S. (kôr′nĭng)	111	36.26N	90.35W
Corning, Ia., U.S.	103	40.58N	94.40W
Corning, N.Y., U.S.	99	42.10N	77.05W
Corno, Monte, mtn., Italy (kôr′nō)	148	42.28N	13.37E
Cornwall, Bah.	122	25.55N	77.15W
Cornwall, Can. (kôrn′wôl)	91	45.05N	74.35W
Coro, Ven. (kō′rō)	130	11.22N	69.43W
Corocoro, Bol. (kō-rō-kō′rō)	130	17.15S	68.21W
Coromandel Coast, cst., India (kŏr-ô-man′dĕl)	183	13.30N	80.30E
Coromandel Peninsula, pen., N.Z.	205	36.50S	176.00E
Corona, Al., U.S. (kō-rō′n*ă*)	114	33.42N	87.28W
Corona, Ca., U.S.	107a	33.52N	117.34W
Coronada, Bahía de, b., C.R. (bä-ē′ä-dĕ-kō-rō-nä′dō)	121	8.47N	84.04W
Corona del Mar, Ca., U.S. (kô-rō′n*ă* dĕl mär)	107a	33.36N	117.53W
Coronado, Ca., U.S. (kŏr-ō-nä′dō)	108a	32.42N	117.12W
Coronation Gulf, b., Can. (kŏr-ō-nā′sh*ŭ*n)	84	68.07N	112.50W
Coronel, Chile (kō-rō-nĕl′)	132	37.00S	73.10W
Coronel Brandsen, Arg. (kŏ-rō-nĕl-brá′nd-sĕn)	129c	35.09S	58.15W
Coronel Dorrego, Arg. (kŏ-rō-nĕl-dŏr-rĕ′gō)	132	38.43S	61.16W
Coronel Oviedo, Para. (kŏ-rō-nĕl-ō-vĕē′dō)	132	25.28S	56.22W

ng-sing; ŋ-baŋk; N-nasalized n; nŏd; c*ŏ*mmit; ōld; ôbey; ôrder; oi-boil; fo͞od; o͝o-as oo in foot; ou-out; s-soft; sh-dish; th-thin; pūre; ůnite; ûrn; stŭd; circ*ŭ*s; ü-as in French tu; ′-indeterminate vowel.

278 Coronel Pringles-Crystal Beach

PLACE (Pronunciation)	PAGE	Lat. °′	Long. °′
Coronel Pringles, Arg. (kō-rō-nĕl-prēn'glĕs)	132	37.54S	61.22W
Coronel Suárez, Arg. (kō-rō-nĕl-swä'rās)	132	37.27S	61.49W
Corowa, Austl. (cŏr-ô*wă*)	204	36.02S	146.23E
Corozal, Belize (cŏr-ŏth-äl')	120a	18.25N	88.23W
Corpus Christi, Tx., U.S. (kôr'pŭs krĭs'tē)	96	27.48N	97.24W
Corpus Christi Bay, b., Tx., U.S.	113	27.47N	97.14W
Corpus Christi Lake, l., Tx., U.S.	112	28.08N	98.20W
Corral, Chile (kō-räl')	132	39.57S	73.15W
Corral de Almaguer, Spain (kō-räl'dā äl-mä-gâr')	158	39.45N	3.10W
Corralillo, Cuba (kō-rä-lē-yō)	122	23.00N	80.40W
Corregidor Island, i., Phil. (kō-rā-hē-dōr')	197a	14.21N	120.25E
Correntina, Braz. (kō-rĕn-tē-n*ă*)	131	13.18S	44.33W
Corrib, Lough, l., Ire. (lŏk kŏr'ĭb)	150	53.25N	9.19W
Corrientes, Arg. (kō-ryĕn'tās)	132	27.25S	58.39W
Corrientes, prov., Arg.	132	28.45S	58.00W
Corrientes, Cabo, c., Col. (kà'bō-kō-ryĕn'tās)	130	5.34N	77.35W
Corrientes, Cabo, c., Cuba (kà'bō-kôr-rē-ĕn'tĕs)	122	21.50N	84.25W
Corrientes, Cabo, c., Mex.	116	20.25N	105.41W
Corringham, Eng., U.K.	235	51.31N	0.28E
Corroios, Port.	238d	38.38N	9.09W
Corry, Pa., U.S. (kŏr'ĭ)	99	41.55N	79.40W
Corse, Cap, c., Fr. (kôrs)	147	42.59N	9.19E
Corsica, i., Fr. (kô'r-sē-kä)	142	42.10N	8.55E
Corsicana, Tx., U.S. (kôr-sĭ-kăn'*ă*)	96	32.06N	96.28W
Corsico, Italy	238c	45.26N	9.07E
Cortazar, Mex. (kôr-tä-zär)	118	20.30N	100.57W
Corte, Fr. (kôr'tā)	160	42.18N	9.10E
Cortegana, Spain (kôr-tā-gä'nä)	158	37.54N	6.48W
Corte Madera, Ca., U.S.	231b	37.55N	122.31W
Cortes, bldg., Spain	238b	40.25N	3.41W
Cortés, Ensenada de, b., Cuba (ĕn-sĕ-nä-dä-dĕ-kôr-tās')	122	22.05N	83.45W
Cortez, Co., U.S.	109	37.21N	108.35W
Cortland, N.Y., U.S. (kôrt'l*ă*nd)	99	42.35N	76.10W
Cortona, Italy (kôr-tō'nä)	160	43.16N	12.00E
Corubal, r., Gui.-B.	214	11.43N	14.40W
Coruche, Port. (kō-rōō'she)	158	38.58N	8.34W
Çoruh, r., Asia (chō-rōōk')	167	40.30N	41.10E
Çorum, Tur. (chō-rōōm')	182	40.34N	34.45E
Corunna, Mi., U.S. (kō-rŭn'*ă*)	98	43.00N	84.05W
Coruripe, Braz. (kō-rō-rē'pĭ)	131	10.09S	36.13W
Corvallis, Or., U.S. (kôr-văl'ĭs)	96	44.34N	123.17W
Corve, r., Eng., U.K. (kôr'vē)	144a	52.28N	2.43W
Corviale, neigh., Italy	239c	41.52N	12.25E
Corydon, In., U.S. (kŏr'ĭ-d*ŭ*n)	98	38.10N	86.05W
Corydon, Ia., U.S.	103	40.45N	93.20W
Corydon, Ky., U.S.	98	37.45N	87.40W
Cosamaloápan, Mex. (kō-sä-mä-lwä'pän)	119	18.21N	95.48W
Coscomatepec, Mex. (kôs'kōmä-tĕ-pĕk')	119	19.04N	97.03W
Cosenza, Italy (kō-zĕnt'sä)	149	39.18N	16.15E
Cosfanero, Canal de, strt., Arg.	233d	34.34S	58.22W
Coshocton, Oh., U.S. (kō-shŏk't*ŭ*n)	98	40.15N	81.55W
Cosigüina, vol., Nic.	120	12.59N	87.35W
Cosmoledo Group, is., Sey. (kŏs-mō-lā'dō)	213	9.42S	47.45E
Cosmopolis, Wa., U.S. (kŏz-mŏp'ō-lĭs)	104	46.58N	123.47W
Cosne-sur-Loire, Fr. (kōn-sür-lwär')	156	47.25N	2.57E
Cosoleacaque, Mex. (kō sō lā-ä-kä'kē)	119	18.01N	94.38W
Costa de Caparica, Port.	159b	38.40N	9.12W
Costa Mesa, Ca., U.S. (kŏs't*ă* mā's*ă*)	107a	33.39N	118.54W
Costa Rica, nation, N.A. (kŏs't*ă* rē'k*ă*)	117	10.30N	84.30W
Cosumnes, r., Ca., U.S. (kŏ-sŭm'nēz)	108	38.21N	121.17W
Cotabambas, Peru (kō-tä-bàm'bäs)	130	13.49S	72.17W
Cotabato, Phil. (kō-tä-bä'tō)	197	7.06N	124.13E
Cotaxtla, Mex. (kō-täs'tlä)	119	18.49N	96.22W
Cotaxtla, r., Mex.	119	18.54N	96.21W
Coteau-du-Lac, Can. (cō-tō'dü-läk)	83a	45.17N	74.11W
Coteau-Landing, Can.	83a	45.15N	74.13W
Coteaux, Haiti	123	18.15N	74.05W
Cote d'Ivoire (Ivory Coast), nation, Afr.	210	7.43N	6.30W
Côte d'Or, reg., Fr.	156	47.02N	4.35E
Côte-Saint-Luc, Can.	227b	45.28N	73.40W
Côte Visitation, neigh., Can.	227b	45.33N	73.36W
Cotija de la Paz, Mex. (kō-tē'-κä-dĕ-lä-pá'z)	118	19.46N	102.43W
Cotonou, Benin (kō-tō-nōō')	210	6.21N	2.26E
Cotopaxi, mtn., Ec. (kō-tō-păk'sē)	130	0.40S	78.26W
Cotorro, Cuba (kō-tôr-rō)	123a	23.03N	82.17W
Cotswold Hills, hills, Eng., U.K. (kŭtz'wōld)	150	51.35N	2.16W
Cottage City, Md., U.S.	229d	38.56N	76.57W
Cottage Grove, Mn., U.S. (kŏt'āj grōv)	107g	44.50N	92.52W
Cottage Grove, Or., U.S.	104	43.48N	123.04W
Cottbus, Ger. (kōt'bōōs)	147	51.47N	14.20E
Cottonwood, r., Mn., U.S. (kŏt'*ŭ*n-wŏod)	102	44.25N	95.35W
Cotulla, Tx., U.S. (kŏ-tŭl'l*ă*)	112	28.26N	99.14W
Coubert, Fr. (kōō-bâr')	157b	48.40N	2.43E
Coudersport, Pa., U.S. (kou'dērz-port)	99	41.45N	78.00W
Coudres, Île aux, i., Can.	92	47.17N	70.12W
Coulommiers, Fr. (kōō-lō-myā')	157b	48.49N	3.05E
Coulsdon, neigh., Eng., U.K.	235	51.19N	0.08W
Coulto, Serra do, mts., Braz. (sĕ'r-rä-dō-kō-ō'tō)	132b	22.33S	43.27W
Council Bluffs, Ia., U.S. (koun'sĭl blŭf)	97	41.16N	95.53W
Council Grove, Ks., U.S. (koun'sĭl grōv)	111	38.39N	96.30W
Coupeville, Wa., U.S. (kōōp'vĭl)	106a	48.13N	122.41W
Courantyne, r., S.A. (kôr'*ă*ntĭn)	131	4.28N	57.42W
Courbevoie, Fr.	237c	48.54N	2.15E
Courcelle, Fr.	237c	48.42N	2.06E
Courtenay, Can. (cōōrt-nā')	84	49.41N	125.00W
Courtleigh, Md., U.S.	229c	39.22N	76.46W
Courtry, Fr.	237c	48.55N	2.36E
Coushatta, La., U.S. (kou-shăt'*ă*)	113	32.02N	93.21W
Coutras, Fr. (kōō-trá')	156	45.02N	0.07W
Cova da Piedade, Port.	238d	38.40N	9.10W
Covelo, Ang.	216	12.06S	13.55E
Cove Neck, N.Y., U.S.	228	40.53N	73.31W
Coventry, Eng., U.K. (kŭv'ĕn-trĭ)	150	52.25N	1.29W
Covina, Ca., U.S. (kō-vē'n*ă*)	107a	34.06N	117.54W
Covington, Ga., U.S. (kŭv'ĭng-t*ŭ*n)	114	33.36N	83.50W
Covington, In., U.S.	98	40.10N	87.15W
Covington, Ky., U.S.	97	39.05N	84.31W
Covington, La., U.S.	113	30.30N	90.06W
Covington, Oh., U.S.	98	40.10N	84.20W
Covington, Ok., U.S.	111	36.18N	97.32W
Covington, Tn., U.S.	114	35.33N	89.40W
Covington, Va., U.S.	98	37.50N	80.00W
Cowal, Lake, l., Austl. (kou'ăl)	204	33.30S	147.10E
Cowan, l., Austl. (kou'*ă*n)	202	32.00S	122.30E
Cowan Heights, Ca., U.S.	232	33.47N	117.47W
Cowansville, Can.	91	45.13N	72.47W
Cow Creek, r., Or., U.S. (kou)	104	42.45N	123.35W
Cowes, Eng., U.K. (kouz)	150	50.43N	1.25W
Cowichan Lake, l., Can.	86	48.54N	124.20W
Cowley, neigh., Eng., U.K.	235	51.32N	0.29W
Cowlitz, r., Wa., U.S. (kou'lĭts)	104	46.30N	122.45W
Cowra, Austl. (kou'r*ă*)	204	33.50S	148.33E
Coxim, Braz. (kō-shēɴ')	131	18.32S	54.43W
Coxquihui, Mex. (kōz-kē-wē')	119	20.10N	97.34W
Cox's Bāzār, Bngl.	186	21.32N	92.00E
Coyaima, Col. (kō-yàē'mä)	130a	3.48N	75.11W
Coyame, Mex. (kō-yä'mā)	112	29.26N	105.05W
Coyanosa Draw, Tx., U.S. (kō yà-nō'sä)	112	30.55N	103.07W
Coyoacán, Mex. (kō-yō-à-kän')	118	19.21N	99.10W
Coyote, r., Ca., U.S. (kī'ōt)	106b	37.37N	121.57W
Coyuca de Benítez, Mex. (kō-yōō'kä dā bā-nē'tāz)	118	17.04N	100.06W
Coyuca de Catalán, Mex. (kō-yōō'kä dā kä-tä-län')	118	18.19N	100.41W
Coyutla, Mex. (kō-yōō'tlä)	119	20.13N	97.40W
Cozad, Ne., U.S. (kō'zăd)	110	40.53N	99.59W
Cozaddale, Oh., U.S. (kō-zăd-dāl)	101f	39.16N	84.09W
Cozoyoapan, Mex. (kō-zō-yō-ä-pá'n)	118	16.45N	98.17W
Cozumel, Mex. (kō-zōō-mĕ'l)	120a	20.31N	86.55W
Cozumel, Isla de, i., Mex. (ē's-lä-dĕ-kō-zōō-mĕ'l)	116	20.26N	87.10W
Crab Creek, r., Wa., U.S. (krăb)	104	46.47N	119.43W
Crab Creek, r., Wa., U.S.	104	47.21N	119.09W
Cradock, S. Afr. (kră'd*ŭ*k)	212	32.12S	25.38E
Crafton, Pa., U.S. (krăf't*ŭ*n)	101e	40.26N	80.04W
Craig, Co., U.S. (krāg)	105	40.32N	107.31W
Craighall Park, neigh., S. Afr.	244b	26.08S	28.01E
Craiova, Rom. (krá-yō'vá)	149	44.18N	23.50E
Cranberry, l., N.Y., U.S. (krăn'bĕr-ĭ)	99	44.10N	74.50W
Cranbourne, Austl.	201a	38.07S	145.16E
Cranbrook, Can. (krăn'brŏok)	84	49.31N	115.46W
Cranbury, N.J., U.S. (krăn'bē-rĭ)	100a	40.19N	74.31W
Crandon, Wi., U.S. (krăn'd*ŭ*n)	103	45.35N	88.55W
Crane Prairie Reservoir, res., Or., U.S.	104	43.50N	121.55W
Cranford, N.J., U.S.	228	40.39N	74.19W
Crank, Eng., U.K.	237a	53.29N	2.45W
Cranston, R.I., U.S. (krăns't*ŭ*n)	100b	41.46N	71.25W
Crater Lake, l., Or., U.S. (krā'tēr)	104	43.00N	122.08W
Crater Lake National Park, rec., Or., U.S.	104	42.58N	122.40W
Craters of the Moon National Monument, rec., Id., U.S. (krā'tēr)	105	43.28N	113.15W
Crateús, Braz. (krä-tå-ōōzh')	131	5.09S	40.35W
Crato, Braz. (krä'tō)	131	7.19S	39.13W
Crawford, Ne., U.S. (krô'fērd)	102	42.41N	103.25W
Crawford, Wa., U.S.	106c	45.49N	122.24W
Crawfordsville, In., U.S. (krô'fērdz-vĭl)	98	40.00N	86.55W
Crazy Mountains, mts., Mt., U.S. (krā'zĭ)	105	46.11N	110.25W
Crazy Woman Creek, r., Wy., U.S.	105	44.08N	106.40W
Crecy, S. Afr. (krĕ-sē)	218d	24.38S	28.52E
Crécy-en-Brie, Fr. (krā-sē'-ĕɴ-brē')	157b	48.52N	2.55E
Crécy-en-Ponthieu, Fr.	156	50.13N	1.48E
Credit, r., Can.	83d	43.41N	79.55W
Cree, l., Can. (krē)	84	57.35N	107.52W
Creekmouth, neigh., Eng., U.K.	235	51.31N	0.06E
Creighton, S. Afr. (cre-tŏn)	213c	30.02S	29.52E
Creighton, Ne., U.S. (krā't*ŭ*n)	102	42.27N	97.54W
Creil, Fr. (krĕ'y')	156	49.18N	2.28E
Crema, Italy (krā'mä)	160	45.21N	9.53E
Cremona, Italy (krā-mō'nä)	148	45.09N	10.02E
Crépy-en-Valois, Fr. (krā-pē'ĕɴ-vä-lwä')	157b	49.14N	2.53E
Cres, Cro. (tsrĕs)	160	44.58N	14.21E
Cres, i., Yugo.	160	44.50N	14.31E
Crescent Beach, Can.	106d	49.03N	122.58W
Crescent City, Ca., U.S. (krĕs'ĕnt)	104	41.46N	124.13W
Crescent City, Fl., U.S.	115	29.26N	81.35W
Crescent Lake, l., Fl., U.S. (krĕs'ĕnt)	115	29.33N	81.30W
Crescent Lake, l., Or., U.S.	104	43.25N	121.58W
Crescentville, neigh., Pa., U.S.	229b	40.02N	75.05W
Cresco, Ia., U.S. (krĕs'kō)	103	43.23N	92.07W
Cresskill, N.J., U.S.	228	40.57N	73.57W
Crested Butte, Co., U.S. (krĕst'ĕd būt)	109	38.50N	107.00W
Crest Haven, Md., U.S.	229d	39.02N	76.59W
Crestline, Ca., U.S. (krĕst-līn)	107a	34.15N	117.17W
Crestline, Oh., U.S.	98	40.50N	82.40W
Crestmore, Ca., U.S. (krĕst'môr)	107a	34.02N	117.23W
Creston, Can. (krĕs't*ŭ*n)	84	49.06N	116.31W
Creston, Ia., U.S.	103	41.04N	94.22W
Creston, Oh., U.S.	101d	40.59N	81.54W
Crestview, Fl., U.S. (krĕst'vū)	114	30.44N	86.35W
Crestwood, Il., U.S.	231a	41.39N	87.44W
Crestwood, Ky., U.S. (krĕst'wŏod)	101h	38.20N	85.28W
Crestwood, Mo., U.S.	107e	38.33N	90.23W
Crete, Il., U.S. (krēt)	101a	41.26N	87.38W
Crete, Ne., U.S.	111	40.38N	96.56W
Crete, i., Grc.	142	35.15N	24.30E
Créteil, Fr.	237c	48.48N	2.28E
Creus, Cabo de, c., Spain (kä'-bō-dĕ-krĕ-ōōs)	159	42.16N	3.18E
Creuse, r., Fr. (krûz)	156	46.51N	0.49E
Creve Coeur, Mo., U.S. (krēv kŏr)	107e	38.40N	90.27W
Crevillente, Spain (krâ-vē-lyĕn'tâ)	159	38.12N	0.48W
Crewe, Eng., U.K. (krōō)	150	53.06N	2.27W
Crewe, Va., U.S.	115	37.09N	78.08W
Crimean Peninsula *see* Kryms'kyy pivostriv, pen., Ukr.	167	45.18N	33.30E
Crimmitschau, Ger. (krĭm'ĭt-shou)	154	50.49N	12.22E
Cripple Creek, Co., U.S. (krĭp''l)	110	38.44N	105.12W
Crisfield, Md., U.S. (krĭs-fēld)	99	38.00N	75.50W
Cristal, Monts de, mts., Gabon	216	0.50N	10.30E
Cristina, Braz. (krĕs-tē'-nä)	129a	22.13S	45.15W
Cristóbal Colón, Pico, mtn., Col. (pē'kō-krēs-tô'bäl-kō-lôn')	130	11.00N	74.00W
Cristo Redentor, Estatua do, hist., Braz.	234c	22.57S	43.13W
Crişul Alb, r., Rom. (krē'shōōl ălb)	155	46.20N	22.15E
Crna, r., Yugo. (ts'r'ná)	161	41.03N	21.46E
Crna Gora (Montenegro), hist. reg., Yugo.	161	42.55N	18.52E
Črnomelj, Slvn. (ch'r'nō-māl')	160	45.35N	15.11E
Croatia, nation, Eur.	160	45.24N	15.18E
Crockenhill, Eng., U.K.	235	51.23N	0.10E
Crockett, Ca., U.S. (krŏk'ĕt)	106b	38.03N	122.14W
Crockett, Tx., U.S.	113	31.19N	95.28W
Crofton, Md., U.S.	100e	39.01N	76.43W
Crofton, Ne., U.S.	102	42.44N	97.32W
Croissy-Beaubourg, Fr.	237c	48.50N	2.40E
Croissy-sur-Seine, Fr.	237c	48.53N	2.09E
Croix, Lac la, l., N.A. (läk lä krōō-ä')	103	48.19N	91.53W
Croker, i., Austl. (krō'k*ă*)	202	10.45S	132.25E
Cromer, Austl.	243a	33.44S	151.17E
Cronenberg, neigh., Ger.	236	51.12N	7.08E
Cronton, Eng., U.K.	237a	53.23N	2.46W
Cronulla, Austl. (krō-nŭl'*ă*)	201b	34.03S	151.09E
Crooked, i., Bah.	123	22.45N	74.10W
Crooked, l., Can.	93	48.25N	56.05W
Crooked, r., Can.	87	54.30N	122.55W
Crooked, r., Or., U.S.	104	44.07N	120.30W
Crooked Creek, r., Il., U.S. (krōōk'ĕd)	111	40.21N	90.49W
Crooked Island Passage, strt., Bah.	123	22.40N	74.50W
Crookston, Mn., U.S. (krŏoks't*ŭ*n)	102	47.44N	96.35W
Crooksville, Oh., U.S. (krŏoks'vĭl)	98	39.45N	82.05W
Crosby, Eng., U.K.	144a	53.30N	3.02W
Crosby, Mn., U.S. (krôz'bĭ)	103	46.29N	93.58W
Crosby, N.D., U.S.	102	48.55N	103.18W
Crosby, Tx., U.S.	113a	29.55N	95.04W
Crosby, neigh., S. Afr.	244b	26.12N	27.59E
Crosne, Fr.	237c	48.43N	2.28E
Cross, l., La., U.S.	113	32.33N	93.58W
Cross, r., Nig.	215	5.35N	8.05E
Cross City, Fl., U.S.	114	29.55N	83.25W
Crossett, Ar., U.S. (krôs'ĕt)	111	33.08N	92.00W
Cross Lake, l., Can.	84	54.45N	97.30W
Cross River Reservoir, res., N.Y., U.S. (krôs)	100a	41.14N	73.34W
Cross Sound, strt., Ak., U.S. (krŏs)	95	58.12N	137.20W
Crosswell, Mi., U.S. (krŏz'wĕl)	98	43.15N	82.35W
Crotch, l., Can.	91	44.55N	76.55W
Crotone, Italy (krō-tō'nĕ)	161	39.05N	17.08E
Croton Falls Reservoir, res., N.Y., U.S. (krōt*ŭ*n)	100a	41.22N	73.44W
Croton-on-Hudson, N.Y., U.S. (krō't*ŭ*n-ŏn hŭd's*ŭ*n)	100a	41.12N	73.53W
Crouse Run, r., Pa., U.S.	230b	40.35N	79.58W
Crow, l., Can.	103	49.13N	93.29W
Crow Agency, Mt., U.S.	105	45.36N	107.27W
Crow Creek, r., Co., U.S.	110	41.08N	104.25W
Crow Creek Indian Reservation, I.R., S.D., U.S.	102	44.17N	99.17W
Crow Indian Reservation, I.R., Mt., U.S. (krō)	105	45.26N	108.12W
Crowle, Eng., U.K. (kroul)	144a	53.36N	0.49W
Crowley, La., U.S. (krou'lē)	113	30.13N	92.22W
Crown Mountain, mtn., Can. (kroun)	106d	49.24N	123.05W
Crown Mountain, mtn., V.I.U.S.	117c	18.22N	64.58W
Crown Point, In., U.S. (kroun point')	101a	41.25N	87.22W
Crown Point, N.Y., U.S.	99	44.00N	73.25W
Crows Nest, Austl.	243a	33.50S	151.12E
Crowsnest Pass, p., Can.	87	49.39N	114.45W
Crow Wing, r., Mn., U.S.	103	46.42N	94.48W
Crow Wing, r., Mn., U.S. (krō)	103	44.50N	94.01W
Crow Wing, North Fork, r., Mn., U.S.	103	45.16N	94.28W
Crow Wing, South Fork, r., Mn., U.S.	103	44.59N	94.42W
Croxley Green, Eng., U.K.	235	51.39N	0.27W
Croydon, Austl.	201a	37.48S	145.17E
Croydon, Austl. (kroi'd*ŭ*n)	203	18.15S	142.15E
Croydon, Eng., U.K.	147	51.22N	0.06W
Croydon, Pa., U.S.	100f	40.05N	74.55W
Crozet, Îles, is., Afr. (krō-zĕ')	3	46.20S	51.30E
Cruces, Cuba (krōō'sås)	122	22.20N	80.20W
Cruces, Arroyo de, r., Mex. (är-rō'yō-dĕ-krōō'sĕs)	112	26.17N	104.32W
Cruillas, Mex. (krōō-ēl'yäs)	112	24.45N	98.31W
Crum Lynne, Pa., U.S.	229b	39.52N	75.20W
Cruz, Cabo, c., Cuba (ká'-bō-krōōz)	117	19.50N	77.45W
Cruz, Cayo, i., Cuba (kä'yō-krōōz)	122	22.15N	77.50W
Cruz Alta, Braz. (krōōz äl'tä)	132	28.41S	54.02W
Cruz del Eje, Arg. (krōō's-dĕl-ĕ-kĕ)	132	30.46S	64.45W
Cruzeiro, Braz. (krōō-zā'rō)	129a	22.36S	44.57W
Cruzeiro do Sul, Braz. (krōō-zā'rō dō sōōl)	130	7.34S	72.40W
Crysler, Can.	83c	45.13N	75.09W
Crystal Beach, Can.	230a	42.52N	79.04W

PRONOUNCING INDEX

Crystal City–Dania 279

PLACE (Pronunciation)	PAGE	Lat. °′	Long. °′
Crystal City, Tx., U.S. (krĭs′tăl sĭ′tĭ)	112	28.40N	99.50W
Crystal Falls, Mi., U.S. (krĭs′tăl fôls)	103	46.06N	88.21W
Crystal Lake, Il., U.S. (krĭs′tăl lăk)	101a	42.15N	88.18W
Crystal Springs, Ms., U.S. (krĭs′tăl sprĭngz)	114	31.58N	90.20W
Crystal Springs, oasis, Ca., U.S.	106b	37.31N	122.26W
Csömör, Hung.	239g	47.33N	19.14E
Csongrád, Hung. (chôn′gräd)	155	46.42N	20.09E
Csorna, Hung. (chôr′nä)	155	47.39N	17.11E
Cúa, Ven. (kōō′ä)	131b	10.10N	66.54W
Cuajimalpa, Mex. (kwä-hē-mäl′pä)	119a	19.21N	99.18W
Cuale, Sierra del, mts., Mex. (sē-ĕ′r-rä-dĕl-kwá′lĕ)	118	20.20N	104.58W
Cuamato, Ang. (kwä-mä′tō)	216	17.05S	15.09E
Cuamba, Moz.	217	14.49S	36.33E
Cuando, Ang. (kwän′dō)	216	16.32S	22.07E
Cuando, r., Afr.	212	14.30S	20.00E
Cuangar, Ang.	216	17.36S	18.39E
Cuango, r., Afr.	212	9.00S	18.00E
Cuanza, r., Ang. (kwän′zä)	212	9.45S	15.00E
Cuarto, r., Arg.	132	33.00S	63.25W
Cuatro Caminos, Cuba (kwä′trô-kä-mē′nôs)	123a	23.01N	82.13W
Cuatro Ciénegas, Mex. (kwä′trō syā′nå-gäs)	112	26.59N	102.03W
Cuauhtemoc, Mex. (kwä-ōō-tē-mōk′)	119	15.43N	91.57W
Cuautepec, Mex. (kwä-ōō-tē-pĕk)	118	16.41N	99.04W
Cuautepec, Mex.	118	20.01N	98.19W
Cuautepec el Alto, Mex.	233a	19.34N	99.08W
Cuautitlán, Mex. (kwä-ōō-tēt-län′)	119a	19.40N	99.12W
Cuautla, Mex. (kwä-ōō′tlä)	118	18.47N	98.57W
Cuba, Port. (kōō′bá)	158	38.10N	7.55W
Cuba, nation, N.A. (kū′bȧ)	117	22.00N	79.00W
Cubagua, Isla, i., Ven. (ē′s-lä-kōō-bä′gwä)	131b	10.48N	64.10W
Cubango (Okavango), r., Afr. (kōō-bäŋ′gō)	212	17.10S	18.20E
Cub Hills, hills, Can. (kŭb)	88	54.20N	104.30W
Cucamonga, Ca., U.S. (kōō-kȧ-mŏŋ′gȧ)	107a	34.05N	117.35W
Cuchi, Ang.	212	14.40S	16.50E
Cuchillo Parado, Mex. (kōō-chē′lyō pä-rä′dō)	112	29.26N	104.52W
Cuchumatanes, Sierra de los, mts., Guat.	120	15.35N	91.10W
Cúcuta, Col. (kōō′kōō-tä)	130	7.56N	72.30W
Cudahy, Wi., U.S. (kŭd′ȧ-hĭ)	101a	42.57N	87.52W
Cuddalore, India (kŭd ȧ-lōr′)	183	11.49N	79.46E
Cuddapah, India (kŭd′ȧ-pä)	183	14.31N	78.52E
Cudham, neigh., Eng., U.K.	235	51.19N	0.05E
Cue, Austl. (kū)	202	27.30S	118.10E
Cuéllar, Spain (kwā′lyär′)	158	41.24N	4.15W
Cuenca, Ec. (kwĕn′kä)	130	2.52S	78.54W
Cuenca, Spain	148	40.05N	2.07W
Cuenca, Sierra de, mts., Spain (sē-ĕ′r-rä-dē-kwĕ′n-kä)	158	40.02N	1.50W
Cuencame, Mex. (kwĕn-kä-mā′)	112	24.52N	103.42W
Cuerámaro, Mex. (kwā-rä′mä-rō)	118	20.39N	101.44W
Cuernavaca, Mex. (kwĕr-nä-vä′kä)	116	18.55N	99.15W
Cuero, Tx., U.S. (kwā′rō)	113	29.05N	97.16W
Cuetzalá del Progreso, Mex. (kwĕt-zä-lä dĕl prō-grā′sō)	118	18.07N	99.51W
Cuetzalan del Progreso, Mex.	119	20.02N	97.33W
Cuevas del Almanzora, Spain (kwĕ′väs-dĕl-äl-män-zō-rä)	148	37.19N	1.54W
Cuffley, Eng., U.K.	235	51.42N	0.07W
Cuglieri, Italy (kōō-lyā′rē)	160	40.11N	8.37E
Cuicatlán, Mex. (kwē-kä-tlän′)	119	17.46N	96.57W
Cuigezhuang, China	240b	40.01N	116.28E
Cuilapa, Guat. (kò-ē-lä′pä)	120	14.16N	90.20W
Cuilo (Kwilu), r., Afr.	216	9.15S	19.30E
Cuito, r., Ang. (kōō-ē-′tō)	212	14.45S	19.00E
Cuitzeo, Mex. (kwēt′zā-ō)	118	19.57N	101.11W
Cuitzeo, Laguna de, l., Mex. (lä-ō′nä-dē-kwēt′zā-ō)	118	19.58N	101.05W
Cul de Sac, pl., Haiti (kōō′l-dĕ-sä′k)	123	18.35N	72.05W
Culebra, i., P.R. (kōō-lā′brä)	117b	18.19N	65.32W
Culebra, Sierra de la, mts., Spain (sē-ĕ′r-rä-dĕ-lä-kōō-lĕ-brä)	158	41.52N	6.21W
Culemborg, Neth.	145a	51.57N	5.14E
Culfa, Azer.	168	38.58N	45.38E
Culgoa, r., Austl. (kŭl-gō′ȧ)	203	29.21S	147.00E
Culiacán, Mex. (kōō-lyä-ká′n)	116	24.45N	107.30W
Culion, Phil. (kōō-lē-ōn′)	196	11.43N	119.58E
Cúllar de Baza, Spain (kōō′l-yär-dē-bá′zä)	158	37.36N	2.35W
Cullera, Spain (kōō-lyā′rä)	148	39.12N	0.15W
Cullinan, S. Afr. (kŏ′lĭ-nán)	218d	25.41S	28.32E
Cullman, Al., U.S. (kŭl′măn)	114	34.10N	86.50W
Culmore, Va., U.S.	229d	38.51N	77.08W
Culpeper, Va., U.S. (kŭl′pĕp-ẽr)	99	38.30N	77.55W
Culross, Can. (kŭl′rôs)	83f	49.43N	97.54W
Culver, In., U.S. (kŭl′vẽr)	98	41.15N	86.25W
Culver City, Ca., U.S.	107a	34.00N	118.23W
Culverstone Green, Eng., U.K.	235	51.20N	0.21E
Cumaná, Ven.	130	10.28N	64.10W
Cumberland, Can. (kŭm′bẽr-lănd)	83c	45.31N	75.25W
Cumberland, Md., U.S.	97	39.40N	78.40W
Cumberland, Wa., U.S.	106a	47.17N	121.55W
Cumberland, Wi., U.S.	103	45.31N	92.01W
Cumberland, r., U.S.	114	36.45N	85.33W
Cumberland, Lake, res., Ky., U.S.	97	36.55N	85.20W
Cumberland Islands, is., Austl.	203	20.20S	149.46E
Cumberland Peninsula, pen., Can.	85	65.59N	64.05W
Cumberland Plateau, plat., U.S.	114	35.25N	85.30W
Cumberland Sound, strt., Can.	85	65.27N	65.44W
Cundinamarca, dept., Col. (kōōn-dē-nä-mä′r-ká)	130a	4.57N	74.27W

PLACE (Pronunciation)	PAGE	Lat. °′	Long. °′
Cunduacán, Mex. (kòn-dōō-á-kän′)	119	18.04N	93.23W
Cunene (Kunene), r., Afr.	212	17.05S	12.35E
Cuneo, Italy (kōō′nā-ō)	160	44.24N	7.31E
Cunha, Braz. (kōō′nyá)	129a	23.05S	44.56W
Cunnamulla, Austl. (kŭn-ȧ-mŭl-ȧ)	203	28.00S	145.55E
Cupula, Pico, mtn., Mex. (pē′kō-kōō′pōō-lä)	116	24.45N	111.10W
Cuquío, Mex. (kōō-kē′ō)	118	20.55N	103.03W
Curaçao, i., Neth. Ant. (kōō-rä-sä′ō)	130	12.12N	68.58W
Curacautín, Chile (kä-rä-käōō-tē′n)	132	38.25S	71.53W
Curaumilla, Punta, c., Chile (kōō-rou-mē′lyä)	129b	33.05S	71.44W
Curepto, Chile (kōō-rĕp-tô)	129b	35.06S	72.02W
Curitiba, Braz. (kōō-rē-tē′bá)	131	25.20S	49.15W
Curly Cut Cays, is., Bah.	122	23.40N	77.40W
Currais Novos, Braz. (kōōr-rä′ēs nō-vōs)	131	6.02S	36.39W
Curran, Can. (kū-răN′)	83c	45.30N	74.59W
Current, i., Bah. (kŭ-rĕnt)	122	25.20N	76.50W
Current, r., Mo., U.S. (kûr′ĕnt)	111	37.18N	91.21W
Currie, Mount, mtn., S. Afr. (kŭ-rē)	213c	30.28S	29.23E
Currituck Sound, strt., N.C., U.S. (kûr′ĭ-tŭk)	115	36.27N	75.42W
Curtis, Ne., U.S. (kûr′tĭs)	110	40.36N	100.29W
Curtis, i., Austl.	203	23.38S	151.43E
Curtis B, Md., U.S.	229c	39.13N	76.35W
Curtisville, Pa., U.S. (kûr′tĭs-vĭl)	101e	40.38N	79.50W
Ćurug, Yugo. (chōō′rŏg)	161	45.27N	20.03E
Curunga, Ang.	216	12.51S	21.12E
Curupira, Serra, mts., S.A. (sĕr′rȧ kōō-rōō-pē′rȧ)	130	1.00N	65.30W
Cururupu, Braz. (kōō-rŏ-rŏ-pōō′)	131	1.40S	44.56W
Curvelo, Braz. (kŏr-vĕl′ō)	131	18.47S	44.14W
Cusano Milanino, Italy	238c	45.33N	9.11E
Cusco, Peru	130	13.36S	71.52W
Cushing, Ok., U.S. (kŭsh′ĭng)	111	35.58N	96.46W
Custer, S.D., U.S. (kŭs′tẽr)	102	43.46N	103.36W
Custer, Wa., U.S.	106d	48.55N	122.39W
Custer Battlefield National Monument, rec., Mt., U.S. (kŭs′tẽr băt′'l-fēld)	105	45.44N	107.15W
Cut Bank, Mt., U.S. (kŭt bănk)	105	48.38N	112.19W
Cuthbert, Ga., U.S. (kŭth′bẽrt)	114	31.47N	84.48W
Cuttack, India (kŭ-tăk′)	183	20.38N	85.53E
Cutzamala, r., Mex. (kōō-tzä-mä-lä′)	118	18.57N	100.41W
Cutzamalá de Pinzón, Mex. (kōō-tzä-mä-lä′dē-pēn-zō′n)	118	18.28N	100.36W
Cuvo, r., Ang. (kōō′vō)	212	11.00S	14.30E
Cuxhaven, Ger. (kŏks′hä-fĕn)	146	53.51N	8.43E
Cuxton, Eng., U.K.	235	51.22N	0.27E
Cuyahoga, r., Oh., U.S. (kī-ȧ-hō′gȧ)	101d	41.22N	81.38W
Cuyahoga Falls, Oh., U.S.	101d	41.08N	81.29W
Cuyahoga Heights, Oh., U.S.	229a	41.26N	81.39W
Cuyapaire Indian Reservation, I.R., Ca., U.S. (kū-yà-pâr)	108	32.46N	116.20W
Cuyo Islands, is., Phil. (kōō′yō)	196	10.54N	120.08E
Cuyotenango, Guat. (kōō-yō-tē-näŋ′gō)	120	14.30N	91.35W
Cuyuni, r., S.A. (kōō-yōō′nē)	131	6.40N	60.44W
Cuyutlán, Mex. (kōō-yōō-tlän′)	118	18.54N	104.04W
Cyclades *see* Kikládhes, is., Grc.	142	37.30N	24.45E
Cynthiana, Ky., U.S. (sĭn-thĭ-ăn′ȧ)	98	38.20N	84.20W
Cypress, Ca., U.S. (sī′prĕs)	107a	33.50N	118.03W
Cypress Hills, hills, Can.	88	49.40N	110.20W
Cypress Lake, l., Can.	88	49.28N	109.43W
Cyprus, nation, Asia (sī′prŭs)	182	35.00N	31.00E
Cyprus, North, nation, Asia	182	35.15N	33.40E
Cyrenaica *see* Barqah, hist. reg., Libya	211	31.09N	21.45E
Cyrildene, neigh., S. Afr.	244b	26.11S	28.06E
Czech Republic, nation, Eur.	142	50.00N	15.00E
Czersk, Pol. (chĕrsk)	155	53.47N	17.58E
Częstochowa, Pol. (chăN-stô κô′vá)	147	50.49N	19.10E

D

PLACE (Pronunciation)	PAGE	Lat. °′	Long. °′
Da'an, China (dä-än)	192	45.25N	124.22E
Dabakala, C. Iv. (dä-bä-kä′lä)	210	8.16N	4.36W
Daba Shan, mts., China (dä-bä shän)	188	32.25N	108.20E
Dabeiba, Col. (dä-bā′bä)	130a	7.01N	76.16W
Dabie Shan, mts., China (dä-bĭē shän)	189	31.40N	114.50E
Dabnou, Niger	215	14.09N	5.22E
Dabob Bay, b., Wa., U.S. (dā′bŏb)	106a	47.50N	122.50W
Dabola, Gui.	214	10.45N	11.07W
Dąbrowa Białostocka, Pol.	155	53.37N	23.18E
Dacca *see* Dhaka, Bngl.	182	23.45N	90.29E
Dachang, China (dä-chäŋ)	191b	31.18N	121.25E
Dachangshan Dao, i., China (dä-chäŋ-shän dou)	190	39.21N	122.31E
Dachau, Ger. (dä′κou)	154	48.16N	11.26E
Dacotah, Can. (dȧ-kō′tȧ)	83f	49.52N	97.38W
Dadar, neigh., India	240e	19.01N	72.50E
Dade City, Fl., U.S. (dād)	115a	28.22N	82.09W
Dadeville, Al., U.S. (dăd′vĭl)	114	32.48N	85.44W
Dādra & Nagar Haveli, India	183	20.00N	73.00E
Dadu, r., China (dä-dōō)	193	29.20N	103.03E
Daet, mtn., Phil. (dä′āt)	197a	14.07N	122.59E
Dafoe, r., Can.	89	55.50N	95.50W
Dafter, Mi., U.S. (dăf′tẽr)	107k	46.21N	84.26W
Dagana, Sen. (dä-gä′nä)	210	16.31N	15.30W
Dagana, reg., Chad	215	12.20N	15.15E

PLACE (Pronunciation)	PAGE	Lat. °′	Long. °′
Dagang, China (dä-gäŋ)	191a	22.48N	113.24E
Dagda, Lat. (dȧg′dȧ)	153	56.04N	27.30E
Dagenham, Eng., U.K. (dăg′ĕn-ăm)	144b	51.32N	0.09E
Dagestan, state, Russia (dä-gĕs-tän′)	167	43.40N	46.10E
Daggafontein, S. Afr.	244b	26.18S	28.28E
Daggett, Ca., U.S. (dăg′ĕt)	108	34.50N	116.52W
Dagu, China (dä-gōō)	192	39.00N	117.42E
Dagu, r., China	190	36.29N	120.06W
Dagupan, Phil. (dä-gōō′pän)	197a	16.02N	120.20E
Daheishan Dao, i., China (dä-hā-shän dou)	190	37.57N	120.37E
Dahīrpur, neigh., India	240d	28.43N	77.12E
Dahl, Ger. (däl)	157c	51.18N	7.33E
Dahlak Archipelago, is., Erit.	211	15.45N	40.30E
Dahlem, neigh., Ger.	238a	52.28N	13.17E
Dahlerau, Ger.	236	51.13N	7.19E
Dahlwitz, Ger.	238a	52.30N	13.38E
Dahomey *see* Benin, nation, Afr.	210	8.00N	2.00E
Dahra, Libya	184	29.34N	17.50E
Daibu, China (dī-bōō)	190	31.22N	119.29E
Daigo, Japan (dī-gō)	195b	34.57N	135.49E
Daimiel Manzanares, Spain (dī-myĕl′män-zä-nä′rĕs)	158	39.05N	3.36W
Dairen *see* Dalian, China	188	38.54N	121.35E
Dairy, r., Or., U.S. (dâr′ĭ)	106c	45.33N	123.04W
Dai-Sen, mtn., Japan (dī′sĕn′)	195	35.22N	133.35E
Dai-Tenjo-dake, mtn., Japan (dī-tĕn′jō dä-κä)	195	36.21N	137.38E
Daiyun Shan, mtn., China (dī-yòn shän)	193	25.40N	118.08E
Dajabón, Dom. Rep. (dä-κä-bō′n)	123	19.35N	71.40W
Dajarra, Austl. (dȧ-jăr′ȧ)	202	21.45S	139.30E
Dakar, Sen. (dȧ-kär′)	210	14.40N	17.26W
Dakhla, W. Sah.	210	23.45N	16.04W
Dakouraoua, Niger	215	13.58N	6.15E
Dakovica, Yugo.	161	42.33N	20.28E
Dalälven, r., Swe.	142	60.26N	15.50E
Dalby, Austl. (dôl′bē)	203	27.10S	151.15E
Dalcour, La., U.S. (dăl-kour)	100d	29.49N	89.59W
Dale, Nor. (dä′lē)	152	60.35N	5.55E
Dale Hollow Lake, res., Tn., U.S. (dāl hŏl′ō)	97	36.33N	85.03W
Dalemead, Can. (dä′lē-mēd)	83e	50.53N	113.38W
Dalen, Nor. (dä′lĕn)	152	59.28N	8.01E
Daleside, S. Afr. (dāl′sīd)	218d	26.30S	28.03E
Dalesville, Can. (dālz′vĭl)	83a	45.42N	74.23W
Daley Waters, Austl. (dā lē)	202	16.15N	133.30E
Dalhart, Tx., U.S. (dăl härt)	110	36.04N	102.32W
Dalhousie, Can. (dăl-hōō′zē)	92	48.04N	66.23W
Dali, China	188	26.00N	100.08E
Dali, China	188	35.00N	109.38E
Dali, China (dä-lē)	191a	23.07N	113.06E
Dalian, China (lů-dä)	189	38.54N	121.35E
Dalian Wan, b., China (dä-lĭĕn wän)	190	38.55N	121.50E
Dalías, Spain (dä-lē′ás)	158	36.49N	2.50W
Dall, i., Ak., U.S. (dăl)	95	54.50N	133.10W
Dallas, Or., U.S. (dăl′lás)	104	44.55N	123.20W
Dallas, S.D., U.S.	102	43.13N	99.34W
Dallas, Tx., U.S.	96	32.45N	96.48W
Dalles Dam, Or., U.S.	104	45.36N	121.08W
Dallgow, Ger.	238a	52.32N	13.05E
Dall Island, i., Ak., U.S.	86	54.50N	132.55W
Dalmacija, hist. reg., Yugo. (dăl-mä′tsē-yä)	160	43.25N	16.37E
Dalnerechensk, Russia	165	46.07N	133.21E
Daloa, C. Iv.	214	6.53N	6.27W
Dalroy, Can. (dăl′roi)	83e	51.07N	113.39W
Dalrymple, Mount, mtn., Austl. (dăl′rĭm-p'l)	203	21.14S	148.46E
Dalton, S. Afr. (dôl′tŏn)	213c	29.21S	30.41E
Dalton, Eng., U.K.	237a	53.34N	2.46W
Dalton, Ga., U.S. (dôl′tŭn)	114	34.46N	84.58W
Daly, r., Austl. (dā′lĭ)	202	14.15S	131.15E
Daly City, Ca., U.S. (dā′lē)	106b	37.42N	122.27W
Damān, India	183	20.32N	72.53E
Damanhūr, Egypt (dä-män-hōōr′)	211	30.59N	30.31E
Damar, Pulau, i., Indon.	197	7.15S	129.15E
Damara, Cen. Afr. Rep.	215	4.58N	18.42E
Damaraland, hist. reg., Nmb. (dă′nȧ-rȧ-lănd)	212	22.15S	16.15E
Damas Cays, is., Bah. (dä′mäs)	122	23.50N	79.50W
Damascus, Syria	182	33.30N	36.18E
Damāvand, Qolleh-ye, mtn., Iran	182	36.05N	52.05E
Damba, Ang. (däm′bä)	212	6.41S	15.08E
Dâmbovița, r., Rom.	161	44.43N	25.41E
Dame Marie, Cap, c., Haiti (dām mȧrē′)	123	18.35N	74.50W
Dāmghān, Iran (dām-gän′)	182	35.50N	54.15E
Daming, China (dä-mĭŋ)	192	36.15N	115.09E
Dammartin-en-Goële, Fr. (dän-mär-tăN-äN-gō-ĕl′)	157b	49.03N	2.40E
Dampier, Selat, strt., Indon. (dăm′pēr)	197	0.40S	131.15E
Dampier Archipielago, is., Austl.	202	20.15S	116.25E
Dampier Land, reg., Austl.	202	17.30S	122.25E
Dan, r., N.C., U.S. (dán)	115	36.26N	79.40W
Dana, Mount, mtn., Ca., U.S.	108	37.54N	119.13W
Da Nang, Viet.	196	16.08N	108.22E
Danbury, Eng., U.K.	144b	51.42N	0.34E
Danbury, Ct., U.S. (dăn′bẽr-ĭ)	100a	41.23N	73.27W
Danbury, Tx., U.S.	113a	29.14N	95.22W
Dandenong, Austl. (dăn′dē-nông)	204	37.59S	145.13E
Dandong, China (dän-dôŋ)	189	40.10N	124.30E
Dane, r., Eng., U.K. (dān)	144a	53.11N	2.14W
Danea, Gui.	214	11.27N	13.12W
Danforth, Me., U.S.	92	45.38N	67.53W
Dan Gora, Nig.	215	11.30N	8.09E
Dangtu, China (däŋ-tōō)	193	31.35N	118.28E
Dani, Burkina	210	13.43N	0.10W
Dania, Fl., U.S. (dă′nĭ-á)	115a	26.01N	80.10W

ng-sing; ŋ-baŋk; N-nasalized n; nŏd; cŏmmit; ōld; ōbey; ôrder; oi-boil; fōōd; ŏŏ-as oo in foot; ou-out; s-soft; sh-dish; th-thin; pūre; ůnite; ûrn; stŭd; circŭs; ü-as in French tu; ′-indeterminate vowel.

280 Daniels–Derbyshire

PLACE (Pronunciation)	PAGE	Lat. °′	Long. °′
Daniels, Md., U.S.	229c	39.26N	77.03W
Danilov, Russia (dä'nê-lôf)	166	58.12N	40.08E
Danissa Hills, hills, Kenya	217	3.20N	40.55E
Dänizkänarı, Azer.	168	40.13N	49.33E
Dankov, Russia (däŋ'kôf)	166	53.17N	39.09E
Dannemora, N.Y., U.S. (dăn-ê-mō'rȧ)	99	44.45N	73.45W
Dannhauser, S. Afr. (dän'hou-zēr)	213c	28.07S	30.04E
Dansville, N.Y., U.S. (dănz'vĭl)	99	42.30N	77.40W
Danube, r., Eur.	142	43.00N	24.00E
Danube, Mouths of the, mth., Rom. (dăn'ūb)	163	45.13N	29.37E
Danvers, Ma., U.S. (dăn'vērz)	93a	42.34N	70.57W
Danville, Ca., U.S. (dăn'vĭl)	106b	37.49N	122.00W
Danville, Il., U.S.	98	40.10N	87.35W
Danville, In., U.S.	98	39.45N	86.30W
Danville, Ky., U.S.	98	37.35N	84.50W
Danville, Pa., U.S.	99	41.00N	76.35W
Danville, Va., U.S.	97	36.35N	79.24W
Danxian, China (dän shyĕn)	193	19.30N	109.38E
Danyang, China (dän-yäŋ)	190	32.01N	119.32E
Danzig see Gdańsk, Pol.	142	54.20N	18.40E
Danzig, Gulf of, b., Eur. (dȧn'tsĭk)	146	54.41N	19.01E
Daoxian, China (dou shyĕn)	193	25.35N	111.27E
Dapango, Togo	214	10.52N	0.12E
Daphnae, hist., Egypt	181a	30.43N	32.12E
Daqin Dao, i., China (dä-chyĭn dou)	190	38.18N	120.50E
Darabani, Rom. (dă-ră-băn'ĭ)	155	48.13N	26.38E
Daraj, Libya	210	30.12N	10.14E
Dār as-Salām, Egypt	244a	29.59N	31.13E
Darāw, Egypt (dȧ-rä'o͞o)	218b	24.24N	32.56E
Darbhanga, India (dŭr-bŭŋ'gä)	183	26.03N	85.09E
Darby, Pa., U.S. (där'bĭ)	100f	39.55N	75.16W
Darby, i., Bah.	122	23.50N	76.20W
Dardanelles see Çanakkale Boğazi, strt., Tur.	149	40.05N	25.50E
Dar es Salaam, Tan. (där ĕs sȧ-läm')	213	6.48S	39.17E
Dārfūr, hist. reg., Sudan (där-fo͞or')	211	13.21N	23.46E
Dargai, Pak. (dŭr-gä'ê)	186	34.35N	72.00E
Darien, Col. (dā-rĭ-ĕn')	130a	3.56N	76.30W
Darien, Ct., U.S. (dâ-rē-ĕn')	100a	41.04N	73.28W
Darién, Cordillera de, mts., Nic.	120	13.00N	85.42W
Darien, Serranía del, mts.	121	8.13N	77.28W
Darjeeling, India (dŭr-jē'lĭng)	183	27.05N	88.16E
Darling, r., Austl.	203	31.50S	143.20E
Darling Downs, reg., Austl.	203	27.22S	150.00E
Darling Range, mts., Austl.	202	30.30S	115.45E
Darlington, Eng., U.K. (där'lĭng-tŭn)	150	54.32N	1.35W
Darlington, S.C., U.S.	115	34.15N	79.52W
Darlington, Wi., U.S.	103	42.41N	90.06W
Darłowo, Pol. (där-lô'vô)	154	54.26N	16.23E
Darmstadt, Ger. (därm'shtät)	147	49.53N	8.40E
Darnah, Libya	211	32.44N	22.41E
Darnley Bay, b., Ak., U.S. (därn'lē)	95	70.00N	124.00W
Daroca, Spain (dä-rō-kä)	158	41.08N	1.24W
Dartford, Eng., U.K.	144b	51.27N	0.14E
Dartmoor, for., Eng., U.K. (därt'mo͞or)	150	50.35N	4.05W
Dartmouth, Can. (därt'mŭth)	85	44.40N	63.34W
Dartmouth, Eng., U.K.	150	50.33N	3.28W
Daru, Pap. N. Gui. (dä'ro͞o)	197	9.04S	143.21E
Daruvar, Cro. (där'o͞o-vär)	161	45.37N	17.16E
Darwen, Eng., U.K. (där'wĕn)	144a	53.42N	2.28W
Darwin, Austl. (där'wĭn)	202	12.25S	131.00E
Darwin, Cordillera, mts., Chile (kôr-dēl-yĕ'rä-där'wĕn)	132	54.40S	69.30W
Dash Point, Wa., U.S. (dăsh)	106a	47.19N	122.25W
Dasht, r., Pak. (dŭsht)	182	25.30N	62.30E
Dasol Bay, b., Phil. (dä-sōl')	197a	15.53N	119.40E
Datchet, Eng., U.K.	235	51.29N	0.34W
Datian Ding, mtn., China (dä-tĭĕn dĭŋ)	193	22.25N	111.20E
Datong, China (dä-tôŋ)	192	40.00N	113.30E
Dattapukur, India	186a	22.45N	88.32E
Datteln, Ger. (dät'tĕln)	157c	51.39N	7.20E
Datu, Tandjung, c., Asia	196	2.08N	110.15E
Datuan, China (dä-tůän)	191b	30.57N	121.43E
Daugava (Zapadnaya Dvina), r., Eur.	153	56.40N	24.40E
Daugavpils, Lat. (dä'ŏ-gäv-pēls)	166	55.52N	26.32E
Dauphin, Can. (dô'fĭn)	84	51.09N	100.00W
Dauphin Lake, l., Can.	89	51.17N	99.48W
Dāvangere, India	187	14.30N	75.55E
Davao, Phil. (dä'vä-ô)	197	7.05N	125.30E
Davao Gulf, b., Phil.	197	6.30N	125.45E
Davenport, Ia., U.S. (dăv'ĕn-pōrt)	97	41.34N	90.38W
Davenport, Wa., U.S.	104	47.39N	118.07W
Daveyton Location, S. Afr.	244b	26.09S	28.25E
David, Pan. (dȧ-vēdh')	117	8.27N	82.27W
David City, Ne., U.S. (dā'vĭd)	102	41.15N	97.10W
David-Gorodok, Bela. (dä-vēt' gô-rō'dôk)	167	52.02N	27.14E
Davis, Ok., U.S. (dā'vĭs)	111	34.34N	97.08W
Davis, W.V., U.S.	99	39.15N	79.25W
Davis Lake, l., Or., U.S.	104	43.38N	121.43W
Davis Mountains, mts., Tx., U.S.	112	30.45N	104.17W
Davis Strait, strt., N.A.	82	66.00N	60.00W
Davlekanovo, Russia	166	54.15N	55.05E
Davos, Switz. (dä'vōs)	154	46.47N	9.50E
Davyhulme, Eng., U.K.	237b	53.27N	2.22W
Dawa, r., Afr.	211	4.30N	40.30E
Dawāsir, Wādī ad, val., Sau. Ar.	182	20.48N	44.07E
Dawei, Myanmar	196	14.04N	98.19E
Dawen, r., China (dä-wŭn)	190	35.58N	116.53E
Dawley, Eng., U.K. (dô'lĭ)	144a	52.38N	2.28W
Dawna Range, mts., Myanmar (dô'nȧ)	196	17.02N	98.01E
Dawson, Can. (dô'sŭn)	84	64.04N	139.22W
Dawson, Ga., U.S.	114	31.45N	84.29W
Dawson, Mn., U.S.	102	44.54N	96.03W
Dawson, r., Austl.	203	24.20S	149.45E
Dawson Bay, b., Can.	89	52.55N	100.50W
Dawson Creek, Can.	84	55.46N	120.14W
Dawson Range, mts., Can.	95	62.15N	138.10W
Dawson Springs, Ky., U.S.	114	37.10N	87.40W
Dawu, China (dä-wo͞o)	190	31.33N	114.07E
Dawuji, China	240b	39.51N	116.30E
Dax, Fr. (dȧks)	147	43.42N	1.06W
Daxian, China (dä-shyĕn)	188	31.12N	107.30E
Daxing, China (dä-shyĭŋ)	192a	39.44N	116.19E
Dayiqiao, China (dä-yē-chyou)	190	31.43N	120.40E
Dayr az Zawr, Syria (dȧ-ērēz-zôr')	182	35.15N	40.01E
Dayton, Ky., U.S. (dā'tŭn)	101f	39.07N	84.28W
Dayton, N.M., U.S.	110	32.44N	104.23W
Dayton, Oh., U.S.	97	39.54N	84.15W
Dayton, Tn., U.S.	114	35.30N	85.00W
Dayton, Tx., U.S.	113	30.03N	94.53W
Dayton, Wa., U.S.	104	46.18N	117.59W
Daytona Beach, Fl., U.S. (dā-tō'nȧ)	97	29.11N	81.02W
Dayu, China (dä-yo͞o)	193	25.20N	114.20E
Da Yunhe (Grand Canal), can., China (dä yòn-hŭ)	189	35.00N	117.00E
Dayville, Ct., U.S. (dā'vĭl)	99	41.50N	71.55W
De Aar, S. Afr. (dē-är')	212	30.45S	24.05E
Dead, l., Mn., U.S. (dĕd)	102	46.28N	96.00W
Dead Sea, l., Asia	182	31.30N	35.30E
Deadwood, S.D., U.S. (dĕd'wòd)	96	44.23N	103.43W
Deal Island, Md., U.S. (dēl-ī'lănd)	99	38.10N	75.55W
Dean, r., Can. (dēn)	86	52.45N	125.30W
Dean Channel, strt., Can.	86	52.33N	127.13W
Deán Funes, Arg. (dĕ-ä'n-fo͞o-nĕs)	132	30.26S	64.12W
Dean Row, Eng., U.K.	237b	53.20N	2.11W
Dearborn, Mi., U.S. (dēr'bŭrn)	101b	42.18N	83.15W
Dearborn Heights, Mi., U.S.	230c	42.19N	83.14W
Dearg, Ben, mtn., Scot., U.K. (bĕn dŭrg)	150	57.48N	4.59W
Dease Strait, strt., Can. (dēz)	84	68.50N	108.20W
Death Valley, Ca., U.S.	108	36.18N	116.26W
Death Valley, val., Ca., U.S.	96	36.30N	117.00W
Death Valley National Monument, rec., Ca., U.S.	108	36.34N	117.00W
Debal'tseve, Ukr.	163	48.23N	38.29E
Debao, China (dŭ-bou)	188	23.18N	106.40E
Debar, Mac. (dĕ'bär) (dá'brä)	161	41.31N	20.32E
Dęblin, Pol. (dăN'blĭn)	155	51.34N	21.49E
Dębno, Pol. (dĕb-nô')	154	52.47N	13.43E
Debo, Lac, l., Mali	214	15.15N	4.40W
Debrecen, Hung. (dĕ'brĕ-tsĕn)	142	47.32N	21.40E
Debre Markos, Eth.	211	10.15N	37.45E
Debre Tabor, Eth.	211	11.57N	38.09E
Decatur, Al., U.S. (dē-kā'tŭr)	114	34.35N	87.00W
Decatur, Ga., U.S.	100c	33.47N	84.18W
Decatur, Il., U.S.	97	39.50N	88.59W
Decatur, In., U.S.	98	40.50N	84.55W
Decatur, Mi., U.S.	98	42.10N	86.00W
Decatur, Tx., U.S.	111	33.14N	97.33W
Decazeville, Fr. (dē-käz'vēl')	147	44.33N	2.16E
Deccan, plat., India (dĕk'ăn)	183	19.05N	76.40E
Deception Lake, l., Can.	88	56.33N	104.15W
Deception Pass, p., Wa., U.S. (dē-sĕp'shŭn)	106a	48.24N	122.44W
Děčín, Czech Rep. (dyĕ'chēn)	154	50.47N	14.14E
Decorah, Ia., U.S. (dē-kō'rȧ)	103	43.18N	91.48W
Dedenevo, Russia (dyĕ-dyĕ'nyĕ-vô)	172b	56.14N	37.31E
Dedham, Ma., U.S. (dĕd'ăm)	93a	42.15N	71.11W
Dedo do Deus, mtn., Braz. (dĕ-dô-dô-dĕ'o͞os)	132b	22.30S	43.02W
Dédougou, Burkina (dā-dô-go͞o')	210	12.38N	3.28W
Dee, r., U.K.	144a	53.15N	3.05E
Dee, r., Scot., U.K.	150	57.05N	2.25W
Deep, r., N.C., U.S. (dēp)	115	35.36N	79.32W
Deep Fork, r., Ok., U.S.	111	35.35N	96.42W
Deep River, Can.	91	46.06N	77.20W
Deepwater, Mo., U.S. (dep-wô-tēr)	111	38.15N	93.46W
Deer, i., Me., U.S.	92	44.07N	68.38W
Deerfield, Il., U.S. (dēr'fēld)	101a	42.10N	87.51W
Deer Island, Or., U.S.	106c	45.56N	122.51W
Deer Lake, Can.	85a	49.10N	57.25W
Deer Lake, l., Can.	89	52.40N	94.30W
Deer Lodge, Mt., U.S. (dēr lŏj)	105	46.23N	112.42W
Deer Park, Oh., U.S.	101f	39.12N	84.24W
Deer Park, Wa., U.S.	104	47.58N	117.28W
Deer River, Mn., U.S.	103	47.20N	93.49W
Dee Why, Austl.	243a	33.45S	151.17E
Dee Why Head, c., Austl.	243a	33.46S	151.19E
Dee Why Lagoon, b., Austl.	243a	33.45S	151.18E
Defiance, Oh., U.S. (dē-fī'ăns)	98	41.15N	84.20W
DeFuniak Springs, Fl., U.S. (dē fū'nĭ-ăk)	114	30.42N	86.06W
Deganga, India	186a	22.41N	88.41E
Degeh Bur, Eth.	218a	8.10N	43.25E
Deggendorf, Ger. (dĕ'ghĕn-dôrf)	154	48.50N	12.59E
Degollado, Mex. (dā-gô-lyä'dō)	118	20.27N	102.11W
DeGrey, r., Austl. (dē grā')	202	20.20S	119.25E
Degtyarsk, Russia (dĕg-ty'arsk)	172a	56.42N	60.05E
Dehiwala-Mount Lavinia, Sri L.	187	6.47N	79.55E
Dehra Dūn, India (dā'rŭ)	183	30.09N	78.07E
Dehua, China (dŭ-hwä)	193	25.30N	118.15E
Dej, Rom. (dāzh)	149	47.09N	23.53E
De Kalb, Il., U.S. (dē kălb')	98	41.54N	88.46W
Dekese, Zaire	216	3.27S	21.24E
Delacour, Can. (dĕ-lä-ko͞or')	83e	51.09N	113.45W
Delagua, Co., U.S. (dĕl-ä'gwä)	110	37.19N	104.42W
Delair, N.J., U.S.	229b	39.59N	75.03W
De Land, Fl., U.S. (dē lănd')	115	29.00N	81.19W
Delano, Ca., U.S. (dĕl'ȧ-nō)	108	35.47N	119.15W
Delano Peak, mtn., Ut., U.S.	96	38.25N	112.25W
Delavan, Wi., U.S. (dĕl'ȧ-văn)	103	42.39N	88.38W
Delaware, Oh., U.S. (dĕl'ȧ-wâr)	98	40.15N	83.05W
Delaware, state, U.S.	97	38.40N	75.30W
Delaware, r., U.S.	99	41.50N	75.20W
Delaware, r., Ks., U.S.	111	39.45N	95.47W
Delaware Bay, b., U.S.	97	39.05N	75.10W
Delaware Reservoir, res., Oh., U.S.	99	40.30N	83.05E
Delémont, Switz. (dē-lā-môN')	154	47.21N	7.18E
De Leon, Tx., U.S. (dē lē-ŏn')	112	32.06N	98.33W
Delft, Neth. (dĕlft)	151	52.01N	4.20E
Delfzijl, Neth.	151	53.20N	6.50E
Delgada, Punta, c., Arg. (po͞o'n-tä-dĕl-gä'dä)	132	43.46S	63.46W
Delgado, Cabo, c., Moz. (kȧ'bô-dĕl-gä'dō)	213	10.40S	40.35E
Delhi, India	183	28.54N	77.13E
Delhi, Il., U.S. (dĕl'hī)	107e	39.03N	90.16W
Delhi, La., U.S.	113	32.26N	91.29W
Delhi, state, India	183	28.30N	76.50E
Delhi Cantonment, India	240d	28.36N	77.08E
Delitzsch, Ger. (dā'lĭch)	154	51.32N	12.18E
Dellansjöarna, l., Swe.	152	61.57N	16.25E
Delles, Alg. (dĕ'lĕs')	210	36.59N	3.40E
Dell Rapids, S.D., U.S. (dĕl)	102	43.50N	96.43W
Dellwig, neigh., Ger.	236	51.29N	6.56E
Dellwood, Mn., U.S. (dĕl'wòd)	107g	45.05N	92.58W
Del Mar, Ca., U.S. (dĕl mär')	108a	32.57N	117.16W
Delmas, S. Afr. (dĕl'mȧs)	218d	26.08S	28.43E
Delmenhorst, Ger. (dĕl'mĕn-hôrst)	154	53.03N	8.38E
Del Norte, Co., U.S. (dĕl nôrt')	109	37.40N	106.25W
De-Longa, i., Russia	165	76.21N	148.56E
De Long Mountains, mts., Ak., U.S. (dē'lŏng)	95	68.38N	162.30W
Deloraine, Austl. (dĕ-lŭ-rān)	204	41.30S	146.40E
Delphi, In., U.S. (dĕl'fī)	98	40.35N	86.40W
Delphos, Oh., U.S. (dĕl'fŏs)	98	40.50N	84.20W
Delran, N.J., U.S.	229b	40.02N	74.58W
Delray Beach, Fl., U.S. (dĕl-rā')	115a	26.27N	80.05W
Del Rio, Tx., U.S. (dĕl rē'ō)	96	29.21N	100.52W
Delson, Can. (dĕl'sŭn)	83a	45.24N	73.32W
Delta, Co., U.S.	109	38.45N	108.05W
Delta, Ut., U.S.	109	39.20N	112.35W
Delta Beach, Can.	83f	50.10N	98.20W
Delvine, Alb. (dĕl'vē-nȧ)	161	39.58N	20.10E
Del Viso, Arg.	233d	34.26S	58.46W
Dëma, r., Russia (dyĕm'ä)	166	53.40N	54.30E
Demarest, N.J., U.S.	228	40.57N	73.58W
Demba, Zaire	216	5.30S	22.16E
Dembi Dolo, Eth.	211	8.46N	34.46E
Demidov, Russia (dzyĕ'mê-dô'f)	162	55.16N	31.32E
Deming, N.M., U.S. (dĕm'ĭng)	96	32.15N	107.45W
Demmeltrath, neigh., Ger.	236	51.11N	7.03E
Demmin, Ger. (dĕm'mēn)	154	53.54N	13.04E
Demnat, Mor. (dĕm-nät)	210	31.58N	7.03W
Demopolis, Al., U.S. (dē-mŏp'ō-lĭs)	114	32.30N	87.50W
Demotte, In., U.S. (dē'mŏt)	101a	41.12N	87.13W
Dempo, Gunung, mtn., Indon. (dĕm'pô)	196	4.04S	103.11E
Dem'yanka, r., Russia (dyĕm-yän'kä)	170	59.07N	72.58E
Demyansk, Russia (dyĕm-yänsk')	162	57.39N	32.26E
Denain, Fr. (dē-năN')	156	50.23N	3.21E
Denakil Plain, pl., Eth.	211	12.45N	41.01E
Denali National Park, rec., Ak., U.S.	96a	63.48N	153.02W
Denbigh, Wales, U.K. (dĕn'bĭ)	150	53.15N	3.25W
Dendermonde, Bel.	145a	51.02N	4.04E
Dendron, Va., U.S. (dĕn'drŭn)	115	37.02N	76.53W
Denenchōfu, neigh., Japan	242a	35.35N	139.41E
Denezhkin Kamen, Gora, mtn., Russia (dzyĕ-ŋĕ'zhkĕn kămĭēŋ)	172a	60.26N	59.35E
Denham, Mount, mtn., Jam.	117	18.20N	77.30W
Den Helder, Neth. (dĕn hĕl'dēr)	151	52.55N	5.45E
Denia, Spain (dā'nyä)	159	38.48N	0.06E
Deniliquin, Austl. (dĕ-nĭl'ĭ-kwĭn)	203	35.20S	144.52E
Denison, Ia., U.S. (dĕn'ĭ-sŭn)	102	42.01N	95.22W
Denison, Tx., U.S.	96	33.45N	97.02W
Denisovka, Kaz. (dĕ-nē'sof-kȧ)	169	52.26N	61.45E
Denizli, Tur. (dĕn-ĭz-lē')	149	37.40N	29.10E
Denklingen, Ger. (dĕn'klēn-gĕn)	157c	50.54N	7.40E
Denmark, S.C., U.S. (dĕn'märk)	115	33.18N	81.09W
Denmark, nation, Eur.	142	56.14N	8.30E
Denmark Strait, strt., Eur.	82	66.30N	27.00W
Dennilton, S. Afr. (dĕn-ĭl-tŭn)	218d	25.18S	29.13E
Dennison, Oh., U.S. (dĕn'ĭ-sŭn)	98	40.25N	81.20W
Denpasar, Indon.	196	8.35S	115.10E
Denshaw, Eng., U.K.	237b	53.35N	2.02W
Denton, Eng., U.K. (dĕn'tŭn)	144a	53.27N	2.07W
Denton, Md., U.S.	99	38.55N	75.50W
Denton, Tx., U.S.	111	33.12N	97.06W
D'Entrecasteaux, Point, c., Austl. (dăN-tr'kȧs-tō')	202	34.50S	114.45E
D'Entrecasteaux Islands, is., Pap. N. Gui. (dăN-tr'-kȧs-tō')	197	9.45S	152.00E
Denver, Co., U.S. (dĕn'vēr)	96	39.44N	104.59W
Deoli, India	186	25.52N	75.23E
De Pere, Wi., U.S. (dē pēr')	103	44.25N	88.04W
Depew, N.Y., U.S. (dē-pū')	101c	42.55N	78.43W
Deping, China (dŭ-pĭŋ)	190	37.28N	116.57E
Deptford, neigh., Eng., U.K.	235	51.28N	0.02W
Depue, Il., U.S. (dē pū)	98	41.15N	89.55W
De Queen, Ar., U.S. (dē kwēn')	111	34.02N	94.21W
De Quincy, La., U.S. (dē kwĭn'sĭ)	113	30.27N	93.27W
Dera, Lach, r., Afr. (läk dā'rä)	218a	0.45N	41.26E
Dera, Lak, r., Afr.	211	0.45N	41.30E
Dera Ghāzi Khān, Pak. (dā'rŭ gä-zē' ĸän')	183	30.09N	70.39E
Dera Ismāīl Khān, Pak. (dā'rŭ ĭs-mä-ēl' ĸän')	186	31.55N	70.51E
Derbent, Russia (dĕr-bĕnt')	167	42.00N	48.10E
Derby, Austl. (där'bē) (dûr'bē)	202	17.20S	123.40E
Derby, S. Afr. (där'bĭ)	218d	25.55S	27.02E
Derby, Eng., U.K. (där'bē)	147	52.55N	1.29W
Derby, Ct., U.S. (dûr'bē)	99	41.20N	73.05W
Derbyshire, co., Eng., U.K.	144a	53.11N	1.30W

ăt; finăl; rāte; senāte; ärm; ȧsk; sofȧ; fâre; ch-choose; dh-as th in other; bē; ėvent; bĕt; recĕnt; cratēr; g-gō; gh-guttural g; bĭt; ĭ-short neutral; rīde; ĸ-guttural k as ch in German ich;

PLACE (Pronunciation)	PAGE	Lat. °'	Long. °'
Derdepoort, S. Afr.	218d	24.39S	26.21E
Derendorf, neigh., Ger.	236	51.15N	6.48E
Derg, Lough, l., Ire. (lŏk dērg)	150	53.00N	8.09W
De Ridder, La., U.S. (dē rĭd′ēr)	113	30.50N	93.18W
Dermott, Ar., U.S. (dûr′mŏt)	111	33.32N	91.24W
Derne, neigh., Ger.	236	51.34N	7.31E
Derry, N.H., U.S. (dâr′ĭ)	93a	42.53N	71.22W
Derventa, Bos. (dĕr′ven-tȧ)	161	44.58N	17.58E
Derwent, r., Austl. (dĕr′wĕnt)	204	42.21S	146.30E
Derwent, r., Eng., U.K.	144a	52.54N	1.24W
Desagüe, Gran Canal del, can., Mex.	233a	19.29N	99.05W
Des Arc, Ar., U.S. (dāz ärk′)	111	34.59N	91.31W
Descalvado, Braz. (dĕs-käl-vȧ-dô)	129a	21.55S	47.37W
Descartes, Fr.	156	46.58N	0.42E
Deschambault Lake, l., Can.	88	54.40N	103.35W
Deschênes, Can.	83c	45.23N	75.47W
Deschenes, Lake, l., Can.	83c	45.25N	75.53W
Deschutes, r., Or., U.S. (dā-shōōt′)	104	44.25N	121.21W
Desdemona, Tx., U.S. (dĕz-dē-mō′nȧ)	112	32.16N	98.33W
Dese, Eth.	211	11.00N	39.51E
Deseado, Río, r., Arg. (rē-ō-dā-sä-ä′dhō)	132	46.50S	67.45W
Desirade Island, i., Guad. (dā-zē-räs′)	121b	16.21N	60.51W
De Smet, S.D., U.S. (dē smĕt′)	102	44.23N	97.33W
Des Moines, Ia., U.S. (dē moin′)	97	41.35N	93.37W
Des Moines, N.M., U.S.	110	36.42N	103.48W
Des Moines, Wa., U.S.	106a	46.24N	122.20W
Des Moines, r., U.S.	97	42.30N	94.20W
Desna, r., Eur. (dyĕs-nȧ′)	167	51.55N	31.45E
Desolación, i., Chile (dĕ-sô-lä-syō′n)	132	53.05S	74.00W
De Soto, Mo., U.S. (dē sō′tō)	111	38.07N	90.32W
Des Peres, Mo., U.S. (dĕs pĕr′ĕs)	107e	38.36N	90.26W
Des Plaines, Il., U.S. (dĕs plānz′)	101a	42.02N	87.54W
Des Plaines, r., U.S.	101a	41.39N	87.56W
Dessau, Ger. (dĕsou)	147	51.50N	12.15E
Detmold, Ger. (dĕt′mōld)	154	51.57N	8.55E
Detroit, Mi., U.S. (dē-troit′)	97	42.22N	83.10W
Detroit, Tx., U.S.	111	33.41N	95.16W
Detroit, r., Mi., U.S.	230c	42.06N	83.08W
Detroit Lake, res., Or., U.S.	104	44.42N	122.10W
Detroit Lakes, Mn., U.S. (dē-troit′lākz)	102	46.48N	95.51W
Detroit Metropolitan-Wayne County Airport, arpt., Mi., U.S.	230c	42.13N	83.22W
Detva, Slvk. (dyĕt′vȧ)	155	48.32N	19.21E
Deuil-la-Barre, Fr.	237c	48.59N	2.20E
Deurne, Bel.	145a	51.13N	4.27E
Deusen, neigh., Ger.	236	51.33N	7.26E
Deutsch Wagram, Aus.	145e	48.19N	16.34E
Deux-Montagnes, Can.	83a	45.33N	73.53W
Deux Montagnes, Lac des, l., Can.	83a	45.28N	74.00W
Deva, Rom. (dā′vä)	149	45.52N	22.52E
Dévaványa, Hung. (dā′vô-vän-yô)	155	47.01N	20.58E
Develi, Tur. (dĕ′vȧ-lē)	167	38.20N	35.10E
Deventer, Neth. (dĕv′ĕn-tēr)	151	52.14N	6.07E
Devils, r., Tx., U.S.	112	29.55N	101.10W
Devils Island see Diable, Île du, i., Fr. Gu.	131	5.15N	52.40W
Devils Lake, N.D., U.S.	96	48.10N	98.55W
Devils Lake, l., N.D., U.S. (dĕv″lz)	102	47.57N	99.04W
Devils Lake Indian Reservation, I.R., N.D., U.S.	102	48.08N	99.40W
Devils Postpile National Monument, rec., Ca., U.S.	108	37.42N	119.12W
Devils Tower National Monument, rec., Wy., U.S.	105	44.38N	105.07W
Devoll, r., Alb.	161	40.55N	20.10E
Devon, Can.	83g	53.23N	113.43W
Devon, S. Afr. (dĕv′ŭn)	218d	26.23S	28.47E
Devonport, Austl. (dĕv′ŭn-pôrt)	203	41.20S	146.30E
Devonport, N.Z.	203a	36.50S	174.45E
Devore, Ca., U.S. (dē-vôr′)	107a	34.13N	117.24W
Dewatto, Wa., U.S. (dē-wät′ō)	106a	47.27N	123.04W
Dewey, Ok., U.S. (dū′ĭ)	111	36.48N	95.55W
De Witt, Ar., U.S. (dē wĭt′)	111	34.17N	91.22W
De Witt, Ia., U.S.	103	41.46N	90.34W
Dewsbury, Eng., U.K. (dūz′bēr-ĭ)	144a	53.42N	1.39W
Dexter, Me., U.S. (dĕks′tēr)	92	45.01N	69.19W
Dexter, Mo., U.S.	111	36.46N	89.56W
Dezfūl, Iran	182	32.14N	48.37E
Dezhnëva, Mys, c., Russia (dyĕzh′nyif)	180	68.00N	172.00W
Dezhou, China (dŭ-jō)	192	37.28N	116.17E
Dháfni, Grc.	239d	38.01N	23.39E
Dhahran see Aẓ Ẓahrān, Sau. Ar.	182	26.13N	50.00E
Dhaka, Bngl. (dă′kä) (dăk′ȧ)	183	23.45N	90.29E
Dharamtar Creek, r., India	187b	18.49N	72.54E
Dharmavaram, India	187	14.32N	77.43E
Dhawalāgiri, mtn., Nepal	183	28.42N	83.31E
Dhenoúsa, i., Grc.	161	37.09N	25.53E
Dhībān, Jord.	181a	31.30N	35.46E
Dhidhimótikhon, Grc.	161	41.20N	26.27E
Dhodhekánisos (Dodecanese), is., Grc.	161	38.00N	26.10E
Dhule, India	183	20.58N	74.43E
Día, i., Grc. (dē′ä)	160a	35.27N	25.17E
Diable, Île du, i., Fr. Gu.	131	5.15N	52.40W
Diablo, Mount, mtn., Ca., U.S. (dyä′blō)	106b	37.52N	121.55W
Diablo Heights, Pan. (dyȧ′blō)	116a	8.58N	79.34W
Diablo Range, mts., Ca., U.S.	106b	37.47N	121.50W
Diablotins, Morne, mtn., Dom.	121b	15.31N	61.24W
Diaca, Moz.	217	11.30S	39.59E
Diaka, r., Mali	215	14.40N	5.00E
Diamantina, Braz.	131	18.14S	43.32W
Diamantina, r., Austl. (dī′man-tē′nȧ)	202	25.38S	139.53E
Diamantino, Braz. (dē-ȧ-män-tē′no)	131	14.22S	56.23W
Diamond Creek, Austl.	243b	37.41S	145.09E
Diamond Peak, mtn., Or., U.S.	104	43.32N	122.08W
Diana Bank, bk. (dī′ăn′ȧ)	123	22.30N	74.45W
Dianbai, China (dĭĕn-bī)	193	21.30N	111.20E
Dian Chi, l., China (dĭĕn chē)	188	24.58N	103.18E

PLACE (Pronunciation)	PAGE	Lat. °'	Long. °'
Diancun, China	240b	39.55N	116.14E
Dickinson, N.D., U.S. (dĭk′ĭn-sŭn)	96	46.52N	102.49W
Dickinson, Tx., U.S. (dĭk′ĭn-sŭn)	113a	29.28N	95.02W
Dickinson Bayou, Tx., U.S.	113a	29.26N	95.08W
Dickson, Tn., U.S. (dĭk′sŭn)	114	36.03N	87.24W
Dickson City, Pa., U.S.	99	41.25N	75.40W
Didcot, Eng., U.K. (dĭd′cŏt)	144b	51.35N	1.15W
Didiéni, Mali	214	13.53N	8.06W
Didsbury, neigh., Eng., U.K.	237b	53.25N	2.14W
Die, Fr. (dē)	157	44.45N	5.22E
Diefenbaker, res., Can.	84	51.20N	108.10W
Diego de Ocampo, Pico, mtn., Dom. Rep. (pē′-kô-dyĕ′gô-dĕ-ô-kä′m-pô)	123	19.40N	70.45W
Diego Ramirez, Islas, is., Chile (dē ä′gō rä-mē′rāz)	132	56.15S	70.15W
Diéma, Mali	214	14.32N	9.12W
Dien Bien Phu, Viet.	188	21.38N	102.49E
Diepensee, Ger.	238a	52.22N	13.31E
Dieppe, Can. (dē-ĕp′)	92	46.06N	64.45W
Dieppe, Fr.	147	49.54N	1.05E
Dierks, Ar., U.S. (dērks)	111	34.06N	94.02W
Diessem, neigh., Ger.	236	51.20N	6.35E
Diessen, Ger. (dēs′sĕn)	145d	47.57N	11.06E
Diest, Bel.	145a	50.59N	5.05E
Digby, Can. (dĭg′bĭ)	85	44.37N	65.46W
Dighton, Ma., U.S. (dī-tŭn)	100b	41.49N	71.05W
Digmoor, Eng., U.K.	237a	53.32N	2.45W
Digne, Fr. (dēn′y′)	157	44.07N	6.16E
Digoin, Fr. (dē-gwăN′)	156	46.28N	4.06E
Digra, India	240a	22.50N	88.20E
Digul, r., Indon.	197	7.00S	140.27E
Dijohan Point, c., Phil. (dē-kō-än)	197a	16.24N	122.25E
Dijon, Fr. (dē-zhôN′)	142	47.21N	5.02E
Dikson, Russia (dĭk′sŏn)	164	73.30N	80.35E
Dikwa, Nig. (dē′kwȧ)	211	12.06N	13.53E
Dili, Indon. (dĭl′ē)	197	8.35S	125.35E
Di Linosa Island, i., Italy (dē-lē-nō′sä)	148	36.01N	12.43E
Dilizhan, Arm.	167	40.45N	45.00E
Dillingham, Ak., U.S. (dĭl′ĕng-hăm)	96a	59.10N	158.38W
Dillon, Mt., U.S. (dĭl′ŭn)	105	45.12N	112.40W
Dillon, S.C., U.S.	115	34.24N	79.28W
Dillon Park, Md., U.S.	229d	38.52N	76.56W
Dillon Reservoir, res., Oh., U.S.	98	40.05N	82.05W
Dilolo, Zaire (dē-lō′lō)	212	10.19S	22.23E
Dimashq see Damascus, Syria	182	33.31N	36.18E
Dimbokro, C. Iv.	214	6.39N	4.42W
Dimitrovo see Pernik, Bul.	149	42.36N	23.04E
Dimlang, mtn., Nig.	215	8.24N	11.47E
Dimona, Isr.	181a	31.03N	35.01E
Dinagat Island, i., Phil.	197	10.15N	126.15E
Dinājpur, Bngl.	186	25.38N	87.39E
Dinan, Fr. (dē-năN′)	156	48.27N	2.03W
Dinant, Bel. (dē-năN′)	151	50.17N	4.50E
Dinara, mts., Yugo. (dē′nä-rä)	149	43.50N	16.15E
Dinard, Fr.	156	48.38N	2.04W
Dindigul, India	187	10.25N	78.03E
Dingalan Bay, b., Phil. (dĭŋ-gä′län)	197a	15.19N	121.33E
Dingle, Ire. (dĭng′′l)	150	52.10N	10.13W
Dingle, neigh., Eng., U.K.	237a	53.23N	2.57W
Dingle Bay, b., Ire.	147	52.02N	10.15W
Dingo, Austl. (dĭŋ′gō)	203	23.45S	149.26E
Dinguiraye, Gui.	214	11.18N	10.43W
Dingwall, Scot., U.K. (dĭng′wôl)	150	57.37N	4.23W
Dingxian, China (dĭŋ shyĕn)	192	38.30N	115.00E
Dingxing, China (dĭŋ-shyĭŋ)	192	39.18N	115.50E
Dingyuan, China (dĭŋ-yüän)	190	32.32N	117.40E
Dingzi Wan, b., China	190	36.33N	121.06E
Dinosaur National Monument, rec., Co., U.S. (dī′nō-sōr)	105	40.45N	109.17W
Dinslaken, Ger. (dēns′lä-kĕn)	157c	51.33N	6.44E
Dinslakener Bruch, Ger.	236	51.35N	6.43E
Dinteloord, Neth.	145a	51.38N	4.21E
Dinuba, Ca., U.S. (dĭ-nū′bȧ)	108	36.33N	119.29W
Dinwiddie, S. Afr.	244b	26.16S	28.10E
Dios, Cayo de, i., Cuba (kä′yō-dĕ-dē-ōs′)	122	22.05N	83.05W
Diourbel, Sen. (dē-ōōr-bĕl′)	210	14.40N	16.15W
Diphu Pass, p., Asia (dĭ-pōō)	188	28.15N	96.45E
Diquis, r., C.R. (dē-kēs′)	121	8.59N	83.24W
Dire Dawa, Eth.	211	9.40N	41.47E
Diriamba, Nic. (dēr-yäm′bä)	120	11.52N	86.15W
Dirk Hartog, i., Austl.	202	26.25S	113.15E
Dirksland, Neth.	145a	51.45N	4.04E
Dirranbandi, Austl. (dĭ-rȧ-băn′dē)	203	28.24S	148.29E
Dirty Devil, r., Ut., U.S. (dûr′tĭ dĕv′′l)	109	38.20N	110.30W
Disappointment, l., Austl.	202	23.20S	123.00E
Disappointment, Cape, c., Wa., U.S. (dĭs′ȧ-point′ment)	106c	46.16N	124.11W
Discovery, S. Afr. (dĭs-kŭv′ēr-ĭ)	213b	26.10S	27.53E
Discovery, is., Can. (dĭs-kŭv′ēr-ē)	106a	48.25N	123.13W
Disko, i., Grnld. (dĭs′kō)	82	70.00N	54.00W
Disna, Bela. (dēs′nȧ)	166	55.34N	28.15E
Disneyland, pt. of i., Ca., U.S.	232	33.48N	117.55W
Dispur, India	186	26.00N	91.50E
Disraëli, Can. (dĭs-rä′lĭ)	91	45.53N	71.23W
Disteln, Ger.	236	51.36N	7.09E
District Heights, Md., U.S.	229d	38.51N	76.53W
District of Columbia, state, U.S.	97	38.50N	77.00W
Distrito Federal, dept., Braz. (dēs-trē′tô-fĕ-dĕ-rä′l)	131	15.49S	47.39W
Distrito Federal, dept., Mex.	118	19.14N	99.08W
Disūq, Egypt (dē-sōōk′)	218b	31.07N	30.41E
Ditton, Eng., U.K.	235	51.18N	0.27E
Diu, India (dē′ōō)	183	20.48N	70.58E
Divilacan Bay, b., Phil. (dē-vē-lä′kän)	197a	17.26N	122.25E
Divinópolis, Braz. (dē-vē-nō′pō-lēs)	131	20.10S	44.53W
Divo, C. Iv.	214	5.50N	5.22W
Dixon, Il., U.S. (dĭks′ŭn)	103	41.50N	89.30W

PLACE (Pronunciation)	PAGE	Lat. °'	Long. °'
Dixon Entrance, strt., N.A.	84	54.25N	132.00W
Diyarbakir, Tur. (dē-yär-bĕk′ĭr)	182	38.00N	40.10E
Dja, r., Afr.	211	2.30N	14.00E
Djakovo, neigh., Russia	239b	55.39N	37.40E
Djambala, Congo	216	2.33S	14.45E
Djanet, Alg.	210	24.29N	9.26E
Djebobo, mtn., Ghana	214	8.20N	0.37E
Djedi, Oued, r., Alg.	148	34.18N	4.39E
Djelo-Binza, Zaire	244c	4.23S	15.16E
Djember, Chad	215	10.25N	17.50E
Djerba, Île de, i., Tun.	148	33.53N	11.26E
Djerid, Chott, l., Tun. (jĕr′ĭd)	210	33.15N	8.29E
Djibasso, Burkina	214	13.07N	4.10W
Djibo, Burkina	214	14.06N	1.38W
Djibouti, Dji. (jē-bōō-tē′)	218a	11.34N	43.00E
Djibouti, nation, Afr.	218a	11.35N	48.08E
Djokoumatombi, Congo	216	0.47N	15.22E
Djokupunda, Zaire	212	5.27S	20.58E
Djoua, r., Afr.	216	1.25N	13.40E
Djursholm, Swe. (djōōrs′hōlm)	152	59.26N	18.01E
Dmitriyev-L′govskiy, Russia (d′mē′trĭ-yĕf l′gôf′skĭ)	162	52.07N	35.05E
Dmitrov, Russia (d′mē′trôf)	162	56.21N	37.32E
Dmitrovsk, Russia (d′mē′trôfsk)	162	52.30N	35.10E
Dmytrivka, Ukr.	163	47.57N	38.56E
Dnepropetrovsk see Dnipropetrovs′k, Ukr.	164	48.15N	34.08E
Dnestrovskiy Liman, l., Ukr.	163	46.13N	29.50E
Dnieper (Dnipro), r., Eur.	167	46.45N	33.40E
Dniester, r., Eur.	167	48.21N	28.10E
Dniprodzerzhyns′k, Ukr.	167	48.32N	34.38E
Dniprodzerzhyns′ke vodoskhovyshche, res., Ukr.	164	49.00N	34.10E
Dnipropetrovs′k, Ukr.	164	48.15N	34.08E
Dnipropetrovs′k, prov., Ukr.	163	48.15N	34.10E
Dniprovs′kyy lyman, b., Ukr.	163	46.33N	31.45E
Dno, Russia (d′nô′)	162	57.49N	29.59E
Do, Lac, l., Mali	214	15.50N	2.20W
Doba, Chad	215	8.39N	16.51E
Dobbs Ferry, N.Y., U.S. (dŏbz′fĕ′rē)	100a	41.01N	73.53W
Dobbyn, Austl. (dŏb′ĭn)	202	19.45S	140.02E
Dobele, Lat. (dô′bĕ-lĕ)	153	56.37N	23.18E
Doberai, Jazirah, pen., Indon.	197	1.25S	133.15E
Döbling, neigh., Aus.	239e	48.15N	16.22E
Dobo, Indon.	197	6.00S	134.18E
Doboj, Bos. (dō′boi)	161	44.42N	18.04E
Dobrich, Bul.	149	43.33N	27.52E
Dobryanka, Russia (dôb-ryän′kȧ)	172a	58.27N	56.26E
Dobšina, Slvk. (dŏp′shē-nä)	155	48.48N	20.25E
Doce, r., Braz. (dō′sȧ)	131	19.01S	42.14W
Doce, Canal Numero, can., Arg.	129c	36.47S	59.00W
Doce Leguas, Cayos de las, is., Cuba	122	20.55N	79.05W
Doctor Arroyo, Mex. (dōk-tōr′ är-rō′yō)	118	23.41N	100.10W
Doddinghurst, Eng., U.K.	235	51.40N	0.18E
Doddington, Eng., U.K. (dŏd′dĭng-tŏn)	144b	51.17N	0.47E
Dodecanese see Dhodhekánisos, is., Grc.	161	38.00N	26.10E
Dodge City, Ks., U.S. (dŏj)	96	37.44N	100.01W
Dodgeville, Wi., U.S. (dŏj′vĭl)	103	42.58N	90.07W
Dodoma, Tan. (dō′dō-mȧ)	212	6.11S	35.45E
Dog, l., Can. (dŏg)	90	48.42N	89.24W
Dogger Bank, bk. (dŏg′gēr)	151	55.07N	2.25E
Dogubayazit, Tur.	167	39.35N	44.00E
Doha see Ad Dawhah, Qatar	182	25.02N	51.28E
Dohad, India	186	22.52N	74.18E
Doiran, l., Grc.	161	41.10N	23.00E
Dokshitsy, Bela. (dôk-shētsē)	162	54.53N	27.49E
Dolbeau, Can.	85	48.52N	72.16W
Dole, Fr. (dōl)	147	47.07N	5.28E
Dolgaya, Kosa, c., Russia (kô′sȧ dôl-gä′yä)	163	46.42N	37.42E
Dolgeville, N.Y., U.S.	99	43.10N	74.45W
Dolgiy, i., Russia	166	69.20N	59.20E
Dolgoprudnyy, Russia	172b	55.57N	37.33E
Dolinsk, Russia (dá-lēnsk′)	171	47.29N	142.31E
Dollard-des-Ormeaux, Can.	227b	45.29N	73.49W
Dollar Harbor, b., Bah.	122	25.30N	79.15W
Dolomite, Al., U.S. (dŏl′ô-mīt)	100h	33.28N	86.57W
Dolomiti, mts., Italy	160	46.16N	11.43E
Dolores, Arg. (dô-lō′rĕs)	132	36.20S	57.42W
Dolores, Col.	130a	3.33N	74.54W
Dolores, Tx., U.S. (dô-lō′rĕs)	112	27.42N	99.47W
Dolores, Ur.	129c	33.32S	58.15W
Dolores, r., Co., U.S.	109	38.35N	108.50W
Dolores Hidalgo, Mex. (dô-lō′rĕs-ē-däl′gō)	118	21.09N	100.56W
Dolphin and Union Strait, strt., Can. (dŏl′fĭn ūn′yŭn)	84	69.22N	117.10W
Dolton, Il., U.S.	231a	41.39N	87.37W
Dolyna, Ukr.	155	48.57N	24.01E
Domažlice, Czech Rep. (dō′mäzh-lē-tsĕ)	154	49.27N	12.55E
Dombasle-sur-Meurthe, Fr. (dôN-bäl′)	157	48.38N	6.18E
Dombóvár, Hung. (dŏm′bō-vär)	155	46.22N	18.08E
Domeyko, Cordillera, mts., Chile (kôr-dēl-yĕ′rä-dô-mä′kō)	130	20.50S	69.02W
Dominguez, Ca., U.S.	232	33.50N	118.31W
Dominica, nation, N.A. (dŏ-mĭ-nē′kȧ)	117	15.30N	60.45W
Dominica Channel, strt., N.A.	121b	15.00N	61.30W
Dominican Republic, nation, N.A. (dô-mĭn′ĭ-kăn)	117	19.00N	70.45W
Dominion, Can. (dô-mĭn′yŭn)	93	46.13N	60.01W
Domiongo, Zaire	216	4.37S	21.15E
Domitilla, Catacombe di, pt. of i., Italy	239c	41.52N	12.31E
Domodedovo, Russia (dô-mô-dyĕ′do-vô)	172b	55.27N	37.45E
Dom Silvério, Braz. (doN-sĕl-vĕ′ryō)	129a	20.09S	42.57W
Don, r., Can.	227c	43.39N	79.21W
Don, r., Russia	164	49.50N	41.30E

282 Don–Dunnellon

PLACE (Pronunciation)	PAGE	Lat. °′	Long. °′
Don, r., Eng., U.K.	144a	53.39N	0.58W
Don, r., Scot., U.K.	150	57.19N	2.39W
Donaldson, Mi., U.S. (dŏn′ăl-sŭn)	107k	46.19N	84.22W
Donaldsonville, La., U.S. (dŏn′ăld-sŭn-vĭl)	113	30.05N	90.58W
Donalsonville, Ga., U.S.	114	31.02N	84.50W
Donaufeld, neigh., Italy	239e	48.15N	16.25E
Donaustadt, neigh., Aus.	239e	48.13N	16.30E
Donauturm, pt. of i., Aus.	239e	48.14N	16.25E
Donawitz, Aus. (dō′na-vĭts)	154	47.23N	15.05E
Don Benito, Spain (dōn′bå-nē′tō)	158	38.55N	5.52W
Dönberg, Ger.	236	51.18N	7.10E
Don Bosco, neigh., Arg.	233d	34.42S	58.19W
Doncaster, Austl. (doŋ′kăs-tẽr)	201a	37.47S	145.08E
Doncaster, Can.	227c	43.48N	79.25W
Doncaster, Eng., U.K. (doŋ′kăs-tẽr)	150	53.32N	1.07W
Doncaster East, Austl.	243b	37.47S	145.10E
Dondo, Ang. (dōn′dō)	212	9.38S	14.25E
Dondo, Moz.	212	19.33S	34.47E
Dondra Head, c., Sri L.	183b	5.52N	80.52E
Donegal, Ire. (dŏn-ê-gôl′)	150	54.44N	8.05W
Donegal Bay, Ire. (dŏn-ē-gôl′)	146	54.35N	8.36W
Donets Coal Basin, reg., Ukr. (dō-nyĕts′)	163	48.15N	38.50E
Donets′k, Ukr.	164	48.00N	37.35E
Donets′k, prov., Ukr.	163	47.55N	37.40E
Dong, r., China (dôŋ)	189	24.13N	115.08E
Dongara, Austl. (dôn-gă′ră)	202	29.15S	115.00E
Dongba, China (dôŋ-bä)	190	31.40N	119.02E
Dongba, China	240b	39.58N	116.32E
Dongbahe, China	240b	39.58N	116.27E
Dong′e, China (dôŋ-ŭ)	190	36.21N	116.14E
Dong′ezhen, China	192	36.11N	116.16E
Dongfang, China (dôŋ-fäŋ)	193	19.08N	108.42E
Donggala, Indon. (dôn-gä′lä)	196	0.45S	119.32E
Dongguan, China (dôŋ-gûän)	191a	23.03N	113.46E
Dongguang, China (dôŋ-gûäŋ)	190	37.54N	116.33E
Donghai, China (dôŋ-hī)	192	34.35N	119.05E
Dong Hoi, Viet. (dông-hô-ē′)	196	17.25N	106.42E
Dongila, Eth.	211	11.17N	37.00E
Dongming, China (dôŋ-miŋ)	190	35.16N	115.06E
Dongo, Ang. (dôŋ′gō)	212	14.45S	15.30E
Dongon Point, c., Phil. (dŏng-ôn′)	197a	12.43N	120.35E
Dongou, Congo (dôŋ-gōō′)	211	2.02N	18.04E
Dongping, China (dôŋ-piŋ)	192	35.50N	116.24E
Dongping Hu, l., China (dôŋ-piŋ hōō)	190	36.06N	116.24E
Dongshan, China (doŋ-shän)	190	31.05N	120.24E
Dongshi, China	240b	39.49N	116.34E
Dongtai, China	190	32.51N	120.20E
Dongting Hu, l., China (dôŋ-tiŋ hōō)	189	29.10N	112.30E
Dongxiang, China (dôŋ-shyän)	193	28.18N	116.38E
Doniphan, Mo., U.S. (dŏn′ĭ-făn)	111	36.37N	90.50W
Donji Vakuf, Bos. (dōn′yĭ väk′ôf)	161	44.08N	17.25E
Don Martin, Presa de, res., Mex. (prĕ′sä-dĕ-dôn-mär-tē′n)	112	27.35N	100.38W
Donnacona, Can.	91	46.40N	71.46W
Donnemarie-en-Montois, Fr. (dôn-mä-rē′ĕN-môN-twä′)	157b	48.29N	3.09E
Donner und Blitzen, r., Or., U.S. (dŏn′ẽr ŏnt′blĭ′tsĕn)	104	42.45N	118.57W
Donnybrook, S. Afr. (dŏ-nĭ-brŏk)	213c	29.56S	29.54E
Donora, Pa., U.S. (dŏ-nō′rä)	101e	40.10N	79.51W
Don Torcuato, Arg.	233d	34.29S	58.37W
Doolow, Som.	218a	4.10N	42.05E
Doonerak, Mount, mtn., Ak., U.S. (dōō′nē-răk)	95	68.00N	150.34W
Doorn, Neth.	145a	52.02N	5.21E
Door Peninsula, pen., Wi., U.S. (dōr)	103	44.40N	87.36W
Dora Baltea, r., Italy (dō′rä bäl′tā-ä)	160	45.40N	7.34E
Doraville, Ga., U.S. (dō′rá-vĭl)	100c	33.54N	84.17W
Dorchester, Eng., U.K. (dôr′chĕs-tẽr)	150	50.45N	2.34W
Dorchester Heights National Historic Site, hist., Ma., U.S.	227a	42.20N	71.03W
Dordogne, r., Fr. (dôr-dôn′yĕ)	142	44.53N	0.16E
Dordrecht, Neth. (dôr′drĕkt)	151	51.48N	4.39E
Dordrecht, S. Afr. (dô′drĕkt)	213c	31.24S	27.06E
Doré Lake, l., Can.	88	54.31N	107.06W
Dorgali, Italy (dôr′gä-lē)	160	40.18N	9.37E
Dörgön Nuur, l., Mong.	188	47.47N	94.01E
Dorion-Vaudreuil, Can. (dôr-yō)	83a	45.23N	74.01W
Dorking, Eng., U.K. (dôr′kĭng)	144b	51.12N	0.20W
Dormont, Pa., U.S. (dôr′mŏnt)	101e	40.24N	80.02W
Dornap, Ger.	236	51.15N	7.04E
Dornbirn, Aus. (dôrn′bêrn)	154	47.24N	9.45E
Dornoch, Scot., U.K. (dôr′nŏk)	146	57.55N	4.01W
Dornoch Firth, b., Scot., U.K. (dôr′nŏk fûrth)	150	57.55N	3.55W
Dorogobuzh, Russia (dôrôgô′-bōō′zh)	162	54.57N	33.18E
Dorohoi, Rom. (dō-rō-hoi′)	155	47.57N	26.28E
Dorre Island, i., Austl. (dôr)	202	25.19S	113.10E
Dorseyville, Pa., U.S.	230b	40.35N	79.53W
Dorstfeld, neigh., Ger.	236	51.31N	7.25E
Dorstsen, Ger.	157c	51.40N	6.58E
Dortmund, Ger. (dôrt′mŏont)	147	51.31N	7.28E
Dortmund-Ems-Kanal, can., Ger. (dōrt′mōōnd-ĕms′kä-näl′)	157c	51.50N	7.25E
Dörtyol, Tur. (dûrt′yôl)	149	36.50N	36.20E
Dorval, Can. (dôr-vál′)	83a	45.26N	73.44W
Dos Bahías, Cabo, c., Arg. (kä′bō-dōs-bä-ē′äs)	132	44.55S	65.35W
Dos Caminos, Ven. (dōs-kä-mē′nōs)	131b	9.38N	67.17W
Dosewallips, r., Wa., U.S. (dō′sē-wäl′lĭps)	106a	47.45N	123.04W
Dos Hermanas, Spain (dōsĕr-mä′näs)	158	37.17N	5.56W
Dosso, Niger (dō-sō′)	210	13.03N	3.12E
Dothan, Al., U.S. (dō′thăn)	97	31.13N	85.23W
Douai, Fr. (dōō-ā′)	147	50.23N	3.04E
Douala, Cam. (dōō-ä′lä)	210	4.03N	9.42E

PLACE (Pronunciation)	PAGE	Lat. °′	Long. °′
Douarnenez, Fr. (dōō-ȧr nĕ-nĕs′)	156	48.06N	4.18W
Double Bayou, Tx., U.S. (dŭb′'l bī′yōō)	113a	29.40N	94.38W
Doubs, r., Eur.	157	46.15N	5.50E
Douentza, Mali	214	15.00N	2.57W
Douglas, I. of Man (dŭg′lăs)	150	54.10N	4.24W
Douglas, Ak., U.S. (dŭg′lăs)	95	58.18N	134.35W
Douglas, Az., U.S.	96	31.20N	109.30W
Douglas, Ga., U.S.	115	31.30N	82.53W
Douglas, Wy., U.S. (dŭg′lăs)	105	42.45N	105.21W
Douglas, r., Eng., U.K. (dŭg′lăs)	144a	53.38N	2.48W
Douglas Channel, strt., Can.	86	53.30N	129.12W
Douglas Lake, res., Tn., U.S. (dŭg′lăs)	114	36.00N	83.35W
Douglas Lake Indian Reserve, I.R., Can.	87	50.10N	120.49W
Douglasville, Ga., U.S. (dŭg′lăs-vĭl)	114	33.45N	84.47W
Dourada, Serra, mts., Braz. (sĕ′r-rä-dōōō-rá′dä)	131	15.11S	49.57W
Dourdan, Fr. (dōōr-däN′)	157b	48.32N	2.01E
Douro, r., Eur. (dwē′rō)	142	41.30N	4.30W
Douro, r., Port. (dô′ō-rō)	158	41.03N	8.12W
Dove, r., Eng., U.K. (dŭv)	144a	52.53N	1.47W
Dover, S. Afr.	218d	27.05S	27.44E
Dover, Eng., U.K.	142	51.08N	1.19E
Dover, De., U.S. (dō vẽr)	97	39.10N	75.30W
Dover, N.H., U.S.	99	43.15N	71.00W
Dover, N.J., U.S.	100a	40.53N	74.33W
Dover, Oh., U.S.	98	40.35N	81.30W
Dover, Strait of, strt., Eur.	142	50.50N	1.15W
Dover-Foxcroft, Me., U.S. (dō′vẽr fôks′krôft)	92	45.10N	69.15W
Dover Heights, Austl.	243a	33.53S	151.17E
Doveton, Austl.	243b	38.00S	145.14E
Dovre Fjell, mts., Nor. (dŏv′rĕ fyĕl′)	142	62.03N	8.36E
Dow, Il., U.S. (dou)	107e	39.01N	90.20W
Dowagiac, Mi., U.S. (dō-wô′jăk)	98	42.00N	86.05W
Dowlatābād, Iran	241h	35.37N	51.27E
Downers Grove, Il., U.S. (dou′nẽrz grōv)	101a	41.48N	88.00W
Downey, Ca., U.S. (dou′nĭ)	107a	33.56N	118.08W
Downieville, Ca., U.S. (dou′nĭ-nĭl)	108	39.35N	120.48W
Downs, Ks., U.S. (dounz)	110	39.29N	98.32W
Doylestown, Oh., U.S. (doilz′toun)	101d	40.58N	81.43W
Drâa, Cap, c., Mor. (drá)	210	28.39N	12.15W
Drâa, Oued, r., Afr.	210	28.00N	9.31W
Drabiv, Ukr.	163	49.57N	32.14E
Drac, r., Fr. (dräk)	157	44.50N	5.47E
Dracut, Ma., U.S. (drā′kŭt)	93a	42.40N	71.19W
Draganovo, Bul. (drä-gä-nō′vō)	161	43.13N	25.45E
Drăgăşani, Rom. (drä-gá-shän′ĭ)	161	44.39N	24.18E
Draguignan, Fr. (drä-gēn-yäN′)	157	43.35N	6.28E
Drakensberg, mts., Afr. (drä′kĕnz-bĕrgh)	212	29.15S	29.07E
Drake Passage, strt. (drāk păs′ĭj)	128	57.00S	65.00W
Dráma, Grc. (drä′mä)	149	41.09N	24.10E
Drammen, Nor. (dräm′ĕn)	146	59.45N	10.15E
Drancy, Fr.	237c	48.56N	2.27E
Drau (Drava), r., Eur. (drou)	154	46.44N	13.45E
Drava, r., Eur. (drä′vä)	142	45.45N	17.30E
Draveil, Fr.	237c	48.41N	2.25E
Dravograd, Slvn. (drä′vō-gräd′)	160	46.37N	15.01E
Dravosburg, Pa., U.S.	230b	40.21N	79.51W
Drawsko Pomorskie, Pol. (dräv′skō pō-môr′skyĕ)	154	53.31N	15.50E
Drayton Harbor, b., Wa., U.S. (drā′tŭn)	106d	48.58N	122.40W
Drayton Plains, Mi., U.S.	101b	42.41N	83.23W
Drayton Valley, Can.	87	53.13N	114.59W
Drensteinfurt, Ger. (drĕn′shtīn-fōōrt)	157c	51.47N	7.44E
Dresden, Ger. (drās′dĕn)	142	51.05N	13.45E
Dreux, Fr. (drû)	156	48.44N	1.24E
Drewitz, neigh., Ger.	238a	52.22N	13.08E
Drexel Hill, Pa., U.S.	229b	39.57N	75.19W
Driefontein, S. Afr.	218d	25.53S	29.10E
Drin, r., Alb. (drēn)	161	42.13N	20.13E
Drina, r., Yugo. (drē′nä)	149	44.09N	19.30E
Drinit, Pellg i, b., Alb.	161	41.42N	19.17E
Dr. Ir. W. J. van Blommestein Meer, res., Sur.	131	4.45N	55.05W
Drissa, Bela. (drĭs′sä)	162	55.48N	27.59E
Drissa, r., Eur.	162	55.44N	28.58E
Driver, Va., U.S.	100g	36.50N	76.30W
Dröbak, Nor. (drû′bäk)	152	59.40N	10.35E
Drobeta-Turnu Severin, Rom. (sĕ-vē-rēn′)	149	43.54N	24.49E
Drogheda, Ire. (drŏ′hĕ-dă)	146	53.43N	6.15W
Drogichin, Bela. (drō-gē′chĭn)	155	52.10N	25.11E
Drohobych, Ukr.	155	49.21N	23.31E
Drôme, r., Fr. (drōm)	156	44.42N	4.53E
Dronfield, Eng., U.K. (drŏn′fēld)	144a	53.18N	1.28W
Droylsden, Eng., U.K.	237b	53.29N	2.10W
Drumheller, Can. (drŭm-hĕl-ẽr)	84	51.28N	112.42W
Drummond, i., Mi., U.S. (drŭm′ŭnd)	98	46.00N	83.50W
Drummondville, Can. (drŭm′ŭnd-vĭl)	85	45.53N	72.33W
Drummoyne, Austl.	243a	33.51S	151.09E
Drumright, Ok., U.S. (drŭm′rīt)	111	35.59N	96.37W
Drunen, Neth.	145a	51.41N	5.10E
Drut′, r., Bela. (drōōt)	162	53.40N	29.45E
Druya, Bela. (drō′yá)	162	55.45N	27.26E
Družba, Russia	239b	55.53N	37.45E
Drwęca, r., Pol. (d′r-vän′tsá)	155	53.06N	19.13E
Dryden, Can. (drī-dĕn)	85	49.47N	92.50W
Drysdale, Austl.	201a	38.11S	144.34E
Dry Tortugas, is., Fl., U.S. (tôr-tōō′gäz)	115a	24.37N	82.45W
Dschang, Cam. (dshäng)	210	5.34N	10.09E
Duabo, Lib.	214	5.40N	8.05W
Duagh, Can.	83g	53.43N	113.24W
Duarte, Ca., U.S.	232	34.08N	117.58W
Duarte, Pico, mtn., Dom. Rep. (dŭŭ′ärtĕh pêcô)	117	19.00N	71.00W
Duas Barras, Braz. (dōō′äs-bä′r-räs)	129a	22.03S	42.30W
Dubai *see* Dubayy, U.A.E.	182	25.18N	55.26E

PLACE (Pronunciation)	PAGE	Lat. °′	Long. °′
Dubăsari, Mol.	163	47.16N	29.11E
Dubawnt, l., Can. (dōō-bônt′)	84	63.27N	103.30W
Dubawnt, r., Can.	84	61.30N	103.49W
Dubayy, U.A.E.	182	25.18N	55.26E
Dubbo, Austl. (dŭb′ō)	203	32.20S	148.42E
Dubie, Zaire	217	8.33S	28.32E
Dublin, Ire.	142	53.20N	6.15W
Dublin, Ca., U.S. (dŭb′lĭn)	106b	37.42N	121.56W
Dublin, Ga., U.S.	115	32.33N	82.55W
Dublin, Tx., U.S.	112	32.05N	98.20W
Dubno, Ukr. (dōō′b-nō)	155	50.24N	25.44E
Du Bois, Pa., U.S. (dō-bois′)	99	41.10N	78.45W
Dubovka, Russia (dō-bôf′ká)	167	49.00N	44.50E
Dubrovka, Russia (dōō-brôf′kå)	172c	59.51N	30.56E
Dubrovnik, Cro. (dō′brôv-nêk) (rä-gōō′sä)	142	42.40N	18.10E
Dubrovno, Bela. (dōō-brôf′nō)	162	54.39N	30.54E
Dubuque, Ia., U.S. (dō-būk′)	97	42.30N	90.43W
Duchesne, Ut., U.S. (dō-shān′)	109	40.12N	110.23W
Duchesne, r., Ut., U.S.	109	40.20N	110.50W
Duchess, Austl. (dŭch′ĕs)	202	21.30S	139.55E
Ducie Island, i., Pit. (dū-sē′)	2	25.30S	126.20W
Duck, r., Tn., U.S.	114	35.55N	87.40W
Duckabush, r., Wa., U.S. (dŭk′ā-bŏsh)	106a	47.41N	123.09W
Duck Lake, Can.	88	52.47N	106.13W
Duck Mountain, mtn., Can.	89	51.35N	101.00W
Ducktown, Tn., U.S. (dŭk′toun)	114	35.03N	84.20W
Duck Valley Indian Reservation, I.R., Id., U.S.	104	42.02N	115.49W
Duckwater Peak, mtn., Nv., U.S. (dŭk-wô-tẽr)	108	39.00N	115.31W
Duda, r., Col. (dōō′dä)	130a	3.25N	74.23W
Dudinka, Russia (dōō-dĭn′kå)	164	69.15N	85.42E
Dudley, Eng., U.K. (dŭd′lĭ)	147	52.28N	2.07E
Dufourspitze, mtn., Eur.	154	45.55N	7.52E
Dugger, In., U.S. (dŭg′ẽr)	98	39.00N887.10	W
Dugi Otok, i., Yugo. (dōō′gē o′tôk)	160	44.03N	14.40E
Dugny, Fr.	237c	48.57N	2.25E
Duisburg, Ger. (dōō′ĭs-bŏrgh)	147	51.26N	6.46E
Duissern, neigh., Ger.	236	51.26N	6.47E
Dukhān, Qatar	185	25.25N	50.48E
Dukhovshchina, Russia (dōō-kôfsh-′chēná)	162	55.13N	32.26E
Dukinfield, Eng., U.K. (dŭk′ĭn-fēld)	144a	53.28N	2.05W
Dukla Pass, p., Eur. (dŏ′klä)	147	49.25N	21.44E
Dulce, Golfo, b., C.R. (gōl′fō dōōl′sä)	117	8.25N	83.13W
Dülken, Ger. (dül′kĕn)	157c	51.15N	6.21E
Dülmen, Ger. (dül′mĕn)	157c	51.50N	7.17E
Duluth, Mn., U.S. (dō-lōōth′)	97	46.50N	92.07W
Dulwich, neigh., Eng., U.K.	235	51.26N	0.05W
Dumai, Indon.	181b	1.39N	101.30E
Dumali Point, c., Phil. (dōō-mä′lē)	197a	13.07N	121.42E
Dumas, Tx., U.S.	110	35.52N	101.58W
Dumbarton, Scot., U.K. (dŭm′bär-tŭn)	150	56.00N	4.35W
Dum-Dum, India	186a	22.37N	88.25E
Dumfries, Scot., U.K. (dŭm-frēs′)	150	55.05N	3.40W
Dumjor, India	186a	22.37N	88.14E
Dumont, N.J., U.S. (dōō′mŏnt)	100a	40.56N	74.00W
Dümpten, neigh., Ger.	236	51.27N	6.54E
Dumyāt, Egypt	211	31.22N	31.50E
Dunaföldvár, Hung. (dŏ′nô-fûld′vär)	155	46.48N	18.55E
Dunajec, r., Pol. (dō-nä′yĕts)	155	49.52N	20.53E
Dunaújváros, Hung.	155	46.57N	18.55E
Dunay, Russia (dōō′nĭ)	172c	59.59N	30.57E
Dunayivtsi, Ukr.	163	48.52N	26.51E
Dunbar, W.V., U.S.	98	38.20N	81.45W
Duncan, Can. (dŭŋ′kăn)	84	48.47N	123.42W
Duncan, Ok., U.S.	111	34.29N	97.56W
Duncan, r., Can.	87	50.30N	116.45W
Duncan Dam, dam, Can.	87	50.15N	116.55W
Duncan Lake, l., Can.	87	50.20N	117.00W
Duncansby Head, c., Scot., U.K. (dŭn′kănz-bĭ)	150	58.40N	3.01W
Duncanville, Tx., U.S. (dŭn′kăn-vĭl)	107c	32.39N	96.55W
Dundalk, Ire. (dŭn′kôk)	146	54.00N	6.18W
Dundalk, Md., U.S.	100e	39.16N	76.31W
Dundalk Bay, b., Ire. (dŭn′dôk)	150	53.55N	6.15W
Dundas, Austl.	243a	33.48S	151.02E
Dundas, Can. (dŭn-dăs′)	91	43.16N	79.58W
Dundas, l., Austl. (dŭn-dăs)	202	32.15S	122.00E
Dundas Island, i., Can.	86	54.33N	130.55W
Dundas Strait, strt., Austl.	202	10.35S	131.15E
Dundedin, Fl., U.S. (dŭn-ē′dĭn)	115a	28.00N	82.43W
Dundee, S. Afr.	213c	28.14S	30.16E
Dundee, Scot., U.K.	142	56.30N	2.55W
Dundee, Il., U.S. (dŭn-dē)	101a	42.06N	88.17W
Dundrum Bay, b., N. Ire., U.K. (dŭn-drŭm′)	150	54.13N	5.47W
Dunedin, N.Z.	203a	45.48S	170.32E
Dunellen, N.J., U.S. (dŭn-ĕl′l′n)	100a	40.36N	74.28W
Dunfermline, Scot., U.K. (dŭn-fĕrm′lĭn)	150	56.05N	3.30W
Dungarvan, Ire. (dŭn-gär′văn)	150	52.06N	7.50W
Dungeness, Wa., U.S. (dŭnj-nĕs′)	106a	48.09N	123.07W
Dungeness, r., Wa., U.S.	106a	48.03N	123.10W
Dungeness Spit, Wa., U.S.	106a	48.11N	123.03W
Dunham Town, Eng., U.K.	237b	53.23N	2.24W
Dunheved, Austl.	243a	33.45S	150.47E
Dunhua, China (dôn-hwä)	189	43.18N	128.10E
Dunkerque, Fr. (dŭN-kĕrk′)	147	51.02N	2.37E
Dunkirk, In., U.S. (dŭn′kûrk)	98	40.20N	85.25W
Dunkwa, Ghana	214	5.22N	1.12W
Dun Laoghaire, Ire. (dŭn-lā′rĕ)	146	53.16N	6.09W
Dunlap, Ia., U.S. (dŭn′lăp)	102	41.53N	95.33W
Dunlap, Tn., U.S.	114	35.23N	85.23W
Dunmore, Pa., U.S. (dŭn′mōr)	99	41.25N	75.30W
Dunn, N.C., U.S. (dŭn)	115	35.18N	78.37W
Dunnellon, Fl., U.S. (dŭn-ĕl′ŏn)	115	29.02N	82.28W

PRONOUNCING INDEX

Dunn Loring–Edremit 283

PLACE (Pronunciation)	PAGE	Lat. °′	Long. °′
Dunn Loring, Va., U.S.	229d	38.53N	77.14W
Dunnville, Can. (dŭn'vĭl)	91	42.55N	79.40W
Dunqulah, Sudan	211	19.21N	30.19E
Dunsmuir, Ca., U.S. (dŭnz'mūr)	104	41.08N	122.17W
Dunton Green, Eng., U.K.	235	51.18N	0.11E
Dunton Wayletts, Eng., U.K.	235	51.35N	0.24E
Dunvegan, S. Afr.	244b	26.09S	28.09E
Dunwoody, Ga., U.S. (dŭn-wŏŏd'ĭ)	100c	33.57N	84.20W
Duolun, China (dwō-lōōn)	189	42.12N	116.15E
Duomo, rel., Italy	238c	45.27N	9.11E
Du Page, r., Il., U.S. (dōō pāj)	101a	41.41N	88.11W
Du Page, East Branch, r., Il., U.S.	101a	41.42N	88.09W
Du Page, West Branch, r., Il., U.S.	101a	41.42N	88.09W
Dupax, Phil. (dōō'päks)	197a	16.16N	121.06E
Dupo, Il., U.S. (dū'pō)	107e	38.31N	90.12W
Duque de Caxias, Braz. (dōō'kĕ-dĕ-kà'shyàs)	129a	22.46S	43.18W
Duquesne, Pa., U.S. (dŏŏ-kān')	101e	40.22N	79.51W
Du Quoin, Il., U.S. (dŏŏ-kwoin')	111	38.01N	89.14W
Durance, r., Fr. (dü-räns')	147	43.46N	5.52E
Durand, Mi., U.S. (dŭ-rănd')	98	42.50N	84.00W
Durand, Wi., U.S.	103	44.37N	91.58W
Durango, Mex. (dōō-rä'n-gō)	116	24.02N	104.42W
Durango, Co., U.S. (dŏŏ-răŋ'gō)	109	37.15N	107.55W
Durango, state, Mex.	116	25.00N	106.00W
Durant, Ms., U.S. (dŭ-rănt')	114	33.05N	89.50W
Durant, Ok., U.S.	111	33.59N	96.23W
Duratón, r., Spain (dōō-rä-tōn')	158	41.30N	3.55W
Durazno, Ur. (dōō-räz'nō)	132	33.21S	56.31W
Durazno, dept., Ur.	129c	33.00S	56.35W
Durban, S. Afr. (dûr'băn)	212	29.48S	31.00E
Durbanville, S. Afr. (dûr-băn'vĭl)	212a	33.50S	18.39E
Durbe, Lat. (dŏŏr'bĕ)	153	56.36N	21.24E
Durchholz, Ger.	236	51.23N	7.17E
Đurđevac, Cro.	149	46.03N	17.03E
Düren, Ger. (dü'rĕn)	157c	50.48N	6.30E
Durham, Eng., U.K. (dûr'ăm)	150	54.47N	1.46W
Durham, N.C., U.S.	97	36.00N	78.55W
Durham Downs, Austl.	204	27.30S	141.55E
Durrës, Alb. (dŏŏr'ĕs)	142	41.19N	19.27E
Duryea, Pa., U.S. (dōōr-yā')	99	41.20N	75.50W
Dushan, China	190	31.38N	116.16E
Dushan, China (dōō-shän)	193	25.50N	107.42E
Dushanbe, Taj.	169	38.30N	68.45E
Düssel, Ger.	236	51.16N	7.03E
Düsseldorf, Ger. (düs'ĕl-dôrf)	147	51.14N	6.47E
Dussen, Neth.	145a	51.43N	4.58E
Dutalan Ula, mts., Mong.	192	49.25N	112.40E
Dutch Harbor, Ak., U.S. (dŭch här'bẽr)	96a	53.58N	166.30W
Duvall, Wa., U.S. (dōō'vâl)	106a	47.44N	121.59W
Duwamish, r., Wa., U.S. (dōō-wăm'ĭsh)	106a	47.24N	122.18W
Duyun, China (dōō-yōn)	188	26.18N	107.40E
Dvinskaya Guba, b., Russia	166	65.10N	38.40E
Dwārka, India	186	22.18N	68.59E
Dwight, Il., U.S. (dwīt)	98	41.00N	88.20W
Dworshak Res, Id., U.S.	104	46.45N	115.50W
Dyat'kovo, Russia (dyät'kō-vō)	162	53.36N	34.19E
Dyer, In., U.S. (dī'ẽr)	101a	41.30N	87.31W
Dyersburg, Tn., U.S. (dī'ẽrz-bûrg)	114	36.02N	89.23W
Dyersville, Ia., U.S. (dī'ẽrz-vĭl)	103	42.28N	91.09W
Dyes Inlet, Wa., U.S. (dīz)	106a	47.37N	122.45W
Dykhtau, Gora, mtn., Russia	168	43.03N	43.08E
Dyment, Can. (dī'mĕnt)	89	49.37N	92.19W
Dzamïn Üüd, Mong.	189	44.38N	111.32E
Dzaoudzi, May. (dzou'dzĭ)	213	12.44S	45.15E
Dzavhan, r., Mong.	188	48.19N	94.08E
Dzerzhinsk, Bela.	162	53.41N	27.14E
Dzerzhinsk, Russia	166	56.20N	43.50E
Dzerzhyns'k, Ukr.	163	48.26N	37.50E
Dzeržinskij, Russia	239b	55.38N	37.50E
Dzhalal-Abad, Kyrg. (jå-läl'å-bät')	169	40.56N	73.00E
Dzhambul see Zhambyl, Kaz.	158	42.51N	71.29E
Dzhankoy, Ukr. (dzhän'koi)	167	45.43N	34.22E
Dzhizak, Uzb. (dzhĕ'zäk)	169	40.13N	67.58E
Dzhugdzhur Khrebet, mts., Russia (jŏŏg-jōōr')	165	56.15N	137.00E
Działoszyce, Pol. (jyä-wō-shĕ'tsĕ)	155	50.21N	20.22E
Dzibalchén, Mex. (zē-bäl-chĕ'n)	120a	19.25N	89.39W
Dzidzantún, Mex. (zēd-zän-tōō'n)	120a	21.18N	89.00W
Dzierżoniów, Pol. (dzyĕr-zhôn'yŭf)	154	50.44N	16.38E
Dzilam González, Mex. (zē-lä'm-gôn-zä'lĕz)	120a	21.21N	88.53W
Dzitás, Mex. (zē-tá's)	120a	20.47N	88.32W
Dzungaria, reg., China (dzŏŏŋ-gä'rĭ-å)	188	44.39N	86.13E
Dzungarian Gate, p., Asia	188	45.00N	88.00E

E

PLACE (Pronunciation)	PAGE	Lat. °′	Long. °′
Eagle, W.V., U.S.	98	38.10N	81.20W
Eagle, r., Co., U.S.	109	39.32N	106.28W
Eaglecliff, Wa., U.S. (ē'gl-klĭf)	106c	46.10N	123.13W
Eagle Creek, r., In., U.S.	101g	39.54N	86.17W
Eagle Grove, Ia., U.S.	103	42.39N	93.55W
Eagle Lake, Me., U.S.	92	47.03N	68.38W
Eagle Lake, Tx., U.S.	113	29.37N	96.20W
Eagle Lake, l., Ca., U.S.	104	40.45N	120.52W
Eagle Mountain, Ca., U.S.	108	33.49N	115.27W
Eagle Mountain L, Tx., U.S.	107c	32.56N	97.27W
Eagle Pass, Tx., U.S.	96	28.49N	100.30W
Eagle Pk, Ca., U.S.	104	41.18N	120.11W
Eagle Rock, neigh., Ca., U.S.	232	34.09N	118.12W
Ealing, Eng., U.K. (ē'lĭng)	144b	51.29N	0.19W
Earle, Ar., U.S. (ûrl)	111	35.14N	90.28W
Earlington, Ky., U.S. (ûr'lĭng-tŭn)	114	37.15N	87.31W
Easley, S.C., U.S. (ēz'lĭ)	115	34.48N	82.37W
East, r., N.Y., U.S.	228	40.48N	73.48W
East, Mount, mtn., Pan.	116a	9.09N	79.46W
East Alton, Il., U.S. (ôl'tŭn)	107e	38.53N	90.08W
East Angus, Can. (ăŋ'gŭs)	91	45.35N	71.40W
East Arlington, Ma., U.S.	227a	42.25N	71.08W
East Aurora, N.Y., U.S. (ô-rō'rå)	101c	42.46N	78.38W
East Barnet, neigh., Eng., U.K.	235	51.38N	0.09W
East Bay, b., Tx., U.S.	113a	29.30N	94.41W
East Bedfont, neigh., Eng., U.K.	235	51.27N	0.26W
East Bernstadt, Ky., U.S. (bûrn'stát)	114	37.09N	84.08W
Eastbourne, Eng., U.K. (ēst'bôrn)	151	50.48N	0.16E
East Braintree, Ma., U.S.	227a	42.13N	70.58W
East Burwood, Austl.	243b	37.51S	145.09E
Eastbury, Eng., U.K.	235	51.37N	0.25W
East Caicos, i., T./C. Is. (kī'kōs)	123	21.40N	71.35W
East Cape, c., N.Z.	203a	37.37S	178.33E
East Cape see Dezhnëva, Mys, c., Russia	180	68.00N	172.00W
East Carondelet, Il., U.S. (kå-rŏn'dĕ-lĕt)	107e	38.33N	90.14W
East Cherokee Indian Reservation, I.R., N.C., U.S.	114	35.33N	83.12W
Eastchester, N.Y., U.S.	228	40.57N	73.49W
East Chicago, In., U.S. (shĭ-kô'gō)	101a	41.39N	87.29W
East China Sea, sea, Asia	189	30.28N	125.52E
East Cleveland, Oh., U.S. (klēv'lănd)	101d	41.33N	81.35W
Eastcote, neigh., Eng., U.K.	235	51.35N	0.24W
East Cote Blanche Bay, b., La., U.S. (kōt blänsh')	113	29.30N	92.07W
East Des Moines, r., Ia., U.S. (dē moin')	103	42.57N	94.17W
East Detroit, Mi., U.S. (dĕ-troit')	101b	42.28N	82.57W
Easter Island see Pascua, Isla de, i., Chile	225	26.50S	109.00W
Eastern Ghāts, mts., India	183	13.50N	78.45E
Eastern Native, neigh., S. Afr.	244b	26.13S	28.05E
Eastern Turkestan, hist. reg., China (tŏŏr-kĕ-stän')(tûr-kĕ-stăn')	188	39.40N	78.20E
East Falls, neigh., Pa., U.S.	229b	40.01N	75.11W
East Grand Forks, Mn., U.S. (grănd fôrks)	102	47.56N	97.02W
East Greenwich, R.I., U.S. (grĭn'ĭj)	100b	41.40N	71.27W
Eastham, Eng., U.K.	237a	53.19N	2.58W
East Ham, neigh., Eng., U.K.	235	51.32N	0.03E
Easthampton, Ma., U.S. (ēst-hămp'tŭn)	99	42.15N	72.45W
East Hartford, Ct., U.S. (härt'fẽrd)	99	41.45N	72.35W
East Helena, Mt., U.S. (hĕ-hē'nå)	105	46.31N	111.50W
East Hills, Austl.	243a	33.58S	150.59E
East Hills, N.Y., U.S.	228	40.47N	73.38W
East Ilsley, Eng., U.K. (ĭl'slē)	144b	51.30N	1.18W
East Jordan, Mi., U.S. (jôr'dăn)	98	45.05N	85.05W
East Kansas City, Mo., U.S. (kăn'zås)	107f	39.09N	94.30W
East Lamma Channel, strt., H.K.	241c	22.15N	114.07E
Eastland, Tx., U.S. (ēst'lănd)	112	32.24N	98.47W
East Lansdowne, Pa., U.S.	229b	39.56N	75.16W
East Lansing, Mi., U.S. (lăn'sĭng)	98	42.45N	84.30W
Eastlawn, Mi., U.S.	101b	42.15N	83.35W
East Leavenworth, Mo., U.S. (lĕv'ĕn-wûrth)	107f	39.18N	94.50W
East Liberty, neigh., Pa., U.S.	230b	40.27N	79.55W
East Lindfield, Austl.	243a	33.46S	151.11E
East Liverpool, Oh., U.S. (lĭv'ẽr-pōōl)	98	40.40N	80.35W
East London, S. Afr. (lŭn'dŭn)	212	33.02S	27.54E
East Los Angeles, Ca., U.S. (lōs ăŋ'hå-lās)	107a	34.01N	118.09W
Eastmain, r., Can. (ēst'măn)	85	52.12N	73.19W
East Malling, Eng., U.K.	235	51.17N	0.26E
Eastman, Ga., U.S. (ēst'măn)	114	32.10N	83.11W
East Meadow, N.Y., U.S.	228	40.43N	73.34W
East Millstone, N.J., U.S. (mĭl'stōn)	100a	40.30N	74.35W
East Molesey, Eng., U.K.	235	51.24N	0.21W
East Moline, Il., U.S. (mō-lēn')	103	41.31N	90.28W
East Newark, N.J., U.S.	228	40.45N	74.10W
East New York, neigh., N.Y., U.S.	228	40.40N	73.53W
East Nishnabotna, r., Ia., U.S. (nĭsh-nå-bŏt'nå)	102	40.53N	95.23W
East Norwich, N.Y., U.S.	228	40.50N	73.32W
Easton, Md., U.S. (ēs'tŭn)	99	38.45N	76.05W
Easton, Pa., U.S.	99	40.45N	75.15W
Easton L, Ct., U.S.	100a	41.18N	73.17W
East Orange, N.J., U.S. (ŏr'ĕnj)	100a	40.46N	74.12W
East Pakistan see Bangladesh, nation, Asia	183	24.15N	90.00E
East Palo Alto, Ca., U.S.	106b	37.27N	122.07W
East Peoria, Il., U.S. (pē-ō'rĭ-å)	98	40.40N	89.30W
East Pittsburgh, Pa., U.S. (pĭts'bûrg)	101e	40.24N	79.50W
East Point, Ga., U.S.	100c	33.41N	84.27W
Eastport, Me., U.S. (ēst'pōrt)	92	44.53N	67.01W
East Providence, R.I., U.S. (prŏv'ĭ-dĕns)	100b	41.49N	71.22W
East Retford, Eng., U.K. (rĕt'fẽrd)	144a	53.19N	0.56W
East Richmond, Ca., U.S.	231b	37.57N	122.19W
East Rochester, N.Y., U.S. (rŏch'ĕs-tẽr)	99	43.10N	77.30W
East Rockaway, N.Y., U.S.	228	40.39N	73.40W
East Saint Louis, Il., U.S.	97	38.38N	90.10W
East Siberian Sea, sea, Russia (sī-bĭr'y'n)	165	73.00N	153.28E
Eastsound, Wa., U.S. (ēst-sound)	106d	48.42N	122.42W
East Stroudsburg, Pa., U.S. (stroudz'bûrg)	99	41.00N	75.10W
East Syracuse, N.Y., U.S. (sĭr'å-kūs)	99	43.05N	76.00W
East Tavaputs Plateau, plat., Ut., U.S. (tă-vă'-pŭts)	109	39.25N	109.45W
East Tawas, Mi., U.S. (tô'wăs)	98	44.15N	83.30W
East Tilbury, Eng., U.K.	235	51.28N	0.26E
East Tustin, Ca., U.S.	232	33.46N	117.49W
East Walker, r., U.S. (wôk'ẽr)	108	38.36N	119.02W
East Walpole, Ma., U.S.	227a	42.10N	71.13W
East Watertown, Ma., U.S.	227a	42.22N	71.10W
East Weymouth, Ma., U.S.	227a	42.13N	70.55W
Eastwick, neigh., Pa., U.S.	229b	39.55N	75.14W
East Wickham, neigh., Eng., U.K.	235	51.28N	0.07E
Eastwood, Austl.	243a	33.48S	151.05E
East York, Can.	83d	43.41S	79.20W
Eaton, Co., U.S. (ē'tŭn)	110	40.31N	104.42W
Eaton, Oh., U.S.	98	39.45N	84.40W
Eaton Estates, Oh., U.S.	101d	41.19N	82.01W
Eaton Rapids, Mi., U.S. (răp'ĭdz)	98	42.30N	84.40W
Eatonton, Ga., U.S. (ē'tŭn-tŭn)	114	33.20N	83.24W
Eatontown, N.J., U.S. (ē'tŭn-toun)	100a	40.18N	74.04W
Eaubonne, Fr.	237c	49.00N	2.17E
Eau Claire, Wi., U.S. (ō klâr')	97	44.47N	91.32W
Ebeltoft, Den. (ĕ'bĕl-tŭft)	152	56.11N	10.39E
Ebensburg, Pa., U.S.	99	40.29N	78.44W
Ebersberg, Ger. (ĕ'bĕrs-bĕrgh)	145d	48.05N	11.58E
Ebina, Japan	242a	35.26N	139.25E
Ebingen, Ger. (ā'bĭng-ĕn)	154	48.13N	9.04E
Eboli, Italy (ĕb'ō-lē)	160	40.38N	15.04E
Ebolowa, Cam.	210	2.54N	11.09E
Ebreichsdorf, Aus.	145e	47.58N	16.24E
Ebrié, Lagune, b., C. Iv.	214	5.20N	4.50W
Ebro, r., Spain (ā'brō)	142	42.00N	2.00W
Ebute-Ikorodu, Nig.	244d	6.37N	3.30E
Eccles, Eng., U.K. (ĕk''lz)	144a	53.29N	2.20W
Eccles, W.V., U.S.	98	37.45N	81.10W
Eccleshall, Eng., U.K.	144a	52.51N	2.15W
Eccleston, Eng., U.K.	237a	53.27N	2.47W
Eccleston, Md., U.S.	229c	39.24N	76.44W
Eceabat, Tur.	161	40.10N	26.21E
Echague, Phil. (ā-chä'gwä)	197a	16.43N	121.40E
Echandi, Cerro, mtn., N.A. (sĕ'r-rô-ĕ-chä'nd)	121	9.05N	82.51W
Ech Cheliff, Alg.	210	36.14N	1.32E
Echimamish, r., Can.	89	54.15N	97.30W
Echmiadzin, Arm.	168	40.10N	44.18E
Echo Bay, Can. (ĕk'ō)	107k	46.29N	84.04W
Echoing, r., Can. (ĕk'ō-ĭng)	89	55.15N	91.30W
Echternach, Lux. (ĕk'tẽr-näk)	157	49.48N	6.25E
Echuca, Austl. (ē-chōō'kå)	203	36.10S	144.47E
Écija, Spain (ā'thē-hä)	148	37.20N	5.07W
Eckernförde, Ger.	154	54.27N	9.51E
Eclipse, Va., U.S. (ē-klĭps')	100g	36.55N	76.29W
Ecorse, Mi., U.S. (ē-kôrs')	101b	42.15N	83.09W
Ecuador, nation, S.A. (ĕk'wå-dôr)	130	0.00N	78.30W
Ed, Erit.	211	13.57N	41.37E
Eda, neigh., Japan	242a	35.34N	139.34E
Eddyville, Ky., U.S. (ĕd'ĭ-vĭl)	114	37.03N	88.03W
Ede, Nig.	215	7.44N	4.27E
Edéa, Cam. (ĕ-dā'ä)	210	3.48N	10.08E
Éden, Braz.	234c	22.48S	43.24W
Eden, Tx., U.S.	112	31.13N	99.51W
Eden, Ut., U.S.	107b	41.18N	111.49W
Eden, r., Eng., U.K. (ē'dĕn)	150	54.40N	2.35W
Edenbridge, Eng., U.K. (ē'dĕn-brĭj)	144b	51.11N	0.05E
Edendale, S. Afr.	244b	26.09S	28.09E
Edenham, Eng., U.K. (ē'd'n-ăm)	144a	52.46N	0.25W
Eden Prairie, Mn., U.S. (prâr'ĭ)	107g	44.51N	93.29W
Edenton, N.C., U.S. (ē'dĕn-tŭn)	115	36.02N	76.37W
Edenton, Oh., U.S.	101f	39.14N	84.02W
Edenvale, S. Afr. (ĕd'ĕn-vāl)	213b	26.09S	28.10E
Edenvale Location, S. Afr.	244b	26.08S	28.11E
Edenville, S. Afr. (ē'd'n-vĭl)	218d	27.33S	27.42E
Eder, r., Ger. (ā'dẽr)	154	51.05N	8.52E
Edgefield, S.C., U.S. (ĕj'fēld)	115	33.52N	81.55W
Edge Hill, neigh., Eng., U.K.	237a	53.24N	2.57W
Edgeley, N.D., U.S. (ĕj'lĭ)	102	46.24N	98.43W
Edgemere, Md., U.S.	229c	39.14N	76.27W
Edgemont, S.D., U.S. (ĕj'mŏnt)	102	43.19N	103.50W
Edgerton, Wi., U.S. (ĕj'ẽr-tŭn)	103	42.49N	89.06W
Edgewater, Al., U.S. (ĕj-wô-tẽr)	100h	33.31N	86.52W
Edgewater, Md., U.S.	100e	38.58N	76.35W
Edgewater, N.J., U.S.	228	40.50N	73.58W
Edgewood, Can. (ĕj'wŏŏd)	87	49.47N	118.08W
Edgware, neigh., Eng., U.K.	235	51.37N	0.17W
Edgwater, N.Y., U.S.	230a	43.03N	78.55W
Edgworth, Eng., U.K.	237b	53.39N	2.24W
Édhessa, Grc.	149	40.48N	22.04E
Edina, Mn., U.S. (ē-dī'nå)	107g	44.55N	93.20W
Edina, Mo., U.S.	111	40.10N	92.11W
Edinburg, In., U.S. (ĕd''n-bûrg)	98	39.20N	85.55W
Edinburg, Tx., U.S.	112	26.18N	98.08W
Edinburgh, Scot., U.K. (ĕd''n-bŭr-ō)	142	55.57N	3.10W
Edirne, Tur.	161	41.41N	26.35E
Edison Park, neigh., Il., U.S.	231a	42.01N	87.49W
Edisto, r., S.C., U.S. (ĕd'ĭs-tō)	115	33.10N	80.50W
Edisto, North Fork, r., S.C., U.S.	115	33.42N	81.24W
Edisto, South Fork, r., S.C., U.S.	115	33.43N	81.35W
Edisto Island, S.C., U.S.	115	32.32N	80.20W
Edmond, Ok., U.S. (ĕd'mŭnd)	111	35.39N	97.29W
Edmonds, Wa., U.S. (ĕd'mŭndz)	106a	47.49N	122.23W
Edmonston, Md., U.S.	229d	38.57N	76.56W
Edmonton, Can.	84	53.33N	113.28W
Edmonton, neigh., Eng., U.K.	235	51.37N	0.04W
Edmundston, Can. (ĕd'mŭn-stŭn)	85	47.22N	68.20W
Edna, Tx., U.S. (ĕd'nå)	113	28.59N	96.39W
Edo, r., Japan	242a	35.41N	139.53E
Edogawa, neigh., Japan	242a	35.42N	139.52E
Edremit, Tur. (ĕd-rē-mĕt')	149	39.35N	27.00E

ng-sing; ŋ-baŋk; N-nasalized n; nŏd; cŏmmit; ōld; ôbey; ôrder; oi-boil; fōōd; ŏŏ-as oo in foot; ou-out; s-soft; sh-dish; th-thin; pūre; ûnite; ûrn; stŭd; circŭs; ü-as in French tu; '-indeterminate vowel.

284 Edremit Körfezi – Emmetsburg

PLACE (Pronunciation)	PAGE	Lat. °′	Long. °′
Edremit Körfezi, b., Tur.	161	39.28N	26.35E
Edson, Can. (ĕd'sŭn)	84	53.35N	116.26W
Edward, i., Can. (ĕd'wẽrd)	90	48.21N	88.29W
Edward, l., Afr.	212	0.25S	29.40E
Edwardsville, Il., U.S. (ĕd'wẽrdz-vĭl)	107e	38.49N	89.58W
Edwardsville, In., U.S.	101h	38.17N	85.53W
Edwardsville, Ks., U.S.	107f	39.04N	94.49W
Eel, r., Ca., U.S. (ēl)	104	40.39N	124.15W
Eel, r., In., U.S.	98	40.50N	85.55W
Efate, i., Vanuatu (å-fä'tä)	203	18.02S	168.29E
Effigy Mounds National Monument, rec., Ia., U.S. (ĕf'ĭ-jü mounds)	103	43.04N	91.15W
Effingham, Il., U.S. (ĕf'ĭng-hăm)	98	39.05N	88.30W
Ega, r., Spain (ā'gä)	158	42.40N	2.20W
Egadi, Isole, is., Italy (ĕ'sō-lĕ-ĕ'gä-dē)	148	38.01N	12.00E
Egea de los Caballeros, Spain	158	42.07N	1.05W
Egegik, Ak., U.S. (ĕg'ĕ-jĭt)	95	58.10N	157.22W
Eger, Hung. (ĕ gĕr)	155	47.53N	20.24E
Egersund, Nor. (ĕ'ghĕr-sōn')	146	58.29N	6.01E
Egg Harbor, N.J., U.S. (ĕg här'bẽr)	99	39.30N	74.35W
Egham, Eng., U.K. (ĕg'ŭm)	144b	51.24N	0.33W
Egiyn, r., Mong.	188	49.41N	100.40E
Egmont, Cape, c., N.Z. (ĕg'mŏnt)	203a	39.18S	173.49E
Egota, neigh., Japan	242a	35.43N	139.40E
Egypt, nation, Afr. (ē'jĭpt)	211	26.58N	27.01E
Eha-Amufu, Nig.	215	6.40N	7.46E
Ehingen, neigh., Ger.	236	51.22N	6.42E
Ehringhausen, Ger.	236	51.11N	7.33E
Ehringhausen, neigh., Ger.	236	51.09N	7.11E
Eibar, Spain (ā'ê-bär)	158	43.12N	2.20W
Eiche, Ger.	238a	52.34N	13.36E
Eichlinghofen, neigh., Ger.	236	51.29N	7.24E
Eichstätt, Ger. (īk'shtät)	154	48.54N	11.14E
Eichwalde, Ger. (īκ'väl-dē)	145b	52.22N	13.37E
Eickerend, Ger.	236	51.13N	6.34E
Eidfjord, Nor. (ĕīd'fyŏr)	152	60.28N	7.04E
Eidsvoll, Nor. (ĭdhs'vôl)	146	60.19N	11.15E
Eifel, mts., Ger. (ī'fĕl)	154	50.08N	6.30E
Eiffel, Tour, pt. of i., Fr.	237c	48.51N	2.18E
Eigen, neigh., Ger.	236	51.33N	6.57E
Eighty Mile Beach, cst., Austl.	202	19.00S	121.00E
Eilenburg, Ger. (ī'lĕn-bòrgh)	154	51.27N	12.38E
Einbeck, Ger. (īn'bĕk)	154	51.49N	9.52E
Eindhoven, Neth. (īnd'hō-vĕn)	151	51.29N	5.20E
Eisenach, Ger. (ī'zĕn-äκ)	147	50.58N	10.18E
Eisenhüttenstadt, Ger.	154	52.08N	14.40E
Ejura, Ghana	214	7.23N	1.22W
Ejutla de Crespo, Mex. (å-hòt'lă dā kräs'pō)	119	16.34N	96.44W
Ekanga, Zaire	216	2.23S	23.14E
Ekenäs, Fin. (ĕ'kĕ-nâs)	153	59.59N	23.25E
Ekeren, Bel.	145a	51.17N	4.27E
Ekoli, Zaire	216	0.23S	24.16E
Eksāra, India	240a	22.38N	88.17E
El Aaiún, W. Sah.	210	26.45N	13.15W
El Affroun, Alg. (ĕl åf-froun')	159	36.28N	2.38E
El Aguacate, Ven.	234a	10.28N	66.59W
Elands, r., S. Afr. (ė̇lånds)	213c	31.48S	26.09E
Elands, r., S. Afr.	218d	25.11S	28.52E
Elandsfontein, S. Afr.	244b	26.10S	28.12E
El Arahal, Spain (ĕl ä-rä-äl')	158	37.17N	5.32W
El Arba, Alg.	159	36.35N	3.10E
Elat, Isr.	182	29.34N	34.57E
Elâziğ, Tur. (ĕl-ä'zĕz)	182	38.40N	39.00E
Elba, Al., U.S. (ĕl'bå)	114	31.25N	86.01W
Elba, Isola d', i., Italy (ĕ-sō lä-d-ĕl'bȧ)	148	42.42N	10.25E
El Banco, Col. (ĕl băn'cō)	130	8.58N	74.01W
Elbansan, Alb. (ĕl-bä-sän')	149	41.08N	20.05E
El Barco de Valdeorras, Spain (ĕl bär'kō)	158	42.26N	6.58W
Elbe (Labe), r., Eur. (ĕl'bĕ)(lä'bĕ)	142	52.30N	11.30E
Elberfeld, neigh., Ger.	236	51.16N	7.08E
Elbert, Mount, mtn., Co., U.S. (ĕl'bẽrt)	96	39.05N	106.25W
Elberton, Ga., U.S. (ĕl'bẽr-tŭn)	115	34.05N	82.53W
Elbeuf, Fr. (ĕl-bûf')	147	49.16N	0.59E
El Beyadh, Alg.	148	33.42N	1.06E
Elbistan, Tur. (ĕl-bē-stän')	149	38.20N	37.10E
Elbląg, Pol. (ĕl'blăng)	146	54.11N	19.25E
El Bonillo, Spain (ĕl bō-nēl'yō)	158	38.56N	2.31W
El Boulaïda, Alg.	210	36.33N	2.45E
Elbow, r., Can. (ĕl'bō)	83e	51.03N	114.24W
Elbow Cay, i., Bah.	122	26.25N	76.55W
Elbow Lake, Mn., U.S.	102	46.00N	95.59W
El'brus, Gora, mtn., Russia (ĕl'brōs')	164	43.20N	42.25E
Elbrus, Mount see El'brus, Gora, mtn., Russia	164	43.20N	42.25E
El Burgo de Osma, Spain	158	41.35N	3.02W
Elburz Mountains, mts., Iran (ĕl'bòrz')	182	36.30N	51.00E
El Cajon, Col. (ĕl-kä-kō'n)	130a	4.50N	76.35W
El Cajon, Ca., U.S.	108a	32.48N	116.58W
El Calvario, neigh., Cuba	233b	23.05N	82.20W
El Cambur, Ven. (käm-bōōr')	131b	10.24N	68.06W
El Campamento, neigh., Spain	238b	40.24N	3.46W
El Campo, Tx., U.S. (kăm'pō)	113	29.13N	96.17W
El Caribe, Ven.	234a	10.37N	66.49W
El Carmen, Chile (kå'r-mĕn)	129b	34.14S	71.23W
El Carmen, Col. (kå'r-mĕn)	130	9.54N	75.12W
El Casco, Ca., U.S. (kăs'kō)	107a	33.59N	117.08W
El Centro, Ca., U.S. (sĕn'trō)	108	32.47N	115.33W
El Cerrito, Ca., U.S. (sĕr-rē'tō)	106b	37.55N	122.19W
Elche, Spain (ĕl'chā)	159	38.15N	0.42W
El Cojo, Ven.	234a	10.37N	66.53W
El Corozo, Ven.	234a	10.35N	66.58W
El Cotorro, Cuba	233b	23.03N	82.16W
El Cuyo, Mex.	120a	21.30N	87.42W
Elda, Spain (ĕl'dä)	159	38.28N	0.44W
Elder Mills, Can.	227c	43.49N	79.38W
El Djelfa, Alg.	210	34.40N	3.17E
El Djouf, des., Afr. (ĕl djōōf)	210	21.45N	7.05W
Eldon, Ia., U.S. (ĕl-dŭn)	103	40.55N	92.15W
Eldon, Mo., U.S.	111	38.21N	92.36W
Eldora, Ia., U.S. (ĕl-dō'rȧ)	103	42.21N	93.08W
El Dorado, Ar., U.S. (ĕl dō-rä'dō)	97	33.13N	92.39W
Eldorado, Il., U.S.	98	37.50N	88.30W
El Dorado, Ks., U.S.	111	37.49N	96.51W
Eldorado Springs, Mo., U.S. (sprĭngz)	111	37.51N	94.02W
Eldoret, Kenya (ĕl-dō-rĕt')	217	0.31N	35.17E
El Ebano, Mex. (ā-bä'nō)	118	22.13N	98.26W
Electra, Tx., U.S. (ė̇-lĕk'trȧ)	110	34.02N	98.54W
Electric Peak, mtn., Mt., U.S. (ė̇-lĕk'trĭk)	105	45.03N	110.52W
Elektrogorsk, Russia (ĕl-yĕk'trô-gôrsk)	172b	55.53N	38.48E
Elektrostal', Russia (ĕl-yĕk'trō-stál)	172b	55.47N	38.27E
Elektrougli, Russia	172b	55.43N	38.13E
El Encantado, Ven.	234a	10.27N	66.47W
Elephanta Island (Ghārāpuri), i., India	240e	18.57N	72.55E
Elephant Butte Reservoir, res., N.M., U.S. (ĕl'ė̇-fănt būt)	96	33.25N	107.10W
El Escorial, Spain (ĕl-ĕs-kō-ryä'l)	159a	40.38N	4.08W
El Espino, Nic. (ĕl-ĕs-pē'nō)	120	13.26N	86.48W
Eleuthera, i., Bah. (ė̇-lū'thẽr-ȧ)	117	25.05N	76.10W
Eleuthera Point, c., Bah.	122	24.35N	76.05W
Eleven Point, r., Mo., U.S. (ė̇-lĕv'ĕn)	111	36.53N	91.39W
El Ferrol, Spain (fā-rōl')	142	43.30N	8.12W
Elgin, Scot., U.K.	150	57.40N	3.30W
Elgin, Il., U.S. (ĕl'jĭn)	101a	42.03N	88.16W
Elgin, Ne., U.S.	102	41.58N	98.04W
Elgin, Or., U.S.	104	45.34N	117.58W
Elgin, Tx., U.S.	113	30.21N	97.22W
Elgin, Wa., U.S.	106a	47.23N	122.42W
Elgon, Mount, mtn., Afr. (ĕl'gōn)	211	1.00N	34.25E
El Granada, Ca., U.S.	231b	37.30N	122.28W
El Grara, Alg.	148	32.50N	4.26E
El Grullo, Mex. (grōōl-yō)	118	19.46N	104.10W
El Guapo, Ven. (gwå'pō)	131b	10.07N	66.00W
El Guarapo, Ven.	234a	10.36N	66.58W
El Hank, reg., Afr.	210	23.44N	6.45W
El Hatillo, Ven. (ä-tē'l-yō)	131b	10.08N	65.13W
Elie, Can. (ē'lē)	83f	49.55N	97.45W
Elila, r., Zaire (ĕ-lē'lå)	212	3.30S	28.00E
Elisa, i., Wa., U.S. (ė̇-lī'så)	106d	48.43N	122.37W
Élisabethville see Lubumbashi, Zaire	212	11.40S	27.28E
Elisenvaara, Russia (ā-lē'sĕn-vä'rå)	153	61.25N	29.46E
Elizabeth, La., U.S. (ė̇-lĭz'ȧ-bĕth)	113	30.50N	92.47W
Elizabeth, N.J., U.S.	100a	40.40N	74.13W
Elizabeth, Pa., U.S.	101e	40.16N	79.53W
Elizabeth City, N.C., U.S.	115	36.15N	76.15W
Elizabethton, Tn., U.S. (ė̇-lĭz-å-bĕth'tŭn)	115	36.19N	82.12W
Elizabethtown, Ky., U.S. (ė̇-lĭz'ȧ-bĕth-toun)	98	37.40N	85.55W
El Jadida, Mor.	210	33.14N	8.34W
Elk, Pol.	146	53.53N	22.23E
Elk, r., Can.	87	50.00N	115.00W
Elk, r., Tn., U.S.	114	35.05N	86.36W
Elk, r., W.V., U.S.	98	38.30N	81.05W
El Kairouan, Tun. (kĕr-ō-än)	210	35.46N	10.04E
Elk City, Ok., U.S. (ĕlk)	110	35.23N	99.23W
El Kef, Tun. (xĕf')	148	36.14N	8.42E
Elkhart, In., U.S. (ĕlk'härt)	98	41.40N	86.00W
Elkhart, Ks., U.S.	110	37.00N	101.54W
Elkhart, Tx., U.S.	113	31.38N	95.35W
Elkhorn, Wi., U.S. (ĕlk'hôrn)	103	42.39N	88.32W
Elkhorn, r., Ne., U.S.	102	42.06N	97.46W
Elkin, N.C., U.S. (ĕl'kĭn)	115	36.15N	80.50W
Elkins Park, Pa., U.S.	229b	40.05N	75.08W
Elk Island, i., Can.	89	50.45N	96.32W
Elk Island National Park, rec., Can. (ĕlk ī'lănd)	84	53.37N	112.45W
Elko, Nv., U.S. (ĕl'kō)	96	40.51N	115.46W
Elk Point, S.D., U.S.	102	42.41N	96.41W
Elk Rapids, Mi., U.S. (răp'ĭdz)	98	44.55N	85.25W
Elkridge, Md., U.S.	229c	39.13N	76.42W
Elk River, Id., U.S. (rĭv'ẽr)	104	46.47N	116.11W
Elk River, Mn., U.S.	103	45.17N	93.33W
Elkton, Ky., U.S. (ĕlk'tŭn)	114	36.47N	87.08W
Elkton, Md., U.S.	99	39.35N	75.50W
Elkton, S.D., U.S.	102	44.15N	96.28W
Elland, Eng., U.K. (el'ănd)	144a	53.41N	1.50W
Ellen, Mount, mtn., Ut., U.S. (ĕl'ĕn)	109	38.05N	110.50W
Ellendale, N.D., U.S. (ĕl'ĕn-dāl)	102	46.01N	98.33W
Ellensburg, Wa., U.S. (ĕl'ĕnz-bûrg)	104	47.00N	120.31W
Ellenville, N.Y., U.S. (ĕl'ĕn-vĭl)	99	41.40N	74.25W
Ellerslie, Can. (ĕl'ẽrz-lė̇)	83g	53.25N	113.30W
Ellesmere, Eng., U.K. (ĕlz'mẽr)	144a	52.55N	2.54W
Ellesmere Island, i., Can.	82	81.00N	80.00W
Ellesmere Park, Eng., U.K.	237b	53.29N	2.20W
Ellesmere Port, Eng., U.K.	144a	53.17N	2.54W
Ellice Islands see Tuvalu, nation, Oc.	3	5.20S	174.00E
Ellicott City, is., Md., U.S. (ĕl'ĭ-kŏt sĭ'tė̇)	100e	39.16N	76.48W
Ellicott Creek, r., N.Y., U.S.	101c	43.00N	78.46W
El Limoncito, Ven.	234a	10.29N	66.47W
Ellinghorst, neigh., Ger.	236	51.34N	6.57E
Elliot, S. Afr.	213c	31.19S	27.52E
Elliot, Wa., U.S. (ĕl'ĭ-ŭt)	106a	47.28N	122.08W
Elliotdale, S. Afr. (ĕl-ĭ-ŏt'dāl)	213c	31.58S	28.42E
Elliot Lake, Can.	90	46.23N	82.39W
Ellis, Ks., U.S. (ĕl'ĭs)	110	38.56N	99.34W
Ellisville, Ms., U.S. (ĕl'ĭs-vĭl)	114	31.37N	89.10W
Ellisville, Mo., U.S.	107e	38.35N	90.35W
Ellsworth, Ks., U.S. (ĕlz'wûrth)	110	38.43N	98.14W
Ellsworth, Me., U.S.	92	44.33N	68.26W
Ellsworth Mountains, mts., Ant.	219	77.00S	90.00W
Ellwangen, Ger. (ĕl'văng-gĕn)	154	48.47N	10.08E
Elm, Ger. (ĕlm)	145c	53.31N	9.13E
Elm, r., S.D., U.S.	102	45.47N	98.28W
Elm, r., W.V., U.S.	98	38.30N	81.05W
Elma, Wa., U.S. (ĕl'må)	104	47.02N	123.20W
El Mahdia, Tun. (mä-dēå)(mä'dė̇-ȧ)	148	35.30N	11.09E
Elmendorf, Tx., U.S. (ĕl'mĕn-dôrf)	107d	29.16N	98.20W
El Menia, Alg.	210	30.39N	2.52E
Elm Fork, Tx., U.S. (ĕlm fôrk)	107c	32.55N	96.56W
Elmhurst, Il., U.S. (ĕlm'hûrst)	101a	41.54N	87.56W
Elmhurst, neigh., N.Y., U.S.	228	40.44N	73.53W
El Miliyya, Alg. (mē'ä)	210	36.30N	6.16E
Elmira, N.Y., U.S. (ĕl-mī'rȧ)	99	42.05N	76.50W
Elmira Heights, N.Y., U.S.	99	42.10N	76.50W
El Modena, Ca., U.S. (mō-dē'nō)	107a	33.47N	117.48W
El Mohammadia, Alg.	159	35.35N	0.05E
El Molinito, Mex.	233a	19.27N	99.15W
Elmont, N.Y., U.S.	228	40.42N	73.42W
El Monte, Ca., U.S. (mŏn'tå)	107a	34.04N	118.02W
El Morro National Monument, rec., N.M., U.S.	109	35.05N	108.20W
Elmshorn, Ger. (ĕlms'hôrn)	154	53.45N	9.39E
Elmwood, neigh., Pa., U.S.	229b	39.56N	75.14W
Elmwood Park, Il., U.S.	231a	41.55N	87.49W
Elmwood Place, Oh., U.S. (ĕlm'wòd plās)	101f	39.11N	84.30W
Elokomin, r., Wa., U.S. (ė̇-lō'kô-mĭn)	106c	46.16N	123.16W
El Oro, Mex. (ō-rō)	118	19.49N	100.04W
El Palmar, Ven.	234a	10.38N	66.52W
El Pao, Ven. (ĕl på'ō)	130	8.08N	62.37W
El Paraíso, Hond. (pä-rä-ē'sō)	120	13.55N	86.35W
El Pardo, Spain (pä'r-dō)	159a	40.31N	3.47W
El Paso, Tx., U.S. (pas'ō)	96	31.47N	106.27W
El Pedregal, neigh., Ven.	234a	10.30N	66.51W
El Pilar, Ven. (pē-lä'r)	131b	9.56N	64.48W
El Plantío, neigh., Spain	238b	40.28N	3.49W
El Porvenir, Pan. (pôr-vä-nēr')	121	9.34N	78.55W
El Puerto de Santa María, Spain	158	36.36N	6.18W
El Qala, Alg.	148	36.52N	8.23E
El Qoll, Alg.	210	37.02N	6.29E
El Real, Pan. (rā-äl)	121	8.07N	77.43W
El Recreo, neigh., Ven.	234a	10.30N	66.53W
El Reloj, Mex.	233a	19.18N	99.08W
El Reno, Ok., U.S. (rē'nō)	111	35.31N	97.57W
El Rincón de la Florida, Chile	234b	33.33S	70.34W
Elroy, Wi., U.S. (ĕl'roi)	103	43.44N	90.17W
Elsa, Can.	95	63.55N	135.25W
Elsah, Il., U.S. (ĕl'zȧ)	107e	38.57N	90.22W
El Salto, Mex. (säl'tō)	118	23.48N	105.22W
El Salvador, nation, N.A.	116	14.00N	89.30W
El Sauce, Nic. (ĕl-så'ō-sĕ)	120	13.00N	86.40W
Elsberry, Mo., U.S. (ĕlz'bĕr-ĭ)	111	39.09N	90.44W
Elsburg, S. Afr.	244b	26.15S	28.12E
Elsdorf, Ger. (ĕls'dōrf)	157c	50.56N	6.35E
El Segundo, Ca., U.S. (sĕgŭn'dō)	107a	33.55N	118.24W
Elsinore, Ca., U.S. (ĕl'sĭ-nôr)	107a	33.40N	117.19W
Elsinore Lake, l., Ca., U.S.	107a	33.38N	117.21W
Elstorf, Ger. (ĕls'tōrf)	145c	53.25N	9.48E
Elstree, Eng., U.K.	235	51.39N	0.16W
Eltham, Austl. (ĕl'thăm)	201a	37.43S	145.08E
Eltham, neigh., Eng., U.K.	235	51.27N	0.04E
El Tigre, Ven. (tē'grĕ)	130	8.49N	64.15W
Elton, Eng., U.K.	237a	53.16N	2.49W
El'ton, l., Russia	167	49.10N	47.00E
El Toreo, pt. of i., Mex.	233a	19.27N	99.13W
El Toro, Ca., U.S. (tō'rō)	107a	33.37N	117.42W
El Triunfo, El Sal.	120	13.17N	88.32W
El Triunfo, Hond. (ĕl-trē-ōō'n-fō)	120	13.06N	87.00W
Elūru, India	183	16.44N	80.09E
El Vado Res, N.M., U.S.	109	36.37N	106.30W
El Valle, neigh., Ven.	234a	10.27N	66.55W
Elvas, Port. (ĕl'väzh)	148	38.53N	7.11W
Elverum, Nor. (ĕl'vĕ-ròm)	152	60.53N	11.33E
El Viejo, Nic. (ĕl-vyĕ'κō)	120	12.10N	87.10W
El Viejo, vol., Nic.	120	12.44N	87.03W
Elvins, Mo., U.S. (ĕl'vĭnz)	111	37.49N	90.31W
El Wad, Alg.	210	33.23N	6.49E
El Wak, Kenya (wäk')	211	3.00N	41.00E
Elwell, Lake, res., Mt., U.S.	105	48.22N	111.17W
Elwood, Il., U.S. (ĕ'wòd)	101a	41.24N	88.07W
Elwood, In., U.S.	98	40.15N	85.50W
Ely, Eng., U.K. (ē'lĭ)	151	52.25N	0.17E
Ely, Mn., U.S.	103	47.54N	91.53W
Ely, Nv., U.S.	96	39.16N	114.53W
Elyria, Oh., U.S. (ė̇-lĭr'ĭ-ȧ)	101d	41.22N	82.07W
El Zamural, Ven.	234a	10.27N	67.00W
El Zig-Zag, Ven.	234a	10.33N	66.58W
Ema, r., Est. (â'må)	153	58.25N	27.00E
Emāmshahr, Iran	182	36.25N	55.01E
Emån, r., Swe.	152	57.15N	15.46E
Embarrass, r., Il., U.S. (ĕm-băr'ăs)	98	39.15N	88.05W
Embrun, Can. (ĕm'brŭn)	83c	45.16N	75.17W
Embrun, Fr. (äɴ-brûɴ')	157	44.35N	6.32E
Embu, Braz.	234d	23.39S	46.51W
Embu, Kenya	217	0.32S	37.27E
Emden, Ger. (ĕm'dĕn)	154	53.21N	7.15E
Émerainville, Fr.	237c	48.49N	2.37E
Emerson, Can. (ĕm'ẽr-sŭn)	84	49.00N	97.12W
Emerson, N.J., U.S.	228	40.58N	74.02W
Emeryville, Ca., U.S. (ĕm'ẽr-ĭ-vĭl)	106b	37.50N	122.17W
Emi Koussi, mtn., Chad (å'mė̇ κōō-sē')	211	19.50N	18.30E
Emiliano Zapata, Mex. (ĕ-mē-lyá'nō-zä-pá'tå)	119	17.45N	91.46W
Emilia-Romagna, hist. reg., Italy (ē-mēl'yä rô-må'n-yä)	160	44.35N	10.48E
Eminence, Ky., U.S. (ĕm'ĭ-nĕns)	98	38.25N	85.15W
Emira Island, i., Pap. N. Gui. (ā-mė̇-rä')	197	1.40S	150.28E
Emmen, Neth. (ĕm'ĕn)	151	52.48N	6.55E
Emmerich, Ger. (ĕm'ẽr-ĭk)	157c	51.51N	6.16E
Emmetsburg, Ia., U.S. (ĕm'ĕts-bûrg)	103	43.07N	94.41W

ăt; finăl; rāte; senāte; ärm; åsk; sofȧ; fâre; ch-choose; dh-as th in other; bē; ėvent; bĕt; recĕnt; cratẽr; g-gō; gh-guttural g; bĭt; ĭ-short neutral; rīde; κ-guttural k as ch in German ich;

PRONOUNCING INDEX

Emmett-Everard Ranges 285

PLACE (Pronunciation)	PAGE	Lat. °'	Long. °'
Emmett, Id., U.S. (ĕm'ĕt)	104	43.53N	116.30W
Emmons, Mount, mtn., Ut., U.S. (ĕm'ŭnz)	96	40.43N	110.20W
Emory Peak, mtn., Tx., U.S. (ĕ'mŏ-rē pēk)	112	29.13N	103.20W
Empoli, Italy (ām'pô-lē)	160	43.43N	10.55E
Emporia, Ks., U.S. (ĕm-pō'rĭ-ȧ)	96	38.24N	96.11W
Emporia, Va., U.S.	115	37.40N	77.34W
Emporium, Pa., U.S. (ĕm-pō'rĭ-ŭm)	99	41.30N	78.15W
Empty Quarter see Ar Rub'al Khālī, des., Asia	182	20.00N	51.00E
Ems, r., Ger. (ĕms)	154	52.52N	7.16E
Emst, neigh., Ger.	236	51.21N	7.30E
Ems-Weser Kanal, can., Ger.	154	52.23N	8.11E
Emsworth, Pa., U.S.	230b	40.30N	80.04W
Enånger, Swe. (ĕn-ôŋ'gĕr)	152	61.36N	16.55E
Encantada, Cerro de la, mtn., Mex. (sĕ'r-rô-dĕ-lä-ĕn-kän-tä'dä)	116	31.58N	115.15W
Encanto, Cape, c., Phil. (ĕn-kän'tō)	197a	15.44N	121.46E
Encarnação, neigh., Port.	238d	38.47N	9.06W
Encarnación, Para. (ĕn-kär-nä-syōn')	132	27.26S	55.52W
Encarnación de Díaz, Mex. (ĕn-kär-nä-syōn dā dē'āz)	118	21.34N	102.15W
Encinal, Tx., U.S. (ĕn'sĭ-nôl)	112	28.02N	99.22W
Encino, neigh., Ca., U.S.	232	34.09N	118.30W
Encontrados, Ven. (ĕn-kōn-trä'dōs)	130	9.01N	72.10W
Encounter Bay, b., Austl. (ĕn-koun'tēr)	202	35.50S	138.45E
Endako, r., Can.	86	54.05N	125.30W
Endau, r., Malay.	181b	2.29N	103.40E
Enderbury, i., Kir. (ĕn'dĕr-bûrĭ)	224	2.00S	171.00W
Enderby Land, reg., Ant. (ĕn'dĕr bĭĭ)	219	72.00S	52.00E
Enderlin, N.D., U.S. (ĕn'dĕr-lĭn)	102	46.38N	97.37W
Endicott, N.Y., U.S. (ĕn'dĭ-kŏt)	99	42.05N	76.00W
Endicott Mountains, mts., Ak., U.S.	95	67.30N	153.45W
Enez, Tur.	161	40.42N	26.05E
Enfer, Pointe d', c., Mart.	121b	14.21N	60.48W
Enfield, Austl.	243a	33.53S	151.06E
Enfield, Eng., U.K.	144b	51.38N	0.06W
Enfield, Ct., U.S. (ĕn'fēld)	99	41.55N	72.35W
Enfield, N.C., U.S.	115	36.10N	77.41W
Engaño, Cabo, c., Dom. Rep. (kä'-bô- ĕn-gä-nô)	117	18.40N	68.30W
Engcobo, S. Afr. (ĕŋg-cô-bô)	213c	31.41S	27.59E
Engel's, Russia (ĕn'gĕls)	167	51.20N	45.40E
Engelskirchen, Ger. (ĕn'gĕls-kĕr'kĕn)	157c	50.59N	7.25E
Engenho de Dentro, neigh., Braz.	234c	22.54S	43.18W
Engenho do Mato, Braz.	234c	22.57S	43.01W
Engenho Nofrvo, neigh., Braz.	234c	22.55S	43.17W
Enggano, Pulau, i., Indon. (ĕng-gä'nō)	196	5.22S	102.18E
Enghien-les-Bains, Fr.	237c	48.58N	2.19E
England, Ar., U.S. (ĭŋ'glănd)	111	34.33N	91.58W
England, , U.K. (ĭŋ'glănd)	142	51.35N	1.40W
Englefield Green, Eng., U.K.	235	51.26N	0.35W
Englewood, Co., U.S. (ĕn'g'l-wŏŏd)	110	39.39N	105.00W
Englewood, N.J., U.S.	100a	40.54N	73.59W
Englewood, neigh., Il., U.S.	231a	41.47N	87.39W
Englewood Cliffs, N.J., U.S.	228	40.53N	73.57W
English, In., U.S. (ĭn'glĭsh)	98	38.15N	86.25W
English, r., Can.	85	50.31N	94.12W
English Channel, strt., Eur.	142	49.45N	3.06W
Enguera, Spain (ān'gārä)	159	38.58N	0.42W
Enid, Ok., U.S. (ē'nĭd)	96	36.25N	97.52W
Enid Lake, res., Ms., U.S.	114	34.13N	89.47W
Enkeldoring, S. Afr. (ĕŋ'k'l-dôr-ĭng)	218d	25.24S	28.43E
Enköping, Swe. (ĕn'kû-pĭng)	152	59.39N	17.05E
Ennedi, mts., Chad (ĕn-nĕd'ē)	211	16.45N	22.45E
Ennepetal, Ger.	236	51.18N	7.22E
Ennis, Ire. (ĕn'ĭs)	150	52.54N	9.05W
Ennis, Tx., U.S.	113	32.20N	96.38W
Enniscorthy, Ire. (ĕn-ĭs-kôr'thĭ)	150	52.33N	6.27W
Enniskillen, N. Ire., U.K. (ĕn-ĭs-kĭl'ĕn)	150	54.20N	7.25W
Ennis Lake, res., Mt., U.S.	105	45.15N	111.30W
Enns, r., Aus. (ĕns)	147	47.37N	14.35E
Enoree, S.C., U.S. (ē-nō'rē)	115	34.43N	81.58W
Enoree, r., S.C., U.S.	115	34.35N	81.55W
Enriquillo, Dom. Rep. (ĕn-rē-kē'l-yō)	123	17.55N	71.15W
Enriquillo, Lago, l., Dom. Rep. (lä'gô-ĕn-rē-kē'l-yō)	123	18.35N	71.35W
Enschede, Neth. (ĕns'kȧ-dĕ)	147	52.10N	6.50E
Enseñada, Arg.	129c	34.50S	57.55W
Ensenada, Mex. (ĕn-sĕ-nä'dä)	116	32.00N	116.30W
Enshi, China (ŭn-shr)	188	30.18N	109.25E
Enshū-Nada, b., Japan (ĕn'shōō nä-dä)	195	34.25N	137.14E
Entebbe, Ug.	211	0.04N	32.28E
Enterprise, Al., U.S. (ĕn'tēr-prīz)	114	31.20N	85.50W
Enterprise, Or., U.S.	104	45.25N	117.16W
Entiat, L, Wa., U.S.	104	45.43N	120.11W
Entraygues, Fr. (ĕN-trĕg')	156	44.39N	2.33E
Entre Rios, prov., Arg.	132	31.30S	59.00W
Enugu, Nig. (ĕ-nōō'gōō)	210	6.27N	7.27E
Enumclaw, Wa., U.S. (ĕn'ŭm-klô)	106a	47.12N	121.59W
Envigado, Col. (ĕn-vē-gá'dŏ)	130a	6.10N	75.34W
Eolie, Isole, is., Italy (ĕ'sō-lĕ-ĕ-ô'lyĕ)	148	38.43N	14.43E
Epe, Nig.	215	6.37N	3.59E
Épernay, Fr. (ā-pĕr-nĕ')	147	49.02N	3.54E
Épernon, Fr. (ā-pĕr-nôN')	157b	48.36N	1.41E
Ephraim, Ut., U.S. (ē'frā-ĭm)	109	39.20N	111.40W
Ephrata, Wa., U.S. (ēfrā'tȧ)	104	47.18N	119.35W
Epi, Vanuatu (ā'pē)	203	16.59S	168.29E
Épila, Spain (ā'pē-lä)	158	41.38N	1.15W
Épinal, Fr. (ā-pē-nál')	147	48.11N	6.27E
Épinay-sous-Sénart, Fr.	237c	48.42N	2.31E
Épinay-sur-Seine, Fr.	237c	48.57N	2.19E
Episkopi, Cyp.	181a	34.38N	32.55E
Eppendorf, neigh., Ger.	236	51.27N	7.11E
Eppenhausen, neigh., Ger.	236	51.21N	7.31E
Epping, Austl.	243a	33.46S	151.05E
Epping, Eng., U.K. (ĕp'ĭng)	144b	51.41N	0.06E
Epping Green, Eng., U.K.	235	51.44N	0.05E
Epping Upland, Eng., U.K.	235	51.43N	0.06E
Epsom, Eng., U.K.	144b	51.20N	0.16W
Epupa Falls, wtfl., Afr.	216	17.00S	13.05E
Epworth, Eng., U.K. (ĕp'wûrth)	144a	53.31N	0.50W
Equatorial Guinea, nation, Afr.	210	2.00N	7.15E
Équilles, Fr.	156a	43.34N	5.21E
Eramosa, r., Can. (ĕr-ȧ-mō'sȧ)	83d	43.39N	80.08W
Erba, Jabal, mtn., Sudan (ĕr-bȧ)	211	20.53N	36.45E
Erciyeş Daği, mtn., Tur.	149	38.30N	35.36E
Erding, Ger. (ĕr'dĕng)	145d	48.19N	11.54E
Erechim, Braz. (ĕ-rĕ-shē'N)	132	27.43S	52.11W
Ereğli, Tur. (ĕ-rā'ĭ-lē)	149	37.40N	34.00E
Ereğli, Tur.	149	41.15N	31.25E
Erenköy, neigh., Tur.	239f	40.58N	29.04E
Erfurt, Ger. (ĕr'fôrt)	147	50.59N	11.04E
Ergene, r., Tur. (ĕr'gĕ-nĕ)	161	41.17N	26.50E
Erges, r., Eur. (ĕr'-zhĕs)	158	39.45N	7.01W
Ērgli, Lat.	153	56.54N	25.38E
Ergste, Ger.	236	51.25N	7.34E
Eria, r., Spain (ā-rē'ä)	158	42.10N	6.08W
Erick, Ok., U.S. (âr'ĭk)	110	35.14N	99.51W
Erie, Ks., U.S. (ē'rĭ)	111	37.35N	95.17W
Erie, Pa., U.S.	97	42.05N	80.05W
Erie, Lake, l., N.A.	97	42.15N	81.25W
Erimo Saki, c., Japan (ā'rē-mō sä-kē)	189	41.53N	143.20E
Erin, Can. (ĕ'rĭn)	83d	43.46N	80.04W
Erith, neigh., Eng., U.K.	235	51.29N	0.10E
Eritrea, nation, Afr. (ā-rē-trā'ȧ)	211	16.15N	38.30E
Erkrath, Ger.	236	51.13N	6.55E
Erlangen, Ger. (ĕr'läng-ĕn)	154	49.36N	11.03E
Erlanger, Ky., U.S. (ĕr'läng-ĕr)	101f	39.01N	84.36W
Erle, neigh., Ger.	236	51.33N	7.05E
Ermont, Fr.	237c	48.59N	2.16E
Ermoúpolis, Grc.	161	37.30N	24.56E
Ernākulam, India	183	9.58N	76.23E
Erne, Lower Lough, l., N. Ire., U.K.	150	54.30N	7.40W
Erne, Upper Lough, l., N. Ire., U.K. (lŏk ûrn)	150	54.20N	7.24W
Erode, India	187	11.20N	77.45E
Eromanga, i., Vanuatu	203	18.58S	169.18E
Eros, La., U.S. (ē'rōs)	113	32.23N	92.22W
Errego, Moz.	217	16.02S	37.14E
Errigal, mtn., Ire. (ĕr-ĭ-gôl')	150	55.02N	8.07W
Errol Heights, Or., U.S.	106c	45.29N	122.38W
Erskine Park, Austl.	243a	33.49S	150.47E
Erstein, Fr. (ĕr'shtīn)	157	48.27N	7.40E
Erwin, N.C., U.S. (ûr'wĭn)	115	35.16N	78.40W
Erwin, Tn., U.S.	115	36.07N	82.25W
Erzgebirge, mts., Eur. (ĕrts'gĕ-bē'gĕ)	142	50.29N	12.40E
Erzincan, Tur. (ĕr-zĭn-jän')	182	39.50N	39.30E
Erzurum, Tur. (ĕrz'rōōm')	182	39.55N	41.10E
Esambo, Zaire	216	3.40S	23.24E
Esashi, Japan (ĕs'ä-shē)	189	41.50N	140.10E
Esbjerg, Den. (ĕs'byĕrgh)	146	55.29N	8.25E
Esborn, Ger.	236	51.23N	7.20E
Escalante, Ut., U.S. (ĕs-kȧ-lăn'tē)	109	37.50N	111.40W
Escalante, r., Ut., U.S.	109	37.40N	111.20W
Escalón, Mex.	112	26.45N	104.20W
Escambia, r., Fl., U.S. (ĕs-kăm'bĭ-ȧ)	114	30.38N	87.20W
Escanaba, Mi., U.S. (ĕs-kȧ-nô'bȧ)	97	45.44N	87.05W
Escanaba, r., Mi., U.S.	103	46.10N	87.22W
Escarpada Point, Phil.	196	18.40N	122.45E
Esch-sur-Alzette, Lux.	157	49.32N	6.21E
Eschwege, Ger. (ĕsh'vā-gĕ)	154	51.11N	10.02E
Eschweiler, Ger. (ĕsh'vī-lĕr)	157c	50.49N	6.15E
Escondido, Ca., U.S. (ĕs-kŏn-dē'dō)	108	33.07N	117.00W
Escondido, r., Nic.	121	12.04N	84.09W
Escondido, Río, r., Mex. (rē'ō-ĕs-kōn-dē'dō)	112	28.30N	100.45W
Escuadrón 201, Mex.	233a	19.22N	99.06W
Escudo de Veraguas, i., Pan. (ĕs-kōō'dä dā vā-rä'gwäs)	121	9.07N	81.25W
Escuinapa, Mex. (ĕs-kwē-nä'pä)	116	22.49N	105.44W
Escuintla, Guat. (ĕs-kwēn'tlä)	120	14.16N	90.47W
Ese, Cayos de, i., Col.	121	12.24N	81.07W
Eşfahān, Iran	182	32.38N	51.30E
Esgueva, r., Spain (ĕs-gĕ'vä)	158	41.48N	4.10W
Esher, Eng., U.K.	144b	51.23N	0.22W
Eshowe, S. Afr. (ĕsh'ō-wē)	213c	28.54S	31.28E
Esiama, Ghana	214	4.56N	2.21W
Eskdale, W.V., U.S. (ĕsk'dāl)	98	38.05N	81.25W
Eskifjördur, Ice. (ĕs'kē-fyûr'dōōr)	142	65.04N	14.01W
Eskilstuna, Swe. (å'shĕl-stū-na)	146	59.23N	16.28E
Eskimo Lakes, l., Can. (ĕs'kĭ-mō)	84	69.40N	130.10W
Eskişehir, Tur. (ĕs-kē-shĕ'h'r)	182	39.40N	30.20E
Esko, Mn., U.S. (ĕs'kō)	107h	46.27N	92.22W
Esla, r., Spain (ĕs-lä)	158	41.50N	5.48W
Eslöv, Swe. (ĕs'lûv)	152	55.50N	13.17E
Esmeraldas, Ec. (ĕs-mā-räl'däs)	130	0.58N	79.45W
Espanola, Can. (ĕs-pȧ-nō'lȧ)	85	46.11N	81.59W
Esparta, C.R. (ĕs-pär'tä)	121	9.59N	84.40W
Esperance, Austl. (ĕs'pē-rȧns)	202	33.45S	122.07E
Esperanza, Cuba (ĕs-pĕ-rä'n-zä)	122	22.30N	80.10W
Espichel, Cabo, c., Port. (kä'bō-ĕs-pē-shĕl')	158	38.25N	9.13W
Espinal, Col. (ĕs-pē-näl')	130	4.10N	74.53W
Espinhaço, Serra do, mts., Braz. (sĕ'r-rä-dō-ĕs-pē-ná-sō)	131	16.00S	44.00W
Espinillo, Punta, c., Ur. (pōō'n-tä-ĕs-pē-nē'l-yō)	129c	34.49S	56.27W
Espírito Santo, Braz. (ĕs-pē'rē-tô-sán'tō)	131	20.27S	40.18W
Espírito Santo, state, Braz.	131	19.57S	40.58W
Espiritu Santo, i., Vanuatu (ĕs-pē'rē-tōō sän'tō)	203	15.45S	166.50E
Espíritu Santo, Bahía del, b., Mex.	120a	19.25N	87.28W
Espita, Mex. (ĕs-pē'tä)	120a	20.57N	88.22W
Esplugas, Spain	238e	41.23N	2.06E
Espoo, Fin.	153	60.13N	24.41E
Esposende, Port. (ĕs-pō-zĕn'dā)	158	41.33N	8.45W
Esquel, Arg. (ĕs-kĕ'l)	132	42.47S	71.22W
Esquimalt, Can. (ĕs-kwī'mŏlt)	86	48.26N	123.24W
Essaouira, Mor.	210	31.34N	9.44W
Essel, neigh., Ger.	236	51.37N	7.15E
Essen, Bel.	145a	51.28N	4.27E
Essen, Ger. (ĕs'sĕn)	142	51.26N	6.59E
Essenberg, Ger.	236	51.26N	6.42E
Essendon, Austl.	201a	37.46S	144.55E
Essequibo, r., Guy. (ĕs-ā-kē'bō)	131	4.26N	58.17W
Essex, Il., U.S.	101a	41.11N	88.11W
Essex, Md., U.S.	100e	39.19N	76.29W
Essex, Ma., U.S.	93a	42.38N	70.47W
Essex, Vt., U.S.	99	44.30N	73.05W
Essex Fells, N.J., U.S. (ĕs'ĕks fĕlz)	100a	40.50N	74.16W
Essexville, Mi., U.S. (ĕs'ĕks-vĭl)	98	43.35N	83.50W
Essington, Pa., U.S.	229b	39.52N	75.18W
Essling, neigh., Aus.	239e	48.13N	16.32E
Esslingen, Ger. (ĕs'slĕn-gĕn)	154	48.45N	9.19E
Estacado, Llano, pl., U.S. (yá-nō ĕs-tȧcȧ-dō')	96	33.50N	103.20W
Estância, Braz. (ĕs-tän'sĭ-ä)	131	11.17S	37.18W
Estarreja, Port. (ĕ-tär-rā'zhä)	158	40.44N	8.39W
Estats, Pique d', mtn., Eur.	159	42.43N	1.30E
Estcourt, S. Afr. (ĕst-coort)	213c	29.04S	29.53E
Este, Italy (ĕs'tä)	160	45.13N	11.40E
Estella, Spain (ĕs-tāl'yä)	158	42.40N	2.01W
Estepa, Spain (ĕs-tā'pä)	158	37.18N	4.54W
Estepona, Spain (ĕs-tā-pō'nä)	158	36.26N	5.08W
Esterhazy, Can. (ĕs'tēr-hä-zē)	89	50.40N	102.08W
Estero Bay, b., Ca., U.S. (ĕs-tā'rōs)	108	35.22N	121.04W
Estevan, Can. (ĕ-stē'vȧn)	84	49.07N	103.05W
Estevan Group, is., Can.	86	53.05N	129.40W
Estherville, Ia., U.S. (ĕs'tēr-vĭl)	103	43.24N	94.49W
Estill, S.C., U.S. (ĕs'tĭl)	115	32.46N	81.15W
Eston, Can.	88	51.10N	108.45W
Estonia, nation, Eur.	164	59.10N	25.00E
Estoril, Port. (ĕs-tô-rēl')	159b	38.45N	9.24W
Estrêla, mtn., Port. (mäl-you'N-dä-ĕs-trĕ'lä)	158	40.20N	7.38W
Estrêla, r., Braz. (ĕs-trĕ'lȧ)	132b	22.39S	43.16W
Estrêla, Serra da, mts., Port. (sĕr'rȧ dä ĕs-trā'lȧ)	158	40.25N	7.45W
Estrella, Cerro de la, mtn., Mex.	233a	19.21N	99.05W
Estremadura, hist. reg., Port. (ĕs-trā-mä-dōō'rȧ)	158	39.00N	8.36W
Estremoz, Port. (ĕs-trā-mōzh')	158	38.50N	7.35W
Estrondo, Serra do, mts., Braz. (sĕr'-rȧ dō ĕs-trōn'-dō)	131	9.52S	48.56W
Esumba, Île, i., Zaire	216	2.00N	21.12E
Esztergom, Hung. (ĕs'tēr-gōm)	155	47.46N	18.45E
Etah, Grnld. (ē'tȧ)	82	78.20N	72.42W
Étampes, Fr. (ā-täNp')	156	48.26N	2.09E
Étaples, Fr. (ā-täp'l')	156	50.32N	1.38E
Etchemin, r., Can. (ĕch'ĕ-mĭn)	83b	46.39N	71.03W
Ethiopa, nation, Afr. (ē-thē-ō'pē-ȧ)	211	7.53N	37.55E
Eticoga, Gui.-B.	214	11.09N	16.08W
Etiwanda, Ca., U.S. (ĕ-tĭ-wăn'dȧ)	107a	34.07N	117.31W
Etna, Pa., U.S. (ĕt'nȧ)	101e	40.30N	79.55W
Etna, Mount, vol., Italy	142	37.48N	15.00E
Etobicoke, Can.	91	43.39N	79.34W
Etobicoke Creek, r., Can.	83d	43.44N	79.48W
Etolin Strait, strt., Ak., U.S. (ĕt ō lĭn)	95	60.35S	165.40W
Eton, Eng., U.K.	235	51.31N	0.37W
Eton College, educ., Eng., U.K.	235	51.30N	0.36W
Etoshapan, pl., Nmb. (ĕtō'shä)	212	19.07S	15.30E
Etowah, Tn., U.S. (ĕt'ō-wä)	114	35.18N	84.31W
Etowah, r., Ga., U.S.	114	34.23N	84.19W
Étréchy, Fr. (ā-trā-shē')	157b	48.29N	2.12E
Etten-Leur, Neth.	145a	51.34N	4.38E
Etterbeek, Bel. (ĕt'ĕr-bāk)	145a	50.51N	4.24E
Etzatlán, Mex. (ĕt-zä-tlän')	118	20.44N	104.04W
Eucla, Austl. (ū'klȧ)	202	31.45S	128.50E
Euclid, Oh., U.S. (ū'klĭd)	101d	41.34N	81.32W
Eudora, Ar., U.S. (u-dō'rȧ)	111	33.07N	91.16W
Eufaula, Al., U.S. (û-fô'lȧ)	114	31.53N	85.09W
Eufaula, Ok., U.S.	111	35.16N	95.35W
Eufaula Reservoir, res., Ok., U.S.	111	35.00N	94.45W
Eugene, Or., U.S. (û-jēn')	96	44.02N	123.06W
Euless, Tx., U.S. (ū'lĕs)	107c	32.50N	97.05W
Eunice, La., U.S. (ū'nĭs)	113	30.30N	92.25W
Eupen, Bel. (oi'pĕn)	151	50.39N	6.05E
Euphrates, r., Asia (û-frā'tēz)	182	36.00N	40.00E
Eure, r., Fr. (ûr)	156	49.03N	1.22E
Eureka, Ca., U.S. (û-rē'kȧ)	96	40.45N	124.10W
Eureka, Ks., U.S.	111	37.48N	96.17W
Eureka, Mt., U.S.	104	48.53N	115.07W
Eureka, Nv., U.S.	108	39.33N	115.58W
Eureka, S.D., U.S.	102	45.46N	99.38W
Eureka, Ut., U.S.	109	39.55N	112.10W
Eureka Springs, Ar., U.S.	111	36.24N	93.43W
Europe, cont. (ū'rŭp)	142	50.00N	15.00E
Eustis, Fl., U.S. (ūs'tĭs)	115	28.50N	81.41W
Eutaw, Al., U.S. (ū-tȧ)	114	32.48N	87.50W
Eutsuk Lake, l., Can. (ōōt'sŭk)	86	53.20N	126.44W
Evanston, Il., U.S. (ĕv'ăn-stŭn)	97	42.03N	87.41W
Evanston, Wy., U.S.	105	41.17N	111.02W
Evansville, In., U.S. (ĕv'ănz-vĭl)	97	38.00N	87.30W
Evansville, Wi., U.S.	103	42.46N	89.19W
Evart, Mi., U.S. (ĕv'ērt)	98	43.55N	85.10W
Evaton, S. Afr. (ĕv'ȧ-tŏn)	218d	26.32S	27.53E
Eveleth, Mn., U.S. (ĕv'ē-lĕth)	103	47.27N	92.35W
Everard, l., Austl. (ĕv'ēr-ård)	202	31.20S	134.10E
Everard Ranges, mts., Austl.	202	27.15S	132.00E

ng-sing; ŋ-baŋk; N-nasalized n; nŏd; cŏmmit; ōld; ôbey; ôrder; oi-boil; fōōd; ŏŏ-as oo in foot; ou-out; s-soft; sh-dish; th-thin; pūre; ûnite; ûrn; stŭd; circŭs; ü-as in French tu; '-indeterminate vowel.

286 Everest–Fertile

PLACE (Pronunciation)	PAGE	Lat. °′	Long. °′
Everest, Mount, mtn., Asia (ĕv′ẽr-ĕst)	183	28.00N	86.57E
Everett, Ma., U.S. (ĕv′ẽr-ĕt)	93a	42.24N	71.03W
Everett, Wa., U.S. (ĕv′ẽr-ĕt)	96	47.59N	122.11W
Everett Mountains, mts., Can.	85	62.34N	68.00W
Everglades, The, sw., Fl., U.S.	115a	25.35N	80.55W
Everglades City, Fl., U.S. (ĕv′ẽr-glādz)	115a	25.50N	81.25W
Everglades National Park, rec., Fl., U.S.	97	25.39N	80.57W
Evergreen, Al., U.S. (ĕv′ẽr-grēn)	114	31.25N	87.56W
Evergreen Park, Il., U.S.	101a	41.44N	87.42W
Everman, Tx., U.S. (ĕv′ẽr-măn)	107c	32.38N	97.17W
Everson, Wa., U.S. (ĕv′ẽr-sŭn)	106d	48.55N	122.21W
Everton, neigh., Eng., U.K.	237a	53.25N	2.58W
Eving, neigh., Ger.	236	51.33N	7.29E
Évora, Port. (ĕv′ō-rä)	148	38.35N	7.54W
Évreux, Fr. (ā-vrû′)	147	49.02N	1.11E
Evrótas, r., Grc. (ĕv-rō′tăs)	161	37.15N	22.17E
Évvoia, i., Grc.	149	38.38N	23.45E
Ewa Beach, Hi., U.S. (ē′wä)	94a	21.17N	158.03E
Ewaso Ng′iro, r., Kenya	211	0.59N	37.47E
Ewell, Eng., U.K.	235	51.21N	0.15W
Ewu, Nig.	244d	6.33N	3.19E
Excelsior, Mn., U.S. (ĕk-sel′sĭ-ŏr)	107g	44.54N	93.35W
Excelsior Springs, Mo., U.S.	111	39.20N	94.13W
Exe, r., Eng., U.K. (ĕks)	150	50.57N	3.37W
Exeter, Eng., U.K.	147	50.45N	3.33W
Exeter, Ca., U.S. (ĕk′sê-tẽr)	108	36.18N	119.09W
Exeter, N.H., U.S.	99	43.00N	71.00W
Exmoor, for., Eng., U.K. (ĕks′mŏr)	150	51.10N	3.55W
Exmouth, Eng., U.K. (ĕks′mŭth)	150	50.40N	3.20W
Exmouth Gulf, b., Austl.	202	21.45S	114.30E
Exploits, r., Can. (ĕks-ploits′)	93	48.50N	56.15W
Extórrax, r., Mex. (ĕx-tó′răx)	118	21.04N	99.39W
Extrema, Braz. (ĕsh-trĕ′mä)	129a	22.52S	46.19W
Extremadura, hist. reg., Spain (ĕks-trā-mä-doo′rä)	158	38.43N	6.30W
Exuma Sound, strt., Bah. (ĕk-sōō′mä)	122	24.20N	76.20W
Eyasi, Lake, l., Tan. (â-yä′sê)	212	3.25S	34.55E
Eyjafjördur, b., Ice.	146	66.21N	18.20W
Eyl, Som.	218a	7.53N	49.45E
Eynsford, Eng., U.K.	235	51.22N	0.13E
Eyrarbakki, Ice.	146	63.51N	20.52W
Eyre, Austl. (âr)	202	32.15S	126.20E
Eyre, l., Austl.	202	28.43S	137.50E
Eyre Peninsula, pen., Austl.	202	33.30S	136.00E
Eyüp, neigh., Tur.	239f	41.03N	28.55E
Ezbekīyah, neigh., Egypt	244a	30.03N	31.15E
Ezeiza, Arg. (ĕ-zā′zä)	132a	34.52S	58.31W
Ezine, Tur. (â′zĭ-nâ)	161	39.47N	26.18E

F

PLACE (Pronunciation)	PAGE	Lat. °′	Long. °′
Fabens, Tx., U.S. (fā′bĕnz)	112	31.30N	106.07W
Fåborg, Den. (fō′bŏrg)	152	55.06N	10.19E
Fabreville, neigh., Can.	227b	45.34N	73.50W
Fabriano, Italy (fä-brē-ä′nō)	160	43.20N	12.55E
Fada, Chad (fä′dä)	211	17.06N	21.18E
Fada Ngourma, Burkina (fä′dä′n gōōr′mä)	210	12.04N	0.21E
Faddeya, i., Russia (fäd-yā′)	165	76.12N	145.00E
Faenza, Italy (fä-ĕnd′zä)	160	44.16N	11.53E
Faeroe Islands, is., Eur. (fā′rō)	142	62.00N	5.45W
Fafe, Port. (fä′fâ)	158	41.30N	8.10W
Fafen, r., Eth.	218a	8.15N	42.40E
Făgăras, Rom. (fă-gă′răsh)	161	45.50N	24.55E
Fagerness, Nor. (fä′ghĕr-nĕs)	146	61.00N	9.10E
Fagnano, l., S.A. (făk-nä′nō)	132	54.35S	68.20W
Faguibine, Lac, l., Mali	214	16.50N	4.20W
Fahrland, Ger.	238a	52.28N	13.01E
Faial, i., Port. (fä-yä′l)	210a	38.40N	29.19W
Fā′id, Egypt (fä-yēd′)	218c	30.19N	32.18E
Failsworth, Eng., U.K.	237b	53.31N	2.09W
Fairbanks, Ak., U.S. (fâr′bănks)	96a	64.50N	147.48W
Fairbury, Il., U.S. (fâr′bĕr-ĭ)	98	40.45N	88.25W
Fairbury, Ne., U.S.	111	40.09N	97.11W
Fairchild Creek, r., Can. (fâr′chīld)	83d	43.18N	80.10W
Fairfax, Mn., U.S. (fâr′făks)	103	44.29N	94.44W
Fairfax, S.C., U.S.	115	32.29N	81.13W
Fairfax, Va., U.S.	100e	38.51N	77.20W
Fairfield, Austl.	201b	33.52S	150.57E
Fairfield, Al., U.S. (fâr′fēld)	100h	33.30N	86.50W
Fairfield, Ct., U.S.	100a	41.08N	73.22W
Fairfield, Il., U.S.	98	38.25N	88.20W
Fairfield, Ia., U.S.	103	41.00N	91.59W
Fairfield, Me., U.S.	92	44.35N	69.38W
Fairfield, N.J., U.S.	228	40.53N	74.17W
Fairhaven, Md., U.S.	229d	38.47N	77.05W
Fairhaven, Ma., U.S. (fâr-hā′vĕn)	99	41.35N	70.55W
Fair Haven, Vt., U.S.	99	43.35N	73.15W
Fair Island, i., Scot., U.K. (fâr)	150a	59.34N	1.41W
Fair Lawn, N.J., U.S.	228	40.56N	74.07W
Fairlee, Md., U.S.	229d	38.52N	77.16W
Fairmont, Mn., U.S. (fâr′mŏnt)	103	43.39N	94.26W
Fairmont, W.V., U.S.	98	39.30N	80.10W
Fairmont City, Il., U.S.	107e	38.39N	90.05W
Fairmount, In., U.S.	98	40.25N	85.45W
Fairmount, Ks., U.S.	107f	39.12N	95.55W
Fairmount Heights, Md., U.S.	229d	38.54N	76.55W

PLACE (Pronunciation)	PAGE	Lat. °′	Long. °′
Fair Oaks, Ga., U.S. (fâr ōks)	100c	33.56N	84.33W
Fairport, N.Y., U.S. (fâr′pōrt)	99	43.05N	77.30W
Fairport Harbor, Oh., U.S.	98	41.45N	81.15W
Fairseat, Eng., U.K.	235	51.20N	0.20E
Fairview, N.J., U.S.	228	40.49N	74.00W
Fairview, Ok., U.S. (fâr′vū)	110	36.16N	98.28W
Fairview, Or., U.S.	106c	45.32N	112.26W
Fairview, Ut., U.S.	109	39.35N	111.30W
Fairview Park, Oh., U.S.	101d	41.27N	81.52W
Fairweather, Mount, mtn., N.A. (fâr-wĕdh′ẽr)	95	59.12N	137.22W
Faisalabad, Pak.	183	31.29N	73.06E
Faith, S.D., U.S. (fāth)	102	45.02N	120.02W
Faizābād, India	183	26.50N	82.17E
Fajardo, P.R.	117b	18.20N	65.40W
Fakfak, Indon.	197	2.56S	132.25E
Faku, China (fä-kōō)	192	42.28N	123.20E
Falcón, dept., Ven. (fäl-kō′n)	131b	11.00N	68.28W
Falconer, N.Y., U.S. (fô′k′n-ẽr)	99	42.10N	79.10W
Falcon Heights, Mn., U.S. (fô′k′n)	107g	44.59N	93.10W
Falcon Reservoir, res., N.A. (fôk′n)	112	26.47N	99.03W
Făleşti, Mol.	163	47.33N	27.46E
Falfurrias, Tx., U.S. (făl′fōō-rē′ás)	112	27.15N	98.08W
Falher, Can. (făl′ẽr)	87	55.44N	117.12W
Falkenberg, Swe. (fäl′kĕn-bĕrgh)	152	56.54N	12.25E
Falkensee, Ger. (fäl′kĕn-zā)	145b	52.34N	13.05E
Falkenthal, Ger. (fäl′kĕn-täl)	145b	52.54N	13.18E
Falkirk, Scot., U.K. (fôl′kûrk)	150	55.59N	3.55W
Falkland Islands, dep., S.A. (fôk′lănd)	132	50.45S	61.00W
Falköping, Swe. (fäl′chûp-ĭng)	152	58.09N	13.30E
Fall City, Wa., U.S.	106a	47.34N	121.53W
Fall Creek, r., In., U.S. (fôl)	101g	39.52N	86.04W
Fallon, Nv., U.S. (făl′ŭn)	108	39.30N	118.48W
Fall River, Ma., U.S.	97	41.42N	71.07W
Falls Church, Va., U.S. (fălz chûrch)	100e	38.53N	77.10W
Falls City, Ne., U.S.	111	40.04N	95.37W
Fallston, Md., U.S. (făls′ton)	100e	39.32N	76.26W
Falmouth, Jam.	122	18.30N	77.40W
Falmouth, Eng., U.K. (făl′mŭth)	150	50.08N	5.04W
Falmouth, Ky., U.S.	98	38.40N	84.20W
False Divi Point, c., India	187	15.45N	80.50E
Falster, i., Den. (fäls′tẽr)	152	54.48N	11.58E
Fălticeni, Rom. (fŭl-tê-chân′y′)	155	47.27N	26.17E
Falun, Swe. (fä-lōōn′)	146	60.38N	15.35E
Famadas, Spain	238e	41.21N	2.05E
Famagusta, N. Cyp. (fä-mä-gōōs′tä)	149	35.08N	33.59E
Famatina, Sierra de, mts., Arg.	132	29.00S	67.50W
Fangxian, China (fäŋ-shyĕn)	192	32.05N	110.45E
Fanning, i., Can.	83f	49.45N	97.46W
Fano, Italy (fä′nō)	160	43.49N	13.01E
Fanø, i., Den. (fän′û)	152	55.24N	8.10E
Fan Si Pan, mtn., Viet.	193	22.25N	103.50E
Farafangana, Madag. (fä-rä-fäŋ-gä′nä)	213	23.18S	47.59E
Farāh, Afg. (fä-rä′)	182	32.15N	62.13E
Farallón, Punta, c., Mex. (pō′n-tä-fä-rä-lōn)	118	19.21N	105.03W
Faranah, Gui. (fä-rä′nä)	210	10.02N	10.44W
Farasān, Jaza′ir, is., Sau. Ar.	182	16.45N	41.08E
Faregh, Wadi al, r., Libya (wädê ĕl fä-rĕg′)	149	30.10N	19.34E
Farewell, Cape, c., N.Z. (fâr-wĕl′)	203a	40.37S	172.40E
Fargo, N.D., U.S. (fär′gō)	96	46.53N	96.48W
Far Hills, N.J., U.S. (fär hĭlz)	100a	40.41N	74.38W
Faribault, Mn., U.S. (fâ′rĭ-bō)	103	44.19N	93.16W
Farilhões, is., Port. (fä-rê-lyôɴzh′)	158	39.28N	9.32W
Faringdon, Eng., U.K. (fă′rĭng-dŏn)	144b	51.38N	1.35W
Fāriskūr, Egypt (fä-rês-kōōr′)	218b	31.19N	31.46E
Farit, Amba, mtn., Eth.	211	10.51N	37.52E
Farley, Mo., U.S. (fär′lē)	107f	39.16N	94.49W
Farmers Branch, Tx., U.S.	107c	32.56N	96.53W
Farmersburg, In., U.S. (fär′mẽrz-bûrg)	98	39.15N	87.25W
Farmersville, Tx., U.S. (fär′mẽrz-vĭl)	111	33.11N	96.22W
Farmingdale, N.J., U.S. (färm′ĕng-dāl)	100a	40.11N	74.10W
Farmingdale, N.Y., U.S.	100a	40.44N	73.26W
Farmingham, Ma., U.S. (färm-ĭng-hăm)	93a	42.17N	71.25W
Farmington, Il., U.S. (färm-ĭng-tŭn)	111	40.42N	90.01W
Farmington, Me., U.S.	92	44.40N	70.10W
Farmington, Mi., U.S.	101b	42.28N	83.23W
Farmington, Mo., U.S.	111	37.46N	90.26W
Farmington, N.M., U.S.	109	36.40N	108.10W
Farmington, Ut., U.S.	107b	40.59N	111.53W
Farmington Hills, Mi., U.S.	230c	42.28N	83.23W
Farmville, N.C., U.S. (färm-vĭl)	115	35.35N	77.35W
Farmville, Va., U.S.	115	37.15N	78.23W
Farnborough, Eng., U.K. (färn′bŭr-ō)	144b	51.15N	0.45W
Farnborough, neigh., Eng., U.K.	235	51.21N	0.04E
Farne Islands, is., Eng., U.K. (färn)	150	55.40N	1.32W
Farnham, Can. (fär′năm)	99	45.15N	72.55W
Farningham, Eng., U.K. (fär′nĭng-ŭm)	144b	51.22N	0.14E
Farnworth, Eng., U.K. (färn′wŭrth)	144a	53.34N	2.24W
Faro, Braz. (fä′rō)	131	2.05S	56.32W
Faro, Port.	148	37.01N	7.57W
Farodofay, Madag.	213	24.59S	46.58E
Fårön, i., Swe.	153	57.57N	19.10E
Farquhar, Cape, c., Austl. (fär′kwär)	202	23.50S	112.55E
Farrell, Pa., U.S. (făr′ĕl)	98	41.10N	80.30W
Far Rockaway, neigh., N.Y., U.S.	228	40.36N	73.45W
Farrukhābād, India (fŭ-rōk-hä-bäd′)	183	27.29N	79.35E
Fársala, Grc.	161	39.18N	22.25E
Farsund, Nor. (fär′sŏn)	152	58.05N	6.47E
Fartak, Ra′s, c., Yemen	182	15.43N	52.17E
Fartura, Serra da, mts., Braz. (sĕ′r-rä-dá-fär-tōō′rä)	132	26.40S	53.15W
Farvel, Kap, c., Grnld.	82	60.00N	44.00W
Farwell, Tx., U.S. (fär′wĕl)	110	34.24N	103.03W
Fasano, Italy (fä-zä′nō)	161	40.50N	17.22E
Fastiv, Ukr.	163	50.04N	29.57E

PLACE (Pronunciation)	PAGE	Lat. °′	Long. °′
Fatëzh, Russia	162	52.06N	35.51E
Fatima, Port.	159	39.36N	9.36E
Fatsa, Tur. (făt′sä)	149	40.50N	37.30E
Faucilles, Monts, mts., Fr. (mōɴ′ fō-sēl′)	157	48.07N	6.13E
Fauske, Nor.	146	67.15N	15.24E
Faust, Can. (foust)	87	55.19N	115.38W
Faustovo, Russia	172b	55.27N	38.29E
Faversham, Eng., U.K. (fă′vẽr-sh′m)	144b	51.19N	0.54E
Favoriten, neigh., Aus.	239e	48.11N	16.23E
Fawkham Green, Eng., U.K.	235	51.22N	0.17E
Fawkner, Austl.	243b	37.43S	144.58E
Fawsett Farms, Md., U.S.	229d	38.59N	77.14W
Faxaflói, b., Ice.	146	64.33N	22.40W
Fayette, Al., U.S. (fâ-yĕt′)	114	33.40N	87.54W
Fayette, Ia., U.S.	103	42.49N	91.49W
Fayette, Ms., U.S.	114	31.43N	91.00W
Fayette, Mo., U.S.	111	39.09N	92.41W
Fayetteville, Ar., U.S. (fâ-yĕt′vĭl)	111	36.03N	94.08W
Fayetteville, N.C., U.S.	115	35.02N	78.54W
Fayetteville, Tn., U.S.	114	35.10N	86.33W
Fazao, Forêt Classée du, for., Togo	214	8.50N	0.40E
Fazilka, India	186	30.30N	74.02E
Fazzān (Fezzan), hist. reg., Libya	211	26.45N	13.01E
Fdérik, Maur.	210	22.45N	12.38W
Fear, Cape, c., N.C., U.S. (fēr)	115	33.52N	77.48W
Feather, r., Ca., U.S. (fĕth′ẽr)	108	38.56N	121.41W
Feather, Middle Fork of, r., Ca., U.S.	108	39.49N	121.10W
Feather, North Fork of, r., Ca., U.S.	108	40.00N	121.20W
Featherstone, Eng., U.K. (fĕdh′ẽr stŭn)	144a	53.39N	1.21W
Fécamp, Fr. (fā-käɴ′)	147	49.45N	0.20E
Federal, Distrito, dept., Ven. (dês-trê′tô-fĕ-dĕ-rä′l)	131b	10.34N	66.55W
Federal Way, Wa., U.S.	106a	47.20N	122.20W
Fëdorovka, Russia (fyô′dō-rôf-kȧ)	172b	56.15N	37.14E
Fehmarn, i., Ger. (fā′märn)	154	54.28N	11.15E
Fehrbellin, Ger. (fĕr′bĕl-lēn)	145b	52.49N	12.46E
Feia, Logoa, l., Braz. (lô-gôä-fĕ′yä)	129a	21.54S	41.15W
Feicheng, China (fā-chŭŋ)	190	36.18N	116.45E
Feidong, China (fā-dôŋ)	190	31.53N	117.28E
Feira de Santana, Braz. (fĕ′ê-rä dä sänt-än′ä)	131	12.16S	38.46W
Feixian, China (fā-shyĕn)	190	35.17N	117.59E
Felanitx, Spain (fā-lä-nēch′)	148	39.29N	3.09E
Feldkirch, Aus. (fĕlt′kĭrk)	154	47.15N	9.36E
Feldkirchen, Ger. (fĕld′kĕr-kĕn)	145d	48.09N	11.44E
Felipe Carrillo Puerto, Mex.	120a	19.36N	88.04W
Feltre, Italy (fĕl′trā)	160	46.02N	11.56E
Femunden, l., Nor.	146	62.17N	11.40E
Fengcheng, China	191b	30.55N	121.38E
Fengcheng, China (fŭŋ-chŭŋ)	192	40.28N	124.03E
Fengdu, China (fŭŋ-dōō)	188	29.58N	107.50E
Fengjie, China (fŭŋ-jyĕ)	188	31.02N	109.30E
Fengming Dao, i., China (fŭŋ-mĭŋ dou)	190	39.19N	121.15E
Fengrun, China (fŭŋ-rŏn)	190	39.51N	118.06E
Fengtai, China (fŭŋ-tī)	192a	39.51N	116.19E
Fengxian, China	190	34.41N	116.36E
Fengxian, China (fŭŋ-shyĕn)	191b	30.55N	121.26E
Fengxiang, China (fŭŋ-shyäŋ)	188	34.25N	107.20E
Fengyang, China (fŭng′yäng′)	192	32.55N	117.32E
Fengzhen, China (fŭŋ-jŭn)	189	40.28N	113.20E
Fennimore Pass, strt., Ak., U.S. (fĕn-ĭ-mōr)	95a	51.40N	175.38W
Fenoarivo Atsinanana, Madag.	213	17.30S	49.31E
Fenton, Mi., U.S. (fĕn-tŭn)	98	42.50N	83.40W
Fenton, Mo., U.S.	107e	38.31N	90.27W
Fenyang, China	189	37.20N	111.48E
Feodosiya, Ukr.	167	45.02N	35.21E
Ferbitz, Ger.	238a	52.30N	13.01E
Ferdows, Iran	182	34.00N	58.13E
Ferencváros, neigh., Hung.	239g	47.28N	19.06E
Ferentino, Italy (fā-rĕn-tē′nō)	160	41.42N	13.18E
Fergana, Uzb.	169	40.23N	71.46E
Fergus Falls, Mn., U.S. (fûr′gŭs)	96	46.17N	96.03W
Ferguson, Mo., U.S. (fûr-gŭ-sŭn)	107e	38.45N	90.18W
Ferkéssédougou, C. Iv.	214	9.36N	5.12W
Fermo, Italy (fĕr′mō)	160	43.10N	13.43E
Fermoselle, Spain (fĕr-mō-sāl′yā)	158	41.20N	6.23W
Fermoy, Ire. (fûr-moi′)	150	52.05N	8.06W
Fernandina Beach, Fl., U.S. (fûr-năn-dē′nȧ)	115	30.38N	81.29W
Fernando de Noronha, , Braz.	131	3.51S	32.25W
Fernando Póo *see* Bioko, i., Eq. Gui.	210	3.35N	7.45E
Fernán-Núñez, Spain (fĕr-nän′nōō′nyăth)	158	37.42N	4.43W
Fernão Veloso, Baia de, b., Moz.	217	14.20S	40.55E
Ferndale, Ca., U.S. (fûrn′dāl)	104	40.34N	124.18W
Ferndale, Md., U.S.	229c	39.11N	76.38W
Ferndale, Mi., U.S.	101b	42.27N	83.08W
Ferndale, Mi., U.S.	230c	42.28N	83.08W
Ferndale, Wa., U.S.	106d	48.51N	122.36W
Fernie, Can. (fûr′nĭ)	84	49.30N	115.03W
Fern Prairie, Wa., U.S. (fûrn prâr′ĭ)	106c	45.38N	122.25W
Ferny Creek, Austl.	243b	37.53S	145.21E
Ferrara, Italy (fĕr-rä′rä)	148	44.50N	11.37E
Ferrat, Cap, c., Alg. (kăp fĕr-rät)	159	35.49N	0.29W
Ferraz de Vasconcelos, Braz.	234d	23.32S	46.22W
Ferreira do Alentejo, Port.	158	38.03N	8.06W
Ferreira do Zezere, Port. (fĕr-rĕ′ê-rä dò zá-zā′rĕ)	158	39.49N	8.17W
Ferrelview, Mo., U.S. (fĕr′rĕl-vū)	107f	39.18N	94.40W
Ferreñafe, Peru (fĕr-rĕn-yä′fĕ)	130	6.38S	79.48W
Ferriday, La., U.S. (fĕr′ĭ-dā)	113	31.38N	91.33W
Ferrieres, Fr.	237c	48.49N	2.42E
Ferry Village, N.Y., U.S.	230a	43.58N	78.57W
Fershampenuaz, Russia (fĕr-shăm′pĕn-wäz)	172a	53.32N	59.50E
Fertile, Mn., U.S. (fur′tĭl)	102	47.33N	96.18W

ăt; finȧl; rāte; senâte; ärm; åsk; sofȧ; fâre; ch-choose; dh-as th in other; bē; ėvent; bĕt; recĕnt; cratẽr; g-gō; gh-guttural g; bĭt; ĭ-short neutral; rīde; ĸ-guttural k as ch in German ich;

PLACE (Pronunciation)	PAGE	Lat. °′	Long. °′
Fès, Mor. (fĕs)	210	34.08N	5.00W
Fessenden, N.D., U.S. (fĕs'ĕn-dĕn)	102	47.39N	99.40W
Festus, Mo., U.S. (fĕst'ŭs)	111	38.12N	90.22W
Fetcham, Eng., U.K.	235	51.17N	0.22W
Fethiye, Tur. (fĕt-hē'yĕ)	149	36.40N	29.05E
Feuilles, Rivière aux, r., Can.	85	58.30N	70.50W
Ffestiniog, Wales, U.K.	150	52.59N	3.58W
Fianarantsoa, Madag. (fyȧ-nä'rȧn-tsō'ȧ)	213	21.21S	47.15E
Fichtenau, Ger.	238a	52.27N	13.42E
Ficksburg, S. Afr. (fĭks'bûrg)	218d	28.53S	27.53E
Fidalgo Island, i., Wa., U.S. (fī-dăl'gō)	106a	48.28N	122.39W
Fiddlers Hamlet, Eng., U.K.	235	51.41N	0.08E
Fieldbrook, Ca., U.S. (fēld'brŏŏk)	104	40.59N	124.02W
Fier, Alb. (fyĕr)	161	40.43N	19.34E
Fife Ness, c., Scot., U.K. (fīf'nes')	150	56.15N	2.19W
Fifth Cataract, wtfl., Sudan	211	18.27N	33.38E
Figeac, Fr. (fē-zhäk')	156	44.37N	2.02E
Figeholm, Swe. (fē-ghĕ-hōlm)	152	57.24N	16.33E
Figueira da Foz, Port. (fē-gwĕy-rä-dä-fō'z)	158	40.10N	8.50W
Figuig, Mor.	210	32.20N	1.30W
Fiji, nation, Oc. (fē'jē)	3	18.40S	175.00E
Filadelfia, C.R. (fĭl-ȧ-dĕl'fĭ-ȧ)	120	10.26N	85.37W
Filatovskoye, Russia (fĭ-lä'tôf-skô-yĕ)	172a	56.49N	62.20E
Filchner Ice Shelf, ice., Ant. (fĭlk'nĕr)	219	80.00S	35.00W
Fili, neigh., Russia	239b	55.45N	37.31E
Filicudi, i., Italy (fē'le-kōō'dē)	160	38.34N	14.39E
Filippovskoye, Russia (fĭ-lĭ-pôf'skô-yĕ)	172b	56.06N	38.38E
Filipstad, Swe. (fĭl'ĭps-städh)	152	59.44N	14.09E
Fillmore, Ut., U.S. (fĭl'môr)	109	39.00N	112.20W
Filsa, Nor.	152	60.35N	12.03E
Fimi, r., Zaire	212	2.43S	17.50E
Finaalspan, S. Afr.	244b	26.17S	28.15E
Finch, Can. (fĭnch)	83c	45.09N	75.06W
Finchley, neigh., Eng., U.K.	235	51.36N	0.10W
Findlay, Oh., U.S. (fĭnd'lå)	98	41.05N	83.40W
Fingoe, Moz.	217	15.12S	31.50E
Finisterre, Cabo de, c., Spain (kä'bô-dĕ-fĭn-ĭs-târ')	142	42.52N	9.48W
Finke, r., Austl. (fĭŋ'kē)	202	25.25S	134.30E
Finkenkrug, Ger.	238a	52.34N	13.03E
Finland, nation, Eur. (fĭn'lănd)	142	62.45N	26.13E
Finland, Gulf of, b., Eur. (fĭn'lănd)	142	59.35N	23.35E
Finlandia, Col. (fēn-lä'n-dēä)	130a	4.38N	75.39W
Finlay, r., Can. (fĭn'lå)	84	57.45N	125.30W
Finow, Ger. (fē'nōv)	145b	52.50N	13.44E
Finowfurt, Ger. (fē'nō-fōōrt)	145b	52.50N	13.41E
Fircrest, Wa., U.S. (fŭr'krĕst)	106a	47.14N	122.31W
Firenze *see* Florence, Italy	142	43.47N	11.15E
Firenzuola, Italy (fē-rĕnt-swô'lä)	160	44.08N	11.21E
Firgrove, Eng., U.K.	237b	53.37N	2.08W
Firozpur, India	183	30.58N	74.39E
Fischa, r., Aus.	145e	48.04N	16.33E
Fischamend Markt, Aus.	145e	48.07N	16.37E
Fischeln, neigh., Ger.	236	51.18N	6.35E
Fish, r., Nmb. (fĭsh)	212	28.00S	17.30E
Fish Cay, i., Bah.	123	22.30N	74.20W
Fish Creek, r., Can. (fĭsh)	83e	50.52N	114.21W
Fisher, La., U.S. (fĭsh'ĕr)	113	31.28N	93.30W
Fisher Bay, b., Can.	89	51.30N	97.16W
Fisher Channel, strt., Can.	86	52.10N	127.42W
Fisherman's Wharf, pt. of i., Ca., U.S.	231b	37.48N	122.25W
Fisher Strait, strt., Can.	85	62.43N	84.28W
Fisherville, Can.	227c	43.47N	79.28W
Fishpool, Eng., U.K.	237b	53.35N	2.17W
Fitchburg, Ma., U.S. (fĭch'bûrg)	99	42.35N	71.48W
Fitri, Lac, l., Chad	215	12.50N	17.28E
Fitzgerald, Ga., U.S. (fĭts-jĕr'ăld)	114	31.42N	83.17W
Fitz Hugh Sound, strt., Can. (fĭts hū)	86	51.40N	127.57W
Fitzroy, Austl.	243b	37.48S	144.59E
Fitzroy, r., Austl. (fĭts-roi')	202	18.00S	124.05E
Fitzroy, r., Austl.	203	23.45S	150.02E
Fitzroy, Monte (Cerro Chaltel), mtn., S.A.	132	48.10S	73.18W
Fitzroy Crossing, Austl.	202	18.08S	126.00E
Fitzwilliam, i., Can. (fĭts-wĭl'yŭm)	90	45.30N	81.45W
Fiume *see* Rijeka, Cro.	148	45.22N	14.24E
Fiumicino, Italy (fyōō-mē-chē'nō)	159d	41.47N	12.19E
Five Dock, Austl.	243a	33.52S	151.08E
Fjällbacka, Swe. (fyĕl'băk-å)	152	58.37N	11.17E
Flagstaff, S. Afr. (flăg'stäf)	213c	31.06S	29.31E
Flagstaff, Az., U.S. (flăg-stäf)	96	35.15N	111.40W
Flagstaff, I., Me., U.S. (flăg-stáf)	99	45.05N	70.30W
Flåm, Nor. (flôm)	152	60.50N	7.00E
Flambeau, r., Wi., U.S. (flăm-bō')	103	45.32N	91.05W
Flaming Gorge Reservoir, res., U.S.	96	41.13N	109.30W
Flamingo, Fl., U.S. (flȧ-mĭŋ'gō)	115	25.10N	80.55W
Flamingo Cay, i., Bah. (flȧ-mĭŋ'gō)	123	22.50N	75.50W
Flamingo Point, c., V.I.U.S.	117c	18.19N	65.00W
Flanders, hist. reg., Fr. (flăn'dĕrz)	151	50.53N	2.29E
Flandreau, S.D., U.S. (flăn'drō)	102	44.02N	96.35W
Flatbush, neigh., N.Y., U.S.	228	40.39N	73.56W
Flathead, r., N.A.	87	49.30N	114.30W
Flathead, Middle Fork, r., Mt., U.S.	105	48.30N	113.47W
Flathead, North Fork, r., N.A.	105	48.45N	114.20W
Flathead, South Fork, r., Mt., U.S.	105	48.05N	113.45W
Flathead Indian Reservation, I.R., Mt., U.S.	105	47.30N	114.25W
Flathead Lake, l., Mt., U.S. (flăt'hĕd)	96	47.57N	114.20W
Flatow, Ger.	145b	52.44N	12.58E
Flat Rock, Mi., U.S. (flăt rŏk)	101b	42.06N	83.17W
Flattery, Cape, c., Wa., U.S. (flăt'ĕr-ĭ)	104	48.22N	124.45W
Flatwillow Creek, r., Mt., U.S. (flat wĭl'ō)	105	46.45N	108.47W
Flaunden, Eng., U.K.	235	51.42N	0.32W
Flehe, neigh., Ger.	236	51.12N	6.47E
Flekkefjord, Nor. (fläk'kĕ-fyôr)	152	58.19N	6.38E
Flemingsburg, Ky., U.S. (flĕm'ĭngz-bûrg)	98	38.25N	83.45W

PLACE (Pronunciation)	PAGE	Lat. °′	Long. °′
Flensburg, Ger. (flĕns'bŏŏrgh)	146	54.48N	9.27E
Flers, Fr. (flĕr)	147	48.43N	0.37W
Fletcher, N.C., U.S.	115	35.26N	82.30W
Fley, neigh., Ger.	236	51.23N	7.30E
Flinders, i., Austl.	203	39.35S	148.10E
Flinders, r., Austl.	203	18.48S	141.07E
Flinders, reg., Austl. (flĭn'dĕrz)	202	32.15S	138.45E
Flinders Reefs, rf., Austl.	203	17.30S	149.02E
Flin Flon, Can. (flĭn flŏn)	84	54.46N	101.53W
Flingern, neigh., Ger.	236	51.14N	6.49E
Flint, Wales, U.K.	144a	53.15N	3.07W
Flint, Mi., U.S.	97	43.00N	83.45W
Flint, r., Ga., U.S. (flĭnt)	97	31.25N	84.15W
Flora, Il., U.S. (flō'rȧ)	98	38.40N	88.25W
Flora, In., U.S.	98	40.25N	86.30W
Florala, Al., U.S. (flŏr-ăl'ȧ)	114	31.01N	86.19W
Floral Park, N.Y., U.S. (flôr'ăl pärk)	100a	40.42N	73.42W
Florence, Italy	142	43.47N	11.15E
Florence, Al., U.S. (flŏr'ĕns)	97	34.46N	87.40W
Florence, Az., U.S.	109	33.00N	111.25W
Florence, Ca., U.S.	232	33.58N	118.15W
Florence, Co., U.S.	110	38.23N	105.08W
Florence, Ks., U.S.	111	38.14N	96.56W
Florence, S.C., U.S.	115	34.10N	79.45W
Florence, Wa., U.S.	106a	48.13N	122.21W
Florencia, Col. (flō-rĕn'sē-ȧ)	130	1.31N	75.13W
Florencio Sánchez, Ur. (flō-rĕn-sēō-sá'n-chĕz)	129c	33.52S	57.24W
Florencio Varela, Arg. (flō-rĕn'sē-o vä-rā'lä)	132a	34.50S	58.16W
Florentia, S. Afr.	244b	26.16S	28.08E
Flores, Braz. (flō'rĕzh)	131	7.57S	37.48W
Flores, Guat.	120a	16.53N	89.54W
Flores, dept., Ur.	129c	33.33S	57.00W
Flores, neigh., Arg.	233d	34.38S	58.28W
Flores, i., Indon.	196	8.14S	121.08E
Flores, r., Arg.	129c	36.13S	60.28W
Flores, Laut (Flores Sea), sea, Indon.	196	7.09S	120.30E
Floresta, neigh., Arg.	233d	34.38S	58.29W
Floresville, Tx., U.S. (flō'rĕs-vĭl)	112	29.10N	98.08W
Floriano, Braz. (flō-rȧ-ä'nō)	131	6.17S	42.58W
Florianópolis, Braz. (flō-rē-ä-nō'pō-lēs)	132	27.30S	48.30W
Florida, Col. (flō-rē'dä)	130a	3.20N	76.12W
Florida, Cuba	122	22.10N	79.50W
Florida, S. Afr.	213b	26.11S	27.56E
Florida, N.Y., U.S. (flŏr'ĭ-dȧ)	100a	41.20N	74.21W
Florida, Ur. (flō-rē-dhä)	132	34.06S	56.14W
Florida, dept., Ur. (flō-rē'dhä)	129c	33.48S	56.15W
Florida, state, U.S. (flŏr'ĭ-dȧ)	97	30.30N	84.40W
Florida, i., Sol.Is.	203	8.56S	159.45E
Florida, Straits of, strt., N.A.	117	24.10N	81.00W
Florida Bay, b., Fl., U.S. (flŏr'ĭ-dȧ)	115a	24.55N	80.55W
Florida Keys, is., Fl., U.S.	97	24.33N	81.20W
Florida Mountains, mts., N.M., U.S.	109	32.10N	107.35W
Florido, Río, r., Mex. (flō-rē'dō)	112	27.21N	104.48W
Floridsdorf, Aus. (flō'rĭds-dôrf)	145e	48.16N	16.25E
Florina, Grc. (flō-rē'nä)	149	40.48N	21.24E
Florissant, Mo., U.S. (flŏr'ĭ-sănt)	107e	38.47N	90.20W
Flotantes, Jardines, rec., Mex.	233a	19.16N	99.06W
Flourtown, Pa., U.S.	229b	40.07N	75.13W
Flower Hill, N.Y., U.S.	228	40.49N	73.41W
Floyd, r., Ia., U.S. (floid)	102	42.38N	96.15W
Floydada, Tx., U.S. (floi-dā'dȧ)	110	33.59N	101.19W
Floyds Fork, r., Ky., U.S. (floi-dz)	101h	38.08N	85.30W
Flumendosa, r., Italy	160	39.45N	9.18E
Flushing, Mi., U.S. (flûsh'ĭng)	98	43.05N	83.50W
Flushing, neigh., N.Y., U.S.	228	40.45N	73.49W
Fly, r. (flī)	197	8.00S	141.45E
Foča, Bos. (fō'chä)	161	43.29N	18.48E
Fochville, S. Afr. (fŏk'vĭl)	218d	26.29S	27.29E
Focşani, Rom. (fŏk-shä'nē)	155	45.41N	27.17E
Fogang, China (fwo-gäŋ)	193	23.50N	113.35E
Foggia, Italy (fôd'jä)	149	41.30N	15.34E
Fogo, Can. (fō'gō)	93	49.43N	54.17W
Fogo, i., Can.	91	49.40N	54.13W
Fogo, i., C.V.	210b	14.46N	24.51W
Fohnsdorf, Aus. (fōns'dôrf)	154	47.13N	14.40E
Föhr, i., Ger. (fûr)	154	54.47N	8.30E
Foix, Fr. (fwä)	156	42.58N	1.34E
Fokku, Nig.	215	11.40N	4.31E
Folcroft, Pa., U.S.	229b	39.54N	75.17W
Folgares, Ang.	216	14.54S	15.08E
Foligno, Italy (fō-lēn'yō)	160	42.58N	12.41E
Folkeston, Eng., U.K.	151	51.05N	1.18E
Folkingham, Eng., U.K. (fō'kĭng-ăm)	144a	52.53N	0.24W
Folkston, Ga., U.S.	115	30.50N	82.01W
Folsom, Ca., U.S.	108	38.40N	121.10W
Folsom, N.M., U.S. (fōl'sŭm)	110	36.47N	103.56W
Folsom, Pa., U.S.	229b	39.54N	75.19W
Fomento, Cuba (fō-mĕ'n-tō)	122	21.35N	78.20W
Fómeque, Col. (fō'mē-kē)	130a	4.29N	73.52W
Fonda, Ia., U.S. (fŏn'dȧ)	103	42.33N	94.51W
Fond du Lac, Wi., U.S. (fŏn dū lăk')	97	43.47N	88.29W
Fond du Lac Indian Reservation, I.R., Mn., U.S.	103	46.44N	93.04W
Fondi, Italy (fōn'dē)	160	41.23N	13.25E
Fonsagrada, Spain (fōn-sä-grä'dhä)	158	43.08N	7.07W
Fonseca, Golfo de, b., N.A. (gôl-fô-dĕ-fôn-sä'kä)	116	13.09N	87.55W
Fontainebleau, Fr. (fôn-tĕn-blō')	147	48.24N	2.42E
Fontainebleau, S. Afr.	244b	26.07S	27.59E
Fontana, Ca., U.S. (fŏn-tă'nȧ)	107a	34.06N	117.27W
Fonte Boa, Braz. (fōn'tå bō'ȧ)	130	2.32S	66.05W
Fontenay-aux-Roses, Fr.	237c	48.47N	2.17E
Fontenay-le-Comte, Fr. (fônt-nĕ'lē-kônt')	156	46.28N	0.53W
Fontenay-le-Fleury, Fr.	237c	48.49N	2.03E
Fontenay-sous-Bois, Fr.	237c	48.51N	2.29E

PLACE (Pronunciation)	PAGE	Lat. °′	Long. °′
Fontenay-Trésigny, Fr. (fôn-te-nā' tra-sēn-yē')	157b	48.43N	2.53E
Fontenelle Reservoir, res., Wy., U.S.	105	42.05N	110.05W
Fontera, Punta, c., Mex. (pōō'n-tä-fôn-tĕ'rä)	119	18.36N	92.43W
Fontibón, Col. (fōn-tē-bōn')	130a	4.42N	74.09W
Fontur, c., Ice.	142	66.21N	14.02W
Foothills, S. Afr. (fŏŏt-hĭls)	213b	25.55S	27.36E
Footscray, Austl.	201a	37.48S	144.54E
Fora, Ponta de, c., Braz.	234c	22.57S	43.07W
Foraker, Mount, mtn., Ak., U.S. (fôr'ȧ-kēr)	95	62.40N	152.40W
Forbach, Fr. (fôr'bäk)	157	49.12N	6.54E
Forbes, Austl. (fôrbz)	203	33.24S	148.05E
Forbes, Mount, mtn., Can.	87	51.52N	116.56W
Forbidden City, bldg., China	240b	39.55N	116.23E
Forchheim, Ger. (fôrk'hīm)	154	49.43N	11.05E
Fordham University, pt. of i., N.Y., U.S.	228	40.51N	73.53W
Fords, N.J., U.S.	228	40.32N	74.19W
Fordsburg, neigh., S. Afr.	244b	26.13S	28.02E
Fordyce, Ar., U.S. (fôr'dīs)	111	33.48N	92.24W
Forécariah, Gui. (fōr-kȧ-rē'ä')	210	9.26N	13.06W
Forel, Mont, mtn., Grnld.	82	65.50N	37.41W
Forest, Ms., U.S. (fŏr'ĕst)	114	32.22N	89.29W
Forest, r., N.D., U.S.	102	48.08N	97.45W
Forest City, Ia., U.S.	103	43.14N	93.40W
Forest City, N.C., U.S.	115	35.20N	81.52W
Forest City, Pa., U.S.	99	41.35N	75.30W
Forest Gate, neigh., Eng., U.K.	235	51.33N	0.02E
Forest Grove, Or., U.S. (grōv)	106c	45.31N	123.07W
Forest Heights, Md., U.S.	229d	38.49N	77.00W
Forest Hill, Austl.	243b	37.50S	145.11E
Forest Hill, Md., U.S.	100e	39.35N	76.26W
Forest Hill, Tx., U.S.	107c	32.40N	97.16W
Forest Hill, neigh., Can.	227c	43.42N	79.24W
Forest Hills, Pa., U.S.	230b	40.26N	79.52W
Forest Hills, neigh., N.Y., U.S.	228	40.42N	73.51W
Forest Park, Il., U.S.	231a	41.53N	87.50W
Forest Park, neigh., Md., U.S.	229c	39.19N	76.41W
Forestville, Austl.	243a	33.46S	151.13E
Forestville, Can. (fŏr'ĕst-vĭl)	92	48.45N	69.06W
Forestville, Md., U.S.	100e	38.51N	76.55W
Forez, Monts du, mts., Fr. (môn dü fō-rā')	156	44.55N	3.43E
Forfar, Scot., U.K. (fôr'fȧr)	150	57.10N	2.55W
Forillon, Parc National, rec., Can.	92	48.50N	64.05W
Forio, mtn., Italy (fō'ryō)	159c	40.29N	13.55E
Forked Creek, r., Il., U.S. (fôrk'd)	101a	41.16N	88.01W
Forked Deer, r., Tn., U.S.	114	35.53N	89.29W
Forli, Italy (fôr-lē')	148	44.13N	12.03E
Formby, Eng., U.K. (fôrm'bē)	144a	53.34N	3.04W
Formby Point, c., Eng., U.K.	144a	53.33N	3.06W
Formentera, Isla de, i., Spain (ē's-lä-dĕ-fôr-mĕn-tā'rä)	148	38.43N	1.25E
Formiga, Braz. (fôr-mē'gȧ)	131	20.27S	45.25W
Formigas Bank, bk. (fôr-mē'gäs)	123	18.30N	75.40W
Formosa, Arg. (fôr-mō'sä)	132	27.25S	58.12W
Formosa, Braz.	131	15.32S	47.10W
Formosa, prov., Arg.	132	24.30S	60.45W
Formosa, Serra, mts., Braz. (sĕ'r-rä)	131	12.59S	55.11W
Formosa Bay, b., Kenya	217	2.45S	40.30E
Formosa Strait *see* Taiwan Strait, strt., Asia	189	24.30N	120.00E
Fornosovo, Russia (fôr-nô'sô vô)	172c	59.35N	30.34E
Forrest City, Ar., U.S. (for'ĕst sĭ'tĭ)	111	35.00N	90.46W
Forsayth, Austl. (fôr-sīth')	203	18.33S	143.42E
Forshaga, Swe. (fōrs'hä'gä)	152	59.34N	13.25E
Forst, Ger. (fôrst)	147	51.45N	14.38E
Forsyth, Ga., U.S. (fôr-sīth')	114	33.02N	83.56W
Forsyth, Mt., U.S.	105	46.15N	106.41W
Fort, neigh., India	240e	18.56N	72.50E
Fort Albany, Can. (fôrt ôl'bȧ nĭ)	85	52.20N	81.30W
Fort Alexander Indian Reserve, I.R., Can.	89	50.27N	96.15W
Fortaleza, Braz. (fôr'tä-lā'zȧ)	131	3.35S	38.31W
Fort Atkinson, Wi., U.S. (ăt'kĭn-sŭn)	103	42.55N	88.46W
Fort Beaufort, S. Afr. (bō'fôrt)	213c	32.47S	26.39E
Fort Belknap Indian Reservation, I.R., Mt., U.S.	105	48.16N	108.38W
Fort Bellefontaine, Mo., U.S. (bĕl-fōn-tān')	107f	38.50N	90.15W
Fort Benton, Mt., U.S. (bĕn'tŭn)	105	47.51N	110.40W
Fort Berthold Indian Reservation, I.R., N.D., U.S. (bĕrth'ôld)	102	47.47N	103.28W
Fort Bragg, Ca., U.S.	108	39.26N	123.48W
Fort Branch, In., U.S. (brănch)	98	38.15N	87.35W
Fort Chipewyan, Can.	84	58.46N	111.15W
Fort Cobb Reservoir, res., Ok., U.S.	110	35.12N	98.28W
Fort Collins, Co., U.S. (kŏl'ĭns)	96	40.36N	105.04W
Fort Crampel, Cen. Afr. Rep. (kräm-pĕl')	211	6.59N	19.11E
Fort-de-France, Mart. (dē fräns)	117	14.37N	61.06W
Fort Deposit, Al., U.S. (dē-pŏz'ĭt)	114	31.58N	86.35W
Fort-de-Possel, Cen. Afr. Rep. (dĕ pô-sĕl')	211	5.03N	19.11E
Fort Dodge, Ia., U.S. (dŏj)	97	42.31N	94.10W
Fort Edward, N.Y., U.S. (wĕrd)	99	43.15N	73.30W
Fort Erie, Can. (ē'rĭ)	101c	42.55N	78.56W
Fortescue, r., Austl. (fôr'tĕs-kū)	202	21.25S	116.50E
Fort Fairfield, Me., U.S. (fâr'fēld)	92	46.46N	67.53W
Fort Fitzgerald, Can. (fĭts-jĕr'ăld)	84	59.48N	111.50W
Fort Frances, Can. (frăn'sĕs)	85	48.36N	93.24W
Fort Frederica National Monument, rec., Ga., U.S. (frĕd'ē-rĭ-kȧ)	114	31.13N	85.25W
Fort Gaines, Ga., U.S. (gānz)	114	31.35N	85.03W
Fort Gibson, Ok., U.S. (gĭb'sŭn)	111	35.50N	95.13W
Fort Good Hope, Can. (gŏŏd hōp)	84	66.19N	128.52W

ng-sing; ŋ-baŋk; ɴ-nasalized n; nŏd; cŏmmit; ōld; ôbey; ôrder; oi-boil; fōōd; ŏŏ-as oo in foot; ou-out; s-soft; sh-dish; th-thin; pūre; ûnite; ûrn; stŭd; circŭs; ü-as in French tu; '-indeterminate vowel.

PLACE (Pronunciation)	PAGE	Lat. °′	Long. °′
Fryerning, Eng., U.K.	235	51.41N	0.22E
Fucheng, China (fo͞o-chŭŋ)	190	37.53N	116.08E
Fuchu, Japan (fo͞o'cho͞o)	195a	35.41N	139.29E
Fuchun, r., China (fo͞o-chòn)	193	29.50N	120.00E
Fuego, vol., Guat. (fwā'gō)	120	14.29N	90.52W
Fuencarral, Spain (fuān-kär-räl')	159a	40.29N	3.42W
Fuensalida, Spain (fwān-sä-lē'dä)	158	40.04N	4.15W
Fuente, Mex. (fwĕ'n-tĕ')	112	28.39N	100.34W
Fuente de Cantos, Spain (fwĕn'tȧ dā kän'tōs)	158	38.15N	6.18W
Fuente el Saz, Spain (fwĕn'tȧ ĕl säth')	159a	40.39N	3.30W
Fuenteobejuna, Spain	158	38.15N	5.30W
Fuentesaúco, Spain (fwēn-tȧ-sä-o͞o'kō)	158	41.18N	5.25W
Fuerte, Río del, r., Mex. (rē'ō-dĕl-fo͞o-ĕ'r-tĕ)	116	26.15N	108.50W
Fuerte Olimpo, Para. (fwĕr'tȧ ō-lēm-pō)	132	21.10S	57.49W
Fuerteventura Island, i., Spain (fwĕr'tȧ-vĕn-to͞o'rä)	210	28.24N	13.21W
Fuhai, China	188	47.01N	87.07E
Fuhlenbrock, neigh., Ger.	236	51.32N	6.54E
Fuji, Japan (jo͞o'jē)	195	35.11N	138.44E
Fuji, r., Japan	195	35.20N	138.23E
Fujian, prov., China (fo͞o-jyĕn)	189	25.40N	117.30E
Fujidera, Japan	195b	34.34N	135.37E
Fujiidera, Japan	242b	34.34N	135.36E
Fujin, China (fo͞o-jyĭn)	189	47.13N	132.11E
Fuji San, mtn., Japan (fo͞o'jē sän)	189	35.23N	138.44E
Fujisawa, Japan (fo͞o'jē-sä'wa)	195a	35.20N	139.29E
Fujiyama see Fuji San, mtn., Japan	189	35.23N	138.44E
Fukagawa, neigh., Japan	242a	35.40N	139.48E
Fukiai, neigh., Japan	242b	34.42N	135.12E
Fukuchiyama, Japan (fō'kō-chē-yä'ma)	195	35.18N	135.07E
Fukue, i., Japan (fō-ko͞o'ā)	194	32.40N	129.02E
Fukui, Japan (fo͞o'ko͞o-ē)	189	36.05N	136.14E
Fukuoka, Japan (fo͞o'kō-ō'kȧ)	189	33.35N	130.23E
Fukuoka, Japan	195a	35.52N	139.31E
Fukushima, Japan (fo͞o'kō-shē'mȧ)	194	37.45N	140.29E
Fukushima, neigh., Japan	242b	34.42N	135.29E
Fukuyama, Japan (fo͞o'kō-yä'mȧ)	194	34.31N	133.21E
Fulda, Ger.	147	50.33N	9.41E
Fulda, r., Ger. (fōl'dä)	154	51.05N	9.40E
Fulerum, neigh., Ger.	236	51.26N	6.57E
Fuling, China (fo͞o-lĭŋ)	188	29.40N	107.30E
Fullerton, Ca., U.S. (fōl'ēr-tŭn)	107a	33.53N	117.56W
Fullerton, La., U.S.	113	31.00N	93.00W
Fullerton, Ne., U.S.	102	41.21N	97.59W
Fulmer, Eng., U.K.	235	51.33N	0.34W
Fulton, Ky., U.S. (fŭl'tŭn)	114	36.30N	88.53W
Fulton, Mo., U.S.	111	38.51N	91.56W
Fulton, N.Y., U.S.	99	43.20N	76.25W
Fultondale, Al., U.S. (fŭl'tŭn-dāl)	100h	33.37N	86.48W
Funabashi, Japan (fo͞o'nȧ-bä'shē)	195	35.43N	139.59E
Funasaka, Japan	242b	34.49N	135.17E
Funaya, Japan (fo͞o-nä'yä)	195b	34.45N	135.52E
Funchal, Port. (fòn-shäl')	210	32.41N	16.15W
Fundación, Col. (fo͞on-dä-syō'n)	130	10.43N	74.13W
Fundão, Port. (fòn-douɴ')	158	40.08N	7.32W
Fundão, Ilha do, i., Braz.	234c	22.51S	43.14W
Funde, India	240e	18.54N	72.58E
Fundy, Bay of, b., Can. (fŭn'dĭ)	85	45.00N	66.00W
Fundy National Park, rec., Can.	85	45.38N	65.00W
Funing, China	190	39.55N	119.16E
Funing, China (fo͞o-nĭŋ)	192	33.55N	119.54E
Funing Wan, b., China	193	26.48N	120.35E
Funtua, Nig.	215	11.31N	7.17E
Furancungo, Moz.	217	14.55S	33.35E
Furbero, Mex. (fo͞or-bĕ'rô)	119	20.21N	97.32W
Furgun, mtn., Iran	182	28.47N	57.00E
Furmanov, Russia (fûr-mä'nôf)	166	57.14N	41.11E
Furnas, Représa de, res., Braz.	131	21.00S	46.00W
Furneaux Group, is., Austl. (fûr'nō)	203	40.15S	146.27E
Fürstenfeld, Aus. (für'stĕn-fĕlt)	154	47.02N	16.03E
Fürstenfeldbruck, Ger. (fur'stēn-fĕld'bro͞ok)	145d	48.11N	11.16E
Fürstenwalde, Ger. (für'stĕn-väl-dĕ)	154	52.21N	14.04E
Fürth, Ger. (fürt)	147	49.28N	11.03E
Furuichi, Japan (fo͞o'rō-ē'chē)	195b	34.33N	135.37E
Fusa, Japan (fo͞o'sä)	195a	35.52N	140.08E
Fuse, Japan	195b	34.40N	135.33E
Fushimi, Japan (fo͞o'shē-mē)	195b	34.57N	135.47E
Fushun, China (fo͞o'sho͞on')	189	41.50N	124.00E
Fusong, China (fo͞o-soŋ)	192	42.12N	127.12E
Futatsubashi, Japan	242a	35.29N	139.30E
Futtsu, Japan (fo͞o'tso͞o')	195a	35.19N	139.49E
Futtsu Misaki, c., Japan (fo͞ot'tso͞o' mē-sä'kē)	195a	35.19N	139.46E
Fuwah, Egypt (fo͞o'wȧ)	218b	31.13N	30.35E
Fuxian, China (fo͞o shyĕn)	190	39.36N	121.59E
Fuxin, China (fo͞o-shyĭn)	192	42.05N	121.40E
Fuyang, China (fo͞o-yäŋ)	189	32.53N	115.48E
Fuyang, China	193	30.10N	119.58E
Fuyang, r., China (fo͞o-yäŋ)	190	36.59N	114.48E
Fuyu, China (fo͞o-yo͞o)	189	45.20N	125.00E
Fuzhou, China (fo͞o-jō)	189	26.02N	119.18E
Fuzhou, r., China	190	39.38N	121.43E
Fuzhoucheng, China (fo͞o-jō-chŭŋ)	190	39.46N	121.44E
Fyfield, Eng., U.K.	235	51.45N	0.16E
Fyn, i., Den. (fü''n)	152	55.24N	10.33E
Fyne, Loch, l., Scot., U.K. (fīn)	150	56.14N	5.10W
Fyresvatn, l., Nor.	152	59.04N	7.55E

G

PLACE (Pronunciation)	PAGE	Lat. °′	Long. °′
Gaalkacyo, Som.	218a	7.00N	47.30E
Gabela, Ang.	216	10.48S	14.20E
Gabès, Tun. (gä'bĕs)	210	33.51N	10.04E
Gabès, Golfe de, b., Tun.	210	32.22N	10.59E
Gabil, Chad	215	11.09N	18.12E
Gąbin, Pol. (gôɴ'bĕn)	155	52.23N	19.47E
Gabon, nation, Afr. (gȧ-bôɴ')	212	0.30S	10.45E
Gaborone, Bots.	212	24.28S	25.59E
Gabriel, r., Tx., U.S. (gā'brĭ-ĕl)	113	30.38N	97.15W
Gabrovo, Bul. (gäb'rô-vō)	161	42.52N	25.19E
Gachsārān, Iran	185	30.12N	50.47E
Gacko, Bos. (gäts'kô)	161	43.10N	18.34E
Gadsden, Al., U.S. (gădz'dĕn)	97	34.00N	86.00W
Gadyach, Ukr. (gäd-yäch')	167	50.22N	33.59E
Găeşti, Rom. (gă-yĕsh'tē)	161	44.43N	25.21E
Gaeta, Italy (gä-ā'tä)	160	41.18N	13.34E
Gaffney, S.C., U.S. (găf'nĭ)	115	35.04N	81.47W
Gafsa, Tun. (găf'sä)	210	34.16N	8.37E
Gagarin, Russia	162	55.32N	34.58E
Gagnoa, C. Iv.	214	6.08N	5.56W
Gagny, Fr.	237c	48.53N	2.32E
Gagra, Geor.	168	43.20N	40.15E
Gahmen, neigh., Ger.	236	51.36N	7.32E
Gaillac-sur-Tarn, Fr. (gȧ-yäk'sür-tärn')	156	43.54N	1.52E
Gaillard Cut, reg., Pan. (gä-ēl-yä'rd)	116a	9.03N	79.42W
Gainesville, Fl., U.S. (gānz'vĭl)	97	29.40N	82.20W
Gainesville, Ga., U.S.	114	34.16N	83.48W
Gainesville, Tx., U.S.	111	33.38N	97.08W
Gainsborough, Eng., U.K. (gānz'bŭr-ō)	144a	53.23N	0.46W
Gairdner, Lake, l., Austl. (gârd'nēr)	202	32.20S	136.30E
Gaithersburg, Md., U.S. (gā'thērs'bûrg)	100e	39.08N	77.13W
Gaixian, China (gī-shyĕn)	192	40.25N	122.20E
Galana, r., Kenya	217	3.00S	39.30E
Galapagar, Spain (gä-lä-pä-gär')	159a	40.36N	4.00W
Galapagos Islands see Colón, Archipiélago de, is., Ec.	130	0.10S	87.45W
Galaria, r., Italy	159d	41.58N	12.21E
Galashiels, Scot., U.K. (găl-ȧ-shēlz)	150	55.40N	2.57W
Galata, neigh., Tur.	239f	41.01N	28.58E
Galaţi, Rom.	142	45.25N	28.05E
Galatina, Italy (gä-lä-tē'nä)	161	40.10N	18.12E
Galátsion, Grc.	239d	38.01N	23.45E
Galaxídhion, Grc.	161	38.26N	22.22E
Galdhøpiggen, mtn., Nor.	152	61.37N	8.17E
Galeana, Mex. (gä-lȧ-ä'nä)	112	24.50N	100.04W
Galena, Il., U.S. (gȧ-lē'nȧ)	103	42.26N	90.27W
Galena, In., U.S.	101h	38.21N	85.55W
Galena Peak, mtn., Tx., U.S.	113a	29.44N	95.14W
Galera, Cerro, mtn., Pan. (sĕ'r-rô-gä-lĕ'rä)	116a	8.55N	79.38W
Galeras, vol., Col. (gä-lĕ'räs)	130	0.57N	77.27W
Gales, r., Or., U.S. (gālz)	106c	45.33N	123.11W
Galesburg, Il., U.S. (gālz'bûrg)	97	40.56N	90.21W
Galesville, Wi., U.S. (gālz'vĭl)	103	44.04N	91.22W
Galeton, Pa., U.S. (gāl'tŭn)	99	41.45N	77.40W
Galich, Russia (gäl'ĭch)	166	58.20N	42.38E
Galicia, hist. reg., Pol. (gȧ-lĭsh'ĭ-ȧ)	155	49.48N	21.05E
Galicia, hist. reg., Spain (gä-lē'thyä)	158	43.35N	8.03W
Galilee, l., Austl. (găl'ĭ-lē)	203	22.23S	145.09E
Galilee, Sea of, l., Isr.	181a	32.53N	35.45E
Galina Point, c., Jam. (gä-lē'nä)	122	18.25N	76.50W
Galion, Oh., U.S. (găl'ĭ-ŭn)	98	40.45N	82.50W
Galisteo, N.M., U.S. (gä-lĭs-tā'ō)	110	35.20N	106.00W
Gallarate, Italy (gäl-lä-rä'tā)	160	45.37N	8.48E
Gallardon, Fr. (gä-lär-dôɴ')	157b	48.31N	1.40E
Gallatin, Mo., U.S. (găl'ȧ-tĭn)	111	39.55N	93.58W
Gallatin, Tn., U.S.	114	36.23N	86.28W
Gallatin, r., Mt., U.S.	105	45.12N	111.10W
Galle, Sri L. (gäl)	183b	6.13N	80.10E
Gállego, r., Spain (gäl-yā'gō)	159	42.27N	0.37W
Gallinas, Punta de, c., Col. (gä-lyē'nās)	130	12.10N	72.10W
Gallipoli, Italy (gäl-lē'pô-lē)	161	40.03N	17.58E
Gallipoli see Gelibolu, Tur.	149	40.25N	26.40E
Gallipoli Peninsula, pen., Tur.	161	40.23N	25.10E
Gallipolis, Oh., U.S. (găl-ĭ-pô-lēs)	98	38.50N	82.10W
Gällivare, Swe. (yĕl-ĭ-vär'ĕ)	146	68.06N	20.29E
Gallo, r., Spain (gäl'yō)	158	40.43N	1.42W
Gallup, N.M., U.S. (găl'ŭp)	96	35.30N	108.45W
Galty Mountains, mts., Ire.	150	52.19N	8.20W
Galva, Il., U.S. (găl'vȧ)	111	41.11N	90.02W
Galveston, Tx., U.S. (găl'vĕs-tŭn)	97	29.18N	94.48W
Galveston Bay, b., Tx., U.S.	97	29.39N	94.45W
Galveston I, Tx., U.S.	113a	29.12N	94.53W
Galvin, Austl.	243b	37.51S	144.49E
Galway, Ire.	142	53.16N	9.05W
Galway Bay, b., Ire. (gôl'wā)	150	53.10N	9.47W
Gamba, China (gäm-bä)	186	28.23N	89.42E
Gambaga, Ghana (gäm-bä'gä)	210	10.32N	0.26W
Gambela, Eth. (găm-bā'lȧ)	211	8.15N	34.33E
Gambia, nation, Afr. (găm'bē-ȧ)	210	13.38N	19.38W
Gambia (Gambie), r., Afr.	214	13.20N	15.55W
Gambie, r., Afr.	210	12.30N	13.00W
Gamboma, Congo (gäm-bō'mä)	212	1.53S	15.51E
Gamleby, Swe. (găm'lĕ-bü)	152	57.54N	16.20E
Gan, r., China (gän)	193	26.50N	115.00E
Gäncä, Azer.	166	40.40N	46.22E
Gandak, r., India	186	26.37N	84.22E
Gander, Can. (găn'dēr)	85	48.57N	54.34W
Gander, r., Can.	93	49.10N	54.35W
Gander Lake, l., Can.	93	48.55N	55.40W
Gandhinagar, India	186	23.30N	72.47E
Gandi, Nig.	215	12.55N	5.49E
Gandía, Spain (gän-dē'ä)	159	38.56N	0.10W
Gangdisê Shan (Trans Himalayas), mts., China	188	30.25N	83.43E
Ganges, r., Asia (găn'jēz)	183	24.00N	89.30E
Ganges, Mouths of the, mth., Asia (găn'jēz)	183	21.18N	88.40E
Gangi, Italy (gän'jē)	160	37.48N	14.15E
Gangtok, India	183	27.15N	88.30E
Gannan, China (gän-nän)	192	47.50N	123.30E
Gannett Peak, mtn., Wy., U.S. (găn'ĕt)	96	43.10N	109.38W
Gano, Oh., U.S. (g'nō)	101f	39.18N	84.24W
Gänserndorf, Aus.	145e	48.21N	16.43E
Gansu, prov., China (gän-so͞o)	188	38.50N	101.10E
Ganwo, Nig.	215	11.13N	4.42E
Ganyu, China (gän-yo͞o)	190	34.52N	119.07E
Ganzhou, China (gän-jō)	189	25.50N	114.30E
Gao, Mali (gä'ō)	210	16.16N	0.03W
Gao'an, China (gou-än)	193	28.30N	115.02E
Gaobaita, China	240b	39.53N	116.30E
Gaobeidian, China	240b	39.54N	116.33E
Gaomi, China (gou-mē)	190	36.23N	119.46E
Gaoqiao, China (gou-chyou)	191b	31.21N	121.35E
Gaoshun, China (gou-shòn)	190	31.22N	118.50E
Gaotang, China (gou-täŋ)	190	36.52N	116.12E
Gaoyao, China (gou-you)	193	23.08N	112.25E
Gaoyi, China (gou-yē)	190	37.37N	114.39E
Gaoyou, China (gou-yō)	192	32.46N	119.26E
Gaoyou Hu, l., China (kä'ō-yo͞o'ho͞o)	189	32.42N	118.40E
Gap, Fr. (gȧp)	147	44.34N	6.08E
Gapan, Phil. (gä-pän)	197a	15.18N	120.56E
Gar, China	188	31.11N	80.35E
Garanhuns, Braz. (gä-rän-yòɴsh')	131	8.49S	36.28W
Garbagnate Milanese, Italy	238c	45.35N	9.05E
Garbatella, neigh., Italy	239c	41.52N	12.29E
Garber, Ok., U.S. (gȧr'bēr)	111	36.28N	97.35W
Garches, Fr.	237c	48.51N	2.11E
Garching, Ger. (gär'ĸĕng)	145d	48.15N	11.39E
Garcia, Mex. (gär-sē'ä)	112	25.50N	100.37W
García de la Cadena, Mex.	118	21.14N	103.26W
Garda, Lago di, l., Italy (lä-gō-dē-gär'dä)	148	45.43N	10.26E
Gardanne, Fr. (gȧr-dȧn')	156a	43.28N	5.29E
Gardelegen, Ger. (gär-dē-lȧ'ghĕn)	154	52.32N	11.22E
Garden, i., Mi., U.S. (gär'd'n)	98	45.50N	85.50W
Gardena, Ca., U.S. (gär-dē'nȧ)	107a	33.53N	118.19W
Garden City, Ks., U.S.	110	37.58N	100.52W
Garden City, Mi., U.S.	101b	42.20N	83.21W
Garden City, N.Y., U.S.	228	40.43N	73.37W
Garden City Park, N.Y., U.S.	228	40.44N	73.40W
Garden Grove, Ca., U.S. (gär'd'n grōv)	107a	33.47N	117.56W
Garden Reach, India	186a	22.33N	88.17E
Garden River, Can.	107k	46.33N	84.10W
Gardēz, Afg.	186	33.43N	69.09E
Gardiner, Me., U.S. (gärd'nēr)	92	44.12N	69.46W
Gardiner, Mt., U.S.	105	45.03N	110.43W
Gardiner, Wa., U.S.	106a	48.03N	122.55W
Gardiner Dam, dam, Can.	88	51.17N	106.51W
Gardner, Ma., U.S.	99	42.35N	72.00W
Gardner Canal, strt., Can.	86	53.28N	128.15W
Gardner Pinnacles, Hi., U.S.	94b	25.10N	167.00W
Gareloi, i., Ak., U.S. (gär-lo͞o-ā')	95a	51.40N	178.48W
Garenfeld, Ger.	236	51.24N	7.31E
Garfield, N.J., U.S. (gär'fēld)	100a	40.53N	74.06W
Garfield, N.J., U.S.	228	40.53N	74.07W
Garfield, Ut., U.S.	107b	40.45N	112.10W
Garfield Heights, Oh., U.S.	101d	41.25N	81.36W
Gargaliánoi, Grc. (gär-gä-lyä'nē)	161	37.07N	21.50E
Garges-lès-Gonesse, Fr.	237c	48.58N	2.25E
Gargždai, Lith. (gärgzh'dī)	153	55.43N	20.09E
Garibaldi, Mount, mtn., Can. (gâr-ĭ-băl'dē)	86	49.51N	123.01W
Garin, Arg. (gä-rē'n)	132a	34.25S	58.44W
Garissa, Kenya	217	0.28S	39.38E
Garland, Md., U.S.	229c	39.11N	76.39W
Garland, Tx., U.S. (gär'lănd)	107c	32.55N	96.39W
Garland, Ut., U.S.	105	41.45N	112.10W
Garm, Taj.	169	39.12N	70.28E
Garmisch-Partenkirchen, Ger. (gär'mēsh pär'tēn-kēr'ĸĕn)	154	47.38N	11.10E
Garnett, Ks., U.S. (gär'nĕt)	111	38.16N	95.15W
Garonne, r., Fr. (gȧ-rôn)	142	44.00N	1.00E
Garoua, Cam. (gär'wä)	211	9.18N	13.24E
Garrett, In., U.S. (găr'ĕt)	98	41.20N	85.10W
Garrison, Md., U.S.	229c	39.24N	76.45W
Garrison, N.Y., U.S. (găr'ĭ-sŭn)	100a	41.23N	73.57W
Garrison, N.D., U.S.	102	47.38N	101.24W
Garrovillas, Spain (gä-rō-vēl'yäs)	158	39.42N	6.30W
Garry, l., Can. (găr'ĭ)	84	66.16N	99.23W
Garsen, Kenya	217	2.16S	40.07E
Garson, Can.	91	46.34N	80.52W
Garstedt, Ger. (gär'shtĕt)	145c	53.40N	9.58E
Garston, Eng., U.K.	235	51.41N	0.23W
Garston, neigh., Eng., U.K.	237a	53.21N	2.53W
Gartenstadt, neigh., Ger.	236	51.30N	7.26E
Garulia, India	186a	22.48N	88.23E
Garwolin, Pol. (gär-vō'lēn)	155	51.54N	21.40E
Garwood, N.J., U.S.	228	40.39N	74.19W
Gary, In., U.S. (gā'rĭ)	97	41.35N	87.21W
Gary, W.V., U.S. (fĭl'bērt)	115	37.21N	81.33W

ng-sing; ŋ-baŋk; ɴ-nasalized n; nŏd; cŏmmit; ōld; ôbey; ôrder; oi-boil; fo͞od; ò-as oo in foot; ou-out; s-soft; sh-dish; th-thin; pūre; ůnite; ûrn; stŭd; circŭs; ü-as in French tu; '-indeterminate vowel.

PLACE (Pronunciation)	PAGE	Lat. °'	Long. °'
Garzón, Col. (gär-thōn')	130	2.13N	75.44W
Gasan, Phil. (gä-sän')	197a	13.19N	121.52E
Gasan-Kuli, Turk.	170	37.25N	53.55E
Gas City, In., U.S. (găs)	98	40.30N	85.40W
Gascogne, reg., Fr. (gäs-kôn'yĕ)	156	43.45N	1.49W
Gasconade, r., Mo., U.S. (găs-kô-nād')	111	37.46N	92.15W
Gascoyne, r., Austl. (găs-koin')	202	25.15S	117.00E
Gashland, Mo., U.S. (găsh'-lănd)	107f	39.15N	94.35W
Gashua, Nig.	215	12.54N	11.00E
Gasny, Fr. (gäs-nē')	157b	49.05N	1.36E
Gaspé, Can.	85	48.50N	64.29W
Gaspé, Péninsule de, pen., Can.	85	48.30N	65.00W
Gasper Hernández, Dom. Rep. (gäs-pär' ĕr-nän'dāth)	123	19.40N	70.15W
Gassaway, W.V., U.S. (găs'á-wā)	98	38.40N	80.45W
Gaston, Or., U.S. (găs'tŭn)	106c	45.26N	123.08W
Gastonia, N.C., U.S. (găs-tô'nĭ-á)	115	35.15N	81.14W
Gastre, Arg. (gäs-trĕ)	132	42.12S	68.50W
Gata, Cabo de, c., Spain (kä'bô-dĕ-gä'tä)	148	36.42N	2.00W
Gata, Sierra de, mts., Spain (syĕr'rä dä gä'tä)	148	40.12N	6.39W
Gatchina, Russia (gä-chē'nà)	166	59.33N	30.08E
Gateacre, neigh., Eng., U.K.	237a	53.23N	2.51W
Gátes, Akrotírion, c., Cyp.	181a	34.30N	33.15E
Gateshead, Eng., U.K. (gāts'hĕd)	150	54.56N	1.38W
Gates of the Arctic National Park, rec., Ak., U.S.	95	67.45N	153.30W
Gatesville, Tx., U.S. (gāts'vĭl)	113	31.26N	97.34W
Gateway of India, hist., India	240e	18.55N	72.50E
Gâtine, Hauteurs de, hills, Fr.	156	46.40N	0.50W
Gatineau, Can. (gá'tē-nō)	83c	45.29N	75.38W
Gatineau, r., Can.	91	45.45N	75.50W
Gatineau, Parc de la, rec., Can.	91	45.32N	75.53W
Gatley, Eng., U.K.	237b	53.23N	2.14W
Gato Negro, Ven.	234a	10.33N	66.57W
Gattendorf, Aus.	145e	48.01N	17.00E
Gatun, Pan. (gä-tōōn')	121	9.16N	79.25W
Gatun, r., Pan.	116a	9.21N	79.40W
Gatún, Lago, l., Pan.	121	9.13N	79.24W
Gatun Locks, trans., Pan.	116a	9.16N	79.57W
Gauhāti, India	183	26.09N	91.51E
Gauja, r., Lat. (gå'ō-yå)	153	57.10N	24.30E
Gaula, r., Nor.	152	62.55N	10.45E
Gāvanpāda, India	240e	18.57N	73.01E
Gávdhos, i., Grc. (gäv'dôs)	149	34.48N	24.08E
Gavins Point Dam, Ne., U.S. (gă'-vĭns)	102	42.47N	97.47W
Gāvkhūnī, Bātlāq-e, l., Iran	182	31.40N	52.48E
Gävle, Swe. (yĕv'lĕ)	142	60.40N	17.07E
Gävlebukten, b., Swe.	152	60.45N	17.30E
Gavrilov Posad, Russia (gá'vrē-lôf'ka po-sát)	162	56.34N	40.09E
Gavrilov-Yam, Russia (gá'vrē-lôf yäm')	162	57.17N	39.49E
Gawler, Austl. (gô'lēr)	202	34.35S	138.47E
Gawler Ranges, mts., Austl.	204	32.35S	136.30E
Gaya, India (gŭ'yä)(gī'á)	183	24.53N	85.00E
Gaya, Nig. (gä'yä)	210	11.58N	9.05E
Gaylord, Mi., U.S. (gā'lôrd)	98	45.00N	84.35W
Gayndah, Austl. (gān'dăh)	204	25.43S	151.33E
Gayton, Eng., U.K.	237a	53.19N	3.06W
Gaza, Gaza	182	31.30N	34.29E
Gaziantep, Tur. (gä-zē-än'tĕp)	182	37.10N	37.30E
Gbarnga, Lib.	214	7.00N	9.29W
Gdańsk, Pol. (g'dänsk)	142	54.20N	18.40E
Gdov, Russia (g'dôf')	166	58.44N	27.51E
Gdynia, Pol. (g'dēn'yà)	146	54.29N	18.30E
Geary, Ok., U.S. (gē'rĭ)	110	35.36N	98.19W
Géba, r., Gui.-B.	214	12.25N	14.35W
Gebo, Wy., U.S. (gĕb'ō)	105	43.49N	108.13W
Ged, La., U.S. (gĕd)	113	30.07N	93.36W
Gediz, r., Tur.	149	38.44N	28.45E
Gedney, i., Wa., U.S. (gĕd-nē)	106a	48.01N	122.18W
Gedser, Den.	152	54.35N	12.08E
Gee Cross, Eng., U.K.	237b	53.26N	2.04W
Geel, Bel.	145a	51.09N	5.01E
Geelong, Austl. (jē-lông')	203	38.06S	144.13E
Gegu, China (gŭ-gōō)	190	39.00N	117.30E
Ge Hu, l., China (gŭ hōō)	190	31.37N	119.57E
Geidam, Nig.	210	12.57N	11.57E
Geikie Range, mts., Austl. (gē'kē)	202	17.35S	125.32E
Geislingen, Ger. (gis'lĭng-ĕn)	154	48.37N	9.52E
Geist Reservoir, res., In., U.S. (gēst)	101g	39.57N	85.59W
Geita, Tan.	217	2.52S	32.10E
Gejiu, China (gŭ-jĭō)	193	23.32N	102.50E
Geldermalsen, Neth.	145a	51.53N	5.18E
Geldern, Ger. (gĕl'dĕrn)	157c	51.31N	6.20E
Gelibolu, Tur. (gĕ-lĭb'ō-lò)	149	40.25N	26.40E
Gellep-Stratum, neigh., Ger.	236	51.20N	6.41E
Gellibrand, Point, c., Austl.	243b	37.52S	144.54E
Gelsenkirchen, Ger. (gĕl-zĕn-kĭrk-ĕn)	154	51.31N	7.05E
Gemas, Malay. (jĕm'ás)	181b	2.35N	102.37E
Gemena, Zaire	211	3.15N	19.46E
Gemlik, Tur. (gĕm'lĭk)	149	40.30N	29.10E
Genale (Jubba), r., Afr.	218a	5.15N	41.00E
General Alvear, Arg. (gĕ-nĕ-räl'äl-vĕ-á'r)	129c	36.04S	60.02W
General Arenales, Arg. (ä-rĕ-nä'lĕs)	129c	34.19S	61.16W
General Belgrano, Arg. (bĕl-grá'nô)	129c	35.45S	58.32W
General Cepeda, Mex. (sĕ-pĕ'dä)	112	25.24N	101.29W
General Conesa, Arg. (kô-nĕ'sä)	129c	36.30S	57.19W
General Guido, Arg. (gē'dô)	129c	36.41S	57.48W
General Lavalle, Arg. (là-vá'l-yĕ)	129c	36.25S	56.55W
General Madariaga, Arg. (män-dá-rēä'gä)	132	36.59S	57.14W
General Pacheco, Arg.	233d	34.28S	58.37W
General Paz, Arg. (pá'z)	129c	35.30S	58.20W
General Pedro Antonio Santos, Mex.	118	21.37N	98.58W
General Pico, Arg. (pē'kô)	132	36.46S	63.44W
General Roca, Arg. (rô-kä)	132	39.01S	67.31W

PLACE (Pronunciation)	PAGE	Lat. °'	Long. °'
General San Martín, Arg. (sän-mär-tē'n)	132a	34.35S	58.32W
General Sarmiento (San Miguel), Arg.	132a	34.33S	58.43W
General Urquiza, neigh., Arg.	233d	34.34S	58.29W
General Viamonte, Arg. (vēá'môn-tĕ)	129c	35.01S	60.59W
General Zuazua, Mex. (zwä'zwä)	112	25.54N	100.07W
Genesee, r., N.Y., U.S. (jĕn-ē-sē')	99	42.25N	78.10W
Geneseo, Il., U.S. (jē-nĕsē̇ō)	98	41.28N	90.11W
Geneva (Genève), Switz.	142	46.14N	6.04E
Geneva, Al., U.S. (jē-nē'vá)	114	31.03N	85.50W
Geneva, Il., U.S.	101a	41.53N	88.18W
Geneva, Ne., U.S.	111	40.32N	97.37W
Geneva, N.Y., U.S.	99	42.50N	77.00W
Geneva, Oh., U.S.	98	41.45N	80.55W
Geneva, Lake, l., Switz.	147	46.28N	6.30E
Genève see Geneva, Switz.	142	46.14N	6.04E
Genil, r., Spain (hå-nēl')	158	37.15N	4.05W
Gennebreck, Ger.	236	51.19N	7.12E
Gennevilliers, Fr.	237c	48.56N	2.18E
Genoa, Italy	142	44.23N	9.52E
Genoa, Ne., U.S. (jen'ō-á)	111	41.26N	97.43W
Genoa City, Wi., U.S.	101a	42.31N	88.19W
Genova, Golfo di, b., Italy (gôl-fô-dē-jĕn'ō-vä)	142	44.10N	8.45E
Genovesa, i., Ec. (ĕ's-lä-gĕ-nō-vĕ-sä)	130	0.08N	90.15W
Gent, Bel.	147	51.05N	3.40E
Genthin, Ger. (gĕn-tēn')	154	52.24N	12.10E
Gentilly, Fr.	237c	48.49N	2.21E
Genzano di Roma, Italy (gzhĕnt-zä'-nō-dē-rō'mä)	159d	41.43N	12.49E
Geographe Bay, b., Austl. (jē-ō-graf')	202	33.00S	114.00E
Geographe Channel, strt., Austl. (jēō'grā-fĭk)	202	24.15S	112.50E
George, l., N.Y., U.S. (jôrj)	99	43.40N	73.30W
George, Lake, l., N.A. (jôrg)	107k	46.26N	84.09W
George, Lake, l., Ug.	217	0.02N	30.25E
George, Lake, l., Fl., U.S. (jôr-ĭj)	115	29.10N	81.50W
George, Lake, l., In., U.S.	101a	41.31N	87.17W
Georges, r., Austl.	201b	33.57S	151.00E
Georges Hall, Austl.	243a	33.55S	150.59E
George Town, Bah.	123	23.30N	75.50W
Georgetown, Can. (jôrg-toun)	83d	43.39N	79.56W
Georgetown, Can. (jôr-ĭj-toun)	93	46.11N	62.32W
George Town, Cay. Is.	122	19.20N	81.20W
Georgetown, Guy. (jôrj'toun)	131	7.45N	58.04W
George Town, Malay.	196	5.21N	100.09E
Georgetown, Ct., U.S.	100a	41.15N	73.25W
Georgetown, De., U.S.	99	38.40N	75.20W
Georgetown, Il., U.S.	98	40.00N	87.40W
Georgetown, Ky., U.S.	98	38.10N	84.35W
Georgetown, Md., U.S.	99	39.25N	75.55W
Georgetown, Ma., U.S. (jôrg-toun)	93a	42.43N	71.00W
Georgetown, S.C., U.S. (jôr-ĭj-toun)	115	33.22N	79.17W
Georgetown, Tx., U.S. (jôrg-toun)	113	30.37N	97.40W
Georgetown, neigh., D.C., U.S.	229d	38.54N	77.03W
Georgetown University, pt. of i., D.C., U.S.	229d	38.54N	77.04W
George Washington Birthplace National Monument, rec., Va., U.S. (jôrj wŏsh'ĭng-tŭn)	99	38.10N	77.00W
George Washington Carver National Monument, rec., Mo., U.S. (jôrg wăsh-ĭng-tŭn kär'vĕr)	111	36.58N	94.21W
George West, Tx., U.S.	112	28.20N	98.07W
Georgia, nation, Asia	164	42.17N	43.00E
Georgia, state, U.S. (jôr'ji-ă)	97	32.40N	83.50W
Georgia, Strait of, strt., N.A.	86	49.20N	124.00W
Georgiana, Al., U.S. (jôr-jē-ăn'á)	114	31.39N	86.44W
Georgian Bay, b., Can.	85	45.15N	80.50W
Georgian Bay Islands National Park, rec., Can.	90	45.20N	81.40W
Georgina, r., Austl. (jôr-jē'ná)	202	22.00S	138.15E
Georgiyevsk, Russia (gyôr-gyĕfsk')	167	44.05N	43.30E
Gera, Ger. (gā'rä)	147	50.52N	12.06E
Geral, Serra, mts., Braz. (sĕr'rá zhä-räl')	132	28.30S	51.00W
Geral de Goiás, Serra, mts., Braz. (zhä-räl'-dĕ-gô-yá's)	131	14.22S	45.40W
Geraldton, Austl. (jĕr'ăld-tŭn)	202	28.40S	114.35E
Geraldton, Can.	85	49.43N	87.00W
Gerdview, S. Afr.	244b	26.10S	28.11E
Gérgal, Spain (gĕr'gäl)	158	37.08N	2.29W
Gering, Ne., U.S. (gē'rĭng)	102	41.49N	103.41W
Gerlachovský štít, mtn., Slvk.	155	49.12N	20.08E
Gerli, neigh., Arg.	233d	34.41S	58.23W
Germantown, Oh., U.S. (jûr'măn-toun)	98	39.35N	84.25W
Germantown, neigh., Pa., U.S.	229b	40.03N	75.11W
Germany, nation, Eur. (jûr'má-nĭ)	142	51.00N	10.00E
Germiston, S. Afr. (jûr'mĭs-tŭn)	212	26.19S	28.11E
Gerona, Phil. (hä-rō'nä)	197a	15.36N	120.36E
Gerona, Spain (hĕ-rō'nä)	148	41.55N	2.48E
Gerrards Cross, Eng., U.K. (jĕrărds krŏs)	144b	51.34N	0.33W
Gers, r., Fr. (zhĕr)	159	43.25N	0.30E
Gersthofen, Ger. (gĕrst-hō'fĕn)	145d	48.26N	10.54E
Getafe, Spain (hä-tä'fä)	158	40.19N	3.44W
Gettysburg, Pa., U.S. (gĕt'ĭs-bûrg)	99	39.50N	77.15W
Gettysburg, S.D., U.S.	102	45.01N	99.59W
Getzville, N.Y., U.S.	230a	43.01N	78.46W
Gevelsberg, Ger. (gĕ-fĕls'bĕrgh)	157c	51.18N	7.20E
Geweke, neigh., Ger.	236	51.22N	7.25E
Ghāghra, r., India	183	26.00N	83.00E
Ghana, nation, Afr. (găn'ä)	210	8.00N	2.00W
Ghanzi, Bots. (găn'zē)	212	21.30S	22.00E
Ghārāpuri, India	240e	18.57N	72.56E
Ghardaïa, Alg. (gär-dä'ē-ä)	210	32.29N	3.38E
Gharo, Pak.	186	24.50N	68.35E
Ghāt, Libya	210	24.52N	10.16E
Ghātkopar, neigh., India	240e	19.05N	72.54E
Ghazāl, Bahr al-, r., Sudan	211	9.30N	30.00E

PLACE (Pronunciation)	PAGE	Lat. °'	Long. °'
Ghazal, Bahr el, r., Chad (bär ĕl ghä-zäl')	215	14.30N	17.00E
Ghāzipur, neigh., India	240d	28.38N	77.19E
Ghazzah see Gaza, Gaza	182	31.30N	34.29E
Gheorgheni, Rom.	149	46.48N	25.30E
Gherla, Rom. (gĕr'lä)	155	47.01N	23.55E
Ghilizane, Alg.	210	35.43N	0.43E
Ghonda, neigh., India	240d	28.41N	77.16E
Ghondi, neigh., India	240d	28.42N	77.16E
Ghost Lake, Can.	83e	51.15N	114.46W
Ghudāmis, Libya	210	30.07N	9.26E
Ghūriān, Afg.	185	34.21N	61.30E
Ghushuri, India	240a	22.37N	88.22E
Gia-dinh, Viet.	241j	10.48N	106.42E
Giannutri, Isola di, i., Italy (jän-nōō'trē)	160	42.15N	11.06E
Gibara, Cuba (hē-bä'rä)	122	21.05N	76.10W
Gibbsboro, N.J., U.S.	229b	39.50N	74.58W
Gibeon, Nmb. (gĭb'ē-ŭn)	212	25.15S	17.30E
Gibraleón, Spain (hē-brä-lå-ōn')	158	37.24N	7.00W
Gibraltar, dep., Eur. (gĭ-brăl-tä'r)	142	36.08N	5.22W
Gibraltar, Strait of, strt.	142	35.55N	5.45W
Gibraltar Point, c., Can.	227c	43.36N	79.23W
Gibson City, Il., U.S. (gĭb'sŭn)	98	40.25N	88.20W
Gibson Desert, des., Austl.	202	24.45S	123.15E
Gibson Island, Md., U.S.	100e	39.05N	76.26W
Gibson Reservoir, res., Ok., U.S.	111	36.07N	95.08W
Giddings, Tx., U.S. (gĭd'ĭngz)	113	30.11N	96.55W
Gidea Park, neigh., Eng., U.K.	235	51.35N	0.12E
Gideon, Mo., U.S. (gĭd'ē-ŭn)	111	36.27N	89.56W
Gien, Fr. (zhē-ăN')	147	47.43N	2.37E
Giessen, Ger. (gēs'sĕn)	154	50.35N	8.40E
Gif-sur-Yvette, Fr.	237c	48.42N	2.08E
Gifu, Japan (gē'fōō)	189	35.25N	136.45E
Gig Harbor, Wa., U.S. (gĭg)	106a	47.20N	122.36W
Giglio, Isola del, i., Italy (jēl'yō)	160	42.23N	10.55E
Gijón, Spain (hē-hōn')	142	43.33N	5.37W
Gila, r., U.S. (hē'lá)	96	33.00N	110.00W
Gila Bend, Az., U.S.	109	32.59N	112.41W
Gila Cliff Dwellings National Monument, rec., N.M., U.S.	109	33.15N	108.20W
Gila River Indian Reservation, I.R., Az., U.S.	109	33.11N	112.38W
Gilbert, Mn., U.S. (gĭl'bērt)	103	47.27N	92.29W
Gilbert, r., Austl. (gĭl-bērt)	203	17.15S	142.09E
Gilbert, Mount, mtn., Can.	86	50.51N	124.20W
Gilbert Islands, is., Kir.	225	0.30S	174.00E
Gilboa, Mount, mtn., S. Afr. (gĭl-bōá)	213c	29.13N	30.17W
Gilford Island, i., Can. (gĭl'fērd)	86	50.45N	126.25W
Gilgit, Pak. (gĭl'gĭt)	183	35.58N	73.48E
Gil Island, i., Can. (gĭl)	86	53.13N	129.15W
Gillen, l., Austl. (jĭl'ĕn)	202	26.15S	125.15E
Gillett, Ar., U.S. (jĭ-lĕt')	111	34.07N	91.22W
Gillette, Wy., U.S.	105	44.17N	105.30W
Gillingham, Eng., U.K. (gĭl'ĭng ăm)	151	51.23N	0.33E
Gilman, Il., U.S. (gĭl'măn)	98	40.45N	87.55W
Gilman Hot Springs, Ca., U.S.	107a	33.49N	116.57W
Gilmer, Tx., U.S. (gĭl'mēr)	113	32.43N	94.57W
Gilmore, Ga., U.S. (gĭl'môr)	100c	33.51N	84.29W
Gilo, r., Eth.	211	7.40N	34.17E
Gilroy, Ca., U.S. (gĭl-roi')	108	37.00N	121.34W
Giluwe, Mount, mtn., Pap. N. Gui.	197	6.04S	144.00E
Gimli, Can. (gĭm'lē)	89	50.39N	97.00W
Gimone, r., Fr. (zhē-mōn')	156	43.26N	0.36E
Ginir, Eth.	211	7.13N	40.44E
Ginosa, Italy (jē-nō'zä)	160	40.35N	16.48E
Ginza, neigh., Japan	242a	35.40N	139.47E
Ginzo, Spain (hēn-thō')	158	42.03N	7.43W
Gioia del Colle, Italy (jō'yä dĕl kôl'lā)	160	40.48N	16.55E
Girard, Ks., U.S. (jĭ-rărd')	111	37.30N	94.50W
Girardot, Col. (hē-rär-dōt')	130	4.19N	74.47W
Giresun, Tur. (ghĕr'ĕ-sōn')	182	40.55N	38.20E
Girgaum, neigh., India	240e	18.57N	72.48E
Giridih, India (jē-rē-dē)	183	24.12N	86.18E
Gironde, r., Fr. (zhē-rôNd')	142	45.31N	1.00W
Girvan, Scot., U.K. (gûr'văn)	150	55.15N	5.01W
Gisborne, N.Z. (gĭz'bŭrn)	203a	38.40S	178.08E
Gisenyi, Rw.	212	1.43S	29.15E
Gisors, Fr. (zhē-zôr')	156	49.19N	1.47E
Gitambo, Zaire	216	4.21N	24.45E
Gitega, Bdi.	212	3.39S	30.05E
Giurgiu, Rom. (jôr'jō)	161	43.53N	25.58E
Givet, Fr. (zhē-vĕ')	156	50.08N	4.47E
Givors, Fr. (zhē-vôr')	156	45.35N	4.46E
Giza see Al Jīzah, Egypt	218b	30.01N	31.12E
Gizhiga, Russia (gē'zhi-gá)	165	61.59N	160.46E
Gizo, Sol.Is.	198e	8.06S	156.51E
Gizycko, Pol. (gĭ'zhĭ-ko)	146	54.03N	21.48E
Gjirokastër, Alb.	149	40.04N	20.10E
Gjøvik, Nor. (gyû'vĕk)	146	60.47N	10.36E
Glabeek-Zuurbemde, Bel.	145a	50.52N	4.59E
Glace Bay, Can. (glās bā)	93	46.12N	59.57W
Glacier Bay National Park, rec., Ak., U.S. (glā'shēr)	96a	58.40N	136.50W
Glacier National Park, rec., Can.	84	51.45N	117.35W
Glacier Peak, mtn., Wa., U.S.	104	48.07N	121.10W
Glacier Point, c., Can.	106a	48.24N	123.59W
Gladbeck, Ger. (gläd'bĕk)	154	51.35N	6.59E
Gladdeklipkop, S. Afr.	218d	24.17S	29.36E
Gladesville, Austl.	243a	33.50S	151.08E
Gladstone, Austl.	202	33.15S	138.20E
Gladstone, Austl. (glăd'stōn)	203	23.45S	152.00E
Gladstone, Mi., U.S.	103	45.50N	87.04W
Gladstone, N.J., U.S.	100a	40.43N	74.39W
Gladstone, Or., U.S.	106c	45.23N	122.36W
Gladwin, Mi., U.S. (glăd'wĭn)	98	44.00N	84.25W
Gladwyne, Pa., U.S.	229b	40.02N	75.17W
Glåma, r., Nor.	142	61.30N	10.30E

ăt; finăl; rāte; senăte; ärm; åsk; sofá; fâre; ch-choose; dh-as th in other; bē; ēvent; bĕt; recĕnt; cratĕr; g-gō; gh-guttural g; bĭt; ĭ-short neutral; rīde; K-guttural k as ch in German ich;

PRONOUNCING INDEX

Glarus–Grand Canal 291

PLACE (Pronunciation)	PAGE	Lat. °′	Long. °′
Glarus, Switz. (glä'rôs)	154	47.02N	9.03E
Glasgow, Scot., U.K. (glås'gō)	142	55.54N	4.25W
Glasgow, Ky., U.S.	114	37.00N	85.55W
Glasgow, Mo., U.S.	111	39.14N	92.48W
Glasgow, Mt., U.S.	105	48.14N	106.39W
Glashütte, neigh., Ger.	236	51.13N	6.52E
Glassmanor, Md., U.S.	229d	38.49N	76.59W
Glassport, Pa., U.S. (glås'pōrt)	101e	40.19N	79.53W
Glassport, Pa., U.S.	230b	40.19N	79.54W
Glauchau, Ger. (glou'kou)	154	50.51N	12.28E
Glazov, Russia (glä'zôf)	164	58.05N	52.52E
Glehn, Ger.	236	51.10N	6.35E
Glen, r., Eng., U.K. (glĕn)	144a	52.44N	0.18W
Glénan, Îles de, is., Fr. (ēl-dē-glā-näN')	156	47.43N	4.42W
Glenarden, Md., U.S.	229d	38.56N	76.52W
Glen Burnie, Md., U.S. (bûr'nē)	100e	39.10N	76.38W
Glen Canyon, val., Ut., U.S.	109	37.10N	110.50W
Glen Canyon Dam, dam, Az., U.S. (glĕn kăn'yŭn)	96	36.57N	111.25W
Glen Canyon National Recreation Area, rec., U.S.	109	37.00N	111.20W
Glen Carbon, Il., U.S. (kär'bŏn)	107e	38.45N	89.59W
Glencoe, S. Afr. (glĕn-cō)	213c	28.14S	30.09E
Glencoe, Il., U.S.	101a	42.08N	87.45W
Glencoe, Mn., U.S. (glĕn'kō)	103	44.44N	94.07W
Glen Cove, N.Y., U.S. (kōv)	100a	40.51N	73.38W
Glendale, Az., U.S. (glĕn'dāl)	109	33.30N	112.15W
Glendale, Ca., U.S.	96	34.09N	118.15W
Glendale, Oh., U.S.	101f	31.16N	84.22W
Glendive, Mt., U.S. (glĕn'dīv)	96	47.08N	104.41W
Glendo, Wy., U.S.	105	42.32N	104.54W
Glendora, Ca., U.S. (glĕn-dō'rȧ)	107a	34.08N	117.52W
Glendora, N.J., U.S.	229b	39.50N	75.04W
Glen Echo, Md., U.S.	229d	38.58N	77.08W
Glenelg, r., Austl.	204	37.20S	141.30E
Glen Ellyn, Il., U.S. (glĕn ĕl'-lĕn)	101a	41.53N	88.04W
Glenfield, Austl.	243a	33.58S	150.54E
Glen Head, N.Y., U.S.	228	40.50N	73.37W
Glenhuntly, Austl.	243b	37.54S	145.03E
Glen Innes, Austl. (ĭn'ĕs)	203	29.45S	152.02E
Glenmore, Md., U.S.	229c	39.11N	76.36W
Glenns Ferry, Id., U.S. (fĕr'ĭ)	104	42.58N	115.21W
Glen Olden, Pa., U.S. (ōl'd'n)	100f	39.54N	75.17W
Glenomra, La., U.S. (glĕn-mō'rȧ)	113	30.58N	92.36W
Glen Ridge, N.J., U.S.	228	40.49N	74.13W
Glen Rock, N.J., U.S.	228	40.58N	74.08W
Glenrock, Wy., U.S. (glĕn'rŏk)	105	42.50N	105.53W
Glenroy, Austl.	243b	37.42S	144.55E
Glens Falls, N.Y., U.S. (glĕnz fôlz)	99	43.20N	73.40W
Glenshaw, Pa., U.S. (glĕn'shô)	101e	40.33N	79.57W
Glenside, Pa., U.S.	229b	40.06N	75.09W
Glen Valley, Can.	106d	49.09N	122.30W
Glenview, Il., U.S. (glĕn'vū)	101a	42.04N	87.48W
Glenville, Ga., U.S. (glĕn'vĭl)	115	31.55N	81.56W
Glen Waverley, Austl.	243b	37.53S	145.10E
Glenwood, Ia., U.S.	102	41.03N	95.44W
Glenwood, Mn., U.S.	102	45.39N	95.23W
Glenwood, N.M., U.S.	109	33.19N	108.52W
Glenwood Landing, N.Y., U.S.	228	40.50N	73.39W
Glenwood Springs, Co., U.S.	109	39.35N	107.20W
Glienicke, Ger. (glē'nē-kĕ)	145b	52.38N	13.19E
Glinde, Ger. (glēn'dĕ)	145c	53.32N	10.13E
Gliwice, Pol. (gwĭ-wĭt'sĕ)	147	50.18N	18.40E
Globe, Az., U.S. (glōb)	96	33.20N	110.50W
Głogów, Pol. (gwō'gōōv)	147	51.40N	16.04E
Glommen, r., Nor. (glôm'ĕn)	152	60.03N	11.15E
Glonn, Ger. (glônn)	145d	47.59N	11.52E
Glorieuses, Îles, is., Reu.	213	11.28S	47.50E
Glossop, Eng., U.K. (glŏs'ŭp)	144a	53.26N	1.57W
Gloster, Ms., U.S. (glŏs'tēr)	114	31.10N	91.00W
Gloucester, Eng., U.K. (glŏs'tēr)	147	51.54N	2.11W
Gloucester, Ma., U.S.	93a	42.37N	70.40W
Gloucester City, N.J., U.S.	100f	39.53N	75.08W
Glouster, Oh., U.S. (glŏs'tēr)	98	39.35N	82.05W
Glover Island, i., Can. (glŭv'ēr)	93	48.44N	57.45W
Gloversville, N.Y., U.S. (glŭv'ērz-vĭl)	99	43.05N	74.20W
Glovertown, Can. (glŭv'ēr-toun)	93	48.41N	54.02W
Glubokoye, Bela. (glōō-bô-kō'yĕ)	166	55.08N	27.44E
Glückstadt, Ger. (glük-shtät)	145c	53.47N	9.25E
Glushkovo, Russia (glōsh'kō-vō)	163	51.21N	34.43E
Gmünden, Aus. (g'mōn'dĕn)	154	47.57N	13.47E
Gniezno, Pol. (g'nyåz'nō)	147	52.32N	17.34E
Gnjilane, Yugo. (gnyē'lå-nĕ)	161	42.28N	21.27E
Goa, , India (gō'ȧ)	183	15.45N	74.00E
Goascorán, Hond. (gō-äs'kō-rän')	120	13.37N	87.43W
Goba, Eth. (gō'bä)	211	7.17N	39.58E
Gobabis, Nmb. (gō-bä'bĭs)	212	22.25S	18.50E
Gobi, des., Asia (gō'be)	188	43.29N	103.15E
Goble, Or., U.S. (gō'b'l)	106c	46.01N	122.53W
Goch, Ger. (gōk)	157c	51.35N	6.10E
Godāvari, r., India (gō-dä'vŭ-rē)	183	19.00N	78.30E
Goddards Soak, sw., Austl. (gŏd'ȧrdz)	202	31.20S	123.30E
Goderich, Can. (gōd'rĭch)	90	43.45N	81.45W
Godfrey, Il., U.S. (gŏd'frē)	107e	38.57N	90.12W
Godhavn, Grnld. (gōdh'håvn)	82	69.15N	53.30W
Gods, r., Can. (gŏdz)	89	55.17N	93.35W
Gods Lake, Can.	85	54.40N	94.09W
Godthåb, Grnld. (gŏt'hōb)	82	64.10N	51.32W
Godwin Austen see K2, mtn., Asia	182	36.06N	76.38E
Goéland, Lac au, l., Can.	91	49.47N	76.41W
Goffs, Ca., U.S. (gôfs)	108	34.57N	115.06W
Goff's Oak, Eng., U.K.	235	51.43N	0.05W
Gogebic, l., Mi., U.S. (gō-gē'bĭk)	103	46.24N	89.25W
Gogebic Range, mts., Mi., U.S.	103	46.37N	89.48W
Göggingen, Ger. (gûg'gĕn-gĕn)	145d	48.21N	10.53E
Gogland, i., Russia	153	60.04N	26.55E
Gogonou, Benin	215	10.50N	2.50E

PLACE (Pronunciation)	PAGE	Lat. °′	Long. °′
Gogorrón, Mex. (gō-gō-rōn')	118	21.51N	100.54W
Goiânia, Braz. (gô-yä'nyä)	131	16.41S	48.57W
Goiás, Braz. (gō-yà's)	131	15.57S	50.10W
Goiás, state, Braz.	131	16.00S	48.00W
Goirle, Neth.	145a	51.31N	5.06E
Gökçeada, i., Tur.	161	40.10N	25.27E
Göksu, r., Tur. (gûk'sōō')	167	36.40N	33.30E
Gol, Nor. (gûl)	152	60.58N	8.54E
Golabāri, India	240a	22.36N	88.20E
Golax, Va., U.S. (gō'lăks)	115	36.41N	80.56W
Golcar, Eng., U.K. (gŏl'kȧr)	144a	53.38N	1.52W
Golconda, Il., U.S. (gŏl-kŏn'dȧ)	111	37.21N	88.32W
Gołdap, Pol. (gôl'dăp)	155	54.17N	22.17E
Golden, Can.	87	51.18N	116.58W
Golden, Co., U.S.	110	39.44N	105.15W
Goldendale, Wa., U.S. (gōl'dĕn-dāl)	104	45.49N	120.48W
Golden Gate, strt., Ca., U.S. (gōl'dĕn gāt)	106b	37.48N	122.32W
Golden Hinde, mtn., Can. (hīnd)	86	49.40N	125.45W
Golden's Bridge, N.Y., U.S.	100a	41.17N	73.41W
Golden Valley, Mn., U.S.	107g	44.58N	93.23W
Golders Green, neigh., Eng., U.K.	235	51.35N	0.12W
Goldfield, Nv., U.S. (gōld'fēld)	108	37.42N	117.15W
Gold Hill, mtn., Pan.	116a	9.03N	79.08W
Gold Mountain, mtn., Wa., U.S. (gōld)	106a	47.33N	122.48W
Goldsboro, N.C., U.S. (gōldz-bûr'ō)	115	35.23N	77.59W
Goldthwaite, Tx., U.S. (gōld'thwāt)	112	31.27N	98.34W
Goleniów, Pol. (gō-lē-nyŭf')	154	53.33N	14.51E
Golets-Purpula, Gora, mtn., Russia	165	59.08N	115.22E
Golf, Il., U.S.	231a	42.03N	87.48W
Golfito, C.R. (gōl-fē'tō)	121	8.40N	83.12W
Golf Park Terrace, Il., U.S.	231a	42.03N	87.51W
Goliad, Tx., U.S. (gō-lĭ-ăd')	113	28.40N	97.12W
Golo, r., Fr.	160	42.28N	9.18E
Golo Island, i., Phil. (gō'lō)	197a	13.38N	120.17E
Golovchino, Russia (gō-lôf'chē-nō)	163	50.34N	35.52E
Golyamo Konare, Bul. (gō'lȧ-mō-kō'nä-rĕ)	161	42.16N	24.33E
Golzow, Ger. (gōl'tsōv)	145b	52.17N	12.36E
Gombe, Nig.	210	10.19N	11.02E
Gomel', Bela. (go'mĕl')	164	52.20N	31.03E
Gomel', prov., Bela. (Oblast)	162	52.18N	29.00E
Gomera Island, i., Spain (gō-mä'rä)	210	28.00N	18.01W
Gomez Farias, Mex. (gō'māz fä-rē'ås)	112	24.59N	101.02W
Gómez Palacio, Mex. (pä-lä'syō)	116	25.35N	103.30W
Gonaïves, Haiti (gō-nå-ēv')	117	19.25N	72.45W
Gonaïves, Golfe des, b., Haiti (gō-nå-ēv')	123	19.20N	73.20W
Gonâve, Île de la, i., Haiti (gō-nàv')	117	18.50N	73.30W
Gonda, India	186	27.13N	82.00E
Gondal, India	186	22.02N	70.47E
Gonder, Eth.	211	12.39N	37.30E
Gonesse, Fr. (gō-nĕs')	157b	48.59N	2.28E
Gongga Shan, mtn., China (gôŋ-gä shän)	188	29.16N	101.46E
Goniri, Nig.	215	11.30N	12.20E
Gonō, r., Japan (gō'nō)	195	35.00N	132.25E
Gonor, Can. (gō'nŏr)	83f	50.04N	96.57W
Gonubie, S. Afr. (gŏn'ōō-bē)	213c	32.56S	28.02E
Gonzales, Mex. (gôn-zá'lĕs)	118	22.47N	98.26W
Gonzales, Tx., U.S. (gŏn-zä'lĕz)	113	29.31N	97.25W
González Catán, Arg. (gōn-zá'lĕz-kä-tá'n)	132a	34.47S	58.39W
Good Hope, Cape of, c., S. Afr. (kāp ov gōōd hōp)	212	34.21S	18.29E
Good Hope Mountain, mtn., Can.	86	51.09N	124.10W
Gooding, Id., U.S. (gŏd'ĭng)	105	42.55N	114.43W
Goodland, In., U.S. (gŏd'lănd)	98	40.50N	87.15W
Goodland, Ks., U.S.	110	39.19N	101.43W
Goodwood, S. Afr. (gŏd'wŏd)	212a	33.54S	18.33E
Goole, Eng., U.K. (gōōl)	144a	53.42N	0.52W
Goose, r., N.D., U.S.	102	47.40N	97.41W
Gooseberry Creek, r., Wy., U.S. (gōōs-bĕr'ĭ)	105	44.04N	108.35W
Goose Creek, r., Id., U.S. (gōōs)	105	42.07N	113.53W
Goose Lake, l., Ca., U.S.	104	41.56N	120.35W
Gorakhpur, India (gō'rŭk-pōōr)	183	26.45N	82.39E
Gorda, Punta, c., Cuba (pōō'n-tä-gôr-dä)	122	22.25N	82.10W
Gorda Cay, i., Bah. (gôr'dä)	122	26.05N	77.30W
Gordon, Can. (gôr'dŭn)	83f	50.00N	97.20W
Gordon, Ne., U.S.	102	42.47N	102.14W
Gordons Corner, Md., U.S.	229d	39.50N	76.57W
Gore, Eth. (gō'rĕ)	211	8.12N	35.34E
Gore Hill, Austl.	243a	33.49S	151.11E
Gorgān, Iran	182	36.44N	54.30E
Gorgona, Isola di, Italy (gôr-gō'nä)	148	43.27N	9.55E
Gori, Geor. (gō'rē)	167	42.00N	44.08E
Gorinchem, Neth. (gō'rĭn-kĕm)	145a	51.50N	4.59E
Goring, Eng., U.K. (gôr'ĭng)	144b	51.30N	1.08W
Gorizia, Italy (gō-rē'tsē-yä)	160	45.56N	13.40E
Gor'kiy see Nizhniy Novgorod, Russia	164	56.15N	44.05E
Gor'kovskoye, res., Russia	164	56.38N	43.40E
Gor'kovskoye, res., Russia	166	57.00N	43.55E
Gorlice, Pol. (gôr-lē'tsĕ)	155	49.38N	21.11E
Görlitz, Ger. (gûr'lĭts)	147	51.10N	15.01E
Gorman, Tx., U.S. (gôr'măn)	112	32.13N	98.40W
Gorna Oryakhovitsa, Bul. (gôr'nä-ôr-yĕk'ō-vē-tsä)	161	43.08N	25.40E
Gornji Milanovac, Yugo. (gôrn'yē-mē'la-nō-väts)	161	44.02N	20.29E
Gorno-Altay, state, Russia	170	51.00N	86.00E
Gorno-Altaysk, Russia (gôr'nŭ'ŭl-tīsk')	164	51.58N	85.58E
Gorodishche, Russia (gō-rô'dĭsh-chĕ)	172a	57.57N	57.03E
Gorodok, Bela.	162	55.27N	29.58E
Gorodok, Russia	165	50.30N	103.58E
Gorontalo, Indon. (gō-rōn-tä'lo)	197	0.40N	123.04E
Gorton, neigh., Eng., U.K.	237b	53.27N	2.10W
Gorzów Wielkopolski, Pol. (gō-zhōōv'vyĕl-ko-pōl'skē)	146	53.44N	15.15E

PLACE (Pronunciation)	PAGE	Lat. °′	Long. °′
Gosely, Eng., U.K.	144a	52.33N	2.10W
Gosen, Ger.	238a	52.24N	13.43E
Goshen, In., U.S. (gō'shĕn)	98	41.35N	85.50W
Goshen, Ky., U.S.	101h	38.24N	85.34W
Goshen, N.Y., U.S.	100a	41.24N	74.19W
Goshen, Oh., U.S.	101f	39.14N	84.09W
Goshute Indian Reservation, I.R., Ut., U.S. (gō-shōōt')	109	39.50N	114.00W
Goslar, Ger. (gôs'lär)	154	51.55N	10.25E
Gospa, r., Ven. (gôs-pä)	131b	9.43N	64.23W
Gostivar, Mac. (gos'tē-vär)	161	41.46N	20.58E
Gostynin, Pol. (gôs-tē'nĭn)	155	52.24N	19.30E
Göta, r., Swe. (gōētä)	152	58.11N	12.03E
Göta Kanal, can., Swe. (yû'tȧ)	152	58.35N	15.24E
Gotanno, neigh., Japan	242a	35.46N	139.49E
Göteborg, Swe. (yû'tē-bôrgh)	142	57.39N	11.56E
Gotel Mountains, mts., Afr.	215	7.05N	11.20E
Gotera, El Sal. (gō-tä'rä)	120	13.41N	88.06W
Gotha, Ger. (gō'tȧ)	147	50.47N	10.43E
Gothenburg see Göteborg, Swe.	142	57.39N	11.56E
Gothenburg, Ne., U.S. (gŏth'ĕn-bûrg)	110	40.57N	100.08W
Gotland, i., Swe.	142	57.35N	17.35E
Gotska Sandön, i., Swe.	153	58.24N	19.15E
Götterswickerhamm, Ger.	236	51.35N	6.40E
Göttingen, Ger. (gût'ĭng-ĕn)	154	51.32N	9.57E
Gouda, Neth. (gou'dä)	145a	52.00N	4.42E
Gough, i., St. Hel. (gŏf)	2	40.00S	10.00W
Gouin, Réservoir, res., Can.	85	48.15N	74.15W
Goukou, China (gō-kō)	189	48.45N	121.42E
Goulais, r., Can.	90	46.45N	84.10W
Goulburn, Austl. (gōl'bŭrn)	203	34.47S	149.40E
Goumbati, mtn., Sen.	214	13.08N	12.06W
Goumbou, Mali (gōōm-bōō')	210	14.59N	7.27W
Gouna, Cam.	215	8.32N	13.34E
Goundam, Mali (gōōn-däN')	210	16.29N	3.37W
Gournay-sur-Marne, Fr.	237c	48.52N	2.34E
Goussainville, Fr.	237c	49.01N	2.28E
Gouverneur, N.Y., U.S. (gŭv-ēr-nōōr')	99	44.20N	75.25W
Go-vap, Viet.	241j	10.49N	106.42E
Govenlock, Can. (gŭvĕn-lŏk)	84	49.15N	109.48W
Governador, Ilha do, i., Braz. (gō-vĕr-nä-dō-'r-ē-lä'dō)	132b	22.48S	43.13W
Governador Portela, Braz. (pōr-tĕ'là)	132b	22.28S	43.30W
Governador Valadares, Braz. (vä-lä-dä'rĕs)	131	18.47S	41.45W
Governor's Harbour, Bah.	122	25.15N	76.15W
Gowanda, N.Y., U.S. (gō-wŏn'dȧ)	99	42.30N	78.55W
Goya, Arg. (gō'yä)	132	29.06S	59.12W
Göyçay, Azer. (gĕ-ôk'chī)	167	40.40N	47.40E
Goyt, r., Eng., U.K. (goit)	144a	53.19N	2.03W
Graaff-Reinet, S. Afr. (gräf'rī'nĕt)	212	32.10S	24.40E
Gračac, Cro. (grä'chäts)	160	44.16N	15.50E
Gračanica, Bos.	161	44.42N	18.18E
Graceville, Fl., U.S. (grās'vĭl)	114	30.57N	85.30W
Graceville, Mn., U.S.	102	45.33N	96.25W
Gracias, Hond. (grä'sē-äs)	120	14.35N	88.37W
Graciosa Island, i., Port. (grä-syō'sä)	210a	39.07N	27.30W
Gradačac, Bos. (gra-dä'chats)	149	44.50N	18.28E
Grado, Spain (grä'dō)	158	43.24N	6.04W
Gräfelfing, Ger. (grä'fĕl-fēng)	145d	48.07N	11.27E
Grafenberg, neigh., Ger.	236	51.14N	6.50E
Grafing bei München, Ger. (grä'fēng)	145d	48.03N	11.58E
Grafton, Austl. (graf'tŭn)	203	29.38S	153.05E
Grafton, Il., U.S.	107e	38.58N	90.26W
Grafton, Ma., U.S.	93a	42.13N	71.41W
Grafton, N.D., U.S.	102	48.24N	97.25W
Grafton, Oh., U.S.	101d	41.16N	82.04W
Grafton, W.V., U.S.	98	39.20N	80.00W
Gragnano, Italy (grän-yä'nō)	159c	40.27N	14.32E
Graham, N.C., U.S. (grā'ăm)	115	36.03N	79.23W
Graham, Tx., U.S.	110	33.07N	98.34W
Graham, Wa., U.S.	106a	47.03N	122.18W
Graham, i., Can.	84	53.50N	132.40W
Grahamstown, S. Afr. (grā'ăms'toun)	213c	33.19S	26.33E
Grajewo, Pol. (grä-yä'vo)	155	53.38N	22.28E
Grama, Serra de, mtn., Braz. (sĕ'r-rä-dĕ-grà'mà)	129a	20.42S	42.28W
Gramada, Bul. (grä'mä-dä)	161	43.46N	22.41E
Gramatneusiedl, Aus.	145e	48.02N	16.29E
Grampian Mountains, mts., Scot., U.K. (grăm'pĭ-ăn)	142	56.30N	4.55W
Granada, Nic. (grä-nä'dhä)	116	11.55N	85.58W
Granada, Spain (grä-nä'dä)	148	37.13N	3.37W
Gran Bajo, reg., Arg. (grän'bä'kō)	132	47.35S	68.45W
Granbury, Tx., U.S. (grăn'bĕr-ĭ)	113	32.26N	97.45W
Granby, Can. (grăn'bĭ)	85	45.30N	72.40W
Granby, Mo., U.S.	111	36.54N	94.15W
Granby, l., Co., U.S.	110	40.07N	105.40W
Gran Canaria Island, i., Spain (grän'kä-nä'rē-ä)	210	27.39N	15.39W
Gran Chaco, reg., S.A. (grän'chà'kō)	132	25.30S	62.15W
Grand, i., Mi., U.S.	103	46.37N	86.38W
Grand, l., Can.	92	45.59N	66.15W
Grand, l., Me., U.S.	92	45.17N	67.42W
Grand, r., Can.	91	43.45N	80.20W
Grand, r., Mi., U.S.	98	42.58N	85.13W
Grand, r., Mo., U.S.	111	39.50N	93.52W
Grand, r., S.D., U.S.	102	45.40N	101.55W
Grand, North Fork, r., U.S.	102	45.52N	102.49W
Grand, South Fork, r., S.D., U.S.	102	45.38N	102.56W
Grand Bahama, i., Bah.	117	26.35N	78.30W
Grand Bank, Can. (grănd băngk)	85a	47.06N	55.47W
Grand Bassam, C. Iv. (grän bå-säN')	210	5.12N	3.44W
Grand Bourg, Guad. (grän bōōr')	121b	15.54N	61.20W
Grand Caicos, i., T./C. Is. (grănd kä-ē'kōs)	123	21.45N	71.50W
Grand Canal see Da Yunhe, can., China	189	35.00N	117.00E

292 Grand Canal-Grey Range

PLACE (Pronunciation)	PAGE	Lat. °′	Long. °′
Grand Canal, can., Ire.	150	53.21N	7.15W
Grand Canyon, Az., U.S.	109	36.05N	112.10W
Grand Canyon, val., Az., U.S.	96	35.50N	113.16W
Grand Canyon National Park, rec., Az., U.S.	96	36.15N	112.20W
Grand Cayman, i., Cay. Is. (kā'măn)	117	19.15N	81.15W
Grand Coulee Dam, dam, Wa., U.S. (ko͞o'lē)	96	47.58N	119.28W
Grande, r., Arg.	129b	35.25S	70.14W
Grande, r., Mex.	119	17.37N	96.41W
Grande, r., Nic. (grän'dĕ)	121	13.01N	84.21W
Grande, r., Ur.	129c	33.19S	57.15W
Grande, Arroyo, r., Mex. (är-rō'yō-grä'n-dĕ)	118	23.30N	98.45W
Grande, Bahía, b., Arg. (bä-ē'ä-grán'dĕ)	132	50.45S	68.00W
Grande, Boca, mth., Ven. (bŏ'kä-grä'n-dĕ)	131	8.46N	60.17W
Grande, Cuchilla, mts., Ur. (ko͞o-chē'l-yä)	132	33.00S	55.15W
Grande, Ilha, i., Braz. (grän'dĕ)	129a	23.11S	44.14W
Grande, Río, r., Bol.	130	16.49S	63.19W
Grande, Rio, r., Braz.	131	19.48S	49.54W
Grande, Rio, r., N.A. (grän'dā)	96	26.50N	99.10W
Grande, Salinas, l., Arg. (sä-lē'näs)	132	29.45S	65.00W
Grande, Salto, wtfl., Braz. (säl-tô)	131	16.18S	39.38W
Grande Cayemite, Île, i., Haiti	123	18.45N	73.45W
Grande de Otoro, r., Hond. (grä'dą dā ô-tō'rō)	120	14.42N	88.21W
Grande de Santiago, Río, r., Mex. (rē'ō-grä'n-dĕ-dĕ-sän-tyá'gô)	116	20.30N	104.00W
Grande Pointe, Can. (grănd point')	83f	49.47N	97.03W
Grande Prairie, Can. (prâr'ĭ)	84	55.10N	118.48W
Grand Erg Occidental, des., Alg.	210	30.00N	1.00E
Grand Erg Oriental, des., Alg.	210	30.00N	7.00E
Grande Rivière du Nord, Haiti (rē-vyâr' dü nôr')	123	19.35N	72.10W
Grande Ronde, r., Or., U.S. (rônd')	104	45.32N	117.52W
Gran Desierto, des., Mex. (grän-dĕ-syĕ'r-tô)	109	32.14N	114.28W
Grande Terre, i., Guad.	121b	16.28N	61.13W
Grande Vigie, Pointe de la, c., Guad. (gräɴd vē-gē')	121b	16.32N	61.25W
Grand Falls, Can. (fôlz)	85a	48.56N	55.40W
Grandfather Mountain, mtn., N.C., U.S. (grănd-fä-thẽr)	115	36.07N	81.48W
Grandfield, Ok., U.S. (grănd'fēld)	110	34.13N	98.39W
Grand Forks, Can. (fôrks)	84	49.02N	118.27W
Grand Forks, N.D., U.S.	96	47.55N	97.05W
Grand Haven, Mi., U.S. (hā'v'n)	98	43.05N	86.15W
Grand I, N.Y., U.S.	101c	43.03N	78.58W
Grand Island, Ne., U.S. (ī'lănd)	96	40.56N	98.20W
Grand Island, N.Y., U.S.	230a	42.49N	78.58W
Grand Junction, Co., U.S. (jŭngk'shŭn)	96	39.05N	108.35W
Grand Lake, l., Can. (lāk)	85a	49.00N	57.10W
Grand Lake, l., La., U.S.	113	29.57N	91.25W
Grand Lake, l., Mn., U.S.	107h	46.54N	92.26W
Grand Ledge, Mi., U.S. (lĕj)	98	42.45N	84.50W
Grand Lieu, Lac de, l., Fr. (grăɴ'-lyû)	156	47.00N	1.45W
Grand Manan, i., Can. (mă-năn)	92	44.40N	66.50W
Grand Mère, Can. (grăɴ mâr')	85	46.36N	72.43W
Grândola, Port. (grän'dô-lă)	158	38.10N	8.36W
Grand Portage Indian Reservation, I.R., Mn., U.S. (pōr'tĭj)	103	47.54N	89.34W
Grand Portage National Monument, rec., Mi., U.S.	103	47.59N	89.47W
Grand Prairie, Tx., U.S. (prĕ'rē)	107c	32.45N	97.00W
Grand Rapids, Can.	89	53.08N	99.20W
Grand Rapids, Mi., U.S. (răp'ĭdz)	97	43.00N	85.45W
Grand Rapids, Mn., U.S.	103	47.16N	93.33W
Grand-Riviere, Can.	92	48.26N	64.30W
Grand Teton, mtn., Wy., U.S.	96	43.46N	110.50W
Grand Teton National Park, Wy., U.S. (tē'tŏn)	105	43.54N	110.15W
Grand Traverse Bay, b., Mi., U.S. (trăv'ẽrs)	98	45.00N	85.30W
Grand Turk, T./C. Is. (tûrk)	123	21.30N	71.10W
Grand Turk, i., T./C. Is.	123	21.30N	71.10W
Grandview, Mo., U.S. (grănd'vyo͞o)	107f	38.53N	94.32W
Grandyle, N.Y., U.S.	230a	43.00N	78.57W
Grange Hill, Eng., U.K.	235	51.37N	0.05E
Granger, Wy., U.S. (grān'jẽr)	105	41.37N	109.58W
Grangeville, Id., U.S. (grānj'vĭl)	104	45.56N	116.08W
Granite, Md., U.S.	229c	39.21N	76.51W
Granite City, Il., U.S. (grăn'ĭt sĭt'ĭ)	107e	38.42N	90.09W
Granite Falls, Mn., U.S. (fôlz)	102	44.46N	95.34W
Granite Falls, N.C., U.S.	115	35.49N	81.25W
Granite Falls, Wa., U.S.	106a	48.05N	121.59W
Granite Lake, l., Can.	93	48.01N	57.00W
Granite Peak, mtn., Mt., U.S.	96	45.13N	109.48W
Graniteville, S.C., U.S. (grăn'ĭt-vĭl)	115	33.35ND1.50	W
Granito, Braz. (grä-nē'tō)	131	7.39S	39.34W
Granma, prov., Cuba	122	20.10N	76.50W
Gränna, Swe. (grĕn'ä)	152	58.02N	14.38E
Granollers, Spain (grä-nôl-yĕrs')	159	41.36N	2.19E
Gran Pajonal, reg., Peru (grä'n-pä-ĸô-näl')	130	11.14S	71.45W
Gran Paradiso, mtn., Italy	160	45.32N	7.16E
Gran Piedra, mtn., Cuba (grän-pyĕ'drä)	123	20.00N	75.40W
Grantham, Eng., U.K. (grăn'tăm)	150	52.54N	0.38W
Grant Park, Il., U.S. (grănt pärk)	101a	41.14N	87.39W
Grant Park, pt. of i., Il., U.S.	231a	41.52N	87.37W
Grants Pass, Or., U.S. (grănts pås)	104	42.26N	123.20W
Granville, Austl.	243a	33.50S	151.01E
Granville, Fr. (grăɴ-vēl')	147	48.52N	1.35W
Granville, N.Y., U.S. (grăn'vĭl)	99	43.25N	73.15W
Granville, l., Can.	84	56.18N	100.30W
Grão Mogol, Braz. (groun' mō-gōl')	131	16.34S	42.35W
Grapevine, Tx., U.S. (grāp'vīn)	107c	32.56N	97.05W
Gräso, i., Swe.	152	60.30N	18.35E
Grass, r., N.Y., U.S.	99	44.45N	75.10W
Grass Cay, i., V.I.U.S.	117c	18.22N	64.50W
Grasse, Fr. (gräs)	157	43.39N	6.57E
Grassendale, neigh., Eng., U.K.	237a	53.21N	2.54W
Grass Mountain, mtn., Wa., U.S. (grås)	106a	47.13N	121.48W
Grates Point, c., Can. (grāts)	93	48.09N	52.57W
Gravelbourg, Can. (grăv'ĕl-bôrg)	84	49.53N	106.34W
Gravesend, Eng., U.K. (grāvz'ĕnd')	144b	51.26N	0.22E
Gravina, Italy (grä-vē'nä)	160	40.48N	16.27E
Gravois, Pointe à, c., Haiti (grȧ-vwä')	123	18.00N	74.20W
Gray, Fr. (grå)	157	47.26N	5.35E
Grayling, Mi., U.S. (grā'lĭng)	98	44.40N	84.40W
Grays, Eng., U.K.	235	51.29N	0.20E
Grays Harbor, b., Wa., U.S. (grās)	96	46.55N	124.23W
Grayslake, Il., U.S. (grāz'lāk)	101a	42.20N	88.20W
Grays Peak, mtn., Co., U.S. (grāz)	110	39.29N	105.52W
Grays Thurrock, Eng., U.K. (thŭ'rŏk)	144b	51.28N	0.19E
Grayvoron, Russia (grȧ-ē'vô-rôn)	163	50.28N	35.41E
Graz, Aus. (gräts)	142	47.05N	15.26E
Greasby, Eng., U.K.	237a	53.23N	3.07W
Great Abaco, i., Bah. (ă'bȧ-kō)	117	26.30N	77.05W
Great Altcar, Eng., U.K.	237a	53.33N	3.01W
Great Artesian Basin, basin, Austl. (är-tēzh-ăn bā-sĭn)	203	23.16S	143.37E
Great Australian Bight, bt., Austl. (ôs-trā'lĭ-ăn bīt)	202	33.30S	127.00E
Great Bahama Bank, bk. (bȧ-hā'mȧ)	122	25.00N	78.50W
Great Barrier, i., N.Z. (băr'ĭ-ẽr)	203a	36.10S	175.30E
Great Barrier Reef, rf., Austl. (bă-rĭ-ẽr rēf)	203	16.43S	146.34E
Great Basin, basin, U.S. (grāt bā's'n)	96	40.08N	117.10W
Great Bear Lake, l., Can. (bâr)	84	66.10N	119.53W
Great Bend, Ks., U.S. (bĕnd)	110	38.41N	98.46W
Great Bitter Lake, l., Egypt	218b	30.24N	32.27E
Great Blasket Island, i., Ire. (blăs'kĕt)	150	52.05N	10.55W
Great Bookham, Eng., U.K.	235	51.16N	0.22W
Great Burstead, Eng., U.K.	235	51.36N	0.25E
Great Corn Island, i., Nic.	121	12.10N	82.54W
Great Crosby, Eng., U.K.	237a	53.29N	3.01W
Great Dismal Swamp, sw., U.S. (dĭz'măl)	115	36.35N	76.34W
Great Divide Basin, basin, Wy., U.S. (dĭ-vīd' bā's'n)	105	42.10N	108.10W
Great Dividing Range, mts., Austl. (dĭ-vī-dĭng rānj)	203	35.16S	146.38E
Great Duck, i., Can. (dŭk)	90	45.40N	83.22W
Greater Antilles, is., N.A.	117	20.30N	79.15W
Greater Khingan Range, mts., China (dä hiŋ-gän lĭŋ)	189	46.30N	120.00E
Greater Leech Indian Reservation, I.R., Mn., U.S. (grāt'ẽr lēch)	103	47.39N	94.27W
Greater Manchester, co., Eng., U.K.	144a	53.34N	2.41W
Greater Sunda Islands, is., Asia	196	4.00S	108.00E
Great Exuma, i., Bah. (ĕk-so͞o'mä)	122	23.35N	76.00W
Great Falls, Mt., U.S. (fôlz)	96	47.30N	111.15W
Great Falls, S.C., U.S.	115	34.32N	80.53W
Great Falls, Va., U.S.	229d	39.00N	77.17W
Great Guana Cay, i., Bah. (gwä'nä)	122	24.00N	76.20W
Great Harbor Cay, i., Bah. (kē)	122	25.45N	77.50W
Great Inagua, i., Bah. (ē-nä'gwä)	117	21.00N	73.15W
Great Indian Desert, des., Asia	183	27.35N	71.37E
Great Isaac, i., Bah. (ī'zȧk)	122	26.05N	79.05W
Great Karroo, plat., S. Afr. (grāt kȧ'ro͞o)	212	32.45S	22.00E
Great Kills, neigh., N.Y., U.S.	228	40.33N	74.10W
Great Namaland, hist. reg., Nmb.	212	25.45S	16.15E
Great Neck, N.Y., U.S. (nĕk)	100a	40.48N	73.44W
Great Nicobar Island, i., India (nĭk-ô-bär')	196	7.00N	94.18E
Great Oxney Green, Eng., U.K.	235	51.44N	0.25E
Great Parndon, Eng., U.K.	235	51.45N	0.05E
Great Pedro Bluff, c., Jam.	122	17.50N	78.05W
Great Pee Dee, r., S.C., U.S. (pē-dē')	97	34.01N	79.26W
Great Plains, pl., N.A. (plāns)	82	45.00N	104.00W
Great Ragged, i., Bah.	123	22.10N	75.45W
Great Ruaha, r., Tan.	212	7.30S	37.00E
Great Salt Lake, l., Ut., U.S. (sôlt lāk)	96	41.19N	112.48W
Great Salt Lake Desert, des., Ut., U.S.	96	41.00N	113.30W
Great Salt Plains Reservoir, res., Ok., U.S.	110	36.56N	98.14W
Great Sand Dunes National Monument, rec., Co., U.S.	110	37.56N	105.25W
Great Sand Hills, hills, Can. (sănd)	88	50.35N	109.05W
Great Sandy Desert, des., Austl. (săn'dē)	202	21.50S	123.10E
Great Sandy Desert, des., Or., U.S. (săn'dĭ)	104	43.43N	120.44W
Great Sitkin, i., Ak., U.S. (sĭt-kĭn)	95a	52.18N	176.22W
Great Slave Lake, l., Can. (slāv)	84	61.37N	114.58W
Great Smoky Mountains National Park, rec., U.S. (smōk-ē)	97	35.43N	83.20W
Great Stirrup Cay, i., Bah. (stĭr-ŭp)	122	25.50N	77.55W
Great Sutton, Eng., U.K.	237a	53.17N	2.56W
Great Victoria Desert, des., Austl. (vĭk-tō'rĭ-ȧ)	202	29.45S	124.30E
Great Wall, hist., China	188	38.00N	109.00E
Great Waltham, Eng., U.K. (wôl'thŭm)	144b	51.47N	0.27E
Great Warley, Eng., U.K.	235	51.35N	0.17E
Great Yarmouth, Eng., U.K. (yär-mŭth)	147	52.35N	1.45E
Grebbestad, Swe. (grĕb-bĕ-städh)	152	58.42N	11.15E
Gréboun, Mont, mtn., Niger	210	20.00N	8.35E
Greco, neigh., Italy	238c	45.30N	9.13E
Gredos, Sierra de, mts., Spain (syĕr'rä dā grā'dōs)	158	40.13N	5.30W
Greece, nation, Eur. (grēs)	142	39.00N	21.30E
Greeley, Co., U.S. (grē'lĭ)	96	40.25N	104.41W
Green, r., U.S.	96	38.30N	110.10W
Green, r., Ky., U.S. (grēn)	114	37.13N	86.30W
Green, r., N.D., U.S.	102	47.05N	103.05W
Green, r., Ut., U.S.	109	38.30N	110.05W
Green, r., Wa., U.S.	106a	47.17N	121.57W
Green, r., Wy., U.S.	105	41.08N	110.27W
Greenbank, Wa., U.S. (grēn'bănk)	106a	48.06N	122.35W
Green Bay, Wi., U.S.	97	44.30N	88.04W
Green Bay, b., U.S.	97	44.55N	87.40W
Green Bayou, Tx., U.S.	113a	29.53N	95.13W
Greenbelt, Md., U.S. (grēn'bĕlt)	100e	38.59N	76.53W
Greenbrae, Ca., U.S.	231b	37.57N	122.31W
Greencastle, In., U.S. (grēn-kȧs''l)	98	39.40N	86.50W
Green Cay, i., Bah.	122	24.05N	77.10W
Green Cove Springs, Fl., U.S. (kōv)	115	29.56N	81.42W
Greendale, Wi., U.S. (grēn'dāl)	101a	42.56N	87.59W
Greenfield, In., U.S. (grēn'fēld)	98	39.45N	85.40W
Greenfield, Ia., U.S.	103	41.16N	94.30W
Greenfield, Ma., U.S.	99	42.35N	72.35W
Greenfield, Mo., U.S.	111	37.23N	93.48W
Greenfield, Oh., U.S.	98	39.15N	83.25W
Greenfield, Tn., U.S.	114	36.08N	88.45W
Greenfield Park, Can.	83a	45.29N	73.29W
Greenhills, Oh., U.S. (grēn-hĭls)	101f	39.16N	84.31W
Greenhithe, Eng., U.K.	235	51.27N	0.17E
Greenland, dep., N.A. (grēn'lănd)	82	74.00N	40.00W
Greenland Sea, sea	220	77.00N	1.00W
Green Meadows, Md., U.S.	229d	38.58N	76.57W
Greenmount, Eng., U.K.	237b	53.37N	2.20W
Green Mountain, mtn., Or., U.S.	106c	45.52N	123.24W
Green Mountain Reservoir, res., Co., U.S.	109	39.50N	106.20W
Green Mountains, mts., N.A.	97	43.10N	73.05W
Greenock, Scot., U.K. (grēn'ŭk)	146	55.55N	4.45W
Green Peter Lake, res., Or., U.S.	104	44.28N	122.30W
Green Pond Mountain, mtn., N.J., U.S. (pŏnd)	100a	41.00N	74.32W
Greenport, N.Y., U.S.	99	41.06N	72.22W
Green River, Ut., U.S. (grēn rĭv'ẽr)	109	39.00N	110.05W
Green River, Wy., U.S.	105	41.32N	109.26W
Green River Lake, res., Ky., U.S.	114	37.15N	85.15W
Greensboro, Al., U.S. (grēnz'bŭro)	114	32.42N	87.36W
Greensboro, Ga., U.S. (grēns-bûr'ô)	114	33.34N	83.11W
Greensboro, N.C., U.S.	97	36.04N	79.45W
Greensborough, Austl.	243b	37.42S	145.06E
Greensburg, In., U.S. (grēnz'bûrg)	98	39.20N	85.30W
Greensburg, Ks., U.S. (grēns-bûrg)	110	37.36N	99.17W
Greensburg, Pa., U.S.	99	40.20N	79.30W
Greenside, neigh., S. Afr.	244b	26.09S	28.01E
Greenstead, Eng., U.K.	235	51.42N	0.14E
Green Street, Eng., U.K.	235	51.40N	0.16W
Green Street Green, neigh., Eng., U.K.	235	51.21N	0.04E
Greenvale, N.Y., U.S.	228	40.49N	73.38W
Greenville, Lib.	210	5.01N	9.03W
Greenville, Al., U.S. (grēn'vĭl)	114	31.49N	86.39W
Greenville, Il., U.S.	111	38.52N	89.22W
Greenville, Ky., U.S.	114	37.11N	87.11W
Greenville, Me., U.S.	92	45.26N	69.35W
Greenville, Mi., U.S.	98	43.10N	85.25W
Greenville, Ms., U.S.	97	33.25N	91.00W
Greenville, N.C., U.S.	115	35.35N	77.22W
Greenville, Oh., U.S.	98	40.05N	84.35W
Greenville, Pa., U.S.	98	41.20N	80.25W
Greenville, S.C., U.S.	97	34.50N	82.25W
Greenville, Tn., U.S.	115	36.08N	82.50W
Greenville, Tx., U.S.	113	33.09N	96.07W
Greenwich, Eng., U.K.	144b	51.28N	0.00
Greenwich, Ct., U.S.	100a	41.01N	73.37W
Greenwich Observatory, pt. of i., Eng., U.K.	235	51.28N	0.00
Greenwich Village, neigh., N.Y., U.S.	228	40.44N	74.00W
Greenwood, Ar., U.S. (grēn-wŏd)	111	35.13N	94.15W
Greenwood, In., U.S.	101g	39.37N	86.07W
Greenwood, Ma., U.S.	227a	42.29N	71.04W
Greenwood, Ms., U.S.	114	33.30N	90.09W
Greenwood, S.C., U.S.	115	34.10N	82.10W
Greenwood, Lake, res., S.C., U.S.	115	34.17N	81.55W
Greenwood Lake, l., N.Y., U.S.	100a	41.13N	74.20W
Greer, S.C., U.S. (grēr)	115	34.55N	81.56W
Grefrath, Ger. (grĕf'rät)	157c	51.20N	6.21E
Gregory, S.D., U.S. (grĕg'ô-rĭ)	102	43.12N	99.27W
Gregory, Lake, l., Austl. (grĕg'ô-rē)	202	28.47S	139.15E
Gregory Range, mts., Austl.	203	19.23S	143.45E
Greifenberg, Ger. (grī'fĕn-bĕrgh)	145d	48.04N	11.06E
Greiffenburg, hist., Ger.	236	51.20N	6.38E
Greifswald, Ger. (grīfs'vält)	154	54.05N	13.24E
Greiz, Ger. (grīts)	154	50.39N	12.14E
Gremyachinsk, Russia (grâ'myȧ-chĭnsk)	172a	58.35N	57.53E
Grenada, Ms., U.S. (grē-nā'dȧ)	114	33.45N	89.47W
Grenada, nation, N.A.	117	12.02N	61.15W
Grenada Lake, res., Ms., U.S.	114	33.52N	89.30W
Grenadines, The, is., N.A. (grĕn'ȧ-dēnz)	121b	12.37N	61.35W
Grenen, c., Den.	146	57.43N	10.31E
Grenoble, Fr. (grē-nŏ'bl')	147	45.14N	5.45E
Grenora, N.D., U.S. (grē-nō'rȧ)	102	48.38N	103.55W
Grenville, Can. (grĕn'vĭl)	99	45.40N	74.35W
Grenville, Gren.	121b	12.07N	61.38W
Gresham, Or., U.S. (grĕsh'ăm)	106c	45.30N	122.25W
Gretna, La., U.S. (grĕt'nȧ)	100d	29.56N	90.03W
Grevel, neigh., Ger.	236	51.34N	7.33E
Grevelingen Krammer, r., Neth.	145a	51.42N	4.03E
Grevenbroich, Ger. (grĕ'fĕn-broik)	157c	51.05N	6.36E
Grey, r., Can. (grā)	93	47.53N	57.00W
Grey, Point, c., Can.	106d	49.22N	123.16W
Greybull, Wy., U.S. (grā'bŏl)	105	44.28N	108.05W
Greybull, r., Wy., U.S.	105	44.13N	108.43W
Greylingstad, S. Afr. (grā-lĭng'shtät)	218d	26.40S	29.13E
Greymouth, N.Z. (grā'mouth)	203a	42.27S	171.17E
Grey Range, mts., Austl.	203	28.40S	142.05E

ăt; finăl; rāte; senāte; ärm; åsk; sofȧ; fâre; ch-choose; dh-as th in other; bē; ēvent; bĕt; recĕnt; cratẽr; g-gō; gh-guttural g; bĭt; ĭ-short neutral; rīde; ĸ-guttural k as ch in German ich;

PRONOUNCING INDEX

Greystanes – Guysborough 293

PLACE (Pronunciation)	PAGE	Lat. °′	Long. °′
Greystanes, Austl.	243a	33.49S	150.58E
Greytown, S. Afr. (grā'toun)	213c	29.07S	30.38E
Grey Wolf Peak, mtn., Wa., U.S. (grā wôlf)	106a	48.53N	123.12W
Gridley, Ca., U.S. (grĭd'lĭ)	108	39.22N	121.43W
Griffin, Ga., U.S. (grĭf'ĭn)	114	33.15N	84.16W
Griffith, Austl. (grĭf-ĭth)	204	34.16S	146.10E
Griffith, In., U.S.	101a	41.31N	87.26W
Grigoriopol', Mol. (grĭ'gor-i-ŏ'pôl)	163	47.09N	29.18E
Grijalva, r., Mex. (grē-häl'vä)	119	17.25N	93.23W
Grim, Cape, c., Austl. (grĭm)	204	40.43S	144.30E
Grimma, Ger. (grĭm'ȧ)	154	51.14N	12.43E
Grimsby, Can. (grĭmz'bĭ)	83d	43.11N	79.33W
Grimsby, Eng., U.K.	146	53.35N	0.05W
Grímsey, i., Ice. (grĭms'ȧ)	146	66.30N	17.50W
Grimstad, Nor. (grĭm-städh)	146	58.21N	8.30E
Grindstone Island, Can.	93	47.25N	61.51W
Grinnel, Ia., U.S. (grĭ-nĕl')	103	41.44N	92.44W
Grinzing, neigh., Aus.	239e	48.15N	16.21E
Griswold, Ia., U.S. (grĭz'wŭld)	102	41.11N	95.05W
Groais Island, i., Can.	93	50.57N	55.35W
Grobina, Lat. (grō'bĭŋĭa)	153	56.35N	21.10E
Groblersdal, S. Afr.	218d	25.11S	29.25E
Grodno, Bela. (grôd'nō)	166	53.40N	23.49E
Grodzisk, Pol. (grō'jēsk)	154	52.14N	16.22E
Grodzisk Masowiecki, Pol. (grō'jēsk mä-zō-vyĕts'ke)	155	52.06N	20.40E
Groesbeck, Tx., U.S. (grōs'bĕk)	113	31.32N	96.31W
Groix, Île de, i., Fr. (ēl dē grwä')	156	47.39N	3.28W
Grójec, Pol. (grò'yĕts)	155	51.53N	20.52E
Gronau, Ger. (grō'nou)	154	52.12N	7.05E
Groningen, Neth. (grō'nĭng-ĕn)	146	53.13N	6.30E
Groote Eylandt, i., Austl. (grō'tē ī'lănt)	202	13.50S	137.30E
Grootfontein, Nmb. (grōt'fōn-tān')	212	19.30S	18.15E
Groot-Kei, r., Afr. (kē)	213c	32.17S	27.30E
Grootkop, mtn., S. Afr.	212a	34.11S	18.23E
Groot Marico, S. Afr.	218d	25.36S	26.23E
Groot Marico, r., Afr.	218d	25.13S	26.20E
Groot-Vis, r., S. Afr.	213c	33.04S	26.08E
Groot Vloer, pl., S. Afr. (grōt' vlôr')	212	30.00S	21.00E
Gros-Mécatina, i., Can.	93	50.50N	58.33W
Gros Morne, mtn., Can. (grō môrn')	93	49.36N	57.48W
Gros Morne National Park, rec., Can.	85a	49.45N	59.15W
Gros Pate, mtn., Can.	93	50.16N	57.25W
Grossbeeren, Ger.	238a	52.21N	13.18E
Grosse Island, i., Mi., U.S. (grōs)	101b	42.08N	83.09W
Grosse Isle, Can. (īl')	83f	50.04N	97.27W
Grossenbaum, neigh., Ger.	236	51.22N	6.47E
Grossenhain, Ger. (grōs'ĕn-hīn)	154	51.17N	13.33E
Gross-Enzersdorf, Aus.	145e	48.13N	16.33E
Grosse Pointe, Mi., U.S. (point')	101b	42.23N	82.54W
Grosse Pointe Farms, Mi., U.S. (färm)	101b	42.25N	82.53W
Grosse Pointe Park, Mi., U.S. (pärk)	101b	42.23N	82.55W
Grosse Pointe Woods, Mi., U.S.	230c	42.27N	82.55W
Grosseto, Italy (grŏs-sā'tō)	160	42.46N	11.09E
Grossglockner, mtn., Aus.	147	47.06N	12.45E
Gross Höbach, Ger. (hû'bäk)	145d	48.21N	11.36E
Grossjedlersdorf, neigh., Aus.	239e	48.17N	16.25E
Gross Kreutz, Ger. (kroitz)	145b	52.24N	12.47E
Gross Schönebeck, Ger. (shō'nĕ-bĕk)	145b	52.54N	13.32E
Gross Ziethen, Ger.	238a	52.24N	13.27E
Gros Ventre, r., Wy., U.S. (grōvĕn't'r)	105	43.38N	110.34W
Groton, Ct., U.S. (grŏt'ŭn)	99	41.20N	72.00W
Groton, Ma., U.S.	93a	42.37N	71.34W
Groton, S.D., U.S.	102	45.25N	98.04W
Grottaglie, Italy (grôt-täl'yā)	161	40.32N	17.26E
Grouard Mission, Can.	84	55.31N	116.09W
Groveland, Ma., U.S. (grōv'land)	93a	42.25N	71.02W
Groveton, N.H., U.S. (grōv'tŭn)	99	44.35N	71.30W
Groveton, Tx., U.S.	113	31.04N	95.07W
Groznyy, Russia (grôz'nĭ)	164	43.20N	45.40E
Grudziądz, Pol. (grò'jyōnts)	146	53.30N	18.48E
Grues, Île aux, i., Can. (ō grü)	83b	47.05N	70.32W
Gruiten, Ger.	236	51.14N	7.01E
Grumme, neigh., Ger.	236	51.30N	7.14E
Grünau, neigh., Ger.	238a	52.25N	13.34E
Grundy Center, Ia., U.S. (grŭn'dĭ sĕn'tĕr)	103	42.22N	92.45W
Grünewald, Ger.	236	51.13N	7.37E
Grunewald, neigh., Ger.	238a	52.30N	13.17E
Gruñidora, Mex. (grōō-nyē-dō'rō)	118	24.10N	101.49W
Grünwald, Ger. (grōōn'väld)	145d	48.04N	11.34E
Gryazi, Russia (gryä'zĭ)	162	52.31N	39.59E
Gryazovets, Russia (gryä'zō-vĕts)	166	58.52N	40.14E
Gryfice, Pol. (grĭ'fĭ-tsĕ)	154	53.55N	15.11E
Gryfino, Pol. (grĭ'fē-nō)	154	53.16N	14.30E
Guabito, Pan. (gwä-bē'tō)	121	9.30N	82.33W
Guacanayabo, Golfo de, b., Cuba (gôl-fô-dē-gwä-kä-nä-yä'bō)	122	20.30N	77.40W
Guacara, Ven. (gwȧ'kä-rä)	131b	10.16N	67.48W
Guadalajara, Mex. (gwä-dhä-lä-hä'rä)	116	20.41N	103.21W
Guadalajara, Spain (gwä-dä-lä-kä'rä)	148	40.37N	3.10W
Guadalcanal, Spain (gwä-dhäl-kä-näl')	158	38.05N	5.48W
Guadalcanal, i., Sol.Is.	203	9.48S	158.43E
Guadalcázar, Mex. (gwä-dhäl-kä'zär)	118	22.38N	100.24W
Guadalete, r., Spain (gwä-dhä-lā'tȧ)	158	36.53N	5.38W
Guadalhorce, r., Spain (gwä-dhäl-ôr'thā)	158	37.05N	4.50W
Guadalimar, r., Spain (gwä-dhä-lē-mär')	158	38.29N	2.53W
Guadalope, r., Spain (gwä-dä-lô-pā)	159	40.48N	0.10W
Guadalquivir, Río, r., Spain (rē'ō-gwä-dhäl-kē-vēr')	142	37.30N	5.00W
Guadalupe, Mex.	112	31.23N	106.06W
Guadalupe, i., Mex.	116	29.00N	118.45W
Guadalupe, r., Tx., U.S. (gwä-dhä-lōō'pä)	112	29.54N	99.03W
Guadalupe, Basílica de, rel., Mex.	233a	19.29N	99.07W
Guadalupe, Sierra de, mts., Spain (syĕr'rä dä gwä-dhä-lōō'pä)	148	39.30N	5.25W
Guadalupe Mountains, mts., N.M., U.S.	112	32.00N	104.55W
Guadalupe Peak, mtn., Tx., U.S.	112	31.55N	104.55W
Guadarrama, r., Spain (gwä-dhär-rä'mä)	159a	40.34N	3.58W
Guadarrama, Sierra de, mts., Spain (gwä-dhär-rä'mä)	142	41.00N	3.40W
Guadatentin, r., Spain	158	37.43N	1.58W
Guadeloupe, dep., N.A. (gwä-dē-lōōp)	117	16.40N	61.10W
Guadeloupe Passage, strt., N.A.	121b	16.26N	62.00W
Guadiana, r., Eur. (gwä-dvä'nä)	142	39.00N	6.00W
Guadiana, Bahía de, b., Cuba (bä-ē'ä-dē-gwä-dhē-ä'nä)	122	22.10N	84.35W
Guadiana Alto, r., Spain (äl'tō)	158	39.02N	2.52W
Guadiana Menor, r., Spain (mä'nôr)	158	37.43N	2.45W
Guadiaro, r., Spain (gwä-dhē-ä rō)	158	36.38N	5.25W
Guadiela, r., Spain (gwä-dhē-ā'lä)	158	40.27N	2.05W
Guadix, Spain (gwä-dēsh')	158	37.18N	3.09W
Guaianazes, neigh., Braz.	234d	23.33S	46.25W
Guaira, Braz. (gwä-ē-rä)	131	24.03S	54.02W
Guaire, r., Ven. (gwī'rē)	131b	10.25N	66.43W
Guajaba, Cayo, i., Cuba (kä'yō-gwä-hä'bä)	122	21.50N	77.35W
Guajará Mirim, Braz. (gwä-zhä-rä'mē-rēn')	130	10.58S	65.12W
Guajira, Península de, pen., S.A.	130	12.35N	73.00W
Gualán, Guat. (gwä-län')	120	15.08N	89.21W
Gualeguay, Arg. (gwä-lĕ-gwä'y)	132	33.10S	59.20W
Gualeguay, r., Arg.	132	32.49S	59.05W
Gualicho, Salina, l., Arg. (sä-lē'nä-gwä-lē'chō)	132	40.20S	65.15W
Guam, i., Oc. (gwäm)	3	14.00N	143.20E
Guamo, Col. (gwä'mō)	130a	4.02N	74.58W
Gu'an, China (gōō-än)	192a	39.25N	116.18E
Guan, r., China (gůän)	190	31.56N	115.19E
Guanabacoa, Cuba (gwä-nä-bä-kō'ä)	117	23.08N	82.19W
Guanabara, Baía de, b., Braz.	129a	22.44S	43.09W
Guanacaste, Cordillera, mts., C.R.	120	10.54N	85.27W
Guanacevi, Mex. (gwä-nä-sĕ-vē')	116	25.30N	105.45W
Guanahacabibes, Península de, pen., Cuba	122	21.55N	84.35W
Guanajay, Cuba (gwänä-hī')	122	22.55N	82.40W
Guanajuato, Mex. (gwä-nä-hwä'tō)	116	21.01N	101.16W
Guanajuato, state, Mex.	116	21.00N	101.00W
Guanape, Ven. (gwä-nä'pē)	131b	9.55N	65.32W
Guanape, r., Ven.	131b	9.52N	65.20W
Guanare, Ven. (gwä-nä'rȧ)	130	8.57N	69.47W
Guanduçu, r., Braz. (gwä'n-dōō'sōō)	132b	22.50S	43.40W
Guane, Cuba (gwä'nȧ)	122	22.10N	84.05W
Guangchang, China (gůäŋ-chäŋ)	193	26.50N	116.18E
Guangde, China (gůäŋ-dŭ)	193	30.40N	119.20E
Guangdong, prov., China (gůäŋ-dôŋ)	189	23.45N	113.15E
Guanglu Dao, i., China (gůäŋ-lōō dou)	190	39.13N	122.21E
Guangping, China (gůäŋ-pĭŋ)	190	36.30N	114.57E
Guangrao, China (gůäŋ-rou)	190	37.04N	118.24E
Guangshan, China (gůäŋ-shän)	190	32.02N	114.53E
Guangxi Zhuangzu, prov., China (gůäŋ-shyē)	188	24.00N	108.30E
Guangzhou, China	188	23.07N	113.15W
Guanhu, China (gůän-hōō)	190	34.26N	117.59E
Guannan, China (gůän-nän)	190	34.17N	119.17E
Guanta, Ven. (gwän'tä)	131b	10.15N	64.35W
Guantánamo, Cuba (gwän-tä'nä-mô)	123	20.10N	75.10W
Guantánamo, prov., Cuba	123	20.10N	75.05W
Guantánamo, Bahía de, b., Cuba	123	19.35N	75.35W
Guantao, China (gůän-tou)	190	36.39N	115.25E
Guanxian, China (gůän-shyĕn)	190	36.30N	115.28E
Guanyao, China (gůän-you)	191a	23.13N	113.04E
Guanyintang, China	240b	39.52N	116.31E
Guanyun, China (gůän-yòn)	190	34.28N	119.16E
Guápiles, C.R. (gwä-pē-lĕs)	121	10.05N	83.54W
Guapimirim, Braz. (gwä-pē-mē-rē'n)	132b	22.31S	42.59W
Guaporé, r., S.A. (gwä-pô-rä')	130	12.11S	63.47W
Guaqui, Bol. (guä'kē)	130	16.42S	68.47W
Guara, Sierra de, mts., Spain (sē-ĕ'r-rä-dē-gwä'rä)	159	42.24N	0.15W
Guarabira, Braz. (gwä-rä-bē'rȧ)	131	6.49S	35.27W
Guaracarumbo, Ven.	234a	10.34N	66.59W
Guaranda, Ec. (gwä-rán'dä)	130	1.39S	78.57W
Guarapari, Braz. (gwä-rä-pä'rē)	131	20.34S	40.31W
Guarapiranga, Represa do, res., Braz.	129a	23.45S	46.44W
Guarapuava, Braz. (gwä-rä-pwä'vȧ)	132	25.29S	51.26W
Guarda, Port. (gwär'dä)	158	40.32N	7.17W
Guardiato, r., Spain	158	38.10N	5.05W
Guarena, Spain (gwä-rā'nyä)	158	38.52N	6.08W
Guaribe, r., Ven. (gwä-rē'bē)	131b	9.48N	65.17W
Guárico, dept., Ven.	131b	9.42N	67.25W
Guarulhos, Braz. (gwä-rō'l-yôs)	129a	23.28S	46.30W
Guarus, Braz. (gwȧ'rōōs)	129a	21.44S	41.19W
Guasca, Col. (gwäs'kä)	130a	4.52N	73.52W
Guasipati, Ven. (gwä-sē-pä'tē)	131	7.26N	61.57W
Guastalla, Italy (gwäs-täl'lä)	160	44.53N	10.39E
Guasti, Ca., U.S. (gwäs'tĭ)	107a	34.04N	117.35W
Guatemala, Guat. (guä-tȧ-mä'lä)	116	14.37N	90.32W
Guatemala, nation, N.A.	116	15.45N	91.45W
Guatire, Ven. (gwä-tē'rē)	131b	10.28N	66.34W
Guaviare, r., Col.	130	3.35N	69.28W
Guayabal, Cuba (gwä-yä-bä'l)	122	20.40N	77.40W
Guayalejo, r., Mex. (gwä-yä-lĕ'hô)	118	23.24N	99.09W
Guayama, P.R. (gwä-yä'mä)	117b	18.00N	66.08W
Guayamouc, r., Haiti	123	19.05N	72.00W
Guayaquil, Ec. (gwī-ä-kēl')	130	2.16S	79.53W
Guayaquil, Golfo de, b., Ec. (gôl-fô-dē)	130	3.03S	82.12W
Guaymas, Mex. (gwä'y-mäs)	116	27.49N	110.58W
Guayubin, Dom. Rep. (gwä-yōō-bē'n)	123	19.40N	71.25W
Guazacapán, Guat. (gwä-zä-kä-pän')	120	14.04N	90.26W
Gubakha, Russia (gōō-bä'kȧ)	164	58.53N	57.35E
Gubbio, Italy (gōōb'byô)	160	43.23N	12.36E
Guben, Ger.	154	51.57N	14.43E
Gucheng, China (gōō-chŭŋ)	190	39.09N	115.43E
Gudar, Sierra de, mts., Spain (syĕr'rä dä gōō'dhär)	159	40.28N	0.47W
Gudena, r., Den.	152	56.20N	9.47E
Gudermes, Russia	168	43.20N	46.08E
Gudvangen, Nor. (gōōdh'väŋ-gĕn)	152	60.52N	6.45E
Guebwiller, Fr. (gĕb-vē-lâr')	157	47.53N	7.10E
Guédi, Mont, mtn., Chad	215	12.14N	18.58E
Guelma, Alg. (gwĕl'mä)	210	36.32N	7.17E
Guelph, Can. (gwĕlf)	91	43.33N	80.15W
Güere, r., Ven. (gwĕ'rē)	131b	9.39N	65.00W
Guéret, Fr. (gā-rĕ')	156	46.09N	1.52E
Guermantes, Fr.	237c	48.51N	2.42E
Guernsey, dep., Eur.	156	49.28N	2.35W
Guernsey, i., Guernsey (gûrn'zĭ)	147	49.27N	2.36W
Guerrero, Mex. (gĕr-rā'rō)	112	26.47N	99.20W
Guerrero, Mex.	112	28.20N	100.24W
Guerrero, state, Mex.	116	17.45N	100.15W
Gueydan, La., U.S. (gā'dăn)	113	30.01N	92.31W
Guia de Pacobaíba, Braz. (gwē'ä-dē-pä'kō-bī'bä)	132b	22.42S	43.10W
Guiana Highlands, mts., S.A.	128	3.20N	60.00W
Guichi, China (gwā-chr)	193	30.35N	117.28E
Guichicovi, Mex. (gwē-chē-kō'vē)	119	16.58N	95.10W
Guidonia, Italy (gwē-dō'nyȧ)	160	42.00N	12.45E
Guiglo, C. Iv.	214	6.33N	7.29W
Guignes-Rabutin, Fr. (gēn'yĕ)	157b	48.38N	2.48E
Güigüe, Ven. (gwē'gwĕ)	131b	10.05N	67.48W
Guija, Lago, l., N.A. (gē'hä)	120	14.16N	89.21W
Guildford, Austl.	243a	33.51S	150.59E
Guildford, Eng., U.K. (gĭl'fērd)	150	51.13N	0.34W
Guilford, In., U.S. (gĭl'fērd)	101f	39.10N	84.55W
Guilin, China (gwā-lĭn)	189	25.18N	110.22E
Guimarães, Port. (gē-mä-ränsh')	158	41.27N	8.22W
Guinea, nation, Afr. (gĭn'ē)	210	10.48N	12.28W
Guinea, Gulf of, b., Afr.	210	2.00N	1.00E
Guinea-Bissau, nation, Afr. (gĭn'ē)	210	12.00N	20.00W
Guingamp, Fr. (găn-gän')	156	48.35N	3.10W
Guir, r., Mor.	148	31.55N	2.48W
Güira de Melena, Cuba (gwē'rä dā mā-lā'nä)	122	22.45N	82.30W
Güiria, Ven. (gwē-rē'ä)	130	10.43N	62.16W
Guise, Fr. (guēz)	156	49.54N	3.37E
Guisisil, vol., Nic. (gē-sē-sēl')	120	12.40N	86.11W
Guiyang, China (gwā-yäŋ)	188	26.45N	107.00E
Guizhou, China (gwā-jō)	191a	22.46N	113.15E
Guizhou, prov., China	188	27.00N	106.10E
Gujānwāla, Pak. (gōj-rän'va-lȧ)	183	32.08N	74.14E
Gujarat, India	183	22.54N	72.00E
Gulbarga, India (gòl-bûr'gȧ)	183	17.25N	76.52E
Gulbene, Lat. (gòl-bă'nĕ)	153	57.09N	26.49E
Gulfport, Ms., U.S. (gŭlf'pōrt)	114	30.24N	89.05W
Gulja *see* Yining, China	188	43.58N	80.40E
Gull Lake, Can.	88	50.10N	108.25W
Gull Lake, l., Can.	87	52.35N	114.00W
Gulph Mills, Pa., U.S.	229b	40.04N	75.21W
Gulu, Ug.	217	2.47N	32.18E
Gumaca, Phil. (gōō-mä-kä')	197a	13.55N	122.06E
Gumbeyka, r., Russia (gòm-bĕy'kȧ)	172a	53.20N	59.42E
Gumel, Nig.	210	12.39N	9.22E
Gummersbach, Ger. (gòm'ĕrs-bäk)	154	51.02N	7.34E
Gummi, Nig.	215	12.09N	5.09E
Gumpoldskirchen, Aus.	145e	48.04N	16.15E
Guna, India	186	24.44N	77.17E
Gunisao, r., Can. (gŭn-ĭ-sā'ō)	89	53.40N	97.35W
Gunisao Lake, l., Can.	89	53.35N	96.10W
Gunnedah, Austl. (gŭ'nē-dä)	204	31.00S	150.10E
Gunnison, Co., U.S. (gŭn'ĭ-sŭn)	109	38.33N	106.56W
Gunnison, Ut., U.S.	109	39.10N	111.50W
Gunnison, r., Co., U.S.	109	38.45N	108.20W
Guntersville, Al., U.S. (gŭn'tĕrz-vĭl)	114	34.20N	86.19W
Guntersville Lake, res., Al., U.S.	114	34.30N	86.20W
Guntramsdorf, Aus.	145e	48.04N	16.19E
Guntūr, India (gòn'tōōr)	183	16.22N	80.29E
Guoyang, China (gwō-yäŋ)	190	33.32N	116.10E
Gurdon, Ar., U.S. (gûr'dŭn)	111	33.56N	93.10W
Gurgueia, r., Braz.	131	8.12S	43.49W
Guri, Embalse, res., Ven.	130	7.30N	63.00W
Gurnee, Il., U.S. (gûr'nē)	101a	42.22N	87.55W
Gurskøy, i., Nor. (gōōrskûē)	152	62.18N	5.20E
Gurupi, Serra do, mts., Braz. (sĕ'r-rä-dô-gōō-rōō-pē')	131	5.32S	47.02W
Guru Sikhar, mtn., India	186	29.42N	72.50E
Gur'yevsk, Russia (gōōr-yĭfsk')	164	54.17N	85.56E
Gusau, Nig. (gōō-zä'ōō)	210	12.12N	6.40E
Gusev, Russia (gōō'sĕf)	153	54.35N	22.15E
Gushi, China (gōō-shr)	190	32.11N	115.39E
Gushiago, Ghana	214	9.55N	0.12W
Gusinje, Yugo. (gōō-sēn'yĕ)	161	42.34N	19.54E
Gus'-Khrustal'nyy, Russia (gōōs-krōō-stäl'ny')	166	55.39N	40.41E
Gustavo A. Madero, Mex. (gōōs-tä'vô-ä-mä-dĕ'rô)	118	19.29N	99.07W
Güstrow, Ger. (güs'trō)	154	53.48N	12.12E
Gütersloh, Ger. (gü'tĕrs-lo)	154	51.54N	8.22E
Guthrie, Ok., U.S. (gŭth'rĭ)	111	35.52N	97.26W
Guthrie Center, Ia., U.S.	103	41.41N	94.33W
Gutiérrez Zamora, Mex. (gōō-tĭ-âr'räz zä-mō'rä)	119	20.27N	97.17W
Guttenberg, Ia., U.S. (gŭt'ĕn-bûrg)	103	42.48N	91.09W
Guttenberg, N.J., U.S.	228	40.48N	74.01W
Guyana, nation, S.A. (gŭy'ănȧ)	131	7.45N	59.00W
Guyancourt, Fr.	237c	48.46N	2.04E
Guyang, China (gōō-yäŋ)	190	34.56N	114.57E
Guye, China (gōō-yŭ)	190	39.46N	118.23E
Guymon, Ok., U.S. (gī'mŏn)	110	36.41N	101.29W
Guysborough, Can. (gīz'bŭr-ô)	93	45.23N	61.30W

ng-sing; ŋ-baŋk; N-nasalized n; nŏd; cŏmmit; ōld; ôbey; ôrder; oi-boil; fōōd; ò-as oo in foot; ou-out; s-soft; sh-dish; th-thin; pūre; ůnite; ûrn; stŭd; circŭs; ü-as in French tu; '-indeterminate vowel.

294 Guzhen – Harmarville

PLACE (Pronunciation)	PAGE	Lat. °′	Long. °′
Guzhen, China (gōō-jŭn)	192	33.20N	117.18E
Gvardeysk, Russia (gvár-dĕysk′)	153	54.39N	21.11E
Gwadabawa, Nig.	215	13.20N	5.15E
Gwādar, Pak. (gwä′dŭr)	182	25.15N	62.29E
Gwalior, India	183	26.13N	78.10E
Gwane, Zaire (gwän)	211	4.43N	25.50E
Gwardafuy, Gees, c., Som.	218a	11.55N	51.30E
Gwda, r., Pol.	154	53.27N	16.52E
Gwembe, Zam.	217	16.30S	27.35E
Gweru, Zimb.	212	19.15S	29.48E
Gwinn, Mi., U.S. (gwĭn)	103	46.15N	87.30W
Gyaring Co, l., China	186	30.37N	88.33E
Gydan, Khrebet (Kolymskiy), mts., Russia	165	61.45N	155.00E
Gydanskiy Poluostrov, pen., Russia	164	70.42N	76.03E
Gympie, Austl. (gĭm′pē)	203	26.20S	152.50E
Gyöngyös, Hung. (dyûn′dyûsh)	149	47.47N	19.55E
Györ, Hung. (dyûr)	149	47.40N	17.37E
Gyōtoku, Japan (gyō′tō-kōō′)	195a	35.42N	139.56E
Gypsumville, Can. (jĭp′sŭm′vĭl)	84	51.45N	98.35W
Gyula, Hung. (dyŏ′lä)	155	46.38N	21.18E
Gyumri, Arm.	167	40.40N	43.50E
H			
Haan, Ger. (hän)	157c	51.12N	7.00E
Haapamäki, Fin. (häp′ä-mĕ-kĕ)	153	62.16N	24.20E
Haapsalu, Est. (häp′sä-lŏ)	153	58.56N	23.33E
Haar, Ger. (här)	145d	48.06N	11.44E
Haar, neigh., Ger.	236	51.26N	7.13E
Ha′Arava (Wādī al Jayb), val., Asia	181a	30.33N	35.10E
Haarlem, Neth. (här′lĕm)	151	52.22N	4.37E
Habana, prov., Cuba (hä-vä′nä)	122	22.45N	82.25W
Haberfield, Austl.	243a	33.53S	151.08E
Hābra, India	186a	22.49N	88.38E
Hachinohe, Japan (hä′chē-nō′hå)	194	40.29N	141.40E
Hachiōji, Japan (hä′chē-ō′jē)	194	35.39N	139.18E
Hacienda Heights, Ca., U.S.	232	33.58N	117.58W
Hackensack, N.J., U.S. (häk′ĕn-säk)	100a	40.54N	74.03W
Hacketts, Eng., U.K.	235	51.45N	0.05W
Hackney, neigh., Eng., U.K.	235	51.33N	0.03W
Ḩadd, Ra′s al, c., Oman	182	22.29N	59.46E
Haddonfield, N.J., U.S. (häd′ŭn-fēld)	100f	39.53N	75.02W
Haddon Heights, N.J., U.S. (häd′ŭn hīts)	100f	39.53N	75.03W
Hadejia, Nig. (hä-dä′jä)	210	12.30N	9.59E
Hadejia, r., Nig.	210	12.15N	10.00E
Ḩadera, Isr. (ка-dĕ′rå)	181a	32.26N	34.55E
Hadersdorf, neigh., Aus.	239e	48.13N	16.14E
Haderslev, Den. (hä′dhĕrs-lĕv)	152	55.17N	9.28E
Hadfield, Austl.	243b	37.42S	144.56E
Ḩadīdū, Yemen	182	12.40N	53.50E
Hadlock, Wa., U.S. (hăd′lŏk)	106a	48.02N	122.46W
Ḩadramawt, reg., Yemen	182	15.22N	48.40E
Ḩadūr Shu′ayb, mtn., Yemen	182	15.45N	43.45E
Haeju, N. Kor. (hä′ĕ-jŭ)	194	38.03N	125.42E
Hafnarfjördur, Ice.	146	64.02N	21.32W
Haft Gel, Iran	185	31.27N	49.27E
Hafun, Ras, c., Som. (hä-fōōn′)	218a	10.15N	51.35E
Hageland, Mt., U.S. (hăge′lănd)	105	48.53N	108.43W
Hagen, Ger. (hä′gĕn)	154	51.21N	7.29E
Hagerstown, In., U.S. (hā′gĕrz-toun)	98	39.55N	85.10W
Hagerstown, Md., U.S.	97	39.40N	77.45W
Hagi, Japan (hä′gĭ)	195	34.25N	131.25E
Hague, Cap de la, c., Fr. (dē lå åg′)	156	49.44N	1.55W
Haguenau, Fr. (åg′nō′)	157	48.47N	7.48E
Hahnenberg, Ger.	236	51.12N	7.24E
Hai′an, China (hī-än)	190	32.35N	120.25E
Haibara, Japan (hä′ē-bä′rä)	195	34.29N	135.57E
Haicheng, China (hī-chŭŋ)	192	40.58N	122.45E
Haidārpur, neigh., India	240d	28.43N	77.09E
Haidian, China (hī-dĭĕn)	190	39.59N	116.17E
Haifa, Isr. (hä′ē-få)	182	32.48N	35.00E
Haifeng, China (hä′ē-fĕng′)	193	23.00N	115.20E
Haifuzhen, China (hī-fōō-jŭn)	190	31.57N	121.48E
Haijima, Japan	242a	35.42N	139.21E
Haikou, China	189	20.03N	110.19E
Haikou, China (hī-kō)	193	20.00N	110.20E
Ḩā′il, Sau. Ar.	182	27.30N	41.47E
Hailar, China	189	49.10N	118.40E
Hailey, Id., U.S. (hā′lĭ)	105	43.31N	114.19W
Haileybury, Can.	91	47.27N	79.38W
Haileyville, Ok., U.S. (hā′lĭ-vĭl)	111	34.51N	95.34W
Hailing Dao, i., China (hī-lĭŋ dou)	193	21.30N	112.15E
Hailong, China (hī-loŋ)	192	42.32N	125.52E
Hailun, China (hä′ē-lōōn′)	189	47.18N	126.50E
Hainan, prov., China	188	19.00N	109.30E
Hainan Dao, i., China (hī-nän dou)	189	19.00N	111.10E
Hainault, neigh., Eng., U.K.	235	51.36N	0.06E
Hainburg, Aus.	154	48.09N	16.57E
Haines, Ak., U.S. (hānz)	95	59.10N	135.38W
Haines City, Fl., U.S.	115a	28.05N	81.38W
Hai Phong, Viet. (hī′fông′)(hä′ēp-hŏng)	196	20.52N	106.40E
Haiti, nation, N.A. (hā′tĭ)	117	19.00N	72.15W
Haizhou, China	190	34.34N	119.11E
Haizhou Wan, b., China	192	34.49N	120.35E
Hajdúböszormény, Hung. (hôl′dō-bû′sûr-män′)	155	47.41N	21.30E
Hajdúhadház, Hung. (hô′ĭ-dō-hôd′häz)	155	47.32N	21.32E
Hajdúnánás, Hung. (hô′ĭ-dō-nä′näsh)	155	47.52N	21.27E
Hakodate, Japan (hä-kō-dä′t å)	189	41.46N	140.42E
Haku-San, mtn., Japan (hä′kōō-sän′)	194	36.11N	136.45E
Halā′ib, Egypt (hä-lä′ēb)	211	22.10N	36.40E
Halbe, Ger. (häl′bē)	145b	52.07N	13.43E
Halberstadt, Ger. (häl′bĕr-shtät)	154	51.54N	11.07E
Halcon, Mount, mtn., Phil. (häl-kōn′)	197a	13.19N	120.55E
Halden, Nor. (häl′dĕn)	146	59.10N	11.21E
Halden, neigh., Ger.	236	51.23N	7.31E
Haldensleben, Ger.	154	52.18N	11.23E
Hale, Eng., U.K. (hāl)	144a	53.22N	2.20W
Haleakala Crater, Hi., U.S. (hä′lā-ä′kä-lä)	94a	20.44N	156.15W
Haleakala National Park, Hi., U.S.	94a	20.46N	156.00W
Halebarns, Eng., U.K.	237b	53.22N	2.19W
Haledon, N.J., U.S.	228	40.56N	74.11W
Hales Corners, Wi., U.S. (hālz kôr′nĕrz)	101a	42.56N	88.03W
Halesowen, Eng., U.K. (hālz′ō-wĕn)	144a	52.26N	2.03W
Halethorpe, Md., U.S. (hāl-thôrp)	100e	39.15N	76.40W
Halewood, Eng., U.K.	237a	53.22N	2.49W
Haleyville, Al., U.S. (hā′lĭ-vĭl)	114	34.11N	87.36W
Half Moon Bay, Ca., U.S. (häf′mōōn)	106b	37.28N	122.26W
Halfway House, S. Afr. (häf-wā hous)	213b	26.00S	28.08E
Halfweg, Neth.	145a	52.23N	4.45E
Halifax, Can. (hăl′ĭ-făks)	85	44.39N	63.36W
Halifax, Eng., U.K.	150	53.44N	1.52W
Halifax Bay, b., Austl. (hăl′ĭ-făx)	203	18.56S	147.07E
Halifax Harbour, b., Can.	92	44.35N	63.31W
Halkett, Cape, c., Ak., U.S.	95	70.50N	151.15W
Hallam, Austl.	243b	38.01S	145.16E
Hallam Peak, mtn., Can.	87	52.11N	118.46E
Halla San, mtn., S. Kor. (häl′lå-sän)	194	33.20N	126.37E
Halle, Bel. (häl′lĕ)	145a	50.45N	4.13E
Halle, Ger.	147	51.30N	11.59E
Hallettsville, Tx., U.S. (hăl′ĕts-vĭl)	113	29.26N	96.55W
Hallock, Mn., U.S. (hăl′ŭk)	102	48.46N	96.57W
Hall Peninsula, pen., Can. (hôl)	85	63.14N	65.40W
Halls Bayou, Tx., U.S.	113a	29.55N	95.23W
Hallsberg, Swe. (häls′bĕrgh)	152	59.04N	15.04E
Halls Creek, Austl. (hôlz)	202	18.15S	127.45E
Halmahera, i., Indon. (häl-mä-hä′rä)	197	0.45N	128.45E
Halmahera, Laut, Indon.	197	1.00S	129.00E
Halmstad, Swe. (hälm′städ)	146	56.40N	12.46E
Halsafjorden, fj., Nor. (häl′sĕ fyōrd)	152	63.03N	8.23E
Halstead, Eng., U.K.	235	51.20N	0.08E
Halstead, Ks., U.S. (hôl′stĕd)	111	38.02N	97.36W
Haltern, Ger. (häl′tĕrn)	157c	51.45N	7.10E
Haltom City, Tx., U.S. (hôl′tŏm)	107c	32.48N	97.13W
Halver, Ger.	157c	51.11N	7.30E
Ham, neigh., Eng., U.K.	235	51.26N	0.19W
Hamada, Japan	194	34.53N	132.05E
Hamadān, Iran (hŭ-mŭ-dän′)	182	34.45N	48.07E
Ḩamāh, Syria (hä′mä)	182	35.08N	36.53E
Hamamatsu, Japan (hä′mä-mät′sŏ)	194	34.41N	137.43E
Hamar, Nor. (hä′mär)	146	60.49N	11.05E
Hamasaka, Japan (hä′må-sä′kå)	195	35.57N	134.27E
Hamberg, S. Afr.	244b	26.11S	27.53E
Hamborn, Ger. (häm′bōrn)	157c	51.30N	6.43E
Hamburg, Ger. (häm′bōōrgh)	142	53.34N	10.02E
Hamburg, S. Afr. (häm′bûrg)	213c	33.18S	27.28E
Hamburg, Ar., U.S. (hăm′bûrg)	111	33.15N	91.49W
Hamburg, N.J., U.S.	100a	41.09N	74.35W
Hamburg, N.Y., U.S.	101c	42.44N	78.51W
Hamburg, state, Ger.	145c	53.35N	10.00E
Hamden, Ct., U.S. (hăm′dĕn)	99	41.20N	72.55W
Hämeenlinna, Fin. (hĕ′mân-lĭn-nå)	146	61.00N	24.29E
Hameln, Ger. (hä′mĕln)	154	52.06N	9.23E
Hamelwörden, Ger. (hä′mĕl-vûr-dĕn)	145c	53.47N	9.19E
Hamersley Range, mts., Austl. (hăm′ērz-lē)	202	22.15S	117.50E
Hamhŭng, N. Kor. (häm′hōng′)	189	39.57N	127.35E
Hamhŭng, N. Kor.	194	39.54N	127.32E
Hami, China (hä-mē)(kō-mōōl′)	188	42.58N	93.14E
Hamilton, Austl. (hăm′ĭl-tŭn)	203	37.50S	142.10E
Hamilton, Can.	85	43.15N	79.52W
Hamilton, N.Z.	203a	37.45S	175.28E
Hamilton, Al., U.S.	114	34.09N	88.01W
Hamilton, Ma., U.S.	93a	42.37N	70.52W
Hamilton, Mo., U.S.	111	39.43N	93.59W
Hamilton, Mt., U.S.	105	46.15N	114.09W
Hamilton, Oh., U.S.	97	39.22N	84.33W
Hamilton, Tx., U.S.	112	31.42N	98.07W
Hamilton, Lake, l., Ar., U.S.	111	34.25N	93.32W
Hamilton Harbour, b., Can.	83d	43.17N	79.50W
Hamilton Inlet, b., Can.	85	54.20N	56.57W
Hamina, Fin. (hä′mē-nå)	153	60.34N	27.15E
Hamlet, N.C., U.S. (hăm′lĕt)	115	35.52N	79.46W
Hamlin, Tx., U.S. (hăm′lĭn)	110	32.54N	100.08W
Hamm, Ger. (häm)	154	51.40N	7.48E
Hamm, neigh., Ger.	236	51.12N	6.44E
Hammanskraal, S. Afr. (hä-måns-kräl′)	218d	25.24S	28.17E
Hamme, Bel.	145a	51.06N	4.07E
Hamme-Oste Kanal, can., Ger. (hä′mĕ-ōs′tĕ kä-näl)	145c	53.20N	8.59E
Hammerfest, Nor. (hä′mĕr-fĕst)	142	70.38N	23.59E
Hammersmith, neigh., Eng., U.K.	235	51.30N	0.14W
Hammond, In., U.S. (hăm′ŭnd)	97	41.37N	87.31W
Hammond, La., U.S.	113	30.30N	90.28W
Hammond, Or., U.S.	106c	46.12N	123.57W
Hammondville, Austl.	243a	33.57S	150.57E
Hammonton, N.J., U.S. (hăm′ŭn-tŭn)	99	39.40N	74.45W
Hampden, Me., U.S. (hăm′dĕn)	92	44.44N	68.51W
Hampstead, Md., U.S.	100e	39.36N	76.54W
Hampstead, neigh., Eng., U.K.	235	51.33N	0.11W
Hampstead Heath, pt. of i., Eng., U.K.	235	51.34N	0.10W
Hampstead Norris, Eng., U.K. (hămp-stĕd nŏ′rĭs)	144b	51.27N	1.14W
Hampton, Austl.	243b	37.56S	145.00E
Hampton, Can. (hămp′tŭn)	92	45.32N	65.51W
Hampton, Ia., U.S.	103	42.43N	93.15W
Hampton, Va., U.S.	99	37.02N	76.21W
Hampton, neigh., Eng., U.K.	235	51.25N	0.22W
Hampton National Historic Site, pt. of i., Md., U.S.	229c	39.25N	76.35W
Hampton Roads, b., Va., U.S.	100g	36.56N	76.23W
Hams Fork, r., Wy., U.S.	105	41.55N	110.40W
Hamtramck, Mi., U.S. (hăm-trăm′ĭk)	101b	42.24N	83.03W
Han, r., China	189	31.40N	112.04E
Han, r., China (hän)	193	25.00N	116.35E
Han, r., S. Kor.	194	37.10N	127.40E
Hana, Hi., U.S. (hä′nä)	94a	20.43N	155.59W
Hanábana, r., Cuba (hä-nä-bä′nä)	122	22.30N	80.55W
Hanalei Bay, b., Hi., U.S. (hä-nä-lā′ē)	94a	22.15N	159.40W
Hanang, mtn., Tan.	217	4.26S	35.24E
Hanau, Ger. (hä′nou)	154	50.08N	8.56E
Hancock, Mi., U.S. (hăn′kŏk)	97	47.08N	88.37W
Handan, China (hän-dän)	190	36.37N	114.30E
Handforth, Eng., U.K.	237b	53.21N	2.13W
Haney, Can. (hā-nē)	87	49.13N	122.36W
Hanford, Ca., U.S. (hăn′fērd)	108	36.20N	119.38W
Hangayn Nuruu, mts., Mong.	188	48.03N	99.45E
Hang Hau Town, H.K.	241c	22.19N	114.16E
Hango, Fin. (häŋ′gû)	142	59.49N	22.56E
Hangzhou, China (hăng′chō′)	189	30.17N	120.12E
Hangzhou Wan, b., China (häŋ-jō wän)	193	30.20N	121.25E
Hankamer, Tx., U.S. (hăn′kå-mēr)	113a	29.52N	94.42W
Hankinson, N.D., U.S. (häŋ′kĭn-sŭn)	102	46.04N	96.54W
Hankou, China (hän-kō)	193	30.42N	114.22E
Hann, Mount, mtn., Austl. (hän)	202	16.05S	126.07E
Hanna, Can. (hăn′å)	84	51.38N	111.54W
Hanna, Wy., U.S.	105	41.51N	106.34W
Hannah, N.D., U.S.	102	48.58N	98.42W
Hannibal, Mo., U.S. (hăn′ĭ bål)	97	39.42N	91.22W
Hannover, Ger. (hän-ō′vĕr)	142	52.22N	9.45E
Hanöbukten, b., Swe.	152	55.54N	14.55E
Hanoi, Viet. (hä-noi′)	196	21.04N	105.50E
Hanover, Can. (hăn′ō-vĕr)	90	44.10N	81.05W
Hanover, Md., U.S.	229c	39.11N	76.42W
Hanover, Ma., U.S.	93a	42.07N	70.49W
Hanover, N.H., U.S.	99	43.45N	72.15W
Hanover, Pa., U.S.	99	39.50N	77.00W
Hanover, i., Chile	132	51.00S	74.45W
Hanshan, China (hän′shän′)	190	31.43N	118.06E
Hans Lollick, i., V.I.U.S. (häns′lôl′ĭk)	117c	18.24N	64.55W
Hanson, Ma., U.S. (hăn′sŭn)	93a	42.04N	70.53W
Hansville, Wa., U.S. (häns′-vĭl)	106a	47.55N	122.33W
Hantengri Feng, mtn., Asia (hän-tŭŋ-rē fŭŋ)	188	42.10N	80.20E
Hantsport, Can. (hănts′pōrt)	92	45.04N	64.11W
Hanworth, neigh., Eng., U.K.	235	51.26N	0.23W
Hanyang, China (hän′yäng′)	189	30.30N	114.10E
Hanzhong, China (hän-jôŋ)	192	33.02N	107.00E
Haocheng, China (hou-chŭŋ)	190	33.19N	117.33E
Haparanda, Swe. (hä-pa-rän′dä)	146	65.54N	23.57E
Hapeville, Ga., U.S. (hāp′vĭl)	100c	33.39N	84.25W
Happy Camp, Ca., U.S.	104	41.47N	123.22W
Happy Valley-Goose Bay, Can.	85	53.19N	60.33W
Hapsford, Eng., U.K.	237a	53.16N	2.48W
Ḩaql, Sau. Ar.	181a	29.15N	34.57E
Ḩar, Laga, r., Kenya	217	2.15N	39.30E
Haramachida, Japan	242a	35.33N	139.27E
Harare, Zimb.	212	17.50S	31.03E
Harbin, China	189	45.40N	126.30E
Harbor Beach, Mi., U.S. (här′bĕr bēch)	98	43.50N	82.40W
Harbor City, neigh., Ca., U.S.	232	33.48N	118.17W
Harbord, Austl.	243a	33.47S	151.17E
Harbor Isle, N.Y., U.S.	228	40.36N	73.40W
Harbor Springs, Mi., U.S.	98	45.25N	85.05W
Harbour Breton, Can. (brĕt′ŭn) (brē-tôN′)	93	47.29N	55.48W
Harbour Grace, Can. (grās)	93	47.32N	53.13W
Harburg, Ger. (här-bōrgh)	145c	53.28N	9.58E
Hardangerfjorden, Nor. (här-däng′ĕr fyōrd)	146	59.58N	6.30E
Hardin, Mt., U.S. (här′dĭn)	105	45.44N	107.36W
Harding, S. Afr. (här′dĭng)	212	30.34S	29.54E
Harding, Lake, res., U.S.	114	32.43N	85.00W
Hardwār, India (hŭr′dvär)	183	29.56N	78.06E
Hardy, r., Mex. (här′dĭ)	108	32.04N	115.10W
Hare Bay, b., Can. (hâr)	93	51.18N	55.50W
Harefield, neigh., Eng., U.K.	235	51.36N	0.29W
Harer, Eth.	211	9.43N	42.10E
Harerge, hist. reg., Eth.	211	8.15N	41.00E
Hargeysa, Som. (här-gā′ē-så)	218a	9.20N	43.57E
Harghita, Munţii, mts., Rom.	155	46.25N	25.40E
Harima-Nada, b., Japan (hä′rē-mä nä-dä)	195	34.34N	134.37E
Haringey, neigh., Eng., U.K.	235	51.35N	0.07W
Haringvliet, r., Neth.	145a	51.49N	4.03E
Hari Rud, r., Asia	182	34.29N	61.16E
Harker Village, N.J., U.S.	229b	39.51N	75.09W
Harlan, Ia., U.S. (här′lăn)	111	41.40N	95.10W
Harlan, Ky., U.S.	114	36.50N	83.19W
Harlan County Reservoir, res., Ne., U.S.	110	40.03N	99.51W
Harlem, Mt., U.S. (hår′lĕm)	105	48.33N	108.50W
Harlem, neigh., N.Y., U.S.	228	40.49N	73.56W
Harlesden, neigh., Eng., U.K.	235	51.32N	0.15W
Harlingen, Neth. (här′lĭng-ĕn)	151	53.10N	5.24E
Harlingen, Tx., U.S.	96	26.12N	97.42W
Harlington, neigh., Eng., U.K.	235	51.29N	0.26W
Harlow, Eng., U.K. (här′lō)	144b	51.46N	0.08E
Harlowton, Mt., U.S. (hår′lō-tŭn)	105	46.26N	109.50W
Harmar Heights, Pa., U.S.	230b	40.33N	79.49W
Harmarville, Pa., U.S.	230b	40.32N	79.51W

PRONOUNCING INDEX

Harmony–Hengyang 295

PLACE (Pronunciation)	PAGE	Lat. °'	Long. °'
Harmony, In., U.S. (här'mȯ-nĭ)	98	39.35N	87.00W
Harney Basin, Or., U.S. (här'nĭ)	104	43.26N	120.19W
Harney Lake, l., Or., U.S.	104	43.11N	119.23W
Harney Peak, mtn., S.D., U.S.	96	43.52N	103.32W
Härnosand, Swe. (hĕr-nû-sänd)	146	62.37N	17.54E
Haro, Spain (ä'rō)	158	42.35N	2.49W
Harola, India	240d	28.36N	77.19E
Harold Hill, neigh., Eng., U.K.	235	51.36N	0.13E
Harold Wood, neigh., Eng., U.K.	235	51.36N	0.14E
Haro Strait, strt., N.A. (hă'rō)	106a	48.27N	123.11W
Harpen, neigh., Ger.	236	51.29N	7.16E
Harpenden, Eng., U.K. (här'pĕn-d'n)	144b	51.48N	0.22W
Harper, Lib.	210	4.25N	7.43W
Harper, Ks., U.S. (här'pēr)	110	37.17N	98.02W
Harper, Wa., U.S.	106a	47.31N	122.32W
Harpers Ferry, W.V., U.S. (här'pērz)	99	39.20N	77.45W
Harper Woods, Mi., U.S.	230c	42.24N	82.55W
Harpurhey, neigh., Eng., U.K.	237b	53.31N	2.13W
Harricana, r., Can.	91	50.10N	78.50W
Harriman, Tn., U.S. (hăr'ĭ-măn)	114	35.55N	84.34W
Harrington, De., U.S. (hăr'ĭng-tŭn)	99	38.55N	75.35W
Harris, i., Scot., U.K. (hăr'ĭs)	150	57.55N	6.40W
Harris, Lake, l., Fl., U.S.	115a	28.43N	81.40W
Harrisburg, Il., U.S. (hăr'ĭs-bûrg)	98	37.45N	88.35W
Harrisburg, Pa., U.S.	97	40.15N	76.50W
Harrismith, S. Afr. (hă-rĭs'mĭth)	218d	28.17S	29.08E
Harrison, Ar., U.S. (hăr'ĭ-sŭn)	111	36.13N	93.06W
Harrison, N.J., U.S.	228	40.45N	74.10W
Harrison, N.Y., U.S.	228	40.58N	73.43W
Harrison, Oh., U.S.	101f	39.16N	84.45W
Harrisonburg, Va., U.S. (hăr'ĭ-sŭn-bûrg)	99	38.30N	78.50W
Harrison Lake, l., Can.	87	49.31N	121.59W
Harrisonville, Md., U.S.	229c	39.23N	77.50W
Harrisonville, Mo., U.S. (hăr-ĭ-sŭn-vĭl)	111	38.39N	94.21W
Harris Park, Austl.	243a	33.49S	151.01E
Harrisville, Ut., U.S. (hăr'ĭs-vĭl)	107b	41.17N	112.00W
Harrisville, W.V., U.S.	98	39.10N	81.05W
Harrodsburg, Ky., U.S. (hăr'ŭdz-bûrg)	98	37.45N	84.50W
Harrods Creek, r., Ky., U.S. (hăr'ŭdz)	101h	38.24N	35.33W
Harrow, Eng., U.K. (hăr'ō)	144b	51.34N	0.21W
Harrow on the Hill, neigh., Eng., U.K.	235	51.34N	0.20W
Harsefeld, Ger. (här'zĕ-fĕld')	145c	53.27N	9.30E
Harstad, Nor. (här'städh)	146	68.49N	16.10E
Hart, Mi., U.S. (härt)	98	43.40N	86.25W
Hartbeesfontein, S. Afr.	218d	26.46S	26.25E
Hartbeespoortdam, res., S. Afr.	213b	25.47S	27.43E
Hartford, Al., U.S. (härt'fērd)	114	31.05N	85.42W
Hartford, Ar., U.S.	111	35.01N	94.21W
Hartford, Ct., U.S.	97	41.45N	72.40W
Hartford, Il., U.S.	107e	38.50N	90.06W
Hartford, Ky., U.S.	114	37.25N	86.50W
Hartford, Mi., U.S.	98	42.15N	86.15W
Hartford, Wi., U.S.	103	43.19N	88.25W
Hartford City, In., U.S.	98	40.35N	85.25W
Hartington, Eng., U.K. (härt'ĭng-tŭn)	144a	53.08N	1.48W
Hartington, Ne., U.S.	102	42.37N	97.18W
Hartland Point, c., Eng., U.K.	150	51.03N	4.40W
Hartlepool, Eng., U.K. (här't'l-po͞ol)	146	54.40N	1.12W
Hartley, Eng., U.K.	235	51.23N	0.19E
Hartley, Ia., U.S. (härt'lĭ)	102	43.12N	95.29W
Hartley Bay, Can.	86	53.25N	129.15W
Hart Mountain, mtn., Can. (härt)	89	52.25N	101.30W
Hartsbeespoort, S. Afr.	213b	25.44S	27.51E
Hartselle, Al., U.S. (härt'sĕl)	114	34.24N	86.55W
Hartshorne, Ok., U.S. (härts'hôrn)	111	34.49N	95.34W
Hartsville, S.C., U.S. (härts'vĭl)	115	34.20N	80.04W
Hartwell, Ga., U.S. (härt'wĕl)	115	34.21N	82.56W
Hartwell Lake, res., U.S.	97	34.30N	83.00W
Hārua, India	186a	22.36N	88.40E
Harvard, Il., U.S. (här'vȧrd)	103	42.25N	88.39W
Harvard, Ma., U.S.	93a	42.30N	71.35W
Harvard, Ne., U.S.	110	40.36N	98.08W
Harvard, Mount, mtn., Co., U.S.	109	38.55N	106.20W
Harvel, Eng., U.K.	235	51.21N	0.22E
Harvey, Can.	92	45.44N	64.46W
Harvey, Il., U.S.	101a	41.37N	87.39W
Harvey, La., U.S.	100d	29.54N	90.05W
Harvey, N.D., U.S.	102	47.46N	99.55W
Harwich, Eng., U.K. (här'wĭch)	151	51.53N	1.13E
Harwick, Pa., U.S.	230b	40.34N	79.48W
Harwood, Eng., U.K.	237b	53.35N	2.23W
Harwood, Md., U.S.	229c	38.52N	76.37W
Harwood Heights, Il., U.S.	231a	41.59N	87.48W
Harwood Park, Md., U.S.	229c	39.12N	76.44W
Haryana, state, India	183	29.00N	75.45E
Harz Mountains, mts., Ger. (härts)	154	51.42N	10.50E
Ḩasanābād, Iran	241h	35.44N	51.19E
Hasbrouck Heights, N.J., U.S.	228	40.52N	74.04W
Hashimoto, Japan (hä'shē-mō'tō)	195	34.19N	135.37E
Haskayne, Eng., U.K.	237a	53.34N	2.58W
Haskell, Ok., U.S. (hăs'kĕl)	111	35.49N	95.41W
Haskell, Tx., U.S.	110	33.09N	99.43W
Hasköy, neigh., Tur.	239f	41.02N	28.58E
Haslingden, Eng., U.K. (hăz'lĭng dĕn)	144a	53.43N	2.19W
Hasselbeck-Schwarzbach, Ger.	236	51.16N	6.53E
Hassels, neigh., Ger.	236	51.10N	6.53E
Hassi Messaoud, Alg.	210	31.17N	6.13E
Hässleholm, Swe. (hĕs'lĕ-hōlm)	152	56.10N	13.44E
Hasslinghausen, Ger.	236	51.20N	7.17E
Hästen, neigh., Ger.	236	51.09N	7.06E
Hasten, neigh., Ger.	236	51.12N	7.09E
Hastings, N.Z.	203a	39.33S	176.53E
Hastings, Eng., U.K. (hās'tĭngz)	147	50.52N	0.28E
Hastings, Mi., U.S.	98	42.40N	85.20W
Hastings, Mn., U.S.	107g	44.44N	92.51W
Hastings, Ne., U.S.	96	40.34N	98.42W
Hastings-on-Hudson, N.Y., U.S. (ŏn-hŭd'sŭn)	100a	40.59N	75.53W
Hastingwood, Eng., U.K.	235	51.45N	0.09E
Hatay, Tur.	182	36.20N	36.10E
Hatchie, r., Tn., U.S. (hăch'ē)	114	35.28N	89.14W
Haţeg, Rom. (kät-säg')	161	45.35N	22.57E
Hatfield Broad Oak, Eng., U.K. (hăt-fēld brôd ōk)	144b	51.50N	0.14E
Hatogaya, Japan (hä'tō-gä-yä)	195a	35.50N	139.45E
Hatsukaichi, Japan (hät'so͞o-kȧ'ē-chē)	195	34.22N	132.19E
Hatteras, Cape, c., N.C., U.S. (hăt'ēr-ȧs)	97	35.15N	75.24W
Hattiesburg, Ms., U.S. (hăt'ĭz-bûrg)	97	31.20N	89.18W
Hattingen, Ger. (hä'tēn-gĕn)	157c	51.24N	7.11E
Hatton, neigh., Eng., U.K.	235	51.28N	0.25W
Hattori, Japan	242b	34.46N	135.27E
Hatvan, Hung. (hôt'vôn)	155	47.39N	19.44E
Hatzfeld, neigh., Ger.	236	51.17N	7.11E
Haugesund, Nor. (hou'gĕ-soon')	146	59.26N	5.20E
Haughton Green, Eng., U.K.	237b	53.27N	2.06W
Haukivesi, l., Fin. (hou'kė-vĕ'sė)	153	62.02N	29.02E
Haultain, r., Can.	88	56.15N	106.35W
Hauptsrus, S. Afr.	218d	26.35S	26.16E
Hauraki Gulf, b., N.Z. (hä-o͞o-rä'kė)	203a	36.30S	175.00E
Haut, Isle au, Me., U.S. (hō)	92	44.03N	68.13W
Haut Atlas, mts., Mor.	148	32.10N	5.49W
Hauterive, Can.	92	49.11N	68.16W
Hauula, Hi., U.S.	94a	21.37N	157.45W
Hauz Rāni, neigh., India	240d	28.32N	77.13E
Havana, Cuba	117	23.08N	82.23W
Havana, Il., U.S. (hȧ-vă'nȧ)	111	40.17N	90.02W
Havasu, Lake, res., U.S. (hăv'ȧ-so͞o)	109	34.26N	114.09W
Havel, r., Ger. (hä'fĕl)	154	53.09N	13.10E
Havel-Kanal, can., Ger.	145b	52.36N	13.12E
Haverford, Pa., U.S.	229b	40.01N	75.18W
Haverhill, Ma., U.S. (hā'vēr-hĭl)	93a	42.46N	71.05W
Haverhill, N.H., U.S.	99	44.00N	72.05W
Havering, neigh., Eng., U.K.	235	51.34N	0.14E
Havering's Grove, Eng., U.K.	235	51.38N	0.23E
Haverstraw, N.Y., U.S. (hā'vĕr-strô)	100a	41.11N	73.58W
Havertown, Pa., U.S.	229b	39.59N	75.18W
Havlíckuv Brod, Czech Rep.	147	49.38N	15.34E
Havre, Mt., U.S. (hăv'ēr)	96	48.34N	109.42W
Havre-Boucher, Can. (hăv'rá-bo͞o-shā')	93	45.42N	61.30W
Havre de Grace, Md., U.S. (hăv'ēr dē grās')	99	39.35N	76.05W
Havre-Saint Pierre, Can.	92	50.15N	63.36W
Haw, r., N.C., U.S. (hô)	115	36.17N	79.46W
Hawaii, state, U.S.	96c	20.00N	157.40W
Hawaii, i., Hi., U.S. (hä wī'ē)	96c	19.50N	157.15W
Hawaiian Gardens, Ca., U.S.	232	33.50N	118.04W
Hawaiian Islands, is., Hi., U.S. (hä-wī'ȧn)	96c	22.00N	158.00W
Hawaii Volcanoes National Park, rec., Hi., U.S.	96c	19.30N	155.25W
Hawarden, Ia., U.S. (hā'wàr-dĕn)	102	43.00N	96.28W
Ḩawf, Jabal, hills, Egypt	244a	29.55N	31.21E
Hawi, Hi., U.S. (hä'wē)	94a	20.16N	155.48W
Hawick, Scot., U.K. (hô'ĭk)	150	55.25N	2.55W
Hawke Bay, b., N.Z. (hôk)	203a	39.17S	177.20E
Hawker, Austl. (hô'kēr)	204	31.58S	138.12E
Hawkesbury, Can. (hôks'bēr-ĭ)	91	45.35N	74.35W
Hawkinsville, Ga., U.S. (hô'kĭnz-vĭl)	114	32.15N	83.30W
Hawks Nest Point, c., Bah.	123	24.05N	75.30W
Hawley, Eng., U.K.	235	51.25N	0.14E
Hawley, Mn., U.S. (hô'lĭ)	102	46.52N	96.18W
Haworth, Eng., U.K. (hä'wûrth)	144a	53.50N	1.57W
Haworth, N.J., U.S.	228	40.58N	73.59W
Hawthorn, Austl.	243b	37.49S	145.02E
Hawthorne, Ca., U.S. (hô'thôrn)	107a	33.55N	118.22W
Hawthorne, Nv., U.S.	108	38.33N	118.39W
Hawthorne, N.J., U.S.	228	40.57N	74.09W
Haxtun, Co., U.S. (hăks'tŭn)	110	40.39N	102.38W
Hay, r., Austl. (hā)	202	23.00S	136.45E
Hay, r., Can.	84	60.21N	117.14W
Hayama, Japan (hä-yä'mä)	195a	35.16N	139.35E
Hayashi, Japan (hä-yä'shē)	195a	35.13N	139.38E
Hayden, Az., U.S. (hā'dĕn)	109	33.00N	110.50W
Hayes, neigh., Eng., U.K.	235	51.23N	0.01E
Hayes, r., Can.	85	55.25N	93.55W
Hayes, Mount, mtn., Ak., U.S. (hāz)	95	63.32N	146.40W
Haynesville, La., U.S. (hānz'vĭl)	113	32.55N	93.08W
Hayrabolu, Tur.	161	41.14N	27.05E
Hay River, Can.	84	60.50N	115.53W
Hays, Ks., U.S. (hāz)	110	38.51N	99.20W
Haystack Mountain, mtn., Wa., U.S. (hā-stăk')	106a	48.26N	122.07W
Haysyn, Ukr.	167	48.46N	29.22E
Hayward, Ca., U.S. (hā'wērd)	106b	37.40N	122.06W
Hayward, Wi., U.S.	103	46.01N	91.31W
Hazard, Ky., U.S. (hăz'ȧrd)	114	37.13N	83.10W
Hazel Grove, Eng., U.K.	237b	53.23N	2.08W
Hazelhurst, Ga., U.S. (hā'z'l-hûrst)	115	31.50N	82.36W
Hazelhurst, Ms., U.S.	114	31.52N	90.23W
Hazel Park, Mi., U.S.	101b	42.28N	83.06W
Hazelton, Can. (hā'z'l-tŭn)	84	55.15N	127.40W
Hazelton Mountains, mts., Can.	86	55.00N	128.00W
Hazleton, Pa., U.S.	99	41.00N	76.00W
Headland, Al., U.S. (hĕd'lănd)	114	31.22N	85.20W
Headley, Eng., U.K.	235	51.17N	0.16W
Heald Green, Eng., U.K.	237b	53.22N	2.14W
Healdsburg, Ca., U.S. (hēldz'bûrg)	108	38.37N	122.52W
Healdton, Ok., U.S. (hēld'tŭn)	111	34.13N	97.28W
Heanor, Eng., U.K. (hēn'ŏr)	144a	53.01N	1.22W
Heard Island, i., Austl. (hûrd)	3	53.10S	74.35E
Hearne, Tx., U.S. (hûrn)	113	30.53N	96.35W
Hearst, Can. (hûrst)	85	49.36N	83.40W
Heart, r., N.D., U.S. (härt)	102	46.46N	102.34W
Heart Lake Indian Reserve, I.R., Can.	87	55.02N	111.30W
Heart's Content, Can. (härts kŏn'tĕnt)	93	47.52N	53.22W
Heathmont, Austl.	243b	37.49S	145.15E
Heaton Moor, Eng., U.K.	237b	53.25N	2.11W
Heavener, Ok., U.S. (hēv'nēr)	111	34.52N	94.36W
Heaverham, Eng., U.K.	235	51.18N	0.15E
Heaviley, Eng., U.K.	237b	53.24N	2.09W
Hebbronville, Tx., U.S. (hē'brŭn-vĭl)	112	27.18N	98.40W
Hebbville, Md., U.S.	229c	39.20N	77.46W
Hebei, prov., China (hŭ-bā)	189	39.15N	115.40E
Heber City, Ut., U.S. (hē'bēr)	109	40.30N	111.25W
Heber Springs, Ar., U.S.	111	35.28N	91.59W
Hebgen Lake, res., Mt., U.S. (hĕb'gĕn)	105	44.47N	111.38W
Hebrides, is., Scot., U.K.	142	57.00N	6.30W
Hebrides, Sea of the, sea, Scot., U.K.	150	57.00N	7.00W
Hebron, Can. (hĕb'rŭn)	85	58.11N	62.56W
Hebron, In., U.S.	101a	41.19N	87.13W
Hebron, Ky., U.S.	101f	39.04N	84.43W
Hebron, Ne., U.S.	111	40.11N	97.36W
Hebron, N.D., U.S.	102	46.54N	102.04W
Hebron see Al Khalīl, W. Bank	181a	31.31N	35.07E
Heby, Swe. (hĭ'bü)	152	59.56N	16.48E
Hecate Strait, strt., Can. (hĕk'ȧ-tē)	84	53.00N	131.00W
Hecelchakán, Mex. (ā-sĕl-chä-kän')	119	20.10N	90.09W
Hechi, China (hŭ-chr)	193	24.50N	108.18E
Hechuan, China (hŭ-chyuän)	188	30.00N	106.20E
Hecla Island, i., Can.	89	51.08N	96.45W
Hedemora, Swe. (hĭ-dĕ-mō'rä)	152	60.16N	15.55E
Hedon, Eng., U.K. (hĕ-dŭn)	144a	53.44N	0.12W
Heemstede, Neth.	145a	52.20N	4.36E
Heerdt, neigh., Ger.	236	51.13N	6.43E
Heerlen, Neth.	151	50.55N	5.58E
Hefei, China (hŭ-fā)	189	31.51N	117.15E
Heflin, Al., U.S. (hĕf'lĭn)	114	33.40N	85.33W
Heide, Ger. (hī'dē)	154	54.13N	9.06E
Heide, neigh., Ger.	236	51.31N	6.52E
Heidelberg, Austl. (hī'dĕl-bûrg)	201a	37.45S	145.04E
Heidelberg, Ger. (hīdĕl-bĕrgh)	147	49.24N	8.43E
Heidelberg, S. Afr.	218d	26.32S	28.22E
Heidelberg, Pa., U.S.	230b	40.23N	80.05W
Heidenheim, Ger. (hī'dĕn-hīm)	154	48.41N	10.09E
Heil, Ger.	236	51.38N	7.35E
Heilbron, S. Afr. (hĭl'brōn)	218d	27.17S	27.58E
Heilbronn, Ger. (hīl'brōn)	147	49.09N	9.16E
Heiligenhaus, Ger. (hī'lē-gĕn-houz)	157c	51.19N	6.58E
Heiligensee, neigh., Ger.	238a	52.36N	13.13E
Heiligenstadt, Ger. (hī'lē-gĕn-shtät)	154	51.21N	10.10E
Heilongjiang, prov., China (hā-lôn-jyäŋ)	189	46.36N	128.07E
Heinersdorf, Ger.	238a	52.23N	13.20E
Heinersdorf, neigh., Ger.	238a	52.34N	13.27E
Heinola, Fin. (hå-nō'lȧ)	153	61.13N	26.03E
Heinsberg, Ger. (hīnz'bĕrgh)	157c	51.04N	6.07E
Heisingen, neigh., Ger.	236	51.25N	7.04E
Heist-op-den-Berg, Bel.	145a	51.05N	4.14E
Hejaz see Al Ḩijāz, reg., Sau. Ar.	182	23.45N	39.08E
Hejian, China (hŭ-jyĕn)	192	38.28N	116.05E
Hekla, vol., Ice.	142	63.53N	19.37W
Hel, Pol. (hāl)	155	54.37N	18.53E
Helagsfjället, mtn., Swe.	146	62.54N	12.24E
Helan Shan, mts., China (hŭ-län shän)	188	38.02N	105.20E
Helena, Ar., U.S. (hē-lē'nȧ)	97	34.33N	90.35W
Helena, Mt., U.S. (hĕ-lē'nȧ)	96	46.35N	112.01W
Helensburgh, Austl. (hĕl'ĕnz-bŭr-ō)	201b	34.11S	150.59E
Helensburgh, Scot., U.K.	150	56.01N	4.53W
Helgoland, i., Ger. (hĕl'gō-lănd)	154	54.13N	7.30E
Heliopolis, hist., Egypt	244a	30.08N	31.17E
Hellier, Ky., U.S. (hĕl'yēr)	115	37.16N	82.27W
Hellín, Spain (ĕl-yén')	148	38.30N	1.40W
Hells Canyon, val., U.S.	104	45.20N	116.45W
Helmand, r., Afg. (hĕl'mŭnd)	182	31.00N	63.48E
Helmond, Neth. (hĕl'mōnt) (ĕl'môɴ')	151	51.35N	5.04E
Helmstedt, Ger. (hĕlm'shtĕt)	154	52.14N	11.03E
Hel'myaziv, Ukr.	163	49.49N	31.54E
Helotes, Tx., U.S. (hē'lōts)	107d	29.35N	98.41W
Helper, Ut., U.S. (hĕlp'ēr)	109	39.40N	110.55W
Helsby, Eng., U.K.	237a	53.16N	2.46W
Helsingborg, Swe. (hĕl'sĭng-bôrgh)	146	56.04N	12.40E
Helsingfors see Helsinki, Fin.	142	60.10N	24.53E
Helsingør, Den. (hĕl-sĭng-ûr')	146	56.03N	12.33E
Helsinki, Fin. (hĕl'sėn-kė)	142	60.10N	24.53E
Hemel Hempstead, Eng., U.K. (hĕm'ĕl hĕmp'stĕd)	144b	51.43N	0.29W
Hemer, Ger.	157c	51.22N	7.46E
Hemet, Ca., U.S. (hĕm'ĕt)	107a	33.45N	116.57W
Hemingford, Ne., U.S. (hĕm'ĭng-fērd)	102	42.21N	103.30W
Hemphill, Tx., U.S. (hĕmp'hĭl)	113	31.20N	93.48W
Hempstead, N.Y., U.S. (hĕmp'stĕd)	100a	40.42N	73.37W
Hempstead, Tx., U.S.	113	30.07N	96.05W
Hemse, Swe. (hĕm'sĕ)	152	57.15N	18.25E
Hemsön, i., Swe.	152	62.43N	18.22E
Henan, prov., China (hŭ-nän)	189	33.58N	112.33E
Henares, r., Spain (å-nä'rås)	158	40.50N	2.55W
Henderson, Ky., U.S. (hĕn'dēr-sŭn)	98	37.50N	87.30W
Henderson, Nv., U.S.	108	36.09N	115.04W
Henderson, N.C., U.S.	115	36.18N	78.24W
Henderson, Tn., U.S.	114	35.25N	88.40W
Henderson, Tx., U.S.	113	32.09N	94.48W
Hendersonville, N.C., U.S. (hĕn'dēr-sŭn-vĭl)	115	35.17N	82.28W
Hendersonville, Tn., U.S.	114	36.18N	86.37W
Hendon, Eng., U.K. (hĕn'dŭn)	144b	51.34N	0.13W
Hendrina, S. Afr. (hĕn-drē'nȧ)	218d	26.10S	29.44E
Hengch'un, Tai. (hĕng'chŭn')	193	22.00N	120.42E
Hengelo, Neth. (hĕŋĕ-lō)	151	52.20N	6.45E
Hengshan, China (hĕng'shän')	193	27.20N	112.40E
Hengshui, China (hĕng'sho͞o-ē')	190	37.43N	115.42E
Hengxian, China (hŭŋ shyĕn)	193	22.40N	109.20E
Hengyang, China	189	26.58N	112.30E

ng-sing; ŋ-baŋk; ɴ-nasalized n; nŏd; cŏmmit; ōld; ôbey; ôrder; oi-boil; fo͞od; ȯ-as oo in foot; ou-out; s-soft; sh-dish; th-thin; pūre; ůnite; ûrn; stŭd; circŭs; ü-as in French tu; '-indeterminate vowel.

296 Heniches'k – Holly

PLACE (Pronunciation)	PAGE	Lat. °'	Long. °'
Heniches'k, Ukr.	167	46.11N	34.47E
Henley on Thames, Eng., U.K. (hĕn'lē ŏn tĕmz)	144b	51.31N	0.54W
Henlopen, Cape, c., De., U.S. (hĕn-lō'pĕn)	99	38.45N	75.05W
Hennebont, Fr. (ĕn-bôN')	156	47.47N	3.16W
Hennenman, S. Afr.	218d	27.59S	27.03E
Hennessey, Ok., U.S. (hĕn'ĕ-sĭ)	111	36.04N	97.53W
Hennigsdorf, Ger. (hĕ'nēngz-dōrf))	145b	52.39N	13.12E
Hennops, r., S. Afr. (hĕn'ŏps)	213b	25.51S	27.57E
Hennopsrivier, S. Afr.	213b	25.50S	27.59E
Henrietta, Ok., U.S. (hĕn-rĭ-ĕt'á)	111	35.25N	95.58W
Henrietta, Tx., U.S. (hen-rĭ-ĕ'tá)	110	33.47N	98.11W
Henrietta Maria, Cape, c., Can. (hĕn-rĭ-ĕt'á)	85	55.10N	82.20W
Henry Mountains, mts., Ut., U.S. (hĕn'rĭ)	96	37.55N	110.45W
Henrys Fork, r., Id., U.S.	105	43.52N	111.55W
Henteyn Nuruu, mtn., Russia	192	49.40N	111.00E
Hentiyn Nuruu, mts., Mong.	188	49.25N	107.51E
Henzada, Myanmar	183	17.38N	95.28E
Heppner, Or., U.S. (hĕp'nẽr)	104	45.21N	119.33W
Hepu, China (hŭ-pōō)	193	21.28N	109.10E
Herāt, Afg. (hĕ-rāt')	182	34.28N	62.13E
Herbede, Ger.	236	51.25N	7.16E
Hercules, Can.	83g	53.27N	113.20W
Herdecke, Ger. (hĕr'dĕ-kĕ)	157c	51.24N	7.26E
Heredia, C.R. (ā-rā'dhē-ä)	121	10.04N	84.06W
Hereford, Eng., U.K. (hĕrĕ'fẽrd)	150	52.05N	2.44W
Hereford, Md., U.S.	100e	39.35N	76.42W
Hereford, Tx., U.S. (hĕr'ĕ-fẽrd)	110	34.47N	102.25W
Hereford and Worcester, co., Eng., U.K.	144a	52.24N	2.15W
Herencia, Spain (å-rān'thē-ä)	158	39.23N	3.22W
Herentals, Bel.	145a	51.10N	4.51E
Herford, Ger. (hĕr'fôrt)	154	52.06N	8.42E
Herington, Ks., U.S. (hĕr'ĭng-tŭn)	111	38.41N	96.57W
Herisau, Switz. (hā'rē-zou)	154	47.23N	9.18E
Herk-de-Stad, Bel.	145a	50.56N	5.13E
Herkimer, N.Y., U.S. (hûr'kĭ-mẽr)	99	43.05N	75.00W
Hermannskogel, mtn., Aus.	239e	48.16N	16.18E
Hermansville, Mi., U.S. (hûr'mǎns-vĭl)	98	45.40N	87.35W
Hermantown, Mn., U.S. (hẽr'mǎn-toun)	107h	46.46N	92.12W
Hermanusdorings, S. Afr.	218d	24.08S	27.46E
Herminie, Pa., U.S. (hûr-mĭ'nē)	101e	40.16N	79.45W
Hermitage Bay, b., Can. (hûr'mĭ-tĕj)	93	47.35N	56.05W
Hermit Islands, is., Pap. N. Gui. (hûr'mĭt)	197	1.48S	144.55E
Hermosa Beach, Ca., U.S. (hẽr-mō'sȧ)	107a	33.51N	118.24W
Hermosillo, Mex. (ĕr-mô-sē'l-yō)	116	29.00N	110.57W
Hermsdorf, neigh., Ger.	238a	52.37N	13.18E
Hernals, neigh., Aus.	239e	48.13N	16.20E
Herndon, Va., U.S. (hĕrn'don)	100e	38.58N	77.22W
Herne, Ger. (hĕr'nĕ)	157c	51.32N	7.13E
Herning, Den. (hĕr'nĭng)	146	56.08N	8.55E
Hernwood Heights, Md., U.S.	229c	39.22N	77.50W
Héroes Chapultepec, Mex.	233a	19.28N	99.04W
Héroes de Churubusco, Mex.	233a	19.22N	99.06W
Heron, l., Mn., U.S. (hĕr'ŭn)	102	43.42N	95.23W
Herongate, Eng., U.K.	235	51.36N	0.21E
Heron Lake, Mn., U.S.	102	43.48N	95.20W
Heronsgate, Eng., U.K.	235	51.38N	0.31W
Herrero, Punta, Mex. (pŏ'n-tä-ĕr-rĕ'rô)	120a	19.18N	87.24W
Herrin, Il., U.S. (hĕr'ĭn)	98	37.50N	89.00W
Herschel, S. Afr. (hĕr'-shĕl)	213c	30.37S	27.12E
Herscher, Il., U.S. (hĕr'shẽr)	101a	41.03N	88.06W
Hersham, Eng., U.K.	235	51.22N	0.23W
Herstal, Bel. (hĕr'stäl)	151	50.42N	5.32E
Herten, Ger.	236	51.35N	7.07E
Hertford, Eng., U.K.	150	51.48N	0.05W
Hertford, N.C., U.S. (hûrt'fẽrd)	115	36.10N	76.30W
Hertfordshire, co., Eng., U.K.	144b	51.46N	0.05W
Hertzberg, Ger. (hĕrtz'bĕrgh)	145b	52.54N	12.58E
Hervás, Spain	158	40.16N	5.51W
Herzliyya, Isr.	181a	32.10N	34.49E
Hessen, hist. reg., Ger. (hĕs'ĕn)	154	50.42N	9.00E
Heswall, Eng., U.K.	237a	53.20N	3.06W
Hetch Hetchy Aqueduct, Ca., U.S. (hĕtch hĕt'chĭ ăk'wē-dŭkt)	108	37.27N	120.54W
Hettinger, N.D., U.S. (hĕt'ĭn-jẽr)	102	45.58N	102.36W
Hetzendorf, neigh., Aus.	239e	48.10N	16.18E
Heuningspruit, S. Afr.	218d	27.28S	27.26E
Heven, neigh., Ger.	236	51.26N	7.17E
Hewlett, N.Y., U.S.	228	40.38N	73.42W
Hewlett Harbor, N.Y., U.S.	228	40.38N	73.41W
Hexian, China	190	31.44N	118.20E
Hexian, China (hŭ shyĕn)	193	24.20N	111.28E
Hextable, Eng., U.K.	235	51.25N	0.11E
Heyang, China (hŭ-yäŋ)	192	35.18N	110.18E
Heystekrand, S. Afr.	218d	25.16S	27.14E
Heyuan, China (hŭ-yůän)	193	23.48N	114.45E
Heywood, Eng., U.K. (hā'wŏd)	144a	53.36N	2.12W
Heze, China (hŭ-dzŭ)	190	35.13N	115.28E
Hialeah, Fl., U.S. (hī-ȧ-lē'ăh)	115a	25.49N	80.18W
Hiawatha, Ks., U.S. (hī-á-wô'thá)	111	39.50N	95.33W
Hiawatha, Ut., U.S.	109	39.25N	111.05W
Hibbing, Mn., U.S. (hĭb'ĭng)	97	47.26N	92.58W
Hickman, Ky., U.S. (hĭk'mǎn)	114	34.33N	89.10W
Hickory, N.C., U.S. (hĭk'ō-rĭ)	115	35.43N	81.21W
Hickory Hills, Il., U.S.	231a	41.43N	87.49W
Hicksville, N.Y., U.S.	98	41.15N	84.45W
Hicksville, N.Y., U.S. (hĭks'vĭl)	100a	40.47N	73.25W
Hico, Tx., U.S. (hī'kō)	112	32.00N	98.02W
Hidalgo, Mex.	112	27.49N	99.53W
Hidalgo, Mex. (ē-dhäl'gō)	118	24.14N	99.25W
Hidalgo, state, Mex.	116	20.45N	99.30W
Hidalgo del Parral, Mex. (ē-dä'l-gō-dĕl-pär-rá'l)	116	26.55N	105.40W

PLACE (Pronunciation)	PAGE	Lat. °'	Long. °'
Hidalgo Yalalag, Mex. (ē-dhäl'gō-yä-lä-läg)	119	17.12N	96.11W
Hiddinghausen, Ger.	236	51.22N	7.17E
Hierro Island, i., Spain (yĕ'r-rô)	210	27.37N	18.29W
Hiesfeld, Ger.	236	51.33N	6.46E
Hietzing, neigh., Aus.	239e	48.11N	16.18E
Higashi, neigh., Japan	242b	34.41N	135.31E
Higashimurayama, Japan	195a	35.46N	139.28E
Higashinada, neigh., Japan	242b	34.43N	135.16E
Higashinakano, Japan	242a	35.38N	139.25E
Higashinari, neigh., Japan	242b	34.40N	135.33E
Higashiōizumi, neigh., Japan	242a	35.45N	139.36E
Higashiōsaka, Japan	195b	34.40N	135.44E
Higashisumiyoshi, neigh., Japan	242b	34.37N	135.32E
Higashiyama, neigh., Japan	241e	35.00N	135.48E
Higashiyodogawa, neigh., Japan	242b	34.44N	135.29E
Higgins, l., Mi., U.S. (hĭg'ĭnz)	98	44.20N	84.45W
Higginsville, Mo., U.S. (hĭg'ĭnz-vĭl)	111	39.05N	93.44W
High, i., Mi., U.S.	98	45.45N	85.45W
Higham, Eng., U.K.	235	51.26N	0.28E
High Beach, Eng., U.K.	235	51.39N	0.02E
High Bluff, Can.	83f	50.01N	98.08W
Highborne Cay, i., Bah. (hībôrn kē)	122	24.45N	76.50W
Highcliff, Pa., U.S.	230b	40.32N	80.03W
Higher Broughton, neigh., Eng., U.K.	237b	53.30N	2.15W
Highgrove, Ca., U.S. (hī'grōv)	107a	34.01N	117.20W
High Island, Tx., U.S.	113a	29.34N	94.24W
Highland, Ca., U.S. (hī'lănd)	107a	34.08N	117.13W
Highland, Il., U.S.	111	38.44N	89.41W
Highland, In., U.S.	101a	41.33N	87.28W
Highland, Mi., U.S.	101b	42.38N	83.37W
Highland, Pa., U.S.	230b	40.33N	80.04W
Highland Park, Il., U.S.	101a	42.11N	87.47W
Highland Park, Md., U.S.	229d	38.54N	76.54W
Highland Park, Mi., U.S.	101b	42.24N	83.06W
Highland Park, N.J., U.S.	100a	40.30N	74.25W
Highland Park, Tx., U.S.	107c	32.49N	96.48W
Highlands, N.J., U.S. (hī-lăndz)	100a	40.24N	73.59W
Highlands, Tx., U.S.	113a	29.49N	95.01W
High Laver, Eng., U.K.	235	51.45N	0.13E
Highmore, S.D., U.S. (hī'mōr)	102	44.30N	99.26W
High Ongar, Eng., U.K. (on'gẽr)	144b	51.43N	0.15E
High Peak, mtn., Phil.	197a	15.38N	120.05E
High Point, N.C., U.S.	115	35.55N	80.00W
High Prairie, Can.	84	55.26N	116.29W
High Ridge, Mo., U.S.	107e	38.27N	90.32W
High River, Can.	84	50.35N	113.52W
High Rock Lake, res., N.C., U.S. (hī'-rŏk)	115	35.40N	80.15W
High Springs, Fl., U.S.	115	29.48N	82.38W
High Tatra Mountains, mts., Eur.	155	49.15N	19.40E
Hightown, Eng., U.K.	237a	53.32N	3.04W
Hightstown, N.J., U.S. (hīts-toun)	100a	40.16N	74.32W
High Wycombe, Eng., U.K. (wĭ-kŭm)	150	51.36N	0.45W
Higuero, Punta, c., P.R.	117b	18.21N	67.11W
Higuerote, Ven. (ē-gĕ-rô'tĕ)	131b	10.29N	66.06W
Higüey, Dom. Rep. (ē-gwĕ'y)	123	18.40N	68.45W
Hiiumaa, i., Est. (hē'ŏm-ô)	166	58.47N	22.05E
Hikone, Japan (hē'kō-nĕ)	195	35.15N	136.15E
Hildburghausen, Ger. (hĭld'bŏrg hou-zĕn)	154	50.26N	10.45E
Hilden, Ger. (hēl'dĕn)	157c	51.10N	6.56E
Hildesheim, Ger. (hĭl'dĕs-hīm)	147	52.08N	9.56E
Hillaby, Mount, mtn., Barb. (hĭl'á-bĭ)	121b	13.15N	59.35W
Hill City, Ks., U.S. (hĭl)	110	39.22N	99.54W
Hill City, Mn., U.S.	103	46.58N	93.38W
Hill Crest, Pa., U.S.	229b	40.05N	75.11W
Hillcrest Heights, Md., U.S.	229d	38.52N	76.57W
Hillegersberg, Neth.	145a	51.57N	4.29E
Hillen, neigh., Ger.	236	51.37N	7.13E
Hillerød, Den. (hē'lĕ-rûdh)	152	55.56N	12.17E
Hillingdon, neigh., Eng., U.K.	235	51.32N	0.27W
Hillsboro, Il., U.S. (hĭlz'bŭr-ō)	111	39.09N	89.28W
Hillsboro, Ks., U.S.	111	38.22N	97.11W
Hillsboro, N.H., U.S.	99	43.05N	71.55W
Hillsboro, N.D., U.S.	102	47.23N	97.05W
Hillsboro, Oh., U.S.	98	39.10N	83.40W
Hillsboro, Or., U.S.	106c	45.31N	122.59W
Hillsboro, Tx., U.S.	113	32.01N	97.06W
Hillsboro, Wi., U.S.	103	43.39N	90.20W
Hillsburgh, Can. (hĭlz'bûrg)	83d	43.48N	80.09W
Hills Creek Lake, res., Or., U.S.	104	43.41N	122.26W
Hillsdale, Mi., U.S. (hĭls-dāl)	109	41.55N	84.35W
Hillside, Md., U.S.	229d	38.52N	76.55W
Hillside, neigh., N.Y., U.S.	228	40.42N	73.47W
Hillwood, Va., U.S.	229d	38.52N	77.10W
Hilo, Hi., U.S. (hē'lō)	96c	19.44N	155.01W
Hiltrop, neigh., Ger.	236	51.30N	7.15E
Hilvarenbeek, Neth.	145a	51.29N	5.10E
Hilversum, Neth. (hĭl'vẽr-sŭm)	145a	52.13N	5.10E
Himachal Pradesh, India	183	32.00N	77.30E
Himalayas, mts., Asia	183	29.30N	85.02E
Himeji, Japan (hē'mȧ-jē)	194	34.50N	134.42E
Himmelgeist, neigh., Ger.	236	51.10N	6.49E
Himmelpforten, Ger. (hē'mĕl-pfōr-tĕn)	145c	53.37N	9.19E
Ḩimş, Syria	182	34.44N	36.43E
Hinche, Haiti (hēn'chȧ) (ăNsh)	123	19.10N	72.05W
Hinchinbrook, i., Austl. (hĭn-chĭn-brŏŏk)	202	18.23S	146.57E
Hinckley, Eng., U.K. (hĭnk'lĭ)	144a	52.32N	1.21W
Hindley, Eng., U.K. (hĭnd'lĭ)	144a	53.32N	2.35W
Hindu Kush, mts., Asia (hĭn'dōō kōōsh')	183	35.15N	68.44E
Hindupur, India (hĭn'dōō-pōōr)	187	13.52N	77.34E
Hingham, Ma., U.S. (hĭng'ăm)	93a	42.14N	70.53W
Hinkley, Oh., U.S. (hĭnk'-lĭ)	101d	41.14N	81.45W
Hino, Japan	242a	35.41N	139.24E
Hinojosa del Duque, Spain (ē-nô-kô'sä)	158	38.30N	5.09W
Hinsdale, Il., U.S. (hĭnz'dāl)	101a	41.48N	87.56W

PLACE (Pronunciation)	PAGE	Lat. °'	Long. °'
Hinsel, neigh., Ger.	236	51.26N	7.05E
Hinton, Can. (hĭn'tŭn)	87	53.25N	117.34W
Hinton, W.V., U.S. (hĭn'tŭn)	98	37.40N	80.55W
Hirado, i., Japan (hē'rä-dō)	194	33.19N	129.18E
Hirakata, Japan (hē'rä-kä'tä)	195b	34.49N	135.40E
Hirara, Japan	198d	24.48N	125.17E
Hiratsuka, Japan (hē-rät-sōō'kȧ)	195	35.20N	139.19E
Hirosaki, Japan (hē'rô-sä'kē)	189	40.31N	140.38E
Hirose, Japan (hē'rô-sā)	195	35.20N	133.11E
Hiroshima, Japan (hē-rô-shē'mȧ)	189	34.22N	132.25E
Hirota, Japan	242b	34.45N	135.21E
Hirschstetten, neigh., Aus.	239e	48.14N	16.29E
Hirson, Fr. (ēr-sôN')	156	49.54N	4.00E
Hisar, India	186	29.15N	75.47E
Hispaniola, i., N.A. (hĭ'spăn-ĭ-ō-lȧ)	117	17.30N	73.15W
Hitachi, Japan (hē-tä'chē)	194	36.42N	140.47E
Hitchcock, Tx., U.S. (hĭch'kŏk)	113a	29.21N	95.01W
Hither Green, neigh., Eng., U.K.	235	51.27N	0.01W
Hitoyoshi, Japan (hē'tô-yō'shē)	195	32.13N	130.45E
Hitra, i., Nor. (hĭträ)	146	63.34N	7.37E
Hittefeld, Ger. (hē'tĕ-fĕld)	145c	53.23N	9.59E
Hiwasa, Japan (hē'wȧ-sä)	195	33.44N	134.31E
Hiwassee, r., Tn., U.S. (hī-wôs'sē)	114	35.10N	84.35W
Hjälmaren, l., Swe.	146	59.07N	16.05E
Hjo, Swe. (yō)	152	58.19N	14.11E
Hjørring, Den. (jûr'ĭng)	146	57.27N	9.59E
Hlobyne, Ukr.	163	49.22N	33.17E
Hlohovec, Slvk. (hlô'ho-vĕts)	155	48.24N	17.49E
Hlukhiv, Ukr.	167	51.42N	33.52E
Hobart, Austl. (hō'bȧrt)	203	43.00S	147.30E
Hobart, In., U.S.	101a	41.31N	87.15W
Hobart, Ok., U.S.	110	35.02N	99.06W
Hobart, Wa., U.S.	106a	47.25N	121.58W
Hobbs, N.M., U.S. (hŏbs)	110	32.41N	103.15W
Hoboken, Bel. (hō'bō-kĕn)	145a	51.11N	4.20E
Hoboken, N.J., U.S.	100a	40.43N	74.03W
Hobro, Den. (hô-brô')	152	56.38N	9.47E
Hobson, Va., U.S. (hŏb'sŭn)	100g	36.54N	76.31W
Hobson's Bay, b., Austl. (hŏb'sŭnz)	201a	37.54S	144.45E
Hobyo, Som.	218a	5.24N	48.28E
Hochdahl, Ger.	236	51.13N	6.56E
Hochheide, Ger.	236	51.27N	6.41E
Ho Chi Minh City, Viet.	196	10.46N	106.34E
Hochlar, neigh., Ger.	236	51.36N	7.10E
Höchsten, Ger.	236	51.27N	7.29E
Hockinson, Wa., U.S. (hŏk'ĭn-sŭn)	106c	45.44N	122.29W
Hoctún, Mex. (ŏk-tōō'n)	120a	20.52N	89.10W
Hodgenville, Ky., U.S. (hŏj'ĕn-vĭl)	98	37.35N	85.45W
Hodges Hill, mtn., Can. (hŏj'ĕz)	93	49.04N	55.53W
Hodgkins, Il., U.S.	231a	41.46N	87.51W
Hódmezővásárhely, Hung. (hōd'mĕ-zû-vô'shôr-hĕl-y')	155	46.24N	20.21E
Hodna, Chott el, l., Alg.	148	35.20N	3.27E
Hodonin, Czech Rep. (hē'dō-nēn)	155	48.50N	17.06E
Hoegaarden, Bel.	145a	50.46N	4.55E
Hoek van Holland, Neth.	145a	51.59N	4.05E
Hoeryŏng, N. Kor. (hwĕr'yŭng)	194	42.28N	129.39E
Hof, Ger. (hōf)	154	50.19N	11.55E
Hofburg, pt. of i., Aus.	239e	48.12N	16.22E
Hofsjökull, ice., Ice. (hôfs'yü'kōōl)	146	64.55N	18.40W
Hog, i., Mi., U.S.	98	45.50N	85.20W
Hogansville, Ga., U.S. (hō'gănz-vĭl)	114	33.10N	84.54W
Hogar y Redención, Mex.	233a	19.22N	99.13W
Hog Cay, i., Bah.	123	23.35N	75.30W
Hogsty Reef, rf., Bah.	123	21.45N	73.50W
Hohenbrunn, Ger. (hō'hĕn-brōōn)	145d	48.03N	11.42E
Hohenlimburg, Ger. (hō'hĕn lĕm'bōōrg)	157c	51.20N	7.35E
Hohen Neuendorf, Ger. (hō'hĕn noi'ĕn-dōrf)	145b	52.40N	13.22E
Hohenschönhausen, neigh., Ger.	238a	52.33N	13.30E
Hohensyburg, hist., Ger.	236	51.25N	7.29E
Hohe Tauern, mts., Aus. (hō'ĕ tou'ĕrn)	154	47.11N	12.12E
Hohhot, China (hŭ-hōō-tŭ)	189	41.05N	111.50E
Hohoe, Ghana	214	7.09N	0.28E
Hohokus, N.J., U.S. (hō-hō-kŭs)	100a	41.01N	74.08W
Höhscheid, neigh., Ger.	236	51.09N	7.04E
Hoi An, Viet.	193	15.48N	108.30E
Hoisington, Ks., U.S. (hoi'zĭng-tŭn)	110	38.30N	98.46W
Hoisten, Ger.	236	51.08N	6.42E
Hojo, Japan (hō'jō)	195	33.58N	132.50E
Hokitika, N.Z. (hō-kĭ-tē'kä)	203a	42.43S	170.59E
Hokkaidō, i., Japan (hŏk'kĭ-dō)	194	43.30N	142.45E
Holbaek, Den. (hōl'bĕk)	152	55.42N	11.40E
Holborn, neigh., Eng., U.K.	235	51.31N	0.07W
Holbox, Mex. (ôl-bŏ'x)	120a	21.33N	87.19W
Holbox, Isla, i., Mex. (ē's-lä-ôl-bŏ'x)	120a	21.40N	87.21W
Holbrook, Az., U.S. (hōl'brŏŏk)	109	34.55N	110.15W
Holbrook, Ma., U.S.	93a	42.10N	71.01W
Holden, Ma., U.S. (hōl'dĕn)	93a	42.21N	71.51W
Holden, Mo., U.S.	111	38.42N	94.00W
Holden, W.V., U.S.	98	37.45N	82.05W
Holdenville, Ok., U.S. (hōl'dĕn-vĭl)	111	35.05N	96.25W
Holdrege, Ne., U.S. (hōl'drĕj)	110	40.25N	99.28W
Holguín, Cuba (ôl-gēn')	117	20.55N	76.15W
Holguín, prov., Cuba	122	20.40N	76.15W
Holidaysburg, Pa., U.S. (hŏl'ĭ-dāz-bûrg)	99	40.30N	78.30W
Hollabrunn, Aus.	154	48.33N	16.04E
Holland, Mi., U.S. (hŏl'ănd)	98	42.45N	86.10W
Hollands Diep, strt., Neth.	145a	51.43N	4.25E
Hollenstedt, Ger. (hō'lĕn-shtĕt)	145c	53.22N	9.43E
Hollins, Eng., U.K.	237b	53.34N	2.17W
Hollis, N.H., U.S. (hŏl'ĭs)	93a	42.30N	71.29W
Hollis, Ok., U.S.	110	34.39N	99.56W
Hollis, neigh., N.Y., U.S.	228	40.43N	73.46W
Hollister, Ca., U.S. (hŏl'ĭs-tẽr)	108	36.50N	121.25W
Holliston, Ma., U.S. (hŏl'ĭs-tŭn)	93a	42.12N	71.25W
Holly, Mi., U.S. (hŏl'ĭ)	98	42.45N	83.30W

PLACE (Pronunciation)	PAGE	Lat. °′	Long. °′
Holly, Wa., U.S.	106a	47.34N	122.58W
Holly Springs, Ms., U.S. (hŏl′ĭ sprĭngz)	114	34.45N	89.28W
Hollywood, Ca., U.S. (hŏl′ē-wo͝od)	107a	34.06N	118.20W
Hollywood, Fl., U.S.	115a	26.00N	80.11W
Hollywood Bowl, pt. of i., Ca., U.S.	232	34.07N	118.20W
Holmes, Pa., U.S.	229b	39.54N	75.19W
Holmes Reefs, rf., Austl. (hōmz)	203	16.33S	148.43E
Holmes Run Acres, Va., U.S.	229d	38.51N	77.13W
Holmestrand, Nor. (hôl′mĕ-strän)	152	59.29N	10.17E
Holmsbu, Nor. (hôlms′bo͞o)	152	59.36N	10.26E
Holmsjön, l., Swe.	152	62.23N	15.43E
Holroyd, Austl.	243a	33.50S	150.58E
Holstebro, Den. (hôl′stĕ-brô)	146	56.22N	8.39E
Holston, r., Tn., U.S. (hōl′stŭn)	114	36.02N	83.42W
Holt, Eng., U.K. (hōlt)	144a	53.05N	2.53W
Holten, neigh., Ger.	236	51.31N	6.48E
Holthausen, neigh., Ger.	236	51.34N	7.26E
Holton, Ks., U.S. (hōl′tŭn)	111	39.27N	95.43W
Holy Cross, Ak., U.S. (hō′lĭ krôs)	95	62.10N	159.40W
Holyhead, Wales, U.K. (hŏl′ē-hĕd)	150	53.18N	4.45W
Holy Island, i., Eng., U.K.	150	55.43N	1.48W
Holy Island, i., Wales, U.K. (hō′lĭ)	150	53.15N	4.45W
Holyoke, Co., U.S. (hōl′yōk)	110	40.36N	102.18W
Holyoke, Ma., U.S.	99	42.10N	72.40W
Holzen, Ger.	236	51.26N	7.31E
Holzheim, Ger.	236	51.09N	6.39E
Holzwickede, Ger.	236	51.30N	7.36E
Homano, Japan (hō-mä′nō)	195a	35.33N	140.08E
Homberg, Ger. (hōm′bĕrgh)	157c	51.27N	6.42E
Hombori, Mali	214	15.17N	1.42W
Home Gardens, Ca., U.S. (hōm gär′d′nz)	107a	33.53N	117.32W
Homeland, Ca., U.S. (hōm′lănd)	107a	33.44N	117.07W
Homer, Ak., U.S. (hō′mẽr)	95	59.42N	151.30W
Homer, La., U.S.	113	32.46N	93.05W
Homer Youngs Peak, mtn., Mt., U.S.	105	45.19N	113.41W
Homestead, Fl., U.S. (hōm′stĕd)	115a	25.27N	80.28W
Homestead, Mi., U.S.	107k	46.20N	84.07W
Homestead, Pa., U.S.	101e	40.29N	79.55W
Homestead National Monument of America, rec., Ne., U.S.	111	40.16N	96.51W
Hometown, Il., U.S.	231a	41.44N	87.44W
Homewood, Al., U.S. (hōm′wo͝od)	100h	33.28N	86.48W
Homewood, Il., U.S.	101a	41.34N	87.40W
Homewood, neigh., Pa., U.S.	230b	40.27N	79.54W
Hominy, Ok., U.S. (hŏm′ĭ-nĭ)	111	36.25N	96.24W
Homochitto, r., Ms., U.S. (hō-mō-chĭt′ō)	114	31.23N	91.15W
Honda, Col. (hōn′dȧ)	130	5.13N	74.45W
Honda, Bahía, b., Cuba (bä-ē′ä-ô′n-dä)	122	23.10N	83.20W
Hondo, Tx., U.S.	112	29.20N	99.08W
Hondo, r., N.M., U.S.	110	33.22N	105.06W
Hondo, Río, r., N.A. (hon-dō′)	120a	18.16N	88.32W
Honduras, nation, N.A. (hŏn-do͞o′rȧs)	116	14.30N	88.00W
Honduras, Gulf of, b., N.A.	116	16.30N	87.30W
Honea Path, S.C., U.S. (hŭn′ĭ păth)	115	34.25N	82.16W
Hönefoss, Nor. (hē′nĕ-fôs)	146	60.10N	10.15E
Honesdale, Pa., U.S. (hōnz′dāl)	99	41.30N	75.15W
Honey Grove, Tx., U.S. (hŭn′ĭ grōv)	111	33.35N	95.54W
Honey Lake, l., Ca., U.S. (hŭn′ĭ)	108	40.11N	120.34W
Honfleur, Can. (ôN-flûr′)	83b	46.39N	70.53W
Honfleur, Fr. (ôN-flûr′)	156	49.26N	0.13E
Hon Gay, Viet.	193	20.58N	107.10E
Hong Kong, dep., Asia (hŏng′ kŏng′)	189	21.45N	115.00E
Hongshui, r., China (hôŋ-shwā)	188	24.30N	105.00E
Honguedo, Détroit d', strt., Can.	92	49.08N	63.45W
Hongze Hu, l., China	189	33.17N	118.37E
Honiara, Sol.Is.	203	9.26S	159.57E
Honiton, Eng., U.K. (hŏn′ĭ-tŏn)	150	50.49N	3.10W
Honolulu, Hi., U.S. (hŏn-ō-lo͞o′lo͞o)	96c	21.18N	157.50W
Honomu, Hi., U.S. (hŏn′ō-mo͞o)	94a	19.50N	155.04W
Honshū, i., Japan	189	36.00N	138.00E
Höntrop, neigh., Ger.	236	51.27N	7.08E
Hood, Mount, mtn., Or., U.S.	96	45.20N	121.43W
Hood Canal, b., Wa., U.S. (ho͝od)	106a	47.45N	122.45W
Hood River, Or., U.S.	96	45.42N	121.30W
Hoodsport, Wa., U.S. (ho͝odz′pōrt)	106a	47.25N	123.09W
Hooghly-Chinsura, India	240a	22.54N	88.24E
Hoogly, r., India (ho͞og′lĭ)	183	21.35N	87.50E
Hoogstraten, Bel.	145a	51.24N	4.46E
Hooker, Ok., U.S. (ho͝ok′ẽr)	110	36.49N	101.13W
Hool, Mex. (o͞o′l)	120a	19.32N	90.22W
Hoonah, Ak., U.S. (ho͞o′nä)	95	58.05N	135.25W
Hoopa Valley Indian Reservation, I.R., Ca., U.S.	104	41.18N	123.35W
Hooper, Ne., U.S. (ho͝op′ẽr)	111	41.37N	96.31W
Hooper, Ut., U.S.	107b	41.10N	112.08W
Hooper Bay, Ak., U.S.	95	61.32N	166.02W
Hoopeston, Il., U.S. (ho͞ops′tŭn)	98	40.35N	87.40W
Hoosick Falls, N.Y., U.S. (ho͞o′sĭk)	99	42.55N	73.15W
Hooton, Eng., U.K.	237a	53.18N	2.57W
Hoover Dam, Nv., U.S. (ho͞o′vẽr)	108	36.00N	115.06W
Hoover Dam, dam, U.S.	96	36.00N	114.27W
Hopatcong, Lake, l., N.J., U.S. (hō-păt′kong)	100a	40.57N	74.38W
Hope, Ak., U.S. (hōp)	95	60.54N	149.48W
Hope, Ar., U.S.	111	33.41N	93.35W
Hope, N.D., U.S.	102	47.17N	97.45W
Hope, Ben, mtn., Scot., U.K. (bĕn hōp)	150	58.25N	4.25W
Hopedale, Can. (hōp′dāl)	85	55.26N	60.11W
Hopedale, Ma., U.S. (hōp′dāl)	93a	42.08N	71.33W
Hopelchén, Mex. (o-pĕl-chĕ′n)	120a	19.47N	89.51W
Hopes Advance, Cap, c., Can. (hōps ăd-vans′)	85	61.05N	69.35W
Hopetoun, Austl. (hōp′toun)	202	33.50S	120.15E
Hopetown, S. Afr. (hōp′toun)	212	29.35S	24.10E
Hopewell, Va., U.S. (hōp′wĕl)	115	37.14N	77.15W

PLACE (Pronunciation)	PAGE	Lat. °′	Long. °′
Hopewell Culture National Historical Park, rec., Oh., U.S.	98	39.25N	83.00W
Hopi Indian Reservation, I.R., Az., U.S. (hō′pē)	109	36.20N	110.30W
Hopkins, Mn., U.S. (hŏp′kĭns)	107g	44.55N	93.24W
Hopkinsville, Ky., U.S. (hŏp′kĭns-vĭl)	97	36.50N	87.28W
Hopkinton, Ma., U.S. (hŏp′kĭn-tŭn)	93a	42.14N	71.31W
Hoppegarten, Ger.	238a	52.31N	13.40E
Hoquiam, Wa., U.S. (hō′kwĭ-ăm)	96	47.00N	123.53W
Horconcitos, Pan. (ŏr-kôn-sē′-tôs)	121	8.18N	82.11W
Hörde, neigh., Ger.	236	51.29N	7.30E
Horgen, Switz. (hôr′gĕn)	154	47.16N	8.35E
Horicon, Wi., U.S. (hŏr′ĭ-kŏn)	103	43.26N	88.40W
Horinouchi, neigh., Japan	242a	35.41N	139.40E
Horlivka, Ukr.	167	48.17N	38.03E
Hormuz, Strait of, strt., Asia (hôr′mŭz′)	182	26.30N	56.30E
Horn, i., Austl. (hôrn)	203	10.30S	143.30E
Horn, Cape *see* Hornos, Cabo de, c., Chile	132	56.00S	67.00W
Hornavan, l., Swe.	146	65.54N	16.17E
Hornchurch, neigh., Eng., U.K.	235	51.34N	0.12E
Horndon on the Hill, Eng., U.K.	235	51.31N	0.25E
Horneburg, Ger. (hôr′nĕ-bŏrgh)	145c	53.30N	9.35E
Horneburg, Ger.	236	51.38N	7.18E
Hornell, N.Y., U.S. (hôr-nĕl′)	99	42.20N	77.40W
Horn Hill, Eng., U.K.	235	51.37N	0.32W
Hornos, Cabo de, c., Chile	132	56.00S	67.00W
Horn Plateau, plat., Can.	84	62.12N	120.29W
Hornsby, Austl. (hôrnz′bĭ)	201b	33.43S	151.06E
Hornsey, neigh., Eng., U.K.	235	51.35N	0.07W
Horodenka, Ukr.	155	48.40N	25.30E
Horodnya, Ukr.	163	51.54N	31.31E
Horodok, Ukr.	155	49.47N	23.39E
Horqueta, Para. (ŏr-kĕ′tä)	132	23.20S	57.00W
Horse Creek, r., Co., U.S. (hôrs)	110	38.49N	103.48W
Horse Creek, r., Wy., U.S.	102	41.33N	104.39W
Horse Islands, is., Can.	93	50.11N	55.45W
Horsell, Eng., U.K.	235	51.19N	0.34W
Horsens, Den. (hôrs′ĕns)	152	55.50N	9.49E
Horseshoe Bay, Can. (hôrs-sho͞o)	106d	49.23N	123.16W
Horsforth, Eng., U.K. (hôrs′fŭrth)	144a	53.50N	1.38W
Horsham, Austl. (hôr′shăm) (hôrs′ăm)	203	36.42S	142.17E
Horsley, Austl.	243a	33.51S	150.51E
Horst, Ger. (hôrst)	145c	53.49N	9.37E
Horst, neigh., Ger.	236	51.32N	7.02E
Horsthausen, neigh., Ger.	236	51.33N	7.13E
Horstmar, neigh., Ger.	236	51.36N	7.33E
Hortaleza, neigh., Spain	238b	40.28N	3.39W
Horten, Nor. (hôr′tĕn)	152	59.26N	10.27E
Horton, Ks., U.S. (hôr′tŭn)	111	39.38N	95.32W
Horton, r., Ak., U.S. (hôr′tŭn)	95	68.38N	122.00W
Horton Kirby, Eng., U.K.	235	51.23N	0.15E
Horwich, Eng., U.K. (hŏr′ĭch)	144a	53.36N	2.33W
Horyn, r., Eur.	155	50.55N	26.07E
Hösel, Ger.	236	51.19N	6.54E
Hososhima, Japan (hō′sō-shē′mä)	194	32.25N	131.40E
Hospitalet, Spain	238e	41.22N	2.08E
Hoste, i., Chile (ôs′tä)	132	55.20S	70.45W
Hostotipaquillo, Mex. (ôs-tō′tĭ-pä-kēl′yō)	118	21.09N	104.05W
Hota, Japan (hō′tä)	195a	35.08N	139.50E
Hotan, China (hwô-tän)	188	37.11N	79.50E
Hotan, r., China	188	39.09N	81.08E
Hoto Mayor, Dom. Rep. (ô-tô-mä-yô′r)	123	18.45N	69.10W
Hot Springs, Ak., U.S. (hŏt sprĭngs)	95	65.00N	150.20W
Hot Springs, Ar., U.S.	97	34.29N	93.02W
Hot Springs, S.D., U.S.	102	43.28N	103.32W
Hot Springs, Va., U.S.	99	38.00N	79.55W
Hot Springs National Park, rec., Ar., U.S.	97	34.30N	93.00W
Hotte, Massif de la, mts., Haiti	123	18.25N	74.00W
Hotville, Ca., U.S. (hŏt′vĭl)	108	32.50N	115.24W
Houdan, Fr. (o͞o-däN′)	157b	48.47N	1.36E
Hough Green, Eng., U.K.	237a	53.23N	2.47W
Houghton, Mi., U.S. (hō′tŭn)	103	47.06N	88.36W
Houghton, l., Mi., U.S.	98	44.20N	84.45W
Houilles, Fr. (o͞o-yĕs′)	157b	48.55N	2.11E
Houjie, China (hwô-jyĕ)	191a	22.58N	113.39E
Houlton, Me., U.S. (hōl′tŭn)	92	46.07N	67.50W
Houma, La., U.S. (ho͞o′mȧ)	113	29.36N	90.43W
Hounslow, neigh., Eng., U.K.	235	51.29N	0.22W
Housatonic, r., U.S. (ho͞o-sȧ-tŏn′ĭk)	99	41.50N	73.25W
House Springs, Mo., U.S. (hous sprĭngs)	107e	38.24N	90.34W
Houston, Ms., U.S. (hūs′tŭn)	114	33.53N	89.00W
Houston, Tx., U.S.	97	29.46N	95.21W
Houston Ship Channel, strt., Tx., U.S.	113a	29.38N	94.57W
Houtbaai, S. Afr.	212a	34.03S	18.22E
Houtman Rocks, is., Austl. (hout′män)	202	28.15S	112.45E
Houzhen, China (hwô-jŭn)	190	36.59N	118.59E
Hovd, Mong.	188	48.08N	91.40E
Hovd Gol, r., Mong.	188	49.06N	91.16E
Hove, Eng., U.K. (hōv)	150	50.50N	0.09W
Hövsgöl Nuur, l., Mong.	188	51.11N	99.11E
Howard, Ks., U.S. (hou′ărd)	111	37.27N	96.10W
Howard, S.D., U.S.	102	44.01N	97.31W
Howard Beach, neigh., N.Y., U.S.	228	40.40N	73.51W
Howden, Eng., U.K. (hou′dĕn)	144a	53.44N	0.52W
Howe, Cape, c., Austl. (hou)	203	37.30S	150.40E
Howell, Mi., U.S. (hou′ĕl)	98	42.40N	84.00W
Howe Sound, strt., Can.	86	49.22N	123.18W
Howick, Can. (hou′ĭk)	83a	45.11N	73.51W
Howick, S. Afr.	213c	29.29S	30.16E
Howland, i., Oc. (hou′lănd)	2	1.00N	176.00W
Howrah, India (hou′rä)	183	22.33N	88.20E
Howrah Bridge, trans., India	240a	22.35N	88.21E
Howse Peak, mtn., Can.	87	51.30N	116.40W
Howson Peak, mtn., Can.	86	54.25N	127.45W
Hoxie, Ar., U.S. (kŏh′sĭ)	111	36.03N	91.00W

PLACE (Pronunciation)	PAGE	Lat. °′	Long. °′
Hoxton Park, Austl.	243a	33.55S	150.51E
Hoy, i., Scot., U.K. (hoi)	150a	58.53N	3.10W
Hōya, Japan	195a	35.45N	139.35E
Hoylake, Eng., U.K. (hoi-lāk′)	144a	53.23N	3.11W
Hoyo, Sierra del, mts., Spain (sē-ĕ′r-rä-dĕl-ô′yô)	159a	40.39N	3.56W
Hradec Králové, Czech Rep.	147	50.12N	15.50E
Hradyz'k, Ukr.	163	49.12N	33.06E
Hranice, Czech Rep. (hrän′yĕ-tsĕ)	155	49.33N	17.45E
Hröby, Swe. (hûr′bü)	152	55.50N	13.41E
Hron, r., Slvk.	155	48.22N	18.42E
Hrubieszów, Pol. (hro͞o-byä′sho͞of)	155	50.48N	23.54E
Hsawnhsup, Myanmar	188	24.29N	94.45E
Hsinchu, Tai. (hsĭn′cho͞o′)	193	24.48N	121.00E
Hsinchuang, Tai.	241d	25.02N	121.26E
Hsinkao Shan, mtn., Tai.	189	23.38N	121.05E
Huadian, China (hwä-dĭĕn)	192	42.38N	126.45E
Huai, r., China (hwī)	189	32.07N	114.38E
Huai'an, China (hwī-än)	192	33.31N	119.11E
Huailai, China	192	40.20N	115.45E
Huailin, China (hwī-lĭn)	190	31.27N	117.36E
Huainan, China	190	32.38N	117.02E
Huaiyang, China (ho͞oăī′yang)	192	33.45N	114.54E
Huaiyuan, China (hwī-yůän)	192	32.53N	117.13E
Huajicori, Mex. (wä-jē-kō′rē)	118	22.41N	105.24W
Huajuapan de León, Mex. (wäj-wä′päm dā lā-ón′)	119	17.46N	97.45W
Hualapai Indian Reservation, I.R., Az., U.S. (wälȧpī)	109	35.41N	113.38W
Hualapai Mountains, mts., Az., U.S.	109	34.53N	113.54W
Hualien, Tai. (hwä′lyĕn′)	193	23.58N	121.58E
Huallaga, r., Peru (wäl-yä′gä)	130	8.12S	76.34W
Huamachuco, Peru (wä-mä-cho͞o′kō)	130	7.52S	78.11W
Huamantla, Mex. (wä-män′tlȧ)	119	19.18N	97.54W
Huambo, Ang.	212	12.44S	15.47E
Huamuxtitlán, Mex. (wä-mo͞os-tē-tlän′)	118	17.49N	98.38W
Huancavelica, Peru (wän′kä-vä-lē′kä)	130	12.47S	75.02W
Huancayo, Peru (wän-kä′yō)	130	12.09S	75.04W
Huanchaca, Bol. (wän-chä′kä)	130	20.09S	66.40W
Huang (Yellow), r., China (hůäŋ)	189	35.06N	113.39E
Huang, Old Beds of the, mth., China	188	40.28N	106.34E
Huang, Old Course of the, r., China	190	34.28N	116.59E
Huangchuan, China (hůäŋ-chůän)	192	32.07N	115.01E
Huangcun, China	240b	39.56N	116.11E
Huanghua, China (hůäŋ-hwä)	190	38.28N	117.18E
Huanghuadian, China (hůäŋ-hwä-dĭĕn)	190	39.22N	116.53E
Huangli, China (ho͞oäNG′lē)	190	31.39N	119.42E
Huangpu, China (hůäŋ-po͞o)	191a	22.44N	113.20E
Huangpu, r., China	191b	30.56N	121.16E
Huangqiao, China (hůän-chyou)	190	32.15N	120.13E
Huangxian, China (hůäŋ shyĕn)	190	37.39N	120.32E
Huangyuan, China (hůäŋ-yůän)	188	37.00N	101.01E
Huanren, China (hůän-rŭn)	192	41.10N	125.30E
Huánuco, Peru (wä-no͞o′kō)	130	9.50S	76.17W
Huánuni, Bol. (wä-no͞o′nē)	130	18.11S	66.43W
Huaquechula, Mex. (wä-kĕ-cho͞o′lä)	118	18.44N	98.37W
Huaral, Peru (wä-rä′l)	130	11.28S	77.11W
Huarás, Peru (öä′rà′s)	130	9.32S	77.29W
Huascarán, Nevados, mts., Peru (wäs-kä-rän′)	130	9.05S	77.50W
Huasco, Chile (wäs′kō)	132	28.32S	71.16W
Huatla de Jiménez, Mex. (wä′tlä-dĕ-KĒ-mĕ′nĕz)	119	18.08N	96.49W
Huatlatlauch, Mex. (wä′tlä-tlä-o͞o′ch)	118	18.40N	98.04W
Huatusco, Mex. (wä-to͞os′kō)	119	19.09N	96.57W
Huauchinango, Mex. (wä-o͞o-chē-näŋ′gō)	118	20.09N	98.03W
Huaunta, Nic. (wä-ô′n-tä)	121	13.30N	83.32W
Huaunta, Laguna, l., Nic. (lä-gō′nä-wä-ô′n-tä)	121	13.35N	83.46W
Huautla, Mex. (wä-o͞o′tlä)	118	21.04N	98.13W
Huaxian, China (hwä shyĕn)	192	35.34N	114.32E
Huaynamota, Río de, r., Mex. (rē′ō-dĕ-wäy-nä-mō′tä)	118	22.10N	104.36W
Huazolotitlán, Mex. (wäzô-lô-tlē-tlän′)	119	16.18N	97.55W
Hubbard, N.H., U.S. (hŭb′ẽrd)	93a	42.53N	71.12W
Hubbard, Tx., U.S.	113	31.53N	96.46W
Hubbard, l., Mi., U.S.	98	44.45N	83.30W
Hubbard Creek Reservoir, res., Tx., U.S.	112	32.50N	98.55W
Hubbelrath, Ger.	236	51.16N	6.55E
Hubei, prov., China (ho͞o-bā)	189	31.20N	111.58E
Hubli, India (ho͞o′blē)	183	15.25N	75.09E
Hückeswagen, Ger. (hü′kĕs-vä′gĕn)	157c	51.09N	7.20E
Hucknall, Eng., U.K. (hŭk′năl)	144a	53.02N	1.12W
Huddersfield, Eng., U.K. (hŭd′ẽrz-fēld)	150	53.39N	1.47W
Hudiksvall, Swe. (ho͞o′dĭks-väl)	146	61.44N	17.05E
Hudson, Can. (hŭd′sŭn)	83a	45.26N	74.08W
Hudson, Ma., U.S.	93a	42.24N	71.34W
Hudson, Mi., U.S.	98	41.50N	84.15W
Hudson, N.Y., U.S.	99	42.15N	73.45W
Hudson, Oh., U.S.	101d	41.15N	81.27W
Hudson, Wi., U.S.	107g	44.59N	92.45W
Hudson, r., U.S.	97	42.30N	73.55W
Hudson Bay, Can.	89	52.52N	102.25W
Hudson Bay, b., Can.	85	60.15N	85.30W
Hudson Falls, N.Y., U.S.	99	43.20N	73.30W
Hudson Heights, Can.	83a	45.28N	74.09W
Hudson Strait, strt., Can.	85	63.25N	74.05W
Hue, Viet. (ü-ā′)	196	16.28N	107.42E
Huebra, r., Spain (wĕ′brä)	158	40.44N	6.17W
Huehuetenango, Guat. (wā-wā-tȧ-näŋ′gō)	120	15.19N	91.26W
Huejotzingo, Mex. (wā-hō-tzĭŋ′gō)	118	19.09N	98.24W
Huejúcar, Mex. (wā-ho͞o′kär)	118	22.26N	103.12W
Huejuquilla el Alto, Mex. (wā-ho͞o-kēl′yä ĕl äl′tō)	118	22.42N	103.54W
Huejutla, Mex. (wā-ho͞o′tlä)	118	21.08N	98.26W

ng-sing; ŋ-baŋk; N-nasalized n; nŏd; cŏmmit; ōld; ôbey; ôrder; oi-boil; fo͞od; ó-as oo in foot; ou-out; s-soft; sh-dish; th-thin; pūre; ûnite; ûrn; stŭd; circŭs; ü-as in French tu; ′-indeterminate vowel.

298 Huelma – Ilo

PLACE (Pronunciation)	PAGE	Lat. °′	Long. °′
Huelma, Spain (wĕl′mä)	158	37.39N	3.36W
Huelva, Spain (wĕl′vä)	148	37.16N	6.58W
Huércal-Overa, Spain (wĕr-käl′ ō-vä′rä)	158	37.12N	1.58W
Huerfano, r., Co., U.S. (wâr′fȧ-nō)	110	37.41N	105.13W
Huésca, Spain (wĕs-kä)	148	42.07N	0.25W
Huéscar, Spain (wās′kär)	158	37.50N	2.34W
Huetamo de Núñez, Mex.	118	18.34N	100.53W
Huete, Spain (wā′tå)	158	40.09N	2.42W
Hueycatenango, Mex. (wĕy-kå-tĕ-nä′n-gô)	118	17.31N	99.10W
Hueytlalpan, Mex. (wā′ī-tläl′păn)	119	20.03N	97.41W
Hueytown, Al., U.S.	100h	33.28N	86.59W
Huffman, Al., U.S. (hŭf′mȧn)	100h	33.36N	86.42W
Hügel, Villa, pt. of i., Ger.	236	51.25N	7.01E
Hugh Butler, l., Ne., U.S.	110	40.21N	100.40W
Hughenden, Austl. (hū′ĕn-dĕn)	203	20.58S	144.13E
Hughes, Austl. (hūz)	202	30.45S	129.30E
Hughesville, Md., U.S.	100e	38.32N	76.48W
Hugo, Mn., U.S. (hū′gō)	107g	45.10N	93.00W
Hugo, Ok., U.S.	111	34.01N	95.32W
Hugoton, Ks., U.S. (hū′gō-tŭn)	110	37.10N	101.28W
Hugou, China (hōō-gō)	190	33.22N	117.07E
Huichapan, Mex. (wē-chä-pän′)	118	20.22N	99.39W
Huila, dept., Col. (wē′lä)	130a	3.10N	75.20W
Huila, Nevado de, mtn., Col. (nĕ-vä-dô-de-wē′lä)	130a	2.59N	76.01W
Huilai, China	193	23.02N	116.18E
Huili, China	188	26.48N	102.20E
Huimanguillo, Mex. (wē-män-gēl′yō)	119	17.50N	93.16W
Huimin, China (hōōi mĭn)	189	37.29N	117.32E
Huipulco, Mex.	233a	19.17N	99.09W
Huitzilac, Mex. (ŏŏ′t-zē-lä′k)	119a	19.01N	99.16W
Huitzitzilingo, Mex. (wē-tzē-tzē-lē′n-go)	118	21.11N	98.42W
Huitzuco, Mex. (wē-tzōō′kō)	118	18.16N	99.20W
Huixquilucan, Mex. (ŏŏē′x-kē-lōō-kä′n)	119a	19.21N	99.22W
Huiyang, China	193	23.05N	114.25E
Hukou, China (hōō-kō)	189	29.58N	116.20E
Hulan, China (hōō′län′)	189	45.58N	126.32E
Hulan, r., China	192	47.20N	126.30E
Hulin, China (hōō′lĭn′)	194	45.45N	133.25E
Hull, Can. (hŭl)	85	45.26N	75.43W
Hull, Ma., U.S.	93a	42.18N	70.54W
Hull, r., Eng., U.K.	144a	53.47N	0.20W
Hülscheid, Ger.	236	51.16N	7.34E
Hulst, Neth. (hōlst)	145a	51.17N	4.01E
Huludao, China (hōō-lōō-dou)	189	40.40N	120.55E
Hulun Nur, l., China (hōō-lŏŏn nŏŏr)	189	48.50N	116.45E
Hulyaypole, Ukr.	163	47.39N	36.12E
Humacao, P.R. (ōō-mä-kä′ō)	117b	18.09N	65.49W
Humansdorp, S. Afr. (hōō′mäns-dôrp)	212	33.57S	24.45E
Humbe, Ang. (hŏm′bâ)	212	16.50S	14.55E
Humber, r., Can.	83d	43.53N	79.40W
Humber, r., Eng., U.K. (hŭm′bẽr)	146	53.30N	0.30E
Humbermouth, Can. (hŭm′bẽr-mŭth)	93	48.58N	57.55W
Humberside, co., Eng., U.K.	144a	53.47N	0.36W
Humble, Tx., U.S. (hŭm′b′l)	113	29.58N	95.15W
Humboldt, Can. (hŭm′bōlt)	84	52.12N	105.07W
Humboldt, Ia., U.S.	103	42.43N	94.11W
Humboldt, Ks., U.S.	111	37.48N	95.26W
Humboldt, Ne., U.S.	111	40.10N	95.57W
Humboldt, r., Nv., U.S.	96	40.30N	116.50W
Humboldt, East Fork, r., Nv., U.S.	104	40.59N	115.21W
Humboldt, North Fork, r., Nv., U.S.	104	41.25N	115.45W
Humboldt, Planetario, bldg., Ven.	234a	10.30N	66.50W
Humboldt Bay, b., Ca., U.S.	104	40.48N	124.25W
Humboldt Range, mts., Nv., U.S.	108	40.12N	118.16W
Humbolt, Tn., U.S.	114	35.47N	88.55W
Humbolt Salt Marsh, Nv., U.S.	108	39.49N	117.41W
Humbolt Sink, Nv., U.S.	108	39.58N	118.54W
Humen, China (hōō-mŭn)	191a	22.49N	113.39E
Humphreys Peak, mtn., Az., U.S. (hŭm′frĭs)	96	35.20N	111.40W
Humpolec, Czech Rep. (hŏŏm′pō-lĕts)	154	49.33N	15.21E
Humuya, r., Hond. (ōō-mōō′yä)	120	14.38N	87.36W
Hunaflói, b., Ice. (hōō′nä-flō′ĭ)	146	65.41N	20.44W
Hunan, prov., China (hōō′nän′)	189	28.08N	111.25E
Hunchun, China (hŏŏn-chŭn)	189	42.53N	130.34E
Hunedoara, Rom. (kōō′nĕd-wä′rȧ)	161	45.45N	22.54E
Hungary, nation, Eur. (hŭŋ′gȧ-rĭ)	142	46.44N	17.55E
Hungerford, Austl. (hŭn′gẽr-fẽrd)	203	28.50S	144.32E
Hungry Horse Reservoir, res., Mt., U.S. (hŭŋ′gȧ-rĭ hôrs)	105	48.11N	113.30W
Hunsrück, mts., Ger. (hōōns′rūk)	154	49.43N	7.12E
Hunte, r., Ger. (hŏn′tĕ)	154	52.45N	8.26E
Hunter Islands, is., Austl. (hŭn-tẽr)	203	40.33S	143.36E
Hunters Hill, Austl.	243a	33.50S	151.09E
Huntingburg, In., U.S. (hŭnt′ĭng-bûrg)	98	38.15N	86.55W
Huntingdon, Can. (hŭnt′ĭng-dŭn)	91	45.10N	74.05W
Huntingdon, Can.	106d	49.00N	122.16W
Huntingdon, Tn., U.S.	114	36.00N	88.23W
Huntington, In., U.S.	98	40.55N	85.30W
Huntington, Pa., U.S.	99	40.30N	78.00W
Huntington, Va., U.S.	229d	38.48N	77.15W
Huntington, W.V., U.S.	97	38.25N	82.25W
Huntington Beach, Ca., U.S.	107a	33.39N	118.00W
Huntington Park, Ca., U.S.	107a	33.59N	118.14W
Huntington Station, N.Y., U.S.	100a	40.51N	73.25W
Huntington Woods, Mi., U.S.	230c	42.29N	83.10W
Huntley, Mt., U.S.	105	45.54N	108.01W
Hunt's Cross, neigh., Eng., U.K.	237a	53.21N	2.51W
Huntsville, Can.	85	45.20N	79.15W
Huntsville, Al., U.S. (hŭnts′vĭl)	114	34.44N	86.36W
Huntsville, Md., U.S.	229d	38.55N	76.54W
Huntsville, Mo., U.S.	111	39.24N	92.32W
Huntsville, Tx., U.S.	113	30.44N	95.34W
Huntsville, Ut., U.S.	107b	41.16N	111.46W
Huolu, China (hŏŏ lōō)	190	38.05N	114.20E
Huon Gulf, b., Pap. N. Gui.	197	7.15S	147.45E
Huoqiu, China (hwō-chyō)	190	32.19N	116.17E
Huoshan, China (hwō-shän)	193	31.30N	116.25E
Ḩuraydin, Wādī, r., Egypt	181a	30.55N	34.12E
Hurd, Cape, c., Can. (hûrd)	90	45.15N	81.45W
Hurdiyo, Som.	218a	10.43N	51.05E
Hurley, Wi., U.S. (hûr′lĭ)	103	46.26N	90.11W
Hurlingham, Arg. (ōō′r-lēn-gäm)	132a	34.36S	58.38W
Huron, Oh., U.S. (hū′rŏn)	98	41.20N	82.35W
Huron, S.D., U.S.	96	44.22N	98.15W
Huron, r., Mi., U.S.	101b	42.12N	83.26W
Huron, Lake, l., N.A. (hū′rŏn)	97	45.15N	82.40W
Huron Mountains, mts., Mi., U.S. (hū′rŏn)	103	46.47N	87.52W
Hurricane, Ak., U.S. (hŭr′ĭ-kān)	95	63.00N	149.30W
Hurricane, Ut., U.S.	109	37.10N	113.20W
Hurricane Flats, bk. (hŭ-rĭ-kȧn flăts)	122	23.35N	78.30W
Hurst, Tx., U.S.	107c	32.48N	97.12W
Hurstville, Austl.	243a	33.58S	151.06E
Húsavik, Ice.	146	66.00N	17.10W
Husen, neigh., Ger.	236	51.33N	7.36E
Huşi, Rom. (kŏsh′)	163	46.52N	28.04E
Huskvarna, Swe. (hŏsk-vär′nȧ)	152	57.48N	14.16E
Husum, Ger. (hōō′zŏom)	154	54.29N	9.04E
Hutchins, Tx., U.S. (hŭch′ĭnz)	107c	32.38N	96.43W
Hutchinson, Ks., U.S. (hŭch′ĭn-sŭn)	96	38.02N	97.56W
Hutchinson, Mn., U.S.	103	44.53N	94.23W
Hütteldorf, neigh., Aus.	239e	48.12N	16.16E
Hüttenheim, neigh., Ger.	236	51.22N	6.43E
Hutton, Eng., U.K.	235	51.38N	0.22E
Huttrop, neigh., Ger.	236	51.27N	7.03E
Hutuo, r., China	192	38.10N	114.00E
Huy, Bel. (ū-ē′) (hŭ′ē)	151	50.33N	5.14E
Huyton, Eng., U.K.	237a	53.24N	2.50W
Hvannadalshnúkur, mtn., Ice.	146	64.09N	16.46W
Hvar, i., Yugo. (κhvär)	160	43.08N	16.28E
Hwange, Zimb.	212	18.22S	26.29E
Hwangju, N. Kor. (hwäng′jōō′)	194	38.39N	125.49E
Hyargas Nuur, l., Mong.	188	48.00N	92.32E
Hyattsville, Md., U.S. (hī′ăt′s-vĭl)	100e	38.57N	76.58W
Hyco Lake, res., N.C., U.S. (rōks′ bŭr-ō)	115	36.22N	78.58W
Hydaburg, Ak., U.S. (hī-dă′bûrg)	95	55.12N	132.49W
Hyde, Eng., U.K. (hīd)	144a	53.27N	2.05W
Hyde Park, neigh., Il., U.S.	231a	41.48N	87.36W
Hyderabad, India	183	18.30N	76.50E
Hyderābād, India (hī-dẽr-å-băd′)	183	17.29N	78.28E
Hyderābād, Pak.	183	25.29N	68.28E
Hyéres, Fr. (ē-âr′)	147	43.09N	6.08E
Hyéres, Îles d′, is., Fr. (ēl′dyâr′)	147	42.57N	6.17E
Hyesanjin, N. Kor. (hyĕ′sän-jĭn′)	194	41.11N	128.12E
Hymera, In., U.S. (hī-mē′rȧ)	98	39.10N	87.20W
Hyndman Peak, mtn., Id., U.S. (hīnd′măn)	96	43.38N	114.04W
Hyōgo, dept., Japan (hĭyō′gō)	195b	34.54N	135.15E
Hyōgo, neigh., Japan	242b	34.47N	135.10E
Hythe End, Eng., U.K.	235	51.27N	0.32W

I

PLACE (Pronunciation)	PAGE	Lat. °′	Long. °′
Ia, r., Japan (ē′ä)	195b	34.54N	135.34E
Ialomiţa, r., Rom.	161	44.37N	26.42E
Iaşi, Rom. (yä′shē)	142	47.10N	27.40E
Iba, Phil. (ē′bä)	197a	15.20N	119.59E
Ibadan, Nig. (ē-bä′dän)	210	7.17N	3.30E
Ibagué, Col.	130	4.27N	75.14W
Ibar, r., Yugo. (ē′bär)	161	43.22N	20.35E
Ibaraki, Japan (ē-bä′rä-gē)	195b	34.49N	135.35E
Ibarra, Ec. (ē-bär′rä)	130	0.19N	78.08W
Ibb, Yemen	185	14.01N	44.10E
Iberoamericana, Universidad, educ., Mex.	233a	19.21N	99.08W
Iberville, Can. (ē-bår-vēl′) (ĭ′bẽr-vĭl)	91	45.14N	73.01W
Ibese, Nig.	244d	6.33N	3.29E
Ibi, Nig. (ē′bē)	210	8.12N	9.45E
Ibiapaba, Serra da, mts., Braz. (sĕ′r-rä-dä-ē-byä-pä′bä)	131	3.30S	40.55W
Ibirapuera, neigh., Braz.	234d	23.37S	46.40W
Ibiza, Spain (ē-bē′thä)	159	38.55N	1.24E
Ibiza (Iviza), i., Spain (ē-bē′zä)	142	39.07N	1.05E
Ibo, Moz. (ē′bō)	213	12.20S	40.35E
Ibrāhīm, Būr, b., Egypt	218c	29.57N	32.33E
Ibrahim, Jabal, mtn., Sau. Ar.	182	20.31N	41.17E
Ibwe Munyama, Zam.	217	16.09S	28.34E
Ica, Peru (ē′kä)	130	14.09S	75.42W
Icá (Putumayo), r., S.A.	130	3.00S	69.00W
Içana, Braz. (ē-sä′nä)	130	0.15N	67.19W
Ice Harbor Dam, Wa., U.S.	104	46.15N	118.54W
İçel, Tur.	182	37.00N	34.40E
Iceland, nation, Eur. (īs′lănd)	142	65.12N	19.45W
Ichāpur, India	240a	22.50N	88.24E
Ichibusayama, mtn., Japan (ē′chē-bōō′sä-yä′mä)	195	32.19N	131.08E
Ichihara, Japan	195a	35.31N	140.05E
Ichikawa, Japan (ē′chē-kä′wä)	195a	35.44N	139.54E
Ichinomiya, Japan (ē′chē-nō-mē′yȧ)	195	35.19N	136.49E
Ichinomoto, Japan (ē-chē′nō-mō-tō)	195b	34.37N	135.50E
Ichnya, Ukr. (ĭch′nyä)	167	50.47N	32.23E
Ickenham, neigh., Eng., U.K.	235	51.34N	0.27W
Ickern, neigh., Ger.	236	51.36N	7.21E
Icy Cape, c., Ak., U.S. (ī′sĭ)	95	70.20N	161.40W
Idabel, Ok., U.S. (ī′dȧ-bĕl)	111	33.52N	94.47W
Idagrove, Ia., U.S. (ī′dȧ-grōv)	102	42.22N	95.29W
Idah, Nig. (ē′dä)	210	7.07N	6.43E
Idaho, state, U.S. (ī′dȧ-hō)	96	44.00N	115.10W
Idaho Falls, Id., U.S.	96	43.30N	112.01W
Idaho Springs, Co., U.S.	110	39.43N	105.32W
Idanha-a-Nova, Port. (ē-dän′yȧ-ä-nō′vȧ)	158	39.58N	7.13W
Iddo, neigh., Nig.	244d	6.28N	3.23E
Ider, r., Mong.	188	48.58N	98.38E
Idhra, i., Grc.	161	37.20N	23.30E
Idi, Indon. (ē′dē)	196	4.58N	97.47E
Idkū Lake, l., Egypt	218b	31.13N	30.22E
Idle, r., Eng., U.K. (īd″l)	144a	53.22N	0.56W
Idlib, Syria	184	35.55N	36.38E
Idriaj, Slvn. (ē′drē-å)	160	46.01N	14.01E
Idutywa, S. Afr. (ē-dŏŏ-tī′wȧ)	213c	32.06S	28.18E
Idylwood, Va., U.S.	229d	38.54N	77.12W
Ieper, Bel.	151	50.50N	2.53E
Ierápetra, Grc.	160a	35.01N	25.48E
Iesi, Italy (yā′sē)	160	43.37N	13.20E
Ife, Nig.	210	7.30N	4.30E
Iferouâne, Niger (ēf′rōō-än′)	210	19.04N	8.24E
Ifôghas, Adrar des, plat., Afr.	210	19.55N	2.00E
Igalula, Tan.	217	5.14S	33.00E
Iganmu, neigh., Nig.	244d	6.29N	3.22E
Igarka, Russia (ē-gär′kȧ)	164	67.22N	86.16E
Igbobi, Nig.	244d	6.32N	3.22E
Ightham, Eng., U.K.	235	51.17N	0.17E
Iglesias, Italy (ē-lĕ′syôs)	148	39.20N	8.34E
Igli, Alg. (ē-glē′)	210	30.32N	2.15W
Igloolik, Can.	85	69.33N	81.18W
Ignacio, Ca., U.S. (ĭg-nā′cĭ-ō)	106b	38.05N	122.32W
Iguaçu, r., Braz. (ē-gwä-sōō′)	132b	22.42S	43.19W
Iguala, Mex. (ē-gwä′lä)	118	18.18N	99.34W
Igualada, Spain (ē-gwä-lä′dä)	159	41.35N	1.38E
Iguassu, r., S.A. (ē-gwä-sōō′)	132	25.45S	52.30W
Iguassu Falls, wtfl., S.A.	131	25.40S	54.16W
Iguatama, Braz. (ē-gwä-tá′mä)	129a	20.13S	45.40W
Iguatu, Braz. (ē-gwä-tōō′)	131	6.22S	39.17W
Iguidi, Erg, Afr.	210	26.22N	6.53W
Iguig, Phil. (ē-gēg′)	197a	17.46N	121.44E
Iharana, Madag.	213	13.35S	50.05E
Ihiala, Nig.	215	5.51N	6.51E
Iida, Japan (ē′ē-dȧ)	195	35.39N	137.53E
Iijoki, r., Fin. (ē′yō′kĭ)	166	65.28N	27.00E
Iizuka, Japan (ē′ē-zŏŏ-kȧ)	195	33.39N	130.39E
Ijebu-Ode, Nig. (ē-jĕ′bōō ōdå)	210	6.50N	3.56E
IJmuiden, Neth.	145a	52.27N	4.36E
IJsselmeer, l., Neth. (ī′sĕl-mār)	151	52.46N	5.14E
Ikaalinen, Fin. (ē′kä-lĭ-nĕn)	153	61.47N	22.55E
Ikaría, i., Grc. (ē-kä′ryȧ)	161	37.43N	26.07E
Ikeda, Japan (ē′kȧ-dä)	195b	34.49N	135.26E
Ikeja, Nig.	244d	6.36N	3.21E
Ikerre, Nig.	215	7.31N	5.14E
Ikhtiman, Bul. (ēk′tē-män)	161	42.26N	23.49E
Iki, i., Japan (ē′kē)	194	33.46N	129.44E
Ikoma, Japan	195b	34.41N	135.43E
Ikoma, Tan. (ē-kō′mä)	212	2.08S	34.47E
Ikorodu, Nig.	244d	6.37N	3.31E
Ikoyi, neigh., Nig.	244d	6.27N	3.26E
Ikoyi Island, i., Nig.	244d	6.27N	3.26E
Iksha, Russia (ĭk′shȧ)	172b	56.10N	37.30E
Ikuno, neigh., Japan	242b	34.39N	135.33E
Ila, Nig.	215	8.01N	4.55E
Ilagan, Phil.	197a	17.09N	121.52E
Ilan, Tai. (ē′län′)	193	24.50N	121.42E
Iława, Pol. (ē-lä′vȧ)	155	53.35N	19.36E
Ilchester, Md., U.S.	229c	39.15N	76.46W
Île, r., Asia	170	44.30N	76.45E
Île-á-la-Crosse, Can.	88	55.34N	108.00W
Ilebo, Zaire	212	4.19S	20.35E
Ilek, Russia (ē′lyĕk)	167	51.30N	53.10E
Île-Perrot, Can. (yl-pĕ-rōt′)	83a	45.21N	73.54W
Ilesha, Nig.	210	7.38N	4.45E
Ilford, Eng., U.K. (ĭl′fẽrd)	144b	51.33N	0.06E
Ilfracombe, Eng., U.K. (ĭl-frȧ-kōōm′)	150	51.13N	4.08W
Ilhabela, Braz. (ē′lä-bĕ′lä)	129a	23.47S	45.21W
Ilha Grande, Baía de, b., Braz. (ēl′yȧ grän′dē)	129a	23.17S	44.25W
Ílhavo, Port. (ēl′yȧ-vō)	148	40.36N	8.41W
Ilhéus, Braz. (ē-lĕ′ōōs)	131	14.52S	39.00W
Iliamna, Ak., U.S. (ē-lē-ăm′nȧ)	95	59.45N	155.05W
Iliamna, Ak., U.S.	95	60.18N	153.25W
Iliamna, l., Ak., U.S.	95	59.25N	155.30W
Ilim, r., Russia (ē-lyēm′)	170	57.28N	103.00E
Ilimsk, Russia (ē-lyēmsk′)	165	56.47N	103.43E
Ilin Island, i., Phil. (ē-lyēn′)	197a	12.16N	120.57E
Ilion, N.Y., U.S. (ĭl′ĭ-ŭn)	99	43.00N	75.05W
Ilioúpolis, Grc.	239d	37.56N	23.45E
Ilkeston, Eng., U.K. (ĭl′kĕs-tŭn)	144a	52.58N	1.19W
Illampu, Nevado, mtn., Bol. (nĕ-vá′dô-ēl-yäm-pōō′)	130	15.50S	68.15W
Illapel, Chile (ē-zhä-pĕ′l)	132	31.37S	71.10W
Iller, r., Ger. (ĭlẽr)	154	47.52N	10.06E
Illimani, Nevado, mtn., Bol. (nĕ-vá′dô-ēl-yē-mä′nē)	130	16.50S	67.38W
Illinois, state, U.S. (ĭl-ĭ-noi′) (ĭl-ĭ-noiz′)	97	40.25N	90.40W
Illinois, r., Il., U.S.	97	39.00N	90.30W
Illintsi, Ukr.	163	49.07N	29.13E
Illizi, Alg.	210	26.35N	8.24E
Illovo, S. Afr.	244b	26.08S	28.03E
Il′men, l., Russia (ô′zē-rô el″men″) (ĭl′mĕn)	166	58.18N	32.00E
Ilo, Peru	130	17.46S	71.13W

ăt; finȧl; rāte; senåte; ärm; ȧsk; sofȧ; fâre; ch-choose; dh-as th in other; bē; ēvent; bĕt; recĕnt; cratẽr; g-gō; gh-guttural g; bĭt; ĭ-short neutral; rīde; κ-guttural k as ch in German ich;

PRONOUNCING INDEX Ilobasco-Istmina 299

PLACE (Pronunciation)	PAGE	Lat. °′	Long. °′
Ilobasco, El Sal. (ē-lô-bäs′kô)	120	13.57N	88.46W
Iloilo, Phil. (ē-lô-ē′lō)	196	10.49N	122.33E
Ilopango, Lago, l., El Sal. (ē-lô-päŋ′gō)	120	13.48N	88.50W
Ilorin, Nig. (ē-lô-rēn′)	210	8.30N	4.32E
Ilūkste, Lat.	153	55.59N	26.20E
Ilverich, Ger.	236	51.17N	6.42E
Ilwaco, Wa., U.S. (ĭl-wā′kô)	106c	46.19N	124.02W
Ilych, r., Russia (ē′l′ĭch)	166	62.30N	57.30E
Imabari, Japan (ē′mä-bä′rē)	194	34.05N	132.58E
Imai, Japan (ē-mī′)	195b	34.30N	135.47E
Iman, r., Russia (ē-män′)	194	45.40N	134.31E
Imandra, l., Russia (ē-män′drá)	166	67.40N	32.30E
Imbābah, Egypt (ēm-bä′bá)	218b	30.06N	31.09E
Imeni Morozova, Russia (ĭm-yĕ′nyĭ mô rô′zô vá)	172c	59.58N	31.02E
Imeni Moskvy, Kanal (Moscow Canal), can., Russia (ká-näl′ĭm-yä′nĭ mŏs-kvĭ)	162	56.33N	37.15E
Imeni Tsyurupy, Russia	172b	55.30N	38.39E
Imeni Vorovskogo, Russia	172b	55.43N	38.21E
Imlay City, Mi., U.S. (ĭm′lā)	98	43.00N	83.15W
Immenstadt, Ger. (ĭm′ĕn-shtät)	154	47.34N	10.12E
Immerpan, S. Afr. (ĭmĕr-pän)	218d	24.29S	29.14E
Imola, Italy (ē′mô-lä)	160	44.19N	11.43E
Imotski, Cro. (ē-môts′kē)	161	43.25N	17.15E
Impameri, Braz.	131	17.44S	48.03W
Impendle, S. Afr. (ĭm-pĕnd′lå)	213c	29.38S	29.54E
Imperia, Italy (ėm-pā′rē-ä)	148	43.52N	8.00E
Imperial, Pa., U.S. (ĭm-pē′rĭ-ăl)	101e	40.27N	80.15W
Imperial Beach, Ca., U.S.	108a	32.34N	117.08W
Imperial Valley, Ca., U.S.	108	33.00N	115.22W
Impfondo, Congo (ĭmp-fōn′dô)	211	1.37N	18.04E
Imphāl, India (ĭmp′hŭl)	183	24.42N	94.00E
Ina, r., Japan (ē-nä′)	195b	34.56N	135.21E
Inagi, Japan	242a	35.38N	139.30E
Inaja Indian Reservation, I.R., Ca., U.S. (ē-nä′hä)	108	32.56N	116.37W
Inari, l., Fin.	146	69.02N	26.22E
Inatsuke, neigh., Japan	242a	35.46N	139.43E
Inca, Spain (ēŋ′kä)	159	39.43N	2.53E
Ince, Eng., U.K.	237a	53.17N	2.49W
Ince Blundell, Eng., U.K.	237a	53.31N	3.02W
Ince Burun, c., Tur. (ĭn′jå)	149	42.00N	35.00E
Inch′ŏn, S. Kor. (ĭn′chŭn)	189	37.26N	126.46E
Incudine, Monte, mtn., Fr. (ēn-kōō-dē′nä) (äN-kü-dēn′)	160	41.53N	9.17E
Indalsälven, r., Swe.	146	62.50N	16.50E
Independence, Ks., U.S. (ĭn-dė-pĕn′dĕns)	111	37.14N	95.42W
Independence, Mo., U.S.	107f	39.06N	94.26W
Independence, Oh., U.S.	101d	41.23N	81.39W
Independence, Or., U.S.	104	44.49N	123.13W
Independence Mountains, mts., Nv., U.S.	104	41.15N	116.02W
Independence National Historical Park, rec., N.J., U.S.	229b	39.57N	75.09W
In der Bredde, Ger.	236	51.20N	7.23E
Inder köli, l., Kaz.	170	48.20N	52.10E
India, nation, Asia (ĭn′dĭ-ă)	183	23.00N	77.30E
India Gate, hist., India	240d	28.37N	77.12E
Indian, l., Mi., U.S. (ĭn′dĭ-ăn)	103	46.04N	86.34W
Indian, r., N.Y., U.S.	99	44.05N	75.45W
Indiana, Pa., U.S. (ĭn-dĭ-ăn′ă)	99	40.40N	79.10W
Indiana, state, U.S.	97	39.50N	86.45W
Indianapolis, In., U.S. (ĭn-dĭ-ăn-ăp′ô-lĭs)	97	39.45N	86.08W
Indian Arm, b., Can. (ĭn′dĭ-ăn ärm)	106d	49.21N	122.55W
Indian Head, Can.	84	50.29N	103.44W
Indian Head Park, Il., U.S.	231a	41.47N	87.54W
Indian Lake, l., Can.	90	47.00N	82.00W
Indian Ocean, o.	5	10.00S	70.00E
Indianola, Ia., U.S. (ĭn-dĭ-ăn-ō′lă)	103	41.22N	93.33W
Indianola, Ms., U.S.	114	33.29N	90.35W
Indianola, Pa., U.S.	230b	40.34N	79.51W
Indianópolis, neigh., Braz.	234d	23.36S	46.38W
Indian Springs, Va., U.S.	229d	38.49N	77.10W
Indigirka, r., Russia (ēn-dė-gēr′kå)	171	67.45N	145.45E
Indio, r., Pan. (ē′n-dyô)	116a	9.13N	79.28W
Indochina, reg., Asia (ĭn-dō-chī′ná)	196	17.22N	105.18E
Indonesia, nation, Asia (ĭn′dô-nē-zhă)	196	4.38S	118.45E
Indonesian Culture, Museum of, bldg., Indon.	241i	6.11S	106.49E
Indore, India (ĭn-dōr′)	183	22.48N	76.51E
Indragiri, r., Indon. (ĭn-drá-jē′rē)	196	0.27S	102.05E
Indrāvati, r., India (ĭn-drŭ-vä′tē)	183	19.00N	82.00E
Indre, r., Fr. (äN′dr′)	156	47.13N	0.29E
Indus, Can. (ĭn′dŭs)	83e	50.55N	113.45W
Indus, r., Asia	183	26.43N	67.41E
Industria, neigh., S. Afr.	244b	26.12S	27.59E
Indwe, S. Afr. (ĭnd′wå)	213c	31.30S	27.21E
Inebolu, Tur. (ē-nå-bō′lōō)	149	41.50N	33.40E
Inego, Tur. (ē′nå-gŭ)	167	40.05N	29.20E
Infanta, Phil. (ēn-fän′tä)	197a	14.44N	121.39E
Infanta, Phil.	197a	15.50N	119.53E
Inferror, Laguna, l., Mex. (lä-gô′nä-ēn-fĕr-rôr)	119	16.18N	94.40W
Infiernillo, Presa de, res., Mex.	118	18.50N	101.50W
Infiesto, Spain (ēn-fyĕ′s-tô)	158	43.21N	5.24W
I-n-Gall, Niger	215	16.47N	6.56E
Ingatestone, Eng., U.K.	235	51.41N	0.22E
Ingeniero Budge, neigh., Arg.	233d	34.43S	58.28W
Ingersoll, Can. (ĭn′gẽr-sŏl)	90	43.05N	81.00W
Ingham, Austl. (ĭng′ăm)	203	18.45S	146.14E
Ingleburn, Austl.	243a	34.00S	150.52E
Ingles, Cayos, is., Cuba (kä-yōs-ē′n-glē′s)	122	21.55N	82.35W
Ingleside, neigh., Ca., U.S.	231b	37.43N	122.28W
Inglewood, Can.	83d	43.48N	79.56W
Inglewood, Ca., U.S. (ĭn′g′l-wŏŏd)	107a	33.57N	118.22W
Ingoda, r., Russia (ēn-gō′dă)	171	51.29N	112.32E
Ingolstadt, Ger. (ĭŋ′gōl-shtät)	154	48.46N	11.27E
Ingomar, Pa., U.S.	230b	40.35N	80.05W
Ingram, Pa., U.S.	230b	40.26N	80.04W
Ingrave, Eng., U.K.	235	51.36N	0.21E
Ingur, r., Geor. (ēn-gŏor′)	167	42.30N	42.00E
Inhambane, Moz. (ēn-äm-bä′-nĕ)	212	23.47S	35.28E
Inhambupe, Braz. (ēn-yäm-bōō′pä)	131	11.47S	38.13W
Inharrime, Moz. (ēn-yär-rē′mä)	212	24.17S	35.07E
Inhomirim, Braz. (ē-nô-mē-rē′N)	132b	22.34S	43.11W
Inhul, r., Ukr.	163	47.22N	32.52E
Inhulets′, r., Ukr.	163	47.12N	33.12E
Inírida, r., Col. (ē-nē-rē′dä)	130	2.25N	70.38W
Injune, Austl. (ĭn′jōn)	204	25.52S	148.30E
Inkeroinem, Fin. (ĭn′kĕr-oi-nĕn)	153	60.42N	26.50E
Inkster, Mi., U.S. (ĭngk′stẽr)	101b	42.18N	83.19W
Inn, r., Eur. (ĭn)	147	48.00N	12.00E
Innamincka, Austl. (ĭnn-ă′mĭn-kă)	204	27.50S	140.48E
Inner Brass, i., V.I.U.S. (bräs)	117c	18.23N	64.58W
Inner Hebrides, is., Scot., U.K.	150	57.20N	6.20W
Inner Mongolia see Nei Monggol, , China	188	40.15N	105.00E
Innisfail, Can.	84	52.02N	113.57W
Innsbruck, Aus. (ĭns′brŏŏk)	147	47.15N	11.25E
Ino, Japan (ē′nô)	195	33.34N	133.23E
Inongo, Zaire (ē-nôŋ′gō)	212	1.57S	18.16E
Inowrocław, Pol. (ē-nô-vrŏts′läf)	155	52.48N	18.16E
In Salah, Alg.	210	27.13N	2.22E
Inscription House Ruin, Az., U.S. (ĭn′skrĭp-shŭn hous rōō′ĭn)	109	36.45N	110.47W
International Falls, Mn., U.S. (ĭn′tẽr-năsh′ŭn-ăl fôlz)	97	48.34N	93.26W
Inuvik, Can.	84	68.40N	134.10W
Inuyama, Japan (ē′nōō-yä′mä)	195	35.24N	137.01E
Invercargil, N.Z. (ĭn-vẽr-kär′gĭl)	205	46.25S	168.27E
Inverel, Austl. (ĭn-vẽr-el′)	203	29.50S	151.32E
Invergrove Heights, Mn., U.S. (ĭn′vẽr-grōv)	107g	44.51N	93.01W
Inverness, Can. (ĭn-vẽr-nĕs′)	93	46.14N	61.18W
Inverness, Scot., U.K.	146	57.30N	4.07W
Inverness, Fl., U.S.	115	28.48N	82.22W
Investigator Strait, strt., Austl. (ĭn-vĕst′ĭ′gā-tôr)	204	35.33S	137.00E
Inwood, N.Y., U.S.	228	40.37N	73.45W
Inyangani, mtn., Zimb. (ēn-yän-gä′nē)	212	18.06S	32.37E
Inyokern, Ca., U.S.	108	35.39N	117.51W
Inyo Mountains, mts., Ca., U.S. (ĭn′yō)	96	36.55N	118.04W
Inzer, r., Russia (ĭn′zẽr)	172a	54.24N	57.17E
Inzersdorf, neigh., Aus.	239e	48.09N	16.21E
Inzia, r., Zaire	216	5.55S	17.50E
Ioánnina, Grc. (yô-ä′nē-nà)	149	39.39N	20.52E
Ioco, Can.	106d	49.18N	122.53W
Iola, Ks., U.S. (ī-ō′lă)	111	37.55N	95.23W
Iôna, Parque Nacional do, rec., Ang.	216	16.35S	12.00E
Ionia, Mi., U.S. (ī-ō′nĭ-ă)	98	43.00N	85.10W
Ionian Islands, is., Grc. (ī-ō′nĭ-ăn)	149	39.10N	20.05E
Ionian Sea, sea, Eur.	142	38.59N	18.48E
Iori, r., Asia	168	41.03N	46.17E
Íos, i., Grc. (ī′ŏs)	161	36.48N	25.25E
Iowa, state, U.S. (ī′ô-wă)	97	42.05N	94.20W
Iowa, r., Ia., U.S.	103	41.55N	92.20W
Iowa City, Ia., U.S.	97	41.39N	91.31W
Iowa Falls, Ia., U.S.	103	42.32N	93.16W
Iowa Park, Tx., U.S.	110	33.57N	98.39W
Ipala, Tan.	217	4.30S	32.53E
Ipanema, neigh., Braz.	234c	22.59S	43.12W
Ipeirus, hist. reg., Grc.	161	39.35N	20.45E
Ipel′, r., Eur. (ē′pĕl)	155	48.08N	19.00E
Ipiales, Col. (ē-pē-ä′lås)	130	0.48N	77.45W
Ipoh, Malay.	196	4.45N	101.05E
Ipswich, Austl. (ĭps′wĭch)	203	27.40S	152.50E
Ipswich, Eng., U.K.	147	52.05N	1.05E
Ipswich, Ma., U.S.	93a	42.41N	70.50W
Ipswich, S.D., U.S.	102	45.26N	99.01W
Ipu, Braz. (ē-pōō)	131	4.11S	40.45W
Iput′, r., Eur. (ē-pŏŏt′)	167	52.53N	31.57E
Iqaluit, Can.	85	63.48N	68.31W
Iquique, Chile (ē-kē′kĕ)	130	20.16S	70.07W
Iquitos, Peru (ē-kē′tōs)	130	3.39S	73.18W
Iráklion, Grc.	142	35.20N	25.10E
Iran, nation, Asia (ē-rän′)	182	31.15N	53.30E
Iran, Plateau of, plat., Iran	182	32.28N	58.00E
Iran Mountains, mts., Asia	196	2.30N	114.30E
Irapuato, Mex. (ē-rä-pwä′tō)	118	20.41N	101.24W
Iraq, nation, Asia (ē-räk′)	182	32.00N	42.30E
Irazú, vol., C.R. (ē-rä-zōō′)	121	9.58N	83.54W
Irbid, Jord. (ēr-bēd′)	184	32.33N	35.51E
Irbīl, Iraq	182	36.10N	44.00E
Irbit, Russia (ēr-bēt′)	164	57.40N	63.10E
Irby, Eng., U.K.	237a	53.21N	3.07W
Irébou, Zaire (ē-rā′bōō)	212	0.40S	17.48E
Ireland, nation, Eur. (īr-lănd)	142	53.33N	8.00W
Iremel′, Gora, mtn., Russia (gá-rä′ĭ-rĕ′mĕl)	172a	54.32N	58.52E
Irene, S. Afr. (ī-rē-nē)	213b	25.53S	28.13E
Irîgui, reg., Mali	214	16.45N	5.35W
Iriklinskoye Vodokhranilishche, res., Russia	167	52.20N	58.50E
Iringa, Tan. (ē-rĭŋ′gä)	212	7.46S	35.42E
Iriomote Jima, i., Japan (ērē′-ō-mō-tä)	189	24.20N	123.30E
Iriona, Hond. (ē-rē-ō′nä)	120	15.53N	85.12W
Irish Sea, sea, Eur. (ī′rĭsh)	142	53.55N	5.25W
Irkutsk, Russia (ĭr-kŏŏtsk′)	165	52.16N	104.00E
Irlam, Eng., U.K. (ûr′lăm)	144a	53.26N	2.26W
Irois, Cap des, c., Haiti	123	18.25N	74.50W
Iron Bottom Sound, strt., Sol.Is.	198e	9.15S	160.00E
Iron Cove, b., Austl.	243a	33.52S	151.10E
Irondale, Al., U.S. (ī′ẽrn-dāl)	100h	33.32N	86.43W
Iron Gate, val., Eur.	161	44.43N	22.32E
Iron Knob, Austl. (ī-ăn nŏb)	204	32.47S	137.10E
Iron Mountain, Mi., U.S. (ī′ẽrn)	103	45.49N	88.04W
Iron River, Mi., U.S.	103	46.09N	88.39W
Ironton, Oh., U.S. (ī′ẽrn-tŭn)	98	38.30N	82.45W
Ironwood, Mi., U.S. (ī′ẽrn-wŏŏd)	103	46.28N	90.10W
Iroquois, r., Il., U.S. (ĭr′ô-kwoi)	98	40.55N	87.20W
Iroquois Falls, Can.	85	48.41N	80.39W
Irō-Saki, c., Japan (ē′rō sä′kē)	194	34.35N	138.54E
Irpen′, r., Ukr. (ĭr-pĕn′)	163	50.13N	29.55E
Irrawaddy, r., Myanmar (ĭr-ă-wäd′ē)	183	23.27N	96.25E
Irtysh, r., Asia (ĭr-tĭsh′)	164	59.00N	69.00E
Irumu, Zaire (ē-rō′mōō)	211	1.30N	29.52E
Irun, Spain (ē-rōōn′)	158	43.20N	1.47W
Irvine, Scot., U.K.	150	55.39N	4.40W
Irvine, Ca., U.S. (ûr′vĭn)	107a	33.40N	117.45W
Irvine, Ky., U.S.	98	37.40N	84.00W
Irving, Tx., U.S. (ûr′vēng)	107c	32.49N	96.57W
Irving Park, neigh., Il., U.S.	231a	41.57N	87.43W
Irvington, N.J., U.S. (ûr′vēng-tŭn)	100a	40.43N	74.15W
Irvington, neigh., Md., U.S.	229c	39.17N	76.41W
Irwin, Pa., U.S. (ûr′wĭn)	101e	40.19N	79.42W
Is, Russia (ēs)	172a	58.48N	59.44E
Isa, Nig.	215	13.14N	6.24E
Isaacs, Mount, mtn., Pan. (ē-sä-á′ks)	116a	9.22N	79.31W
Isabela, i., Ec. (ē-sä-bā′lä)	130	0.47S	91.35W
Isabela, Cabo, c., Dom. Rep. (ká′bô-ē-sä-bĕ′lä)	123	20.00N	71.00W
Isabella, Cordillera, mts., Nic. (kôr-dēl-yĕ′rä-ē-sä-bĕlä)	120	13.20N	85.37W
Isabella Indian Reservation, I.R., Mi., U.S. (ĭs-á-bĕl′-lå)	98	43.35N	84.55W
Isaccea, Rom. (ė-säk′chä)	163	45.16N	28.26E
Ísafjördur, Ice. (ēs′ä-fÿr-dŏr)	146	66.09N	22.39W
Isando, S. Afr.	244b	26.09S	28.12E
Isangi, Zaire (ē-säŋ′gē)	188	0.46N	24.15E
Isar, r., Ger. (ē′zär)	147	48.30N	12.30E
Isarco, r., Italy (ė-sär′kō)	160	46.37N	11.25E
Isarog, Mount, mtn., Phil. (ē-sä-rô-g)	197a	13.40N	123.23E
Ischia, Italy (ēs′kyä)	159c	40.29N	13.58E
Ischia, Isola d′, i., Italy (dē′sh-kyä)	148	40.26N	13.55E
Ise, Japan (ĭs′hē) (ĭ′gē-yä′mä′dá)	194	34.30N	136.43E
Iselin, N.J., U.S.	228	40.34N	74.19W
Iseo, Lago d′, l., Italy (lä-′gō-dē-ē-zĕ′ō)	160	45.50N	9.55E
Isére, r., Fr. (ē-zâr′)	147	45.15N	5.15E
Iserlohn, Ger. (ē′zĕr-lōn)	157c	51.22N	7.42E
Isernia, Italy (ē-zĕr′nyä)	160	41.35N	14.14E
Ise-Wan, b., Japan (ē′sē wän)	194	34.49N	136.44E
Iseyin, Nig.	210	7.58N	3.36E
Ishigaki, Japan	198d	24.20N	124.09E
Ishikari Wan, b., Japan (ē′shē-kä-rē wän)	194	43.30N	141.05E
Ishim, Russia (ĭsh-ėm′)	164	56.07N	69.13E
Ishim, r., Asia	164	53.17N	67.45E
Ishimbay, Russia (ē-shĕm-bī′)	172a	53.28N	56.02E
Ishinomaki, Japan (ĭsh-nō-mä′kē)	189	38.22N	141.22E
Ishinomaki Wan, b., Japan (ē-shē-nō-mä′kē wän)	194	38.10N	141.40E
Ishly, Russia (ĭsh′lĭ)	172a	54.13N	55.55E
Ishlya, Russia (ĭsh′lyå)	172a	53.54N	57.48E
Ishmant, Egypt	218b	29.17N	31.15E
Ishpeming, Mi., U.S. (ĭsh′pė-mĭng)	103	46.28N	87.42W
Isidro Casanova, Arg.	233d	34.42S	58.35W
Isipingo, S. Afr. (ĭs-ĭ-pĭŋ-gô)	213c	29.59S	30.58E
Isiro, Zaire	211	2.47N	27.37E
İskenderun, Tur. (ĭs-kĕn′dĕr-ōōn)	182	36.45N	36.15E
İskenderun Körfezi, b., Tur.	149	36.22N	35.25E
İskilip, Tur. (ĕs′kĭ-lĕp′)	149	40.40N	34.30E
Iskŭr, r., Bul. (ĭs′k′r)	161	43.05N	23.37E
Isla-Cristina, Spain (ĭ′lä-krē-stē′nä)	158	37.13N	7.20W
Islāmābād, Pak.	183	33.55N	73.05E
Isla Mujeres, Mex. (ē′s-lä-mōō-kĕ′rĕs)	120a	21.25N	86.53W
Island Lake, l., Can.	85	53.47N	94.25W
Island Park, N.Y., U.S.	228	40.36N	73.40W
Islands, Bay of, b., Can. (ī′lăndz)	93	49.10N	58.15W
Islay, i., Scot., U.K. (ī′lā)	146	55.55N	6.35W
Isle, r., Fr. (ēl)	156	45.02N	0.29E
Isle of Axholme, reg., Eng., U.K. (äks′-hôm)	144a	53.33N	0.48W
Isle of Man, dep., Eur. (măn)	150	54.26N	4.21W
Isle Royale National Park, rec., Mi., U.S. (ĭl′roi-ăl′)	97	47.57N	88.37W
Isleta, N.M., U.S. (ēs-lā′tă) (ī-lē′tă)	109	34.55N	106.45W
Isleta Indian Reservation, I.R., N.M., U.S.	109	34.55N	106.45W
Isleworth, neigh., Eng., U.K.	235	51.28N	0.20W
Islington, neigh., Can.	227c	43.39N	79.32W
Islington, neigh., Eng., U.K.	235	51.34N	0.06W
Ismailia, Egypt (ēs-mä-ēl′ēä)	218b	30.35N	32.17E
Ismā′īlīyah, neigh., Egypt	244a	30.03N	31.14E
Ismā′īlīyah Canal, can., Egypt	218b	30.25N	31.45E
Ismaning, Ger. (ēz′mä-nēng)	145d	48.14N	11.41E
Isparta, Tur. (ė-spär′tà)	182	37.50N	30.40E
Israel, nation, Asia	182	32.40N	34.00E
Issaquah, Wa., U.S. (ĭz′sä-kwäh)	106a	47.32N	122.02W
Isselburg, Ger. (ē′sĕl-bōōrg)	157c	51.50N	6.28E
Issoire, Fr. (ē-swár′)	156	45.32N	3.13E
Issoudun, Fr. (ē-sōō-dăN′)	156	46.56N	2.00E
Issum, Ger. (ē′sōōm)	157c	51.32N	6.24E
Issyk-Kul, Ozero, l., Kyrg.	169	42.13N	76.12E
Issy-les-Moulineaux, Fr.	237c	48.49N	2.17E
Īstādeh-ye Moqor, Āb-e, l., Afg.	186	32.35N	68.00E
İstanbul, Tur. (ė-stän-bōōl′)	182	41.02N	29.00E
İstanbul Boğazi (Bosporus), strt., Tur.	182	41.10N	29.10E
Istead Rise, Eng., U.K.	235	51.24N	0.22E
Istiaía, Grc. (ĭs-tyī′yä)	161	38.58N	23.11E
Istmina, Col. (ēst-mē′nä)	130a	5.10N	76.40W

ng-sing; ŋ-baŋk; N-nasalized n; nŏd; cŏmmit; ōld; ôbey; ôrder; oi-boil; fōōd; ŏŏ-as oo in foot; ou-out; s-soft; sh-dish; th-thin; pūre; ûnite; ûrn; stŭd; circŭs; ü-as in French tu; ′-indeterminate vowel.

300 Istokpoga–Jelgava

PLACE (Pronunciation)	PAGE	Lat. °′	Long. °′
Istokpoga, Lake, l., Fl., U.S. (ĭs-tŏk-pō'gȧ)	115a	27.20N	81.33W
Istra, pen., Yugo. (ē-strä)	160	45.18N	13.48E
Istranca Dağlari, mts., Eur. (ĭ-strän'jȧ)	161	41.50N	27.25E
Istres, Fr. (ēs'tr')	156a	43.30N	5.00E
Itabaiana, Braz. (ē-tä-bä-yȧ-nä)	131	10.42S	37.17W
Itabapoana, Braz. (ē-tä'-bä-pôä'nä)	129a	21.19S	40.58W
Itabapoana, r., Braz.	129a	21.11S	41.18W
Itabirito, Braz. (ē-tä-bē-rē'tô)	129a	20.15S	43.46W
Itabuna, Braz. (ē-tä-bōō'nȧ)	131	14.47S	39.17W
Itacoara, Braz. (ē-tä-kō'ä-rä)	129a	21.41S	42.04W
Itacoatiara, Braz. (ē-tȧ-kwȧ-tyä'rȧ)	131	3.03S	58.18W
Itagüí, Col. (ē-tä'gwê)	130a	6.11N	75.36W
Itaguí, r., Braz.	132b	22.53S	43.43W
Itaipava, Braz. (ē-tī-pȧ'-vä)	132b	22.23S	43.09W
Itaipu, Braz. (ē-tī'pōō)	132b	22.58S	43.02W
Itaipu, Ponta de, c., Braz.	234c	22.59S	43.03W
Itaituba, Braz. (ē-tä'ĭ-tōō'bȧ)	131	4.12S	56.00W
Itajái, Braz. (ē-tä-zhī')	132	26.52S	48.39W
Italy, Tx., U.S.	113	32.11N	96.51W
Italy, nation, Eur. (ĭt'ȧ-lē)	142	43.58N	11.14E
Itambi, Braz. (ē-tä'm-bē)	132b	22.44S	42.57W
Itami, Japan (ē'tä'mē')	195b	34.47N	135.25E
Itapecerica, Braz. (ē-tä-pĕ-sĕ-rē'kȧ)	129a	20.29S	45.08W
Itapecuru-Mirim, Braz. (ē-tä-pĕ'kōō-rōō-mē-rēɴ')	131	3.17S	44.15W
Itaperuna, Braz. (ē-tä'pâ-rōō'nä)	131	21.12S	41.53W
Itapetininga, Braz. (ē-tä-pē-tē-nē'ɴ-gä)	131	23.37S	48.03W
Itapira, Braz.	129a	22.27S	46.47W
Itapira, Braz. (ē-tȧ-pē'rȧ)	131	20.42S	51.19W
Itaquaquecetuba, Braz.	234d	23.29S	46.21W
Itarsi, India	186	22.43N	77.45E
Itasca, Tx., U.S. (ī-tăs'kȧ)	113	32.09N	97.08W
Itasca, l., Mn., U.S.	102	47.13N	95.14W
Itatiaia, Pico da, mtn., Braz. (pē'-kô-dȧ-ē-tä-tyȧ'ēä)	131	22.18S	44.41W
Itatiba, Braz. (ē-tä-tē'bä)	129a	23.01S	46.48W
Itaúna, Braz. (ē-tä-ōō'nä)	129a	20.05S	44.35W
Ithaca, Mi., U.S. (ĭth'ȧ-kȧ)	98	43.20N	84.35W
Ithaca, N.Y., U.S.	97	42.25N	76.30W
Itháka, i., Grc. (ē'thä-kē)	161	38.27N	20.48E
Itigi, Tan.	217	5.42S	34.29E
Itimbiri, r., Zaire	216	2.40N	23.30E
Itire, Nig.	244d	6.31N	3.21E
Itoko, Zaire (ē-tō'kō)	212	1.13S	22.07E
Itu, Braz. (ē-tōō')	129a	23.16S	47.16W
Ituango, Col. (ē-twäŋ'gō)	130	7.07N	75.44W
Ituiutaba, Braz. (ē-tōō-ēōō-tä'bä)	131	18.56S	49.17W
Itumirim, Braz. (ē-tōō-mē-rē'ɴ)	129a	21.20S	44.51W
Itundujia Santa Cruz, Mex. (ē-tōōn-dōō-hē'ȧ sä'n-tä krōō'z)	119	16.50N	97.43W
Iturbide, Mex. (ē'tōōr-bē'dhȧ)	120a	19.38N	89.31W
Iturup, i., Russia (ē-tōō-rōōp')	171	45.35N	147.15E
Ituzaingo, Arg. (ē-tōō-zä-ē'n-gō)	132a	34.40S	58.40W
Itzehoe, Ger. (ē'tzē-hō)	154	53.55N	9.31E
Iuka, Ms., U.S. (ī-ū'kȧ)	114	34.47N	88.10W
Iúna, Braz. (ē-ōō'-nä)	129a	20.22S	41.32W
Iupeba, Braz.	234d	23.41S	46.22W
Ivanhoe, Austl. (ĭv'ăn-hō)	204	32.53S	144.10E
Ivanhoe, Austl.	243b	37.46S	145.03E
Ivanivka, Ukr.	162	46.43N	34.33E
Ivano-Frankivs'k, Ukr.	167	48.53N	24.46E
Ivanopil', Ukr.	163	49.51N	28.11E
Ivanovo, Russia (ē-vä'nô-vō)	164	57.02N	41.54E
Ivanovo, prov., Russia	162	56.55N	40.30E
Ivanteyevka, Russia (ē-ván-tyĕ'yĕf-kȧ)	172b	55.58N	37.56E
Ivdel', Russia (ĭv'dyĕl)	172a	60.42N	60.27E
Iver, Eng., U.K.	235	51.31N	0.30W
Iver Heath, Eng., U.K.	235	51.32N	0.31W
Iviza see Ibiza, i., Spain	142	38.55N	1.24E
Ivohibé, Madag. (ē-vô-hē-bā')	213	22.28S	46.59E
Ivory Coast see Cote d'Ivoire, nation, Afr.	210	7.43N	6.30W
Ivrea, Italy (ē-vrĕ'ä)	148	45.25N	7.54E
Ivry-sur-Seine, Fr.	157b	48.49N	2.23E
Ivujivik, Can.	85	62.17N	77.52W
Iwaki, Japan	194	37.03N	140.57E
Iwate Yama, mtn., Japan (ē-wä-tē-yä'mä)	194	39.50N	140.56E
Iwatsuki, Japan	195a	35.48N	139.43E
Iwaya, Japan (ē'wȧ-yȧ)	195b	34.35N	135.01E
Iwo, Nig.	210	7.38N	4.11E
Ixcateopán, Mex. (ēs-kä-tä-ō-pän')	118	18.29N	99.49W
Ixelles, Bel.	145a	50.49N	4.23E
Ixhautlán, Mex. (ēs-wȧt-län')	118	20.41N	98.01W
Ixhuatán, Mex. (ēs-hwä-tän')	119	16.19N	94.30W
Ixmiquilpan, Mex. (ēs-mē-kēl'pän)	118	20.30N	99.12W
Ixopo, S. Afr.	213c	30.10S	30.04E
Ixtacalco, Mex. (ēs-tȧ-käl'kō)	119a	19.23N	99.07W
Ixtaltepec, Mex. (ēs-täl-tē-pĕk')	119	16.33N	95.04W
Ixtapalapa, Mex. (ēs'tä-pä-lä'pä)	119a	19.21N	99.06W
Ixtapaluca, Mex. (ēs'tä-pä-lōō'kä)	119a	19.18N	98.53W
Ixtepec, Mex. (ēks-tē'pĕk)	119	16.37N	95.09W
Ixtlahuaca, Mex. (ēs-tlä-wä'kä)	118	19.34N	99.46W
Ixtlán de Juárez, Mex. (ēs-tlän' dā hwä'rȧz)	119	17.20N	96.29W
Ixtlán del Río, Mex. (ēs-tlän'dĕl rē'ō)	118	21.05N	104.22W
Iya, r., Russia	170	53.45N	99.30E
Iyo-Nada, b., Japan (ē'yō nä-dä)	195	33.33N	132.07E
Izabal, Guat. (ē'zä-bäl')	120	15.23N	89.10W
Izabal, Lago, l., Guat.	120	15.30N	89.04W
Izalco, El Sal. (ē-zäl'kō)	120	13.50N	89.40W
Izamal, Mex. (ē-zä-mä'l)	120a	20.55N	89.00W
Izberbash, Russia	168	42.33N	47.52E
Izhevsk, Russia (ē-zhyĕfsk')	164	56.50N	53.15E
Izhma, Russia (ĭzh'mȧ)	166	65.00N	54.05E
Izhma, r., Russia	166	64.00N	53.00E
Izhora, r., Russia (ēz'hô-rȧ)	172c	59.36N	30.20E
Izmayil, Ukr.	167	45.00N	28.49E
İzmir, Tur. (ĭz-mēr')	182	38.25N	27.05E
Izmit, Tur. (ĭz-mēt')	149	40.45N	29.45E
Iznajar, Embalse de, res., Spain	158	37.15N	4.30W
Iztaccíhuatl, mtn., Mex.	118	19.10N	98.38W
Izuhara, Japan (ē'zōō-hä'rä)	195	34.11N	129.18E
Izumi-Ōtsu, Japan (ē'zōō-mōō ō'tsōō)	195b	34.30N	135.24E
Izumo, Japan (ē'zōō-mō)	195	35.22N	132.45E
Izu Shichitō, is., Japan	189	34.32N	139.25E

J

PLACE (Pronunciation)	PAGE	Lat. °′	Long. °′
Jabal, Bahr al, r., Sudan	211	7.30N	31.00E
Jabalpur, India	183	23.18N	79.59E
Jabavu, S. Afr.	244b	26.15S	27.53E
Jablonec nad Nisou, Czech Rep. (yäb'lô-nyĕts)	154	50.43N	15.12E
Jablunkov Pass, p., Eur. (yäb'lòn-kôf)	155	49.31N	18.35E
Jaboatão, Braz. (zhä-bô-ȧ-touɴ)	131	8.14S	35.08W
Jaca, Spain (hä'kä)	159	42.35N	0.30W
Jacala, Mex. (hä-kȧ'lä)	118	21.01N	99.11W
Jacaltenango, Guat. (hä-kȧl-tē-näŋ'gō)	120	15.39N	91.41W
Jacarézinho, Braz. (zhä-kä-rē'zē-nyō)	131	23.13S	49.58W
Jachymov, Czech Rep. (yä'chĭ-môf)	154	50.22N	12.51E
Jacinto City, Tx., U.S. (hä-sēn'tō) (jȧ-sĭn'tō)	113a	29.45N	95.14W
Jacksboro, Tx., U.S. (jăks'bŭr-ô)	110	33.13N	98.11W
Jackson, Al., U.S. (jăk'sŭn)	114	31.31N	87.52W
Jackson, Ca., U.S.	108	38.22N	120.47W
Jackson, Ga., U.S.	114	33.19N	83.55W
Jackson, Ky., U.S.	114	37.32N	83.17W
Jackson, La., U.S.	113	30.50N	91.13W
Jackson, Mi., U.S.	97	42.15N	84.25W
Jackson, Mn., U.S.	102	43.37N	95.00W
Jackson, Ms., U.S.	97	32.17N	90.10W
Jackson, Mo., U.S.	111	37.23N	89.40W
Jackson, Oh., U.S.	98	39.00N	82.40W
Jackson, Tn., U.S.	97	35.37N	88.49W
Jackson, Port, b., Austl.	201b	33.50S	151.18E
Jackson Heights, neigh., N.Y., U.S.	228	40.45N	73.53W
Jackson Lake, l., Wy., U.S.	105	43.57N	110.28W
Jacksonville, Al., U.S. (jăk'sŭn-vĭl)	114	33.52N	85.45W
Jacksonville, Fl., U.S.	97	30.20N	81.40W
Jacksonville, Il., U.S.	97	39.43N	90.12W
Jacksonville, Tx., U.S.	113	31.58N	95.18W
Jacksonville Beach, Fl., U.S.	115	31.18N	81.25W
Jacmel, Haiti (zhȧk-mĕl')	123	18.15N	72.30W
Jaco, l., Mex. (hä'kō)	112	27.51N	103.50W
Jacobābad, Pak.	186	28.22N	68.30E
Jacobina, Braz. (zhä-kô-bē'nȧ)	131	11.13S	40.30W
Jacomino, Cuba	233b	23.06N	82.20W
Jacques-Cartier, r., Can.	83b	47.04N	71.28W
Jacques Cartier, Détroit de, strt., Can.	92	50.07S	63.58W
Jacques-Cartier, Mont, mtn., Can.	92	48.59N	66.00W
Jacquet River, Can. (zhȧ-kĕ') (jăk'ĕt)	92	47.55N	66.00W
Jacutinga, Braz. (zhȧ-kōō-tēn'gä)	129a	22.17S	46.36W
Jade Buddha, Temple of the (Yufosi), rel., China	241a	31.14N	121.26E
Jadebusen, b., Ger.	154	53.28N	8.17E
Jadotville see Likasi, Zaire	212	10.59S	26.44E
Jaén, Peru (kä-ĕ'n)	130	5.38S	78.49W
Jaen, Spain	148	37.45N	3.48W
Jaffa, Cape, c., Austl. (jăf'ȧ)	202	36.58S	139.29E
Jaffna, Sri L. (jäf'nȧ)	183b	9.44N	80.09E
Jagüey Grande, Cuba (hä'gwā grän'dā)	122	22.35N	81.05W
Jahore Strait, strt., Asia	181b	1.22N	103.37E
Jahrom, Iran	182	28.30N	53.28E
Jaibo, r., Cuba (hä-ē'bō)	123	20.10N	75.20W
Jaipur, India	183	27.00N	75.50E
Jaisalmer, India	186	27.00N	70.54E
Jajce, Bos. (yī'tsĕ)	161	44.20N	17.19E
Jajpur, India	183	20.49N	86.37E
Jakarta, Indon. (yä-kär'tä)	196	6.17S	106.45E
Jakobstad, Fin. (yȧ'kôb-stȧdh)	146	63.33N	22.31E
Jalacingo, Mex. (hä-lä-sĭŋ'gō)	119	19.47N	97.16W
Jalālābād, Afg. (jŭ-lä-lȧ-bȧd)	183a	34.25N	70.27E
Jalālah al Baḩrīyah, Jabal, mts., Egypt	218b	29.20N	32.00E
Jalapa, Guat. (hä-lä'pä)	120	14.38N	89.58W
Jalapa de Díaz, Mex.	119	18.06N	96.33W
Jalapa del Marqués, Mex. (dĕl mär-kās')	119	16.30N	95.29W
Jaleswar, Nepal	186	26.50N	85.55E
Jalgaon, India	186	21.08N	75.33E
Jalisco, Mex. (hä-lēs'kō)	118	21.27N	104.54W
Jalisco, state, Mex.	116	20.07N	104.45W
Jalón, r., Spain (hä-lōn')	158	41.22N	1.46W
Jalostotitlán, Mex. (hä-lōs-tē-tlán')	118	21.09N	102.30W
Jalpa, Mex. (häl'pä)	118	21.40N	103.04W
Jalpa, Mex. (häl'pä)	119	18.12N	93.06W
Jalpan, Mex. (häl'pän)	118	21.13N	99.31W
Jaltepec, Mex. (häl-tȧ-pĕk')	119	17.20N	95.15W
Jaltipan, Mex. (häl-tä-pän')	119	17.59N	94.42W
Jaltocan, Mex. (häl-tô-kän')	118	21.08N	98.32W
Jamaare, r., Nig.	215	11.50N	10.10E
Jamaica, nation, N.A.	117	17.45N	78.00W
Jamaica Bay, b., N.Y., U.S.	228	40.36N	73.51W
Jamaica Cay, i., Bah.	123	22.45N	75.55W
Jamālīyah, neigh., Egypt	244a	30.03N	31.16E
Jamālpur, Bngl.	186	24.56N	89.58E
Jamay, Mex. (hä-mī')	118	20.16N	102.43W
Jambi, Indon. (mäm'bē)	196	1.45S	103.28E
James, r., U.S.	96	46.25N	98.55W
James, r., Mo., U.S.	111	36.51N	93.22W
James, r., Va., U.S.	97	37.35N	77.50W
James, Lake, res., N.C., U.S.	115	36.07N	81.48W
James Bay, b., Can. (jāmz)	85	53.53N	80.40W
Jamesburg, N.J., U.S. (jāmz'bûrg)	100a	40.21N	74.26W
Jameson Raid Memorial, hist., S. Afr.	244b	26.11S	27.49E
James Point, c., Bah.	122	25.20N	76.30W
James Range, mts., Austl.	202	24.15S	133.30E
James Ross, i., Ant.	128	64.20S	58.20W
Jamestown, S. Afr.	213c	31.07S	26.49E
Jamestown, N.Y., U.S. (jāmz'toun)	97	42.05N	79.15W
Jamestown, N.D., U.S.	96	46.54N	98.42W
Jamestown, R.I., U.S.	100b	41.30N	71.21W
Jamestown Reservoir, res., N.D., U.S.	102	47.16N	98.40W
Jamiltepec, Mex. (hä-mēl-tȧ-pĕk)	119	16.16N	97.54W
Jammerbugten, b., Den.	152	57.20N	9.28E
Jammu, India	183	32.50N	74.52E
Jammu and Kashmīr, hist. reg., Asia (kȧsh-mēr')	183	39.10N	75.05E
Jāmnagar, India (jäm-nŭ'gŭr)	183	22.33N	70.03E
Jamshedpur, India (jäm'shĕd-pōōr)	183	22.52N	86.11E
Jándula, r., Spain (hän'dōō-lȧ)	158	38.28N	3.52W
Janesville, Wi., U.S. (jānz'vĭl)	103	42.41N	89.03W
Janin, W. Bank	181a	32.27N	35.19E
Jan Mayen, i., Nor. (yän mī'ĕn)	146	70.59N	8.05W
Jánoshalma, Hung. (yä'nòsh-hôl-mô)	155	46.17N	19.18E
Janów Lubelski, Pol. (yä'nōōf lū-bĕl'skĭ)	155	50.40N	22.25E
Januária, Braz. (zhä-nwä'rē-ä)	131	15.31S	44.17W
Japan, nation, Asia (jȧ-păn')	189	36.30N	133.30E
Japan, Sea of, sea, Asia (jȧ-păn')	189	40.08N	132.55E
Japeri, Braz. (zhȧ-pĕ'rē)	132b	22.38S	43.40W
Japurá (Caquetá), r., S.A.	130	2.00S	68.00W
Jarabacoa, Dom. Rep. (ĸä-rä-bä-kô'ä)	123	19.05N	70.40W
Jaral del Progreso, Mex. (hä-räl dĕl prô-grā'sō)	118	20.21N	101.05W
Jarama, r., Spain (hä-rä'mä)	158	40.33N	3.30W
Jarash, Jord.	181a	32.17N	35.53E
Jardim Paulista, neigh., Braz.	234d	23.35S	46.40W
Jardines, Banco, bk., Cuba (bä'n-kō-här-dē'nȧs)	122	21.45N	81.40W
Jargalant, Mong.	192	46.28N	115.10E
Jari, r., Braz. (zhä-rē)	131	0.28N	53.00W
Jarocin, Pol. (yä-rō'tsēn)	155	51.58N	17.31E
Jarosław, Pol. (yȧ-rôs-wȧf)	147	50.01N	22.41E
Jarud Qi, China (jya-lōō-tŭ shyē)	189	44.35N	120.40E
Jasenevo, neigh., Russia	239b	55.36N	37.33E
Jasin, Malay.	181b	2.19N	102.26E
Jašiūnai, Lith. (dzȧ-shōō-nȧ'yē)	153	54.27N	25.25E
Jāsk, Iran (jäsk)	182	25.46N	57.48E
Jasło, Pol. (yäs'wō)	155	49.44N	21.28E
Jason Bay, b., Malay.	181b	1.53N	104.14E
Jasonville, In., U.S. (jā'sŭn-vĭl)	98	39.10N	87.15W
Jasper, Can.	84	52.53N	118.05W
Jasper, Al., U.S. (jăs'pēr)	114	33.50N	87.17W
Jasper, Fl., U.S.	115	30.30N	82.56W
Jasper, In., U.S.	98	38.20N	86.55W
Jasper, Mn., U.S.	102	43.51N	96.22W
Jasper, Tx., U.S.	113	30.55N	93.59W
Jasper National Park, rec., Can.	84	53.09N	117.45W
Jászapáti, Hung. (yäs'ô-pä-tē)	155	47.29N	20.10E
Jászberény, Hung.	155	47.30N	19.56E
Jatibonico, Cuba (hä-tē-bō-nē'kō)	122	22.00N	79.15W
Játiva, Spain (hä'tē-vä)	148	38.58N	0.31W
Jauja, Peru (ĸä-ō'ĸ)	130	11.43S	75.32W
Jaumave, Mex. (hou-mä'vȧ)	118	23.23N	99.24W
Jaunjelgava, Lat. (youn'yĕl'gȧ-vȧ)	166	56.37N	25.06E
Java (Jawa), i., Indon.	196	8.35S	111.11E
Javari, r., S.A. (kȧ-vä-rē)	130	4.25S	72.07W
Java Trench, deep	196	9.45S	107.30E
Jávea, Spain (hȧ-vā'ä)	159	38.45N	0.07E
Jawa, Laut (Java Sea), sea, Indon.	196	5.10S	110.30E
Jawor, Pol. (yä'vôr)	154	51.04N	16.12E
Jaworzno, Pol. (yä-vôzh'nô)	155	50.11N	19.18E
Jaya, Puncak, mtn., Indon.	197	4.00S	137.00E
Jayapura, Indon.	196	2.30S	140.45W
Jayb, Wādī al (Ha'Arava), val., Asia	181a	30.33N	35.10E
Jazīrat Muhammad, Egypt	244a	30.07N	31.12E
Jazzīn, Leb.	181a	33.34N	35.37E
Jeanerette, La., U.S. (jĕn-ēr-et') (zhän-rĕt')	113	29.54N	91.41W
Jebba, Nig. (jĕb'ȧ)	210	9.07N	4.46E
Jeddore Lake, l., Can.	93	48.07N	55.35W
Jedlesee, neigh., Aus.	239e	48.16N	16.23E
Jędrzejów, Pol. (yăɴ-dzhā'yòf)	155	50.38N	20.18E
Jefferson, Ga., U.S. (jĕf'ēr-sŭn)	114	34.05N	83.35W
Jefferson, Ia., U.S.	103	42.10N	94.22W
Jefferson, La., U.S.	100d	29.57N	90.04W
Jefferson, Pa., U.S.	230b	39.56N	80.04W
Jefferson, Tx., U.S.	113	32.47N	94.21W
Jefferson, Wi., U.S.	103	42.59N	88.45W
Jefferson, r., Mt., U.S.	105	45.37N	112.22W
Jefferson, Mount, mtn., Or., U.S.	104	44.41N	121.50W
Jefferson City, Mo., U.S.	97	38.34N	92.10W
Jefferson Park, neigh., Il., U.S.	231a	41.59N	87.46W
Jeffersontown, Ky., U.S. (jĕf'ēr-sŭn-toun)	101h	38.11N	85.34W
Jeffersonville, In., U.S. (jĕf'ēr-sŭn-vĭl)	101h	38.17N	85.44W
Jega, Nig.	215	12.15N	4.23E
Jehol, hist. reg., China (jĕ-hŏl)	189	42.31N	118.12E
Jēkabpils, Lat. (yĕk'ȧb-pĭls)	166	56.29N	25.50E
Jelenia Góra, Pol. (yĕ-lĕn'yȧ gò'rȧ)	154	50.53N	15.43E
Jelgava, Lat.	153	56.39N	23.42E

PRONOUNCING INDEX

Jellico–Južna Morava 301

PLACE (Pronunciation)	PAGE	Lat. °′	Long. °′
Jellico, Tn., U.S. (jĕl'ĭ-kō)	114	36.34N	84.06W
Jemez Indian Reservation, I.R., N.M., U.S.	109	35.35N	106.45W
Jena, Ger. (yā'nä)	147	50.55N	11.37E
Jenkins, Ky., U.S. (jĕŋ'kĭnz)	115	37.09N	82.38W
Jenkintown, Pa., U.S. (jĕŋ'kĭn-toun)	100f	40.06N	75.08W
Jennings, La., U.S. (jĕn'ĭngz)	113	30.14N	92.40W
Jennings, Mi., U.S.	98	44.20N	85.20W
Jennings, Mo., U.S.	107e	38.43N	90.16W
Jequitinhonha, r., Braz. (zhĕ-kē-tēŋ-ō'n-yä)	131	16.47S	41.19W
Jérémie, Haiti (zhā-rā-mē')	123	18.40N	74.10W
Jeremoabo, Braz. (zhĕ-rā-mō-á'bō)	131	10.03S	38.13W
Jerez, Punta, c., Mex. (pōō'n-tä-ĸĕ-rāz')	119	23.04N	97.44W
Jerez de la Frontera, Spain	148	36.42N	6.09W
Jerez de los Caballeros, Spain	158	38.20N	6.45W
Jericho, Austl. (jĕr'ĭ-kō)	203	23.38S	146.24E
Jericho, S. Afr. (jĕr-ĭkô)	218d	25.16S	27.47E
Jericho, N.Y., U.S.	228	40.48N	73.32W
Jericho see Arīḥā, W. Bank	181a	31.51N	35.28E
Jerome, Az., U.S. (jė-rōm')	96	34.45N	112.10W
Jerome, Id., U.S.	105	42.44N	114.31W
Jersey, dep., Eur.	156	49.15N	2.10W
Jersey, i., Jersey (jûr'zĭ)	147	49.13N	2.07W
Jersey City, N.J., U.S.	97	40.43N	74.05W
Jersey Shore, Pa., U.S.	99	41.10N	77.15W
Jerseyville, Il., U.S. (jĕr'zē-vĭl)	111	39.07N	90.18W
Jerusalem, Isr. (jė-rōō'sȧ-lĕm)	182	31.46N	35.14E
Jesup, Ga., U.S. (jĕs'ŭp)	115	31.36N	81.53W
Jésus, Île, i., Can.	227b	45.35N	73.45W
Jesús Carranza, Mex. (hĕ-sōō's-kär-rá'n-zä)	119	17.26N	95.01W
Jesús del Monte, neigh., Cuba	233b	23.06N	82.22W
Jesús María, Peru	233c	12.04S	77.04W
Jewel, Or., U.S. (jū'ĕl)	106c	45.56N	123.30W
Jewel Cave National Monument, rec., S.D., U.S.	102	43.44N	103.52W
Jhālawār, India	183	24.30N	76.00E
Jhang Maghiāna, Pak.	186	31.21N	72.19E
Jhānsi, India (jän'sē)	183	25.29N	78.32E
Jhārsuguda, India	186	22.51N	84.13E
Jhelum, Pak.	183	32.59N	73.43E
Jhelum, r., Asia (jā'lŭm)	183	31.40N	71.51E
Jhenkāri, India	240a	22.46N	88.18E
Jhil Kuranga, neigh., India	240d	28.40N	77.17E
Jiading, China (jyä-dĭŋ)	190	31.23N	121.15E
Jialing, r., China (jyä-lĭŋ)	188	32.30N	105.30E
Jiamusi, China	194	46.50N	130.21E
Ji'an, China (jyē-än)	189	27.15N	115.10E
Ji'an, China	192	41.00N	126.04E
Jianchangying, China (jyĕn-chäŋ-yĭŋ)	190	40.09N	118.47E
Jiangcun, China (jyän-tsōn)	191a	23.16N	113.14E
Jiangling, China (jyäŋ-lĭŋ)	189	30.30N	112.10E
Jiangshanzhen, China (jyäŋ-shän-jŭn)	190	36.39N	120.31E
Jiangsu, prov., China (jyäŋ-sōō)	189	33.45N	120.30E
Jiangwan, China (jyäŋ-wän)	191b	31.18N	121.29E
Jiangxi, prov., China (jyäŋ-shyē)	189	28.15N	116.00E
Jiangyin, China (jyäŋ-yĭn)	193	31.54N	120.15E
Jianli, China (jyĕn-lē)	193	29.50N	112.52E
Jianning, China (jyĕn-nĭŋ)	193	26.50N	116.55E
Jian'ou, China (jyĕn-ō)	193	27.10N	118.18E
Jianshi, China (jyĕn-shr)	193	30.40N	109.45E
Jiaohe, China	190	38.03N	116.18E
Jiaohe, China (jyou-hŭ)	192	43.40N	127.20E
Jiaoxian, China (jyou shyĕn)	189	36.18N	120.01E
Jiaozuo, China (jyou-dzwô)	190	35.15N	113.18E
Jiashan, China (jyä-shän)	190	32.41N	118.00E
Jiaxing, China (jyä-shyĭŋ)	189	30.45N	120.50E
Jiayu, China (jyä-yōō)	193	30.00N	114.00E
Jiazhou Wan, b., China (jyä-jō wän)	189	36.10N	119.55E
Jicarilla Apache Indian Reservation, I.R., N.M., U.S. (ĸē-kȧ-rēl'yȧ)	109	36.45N	107.00W
Jicarón, Isla, i., Pan. (ĸē-kä-rōn')	121	7.14N	81.41W
Jiddah, Sau. Ar.	182	21.30N	39.15E
Jieshou, China	190	33.17N	115.20E
Jieyang, China (jyĕ-yäŋ)	189	23.38N	116.20E
Jiggalong, Austl. (jĭg'ȧ-lông)	202	23.20S	120.45E
Jiguani, Cuba (ĸē-gwä-nē')	122	20.20N	76.30W
Jigüey, Bahía, b., Cuba (bä-ē'ä-ĸē'gwā)	122	22.15N	78.10W
Jihlava, Czech Rep. (yē'hlȧ-vȧ)	147	49.23N	15.33E
Jijel, Alg.	147	36.49N	5.47E
Jijia, r., Rom.	155	47.35N	27.02E
Jijiashi, China (jyē-jyä-shr)	190	32.10N	120.17E
Jijiga, Eth.	218a	9.15N	42.48E
Jijona, Spain (ĸē-hō'nä)	159	38.31N	0.29W
Jilin, China (jyē-lĭn)	189	43.58N	126.40E
Jilin, prov., China	189	44.20N	124.50E
Jiloca, r., Spain (ĸē-lō'kȧ)	158	41.13N	1.30W
Jilotepeque, Guat. (ĸē-lō-tĕ-pĕ'kĕ)	120	14.39N	89.36W
Jima, Eth.	211	7.41N	36.52E
Jimbolia, Rom. (zhĭm-bô'lyä)	161	45.45N	20.44E
Jiménez, Mex.	112	27.09N	104.55W
Jiménez, Mex.	112	29.03N	100.42W
Jiménez, Mex. (ĸē-mā'nāz)	118	24.12N	98.29W
Jiménez del Téul, Mex. (tĕ-ōō'l)	118	21.28N	103.51W
Jimo, China (jyē-mwo)	192	36.22N	120.28E
Jim Thorpe, Pa., U.S. (jĭm' thôrp')	99	40.50N	75.45W
Jinan, China (jyē-nän)	189	36.40N	117.01E
Jincheng, China (jyĭn-chŭŋ)	192	35.30N	112.50E
Jindřichův Hradec, Czech Rep. (yēn'd'r-zhĭ-kōōf hrä'dĕts)	154	49.09N	15.02E
Jing, r., China (jyĭŋ)	192	34.40N	108.20E
Jing'anji, China (jyĭŋ-än-jē)	190	34.30N	116.55E
Jingdezhen, China (jyĭn-dŭ-jŭn)	193	29.18N	117.18E
Jingjiang, China (jyĭŋ-jyäŋ)	190	32.02N	120.15E
Jingning, China (jyĭŋ-nĭŋ)	192	35.28N	105.50E
Jingpo Hu, l., China (jyĭŋ-pwo hōō)	192	44.10N	129.00E
Jingxian, China	190	37.43N	116.17E
Jingxian, China (jyĭŋ shyĕn)	193	26.32N	109.45E
Jingxing, China (jyĭŋ-shyĭŋ)	192	47.00N	123.00E
Jingzhi, China (jyĭŋ-jr)	190	36.19N	119.23E
Jinhua, China (jyĭn-hwä)	189	29.10N	119.42E
Jining, China (jyē-nĭŋ)	189	35.26N	116.34E
Jining, China	192	41.00N	113.10E
Jinja, Ug. (jĭn'jä)	211	0.26N	33.12E
Jinotega, Nic. (ĸē-nô-tā'gä)	120	13.07N	86.00W
Jinotepe, Nic. (ĸē-nô-tā'pȧ)	120	11.52N	86.12W
Jinqiao, China (jyĭn-chyou)	190	31.46N	116.46E
Jinshan, China (jyĭn-shän)	191b	30.53N	121.09E
Jinta, China (jyĭn-tä)	188	40.11N	98.45E
Jintan, China (jyĭn-tän)	190	31.47N	119.34E
Jin Xian, China (jyĭn shyĕn)	192	39.04N	121.40E
Jinxiang, China (jyĭn-shyäŋ)	190	35.03N	116.20E
Jinyun, China (jyĭn-yòn)	193	28.40N	120.08E
Jinzhai, China (jyĭn-jī)	190	31.41N	115.51E
Jinzhou, China (jyĭn-jō)	189	41.00N	121.00E
Jinzhou Wan, b., China (jyĭn-jō wän)	190	39.07N	121.17E
Jinzū-Gawa, r., Japan (jĕn'zōō gä'wä)	195	36.26N	137.18E
Jipijapa, Ec. (ĸē-pē-hä'pä)	130	1.36S	80.52W
Jiquilisco, El Sal. (ĸē-kē-lē's-kô)	120	13.18N	88.32W
Jiquilpan de Juárez, Mex. (ĸē-kēl'pän dā hwä'räz)	118	20.00N	102.43W
Jiquipilco, Mex. (hē-kē-pē'l-kô)	119a	19.32N	99.37W
Jitotol, Mex. (ĸē-tô-tōl')	119	17.03N	92.54W
Jiu, r., Rom.	161	44.45N	23.17E
Jiugang, China	240b	39.49N	116.27E
Jiujiang, China	189	29.43N	116.00E
Jiujiang, China (jyô-jyän)	191a	22.50N	113.02E
Jiuquan, China (jyô-chyän)	188	39.46N	98.26E
Jiurongcheng, China (jyô-rôŋ-chŭŋ)	190	37.23N	122.31E
Jiushouzhang, China (jyô-shō-jäŋ)	190	35.59N	115.52E
Jiuwuqing, China (jyô-wōō-chyĭŋ)	192a	32.31N	116.51E
Jiuyongnian, China (jyô-yôŋ-nĭĕn)	190	36.41N	114.46E
Jixian, China (jyē shyĕn)	190	35.25N	114.03E
Jixian, China	190	37.37N	115.33E
Jixian, China	190	40.03N	117.25E
Jiyun, r., China (jyē-yōōm)	190	39.35N	117.34E
Joachimsthal, Ger.	145b	52.58N	13.45E
João Pessoa, Braz.	131	7.09S	34.45W
João Ribeiro, Braz. (zhô-un-rē-bā'rō)	129a	20.42S	44.03W
Jobabo, r., Cuba (hō-bä'bä)	122	20.50N	77.15W
Jock, r., Can. (jŏk)	83c	45.08N	75.51W
Jocotepec, Mex. (jō-kō-tȧ-pĕk')	118	20.17N	103.26W
Jodar, Spain (hō'där)	158	37.54N	3.20W
Jodhpur, India (hŏd'pōōr)	183	26.23N	73.00E
Joensuu, Fin. (yō-ĕn'sōō)	153	62.35N	29.46E
Joffre, Mount, mtn., Can. (jŏ'f'r)	87	50.32N	115.13W
Jõgeva, Est. (yû'gĕ-vȧ)	153	58.45N	26.23E
Joggins, Can. (jŏ'gĭnz)	92	45.42N	64.27W
Johannesburg, S. Afr. (yō-hän'ĕs-bôrgh)	212	26.08S	27.54E
Johannisthal, neigh., Ger.	238a	52.26N	13.30E
John Carroll University, pt. of i., Oh., U.S.	229a	41.29N	81.32W
John Day, r., Or., U.S. (jŏn'dā)	104	44.46N	120.15W
John Day, Middle Fork, r., Or., U.S.	104	44.53N	119.04W
John Day, North Fork, r., Or., U.S.	104	45.03N	118.50W
John Day Dam, Or., U.S.	104	45.40N	120.15W
John F. Kennedy International Airport, arpt., N.Y., U.S.	228	40.38N	73.47W
John H. Kerr Reservoir, res., U.S.	97	36.30N	78.38W
John Martin Reservoir, res., Co., U.S. (jŏn mär'tĭn)	110	37.57N	103.04W
Johns Hopkins University, pt. of i., Md., U.S.	229c	39.20N	76.37W
Johnson, r., Or., U.S. (jŏn'sŭn)	106c	45.27N	122.20W
Johnsonburg, Pa., U.S. (jŏn'sŭn-bûrg)	99	41.30N	78.40W
Johnson City, Il., U.S. (jŏn'sŭn)	98	37.50N	88.55W
Johnson City, N.Y., U.S.	99	42.10N	76.00W
Johnson City, Tn., U.S.	97	36.17N	82.23W
Johnston, i., Oc. (jŏn'stŭn)	2	17.00N	168.00W
Johnstone Strait, strt., Can.	86	50.25N	126.00W
Johnston Falls, wtfl., Afr.	217	10.35S	28.50E
Johnstown, N.Y., U.S. (jonz'toun)	99	43.00N	74.20W
Johnstown, Pa., U.S.	97	40.20N	78.50W
Johor, r., Malay. (jŭ-hōr')	181b	1.39N	103.52E
Johor Baharu, Malay.	196	1.28N	103.46E
Jõhvi, Est. (yû'vĭ)	153	59.21N	27.21E
Joigny, Fr. (zhwȧn-yē')	156	47.58N	3.26E
Joinville, Braz. (zhwăn-vĕl')	132	26.18S	48.47W
Joinville, Fr.	157	48.28N	5.05E
Joinville, i., Ant.	128	63.00S	53.30W
Joinville-le-Pont, Fr.	237c	48.49N	2.28E
Jojutla, Mex. (hō-hōō'tlä)	118	18.39N	99.11W
Jola, Mex. (ĸô'lä)	118	21.08N	104.26W
Joliet, Il., U.S. (jō-lĭ-ĕt')	101a	41.32N	88.05W
Joliette, Can. (zhō-lyĕt')	85	46.01N	73.30W
Jolo, Phil. (hō-lō)	196	5.59N	121.05E
Jolo Island, i., Phil.	196	5.55N	121.15E
Jomalig, i., Phil. (hō-mä'lēg)	197a	14.44N	122.34E
Jomulco, Mex. (hô-mōōl'kô)	118	21.08N	104.24W
Jonacatepec, Mex.	118	18.39N	98.46W
Jonava, Lith. (yō-nä'vȧ)	153	55.05N	24.15E
Jones, Phil. (jōnz)	197a	12.56N	122.05E
Jones, Phil.	197a	16.35N	121.39E
Jonesboro, Ar., U.S. (jōnz'bûro)	97	35.49N	90.42W
Jonesboro, La., U.S.	113	32.14N	92.43W
Jonesville, La., U.S. (jōnz'vĭl)	113	31.35N	91.50W
Jonesville, Mi., U.S.	98	42.00N	84.45W
Jong, r., S.L.	214	8.10N	12.10W
Joniškis, Lith. (yô'nĭsh-kĭs)	153	56.14N	23.36E
Jönköping, Swe. (yûn'chû-pĭng)	146	57.47N	14.10E
Jonquiere, Can. (zhôn-kyâr')	85	48.25N	71.15W
Jonuta, Mex. (hô-nōō'tä)	119	18.07N	92.09W
Jonzac, Fr. (zhôn-zák')	156	45.27N	0.27W
Joplin, Mo., U.S. (jŏp'lĭn)	97	37.05N	94.31W
Jordan, nation, Asia (jôr'dăn)	182	30.15N	38.00E
Jordan, r., Asia	181a	32.05N	35.35E
Jordan, r., Ut., U.S.	107b	40.42N	111.56W
Jorhāt, India (jòr-hät')	183	26.43N	94.16E
Jorullo, Volcán de, vol., Mex. (vôl-kä'n-dĕ-hô-rōōl'yō)	118	18.54N	101.38W
José C. Paz, Arg.	132a	34.32S	58.44W
Joseph Bonaparte Gulf, b., Austl. (jō'sĕf bō'nȧ-pärt)	202	13.30S	128.40E
Josephburg, Can.	83g	53.45N	113.06W
Joseph Lake, l., Can. (jō'sĕf läk)	83g	53.18N	113.06W
Joshua Tree National Monument, rec., Ca., U.S. (jō'shū-ȧ trē)	108	34.02N	115.53W
Jos Plateau, plat., Nig. (jŏs)	215	9.53N	9.05E
Jostedalsbreen, ice., Nor. (yŏstĕ-däls-brēĕn)	146	61.40N	6.55E
Jotunheimen, mts., Nor.	146	61.44N	8.11E
Joulter's Cays, is., Bah. (jōl'tĕrz)	122	25.20N	78.10W
Jouy-en-Josas, Fr.	237c	48.46N	2.10E
Jouy-le-Chatel, Fr. (zhwē-lĕ-shä-tĕl')	157b	48.40N	3.07E
Jovellanos, Cuba (hō-vĕl-yä'nōs)	122	22.50N	81.10W
J. Percy Priest Lake, res., Tn., U.S.	114	36.00N	86.45W
Juan Aldama, Mex. (kòá'n-äl-dá'mä)	118	24.16N	103.21W
Juan Anchorena, neigh., Arg.	233d	34.29S	58.30W
Juan de Fuca, Strait of, strt., N.A. (hwän' dā fōō'kä)	84	48.25N	124.37W
Juan de Nova, Île, i., Reu.	213	17.18S	43.07E
Juan Diaz, r., Pan. (ĸōōá'n-dē'äz)	116a	9.05N	79.30W
Juan Fernández, Islas de, is., Chile	128	33.30S	79.00W
Juan González Romero, Mex.	233a	19.30N	99.04W
Juan L. Lacaze, Ur. (hōōá'n-ĕ'lĕ-lä-kä'zĕ)	129c	34.25S	57.28W
Juan Luis, Cayos de, is., Cuba (ka-yōs-dĕ-hwän lōō-ēs')	122	22.15N	82.00W
Juárez, Arg. (hōōá'rĕz)	132	37.42S	59.46W
Juázeiro, Braz. (zhōōá'zā'rō)	131	9.27S	40.28W
Juazeiro do Norte, Braz. (zhōōá'zā'rō-dō-nôr-tĕ)	131	7.16S	38.57W
Jubayl, Leb. (jōō-bīl')	181a	34.07N	35.38E
Jubba (Genale), r., Afr.	218a	1.30N	42.25E
Juby, Cap, c., Mor. (yōō'bē)	210	28.01N	13.21W
Júcar, r., Spain (hōō'kär)	148	39.10N	1.22W
Júcaro, Cuba (hōō'kä-rō)	122	21.40N	78.50W
Juchipila, Mex. (hōō-chē-pē'lä)	118	21.26N	103.09W
Juchitán, Mex. (hōō-chē-tän')	116	16.15N	95.00W
Juchitlán, Mex. (hōō-chē-tlän)	118	20.05N	104.07W
Jucuapa, El Sal. (ĸōō-kwä'pä)	120	13.30N	88.24W
Judenburg, Aus. (jōō'dĕn-bûrg)	154	47.10N	14.40E
Judith, r., Mt., U.S. (jōō'dĭth)	105	47.20N	109.36W
Jugo-Zapad, neigh., Russia	239b	55.40N	37.32E
Juhua Dao, i., China (jyōō-hwä dou)	190	40.30N	120.47E
Juigalpa, Nic. (hwē-gäl'pä)	120	12.02N	85.24W
Juilly, Fr.	237c	49.01N	2.42E
Juiz de Fora, Braz. (zhò-ēzh' dā fō'rä)	131	21.47S	43.20W
Jujuy, Arg. (hōō-hwē')	132	24.14S	65.15W
Jujuy, prov., Arg. (hōō-hwē')	132	23.00S	65.45W
Jukskei, r., S. Afr.	213b	25.58S	27.58E
Julesburg, Co., U.S. (jōōlz'bûrg)	110	40.59N	102.16W
Juliaca, Peru (hōō-lē-ä'kä)	130	15.26S	70.12W
Julian Alps, mts., Yugo.	148	46.05N	14.05E
Julianehåb, Grnld.	82	60.07N	46.20W
Jülich, Ger. (yü'lĕk)	157c	50.55N	6.22E
Jullundur, India	183	31.29N	75.39E
Julpaiguri, India	186	26.35N	88.48E
Jumento Cays, is., Bah. (hōō-mĕn'tō)	123	23.05N	75.40W
Jumilla, Spain (hōō-mēl'yä)	158	38.28N	1.20W
Jump, r., Wi., U.S. (jŭmp)	103	45.18N	90.53W
Jumpingpound Creek, r., Can. (jŭmp-ĭng-pound)	83e	51.01N	114.34W
Jumrah, Indon.	181b	1.48N	101.04E
Junagādh, India (jò-nä'gŭd)	183	21.33N	70.25E
Junayfah, Egypt	218c	30.11N	32.26E
Junaynah, Ra's al, mtn., Egypt	181a	29.02N	33.58E
Junction, Tx., U.S. (jŭŋk'shŭn)	112	30.29N	99.48W
Junction City, Ks., U.S.	111	39.01N	96.49W
Jundiaí, Braz.	131	23.11S	46.52W
Juneau, Ak., U.S. (jōō'nō)	96a	58.25N	134.30W
Jungfrau, mtn., Switz. (yòng'frou)	154	46.30N	7.59E
Juniata, neigh., Pa., U.S.	229b	40.01N	75.07W
Junín, Arg. (hōō-nē'n)	132	34.35S	60.56W
Junín, Col.	130a	4.47N	73.39W
Juniyah, Leb. (jōō-nē'ē)	181a	33.59N	35.38E
Jupiter, r., Can.	92	49.40N	63.20W
Jupiter, Mount, mtn., Wa., U.S.	106a	47.42N	123.04W
Jur, r., Sudan (jòr)	211	6.38N	27.52E
Jura, mts., Eur. (zhü-rá')	147	46.55N	6.49E
Jura, i., Scot., U.K. (jōō'rá)	150	56.09N	6.45W
Jura, Sound of, strt., Scot., U.K. (jōō'rȧ)	150	55.45N	5.55W
Jurbarkas, Lith. (yōōr-bär'käs)	153	55.06N	22.50E
Jūrmala, Lat.	153	56.57N	23.37E
Jurong, China (jyōō-roŋ)	190	31.58N	119.12E
Jurong, Sing.	240c	1.21N	103.42E
Juruá, r., S.A.	130	5.30S	67.30W
Juruena, r., Braz. (zhōō-rōōĕ'nä)	131	12.22S	58.34W
Justice, Il., U.S.	231a	41.45N	87.50W
Jutiapa, Guat. (hōō-tē-ä'pä)	120	14.16N	89.55W
Juticalpa, Hond. (hōō-tē-käl'pä)	116	14.35N	86.17W
Jutland see Jylland, reg., Den.	146	56.04N	9.00E
Juventino Rosas, Mex.	118	20.38N	101.02W
Juventud, Isla de la, i., Cuba	117	21.40N	82.45W
Juvisy-sur-Orge, Fr.	237c	48.41N	2.23E
Juxian, China (jyōō shyĕn)	192	35.35N	118.50E
Juxtlahuaca, Mex. (hōōs-tlä-hwä'kä)	118	17.20N	98.02W
Juye, China (jyōō-yü)	190	35.25N	116.05E
Južna Morava, r., Yugo. (ù'zhnä mô'rä-vä)	161	42.30N	22.00E

PLACE (Pronunciation)	PAGE	Lat. ° '	Long. ° '

Jwālahari, neigh., India — 240d — 28.40N 77.06E
Jylland, reg., Den. — 146 — 56.04N 9.00E

K

K2, mtn., Asia — 183 — 36.06N 76.38E
Kaabong, Ug. — 217 — 3.31N 34.08E
Kaalfontein, S. Afr. (kärl-fōn-tān) — 213b — 26.02S 28.16E
Kaappunt, c., S. Afr. — 212a — 34.21S 18.30E
Kaarst, Ger. — 236 — 51.14N 6.37E
Kabaena, Pulau, i., Indon. (kä-bá-ä'ná) — 196 — 5.35S 121.07E
Kabala, S.L. (ká-bä'lá) — 210 — 9.43N 11.39W
Kabale, Ug. — 217 — 1.15S 29.59E
Kabalega Falls, wtfl., Ug. — 211 — 2.15N 31.41E
Kabalo, Zaire (kä-bä'lō) — 212 — 6.03S 26.55E
Kabambare, Zaire — 212 — 4.47S 27.45E
Kabardino-Balkaria, state, Russia — 166 — 43.30N 43.30E
Kabba, Nig. — 215 — 7.50N 6.03E
Kabe, Japan (kä'bā) — 195 — 34.32N 132.30E
Kabel, neigh., Ger. — 236 — 51.24N 7.29E
Kabinakagami, r., Can. — 90 — 49.00N 84.15W
Kabinda, Zaire (kä-bēn'dä) — 212 — 6.08S 24.29E
Kabompo, r., Zam. (ká-bôm'pò) — 212 — 14.00S 23.40E
Kabongo, Zaire (ká-bông'ō) — 212 — 7.58S 25.10E
Kabot, Gui. — 214 — 10.48N 14.57W
Kaboudia, Ra's, c., Tun. — 148 — 35.17N 11.28E
Kābul, Afg. (kä'bŏl) — 183 — 34.39N 69.14E
Kabul, r., Asia (kä'bŏl) — 183 — 34.44N 69.43E
Kabunda, Zaire — 217 — 12.25S 29.22E
Kabwe, Zam. — 212 — 14.27S 28.27E
Kachuga, Russia (ká-chōō-gá) — 165 — 54.09N 105.43E
Kadei, r., Afr. — 215 — 4.00N 15.10E
Kadıköy, neigh., Tur. — 239f — 40.59N 29.01E
Kadnikov, Russia (käd'nĕ-kôf) — 166 — 59.30N 40.10E
Kadoma, Japan — 195b — 34.43N 135.36E
Kadoma, Zimb. — 212 — 18.21S 29.55E
Kaduna, Nig. (kä-dōō'nä) — 210 — 10.33N 7.27E
Kaduna, r., Nig. — 215 — 9.30N 6.00E
Kaédi, Maur. (kä-ā-dē') — 210 — 16.09N 13.30W
Kaena Point, c., Hi., U.S. (kä'á-nä) — 96d — 21.33N 158.19W
Kaesŏng, N. Kor. (kä'ē-sŭng) (kī'jŏ) — 189 — 38.00N 126.35E
Kafanchan, Nig. — 215 — 9.36N 8.17E
Kafia Kingi, Sudan (kä'fē-à kĭŋ'gē) — 211 — 9.17N 24.28E
Kafue, Zam. (kä'fōō) — 212 — 15.45S 28.17E
Kafue, r., Zam. — 212 — 15.45S 26.30E
Kafue Flats, sw., Zam. — 217 — 16.15S 26.30E
Kafue National Park, rec., Zam. — 217 — 15.00S 25.35E
Kafwira, Zaire — 217 — 12.10S 27.33E
Kagal'nik, r., Russia (kä-gäl'nĕk) — 163 — 46.58N 39.25E
Kagera, r., Afr. (kä-gä'rä) — 211 — 1.10S 31.10E
Kagoshima, Japan (kä'gồ-shē'má) — 189 — 31.35N 130.31E
Kagoshima-Wan, b., Japan (kä'gồ-shē'mä wän) — 194 — 31.24N 130.39E
Kagran, neigh., Aus. — 239e — 48.15N 16.27E
Kahayan, r., Indon. — 196 — 1.45S 113.40E
Kahemba, Zaire — 216 — 7.17S 19.00E
Kahia, Zaire — 217 — 6.21S 28.24E
Kahoka, Mo., U.S. (ká-hō'ká) — 111 — 40.26N 91.42W
Kahoolawe, Hi., U.S. (kä-hōō-lä'wē) — 94a — 20.28N 156.48W
Kahramanmaraş, Tur. — 182 — 37.40N 36.50W
Kahshahpiwi, r., Can. — 103 — 48.24N 90.56W
Kahuku Point, c., Hi., U.S. (kä-hōō'kōō) — 96d — 21.50N 157.50W
Kahului, Hi., U.S. — 96c — 20.53N 156.28W
Kai, Kepulauan, is., Indon. — 197 — 5.35S 132.45E
Kaiang, Malay. — 181b — 3.00N 101.47E
Kaiashk, r., Can. — 90 — 49.40N 89.30W
Kaibab Indian Reservation, I.R., Az., U.S. (kä'ē-báb) — 109 — 36.55N 112.45W
Kaibab Plat, Az., U.S. — 109 — 36.30N 112.10W
Kaidori, Japan — 242a — 35.37N 139.27E
Kaidu, r., China (kī-dōō) — 188 — 42.35N 84.04E
Kaieteur Fall, wtfl., Guy. (kī-ē-tōōr') — 131 — 4.48N 59.24W
Kaifeng, China (kī-fŭŋ) — 189 — 34.48N 114.22E
Kai Kecil, i., Indon. — 197 — 5.45S 132.40E
Kailua, Hi., U.S. (kä'ē-lōō'á) — 96c — 21.18N 157.43W
Kailua Kona, Hi., U.S. — 94a — 19.49N 155.59W
Kaimana, Indon. — 197 — 3.32S 133.47E
Kaimanawa Mountains, mts., N.Z. — 205 — 39.10S 176.00E
Kainan, Japan (kä'ē-nän') — 195 — 34.09N 135.14E
Kainji Lake, res., Nig. — 210 — 10.25N 4.50E
Kaisermühlen, neigh., Aus. — 239e — 48.14N 16.26E
Kaiserslautern, Ger. (kī-zĕrs-lou'tĕrn) — 147 — 49.26N 7.46E
Kaiserwerth, neigh., Ger. — 236 — 51.18N 6.44E
Kaitaia, N.Z. (kä-ē-tä'ē-ä) — 203a — 35.30S 173.28E
Kaiwi Channel, strt., Hi., U.S. (käĕ-wē) — 96c — 21.10N 157.38W
Kaiyuan, China — 192 — 42.30N 124.00E
Kaiyuan, China (kū-yuän) — 193 — 23.42N 103.20E
Kaiyuh Mountains, mts., Ak., U.S. (kī-yōō') — 95 — 64.25N 157.38W
Kajaani, Fin. (kä'yá-nĕ) — 146 — 64.15N 27.16E
Kajang, neigh., Malay. — 181b — 2.47N 104.05E
Kajiki, Japan (kä'jē-kē) — 194 — 31.44N 130.41E
Kakhovka, Russia — 163 — 46.46N 33.32E
Kakhovs'ke vodoskhovyshche, res., Ukr. — 164 — 47.21N 33.33E
Kākināda, India — 183 — 16.58N 82.18E

Kaktovik, Ak., U.S. (käk-tŏ'vĭk) — 95 — 70.08N 143.51W
Kakwa, r., Can. (käk'wá) — 87 — 54.00N 118.55W
Kalach, Russia (kä-lách') — 167 — 50.15N 40.55E
Kaladan, r., Asia — 188 — 21.07N 93.04E
Ka Lae, c., Hi., U.S. — 94a — 18.55N 155.41W
Kalahari Desert, des., Afr. (kä-lä-hä'rĕ) — 212 — 23.00S 22.03E
Kalama, Wa., U.S. (ká-läm'á) — 106c — 46.01N 122.50W
Kalama, r., Wa., U.S. — 106c — 46.03N 122.47W
Kalámai, Grc. (kä-lä-mī') — 142 — 37.04N 22.08E
Kalamákion, Grc. — 239d — 37.55N 23.43E
Kalamazoo, Mi., U.S. (kăl-á-má-zōō') — 97 — 42.20N 85.40W
Kalamazoo, r., Mi., U.S. — 98 — 42.35N 86.00W
Kalanchak, Ukr. (kä-län-chäk') — 163 — 46.17N 33.14E
Kalandula, Ang. (dōō'ká dá brä-gän'sä) — 212 — 9.06S 15.57E
Kalaotoa, Pulau, i., Indon. — 196 — 7.22S 122.30E
Kalapana, Hi., U.S. (kä-lä-pá'nä) — 94a — 19.25N 155.00W
Kalar, mtn., Iran — 182 — 31.43N 51.41E
Kalāt, Pak. (kū-lät') — 183 — 29.05N 66.36E
Kalemie, Zaire — 212 — 5.56S 29.12E
Kalgan see Zhangjiakou, China — 189 — 40.45N 114.58E
Kalgoorlie-Boulder, Austl. (kăl-gōōr'lĕ) — 202 — 30.45S 121.35E
Kaliakra, Nos, c., Bul. — 149 — 43.25N 28.42E
Kalima, Zaire — 217 — 2.34S 26.37E
Kalina, neigh., Zaire — 244c — 4.18S 15.16E
Kaliningrad, Russia — 164 — 54.42N 20.32E
Kaliningrad, Russia (kä-lē-nēn'grät) — 172b — 55.55N 37.49E
Kalinkovichi, Bela. (kä-lēn-ko-vē'chē) — 162 — 52.07N 29.19E
Kalispel Indian Reservation, I.R., Wa., U.S. (kăl-ĭ-spĕl') — 104 — 48.25N 117.30W
Kalispell, Mt., U.S. (kăl'ĭ-spĕl) — 96 — 48.12N 114.18W
Kalisz, Pol. (kä'lēsh) — 147 — 51.45N 18.05E
Kaliua, Tan. — 217 — 5.04S 31.48E
Kalixälven, r., Swe. — 146 — 67.12N 22.00E
Kālkāji, neigh., India — 240d — 28.33N 77.16E
Kalksburg, neigh., Aus. — 239e — 48.08N 16.15E
Kalkum, Ger. — 236 — 51.18N 6.46E
Kallithéa, Grc. — 239d — 37.57N 23.42E
Kalmar, Swe. (käl'mär) — 146 — 56.40N 16.19E
Kalmarsund, strt., Swe. (käl'mär) — 152 — 56.30N 16.17E
Kal'mius, r., Ukr. (käl'myōōs) — 163 — 47.15N 37.38E
Kalmykia, state, Russia — 167 — 46.56N 46.00E
Kalocsa, Hung. (kä'lō-chä) — 155 — 46.32N 19.00E
Kalohi Channel, strt., Hi., U.S. (kä-lō'hĭ) — 94a — 20.55N 157.15W
Kaloko, Zaire — 217 — 6.47S 25.48E
Kalomo, Zam. (kä-lō'mō) — 212 — 17.02S 26.30E
Kalsubai Mount, mtn., India — 186 — 19.43N 73.47E
Kaltenkirchen, Ger. (käl'tĕn-kēr-ĸĕn) — 145c — 53.50N 9.57E
Kālu, r., India — 187b — 19.18N 73.14E
Kaluga, Russia (kä-lō'gä) — 164 — 54.29N 36.12E
Kaluga, prov., Russia — 162 — 54.10N 35.00E
Kalundborg, Den. (ká-lŏn'bôr') — 152 — 55.42N 11.07E
Kalush, Ukr. (kä'lŏsh) — 155 — 49.02N 24.24E
Kalvarija, Lith. (käl-vä-rē'yä) — 153 — 54.24N 23.17E
Kalwa, India — 187b — 19.12N 72.59E
Kal'ya, Russia (käl'yá) — 172a — 60.17N 59.58E
Kalyān, India — 186 — 19.16N 73.07E
Kalyazin, Russia (kál-yá'zēn) — 162 — 57.13N 37.55E
Kama, r., Russia (kä'mä) — 164 — 56.10N 53.50E
Kamaishi, Japan (kä'mä-ē'shē) — 194 — 39.16N 142.03E
Kamakura, Japan (kä'mä-kōō'rä) — 195 — 35.19N 139.33E
Kamarān, i., Yemen — 182 — 15.19N 41.47E
Kāmārhāti, India — 186a — 22.41N 88.23E
Kamata, neigh., Japan — 242a — 35.33N 139.43E
Kambove, Zaire (käm-bō'vĕ) — 212 — 10.58S 26.43E
Kamchatka, r., Russia — 171 — 54.15N 158.38E
Kamchatka, Poluostrov, pen., Russia — 171 — 55.19N 157.45E
Kāmdebpur, India — 240a — 22.54N 88.20E
Kameari, neigh., Japan — 242a — 35.46N 139.51E
Kameido, neigh., Japan — 242a — 35.42N 139.50E
Kamen, Ger. (kä'mĕn) — 157c — 51.35N 7.40E
Kamenjak, Rt, c., Cro. (kä'mĕ-nyäk) — 160 — 44.45N 13.57E
Kamen'-na-Obi, Russia (kä-mĭny'nŭ ồ'bĕ) — 164 — 53.43N 81.28E
Kamensk-Shakhtinskiy, Russia (kä'mĕnsk shäk'tĭn-skī) — 163 — 48.17N 40.16E
Kamensk-Ural'skiy, Russia (kä'mĕnsk ōō-räl'skī) — 166 — 56.27N 61.55E
Kamenz, Ger. (kä'mĕnts) — 154 — 51.16N 14.05E
Kameoka, Japan (kä'mä-ōkä) — 195b — 35.01N 135.35E
Kāmet, mtn., Asia — 186 — 30.50N 79.42E
Kamiakatsuka, neigh., Japan — 242a — 35.46N 139.39E
Kamiasao, Japan — 242a — 35.35N 139.30E
Kamień Pomorski, Pol. — 154 — 53.57N 14.48E
Kamiishihara, Japan — 242a — 35.39N 139.32E
Kamikitazawa, neigh., Japan — 242a — 35.40N 139.38E
Kamikoma, Japan — 195b — 34.45N 135.50E
Kamina, Zaire — 212 — 8.44S 25.00E
Kaministikwia, r., Can. (ká-mĭ-nĭ-stĭk'wĭ-á) — 103 — 48.40N 89.41W
Kamioyamada, neigh., Japan — 242a — 35.35N 139.24E
Kamitsuruma, Japan — 242a — 35.31N 139.25E
Kamituga, Zaire — 217 — 3.04S 28.11E
Kamloops, Can. (käm'lōōps) — 84 — 50.40N 120.20W
Kamoshida, neigh., Japan — 242a — 35.34N 139.30E
Kamp, r., Aus. (kämp) — 154 — 48.30N 15.45E
Kampala, Ug. (käm-pä'lä) — 211 — 0.19N 32.25E
Kampar, r., Indon. (käm'pär) — 196 — 0.30N 101.30E
Kampene, Zaire — 217 — 3.36S 26.40E
Kampenhout, Bel. — 145a — 50.56N 4.33E
Kamp-Lintfort, Ger. (kämp-lēnt'fồrt) — 157c — 51.30N 6.34E
Kampong Kranji, Sing. — 240c — 1.26N 103.46E
Kampong Loyang, Sing. — 240c — 1.22N 103.58E
Kampong Tanjong Keling, Sing. — 240c — 1.18N 103.42E
Kâmpóng Thum, Camb. (kŏm'pŏng-tồm) — 196 — 12.41N 104.29E

Kâmpôt, Camb. (käm'pŏt) — 196 — 10.41N 104.07E
Kampuchea see Cambodia, nation, Asia — 196 — 12.15N 104.00E
Kamsack, Can. (käm'säk) — 84 — 51.34N 101.54W
Kamskoye, res., Russia — 164 — 59.08N 56.30E
Kamudilo, Zaire — 217 — 7.42S 27.18E
Kamuela, Hi., U.S. — 94a — 20.01N 155.40W
Kamui Misaki, c., Japan — 194 — 43.25N 139.35E
Kámuk, Cerro, mtn., C.R. (sě'r-rồ-kä-mōō'k) — 121 — 9.18N 83.02W
Kam'yanets'-Podil's'kyy, Ukr. — 167 — 48.41N 26.34E
Kam'yanka-Buz'ka, Ukr. — 155 — 50.06N 24.20E
Kamyshevatskaya, Russia — 163 — 46.24N 37.58E
Kamyshin, Russia (kä-mwĕsh'ĭn) — 164 — 50.08N 45.20E
Kamyshlov, Russia (kä-mĕsh'lồf) — 164 — 56.50N 62.32E
Kan, r., Russia (kän) — 170 — 56.30N 94.91E
Kanab, Ut., U.S. (kän'áb) — 109 — 37.00N 112.30W
Kanabeki, Russia (ká-nä'byĕ-kī) — 172a — 57.48N 57.16E
Kanab Plateau, plat., Az., U.S. — 109 — 36.31N 112.55W
Kanaga, i., Ak., U.S. (kä-nä'gä) — 95a — 52.02N 177.38W
Kanagawa, dept., Japan (kä'nä-gä'wä) — 195a — 35.29N 139.32E
Kanai, Japan — 242a — 35.35N 139.28E
Kanā'is, Ra's al, c., Egypt — 149 — 31.14N 28.08E
Kanamachi, Japan (kä-nä-mä'chē) — 195a — 35.46N 139.52E
Kanamori, Japan — 242a — 35.32N 139.28E
Kananga, Zaire — 212 — 6.14S 22.17E
Kananikol'skoye, Russia — 172a — 52.48N 57.29E
Kanasín, Mex. (kä-nä-sē'n) — 120a — 20.54N 89.31W
Kanatak, Ak., U.S. — 95 — 57.35N 155.48W
Kanawha, r., W.V., U.S. (ká-nô'wá) — 97 — 37.55N 81.50W
Kanaya, Japan (kä-nä'yä) — 195a — 35.10N 139.49E
Kanazawa, Japan (kä'nä-zä'wä) — 189 — 36.34N 136.38E
Kānchenjunga, mtn., Asia (kŭn-chĭn-jón'gä) — 183 — 27.30N 88.18E
Kānchipuram, India — 183 — 12.55N 79.43E
Kanda Kanda, Zaire (kän'dá kän'dá) — 212 — 6.56S 23.36E
Kandalaksha, Russia (kän-dä-läk'shä) — 164 — 67.10N 33.05E
Kandalakshskiy Zaliv, b., Russia — 166 — 66.20N 35.00E
Kandava, Lat. (kän'dä-vá) — 153 — 57.03N 22.45E
Kandi, Benin — 210 — 11.08N 2.56E
Kandiāro, Pak. — 186 — 27.09N 68.12E
Kandla, India (kŭnd'lŭ) — 186 — 23.00N 70.20E
Kandy, Sri L. (kän'dĕ) — 183b — 7.18N 80.42E
Kane, Pa., U.S. (kān) — 99 — 41.40N 78.50W
Kaneohe, Hi., U.S. (kä-nä-ō'hä) — 94a — 21.25N 157.47W
Kaneohe Bay, b., Hi., U.S. — 96d — 21.32N 157.40W
Kanevskaya, Russia (kä-nyĕf'ská) — 163 — 46.07N 38.58E
Kangaroo, i., Austl. (käŋ-gá-rò') — 202 — 36.05S 137.05E
Kangaroo Ground, Austl. — 243b — 37.41S 145.13E
Kangāvar, Iran (kŭŋ'gä-vär) — 182 — 34.37N 46.45E
Kangean, Kepulauan, is., Indon. (käŋ'gĕ-än) — 196 — 6.50S 116.22E
Kanggye, N. Kor. (käŋ'gyĕ) — 189 — 40.55N 126.40E
Kanghwa, i., S. Kor. (käng'hwä) — 194 — 37.38N 126.00E
Kangnŭng, S. Kor. (käng'nồ ng) — 194 — 37.42N 128.50E
Kango, Gabon (käN-gō) — 212 — 0.09N 10.08E
Kangowa, Zaire — 216 — 9.55S 22.48E
Kanin, Poluostrov, pen., Russia — 164 — 68.00N 45.00E
Kaningo, Kenya — 217 — 0.49S 38.32E
Kanin Nos, Mys, c., Russia — 166 — 68.40N 44.00E
Kaniv, Ukr. — 163 — 49.46N 31.27E
Kanivs'ke vodoskhovyshche, res., Ukr. — 164 — 50.10N 30.40E
Kanjiža, Yugo. (kä'nyĕ-zhä) — 161 — 46.05N 20.02E
Kankakee, Il., U.S. (käŋ-ká-kē') — 98 — 41.07N 87.53W
Kankakee, r., Il., U.S. — 98 — 41.15N 88.15W
Kankan, Gui. (käN-kän) (kän-kän') — 210 — 10.23N 9.18W
Kannapolis, N.C., U.S. (kän-äp'ỏ-lĭs) — 115 — 35.30N 80.38W
Kannoura, Japan — 195 — 33.34N 134.18E
Kano, Nig. (kä'nō) — 210 — 12.00N 8.30E
Kanokop, mtn., S. Afr. — 212a — 33.49S 18.37E
Kanopolis Reservoir, res., Ks., U.S. (kän-ŏp'ỏ-lĭs) — 110 — 38.44N 98.01W
Kānpur, India (kän'pûr) — 186 — 26.30N 80.10E
Kansas, state, U.S. (kän'zás) — 96 — 38.30N 99.40W
Kansas, r., Ks., U.S. — 111 — 39.00N 95.52W
Kansas City, Ks., U.S. — 97 — 39.06N 94.39W
Kansas City, Mo., U.S. — 97 — 39.05N 94.35W
Kansk, Russia — 165 — 56.14N 95.43E
Kansŏng, S. Kor. — 194 — 38.09N 128.29E
Kantang, Thai. (kän'täng') — 196 — 7.26N 99.28E
Kantchari, Burkina — 214 — 12.29N 1.31E
Kanton, i., Kir. — 224 — 5.00S 174.00W
Kantunilkin, Mex. (kän-tōō-nēl-kē'n) — 120a — 21.07N 87.30W
Kanzaki, r., Japan — 242b — 34.42N 135.25E
Kanzhakovskiy Kamen, Gora, mtn., Russia (kän-zhä'kồvs-kēē kämĕn) — 172a — 59.38N 59.12E
Kaohsiung, Tai. (kä-ō-syóng') — 189 — 22.35N 120.25E
Kaolack, Sen. — 210 — 14.09N 16.04W
Kaouar, oasis, Niger — 211 — 19.16N 13.09E
Kapaa, Hi., U.S. — 94a — 22.06N 159.20W
Kapanga, Zaire — 216 — 8.21S 22.35E
Kapellen, Ger. — 236 — 51.25N 6.35E
Kapfenberg, Aus. (käp'fän-bĕrgh) — 154 — 47.27N 15.16E
Kapiri Mposhi, Zam. — 217 — 13.58S 28.41E
Kapoeta, Sudan — 211 — 4.45N 33.35E
Kaposvár, Hung. (kồ'pòsh-vär) — 155 — 46.21N 17.45E
Kapotn'a, neigh., Russia — 239b — 55.38N 37.48E
Kapsan, N. Kor. (käp'sän') — 194 — 40.59N 128.22E
Kapuskasing, Can. — 85 — 49.28N 82.22W
Kapuskasing, r., Can. — 90 — 48.55N 82.55W
Kapustin Yar, Russia (kä'pòs-tĕn yär') — 167 — 48.30N 45.40E
Kaputar, Mount, mtn., Austl. (kä-pû-tär) — 204 — 30.15S 150.11E
Kaputir, Kenya — 217 — 47.35N 17.02E
Kara, Russia (kärá) — 164 — 68.42N 65.30E
Kara, r., Russia — 166 — 68.30N 65.20E
Karabalā', Iraq (kŭr'bá-lä) — 182 — 32.31N 43.58E

ăt; fĭnàl; rāte; senàte; ârm; àsk; sofà; fâre; ch-choose; dh-as th in other; bē; ĕvent; bĕt; recĕnt; cratĕr; g-gō; gh-guttural g; bĭt; ī-short neutral; rīde; ĸ-guttural k as ch in German ich;

PRONOUNCING INDEX

Karabanovo-Kentucky 303

PLACE (Pronunciation)	PAGE	Lat. °'	Long. °'
Karabanovo, Russia (kä'rá-bá-nō-vô)	162	56.19N	38.43E
Karabash, Russia (kó-rá-bäsh')	172a	55.27N	60.14E
Kara-Bogaz-Gol, Zaliv, b., Turk. (kȧ-rä' bŭ-gäs')	169	41.30N	53.40E
Karachay-Cherkessia, state, Russia	168	44.00N	42.00E
Karachev, Russia (ká-rá-chôf')	166	53.08N	34.54E
Karāchi, Pak.	183	24.59N	68.56E
Karaganda see Qaraghandy, Kaz.	169	49.42N	73.18E
Karaidel', Russia (kä'rī-dĕl)	172a	55.52N	56.54E
Kara-Khobda, r., Kaz. (kä-rá кôb'dá)	170	50.40N	55.00E
Karakoram Pass, p., Asia	183	35.35N	77.45E
Karakoram Range, mts., India (kä'rä kō'rŏm)	183	35.24N	76.38E
Karakorum, hist., Mong.	188	47.25N	102.22E
Kara Kum Canal, can., Turk.	169	37.35N	61.50E
Karakumy, des., Turk. (kara-kum)	169	40.00N	57.00E
Karaman, Tur. (kä-rä-män')	149	37.10N	33.00E
Karamay, China (kär-äm-ä)	188	45.37N	84.53E
Karamea Bight, bt., N.Z. (kȧ-rá-mē'á bīt)	203a	41.20S	171.30E
Kara Sea see Karskoye More, sea, Russia	164	74.00N	68.00E
Karashahr (Yanqui), China (kä-rä-shä-är) (yän-chyē)	188	42.14N	86.28E
Karatsu, Japan (kä'rá-tso͞o)	195	33.28N	129.59E
Karaul, Russia (kä-rä-ól')	170	70.13N	83.46E
Karave, India	240e	19.01N	73.01E
Karawanken, mts., Eur.	154	46.32N	14.07E
Karcag, Hung. (kär'tsäg)	155	47.18N	20.58E
Kardhítsa, Grc.	161	39.23N	21.57E
Kärdla, Est. (kĕrd'là)	153	58.59N	22.44E
Karelia, state, Russia	170	62.30N	32.35E
Karema, Tan.	212	6.49S	30.26E
Kargat, Russia (kär-gät')	164	55.17N	80.07E
Karghalik see Yecheng, China	188	37.54N	77.25E
Kargopol', Russia (kär-gō-pōl'')	164	61.30N	38.50E
Kariba, Lake, res., Afr.	212	17.15S	27.55E
Karibib, Nmb. (kar'á-bĭb)	212	21.55S	15.50E
Kārikāl, India (kä-rē-käl')	187	10.58N	79.49E
Karimata, Kepulauan, is., Indon. (kä-rē-mä'tá)	196	1.08S	108.10E
Karimata, Selat, strt., Indon.	196	1.00S	107.10E
Karimun Besar, i., Indon.	181b	1.10N	103.28E
Karimunjawa, Kepulauan, is., Indon. (kä'rē-mo͞on-yä'vä)	196	5.36S	110.15E
Karin, Som. (kár'ĭn)	218a	10.43N	45.50E
Karkar Dūmān, neigh., India	240d	28.39N	77.18E
Karkar Island, i., Pap. N. Gui. (kär'kär)	197	4.50S	146.45E
Karkheh, r., Iran	182	32.45N	47.50E
Karkinits'ka zatoka, b., Ukr.	163	45.50N	32.45E
Karlivka, Ukr.	163	49.26N	35.08E
Karlobag, Cro. (kär-lō-bäg')	160	44.30N	15.03E
Karlovac, Cro. (kär'lō-váts)	149	45.29N	15.16E
Karlovo, Bul. (kär'lō-vō)	161	42.39N	24.48E
Karlovy Vary, Czech Rep. (kär'lō-vē vä'rē)	147	50.13N	12.53E
Karlshamn, Swe. (kärls'häm)	152	56.11N	14.50E
Karlskrona, Swe. (kärls'krō-nä)	146	56.10N	15.33E
Karlsruhe, Ger. (kärls'ro͞o-ē)	147	49.00N	8.23E
Karlstad, Swe. (kärl'städ)	142	59.25N	13.28E
Karluk, Ak., U.S. (kär'lŭk)	95	57.30N	154.22W
Karmøy, i., Nor. (kärm-ûe)	152	59.14N	5.00E
Karnataka, state, India	183	14.55N	75.00E
Karnobat, Bul. (kär-nó'bät)	161	42.39N	26.59E
Kärnten (Carinthia), prov., Aus. (kĕrn'tĕn)	154	46.55N	13.42E
Karolinenhof, neigh., Ger.	238a	52.23N	13.38E
Karonga, Mwi. (ká-rōŋ'gá)	212	9.52S	33.57E
Kárpathos, i., Grc.	149	35.34N	27.26E
Karpinsk, Russia (kär'pĭnsk)	172a	59.46N	60.00E
Kars, Tur. (kärs)	182	40.35N	43.00E
Kārsava, Lat. (kär'sä-vä)	153	56.46N	27.39E
Karshi, Uzb. (kär'shē)	169	38.30N	66.08E
Karskiye Vorota, Proliv, strt., Russia	164	70.30N	58.07E
Karskoye More (Kara Sea), sea, Russia	164	74.00N	68.00E
Kartaly, Russia (kȧr'tá lē)	164	53.05N	60.40E
Karunagapalli, India	187	9.09N	76.34E
Karvina, Czech Rep.	155	49.50N	18.30E
Kasaan, Ak., U.S.	87	55.32N	132.24E
Kasai, neigh., Japan	242a	35.39N	139.53E
Kasai (Cassai), r., Afr.	212	3.45S	19.10E
Kasama, Zam. (ká-sä'mä)	212	10.13S	31.12E
Kasanga, Tan. (ká-säŋ'gá)	212	8.28S	31.09E
Kasaoka, Japan (kä'sȧ-ō'ká)	195	34.33N	133.29E
Kasba-Tadla, Mor. (käs'bá-täd'lá)	210	32.37N	5.57W
Kasempa, Zam. (ká-sĕm'pá)	212	13.27S	25.50E
Kasenga, Zaire (ká-seŋ'gá)	212	10.22S	28.38E
Kasese, Ug.	217	0.10N	30.05E
Kasese, Zaire	217	1.38S	27.07E
Kāshān, Iran (kä-shän')	182	33.52N	51.15E
Kashgar see Kashi, China	188	39.29N	76.00E
Kashi (Kashgar), China (kä-shr) (käsh-gär)	188	39.29N	76.00E
Kashihara, Japan (kä'shē-hä'rä)	195b	34.31N	135.48E
Kashiji Plain, pl., Zam.	216	13.25S	22.30E
Kashin, Russia (kä-shēn')	162	57.20N	37.38E
Kashira, Russia (kä-shē'rá)	162	54.49N	38.11E
Kashiwa, Japan (kä'shē-wä)	195a	35.51N	139.58E
Kashiwara, Japan	195b	34.35N	135.38E
Kashiwazaki, Japan (kä'shē-wä-zä'kē)	194	37.06N	138.17E
Kāshmar, Iran	185	35.12N	58.27E
Kashmir see Jammu and Kashmir, hist. reg., Asia	183	39.10N	75.05E
Kashmor, Pak.	186	28.33N	69.34E
Kashtak, Russia (käsh'ták)	172a	55.18N	61.25E
Kasimov, Russia (ká-sē'môf)	166	54.56N	41.23E
Kaskanak, Ak., U.S. (käs-kă'năk)	95	60.00N	158.00W
Kaskaskia, r., Il., U.S. (kăs-kăs'kĭ-ȧ)	98	39.10N	88.50W
Kaskattama, r., Can. (kăs-kȧ-tä'mȧ)	89	56.28N	90.55W
Kaskö (Kaskinen), Fin. (käs'kû) (käs'kē-nĕn)	153	62.24N	21.18E
Kasli, Russia (käs'lĭ)	166	55.53N	60.46E
Kasongo, Zaire (kä-sôŋ'gō)	212	4.31S	26.42E
Kásos, i., Grc.	149	35.20N	26.55E
Kaspiysk, Russia	168	42.52N	47.38E
Kassándras, Kólpos, b., Grc.	161	40.10N	23.35E
Kassel, Ger. (käs'ĕl)	147	51.19N	9.30E
Kasslerfeld, neigh., Ger.	236	51.26N	6.45E
Kasson, Mn., U.S. (kăs'ŭn)	103	44.01N	92.45W
Kastamonu, Tur. (kä-stá-mō'no͞o)	182	41.20N	33.50E
Kastoría, Grc. (kás-tō'rĭ-á)	149	40.28N	21.17E
Kasūr, Pak.	186	31.10N	74.29E
Kataba, Zam.	217	16.05S	25.10E
Katahdin, Mount, mtn., Me., U.S. (kȧ-tä'dĭn)	92	45.56N	68.57W
Katanga, hist. reg., Zaire (ká-täŋ'gá)	212	8.30S	25.00E
Katanning, Austl. (ká-tăn'ĭng)	202	33.45S	117.45E
Katano, Japan	242b	34.48N	135.42E
Katav-Ivanovsk, Russia (kä'tăf ĭ-vä'nôfsk)	172a	54.46N	58.13E
Katayama, neigh., Japan	242a	35.46N	139.34E
Kateninskiy, Russia (kátyĕ'nĭs-kĭ)	172a	53.12N	61.05E
Kateríni, Grc.	161	40.18N	22.36E
Katernberg, neigh., Ger.	236	51.29N	7.04E
Katete, Zam.	217	14.05S	32.07E
Katherine, Austl. (käth'ēr-ĭn)	202	14.15S	132.20E
Kāthiāwār, pen., India (kä'tyȧ-wär')	183	22.10N	70.20E
Kathmandu, Nepal (kāt-män-do͞o')	183	27.49N	85.21E
Kathryn, Can. (kăth'rĭn)	83e	51.13N	113.42W
Kathryn, Ca., U.S.	107a	33.42N	117.45W
Katihār, India	186	25.39N	87.39E
Katiola, C. Iv.	214	8.08N	5.06W
Katmai National Park, rec., Ak., U.S. (kăt'mī)	96a	58.38N	155.00W
Katompi, Zaire	217	6.11S	26.20E
Katopa, Zaire	217	2.45S	25.06E
Katowice, Pol.	142	50.15N	19.00E
Katrineholm, Swe. (ká-trē'nĕ-hōlm)	152	59.01N	16.10E
Katsbakhskiy, Russia (kȧts-băk'skĭ)	172a	52.57N	59.37E
Katsina, Nig. (kăt'sē-ná)	210	13.00N	7.32E
Katsina Ala, Nig.	210	7.10N	9.17E
Katsura, r., Japan (kä'tsó-rä)	195b	34.55N	135.43E
Katsushika, neigh., Japan	242a	35.43N	139.51E
Katta-Kurgan, Uzb. (kȧ-tá-kór-gän')	169	39.45N	66.42E
Kattegat, strt., Eur. (kăt'ĕ-gät)	142	56.57N	11.25E
Katternberg, neigh., Ger.	236	51.09N	7.02E
Katumba, Zaire	217	7.45S	25.18E
Katun', r., Russia (ká-tón')	170	51.30N	86.18E
Katwijk aan Zee, Neth.	145a	52.12N	4.23E
Kauai, i., Hi., U.S.	96c	22.09N	159.15W
Kauai Channel, strt., Hi., U.S. (kä-o͞o-ä'ē)	96c	21.35N	158.52W
Kaufbeuren, Ger. (kouf'boi-rĕn)	154	47.52N	10.38E
Kaufman, Tx., U.S. (kôf'măn)	113	32.36N	96.18W
Kaukauna, Wi., U.S. (kô-kô'nȧ)	103	44.17N	88.15W
Kaulakahi Channel, strt., Hi., U.S. (kä'o͞o-lá-kä'hē)	94a	22.00N	159.55W
Kaulsdorf-Süd, neigh., Ger.	238a	52.29N	13.34E
Kaunakakai, Hi., U.S. (kä'o͞o-ná-kä'kī)	94a	21.06N	156.59W
Kaunas, Lith. (kou'nás) (kôv'nō)	164	54.42N	23.54E
Kaura Namoda, Nig.	210	12.35N	6.35E
Kavála, Grc. (kä-vä'lä)	149	40.55N	24.24E
Kavieng, Pap. N. Gui. (kä-vē-ĕng')	197	2.44S	151.02E
Kavīr, Dasht-e, des., Iran (dŭsht-ē-ka-vēr')	182	34.41N	53.30E
Kawagoe, Japan (kä-wä-gō'á)	195	35.55N	139.29E
Kawaguchi, Japan (kä-wä-go͞o-chē)	195a	35.48N	139.44E
Kawaikini, mtn., Hi., U.S. (kä-wä'ē-kĭ-nĭ)	94a	22.05N	159.33W
Kawanishi, Japan (kä-wä'nē-shē)	195b	34.49N	135.26E
Kawasaki, Japan (kä-wä-sä'kē)	194	35.32N	139.43E
Kawashima, neigh., Japan	242a	35.28N	139.35E
Kaxgar, r., China	188	39.30N	75.00E
Kaya, Burkina (kä'yä)	210	13.05N	1.05W
Kayan, r., Indon.	196	1.45N	115.38E
Kaycee, Wy., U.S. (kā-sē')	105	43.43N	106.38W
Kayes, Mali (kāz)	210	14.27N	11.26W
Kayseri, Tur. (kī'sĕ-rē)	182	38.45N	35.20E
Kazach'ye, Russia	165	70.46N	135.47E
Kazakhstan, nation, Asia	164	48.45N	59.00E
Kazan', Russia (ká-zän')	164	55.50N	49.18E
Kazanka, Ukr. (kä-zän'kä)	163	47.49N	32.50E
Kazanlŭk, Bul. (kä'zán-lêk)	161	42.47N	25.23E
Kazbek, Gora, mtn. (káz-bĕk')	167	42.42N	44.31E
Kāzerūn, Iran	182	29.37N	51.44E
Kazincbarcika, Hung. (kô'zĭnts-bôr-tsĭ-ko)	155	48.15N	20.39E
Kazungula, Zam.	217	17.45S	25.20E
Kazusa Kameyama, Japan (kä-zo͞o-sä kä-mâ'yä-mä)	195a	35.14N	140.06E
Kazym, r., Russia (kä-zēm')	170	63.30N	67.41E
Kéa, i., Grc.	161	37.36N	24.13E
Kealaikahiki Channel, strt., Hi., U.S. (kā-ä'lä-ē-kä-hē'kē)	94a	20.38N	157.00W
Keansburg, N.J., U.S. (kēnz'bûrg)	100a	40.26N	74.08W
Kearney, Ne., U.S. (kär'nĭ)	102	40.42N	99.05W
Kearny, N.J., U.S.	100a	40.46N	74.09W
Kearsley, Eng., U.K.	237b	53.32N	2.23W
Keasey, Or., U.S. (kēz'ĭ)	106c	45.51N	123.20W
Kebayoram, neigh., Indon.	241i	6.14S	106.46E
Kebnekaise, mtn., Swe. (kĕp'nĕ-kä-ēs'ĕ)	142	67.53N	18.10E
Kecskemét, Hung. (kĕch'kĕ-māt)	149	46.52N	19.42E
Kedah, hist. reg., Malay. (kĕ'dä)	196	6.00N	100.31E
Kédainiai, Lith. (kē-dī'nĭ-ī)	153	55.16N	23.58E
Kedgwick, Can. (kĕdj'wĭk)	92	47.39N	67.21W
Keenbrook, Ca., U.S. (kēn'brók)	107a	34.16N	117.29W
Keene, N.H., U.S. (kēn)	99	42.55N	72.15W
Keetmanshoop, Nmb. (kāt'mȧns-hōp)	212	26.30S	18.05E
Keet Seel Ruin, Az., U.S. (kēt sēl)	109	36.46N	110.32W
Keewatin, Mn., U.S. (kē-wä'tĭn)	103	47.24N	93.03W
Kefallinía, i., Grc.	149	38.08N	20.58E
Keffi, Nig. (kĕf'ē)	210	8.51N	7.52E
Ke Ga, Mui, c., Viet.	196	12.58N	109.50E
Kei, r., Afr. (kā)	213c	32.57S	26.50E
Keila, Est. (kā'lá)	153	59.19N	24.25E
Keilor, Austl.	201a	37.43S	144.50E
Kei Mouth, S. Afr.	213c	32.40S	28.23E
Keiskammahoek, S. Afr. (kās'kämä-ho͞ok')	213c	32.42S	27.11E
Kéita, Bahr, r., Chad	215	9.30N	19.17E
Keitele, l., Fin. (kā'tĕ-lĕ)	153	62.50N	25.40E
Kekaha, Hi., U.S.	94a	21.57N	159.42W
Kelafo, Eth.	218a	5.40N	44.00E
Kelang, Malay.	196	3.20N	101.27E
Kelang, r., Malay.	181b	3.00N	101.40E
Kelenföld, neigh., Hung.	239g	47.28N	19.03E
Kelkit, r., Tur.	149	40.38N	37.03E
Keller, Tx., U.S. (kĕl'ēr)	107c	32.56N	97.15W
Kellinghusen, Ger. (kĕ'lĕng-ho͞o-zĕn)	145c	53.57N	9.43E
Kellogg, Id., U.S. (kĕl'ŏg)	104	47.32N	116.07W
Kellyville, Austl.	243a	33.43S	150.57E
Kelme', Lith. (kĕl-mâ)	153	55.36N	22.53E
Kélo, Chad	215	9.19N	15.48E
Kelowna, Can.	84	49.53N	119.29W
Kelsey Bay, Can. (kĕl'sē)	86	50.24N	125.57W
Kelso, Wa., U.S.	106c	46.09N	122.54W
Keluang, Malay.	181b	2.01N	103.19E
Kelvedon Hatch, Eng., U.K.	235	51.40N	0.16E
Kem', Russia (kĕm)	164	65.00N	34.48E
Kemah, Tx., U.S. (kē'má)	113a	29.32N	95.01W
Kemerovo, Russia	164	55.31N	86.05E
Kemi, Fin. (kā'mē)	146	65.48N	24.38E
Kemi, r., Fin.	146	67.02N	27.50E
Kemigawa, Japan (kĕ'mē-gä'wä)	195a	35.38N	140.07E
Kemijarvi, Fin. (kā'mē-yĕr-vē)	146	66.48N	27.21E
Kemi-joki, l., Fin.	146	66.37N	28.13E
Kemmerer, Wy., U.S. (kĕm'ēr-ēr)	105	41.48N	110.36W
Kemp, l., Tx., U.S. (kĕmp)	110	33.55N	99.22W
Kempen, Ger. (kĕm'pĕn)	157c	51.22N	6.25E
Kempsey, Austl. (kĕmp'sē)	203	30.59S	152.50E
Kempt, l., Can. (kĕmpt)	91	47.28N	74.00W
Kempten, Ger. (kĕmp'tĕn)	147	47.44N	10.17E
Kempton Park, S. Afr. (kĕmp'tŏn pärk)	218d	26.07S	28.29E
Kemsing, Eng., U.K.	235	51.18N	0.14E
Ken, r., India	186	25.00N	79.55E
Kenai, Ak., U.S. (kĕ-nī')	95	60.38N	151.18W
Kenai Fjords National Park, rec., Ak., U.S.	95	59.45N	150.00W
Kenai Mountains, mts., Ak., U.S.	95	60.00N	150.00W
Kenai Pen, Ak., U.S.	95	64.40N	150.18W
Kenberma, Ma., U.S.	227a	42.17N	70.52W
Kendal, S. Afr.	218d	26.03S	28.58E
Kendal, Eng., U.K. (kĕn'dăl)	150	54.20N	1.48W
Kendallville, In., U.S. (kĕn'dăl-vĭl)	98	41.25N	85.20W
Kenedy, Tx., U.S. (kĕn'ĕ-dĭ)	113	28.49N	97.50W
Kenema, S.L.	214	7.52N	11.12W
Kenilworth, Il., U.S.	231a	42.05N	87.43W
Kenilworth, N.J., U.S.	228	40.41N	74.18W
Kenitra, Mor. (kĕ-nē'trá)	148	34.21N	6.34W
Kenley, neigh., Eng., U.K.	235	51.19N	0.06W
Kenmare, N.D., U.S. (kĕn-mâr')	102	48.41N	102.05W
Kenmore, N.Y., U.S. (kĕn'mōr)	101c	42.58N	78.53W
Kennebec, r., Me., U.S. (kĕn-ē-bĕk')	92	44.23N	69.48W
Kennebunk, Me., U.S. (kĕn-ē-buŋk')	92	43.24N	70.33W
Kennedale, Tx., U.S. (kĕn'-ē-dāl)	107c	32.38N	97.13W
Kennedy, Cape see Canaveral, Cape, c., Fl., U.S.	97	28.30N	80.23W
Kennedy, Mount, mtn., Can.	95	60.25N	138.50W
Kenner, La., U.S. (kĕn'ēr)	113	29.58N	90.15W
Kennett, Mo., U.S. (kĕn'ĕt)	111	36.14N	90.01W
Kennewick, Wa., U.S. (kĕn'ē-wĭk)	104	46.12N	119.06W
Kenney Dam, dam, Can.	86	53.37N	124.58W
Kennydale, Wa., U.S. (kĕn-nĕ'dāl)	106a	47.31N	122.12W
Kénogami, Can. (kĕn-ō'gä-mē)	85	48.26N	71.14W
Kenogamissi Lake, l., Can.	90	48.15N	81.31W
Keno Hill, Can.	95	63.58N	135.18W
Kenora, Can. (kē-nō'rȧ)	85	49.47N	94.29W
Kenosha, Wi., U.S. (kĕ-nō'shȧ)	97	42.34N	87.50W
Kenova, W.V., U.S. (kē-nō'vȧ)	98	38.20N	82.35W
Kensico Reservoir, res., N.Y., U.S. (kĕn'sĭ-kō)	100a	41.08N	73.45W
Kensington, Austl.	243a	33.55S	151.14E
Kensington, Ca., U.S.	231b	37.54N	122.16W
Kensington, Md., U.S.	229d	39.02N	77.03W
Kensington, neigh., S. Afr.	244b	26.12S	28.06E
Kensington, neigh., N.Y., U.S.	228	40.39N	73.58W
Kensington, neigh., Pa., U.S.	229b	39.58N	75.08W
Kensington and Chelsea, neigh., Eng., U.K.	235	51.29N	0.11W
Kent, Oh., U.S. (kĕnt)	98	41.05N	81.20W
Kent, Wa., U.S.	106a	47.23N	122.14W
Kentani, S. Afr. (kĕnt-änĭ')	213c	32.31S	28.19E
Kentland, In., U.S. (kĕnt'lănd)	98	40.50N	87.25W
Kentland, Md., U.S.	229d	38.55N	76.53W
Kenton, Oh., U.S. (kĕn'tŭn)	98	40.40N	83.35W
Kent Peninsula, pen., Can.	84	68.28N	108.10W
Kentucky, state, U.S. (kĕn-tŭk'ĭ)	97	37.30N	87.35W
Kentucky, res., U.S.	97	36.20N	88.50W

304 Kentucky–Kirchhörde

PLACE (Pronunciation)	PAGE	Lat. °′	Long. °′
Kentucky, r., Ky., U.S.	97	38.15N	85.01W
Kentwood, La., U.S. (kĕnt'wood)	113	30.56N	90.31W
Kenya, nation, Afr. (kĕn'yȧ)	212	1.00N	36.53E
Kenya, Mount (Kirinyaga), mtn., Kenya	213	0.10S	37.20E
Kenyon, Mn., U.S. (kĕn'yŭn)	103	44.15N	92.58W
Keokuk, Ia., U.S. (kē'ô-kŭk)	97	40.24N	91.34W
Keoma, Can. (kē-ō'mȧ)	83e	51.13N	113.39W
Keon Park, Austl.	243b	37.42S	145.01E
Kepenkeck Lake, l., Can.	93	48.13N	54.45W
Kępno, Pol. (kaṉ'pnō)	155	51.17N	17.59E
Kerala, state, India	183	16.38N	76.00E
Kerang, Austl. (kē-răng')	203	35.32S	143.58E
Keratsínion, Grc.	239d	37.58N	23.37E
Kerch, Ukr. (kĕrch)	164	45.20N	36.26E
Kerchenskiy Proliv, strt., Eur. (kĕr-chĕn'skĭ prô'lĭf)	163	45.08N	36.35E
Kerempe Burun, c., Tur.	149	42.00N	33.20E
Keren, Erit.	211	15.46N	38.28E
Kerguélen, Îles, is., Afr. (kĕr'gā-lĕn)	3	49.50S	69.30E
Kericho, Kenya	217	0.22S	35.17E
Kerinci, Gunung, mtn., Indon.	196	1.45S	101.18E
Keriya see Yutian, China	188	36.55N	81.39E
Keriya, r., China (kē'rē-yä)	188	37.13N	81.59E
Kerkebet, Erit.	184	16.18N	37.24E
Kerkenna, Îles, i., Tun. (kĕr'kĕn-nä)	210	34.49N	11.37E
Kerki, Turk. (kĕr'kē)	170	37.52N	65.15E
Kérkira, Grc.	149	39.36N	19.56E
Kérkira, i., Grc.	142	39.33N	19.36E
Kermadec Islands, is., N.Z. (kĕr-măd'ĕk)	3	30.30S	177.00E
Kermān, Iran (kĕr-män')	182	30.23N	57.08E
Kermānshāh see Bakhtarān, Iran	182	34.01N	47.00E
Kern, r., Ca., U.S.	108	35.31N	118.37W
Kern, South Fork, r., Ca., U.S.	108	35.40N	118.15W
Kerpen, Ger. (kĕr'pĕn)	157c	50.52N	6.42E
Kerrobert, Can.	88	51.53N	109.13W
Kerrville, Tx., U.S. (kûr'vĭl)	112	30.02N	99.07W
Kerulen, r., Asia (kĕr'ōō-lĕn)	189	47.52N	113.22E
Kesagami Lake, l., Can.	91	50.23N	80.15W
Keşan, Tur. (kĕ'shăn)	161	40.50N	26.37E
Keshan, China (kŭ-shän)	189	48.00N	126.30E
Kesour, Monts des, mts., Alg.	148	32.51N	0.30W
Kestell, S. Afr. (kĕs'tĕl)	218d	28.19S	28.43E
Keszthely, Hung. (kĕst'hĕl-lĭ)	155	46.46N	17.12E
Ket', r., Russia (kyĕt)	170	58.30N	84.15E
Keta, Ghana	210	6.00N	1.00E
Ketamputih, Indon.	181b	1.25N	102.19E
Ketapang, Indon. (kĕ-tȧ-päng')	196	2.00S	109.57E
Ketchikan, Ak., U.S. (kĕch-ĭ-kăn')	96a	55.21N	131.35W
Kętrzyn, Pol. (kaṉ't'r-zĭn)	155	54.04N	21.24E
Kettering, Eng., U.K. (kĕt'ĕr-ĭng)	144a	52.23N	0.43W
Kettering, Oh., U.S.	98	39.40N	84.15W
Kettle, r., Can.	87	49.40N	119.00W
Kettle, r., Mn., U.S. (kĕt''l)	103	46.20N	92.57W
Kettwig, Ger. (kĕt'vĕg)	157c	51.22N	6.56E
Kęty, Pol. (kaṉ tĭ)	155	49.54N	19.16E
Ketzin, Ger. (kĕ'tzĕn)	145b	52.29N	12.51E
Keuka, l., N.Y., U.S. (kē-ū'kȧ)	99	42.30N	77.10W
Kevelaer, Ger. (kĕ'fĕ-lär)	157c	51.35N	6.15E
Kew, Austl.	201a	37.49S	145.02E
Kew, S. Afr.	244b	26.08S	28.06E
Kewanee, Il., U.S. (kē-wä'nē)	103	41.15N	89.55W
Kewaunee, Wi., U.S. (kē-wô'nē)	103	44.27N	87.33W
Keweenaw Bay, b., Mi., U.S. (kē'wē-nô)	103	46.59N	88.15W
Keweenaw Peninsula, pen., Mi., U.S.	103	47.28N	88.12W
Kew Gardens, pt. of i., Eng., U.K.	235	51.28N	0.18W
Keya Paha, r., S.D., U.S. (kē-yȧ pä'hä)	102	43.11N	100.10W
Key Largo, i., Fl., U.S.	115a	25.11N	80.15W
Keyport, N.J., U.S. (kē'pōrt)	100a	40.26N	74.12W
Keyport, Wa., U.S.	106a	47.42N	122.38W
Keyser, W.V., U.S. (kī'sĕr)	99	39.25N	79.00W
Key West, Fl., U.S. (kē wĕst')	97	24.31N	81.47W
Kežmarok, Slvk. (kĕzh'mȧ-rôk)	155	49.10N	20.27E
Khabarovo, Russia (kŭ-bár-ôvŏ)	164	69.31N	60.41E
Khabarovsk, Russia (kä-bä'rôfsk)	165	48.35N	135.12E
Khaïdhárion, Grc.	239d	38.01N	23.39E
Khajuri, neigh., India	240d	28.43N	77.16E
Khakassia, state, Russia	170	52.32N	89.33E
Khalándrion, Grc.	239d	38.01N	23.48E
Khālāpur, India	187b	18.48N	73.17E
Khalkidhiki, pen., Grc.	161	40.30N	23.18E
Khalkís, Grc. (käl'kĭs)	149	38.28N	23.38E
Khal'mer-Yu, Russia (kŭl-myĕr'-yōō')	164	67.52N	64.25E
Khalturin, Russia (käl'tōō-rĕn)	166	58.28N	49.00E
Khambhāt, Gulf of, b., India	183	21.20N	72.27E
Khammam, India	187	17.09N	80.13E
Khānābād, Afg.	186	36.43N	69.11E
Khānaqīn, Iraq	185	34.21N	45.22E
Khandwa, India	186	21.53N	76.22E
Khaníon, Kólpos, b., Grc.	160a	35.35N	23.55E
Khanka, l., Asia (kän'kȧ)	165	45.09N	133.28E
Khānpur, Pak.	186	28.42N	70.42E
Khanty-Mansiysk, Russia (kŭn-te'mŭn-sēsk')	164	61.02N	69.01E
Khān Yūnus, Gaza	181a	31.21N	34.19E
Kharagpur, India (kŭ-rŭg'pŏr)	183	22.26N	87.21E
Khardah, India	240a	22.44N	88.22E
Kharkiv, Ukr.	164	50.00N	36.10E
Kharkiv, prov., Ukr.	163	49.33N	35.55E
Kharkov see Kharkiv, Ukr.	164	50.00N	36.10E
Kharlovka, Russia	166	68.47N	37.20E
Kharmanli, Bul. (kár-män'lē)	161	41.54N	25.55E
Khartoum, Sudan	211	15.34N	32.36E
Khasavyurt, Russia	168	43.15N	46.37E
Khāsh, Iran	182	28.08N	61.08E
Khāsh, r., Afg.	182	32.30N	64.27E

PLACE (Pronunciation)	PAGE	Lat. °′	Long. °′
Khasi Hills, hills, India	183	25.38N	91.55E
Khaskovo, Bul. (käs'kô-vô)	149	41.56N	25.32E
Khatanga, Russia (kȧ-tän'gȧ)	165	71.48N	101.47E
Khatangskiy Zaliv, b., Russia (kä-täṉ'g-skē)	165	73.45N	108.30E
Khayāla, neigh., India	240d	28.40N	77.06E
Khaybār, Sau. Ar.	182	25.45N	39.28E
Kherson, Ukr. (kĕr-sôn')	167	46.38N	32.34E
Kherson, prov., Ukr.	163	46.32N	32.55E
Khichripur, neigh., India	240d	28.37N	77.19E
Khiitola, Russia (khē'tō-lȧ)	153	61.14N	29.40E
Khimki, Russia (kēm'kĭ)	172b	55.54N	37.27E
Khíos, Grc. (kē'ôs)	149	38.23N	26.09E
Khíos, i., Grc.	149	38.20N	25.45E
Khmel'nyts'kyy, Ukr.	167	49.29N	26.54E
Khmel'nyts'kyy, prov., Ukr.	163	49.27N	26.30E
Khmil'nyk, Ukr.	163	49.34N	27.58E
Kholargós, Grc.	239d	38.00N	23.48E
Kholm, Russia (kôlm)	162	57.09N	31.07E
Kholmsk, Russia (kŭlmsk)	165	47.09N	142.33E
Khomeynīshahr, Iran	185	32.41N	51.31E
Khon Kaen, Thai.	196	16.37N	102.41E
Khopër, r., Russia (kô'pēr)	167	52.00N	43.00E
Khor, Russia (kôr')	194	47.50N	134.52E
Khor, r., Russia	194	47.23N	135.20E
Khóra Sfakíon, Grc.	160a	35.12N	24.10E
Khorel, India	240a	22.42N	88.19E
Khorog, Taj.	169	37.30N	71.36E
Khorol, Ukr. (kō'rôl)	163	49.48N	33.17E
Khorol, r., Ukr.	163	49.50N	33.21E
Khorramābād, Iran	185	33.30N	48.20E
Khorramshahr, Iran (kô-ram'shär)	182	30.36N	48.15E
Khot'kovo, Russia	172b	56.15N	38.00E
Khotyn, Ukr.	167	48.29N	26.32E
Khoyniki, Bela.	163	51.54N	30.00E
Khudzhand, Taj.	169	40.17N	69.37E
Khulna, Bngl.	183	22.50N	89.38E
Khūryān Mūryān, is., Oman	182	17.27N	56.02E
Khust, Ukr. (kôst)	155	48.10N	23.18E
Khvalynsk, Russia (kvá-lĭnsk')	167	52.30N	48.00E
Khvoy, Iran	182	38.32N	45.01E
Khyber Pass, p., Asia (kī'bēr)	183	34.28N	71.18E
Kialwe, Zaire	217	9.22S	27.08E
Kiambi, Zaire (kyäm'bē)	212	7.20S	28.01E
Kiamichi, r., Ok., U.S. (kyȧ-mē'chē)	111	34.31N	95.34W
Kianta, l., Fin. (kyän'tȧ)	166	65.00N	28.15E
Kibenga, Zaire	216	7.55S	17.35E
Kibiti, Tan.	217	7.44S	38.57E
Kibombo, Zaire	217	3.54S	25.55E
Kibondo, Tan.	217	3.35S	30.42E
Kičevo, Mac. (kē'chĕ-vô)	161	41.30N	20.59E
Kichijōji, Japan	242a	35.42N	139.35E
Kickapoo, r., Wi., U.S. (kĭk'ȧ-pōō)	103	43.20N	90.55W
Kicking Horse Pass, p., Can.	87	51.25N	116.10W
Kidal, Mali (kē-dál')	210	18.33N	1.00E
Kidderminster, Eng., U.K. (kĭd'ēr-mĭn-stēr)	144a	52.23N	2.14W
Kidderpore, neigh., India	240a	22.31N	88.19E
Kidd's Beach, S. Afr. (kĭdz)	213c	33.09S	27.43E
Kidsgrove, Eng., U.K. (kĭdz'grōv)	144a	53.05N	2.15W
Kiel, Ger. (kēl)	142	54.19N	10.08E
Kiel, Wi., U.S.	103	43.52N	88.04W
Kiel Bay, b., Ger.	154	54.33N	10.19E
Kiel Canal see Nord-Ostsee Kanal, can., Ger.	154	54.03N	9.23E
Kielce, Pol. (kyĕl'tsĕ)	155	50.50N	20.41E
Kieldrecht, Bel. (kēl'drĕkt)	145a	51.17N	4.09E
Kierspe, Ger.	236	51.08N	7.35E
Kiev (Kyyiv), Ukr. (kē'yĕf)	164	50.27N	30.30E
Kiffa, Maur. (kēf'ȧ)	210	16.37N	11.24W
Kigali, Rw. (kē-gä'lē)	212	1.59S	30.05E
Kigoma, Tan. (kē-gō'mä)	212	4.57S	29.38E
Kii-Suido, strt., Japan (kē sōō-ē'dō)	194	33.53N	134.55E
Kikaiga, i., Japan	194	28.25N	130.10E
Kikinda, Yugo. (kĕ'kĕn-dä)	161	45.49N	20.30E
Kikládhes, is., Grc.	142	37.30N	24.45E
Kikwit, Zaire (kē'kwēt)	212	5.02S	18.49E
Kil, Swe. (kĕl)	152	59.30N	13.15E
Kilauea, Hi., U.S. (kē-lä-ōō-ā'ä)	94a	22.12N	159.25W
Kilauea Crater, Hi., U.S.	94a	19.28N	155.18W
Kilbuck Mountains, mts., Ak., U.S. (kĭl-bŭk)	95	60.05N	160.00W
Kilchu, N. Kor. (kĭl'chō)	194	40.59N	129.23E
Kildare, Ire. (kĭl-dār')	150	53.09N	7.05W
Kilembe, Zaire	216	5.42S	19.55E
Kilgore, Tx., U.S.	113	32.23N	94.53W
Kilifi, Kenya	217	3.38S	39.51E
Kilimanjaro, mtn., Tan. (kyl-ē-măn-jä'rō)	213	3.09S	37.19E
Kilimatinde, Tan. (kĭl-ē-mä-tĭn'dȧ)	212	5.48S	34.58E
Kilindoni, Tan.	217	7.55S	39.39E
Kilingi-Nõmme, Est. (kē'lĭn-gē-nôm'mĕ)	153	58.08N	25.03E
Kilis, Tur. (kē'lĕs)	149	36.50N	37.20E
Kiliya, Ukr. (kē'lyȧ)	163	45.28N	29.17E
Kilkenny, Ire. (kĭl-kĕn-ĭ)	147	52.40N	7.30W
Kilkis, Grc. (kĭl'kĭs)	161	40.59N	22.51E
Killala, Ire. (kĭ-lă'lȧ)	150	54.11N	9.10W
Killara, Austl.	243a	33.46S	151.09E
Killarney, Ire.	150	52.03N	9.05W
Killarney Heights, Austl.	243a	33.46S	151.13E
Killdeer, N.D., U.S. (kĭl'dēr)	102	47.22N	102.45W
Killiniq Island, i., Can.	85	60.32N	63.56W
Kilmarnock, Scot., U.K. (kĭl-mär'nŭk)	150	55.38N	4.25W
Kilrush, Ire. (kĭl'rŭsh)	150	52.40N	9.16W
Kilwa Kisiwani, Tan.	217	8.58S	39.30E
Kilwa Kivinje, Tan.	213	8.43S	39.18E

PLACE (Pronunciation)	PAGE	Lat. °′	Long. °′
Kim, r., Cam.	215	5.40N	11.17E
Kimamba, Tan.	217	6.47S	37.08E
Kimba, Austl. (kĭm'bȧ)	204	33.08S	136.25E
Kimball, Ne., U.S. (kĭm-bȧl)	102	41.14N	103.41W
Kimball, S.D., U.S.	102	43.44N	98.58W
Kimberley, Can. (kĭm'bēr-lĭ)	84	49.41N	115.59W
Kimberley, S. Afr.	212	28.40S	24.50E
Kimi, Cam.	215	6.05N	11.30E
Kími, Grc.	161	38.38N	24.05E
Kímolos, i., Grc. (kē'mô-lôs)	161	36.52N	24.20E
Kimry, Russia (kĭm'rē)	166	56.53N	37.24E
Kimvula, Zaire	216	5.44S	15.58E
Kinabalu, Gunong, mtn., Malay.	196	5.45N	115.26E
Kincardine, Can. (kĭn-kär'dĭn)	85	44.10N	81.15W
Kinda, Zaire	217	9.18S	25.04E
Kindanba, Congo	216	3.44S	14.31E
Kinder, La., U.S. (kĭn'dēr)	113	30.30N	92.50W
Kindersley, Can. (kĭn'dērz-lē)	84	51.27N	109.10W
Kindia, Gui. (kĭn'dē-ȧ)	210	10.04N	12.51W
Kindu, Zaire	212	2.57S	25.56E
Kinel'-Cherkassy, Russia	166	53.32N	51.32E
Kineshma, Russia (kē-nĕsh'mȧ)	166	57.27N	41.02E
King, i., Austl. (kĭng)	203	39.35S	143.40E
Kingaroy, Austl. (kĭṉ'gă-roi)	204	26.37S	151.50E
King City, Can.	83d	43.56N	79.32W
King City, Ca., U.S. (kĭng sĭ'tĭ)	108	36.12N	121.08W
Kingcome Inlet, b., Can. (kĭng'kŭm)	86	50.50N	126.10W
Kingfisher, Ok., U.S. (kĭng'fĭsh-ēr)	111	35.51N	97.55W
King George Sound, strt., Austl. (jôrj)	202	35.17S	118.30E
King George's Reservoir, res., Eng., U.K.	235	51.39N	0.01W
Kingisepp, Russia (kĭṉ-gē-sep')	166	59.22N	28.38E
King Leopold Ranges, mts., Austl. (lē'ô-pōld)	202	16.25S	125.00E
Kingman, Az., U.S. (kĭng'măn)	109	35.10N	114.05W
Kingman, Ks., U.S. (kĭng'măn)	110	37.38N	98.07W
King of Prussia, Pa., U.S.	229b	40.05N	75.23W
Kings, r., Ca., U.S.	108	36.28N	119.43W
Kingsbury, neigh., Eng., U.K.	235	51.35N	0.17W
Kings Canyon National Park, rec., Ca., U.S. (kăn'yŭn)	96	36.52N	118.53W
Kingsclere, Eng., U.K. (kĭngs-clēr)	144b	51.18N	1.15W
Kingscote, Austl. (kĭngz'kŭt)	204	35.45S	137.32E
Kingsdown, Eng., U.K.	235	51.21N	0.17E
Kingsford, Austl.	243a	33.56S	151.14E
Kingsgrove, Austl.	243a	33.57S	151.06E
Kings Langley, Eng., U.K.	235	51.43N	0.28W
King's Lynn, Eng., U.K. (kĭngz lĭn')	151	52.45N	0.20E
Kings Mountain, N.C., U.S.	115	35.13N	81.30W
Kings Norton, Eng., U.K. (nôr'tŭn)	144a	52.25N	1.54W
King Sound, strt., Austl.	202	16.50S	123.35E
Kings Park, N.Y., U.S. (kĭngz pärk)	100a	40.53N	73.16W
Kings Park, Va., U.S.	229d	38.48N	77.15W
Kings Peak, mtn., Ut., U.S.	96	40.46N	110.20W
Kings Point, N.Y., U.S.	228	40.49N	73.45W
Kingsport, Tn., U.S. (kĭngz'pōrt)	115	36.33N	82.36W
Kingston, Austl. (kĭngz'tŭn)	202	37.52S	139.52E
Kingston, Can.	85	44.15N	76.30W
Kingston, Jam.	117	18.00N	76.45W
Kingston, N.Y., U.S.	97	42.00N	74.00W
Kingston, Pa., U.S.	99	41.15N	75.50W
Kingston, Wa., U.S.	106a	47.04N	122.29W
Kingston upon Hull, Eng., U.K.	142	53.45N	0.25W
Kingston upon Thames, neigh., Eng., U.K.	235	51.25N	0.19W
Kingstown, St. Vin. (kĭngz'toun)	117	13.10N	61.14W
Kingstree, S.C., U.S. (kĭngz'trē)	115	33.30N	79.50W
Kingsville, Tx., U.S. (kĭngz'vĭl)	113	27.32N	97.52W
King William Island, i., Can. (kĭng wĭl'yăm)	84	69.25N	97.00W
King William's Town, S. Afr. (kĭng-wĭl'-yŭmz-toun)	213c	32.53S	27.24E
Kinira, r., S. Afr.	213c	30.37S	28.52E
Kinloch, Mo., U.S. (kĭn-lŏk)	107e	38.44N	90.19W
Kinnaird, Can. (kĭn-ärd')	87	49.17N	117.39W
Kinnairds Head, c., Scot., U.K. (kĭn-ârds'hĕd)	146	57.42N	3.55W
Kinomoto, Japan (kē'nō-mōtō)	195	33.53N	136.07E
Kinosaki, Japan (kē'nō-sä'kē)	195	35.38N	134.47E
Kinshasa, Zaire	212	4.18S	15.18E
Kinshasa-Est, neigh., Zaire	244c	4.18S	15.18E
Kinshasa-Ouest, neigh., Zaire	244c	4.20S	15.15E
Kinsley, Ks., U.S. (kĭnz'lĭ)	110	37.55N	99.24W
Kinston, N.C., U.S. (kĭnz'tŭn)	115	35.15N	77.35W
Kintamo, Rapides de, wtfl., Afr.	244c	4.19S	15.15E
Kintampo, Ghana (kĕn-tăm'pō)	210	8.03N	1.43W
Kintsana, Congo	244c	4.19S	15.10E
Kintyre, pen., Scot., U.K.	150	55.50N	5.40W
Kiowa, Ks., U.S. (kī'ô-wȧ)	110	37.01N	98.30W
Kiowa, Ok., U.S.	111	34.42N	95.53W
Kiparissia, Grc.	149	37.17N	21.43E
Kiparissiakós Kólpos, b., Grc.	161	37.28N	21.15E
Kipawa, Lac, l., Can.	91	46.55N	79.00W
Kipembawe, Tan. (kē-pĕm-bä'wȧ)	212	7.39S	33.24E
Kipengere Range, mts., Tan.	217	9.10S	34.00E
Kipili, Tan.	217	7.26S	30.36E
Kipushi, Zaire	217	11.46S	27.14E
Kirakira, Sol.Is.	198e	10.27S	161.55E
Kirby, Tx., U.S. (kŭr'bĭ)	107d	29.29N	98.23W
Kirbyville, Tx., U.S. (kŭr'bĭ-vĭl)	113	30.39N	93.54W
Kirchderne, neigh., Ger.	236	51.33N	7.30E
Kirchende, Ger.	236	51.25N	7.26E
Kirchhellen, Ger.	236	51.36N	6.55E
Kirchheller Heide, for., Ger.	236	51.36N	6.53E
Kirchhörde, neigh., Ger.	236	51.27N	7.27E

ăt; finăl; rāte; senāte; ärm; ȧsk; sofȧ; fâre; ch-choose; dh-as th in other; bē; ēvent; bĕt; recĕnt; cratēr; g-gō; gh-guttural g; bĭt; ĭ-short neutral; rīde; ᴋ-guttural k as ch in German ich;

PRONOUNCING INDEX

Kirchlinde–Konstanz 305

PLACE (Pronunciation)	PAGE	Lat. °′	Long. °′
Kirchlinde, neigh., Ger.	236	51.32N	7.22E
Kirdāsah, Egypt	244a	30.02N	31.07E
Kirenga, r., Russia (kê-rĕŋ'gá)	171	56.30N	108.18E
Kirensk, Russia (kē-rĕnsk')	165	57.47N	108.22E
Kirghiz Steppe, plat., Kyrg.	169	49.28N	57.07E
Kiri, Zaire	216	1.27S	19.00E
Kiribati, nation, Oc.	3	1.30S	173.00E
Kirin *see* Chilung, Tai.	189	25.02N	121.48E
Kiritimati, i., Kir.	2	2.20N	157.40W
Kirkby, Eng., U.K.	144a	53.29N	2.54W
Kirkby-in-Ashfield, Eng., U.K. (kûrk'bē-ĭn-ăsh'fēld)	144a	53.06N	1.16W
Kirkcaldy, Scot., U.K. (kĕr-kô'dĭ)	150	56.06N	3.15W
Kirkdale, neigh., Eng., U.K.	237a	53.26N	2.59W
Kirkenes, Nor.	146	69.40N	30.03E
Kirkham, Eng., U.K. (kûrk'ăm)	144a	53.47N	2.53W
Kirkland, Can.	227b	45.27N	73.52W
Kirkland, Wa., U.S. (kûrk'lănd)	106a	47.41N	122.12W
Kirklareli, Tur. (kėrk'lår-ĕ'lė)	149	41.44N	27.15E
Kirksville, Mo., U.S. (kûrks'vĭl)	97	40.12N	92.35W
Kirkūk, Iraq (kĭr-ko͞ok')	182	35.28N	44.22E
Kirkwall, Scot., U.K. (kûrk'wôl)	146	58.58N	2.59W
Kirkwood, S. Afr.	213c	33.26S	25.24E
Kirkwood, Md., U.S.	229d	38.57N	76.58W
Kirkwood, Mo., U.S. (kûrk'wo̤od)	107e	38.35N	90.24W
Kirn, Ger. (kērn)	154	49.47N	7.23E
Kirov, Russia	162	54.04N	34.19E
Kirov, Russia	164	58.35N	49.35E
Kirovakan, Arm.	168	40.48N	44.30E
Kirovgrad, Russia (kē'rŭ-vŭ-grad)	172a	57.26N	60.03E
Kirovohrad, Ukr.	167	48.33N	32.17E
Kirovohrad, prov., Ukr.	163	48.23N	31.10E
Kirovsk, Russia	164	67.40N	33.58E
Kirovsk, Russia (kė-rôfsk')	172c	59.52N	30.59E
Kirsanov, Russia (kēr-sá'nôf)	167	52.40N	42.40E
Kirşehir, Tur. (kėr-shĕ'hēr)	182	39.10N	34.00E
Kirtachi Seybou, Niger	215	12.48N	2.29E
Kīrthar Range, mts., Pak. (kĭr-tŭr)	183	27.00N	67.10E
Kirton, Eng., U.K. (kûr'tŭn)	144a	53.29N	0.35W
Kiruna, Swe. (kē-ro͞o'nä)	146	67.49N	20.08E
Kirundu, Zaire	217	0.44S	25.32E
Kirwan Heights, Pa., U.S.	230b	40.22N	80.06W
Kirwin Reservoir, res., Ks., U.S. (kûr'wĭn)	110	39.34N	99.04W
Kiryū, Japan	194	36.24N	139.20E
Kirzhach, Russia (kėr-zhák')	162	56.08N	38.53E
Kisaki, Tan. (kē-sá'kē)	213	7.37S	37.43E
Kisangani, Zaire	211	0.30N	25.12E
Kisarazu, Japan (kē'sá-rá'zo͞o)	195a	35.23N	139.55E
Kiselëvsk, Russia (kē-sĭ-lyôfsk')	164	54.00N	86.39E
Kishinev *see* Chişinău, Mol.	164	47.02N	28.52E
Kishiwada, Japan (kē'shė-wä'dä)	194	34.25N	135.18E
Kishkino, Russia (kēsh'kĭ-nô)	172b	55.15N	38.04E
Kisiwani, Tan.	217	4.08S	37.57E
Kiska, i., Ak., U.S. (kĭs'kä)	96b	52.08N	177.10E
Kiskatinaw, r., Can.	87	55.10N	120.20W
Kiskittogisu Lake, l., Can.	89	54.05N	99.00W
Kiskitto Lake, l., Can. (kĭs-kĭ'tō)	89	54.16N	98.34W
Kiskunfélegyháza, Hung. (kĭsh'ko̤n-fā'lĕd-y'hä'zô)	155	46.42N	19.52E
Kiskunhalas, Hung. (kĭsh'ko̤n-hô'lôsh)	155	46.24N	19.26E
Kiskunmajsa, Hung. (kĭsh'ko̤n-mĭ'shô)	155	46.29N	19.42E
Kislovodsk, Russia	168	43.55N	42.44E
Kismaayo, Som.	213	0.18S	42.30E
Kiso, Japan	242a	35.34N	139.26E
Kiso-Gawa, r., Japan (kē'sō-gä'wä)	195	35.29N	137.12E
Kiso-Sammyaku, mts., Japan (kē'sō säm'myá-ko͞o)	195	35.47N	137.39E
Kissamos, Grc.	160a	35.13N	23.35E
Kissidougou, Gui. (kē'sē-do͞o'go͞o)	210	9.11N	10.06W
Kissimmee, Fl., U.S. (kĭ-sĭm'ē)	115a	28.17N	81.25W
Kissimmee, r., Fl., U.S.	115a	27.45N	81.07W
Kissimmee, Lake, l., Fl., U.S.	115a	27.58N	81.17W
Kistarcsa, Hung.	239g	47.33N	19.16E
Kisujszallás, Hung.	155	47.12N	20.47E
Kisumu, Kenya (kē'so͞o-mo͞o)	212	0.06S	34.45E
Kita, Mali (kē'tà)	210	13.03N	9.29W
Kita, neigh., Japan	242a	35.45N	139.44E
Kitakami Gawa, r., Japan	194	39.20N	141.10E
Kitakyūshū, Japan	189	33.53N	130.50E
Kitale, Kenya	217	1.01N	35.00E
Kitamachi, neigh., Japan	242a	35.46N	139.39E
Kitamba, neigh., Zaire	244c	4.19S	15.14E
Kitatawara, Japan	242b	34.44N	135.42E
Kit Carson, Co., U.S.	110	38.46N	102.48W
Kitchener, Can. (kĭch'ĕ-nēr)	85	43.25N	80.35W
Kitenda, Zaire	216	6.53S	17.21E
Kitgum, Ug. (kĭt'go̤m)	211	3.29N	33.04E
Kíthira, i., Grc.	149	36.15N	22.56E
Kíthnos, i., Grc.	161	37.24N	24.10E
Kitimat, Can. (kĭ'tĭ-măt)	84	54.03N	128.33W
Kitimat, r., Can.	86	53.50N	129.00W
Kitimat Ranges, mts., Can.	86	53.30N	128.50W
Kitlope, r., Can. (kĭt'lōp)	86	53.00N	128.00W
Kitsuki, Japan (kėt'so̤-kė)	195	33.24N	131.35E
Kittanning, Pa., U.S. (kĭ-tăn'ĭng)	99	40.50N	79.30W
Kittatinny Mountains, mts., N.J., U.S. (kĭ-tă-tĭ'nē)	100a	41.16N	74.44W
Kittery, Me., U.S. (kĭt'ēr-ĭ)	92	43.07N	70.45W
Kittsee, Aus.	145e	48.05N	17.05E
Kitty Hawk, N.C., U.S. (kĭt'ė hôk)	115	36.04N	75.42W
Kitunda, Tan.	217	6.48S	33.13E
Kitwe, Zam.	217	12.49S	28.13E
Kitzingen, Ger. (kĭt'zĭng-ĕn)	154	49.44N	10.08E
Kiunga, Kenya	217	1.45S	41.29E
Kivu, Lac, l., Afr.	212	1.45S	28.55E
Kiyev *see* Kiev, Ukr.	164	50.27N	30.30E
Kīyose, Japan	195a	35.47N	139.32E
Kizel, Russia (kē'zĕl)	166	59.05N	57.42E
Kızıl, r., Tur.	182	40.00N	34.00E
Kizil'skoye, Russia (kĭz'ĭl-skô-yĕ)	172a	52.43N	58.53E
Kizlyar, Russia (kĭz-lyär')	167	44.00N	46.50E
Kizlyarskiy Zaliv, b., Russia	168	44.33N	46.55E
Kizu, Japan (kē'zo͞o)	195	34.43N	135.49E
Kizuki, Japan	242a	35.34N	139.40E
Kizuri, Japan	242b	34.39N	135.34E
Kizyl-Arvat, Turk. (kē'zĭl-ŭr-vät')	169	38.55N	56.33E
Klaas Smits, r., S. Afr.	213c	31.45S	26.33E
Klaaswaal, Neth.	145a	51.46N	4.25E
Kladno, Czech Rep. (kläd'nō)	154	50.10N	14.05E
Klagenfurt, Aus. (klä'gĕn-fo̤rt)	147	46.38N	14.19E
Klaipėda, Lith. (klī'pā-dá)	166	55.43N	21.10E
Klamath, r., U.S.	104	41.40N	123.25W
Klamath Falls, Or., U.S.	96	42.13N	121.49W
Klamath Mountains, mts., Ca., U.S.	104	42.00N	123.25W
Klarälven, r., Swe.	146	60.40N	13.00E
Klaskanine, r., Or., U.S. (klăs'kā-nīn)	106c	46.02N	123.43W
Klatovy, Czech Rep. (klá'tô-vė)	147	49.23N	13.18E
Klawock, Ak., U.S. (klā'wăk)	95	55.32N	133.10W
Kleef, Ger.	236	51.11N	6.56E
Kleinebroich, Ger.	236	51.12N	6.35E
Kleinmachnow, Ger. (klīn-mäĸ'nō)	145b	52.22N	13.12E
Klein Ziethen, Ger.	238a	52.23N	13.27E
Klerksdorp, S. Afr. (klērks'dôrp)	218d	26.52S	26.40E
Klerksraal, S. Afr. (klērks'kräl)	218d	26.15N	27.10E
Kletnya, Russia (klyĕt'nyá)	162	53.19N	33.14E
Kletsk, Bela. (klĕtsk)	162	53.04N	26.43E
Kleve, Ger. (klĕ'fĕ)	154	51.47N	6.09E
Kley, neigh., Ger.	236	51.30N	7.22E
Klickitat, r., Wa., U.S.	104	46.01N	121.07W
Klimovichi, Bela. (klē-mô-vē'chė)	162	53.37N	31.21E
Klimovsk, Russia (klĭ'môfsk)	172b	55.21N	37.32E
Klin, Russia (klēn)	162	56.18N	36.43E
Klintehamn, Swe. (klēn'tē-häm)	152	57.24N	18.14E
Klintsy, Russia (klĭn'tsĭ)	167	52.46N	32.14E
Klip, r., S. Afr. (klĭp)	218d	27.18N	29.25E
Klipgat, S. Afr.	218d	25.26S	27.57E
Klippan, Swe. (klyp'pán)	152	56.08N	13.09E
Klippoortje, S. Afr.	244b	26.17S	28.14E
Kliptown, S. Afr.	244b	26.17S	27.53E
Kłodzko, Pol. (klôd'skô)	154	50.26N	16.38E
Klondike Region, hist. reg., N.A. (klŏn'dīk)	84	64.12N	142.38W
Klosterfelde, Ger. (klōs'tĕr-fĕl-dĕ)	145b	52.47N	13.29E
Klosterneuburg, Aus. (klōs-tĕr-noi'bo͞orgh)	145e	48.19N	16.20E
Kluane, l., Can.	84	61.15N	138.40W
Kluane National Park, rec., Can.	84	60.25N	137.53W
Kluczbork, Pol. (klo͞och'bo̤rk)	155	50.59N	18.15E
Klyaz'ma, r., Russia (klyäz'má)	162	55.49N	39.19E
Klyuchevskaya, vol., Russia (klyo͞o-chĕfskä'yä)	165	56.13N	160.00E
Klyuchi, Russia (klyo͞o'chĭ)	172a	57.03N	57.20E
Knezha, Bul. (knyā'zhá)	149	43.27N	24.03E
Knife, r., N.D., U.S. (nīf)	102	47.06N	102.33W
Knight Inlet, b., Can. (nīt)	86	50.41N	125.40W
Knightstown, In., U.S. (nīts'toun)	98	39.45N	85.30W
Knin, Cro. (knēn)	160	44.02N	16.14E
Knittelfeld, Aus.	147	47.13N	14.50E
Knob Peak, mtn., Phil. (nŏb)	197a	12.30N	121.20E
Knockholt, Eng., U.K.	235	51.18N	0.06E
Knockholt Pound, Eng., U.K.	235	51.19N	0.08E
Knoppiesfontein, S. Afr.	244b	26.05S	28.25E
Knottingley, Eng., U.K. (nŏt'ĭng-lĭ)	144a	53.42N	1.14W
Knott's Berry Farm, pt. of i., Ca., U.S.	232	33.50N	118.00W
Knotty Ash, neigh., Eng., U.K.	237a	53.25N	2.54W
Knowsley, Eng., U.K.	237a	53.27N	2.51W
Knox, Austl.	243b	37.53S	145.18E
Knox, In., U.S. (nŏks)	98	41.15N	86.40W
Knox, Cape, c., Can.	86	54.12N	133.20W
Knoxville, Ia., U.S. (nŏks'vĭl)	103	41.19N	93.05W
Knoxville, Tn., U.S.	97	35.58N	83.55W
Knutsford, Eng., U.K. (nŭts'fērd)	144a	53.18N	2.22W
Knyszyn, Pol. (knĭ'shĭn)	155	53.16N	22.59E
Kobayashi, Japan (kō'bá-yä'shė)	195	31.58N	130.59E
Kōbe, Japan (kō'bė)	189	34.30N	135.10E
Kobelyaky, Ukr.	167	49.11N	34.12E
København *see* Copenhagen, Den.	142	55.43N	12.27E
Koblenz, Ger. (kō'blĕntz)	147	50.18N	7.36E
Kobozha, r., Russia (kô-bō'zhá)	162	58.55N	35.18E
Kobrin, Bela. (kō'brĕn')	167	52.13N	24.23E
Kobrinskoye, Russia (kô-brĭn'skô-yĕ)	172c	59.25N	30.07E
Kobuk, r., Ak., U.S. (kō'bŭk)	95	66.58N	158.48W
Kobuk Valley National Park, rec., Ak., U.S.	95	67.20N	159.00W
Kobuleti, Geor. (kô-bo̤-lyā'tė)	167	41.50N	41.40E
Kočani, Mac. (kô'chä-nĕ)	161	41.54N	22.25E
Kočevje, Slvn. (kô'chāv-ye)	160	45.38N	14.51E
Kocher, r., Ger. (kôĸ'ēr)	154	49.00N	9.52E
Kōchi, Japan (kō'chė)	189	33.35N	133.32E
Kodaira, Japan	195a	35.43N	139.29E
Kodiak, Ak., U.S. (kō'dyăk)	96a	57.50N	152.30W
Kodiak Island, i., Ak., U.S.	95	57.24N	153.32W
Kodok, Sudan (ko'dŏk)	211	9.57N	32.08E
Koforidua, Ghana (kō fō-rĭ-do͞o'á)	210	6.03N	0.17W
Kōfu, Japan (kō'fo͞o')	194	35.41N	138.34E
Koga, Japan (kō'gá)	195	36.13N	139.40E
Kogan, r., Gui.	214	11.30N	14.05W
Kogane, Japan (kō'gä-nā)	195a	35.50N	139.56E
Koganei, Japan (kō'gä-nā)	195a	35.42N	139.31E
Kogarah, Austl.	243a	33.58S	151.08E
Køge, Den. (kû'gĕ)	152	55.27N	12.09E
Køge Bugt, b., Den.	152	55.30N	12.25E
Kogil'nik, r., Eur. (kô-gėl-nĕk')	163	46.08N	29.10E
Kogoni, Mali	214	14.44N	6.02W
Kohīma, India (kô-ē'mà)	183	25.45N	94.41E
Koito, r., Japan (kô'ē-tō)	195a	35.19N	139.58E
Kōje, i., S. Kor. (kû'jĕ)	194	34.53N	129.00E
Kokand, Uzb. (kô-känt')	169	40.27N	71.07E
Kokemäenjoki, r., Fin.	153	61.23N	22.03E
Kokhma, Russia (kôĸ'má)	162	56.57N	41.08E
Kokkola, Fin. (kô'kô-lá)	146	63.47N	22.58E
Kokomo, In., U.S. (kō'kô-mō)	98	40.30N	86.20W
Koko Nor (Qinghai Hu), l., China (kō'kō nor) (chyĭŋ-hī ho͞o)	188	37.26N	98.30E
Kokopo, Pap. N. Gui. (kô-kō'pō)	197	4.25S	152.27E
Kokshetau, Kaz.	169	53.15N	69.13E
Koksoak, r., Can. (kôk'sō-ăk)	85	57.42N	69.50W
Kokstad, S. Afr. (kôk'shtät)	213c	30.33S	29.27E
Kokubu, Japan (kō'ko͞o-bo͞o)	195	31.42N	130.46E
Kokubunji, Japan	242a	35.42N	139.29E
Kokuou, Japan (kō'ko͞o-ō'o͞o)	195b	34.34N	135.39E
Kola Peninsula *see* Kol'skiy Poluostrov, pen., Russia	164	67.15N	37.40E
Kolār (Kolār Gold Fields), India (kōl-är')	183	13.39N	78.33E
Kolárvo, Slvk. (kōl-árōvō)	155	47.54N	17.59E
Kolbio, Kenya	217	1.10S	41.15E
Kol'chugino, Russia (kôl-cho̤'gē-nô)	162	56.19N	39.29E
Kolda, Sen.	214	12.53N	14.57W
Kolding, Den. (kŭl'dĭng)	152	55.29N	9.24E
Kole, Zaire (kō'lā)	212	3.19S	22.46E
Kolguyev, i., Russia (kôl-go̤'yĕf)	164	69.00N	49.00E
Kolhāpur, India	187	16.48N	74.15E
Kolín, Czech Rep. (kō'lēn)	154	50.01N	15.11E
Kolkasrags, c., Lat. (kôl-käs'rágz)	153	57.46N	22.39E
Köln *see* Cologne, Ger.	157c	50.56N	6.57E
Kolno, Pol. (kōw'nō)	155	53.23N	21.56E
Koło, Pol. (kô'wō)	155	52.11N	18.37E
Kołobrzeg, Pol. (kô-lôb'zhĕk)	146	54.10N	15.35E
Kolomenskoje, neigh., Russia	239b	55.40N	37.41E
Kolomna, Russia (kál-ôm'ná)	166	55.06N	38.47E
Kolomyya, Ukr. (kō'lô-mē'yá)	155	48.32N	25.04E
Kolonie Stolp, Ger.	238a	52.28N	13.46E
Kolp', r., Russia (kôlp)	162	59.18N	35.32E
Kolpashevo, Russia (kŭl pá shô'vá)	164	58.16N	82.43E
Kolpino, Russia (kôl'pē-nô)	166	59.45N	30.37E
Kolpny, Russia (kôlp'nyē)	162	52.14N	36.54E
Kol'skiy Poluostrov, pen., Russia	164	67.15N	37.40E
Kolva, r., Russia	166	61.00N	57.00E
Kolwezi, Zaire (kōl-wē'zē)	212	10.43S	25.28E
Kolyberovo, Russia (kô-lĭ-byâ'rô-vô)	172b	55.16N	38.45E
Kolyma, r., Russia	165	66.30N	151.45E
Kolymskiy Mountains *see* Gydan, Khrebet, mts., Russia	165	61.45N	155.00E
Kom, r., Afr.	216	2.15N	12.05E
Komadugu Gana, r., Nig.	215	12.15N	11.10E
Komae, Japan	195a	35.37N	139.35E
Komagome, neigh., Japan	242a	35.44N	139.45E
Komandorskiye Ostrova, is., Russia	181	55.40N	167.13E
Komárno, Slvk. (kō'mär-nô)	155	47.46N	18.08E
Komarno, Ukr.	155	49.38N	23.42E
Komárom, Hung. (kō'mä-rôm)	155	47.45N	18.06E
Komatipoort, S. Afr. (kō-mä'tē-pōrt)	212	25.21S	32.00E
Komatsu, Japan (kō-mät'so͞o)	194	36.23N	136.26E
Komatsushima, Japan (kō-mät'so͞o-shē'mä)	195	34.04N	134.32E
Komeshia, Zaire	217	8.01S	27.07E
Komga, S. Afr. (kōm'gá)	213c	32.36S	27.54E
Komi, state, Russia (kô'mė)	170	63.00N	55.00E
Kommetijie, S. Afr.	212a	34.09S	18.19E
Kommunizma, Pik, mtn., Taj.	169	38.57N	72.01E
Komoé, r., C. Iv.	214	5.40N	3.40W
Komsomol, Kaz.	169	53.45N	62.04E
Komsomol's'ke, Ukr.	163	49.42N	28.44E
Komsomol'sk-na-Amure, Russia	165	50.46N	137.14E
Kona, Mali	214	14.57N	3.53W
Konda, r., Russia (kôn'dá)	166	60.50N	64.00E
Kondas, r., Russia (kôn'dás)	172a	59.30N	56.28E
Kondli, neigh., India	240d	28.37N	77.19E
Kondoa, Tan. (kôn-dō'á)	212	4.52S	36.00E
Kondolole, Zaire	217	1.20N	25.58E
Koné, N. Cal.	198f	21.04S	164.52E
Kong, C. Iv. (kông)	210	9.05N	4.41W
Kongbo, Cen. Afr. Rep.	216	4.44N	21.23E
Kongolo, Zaire (kōŋ'gō'lō)	212	5.23S	27.00E
Kongsberg, Nor. (kŭngs'bĕrg)	152	59.40N	9.36E
Kongsvinger, Nor. (kŭngs'vĭŋ-gĕr)	152	60.12N	12.00E
Koni, Zaire (kō'nē)	212	10.32S	27.27E
Königsberg *see* Kaliningrad, Russia	164	54.42N	20.32E
Königsbrunn, Ger. (kû'nĕgs-bro͞on)	145d	48.16N	10.53E
Königshardt, neigh., Ger.	236	51.33N	6.51E
Königs Wusterhausen, Ger. (kû'nĕgs vo͞os'tĕr-hou-zĕn)	145b	52.18N	13.38E
Konin, Pol. (kō'nyĕn)	147	52.11N	18.17E
Kónitsa, Grc. (kō'nyē'tsá)	161	40.03N	20.46E
Konjic, Bos. (kôn'yēts)	161	43.38N	17.59E
Konju, S. Kor.	194	36.21N	127.05E
Konnagar, India	186a	22.41N	88.22E
Konohana, neigh., Japan	242b	34.41N	135.26E
Kōnoike, Japan	242b	34.42N	135.37E
Konotop, Ukr. (kô-nô-tôp')	167	51.13N	33.14E
Konpienga, r., Burkina	214	11.15N	0.35E
Konqi, r., China (kôn-chyē)	188	41.09N	87.46E
Końskie, Pol. (koin''skyĕ)	155	51.12N	20.26E
Konstanz, Ger. (kôn'shtänts)	154	47.39N	9.10E

306 Kontagora–Kup'yans'k

PLACE (Pronunciation)	PAGE	Lat. °'	Long. °'
Kontagora, Nig. (kōn-tá-gō'rä)	210	10.24N	5.28E
Konya, Tur. (kōn'yá)	182	36.55N	32.25E
Koocanusa, Lake, res., N.A.	104	49.00N	115.10W
Kootenay (Kootenai), r., N.A.	87	49.45N	117.05W
Kootenay Lake, l., Can.	87	49.35N	116.50W
Kootenay National Park, Can. (ko͞o'tė-nå)	84	51.06N	117.02W
Kooyong, Austl.	243b	37.50S	145.02E
Kōō-zan, mtn., Japan (ko͞o'zän)	195b	34.53N	135.32E
Kopervik, Nor. (kô'pĕr-vėk)	152	59.18N	5.20E
Kopeysk, Russia (kô-pāsk')	170	55.07N	61.37E
Köping, Swe. (chû'pĭng)	152	59.32N	15.58E
Kopparberg, Swe. (kŏp'pår-bĕrgh)	152	59.53N	15.00E
Koppeh Dāgh, mts., Asia	182	37.28N	58.29E
Koppies, S. Afr.	218d	27.15S	27.35E
Koprivnica, Cro. (kô'prēv-nė'tsá)	160	46.10N	16.48E
Kopychyntsi, Ukr.	155	49.06N	25.55E
Korčula, i., Yugo. (kôr'cho͞o-lá)	161	42.50N	17.05E
Korea, North, nation, Asia	189	40.00N	127.00E
Korea, South, nation, Asia	189	36.30N	128.00E
Korea Bay, b., Asia	192	39.18N	123.50E
Korean Archipelago, is., S. Kor.	189	34.05N	125.35E
Korea Strait, strt., Asia	189	33.30N	128.30E
Korets', Ukr.	155	50.35N	27.13E
Korhogo, C. Iv. (kôr-hō'gō)	210	9.27N	5.38W
Kōri, Japan	242b	34.47N	135.39E
Koridhallós, Grc.	239d	37.59N	23.39E
Korinthiakós Kólpos, b., Grc.	149	38.15N	22.33E
Kórinthos, Grc. (kô-rēn'thôs) (kŏr'ĭnth)	142	37.56N	22.54E
Kōriyama, Japan (kō'rė-yä'mä)	194	37.18N	140.25E
Korkino, Russia (kôr'kē-nŭ)	172a	54.53N	61.25E
Korla, China (kōr-lä)	188	41.37N	86.03E
Körmend, Hung. (kûr'mĕnt)	154	47.02N	16.36E
Kornat, i., Yugo. (kôr-nät')	160	43.46N	15.10E
Korneuburg, Aus. (kôr'noi-bôrgh)	145e	48.22N	16.21E
Koro, Mali	214	14.04N	3.05W
Korocha, Russia (kô-rō'chá)	163	50.50N	37.13E
Korop, Ukr. (kō'rôp)	163	51.33N	32.54E
Koro Sea, sea, Fiji	198g	18.00S	179.50E
Korosten', Ukr. (kô'rôs-tĕn)	167	50.51N	28.39E
Korostyshiv, Ukr.	163	50.19N	29.05E
Koro Toro, Chad	215	16.05N	18.30E
Korotoyak, Russia (kô'rô-tô-yák')	163	51.00N	39.06E
Korsakov, Russia (kôr'sá-kôf')	165	46.42N	143.16E
Korsnäs, Fin. (kôrs'nĕs)	153	62.51N	21.17E
Korsør, Den. (kôrs'ûr')	152	55.19N	11.08E
Kortrijk, Bel.	151	50.49N	3.10E
Koryakskiy Khrebet, mts., Russia	165	62.00N	168.45E
Koryukivka, Ukr. (kôr-yo͞o-kôf'ká)	163	51.44N	32.24E
Kosa Byryuchyy ostriv, i., Ukr.	163	46.07N	35.12E
Kościan, Pol. (kŭsh'tsyán)	154	52.05N	16.38E
Kościerzyna, Pol. (kŭsh-tsyĕ-zhē'ná)	155	54.08N	17.59E
Kosciusko, Ms., U.S. (kŏs-ĭ-ŭs'kō)	114	33.04N	89.35W
Kosciusko, Mount, mtn., Austl.	203	36.26S	148.20E
Kosha, Sudan	211	20.49N	30.27E
Koshigaya, Japan (kô'shė-gä'yä)	195a	35.53N	139.48E
Koshim, r., Kaz.	170	50.30N	50.40E
Kosi, r., India (kô'sē)	186	26.00N	86.20E
Košice, Slvk. (kō'shė-tsĕ')	147	48.43N	21.17E
Kosino, Russia	239b	55.43N	37.52E
Kosmos, S. Afr. (kŏz'mŏs)	213b	25.45S	27.51E
Kosmosa, Monument, hist., Russia	239b	55.49N	37.38E
Kosobrodskiy, Russia (kä-sô'brôd-skĭ)	172a	54.14N	60.53E
Kosovo, hist. reg., Yugo.	161	42.35N	21.00E
Kosovska Mitrovica, Yugo. (kô'sôv-skä' mė'trô-vė-tsä')	161	42.51N	20.50E
Kostajnica, Cro. (kôs'tä-ė-nē'tsá)	160	45.14N	16.32E
Koster, S. Afr.	218d	25.52S	26.52E
Kostino, Russia (kôs'tĭ-nô)	172b	55.54N	37.51E
Kostroma, Russia (kôs-trô-má')	164	57.46N	40.55E
Kostroma, prov., Russia	162	57.50N	41.10E
Kostrzyn, Pol. (kôst'chėn)	147	52.35N	14.38E
Kostyantynivka, Ukr.	163	48.33N	37.42E
Kos'va, r., Russia (kôs'vá)	172a	58.44N	57.08E
Koszalin, Pol. (kô-shä'lĭn)	146	54.12N	16.10E
Köszeg, Hung. (kû'sĕg)	154	47.21N	16.32E
Kota, India	183	25.17N	75.49E
Kota Baharu, Malay. (kō'tä bä'ro͞o)	196	6.15N	102.23E
Kotabaru, Indon.	196	3.22S	116.15E
Kota Kinabalu, Malay.	196	5.55N	116.05E
Kota Tinggi, Malay.	181b	1.43N	103.54E
Kotel, Bul. (kō-tĕl')	161	42.54N	26.28E
Kotel'nich, Russia (kô-tyĕl'nėch)	166	58.15N	48.20E
Kotel'nyy, i., Russia (kô-tyĕl'nė)	165	74.51N	134.09E
Kotka, Fin. (kŏt'ká)	146	60.28N	26.56E
Kotlas, Russia (kôt'lás)	166	61.10N	46.50E
Kotlin, Ostrov, i., Russia (ôs-trôf' kôt'lĭn)	172c	60.02N	29.49E
Kōtō, neigh., Japan	242a	35.41N	139.48E
Kotor, Yugo.	161	42.25N	18.46E
Kotorosl', r., Russia (kô-tô'rôsl)	162	57.18N	39.08E
Kotovs'k, Ukr.	163	47.49N	29.31E
Kotte, Sri L.	187	6.50N	80.05E
Kotto, r., Cen. Afr. Rep.	211	5.17N	22.04E
Kotuy, r., Russia (kô-to͞o')	170	71.00N	103.15E
Kotzebue, Ak., U.S. (kôt'sē-bo͞o)	96a	66.48N	162.42W
Kotzebue Sound, strt., Ak., U.S.	95	67.00N	164.28W
Kouchibouguac National Park, rec., Can.	92	46.53N	65.35W
Koudougou, Burkina (ko͞o-do͞o'go͞o)	210	12.15N	2.22W
Kouilou, r., Congo	212	4.30S	12.00E
Koula-Moutou, Gabon	216	1.08S	12.29E
Koulikoro, Mali (ko͞o-lė-kō'rô)	210	12.53N	7.33W
Koulouguidi, Mali	215	13.27N	17.33E
Koumac, N. Cal.	198f	20.33S	164.17E
Koumra, Chad	215	8.55N	17.33E

PLACE (Pronunciation)	PAGE	Lat. °'	Long. °'
Koundara, Gui.	214	12.29N	13.18W
Kouroussa, Gui. (ko͞o-ro͞o'sä)	210	10.39N	9.53W
Koutiala, Mali (ko͞o-tė-ä'lä)	210	12.29N	5.29W
Kouvola, Fin. (kō'ô-vô-lä)	153	60.51N	26.40E
Kouzhen, China (kō-jŭn)	190	36.19N	117.37E
Kovda, l., Russia (kôv'dá)	166	66.45N	32.00E
Kovel', Ukr. (kō'vĕl)	167	51.13N	24.45E
Kovno *see* Kaunas, Lith.	164	54.42N	23.54E
Kovrov, Russia (kôv-rôf')	166	56.23N	41.21E
Kowloon (Jiulong), H.K.	189	22.18N	114.10E
Kowloon City, H.K.	241c	22.19N	114.11E
Koyuk, Ak., U.S. (kô-yo͞ok')	95	65.00N	161.18W
Koyukuk, r., Ak., U.S. (kô-yo͞o'kôk)	95	66.25N	153.50W
Kozáni, Grc.	149	40.16N	21.51E
Kozelets', Ukr. (kôzĕ-lyĕts)	163	50.53N	31.07E
Kozel'sk, Russia (kô-zĕlsk')	162	54.01N	35.49E
Kozienice, Pol. (kō-zyĕ-nē'tsĕ)	155	51.34N	21.35E
Koźle, Pol. (kôzh'lĕ)	155	50.19N	18.10E
Kozloduy, Bul. (kŭz'lô-dwē)	161	43.45N	23.42E
Kōzu, i., Japan (kō'zo͞o)	195	34.16N	139.03E
Kozyatyn, Ukr.	167	49.43N	28.50E
Kra, Isthmus of, isth., Asia	196	9.30S	99.45E
Kraai, r., S. Afr. (krä'ė)	213c	30.50S	27.03E
Krabbendijke, Neth.	145a	51.26N	4.05E
Krâchéh, Camb.	196	12.28N	106.06E
Kragujevac, Yugo. (krä'go͞o'yĕ-váts)	149	44.01N	20.55E
Krahenhöhe, neigh., Ger.	236	51.10N	7.06E
Kraków, Pol. (krä'kôf)	142	50.05N	20.00E
Kraljevo, Yugo. (kräl'ye-vô)	149	43.39N	20.48E
Kramators'k, Ukr.	163	48.43N	37.32E
Kramfors, Swe. (kräm'fôrs)	152	62.54N	17.49E
Krampnitz, Ger.	238a	52.28N	13.04E
Kranj, Slvn. (krän')	148	46.16N	14.23E
Kranskop, S. Afr. (kränz'kŏp)	213c	28.57S	30.54E
Krāslava, Lat. (kräs'lä-vä)	153	55.53N	27.12E
Kraslice, Czech Rep. (kräs'lė-tsĕ)	154	50.19N	12.30E
Krasnaya Gorka, Russia	172a	55.12N	56.40E
Krasnaya Sloboda, Russia	167	48.25N	44.35E
Kraśnik, Pol. (kräsh'nĭk)	155	50.53N	22.15E
Krasnoarmeysk, Russia (kräs'nô-ár-maśk')	172b	56.06N	38.09E
Krasnoarmiys'k, Ukr.	163	48.19N	37.04E
Krasnodar, Russia (kräs'nô-dár)	164	45.03N	38.55E
Krasnodarskiy, prov., Russia (krás-nô-där'skĭ ôb'lást)	163	45.25N	38.10E
Krasnogorsk, Russia	172b	55.49N	37.20E
Krasnogorskiy, Russia (kräs-nô-gôr'skĭ)	172a	54.36N	61.15E
Krasnogvardeyskiy, Russia (krå'sno-gvăr-dzyē ės-kēė)	172a	57.17N	62.05E
Krasnohrad, Ukr.	163	49.23N	35.26E
Krasnokamsk, Russia (kräs-nô-kämsk')	166	58.00N	55.45E
Krasnokuts'k, Ukr.	163	50.03N	35.05E
Krasnoslobodsk, Russia (kräs'nô-slôbôtsk')	166	54.20N	43.50E
Krasnotur'insk, Russia (krŭs-nŭ-to͞o-rensk')	164	59.47N	60.15E
Krasnoufimsk, Russia (krŭs-nŭ-o͞o-fēmsk')	164	56.38N	57.46E
Krasnoural'sk, Russia (kräs'nô-o͞o-rälsk')	166	58.21N	60.05E
Krasnousol'skiy, Russia (kräs-nô-ô-sôl'skĭ)	172a	53.54N	56.27E
Krasnovishersk, Russia (kräs-nô-vėshersk')	166	60.22N	57.20E
Krasnovodsk, Turk.	169	40.00N	52.50E
Krasnoyarsk, Russia (kräs-nô-yársk')	165	56.13N	93.12E
Krasnoye Selo, Russia (kräs'nŭ-yŭ sâ'lō)	172c	59.44N	30.06E
Krasnyj Stroitel', neigh., Russia	239b	55.35N	37.37E
Krasny Kholm, Russia (kräs'nė ĸōlm)	162	58.03N	37.11E
Krasnystaw, Pol. (kräs-nė-stáf')	155	50.59N	23.11E
Krasnyy Bor, Russia (kräs'nė bôr)	172c	59.41N	30.40E
Krasnyy Klyuch, Russia (kräs'nė'klyûch')	172a	55.24N	56.43E
Krasnyy Kut, Russia (krás-nė ko͞ot')	167	50.50N	47.00E
Kratovo, Mac. (krä'tô-vô)	161	42.04N	22.12E
Kratovo, Russia (krä'tô-vô)	172b	55.35N	38.10E
Kray, neigh., Ger.	236	51.28N	7.05E
Krefeld, Ger. (krā'fĕlt)	157c	51.20N	6.34E
Kremenchuk, Ukr.	167	49.04N	33.26E
Kremenchuk vodoskhovyshche, res., Ukr.	167	49.20N	32.45E
Kremenets', Ukr.	155	50.06N	25.43E
Kreml', bldg., Russia	239b	55.45N	37.37E
Kremmen, Ger. (krĕ'mĕn)	145b	52.45N	13.02E
Krempe, Ger. (krĕm'pĕ)	145c	53.50N	9.29E
Krems, Aus. (krĕms)	154	48.25N	15.36E
Krestovyy, Pereval, p., Geor.	168	42.32N	44.28E
Kresttsy, Russia (kråst'sė)	162	58.16N	32.25E
Kretinga, Lith. (krĕ-tĭŋ'gá)	153	55.55N	21.17E
Kreuzberg, Ger.	236	51.09N	7.27E
Kreuzberg, neigh., Ger.	238a	52.30N	13.23E
Kribi, Cam. (krē'bė)	210	2.57N	9.55E
Krichëv, Bela. (krē'chôf)	162	53.44N	31.39E
Krilon, Mys, c., Russia (mĭs krĭl'ôn)	194	45.58N	142.00E
Krimpen aan de IJssel, Neth.	145a	51.55N	4.34E
Krishna, r., India	183	16.00N	79.00E
Krishnanagar, India	186	23.29N	88.33E
Krishnapur, India	240a	22.36N	88.26E
Kristiansand, Nor. (krĭs-tyán-sän'')	142	58.09N	7.59E
Kristianstad, Swe. (krĭs-tyán-städ')	146	56.02N	14.09E
Kristiansund, Nor. (krĭs-tyán-sôn'')	146	63.07N	7.49E
Kristinehamn, Swe. (krēs-tē'nĕ-häm')	146	59.20N	14.05E
Kristinestad, Fin. (krĭs-tē'nĕ-städh)	153	62.16N	21.28E
Kriva-Palanka, Mac. (krē-vá-pá-läŋ'ká)	161	42.12N	22.21E
Krivoy Rog *see* Kryvyy Rih, Ukr.	164	47.54N	33.22E
Križevci, Cro. (krē'zhĕv-tsĭ)	160	46.02N	16.30E
Krk, i., Yugo. (k'rk)	160	45.06N	14.33E

PLACE (Pronunciation)	PAGE	Lat. °'	Long. °'
Krnov, Czech Rep. (k'r'nôf)	155	50.05N	17.41E
Krokodil, r., S. Afr. (krŏ'kŏ-dī)	218d	24.25S	27.08E
Krolevets', Ukr.	167	51.33N	33.21E
Kromy, Russia (krô'mė)	162	52.44N	35.41E
Kronshtadt, Russia (krōn'shtät)	166	59.59N	29.47E
Kroonstad, S. Afr. (krōn'shtät)	212	27.40S	27.15E
Kropotkin, Russia (krá-pôt'kĭn)	167	45.25N	40.30E
Krosno, Pol. (krôs'nô)	155	49.41N	21.46E
Krotoszyn, Pol. (krô-tō'shĭn)	155	51.41N	17.25E
Krško, Slvn. (k'rsh'kô)	160	45.58N	15.30E
Kruger National Park, rec., S. Afr. (kro͞o'gĕr) (krü'gĕr)	212	23.22S	30.18E
Krugersdorp, S. Afr. (kro͞o'gĕrz-dôrp)	212	26.06S	27.46E
Krugersdorp West, S. Afr.	244b	26.06S	27.45E
Krummensee, Ger.	238a	52.36N	13.42E
Krung Thep *see* Bangkok, Thai.	196	13.50N	100.29E
Kruševac, Yugo. (krô'shĕ-váts)	161	43.34N	21.21E
Kruševo, Mac.	161	41.20N	21.15E
Krylatskoje, neigh., Russia	239b	55.45N	37.26E
Krylbo, Swe. (krŭl'bô)	152	60.07N	16.14E
Krym, Respublika, prov., Ukr.	163	45.08N	34.05E
Krymskaya, Russia (krĭm'ská-yá)	163	44.58N	38.01E
Kryms'kyy pivostriv (Crimean Peninsula), pen., Ukr.	167	45.18N	33.30E
Krynki, Pol. (krĭn'kė)	155	53.15N	23.47E
Kryve Ozero, Ukr.	163	47.57N	30.21E
Kryvyy Rih, Ukr.	164	47.54N	33.22E
Ksar Chellala, Alg.	159	35.12N	2.20E
Ksar-el-Kebir, Mor.	148	35.01N	5.48W
Ksar-es-Souk, Mor.	148	31.58N	4.25W
Kuai, r., China (ko͞o-ī)	190	33.30N	116.56E
Kuala Klawang, Malay.	181b	2.57N	102.04E
Kuala Lumpur, Malay. (kwä'lä lôm-po͞or')	196	3.08N	101.42E
Kuandian, China (kůän-dĭĕn)	192	40.40N	124.50E
Kuban, r., Russia	167	45.20N	40.05E
Kubenskoye, l., Russia	166	59.40N	39.40E
Kuching, Malay. (ko͞o'chĭng)	196	1.30N	110.26E
Kuchinoerabo, i., Japan (ko͞o'chė nō ĕr'á-bō)	195	30.31N	129.53E
Kudamatsu, Japan (ko͞o'dá-mä'tso͞o)	195	34.00N	131.51E
Kudap, Indon.	181b	1.14N	102.30E
Kudat, Malay. (ko͞o-dät')	196	6.56N	116.48E
Kudbrooke, neigh., Eng., U.K.	235	51.28N	0.03E
Kudirkos Naumietis, Lith. (ko͞odĭr-kôs nå'ô-mĕ'tĭs)	153	54.51N	23.00E
Kudymkar, Russia (ko͞o-dĭm-kär')	164	58.43N	54.52E
Kufstein, Aus. (ko͞of'shtīn)	154	47.34N	12.11E
Kuhstedt, Ger. (ko͞o'shtĕ)	145c	53.23N	8.58E
Kuibyshev *see* Kuybyshev, Russia	164	53.10N	50.05E
Kuilsrivier, S. Afr.	212a	33.56S	18.41E
Kuito, Ang.	212	12.22S	16.56E
Kuji, Japan	189	40.11N	141.46E
Kujū-san, mtn., Japan (ko͞o'jô-sän')	195	33.07N	131.14E
Kukës, Alb. (ko͞o'kĕs)	161	42.03N	20.25E
Kula, Bul. (ko͞o'lá)	161	43.52N	23.13E
Kula, Tur.	149	38.32N	28.30E
Kula Kangri, mtn., Bhu.	183	33.11N	90.36E
Kular, Khrebet, mts., Russia (kô-lär')	171	69.00N	131.45E
Kuldīga, Lat. (kôl'dė-gá)	153	56.59N	21.59E
Kulebaki, Russia (ko͞o-lĕ-bäk'ĭ)	166	55.22N	42.30E
Küllenhahn, neigh., Ger.	236	51.14N	7.08E
Kulmbach, Ger. (klôlm'bäĸ)	154	50.07N	11.28E
Kulunda, Russia (kô-lôn'dá)	164	52.38N	79.00E
Kulundinskoye, l., Russia	170	52.45N	77.18E
Kum, r., S. Kor. (kôm)	194	36.50N	127.30E
Kuma, r., Russia (ko͞o'mä)	167	44.50N	45.10E
Kumamoto, Japan (ko͞o'mä-mō'tô)	189	32.49N	130.40E
Kumano-Nada, b., Japan (ko͞o-mä'nō nä-dä)	195	34.03N	136.36E
Kumanovo, Mac. (kô-mä'nô-vô)	161	42.10N	21.41E
Kumasi, Ghana (ko͞o-mä'sė)	210	6.41N	1.35W
Kumba, Cam. (kôm'bá)	210	4.38N	9.25E
Kumbakonam, India (kôm'bŭ-kō'nŭm)	183	10.59N	79.25E
Kumkale, Tur.	161	39.59N	26.10E
Kumo, Nig.	215	10.03N	11.13E
Kumta, India	187	14.19N	75.28E
Kumul *see* Hami, China	188	42.58N	93.14E
Kunashak, Russia (kû-nä'shák)	172a	55.43N	61.35E
Kunashir (Kunashiri), i., Russia (ko͞o-nŭ-shēr')	189	44.00N	145.45E
Kunda, Est.	153	59.30N	26.28E
Kundravy, Russia (ko͞on'drá-vĭ)	172a	54.50N	60.14E
Kundur, i., Indon.	181b	0.49N	103.20E
Kunene (Cunene), r., Afr.	212	17.05S	12.35E
Kungälv, Swe. (kŭng'ĕlf)	152	57.53N	12.01E
Kungsbacka, Swe. (kŭngs'bä-ká)	152	57.31N	12.04E
Kungur, Russia (kôn-go͞or')	164	57.27N	56.53E
Kunitachi, Japan	242a	35.41N	139.26E
Kunlun Shan, mts., China (ko͞on-lo͞on shän)	188	35.26N	83.09E
Kunming, China (ko͞on-mĭŋ)	188	25.10N	102.50E
Kunsan, S. Kor. (kôn'sän')	189	35.54N	126.46E
Kunshan, China (ko͞onshän)	191b	31.23N	120.57E
Kuntsëvo, Russia (kôn-tsyô'vô)	162	55.43N	37.27E
Kun'ya, Russia	172a	58.42N	56.47E
Kun'ya, r., Russia (kôn'yá)	162	56.45N	30.53E
Kuopio, Fin. (kô-ô'pė-ŏ)	146	62.48N	28.30E
Kupa, r., Yugo.	160	45.32N	14.50E
Kupang, Indon.	197	10.14S	123.37E
Kupavna, Russia	172b	55.49N	38.11E
Kupferdreh, neigh., Ger.	236	51.23N	7.05E
Kupino, Russia (ko͞o-pĭ'nô)	164	54.00N	77.47E
Kupiškis, Lith. (kô-pĭsh'kĭs)	153	55.50N	24.55E
Kup'yans'k, Ukr.	167	49.44N	37.38E

ăt; finăl; rāte; senåte; ärm; åsk; sofȧ; fâre; ch-choose; dh-as th in other; bē; ėvent; bĕt; recĕnt; cratẽr; g-gō; gh-guttural g; bĭt; ĭ-short neutral; rīde; ĸ-guttural k as ch in German ich;

PLACE (Pronunciation)	PAGE	Lat. °′	Long. °′
Kuqa, China (kōō-chyä)	188	41.34N	82.44E
Kür, r., Asia	167	41.10N	45.40E
Kurashiki, Japan (kōō'rä-shē'kė)	195	34.37N	133.44E
Kuraymah, Sudan	211	18.34N	31.49E
Kurayoshi, Japan (kōō'rá-yō'shė)	195	35.25N	133.49E
Kurdistan, hist. reg., Asia (kûrd'ĭ-stăn)	182	37.40N	43.30E
Kurdufān, hist. reg., Sudan (kôr-dò-făn')	211	14.08N	28.39E
Kŭrdzhali, Bul.	161	41.39N	25.21E
Kure, Japan (kōō'rĕ)	189	34.17N	132.35E
Kuressaare, Est. (kò'rĕ-sä'rĕ)	153	58.15N	22.26E
Kurgan, Russia (kòr-gän')	164	55.28N	65.14E
Kurgan-Tyube, Taj. (kòr-gän' tyò'bĕ)	169	38.00N	68.49E
Kurihama, Japan (kōō-rē-hä'mä)	195a	35.14N	139.42E
Kuril Islands, is., Russia (kōō'rĭl)	171	46.20N	149.30E
Ku-ring-gai, Austl.	243a	33.45S	151.08E
Kurisches Haff, b., Eur.	153	55.10N	21.08E
Kurl, neigh., Ger.	236	51.35N	7.35E
Kurla, neigh., India	187b	19.03N	72.53E
Kurmuk, Sudan (kòr'mōōk)	211	10.40N	34.13E
Kurnell, Austl.	243a	34.01S	151.13E
Kurnool, India (kòr-nōōl')	183	16.00N	78.04E
Kurrajong, Austl.	201b	33.33S	150.40E
Kuršenai, Lith. (kòr'shä-nī)	153	56.01N	22.56E
Kursk, Russia (kòrsk)	164	51.44N	36.08E
Kuršumlija, Yugo. (kòr'shòm'lĭ-yà)	161	43.08N	21.18E
Kuruçeşme, neigh., Tur.	239f	41.03N	29.02E
Kuruman, S. Afr. (kōō-rōō-män')	212	27.25S	23.30E
Kurume, Japan (kōō'rò-mĕ)	189	33.10N	130.30E
Kurume, Japan	242a	35.45N	139.32E
Kururi, Japan (kōō'rò-rė)	195a	35.17N	140.05E
Kusa, Russia (kōō'sà)	172a	55.19N	59.27E
Kushchëvskaya, Russia	163	46.34N	39.40E
Kushikino, Japan (kōō'shĭ-kē'nō)	195	31.44N	130.19E
Kushimoto, Japan (kōō'shĭ-mō'tō)	195	33.29N	135.47E
Kushiro, Japan (kōō'shē-rō)	189	43.00N	144.22E
Kushva, Russia (kōōsh'và)	164	58.18N	59.51E
Kuskokwim, r., Ak., U.S.	95	61.32N	160.36W
Kuskokwim Bay, b., Ak., U.S. (kŭs'kò-kwĭm)	95	59.25N	163.14W
Kuskokwim Mountains, mts., Ak., U.S.	95	62.08N	158.00W
Kuskovak, Ak., U.S. (kŭs-kō'văk)	95	60.10N	162.50W
Kuskovo, neigh., Russia	239b	55.44N	37.49E
Kütahya, Tur. (kû-tä'hyà)	182	39.20N	29.50E
Kutaisi, Geor. (kōō-tŭ-ē'sē)	167	42.15N	42.40E
Kutch, Gulf of, b., India	183	22.45N	68.33E
Kutch, Rann of, sw., Asia	183	23.59N	69.13E
Kutenholz, Ger. (kōō'tĕn-hōlts)	145c	53.29N	9.20E
Kutim, Russia (kōō'tĭm)	172a	60.22N	58.51E
Kutina, Cro. (kōō'tē-nà)	160	45.29N	16.48E
Kutno, Pol. (kòt'nô)	147	52.14N	19.22E
Kutno, l., Russia	166	65.15N	31.30E
Kutulik, Russia (kò tōō'lyĭk)	165	53.12N	102.51E
Kuty, Ukr. (kōō'tė)	155	48.16N	25.12E
Kuujjuaq, Can.	85	58.06N	68.25W
Kuusamo, Fin. (kōō'sà-mò)	146	65.59N	29.10E
Kuvshinovo, Russia (kòv-shē'nô-vò)	162	57.01N	34.09E
Kuwait see Al Kuwait, Kuw.	182	29.04N	47.59E
Kuwait, nation, Asia	182	29.00N	48.45E
Kuwana, Japan (kōō'wà-nà)	195	35.02N	136.40E
Kuybyshev see Samara, Russia	166	53.10N	50.05E
Kuybyshevskoye, res., Russia	164	53.40N	49.00E
Kuz'minki, neigh., Russia	239b	55.42N	37.48E
Kuzneckovo, Russia	172b	55.29N	38.22E
Kuznetsk, Russia (kōōz-nyĕtsk')	166	53.00N	46.30E
Kuznetsk Basin, basin, Russia	164	56.30N	86.15E
Kuznetsovka, Russia (kòz-nyĕt'sôf-kȧ)	172a	54.41N	56.40E
Kuznetsovo, Russia (kòz-nyĕt-sô'vò)	162	56.39N	36.55E
Kuznetsy, Russia	172b	55.50N	38.39E
Kvarner Zaliv, b., Yugo. (kvär'nĕr)	160	44.41N	14.05E
Kwa, r., Zaire	216	3.00S	16.45E
Kwahu Plateau, plat., Ghana	214	7.00N	1.35W
Kwando (Cuando), r., Afr.	216	16.50S	22.40E
Kwangju, S. Kor.	194	35.09N	126.54E
Kwango (Cuango), r., Afr. (kwäng'ō')	216	6.35S	16.50E
Kwangwazi, Tan.	217	7.47S	38.15E
Kwa-Thema, S. Afr.	244b	26.18S	28.23E
Kwekwe, Zimb.	212	18.49S	29.45E
Kwenge, r., Afr. (kwĕŋ'gė)	212	6.45S	18.23E
Kwilu, r., Afr. (kwē'lōō)	212	4.00S	18.00E
Kyakhta, Russia (kyäk'ta)	165	51.00N	107.30E
Kyaukpyu, Myanmar (chouk'pyoo')	183	19.19N	93.33E
Kybartai, Lith. (kē'bär-tī')	153	54.40N	22.46E
Kyn, Russia (kĭn')	172a	57.52N	58.42E
Kynuna, Austl. (kĭ-nōō'nà)	203	21.30S	142.12E
Kyoga, Lake, l., Ug.	211	1.30N	32.45E
Kyōga-Saki, c., Japan (kyō'gä sa'kė)	195	35.46N	135.14E
Kyŏngju, S. Kor. (kyŭng'yōō)	189	35.48N	129.12E
Kyŏngju, S. Kor.	194	35.51N	129.14E
Kyōto, Japan (kyō'tō')	189	35.00N	135.46E
Kyōto, dept., Japan	195b	34.56N	135.42E
Kyren, Russia (kĭ-rĕn')	165	51.46N	102.13E
Kyrgyzstan, nation, Asia	164	41.45N	74.38E
Kyrönjoki, r., Fin.	153	63.03N	22.20E
Kyrya, Russia (kēr'yà)	172a	59.18N	59.03E
Kyshtym, Russia (kĭsh-tĭm')	166	55.42N	60.34E
Kytlym, Russia (kĭt'lĭm)	172a	59.30N	59.15E
Kyūhōji, neigh., Japan	242b	34.38N	135.35E
Kyūshū, i., Japan	189	33.00N	131.00E
Kyustendil, Bul. (kyòs-tĕn-dĭl')	149	42.16N	22.39E
Kyyiv, prov., Ukr.	163	50.05N	30.40E
Kyyivs'ke vodoskhovyshche, res., Ukr.	164	51.00N	30.20E
Kyzyl, Russia (kĭ zĭl)	165	51.37N	93.38E

L

PLACE (Pronunciation)	PAGE	Lat. °′	Long. °′
Laa, Aus.	154	48.42N	16.23E
Laab im Walde, Aus.	239e	48.09N	16.11E
La Almunia de Doña Godina, Spain	158	41.29N	1.22W
Laas Caanood, Som.	218a	8.24N	47.20E
La Asunción, Ven. (lä ä-sōōn-syōn')	130	11.02N	63.57W
La Baie, Can.	91	48.21N	70.53W
La Banda, Arg. (lä bän'dä)	132	27.48S	64.12W
La Bandera, Chile	234b	33.34S	70.39W
La Barca, Mex. (lä bär'kà)	118	20.17N	102.33W
Laberge, Lake, l., Can. (lȧ-bĕrzh')	84	61.08N	136.42W
Laberinto de las Doce Leguas, is., Cuba	122	20.40N	78.35W
Labinsk, Russia	167	44.30N	40.40E
Labis, Malay. (läb'ĭs)	181b	2.23N	103.01E
La Bisbal, Spain (lä bēs-bäl')	159	41.55N	3.00E
Labo, Phil. (lä'bò)	197a	14.11N	122.49E
Labo, Mount, mtn., Phil.	197a	14.00N	122.47E
Labouheyre, Fr. (lȧ-bōō-âr')	156	44.14N	0.58W
Laboulaye, Arg. (lä-bô'ōō-lä-yĕ)	132	34.01S	63.10W
Labrador, reg., Can. (lăb'rȧ-dôr)	85	53.05N	63.30W
Labrador Sea, sea, Can.	93	50.38N	55.00W
Lábrea, Braz. (lä-brā'ä)	130	7.28S	64.39W
Labuan, Pulau, i., Malay. (lä-bò-än')	196	5.28N	115.11E
Labuha, Indon.	197	0.43S	127.35E
L'Acadie, Can. (lȧ-kȧ-dē')	83a	45.18N	73.22W
L'Acadie, r., Can.	83a	45.24N	73.21W
La Calera, Chile (lä-kä-lĕ-rä)	129b	32.47S	71.11W
La Calera, Col.	130a	4.43N	73.58W
Lac Allard, Can.	92	50.38N	63.28W
La Canada, Ca., U.S. (lä kän-yä'dä)	107a	34.13N	118.12W
La Candelaria, Mex.	233a	19.20N	99.09W
Lacantum, r., Mex. (lä-kän-tōō'm)	119	16.13N	90.52W
La Carolina, Spain (lä kä-rô-lē'nä)	158	38.16N	3.48W
La Catedral, Cerro, mtn., Mex. (sĕ'r-rô-lä-kä-tĕ-drà'l)	119a	19.32N	99.31W
Lac-Beauport, Can. (läk-bō-pōr')	83b	46.58N	71.17W
Laccadive Islands see Lakshadweep, is., India	183	11.00N	73.02E
Laccadive Sea, sea, Asia	187	9.10N	75.17E
Lac Court Oreille Indian Reservation, I.R., Wi., U.S.	103	46.04N	91.18W
Lac du Flambeau Indian Reservation, I.R., Wi., U.S.	103	46.12N	89.50W
La Ceiba, Hond. (lä sēbä)	116	15.45N	86.52W
La Ceja, Col. (lä-sĕ-kä)	130a	6.02N	75.25W
Lac-Frontière, Can.	85	46.42N	70.00W
Lacha, l., Russia (lá'chä)	166	61.15N	39.05E
La Chaux de Fonds, Switz. (lȧ shō dē-fôn')	154	47.07N	6.47E
L'Achigan, r., Can. (lä-shē-gän)	83a	45.49N	73.48W
Lachine, Can. (lȧ-shēn')	83a	45.26N	73.40W
Lachlan, r., Austl. (läk'lăn)	203	34.00S	145.00E
La Chorrera, Pan. (làchôr-rā'rä)	121	8.54N	79.47W
Lachta, neigh., Russia	239a	60.00N	30.10E
Lachute, Can. (lȧ-shōōt')	91	45.39N	74.20W
La Ciotat, Fr. (lä syò-tá')	157	43.13N	5.35E
La Cisterna, Chile	234b	33.33S	70.41W
Lackawanna, N.Y., U.S. (lak-ȧ-wŏn'ȧ)	101c	42.49N	78.50W
Lac La Biche, Can.	84	54.46N	112.58W
Lacombe, Can.	84	52.28N	113.44W
Laconia, N.H., U.S. (lȧ-kō'nĭ-ȧ)	99	43.30N	71.30W
La Conner, Wa., U.S. (lȧ kŏn'ĕr)	106a	48.23N	122.30W
La Coruña, Spain (lä kò-rōōn'yä)	142	43.20N	8.20W
La Courneuve, Fr.	237c	48.56N	2.23E
Lacreek, l., S.D., U.S. (lă'krēk)	102	43.04N	101.46W
La Cresenta, Ca., U.S. (lȧ krĕs'ĕnt-ȧ)	107a	34.14N	118.13W
La Cross, Ks., U.S. (lȧ-krôs')	110	38.30N	99.20W
La Crosse, Wi., U.S.	97	43.48N	91.14W
La Cruz, Col. (lä krōōz')	130	1.37N	77.00W
La Cruz, C.R. (lä-krōō'z)	120	11.05N	85.37W
Lacs, Riviere des, r., N.D., U.S. (rē-vyĕr' de läk)	102	48.30N	101.45W
La Cuesta, C.R. (lä-kwĕ's-tä)	121	8.32N	82.51W
La Cygne, Ks., U.S. (lȧ-sēn'y') (lȧ-sēn')	111	38.20N	94.45W
Ladd, Il., U.S. (lăd)	98	41.25N	89.25W
Ladíspoli, Italy (lä-dē's-pô-lē)	159d	41.57N	12.05E
Lādīz, Iran	185	28.56N	61.19E
Ladner, Can. (lăd'nĕr)	86	49.05N	123.05W
Lādnun, India (läd'nòn)	186	27.45N	74.20E
Ladoga, Lake see Ladozhskoye Ozero, l., Russia	164	60.59N	31.30E
La Dolorita, Ven.	234a	10.29N	66.47W
La Dorado, Col. (lä dò-rä'dä)	130	5.28N	74.42W
Ladozhskoye Ozero, Russia (lȧ-dôsh'skô-yē ô'zĕ-rô)	164	60.59N	31.30E
La Durantaye, Can. (lä dü-rän-tā')	83b	46.51N	70.51W
Lady Frere, S. Afr. (lā-dē frâ'r')	213c	31.48S	27.16E
Lady Grey, S. Afr.	213c	30.44S	27.17E
Ladysmith, Can. (lā'dĭ-smĭth)	86	48.58N	123.49W
Ladysmith, S. Afr.	212	28.38S	29.48E
Ladysmith, Wi., U.S.	103	45.27N	91.07W
Lae, Pap. N. Gui. (lä'å)	197	6.15S	146.57E
Laerdalsøyri, Nor.	152	61.08N	7.26E
La Esperanza, Hond. (lä ĕs-pā-rän'zä)	120	14.20N	88.21W
La Estrada, Spain (lä ĕs-trä'dä)	158	42.42N	8.29W
Lafayette, Al., U.S.	114	32.52N	85.25W
Lafayette, Ca., U.S.	106b	37.53N	122.07W
Lafayette, Ga., U.S. (lä-fā-yĕt')	114	34.41N	85.19W
Lafayette, In., U.S.	97	40.25N	86.55W
Lafayette, La., U.S.	97	30.15N	92.02W
La Fayette, R.I., U.S.	100b	41.34N	71.29W
Lafayette Hill, Pa., U.S.	229b	40.05N	75.15W
Laferrere, Arg.	233d	34.45S	58.35W
La Ferté-Alais, Fr. (lä-fĕr-tā'ā-lā')	157b	48.29N	2.19E
La Ferté-sous-Jouarre, Fr. (lȧ fĕr-tā'sōō-zhōō-är')	157b	48.56N	3.07E
Lafia, Nig.	215	8.30N	8.30E
Lafiagi, Nig.	215	8.52N	5.25E
Laflèche, Can.	227b	45.30N	73.28W
La Flèche, Fr. (lä flāsh')	156	47.43N	0.03W
La Floresta, Spain	238e	41.27N	2.04E
La Florida, Chile	234b	33.32S	70.33W
La Follete, Tn., U.S. (lä-fŏl'ĕt)	114	36.23N	84.07W
Lafourche, Bayou, r., La., U.S. (bȧ-yōō'lȧ-fōōrsh')	113	29.25N	90.15W
La Frette-sur-Seine, Fr.	237c	48.58N	2.11E
La Gaiba, Braz. (lä-gī'bä)	131	17.54S	57.32W
La Galite, i., Tun. (gä-lēt)	148	37.36N	8.03E
Lågan, r., Nor. (lô'ghĕn)	142	61.00N	10.00E
Lagan, r., Swe.	152	56.34N	13.25E
Lagan, r., N. Ire., U.K. (lă'găn)	150	54.30N	6.00W
La Garenne-Colombes, Fr.	237c	48.55N	2.15E
Lagarto, r., Pan. (lä-gä'r-tô)	116a	9.08N	80.05W
Lagartos, l., Mex. (lä-gä'r-tôs)	120a	21.32N	88.15W
Laghouat, Alg. (lä-gwät')	210	33.45N	2.49E
Lagny, Fr. (län-yē')	157b	48.53N	2.41E
Lagoa da Prata, Braz. (lȧ-gô'ä-dȧ-prä'tȧ)	129a	20.04S	45.33W
Lagoa Dourada, Braz. (lȧ-gô'ä-dò-rä'dä)	129a	20.55S	44.03W
Lagogne, Fr. (lan-gōn'y')	156	44.43N	3.50E
Lagonay, Phil.	197a	13.44N	123.31E
Lagos, Nig. (lä'gōs)	210	6.27N	3.24E
Lagos, Port. (lä'gôzh)	158	37.08N	8.43W
Lagos de Moreno, Mex. (lä'gōs dā mô-rā'nō)	116	21.21N	101.55W
La Grand' Combe, Fr. (lȧ grän kanb')	156	44.12N	4.03E
La Grande, Or., U.S. (lȧ grănd')	96	45.20N	118.06W
La Grande, r., Can.	85	53.55N	77.30W
La Grange, Austl. (lä grānj)	202	18.40S	122.00E
La Grange, Ga., U.S. (lȧ-grānj')	97	33.01N	85.00W
La Grange, Il., U.S.	101a	41.49N	87.53W
Lagrange, In., U.S.	98	41.40N	85.25W
La Grange, Ky., U.S.	98	38.20N	85.25W
La Grange, Mo., U.S.	111	40.04N	91.30W
Lagrange, Oh., U.S.	101d	41.14N	82.07W
Lagrange, Tx., U.S.	113	29.55N	96.50W
La Grange Highlands, Il., U.S.	231a	41.48N	87.53W
La Grange Park, Il., U.S.	231a	41.50N	87.52W
La Granja, Chile	234b	33.32S	70.39W
La Grita, Ven. (lä grē'tä)	130	8.02N	71.59W
La Guaira, Ven. (lä gwä'ē-rä)	130	10.36N	66.54W
La Guardia, Spain (lä gwär'dē-ä)	158	41.55N	8.48W
La Guardia Airport, arpt., N.Y., U.S.	228	40.46N	73.53W
Laguna, Braz. (lä-gōō'nä)	132	28.19S	48.42W
Laguna, Cayos, is., Cuba (kä'yōs-lä-gò'nä)	122	22.15N	82.45W
Laguna Indian Reservation, I.R., N.M., U.S.	109	35.00N	107.30W
Lagunillas, Bol. (lä-gōō-nēl'yäs)	130	19.42S	63.38W
Lagunillas, Mex. (lä-gōō-nē'l-yäs)	118	21.34N	99.41W
La Habana see Havana, Cuba	117	23.08N	82.23W
La Habra, Ca., U.S. (lȧ hăb'rȧ)	107a	34.56N	117.57W
La Habra Heights, Ca., U.S.	232	33.57N	117.57W
Lahaina, Hi., U.S. (lä-hä'ē-nä)	94a	20.52N	156.39W
La Häy-les-Roses, Fr.	237c	48.47N	2.21E
Lāhījān, Iran	185	37.12N	50.01E
Laholm, Swe. (lä'hòlm)	152	56.30N	13.00E
La Honda, Ca., U.S. (lä hŏn'dȧ)	106b	37.20N	122.16W
Lahore, Pak. (lä-hōr')	183	32.00N	74.18E
Lahr, Ger. (lär)	154	48.19N	7.52E
Lahti, Fin. (lä'tė)	146	60.59N	27.39E
Lai, Chad	211	9.29N	16.18E
Lai'an, China (lī-än)	190	32.27N	118.25E
Laibin, China (lī-bĭn)	193	23.42N	109.20E
L'Aigle, Fr. (lĕ'gl')	156	48.45N	0.37E
Lainate, Italy	238c	45.34N	9.02E
Lainz, neigh., Aus.	239e	48.11N	16.17E
Laisamis, Kenya	217	1.36N	37.48E
Laiyang, China (läī'yäng)	192	36.59N	120.42E
Laizhou Wan, b., China (lī-jō wän)	189	37.22N	119.19E
Laja, Río de la, r., Mex. (rē'ō-dĕ-lä-lä'kä)	118	21.17N	100.57W
Lajas, Cuba (lä'häs)	122	22.25N	80.20W
Laje, Ponta da, c., Port.	238d	38.40N	9.19W
Lajeado, Braz. (lä-zheä'dò)	132	29.24S	51.46W
Lajeado Velho, neigh., Braz.	234d	23.32S	46.23W
Lajes, Braz. (lä'zhĕs)	132	27.47S	50.17W
Lajinha, Braz. (lä-zhē'nyä)	129a	20.08S	41.36W
La Jolla, Ca., U.S. (lȧ hoi'yȧ)	108a	32.51N	117.16W
La Jolla Indian Reservation, I.R., Ca., U.S.	108	33.19N	116.21W
La Junta, Co., U.S. (lȧ hōōn'tȧ)	110	37.59N	103.35W
Lake Arrowhead, Ca., U.S.	232	33.52N	118.05W
Lake Arthur, La., U.S. (är'thŭr)	113	30.06N	92.40W
Lake Barcroft, Va., U.S.	229d	38.51N	77.09W
Lake Barkley, res., U.S.	114	36.45N	88.00W
Lake Benton, Mn., U.S. (bĕn'tŭn)	102	44.15N	96.17W
Lake Bluff, Il., U.S. (blŭf)	101a	42.17N	87.50W
Lake Brown, Austl. (broun)	202	31.03S	118.30E
Lake Charles, La., U.S. (chärlz')	97	30.15N	93.14W

PLACE (Pronunciation)	PAGE	Lat. °'	Long. °'
Lake City, Fl., U.S.	115	30.09N	82.40W
Lake City, Ia., U.S.	103	42.14N	94.43W
Lake City, Mn., U.S.	103	44.28N	92.19W
Lake City, S.C., U.S.	115	33.57N	79.45W
Lake Clark National Park, rec., Ak., U.S.	95	60.30N	153.15W
Lake Cowichan, Can. (kou'ĭ-chăn)	86	48.50N	124.03W
Lake Crystal, Mn., U.S. (krĭs'tăl)	103	44.05N	94.12W
Lake District, reg., Eng., U.K. (lăk)	150	54.25N	3.20W
Lake Elmo, Mn., U.S. (ĕlmō)	107g	45.00N	92.53W
Lake Forest, Il., U.S. (fŏr'ĕst)	101a	42.16N	87.50W
Lake Fork, r., Ut., U.S.	109	40.30N	110.25W
Lake Geneva, Wi., U.S. (jĕ-nē'vá)	103	42.36N	88.28W
Lake Harbour, Can. (här'bẽr)	85	62.43N	69.40W
Lake Havasu City, Az., U.S.	109	34.27N	114.22W
Lake June, Tx., U.S. (jōōn)	107c	32.43N	96.45W
Lakeland, Fl., U.S. (lāk'lănd)	97	28.02N	81.58W
Lakeland, Ga., U.S.	114	31.02N	83.02W
Lakeland, Mn., U.S.	107g	44.57N	92.47W
Lake Linden, Mi., U.S. (lĭn'dĕn)	103	47.11N	88.26W
Lake Louise, Can. (lōō-ēz')	87	51.26N	116.11W
Lakemba, Austl.	243a	33.55S	151.05E
Lake Mead National Recreation Area, rec., U.S.	109	36.00N	114.30W
Lake Mills, Ia., U.S. (mĭlz')	103	43.25N	93.32W
Lakemore, Oh., U.S. (lāk-mōr)	101d	41.01N	81.24W
Lake Odessa, Mi., U.S.	98	42.50N	85.15W
Lake Oswego, Or., U.S. (ŏs-wē'go)	106c	45.25N	122.40W
Lake Placid, N.Y., U.S.	99	44.17N	73.59W
Lake Point, Ut., U.S.	107b	40.41N	112.16W
Lakeport, Ca., U.S. (lāk'pōrt)	108	39.03N	122.54W
Lake Preston, S.D., U.S. (prēs'tŭn)	102	44.21N	97.23W
Lake Providence, La., U.S. (prŏv'ĭ-dĕns)	113	32.48N	91.12W
Lake Red Rock, res., Ia., U.S.	103	41.30N	93.15W
Lake Sharpe, res., S.D., U.S.	102	44.30N	100.00W
Lakeside, S. Afr.	244b	26.06S	28.09E
Lakeside, Ca., U.S. (lāk'sīd)	108a	32.52N	116.55W
Lake Station, In., U.S.	101a	41.34N	87.15W
Lake Stevens, Wa., U.S.	106a	48.01N	122.04W
Lake Success, N.Y., U.S. (sŭk-sĕs')	100a	40.46N	73.43W
Lakeview, Or., U.S.	104	42.11N	120.21W
Lakeview, neigh., Il., U.S.	231a	41.57N	87.39W
Lake Village, Ar., U.S.	111	33.20N	91.17W
Lake Wales, Fl., U.S. (wālz')	115a	27.54N	81.35W
Lakewood, Ca., U.S. (lāk'wŏŏd)	107a	33.50N	118.09W
Lakewood, Co., U.S.	110	39.44N	105.06W
Lakewood, Oh., U.S.	97	41.29N	81.48W
Lakewood, Pa., U.S.	99	40.05N	74.10W
Lakewood, Wa., U.S.	106a	48.09N	122.13W
Lakewood Center, Wa., U.S.	106a	47.10N	122.31W
Lake Worth, Fl., U.S. (wûrth')	115a	26.37N	80.04W
Lake Worth Village, Tx., U.S.	107c	32.49N	97.26W
Lake Zurich, Il., U.S. (tsü'rĭk)	101a	42.11N	88.05W
Lakhdenpokh'ya, Russia (l'äk-dīe'npōkyá)	153	61.33N	30.10E
Lakhtinskiy, Russia (lák-tĭn'skĭ)	172c	59.59N	30.10E
Lakota, N.D., U.S. (lȧ-kō'tȧ)	102	48.04N	98.21W
Lakshadweep, state, India	183	10.10N	72.50E
Lakshadweep, is., India	183	11.00N	73.02E
Laleham, Eng., U.K.	235	51.25N	0.30W
La Libertad, El Sal.	120	13.29N	89.20W
La Libertad, Guat. (lä lē-bĕr-tädh')	120	15.31N	91.44W
La Libertad, Guat.	120a	16.46N	90.12W
La Ligua, Chile (lä lē'gwä)	129b	32.21S	71.13W
Lalín, Spain (lä-lē'n)	158	42.40N	8.05W
La Línea, Spain (lä lē'nå-ä)	148	36.11N	5.22W
La Lisa, Cuba	233b	23.04N	82.26W
Lalitpur, Nepal	183	27.23N	85.24E
La Louviere, Bel. (lá lōō-vyâr')	151	50.30N	4.10E
La Luz, Mex. (lä lōōz')	118	21.04N	101.19W
Lama-Kara, Togo	214	9.33N	1.12E
La Malbaie, Can. (lá mäl-bå')	85	47.39N	70.10W
La Mancha, reg., Spain (lä män'chä)	158	38.55N	4.20W
Lamar, Co., U.S. (lȧ-mär')	110	38.04N	102.44W
Lamar, Mo., U.S.	111	37.28N	94.15W
La Marmora, Punta, mtn., Italy (lä-mä'r-mô-rä)	148	40.00N	9.28E
La Marque, Tx., U.S. (lå-märk)	113a	29.23N	94.58W
Lamas, Peru (lä'más)	130	6.24S	76.41W
Lamballe, Fr. (län-bäl')	156	48.29N	2.36W
Lambari, Braz. (läm-bá'rē)	129a	21.58S	45.22W
Lambasa, Fiji	198g	16.26S	179.24E
Lambayeque, Peru (läm-bä-yā'kå)	130	6.41S	79.58W
Lambert, Ms., U.S. (lăm'bẽrt)	114	34.10N	90.16W
Lambertville, N.J., U.S. (lăm'bẽrt-vĭl)	99	40.20N	75.00W
Lambeth, neigh., Eng., U.K.	235	51.28N	0.07W
Lambourne End, Eng., U.K.	235	51.38N	0.08E
Lambrate, neigh., Italy	238c	45.29N	9.15E
Lambro, r., Italy	238c	45.26N	9.16E
Lambton, S. Afr.	244b	26.15S	28.10E
Lame Deer, Mt., U.S. (lām dēr')	105	45.36N	106.40W
Lamego, Port. (lä-mā'gō)	158	41.07N	7.47W
La Mesa, Col.	130a	4.38N	74.27W
La Mesa, Ca., U.S. (lä mā'sä)	108a	32.46N	117.01W
Lamesa, Tx., U.S.	110	32.44N	101.54W
Lamía, Grc. (lá-mē'á)	149	38.54N	22.25E
La Mirada, Ca., U.S.	232	33.54N	118.01W
Lamon Bay, b., Phil. (lä-mōn')	196	14.35N	121.52E
La Mora, Chile (lä-mō'rä)	129b	32.28S	70.56W
La Mott, Pa., U.S.	229b	40.04N	75.08W
La Moure, N.D., U.S. (lȧ mōōr')	102	46.23N	98.17W
Lampa, r., Chile (lá'm-pä)	129b	33.15S	70.55W
Lampasas, Tx., U.S. (lăm-păs'ȧs)	112	31.06N	98.10W
Lampasas, r., Tx., U.S.	112	31.18N	98.08W
Lampazos, Mex. (läm-pä'zōs)	116	27.03N	100.30W
Lampedusa, i., Italy (läm-pĕ-dōō'sä)	148	35.29N	12.58E
Lamstedt, Ger. (läm'shtĕt)	145c	53.38N	9.06E
Lamu, Kenya (lä'mōō)	213	2.16S	40.54E
Lamu Island, i., Kenya	217	2.25S	40.50E
La Mure, Fr. (lá mür')	157	44.55N	5.50E
Lan', r., Bela. (lán')	162	52.38N	27.05E
Lanai, i., Hi., U.S. (lä-nä'ē)	96c	20.48N	157.06W
Lanai City, Hi., U.S.	94a	20.50N	156.56W
Lanak La, p., China	188	34.40N	79.50E
Lanark, Scot., U.K. (lăn'ȧrk)	150	55.40N	3.50W
Lancashire, co., Eng., U.K. (lăŋ'kȧ-shĭr)	144a	53.49N	2.42W
Lancaster, Eng., U.K.	146	54.04N	2.55W
Lancaster, Ky., U.S.	98	37.35N	84.30W
Lancaster, Ma., U.S.	93a	42.28N	71.40W
Lancaster, N.H., U.S.	99	44.25N	71.30W
Lancaster, N.Y., U.S.	101c	42.54N	78.42W
Lancaster, Oh., U.S.	98	39.40N	82.35W
Lancaster, Pa., U.S.	97	40.05N	76.20W
Lancaster, Tx., U.S.	107c	32.36N	96.45W
Lancaster, Wi., U.S.	103	42.51N	90.44W
Lândana, Ang. (län-dä'nä)	212	5.15S	12.07E
Landau, Ger. (län'dou)	154	49.13N	8.07E
Lander, Wy., U.S. (lăn'dẽr)	105	42.49N	108.24W
Landerneau, Fr. (län-dĕr-nō')	156	48.28N	4.14W
Landes, reg., Fr. (länd)	156	44.22N	0.52W
Landover, Md., U.S.	229d	38.56N	76.54W
Landsberg, Ger. (länds'bōōrgh)	154	48.03N	10.53E
Lands End, c., Eng., U.K.	142	50.03N	5.45W
Landshut, Ger. (länts'hōōt)	147	48.32N	12.09E
Landskrona, Swe. (låns-krô'ná)	152	55.51N	12.47E
Lane Cove, Austl.	243a	33.49S	151.10E
Lanett, Al., U.S. (lȧ-nĕt')	114	32.52N	85.13W
Langadhás, Grc.	161	40.44N	23.10E
Langat, r., Malay.	181b	2.46N	101.33E
Langdon, Can. (lăng'dŭn)	83e	50.58N	113.40W
Langdon, Mn., U.S.	107g	44.49N	92.56W
Langdon Hills, Eng., U.K.	235	51.34N	0.25E
L'Ange-Gardien, Can. (länzh gàr-dyăn')	83b	46.55N	71.06W
Langeland, i., Den.	152	54.52N	10.46E
Langenberg, Ger.	236	51.21N	7.09E
Langenbochum, Ger.	236	51.37N	7.07E
Langendreer, neigh., Ger.	236	51.28N	7.19E
Langenhorst, Ger.	236	51.22N	7.02E
Langenzersdorf, Aus.	145e	48.30N	16.22E
Langesund, Nor. (läng'ĕ-sòn')	152	58.59N	9.38E
Langfjorden, fj., Nor.	152	62.40N	7.45E
Langhorne, Pa., U.S. (lăng'hôrn)	100f	40.10N	74.55W
Langhorne Acres, Md., U.S.	229d	38.51N	77.16W
Langia Mountains, mts., Ug.	217	3.35N	33.35E
Langjökoll, ice., Ice. (läng-yû'kōōl)	146	64.40N	20.31W
Langla Co, l., China (läŋ-lä tswo)	186	30.42N	80.40E
Langley, Can. (lăng'lĭ)	87	49.06N	122.39W
Langley, Md., U.S.	229d	38.57N	77.10W
Langley, S.C., U.S.	115	33.32N	81.52W
Langley, Wa., U.S.	106a	48.02N	122.25W
Langley Indian Reserve, I.R., Can.	106d	49.12N	122.31W
Langley Park, Md., U.S.	229d	38.59N	76.59W
Langnau, Switz. (läng'nou)	154	46.56N	7.46E
Langon, Fr. (län-gôn')	156	44.34N	0.16W
Langres, Fr. (län'gr')	157	47.53N	5.20E
Langres, Plateau de, plat., Fr. (plä-tō'dē-län'grĕ)	156	47.39N	5.00E
Langsa, Indon. (läng'sá)	196	4.33N	97.52E
Lang Son, Viet. (läng'sŏn')	196	21.52N	106.42E
Langst-Kierst, Ger.	236	51.18N	6.43E
L'Anguille, r., Ar., U.S. (län-gē'y')	111	35.23N	90.52W
Langxi, China (läŋ-shyē)	190	31.10N	119.09E
Langzhong, China (läŋ-jōŋ)	188	31.40N	106.05E
Lanham, Md., U.S. (lăn'ăm)	100e	38.58N	76.54W
Lanigan, Can. (lăn'ĭ-găn)	84	51.52N	105.02W
Länkäran, Azer. (lĕn-kô-rän')	164	38.52N	48.58E
Lank-Latum, Ger.	236	51.18N	6.41E
Lankoviri, Nig.	215	9.00N	11.25E
Lankwitz, neigh., Ger.	238a	52.26N	13.21E
Lansdale, Pa., U.S. (lănz'dāl)	99	40.20N	75.15W
Lansdowne, Austl.	243a	33.54S	150.59E
Lansdowne, Md., U.S.	229c	39.15N	76.40W
Lansdowne, Pa., U.S.	100f	39.57N	75.17W
L'Anse, Mi., U.S. (lăns)	103	46.43N	88.28W
L'Anse and Vieux Desert Indian Reservation, I.R., Mi., U.S.	103	46.41N	88.12W
Lansford, Pa., U.S. (lănz'fẽrd)	99	40.50N	75.50W
Lansing, Il., U.S.	101a	41.34N	87.33W
Lansing, Ia., U.S.	103	43.22N	91.16W
Lansing, Ks., U.S.	107f	39.15N	94.53W
Lansing, Mi., U.S.	97	42.45N	84.35W
Lansing, neigh., Can.	227c	43.45N	79.25W
Lantianchang, China	240b	39.58N	116.17E
Lanús, Arg. (lä-nōōs')	132a	34.42S	58.24W
Lanusei, Italy (lä-nōō-sĕ'y)	160	39.51N	9.34E
Lanúvio, Italy (lä-nōō'vyô)	159d	41.41N	12.42E
Lanzarote Island, i., Spain (län-zá-rō'tä)	210	29.04N	13.03W
Lanzhou, China (län-jō)	188	35.55N	103.55E
Laoag, Phil. (lä-wäg')	196	18.13N	120.38E
Laohumiao, China	240b	39.58N	116.20E
Laon, Fr. (län)	156	49.36N	3.35E
La Oroya, Peru (lä-ô-rō'yä)	130	11.30S	76.00W
Laos, nation, Asia (lä-ōs) (lá-ōs')	196	20.15N	102.00E
Laoshan Wan, b., China (lou-shän wän)	190	36.21N	120.48E
Lapa, neigh., Braz.	234c	22.55S	43.11W
La Palma, Pan. (lä-päl'mä)	121	8.25N	78.07W
La Palma, Spain	158	37.24N	6.36W
La Palma Island, i., Spain	210	28.42N	19.03W
La Pampa, prov., Arg.	132	37.25S	67.00W
Lapa Rio Negro, Braz. (lä-pä-rē'ō-nĕ'grô)	132	26.12S	49.56W
La Paternal, neigh., Arg.	233d	34.36S	58.28W
La Paz, Arg. (lä päz')	132	30.48S	59.47W
La Paz, Bol.	130	16.31S	68.03W
La Paz, Hond.	120	14.15N	87.40W
La Paz, Mex.	116	24.00N	110.15W
La Paz, Mex. (lä-pá'z)	118	23.39N	100.44W
Lapeer, Mi., U.S. (lȧ-pēr')	98	43.05N	83.15W
La-Penne-sur-Huveaune, Fr. (la-pĕn'sür-ü-vōn')	156a	43.18N	5.33E
La Perouse, Austl.	201b	33.59S	151.14E
La Piedad Cabadas, Mex. (lä pyå-dhädh' kä-bä'dhäs)	118	20.20N	102.04W
Lapland, hist. reg., Eur. (lăp'lănd)	142	68.20N	22.00E
La Plata, Arg. (lä plä'tä)	132	34.54S	57.57W
La Plata, Mo., U.S. (lȧ plä'tȧ)	111	40.03N	92.28W
La Plata Peak, mtn., Co., U.S.	109	39.00N	106.25W
La Playa, Cuba	233b	23.06N	82.27W
La Pocatière, Can. (lá pō-ká-tyâr')	91	47.24N	70.01W
La Poile Bay, b., Can. (lá pwäl')	93	47.38N	58.20W
La Porte, In., U.S. (lȧ pōrt')	98	41.35N	86.45W
Laporte, Oh., U.S.	101d	41.19N	82.05W
La Porte, Tx., U.S.	113a	29.40N	95.01W
La Porte City, Ia., U.S.	103	42.20N	92.10W
Lappeenranta, Fin. (lä'pēn-rän'tä)	153	61.04N	28.08E
La Prairie, Can. (lä-prå-rē')	83a	45.24N	73.30W
Lâpseki, Tur. (läp'sá-kē)	161	40.20N	26.41E
Laptev Sea, sea, Russia (läp'tyĭf)	165	75.39N	120.00E
La Puebla, Spain (lä pwā'blä)	159	39.46N	3.02E
La Puebla de Montalbán, Spain	158	39.54N	4.21W
La Puente, Ca., U.S. (pwĕn'tē)	107a	34.01N	117.57W
La Punta, Peru	233c	12.05S	77.10W
Lapuşul, r., Rom. (lä'pōō-shōōl)	155	47.29N	23.46E
La Queue-en-Brie, Fr.	237c	48.47N	2.35E
La Quiaca, Arg. (lä kē-ä'kä)	132	22.15S	65.44W
L'Aquila, Italy (lá'kē-lä)	148	42.22N	13.24E
Lār, Iran (lär)	182	27.31N	54.12E
Lara, Austl.	201a	38.02S	144.24E
Larache, Mor. (lä-räsh')	210	35.15N	6.09W
Laramie, Wy., U.S. (lăr'ȧ-mĭ)	96	41.20N	105.40W
Laramie, r., Co., U.S.	110	40.56N	105.55W
Laranjeiras, neigh., Braz.	234c	22.56S	43.11W
Larchmont, N.Y., U.S. (lärch'mŏnt)	100a	40.56N	73.46W
Larch Mountain, mtn., Or., U.S. (lärch)	106c	45.32N	122.06W
Laredo, Spain (lå-rā'dhō)	158	43.24N	3.24W
Laredo, Tx., U.S.	96	27.31N	99.29W
La Reina, Chile	234b	33.27S	70.33W
La Réole, Fr. (lá rå-ōl')	156	44.37N	0.03W
Largeau, Chad (lär-zhō')	211	17.55N	19.07E
Largo, Cayo, Cuba (kä'yō-lär'gō)	122	21.40N	81.30W
Larimore, N.D., U.S. (lăr'ĭ-môr)	102	47.53N	97.38W
Larino, Italy (lä-rē'nô)	160	41.48N	14.54E
La Rioja, Arg. (lä rē-ōhä)	132	29.18S	67.42W
La Rioja, prov., Arg. (lä-rē-ô'kä)	132	28.45S	68.00W
Lárisa, Grc. (lä'rē-sá)	149	39.38N	22.25E
Lārkāna, Pak.	186	27.40N	68.12E
Larkspur, Ca., U.S.	231b	37.56N	122.32W
Larnaca, Cyp.	149	34.55N	33.37E
Lárnakos, Kólpos, b., Cyp.	181a	36.50N	33.45E
Larned, Ks., U.S. (lär'nĕd)	110	38.09N	99.07W
La Robla, Spain (lä rōb'lä)	158	42.48N	5.36W
La Rochelle, Fr. (lá rō-shĕl')	142	46.10N	1.09W
La Roche-sur-Yon, Fr. (lȧ rôsh'sûr-yôn')	147	46.39N	1.27W
La Roda, Spain (lä rō'dä)	158	39.13N	2.08W
La Romona, Dom. Rep. (lä-rä-mô'nä)	123	18.25N	69.00W
Larrey Point, c., Austl. (lăr'ē)	202	19.15S	118.15E
Laruns, Fr. (lá-räns')	156	42.58N	0.28W
Larvik, Nor. (lär'vēk)	146	59.06N	10.03E
La Sabana, Ven. (lä-sä-bá'nä)	131b	10.38N	66.24W
La Sabina, Cuba (lä-sä-bē'nä)	123a	22.51N	82.05W
La Sagra, mtn., Spain (lä sä'grä)	148	37.56N	2.35W
La Sal, Ut., U.S. (lȧ sál')	109	38.10N	109.20W
La Salle, Can.	83a	45.26N	73.39W
La Salle, Can.	83f	49.41N	97.16W
La Salle, Can. (lȧ săl')	101b	42.14N	83.06W
La Salle, Il., U.S.	98	41.20N	89.05W
Las Animas, Co., U.S. (lás ă'nĭ-măs)	110	38.03N	103.16W
La Sarre, Can.	85	48.43N	79.12W
Lascahobas, Haiti (läs-kä-ō'bás)	123	19.00N	71.55W
Las Cruces, Mex. (läs-krōō'sĕs)	119	16.37N	93.54W
Las Cruces, N.M., U.S.	96	32.20N	106.50W
La Selle, Massif de, mtn., Haiti (lá'sĕl')	123	18.25N	72.05W
La Serena, Chile (lä-sĕ-rē'nä)	132	29.55S	71.24W
La Seyne, Fr. (lä-sån')	147	43.07N	5.52E
Las Flores, Arg. (läs flō'rĕs)	132	36.01S	59.07W
Las Flores, Ven.	234a	10.34N	66.56W
Lashio, Myanmar (lăsh'ē-ō)	188	22.58N	98.03E
Las Juntas, C.R. (läs-kōō'n-täs)	120	10.15N	85.00W
Las Maismas, sw., Spain (läs-mī's-mäs)	158	37.05N	6.25W
Las Minas, Ven.	234a	10.27N	66.52W
La Solana, Spain (lä-sō-lä-nä)	158	38.56N	3.13W
Las Palmas, Pan.	121	8.08N	81.30W
Las Palmas de Gran Canaria, Spain (läs päl'mäs)	210	28.07N	15.28W
La Spezia, Italy (lä-spĕ'zyä)	142	44.07N	9.48E
Las Piedras, Ur. (läs-pyĕ'drás)	129c	34.42S	56.08W
Las Pilas, vol., Nic. (läs-pē'läs)	120	12.32N	86.43W
Las Rejas, Chile	234b	33.28S	70.44W
Las Rosas, Mex. (läs rō thäs)	119	16.24N	92.23W
Las Rozas de Madrid, Spain (läs rō'thas dā mä-dhrēd')	159a	40.29N	3.53W
Lassee, Aus.	145e	48.14N	16.50E
Lassen Peak, mtn., Ca., U.S. (lăs'ĕn)	96	40.30N	121.32W
Lassen Volcanic National Park, rec., Ca., U.S.	96	40.43N	121.35W
L'Assomption, Can. (lás-sôm-syôn)	83a	45.50N	73.25W

ăt; finăl; rāte; senåte; ärm; ásk; sofȧ; fâre; ch-choose; dh-as th in other; bē; ēvent; bĕt; recĕnt; cratẽr; g-gō; gh-guttural g; bĭt; ĭ-short neutral; rīde; κ-guttural k as ch in German ich;

PRONOUNCING INDEX
Lass Qoray–Les Grésillons 309

PLACE (Pronunciation)	PAGE	Lat. °′	Long. °′
Lass Qoray, Som.	218a	11.13N	48.19E
Las Tablas, Pan. (läs tä'bläs)	121	7.48N	80.16W
Last Mountain, l., Can. (last moun'tĭn)	84	51.05N	105.10W
Lastoursville, Gabon (làs-to͞or-vēl')	212	1.00S	12.49E
Las Tres Vírgenes, Volcán, vol., Mex. (vē'r-hĕ-nĕs)	116	26.00N	111.45W
Las Tunas, prov., Cuba	122	21.05N	77.00W
Las Vacas, Mex. (läs-vá'käs)	119	16.24N	95.48W
Las Vegas, Chile (läs-vĕ'gäs)	129b	32.50S	70.59W
Las Vegas, Nv., U.S. (läs vā'gäs)	96	36.12N	115.10W
Las Vegas, N.M., U.S.	96	35.36N	105.13W
Las Vegas, Ven. (läs-vĕ'gäs)	131b	10.26N	64.08W
Las Vigas, Mex.	119	19.38N	97.03W
Las Vizcachas, Meseta de, plat., Arg.	132	49.35S	71.00W
Latacunga, Ec. (lä-tä-ko͝oŋ'gä)	130	1.02S	78.33W
Latakia see Al Lādhiqīyah, Syria	182	35.32N	35.51E
La Teste-de-Buch, Fr. (lä-tĕst-dē-büsh)	156	44.38N	1.11W
Lathrop, Mo., U.S. (lā'thrŭp)	111	39.32N	94.21W
Latimer, Eng., U.K.	235	51.41N	0.33W
La Tortuga, Isla, i., Ven. (ē's-lä-lä-tôr-to͞o'gä)	130	10.55N	65.18W
Latorytsya, r., Eur.	155	48.27N	22.30E
Latourell, Or., U.S. (lá-tou'rĕl)	106c	45.32N	122.13W
La Tremblade, Fr. (lä-trĕN-bläd')	156	45.45N	1.12W
Latrobe, Pa., U.S. (lá-trōb')	99	40.25N	79.15W
Lattingtown, N.Y., U.S.	228	40.54N	73.36W
La Tuque, Can. (lá'tük')	85	47.27N	72.49W
Lātūr, India (lä-to͞or')	186	18.20N	76.35E
Latvia, nation, Eur.	164	57.28N	24.29E
Lau Group, is., Fiji	198g	18.20S	178.30W
Launceston, Austl. (lôn'sĕs-tŭn)	203	41.35S	147.22E
Launceston, Eng., U.K. (lôrn'stŏn)	150	50.38N	4.26W
La Unión, Chile (lä-o͞o-nyô'n)	132	40.15S	73.04W
La Unión, El Sal.	120	13.18N	87.51W
La Unión, Mex. (lä o͞on-nyōn')	118	17.59N	101.48W
La Unión, Spain	148	37.38N	0.50W
Laupendahl, Ger.	236	51.21N	6.56E
Laura, Austl. (lôrá)	203	15.40S	144.45E
Laurel, De., U.S. (lô'rĕl)	99	38.30N	75.40W
Laurel, Md., U.S.	100e	39.06N	76.51W
Laurel, Ms., U.S.	97	31.42N	89.07W
Laurel, Mt., U.S.	105	45.41N	108.45W
Laurel, Wa., U.S.	106d	48.52N	122.29W
Laurel Gardens, Pa., U.S.	230b	40.31N	80.01W
Laurel Hollow, N.Y., U.S.	228	40.52N	73.28W
Laurelwood, Or., U.S. (lô'rĕl-wo͝od)	106c	45.25N	123.05W
Laurens, S.C., U.S. (lô'rĕnz)	115	34.29N	82.03W
Laurentian Highlands, hills, Can. (lô'rĕn-tĭ-ăn)	82	49.00N	74.50W
Laurentides, Can. (lô'rĕn-tīdz)	83a	45.51N	73.46W
Lauria, Italy (lou'rē-ä)	149	40.03N	15.02E
Laurinburg, N.C., U.S. (lô'rĭn-bûrg)	115	34.45N	79.27W
Laurium, Mi., U.S. (lô'rĭ-ŭm)	103	47.13N	88.28W
Lausanne, Switz. (lō-zán')	142	46.32N	6.35E
Laut, Pulau, i., Indon.	196	3.39S	116.07E
Lautaro, Chile (lou-tä'rō)	132	38.40S	72.24W
Laut Kecil, Kepulauan, is., Indon.	196	4.44S	115.43E
Lautoka, Fiji	198g	17.37S	177.27E
Lauzon, Can. (lō-zōN')	83b	46.50N	71.10W
Lava Beds National Monument, rec., Ca., U.S. (lä'vá bĕds)	104	41.38N	121.44W
Lavaca, r., Tx., U.S. (lá-vák'á)	113	29.05N	96.50W
Lava Hot Springs, Id., U.S.	105	42.37N	111.58W
Laval, Can.	85	45.31N	73.44W
Laval, Fr. (lä-väl')	147	48.05N	0.47W
Laval-des-Rapides, neigh., Can.	227b	45.33N	73.42W
Laval-Ouest, neigh., Can.	227b	45.33N	73.52W
La Vecilla de Curueno, Spain	158	42.53N	5.18W
La Vega, Dom. Rep. (lä-vĕ'gä)	123	19.15N	70.35W
La Vega, neigh., Ven.	234a	10.28N	66.57W
Lavello, Italy (lä-vĕl'lō)	160	41.05N	15.50E
La Verne, Ca., U.S. (lá vûrn')	107a	34.06N	117.46W
Laverton, Austl. (lā'vẽr-tŭn)	202	28.45S	122.30E
La Victoria, Peru	233c	12.04S	77.02W
La Victoria, Ven. (lä vēk-tō'rē-ä)	130	10.14N	67.20W
Lavonia, Ga., U.S. (lá-vō'nĭ-á)	114	34.26N	83.05W
Lavon Reservoir, res., Tx., U.S.	113	33.06N	96.20W
Lavras, Braz. (lä'vräzh)	129a	21.15S	44.59W
Lávrion, Grc. (läv'rĭ-ōn)	161	37.44N	24.05E
Lavry, Russia (lou'rá)	162	57.35N	27.28E
Lawndale, Ca., U.S. (lôn'dāl)	107a	33.54N	118.22W
Lawndale, neigh., Il., U.S.	231a	41.51N	87.43W
Lawndale, neigh., Pa., U.S.	229b	40.03N	75.05W
Lawnside, N.J., U.S.	229b	39.52N	75.03W
Lawra, Ghana	214	10.39N	2.52W
Lawrence, In., U.S. (lô'rĕns)	101g	39.59N	86.01W
Lawrence, Ks., U.S.	97	38.57N	95.13W
Lawrence, Ma., U.S.	93a	42.42N	71.09W
Lawrence, Pa., U.S.	101e	40.18N	80.07W
Lawrenceburg, In., U.S. (lô'rĕns-bûrg)	101f	39.06N	84.47W
Lawrenceburg, Ky., U.S.	98	38.00N	85.00W
Lawrenceburg, Tn., U.S.	114	35.13N	87.20W
Lawrenceville, Ga., U.S. (lô-rĕns-vĭl)	114	33.56N	83.57W
Lawrenceville, Il., U.S.	98	38.45N	87.45W
Lawrenceville, N.J., U.S.	100a	40.17N	74.44W
Lawrenceville, Va., U.S.	115	36.43N	77.52W
Lawrenceville, neigh., Pa., U.S.	230b	40.28N	79.57W
Lawsonia, Md., U.S. (lô-sō'nĭ-á)	99	38.00N	75.50W
Lawton, Ok., U.S. (lô'tŭn)	96	34.36N	98.25W
Lawz, Jabal al, mtn., Sau. Ar.	182	28.46N	35.37E
Layang Layang, Malay. (lä-yäng' lä-yäng')	181b	1.49N	103.28E
Laysan, i., Hi., U.S.	94b	26.00N	171.00W
Layton, Ut., U.S. (lā'tŭn)	107b	41.04N	111.58W
Lazdijai, Lith. (läzh'dē-yī')	153	54.12N	23.35E

PLACE (Pronunciation)	PAGE	Lat. °′	Long. °′
Lazio (Latium), hist. reg., Italy	160	42.05N	12.25E
Lead, S.D., U.S. (lēd)	96	44.22N	103.47W
Leader, Can.	88	50.55N	109.32W
Leadville, Co., U.S. (lĕd'vĭl)	110	39.14N	106.18W
Leaf, r., Ms., U.S. (lēf)	114	31.43N	89.20W
League City, Tx., U.S. (lēg)	113a	29.31N	95.05W
Leamington, Can. (lĕm'ĭng-tŭn)	90	42.05N	82.35W
Leamington, Eng., U.K. (lĕ'mĭng-tŭn)	150	52.17N	1.25W
Leatherhead, Eng., U.K. (lĕdh'ẽr-hĕd')	144b	51.17N	0.20W
Leavenworth, Ks., U.S. (lĕv'ĕn-wûrth)	97	39.19N	94.54W
Leavenworth, Wa., U.S.	104	47.35N	120.39W
Leawood, Ks., U.S. (lē'wo͝od)	107f	38.58N	94.37W
Łeba, Pol. (lā'bä)	155	54.45N	17.34E
Lebam, r., Malay.	181b	1.35N	104.09E
Lebango, Congo	216	0.22N	14.49E
Lebanon, Il., U.S. (lĕb'á-nŭn)	107e	38.36N	89.49W
Lebanon, In., U.S.	98	40.00N	86.30W
Lebanon, Ky., U.S.	114	37.32N	85.15W
Lebanon, Mo., U.S.	111	37.40N	92.43W
Lebanon, N.H., U.S.	99	43.40N	72.15W
Lebanon, Oh., U.S.	98	39.25N	84.10W
Lebanon, Or., U.S.	104	44.31N	122.53W
Lebanon, Pa., U.S.	99	40.20N	76.20W
Lebanon, Tn., U.S.	114	36.10N	86.16W
Lebanon, nation, Asia	182	34.00N	34.00E
Lebedyan', Russia (lyĕ'bĕ-dyän')	166	53.03N	39.08E
Lebedyn, Ukr.	163	48.56N	31.35E
Lebedyn, Ukr.	167	50.34N	34.27E
Le Blanc, Fr. (lĕ-bläN')	156	46.38N	0.59E
Le Blanc-Mesnil, Fr.	237c	48.56N	2.28E
Leblon, neigh., Braz.	234c	22.59S	43.13W
Le Borgne, Haiti (lĕ bôrn'y')	123	19.50N	72.30W
Lębork, Pol. (lăN-bo͝ork')	155	54.33N	17.46E
Le Bourget, Fr.	237c	48.56N	2.26E
Lebrija, Spain (lå-brē'hä)	158	36.55N	6.06W
Lecce, Italy (lĕt'chā)	149	40.22N	18.11E
Lecco, Italy (lĕk'kō)	160	45.52N	9.28E
Lech, r., Ger. (lĕk)	154	47.41N	10.52E
Le Châtelet-en-Brie, Fr. (lĕ-shä-tĕ-lā'ĕN-brē')	157b	48.29N	2.50E
Leche, Laguna de, l., Cuba (lä-go͞o'nä-dĕ-lĕ'chĕ)	122	22.10N	78.30W
Leche, Laguna de la, l., Mex.	112	27.16N	102.45W
Lecompte, La., U.S.	113	31.06N	92.25W
Le Creusot, Fr. (lĕkrû-zô)	147	46.48N	4.23E
Ledesma, Spain (lå-dĕs'mä)	158	41.05N	5.59W
Ledsham, Eng., U.K.	237a	53.16N	2.58W
Leduc, Can. (lĕ-do͞ok')	87	53.16N	113.33W
Leech, l., Mn., U.S. (lēch)	103	47.06N	94.16W
Leeds, Eng., U.K.	142	53.48N	1.33W
Leeds, Al., U.S. (lēdz)	100h	33.33N	86.33W
Leeds, N.D., U.S.	102	48.18N	99.24W
Leeds and Liverpool Canal, can., Eng., U.K. (lĭv'ẽr-po͞ol)	144a	53.36N	2.38W
Leegebruch, Ger. (lĕh'gĕn-bro͞ok)	145b	52.43N	13.12E
Leek, Eng., U.K. (lēk)	144a	53.06N	2.01W
Lee Manor, Va., U.S.	229d	38.52N	77.15W
Leer, Ger. (lār)	154	53.14N	7.27E
Lees, Eng., U.K.	237b	53.32N	2.04W
Leesburg, Fl., U.S. (lēz'bûrg)	115	28.49N	81.53W
Leesburg, Va., U.S.	99	39.10N	77.30W
Lees Summit, Mo., U.S.	107f	38.55N	94.23W
Lee Stocking, i., Bah.	122	23.45N	76.05W
Leesville, La., U.S. (lēz'vĭl)	113	31.09N	93.17W
Leetonia, Oh., U.S. (lē-tō'nĭ-á)	98	40.50N	80.45W
Leeuwarden, Neth. (lā'wär-dĕn)	147	52.12N	5.50E
Leeuwin, Cape, c., Austl. (lo͞o'wĭn)	202	34.15S	114.30E
Leeward Islands, is., N.A. (lē'wẽrd)	113	17.00N	62.15W
Le François, Mart.	121b	14.37N	60.55W
Lefroy, l., Austl. (lē-froi')	202	31.30S	122.00E
Leganés, Spain (lå-gä'nås)	159a	40.20N	3.46W
Legazpi, Phil. (lå-gäs'pē)	197	13.09N	123.44E
Legge Peak, mtn., Austl. (lĕg)	204	41.33S	148.10E
Leggett, Ca., U.S.	108	39.51N	123.42W
Leghorn see Livorno, Italy	142	43.32N	11.18E
Legnano, Italy (lå-nyä'nō)	160	45.35N	8.53E
Legnica, Pol. (lĕk-nĭt'sá)	147	51.13N	16.10E
Leh, India (lā)	186	34.10N	77.40E
Le Havre, Fr. (lĕ áv'r')	142	49.31N	0.07E
Lehi, Ut., U.S. (lē'hī)	109	40.25N	111.55W
Lehman Caves National Monument, rec., Nv., U.S. (lē'măn)	109	38.54N	114.08W
Lehnin, Ger. (lĕh'nēn)	145b	52.19N	12.45E
Leião, Port.	238d	38.44N	9.18W
Leicester, Eng., U.K. (lĕs'tẽr)	142	52.37N	1.08W
Leicestershire, co., Eng., U.K.	144a	52.40N	1.12W
Leichhardt, Austl.	243a	33.53S	151.09E
Leichhardt, r., Austl. (līk'härt)	202	18.30S	139.45E
Leiden, Neth. (lī'dĕn)	151	52.09N	4.29E
Leigh Creek, Austl. (lē krēk)	204	30.33S	138.30E
Leikanger, Nor. (lī'käŋ'gẽr)	152	61.11N	6.51E
Leimuiden, Neth.	145a	52.13N	4.40E
Leine, r., Ger. (lī'nĕ)	154	51.58N	9.56E
Leinster, hist. reg., Ire. (lĕn-stẽr)	150	52.45N	7.19W
Leipsic, Oh., U.S. (lĭp'sĭk)	98	41.05N	84.00W
Leipzig, Ger. (līp'tsĭk)	142	51.20N	12.24E
Leiria, Port. (lā-rē'ä)	158	39.45N	8.50W
Leitchfield, Ky., U.S. (lēch'fēld)	114	37.28N	86.20W
Leitha, r., Aus.	145e	48.04N	16.57E
Leithe, neigh., Ger.	236	51.29N	7.06E
Leitrim, Can.	83c	45.20N	75.36W
Leizhou Bandao, pen., China (lā-jō bän-dou)	188	20.42N	109.10E
Le Kremlin-Bicêtre, Fr.	237c	48.49N	2.21E
Leksand, Swe. (lĕk'sänd)	152	60.45N	14.56E

PLACE (Pronunciation)	PAGE	Lat. °′	Long. °′
Leland, Wa., U.S. (lē'lănd)	106a	47.54N	122.53W
Leliu, China (lŭ-lĭō)	191a	22.52N	113.09E
Le Locle, Switz. (lĕ lô'kl')	154	47.03N	6.43E
Le Maire, Estrecho de, strt., Arg. (ĕs-trĕ'chô-dĕ-lĕ-mī'rĕ)	132	55.15S	65.30W
Le Mans, Fr. (lĕ mäN')	147	48.01N	0.12E
Le Marin, Mart.	121b	14.28N	60.55W
Le Mars, Ia., U.S. (lē märz')	102	42.46N	96.09W
Lemay, Mo., U.S.	107e	38.32N	90.17W
Lemdiyya, Alg.	210	36.18N	2.40E
Leme, Morro do, mtn., Braz.	234c	22.58S	43.10W
Lemery, Phil. (lā-mā-rē')	197a	13.51S	120.55E
Le Mesnil-Amelot, Fr.	237c	49.01N	2.36E
Le Mesnil-le-Roi, Fr.	237c	48.56N	2.08E
Lemhi, r., Id., U.S.	105	44.40N	113.27W
Lemhi Range, mts., Id., U.S. (lĕm'hī)	105	44.35N	113.33W
Lemmon, S.D., U.S. (lĕm'ŭn)	102	45.55N	102.10W
Le Môle, Haiti (lĕ mōl')	123	19.50N	73.20W
Lemon Grove, Ca., U.S. (lĕm'ŭn-grōv)	108a	32.44N	117.02W
Lemon Heights, Ca., U.S.	232	33.46N	117.48W
Le Moule, Guad. (lĕ mo͞ol')	121b	16.19N	61.22W
LeMoyne, Can.	227b	45.31N	73.29W
Lempa, r., N.A. (lĕm'pä)	120	13.20N	88.46W
Lemvig, Den. (lĕm'vēgh)	152	56.33N	8.16E
Lena, r., Russia	165	68.00N	123.00E
Lençóes Paulista, Braz. (lĕN-sôNs' pou-lēs'tá)	132	22.30S	48.45W
Lençóis, Braz. (lĕn-sóis)	131	12.38S	41.28W
Lenexa, Ks., U.S. (lē'nĕx-á)	107f	38.58N	99.44W
Lengyandong, China (lŭŋ-yän-dôŋ)	191a	23.12N	113.21E
Lenik, r., Malay.	181b	1.59N	102.51E
Lenina, Gora, hill, Russia	239b	55.42N	37.31E
Leningrad see Saint Petersburg, Russia	164	59.57N	30.20E
Leningrad, prov., Russia	162	59.15N	30.30E
Leningradskaya, Russia (lyĕ-nĭn-gräd'ská-yá)	163	46.19N	39.23E
Lenino, Russia (lyĕ'nĭ-nô)	172b	55.37N	37.41E
Leninogor, Kaz.	169	50.29N	83.25E
Leninsk, Russia (lyĕ-nēnsk')	167	48.40N	45.10E
Leninsk-Kuznetski, Russia (lyĕ-nēnsk'ko͞oz-nyĕt'skĭ)	164	54.28N	86.48E
Lennox, Ca., U.S.	232	33.56N	118.21W
Lennox, S.D., U.S. (lĕn'ŭks)	102	43.22N	96.53W
Lenoir, N.C., U.S. (lē-nōr')	115	35.54N	81.35W
Lenoir City, Tn., U.S.	114	35.47N	84.16W
Lenox, Ia., U.S.	103	40.51N	94.29W
Lenz, S. Afr.	244b	26.19S	27.49E
Léo, Burkina	214	11.06N	2.06W
Leoben, Aus. (lå-ō'bĕn)	154	47.22N	15.09E
Léogane, Haiti (lā-ô-gan')	123	18.30N	72.35W
Leola, S.D., U.S. (lē-ō'lá)	102	45.43N	99.55W
Leominster, Ma., U.S. (lĕm'ĭn-stẽr)	99	42.32N	71.45W
León, Mex. (lå-ōn')	116	21.08N	101.41W
León, Nic. (lĕ-ô'n)	116	12.28N	86.53W
León, Spain (lĕ-ô'n)	148	42.38N	5.33W
Leon, Ia., U.S. (lē'ŏn)	103	40.43N	93.44W
Leon, hist. reg., Spain (lĕ-ô'n)	158	41.18N	5.50W
Leon, r., Tx., U.S. (lē'ŏn)	112	31.54N	98.20W
Leonforte, Italy (lā-ôn-fôr'tä)	160	37.40N	14.27E
Leonia, N.J., U.S.	228	40.52N	73.59W
Léopold, Mont, Zaire	244c	4.19S	15.15E
Leopoldau, neigh., Aus.	239e	48.16N	16.27E
Leopold II, Lac see Mai-Ndombe, Lac, l., Zaire	212	2.16S	19.00E
Leopoldina, Braz. (lā-ô-pôl-dē'nä)	129a	21.32S	42.38W
Leopoldsburg, Bel.	145a	51.07N	5.18E
Leopoldsdorf im Marchfelde, Aus. (lā'ō-pōlts-dôrf')	145e	48.14N	16.42E
Leopoldstadt, neigh., Aus.	239e	48.13N	16.23E
Léopoldville see Kinshasa, Zaire	212	4.18S	15.18E
Leova, Mol.	163	46.30N	28.16E
Lepe, Spain (lā'pä)	158	37.15N	7.12W
Le Pecq, Fr.	237c	48.54N	2.07E
Lepel', Bela. (lyĕ-pĕl')	162	54.52N	28.41E
Le Perreux-sur-Marne, Fr.	237c	48.51N	2.30E
Leping, China (lŭ-pĭŋ)	193	29.02N	117.12E
L'Épiphanie, Can. (lā-pē-fä-nē')	83a	45.51N	73.29W
Le Plessis-Belleville, Fr. (lĕ-plĕ-sē'bĕl-vēl')	157b	49.05N	2.46E
Le Plessis-Bouchard, Fr.	237c	49.00N	2.14E
Le Plessis-Trévise, Fr.	237c	48.49N	2.34E
Le Port-Marly, Fr.	237c	48.53N	2.06E
Lepreau, Can. (lē-prō')	92	45.10N	66.28W
Le Pré-Saint-Gervais, Fr.	237c	48.53N	2.25E
Lepsinsk, Kaz.	169	45.32N	80.47E
Le Puy, Fr. (lĕ pwē')	147	45.02N	3.54E
Le Raincy, Fr.	237c	48.54N	2.31E
Lercara Friddi, Italy (lĕr-kä'rä)	160	37.47N	13.36E
Lerdo, Mex. (lĕr'dō)	116	25.31N	103.30W
Leribe, Leso.	213c	28.53S	28.02E
Lérida, Spain (lā'rē-dhä)	148	41.38N	0.37E
Lerma, Mex. (lĕr'mä)	119	19.49N	90.34W
Lerma, Mex.	119a	19.17N	99.30W
Lerma, Spain (lĕ'r-mä)	158	42.03N	3.45W
Lerma, r., Mex.	118	20.14N	101.50W
Le Roy, N.Y., U.S. (lē roi')	99	43.00N	78.00W
Lerwick, Scot., U.K. (lĕr'ĭk) (lûr'wĭk)	142	60.08N	1.27W
Léry, Can. (lā-rī')	83a	45.21N	73.49W
Lery, Lake, l., La., U.S. (lĕ'rē)	100d	29.48N	89.45W
Les Andelys, Fr. (lä-zäN-dē-lē')	157b	49.15N	1.25E
Lesbos see Lésvos, i., Grc.	142	39.15N	25.40E
Les Cayes, Haiti	123	18.15N	73.45W
Les Cèdres, Can. (lā-sĕdr'')	83a	45.18N	74.03W
Les Clayes-sous-Bois, Fr.	237c	48.49N	1.59E
Les Grésillons, Fr.	237c	48.56N	2.01E

310 Lesh–Linksfield

PLACE (Pronunciation)	PAGE	Lat. °'	Long. °'
Lesh, Alb. (lĕshĕ) (ä-lä'sē-ō)	161	41.47N	19.40E
Leshan, China (lŭ-shän)	188	29.40N	103.40E
Lésigny, Fr.	237c	48.45N	2.37E
Lésina, Lago di, l., Italy (lä'gō dē lä'zē-nä)	160	41.48N	15.12E
Leskovac, Yugo. (lĕs'kō-váts)	149	43.00N	21.58E
Leslie, S. Afr.	218d	26.23S	28.57E
Leslie, Ar., U.S. (lĕz'lĭ)	111	35.49N	92.32W
Les Lilas, Fr.	237c	48.53N	2.25E
Les Loges-en-Josas, Fr.	237c	48.46N	2.09E
Lesnoj, neigh., Russia	239a	60.00N	30.20E
Lesnoy, Russia (lĕs'noi)	166	66.45N	34.45E
Lesogorsk, Russia (lyĕs'ō-gôrsk)	194	49.28N	141.59E
Lesotho, nation, Afr. (lĕsō'thō)	212	29.45S	28.07E
Lesozavodsk, Russia (lyĕ-sô-zá-vôdsk')	194	45.21N	133.19E
Les Pavillons-sous-Bois, Fr.	237c	48.55N	2.30E
Les Sables-d'Olonne, Fr. (lā sá'bl'dō-lŭn')	147	46.30N	1.47W
Les Saintes Islands, is., Guad. (lā-sănt')	121b	15.50N	61.40W
Lesser Antilles, is.	117	12.15N	65.00W
Lesser Caucasus, mts., Asia	168	41.00N	44.35E
Lesser Khingan Range, mts., China	189	49.50N	129.26E
Lesser Slave, r., Can.	87	55.15N	114.30W
Lesser Slave Lake, l., Can. (lĕs'ẽr slāv)	84	55.25N	115.30W
Lesser Sunda Islands, is., Indon.	196	9.00S	120.00E
L'Estaque, Fr. (lĕs-täl)	156a	43.22N	5.20E
Lester, Pa., U.S.	229b	39.52N	75.17W
Les Thilliers-en-Vexin, Fr. (lā-tē-yā'ĕɴ-vĕ-săɴ')	157b	49.19N	1.36E
Le Sueur, Mn., U.S. (lē sōōr')	103	44.27N	93.53W
Lésvos, i., Grc.	142	39.15N	25.40E
Leszno, Pol. (lĕsh'nô)	147	51.51N	16.35E
L'Étang-la-Ville, Fr.	237c	48.52N	2.05E
Letchmore Heath, Eng., U.K.	235	51.40N	0.20W
Le Teil, Fr. (lē tā'y')	156	44.34N	4.39E
Lethbridge, Austl.	243a	33.44S	150.48E
Lethbridge, Can. (lĕth'brĭj)	84	49.42N	112.50W
Le Thillay, Fr.	237c	49.00N	2.28E
Leticia, Col. (lĕ-tē'syá)	130	4.04S	69.57W
Leting, China (lŭ-tĭŋ)	190	39.26N	118.53E
Le Tréport, Fr. (lĕ-trā'pôr')	156	50.03N	1.21E
Letychiv, Ukr.	163	49.22N	27.29E
Leuven, Bel.	151	50.53N	4.42E
Levack, Can.	90	46.38N	81.23W
Levádhia, Grc.	161	38.25N	22.51E
Le Val-d'Albian, Fr.	237c	48.45N	2.11E
Levallois-Perret, Fr. (lē-vál-wä'pĕ-rĕ')	157b	48.53N	2.17E
Levanger, Nor. (lĕ-väng'ẽr)	146	63.42N	11.01E
Levanna, mtn., Eur. (lå-vä'nä)	160	45.25N	7.14E
Levenshulme, neigh., Eng., U.K.	237b	53.27N	2.10W
Leveque, Cape, c., Austl. (lē-vĕk')	202	16.26S	123.08E
Leverkusen, Ger. (lĕ'fĕr-kōō-zĕn)	157c	51.01N	6.59E
Le Vésinet, Fr.	237c	48.54N	2.08E
Levice, Slvk. (lā'vĕt-sĕ)	155	48.13N	18.37E
Levico, Italy (lā'vē-kō)	160	46.02N	11.20E
Le Vigan, Fr. (lē vē-gäɴ')	156	43.59N	3.36E
Lévis, Can. (lā-vē') (lē'vĭs)	85	46.49N	71.11W
Levittown, N.Y., U.S.	228	40.41N	73.31W
Levittown, Pa., U.S. (lĕ'vĭt-toun)	100f	40.08N	74.50W
Levkás, Grc. (lyĕf'käs')	161	38.49N	20.43E
Levkás, i., Grc.	149	38.42N	20.22E
Levoča, Slvk. (lā'vô-chá)	155	49.03N	20.38E
Levuka, Fiji	198g	17.41S	178.50E
Lewes, Eng., U.K.	151	50.51N	0.01E
Lewes, De., U.S. (lōō'ĭs)	99	38.45N	75.10W
Lewinsville, Va., U.S.	229d	38.54N	77.12W
Lewinsville Heights, Va., U.S.	229d	38.53N	77.12W
Lewis, r., Wa., U.S.	104	46.05N	122.09W
Lewis, East Fork, r., Wa., U.S.	106c	45.52N	122.40W
Lewis, Island of, i., Scot., U.K. (lōō'ĭs)	150	58.05N	6.07W
Lewisburg, Tn., U.S. (lū'ĭs-bûrg)	114	35.27N	86.47W
Lewisburg, W.V., U.S.	98	37.50N	80.20W
Lewisdale, Md., U.S.	229d	38.58N	76.58W
Lewisham, S. Afr.	244b	26.07S	27.49E
Lewisham, neigh., Eng., U.K.	235	51.27N	0.01E
Lewis Hills, hills, Can.	93	48.48N	58.30W
Lewisporte, Can. (lū'ĭs-pōrt)	93	49.15N	55.04W
Lewis Range, mts., Mt., U.S. (lū'ĭs)	105	48.15N	113.20W
Lewis Smith Lake, res., Al., U.S.	114	34.05N	87.07W
Lewiston, Id., U.S. (lū'ĭs-tŭn)	96	46.24N	116.59W
Lewiston, Me., U.S.	97	44.05N	70.14W
Lewiston, N.Y., U.S.	101c	43.11N	79.02W
Lewiston, Ut., U.S.	105	41.58N	111.51W
Lewistown, Il., U.S. (lū'ĭs-toun)	111	40.23N	90.06W
Lewistown, Mt., U.S.	96	47.05N	109.25W
Lewistown, Pa., U.S.	99	40.35N	77.30W
Lexington, Ky., U.S. (lĕk'sĭng-tŭn)	97	38.05N	84.30W
Lexington, Ma., U.S.	93a	42.27N	71.14W
Lexington, Ms., U.S.	114	33.08N	90.02W
Lexington, Mo., U.S.	111	39.11N	93.52W
Lexington, Ne., U.S.	110	40.46N	99.44W
Lexington, N.C., U.S.	115	35.47N	80.15W
Lexington, Tn., U.S.	114	35.37N	88.24W
Lexington, Va., U.S.	99	37.45N	79.20W
Leybourne, Eng., U.K.	235	51.18N	0.25E
Leyte, i., Phil. (lā'tā)	197	10.35N	125.35E
Leżajsk, Pol. (lĕ'zhä-ĭsk)	155	50.14N	22.25E
Lezha, r., Russia (lĕ-zhä')	162	58.59N	40.27E
L'gov, Russia (lgôf)	163	51.42N	35.15E
Lhasa, China (läs'ä)	188	29.41N	91.12E
L'Hautil, Fr.	237c	49.00N	2.01E
Liangxiangzhen, China (lĭäŋ-shyäŋ-jŭn)	192a	39.43N	116.08E
Lianjiang, China (lĭĕn-jyäŋ)	193	21.38N	110.15E
Lianozovo, Russia (lĭ-a-nô'zō-vô)	172b	55.54N	37.36E
Lianshui, China (lĭĕn-shwā)	190	33.46N	119.15E
Lianyungang, China (lĭĕn-yòn-gäŋ)	189	34.35N	119.09E
Liao, r., China	189	43.37N	120.05E
Liaocheng, China (lĭou-chŭŋ)	192	36.27N	115.56E
Liaodong Bandao, pen., China (lĭou-dôŋ bän-dou)	189	39.45N	122.22E
Liaodong Wan, b., China (lĭou-dôŋ wäŋ)	192	40.25N	121.15E
Liaoning, prov., China	189	41.31N	122.11E
Liaoyang, China (lyä'ō-yäng')	189	41.18N	123.10E
Liaoyuan, China (lĭou-yůän)	192	43.00N	124.59E
Liard, r., Can. (lē-är')	84	59.43N	126.42W
Libano, Col. (lē'bá-nō)	130a	4.55N	75.05W
Libby, Mt., U.S. (lĭb'ē)	104	48.27N	115.35W
Libenge, Zaire (lē-bĕŋ'gä)	211	3.39N	18.40E
Liberal, Ks., U.S. (lĭb'ẽr-ăl)	110	37.01N	100.56W
Liberdade, neigh., Braz.	234d	23.35S	46.37W
Liberec, Czech Rep. (lē'bĕr-ĕts)	147	50.45N	15.06E
Liberia, C.R.	120	10.38N	85.28W
Liberia, nation, Afr. (lī-bē'rĭ-ȧ)	210	6.30N	9.55W
Libertad, Arg.	132a	34.42S	58.42W
Libertad de Orituco, Ven. (lē-bĕr-tä'd-dĕ-ō-rē-tōō'kō)	131b	9.32N	66.24W
Liberty, In., U.S. (lĭb'ẽr-tĭ)	98	39.35N	84.55W
Liberty, Mo., U.S.	107f	39.15N	94.25W
Liberty, Pa., U.S.	230b	40.20N	79.51W
Liberty, S.C., U.S.	115	34.47N	82.41W
Liberty, Tx., U.S.	113	30.03N	94.46W
Liberty, Ut., U.S.	107b	41.20N	111.52W
Liberty Bay, b., Wa., U.S.	106a	47.43N	122.41W
Liberty Lake, l., Md., U.S.	100e	39.25N	76.56W
Liberty Manor, Md., U.S.	229c	39.21N	76.47W
Libertyville, Il., U.S. (lĭb'ẽr-tĭ-vĭl)	101a	42.17N	87.57W
Libode, S. Afr. (lĭ-bō'dē)	213c	31.33S	29.03E
Libón, r., N.A.	123	19.30N	71.45W
Libourne, Fr. (lē-bōōrn')	147	44.55N	0.12W
Library, Pa., U.S.	230b	40.18N	80.02W
Libres, Mex. (lē'brās)	119	19.26N	97.41W
Libreville, Gabon (lē-br'vēl')	212	0.23N	9.27E
Liburn, Ga., U.S. (lĭb'ûrn)	100c	33.53N	84.09W
Libya, nation, Afr. (lĭb'ē-ä)	211	27.38N	15.00E
Libyan Desert, des., Afr. (lĭb'ē-ăn)	211	28.23N	23.34E
Libyan Plateau, plat., Afr.	184	30.58N	26.20E
Licancábur, Cerro, mtn., S.A. (sĕ'r-rō-lē-kän-kä'bōōr)	132	22.45S	67.45W
Licanten, Chile (lē-kän-tĕ'n)	129b	34.58S	72.00W
Lichfield, Eng., U.K. (lĭch'fēld)	144a	52.41N	1.49W
Lichinga, Moz.	217	13.18S	35.14E
Lichtenberg, neigh., Ger.	238a	52.31N	13.29E
Lichtenburg, S. Afr. (lĭk'tĕn-bĕrgh)	218d	26.09S	26.10E
Lichtendorf, Ger.	236	51.28N	7.37E
Lichtenplatz, neigh., Ger.	236	51.15N	7.12E
Lichtenrade, neigh., Ger.	238a	52.23N	13.25E
Lichterfelde, neigh., Ger.	238a	52.26N	13.19E
Lick Creek, r., In., U.S. (lĭk)	101g	39.43N	86.06W
Licking, r., Ky., U.S. (lĭk'ĭng)	98	38.30N	84.10W
Lida, Bela. (lē'dá)	155	53.53N	25.19E
Lidcombe, Austl.	243a	33.52S	151.03E
Lidgerwood, N.D., U.S. (lĭj'ẽr-wood)	102	46.04N	97.10W
Lidköping, Swe. (lēt'chû-pĭng)	152	58.31N	13.06E
Lido Beach, N.Y., U.S.	228	40.35N	73.38W
Lido di Roma, Italy (lē'dō-dē-rō'mä)	159d	41.19N	12.17E
Lidzbark, Pol. (lĭts'bärk)	155	54.07N	20.36E
Liebenbergsvlei, r., S. Afr.	218d	27.35S	28.25E
Liebenwalde, Ger. (lē'bĕn-väl-dĕ)	145b	52.52N	13.24E
Liechtenstein, nation, Eur. (lĕk'tĕn-shtīn)	147	47.10N	10.00E
Liège, Bel.	147	50.38N	5.34E
Lienz, Aus. (lē-ĕnts')	154	46.49N	12.45E
Liepāja, Lat. (le'pä-yä')	166	56.31N	20.59E
Lier, Bel.	145a	51.08N	4.34E
Lierenfeld, neigh., Ger.	236	51.13N	6.51E
Liesing, Aus. (lē'sĭng)	145e	48.09N	16.17E
Liestal, Switz. (lēs'täl)	154	47.28N	7.44E
Lifanga, Zaire	216	0.19N	21.57E
Lifou, i., N. Cal.	203	21.15S	167.32E
Ligao, Phil. (lē-gä'ō)	197a	13.14N	123.33E
Lightning Ridge, Austl.	204	29.23S	147.50E
Ligonha, r., Moz. (lē-gō'nyȧ)	213	16.14S	39.00E
Ligonier, In., U.S. (lĭg-ō-nēr)	98	41.30N	85.35W
Ligovo, Russia (lĕ'gô-vô)	172c	59.51N	30.13E
Liguria, hist. reg., Italy (lē-gōō-rē-ä)	160	44.24N	8.27E
Ligurian Sea, sea, Eur. (lĭ-gū'rĭ-ăn)	148	43.42N	8.32E
Lihou Reef, rf., Austl. (lē-hōō')	203	17.23S	152.43E
Lihuang, China (lē'hōōäng)	190	31.32N	115.46E
Lihue, Hi., U.S. (lē-hōō'ā)	96c	21.59N	159.23W
Lihula, Est. (lē'hò-lá)	153	58.41N	23.50E
Liji, China (lē-jyē)	190	33.47N	117.47E
Lijiang, China (lē-jyäŋ)	188	27.00N	100.08E
Lijin, China (lē-jyĭn)	192	37.30N	118.15E
Likasi, Zaire	212	10.59S	26.44E
Likhoslavl', Russia (lyē-kôsläv''l)	162	57.07N	35.27E
Likhovka, Ukr. (lyē-kôf'ká)	163	48.52N	33.57E
Likouala, r., Congo	216	0.10S	16.30E
Lille, Fr. (lēl)	142	50.38N	3.01E
Lille Baelt, strt., Den.	152	55.09N	9.53E
Lillehammer, Nor. (lēl'ĕ-häm'mĕr)	146	61.07N	10.25E
Lillesand, Nor. (lēl'ĕ-sän')	152	58.16N	8.19E
Lilleström, Nor. (lēl'ĕ-strûm)	152	59.56N	11.04E
Lilliwaup, Wa., U.S. (lĭl'ĭ-wŏp)	106a	47.28N	123.07W
Lillooet, Can. (lĭ'lōō-ĕt)	84	50.30N	121.55W
Lillooet, r., Can.	87	49.50N	122.10W
Lilongwe, Mwi. (lē-lō-än)	212	13.59S	33.44E
Liluāh, India	240a	22.37N	88.20E
Lilydale, Austl.	243b	37.45S	145.21E
Lilyfield, Austl.	243a	33.52S	151.10E
Lima, Peru (lē'mä)	130	12.06S	76.55W
Lima, Swe.	152	60.54N	13.24E
Lima, Oh., U.S. (lī'mȧ)	97	40.40N	84.05W
Lima, r., Eur.	158	41.45N	8.22W
Lima Duarte, Braz. (dwä'r-tē)	129a	21.52S	43.47W
Limão, neigh., Braz.	234d	23.30S	46.40W
Lima Reservoir, res., Mt., U.S.	105	44.45N	112.15W
Limassol, Cyp.	149	34.39N	33.02E
Limay, r., Arg. (lē-mä'ē)	132	39.50S	69.15W
Limbazi, Lat. (lēm'bä-zĭ)	153	57.32N	24.44E
Limbdi, India	186	22.37N	71.52E
Limbe, Cam.	210	4.01N	9.12E
Limburg an der Lahn, Ger. (lem-bòrg')	154	50.22N	8.03E
Limefield, Eng., U.K.	237b	53.37N	2.18W
Limeira, Braz. (lē-mā'rä)	129a	22.34S	47.24W
Limerick, Ire. (lĭm'nák)	147	52.39N	8.35W
Limestone Bay, b., Can. (lĭm'stōn)	89	53.50N	98.50W
Limfjorden, Den.	146	56.55N	8.56E
Limmen Bight, bt., Austl. (lĭm'ĕn)	202	14.45S	136.00E
Limni, Grc. (lēm'nē)	161	38.47N	23.22E
Limnos, i., Grc.	149	39.58N	24.48E
Limoges, Can. (lē-môzh')	83c	45.20N	75.15W
Limoges, Fr.	147	45.50N	1.15E
Limón, C.R. (lē-mōn')	117	10.01N	83.02W
Limón, Hond. (lē-mô'n)	120	15.53N	85.34W
Limon, Co., U.S. (lī'mŏn)	110	39.15N	103.41W
Limon, r., Dom. Rep.	123	18.20N	71.40W
Limón, Bahía, b., Pan.	116a	9.21N	79.58W
Limours, Fr. (lē-mōōr')	157b	48.39N	2.05E
Limousin, Plateaux du, plat., Fr. (plä-tō' dü lē-mōō-zăɴ')	156	45.44N	1.09E
Limoux, Fr. (lē-mōō')	156	43.03N	2.14E
Limpopo, r., Afr. (lĭm-pō'pō)	212	23.15S	27.46E
Linares, Chile (lē-nä'rās)	132	35.51S	71.35W
Linares, Mex.	116	24.53N	99.34W
Linares, Spain (lē-nä'rĕs)	148	38.07N	3.38W
Linares, prov., Chile	129b	35.53S	71.30W
Linaro, Cape, c., Italy (lē-nä'rä)	160	42.02N	11.53E
Lince, Peru	233c	12.05S	77.03W
Linchuan, China (lĭn-chůän)	189	27.58N	116.18E
Lincoln, Arg. (lĭŋ'kŭn)	132	34.51S	61.29W
Lincoln, Can.	83d	43.10N	79.29W
Lincoln, Eng., U.K.	146	53.14N	0.33W
Lincoln, Ca., U.S.	108	38.51N	121.19W
Lincoln, Il., U.S.	111	40.09N	89.21W
Lincoln, Ks., U.S.	110	39.02N	98.08W
Lincoln, Me., U.S.	92	45.23N	68.31W
Lincoln, Ma., U.S.	93a	42.25N	71.19W
Lincoln, Ne., U.S.	96	40.49N	96.43W
Lincoln, Pa., U.S.	230b	40.18N	79.51W
Lincoln, Mount, mtn., Co., U.S.	110	39.20N	106.19W
Lincoln Center, pt. of i., N.Y., U.S.	228	40.46N	73.59W
Lincoln Heath, reg., Eng., U.K.	144a	53.23N	0.39W
Lincolnia Heights, Va., U.S.	229d	38.50N	77.09W
Lincoln Park, Mi., U.S.	101b	42.14N	83.11W
Lincoln Park, N.J., U.S.	100a	40.56N	74.18W
Lincoln Park, pt. of i., Il., U.S.	231a	41.56N	87.38W
Lincoln Place, neigh., Pa., U.S.	230b	40.22N	79.55W
Lincolnshire, co., Eng., U.K.	144a	53.12N	0.29W
Lincolnshire Wolds, Eng., U.K. (woldz')	150	53.25N	0.23W
Lincolnton, N.C., U.S. (lĭŋ'kŭn-tŭn)	115	35.27N	81.15W
Lincolnwood, Il., U.S.	231a	42.00N	87.46W
Linda-a-Velha, Port.	238d	38.43N	9.14W
Lindale, Ga., U.S. (lĭn'dāl)	114	34.10N	85.10W
Lindau, Ger. (lĭn'dou)	154	47.33N	9.40E
Linden, Al., U.S. (lĭn'dĕn)	114	32.16N	87.47W
Linden, Ma., U.S.	227a	42.26N	71.02W
Linden, Mo., U.S.	107f	39.13N	94.35W
Linden, N.J., U.S.	100a	40.39N	74.14W
Linden, neigh., S. Afr.	244b	26.08S	28.00E
Lindenberg, Ger.	238a	52.36N	13.31E
Linden-Dahlhausen, neigh., Ger.	236	51.26N	7.09E
Lindenhorst, neigh., Ger.	236	51.33N	7.27E
Lindenhurst, N.Y., U.S. (lĭn'dĕn-hûrst)	100a	40.41N	73.23W
Lindenwold, N.J., U.S. (lĭn'dĕn-wôld)	100f	39.50N	75.00W
Linderhausen, Ger.	236	51.18N	7.17E
Lindesberg, Swe. (lĭn'dĕs-bĕrgh)	152	59.37N	15.14E
Lindesnes, c., Nor. (lĭn'ĕs-nĕs)	142	58.00N	7.05E
Lindfield, Austl.	243a	33.47S	151.10E
Lindi, Tan. (lĭn'dē)	213	10.00S	39.43E
Lindi, r., Zaire	211	1.00N	27.13E
Lindian, China (lĭn-dĭĕn)	192	47.08N	124.59E
Lindley, S. Afr. (lĭnd'lē)	218d	27.52S	27.55E
Lindow, Ger. (lēn'dōv)	145b	52.58N	12.59E
Lindsay, Can. (lĭn'zē)	91	44.20N	78.45W
Lindsay, Ok., U.S.	111	34.50N	97.38W
Lindsborg, Ks., U.S. (lĭnz'bôrg)	111	38.34N	97.42W
Lineville, Al., U.S. (lĭn'vĭl)	114	33.18N	85.45W
Linfen, China	189	36.00N	111.38E
Linga, Kepulauan, is., Indon.	196	0.35S	105.05E
Lingao, China (lĭn-gou)	193	19.58N	109.40E
Lingayen, Phil. (lĭŋ'gä-yän')	196	16.01N	120.13E
Lingayen Gulf, b., Phil.	197a	16.18N	120.11E
Lingdianzhen, China	190	31.52N	121.28E
Lingen, Ger. (lĭŋ'gĕn)	154	52.32N	7.20E
Lingling, China (lĭŋ-lĭŋ)	193	26.10N	111.40E
Lingshou, China (lĭŋ-shō)	190	38.21N	114.41E
Linguère, Sen. (lĭŋ-gĕr')	210	15.24N	15.07W
Lingwu, China	192	38.05N	106.18E
Lingyuan, China (lĭŋ-yůän)	192	41.12N	119.20E
Linhai, China	193	28.52N	121.08E
Linhe, China (lĭn-hŭ)	192	40.49N	107.45E
Linhuaiguan, China (lĭn-hwī-gůän)	190	32.55N	117.38E
Linhuanji, China	190	33.42N	116.33E
Linjiang, China (lĭn-jyäŋ)	192	41.45N	127.00E
Linköping, Swe. (lĭn'chû-pĭng)	146	58.25N	15.35E
Linksfield, neigh., S. Afr.	244b	26.10S	28.06E

ăt; finăl; rāte; senāte; ärm; ȧsk; sofȧ; fâre; ch-choose; dh-as th in other; bē; ēvent; bĕt; recĕnt; cratẽr; g-gō; gh-guttural g; bĭt; ĭ-short neutral; rīde; ᴋ-guttural k as ch in German ich;

PRONOUNCING INDEX

Linmeyer-London 311

PLACE (Pronunciation)	PAGE	Lat. °′	Long. °′
Linmeyer, S. Afr.	244b	26.16S	28.04E
Linn, neigh., Ger.	236	51.20N	6.38E
Linnhe, Loch, b., Scot., U.K. (lĭn′ė)	150	56.35N	4.30W
Linqing, China (lĭn-chyĭŋ)	189	36.49N	115.42E
Linqu, China (lĭn-chyōō)	190	36.31N	118.33E
Lins, Braz. (lė′ns)	131	21.42S	49.41W
Linthicum Heights, Md., U.S. (lĭn′thĭ-kŭm)	100e	39.12N	76.39W
Linton, In., U.S. (lĭn′tŭn)	98	39.05N	87.15W
Linton, N.D., U.S.	102	46.16N	100.15W
Lintorf, Ger.	236	51.20N	6.49E
Linwu, China (lĭn′wōō′)	193	25.20N	112.30E
Linxi, China (lĭn-shyē)	192	43.30N	118.02E
Linyi, China (lĭn-yē)	189	35.04N	118.21E
Linying, China (lĭn′yĭng′)	190	33.48N	113.56E
Linz, Aus. (lĭnts)	147	48.18N	14.18E
Linzhang, China (lĭn-jäŋ)	190	36.19N	114.40E
Lion, Golfe du, b., Fin.	142	43.00N	4.00E
Lipa, Phil. (lė-pä′)	196	13.55N	121.10E
Lipari, Italy (lē′pä-rė)	160	38.29N	15.00E
Lipari, i., Italy	160	38.32N	15.04E
Lipetsk, Russia (lyē′pĕtsk)	164	52.26N	39.34E
Lipetsk, prov., Russia	162	52.18N	38.30E
Liping, China (lē-pĭŋ)	188	26.18N	109.00E
Lipno, Pol. (lēp′nỏ)	155	52.50N	19.12E
Lippe, r., Ger. (lĭp′ĕ)	157b	51.36N	6.45E
Lippolthausen, neigh., Ger.	236	51.37N	7.29E
Lippstadt, Ger. (lĭp′shtät)	154	51.39N	8.20E
Lipscomb, Al., U.S. (lĭp′skŭm)	100h	33.26N	86.56W
Lipu, China (lē-pōō)	193	24.38N	110.35E
Lira, Ug.	217	2.15N	32.54E
Liri, r., Italy (lē′rē)	160	41.49N	13.30E
Liria, Spain (lė′ryä)	159	39.35N	0.34W
Lisala, Zaire (lė-sä′lä)	211	2.09N	21.31E
Lisboa *see* Lisbon, Port.	142	38.42N	9.05W
Lisbon (Lisboa), Port.	142	38.42N	9.05W
Lisbon, N.D., U.S.	102	46.21N	97.43W
Lisbon, Oh., U.S.	98	40.45N	80.50W
Lisbon Falls, Me., U.S.	92	43.59N	70.03W
Lisburn, N. Ire., U.K. (lĭs′bŭrn)	150	54.35N	6.05W
Lisburne, Cape, c., Ak., U.S.	96a	68.20N	165.40W
Lishi, China (lē-shr)	192	37.32N	111.12E
Lishu, China	192	43.12N	124.18E
Lishui, China	189	28.28N	120.00E
Lishui, China (lĭ′shwĭ′)	190	31.41N	119.01E
Lisianski Island, i., Hi., U.S.	94b	25.30N	174.00W
Lisieux, Fr. (lē-zyû′)	156	49.10N	0.13E
Lisiy Nos, Russia (lĭ′sĭy-nôs)	172c	60.01N	30.00E
Liski, Russia (lyēs′kė)	163	50.56N	39.28E
Lisle, Il., U.S. (līl)	101a	41.48N	88.04W
L'Isle-Adam, Fr. (lēl-ädän′)	157b	49.05N	2.13E
Lismore, Austl. (lĭz′môr)	203	28.48S	153.18E
Litani, r., Leb.	181a	33.28N	35.42E
Litchfield, Il., U.S. (lĭch′fēld)	111	39.10N	89.38W
Litchfield, Mn., U.S.	103	45.08N	94.34W
Litchfield, Oh., U.S.	101d	41.10N	82.01W
Litherland, Eng., U.K.	237a	53.28N	2.59W
Lithgow, Austl. (lĭth′gō)	203	33.23S	149.31E
Lithinon, Akra, c., Grc.	160a	34.59N	24.35E
Lithonia, Ga., U.S. (lĭ-thō′nĭ-*ȧ*)	100c	33.43N	84.07W
Lithuania, nation, Eur. (lĭth-ů-ā-′nĭ-*ȧ*)	164	55.42N	23.30E
Litókhoron, Grc. (lē′tỏ-kō′rỏn)	161	40.05N	22.29E
Litoko, Zaire	216	1.13S	24.47E
Litoměřice, Czech Rep. (lē′tỏ-myĕr′zhĭ-tsĕ)	154	50.33N	14.10E
Litomyšl, Czech Rep. (lē′tỏ-mėsh'l)	154	49.52N	16.14E
Litoo, Tan.	217	9.45S	38.24E
Little, r., Austl.	201a	37.54S	144.27E
Little, r., Tn., U.S.	114	36.28N	89.39W
Little, r., Tx., U.S.	113	30.48N	96.50W
Little Abaco, i., Bah. (ä′bä-kō)	122	26.55N	77.45W
Little Abitibi, r., Can.	90	50.15N	81.30W
Little America, sci., Ant.	219	78.30S	161.30W
Little Andaman, i., India (ăn-d*ȧ*-măn′)	196	10.39N	93.08E
Little Bahama Bank, bk. (b*ȧ*-hā′m*ȧ*)	122	26.55N	78.40W
Little Belt Mountains, mts., Mt., U.S. (bĕlt)	96	47.00N	110.50W
Little Berkhamsted, Eng., U.K.	235	51.45N	0.08W
Little Bighorn, r., Mt., U.S. (bĭg-hôrn)	105	45.08N	107.30W
Little Bitter Lake, l., Egypt	218b	30.10N	32.36E
Little Bitterroot, r., Mt., U.S. (bĭt′ẽr-ōōt)	105	47.45N	114.45W
Little Blue, r., Ia., U.S. (blōō)	107f	38.52N	94.25W
Little Blue, r., Ne., U.S.	110	40.15N	98.01W
Littleborough, Eng., U.K. (lĭt''l-bŭr-ỏ)	144a	53.39N	2.06W
Little Burstead, Eng., U.K.	235	51.36N	0.24E
Little Calumet, r., Il., U.S. (kăl-ů-mĕt′)	101a	41.38N	87.38W
Little Cayman, i., Cay. Is. (kā′m*ȧ*n)	122	19.40N	80.05W
Little Chalfont, Eng., U.K.	235	51.40N	0.34W
Little Colorado, r., Az., U.S. (kŏl-ỏ-rā′dō)	96	36.05N	111.35W
Little Compton, R.I., U.S. (kŏmp′tŏn)	100b	41.31N	71.07W
Little Corn Island, i., Nic.	121	12.19N	82.50W
Little End, Eng., U.K.	235	51.41N	0.14E
Little Exuma, i., Bah. (ĕk-sōō′mä)	123	23.25N	75.40W
Little Falls, Mn., U.S. (fôlz)	103	45.58N	94.23W
Little Falls, N.J., U.S.	228	40.53N	74.14W
Little Falls, N.Y., U.S.	99	43.05N	74.55W
Little Ferry, N.J., U.S.	228	40.51N	74.03W
Littlefield, Tx., U.S. (lĭt''l-fēld)	110	33.55N	102.17W
Little Fork, r., Mn., U.S. (fôrk)	103	48.24N	93.30W
Little Goose Dam, dam, Wa., U.S.	104	46.35N	118.02W
Little Hans Lollick, i., V.I.U.S. (häns lôl′lĭk)	117c	18.25N	64.54W
Little Hulton, Eng., U.K.	237b	53.32N	2.25W
Little Humboldt, r., Nv., U.S. (hŭm′bōlt)	104	41.10N	117.40W
Little Inagua, i., Bah. (ė-nä′gwä)	123	21.30N	73.00W

PLACE (Pronunciation)	PAGE	Lat. °′	Long. °′
Little Isaac, i., Bah. (ī′z*ȧ*k)	122	25.55N	79.00W
Little Kanawha, r., W.V., U.S. (k*ȧ*-nô′w*ȧ*)	98	39.05N	81.30W
Little Karroo, plat., S. Afr. (kä-rōō)	212	33.50S	21.02E
Little Lever, Eng., U.K.	237b	53.34N	2.22W
Little Mecatina, r., Can. (mĕ c*ȧ* tī nå)	85	52.40N	62.21W
Little Miami, r., Oh., U.S. (mī-ăm′ĭ)	101f	39.19N	84.15W
Little Minch, strt., Scot., U.K.	150	57.35N	6.45W
Little Missouri, r., U.S.	96	46.00N	104.00W
Little Missouri, r., Ar., U.S. (mĭ-sōō′rĭ)	111	34.15N	93.54W
Little Nahant, Ma., U.S.	227a	42.25N	70.56W
Little Neck, neigh., N.Y., U.S.	228	40.46N	73.44W
Little Pee Dee, r., S.C., U.S. (pē-dē′)	115	34.35N	79.21W
Little Powder, r., Wy., U.S. (pou′dẽr)	105	44.51N	105.20W
Little Red, r., Ar., U.S. (rĕd)	111	35.25N	91.55W
Little Red, r., Ok., U.S.	111	33.53N	94.38W
Little Rock, Ar., U.S. (rôk)	97	34.42N	92.16W
Little Sachigo Lake, l., Can. (să′chĭ-gō)	89	54.09N	92.11W
Little Salt Lake, l., Ut., U.S.	109	37.55N	112.53W
Little San Salvador, i., Bah. (săn săl′vȧ-dôr)	123	24.35N	75.55W
Little Satilla, r., Ga., U.S. (sȧ-tĭl′*ȧ*)	115	31.43N	82.47W
Little Sioux, r., Ia., U.S. (sōō)	102	42.22N	95.47W
Little Smoky, r., Can. (smōk′ĭ)	87	55.10N	116.55W
Little Snake, r., Co., U.S. (snāk)	105	40.40N	108.21W
Little Stanney, Eng., U.K.	237a	53.15N	2.53W
Little Sutton, Eng., U.K.	237a	53.17N	2.57W
Little Tallapoosa, r., Al., U.S. (tăl-ȧ-pỏ′să)	114	32.25N	85.28W
Little Tennessee, r., Tn., U.S. (tĕn-ĕ-sē′)	114	35.36N	84.05W
Little Thurrock, Eng., U.K.	235	51.28N	0.21E
Littleton, Eng., U.K.	235	51.24N	0.28W
Littleton, Co., U.S. (lĭt''l-tŭn)	110	39.34N	105.01W
Littleton, Ma., U.S.	93a	42.32N	71.29W
Littleton, N.H., U.S.	99	44.15N	71.45W
Little Wabash, r., Il., U.S. (wô′băsh)	98	38.50N	88.30W
Little Warley, Eng., U.K.	235	51.35N	0.19E
Little Wood, r., Id., U.S. (wȯd)	105	43.00N	114.08W
Lityn, Ukr.	163	49.16N	28.11E
Liuhe, China	192	42.10N	125.38E
Liuli, Tan.	217	11.05S	34.38E
Liulicun, China	240b	39.56N	116.28E
Liupan Shan, mts., China	192	36.20N	105.30E
Liuwa Plain, pl., Zam.	216	14.30S	22.40E
Liuyang, China (lyōō′yäng′)	193	28.10N	113.35E
Liuyuan, China (lĭỏ-yůän)	190	36.09N	114.37E
Liuzhou, China (lĭỏ-jō)	188	24.25N	109.30E
Līvāni, Lat. (lē′vȧ-nė)	153	56.24N	26.12E
Lively, Can.	90	46.26N	81.09W
Livengood, Ak., U.S. (līv′ĕn-gȯd)	95	65.30N	148.35W
Live Oak, Fl., U.S. (līv′ōk)	114	30.15N	83.00W
Livermore, Ca., U.S. (lĭv′ẽr-mōr)	106b	37.41N	121.46W
Livermore, Ky., U.S.	98	37.30N	87.05W
Liverpool, Austl. (lĭv′ẽr-pōōl)	201b	33.55S	150.56E
Liverpool, Can.	85	44.02N	64.41W
Liverpool, Eng., U.K.	142	53.25N	2.52W
Liverpool, Tx., U.S.	113a	29.18N	95.17W
Liverpool Bay, b., Can.	95	69.45N	130.00W
Liverpool Range, mts., Austl.	203	31.47S	151.00E
Livindo, r., Afr.	211	1.09N	13.30E
Livingston, Guat.	120	15.50N	88.45W
Livingston, Al., U.S. (lĭv′ĭng-stŭn)	114	32.35N	88.09W
Livingston, Il., U.S.	107e	38.58N	89.51W
Livingston, Mt., U.S.	96	45.40N	110.35W
Livingston, N.J., U.S.	100a	40.47N	74.20W
Livingston, Tn., U.S.	114	36.23N	85.20W
Livingstone, Zam. (lĭv-ĭng-stỏn)	212	17.50S	25.53E
Livingstone, Chutes de, wtfl., Afr.	216	4.50S	14.30E
Livingstonia, Mwi. (lĭv-ĭng-stō′nĭ-*ȧ*)	212	10.36S	34.07E
Livno, Bos. (lēv′nỏ)	149	43.50N	17.03E
Livny, Russia (lēv′nė)	167	52.28N	37.36E
Livonia, Mi., U.S. (lĭ-vō-nĭ-*ȧ*)	101b	42.25N	83.23W
Livorno, Italy (lė-vôr′nō) (lĕg′hỏrn)	142	43.32N	11.18E
Livramento, Braz. (lē-vrȧ-mĕ′n-tô)	132	30.46S	55.21W
Livry-Gargan, Fr.	237c	48.56N	2.33E
Lixian, China	190	38.30N	115.38E
Lixian, China (lē shyĕn)	193	29.42N	111.40E
Liyang, China (lē′yäng′)	193	31.30N	119.29E
Lizard Point, c., Eng., U.K. (lĭz′*ȧ*rd)	147	49.55N	5.09W
Lizy-sur-Ourcq, Fr. (lēk-sē′sür-ōōrk′)	157b	49.01N	3.02E
Ljubljana, Slvn. (lyōō′blyä′na)	142	46.04N	14.29E
Ljubuški, Bos. (lyōō′bȯsh-kė)	161	43.11N	17.29E
Ljungan, r., Swe.	152	62.50N	13.45E
Ljungby, Swe. (lyȯng′bü)	152	56.49N	13.56E
Ljusdal, Swe. (lyōōs′däl)	152	61.50N	16.11E
Ljusnan, r., Swe.	146	61.55N	15.33E
Llandudno, Wales, U.K. (lăn-düd′nō)	150	53.20N	3.46W
Llanelli, Wales, U.K. (lȧ-nĕl′ĭ)	147	51.44N	4.09W
Llanes, Spain (lyä′nȧs)	148	43.25N	4.41W
Llano, Tx., U.S. (lä′nō) (lyä′nō)	112	30.45N	98.41W
Llano, r., Tx., U.S.	112	30.38N	99.04W
Llanos, reg., S.A. (lyȧ′nōs)	130	4.00N	71.15W
Llera, Mex. (lyā′rä)	118	23.16N	99.03W
Llerena, Spain (lyā-rā′nä)	158	38.14N	6.02W
Llobregat, r., Spain (lyỏ-brĕ-gät′)	159	41.55N	1.55E
Lloyd Lake, l., Can. (loid)	83e	50.52N	114.13W
Lloydminster, Can.	84	53.17N	110.00W
Lluchmayor, Spain (lyōōch-mä-yỏr′)	159	39.28N	2.53E
Llullaillaco, Volcán, vol., S.A. (lyōō-lyī-lyä′kō)	132	24.50S	68.30W
Loange, r., Afr. (lỏ-äŋ′gä)	212	5.00S	20.15E
Lo Aranguiz, Chile	234b	33.23S	70.40W
Lobamba, Swaz.	212	26.27S	31.12E
Lobatse, Bots. (lō-bä′tsē)	212	25.13S	25.35E
Lobau, reg., Aus.	239e	48.10N	16.32E

PLACE (Pronunciation)	PAGE	Lat. °′	Long. °′
Lobería, Arg. (lô-bĕ'rē′ä)	132	38.13S	58.48W
Lobito, Ang. (lỏ-bē′tō)	212	12.30S	13.34E
Lobnya, Russia (lôb′nyȧ)	172b	56.01N	37.29E
Lobo, Phil.	197a	13.39N	121.14E
Lobos, Arg. (lō′bỏs)	129c	35.10S	59.08W
Lobos, Cayo, i., Bah. (lō′bỏs)	122	22.25N	77.40W
Lobos, Isla de, i., Mex. (ė′s-lä-dĕ-lô′bōs)	119	21.24N	97.11W
Lobos de Tierra, i., Peru (lô′bō-dĕ-tyĕ′r-rä)	130	6.29S	80.55W
Lobva, Russia (lôb′vȧ)	172a	59.12N	60.28E
Lobva, r., Russia	172a	59.14N	60.17E
Locarno, Switz. (lỏ-kär′nō)	154	46.10N	8.43E
Lochearn, Md., U.S.	229c	39.21N	76.43W
Loches, Fr. (lỏsh)	156	47.08N	0.56E
Loch Raven Reservoir, res., Md., U.S.	100e	39.28N	76.38W
Lockeport, Can.	92	43.42N	65.07W
Lockhart, S.C., U.S. (lŏk′hȧrt)	115	34.47N	81.30W
Lockhart, Tx., U.S.	113	29.54N	97.40W
Lock Haven, Pa., U.S. (lŏk′hā-vĕn)	99	41.05N	77.30W
Lockland, Oh., U.S. (lŏk′lănd)	101f	39.14N	84.27W
Lockport, Il., U.S.	101a	41.35N	88.04W
Lockport, N.Y., U.S.	99	43.11N	78.43W
Lockwillow, S. Afr.	244b	26.17S	27.50E
Loc Ninh, Viet. (lōk′nĭng′)	196	12.00N	106.30E
Locust Grove, N.Y., U.S.	228	40.48N	73.30W
Locust Valley, N.Y., U.S.	228	40.53N	73.36W
Lod, Isr. (lôd)	181a	31.57N	34.55E
Lodève, Fr. (lỏ-dĕv′)	156	43.43N	3.18E
Lodeynoye Pole, Russia (lỏ-dĕy-nô′yĕ)	166	60.43N	33.24E
Lodge Creek, r., N.A. (lŏj)	105	49.20N	110.20W
Lodge Creek, r., Mt., U.S.	105	48.51N	109.30W
Lodgepole Creek, r., Wy., U.S. (lŏj′pōl)	102	41.22N	104.48W
Lodhran, Pak.	186	29.40N	71.39E
Lodi, Italy (lô′dē)	160	45.18N	9.30E
Lodi, Ca., U.S. (lō′dī)	108	38.07N	121.17W
Lodi, N.J., U.S.	228	40.53N	74.05W
Lodi, Oh., U.S. (lō′dī)	101d	41.02N	82.01W
Lodosa, Spain (lỏ-dô′sä)	158	42.27N	2.04W
Lodwar, Kenya	217	3.07N	35.36E
Łódź, Pol.	142	51.46N	19.30E
Loeches, Spain (lỏ-āch′ĕs)	159a	40.22N	3.25W
Loffa, r., Afr.	214	7.10N	10.35W
Lofoten, is., Nor. (lỏ′fō-tĕn)	142	68.26N	13.42E
Logăn, Oh., U.S. (lō′g*ȧ*n)	98	39.35N	82.25W
Logan, Ut., U.S.	96	41.46N	111.51W
Logan, W.V., U.S.	98	37.50N	82.00W
Logan, Mount, mtn., Can.	84	60.54N	140.33W
Logansport, In., U.S. (lō′gănz-pōrt)	97	40.45N	86.25W
Logan Square, neigh., Il., U.S.	231a	41.56N	87.42W
Lognes, Fr.	237c	48.50N	2.38E
Logone, r., Afr. (lō-gō′nā) (lỏ-gỏn′)	211	10.20N	15.30E
Logroño, Spain (lỏ-grō′nyō)	148	42.28N	2.25W
Logrosán, Spain (lỏ-grỏ-sän′)	158	39.22N	5.29W
Løgstør, Den. (lügh-stûr′)	152	56.56N	9.15E
Lohausen, neigh., Ger.	236	51.16N	6.44E
Lohberg, Ger.	236	51.35N	6.46E
Lo Hermida, Chile	234b	33.29S	70.33W
Lohheide, Ger.	236	51.30N	6.40E
Löhme, Ger.	238a	52.37N	13.40E
Lohmühle, Ger.	236	51.31N	6.40E
Löhnen, Ger.	236	51.36N	6.39E
Loir, r., Fr. (lwȧr)	156	47.40N	0.07E
Loire, r., Fr.	142	47.30N	2.00E
Loja, Ec. (lō′hä)	130	3.49S	79.13W
Loja, Spain (lỏ′-kä)	158	37.10N	4.11W
Loka, Zaire	216	0.20N	17.57E
Lokala Drift, Bots. (lỏ′kä-l*ȧ* drĭft)	218d	24.00S	26.38E
Lokandu, Zaire	217	2.31S	25.47E
Lokhvytsya, Ukr.	167	50.21N	33.16E
Lokichar, Kenya	217	2.23N	35.39E
Lokitaung, Kenya	217	4.16N	35.45E
Lokofa-Bokolongo, Zaire	216	0.12N	19.22E
Lokoja, Nig. (lỏ-kō′yä)	210	7.47N	6.45E
Lokolama, Zaire	216	2.34S	19.53E
Lokosso, Burkina	214	10.19N	3.40W
Lol, r., Sudan (lōl)	211	9.06N	28.09E
Loliondo, Tan.	217	2.03S	35.37E
Lolland, i., Den. (lôl′än')	152	54.41N	11.00E
Lolo, Mt., U.S.	105	46.45N	114.05W
Lom, Bul. (lōm)	149	43.48N	23.15E
Loma Linda, Ca., U.S. (lō′m*ȧ* lĭn′d*ȧ*)	107a	34.04N	117.16W
Lomami, r., Zaire	212	0.50S	24.40E
Lomas Chapultepec, neigh., Mex.	233a	19.26N	99.13W
Lomas de Zamora, Arg. (lō′mäs dā zä-mō′rä)	129c	34.46S	58.24W
Lombard, Il., U.S. (lŏm-bärd)	101a	41.53N	88.01W
Lombardia, hist. reg., Italy (lỏm-bär-dė′ä)	160	45.20N	9.30E
Lombardy, S. Afr.	244b	26.07S	28.08E
Lomblen, Pulau, i., Indon. (lŏm-blĕn′)	197	8.08S	123.45E
Lombok, i., Indon. (lŏm-bŏk′)	196	9.15S	116.15E
Lomé, Togo	210	6.08N	1.13E
Lomela, Zaire (lỏ-mā′lȧ)	212	2.19S	23.33E
Lomela, r., Zaire	212	0.35S	21.20E
Lometa, Tx., U.S. (lỏ-mē′t*ȧ*)	112	31.10N	98.25W
Lomié, Cam. (lỏ-mė-ā′)	215	3.10N	13.37E
Lomita, Ca., U.S. (lō-mē′t*ȧ*)	107a	33.48N	118.20W
Lommel, Bel.	145a	51.14N	5.21E
Lommond, Loch, l., Scot., U.K. (lôk lō′mŭnd)	150	56.15N	4.40W
Lomonosov, Russia (lô-mô′nô-sof)	172c	59.54N	29.47E
Lompoc, Ca., U.S. (lŏm-pōk′)	108	34.39N	120.30W
Łomża, Pol. (lôm′zhȧ)	155	53.11N	22.04E
Lonaconing, Md., U.S. (lō-nă-kō′nĭng)	99	39.35N	78.55W
London, Can. (lŭn′dŭn)	85	43.00N	81.20W

ng-sing; ŋ-baŋk; n-nasalized n; nŏd; cŏmmit; ōld; ỏbey; ôrder; oi-boil; fōōd; ȯ-as oo in foot; ou-out; s-soft; sh-dish; th-thin; pūre; ůnite; ûrn; stŭd; circŭs; ü-as in French tu; '-indeterminate vowel.

312 London – Luling

PLACE (Pronunciation)	PAGE	Lat. °'	Long. °'
London, Eng., U.K.	142	51.30N	0.07W
London, Ky., U.S.	114	37.07N	84.06W
London, Oh., U.S.	98	39.50N	83.30W
London (Heathrow) Airport, arpt., Eng., U.K.	235	51.27N	0.28W
London Colney, Eng., U.K.	235	51.43N	0.18W
Londonderry, Can. (lŭn'dŭn-dĕr-ĭ)	92	45.29N	63.36W
Londonderry, N. Ire., U.K.	146	55.00N	7.19W
Londonderry, Cape, c., Austl.	202	13.30S	127.00E
London Zoo, pt. of i., Eng., U.K.	235	51.32N	0.09W
Londrina, Braz. (lôn-drē'nä)	131	21.53S	51.17W
Lonely, i., Can. (lōn'lĭ)	85	45.35N	81.30W
Lone Pine, Ca., U.S.	108	36.36N	118.03W
Lone Star, Nic.	121	13.58N	84.25W
Long, i., Bah.	117	23.25N	75.10W
Long, i., Can.	92	44.21S	66.25W
Long, l., N.D., U.S.	102	46.47N	100.14W
Long, l., Wa., U.S.	106a	47.29N	122.36W
Longa, r., Ang. (lôŋ'gȧ)	212	10.20S	15.15E
Long Bay, b., S.C., U.S.	115	33.30N	78.54W
Long Beach, Ca., U.S. (lông bēch)	96	33.46N	118.12W
Long Beach, N.Y., U.S.	100a	40.35N	73.38W
Long Branch, N.J., U.S. (lông brȧnch)	100a	40.18N	73.59W
Long Ditton, Eng., U.K.	235	51.23N	0.20W
Longdon, N.D., U.S. (lông'-dŭn)	102	48.45N	98.23W
Long Eaton, Eng., U.K. (ē'tŭn)	144a	52.54N	1.16W
Longfield, Eng., U.K.	235	51.24N	0.18E
Longford, Ire. (lŏng'fērd)	150	53.43N	7.40W
Longgu, China (lôŋ-gōō)	190	34.52N	116.48E
Longhorn, Tx., U.S. (lông-hôrn)	107d	29.33N	98.23W
Longhua, China	241a	31.09N	121.26E
Longido, Tan.	217	2.44S	36.41E
Long Island, i., Pap. N. Gui.	197	5.10S	147.30E
Long Island, i., Ak., U.S.	86	54.54N	132.45W
Long Island, i., N.Y., U.S. (lông)	97	40.50N	72.50W
Long Island City, neigh., N.Y., U.S.	228	40.45N	73.56W
Long Island Sound, strt., U.S. (lông ī'lănd)	97	41.05N	72.45W
Longjumeau, Fr. (lôN-zhü-mō')	157b	48.42N	2.17E
Longkou, China (lôŋ-kō)	190	37.39N	120.21E
Longlac, Can. (lông'lăk)	85	49.41N	86.28W
Longlake, S.D., U.S. (lông-lāk)	102	45.52N	99.06W
Long Lake, l., Can.	90	49.10N	86.45W
Longmont, Co., U.S. (lông'mŏnt)	110	40.11N	105.07W
Longnor, Eng., U.K. (lông'nôr)	144a	53.11N	1.52W
Long Pine, Ne., U.S. (lông pīn)	102	42.31N	99.42W
Long Point, Austl.	243a	34.01S	150.54E
Long Point, c., Can.	89	53.02N	98.40W
Long Point, c., Can.	91	42.35N	80.05W
Long Point, c., Can.	93	48.48N	58.46W
Long Point Bay, b., Can.	91	42.40N	80.10W
Long Range Mountains, mts., Can.	85a	48.00N	58.30W
Longreach, Austl. (lông'rēch)	203	23.32S	144.17E
Long Reach, r., Can.	92	45.26N	66.05W
Long Reef, c., Austl.	201b	33.45S	151.22E
Longridge, Eng., U.K. (lông'rĭj)	144a	53.51N	2.37W
Longs Peak, mtn., Co., U.S. (lôngz)	96	40.17N	105.37W
Longtansi, China (lôŋ-tä-sz)	190	32.12N	115.53E
Longton, Eng., U.K. (lông'tŭn)	144a	52.59N	2.08W
Longueuil, Can. (lôN-gû'y')	91	45.32N	73.30W
Longueville, Austl.	243a	33.50S	151.10E
Longview, Tx., U.S.	113	32.29N	94.44W
Longview, Wa., U.S. (lông-vū)	104	46.06N	123.02W
Longville, La., U.S. (lông'vĭl)	113	30.36N	93.14W
Longwy, Fr. (lôN-wē')	157	49.32N	6.14E
Longxi, China (lôŋ-shyē)	188	35.00N	104.40E
Long Xuyen, Viet. (loung' sōō'yĕn)	196	10.31N	105.28E
Longzhou, China (lôŋ-jō)	188	22.20N	107.02E
Lonoke, Ar., U.S. (lō'nōk)	111	34.48N	91.52W
Lons-le-Saunier, Fr. (lôN-lē-sō-nyā')	157	46.40N	5.33E
Lontue, r., Chile (lōn-tòĕ')	129b	35.20S	70.45W
Looc, Phil. (lô-ōk')	197a	12.16N	121.59E
Loogootee, In., U.S.	98	38.40N	86.55W
Lookout, Cape, c., N.C., U.S. (lòk'out)	115	34.34N	76.38W
Lookout Point Lake, res., Or., U.S.	104	43.51N	122.38W
Loolmalasin, mtn., Tan.	217	3.03S	35.46E
Looma, Can. (ōō'mä)	83g	53.22N	113.15W
Loop, neigh., Il., U.S.	231a	41.53N	87.38W
Loop Head, c., Ire. (lōōp)	150	52.32N	9.59W
Loosahatchie, r., Tn., U.S. (lōz-á-hă'chē)	114	35.20N	89.45W
Loosdrechtsche Plassen, l., Neth.	145a	52.11N	5.09E
Lopatka, Mys, c., Russia (lō-pät'kȧ)	181	51.00N	156.52E
Lopez, Cap, c., Gabon	216	0.37S	8.43E
Lopez Bay, b., Phil. (lō'pāz)	197a	14.04N	122.00E
Lopez I, Wa., U.S.	106a	48.25N	122.53W
Lopori, r., Zaire (lō-pō'rē)	211	1.35N	20.43E
Lo Prado Arriba, Chile	234b	33.26S	70.45W
Lora, Spain (lō'rä)	158	37.40N	5.31W
Lorain, Oh., U.S. (lō-rān')	101d	41.28N	82.10W
Loralai, Pak. (lō-rŭ-lī')	183	30.31N	68.35E
Lorca, Spain (lôr'kä)	148	37.39N	1.40W
Lord Howe, i., Austl. (lôrd hou)	202	31.44S	157.56W
Lordsburg, N.M., U.S. (lôrdz'bûrg)	109	32.20N	108.45W
Lorena, Braz. (lō-rā'nȧ)	129a	22.45S	45.07W
Loreto, Braz. (lō-rā'tō)	131	7.09S	45.10W
Loretteville, Can. (lō-rĕt-vĕl')	83b	46.51N	71.21W
Lorica, Col. (lō-rē'kä)	130	9.14N	75.54W
Lorient, Fr. (lō-rē'äN')	147	47.45N	3.22W
Lorn, Firth of, b., Scot., U.K. (fûrth ŏv lôrn')	150	56.10N	6.09W
Lörrach, Ger. (lûr'äK)	154	47.36N	7.38E
Lorraine, hist. reg., Fr.	157	49.00N	6.00E
Los Alamitos, Ca., U.S. (lōs ăl-ȧ-mē'tōs)	107a	33.48N	118.04W
Los Alamos, N.M., U.S. (ăl-ȧ-mōs')	109	35.53N	106.20W
Los Altos, Ca., U.S. (ăl-tōs')	106b	37.23N	122.06W
Los Andes, Chile (ȧn'dēs)	129b	32.44S	70.36W
Los Angeles, Chile (äŋ'hȧ-lās)	132	37.27S	72.15W
Los Angeles, Ca., U.S.	108	34.03N	118.14W
Los Angeles, r., Ca., U.S.	107a	33.50N	118.13W
Los Angeles Aqueduct, Ca., U.S.	108	35.12N	118.02W
Los Angeles International Airport, arpt., Ca., U.S.	232	33.56N	118.24W
Los Bronces, Chile (lōs brō'n-sĕs)	129b	33.09S	70.18W
Loscha, r., Id., U.S. (lŏs'chă)	104	46.20N	115.11W
Los Cuatro Álamos, Chile	234b	33.32S	70.44W
Los Dos Caminos, Ven.	234a	10.31N	66.50W
Los Estados, Isla de, i., Arg. (ē's-lä dĕ lōs ĕs-dōs)	132	54.45S	64.25W
Los Gatos, Ca., U.S. (gă'tōs)	108	37.13N	121.59W
Los Herreras, Mex. (ĕr-rā-räs)	112	25.55N	99.23W
Los llanos, Dom. Rep. (lōs ē-lä'nōs)	123	18.35N	69.30W
Los Indios, Cayos de, is., Cuba (kä'vōs dē lōs ē'n-dvō's)	122	21.50N	83.10W
Lošinj, i., Yugo.	160	44.35N	14.34E
Losino Petrovskiy, Russia	172b	55.52N	38.12E
Los Nietos, Ca., U.S. (nyā'tōs)	107a	33.57N	118.05W
Los Palacios, Cuba	122	22.35N	83.15W
Los Pinos, r., Co., U.S. (pē'nōs)	109	36.58N	107.35W
Los Reyes, Mex.	116	19.35N	102.29W
Los Reyes, Mex.	119a	19.21N	98.58W
Los Santos, Pan. (săn'tōs)	121	7.57N	80.24W
Los Santos de Maimona, Spain (săn'tōs)	158	38.38N	6.30W
Lost, r., Or., U.S.	104	42.07N	121.30W
Los Teques, Ven. (tē'kēs)	130	10.22N	67.04W
Lost River Range, mts., Id., U.S. (rĭ'vẽr)	105	44.23N	113.48W
Los Vilos, Chile (vē'lōs)	132	31.56S	71.29W
Lot, r., Fr. (lôt)	147	44.30N	1.30E
Lota, Chile (lō'tä)	132	37.11S	73.14W
Lothian, Md., U.S. (lōth'ĭăn)	100e	38.50N	76.38W
Lotikipi Plain, pl., Afr.	217	4.25N	34.55E
Lötschberg Tunnel, trans., Switz.	154	46.26N	7.54E
Louangphrabang, Laos (lōō-ang'prä-bäng')	196	19.47N	102.15E
Loudon, Tn., U.S. (lou'dŭn)	114	35.43N	84.20W
Loudonville, Oh., U.S. (lou'dŭn-vĭl)	98	40.40N	82.15W
Loudun, Fr.	156	47.03N	0.00
Loughborough, Eng., U.K. (lŭf'bŭr-ō)	144a	52.46N	1.12W
Loughton, Eng., U.K.	235	51.39N	0.03E
Louisa, Ky., U.S. (lōō'ēz-ȧ)	98	38.05N	82.40W
Louisade Archipelago, is., Pap. N. Gui.	203	10.44S	153.58E
Louisberg, N.C., U.S. (lōō'ĭs-bûrg)	115	36.05N	79.19W
Louisburg, Can. (lōō'ĭs-bourg)	93	45.55N	59.58W
Louiseville, Can.	91	46.17N	72.58W
Louisiana, Mo., U.S. (lōō-ē-zē-ăn'ȧ)	111	39.24N	91.03W
Louisiana, state, U.S.	97	30.50N	92.50W
Louis Trichardt, S. Afr. (lōō'ĭs trĭchȧrt)	212	22.52S	29.53E
Louisville, Co., U.S. (lōō'ĭs-vĭl) (lōō'ē-vĭl)	110	39.58N	105.08W
Louisville, Ga., U.S.	115	33.00N	82.25W
Louisville, Ky., U.S.	97	38.15N	85.45W
Louisville, Ms., U.S.	114	33.07N	89.02W
Louis XIV, Pointe, c., Can.	85	54.35N	79.51W
Louny, Czech Rep. (lō'nē)	154	50.20N	13.47E
Loup, r., Ne., U.S. (lōōp)	102	41.17N	97.58W
Loup City, Ne., U.S.	102	41.15N	98.59W
Lourdes, Fr. (lōōrd)	147	43.06N	0.03W
Lourenço Marques see Maputo, Moz.	212	26.50S	32.30E
Loures, Port. (lō'rĕzh)	159b	38.49N	9.10W
Lousa, Port. (lō'zȧ)	158	40.05N	8.12W
Louth, Eng., U.K. (louth)	150	53.27N	0.02W
Louvain see Leuven, Bel.	151	50.53N	4.42E
Louveciennes, Fr.	237c	48.52N	2.07E
Louviers, Fr. (lōō-vyā')	156	49.13N	1.11E
Louvre, bldg., Fr.	237c	48.52N	2.20E
Lovech, Bul. (lō'vĕts)	161	43.10N	24.40E
Lovedale, Pa., U.S.	230b	40.17N	79.52W
Loveland, Co., U.S. (lŭv'lănd)	110	40.24N	105.04W
Loveland, Oh., U.S.	101f	39.16N	84.15W
Lovell, Wy., U.S. (lŭv'ĕl)	105	44.50N	108.23W
Lovelock, Nv., U.S. (lŭv'lŏk)	108	40.10N	118.37W
Loves Green, Eng., U.K.	235	51.43N	0.24E
Lovick, Al., U.S. (lŭ'vĭk)	100h	33.34N	86.38W
Loviisa, Fin. (lô'vē-sȧ)	153	60.28N	26.10E
Low, Cape, c., Can. (lō)	85	62.58N	86.50W
Lowa, r., Zaire (lō'wȧ)	212	1.30S	27.18E
Lowell, In., U.S.	101a	41.17N	87.26W
Lowell, Ma., U.S.	97	42.38N	71.18W
Lowell, Mi., U.S.	98	42.55N	85.20W
Löwenberg, Ger. (lû'vĕn-bĕrgh)	145b	52.53N	13.09E
Lower Broughton, neigh., Eng., U.K.	237b	53.29N	2.15W
Lower Brule Indian Reservation, I.R., S.D., U.S. (brü'lā)	102	44.15N	100.21W
Lower California see Baja California, pen., Mex.	82	28.00N	113.30W
Lower Granite Dam, dam, Wa., U.S.	104	46.40N	117.26W
Lower Higham, Eng., U.K.	235	51.26N	0.28E
Lower Hutt, N.Z. (hŭt)	203a	41.10S	174.55E
Lower Klamath Lake, l., Ca., U.S. (klăm'ȧth)	104	41.55N	121.50W
Lower Lake, l., Ca., U.S.	104	41.21N	119.53W
Lower Marlboro, Md., U.S. (lō'ēr märl'bōrō)	100e	38.40N	76.42W
Lower Monumental Dam, dam, Wa., U.S.	104	46.34N	118.32W
Lower Nazeing, Eng., U.K.	235	51.44N	0.01E
Lower New York Bay, b., N.Y., U.S.	228	40.33N	74.02W
Lower Otay Lake, res., Ca., U.S. (ō'tā)	108a	32.37N	116.46W
Lower Place, Eng., U.K.	237b	53.36N	2.09W
Lower Red Lake, l., Mn., U.S.	103	47.58N	94.31W
Lower Saxony see Niedersachsen, hist. reg., Ger.	154	52.52N	8.27E
Lowestoft, Eng., U.K. (lō'stŏf)	151	52.31N	1.45E
Łowicz, Pol. (lô'vĭch)	155	52.06N	19.57E
Lowville, N.Y., U.S. (lou'vĭl)	99	43.45N	75.30W
Loxicha, Mex.	119	16.03N	96.46W
Loxton, Austl. (lôks'tŭn)	204	34.25S	140.38E
Loyauté, Îles, is., N. Cal.	203	21.00S	167.00E
Loznica, Yugo. (lōz'nē-tsȧ)	149	44.31N	19.16E
Lozova, Ukr.	167	48.53N	36.23E
Luama, r., Zaire (lōō'ä-mȧ)	212	4.17S	27.45E
Lu'an, China (lōō-än)	193	31.45N	116.29E
Luan, r., China	189	41.25N	117.15E
Luanda, Ang. (lōō-än'dä)	212	8.48S	13.14E
Luanguinga, r., Afr. (lōō-ä-gĭŋ'gȧ)	212	14.00S	20.45E
Luanshya, Zam.	217	13.08S	28.24E
Luanxian, China (luăn shyĕn)	190	39.47N	118.40E
Luao, Ang.	216	10.42S	22.12E
Luarca, Spain (lwä'kä)	148	43.33N	6.30W
Lubaczów, Pol. (lōō-bä'chôf)	155	50.08N	23.10E
Lubán, Pol. (lōō'bän')	154	51.08N	15.17E
Lubānas Ezers, l., Lat. (lōō-bä'nȧs ä'zĕrs)	153	56.48N	26.30E
Lubang, Phil. (lōō-bäng')	197a	13.49N	120.07E
Lubang Islands, is., Phil.	196	13.47N	119.56E
Lubango, Ang.	212	14.55S	13.30E
Lubartów, Pol. (lōō-bär'tòf)	155	51.27N	22.37E
Lubawa, Pol. (lōō-bä'vä)	155	53.31N	19.47E
Lübben, Ger. (lüb'ĕn)	154	51.56N	13.53E
Lubbock, Tx., U.S.	97	33.35N	101.50E
Lubec, Me., U.S. (lū'bĕk)	92	44.49N	67.01W
Lübeck, Ger. (lü'bĕk)	142	53.53N	10.42E
Lübecker Bucht, b., Ger. (lü'bĕ-kĕr bōōKt)	146	54.10N	11.20E
Lubilash, r., Zaire (lōō-bē-lȧsh')	212	7.35S	23.55E
Lubin, Pol. (lyò'bĭn)	154	51.24N	16.14E
Lublin, Pol. (lyò'blēn')	142	51.14N	22.33E
Lubny, Ukr. (lòb'nē)	167	50.01N	33.02E
Lubuagan, Phil. (lō-bwä-gä'n)	197a	17.24N	121.11E
Lubudi, Zaire	217	9.57S	25.58E
Lubudi, r., Zaire (lō-bō'dē)	212	10.00S	24.30E
Lubumbashi, Zaire	212	11.40S	27.28E
Lucano, Ang.	216	11.16S	21.38E
Lucca, Italy (lōōk'kä)	148	43.51N	10.29E
Lucea, Jam.	122	18.25N	78.10W
Luce Bay, b., Scot., U.K. (lūs)	150	54.45N	4.45W
Lucena, Phil. (lōō-sā'nä)	197a	13.55N	121.36E
Lucena, Spain (lōō-thā'nä)	148	37.25N	4.28W
Lucena del Cid, Spain	159	40.08N	0.18W
Lučenec, Slvk. (lōō'châ-nyĕts)	147	48.19N	19.41E
Lucera, Italy (lōō-châ'rä)	160	41.31N	15.22E
Luchi, China	193	28.18N	110.10E
Luchou, Tai.	241d	25.05N	121.28E
Lucin, Ut., U.S. (lů-sēn')	105	41.23N	113.59W
Lucipara, Kepulauan, is., Indon.	197	5.45S	128.15E
Luckenwalde, Ger.	154	52.05N	13.10E
Lucknow, India (lŭk'nou)	183	26.54N	80.58E
Lucky Peak Lake, res., Id., U.S.	104	43.33N	116.00W
Luçon, Fr. (lü-sôN')	156	46.27N	1.12W
Lucrecia, Cabo, c., Cuba	123	21.05N	75.30W
Luda Kamchiya, r., Bul.	161	42.46N	27.13E
Luddesdown, Eng., U.K.	235	51.22N	0.24E
Lüdenscheid, Ger. (lü'dĕn-shīt)	157c	51.13N	7.38E
Lüderitz, Nmb. (lü'dēr-ĭts) (lü'dĕ-rĭts)	212	26.35S	15.15E
Lüderitz Bucht, b., Nmb.	212	26.35S	14.30E
Ludhiāna, India	183	31.00N	75.52E
Lüdinghausen, Ger.	157c	51.46N	7.27E
Ludington, Mi., U.S. (lŭd'ĭng-tŭn)	98	44.00N	86.25W
Ludlow, Eng., U.K. (lŭd'lō)	144a	52.22N	2.43W
Ludlow, Ky., U.S.	101f	39.05N	84.33W
Ludvika, Swe. (loodh-vē'kȧ)	152	60.10N	15.09E
Ludwigsburg, Ger.	154	48.53N	9.14E
Ludwigsfelde, Ger.	145b	52.18N	13.16E
Ludwigshafen, Ger.	154	49.29N	8.26E
Ludwigslust, Ger.	154	53.18N	11.31E
Ludza, Lat. (lōōd'zȧ)	153	56.33N	27.45E
Luebo, Zaire (lōō-ā'bō)	212	5.15S	21.22E
Luena, Ang.	212	11.45S	19.55E
Luena, Zaire	217	9.27S	25.47E
Lufira, r., Zaire (lōō-fē'rȧ)	212	9.32S	27.15E
Lufkin, Tx., U.S. (lŭf'kĭn)	113	31.21N	94.43W
Luga, Russia (lōō'gȧ)	166	58.43N	29.52E
Luga, r., Russia	162	59.00N	29.25E
Lugano, Switz. (lōō-gä'nō)	154	46.01N	8.52E
Lugarno, Austl.	243a	33.59S	151.03E
Lugenda, r., Moz.	213	12.05S	38.15E
Lugo, Italy (lōō'gô)	160	44.28N	11.57E
Lugo, Spain (lōō'gō)	148	43.01N	7.32W
Lugoj, Rom.	149	45.51N	21.56E
Lugouqiao, China	240b	39.51N	116.13E
Luhans'k, Ukr.	164	48.34N	39.18E
Luhans'k, prov., Ukr.	163	49.30N	38.35E
Luhe, China (lōō-hŭ)	190	32.22N	118.50E
Luiana, Ang.	216	17.23S	23.03E
Luilaka, r., Zaire (lōō-ē-lä'kȧ)	212	2.18S	21.15E
Luis Moya, Mex. (lōōē's-mô-yä)	118	22.26N	102.14W
Luján, Arg. (lōō'hän')	129c	34.36S	59.07W
Luján, r., Arg.	129c	34.33S	58.59W
Lujia, China (lōō-jyä)	190	31.17N	120.54W
Lukanga Swamp, sw., Zam. (lōō-käŋ'gȧ)	212	14.30S	27.25E
Lukenie, r., Zaire (lōō-kā'ynȧ)	212	3.10S	19.05E
Lukolela, Zaire	212	1.03S	17.01E
Lukovit, Bul. (lōō'kō-vēt')	161	43.13N	24.07E
Łuków, Pol. (wò'kòf)	155	51.57N	22.25E
Lukuga, r., Zaire (lōō-kōō'gȧ)	212	5.50S	27.35E
Lüleburgaz, Tur. (lü'lē-bòr-gäs')	161	41.25N	27.23E
Luling, Tx., U.S. (lū'lĭng)	113	29.41N	97.38W

ăt; finȧl; rāte; senȧte; ärm; ȧsk; sofȧ; fâre; ch-choose; dh-as th in other; bē; ēvent; bĕt; recĕnt; cratẽr; g-gō; gh-guttural g; bĭt; ĭ-short neutral; rīde; K-guttural k as ch in German ich;

PRONOUNCING INDEX

Lulong–Magiscatzin 313

PLACE (Pronunciation)	PAGE	Lat. °′	Long. °′
Lulong, China (lo͞o-lôŋ)	189	39.54N	118.53E
Lulonga, r., Zaire	216	1.00N	18.37E
Luluabourg *see* Kananga, Zaire	212	6.14S	22.17E
Lulu Island, i., Can.	106d	49.09N	123.05W
Lulu Island, i., Ak., U.S.	84	55.28N	133.30W
Lumajangdong Co, l., China	186	34.00N	81.47E
Lumber, r., N.C., U.S. (lŭm′bẽr)	115	34.45N	79.10W
Lumberton, Ms., U.S. (lŭm′bẽr-tŭn)	114	31.00N	89.25W
Lumberton, N.C., U.S.	115	34.47N	79.00W
Luminárias, Braz. (lo͞o-mē-nä′ryäs)	129a	21.32S	44.53W
Lummi, i., Wa., U.S.	106d	48.42N	122.43W
Lummi Bay, b., Wa., U.S. (lŭm′ĭ)	106d	48.47N	122.44W
Lummi Island, Wa., U.S.	106d	48.44N	122.42W
Lumwana, Zam.	217	11.50S	25.10E
Lün, Mong.	188	47.58N	104.52E
Luna, Phil. (lo͞o′nȧ)	197a	16.51N	120.22E
Lund, Swe. (lŭnd)	146	55.42N	13.10E
Lundy, i., Eng., U.K. (lŭn′dē)	150	51.12N	4.50W
Lüneburg, Ger. (lü′nē-bòrgh)	154	53.16N	10.25E
Lunel, Fr. (lü-nĕl′)	156	43.41N	4.07E
Lünen, Ger. (lü′nĕn)	157c	51.36N	7.30E
Lunenburg, Can. (lo͞o′nĕn-bûrg)	85	44.23N	64.19W
Lunenburg, Ma., U.S.	93a	42.36N	71.44W
Lunéville, Fr. (lü-nå-vel′)	157	48.37N	6.29E
Lunga, Ang.	216	14.42S	18.32E
Lungué-Bungo, r., Afr.	212	13.00S	20.30E
Lunsar, S.L.	214	8.41N	12.32W
Lunt, Eng., U.K.	237a	53.31N	2.59W
Luodian, China (lwô-diĕn)	190	31.25N	121.20E
Luoding, China (lwô-dĭŋ)	193	23.42N	111.35E
Luohe, China (lwô-hŭ)	190	33.35N	114.02E
Luoyang, China (lwô-yäŋ)	189	34.45N	112.32E
Luozhen, China (lwô-jŭn)	190	37.45N	118.29E
Luque, Para. (loo′kā)	132	25.18S	57.17W
Luray, Va., U.S. (lū-rā′)	99	38.40N	78.25W
Lurgan, N. Ire., U.K. (lûr′găn)	146	54.27N	6.28W
Lurigancho, Peru	233c	12.02S	77.01W
Lúrio, Moz. (lo͞o′rē-ô)	213	13.17S	40.29E
Lúrio, Moz.	213	14.00S	38.45E
Lurnea, Austl.	243a	33.56S	150.54E
Lusaka, Zaire	217	7.10S	29.27E
Lusaka, Zam. (lò-sä′kȧ)	212	15.25S	28.17E
Lusambo, Zaire (lo͞o-säm′bō)	212	4.58S	23.27E
Lusanga, Zaire	212	5.13S	18.43E
Lusangi, Zaire	217	4.37S	27.08E
Lushan, China	192	33.45N	113.00E
Lushiko, r., Afr.	216	6.35S	19.45E
Lushoto, Tan. (lo͞o-shō′tō)	213	4.47S	38.17E
Lüshun, China (lü-shūn)	189	38.49N	121.15E
Lusikisiki, S. Afr. (lo͞o-sē-kē-sē′kē)	213c	31.22S	29.37E
Lusk, Wy., U.S. (lŭsk)	102	42.46N	104.27W
Lūt, Dasht-e, des., Iran (dă′sht-ē-lo͞ot)	182	31.47N	58.38E
Lutcher, La., U.S. (lŭch′ẽr)	113	30.03N	90.43W
Lütgendortmund, neigh., Ger.	236	51.30N	7.21E
Luton, Eng., U.K. (lū′tŭn)	150	51.55N	0.28W
Luts′k, Ukr.	167	50.45N	25.20E
Lüttringhausen, neigh., Ger.	236	51.13N	7.14E
Luuq, Som.	218a	3.38N	42.35E
Luverne, Al., U.S. (lū-vûn′)	114	31.42N	86.15W
Luverne, Mn., U.S.	102	43.40N	96.13W
Luwingu, Zam.	217	10.15S	29.55E
Luxapallila Creek, r., U.S. (lŭk-sȧ-pôl′ĭ-lȧ)	114	33.36N	88.08W
Luxembourg, Lux.	142	49.38N	6.30E
Luxembourg, nation, Eur.	142	49.30N	6.22E
Luxeuil-les-Baines, Fr.	157	47.49N	6.19E
Luxomni, Ga., U.S. (lŭx′ôm-nī)	100c	33.54N	84.07W
Luxor *see* Al Uqṣur, Egypt	211	25.38N	32.59E
Lu Xun Museum, bldg., China	241a	31.16N	121.28E
Luya Shan, mtn., China	192	38.50N	111.40E
Luyi, China (lo͞o-yē)	190	33.52N	115.32E
Luyuan, China	240b	39.54N	116.27E
Luz, Braz.	234c	22.48S	43.05W
Luz, neigh., Port.	238d	38.46N	9.10W
Luzern, Switz. (lò-tsĕrn)	147	47.03N	8.18E
Luzhou, China (lo͞o-jō)	188	28.58N	105.25E
Luziânia, Braz. (lo͞o-zyȧ′nēȧ)	131	16.17S	47.44W
Lužniki, neigh., Russia	239b	55.43N	37.33E
Luzon, i., Phil. (lo͞o-zŏn′)	196	17.10N	119.45E
Luzon Strait, strt., Asia	193	20.40N	121.00E
L′viv, Ukr.	164	49.50N	24.00E
L′vov *see* L′viv, Ukr.	164	49.50N	24.00E
Lyalta, Can.	83e	51.07N	113.36W
Lyalya, r., Russia (lyä′lyȧ)	172a	58.58N	60.17E
Lyaskovets, Bul.	161	43.07N	25.41E
Lydenburg, S. Afr. (lī′dĕn-bûrg)	212	25.06S	30.21E
Lydiate, Eng., U.K.	237a	53.32N	2.57W
Lye Green, Eng., U.K.	235	51.43N	0.35W
Lyell, Mount, mtn., Ca., U.S. (lī′ĕl)	108	37.44N	119.22W
Lykens, Pa., U.S. (lī′kĕnz)	99	40.35N	76.45W
Lyna, r., Eur. (lĭn′ȧ)	155	53.56N	20.30E
Lynbrook, N.Y., U.S.	228	40.39N	73.41W
Lynch, Ky., U.S. (lĭnch)	115	36.56N	82.55W
Lynchburg, Va., U.S. (lĭnch′bûrg)	97	37.23N	79.08W
Lynch Cove, Wa., U.S. (lĭnch)	106a	47.26N	122.54W
Lynden, Can. (lĭn′dĕn)	83d	43.14N	80.08W
Lynden, Wa., U.S.	106d	48.56N	122.27W
Lyndhurst, Austl.	201a	38.03S	145.14E
Lyndhurst, N.J., U.S.	228	40.49N	74.07W
Lyndhurst, Oh., U.S.	229a	41.31N	81.30W
Lyndon, Ky., U.S. (lĭn′dŭn)	101h	38.15N	85.36W
Lyndonville, Vt., U.S. (lĭn′dŭn-vĭl)	99	44.35N	72.00W
Lyne, Eng., U.K.	235	51.23N	0.33W
Lynn, Ma., U.S. (lĭn)	97	42.28N	70.57W
Lynnewood Gardens, Pa., U.S.	229b	40.04N	75.09W

PLACE (Pronunciation)	PAGE	Lat. °′	Long. °′
Lynnfield, Ma., U.S.	227a	42.32N	71.03W
Lynn Lake, Can. (lăk)	84	56.51N	101.05W
Lynwood, Ca., U.S. (lĭn′wòd)	107a	33.56N	118.13W
Lyon, Fr. (lē-ôN′)	142	45.44N	4.52E
Lyons, Ga., U.S. (lī′ŭnz)	115	32.08N	82.19W
Lyons, Il., U.S.	231a	41.49N	87.50W
Lyons, Ks., U.S.	110	38.20N	98.11W
Lyons, Ne., U.S.	102	41.57N	96.28W
Lyons, N.J., U.S.	100a	40.41N	74.33W
Lyons, N.Y., U.S.	99	43.05N	77.00W
Lyptsi, Ukr.	163	50.11N	36.25E
Lysefjorden, fj., Nor.	152	58.59N	6.35E
Lysekil, Swe. (lü′sĕ-kĕl)	152	58.17N	11.22E
Lysterfield, Austl.	243b	37.56S	145.18E
Lys′va, Russia (lĭs′vȧ)	166	58.07N	57.47E
Lytham, Eng., U.K. (lĭth′ăm)	144a	53.44N	2.58W
Lytkarino, Russia	172b	55.35N	37.55E
Lyttelton, S. Afr. (lĭt′l′ton)	213b	25.51S	28.13E
Lyuban′, Russia (lyo͞o′bȧn)	162	59.21N	31.15E
Lyubar, Ukr. (lyo͞o′bär)	163	49.56N	27.44E
Lyubertsy, Russia (lyo͞o′bĕr-tsē)	162	55.40N	37.55E
Lyubim, Russia (lyo͞o-bēm′)	162	58.24N	40.39E
Lyublino, Russia (lyo͞ob′lĭ-nô)	172b	55.41N	37.45E
Lyudinovo, Russia (lū-dē′novō)	162	53.52N	34.28E

M

PLACE (Pronunciation)	PAGE	Lat. °′	Long. °′
Ma′ān, Jord. (mä-än′)	182	30.12N	35.45E
Maartensdijk, Neth.	145a	52.09N	5.10E
Maas (Meuse), r., Eur.	151	51.50N	5.40E
Maastricht, Neth. (mäs′trĭkt)	151	50.51N	5.35E
Mabaia, Ang.	216	7.13S	14.03E
Mabana, Wa., U.S. (mä-bä-nä)	106a	48.06N	122.25W
Mabank, Tx., U.S. (mā′bănk)	113	32.21N	96.05W
Mabeskraal, S. Afr.	218d	25.12S	26.47E
Mableton, Ga., U.S. (mā′b′l-tŭn)	100c	33.49N	84.34W
Mabrouk, Mali	210	19.27N	1.16W
Mabula, S. Afr. (mä′bo͞o-la)	218d	24.49S	27.59E
Macalelon, Phil. (mä-kä-lä-lōn′)	197a	13.46N	122.09E
Macao, dep., Asia	189	22.00N	113.00E
Macau, Braz. (mä-kà′ò)	131	5.12S	36.34W
Macaya, Pico de, mtn., Haiti	123	18.25N	74.00W
Macclesfield, Eng., U.K. (măk″lz-fēld)	144a	53.15N	2.07W
Macclesfield Canal, can., Eng., U.K. (măk″lz-fēld)	144a	53.14N	2.07W
Macdona, Tx., U.S. (măk-dō′nȧ)	107d	29.20N	98.42W
Macdonald, l., Austl. (măk-dŏn′ăld)	202	23.40S	127.40E
Macdonnell Ranges, mts., Austl. (măk-dŏn′ĕl)	202	23.40S	131.30E
MacDowell Lake, l., Can. (măk-dou ĕl)	89	52.15N	92.45W
Macdui, Ben, mtn., Scot., U.K. (bĕn măk-do͞o′ē)	146	57.06N	3.45W
Macedonia, Oh., U.S. (măs-ē-dō′nĭ-ȧ)	101d	41.19N	81.30E
Macedonia, hist. reg., Eur. (măs-ē-dō′nĭ-ȧ)	149	41.05N	22.15E
Macedonia, nation, Eur.	161	41.50N	22.00E
Maceió, Braz.	131	9.40S	35.43W
Macerata, Italy (mä-chā-rä′tä)	160	43.18N	13.28E
Macfarlane, Lake, l., Austl. (măc′fär-lān)	204	32.10S	137.00E
Machache, mtn., Leso.	213c	29.22S	27.53E
Machado, Braz. (mä-shȧ-dô)	129a	21.42S	45.55W
Machakos, Kenya	217	1.31S	37.16E
Machala, Ec. (mä-chȧ′lä)	130	3.18S	78.54W
Machens, Mo., U.S. (măk′ĕns)	107e	38.54N	90.20W
Machias, Me., U.S. (mȧ-chī′ȧs)	92	44.22N	67.29W
Machida, Japan (mä-chē′dä)	195a	35.32N	139.28E
Machilīpatnam, India	183	16.22N	81.10E
Machu Picchu, Peru (mä′chò-pē′k-chò)	130	13.07S	72.34W
Măcin, Rom. (mä-chēn′)	163	45.15N	28.09E
Macina, reg., Mali	214	14.50N	4.40W
Mackay, Austl. (mȧ-kī′)	203	21.15S	149.08E
Mackay, Id., U.S. (măk-kā′)	105	43.55N	113.38W
Mackay, l., Austl. (mă-kī′)	202	22.30S	127.45E
MacKay, l., Can. (măk-kā′)	84	64.10N	112.35W
Mackenzie, r., Can.	84	63.38N	124.23W
Mackenzie Bay, b., Can.	95	69.20N	137.10W
Mackenzie Mountains, mts., Can. (mȧ-kĕn′zĭ)	84	63.41N	129.27W
Mackinaw, r., Il., U.S.	98	40.35N	89.25W
Mackinaw City, Mi., U.S. (măk′ĭ-nô)	98	45.45N	84.45W
Mackinnon Road, Kenya	217	3.44S	39.03E
Macleantown, S. Afr. (măk-lăn′toun)	213c	32.48S	27.48E
Maclear, S. Afr. (mȧ-klēr′)	212	31.06S	28.23E
Macleod, Austl.	243b	37.43S	145.04E
Macomb, Il., U.S. (mȧ-ko͞om′)	111	40.27N	90.40W
Mâcon, Fr. (mä-kôN)	147	46.19N	4.51E
Macon, Ga., U.S. (mā′kŏn)	97	32.49N	83.39W
Macon, Ms., U.S.	114	32.07N	88.31W
Macon, Mo., U.S.	111	39.42N	92.29W
Macquarie, r., Austl.	203	31.43S	148.04E
Macquarie Fields, Austl.	243a	33.59S	150.53E
Macquarie Islands, is., Austl. (mȧ-kwŏr′ē)	3	54.36S	158.45E
Macquarie University, educ., Austl.	243a	33.46S	151.06E
Macritchie Reservoir, res., Sing.	240c	1.21N	103.50E
Macuelizo, Hond. (mä-kwē-lē′zô)	120	15.22N	88.32W

PLACE (Pronunciation)	PAGE	Lat. °′	Long. °′
Macuto, Ven.	234a	10.37N	66.53W
Mad, r., Ca., U.S. (măd)	104	40.38N	123.37W
Madagascar, nation, Afr. (măd-ȧ-găs′kȧr)	213	18.05S	43.12E
Madame, i., Can. (mȧ-dȧm′)	93	45.33N	61.02W
Madanapalle, India	187	13.06N	78.09E
Madang, Pap. N. Gui. (mä-däng′)	197	5.15S	145.45E
Madaoua, Niger (mȧ-dou′ȧ)	210	14.04N	6.03E
Madawaska, r., Can. (măd-ȧ-wôs′kȧ)	91	45.20N	77.25W
Madeira, r., S.A.	130	6.48S	62.43W
Madeira, Arquipélago da, is., Port.	209	33.26N	16.44W
Madeira, Ilha da, i., Port. (mä-dā′rä)	210	32.41N	16.15W
Madelia, Mn., U.S. (mȧ-dē′lĭ-ȧ)	103	44.03N	94.23W
Madeline, i., Wi., U.S. (măd′ĕ-lĭn)	103	46.47N	91.30W
Madera, Ca., U.S. (mȧ-dā′rȧ)	108	36.57N	120.04W
Madera, vol., Nic.	120	11.27N	85.30W
Madgaon, India	187	15.09N	73.58E
Madhya Pradesh, state, India (mŭd′vŭ prŭ-dăsh′)	183	22.04N	77.48E
Madill, Ok., U.S. (mȧ-dĭl′)	111	34.04N	96.45W
Madīnat ash Sha′b, Yemen	182	12.45N	44.00E
Madingo, Congo	216	4.07S	11.22E
Madingou, Congo	216	4.09S	13.34E
Madison, Fl., U.S. (măd′ĭ-sŭn)	114	30.28N	83.25W
Madison, Ga., U.S.	114	33.34N	83.29W
Madison, Il., U.S.	107e	38.40N	90.09W
Madison, In., U.S.	98	38.45N	85.25W
Madison, Ks., U.S.	111	38.08N	96.07W
Madison, Me., U.S.	92	44.47N	69.52W
Madison, Mn., U.S.	102	44.59N	96.13W
Madison, Ne., U.S.	102	41.49N	97.27W
Madison, N.J., U.S.	100a	40.46N	74.25W
Madison, N.C., U.S.	115	36.22N	79.59W
Madison, S.D., U.S.	102	44.01N	97.08W
Madison, Wi., U.S.	97	43.05N	89.23W
Madison Heights, Mi., U.S.	230c	42.30N	83.06W
Madison Res, Mt., U.S.	105	45.25N	111.28W
Madisonville, Ky., U.S. (măd′ĭ-sŭn-vĭl)	98	37.20N	87.30W
Madisonville, La., U.S.	113	30.22N	90.10W
Madisonville, Tx., U.S.	113	30.57N	95.55W
Madjori, Burkina	214	11.26N	1.15E
Mado Gashi, Kenya	217	0.44N	39.10E
Madona, Lat. (mȧ′dō′nȧ)	153	56.50N	26.14E
Madrakah, Ra′s al, c., Oman	182	18.53N	57.48E
Madras, India (mȧ-drȧs′) (mŭ-drŭs′)	183	13.08N	80.15E
Madre, Laguna, l., Mex. (lä-go͞o′nä mä′drå)	113	25.08N	97.41W
Madre, Sierra, mts., N.A. (sē-ĕ′r-rä-mȧ′drē)	119	15.55N	92.40W
Madre, Sierra, mts., Phil.	197a	16.40N	122.10E
Madre de Dios, Archipiélago, is., Chile (mȧ′drå dä dē-ōs′)	132	50.40S	76.30W
Madre de Dios, Río, r., S.A. (rē′ō-mä′drå dä dē-ōs′)	130	12.07S	68.02W
Madre del Sur, Sierra, mts., Mex. (sē-ĕ′r-rä-mä′drå dĕlsōor′)	116	17.35N	100.35W
Madre Occidental, Sierra, mts., Mex.	116	29.30N	107.30W
Madre Oriental, Sierra, mts., Mex.	116	25.30N	100.45W
Madrid, Spain (mȧ-drē′d)	142	40.26N	3.42W
Madrid, Ia., U.S. (măd′rĭd)	103	41.51N	93.48W
Madridejos, Spain (mä-dhrē-dhā′hōs)	158	39.29N	3.32W
Madrillon, Va., U.S.	229d	38.55N	77.14W
Madura, i., Indon. (mȧ-do͞o′rä)	196	6.45S	113.30E
Madurai, India (mä-do͞o′rä)	183	9.57N	78.04E
Madureira, neigh., Braz.	234c	22.53S	43.21W
Madureira, Serra do, mtn., Braz. (sĕ′r-rä-dô-mä-do͞o-rā′rȧ)	132b	22.49S	43.30W
Maebashi, Japan (mä-ĕ-bä′shē)	189	36.26N	139.04E
Maeno, neigh., Japan	242a	35.46N	139.42E
Maestra, Sierra, mts., Cuba (sē-ĕ′r-rȧ-mä-ās′trä)	117	20.05N	77.05W
Maewo, i., Vanuatu	203	15.17S	168.16E
Mafeking, S. Afr. (mäf′ê′kĭng)	212	25.46S	24.45E
Mafra, Braz. (mä′frä)	132	26.21N	49.59W
Mafra, Port. (mäf′rȧ)	159b	38.56N	9.20W
Magadan, Russia (mä-gȧ-dän′)	165	59.39N	150.43E
Magadan Oblast, Russia	171	65.00N	160.00E
Magadi, Kenya	217	1.54S	36.17E
Magalhães Bastos, neigh., Braz.	234c	22.53S	43.23W
Magalies, r., S. Afr. (mä-gä′lyĕs)	213b	25.51S	27.42E
Magaliesberg, mts., S. Afr.	213b	25.45S	27.43E
Magaliesburg, S. Afr.	218d	26.01S	27.32E
Magallanes, Estrecho de, strt., S.A.	132	52.30S	68.45W
Magat, r., Phil. (mä-gät′)	197a	16.45N	121.16E
Magdalena, Arg. (mäg-dä-lä′nä)	129c	35.05S	57.32W
Magdalena, Bol.	130	13.17S	63.57W
Magdalena, Mex.	96	30.34N	110.50W
Magdalena, N.M., U.S.	109	34.10N	107.45W
Magdalena, i., Chile	132	44.45S	73.15W
Magdalena, Bahía, b., Mex. (bä-ē′ä-mäg-dä-lä′nä)	116	24.30N	114.00W
Magdalena, Río, r., Col.	130	7.45N	74.04W
Magdalena del Mar, Peru	233c	12.06S	77.05W
Magdalen Laver, Eng., U.K.	235	51.45N	0.11E
Magdeburg, Ger. (mäg′dĕ-bòrgh)	142	52.07N	11.39E
Magellan, Strait of *see* Magallanes, Estrecho de, strt., S.A.	132	52.30S	68.45W
Magenta, Italy (mȧ-jĕn′tȧ)	160	45.26N	8.53E
Magerøya, i., Nor.	146	71.10N	24.11E
Maggiore, Lago, l., Italy	148	46.03N	8.25E
Maghāghah, Egypt	218b	28.38N	30.50W
Maghniyya, Alg.	148	34.52N	1.40W
Maghull, Eng., U.K.	237a	53.32N	2.57W
Maginu, Japan	242a	35.35N	139.36E
Magiscatzin, Mex. (mä-kēs-kät-zēn′)	118	22.48N	98.42W

PLACE (Pronunciation)	PAGE	Lat. °′	Long. °′
Maglaj, Bos. (má'glä-ê)	161	44.34N	18.12E
Magliana, neigh., Italy	239c	41.50N	12.25E
Maglie, Italy (mäl'yā)	161	40.06N	18.20E
Magna, Ut., U.S. (măg'nȧ)	107b	40.43N	112.06W
Magnitogorsk, Russia (mág-nyĕ'tô-gôrsk)	164	53.26N	59.05E
Magnolia, Ar., U.S. (măg-nō'lĭ-ȧ)	111	33.16N	93.13W
Magnolia, Ms., U.S.	114	31.08N	90.27W
Magnolia, N.J., U.S.	229b	39.51N	75.02W
Magny-en-Vexin, Fr. (mä-nyē'ĕN-vĕ-sȧN')	157b	49.09N	1.45E
Magny-les-Hameaux, Fr.	237c	48.44N	2.04E
Magog, Can. (mȧ-gŏg')	91	45.15N	72.10W
Magome, neigh., Japan	242a	35.35N	139.43E
Magpie, r., Can.	90	48.13N	84.50W
Magpie, r., Can.	92	50.40N	64.30W
Magpie, Lac, l., Can.	92	50.55N	64.39W
Magrath, Can.	84	49.25N	112.52W
Maguanying, China	240b	39.52N	116.17E
Magude, Moz. (mä-gōō'dȧ)	212	24.58S	32.39E
Magwe, Myanmar (mŭg-wā')	183	20.19N	94.57E
Mahābād, Iran	185	36.55N	45.50E
Mahahi Port, Zaire (mä-hä'gē)	211	2.14N	31.12E
Mahajanga, Madag.	213	15.12S	46.26E
Mahakam, r., Indon.	196	0.30S	116.15E
Mahali Mountains, mts., Tan.	217	6.20S	30.00E
Mahaly, Madag. (mȧ-hȧl-ē')	213	24.09S	46.20E
Mahanoro, Madag. (mȧ-hȧ-nô'rō)	213	19.57S	48.47E
Mahanoy City, Pa., U.S. (mä-hȧ-noi')	99	40.50N	76.10W
Mahaṭṭat al-Hilmīyah, neigh., Egypt	244a	30.07N	31.19E
Mahaṭṭat al Qaṭrānah, Jord.	181a	31.15N	36.04E
Mahaṭṭat 'Aqabat al Ḥijāzīyah, Jord.	181a	29.45N	35.55E
Mahaṭṭat ar Ramlah, Jord.	181a	29.31N	35.57E
Mahaṭṭat Jurf ad Darāwīsh, Jord.	181a	30.41N	35.51E
Mahd adh-Dhahab, Sau. Ar.	185	23.30N	40.52E
Mahe, India (mä-ā')	183	11.42N	75.39E
Mahenge, Tan. (mä-hĕŋ'gȧ)	212	7.38S	36.16E
Mahi, r., India	186	23.16N	73.20E
Māhīm, neigh., India	240e	19.03N	72.49E
Māhīm Bay, b., India	187b	19.03N	72.45E
Mahlabatini, S. Afr. (mä'lȧ-bȧ-tē'nê)	213c	28.15S	31.29E
Mahlow, Ger. (mä'lōv)	145b	52.23N	13.24E
Mahlsdorf, neigh., Ger.	238a	52.31N	13.37E
Mahlsdorf-Süd, neigh., Ger.	238a	52.29N	13.36E
Mahnomen, Mn., U.S. (mô-nō'mĕn)	102	47.18N	95.58W
Mahón, Spain (mä-ōn')	148	39.52N	4.15E
Mahone Bay, Can. (mȧ-hōn')	92	44.27N	64.23W
Mahone Bay, b., Can.	92	44.30N	64.15W
Mahopac, Lake, l., N.Y., U.S. (mā-hō'păk)	100a	41.24N	73.45W
Mahrauli, neigh., India	240d	28.31N	77.11E
Māhul, neigh., India	240e	19.01N	72.53E
Mahwah, N.J., U.S. (mȧ-wä')	100a	41.05N	74.09W
Maidenhead, Eng., U.K. (mād'ĕn-hĕd)	144b	51.30N	0.44W
Maidstone, Austl.	243b	37.47S	144.52E
Maidstone, Eng., U.K.	151	51.17N	0.32E
Maiduguri, Nig. (mä'ē-dȧ-gōō'rê)	211	11.51N	13.10E
Maigualida, Sierra, mts., Ven. (sē-ĕ'r-rȧ-mī-gwä'lē-dĕ)	130	6.30N	65.50W
Maijdi, Bngl.	186	22.59N	91.08E
Maikop *see* Maykop, Russia	164	44.35N	40.07E
Main, r., Ger. (mīn)	154	49.49N	9.20E
Main Barrier Range, mts., Austl. (băr''ēr)	203	31.25S	141.40E
Mai-Ndombe, Lac, l., Zaire	212	2.16S	19.00E
Maine, state, U.S. (mān)	97	45.25N	69.50W
Mainland, i., Scot., U.K. (mān-lănd)	146	60.19N	2.40W
Maintenon, Fr. (mäN-tĕ-nôN')	157b	48.35N	1.35E
Maintirano, Madag. (mä'ēn-tē-rä'nō)	213	18.05S	44.08E
Mainz, Ger. (mīnts)	142	49.59N	8.16E
Maio, i., C.V. (mä'yo)	210b	15.15N	22.50W
Maipo, S.A.	132	34.08S	69.51W
Maipo, r., Chile (mī'pō)	129b	33.45S	71.08W
Maiquetía, Ven. (mī-kĕ-tē'ä)	130	10.37N	66.56W
Maison-Rouge, Fr. (mā-zôN-rōōzh')	157b	48.34N	3.09E
Maisons-Alfort, Fr.	237c	48.48N	2.26E
Maisons-Laffitte, Fr.	157b	48.57N	2.09E
Maitani, Japan	242b	34.49N	135.22E
Maitland, Austl. (māt'lănd)	203	32.45S	151.40E
Maizuru, Japan (mä-ĭ'zōō-rōō)	195	35.26N	135.15E
Majene, Indon.	196	3.34S	119.00E
Maji, Eth.	211	6.14N	35.34E
Majorca *see* Mallorca, i., Spain	142	39.18N	2.22E
Makah Indian Reservation, I.R., Wa., U.S.	104	48.17N	124.52W
Makala, Zaire	244c	4.25S	15.15E
Makanya, Tan. (mä-kän'yä)	213	4.15S	37.49E
Makanza, Zaire	211	1.42N	19.08E
Makarakomburu, Mount, mtn., Sol.Is.	198e	9.43S	160.02E
Makarska, Cro. (mä'kär-skȧ)	161	43.17N	17.05E
Makar'yev, Russia	166	57.50N	43.48E
Makasar *see* Ujung Pandang, Indon.	196	5.08S	119.28E
Makasar, Selat (Makassar Strait), strt., Indon.	196	2.00S	118.07E
Makati, Phil.	241g	14.34N	121.01E
Makaw, Zaire	216	3.29S	18.19E
Make, i., Japan (mä'kȧ)	195	30.43N	130.49E
Makeni, S.L.	210	8.53N	12.03W
Makgadikgadi Pans, pl., Bots.	212	20.38S	21.31E
Makhachkala, Russia (mäк'äch-kä'lä)	167	43.00N	47.40E
Makhaleng, r., Leso.	213c	29.53S	27.33E
Makindu, Kenya	217	2.17S	37.49E
M'akino, Russia	239b	55.48N	37.22E
Makiyivka, Ukr.	167	48.03N	38.00E
Makkah *see* Mecca, Sau. Ar.	182	21.27N	39.45E
Makkovik, Can.	85	55.01N	59.10W
Makokou, Gabon (mȧ-kô-kōō')	210	0.34N	12.52E
Maków Mazowiecki, Pol. (mä'kōov mä-zō-vyĕts'kē)	155	52.51N	21.07E
Makuhari, Japan (mä-kōō-hä'rē)	195a	35.39N	140.04E
Makurazaki, Japan (mä'kó-rä-zä'kê)	195	31.16N	130.18E
Makurdi, Nig.	210	7.45N	8.32E
Makushin, Ak., U.S. (mȧ-kö'shĭn)	95	53.57N	166.28W
Makushino, Russia (mȧ-kö-shēn'ô)	164	55.03N	67.43E
Mala, Punta, c., Pan. (pōō'n-tä-mä'lä)	121	7.32N	79.44W
Malabar Coast, cst., India (măl'ȧ-bär)	187	11.19N	75.33E
Malabar Point, c., India	187b	18.57N	72.47E
Malabo, Eq. Gui.	210	3.45N	8.47E
Malabon, Phil.	197a	14.39N	120.57E
Malacca, Strait of, strt., Asia (mȧ-lăk'ȧ)	196	4.15N	99.44E
Malad City, Id., U.S. (mȧ-lăd')	105	42.11N	112.15W
Málaga, Col. (má'lä-gȧ)	130	6.41N	72.46W
Málaga, Spain	142	36.45N	4.25W
Malagón, Spain (mä-lä-gōn')	158	39.12N	3.52W
Malaita, i., Sol.Is. (mȧ-lä'ē-tȧ)	203	8.38S	161.15E
Malakāl, Sudan (mȧ-lȧ-käl')	211	9.46N	31.54E
Malakhovka, Russia (mȧ-lăk'ôf-kȧ)	172b	55.38N	38.01E
Malakoff, Fr.	237c	48.49N	2.19E
Malakpur, neigh., India	240d	28.42N	77.12E
Malang, Indon.	196	8.06S	112.50E
Malanje, Ang. (mä-läŋ-gȧ)	212	9.32S	16.20E
Malanville, Benin	210	12.04N	3.09E
Mälaren, l., Swe.	146	59.38N	16.55E
Malartic, Can.	85	48.07N	78.11W
Malatya, Tur. (mȧ-lä'tyȧ)	182	38.30N	38.15E
Malawi, nation, Afr.	212	11.15S	33.45E
Malawi, Lake *see* Nyasa, Lake, l., Afr.	212	10.45S	34.30E
Malaya Vishera, Russia (vê-shä'rä)	164	58.51N	32.13E
Malay Peninsula, pen., Asia (mȧ-lā') (mā'lā)	196	6.00N	101.00E
Malaysia, nation, Asia (mȧ-lā'zhȧ)	196	4.10N	101.22E
Malbon, Austl. (măl'bŭn)	202	21.15S	140.30E
Malbork, Pol. (mäl'bōrk)	146	54.02N	19.04E
Malcabran, r., Port. (mäl-kä-brän')	159b	38.47N	8.46W
Malden, Ma., U.S. (môl'dĕn)	93a	42.26N	71.04W
Malden, Mo., U.S.	111	36.32N	89.56W
Malden, i., Kir.	2	4.20S	154.30W
Maldives, nation, Asia	180	4.30N	71.30E
Maldon, Eng., U.K. (môrl'dŏn)	144b	51.44N	0.39E
Maldonado, Ur. (mäl-dō-nä'dō)	132	34.54S	54.57W
Maldonado, Punta, c., Mex. (pōō'n-tä)	118	16.18N	98.34W
Maléa, Ákra, c., Grc.	149	36.31N	23.13E
Mālegaon, India	186	20.35N	74.30E
Malé Karpaty, mts., Slvk.	155	48.31N	17.15E
Malekula, i., Vanuatu (mä-lā-kōō'lä)	203	16.44S	167.45E
Malema, Moz.	217	14.57S	37.20E
Malheur, r., Or., U.S. (mȧ-lōōr')	104	43.45N	117.41W
Malheur Lake, l., Or., U.S. (mȧ-lōōr')	104	43.16N	118.37W
Mali, nation, Afr.	210	15.45N	0.15W
Malibu, Ca., U.S. (mă'lĭ-bōō)	107a	34.03N	118.38W
Malik, Wādī al, r., Sudan	211	16.48N	29.30E
Malimba, Monts, mts., Zaire	217	7.45S	29.15E
Malinalco, Mex. (mä-lē-näl'kō)	118	18.54N	99.31W
Malinaltepec, Mex. (mä-lē-näl-tȧ-pĕk')	118	17.01N	98.41W
Malindi, Kenya (mä-lēn'dē)	213	3.14S	40.04E
Malin Head, c., Ire.	146	55.23N	7.24W
Malino, Russia (mä'lĭ-nô)	172b	55.07N	38.12E
Malkara, Tur. (mäl'kȧ-rȧ)	161	40.51N	26.52E
Malko Tŭrnovo, Bul. (mäl'kō-t'r'nô-vȧ)	161	41.59N	27.28E
Mallaig, Scot., U.K.	150	56.59N	5.55W
Mallet Creek, Oh., U.S. (măl'ĕt)	101d	41.10N	81.55W
Mallorca, i., Spain	142	39.30N	3.00E
Mallorquinas, Spain	238e	41.28N	2.16E
Mallow, Ire. (măl'ō)	150	52.07N	9.04W
Malmédy, Bel. (mȧl-mā-dē')	151	50.25N	6.01E
Malmesbury, S. Afr. (mämz'bēr-ĭ)	212	33.30S	18.35E
Malmköping, Swe. (mälm'chû'pĭng)	152	59.09N	16.39E
Malmö, Swe.	142	55.36N	13.00E
Malmyzh, Russia (mȧl-mēzh')	165	49.58N	137.07E
Malmyzh, Russia	166	56.30N	50.48E
Malnoue, Fr.	237c	48.50N	2.36E
Maloarkhangelsk, Russia (mä'lô-ȧr-кäŋ'gĕlsk)	162	52.26N	36.29E
Malolos, Phil. (mä-lō'lōs)	197a	14.51N	120.49E
Malomal'sk, Russia (mȧ-lô-mälsk'')	172a	58.47N	59.55E
Malone, N.Y., U.S. (mȧ-lōn')	99	44.50N	74.20W
Malonga, Zaire	216	10.24S	23.10E
Maloti Mountains, mts., Leso.	213c	29.00S	28.29E
Maloyaroslavets, Russia (mä'lô-yä-rô-slä-vyĕts)	162	55.01N	36.25E
Malozemel'skaya Tundra, reg., Russia	166	67.30N	50.00E
Malpas, Eng., U.K. (mäl'pȧz)	144a	53.01N	2.46W
Malpelo, Isla de, i., Col. (mäl-pä'lō)	130	3.55N	81.30W
Malpeque Bay, b., Can. (môl-pĕk')	92	46.30N	63.47W
Malta, Mt., U.S. (môl'tȧ)	105	48.20N	107.50W
Malta, nation, Eur.	142	35.52N	13.30E
Maltahöhe, Nmb. (mäl'tä-hō'ē)	212	24.45S	16.45E
Maltrata, Mex. (mäl-trä'tä)	119	18.48N	97.16W
Maluku (Moluccas), is., Indon.	197	2.22S	128.25E
Maluku, Laut (Molucca Sea), sea, Indon.	197	0.15N	125.41E
Malūṭ, Sudan	211	10.30N	32.17E
Mālvan, India	187	16.08N	73.32E
Malvern, Austl.	243b	37.52S	145.02E
Malvern, Ar., U.S. (măl'vērn)	111	34.21N	92.47W
Malvern, neigh., S. Afr.	244b	26.12S	28.06E
Malverne, N.Y., U.S.	228	40.40N	73.40W
Malvern East, S. Afr.	244b	26.12S	28.08E
Malyn, Ukr.	163	50.44N	29.15E
Malynivka, Ukr.	163	49.50N	36.43E
Malyy Anyuy, r., Russia	171	67.52N	164.30E
Malyy Tamir, i., Russia	171	78.10N	107.30E
Mamantel, Mex. (mä-mȧn-tĕl')	119	18.36N	91.06W
Mamaroneck, N.Y., U.S. (măm'ȧ-rō-nĕk)	100a	40.57N	73.44W
Mambasa, Zaire	217	1.21N	29.03E
Mamburao, Phil. (mäm-bōō'rä-ō)	197a	13.14N	120.35E
Mamera, Ven.	234a	10.27N	66.59W
Mamfe, Cam. (mäm'fĕ)	210	5.46N	9.17E
Mamihara, Japan (mä'mê-hä-rä)	195	32.41N	131.12E
Mammoth Cave, Ky., U.S. (măm'ŏth)	114	37.10N	86.04W
Mammoth Cave National Park, rec., Ky., U.S.	97	37.20N	86.21W
Mammoth Hot Springs, Wy., U.S. (măm'ŭth hôt sprĭngz)	105	44.55N	110.50W
Mamnoli, India	187b	19.17N	73.15E
Mamoré, r., S.A.	130	13.00S	65.20W
Mamou, Gui.	210	10.26N	12.07W
Mampong, Ghana	214	7.04N	1.24W
Mamry, Jezioro, l., Pol. (mäm'rĭ)	155	54.10N	21.28E
Man, C. Iv.	214	7.24N	7.33W
Manacor, Spain (mä-nä-kôr')	159	39.35N	3.15E
Manado, Indon.	197	1.29N	124.50E
Managua, Cuba (mä-nä'gwä)	123a	22.58N	82.17W
Managua, Nic.	116	12.10N	86.16W
Managua, Lago de, l., Nic. (lá'gô-dĕ)	120	12.28N	86.10W
Manakara, Madag. (mä-nä-kä'rŭ)	213	22.17S	48.06E
Manama *see* Al Manāmah, Bahr.	182	26.01N	50.33E
Mananara, r., Madag. (mä-nä-nä'rŭ)	213	23.15S	48.15E
Mananjary, Madag. (mä-nän-zhä'rê)	213	20.16S	48.13E
Manas, China	188	44.30N	86.00E
Manassas, Va., U.S. (mȧ-năs'ȧs)	99	38.45N	77.30W
Manaus, Braz. (mä-nä'ōōzh)	131	3.01S	60.00W
Manayunk, neigh., Pa., U.S.	229b	40.01N	75.13W
Mancelona, Mi., U.S. (măn-sē-lō'nȧ)	98	44.50N	85.05W
Mancha Real, Spain (män'chä rā-äl')	158	37.48N	3.37W
Manchazh, Russia (män'chȧsh)	172a	56.30N	58.10E
Manchester, Eng., U.K.	142	53.28N	2.14W
Manchester, Ct., U.S. (măn'chĕs-tēr)	99	41.45N	72.30W
Manchester, Ga., U.S.	114	32.50N	84.37W
Manchester, Ia., U.S.	103	42.30N	91.30W
Manchester, Ma., U.S.	93a	42.35N	70.47W
Manchester, Mo., U.S.	107e	38.36N	90.31W
Manchester, N.H., U.S.	97	43.00N	71.30W
Manchester, Oh., U.S.	98	38.40N	83.35W
Manchester Docks, pt. of i., Eng., U.K.	237b	53.28N	2.17W
Manchester Ship Canal, Eng., U.K.	144a	53.20N	2.40W
Manchuria, hist. reg., China (măn-chōō'rē-ȧ)	189	48.00N	124.58E
Mandal, Nor. (män'däl)	152	58.03N	7.28E
Mandalay, Myanmar (măn'dȧ-lā)	183	22.00N	96.08E
Mandalselva, r., Nor.	152	58.25N	7.30E
Mandaluyong, Phil.	241g	14.35N	121.02E
Mandan, N.D., U.S. (măn'dăn)	96	46.49N	100.54W
Mandāoli, neigh., India	240d	28.38N	77.18E
Mandara Mountains, mts., Afr. (män-dä'rä)	211	10.15N	13.23E
Mandau Siak, r., Indon.	181b	1.03N	101.25E
Mandeb, Bab-el-, strt. (bäb'ĕl män-dĕb')	182	13.17N	42.49E
Mandimba, Moz.	217	14.21S	35.39E
Mandinga, Pan. (män-dĭŋ'gä)	121	9.32N	79.04W
Mandla, India	186	22.43N	80.23E
Mándra, Grc. (män'drä)	161	38.06N	23.32E
Mandres-les-Roses, Fr.	237c	48.42N	2.33E
Mandritsara, Madag. (mȧn-drēt-sä'rȧ)	213	15.49S	48.47E
Manduria, Italy (män-dōō'rē-ä)	161	40.23N	17.41E
Mandve, India	187b	18.47N	72.52E
Māndvi, India (mŭnd'vē)	183	22.54N	69.23E
Māndvi, India (mŭnd'vē)	187b	19.29N	72.53E
Mandvi, neigh., India	240e	18.57N	72.50E
Mandya, India	187	12.40N	77.00E
Manfredonia, Italy (män-frȧ-dô'nyä)	160	41.39N	15.55E
Manfredónia, Golfo di, b., Italy (gôl-fô-dē)	160	41.34N	16.05E
Mangabeiras, Chapada das, pl., Braz.	131	8.05S	47.32W
Mangalore, India (mŭŋ-gŭ-lōr')	183	12.53N	74.52E
Manganji, Japan	242a	35.40N	139.26E
Mangaratiba, Braz. (män-gä-rä-tē'bȧ)	129a	22.56S	44.03W
Mangatarem, Phil. (män'gȧ-tä'rĕm)	197a	15.48N	120.18E
Mange, Zaire	216	0.54N	20.30E
Mangkalihat, Tanjung, c., Indon.	196	1.25N	119.55E
Mangles, Islas de, Cuba (ē's-läs-dĕ-mäŋ'gläs) (măn'g'lz)	122	22.05N	82.50W
Mangoche, Mwi.	212	14.16S	35.14E
Mangoky, r., Madag. (män-gō'kē)	213	22.02S	44.11E
Mangole, Pulau, i., Indon.	197	1.35S	126.22E
Mangualde, Port. (män-gwäl'dĕ)	158	40.38N	7.44W
Mangueira, Lagoa da, l., Braz.	132	33.15S	52.45W
Mangum, Ok., U.S. (măŋ'gŭm)	110	34.52N	99.31W
Mangzhangdian, China (mäŋ-jäŋ-dĭĕn)	190	32.07N	114.44E
Manhasset, N.Y., U.S.	228	40.48N	73.42W
Manhattan, Il., U.S.	101a	41.25N	87.29W
Manhattan, Ks., U.S. (măn-hăt'ăn)	96	39.11N	96.34W
Manhattan Beach, Ca., U.S.	107a	33.53N	118.24W
Manhuaçu, Braz. (män-ōōȧ'sōō)	129a	20.17S	42.01W
Manhumirim, Braz. (män-ōō-mê-rē'N)	129a	22.30S	41.57W
Manicouagane, r., Can.	85	50.00N	68.35W
Manicouagane, Lac, res., Can.	85	51.30N	68.19W
Manicuare, Ven. (mä-nē-kwä'rē)	131b	10.35N	64.10W
Manihiki Islands, is., Cook Is. (mä'nē-hē'kê)	225	9.40S	158.00W
Manila, Phil.	196	14.37N	121.00E
Manila Bay, b., Phil. (mȧ-nĭl'ȧ)	197a	14.38N	120.46E
Manique de Baixo, Port.	238d	38.44N	9.22W
Manisa, Tur. (mä'nê-sȧ)	149	38.40N	27.30E
Manistee, Mi., U.S. (măn-ĭs-tē')	98	44.15N	86.20W
Manistee, r., Mi., U.S.	98	44.25N	85.45W
Manistique, Mi., U.S. (măn-ĭs-tēk')	103	45.58N	86.16W
Manistique, l., Mi., U.S.	103	46.14N	85.30W

ăt; finăl; rāte; senâte; ärm; ȧsk; sofȧ; fâre; ch-choose; dh-as th in other; bē; ēvent; bĕt; recĕnt; cratēr; g-gō; gh-guttural g; bĭt; ĭ-short neutral; rīde; к-guttural k as ch in German ich;

PRONOUNCING INDEX

Manistique–Marquette 315

PLACE (Pronunciation)	PAGE	Lat. °'	Long. °'
Manistique, r., Mi., U.S.	103	46.05N	86.09W
Manitoba, prov., Can. (măn-ĭ-tō'bȧ)	84	55.12N	97.29W
Manitoba, Lake, l., Can.	84	51.00N	98.45W
Manito Lake, l., Can. (măn'ĭ-tō)	88	52.45N	109.45W
Manitou, i., Mi., U.S. (măn'ĭ-tōō)	103	47.21N	87.33W
Manitou, l., Can.	103	49.21N	93.01W
Manitou Islands, is., Mi., U.S.	98	45.05N	86.00W
Manitoulin Island, i., Can. (măn-ĭ-tōō'lĭn)	85	45.45N	81.30W
Manitou Springs, Co., U.S.	110	38.51N	104.58W
Manitowoc, Wi., U.S. (măn-ĭ-tō-wŏk')	103	44.05N	87.42W
Manitqueira, Serra da, mts., Braz.	129a	22.40S	45.12W
Maniwaki, Can.	91	46.23N	76.00W
Manizales, Col. (mä-nē-zä'lås)	130	5.05N	75.31W
Manjacaze, Moz. (man'yä-kä'zē)	212	24.37S	33.49E
Mankato, Ks., U.S. (măn-kā'tō)	110	39.45N	98.12W
Mankato, Mn., U.S.	97	44.10N	93.59W
Mankim, Cam.	215	5.01N	12.00E
Manlléu, Spain (män-lyā'ōō)	159	42.00N	2.16E
Manly, Austl.	243a	33.48S	151.17E
Mannar, Sri L. (må-när')	183b	9.48N	80.03E
Mannar, Gulf of, b., Asia	183	8.47N	78.33E
Mannheim, Ger. (män'hīm)	147	49.30N	8.31E
Manning, Ia., U.S. (măn'ĭng)	102	41.53N	95.04W
Manning, S.C., U.S.	115	33.41N	80.12W
Mannington, W.V., U.S. (măn'ĭng-tŭn)	98	39.30N	80.55W
Mannswörth, neigh., Aus.	239e	48.09N	16.31E
Mano, r., Afr.	214	7.00N	11.25W
Man of War Bay, b., Bah.	123	21.05N	74.05W
Man of War Channel, strt., Bah.	122	22.45N	76.10W
Manokwari, Indon. (må-nŏk-wä'rē)	197	0.56S	134.10E
Manono, Zaire	217	7.18S	27.25E
Manor, Can. (măn'ēr)	89	49.36N	102.05W
Manor, Wa., U.S.	106c	45.45N	122.36W
Manorhaven, N.Y., U.S.	228	40.50N	73.42W
Manori, neigh., India	187b	19.13N	72.43E
Manosque, Fr. (må-nōsh')	157	43.51N	5.48E
Manotick, Can.	83c	45.13N	75.41W
Manouane, r., Can.	91	50.15N	70.30W
Manouane, Lac, l., Can. (mä-nōō'án)	92	50.36N	70.50W
Manresa, Spain (män-rā'sä)	148	41.44N	1.52E
Mansa, Zam.	212	11.12S	28.53E
Mansel, i., Can. (măn'sĕl)	85	61.56N	81.10W
Manseriche, Pongo de, reg., Peru (pŏ'n-gō-dĕ-män-sĕ-rē'chĕ)	130	4.15S	77.45W
Mansfield, Eng., U.K. (mănz'fēld)	144a	53.08N	1.12W
Mansfield, La., U.S.	113	32.02N	93.43W
Mansfield, Oh., U.S.	98	40.45N	82.30W
Mansfield, Wa., U.S.	104	47.48N	119.39W
Mansfield, Mount, mtn., Vt., U.S.	99	44.30N	72.45W
Mansfield Woodhouse, Eng., U.K. (wŏŏd-hous)	144a	53.08N	1.12W
Manta, Ec. (män'tä)	130	1.03S	80.16W
Manteno, Il., U.S. (măn-tē-nō)	101a	41.15N	87.50W
Manteo, N.C., U.S.	115	35.55N	75.40W
Mantes-la-Jolie, Fr. (mäɴt-ĕ-lä-zhō-lē')	156	48.59N	1.42E
Manti, Ut., U.S. (măn'tī)	109	39.15N	11.40W
Mantilla, neigh., Cuba	233b	23.04N	82.20W
Mantova, Italy (män'tō-vä) (măn'tū-ȧ)	148	45.09N	10.47E
Mantua, Cuba (män-tōō'å)	122	22.20N	84.15W
Mantua *see* Mantova, Italy	148	45.09N	10.47E
Mantua, Md., U.S.	229d	38.51N	77.15W
Mantua, Ut., U.S. (măn'tū-ȧ)	107b	41.30N	111.57W
Manua Islands, is., Am. Sam.	198a	14.13S	169.35W
Manui, Pulau, i., Indon. (mä-nōō'ē)	197	3.35S	123.38E
Manus Island, i., Pap. N. Gui. (mä'nōōs)	197	2.22S	146.22E
Manvel, Tx., U.S. (măn'vel)	113a	29.28N	95.22W
Manville, N.J., U.S. (măn'vĭl)	100a	40.33N	74.36W
Manville, R.I., U.S.	100b	41.57N	71.27W
Manyal Shīhah, Egypt	244a	29.57N	31.14E
Manzala Lake, l., Egypt	218b	31.14N	32.04E
Manzanares, Col. (män-sä-nä'rĕs)	130a	5.15N	75.09W
Manzanares, r., Spain (mänz-nä'rĕs)	159a	40.36N	3.48W
Manzanares, Canal del, Spain (kä-nä'l-dĕl-män-thä-nä'rĕs)	159a	40.20N	3.38W
Manzanillo, Cuba (män'zä-nēl'yō)	117	20.20N	77.05W
Manzanillo, Mex.	116	19.02N	104.21W
Manzanillo, Bahía de, b., Mex. (bä-ē'ä-dĕ-män-zä-nē'l-yō)	118	19.00N	104.38W
Manzanillo, Bahía de, b., N.A.	123	19.55N	71.50W
Manzanillo, Punta, c., Pan.	121	9.40N	79.33W
Manzhouli, China (män-jō-lē)	189	49.25N	117.15E
Manzovka, Russia (mán-zhô'f-kå)	194	44.16N	132.13E
Mao, Chad (mä'ô)	211	14.07N	15.19E
Mao, Dom. Rep.	123	19.35N	71.10W
Maoke, Pegunungan, mts., Indon.	197	4.00S	138.00E
Maoming, China	189	21.55N	110.40E
Maoniu Shan, mtn., China (mou-nĭō shän)	192	32.45N	104.09E
Mapastepec, Mex. (ma-päs-tå-pĕk')	119	15.24N	92.52W
Mapia, Kepulauan, i., Indon.	197	0.57N	134.22E
Mapimí, Mex. (mä-pē-mē')	112	25.50N	103.50W
Mapimí, Bolsón de, des., Mex. (bôl-sŏ'n-dĕ-mä-pē'mē)	112	27.27N	103.20W
Maple Creek, Can. (mā'p'l) (crēk)	84	49.55N	109.27W
Maple Cross, Eng., U.K.	235	51.37N	0.30W
Maple Grove, Can. (grōv)	83a	45.19N	73.51W
Maple Heights, Oh., U.S.	101d	41.25N	81.34W
Maple Leaf Gardens, rec., Can.	227c	43.40N	79.23W
Maple Shade, N.J., U.S. (shād)	100f	39.57N	75.01W
Maple Valley, Wa., U.S. (văl'ē)	106a	47.24N	122.02W
Maplewood, Mn., U.S. (wŏŏd)	107g	45.00N	93.03W
Maplewood, Mo., U.S.	107e	38.37N	90.20W
Maplewood, N.J., U.S.	228	40.44N	74.17W
Mapocho, r., Chile	234b	33.25S	70.47W
Mapumulo, S. Afr. (mä-pä-mōō'lō)	213c	29.12S	31.05E
Maputo, Moz.	212	26.50S	32.30E
Maquela do Zombo, Ang. (må-kā'lȧ dò zôm'bò)	212	6.08S	15.15E
Maquoketa, Ia., U.S. (mȧ-kō-kē-tȧ)	103	42.04N	90.42W
Maquoketa, r., Ia., U.S.	103	42.08N	90.40W
Mar, Serra do, mts., Braz. (sĕr'rȧ dò mär')	132	26.30S	49.15W
Maracaibo, Ven. (mä-rä-kī'bō)	130	10.38N	71.45W
Maracaibo, Lago de, l., Ven. (lä'gô-dĕ-mä-rä-kī'bō)	130	9.55N	72.13W
Maracay, Ven. (mä-rä-käy')	130	10.15N	67.35W
Marādah, Libya	211	29.10N	19.07E
Maradi, Niger (mȧ-rȧ-dē')	210	13.29N	7.06E
Marāgheh, Iran	185	37.20N	46.10E
Maraisburg, S. Afr.	213b	26.12S	27.57E
Marais des Cygnes, r., Ks., U.S.	111	38.30N	95.30W
Marajó, Ilha de, i., Braz.	131	1.00S	49.30W
Maralal, Kenya	217	1.06N	36.42E
Marali, Cen. Afr. Rep.	215	6.01N	18.24E
Marand, Iran	185	38.26N	45.46E
Maranguape, Braz. (mä-rán-gwä'pĕ)	131	3.48S	38.38W
Maranhão, state, Braz. (mä-rän-youɴ)	131	5.15S	45.52W
Maranoa, r., Austl. (mä-rä-nō'ä)	203	27.01S	148.03E
Marano di Napoli, Italy (mä-rä'nô-dē-nä'pô-lē)	159c	40.39N	14.12E
Marañón, Río, r., Peru (rē'ō-mä-rä-nyōn')	130	4.26S	75.08W
Maraoli, neigh., India	240e	19.03N	72.54E
Marapanim, Braz. (mä-rä-pä-nē'ɴ)	131	0.45S	47.42W
Marathon, Can.	85	48.50N	86.10W
Marathon, Fl., U.S. (mär'ȧ-thŏn)	115a	24.41N	81.06W
Marathon, Oh., U.S.	101f	39.09N	83.59W
Maravatio, Mex. (mä-rȧ-vä'tē-ō)	118	19.54N	100.25W
Marawi, Sudan	211	18.07N	31.57E
Marayong, Austl.	243a	33.45S	150.54E
Marble Bar, Austl. (märb''l bär)	202	21.15S	119.15E
Marble Canal, can., Az., U.S. (mär'b'l)	109	36.21N	111.48W
Marblehead, Ma., U.S. (mär'b'l-hĕd)	93a	42.30N	70.51W
Marburg an der Lahn, Ger.	154	50.49N	8.46E
Marca, Ponta da, c., Ang.	216	16.31S	11.42E
Marcala, Hond. (mär-kä-lä)	120	14.08N	88.01W
Marceline, Mo., U.S. (mär-sē-lēn')	111	39.42N	92.56W
Marche, hist. reg., Italy (mär'kā)	160	43.35N	12.33E
Marchegg, Aus.	145e	48.18N	16.55E
Marchena, Spain (mär-chā'nä)	148	37.20N	5.25W
Marchena, i., Ec. (ĕ's-lä-mär-chĕ'nä)	130	0.29N	90.31W
Marchfeld, reg., Aus.	145e	48.14N	16.37E
Mar Chiquita, Laguna, l., Arg. (lä-gōō'nä-mär-chē-kē'tä)	129c	34.25S	61.10W
Marco Polo Bridge, trans., China	240b	39.52N	116.12E
Marcos Paz, Arg. (mär-kōs' päz)	129c	34.49S	58.51W
Marcus, i., Japan (mär'kŭs)	225	24.00N	155.00E
Marcus Hook, Pa., U.S. (mär'kŭs hŏŏk)	100f	39.49N	75.25W
Marcy, Mount, mtn., N.Y., U.S. (mär'sē)	99	44.10N	73.55W
Mar de Espanha, Braz. (mär-dĕ-ĕs-pá'nyȧ)	129a	21.53S	43.00W
Mar del Plata, Arg. (mär dĕl- plä'ta)	132	37.59S	57.35W
Mardin, Tur. (mär-dēn')	182	37.25N	40.40E
Maré, i., N. Cal. (mä-rā')	203	21.53S	168.30E
Maree, Loch, b., Scot., U.K. (mȧ-rē')	150	57.40N	5.44W
Mareil-Marly, Fr.	237c	48.53N	2.05E
Marengo, Ia., U.S. (mȧ-rĕŋ'gō)	103	41.47N	92.04W
Marennes, Fr. (mȧ-rĕn')	156	45.49N	1.08W
Marfa, Tx., U.S. (mär'fȧ)	112	30.19N	104.01W
Margarethenhöhe, neigh., Ger.	236	51.26N	6.58E
Margaretting, Eng., U.K.	235	51.41N	0.25E
Margarita, Pan. (mär-gōō-rē'tä)	116a	9.20N	79.55W
Margarita, Isla de, i., Ven. (mä-gȧ-rē'tä)	130	11.00N	64.15W
Margate, S. Afr. (mä-gāt')	213c	30.52S	30.21E
Margate, Eng., U.K. (mär'gāt)	151	51.21N	1.17E
Margherita Peak, mtn., Afr.	211	0.22N	29.51E
Marguerite, r., Can.	92	50.39N	66.42W
Marhanets', Ukr.	163	47.41N	34.33E
Maria, Can. (mȧ-rē'ȧ)	92	48.10N	66.04W
Mariager, Den. (mä-rē-ägh'ēr)	152	56.38N	10.00E
Mariana, Braz. (mä-ryä'nä)	129a	20.23S	43.24W
Mariana Islands, is., Oc.	5	16.00N	145.30E
Marianao, Cuba (mä-rē-ä-nä'ō)	117	23.05N	82.26W
Mariana Trench, deep	225	12.00N	144.00E
Marianna, Ar., U.S. (mā-rĭ-ăn'ȧ)	111	34.45N	90.45W
Marianna, Fl., U.S.	114	30.46N	85.14W
Marianna, Pa., U.S.	101e	40.01N	80.05W
Mariano Acosta, Arg. (mä-rē-ä'nō-ȧ-kōs'tä)	132a	34.28S	58.48W
Mariano J. Haedo, Arg.	233d	34.39S	58.36W
Mariánské Lázně, Czech Rep. (mär'yán-skĕ'läz'nyĕ)	154	49.58N	12.42E
Maria Paula, Braz.	234c	22.54S	43.02W
Marias, r., Mt., U.S. (mȧ-rī'ȧz)	105	48.15N	110.50W
Marías, Islas, is., Mex. (mä-rē'äs)	116	21.30N	106.40W
Mariato, Punta, c., Pan.	121	7.17N	81.09W
Maribo, Den. (mä'rē-bô)	152	54.46N	11.29E
Maribor, Slvn. (mä're-bôr)	142	46.33N	15.37E
Maribyrnong, Austl.	243b	37.46S	144.54E
Maricaban, i., Phil. (mä-rē-kä-bän')	197a	13.40N	120.44E
Mariefred, Swe. (mä-rē'ĕ-frĭd)	152	59.17N	17.09E
Marie Galante, i., Guad. (mȧ-rē' gȧ-läɴt')	121b	15.58N	61.05W
Mariehamn, Fin. (mä-rē'ê-häm''n)	153	60.07N	19.57E
Mari El, state, Russia	166	56.30N	48.00E
Mariendorf, neigh., Ger.	238a	52.26N	13.23E
Marienfelde, neigh., Ger.	238a	52.25N	13.22E
Mariestad, Swe. (mä-rē'ĕ-städ')	152	58.43N	13.45E
Marietta, Ga., U.S. (mā-rĭ-ĕt'ȧ)	100c	33.57N	84.33W
Marietta, Oh., U.S.	98	39.25N	81.30W
Marietta, Ok., U.S.	111	33.53N	97.07W
Marietta, Wa., U.S.	106d	48.48N	122.35W
Mariinsk, Russia (mȧ-re'ĭnsk)	170	56.15N	87.28E
Marijampole, Lith. (mä-rê-yäm-pô'lê)	153	54.33N	23.26E
Marikana, S. Afr. (mä'-rĭ-kä-nȧ)	218d	25.40S	27.28E
Marikina, Phil.	241g	14.37N	121.06E
Marília, Braz. (mä-rē'lyȧ)	131	22.02S	49.48W
Marimba, Ang.	216	8.28S	17.08E
Marín, Spain	158	42.24N	8.40W
Marina del Rey, Ca., U.S.	232	33.59N	118.28W
Marina del Rey, b., Ca., U.S.	232	33.58N	118.27W
Marin City, Ca., U.S.	231b	37.52N	122.21W
Marinduque Island, i., Phil. (mä-rēn-dōō'kä)	197a	13.14N	121.45E
Marine, Il., U.S. (mȧ-rēn')	107e	38.48N	89.47W
Marine City, Mi., U.S.	98	42.45N	82.30W
Marine Lake, l., Mn., U.S.	107g	45.13N	92.55W
Marineland of the Pacific, pt. of i., Ca., U.S.	232	33.44N	118.24W
Marine on Saint Croix, Mn., U.S.	107g	45.11N	92.47W
Marinette, Wi., U.S. (mär-ĭ-nĕt')	97	45.04N	87.40W
Maringa, r., Zaire (mä-riŋ'gä)	211	0.30N	21.00E
Marinha Grande, Port. (mä-rēn'yȧ grän'dĕ)	158	39.49N	8.53W
Marion, Al., U.S. (măr'ĭ-ŭn)	114	32.36N	87.19W
Marion, Il., U.S.	98	37.40N	88.55W
Marion, In., U.S.	97	40.35N	85.45W
Marion, Ia., U.S.	103	42.01N	91.39W
Marion, Ks., U.S.	111	38.21N	97.02W
Marion, Ky., U.S.	114	37.19N	88.05W
Marion, N.C., U.S.	115	35.40N	82.00W
Marion, N.D., U.S.	102	46.37N	98.20W
Marion, Oh., U.S.	98	40.35N	83.10W
Marion, S.C., U.S.	115	34.08N	79.23W
Marion, Va., U.S.	115	36.48N	81.33W
Marion, Lake, res., S.C., U.S.	115	33.25N	80.35W
Marion Reef, rf., Austl.	203	18.57S	151.31E
Mariposa, Chile (mä-rê-pô'sä)	129b	35.33S	71.21W
Mariposa Creek, r., Ca., U.S.	108	37.14N	120.30W
Mariquita, Col. (mä-rē-kē'tä)	130a	5.13N	74.52W
Mariscal Estigarribia, Para.	132	22.03S	60.28W
Marisco, Ponta do, c., Braz. (pô'n-tä-dô-mä-rē's-kō)	132b	23.01S	43.17W
Maritime Alps, mts., Eur. (mă'rĭ-tīm ălps)	147	44.20N	7.02E
Mariupol', Ukr.	164	47.07N	37.32E
Mariveles, Phil.	197a	14.27N	120.29E
Marj Uyan, Leb.	181a	33.21N	35.36E
Marka, Som.	218a	1.45N	44.47E
Markaryd, Swe. (mär'kä-rüd)	152	56.30N	13.34E
Marked Tree, Ar., U.S. (märkt trē)	111	35.31N	90.26W
Marken, i., Neth.	145a	52.26N	5.08E
Market Bosworth, Eng., U.K. (bŏz'wûrth)	144a	52.37N	1.23W
Market Deeping, Eng., U.K. (dēp'ĭng)	144a	52.40N	0.19W
Market Drayton, Eng., U.K. (drā'tŭn)	144a	52.54N	2.29W
Market Harborough, Eng., U.K. (här'bŭr-ô)	144a	52.28N	0.55W
Market Rasen, Eng., U.K. (rā'zĕn)	144a	53.23N	0.21W
Markham, Can. (märk'ȧm)	91	43.53N	79.15W
Markham, Mount, mtn., Ant.	219	82.59S	159.30E
Markivka, Ukr.	163	49.32N	39.34E
Markovo, Russia (mär'kô-vô)	165	64.46N	170.48E
Markrāna, India	186	27.08N	74.43E
Marks, Russia	167	51.42N	46.46E
Marksville, La., U.S. (märks'vĭl)	113	31.09N	92.05W
Markt Indersdorf, Ger. (märkt ēn'dĕrs-dōrf)	145d	48.22N	11.23E
Marktredwitz, Ger. (märk-rĕd'vēts)	154	50.02N	12.05E
Markt Schwaben, Ger. (märkt shvä'bĕn)	145d	48.12N	11.52E
Marl, Ger. (märl)	157c	51.40N	7.05E
Marlboro, N.J., U.S.	100a	40.18N	74.15W
Marlborough, Ma., U.S.	93a	42.21N	71.33W
Marlette, Mi., U.S. (mär-lĕt')	98	43.25N	83.05W
Marlin, Tx., U.S. (mär'lĭn)	113	31.18N	96.52W
Marlinton, W.V., U.S. (mär'lĭn-tŭn)	98	38.15N	80.10W
Marlow, Eng., U.K. (mär'lō)	144b	51.33N	0.46W
Marlow, Ok., U.S.	111	34.38N	97.56W
Marls, The, b., Bah. (märls)	122	26.30N	77.15W
Marly-le-Roi, Fr.	237c	48.52N	2.05E
Marmande, Fr. (mȧr-mäɴd')	156	44.30N	0.10E
Marmara Denizi, sea, Tur.	182	40.40N	28.00E
Marmarth, N.D., U.S. (mär'mȧrth)	102	46.19N	103.57W
Mar Muerto, l., Mex. (mär-mōē'r-tô)	119	16.13N	94.22W
Marne, Ger. (mär'nē)	145c	53.57N	9.01E
Marne, r., Fr. (märn)	147	49.00N	4.30E
Maroa, Ven. (mä-rō'ä)	130	2.43N	67.37W
Maroantsetra, Madag. (mä-rō-äŋ-tsā'trȧ)	213	15.18S	49.48E
Maro Jarapeto, mtn., Col. (mä-rô-hä-rä-pĕ'tô)	130a	6.29N	76.39W
Marolles-en-Brie, Fr.	237c	48.44N	2.33E
Maromokotro, mtn., Madag.	213	14.00S	49.11E
Marondera, Zimb.	212	18.10S	31.36E
Maroni, r., S.A. (mȧ-rō'nē)	131	3.02N	53.54W
Maro Reef, rf., Hi., U.S.	94b	25.15N	170.00W
Maroua, Cam. (mär'wä)	211	10.36N	14.20E
Maroubra, Austl.	243a	33.57S	151.16E
Marple, Eng., U.K. (mär'p'l)	144a	53.24N	2.04W
Marquard, S. Afr.	218d	28.41S	27.26E
Marquesas Islands, is., Fr. Poly. (mär-kĕ'säs)	2	8.50S	141.00W
Marquesas Keys, is., Fl., U.S. (mȧr-kē'zȧs)	115a	24.37N	82.15W
Marquês de Valença, Braz. (mär-kĕ's-dĕ-vä-lĕ'n-sä)	129a	22.16S	43.42W
Marquette, Can. (mȧr-kĕt')	83f	50.04N	97.43W

ng-sing; ŋ-baŋk; ɴ-nasalized n; nŏd; cŏmmit; ōld; ôbey; ôrder; oi-boil; fōōd; ŏŏ-as oo in foot; ou-out; s-soft; sh-dish; th-thin; pūre; ûnite; ûrn; stŭd; circŭs; ü-as in French tu; '-indeterminate vowel.

316 Marquette–McCormick Place

PLACE (Pronunciation)	PAGE	Lat. °′	Long. °′
Marquette, Mi., U.S.	97	46.32N	87.25W
Marquez, Tx., U.S. (mär-käz′)	113	31.14N	96.15W
Marra, Jabal, mtn., Sudan (jĕb′ĕl mär′ä)	211	13.00N	23.47E
Marrakech, Mor. (mȧr-rä′kĕsh)	210	31.38N	8.00W
Marree, Austl. (măr′rē)	202	29.38S	137.55E
Marrero, La., U.S.	100d	29.55N	90.06W
Marrickville, Austl.	243a	33.55S	151.09E
Marrupa, Moz.	217	13.08S	37.30E
Mars, Pa., U.S. (märz)	101e	40.42N	80.01W
Marsabit, Kenya	217	2.20N	37.59E
Marsala, Italy (mär-sä′lä)	148	37.48N	12.28E
Marscheid, neigh., Ger.	236	51.14N	7.14E
Marsden, Eng., U.K. (märz′dĕn)	144a	53.36N	1.55W
Marseille, Fr. (mȧr-sâ′y′)	142	43.18N	5.25E
Marseilles, Il., U.S. (mär-sĕlz′)	98	41.20N	88.40W
Marsfield, Austl.	243a	33.47S	151.07E
Marshall, Il., U.S. (mär′shăl)	98	39.20N	87.40W
Marshall, Mi., U.S.	98	42.20N	84.55W
Marshall, Mn., U.S.	102	44.28N	95.49W
Marshall, Mo., U.S.	111	39.07N	93.12W
Marshall, Tx., U.S.	97	32.33N	94.22W
Marshall Islands, nation, Oc.	3	10.00N	165.00E
Marshalltown, Ia., U.S. (mär′shăl-toun)	103	42.02N	92.55W
Marshallville, Ga., U.S. (mär′shăl-vĭl)	114	32.29N	83.55W
Marshfield, Ma., U.S. (märsh′fēld)	93a	42.06N	70.43W
Marshfield, Mo., U.S.	111	37.20N	92.53W
Marshfield, Wi., U.S.	103	44.40N	90.10W
Marsh Harbour, Bah.	122	26.30N	77.00W
Mars Hill, In., U.S. (märz′hĭl′)	101g	39.43N	86.15W
Mars Hill, Me., U.S.	92	46.34N	67.54W
Marstrand, Swe. (mär′stränd)	152	57.54N	11.33E
Marsyaty, Russia (märs′yȧ-tĭ)	172a	60.03N	60.28E
Mart, Tx., U.S. (märt)	113	31.32N	96.49W
Martaban, Gulf of, b., Myanmar (mär-tŭ-bän′)	196	16.34N	96.58E
Martapura, Indon.	196	3.19S	114.45E
Marten, neigh., Ger.	236	51.31N	7.23E
Martha's Vineyard, i., Ma., U.S. (mär′thȧz vĭn′yȧrd)	99	41.25N	70.35W
Martigny, Switz. (mȧr-tē-nyē′)	154	46.06N	7.00E
Martigues, Fr.	157	43.24N	5.05E
Martin, Tn., U.S. (mär′tĭn)	114	36.20N	88.45W
Martina Franca, Italy (mär-tē′nä fräŋ′kä)	161	40.43N	17.21E
Martinez, Ca., U.S. (mär-tē′nĕz)	106b	38.01N	122.08W
Martinez, Tx., U.S.	107d	29.25N	98.20W
Martínez, neigh., Arg.	233d	34.29S	58.30W
Martinique, dep., N.A. (mȧr-tē-nēk′)	117	14.50N	60.40W
Martin Lake, res., Al., U.S.	114	32.40N	86.05W
Martin Point, c., Ak., U.S.	95	70.10N	142.00W
Martinsburg, W.V., U.S. (mär′tĭnz-bûrg)	99	39.30N	78.00W
Martins Ferry, Oh., U.S. (mär′tĭnz)	98	40.05N	80.45W
Martinsville, In., U.S. (mär′tĭnz-vĭl)	98	39.25N	86.25W
Martinsville, Va., U.S.	115	36.40N	79.53W
Martos, Spain (mär′tōs)	158	37.43N	3.58W
Martre, Lac la, l., Can. (läk la märtr)	84	63.24N	119.58W
Marugame, Japan (mä′rōō-gä′mä)	195	34.19N	133.48E
Marungu, mts., Zaire	217	7.50S	29.50E
Marve, neigh., India	187b	19.12N	72.43E
Marwitz, Ger.	238a	52.41N	13.09E
Mary, Turk. (mä′rē)	169	37.45N	61.47E
Mar′yanskaya, Russia (mȧr-yän′skȧ-yȧ)	163	45.04N	38.39E
Maryborough, Austl. (mă′rĭ-bŭr-ō)	203	25.35S	152.40E
Maryborough, Austl.	203	37.00S	143.50E
Maryland, state, U.S. (mĕr′ĭ-lănd)	97	39.10N	76.25W
Maryland Park, Md., U.S.	229d	38.53N	76.54W
Marys, r., Nv., U.S. (mā′rĭz)	104	41.25N	115.10W
Marystown, Can. (mâr′ĭz-toun)	93	47.11N	55.10W
Marysville, Can.	92	45.59N	66.35W
Marysville, Ca., U.S.	108	39.09N	121.37W
Marysville, Oh., U.S.	98	40.15N	83.25W
Marysville, Wa., U.S.	106a	48.03N	122.11W
Maryville, Il., U.S. (mā′rĭ-vĭl)	107e	38.44N	89.57W
Maryville, Mo., U.S.	111	40.21N	94.51W
Maryville, Tn., U.S.	114	35.44N	83.59W
Marzahn, neigh., Ger.	238a	52.33N	13.33E
Mārzuq, Libya	211	26.00N	14.09E
Marzūq, Idehan, des., Libya	210	24.30N	13.00E
Masai Steppe, plat., Tan.	217	4.30S	36.40E
Masaka, Ug.	217	0.20S	31.44E
Masalasef, Chad	215	11.43N	17.08E
Masalembo-Besar, i., Indon.	196	5.40S	114.28E
Masan, S. Kor. (mä-sän′)	189	35.10N	128.31E
Masangwe, Tan.	217	5.28S	30.05E
Masasi, Tan. (mä-sä′sē)	213	10.43S	38.48E
Masatepe, Nic. (mä-sä-tĕ′pĕ)	120	11.57N	86.10W
Masaya, Nic. (mä-sä′yä)	120	11.58N	86.05W
Masbate, Phil. (mäs-bä′tä)	197a	12.21N	123.38E
Masbate, i., Phil.	197	12.19N	123.03E
Mascarene Islands, is., Afr.	5	20.20S	56.40E
Mascot, Austl.	243a	33.56S	151.12E
Mascot, Tn., U.S. (măs′kŏt)	114	36.04N	83.45W
Mascota, Mex. (mäs-kō′tä)	118	20.33N	104.45W
Mascota, r., Mex.	118	20.33N	104.52W
Mascouche, Can. (mȧs-kōōsh′)	83a	45.45N	73.36W
Mascouche, r., Can.	83a	45.44N	73.45W
Mascoutah, Il., U.S. (măs-kū′tā)	107e	38.29N	89.48W
Maseru, Leso. (măz′ĕr-ōō)	212	29.09S	27.11E
Mashhad, Iran	182	36.17N	59.30E
Māshkel, Hāmūn-i-, l., Asia (hä-mōōn′ē mäsh-kĕl′)	182	28.28N	64.13E
Mashra′ar Raqq, Sudan	211	8.28N	29.15E
Masi-Manimba, Zaire	216	4.46S	17.55E
Masindi, Ug. (mä-sēn′dē)	211	1.44N	31.43E
Masjed Soleymān, Iran	182	31.45N	49.17E
Mask, Lough, b., Ire. (lŏk mȧsk)	150	53.35N	9.23W
Maslovo, Russia (mäs′lô-vô)	172a	60.08N	60.28E
Mason, Mi., U.S. (mā′sŭn)	98	42.35N	84.25W
Mason, Oh., U.S.	101f	39.22N	84.18W
Mason, Tx., U.S.	112	30.46N	99.14W
Mason City, Ia., U.S.	97	43.08N	93.14W
Masonville, Va., U.S.	229d	38.51N	77.12W
Maspeth, neigh., N.Y., U.S.	228	40.43N	73.55W
Massa, Italy (mäs′sä)	160	44.02N	10.08E
Massachusetts, state, U.S. (măs-ȧ-chōō′sĕts)	97	42.20N	72.30W
Massachusetts Bay, b., Ma., U.S.	92	42.26N	70.20W
Massafra, Italy (mäs-sä′frä)	161	40.35N	17.05E
Massa Marittima, Italy	160	43.03N	10.55E
Massapequa, N.Y., U.S.	100a	40.41N	73.28W
Massaua see Mitsiwa, Erit.	211	15.40N	39.19E
Massena, N.Y., U.S. (mă-sē′nȧ)	99	44.55N	74.55W
Masset, Can. (măs′ĕt)	84	54.02N	132.09W
Masset Inlet, b., Can.	87	53.42N	132.20E
Massif Central, Fr. (mȧ-sēf′ säN-trȧl′)	142	45.12N	3.02E
Massillon, Oh., U.S. (măs′ĭ-lŏn)	98	40.50N	81.35W
Massinga, Moz. (mä-sĭn′gä)	212	23.18S	35.18E
Massive, Mount, mtn., Co., U.S. (măs′ĭv)	96	39.05N	106.30W
Masson, Can. (măs-sŭn)	83c	45.33N	75.25W
Massy, Fr.	237c	48.44N	2.17E
Masuda, Japan (mä-sōō′dȧ)	195	34.42N	131.53E
Masuria, reg., Pol.	155	53.40N	21.10E
Masvingo, Zimb.	212	20.07S	30.47E
Matadi, Zaire (mȧ-tä′dē)	212	5.49S	13.27E
Matagalpa, Nic. (mä-tä-gäl′pä)	116	12.52N	85.57W
Matagami, l., Can. (mȧ-tä-gä′mē)	85	50.10N	78.28W
Matagorda Bay, b., Tx., U.S. (măt-ȧ-gôr′dȧ)	113	28.32N	96.13W
Matagorda Island, i., Tx., U.S.	113	28.13N	96.27W
Matam, Sen. (mä-täm′)	210	15.40N	13.15W
Matamoros, Mex. (mä-tä-mō′rôs)	112	25.32N	103.13W
Matamoros, Mex.	116	25.52N	97.30W
Matane, Can. (mȧ-tȧn′)	85	48.51N	67.32W
Matanzas, Cuba (mä-tän′zäs)	117	23.05N	81.35W
Matanzas, prov., Cuba	122	22.45N	81.20W
Matanzas, Bahía, b., Cuba (bä-ē′ä)	122	23.10N	81.30W
Matapalo, Cabo, c., C.R. (kȧ′bō-mä-tä-pä′lō)	121	8.22N	83.25W
Matapédia, Can. (mä-tȧ-pā′dē-ȧ)	92	47.58N	66.56W
Matapédia, l., Can.	92	48.33N	67.32W
Matapédia, r., Can.	92	48.10N	67.10W
Mataquito, r., Chile (mä-tä-kē′tō)	129b	35.08S	71.35W
Matara, Sri L. (mä-tä′rä)	183b	5.59N	80.35E
Mataram, Indon.	196	8.45S	116.15E
Matatiele, S. Afr. (mä-tä-tyā′lā)	213c	30.21S	28.49E
Matawan, N.J., U.S.	100a	40.24N	74.13W
Matehuala, Mex. (mä-tȧ-wä′lä)	116	23.38N	100.39W
Matera, Italy (mä-tâ′rä)	160	40.42N	16.37E
Mateur, Tun. (mȧ-tûr′)	148	37.09N	9.43E
Mātherān, India	187b	18.58N	73.16E
Matheson, Can.	91	48.35N	80.33W
Mathews, Lake, l., Ca., U.S. (măth ūz)	107a	33.50N	117.24W
Mathura, India (mu-tǒ′rū)	183	27.39N	77.39E
Matias Barbosa, Braz. (mä-tē′äs-bär-bô-sä)	129a	21.53S	43.19W
Matillas, Laguna, l., Mex. (lä-gò′nä-mä-tē′l-yäs)	119	18.02N	92.36W
Matina, C.R. (mä-tē′nä)	121	10.06N	83.20W
Matiši, Lat. (mä′tē-sē)	153	57.43N	25.09E
Matlalcueyetl, Cerro, mtn., Mex. (sĕ′r-rä-mä-tläl-kwĕ′yĕtl)	118	19.13N	98.02W
Matlock, Eng., U.K. (măt′lŏk)	144a	53.08N	1.33W
Matochkin Shar, Russia (mä′tŏch-kĭn)	164	73.57N	56.16E
Mato Grosso, Braz. (mät′ò grōs′ò)	131	15.04S	59.58W
Mato Grosso, state, Braz.	131	14.38S	55.36W
Mato Grosso, Chapada de, hills, Braz. (shä-pä′dä-dĕ)	131	13.39S	55.42W
Mato Grosso do Sul, state, Braz.	131	20.00S	56.00W
Matosinhos, Port.	158	41.10N	8.48W
Maṭraḥ, Oman (mȧ-trä′)	182	23.36N	58.27E
Matsubara, Japan	195b	34.34N	135.34E
Matsudo, Japan (mät′sò-dò)	195a	35.48N	139.55E
Matsue, Japan (mät′sò-ĕ)	189	35.29N	133.04E
Matsumoto, Japan (mät′sò-mō′tò)	194	36.15N	137.59E
Matsuyama, Japan (mät′sò-yä′mä)	189	33.48N	132.45E
Matsuzaka, Japan (mät′sò-zä′kä)	195	34.35N	136.34E
Mattamuskeet, Lake, l., N.C., U.S. (măt-tȧ-mŭs′kēt)	115	35.34N	76.03W
Mattaponi, r., Va., U.S. (măt′ȧ-poni′)	99	37.45N	77.00W
Mattawa, Can. (măt′ȧ-wȧ)	85	46.15N	78.49W
Matterhorn, mtn., Eur. (mät′ĕr-hôrn)	154	45.57N	7.36E
Matteson, Il., U.S. (mătt′ĕ-sŭn)	101a	41.30N	87.42W
Matthew Town, Bah. (măth′ū toun)	123	21.00N	73.40W
Mattoon, Il., U.S. (mă-tōōn′)	97	39.30N	88.20W
Maturín, Ven. (mä-tōō-rēn′)	130	9.48N	63.16W
Mátyásföld, neigh., Hung.	239g	47.31N	19.13E
Mátyas-Templom, rel., Hung.	239g	47.30N	19.02E
Maúa, Moz.	217	13.51S	37.10E
Mauban, Phil. (mä′ōō-bän′)	197a	14.11N	121.44E
Maubeuge, Fr. (mò-bûzh′)	156	50.18N	3.57E
Maud, Oh., U.S. (môd)	101f	39.21N	84.23W
Mauer, Aus. (mou′ĕr)	145e	48.09N	16.16E
Maués, Braz. (mȧ-wĕ′s)	131	3.34S	57.30W
Mau Escarpment, cliff, Kenya	217	0.45S	35.50E
Maui, i., Hi., U.S. (mä′ōō-ē)	96c	20.52N	156.02W
Maule, r., Chile (mä′ò-lĕ)	129b	35.45S	70.50W
Maumee, Oh., U.S. (mô-mē′)	98	41.30N	83.40W
Maumee, r., In., U.S.	98	41.10N	84.50W
Maumee Bay, b., Oh., U.S.	98	41.50N	83.20W
Maun, Bots. (mä-ôn′)	212	19.52S	23.40E
Mauna Kea, mtn., Hi., U.S. (mä′ò-nākā′ä)	96c	19.52N	155.30W
Mauna Loa, mtn., Hi., U.S. (mä′ò-nälō′ä)	96c	19.28N	155.38W
Maurecourt, Fr.	237c	49.00N	2.04E
Maurepas Lake, l., La., U.S. (mō-rē-pä′)	113	30.18N	90.40W
Mauricie, Parc National de la, rec., Can.	91	46.46N	73.00W
Mauritania, nation, Afr. (mô-rē-tā′nĭ-ȧ)	210	19.38N	13.30W
Mauritius, nation, Afr. (mô-rĭsh′ĭ-ŭs)	3	20.18S	57.36E
Maury, Wa., U.S. (mô′rĭ)	106a	47.22N	122.23W
Mauston, Wi., U.S. (môs′tŭn)	103	43.46N	90.05W
Maverick, r., Az., U.S. (mă-vûr′ĭk)	109	33.40N	109.30W
Mavinga, Ang.	216	15.50S	20.21E
Mawlamyine, Myanmar	196	16.30N	97.39E
Maxville, Can. (măks′vĭl)	83c	45.17N	74.52W
Maxville, Mo., U.S.	107e	38.26N	90.24W
Maya, r., Russia (mä′yä)	171	58.00N	135.45E
Mayaguana, i., Bah.	123	22.25N	73.00W
Mayaguana Passage, strt., Bah.	123	22.20N	73.25W
Mayagüez, P.R. (mä-yä-gwāz′)	117	18.12N	67.10W
Mayari, r., Cuba	123	20.25N	75.35W
Mayas, Montañas, mts., N.A. (mŏntăŋ′äs mä′äs)	120a	16.43N	89.00W
Mayd, i., Som.	218a	11.24N	46.38E
Mayen, Ger. (mī′ĕn)	154	50.19N	7.14E
Mayenne, r., Fr. (mȧ-yĕn)	156	48.14N	0.45W
Mayfair, neigh., S. Afr.	244b	26.12S	28.01E
Mayfair, neigh., Pa., U.S.	229b	40.02N	75.03W
Mayfield, Ky., U.S. (mā′fēld)	114	36.44N	88.19W
Mayfield Creek, r., Ky., U.S.	114	36.54N	88.47W
Mayfield Heights, Oh., U.S.	101d	41.31N	81.26W
Mayfield Lake, res., Wa., U.S.	104	46.31N	122.34W
Maykop, Russia	164	44.35N	40.07E
Maykor, Russia (mī-kôr′)	172a	59.01N	55.52E
Maymyo, Myanmar (mī′myō)	188	22.14N	96.32E
Maynard, Ma., U.S. (mā′nȧrd)	93a	42.25N	71.27W
Mayne, Can. (mān)	106d	48.51N	123.18W
Mayne, i., Can.	106d	48.52N	123.14W
Mayo, Can. (mä-yō′)	84	63.40N	135.51W
Mayo, Fl., U.S.	114	30.02N	83.08W
Mayo, Md., U.S.	100e	38.54N	76.31W
Mayodan, N.C., U.S. (mā-yō′dăn)	115	36.25N	79.59W
Mayon Volcano, vol., Phil. (mä-yōn′)	197a	13.21N	123.43E
Mayotte, dep., Afr. (mȧ-yôt′)	213	13.07S	45.32E
May Pen, Jam.	122	18.00N	77.25W
Mayraira Point, c., Phil.	193	18.40N	120.45E
Mayran, Laguna de, l., Mex. (lä-ò′nä-dē-mī-rän′)	116	25.40N	102.35W
Mayskiy, Russia	168	43.38N	44.04E
Maysville, Ky., U.S. (māz′vĭl)	98	38.35N	83.45W
Mayumba, Gabon	212	3.25S	10.39E
Mayville, N.Y., U.S. (mā′vĭl)	99	42.15N	79.30W
Mayville, N.D., U.S.	102	47.30N	97.20W
Mayville, Wi., U.S.	103	43.30N	88.45W
Maywood, Ca., U.S. (mā′wòd)	107a	33.59N	118.11W
Maywood, Il., U.S.	101a	41.53N	87.51W
Maywood, N.J., U.S.	228	40.56N	74.04W
Mazabuka, Zam. (mä-zä-bōō′kä)	212	15.51S	27.46E
Mazagão, Braz. (mä-zȧ-gou′N)	131	0.05S	51.27W
Mazapil, Mex. (mä-zä-pēl′)	112	24.40N	101.30W
Mazara del Vallo, Italy (mät-sä′rä dĕl väl′lō)	160	37.40N	12.37E
Mazār-i-Sharīf, Afg. (mȧ-zär′-ē-shȧ-rēf′)	183	36.48N	67.12E
Mazarrón, Spain (mä-zär-rō′n)	158	37.37N	1.29W
Mazatenango, Guat. (mä-zä-tȧ-näŋ′gō)	116	14.30N	91.30W
Mazatla, Mex.	119a	19.30N	99.24W
Mazatlán, Mex.	116	23.14N	106.27W
Mazatlán (San Juan), Mex. (mä-zä-tlän′) (säṅ hwän′)	119	17.05N	95.26W
Mažeikiai, Lith. (mȧ-zhā′kē-ĭ)	153	56.19N	22.24E
Mazhafah, Jabal, mtn., Sau. Ar.	181a	28.56N	35.05E
Mazilovo, neigh., Russia	239b	55.44N	37.26E
Mazorra, Cuba	233b	23.01N	82.24W
Mbabane, Swaz. (m′bä-bä′nē)	212	26.18S	31.14E
Mbaiki, Cen. Afr. Rep. (m′bȧ-ē′kē)	211	3.53N	18.00E
Mbakana, Montagne de, mts., Cam.	215	7.55N	14.40E
Mbakaou, Barrage de, dam, Cam.	215	6.10N	12.55E
Mbala, Zam.	212	8.50S	31.22E
Mbale, Ug.	217	1.05N	34.10E
Mbamba Bay, Tan.	217	11.17S	34.46E
Mbandaka, Zaire	212	0.04N	18.16E
M′banza Congo, Ang.	212	6.30S	14.10E
Mbanza-Ngungu, Zaire	212	5.20S	10.55E
Mbarara, Ug.	217	0.37S	30.39E
Mbasay, Chad	215	7.39N	15.40E
Mbigou, Gabon (m-bē-gōō′)	212	2.07S	11.30E
Mbinda, Congo	216	2.00S	12.55E
Mbogo, Tan.	217	7.26S	33.26E
Mbomou (Bomu), r., Afr. (m′bō′mōō)	211	4.50N	24.00E
Mbout, Maur. (m′bōō′)	210	16.03N	12.31W
Mbuji-Mayi, Zaire	216	6.09S	23.38E
McAdam, Can. (măk-ăd′ăm)	92	45.36N	67.20W
McAfee, N.J., U.S. (măk-ă′fē)	100a	41.10N	74.32W
McAlester, Ok., U.S. (măk ăl′ĕs-tĕr)	97	34.55N	95.45W
McAllen, Tx., U.S. (măk-ăl′ĕn)	112	26.12N	98.14W
McBride, Can. (măk-brīd′)	84	53.18N	120.10W
McCalla, Al., U.S. (măk-kăl′lȧ)	100h	33.20N	87.00W
McCamey, Tx., U.S. (mȧ-kā′mĭ)	112	31.08N	102.13W
McColl, S.C., U.S. (mȧ-kōl′)	115	34.40N	79.34W
McComb, Ms., U.S. (mȧ-kōm′)	114	31.14N	90.27W
McConaughy, Lake, l., Ne., U.S. (măk kŏ′nō ĭ′)	102	41.24N	101.40W
McCook, Il., U.S.	231a	41.48N	87.50W
McCook, Ne., U.S. (mȧ-kòk′)	110	40.13N	100.37W
McCormick, S.C., U.S. (mȧ-kôr′mĭk)	115	33.56N	82.20W
McCormick Place, pt. of i., Il., U.S.	231a	41.51N	87.37W

PRONOUNCING INDEX

McDonald - Merrimack 317

PLACE (Pronunciation)	PAGE	Lat. °′	Long. °′
McDonald, Pa., U.S. (măk-dŏn'ăld)	101e	40.22N	80.13W
McDonald Island, i., Austl.	219	53.00S	72.45E
McDonald Lake, l., Can. (măk-dŏn-ăld)	83e	51.12N	113.53W
McGehee, Ar., U.S. (mȧ-gē')	111	33.39N	91.22W
McGill, Nv., U.S. (mȧ-gĭl')	109	39.25N	114.47W
McGill University, educ., Can.	227b	45.30N	73.35W
McGowan, Wa., U.S. (măk-gou'ăn)	106c	46.15N	123.55W
McGrath, Ak., U.S. (măk'grȧth)	96a	62.58N	155.20W
McGregor, Can. (măk-grĕg'ẽr)	101b	42.08N	82.58W
McGregor, Ia., U.S.	103	42.58N	91.12W
McGregor, Tx., U.S.	113	31.26N	97.23W
McGregor, r., Can.	87	54.10N	121.00W
McGregor Lake, l., Can. (măk-grĕg'ẽr)	83c	45.38N	75.44W
McHenry, Il., U.S. (măk-hĕn'rĭ)	101a	42.21N	88.16W
Mchinji, Mwi.	212	13.42S	32.50E
McIntosh, S.D., U.S. (măk'ĭn-tŏsh)	102	45.54N	101.22W
McKay, r., Or., U.S.	106c	45.43N	123.00W
McKeesport, Pa., U.S. (mȧ-kez'pōrt)	101e	40.21N	79.51W
McKees Rocks, Pa., U.S. (mȧ-kēz' rŏks)	101e	40.29N	80.05W
McKenzie, Tn., U.S. (mȧ-kĕn'zĭ)	114	36.07N	88.30W
McKenzie, r., Or., U.S.	104	44.07N	122.20W
McKinley, Mount, mtn., Ak., U.S. (mȧ-kĭn'lĭ)	96a	63.00N	151.02W
McKinney, Tx., U.S. (mȧ-kĭn'ĭ)	111	33.12N	96.35W
McKnight Village, Pa., U.S.	230b	40.31N	80.00W
McLaughlin, S.D., U.S. (mȧk-lŏf'lĭn)	102	45.48N	100.45W
McLean, Va., U.S. (măc'lān)	100e	38.56N	77.11W
McLeansboro, Il., U.S. (mȧ-klānz'bŭr-ō)	98	38.10N	88.35W
McLennan, Can. (măk-lĭn'năn)	84	55.42N	116.54W
McLeod, r., Can.	87	53.45N	115.55W
McLeod Lake, Can.	86	54.59N	123.02W
McLoughlin, Mount, mtn., Or., U.S. (măk-lŏk'lĭn)	104	42.27N	122.20W
McMillan Lake, l., Tx., U.S. (măk-mĭl'ăn)	112	32.40N	104.09W
McMillin, Wa., U.S. (măk-mĭl'ĭn)	106a	47.08N	122.14W
McMinnville, Or., U.S. (măk-mĭn'vĭl)	104	45.13N	123.13W
McMinnville, Tn., U.S.	114	35.41N	85.47W
McMurray, Pa., U.S.	230b	40.17N	80.05W
McMurray, Wa., U.S. (măk-mŭr'ĭ)	106a	48.19N	122.15W
McNary, Az., U.S. (măk-nâr'ē)	109	34.10N	109.55W
McNary, La., U.S.	113	30.58N	92.32W
McNary Dam, Or., U.S.	104	45.57N	119.15W
McPherson, Ks., U.S. (măk-fŭr's'n)	111	38.21N	97.41W
McRae, Ga., U.S. (măk-rā')	115	32.02N	82.55W
McRoberts, Ky., U.S. (măk-rŏb'ẽrts)	115	37.12N	82.40W
Mead, Ks., U.S. (mēd)	110	37.17N	100.21W
Mead, Lake, l., U.S.	96	36.20N	114.14W
Meade Peak, mtn., Id., U.S.	105	42.19N	111.16W
Meadow Lake, Can. (mĕd'ō lăk)	84	54.08N	108.26W
Meadowlands, S. Afr.	244b	26.13S	27.54E
Meadows, Can. (mĕd'ōz)	83f	50.02N	97.35W
Meadville, Pa., U.S. (mēd'vĭl)	98	41.40N	80.10W
Meaford, Can. (mē'fẽrd)	91	44.35N	80.40W
Mealy Mountains, mts., Can. (mē'lē)	85	53.32N	57.58W
Meandarra, Austl. (mē-ăn-dă'rȧ)	204	27.47S	149.40E
Meaux, Fr. (mō)	156	48.58N	2.53E
Mecapalapa, Mex. (mā-kä-pä-lä'pä)	119	20.32N	97.52W
Mecatina, r., Can. (mā-kȧ-tē'nȧ)	93	50.50N	59.45W
Mecca (Makkah), Sau. Ar. (mĕk'ȧ)	182	21.27N	39.45E
Mechanic Falls, Me., U.S. (mē-kăn'ĭk)	92	44.05N	70.23W
Mechanicsburg, Pa., U.S. (mē-kăn'ĭks-bûrg)	99	40.15N	77.00W
Mechanicsville, Md., U.S. (mē-kăn'ĭks-vĭl)	100e	38.27N	76.45W
Mechanicville, N.Y., U.S. (mēkăn'ĭk-vĭl)	99	42.55N	73.45W
Mechelen, Bel.	151	51.01N	4.28E
Mechriyya, Alg.	148	33.30N	0.13W
Mecicine Bow Range, mts., Co., U.S. (mĕd'ĭ-sĭn bō)	110	40.55N	106.02W
Meckinghoven, Ger.	236	51.37N	7.19E
Mecklenburg, hist. reg., Ger.	154	53.30N	13.00E
Medan, Indon. (mā-dän')	196	3.35N	98.35E
Medanosa, Punta, c., Arg. (pōō'n-tä-mē-dä-nō'sä)	132	47.50S	65.53W
Medden, r., Eng., U.K. (mĕd'ĕn)	144a	53.14N	1.05W
Medellín, Col. (mā-dhĕl-yēn')	130	6.15N	75.34W
Medellín, Mex. (mĕ-dĕl-yĕ'n)	119	19.03N	96.08W
Medenine, Tun. (mā-dĕ-nēn')	148	33.22N	10.33E
Medfeld, Ma., U.S. (mĕd'fēld)	93a	42.11N	71.19W
Medford, Ma., U.S. (mĕd'fẽrd)	93a	42.25N	71.07W
Medford, N.J., U.S.	100f	39.54N	74.50W
Medford, Ok., U.S.	111	36.47N	97.44W
Medford, Or., U.S.	96	42.19N	122.52W
Medford, Wi., U.S.	103	45.09N	90.22W
Medford Hillside, Ma., U.S.	227a	42.24N	71.07W
Media, Pa., U.S. (mē'dĭ-ȧ)	100f	39.55N	75.24W
Mediaş, Rom. (mĕd-yäsh')	155	46.09N	24.21E
Medical Lake, Wa., U.S. (mĕd'ĭ-kăl)	104	47.34N	117.40W
Medicine Bow, r., Wy., U.S.	105	41.58N	106.30W
Medicine Hat, Can. (mĕd'ĭ-sĭn hăt)	84	50.03N	110.40W
Medicine Lake, l., Mt., U.S. (mĕd'ĭ-sĭn)	105	48.24N	104.15W
Medicine Lodge, Ks., U.S.	110	37.17N	98.37W
Medicine Lodge, r., Ks., U.S.	110	37.20N	98.57W
Medina *see* Al Madīnah, Sau. Ar.	182	24.26N	39.42E
Medina, N.Y., U.S. (mē-dī'nȧ)	99	43.15N	78.20W
Medina, Oh., U.S.	101d	41.08N	81.52W
Medina, r., Tx., U.S.	112	29.45N	99.13W
Medina del Campo, Spain (mā-dē'nä dĕl käm'pō)	148	41.18N	4.54W
Medina de Ríoseco, Spain (mā-dē'nä dā rē-ō-sā'kō)	158	41.53N	5.05W
Medina Lake, l., Tx., U.S.	112	29.36N	98.47W
Medina Sidonia, Spain	158	36.28N	5.58W
Mediterranean Sea, sea (mĕd-ĭ-tẽr-ā'nē-ăn)	148	36.22N	13.25E
Medjerda, Oued, r., Afr.	148	36.43N	9.54E
Mednogorsk, Russia	164	51.27N	57.22E
Medveditsa, r., Russia (mĕd-vyĕ'dē tsȧ)	167	50.10N	43.40E
Medvedkovo, neigh., Russia	239b	55.53N	37.38E
Medvezhegorsk, Russia (mĕd-vyĕzh'yĕ-gôrsk')	166	63.00N	34.20E
Medway, Ma., U.S. (mĕd'wā)	93a	42.08N	71.23W
Medyn', Russia (mĕ-dēn')	162	54.58N	35.53E
Medzhybizh, Ukr.	163	49.23N	27.29E
Meekatharra, Austl. (mē-kȧ-thär'ȧ)	202	26.30S	118.38E
Meeker, Co., U.S. (mēk'ẽr)	109	40.00N	107.55W
Meelpaeg Lake, l., Can. (mēl'pȧ-ĕg)	93	48.22N	56.52W
Meerane, Ger. (mā-rä'nĕ)	154	50.51N	12.27E
Meerbusch, Ger.	157c	51.15N	6.41E
Meerut, India (mē'rŏt)	183	28.59N	77.43E
Megalópolis, Grc. (mĕg-ȧ lŏ'pō-lĭs)	161	37.22N	22.08E
Meganom, Mys, c., Ukr.	163	44.48N	35.17E
Mégara, Grc. (mĕg'ȧ-rȧ)	161	37.59N	23.21E
Megget, S.C., U.S. (mĕg'ĕt)	115	32.44N	80.15W
Megler, Wa., U.S. (mĕg'lẽr)	106c	46.15N	123.52W
Meguro, neigh., Japan	242a	35.38N	139.42E
Meherrin, r., Va., U.S. (mē-hĕr'ĭn)	115	36.40N	77.49W
Mehlville, Mo., U.S.	107e	38.30N	90.19W
Mehpālpur, neigh., India	240d	28.33N	77.08E
Mehrābād, Iran	241h	35.40N	51.20E
Mehram Nagar, neigh., India	240d	28.34N	77.07E
Mehrow, Ger.	238a	52.34N	13.37E
Mehrum, Ger.	236	51.35N	6.37E
Mehsāna, India	186	23.42N	72.23E
Mehun-sur-Yèvre, Fr. (mē-ŭN-sür-yĕvr')	156	47.11N	2.14E
Meide, Ger.	236	51.11N	6.55E
Meiderich, neigh., Ger.	236	51.28N	6.46E
Meidling, neigh., Aus.	239e	48.11N	16.20E
Meiersberg, Ger.	236	51.17N	6.57E
Meiji Shrine, rel., Japan	242a	35.41N	139.42E
Meiling Pass, p., China (mā'lĭng')	189	25.22N	115.00E
Meinerzhagen, Ger. (mī'nĕrts-hä-gĕn)	157c	51.06N	7.39E
Meiningen, Ger. (mī'nĭng-ĕn)	154	50.35N	10.25E
Meiringen, Switz.	154	46.45N	8.11E
Meissen, Ger.	154	51.11N	13.28E
Meizhu, China (mā-jōō)	190	31.17N	119.12E
Mejillones, Chile (mā-ĸē-lyō'nås)	132	23.07S	70.31W
Mekambo, Gabon	216	1.01N	13.56E
Mekele, Eth.	211	13.31N	39.19E
Meknés, Mor. (mĕk'nĕs) (mĕk-nĕs')	210	33.56N	5.44W
Mekong, r., Asia	196	18.00N	104.30E
Melaka, Malay.	196	2.11N	102.15E
Melaka, state, Malay.	181b	2.19N	102.09E
Melanesia, is., Oc.	224	13.00S	164.00E
Melbourne, Austl. (mĕl'bŭrn)	203	37.52S	145.08E
Melbourne, Eng., U.K.	144a	52.49N	1.26W
Melbourne, Fl., U.S.	115a	28.05N	80.37W
Melbourne, Ky., U.S.	101f	39.02N	84.22W
Melcher, Ia., U.S. (mĕl'chẽr)	103	41.13N	93.11W
Melekess, Russia (mĕl-yĕk-ĕs)	166	54.14N	49.39E
Melenki, Russia (mĕ-lyĕŋ'kē)	166	55.25N	41.34E
Melfort, Can. (mĕl'fôrt)	84	52.52N	104.36W
Melghir, Chott, l., Alg.	210	33.52N	5.22E
Melilla, Sp. N. Afr. (mā-lēl'yä)	210	35.24N	3.30W
Melipilla, Chile (mā-lē-pē'lyä)	132	33.40S	71.12W
Melita, Can.	89	49.11N	101.09W
Melitopol', Ukr. (mā-lē-tô'pôl-y')	167	46.49N	35.19E
Melívoia, Grc.	161	39.42N	22.47E
Melkrivier, S. Afr.	218d	24.01S	28.23E
Mellen, Wi., U.S. (mĕl'ĕn)	103	46.20N	90.40W
Mellerud, Swe. (mäl'ĕ-rōōdh)	152	58.43N	12.25E
Melling, Eng., U.K.	237a	53.30N	2.56W
Melmoth, S. Afr.	213c	28.38S	31.26E
Melo, Ur. (mā'lō)	132	32.18S	54.07W
Melocheville, Can. (mĕ-lŏsh-vēl')	83a	45.24N	73.56W
Melozha, r., Russia (myĕ'lô-zhȧ)	172b	56.06N	38.34E
Melrose, Ma., U.S. (mĕl'rōz)	93a	42.29N	71.06W
Melrose, Mn., U.S.	103	45.39N	94.49W
Melrose Highlands, Ma., U.S.	227a	42.28N	71.04W
Melrose Park, Il., U.S.	101a	41.54N	87.52W
Meltham, Eng., U.K. (mĕl'thăm)	144a	53.35N	1.51W
Melton, Austl. (mĕl'tŭn)	201a	37.41S	144.35E
Melton Mowbray, Eng., U.K. (mō'brâ)	144a	52.45N	0.52W
Melúli, r., Moz.	217	16.10S	39.30E
Melun, Fr. (mĕ-lŭN')	147	48.32N	2.40E
Melunga, Ang.	216	17.16S	16.24E
Melville, Can. (mĕl'vĭl)	84	50.55N	102.48W
Melville, La., U.S.	113	30.39N	91.45W
Melville, i., Austl.	202	11.30S	131.12E
Melville, l., Can.	85	53.46N	59.31W
Melville, Cape, c., Austl.	203	14.15S	145.50E
Melville Hills, hills, Can.	84	69.18N	124.57W
Melville Peninsula, pen., Can.	85	67.44N	84.09W
Melvindale, Mi., U.S. (mĕl'vĭn-dāl)	101b	42.17N	83.11W
Melyana, Alg.	147	36.19N	1.56E
Mélykút, Hung. (mā'l'kōōt)	155	46.14N	19.21E
Memba, Moz. (mĕm'bȧ)	213	14.12N	40.35E
Memel *see* Klaipėda, Lith.	166	55.43N	21.10E
Memel, S. Afr. (mĕ'mĕl)	218d	27.42S	29.35E
Memmingen, Ger. (mĕm'ĭng-ĕn)	154	47.59N	10.10E
Memo, r., Ven. (mĕ'mō)	131b	9.32N	66.30W
Memphis, Mo., U.S. (mĕm'fĭs)	111	40.27N	92.11W
Memphis, Tn., U.S. (mĕm'fĭs)	97	35.07N	90.03W
Memphis, Tx., U.S.	110	34.42N	100.33W
Memphis, hist., Egypt	218b	29.50N	31.12E
Mena, Ukr. (mē-nä')	163	51.31N	32.14E
Mena, Ar., U.S. (mē'nȧ)	111	34.35N	94.09W
Menangle, Austl.	201b	34.08S	150.48E
Menard, Tx., U.S. (mē-närd')	112	30.56N	99.48W
Menasha, Wi., U.S. (mē-năsh'ȧ)	103	44.12N	88.29W
Mende, Fr. (mäNd)	156	44.31N	3.30E
Menden, Ger. (mĕn'dĕn)	157c	51.26N	7.47E
Menden, neigh., Ger.	236	51.24N	6.54E
Mendes, Braz. (mĕ'n-dĕs)	132b	22.32S	43.44W
Mendocino, Ca., U.S.	108	39.18N	123.47W
Mendocino, Cape, c., Ca., U.S. (mĕn'dō-sē'nō)	97	40.25N	12.42W
Mendota, Il., U.S. (mĕn-dō'tȧ)	103	41.34N	89.06W
Mendota, l., Wi., U.S.	103	43.09N	89.41W
Mendoza, Arg. (mĕn-dō'sä)	132	32.48S	68.45W
Mendoza, prov., Arg.	132	35.10S	69.00W
Mengcheng, China (mŭŋ-chŭŋ)	190	33.15N	116.34E
Mengede, neigh., Ger.	236	51.34N	7.23E
Menglinghausen, neigh., Ger.	236	51.28N	7.25E
Meng Shan, mts., China (mŭŋ shän)	190	35.47N	117.23E
Mengzi, China	188	23.22N	103.20E
Menindee, Austl. (mĕ-nĭn-dē)	204	32.23S	142.30E
Menlo Park, Ca., U.S. (mĕn'lō pärk)	106b	37.27N	122.11W
Menlo Park Terrace, N.J., U.S.	228	40.32N	74.20W
Menno, S.D., U.S. (mĕn'ō)	102	43.14N	97.34W
Menominee, Mi., U.S. (mē-nŏm'ĭ-nē)	103	45.08N	87.40W
Menominee, r., Mi., U.S.	103	45.37N	87.54W
Menominee Falls, Wi., U.S. (fôls)	101a	43.11N	88.06W
Menominee Ra, Mi., U.S.	103	46.07N	88.53W
Menomonee, r., Wi., U.S.	101a	43.09N	88.06W
Menomonie, Wi., U.S.	103	44.53N	91.55W
Menongue, Ang.	216	14.36S	17.48E
Menorca (Minorca), i., Spain (mē-nô'r-kä)	142	40.05N	3.58E
Mentana, Italy (mĕn-tȧ'nä)	159d	42.02N	12.40E
Mentawai, Kepulauan, is., Indon. (mĕn-tä-vī')	196	1.08S	98.10E
Menton, Fr. (mäN-tôN')	157	43.46N	7.37E
Mentone, Austl.	243b	37.59S	145.05E
Mentone, Ca., U.S. (mĕn'tōne)	107a	34.05N	117.08W
Mentz, l., S. Afr. (mĕnts)	213c	33.13S	25.15E
Menzel Bourguiba, Tun.	148	37.12N	9.51E
Menzelinsk, Russia (mĕn'zyĕ-lĕnsk')	166	55.40N	53.15E
Menzies, Austl. (mĕn'zēz)	202	29.45S	122.15E
Meogui, Mex. (mā-ō'gē)	112	28.17N	105.28W
Meopham, Eng., U.K.	235	51.22N	0.22E
Meopham Station, Eng., U.K.	235	51.23N	0.21E
Meppel, Neth. (mĕp'ĕl)	151	52.41N	6.08E
Meppen, Ger. (mĕp'ĕn)	154	52.40N	7.18E
Merabéllou, Kólpos, b., Grc.	160a	35.16N	25.55E
Meramec, r., Mo., U.S. (mĕr'ȧ-mĕk)	111	38.06N	91.06W
Merano, Italy (mā-rä'nō)	148	46.39N	11.10E
Merasheen, i., Can. (mĕ'rȧ-shēn)	93	47.30N	54.15W
Merauke, Indon. (mā-rou'kä)	197	8.32S	140.17E
Meraux, La., U.S. (mĕ-ro')	100d	29.56N	89.56W
Mercader y Millás, Spain	238e	41.21N	2.05E
Mercato San Severino, Italy	159c	40.34N	14.38E
Merced, Ca., U.S. (mẽr-sĕd')	108	37.17N	120.30W
Merced, Ca., U.S.	108	37.25N	120.31W
Mercedario, Cerro, mtn., Arg. (mĕr-så-dhä'rē-ō)	132	31.58S	70.07W
Mercedes, Arg.	129c	34.41S	59.26W
Mercedes, Arg. (mĕr-sā'dhās)	132	29.04S	58.01W
Mercedes, Tx., U.S.	113	26.09N	97.55W
Mercedes, Ur.	132	33.17S	58.04W
Mercedita, Chile (mĕr-sĕ-dē'tä)	129b	33.51S	71.10W
Mercer Island, Wa., U.S. (mûr'sẽr)	106a	47.35N	122.15W
Mercês, Braz. (mĕ-sĕ's)	129a	21.13S	43.20W
Mercês, Port.	238d	38.47N	9.19W
Merchtem, Bel.	145a	50.57N	4.13E
Mercier, Can.	83a	45.19N	73.45W
Mercy, Cape, c., Can.	85	64.48N	63.22W
Merdeka Palace, bldg., Indon.	241i	6.10S	106.49E
Mere, Eng., U.K.	237b	53.20N	2.25W
Meredale, S. Afr.	244b	26.17S	27.59E
Meredith, N.H., U.S. (mĕr'ē-dĭth)	99	43.35N	71.35W
Merefa, Ukr. (mā-rĕf'ȧ)	163	49.49N	36.04E
Merendón, Serranía de, mts., Hond.	120	15.01N	89.05W
Mereworth, Eng., U.K. (mĕ-rē wûrth)	144b	51.15N	0.23E
Mergui, Myanmar (mẽr-gē')	196	12.29N	98.39E
Mergui Archipelago, is., Myanmar	196	12.04N	97.02E
Meric (Maritsa), r., Eur.	153	40.43N	26.19E
Mérida, Mex.	116	20.58N	89.37W
Mérida, Ven.	130	8.30N	71.15W
Mérida, Cordillera de, mts., Ven. (mĕ'rē-dhä)	130	8.30N	70.45W
Meriden, Ct., U.S. (mĕr'ĭ-dĕn)	99	41.30N	72.50W
Meridian, Ms., U.S. (mē-rĭd-ĭ-ăn)	97	32.21N	88.41W
Meridian, Tx., U.S.	113	31.56N	97.37W
Mérignac, Fr.	156	44.50N	0.40W
Merikarvia, Fin. (mā'rē-kàr'vē-ȧ)	153	61.51N	21.30E
Mering, Ger. (mĕ'rĕng)	145d	48.16N	11.00E
Merion Station, Pa., U.S.	229b	40.00N	75.15W
Merkel, Tx., U.S. (mûr'kĕl)	112	32.26N	100.02W
Merkinė, Lith.	153	54.10N	24.10E
Merksem, Bel.	145a	51.15N	4.27E
Merkys, r., Lith. (mär'kĭs)	155	54.23N	25.00E
Merlo, Arg. (mĕr-lō)	132a	34.40S	58.44W
Merlynston, Austl.	243b	37.43S	144.58E
Meron, Hare, mtn., Isr.	181a	32.58N	35.25E
Merriam, Ks., U.S. (mĕr-rĭ-yăm)	107f	39.01N	94.42W
Merriam, Mn., U.S.	107g	44.44N	93.36W
Merrick, N.Y., U.S. (mĕr'ĭk)	100a	40.40N	73.33W
Merri Creek, r., Austl.	243b	37.48S	144.59E
Merrifield, Va., U.S. (mĕr'ĭ-fēld)	100e	38.50N	77.12W
Merrill, Wi., U.S. (mĕr'ĭl)	103	45.11N	89.42W
Merrimac, Ma., U.S. (mĕr'ĭ-măk)	93a	45.20N	71.00W
Merrimack, N.H., U.S.	93a	42.51N	71.25W

318 Merrimack–Minato

PLACE (Pronunciation)	PAGE	Lat. °'	Long. °'
Merrimack, r., Ma., U.S. (měr'ĭ-măk)	99	43.10N	71.30W
Merrionette Park, Il., U.S.	231a	41.41N	87.42W
Merritt, Can. (měr'ĭt)	84	50.07N	120.47W
Merrylands, Austl.	243a	33.50S	150.59E
Merryville, La., U.S. (měr'ĭ-vĭl)	113	30.46N	93.34W
Mersa Fatma, Erit.	211	14.54N	40.14E
Merscheid, neigh., Ger.	236	51.10N	7.01E
Merseburg, Ger. (měr'zē-bŏŏrgh)	154	51.21N	11.59E
Mersey, r., Eng., U.K. (mûr'zė)	144a	53.20N	2.55W
Merseyside, co., Eng., U.K.	144a	53.29N	2.59W
Mersing, Malay.	181b	2.25N	103.51E
Merta Road, India (mär'tŭ rōd)	186	26.50N	73.54E
Merthyr Tydfil, Wales, U.K. (mûr'thẽr tĭd'vĭl)	150	51.46N	3.30W
Mértola Almodóvar, Port. (měr-tō-la-äl-mō-dô'vär)	158	37.39N	8.04W
Merton, neigh., Eng., U.K.	235	51.25N	0.12W
Méru, Fr. (mā-rü')	156	49.14N	2.08E
Meru, Kenya (mā'rōō)	211	0.01N	37.45E
Meru, Mount, mtn., Tan.	217	3.15S	36.43E
Merume Mountains, mts., Guy. (měr-ü'mĕ)	131	5.45N	60.15W
Merwede Kanaal, can., Neth.	145a	52.15N	5.01E
Merwin, l., Wa., U.S. (měr'wĭn)	106c	45.58N	122.27W
Merzifon, Tur. (měr'ze-fōn)	182	40.50N	35.30E
Mesa, Az., U.S. (mā'sa)	109	33.25N	111.50W
Mesabi Range, mts., Mn., U.S. (mā-sŏb'bē)	103	47.17N	93.04W
Mesagne, Italy (mā-sän'yå)	161	40.34N	17.51E
Mesa Verde National Park, rec., Co., U.S. (vēr'dē)	96	37.22N	108.27W
Mescalero Apache Indian Reservation, I.R., N.M., U.S. (mĕs-kä-lā'rō)	109	33.10N	105.45W
Meščerskij, Russia	239b	55.40N	37.25E
Meshchovsk, Russia (myĕsh'chĕfsk)	162	54.17N	35.19E
Mesilla, N.M., U.S. (mā-sē'yä)	109	32.15N	106.45W
Meskine, Chad	215	11.25N	15.21E
Mesolóngion, Grc. (mē-sō-lôŋ'gē-ŏn)	161	38.23N	21.28E
Mesopotamia, hist. reg., Asia	185	34.00N	44.00E
Mesquita, Braz.	132b	22.48S	43.26W
Messina, Italy (mĕ-sē'na)	142	38.11N	15.34E
Messina, S. Afr.	212	22.17S	30.13E
Messina, Stretto di, strt., Italy (stě't-tô dē)	149	38.10N	15.34E
Messíni, Grc.	161	37.05N	22.00E
Messy, Fr.	237c	48.58N	2.42E
Mestaganem, Alg.	210	36.04N	0.11E
Mestre, Italy (mĕs'trā)	160	45.29N	12.15E
Meta, dept., Col. (mĕ'tä)	130a	3.28N	74.07W
Meta, r., S.A.	130	4.33N	72.09W
Métabetchouane, r., Can. (mĕ-tá-bĕt-chōō-än')	91	47.45N	72.00W
Metairie, La., U.S.	113	30.00N	90.11W
Metán, Arg. (mĕ-tá'n)	132	25.32S	64.51W
Metangula, Moz.	212	12.42S	34.48E
Metapán, El Sal. (må-täpän')	120	14.21N	89.26W
Metcalfe, Can. (mĕt-käf)	83c	45.14N	75.27W
Metchosin, Can.	106a	48.22N	123.33W
Metepec, Mex. (må-tĕ-pĕk')	118	18.56N	98.31W
Metepec, Mex.	118	19.15N	99.36W
Methow, r., Wa., U.S. (mĕt'hou) (mĕt hou')	104	48.26N	120.15W
Methuen, Ma., U.S. (mē-thū'ĕn)	93a	42.44N	71.11W
Metković, Cro. (mĕt'kō-vĭch)	161	43.02N	17.40E
Metlakatla, Ak., U.S. (mĕt-la-kăt'la)	95	55.08N	131.35W
Metropolis, Il., U.S. (mē-trŏp'ō-lĭs)	111	37.09N	88.46W
Metropolitan Museum of Art, pt. of i., N.Y., U.S.	228	40.47N	73.58W
Metter, Ga., U.S. (mĕt'ẽr)	115	32.21N	82.05W
Mettmann, Ger. (mĕt'män)	157c	51.15N	6.58E
Metuchen, N.J., U.S. (mĕ-tŭ'chĕn)	100a	40.32N	74.21W
Metz, Fr. (mĕtz)	147	49.08N	6.10E
Metztitlán, Mex. (mĕtz-tĕt-län)	118	20.36N	98.45W
Meuban, Cam.	215	2.27N	12.41E
Meudon, Fr.	237c	48.48N	2.14E
Meuse (Maas), r., Eur. (mûz) (müz)	151	50.32N	5.22E
Mexborough, Eng., U.K. (mĕks'bŭr-ô)	144a	53.30N	1.17W
Mexia, Tx., U.S. (må-hē'ä)	113	31.32N	96.29W
Mexian, China	189	24.20N	116.10E
Mexicalcingo, Mex. (mĕ-kē-käl-sĕn'gō)	119a	19.13N	99.34W
Mexicali, Mex. (mäk-sē-kä'lē)	116	32.28N	115.29W
Mexicana, Altiplanicie, plat., Mex.	118	22.38N	102.33W
Mexican Hat, Ut., U.S. (mĕk'sĭ-kăn hăt)	109	37.10N	109.55W
Mexico, Me., U.S. (mĕk'sĭ-kō)	92	44.34N	70.33W
Mexico, Mo., U.S.	111	39.09N	91.51W
Mexico, nation, N.A.	116	23.45N	104.00W
Mexico, Gulf of, b., N.A.	116	25.15N	93.45W
Mexico City, Mex. (mĕk'sĭ-kō)	116	19.28N	99.09W
Mexticacán, Mex. (mĕs'tē-kä-kän')	118	21.12N	102.43W
Meyers Chuck, Ak., U.S.	86	55.44N	132.15W
Meyersdale, Pa., U.S. (mī'ẽrz-dāl)	99	39.55N	79.00W
Meyerton, S. Afr. (mī'ẽr-tŭn)	218d	26.35S	28.01E
Meymaneh, Afg.	182	35.53N	64.38E
Mezen', Russia	164	65.50N	44.05E
Mezen', r., Russia	166	65.20N	44.45E
Mézenc, Mont, mtn., Fr. (mōn-mā-zĕn')	156	44.55N	4.12E
Mezha, r., Eur. (myā'zhá)	162	55.53N	31.44E
Mézieres-sur-Seine, Fr. (mā-zyâr'sür-sån')	157b	48.58N	1.49E
Mezőkövesd, Hung. (mĕ'zû-kû'vĕsht)	155	47.49N	20.36E
Mezőtur, Hung. (mĕ'zû-tōōr)	155	47.00N	20.36E
Mezquital, Mex. (måz-kē-täl')	118	23.30N	104.20W
Mezquitic, Mex. (måz-kē-tēk')	118	22.25N	103.43W
Mezquitic, r., Mex.	118	22.25N	103.45W
Mfangano Island, i., Kenya	217	0.28S	33.35E

PLACE (Pronunciation)	PAGE	Lat. °'	Long. °'
Mga, Russia (m'gá)	172c	59.45N	31.04E
Mglin, Russia (m'glĕn')	162	53.03N	32.52W
Mia, Oued, r., Alg.	148	29.26N	3.15E
Miacatlán, Mex. (mē'ä-kä-tlän')	118	18.42N	99.17W
Mia-dong, neigh., S. Kor.	241b	37.37N	127.01E
Miahuatlán, Mex. (mē'ä-wä-tlän')	119	16.20N	96.38W
Miajadas, Spain (mē-ä-hä'däs)	158	39.10N	5.53W
Miami, Az., U.S.	96	33.20N	110.55W
Miami, Fl., U.S.	97	25.45N	80.11W
Miami, Ok., U.S.	111	36.51N	94.51W
Miami, Tx., U.S.	110	35.41N	100.39W
Miami Beach, Fl., U.S.	115a	25.47N	80.07W
Miamisburg, Oh., U.S. (mī-ăm'iz-bûrg)	98	39.40N	84.20W
Miamitown, Oh., U.S. (mī-ăm'ĭ-toun)	101f	39.13N	84.43W
Mīāneh, Iran	182	37.15N	47.13E
Miangas, Pulau, i., Indon.	197	5.30N	127.00E
Miaoli, Tai. (mē-ou'lĭ)	193	24.30N	120.48E
Miaozhen, China (miou-jŭn)	190	31.44N	121.28E
Miass, Russia (mī-äs')	170	54.59N	60.06E
Miastko, Pol. (myäst'kô)	154	54.01N	17.00E
Miccosukee Indian Reservation, I.R., Fl., U.S.	115a	26.10N	80.50W
Michajlovskoje, Russia	239b	55.35N	37.35E
Michalovce, Slvk. (mē'ĸä-lôf'tsĕ)	155	48.44N	21.56E
Michel Peak, mtn., Can.	86	53.35N	126.25W
Michelson, Mount, mtn., Ak., U.S. (mĭch'ĕl-sŭn)	95	69.11N	144.12W
Michendorf, Ger. (mē'ĸĕn-dōrf)	145b	52.19N	13.02E
Miches, Dom. Rep. (mē'chĕs)	123	19.00N	69.05W
Michigan, state, U.S. (mĭsh-'ĭ-găn)	97	45.55N	87.00W
Michigan, Lake, l., U.S.	97	43.20N	87.10W
Michigan City, In., U.S.	98	41.40N	86.55W
Michillinda, Ca., U.S.	232	34.07N	118.05W
Michipicoten, r., Can.	103	47.56N	84.42W
Michipicoten Harbour, Can.	103	47.58N	84.58W
Michurinsk, Russia (mĭ-chōō-rĭnsk')	167	52.53N	40.32E
Mico, Punta, c., Nic. (pōō'n-tä-mē'kô)	121	11.38N	83.24W
Micronesia, is., Oc.	224	11.00N	159.00E
Micronesia, Federated States of, nation, Oc.	3	5.00N	152.00E
Midas, Nv., U.S. (mī'dås)	104	41.15N	116.50W
Middelfart, Den. (mēd''l-färt)	152	55.30N	9.45E
Middle, r., Can.	86	55.00N	125.50W
Middle Andaman, i., India (ăn-dȧ-măn')	196	12.44N	93.21E
Middle Bayou, Tx., U.S.	113a	29.38N	95.06W
Middleburg, S. Afr. (mĭd'ĕl-bûrg)	212	31.30S	25.00E
Middleburg, S. Afr.	218d	25.47S	29.30E
Middleburgh Heights, Oh., U.S.	229a	41.22N	81.48W
Middlebury, Vt., U.S. (mĭd''l-bĕr-ĭ)	99	44.00N	73.10W
Middle Concho, Tx., U.S. (kōn'chō)	112	31.21N	100.50W
Middle River, Md., U.S.	100e	39.20N	76.27W
Middlesboro, Ky., U.S. (mĭd''lz-bŭr-ō)	114	36.36N	83.42W
Middlesbrough, Eng., U.K. (mĭd''lz-brŭ)	146	54.35N	1.18W
Middlesex, N.J., U.S. (mĭd''l-sĕks)	100a	40.34N	74.30W
Middleton, Can. (mĭd''l-tŭn)	92	44.57N	65.04W
Middleton, Eng., U.K.	144a	53.34N	2.12W
Middletown, Ct., U.S.	99	41.35N	72.40W
Middletown, De., U.S.	99	39.30N	75.40W
Middletown, Ma., U.S.	93a	42.35N	71.01W
Middletown, N.Y., U.S.	99	41.26N	74.25W
Middletown, Oh., U.S.	98	39.30N	84.25W
Middlewich, Eng., U.K. (mĭd''l-wĭch)	144a	53.11N	2.27W
Middlewit, S. Afr. (mĭd'l'wĭt)	218d	24.50S	27.00E
Midfield, Al., U.S.	100h	33.28N	86.54W
Midi, Canal du, Fr. (kä-näl-dü-mē-dē')	147	43.22N	1.35E
Mid Illovo, S. Afr. (mĭd ĭl'ō-vō)	213c	29.59S	30.32E
Midland, Can. (mĭd'lănd)	85	44.45N	79.50W
Midland, Mi., U.S.	98	43.40N	84.20W
Midland, Tx., U.S.	112	32.05N	102.05W
Midland Beach, neigh., N.Y., U.S.	228	40.34N	74.05W
Midlothian, Il., U.S.	231a	41.38N	87.42W
Midvale, Ut., U.S. (mĭd'vāl)	107b	40.37N	111.54W
Midway, S. Afr.	244b	26.18S	27.51E
Midway, Al., U.S. (mĭd'wā)	114	32.03N	85.30W
Midway City, Ca., U.S.	232	33.45N	118.00W
Midway Islands, is., Oc.	2	28.00N	179.00W
Midwest, Wy., U.S. (mĭd-wĕst')	105	43.25N	106.15W
Midye, Tur. (mēd'yĕ)	167	41.35N	28.10E
Międzyrzecz, Pol. (myăn-dzû'zhĕch)	154	52.26N	15.35E
Mielec, Pol. (myĕ'lĕts)	155	50.17N	21.27E
Mier, Mex. (myâr)	112	26.26N	99.08W
Mieres, Spain (myā'rās)	158	43.14N	5.45W
Mier y Noriega, Mex. (myâr'ē nō-rē-ā'gä)	118	23.28N	100.08W
Miguel Auza, Mex.	118	24.17N	103.27W
Miguel Pereira, Braz.	132b	22.27S	43.28W
Mijares, r., Spain	159	39.55N	0.01W
Mikage, Japan (mē'ká-gä)	195b	34.42N	135.15E
Mikawa-Wan, b., Japan (mē'kä-wä wän)	195	34.43N	137.09E
Mikhaylov, Russia (mē-ĸäy'lôf)	166	54.14N	39.03E
Mikhaylovka, Russia	167	50.05N	43.10E
Mikhaylovka, Russia	172a	55.35N	57.57E
Mikhaylovka, Russia	172c	59.20N	30.21E
Mikhnëvo, Russia (mĭk-nyô'vô)	172b	55.08N	37.57E
Miki, Japan (mē'kē)	195b	34.47N	134.59E
Mikindani, Tan. (mē-kēn-dä'nē)	213	10.17S	40.07E
Mikkeli, Fin. (mĭk'ĕ-lĭ)	146	61.42N	27.14E
Míkonos, i., Grc.	161	37.26N	25.30E
Mikulov, Czech Rep. (mĭ'kōō-lôf)	154	48.47N	16.39E
Mikumi, Tan.	217	7.24S	36.59E
Mikuni, Japan (mē'kōō-nē)	195	36.09N	136.14E
Mikuni-Sammyaku, mts., Japan (säm'myä-kōō)	195	36.51N	138.38E
Mikura, i., Japan (mē'kōō-rä)	195	33.53N	139.26E
Milaca, Milaca, Mn., U.S. (mē-lăk'ȧ)	103	45.45N	93.41W
Milan (Milano), Italy (mē-lä'nō)	160	45.29N	9.12E

PLACE (Pronunciation)	PAGE	Lat. °'	Long. °'
Milan, Mi., U.S. (mĭ'lăn)	98	42.05N	83.40W
Milan, Mo., U.S.	111	40.13N	93.07W
Milan, Tn., U.S.	114	35.54N	88.47W
Milâs, Tur. (mē'läs)	149	37.10N	27.25E
Milazzo, Italy	160	38.13N	15.17E
Milbank, S.D., U.S. (mĭl'băŋĸ)	102	45.13N	96.38W
Mildura, Austl. (mĭl-dū'rȧ)	203	34.10S	142.18E
Miles City, Mt., U.S. (mīlz)	96	46.24N	105.50W
Milford, Ct., U.S. (mĭl'fẽrd)	99	41.15N	73.05W
Milford, De., U.S.	99	38.55N	75.25W
Milford, Md., U.S.	229c	39.21N	76.44W
Milford, Ma., U.S.	93a	42.09N	71.31W
Milford, Mi., U.S.	101b	42.35N	83.36W
Milford, N.H., U.S.	99	42.50N	71.40W
Milford, Oh., U.S.	101f	39.11N	84.18W
Milford, Ut., U.S.	109	38.20N	113.05W
Milford Sound, strt., N.Z.	205	44.35S	167.47E
Miling, Austl. (mĭl''ng)	202	30.30S	116.25E
Milipitas, Ca., U.S. (mĭl-ĭ-pĭ'tăs)	106b	37.26N	121.54W
Milk, r., N.A.	96	48.30N	107.00W
Millau, Fr. (mē-yō')	147	44.06N	3.04E
Millbourne, Pa., U.S.	229b	39.58N	75.15W
Millbrae, Ca., U.S. (mĭl'brā)	106b	37.36N	122.23W
Millburn, N.J., U.S.	228	40.44N	74.20W
Millbury, Ma., U.S. (mĭl'bĕr-ĭ)	93a	42.12N	71.46W
Mill Creek, r., Can. (mĭl)	83g	53.28N	113.25W
Mill Creek, r., Ca., U.S.	108	40.07N	121.55W
Milledgeville, Ga., U.S. (mĭl'ĕj-vĭl)	114	33.05N	83.15W
Mille Îles, Rivière des, r., Can. (rē-vyâr' dā mĭl'ĭl')	83a	45.41N	73.40W
Mille Lac Indian Reservation, I.R., Mn., U.S. (mĭl lăk')	103	46.14N	94.13W
Mille Lacs, l., Mn., U.S.	103	46.25N	93.22W
Mille Lacs, Lac des, l., Can. (läk dĕ mēl läks)	90	48.52N	90.53W
Millen, Ga., U.S. (mĭl'ĕn)	115	32.47N	81.55W
Miller, S.D., U.S. (mĭl'ẽr)	102	44.31N	99.00W
Millerovo, Russia (mĭl'ĕ-rô-vô)	167	48.58N	40.27E
Millersburg, Ky., U.S. (mĭl'ẽrz-bûrg)	98	38.15N	84.10W
Millersburg, Oh., U.S.	98	40.35N	81.55W
Millersburg, Pa., U.S.	99	40.35N	76.55W
Millerton, Can. (mĭl'ẽr-tŭn)	92	46.56N	65.40W
Millertown, Can. (mĭl'ẽr-toun)	93	48.49N	56.32W
Mill Green, Eng., U.K.	235	51.41N	0.22E
Mill Hill, neigh., Eng., U.K.	235	51.37N	0.13W
Millicent, Austl. (mĭl-ĭ-sĕnt)	204	37.30S	140.20E
Millinocket, Me., U.S. (mĭl-ĭ-nŏk'ĕt)	92	45.40N	68.44W
Millis, Ma., U.S. (mĭl-ĭs)	93a	42.10N	71.22W
Mill Neck, N.Y., U.S.	228	40.52N	73.34W
Millstadt, Il., U.S. (mĭl'stăt)	107e	38.27N	90.06W
Millstone, r., N.J., U.S. (mĭl'stōn)	100a	40.27N	74.38W
Millstream, Austl. (mĭl'strēm)	202	21.45S	117.10E
Milltown, Can. (mĭl'toun)	92	45.13N	67.19W
Millvale, Pa., U.S.	230b	40.29N	79.58W
Mill Valley, Ca., U.S. (mĭl)	106b	37.54N	122.32W
Millwood Reservoir, res., Ar., U.S.	111	33.00N	94.00W
Milly-la-Forêt, Fr. (mē-yĕ'-la-fō-rĕ')	157b	48.24N	2.28E
Milmont Park, Pa., U.S.	229b	39.53N	75.20W
Milnerton, S. Afr. (mĭl'nẽr-tŭn)	212a	33.52S	18.30E
Milnor, N.D., U.S. (mĭl'nẽr)	102	46.17N	97.29W
Milnrow, Eng., U.K.	237b	53.37N	2.06W
Milo, Me., U.S.	92	44.16N	69.01W
Milon-la-Chapelle, Fr.	237c	48.44N	2.03E
Milos, i., Grc. (mē'lŏs)	149	36.45N	24.35E
Milpa Alta, Mex. (mē'l-pä-á'l-tä)	119a	19.11N	99.01W
Milspe, Ger.	236	51.18N	7.21E
Milton, Can.	83d	43.31N	79.53W
Milton, Fl., U.S. (mĭl'tŭn)	114	30.37N	87.02W
Milton, Pa., U.S.	99	41.00N	76.50W
Milton, Ut., U.S.	107b	41.04N	111.44W
Milton, Wa., U.S.	106a	47.15N	122.20W
Milton, Wi., U.S.	103	42.45N	89.00W
Milton-Freewater, Or., U.S.	104	45.57N	118.25W
Milvale, Pa., U.S. (mĭl'vāl)	101e	40.29N	79.58W
Milville, N.J., U.S. (mĭl'vĭl)	99	39.25N	75.00W
Milwaukee, Wi., U.S.	97	43.03N	87.55W
Milwaukee, r., Wi., U.S.	101a	43.10N	87.56W
Milwaukie, Or., U.S. (mĭl-wô'kē)	104	45.27N	122.38W
Mimiapan, Mex. (mē-myä-pán')	119a	19.26N	99.28W
Mimoso do Sul, Braz. (mē-mô'sō-dō-sōō'l)	129a	21.03S	41.21W
Min, r., China (mēn)	189	26.03N	118.30E
Min, r., China	193	29.30N	104.00E
Mina, r., Alg. (mē'ná)	159	35.24N	0.51E
Minago, r., Can. (mĭ-nä'gō)	89	54.25N	98.45W
Minakuchi, Japan (mē'ná-kōō'chē)	195	34.59N	136.06E
Minami, neigh., Japan	241e	34.58N	135.45E
Minamisenju, neigh., Japan	242a	35.44N	139.48E
Minas, Cuba (mē'näs)	122	21.30N	77.35W
Minas, Indon.	181b	0.52N	101.29E
Minas, Ur. (mē'näs)	132	34.18S	55.12W
Minas, Sierra de las, mts., Guat. (syĕr'rä dā läs mē'näs)	120	15.08N	90.25W
Minas Basin, b., Can. (mī'nȧs)	92	45.20N	64.00W
Minas Channel, strt., Can.	92	45.15N	64.45W
Minas de Oro, Hond. (mē'näs-dĕ-dĕ-ŏ-rô)	120	14.52N	87.19W
Minas de Riotinto, Spain (mē'näs dä rē-ō-tēn'tō)	158	37.43N	6.35W
Minas Novas, Braz. (mē'näzh nō'väzh)	131	17.20S	42.19W
Minatare, l., Ne., U.S. (mĭn'ȧ-târ)	102	41.56N	103.07W
Minatitlán, Mex. (mē-nä-tē-tlän')	116	17.59N	94.33W
Minatitlán, Mex.	118	19.21N	104.02W
Minato, Japan (mē'ná-tô)	195	35.13N	139.52E
Minato, neigh., Japan	242a	35.39N	139.45E

ăt; finȧl; rāte; senåte; ärm; åsk; sofȧ; fâre; ch-choose; dh-as th in other; bē; ėvent; bĕt; recĕnt; cratẽr; g-gō; gh-guttural g; bĭt; ĭ-short neutral; rīde; ĸ-guttural k as ch in German ich;

PLACE (Pronunciation)	PAGE	Lat. °′	Long. °′
Minato, neigh., Japan	242b	34.39N	135.26E
Minch, The, strt., Scot., U.K.	142	58.04N	6.04W
Mindanao, i., Phil.	197	8.00N	125.00E
Mindanao Sea, sea, Phil.	197	8.55N	124.00E
Minden, Ger. (mĭn'dĕn)	154	52.17N	8.58E
Minden, La., U.S.	113	32.36N	93.19W
Minden, Ne., U.S.	110	40.30N	98.54W
Mindoro, i., Phil.	196	12.50N	121.05E
Mindoro Strait, strt., Phil.	197a	12.28N	120.33E
Mindyak, Russia (mēn'dyák)	172a	54.01N	58.48E
Mineola, N.Y., U.S. (mĭn-ē-ō'lȧ)	100a	40.43N	73.38W
Mineola, Tx., U.S.	113	32.39N	95.31W
Mineral del Chico, Mex. (mē-nä-räl'dĕl chē'kō)	118	20.13N	98.46W
Mineral del Monte, Mex. (mē-nä-räl dĕl mōn'tå)	118	20.18N	98.39W
Mineral'nyye Vody, Russia	167	44.10N	43.15E
Mineral Point, Wi., U.S. (mĭn'ẽr-ăl)	103	42.50N	90.10W
Minerál Wells, Tx., U.S. (mĭn'ẽr-ăl wĕlz)	112	32.48N	98.06W
Minerva, Oh., U.S. (mĭ-nur'vá)	98	40.45N	81.10W
Minervino, Italy (mē-nĕr-vē'nō)	160	41.07N	16.05E
Mineyama, Japan (mē-nĕ-yä'mä)	195	35.38N	135.05E
Mingäçevir, Azer.	168	40.45N	47.03E
Mingäçevir su anbarı, res., Azer.	168	40.50N	46.50E
Mingan, Can.	85	50.18N	64.02W
Mingenew, Austl. (mĭn'gĕ-nû)	202	29.15S	115.45E
Mingo Junction, Oh., U.S. (mĭŋ'gō)	98	40.15N	80.40W
Minho, hist. reg., Port. (mēn yō)	158	41.32N	8.13W
Minho (Miño), r., Eur. (mē'n-yō)	158	41.28N	9.05W
Ministik Lake, l., Can. (mĭ-nĭs'tĭk)	83g	53.23N	113.05W
Minna, Nig. (mĭn'á)	210	9.37N	6.33E
Minneapolis, Ks., U.S. (mĭn-ē-ăp'ō-lĭs)	111	39.07N	97.41W
Minneapolis, Mn., U.S.	97	44.58N	93.15W
Minnedosa, Can. (mĭn-ē-dō'sȧ)	84	50.14N	99.51W
Minneota, Mn., U.S. (mĭn-ē-ō'tȧ)	102	44.34N	95.59W
Minnesota, state, U.S. (mĭn-ē-sō'tȧ)	97	46.10N	90.20W
Minnesota, r., Mn., U.S.	97	44.30N	95.00W
Minnetonka, l., Mn., U.S. (mĭn-ē-tôŋ'kȧ)	103	44.52N	93.34W
Minnitaki Lake, l., Can. (mĭ'nĭ-tä'kē)	89	49.58N	92.00W
Mino, r., Japan	195b	34.56N	135.06E
Minonk, Il., U.S. (mĭ'nŏnk)	98	40.55N	89.00W
Minooka, Il., U.S. (mĭ-nōō'kȧ)	101a	41.27N	88.15W
Minot, N.D., U.S.	96	48.13N	101.17W
Minsk, Bela. (mênsk)	164	53.54N	27.35E
Minsk, prov., Bela.	162	53.50N	27.43E
Mińsk Mazowiecki, Pol. (mēn'sk mä-zō-vyĕt'skĭ)	155	52.10N	21.35E
Minsterley, Eng., U.K. (mĭnstẽr-lē)	144a	52.38N	2.55W
Mintard, Ger.	236	51.22N	6.54E
Minto, Austl.	243a	34.01S	150.51E
Minto, Can.	92	46.05N	66.05W
Minto, l., Can.	85	57.18N	75.50W
Minturno, Italy (mēn-tōōr'nō)	160	41.17N	13.44E
Minūf, Egypt (mē-nōōf')	218b	30.26N	30.55E
Minusinsk, Russia (mē-nō-sēnsk')	165	53.47N	91.45E
Min'yar, Russia	172a	55.06N	57.33E
Miquelon Lake, l., Can. (mĭ'kē-lôn)	83g	53.16N	112.55W
Miquihuana, Mex. (mē-kē-wä'nä)	118	23.36N	99.45W
Miquon, Pa., U.S.	229b	40.04N	75.16W
Mir, Bela. (mēr)	155	53.27N	26.25E
Miracema, Braz. (mē-rä-sĕ'mä)	129a	21.24S	42.10W
Miracema do Tocantins, Braz.	131	9.34S	48.24W
Mirador, Braz. (mē-rá-dōr')	131	6.19S	44.12W
Miraflores, Col. (mē-rä-flō'räs)	130	5.10N	73.13W
Miraflores, Peru	130	16.19S	71.20W
Miraflores, Peru	233c	12.08S	77.03W
Miraflores Locks, trans., Pan.	116a	9.00N	79.35W
Miragoâne, Haiti (mē-rá-gwän')	123	18.25N	73.05W
Mira Loma, Ca., U.S. (mĭ'rȧ lō'mȧ)	107a	34.01N	117.32W
Miramar, Ca., U.S. (mĭr'ȧ-mär)	108a	32.53N	117.08W
Miramar, neigh., Cuba	233b	23.07N	82.25W
Miramas, Fr.	156	43.35N	5.00E
Miramichi Bay, b., Can. (mĭr'ȧ-mē'shē)	92	47.08N	65.08W
Miranda, Austl.	243a	34.02S	151.06E
Miranda, Col. (mē-rä'n-dä)	130a	3.14N	76.11W
Miranda, Ca., U.S.	108	40.14N	123.49W
Miranda, Ven.	131b	10.09N	68.24W
Miranda, dept., Ven.	131b	10.17N	66.41W
Miranda de Ebro, Spain (mē-rä'n-dä-dĕ-ĕ'brō)	158	42.42N	2.59W
Miranda do Douro, Port. (mē-rän'dä dō-dwĕ'rō)	158	41.30N	6.17W
Mirandela, Port. (mē-rän-dä'lȧ)	158	41.28N	7.10W
Mirando City, Tx., U.S. (mĭr-ȧn'dō)	112	27.25N	99.03W
Mira Por Vos Islets, is., Bah. (mē'rä pōr vōs)	123	22.05N	74.30W
Mira Por Vos Pass, strt., Bah.	123	22.10N	74.35W
Mirbāṭ, Oman	182	16.58N	54.42E
Mirebalais, Haiti (mēr-bá-lĕ')	123	18.50N	72.05W
Mirecourt, Fr. (mēr-kōōr')	157	48.20N	6.08E
Mirfield, Eng., U.K. (mûr'fēld)	144a	53.41N	1.42W
Miri, Malay. (mē'rē)	196	4.13N	113.56E
Mirim, Lagoa, l., S.A. (mē-rêɴ')	132	33.00S	53.15W
Mírina, Grc.	161	39.52N	25.01E
Miropol'ye, Ukr. (mē-rō-pôl'yĕ)	163	51.02N	35.13E
Mīrpur Khās, Pak. (mēr'pōōr ᴋäs)	186	25.36N	69.10E
Mirzāpur, India (mēr'zä-pōōr)	183	25.12N	82.38E
Mirzāpur, India	240a	22.50N	88.24E
Misailovo, Russia	239b	55.34N	37.49E
Misantla, Mex. (mē-sän'tlä)	119	19.55N	96.49W
Miscou, i., Can. (mĭs'kō)	92	47.58N	64.35W
Miscou Point, c., Can.	92	48.04N	64.32W
Miseno, Cape, c., Italy (mē-zĕ'nō)	159c	40.33N	14.12E
Misery, Mount, mtn., St. K./N. (mĭz'rē-ĭ)	121b	17.28N	62.47W
Mishan, China (mĭ'shäɴ)	194	45.32N	132.19E
Mishawaka, In., U.S. (mĭsh-ȧ-wôk'ȧ)	98	41.45N	86.15W
Mishina, Japan (mē'shē-mä)	195	35.09N	138.56E
Misiones, prov., Arg. (mē-syō'nās)	132	27.00S	54.30W
Miskito, Cayos, is., Nic.	121	14.34N	82.30W
Miskolc, Hung. (mĭsh'kōlts)	142	48.07N	20.50E
Misool, Pulau, i., Indon. (mē-sōl')	197	2.00S	130.05E
Misquah Hills, Mn., U.S. (mĭs-kwä' hĭlz)	103	47.50N	90.30W
Miṣr al Jadīdah, Egypt	218b	30.06N	31.35E
Miṣr al-Qadīmah (Old Cairo), neigh., Egypt	244a	30.00N	31.14E
Misrātah, Libya	211	32.23N	14.58E
Missinaibi, r., Can. (mĭs'ĭn-ä'ē-bē)	85	50.27N	83.01W
Missinaibi Lake, l., Can.	90	48.23N	83.40W
Mission, Ks., U.S. (mĭsh'ŭn)	107f	39.02N	94.39W
Mission, Tx., U.S.	112	26.14N	98.19W
Mission City, Can. (sĭ'tĭ)	87	49.08N	112.18W
Mississagi, r., Can.	90	46.35N	83.30W
Mississauga, Can.	91	43.34N	79.37W
Mississippi, state, U.S. (mĭs-ĭ-sĭp'ē)	97	32.30N	89.45W
Mississippi, l., Can.	91	45.05N	76.15W
Mississippi, r., U.S.	97	32.00N	91.30W
Mississippi Sound, strt., Ms., U.S.	114	34.16N	89.10W
Missoula, Mt., U.S. (mĭ-zōō'lȧ)	96	46.55N	114.00W
Missouri, state, U.S. (mĭ-sōō'rē)	97	38.00N	93.40W
Missouri, r., U.S.	96	40.40N	96.00W
Missouri City, Tx., U.S.	113a	29.37N	95.32W
Missouri Coteau, hills, U.S.	96	47.30N	101.00W
Missouri Valley, Ia., U.S.	102	41.35N	95.53W
Mist, Or., U.S. (mĭst)	106c	46.00N	123.15W
Mistassini, Can. (mĭs-tȧ-sĭ'nē)	91	48.56N	71.55W
Mistassini, l., Can. (mĭs-tȧ-sĭ'nē)	85	50.48N	73.30W
Mistelbach, Aus. (mĭs'tĕl-bäk)	154	48.34N	16.33E
Misteriosa, Lago, l., Mex. (mēs-tē-ryō'sä)	120a	18.05N	90.15W
Misti, Volcán, vol., Peru	130	16.04S	71.20W
Mistretta, Italy (mē-strĕt'tä)	160	37.54N	14.22E
Misty Fjords National Monument, rec., Ak., U.S.	95	51.00N	131.00W
Mita, Punta de, c., Mex. (pōō'n-tä-dĕ-mē'tä)	118	20.44N	105.34W
Mitaka, Japan (mē'tä-kä)	195a	35.42N	139.34E
Mitcham, Austl.	243b	37.49S	145.12E
Mitcham, neigh., Eng., U.K.	235	51.24N	0.10W
Mitchell, Il., U.S. (mĭch'ĕl)	107e	38.46N	90.05W
Mitchell, In., U.S.	98	38.45N	86.25W
Mitchell, Ne., U.S.	102	41.56N	103.49W
Mitchell, S.D., U.S.	96	43.42N	98.01W
Mitchell, Mount, mtn., N.C., U.S.	97	35.47N	82.15W
Mīt Ghamr, Egypt	218b	30.43N	31.20E
Mitilíni, Grc.	149	39.09N	26.35E
Mitla Pass, p., Egypt	181a	30.03N	32.40E
Mito, Japan (mē'tō)	194	36.20N	140.23E
Mitry-Mory, Fr.	237c	48.59N	2.37E
Mitsiwa, Erit.	211	15.40N	39.19E
Mitsu, Japan (mēt'sō)	195	34.21N	132.49E
Mitte, neigh., Ger.	238a	52.31N	13.24E
Mittelland Kanal, can., Ger. (mĭt'ĕl-länd)	154	52.18N	10.42E
Mittenwalde, Ger. (mē'tĕn-väl-dĕ)	145b	52.16N	13.33E
Mittweida, Ger. (mĭt-vī'dä)	154	50.59N	12.58E
Mitumba, Monts, mts., Zaire	217	10.50S	27.00E
Mityayevo, Russia (mĭt-yä'yĕ-vô)	172a	60.17N	61.02E
Miura, Japan	195a	35.08N	139.37E
Miwa, Japan (mē'wä)	195b	34.32N	135.51E
Mixcoac, neigh., Mex.	233a	19.23N	99.12W
Mixico, Guat. (mēs'kō)	120	14.37N	90.37W
Mixquiahuala, Mex. (mēs-kē-wä'lä)	118	20.12N	99.13W
Mixteco, r., Mex. (mēs-tā'kō)	118	17.45N	98.10W
Miyake, Japan (mē'yä-kå)	195b	34.35N	135.34E
Miyake, i., Japan (mē'yä-kå)	195	34.06N	139.21E
Miyakojima, neigh., Japan	242b	34.43N	135.33E
Miyakonojō, Japan	194	31.44N	131.04E
Miyazaki, Japan (mē'yä-zä'kē)	194	31.55N	131.27E
Miyoshi, Japan (mē-yō'shē')	194	34.48N	132.49E
Mizdah, Libya (mēz'dä)	184	31.29N	13.09E
Mizil, Rom. (mē'zēl)	161	45.01N	26.30E
Mizonuma, Japan	242a	35.48N	139.36E
Mizoram, state, India	183	23.25N	92.45E
Mizue, neigh., Japan	242a	35.41N	139.54E
Mizuho, Japan	242a	35.46N	139.21E
Mjölby, Swe. (myûl'bü)	152	58.20N	15.09E
Mjörn, l., Swe.	152	57.55N	12.22E
Mjösa, l., Nor. (myûsä)	146	60.41N	11.25E
Mkalama, Tan.	212	4.07S	34.38E
Mkushi, Zam.	217	13.40S	29.20E
Mkwaja, Tan.	217	5.47S	38.51E
Mladá Boleslav, Czech Rep. (mlä'dä bō'lĕ-slȧf)	154	50.26N	14.52E
Mlala Hills, hills, Tan.	217	6.47S	31.45E
Mlanje Mountains, mts., Mwi.	217	15.55S	35.30E
Mława, Pol. (mwä'vá)	146	53.07N	20.25E
Mmabatho, S. Afr.	212	25.42S	25.43E
Mnevniki, neigh., Russia	239b	55.45N	37.28E
Moa, r., Afr.	214	7.40N	11.15W
Moa, Pulau, i., Indon.	197	8.30S	128.30E
Moab, Ut., U.S. (mō'ăb)	109	38.35N	109.35W
Moanda, Gabon	212	1.37S	13.09E
Moar Lake, l., Can. (môr)	89	52.00N	95.09W
Moba, Nig.	244d	6.27N	3.28E
Moba, Zaire	212	7.12S	29.39E
Mobaye, Cen. Afr. Rep. (mō-bä'y')	211	4.19N	21.11E
Mobayi-Mbongo, Zaire	211	4.14N	21.11E
Moberly, Mo., U.S. (mō'bẽr-lĭ)	97	39.24N	92.25W
Mobile, Al., U.S. (mō-bēl')	97	30.42N	88.03W
Mobile, r., Al., U.S.	114	31.15N	88.00W
Mobile Bay, b., Al., U.S.	97	30.26N	87.56W
Mobridge, S.D., U.S. (mō'brĭj)	102	45.32N	100.26W
Moca, Dom. Rep. (mô'kä)	123	19.25N	70.35W
Moçambique, Moz. (mō-säɴ-bē'kĕ)	217	15.03S	40.42E
Moçâmedes, Ang. (mô-zá-mĕ-dĕs)	212	15.10S	12.09E
Moçâmedes, hist. reg., Ang.	212	16.00S	12.15E
Mochitlán, Mex. (mō-chē-tlän')	118	17.10N	99.19W
Mochudi, Bots. (mō-chōō'dē)	212	24.13S	26.07E
Mocímboa da Praia, Moz. (mō-sē'êm-bō-á prä'ēá)	213	11.20S	40.21E
Moclips, Wa., U.S.	104	47.14N	124.13W
Môco, Serra do, mtn., Ang.	216	12.25S	15.10E
Mococa, Braz. (mō-kō'kȧ)	129a	21.29S	46.58W
Moctezuma, Mex. (mōk'tā-zōō'mä)	118	22.44N	101.06W
Mocuba, Moz.	217	16.50S	36.59E
Modderbee, S. Afr.	244b	26.10S	28.24E
Modderfontein, S. Afr.	213b	26.06S	28.10E
Modena, Italy (mô'dĕ-nä)	148	44.38N	10.54E
Modesto, Ca., U.S. (mō-dĕs'tō)	108	37.39N	121.00W
Modjeska, Ca., U.S.	232	33.43N	117.37W
Mödling, Aus. (mûd'lĭng)	145e	48.06N	16.17E
Moelv, Nor.	152	60.55N	10.40E
Moengo, Sur.	131	5.43N	54.19W
Moenkopi, Az., U.S.	109	36.07N	111.13W
Moers, Ger. (mûrs)	157c	51.27N	6.38E
Moffat Tunnel, trans., Co., U.S. (môf'ăt)	110	39.52N	106.20W
Mofolo, S. Afr.	244b	26.14S	27.53E
Mogadishu (Muqdisho), Som.	218a	2.08N	45.22E
Mogadore, Oh., U.S. (mŏg-á-dōr')	101d	41.04N	81.23E
Mogaung, Myanmar (mō-gä'ŏng)	183	25.30N	96.52E
Mogi das Cruzes, Braz. (mō-gē-däs-krōō'sĕs)	131	23.33S	46.10W
Mogi-Guaçu, r., Braz. (mō-gē-gwá'sōō)	129a	22.06S	47.12W
Mogilëv, Bela. (mō-gē-lyôf')	164	53.53N	30.22E
Mogilëv, prov., Bela. (mō-gē-lyôf')	162	53.28N	30.15E
Mogilno, Pol. (mō-gēl'nō)	154	52.38N	17.58W
Mogi-Mirim, Braz. (mō-gē-mē-rē'ɴ)	129a	22.26S	46.57W
Mogok, Myanmar (mō-gōk')	183	23.14N	96.38E
Mogol, r., S. Afr. (mō-gōl)	218d	24.12S	27.55E
Mogollon Plateau, plat., Az., U.S.	96	34.15N	110.45W
Mogollon Rim, cliff, Az., U.S. (mō-gō-yōn')	109	34.26N	111.17W
Moguer, Spain (mō-gĕr')	158	37.15N	6.50W
Mohács, Hung. (mō'häch)	155	45.59N	18.38E
Mohale's Hoek, Leso.	213c	30.09S	27.28E
Mohall, N.D., U.S. (mō'hôl)	102	48.46N	101.29W
Mohave, l., Nv., U.S. (mō-hä'vä)	109	35.23N	114.40W
Mohe, China (mwo-hŭ)	189	53.33N	122.30E
Mohenjo-Dero, hist., Pak.	183	27.20N	68.10E
Mohili, neigh., India	240e	19.06N	72.53E
Mohyliv-Podil's'kyy, Ukr.	167	48.27N	27.51E
Mõisaküla, Est. (mẽē'sá-kü'lä)	153	58.07N	25.12E
Moissac, Fr. (mwä-sák')	156	44.07N	1.05E
Moita, Port. (mō-ē'tȧ)	159b	38.39N	9.00W
Mojave, Ca., U.S.	108	35.06N	118.09W
Mojave, r., Ca., U.S. (mō-hä'vä)	108	34.46N	117.24W
Mojave Desert, Ca., U.S.	108	35.05N	117.30W
Mojave Desert, des., Ca., U.S.	96	35.00N	117.00W
Mokhotlong, Leso.	213c	29.18S	29.06E
Mokp'o, S. Kor. (mōk'pō')	189	34.50N	126.30E
Mol, Bel.	145a	51.21N	5.09E
Moldavia, hist. reg., Rom.	155	47.20N	27.12E
Moldavia *see* Moldova, nation, Eur.	164	48.00N	28.00E
Molde, Nor. (môl'dĕ)	146	62.44N	7.15E
Moldova, nation, Eur.	164	48.00N	28.00E
Moldova, r., Rom.	155	47.17N	26.27E
Moldoveanu, Vârful, mtn., Rom.	161	45.33N	24.38E
Molepolole, Bots. (mō-lō-pō-lō'lā)	212	24.15S	25.33W
Molfetta, Italy (mōl-fĕt'tä)	149	41.11N	16.38E
Molina, Chile (mŏ-lē'nä)	129b	35.07S	71.17W
Molina de Aragón, Spain (mō-lē'nä dĕ ä-rä-gō'n)	158	40.40N	1.54W
Molína de Segura, Spain (mō-lē'nä dĕ sĕ-gōō'rä)	158	38.03N	1.07W
Moline, Il., U.S. (mō-lēn')	111	41.31N	90.34W
Molino de Rosas, Mex.	233a	19.22N	99.13W
Molíns de Rey, Spain	238e	41.25N	2.01E
Moliro, Zaire	212	8.13S	30.34E
Moliterno, Italy (mōl-ē-tĕr'nō)	160	40.13N	15.54W
Möllen, Ger.	236	51.35N	6.42E
Mollendo, Peru (mō-lyĕn'dō)	130	17.02S	71.59W
Moller, Port, Ak., U.S. (pōrt mōl'ẽr)	95	56.18N	161.30W
Mölndal, Swe. (mûln'däl)	152	57.39N	12.01E
Molochna, r., Ukr.	163	47.05N	35.22E
Molochnyy lyman, l., Ukr.	163	46.35N	35.32E
Molodechno, Bela. (mō-lō-dĕch'nō)	166	54.18N	26.57E
Molody Tud, Russia (mō-lō-dô'ē tōō'd)	172b	55.17N	37.31E
Molokai, i., Hi., U.S. (mō-lō kä'ē)	96c	21.15N	157.05E
Molokcha, r., Russia (mō'lôk-chä)	172b	56.15N	38.29E
Molopo, r., Afr. (mō-lō-pō)	212	27.45S	20.45E
Molson Lake, l., Can. (mōl'sŭn)	89	54.12N	96.45W
Molteno, S. Afr. (môl-tā'nō)	213c	31.24S	26.23E
Moluccas *see* Maluku, is., Indon.	197	2.22S	128.25E
Moma, Moz.	217	16.44S	39.14E
Mombasa, Kenya (mōm-bä'sä)	213	4.03S	39.40E
Mombetsu, Japan (mōm'bĕt-sōō')	194	44.21N	142.48E
Momence, Il., U.S. (mō-mĕns')	101a	41.09N	87.40W
Momostenango, Guat. (mō-mōs-tā-näŋ'gō)	120	15.02N	91.25W
Momotombo, Nic.	120	12.25N	86.43W
Mompog Passage, strt., Phil. (mōm-pŏg')	197a	13.35N	122.09E
Mompos, Col. (mōm-pōs')	130	9.05N	74.30W
Møn, i., Den. (mûn)	152	54.54N	12.30E
Monaca, Pa., U.S. (mō-nȧ'kō)	101e	40.41N	80.17W
Monaco, nation, Eur. (mŏn'ȧ-kō)	142	43.43N	7.47E
Monaghan, Ire. (mŏ'ȧ-găn)	150	54.16N	7.20W
Mona Passage, strt., N.A. (mō'nä)	117	18.00N	68.10W

PLACE (Pronunciation)	PAGE	Lat. ° '	Long. ° '
Monarch Mountain, mtn., Can. (mŏn'ĕrk)	86	51.41N	125.53W
Monashee Mountains, mts., Can. (mŏ-nä'shē)	87	50.30N	118.30W
Monastir *see* Bitola, Mac.	160	41.02N	21.22E
Monastir, Tun. (mŏn-ás-tēr')	148	35.49N	10.56E
Monastyrshchina, Russia (mŏ-nás-tērsh'chī-ná)	162	54.19N	31.49E
Monastyryshche, Ukr.	163	48.57N	29.53E
Moncada, Spain	238e	41.29N	2.11E
Monção, Braz. (mon-souɴ')	131	3.39S	45.23W
Moncayo, mtn., Spain (mŏn-kä'yō)	158	41.44N	1.48W
Monchegorsk, Russia (mŏn'chĕ-gŏrsk)	166	69.00N	33.35E
Mönchengladbach, Ger. (mûn'kĕn gläd'bäk)	154	51.12N	6.28E
Moncique, Serra de, mts., Port. (sĕr'rä dĕ mŏn-chē'kē)	158	37.22N	8.37W
Monclova, Mex. (mŏn-klō'vä)	116	26.53N	101.25W
Moncton, Can. (mŭngk'tŭn)	85	46.06N	64.47W
Mondego, r., Port. (mŏn-dĕ'gō)	158	40.10N	8.36W
Mondego, Cabo, c., Port. (ká'bō mŏn-dá'gó)	158	40.12N	8.55W
Mondeor, S. Afr.	244b	26.17S	28.00E
Mondombe, Zaire (mŏn-dôm'bâ)	212	0.45S	23.06E
Mondoñedo, Spain (mŏn-dô-nyä'dō)	158	43.35N	7.18W
Mondovi, Wi., U.S. (mŏn-dō'vī)	103	44.35N	91.42W
Monee, Il., U.S. (mō-nī)	101a	41.25N	87.45W
Monessen, Pa., U.S. (mô-nĕs'sen)	101e	40.09N	79.53W
Monett, Mo., U.S. (mô-nĕt')	111	36.55N	93.55W
Monfalcone, Italy	160	45.49N	13.30E
Monforte de Lemos, Spain (mŏn-fōr'tä dĕ lĕ'mós)	158	42.30N	7.30W
Mongala, r., Zaire (mŏn-gál'á)	211	3.20N	21.30E
Mongalla, Sudan	211	5.11N	31.46E
Mongat, Spain	238e	41.28N	2.17E
Monghyr, India (mŏn-gēr')	183	25.23N	86.34E
Mongo, r., Afr.	214	9.50N	11.50W
Mongolia, nation, Asia	188	46.00N	100.00E
Mongos, Chaîne des, mts., Cen. Afr. Rep.	211	8.04N	21.59E
Mongoumba, Cen. Afr. Rep. (mŏn-gōōm'bä)	211	3.38N	18.36E
Mongu, Zam. (mŏn-gōō')	212	15.15S	23.09E
Monken Hadley, neigh., Eng., U.K.	235	51.40N	0.11W
Monkey Bay, Mwi.	217	14.05S	34.55E
Monkey River, Belize (mŭŋ'kĭ)	120a	16.22N	88.33W
Monkland, Can. (mŭngk-lănd)	83c	45.12N	74.52W
Monkoto, Zaire (mŏn-kō'tō)	212	1.38S	20.39E
Monmouth, Il., U.S. (mŏn'mŭth)(mŏn'mouth)	111	40.54N	90.38W
Monmouth Junction, N.J., U.S. (mŏn'mouth jŭngk'shŭn)	100a	40.23N	74.33W
Monmouth Mountain, mtn., Can. (mŏn'mŭth)	86	51.00N	123.47W
Mono, r., Afr.	214	7.20N	1.25E
Mono Lake, l., Ca., U.S. (mō'nō)	108	38.04N	119.00W
Monon, In., U.S. (mō'nŏn)	98	40.55N	86.55W
Monongah, W.V., U.S. (mô-nŏn'gá)	98	39.25N	80.10W
Monongahela, Pa., U.S. (mô-nŏn-gá-hē'lá)	101a	40.11N	79.55W
Monongahela, r., W.V., U.S.	98	39.30N	80.10W
Monopoli, Italy	161	40.55N	17.17E
Monóvar, Spain (mō-nō'vär)	159	38.26N	0.50W
Monreale, Italy (mŏn-rä-ā'lä)	160	38.04N	13.15E
Monroe, Ga., U.S. (mŭn-rō')	114	33.47N	83.43W
Monroe, La., U.S.	97	32.30N	92.06W
Monroe, Mi., U.S.	98	41.55N	83.25W
Monroe, N.Y., U.S.	100a	41.19N	74.11W
Monroe, N.C., U.S.	115	34.58N	80.34W
Monroe, Ut., U.S.	109	38.35N	112.10W
Monroe, Wa., U.S.	106a	47.52N	121.58W
Monroe, Wi., U.S.	103	42.35N	89.40W
Monroe, Lake, l., Fl., U.S.	115	28.50N	81.15W
Monroe City, Mo., U.S.	111	39.38N	91.41W
Monroeville, Al., U.S. (mŭn-rō'vĭl)	114	31.33N	87.19W
Monrovia, Lib.	210	6.18N	10.47W
Monrovia, Ca., U.S. (mŏn-rō'vĭ-á)	107a	34.09N	118.00W
Mons, Bel. (môɴ')	154	50.29N	3.55E
Monson, Me., U.S. (mŏn'sŭn)	92	45.17N	69.28W
Mönsterås, Swe. (mün'stēr-ôs)	152	57.04N	16.24E
Montagne Tremblant Provincial Park, rec., Can.	97	46.30N	75.51W
Montague, Ca., U.S. (mŏn'tá-gū)	93	46.10N	62.39W
Montague, Mi., U.S.	98	43.30N	86.25W
Montague, i., Ak., U.S.	95	60.10N	147.00W
Montalbán, Ven. (mōnt-äl-bän)	131b	10.14N	68.19W
Montalbancito, Ven.	234a	10.28N	66.59W
Montalegre, Port. (mōn-tä-lā'grĕ)	158	41.49N	7.48W
Montana, state, U.S. (mŏn-tăn'á)	96	47.10N	111.50W
Montánchez, Spain (mŏn-tän'cháth)	158	39.18N	6.09W
Montara, Ca., U.S.	231b	37.33N	122.31W
Montargis, Fr. (môɴ-tàr-zhē')	147	47.59N	2.42E
Montataire, Fr. (mōɴ-tá-târ')	157b	49.15N	2.26E
Montauban, Fr. (mōɴ-tō-bäɴ')	147	44.01N	1.22E
Montauk, N.Y., U.S. (mŏn-tôk')	99	41.03N	71.57W
Montauk Point, c., N.Y., U.S. (mŏn-tôk')	99	41.05N	71.55W
Montbanch, Spain (mŏnt-bän'ch)	159	41.20N	1.08E
Montbard, Fr. (môɴ-bàr')	156	47.40N	4.19E
Montbéliard, Fr. (môɴ-bā-lyàr')	157	47.32N	6.45E
Mont Belvieu, Tx., U.S. (mŏnt bĕl'vū)	113a	29.51N	94.53W
Montbrison, Fr. (môɴ-brē-zōɴ')	156	45.38N	4.06E
Montceau, Fr. (mōɴ-sō')	156	46.39N	4.22E
Montclair, Ca., U.S.	232	34.06N	117.41W
Montclair, N.J., U.S. (mŏnt-klâr')	100a	40.49N	74.13W
Mont-de-Marsan, Fr. (môɴ-dĕ-már-säɴ')	147	43.54N	0.32W
Montdidier, Fr. (môɴ-dē-dyä')	156	49.42N	2.33E
Monte, Arg. (mō'n-tĕ)	129c	35.25S	58.49W
Monteagudo, Bol. (mŏn'tä-ä-gōō'dhō)	130	19.49S	63.48W
Montebello, Can.	83c	45.40N	74.56W
Montebello, Ca., U.S. (mŏn-tĕ-bĕl'ō)	107a	34.01N	118.06W
Monte Bello Islands, is., Austl.	202	20.30S	114.10E
Monte Caseros, Arg. (mō'n-tĕ-kä-sĕ'rós)	132	30.16S	57.39W
Monte Chingolo, neigh., Arg.	233d	34.45S	58.20W
Montecillos, Cordillera de, mts., Hond.	120	14.19N	87.52W
Monte Cristi, Dom. Rep. (mŏ'n-tĕ-krē's-tĕ)	123	19.50N	71.40W
Montecristo, Isola di, i., Italy	160	42.20N	10.19E
Monte Escobedo, Mex. (mŏn'tä ĕs-kō-bä'dhō)	118	22.18N	103.34W
Monteforte Irpino, Italy (mŏn-tĕ-fôr'tĕ ē'r-pē'nō)	159c	40.39N	14.42E
Montefrío, Spain (mŏn-tä-frē'ō)	158	37.20N	4.02W
Montego Bay, Jam. (mŏn-tē'gō)	117	18.30N	77.55W
Montelavar, Port. (mŏn-tĕ-lä-vär')	159b	38.51N	9.20W
Montélimar, Fr. (mŏɴ-tä-lē-mär')	147	44.33N	4.47E
Montellano, Spain (mŏn-tĕ-lyä'nō)	158	37.00N	5.34W
Montello, Wi., U.S. (mŏn-tĕl'ō)	103	43.47N	89.20W
Montemorelos, Mex. (mŏn'tä-mō-rā'lōs)	116	25.14N	99.50W
Montemor-o-Novo, Port. (mōn-tĕ-môr'ô-nô'vō)	158	38.39N	8.11W
Montenegro *see* Crna Gora, state, Yugo.	161	42.55N	18.52E
Montenegro, reg., Moz.	217	13.07S	39.00E
Montepulciano, Italy (mŏn'tä-pōōl-chä'nō)	160	43.05N	11.48E
Montereau-faut-Yonne, Fr. (mŏɴ-t'rō'fō-yòn')	156	48.24N	2.57E
Monterey, Ca., U.S. (mŏn-tĕ-rä')	96	36.36N	121.53W
Monterey, Tn., U.S.	114	36.06N	85.15W
Monterey Bay, b., Ca., U.S.	96	36.48N	122.01W
Monterey Park, Ca., U.S.	107a	34.04N	118.08W
Montería, Col. (mŏn-tä-rä'ä)	130	8.47N	75.57W
Monteros, Arg. (mŏn-tĕ'rós)	132	27.14S	65.29W
Monterotondo, Italy (mŏn-tĕ-rŏ-tô'n-dō)	159d	42.03N	12.39E
Monterrey, Mex. (mŏn-tĕr-rä')	116	25.43N	100.19W
Montesano, Wa., U.S. (mŏn-tĕ-sä'nō)	104	46.59N	123.35W
Monte Sant'Angelo, Italy (mŏ'n-tĕ sän ä'n-gzhĕ-lō)	149	41.43N	15.59E
Montes Claros, Braz. (môn-tĕs-klä'rós)	131	16.44S	43.41W
Montespaccato, neigh., Italy	239c	41.54N	12.23E
Montevallo, Al., U.S. (mŏn-tĕ-väl'ō)	114	33.05N	86.49W
Montevarchi, Italy (mŏn-tä-vär'kē)	160	43.30N	11.45E
Monteverde Nuovo, neigh., Italy	239c	41.51N	12.27E
Montevideo, Mn., U.S. (mŏn'tä-vĕ-dhá'ō)	102	44.56N	95.42W
Montevideo, Ur. (mŏn'tä-vĕ-dhá'ō)	132	34.50S	56.10W
Monte Vista, Co., U.S. (mŏn'tĕ vĭs'tá)	109	37.35N	106.10W
Montezuma, Ga., U.S. (mŏn-tĕ-zōō'má)	114	32.17N	84.00W
Montezuma Castle National Monument, rec., Az., U.S.	109	34.38N	111.50W
Montfermeil, Fr.	237c	48.54N	2.34E
Montflorit, Spain	238e	41.29N	2.08E
Montfoort, Neth.	145a	52.02N	4.56E
Montfor-l'Amaury, Fr. (mŏɴ-fŏr'lä-mō-rē')	157b	48.47N	1.49E
Montfort, Fr. (mŏn-fŏr')	156	48.09N	1.58W
Montgeron, Fr.	237c	48.42N	2.27E
Montgomery, Al., U.S. (mŏnt-gŭm'ēr-ĭ)	97	32.23N	86.17W
Montgomery, W.V., U.S.	98	38.10N	81.25W
Montgomery City, Mo., U.S.	111	38.58N	91.29W
Montgomery Knolls, Md., U.S.	229c	39.14N	76.48W
Monticello, Ar., U.S. (mŏn-tĭ-sĕl'ō)	111	33.38N	91.47W
Monticello, Fl., U.S.	114	30.32N	83.53W
Monticello, Ga., U.S.	114	33.00N	83.11W
Monticello, Il., U.S.	98	40.05N	88.35W
Monticello, In., U.S.	98	40.40N	86.50W
Monticello, Ia., U.S.	103	42.14N	91.13W
Monticello, Ky., U.S.	114	36.47N	84.50W
Monticello, Me., U.S.	92	46.19N	67.53W
Monticello, Mn., U.S.	103	45.18N	93.48W
Monticello, N.Y., U.S.	99	41.35N	74.40W
Monticello, Ut., U.S.	109	37.55N	109.25W
Montigny-le-Bretonneux, Fr.	237c	48.46N	2.02E
Montigny-lés-Cormeilles, Fr.	237c	48.59N	2.12E
Montijo, Port. (mŏn-tē'zhō)	159b	38.42N	8.58W
Montijo, Spain (mŏn-tē'hō)	158	38.55N	6.35W
Montijo, Bahía, b., Pan. (bä-ē'ä mŏn-tē'hō)	117	7.36N	81.11W
Mont-Joli, Can. (mŏɴ zhó-lē')	85	48.35N	68.11W
Montjuich, Castillo de, hist., Spain	238e	41.22N	2.10E
Montluçon, Fr. (môɴ-lü-sôɴ')	147	46.20N	2.35E
Montmagny, Can. (mŏn-mán-yē')	91	46.59N	70.33W
Montmagny, Fr.	237c	48.58N	2.21E
Montmartre, neigh., Fr.	237c	48.53N	2.21E
Montmorency, Austl.	243b	37.43S	145.07E
Montmorency, Fr. (môɴ'mô-rän-sē')	157b	48.59N	2.19E
Montmorency, r., Can. (mŏnt-mô-rĕn'sĭ)	83b	47.03N	71.10W
Montmorillon, Fr. (môɴ-mô-rē-yôn')	156	46.26N	0.50E
Montone, r., Italy (mŏn-tō'nĕ)	160	44.03N	11.45E
Montoro, Spain (mŏn-tō'rō)	158	38.01N	4.22W
Montpelier, Id., U.S. (mŏnt-pēl'yĕr)	105	42.19N	111.19W
Montpelier, In., U.S.	98	40.35N	85.20W
Montpelier, Oh., U.S.	98	41.35N	84.35W
Montpelier, Vt., U.S.	97	44.20N	72.35W
Montpellier, Fr. (môɴ-pĕ-lyà')	147	43.38N	3.53E
Montréal, Can. (mŏn-trē-ôl')	85	45.30N	73.35W
Montreal, r., Can.	90	47.15N	84.20W
Montreal, r., Can.	91	47.50N	80.30W
Montreal Lake, l., Can.	88	54.20N	105.40W
Montréal-Nord, Can.	83a	45.36N	73.38W
Montréal-Ouest, Can.	227b	45.27N	73.39W
Montreuil, Fr.	157b	48.52N	2.27E
Montreux, Switz. (môn-trû')	154	46.26N	6.52E
Montrose, Austl.	243b	37.49S	145.21E
Montrose, Scot., U.K.	150	56.45N	2.25W
Montrose, Ca., U.S. (mŏnt-rōz)	107a	34.13N	118.13W
Montrose, Co., U.S. (mŏnt-trōz')	109	38.30N	107.55W
Montrose, Oh., U.S.	101d	41.08N	81.38W
Montrose, Pa., U.S. (mŏnt-rōz')	99	41.50N	75.50W
Montrose Hill, Pa., U.S.	230b	40.30N	79.51W
Montrouge, Fr.	157b	48.49N	2.19E
Mont-Royal, Can.	83a	47.31N	73.39W
Monts, Pointe des, c., Can. (pwăɴt' dä môɴ')	92	49.19N	67.22W
Mont Saint Martin, Fr. (mŏɴ säɴ mär-täɴ')	157	49.34N	6.13E
Montserrat, dep., N.A.	117	16.48N	63.15W
Montvale, N.J., U.S. (mŏnt-väl')	100a	41.02N	74.01W
Monywa, Myanmar (mŏn'yōō-wä)	183	22.02N	95.16E
Monza, Italy (mŏn'tsä)	160	45.34N	9.17E
Monzón, Spain (mŏn-thōn')	159	41.54N	0.09E
Moóca, neigh., Braz.	234d	23.33S	46.35W
Moody, Tx., U.S. (mōō'dĭ)	113	31.18N	97.20W
Mooi, r., S. Afr.	213c	29.00S	30.15E
Mooi, r., S. Afr. (mōō'ĭ)	218d	26.34S	27.03E
Mooirivier, S. Afr.	213c	29.14S	29.59E
Moolap, Austl.	201a	38.11S	144.26E
Moonachie, N.J., U.S.	228	40.50N	74.03W
Moonta, Austl. (mōōn'tä)	202	34.05S	137.42E
Moora, Austl. (mōō'rá)	202	30.35S	116.12E
Moorabbin, Austl.	201a	37.56S	145.02E
Moore, l., Austl. (mōr)	202	29.50S	118.12E
Moorebank, Austl.	243a	33.56S	150.56E
Moorenweis, Ger. (mō'rĕn-vīz)	145d	48.10N	11.05E
Moore Reservoir, res., Vt., U.S.	99	44.20N	72.10W
Moorestown, N.J., U.S. (morz'toun)	100f	39.58N	74.56W
Mooresville, In., U.S. (mòrz'vĭl)	101g	39.37N	86.22W
Mooresville, N.C., U.S.	115	35.34N	80.48W
Moorhead, Mn., U.S. (mōr'hĕd)	102	46.52N	96.44W
Moorhead, Ms., U.S.	114	33.25N	90.30W
Mooroolbark, Austl.	243b	37.47S	145.19E
Moorside, Eng., U.K.	237b	53.34N	2.04W
Moose, r., Can.	85	51.01N	80.42W
Moose Creek, Can.	83c	45.16N	74.58W
Moosehead, Me., U.S. (mōōs'hĕd)	92	45.37N	69.15W
Moose Island, i., Can.	89	51.50N	97.09W
Moose Jaw, Can. (mōōs jô)	84	50.23N	105.32W
Moose Jaw, r., Can.	88	50.34N	105.17W
Moose Lake, Can.	89	53.40N	100.28W
Moose Mountain, mtn., Can.	89	49.45N	102.37W
Moose Mountain Creek, r., Can.	89	49.12N	102.10W
Moosilauke, mtn., N.H., U.S. (mōō-sĭ-lá'kē)	99	44.00N	71.50W
Moosinning, Ger. (mō'zĕ-nĕng)	145d	48.17N	11.51E
Moosomin, Can. (mōō'só-mĭn)	89	50.07N	101.40W
Moosonee, Can. (mōōs'ó-nē)	85	51.20N	80.44W
Mopti, Mali (mŏp'tē)	210	14.30N	4.12W
Moquegua, Peru (mō-kā'gwä)	130	17.15S	70.54W
Mór, Hung. (mōr)	155	47.25N	18.14E
Mora, India	187b	18.54N	72.56E
Mora, Spain (mō-rä)	158	39.42N	3.45W
Mora, Swe. (mō'rä)	152	61.00N	14.29E
Mora, Mn., U.S. (mō'rá)	103	45.52N	93.18W
Mora, N.M., U.S.	110	35.58N	105.17W
Morādābād, India (mō-rä-dä-bäd')	183	28.57N	78.48E
Morales, Guat. (mō-rä'lĕs)	120	15.29N	88.46W
Moramanga, Madag. (mō-rä-mäŋ'gä)	213	18.48S	48.09E
Morangis, Fr.	237c	48.42N	2.20E
Morant Point, c., Jam. (mō-ränt')	122	17.55N	76.10W
Morata de Tajuña, Spain (mō-rä'tä dä tä-hōō'nyä)	159a	40.14N	3.27W
Moratuwa, Sri L.	187	6.35N	79.59E
Morava (Moravia), hist. reg., Czech Rep.	154	49.21N	16.57E
Morava, r., Eur.	147	49.00N	17.30E
Moravia *see* Morava, hist. reg., Czech Rep.	154	49.21N	16.57E
Morawhanna, Guy. (mō-rä-hwä'ná)	131	8.12N	59.33W
Moray Firth, b., Scot., U.K. (mûr'á)	142	57.41N	3.55W
Mörbylånga, Swe. (mûr'bü-lôŋ'gä)	152	56.32N	16.23E
Morden, Can. (mōr'dĕn)	84	49.11N	98.05W
Mordialloc, Austl. (mōr-dĭ-äl'ŏk)	201a	38.00S	145.05E
Mordvinia, state, Russia	166	54.18N	43.50E
More, Ben, mtn., Scot., U.K. (bĕn mōr)	150	58.09N	5.01W
Moreau, r., S.D., U.S. (mō-rō')	102	45.13N	102.22W
Moree, Austl. (mō'rē)	203	29.20S	149.50E
Morehead, Ky., U.S.	98	38.10N	83.25W
Morehead City, N.C., U.S. (mōr'hĕd)	115	34.43N	76.43W
Morehouse, Mo., U.S. (mōr'hous)	111	36.49N	89.41W
Morelia, Mex. (mō-rä'lyä)	116	19.43N	101.12W
Morella, Spain (mō-rĕl'yä)	159	40.38N	0.07W
Morelos, Mex.	112	28.24N	100.51W
Morelos, Mex. (mō-rä'lōs)	116	22.46N	102.36W
Morelos, Mex.	119a	19.41N	99.29W
Morelos, neigh., Mex.	233a	19.27N	99.07W
Morelos, r., Mex.	112	25.27N	99.35W
Morena, Sierra, mtn., Ca., U.S. (syĕr'rä dă rä'nä)	106b	37.24N	122.19W
Morena, Sierra, mts., Spain (syĕr'rä mō-rĕn'sĭ)	142	38.15N	5.45W
Morenci, Mi., U.S.	98	41.50N	84.50W
Moreno, Arg. (mō-rĕ'nō)	233a	34.39S	58.47W
Moreno, Ca., U.S.	107a	33.55N	117.09W
Mores, i., Bah. (mōrz)	122	26.20N	77.35W

PRONOUNCING INDEX

Moresby–Mullins 321

PLACE (Pronunciation)	PAGE	Lat. °′	Long. °′
Moresby, i., Can. (mōrz′bĭ)	106d	48.43N	123.15W
Moresby Island, i., Can.	84	52.50N	131.55W
Moreton, Eng., U.K.	237a	53.24N	3.07W
Moreton, i., Austl. (môr′tŭn)	204	26.53S	152.42E
Moreton Bay, b., Austl. (môr′tŭn)	204	27.12S	153.10E
Morewood, Can. (mōr′wȯd)	83c	45.11N	75.17W
Morgan, Mt., U.S. (môr′găn)	105	48.55N	107.56W
Morgan, Ut., U.S.	105	41.04N	111.42W
Morgan City, La., U.S.	113	29.41N	91.11W
Morganfield, Ky., U.S. (môr′găn-fēld)	98	37.40N	87.55W
Morgan's Bay, S. Afr.	213c	32.42S	28.19E
Morganton, N.C., U.S. (môr′găn-tŭn)	115	35.44N	81.42W
Morgantown, W.V., U.S. (môr′găn-toun)	99	39.40N	79.55W
Morga Range, mts., Afg.	183a	34.02N	70.38E
Morgenzon, S. Afr. (môr′gănt-sŏn)	218d	26.44S	29.39E
Moriac, Austl.	201a	38.15S	144.20E
Morice Lake, l., Can.	86	54.00N	127.37W
Moriguchi, Japan (mō′rė-go͞o′chė)	195b	34.44N	135.34E
Morinville, Can. (mō′rĭn-vĭl)	83g	53.48N	113.39W
Morioka, Japan (mō′rė-ō′kȧ)	189	39.40N	141.21E
Morivione, neigh., Italy	238c	45.26N	9.12E
Morkoka, r., Russia (mȯr-kô′kȧ)	171	65.35N	111.00E
Morlaix, Fr. (mŏr-lĕ′)	147	48.36N	3.48W
Morley, Can. (mŏr′lė)	83e	51.10N	114.51W
Morley Green, Eng., U.K.	237b	53.20N	2.16W
Mormant, Fr.	157b	48.35N	2.54E
Morne Gimie, St. Luc. (mȯrn′ zhė-mē′)	121b	13.53N	61.03W
Morningside, Md., U.S.	229d	38.50N	76.53W
Mornington, Austl.	201a	38.13S	145.02E
Morobe, Pap. N. Gui.	197	8.03S	147.45E
Morocco, nation, Afr. (mȯ-rŏk′ō)	210	32.00N	7.00W
Morogoro, Tan. (mō-rȯ-gō′rō)	213	6.49S	37.40E
Moroleón, Mex. (mȯ-rō-lā-ōn′)	118	20.07N	101.15W
Morombe, Madag. (mo͞o-ro͞om′bā)	213	21.39S	43.34E
Morón, Arg. (mo-rŏ′n)	129c	34.39S	58.37W
Morón, Cuba (mȯ-rōn′)	122	22.05N	78.35W
Morón, Ven. (mȯ-rŏ′n)	131b	10.29N	68.11W
Morondava, Madag. (mȯ-rōn-dȧ′vȧ)	213	20.17S	44.18E
Morón de la Frontera, Spain (mȯ-rōn′dā läf rȯn-tā′rä)	158	37.08N	5.20W
Morongo Indian Reservation, I.R., Ca., U.S. (mō-rôŋ′gō)	108	33.54N	116.47W
Moroni, Com.	213	11.41S	43.16E
Moroni, Ut., U.S. (mȯ-rō′nĭ)	109	39.30N	111.40W
Morotai, i., Indon. (mō-rȯ-tä′ė)	197	2.12N	128.30E
Moroto, Ug.	217	2.32N	34.39E
Morozovsk, Russia	167	48.20N	41.50E
Morrill, Ne., U.S. (mŏr′ĭl)	102	41.59N	103.54W
Morrilton, Ar., U.S. (mŏr′ĭl-tŭn)	111	35.09N	92.42W
Morrinhos, Braz. (mȯ-rēn′yōzh)	131	17.45S	48.56W
Morris, Can. (mŏr′ĭs)	84	49.21N	97.22W
Morris, Il., U.S.	98	41.20N	88.25W
Morris, Mn., U.S.	102	45.35N	95.53W
Morris, r., Can.	89	49.30N	97.30W
Morrison, Il., U.S. (mŏr′ĭ-sŭn)	103	41.48N	89.58W
Morris Reservoir, res., Ca., U.S.	107a	34.11N	117.49W
Morristown, N.J., U.S. (mŏr′rĭs-toun)	100a	40.48N	74.29W
Morristown, Tn., U.S.	114	36.10N	83.18W
Morrisville, Pa., U.S. (mŏr′ĭs-vĭl)	100f	40.12N	74.46W
Morro, Castillo del, hist., Cuba	233b	23.09N	82.21W
Morro do Chapéu, Braz. (mȯr-ō dȯ-shä-pĕ′o͞o)	131	11.34S	41.03W
Morrow, Oh., U.S. (mŏr′ō)	101f	39.21N	84.07W
Mors, i., Den.	152	56.46N	8.38E
Mörsenbroich, neigh., Ger.	236	51.15N	6.48E
Morshansk, Russia (môr-shȧnsk′)	166	53.25N	41.35E
Mortara, Italy (mȯr-tä′rä)	160	45.13N	8.47E
Morteros, Arg. (mȯr-tĕ′tȯs)	132	30.47S	62.00W
Mortes, Rio das, r., Braz. (rēȯ-däs-mô′r-tĕs)	129a	21.04S	44.29W
Mortlake, Austl.	243a	33.51S	151.07E
Mortlake, neigh., Eng., U.K.	235	51.28N	0.16W
Morton, Pa., U.S.	229b	39.55N	75.20W
Morton Grove, Il., U.S.	231a	42.02N	87.47W
Morton Indian Reservation, I.R., Mn., U.S. (mŏr′tŭn)	103	44.35N	94.48W
Mortsel, Bel. (mȯr-sĕl′)	145a	51.10N	4.28E
Morvan, mts., Fr. (mōr-väN′)	156	47.11N	4.10E
Morzhovets, i., Russia (mȯr′zhô-vyĕts′)	166	66.40N	42.30E
Mosal'sk, Russia (mō-zȧlsk′)	162	54.27N	34.57E
Moscavide, Port.	159b	38.47N	9.06W
Moscow (Moskva), Russia	164	55.45N	37.37E
Moscow, Id., U.S. (mŏs′kō)	96	46.44N	116.57W
Mosel (Moselle), r., Eur. (mō′sĕl) (mȯ-zĕl)	154	49.49N	7.00E
Moses, r., S. Afr.	218d	25.17S	29.04E
Moses Lake, Wa., U.S.	104	47.08N	119.15W
Moses Lake, l., Wa., U.S. (mō′zĕz)	104	47.09N	119.30W
Moshchnyy, is., Russia (môsh′chnĭ)	153	59.56N	28.07E
Moshi, Tan. (mō′shė)	213	3.21S	37.20E
Mosjøen, Nor.	146	65.50N	13.10E
Moskháton, Grc.	239d	37.57N	23.41E
Moskva *see* Moscow, Russia	164	55.45N	37.37E
Moskva, prov., Russia	162	55.38N	36.48E
Moskva, r., Russia	166	55.30N	37.05E
Mosman, Austl.	243a	33.49S	151.14E
Mosonmagyaróvár, Hung.	155	47.51N	17.16E
Mosquitos, Costa de, cst., Nic. (kȯs-tä-dĕ-mŏs-kē′tō)	121	12.05N	83.49W
Mosquitos, Gulfo de los, b., Pan. (go͞o′l-fô-dĕ-lȯs-mŏs-kē′tōs)	117	9.17N	80.59W
Moss, Nor. (môs)	146	59.29N	10.39E
Moss Bank, Eng., U.K.	237a	53.29N	2.44W
Moss Beach, Ca., U.S. (môs bēch)	106b	37.32N	122.31W
Moss Crest, mtn., Va., U.S.	229d	38.55N	77.15W
Mosselbaai, S. Afr. (mô′s*ul* bā)	212	34.06S	22.23E
Mossendjo, Congo	216	2.57S	12.44E
Mossley, Eng., U.K. (môs′lĭ)	144a	53.31N	2.02W
Mossley Hill, neigh., Eng., U.K.	237a	53.23N	2.55W
Moss Point, Ms., U.S. (môs)	114	30.25N	88.32W
Most, Czech Rep. (mȯst)	154	50.32N	13.37E
Mostar, Bos. (môs′tär)	149	43.20N	17.51E
Móstoles, Spain (mȯs-tō′lās)	159a	40.19N	3.52W
Mostoos Hills, hills, Can. (mŏs′to͞os)	88	54.50N	108.45W
Mosvatnet, l., Nor.	152	59.55N	7.50E
Motagua, r., N.A. (mȯ-tä′gwä)	120	15.29N	88.39W
Motala, Swe. (mȯ-tô′lä)	152	58.34N	15.00E
Motherwell, Scot., U.K. (mŭdh′ēr-wĕl)	146	55.45N	4.05W
Motril, Spain (mȯ-trēl′)	148	36.44N	3.32W
Mottingham, neigh., Eng., U.K.	235	51.26N	0.03E
Motul, Mex. (mō-to͞o′l)	120a	21.07N	89.14W
Mouaskar, Alg.	210	35.25N	0.08E
Mouchoir Bank, bk. (mo͞o-shwȧr′)	123	21.35N	70.40W
Mouchoir Passage, strt., T./C. Is.	123	21.05N	71.05W
Moudjéria, Maur.	214	17.53N	12.20W
Mouila, Gabon	216	1.52S	11.01E
Mouille Point, c., S. Afr.	212a	33.54S	18.19E
Moulins, Fr. (mo͞o-lăN′)	147	46.34N	3.19E
Moulouya, Oued, r., Mor. (mo͞o-lo͞o′yȧ)	210	34.00N	4.00W
Moultrie, Ga., U.S. (mōl′trĭ)	114	31.10N	83.48W
Moultrie, Lake, l., S.C., U.S.	115	33.12N	80.00W
Mound City, Il., U.S.	111	37.06N	89.13W
Mound City, Mo., U.S.	111	40.08N	95.13W
Moundou, Chad	215	8.34N	16.05E
Moundsville, W.V., U.S. (moundz′vĭl)	98	39.50N	80.50W
Mount, Cape, c., Lib.	214	6.47N	11.20W
Mountain Brook, Al., U.S. (moun′tĭn brȯk)	100h	33.30N	86.45W
Mountain Creek Lake, l., Tx., U.S.	107c	32.43N	97.03W
Mountain Grove, Mo., U.S. (grōv)	111	37.07N	92.16W
Mountain Home, Id., U.S. (hōm)	104	43.08N	115.43W
Mountain Park, Can. (pärk)	84	52.55N	117.14W
Mountain View, Ca., U.S. (moun′tĭn vū)	106b	37.25N	122.07W
Mountain View, Mo., U.S.	111	36.59N	91.46W
Mount Airy, N.C., U.S. (âr′ĭ)	115	36.28N	80.37W
Mount Ayliff, S. Afr. (ā′lĭf)	213c	30.48S	29.24E
Mount Ayr, Ia., U.S. (âr)	103	40.43N	94.06W
Mount Baldy, Ca., U.S.	232	34.14N	117.40W
Mount Carmel, Il., U.S. (kär′mĕl)	98	38.25N	87.45W
Mount Carmel, Pa., U.S.	99	40.50N	76.25W
Mount Carooll, Il., U.S.	103	42.05N	89.55W
Mount Clemens, Mi., U.S. (klĕm′ĕnz)	101b	42.36N	82.52W
Mount Dennis, neigh., Can.	227c	43.42N	79.30W
Mount Desert, i., Me., U.S. (dė-zûrt′)	92	44.15N	68.08W
Mount Dora, Fl., U.S. (dō′rȧ)	115a	28.45N	81.38W
Mount Druitt, Austl.	243a	33.46S	150.49E
Mount Duneed, Austl.	201a	38.15S	144.20E
Mount Eliza, Austl.	201a	38.11S	145.05E
Mount Ephraim, N.J., U.S.	229b	39.53N	75.06W
Mount Fletcher, S. Afr. (flĕ′chẽr)	213c	30.42S	28.32E
Mount Forest, Can. (fŏr′ĕst)	91	44.00N	80.45W
Mount Frere, S. Afr. (frâr′)	213c	30.54S	29.02E
Mount Gambier, Austl. (găm′bēr)	202	37.30S	140.53E
Mount Gilead, Oh., U.S. (gĭl′ėăd)	98	40.30N	82.50W
Mount Greenwood, neigh., Il., U.S.	231a	41.42N	87.43W
Mount Healthy, Oh., U.S. (hĕlth′ė)	101f	39.14N	84.32W
Mount Hebron, Md., U.S.	229c	39.18N	76.50W
Mount Holly, N.J., U.S. (hŏl′ĭ)	100f	39.59N	74.47W
Mount Hope, Can.	83d	43.09N	79.55W
Mount Hope, N.J., U.S. (hōp)	100a	40.55N	74.32W
Mount Hope, W.V., U.S.	98	37.55N	81.10W
Mount Isa, Austl. (ī′zȧ)	202	21.00S	139.45E
Mount Kisco, N.Y., U.S. (kĭs′ko)	100a	41.12N	73.44W
Mountlake Terrace, Wa., U.S. (mount lāk tĕr′ĭs)	106a	47.48N	122.19W
Mount Lebanon, Pa., U.S. (lĕb′ȧ-nŭn)	101e	40.22N	80.03W
Mount Magnet, Austl. (măg-nĕt)	202	28.00S	118.00E
Mount Martha, Austl.	201a	38.17S	145.01E
Mount Morgan, Austl. (môr-găn)	203	23.42S	150.45E
Mount Moriac, Austl.	201a	38.13S	144.12E
Mount Morris, Mi., U.S. (mĭr′ĭs)	98	43.10N	83.45W
Mount Morris, N.Y., U.S.	99	42.45N	77.50W
Mountnessing, Eng., U.K.	235	51.39N	0.21E
Mount Nimba National Park, rec., C. Iv.	214	7.35N	8.10W
Mount Olive, N.C., U.S. (ŏl′ĭv)	115	35.11N	78.05W
Mount Oliver, Pa., U.S.	230b	40.28N	79.59W
Mount Peale, Ut., U.S.	109	38.26N	109.16W
Mount Pleasant, Ia., U.S. (plĕz′ănnt)	103	40.59N	91.34W
Mount Pleasant, Mi., U.S.	98	43.35N	84.45W
Mount Pleasant, S.C., U.S.	115	32.46N	79.51W
Mount Pleasant, Tn., U.S.	114	35.31N	87.12W
Mount Pleasant, Tx., U.S.	113	33.10N	94.56W
Mount Pleasant, Ut., U.S.	109	39.35N	111.20W
Mount Pritchard, Austl.	243a	33.54S	150.54E
Mount Prospect, Il., U.S. (prŏs′pĕkt)	101a	42.03N	87.56W
Mount Rainier, Md., U.S.	229d	38.56N	76.58W
Mount Rainier National Park, rec., Wa., U.S. (rȧ-nēr′)	96	46.47N	121.17W
Mount Revelstoke National Park, Can. (rĕv′ĕl-stōk)	84	51.22N	120.15W
Mount Savage, Md., U.S. (săv′ȧj)	99	39.45N	78.55W
Mount Shasta, Ca., U.S. (shăs′tȧ)	104	41.18N	122.17W
Mount Sterling, Il., U.S. (stûr′lĭng)	111	39.59N	90.44W
Mount Sterling, Ky., U.S.	98	38.05N	84.00W
Mount Stewart, Can. (stū′ărt)	93	46.22N	62.52W
Mount Union, Pa., U.S. (ūn′yŭn)	99	40.25N	77.50W
Mount Vernon, Il., U.S. (vûr′nŭn)	98	38.20N	88.50W
Mount Vernon, In., U.S.	98	37.55N	87.50W
Mount Vernon, Mo., U.S.	111	37.09N	93.48W
Mount Vernon, N.Y., U.S.	100a	40.55N	73.51W
Mount Vernon, Oh., U.S.	98	40.25N	82.30W
Mount Vernon, Pa., U.S.	230b	40.17N	79.48W
Mount Vernon, Va., U.S.	100e	38.43N	77.06W
Mount Vernon, Wa., U.S.	104	48.25N	122.20W
Mount Washington, neigh., Md., U.S.	229c	39.22N	76.40W
Mount Washington Summit, Md., U.S.	229c	39.23N	76.40W
Mount Waverley, Austl.	243b	37.53S	145.08E
Moura, Braz. (mō′rȧ)	131	1.33S	61.38W
Moura, Port.	158	38.08N	7.28W
Mourne Mountains, mts., N. Ire., U.K. (mȯrn)	150	54.10N	6.09W
Moussoro, Chad	215	13.39N	16.29E
Moûtiers, Fr. (mo͞o-tyâr′)	157	45.31N	6.34E
Mowbullan, Mount, mtn., Austl.	204	26.50S	151.34E
Moyahua, Mex. (mȯ-yä′wä)	118	21.16N	103.10W
Moyale, Kenya (mȯ-yä′lä)	211	3.28N	39.04E
Moyamba, S.L. (mȯ-yäm′bä)	210	8.10N	12.26W
Moyen Atlas, mts., Mor.	148	32.49N	5.28W
Moyeuvre-Grande, Fr.	157	49.15N	6.26E
Moyie, r., Id., U.S. (moi′yė)	104	38.50N	116.10W
Moylan, Pa., U.S.	229b	39.54N	75.23W
Moyobamba, Peru (mō-yȯ-bäm′bä)	130	6.12S	76.56W
Moyuta, Guat. (mȯ-ē-o͞o′tä)	120	14.01N	90.05W
Moyyero, r., Russia	170	67.15N	104.10E
Moyynqūm, des., Kaz.	169	44.30N	70.00E
Mozambique, nation, Afr. (mō-zăm-bēk′)	212	20.15S	33.53E
Mozambique Channel, strt., Afr. (mō-zăm-bek′)	213	24.00S	38.00E
Mozdok, Russia (mȯz-dôk′)	167	43.45N	44.35E
Mozhaysk, Russia (mȯ-zhäysk′)	162	55.31N	36.02E
Mozhayskiy, Russia (mȯ-zhȧy′skĭ)	172c	59.42N	30.08E
Mozyr', Bela. (mȯ-zür′)	167	52.03N	29.14E
Mpanda, Tan.	217	6.22S	31.02E
Mpika, Zam.	217	11.54S	31.26E
Mpimbe, Mwi.	217	15.18S	35.04E
Mporokoso, Zam. ('m-pō-rȯ-kō′sō)	212	9.23S	30.05E
Mpwapwa, Tan. ('m-pwä′pwä)	212	6.21S	36.29E
Mqanduli, S. Afr. ('m-kän′do͞o-lė)	213c	31.50S	28.42E
Mrągowo, Pol. (mräŋ′gô-vȯ)	155	53.52N	21.18E
M'Sila, Alg. (m'sē′lȧ)	210	35.47N	4.34E
Msta, r., Russia (m'stȧ′)	166	58.30N	33.00E
Mstislavl', Bela. (m'stē-slävl′)	162	54.01N	31.42E
Mtakataka, Mwi.	217	14.12S	34.32E
Mtamvuna, r., Afr.	213c	30.43S	29.53E
Mtata, r., S. Afr.	213c	31.48S	29.03E
Mtsensk, Russia (m'tsĕnsk)	166	53.17N	36.33E
Mtwara, Tan.	217	10.16S	40.11E
Muar, r., Malay.	181b	2.18N	102.43E
Mubende, Ug.	217	0.35N	31.23E
Mubi, Nig.	215	10.18N	13.20E
Mucacata, Moz.	217	13.20S	39.59E
Much, Ger. (mo͞oK)	157c	50.54N	7.24E
Muchinga Mountains, mts., Zam.	217	12.40S	30.50E
Much Wenlock, Eng., U.K. (mŭch wĕn′lŏk)	144a	52.35N	2.33W
Muckalee Creek, r., Ga., U.S. (mŭk′ă lē)	114	31.55N	84.10W
Mucking, Eng., U.K.	235	51.30N	0.26E
Muckleshoot Indian Reservation, I.R., Wa., U.S. (mŭck′′l-sho͞ot)	106a	47.21N	122.04W
Mucubela, Moz.	217	16.55S	37.52E
Mud, l., Mi., U.S. (mŭd)	103	46.12N	84.32W
Mudan, r., China (mo͞o-dän)	192	45.30N	129.40E
Mudanjiang, China (mo͞o-dän-jyäŋ)	192	44.28N	129.38E
Muddy, r., Nv., U.S. (mŭd′ĭ)	109	36.56N	114.42W
Muddy Boggy Creek, r., Ok., U.S. (mud′ĭ bôg′ĭ)	111	34.42N	96.11W
Muddy Creek, r., Ut., U.S. (mŭd′ĭ)	109	38.45N	111.10W
Mudgee, Austl. (mŭ-jē)	204	32.47S	149.10E
Mudjatik, r., Can.	88	56.23N	107.40W
Mufulira, Zam.	217	12.33S	28.14E
Muğla, Tur. (mo͞og′lä)	182	37.10N	28.20E
Mühileiten, Aus.	239e	48.10N	16.34E
Mühldorf, Ger. (mül-dôrf)	154	48.15N	12.33E
Mühlenbeck, Ger.	238a	52.40N	13.22E
Mühlhausen, Ger. (mül′hou-zĕn)	154	51.13N	10.25E
Muhu, i., Est. (mo͞o′ho͞o)	153	58.41N	22.55E
Muir Woods National Monument, rec., Ca., U.S. (mūr)	108	37.54N	123.22W
Muizenberg, S. Afr. (mwĭz-ĕn-bûrg′)	212a	34.07S	18.28E
Mujāhidpur, neigh., India	240d	28.34N	77.13E
Mukacheve, Ukr.	155	48.25N	22.43E
Mukden *see* Shenyang, China	188	41.45N	123.22E
Mukhtuya, Russia (mȯk-to͞o′yȧ)	165	61.00N	113.00E
Mukilteo, Wa., U.S. (mū-kĭl-tā′ō)	106a	47.57N	122.18W
Muko, Japan (mo͞o′kȯ)	195b	34.57N	135.43E
Muko, r., Japan (mo͞o′kȯ)	195b	34.52N	135.17E
Mukutawa, r., Can.	89	53.10N	97.28W
Mukwonago, Wi., U.S. (mū-kwō-nȧ′gō)	101a	42.52N	88.19W
Mula, Spain (mo͞o′lä)	158	38.05N	1.12W
Mula, Al., U.S. (mŭl′gȧ)	100h	33.33N	86.59W
Mulde, r., Ger. (mȯl′dĕ)	154	50.30N	12.30E
Muleros, Mex. (mo͞o-lā′rōs)	118	23.44N	104.00W
Muleshoe, Tx., U.S.	110	34.13N	102.43W
Mulgrave, Can. (mŭl′grāv)	93	45.37N	61.23W
Mulhacén, mtn., Spain	148	37.04N	3.18W
Mülheim, Ger. (mül′hīm)	157c	51.25N	6.53E
Mulhouse, Fr. (mü-lo͞oz′)	147	47.46N	7.20E
Muling, China (mo͞o-lĭŋ)	192	44.32N	130.18E
Muling, r., China	192	44.40N	130.30E
Mull, Island of, i., Scot., U.K. (mŭl)	150	56.40N	6.19W
Mullan, Id., U.S. (mŭl′ăn)	104	47.26N	115.50W
Müller, Pegunungan, mts., Indon. (mül′ẽr)	196	0.22N	113.05E
Mullingar, Ire. (mŭl-ĭn-gär)	150	53.31N	7.26W
Mullins, S.C., U.S. (mŭl′ĭnz)	115	34.11N	79.13W

ng-sing; ŋ-baŋk; N-nasalized n; nŏd; cŏmmit; ōld; ôbey; ôrder; oi-boil; fo͞od; ȯ-as oo in foot; ou-out; s-soft; sh-dish; th-thin; pūre; ůnite; ûrn; stŭd; circŭs; ü-as in French tu; '-indeterminate vowel.

322 Mullins River–Nanga Parbat

PLACE (Pronunciation)	PAGE	Lat. °′	Long. °′
Mullins River, Belize	120a	17.08N	88.18W
Multān, Pak. (mó-tän')	183	30.17N	71.13E
Multnomah Channel, strt., Or., U.S. (mŭl nō mȧ)	106c	45.41N	122.53W
Mulumbe, Monts, mts., Zaire	217	8.47S	27.20E
Mulvane, Ks., U.S. (mŭl-vān')	111	37.30N	97.13W
Mumbwa, Zam. (mōm'bwä)	212	14.59S	27.04E
Mumias, Kenya	217	0.20N	34.29E
Muna, Mex. (mōō'nȧ)	120a	20.28N	89.42W
Münchehofe, Ger.	238a	52.30N	13.40E
München *see* Munich, Ger.	142	48.08N	11.35E
Muncie, In., U.S. (mŭn'sĭ)	97	40.10N	85.30W
Mundelein, Il., U.S. (mŭn-dē-līn')	101a	42.16N	88.00W
Mündelheim, neigh., Ger.	236	51.21N	6.41E
Mundonueva, Pico de, mtn., Col. (pē'kō-dĕ-mōō'n-dō-nwĕ'vä)	130a	4.18N	74.12W
Muneco, Cerro, mtn., Mex. (sĕ'r-rō-mōō-nĕ'kō)	119a	19.13N	99.20W
Mungana, Austl. (mŭn-găn'ȧ)	203	17.15S	144.18E
Mungbere, Zaire	217	2.38N	28.30E
Munger, Mn., U.S. (mŭn'gẽr)	107h	46.48N	92.20W
Mungindi, Austl. (mŭn-gĭn'dē)	203	29.00S	148.45E
Munhall, Pa., U.S. (mŭn'hôl)	101e	40.24N	79.53W
Munhango, Ang. (mōn-häŋ'gȧ)	212	12.15S	18.55E
Munich, Ger.	142	48.08N	11.35E
Munirka, neigh., India	240d	28.34N	77.10E
Munising, Mi., U.S. (mū'nĭ-sĭng)	103	46.24N	86.41W
Muniz Freire, Braz.	129a	20.29S	41.25W
Munku Sardyk, mtn., Asia (mòn'kò sär-dĭk')	165	51.45N	100.30E
Muñoz, Phil. (mōōn-nyōth')	197a	15.44N	120.53E
Munro, neigh., Arg.	233d	34.32S	58.31W
Münster, Ger. (mün'stĕr)	147	51.57N	7.38E
Munster, In., U.S. (mŭn'stẽr)	101a	41.34N	87.31W
Munster, hist. reg., Ire. (mŭn-stẽr)	150	52.30N	9.24W
Muntok, Indon. (mòn-tŏk')	196	2.05S	105.11E
Muong Sing, Laos (mōō'ông-sĭng')	196	21.06N	101.17E
Muping, China (mōō-pĭŋ)	190	37.23N	121.36E
Muqui, Braz. (mōō-kòē)	129a	20.56S	41.20W
Mur, r., Eur. (mōōr)	147	47.00N	15.00E
Muradiye, Tur. (mōō-rä'dē-yĕ)	167	39.00N	43.40E
Murat, Fr. (mü-rä')	156	45.05N	2.56E
Murat, r., Tur. (mōō-rát')	182	39.00N	42.00E
Murayama, Japan	242a	35.45N	139.23E
Murchison, r., Austl. (mûr'chĭ-sŭn)	202	26.45S	116.15E
Murcia, Spain (mōōr'thyä)	142	38.00N	1.10W
Murcia, hist. reg., Spain	158	38.35N	1.51W
Murdo, S.D., U.S. (mûr'dō)	102	43.53N	100.42W
Mureş, r., Rom. (mōō'rĕsh)	149	46.02N	21.50E
Muret, Fr. (mü-rĕ')	156	43.28N	1.17E
Murfreesboro, Tn., U.S. (mûr'frēz-bŭr-ō)	114	35.50N	86.19W
Murgab, Taj.	169	38.10N	73.59E
Murgab, r., Asia (mōōr-gäb')	182	37.07N	62.32E
Muriaé, r., Braz.	129a	21.20S	41.40W
Murino, Russia (mōō'rĭ-nō)	172c	60.03N	30.28E
Müritz, l., Ger. (mür'its)	154	53.20N	12.33E
Murmansk, Russia (mōōr-mänsk')	164	69.00N	33.20E
Murom, Russia (mōō'rŏm)	164	55.30N	42.00W
Muroran, Japan (mōō'rō-rän)	189	42.21N	141.05E
Muros, Spain (mōō'rōs)	158	42.48N	9.00W
Muroto-Zaki, c., Japan (mōō'rō-tō zä'kē)	194	33.14N	134.12E
Murphy, Mo., U.S. (mûr'fĭ)	107e	38.29N	90.29W
Murphy, N.C., U.S.	114	35.05N	84.00W
Murphysboro, Il., U.S. (mûr'fĭz-bŭr-ō)	111	37.46N	89.21W
Murray, Ky., U.S. (mŭr'ĭ)	114	36.39N	88.17W
Murray, Ut., U.S.	107b	40.40N	111.53W
Murray, r., Austl.	202	34.20S	140.00E
Murray, r., Can.	87	55.00N	121.00W
Murray, Lake, res., S.C., U.S. (mŭr'ĭ)	115	34.07N	81.18W
Murray Bridge, Austl.	202	35.10S	139.35E
Murray Harbour, Can.	93	46.00N	62.31W
Murray Region, reg., Austl. (mŭ'rē)	203	33.20S	142.30E
Murrumbidgee, r., Austl. (mŭr-ŭm-bĭd'jē)	203	34.30S	145.20E
Murrupula, Moz.	217	15.27S	38.47E
Murshidābād, India (mòr'shē-dä-bäd')	186	24.08N	88.11E
Murska Sobota, Slvn. (mōōr'skä sô'bô-tä)	160	46.40N	16.14E
Murtal, Port.	238d	38.42N	9.22W
Muruasigar, mtn., Kenya	217	3.08N	35.02E
Murwāra, India	183	23.54N	80.23E
Murwillumbah, Austl. (mŭr-wĭl'lŭm-bŭ)	204	28.15S	153.30E
Mürz, r., Aus. (mürts)	154	47.30N	15.21E
Mürzzuschlag, Aus. (mürts'tsōō-shlägh)	154	47.37N	15.41E
Mus, Tur. (mōōsh)	167	38.55N	41.30E
Musala, mtn., Bul.	161	42.05N	23.24E
Musan, N. Kor. (mò'sän)	189	41.11N	129.10E
Musashino, Japan (mōō-sä'shē-nō)	195a	35.43N	139.35E
Muscat, Oman (mŭs-kăt')	182	23.23N	58.30E
Muscat and Oman *see* Oman, nation, Asia	182	20.00N	57.45E
Muscatine, Ia., U.S. (mŭs-kȧ-tēn)	103	41.26N	91.00W
Muscle Shoals, Al., U.S. (mŭs''l shōlz)	114	34.44N	87.38W
Musgrave Ranges, mts., Austl. (mŭs'grāv)	202	26.15S	131.15E
Mushie, Zaire (mŭsh'ē)	212	3.04S	16.50E
Mushin, Nig.	215	6.32N	3.22E
Musi, r., Indon. (mōō'sē)	196	2.40S	103.42E
Musinga, Alto, mtn., Col. (ä'l-tō-mōō-sē'n-gä)	130a	6.40N	76.13W
Muskego Lake, l., Wi., U.S. (mŭs-kē'gō)	101a	42.53N	88.10W
Muskegon, Mi., U.S. (mŭs-kē'gŭn)	97	43.15N	86.20W
Muskegon, r., Mi., U.S.	98	43.20N	85.55W
Muskegon Heights, Mi., U.S.	98	43.10N	86.20W
Muskingum, r., Oh., U.S. (mŭs-kĭŋ'gŭm)	98	39.45N	81.55W
Muskogee, Ok., U.S. (mŭs-kō'gē)	97	35.44N	95.21W
Muskoka, l., Can. (mŭs-kō'kȧ)	91	45.00N	79.30W
Musoma, Tan.	217	1.30S	33.48E
Mussau Island, i., Pap. N. Gui. (mōō-sä'ōō)	197	1.30S	149.32E
Musselshell, r., Mt., U.S. (mŭs''l-shĕl)	105	46.25N	108.20W
Mussende, Ang.	216	10.32S	16.05E
Mussuma, Ang.	216	14.14S	21.59E
Mustafakemalpaşa, Tur.	149	40.05N	28.30E
Mustang Bayou, Tx., U.S.	113a	29.22N	95.12W
Mustang Creek, r., Tx., U.S. (mŭs'tăng)	110	36.22N	102.46W
Mustang Island, i., Tx., U.S.	113	27.43N	97.00W
Mustique, i., St. Vin. (müs-tēk')	121b	12.53N	61.03W
Musturud, Egypt	244a	30.08N	31.17E
Mustvee, Est. (mōōst'vĕ-ĕ)	153	58.50N	26.54E
Musu Dan, c., N. Kor. (mò'sò dän)	189	40.51N	130.00E
Muswellbrook, Austl. (mŭs'wŭnl-bròk)	204	32.15S	150.50E
Mutare, Zimb.	212	18.49S	32.39E
Mutombo Mukulu, Zaire (mōō-tôm'bō mōō-kōō'lōō)	212	8.12S	23.56E
Mutsu Wan, b., Japan (mōōt'sōō wän)	194	41.20N	140.55E
Mutton Bay, Can. (mŭt''n)	93	50.48N	59.02W
Mutum, Braz. (mōō-tōō'm)	129a	19.48S	41.24W
Muzaffargarh, Pak.	186	30.09N	71.15E
Muzaffarpur, India	186	26.13N	85.20E
Muzon, Cape, c., Ak., U.S.	86	54.41N	132.44W
Muzquiz, Mex. (mōōz'kēz)	112	27.53N	101.31W
Muztagata, mtn., China	188	38.20N	75.28E
Mvomero, Tan.	217	6.20S	37.25E
Mvoti, r., S. Afr.	213c	29.18S	30.52E
Mwali, i., Com.	213	12.15S	43.45E
Mwanza, Tan. (mwän'zä)	212	2.31S	32.54E
Mwaya, Tan. (mwä'yä)	212	9.19S	33.51E
Mwenga, Zaire	217	3.02S	28.26E
Mweru, l., Afr.	212	8.50S	28.50E
Mwingi, Kenya	217	0.56S	38.04E
Myanmar (Burma), nation, Asia	180	21.00N	95.15E
Myingyan, Myanmar (myĭng-yŭn')	183	21.37N	95.26E
Myitkyina, Myanmar (myĭ'chē-nȧ)	183	25.33N	97.25E
Myjava, Slvk. (mûê'yȧ-vä)	155	48.45N	17.33E
Mykhaylivka, Ukr.	163	47.16N	35.12E
Mykolayiv, Ukr.	164	46.58N	32.02E
Mykolayiv, prov., Ukr.	163	47.27N	31.25E
Mymensingh, Bngl.	183	24.48N	90.28E
Mynämäki, Fin.	153	60.41N	21.58E
Myohyang San, mtn., N. Kor. (myō'hyang)	194	40.00N	126.12E
Mýrdalsjökull, ice., Ice. (mür'däls-yû'kòl)	146	63.34N	18.04W
Myrhorod, Ukr.	167	49.56N	33.36E
Myrtle Beach, S.C., U.S. (mûr't'l)	115	33.42N	78.53W
Myrtle Point, Or., U.S.	104	43.04N	124.08W
Mysen, Nor.	152	59.32N	11.16E
Myshikino, Russia (mēsh'kē-nō)	162	57.48N	38.21E
Mysore, India (mī-sōr')	183	12.31N	76.42E
Mysovka, Russia (mē' sôf-kȧ)	153	55.11N	21.17E
Mystic, Ia., U.S. (mĭs'tĭk)	103	40.47N	92.54W
Mytishchi, Russia (mē-tēsh'chi)	172b	55.55N	37.46E
Mziha, Tan.	217	5.54S	37.47E
Mzimba, Mwi. ('m-zĭm'bä)	212	11.52S	33.34E
Mzimkulu, r., Afr.	213c	30.12S	29.57E
Mzimvubu, r., S. Afr.	213c	31.22S	29.20E
Mzuzu, Mwi.	217	11.30S	34.10E

N

PLACE (Pronunciation)	PAGE	Lat. °′	Long. °′
Naab, r., Ger. (näp)	154	49.38N	12.15E
Naaldwijk, Neth.	145a	52.00N	4.11E
Naalehu, Hi., U.S.	94a	19.00N	155.35W
Naantali, Fin. (nän'tȧ-lē)	153	60.29N	22.03E
Nabberu, l., Austl. (năb'ẽr-ōō)	202	26.05S	120.35E
Naberezhnyye Chelny, Russia	164	55.42N	52.19E
Nabeul, Tun. (nā-bûl')	210	36.34N	10.45E
Nabiswera, Ug.	217	1.28N	32.16E
Naboomspruit, S. Afr.	218d	24.32S	28.43E
Nābulus, W. Bank	181a	32.13N	35.16E
Nacala, Moz. (nă-ká'lȧ)	213	14.34S	40.41E
Nacaome, Hond. (nä-kä-ō'mȧ)	120	13.32N	87.28W
Na Cham, Viet. (nä chäm')	193	22.02N	106.30E
Naches, r., Wa., U.S. (năch'ĕz)	104	46.51N	121.03W
Náchod, Czech Rep. (näk'ôt)	154	50.25N	16.08E
Nächstebreck, neigh., Ger.	236	51.18N	7.14E
Nacimiento, Lake, res., Ca., U.S. (nȧ-sĭ-myĕn'tō)	108	35.50N	121.00W
Nacogdoches, Tx., U.S. (năk'ō-dō'chĕz)	113	31.36N	94.40W
Nadadores, Mex. (nä-dä-dō'räs)	112	27.04N	101.36W
Nadiād, India	186	22.45N	72.51E
Nadir, V.I.U.S.	117c	18.19N	64.53W
Nădlac, Rom.	161	46.09N	20.52E
Nadvirna, Ukr.	155	48.37N	24.35E
Nadym, r., Russia (ná'dĭm)	170	64.30N	72.48E
Naestved, Den. (nĕst'vĭdh)	146	55.14N	11.46E
Nafada, Nig.	215	11.08N	11.20E
Nafishah, Egypt	218c	30.34N	32.15E
Nafūd ad Dahy, des., Sau. Ar.	182	22.15N	44.15E
Nag, Co, l., China	186	31.38N	91.18E
Naga, Phil. (nä'gä)	197	13.37N	123.12E
Naga, i., Japan	195	32.09N	130.16E
Nagahama, Japan (nä'gä-hä'mä)	195	33.32N	132.29E
Nagahama, Japan	195	35.23N	136.16E
Nagaland, India	183	25.47N	94.15E
Nagano, Japan (nä'gä-nō)	189	36.42N	138.12E
Nagao, Japan	242b	34.50N	135.43E
Nagaoka, Japan (nä'gȧ-ō'kȧ)	189	37.22N	138.49E
Nagaoka, Japan	195b	34.54N	135.42E
Nāgappattinam, India	183	10.48N	79.51E
Nagarote, Nic. (nä-gä-rō'tē)	120	12.17N	86.35W
Nagasaki, Japan (nä'gȧ-sä'kē)	189	32.48N	129.53E
Nagata, neigh., Japan	242b	34.40N	135.09E
Nagatino, neigh., Russia	239b	55.41N	37.41E
Nagatsuta, neigh., Japan	242a	35.32N	139.30E
Nāgaur, India	186	27.19N	73.41E
Nagaybakskiy, Russia (nȧ-gáy-bäk'skĭ)	172a	53.33N	59.33E
Nagcarlan, Phil. (näg-kär-län')	197a	14.07N	121.24E
Nāgercoil, India	187	8.15N	77.29E
Nagorno Karabakh, hist. reg., Azer. (nu-gôr'nŭ-kŭ-rŭ-bäk')	167	40.10N	46.50E
Nagoya, Japan	189	35.09N	136.53E
Nāgpur, India (näg'pōōr)	183	21.12N	79.09E
Nagua, Dom. Rep. (nä'gwä)	123	19.20N	69.40W
Nagykanizsa, Hung. (nôd'y'kô'nē-shô)	149	46.27N	17.00E
Nagykōrōs, Hung. (nôd'y'kū-rūsh)	155	47.02N	19.46E
Nagytarcsa, Hung.	239g	47.32N	19.17E
Naha, Japan (nä'hä)	189	26.02N	127.43E
Nahanni National Park, rec., Can.	84	62.10N	125.15W
Nahant, Ma., U.S. (nȧ-hănt)	93a	42.26N	70.55W
Nahant Bay, b., Ma., U.S.	227a	42.27N	70.55W
Nahariyya, Isr.	181a	33.01N	35.06E
Nahaut, Ma., U.S.	227a	42.25N	70.55W
Nahmer, Ger.	236	51.20N	7.35E
Nahuel Huapi, l., Arg. (nä'wĕl wä'pē)	132	41.00S	71.30W
Nahuizalco, El Sal. (nä-wē-zäl'kō)	120	13.50N	89.43W
Naic, Phil. (nä-ēk)	197a	14.20N	120.46E
Naica, Mex. (nä-ē'kä)	112	27.53N	105.30W
Naiguata, Pico, mtn., Ven. (pē'kō)	131b	10.32N	66.44W
Naihāti, India	240a	22.54N	88.25E
Nain, Can. (nīn)	85	56.29N	61.52W
Nā'īn, Iran	185	32.52N	53.05E
Nairn, Scot., U.K. (nârn)	150	57.35N	3.54W
Nairobi, Kenya (nī-rō'bē)	212	1.17S	36.49E
Naivasha, Kenya (nī-vä'shȧ)	212	0.47S	36.29E
Najd, hist. reg., Sau. Ar.	182	25.18N	42.38E
Najin, N. Kor. (nä'jĭn)	189	42.04N	130.35E
Najran, des., Sau. Ar. (nŭj-rän')	182	17.29N	45.30E
Naju, S. Kor. (nä'jōō')	194	35.02N	126.42E
Najusa, r., Cuba (nä-hōō'sä)	122	20.55N	77.55W
Naka, r., Japan	242a	35.39N	139.51E
Nakajima, Japan	242a	35.26N	139.56E
Nakanobu, neigh., Japan	242a	35.36N	139.43E
Nakatsu, Japan (nä'käts-ōō)	194	33.34N	131.10E
Nakhodka, Russia (nŭ-kôt'kŭ)	165	43.03N	133.08E
Nakhon Ratchasima, Thai.	196	14.56N	102.14E
Nakhon Sawan, Thai.	196	15.42N	100.06E
Nakhon Si Thammarat, Thai.	196	8.27N	99.58E
Nakło nad Notecia, Pol.	155	53.10N	17.35E
Nakskov, Den. (näk'skou)	146	54.51N	11.06E
Naktong, r., S. Kor. (näk'tŭng)	194	36.10N	128.30E
Nal'chik, Russia (nál-chĕk')	167	43.30N	43.35E
Nalón, r., Spain (nä-lōn')	158	43.15N	5.38W
Nālūt, Libya (nä-lōōt')	210	31.51N	10.49E
Namak, Daryacheh-ye, l., Iran	182	34.58N	51.33E
Namakan, l., Mn., U.S. (nä'mȧ-kȧn)	103	48.20N	92.43W
Namamugi, neigh., Japan	242a	35.29N	139.41E
Namangan, Uzb. (nȧ-män-gän')	169	41.08N	71.59E
Namao, Can.	83g	53.43N	113.30W
Namatanai, Pap. N. Gui. (nä'mä-tȧ-nä'ē)	197	3.43S	152.26E
Nambour, Austl. (năm'bòr)	204	26.48S	153.00E
Nam Co, l., China (näm tswo)	188	30.30N	91.10E
Nam Dinh, Viet. (näm dēnk')	196	20.30N	106.10E
Nametil, Moz.	217	15.43S	39.21E
Namhae, i., S. Kor. (näm'hī')	194	34.23N	128.05E
Namib Desert, des., Nmb. (nä-mēb')	212	18.45S	12.45E
Namibia, nation, Afr.	212	19.30S	16.13E
Namoi, r., Austl. (nămoi)	203	30.10S	148.43E
Namous, Oued en, r., Alg. (nȧ-mōōs')	148	31.48N	0.19W
Nampa, Id., U.S. (năm'pȧ)	96	43.35N	116.35W
Namp'o, N. Kor.	189	38.47N	125.28E
Nampuecha, Moz.	217	13.59S	40.18E
Nampula, Moz.	217	15.07S	39.15E
Namsos, Nor. (näm'sôs)	146	64.28N	11.14E
Namu, Can.	86	51.53N	127.50W
Namuli, Serra, mts., Moz.	217	15.05S	37.05E
Namur, Bel. (nä-mür')	147	50.29N	4.55E
Namutoni, Nmb. (nȧ-mōō-tō'nē)	212	18.45S	17.00E
Nan, r., Thai.	196	18.11N	100.29E
Nanacamilpa, Mex. (nä-nä-kä-mē'l-pä)	119a	19.30N	98.33W
Nanaimo, Can. (nȧ-nī'mō)	84	49.10N	123.56W
Nanam, N. Kor. (nä'nän')	194	41.38N	129.37E
Nanao, Japan (nä'nä-ō)	194	37.03N	136.59E
Nan'ao Dao, i., China (nän-ou dou)	193	23.30N	117.30E
Nancefield, S. Afr.	244b	26.17S	27.53E
Nanchang, China (nän'chäng')	189	28.38N	115.48E
Nanchangshan Dao, i., China (nän-chäŋ-shän dou)	190	37.56N	120.42E
Nancheng, China (nän-chäŋ)	189	26.50N	116.40E
Nanchong, China (nän-chôŋ)	188	30.45N	106.05E
Nancy, Fr. (näN-sē')	147	48.42N	6.11E
Nancy Creek, r., Ga., U.S. (năn'cē)	100c	33.51N	84.25W
Nanda Devi, mtn., India (nän'dä dā'vē)	183	30.30N	80.25E
Nānded, India	186	19.13N	77.21E
Nandurbār, India	186	21.29N	74.13E
Nandyāl, India	187	15.54N	78.09E
Nanga Parbat, mtn., Pak.	186	35.20N	74.35E

PRONOUNCING INDEX

Nangi – Nerchinskiy Zavod 323

PLACE (Pronunciation)	PAGE	Lat. °′	Long. °′
Nangi, India	186a	22.30N	88.14E
Nangis, Fr. (näN-zhē′)	157b	48.33N	3.01E
Nangong, China (nän-gôŋ)	192	37.22N	115.22E
Nangweshi, Zam.	216	16.26S	23.17E
Nanhuangcheng Dao, i., China (nän-hüäŋ-chŭŋ dou)	190	38.22N	120.54E
Nanhui, China	190	31.03N	121.45E
Naniwa, neigh., Japan	242b	34.39N	135.30E
Nanjing, China (nän-jyĭŋ)	189	32.04N	118.46E
Nanjuma, r., China (nän-jyōō-mä)	190	39.37N	115.45E
Nanking see Nanjing, China	188	32.04N	118.46E
Nanle, China (nän-lŭ)	190	36.03N	115.13E
Nan Ling, mts., China	189	25.15N	111.40E
Nanliu, r., China (nän-lĭō)	193	22.00N	109.18E
Nannine, Austl. (nă-nēn′)	202	25.50S	118.30E
Nanning, China (nän′nĭng′)	188	22.56N	108.10E
Nānole, neigh., India	240e	19.01N	72.55E
Nanpan, r., China (nän-pän)	193	24.50N	105.30E
Nanping, China (nän-pĭŋ)	189	26.40N	118.05E
Nansei-shotō, is., Japan	189	27.30N	127.00E
Nansemond, Va., U.S. (năn′sē-mŭnd)	100g	36.46N	76.32W
Nantai Zan, mtn., Japan (nän-täē zän)	194	36.47N	139.28E
Nanterre, Fr.	237c	48.53N	2.12E
Nantes, Fr. (näNt′)	142	47.13N	1.37W
Nanteuil-le-Haudouin, Fr. (näN-tû-lĕ-ō-dwăN′)	157b	49.08N	2.49E
Nanticoke, Pa., U.S. (năn′tĭ-kōk)	99	41.10N	76.00W
Nantong, China (nän-tôŋ)	190	32.02N	120.51E
Nantong, China	190	32.08N	121.06E
Nantouillet, Fr.	237c	49.00N	2.42E
Nantucket, i., Ma., U.S. (năn-tŭk′ĕt)	97	41.15N	70.05W
Nantwich, Eng., U.K. (nănt′wĭch)	144a	53.04N	2.31W
Nanxiang, China (nän-shyäŋ)	190	31.17N	121.17E
Nanxiong, China (nän-shôŋ)	193	25.10N	114.20E
Nanyang, China	189	33.00N	112.42E
Nanyang Hu, l., China (nän-yäŋ hōō)	190	35.14N	116.24E
Nanyuan, China (nän-yůän)	192a	39.48N	116.24E
Nao, Cabo de la, c., Spain (kå′bô-dĕ-lä-nä′ō)	142	38.43N	0.14E
Naoābād, India	240a	22.28N	88.27E
Naolinco, Mex. (nä-o-lēŋ′kō)	119	19.39N	96.50W
Naopukuria, India	240a	22.55N	88.16E
Náousa, Grc. (nä′ōō-så)	161	40.38N	22.05E
Naozhou Dao, i., China (nou-jō dou)	193	20.58N	110.58E
Napa, Ca., U.S. (năp′ȧ)	96	38.20N	122.17W
Napanee, Can. (năp′ȧ-nē)	91	44.15N	77.00W
Naperville, Il., U.S. (nā′pẽr-vĭl)	101a	41.46N	88.09W
Napier, N.Z. (nā′pĭ-ẽr)	203a	39.30S	177.00E
Napierville, Can. (nā′pĭ-ē-vĭl)	83a	45.11N	73.24W
Naples (Napoli), Italy	142	40.37N	14.12E
Naples, Fl., U.S. (nā′p′lz)	115a	26.07N	81.46W
Napo, r., S.A. (nä′pō)	130	1.49S	74.20W
Napoleon, Oh., U.S. (nȧ-pō′lē-ŭn)	98	41.20N	84.10W
Napoleonville, La., U.S. (nȧ-pō′lē-ŭn-vĭl)	113	29.56N	91.03W
Napoli see Naples, Italy	142	40.37N	14.12E
Napoli, Golfo di, b., Italy	148	40.29N	14.08E
Nappanee, In., U.S. (năp′ȧ-nē)	98	41.30N	86.00W
Nara, Japan (nä′rä)	189	34.41N	135.50E
Nara, Mali	210	15.09N	7.27W
Nara, dept., Japan	195b	34.36N	135.49E
Nara, r., Russia	162	55.05N	37.16E
Naracoorte, Austl. (nă-rå-kōōn′tē)	202	36.50S	140.50E
Narashino, Japan	195a	35.41N	140.01E
Naraspur, India	187	16.32N	81.43E
Nārāyanpāra, India	240a	22.54N	88.19E
Narberth, Pa., U.S. (när′bûrth)	100f	40.01N	75.17W
Narbonne, Fr. (når-bôn′)	147	43.12N	3.00E
Nare, Col. (nä′rē)	130a	6.12N	74.37W
Narew, r., Pol. (när′ĕf)	155	52.43N	21.19E
Narmada, r., India	183	22.30N	75.30E
Naroch′, l., Bela. (nä′rôch)	162	54.51N	27.00E
Narodnaya, Gora, mtn., Russia (ná-rôd′ná-yà)	164	65.10N	60.10E
Naro-Fominsk, Russia (nä′rô-mēnsk′)	166	55.23N	36.43E
Narrabeen, Austl. (năr-ȧ-bĭn)	201b	33.44S	151.18E
Narragansett, R.I., U.S. (năr-ă-găn′sĕt)	100b	41.26N	71.27W
Narragansett Bay, b., R.I., U.S.	99	41.20N	71.15W
Narrandera, Austl. (nå-rån-dē′rå)	203	34.40S	146.40E
Narraweena, Austl.	243a	33.45S	151.16E
Narre Warren North, Austl.	243b	37.59S	145.19E
Narrogin, Austl. (năr′ô-gĭn)	202	33.00S	117.15E
Naruo, Japan	242b	34.43N	135.23E
Narva, Est. (når′vå)	166	59.24N	28.12E
Narvacan, Phil. (när-vä-kän′)	197a	17.27N	120.29E
Narva Jõesuu, Est. (når′vå ô-ô-ä′sōō-ō)	153	59.26N	28.02E
Narvik, Nor. (när′vĕk)	142	68.21N	17.18E
Narvskiy Zaliv, b., Eur. (nár′vskĭ zä′lĭf)	153	59.35N	27.25E
Narvskoye, res., Eur.	153	59.18N	28.14E
Nar′yan-Mar, Russia (när′yán mär′)	164	67.42N	53.30E
Naryilco, Austl. (năr-ĭl′kô)	204	28.40S	141.50E
Narym, Russia (nä-rēm′)	164	58.47N	82.05E
Naryn, r., Asia (nŭ-rĭn′)	170	41.20N	76.00E
Naseby, Eng., U.K. (nāz′bĭ)	144a	52.23N	0.59W
Nashua, Mo., U.S. (năsh′ŭ-ȧ)	107f	39.18N	94.34W
Nashua, N.H., U.S.	97	42.47N	71.23W
Nashville, Ar., U.S. (năsh′vĭl)	111	33.56N	93.50W
Nashville, Ga., U.S.	114	31.12N	83.15W
Nashville, Il., U.S.	111	38.21N	89.42W
Nashville, Mi., U.S.	98	42.35N	85.50W
Nashville, Tn., U.S.	97	36.10N	86.48W
Nashwauk, Mn., U.S. (năsh′wôk)	103	47.21N	93.12W
Näsi, l., Fin.	146	61.42N	24.05E
Našice, Cro. (nä′shē-tsĕ)	149	45.29N	18.06E
Nasielsk, Pol. (nä′syĕlsk)	155	52.35N	20.50E
Nāsik, India (nä′sĭk)	183	20.02N	73.49E
Nāşir, Sudan (nä-zēr′)	211	8.30N	33.06E
Nasirabād, India	186	26.13N	74.48E
Naskaupi, r., Can. (năs′kô-pĭ)	85	53.59N	61.10W
Nasondoye, Zaire	217	10.22S	25.06E
Nass, r., Can. (năs)	86	55.00N	129.30W
Nassau, Bah. (năs′ô)	117	25.05N	77.20W
Nassenheide, Ger. (nä′sĕn-hī-dĕ)	145b	52.49N	13.13E
Nasser, Lake, res., Egypt	211	23.50N	32.50E
Nasugbu, Phil. (ná-sóg-bōō′)	197a	14.05N	120.37E
Nasworthy Lake, l., Tx., U.S. (năz′wûr-thē)	112	31.17N	100.30W
Natagaima, Col. (nä-tä-gī′mä)	130a	3.38N	75.07W
Nātāgarh, India	240a	22.42N	88.25E
Natal, Braz. (nä-täl′)	131	6.00S	35.13W
Natalspruit, S. Afr.	244b	26.19S	28.09E
Natashquan, Can. (nä-täsh′kwän)	85	50.11N	61.49W
Natashquan, r., Can.	93	50.35N	61.35W
Natchez, Ms., U.S. (năch′ĕz)	97	31.35N	91.20W
Natchitoches, La., U.S. (năk′ĭ-tŏsh)(nách-ĭ-tōsh′)	113	31.46N	93.06W
Natick, Ma., U.S. (nā′tĭk)	93a	42.17N	71.21W
National Bison Range, I.R., Mt., U.S. (năsh′ŭn-ăl bī′s′n)	105	47.18N	113.58W
National City, Ca., U.S.	108a	32.38N	117.01W
National Park, Pa., U.S.	229b	39.51N	75.12W
Natitingou, Benin	210	10.19N	1.22E
Natividade, Braz. (nä-tē-vē-dä′dĕ)	131	11.43S	47.34W
Natron, Lake, l., Tan. (nā′trŏn)	212	2.17S	36.10E
Natrona Heights, Pa., U.S. (nā′trō nā)	101e	40.38N	79.43W
Naţrūn, Wādī an, val., Egypt	218b	30.33N	30.12E
Natuna Besar, i., Indon.	196	4.00N	106.50E
Natural Bridges National Monument, rec., Ut., U.S. (năt′ŭ-răl brĭj′ĕs)	109	37.20N	110.20W
Naturaliste, Cape, c., Austl. (năt-ū-rá-lĭst′)	202	33.30S	115.10E
Naucalpan de Juárez, Mex.	119a	19.28N	99.14W
Nauchampatepetl, mtn., Mex. (näōō-chäm-pä-tĕ′pĕtl)	119	19.32N	97.09W
Nauen, Ger. (nou′ĕn)	145b	52.36N	12.53E
Naugatuck, Ct., U.S. (nô′gȧ-tŭk)	99	41.25N	73.05W
Naujan, Phil. (nä-ō-hän′)	197a	13.19N	121.17E
Naumburg, Ger. (noum′bŏrgh)	154	51.10N	11.50E
Naupada, neigh., India	240e	19.04N	72.50E
Nauru, nation, Oc.	3	0.30S	167.00E
Nautla, Mex. (nä-ōōt′lä)	116	20.14N	96.44W
Nava, Mex. (nä′vä)	112	28.25N	100.44W
Nava del Rey, Spain (nä-vä dĕl rā′ē)	158	41.22N	5.04W
Navahermosa, Spain (nä-vä-ĕr-mō′sä)	158	39.39N	4.28W
Navajas, Cuba (nä-vä-häs′)	122	22.40N	81.20W
Navajo Hopi Joint Use Area, I.R., U.S.	109	36.15N	110.30W
Navajo Indian Reservation, I.R., U.S. (năv′á-hō)	109	36.31N	109.24W
Navajo National Monument, rec., Az., U.S.	109	36.43N	110.39W
Navajo Reservoir, res., N.M., U.S.	109	36.57N	107.26W
Navalcarnero, Spain (nä-väl′kär-nā′rō)	159a	40.17N	4.05W
Navalmoral de la Mata, Spain	158	39.53N	5.32W
Navan, Can. (nă′văn)	83c	45.25N	75.26W
Navarino, i., Chile (nä-vä-rē′nô)	132	55.30S	68.15W
Navarra, hist. reg., Spain (nä-vär′rä)	158	42.40N	1.35W
Navarro, Arg. (nä-vá′r-rō)	129c	35.00S	59.16W
Navasota, Tx., U.S. (năv-ȧ-sō′tȧ)	113	30.24N	96.05W
Navasota, r., Tx., U.S.	113	31.03N	96.11W
Navassa, i., N.A. (nȧ-văs′ȧ)	123	18.25N	75.15W
Navestock, Eng., U.K.	235	51.39N	0.13E
Navestock Side, Eng., U.K.	235	51.39N	0.16E
Navia, r., Spain (nä-vē′ä)	158	43.10N	6.45W
Navidad, Chile (nä-vē-dä′d)	129b	33.57S	71.51W
Navidad Bank, bk. (nä-vē-dädh′)	123	20.05N	69.00W
Navidade do Carangola, Braz. (nä-vē-dä′dō-kå-rän-gō′la)	129a	21.04S	41.58W
Navojoa, Mex. (nä-vô-kô′ä)	116	27.00N	109.40W
Navotas, Phil.	241g	14.40N	120.57E
Návplion, Grc.	161	37.33N	22.46E
Nawābshāh, Pak. (nȧ-wäb′shä)	186	26.20N	68.30E
Naxçıvan, Azer.	167	39.10N	45.30E
Naxçıvan Muxtar, state, Azer.	168	39.20N	45.30E
Náxos, i., Grc. (nák′sôs)	149	37.15N	25.20E
Nayābās, India	240d	28.35N	77.19E
Nayarit, state, Mex. (nä-yä-rēt′)	116	22.00N	105.15W
Nayarit, Sierra de, mts., Mex. (sē-ĕ′r-rä-dĕ)	118	23.20N	105.07W
Naye, Sen.	214	14.25N	12.12W
Naylor, Md., U.S. (nā′lŏr)	100e	38.43N	76.46W
Nazaré da Mata, Braz. (dä-mä-tä)	131	7.46S	35.13W
Nazas, Mex. (nä′zäs)	112	25.14N	104.08W
Nazas, r., Mex.	116	25.30N	104.40W
Nazerat, Isr.	181a	32.43N	35.19E
Nazilli, Tur. (ná-zĭ-lē′)	167	37.40N	28.10E
Naziya, r., Russia (ná-zē′yå)	172c	59.48N	31.18E
Nazko, r., Can.	86	52.35N	123.10W
Nazlat as-Sammān, Egypt	244a	29.59N	31.08E
Nazlat Khalīfah, Egypt	244a	30.01N	31.10E
N′dalatando, Ang.	216	9.18S	14.54E
Ndali, Benin	215	9.51N	2.43E
Ndikiniméki, Cam.	215	4.46N	10.50E
N′Djamena, Chad	211	12.07N	15.03E
Ndjili, neigh., Zaire	244c	4.21S	15.19E
Ndola, Zam. (n′dō′lä)	212	12.58S	28.38E
Ndoto Mountains, mts., Kenya	217	1.55N	37.05E
Ndrhamcha, Sebkha de, l., Maur.	214	18.50N	15.15W
Nduye, Zaire	217	1.50N	29.01E
Neagh, Lough, l., N. Ire., U.K. (lŏk nā)	146	54.40N	6.47W
Néa Ionía, Grc.	239d	38.02N	23.45E
Néa Liósia, Grc.	239d	38.02N	23.42E
Néa Páfos, Cyp.	181a	34.46N	32.27E
Neapean, r., Austl.	201b	33.40S	150.39E
Neápolis, Grc.	160a	35.17N	25.37E
Neápolis, Grc. (nā-ŏp′ ô-lĭs)	161	36.35N	23.08E
Near Islands, is., Ak., U.S. (nēr)	95a	52.20N	172.40E
Near North Side, neigh., Il., U.S.	231a	41.54N	87.38W
Néa Smírni, Grc.	239d	37.57N	23.43E
Neath, Wales, U.K. (nēth)	150	51.41N	3.50W
Nebine Creek, r., Austl. (nĕ-bēne′)	204	27.50S	147.00E
Nebit-Dag, Turk. (nyĕ-bĕt′däg′)	170	39.30N	54.20E
Nebraska, state, U.S. (nē-brăs′kȧ)	96	41.45N	101.30W
Nebraska City, Ne., U.S.	111	40.40N	95.50W
Nechako, r., Can.	86	53.45N	124.55W
Nechako Plateau, plat., Can. (nĭ-chă′kō)	86	54.00N	124.30W
Nechako Range, mts., Can.	86	53.20N	124.30W
Nechako Reservoir, res., Can.	86	53.25N	125.10W
Neches, r., Tx., U.S. (nĕch′ĕz)	113	31.03N	94.40W
Neckar, r., Ger. (nĕk′är)	154	49.16N	9.06E
Necker Island, i., Hi., U.S.	94b	24.00N	164.00W
Necochea, Arg. (nā-kô-chā′ä)	132	38.30S	58.45W
Nedlitz, neigh., Ger.	238a	52.26N	13.03E
Nedryhayliv, Ukr.	163	50.49N	33.52E
Needham, Ma., U.S. (nēd′ăm)	93a	42.17N	71.14W
Needham Heights, Ma., U.S.	227a	41.28N	71.14W
Needles, Ca., U.S. (nē′d′lz)	109	34.51N	114.39W
Neenah, Wi., U.S. (nē′nȧ)	103	44.10N	88.30W
Neepawa, Can.	84	50.13N	99.29W
Nee Reservoir, res., Co., U.S. (nee)	110	38.26N	102.56W
Nee Soon, Sing.	240c	1.24N	103.49E
Negareyama, Japan (nå′gä-rä-yä′mä)	195a	35.52N	139.54E
Negaunee, Mi., U.S. (nē-gô′nē)	103	46.30N	87.37W
Negeri Sembilan, state, Malay. (nă′grē-sĕm-bē-län′)	181b	2.46N	101.54E
Negev, des., Isr. (nĕ′gĕv)	181a	30.34N	34.43E
Negombo, Sri L.	187	7.39N	79.49E
Negotin, Yugo. (nĕ′gô-tēn)	161	44.13N	22.33E
Negro, r., Arg.	132	39.50S	65.00W
Negro, r., N.A.	120	13.01N	87.10W
Negro, r., S.A.	129c	33.17S	58.18W
Negro, Cerro, mtn., Pan. (sĕ′-rrō-nā′grô)	121	8.44N	80.37W
Negro, Rio, r., S.A. (rē′ō nā′grô)	130	0.18S	63.21W
Negros, i., Phil. (nā′grōs)	196	9.50N	121.45E
Nehalem, r., Or., U.S. (nē-hăl′ĕm)	104	45.52N	123.37W
Nehaus an der Oste, Ger. (noi′houz)(ōz′tĕ)	145c	53.48N	9.02E
Nehbandān, Iran	185	31.32N	60.02E
Nehe, China (nŭ-hŭ)	192	48.23N	124.58E
Neheim-Hüsten, Ger. (nĕ′hīm)	157c	51.28N	7.58E
Neiba, Dom. Rep. (nå-ē′bä)	123	18.30N	71.20W
Neiba, Bahía de, b., Dom. Rep.	123	18.10N	71.00W
Neiba, Sierra de, mts., Dom. Rep. (sē-ĕr′rä-dĕ)	123	18.40N	71.40W
Neihart, Mt., U.S. (nī′hárt)	105	46.54N	110.39W
Neijiang, China (nā-jyäŋ)	193	29.38N	105.01E
Neillsville, Wi., U.S. (nēlz′vĭl)	103	44.35N	90.37W
Neiqiu, China (nā-chyō)	190	37.17N	114.32E
Neira, Col. (nā′rä)	130a	5.10N	75.32W
Neisse, r., Eur. (nēs)	154	51.30N	15.00E
Neiva, Col. (nå-ē′vä)(nā′vä)	130	2.55N	75.16W
Neixiang, China (nā-shyäŋ)	192	33.00N	111.38E
Nekemte, Eth.	211	9.09N	36.29E
Nekoosa, Wi., U.S. (nē-kōō′sȧ)	103	44.19N	89.54W
Neligh, Ne., U.S. (nē′-lē)	102	42.06N	98.02W
Nel′kan, Russia (nĕl-kän′)	165	57.45N	136.36E
Nellore, India (nĕl-lōr′)	183	14.28N	79.59E
Nel′ma, Russia (nĕl-mä′)	194	47.34N	139.05E
Nelson, Can. (nĕl′sŭn)	84	49.29N	117.17W
Nelson, N.Z.	203a	41.15S	173.22E
Nelson, Eng., U.K.	144a	53.50N	2.13W
Nelson, i., Ak., U.S.	95	60.38N	164.42W
Nelson, r., Can.	89	56.50N	93.40W
Nelson, Cape, c., Austl.	204	38.29S	141.20E
Nelsonville, Oh., U.S. (nĕl′sŭn-vĭl)	98	39.30N	82.15W
Néma, Maur. (nā′mä)	210	16.37N	7.15W
Nemadji, r., Wi., U.S. (nē-măd′jē)	107h	46.33N	92.16W
Neman, Russia (ŋĕ′-mån)	153	55.02N	22.01E
Neman, r., Eur.	166	53.28N	24.45E
Nematābād, Iran	241h	35.38N	51.21E
Nembe, Nig.	215	4.35N	6.26E
Nemčinovka, Russia	239b	55.43N	37.23E
Nemeiben Lake, l., Can. (nĕ-mē′bȧn)	88	55.20N	105.20W
Nemours, Fr.	156	48.16N	2.41E
Nemuro, Japan (nā′mô-rō)	189	43.13N	145.10E
Nemuro Strait, strt., Asia	194	43.07N	145.10E
Nemyriv, Ukr.	163	48.56N	28.51E
Nen, r., China (nŭn)	189	47.07N	123.28E
Nen, r., Eng., U.K. (nĕn)	144a	52.32N	0.19W
Nenagh, Ire. (nē′nȧ)	150	52.50N	8.05W
Nenana, Ak., U.S. (nā-nä′nȧ)	95	64.28N	149.18W
Nenets, state, Russia	166	67.30N	54.00E
Nenikyul′, Russia (nĕ-nyĕ′kyûl)	172c	59.26N	30.40E
Nenjiang, China (nŭn-jyäŋ)	189	49.02N	125.15E
Neodesha, Ks., U.S. (nē-ō-dĕ-shô′)	111	37.24N	95.41W
Neosho, Mo., U.S.	111	36.51N	94.22W
Neosho, r., Ks., U.S. (nē-ō′shō)	111	38.07N	95.40W
Nepal, nation, Asia (nĕ-pôl′)	183	28.45N	83.00E
Nephi, Ut., U.S. (nē′fī)	109	39.40N	111.50W
Nepomuceno, Braz. (nĕ-pô-mōō-sĕ′no)	129a	21.15S	45.13W
Nera, r., Italy (nā′rä)	160	42.45N	12.54E
Nérac, Fr. (nā-räk′)	156	44.08N	0.19E
Nerchinsk, Russia (nyĕr′ chĕnsk)	165	51.47N	116.17E
Nerchinskiy Khrebet, mts., Russia	165	50.30N	118.30E
Nerchinskiy Zavod, Russia (nyĕr′chĕn-skĭzá-vôt′)	165	51.35N	119.46E

ng-sing; ŋ-baŋk; N-nasalized n; nŏd; cŏmmit; ōld; ôbey; ôrder; oi-boil; fōōd; ŏ-as oo in foot; ou-out; s-soft; sh-dish; th-thin; pūre; ůnite; ûrn; stŭd; circŭs; ü-as in French tu; ′-indeterminate vowel.

324 Nerekhta – Niangara

PLACE (Pronunciation)	PAGE	Lat. °′	Long. °′
Nerekhta, Russia (nyě-rěĸ'tá)	162	57.29N	40.34E
Neretva, r., Yugo. (ně'rět-vȧ)	161	43.08N	17.50E
Nerja, Spain (něr'hä)	158	36.45N	3.53W
Nerl', r., Russia (nyěrl)	162	56.59N	37.57E
Nerskaya, r., Russia (nyěr'ská-yȧ)	172b	55.31N	38.46E
Nerussa, r., Russia (nyȧ-rōō'sȧ)	162	52.24N	34.20E
Ness, Eng., U.K.	237a	53.17N	3.03W
Ness, Loch, l., Scot., U.K. (lŏĸ něs)	150	57.23N	4.20W
Ness City, Ks., U.S. (něs)	110	38.27N	99.55W
Nesterov, Russia (nyěs-tă'rôf)	153	54.39N	22.38E
Neston, Eng., U.K.	237a	53.18N	3.04W
Néstos (Mesta), r., Eur. (nās'tōs)	161	41.25N	24.12E
Nesvizh, Bela. (nyěs'vēsh)	162	53.13N	26.44E
Netanya, Isr.	181a	32.19N	34.52E
Netcong, N.J., U.S. (nět'cŏnj)	100a	40.54N	74.42W
Netherlands, nation, Eur. (nědh'ěr-lăndz)	142	53.01N	3.57E
Netherlands Guiana see Suriname, nation, S.A.	131	4.00N	56.00W
Netherton, Eng., U.K.	237a	53.30N	2.58W
Nette, neigh., Ger.	236	51.33N	7.25E
Nettilling, l., Can.	85	66.30N	70.40W
Nett Lake Indian Reservation, I.R., Mn., U.S. (nět lāk)	103	48.23N	93.19W
Nettuno, Italy (nět-tōō'nô)	159d	41.28N	12.40E
Neubeckum, Ger. (noi'bě-kōōm)	157c	51.48N	8.01E
Neubrandenburg, Ger. (noi-brän'děn-bòrgh)	154	53.33N	13.16E
Neuburg, Ger. (noi'bòrgh)	154	48.43N	11.12E
Neuchâtel, Switz. (nû-shȧ-těl')	147	47.00N	6.52E
Neuchâtel, Lac de, l., Switz.	154	46.48N	6.53E
Neudorf, neigh., Ger.	236	51.25N	6.47E
Neuenhagen, Ger. (noi'ěn-hä-gěn)	145b	52.31N	13.41E
Neuenhof, neigh., Ger.	236	51.10N	7.13E
Neuenkamp, neigh., Ger.	236	51.26N	6.44E
Neuenrade, Ger. (noi'ěn-rä-dě)	157c	51.17N	7.47E
Neu-Erlaa, neigh., Aus.	239e	48.08N	16.19E
Neu Fahrland, Ger.	238a	52.26N	13.03E
Neufchâtel-en-Bray, Fr. (nû-shä-těl'ěɴ-brā')	156	49.43N	1.25E
Neuilly-sur-Marne, Fr.	237c	48.51N	2.32E
Neuilly-sur-Seine, Fr.	237c	48.53N	2.16E
Neukirchen, Ger.	236	51.27N	6.33E
Neulengbach, Aus.	145e	48.13N	15.55E
Neumarkt, Ger. (noi'märkt)	154	49.17N	11.30E
Neumünster, Ger. (noi'münstěr)	146	54.04N	10.00E
Neunkirchen, Aus. (noin'kĭrĸ-ĕn)	154	47.43N	16.05E
Neuquén, Arg. (ně-ò-kān')	132	38.52S	68.12W
Neuquén, prov., Arg.	132	39.40S	70.45W
Neuquén, r., Arg.	132	38.45S	69.00W
Neuruppin, Ger. (noi'rōō-pēn)	154	52.55N	12.48E
Neuse, r., N.C., U.S. (nūz)	115	36.12N	78.50W
Neusiedler See, l., Eur. (noi-zēd'lēr)	154	47.54N	16.31E
Neuss, Ger. (nois)	157c	51.12N	6.41E
Neusserweyhe, neigh., Ger.	236	51.13N	6.39E
Neustadt, Ger. (noi'shtät)	154	49.21N	8.08E
Neustadt bei Coburg, Ger. (bī kō'bōōrgh)	154	50.20N	11.09E
Neustadt in Holstein, Ger.	154	54.06N	10.50E
Neustift am Walde, neigh., Aus.	239e	48.15N	16.18E
Neustrelitz, Ger. (noi-strä'lĭts)	154	53.21N	13.05E
Neutral Hills, hills, Can. (nū'trăl)	88	52.10N	110.50W
Neu Ulm, Ger. (noi ò lm')	154	48.23N	10.01E
Neuva Pompeya, neigh., Arg.	233d	34.39S	58.25W
Neuville, Can. (nū'vĭl)	83b	46.39N	71.35W
Neuville-sur-Oise, Fr.	237c	49.01N	2.04E
Neuwaldegg, neigh., Aus.	239e	48.14N	16.17E
Neuwied, Ger. (noi'vēdt)	154	50.26N	7.28E
Neva, r., Russia (nyě-vȧ')	162	59.49N	30.54E
Nevada, Ia., U.S. (nė-vā'dȧ)	103	42.01N	93.27W
Nevada, Mo., U.S.	111	37.49N	94.21W
Nevada, state, U.S. (nė vä'dȧ)	96	39.30N	117.00W
Nevada, Sierra, mts., Spain (syěr'rä nä-vä'dhä)	142	37.01N	3.28W
Nevada, Sierra, mts., U.S. (sē-ě'r-rä nė-vä'dȧ)	96	39.20N	120.05W
Nevado, Cerro el, mtn., Col. (sě'r-rô-ěl-ně-vä'dô)	130a	4.02N	74.08W
Neva Stantsiya, Russia (nyě-vä' stän'tsĭ-yȧ)	172c	59.53N	30.30E
Neve, Serra da, mts., Ang.	216	13.40S	13.20E
Nevel', Russia (nyě'věl)	166	56.03N	29.57E
Neveri, r., Ven. (nē-vē-rē)	131b	10.13N	64.18W
Nevers, Fr. (nē-vȧr')	147	46.59N	3.10E
Neves, Braz.	132b	22.51S	43.06W
Nevesinje, Bos. (ně-vě'sěn-yě)	161	43.15N	18.08E
Neviges, Ger.	236	51.19N	7.05E
Neville Island, i., Pa., U.S.	230b	40.31N	80.08W
Nevinnomyssk, Russia	168	44.38N	41.56E
Nevis, i., St. K./N. (nē'vĭs)	117	17.05N	62.38W
Nevis, Ben, mtn., Scot., U.K. (běn)	146	56.47N	5.00W
Nevis Peak, mtn., St. K./N.	121b	17.11N	62.33W
Nevşehir, Tur. (něv-shě'hêr)	149	38.40N	34.35E
Nev'yansk, Russia (něv-yänsk')	164	57.29N	60.14E
New, r., Va., U.S. (nū)	115	37.20N	80.35W
Newabāgam, India	240a	22.48N	88.24E
New Addington, neigh., Eng., U.K.	235	51.21N	0.01W
Newala, Tan.	217	10.56S	39.18E
New Albany, In., U.S. (nū ôl'bȧ-nĭ)	101h	38.17N	85.49W
New Albany, Ms., U.S.	115	34.28N	39.00W
New Amsterdam, Guy. (ăm'stēr-dăm)	131	6.14N	57.30W
Newark, Eng., U.K. (nū'ěrk)	144a	53.04N	0.49W
Newark, Ca., U.S. (nū'ěrk)	106b	37.32N	122.02W
Newark, De., U.S. (nōō'ärk)	99	39.40N	75.45W
Newark, N.J., U.S. (nōō'ûrk)	97	40.44N	74.10W
Newark, N.Y., U.S. (nū'ěrk)	99	43.05N	77.10W
Newark, Oh., U.S.	98	40.05N	82.25W
Newaygo, Mi., U.S. (nū'wā-go)	98	43.25N	85.50W
New Bedford, Ma., U.S. (běd'fērd)	97	41.35N	70.55W
Newberg, Or., U.S. (nū'bûrg)	98	45.17N	122.58W
New Bern, N.C., U.S. (bûrn)	97	35.05N	77.05W
Newbern, Tn., U.S.	114	36.05N	89.12W
Newberry, Mi., U.S. (nū'běr-ĭ)	103	46.22N	85.31W
Newberry, S.C., U.S.	115	34.15N	81.40W
New Boston, Mi., U.S. (bôs'tŭn)	101b	42.10N	83.24W
New Boston, Oh., U.S.	98	38.45N	82.55W
New Braunfels, Tx., U.S. (nū broun'fěls)	112	29.43N	98.07W
New Brighton, Eng., U.K.	237a	53.26N	3.03W
New Brighton, Mn., U.S. (brī'tŭn)	107g	45.04N	93.12W
New Brighton, Pa., U.S.	101e	40.34N	80.18W
New Brighton, neigh., N.Y., U.S.	228	40.38N	74.06W
New Britain, Ct., U.S. (brĭt''n)	99	41.40N	72.45W
New Britain, i., Pap. N. Gui.	197	6.45S	149.38E
New Brunswick, N.J., U.S. (brŭnz'wĭk)	100a	40.29N	74.27W
New Brunswick, prov., Can.	85	47.14N	66.30W
Newburg, In., U.S.	98	38.00N	87.25W
Newburg, Mo., U.S.	111	37.54N	91.53W
Newburgh, N.Y., U.S.	99	41.30N	74.00W
Newburgh Heights, Oh., U.S.	101d	41.27N	81.40W
Newbury, Eng., U.K. (nū'běr-ĭ)	150	51.24N	1.26W
Newbury, Ma., U.S.	93a	42.48N	70.52W
Newburyport, Ma., U.S. (nū'běr-ĭ-pōrt)	93a	42.48N	70.53W
New Caledonia, dep., Oc.	203	21.28S	164.40E
New Canaan, Ct., U.S. (kā-năn)	100a	41.06N	73.30W
New Carlisle, Can. (kär-līl')	85	48.01N	65.20W
New Carrollton, Md., U.S.	229d	35.58N	76.53W
Newcastle, Austl. (nū-kȧs''l)	204	33.00S	151.55E
Newcastle, Can.	85	47.00N	65.34W
New Castle, De., U.S.	99	39.40N	75.35W
New Castle, In., U.S.	98	39.55N	85.25W
New Castle, Oh., U.S.	98	40.20N	82.10W
New Castle, Pa., U.S.	98	41.00N	80.25W
Newcastle, Tx., U.S.	110	33.13N	98.44W
Newcastle, Wy., U.S.	102	43.51N	104.11W
Newcastle under Lyme, Eng., U.K. (nů-kȧs''l) (nů-käs''l)	144a	53.01N	2.14W
Newcastle upon Tyne, Eng., U.K.	142	55.00N	1.45W
Newcastle Waters, Austl. (wô'těrz)	202	17.10S	133.25E
Newclare, neigh., S. Afr.	244b	26.11S	27.58E
Newcomerstown, Oh., U.S. (nū'kŭm-ěrz-toun)	98	40.15N	81.40W
New Croton Reservoir, res., N.Y., U.S. (krŏ'tôn)	100a	41.15N	73.47W
New Delhi, India (děl'hī)	183	28.43N	77.18E
Newell, S.D., U.S. (nū'ěl)	102	44.43N	103.26W
New Eltham, neigh., Eng., U.K.	235	51.26N	0.04E
New England Range, mts., Austl. (nů ĭŋ'glănd)	203	29.32S	152.30E
Newenham, Cape, c., Ak., U.S. (nū-ěn-hăm)	95	58.40N	162.32W
Newfane, N.Y., U.S. (nū-fān)	101c	43.17N	78.44W
New Ferry, Eng., U.K.	237a	53.22N	2.59W
Newfoundland, prov., Can.	85a	48.15N	56.53W
Newgate, Can. (nū'gāt)	87	49.01N	115.10W
Newgate Street, Eng., U.K.	235	51.44N	0.07W
New Georgia, i., Sol.Is. (jôr'jĭ-ȧ)	203	8.08S	158.00E
New Georgia Group, is., Sol.Is.	198e	8.30S	157.20E
New Georgia Sound, strt., Sol.Is.	198e	8.00S	158.10E
New Glasgow, Can. (glȧs'gō)	85	45.35N	62.36W
New Guinea, i. (gĭne)	197	5.45S	140.00E
Newhalem, Wa., U.S. (nū hā'lŭm)	104	48.44N	121.11W
Newham, neigh., Eng., U.K.	235	51.32N	0.03E
New Hampshire, state, U.S. (hămp'shĭr)	97	43.55N	71.40W
New Hampton, Ia., U.S. (hămp'tŭn)	103	43.03N	92.20W
New Hanover, S. Afr. (hăn'ôvěr)	213c	29.23S	30.32E
New Hanover, i., Pap. N. Gui.	197	2.37S	150.15E
New Harmony, In., U.S. (nū här'mô-nĭ)	98	38.10N	87.55W
New Haven, Ct., U.S. (hā'věn)	97	41.20N	72.55W
New Haven, In., U.S. (nū hāv''n)	98	41.05N	85.00W
New Hebrides, is., Vanuatu	203	16.00S	167.00E
New Hey, Eng., U.K.	237b	53.36N	2.06W
New Holland, Eng., U.K. (hŏl'ănd)	144a	53.42N	0.21W
New Holland, N.C., U.S.	115	35.27N	76.14W
New Hope Mountain, mtn., Al., U.S. (hōp)	100h	33.23N	86.45W
New Hudson, Mi., U.S. (hŭd'sŭn)	101b	42.30N	83.36W
New Hyde Park, N.Y., U.S.	228	40.44N	73.41W
New Hythe, Eng., U.K.	235	51.19N	0.27E
New Iberia, La., U.S. (ī-bē'rĭ-ȧ)	113	30.00N	91.50W
Newington, Can. (nū'ĕng-tŏn)	83c	45.07N	75.00W
New Ireland, i., Pap. N. Gui. (ĭr'lănd)	197	3.15S	152.30E
New Jersey, state, U.S. (jûr'zĭ)	97	40.30N	74.50W
New Kensington, Pa., U.S. (kěn'zĭng-tŭn)	101e	40.34N	79.35W
Newkirk, Ok., U.S. (nū'kûrk)	111	36.52N	97.03W
New Kowloon (Xinjiulong), H.K.	241c	22.20N	114.10E
New Lagos, neigh., Nig.	244d	6.30N	3.22E
New Lenox, Il., U.S. (lěn'ŭk)	101a	41.31N	87.58W
New Lexington, Oh., U.S. (lěk'sĭng-tŭn)	98	39.40N	82.10W
New Lisbon, Wi., U.S. (lĭz'bŭn)	103	43.52N	90.11W
New Liskeard, Can.	91	47.30N	79.40W
New London, Ct., U.S. (lŭn'dŭn)	99	41.20N	72.05W
New London, Wi., U.S.	103	44.24N	88.45W
New Madrid, Mo., U.S. (măd'rĭd)	111	36.34N	89.31W
Newman's Grove, Ne., U.S. (nū'măn grōv)	102	41.46N	97.44W
Newmarket, Can. (nū'mär-kět)	91	44.00N	79.30W
Newmarket, S. Afr.	244b	26.17S	28.08E
New Martinsville, W.V., U.S. (mär'tĭnz-vĭl)	98	39.35N	80.50W
New Meadows, Id., U.S.	104	44.58N	116.20W
New Mexico, state, U.S. (měk'sĭ-kō)	96	34.30N	107.10W
New Milford, N.J., U.S.	228	40.56N	74.01W
New Mills, Eng., U.K. (mĭlz)	144a	53.22N	2.00W
New Munster, Wi., U.S. (mŭn'stēr)	101a	42.35N	88.13W
Newnan, Ga., U.S. (nū'năn)	114	33.22N	84.47W
New Norfolk, Austl. (nôr'fŏk)	203	42.50S	147.17E
New Orleans, La., U.S. (ôr'lê-ănz)	97	30.00N	90.05W
New Philadelphia, Oh., U.S. (fĭl-ȧ-děl'fĭ-ȧ)	98	40.30N	81.30W
New Plymouth, N.Z. (plĭm'ŭth)	203a	39.04S	174.13E
Newport, Austl.	201b	33.39S	151.19E
Newport, Austl.	243b	37.51S	144.53E
Newport, Eng., U.K.	144a	52.46N	2.22W
Newport, Eng., U.K. (nū-pôrt)	150	50.41N	1.25W
Newport, Wales, U.K.	147	51.36N	3.05W
Newport, Ar., U.S. (nū'pōrt)	111	35.35N	91.16W
Newport, Ky., U.S.	97	39.05N	84.30W
Newport, Me., U.S.	92	44.49N	69.20W
Newport, Mn., U.S.	107g	44.52N	92.59W
Newport, N.H., U.S.	99	43.20N	72.10W
Newport, Or., U.S.	104	44.39N	124.02W
Newport, R.I., U.S.	99	41.29N	71.16W
Newport, Tn., U.S.	114	35.55N	83.12W
Newport, Vt., U.S.	99	44.55N	72.15W
Newport, Wa., U.S.	104	48.12N	117.01W
Newport Beach, Ca., U.S. (bēch)	107a	33.36N	117.55W
Newport News, Va., U.S.	97	36.59N	76.24W
New Prague, Mn., U.S. (nū prāg)	103	44.33N	93.35W
New Providence, i., Bah. (prŏv'ĭ-děns)	122	25.00N	77.25W
New Redruth, S. Afr.	244b	26.16S	28.07E
New Richmond, Oh., U.S. (rĭch'mŭnd)	98	38.55N	84.15W
New Richmond, Wi., U.S.	103	45.07N	92.34W
New Roads, La., U.S. (rōds)	113	30.42N	91.26W
New Rochelle, N.Y., U.S. (rū-shěl')	100a	40.55N	73.47W
New Rockford, N.D., U.S. (rŏk'fōrd)	102	47.40N	99.08W
New Ross, Ire. (rôs)	150	52.25N	6.55W
New Sarepta, Can.	83g	53.17N	113.09W
New Siberian Islands see Novosibirskiye Ostrova, is., Russia	165	74.00N	140.30E
New Smyrna Beach, Fl., U.S. (smûr'nȧ)	115	29.00N	80.57W
New South Wales, state, Austl. (wālz)	203	32.45S	146.14E
Newton, Can. (nū'tŭn)	83f	49.56N	98.04W
Newton, Eng., U.K.	144a	53.27N	2.37W
Newton, Il., U.S.	98	39.00N	88.10W
Newton, Ia., U.S.	103	41.42N	93.04W
Newton, Ks., U.S.	111	38.03N	97.22W
Newton, Ma., U.S.	93a	42.21N	71.13W
Newton, Ms., U.S.	114	32.18N	89.10W
Newton, N.J., U.S.	100a	41.03N	74.45W
Newton, N.C., U.S.	115	35.40N	81.19W
Newton, Tx., U.S.	113	30.47N	93.45W
Newton Brook, neigh., Can.	227c	43.48N	79.24W
Newton Highlands, Ma., U.S.	227a	41.19N	71.13W
Newton Lower Falls, Ma., U.S.	227a	42.19N	71.23W
Newtonsville, Oh., U.S. (nū'tŭnz-vĭl)	101f	39.11N	84.04W
Newton Upper Falls, Ma., U.S.	227a	42.19N	71.13W
Newtonville, Ma., U.S.	227a	42.21N	71.13W
Newtown, N.D., U.S. (nū'toun)	102	47.57N	102.25W
Newtown, Oh., U.S.	101f	39.08N	84.22W
Newtown, Pa., U.S.	100f	40.13N	74.56W
Newtown, neigh., Austl.	243a	33.54S	151.11E
Newtownards, N. Ire., U.K. (nu-t'n-ardz')	150	54.35N	5.39W
New Ulm, Mn., U.S. (ŭlm)	103	44.18N	94.27W
New Utrecht, neigh., N.Y., U.S.	228	40.36N	73.59W
New Waterford, Can. (wô'těr-fērd)	85	46.15N	60.05W
New Westminster, Can. (wěst'mĭn-stēr)	87	49.12N	122.55W
New York, N.Y., U.S. (yôrk)	97	40.40N	73.58W
New York, state, U.S.	97	42.45N	78.05W
New Zealand, nation, Oc. (zē'lȧnd)	203a	42.00S	175.00E
Nexapa, r., Mex. (něks-ä'pä)	118	18.32N	98.29W
Neya-gawa, Japan (nā'yä gä'wä)	195b	34.47N	135.38E
Neyshābūr, Iran	182	36.06N	58.45E
Neyva, r., Russia (něy'vȧ)	172a	57.39N	60.37E
Nezahualcóyotl, Mex.	119a	19.27N	99.03W
Nez Perce, Id., U.S. (něz' pûrs')	104	46.16N	116.15W
Nez Perce Indian Reservation, I.R., Id., U.S.	104	46.20N	116.30W
Ngami, l., Bots. (n'gä'mē)	212	20.56S	22.31E
Ngamouéri, Congo	244c	4.14S	15.14E
Ngangerabeli Plain, pl., Kenya	217	1.20S	40.10E
Ngangla Ringco, l., China (ŋäŋ-lä rĭŋ-tswo)	186	31.42N	82.53E
Ngarimbi, Tan.	217	8.28S	38.36E
Ngoko, r., Afr.	216	1.55N	15.53E
Ngol-Kedju Hill, mtn., Cam.	215	6.20N	9.45E
Ngombe, Zaire	244c	4.24S	15.11E
Ngong, Kenya ('n-gông)	212	1.27S	36.39E
Ngounié, r., Gabon	216	1.15S	10.43E
Ngoywa, Tan.	217	5.56S	32.48E
Ngqeleni, S. Afr. ('ng-kě-lā'nē)	213c	31.41S	29.04E
Nguigmi, Niger ('n-gēg'mē)	211	14.15N	13.07E
Ngurore, Nig.	215	9.18N	12.14E
Nguru, Nig. ('n-gōō'rōō)	210	12.53N	10.26E
Nguru Mountains, mts., Tan.	217	6.10S	37.35E
Nha Trang, Viet. (nyä-träng')	196	12.08N	108.56E
Niafounke, Mali	210	16.03N	4.17W
Niagara, Wi., U.S. (nī-ăg'ȧ-rȧ)	103	45.45N	88.05W
Niagara, r., N.A.	101c	43.12N	79.03W
Niagara Falls, Can.	101c	43.05N	79.05W
Niagara Falls, N.Y., U.S.	97	43.06N	79.02W
Niagara-on-the-Lake, Can.	83d	43.16N	79.05W
Niakaramandougou, C. Iv.	214	8.40N	5.17W
Niamey, Niger (nē-ä-mā')	210	13.31N	2.07E
Niamtougou, Togo	214	9.46N	1.06E
Niangara, Zaire (nē-äŋ-gá'rȧ)	211	3.42N	27.52E

PRONOUNCING INDEX Niangua-North Borneo 325

PLACE (Pronunciation)	PAGE	Lat. °′	Long. °′
Niangua, r., Mo., U.S. (nī-ăŋ'gwȧ)	111	37.30N	93.05W
Nias, Pulau, i., Indon. (nē'äs')	196	0.58N	97.43E
Nibe, Den. (nē'bĕ)	152	56.57N	9.36E
Nicaragua, nation, N.A. (nĭk-ȧ-rä'gwȧ)	116	12.45N	86.15W
Nicaragua, Lago de, l., Nic. (lä'gō dĕ)	116	11.45N	85.28W
Nicastro, Italy (nē-käs'trō)	149	38.39N	16.15E
Nicchehabin, Punta, c., Mex. (pōō'n-tä-nĕk-chĕ-ä-bē'n)	120a	19.50N	87.20W
Nice, Fr. (nēs)	142	43.42N	7.21E
Nicheng, China (nē-chŭŋ)	191b	30.54N	121.48E
Nichicun, l., Can. (nĭch'ĭ-kŭn)	85	53.07N	72.10W
Nicholas Channel, strt., N.A. (nĭk'ō-lȧs)	122	23.30N	80.20W
Nicholasville, Ky., U.S. (nĭk'ō-lȧs-vĭl)	98	37.55N	84.35W
Nicobar Islands, is., India (nĭk-ō-bär')	196	8.28N	94.04E
Nicolai Mountain, mtn., Or., U.S. (nē-cō lī')	106c	46.05N	123.27W
Nicolás Romero, Mex. (nē-kō-lä's rô-mĕ'rô)	119a	19.38N	99.20W
Nicolet, Lake, l., Mi., U.S. (nĭ'kŏ-lĕt)	107k	46.22N	84.14W
Nicolls Town, Bah.	122	25.10N	78.00W
Nicols, Mn., U.S. (nĭk'ĕls)	107g	44.50N	93.12W
Nicomeki, r., Can.	106d	49.04N	122.47W
Nicosia, Cyp. (nē-kô-sē'ä)	182	35.10N	33.22E
Nicoya, C.R. (nē-kō'yä)	120	10.08N	85.27W
Nicoya, Golfo de, b., C.R. (gôl-fô-dĕ)	120	10.03N	85.04W
Nicoya, Península de, pen., C.R.	120	10.05N	86.00W
Nidzica, Pol. (nē-jēt'sȧ)	155	53.21N	20.30E
Niederaden, neigh., Ger.	236	51.36N	7.34E
Niederbonsfeld, Ger.	236	51.23N	7.08E
Niederdonk, Ger.	236	51.14N	6.41E
Niederelfringhausen, Ger.	236	51.21N	7.10E
Niedere Tauern, mts., Aus.	154	47.15N	13.41E
Niederkrüchten, Ger. (nē'dĕr-krük-tĕn)	157c	51.12N	6.14E
Nieder-Neuendorf, Ger.	238a	52.37N	13.12E
Niederösterreich, prov., Aus.	145e	48.24N	16.20E
Niedersachsen (Lower Saxony), hist. reg., Ger. (nē'dĕr-zäκ-sĕn)	154	52.52N	8.27E
Niederschöneweide, neigh., Ger.	238a	52.27N	13.31E
Niederschönhausen, neigh., Ger.	238a	52.35N	13.23E
Niellim, Chad	215	9.42N	17.49E
Niemeyer, neigh., Braz.	234c	23.00S	43.15W
Nienburg, Ger. (nē'ĕn-bòrgh)	154	52.40N	9.15E
Nierst, Ger.	236	51.19N	6.43E
Nietverdiend, S. Afr.	218d	25.02S	26.10E
Nieuw Nickerie, Sur. (nē-nē'kĕ-rē')	131	5.51N	57.00W
Nieves, Mex. (nyā'vås)	118	24.00N	102.57W
Niğde, Tur. (nĭg'dĕ)	149	37.55N	34.40E
Nigel, S. Afr. (nī'jĕl)	218d	26.26S	28.27E
Niger, nation, Afr. (nī'jẽr)	210	18.02N	8.30E
Niger, r., Afr.	210	8.00N	6.00E
Niger Delta, d., Nig.	215	4.45N	5.20E
Nigeria, nation, Afr. (nī-jē'rĭ-ȧ)	210	8.57N	6.30E
Nihoa, i., Hi., U.S.	94b	23.15N	161.30W
Nihonbashi, neigh., Japan	242a	35.41N	139.47E
Nii, i., Japan (nē)	195	34.26N	139.23E
Niigata, Japan (nē'ē-gä'tȧ)	189	37.47N	139.04E
Niihau, i., Hi., U.S. (nē'ē-ha'ōō)	96c	21.50N	160.05W
Niimi, Japan (nē'mē)	195	34.59N	133.28E
Niiza, Japan	195a	35.48N	139.34E
Nijmegen, Neth. (nī'mȧ-gĕn)	151	51.50N	5.52E
Níkaia, Grc.	239d	37.58N	23.39E
Nikitinka, Russia (nĕ-kĭ'tĭn-kȧ)	162	55.33N	33.19E
Nikolayevka, Russia (nē-kô-lä'yĕf-kȧ)	172c	59.29N	29.48E
Nikolayevka, Russia	194	48.37N	134.09E
Nikolayevskiy, Russia	167	50.00N	45.30E
Nikolayevsk-na-Amure, Russia	165	53.18N	140.49E
Nikolo-Chovanskoje, Russia	239b	55.36N	37.27E
Nikol'sk, Russia (nē-kôlsk')	164	59.30N	45.40E
Nikol'skoye, Russia (nē-kôl'skô-yĕ)	172c	59.27N	30.00E
Nikopol, Bul. (nē'kô-pōl')	149	43.41N	24.52E
Nikopol', Ukr.	167	47.36N	34.24E
Nilahue, r., Chile (nē-lȧ'wĕ)	129b	34.36S	71.50W
Nile, r., Afr. (nīl)	211	27.30N	31.00E
Niles, Il., U.S.	231a	42.01N	87.49W
Niles, Mi., U.S. (nīlz)	98	41.50N	86.15W
Niles, Oh., U.S.	98	41.15N	80.45W
Nileshwar, India	187	12.08N	74.14E
Nilgani, India	240a	22.46N	88.26E
Nilgiri Hills, hills, India	187	12.05N	76.22E
Nilópolis, Braz. (nē-lô'pō-lēs)	129a	22.48S	43.25W
Nīmach, India	186	24.32N	74.51E
Nimba, Mont, mtn., Afr. (nĭm'bȧ)	210	7.40N	8.33W
Nimba Mountains, mts., Afr.	214	7.30N	8.35W
Nîmes, Fr. (nēm)	142	43.49N	4.22E
Nimrod Reservoir, res., Ar., U.S. (nĭm'rŏd)	111	34.58N	93.46W
Nimule, Sudan (nē-mōō'lȧ)	211	3.38N	32.12E
Ninda, Ang.	216	14.47S	21.24E
Nine Ashes, Eng., U.K.	235	51.42N	0.18E
Nine Mile Creek, r., Ut., U.S. (mīn'ĭmōd')	109	39.50N	110.30W
Ninety Mile Beach, cst., Austl.	203	38.20S	147.30E
Nineveh, Iraq (nĭn'ē-vȧ)	182	36.30N	43.10E
Ning'an, China (nĭŋ-än)	189	44.20N	129.20E
Ningbo, China (nĭŋ-bwo)	189	29.56N	121.30E
Ningde, China (nĭŋ-dŭ)	189	26.38N	119.33E
Ninghai, China (nĭng'hī')	193	29.20N	121.20E
Ninghe, China (nĭŋ-hŭ)	190	39.20N	117.50E
Ningjin, China (nĭŋ-jyĭn)	190	37.39N	116.47E
Ningjin, China	190	37.37N	114.55E
Ningming, China	193	22.22N	107.06E
Ningwu, China (nĭng'wōō')	189	39.00N	112.12E
Ningxia Huizu, prov., China (nĭŋ-shyä)	188	37.10N	106.00E
Ningyang, China (nĭng'yäng')	190	35.46N	116.48E
Ninh Binh, Viet. (nĕn bēnk')	196	20.22N	106.00E
Ninigo Group, is., Pap. N. Gui.	197	1.15S	143.30E
Ninnescah, r., Ks., U.S. (nĭn'ĕs-kä)	110	37.37N	98.31W
Nioaque, Braz. (nēô-ä'-kĕ)	131	21.14S	55.41W
Niobrara, r., U.S. (nī-ō-brâr'ȧ)	96	42.46N	98.46W
Niokolo Koba, Parc National du, rec., Sen.	214	13.05N	13.00W
Nioro du Sahel, Mali (nē-ō'rō)	210	15.15N	9.35W
Nipawin, Can.	84	53.22N	104.00W
Nipe, Bahía de, b., Cuba (bä-ē'ä-dĕ-nē'pā)	123	20.50N	75.30W
Nipe, Sierra de, mts., Cuba (sē-ĕ'r-rȧ-dĕ)	123	20.20N	75.50W
Nipigon, Can. (nĭp'ĭ-gŏn)	85	48.58N	88.17W
Nipigon, l., Can.	85	49.37N	89.55W
Nipigon Bay, b., Can.	90	48.56N	88.00W
Nipisiguit, r., Can. (nĭ-pĭ'sĭ-kwĭt)	92	47.26N	66.15W
Nipissing, l., Can. (nĭp'ĭ-sĭng)	85	45.59N	80.19W
Niquero, Cuba (nē-kä'rō)	122	20.00N	77.35W
Nirmali, India	186	26.30N	86.43E
Niš, Yugo.	142	43.19N	21.54E
Nisa, Port. (nē'sȧ)	158	39.32N	7.41W
Nišava, r., Eur. (nē'shȧ-vȧ)	161	43.17N	22.17E
Nishi, Japan	242b	34.41N	135.30E
Nishinari, neigh., Japan	242b	34.38N	135.28E
Nishino, i., Japan (nēsh'ē-nô)	195	36.06N	132.49E
Nishinomiya, Japan (nēsh'ē-nô-mē'yȧ)	195b	34.44N	135.21E
Nishio, Japan (nēsh'ē-ô)	195	34.50N	137.01E
Nishiyodogawa, neigh., Japan	242b	34.42N	135.27E
Niska Lake, l., Can. (nĭs'kȧ)	88	55.35N	108.38W
Nisko, Pol. (nēs'kô)	155	50.30N	22.07E
Nisku, Can. (nĭs-kū')	83g	53.21N	113.33W
Nisqually, r., Wa., U.S. (nĭs-kwôl'ĭ)	104	46.51N	122.33W
Nissan, r., Swe.	152	57.06N	13.22E
Nisser, l., Nor. (nĭs'ĕr)	152	59.14N	8.35E
Nissum Fjord, fj., Den.	152	56.24N	7.35E
Niterói, Braz. (nē-tĕ-rô'ĭ)	131	22.53S	43.07W
Nith, r., Scot., U.K. (nĭth)	150	55.13N	3.55W
Nitra, Slvk. (nē'trȧ)	155	48.18N	18.04E
Nitra, r., Slvk.	155	48.13N	18.14E
Nitro, W.V., U.S. (nī'trō)	98	38.25N	81.50W
Niue, dep., Oc. (nĭ'ō)	225	19.50S	167.00W
Nivelles, Bel. (nē'vĕl')	151	50.33N	4.17E
Nixon, Tx., U.S. (nĭk'sŭn)	113	29.16N	97.48W
Nizāmābād, India	183	18.48N	78.07E
Nizhne-Angarsk, Russia (nyēzh'nyĭ-ŭngärsk')	165	55.49N	108.46E
Nizhne-Chirskaya, Russia	167	48.20N	42.50E
Nizhne-Kolymsk, Russia (kō-lĕmsk')	165	68.32N	160.56E
Nizhneudinsk, Russia (nēzh'nyĭ-ōōdēnsk')	165	54.58N	99.15E
Nizhniye Sergi, Russia (nyēzh' nyē sĕr'gē)	166	56.41N	59.19E
Nizhniy Novgorod (Gor'kiy), Russia	164	56.15N	44.05E
Nizhniy Tagil, Russia (tŭgĕl')	164	57.54N	59.59E
Nizhnyaya Kur'ya, Russia (nyē'zhnyȧ-yȧ koor'yȧ)	172a	58.01N	56.00E
Nizhnyaya Salda, Russia (nyē'zhnya'ya säl'da')	172a	58.05N	60.43E
Nizhnyaya Taymyra, r., Russia	170	72.30N	95.18E
Nizhnyaya Tunguska, r., Russia	165	64.13N	91.30E
Nizhnyaya Tura, Russia (tōō'rȧ)	172a	58.38N	59.50E
Nizhnyaya Us'va, Russia (ōō'vȧ)	172a	59.05N	58.53E
Nizhyn, Ukr.	167	51.03N	31.52E
Nízke Tatry, mts., Slvk.	155	48.57N	19.18E
Njazidja, i., Com.	213	11.44S	42.38E
Njombe, Tan.	217	9.20S	34.46E
Njurunda, Swe. (nyōō-rŏn'dȧ)	152	62.15N	17.24E
Nkala Mission, Zam.	217	15.55S	26.00E
Nkandla, S. Afr. ('n-känd'lȧ)	213c	28.40S	31.06E
Nkawkaw, Ghana	214	6.33N	0.47W
Nkhota, Mwi. (kō-tȧ kō-tȧ)	212	12.52S	34.16E
Noākhāli, Bngl.	183	22.52N	91.08E
Noatak, Ak., U.S. (nô-ȧ'tȧk)	95	67.22N	163.28W
Noatak, r., Ak., U.S.	95	67.58N	162.15W
Nobeoka, Japan (nō-bȧ-ō'kȧ)	194	32.36N	131.41E
Noblesville, In., U.S. (nō'bl'z-vĭl)	98	40.00N	86.00W
Nobleton, Can. (nō'bl'tŭn)	83d	43.54N	79.39W
Noborito, Japan	242a	35.37N	139.34E
Nocera Inferiore, Italy (ĕn-fĕ-ryō'rĕ)	159c	40.30N	14.38E
Nochistlán, Mex. (nô-chēs-tlän')	118	21.23N	102.52W
Nochixtlón, Mex. (ä-sôn-syōn')	119	17.28N	97.12W
Nogales, Mex.	116	31.15N	111.00W
Nogales, Mex. (nō-gä'lĕs)	119	18.49N	97.09W
Nogales, Az., U.S. (nô-gä'lĕs)	96	31.20N	110.55W
Nogal Valley, val., Som. (nô'gäl)	218a	8.30N	47.50E
Nogent-le-Roi, Fr. (nō-zhŏn-lĕ-rwä')	157b	48.39N	1.32E
Nogent-le-Rotrou, Fr. (rō-trōō')	156	48.22N	0.47E
Nogent-sur-Marne, Fr.	237c	48.50N	2.29E
Noginsk, Russia (nô-gēnsk')	166	55.52N	38.28E
Noguera Pallares, r., Spain	159	42.18N	1.03E
Noirmoutier, Île de, i., Fr. (nwȧr-mōō-tyā')	147	47.03N	3.08W
Noisy-le-Grand, Fr.	237c	48.51N	2.33E
Noisy-le-Roi, Fr.	237c	48.51N	2.04E
Noisy-le-Sec, Fr.	237c	48.53N	2.28E
Nojima-Zaki, c., Japan (nō'jē-mä zä-kē)	195	34.54N	139.48E
Nokomis, Il., U.S. (nô-kō'mĭs)	98	39.15N	89.10W
Nola, Italy (nô'lä)	160	40.41N	14.32E
Nolinsk, Russia (nô-lēnsk')	166	57.32N	49.50E
Noma Misaki, c., Japan (nô'mä mē'sä-kē)	195	31.25N	130.09E
Nombre de Dios, Mex. (nôm-brĕ-dĕ-dyō's)	118	23.50N	104.14W
Nombre de Dios, Pan. (nô'm-brĕ)	121	9.34N	79.28W
Nome, Ak., U.S. (nōm)	96a	64.30N	165.20W
Nonacho, l., Can.	84	61.48N	111.20W
Nonantum, Ma., U.S.	227a	42.20N	71.12W
Nong'an, China (nôŋ-än)	192	44.25N	125.10E
Nongoma, S. Afr. (nôn-gō'mȧ)	212	27.48S	31.45E
Nooksack, Wa., U.S. (nòk'săk)	106d	48.55N	122.19W
Nooksack, r., Wa., U.S.	106d	48.54N	122.31W
Noordwijk aan Zee, Neth.	145a	52.14N	4.25E
Noordzee Kanaal, can., Neth.	145a	52.27N	4.42E
Nootka, i., Can. (nōōt'kȧ)	84	49.32N	126.42W
Nootka Sound, strt., Can.	86	49.33N	126.38W
Nóqui, Ang. (nō-kē')	212	5.51S	13.25E
Nor, r., China (nou')	194	46.55N	132.45E
Nora, Swe.	152	59.32N	14.56E
Nora, In., U.S. (nō'rä)	101g	39.54N	86.08W
Noranda, Can.	91	48.15N	79.01W
Norbeck, Md., U.S. (nōr'bĕk)	100e	39.06N	77.05W
Norborne, Mo., U.S. (nōr'bôrn)	111	39.17N	93.39W
Norco, Ca., U.S. (nôr'kô)	107a	33.57N	117.33W
Norcross, Ga., U.S. (nôr'krôs)	100c	33.56N	84.13W
Nord, Riviere du, Can. (rēv-yĕr' dü nōr)	83a	45.45N	74.02W
Nordegg, Can. (nûr'dĕg)	87	52.28N	116.04W
Norden, Ger. (nôr'dĕn)	154	53.35N	7.14E
Norden, Eng., U.K.	237b	53.38N	2.13W
Norderney, i., Ger. (nōr'dĕr-nĕy)	154	53.45N	6.58E
Nordfjord, fj., Nor. (nō'fyōr)	152	61.50N	5.35E
Nordhausen, Ger. (nôrt'hau-zĕn)	147	51.30N	10.48E
Nordhorn, Ger. (nôrt'hôrn)	154	52.26N	7.05E
Nord Kapp, c., Nor.	166	71.11N	25.48E
Nordland, Wa., U.S. (nôrd'lȧnd)	106a	48.03N	122.41W
Nördlingen, Ger. (nûrt'lĭng-ĕn)	154	48.51N	10.30E
Nord-Ostsee Kanal (Kiel Canal), can., Ger. (nōrd-ōzt-zā) (kēl)	154	54.03N	9.23E
Nordrhein-Westfalen (North Rhine-Westphalia), hist. reg., Ger. (nōrd'hīn-vĕst-fä-lĕn)	154	50.50N	6.53E
Nordvik, Russia (nôrd'vĕk)	165	73.57N	111.15E
Nore, r., Ire. (nōr)	150	52.34N	7.15W
Norf, Ger.	236	51.09N	6.43E
Norfolk, Ma., U.S. (nôr'fŏk)	93a	42.07N	71.19W
Norfolk, Ne., U.S.	96	42.10N	97.25W
Norfolk, Va., U.S.	97	36.55N	76.15W
Norfolk, i., Oc.	225	27.10S	166.50E
Norfork, Lake, l., Ar., U.S.	111	36.25N	92.09W
Noril'sk, Russia (nô rēlsk')	164	69.00N	87.11E
Normal, Il., U.S. (nôr'mȧl)	98	40.35N	89.00W
Norman, r., Austl.	203	18.27S	141.29E
Norman, Lake, res., N.C., U.S.	97	35.30N	80.53W
Normandie, hist. reg., Fr. (nōr-män-dē')	156	49.02N	0.17E
Normandie, Collines de, hills, Fr. (kō-lēn'dĕ-nōr-män-dē')	156	48.46N	0.50W
Normandy see Normandie, hist. reg., Fr.	156	49.02N	0.17E
Normandy Heights, Md., U.S.	229c	39.17N	76.48W
Normanhurst, Austl.	243a	33.43S	151.06E
Normanton, Austl. (nôr'mȧn-tŭn)	203	17.45S	141.10E
Normanton, Eng., U.K.	144a	53.40N	1.21W
Norman Wells, Can.	84	65.26N	127.00W
Nornalup, Austl. (nôr-năl'ŭp)	202	35.00S	117.00E
Nørresundby, Den. (nû-rĕ-sòn'bü)	152	57.04N	9.55E
Norridge, Il., U.S.	231a	41.57N	87.49W
Norris, Tn., U.S. (nŏr'ĭs)	114	36.09N	84.05W
Norris Lake, res., Tn., U.S.	97	36.17N	84.10W
Norristown, Pa., U.S. (nŏr'ĭs-town)	100f	40.07N	75.21W
Norrköping, Swe. (nôr'chûp'ĭng)	142	58.37N	16.10E
Norrtälje, Swe. (nôr-tĕl'yĕ)	146	59.47N	18.39E
Norseman, Austl. (nôrs'mȧn)	202	32.15S	122.00E
Norte, Punta, c., Arg. (pōō'n-tä-nŏr'tĕ)	129c	36.17S	56.46W
Norte, Serra do, mts., Braz. (sĕ'r-rä-dô-nôr'te)	131	12.04S	59.08W
North, Cape, c., Can.	93	47.02N	60.25W
North Abington, Ma., U.S.	227a	42.08N	70.57W
North Adams, Ma., U.S. (ăd'ămz)	99	42.40N	73.05W
Northam, Austl. (nôr-dhȧm)	202	31.50S	116.45E
Northam, S. Afr. (nôr'thȧm)	218d	24.52S	27.16E
North America, cont.	82	45.00N	100.00W
North American Basin, deep (ȧ-mĕr'ĭ-kȧn)	4	23.45N	62.45W
Northampton, Austl. (nôr-thămp'tŭn)	202	28.22S	114.45E
Northampton, Eng., U.K. (nôrth-ămp'tŭn)	147	52.14N	0.56W
Northampton, Ma., U.S.	99	42.20N	72.45W
Northampton, Pa., U.S.	99	40.45N	75.30W
Northamptonshire, co., Eng., U.K.	144a	52.25N	0.47W
North Andaman Island, i., India (ăn-dȧ-măn')	196	13.15N	93.30E
North Andover, Ma., U.S. (ăn'dô-vẽr)	93a	42.42N	71.07W
North Arlington, N.J., U.S.	228	40.47N	74.08W
North Arm, mth., Can. (ärm)	106d	49.13N	123.01W
North Atlanta, Ga., U.S. (ăt-lăn'tȧ)	100c	33.52N	84.20W
North Attleboro, Ma., U.S. (ăt'l-bŭr-ô)	100b	41.59N	71.18W
North Auburn, Austl.	243a	33.50S	151.02E
North Baltimore, Oh., U.S. (bôl'tĭ-mōr)	98	41.10N	83.40W
North Balwyn, Austl.	243b	37.48S	145.05E
North Barnaby, Md., U.S.	229d	38.49N	76.57W
North Barrackpore, India	240a	22.46N	88.22E
North Basque, Tx., U.S. (băsk)	112	31.56N	98.01W
North Battleford, Can. (băt''l-fẽrd)	84	52.47N	108.17W
North Bay, Can.	85	46.13N	79.26W
North Beach, neigh., Ca., U.S.	231b	37.48N	122.25W
North Bellmore, N.Y., U.S.	228	40.41N	73.32W
North Bend, Or., U.S. (bĕnd)	104	43.23N	124.13W
North Bergen, N.J., U.S.	228	40.48N	74.01W
North Berwick, Me., U.S. (bûr'wĭk)	92	43.18N	70.46W
North Bight, bt., Bah. (bĭt)	122	24.30N	77.40W
North Bimini, i., Bah. (bĭ'mĭ-nē)	122	25.45N	79.20W
North Borneo see Sabah, hist. reg., Malay.	196	5.10N	116.25E

PLACE (Pronunciation)	PAGE	Lat. °′	Long. °′
Northborough, Ma., U.S.	93a	42.19N	71.39W
North Box Hill, Austl.	243b	37.48S	145.07E
North Braddock, Pa., U.S.	230b	40.24N	79.52W
Northbridge, Austl.	243a	33.49S	151.13E
Northbridge, Ma., U.S. (nôrth'brĭj)	93a	42.09N	71.39W
North Caicos, i., T./C. Is. (kī'kōs)	123	21.55N	72.00W
North Caldwell, N.J., U.S.	228	40.52N	74.16W
North Cape, c., N.Z.	203a	34.31S	173.02E
North Carolina, state, U.S. (kăr-ō-lī'nȧ)	97	35.40N	81.30W
North Cascades National Park, rec., Wa., U.S.	87	48.50N	120.50W
North Cat Cay, i., Bah.	122	25.35N	79.20W
North Channel, strt., Can.	90	46.10N	83.20W
North Channel, strt., U.K.	142	55.15N	7.56W
North Charleston, S.C., U.S. (chärlz'tŭn)	115	32.49N	79.57W
North Chicago, Il., U.S. (shĭ-kô'gō)	101a	42.19N	87.51W
Northcliff, neigh., S. Afr.	244b	26.09S	27.58E
North College Hill, Oh., U.S. (kŏl'ĕj hĭl)	101f	39.13N	84.33W
North Concho, Tx., U.S. (kŏn'chō)	112	31.40N	100.48W
North Cooking Lake, Can. (kŏk'ĭng lāk)	83g	53.28N	112.57W
Northcote, Austl.	243b	37.46S	145.00E
North Cyprus, nation, Asia	182	35.15N	33.40E
North Dakota, state, U.S. (dȧ-kō'tȧ)	96	47.20N	101.55W
North Downs, Eng., U.K. (dounz)	150	51.11N	0.01W
North Dum-Dum, India	186a	22.38N	88.23E
Northeast Cape, c., Ak., U.S. (nôrth-ēst)	95	63.15N	169.04W
Northeast Point, c., Bah.	123	22.45N	73.50W
Northeast Point, c., Bah.	123	21.25N	73.00W
Northeast Providence Channel, strt., Bah. (prŏv'ĭ-dĕns)	122	25.45N	77.00W
Northeim, Ger. (nôrt'hīm)	154	51.42N	9.59E
North Elbow Cays, is., Bah.	122	23.55N	80.30W
North Englewood, Md., U.S.	229d	38.55N	76.55W
Northern Cheyenne Indian Reservation, I.R., Mt., U.S.	105	45.32N	106.43W
Northern Dvina *see* Severnaya Dvina, r., Russia	164	63.00N	42.40E
Northern Ireland, , U.K. (īr'lănd)	142	54.48N	7.00W
Northern Land *see* Severnaya Zemlya, is., Russia	165	79.33N	101.15E
Northern Mariana Islands, dep., Oc. (mä-rē-ä'nȧ)	3	17.20N	145.00E
Northern Territory, , Austl.	202	18.15S	133.00E
Northern Yukon National Park, rec., Can.	95	69.00N	140.00W
North Essendon, Austl.	243b	37.45S	144.54E
Northfield, Il., U.S.	231a	42.06N	87.46W
Northfield, Mn., U.S. (nôrth'fēld)	103	44.28N	93.11W
North Fitzroy, Austl.	243b	37.47S	144.59E
Northfleet, Eng., U.K.	235	51.27N	0.21E
North Flinders Ranges, mts., Austl. (flĭn'dẽrz)	204	31.55S	138.45E
North Foreland, Eng., U.K. (nôrth-fōr'lănd)	151	51.20N	1.30E
North Franklin Mountain, mtn., Tx., U.S. (frăŋ'klĭn)	112	31.55N	106.30W
North Frisian Islands, is., Eur.	146	55.16N	8.15E
North Gamboa, Pan. (gäm-bô'ä)	121	9.07N	79.40W
North Germiston, S. Afr.	244b	26.14S	28.09E
North Gower, Can. (gŏw'ẽr)	83c	45.08N	75.43W
North Haledon, N.J., U.S.	228	40.58N	74.11W
North Hanover, Ma., U.S.	227a	42.09N	70.52W
North Hills, N.Y., U.S.	228	40.47N	73.41W
North Hollywood, Ca., U.S. (hŏl'ē-wŏd)	107a	34.10N	118.23W
North Island, i., N.Z.	203a	37.20S	173.30E
North Island, i., Ca., U.S.	108a	32.39N	117.14W
North Judson, In., U.S. (jŭd'sŭn)	98	41.15N	86.50W
North Kansas City, Mo., U.S. (kăn'zȧs)	107f	39.08N	94.34W
North Kingstown, R.I., U.S.	100b	41.34N	71.26W
Northlake, Il., U.S.	231a	41.55N	87.54W
North Little Rock, Ar., U.S. (lĭt''l rŏk)	111	34.46N	92.13W
North Loup, r., Ne., U.S. (lo͞op)	102	42.05N	100.10W
North Magnetic Pole, pt. of i.	220	77.19N	101.49W
North Manchester, In., U.S. (măn'chĕs-tẽr)	98	41.00N	85.45W
North Manly, Austl.	243a	33.46S	151.16E
Northmead, Austl.	243a	33.47S	151.00E
Northmead, S. Afr.	244b	26.10S	28.20E
North Merrick, N.Y., U.S.	228	40.41N	73.34W
Northmoor, Mo., U.S. (nôth'mo͞or)	107f	39.10N	94.37W
North Moose Lake, l., Can.	89	54.09N	100.20W
North Mount Lofty Ranges, mts., Austl.	204	33.50S	138.30E
North Ockendon, neigh., Eng., U.K.	235	51.32N	0.18E
North Ogden, Ut., U.S. (ŏg'dĕn)	107b	41.18N	111.58W
North Ogden Peak, mtn., Ut., U.S.	107b	41.23N	111.59W
North Olmsted, Oh., U.S. (ōlm-stĕd)	101d	41.25N	81.55W
North Ossetia, state, Russia	166	43.00N	44.15E
North Parramatta, Austl.	243a	33.48S	151.00E
North Pease, r., Tx., U.S. (pēz)	110	34.19N	100.58W
North Pender, i., Can. (pĕn'dẽr)	106d	48.48N	123.16W
North Philadelphia, neigh., Pa., U.S.	229b	39.58N	75.09W
North Plains, Or., U.S. (plānz)	106c	45.36N	123.00W
North Platte, Ne., U.S. (plăt)	96	41.08N	100.45W
North Platte, r., U.S.	96	41.20N	102.40W
North Point, H.K.	241c	22.17N	114.12E
North Point, c., Barb.	121b	13.22N	59.36W
North Point, c., Mi., U.S.	98	45.00N	83.20W
North Pole, pt. of i.	220	90.00N	0.00
Northport, Al., U.S. (nôrth'pōrt)	114	33.12N	87.35W
Northport, N.Y., U.S.	100a	40.53N	73.20W
Northport, Wa., U.S.	104	48.53N	117.47W
North Quincy, Ma., U.S.	227a	42.17N	71.01W
North Randolph, Ma., U.S.	227a	42.12N	71.04W
North Reading, Ma., U.S. (rĕd'ĭng)	93a	42.34N	71.04W
North Richland Hills, Tx., U.S.	107c	32.50N	97.13W

PLACE (Pronunciation)	PAGE	Lat. °′	Long. °′
North Richmond, Ca., U.S.	231b	37.57N	122.22W
Northridge, Ca., U.S. (nôrth'rĭdj)	107a	34.14N	118.32W
North Ridgeville, Oh., U.S. (rĭj-vĭl)	101d	41.23N	82.01W
North Riverside, Il., U.S.	231a	41.51N	87.49W
North Ronaldsay, i., Scot., U.K.	150a	59.21N	2.23W
North Royalton, Oh., U.S. (roi'ăl-tŭn)	101d	41.19N	81.44W
North Ryde, Austl.	243a	33.48S	151.07E
North Saint Paul, Mn., U.S. (sȧnt pôl')	103	45.01N	92.59W
North Santiam, r., Or., U.S. (săn'tyăm)	104	44.42N	122.50W
North Saskatchewan, r., Can. (săn-kăch'ē-wän)	84	54.00N	111.30W
North Sea, Eur.	142	56.09N	3.16E
North Side, neigh., Pa., U.S.	230b	40.28N	80.01W
North Skunk, r., Ia., U.S. (skŭnk)	103	41.39N	92.46W
North Springfield, Va., U.S.	229d	38.48N	77.13W
North Stradbroke Island, i., Austl. (străd'brōk)	203	27.45S	154.18E
North Sydney, Austl.	243a	33.50S	151.13E
North Sydney, Can. (sĭd'nē)	93	46.13N	60.15W
North Taranaki Bight, N.Z. (tȧ-rȧ-nä'kĭ bīt)	203a	38.40S	174.00E
North Tarrytown, N.Y., U.S. (tăr'ĭ-toun)	100a	41.05N	73.52W
North Thompson, r., Can.	87	50.50N	120.10W
North Tonawanda, N.Y., U.S. (tŏn-ȧ-wŏn'dȧ)	101c	43.02N	78.53W
North Truchas Peaks, mtn., N.M., U.S. (tro͞o'chäs)	96	35.58N	105.40W
North Twillingate, i., Can. (twĭl'ĭn-gāt)	92	35.58N	105.37W
North Uist, i., Scot., U.K. (ū'ĭst)	150	57.37N	7.22W
Northumberland, N.H., U.S.	99	44.30N	71.30W
Northumberland Islands, is., Austl.	203	21.42S	151.30E
Northumberland Strait, strt., Can. (nôr thŭm'bẽr-lănd)	92	46.25N	64.20W
North Umpqua, r., Or., U.S. (ŭmp'kwȧ)	104	43.20N	122.50W
North Valley Stream, N.Y., U.S.	228	40.41N	73.41W
North Vancouver, Can. (văn-ko͞o'vẽr)	84	49.19N	123.04W
North Vernon, In., U.S. (vûr'nŭn)	98	39.05N	85.45W
North Versailles, Pa., U.S.	230b	40.22N	79.48W
Northville, Mi., U.S. (nôrth-vĭl)	101b	42.26N	83.28W
North Wales, Pa., U.S. (wālz)	100f	40.12N	75.16W
North Weald Bassett, Eng., U.K.	235	51.43N	0.10E
North West Cape, c., Austl. (nôrth'wĕst)	202	21.50S	112.25E
Northwest Cape Fear, r., N.C., U.S. (cāp fēr)	115	34.34N	79.46W
Northwestern University, pt. of i., Il., U.S.	231a	42.04N	87.40W
North West Gander, r., Can. (găn'dẽr)	93	48.40N	55.15W
Northwest Harbor, b., Md., U.S.	229c	39.16N	76.35W
Northwest Providence Channel, strt., Bah. (prŏv'ĭ-dĕns)	122	26.15N	78.45W
Northwest Territories, , Can. (tĕr'ĭ-tō'rĭs)	84	64.42N	119.09W
North Weymouth, Ma., U.S.	227a	42.15N	70.57W
Northwich, Eng., U.K. (nôrth'wĭch)	144a	53.15N	2.31W
North Wilkesboro, N.C., U.S. (wĭlks'bûrō)	115	36.08N	81.10W
North Wilmington, Ma., U.S.	227a	42.34N	71.10W
Northwood, Ia., U.S. (nôrth'wŏd)	103	43.26N	93.13W
Northwood, N.D., U.S.	102	47.44N	97.36W
Northwood, neigh., Eng., U.K.	235	51.37N	0.25W
North Yamhill, r., Or., U.S. (yăm' hĭl)	106c	45.22N	123.21W
North York, Can.	91	43.47N	79.25W
North York Moors, for., Eng., U.K. (yôrk mŏrz')	150	54.20N	0.40W
North Yorkshire, co., Eng., U.K.	144a	53.50N	1.10W
Norton, Ks., U.S. (nôr'tŭn)	110	39.40N	99.54W
Norton, Ma., U.S.	100b	41.58N	71.08W
Norton, Va., U.S.	115	36.54N	82.36W
Norton Bay, b., Ak., U.S.	95	64.22N	162.18W
Norton Heath, Eng., U.K.	235	51.43N	0.19E
Norton Reservoir, res., Ma., U.S.	100b	42.01N	71.07W
Norton Sound, strt., Ak., U.S.	95	63.48N	164.50W
Norval, Can. (nôr'vȧl)	83d	43.39N	79.52W
Norwalk, Ca., U.S. (nôr'wôk)	107a	33.54N	118.05W
Norwalk, Ct., U.S.	100a	41.06N	73.25W
Norwalk, Oh., U.S.	98	41.15N	82.35W
Norway, Me., U.S.	92	44.11N	70.35W
Norway, Mi., U.S.	103	45.47N	87.55W
Norway, nation, Eur. (nôr'wā)	142	63.48N	11.17E
Norway House, Can.	84	53.59N	97.50W
Norwegian Sea, sea, Eur. (nôr-wē'jăn)	146	66.54N	1.43E
Norwell, Ma., U.S. (nôr'wĕl)	93a	42.10N	70.47W
Norwich, Eng., U.K.	147	52.40N	1.15E
Norwich, Ct., U.S. (nôr'wĭch)	99	41.20N	72.00W
Norwich, N.Y., U.S.	99	42.35N	75.30W
Norwood, Ma., U.S. (nôr'wo͝od)	93a	42.11N	71.13W
Norwood, N.C., U.S.	115	35.15N	80.08W
Norwood, Oh., U.S.	101f	39.10N	84.27W
Norwood, Pa., U.S.	229b	39.53N	75.18W
Norwood Park, neigh., Il., U.S.	231a	41.59N	87.48W
Nose, neigh., Japan	242b	34.49N	135.09E
Nose Creek, r., Can. (nōz)	83e	51.09N	114.02W
Noshiro, Japan (nō'shē-rō)	194	40.09N	140.02E
Nosivka, Ukr. (nô'sôf-kȧ)	163	50.54N	31.35E
Nossob, r., Afr. (nŏ'sŏb)	212	24.15S	19.10E
Noteć, r., Pol. (nô'tĕcn)	154	52.50N	16.19E
Notodden, Nor. (nōt'ôd'n)	152	59.35N	9.15E
Notre-Dame, rel., Fr.	237c	48.51N	2.21E
Notre Dame, Monts, mts., Can.	92	46.35N	70.35W
Notre Dame Bay, b., Can. (nō't'r dȧm')	85a	49.45N	55.15W
Notre-Dame-des-Victoires, neigh., Can.	227b	45.35N	73.34W
Notre-Dame-du-Lac, Can.	92	47.37N	68.51W
Nottawasaga Bay, b., Can. (nŏt'ȧ-wȧ-sä'gȧ)	91	44.45N	80.35W
Nottaway, r., Can. (nôt'ȧ-wā)	85	50.58N	78.02W
Nottingham, Eng., U.K. (nŏt'ĭng-ăm)	147	52.58N	1.09W

PLACE (Pronunciation)	PAGE	Lat. °′	Long. °′
Nottingham, Pa., U.S.	229b	40.07N	74.58W
Nottingham Island, i., Can.	85	62.58N	78.53W
Nottingham Park, Il., U.S.	231a	41.46N	87.48W
Nottinghamshire, co., Eng., U.K.	144a	53.03N	1.05W
Notting Hill, Austl.	243b	37.54S	145.08E
Nottoway, r., Va., U.S. (nôt'ȧ-wā)	115	36.53N	77.47W
Notukeu Creek, r., Can.	88	49.55N	106.30W
Nouadhibou, Maur.	210	21.02N	17.09W
Nouakchott, Maur.	210	18.06N	15.57W
Nouamrhar, Maur.	210	19.22N	16.31W
Nouméa, N. Cal. (no͞o-mā'ä)	203	22.16S	166.27E
Nouvelle, Can. (no͞o-vĕl')	92	48.09N	66.22W
Nouvelle-France, Cap de, c., Can.	85	62.03N	74.00W
Nouzonville, Fr. (no͞o-zôɴ-vēl')	156	49.51N	4.43E
Nova Cachoeirinha, neigh., Braz.	234d	23.28S	46.40W
Nova Cruz, Braz. (nō'vȧ-kro͞o'z)	131	6.22S	35.20W
Nova Friburgo, Braz. (frē-bo͞or'gŏ)	131	22.18S	42.31W
Nova Iguaçu, Braz. (nō'vä-ē-gwä-so͞o')	131	22.45S	43.27W
Nova Lima, Braz. (lē'mä)	129a	19.59S	43.51W
Nova Lisboa *see* Huambo, Ang.	212	12.44S	15.47E
Nova Mambone, Moz. (nō'vȧ-mȧm-bŏ'nĕ)	212	21.04S	35.13E
Nova Odesa, Ukr.	163	47.18N	31.48E
Nova Praha, Ukr.	163	48.34N	32.54E
Novara, Italy (nō-vä'rä)	148	45.24N	8.38E
Nova Resende, Braz.	129a	21.12S	46.25W
Nova Scotia, prov., Can. (skō'shȧ)	85	44.28N	65.00W
Novate Milanese, Italy	238c	45.32N	9.08E
Nova Vodolaha, Ukr.	163	49.43N	35.51E
Novaya Ladoga, Russia (nô'vȧ-ya lȧ-dô-gȧ)	153	60.06N	32.16E
Novaya Lyalya, Russia (lyȧ'lyȧ)	172a	59.03N	60.36E
Novaya Sibir, i., Russia (sē-bēr')	165	75.00N	149.00E
Novaya Zemlya, i., Russia (zĕm-lyȧ')	164	72.00N	54.46E
Nova Zagora, Bul. (zä'gô-rȧ)	161	42.30N	26.01E
Novelda, Spain (nô-vĕl'dȧ)	159	38.22N	0.46W
Nové Mesto nad Váhom, Slvk. (nô'vĕ myĕs'tō)	155	48.44N	17.47E
Nové Zámky, Slvk. (zȧm'kĕ)	147	47.58N	18.10E
Novgorod, Russia (nôv'gô-rŏt)	166	58.32N	31.16E
Novgorod, prov., Russia	162	58.27N	31.55E
Novhorod-Sivers'kyy, Ukr.	167	52.01N	33.14E
Novi, Mi., U.S. (nō'vĭ)	101b	42.29N	83.28W
Novigrad, Cro. (nō'vĭ grȧd)	160	44.09N	15.34E
Novi Ligure, Italy (nô'vē)	160	44.43N	8.48E
Novinger, Mo., U.S. (nŏv'ĭn-jẽr)	111	40.14N	92.43W
Novi Pazar, Bul. (pä-zär')	161	43.22N	27.26E
Novi Pazar, Yugo. (pȧ-zär')	149	43.08N	20.30E
Novi Sad, Yugo. (säd')	142	45.15N	19.53E
Novoarchangel'skoje, Russia	239b	55.55N	37.33E
Novoasbest, Russia (nô-vô-ăs-bĕst')	172a	57.43N	60.14E
Novoaydar, Ukr. (nô'vô-ī-där')	163	48.57N	39.01E
Novocherkassk, Russia (nô'vô-chĕr-kȧsk')	167	47.25N	40.04E
Novochovrino, neigh., Russia	239b	55.52N	37.30E
Novogirejevo, neigh., Russia	239b	55.45N	37.49E
Novokuznetsk, Russia (nô'vô-kô'z-nyĕ'tsk) (stȧ'lênsk)	164	53.43N	86.59E
Novo-Ladozhskiy Kanal, can., Russia (nô-vô-lä'dôzh-skĭ kȧ-näl')	153	59.54N	31.19E
Novo Mesto, Slvn. (nôvô mâs'tô)	160	45.48N	15.13E
Novomoskovsk, Russia (nô'vô-môs-kôfsk')	164	54.06N	38.08E
Novomoskovs'k, Ukr.	167	48.37N	35.12E
Novomyrhorod, Ukr.	163	48.46N	31.44E
Novonikol'skiy, Russia (nô'vô-nyĭ-kôl'skĭ)	172a	52.28N	57.12E
Novorossiysk, Russia (nô'vô-rô-sēsk')	164	44.43N	37.48E
Novorzhev, Russia (nô'vô-rzhêv')	162	57.01N	29.17E
Novo-Selo, Bul. (nô'vô-sĕ'lô)	161	44.09N	22.46E
Novosibirsk, Russia (nô'vô-sē-bērsk')	164	55.09N	82.58E
Novosibirskiye Ostrova (New Siberian Islands), is., Russia	165	74.00N	140.30E
Novosil', Russia (nô'vô-sĭl)	162	52.58N	37.03E
Novosokol'niki, Russia (nô'vô-sô-kôl'nē-kē)	162	56.18N	30.07E
Novotatishchevskiy, Russia (nô'vô-tȧ-tyĭsh'chĕv-skĭ)	172a	53.22N	60.24E
Novoukrayinka, Ukr.	167	48.18N	31.33E
Novouzensk, Russia (nô-vô-ô-zĕnsk')	167	50.40N	48.08E
Novozybkov, Russia (nô'vô-zĕp'kôf)	167	52.31N	31.54E
Nový Jičín, Czech Rep. (nô'vē yē'chēn)	155	49.36N	18.02E
Novyy Buh, Ukr.	163	47.43N	32.33E
Novyy Oskol, Russia (ôs-kôl')	163	50.46N	37.53E
Novyy Port, Russia (nô'vē)	164	67.19N	72.28E
Nowa Sól, Pol. (nô'vȧ sŭl')	154	51.49N	15.41E
Nowata, Ok., U.S. (nô-wä'tȧ)	111	36.42N	95.38W
Nowood Creek, r., Wy., U.S.	105	44.02N	107.37W
Nowra, Austl. (nou'rȧ)	204	34.55S	150.45E
Nowy Dwór Mazowiecki, Pol. (nô'vĭ dvo͞or mä-zo-vyĕts'ke)	155	52.26N	20.46E
Nowy Sącz, Pol. (nô'vē sôɴch')	155	49.36N	20.42E
Nowy Targ, Pol. (tärk')	155	49.29N	20.02E
Noxon Reservoir, res., Mt., U.S.	104	47.50N	115.40W
Noxubee, r., Ms., U.S. (nŏks'ū-bē)	114	33.20N	88.55W
Noya, Spain (no'yä)	158	42.46N	8.50W
Noyes Island, i., Ak., U.S. (noiz)	86	55.30N	133.40W
Nozaki, Japan (nō'zä-kē)	195b	34.43N	135.39E
Nozuta, Japan	242a	35.35N	139.27E
Nqamakwe, S. Afr. ('n-gä-mä'kwȧ)	213c	32.13S	27.57E
Nqutu, S. Afr. ('n-ko͞o'to͞o)	213c	28.17S	30.41E
Nsawam, Ghana	214	5.50N	0.20W
Ntshoni, mtn., S. Afr.	213c	29.34S	30.03E
Ntwetwe Pan, pl., Bots.	212	20.00S	24.18E
Nubah, Jibāl an, mts., Sudan	211	12.22N	30.39E

ăt; finăl; rāte; senȧte; ärm; ȧsk; sofȧ; fâre; ch-choose; dh-as th in other; bē; ēvent; bĕt; recĕnt; cratẽr; g-gō; gh-guttural g; bĭt; ĭ-short neutral; rīde; ĸ-guttural k as ch in German ich;

PRONOUNCING INDEX
Nubian Desert–Ogoyo 327

PLACE (Pronunciation)	PAGE	Lat. °'	Long. °'
Nubian Desert, des., Sudan (no͞o'bĭ-ǎn)	211	21.13N	33.09E
Nudo Coropuna, mtn., Peru (no͞o'dô kō-rō-po͞o'nä)	130	15.53S	72.04W
Nudo de Pasco, mtn., Peru (dĕ pás'kô)	130	10.34S	76.12W
Nueces, r., Tx., U.S. (nů-ā'sås)	96	28.20N	98.08W
Nueltin, l., Can. (nwĕl'tin)	84	60.14N	101.00W
Nueva Armenia, Hond. (nwä'vä är-mā'nē-à)	120	15.47N	86.32W
Nueva Atzacoalco, Mex.	233a	19.29N	99.05W
Nueva Chicago, neigh., Arg.	233d	34.40S	58.30W
Nueva Coronela, Cuba	233b	23.04N	82.28W
Nueva Esparta, dept., Ven. (nwĕ'vä ĕs-pä'r-tä)	131b	10.50N	64.35W
Nueva Gerona, Cuba (ĸĕ-rō'nä)	122	21.55N	82.45W
Nueva Palmira, Ur. (päl-mē'rä)	129c	33.53S	58.23W
Nueva Rosita, Mex. (nòĕ'vä rô-sē'tä)	96	27.55N	101.10W
Nueva San Salvador, El Sal.	120	13.41N	89.16W
Nueve, Canal Numero, can., Arg.	129c	36.22S	58.19W
Nueve de Julio, Arg. (nwā'vå dā ho͞o'lyô)	132	35.26S	60.51W
Nuevitas, Cuba (nwā-vē'täs)	117	21.35N	77.15W
Nuevitas, Bahía de, b., Cuba (bä-ē'ä dē nwā-vē'täs)	122	21.30N	77.05W
Nuevo, Ca., U.S. (nwā'vō)	107a	33.48N	117.09W
Nuevo Laredo, Mex. (lä-rā'dhō)	116	27.29N	99.30W
Nuevo Leon, state, Mex. (lå-ōn')	116	26.00N	100.00W
Nuevo San Juan, Pan. (nwĕ'vô sän ĸo͞o-ä'n)	116a	9.14N	79.43W
Nugumanovo, Russia (nû-gû-mä'nô-vô)	172a	55.28N	61.50E
Nulato, Ak., U.S. (no͞o-lä'tō)	95	64.40N	158.18W
Nullagine, Austl. (nŭ-lă'jēn)	202	22.00S	120.07E
Nullarbor Plain, pl., Austl. (nŭ-lär'bôr)	202	31.45S	126.30E
Numabin Bay, b., Can. (no͞o-mä'bĭn)	88	56.30N	103.08W
Numansdorp, Neth.	145a	51.43N	4.25E
Numazu, Japan (no͞o'mä-zo͞o)	194	35.06N	138.55E
Numfoor, Pulau, i., Indon.	197	1.20S	134.48E
Nun, r., Nig.	215	5.05N	6.10E
Nunawading, Austl.	201a	37.49S	145.10E
Nuneaton, Eng., U.K. (nŭn'ē-tǔn)	150	52.31N	1.28W
Nunivak, i., Ak., U.S. (no͞o'nĭ-văk)	96a	60.25N	167.42W
Ñuñoa, Chile	234b	33.28S	70.36W
Nunyama, Russia (nûn-yä'må)	95	65.49N	170.32W
Nuoro, Italy (nwô'rō)	160	40.29N	9.20E
Nūra, r., Kaz.	169	49.48N	73.54E
Nurata, Uzb. (no͞or'ät'á)	169	40.33N	65.28E
Nuremberg *see* Nürnberg, Ger.	142	49.28N	11.07E
Nürnberg, Ger. (nürn'bĕrgh)	142	49.28N	11.07E
Nurse Cay, i., Bah.	123	22.30N	75.50W
Nusabyin, Tur. (no͞o'sĭ-bēn)	167	37.05N	41.10E
Nushagak, r., Ak., U.S. (nū-shă-găk')	95	59.28N	157.40W
Nushan Hu, l., China	190	32.50N	117.59E
Nushki, Pak. (nŭsh'kē)	183	29.30N	66.02E
Nussdorf, neigh., Aus.	239e	48.15N	16.22E
Nuthe, r., Ger. (no͞o'tē)	145b	52.15N	13.11E
Nutley, N.J., U.S. (nŭt'lē)	100a	40.49N	74.09W
Nutter Fort, W.V., U.S. (nŭt'ēr fôrt)	98	39.15N	80.15W
Nutwood, Il., U.S. (nŭt'wòd)	107e	39.05N	90.34W
Nuwaybi 'al Muzayyinah, Egypt	181a	28.59N	34.40E
Nuweland, S. Afr.	212a	33.58S	18.28E
Nyack, N.Y., U.S. (nī'ăk)	100a	41.05N	73.55W
Nyainqêntanglha Shan, mts., China (nyä-ĭn-chyŭn-täŋ-lä shän)	188	29.55N	88.08E
Nyakanazi, Tan.	217	3.00S	31.15E
Nyala, Sudan	211	12.00N	24.52E
Nyanga, r., Gabon	216	2.45S	10.30E
Nyanza, Rw.	217	2.21S	29.45E
Nyasa, Lake, l., Afr. (nyä'sä)	212	10.45S	34.30E
Nyazepetrovsk, Russia (nyä'zĕ-pĕ-trôvsk')	172a	56.04N	59.38E
Nyborg, Den. (nü'bôr'')	152	55.20N	10.45E
Nybro, Swe. (nü'brô)	152	56.44N	15.56E
Nyeri, Kenya	217	0.25S	36.57E
Nyika Plateau, plat., Mwi.	217	10.30S	35.50E
Nyíregyháza, Hung. (nyē'rĕd-y'hä'zä)	149	47.58N	21.45E
Nykøbing, Den. (nü'kû-bĭng)	146	56.46N	8.47E
Nykøbing, Den.	152	54.45N	11.54E
Nykøbing Sjaelland, Den.	152	55.55N	11.37E
Nyköping, Swe. (nü'chû-pĭng)	146	58.46N	16.58E
Nylstroom, S. Afr. (nĭl'strōm)	212	24.42S	28.25E
Nymagee, Austl. (nī-mà-gē')	203	32.17S	146.18E
Nymburk, Czech Rep. (nêm'bòrk)	147	50.12N	15.03E
Nynäshamn, Swe. (nü-nĕs-häm'n)	152	58.53N	17.55E
Nyngan, Austl. (nĭŋ'gǎn)	203	31.31S	147.25E
Nyong, r., Cam. (nyông)	210	4.00N	12.00E
Nyou, Burkina	214	12.46N	1.56W
Nýřany, Czech Rep. (nêr-zhä'nē)	154	49.43N	13.13E
Nysa, Pol. (nē'sà)	155	50.29N	17.20E
Nytva, Russia	166	58.00N	55.10E
Nyungwe, Mwi.	217	10.16S	34.07E
Nyunzu, Zaire	217	5.57S	28.01E
Nyuya, r., Russia (nyo͞o'yá)	171	60.30N	111.45E
Nyzhni Sirohozy, Ukr.	163	46.51N	34.25E
Nzega, Tan.	217	4.13S	33.11E
N'zeto, Ang.	212	7.14S	12.52E
Nzi, r., C. Iv.	214	7.00N	4.27W

PLACE (Pronunciation)	PAGE	Lat. °'	Long. °'
Nzwani, i., Com. (äɴ-zhwäɴ)	213	12.14S	44.47E

O

PLACE (Pronunciation)	PAGE	Lat. °'	Long. °'
Oahe, Lake, res., U.S.	96	45.20N	100.00W
Oahu, i., Hi., U.S. (ō-ä'ho͞o) (ō-ä'hū)	96c	21.38N	157.48W
Oak Bay, Can.	86	48.27N	123.18W
Oak Bluff, Can. (ōk blŭf)	83f	49.47N	97.21W
Oak Creek, Co., U.S. (ōk krēk')	105	40.20N	106.50W
Oakdale, Ca., U.S. (ōk'dāl)	108	37.45N	120.52W
Oakdale, Ky., U.S.	98	38.15N	85.50W
Oakdale, La., U.S.	113	30.49N	92.40W
Oakdale, Pa., U.S.	101e	40.24N	80.11W
Oakengates, Eng., U.K. (ōk'ĕn-gāts)	144a	52.41N	2.27W
Oakes, N.D., U.S. (ōks)	102	46.10N	98.50W
Oakfield, Me., U.S. (ōk'fēld)	92	46.08N	68.10W
Oakford, Pa., U.S. (ōk'fōrd)	100f	40.08N	74.58W
Oak Forest, Il., U.S.	231a	41.36N	87.45W
Oak Grove, Or., U.S. (grōv)	106c	45.25N	122.38W
Oakham, Eng., U.K. (ōk'ǎm)	144a	52.40N	0.38W
Oak Harbor, Oh., U.S. (ōk'här'bēr)	98	41.30N	83.05W
Oak Harbor, Wa., U.S.	106a	48.18N	122.39W
Oakland, Ca., U.S. (ōk'lănd)	96	37.48N	122.16W
Oakland, Md., U.S.	229d	38.52N	76.55W
Oakland, Ne., U.S.	102	41.50N	96.28W
Oakland, neigh., Pa., U.S.	230b	40.26N	79.58W
Oakland City, In., U.S.	98	38.20N	87.20W
Oakland Gardens, neigh., N.Y., U.S.	228	40.45N	73.45W
Oaklawn, Il., U.S. (ōk'lôn)	101a	41.43N	87.45W
Oakleigh, Austl. (ōk'lå)	201a	37.54S	145.05E
Oakleigh South, Austl.	243b	37.56S	145.05E
Oakley, Id., U.S. (ōk'lĭ)	104	42.15N	135.53W
Oakley, Ks., U.S.	110	39.08N	100.49W
Oakman, Al., U.S. (ōk'măn)	114	33.42N	87.20W
Oakmont, Pa., U.S. (ōk'mōnt)	101e	40.31N	79.50W
Oak Mountain, mtn., Al., U.S.	100h	33.22N	86.42W
Oak Park, Il., U.S. (pärk)	101a	41.53N	87.48W
Oak Park, Mi., U.S.	230c	42.28N	83.11W
Oak Point, Wa., U.S.	106c	46.11N	123.11W
Oak Ridge, Tn., U.S. (rĭj)	114	36.01N	84.15W
Oak View, Md., U.S.	229d	39.01N	76.59W
Oakview, N.J., U.S.	229b	39.51N	75.09W
Oakville, Can.	83f	49.56N	97.58W
Oakville, Can. (ōk'vĭl)	91	43.27N	79.40W
Oakville, Mo., U.S.	107e	38.27N	90.18W
Oakville Creek, r., Can.	83d	43.34N	79.54W
Oakwood, Oh., U.S.	229a	41.06N	84.23W
Oakwood, Tx., U.S. (ōk'wòd)	113	31.36N	95.48W
Oatley, Austl.	243a	33.59S	151.05E
Oatman, Az., U.S. (ōt'măn)	109	34.00N	114.25W
Oaxaca, Mex.	116	17.03N	96.42W
Oaxaca, state, Mex. (wä-hä'kä)	116	16.45N	97.00W
Oaxaca, Sierra de, mts., Mex. (sē-ĕ'r-rä dĕ)	119	16.15N	97.25W
Ob', r., Russia	164	62.15N	67.00E
Oba, Can. (ō'bá)	85	48.58N	84.09W
Obama, Japan (ō'bá-mä)	195	35.29N	135.44E
Oban, Scot., U.K. (ō'băn)	150	56.25N	5.35W
Oban Hills, hills, Nig.	215	5.35N	8.30E
O'Bannon, Ky., U.S. (ō-băn'nŏn)	101h	38.17N	85.30W
Obatogamau, l., Can. (ō-bá-tō'găm-ô)	91	49.38N	74.10W
Oberbauer, Ger.	236	51.17N	7.26E
Oberbonsfeld, Ger.	236	51.22N	7.08E
Oberelfringhausen, Ger.	236	51.20N	7.11E
Oberhaan, Ger.	236	51.13N	7.02E
Oberhausen, Ger. (ō'bĕr-hou'zĕn)	157c	51.27N	6.51E
Oberkassel, neigh., Ger.	236	51.14N	6.46E
Ober-kirchbach, Aus.	239e	48.17N	16.12E
Oberlaa, neigh., Aus.	239e	48.08N	16.24E
Oberlin, Ks., U.S. (o'bĕr-lĭn)	110	39.49N	100.30W
Oberlin, Oh., U.S.	98	41.15N	82.15W
Oberösterreich, prov., Aus.	154	48.05N	13.15E
Oberroth, Ger. (ō'bĕr-rōt)	145d	48.19N	11.20E
Ober Sankt Veit, neigh., Aus.	239e	48.11N	16.16E
Oberschöneweide, neigh., Ger.	238a	52.28N	13.31E
Oberwengern, Ger.	236	51.23N	7.22E
Obgruiten, Ger.	236	51.13N	7.01E
Obi, Kepulauan, is., Indon. (ō'bē)	197	1.25S	128.15E
Obi, Pulau, i., Indon.	197	1.30S	127.45E
Óbidos, Braz. (ō'bē-dòzh)	131	1.57S	55.32W
Obihiro, Japan (ō'bē-hē'rō)	194	42.55N	142.50E
Obion, r., Tn., U.S.	114	36.10N	89.25W
Obion, North Fork, r., Tn., U.S. (ô-bī'ŏn)	114	35.49N	89.06W
Obitsu, r., Japan (ō'bĕt'so͞o)	195a	35.19N	140.03E
Obock, Dji. (ō-bŏk')	218a	11.55N	43.15E
Obol', r., Bela. (ō-bŏl')	162	55.24N	29.24E
Oboyan', Russia (ō-bô-yän')	167	51.14N	36.16E
Obskaya Guba, b., Russia	164	67.13N	73.45E
Obu, neigh., Japan	242b	34.44N	135.09E
Obuasi, Ghana	214	6.14N	1.39W
Óbuda, neigh., Hung.	239g	47.33N	19.02E
Obukhiv, Ukr.	163	50.07N	30.36E
Obukhovo, Russia	172b	55.50N	38.17E
Obytichna kosa, spit, Ukr.	163	46.32N	36.07E
Očakovo, neigh., Russia	239b	55.41N	37.27E
Ocala, Fl., U.S. (ô-kä'lá)	115	29.11N	82.09W

PLACE (Pronunciation)	PAGE	Lat. °'	Long. °'
Ocampo, Mex. (ō-käm'pō)	118	22.49N	99.23W
Ocaña, Col. (ō-kän'yä)	130	8.15N	73.37W
Ocaña, Spain (ō-kä'n-yä)	158	39.58N	3.31W
Occidental, Cordillera, mts., Col.	130a	5.05N	76.04W
Occidental, Cordillera, mts., Peru	130	10.12S	76.58W
Ocean Beach, Ca., U.S. (ō'shăn bēch)	108a	32.44N	117.14W
Ocean Bight, bt., Bah.	123	21.15N	73.15W
Ocean City, Md., U.S.	99	38.20N	75.10W
Ocean City, N.J., U.S.	99	39.15N	74.35W
Ocean Falls, Can. (Fôls)	84	52.21N	127.40W
Ocean Grove, Austl.	201a	38.16S	144.32E
Ocean Grove, N.J., U.S. (grōv)	99	40.10N	74.00W
Oceanside, Ca., U.S. (ō'shăn-sīd)	108	33.11N	117.22W
Oceanside, N.Y., U.S.	100a	40.38N	73.39W
Ocean Springs, Ms., U.S. (sprĭngs)	114	30.25N	88.49W
Ochakiv, Ukr.	163	46.38N	31.33E
Ochamchira, Geor.	168	42.44N	41.28E
Ochiai, neigh., Japan	242a	35.43N	139.42E
Ochlockonee, r., Fl., U.S. (ŏk-lô-kō'nē)	114	30.10N	84.38W
Ocilla, Ga., U.S. (ô-sĭl'á)	114	31.36N	83.15W
Ockelbo, Swe. (ôk'ĕl-bô)	152	60.54N	16.35E
Ockham, Eng., U.K.	235	51.18N	0.27W
Ocklawaha, Lake, res., Fl., U.S.	115	29.30N	81.50W
Ocmulgee, r., Ga., U.S.	114	32.25N	83.30W
Ocmulgee National Monument, rec., Ga., U.S. (ôk-mŭl'gē)	114	32.45N	83.28W
Ocoa, Bahía de, b., Dom. Rep.	123	18.20N	70.40W
Ococingo, Mex. (ô-kô-sē'n-gô)	119	17.03N	92.18W
Ocom, Lago, l., Mex. (ô-kô'm)	120a	19.26N	88.18W
Oconee, r., Ga., U.S. (ô-kō'nē)	97	32.45N	83.00W
Oconee, Lake, res., Ga., U.S.	114	33.30N	83.15W
Oconomowoc, Wi., U.S. (ô-kŏn'ô-mô-wŏk')	103	43.06N	88.24W
Oconto, Wi., U.S. (ô-kŏn'tō)	103	44.54N	87.55W
Oconto, r., Wi., U.S.	103	45.08N	88.24W
Oconto Falls, Wi., U.S.	103	44.53N	88.11W
Ocós, Guat. (ô-kōs')	120	14.31N	92.12W
Ocotal, Nic. (ō-kô-täl')	120	13.36N	86.31W
Ocotepeque, Hond. (ô-kô-tå-pā'kå)	120	14.25N	89.13W
Ocotlán, Mex. (ō-kô-tlän')	118	20.19N	102.44W
Ocotlán de Morelos, Mex. (dā mô-rā'lōs)	119	16.46N	96.41W
Ocozocoautla, Mex. (ô-kō'zô-kwä-o͞o'tlä)	119	16.44N	93.22W
Ocumare del Tuy, Ven. (ô-ko͞o-mä'ra del twē')	130	10.07N	66.47W
Oda, Ghana	214	5.55N	0.59W
Odawara, Japan (ō'dá-wä'rä)	195	35.15N	139.10E
Odda, Nor. (ôdh-á)	152	60.04N	6.30E
Odebolt, Ia., U.S. (ō'dē-bōlt)	102	42.20N	95.14W
Odemira, Port. (ō-dá-mē'rá)	158	37.35N	8.40W
Ödemiş, Tur. (û'dē-mēsh)	149	38.12N	28.00E
Odendaalsrus, S. Afr. (ō'dĕn-däls-rûs')	218d	27.52S	26.41E
Odense, Den. (ō'dhĕn-sĕ)	146	55.24N	10.20E
Odenton, Md., U.S. (ō'dĕn-tǔn)	100e	39.05N	76.43W
Odenwald, for., Ger. (ō'dĕn-väld)	154	49.39N	8.55E
Oder, r., Eur. (ō'dĕr)	142	52.40N	14.19E
Oderhaff, l., Eur.	154	53.47N	14.02E
Odesa, Ukr.	164	46.28N	30.44E
Odesa, prov., Ukr.	163	46.05N	29.48E
Odessa, Tx., U.S. (ô-dĕs'á)	112	31.52N	102.21W
Odessa, Wa., U.S.	104	47.20N	118.42W
Odiel, r., Spain (ō-dê-ĕl')	158	37.47N	6.42W
Odiham, Eng., U.K. (ŏd'ē-ǎm)	144b	51.14N	0.56W
Odintsovo, Russia (ô-dĕn'tsô-vô)	172b	55.40N	37.16E
Odiongan, Phil. (ō-dē-ôŋ'gän)	197a	12.24N	121.59E
Odivelas, Port. (ō-dē-vä'lyäs)	159b	38.47N	9.11W
Odobeşti, Rom. (ō-dô-bĕsh't')	155	45.46N	27.08E
O'Donnell, Tx., U.S. (ō-dŏn'ĕl)	110	32.59N	101.51W
Odorhei, Rom. (ō-dôr-hā')	155	46.18N	25.17E
Odra *see* Oder, r., Eur. (ô'drà)	142	52.40N	14.19E
Oeiras, Braz. (wå-ē-räzh')	131	7.05S	42.01W
Oeirás, Port. (ō-ĕ'y-rä's)	159b	38.42N	9.18W
Oella, Md., U.S.	229c	39.16N	76.47W
Oelwein, Ia., U.S. (ōl'wīn)	103	42.40N	91.56W
Oespel, neigh., Ger.	236	51.30N	7.23E
Oestrich, Ger.	236	51.22N	7.38E
Oestrich, neigh., Ger.	236	51.34N	7.22E
Oestrum, Ger.	236	51.25N	6.40E
O'Fallon, Il., U.S. (ō-făl'ǔn)	107e	38.36N	89.55W
O'Fallon Creek, r., Mt., U.S.	105	46.25N	104.47W
Ofanto, r., Italy (ô-fän'tō)	160	41.08N	15.33E
Offa, Nig.	215	8.09N	4.44E
Offenbach, Ger. (ôf'ĕn-bäk)	154	50.06N	8.50E
Offenburg, Ger. (ôf'ĕn-bòrgh)	154	48.28N	7.57E
Ofin, Nig.	244d	6.33N	3.30E
Ofomori, neigh., Japan	242a	35.34N	139.44E
Ofuna, Japan (ō'fo͞o-nä)	195a	35.21N	139.32E
Ogaden Plateau, plat., Eth.	218a	6.45N	44.53E
Ogaki, Japan	194	35.21N	136.36E
Ogallala, Ne., U.S. (ō-gä-lä'lä)	102	41.08N	101.44W
Ogawa, Japan	242a	35.44N	139.28E
Ogbomosho, Nig. (ŏg-bô-mō'shō)	210	8.08N	4.15E
Ogden, Ia., U.S. (ŏg'dĕn)	103	42.10N	94.20W
Ogden, Ut., U.S.	96	41.14N	111.58W
Ogden, r., Ut., U.S.	107b	41.16N	111.54W
Ogden Peak, mtn., Ut., U.S.	107b	41.11N	111.51W
Ogdensburg, N.J., U.S. (ŏg'dĕnz-bûrg)	100a	41.05N	74.36W
Ogdensburg, N.Y., U.S.	97	44.40N	75.30W
Ogeechee, r., Ga., U.S. (ô-gē'chē)	115	32.35N	81.50W
Ogies, S. Afr.	218d	26.03S	29.04E
Ogilvie Mountains, mts., Can. (ō'g'l-vĭ)	84	64.45N	138.10W
Oglesby, Il., U.S. (ō'g'lz-bĭ)	98	41.20N	89.00W
Oglio, r., Italy (ôl'yō)	160	45.15N	10.19E
Ōgo, Japan (ō'gô)	195b	34.49N	135.06E
Ogou, r., Togo	214	8.05N	1.30E
Ogoyo, Nig.	244d	6.26N	3.29E

PLACE (Pronunciation)	PAGE	Lat. °′	Long. °′
Ogudnëvo, Russia (ŏg-ŏd-nyô′vô)	172b	56.04N	38.17E
Ogudu, Nig.	244d	6.34N	3.24E
Ogulin, Cro. (ō-gōō-lēn′)	160	45.17N	15.11E
Ogwashi-Uku, Nig.	215	6.10N	6.31E
O'Higgins, prov., Chile (ō-kē′gēns)	129b	34.17S	70.52W
Ohio, state, U.S. (ō′hī′ō)	97	40.30N	83.15W
Ohio, r., U.S.	97	37.25N	88.05W
Ohoopee, r., Ga., U.S. (ō-hōō′pe-mc)	115	32.32N	82.38W
Ohře, r., Eur. (ŏr′zhě)	154	50.08N	12.45E
Ohrid, Mac. (ō′krēd)	161	41.08N	20.46E
Ohrid, Lake, l., Eur.	161	40.58N	20.35E
Ōi, Japan (oi′)	195a	35.51N	139.31E
Oi-Gawa, r., Japan (ō′ē-gä′wȧ)	195	35.09N	138.05E
Oil City, Pa., U.S. (oil sĭ′tĭ)	99	41.25N	79.40W
Oirschot, Neth.	145a	51.30N	5.20E
Oise, r., Fr. (wäz)	147	49.30N	2.56E
Oisterwijk, Neth.	145a	51.34N	5.13E
Oita, Japan (ō′ē-tä)	194	33.14N	131.38E
Oji, Japan (ō′jē)	195b	34.36N	135.43E
Ojinaga, Mex. (ō-kē-nä′gä)	116	29.34N	104.26W
Ojitlán, Mex. (ōkē-tlän′) (sän-lōō′käs)	119	18.04N	96.23W
Ojo Caliente, Mex. (ōkō käl-yĕn′tä)	118	21.50N	100.43W
Ojocaliente, Mex. (ō-kō-kä-lyĕ′n-tĕ)	118	22.39N	102.15W
Ojo del Toro, Pico, mtn., Cuba (pē′kō-ō-kō-dĕl-tō′rō)	122	19.55N	77.25W
Oka, Can. (ō-kä)	83a	45.28N	74.05W
Oka, r., Russia (ô-kä′)	166	55.10N	42.10E
Oka, r., Russia (ô-kä′)	167	52.10N	35.20E
Oka, r., Russia (ō-kä′)	170	53.28N	101.09E
Okahandja, Nmb.	212	21.50S	16.45E
Okanagan (Okanogan), r., N.A. (ō′kā-näg′ān)	87	49.06N	119.43W
Okanagan Lake, l., Can.	84	50.00N	119.28W
Okano, r., Gabon (ō′kä′nō)	210	0.15N	11.08E
Okanogan, Wa., U.S.	104	48.20N	119.34W
Okanogan, r., Wa., U.S.	104	48.36N	119.33W
Okatibbee, r., Ms., U.S. (ō′kä-tĭb′ē)	114	32.37N	88.54W
Okatoma Creek, r., Ms., U.S. (ō-kȧ-tō′mä)	114	31.43N	89.34W
Okavango (Cubango), r., Afr.	212	18.00S	20.00E
Okavango Swamp, sw., Bots.	212	19.30S	23.02E
Okaya, Japan (ō′kȧ-yȧ)	195	36.04N	138.01E
Okayama, Japan (ō′kȧ-yä′mȧ)	189	34.39N	133.54E
Okazaki, Japan (ō′kȧ-zä′kē)	194	34.58N	137.09E
Okeechobee, Fl., U.S. (ō-kē-chō′bē)	115	27.15N	80.50W
Okeechobee, Lake, l., Fl., U.S.	97	27.00N	80.49W
O'Keefe Centre, bldg., Can.	227c	43.37N	79.22W
Okeene, Ok., U.S. (ō-kēn′)	110	36.06N	98.19W
Okefenokee Swamp, sw., U.S. (ō′kē-fē-nō′kē)	115	30.54N	82.20W
Okemah, Ok., U.S. (ō-kē′mä)	111	35.26N	96.18W
Okene, Nig.	215	7.33N	6.15E
Oke Ogbe, Nig.	244d	6.24N	3.23E
Okha, Russia (ŭ-kä′)	165	53.44N	143.12E
Okhotino, Russia (ô-kô′tĭ-nô)	172b	56.14N	38.24E
Okhotsk, Russia (ô-kôtsk′)	165	59.28N	143.32E
Okhotsk, Sea of, sea, Asia (ō-kôtsk′)	165	56.45N	146.00E
Okhtyrka, Ukr.	167	50.18N	34.53E
Okinawa, i., Japan	189	26.30N	128.00E
Okino, i., Japan (ō′kē-nō)	195	36.22N	133.27E
Ōkino Erabu, i., Japan (ō-kē′nō-ȧ-rä′bōō)	194	27.18N	129.00E
Oklahoma, state, U.S. (ō-klȧ-hō′mȧ)	96	36.00N	98.20W
Oklahoma City, Ok., U.S.	96	35.27N	97.32W
Oklawaha, r., Fl., U.S. (ōk-lȧ-wô′hô)	115	29.13N	82.00W
Okmulgee, Ok., U.S. (ōk-mŭl′gē)	111	35.37N	95.58W
Okolona, Ky., U.S. (ō-kō-lō′nȧ)	101h	38.08N	85.41W
Okolona, Ms., U.S.	114	33.59N	88.43W
Oktemberyan, Arm.	168	40.09N	44.02E
Okushiri, i., Japan (ō′koo-shē′rē)	194	42.12N	139.30E
Okuta, Nig.	215	9.14N	3.15E
Olalla, Wa., U.S. (ō-lă′lȧ)	106a	47.26N	122.33W
Olanchito, Hond. (ō′län-chē′tō)	120	15.28N	86.35W
Öland, i., Swe. (û-länd′)	142	57.03N	17.15E
Olathe, Ks., U.S. (ō-lā′thē)	107f	38.53N	94.49W
Olavarría, Arg. (ō-lä-vär-rē′ä)	132	36.49N	60.15W
Oława, Pol. (ô-lä′vȧ)	155	50.57N	17.18E
Olazoago, Arg. (ō-läz-kōä′gō)	129c	35.14S	60.37W
Olbia, Italy (ō′l-byä)	160	40.55N	9.28E
Olching, Ger. (ōl′kĕng)	145d	48.13N	11.21E
Old Bahama Channel, strt., N.A. (bȧ-hā′mȧ)	122	22.45N	78.30W
Old Bight, Bah.	123	24.15N	75.20W
Old Bridge, N.J., U.S. (brĭj)	100a	40.24N	74.22W
Old Brookville, N.Y., U.S.	228	40.49N	73.36W
Old Crow, Can. (crō)	84	67.51N	139.58W
Oldenburg, Ger. (ōl′dĕn-bōrgh)	146	53.09N	8.13E
Old Forge, Pa., U.S. (fôrj)	99	41.20N	75.50W
Oldham, Eng., U.K. (ōld′ăm)	150	53.32N	2.07W
Oldham Pond, l., Ma., U.S.	227a	42.03N	70.51W
Old Harbor, Ak., U.S. (här′bĕr)	95	57.18N	153.20W
Old Head of Kinsale, c., Ire. (ōld hĕd ŏv kĭn-sāl)	150	51.35N	8.35W
Old Malden, neigh., Eng., U.K.	235	51.23N	0.15W
Old North Church, pt. of i., Ma., U.S.	227a	42.22N	71.03W
Old R, Tx., U.S.	113a	29.54N	94.52W
Olds, Can. (ōldz)	84	51.47N	114.06W
Old Tate, Bots.	212	21.18S	27.43E
Old Town, Me., U.S. (toun)	92	44.55N	68.42W
Old Westbury, N.Y., U.S.	228	40.47N	73.37W
Old Windsor, Eng., U.K.	235	51.28N	0.35W
Old Wives Lake, l., Can. (wīvz)	88	50.05N	106.00W
Olean, N.Y., U.S. (ō-lē-ăn′)	97	42.05N	78.25W
Olecko, Pol. (ō-lĕt′skō)	155	54.02N	22.29E
Olekma, r., Russia (ō-lyĕk-mȧ′)	171	55.41N	120.33E
Olëkminsk, Russia (ō-lyĕk-mênsk′)	165	60.39N	120.40E
Oleksandriya, Ukr.	162	48.40N	33.07E
Olenëk, r., Russia (ō-lyĕ-nyôk′)	165	68.00N	113.00E
Oléron Île, d', i., Fr. (ēl′ dō lā-rôN′)	147	45.52N	1.58W
Oleśnica, Pol. (ô-lĕsh-nĭ′tsȧ)	147	51.13N	17.24E
Olfen, Ger. (ōl′fĕn)	157c	51.43N	7.22E
Ol'ga, Russia (ôl′gȧ)	165	43.48N	135.44E
Ol'gi, Zaliv, b., Russia (zä′lĭf ôl′gĭ)	194	43.43N	135.25E
Olhão, Port. (ōl-youN′)	148	37.02N	7.54W
Ol'hopil', Ukr.	163	48.11N	29.28E
Olievenhoutpoort, S. Afr.	213b	25.58S	27.55E
Ólimbos, Grc.	149	40.03N	22.22E
Ólimbos, mtn., Cyp.	181a	34.56N	32.52E
Olinda, Austl.	243b	37.51S	145.22E
Olinda, Braz. (ô-lē′n-dä)	131	8.00S	34.58W
Olinda, Braz.	132b	22.49S	43.25W
Oliva, Spain (ô-lē′vä)	159	38.54N	0.07W
Oliva de la Frontera, Spain (ô-lē′vä dā)	158	38.33N	6.55W
Olivais, neigh., Port.	238d	34.46N	9.06W
Olive Hill, Ky., U.S. (ŏl′ĭv)	98	38.15N	83.10W
Oliveira, Braz. (ō-lē-vā′rä)	129a	20.42S	44.49W
Olive Mount, neigh., Eng., U.K.	237a	53.24N	2.55W
Olivenza, Spain (ō-lē-vĕn′thä)	158	38.42N	7.06W
Oliver, Can.	83g	53.38N	113.21W
Oliver, Can. (ŏ′lĭ-vĕr)	84	49.11N	119.33W
Oliver, Wi., U.S. (ŏ′lĭvĕr)	107h	46.39N	92.12W
Oliver Lake, l., Can.	83g	53.19N	113.00W
Olivia, Mn., U.S. (ō-lĭv′ē-ȧ)	102	44.46N	95.00W
Olivos, Arg. (ōlē′vōs)	132a	34.30S	58.29W
Ollagüe, Chile (ō-lyä′gȧ)	130	21.17S	68.17W
Ollerton, Eng., U.K. (ŏl′ĕr-tŭn)	144a	53.12N	1.02W
Olmos Park, Tx., U.S. (ōl′mŭs pärk′)	107d	29.27N	98.32W
Olmsted, Oh., U.S.	229a	41.24N	81.44W
Olmsted Falls, Oh., U.S.	229a	41.22N	81.55W
Olney, Il., U.S. (ŏl′nĭ)	98	38.45N	88.05W
Olney, Or., U.S. (ŏl′nē)	106c	46.06N	123.45W
Olney, Tx., U.S.	110	33.24N	98.43W
Olney, neigh., Pa., U.S.	229b	40.02N	75.08W
Olomane, r., Can. (ō′lō mȧ′nē)	93	51.05N	60.50W
Olomouc, Czech Rep. (ō′lō-mōts)	147	49.37N	17.15E
Olonets, Russia (ô-lô′nĕts)	153	60.58N	32.54E
Olongapo, Phil.	196	14.49S	120.17E
Oloron, Gave d', r., Fr. (gäv-dō-lō-rôN′)	156	43.21N	0.44W
Oloron-Sainte Marie, Fr. (ō-lō-rôNt′sǎNt mȧ-rē′)	156	43.11N	1.37W
Olot, Spain (ô-lōt′)	148	42.09N	2.30E
Olpe, Ger. (ōl′pĕ)	157c	51.02N	7.51E
Olsnitz, Ger. (ōlz′nētz)	154	50.25N	12.11E
Olsztyn, Pol. (ôl′shtĭn)	146	53.47N	20.28E
Olt, r., Rom.	149	44.09N	24.40E
Olten, Switz. (ōl′tĕn)	154	47.20N	7.53E
Oltenita, Rom. (ōl-tä′nĭ-tsȧ)	161	44.05N	26.39E
Olvera, Spain (ōl-vĕ′rä)	158	36.55N	5.16W
Olympia, Wa., U.S. (ō-lĭm′pĭ-ȧ)	96	47.02N	122.52W
Olympic Mountains, mts., Wa., U.S.	104	47.54N	123.58W
Olympic National Park, rec., Wa., U.S. (ō-lĭm′pĭk)	96	47.54N	123.00W
Olympieion, pt. of i., Grc.	239d	37.58N	23.44E
Olympus, Mount, mtn., Wa., U.S. (ō-lĭm′pŭs)	104	47.43N	123.30W
Olyphant, Pa., U.S. (ŏl′ĭ-fănt)	99	41.30N	75.40W
Olyutorskiy, Mys, c., Russia (ŭl-yōō′tŏr-skē)	165	59.49N	167.16E
Omae-Zaki, c., Japan (ō′mä-ȧ zä′kē)	195	34.37N	138.15E
Omagh, N. Ire., U.K. (ō′mä)	150	54.35N	7.25W
Omaha, Ne., U.S. (ō′mȧ-hä)	97	41.18N	95.57W
Omaha Indian Reservation, I.R., Ne., U.S.	102	42.09N	96.08W
Oman, nation, Asia	182	20.00N	57.45E
Oman, Gulf of, b., Asia	182	24.24N	58.58E
Omaruru, Nmb. (ō-mä-rōō′rōō)	212	21.25S	16.50E
Ombrone, r., Italy (ōm-brō′nā)	160	42.48N	11.18E
Omdurman, Sudan	211	15.45N	32.30E
Omealca, Mex. (ōmȧ-äl′kō)	119	18.44N	96.45W
Ometepec, Mex. (ō-mä-tȧ-pĕk′)	118	16.41N	98.27W
Om Hajer, Eth.	211	14.06N	36.46E
Omineca, r., Can. (ō-mĭ-nĕk′ȧ)	86	55.50N	125.45W
Omineca Mountains, mts., Can.	86	56.00N	125.00W
Ōmiya, Japan (ō′mē-yȧ)	195	35.54S	139.38E
Omo, r., Eth. (ō′mō)	211	5.54N	36.09E
Omoa, Hond. (ō-mō′rä)	120	15.43N	88.03W
Omoko, Nig.	215	5.20N	6.39E
Omolon, r., Russia (ō′mō)	171	67.43N	159.15E
Ōmori, Japan (ō′mō-rē)	195a	35.50N	140.09E
Omotepe, Isla de, i., Nic. (ē′s-lä-dĕ-ō-mō-tā′pȧ)	120	11.32N	85.30W
Omro, Wi., U.S. (ŏm′rō)	103	44.01N	89.46W
Omsk, Russia (ōmsk)	164	55.12N	73.19E
Ōmura, Japan (ō′mōō-rȧ)	195	32.56N	129.57E
Ōmuta, Japan (ō-mō-tȧ)	195	33.02N	130.28E
Omutninsk, Russia (ō′mōō-tnēnsk)	166	58.38N	52.10E
Onawa, Ia., U.S. (ŏn-ȧ-wȧ)	102	42.02N	96.05W
Onaway, Mi., U.S.	98	45.25N	84.10W
Once, neigh., Arg.	233d	34.36S	58.24W
Oncócua, Ang.	216	16.34S	13.28E
Onda, Spain (ōn′dä)	159	39.58N	0.13W
Ondava, r., Slvk. (ōn′dȧ-vȧ)	155	48.51N	21.40E
Ondo, Nig.	215	7.04N	4.47E
Öndörhaan, Mong.	189	47.20N	110.40E
Onega, Russia (ô-nyĕ′gȧ)	164	63.50N	38.08E
Onega, r., Russia	166	63.20N	39.20E
Onega, Lake *see* Onezhskoye Ozero, l., Russia	166	62.02N	34.35E
Oneida, N.Y., U.S. (ō-nī′dȧ)	99	43.05N	75.40W
Oneida, l., N.Y., U.S.	99	43.10N	76.00W
O'Neill, Ne., U.S. (ō-nēl′)	102	42.28N	98.38W
Oneonta, N.Y., U.S. (ō-nē-ŏn′tȧ)	99	42.25N	75.05W
Onezhskaja Guba, b., Russia	166	64.30N	36.00E
Onezhskiy, Poluostrov, pen., Russia	166	64.30N	37.40E
Onezhskoye Ozero, Russia (ô-năsh′skô-yĕ ô′zĕ-rô)	166	62.02N	34.35E
Ongiin Hiid, Mong.	188	46.00N	102.46E
Ongole, India	187	15.36N	80.03E
Onilahy, r., Madag.	213	23.41S	45.00E
Onitsha, Nig. (ō-nĭt′shȧ)	210	6.09N	6.47W
Onomichi, Japan (ō′nō-mē′chē)	194	34.27N	133.12E
Onon, r., Asia (ô′nôn)	165	49.00N	112.00E
Onoto, Ven. (ô-nō′tō)	131b	9.38N	65.03W
Onslow, Austl. (ŏnz′lō)	202	21.53S	115.00E
Onslow B, N.C., U.S. (ŏnz′lō)	115	34.22N	77.35W
Ontake San, mtn., Japan (ōn′tä-kȧ sän)	194	35.55N	137.29E
Ontario, Ca., U.S. (ŏn-tā′rĭ-ō)	107a	34.04N	117.39E
Ontario, Or., U.S.	104	44.02N	116.57W
Ontario, prov., Can.	85	50.47N	88.50W
Ontario, Lake, l., N.A.	97	43.35N	79.05W
Ontario Science Centre, bldg., Can.	227c	43.43N	79.21W
Onteniente, Spain (ōn-tȧ-nyĕn′tā)	159	38.48N	0.35W
Ontonagon, Mi., U.S. (ŏn-tō-năg′ŏn)	103	46.50N	89.20W
Ōnuki, Japan (ō′nōō-kē)	195a	35.17N	139.51E
Oodnadatta, Austl. (ōōd′nȧ-dȧ′tȧ)	202	27.38S	135.40E
Ooldea Station, Austl. (ōōl-dā′ä)	202	30.35S	132.08E
Oologah Reservoir, res., Ok., U.S.	97	36.43N	95.32W
Ooltgensplaat, Neth.	145a	51.41N	4.19E
Oostanaula, r., Ga., U.S. (ōō-stȧ-nô′lȧ)	114	34.25N	85.10W
Oostende, Bel. (ōst-ĕn′dē)	147	51.14N	2.55E
Oosterhout, Neth.	145a	51.38N	4.52E
Ooster Schelde, r., Neth.	145a	51.40N	3.40E
Ootsa Lake, l., Can.	86	53.49N	126.18W
Opalaca, Sierra de, mts., Hond. (sē-sĕ′r-rä-dĕ-ô-pä-lä′kä)	120	14.30N	88.29W
Opasquia, Can. (ō-păs′kwē-ȧ)	89	53.16N	93.53W
Opatów, Pol. (ō-pä′tôf)	155	50.47N	21.25E
Opava, Czech Rep. (ō′pä-vä)	155	49.56N	17.52E
Opelika, Al., U.S. (ŏp-ē-lī′kȧ)	114	32.39N	85.23W
Opelousas, La., U.S. (ŏp-ē-lōō′sȧs)	113	30.33N	92.04W
Opeongo, l., Can. (ŏp-ē-ōn′gō)	91	45.40N	78.20W
Opheim, Mt., U.S. (ō-fīm′)	105	48.51N	106.19W
Ophir, Ak., U.S. (ō′fēr)	95	63.10N	156.28W
Ophir, Mount, mtn., Malay.	181b	2.22N	102.37E
Ophirton, neigh., S. Afr.	244b	26.14S	28.01E
Opico, El Sal. (ō-pē′kō)	120	13.50N	89.23W
Opinaca, r., Can. (ŏp-ĭ-nä′kȧ)	85	52.28N	77.40W
Opishnya, Ukr.	163	49.57N	34.34E
Opladen, Ger. (ŏp′lä-dĕn)	157c	51.04N	7.00E
Opobo, Nig.	215	4.34N	7.27E
Opochka, Russia (ō-pôch′kȧ)	166	56.43N	28.39E
Opoczno, Pol. (ō-pôch′nō)	155	51.22N	20.18E
Opole, Pol. (ō-pôl′ȧ)	147	50.42N	17.55E
Opole Lubelskie, Pol. (ō-pō′lā lōō-bĕl′skyĕ)	155	51.09N	21.58E
Opp, Al., U.S. (ŏp)	114	31.18N	86.15W
Oppdal, Nor. (ōp′däl)	152	62.37N	9.41E
Opportunity, Wa., U.S. (ŏp-ŏr tū′nĭ tĭ)	104	47.37N	117.20W
Oppum, neigh., Ger.	236	51.19N	6.37E
Oquirrh Mountains, mts., Ut., U.S. (ō′kwēr)	107b	40.38N	112.11W
Oradea, Rom. (ō-räd′yä)	142	47.02N	21.55E
Oradell, N.J., U.S.	228	40.57N	74.02W
Oral, Kaz.	169	51.14N	51.22E
Oran, Alg. (ō-rän)(ō-räN′)	210	35.46N	0.45W
Orán, Arg. (ō-rá′n)	132	23.13S	64.17W
Oran, Mo., U.S. (ŏr′ăn)	111	37.05N	89.39W
Oran, Sebkha d', l., Alg.	159	35.28N	0.28W
Orange, Austl. (ŏr′ĕnj)	203	33.15S	149.08E
Orange, Fr. (ō-raNzh′)	147	44.08N	4.48E
Orange, Ca., U.S.	107a	33.48N	117.51W
Orange, Ct., U.S.	99	41.15N	73.00W
Orange, N.J., U.S.	100a	40.46N	74.14W
Orange, Tx., U.S.	111	30.07N	93.44W
Orange, r., Afr.	212	29.15S	17.30E
Orange, Cabo, c., Braz. (kȧ-bô-rȧ′n-zhĕ)	131	4.25N	51.30W
Orangeburg, S.C., U.S. (ŏr′ĕnj-bûrg)	115	33.30N	80.50W
Orange Cay, i., Bah. (ŏr-ĕnj kē)	122	24.55N	79.05W
Orange City, Ia., U.S.	102	43.01N	96.06W
Orange Grove, neigh., S. Afr.	244b	26.10S	28.05E
Orange Lake, l., Fl., U.S.	115	29.30N	82.12W
Orangeville, Can. (ŏr′ĕnj-vĭl)	91	43.55N	80.06W
Orangeville, S. Afr.	218d	27.05S	28.13E
Orange Walk, Belize (wôl″k)	120a	18.09N	88.32W
Orani, Phil. (ō-rä′nē)	197a	14.47N	120.32E
Oranienburg, Ger. (ō-rä′nē-ĕn-bōrgh)	154	52.45N	13.14E
Oranjemund, Nmb.	212	28.33S	16.20E
Orăştie, Rom. (ō-rûsh′tyȧ)	161	45.50N	23.14E
Orbetello, Italy (ôr-bȧ-tĕl′lō)	160	42.27N	11.15E
Orbigo, r., Spain (ôr-bē′gō)	158	42.30N	5.55W
Orbost, Austl. (ôr′bŭst)	204	37.43S	148.20E
Orcas, i., Wa., U.S. (ôr′kȧs)	106d	48.43N	122.52W
Orchard Farm, Mo., U.S. (ôr′chĕrd färm)	107e	38.53N	90.27W
Orchard Park, N.Y., U.S.	101c	42.46N	78.46W
Orchards, Wa., U.S. (ôr′chĕdz)	106c	45.40N	122.33W
Orchila, Isla, i., Ven.	130	11.47N	66.34W
Ord, Ne., U.S. (ôrd)	102	41.35N	98.57W
Ord, r., Austl.	202	17.30S	128.40E
Ord, Mount, mtn., Az., U.S.	109	33.55N	109.40W
Orda, Russia (ôr′dȧ)	172a	57.10N	57.12E
Órdenes, Spain (ôr′dȧ-nās)	158	43.00N	8.24W
Ordos Desert, des., China	188	39.12N	108.10E
Ordu, Tur. (ôr′dō)	149	41.00N	37.50E
Ordway, Co., U.S. (ôrd′wā)	110	38.11N	103.46W
Örebro, Swe. (û′rē-brō)	146	59.16N	15.11E
Oredezh, r., Russia (ô′rē-dĕzh)	172c	59.23N	30.21E

ăt; finăl; rāte; senāte; ärm; ȧsk; sofȧ; fâre; ch-choose; dh-as th in other; bē; ēvent; bĕt; recĕnt; cratēr; g-gō; gh-guttural g; bĭt; ĭ-short neutral; rīde; K-guttural k as ch in German ich;

PLACE (Pronunciation)	PAGE	Lat. °′	Long. °′
Oregon, Il., U.S.	103	42.01N	89.21W
Oregon, state, U.S.	96	43.40N	121.50W
Oregon Caves National Monument, rec., Or., U.S. (căvz)	104	42.05N	123.13W
Oregon City, Or., U.S.	106c	45.21N	122.36W
Öregrund, Swe. (û-rē-grȯnd)	152	60.20N	18.26E
Orekhovo, Bul.	161	43.43N	23.59E
Orekhovo-Zuyevo, Russia (ôr-yě′kô-vô zô′yě-vô)	164	55.46N	39.00E
Orël, Russia (ôr-yôl′)	164	52.59N	36.05E
Orël, prov., Russia	162	52.35N	36.08E
Orel′, r., Ukr.	163	49.08N	34.55E
Oreland, Pa., U.S.	229b	40.07N	75.11W
Orem, Ut., U.S. (ŏ′rĕm)	109	40.15N	111.50W
Ore Mountains *see* Erzgebirge, mts., Eur.	142	50.29N	12.40E
Orenburg, Russia (ô′rĕn-bōōrg)	164	51.50N	55.05E
Orense, Spain (ô-rĕn′sā)	158	42.20N	7.52W
Øresund, strt., Eur.	152	55.50N	12.40E
Órganos, Sierra de los, mts., Cuba (sē-ĕ′r-rä-dĕ-lôs-ŏ′r-gä-nôs)	122	22.20N	84.10W
Organ Pipe Cactus National Monument, rec., Az., U.S. (ôr′găn pīp kăk′tŭs)	109	32.14N	113.05W
Orgãos, Serra das, mtn., Braz. (sĕ′r-rä-däs-ôr-gouɴ′s)	129a	22.30S	43.01W
Orhei, Mol.	167	47.27N	28.49E
Orhon, r., Mong.	188	48.33N	103.07E
Oriental, Cordillera, mts., Col. (kôr-dēl-yĕ′rä)	130a	3.30N	74.27W
Oriental, Cordillera, mts., Dom. Rep. (kôr-dēl-yĕ′rä-ô-ryĕ′n-täl)	123	18.55N	69.40W
Oriental, Cordillera, mts., S.A. (kôr-dēl-yĕ′rä ō-rē-ĕn-täl′)	130	14.00S	68.33W
Orihuela, Spain (ō′rē-wā′lä)	159	38.04N	0.55W
Orikhiv, Ukr.	163	47.34N	35.51E
Orillia, Can. (ô-rĭl′ĭ-ȧ)	85	44.35N	79.25W
Orin, Wy., U.S.	105	42.40N	105.10W
Orinda, Ca., U.S.	106b	37.53N	122.11W
Orinoco, Río, r., Ven. (rē′ō-ō-rĭ-nō′kō)	130	8.32N	63.13W
Orion, Phil. (ō-rē-ōn′)	197a	14.37N	120.34E
Orissa, state, India (ŏ-rĭs′ȧ)	183	25.09N	83.50E
Oristano, Italy (ō-rēs-tä′nō)	148	39.53N	8.38E
Oristano, Golfo di, b., Italy (gôl-fô-dē-ô-rēs-tä′nō)	160	39.53N	8.12E
Orituco, r., Ven. (ô-rē-tōō′kō)	131b	9.37N	66.25W
Oriuco, r., Ven. (ô-rēōō′kō)	131b	9.36N	66.25W
Orivesi, l., Fin.	153	62.15N	29.55E
Orizaba, Mex. (ô-rē-zä′bä)	117	18.52N	97.05E
Orizaba, Pico de, vol., Mex.	116	19.04N	97.14W
Orkanger, Nor.	152	63.19N	9.54W
Orkla, r., Nor. (ôr′klȧ)	152	62.55N	9.50E
Orkney, S. Afr. (ôrk′nĭ)	218d	26.58S	26.39E
Orkney Islands, is., Scot., U.K.	142	59.01N	2.08W
Orlando, S. Afr. (ôr-lăn-dô)	213b	26.15S	27.56E
Orlando, Fl., U.S. (ôr-lăn′dō)	97	28.32N	81.22W
Orlando West Extension, S. Afr.	244b	26.15S	27.54E
Orland Park, Il., U.S. (ôr-lăn′)	101a	41.38N	87.52W
Orleans, Can. (ôr-lâ-äɴ′)	83c	45.28N	75.31W
Orléans, Fr. (ôr-lā-äɴ′)	142	47.55N	1.56E
Orleans, In., U.S. (ôr-lēnz′)	98	38.40N	86.25W
Orléans, Île d′, i., Can.	91	46.56N	70.57W
Orly, Fr.	157b	48.45N	2.24E
Ormond, Austl.	243b	37.54S	145.03E
Ormond Beach, Fl., U.S. (ôr′mŏnd)	115	29.15N	81.05W
Ormskirk, Eng., U.K. (ôrms′kērk)	144a	53.34N	2.53W
Ormstown, Can. (ôrms′toun)	83a	45.07N	74.00W
Orneta, Pol. (ôr-nyĕ′tä)	155	54.07N	20.10E
Örnsköldsvik, Swe. (ûrn′skôlts-vēk)	146	63.10N	18.32E
Oro, Río del, r., Mex.	109	26.04N	105.40W
Oro, Río del, r., Mex. (rē′ō dĕl ō′rō)	118	18.04N	100.59W
Orobie, Alpi, mts., Italy (äl′pē-ō-rō′byĕ)	160	46.05N	9.47E
Oron, Nig.	215	4.48N	8.14E
Orosei, Golfo di, b., Italy (gôl-fô-dē-ō-rō-sā′ē)	160	40.12N	9.45E
Orosháza, Hung. (ô-rôsh-hä′sô)	155	46.33N	20.31E
Orosi, vol., C.R. (ō-rō′sē)	120	11.00N	85.30W
Oroville, Ca., U.S. (ōr′ō-vĭl)	108	39.29N	121.34W
Oroville, Wa., U.S.	104	48.55N	119.25W
Oroville, Lake, res., Ca., U.S.	108	39.32N	121.25W
Orpington, neigh., Eng., U.K.	235	51.23N	0.06E
Orrville, Oh., U.S. (ôr′vĭl)	98	40.45N	81.50W
Orsa, Swe. (ōr′sä)	152	61.08N	14.35E
Orsay, Fr.	237c	48.42N	2.11E
Orsett, Eng., U.K.	235	51.31N	0.22E
Orsha, Bela. (ôr′shȧ)	166	54.29N	30.28E
Orsk, Russia (ôrsk)	164	51.15N	58.50E
Orşova, Rom. (ôr′shô-vä)	161	44.43N	22.26E
Orsoy, Ger.	236	51.31N	6.41E
Ortega, Col. (ôr-tĕ′gä)	130a	3.56N	75.12W
Ortegal, Cabo, c., Spain (kä′bô-ôr-tä-gäl′)	148	43.46N	8.15W
Orth, Aus.	145e	48.09N	16.42E
Orthez, Fr. (ôr-tĕz′)	157	43.29N	0.43W
Ortigueira, Spain (ôr-tē-gā′ê-rä)	148	43.40N	7.50W
Orting, Wa., U.S. (ôrt′ĭng)	106a	47.06N	122.12W
Ortona, Italy (ôr-tō′nä)	160	42.22N	14.22E
Ortonville, Mn., U.S. (ôr-tŭn-vĭl)	102	45.18N	96.26W
Oruba, Nig.	244d	6.35N	3.25E
Orūmīyeh, Iran	182	37.30N	45.15E
Orūmīyeh, Daryacheh-ye, l., Iran	182	38.01N	45.17E
Oruro, Bol. (ō-rōō′rō)	130	17.57S	66.59W
Orvieto, Italy (ôr-vyâ′tō)	160	42.43N	12.08E
Oryu-dong, neigh., S. Kor.	241b	37.29N	126.51E
Osa, Russia (ō′sȧ)	166	57.18N	55.25E
Osa, Península de, pen., C.R. (ō′sä)	121	8.30N	83.25W
Osage, Ia., U.S. (ō′sāj)	103	43.16N	92.49W
Osage, N.J., U.S.	229b	39.51N	75.01W
Osage, r., Mo., U.S.	111	38.10N	93.12W
Osage City, Ks., U.S. (ō′sāj sĭ′tĭ)	111	38.28N	95.53W
Ōsaka, Japan (ō′sä-kä)	189	34.40N	135.27E
Ōsaka, dept., Japan	195b	34.45N	135.36E
Osaka Castle, hist., Japan	242b	34.41N	135.32E
Ōsaka-Wan, b., Japan (wän)	194	34.34N	135.16E
Osakis, Mn., U.S. (ô-sā′kĭs)	102	45.51N	95.09W
Osakis, l., Mn., U.S.	103	45.55N	94.55W
Osasco, Braz.	234d	23.32S	46.46W
Osawatomie, Ks., U.S. (ŏs-ȧ-wăt′ô-mē)	111	38.29N	94.57W
Osborne, Ks., U.S. (ŏz′bŭrn)	110	39.25N	98.42W
Osceola, Ar., U.S. (ŏs-ē-ō′lȧ)	111	35.42N	89.58W
Osceola, Ia., U.S.	103	41.04N	93.45W
Osceola, Mo., U.S.	111	38.02N	93.41W
Osceola, Ne., U.S.	102	41.11N	97.34W
Oscoda, Mi., U.S. (ŏs-kō′dȧ)	98	44.25N	83.20W
Osëtr, r., Russia (ô′sĕt′r)	162	54.27N	38.15E
Osgood, In., U.S. (ŏz′gŏŏd)	98	39.10N	85.20W
Osgoode, Can.	83c	45.09N	75.37W
Osh, Kyrg. (ôsh)	169	40.33N	72.48E
Oshawa, Can. (ŏsh′ȧ-wȧ)	85	43.50N	78.50W
Ōshima, i., Japan (ō′shē′mä)	195	34.47N	139.35E
Oshkosh, Ne., U.S. (ŏsh′kŏsh)	102	41.24N	102.22W
Oshkosh, Wi., U.S.	97	44.01N	88.35W
Oshmyany, Bela. (ôsh-myä′nĭ)	153	54.27N	25.55E
Oshodi, Nig.	244d	6.34N	3.21E
Oshogbo, Nig.	210	7.47N	4.34E
Osijek, Cro. (ôs′ĭ-yĕk)	149	45.33N	18.48E
Osinniki, Russia (ŭ-sē′nyĭ-kē)	170	53.37N	87.21E
Oskaloosa, Ia., U.S. (ŏs-kȧ-lōō′sȧ)	103	41.16N	92.40W
Oskarshamn, Swe. (ôs′kärs-häm′n)	152	57.16N	16.24E
Oskarström, Swe. (ôs′kärs-strûm)	152	56.48N	12.55E
Oskemen, Kaz.	169	49.58N	82.38E
Oskol, r., Eur. (ôs-kôl′)	167	51.00N	37.41E
Oslo, Nor. (ŏs′lō)	142	59.56N	10.41E
Oslofjorden, fj., Nor.	152	59.03N	10.35E
Osmaniye, Tur.	149	37.10N	36.30E
Osnabrück, Ger. (ôs-nä-brük′)	154	52.16N	8.05E
Osorno, Chile (ô-sō′r-nō)	132	40.42S	73.13W
Osorun, Nig.	244d	6.33N	3.29E
Osøyra, Nor.	152	60.24N	5.22E
Osprey Reef, rf., Austl. (ŏs′prā)	203	14.00S	146.45E
Ossa, Mount, mtn., Austl. (ŏsȧ)	203	41.45S	146.05E
Ossenberg, Ger.	236	51.34N	6.35E
Osseo, Mn., U.S. (ŏs′sē-ō)	107g	45.07N	93.24W
Ossining, N.Y., U.S. (ŏs′ĭ-nĭng)	100a	41.09N	73.51W
Ossipee, N.H., U.S. (ŏs′ĭ-pē)	92	43.42N	71.08W
Ossjøen, l., Nor. (ôs-syûēn)	152	61.20N	12.00E
Ossum-Bösinghoven, Ger.	236	51.18N	6.39E
Ostankino, neigh., Russia	239b	55.49N	37.37E
Ostashkov, Russia (ôs-täsh′kôf)	166	57.07N	33.04E
Oster, Ukr. (ōs′tĕr)	163	50.55N	30.52E
Österdalälven, r., Swe.	146	61.40N	13.00E
Osterfeld, neigh., Ger.	236	51.30N	6.53E
Österfjord, fj., Nor. (ûs′tĕr fyôr′)	152	60.40N	5.25E
Östersund, Swe. (ûs′tĕr-sōōnd)	146	63.09N	14.49E
Östhammar, Swe. (ûst′häm′är)	152	60.16N	18.21E
Ostrava, Czech Rep.	142	49.51N	18.18E
Ostróda, Pol. (ôs′trŏt-ȧ)	155	53.41N	19.58E
Ostrogozhsk, Russia (ôs-tr-gôzhk′)	167	50.53N	39.03E
Ostroh, Ukr.	167	50.21N	26.40E
Ostrołęka, Pol. (ôs-trô-woɴ′kȧ)	155	53.04N	21.35E
Ostrov, Russia (ôs-trôf′)	166	57.21N	28.22E
Ostrov, Russia	239b	55.35N	37.51E
Ostrowiec Świętokrzyski, Pol. (ôs-trō′vyĕts shvyĕɴ-tō-kzhĭ′ske)	147	50.55N	21.24E
Ostrów Lubelski, Pol. (ôs′trōf lōō′bĕl-skĭ)	155	51.32N	22.49E
Ostrów Mazowiecka, Pol. (mä-zô-vyĕt′skä)	147	52.47N	21.54E
Ostrów Wielkopolski, Pol. (ôs′trōōf vyĕl-kō-pōl′skē)	147	51.38N	17.49E
Ostrzeszów, Pol. (ôs-tzhā′shōf)	155	51.26N	17.56E
Ostuni, Italy (ôs-tōō′nē)	161	40.44N	17.35E
Osum, r., Alb. (ō′sōm)	161	40.37N	20.00E
Osuna, Spain (ô-sōō′nä)	158	37.18N	5.05W
Osveya, Bela. (ôs′vē-yȧ)	162	56.00N	28.08E
Oswaldtwistle, Eng., U.K. (ŏz-wăld-twĭs′'l)	144a	53.44N	2.23W
Oswegatchie, r., N.Y., U.S. (ŏs-wē-găch′ĭ)	99	44.15N	75.20W
Oswego, Ks., U.S. (ŏs-wē′gō)	111	37.10N	95.08W
Oswego, N.Y., U.S.	97	43.25N	76.30W
Oświęcim, Pol. (ôsh-vyăɴ′tsyĭm)	155	50.02N	19.17E
Otaru, Japan (ō′tȧ-rō)	189	43.07N	141.00E
Otavalo, Ec. (ōtä-vä′lō)	130	0.14N	78.16W
Otavi, Nmb. (ô-tä′vē)	212	19.35S	17.20E
Otay, Ca., U.S. (ō′tā)	108a	32.36N	117.04W
Otepää, Est.	153	58.03N	26.30E
Otford, Eng., U.K.	235	51.19N	0.12E
Óthris, Óros, mtn., Grc.	161	39.00N	22.15E
Oti, r., Afr.	214	9.00N	0.10E
Otish, Monts, mts., Can. (ô-tĭsh′)	85	52.15N	70.20W
Otjiwarongo, Nmb. (ŏt-jē-wȧ-rôn′gō)	212	20.20S	16.25E
Otočac, Cro. (ō′tô-chäts)	160	44.53N	15.15E
Otra, r., Nor.	152	59.13N	7.20E
Otra, r., Russia (ôt′rȧ)	172b	55.22N	38.20E
Otradnoye, Russia (ô-trȧ′d-nôyĕ)	172c	59.46N	30.50E
Otranto, Italy (ō′trän-tô) (ô-trän′tō)	161	40.07N	18.30E
Otranto, Strait of, strt., Eur.	142	40.30N	18.45E
Otsego, Mi., U.S. (ŏt-sē′gō)	98	42.25N	85.45W
Otsu, Japan (ō′tsō)	194	35.00N	135.54E
Otta, l., Nor. (ôt′tȧ)	152	61.53N	8.40E
Ottakring, neigh., Aus.	239e	48.12N	16.19E
Ottavia, neigh., Italy	239c	41.58N	12.24E
Ottawa, Can. (ŏt′ȧ-wȧ)	85	45.25N	75.43W
Ottawa, Il., U.S.	98	41.20N	88.50W
Ottawa, Ks., U.S.	111	38.37N	95.16W
Ottawa, Oh., U.S.	98	41.00N	84.00W
Ottawa, r., Can.	85	46.05N	77.20W
Otter Creek, r., Ut., U.S. (ŏt′ēr)	109	38.20N	111.55W
Otter Creek, r., Vt., U.S.	99	44.05N	73.15W
Otter Point, c., Can.	106a	48.21N	123.50W
Ottershaw, Eng., U.K.	235	51.22N	0.32W
Otter Tail, l., Mn., U.S.	102	46.21N	95.52W
Otterville, Il., U.S. (ŏt′ēr-vĭl)	107e	39.03N	90.24W
Ottery, S. Afr. (ŏt′ēr-ĭ)	212a	34.02S	18.31E
Ottumwa, Ia., U.S. (ô-tŭm′wȧ)	97	41.00N	92.26W
Otukpa, Nig.	215	7.09N	7.41E
Otumba, Mex. (ô-tŭm′bä)	118	19.41N	98.46W
Otway, Cape, c., Austl. (ŏt′wā)	203	38.55S	153.40E
Otway, Seno, b., Chile (sĕ′nō-ō′t-wä′y)	132	53.00S	73.00W
Otwock, Pol. (ôt′vôtsk)	155	52.05N	21.18E
Ouachita, r., U.S.	97	33.25N	92.30W
Ouachita Mountains, mts., U.S. (wŏsh′ĭ-tô)	97	34.29N	95.01W
Ouagadougou, Burkina (wä′gȧ-dōō′gōō)	210	12.22N	1.31W
Ouahigouya, Burkina (wä-ē-gōō′yä)	210	13.35N	2.25W
Oualâta, Maur. (wä-lä′tä)	210	17.11N	6.50W
Ouallene, Alg. (wäl-lĕn′)	210	24.43N	1.15E
Ouanaminthe, Haiti	123	19.35N	71.45W
Ouarane, reg., Maur.	210	20.44N	10.27W
Ouarkoye, Burkina	214	12.05N	3.40W
Ouassel, r., Alg.	159	35.30N	1.55E
Oubangui (Ubangi), r., Afr. (ōō-băŋ′gē)	216	4.30N	20.35E
Oude Rijn, r., Neth.	145a	52.09N	4.33E
Oudewater, Neth.	145a	52.01N	4.52E
Oud-Gastel, Neth.	145a	51.35N	4.27E
Oudtshoorn, S. Afr. (outs′hōrn)	212	33.33S	23.36E
Oued Rhiou, Alg.	159	35.55N	0.57E
Oued Tlelat, Alg.	159	35.33N	0.28W
Oued-Zem, Mor. (wĕd-zĕm′)	210	33.05N	5.49W
Ouessant, Island d′, i., Fr. (ēl-dwĕ-säɴ′)	147	48.28N	5.00W
Ouesso, Congo	211	1.37N	16.04E
Ouest, Point, c., Haiti	123	19.00N	73.25W
Ouezzane, Mor. (wĕ-zan′)	210	34.48N	5.40W
Ouham, r., Afr.	215	8.30N	17.50E
Ouidah, Benin (wē-dä′)	210	6.25N	2.05E
Oujda, Mor.	210	34.41N	1.45W
Oulins, Fr. (ōō-lăɴ′)	157b	48.52N	1.27E
Oullins, Fr. (ōō-lăɴ′)	156	45.44N	4.46E
Oulu, Fin. (ō′lō)	142	64.58N	25.43E
Oulujärvi, l., Fin.	146	64.20N	25.48E
Oum Chalouba, Chad (ōōm shä-lōō′bä)	211	15.48N	20.30E
Oum Hadjer, Chad	215	13.18N	19.41E
Ounas, r., Fin. (ō′nȧs)	146	67.46N	24.40E
Oundle, Eng., U.K. (ōn′d'l)	144a	52.28N	0.28W
Ounianga Kébir, Chad (ōō-nē-äŋ′gȧ kē-bēr′)	211	19.04N	20.22E
Ouray, Co., U.S. (ōō-rā′)	110	38.00N	107.40W
Ourinhos, Braz. (ôô-rē′nyôs)	131	23.04S	49.45W
Ourique, Port. (ō-rē′kĕ)	158	37.39N	8.10W
Ouro Fino, Braz. (ōū-rô-fē′nō)	129a	22.18S	46.21W
Ouro Prêto, Braz. (ō′rò prā′tò)	132	20.24S	43.30W
Outardes, Rivière aux, r., Can.	85	50.53N	68.50W
Outer, i., Wi., U.S. (out′ēr)	103	47.03N	90.20W
Outer Brass, i., V.I.U.S. (bräs)	117c	18.24N	64.58W
Outer Hebrides, is., Scot., U.K.	150	57.20N	7.50W
Outjo, Nmb. (ōt′yō)	212	20.05S	17.10E
Outlook, Can.	88	51.31N	107.05W
Outremont, Can. (ōō-trē-môɴ′)	83a	45.31N	73.36W
Ouvéa, i., N. Cal.	203	20.43S	166.48E
Ouyen, Austl. (ōō-ĕn)	204	35.05S	142.10E
Ovalle, Chile (ō-väl′yä)	132	30.43S	71.16W
Ovando, Bahía de, b., Cuba (bä-ē′ä-dē-ô-vä′n-dō)	123	20.10N	74.05W
Ovar, Port. (ô-vär′)	158	40.52N	8.38W
Overbrook, neigh., Pa., U.S.	229b	39.58N	75.16W
Overbrook, neigh., Pa., U.S.	230b	40.24N	79.59W
Overijse, Bel.	145a	50.46N	4.32E
Overland, Mo., U.S. (ō-vēr-lănd)	107e	38.42N	90.22W
Overland Park, Ks., U.S.	107f	38.59N	94.40W
Overlea, Md., U.S. (ō′vēr-lā)(ō′vēr-lē)	100e	39.21N	76.31W
Övertornea, Swe.	146	66.19N	23.31E
Ovidiopol′, Ukr.	163	46.15N	30.28E
Oviedo, Dom. Rep. (ō-vyĕ′dō)	123	17.50N	71.25W
Oviedo, Spain (ō-vē-ā′dhō)	142	43.22N	5.50W
Ovrych, Ukr.	163	51.19N	28.51E
Owada, Japan (ō′wä-dȧ)	195a	35.49N	139.33E
Owambo, hist. reg., Nmb.	212	18.10S	15.00E
Owando, Congo	212	0.29S	15.55E
Owasco, l., N.Y., U.S. (ō-wăsk′kō)	99	42.50N	76.30W
Owase, Japan (ō′wä-shē)	195	34.03N	136.12E
Owego, N.Y., U.S. (ō-wē′gō)	99	42.05N	76.15W
Owen, Wi., U.S. (ō′ĕn)	103	44.56N	90.35W
Owensboro, Ky., U.S. (ō′ĕnz-bŭr-ô)	97	37.45N	87.05W
Owens Lake, l., Ca., U.S.	108	37.13N	118.20W
Owen Sound, Can. (ō′ĕn)	85	44.30N	80.55W
Owen Stanley Range, mts., Pap. N. Gui. (stăn′lē)	197	9.00S	147.30E
Owensville, In., U.S. (ō′ĕnz-vĭl)	98	38.15N	87.40W
Owensville, Mo., U.S.	111	38.20N	91.29W
Owensville, Oh., U.S.	101f	39.08N	84.07W
Owenton, Ky., U.S. (ō′ĕn-tŭn)	98	38.35N	84.55W
Owerri, Nig. (ô-wĕr′ē)	210	5.26N	7.04E
Owings Mill, Md., U.S. (ōwĭngz mĭl)	100e	39.25N	76.50W
Owl Creek, r., Wy., U.S. (oul)	105	43.45N	108.46W
Owo, Nig.	215	7.15N	5.37E

ng-sing; ŋ-baŋk; ɴ-nasalized n; nŏd; cŏmmit; ōld; ôbey; ôrder; oi-boil; fōōd; ŏŏ-as oo in foot; ou-out; s-soft; sh-dish; th-thin; pūre; ûnite; ûrn; stŭd; circŭs; ü-as in French tu; ′-indeterminate vowel.

330 Oworonsoki–Paracel Islands

PLACE (Pronunciation)	PAGE	Lat. °′	Long. °′
Oworonsoki, Nig.	244d	6.33N	3.24E
Owosso, Mi., U.S. (ȯ-wŏs′ō)	98	43.00N	84.15W
Owyhee, r., U.S.	96	43.04N	117.45W
Owyhee, Lake, res., Or., U.S.	96	43.27N	117.30W
Owyhee, South Fork, r., Id., U.S.	104	42.07N	116.43W
Owyhee Mountains, mts., Id., U.S. (ȯ-wī′hė)	96	43.15N	116.48W
Oxbow, Can.	89	49.12N	102.11W
Oxchuc, Mex. (ȯs-cho͞ok′)	119	16.47N	92.24W
Oxford, Can. (ŏks′fẽrd)	92	45.44N	63.52W
Oxford, Eng., U.K.	147	51.43N	1.16W
Oxford, Al., U.S. (ŏks′fẽrd)	115	33.38N	80.46W
Oxford, Ma., U.S.	93a	42.07N	71.52W
Oxford, Mi., U.S.	98	42.50N	83.15W
Oxford, Ms., U.S.	114	34.22N	89.30W
Oxford, N.C., U.S.	115	36.17N	78.35W
Oxford, Oh., U.S.	98	39.30N	84.45W
Oxford Falls, Austl.	243a	33.44S	151.15E
Oxford Lake, l., Can.	89	54.51N	95.37W
Oxfordshire, co., Eng., U.K.	144b	51.36N	1.30W
Oxkutzcab, Mex. (ȯx-ko͞o′tz-käb)	120a	20.18N	89.22W
Oxmoor, Al., U.S. (ŏks′mȯr)	100h	33.25N	86.52W
Oxnard, Ca., U.S. (ŏks′närd)	108	34.08N	119.12W
Oxon Hill, Md., U.S. (ōks′ōn hĭl)	100e	38.48N	77.00W
Oxshott, Eng., U.K.	235	51.20N	0.21W
Oyama, Japan	242a	35.36N	139.22E
Oyapock, r., S.A. (ō-yȧ-pŏk′)	131	2.45N	52.15W
Oyem, Gabon	210	1.37N	11.35E
Øyeren, l., Nor. (ûĭĕrĕn)	152	59.50N	11.25E
Oymyakon, Russia (oi-myŭ-kôn′)	165	63.14N	142.58E
Oyo, Nig. (ō′yō)	210	7.51N	3.56E
Oyodo, neigh., Japan	242b	34.43N	135.30E
Oyonnax, Fr. (ȯ-yȯ-nȧks′)	157	46.16N	5.40E
Oyster Bay, N.Y., U.S.	100a	40.52N	73.32W
Oyster Bay Cove, N.Y., U.S.	228	40.52N	73.31W
Oyster Bayou, Tx., U.S.	113a	29.41N	94.33W
Oyster Creek, r., Tx., U.S. (ois′tẽr)	113a	29.13N	95.29W
Oyyl, r., Kaz.	170	49.30N	55.10E
Ozama, r., Dom. Rep. (ȯ-zä′mä)	123	18.45N	69.55W
Ozamiz, Phil. (ȯ-zä′mėz)	197	8.06N	123.43E
Ozark, Al., U.S. (ō′zärk)	114	31.28N	85.28W
Ozark, Ar., U.S.	111	35.29N	93.49W
Ozark Plateau, plat., U.S.	97	36.37N	93.56W
Ozarks, Lake of the, l., Mo., U.S. (ō′zärksz)	97	38.06N	93.26W
Ozëry, Russia (ȯ-zyô′rė)	162	54.53N	38.31E
Ozieri, Italy	148	40.38N	8.53E
Ozoir-la-Ferrière, Fr.	237c	48.46N	2.40E
Ozone Park, neigh., N.Y., U.S.	228	40.40N	73.51W
Ozorków, Pol. (ȯ-zȯr′kȯf)	155	51.58N	19.20E
Ozuluama, Mex.	119	21.34N	97.52W
Ozumba, Mex.	119a	19.02N	98.48W
Ozurgeti, Geor.	168	41.56N	42.00E

P

PLACE (Pronunciation)	PAGE	Lat. °′	Long. °′
Paarl, S. Afr. (pärl)	212	33.45S	18.55E
Paarlshoop, neigh., S. Afr.	244b	26.13S	27.59E
Paauilo, Hi., U.S. (pä-ä-o͞o′ė-lō)	94a	20.03N	155.25W
Pabianice, Pol. (pä-byȧ-nē′tsĕ)	155	51.40N	19.29E
Pacaás Novos, Massiço de, mts., Braz.	130	11.03S	64.02W
Pacaraima, Serra, mts., S.A. (sĕr′rȧ pä-kä-rä-ē′mȧ)	130	3.45N	62.30W
Pacasmayo, Peru (pä-käs-mä′yō)	130	7.24S	79.30W
Pachuca, Mex. (pä-cho͞o′kä)	116	20.07N	98.43W
Pacific, Wa., U.S. (pȧ-sĭf′ĭk)	106a	47.16N	122.15W
Pacifica, Ca., U.S. (pȧ-sĭf′ĭ-kä)	106b	37.38N	122.29W
Pacific Beach, Ca., U.S.	108a	32.47N	117.22W
Pacific Grove, Ca., U.S.	108	36.37N	121.54W
Pacific Ocean, o.	2	0.00	170.00W
Pacific Palisades, neigh., Ca., U.S.	232	34.03N	118.32W
Pacific Ranges, mts., Can.	86	51.00N	125.30W
Pacific Rim National Park, rec., Can.	86	49.00N	126.00W
Paço de Arcos, Port.	238d	38.42N	9.17W
Pacolet, r., S.C., U.S. (pā′cō-lĕt)	115	34.55N	81.49W
Pacy-sur-Eure, Fr. (pä-sē-sür-ûr′)	157b	49.01N	1.24E
Padang, Indon. (pä-däng′)	196	1.01S	100.28E
Padang, i., Indon.	181b	1.12N	102.21E
Padang Endau, Malay.	181b	2.39N	103.38E
Paddington, neigh., Eng., U.K.	235	51.31N	0.10W
Paden City, W.V., U.S. (pā′dĕn)	98	39.30N	80.55W
Paderborn, Ger. (pä-dĕr-bȯrn′)	154	51.43N	8.46E
Paderno Dugnano, Italy	238c	45.34N	9.10E
Padibe, Ug.	217	3.28N	32.50E
Padiham, Eng., U.K. (păd′ĭ-hăm)	144a	53.48N	2.19W
Padilla, Mex. (pä-dēl′yä)	118	24.00N	98.45W
Padilla Bay, b., Wa., U.S. (pä-dĕl′lȧ)	106a	48.31N	122.34W
Padova, Italy (pä′dȯ-vä)(păd′û-ȧ)	148	45.24N	11.53E
Padre Island, i., Tx., U.S. (pä′drā)	113	27.09N	97.15W
Padre Miguel, neigh., Braz.	234c	22.53S	43.26W
Padua *see* Padova, Italy	148	45.24N	11.53E
Paducah, Ky., U.S.	97	37.05N	88.36W
Paducah, Tx., U.S.	110	34.01N	100.18W
Paektu-san, mtn., Asia (pâk′to͞o-sän′)	194	42.00N	128.03E
Pag, i., Yugo. (päg)	160	44.30N	14.48E
Pagai Selatan, Pulau, i., Indon.	196	2.48S	100.22E
Pagai Utara, Pulau, i., Indon.	196	2.45S	100.02E
Pagasitikós Kólpos, b., Grc.	161	39.15N	23.00E
Page, Az., U.S.	109	36.57N	111.27W
Pago Pago, Am. Sam.	198a	14.16S	170.42W
Pagosa Springs, Co., U.S. (pȧ-gō′sȧ)	110	37.15N	107.05W
Pagote, India	240e	18.54N	72.59E
Pahala, Hi., U.S. (pä-hä′lä)	94a	19.11N	155.28W
Pahang, state, Malay.	181b	3.02N	102.57E
Pahang, r., Malay.	196	3.39N	102.41E
Pahokee, Fl., U.S. (pȧ-hō′kē)	115a	26.45N	80.40W
Paide, Est. (pī′dĕ)	153	58.54N	25.30E
Päijänne, l., Fin. (pĕ′ē-yĕn-nĕ)	146	61.38N	25.05E
Pailolo Channel, strt., Hi., U.S. (pä-ė-lō′lō)	94a	21.05N	156.41W
Paine, Chile (pī′nĕ)	129b	33.49S	70.44W
Painesville, Oh., U.S. (pānz′vĭl)	98	41.40N	81.15W
Painted Desert, des., Az., U.S. (pānt′ēd)	110	36.15N	111.35W
Painted Rock Reservoir, res., Az., U.S.	109	33.00N	113.05W
Paintsville, Ky., U.S. (pānts′vĭl)	98	37.50N	82.50W
Paisley, Austl.	243b	37.51S	144.51E
Paisley, Scot., U.K. (pāz′lĭ)	146	55.50N	4.30W
Paita, Peru (pä-ē′tä)	130	5.11S	81.12W
Pai T'ou Shan, mts., N. Kor.	189	40.30N	127.20E
Paiute Indian Reservation, I.R., Ut., U.S.	109	38.17N	113.50W
Pajápan, Mex. (pä-hä′pän)	119	18.16N	94.41W
Pakanbaru, Indon.	196	0.43N	101.15E
Pakhra, r., Russia (päκ′rá)	172b	55.29N	37.51E
Pakistan, nation, Asia	183	28.00N	67.30E
Pakokku, Myanmar (pȧ-kŏk′kȯ)	188	21.29N	95.00E
Paks, Hung. (pôksh)	155	46.38N	18.53E
Pala, Chad	215	9.22N	14.54E
Palacios, Tx., U.S. (pä-lä′syōs)	113	28.42N	96.12W
Palagruža, Otoci, is., Cro.	160	42.20N	16.23E
Palaión Fáliron, Grc.	239d	37.55N	23.41E
Palaiseau, Fr. (pȧ-lĕ-zō′)	157b	48.44N	2.16E
Palana, Russia	165	59.07N	159.58E
Palanan Bay, b., Phil. (pä-lä′nän)	197a	17.14N	122.35E
Palanan Point, c., Phil.	197a	17.12N	122.40E
Pālanpur, India (pä′lŭn-po͞or)	183	24.08N	73.29E
Palapye, Bots. (pȧ-läp′yĕ)	212	22.34S	27.28E
Palatine, Il., U.S. (păl′ȧ-tīn)	101a	42.07N	88.03W
Palatka, Fl., U.S. (pȧ-lăt′kȧ)	115	29.39N	81.40W
Palau (Belau), dep., Oc. (pä-lä′ȯ)	3	7.15N	134.30E
Palauig, Phil. (pȧ-lou′ėg)	197a	15.27N	119.54E
Palawan, i., Phil. (pä-lä′wȧn)	196	9.50N	117.38E
Pālayankottai, India	187	8.50N	77.50E
Paldiski, Est. (päl′dĭ-skĭ)	153	59.22N	24.04E
Palembang, Indon. (pä-lĕm-bäng′)	196	2.57S	104.40E
Palencia, Guat. (pä-lĕn′sė-ȧ)	120	14.40N	90.22W
Palencia, Spain (pä-lĕ′n-syä)	148	42.02N	4.32W
Palenque, Mex. (pä-lĕŋ′kȧ)	119	17.34N	91.58W
Palenque, Punta, c., Dom. Rep. (po͞o′n-tä)	123	18.10N	70.10W
Palermo, Col. (pä-lĕr′mô)	130a	2.53N	75.26W
Palermo, Italy	142	38.08N	13.24E
Palermo, neigh., Arg.	233d	34.35S	58.25W
Palestine, Tx., U.S.	97	31.46N	95.38W
Palestine, hist. reg., Asia (păl′ĕs-tīn)	181a	31.33N	35.00E
Paletwa, Myanmar (pŭ-lĕt′wä)	183	21.19N	92.52E
Palghāt, India	187	10.49N	76.40E
Pāli, India	186	25.53N	73.18E
Palín, Guat. (pä-lēn′)	120	14.42N	90.42W
Palisades Park, N.J., U.S.	228	40.51N	74.00W
Palizada, Mex. (pä-lė-zä′dä)	119	18.17N	92.04W
Palk Strait, strt., Asia (pôk)	183	10.00N	79.23E
Palma, Braz. (päl′mä)	129a	21.23S	42.18W
Palma, Spain	142	39.35N	2.38E
Palma, Bahía de, b., Spain	159	39.24N	2.37E
Palma del Río, Spain	158	37.43N	5.19W
Palmar de Cariaco, Ven.	234a	10.34N	66.55W
Palmares, Braz. (päl-mȧ′rĕs)	131	8.46S	35.28W
Palmas, Braz.	131	10.08S	48.18W
Palmas, Braz. (päl′mäs)	132	26.20S	51.56W
Palmas, Cape, c., Lib.	210	4.22N	7.44W
Palma Soriano, Cuba (sȯ-ré-ä′nō)	122	20.15N	76.00W
Palm Beach, Fl., U.S. (päm bēch′)	115a	26.43N	80.03W
Palmeira dos Índios, Braz. (pä-mā′rä-dȯs-ē′n-dyȯs)	131	9.26S	36.33W
Palmeirinhas, Ponta das, c., Ang.	216	9.05S	13.00E
Palmela, Port. (päl-mā′lä)	158	38.34N	8.54W
Palmer, Ak., U.S. (päm′ẽr)	95	61.38N	149.15W
Palmer, Wa., U.S.	106a	47.19N	121.53W
Palmer Park, Md., U.S.	229d	38.55N	76.52W
Palmerston North, N.Z. (päm′ẽr-stŭn)	203a	40.20S	175.35E
Palmerville, Austl. (päm′ẽr-vĭl)	203	16.08S	144.15E
Palmetto, Fl., U.S. (pȧl-mĕt′ȯ)	115a	27.32N	82.34W
Palmetto Point, c., Bah.	123	21.15N	73.25W
Palmi, Italy (päl′mē)	160	38.21N	15.54E
Palmira, Col. (päl-mē′rä)	130	3.33N	76.17W
Palmira, Cuba	122	22.15N	80.25W
Palmyra, Mo., U.S. (păl-mī′rȧ)	111	39.45N	91.32W
Palmyra, N.J., U.S.	100f	40.01N	75.00W
Palmyra, i., Oc.	2	6.00N	162.20W
Palmyra, hist., Syria	182	34.25N	38.28E
Palmyras Point, c., India	186	20.42N	87.45E
Palo Alto, Ca., U.S. (pä′lō äl′tō)	106b	37.27N	122.09W
Paloduro Creek, r., Tx., U.S. (pā-lȯ-do͞o′rȯ)	110	36.16N	101.12W
Paloh, Malay.	181b	2.11N	103.12E
Paloma, l., Mex. (pä-lō′mä)	112	26.53N	104.02W
Palomar Park, Ca., U.S.	231b	37.29N	122.16W
Palomo, Cerro el, mtn., Chile (sĕ′r-rȯ-ĕl-pä-lô′mȯ)	129b	34.36S	70.20W
Palos, Cabo de, c., Spain (kȧ′bȯ-dĕ-pä′lȯs)	148	39.38N	0.43W
Palos Heights, Il., U.S.	231a	41.40N	87.48W
Palos Hills, Il., U.S.	231a	41.41N	87.49W
Palos Park, Il., U.S.	231a	41.40N	87.50W
Palos Verdes Estates, Ca., U.S. (pă′lŭs vûr′dĭs)	107a	33.48N	118.24W
Palouse, Wa., U.S. (pȧ-lo͞oz′)	104	46.54N	117.04W
Palouse, r., Wa., U.S.	104	47.02N	117.35W
Palu, Tur. (pä-loo′)	167	38.55N	40.10E
Paluan, Phil. (pä-lo͞o′än)	197a	13.25N	120.29E
Pamiers, Fr. (pȧ-myā′)	147	43.07N	1.34E
Pamirs, mts., Asia	183	38.14N	72.27E
Pamlico, r., N.C., U.S. (păm′lĭ-kō)	115	35.25N	76.59W
Pamlico Sound, strt., N.C., U.S.	97	35.10N	76.10W
Pampa, Tx., U.S. (păm′pȧ)	96	35.32N	100.56W
Pampa de Castillo, pl., Arg. (pä′m-pä-dĕ-käs-tė′l-yȯ)	132	45.30S	67.30W
Pampana, r., S.L.	214	8.35N	11.55W
Pampanga, r., Phil. (päm-päŋ′gä)	197a	15.20N	120.48E
Pampas, reg., Arg. (päm′päs)	132	37.00S	64.30W
Pampilhosa do Botão, Port. (päm-pė-lyō′sȧ-dȯ-bō-toun)	158	40.21N	8.32W
Pamplona, Col. (päm-plō′nä)	130	7.19N	72.41W
Pamplona, Spain (päm-plȯ′nä)	148	42.49N	1.39W
Pamunkey, r., Va., U.S. (pȧ-mŭŋ′kĭ)	99	37.40N	77.20W
Pana, Il., U.S. (pā′nȧ)	98	39.25N	89.05W
Panagyurishte, Bul. (pȧ-nȧ-gyo͞o′rėsh-tĕ)	161	42.30N	24.11E
Panaji (Panjim), India	183	15.33N	73.52E
Panamá, Pan.	117	8.58N	79.32W
Panama, nation, N.A.	117	9.00N	80.00W
Panamá, Istmo de, isth., Pan.	117	9.00N	80.00W
Panama Canal, can., Pan.	116a	9.20N	79.55W
Panama City, Fl., U.S. (păn-ȧ mä′ sĭ′tĭ)	114	30.08N	85.39W
Panamint Range, mts., Ca., U.S. (păn-ȧ-mĭnt′)	108	36.40N	117.30W
Panarea, i., Italy (pä-nä′rė-a)	160	38.37N	15.05E
Panaro, r., Italy (pä-nä′rȯ)	160	44.47N	11.06E
Panay, i., Phil. (pä-nī′)	196	11.15N	121.38E
Pančevo, Yugo. (pȧn′chĕ-vȯ)	149	44.52N	20.42E
Pānchghara, India	240a	22.44N	88.16E
Panch'iao, Tai.	241d	25.01N	121.27E
Panchor, Malay.	181b	2.11N	102.43E
Pānchur, India	186a	22.31N	88.17E
Panda, Zaire (pän′dä′)	212	10.59S	27.24E
Pan de Guajaibon, mtn., Cuba (pän dā gwä-jȧ-bōn′)	122	22.50N	83.20W
Panevėžys, Lith. (pä′nyĕ-vāzh′ēs)	166	55.44N	24.21E
Panfilov, Kaz. (pŭn-fē′lŏf)	169	44.12N	79.58E
Panga, Zaire (päŋ′gä)	211	1.51N	26.25E
Pangani, Tan. (pän-gä′nē)	213	5.28S	38.58E
Pangani, r., Tan.	217	4.40S	37.45E
Pangkalpinang, Indon. (päng-käl′pė-näng′)	196	2.11S	106.04E
Pangnirtung, Can.	85	66.08N	65.26W
Panguitch, Ut., U.S. (pän′gwĭch)	109	37.50N	112.30W
Panié, Mont, mtn., N. Cal.	198f	20.36S	164.46E
Pānihāti, India	186a	22.42N	88.23E
Panimávida, Chile (pä-nē-mȧ′vē-dä)	129b	35.44S	71.26W
Panje, India	240e	18.54N	72.57E
Pankow, neigh., Ger.	238a	52.34N	13.24E
Panshi, China (pän-shē)	192	42.50N	126.48E
Pantar, Pulau, i., Indon. (pän′tär)	197	8.40N	123.45E
Pantelleria, i., Italy (pän-tĕl-lȧ-rē′ä)	148	36.43N	11.59E
Pantepec, Mex. (pän-tȧ-pĕk′)	119	17.11N	93.04W
Pantheon, hist., Italy	239c	41.55N	12.29E
Pantin, Fr.	237c	48.54N	2.24E
Pantitlán, Mex.	233a	19.25N	99.05W
Panuco, Mex. (pä′no͞o-kȯ)	118	22.04N	98.11W
Pánuco, Mex. (pä′no͞o-kȯ)	118	23.25N	105.55W
Panuco, r., Mex.	116	21.59N	98.20W
Pánuco de Coronado, Mex. (pä′no͞o-kȯ dā kō-rȯ-nä′dhō)	112	24.33N	104.20W
Panvel, India	187b	18.59N	73.06E
Panyu, China (pä-yo͞o)	191a	22.56N	113.22E
Panzós, Guat. (pä-zós′)	120	15.26N	89.40W
Pao, r., Ven. (pȧ′ō)	131b	9.52N	67.57W
Paola, Ks., U.S. (pȧ-ō′lȧ)	111	38.34N	94.51W
Paoli, In., U.S. (pȧ-ō′lī)	98	38.35N	86.30W
Paoli, Pa., U.S.	100f	40.03N	75.29W
Paonia, Co., U.S. (pā-ō′nyȧ)	109	38.50N	107.40W
Pápa, Hung. (pä′pô)	149	47.18N	17.27E
Papagayo, r., Mex. (pä-pä-gä′yō)	118	16.52N	99.41W
Papagayo, Golfo del, b., C.R. (gȯl-fô-dĕl-pä-pä-gȧ′yō)	120	10.44N	85.56W
Papagayo, Laguna, l., Mex. (lä-ȯ-nä)	118	16.44N	99.44W
Papago Indian Reservation, I.R., Az., U.S. (pä′pä′gō)	109	32.33N	112.12W
Papantla de Olarte, Mex. (pä-pän′tlä dā-ô-lä′r-tĕ)	116	20.30N	97.15W
Papatoapan, r., Mex. (pä-pä-tô-ā-pȧ′n)	119	18.00N	96.22W
Papelón, Ven.	234a	10.27N	66.47W
Papenburg, Ger. (päp′ĕn-bȯrgh)	154	53.05N	7.23E
Papinas, Arg. (pä-pė′näs)	129c	35.30S	57.19W
Papineauville, Can. (pä-pē-nō′vēl)	83c	45.38N	75.01W
Papua, Gulf of, b., Pap. N. Gui. (păp-o͞o-ȧ)	197	8.20S	144.45E
Papua New Guinea, nation, Oc. (păp-o͞o-ȧ)(gĭne)	197	7.00S	142.15E
Papudo, Chile (pä-po͞o′dȯ)	129b	32.30S	71.25W
Paquequer Pequeno, Braz. (pä-kĕ-kĕ′r-pĕ-kĕ′nȯ)	132b	22.19S	43.02W
Para, r., Russia	162	53.45N	40.58E
Paracale, Phil. (pä-rä-kä′lȧ)	197a	14.17N	122.47E
Paracambi, Braz.	132b	22.36S	43.43W
Paracatu, Braz. (pä-rä-kä-to͞o′)	131	17.17S	46.43W
Paracel Islands, is., Asia	196	16.40N	113.00E

ăt; fināl; rāte; senȧte; ärm; ȧsk; sofȧ; fâre; ch-choose; dh-as th in other; bē; ėvent; bĕt; recĕnt; cratẽr; g-gō; gh-guttural g; bĭt; ĭ-short neutral; rīde; κ-guttural k as ch in German ich;

PRONOUNCING INDEX   Paraćin–Peebles 331

PLACE (Pronunciation)	PAGE	Lat. °′	Long. °′
Paraćin, Yugo. (pá'rä-chên)	149	43.51N	21.26E
Para de Minas, Braz. (pä-rä-dē-mē'näs)	131	19.52S	44.37W
Paradise, i., Bah.	122	25.05N	77.20W
Paradise Valley, Nv., U.S. (păr'á-dīs)	104	41.28N	117.32W
Parados, Cerro de los, mtn., Col. (sĕ'r-rô-dĕ-lôs-pä-rä'dôs)	130a	5.44N	75.13W
Paragould, Ar., U.S. (păr'á-gōōld)	111	36.03N	90.29W
Paraguaçu, r., Braz. (pä-rä-gwä-zōō')	131	12.25S	39.46W
Paraguay, nation, S.A. (păr'á-gwā)	132	24.00S	57.00W
Paraguay, Río, r., S.A. (rē'ō-pä-rä-gwä'y)	132	21.12S	57.31W
Paraíba, state, Braz. (pä-rä-ē'bä)	131	7.11S	37.05W
Paraíba, r., Braz.	129a	23.02S	45.43W
Paraíba do Sul, Braz. (dô-sōō'l)	129a	22.10S	43.18W
Paraibuna, Braz. (pä-rä-ē-bōō'nä)	129a	23.23S	45.38W
Paraíso, C.R.	121	9.50N	83.53W
Paraíso, Mex.	119	18.24N	93.11W
Paraiso, Pan. (pä-rä-ē'sō)	116a	9.02N	79.38W
Paraisópolis, Braz. (pä-rä-ē-sô'pō-lēs)	129a	22.35S	45.45W
Paraitinga, r., Braz. (pä-rä-ē-tē'n-gä)	129a	23.15S	45.24W
Parakou, Benin (pá-rá-kōō')	210	9.21N	2.37E
Paramaribo, Sur. (pá-rá-má'rê-bō)	131	5.50N	55.15W
Paramatta, Austl. (păr-á-măt'á)	201b	33.49S	150.59E
Paramillo, mtn., Col. (pä-rä-mê'l-yō)	130a	7.06N	75.55W
Paramount, Ca., U.S.	232	33.53N	118.09W
Paramus, N.J., U.S.	100a	40.56N	74.04W
Paran, r., Asia	181a	30.05N	34.50E
Paraná, Arg.	132	31.44S	60.32W
Paraná, Río, r., S.A.	132	24.00S	54.00W
Paranaíba, Braz. (pä-rä-ná-ē'bá)	131	19.43S	51.13W
Paranaíba, r., Braz.	131	18.58S	50.44W
Paraná Ibicuy, r., Arg.	129c	33.27S	59.26W
Paranam, Sur.	131	5.39N	55.13W
Paranápanema, r., Braz. (pä-rä'ná'pä-nĕ-mä)	131	22.28S	52.15W
Parañaque, Phil.	241g	14.30N	120.59E
Paraopeda, r., Braz. (pä-rä-o-pĕ'dä)	129a	20.09S	44.14W
Parapara, Ven. (pä-rä-pä-rä)	131b	9.44N	67.17W
Parati, Braz. (pä-rätē)	129a	23.14S	44.43W
Paray-le-Monial, Fr. (pá-rĕ'lē-mô-nyäl')	156	46.27N	4.14E
Pārbati, r., India	186	24.50N	76.44E
Parchim, Ger. (par'kĭm)	154	53.25N	11.52E
Parczew, Pol. (pär'chĕf)	155	51.38N	22.53E
Pardo, r., Braz.	129a	21.32S	46.40W
Pardo, r., Braz. (pär'dō)	131	15.25S	39.40W
Pardubice, Czech Rep. (pär'dò-bĭt-sĕ)	154	50.02N	15.47E
Parecis, Serra dos, mts., Braz. (sĕr'rá dōs pä-rá-sēzh')	131	13.45S	59.28W
Paredes de Nava, Spain (pä-rā'dās dä nä'vä)	158	42.10N	4.41W
Paredón, Mex.	112	25.56N	100.58W
Parent, Can.	85	47.59N	74.30W
Parent, Lac, l., Can.	91	48.40N	77.00W
Parepare, Indon.	196	4.01S	119.38E
Pargolovo, Russia (pár-gô'lô vô)	172c	60.04N	30.18E
Pari, neigh., Braz.	234d	23.32S	46.37W
Paria, r., Az., U.S.	109	37.07N	111.51W
Paria, Golfo de, b. (gôl-fô-dĕ-br-pä-rê-ä)	130	10.33N	62.14W
Paricutín, Volcán, vol., Mex.	118	19.27N	102.14W
Parida, Río de la, r., Mex. (rê'ō-dĕ-lä-pä-rē'dä)	112	26.23N	104.40W
Parima, Serra, mts., S.A. (sĕr'rá pä-rē'má)	130	3.45N	64.00W
Pariñas, Punta, c., Peru (pōō'n-tä-pä-rē'n-yäs)	130	4.30S	81.23W
Parintins, Braz. (pä-rīn-tĭɴzh')	131	2.34S	56.30W
Paris, Can.	91	43.15N	80.23W
Paris, Fr. (pá-rē')	142	48.51N	2.20E
Paris, Ar., U.S. (păr'ĭs)	111	35.17N	93.43W
Paris, Il., U.S.	98	39.35N	87.40W
Paris, Ky., U.S.	98	38.15N	84.15W
Paris, Mo., U.S.	111	39.27N	91.59W
Paris, Tn., U.S.	114	36.16N	88.20W
Paris, Tx., U.S.	97	33.39N	95.33W
Paris-le-Bourget, Aéroport de, arpt., Fr.	237c	48.57N	2.25E
Paris-Orly, Aéroport de, arpt., Fr.	237c	48.45N	2.25E
Parita, Golfo de, b., Pan. (gôl-fô-dĕ-pä-rē'tä)	121	8.06N	80.10W
Park City, Ut., U.S.	105	40.39N	111.33W
Parkdene, S. Afr.	244b	26.14S	28.16E
Parker, S.D., U.S. (pär'kẽr)	102	43.24N	97.10W
Parker Dam, dam, U.S.	96	34.20N	114.00W
Parkersburg, W.V., U.S. (pär'kẽrz-bûrg)	97	39.15N	81.35W
Parkes, Austl. (pärks)	204	33.10S	148.10E
Park Falls, Wi., U.S. (pärk)	103	45.55N	90.29W
Park Forest, Il., U.S.	101a	41.29N	87.41W
Parkgate, Eng., U.K.	237a	53.18N	3.05W
Parkhill Gardens, S. Afr.	244b	26.14S	28.11E
Parkland, Wa., U.S. (pärk'lănd)	106a	47.09N	122.26W
Parklawn, Va., U.S.	229d	38.50N	77.09W
Parklea, Austl.	243a	33.44S	150.57E
Park Orchards, Austl.	243b	37.46S	145.13E
Park Range, mts., Co., U.S.	105	40.54N	106.40W
Park Rapids, Mn., U.S.	102	46.53N	95.05W
Park Ridge, Il., U.S.	101a	42.00N	87.50W
Park Ridge Manor, Il., U.S.	231a	42.02N	87.50W
Park River, N.D., U.S.	102	48.22N	97.43W
Parkrose, Or., U.S. (pärk'rōz)	106c	45.33N	122.33W
Park Rynie, S. Afr.	213c	30.22S	30.43E
Parkston, S.D., U.S. (pärks'tŭn)	102	43.22N	97.59W
Park Town, neigh., S. Afr.	244b	26.11S	28.03E
Parktown North, neigh., S. Afr.	244b	26.09S	28.02E
Parkview, Pa., U.S.	230b	40.30N	79.56W
Parkville, Md., U.S.	100e	39.22N	76.32W
Parkville, Mo., U.S.	107f	39.12N	94.41W
Parkwood, Md., U.S.	229d	39.01N	77.05W

PLACE (Pronunciation)	PAGE	Lat. °′	Long. °′
Parla, Spain (pär'lä)	159a	40.14N	3.46W
Parliament, Houses of, pt. of i., Eng., U.K.	235	51.30N	0.07W
Parma, Italy (pär'mä)	148	44.48N	10.20E
Parma, Oh., U.S.	101d	41.23N	81.44W
Parma Heights, Oh., U.S.	101d	41.23N	81.36W
Parnaíba, Braz. (pär-nä-ē'bä)	131	3.00S	41.42W
Parnaiba, r., Braz.	131	3.57S	42.30W
Parnassós, mtn., Grc.	161	38.36N	22.35E
Parndorf, Aus.	145e	48.00N	16.52E
Pärnu, Est. (pĕr'nōō)	166	58.24N	24.29E
Pärnu, r., Est.	153	58.40N	25.05E
Pärnu Laht, b., Est. (läкt)	153	58.15N	24.17E
Paro, Bhu. (pä'rô)	186	27.30N	89.30E
Paroo, r., Austl. (pä'rōō)	203	30.00S	144.00E
Paropamisus, mts., Afg.	182	34.45N	63.58E
Páros, Grc. (pä'rôs) (pā'rŏs)	161	37.05N	25.14E
Páros, i., Grc.	149	37.11N	25.00E
Parow, S. Afr. (pä'rô)	212a	33.54S	18.36E
Parowan, Ut., U.S. (păr'ô-wăn)	109	37.50N	112.50W
Parral, Chile (pär-rä'l)	132	36.07S	71.47W
Parral, r., Mex.	112	27.25N	105.08W
Parramatta, r., Austl. (păr-á-măt'á)	201b	33.42S	150.58E
Parras, Mex. (pär-räs')	112	25.28N	102.08W
Parrita, C.R. (pär-rē'tä)	121	9.32N	84.17W
Parrsboro, Can. (pärz'bŭr-ô)	92	45.24N	64.20W
Parry, i., Can. (păr'ĭ)	91	45.15N	80.00W
Parry, Mount, mtn., Can.	86	52.53N	128.45W
Parry Islands, is., Can.	82	75.30N	110.00W
Parry Sound, Can.	85	45.20N	80.00W
Parsnip, r., Can. (pärs'nĭp)	87	54.45N	122.20W
Parsons, Ks., U.S. (pär's'nz)	97	37.20N	95.16W
Parsons, W.V., U.S.	99	39.05N	79.40W
Parthenay, Fr. (pår-t'nĕ')	156	46.39N	0.16W
Partington, Eng., U.K.	237b	53.25N	2.26W
Partinico, Italy (pär-tē'nê-kô)	160	38.02N	13.11E
Partizansk, Russia	165	43.15N	133.19E
Parys, S. Afr. (pá-rīs')	218d	26.53S	27.28E
Pasadena, Ca., U.S. (păs-á-dē'ná)	96	34.09N	118.09W
Pasadena, Md., U.S.	100e	39.06N	76.35W
Pasadena, Tx., U.S.	113a	29.43N	95.13W
Pasay, Phil.	241g	14.33N	121.00E
Pascagoula, Ms., U.S. (păs-ká-gōō'lá)	114	30.22N	88.33W
Pascagoula, r., Ms., U.S.	114	30.52N	88.48W
Paşcani, Rom. (päsh-kän')	155	47.46N	26.42E
Pasco, Wa., U.S. (păs'kō)	104	46.13N	119.04W
Pascoe Vale, Austl.	243b	37.44S	144.56E
Pascua, Isla de (Easter Island), i., Chile	225	26.50S	109.00W
Pasewalk, Ger. (pä'zē-välk)	154	53.31N	14.01E
Pashiya, Russia (pä'shĭ-yá)	172a	58.27N	58.17E
Pashkovo, Russia (pásh-kô'vô)	194	48.52N	131.09E
Pashkovskaya, Russia (pásh-kôf'ská-yá)	163	45.00N	39.04E
Pasig, Phil.	197a	14.34N	121.05E
Pasión, Río de la, r., Guat. (rē'ō-dĕ-lä-pä-syōn')	120a	16.31N	90.11W
Pasir Gudang, Malay.	240c	1.27N	103.53E
Pasir Panjang, Sing.	240c	1.17N	103.47E
Pasir Puteh, Malay.	240c	1.26N	103.56E
Paso de los Libres, Arg. (pä-sô-dĕ-lôs-lē'brĕs)	132	29.33S	57.05W
Paso de los Toros, Ur. (tŏ'rôs)	129c	32.43S	56.33W
Paso del Rey, Arg.	233d	34.39S	58.45W
Paso Robles, Ca., U.S. (pä'sō rō'blĕs)	108	35.38N	120.44W
Pasquia Hills, hills, Can. (päs'kwê-á)	89	53.13N	102.37W
Passaic, N.J., U.S. (pă-sā'ĭk)	100a	40.52N	74.08W
Passaic, r., N.J., U.S.	100a	40.42N	74.26W
Passamaquoddy Bay, b., N.A. (păs'á-má-kwŏd'ĭ)	92	45.06N	66.59W
Passa Tempo, Braz. (pä's-sä-tĕ'm-pô)	129a	20.40S	44.29W
Passau, Ger. (päsou)	147	48.34N	13.27E
Pass Christian, Ms., U.S. (pås krĭs'tyĕn)	114	30.20N	89.15W
Passero, Cape, c., Italy (päs-sĕ'rô)	142	36.34N	15.13E
Passo Fundo, Braz. (pä'sō fōn'dò)	132	28.16S	52.13W
Passos, Braz. (pä's-sōs)	131	20.45S	46.37W
Pastaza, r., S.A. (päs-tä'zä)	130	3.05S	76.18W
Pasto, Col. (päs'tô)	130	1.15N	77.19W
Pastora, Mex. (päs-tō-rä)	118	22.08N	100.04W
Pasuruan, Indon.	196	7.45S	112.50E
Pasvalys, Lith. (päs-vä-lēs')	153	56.04N	24.23E
Patagonia, reg., Arg. (păt-á-gō'nĭ-á)	132	46.45S	69.30W
Pātālganga, r., India	187b	18.52N	73.08E
Patapsco, r., Md., U.S. (pá-tăps'kō)	100e	39.12N	76.30W
Pateros, Lake, res., Wa., U.S.	104	48.05N	119.45W
Paterson, N.J., U.S. (păt'ẽr-sŭn)	100a	40.55N	74.10W
Pathein, Myanmar	183	16.46N	94.47E
Pathfinder Reservoir, res., Wy., U.S. (păth'fīn-dẽr)	105	42.22N	107.10W
Patiāla, India (pŭt-ē-ä'lŭ)	183	30.25N	76.28E
Pati do Alferes, Braz. (pä-tē-dô-ál-fĕ'rĕs)	132b	22.25S	43.25W
Patna, India (pŭt'nŭ)	183	25.33N	85.18E
Patnanongan, i., Phil. (pät-nä-nôŋ'gän)	197a	14.50N	122.25E
Patoka, r., In., U.S. (pá-tō'ká)	98	38.25N	87.25W
Patom Plateau, plat., Russia	165	59.30N	115.00E
Patos, Braz. (pä'tōzh)	131	7.03S	37.14W
Patos, Wa., U.S. (pä'tōs)	106d	48.47N	122.57W
Patos, Lagoa dos, l., Braz. (lä'gō-á dozh pä'tōzh)	132	31.15S	51.30W
Patos de Minas, Braz. (dē-mē'näzh)	131	18.39S	46.31W
Pátrai, Grc. (pä-trī') (pä-träs')	149	38.15N	21.48E
Patraïkós Kólpos, b., Grc.	161	38.16N	21.19E
Patras *see* Pátrai, Grc.	149	38.15N	21.48E
Patrocínio, Braz. (pä-trō-sē'nê-ō)	131	18.48S	46.47W
Pattani, Thai. (pät'á-nê)	196	6.56N	101.13E
Patten, Me., U.S. (păt''n)	92	45.59N	68.27W
Patterson, La., U.S. (păt'ẽr-sŭn)	113	29.41N	91.20W

PLACE (Pronunciation)	PAGE	Lat. °′	Long. °′
Patterson, i., Can.	90	48.38N	87.14W
Patton, Pa., U.S.	99	40.40N	78.45W
Patuca, r., Hond.	121	15.22N	84.31W
Patuca, Punta, c., Hond. (pōō'n-tä-pä-tōō'kä)	121	15.55N	84.05W
Patuxent, r., Md., U.S. (pá-tŭk'sĕnt)	99	39.10N	77.10W
Pátzcuaro, Mex. (päts'kwä-rô)	118	19.30N	101.36W
Pátzcuaro, Lago de, l., Mex. (lä'gô-dē)	118	19.36N	101.38W
Patzicia, Guat. (pät-zê'syä)	120	14.36N	90.57W
Patzún, Guat. (pät-zōōn')	120	14.40N	91.00W
Pau, Fr. (pō)	147	43.18N	0.23W
Pau, Gave de, r., Fr. (gäv-dē)	156	43.33N	0.51W
Paulding, Oh., U.S. (pôl'dĭng)	98	41.05N	84.35W
Paulinenaue, Ger. (pou'lē-nĕ-nou-ĕ)	145b	52.40N	12.43E
Paulistano, Braz. (pá'ō-lēs-tá-nä)	131	8.13S	41.06W
Paulo Afonso, Salto, wtfl., Braz. (säl-tô-pou'lô äf-fôɴ'sô)	131	9.33S	38.32W
Paul Roux, S. Afr. (pôrl rōō)	218d	28.18S	27.57E
Paulsboro, N.J., U.S. (pôlz'bē-rô)	100f	39.50N	75.16W
Pauls Valley, Ok., U.S. (pôlz văl'ē)	111	34.43N	97.13W
Pavarandocito, Col. (pä-vä-rän-dô-sē'tô)	130a	7.18N	76.32W
Pavda, Russia (päv'da)	172a	59.16N	59.32E
Pavia, Italy (pä-vē'ä)	148	45.12N	9.11E
Pavlodar, Kaz. (páv-lô-dár')	169	52.17N	77.23E
Pavlof Bay, b., Ak., U.S. (păv-lŏf)	95	55.20N	161.20W
Pavlohrad, Ukr.	167	48.32N	35.52E
Pavlovsk, Russia (páv-lôfsk')	163	50.28N	40.05E
Pavlovsk, Russia	172c	59.41N	30.27E
Pavlovskiy Posad, Russia (páv-lôf'skĭ pô-sát')	166	55.47N	38.39E
Pavuna, Braz. (pä-vōō'ná)	132b	22.48S	43.21W
Päwesin, Ger. (pă'vĕ-zēn)	145b	52.31N	12.44E
Pawhuska, Ok., U.S. (pô-hŭs'ká)	111	36.41N	96.20W
Pawnee, Ok., U.S. (pô-nē')	111	36.20N	96.47W
Pawnee, r., Ks., U.S.	110	38.18N	99.42W
Pawnee City, Ne., U.S.	111	40.08N	96.09W
Paw Paw, Mi., U.S. (pô'pô)	98	42.15N	85.55W
Paw Paw, r., Mi., U.S.	103	42.14N	86.21W
Pawtucket, R.I., U.S. (pô-tŭk'ĕt)	99	41.53N	71.23W
Paxoi, i., Grc.	161	39.14N	20.15E
Paxton, Il., U.S. (păks'tŭn)	98	40.35N	88.00W
Paya Lebar, Sing.	240c	1.22N	103.53E
Payette, Id., U.S. (pâ-ĕt')	104	44.05N	116.55W
Payette, r., Id., U.S.	104	43.57N	116.26W
Payette, North Fork, r., Id., U.S.	104	44.10N	116.10W
Payette, South Fork, r., Id., U.S.	104	44.07N	115.43W
Pay-Khoy, Khrebet, mts., Russia	166	68.08N	63.04E
Payne, l., Can. (pān)	85	59.22N	73.16W
Paynesville, S. Afr.	244b	26.14S	28.28E
Paynesville, Mn., U.S. (pānz'vĭl)	103	45.23N	94.43W
Paysandú, Ur. (pī-sän-dōō')	132	32.16S	57.55W
Payson, Ut., U.S. (pā's'n)	109	40.05N	111.45W
Pazardzhik, Bul. (pä-zár-dzhek')	149	42.10N	24.22E
Pazin, Cro. (pä'zēn)	160	45.14N	13.57E
Peabody, Ks., U.S. (pē'bŏd-ĭ)	111	38.09N	97.09W
Peabody, Ma., U.S.	93a	42.32N	70.56W
Peabody Institute, pt. of i., Md., U.S.	229c	39.18N	76.37W
Peace, r., Can.	84	57.30N	117.30W
Peace Creek, r., Fl., U.S. (pēs)	115a	27.16N	81.53W
Peace Dale, R.I., U.S. (dāl)	100b	41.27N	71.30W
Peace River, Can. (rĭv'ẽr)	84	56.14N	117.17W
Peacock Hills, hills, Can. (pē-kŏk' hĭlz)	84	66.08N	109.55W
Peak Hill, Austl.	202	25.38S	118.50E
Peakhurst, Austl.	243a	33.58S	151.04E
Pearl, r., U.S. (pûrl)	97	30.30N	89.45W
Pearland, Tx., U.S. (pûrl'ănd)	113a	29.34N	95.17W
Pearl Harbor, Hi., U.S.	94a	21.20N	157.53W
Pearl Harbor, b., Hi., U.S.	96d	21.22N	157.58W
Pearsall, Tx., U.S. (pēr'sôl)	112	28.53N	99.06W
Pearse Island, i., Can. (pērs)	86	54.51N	130.21W
Pearston, S. Afr. (pē'ẽrstŏn)	213c	32.36S	25.09E
Peary Land, reg., Grnld. (pēr'ĭ)	220	82.00N	40.00W
Pease, r., Tx., U.S. (pēz)	110	34.07N	99.53W
Peason, La., U.S. (pēz''n)	113	31.25N	93.19W
Pebane, Moz. (pĕ-bá'nē)	213	17.10S	38.08E
Pecan Bay, Tx., U.S. (pê-kăn')	112	32.04N	99.15W
Peçanha, Braz. (pā-kän'yá)	131	18.37S	42.26W
Pecatonica, r., Il., U.S. (pĕk-á-tŏn-ĭ-ká)	103	42.21N	89.28W
Pechenga, Russia (pyĕ'chĕŋ-gá)	166	69.30N	31.10E
Pechincha, neigh., Braz.	234c	22.56S	43.21W
Pechora, r., Russia	164	66.00N	54.00E
Pechora Basin, Russia (pyĕ-chô'rá)	164	67.55N	58.37E
Pechori, Russia (pĕt'sĕ-rĕ)	162	57.48N	27.33E
Pecos, N.M., U.S. (pā'kôs)	109	35.29N	105.41W
Pecos, Tx., U.S.	112	31.26N	103.30W
Pecos, r., U.S.	96	31.10N	103.10W
Pécs, Hung. (pāch)	149	46.04N	18.15E
Peddie, S. Afr.	213c	33.13S	27.09E
Pedley, Ca., U.S. (pĕd'lē)	107a	33.59N	117.29W
Pedra Azul, Braz. (pā'drä-zōō'l)	131	16.03S	41.13W
Pedreiras, Braz. (pĕ-drā'räs)	131	4.30S	44.31W
Pedro, Point, c., Sri L. (pē'drô)	187	9.50N	80.14E
Pedro Antonio Santos, Mex.	120a	18.55N	88.13W
Pedro Betancourt, Cuba (bā-tăŋ-kōrt')	122	22.40N	81.15W
Pedro de Valdivia, Chile (pĕ'drô-dē-väl-dē'vê-ä)	132	22.32S	69.55W
Pedro do Rio, Braz. (dô-rē'rô)	132b	22.20S	43.09W
Pedro II, Braz. (pā'drô sā-gôn'dô)	131	4.20S	41.27W
Pedro Juan Caballero, Para. (hôá'n-kä-bäl-yē'rō)	132	22.40S	55.42W
Pedro Miguel, Pan. (mê-gāl')	116a	9.01N	79.36W
Pedro Miguel Locks, trans., Pan. (mê-gāl')	116a	9.01N	79.36W
Peebinga, Austl. (pē-bĭng'á)	202	34.43S	140.55E
Peebles, Scot., U.K. (pē'b'lz)	150	55.40N	3.15W

ng-sing; ŋ-baŋk; ɴ-nasalized n; nŏd; cŏmmit; ōld; ôbey; ôrder; oi-boil; fōōd; ó-as oo in foot; ou-out; s-soft; sh-dish; th-thin; pūre; ûnite; ûrn; stŭd; circŭs; ü-as in French tu; '-indeterminate vowel.

332 Peekskill – Philipsburg

PLACE (Pronunciation)	PAGE	Lat. °′	Long. °′
Peekskill, N.Y., U.S. (pēks′kĭl)	100a	41.17N	73.55W
Pegasus Bay, b., N.Z. (pĕg′ȧ-sŭs)	203a	43.18S	173.25E
Pegnitz, r., Ger. (pĕgh-nēts)	154	49.38N	11.40E
Pego, Spain (pā′gō)	159	38.50N	0.09W
Peguis Indian Reserve, I.R., Can.	89	51.20N	97.35W
Pegu Yoma, mts., Myanmar (pĕ-gōō′yō′mä)	183	19.16N	95.59E
Pehčevo, Mac. (pĕκ′chĕ-vō)	161	41.42N	22.57E
Pehladpur, neigh., India	240d	28.35N	77.06E
Peigan Indian Reserve, I.R., Can.	87	49.35N	113.40W
Peipus, Lake *see* Chudskoye Ozero, l., Eur.	166	58.43N	26.45E
Peit′ou, Tai.	241d	25.08N	121.29E
Pekin, Il., U.S. (pē′kĭn)	98	40.35N	89.30W
Peking *see* Beijing, China	189	39.55N	116.23E
Pelagie, Isole, is., Italy	148	35.46N	12.32E
Pélagos, i., Grc.	161	39.17N	24.05E
Pelahatchie, Ms., U.S. (pĕl-á-hăch′ė)	114	32.17N	89.48W
Pelat, Mont, mtn., Fr. (pē-lá′)	147	44.16N	6.43E
Peleduy, Russia (pyĕl-yĭ-dōō′ē)	165	59.50N	112.47E
Pelée, Mont, mtn., Mart. (pē-lā′)	121b	14.49N	61.10W
Pelee, Point, c., Can.	90	41.55N	82.30W
Pelee Island, i., Can. (pē′lė)	90	41.45N	82.30W
Pelequén, Chile (pĕ-lĕ-kĕ′n)	129b	34.26S	71.52W
Pelham, Ga., U.S. (pĕl′hăm)	114	31.07N	84.10W
Pelham, N.H., U.S.	93a	42.43N	71.22W
Pelham, N.Y., U.S.	228	40.55N	73.49W
Pelham Manor, N.Y., U.S.	228	40.54N	73.48W
Pelican, l., Mn., U.S.	103	46.36N	94.00W
Pelican Bay, b., Can.	89	52.45N	100.20W
Pelican Harbor, b., Bah. (pĕl′ĭ-kăn)	122	26.20N	76.45W
Pelican Rapids, Mn., U.S. (pĕl′ĭ-kăn)	102	46.34N	96.05W
Pella, Ia., U.S. (pĕl′ȧ)	103	41.25N	92.50W
Pellworm, i., Ger. (pĕl′vôrm)	154	54.33N	8.25E
Pelly, l., Can.	84	66.08N	102.57W
Pelly, r., Can.	84	62.20N	133.00W
Pelly Bay, b., Can. (pĕl′ĭ)	85	68.57N	91.05W
Pelly Crossing, Can.	95	62.50N	136.50W
Pelly Mountains, mts., Can.	84	61.50N	133.05W
Peloncillo Mountains, mts., Az., U.S. (pĕl-ôn-sĭl′lō)	109	32.40N	109.20W
Pelopónnisos, pen., Grc.	161	37.28N	22.14E
Pelotas, Braz. (pā-lō′tázh)	132	31.45S	52.18W
Pelton, Can. (pĕl′tŭn)	101b	42.15N	82.57W
Pelym, r., Russia	166	60.20N	63.05E
Pelzer, S.C., U.S. (pĕl′zẽr)	115	34.38N	82.30W
Pemanggil, i., Malay.	181b	2.37N	104.41E
Pematangsiantar, Indon.	196	2.58N	99.03E
Pemba, Moz. (pĕm′bá)	213	12.58S	40.30E
Pemba, Zam.	212	15.29S	27.22E
Pemba Channel, strt., Afr.	217	5.10S	39.30E
Pemba Island, i., Tan.	217	5.20S	39.57E
Pembina, N.D., U.S. (pĕm′bĭ-ná)	102	48.58N	97.15W
Pembina, r., Can.	87	53.05N	114.30W
Pembina, r., N.A.	89	49.08N	98.20W
Pembroke, Can. (pĕm′ brōk)	85	45.50N	77.00W
Pembroke, Wales, U.K.	150	51.40N	5.00W
Pembroke, Ma., U.S. (pĕm′brōk)	93a	42.05N	70.49W
Pen, India	187b	18.44N	73.06E
Penafiel, Port. (pā-ná-fyĕl′)	158	41.12N	8.19W
Peñafiel, Spain (pā-nyá-fyĕl′)	158	41.38N	4.08W
Peña Grande, neigh., Spain	238b	40.23N	3.44W
Peñalara, mtn., Spain (pā-nyä-lä′rä)	148	40.52N	3.57W
Pena Nevada, Cerro, Mex.	118	23.47N	99.52W
Peñaranda de Bracamonte, Spain	158	40.54N	5.11W
Peñarroya-Pueblonuevo, Spain (pĕn-yär-rō′yä-pwĕ′blō-nwĕ′vō)	158	38.18N	5.18W
Peñas, Cabo de, c., Spain (kā′bō-dĕ-pā′nyäs)	158	43.42N	6.12W
Penas, Golfo de, b., Chile (gôl-fô-dĕ-pĕ′n-äs)	132	47.15S	77.30W
Penasco, r., Tx., U.S. (pā-nás′kō)	112	32.50N	104.45W
Pendembu, S.L. (pĕn-dĕm′bōō)	210	8.06N	10.42W
Pender, Ne., U.S. (pĕn′dẽr)	102	42.08N	96.43W
Penderisco, r., Col. (pĕn-dĕ-rē′s-kō)	130a	6.30N	76.21W
Pendjari, Parc National de la, rec., Benin	214	11.25N	1.30E
Pendlebury, Eng., U.K.	237b	53.31N	2.20W
Pendleton, Or., U.S. (pĕn′d′l-tŭn)	96	45.41N	118.47W
Pend Oreille, r., Wa., U.S.	104	48.44N	117.20W
Pend Oreille, Lake, l., Id., U.S. (pŏn-dô-rā′) (pĕn-dô-rĕl′)	96	48.09N	116.38W
Penedo, Braz. (pā-nā′dò)	131	10.17S	36.28W
Penetanguishene, Can. (pĕn′ē-tăŋ-gĭ-shēn′)	91	44.45N	79.55W
Pengcheng, China (pŭŋ-chŭŋ)	190	36.24N	114.11E
Penglai, China (pŭŋ-lī)	192	37.49N	120.45E
Penha, neigh., Braz.	234c	22.49S	43.17W
Penha de França, neigh., Braz.	234d	23.32S	46.32W
Peniche, Port. (pĕ-nē′chå)	158	39.22N	9.24W
Peninsula, Oh., U.S. (pĕn-ĭn′sū-lȧ)	101d	41.14N	81.32W
Penistone, Eng., U.K. (pĕn′ĭ-stŭn)	144a	53.31N	1.38W
Penjamillo, Mex. (pĕn-hä-mēl′yō)	118	20.06N	101.56W
Pénjamo, Mex. (pān′hä-mō)	118	20.27N	101.43W
Penk, r., Eng., U.K. (pĕnk)	144a	52.41N	2.10W
Penkridge, Eng., U.K. (pĕnk′rĭj)	144a	52.43N	2.07W
Pennant Hills, Austl.	243a	33.44S	151.04E
Penne, Italy (pĕn′nā)	160	42.28N	13.57E
Penner, r., India (pĕn′ẽr)	183	14.43N	79.09E
Penn Hills, Pa., U.S.	230b	40.28N	79.53W
Pennines, hills, Eng., U.K. (pĕn-īn′)	150	54.30N	2.10W
Pennines, Alpes, mts., Eur.	154	46.02N	7.07E
Pennsauken, N.J., U.S.	229b	39.58N	75.04W
Pennsboro, W.V., U.S. (pĕnz′bŭr-ô)	98	39.10N	81.00W
Penns Grove, N.J., U.S. (pĕnz grōv)	100f	39.44N	75.28W

PLACE (Pronunciation)	PAGE	Lat. °′	Long. °′
Pennsylvania, state, U.S. (pĕn-sĭl-vā′nĭ-ȧ)	97	41.00N	78.10W
Penn Valley, Pa., U.S.	229b	40.01N	75.16W
Penn Wynne, Pa., U.S.	229b	39.59N	75.16W
Penn Yan, N.Y., U.S. (pĕn yăn′)	99	42.40N	77.00W
Pennycutaway, r., Can.	89	56.10N	93.25W
Peno, l., Russia (pā′nō)	162	56.55N	32.28E
Penobscot, r., Me., U.S.	97	45.00N	68.36W
Penobscot Bay, b., Me., U.S. (pė-nŏb′skŏt)	92	44.20N	69.00W
Penong, Austl. (pė-nông′)	202	32.00S	133.00E
Penrith, Austl.	201b	33.45S	150.42E
Pensacola, Fl., U.S. (pĕn-sȧ-kō′lȧ)	97	30.25N	87.13W
Pensacola Dam, Ok., U.S.	111	36.27N	95.02W
Pensby, Eng., U.K.	237a	53.21N	3.06W
Pensilvania, Col. (pĕn-sĕl-vá′nyä)	130a	5.31N	75.05W
Pentagon, pt. of i., Va., U.S.	229d	38.52N	77.03W
Pentecost, i., Vanuatu (pĕn′tė-kŏst)	203	16.05S	168.28E
Penticton, Can.	84	49.30N	119.35W
Pentland Firth, strt., Scot., U.K. (pĕnt′lănd)	150	58.44N	3.25W
Penza, Russia (pĕn′zá)	164	53.10N	45.00E
Penzance, Eng., U.K. (pĕn-zăns′)	150	50.07N	5.40W
Penzberg, Ger. (pĕnts′bĕrgh)	154	47.43N	11.21E
Penzhina, r., Russia (pyĭn-zē-nŭ)	171	62.15N	166.30E
Penzhino, Russia	165	63.42N	168.00E
Penzhinskaya Guba, b., Russia	171	60.30N	161.30E
Penzing, neigh., Aus.	239e	48.12N	16.18E
Peoria, Il., U.S. (pē-ō′rĭ-ȧ)	97	40.45N	89.35W
Peotillos, Mex. (pā-ō-tel′yōs)	118	22.30N	100.39W
Peotone, Il., U.S. (pē′ō-tôn)	101a	41.20N	87.47W
Pepacton Reservoir, res., N.Y., U.S. (pĕp-ác′tŭn)	99	42.05N	74.40W
Pepe, Cabo, c., Cuba (kä′bō-pĕ′pĕ)	122	21.30N	83.10W
Pepperell, Ma., U.S. (pĕp′ẽr-ĕl)	93a	42.40N	71.36W
Peqin, Alb. (pĕ-kēn′)	161	41.03N	19.48E
Pequannock, N.J., U.S.	228	40.57N	74.18W
Perales, r., Spain (pā-rä′läs)	159a	40.24N	4.07W
Perales de Tajuña, Spain (dā tä-hōō′nyä)	159a	40.14N	3.22W
Perche, Collines du, hills, Fr.	156	48.25N	0.40E
Perchtoldsdorf, Aus. (pĕrk′tôlts-dôrf)	145e	48.07N	16.17E
Perdekop, S. Afr.	218d	27.11S	29.38E
Perdido, r., Al., U.S. (pĕr-dī′dō)	114	30.45N	87.38W
Perdido, Monte, mtn., Spain (pĕr-dē′dō)	159	42.40N	0.00
Perdões, Braz. (pĕr-dô′ĕs)	129a	21.05S	45.05W
Pereira, Col. (pā-rā′rä)	130	4.49N	75.42W
Pere Marquette, Mi., U.S.	98	43.55N	86.10W
Pereshchepyne, Ukr.	163	49.02N	35.19E
Pereslavl′-Zalesskiy, Russia (pâ-râ-släv′′l zá-lyĕs′kĭ)	166	56.43N	38.52E
Pereyaslav-Khmel′nyts′kyy, Ukr.	167	50.05N	31.25E
Pergamino, Arg. (pĕr-gä-mē′nō)	132	33.53S	60.36W
Perham, Mn., U.S. (pẽr′hăm)	102	46.37N	95.35W
Peribonca, r., Can. (pĕr-ĭ-bŏŋ′kȧ)	85	50.30N	71.00W
Périgueux, Fr. (pā-rė-gû′)	147	45.12N	0.43E
Perija, Sierra de, mts., Col. (sē-ĕ′r-rá-dĕ-pĕ-rē′κä)	130	9.25N	73.30W
Peristérion, Grc.	239d	38.01N	23.42E
Perivale, neigh., Eng., U.K.	235	51.32N	0.19W
Perkam, Tanjung, c., Indon.	197	1.20S	138.45E
Perkins, Can. (pĕr′kĕns)	83c	45.37N	75.37W
Perlas, Archipiélago de las, is., Pan.	121	8.29N	79.15W
Perlas, Laguna las, l., Nic. (lä-gō′nä-dĕ-läs)	121	12.34N	83.19W
Perleberg, Ger. (pĕr′lĕ-bĕrg)	154	53.06N	11.51E
Perm′, Russia (pĕrm)	164	58.00N	56.15E
Pernambuco *see* Recife, Braz.	131	8.09S	34.59W
Pernambuco, state, Braz. (pĕr-näm-bōō′kō)	131	8.08S	38.54W
Pernik, Bul. (pĕr-nēk′)	149	42.36N	23.04E
Péronne, Fr. (pā-rōn′)	156	49.57N	2.49E
Perote, Mex. (pĕ-rō′tĕ)	119	19.33N	97.13W
Perovo, Russia (pâ′rô-vô)	172b	55.43N	37.47E
Perpignan, Fr. (pĕr-pē-nyäN′)	147	42.42N	2.48E
Perris, Ca., U.S. (pĕr′ĭs)	107a	33.46N	117.14W
Perros, Bahía, b., Cuba (bä-ē′ä-pā′rōs)	122	22.25N	78.35W
Perrot, Île, i., Can.	83a	45.23N	73.57W
Perry, Fl., U.S. (pĕr′ĭ)	114	30.06N	83.35W
Perry, Ga., U.S.	114	32.27N	83.44W
Perry, Ia., U.S.	103	41.49N	94.40W
Perry, N.Y., U.S.	99	42.45N	78.00W
Perry, Ok., U.S.	111	36.17N	97.18W
Perry, Ut., U.S.	107b	41.27N	112.02W
Perry Hall, Md., U.S.	100e	39.24N	76.29W
Perrymont, Pa., U.S.	230b	40.33N	80.02W
Perryopolis, Pa., U.S. (pĕr-rė-ŏ′pō-lĭs)	101e	40.05N	79.45W
Perrysburg, Oh., U.S. (pĕr ĭz-bûrg)	98	41.35N	83.35W
Perryton, Tx., U.S. (pĕr′ĭ-tŭn)	110	36.23N	100.48W
Perryville, Ak., U.S. (pĕr-ĭ-vĭl)	95	55.58N	159.28W
Perryville, Mo., U.S.	111	37.41N	89.52W
Persan, Fr. (pĕr-säN′)	157b	49.09N	2.15E
Persepolis, hist., Iran (pẽr-sĕpō-lĭs)	182	30.15N	53.08E
Persian Gulf, b., Asia (pûr′zhȧn)	182	27.38N	50.30E
Perth, Austl. (pûrth)	202	31.50S	116.10E
Perth, Can.	91	44.40N	76.15W
Perth, Scot., U.K.	146	56.24N	3.25W
Perth Amboy, N.J., U.S. (ăm′boi)	100a	40.31N	74.16W
Pertuis, Fr. (pĕr-tüē′)	157	43.43N	5.29E
Peru, Il., U.S. (pė-rōō′)	98	41.20N	89.10W
Peru, In., U.S.	98	40.45N	86.00W
Peru, nation, S.A.	130	10.00S	75.00W
Perugia, Italy (pā-rōō′jä)	148	43.08N	12.24E
Peruque, Mo., U.S. (pĕ rō′kĕ)	107e	38.52N	90.36W
Pervomays′k, Ukr.	167	48.04N	30.52E

PLACE (Pronunciation)	PAGE	Lat. °′	Long. °′
Pervoural′sk, Russia (pĕr-vô-ô-rálsk′)	172a	56.54N	59.58E
Perwenitz, Ger.	238a	52.40N	13.01E
Pesaro, Italy (pā′zä-rō)	148	43.54N	12.55E
Pescado, r., Ven. (pĕs-kä′dō)	131b	9.33N	65.32W
Pescara, Italy (pās-kä′rä)	160	42.26N	14.15E
Pescara, r., Italy	160	42.18N	13.22E
Peschanyy mûïs, c., Kaz.	170	43.10N	51.20E
Pescia, Italy (pā′shä)	160	43.53N	11.42E
Peshāwar, Pak. (pĕ-shä′wŭr)	183	34.01N	71.34E
Peshtera, Bul.	161	42.03N	24.19E
Peshtigo, Wi., U.S. (pĕsh′tė-gō)	103	45.03N	87.46W
Peshtigo, r., Wi., U.S.	103	45.15N	88.14W
Peski, Russia (pyâs′kĭ)	172b	55.13N	38.48E
Pêso da Régua, Port. (pā-sò-dä-rā′gwä)	158	41.09N	7.47W
Pespire, Hond. (pås-pē′rå)	120	13.35N	87.20W
Pesqueria, r., Mex. (pås-kå-rē′ȧ)	112	25.55N	100.25W
Pessac, Fr.	156	44.48N	0.38W
Pesterzsébet, neigh., Hung.	239g	47.26N	19.07E
Pestlorinc, neigh., Hung.	239g	47.26N	19.12E
Pestújhely, neigh., Hung.	239g	47.32N	19.07E
Petacalco, Bahía de, b., Mex. (bä-ē′ä-dĕ-pĕ-tä-kál′kō)	118	17.55N	102.00W
Petah Tiqwa, Isr.	181a	32.05N	34.53E
Petaluma, Ca., U.S. (pét-ȧ-lō′mȧ)	108	38.15N	122.38W
Petare, Ven. (pĕ-tä′rĕ)	131b	10.28N	66.48W
Petatlán, Mex. (pā-tä-tlän′)	118	17.31N	101.17W
Petawawa, Can.	91	45.54N	77.17W
Petén, Laguna de, l., Guat. (lä-gò′nä-dĕ-på-tān′)	120a	17.05N	89.54W
Petenwell Reservoir, res., Wi., U.S.	103	44.10N	89.55W
Peterborough, Austl.	202	32.53S	138.58E
Peterborough, Can. (pē′tẽr-bŭr-ô)	85	44.20N	78.20W
Peterborough, Eng., U.K.	150	52.35N	0.14W
Peterhead, Scot., U.K. (pē-tẽr-hĕd′)	150	57.36N	3.47W
Peter Pond Lake, l., Can. (pŏnd)	84	55.55N	108.44W
Petersburg, Ak., U.S. (pē′tẽrz-bûrg)	95	56.52N	133.10W
Petersburg, Il., U.S.	111	40.01N	89.51W
Petersburg, In., U.S.	98	38.30N	87.15W
Petersburg, Ky., U.S.	101f	39.04N	84.52W
Petersburg, Va., U.S.	97	37.12N	77.30W
Peters Creek, r., Pa., U.S.	230b	40.18N	79.52W
Petershagen, Ger. (pĕ′tĕrs-hä-gĕn)	145b	52.32N	13.46E
Petersham, Austl.	243a	33.54S	151.09E
Petershausen, Ger. (pĕ′tĕrs-hou-zĕn)	145d	48.25N	11.29E
Pétionville, Haiti	123	18.30N	72.20W
Petit, S. Afr.	244b	26.06S	28.22E
Petitcodiac, Can. (pē-tē-kō-dyák′)	92	45.56N	65.10W
Petite Terre, i., Guad. (pē-tēt′târ′)	121b	16.12N	61.00W
Petit Goâve, Haiti (pē-tē′ gô-áv′)	123	18.25N	72.50W
Petit Jean Creek, r., Ar., U.S. (pē-tē′zhäN′)	111	35.05N	93.55W
Petit Loango, Gabon	216	2.16S	9.35E
Petlalcingo, Mex. (pĕ-tläl-sēŋ′gō)	119	18.05N	97.53W
Peto, Mex. (pĕ′tô)	120a	20.07N	88.49W
Petorca, Chile (pā-tōr′kȧ)	129b	32.14S	70.55W
Petoskey, Mi., U.S. (pė-tŏs-kĭ)	98	45.25N	84.55W
Petra, hist., Jord.	181a	30.21N	35.25E
Petra Velikogo, Zaliv, b., Russia	194	42.40N	131.50E
Petre, Point, c., Can.	91	43.50N	77.00W
Petrich, Bul. (pā′trĭch)	149	41.24N	23.13E
Petrified Forest National Park, rec., Az., U.S. (pĕt′rĭ-fīd fôr′ĕst)	109	34.58N	109.35W
Petrikov, Bela. (pyĕ′trē-kô-v)	162	52.09N	28.30E
Petrinja, Cro. (pā′trēn-yȧ)	160	45.25N	16.17E
Petrodvorets, Russia (pyĕ-trô-dvô-ryĕts′)	172c	59.53N	29.55E
Petrokrepost′, Russia (pyĕ′trô-krĕ-pôst)	166	59.56N	31.03E
Petrolia, Can. (pė-trō′lĭ-ȧ)	90	42.50N	82.10W
Petrolina, Braz. (pĕ-trō-lē′nȧ)	131	9.18S	40.28W
Petronell, Aus.	145e	48.07N	16.52E
Petropavl, Kaz.	169	54.44N	69.07E
Petropavlivka, Ukr.	163	48.24N	36.23E
Petropavlovka, Russia	172a	54.10N	59.50E
Petropavlovsk-Kamchatskiy, Russia (käm-chät′skĭ)	165	53.13N	158.56E
Petrópolis, Braz. (pā-trō-pō-lēzh′)	131	22.31S	43.10W
Petroşani, Rom.	161	45.24N	23.24E
Petrovsk, Russia (pyĕ-trôfsk′)	167	52.20N	45.15E
Petrovskaya, Russia (pyĕ-trôf′ská-yá)	163	45.25N	37.50E
Petrovsko-Razumovskoje, neigh., Russia	239b	55.50N	37.34E
Petrovskoye, Russia	167	45.20N	43.00E
Petrovsk-Zabaykal′skiy, Russia (pyĕ-trôfskzä-bī-käl′skĭ)	165	51.13N	109.08E
Petrozavodsk, Russia (pyā′trō-zá-vôtsk′)	164	61.46N	34.25E
Petrus Steyn, S. Afr.	218d	27.40S	28.09E
Petrykivka, Ukr.	163	48.43N	34.29E
Pewaukee, Wi., U.S. (pĭ-wô′kė)	101a	43.05N	88.15W
Pewaukee Lake, l., Wi., U.S.	101a	43.03N	88.18W
Pewee Valley, Ky., U.S. (pe wē)	101h	38.19N	85.29W
Peza, r., Russia (pyá′zá)	166	65.35N	46.50E
Pézenas, Fr. (pā-zē-nä′)	156	43.26N	3.24E
Pforzheim, Ger. (pfôrts′hīm)	147	48.52N	8.43E
Phalodi, India	186	27.13N	72.22E
Phan Thiet, Viet. (p′hän′)	196	11.30N	108.43E
Phelps Corner, Md., U.S.	229d	38.48N	76.58W
Phelps Lake, l., N.C., U.S.	115	35.46N	76.27W
Phenix City, Al., U.S. (fē′nĭks)	114	32.29N	85.00W
Philadelphia, Ms., U.S. (fĭl-ȧ-dĕl′phĭ-ȧ)	114	32.45N	89.07W
Philadelphia, Pa., U.S.	97	40.00N	75.13W
Philip, S.D., U.S. (fĭl′ĭp)	102	44.03N	101.35W
Philippeville *see* Skikda, Alg.	210	36.58N	6.51E
Philippines, nation, Asia (fĭl′ĭ-pēnz)	197	14.25N	125.00E
Philippine Sea, sea (fĭl′ĭ-pēn)	225	16.00N	133.00E
Philippine Trench, deep	197	10.30N	127.15E
Philipsburg, Pa., U.S. (fĭl′lĭps-bĕrg)	99	40.55N	78.10W

ăt; finăl; rāte; senāte; ärm; åsk; sofȧ; fâre; ch-choose; dh-as th in other; bē; ėvent; bĕt; recĕnt; cratẽr; g-gō; gh-guttural g; bĭt; ĭ-short neutral; rīde; κ-guttural k as ch in German ich;

PRONOUNCING INDEX

Philipsburg-Playas Lake 333

PLACE (Pronunciation)	PAGE	Lat. °′	Long. °′
Philipsburg, Wy., U.S.	105	46.19N	113.19W
Phillip, i., Austl. (fĭl'ĭp)	204	38.32S	145.10E
Phillip Channel, strt., Indon.	181b	1.04N	103.40E
Phillipi, W.V., U.S. (fĭ-lĭp'ĭ)	98	39.10N	80.00W
Phillips, Wi., U.S. (fĭl'ĭps)	103	45.41N	90.24W
Phillipsburg, Ks., U.S. (fĭl'lĭps-bĕrg)	110	39.44N	99.19W
Phillipsburg, N.J., U.S.	99	40.45N	75.10W
Phinga, India	240a	22.41N	88.25E
Phitsanulok, Thai.	196	16.51N	100.15E
Phnom Penh see Phnum Pénh, Camb.	196	11.39N	104.53E
Phnum Pénh, Camb. (nŏm'pĕn')	196	11.39N	104.53E
Phoenix, Az., U.S. (fē'nĭks)	96	33.30N	112.00W
Phoenix, Md., U.S.	100e	39.31N	76.40W
Phoenix Islands, is., Kir.	2	4.00S	174.00W
Phoenixville, Pa., U.S. (fē'nĭks-vĭl)	100f	40.08N	75.31W
Phou Bia, mtn., Laos	196	19.36N	103.00E
Phra Nakhon Si Ayutthaya, Thai.	196	14.16N	100.37E
Phuket, Thai.	196	7.57N	98.19E
Phu Quoc, Dao, i., Viet.	196	10.13N	104.00E
Phu-tho-hoa, Viet.	241j	10.46N	106.39E
Pi, r., China (bē)	190	32.06N	116.31E
Piacenza, Italy (pyä-chĕnt'sä)	148	45.02N	9.42E
Pianosa, i., Italy (pyä-nō'sä)	160	42.13N	15.45E
Piave, r., Italy (pyä'vā)	160	45.45N	12.15E
Piazza Armerina, Italy (pyät'sä är-mā-rē'nä)	160	37.23N	14.26E
Pibor, r., Sudan (pē'bôr)	211	7.21N	32.54E
Pic, r., Can. (pĕk)	90	48.48N	86.28W
Picara Point, c., V.I.U.S. (pē-kä'rä)	117c	18.23N	64.57W
Picayune, Ms., U.S. (pĭk'á yōōn)	114	30.32N	89.41W
Picher, Ok., U.S. (pĭch'ēr)	111	36.58N	94.49W
Pichilemu, Chile (pē-chē-lĕ'mōō)	129b	34.22S	72.01W
Pichucalco, Mex. (pē-chōō-käl'kō)	119	17.34N	93.06W
Pickerel, l., Can. (pĭk'ēr-ĕl)	90	48.35N	91.10W
Pickwick Lake, res., U.S. (pĭk'wĭck)	114	35.04N	88.05W
Pico, Ca., U.S. (pē'kō)	107a	34.01N	118.05W
Pico Island, i., Port. (pē'kō)	210a	38.16N	28.49W
Pico Rivera, Ca., U.S.	107a	34.01N	118.05W
Picos, Braz. (pē'kōzh)	131	7.13S	41.23W
Picton, Austl. (pĭk'tŭn)	201b	34.11S	150.37E
Picton, Can.	91	44.00N	77.15W
Pictou, Can. (pĭk-tōō')	93	45.41N	62.43W
Pidálion, Akrotírion, c., Cyp.	181a	34.50N	34.05E
Pidurutalagala, mtn., Sri L. (pē'dō-rō-tä'lá-gä'lá)	183	7.00N	80.46E
Pidvolochys'k, Ukr.	163	49.32N	26.16E
Pie, i., Can. (pī)	90	48.10N	89.07W
Piedade, Braz. (pyä-dä'dĕ)	129a	23.42S	47.25W
Piedade do Baruel, Braz.	234d	23.37S	46.18W
Piedmont, Al., U.S. (pēd'mŏnt)	114	33.54N	85.36W
Piedmont, Ca., U.S.	106b	37.50N	122.14W
Piedmont, Mo., U.S.	111	37.09N	90.42W
Piedmont, S.C., U.S.	115	34.40N	82.27W
Piedmont, W.V., U.S.	99	39.30N	79.05W
Piedrabuena, Spain (pyā-drä-bwā'nä)	158	39.01N	4.10W
Piedras, Punta, c., Arg. (pōō'n-tä-pyĕ'dräs)	129c	35.25S	57.10W
Piedras Negras, Mex. (pyā'dräs nā'gräs)	116	28.41N	100.33W
Pieksämäki, Fin. (pyĕk'sĕ-mĕ-kĕ)	153	62.18N	27.14E
Piemonte, hist. reg., Italy (pyĕ-mô'n-tĕ)	160	44.30N	7.42E
Pienaars, r., S. Afr.	218d	25.13S	28.05E
Pienaarsrivier, S. Afr.	218d	25.12S	28.18E
Pierce, Ne., U.S. (pērs)	102	42.11N	97.33W
Pierce, W.V., U.S.	99	39.15N	79.30W
Piermont, N.Y., U.S. (pēr'mŏnt)	100a	41.03N	73.55W
Pierre, S.D., U.S. (pēr)	96	44.22N	100.20W
Pierrefitte-sur-Seine, Fr.	237c	48.58N	2.22E
Pierrefonds, Can.	83a	45.29N	73.52W
Piešt'any, Slvk.	155	48.36N	17.48E
Pietermaritzburg, S. Afr. (pē-tēr-mä-rĭts-bûrg)	212	29.36S	30.23E
Pietersburg, S. Afr. (pē'tērz-bûrg)	212	23.56S	29.30E
Pietersfield, S. Afr.	244b	26.14S	28.26E
Piet Retief, S. Afr. (pēt rĕ-tēf')	212	27.00S	30.58E
Pietrosu, Vârful, mtn., Rom.	155	47.35N	24.49E
Pieve di Cadore, Italy (pyā'vā dē kä-dō'rā)	148	46.26N	12.22E
Pigeon, r., N.A. (pĭj'ŭn)	103	48.05N	90.13W
Pigeon Lake, Can.	83f	49.57N	97.36W
Pigeon Lake, l., Can.	87	53.00N	114.00W
Piggott, Ar., U.S. (pĭg-ŭt)	111	36.22N	90.10W
Pijijiapan, Mex. (pēkē-kē-ä'pän)	119	15.40N	93.12W
Pijnacker, Neth.	145a	52.01N	4.25E
Pikes Peak, mtn., Co., U.S. (pīks)	96	38.49N	105.03W
Pikesville, Md., U.S.	229c	39.23N	76.44W
Pikeville, Ky., U.S. (pīk'vĭl)	98	37.28N	82.31W
Pikou, China (pē-kō)	192	39.25N	122.19E
Pikwitonei, Can. (pĭk'wĭ-tōn)	89	55.35N	97.09W
Piła, Pol. (pē'lá)	154	53.09N	16.44E
Pilansberg, mtn., S. Afr. (pē'ăns'bûrg)	218d	25.08S	26.55E
Pilar, Arg. (pē'lär)	129c	34.27S	58.55W
Pilar, Para.	132	27.00S	58.15W
Pilar de Goiás, Braz. (dĕ-gô'yá's)	131	14.47S	49.33W
Pilchuck, r., Wa., U.S.	106a	48.03N	121.58W
Pilchuck Creek, r., Wa., U.S. (pĭl'chŭck)	106a	48.19N	122.11W
Pilchuck Mountain, mtn., Wa., U.S.	106a	48.03N	121.48W
Pilcomayo, r., S.A. (pēl-cō-mī'ō)	132	24.45S	59.15W
Pilgrim Gardens, N.J., U.S.	229b	39.57N	75.19W
Pilgrims Hatch, Eng., U.K.	235	51.38N	0.17E
Pili, Phil. (pē'lē)	197a	13.34N	123.17E
Pilica, r., Pol. (pē-lēt'sä)	155	51.00N	19.48E
Pillar Point, c., Wa., U.S. (pĭl'ăr)	106a	48.14N	124.06W
Pillar Rocks, Wa., U.S.	106c	46.16N	123.35W
Pilón, r., Mex. (pē-lōn')	118	24.13N	99.03W
Pilot Point, Tx., U.S. (pī'lŭt)	111	33.24N	97.00W

PLACE (Pronunciation)	PAGE	Lat. °′	Long. °′
Pilsen see Plzeň, Czech Rep.	142	49.46N	13.25E
Piltene, Lat. (pĭl'tĕ-nĕ)	153	57.17N	21.40E
Pimal, Cerra, mtn., Mex. (sĕ'r-rä-pē-mäl')	118	22.58N	104.19W
Pimba, Austl. (pĭm'bá)	202	31.15S	137.50E
Pimville, neigh., S. Afr. (pĭm'vĭl)	213b	26.17S	27.54E
Pinacate, Cerro, mtn., Mex. (sĕ'r-rô-pē-nä-kä'tĕ)	116	31.45N	113.30W
Pinamalayan, Phil. (pē-nä-mä-lä'yän)	197a	13.04N	121.31E
Pinang see George Town, Malay.	196	5.21N	100.09E
Pinarbaşi, Tur. (pē'när-bä'shĭ)	149	38.50N	36.10E
Pinar del Río, Cuba (pē-när' dĕl rē'ō)	117	22.25N	83.35W
Pinar del Río, prov., Cuba	122	22.45N	83.25W
Pinatubo, mtn., Phil. (pē-nä-tōō'bō)	197a	15.09N	120.19E
Pincher Creek, Can. (pĭn'chēr krēk)	87	49.29N	113.57W
Pinckneyville, Il., U.S. (pĭnk'nĭ-vĭl)	111	38.06N	89.22W
Pińczów, Pol. (pēn''chôf)	155	50.32N	20.33E
Pindamonhangaba, Braz. (pē'n-dä-mōnyä'n-gä-bä)	129a	22.56S	45.26W
Pinder Point, c., Bah.	122	26.35N	78.35W
Píndhos Oros, mts., Grc.	142	39.48N	21.19E
Pindiga, Nig.	215	9.59N	10.54E
Pine, r., Can. (pīn)	87	55.30N	122.20W
Pine, r., Wi., U.S.	103	45.50N	88.37W
Pine Bluff, Ar., U.S. (pīn blŭf)	97	34.13N	92.01W
Pine Brook, N.J., U.S.	228	40.52N	74.20W
Pine City, Mn., U.S. (pīn)	103	45.50N	93.01W
Pine Creek, Austl.	202	13.45S	132.00E
Pine Creek, r., Nv., U.S.	108	40.15N	116.17W
Pinecrest, Va., U.S.	229d	38.50N	77.09W
Pine Falls, Can.	89	50.35N	96.15W
Pine Flat Lake, res., Ca., U.S.	108	36.52N	119.18W
Pine Forest Range, mts., Nv., U.S.	104	41.35N	118.45W
Pinega, Russia (pê-nyĕ'gá)	164	64.40N	43.30E
Pinega, r., Russia	166	64.10N	42.30E
Pine Grove, Can.	227c	43.48N	79.35W
Pine Hill, N.J., U.S. (pīn hĭl)	100f	39.47N	74.59W
Pinehurst, Ma., U.S.	227a	42.32N	71.14W
Pine Island Sound, strt., Fl., U.S.	115a	26.32N	82.30W
Pine Lake Estates, Ga., U.S. (lāk ĕs-tāts')	100c	33.47N	84.13W
Pinelands, S. Afr. (pīn'lănds)	212a	33.57S	18.30E
Pine Lawn, Mo., U.S. (lôn)	107e	38.42N	90.17W
Pine Pass, p., Can.	87	55.22N	122.40W
Pine Ridge, Va., U.S.	229d	38.52N	77.14W
Pinerolo, Italy (pē-nå-rô'lō)	160	44.47N	7.18E
Pines, Lake o' the, Tx., U.S.	113	32.50N	94.40W
Pinetown, S. Afr. (pīn'toun)	213c	29.47S	30.52E
Pine View Reservoir, res., Ut., U.S. (vū)	107b	41.17N	111.54W
Pineville, Ky., U.S. (pīn'vĭl)	114	36.48N	83.43W
Pineville, La., U.S.	113	31.20N	92.25W
Ping, r., Thai.	196	17.54N	98.29E
Pingding, China (pĭŋ-dĭŋ)	192	37.50N	113.30E
Pingdu, China (pĭŋ-dōō)	192	36.46N	119.57E
Pingfang, China	240b	39.56N	116.33E
Pinggir, Indon.	181b	1.05N	101.12E
Pinghe, China (pĭŋ-hŭ)	193	24.30N	117.02E
Pingle, China (pĭŋ-lŭ)	193	24.30N	110.22E
Pingliang, China (pĭng'lyăng')	188	35.12N	106.50E
Pingquan, China (pĭŋ-chyůän)	192	40.58N	118.40E
Pingtan, China (pĭŋ-tän)	193	25.30N	119.45E
Pingtan Dao, i., China (pĭŋ-tän dou)	193	25.40N	119.45E
P'ingtung, Tai.	193	22.40N	120.35E
Pingwu, China (pĭŋ-wōō)	192	32.20N	104.40E
Pingxiang, China (pĭŋ-shyäŋ)	193	27.40N	113.50E
Pingyi, China (pĭŋ-yē)	190	35.30N	117.38E
Pingyuan, China (pĭŋ-yůän)	190	37.11N	116.26E
Pingzhou, China (pĭŋ-jō)	191a	23.01N	113.11E
Pinhal, Braz. (pē-nyá'l)	129a	22.11S	46.43W
Pinhal Novo, Port. (nô vô)	159b	38.38N	8.54W
Pinheiros, r., Braz.	234d	23.38S	46.43W
Pinhel, Port.	158	40.46N	7.04W
Pinhel, Port. (pēn-yĕl')	158	40.45N	7.03W
Pini, Pulau, i., Indon.	196	0.07S	98.38E
Piniós, r., Grc.	161	39.30N	21.40E
Pinnacles National Monument, rec., Ca., U.S. (pĭn'á-k'lz)	108	36.30N	121.00W
Pinneberg, Ger. (pĭn'ĕ-bĕrg)	145c	53.40N	9.48E
Pinner, neigh., Eng., U.K.	235	51.36N	0.23W
Pinole, Ca., U.S. (pĭ-nō'lē)	106b	38.01N	122.17W
Pinos-Puente, Spain (pwān'tå)	158	37.15N	3.43W
Pinotepa Nacional, Mex. (pē-nô-tä'pä nä-syô-näl')	118	16.21N	98.04W
Pins, Île des, i., N. Cal.	203	22.44S	167.44E
Pinsk, Bela. (pēn'sk)	164	52.07N	26.05E
Pinta, i., Ec.	130	0.41N	90.47W
Pintendre, Can. (pĕN-tändr')	83b	46.45N	71.07W
Pinto, Spain (pēn'tō)	159a	40.14N	3.42W
Pinto Butte, Can. (pĭn'tō)	88	49.22N	107.25W
Pioche, Nv., U.S. (pī-ō'chē)	109	37.56N	114.28W
Piombino, Italy (pyôm-bē'nō)	148	42.56N	10.33E
Pioneer Mountains, mts., Mt., U.S. (pī'ō-nēr')	105	45.23N	112.51W
Piotrków Trybunalski, Pol. (pyōtr'kōōv trĭ-bōō-nal'skē)	147	51.23N	19.44E
Piper, Al., U.S. (pī'pēr)	114	33.04N	87.00W
Piper, Ks., U.S.	107f	39.09N	94.51W
Pipéri, i., Grc. (pē'per-ē)	161	39.19N	24.20E
Pipe Spring National Monument, rec., Az., U.S. (pīp sprĭng)	109	36.50N	112.45W
Pipestone, Mn., U.S. (pīp'stōn)	102	44.00N	96.19W
Pipestone National Monument, rec., Mn., U.S.	102	44.03N	96.24W
Pipmuacan, Réservoir, res., Can. (pĭp-mä-kän')	91	49.45N	70.00W

PLACE (Pronunciation)	PAGE	Lat. °′	Long. °′
Piqua, Oh., U.S. (pĭk'wá)	98	40.10N	84.15W
Piracaia, Braz. (pē-rä-ká'yä)	129a	23.04S	46.20W
Piracicaba, Braz. (pē-rä-sē-kä'bä)	131	22.43S	47.39W
Piraíba, r., Braz. (pä-rä-ē'bá)	129a	21.38S	41.29W
Piraiévs, Grc.	149	37.57N	23.38E
Piramida, mtn., Russia	165	54.00N	96.00E
Pirámide de Cuicuilco, hist., Mex.	233a	19.18N	99.11W
Piran, Slvn. (pē-rá'n)	160	45.31N	13.34E
Piranga, Braz. (pē-rä'n-gä)	129a	20.41S	43.17W
Pirapetinga, Braz. (pē-rä-pē-tē'n-gä)	129a	21.40S	42.20W
Pirapora, Braz. (pē-rá-pō'rá)	131	17.39S	44.54W
Pirassununga, Braz. (pē-rä-sōō-nōō'n-gä)	129a	22.00S	47.24W
Pirenópolis, Braz. (pē-rē-nô'pō-lēs)	131	15.56S	48.49W
Pírgos, Grc.	149	37.51N	21.28E
Piritu, Laguna de, l., Ven. (lä-gō'nä-dĕ-pē-rē'tōō)	131b	10.00N	64.57W
Pirmasens, Ger. (pĭr-mä-zĕns')	154	49.12N	7.34E
Pirna, Ger. (pĭr'nä)	154	50.57N	13.56E
Pirot, Yugo. (pē'rōt)	149	43.09N	22.35E
Pirtleville, Az., U.S. (pûr't'l-vĭl)	109	31.25N	109.35W
Piru, Indon. (pē-rōō')	197	3.15S	128.25E
Pisa, Italy (pē'sä)	148	43.52N	10.24E
Pisagua, Chile (pē-sä'gwä)	130	19.43S	70.12W
Piscataway, Md., U.S. (pĭs-kă-tă-wā)	100e	38.42N	76.59W
Piscataway, N.J., U.S.	100a	40.35N	74.27W
Pisco, Peru (pēs'kō)	130	13.43S	76.07W
Pisco, Bahía de, b., Peru	130	13.43S	77.48W
Piseco, l., N.Y., U.S. (pĭ-sā'kō)	99	43.25N	74.35W
Pisek, Czech Rep. (pē'sĕk)	147	49.18N	14.08E
Pisticci, Italy (pēs-tē'chē)	160	40.24N	16.34E
Pistoia, Italy (pēs-tô'yä)	148	43.57N	11.54E
Pisuerga, r., Spain (pē-swĕr'gä)	158	41.48N	4.28W
Pit, r., Ca., U.S. (pĭt)	104	40.58N	121.42W
Pitalito, Col. (pē-tä-lē'tō)	130	1.45N	75.09W
Pitampura Kālan, neigh., India	240d	28.42N	77.08E
Pitcairn, Pa., U.S. (pĭt'kârn)	101e	40.29N	79.47W
Pitcairn, dep., Oc.	2	25.04S	130.05W
Piteälven, r., Swe.	146	66.08N	18.51E
Piteşti, Rom. (pē-tĕsht'')	161	44.51N	24.51E
Pithara, Austl. (pĭt'ără)	202	30.27S	116.45E
Pithiviers, Fr. (pē-tē-vyā')	156	48.12N	2.14E
Pitman, N.J., U.S. (pĭt'măn)	100f	39.44N	75.08W
Pitseng, Leso.	213c	29.03S	28.13E
Pitt, r., Can.	106d	49.19N	122.39W
Pitt Island, i., Can.	86	53.35N	129.45W
Pittsburg, Ca., U.S. (pĭts'bûrg)	106b	38.01N	121.52W
Pittsburg, Ks., U.S.	97	37.25N	94.43W
Pittsburg, Tx., U.S.	111	32.00N	94.57W
Pittsburgh, Pa., U.S.	97	40.26N	80.01W
Pittsfield, Il., U.S. (pĭts'fēld)	111	39.37N	90.47W
Pittsfield, Me., U.S.	92	44.45N	69.44W
Pittsfield, Ma., U.S.	99	42.25N	73.15W
Pittston, Pa., U.S. (pĭts'tŭn)	99	41.20N	75.50W
Piũi, Braz. (pē-ōō'ē)	129a	20.27S	45.57W
Piura, Peru (pē-ōō'rä)	130	5.13S	80.46W
Pivdennyy Buh, r., Ukr.	167	48.12N	30.13E
Piya, Russia (pē'yá)	172a	58.34N	61.12E
Placentia, Can.	93	47.15N	53.58W
Placentia, Ca., U.S. (plă-sĕn'shĭ-á)	107a	33.52N	117.50W
Placentia Bay, b., Can.	85a	47.14N	54.30W
Placerville, Ca., U.S. (plăs'ēr-vĭl)	108	38.43N	120.47W
Placetas, Cuba (plä-thä'täs)	122	22.10N	79.40W
Placid, l., N.Y., U.S. (plăs'ĭd)	99	44.20N	74.00W
Plain City, Ut., U.S. (plān)	107b	41.18N	112.06W
Plainfield, Il., U.S. (plān'fēld)	101a	41.37N	88.12W
Plainfield, In., U.S.	101g	39.42N	86.23W
Plainfield, N.J., U.S.	100a	40.38N	74.25W
Plainview, Ar., U.S. (plān'vū)	111	34.59N	93.15W
Plainview, Mn., U.S.	103	44.09N	93.12W
Plainview, Ne., U.S.	102	42.20N	97.47W
Plainview, Tx., U.S.	110	34.11N	101.42W
Plainwell, Mi., U.S. (plan'wĕl)	98	42.25N	85.40W
Plaisance, Can. (plĕ-zäNs')	83c	45.37N	75.07W
Plana or Flat Cays, is., Bah. (plä'nä)	123	22.35N	73.35W
Plandome Manor, N.Y., U.S.	228	40.49N	73.42W
Planegg, Ger. (plä'nĕg)	145d	48.06N	11.27E
Plano, Tx., U.S. (plā'nō)	111	33.01N	96.42W
Plantagenet, Can. (plän-tàzh-nĕ')	83c	45.33N	75.00W
Plant City, Fl., U.S. (plánt sĭ'tĭ)	115a	28.00N	82.07W
Plaquemine, La., U.S. (plăk'mēn')	113	30.17N	91.14W
Plasencia, Spain (plä-sĕn'thē-ä)	158	40.02N	6.07W
Plast, Russia (plást)	166	54.22N	60.48E
Plaster Rock, Can. (plás'tēr rŏk)	92	46.54N	67.24W
Plastun, Russia (plás-tōōn')	194	44.41N	136.08E
Plata, Río de la, est., S.A. (dālā plā'tä)	132	34.35S	58.15W
Platani, r., Italy (plä-tä'nē)	160	37.26N	13.28E
Plateforme, Pointe, c., Haiti	123	19.35N	73.50W
Platinum, Ak., U.S. (plăt'ĭ-nŭm)	95	59.00N	161.27W
Plato, Col. (plä'tō)	130	9.49N	74.48W
Platón Sánchez, Mex. (plä-tōn' sän'chĕz)	118	21.14N	98.20W
Platt, Eng., U.K.	235	51.17N	0.20E
Platte, S.D., U.S. (plăt)	102	43.22N	98.51W
Platte, r., Mo., U.S.	111	40.09N	94.40W
Platte, r., Ne., U.S.	96	40.50N	100.40W
Platteville, Wi., U.S. (plăt'vĭl)	103	42.44N	90.31W
Plattsburg, Mo., U.S. (plăts'bûrg)	111	39.33N	94.26W
Plattsburg, N.Y., U.S.	99	44.40N	73.30W
Plattsmouth, Ne., U.S. (plăts'mŭth)	102	41.00N	95.53W
Plauen, Ger. (plou'ĕn)	147	50.30N	12.08E
Playa de Guanabo, Cuba (plä-yä-dĕ-gwä-nä'bô)	123a	23.10N	82.07W
Playa del Rey, neigh., Ca., U.S.	232	33.58N	118.26W
Playa de Santa Fé, Cuba	123a	23.05N	82.31W
Playas Lake, l., N.M., U.S. (plä'yás)	109	31.50N	108.30W

ng-sing; ŋ-baŋk; N-nasalized n; nŏd; cŏmmit; ōld; ōbey; ôrder; oi-boil; fōōd; ŏŏ-as oo in foot; ou-out; s-soft; sh-dish; th-thin; pūre; ûnite; ûrn; stŭd; circŭs; ü-as in French tu; '-indeterminate vowel.

334 Playa Vicente-Porto Mendes

PLACE (Pronunciation)	PAGE	Lat. °'	Long. °'
Playa Vicente, Mex. (vē-sĕn'tå)	119	17.49N	95.49W
Playa Vicente, r., Mex.	119	17.36N	96.13W
Playgreen Lake, l., Can. (plā'grēn)	89	54.00N	98.10W
Plaza de Toros Monumental, rec., Spain	238e	41.24N	2.11E
Pleasant, l., N.Y., U.S. (plĕz'ănt)	99	43.25N	74.25W
Pleasant Grove, Al., U.S.	100h	33.29N	86.57W
Pleasant Hill, Ca., U.S.	106b	37.57N	122.04W
Pleasant Hill, Mo., U.S.	111	38.46N	94.18W
Pleasant Hills, Pa., U.S.	230b	40.20N	79.58W
Pleasanton, Ca., U.S. (plĕz'ăn-tŭn)	106b	37.40N	121.53W
Pleasanton, Ks., U.S.	111	38.10N	94.41W
Pleasanton, Tx., U.S.	112	28.58N	98.30W
Pleasant Plain, Oh., U.S. (plĕz'ănt)	101f	39.17N	84.06W
Pleasant Ridge, Mi., U.S.	101b	42.28N	83.09W
Pleasant View, Ut., U.S. (plĕz'ănt vū)	107b	41.20N	112.02W
Pleasantville, Md., U.S.	229c	39.11N	76.38W
Pleasantville, N.Y., U.S. (plĕz'ănt-vĭl)	100a	41.08N	73.47W
Pleasure Ridge Park, Ky., U.S. (plĕzh'ēr rĭj)	101h	38.09N	85.49W
Plenty, Bay of, b., N.Z. (plĕn'tē)	203a	37.30S	177.10E
Plentywood, Mt., U.S. (plĕn'tē-wŏod)	105	48.47N	104.38W
Ples, Russia (plyĕs)	162	57.26N	41.29E
Pleshcheyevo, l., Russia (plĕsh-chā'yĕ-vô)	162	56.50N	38.22E
Plessisville, Can. (plĕ-sē'vēl')	91	46.12N	71.47W
Pleszew, Pol. (plĕ'zhĕf)	155	51.54N	17.48E
Plettenberg, Ger. (plĕ'tĕn-bĕrgh)	157c	51.13N	7.53E
Pleven, Bul. (plĕ'vĕn)	149	43.24N	24.26E
Pljevlja, Yugo. (plĕv'lyä)	149	43.20N	19.21E
Płock, Pol. (pwôtsk)	147	52.32N	19.44E
Ploërmel, Fr. (plô-ĕr-mĕl')	156	47.56N	2.25W
Ploieşti, Rom. (plô-yĕsht')	142	44.56N	26.01E
Plomárion, Grc. (plô-mä'rĭ-ŏn)	161	38.51N	26.24E
Plomb du Cantal, mtn., Fr. (plôn'dükän-täl')	147	45.30N	2.49E
Plonge, Lac la, l., Can. (plōnzh)	88	55.08N	107.25W
Plovdiv, Bul. (plôv'dĭf) (fĭl-ĭp-ŏp'ô-lĭs)	142	42.09N	24.43E
Pluma Hidalgo, Mex. (plōō'mä ē-däl'gō)	119	15.54N	96.23W
Plumpton, Austl.	243a	33.45S	150.50E
Plunge, Lith. (plòn'gä)	153	55.56N	21.45E
Plymouth, Monts.	121b	16.43N	62.12W
Plymouth, Eng., U.K. (plĭm'ŭth)	147	50.25N	4.14W
Plymouth, In., U.S.	98	41.20N	86.20W
Plymouth, Ma., U.S.	99	42.00N	70.45W
Plymouth, Mi., U.S.	101b	42.23N	83.27W
Plymouth, N.H., U.S.	99	43.50N	71.40W
Plymouth, N.C., U.S.	115	35.50N	76.44W
Plymouth, Pa., U.S.	99	41.15N	75.55W
Plymouth, Wi., U.S.	103	43.45N	87.59W
Plyussa, r., Russia (plyōō'sá)	162	58.33N	28.30E
Plzeň, Czech Rep.	142	49.45N	13.23E
Po, r., Italy	142	45.10N	11.00E
Pocahontas, Ar., U.S. (pō-kȧ-hŏn'tȧs)	111	36.15N	91.01W
Pocahontas, Ia., U.S.	103	42.43N	94.41W
Pocatello, Id., U.S. (pō-kȧ-tĕl'ō)	96	42.54N	112.30W
Pochëp, Russia (pō-chĕp')	167	52.56N	33.27E
Pochinok, Russia (pō-chē'nôk)	162	54.14N	32.27E
Pochinski, Russia	166	54.40N	44.50E
Pochotitán, Mex. (pô-chô-tē-tä'n)	118	21.37N	104.33W
Pochutla, Mex.	119	15.46N	96.28W
Pocomoke City, Md., U.S. (pō-kō-mōk')	99	38.05N	75.35W
Pocono Mountains, mts., Pa., U.S. (pō-cō'nō)	99	41.10N	75.30W
Poços de Caldas, Braz. (pō-sôs-dĕ-käl'dás)	131	21.48S	46.34W
Poder, Sen. (pô-dôr')	210	16.35N	15.04W
Podgorica, Yugo.	161	42.25N	19.15E
Podkamennaya Tunguska, r., Russia	165	61.43N	93.45E
Podol'sk, Russia (pô-dôl''sk)	166	55.26N	37.33E
Poggibonsi, Italy (pôd-jē-bôn'sē)	160	43.27N	11.12E
Pogodino, Bela. (pô-gô'dē-nô)	166	54.17N	31.00E
P'ohangdong, S. Kor.	194	35.57N	129.23E
Point Cook, Austl.	243b	37.56S	144.45E
Pointe-à-Pitre, Guad. (pwănt' á pē-tr')	117	16.15N	61.32W
Pointe-aux-Trembles, Can. (pōō-ănt' ō-tränbl)	83a	45.39N	73.30W
Pointe Claire, Can. (pōō-ănt' klĕr)	83a	45.27N	73.48W
Pointe-des-Cascades, Can. (käs-kädz')	83a	45.19N	73.58W
Pointe Fortune, Can. (fôr'tūn)	83a	45.34N	74.23W
Pointe-Gatineau, Can. (pōō-ănt'gä-tē-nō')	83c	45.28N	75.42W
Pointe Noire, Congo	212	4.48S	11.51E
Point Hope, Ak., U.S. (hōp)	95	68.18N	166.38W
Point Pleasant, Md., U.S.	229c	39.11N	76.35W
Point Pleasant, W.V., U.S. (plĕz'ănt)	98	38.50N	82.10W
Point Roberts, Wa., U.S. (rŏb'ērts)	106d	48.59N	123.04W
Poissy, Fr. (pwá-sē')	157b	48.55N	2.02E
Poitiers, Fr. (pwá-tyā')	147	46.35N	0.18E
Pokaran, India (pō'kŭr-ŭn)	186	27.00N	72.05E
Pokrov, Russia (pô-krôf)	162	55.56N	39.09E
Pokrovsko-Strešnevo, neigh., Russia	239b	55.49N	37.29E
Pokrovskoye, Russia (pô-krôf'skô-yĕ)	163	47.27N	38.54E
Pola, r., Russia (pō'lä)	162	57.44N	31.53E
Pola de Laviana, Spain (dĕ-lä-vyä'nä)	158	43.15N	5.29W
Pola de Siero, Spain	158	43.24N	5.39W
Poland, nation, Eur. (pō'lănd)	142	52.37N	17.01E
Polangui, Phil. (pô-läŋ'gē)	197a	13.18N	123.29E
Polazna, Russia (pô'láz-ná)	172a	58.18N	56.25E
Polessk, Russia (pô'lĕsk)	153	54.50N	21.14E
Poles'ye (Pripyat Marshes), sw., Eur.	167	52.10N	27.30E
Polevskoy, Russia (pô-lĕ'vs-kô'ĕ)	172a	56.28N	60.14E
Polgár, Hung. (pôl'gär)	155	47.54N	21.10E
Policastro, Golfo di, b., Italy	160	40.00N	13.23E
Poligny, Fr. (pō-lē-nyē')	157	46.48N	5.42E
Polikhnitos, Grc.	161	39.05N	26.11E

PLACE (Pronunciation)	PAGE	Lat. °'	Long. °'
Polillo, Phil. (pô-lēl'yō)	197a	14.42N	121.56W
Polillo Islands, is., Phil.	183	15.05N	122.15E
Polillo Strait, strt., Phil.	197a	15.02N	121.40E
Polist', r., Russia (pô'lĭst)	162	57.42N	31.02E
Polistena, Italy (pō-lēs-tā'nä)	160	38.25N	16.05E
Políyiros, Grc.	161	40.23N	23.27E
Polkan, Gora, mtn., Russia	165	60.18N	92.08E
Pollensa, Spain (pōl-yĕn'sä)	159	39.50N	3.00E
Polochic, r., Guat. (pō-lô-chēk')	120	15.19N	89.45W
Polonne, Ukr.	163	50.07N	27.31E
Polotsk, Bela. (pô'lôtsk)	166	55.30N	28.48E
Polpaico, Chile (pôl-pá'y-kô)	129b	33.10S	70.53W
Polson, Mt., U.S. (pōl'sŭn)	105	47.40N	114.10W
Polsum, Ger.	236	51.37N	7.03E
Poltava, Ukr. (pôl-tä'vä)	164	49.35N	34.33E
Poltava, prov., Ukr.	163	49.53N	32.58E
Põltsamaa, Est. (põlt'sá-mä)	153	58.39N	26.00E
Polunochnoye, Russia (pô-lōō-nô'ch-nô'yĕ)	172a	60.52N	60.27E
Poluy, r., Russia (pôl'wē)	170	65.45N	68.15E
Polyakovka, Russia (pŭl-yä'kôv-kȧ)	172a	54.38N	59.42E
Polyarnyy, Russia (pŭl-yär'nē)	164	69.10N	33.30E
Polynesia, is., Oc.	224	4.00S	156.00W
Pomba, r., Braz. (pô'm-bá)	129a	21.28S	42.28W
Pomerania, hist. reg., Pol. (pŏm-ē-rā'nĭ-ȧ)	154	53.50N	15.20E
Pomeroy, S. Afr. (pŏm'ēr-roi)	213c	28.36S	30.26E
Pomeroy, Wa., U.S. (pŏm'ēr-oi)	104	46.28N	117.35W
Pomezia, Italy (pô-mĕ't-zyä)	159d	41.41N	12.31E
Pomigliano d'Arco, Italy (pô-mē-lyä'nô-d-ä'r-kô)	159c	40.39N	14.23E
Pomme de Terre, Mn., U.S. (pôm dē tĕr')	102	45.22N	95.52W
Pomona, Ca., U.S. (pō-mō'nȧ)	96	34.04N	117.45W
Pomona Estates, S. Afr.	244b	26.06S	28.15E
Pomorie, Bul.	149	42.24N	27.41E
Pompano Beach, Fl., U.S. (pŏm'pȧ-nō)	115a	26.12N	80.07W
Pompeii Ruins, hist., Italy	159c	40.31N	14.29E
Pomponne, Fr.	237c	48.53N	2.41E
Pompton Lakes, N.J., U.S. (pŏmp'tŏn)	100a	41.01N	74.16W
Pompton Plains, N.J., U.S.	228	40.58N	74.18W
Pomuch, Mex. (pô-mōō'ch)	120a	20.12N	90.10W
Ponca, Ne., U.S. (pŏn'kȧ)	102	42.34N	96.43W
Ponca City, Ok., U.S.	111	36.42N	97.07W
Ponce, P.R. (pōn'sā)	117	18.01N	66.43W
Ponders End, neigh., Eng., U.K.	235	51.39N	0.03W
Pondicherry, India	183	11.58N	79.48E
Pondicherry, state, India	183	11.50N	74.50E
Ponferrada, Spain (pôn-fĕr-rä'dhä)	148	42.33N	6.38W
Ponoka, Can. (pŏ-nō'kȧ)	84	52.42N	113.35W
Ponoy, Russia	166	66.58N	41.00E
Ponoy, r., Russia	166	67.00N	39.00E
Ponta Delgada, Port. (pōn'tȧ dĕl-gä'dȧ)	210a	37.40N	25.45W
Ponta Grossa, Braz. (grō'sȧ)	131	25.09S	50.05W
Pont-à-Mousson, Fr. (pôn'tá-mōōsôn')	157	48.55N	6.02E
Pontarlier, Fr. (pôn'tár-lyā')	157	46.53N	6.22E
Pont-Audemer, Fr. (pôn'tōd'mâr')	156	49.23N	0.28E
Pontault-Combault, Fr.	237c	48.47N	2.36E
Pontchartrain Lake, l., La., U.S. (pôn-shár-trăn')	113	30.10N	90.10W
Pontedera, Italy (pōn-tå-dā'rä)	160	43.37N	10.37E
Ponte de Sor, Port.	158	39.14N	8.03W
Pontefract, Eng., U.K. (pŏn'tē-frăkt)	144a	53.41N	1.18W
Ponte Nova, Braz. (pô'n-tĕ-nô'vá)	131	20.26S	42.52W
Pontevedra, Arg.	233d	34.46S	58.43W
Pontevedra, Spain (pôn-tĕ-vĕ-drä)	148	42.28N	8.38W
Ponthierville see Ubundi, Zaire	212	0.21S	25.29E
Pontiac, Il., U.S. (pŏn'tĭ-ăk)	98	40.55N	88.35W
Pontiac, Mi., U.S.	97	42.37N	83.17W
Pontianak, Indon. (pôn-tē-ä'nák)	196	0.04S	109.20E
Pontian Kechil, Malay.	181b	1.29N	103.24E
Pontic Mountains, mts., Tur.	167	41.20N	34.30E
Pontinha, neigh., Port.	238d	38.46N	9.11W
Pontivy, Fr. (pôn-tē-vē')	156	48.05N	2.57W
Pontoise, Fr. (pôn-twáz')	156	49.03N	2.05E
Pontonnyy, Russia (pôn'tôn-nyĭ)	172c	59.47N	30.39E
Pontotoc, Ms., U.S. (pŏn-tô-tŏk')	114	34.11N	88.59W
Pontremoli, Italy (pôn-trĕm'ô-lē)	160	44.21N	9.50E
Ponziane, Isole, i., Italy (ē'sō-lĕ)	148	40.55N	12.58E
Poole, Eng., U.K. (pōōl)	150	50.43N	2.00W
Poolesville, Md., U.S. (poolĕs-vĭl)	100e	39.08N	77.26W
Pooley Island, i., Can. (pōō'lē)	86	52.44N	128.16W
Poopó, Lago de, l., Bol.	130	18.45S	67.07W
Popayán, Col. (pō-pä-yän')	130	2.21N	76.43W
Popivka, Ukr.	163	50.03N	33.41E
Popivka, Ukr.	163	51.13N	33.08E
Poplar, Mt., U.S. (pŏp'lēr)	105	48.08N	105.10W
Poplar, neigh., Eng., U.K.	235	51.31N	0.01W
Poplar, r., Mt., U.S.	105	48.34N	105.20W
Poplar, West Fork, r., Mt., U.S.	105	48.59N	106.06W
Poplar Bluff, Mo., U.S. (blŭf)	111	36.43N	90.22W
Poplar Heights, Va., U.S.	229d	38.53N	77.12W
Poplar Plains, Ky., U.S. (plāns)	98	38.20N	83.40W
Poplar Point, Can.	83f	50.04N	97.57W
Poplarville, Ms., U.S. (pŏp'lēr-vĭl)	114	30.50N	89.33W
Popocatépetl Volcán, Mex. (pô-pô-kä-tä'pĕ't'l)	116	19.01N	98.38W
Popokabaka, Zaire (pō'pô-kȧ-bä'kȧ)	212	5.42S	16.35E
Popovo, Bul. (pô'pô-vô)	161	43.23N	26.17E
Porbandar, India (pōr-bŭn'dŭr)	183	21.44N	69.40E
Porce, r., Col. (pôr-sĕ)	130a	7.11N	74.55W
Porcher Island, i., Can. (pôr'kēr)	86	53.57N	130.30W
Porcuna, Spain (pôr-kōō'nä)	158	37.54N	4.10W
Porcupine, r., N.A.	95	67.38N	140.07W
Porcupine Creek, r., Mt., U.S.	105	48.27N	106.24W

PLACE (Pronunciation)	PAGE	Lat. °'	Long. °'
Porcupine Hills, hills, Can.	89	52.30N	101.45W
Pordenone, Italy (pōr-då-nō'nå)	160	45.58N	12.38E
Pori, Fin. (pô'rē)	146	61.29N	21.45E
Poriúncula, Braz.	129a	20.58S	42.02W
Porkhov, Russia (pôr'κôf)	166	57.46N	29.33E
Porlamar, Ven. (pōr-lä-mär')	130	11.00N	63.55W
Pornic, Fr. (pôr-nēk')	156	47.08N	2.07W
Poronaysk, Russia (pô'rô-nīsk)	165	49.21N	143.23E
Porrentruy, Switz. (pô-răn-trüē')	154	47.25N	7.02E
Porsgrunn, Nor. (pôrs'grôn')	152	59.09N	9.36E
Portachuelo, Bol. (pôrt-ä-chwā'lô)	130	17.20S	63.12W
Portage, Pa., U.S. (pôr'tȧj)	99	40.25N	78.35W
Portage, Wi., U.S.	103	43.33N	89.29W
Portage Des Sioux, Mo., U.S. (dē sōō)	107e	38.56N	90.21W
Portage la Prairie, Can. (lä-prā'rĭ)	84	49.57N	98.25W
Port Alberni, Can. (pōr äl-bĕr-nē')	84	49.14N	124.48W
Portalegre, Port. (pôr-tä-lā'grĕ)	148	39.18N	7.26W
Portales, N.M., U.S. (pôr-tä'lĕs)	110	34.10N	103.11W
Port Alfred, S. Afr.	212	33.36S	26.55E
Port Alice, Can. (ăl'ĭs)	84	50.23N	127.27W
Port Allegany, Pa., U.S. (ăl-ē-gā'nĭ)	99	41.50N	78.10W
Port Angeles, Wa., U.S. (ăn'jē-lĕs)	96	48.07N	123.26W
Port Antonio, Jam.	117	18.10N	76.25W
Portarlington, Austl.	201a	38.07S	144.39E
Port Arthur, Tx., U.S.	97	29.52N	93.59W
Port Augusta, Austl. (ô-gŭs'tȧ)	204	32.28S	137.50E
Port au Port Bay, b., Can. (pôr'tō pōr')	93	48.41N	58.45W
Port-au-Prince, Haiti (prăns')	117	18.35N	72.20W
Port Austin, Mi., U.S. (ôs'tĭn)	98	44.00N	83.00W
Port Blair, India (blâr)	196	12.07N	92.45E
Port Bolivar, Tx., U.S. (bŏl'ĭ-vár)	113a	29.22N	94.46W
Port Borden, Can. (bôr'dĕn)	92	46.15N	63.42W
Port-Bouët, C. Iv.	210	5.24N	3.56W
Port-Cartier, Can.	92	50.01N	66.53W
Port Chester, N.Y., U.S. (chĕs'tēr)	100a	40.59N	73.40W
Port Chicago, Ca., U.S. (shĭ-kô'gō)	106b	38.03N	122.01W
Port Clinton, Oh., U.S. (klĭn'tŭn)	98	41.30N	83.00W
Port Colborne, Can.	91	42.53N	79.13W
Port Coquitlam, Can. (kô-kwĭt'lȧm)	87	49.16N	122.46W
Port Credit, Can. (krĕd'ĭt)	83d	43.33N	79.35W
Port-de-Bouc, Fr. (pôr-dē-bōōk')	156a	43.24N	5.00E
Port de Paix, Haiti (pĕ)	123	19.55N	72.50W
Port Dickson, Malay. (dĭk'sŭn)	181b	2.33N	101.49E
Port Discovery, b., Wa., U.S. (dĭs-kŭv'ēr-ĭ)	106a	48.05N	122.55W
Port Edward, S. Afr. (ĕd'wērd)	213c	31.04S	30.14E
Port Elgin, Can. (ĕl'jĭn)	92	46.03N	64.05W
Port Elizabeth, S. Afr. (ē-lĭz'ȧ-bĕth)	212	33.57S	25.37E
Porterdale, Ga., U.S. (pōr'tēr-dāl)	114	33.34N	83.53W
Porterville, Ca., U.S. (pōr'tēr-vĭl)	108	36.03N	119.05W
Port Francqui see Ilebo, Zaire	212	4.19S	20.35E
Port Gamble, Wa., U.S. (găm'bŭl)	106a	47.52N	122.36W
Port Gamble Indian Reservation, I.R., Wa., U.S.	106a	47.54N	122.33W
Port-Gentil, Gabon (zhän-tē')	212	0.43S	8.47E
Port Gibson, Ms., U.S.	114	31.56N	90.57W
Port Harcourt, Nig. (här'kŭrt)	210	4.43N	7.05E
Port Hardy, Can. (här'dĭ)	86	50.43N	127.29W
Port Hawkesbury, Can.	93	45.37N	61.21W
Port Hedland, Austl. (hĕd'lănd)	202	20.30S	118.30E
Porthill, Id., U.S.	104	49.00N	116.30W
Port Hood, Can. (hŏŏd)	93	46.01N	61.32W
Port Hope, Can. (hōp)	91	43.55N	78.10W
Port Huron, Mi., U.S. (hū'rŏn)	97	43.00N	82.30W
Portici, Italy (pôr'tē-chē)	159c	40.34N	14.20E
Portillo, Chile (pôr-tē'l-yô)	129b	32.51S	70.09W
Portimão, Port. (pôr-tē-mouN)	158	37.09N	8.34W
Port Jervis, N.Y., U.S. (jŭr'vĭs)	100a	41.22N	74.41W
Portland, Austl. (pōrt'lănd)	203	38.20S	142.40E
Portland, In., U.S.	98	40.25N	85.00W
Portland, Me., U.S.	97	43.40N	70.16W
Portland, Mi., U.S.	98	42.50N	85.00W
Portland, Or., U.S.	96	45.31N	122.41W
Portland, Tx., U.S.	113	27.53N	97.20W
Portland Bight, bt., Jam.	122	17.45N	77.05W
Portland Canal, can., Ak., U.S.	86	55.10N	130.08W
Portland Inlet, b., Can.	86	54.50N	130.15W
Portland Point, c., Jam.	122	17.40N	77.20W
Port Lavaca, Tx., U.S. (lȧ-vä'kȧ)	113	28.36N	96.38W
Port Lincoln, Austl. (lĭŋ-kŭn)	202	34.39S	135.50E
Port Ludlow, Wa., U.S. (lŭd'lō)	106a	47.26N	122.41W
Port Macquarie, Austl. (mȧ-kwŏ'rĭ)	203	31.25S	152.45E
Port Madison Indian Reservation, I.R., Wa., U.S. (măd'ĭ-sŭn)	106a	47.46N	122.38W
Port Maria, Jam. (mȧ-rī'ȧ)	122	18.20N	76.55W
Port Melbourne, Austl.	243b	37.51S	144.56E
Port Moody, Can. (mōōd'ĭ)	87	49.17N	122.51W
Port Moresby, Pap. N. Gui. (môrz'bē)	197	9.34S	147.20E
Port Neches, Tx., U.S. (nĕch'ĕz)	113	29.59N	93.57W
Port Nelson, Can. (nĕl'sŭn)	89	57.03N	92.36W
Portneuf-Sur-Mer, Can. (pôr-nûf'sür mĕr)	92	48.36N	69.06W
Port Nolloth, S. Afr. (nŏl'ŏth)	212	29.10S	17.00E
Porto (Oporto), Port. (pôr'tō)	142	41.10N	8.38W
Porto Acre, Braz. (ä'krĕ)	130	9.38S	67.34W
Porto Alegre, Braz. (ä-lā'grĕ)	132	29.58S	51.11W
Porto Amboim, Ang.	212	11.01S	13.45E
Portobelo, Pan. (pôr'tô-bā'lô)	117	9.32N	79.40W
Pôrto de Pedras, Braz. (pā'drăzh)	131	9.09S	35.20W
Pôrto Feliz, Braz. (fē-lē's)	129a	23.12S	47.30W
Portoferraio, Italy (pōr'tō-fĕr-rä'yō)	160	42.47N	10.20E
Port of Spain, Trin. (spān)	131	10.44N	61.24W
Portogruaro, Italy (pōr'tō-grō-ä'rō)	160	45.48N	12.49E
Portola, Ca., U.S. (pôr'tō-lȧ)	108	39.47N	120.29W
Porto Mendes, Braz. (mĕ'n-dĕs)	131	24.41S	54.13W

PLACE (Pronunciation)	PAGE	Lat. °′	Long. °′
Porto Murtinho, Braz. (mòr-tēn'yò)	131	21.43S	57.43W
Porto Nacional, Braz. (nà-syô-näl')	131	10.43S	48.14W
Porto Novo, Benin (pōr'tô-nō'vō)	210	6.29N	2.37E
Port Orchard, Wa., U.S. (ôr'chẽrd)	106a	47.32N	122.38W
Port Orchard, b., Wa., U.S.	106a	47.40N	122.39W
Porto Salvo, Port.	238d	38.43N	9.18W
Porto Santo, Ilha de, i., Port. (säN'tò)	210	32.41N	16.15W
Porto Seguro, Braz. (sā-gōō'rò)	131	16.26S	38.59W
Porto Torres, Italy (tôr'rĕs)	160	40.49N	8.25E
Porto-Vecchio, Fr. (vĕk'ē-ô)	160	41.36N	9.17E
Porto Velho, Braz. (väl'yò)	130	8.45S	63.43W
Portoviejo, Ec. (pôr-tō-vyā'hō)	130	1.11S	80.28W
Port Phillip Bay, b., Austl. (fĭl'ĭp)	203	37.57S	144.50E
Port Pirie, Austl. (pĭ'rē)	202	33.10S	138.00E
Port Reading, N.J., U.S.	228	40.34N	74.16W
Port Royal, b., Jam. (roi'ăl)	122	17.50N	76.45W
Port Said, Egypt	218c	31.15N	32.19E
Port Saint Johns, S. Afr. (sånt jŏnz)	212	31.37S	29.32E
Port Shepstone, S. Afr. (shĕps'tŭn)	212	30.45S	30.23E
Portsmouth, Dom.	121b	15.33N	61.28W
Portsmouth, Eng., U.K. (pôrts'mŭth)	142	50.45N	1.03W
Portsmouth, N.H., U.S.	97	43.05N	70.50W
Portsmouth, Oh., U.S.	97	38.45N	83.00W
Portsmouth, Va., U.S.	97	36.50N	76.19W
Port Sulphur, La., U.S. (sŭl'fẽr)	114	29.28N	89.41W
Port Sunlight, Eng., U.K.	237a	53.21N	2.59W
Port Susan, b., Wa., U.S. (sū-zán')	106a	48.11N	122.25W
Port Townsend, Wa., U.S. (tounz'ĕnd)	106a	48.07N	122.46W
Port Townsend, b., Wa., U.S.	106a	48.05N	122.47W
Portugal, nation, Eur. (pōr'tu-găl)	142	38.15N	8.08W
Portugalete, Spain (pōr-tōō-gä-lā'tä)	158	43.18N	3.05W
Portuguese West Africa see Angola, nation, Ang.	212	14.15S	16.00E
Port Vendres, Fr.	156	42.32N	3.07E
Port Vila, Vanuatu	203	17.44S	168.19E
Port Vue, Pa., U.S.	230b	40.20N	79.52W
Port Wakefield, Austl. (wāk'fēld)	202	34.12S	138.10E
Port Washington, N.Y., U.S. (wôsh'ĭng-tŭn)	100a	40.49N	73.42W
Port Washington, Wi., U.S.	103	43.24N	87.52W
Posadas, Arg. (pō-sä'dhäs)	132	27.32S	55.56W
Posadas, Spain (pō-sä-däs)	158	37.48N	5.09W
Poshekhon'ye Volodarsk, Russia (pô-shyĕ'kôn-yĕ vôl'ô-dársk)	162	58.31N	39.07E
Poso, Danau, l., Indon. (pō'sō)	196	2.00S	119.40E
Pospelokova, Russia (pôs-pyĕl'kô-vá)	172a	59.25N	60.50E
Possession Sound, strt., Wa., U.S. (pŏ-zĕsh-ŭn)	106a	47.59N	122.17W
Possum Kingdom Reservoir, res., Tx., U.S. (pŏs'ŭm kĭng'dŭm)	112	32.58N	98.12W
Post, Tx., U.S. (pōst)	110	33.12N	101.21W
Postojna, Slvn. (pōs-tōyná)	160	45.45N	14.13E
Pos'yet, Russia (pos-yĕt')	194	42.27N	130.47E
Potawatomi Indian Reservation, I.R., Ks., U.S. (pŏt-å-wä'tō mē)	111	39.30N	96.11W
Potchefstroom, S. Afr. (pŏch'ĕf-strōm)	212	26.42S	27.06E
Poteau, Ok., U.S. (pò-tō')	111	35.03N	94.37W
Poteet, Tx., U.S. (pò-tēt)	112	29.05N	98.35W
Potenza, Italy (pò-tĕnt'sä)	149	40.39N	15.49E
Potenza, r., Italy	160	43.09N	13.00E
Potgietersrus, S. Afr. (pŏt-kē'tẽrs-rûs)	212	24.09S	29.04E
Potholes Reservoir, res., Wa., U.S.	104	47.00N	119.20W
Poti, Geor. (pô'tē)	167	42.10N	41.40E
Potiskum, Nig.	210	11.43N	11.05E
Potomac, Md., U.S. (pò-tō'măk)	100e	39.01N	77.13W
Potomac, r., U.S. (pò-tō'măk)	97	38.15N	76.55W
Poto Poto, neigh., Congo	244c	4.15S	15.18E
Potosí, Bol.	130	19.35S	65.45W
Potosi, Mo., U.S. (pō-tō'sĭ)	111	37.56N	90.46W
Potosi, r., Mex. (pō-tô-sē')	112	25.04N	99.36W
Potrerillos, Hond. (pō-trä-rēl'yōs)	120	15.13N	87.58W
Potsdam, Ger. (pôts'däm)	147	52.24N	13.04E
Potsdam, N.Y., U.S. (pŏts'dăm)	99	44.40N	75.00W
Pottenstein, Aus.	145e	47.58N	16.06E
Potters Bar, Eng., U.K. (pŏt'ĕz bär)	144b	51.41N	0.12W
Potter Street, Eng., U.K.	235	51.46N	0.08E
Pottstown, Pa., U.S. (pŏts'toun)	99	40.15N	75.40W
Pottsville, Pa., U.S. (pôts'vĭl)	99	40.40N	76.15W
Poughkeepsie, N.Y., U.S. (pŏ-kĭp'sē)	97	41.45N	73.55W
Poulsbo, Wa., U.S. (pōlz'bò)	106a	47.44N	122.38W
Poulton-le-Fylde, Eng., U.K. (pōl'tŭn-lē-fīld')	144a	53.52N	2.59W
Pouso Alegre, Braz. (pō'zò ä-lā'grĕ)	131	22.13S	45.56W
Póvoa de Varzim, Port. (pō-vō'á dā vär'zēN)	148	41.23N	8.44W
Powder, r., U.S. (pou'dẽr)	96	45.18N	105.37W
Powder, r., Or., U.S.	104	44.55N	117.35W
Powder, South Fork, r., Wy., U.S.	105	43.13N	106.54W
Powder River, Wy., U.S.	105	43.06N	106.55W
Powell, Wy., U.S. (pou'ĕl)	105	44.44N	108.44W
Powell, Lake, res., U.S.	96	37.26N	110.25W
Powell Lake, l., Can.	86	50.10N	124.13W
Powell Point, c., Bah.	122	24.50N	76.20W
Powell Reservoir, res., Ky., U.S.	114	36.30N	83.35W
Powell River, Can.	84	49.52N	124.33W
Poyang Hu, l., China	189	29.20N	116.28E
Poygan, r., Wi., U.S. (poi'găn)	103	44.10N	89.05W
Poyle, Eng., U.K.	235	51.28N	0.31W
Poynton, Eng., U.K.	237b	53.21N	2.07W
Požarevac, Yugo. (pô'zhá'rĕ-váts)	161	44.38N	21.12E
Poza Rica, Mex. (pô-zô-rē'kä)	119	20.32N	97.25W
Poznań, Pol.	142	52.25N	16.55E
Pozoblanco, Spain (pô-thō-blän'kō)	158	38.23N	4.50W
Pozos, Mex. (pó'zōs)	118	22.05N	100.50W
Pozuelo de Alarcón, Spain (pô-thwā'lō dā ä-lär-kōn')	159a	40.27N	3.49W
Pozzuoli, Italy (pôt-swô'lē)	160	40.34N	14.08E
Pra, r., Ghana (prá)	214	5.45N	1.35W
Pra, r., Russia	162	55.00N	40.13E
Prachin Buri, Thai. (prä'chēn)	196	13.59N	101.15E
Pradera, Col. (prä-dĕ'rä)	130a	3.24N	76.13W
Prades, Fr. (pråd)	156	42.37N	2.23E
Prado, Col. (prädô)	130a	3.44N	74.55W
Prado, Museo del, bldg., Spain	238b	40.25N	3.41W
Prado Churubusco, Mex.	233a	19.21N	99.07W
Prado Reservoir, res., Ca., U.S. (prä'dō)	107a	33.45N	117.40W
Prados, Braz. (prá'dôs)	129a	21.05S	44.04W
Prague, Czech Rep.	154	50.05N	14.26E
Praha see Prague, Czech Rep.	142	50.05N	14.26E
Prahran, Austl.	243b	37.51S	144.59E
Praia, C.V. (prä'yá)	210b	15.00N	23.30W
Praia Funda, Ponta da, c., Braz. (pôn'tä-då-prä'yá-fōō'n-dä)	132b	23.04S	43.34W
Prairie du Chien, Wi., U.S. (prā'rĭ dò shēn')	103	43.02N	91.10W
Prairie Grove, Can. (prā'rĭ grōv)	83f	49.48N	96.57W
Prairie Island Indian Reservation, I.R., Mn., U.S.	103	44.42N	92.32W
Prairies, Rivière des, r., Can. (rē-vyâr' dā prâ-rē')	83a	45.40N	73.34W
Pratas Island, i., Asia	193	20.40N	116.30E
Prat del Llobregat, Spain	238e	41.20N	2.06E
Prato, Italy (prä'tō)	160	43.53N	11.03E
Pratt, Ks., U.S. (prăt)	110	37.37N	98.43W
Pratt's Bottom, neigh., Eng., U.K.	235	51.20N	0.07E
Prattville, Al., U.S. (prăt'vĭl)	114	32.28N	86.27W
Pravdinsk, Russia	153	54.26N	21.00E
Pravdinskiy, Russia (práv-dĕn'skĭ)	172b	56.03N	37.52E
Pravia, Spain (prä'vē-ä)	158	43.30N	6.08W
Pregolya, r., Russia (prĕ-gô'lă)	153	54.37N	20.50E
Premont, Tx., U.S. (prē-mŏnt')	112	27.20N	98.07W
Prenton, Eng., U.K.	237a	53.22N	3.03W
Prenzlau, Ger. (prĕnts'lou)	154	53.19N	13.52E
Prenzlauer Berg, neigh., Ger.	238a	52.32N	13.26E
Přerov, Czech Rep. (przhĕ'rôf)	147	49.28N	17.28E
Prescot, Eng., U.K. (prĕs'kŭt)	144a	53.25N	2.48W
Prescott, Can. (prĕs'kŭt)	99	44.45N	75.35W
Prescott, Az., U.S. (prĕs'kŏt)	96	34.30N	112.30W
Prescott, Ar., U.S.	111	33.47N	93.23W
Prescott, Wi., U.S. (prĕs'kŏt)	107g	44.45N	92.48W
Presho, S.D., U.S. (prĕsh'ô)	102	43.56N	100.04W
Presidencia Rogue Sáenz Peña, Arg.	132	26.52S	60.15W
Presidente Epitácio, Braz. (prā-sē-dĕn'tē å-pē-tä'syò)	131	21.56S	52.01W
Presidente Roosevelt, Estação, trans., Braz.	234d	23.33S	46.36W
Presidio, Tx., U.S. (prĕ-sĭ'dĭ-ô)	112	29.33N	104.23W
Presidio, Río del, r., Mex. (rē'ō-dĕl-prĕ-sē'dyô)	118	23.54N	105.44W
Presidio of San Francisco, pt. of i., Ca., U.S.	231b	37.48N	122.28W
Prešov, Slvk. (prĕ'shôf)	147	49.00N	21.18E
Prespa, Lake, l., Eur. (prĕs'pä)	161	40.49N	20.50E
Prespuntal, r., Ven.	131b	9.55N	64.32W
Presque Isle, Me., U.S. (prĕsk'ēl')	92	46.41N	68.03W
Pressbaum, Aus.	145e	48.12N	16.06E
Prestea, Ghana	214	5.27N	2.08W
Preston, Austl.	201a	37.45S	145.01E
Preston, Eng., U.K. (prĕs'tŭn)	150	53.46N	2.42W
Preston, Id., U.S. (pres'tŭn)	105	42.05N	111.54W
Preston, Mn., U.S. (prĕs'tŭn)	103	43.42N	92.06W
Preston, Wa., U.S.	106a	47.31N	121.56W
Prestonburg, Ky., U.S. (prĕs'tŭn-bûrg)	98	37.35N	82.50W
Prestwich, Eng., U.K. (prĕst'wĭch)	144a	53.32N	2.17W
Pretoria, S. Afr. (prĕ-tō'rĭ-ȧ)	212	25.43S	28.16E
Pretoria North, S. Afr. (prĕ-tō'rĭ-ȧ nōōrd)	218d	25.41S	28.11E
Préveza, Grc. (prĕ'vå-zä)	161	38.58N	20.44E
Pribilof Islands, is., Ak., U.S. (prĭ'bĭ-lof)	95	57.00N	169.20W
Priboj, Yugo. (prē'boi)	161	43.33N	19.33E
Price, Ut., U.S. (prīs)	109	39.35N	110.50W
Price, r., Ut., U.S.	109	39.21N	110.35W
Prichard, Al., U.S. (prĭt'chârd)	114	30.44N	88.04W
Priddis, Can. (prĭd'dĭs)	83e	50.53N	114.20W
Priddis Creek, r., Can.	83e	50.56N	114.32W
Priego, Spain (prē-ā'gō)	158	37.27N	4.13W
Prienai, Lith. (prē-ĕn'ī)	153	54.38N	23.56E
Prieska, S. Afr. (prē-ĕs'kȧ)	212	29.40S	22.50E
Priest Lake, l., Id., U.S. (prēst)	104	48.30N	116.43W
Priest Rapids Dam, Wa., U.S.	104	46.39N	119.55W
Priest Rapids Lake, res., Wa., U.S.	104	46.42N	119.58W
Priiskovaya, Russia (prĭ-ĕs'kô-va-yá)	172a	60.50N	58.55E
Prijedor, Bos. (prē'yĕ-dôr)	160	44.58N	16.43E
Prijepolje, Yugo. (prē'yĕ-pô'lyĕ)	161	43.22N	19.41E
Prilep, Mac. (prē'lĕp)	149	41.20N	21.35E
Primorsk, Russia (prē-môrsk')	153	60.24N	28.35E
Primorsko-Akhtarskaya, Russia (prē-môr'skô äk-tär'skĭ-ê)	167	46.03N	38.09E
Primos, Pa., U.S.	229b	39.55N	75.18W
Primrose, S. Afr.	213b	26.11S	28.11E
Primrose Lake, l., Can.	88	54.55N	109.45W
Prince Albert, Can. (prĭns ăl'bẽrt)	84	53.12N	105.46W
Prince Albert National Park, rec., Can.	84	54.10N	105.25W
Prince Albert Sound, strt., Can.	84	70.23N	116.57W
Prince Charles Island, i., Can. (chärlz)	85	67.41N	74.10W
Prince Edward Island, prov., Can.	85	46.45N	63.10W
Prince Edward Islands, is., S. Afr.	219	46.36S	37.57E
Prince Edward National Park, rec., Can. (ĕd'wẽrd)	85	46.33N	63.35W
Prince Edward Peninsula, pen., Can.	99	44.00N	77.15W
Prince Frederick, Md., U.S. (prĭnce frĕdĕrĭk)	100e	38.33N	76.35W
Prince George, Can. (jôrj)	84	53.51N	122.57W
Prince of Wales, i., Austl.	203	10.47S	142.15E
Prince of Wales, i., Ak., U.S.	95	55.47N	132.50W
Prince of Wales, Cape, c., Ak., U.S. (wālz)	95	65.48N	169.08W
Prince Rupert, Can. (roo'pĕrt)	84	54.19N	130.19W
Princes Risborough, Eng., U.K. (prĭns'ĕz rĭz'brŭ)	144b	51.41N	0.51W
Princess Charlotte Bay, b., Austl. (shär'lŏt)	203	13.45S	144.15E
Princess Royal Channel, strt., Can. (roi'ăl)	86	53.10N	128.37W
Princess Royal Island, i., Can.	86	52.57N	128.49W
Princeton, Can. (prĭns'tŭn)	84	49.27N	120.31W
Princeton, Il., U.S.	98	41.20N	89.25W
Princeton, In., U.S.	98	38.20N	87.35W
Princeton, Ky., U.S.	114	37.07N	87.52W
Princeton, Mi., U.S.	103	46.16N	87.33W
Princeton, Mn., U.S.	103	45.34N	93.36W
Princeton, Mo., U.S.	111	40.23N	93.34W
Princeton, N.J., U.S.	99	40.21N	74.40W
Princeton, W.V., U.S.	115	37.21N	81.05W
Princeton, Wi., U.S.	103	43.50N	89.09W
Prince William Sound, strt., Ak., U.S. (wĭl'yăm)	95	60.40N	147.10W
Príncipe, i., S. Tom./P. (prēn'sē-pĕ)	210	1.37N	7.25E
Principe Channel, strt., Can. (prĭn'sĭ-pē)	86	53.28N	129.45W
Prineville, Or., U.S. (prīn'vĭl)	104	44.17N	120.48W
Prineville Reservoir, res., Or., U.S.	104	44.07N	120.45W
Prinzapolca, Nic. (prēn-zä-pōl'kä)	121	13.18N	83.35W
Prinzapolca, r., Nic.	121	13.23N	84.23W
Prior Lake, Mn., U.S. (prī'ẽr)	107g	44.43N	93.26W
Priozërsk, Russia (prĭ-ô'zĕrsk)	153	61.03N	30.08E
Pripet, r., Eur.	167	51.50N	29.45E
Pripyat Marshes see Poles'ye, sw., Eur.	167	52.10N	27.30E
Priština, Yugo. (prēsh'tĭ-nä)	149	42.39N	21.12E
Pritzwalk, Ger. (prēts'välk)	154	53.09N	12.12E
Privas, Fr. (prē-väs')	156	44.44N	4.37E
Prizren, Yugo. (prē'zrĕn)	149	42.11N	20.45E
Procida, Italy (prô'chē-dä)	159c	40.31N	14.02E
Procida, Isola di, i., Italy	159c	40.32N	13.57E
Proctor, Mn., U.S. (prŏk'tẽr)	107h	46.45N	92.14W
Proctor, Vt., U.S.	99	43.40N	73.00W
Proebstel, Wa., U.S. (prōb'stĕl)	106c	45.40N	122.29W
Proenca-a-Nova, Port. (prô-ān'så-ä-nō'vȧ)	158	39.44N	7.55W
Progreso, Hond. (prò-grĕ'sò)	120	15.28N	87.49W
Progreso, Mex.	112	27.29N	101.05W
Progreso, Mex. (prò-grā'sō)	116	21.14N	89.39W
Prokhladnyy, Russia	168	43.46N	44.00E
Prokop'yevsk, Russia	170	53.53N	86.45E
Prokuplje, Yugo. (prô'kōp'l-yĕ)	161	43.16N	21.40E
Prome, Myanmar	196	18.46N	95.15E
Pronya, r., Bela. (prô'nyä)	162	54.08N	30.58E
Pronya, r., Russia	162	54.08N	39.30E
Prospect, Austl.	243a	33.48S	150.56E
Prospect, Ky., U.S. (prŏs'pĕkt)	101h	38.21N	85.36W
Prospect Heights, Il., U.S.	231a	42.06N	87.56W
Prospect Park, N.J., U.S.	228	40.56N	74.10W
Prospect Park, Pa., U.S. (prŏs'pĕkt pärk)	100f	39.53N	75.18W
Prosser, Wa., U.S. (prŏs'ẽr)	104	46.10N	119.46W
Prostějov, Czech Rep. (prôs'tyĕ-yôf)	155	49.28N	17.08E
Protea, S. Afr.	244b	26.17S	27.51E
Protection, i., Wa., U.S. (prô-tĕk'shŭn)	106a	48.07N	122.56W
Protoka, r., Russia (prôt'ô-kå)	162	55.00N	36.42E
Provadiya, Bul. (prō-väd'ē-yȧ)	161	43.13N	27.28E
Providence, Ky., U.S. (prŏv'ĭ-dĕns)	98	37.25N	87.45W
Providence, R.I., U.S.	97	41.50N	71.23W
Providence, Ut., U.S.	105	41.42N	111.50W
Providencia, Chile	234b	33.26S	70.37W
Providencia, Isla de, i., Col.	121	13.21N	80.55W
Providenciales, i., T./C. Is.	123	21.50N	72.15W
Provideniya, Russia (prô-vĭ-dä'nĭ-yá)	95	64.30N	172.54W
Provincetown, Ma., U.S.	99	42.03N	70.11W
Provo, Ut., U.S. (prō'vō)	96	40.15N	111.40W
Prozor, Bos. (prô'zôr)	161	43.48N	17.59E
Prudence Island, i., R.I., U.S. (prōō'dĕns)	100b	41.38N	71.20W
Prudhoe Bay, b., Ak., U.S.	95	70.40N	147.25W
Prudnik, Pol. (prŏd'nĭk)	155	50.19N	17.34E
Prussia, hist. reg., Eur. (prŭsh'ȧ)	154	50.43N	8.35E
Pruszków, Pol. (pròsh'kôf)	155	52.09N	20.50E
Prut, r., Eur. (prōōt)	142	48.05N	27.07E
Pryluky, Ukr.	167	50.36N	32.21E
Prymors'k, Ukr.	163	46.43N	36.21E
Pryor, Ok., U.S. (prī'ẽr)	111	36.16N	95.19W
Pryvil'ne, Ukr.	163	47.30N	32.21E
Przedbórz, Pol.	155	51.05N	19.53E
Przemyśl, Pol. (pzhĕ'mĭsh'l)	142	49.47N	22.45E
Przheval'sk, Kyrg. (p'r-zhĭ-välsk')	169	42.29N	78.24E
Psikhikón, Grc.	239d	38.00N	23.47E
Pskov, Russia (pskôf)	164	57.48N	28.19E
Pskov, prov., Russia	162	57.33N	29.05E
Pskovskoye Ozero, l., Eur. (p'skôv'skō'yĕ ôzĕ-rô)	166	58.05N	28.15E
Ps'ol, r., Eur.	167	49.45N	33.42E
Ptich', r., Bela. (p'tēch)	166	53.17N	28.16E
Ptuj, Slvn. (ptōō'ē)	160	46.24N	15.54E
Pucheng, China (pōō-chŭŋ)	190	35.43N	115.22E
Pucheng, China (pōō'chĕng')	193	28.02N	118.25E
Puck, Pol. (pôtsk)	155	54.43N	18.23E

336 Puddington – Querenburg

PLACE (Pronunciation)	PAGE	Lat. °'	Long. °'
Puddington, Eng., U.K.	237a	53.15N	3.00W
Pudozh, Russia (pōō'dôzh)	166	61.50N	36.50E
Puebla, Mex. (pwā'blä)	116	19.02N	98.11W
Puebla, state, Mex.	119	19.00N	97.45W
Puebla de Don Fadrique, Spain	158	37.55N	2.55W
Pueblo, Co., U.S. (pwā'blō)	96	38.15N	104.36W
Pueblo Libre, Peru	233c	12.05S	77.05W
Pueblo Nuevo, Mex. (nwā'vô)	118	23.23N	105.21W
Pueblo Nuevo, neigh., Spain	238b	40.26N	3.39W
Pueblo Viejo, Mex. (vyā'hô)	119	17.23N	93.46W
Puente Alto, Chile (pwĕ'n-tĕ äl'tô)	129b	33.36S	70.34W
Puenteareas, Spain (pwĕn-tä-ä-rā'äs)	158	42.09N	8.23W
Puentedeume, Spain (pwĕn-tå-dhå-ōō'må)	158	43.28N	8.09W
Puente-Genil, Spain (pwĕn'tå-hå-nēl')	158	37.25N	4.18W
Puerco, Rio, r., N.M., U.S. (pwĕr'kō)	109	35.15N	107.05W
Puerto Aisén, Chile (pwĕ'r-tō ä'y-sĕ'n)	132	45.28S	72.44W
Puerto Angel, Mex. (pwĕ'r-tō äŋ'hål)	119	15.42N	96.32W
Puerto Armuelles, Pan. (pwe'r-tō är-mōō-ā'lyās)	121	8.18N	82.52W
Puerto Barrios, Guat. (pwĕ'r-tô bär'rê-ôs)	116	15.43N	88.36W
Puerto Bermúdez, Peru (pwĕ'r-tō bĕr-mōō'dāz)	130	10.17S	74.57W
Puerto Berrío, Col. (pwĕ'r-tō bĕr-rē'ō)	130	6.29N	74.27W
Puerto Cabello, Ven. (pwĕ'r-tō kä-bĕl'yō)	130	10.28N	68.01W
Puerto Cabezas, Nic. (pwĕ'r-tô kä-bā'zäs)	121	14.01N	83.26W
Puerto Casado, Para. (pwĕ'r-tō kä-sä'dō)	132	22.16S	57.57W
Puerto Castilla, Hond. (pwĕ'r-tô käs-tēl'yō)	120	16.01N	86.01W
Puerto Chicama, Peru (pwĕ'r-tō chē-kä'mä)	130	7.46S	79.18W
Puerto Colombia, Col. (pwĕr'tô kô-lôm'bê-ä)	130	11.08N	75.09W
Puerto Cortés, C.R. (pwĕ'r-tô kôr-tās')	121	9.00N	83.37W
Puerto Cortés, Hond. (pwĕ'r-tô kôr-tās')	116	15.48N	87.57W
Puerto Cumarebo, Ven. (pwĕ'r-tō kōō-mä-rĕ'bô)	130	11.25N	69.17W
Puerto de Luna, N.M., U.S. (pwĕr'tô då lōō'nä)	110	34.49N	104.36W
Puerto de Nutrias, Ven. (pwĕ'r-tô dĕ nōō-trê-äs')	130	8.02N	69.19W
Puerto Deseado, Arg. (pwĕ'r-tō dā-så-ä'dhō)	132	47.38S	66.00W
Puerto de Somport, p., Eur.	159	42.51N	0.25W
Puerto Eten, Peru (pwĕ'r-tō ĕ-tĕ'n)	130	6.59S	79.51W
Puerto Jiménez, C.R. (pwĕ'r-tô ĸê-mĕ'nĕz)	121	8.35N	83.23W
Puerto La Cruz, Ven. (pwĕ'r-tō lä krōō'z)	130	10.14N	64.38W
Puertollano, Spain (pwĕ-tôl-yä'nō)	148	38.41N	4.05W
Puerto Madryn, Arg. (pwĕ'r-tō mä-drĕn')	132	42.45S	65.01W
Puerto Maldonado, Peru (pwĕ'r-tō mäl-dō-nä'dô)	130	12.43S	69.01W
Puerto Miniso, Mex. (pwĕ'r-tō mē-nê'sô)	118	16.06N	98.02W
Puerto Montt, Chile (pwĕ'r-tō mô'nt)	132	41.29S	73.00W
Puerto Natales, Chile (pwĕ'r-tō nä-tá'lĕs)	132	51.48S	72.01W
Puerto Niño, Col. (pwĕ'r-tō nê'n-yô)	130a	5.57N	74.36W
Puerto Padre, Cuba (pwĕ'r-tō pä'drā)	122	21.10N	76.40W
Puerto Peñasco, Mex. (pwĕ'r-tô pĕn-yä's-kô)	116	31.39N	113.15W
Puerto Pinasco, Para. (pwĕ'r-tō pê-nä's-kô)	132	22.31S	57.50W
Puerto Píritu, Ven. (pwĕ'r-tō pē'rē-tōō)	131b	10.05N	65.04W
Puerto Plata, Dom. Rep. (pwĕ'r-tô plä'tä)	117	19.50N	70.40W
Puerto Princesa, Phil. (pwĕr-tô prên-sä'sä)	196	9.45N	118.41E
Puerto Rico, dep., N.A. (pwĕr'tô rē'kō)	117	18.16N	66.50W
Puerto Rico Trench, deep	117	19.45N	66.30W
Puerto Salgar, Col. (pwĕ'r-tō säl-gär')	130a	5.30N	74.39W
Puerto Santa Cruz, Arg. (pwĕ'r-tō sän'tä krōōz')	132	50.04S	68.32W
Puerto Suárez, Bol. (pwĕ'r-tō swä'räz)	131	18.55S	57.39W
Puerto Tejada, Col. (pwĕ'r-tō tĕ-ĸä'dä)	130	3.13N	76.23W
Puerto Vallarta, Mex. (pwĕ'r-tō väl-yär'tä)	118	20.36N	105.13W
Puerto Varas, Chile (pwĕ'r-tō vä'räs)	132	41.16S	73.03W
Puerto Wilches, Col. (pwĕ'r-tō vĕl'c-hĕs)	130	7.19N	73.54W
Pugachëv, Russia (pōō'gá-chyôf)	167	52.00N	48.40E
Puget, Wa., U.S. (pū'jĕt)	106c	46.10N	123.23W
Puget Sound, strt., Wa., U.S.	104	47.49N	122.26W
Puglia (Apulia), hist. reg., Italy (pōō'lyä) (ä-pōō'lyä)	160	41.13N	16.10E
Pukaskwa National Park, rec., Can.	85	48.22N	85.55W
Pukeashun Mountain, mtn., Can.	87	51.12N	119.14W
Pukin, r., Malay.	181b	2.53N	102.54E
Pula, Cro. (pōō'lä)	148	44.52N	13.55E
Pulacayo, Bol. (pōō-lä-kä'yō)	130	20.12N	66.33W
Pulaski, Tn., U.S. (pů-lăs'kĭ)	114	35.11N	87.03W
Pulaski, Va., U.S.	115	37.00N	81.45W
Puławy, Pol. (pò-wä'vê)	155	51.24N	21.59E
Pulicat, r., India	187	13.58N	79.52E
Pullman, Wa., U.S. (pòl'măn)	104	46.44N	117.10W
Pullman, neigh., Il., U.S.	231a	41.43N	87.36W
Pulog, Mount, mtn., Phil. (pōō'lôg)	197a	16.38N	120.53E
Puma Yumco, l., China (pōō-mä yōōm-tswo)	186	28.30N	90.10E
Pumphrey, Md., U.S.	229c	39.13N	76.38W
Pumpkin Creek, r., Mt., U.S. (pŭmp'kĭn)	105	45.47N	105.35W
Punakha, Bhu. (pōō-nŭk'ŭ)	183	27.45N	89.59E
Punata, Bol. (pōō-nä'tä)	130	17.43S	65.43W
Punchbowl, Austl.	243a	33.56S	151.03E
Pune, India	183	18.38N	73.53E
Punggol, Sing.	240c	1.25N	103.55E
Punjab, state, India (pŭn'jäb')	183	31.00N	75.30E
Puno, Peru (pōō'nô)	130	15.58S	70.02W
Punta Arenas, Chile (pōō'n-tä-rĕ'näs)	132	53.09S	70.48W
Punta Brava, Cuba	233b	23.01N	82.30W
Punta de Piedras, Ven. (pōō'n-tä dĕ pyĕ'dräs)	131b	10.54N	64.06W
Punta Gorda, Belize (pòn'tä gôr'dä)	120	16.07N	88.50W
Punta Gorda, Fl., U.S. (pŭn'tȧ gôr'dȧ)	115a	26.55N	82.02W
Punta Gorda, Río, r., Nic. (pōō'n-tä gô'r-dä)	121	11.34N	84.13W
Punta Indio, Canal, strt., Arg. (pōō'n-tä- ê'n-dyô)	129c	34.56S	57.20W
Puntarenas, C.R. (pònt-ä-rā'näs)	117	9.59N	84.49W
Punto Fijo, Ven. (pōō'n-tô fē'κô)	130	11.48N	70.14W
Punxsutawney, Pa., U.S. (pŭnk-sŭ-tô'nê)	99	40.55N	79.00W
Puquio, Peru (pōō'kyô)	130	14.43S	74.02W
Pur, r., Russia	170	65.30N	77.30E
Purcell, Ok., U.S. (pûr-sĕl')	111	35.01N	97.22W
Purcell Mountains, mts., N.A. (pûr-sĕl')	87	50.00N	116.30W
Purdy, Wa., U.S. (pûr'dē)	106a	47.23N	122.37W
Purépero, Mex. (pōō-rā'pâ-rō)	118	19.56N	102.02W
Purfleet, Eng., U.K.	235	51.29N	0.15E
Purgatoire, r., Co., U.S. (pûr-gá-twär')	110	37.25N	103.53W
Puri, India (pò'rê)	183	19.52N	85.51E
Purial, Sierra de, mts., Cuba (sē-ĕ'r-rä-dĕ-pōō-rê-äl')	123	20.15N	74.40W
Purificación, Col. (pōō-rê-fê-kä-syōn')	130	3.52N	74.54W
Purificación, Mex. (pōō-rē-fê-kä-syô'n)	118	19.44N	104.38W
Purificación, r., Mex.	118	19.30N	104.54W
Purkersdorf, Aus.	145e	48.13N	16.11E
Purley, neigh., Eng., U.K.	235	51.20N	0.07W
Puruandiro, Mex. (pò-rōō-än'dê-rō)	118	20.04N	101.33W
Purús, r., S.A. (pōō-rōō's)	130	6.45S	64.34W
Pusan, S. Kor.	189	35.08N	129.05E
Pushkin, Russia (pòsh'kĭn)	166	59.43N	30.25E
Pushkino, Russia (pōōsh'kê-nô)	162	56.01N	37.51E
Pustoshka, Russia (pûs-tôsh'ká)	162	56.20N	29.33E
Pustunich, Mex. (pōōs-tōō'nêch)	119	19.10N	90.29W
Putaendo, Chile (pōō-tä-ĕn-dô)	129b	32.37S	70.42W
Puteaux, Fr. (pü-tō')	157b	48.52N	2.12E
Putfontein, S. Afr. (pòt'fŏn-tān)	213b	26.08S	28.24E
Puth Kalān, neigh., India	240d	28.43N	77.05E
Putian, China (pōō-tĭĕn)	193	25.40N	119.02E
Putilkovo, Russia	239b	55.52N	37.23E
Putla de Guerrero, Mex. (pōō'tlä-dĕ-gĕr-rĕ'rō)	119	17.03N	97.55W
Putnam, Ct., U.S. (pŭt'nȧm)	99	41.55N	71.55W
Putney, neigh., Eng., U.K.	235	51.28N	0.13W
Putorana, Gory, mts., Russia	165	68.45N	93.15E
Pütt, Ger.	236	51.11N	6.59E
Puttalam, Sri L.	183b	8.02N	79.44E
Putumayo, r., S.A. (pò-tōō-mä'yō)	130	1.02S	73.50W
Putung, Tanjung, c., Indon.	196	3.35S	111.50E
Putyvl', Ukr.	163	51.21N	33.52E
Puulavesi, l., Fin.	153	61.49N	27.10E
Puyallup, Wa., U.S. (pū-äl'ŭp)	106a	47.12N	122.18W
Puyang, China (pōō-yäŋ)	192	35.42N	114.58E
Pweto, Zaire (pwä'tō)	212	8.29S	28.58E
Pyasina, r., Russia (pyä-sē'ná)	170	72.45N	87.37E
Pyatigorsk, Russia (pyá-tê-gôrsk')	167	44.00N	43.00E
Pyhäjärvi, l., Fin.	153	60.57N	21.50E
Pyinmana, Myanmar (pyĕn-mä'nŭ)	183	19.47N	96.15E
Pymatuning Reservoir, res., Pa., U.S. (pī-mȧ-tŭn'ĭng)	98	41.40N	80.30W
Pymble, Austl.	243a	33.45S	151.09E
Pyŏnggang, N. Kor. (pyŭng'gäng')	194	38.21N	127.18E
P'yŏngyang, N. Kor.	189	39.03N	125.48E
Pyramid, l., Nv., U.S. (pĭ'rȧ-mĭd)	108	40.02N	119.50W
Pyramid Lake Indian Reservation, I.R., Nv., U.S.	108	40.17N	119.52W
Pyramids, hist., Egypt	218b	29.53N	31.10E
Pyrenees, mts., Eur. (pĭr-e-nēz')	142	43.00N	0.05E
Pyrford, Eng., U.K.	235	51.19N	0.30W
Pyryatyn, Ukr.	167	50.13N	32.31E
Pyrzyce, Pol. (pĕzhĭ'tsĕ)	154	53.09N	14.53E

Q

PLACE (Pronunciation)	PAGE	Lat. °'	Long. °'
Qal'at Bishah, Sau. Ar.	182	20.01N	42.30E
Qamdo, China (chyäm-dwō)	188	31.06N	96.30E
Qandahār, Afg.	183	31.43N	65.58E
Qandala, Som.	185	11.28N	49.52E
Qapal, Kaz.	169	45.13N	79.08E
Qaraghandy, Kaz.	169	49.42N	73.18E
Qarqan see Qiemo, China	188	38.02N	85.16E
Qarqan, r., China	188	38.55N	87.15E
Qarqaraly, Kaz.	169	49.18N	75.28E
Qārūn, Birket, l., Egypt	211	29.34N	30.34E
Qaşr al Burayqah, Libya	211	30.25N	19.20E
Qasr al-Farāfirah, Egypt	211	27.04N	28.13E
Qaşr Banī Walīd, Libya	211	31.45N	14.04E
Qasr-e Fīrūzeh, Iran	241h	35.40N	51.32E
Qasr el Boukhari, Alg.	148	35.50N	2.48E
Qatar, nation, Asia (kä'tár)	182	25.00N	52.45E
Qaţārah, Munkhafaḑ al, depr., Egypt	211	30.07N	27.30E
Qāyen, Iran	182	33.45N	59.08E
Qazvīn, Iran	182	36.10N	49.59E
Qeshm, Iran	182	26.51N	56.10E
Qeshm, i., Iran	182	26.52N	56.15E
Qezel Owzan, r., Iran	182	36.30N	49.00E
Qezi'ot, Isr.	181a	30.53N	34.28E
Qianwei, China (chyĕn-wā)	190	40.11N	120.05E
Qi'anzhen, China (chyē-än-jŭn)	190	32.16N	120.59E
Qibao, China (chyē-bou)	191b	31.06N	121.16E
Qiblīyah, Jabal al Jalālat al, mts., Egypt	181a	28.49N	32.21E
Qieshikou, China	240b	39.59N	116.24E
Qijiang, China (chyē-jyäŋ)	193	29.05N	106.40E
Qikou, China (chyē-kō)	190	38.37N	117.33E
Qilian Shan, mts., China (chyē-lĭĕn shän)	188	38.43N	98.00E
Qiliping, China (chyē-lē-piŋ)	190	31.28N	114.41E
Qindao, China (chyĭn-dou)	189	36.05N	120.10E
Qing'an, China (chyĭŋ-än)	192	46.50N	127.30E
Qingcheng, China (chyĭŋ-chŭŋ)	190	37.12N	117.43E
Qingfeng, China (chyĭŋ-fŭŋ)	190	35.52N	115.05E
Qinghai, prov., China (chyĭŋ-hī)	188	36.14N	95.30E
Qinghai Hu see Koko Nor, l., China	188	37.26N	98.30E
Qinghe, China (chyĭŋ-hŭ)	192a	40.08N	116.16E
Qinghuayuan, China	240b	40.00N	116.19E
Qingjiang, China	190	33.34N	118.58E
Qingjiang, China (chyĭŋ-jyäŋ)	193	28.00N	115.30E
Qingliu, China (chyĭŋ-lĭō)	193	26.15N	116.50E
Qingningsi, China (chyĭŋ-nĭŋ-sz)	191b	31.16N	121.33E
Qingping, China (chyĭŋ-pĭŋ)	190	36.46N	116.03E
Qingpu, China (chyĭŋ-pōō)	193	31.08N	121.06E
Qingxian, China (chyĭŋ shyĕn)	190	38.37N	116.48E
Qingyang, China (chyĭŋ-yäŋ)	188	36.02N	107.42E
Qingyuan, China	192	42.05N	125.00E
Qingyuan, China (chyĭŋ-yòän)	193	23.43N	113.10E
Qingyun, China (chyĭŋ-yòn)	190	37.52N	117.26E
Qingyundian, China (chĭŋ-yòn-dĭĕn)	192a	39.41N	116.31E
Qinhuangdao, China (chyĭn-huaŋ-dou)	189	39.57N	119.34E
Qin Ling, mts., China (chyĭn lĭŋ)	188	33.25N	108.58E
Qinyang, China (chyĭn-yäŋ)	192	35.00N	112.55E
Qinzhou, China (chyĭn-jō)	193	22.00N	108.35E
Qionghai, China (chyôŋ-hī)	193	19.10N	110.28E
Qiqian, China (chyē-chyĕn)	189	52.23N	121.04E
Qiqihar, China	189	47.18N	124.00E
Qiryat Gat, Isr.	181a	31.38N	34.36E
Qiryat Shemona, Isr.	181a	33.12N	35.34E
Qitai, China (chyē-tī)	188	44.07N	89.04E
Qiuxian, China (chyô shyĕn)	190	36.43N	115.13E
Qixian, China (chyē-shyĕn)	190	34.33N	114.47E
Qixian, China	192	35.36N	114.13E
Qiyang, China (chyē-yäŋ)	193	26.40N	112.00E
Qom, Iran	182	34.28N	50.53E
Qostanay, Kaz.	169	53.10N	63.39E
Quabbin Reservoir, res., Ma., U.S. (kwā'bĭn)	99	42.20N	72.10W
Quachita, Lake, l., Ar., U.S. (kwä shĭ'tô)	111	34.47N	93.37W
Quadra Island, i., Can.	86	50.08N	125.16W
Quadraro, neigh., Italy	239c	41.51N	12.33E
Quakers Hill, Austl.	243a	33.43S	150.53E
Quakertown, Pa., U.S. (kwā'kēr-toun)	99	40.30N	75.20W
Quanah, Tx., U.S. (kwä'nȧ)	110	34.19N	99.43W
Quang Ngai, Viet. (kwäng n'gä'ê)	196	15.05N	108.58E
Quang Ngai, mtn., Viet.	193	15.10N	108.20E
Quanjiao, China (chyuän-jyou)	190	32.06N	118.17E
Quanzhou, China (chyuän-jō)	189	24.58N	118.40E
Quanzhou, China	193	25.58N	111.02E
Qu'Appelle, r., Can.	84	50.30N	104.00W
Qu'Appelle Dam, dam, Can.	88	51.00N	106.25W
Quartu Sant'Elena, Italy (kwär-tōō' sänt a'lå-nä)	160	39.16N	9.12E
Quartzsite, Az., U.S.	109	33.40N	114.13W
Quatsino Sound, strt., Can. (kwŏt-sē'nō)	86	50.25N	128.10W
Quba, Azer. (kōō'bä)	167	41.05N	48.30E
Qūchān, Iran	185	37.06N	58.30E
Qudi, China	190	37.06N	117.15E
Québec, Can. (kwê-bĕk') (kå-bĕk')	83b	46.49N	71.13W
Quebec, prov., Can.	85	51.07N	70.25W
Quedlinburg, Ger. (kvĕd'lĕn-bōōrgh)	154	51.45N	11.10E
Queen Bess, Can.	86	51.16N	124.34W
Queen Charlotte Islands, is., Can. (kwēn shär'lŏt)	84	53.30N	132.25W
Queen Charlotte Ranges, mts., Can.	86	53.00N	132.00W
Queen Charlotte Sound, strt., Can.	86	51.30N	129.30W
Queen Charlotte Strait, strt., Can. (strāt)	84	50.40N	127.25W
Queen Elizabeth Islands, is., Can. (ê-lĭz'á-bĕth)	82	78.20N	110.00W
Queen Maud Gulf, b., Can. (mäd)	84	68.27N	102.55W
Queen Maud Land, reg., Ant.	219	75.00S	10.00E
Queen Maud Mountains, mts., Ant.	219	85.00S	179.00W
Queens Channel, strt., Austl. (kwēnz)	202	14.25S	129.10E
Queenscliff, Austl.	201a	38.16S	144.39E
Queensland, state, Austl. (kwēnz'lănd)	203	22.45S	141.01E
Queenstown, Austl. (kwēnz'toun)	204	42.00S	145.40E
Queenstown, S. Afr.	213c	31.54S	26.53E
Queimados, Braz. (kā-mȧ'dôs)	132b	22.42S	43.34W
Quela, Ang.	216	9.16S	17.02E
Quelimane, Moz. (kā-lê-mä'nĕ)	213	17.48S	37.05E
Queluz, Port.	159b	38.45N	9.15W
Quemado de Güines, Cuba (kä-mä'dhä-dĕ-gwĕ'nĕs)	122	22.45N	80.20W
Quemoy, Tai.	193	24.30N	118.20E
Quemoy, i., Tai.	193	24.27N	118.23E
Quepos, C.R. (kā'pôs)	121	9.26N	84.10W
Quepos, Punta, c., C.R. (pōō'n-tä)	121	9.23N	84.20W
Querenburg, neigh., Ger.	236	51.27N	7.16E

PRONOUNCING INDEX
Querétaro–Razorback Mountain 337

PLACE (Pronunciation)	PAGE	Lat. °′	Long. °′
Querétaro, Mex. (kå-rā'tä-rō)	116	20.37N	100.25W
Querétaro, state, Mex.	118	21.00N	100.00W
Quesada, Spain (kå-sä'dhä)	158	37.51N	3.04W
Quesnel, Can. (kā-nĕl')	84	52.59N	122.30W
Quesnel, r., Can.	87	52.15N	122.00W
Quesnel Lake, l., Can.	84	52.32N	121.05W
Quetame, Col. (kĕ-tä'mĕ)	130a	4.20N	73.50W
Quetta, Pak. (kwĕt'ä)	183	30.19N	67.01E
Quezaltenango, Guat. (kå-zäl'tå-näŋ'gō)	116	14.50N	91.30W
Quezaltepeque, El Sal. (kĕ-zäl'tĕ'pĕ-kĕ)	120	13.50N	89.17W
Quezaltepeque, Guat. (kå-zäl'tå-pä'kå)	120	14.39N	89.26W
Quezon City, Phil. (kā-zōn)	196	14.40N	121.02E
Qufu, China (chyōō-fōō)	190	35.37N	116.54E
Quibdo, Col. (kēb'dō)	130	5.42N	76.41W
Quiberon, Fr. (kē-bē-rôN')	156	47.29N	3.08W
Quiçama, Parque Nacional de, rec., Ang.	216	10.00S	13.25E
Quicksborn, Ger. (kvēks'bōrn)	145c	53.44N	9.54E
Quilcene, Wa., U.S. (kwĭl-sēn')	106a	47.50N	122.53W
Quilimari, Chile (kē-lē-mä'rē)	129b	32.06S	71.28W
Quillan, Fr. (kē-yäN')	156	42.53N	2.13E
Quillota, Chile (kēl-yō'tä)	132	32.52S	71.14W
Quilmes, Arg. (kēl'mās)	129c	34.43S	58.16W
Quilon, India (kwē-lōn')	183b	8.58N	76.16E
Quilpie, Austl. (kwĭl'pē)	203	26.34S	149.20E
Quimbaya, Col. (kēm-bä'yä)	130a	4.38N	75.46W
Quimbele, Ang.	216	6.28S	16.13E
Quimbonge, Ang.	216	8.36S	18.30E
Quimper, Fr. (kăN-pĕr')	147	47.59N	4.04W
Quinalt, r., Wa., U.S.	104	47.23N	124.10W
Quinault Indian Reservation, I.R., Wa., U.S.	104	47.27N	124.34W
Quincy, Fl., U.S. (kwĭn'sē)	114	30.35N	84.35W
Quincy, Il., U.S.	97	39.55N	91.23W
Quincy, Ma., U.S.	93a	42.15N	71.00W
Quincy, Mi., U.S.	98	42.00N	84.50W
Quincy, Or., U.S.	106c	46.08N	123.10W
Quincy Bay, b., Ma., U.S.	227a	42.17N	70.58W
Qui Nhon, Viet. (kwĭnyŏn)	196	13.51N	109.03E
Quinn, r., Nv., U.S. (kwĭn)	104	41.42N	117.45W
Quintanar de la Orden, Spain (kēn-tä-när')	158	39.36N	3.02W
Quintana Roo, state, Mex. (rô'ô)	116	19.30N	88.30W
Quinta Normal, Chile	234b	33.27S	70.42W
Quintero, Chile (kēn-tĕ'rô)	129b	32.48S	71.30W
Quinto Romano, neigh., Italy	238c	45.29N	9.05E
Quionga, Moz.	217	10.37S	40.30E
Quiroga, Mex. (kē-rō'gä)	118	19.39N	101.30W
Quiroga, Spain (kē-rô'gä)	158	42.28N	7.18W
Quitaúna, Braz.	234d	23.31S	46.47W
Quitman, Ga., U.S. (kwĭt'măn)	114	30.46N	83.35W
Quitman, Ms., U.S.	114	33.02N	88.43W
Quito, Ec. (kē'tō)	130	0.17S	78.32W
Qumbu, S. Afr. (kŏm'bōō)	213c	31.10S	28.48E
Quorn, Austl. (kwôrn)	204	32.20S	138.00E
Qurayyah, Wādī, r., Egypt	181a	30.08N	34.27E
Qūsmūryn Kölï, l., Kaz.	169	52.30N	64.15E
Qutang, China (chyōō-täŋ)	190	32.33N	120.07E
Quthing, Leso.	213c	30.35S	27.42E
Quxian, China (chyōō-shyĕn)	189	28.58N	118.58E
Quxian, China	193	30.40N	106.48E
Quzhou, China (chyoŏ-jō)	190	36.47N	114.58E
Qyrghyz zhot, mts., Asia	168	37.58N	72.23E
Qyzylorda, Kaz.	169	44.58N	65.45E

R

PLACE (Pronunciation)	PAGE	Lat. °′	Long. °′
Raab (Raba), r., Eur. (räp)	154	46.55N	15.55E
Raadt, neigh., Ger.	236	51.24N	6.56E
Raahe, Fin. (rä'ĕ)	146	64.39N	24.22E
Raasdorf, Aus.	239e	48.15N	16.34E
Rab, i., Yugo. (räb)	160	44.45N	14.40E
Raba, Indon.	196	8.32S	118.49E
Raba (Raab), r., Eur.	155	47.28N	17.12E
Rabat, Mor. (rå-bät')	210	33.59N	6.47W
Rabaul, Pap. N. Gui. (rä'boul)	197	4.15S	152.19E
Rābigh, Sau. Ar.	185	22.48N	39.01E
Raby, Eng., U.K.	237a	53.19N	3.02W
Raccoon, r., Ia., U.S. (ră-kōōn')	103	42.07N	94.45W
Raccoon Cay, i., Bah.	123	22.25N	75.50W
Race, Cape, c., Can. (rās)	93	46.40N	53.10W
Raceview, S. Afr.	244b	26.17S	28.08E
Rachado, Cape, c., Malay.	181b	2.26N	101.29E
Racibórz, Pol. (rä-chē'bōōzh)	155	50.06N	18.14E
Racine, Wi., U.S. (rá-sēn')	97	42.43N	87.49W
Raco, Mi., U.S. (rá cō)	107k	46.22N	84.43W
Rădăuţi, Rom.	149	47.53N	25.55E
Radcliffe, Eng., U.K. (răd'klĭf)	144a	53.34N	2.20W
Radevormwald, Ger. (rä'dē-fōrm-väld)	157c	51.12N	7.22E
Radford, Va., U.S. (răd'fērd)	115	37.06N	81.33W
Rādhanpur, India	186	23.57N	71.38E
Radium, S. Afr. (rā'dĭ-ŭm)	218d	25.06S	28.18E
Radlett, Eng., U.K.	235	51.42N	0.20W
Radnor, Pa., U.S.	229b	40.02N	75.21W
Radom, Pol. (rä'dŏm)	147	51.24N	21.11E
Radomir, Bul. (rä'dō-mēr)	161	42.33N	22.58E
Radomsko, Pol. (rä-dôm'skô)	147	51.04N	19.27E
Radomyshl, Ukr. (rä-dô-mēsh''l)	167	50.30N	29.13E
Radul', Ukr. (rá'dōōl)	163	51.52N	30.46E
Radviliškis, Lith. (rád'vē-lēsh'kēs)	153	55.49N	23.31E
Radwah, Jabal, mtn., Sau. Ar.	182	24.44N	38.14E
Radzyń Podlaski, Pol. (räd'zēn-y' pŭd-lä'skĭ)	155	51.49N	22.40E
Raeford, N.C., U.S. (rā'fērd)	115	34.57N	79.15W
Raesfeld, Ger. (răz'fĕld)	157c	51.46N	6.50E
Raeside, l., Austl. (rā'sīd)	202	29.20S	122.30E
Rae Strait, strt., Can. (rā)	84	68.40N	95.03W
Rafaela, Arg. (rä-fä-å'lä)	132	31.15S	61.21W
Rafael Castillo, Arg.	233d	34.42S	58.37W
Rafah, Pak. (rä'fä)	181a	31.14N	34.12E
Rafsanjān, Iran	182	30.45N	56.30E
Raft, r., Id., U.S. (răft)	105	42.20N	113.17W
Ragay, Phil. (rä-gī')	197a	13.49N	122.45E
Ragay Gulf, b., Phil.	197a	13.44N	122.38E
Ragunda, Swe. (rä-gòn'dä)	152	63.07N	16.24E
Ragusa, Italy (rä-gōō'sä)	148	36.58N	14.41E
Rahm, neigh., Ger.	236	51.21N	6.47E
Rahnsdorf, neigh., Ger.	238a	52.26N	13.42E
Rahway, N.J., U.S. (rô'wā)	100a	40.37N	74.16W
Rāichūr, India (rä'ē-chōōr')	183	16.23N	77.18E
Raigarh, India (rī'gŭr)	183	21.57N	83.32E
Rainbow Bridge National Monument, rec., Ut., U.S. (rān'bō)	109	37.05N	111.00W
Rainbow City, Pan.	116a	9.20N	79.53W
Rainford, Eng., U.K.	237a	53.30N	2.48W
Rainhill, Eng., U.K.	237a	53.26N	2.46W
Rainhill Stoops, Eng., U.K.	237a	53.24N	2.45W
Rainier, Or., U.S.	106c	46.05N	122.56W
Rainier, Mount, mtn., Wa., U.S. (rā-nēr')	96	46.52N	121.46W
Rainy, r., N.A.	97	48.50N	94.41W
Rainy Lake, l., N.A. (rān'ē)	85	48.43N	94.29W
Rainy River, Can.	85	48.43N	94.29W
Raipur, India (rä'jū-bōō-rē')	186	21.25N	81.37E
Raisin, r., Mi., U.S. (rā'zĭn)	98	42.00N	83.35W
Raitan, N.J., U.S. (rā-tăn)	100a	40.34N	74.40W
Rājahmundry, India (räj-ŭ-mŭn'drē)	183	17.03N	81.51E
Rajang, r., Malay.	196	2.10N	113.30E
Rājapālaiyam, India	187	9.30N	77.33E
Rājasthān, state, India (rä'jŭs-tän)	183	26.00N	72.00E
Rājkot, India (räj'kôt)	183	22.20N	70.48E
Rājpur, India	186a	22.24N	88.25E
Rājpur, neigh., India	240d	28.41N	77.12E
Rājshāhi, Bngl.	183	24.26S	88.39E
Rakhiv, Ukr.	155	48.02N	24.13E
Rakh'oya, Russia (räk'yá)	172c	60.06N	30.50E
Rakitnoye, Russia (rá-kēt'nô-yĕ)	167	50.51N	35.53E
Rákoscsaba, neigh., Hung.	239g	47.29N	19.17E
Rákoshegy, neigh., Hung.	239g	47.28N	19.14E
Rákoskeresztúr, neigh., Hung.	239g	47.29N	19.15E
Rákosliget, neigh., Hung.	239g	47.30N	19.16E
Rákospalota, neigh., Hung.	239g	47.34N	19.08E
Rákosszentmihály, neigh., Hung.	239g	47.32N	19.11E
Rakovník, Czech Rep.	154	50.07N	13.45E
Rakvere, Est. (rák'vĕ-rĕ)	166	59.22N	26.14E
Raleigh, N.C., U.S.	97	35.45N	78.39W
Ram, r., Can.	87	52.10N	115.05W
Rama, Nic. (rä'mä)	121	12.11N	84.14W
Ramallo, Arg. (rä-mä'l-yô)	129c	33.28S	60.02W
Ramanāthapuram, India	187	9.13N	78.52E
Rambouillet, Fr. (räN-bōō-yĕ')	156	48.39N	1.49E
Rame Head, c., S. Afr.	213c	31.48S	29.22E
Ramenka, neigh., Russia	239b	55.41N	37.30E
Ramenskoye, Russia (rá'mĕn-skô-yĕ)	162	55.34N	38.15E
Ramlat as Sab'atayn, reg., Asia	182	16.08N	45.15E
Ramm, Jabal, mtn., Jord.	181a	29.37N	35.32E
Râmnicu Sărat, Rom.	149	45.24N	27.06E
Râmnicu Vâlcea, Rom.	161	45.07N	24.22E
Ramos, Mex. (rä'mōs)	118	22.46N	101.52W
Ramos, r., Nig.	215	5.10N	5.40E
Ramos Arizpe, Mex. (ä-rēz'pā)	112	25.33N	100.57W
Rampart, Ak., U.S. (răm'pärt)	95	65.28N	150.18W
Rampo Mountains, mts., N.J., U.S. (răm'pō)	100a	41.06N	72.12W
Rāmpur, India (räm'pōōr)	183	28.53N	79.03E
Ramree Island, i., Myanmar (räm'rē')	196	19.01N	93.23E
Ramsayville, Can. (răm'zē vĭl)	83c	45.23N	75.34W
Ramsbottom, Eng., U.K. (rămz'bŏt-ŭm)	144a	53.39N	2.20W
Ramsden Heath, Eng., U.K.	235	51.38N	0.28E
Ramsey, I. of Man (răm'zē)	150	54.20N	4.25W
Ramsey, N.J., U.S.	100a	41.03N	74.09W
Ramsey Lake, l., Can.	90	47.15N	82.16W
Ramsgate, Austl.	243a	33.59S	151.08E
Ramsgate, Eng., U.K. (rămz''gāt)	151	51.19N	1.20E
Ramu, r., Pap. N. Gui. (rä'mōō)	197	5.35S	145.16E
Rancagua, Chile (rän-kä'gwä)	132	34.10S	70.43W
Rance, r., Fr. (räNs)	156	48.17N	2.30W
Rānchī, India	183	23.21N	85.20E
Ranchleigh, Md., U.S.	229c	39.22N	76.40W
Rancho Boyeros, Cuba (rä'n-chô-bô-yĕ'rôs)	123a	23.00N	82.23W
Rancho Palos Verdes, Ca., U.S.	232	33.45N	118.24W
Randallstown, Md., U.S. (răn'dălz-toun)	100e	39.22N	76.48W
Randburg, S. Afr.	244b	26.06S	27.59E
Randers, Den. (rän'ĕrs)	146	56.28N	10.03E
Randfontein, S. Afr. (rănt'fŏn-tān)	213b	26.10S	27.42E
Randleman, N.C., U.S. (răn'd'l-măn)	115	35.49N	79.50W
Randolph, Ma., U.S. (răn'dôlf)	93a	42.10N	71.03W
Randolph, Ne., U.S.	102	42.22N	97.22W
Randolph, Vt., U.S.	99	43.55N	72.40W
Random Island, i., Can. (răn'dŭm)	93	48.12N	53.25W
Randsfjorden, Nor.	152	60.35N	10.10E
Randwick, Austl.	201b	33.55S	151.15E
Ranérou, Sen.	214	15.18N	13.58W
Rangeley, Me., U.S. (rānj'lē)	92	44.56N	70.38W
Rangeley, l., Me., U.S.	92	45.00N	70.25W
Ranger, Tx., U.S. (rān'jēr)	96	32.26N	98.41W
Rangia, India	186	26.32N	91.39E
Rangoon (Yangon), Myanmar (räŋ-gōōn')	183	16.46N	96.09E
Rangpur, Bngl. (rŭng'pōōr)	183	25.48N	89.19E
Rangsang, i., Indon. (räng'säng')	181b	0.53N	103.05E
Rangsdorf, Ger. (rängs'dōrf)	145b	52.17N	13.25E
Ranholas, Port.	238d	38.47N	9.22W
Rānīganj, India (rä-nē-gŭnj')	186	23.40N	87.08E
Rankin, Pa., U.S.	230b	40.25N	79.53W
Rankin Inlet, b., Can. (răŋ'kĕn)	85	62.45N	94.27W
Ranova, r., Russia (rä'nô-vá)	162	53.55N	40.03E
Rantau, Malay.	181b	2.35N	101.58E
Rantekombola, Bulu, mtn., Indon.	196	3.22S	119.50E
Rantoul, Il., U.S. (răn-tōōl')	98	40.25N	88.05W
Raoyang, China (rou-yäŋ)	190	38.16N	115.45E
Rapallo, Italy (rä-päl'lô)	160	44.21N	9.14E
Rapel, r., Chile (rä-pål')	129b	34.05S	71.30W
Rapid, r., Mn., U.S. (răp'ĭd)	103	48.21N	94.50W
Rapid City, S.D., U.S.	96	44.06N	103.14W
Rapla, Est. (räp'lå)	153	59.02N	24.46E
Rappahannock, r., Va., U.S. (răp'ă-hăn'ŭk)	99	38.20N	75.25W
Raquette, l., N.Y., U.S. (răk'ĕt)	99	43.50N	74.35W
Raritan, r., N.J., U.S. (răr'ĭ-tăn)	100a	40.32N	74.27W
Rarotonga, Cook Is. (rä'rô-tŏŋ'gá)	2	20.40S	163.00W
Ra's an Naqb, Jord.	181a	30.00N	35.29E
Raşcov, Mol.	163	47.55N	28.51E
Ras Dashen Terara, mtn., Eth. (räs dä-shän')	211	12.49N	38.14E
Raseiniai, Lith. (rä-syā'nyĭ)	153	55.23N	23.04E
Rashayya, Leb.	181a	33.30N	35.50E
Rashīd, Egypt (rá-shēd') (rô-zĕt'á)	184	31.22N	30.25E
Rashīd, Masabb, mth., Egypt	218b	31.30N	29.58E
Rashkina, Russia (rásh'kĭ-ná)	172a	59.57N	61.30E
Rasht, Iran	182	37.13N	49.45E
Raška, Yugo. (räsh'ká)	161	43.16N	20.40E
Rasskazovo, Russia (räs-kä'sô-vô)	167	52.40N	41.40E
Rastatt, Ger. (rä-shtät)	154	48.51N	8.12E
Rastes, Russia (rås'tĕs)	172a	59.24N	58.49E
Rastunovo, Russia (rás-tōō'nô-vô)	172b	55.15N	37.50E
Ratangarh, India (rŭ-tŭn'gŭr)	186	28.10N	74.30E
Ratcliff, Tx., U.S. (răt'klĭf)	113	31.22N	95.09W
Rath, neigh., Ger.	236	51.17N	6.49E
Rathenow, Ger. (rä'tĕ-nō)	154	52.36N	12.20E
Rathlin Island, i., N. Ire., U.K. (răth-lĭn)	150	55.18N	6.13W
Rathmecke, Ger.	236	51.15N	7.38E
Ratingen, Ger. (rä'tĕn-gĕn)	157c	51.18N	6.51E
Rat Islands, is., Ak., U.S. (răt)	95a	51.35N	176.48E
Ratlām, India	186	23.19N	75.05E
Ratnāgiri, India	187	17.04N	73.24E
Raton, N.M., U.S. (rá-tōn')	96	36.52N	104.26W
Rattlesnake Creek, r., Or., U.S. (răt''l snāk)	104	42.38N	117.39W
Rättvik, Swe. (rĕt'vĕk)	152	60.54N	15.07E
Rauch, Arg. (rá'ōōch)	132	36.47S	59.05W
Raufoss, Nor. (rou'fôs)	152	60.44N	10.30E
Raúl Soares, Braz. (rä-ōō'l-sôä'rĕs)	129a	20.05S	42.28W
Rauma, Fin. (rä'ô-mä)	146	61.07N	21.31E
Rauna, Lat. (råŭ'nå)	153	57.21N	25.31E
Raurkela, India	183	22.15N	84.53E
Rautalampi, Fin. (rä'ōō-tē-läm'pô)	153	62.39N	26.25E
Rava-Rus'ka, Ukr.	155	50.14N	23.40E
Ravenna, Italy (rä-vĕn'nä)	148	44.27N	12.13E
Ravenna, Ne., U.S. (rá-vĕn'á)	102	41.20N	98.50W
Ravenna, Oh., U.S.	98	41.10N	81.20W
Ravensburg, Ger. (rä'vĕns-bōōrgh)	154	47.48N	9.35E
Ravensdale, Wa., U.S. (rā'vĕnz-dāl)	106a	47.22N	121.58W
Ravensthorpe, Austl. (rā'vĕns-thôrp)	202	33.30S	120.20E
Ravenswood, S. Afr.	244b	26.11S	28.15E
Ravenswood, W.V., U.S. (rā'vĕnz-wŏd)	98	38.55N	81.50W
Ravensworth, Va., U.S.	229d	38.48N	77.13W
Ravenwood, Va., U.S.	229d	38.52N	77.09W
Rāwalpindi, Pak. (rä-wŭl-pēn'dē)	183	33.40N	73.10E
Rawa Mazowiecka, Pol.	155	51.46N	20.17E
Rawāndūz, Iraq	182	36.37N	44.30E
Rawicz, Pol. (rä'vēch)	154	51.36N	16.51E
Rawlina, Austl. (rôr-lēn á)	202	31.13S	125.45E
Rawlins, Wy., U.S. (rô'lĭnz)	96	41.46N	107.15W
Rawson, Arg.	129c	34.36S	60.03W
Rawson, Arg. (rô'sŭn)	132	43.16S	65.09W
Rawtenstall, Eng., U.K. (rô'tĕn-stôl)	144a	53.42N	2.17W
Ray, Cape, c., Can. (rā)	85a	47.40N	59.18W
Raya, Bukit, mtn., Indon.	196	0.45S	112.11E
Raychikinsk, Russia (rī'chĭ-kēnsk)	171	49.52N	129.17E
Rayleigh, Eng., U.K. (rā'lē)	144b	51.35N	0.36E
Raymond, Can. (rā'mŭnd)	87	49.27N	112.39W
Raymond, Wa., U.S.	104	46.41N	123.42W
Raymondville, Tx., U.S. (rā'mŭnd-vĭl)	111	26.30N	97.46W
Ray Mountains, mts., Ak., U.S.	95a	65.40N	151.45W
Rayne, La., U.S. (rān)	113	30.12N	92.15W
Rayón, Mex. (rä-yōn')	118	21.49N	99.39W
Rayton, S. Afr. (rā'tŭn)	213b	25.45S	28.33E
Raytown, Mo., U.S. (rā'toun)	107f	39.01N	94.48W
Rayville, La., U.S. (rā-vĭl)	113	32.28N	91.46W
Raz, Pointe du, c., Fr. (pwăNt dü rä)	147	48.02N	4.43W
Razdan, Arm.	168	40.30N	44.46E
Razdol'noye, Russia (räz-dôl'nô-yĕ)	194	43.38N	131.58E
Razgrad, Bul.	149	43.32N	26.32E
Razlog, Bul. (räz'lôk)	161	41.54N	23.32E
Razorback Mountain, mtn., Can. (rā'zēr-băk)	86	51.35N	124.42W

ng-sing; ŋ-baŋk; N-nasalized n; nŏd; cŏmmit; ōld; ôbey; ôrder; oi-boil; fōōd; ŏ-as oo in foot; ou-out; s-soft; sh-dish; th-thin; pūre; ûnite; ûrn; stŭd; circŭs; ü-as in French tu; '-indeterminate vowel.

338 Rea – Ridgefield

PLACE (Pronunciation)	PAGE	Lat. °'	Long. °'
Rea, r., Eng., U.K. (rē)	144a	52.25N	2.31W
Reaburn, Can. (rā'bûrn)	83f	50.06N	97.53W
Reading, Eng., U.K. (rĕd'ĭng)	147	51.25N	0.58W
Reading, Ma., U.S.	93a	42.32N	71.07W
Reading, Mi., U.S.	98	41.45N	84.45W
Reading, Oh., U.S.	101f	39.14N	84.26W
Reading, Pa., U.S.	97	40.20N	75.55W
Readville, neigh., Ma., U.S.	227a	42.14N	71.08W
Realengo, Braz. (rĕ-ä-län-gō)	129a	23.50S	43.25W
Real Felipe, Castillo, hist., Peru	233c	12.04S	77.09W
Rebel Hill, Pa., U.S.	229b	40.04N	75.20W
Rebiana, Libya	211	24.10N	22.03E
Rebun, i., Japan (rē'bo͞on)	194	45.25N	140.54E
Recanati, Italy (rā-kä-nä'tē)	160	43.25N	13.35E
Recherche, Archipelago of the, is., Austl. (rē-shârsh')	202	34.17S	122.30E
Rechitsa, Bela. (ryĕ'chēt-sȧ)	167	52.22N	30.24E
Recife, Braz. (rå-sē'fĕ)	131	8.09S	34.59W
Recife, Kapp, c., S. Afr. (rå-sē'fĕ)	213c	34.03S	25.43E
Recklinghausen, Ger. (rĕk'lĭng-hou-zĕn)	157c	51.36N	7.13E
Recklinghausen Süd, neigh., Ger.	236	51.34N	7.13E
Reconquista, Arg. (rā-kôn-kēs'tä)	132	29.01S	59.41W
Reconquista, r., Arg.	233d	34.39S	58.45W
Rector, Ar., U.S. (rĕk'tẽr)	111	36.16N	90.21W
Red, r., Asia	196	21.00N	103.00E
Red, r., N.A. (rĕd)	96	48.00N	97.00W
Red, r., U.S.	97	31.40N	92.55W
Red, r., Tn., U.S.	114	36.35N	86.55W
Red, North Fork, r., U.S.	110	35.20N	100.08W
Red, Prairie Dog Town Fork, r., U.S. (prā'rĭ)	110	34.54N	101.31W
Red, Salt Fork, r., U.S.	110	35.04N	100.31W
Redan, Ga., U.S. (rē-dăn') (rĕd'ăn)	100c	33.44N	84.09W
Red Bank, N.J., U.S. (băngk)	100a	40.21N	74.06W
Red Bank National Park, N.J., U.S.	229b	39.52N	75.10W
Red Bluff Reservoir, res., Tx., U.S.	112	32.03N	103.52W
Redbridge, neigh., Eng., U.K.	235	51.34N	0.05E
Redby, Mn., Mn., U.S. (rĕd'bē)	103	47.52N	94.55W
Red Cedar, r., Wi., U.S. (sē'dẽr)	103	45.03N	91.48W
Redcliff, Can. (rĕd'clĭf)	84	50.05N	110.47W
Redcliffe, Austl. (rĕd'clĭf)	204	27.20S	153.12E
Red Cliff Indian Reservation, I.R., Wi., U.S.	103	46.48N	91.22W
Red Cloud, Ne., U.S. (kloud)	110	40.06N	98.32W
Red Deer, Can. (dēr)	84	52.16N	113.48W
Red Deer, r., Can.	84	51.00N	111.00W
Red Deer, r., Can.	89	52.55N	102.10W
Red Deer Lake, l., Can.	89	52.58N	101.28W
Reddick, Il., U.S. (rĕd'dĭk)	101a	41.06N	88.16W
Redding, Ca., U.S. (rĕd'ĭng)	104	40.36N	122.25W
Reddish, Eng., U.K.	237b	53.26N	2.09W
Redenção da Serra, Braz. (rĕ-dĕn-souɴ-dä-sĕ'r-rä)	129a	23.17S	45.31W
Redfield, S.D., U.S. (rĕd'fēld)	102	44.53N	98.30W
Red Fish Bar, Tx., U.S.	113a	29.29N	94.53W
Redford, neigh., Mi., U.S.	230c	42.25N	83.16W
Redford Township, Mi., U.S.	230c	42.25N	83.16W
Red Hill, Ca., U.S.	232	33.45N	117.48W
Red Indian Lake, l., Can. (ĭn'dĭ-ăn)	85a	48.40N	56.50W
Red Lake, Can. (lāk)	85	51.02N	93.49W
Red Lake, r., Mn., U.S.	102	48.02N	96.04W
Red Lake Falls, Mn., U.S. (lāk fôls)	102	47.52N	96.17W
Red Lake Indian Reservation, I.R., Mn., U.S.	102	48.09N	95.55W
Redlands, Ca., U.S. (rĕd'lăndz)	107a	34.04N	117.11W
Red Lion, Pa., U.S. (lī'ŭn)	99	39.55N	76.30W
Red Lodge, Mt., U.S.	105	45.13N	107.16W
Redmond, Wa., U.S. (rĕd'mŭnd)	106a	47.40N	122.07W
Rednitz, r., Ger. (rĕd'nĕtz)	154	49.10N	11.00E
Red Oak, Ia., U.S. (ōk)	102	41.00N	95.12W
Redon, Fr. (rē-dôɴ')	156	47.42N	2.03W
Redonda, Isla, i., Braz. (ē's-lä-rĕ-dô'n-dä)	132b	23.05S	43.11W
Redonda Island, i., Antig. (rĕ-dŏn'dȧ)	121b	16.55N	62.28W
Redondela, Spain (rā-dhôn-dā'lä)	158	42.16N	8.34W
Redondo, Port. (rā-dôn'dō)	158	38.40N	7.32W
Redondo, Wa., U.S. (rē-dŏn'dō)	106a	47.21N	122.19W
Redondo Beach, Ca., U.S.	107a	33.50N	118.23W
Red Pass, Can. (pȧs)	87	52.59N	118.59W
Red Rock, r., Mt., U.S.	105	44.54N	112.44W
Red Sea, sea	182	23.15N	37.00E
Redstone, Can. (rĕd'stōn)	86	52.08N	123.42W
Red Sucker Lake, l., Can. (sŭk'ẽr)	89	54.09N	93.40W
Redwater, r., Mt., U.S.	105	47.37N	105.25W
Red Willow Creek, r., Ne., U.S.	110	40.34N	100.48W
Red Wing, Mn., U.S.	103	44.34N	92.35W
Redwood City, Ca., U.S. (rĕd' wo͝od)	106b	37.29N	122.13W
Redwood Falls, Mn., U.S.	102	44.32N	95.06W
Redwood Valley, Ca., U.S.	108	39.15N	123.12W
Ree, Lough, l., Ire. (lŏĸ'rē')	146	53.30N	7.45W
Reed City, Mi., U.S. (rēd)	98	43.50N	85.35W
Reed Lake, l., Can.	89	54.37N	100.30W
Reedley, Ca., U.S. (rēd'lē)	108	36.37N	119.27W
Reedsburg, Wi., U.S. (rēdz'bûrg)	103	43.32N	90.01W
Reedsport, Or., U.S. (rēdz'pôrt)	104	43.42N	124.08W
Reelfoot Lake, res., Tn., U.S. (rēl'fo͝ot)	114	36.18N	89.20W
Rees, Ger. (rĕz)	157c	51.46N	6.25E
Reeves, Mount, mtn., Austl. (rēv's)	204	33.50S	149.56E
Reform, Al., U.S. (rē-fôrm')	114	33.23N	88.00W
Refugio, Tx., U.S. (rå-fo͞o'hyō) (rē-fū'jō)	113	28.18N	97.15W
Rega, r., Pol. (rĕ-gä)	154	53.48N	15.30E
Regen, r., Ger. (rā'ghĕn)	154	49.09N	12.21E
Regensburg, Ger. (rā'ghĕns-bôrgh)	147	49.02N	12.06E
Regents Park, Austl.	243a	33.53S	151.02E
Regent's Park, pt. of i., Eng., U.K.	235	51.32N	0.09W
Reggio, La., U.S. (rĕg'jĭ-ō)	100d	29.50N	89.46W
Reggio di Calabria, Italy (rĕ'jō dē kä-lä'brē-ä)	149	38.07N	15.42E
Reggio nell' Emilia, Italy	148	44.43N	10.34E
Reghin, Rom. (rå-gēn')	155	46.47N	24.44E
Regina, Can. (rē-jī'nȧ)	88	50.25N	104.39W
Regla, Cuba (răg'lä)	122	23.08N	82.20W
Regnitz, r., Ger. (rĕg'nētz)	154	49.50N	10.55E
Rego Park, neigh., N.Y., U.S.	228	40.44N	73.52W
Reguengos de Monsaraz, Port.	158	38.26N	7.30W
Rehoboth, Nmb.	212	23.10S	17.15E
Reḥovot, Isr.	181a	31.53N	34.49E
Reichenbach, Ger. (rī'ĸĕn-bäĸ)	154	50.36N	12.18E
Reidsville, N.C., U.S. (rēdz'vĭl)	115	36.20N	79.37W
Reigate, Eng., U.K. (rī'gāt)	150	51.12N	0.12W
Reims, Fr. (răɴs)	142	49.16N	4.00E
Reina Adelaida, Archipiélago, is., Chile	132	52.00S	74.15W
Reinbeck, Ia., U.S. (rīn'bĕk)	103	42.22N	92.34W
Reindeer, l., Can. (rān'dēr)	84	57.36N	101.23W
Reindeer, r., Can.	88	55.45N	103.30W
Reindeer Island, i., Can.	89	52.25N	98.00W
Reinosa, Spain (rå-ē-nō'sä)	158	43.01N	4.08W
Reisholz, neigh., Ger.	236	51.11N	6.52E
Reistertown, Md., U.S. (rēs'tẽr-toun)	100e	39.28N	76.50W
Reitz, S. Afr.	218d	27.48S	28.25E
Rema, Jabal, mtn., Yemen	182	14.13N	44.38E
Rembau, Malay.	181b	2.36N	102.06E
Remedios, Col. (rĕ-mĕ'dyôs)	130a	7.03N	74.42W
Remedios, Cuba (rā-mā'dhē-ōs)	122	22.30N	79.35W
Remedios, Pan. (rĕ-mĕ'dyōs)	121	8.14N	81.46W
Remedios de Escalada, neigh., Arg.	233d	34.43S	58.23W
Remiremont, Fr. (rē-mēr-môɴ')	157	48.01N	6.35E
Rempang, i., Indon.	181b	0.51N	104.04E
Remscheid, Ger. (rĕm'shīt)	157c	51.10N	7.11E
Rena, Nor.	152	61.08N	11.17E
Renca, Chile	234b	33.24S	70.44W
Renca, Cerro, mtn., Chile	234b	33.23S	70.43W
Rendova, i., Sol.Is. (rĕn'dō-vȧ)	203	8.38S	156.26E
Rendsburg, Ger. (rĕnts'bôrgh)	154	54.19N	9.39E
Renfrew, Can. (rĕn'fro͞o)	85	45.30N	76.30W
Rengam, Malay. (rĕn'găm')	181b	1.53N	103.24E
Rengo, Chile (rĕn'gō)	129b	34.22S	70.50W
Reni, Ukr. (ran')	163	45.26N	28.18E
Renmark, Austl. (rĕn'märk)	202	34.10S	140.50E
Rennel, i., Sol.Is. (rĕn-nĕl')	203	11.50S	160.38E
Rennes, Fr. (rĕn)	142	48.07N	1.02W
Reno, Nv., U.S. (rē'nō)	96	39.32N	119.49W
Reno, r., Italy (rā'nō)	160	44.10N	10.55E
Renovo, Pa., U.S. (rē-nō'vō)	99	41.20N	77.50W
Renqiu, China (rŭn-chyō)	190	38.44N	116.05E
Rensselaer, In., U.S. (rĕn'sē-lâr)	98	41.00N	87.10W
Rensselaer, N.Y., U.S. (rĕn'sē-lâr)	99	42.40N	73.45W
Rentchler, Il., U.S. (rĕnt'chlẽr)	107e	38.30N	89.52W
Renton, Wa., U.S. (rĕn'tŭn)	106a	47.29N	122.13W
Repentigny, Can.	83a	45.47N	73.26W
Republic, Al., U.S. (rē-pŭb'lĭk)	100h	33.37N	86.54W
Republic, Wa., U.S.	104	48.38N	118.44W
Republican, r., U.S.	96	40.15N	100.00W
Republican, South Fork, r., Co., U.S. (rē-pŭb'lĭ-kăn)	110	39.35N	102.28W
Repulse Bay, b., Austl. (rē-pŭls')	203	20.56S	149.22E
Requena, Spain (rå-kā'nä)	148	39.29N	1.03W
Reseda, neigh., Ca., U.S.	232	34.12N	118.31W
Resende, Braz. (rĕ-sĕ'n-dĕ)	129a	22.30S	44.26W
Resende Costa, Braz. (kôs-tä)	129a	20.55S	44.12W
Reservoir, Austl.	243b	37.43S	145.00E
Reshetylivka, Ukr.	163	49.34N	34.04E
Resistencia, Arg. (rā-sēs-tĕn'syä)	132	27.24S	58.54W
Reşiţa, Rom. (rå'shē-tȧ)	161	45.18N	21.56E
Resolute, Can. (rĕz-ō-lūt')	82	74.41N	95.00W
Resolution, i., Can. (rĕz-ō-lū'shŭn)	85	61.30N	63.58W
Resolution Island, i., N.Z. (rĕz-ŏl-ûshûn)	203a	45.43S	166.20E
Resse, neigh., Ger.	236	51.34N	7.07E
Restigouche, r., Can.	92	47.35N	67.35W
Restrepo, Col. (rĕs-trĕ'pô)	130a	3.49N	76.31W
Restrepo, Col.	130a	4.16N	73.32W
Retalhuleu, Guat. (rā-täl-o͞o-lān')	120	14.31N	91.41W
Rethel, Fr. (r-tl')	156	49.34N	4.20E
Réthimnon, Grc.	160a	35.21N	24.30E
Retie, Bel.	145a	51.16N	5.08E
Retiro, Parque del, rec., Spain	238b	40.25N	3.41W
Retsil, Wa., U.S. (rĕt'sĭl)	106a	47.33N	122.37W
Reunion, dep., Afr. (rā-ü-nyôn')	3	21.06S	55.36E
Reus, Spain (rā'o͞os)	148	41.08N	1.05E
Reutlingen, Ger. (roit'lĭng-ĕn)	154	48.29N	9.14E
Reutov, Russia (rē-o͞o'ôf)	172b	55.45N	37.52E
Revda, Russia (ryâv'dȧ)	172a	56.48N	59.57E
Revelstoke, Can. (rĕv'ĕl-stōk)	84	51.00N	118.12W
Reventazón, Río, r., C.R. (rā-vĕn-tä-zōn')	121	10.10N	83.30W
Revere, Ma., U.S. (rē-vēr')	93a	42.24N	71.01W
Revesby, Austl.	243a	33.57S	151.01E
Revillagigedo, Islas, is., Mex. (ē's-läs-rĕ-vēl-yä-hĕ'gĕ-dō)	116	18.45N	111.00W
Revillagigedo Chan, Ak., U.S. (rĕ-vĭl'ȧ-gĭ-gē'dō)	86	55.10N	131.13W
Revillagigedo Island, i., Ak., U.S.	86	55.35N	131.23W
Revin, Fr. (rē-văɴ)	156	49.56N	4.34E
Rewa, India (rā'wä)	183	24.41N	81.11E
Rewāri, India	186	28.19N	76.39E
Rexburg, Id., U.S. (rĕks'bûrg)	105	43.50N	111.48W
Rey, Iran	185	35.35N	51.25E
Rey, l., Mex. (rā)	112	27.00N	103.33W
Rey, Isla del, i., Pan. (ē's-lä-dĕl-rā'ē)	121	8.20N	78.40W
Reyes, Bol. (rā'yĕs)	130	14.19S	67.16W
Reyes, Point, c., Ca., U.S.	108	38.00N	123.00W
Reykjanes, c., Ice. (rā'kyȧ-nĕs)	142	63.37N	24.33W
Reykjavík, Ice. (rā'kyȧ-vēk)	142	64.09N	21.39W
Reynosa, Mex. (rā-ē-nō'sä)	112	26.05N	98.21W
Rēzekne, Lat. (rå'zĕk-nĕ)	166	56.31N	27.19E
Rezh, Russia (rĕzh')	172a	57.22N	61.23E
Rezina, Mol. (ryĕzh'ĕ-nĭ)	163	47.44N	28.56E
Rhaetian Alps, mts., Eur.	154	46.30N	10.00E
Rhaetien Alps, mts., Eur.	160	46.22N	10.33E
Rheinberg, Ger. (rīn'bĕrgh)	157c	51.33N	6.37E
Rheine, Ger. (rī'nĕ)	154	52.16N	7.26E
Rheinen, Ger.	236	51.27N	7.38E
Rheinhausen, Ger.	236	51.24N	6.44E
Rhein-Herne-Kanal, can., Ger.	236	51.27N	6.47E
Rheinkamp, Ger.	157c	51.30N	6.37E
Rheinland-Pfalz (Rhineland-Palatinate), hist. reg., Ger.	154	50.05N	6.40E
Rheydt, Ger. (rĕ'yt)	157c	51.10N	6.28E
Rhin, r., Ger. (rēn)	145b	52.52N	12.49E
Rhine, r., Eur.	142	50.34N	7.21E
Rhinelander, Wi., U.S. (rīn'lăn-dẽr)	103	45.39N	89.25W
Rhin Kanal, can., Ger. (rēn kä-näl')	145b	52.47N	12.40E
Rhiou, r., Alg.	159	35.45N	1.18E
Rho, Italy	238c	45.32N	9.02E
Rhode Island, state, U.S. (rōd ī'lȧnd)	97	41.35N	71.40W
Rhode Island, i., R.I., U.S.	100b	41.31N	71.14W
Rhodes, Austl.	243a	33.50S	151.05E
Rhodes, S. Afr. (rōdz)	213c	30.48S	27.56E
Rhodes, Eng., U.K.	237b	53.33N	2.14W
Rhodes *see* Ródhos, i., Grc.	142	36.00N	28.29E
Rhodesia *see* Zimbabwe, nation, Afr.	212	17.50S	29.30E
Rhodon, Fr.	237c	48.43N	2.04E
Rhodope Mountains, mts., Eur. (rô'dô-pĕ)	142	42.00N	24.08E
Rhondda, Wales, U.K. (rŏn'dhȧ)	150	51.40N	3.40W
Rhône, r., Fr. (rōn)	142	44.30N	4.45E
Rhoon, Neth.	145a	51.52N	4.24E
Rhum, i., Scot., U.K. (rŭm)	150	57.00N	6.20W
Riachão, Braz. (rē-ä-chouɴ')	131	7.15S	46.30W
Rialto, Ca., U.S. (rē-ăl'tō)	107a	34.06N	117.23W
Riau, prov., Indon.	181b	0.56N	101.25E
Riau, Kepulauan, i., Indon.	196	0.30N	104.55E
Riau, Selat, strt., Indon.	181b	0.40N	104.27E
Riaza, r., Spain (rē-ä'thä)	158	41.25N	3.25W
Ribadavia, Spain (rē-bä-dhä'vē-ä)	158	42.18N	8.06W
Ribadeo, Spain (rē-bä-dhā'ō)	158	43.32N	7.05W
Ribadesella, Spain (rē'bä-dā-sāl'yä)	158	43.30N	5.02W
Ribe, Den. (rē'bĕ)	152	55.20N	8.45E
Ribeirão Prêto, Braz. (rē-bā-rouɴ-prĕ'tô)	131	21.11S	47.47W
Ribera, N.M., U.S. (rē-bĕ'rä)	110	35.23N	105.27W
Riberalta, Bol. (rē-bå-räl'tä)	130	11.06S	66.02W
Rib Lake, Wi., U.S. (rĭb lāk)	103	45.20N	90.11W
Rîbniţa, Mol.	163	47.45N	29.02E
Rice, l., Can.	91	44.05N	78.10W
Rice Lake, Wi., U.S.	103	45.30N	91.44W
Rice Lake, l., Mn., U.S.	107g	45.10N	93.09W
Richards Island, i., Can. (rĭch'ẽrds)	95	69.45N	135.30W
Richards Landing, Can. (lănd'ĭng)	107k	46.18N	84.02W
Richardson, Tx., U.S. (rĭch'ẽrd-sŭn)	107c	32.56N	96.44W
Richardson, Wa., U.S.	106a	48.27N	122.54W
Richardson Mountains, mts., Can.	84	66.58N	136.19W
Richardson Mountains, mts., N.Z.	205	44.50S	168.30E
Richardson Park, De., U.S. (pärk)	99	39.45N	75.35W
Richelieu, r., Can. (rēsh'lyû')	91	45.05N	73.25W
Richfield, Mn., U.S.	107g	44.53N	93.17W
Richfield, Oh., U.S.	101d	41.14N	81.38W
Richfield, Ut., U.S.	109	38.45N	112.05W
Richford, Vt., U.S. (rĭch'fẽrd)	99	45.00N	72.35W
Rich Hill, Mo., U.S. (rĭch hĭl)	111	38.05N	94.21W
Richibucto, Can. (rĭ-chĭ-bŭk'tō)	85	46.41N	64.52W
Richland, Ga., U.S. (rĭch'lănd)	114	32.05N	84.40W
Richland, Wa., U.S.	104	46.17N	119.19W
Richland Center, Wi., U.S. (sĕn'tẽr)	103	43.20N	90.25W
Richmond, Austl.	201b	33.36S	150.45E
Richmond, Austl. (rĭch'mŭnd)	203	20.47S	143.14E
Richmond, Austl.	243b	37.49S	145.00E
Richmond, Can.	83c	45.12N	75.49W
Richmond, Can.	91	45.40N	72.07W
Richmond, S. Afr.	213c	29.52S	30.17E
Richmond, Il., U.S.	101a	42.29N	88.18W
Richmond, In., U.S.	98	39.50N	85.00W
Richmond, Ky., U.S.	98	37.45N	84.20W
Richmond, Mo., U.S.	111	39.16N	93.58W
Richmond, Tx., U.S.	113	29.35N	95.45W
Richmond, Ut., U.S.	105	41.55N	111.50W
Richmond, Va., U.S.	97	37.35N	77.30W
Richmond, neigh., Eng., U.K.	235	51.28N	0.18W
Richmond, neigh., N.J., U.S.	229b	39.59N	75.06W
Richmond Beach, Wa., U.S.	106a	47.47N	122.23W
Richmond Heights, Mo., U.S.	107e	38.38N	90.20W
Richmond Heights, Oh., U.S.	229a	41.33N	81.29W
Richmond Highlands, Wa., U.S.	106a	47.46N	122.22W
Richmond Hill, Can. (hĭl)	91	43.53N	79.26W
Richmondtown Restoration, pt. of i., N.Y., U.S.	228	40.34N	74.09W
Richmond Valley, neigh., N.Y., U.S.	228	40.31N	74.13W
Richton, Ms., U.S. (rĭch'tŭn)	114	31.20N	89.54W
Richwood, W.V., U.S. (rĭch'wo͝od)	98	38.10N	80.30W
Ricketts Point, c., Austl.	243b	38.00S	145.02E
Rickmansworth, Eng., U.K.	235	51.39N	0.29W
Ridderkerk, Neth.	145a	51.52N	4.35E
Rideau, r., Can.	83c	45.17N	75.41W
Rideau Lake, l., Can. (rē-dō')	91	44.40N	76.20W
Ridge, Eng., U.K.	235	51.41N	0.15W
Ridgefield, Ct., U.S. (rĭj'fēld)	100a	41.16N	73.30W

ăt; finăl; rāte; senăte; ärm; ȧsk; sofȧ; fâre; ch-choose; dh-as th in other; bē; ēvent; bĕt; recĕnt; cratẽr; g-gō; gh-guttural g; bĭt; ĭ-short neutral; rīde; ĸ-guttural k as ch in German ich;

PRONOUNCING INDEX

Ridgefield-Rohrbeck 339

PLACE (Pronunciation)	PAGE	Lat. °'	Long. °'
Ridgefield, N.J., U.S.	228	40.50N	74.00W
Ridgefield, Wa., U.S.	106c	45.49N	122.40W
Ridgefield Park, N.J., U.S.	228	40.51N	74.01W
Ridgeway, Can. (rĭj'wā)	101c	42.53N	79.02W
Ridgewood, N.J., U.S. (ridj'wo͝od)	100a	40.59N	74.08W
Ridgewood, neigh., N.Y., U.S.	228	40.42N	73.53W
Ridgway, Pa., U.S.	99	41.25N	78.40W
Riding Mountain, mtn., Can. (rīd'ĭng)	89	50.37N	99.37W
Riding Mountain National Park, rec., Can. (rīd'ĭng)	84	50.59N	99.19W
Riding Rocks, is., Bah.	122	25.20N	79.10W
Ridley Park, Pa., U.S.	229b	39.53N	75.19W
Riebeek-Oos, S. Afr.	213c	33.14S	26.09E
Ried, Aus. (rēd)	154	48.13N	13.30E
Riemke, neigh., Ger.	236	51.30N	7.13E
Riesa, Ger. (rē'zȧ)	154	51.17N	13.17E
Rieti, Italy (rē-ā'tē)	148	42.25N	12.51E
Rietvlei, S. Afr.	244b	26.18S	28.03E
Rievleidam, res., S. Afr.	213b	25.52S	28.18E
Riffe Lake, res., Wa., U.S.	104	46.20N	122.10W
Rifle, Co., U.S. (rī'f'l)	109	39.35N	107.50W
Rīga, Lat. (rē'gȧ)	164	56.55N	24.05E
Riga, Gulf of, b., Eur.	166	57.56N	23.05E
Rīgān, Iran	182	28.45N	58.55E
Rigaud, Can. (rē-gō')	83a	45.29N	74.18W
Rigby, Id., U.S. (rĭg'bē)	105	43.40N	111.55W
Rigeley, W.V., U.S. (rĭj'lē)	99	39.40N	78.45W
Rīgestān, des., Afg.	182	30.53N	64.42E
Rigolet, Can. (rĭg-ō-lā')	85	54.10N	58.40W
Riihimäki, Fin.	153	60.44N	24.44E
Rijeka, Cro. (rī-yĕ'kä)	148	45.22N	14.24E
Rijkevorsel, Bel.	145a	51.21N	4.46E
Rijswijk, Neth.	145a	52.03N	4.19E
Rika, r., Ukr. (rē'kȧ)	155	48.21N	23.37E
Rima, r., Nig.	215	13.30N	5.50E
Rímac, Peru	233c	12.02S	77.03W
Rímac, r., Peru	233c	12.02S	77.09W
Rimavska Sobota, Slvk. (rē'máf-ská sô'bô-tá)	155	48.25N	20.01E
Rimbo, Swe. (rēm'bō)	152	59.45N	18.22E
Rimini, Italy (rē'mē-nē)	148	44.03N	12.33E
Rimouski, Can. (rē-mo͞os'kē)	85	48.27N	68.32W
Rincón de Romos, Mex. (rēn-kōn dā rō-mōs')	118	22.13N	102.21W
Ringkøbing, Den. (rĭng'kûb-ĭng)	146	56.06N	8.14E
Ringkøbing Fjord, fj., Den.	152	55.55N	8.04E
Ringsted, Den. (rĭng'stĕdh)	152	55.27N	11.49E
Ringvassøya, i., Nor. (rĭng'väs-ûē)	146	69.58N	16.43E
Ringwood, Austl.	201a	37.49S	145.14E
Ringwood North, Austl.	243b	37.48S	145.14E
Rinjani, Gunung, mtn., Indon.	196	8.39S	116.22E
Río Abajo, Pan. (rē'ō-ä-bä'kō)	116a	9.01N	78.30W
Río Balsas, Mex. (rē'ō-bäl-säs)	118	17.59N	99.45W
Riobamba, Ec. (rē'ō-bäm-bä)	130	1.45S	78.37W
Rio Bonito, Braz. (rē'ō bō-nē'tō)	129a	22.44S	42.38W
Rio Branco, Braz. (rē'ō brän'kō)	130	9.57S	67.50W
Río Branco, Ur. (riō brănco)	132	32.33S	53.29W
Rio Casca, Braz. (rē'ō-kà's-kä)	129a	20.15S	42.39W
Río Chico, Ven. (rē'ō chē'kō)	131b	10.20N	65.58W
Rio Claro, Braz. (rē'ō klä'rō)	131	22.25S	47.33W
Rio Comprido, neigh., Braz.	234c	22.55S	43.12W
Río Cuarto, Arg. (rē'ō kwär'tō)	132	33.05S	64.15W
Rio das Flores, Braz. (rē'ō-däs-flô-rĕs)	129a	22.10S	43.35W
Rio de Janeiro, Braz. (rē'ō dā zhä-nā'ê-rō)	132b	22.50S	43.20W
Rio de Janeiro, state, Braz.	131	22.27S	42.43W
Río de Jesús, Pan.	121	7.54N	80.59W
Rio de Mouro, Port.	238d	38.46N	9.20W
Río Frío, Mex. (rē'ō-frē'ō)	119a	19.21N	98.40W
Río Gallegos, Arg. (rē'ō gä-lā'gōs)	132	51.43S	69.15W
Rio Grande, Braz. (rē'ō grän'dĕ)	132	31.04S	52.14W
Río Grande, Mex. (rē'ō grän'dā)	118	23.51N	102.59W
Riogrande, Tx., U.S. (rē'ō grán-dā)	112	26.23N	98.48W
Río Grande, Ven.	234a	10.35N	66.57W
Rio Grande do Norte, state, Braz.	131	5.26S	37.20W
Rio Grande do Sul, state, Braz. (rē'ō grän'dĕ-dō-so͞o'l)	132	29.00S	54.00W
Ríohacha, Col. (rē'ō-ä'chä)	130	11.30N	72.54W
Río Hato, Pan. (rē'ō-ä'tō)	121	8.19N	80.11W
Riom, Fr. (rē-ôN')	156	45.54N	3.08E
Rio Muni, hist. reg., Eq. Gui. (rē'ō mo͞o'nē)	210	1.47N	8.33E
Ríonegro, Col. (rē'ō-nĕ'grō)	130a	6.09N	75.22W
Río Negro, prov., Arg. (rē'ō nā'grō)	132	40.15S	68.15W
Río Negro, dept., Ur. (rē'ō-nĕ'grō)	129c	32.48S	57.45W
Río Negro, Embalse del, res., Ur.	132	32.45S	55.50W
Rionero, Italy (rē-ō-nā'rō)	160	40.55N	15.42E
Rioni, r., Geor.	168	42.08N	41.39E
Rio Novo, Braz. (rē'ō-nô'vō)	129a	21.30S	43.08W
Rio Pardo de Minas, Braz. (rē'ō pär'dō-dĕ-mē'näs)	131	15.43S	42.24W
Rio Pombo, Braz. (rē'ō pôm'bä)	129a	21.17S	43.09W
Rio Sorocaba, Represa do, res., Braz.	129a	23.37S	47.19W
Ríosucio, Col. (rē'ō-so͞o'syō)	130a	5.25N	75.41W
Río Tercero, Arg. (rē'ō dĕr-sĕ'rō)	132	32.12S	63.59W
Rio Verde, Braz. (vĕr'dĕ)	131	17.47S	50.49W
Ríoverde, Mex. (rē'ō-vĕr'dā)	116	21.54N	99.59W
Ripley, Eng., U.K. (rĭp'lē)	144a	53.03N	1.24W
Ripley, Eng., U.K.	235	51.18N	0.29W
Ripley, Ms., U.S.	114	34.44N	88.55W
Ripley, Tn., U.S.	114	35.44N	89.34W
Ripoll, Spain (rē-pōl'')	159	42.10N	2.10E
Ripon, Wi., U.S. (rĭp'ŏn)	103	43.49N	88.50W
Ripon, i., Austl.	202	20.05S	118.10E
Ripon Falls, wtfl., Ug.	212	0.38N	33.02E
Risaralda, dept., Col.	130a	5.15N	76.00W
Risdon, Austl. (rĭz'dŭn)	203	42.37S	147.32E
Rishiri, i., Japan (rē-shē'rē)	194	45.10N	141.08E
Rishon le Ẕiyyon, Isr.	181a	31.57N	34.48E
Rishra, India	186a	22.42N	88.22E
Rising Sun, In., U.S. (rīz'ĭng sŭn)	98	38.55N	84.55W
Risor, Nor. (rēs'ûr)	146	58.44N	9.10E
Ritacuva, Alto, mtn., Col. (ä'l-tô-rē-tä-ko͞o'vä)	130	6.22N	72.13W
Ritchie, Va., U.S.	229d	38.52N	76.52W
Rithāla, neigh., India	240d	28.43N	77.06E
Rittman, Oh., U.S. (rĭt'năn)	101d	40.58N	81.47W
Ritzville, Wa., U.S. (rĭts'vĭl)	104	47.08N	118.23W
Riva, Dom. Rep. (rē'vä)	123	19.10N	69.55W
Riva, Italy (rē'vä)	160	45.54N	10.49E
Riva, Md., U.S. (rĭ'vä)	100e	38.57N	76.36W
Rivas, Nic. (rē'väs)	120	11.25N	85.51W
Rive-de-Gier, Fr. (rēv-dē-zhē-ā')	156	45.32N	4.37E
Rivera, Ur. (rē-vä'rä)	132	30.52S	55.32W
River Cess, Lib. (rĭv'ēr sĕs)	210	5.46N	9.52W
Riverdale, Il., U.S. (rĭv'ēr dāl)	101a	41.38N	87.36W
Riverdale, Md., U.S.	229d	38.58N	76.55W
Riverdale, Ut., U.S.	107b	41.11N	112.00W
Riverdale, neigh., N.Y., U.S.	228	40.54N	73.54W
River Edge, N.J., U.S.	228	40.56N	74.02W
River Falls, Al., U.S.	114	31.20N	86.25W
River Falls, Wi., U.S.	103	44.48N	92.38W
River Forest, Il., U.S.	231a	41.53N	87.49W
River Grove, Il., U.S.	231a	41.56N	87.50W
Riverhead, Eng., U.K.	235	51.17N	0.10E
Riverhead, N.Y., U.S. (rĭv'ēr hĕd)	99	40.55N	72.40W
Riverina, reg., Austl. (rĭv-ēr-ē'nä)	203	34.55S	144.30E
River Jordan, Can. (jôr'dăn)	106a	48.25N	124.03W
River Oaks, Tx., U.S. (ōkz)	107c	32.47N	97.24W
River Rouge, Mi., U.S. (ro͞ozh)	101b	42.16N	83.09W
Rivers, Can.	89	50.01N	100.15W
Riverside, Ca., U.S. (rĭv'ēr-sīd)	96	33.59N	117.21W
Riverside, Il., U.S.	231a	41.50N	87.49W
Riverside, N.J., U.S.	100f	40.02N	74.58W
Rivers Inlet, Can.	86	51.45N	127.15W
Riverstone, Austl.	201b	33.41S	150.52E
Riverton, Va., U.S.	99	39.00N	78.15W
Riverton, Wy., U.S.	105	43.02N	108.24W
Rivesaltes, Fr. (rēv'zält')	156	42.48N	2.48E
Riviera Beach, Fl., U.S. (rĭv-ĭ-ĕr'ȧ bēch)	115a	26.46N	80.04W
Riviera Beach, Md., U.S.	100e	39.10N	76.32W
Rivière-Beaudette, Can.	83a	45.14N	74.20W
Rivière-du-Loup, Can. (rē-vyâr' dü lo͞o')	85	47.50N	69.32W
Rivière Qui Barre, Can. (rēv-yĕr' kē-bär)	83g	53.47N	113.51W
Rivière-Trois-Pistoles, Can. (trwä'pēs-tōl')	92	48.07N	69.10W
Rivne, Ukr.	163	48.11N	31.46E
Rivne, Ukr.	167	50.37N	26.17E
Rivne, prov., Ukr.	163	50.55N	27.00E
Riyadh, Sau. Ar.	182	24.31N	46.47E
Rize, Tur. (rē'zĕ)	149	41.00N	40.30E
Rizhao, China (rē-jou)	192	35.27N	119.28E
Rizzuto, Cape, c., Italy (rēt-so͞o'tō)	161	38.53N	17.05E
Rjukan, Nor. (ryo͞o'kän)	146	59.53N	8.30E
Roanne, Fr. (rō-än')	147	46.02N	4.04E
Roanoke, Al., U.S. (rō'ȧ-nōk)	114	33.08N	85.21W
Roanoke, Va., U.S.	97	37.16N	79.55W
Roanoke, r., U.S.	97	36.17N	77.22W
Roanoke Rapids, N.C., U.S.	115	36.25N	77.40W
Roanoke Rapids Lake, res., N.C., U.S.	115	36.28N	77.37W
Roan Plateau, plat., Co., U.S. (rōn)	109	39.25N	110.00W
Roatan, Hond. (rō-ä-tän')	120	16.18N	86.33W
Roatán, i., Hond.	120	16.19N	86.46W
Robbeneiland, i., S. Afr.	212a	33.48S	18.22E
Robbins, Il., U.S. (rŏb'ĭnz)	101a	41.39N	87.42W
Robbinsdale, Mn., U.S. (rŏb'ĭnz-dāl)	107g	45.03N	93.22W
Robe, Wa., U.S. (rōb)	106a	48.06N	121.50W
Roberts, Mount, mtn., Austl. (rŏb'ērts)	203	28.05S	152.30E
Roberts, Point, c., Wa., U.S. (rŏb'ērts)	106d	48.58N	123.05W
Robertsham, neigh., S. Afr.	244b	26.15S	28.00E
Robertson, Lac, l., Can.	93	51.00N	59.10W
Robertsport, Lib. (rŏb'ērts-pōrt)	210	6.45N	11.22W
Roberval, Can. (rŏb'ēr-văl) (rō-bĕr-vál')	85	48.32N	72.15W
Robinson, Can.	93	48.16N	58.50W
Robinson, S. Afr.	244b	26.09S	27.43E
Robinson, Il., U.S. (rŏb'ĭn-sŭn)	98	39.00N	87.45W
Robinvale, Austl. (rŏb-ĭn'văl)	204	34.45S	142.45E
Roblin, Can.	89	51.15N	101.25W
Robson, Mount, mtn., Can. (rŏb'sŭn)	87	53.07N	119.09W
Robstown, Tx., U.S. (rŏbz'toun)	113	27.46N	97.41W
Roby, Eng., U.K.	237a	53.25N	2.51W
Roca, Cabo da, c., Port. (kȧ'bō-dä-rō'kă)	158	38.47N	9.30W
Rocas, Atol das, atoll, Braz. (ä-tōl-däs-rō'kás)	131	3.50S	33.46W
Rocha, Ur. (rō'chás)	132	34.26S	54.14W
Rocha Miranda, neigh., Braz.	234c	22.52S	43.22W
Rocha Sobrinho, Braz.	234c	22.47S	43.25W
Rochdale, Eng., U.K. (rŏch'dāl)	150	53.37N	2.09W
Roche à Bateau, Haiti (rôsh á bá-tō')	123	18.10N	74.00W
Rochefort, Fr. (rôsh-fôr')	147	45.55N	0.57W
Rochelle, Il., U.S. (rō-shĕl')	103	41.53N	89.06W
Rochelle Park, N.J., U.S.	228	40.55N	74.04W
Rochester, Eng., U.K.	144a	51.24N	0.30E
Rochester, In., U.S. (rŏch'ĕs-tēr)	98	41.05N	86.20W
Rochester, Mi., U.S.	101b	42.41N	83.09W
Rochester, Mn., U.S.	97	44.01N	92.30W
Rochester, N.H., U.S.	99	43.20N	71.00W
Rochester, N.Y., U.S.	97	43.15N	77.35W
Rochester, Pa., U.S.	101e	40.42N	80.16W
Rock, r., U.S.	97	41.40N	90.00W
Rock, r., Ia., U.S.	102	43.17N	96.13W
Rock, r., Or., U.S.	106c	45.34N	122.52W
Rock, r., Or., U.S.	106c	45.52N	123.14W
Rockaway, N.J., U.S. (rŏck'ȧ-wā)	100a	40.54N	74.30W
Rockaway Park, neigh., N.Y., U.S.	228	40.35N	73.50W
Rockaway Point, neigh., N.Y., U.S.	228	40.33N	73.55W
Rockbank, Austl.	201a	37.44S	144.40E
Rockcliffe Park, Can. (rok'klĭf pärk)	83c	45.27N	75.40W
Rock Creek, r., Can. (rŏk)	105	49.01N	107.00W
Rock Creek, r., Il., U.S.	101a	41.16N	87.54W
Rock Creek, r., Mt., U.S.	105	46.25N	113.40W
Rock Creek, r., Or., U.S.	104	45.30N	120.06W
Rock Creek, r., Wa., U.S.	104	47.09N	117.50W
Rock Creek Park, pt. of i., D.C., U.S.	229d	38.58N	77.03W
Rockdale, Austl.	201b	33.57S	151.08E
Rockdale, Md., U.S.	100e	39.22N	76.49W
Rockdale, Tx., U.S. (rŏk'dāl)	113	30.39N	97.00W
Rockefeller Center, pt. of i., N.Y., U.S.	228	40.45N	74.00W
Rock Falls, Il., U.S. (rŏk fôlz)	103	41.45N	89.42W
Rock Ferry, Eng., U.K.	237a	53.22N	3.00W
Rockford, Il., U.S. (rŏk'fērd)	97	42.16N	89.07W
Rockhampton, Austl. (rŏk-hămp'tŭn)	203	23.26S	150.29E
Rock Hill, S.C., U.S. (rŏk'hĭl)	97	34.55N	81.01W
Rockingham, N.C., U.S. (rŏk'ĭng-hăm)	115	34.54N	79.45W
Rockingham Forest, for., Eng., U.K. (rok'ĭng-hăm)	144a	52.29N	0.43W
Rock Island, Il., U.S.	97	41.31N	90.37W
Rock Island Dam, Wa., U.S. (ī lănd)	104	47.17N	120.33W
Rockland, Can. (rŏk'lănd)	83c	45.33N	75.17W
Rockland, Me., U.S.	92	44.06N	69.09W
Rockland, Ma., U.S.	93a	42.07N	70.55W
Rockland Reservoir, res., Austl.	204	36.55S	142.20E
Rockledge, Pa., U.S.	229b	40.03N	75.05W
Rockmart, Ga., U.S. (rŏk'märt)	114	33.58N	85.00W
Rockmont, Wi., U.S. (rŏk'mŏnt)	107h	46.34N	91.54W
Rockport, In., U.S. (rŏk'pōrt)	98	38.20N	87.00W
Rockport, Ma., U.S.	93a	42.39N	70.37W
Rockport, Mo., U.S.	111	40.25N	95.30W
Rockport, Tx., U.S.	113	28.03N	97.03W
Rock Rapids, Ia., U.S. (răp'ĭdz)	102	43.26N	96.10W
Rock Sound, strt., Bah.	122	24.50N	76.05W
Rocksprings, Tx., U.S. (rŏk sprĭngs)	112	30.02N	100.12W
Rock Springs, Wy., U.S.	96	41.35N	109.13W
Rockstone, Guy. (rŏk'stōn)	131	5.55N	57.27W
Rock Valley, Ia., U.S. (văl'ĭ)	102	43.13N	96.17W
Rockville, In., U.S. (rŏk'vĭl)	98	39.45N	87.15W
Rockville, Md., U.S.	100e	39.05N	77.11W
Rockville Centre, N.Y., U.S. (sĕn'tēr)	100a	40.39N	73.39W
Rockwall, Tx., U.S. (rŏk'wôl)	111	32.55N	96.23W
Rockwell City, Ia., U.S. (rŏk'wĕl)	103	42.22N	94.37W
Rockwood, Can. (rŏk-wo͝od)	83d	43.37N	80.08W
Rockwood, Me., U.S.	92	45.39N	69.45W
Rockwood, Tn., U.S.	114	35.51N	84.41W
Rocky, r., Oh., U.S.	229a	41.30N	81.49W
Rocky, East Branch, r., Oh., U.S.	101d	41.13N	81.43W
Rocky, West Branch, r., Oh., U.S.	101d	41.17N	81.54W
Rocky Boys Indian Reservation, I.R., Mt., U.S.	105	48.08N	109.34W
Rocky Ford, Co., U.S.	110	38.02N	103.43W
Rocky Hill, N.J., U.S. (hĭl)	100a	40.24N	74.38W
Rocky Island Lake, l., Can.	90	46.56N	83.04W
Rocky Mount, N.C., U.S.	115	35.55N	77.47W
Rocky Mountain House, Can.	87	52.22N	114.55W
Rocky Mountain National Park, rec., Co., U.S.	96	40.29N	106.06W
Rocky Mountains, mts., N.A.	82	50.00N	114.00W
Rocky River, Oh., U.S.	101d	41.29N	81.51W
Rocky River, Oh., U.S.	229a	41.30N	81.40W
Rocquencourt, Fr.	237c	48.50N	2.07E
Rodas, Cuba (rō'dhás)	122	22.20N	80.35W
Roden, r., Eng., U.K. (rō'dĕn)	144a	52.49N	2.38W
Rodeo, Mex. (rō-dā'ō)	112	25.12N	104.34W
Rodeo, Ca., U.S. (rō'dĕō)	106b	38.02N	122.16W
Roderick Island, i., Can. (rŏd'ē-rĭk)	86	52.40N	128.22W
Rodez, Fr. (rō-dĕz')	147	44.22N	2.34E
Rōdhos, Grc.	149	36.24N	28.15E
Ródhos, i., Grc.	142	36.00N	28.29E
Rodnei, Munții, mts., Rom.	155	47.41N	24.05E
Rodniki, Russia (rôd'nē-kē)	166	57.08N	41.48E
Rodonit, Kep I, c., Alb.	161	41.38N	19.01E
Roebling, N.J., U.S. (rōb'lĭng)	100f	40.07N	74.48W
Roebourne, Austl. (rō'bŭrn)	202	20.50S	117.15E
Roebuck Bay, b., Austl. (rō'bŭck)	202	18.15S	121.10E
Roedtan, S. Afr.	218d	24.37S	29.08E
Roehampton, neigh., Eng., U.K.	235	51.27N	0.14W
Roeselare, Bel.	151	50.55N	3.05E
Roesiger, l., Wa., U.S. (rōz'ĭ-gēr)	106a	47.59N	121.56W
Roes Welcome Sound, strt., Can. (rōz)	85	64.10N	87.23W
Rogachëv, Bela. (rôg'á-chyôf)	166	53.07N	30.04E
Rogans Hill, Austl.	243a	33.44S	151.01E
Rogatica, Bos. (rô-gä'tē-tsä)	161	43.46N	19.00E
Rogers, Ar., U.S. (rŏj-ērz)	111	36.19N	94.07W
Rogers City, Mi., U.S.	98	45.30N	83.50W
Rogers Park, neigh., Il., U.S.	231a	42.01N	87.40W
Rogersville, Tn., U.S.	114	36.21N	83.00W
Rognac, Fr. (rōn-yäk')	156a	43.29N	5.15E
Rogoaguado, l., Bol. (rō'gō-ä-gwä-dō)	130	12.42S	66.46W
Rogovskaya, Russia (rô-gôf'ská-yá)	163	45.43N	38.42E
Rogózno, Pol. (rô'gôzh-nō)	154	52.44N	16.53E
Rogue, r., Or., U.S. (rōg)	104	42.32N	124.13W
Rohatyn, Ukr.	155	49.22N	24.37E
Rohdenhaus, Ger.	236	51.18N	7.01E
Röhlinghausen, neigh., Ger.	236	51.31N	7.08E
Rohrbeck, Ger.	238a	52.32N	13.02E

340 Roissy–Ruse

PLACE (Pronunciation)	PAGE	Lat. °'	Long. °'
Roissy, Fr.	237c	48.47N	2.39E
Roissy-en-France, Fr.	237c	49.00N	2.31E
Rojas, Arg. (rō'häs)	129c	34.11S	60.42W
Rojo, Cabo, c., Mex. (rō'hō)	119	21.35N	97.16W
Rojo, Cabo, c., P.R. (rō'hō)	117b	17.55N	67.14W
Rokel, r., S.L.	214	9.00N	11.55W
Rokkō-Zan, mtn., Japan (rōk'kō zän)	195b	34.46N	135.16E
Roksana, S. Afr.	244b	26.07S	28.24E
Rokycany, Czech Rep. (rō'kĭ'tsȧ-nĭ)	154	49.44N	13.37E
Roldanillo, Col. (rôl-dä-nē'l-yō)	130a	4.24N	76.09W
Rolla, Mo., U.S.	111	37.56N	91.45W
Rolla, N.D., U.S.	102	48.52N	99.32W
Rolleville, Bah.	122	23.40N	76.00W
Rolling Acres, Md., U.S.	229c	39.17N	76.52W
Röllinghausen, neigh., Ger.	236	51.36N	7.14E
Rolling Hills, Ca., U.S.	232	33.46N	118.21W
Roma, Austl. (rō'mȧ)	203	26.30S	148.48E
Roma *see* Rome, Italy	142	41.52N	12.37E
Roma, Leso.	213c	29.28S	27.43E
Romaine, r., Can. (rō-mĕn')	85	51.22N	63.23W
Romainville, Fr.	237c	48.53N	2.26E
Roman, Rom. (rō'män)	155	46.56N	26.57E
Romania, nation, Eur. (rō-mā'nē-ȧ)	152	46.18N	22.53E
Romano, Cape, c., Fl., U.S. (rō-mä'nō)	115a	25.48N	82.00W
Romano, Cayo, i., Cuba (kä'yō-rô-mä'nō)	122	22.15N	78.00W
Romanovo, Russia (rô-mä'nô-vô)	172a	59.09N	61.24E
Romans, Fr. (rō-mäɴ')	156	45.04N	4.49E
Romblon, Phil. (rōm-blōn')	197a	12.34N	122.16E
Romblon Island, i., Phil.	197a	12.33N	122.17E
Rome (Roma), Italy	142	41.52N	12.37E
Rome, Ga., U.S. (rōm)	97	34.14N	85.10W
Rome, N.Y., U.S.	99	43.15N	75.25W
Romeo, Mi., U.S. (rō'mē-ō)	98	42.50N	83.00W
Romford, Eng., U.K. (rŭm'fērd)	144b	51.35N	0.11E
Romiley, Eng., U.K.	237b	53.25N	2.05W
Romilly-sur-Seine, Fr. (rō-mē-yē'sür-sān')	156	48.32N	3.41E
Romita, Mex. (rō-mē'tä)	118	20.53N	101.32W
Romny, Ukr. (rôm'nĭ)	167	50.46N	33.31E
Rømø, i., Den. (rûm'û)	152	55.08N	8.17E
Romoland, Ca., U.S. (rō'mō'lănd)	107a	33.44N	117.11W
Romorantin-Lanthenay, Fr. (rō-mō-rän-tăɴ')	156	47.24N	1.46E
Rompin, Malay.	181b	2.42N	102.30E
Rompin, r., Malay.	181b	2.54N	103.10E
Romsdalsfjorden, Nor.	152	62.40N	7.05W
Romulus, Mi., U.S. (rom'ū lŭs)	101b	42.14N	83.24W
Ron, Mui, c., Viet.	193	18.05N	106.45E
Ronan, Mt., U.S. (rō'năn)	105	47.28N	114.03W
Roncador, Serra do, mts., Braz. (sĕr'rȧ dō rôn-kä-dôr')	131	12.44S	52.19W
Roncesvalles, Spain (rôn-sĕs-vä'l-yĕs)	158	43.00N	1.17W
Ronceverte, W.V., U.S. (rŏn'sē-vûrt)	98	37.45N	80.30W
Ronda, Spain (rōn'dä)	167	36.45N	5.10W
Ronda, Sierra de, mts., Spain	158	36.35N	5.03W
Rondebult, S. Afr.	244b	26.18S	28.14E
Rondônia, , Braz.	130	10.15S	63.07W
Ronge, Lac la, l., Can. (rōnzh)	84	55.10N	105.00W
Rongjiang, China (rôŋ-jyäŋ)	193	25.52N	108.45E
Rongxian, China	193	22.50N	110.32E
Rønne, Den. (rûn'ĕ)	146	55.08N	14.46E
Ronneby, Swe. (rōn'ĕ-bü)	152	56.13N	15.17E
Ronne Ice Shelf, ice., Ant.	219	77.30S	38.00W
Ronsdorf, neigh., Ger.	236	51.14N	7.12E
Roodepoort, S. Afr. (rō'dē-pōrt)	213b	26.10S	27.52E
Roodhouse, Il., U.S. (rōōd'hous)	111	39.29N	90.21W
Rooiberg, S. Afr.	218d	24.46S	27.42E
Roosendaal, Neth. (rō'zĕn-däl)	145a	51.32N	4.27E
Roosevelt, N.Y., U.S.	228	40.41N	73.36W
Roosevelt, Ut., U.S. (rō'z'vĕlt)	109	40.20N	110.00W
Roosevelt, r., Braz. (rô'sē-vĕlt)	131	9.22S	60.28W
Roosevelt Island, i., Ant.	219	79.30S	168.00W
Root, r., Wi., U.S.	101a	42.49N	87.54W
Rooty Hill, Austl.	243a	33.46S	150.50E
Roper, r., Austl. (rōp'ēr)	202	14.50S	134.00E
Ropsha, Russia (rôp'shȧ)	172c	59.44N	29.53E
Roque Pérez, Arg. (rô'kĕ-pĕ'rĕz)	129c	35.23S	59.22W
Roques, Islas los, is., Ven.	130	12.25N	67.40W
Roraima, , Braz. (rō'rĭ-mȧ)	130	2.00N	62.15W
Roraima, Mount, mtn., S.A. (rō-rä-ē'mä)	131	5.12N	60.52W
Røros, Nor. (rûr'ōs)	146	62.36N	11.25E
Ros', r., Ukr. (rôs)	163	49.40N	30.22E
Rosa, Monte, mtn., Italy (mōn'tä rō'zä)	148	45.56N	7.51E
Rosales, Mex. (rō-zä'läs)	112	28.15N	100.43W
Rosales, Phil. (rō-sä'lĕs)	197a	15.54N	120.38E
Rosamorada, Mex. (rō'zä-mō-rä'dhä)	118	22.06N	105.16W
Rosanna, Austl.	243b	37.45S	145.04E
Rosaria, Laguna, l., Mex. (lä-gō'nä-rō-sȧ'ryä)	119	17.50N	93.51W
Rosario, Arg. (rō-zä'rē-ō)	132	32.58S	60.42W
Rosario, Braz. (rō-zä'rē-ō)	131	2.49S	44.15W
Rosario, Mex.	112	26.31N	105.40W
Rosario, Mex.	118	22.58N	105.54W
Rosario, Phil.	197a	13.49N	121.13W
Rosario, Ur.	129c	34.19S	57.24E
Rosario, Cayo, i., Cuba (kä'yō-rō-sä'ryō)	122	21.40N	81.55W
Rosário do Sul, Braz. (rō-zä'rē-ō-dō-sōō'l)	132	30.17S	54.52W
Rosário Oeste, Braz. (ō'ĕst'ĕ)	131	14.47S	56.20W
Rosario Strait, strt., Wa., U.S.	106a	48.27N	122.45W
Rosas, Golfo de, b., Spain (gôl-fô-dĕ-rō'zäs)	159	42.10N	3.20E
Rosbach, Ger. (rōz'bäĸ)	157c	50.47N	7.38E
Roscoe, Tx., U.S. (rôs'kō)	112	32.26N	100.38W
Roseau, Dom.	121b	15.17N	61.23W
Roseau, Mn., U.S. (rō-zō')	102	48.52N	95.47W
Roseau, r., Mn., U.S.	102	48.52N	96.11W
Rosebank, neigh., S. Afr.	244b	26.09S	28.02E
Roseberg, Or., U.S. (rōz'bûrg)	96	43.13N	123.30W
Rosebery, neigh., Austl.	243a	33.55S	151.12E
Rosebud, r., Can. (rōz'bŭd)	87	51.20N	112.20W
Rosebud Creek, r., Mt., U.S.	105	45.48N	106.34W
Rosebud Indian Reservation, I.R., S.D., U.S.	102	43.13N	100.42W
Rosedale, Ms., U.S.	114	33.49N	90.56W
Rosedale, Wa., U.S.	106a	47.20N	122.39W
Rosedale, neigh., Can.	227c	43.41N	79.22W
Rosedale, neigh., N.Y., U.S.	228	40.39N	73.45W
Roseires Reservoir, res., Sudan	211	11.15N	34.45E
Roseland, neigh., Il., U.S.	231a	41.42N	87.38W
Roselle, Il., U.S. (rō-zĕl')	101a	41.59N	88.05W
Roselle, N.J., U.S.	228	40.40N	74.16W
Rosemead, Ca., U.S.	232	34.04N	118.03W
Rosemère, Can. (rōz'mĕr)	83a	45.38N	73.48W
Rosemont, Il., U.S.	231a	41.59N	87.52W
Rosemont, Pa., U.S.	229b	40.01N	75.19W
Rosemount, Mn., U.S. (rōz'mount)	107g	44.44N	93.08W
Rosendal, S. Afr. (rō-sĕn'täl)	218d	28.32S	27.56E
Roseneath, S. Afr.	244b	26.17S	28.11E
Rosenheim, Ger. (rō'zĕn-hīm)	147	47.52N	12.06E
Rosenthal, neigh., Ger.	238a	52.36N	13.23E
Rosetown, Can. (rōz'toun)	84	51.33N	108.00W
Rose Tree, Pa., U.S.	229b	39.56N	75.23W
Rosetta *see* Rashīd, Egypt	184	31.22N	30.25E
Rosettenville, neigh., S. Afr.	213b	26.15S	28.04E
Roseville, Austl.	243a	33.47S	151.11E
Roseville, Ca., U.S. (rōz'vĭl)	108	38.44N	121.19W
Roseville, Mi., U.S.	101b	42.30N	82.55W
Roseville, Mn., U.S.	107g	45.01N	93.10W
Rosiclare, Il., U.S. (rōz'y-klâr)	98	37.30N	88.15W
Rosignol, Guy. (rŏs-ĭg-nŏl)	131	6.16N	57.37W
Roşiori de Vede, Rom. (rō-shôr'ĕ dĕ vĕ-dĕ)	161	44.06N	25.00E
Roskilde, Den. (rôs'kĕl-dĕ)	152	55.39N	12.04E
Roslavl', Russia (rôs'läv'l)	166	53.56N	32.52E
Roslyn, N.Y., U.S.	228	40.48N	73.39W
Roslyn, Wa., U.S. (rŏz'lĭn)	104	47.14N	121.00W
Roslyn Estates, N.Y., U.S.	228	40.47N	73.40W
Roslyn Heights, N.Y., U.S.	228	40.47N	73.39W
Rosny-sous-Bois, Fr.	237c	48.53N	2.29E
Rösrath, Ger. (rûz'rät)	157c	50.53N	7.11E
Ross, Oh., U.S. (rôs)	101f	39.19N	84.39W
Rossano, Italy (rô-sä'nō)	149	39.34N	16.38E
Rossan Point, c., Ire.	150	54.45N	8.30W
Ross Creek, r., Can.	83g	53.40N	113.08W
Rosseau, l., Can. (rôs-sō')	91	45.15N	79.30W
Rossel, i., Pap. N. Gui. (rō-sĕl')	203	11.31S	154.00E
Rosser, Can. (rŏs'sēr)	83f	49.59N	97.27W
Ross Ice Shelf, ice., Ant.	219	81.30S	175.00W
Rossignol, Lake, l., Can.	92	44.10N	65.10W
Ross Island, i., Can.	89	54.14N	97.45W
Ross Lake, res., Wa., U.S.	104	48.40N	121.07W
Rossland, Can. (rôs'lănd)	84	49.05N	118.48W
Rossmore, Austl.	243a	33.57S	150.46E
Rossosh', Russia (rôs'sŭsh)	167	50.12N	39.32E
Rossouw, S. Afr.	213c	31.12S	27.18E
Ross Sea, sea, Ant.	219	76.00S	178.00W
Rossvatnet, l., Nor.	146	65.36N	13.08E
Rossville, Ga., U.S. (rôs'vĭl)	114	34.57N	85.22W
Rossville, Md., U.S.	229c	39.20N	76.29W
Rosthern, Can.	88	52.41N	106.25W
Rostherne, Eng., U.K.	237b	53.21N	2.23W
Rostock, Ger. (rôs'tŭk)	146	54.04N	12.06E
Rostov, Russia	166	57.13N	39.23E
Rostov, prov., Russia	163	47.38N	39.15E
Rostov-na-Donu, Russia (rôstôv-nȧ-dô-nōō)	164	47.16N	39.47E
Roswell, Ga., U.S. (rôz'wĕl)	114	34.02N	84.21W
Roswell, N.M., U.S.	96	33.23N	104.32W
Rosyln, Pa., U.S.	229b	40.07N	75.08W
Rotan, Tx., U.S. (rō-tăn')	110	32.51N	100.27W
Rothenburg, Ger.	154	49.20N	10.10E
Rotherham, Eng., U.K. (rŏdh'ēr-ăm)	144a	53.26N	1.21W
Rothesay, Can. (rôth'sȧ)	92	45.23N	66.00W
Rothesay, Scot., U.K.	150	55.50N	3.14W
Rothneusiedl, neigh., Aus.	239e	48.08N	16.23E
Rothwell, Eng., U.K.	144a	53.44N	1.30W
Roti, Pulau, i., Indon. (rō'tē)	196	10.30S	122.52E
Roto, Austl. (rō'tō)	204	33.07S	145.30E
Rotorua, N.Z.	205	38.07S	176.17E
Rotterdam, Neth. (rŏt'ēr-däm')	142	51.55N	4.27E
Rottweil, Ger. (rōt'vĭl)	154	48.10N	8.36E
Roubaix, Fr. (rōō-bĕ')	156	50.42N	3.10E
Rouen, Fr. (rōō-äɴ')	142	49.25N	1.05E
Rouge, r., Can. (rōōzh)	83d	43.53N	79.21W
Rouge, r., Can.	91	46.40N	74.50W
Rouge, r., Mi., U.S.	101b	42.30N	83.15W
Rough River Reservoir, res., Ky., U.S.	98	37.45N	86.10W
Round Lake, Il., U.S.	101a	42.21N	88.05W
Round Pond, l., Can.	93	48.15N	55.57W
Round Rock, Tx., U.S.	113	30.31N	97.41W
Round Top, mtn., Or., U.S. (tŏp)	106c	45.41N	123.22W
Roundup, Mt., U.S. (round'ŭp)	105	46.25N	108.35W
Rousay, i., Scot., U.K. (rōō'zȧ)	150a	59.10N	3.04W
Rouyn, Can. (rōōn)	85	48.22N	79.03W
Rovaniemi, Fin. (rô'vȧ-nyĕ'mĭ)	146	66.29N	25.45E
Rovato, Italy (rō-vä'tō)	160	45.33N	10.00E
Roven'ki, Russia	163	49.54N	38.54E
Roven'ky, Ukr.	163	48.06N	39.44E
Rovereto, Italy (rō-vå-rā'tō)	160	45.53N	11.05E
Rovigo, Italy (rô-vē'gô)	160	45.05N	11.48E
Rovinj, Cro. (rô'ēn')	160	45.05N	13.40E
Rovira, Col. (rō-vē'rä)	130a	4.14N	75.13W
Rovuma (Ruvuma), r., Afr.	217	10.50S	39.50E
Rowland Heights, Ca., U.S.	232	33.59N	117.54W
Rowley, Ma., U.S. (rou'lē)	93a	42.43N	70.53W
Rowville, Austl.	243b	37.56S	145.14E
Roxana, Il., U.S. (rŏks'ăn-nȧ)	107e	38.51N	90.05W
Roxas, Phil. (rô-xäs)	196	11.30N	122.47E
Roxboro, Can.	227b	45.31N	73.48W
Roxborough, neigh., Pa., U.S.	229b	40.02N	75.13W
Roxbury, neigh., N.Y., U.S.	228	40.34N	73.54W
Roxo, Cap, c., Sen.	214	12.20N	16.43W
Roy, N.M., U.S. (roi)	110	35.54N	104.09W
Roy, Ut., U.S.	107b	41.10N	112.02W
Royal, i., Bah.	122	25.30N	76.50W
Royal Albert Hall, pt. of i., Eng., U.K.	235	51.30N	0.11W
Royal Canal, can., Ire. (roi-ăl)	150	53.28N	6.45W
Royal Natal National Park, rec., S. Afr.	213c	28.35S	28.54E
Royal Naval College, pt. of i., Eng., U.K.	235	51.29N	0.01W
Royal Oak, Can. (roi'ăl ōk)	106a	48.30N	123.24W
Royal Oak, Mi., U.S.	101b	42.29N	83.09W
Royal Oak Township, Mi., U.S.	230c	42.27N	83.10W
Royal Ontario Museum, bldg., Can.	227c	43.40N	79.24W
Royalton, Mi., U.S. (roi'ăl-tŭn)	98	42.00N	86.25W
Royan, Fr. (rwä-yäɴ')	156	45.40N	1.02W
Roye, Fr. (rwä)	156	49.43N	2.40E
Royersford, Pa., U.S. (rô' yērz-fērd)	100f	40.11N	75.32W
Royston, Ga., U.S. (roiz'tŭn)	114	34.15N	83.06W
Royton, Eng., U.K. (roi'tŭn)	144a	53.34N	2.07W
Rozay-en-Brie, Fr. (rō-zā-ĕɴ-brē')	157b	48.41N	2.57E
Rozdil'na, Ukr.	163	46.47N	30.08E
Rozelle, Austl.	243a	33.52S	151.10E
Rozhaya, r., Russia (rô'zhȧ-yȧ)	172b	55.20N	37.37E
Rozivka, Ukr.	163	47.14N	36.35E
Rožňava, Slvk. (rôzh'nyȧ-vȧ)	155	48.39N	20.32E
Rtishchevo, Russia ('r-tĭsh'chĕ-vô)	167	52.15N	43.40E
Ru, r., China (rōō)	190	33.07N	114.18E
Ruacana Falls, wtfl., Afr.	212	17.15S	14.45E
Ruaha National Park, rec., Tan.	217	7.15S	34.50E
Ruapehu, vol., N.Z. (rō-ȧ-pā'hōō)	203a	39.15S	175.37E
Rubʿ al Khali *see* Ar Rubʿ al Khālī, des., Asia	182	20.00N	51.00E
Rubeho Mountains, mts., Tan.	217	6.45S	36.15E
Rubidoux, Ca., U.S.	107a	33.59N	117.24W
Rubondo Island, i., Tan.	217	2.10S	31.55E
Rubtsovsk, Russia	164	51.31N	81.17E
Ruby, Ak., U.S. (rōō'bē)	96a	64.38N	155.22W
Ruby, l., Nv., U.S.	108	40.11N	115.20W
Ruby, r., Mt., U.S.	105	45.06N	112.10W
Ruby Mountains, mts., Nv., U.S.	108	40.11N	115.36W
Rüdersdorf, Ger.	238a	52.29N	13.47E
Rudge Ramos, Braz.	234d	23.41S	46.34W
Rüdinghausen, neigh., Ger.	236	51.27N	7.25E
Rudkøbing, Den. (rōōdh'kûb-ĭng)	152	54.56N	10.44E
Rüdnitz, Ger. (rüd'nētz)	145b	52.44N	13.38E
Rudolf, Lake, l., Afr. (rōō'dŏlf)	211	3.30N	36.05E
Rudow, neigh., Ger.	238a	52.25N	13.30E
Rueil-Malmaison, Fr.	237c	48.53N	2.11E
Rufāʿah, Sudan (rōō-fä'ä)	211	14.52N	33.30E
Ruffec, Fr. (rü-fĕk')	156	46.03N	0.11E
Rufiji, r., Tan. (rō-fē'jē)	213	8.00S	38.00E
Rufisque, Sen. (rü-fēsk')	210	14.43N	17.17W
Rufunsa, Zam.	217	15.05S	29.40E
Rufus Woods, Wa., U.S.	104	48.02N	119.33W
Rugao, China (rōō-gou)	192	32.24N	120.33E
Rugby, Eng., U.K. (rŭg'bē)	144a	52.22N	1.15W
Rugby, N.D., U.S.	102	48.22N	100.00W
Rugeley, Eng., U.K. (rōōj'lē)	144a	52.46N	1.56W
Rügen, i., Ger. (rü'ghĕn)	142	54.28N	13.47E
Rüggeberg, Ger.	236	51.16N	7.22E
Ruhlsdorf, Ger.	238a	52.23N	13.16E
Ruhnu-Saar, i., Est. (rōōnō-sȧ'ăr)	153	57.46N	23.15E
Ruhr, r., Ger. (rōr)	154	51.18N	8.17E
Ruhrort, neigh., Ger.	236	51.26N	6.45E
Rui'an, China (rwā-än)	193	27.48N	120.40E
Ruislip, neigh., Eng., U.K.	235	51.34N	0.25W
Ruiz, Mex. (rōē'z)	118	21.55N	105.09W
Ruiz, Nevado del, vol., Col. (nĕ-vȧ'dô-dĕl-rōōē'z)	130a	4.52N	75.20W
Rūjiena, Lat. (rō'yĭ-ă-nȧ)	153	57.54N	25.19E
Ruki, r., Zaire	216	0.05S	18.55E
Rukwa, Lake, l., Tan. (rōōk-wä')	212	8.00S	32.25E
Rum, r., Mn., U.S. (rŭm)	103	45.52N	93.45W
Ruma, Yugo. (rōō'mȧ)	161	45.00N	19.53E
Rum'ancevo, Russia	239b	55.38N	37.26E
Rumbek, Sudan (rŭm'bĕk)	211	6.52N	29.43E
Rum Cay, i., Bah.	123	23.40N	74.50W
Rumelihisari, neigh., Tur.	239f	41.05N	29.03E
Rumford, Me., U.S. (rŭm'fērd)	92	44.32N	70.35W
Rummah, Wādī ar, val., Sau. Ar.	182	26.17N	41.45E
Rummānah, Egypt	181a	31.01N	32.39E
Rummelsburg, neigh., Ger.	238a	52.30N	13.29E
Rummenohl, Ger.	236	51.17N	7.32E
Runan, China (rōō-nän)	192	32.59N	114.22E
Runcorn, Eng., U.K. (rŭŋ'kôrn)	144a	53.20N	2.44W
Runnemede, N.J., U.S.	229b	39.51N	75.04W
Runnymede, pt. of i., Eng., U.K.	235	51.26N	0.34W
Ruo, r., China (rwō)	188	41.15N	100.46E
Rupat, i., Indon. (rōō'pät)	181b	1.55N	101.35E
Rupat, Selat, strt., Indon.	181b	1.55N	101.17E
Rupert, Id., U.S. (rōō'pērt)	105	42.36N	113.41W
Rupert, Rivière de, r., Can.	85	51.35N	76.30W
Rural Ridge, Pa., U.S.	230b	40.35N	79.50W
Ruse, Bul. (rōō'sĕ) (rō'sĕ)	142	43.50N	25.59E

ăt; finăl; rāte; senăte; ärm; ȧsk; sofȧ; fâre; ch-choose; dh-as th in other; bē; ēvent; bĕt; recĕnt; cratēr; g-gō; gh-guttural g; bĭt; ĭ-short neutral; rīde; ĸ-guttural k as ch in German ich;

PLACE (Pronunciation)	PAGE	Lat. °	Long. °
Rushan, China (rōō-shän)	190	36.54N	121.31E
Rush City, Mn., U.S.	103	45.40N	92.59W
Rusholme, neigh., Eng., U.K.	237b	53.27N	2.12W
Rushville, Il., U.S. (rŭsh'vïl)	111	40.08N	90.34W
Rushville, In., U.S.	98	39.35N	85.30W
Rushville, Ne., U.S.	102	42.43N	102.27W
Rusizi, r., Afr.	217	3.00S	29.05E
Rusk, Tx., U.S. (rŭsk)	113	31.49N	95.09W
Ruskin, Can. (rŭs'kin)	106d	49.10N	122.25W
Russ, r., Aus.	145e	48.12N	16.55E
Russas, Braz. (rōō's-säs)	131	4.48S	37.50W
Russell, Can.	83c	45.15N	75.22W
Russell, Can. (rŭs'ĕl)	84	50.47N	101.15W
Russell, Ca., U.S.	106b	37.39N	122.08W
Russell, Ks., U.S.	110	38.51N	98.51W
Russell, Ky., U.S.	98	38.30N	82.45W
Russel Lake, l., Can.	89	56.15N	101.30W
Russell Gardens, N.Y., U.S.	228	40.47N	73.43W
Russell Islands, is., Sol.Is.	203	9.16S	158.30E
Russellville, Al., U.S. (rŭs'ĕl-vïl)	114	34.29N	87.44W
Russellville, Ar., U.S.	111	35.16N	93.08W
Russellville, Ky., U.S.	114	36.48N	86.51W
Russia, nation, Russia	164	61.00N	60.00E
Russian, r., Ca., U.S. (rŭsh'ăn)	108	38.59N	123.10W
Rustavi, Geor.	168	41.33N	45.02E
Rustenburg, S. Afr. (rŭs'tĕn-bûrg)	218d	25.40S	27.15E
Ruston, La., U.S. (rŭs'tŭn)	113	32.32N	92.39W
Ruston, Wa., U.S.	106a	47.18N	122.30W
Rusville, S. Afr.	244b	26.10S	28.18E
Rute, Spain (rōō'tä)	158	38.20N	4.34W
Ruth, Nv., U.S. (rōōth)	108	39.17N	115.00W
Ruthenia, hist. reg., Ukr.	155	48.25N	23.00E
Rutherford, N.J., U.S.	228	40.49N	74.07W
Rutherfordton, N.C., U.S. (rŭdh'ẽr-fẽrd-tŭn)	115	35.23N	81.58W
Rutland, Vt., U.S.	99	43.35N	72.55W
Rutledge, Md., U.S. (rŭt'lĕdj)	100e	39.34N	76.33W
Rutledge, Pa., U.S.	229b	39.54N	75.20W
Rutog, China	188	33.29N	79.26E
Rutshuru, Zaire (rōōt-shōō'rōō)	212	1.11S	29.27E
Rüttenscheid, neigh., Ger.	236	51.26N	7.00E
Ruvo, Italy (rōō'vö)	160	41.07N	16.32E
Ruvuma, r., Afr.	212	11.30S	37.00E
Ruza, Russia (rōō'zä)	162	55.42N	36.12E
Ruzhany, Bela. (rö-zhän'ĭ)	155	52.49N	24.54E
Rwanda, nation, Afr.	212	2.10S	29.37E
Ryabovo, Russia (ryä'bô-vô)	172c	59.24N	31.08E
Ryarsh, Eng., U.K.	235	51.19N	0.24E
Ryazan', Russia (ryä-zän'')	164	54.37N	39.43E
Ryazan', prov., Russia	162	54.10N	39.37E
Ryazhsk, Russia (ryäzh'sk')	166	53.43N	40.04E
Rybachiy, Poluostrov, pen., Russia	166	69.50N	33.20E
Rybatskoye, Russia	172c	59.50N	30.31E
Rybinsk, Russia	164	58.02N	38.52E
Rybinskoye, res., Russia	164	58.23N	38.15E
Rybnik, Pol.	155	50.06N	18.37E
Rydal, Pa., U.S.	229b	40.06N	75.06W
Rydalmere, Austl.	243a	33.49S	151.02E
Ryde, Austl.	243a	33.49S	151.06E
Ryde, Eng., U.K. (rīd)	150	50.43N	1.16W
Rye, N.Y., U.S. (rī)	100a	40.58N	73.42W
Ryl'sk, Russia (rĕl''sk)	167	51.33N	34.42E
Rynfield, S. Afr.	244b	26.09S	28.20E
Ryōtsu, Japan (ryŏt'sōō)	194	38.02N	138.23E
Rypin, Pol. (ri'pĕn)	155	53.04N	19.25E
Rysy, mtn., Eur.	155	49.12N	20.04E
Ryukyu Islands see Nansei-shotō, is., Japan	189	27.30N	127.00E
Rzeszów, Pol. (zhä-shóf)	147	50.02N	22.00E
Rzhev, Russia ('r-zhĕf)	164	56.16N	34.17E
Rzhyshchiv, Ukr.	163	49.58N	31.05E

S

PLACE (Pronunciation)	PAGE	Lat. °	Long. °
Saale, r., Ger. (sä-lĕ)	154	51.14N	11.52E
Saalfeld, Ger. (säl'fĕlt)	154	50.38N	11.20E
Saarbrücken, Ger. (zähr'brü-kĕn)	147	49.15N	7.01E
Saaremaa, i., Est.	166	58.25N	22.30E
Saarland, state, Ger.	154	49.25N	6.50E
Saarn, neigh., Ger.	236	51.24N	6.53E
Saarnberg, neigh., Ger.	236	51.25N	6.53E
Saavedra, Arg. (sä-ä-vä'drä)	132	37.45S	62.23W
Şaba, i., Neth. Ant. (sä'bä)	121b	17.39N	63.20W
Šabac, Yugo. (shä'bäts)	149	44.45N	19.49E
Sabadell, Spain (sä-bä-dhäl')	148	41.32N	2.07E
Sabah, hist. reg., Malay.	196	5.10N	116.25E
Sabana, Archipiélago de, is., Cuba	122	23.05N	80.00W
Sabana, Río, r., Pan. (sä-bä'nä)	121	8.40N	78.02W
Sabana de la Mar, Dom. Rep. (sä-bä'nä dä lä mär')	123	19.05N	69.30W
Sabana de Uchire, Ven. (sä-bá'nä dĕ ōō-chē'rĕ)	131b	10.02N	65.32W
Sabanagrande, Hond. (sä-bä-grä'n-dĕ)	120	13.47N	87.16W
Sabanalarga, Col. (sä-bä'nä-lär'gä)	130	10.38N	75.02W

PLACE (Pronunciation)	PAGE	Lat. °	Long. °
Sabanas Páramo, mtn., Col. (sä-bá'näs pá'rä-mö)	130a	6.28N	76.08W
Sabancuy, Mex. (sä-bän-kwĕ')	119	18.58N	91.09W
Sabang, Indon. (sä'bäng)	196	5.52N	95.26E
Sabaudia, Italy (sá-bou'dĕ-ä)	160	41.19N	13.00E
Sabetha, Ks., U.S. (sá-bĕth'ä)	111	39.54N	95.49W
Sabi (Rio Save), r., Afr. (sä'bĕ)	212	20.18S	32.07E
Sabile, Lat. (sá'bĕ-lĕ)	153	57.03N	22.34E
Sabinal, Tx., U.S. (sá-bĭ'näl)	112	29.19N	99.27W
Sabinal, Cayo, i., Cuba (kä'yö sä-bĕ-näl')	122	21.40N	77.20W
Sabinas, Mex.	116	28.05N	101.30W
Sabinas, r., Mex. (sä-bē'näs)	112	26.37N	99.52W
Sabinas, Río, r., Mex. (rĕ'ö sä-bē'näs)	112	27.25N	100.33W
Sabinas Hidalgo, Mex. (ē-däl'gó)	112	26.30N	100.10W
Sabine, Tx., U.S. (sá-bēn')	113	29.44N	93.54W
Sabine, r., U.S.	97	32.00N	94.30W
Sabine, Mount, mtn., Ant.	219	72.05S	169.10E
Sabine Lake, l., La., U.S.	113	29.53N	93.41W
Sablayan, Phil. (säb-lä-yän')	197a	12.49N	120.47E
Sable, Cape, c., Can. (sä'b'l)	85	43.25N	65.24W
Sable, Cape, c., Fl., U.S.	97	25.12N	81.10W
Sables, Rivière aux, r., Can.	91	49.00N	70.20W
Sablé-sur-Sarthe, Fr. (säb-lä-sür-särt')	156	47.50N	0.17W
Sablya, Gora, mtn., Russia	166	64.50N	59.00E
Sàbor, r., Port. (sä-bôr')	158	41.18N	6.54W
Sabunchu, Azer.	168	40.26N	49.56E
Saburovo, neigh., Russia	239b	55.38N	37.42E
Sabzevār, Iran	185	36.13N	57.42E
Sac, r., Mo., U.S. (sôk)	111	38.11N	93.45W
Sacandaga Reservoir, res., N.Y., U.S. (sá-kän-dâ'gá)	99	43.10N	74.15W
Sacavém, Port. (sä-kä-vĕn')	159b	38.47N	9.06W
Sacavém, r., Port.	159b	38.52N	9.06W
Sac City, Ia., U.S. (sôk)	102	42.25N	95.00W
Sachigo Lake, l., Can. (sách'ĭ-gö)	89	53.49N	92.08W
Sachsen, hist. reg., Ger. (zäk'sĕn)	154	50.45N	12.17E
Sacketts Harbor, N.Y., U.S. (săk'ĕts)	99	43.55N	76.05W
Sackville, Can. (säk'vïl)	92	45.54N	64.22W
Saco, Me., U.S. (sô'kô)	92	43.30N	70.28W
Saco, r., Braz. (sä'kô)	132b	22.20S	43.26W
Saco, r., Me., U.S.	92	43.53N	70.46W
Sacramento, Mex.	112	25.45N	103.22W
Sacramento, Mex.	112	27.05N	101.45W
Sacramento, Ca., U.S. (săk-rá-mĕn'tô)	96	38.35N	121.30W
Sacramento, r., Ca., U.S.	108	40.20N	122.07W
Sacrow, neigh., Ger.	238a	52.26N	13.06E
Şa'dah, Yemen	182	16.50N	43.45E
Saddle Brook, N.J., U.S.	228	40.54N	74.06W
Saddle Lake Indian Reserve, I.R., Can.	87	54.00N	111.40W
Saddle Mountain, mtn., Or., U.S. (săd''l)	106c	45.58N	123.40W
Saddle Rock, N.Y., U.S.	228	40.48N	73.45W
Sadiya, India (sŭ-dē'yä)	183	27.53N	95.35E
Sado, i., Japan (sä'dô)	189	38.05N	138.26E
Sado, r., Port. (sä'dó)	158	38.15N	8.20W
Saeby, Den. (sĕ'bü)	152	57.21N	10.29E
Saeki, Japan (sä'á-kē)	194	32.56N	131.51E
Safdar Jang's Tomb, rel., India	240d	28.36N	77.13E
Säffle, Swe.	152	59.10N	12.55E
Safford, Az., U.S. (săf'fĕrd)	109	32.50N	109.45W
Safi, Mor. (sä'fĕ) (äs'fĕ)	210	32.24N	9.09W
Saga, Japan (sä'gä)	195	33.15N	130.18E
Sagamihara, Japan	242a	35.34N	139.23E
Sagami-Nada, b., Japan (sä'gä'mĕ nä-dä)	195	35.06N	139.24E
Sagamore Hills, Oh., U.S. (săg'á-môr hĭlz)	101d	41.19N	81.34W
Saganaga, l., N.A. (să-gä-nä'gá)	103	48.13N	91.17W
Sāgar, India	183	23.55N	78.45E
Saghyz, r., Kaz.	170	48.30N	56.10E
Saginaw, Mi., U.S. (săg'ĭ-nô)	97	43.26N	84.00W
Saginaw, Mn., U.S.	107h	46.51N	92.26W
Saginaw, Tx., U.S.	107c	32.52N	97.22W
Saginaw Bay, b., Mi., U.S.	97	43.50N	83.40W
Saguache, Co., U.S. (sá-wäch') (sá-gwä'chĕ)	109	38.05N	106.10W
Saguache Creek, r., Co., U.S.	98	38.05N	106.40W
Sagua de Tánamo, Cuba (sä-gwä dĕ tá'nä-mö)	123	20.40N	75.15W
Sagua la Grande, Cuba (sä-gwä lä grä'n-dĕ)	122	22.45N	80.05W
Saguaro National Monument, rec., Az., U.S. (säg-wä'rō)	109	32.12N	110.40W
Saguenay, r., Can. (säg-ē-nä')	85	48.20N	70.15W
Sagunto, Spain (sä-gón'tö)	148	39.40N	0.17W
Sahara, des., Afr. (sá-hä'rá)	210	23.44N	1.40W
Saharan Atlas, mts., Afr.	148	32.51N	1.02W
Sahāranpur, India (sü-hä'rŭn-pōōr')	183	29.58N	77.41E
Sahara Village, Ut., U.S. (sá-hä'rá)	107b	41.06N	111.58W
Sahel see Sudan, reg., Afr.	210	15.00N	7.00E
Sāhiwāl, Pak.	186	30.43N	73.04E
Sahuayo de Dias, Mex.	118	20.03N	102.43W
Saigon see Ho Chi Minh City, Viet.	196	10.46N	106.34E
Saijō, Japan (sä'è-jô)	195	33.55N	133.13E
Saimaa, l., Fin. (sä'ĭ-mä)	146	61.24N	28.45E
Sain Alto, Mex. (sä-ēn' äl'tö)	118	23.35N	103.13W
Saint Adolphe, Can. (sänt a'dólf) (sän' tá-dôlf')	83f	49.40N	97.07W
Saint Afrique, Fr. (săn' tá-frēk')	156	43.58N	2.52E
Saint Albans, Austl. (sänt ôl'bǎnz)	201a	37.44S	144.47E
Saint Albans, Eng., U.K.	150	51.44N	0.20W
Saint Albans, Vt., U.S.	99	44.49N	73.05W
Saint Albans, W.V., U.S.	98	38.20N	81.50W
Saint Albans, neigh., N.Y., U.S.	228	40.42N	73.46W
Saint Albans Cathedral, pt. of i., Eng., U.K.	235	51.45N	0.20W

PLACE (Pronunciation)	PAGE	Lat. °	Long. °
Saint Albert, Can. (sänt äl'bĕrt)	87	53.38N	113.38W
Saint Amand-Mont Rond, Fr. (sän't à-män' môn-rôn')	156	46.44N	2.28E
Saint André-Est, Can.	83a	45.33N	74.19W
Saint Andrews, Can.	85	45.05N	67.03W
Saint Andrews, Scot., U.K.	150	56.20N	2.40W
Saint Andrew's Channel, strt., Can.	93	46.06N	60.28W
Saint Anicet, Can. (sĕnt ä-nē-sĕ')	83a	45.07N	74.23W
Saint Ann, Mo., U.S. (sänt än')	107e	38.44N	90.23W
Sainte Anne, Guad.	121b	16.15N	61.23W
Sainte-Anne, Il., U.S.	101a	41.01N	87.44W
Sainte-Anne, r., Can.	83b	47.07N	70.50W
Sainte Anne, r., Can. (sänt än') (sänt än')	91	46.55N	71.46W
Sainte Anne-des-Plaines, Can. (dä plĕn)	83a	45.46N	73.49W
Saint Anne of the Congo, rel., Congo	244c	4.16S	15.17E
Saint Ann's Bay, Jam.	122	18.25N	77.15W
Saint Anns Bay, b., Can. (änz)	93	46.20N	60.30W
Saint Anselme, Can. (sän' täv-sĕlm')	83b	46.37N	70.58W
Saint Anthony, Can. (sän än'thô-nĕ)	85	51.24N	55.35W
Saint Anthony, Id., U.S. (sänt än'thô-nĕ)	105	43.59N	111.42W
Saint Antoine-de-Tilly, Can.	83b	46.40N	71.31W
Saint Apollinaire, Can. (sän' tá-pôl-ê-nâr')	83b	46.36N	71.30W
Saint Arnoult-en-Yvelines, Fr. (sän-tär-nōō'ĕn-nēv-lēn')	157b	48.33N	1.55E
Saint Augustin-de-Québec, Can.	83b	46.45N	71.27W
Saint Augustin-Deux-Montagnes, Can.	83a	45.38N	73.59W
Saint Augustine, Fl., U.S. (sänt ô'gŭs-tēn)	97	29.53N	81.21W
Sainte Barbe, Can. (sänt bärb')	83a	45.14N	74.12W
Saint Barthélemy, i., Guad.	121b	17.55N	62.32W
Saint Bees Head, c., Eng., U.K. (sänt bĕz' hĕd)	150	54.30N	3.40W
Saint Benoit, Can. (sĕn bĕ-nōō-ä')	83a	45.34N	74.05W
Saint Bernard, La., U.S. (bĕr-närd')	100d	29.52N	89.52W
Saint Bernard, Oh., U.S.	101f	39.10N	84.30W
Saint Bride, Mount, mtn., Can. (sänt brĭd)	87	51.30N	115.57W
Saint Brieuc, Fr. (săn' brēs')	147	48.32N	2.47W
Saint Bruno, Can. (brü'nô)	83a	45.31N	73.20W
Saint Canut, Can. (sän' tá-nü')	83a	45.43N	74.04W
Saint Casimir, Can. (ká-zĕ-mēr')	91	46.45N	72.34W
Saint Catharines, Can. (kăth'á-rĭnz)	85	43.10N	79.14W
Saint Catherine, Mount, mtn., Gren.	121b	12.10N	61.42W
Saint Chamas, Fr. (săn-shä-mä')	156a	43.32N	5.03E
Saint Chamond, Fr. (săn' shä-môn')	147	45.30N	4.17E
Saint Charles, Can. (sän' shärlz')	83b	46.47N	70.57W
Saint Charles, Il., U.S. (sänt chärlz')	101a	41.55N	88.19W
Saint Charles, Mi., U.S.	98	43.20N	84.10W
Saint Charles, Mn., U.S.	103	43.56N	92.05W
Saint Charles, Mo., U.S.	107e	38.47N	90.29W
Saint Charles, Lac, l., Can.	83b	46.56N	71.21W
Saint Christopher-Nevis see Saint Kitts and Nevis, nation, N.A.	116	17.24N	63.30W
Saint Clair, Mi., U.S. (sänt klâr')	98	42.55N	82.30W
Saint Clair, l., Can.	97	42.25N	82.30W
Saint Clair, r., Can.	90	42.45N	82.25W
Sainte Claire, Can.	83b	46.36N	70.52W
Saint Clair Shores, Mi., U.S.	101b	42.30N	82.54W
Saint Claude, Fr. (săn' klôd')	157	46.24N	5.53E
Saint Clet, Can. (sänt' klä')	83a	45.22N	74.21W
Saint-Cloud, Fr.	237c	48.51N	2.13E
Saint Cloud, Fl., U.S. (sänt kloud')	115a	28.13N	81.17W
Saint Cloud, Mn., U.S.	97	45.33N	94.08W
Saint Constant, Can. (kôn'stănt)	83a	45.23N	73.34W
Saint Croix, r., N.A. (sänt kroi')	117	17.40N	64.43W
Saint Croix, r., N.A.	92	45.28N	67.32W
Saint Croix, r., U.S. (sänt kroi')	97	45.45N	93.00W
Saint Croix Indian Reservation, I.R., Wi., U.S.	103	45.40N	92.21W
Saint Croix Island, i., S. Afr. (sän krwä)	213c	33.48S	25.45E
Saint-Cyr-l'Ecole, Fr.	237c	48.48N	2.04E
Saint Damien-de-Buckland, Can. (sänt dä'mē-ĕn)	83b	46.37N	70.39W
Saint David, Can. (dä'vïd)	83b	46.47N	71.11W
Saint Davids, Ca., U.S.	229b	40.02N	75.22W
Saint David's Head, c., Wales, U.K.	150	51.54N	5.25W
Saint-Denis, Fr. (săn'dĕ-nē')	147	48.26N	2.22E
Saint Dizier, Fr. (săn' dē-zyä')	147	48.49N	4.55E
Saint Dominique, Can. (sĕn dô-mē-nēk')	83a	45.19N	74.09W
Sainte-Dorothée, neigh., Can.	227b	45.32N	73.49W
Saint Edouard-de-Napierville, Can. (sĕn-tĕ-dōō-är')	83a	45.14N	73.31W
Saint Elias, Mount, mtn., N.A.	84	60.25N	141.00W
Saint Étienne, Fr.	147	45.26N	4.22E
Saint Étienne-de-Lauzon, Can. (sän' tä-tyĕn')	83b	46.39N	71.19W
Sainte Euphémie, Can. (sĕnt û-fĕ-mē')	83b	46.47N	70.27W
Saint Eustache, Can. (sän' tü-stásh')	83a	45.34N	73.54W
Saint Eustache, Can.	83f	49.58N	97.47W
Sainte Famille, Can. (sän't fä-mē'y)	83b	46.58N	70.58W
Saint Félicien, Can. (săn fä-lē-syän')	85	48.39N	72.28W
Sainte Felicite, Can.	92	48.54N	67.20W
Saint Féréol, Can. (fa-rä-ôl')	83b	47.07N	70.52W
Saint Florent-sur-Cher, Fr. (sän' flô-rän'sür-shär')	156	46.58N	2.15E
Saint Flour, Fr. (săn flōōr')	156	45.02N	3.09E
Saint Foy, Can. (sän fwä')	83b	46.47N	71.18W
Saint Francis, r., Ar., U.S.	111	35.56N	90.27W
Saint Francis Lake, l., Can. (sän'frän'sĭs)	91	45.00N	74.20W
Saint Francis, r., U.S. (sän'frän-swä')	85	47.01N	70.49W
Saint François de Boundji, Congo	216	1.03S	15.22E

PLACE (Pronunciation)	PAGE	Lat. °′	Long. °′
Saint Francois Xavier, Can.	83f	49.55N	97.32W
Saint Gaudens, Fr. (gō-däNs')	156	43.07N	0.43E
Sainte-Geneviève, Can.	227b	45.29N	73.52W
Sainte Genevieve, Mo., U.S. (sånt jĕn'ĕ-vēv)	111	37.58N	90.02W
Saint George, Austl. (sånt jôrj')	203	28.02S	148.40E
Saint George, Can. (săN'zhôrzh')	83d	43.14N	80.15W
Saint George, Can. (săN jôrj')	85	45.08N	66.49W
Saint George, S.C., U.S. (sånt jôrj')	115	33.11N	80.35W
Saint George, Ut., U.S.	109	37.05N	113.40W
Saint George, neigh., N.Y., U.S.	228	40.39N	74.05W
Saint George, i., Ak., U.S.	95	56.30N	169.40W
Saint George, Cape, c., Can.	85a	48.28N	59.15W
Saint George, Cape, c., Fl., U.S.	114	29.30N	85.20W
Saint George's, Can. (jôrj'ĕs)	85	48.26N	58.29W
Saint Georges, Fr. Gu.	131	3.48N	51.47W
Saint George's, Gren.	121b	12.02N	61.57W
Saint George's Bay, b., Can.	85a	48.20N	59.00W
Saint Georges Bay, b., Can.	93	45.49N	61.45W
Saint George's Channel, strt., Eur. (jôr-jĕz)	142	51.45N	6.30W
Saint Germain-en-Laye, Fr. (săN' zhĕr-măN-äN-lā')	156	48.53N	2.05E
Saint Gervais, Can. (zhĕr-vĕ')	83b	46.43N	70.53W
Saint Girons, Fr. (zhē-rôN')	156	42.58N	1.08E
Saint Gotthard Pass, p., Switz.	154	46.33N	8.34E
Saint-Gratien, Fr.	237c	48.58N	2.17E
Saint Gregory, Mount, mtn., Can. (sånt grĕg'ẽr-ê)	93	49.19N	58.13W
Saint Helena, i., St. Hel.	209	16.01S	5.16W
Saint Helenabaai, b., S. Afr.	212	32.25S	17.15E
Sainte-Hélène, Île, i., Can.	227b	45.31N	73.32W
Saint Helens, Eng., U.K. (sånt hĕl'ĕnz)	144a	53.27N	2.44W
Saint Helens, Or., U.S. (hĕl'ĕnz)	106c	45.52N	122.49W
Saint Helens, Mount, vol., Wa., U.S.	104	46.13N	122.10W
Saint Helier, Jersey (hyĕl'yẽr)	156	49.12N	2.06W
Saint Henri, Can. (săN' hĕN'rê)	83b	46.41N	71.04W
Saint Hubert, Can.	83a	45.29N	73.24W
Saint Hyacinthe, Can.	85	45.35N	72.55W
Saint Ignace, Mi., U.S. (sånt ĭg'nås)	103	45.51N	84.39W
Saint Ignace, i., Can. (săN' ĭg'nås)	90	48.47N	88.14W
Saint Irenee, Can. (săN' tē-rå-nā')	91	47.34N	70.15W
Saint Isidore-de-Laprairie, Can.	83a	45.18N	73.41W
Saint Isidore-de-Prescott, Can. (săN' ĭz'ĭ-dôr-prĕs-kŏt)	83c	45.23N	74.54W
Saint Isidore-Dorchester, Can. (dŏr-chĕs'tẽr)	83b	46.35N	71.05W
Saint Ives, Austl.	243a	33.44S	151.10E
Saint Jacob, Il., U.S. (jā-kŏb)	107e	38.43N	89.46W
Saint James, Mn., U.S. (sånt jāmz')	103	43.58N	94.37W
Saint James, Mo., U.S.	111	37.59N	91.37W
Saint James, Cape, c., Can.	86	51.58N	131.00W
Saint Janvier, Can. (săN' zhäN-vyā')	83a	45.43N	73.56W
Saint Jean, Can.	83b	46.55N	70.54W
Saint Jean, Can. (săN' zhäN')	85	45.20N	73.15W
Saint Jean, Lac, l., Can.	85	48.35N	72.00W
Saint Jean-Chrysostome, Can. (krĭ-zōs-tōm')	83b	46.43N	71.12W
Saint Jean-d'Angely, Fr. (däN-zhå-lē')	156	45.56N	0.33W
Saint Jean-de-Luz, Fr. (dē lüz')	156	43.23N	1.40W
Saint Jérôme, Can. (sånt jĕ-rōm') (săN zhā-rōm')	83a	45.47N	74.00W
Saint Joachim-de-Montmorency, Can. (sånt jō'å-kĭm)	83b	47.04N	70.51W
Saint John, Can. (sånt jŏn)	85	45.16N	66.03W
Saint John, In., U.S.	101a	41.27N	87.29W
Saint John, Ks., U.S.	110	37.59N	98.44W
Saint John, N.D., U.S.	102	48.57N	99.42W
Saint John, i., V.I.U.S.	117b	18.16N	64.48W
Saint John, r., N.A.	85	47.00N	68.00W
Saint John, Cape, c., Can.	93	50.00N	55.32W
Saint Johns, Antig.	121b	17.07N	61.50W
Saint John's, Can. (jŏns)	85a	47.34N	52.43W
Saint Johns, Az., U.S. (jŏnz)	109	34.30N	109.25W
Saint Johns, Mi., U.S.	98	43.05N	84.35W
Saint Johns, r., Fl., U.S.	97	29.54N	81.32W
Saint Johnsburg, N.Y., U.S.	230a	43.05N	78.53W
Saint Johnsbury, Vt., U.S. (jŏnz'bĕr-ê)	99	44.25N	72.00W
Saint John's University, pt. of i., N.Y., U.S.	228	40.43N	73.48W
Saint Joseph, Dom.	121b	15.25N	61.26W
Saint Joseph, Mi., U.S.	98	42.05N	86.30W
Saint Joseph, Mo., U.S. (sånt jô-sĕf)	97	39.44N	94.49W
Saint Joseph, i., Can.	98	46.15N	83.55W
Saint Joseph, l., Can. (jō'zhûf)	85	51.31N	90.40W
Saint Joseph, r., Mi., U.S. (sånt jō'sĕf)	98	41.45N	85.50W
Saint Joseph Bay, b., Fl., U.S. (jō'zhûf)	114	29.48N	85.26W
Saint Joseph-de-Beauce, Can. (sĕN zhō-zĕf'dē bōs)	91	46.18N	70.52W
Saint Joseph-du-Lac, Can. (sĕN zhō-zĕf' dü läk)	83a	45.32N	74.00W
Saint Joseph Island, i., Tx., U.S. (sånt jô-sĕf)	113	27.58N	96.50W
Saint Junien, Fr. (săN'zhü-nyăN')	156	45.53N	0.54E
Sainte Justine-de-Newton, Can. (sånt jŭs-tēn')	83a	45.22N	74.22W
Saint Kilda, Austl.	201a	37.52S	144.59E
Saint Kilda, i., Scot., U.K. (kĭl'då)	150	57.50N	8.32W
Saint Kitts, i., St. K./N. (sănt kĭtts)	117	17.24N	63.30W
Saint Kitts and Nevis, nation, N.A.	117	17.24N	63.30W
Saint Lambert, Can.	99	45.29N	73.29W
Saint Lambert-de-Lévis, Can.	83b	46.35N	71.12W
Saint Laurent, Can. (săN'lō-räN)	83a	45.31N	73.41W
Saint Laurent, Fr. Gu.	131	5.27N	53.56W
Saint Laurent-d'Orleans, Can.	83b	46.52N	71.00W
Saint Lawrence, Can. (sānt lô'rĕns)	93	46.55N	55.23W
Saint Lawrence, i., Ak., U.S. (sånt lô'rĕns)	96a	63.10N	172.12W
Saint Lawrence, r., N.A.	85	48.24N	69.30W
Saint Lawrence, Gulf of, b., Can.	85	48.00N	62.00W
Saint Lazare, Can. (săN'lå-zår')	83b	46.39N	70.48W
Saint Lazare-de-Vaudreuil, Can.	83a	45.24N	74.08W
Saint Léger-en-Yvelines, Fr. (såN-lā-zhĕ'ĕN-nēv-lēn')	157b	48.43N	1.45E
Saint Léonard, Can.	83a	45.36N	73.35W
Saint Leonard, Can. (sånt lĕn'ård)	92	47.10N	67.56W
Saint Leonard, Md., U.S.	100e	38.29N	76.31W
Saint Lô, Fr.	147	49.07N	1.05W
Saint-Louis, Sen.	210	16.02N	16.30W
Saint Louis, Mi., U.S. (sånt lo͞o'ĭs)	98	43.25N	84.35W
Saint Louis, Mo., U.S. (sånt lo͞o'ĭs) (lo͞o'ê)	97	38.39N	90.15W
Saint Louis, r., Mn., U.S. (sånt lo͞o'ĭs)	103	46.57N	92.58W
Saint Louis, Lac, l., Can. (săN' lo͞o-ē')	83a	45.24N	73.51W
Saint Louis-de-Gonzague, Can. (săN' lo͞o ē')	83a	45.13N	74.00W
Saint Louis Park, Mn., U.S.	107g	44.56N	93.21W
Saint Lucia, nation, N.A.	117	13.54N	60.40W
Saint Lucia Channel, strt., N.A. (lū'shĭ-å)	121b	14.15N	61.00W
Saint Lucie Canal, can., Fl., U.S. (lū'sê)	115a	26.57N	80.25W
Saint Magnus Bay, b., Scot., U.K. (măg'nŭs)	150a	60.25N	2.09W
Saint Malo, Fr. (săN' må-lō')	147	48.40N	2.02W
Saint Malo, Golfe de, b., Fr. (gôlf-dē-såN-mä-lō')	147	48.50N	2.49W
Saint Marc, Haiti (săN' mårk')	123	19.10N	72.40W
Saint-Marc, Canal de, strt., Haiti	123	19.05N	73.15W
Saint Marcellin, Fr. (mär-sĕ-lăN')	157	45.08N	5.15E
Saint Margarets, Md., U.S.	100e	39.02N	76.30W
Sainte Marie, Cap, c., Madag.	213	25.31S	45.00E
Sainte-Marie-aux-Mines, Fr. (săN'tĕ-mä-rē'ō-mēn')	157	48.14N	7.08E
Sainte Marie-Beauce, Can. (săNt'må-rē')	91	46.27N	71.03W
Saint Maries, Id., U.S. (sånt mā'rēs)	104	47.18N	116.34W
Saint Martin, i., N.A. (mär'tĭn)	121b	18.06N	62.54W
Sainte Martine, Can.	83a	45.14N	73.37W
Saint Martins, Can. (mär'tĭnz)	92	45.21N	65.32W
Saint Martinville, La., U.S. (mär'tĭn-vĭl)	113	30.08N	91.50W
Saint Mary, r., Can. (mā'rê)	87	49.25N	113.00W
Saint Mary, Cape, c., Gam.	214	13.28N	16.40W
Saint Mary Cray, neigh., Eng., U.K.	235	51.23N	0.07E
Saint Marylebone, neigh., Eng., U.K.	235	51.31N	0.10W
Saint Mary Reservoir, res., Can.	87	49.30N	113.00W
Saint Marys, Austl. (mā'rēz)	204	41.40S	148.10E
Saint Marys, Austl.	243a	33.47S	150.47E
Saint Marys, Can.	90	43.15N	81.10W
Saint Marys, Ga., U.S.	115	30.43N	81.35W
Saint Mary's, Ks., U.S.	111	39.12N	96.03W
Saint Mary's, Oh., U.S.	98	40.30N	84.25W
Saint Marys, Pa., U.S.	99	41.25N	78.30W
Saint Marys, W.V., U.S.	98	39.20N	81.15W
Saint Marys, r., N.A.	107k	46.27N	84.33W
Saint Marys, r., U.S.	115	30.37N	82.05W
Saint Mary's Bay, b., Can.	92	44.20N	66.10W
Saint Mary's Bay, b., Can.	93	46.50N	53.47W
Saint Mathew, S.C., U.S. (măth'ū)	115	33.40N	80.46W
Saint Matthew, i., Ak., U.S.	95	60.25N	172.10W
Saint Matthews, Ky., U.S. (măth'ūz)	101h	38.15N	85.39W
Saint Maur-des-Fossés, Fr.	157b	48.48N	2.29E
Saint-Maurice, Fr.	237c	48.49N	2.25E
Saint Maurice, r., Can. (săN' mô-rēs') (sånt mô'rĭs)	85	47.20N	72.55W
Saint-Mesmes, Fr.	237c	48.59N	2.42E
Saint Michael, Ak., U.S. (sånt mī'kĕl)	95	63.22N	162.20W
Saint Michel, Can. (săN'mê-shĕl')	83b	46.52N	70.54W
Saint-Michel, neigh., Can.	227b	45.35N	73.35W
Saint Michel, Bras, r., Can.	83b	46.47N	70.51W
Saint Michel-de-l'Atalaye, Haiti	123	19.25N	72.20W
Saint Michel-de-Napierville, Can.	83a	45.14N	73.34W
Saint Mihiel, Fr. (săN' mē-yĕl')	157	48.53N	5.30E
Saint Nazaire, Fr. (săN'nå-zâr')	142	47.18N	2.13W
Saint Nérée, Can. (nā-rā')	83b	46.43N	70.43W
Saint Nicolas, Can. (ne-kô-lä')	83b	46.42N	71.22W
Saint Nicolas, Cap, c., Haiti	123	19.45N	73.35W
Saint Omer, Fr. (săN'tô-mâr')	156	50.44N	2.16E
Saint-Ouen, Fr.	237c	48.54N	2.20E
Saint Pancras, neigh., Eng., U.K.	235	51.32N	0.07W
Saint Pascal, Can. (sĕN pä-skål')	92	47.32N	69.48W
Saint Paul, Can. (sånt pôl')	84	53.59N	111.17W
Saint Paul, Mn., U.S.	97	44.57N	93.05W
Saint Paul, Ne., U.S.	102	41.13N	98.28W
Saint Paul, i., Can.	93	47.15N	60.10W
Saint Paul, i., Ak., U.S.	95	57.10N	170.20W
Saint Paul, r., Lib.	214	7.10N	10.00W
Saint Paul, Île, i., Afr.	3	38.43S	77.31E
Saint Paul Park, Mn., U.S. (pärk)	107g	44.51N	93.00W
Saint Pauls, N.C., U.S. (pôls)	115	34.47N	78.57W
Saint Paul's Cathedral, pt. of i., Eng., U.K.	235	51.31N	0.06W
Saint Paul's Cray, neigh., Eng., U.K.	235	51.24N	0.07E
Saint Peter, Mn., U.S. (pē tẽr)	103	44.20N	93.56W
Saint Peter Port, Guernsey	156	49.27N	2.35W
Saint Petersburg (Sankt-Peterburg) (Leningrad), Russia	164	59.57N	30.20E
Saint Petersburg, Fl., U.S. (pē'tẽrz-bûrg)	97	27.47N	82.38W
Sainte Pétronille, Can. (sĕNt pĕt-rō-nēl')	83b	46.51N	71.08W
Saint Philémon, Can. (sĕN fēl-mōN')	83b	46.41N	70.28W
Saint Philippe-d'Argenteuil, Can. (săN'fe-lēp')	83a	45.38N	74.25W
Saint Philippe-de-Lapairie, Can.	83a	45.20N	73.28W
Saint-Pierre, Can.	227b	45.27N	73.39W
Saint Pierre, Mart. (săN'pyâr')	121b	14.45N	61.12W
Saint Pierre, St. P./M.	93	46.47N	56.11W
Saint Pierre, i., St. P./M.	93	46.47N	56.11W
Saint Pierre, Lac, l., Can.	91	46.07N	72.45W
Saint Pierre and Miquelon, dep., N.A.	85a	46.53N	56.40W
Saint Pierre-d'Orléans, Can.	83b	46.53N	71.04W
Saint Pierre-Montmagny, Can.	83b	46.55N	70.37W
Saint Placide, Can. (plăs'ĭd)	83a	45.32N	74.11W
Saint Pol-de-Léon, Fr. (săN-pô'dē-lā-ôN')	156	48.41N	4.00W
Saint-Prix, Fr.	237c	49.01N	2.16E
Saint Quentin, Fr. (săN'kāN-tăN')	147	49.52N	3.16E
Saint Raphaël, Can. (rä-fā-ĕl')	83b	46.48N	70.46W
Saint Raymond, Can.	91	46.50N	71.51W
Saint Rédempteur, Can. (săN rā-däNp-tûr')	83b	46.42N	71.18W
Saint Rémi, Can. (sĕN rĕ-mē')	83a	45.15N	73.36W
Saint-Rémy-lès-Chevreuse, Fr.	237c	48.42N	2.04E
Saint Romuald-d'Etchemin, Can. (sĕN rō'mo͞o-äl)	91	46.45N	71.14W
Sainte Rose, Guad.	121b	16.19N	61.45W
Sainte-Rose, neigh., Can.	227b	45.36N	73.47W
Saintes, Fr.	156	45.44N	0.41W
Sainte Scholastique, Can. (skô-lás-tēk')	83a	45.39N	74.05W
Saint Siméon, Can.	91	47.51N	69.55W
Saint Stanislas-de-Kostka, Can.	83a	45.11N	74.08W
Saint Stephen, Can. (stē'vĕn)	85	45.12N	66.17W
Saint Sulpice, Can.	83a	45.50N	73.21W
Saint Thérèse-de-Blainville, Can. (tē-rēz' dē blĕN-vēl')	91	45.38N	73.51W
Saint-Thibault-des-Vignes, Fr.	237c	48.52N	2.41E
Saint Thomas, Can. (tŏm'ås)	85	42.45N	81.15W
Saint Thomas, i., V.I.U.S.	117	18.22N	64.57W
Saint Thomas Harbor, b., V.I.U.S. (tŏm'ås)	117c	18.19N	64.56W
Saint Timothée, Can. (tē-mô-tā')	83a	45.17N	74.03W
Saint Tropez, Fr. (trô-pē')	157	43.15N	6.42E
Saint Valentin, Can. (văl-ĕn-tīn)	83a	45.07N	73.19W
Saint Valéry-sur-Somme, Fr. (vå-lå-rē')	156	50.10N	1.39E
Saint Vallier, Can. (väl-yā')	83b	46.54N	70.49W
Saint Victor, Can. (vĭk'tẽr)	91	46.09N	70.56W
Saint Vincent, Gulf, b., Austl. (vĭn'sĕnt)	204	34.55S	138.00E
Saint Vincent and the Grenadines, nation, N.A.	117	13.20N	60.50W
Saint-Vincent-de-Paul, neigh., Can.	227b	45.37N	73.39W
Saint Vincent Passage, strt., N.A.	121b	13.35N	61.10W
Saint Walburg, Can.	84	53.39N	109.12W
Saint Yrieix-la-Perche, Fr. (ē-rē-ĕ)	156	45.30N	1.08E
Saitama, dept., Japan (sī'tä-mä)	195a	35.52N	139.40E
Saitbaba, Russia (så-ĕt'bá-bå)	172a	54.06N	56.42E
Sajama, Nevada, mtn., Bol. (nĕ-vå'dä-sä-hä'mä)	130	18.13S	68.53W
Sakai, Japan (sä'kä-ê)	194	34.34N	135.28E
Sakaiminato, Japan	195	35.33N	133.15E
Sakākah, Sau. Ar.	182	29.58N	40.03E
Sakakawea, Lake, res., N.D., U.S.	96	47.49N	101.58W
Sakania, Zaire (så-kä'nĭ-å)	212	12.45S	28.34E
Sakarya, r., Tur. (så-kär'yå)	182	40.10N	31.00E
Sakata, Japan (sä'kä-tä)	189	38.56N	139.57E
Sakchu, N. Kor. (säk'chô)	194	40.29N	125.09E
Sakha (Yakutia), state, Russia	171	65.21N	117.13E
Sakhalin, i., Russia (så-kå-lēn')	165	52.00N	143.00E
Šakiai, Lith. (shä'kĭ-ī)	153	54.59N	23.05E
Sakishima-guntō, is., Japan (sä'kê-shē'ma gòn'tō')	189	24.25N	125.00E
Sakmara, r., Russia	167	52.00N	56.10E
Sakomet, r., R.I., U.S. (så-kō'mĕt)	100b	41.32N	71.11W
Sakurai, Japan	195b	34.31N	135.51E
Sakwaso Lake, l., Can. (så-kwå'sō)	89	53.01N	91.55W
Sal, i., C.V. (säal)	210b	16.45N	22.39W
Sal, r., Russia (säl)	167	47.30N	43.00E
Sal, Cay, i., Bah. (kē săl)	122	23.45N	80.25W
Sala, Swe. (sô'lă)	152	59.56N	16.34E
Sala Consilina, Italy (sä'lä kōn-sē-lē'nä)	160	40.24N	15.38E
Salada, Laguna, l., Mex. (lä-gò'nä-sä-lä'dä)	108	32.34N	115.45W
Saladillo, Arg. (sä-lä-dēl'yō)	132	35.38S	59.48W
Salado, Hond. (sä-lä'dhō)	120	15.44N	87.03W
Salado, r., Arg.	129c	35.53S	58.12W
Salado, r., Arg. (sä-lä'dô)	132	26.05S	63.35W
Salado, r., Arg.	132	37.00S	67.00W
Salado, r., Mex.	116	28.00N	102.00W
Salado, r., Mex. (sä-lä'dô)	119	18.30N	97.29W
Salado Creek, r., Tx., U.S.	107d	29.23N	98.25W
Salado de los Nadadores, Río, r., Mex. (dē-lôs-nä-dä-dō'rēs)	112	27.26N	101.35W
Salal, Chad	215	14.51N	17.13E
Salamanca, Chile (sä-lä-mä'n-kä)	129b	31.48S	70.57W
Salamanca, Mex.	116	20.36N	101.10W
Salamanca, Spain (sä-lä-mä'n-kå)	142	40.54N	5.42W
Salamanca, N.Y., U.S. (săl-å-măn'kå)	99	42.10N	78.45W
Salamat, Bahr, r., Chad (bär sä-lä-mät')	211	10.06N	19.16E
Salamina, Col. (sä-lä-mē'-nä)	130a	5.25N	75.29W
Salamis, Grc. (săl'å-mĭs)	161	37.58N	23.30E
Salat-la-Canada, Fr.	156	44.52N	1.13E
Salaverry, Peru (sä-lä-vā'rē)	130	8.16S	78.54W
Salawati, i., Indon. (sä-lä-wä'tê)	197	1.07S	130.52E
Salawe, Tan.	217	3.19S	32.52E
Sala y Gómez, Isla, i., Chile	225	26.50S	105.50W
Salcedo, Dom. Rep. (säl-sä'dō)	123	19.25N	70.30W
Saldaña, r., Col. (säl-dá'n-yä)	130a	3.42N	75.16W
Saldanha, S. Afr.	212	32.55S	18.05E
Saldus, Lat. (sål'dòs)	153	56.39N	22.30E
Sale, Austl. (sāl)	204	38.10S	147.07E
Sale, Eng., U.K.	144a	53.24N	2.20W

ăt; finăl; rāte; senåte; ärm; åsk; sofå; fâre; ch-choose; dh-as th in other; bē; êvent; bĕt; recĕnt; cratẽr; g-gō; gh-guttural g; bĭt; ĭ-short neutral; rīde; K-guttural k as ch in German ich;

PLACE (Pronunciation)	PAGE	Lat. °′	Long. °′
Sale, r., Can. (sàl'rē-vyâr')	83f	49.44N	97.11W
Salekhard, Russia (sŭ-lyĭ-kärt)	166	66.35N	66.50E
Salem, India	183	11.39N	78.11E
Salem, S. Afr.	213c	33.29S	26.30E
Salem, Il., U.S. (sā'lĕm)	98	38.40N	89.00W
Salem, In., U.S.	98	38.35N	86.00W
Salem, Ma., U.S.	93a	42.31N	70.54W
Salem, Mo., U.S.	111	37.36N	91.33W
Salem, N.H., U.S.	93a	42.46N	71.16W
Salem, N.J., U.S.	99	39.35N	75.30W
Salem, Oh., U.S.	98	40.55N	80.50W
Salem, Or., U.S.	96	44.55N	123.03W
Salem, S.D., U.S.	102	43.43N	97.23W
Salem, Va., U.S.	115	37.16N	80.05W
Salem, W.V., U.S.	98	39.15N	80.35W
Salemi, Italy (sä-lâ'mē)	160	37.49N	12.48E
Salerno, Italy (sä-lĕr'nô)	148	40.27N	14.46E
Salerno, Golfo di, b., Italy (gôl-fô-dē)	148	40.30N	14.40E
Salford, Eng., U.K. (săl'fērd)	150	53.26N	2.19W
Salgótarján, Hung. (shôl'gô-tôr-yän)	155	48.06N	19.50E
Salhyr, r., Ukr.	163	45.25N	34.22E
Salida, Co., U.S. (sȧ-lī'dȧ)	110	38.31N	106.01W
Salies-de-Béan, Fr.	156	43.27N	0.58W
Salima, Mwi.	217	13.47S	34.26E
Salina, Ks., U.S. (sȧ-lī'nȧ)	96	38.50N	97.37W
Salina, Ut., U.S.	109	39.00N	111.55W
Salina, i., Italy (sä-lē'nä)	160	38.35N	14.48E
Salina Cruz, Mex. (sä-lē'nä krōōz')	116	16.10N	95.12W
Salina Point, c., Bah.	123	22.10N	74.20W
Salinas, Mex.	116	22.38N	101.42W
Salinas, P.R.	117b	17.58N	66.16W
Salinas, Ca., U.S. (sȧ-lē'nȧs)	108	36.41N	121.40W
Salinas, r., Mex. (sä-lē'näs)	119	16.15N	90.31W
Salinas, r., Ca., U.S.	108	36.33N	121.29W
Salinas, Bahía de, b., N.A. (bä-ē'ä-dē-sȧ-lē'nȧs)	120	11.05N	85.55W
Salinas, Cape, c., Spain (sä-lēnäs)	159	39.14N	1.02E
Salinas National Monument, rec., N.M., U.S.	109	34.10N	106.05W
Salinas Victoria, Mex. (sä-lē'näs vēk-tō'rē-ä)	112	25.59N	100.19W
Saline, r., Ar., U.S. (sȧ-lēn')	111	34.06N	92.30W
Saline, r., Ks., U.S.	110	39.05N	99.43W
Salins-les-Bains, Fr. (sȧ-lăN'-lā-băN')	157	46.55N	5.54E
Salisbury, Can.	92	46.03N	65.05W
Salisbury, Eng., U.K. (sôlz'bē-rē)	147	50.35N	1.51W
Salisbury, Md., U.S.	99	38.20N	75.40W
Salisbury, Mo., U.S.	111	39.24N	92.47W
Salisbury, N.C., U.S.	115	35.40N	80.29W
Salisbury see Harare, Zimb.	212	17.50S	31.03E
Salisbury Island, i., Can.	85	63.36N	76.20W
Salisbury Plain, pl., Eng., U.K.	150	51.15N	1.52W
Salkehatchie, r., S.C., U.S. (sô-kē-hăch'ē)	115	33.09N	81.10W
Salkhia, India	240a	22.35N	88.21E
Sallisaw, Ok., U.S. (săl'ĭ-sô)	111	35.27N	94.48W
Salmon, Id., U.S. (săm'ŭn)	105	45.11N	113.54W
Salmon, r., Can.	86	54.00N	123.50W
Salmon, r., Can.	92	46.19N	65.36W
Salmon, r., Id., U.S.	96	45.30N	115.45W
Salmon, r., Id., U.S.	104	44.51N	115.47W
Salmon, r., Id., U.S.	105	44.54N	114.50W
Salmon, r., N.Y., U.S.	99	44.35N	74.15W
Salmon, r., Wa., U.S.	106c	45.44N	122.36W
Salmon Arm, Can.	87	50.42N	119.16W
Salmon Falls Creek, r., Id., U.S.	105	42.22N	114.53W
Salmon Gums, Austl. (gŭmz)	202	33.00S	122.00E
Salmon River Mountains, mts., Id., U.S.	96	44.15N	115.44W
Salon-de-Provence, Fr. (sȧ-lôN-dē-prô-văNs')	157	43.48N	5.09E
Salonika see Thessaloníki, Grc.	142	40.38N	22.59E
Salonta, Rom. (sä-lôn'tä)	155	46.46N	21.38E
Salop, co., Eng., U.K.	144a	52.36N	2.45W
Saloum, r., Sen.	214	14.10N	15.45W
Salsette Island, i., India	187b	19.12N	72.52E
Sal'sk, Russia (sälsk)	167	46.30N	41.20E
Salt, r., Az., U.S. (sôlt)	96	33.28N	111.35W
Salt, r., Mo., U.S.	111	39.54N	92.11W
Salta, Arg. (säl'tä)	132	24.50S	65.16W
Salta, prov., Arg.	132	25.15S	65.00W
Saltair, Ut., U.S. (sôlt'âr)	107b	40.46N	112.09W
Salt Cay, i., T./C. Is.	123	21.20N	71.15W
Salt Creek, r., Il., U.S. (sôlt)	101a	42.01N	88.01W
Saltillo, Mex. (säl-tēl'yō)	116	25.24N	100.59W
Salt Lake City, Ut., U.S. (sôlt lāk sĭ'tĭ)	96	40.45N	111.52W
Salto, Arg. (säl'tō)	129c	34.17S	60.15W
Salto, Ur.	132	31.18S	57.45W
Salto, r., Mex.	118	22.16N	99.18W
Salto, Serra do, mtn., Braz. (sĕ'r-rä-dô)	129a	20.26S	43.28W
Salto Grande, Braz. (grän'dä)	131	22.57S	49.58W
Salton Sea, Ca., U.S. (sôlt'ŭn)	108	33.28N	115.43W
Salton Sea, l., Ca., U.S.	96	33.19N	115.50W
Saltpond, Ghana	210	5.16N	1.07W
Salt River Indian Reservation, I.R., Az., U.S. (sôlt rĭv'ēr)	109	33.40N	112.01W
Saltsjöbaden, Swe. (sält'shû-bäd'ĕn)	152	59.15N	18.20E
Saltspring Island, i., Can. (sält'sprĭng)	86	48.47N	123.30W
Saltville, Va., U.S. (sôlt'vĭl)	115	36.50N	81.45W
Saltykovka, Russia (sȧl-tē'kôf-kȧ)	172b	55.45N	37.56E
Salud, Mount, mtn., Pan. (sä-lōō'th)	116a	9.14N	79.42W
Saluda, S.C., U.S. (sȧ-lōō'dȧ)	115	34.02N	81.46W
Saluda, r., S.C., U.S.	115	34.07N	81.48W
Saluzzo, Italy (sä-lōōt'sō)	160	44.39N	7.31E
Salvador, Braz. (säl-vä-dōr') (bä-ē'ä)	131	12.59S	38.27W
Salvador Lake, l., La., U.S.	113	29.45N	90.20W
Salvador Point, c., Bah.	122	24.30N	77.45W
Salvatierra, Mex. (säl-vä-tyĕr'rä)	118	20.13N	100.52W
Salween, r., Asia	180	21.00N	98.00E
Salyan, Azer.	167	39.40N	49.10E
Salzburg, Aus. (sälts'bŏorgh)	147	47.48N	13.04E
Salzburg, state, Aus.	154	47.30N	13.18E
Salzwedel, Ger. (sälts-vă'dĕl)	154	52.51N	11.10E
Samāika, neigh., India	240d	28.32N	77.05E
Samālūt, Egypt (sä-mä-lōōt')	184	28.17N	30.43E
Samana, Cabo, c., Dom. Rep.	117	19.20N	69.00W
Samana or Atwood Cay, i., Bah.	123	23.05N	73.45W
Samar, i., Phil. (sä'mär)	197	11.30N	126.07E
Samara (Kuybyshev), Russia	166	53.10N	50.05E
Samara, r., Russia	167	52.50N	50.35E
Samara, r., Ukr. (sȧ-mä'rȧ)	163	48.47N	35.30E
Samarai, Pap. N. Gui. (sä-mä-rä'ē)	197	10.45S	150.49E
Samarinda, Indon.	196	0.30S	117.10E
Samarkand, Uzb. (sȧ-mȧr-känt')	169	39.42N	67.00E
Şamaxı, Azer.	167	40.35N	48.40E
Samba, Zaire	217	4.38S	26.22E
Sambalpur, India (sŭm'bŭl-pŏor)	183	21.30N	84.05E
Sāmbhar, r., India	186	27.00N	74.58E
Sambir, Ukr.	155	49.31N	23.12E
Samborombón, r., Arg.	129c	35.20S	57.52W
Samborombón, Bahía, b., Arg. (bä-ē'ä-säm-bô-rôm-bô'n)	129c	35.57S	57.05W
Sambre, r., Eur. (säN'br')	151	50.20N	4.15E
Sambungo, Ang.	216	8.39S	20.43E
Sammamish, r., Wa., U.S.	106a	47.43N	122.08W
Sammamish, Lake, l., Wa., U.S. (sȧ-măm'ĭsh)	106a	47.35N	122.02W
Samoa Islands, is., Oc.	198a	14.00S	171.00W
Samokov, Bul. (sä'mô-kôf)	161	42.20N	23.33E
Samora Correia, Port. (sä-mō'rä-kôr-rē'yä)	159b	38.55N	8.52W
Samorovo, Russia (sȧ-mȧ-rô'vô)	170	60.47N	69.13E
Sámos, i., Grc. (să'mŏs)	149	37.53N	26.35E
Samothráki, i., Grc.	149	40.23N	25.10E
Sampaloc Point, c., Phil. (säm-pä'lôk)	197a	14.43N	119.56E
Sam Rayburn Reservoir, res., Tx., U.S.	113	31.10N	94.15W
Samson, Al., U.S. (săm'sŭn)	114	31.06N	86.02W
Samsu, N. Kor. (säm'sōō')	194	41.12N	128.00E
Samsun, Tur. (sȧm'sōōn')	182	41.20N	36.05E
Samtredia, Geor. (sȧm'trĕ-dē)	167	42.18N	42.25E
Samuel, i., Can. (săm'ū-ĕl)	106d	48.50N	123.10W
Samur, r. (sä-mōōr')	167	41.40N	47.20E
San, Mali (sän)	210	13.18N	4.54W
San, r., Eur.	147	50.33N	22.12E
Şan'ā', Yemen (sän'ä)	182	15.17N	44.05E
Sanaga, r., Cam. (sä-nä'gä)	210	4.30N	12.00E
San Ambrosio, Isla, i., Chile (ē's-lä-dē-sän äm-brō'zē-ō)	128	26.40S	80.00W
Sanana, Pulau, i., Indon.	197	2.15S	126.38E
Sanandaj, Iran	182	36.44N	46.43E
San Andreas, Ca., U.S. (săn ăn'drē-ăs)	108	38.10N	120.42W
San Andreas, l., Ca., U.S.	106b	37.36N	122.26W
San Andrés, Col. (sän-än-drĕ's)	130a	6.57N	75.41W
San Andrés, Mex. (sän än-drās')	119a	19.15N	99.10W
San Andrés, i., Col.	121	12.32N	81.34W
San Andres, Laguna de, l., Mex.	119	22.40N	97.50W
San Andres Mountains, mts., N.M., U.S. (săn ăn'drē-ăs)	96	33.00N	106.40W
San Andrés Tuxtla, Mex. (sän-än-drā's-tōōs'tlä)	116	18.27N	95.12W
San Angelo, Tx., U.S. (săn ăn-jĕ-lō)	96	31.28N	100.22W
San Antioco, Isola di, i., Italy (ē'sō-lä-dē-sän-än-tyŏ'kō)	160	39.00N	8.25E
San Antonio, Chile (sän-ȧn-tō'nyō)	132	33.34S	71.36W
San Antonio, Col.	130a	2.57N	75.06W
San Antonio, Col.	130a	3.55N	75.28W
San Antonio, Phil.	197a	14.57N	120.05E
San Antonio, Tx., U.S. (săn ăn-tō'nē-ô)	96	29.25N	98.30W
San Antonio, r., Tx., U.S.	113	29.00N	97.58W
San Antonio, Cabo, c., Cuba (kȧ'bô-sän-än-tô'nyô)	117	21.55N	84.55W
San Antonio, Lake, res., Ca., U.S.	108	36.00N	121.13W
San Antonio Abad, Spain (sän än-tō'nyô ä-bädh')	159	38.59N	1.17E
San Antonio Bay, b., Tx., U.S.	113	28.20N	97.08W
San Antonio de Areco, Arg. (dā ä-rä'kô)	129c	34.16S	59.30W
San Antonio de Galipán, Ven.	234a	10.33N	66.53W
San Antonio de las Vegas, Cuba	123a	22.51N	82.23W
San Antonio de los Baños, Cuba (dā lōs bän'yōs)	122	22.54N	82.30W
San Antonio de los Cobres, Arg. (dā lōs kō'brås)	132	24.15S	66.29W
San Antônio de Pádua, Braz. (dē-pȧ'dwä)	129a	21.32S	42.09W
San Antonio de Tamanaco, Ven.	131b	9.42N	66.03W
San Antonio Heights, Ca., U.S.	232	34.10N	117.40W
San Antonio Oeste, Arg. (sän-nä-tō'nyō ō-ĕs'tā)	132	40.49S	64.56W
San Antonio Peak, mtn., Ca., U.S. (săn ăn-tō'nĭ-ō)	107a	34.17N	117.39W
Sanarate, Guat. (sä-nä-rä'tē)	120	14.47N	90.12W
San Augustine, Tx., U.S. (săn ô'gŭs-tēn)	113	31.33N	94.08W
San Bartolo, Mex.	112	24.43N	103.12W
San Bartolo, Mex. (sän bär-tō'lō)	119a	19.36N	99.43W
San Bartolomé de la Cuadra, Spain	238e	41.26N	2.02E
San Bartolomeo, Italy (bär-tô-lô-mā'ō)	160	41.25N	15.04E
San Baudilio de Llobregat, Spain	238e	41.21N	2.03E
San Benedetto del Tronto, Italy (bā'nā-dĕt'tō dĕl trōn'tō)	160	42.58N	13.54E
San Benito, Tx., U.S. (săn bĕ-nē'tō)	113	26.07N	97.37W
San Benito, r., Ca., U.S.	108	36.40N	121.20W
San Bernardino, Ca., U.S. (bûr-när-dē'nō)	96	34.07N	117.19W
San Bernardino Mountains, mts., Ca., U.S.	108	34.05N	116.23W
San Bernardo, Chile (sän bĕr-när'dô)	129b	33.35S	70.42W
San Blas, Mex. (sän bläs')	116	21.33N	105.19W
San Blas, Cape, c., Fl., U.S.	97	29.38N	85.38W
San Blas, Cordillera de, mts., Pan.	121	9.17N	78.20W
San Blas, Golfo de, b., Pan.	121	9.33N	78.42W
San Blas, Punta, c., Pan.	121	9.35N	78.55W
San Bruno, Ca., U.S. (săn brū-nô)	106b	37.38N	122.25W
San Buenaventura, Mex. (bwā'nȧ-vĕn-tōō'rȧ)	112	27.07N	101.30W
San Carlos, Chile (sän-kȧ'r-lŏs)	132	36.23S	71.58W
San Carlos, Col.	130a	6.11N	74.58W
San Carlos, Eq. Gui.	216	3.27N	8.33E
San Carlos, Mex.	112	24.36N	98.52W
San Carlos, Mex. (sän kär'lŏs)	119	17.49N	92.33W
San Carlos, Nic. (sän-kä'r-lôs)	121	11.08N	84.48W
San Carlos, Phil.	197a	15.56N	120.20E
San Carlos, Ca., U.S. (săn kär'lōs)	106b	37.30N	122.15W
San Carlos, Ven.	130	9.36N	68.35W
San Carlos, r., C.R.	121	10.36N	84.18W
San Carlos de Bariloche, Arg.	132	41.15S	71.26W
San Carlos Indian Reservation, I.R., Az., U.S. (săn kär'lōs)	109	33.27N	110.15W
San Carlos Lake, res., Az., U.S.	109	33.05N	110.29W
San Casimiro, Ven. (kä-sē-mē'rô)	131b	10.01N	67.02W
San Cataldo, Italy (kä-täl'dō)	160	37.30N	13.59E
Sánchez, Dom. Rep. (sän'chĕz)	117	19.15N	69.40W
Sanchez, Río de los, r., Mex. (rē'ō-dĕ-lôs)	118	20.31N	102.29W
Sánchez Román, Mex. (rô-mȧ'n)	118	21.48N	103.20W
Sanchung, Tai.	241d	25.04N	121.29E
San Clemente, Spain (sän klȧ-mĕn'tȧ)	158	39.25N	2.24W
San Clemente de Llobregat, Spain	238e	41.20N	2.00E
San Clemente Island, i., Ca., U.S.	96	32.54N	118.29W
San Cristóbal, Dom. Rep. (krēs-tô'bäl)	123	18.25N	70.05W
San Cristóbal, Guat.	120	15.22N	90.26W
San Cristóbal, Ven.	130	7.43N	72.15W
San Cristobal, i., Sol.Is.	203	10.47S	162.17E
San Cristóbal de las Casas, Mex.	116	16.44N	92.39W
Sancti Spíritus, Cuba (säŋk'tē spē'rē-tōōs)	117	21.55N	79.25W
Sancti Spíritus, prov., Cuba	122	22.05N	79.20W
San Cugat del Vallés, Spain	238e	41.28N	2.05E
Sancy, Puy de, mtn., Fr. (pwē-dē-säN-sē')	147	45.30N	2.53E
Sand, i., Or., U.S. (sănd)	106c	46.16N	124.01W
Sand, i., Wi., U.S.	103	46.03N	91.09W
Sand, r., S. Afr.	213c	28.30S	29.30E
Sand, r., S. Afr.	218d	28.09S	26.46E
Sanda, Japan (sän'dä)	195	34.53N	135.14E
Sandakan, Malay. (sȧn-dä'kȧn)	196	5.51N	118.03E
Sanday, i., Scot., U.K. (sănd'ā)	150a	59.17N	2.25W
Sandbach, Eng., U.K. (sănd'băch)	144a	53.08N	2.22W
Sandefjord, Nor. (sän'dē-fyôr')	152	59.09N	10.14E
San de Fuca, Wa., U.S. (de-fōō-cä)	106a	48.14N	122.44W
Sanders, Az., U.S.	109	35.13N	109.20W
Sanderson, Tx., U.S. (săn'dēr-sŭn)	112	30.09N	102.24W
Sanderstead, neigh., Eng., U.K.	235	51.20N	0.05W
Sandersville, Ga., U.S. (săn'dērz-vĭl)	115	32.57N	82.50W
Sandhammaren, c., Swe. (sänt'häm-mȧr)	146	55.24N	14.37E
Sand Hills, reg., Ne., U.S. (sănd)	102	41.57N	101.29W
Sand Hook, N.J., U.S. (sănd hŏŏk)	100a	40.29N	74.05W
Sandhurst, Eng., U.K. (sănd'hûrst)	144b	51.20N	0.48W
Sandia Indian Reservation, I.R., N.M., U.S.	109	35.15N	106.30W
San Diego, Ca., U.S. (săn dē-ā'gō)	96	32.43N	117.10W
San Diego, Tx., U.S.	110	27.47N	98.13W
San Diego, r., Ca., U.S.	108	32.53N	116.57W
San Diego de la Unión, Mex. (sän dē-ā-gō dā lä ōō-nyōn')	118	21.27N	100.52W
Sandies Creek, r., Tx., U.S. (sănd'ēz)	113	29.13N	97.34W
San Dimas, Mex. (dē-mäs')	118	24.08N	105.57W
San Dimas, Ca., U.S. (săn dē-mȧs)	107a	34.07N	117.49W
Sandnes, Nor. (sänd'nĕs)	152	58.52N	5.44E
Sandoa, Zaire (sän-dō'ȧ)	212	9.39S	23.00E
Sandomierz, Pol. (sȧn-dô'myĕzh)	155	50.39N	21.45E
San Doná di Piave, Italy (sän dô nȧ' dē pyä'vē)	160	45.38N	12.34E
Sandoway, Myanmar (sän-dō-wī')	183	18.24N	94.28E
Sandpoint, Id., U.S. (sănd point)	104	48.17N	116.34W
Sandringham, Austl. (săn'drĭng-ăm)	201a	37.57S	145.01E
Sandringham, neigh., S. Afr.	244b	26.09S	28.07E
Sandrio, Italy (sä'n-dryô)	160	46.11N	9.53E
Sands Point, N.Y., U.S.	228	40.51N	73.43W
Sand Springs, Ok., U.S. (sănd sprĭnz)	111	36.08N	96.06W
Sandstone, Austl. (sănd'stōn)	202	28.00S	119.25E
Sandstone, Mn., U.S.	103	46.08N	92.53W
Sanduo, China (sän-dwô)	190	32.49N	119.39E
Sandusky, Al., U.S. (săn-dŭs'kē)	100h	33.32N	86.50W
Sandusky, Mi., U.S.	98	43.25N	82.50W
Sandusky, Oh., U.S.	97	41.25N	82.45W
Sandusky, r., Oh., U.S.	98	41.10N	83.20W
Sandwich, Il., U.S. (sănd'wĭch)	98	42.35N	88.53W
Sandy, Or., U.S. (sănd'ē)	106c	45.24N	122.16W
Sandy, Ut., U.S.	107b	40.36N	111.53W
Sandy, r., Or., U.S.	106c	45.28N	122.17W
Sandy Cape, c., Austl.	203	24.25S	153.10E
Sandy Hook, Ct., U.S. (hŏŏk)	100a	41.25N	73.17W
Sandy Lake, l., Can.	83g	53.46N	113.58W
Sandy Lake, l., Can.	89	53.00N	93.07W
Sandy Lake, l., Can.	93	49.16N	57.00W

PLACE (Pronunciation)	PAGE	Lat. °′	Long. °′
Sandy Point, Tx., U.S.	113a	29.22N	95.27W
Sandy Point, c., Wa., U.S.	106d	48.48N	122.42W
Sandy Springs, Ga., U.S. (springz)	100c	33.55N	84.23W
San Estanislao, Para. (ĕs-tä-nĕs-lä′ô)	132	24.38S	56.20W
San Esteban, Hond. (ĕs-tĕ′bän)	120	15.13N	85.53W
San Fabian, Phil. (fä-byä′n)	197a	16.14N	120.28E
San Felipe, Chile (fā-lē′pā)	132	32.45S	70.43W
San Felipe, Mex. (fē-lē′pē)	118	21.29N	101.13W
San Felipe, Mex.	118	22.21N	105.26W
San Felipe, Ven. (fē-lē′pē)	130	10.13N	68.45W
San Felipe, Cayos de, is., Cuba (kä′yōs-dĕ-sän-fē-lē′pĕ)	122	22.00N	83.30W
San Felipe Creek, r., Ca., U.S. (săn fē-lēp′ā)	108	33.10N	116.03W
San Felipe Indian Reservation, I.R., N.M., U.S.	109	35.26N	106.26W
San Felíu de Guixols, Spain (sän fā-lē′ò dā gē-hôls)	159	41.45N	3.01E
San Félix, Isla, i., Chile (ē′s-lä-dĕ-sän fā-lēks′)	128	26.20S	80.10W
San Fernanda, Spain (fĕr-nä′n-dä)	158	36.28N	6.13W
San Fernando, Arg. (fĕr-nà′n-dô)	132a	34.26S	58.34W
San Fernando, Chile	129b	35.36S	70.58W
San Fernando, Mex. (fĕr-nän′dô)	112	24.52N	98.10W
San Fernando, Phil. (sän fĕr-nä′n-dô)	196	16.38N	120.19E
San Fernando, Ca., U.S. (fĕr-nän′dô)	107a	34.17N	118.27W
San Fernando, r., Mex. (sän fĕr-nän′dô)	112	25.07N	98.25W
San Fernando de Apure, Ven. (sän-fĕr-nä′n-dō-dĕ-ä-pōō′rå)	130	7.46N	67.29W
San Fernando de Atabapo, Ven. (dĕ-ä-tä-bä′pô)	130	3.58N	67.41W
San Fernando de Henares, Spain (dĕ-ā-nä′rås)	159a	40.23N	3.31W
Sånfjället, mtn., Swe.	146	62.19N	13.30E
Sanford, Can. (săn′fĕrd)	83f	49.41N	97.27W
Sanford, Fl., U.S. (săn′fôrd)	97	28.46N	81.18W
Sanford, Me., U.S. (săn′fĕrd)	92	43.26N	70.47W
Sanford, N.C., U.S.	115	35.26N	79.10W
San Francisco, Arg. (săn frăn′sĭs′kô)	132	31.23S	62.09W
San Francisco, El Sal.	120	13.48N	88.11W
San Francisco, Ca., U.S.	96	37.45N	122.26W
San Francisco, r., N.M., U.S.	109	33.35N	108.55W
San Francisco Bay, b., Ca., U.S. (săn frăn′sĭs′kô)	108	37.45N	122.21W
San Francisco Culhuacán, Mex.	233a	19.20N	99.06W
San Francisco del Oro, Mex. (dĕl ō′rō)	116	27.00N	106.37W
San Francisco del Rincón, Mex. (dĕl rēn-kōn′)	118	21.01N	101.51W
San Francisco de Macaira, Ven. (dĕ-mä-kī′rä)	131b	9.58N	66.17W
San Francisco de Macoris, Dom. Rep. (dā-mä-kō′rēs)	123	19.20N	70.15W
San Francisco de Paula, Cuba (dā pou′lä)	123a	23.04N	82.18W
San Francisco el Grande, Iglesia de, rel., Spain	238b	40.25N	3.43W
San Gabriel, Ca., U.S. (săn gä-brē-ĕl′) (gā′brē-ĕl)	107a	34.06N	118.06W
San Gabriel, r., Ca., U.S.	107a	33.47N	118.06W
San Gabriel Chilac, Mex. (sän-gä-brē-ĕl-chē-läk′)	119	18.19N	97.22W
San Gabriel Mts, Ca., U.S.	107a	34.17N	118.03W
San Gabriel Reservoir, res., Ca., U.S.	107a	34.14N	117.48W
Sangamon, r., Il., U.S. (săn′gȧ-msion)	111	40.08N	90.08W
Sangenjaya, neigh., Japan	242a	35.38N	139.40E
Sanger, Ca., U.S. (săng′ẽr)	108	36.42N	119.33W
Sangerhausen, Ger. (säng′ĕr-hou-zĕn)	154	51.28N	11.17E
Sangha, r., Afr.	211	2.40N	16.10E
Sangihe, Pulau, i., Indon.	197	3.30N	125.30E
San Gil, Col. (sän-кē′l)	130	6.32N	73.13W
San Giovanni in Fiore, Italy (sän jô-vän′nē ēn fyō′rå)	160	39.15N	16.40E
San Giuseppe Vesuviano, Italy	159c	40.36N	14.31E
Sangju, S. Kor. (säng′jōō′)	194	36.20N	128.07E
Sāngli, India	183	16.56N	74.38E
Sangmélima, Cam.	215	2.56N	11.59E
San Gorgonio Mountain, mtn., Ca., U.S. (săn gôr-gō′nĭ-ō)	107a	34.06N	116.50W
Sangre de Cristo Mountains, mts., U.S.	96	37.45N	105.50W
San Gregoria, Ca., U.S. (săn grĕ-gôr′ä)	106b	37.20N	122.23W
San Gregorio Atlapulco, Mex.	233a	19.15N	99.03W
Sangro, r., Italy (säŋ′grô)	160	41.38N	13.56E
Sangüesa, Spain (sän-gwĕ′sä)	158	42.36N	1.15W
Sanhe, China (sän-hŭ)	190	39.59N	117.06E
Sanibel Island, i., Fl., U.S. (săn′ĭ-bĕl)	115a	26.26N	82.15W
San Ignacio, Belize	120a	17.11N	89.04W
San Ildefonso, Cape, c., Phil. (sän-ēl-dĕ-fôn-sô)	197a	16.03N	122.10E
San Ildefonso o la Granja, Spain (ō lä grän′khä)	158	40.54N	4.02W
San Isidro, Arg. (ē-sē′drô)	129c	34.28S	58.31W
San Isidro, C.R.	121	9.24N	83.43W
San Isidro, Peru	233c	12.07S	77.03W
San Jacinto, Phil. (sän hä-sēn′tô)	197a	12.33N	123.43E
San Jacinto, Ca., U.S. (săn jȧ-sĭn′tô)	107a	33.47N	116.57W
San Jacinto, r., Ca., U.S. (săn jȧ-sĭn′tô)	107a	33.44N	117.14W
San Jacinto, r., Tx., U.S.	113	30.25N	95.05W
San Jacinto, West Fork, r., Tx., U.S.	113	30.35N	95.37W
San Javier, Chile (sän-hà-vē′ĕr)	129b	35.35S	71.43W
San Jerónimo, Mex.	119a	19.31N	98.46W
San Jerónimo de Juárez, Mex. (hå-rō′nē-mô dā hwä′râz)	118	17.08N	100.30W
San Jerónimo Lídice, Mex.	233a	19.20N	99.13W
San Joaquin, Ven.	131b	10.16N	67.47W
San Joaquin, r., Ca., U.S. (săn hwä-kēn′)	108	37.10N	120.51W
San Joaquin Valley, Ca., U.S.	108	36.45N	120.30W
San Jorge, Golfo, b., Arg. (gôl-fô-sän-кô′r-кĕ)	132	46.15S	66.45W
San José, C.R. (sän hô-sā′)	117	9.57N	84.05W
San Jose, Phil.	197a	12.22N	121.04E
San Jose, Phil.	197a	15.49N	120.57E
San Jose, Ca., U.S. (săn hô-zā′)	96	37.20N	121.54W
San José, i., Mex. (кô-sĕ′)	116	25.00N	110.35W
San José, Isla de, i., Pan. (ē′s-lä-dĕ-sän hô-sā′)	121	8.17N	79.20W
San Jose, Rio, r., N.M., U.S. (săn hô-zā′)	109	35.15N	108.10W
San José de Feliciano, Arg. (dā lä ĕs-kē′nä)	132	30.26S	58.44W
San José de Galipán, Ven.	234a	10.35N	66.54W
San José de Gauribe, Ven. (sän-hô-sĕ′dĕ-gäōō-rē′bĕ)	131b	9.51N	65.49W
San José de las Lajas, Cuba (sän-кô-sĕ′dĕ-läs-lä′käs)	123a	22.58N	82.10W
San José Iturbide, Mex. (ē-tōōr-bē′dĕ)	118	21.00N	100.24W
San Juan, Arg. (hwän′)	132	31.36S	68.29W
San Juan, Col. (hòä′n)	130a	3.23N	73.48W
San Juan, Dom. Rep. (sän hwän′)	123	18.50N	71.15W
San Juan, Phil.	197a	16.41N	120.20E
San Juan, P.R. (sän hwän′)	117	18.30N	66.10W
San Juan, prov., Arg.	132	31.00S	69.30W
San Juan, r., Mex. (sän-hōō-än′)	119	18.10N	95.23W
San Juan, r., N.A.	117	10.58N	84.18W
San Juan, r., U.S.	96	36.30N	109.00W
San Juan, Cabezas de, c., P.R.	117b	18.29N	65.30W
San Juan, Cabo, c., Eq. Gui.	216	1.08N	9.23E
San Juan, Pico, mtn., Cuba (pē′kô-sän-kòä′n)	122	21.55N	80.00W
San Juan, Río, r., Mex. (rē′ō-sän-hwän)	112	25.35N	99.15W
San Juan Bautista, Para. (sän hwän′ bou-tēs′tä)	132	26.48S	57.09W
San Juan Capistrano, Mex. (sän-hōō-än′ kä-pēs-trä′nô)	118	22.41N	104.07W
San Juan Creek, r., Ca., U.S. (săn hwän′)	108	35.24N	120.12W
San Juan de Aragón, Mex.	233a	19.28N	99.05W
San Juan de Aragón, Bosque, rec., Mex.	233a	19.28N	99.04W
San Juan de Aragón, Zoológico de, rec., Mex.	233a	19.28N	99.05W
San Juan de Dios, Ven.	234a	10.35N	66.57W
San Juan de Guadalupe, Mex. (sän hwan dā gwä-dhä-lōō′pä)	112	24.37N	102.43W
San Juan del Monte, Phil.	241g	14.36N	121.02E
San Juan del Norte, Nic.	121	10.55N	83.44W
San Juan del Norte, Bahía de, b., Nic.	121	11.12N	83.40W
San Juan de los Lagos, Mex. (sän-hōō-än′dā los lä′gôs)	118	21.15N	102.18W
San Juan de los Lagos, r., Mex. (dā lōs lä′gôs)	118	21.13N	102.12W
San Juan de los Morros, Ven. (dĕ-lôs-mô′r-rōs)	131b	9.54N	67.22W
San Juan del Río, Mex. (sän hwän del rē′ô)	112	24.47N	104.29W
San Juan del Río, Mex.	118	20.21N	99.59W
San Juan del Sur, Nic. (dĕl sōōr)	116	11.15N	85.53W
San Juan Evangelista, Mex. (sän-hōō-ä′n-å-väŋ-kå-lēs′ta′)	119	17.57N	95.08W
San Juan Island, i., Wa., U.S.	106a	48.28N	123.08W
San Juan Islands, is., Can. (săn hwän)	86	48.49N	123.14W
San Juan Islands, is., Wa., U.S.	172a	48.36N	122.50W
San Juan Ixtenco, Mex. (ēx-tĕ′n-kô)	119	19.14N	97.52W
San Juan Martínez, Cuba	122	22.15N	83.50W
San Juan Mountains, mts., Co., U.S. (san hwän′)	96	37.50N	107.30W
San Julián, Arg. (sän hōō-lyá′n)	132	49.17S	68.02W
San Justo, Arg. (hōōs′tô)	132a	34.40S	58.33W
San Justo Desvern, Spain	238e	41.23N	2.05E
Sankanbiriwa, mtn., S.L.	214	8.56N	10.48W
Sankarani, r., Afr. (sän′kä-rä′nē)	210	11.10N	8.35W
Sankt Gallen, Switz.	147	47.25N	9.22E
Sankt Moritz, Switz. (sånt mô′rĭts) (zäŋkt mō′rēts)	154	46.31N	9.50E
Sankt Pölten, Aus. (zäŋkt-pûl′tĕn)	154	48.12N	15.38E
Sankt Veit, Aus. (zäŋkt vīt′)	154	46.46N	14.20E
Sankuru, r., Zaire (säŋ-kōō′rōō)	212	4.00S	22.35E
San Lázaro, Cabo, c., Mex. (sän-là′zä-rō)	116	24.58N	113.30W
San Leandro, Ca., U.S. (săn lē-ăn′drô)	106b	37.43N	122.10W
Şanlıurfa, Tur.	182	37.20N	38.45E
San Lorenzo, Arg. (sän lô-rĕn′zô)	132	32.46S	60.44W
San Lorenzo, Hond. (sän lô-rĕn′zô)	120	13.24N	87.24W
San Lorenzo, Ca., U.S. (săn lô-rĕn′zô)	106b	37.41N	122.08W
San Lorenzo de El Escorial, Spain	158	40.36N	4.09W
San Lorenzo Tezonco, Mex.	233a	19.18N	99.04W
Sanlúcar de Barrameda, Spain (sän-lōō′kär)	148	36.46N	6.21W
San Lucas, Bol. (lōō′kás)	130	20.12S	65.06W
San Lucas, Cabo, c., Mex.	116	22.45N	109.45W
San Luis, Arg. (lò-ēs′)	132	33.16S	66.15W
San Luis, Col. (lòē′s)	130a	6.03N	74.57W
San Luis, Cuba	123	20.15N	75.50W
San Luis, Guat.	120	14.38N	89.42W
San Luis, prov., Arg.	132	32.45S	66.00W
San Luis, neigh., Cuba	233b	23.05N	82.20W
San Luis de la Paz, Mex. (dā lä päz′)	118	21.17N	100.32W
San Luis del Cordero, Mex. (dĕl kôr-dä′rō)	112	25.25N	104.20W
San Luis Obispo, Ca., U.S. (ô-bĭs′pō)	96	35.18N	120.40W
San Luis Obispo Bay, b., Ca., U.S.	108	35.07N	121.05W
San Luis Potosí, Mex.	116	22.08N	100.58W
San Luis Potosí, state, Mex.	116	22.45N	101.45W
San Luis Rey, r., Ca., U.S. (rā′ē)	108	33.22N	117.06W
San Luis Tlaxialtemalco, Mex.	233a	19.15N	99.03W
San Manuel, Az., U.S. (săn măn′ū-ĕl)	109	32.30N	110.45W
San Marcial, N.M., U.S. (săn mär-shäl′)	109	33.40N	107.00W
San Marco, Italy (sän mär′kô)	160	41.53N	15.50E
San Marcos, Guat. (mär′kôs)	120	14.57N	91.49W
San Marcos, Mex.	118	16.46N	99.23W
San Marcos, Tx., U.S. (săn mär′kôs)	113	29.53N	97.56W
San Marcos, r., Tx., U.S.	112	30.08N	98.15W
San Marcos, Universidad de, educ., Peru	233c	12.03S	77.05W
San Marcos de Colón, Hond. (sän-mà′r-kōs-dĕ-kô-lô′n)	120	13.17N	86.50W
San Maria di Léuca, Cape, c., Italy (dē-lĕ′ōō-kä)	149	39.47N	18.20E
San Marino, S. Mar. (sän mä-rē′nô)	160	44.55N	12.26E
San Marino, Ca., U.S. (săn mẽr-ē′nô)	107a	34.07N	118.06W
San Marino, nation, Eur.	142	43.40N	13.00E
San Martín, Col. (sän mär-tē′n)	130a	3.42N	73.44W
San Martín, vol., Mex. (mär-tē′n)	119	18.36N	95.11W
San Martín, l., S.A.	132	48.15S	72.30W
San Martín Chalchicuautla, Mex.	118	21.22N	98.39W
San Martin de la Vega, Spain (sän mär ten′ dā lä vā′gä)	159a	40.12N	3.34W
San Martín Hidalgo, Mex. (sän mär-tē′n-ē-däl′gô)	118	20.27N	103.55W
San Mateo, Mex.	119	16.59N	97.04W
San Mateo, Spain (sän mä-tā′ô)	159	40.26N	0.09E
San Mateo, Ca., U.S. (săn mä-tā′ô)	106b	37.34N	122.20W
San Mateo, Ven. (sän mȧ-tĕ′ô)	131b	9.45N	64.34W
San Matías, Golfo, b., Arg. (sän mä-tē′äs)	132	41.30S	63.45W
Sanmen Wan, b., China	193	29.00N	122.15E
San Miguel, Chile	234b	33.30S	70.40W
San Miguel, El Sal. (sän mē-gāl′)	116	13.28N	88.11W
San Miguel, Mex. (sän mē-gāl′)	119	18.18N	97.09W
San Miguel, Pan.	121	8.26N	78.55W
San Miguel, Peru	233c	12.06S	77.06W
San Miguel, Phil. (sän mē-gĕ′l)	197a	15.09N	120.56E
San Miguel, Ven. (sän mē-gĕ′l)	131b	9.56N	64.58W
San Miguel, vol., El Sal.	120	13.27N	88.17W
San Miguel, i., Ca., U.S.	108	34.03N	120.23W
San Miguel, r., Bol. (sän-mē-gĕl′)	130	13.34S	63.58W
San Miguel, r., N.A. (sän mē-gāl′)	119	15.27N	92.00W
San Miguel, r., Co., U.S. (săn mē-gĕl′)	109	38.15N	108.40W
San Miguel, Bahía, b., Pan. (bä-ē′ä-sän mē-gāl′)	121	8.17N	78.26W
San Miguel Bay, b., Phil.	197a	13.55N	123.12E
San Miguel de Allende, Mex. (dā ä-lyĕn′dā)	118	20.54N	100.44W
San Miguel del Padrón, Cuba	233b	23.05N	82.19W
San Miguel el Alto, Mex. (ĕl äl′tô)	118	21.03N	102.26W
Sannār, Sudan	211	14.25N	33.30E
San Narcisco, Phil. (sän när-sē′sô)	197a	15.01N	120.05E
San Narcisco, Phil.	197a	13.34N	122.33E
San Nicolás, Arg. (sän nē-kô-lä′s)	132	33.20S	60.14W
San Nicolas, Phil. (nē-kô-läs′)	197a	16.05N	120.45E
San Nicolas, i., Ca., U.S. (săn nĭ′kô-lȧ)	108	33.14N	119.10W
San Nicolás, r., Mex.	118	19.40N	105.08W
Sanniquellie, Lib.	214	7.22N	8.43W
Sannois, Fr.	237c	48.58N	2.15E
Sannūr, Wādī, Egypt	218b	28.48N	31.12E
Sanok, Pol. (sä′nôk)	155	49.31N	22.13E
San Pablo, Phil. (sän-pä-blô)	197a	14.05N	121.20E
San Pablo, Ca., U.S. (săn păb′lô)	106b	37.58N	122.21W
San Pablo, Ven. (sän-pà′blô)	131b	9.46N	65.04W
San Pablo, r., Pan. (sän päb′lô)	121	8.12N	81.12W
San Pablo Bay, b., Ca., U.S. (săn păb′lô)	106b	38.04N	122.25W
San Pablo Res, Ca., U.S.	106b	37.55N	122.12W
San Pascual, Phil. (päs-kwäl′)	197a	13.08N	122.59E
San Pedro, Arg.	129c	33.41S	59.42W
San Pedro, Arg. (sän pä′drô)	132	24.15S	64.15W
San Pedro, Chile (sän pĕ′drô)	129b	33.54S	71.27W
San Pedro, El Sal. (sän pä′drô)	120	13.49N	88.58W
San Pedro, Mex. (sän pä′drô)	119	18.38N	92.25W
San Pedro, Para. (sän-pĕ′drô)	132	24.13S	57.00W
San Pedro, Ca., U.S. (săn pē′drô)	107a	33.44N	118.17W
San Pedro, r., Cuba (sän-pĕ′drô)	122	21.05N	78.15W
San Pedro, r., Mex.	112	27.56N	105.50W
San Pedro, r., Mex. (sän pä′drô)	118	22.08N	104.59W
San Pedro, r., Az., U.S.	109	32.48N	110.37W
San Pedro, Río de, r., Mex.	118	21.51N	102.24W
San Pedro, Río de, r., N.A.	119	18.23N	92.13W
San Pedro Bay, b., Ca., U.S. (săn pē′drô)	107a	33.42N	118.12W
San Pedro de las Colonias, Mex. (dĕ-läs-kô-lô′nyäs)	112	25.47N	102.58W
San Pedro de Macorís, Dom. Rep. (sän-pĕ′drō-dā mä-kô-rēs′)	123	18.30N	69.30W
San Pedro Lagunillas, Mex. (sän pä′drô lä-gōō-nēl′yäs)	118	21.12N	104.47W
San Pedro Sula, Hond. (sän pä′drô sōō′lä)	120	15.29N	88.01W
San Pedro Xalostoc, Mex.	233a	19.32N	99.05W
San Pedro Zacatenco, Mex.	233a	19.31N	99.08W
San Pietro, Isola di, i., Italy (ē′sō-lä-dē-sän pyā′trô)	160	39.09N	8.15E
San Pietro in Vaticano, rel., Vat.	239c	41.54N	12.28E
San Quentin, Ca., U.S. (săn kwĕn-tĕn′)	106b	37.57N	122.29W
San Quintin, Phil. (sän kēn-tēn′)	197a	15.59N	120.47E
San Rafael, Arg. (sän rä-fä-āl′)	132	34.30S	68.13W
San Rafael, Col. (sän-rä-fä-ĕ′l)	130a	6.18N	75.02W

ăt; finȧl; rāte; senȧte; ärm; ȧsk; sofȧ; fâre; ch-choose; dh-as th in other; bē; ėvent; bĕt; recĕnt; cratẽr; g-gō; gh-guttural g; bĭt; ĭ-short neutral; rīde; κ-guttural k as ch in German ich;

PRONOUNCING INDEX San Rafael-São Pedro e São Paulo 345

PLACE (Pronunciation)	PAGE	Lat. °′	Long. °′
San Rafael, Ca., U.S. (săn rá-fĕl)	106b	37.58N	122.31W
San Rafael, r., Ut., U.S. (săn rá-fĕl′)	109	39.05N	110.50W
San Rafael, Cabo, c., Dom. Rep. (ká′bô)	123	19.00N	68.50W
San Ramón, C.R.	121	10.07N	84.30W
San Ramon, Ca., U.S. (săn rä-mōn′)	106b	37.47N	122.59W
San Remo, Italy (săn rā′mô)	160	43.48N	7.46E
San Roque, Col. (săn-rô′kĕ)	130a	6.29N	75.00W
San Roque, Spain	158	36.13N	5.23W
San Saba, Tx., U.S. (săn să′bá)	112	31.12N	98.43W
San Saba, r., Tx., U.S.	112	30.58N	99.12W
San Salvador, El Sal. (săn säl-vä-dōr′)	116	13.45N	89.11W
San Salvador (Watling), i., Bah. (săn săl′vá-dôr)	123	24.05N	74.30W
San Salvador, i., Ec.	130	0.14S	90.50W
San Salvador, r., Ur. (săn-säl-vä-dô′r)	129c	33.42S	58.04W
Sansanné-Mango, Togo (săn-sá-nā′ mäN′gô)	210	10.21N	0.28E
San Sebastián, Spain	142	43.19N	1.59W
San Sebastian, Spain (săn sá-bás-tyän′)	210	28.09N	17.11W
San Sebastián, Ven. (săn-sĕ-bäs-tyá′n)	131b	9.58N	67.11W
San Sebastiàn de los Reyes, Spain	159a	40.33N	3.38W
San Severo, Italy (săn sĕ-vâ′rō)	149	41.43N	15.24E
Sanshui, China (săn-shwā)	189	23.14N	112.51E
San Simon Creek, r., Az., U.S. (săn sī-mōn′)	109	32.45N	109.30W
San Siro, neigh., Italy	238c	45.29S	9.07E
Sanssouci, Schloss, hist., Ger.	238a	52.24N	13.02E
Santa Ana, El Sal.	116	14.02N	89.35W
Santa Ana, Mex. (săn′tä ä′nä)	118	19.18N	98.10W
Santa Ana, Ca., U.S. (săn′tá ăn′á)	96	33.45N	117.52W
Santa Ana, r., Ca., U.S.	107a	33.41N	117.57W
Santa Ana Mountains, mts., Ca., U.S.	107a	33.44N	117.36W
Santa Anna, Tx., U.S.	112	31.44N	99.18W
Santa Antão, i., C.V. (sä-tä-ă′n-zhĕ-lô)	210b	17.20N	26.05W
Santa Bárbara, Braz. (săn-tä-bá′r-bä-rä)	131	19.57S	43.25W
Santa Bárbara, Hond.	120	14.52N	88.20W
Santa Barbara, Mex.	112	26.48N	105.50W
Santa Barbara, Ca., U.S.	96	34.26N	119.43W
Santa Barbara, i., Ca., U.S.	108	33.30N	118.44W
Santa Barbara Channel, strt., Ca., U.S.	108	34.15N	120.00W
Santa Branca, Braz. (săn-tä-brä′N-kä)	129a	23.25S	45.52W
Santa Catalina, i., Ca., U.S.	96	33.29N	118.37W
Santa Catalina, Cerro de, mtn., Pan.	121	8.39N	81.36W
Santa Catalina, Gulf of, b., Ca., U.S. (săn′tȧ kă-tȧ-lē′nȧ)	108	33.00N	117.58W
Santa Catarina, Mex. (săn′tä kä-tä-rē′nä)	112	25.41N	100.27W
Santa Catarina, state, Braz. (săn-tä-kä-tä-rē′ná)	132	27.15S	50.30W
Santa Catarina, r., Mex.	118	16.31N	98.39W
Santa Clara, Cuba (săn′t klä′rá)	117	22.25N	80.00W
Santa Clara, Mex.	112	24.29N	103.22W
Santa Clara, Ca., U.S. (săn′tȧ klârȧ)	104	37.21N	121.56W
Santa Clara, Ur.	132	32.46S	54.51W
Santa Clara, vol., Nic.	120	12.44N	87.00W
Santa Clara, r., Ca., U.S. (săn′tȧ klă′rȧ)	108	34.22N	118.53W
Santa Clara, Bahía de, b., Cuba (bä-ē′ä-dĕ-săn-tä-klä-rä)	122	23.05N	80.50W
Santa Clara, Sierra, mts., Mex. (sē-ĕ′r-rä-săn′tä klä′rá)	116	27.30N	113.50W
Santa Clara Indian Reservation, I.R., N.M., U.S.	109	35.59N	106.10W
Santa Coloma de Gramanet, Spain	238e	41.27N	2.13E
Santa Cruz, Bol. (săn′tá krōōz′)	130	17.45S	63.03W
Santa Cruz, Braz. (săn-tä-krōō′s)	132	29.43S	52.15W
Santa Cruz, Braz.	132b	22.55S	43.41W
Santa Cruz, Chile	129b	34.38S	71.21W
Santa Cruz, C.R.	120	10.16N	85.37W
Santa Cruz, Mex.	112	25.50N	105.25W
Santa Cruz, Phil.	197a	13.28N	122.02E
Santa Cruz, Phil.	197a	14.17N	121.25E
Santa Cruz, Phil.	197a	15.46N	119.53E
Santa Cruz, Ca., U.S.	96	36.59N	122.02W
Santa Cruz, prov., Arg.	132	48.00S	70.00W
Santa Cruz, i., Ec. (săn-tä-krōō′z)	130	0.38S	90.20W
Santa Cruz, r., Arg. (săn′tá krōōz′)	132	50.05S	71.00W
Santa Cruz, r., Az., U.S. (săn′tȧ krōōz′)	109	32.30N	111.30W
Santa Cruz Barillas, Guat. (săn-tä-krōō′z-bä-rē′l-yäs)	120	15.47N	91.22W
Santa Cruz del Sur, Cuba (săn-tä-krōō′s-dĕl-sō′r)	122	20.45N	78.00W
Santa Cruz de Tenerife, Spain (săn′tä krōōz dā tā-nâ-rē′fā)	209	28.07N	15.27W
Santa Cruz Islands, is., Sol.Is.	203	10.58S	166.47E
Santa Cruz Meyehualco, Mex.	233a	19.20N	99.03W
Santa Cruz Mountains, mts., Ca., U.S. (săn′tá krōōz′)	106b	37.30N	122.19W
Santa Domingo, Cay, i., Bah.	123	21.50N	75.45W
Santa Eduviges, Chile	234b	33.33S	70.39W
Santa Elena del Gomero, Chile	234b	33.29S	70.46W
Santa Eugenia de Ribeira, Spain	158	42.34N	8.55W
Santa Eulalia del Río, Spain	159	38.58N	1.29E
Santa Fe, Arg. (săn′tä fā′)	132	31.33S	60.45W
Santa Fé, Cuba (săn-tä-fē′)	122	21.45N	82.40W
Santa Fe, Mex.	233a	19.23N	99.14W
Santa Fe, Spain (săn′tä-fā′)	158	37.12N	3.43W
Santa Fe, N.M., U.S. (săn′tȧ fā′)	96	35.40N	106.00W
Santa Fe, prov., Arg. (săn′tä fā′)	132	32.00S	61.15W
Santa Fe de Bogotá, Col.	130	4.36N	74.05W
Santa Filomena, Braz. (săn-tä-fē-lô-mĕ′nä)	131	9.09S	44.45W
Santa Genoveva, mtn., Mex. (săn-tä-hĕ-nō-vĕ′vä)	116	23.30N	110.00W
Santai, China (san-tī)	188	31.02N	105.02E
Santa Inés, Ven. (săn′tä ē-nĕ′s)	131b	9.54N	64.21W
Santa Inés, i., Chile (săn′tä ē-nās′)	132	53.45S	74.15W
Santa Isabel, i., Sol.Is.	203	7.57S	159.28E
Santa Isabel, Pico de, mtn., Eq. Gui.	215	3.35N	8.46E
Santa Lucia, Cuba (săn′tá lōō-sē′á)	122	21.15N	77.30W
Santa Lucia, Ur. (săn-tä-lōō-sē′ä)	132	34.27S	56.23W
Santa Lucia, Ven.	131b	10.18N	66.40W
Santa Lucia, r., Ur.	129c	34.19S	56.13W
Santa Lucia Bay, b., Cuba (săn′tá lōō-sē′á)	122	22.55N	84.20W
Santa Margarita, i., Mex. (săn′tá mär-gá-rē′tá)	116	24.15N	112.00W
Santa Maria, Braz. (săn′tá mä-rē′á)	132	29.40S	54.00W
Santa Maria, Italy (săn-tä mä-rē′ä)	160	41.05N	14.15E
Santa Maria, Phil. (săn-tä-mä-rē′ä)	197a	14.48N	120.57E
Santa Maria, Ca., U.S. (săn-tȧ mȧ-rē′ȧ)	108	34.57N	120.28W
Santa María, vol., Guat.	120	14.45N	91.33W
Santa María, r., Mex. (săn′tá mä-rē′ä)	118	21.33N	100.17W
Santa Maria, Cabo de, c., Port. (ká′bō-dĕ-săn-tä-mä-rē′ä)	158	36.58N	7.54W
Santa Maria, Cape, c., Bah.	123	23.45N	75.30W
Santa Maria, Cayo, i., Cuba	122	22.40N	79.00W
Santa María del Oro, Mex. (săn′tä-mä-rē′ä-dĕl-ô-rō)	118	21.21N	104.35W
Santa María de los Angeles, Mex. (dĕ-lôs-á′n-hĕ-lĕs)	118	22.10N	103.34W
Santa María del Río, Mex.	118	21.46N	100.43W
Santa María del Rosario, Cuba	233b	23.04N	82.15W
Santa María de Ocotán, Mex.	118	22.56N	104.30W
Santa Maria Island, i., Port. (săn-tä-mä-rē′ä)	210a	37.09N	26.02W
Santa Maria Madalena, Braz.	129a	22.00S	42.00W
Santa Marta, Col. (săn′tá mär′tá)	130	11.15N	74.13W
Santa Marta, Peru	233c	12.02S	76.56W
Santa Marta, Cabo de, c., Ang.	216	13.52S	12.25E
Santa Martha Acatitla, Mex.	233a	19.22N	99.01W
Santa Monica, Ca., U.S. (săn′tȧ mŏn′ĭ-kȧ)	96	34.01N	118.29W
Santa Mónica, neigh., Ven.	234a	10.29N	66.53W
Santa Monica Bay, b., Ca., U.S.	232	33.54N	118.25W
Santa Monica Mountains, mts., Ca., U.S.	107a	34.08N	118.38W
Santana, r., Braz. (săn-tä′nä)	132b	22.33S	43.37W
Santander, Col. (săn-tän-dĕr′)	130a	3.00N	76.25W
Santander, Spain (săn-tän-dâr′)	142	43.27N	3.50W
Santa Paula, Ca., U.S. (săn′tȧ pô′lȧ)	108	34.24N	119.05W
Santarém, Braz. (săn-tä-rĕN′)	131	2.28S	54.37W
Santarém, Port.	158	39.18N	8.48W
Santaren Channel, strt., Bah. (săn-tȧ-rĕn′)	122	24.15N	79.30W
Santa Rita do Sapucai, Braz. (sá-pô-ká′ĕ)	129a	22.15S	45.41W
Santa Rosa, Arg. (săn-tä-rô-sä)	132	36.45S	64.10W
Santa Rosa, Col. (săn-tä-rô-sä)	130a	6.38N	75.26W
Santa Rosa, Ec.	130	3.29S	79.55W
Santa Rosa, Guat. (săn′tá rō′sȧ)	120	14.21N	90.16W
Santa Rosa, Hond.	120	14.45N	88.51W
Santa Rosa, Ca., U.S. (săn′tȧ rō′zȧ)	96	38.27N	122.42W
Santa Rosa, N.M., U.S. (săn′tȧ rō′sȧ)	110	34.55N	104.41W
Santa Rosa, Ven. (săn-tä-rô-sä)	131b	9.37N	64.10W
Santa Rosa de Cabal, Col. (săn-tä-rô-sä-dĕ-kä-bä′l)	130a	4.53N	75.38W
Santa Rosa de Huechuraba, Chile	234b	33.21S	70.41W
Santa Rosa de Viterbo, Braz. (săn-tä-rô-sá-dĕ-vē-tĕr′-bô)	129a	21.30S	47.21W
Santa Rosa Indian Reservation, I.R., Ca., U.S. (săn′tȧ rō′zȧ′)	108	33.28N	116.50W
Santa Rosalía, Mex. (săn′tá rô-zä′lē-á)	116	27.13N	112.15W
Santa Rosa Range, mts., Nv., U.S. (săn′tȧ rō′zȧ)	104	41.33N	117.50W
Santa Susana, Ca., U.S. (săn′tȧ sōō-ză′nȧ)	107a	34.16N	118.42W
Santa Teresa, Arg. (săn-tä-tĕ-rĕ′sä)	129c	33.27S	60.47W
Santa Teresa, Ven.	131b	10.14N	66.40W
Santa Teresa de lo Ovalle, Chile	234b	33.23S	70.47W
Santa Úrsula Coapa, Mex.	233a	19.17N	99.11W
Santa Vitória do Palmar, Braz. (săn-tä-vē-tō′ryä-dô-päl-màr)	132	33.30S	53.16W
Santa Ynez, r., Ca., U.S. (săn′tȧ ē-nĕz′)	108	34.40N	120.20W
Santa Ysabel Indian Reservation, I.R., Ca., U.S. (săn-tȧ ĭ-zȧ-bĕl′)	108	33.05N	116.46W
Santee, Ca., U.S. (săn tē′)	108a	32.50N	116.58W
Santee, r., S.C., U.S.	97	33.00N	79.45W
Santeny, Fr.	237c	48.43N	2.34E
Sant' Eufemia, Golfo di, b., Italy (gôl-fō-dē-săn-tĕ′ŏ-fĕ′myä)	160	38.53N	15.53E
Santiago, Braz. (săn-tyà′gô)	132	29.05S	54.46W
Santiago, Chile (săn-tē-ä′gô)	132	33.26S	70.40W
Santiago, Pan.	117	8.07N	80.58W
Santiago, Phil. (săn-tyä′gô)	197a	16.42N	121.33E
Santiago, prov., Chile (săn-tyà′gô)	129b	33.28S	70.55W
Santiago, i., Phil.	197a	16.29N	120.03E
Santiago de Compostela, Spain	148	42.52N	8.32W
Santiago de Cuba, Cuba (săn-tyà′gô-dā kōō′bá)	117	20.00N	75.50W
Santiago de Cuba, prov., Cuba	122	20.20N	76.05W
Santiago de las Vegas, Cuba (săn-tyà′gō-dĕ-läs-vĕ′gäs)	123a	22.58N	82.23W
Santiago del Estero, Arg.	132	27.50S	64.14W
Santiago del Estero, prov., Arg. (săn-tē-à′gō-dĕl ĕs-tā-rō)	132	27.15S	63.30W
Santiago de los Cabelleros, Dom. Rep.	117	19.30N	70.45W
Santiago Mountains, mts., Tx., U.S. (săn-tē-ä′gô)	96	30.00N	103.30W
Santiago Reservoir, res., Ca., U.S.	107a	33.47N	117.42W
Santiago Rodriguez, Dom. Rep. (săn-tyà′gô-rō-drē′gĕz)	123	19.30N	71.25W
Santiago Tepalcatlalpan, Mex.	233a	19.15N	99.08W
Santiago Tuxtla, Mex. (săn-tyà′gô-tōō′x-tlä)	119	18.28N	95.18W
Santiaguillo, Laguna de, l., Mex. (lä-oō′nä-dĕ-săn-tē-a-gēl′yô)	112	24.51N	104.43W
Santissimo, neigh., Braz.	234c	22.53S	43.31W
Santisteban del Puerto, Spain (săn′tē stá-bän′dĕl pwĕr′tô)	158	38.15N	3.12W
Santo Amaro, Braz. (săn′tô ä-mä′rô)	131	12.32S	38.33W
Santo Amaro, neigh., Braz.	234d	23.39S	46.42W
Santo Amaro de Campos, Braz.	129a	22.01S	41.05W
Santo André, Braz.	129a	23.40S	46.31W
Santo Angelo, Braz. (săn-tô-ä′n-zhĕ-lô)	132	28.16S	53.59W
Santo Antônio do Monte, Braz. (săn-tô-än-tô′nyô-dô-môn-tĕ)	129a	20.06S	45.18W
Santo Domingo, Cuba (săn′tô-dōmīŋ′gô)	122	22.35N	80.20W
Santo Domingo, Dom. Rep. (săn′tô dô-mĭn′gô)	117	18.30N	69.55W
Santo Domingo, Nic. (săn-tô-dô-mē′n-gō)	121	12.15N	84.56W
Santo Domingo de la Caizada, Spain (dā lä käl-thä′dä)	158	42.27N	2.55W
Santoña, Spain (săn-tō′nyä)	158	43.25N	3.27W
Sant' Onofrio, neigh., Italy	239c	41.56N	12.25E
Santos, Braz. (săn′tozh)	131	23.58S	46.20W
Santos Dumont, Braz. (săn′tôs-dô-mô′nt)	131	21.28S	43.33W
Sanuki, Japan (sä′nōō-kē)	195a	35.16N	139.53E
San Urbano, Arg. (săn-ōr-bä′nô)	129c	33.39S	61.28W
San Valentin, Monte, mtn., Chile (săn-vä-lĕn-tē′n)	132	46.41S	73.30W
San Vicente, Arg. (săn-vē-sĕn′tĕ)	129c	35.00S	58.26W
San Vicente, Chile	129b	34.25S	71.06W
San Vicente, El Sal. (săn vē-sĕn′tá)	120	13.41N	88.43W
San Vicente de Alcántara, Spain	158	39.24N	7.08W
San Vicente dels Horts, Spain	238e	41.24N	2.01E
San Vito al Tagliamento, Italy (san vē′tô)	160	45.53N	12.52E
San Xavier Indian Reservation, I.R., Az., U.S. (x-ā′vī-ĕr)	109	32.07N	111.12W
San Ysidro, Ca., U.S. (săn ysĭ-drō′)	108a	32.33N	117.02W
Sanyuanli, China (săn-yüän-lē)	191a	23.11N	113.16E
São Bernardo do Campo, Braz. (souN-bĕr-nár′dô-dô-kä′m-pô)	129a	23.44S	46.33W
São Borja, Braz. (souN-bôr-zhä)	132	28.44S	55.59W
São Caetano do Sul, Braz.	234d	23.37S	46.34W
São Carlos, Braz. (souN kär′lōzh)	131	22.02S	47.54W
São Cristovão, Braz. (souN-krĕs-tō-vouN)	131	11.04S	37.11W
São Cristóvão, neigh., Braz.	234c	22.54S	43.14W
São Fidélis, Braz. (souN-fē-dĕ′lēs)	129a	21.41S	41.45W
São Francisco, Braz. (souN fräN-sĕsh′kô)	131	15.59S	44.42W
São Francisco, Rio, r., Braz. (rē′ō-săn-frăn-sē′s-kō)	131	8.56S	40.20W
São Francisco do Sul, Braz. (souN fräN-sĕsh′kô-dô-sōō′l)	132	26.15S	48.42W
São Gabriel, Braz. (souN′gä-brē-ĕl′)	132	30.28S	54.11W
São Geraldo, Braz. (souN-zhĕ-rä′l-dô)	129a	21.01S	42.49W
São Gonçalo, Braz. (souN′gōŋ-sä′lô)	129a	22.55S	43.04W
Sao Hill, Tan.	217	8.20S	35.12E
São João, Gui.-B.	214	11.32N	15.26W
São João da Barra, Braz. (souN-zhôuN-dä-bà′rä)	129a	21.40S	41.03W
São João da Boa Vista, Braz. (souN-zhôuN-dä-bôä-vē′s-tä)	129a	21.58S	46.45W
São João del Rei, Braz. (souN zhô-ouN′dĕl-rā)	132	21.08S	44.14W
São João de Meriti, Braz. (souN-zhôuN-dĕ-mĕ-rē-tē)	132b	22.47S	43.22W
São João do Araguaia, Braz. (souN zhô-ouN′dô-ä-rä-gwä′yä)	131	5.29S	48.44W
São João dos Lampas, Port. (souN′ zhô-ouN′ dōzh län-päzh′)	159b	38.52N	9.24W
São João Nepomuceno, Braz. (souN-zhôuN-nĕ-pô-mōō-sĕ-nō)	129a	21.33S	43.00W
São Jorge Island, i., Port. (souN zhôr′zhĕ)	210a	38.28N	27.34W
São José do Rio Pardo, Braz. (souN-zhô-sĕ′dô-rē′ō-pá′r-dō)	129a	21.36S	46.50W
São José do Rio Prêto, Braz. (souN zhô-zĕ′dô-rē′ō-prē-tō)	131	20.57S	49.12W
São José dos Campos, Braz. (souN zhô-zā′dōzh käN pōzh′)	129a	23.12S	45.53W
São Julião da Barra, Port.	238d	38.40N	9.21W
São Leopoldo, Braz. (souN-lĕ-ô-pôl′dô)	132	29.46S	51.09W
São Luis, Braz.	131	2.31S	43.14W
São Luis do Paraitinga, Braz. (souN-lōōē′s-dô-pä-rä-ē-tē′n-gä)	129a	23.15S	45.18W
São Manuel, r., Braz.	131	8.28S	57.07E
São Mateus, Braz. (souN mä-tā′ōzh)	131	18.44S	39.45W
São Mateus, Braz.	132b	22.49S	43.23W
São Miguel Arcanjo, Braz. (souN-mē-gĕ′l-ár-kän-zhō)	129a	23.54S	47.59W
São Miguel Island, i., Port.	210a	37.59N	26.38W
Saona, i., Dom. Rep. (sä-ō′nä)	123	18.10N	68.55W
Saône, r., Fr. (sōn)	142	47.00N	5.30E
São Nicolau, i., C.V. (souN′ nĕ-kô-louN′)	210b	16.19N	25.19W
São Paulo, Braz. (souN′ pou′lô)	131	23.34S	46.38W
São Paulo, state, Braz. (souN pou′lô)	131	21.45S	50.47W
São Paulo de Olivença, Braz. (souN′pou′lôdâ ô-lē-vĕn′sȧ)	130	3.32S	68.46W
São Pedro, Braz. (souN-pĕ′drô)	129a	22.34S	47.54W
São Pedro de Aldeia, Braz. (souN-pĕ′drô-dĕ-äl-dĕ′yä)	129a	22.50S	42.04W
São Pedro e São Paulo, Rocedos, rocks, Braz.	128	1.50N	30.00W

ng-sing; ŋ-baŋk; N-nasalized n; nŏd; cŏmmit; ōld; ôbey; ôrder; oi-boil; fōōd; ŏ-as oo in foot; ou-out; s-soft; sh-dish; th-thin; pūre; ûnite; ûrn; stŭd; circŭs; ü-as in French tu; ′-indeterminate vowel.

PLACE (Pronunciation)	PAGE	Lat. ° '	Long. ° '
São Raimundo Nonato, Braz.			
(soun' rī-mó'n-do nó-nä'tó)	131	9.09S	42.32W
São Roque, Braz. (soun' rō'kě)	129a	23.32S	47.08W
São Roque, Cabo de, c., Braz.			
(kä'bo-dě-soun' rō'kě)	131	5.06S	35.11W
São Sebastião, Braz.			
(soun så-bäs-tě-oun')	129a	23.48S	45.25W
São Sebastião, Ilha de, i., Braz.	129a	23.52S	45.22W
São Sebastião do Paraíso, Braz.	129a	20.54S	46.58W
São Simão, Braz. (soun-sě-moun')	129a	21.30S	47.33W
São Tiago, i., C.V. (soun tě-ä'gò)	210b	15.09N	24.45W
São Tomé, S. Tom./P.	210	0.20N	6.44E
Sao Tome and Principe, nation, Afr.			
(prěn'sě-pě)	210	1.00N	6.00E
Saoura, Oued, r., Alg.	210	29.39N	1.42W
São Vicente, Braz. (soun ve-se'n-tě)	131	23.57S	46.25W
São Vicente, i., C.V. (soun vě-sěn'tä)	210b	16.51N	24.35W
São Vicente, Cabo de, c., Port.			
(kä'bo-dě-sän-vě-sě'n-tě)	142	37.03N	9.31W
Sapele, Nig. (sä-pā'lā)	210	5.54N	5.41E
Sapitwa, mtn., Mwi.	217	15.58S	35.38E
Sapozhok, Russia (sä-pô-zhôk')	162	53.58N	40.44E
Sapporo, Japan (säp-pô'rô)	189	43.02N	141.29E
Sapronovo, Russia (säp-rô'nô-vô)	172b	55.13N	38.25E
Sapucaí, r., Braz. (sä-pōō-kä-ē')	129a	22.20S	45.53W
Sapucaia, Braz. (sä-pōō-kä'yä)	129a	22.01S	42.54W
Sapucaí Mirim, r., Braz.			
(sä-pōō-kä-ě'mē-rěn)	129a	21.06S	47.03W
Sapulpa, Ok., U.S. (så-pŭl'på)	111	36.01N	96.05W
Saqqez, Iran	185	36.14N	46.16E
Saquarema, Braz. (sä-kwä-rě-mä)	129a	22.56S	42.30W
Sara, Wa., U.S. (sā'rä)	106c	45.45N	122.42W
Sara, Bahr, r., Chad (bär)	211	8.19N	17.44E
Sarajevo, Bos. (sä-rä-yěv'ô) (sä-rä'ya-vô)	142	43.50N	18.26E
Sarakhs, Iran	185	36.32N	61.11E
Sarana, Russia (sä-rä'nä)	172a	56.31N	57.44E
Saranac Lake, N.Y., U.S.	99	44.20N	74.05W
Saranac Lake, l., N.Y., U.S.	99	44.15N	74.20W
Sarandí, Arg. (sä-rän'dě)	132a	34.41S	58.21W
Sarandi Grande, Ur. (sä-rän'dě-grän'dě)	129c	33.42S	56.21W
Saranley, Som.	218a	2.28N	42.15E
Saransk, Russia (så-ränsk')	164	54.10N	45.10E
Sarany, Russia (sä-rá'nĭ)	172a	58.33N	58.48E
Sara Peak, mtn., Nig.	215	9.37N	9.25E
Sarapul, Russia (sä-räpôl')	166	56.28N	53.50E
Sarasota, Fl., U.S. (săr-á-sōtá)	115a	27.27N	82.30W
Saratoga, Tx., U.S. (săr-á-tō'gá)	113	30.17N	94.31W
Saratoga, Wa., U.S.	106a	48.04N	122.29W
Saratoga Pass, Wa., U.S.	106a	48.09N	122.33W
Saratoga Springs, N.Y., U.S. (springz)	99	43.05N	74.50W
Saratov, Russia (så rä'tôf)	164	51.30N	45.30E
Saravane, Laos	193	15.48N	106.40E
Sarawak, hist. reg., Malay. (sá-rä'wäk)	196	2.30N	112.45E
Sárbogárd, Hung. (shär'bô-gärd)	155	46.53N	18.38E
Sarcee Indian Reserve, I.R., Can. (sär'sě)	83e	50.58N	114.23W
Sarcelles, Fr.	157b	49.00N	2.23E
Sardalas, Libya	210	25.59N	10.33E
Sardinia, i., Italy (sär-dĭn'ĭá)	142	40.08N	9.05E
Sardis, Ms., U.S. (sär'dĭs)	114	34.26N	89.55W
Sardis Lake, res., Ms., U.S.	114	34.27N	89.43W
Sargent, Ne., U.S. (sär'jěnt)	102	41.40N	99.38W
Sarh, Chad (är-chan-bô')	211	9.09N	18.23E
Sarikamis, Tur.	167	40.30N	42.40E
Sariñena, Spain (sä-rěn-yě'nä)	159	41.46N	0.11W
Sark, i., Guernsey (särk)	156	49.28N	2.22W
Şarköy, Tur. (shär'kû-ě)	161	40.39N	27.07E
Sarmiento, Monte, mtn., Chile			
(mó'n-tě-sär-myěn'tô)	132	54.28S	70.40W
Sarnia, Can. (sär'ně-á)	85	43.00N	82.25W
Sarno, Italy (sä'r-nô)	159c	40.35N	14.38E
Sarny, Ukr. (sär'ně)	167	51.17N	26.39E
Saronikós Kólpos, b., Grc.	161	37.51N	23.30E
Saros Körfezi, b., Tur. (sä'rôs)	161	40.30N	26.20E
Sárospatak, Hung. (shä'rôsh-pô'tôk)	155	48.19N	21.35E
Šar Planina, mts., Yugo. (shär plä'ně-na)	161	42.07N	21.54E
Sarpsborg, Nor. (särps'bôrg)	152	59.17N	11.07E
Sarratt, Eng., U.K.	235	51.41N	0.29W
Sarrebourg, Fr. (sär-bōōr')	157	48.44N	7.02E
Sarreguemines, Fr. (sär-gě-mēn')	147	49.06N	7.05E
Sarria, Spain (sär'ě-ä)	148	42.14N	7.17W
Sarstun, r., N.A. (särs-tōō'n)	120	15.50N	89.26W
Sartène, Fr. (sär-těn')	160	41.36N	8.59E
Sarthe, r., Fr. (särt)	147	47.44N	0.32W
Sartrouville, Fr.	237c	48.57N	2.10E
Şärur, Azer.	168	39.33N	44.58E
Sárvár, Hung. (shär'vär)	154	47.14N	16.55E
Sarych, Mys., c., Ukr. (mĭs sä-rěch')	167	44.25N	33.00E
Sary-Ishikotrau, Peski, des., Kyrg.			
(sä'rě ě' shěk-ō'trou)	169	46.12N	75.30E
Sarysu, r., Kaz. (sä'rě-sōō)	169	47.47N	69.14E
Sasarām, India (sŭs-ü-räm')	183	25.00N	84.00E
Sasayama, Japan (sä'sä-yä'mä)	195	35.05N	135.14E
Sasebo, Japan (sä'sä-bô)	189	33.12N	129.43E
Sashalom, neigh., Hung.	239g	47.31N	19.11E
Saskatchewan, prov., Can.	84	54.46N	107.40W
Saskatchewan, r., Can.	84	53.45N	103.20W
Saskatoon, Can. (säs-ká-tōōn')	84	52.07N	106.38W
Sasolburg, S. Afr.	218d	26.52S	27.47E
Sasovo, Russia (sás'ô-vô)	166	54.20N	42.00E
Saspamco, Tx., U.S. (säs-păm'cō)	107d	29.13N	98.18W
Sassafras, Austl.	243b	37.52S	145.21E
Sassandra, C. Iv.	214	4.58N	6.05W
Sassandra, r., C. Iv. (säs-sän'drá)	210	5.35N	6.25W
Sassari, Italy (säs'sä-rě)	148	40.44N	8.33E
Sassnitz, Ger. (säs'něts)	154	54.31N	13.37E
Satadougou, Mali (sä-tá-dōō-goò')	214	12.21N	12.07W
Säter, Swe. (sě'těr)	152	60.21N	15.50E
Sätghara, India	240a	22.44N	88.21E
Satilla, r., Ga., U.S. (sá-tĭl'á)	115	31.15N	82.13W
Satka, Russia (sät'ká)	166	55.03N	59.02E
Sátoraljaujhely, Hung.			
(shä'tô-rô-lyô-ōō'yěl')	155	48.24N	21.40E
Satu Mare, Rom. (sá'tōō-mä'rě)	149	47.50N	22.53E
Saturna, Can. (sä-tûr'ná)	106d	48.48N	123.12W
Saturna, i., Can.	106d	48.47N	123.03W
Sauda, Nor.	146	59.40N	6.21E
Saudi Arabia, nation, Asia			
(sá-ō'dǐ á-rä'bǐ-á)	182	22.40N	46.00E
Sauerlach, Ger. (zou'ěr-läk)	145d	47.58N	11.39E
Saugatuck, Mi., U.S. (sô'gá-tŭk)	98	42.40N	86.10W
Saugeen, r., Can.	90	44.20N	81.20W
Saugerties, N.Y., U.S. (sô'gěr-tēz)	99	42.05N	73.55W
Saugus, Ma., U.S. (sô'gŭs)	93a	42.28N	71.01W
Sauk, r., Mn., U.S. (sôk)	103	45.30N	94.45W
Sauk Centre, Mn., U.S.	103	45.43N	94.58W
Sauk Rapids, Mn., U.S. (răp'ĭd)	103	45.35N	94.08W
Sault Sainte Marie, Can.	85	46.31N	84.20W
Sault Sainte Marie, Mi., U.S.			
(sōō sånt má-rē')	97	46.29N	84.21W
Saumatre, Étang, l., Haiti	123	18.40N	72.10W
Saunders Lake, l., Can. (sän'děrs)	83g	53.18N	113.25W
Saurimo, Ang.	212	9.39S	20.24E
Sausalito, Ca., U.S. (sô-sá-lē'tô)	106b	37.51N	122.29W
Sausset-les-Pins, Fr. (sō-sě'lä-pàn')	156a	43.20N	5.08E
Saútar, Ang.	216	11.06S	18.27E
Sauvie Island, i., Or., U.S. (sô'vē)	106c	45.43N	123.49W
Sava, r., Yugo. (sä'vä)	142	44.50N	18.30E
Savage, Md., U.S. (sá'věj)	100e	39.07N	76.49W
Savage, Mn., U.S.	107g	44.47N	93.20W
Savai'i, i., W. Sam.	198a	13.35S	172.25W
Savalen, l., Nor.	152	62.19N	10.15E
Savalou, Benin	210	7.56N	1.58E
Savanna, Il., U.S. (sá-vän'á)	103	42.05N	90.09W
Savannah, Ga., U.S. (sá-vän'á)	97	32.04N	81.07W
Savannah, Mo., U.S.	111	39.58N	94.49W
Savannah, Tn., U.S.	114	35.13N	88.14W
Savannah, r., U.S.	97	33.11N	81.51W
Savannakhét, Laos	196	16.33N	104.45E
Savanna la Mar, Jam. (sá-vän'á lá mär')	122	18.10N	78.10W
Save, r., Fr.	156	43.32N	0.50E
Save, Rio (Sabi), r., Afr. (rě'ō-sä'vě)	212	21.28S	34.14E
Sáveh, Iran	185	35.01N	50.20E
Saverne, Fr. (sá-věrn')	157	48.40N	7.22E
Savigliano, Italy (sä-vēl-yä'nô)	160	44.38N	7.42E
Savigny-sur-Orge, Fr.	157b	48.41N	2.22E
Savona, Italy (sä-nō'nä)	148	44.19N	8.28E
Savonlinna, Fin. (sä'vôn-lěn'ná)	153	61.53N	28.49E
Savran', Ukr. (säv-rän')	163	48.07N	30.09E
Sawahlunto, Indon.	196	0.37S	100.50E
Sawākin, Sudan	211	19.02N	37.19E
Sawda, Jabal as, mts., Libya	211	28.14N	13.46E
Sawhāj, Egypt	211	26.34N	31.40E
Sawknah, Libya	211	29.04N	15.53E
Sawu, Laut (Savu Sea), sea, Indon.	196	9.15S	122.15E
Sawyer, l., Wa., U.S. (sô'yěr)	106a	47.20N	122.02W
Saxony see Sachsen, hist. reg., Ger.	154	50.45N	12.17E
Say, Niger (sä'yer)	210	13.09N	2.16E
Sayan Khrebet, mts., Russia (sŭ-yän')	165	51.30N	90.00E
Sayhūt, Yemen	182	15.23N	51.28E
Sayre, Ok., U.S. (sā'ěr)	110	35.19N	99.40W
Sayre, Pa., U.S.	99	41.55N	76.30W
Sayreton, Al., U.S. (sä'ěr-tŭn)	100h	33.34N	86.51W
Sayreville, N.J., U.S. (sâr'vĭl)	100a	40.28N	74.21W
Sayr Usa, Mong.	188	44.15N	107.00E
Sayula, Mex.	118	19.50N	103.33W
Sayula, Mex. (sä-yōō'lä)	119	17.51N	94.56W
Sayula, Laguna de, l., Mex. (lä-gó'nä-dě)	118	20.00N	103.33W
Say'un, Yemen	182	16.00N	48.59E
Sayville, N.Y., U.S. (sā'vĭl)	99	40.45N	73.10W
Sazanit, i., Alb.	149	40.30N	19.17E
Sázava, r., Czech Rep.	154	49.36N	15.24E
Sazhino, Russia (säz-hě'nô)	172a	56.20N	58.15E
Scala, Teatro alla, bldg., Italy	238c	45.28N	9.11E
Scandinavian Peninsula, pen., Eur.	180	62.00N	14.00E
Scanlon, Mn., U.S. (skän'lôn)	107h	46.27N	92.26W
Scappoose, Or., U.S. (skä-pōōs')	106c	45.46N	122.53W
Scappoose, r., Or., U.S.	106c	45.47N	122.57W
Scarborough, Can. (skär'běr-ô)	91	43.45N	79.12W
Scarborough, Eng., U.K. (skär'bŭr-ô)	150	54.16N	0.19W
Scarsdale, N.Y., U.S. (skärz'dál)	100a	41.01N	73.47W
Scarth Hill, Eng., U.K.	237a	53.33N	2.52W
Scatari I, Can. (skät'á-rē)	93	46.00N	59.44W
Sceaux, Fr.	237c	48.47N	2.17E
Schaerbeek, Bel. (skär'bäk)	145a	50.50N	4.23E
Schaffhausen, Switz. (shäf'hou-zěn)	147	47.42N	8.38E
Schalksmühle, Ger.	236	51.14N	7.31E
Schapenrust, S. Afr.	244b	26.16S	28.22E
Scharnhorst, neigh., Ger.	236	51.32N	7.32E
Schefferville, Can.	85	54.52N	67.01W
Scheiblingstein, Aus.	239e	48.16N	16.13E
Schelde, r., Eur.	151	51.04N	3.55E
Schenectady, N.Y., U.S. (skě-někt'tá-dē)	97	42.50N	73.55W
Scheveningen, Neth.	145a	52.06N	4.15E
Schiedam, Neth.	145a	51.55N	4.23E
Schildow, Ger.	238a	52.38N	13.23E
Schiller Park, Il., U.S.	231a	41.58N	87.52W
Schiltigheim, Fr. (shěl'tegh-hīm)	157	48.48N	7.47E
Schio, Italy (skě'ō)	160	45.43N	11.23E
Schleswig, Ger. (shěls'věgh)	146	54.32N	9.32E
Schleswig-Holstein, hist. reg., Ger.			
(shlěs'věgh-hōl'shtīn)	154	54.40N	9.10E
Schmalkalden, Ger. (shmäl'käl-děn)	154	50.41N	10.25E
Schneider, In., U.S. (schnīd'ěr)	101a	41.12N	87.26W
Schofield, Wi., U.S. (skō'fěld)	103	44.52N	89.37W
Schöller, Ger.	236	51.14N	7.01E
Scholven, neigh., Ger.	236	51.36N	7.01E
Schönbrunn, Schloss, pt. of i., Aus.	239e	48.11N	16.19E
Schönebeck, Ger. (shû'ně-bergh)	154	52.01N	11.44E
Schönebeck, neigh., Ger.	236	51.28N	6.56E
Schöneberg, neigh., Ger.	238a	52.29N	13.21E
Schönefeld, Ger.	238a	52.23N	13.30E
Schöneiche, Ger.	238a	52.28N	13.41E
Schönerlinde, Ger.	238a	52.39N	13.27E
Schonnebeck, neigh., Ger.	236	51.29N	7.04E
Schönow, Ger.	238a	52.40N	13.32E
Schönwalde, Ger.	238a	52.37N	13.07E
Schoonhoven, Neth.	145a	51.56N	4.51E
Schramberg, Ger. (shräm'běrgh)	154	48.14N	8.24E
Schreiber, Can.	90	48.50N	87.10W
Schroon, l., N.Y., U.S. (skrōōn)	99	43.50N	73.50W
Schultzendorf, Ger. (shōōl'tzěn-dörf)	145b	52.21N	13.55E
Schumacher, Can.	90	48.30N	81.30W
Schüren, neigh., Ger.	236	51.30N	7.32E
Schuyler, Ne., U.S. (slī'ler)	102	41.28N	97.05W
Schuylkill, r., Pa., U.S. (skōōl'kil)	100f	40.10N	75.31W
Schuylkill-Haven, Pa., U.S.			
(skōōl'kil hä-věn)	99	40.35N	76.10W
Schwabach, Ger. (shvä'bäk)	154	49.19N	11.02E
Schwäbische Alb, mts., Ger.			
(shvä'bě-shě älb)	154	48.11N	9.09E
Schwäbisch Gmünd, Ger.			
(shvä'běsh gmünd)	154	48.47N	9.49E
Schwäbisch Hall, Ger. (häl)	154	49.08N	9.44E
Schwafheim, Ger.	236	51.25N	6.39E
Schwandorf, Ger. (shvän'dörf)	154	49.19N	12.08E
Schwanebeck, Ger.	238a	52.37N	13.32E
Schwanewerder, neigh., Ger.	238a	52.27N	13.10E
Schwaner, Pegunungan, mts., Indon.			
(skvän'ěr)	196	1.05S	112.30E
Schwarzenberg, Ger.	236	51.24N	6.42E
Schwarzwald, for., Ger. (shvärts'väld)	154	47.54N	7.57E
Schwaz, Aus.	154	47.20N	11.45E
Schwechat, Aus. (shvěk'át)	154	48.09N	16.29E
Schwedt, Ger. (shvět)	154	53.04N	14.17E
Schweflinghausen, Ger.	236	51.16N	7.25E
Schweinfurt, Ger. (shvīn'fôrt)	154	50.03N	10.14E
Schwelm, Ger. (shvělm)	157c	51.17N	7.18E
Schwenke, Ger.	236	51.11N	7.26E
Schwerin, Ger. (shvě-rēn')	154	53.36N	11.25E
Schwerin, neigh., Ger.	236	51.33N	7.20E
Schweriner See, l., Ger. (shvě'rě-něr zä)	154	53.40N	11.06E
Schwerte, Ger. (shvěr'tě)	157c	51.26N	7.34E
Schwielowsee, l., Ger. (shvě'lōv zä)	145b	52.20N	12.52E
Schwyz, Switz. (shěts)	154	47.01N	8.38E
Sciacca, Italy (shě-äk'kä)	160	37.30N	13.09E
Science and Industry, Museum of, pt. of i.,			
Il., U.S.	231a	41.47N	87.35W
Scilly, Isles of, is., Eng., U.K. (sil'ě)	142	49.56N	6.50W
Scioto, r., Oh., U.S. (sī-ō'tō)	97	39.10N	82.55W
Scituate, Ma., U.S. (sĭt'ū-āt)	93a	42.12N	70.45W
Scobey, Mt., U.S. (skō'bē)	105	48.48N	105.29W
Scoggin, Or., U.S. (skō'gǐn)	106c	45.28N	123.14W
Scoresby, Austl.	243b	37.54S	145.14E
Scotch, r., Can. (skŏch)	83c	45.21N	74.56W
Scotia, Can., U.S. (skō'shá)	104	40.29N	124.06W
Scotland, S.D., U.S.	102	43.08N	97.43W
Scotland, U.K. (skŏt'lánd)	142	57.05N	5.10W
Scotland Neck, N.C., U.S. (něk)	115	36.06N	77.25W
Scotstown, Can. (skŏts'toun)	99	45.35N	71.15W
Scott, r., Ca., U.S.	104	41.20N	122.55W
Scott, Cape, c., Can. (skŏt)	84	50.47N	128.26W
Scott, Mount, mtn., Or., U.S.	104	42.55N	122.00W
Scott, Mount, mtn., Or., U.S.	106c	45.27N	122.33W
Scott Air Force Base, Il., U.S.	107e	38.33N	89.52W
Scottburgh, S. Afr. (skŏt'bŭr-ô)	212	30.18S	30.42E
Scott City, Ks., U.S.	110	38.28N	100.54W
Scottdale, Ga., U.S. (skŏt'dál)	100c	33.47N	84.16W
Scott Islands, is., Ant.	219	67.00S	178.00E
Scottsbluff, Ne., U.S. (skŏts'blŭf)	102	41.52N	103.40W
Scottsboro, Al., U.S. (skŏts'būro)	114	34.40N	86.03W
Scottsburg, In., U.S. (skŏts'bûrg)	98	38.40N	85.50W
Scottsdale, Austl. (skŏts'dál)	204	41.12S	147.37E
Scottsville, Ky., U.S.	114	36.45N	86.10W
Scott Township, Pa., U.S.	230b	40.24N	80.06W
Scottville, Mi., U.S.	98	44.00N	86.20W
Scranton, Pa., U.S. (skrăn'tǔn)	97	41.15N	75.45W
Scugog, l., Can. (skū'gŏg)	91	44.05N	78.55W
Scunthorpe, Eng., U.K. (skŭn'thôrp)	144a	53.36N	0.38W
Scutari see Shkodër, Alb.	142	42.04N	19.30E
Scutari, Lake, l., Eur. (skōō'tä-rě)	149	42.14N	19.33E
Seabeck, Wa., U.S. (sē'běck)	106a	47.38N	122.50W
Sea Bright, N.J., U.S. (sē brīt)	100a	40.22N	73.58W
Seabrook, Md., U.S.	229d	38.58N	76.51W
Seabrook, Tx., U.S. (sē'brók)	113	29.34N	95.01W
Sea Cliff, N.Y., U.S.	228	40.51N	73.38W
Seacombe, Eng., U.K.	237a	53.25N	3.01W
Seaford, De., U.S. (sē'fěrd)	99	38.35N	75.40W
Seaford, Eng., U.K.	235	50.46N	0.06E
Seaforth, Austl.	243a	33.48S	151.15E
Seaforth, Eng., U.K.	237a	53.28N	3.01W
Seagraves, Tx., U.S. (sē'grāvs)	110	32.51N	102.38W
Sea Islands, is., Ga., U.S. (sē)	115	31.21N	81.05W
Seal, Eng., U.K.	235	51.17N	0.14E

PLACE (Pronunciation)	PAGE	Lat. °′	Long. °′
Seal, r., Can.	84	59.08N	96.37W
Seal Beach, Ca., U.S.	107a	33.44N	118.06W
Seal Cays, is., Bah.	123	22.40N	75.55W
Seal Cays, is., T./C. Is.	123	21.10N	71.45W
Seal Island, i., S. Afr. (sēl)	212a	34.07S	18.36E
Seal Rocks, Ca., U.S.	231b	37.47N	122.31W
Sealy, Tx., U.S. (sē'lē)	113	29.46N	96.10W
Searcy, Ar., U.S. (sûr'sē)	111	35.13N	91.43W
Searles, l., Ca., U.S. (sûrl's)	108	35.44N	117.22W
Searsport, Me., U.S. (sērz'pōrt)	92	44.28N	68.55W
Seaside, Or., U.S. (sē'sīd)	104	45.59N	123.55W
Seat Pleasant, Md., U.S.	229d	38.53N	76.52W
Seattle, Wa., U.S. (sē-ăt''l)	96	47.36N	122.20W
Sebaco, Nic. (sē-bä'kō)	120	12.50N	86.03W
Sebago, Me., U.S. (sē-bā'gō)	92	43.52N	70.20W
Sebastián Vizcaíno, Bahía, b., Mex.	116	28.45N	115.15W
Sebastopol, Ca., U.S. (sē-bás'tō-pōl)	108	38.27N	122.50W
Sebderat, Erit.	211	15.30N	36.45E
Sebewaing, Mi., U.S. (se'bē-wăng)	98	43.45N	83.25W
Sebezh, Russia (syĕ'bĕzh)	162	56.16N	28.29E
Sebinkarahisar, Tur.	149	40.15N	38.10E
Sebnitz, Ger. (zĕb'nēts)	154	51.01N	14.16E
Sebou, Oued, r., Mor.	210	34.23N	5.18W
Sebree, Ky., U.S. (sē-brē')	98	37.35N	87.30W
Sebring, Fl., U.S. (sē'brĭng)	115a	27.30N	81.26W
Sebring, Oh., U.S.	98	40.55N	81.05W
Secane, Pa., U.S.	229b	39.55N	75.18W
Secaucus, N.J., U.S.	228	40.47N	74.04W
Secchia, r., Italy (sĕ'kyä)	160	44.25N	10.25E
Seco, r., Mex. (sĕ'kō)	119	18.11N	93.18W
Sedalia, Mo., U.S.	97	38.42N	93.12W
Sedan, Fr. (sē-däN)	147	49.49N	4.55E
Sedan, Ks., U.S. (sē-dăn')	111	37.07N	96.08W
Sedom, Isr.	181a	31.04N	35.24E
Sedro Woolley, Wa., U.S. (sē'drō-wŏol'ē)	106a	48.30N	122.14W
Šeduva, Lith. (shĕ'dō-vá)	153	55.46N	23.45E
Seeberg, Ger.	238a	52.33N	13.41E
Seeburg, Ger.	238a	52.31N	13.07E
Seefeld, Ger.	238a	52.37N	13.40E
Seer Green, Eng., U.K.	235	51.37N	0.36W
Seestall, Ger. (zā'shtäl)	145d	47.58N	10.52E
Sefrou, Mor. (sē-frōō')	148	33.49N	4.46W
Sefton, Eng., U.K.	237a	53.30N	2.58W
Seg, l., Russia (syĕgh)	166	63.20N	33.30E
Segamat, Malay. (sā'gá-mát)	181b	2.30N	102.49E
Segang, China (sŭ-gäŋ)	190	31.59N	114.13E
Segbana, Benin	215	10.56N	3.42E
Segorbe, Spain (sĕ-gôr-bē)	159	39.50N	0.30W
Ségou, Mali (sā-gōō')	210	13.27N	6.16W
Segovia, Col. (sĕ-gō'vēä)	130a	7.08N	74.42W
Segovia, Spain (så-gō'vē-ä)	148	40.58N	4.05W
Segre, r., Spain (så'grä)	159	41.54N	1.10E
Seguam, i., Ak., U.S. (sē'gwäm)	95a	52.16N	172.10W
Seguam Passage, strt., Ak., U.S.	95a	52.20N	173.00W
Séguédine, Niger	215	20.12N	12.59E
Séguéla, C. Iv. (sā-gā-lä')	210	7.57N	6.40W
Seguin, Tx., U.S. (sĕ-gēn')	113	29.35N	97.58W
Segula, i., Ak., U.S. (sē-gū'lá)	95a	52.08N	178.35E
Segura, r., Spain	148	38.24N	2.12W
Segura, Sierra de, mts., Spain (sē-ĕ'r-rä-dĕ)	158	38.05N	2.45W
Sehwān, Pak.	186	26.33N	67.51E
Seibeeshiden, Japan	242a	35.34N	139.22E
Seibo, Dom. Rep. (sĕ'y-bō)	123	18.45N	69.05W
Seiling, Ok., U.S.	110	36.09N	98.56W
Seinäjoki, Fin. (så'ē-nē-yō'kē)	153	62.47N	22.50E
Seine, r., Can. (sān)	83f	49.48N	97.03W
Seine, r., Can. (sān)	90	49.04N	91.00W
Seine, r., Fr.	142	48.00N	4.30E
Seine, Baie de la, b., Fr. (bī dĕ lä sån)	156	49.37N	0.53W
Seio do Venus, mtn., Braz. (sē-yō-dō-vē'nōōs)	132b	22.28S	43.12W
Seixal, Port. (så-ē-shäl')	159b	38.38N	9.06W
Sekenke, Tan.	217	4.16S	34.10E
Şeki, Azer.	168	41.12N	47.12E
Sekondi-Takoradi, Ghana (sĕ-kōn'dē tä-kō-rä'dē)	210	4.59N	1.43W
Sekota, Eth.	211	12.47N	38.59E
Selangor, state, Malay. (så-län'gōr)	181b	2.53N	101.29E
Selanovtsi, Bul. (sål'á-nôv-tsĭ)	161	43.42N	24.05E
Selaru, Pulau, i., Indon.	197	8.30S	130.30E
Selatan, Tanjung, c., Indon. (så-lä'tän)	196	4.09S	114.40E
Selawik, Ak., U.S. (sē-lá-wĭk)	95	66.30N	160.09W
Selayar, Pulau, i., Indon.	196	6.15S	121.15E
Selbecke, neigh., Ger.	236	51.20N	7.28E
Selbusjøen, l., Nor. (sĕl'bōō)	152	63.18N	11.55E
Selby, Eng., U.K. (sĕl'bē)	144a	53.47N	1.03W
Selby, neigh., S. Afr.	244b	26.13S	28.02E
Seldovia, Ak., U.S. (sĕl-dō'vē-ȧ)	95	59.26N	151.42W
Selection Park, S. Afr.	244b	26.18S	28.27E
Selemdzha, r., Russia (sâ-lĕmt-zhä')	171	52.28N	131.50E
Selenga (Selenge), r., Asia (sĕ lĕŋ gä')	165	49.00N	102.00E
Selenge, r., Asia	188	49.04N	102.23E
Selennyakh, r., Russia (sĕl-yĭn-yäk)	171	67.42N	141.45E
Sélestat, Fr. (sĕ-lĕ-stä')	157	48.16N	7.27E
Seletar, Sing.	240c	1.25N	103.53E
Sélibaby, Maur. (så-lē-bá-bē')	210	15.21N	12.11W
Seliger, l., Russia (sĕl'lē-gĕr)	166	57.14N	33.18E
Selizharovo, Russia (så'lē-zhä'rō-vō)	162	56.51N	33.28E
Selkirk, Can. (sĕl'kûrk)	84	50.09N	96.52W
Selkirk Mountains, mts., Can.	84	51.00N	117.40W
Selleck, Wa., U.S. (sĕl'ĕck)	106a	47.22N	121.52W
Sellersburg, In., U.S. (sĕl'ērs-bûrg)	101h	38.25N	85.45W
Sellya Khskaya, Guba, b., Russia (sĕl-yäk'skȧ-yȧ)	171	72.30N	136.00E
Selma, Al., U.S. (sĕl'mȧ)	97	32.25N	87.00W
Selma, Ca., U.S.	108	36.34N	119.37W
Selma, N.C., U.S.	115	35.33N	78.16W
Selma, Tx., U.S.	107d	29.33N	98.19W
Selmer, Tn., U.S.	114	35.11N	88.36W
Selsingen, Ger. (zĕl'zēn-gĕn)	145c	53.22N	9.13E
Selway, r., Id., U.S. (sĕl'wā)	104	46.07N	115.12W
Selwyn, l., Can. (sĕl'wĭn)	84	59.41N	104.30W
Seman, r., Alb.	161	40.48N	19.53E
Semarang, Indon. (sĕ-mä'räng)	196	7.03S	110.27E
Sembawang, Sing.	240c	1.27N	103.50E
Semenivka, Ukr.	167	52.10N	32.34E
Semeru, Gunung, mtn., Indon.	196	8.06S	112.55E
Semey (Semipalatinsk), Kaz.	169	50.28N	80.29E
Semiahmoo Indian Reserve, I.R., Can.	106d	49.01N	122.43W
Semiahmoo Spit, Wa., U.S. (sĕm'ĭ-â-mōō)	106d	48.59N	122.52W
Semichi Islands, is., Ak., U.S. (sē-mē'chī)	95a	52.40N	174.50E
Seminoe Reservoir, res., Wy., U.S. (sĕm'ĭ nō)	105	42.08N	107.10W
Seminole, Ok., U.S. (sĕm'ĭ-nōl)	111	35.13N	96.41W
Seminole, Tx., U.S.	112	32.43N	102.39W
Seminole, Lake, res., U.S.	114	30.57N	84.46W
Semisopochnoi, i., Ak., U.S. (sĕ-mē-sá-pōsh' noi)	95a	51.45N	179.25E
Semliki, r., Afr. (sĕm'lē-kē)	211	0.45N	29.36E
Semmering Pass, p., Aus. (sĕm'ĕr-ĭng)	154	47.39N	15.50E
Senador Pompeu, Braz. (sĕ-nä-dōr-pôm-pĕ'ō)	131	5.34S	39.18W
Senaki, Geor.	168	42.17N	42.04E
Senatobia, Ms., U.S. (sĕ-ná-tō'bē-ȧ)	114	34.36N	89.56W
Send, Eng., U.K.	235	51.17N	0.31W
Sendai, Japan (sĕn-dī')	189	38.18N	141.02E
Seneca, Ks., U.S. (sĕn'ĕ-kȧ)	111	39.49N	96.03W
Seneca, Md., U.S.	100e	39.04N	77.20W
Seneca, S.C., U.S.	115	34.40N	82.58W
Seneca, l., N.Y., U.S.	99	42.30N	76.55W
Seneca Falls, N.Y., U.S.	99	42.55N	76.55W
Senegal, nation, Afr. (sĕn-ĕ-gôl')	210	14.53N	14.58W
Sénégal, r., Afr.	210	16.00N	14.00W
Senekal, S. Afr. (sĕn'ĕ-kȧl)	218d	28.20S	27.37E
Senftenberg, Ger. (zĕnf'tĕn-bĕrgh)	154	51.32N	14.00E
Sengunyane, r., Leso.	213c	29.35S	28.08E
Senhor do Bonfim, Braz. (sĕn-yôr dŏ bôN-fē'N)	131	10.21S	40.09W
Senigallia, Italy (sā-nē-gäl'lyä)	160	43.42N	13.16E
Senj, Cro. (sĕn')	160	44.58N	14.55E
Senja, i., Nor. (sĕnyä)	146	69.28N	16.10E
Senlis, Fr. (säN-lēs')	157b	49.13N	2.35E
Sennar Dam, dam, Sudan	211	13.38N	33.38E
Senneterre, Can.	85	48.20N	77.22W
Senno, Bela. (syĕ'nō)	162	54.48N	29.43E
Senriyama, Japan	242b	34.47N	135.30E
Sens, Fr. (säNs)	156	48.05N	3.18E
Sensuntepeque, El Sal. (sĕn-sōōn-tā-pā'kā)	120	13.53N	88.34W
Senta, Yugo. (sĕn'tä)	149	45.54N	20.05E
Sentosa, i., Sing.	240c	1.15N	103.50E
Senzaki, Japan (sĕn'zä-kē)	195	34.22N	131.09E
Seoul (Sŏul), S. Kor.	189	37.35N	127.03E
Sepang, Malay.	181b	2.43N	101.45E
Sepetiba, Baía de, b., Braz. (bäē'ä dĕ så-pā-tē'bȧ)	132b	23.01S	43.42W
Sepik, r. (sĕp-ĕk')	197	4.07S	142.40E
Septentrional, Cordillera, mts., Dom. Rep.	123	19.50N	71.15W
Septeuil, Fr. (sĕ-tû')	157b	48.53N	1.40E
Sept-Îles, Can. (sĕ-tēl')	92	50.12N	66.23W
Sequatchie, r., Tn., U.S. (sē-kwăch'ē)	114	35.33N	85.14W
Sequim, Wa., U.S. (sē'kwĭm)	106a	48.05N	123.07W
Sequim Bay, b., Wa., U.S.	106a	48.04N	122.58W
Sequoia National Park, rec., Ca., U.S. (sē-kwoi'ȧ)	96	36.34N	118.37W
Seraing, Bel. (sĕ-räN')	151	50.38N	5.28E
Serāmpore, India	186a	22.44N	88.21E
Serang, Indon. (så-räng')	196	6.13S	106.10E
Seranggung, Indon.	181b	0.49N	104.11E
Serangoon, Sing.	240c	1.22N	103.54E
Serangoon Harbour, b., Sing.	240c	1.23N	103.57E
Serbia *see* Srbija, hist. reg., Yugo.	161	44.05N	20.35E
Serdobsk, Russia (sĕr-dôpsk')	167	52.30N	44.20E
Serebr'anyj Bor, neigh., Russia	239b	55.47N	37.25E
Sered', Slvk.	155	48.17N	17.43E
Seredyna-Buda, Ukr.	162	52.11N	34.03E
Seremban, Malay. (sĕr-ĕm-băn')	181b	2.44N	101.57E
Serengeti National Park, rec., Tan.	217	2.20S	34.50E
Serengeti Plain, pl., Tan.	217	2.40S	34.55E
Serenje, Zam. (sē-rĕn'yē)	212	13.12S	30.49E
Seret, r., Ukr. (sĕr'ĕt)	155	49.45N	25.30E
Sergeya Kirova, i., Russia (sĕr-gyē'yȧ kē'rō-vȧ)	170	77.30N	86.10E
Sergipe, state, Braz. (sĕr-zhē'pĕ)	131	10.27S	37.04W
Sergiyev Posad, Russia	172b	56.18N	38.08E
Sergiyevsk, Russia	166	53.58N	51.00E
Sérifos, Grc.	161	37.10N	24.32E
Sérifos, i., Grc.	161	37.42N	24.17E
Serodino, Arg. (sĕ-rō-dē'nō)	129c	32.36S	60.56W
Seropédica, Braz. (sĕ-rō-pĕ'dē-kä)	132b	22.44S	43.43W
Serov, Russia (syĕ-rôf')	170	59.36N	60.30E
Serowe, Bots. (sĕ-rō'wĕ)	212	22.18S	26.39E
Serpa, Port. (sĕr-pä)	158	37.56N	7.38W
Serpukhov, Russia (syĕr'pō-kôf)	164	54.53N	37.27E
Sérrai, Grc. (sĕr'rĕ) (sĕr'ĕs)	149	41.06N	23.36E
Serrinha, Braz. (sĕr-rēn'yȧ)	131	11.43S	38.49W
Serta, Port. (sĕr'tȧ)	158	39.48N	8.01W
Sertânia, Braz. (sĕr-tá'nyä)	131	8.28S	37.13W
Sertãozinho, Braz. (sĕr-touN-zē'n-yō)	129a	21.10S	47.58W
Serting, r., Malay.	181b	3.01N	102.32E
Servon, Fr.	237c	48.43N	2.35E
Sese Islands, is., Ug.	217	0.30S	32.30E
Sesia, r., Italy (såz'yä)	160	45.33N	8.25E
Sesimbra, Port. (sĕ-sė'm-brä)	159b	38.27N	9.06W
Sesmyl, r., S. Afr.	213b	25.51S	28.06E
Sesto San Giovanni, Italy	238c	45.32N	9.14E
Sestri Levante, Italy (sĕs'trė lå-vän'tå)	160	44.15N	9.24E
Sestroretsk, Russia (sĕs-trô-rĕtsk)	166	60.06N	29.58E
Sestroretskiy Razliv, Ozero, l., Russia	172c	60.05N	30.07E
Seta, Japan (sĕ'tä)	195b	34.58N	135.56W
Setagaya, neigh., Japan	242a	35.39N	139.40E
Séte, Fr. (sĕt)	147	43.24N	3.42E
Sete Lagoas, Braz. (sĕ-tĕ lä-gô'äs)	131	19.23S	43.58W
Sete Pontes, Braz.	132b	22.51S	43.05W
Seto, Japan (sē'tō)	195	35.11N	137.07E
Seto-Naikai, sea, Japan (sĕ'tȯ nī'kī)	195	33.50N	132.25E
Seton Hall University, pt. of i., N.Y., U.S.	228	40.45N	74.15W
Settat, Mor. (sĕt-ät') (sĕ-tá')	210	33.02N	7.30W
Sette-Cama, Gabon (sĕ-tĕ-kä-mä')	212	2.29S	9.40E
Settecamini, neigh., Italy	239c	41.56N	12.37E
Settimo Milanese, Italy	238c	45.29N	9.03E
Settlement Point, c., Bah. (sĕt'l-mĕnt)	122	26.40N	79.00W
Settlers, S. Afr. (sĕt'lērs)	218d	24.57S	28.33E
Settsu, Japan	195b	34.46N	135.33E
Setúbal, Port. (så-tōō'bäl)	148	38.32N	8.54W
Setúbal, Baía de, b., Port.	158	38.27N	9.08W
Seul, Lac, l., Can. (lák sûl)	85	50.20N	92.30W
Sevan, l., Arm. (syĭ-vän')	167	40.10N	45.20E
Sevastopol', Ukr. (syĕ-vás-tô'pôl'')	164	44.34N	33.34E
Seven Hills, Austl.	243a	33.46S	150.57E
Seven Hills, Oh., U.S.	229a	41.22N	81.41W
Seven Kings, neigh., Eng., U.K.	235	51.34N	0.05E
Sevenoaks, Eng., U.K. (sĕ-vĕn-ōks')	144b	51.16N	0.12E
Severka, r., Russia (sâ'vĕr-kȧ)	172b	55.11N	38.41E
Severn, r., Can. (sĕv'ērn)	85	55.21N	88.42W
Severn, r., U.K.	150	51.50N	2.25W
Severna Park, Md., U.S. (sĕv'ērn-â)	100e	39.04N	76.33W
Severnaya Dvina, r., Russia	164	63.00N	42.40E
Severnaya Zemlya (Northern Land), is., Russia (sĕ-vyĭr-nīŭ zĭ-m'lyä')	165	79.33N	101.15E
Severoural'sk, Russia (sĕ-vyĭ-rŭ-ōō-rälsk')	170	60.08N	59.53E
Sevier, r., Ut., U.S.	96	39.25N	112.20W
Sevier, East Fork, r., Ut., U.S.	109	37.45N	112.10W
Sevier Lake, l., Ut., U.S. (sĕ-vēr')	109	38.55N	113.10W
Sevilla, Col. (sĕ-vē'l-yä)	130a	4.16N	75.56W
Sevilla, Spain (så-vēl'yä)	142	37.29N	5.58W
Seville, Oh., U.S. (sĕ'vĭl)	101d	41.01N	81.45W
Sevlievo, Bul. (sĕv'lyĕ-vō)	149	43.02N	25.05E
Sevran, Fr.	237c	48.56N	2.32E
Sèvres, Fr.	237c	48.49N	2.12E
Sevsk, Russia (syĕfsk)	162	52.08N	34.28E
Seward, Ak., U.S. (sū'ârd)	96a	60.18N	149.28W
Seward, Ne., U.S.	111	40.55N	97.06W
Seward Peninsula, pen., Ak., U.S.	95	65.40N	164.00W
Sewell, Chile (sĕ'ŏ-ĕl)	132	34.01S	70.18W
Sewickley, Pa., U.S. (sē-wĭk'lē)	101e	40.33N	80.11W
Seybaplaya, Mex. (sā-ē-bä-plä'yä)	119	19.38N	90.40W
Seychelles, nation, Afr. (sā-shĕl')	3	5.20S	55.10E
Seydisfjördur, Ice. (sā'dēs-fyûr-dŏr)	146	65.21N	14.08W
Seyhan, r., Tur.	149	37.28N	35.40E
Seylac, Som.	218a	11.19N	43.20E
Seym, r., Eur. (sĕym)	167	51.23N	33.22E
Seymour, S. Afr. (sē'môr)	213c	32.33S	26.48E
Seymour, In., U.S. (sē'mōr)	98	38.55N	85.55W
Seymour, Ia., U.S.	103	40.41N	93.03W
Seymour, Tx., U.S.	110	33.35N	99.16W
Sezela, S. Afr.	213c	30.33S	30.37W
Sezze, Italy (sĕt'sā)	160	41.32N	13.00E
Sfântu Gheorghe, Rom.	149	45.53N	25.49E
Sfax, Tun. (sfäks)	210	34.51N	10.45E
's-Gravenhage *see* The Hague, Neth. ('s krä'vĕn-hä'kē) (häg)	142	52.05N	4.16E
Sha, r., China (shä)	189	33.33N	114.30E
Shaanxi, prov., China (shän-shyē)	188	35.30N	109.10E
Shabeelle (Shebele), r., Afr.	218a	1.38N	43.50E
Shache, China (shä-chŭ)	188	38.15N	77.15E
Shackleton Ice Shelf, ice., Ant. (shăk''l-tŭn)	219	65.00S	100.00E
Shades Creek, r., Al., U.S. (shādz)	100h	33.20N	86.55W
Shades Mountain, mtn., Al., U.S.	100h	33.22N	86.51W
Shagamu, Nig.	215	6.51N	3.39E
Shāhdād, Namakzār-e, l., Iran (nŭ-mŭk-zär')	182	31.00N	58.30E
Shāhdara, neigh., India	240d	28.40N	77.18E
Shāhjahānpur, India (shä-jŭ-hän'pōōr)	183	27.58N	79.58E
Shah Mosque, rel., Iran	241h	35.40N	51.25E
Shajing, China (shä-jyĭŋ)	191a	22.44N	113.48E
Shakarpur Khās, neigh., India	240d	28.38N	77.17E
Shaker Heights, Oh., U.S. (shā'kēr)	101d	41.28N	81.34W
Shakhty, Russia (shäk'tē)	164	47.41N	40.11E
Shaki, Nig.	215	8.39N	3.25E
Shakopee, Mn., U.S. (shăk'ō-pe)	107g	44.48N	93.31W
Shakūrpur, neigh., India	240d	28.41N	77.09E
Shala Lake, l., Eth. (shä'lá)	211	7.34N	39.00E
Shalqar, Kaz.	169	47.52N	59.41E
Shalqar kölï, l., Kaz.	170	50.30N	51.30E
Shām, Jabal ash, mtn., Oman	182	23.01N	57.45E
Shambe, Sudan (shäm'bá)	211	7.08N	30.46E
Shammar, Jabal, mts., Sau. Ar. (jĕb'ĕl shŭm'âr)	182	27.13N	40.16E

PLACE (Pronunciation)	PAGE	Lat. °′	Long. °′
Shamokin, Pa., U.S. (shȧ-mō′kĭn) . . .	99	40.45N	76.30W
Shamrock, Tx., U.S. (shăm′rŏk)	110	35.14N	100.12W
Shamva, Zimb. (shäm′vȧ)	212	17.18S	31.35E
Shandon, Oh., U.S. (shăn-dŭn)	101f	39.20N	84.13W
Shandong, prov., China (shän-dôŋ) . .	189	36.08N	117.09E
Shandong Bandao, pen., China (shän-dôŋ bän-dou)	189	37.00N	120.10E
Shangcai, China (shäŋ-tsī)	190	33.16N	114.16E
Shangcheng, China (shäŋ-chŭŋ)	190	31.47N	115.22E
Shangdu, China (shäŋ-do͞o)	192	41.38N	113.22E
Shanghai, China (shăng′hī′)	189	31.14N	121.27E
Shanghai-Shi, prov., China (shäŋ-hī shr)	189	31.30N	121.45E
Shanghe, China (shäŋ-hŭ)	190	37.18N	117.10E
Shanglin, China (shäŋ-lĭn)	190	38.20N	116.05E
Shangqiu, China (shäŋ-chyō)	192	34.24N	115.39E
Shangrao, China (shäŋ-rou)	193	28.25N	117.58E
Shangzhi, China (shäŋ-jr)	192	45.18N	127.52E
Shanhaiguan, China	192	40.01N	119.45E
Shannon, Al., U.S. (shăn′ŭn)	100h	33.23N	86.52W
Shannon, r., Ire. (shăn′ŏn)	147	52.30N	10.15W
Shanshan, China (shän′shän′)	188	42.51N	89.53E
Shantar, i., Russia (shän′tär)	171	55.13N	138.42E
Shantou, China (shän-tō)	189	23.20N	116.40E
Shanxi, prov., China (shän-shyē)	189	37.30N	112.00E
Shan Xian, China (shän shyĕn)	190	34.47N	116.04E
Shaobo, China (shou-bwo)	192	32.33N	119.30E
Shaobo Hu, l., China (shou-bwo ho͞o)	190	32.47N	119.13E
Shaoguan, China (shou-gūän)	189	24.58N	113.42E
Shaoxing, China (shou-shyĭŋ)	189	30.00N	120.40E
Shaoyang, China	189	27.15N	111.28E
Shapki, Russia (shäp′kĭ)	172c	59.36N	31.11E
Shark Bay, b., Austl. (shärk)	202	25.30S	113.00E
Sharon, Ma., U.S. (shâr′ŏn)	93a	42.07N	71.11W
Sharon, Pa., U.S.	98	41.15N	80.30W
Sharon Hill, Pa., U.S.	229b	39.55N	75.16W
Sharon Springs, Ks., U.S.	110	38.51N	101.45W
Sharonville, Oh., U.S. (shăr′ŏn vĭl) . . .	101f	39.16N	84.24W
Sharpsburg, Pa., U.S. (shärps′bûrg) . .	101e	40.30N	79.54W
Sharps Hill, Pa., U.S.	230b	40.30N	79.56W
Sharr, Jabal, mtn., Sau. Ar.	182	28.00N	36.07E
Shashi, China (shä-shē)	189	30.20N	112.18E
Shasta, Mount, mtn., Ca., U.S.	96	41.35N	122.12W
Shasta Lake, res., Ca., U.S. (shăs′tȧ)	96	40.51N	122.32W
Shatsk, Russia (shȧtsk)	166	54.00N	41.40E
Shattuck, Ok., U.S. (shăt′ŭk)	110	36.16N	99.53W
Shaunavon, Can.	84	49.40N	108.25W
Shaw, Eng., U.K.	237b	53.35N	2.06W
Shaw, Ms., U.S. (shô)	114	33.36N	90.44W
Shawano, Wi., U.S. (shȧ-wô′nō)	103	44.41N	88.13W
Shawinigan, Can.	85	46.32N	72.46W
Shawnee, Ks., U.S. (shô-nē′)	107f	39.01N	94.43W
Shawnee, Ok., U.S.	96	35.20N	96.54W
Shawneetown, Il., U.S. (shô′nē-toun)	98	37.40N	88.05W
Shayang, China	193	31.00N	112.38E
Shchara, r., Bela. (sh-chä′rȧ)	155	53.17N	25.12E
Shchëlkovo, Russia (shchĕl′kô-vô) . . .	162	55.55N	38.00E
Shchigry, Russia (shchē′grē)	163	51.52N	36.54E
Shchors, Ukr. (shchôrs)	163	51.38N	31.58E
Shchuch′ye Ozero, Russia (shcho͞och′yĕ ô′zĕ-rō)	172a	56.31N	56.35E
Sheakhala, India	186a	22.47N	88.10E
Shebele (Shabeelle), r., Afr. (shā′bā-lē)	218a	6.07N	43.10E
Sheboygan, Wi., U.S. (shē-boi′gȧn) . .	97	43.45N	87.44W
Sheboygan Falls, Wi., U.S.	103	43.43N	87.51W
Shechem, hist., W. Bank	181a	32.15N	35.22E
Shedandoah, Pa., U.S.	99	40.50N	76.15W
Shediac, Can. (shē′dē-ăk)	92	46.13N	64.32W
Shedin Peak, mtn., Can. (shĕd′ĭn) . . .	86	55.55N	127.32W
Sheepshead Bay, neigh., N.Y., U.S. . .	228	40.35N	73.56W
Sheerness, Eng., U.K. (shēr′nĕs)	144b	51.26N	0.46E
Sheffield, Can.	83d	43.20N	80.13W
Sheffield, Eng., U.K.	146	53.23N	1.28W
Sheffield, Al., U.S. (shĕf′fēld)	114	35.42N	87.42W
Sheffield, Oh., U.S.	101d	41.26N	82.05W
Sheffield Lake, Oh., U.S.	101d	41.30N	82.03W
Sheksna, r., Russia (shĕks′nȧ)	166	59.50N	38.40E
Shelagskiy, Mys, c., Russia (shĭ-läg′skē)	165	70.08N	170.52E
Shelbina, Ar., U.S. (shĕl-bī′nȧ)	111	39.41N	92.03W
Shelburn, In., U.S. (shĕl′bŭrn)	98	39.10N	87.30W
Shelburne, Can.	85	43.46N	65.19W
Shelburne, Can.	91	44.04N	80.12W
Shelby, In., U.S. (shĕl′bē)	101a	41.12N	87.21W
Shelby, Mi., U.S.	98	43.35N	86.20W
Shelby, Ms., U.S.	114	33.56N	90.44W
Shelby, Mt., U.S.	105	48.35N	111.55W
Shelby, N.C., U.S.	115	35.16N	81.35W
Shelby, Oh., U.S.	98	40.50N	82.40W
Shelbyville, Il., U.S. (shĕl′bē-vĭl)	98	39.20N	88.45W
Shelbyville, In., U.S.	98	39.30N	85.45W
Shelbyville, Ky., U.S.	98	38.10N	85.15W
Shelbyville, Tn., U.S.	114	35.30N	86.28W
Shelbyville Reservoir, res., Il., U.S. . .	98	39.30N	88.45W
Sheldon, Ia., U.S. (shĕl′dŭn)	102	43.10N	95.50W
Sheldon, Tx., U.S.	113a	29.52N	95.07W
Shelekhova, Zaliv, b., Russia	165	60.00N	156.00E
Shelikof Strait, strt., Ak., U.S. (shĕ′lē-kôf)	95	57.56N	154.20W
Shellbrook, Can.	88	53.15N	106.22W
Shelley, Id., U.S. (shĕl′lē)	105	43.24N	112.06W
Shellow Bowells, Eng., U.K.	235	51.45N	0.20E
Shellrock, r., Ia., U.S. (shĕl′rŏk)	103	43.25N	93.19W
Shelon′, r., Russia (shä′lôn)	162	57.50N	29.40E
Shelter, Port, b., H.K.	241c	22.21N	114.17E
Shelton, Ct., U.S. (shĕl′tŭn)	99	41.15N	73.05W
Shelton, Ne., U.S.	110	40.46N	98.41W

PLACE (Pronunciation)	PAGE	Lat. °′	Long. °′
Shelton, Wa., U.S.	104	47.14N	123.05W
Shemakha, Russia (shĕ-mȧ-kä′)	172a	56.16N	59.19E
Shenandoah, Ia., U.S. (shĕn-ăn-dō′ȧ)	111	40.46N	95.23W
Shenandoah, Va., U.S.	99	38.30N	78.30W
Shenandoah, r., Va., U.S.	99	38.55N	78.05W
Shenandoah National Park, rec., Va., U.S.	97	38.35N	78.25W
Shendam, Nig.	215	8.53N	9.32E
Shenfield, Eng., U.K.	235	51.38N	0.19E
Shengfang, China (shengfäng)	190	39.05N	116.40E
Shenkursk, Russia (shĕn-ko͞orsk′) . . .	164	62.10N	43.08E
Shenmu, China	192	38.55N	110.35E
Shenqiu, China	192	33.11N	115.06E
Shenxian, China (shŭn shyän)	190	38.02N	115.33E
Shenxian, China (shŭn shyĕn)	190	36.14N	115.38E
Shenyang, China (shŭn-yäŋ)	189	41.45N	123.22E
Shenze, China (shŭn-dzŭ)	190	38.12N	115.12E
Shenzhen, China	193	22.32N	114.08E
Sheopur, India	183	25.37N	77.10E
Shepard, Can. (shĕ′pärd)	83e	50.57N	113.55W
Shepetivka, Ukr.	167	50.10N	27.01E
Shepparton, Austl. (shĕp′ȧr-tŭn)	204	36.15S	145.25E
Shepperton, Eng., U.K.	235	51.24N	0.27W
Sherborn, Ma., U.S. (shûr′bŭrn)	93a	42.15N	71.22W
Sherbrooke, Can.	85	45.24N	71.54W
Sherburn, Eng., U.K. (shûr′bŭrn) . . .	144a	53.47N	1.15W
Shereshevo, Bela. (shĕ-rĕ-shĕ-vô) . . .	155	52.31N	24.08E
Sheridan, Ar., U.S. (shĕr′ĭ-dăn)	111	34.19N	92.21W
Sheridan, Or., U.S.	104	45.06N	123.22W
Sheridan, Wy., U.S.	96	44.48N	106.56W
Sherman, Tx., U.S. (shĕr′măn)	96	33.39N	96.37W
Sherman Oaks, neigh., Ca., U.S. . . .	232	34.09N	118.26W
Sherna, r., Russia (shĕr′nȧ)	172b	56.08N	38.45E
Sherridon, Can.	89	55.10N	101.10W
′s Hertogenbosch, Neth. (sĕr-tō′ghĕn-bôs)	151	51.41N	5.19E
Sherwood, Or., U.S.	106c	45.21N	122.50W
Sherwood Forest, for., Eng., U.K. . . .	144a	53.11N	1.07W
Sherwood Park, Can.	87	53.31N	113.19W
Shetland Islands, is., Scot., U.K. (shĕt′lănd)	142	60.35N	2.10W
Sheva, India	240e	18.56N	72.57E
Shewa Gimira, Eth.	211	7.13N	35.49E
Shexian, China (shŭ shyĕn)	190	36.34N	113.42E
Sheyang, r., China (she-yäŋ)	190	33.42N	119.40E
Sheyenne, r., N.D., U.S. (shī-ĕn′) . . .	102	46.42N	97.52W
Shi, r., China (shr)	190	31.58N	115.50E
Shi, r., China	190	32.09N	114.11E
Shiawassee, r., Mi., U.S. (shī-ȧ-wôs′ē)	98	43.15N	84.05W
Shibām, Yemen (shē′bäm)	182	16.02N	48.40E
Shibīn al Kawn, Egypt (shē-bēn′ĕl kōm′)	218b	30.31N	31.01E
Shibīn al Qanāṭir, Egypt (kȧ-nä′tēr) . . .	218b	30.18N	31.21E
Shibuya, neigh., Japan	242a	35.40N	139.42E
Shicun, China (shr-tsŏn)	190	33.47N	117.18E
Shields, r., Mt., U.S. (shēldz)	105	45.54N	110.40W
Shifnal, Eng., U.K. (shĭf′năl)	144a	52.40N	2.22W
Shihlin, Tai.	241d	25.05N	121.31E
Shijian, China (shr-jyĕn)	190	31.27N	117.51E
Shijiazhuang, China (shr-jyä-jŭäŋ) . . .	189	38.04N	114.31E
Shijiu Hu, l., China (shr-jyō ho͞o) . . .	190	31.29N	119.07E
Shijōnawate, Japan	242b	34.45N	135.39E
Shikārpur, Pak.	183	27.51N	68.52E
Shiki, Japan (shē′kē)	195a	35.50N	139.35E
Shikoku, i., Japan (shē′kō′ko͞o)	189	33.43N	133.33E
Shilibao, China	240b	39.55N	116.29E
Shilka, r., Russia (shĭl′kȧ)	171	53.00N	118.45E
Shilla, mtn., India	186	32.18N	78.17E
Shillong, India (shĕl-lông′)	183	25.39N	91.58E
Shiloh, Il., U.S. (shī′lō)	107e	38.34N	89.54W
Shilong, China (shr-lôŋ)	193	23.05N	113.58E
Shilou, China	191a	22.58N	113.29E
Shimabara, Japan (shē′mä-bä′rä)	195	32.46N	130.22E
Shimada, Japan (shē′mä-dä)	195	34.49N	138.13E
Shimbiris, mtn., Som.	218a	10.40N	47.23E
Shimizu, Japan (shē′mē-zo͞o)	194	35.00N	138.29E
Shimminato, Japan (shēm′mē′nä-tō) . .	195	36.47N	137.05E
Shimoda, Japan (shē′mō-dȧ)	195	34.41N	138.58E
Shimoga, India	187	13.59N	75.38E
Shimohōya, Japan	242a	35.45N	139.34E
Shimoigusa, neigh., Japan	242a	35.43N	139.37E
Shimomizo, Japan	242a	35.31N	139.23E
Shimoni, Kenya	217	4.39S	39.23E
Shimonoseki, Japan	189	33.58N	130.55E
Shimo-Saga, Japan (shē′mō sä′gä) . . .	195b	35.01N	135.41E
Shimo-shakujii, neigh., Japan	242a	35.45N	139.37E
Shimotsuruma, Japan	242a	35.29N	139.28E
Shimoyugi, Japan	242a	35.38N	139.23E
Shin, Loch, l., Scot., U.K. (lŏκ shĭn) . .	150	58.08N	4.02W
Shinagawa-Wan, b., Japan (shē′nä-gä′wä wän)	195a	35.37N	139.49E
Shinano-Gawa, r., Japan (shē-nä′nō gä′wä)	195	36.43N	138.22E
Shīndand, Afg.	185	33.18N	62.08E
Shinji, l., Japan (shĭn′jē)	195	35.23N	133.05E
Shinjuku, neigh., Japan	242a	35.41N	139.42E
Shinkolobwe, Zaire	217	11.02S	26.35E
Shinyanga, Tan. (shĭn-yäŋ′gä)	212	3.40S	33.26E
Shiono Misaki, c., Japan (shē-ô′nō mē′sä-kē)	194	33.20N	136.10E
Shipai, China (shr-pī)	191a	23.07N	113.23E
Ship Channel Cay, i., Bah. (shĭp chă-nĕl kē)	122	24.50N	76.50W
Shipley, Eng., U.K. (shĭp′lē)	144a	53.50N	1.47W
Shippegan, Can. (shĭ′pē-găn)	92	47.45N	64.42W
Shippegan Island, i., Can.	92	47.50N	64.38W

PLACE (Pronunciation)	PAGE	Lat. °′	Long. °′
Shippenburg, Pa., U.S. (shĭp′ĕn bûrg)	99	40.00N	77.30W
Shipshaw, r., Can. (shĭp′shô)	91	48.50N	71.03W
Shiqma, r., Isr.	181a	31.31N	34.40E
Shirane-san, mtn., Japan (shē′rä′nȧ-sän′)	195	35.44N	138.14E
Shirati, Tan. (shē-rä′tē)	212	1.15S	34.02E
Shīrāz, Iran (shē-räz′)	182	29.32N	52.27E
Shire, r., Afr. (shē′rȧ)	212	15.00S	35.00E
Shiriya Saki, c., Japan (shē′rē-yä sä′kē) . .	194	41.25N	142.10E
Shirley, Ma., U.S. (shûr′lē)	93a	42.33N	71.39W
Shishaldin Volcano, vol., Ak., U.S. (shī-shăl′dĭn)	95a	54.48N	164.00W
Shively, Ky., U.S. (shīv′lē)	101h	38.11N	85.47W
Shivpuri, India	183	25.31N	77.46E
Shivta, Horvot, hist., Isr.	181a	30.54N	34.36E
Shivwits Plateau, plat., Az., U.S. . . .	109	36.13N	113.42W
Shiwan, China (shr-wän)	191a	23.01N	113.04E
Shiwan Dashan, mts., China (shr-wän dä-shän)	193	22.10N	107.30E
Shizuki, Japan (shē′zo͞o-kē)	195	34.29N	134.51E
Shizuoka, Japan (shē′zo͞o′ōkȧ)	194	34.58N	138.24E
Shklov, Bela. (shklôf)	162	54.11N	30.23E
Shkodër, Alb. (shkô′dûr) (sko͞o′tȧrē) . .	142	42.04N	19.30E
Shkotovo, Russia (shkô′tô-vô)	194	43.15N	132.21E
Shoal Creek, r., Il., U.S. (shōl)	111	38.37N	89.25W
Shoal Lake, l., Can.	89	49.32N	95.00W
Shoals, In., U.S. (shōlz)	98	38.40N	86.45W
Shōdai, Japan	242b	34.51N	135.42E
Shōdo, i., Japan (shō′dō)	195	34.27N	134.27E
Shogunle, Nig.	244d	6.35N	3.21E
Sholāpur, India (shō′lä-po͞or)	183	17.42N	75.51E
Shomolu, Nig.	244d	6.32N	3.23E
Shoreham, Eng., U.K.	235	51.20N	0.11E
Shorewood, Wi., U.S. (shōr′wŏŏd)	101a	43.05N	87.54W
Shoshone, Id., U.S. (shō-shōn′tē)	105	42.56N	114.24W
Shoshone, r., Wy., U.S.	105	44.35N	108.50W
Shoshone Lake, l., Wy., U.S.	105	44.17N	110.50W
Shoshoni, Wy., U.S.	105	43.14N	108.05W
Shostka, Ukr. (shôst′kȧ)	163	51.51N	33.31E
Shouguang, China (shō-gŭäŋ)	190	36.53N	118.45E
Shouxian, China (shō shyĕn)	190	32.36N	116.45E
Shpola, Ukr. (shpô′lȧ)	167	49.01N	31.36E
Shreveport, La., U.S. (shrēv′pôrt) . . .	97	32.30N	93.46W
Shrewsbury, Eng., U.K. (shro͞oz′bēr-ĭ)	150	52.43N	2.44W
Shrewsbury, Ma., U.S.	93a	42.18N	71.43W
Shroud Cay, i., Bah.	122	24.20N	76.40W
Shuangcheng, China (shŭäŋ-chŭŋ) . . .	192	45.18N	126.18E
Shuanghe, China (shŭäŋ-hŭ)	190	31.33N	116.48E
Shuangliao, China	189	43.37N	123.30E
Shuangyang, China	192	43.28N	125.45E
Shubrā al-Khaymah, Egypt	244a	30.06N	31.15E
Shuhedun, China (shō͞o-hŭ-dōn)	190	31.33N	117.01E
Shuiye, China (shwā-yŭ)	190	36.08N	114.07E
Shule, r., China (sho͞o-lŭ)	188	40.53N	94.55E
Shullsburg, Wi., U.S. (shŭlz′bûrg) . . .	103	42.35N	90.16W
Shumagin, is., Ak., U.S. (sho͞o′mȧ-gĕn)	95	55.22N	159.20W
Shumen, Bul.	149	43.15N	26.54E
Shunde, China (shōn-dŭ)	191a	22.50N	113.15E
Shungnak, Ak., U.S. (shŭng′nȧk)	95	66.55N	157.20W
Shunut, Gora, mtn., Russia (gȧ-rä sho͞o′nŏt)	172a	56.33N	59.45E
Shunyi, China (shōn-yē)	190	40.09N	116.38E
Shuqrah, Yemen	182	13.32N	46.02E
Shūrāb, r., Iran (sho͞o rāb)	182	31.08N	55.30E
Shuri, Japan (sho͞o′rē)	194	26.10N	127.48E
Shurugwi, Zimb.	212	19.34S	30.03E
Shūshtar, Iran (sho͞osh′tŭr)	182	31.50N	48.46E
Shuswap Lake, l., Can. (sho͞os′wŏp) . .	87	50.57N	119.15W
Shuya, Russia (sho͞o′yȧ)	164	56.52N	41.23E
Shuyang, China (sho͞o yäng)	190	34.09N	118.47E
Shweba, Myanmar	183	22.23N	96.13E
Shyghys Qongyrat, Kaz.	169	47.25N	75.10E
Shymkent, Kaz.	169	42.17N	69.42E
Shyroke, Ukr.	163	47.40N	33.18E
Siak Kecil, r., Indon.	181b	1.01N	101.45E
Siaksriinderapura, Indon. (sē-äks′rĭ ĕn′drȧ-po͞o′rä)	181b	0.48N	102.05E
Siālkot, Pak. (sē-äl′kōt)	183	32.39N	74.30E
Siátista, Grc. (syä′tĭs-ta)	161	40.15N	21.32E
Şiau, Pulau, i., Indon.	197	2.40N	126.00E
Šiauliai, Lith. (shē-ou′lē-ī)	166	55.57N	23.19E
Şibay, Russia (sē′báy)	172a	52.41N	58.40E
Šibenik, Cro. (shē-bä′nĕk)	149	43.44N	15.55E
Siberia, reg., Russia	180	57.00N	97.00E
Siberut, Pulau, i., Indon. (sē′bȧ-ro͞ot) .	196	1.22S	99.45E
Sibiti, Congo (sē-bē-tē′)	212	3.41S	13.21E
Sibiu, Rom. (sē-bē-o͞o′)	149	45.47N	24.09E
Sibley, Ia., U.S. (sĭb′lē)	102	43.24N	95.33W
Sibolga, Indon. (sē-bō′gä)	196	1.45N	98.45E
Sibpur, India	240a	22.34N	88.19E
Sibsāgar, India (sēb-sŭ′gŭr)	183	26.47N	94.45E
Sibutu Island, i., Phil.	196	4.40N	119.30E
Sibuyan, i., Phil. (sē-bo͞o-yän′)	197a	12.19N	122.25E
Sibuyan Sea, sea, Phil.	196	12.43N	122.38E
Sichuan, prov., China (sz-chŭän)	188	31.20N	103.00E
Sicily, i., Italy (sĭs′ĭ-lē)	142	37.38N	13.30E
Sico, r., Hond. (sē-kō)	120	15.32N	85.42W
Sidamo, hist. reg., Eth. (sē-dä′mō) . . .	211	5.08N	37.45E
Sidao, China	240b	39.51N	116.26E
Sidcup, neigh., Eng., U.K.	235	51.25N	0.06E
Siderno Marina, Italy (sē-dĕr′nō mä-rē′nä)	160	38.18N	16.19E
Sídheros, Ákra, c., Grc.	160a	35.19N	26.20E
Sidhirókastron, Grc.	161	41.13N	23.27E
Sidi Aïssa, Alg.	159	35.53N	3.44E
Sidi bel Abbès, Alg. (sē′dē-bĕl ȧ-bĕs′)	210	35.15N	0.43W

PRONOUNCING INDEX

Sidi Ifni–Slobodka 349

PLACE (Pronunciation)	PAGE	Lat. °′	Long. °′
Sidi Ifni, Mor. (ēf'nē)	210	29.22N	10.15W
Sidley, Mount, mtn., Ant. (sĭd'lē)	219	77.25S	129.00W
Sidney, Can.	86	48.39N	123.24W
Sidney, Mt., U.S. (sĭd'nē)	105	47.43N	104.07W
Sidney, Ne., U.S.	102	41.10N	103.00W
Sidney, Oh., U.S.	98	40.20N	84.10W
Sidney Lanier, Lake, res., Ga., U.S. (lăn'yēr)	97	34.27N	83.56W
Sido, Mali	214	11.40N	7.36W
Sidon *see* Saydā, Leb.	182	33.34N	35.23E
Sidr, Wādī, r., Egypt	181a	29.43N	32.58E
Sidra, Gulf of *see* Surt, Khalīj, b., Libya	211	31.30N	18.28E
Siedlce, Pol. (syĕd''l-tsĕ)	155	52.09N	22.20E
Siegburg, Ger. (zēg'bōōrgh)	154	50.48N	7.13E
Siegen, Ger. (zē'ghĕn)	154	50.52N	8.01E
Sieghartskirchen, Aus.	145e	48.16N	16.00E
Siemensstadt, neigh., Ger.	238a	52.32N	13.17E
Siemiatycze, Pol. (syĕm'yä'tē-chĕ)	155	52.26N	22.52E
Siemionówka, Pol. (sĕè-mēō'nôf-kä)	155	52.53N	23.50E
Siem Reap, Camb. (syĕm'rā'áp)	196	13.32N	103.54E
Siena, Italy (sê-ĕn'ä)	148	43.19N	11.21E
Sieradz, Pol. (syĕ'rädz)	155	51.35N	18.45E
Sierpc, Pol. (syĕrpts)	155	52.51N	19.42E
Sierra Blanca, Tx., U.S. (sē-ĕ'rȧ blaŋ-kä)	112	31.10N	105.20W
Sierra Blanca Peak, mtn., N.M., U.S. (blăn'kȧ)	96	33.25N	105.50W
Sierra Leone, nation, Afr. (sê-ĕr'rä lȧ-ō'nȧ)	210	8.48N	12.30W
Sierra Madre, Ca., U.S. (mä'drē)	107a	34.10N	118.03W
Sierra Mojada, Mex. (sē-ĕ'r-rä-mô-κä'dä)	112	27.22N	103.42W
Sífnos, i., Grc.	161	36.58N	24.30E
Sigean, Fr. (sē-zhŏN')	156	43.02N	2.56E
Sigeurney, Ia., U.S. (sē-gûr-nĭ)	103	41.16N	92.10W
Sighetu Marmaţiei, Rom.	155	47.57N	23.55E
Sighişoara, Rom. (sē-gê-shwä'rȧ)	155	46.11N	24.48E
Siglufjördur, Ice.	146	66.06N	18.45W
Signakhi, Geor.	167	41.45N	45.50E
Signal Hill, Ca., U.S. (sĭg'nȧl hĭl)	107a	33.48N	118.11W
Sigsig, Ec. (sēg-sēg')	130	3.04S	78.44W
Sigtuna, Swe. (sēgh-tōō'nȧ)	152	59.40N	17.39E
Siguanea, Ensenada de la, b., Cuba	122	21.45N	83.15W
Siguatepeque, Hond. (sē-gwȧ'tē-pĕ-kĕ)	120	14.33N	87.51W
Sigüenza, Spain (sē-gwĕ'n-zä)	148	41.03N	2.38W
Siguiri, Gui. (sē-gē-rē')	210	11.25N	9.10W
Sihong, China (sz-hôŋ)	190	33.25N	118.13E
Siirt, Tur. (sĭ-ērt')	167	38.00N	42.00E
Sikalongo, Zam.	217	16.46S	27.07E
Sikasso, Mali (sē-käs'sō)	210	11.19N	5.40W
Sikeston, Mo., U.S. (sīks'tŭn)	111	36.50N	89.35W
Sikhote Alin', Khrebet, mts., Russia (se-kô'ta a-lēn')	165	45.00N	135.45E
Sikinos, i., Grc. (sĭ'kĭ-nōs)	161	36.45N	24.55E
Sikkim, state, India	183	27.42N	88.25E
Siklós, Hung. (sĭ'klōsh)	155	45.51N	18.18E
Sil, r., Spain (sē'l)	158	42.20N	7.13W
Silāmpur, neigh., India	240d	28.40N	77.16E
Silang, Phil. (sē-läng')	197a	14.14N	120.58E
Silao, Mex. (sē-lä'ō)	118	20.56N	101.25W
Silchar, India (sĭl-chär')	183	24.52N	92.50E
Silent Valley, S. Afr. (sī'lĕnt vă'lē)	218d	24.32S	26.40E
Siler City, N.C., U.S. (sī'lēr)	115	35.45N	79.29W
Silesia, hist. reg., Pol. (sĭ-lē'shȧ)	154	50.58N	16.53E
Silifke, Tur.	149	36.20N	34.00E
Siling Co, l., China	188	32.05N	89.10E
Silistra, Bul. (sê-lēs'trȧ)	149	44.01N	27.13E
Siljan, l., Swe. (sĕl'yän)	146	60.48N	14.28E
Silkeborg, Den. (sĭl'kĕ-bôr')	152	56.10N	9.33E
Sillery, Can. (sēl'-re')	83b	46.46N	71.15W
Siloam Springs, Ar., U.S. (sĭ-lōm)	111	36.10N	94.32W
Siloana Plains, pl., Zam.	216	16.55S	23.10E
Silocayoápan, Mex. (sē-lô-kä-yô-ȧ'pän)	118	17.29N	98.09W
Silsbee, Tx., U.S. (sĭlz' bē)	113	30.19N	94.09W
Šilschede, Ger.	236	51.21N	7.19E
Šilutė, Lith.	153	55.21N	21.29E
Silva Jardim, Braz. (sē'l-vä-zhär-dēN)	129a	22.40N	42.24W
Silvana, Wa., U.S. (sĭ-văn'ȧ)	106a	48.12N	122.16W
Silvânia, Braz. (sēl-vȧ'nyä)	131	16.43S	48.33W
Silvassa, India	186	20.10N	73.00E
Silver, l., Mo., U.S.	111	39.38N	93.12W
Silverado, Ca., U.S. (sĭl-vēr-ä'dō)	107a	33.45N	117.40W
Silver Bank, bk.	123	20.40N	69.40W
Silver Bank Passage, strt., N.A.	123	20.40N	70.20W
Silver Bay, Mn., U.S.	103	47.24N	91.07W
Silver City, Pan.	121	9.20N	79.54W
Silver City, N.M., U.S. (sĭl'vēr sĭ'tĭ)	109	32.45N	108.20W
Silver Creek, N.Y., U.S. (crēk)	99	42.35N	79.10W
Silver Creek, r., Az., U.S.	109	34.30N	110.05W
Silver Creek, r., In., U.S.	101h	38.20N	85.45W
Silver Creek, Muddy Fork, r., In., U.S.	101h	38.26N	85.52W
Silverdale, Wa., U.S. (sĭl'vēr-dāl)	106a	49.39N	122.42W
Silver Hill, Md., U.S.	229d	38.51N	76.57W
Silver Lake, Ma., U.S.	227a	42.00N	70.48W
Silver Lake, Wi., U.S. (lāk)	101a	42.33N	88.10W
Silver Lake, l., Wi., U.S.	101a	42.35N	88.08W
Silver Spring, Md., U.S. (sprĭng)	100e	39.00N	77.00W
Silver Star Mountain, mtn., Wa., U.S.	106c	45.45N	122.15W
Silverthrone Mountain, mtn., Can. (sĭl'vēr-thrōn)	86	51.31N	126.06W
Silverton, S. Afr.	218d	25.45S	28.13E
Silverton, Co., U.S. (sĭl'vēr-tŭn)	109	37.50N	107.40W
Silverton, Oh., U.S.	101f	39.12N	84.24W
Silverton, Or., U.S.	104	45.02N	122.46W
Silves, Port. (sēl'vĕzh)	148	37.15N	8.24W
Silvies, r., Or., U.S. (sĭl'vēz)	104	43.44N	119.15W
Sim, Russia (sĭm)	172a	55.00N	57.42E

PLACE (Pronunciation)	PAGE	Lat. °′	Long. °′
Sim, r., Russia	172a	54.50N	56.50E
Simao, China (sz-mou)	188	22.56N	101.07E
Simard, Lac, l., Can.	91	47.38N	78.40W
Simba, Zaire	216	0.36N	22.55E
Simcoe, Can. (sĭm'kō)	150	42.50N	80.20W
Simcoe, l., Can.	85	44.30N	79.20W
Simeulue, Pulau, i., Indon.	196	2.27N	95.30E
Simferopol', Ukr.	164	44.58N	34.04E
Simi, i., Grc.	149	36.27N	27.41E
Similk Beach, Wa., U.S. (sē'mĭlk)	106a	48.27N	122.35W
Simla, India (sĭm'lȧ)	183	31.09N	77.15E
Simla, neigh., India	240a	22.35N	88.22E
Şimleu Silvaniei, Rom.	149	47.14N	22.46E
Simms Point, c., Bah.	122	25.00N	77.40W
Simojovel, Mex. (sē-mō-hô-vĕl')	119	17.12N	92.43W
Simonésia, Braz. (sē-mô-nĕ'syä)	129a	20.04S	41.53W
Simonette, r., Can. (sī-mŏn-ĕt')	87	54.15N	118.00W
Simonstad, S. Afr.	212a	34.11S	18.25E
Simood Sound, Can.	86	50.45N	126.25W
Simplon Pass, p., Switz. (sĭm'plŏn) (säN-plôN')	154	46.13N	7.53E
Simpson, i., Can.	103	48.43N	87.44W
Simpson Desert, des., Austl. (sĭmp-sŭn)	202	24.40S	136.40E
Simrishamn, Swe. (sēm'rēs-häm'n)	152	55.35N	14.19E
Sims Bayou, Tx., U.S. (sĭmz bī-yōō')	113a	29.37N	95.23W
Simushir, i., Russia (se-mōō'shēr)	189	47.15N	150.47E
Sinaia, Rom. (sĭ-nä'yȧ)	161	45.20N	25.30E
Sinai Peninsula, pen., Egypt (sī'nī)	211	29.24N	33.29E
Sinaloa, state, Mex. (sē-nä-lô-ä)	116	25.15N	107.45W
Sinan, China (sz-nän)	188	27.50N	108.30E
Sinanju, N. Kor. (sĭ'nän-jŏ')	194	39.39N	125.41E
Sincelejo, Col. (sēn-sȧ-lā'hō)	130	9.12N	75.30W
Sinclair Inlet, Wa., U.S. (sĭn-klâr')	106a	47.31N	122.41W
Sinclair Mills, Can.	87	54.02N	121.41W
Sindi, Est. (sēn'dē)	153	58.20N	24.40E
Sines, Port. (sē'nȧzh)	158	37.57N	8.50W
Singapore, Sing. (sĭn'gȧ-pōr')	196	1.18N	103.52E
Singapore, nation, Asia	196	1.22N	103.45E
Singapore Strait, strt., Asia	181b	1.14N	104.20E
Singlewell or Ifield, Eng., U.K.	235	51.25N	0.23E
Singu, Myanmar (sĭn'gŭ)	188	22.37N	96.04E
Siniye Lipyagi, Russia (sēn'ê lēp'yä-gê)	163	51.24N	38.29E
Sinj, Cro. (sēn')	160	43.42N	16.39E
Sinjah, Sudan	211	13.09N	33.52E
Sinkāt, Sudan	184	18.50N	36.50E
Sinkiang *see* Xinjiang Uygur, , China	188	40.15N	82.15E
Sin'kovo, Russia (sĭn-kô'vô)	172b	56.23N	37.19E
Sinnamary, Fr. Gu.	131	5.15N	52.52W
Sinni, r., Italy (sēn'nē)	160	40.05N	16.15E
Sinnūris, Egypt	218b	29.25N	30.52E
Sino, Pedra de, mtn., Braz. (pĕ'drä-dô-sē'nô)	132b	22.27S	43.02W
Sinop, Tur.	182	42.00N	35.05E
Sint Eustatius, i., Neth. Ant.	121b	17.32N	62.45W
Sint Niklaas, Bel.	145a	51.10N	4.07E
Sinton, Tx., U.S. (sĭn'tŭn)	113	28.03N	97.30W
Sintra, Port. (sēn'trȧ)	158	38.48N	9.23W
Sint Truiden, Bel.	145a	50.49N	5.14E
Sinŭiju, N. Kor. (sĭ'noĭ-jōō)	189	40.04N	124.33E
Sinyavino, Russia (sĭn-yä'vĭ-nô)	172c	59.50N	31.07E
Sinyaya, r., Eur. (sēn'yȧ-yȧ)	162	56.40N	28.20E
Sinyukha, r., Ukr. (sē-nyō-κȧ)	163	48.34N	30.49E
Sion, Switz. (sē'ôN')	154	46.15N	7.17E
Sioux City, Ia., U.S. (sōō sĭ'tĭ)	96	42.30N	96.25W
Sioux Falls, S.D., U.S. (fôlz)	96	43.33N	96.43W
Sioux Lookout, Can.	85	50.06N	91.55W
Siping, China (sz-pĭŋ)	189	43.05N	124.24E
Sipiwesk, Can.	84	55.27N	97.24W
Sipsey, r., Al., U.S. (sĭp'sē)	114	33.26N	87.42W
Sipura, Pulau, i., Indon.	196	2.15S	99.33E
Siqueros, Mex. (sê-kä'rōs)	118	23.19N	106.14W
Siquia, Río, r., Nic. (sē-kē'ä)	121	12.23N	84.36W
Siracusa, Italy (sē-rä-koo'sä)	149	37.02N	15.19E
Sirājganj, Bngl. (sĭ-räj'gŭnj)	183	24.23N	89.43E
Sirama, El Sal. (Sē-rä-mä)	120	13.23N	87.55W
Sir Douglas, Mount, mtn., Can. (sûr dŭg'lăs)	87	50.44N	115.20W
Sir Edward Pellew Group, is., Austl. (pĕl'ū)	202	15.15S	137.15E
Siret, Rom.	155	47.58N	26.01E
Siret, r., Eur.	149	47.00N	27.00E
Sirhān, Wadi, depr., Sau. Ar.	182	31.02N	37.16E
Síros, i., Grc.	149	37.23N	24.55E
Sirsa, India	186	29.39N	75.02E
Sir Sandford, Mount, mtn., Can. (sûr sănd'fērd)	87	51.40N	117.52W
Širvintos, Lith. (shēr'vĭn-tôs)	153	55.02N	24.59E
Sir Wilfrid Laurier, Mount, mtn., Can. (sûr wĭl'frĭd lôr'yēr)	87	52.47N	119.45W
Sisak, Cro. (sē'sȧk)	149	45.29N	16.20E
Sisal, Mex. (sē-säl')	116	21.09N	90.03W
Sishui, China (sz-shwä)	190	35.40N	117.17E
Sisquoc, r., Ca., U.S. (sĭs'kwŏk)	108	34.47N	120.13W
Sisseton, S.D., U.S. (sĭs'tŭn)	102	45.39N	97.04W
Sistān, Daryacheh-ye, l., Asia	182	31.45N	61.15E
Sisteron, Fr. (sēst'rôN')	157	44.10N	5.55E
Sisterville, W.V., U.S. (sĭs'tēr-vĭl)	98	39.30N	81.00W
Sitía, Grc. (sē'tĭ-ȧ)	160a	35.09N	26.10E
Sitka, Ak., U.S. (sĭt'kȧ)	96a	57.08N	135.18W
Sittingbourne, Eng., U.K. (sĭt-ĭng-bôrn)	144b	51.20N	0.44E
Sittwe, Myanmar	183	20.09N	92.54E
Sivas, Tur. (sē'väs)	182	39.50N	36.50E
Siverek, Tur. (sē'vĕ-rĕk)	182	37.50N	39.20E
Siverskaya, Russia (sē'vĕr-skȧ-yȧ)	153	59.17N	30.03E
Sivers'kyy Donec', r., Eur.	163	48.48N	38.42E

PLACE (Pronunciation)	PAGE	Lat. °′	Long. °′
Sīwah, Egypt	184	29.12N	25.31E
Siwah, oasis, Egypt (sē'wä)	211	29.33N	25.11E
Sixaola, r., C.R.	121	9.31N	83.07W
Sixian, China (sz shyĕn)	190	33.37N	117.51E
Sixth Cataract, wtfl., Sudan	211	16.26N	32.44E
Siyang, China (sz-yäŋ)	190	33.43N	118.42E
Sjaelland, i., Den. (shĕl'lăn')	152	55.34N	11.35E
Sjenica, Yugo. (syĕ'nē-tsȧ)	161	43.15N	20.02E
Skadovs'k, Ukr.	163	46.08N	32.54E
Skagen, Den. (skä'ghĕn)	152	57.43N	10.32E
Skagerrak, strt., Eur. (skä-ghĕ-räk')	142	57.43N	8.28E
Skagit, r., Wa., U.S.	104	48.29N	121.52W
Skagit Bay, b., Wa., U.S. (skăg'ĭt)	106a	48.20N	122.32W
Skagway, Ak., U.S. (skăg-wā)	96a	59.30N	135.28W
Skälderviken, b., Swe.	152	56.20N	12.25E
Skalistyy, Golets, mtn., Russia	165	57.28N	119.48E
Skalistyy Khrebet, mts., Russia	168	43.15N	43.00E
Skamania, Wa., U.S. (skȧ-mā'nĭ-ȧ)	106c	45.37N	112.03W
Skamokawa, Wa., U.S.	106c	46.16N	123.27W
Skanderborg, Den. (skän-ĕr-bôr')	152	56.04N	9.55E
Skaneateles, N.Y., U.S. (skăn-ĕ-ăt'lĕs)	99	42.55N	76.25W
Skaneateles, l., N.Y., U.S.	99	42.50N	76.20W
Skänninge, Swe. (shĕn'ĭng-ĕ)	152	58.24N	15.02E
Skanör-Falseterbo, Swe. (skän'ûr)	152	55.24N	12.49E
Skara, Swe. (skä'rȧ)	152	58.25N	13.24E
Skeena, r., Can. (skē'nă)	84	54.30N	129.00W
Skeena Mountains, mts., Can.	86	56.00N	128.00W
Skeerpoort, S. Afr.	213b	25.49S	27.45E
Skeerpoort, r., S. Afr.	213b	25.58S	27.41E
Skeldon, Guy. (skĕl'dŭn)	131	5.49N	57.15W
Skellefteå, Swe. (shĕl'ĕf-tē-a')	146	64.47N	20.48E
Skellefteälven, r., Swe.	146	65.15N	19.30E
Skelmersdale, Eng., U.K.	237a	53.33N	2.48W
Skhodnya, Russia (skôd'nyȧ)	172b	55.57N	37.21E
Skhodnya, r., Russia	172b	55.55N	37.16E
Skíathos, i., Grc. (skē'á-thôs)	161	39.15N	23.25E
Skibbereen, Ire. (skĭb'ēr-ēn)	150	51.32N	9.25W
Skidegate, b., Can. (skĭ'-dē-gāt')	86	53.15N	132.00W
Skidmore, Tx., U.S. (skĭd'mōr)	113	28.16N	97.40W
Skien, Nor. (skē'ĕn)	146	59.13N	9.35E
Skierniewice, Pol. (skyĕr-nyĕ-vēt'sĕ)	155	51.58N	20.13E
Skihist Mountain, mtn., Can.	87	50.11N	121.54W
Skikda, Alg.	210	36.58N	6.51E
Skilpadfontein, S. Afr.	218d	25.02S	28.50E
Skíros, Grc.	161	38.53N	24.32E
Skiros, i., Grc.	149	38.50N	24.43E
Skive, Den. (skē'vĕ)	152	56.34N	8.56E
Skjálfandafljót, r., Ice. (skyäl'fänd-ô)	146	65.24N	16.40W
Skjerstad, Nor. (skyĕr-städ)	146	67.12N	15.37E
Škofja Loka, Slvn. (shkôf'yȧ lō'kȧ)	160	46.10N	14.20E
Skokie, Il., U.S. (skō'kē)	101a	42.02N	87.45W
Skokomish Indian Reservation, I.R., Wa., U.S. (Skō-kō'mĭsh)	106a	47.22N	123.07W
Skole, Ukr. (skô'lē)	155	49.03N	23.32E
Skópelos, i., Grc. (skô'pȧ-lôs)	161	39.04N	23.31E
Skopin, Russia (skô'pēn)	166	53.49N	39.35E
Skopje, Mac. (skôp'yĕ)	160	42.02N	21.26E
Skövde, Swe. (shûv'dĕ)	146	58.25N	13.48E
Skovorodino, Russia (skô'vô-rô'dĭ-nô)	165	53.53N	123.56E
Skowhegan, Me., U.S. (skou-hē'găn)	92	44.45N	69.27W
Skradin, Cro. (skrä'dēn)	161	43.49N	17.58E
Skreia, Nor. (skrā'ȧ)	152	60.40N	10.55E
Skudeneshavn, Nor. (skōō'dĕ-nes-houn')	152	59.10N	5.19E
Skuilte, S. Afr.	244b	26.07S	28.19E
Skull Valley Indian Reservation, I.R., Ut., U.S. (skŭl)	109	40.25N	112.50W
Skuna, r., Ms., U.S. (skŭ'nȧ)	114	33.57N	89.36W
Skunk, r., Ia., U.S. (skŭnk)	103	41.12N	92.14W
Skuodas, Lith. (skwô'dȧs)	153	56.16N	21.32E
Skurup, Swe. (skû'rŏp)	152	55.29N	13.27E
Skvyra, Ukr.	167	49.43N	29.41E
Skwierzyna, Pol. (skvê-ĕr'zhĭ-nȧ)	154	52.35N	15.30E
Skye, Island of, i., Scot., U.K. (skī)	146	57.25N	6.17W
Skykomish, r., Wa., U.S. (skī'kō-mĭsh)	106a	47.50N	121.55W
Skyring, Seno de, b., Chile (sĕ'nô-s-krē'ng)	132	52.35S	72.30W
Slade Green, neigh., Eng., U.K.	235	51.28N	0.12E
Slagese, Den.	152	55.25N	11.19E
Slamet, Gunung, mtn., Indon. (slä'mĕt)	196	7.15S	109.15E
Slănic, Rom. (slŭ'nēk)	161	45.13N	25.56E
Slater, Mo., U.S. (slāt'ēr)	111	39.13N	93.03W
Slatina, Rom. (slä'tē-nä)	161	44.26N	24.21E
Slaton, Tx., U.S. (slā'tŭn)	110	33.26N	101.38W
Slattocks, Eng., U.K.	237b	53.35N	2.10W
Slave, r., Can. (slāv)	84	59.40N	111.21W
Slavgorod, Russia (sláf'gô-rôt)	164	52.58N	78.43E
Slavonija, hist. reg., Yugo. (slä-vô'nē-yä)	161	45.29N	17.31E
Slavonska Požega, Cro. (slä-vôn'skä pô'zhĕ-gä)	161	45.18N	17.42E
Slavonski Brod, Cro. (skä-vôn'skē brôd)	149	45.10N	18.01E
Slavuta, Ukr. (slȧ-vōō'tȧ)	163	50.18N	27.01E
Slavyanskaya, Russia (sláv-yȧn'skȧ-yȧ)	163	45.14N	38.09E
Sławno, Pol. (swav'nō)	154	54.21N	16.38E
Slayton, Mn., U.S. (slā'tŭn)	102	44.00N	95.44W
Sleaford, Eng., U.K. (slē'fērd)	144a	53.00N	0.25W
Sleepy Eye, Mn., U.S. (slēp'ĭ ī)	103	44.17N	94.44W
Sleepy Hollow, Ca., U.S.	232	33.57N	117.47W
Slidell, La., U.S. (slī-dĕl')	113	30.17N	89.47W
Sliedrecht, Neth.	145a	51.49N	4.46E
Sligo, Ire. (slī'gō)	146	54.17N	8.19W
Slite, Swe. (slē'tē)	152	57.41N	18.47E
Sliven, Bul. (slē'vĕn)	149	42.41N	26.20E
Sloan, N.Y., U.S.	230a	42.54N	78.47W
Sloatsburg, N.Y., U.S. (slōts'bûrg)	100a	41.09N	74.11W
Slobodka, Bela. (slô'bôd-kȧ)	153	54.34N	26.12E

ng-sing; ŋ-baŋk; N-nasalized n; nŏd; cŏmmit; ōld; ôbey; ôrder; oi-boil; fōōd; ŏ-as oo in foot; ou-out; s-soft; sh-dish; th-thin; pūre; ûnite; ûrn; stŭd; circŭs; ü-as in French tu; '-indeterminate vowel.

ăt; fīnăl; rāte; senāte; ärm; ásk; sofá; fâre;   ch-choose;   dh-as th in other;   bē; ĕvent; bĕt; recĕnt; crātēr;   g-gō; gh-guttural g;   bĭt; ĭ-short neutral; rīde;   κ-guttural k as ch in German ich;

PRONOUNCING INDEX

South Haven-Start Point 351

PLACE (Pronunciation)	PAGE	Lat. °′	Long. °′
South Haven, Mi., U.S. (hāv′'n)	98	42.25N	86.15W
South Head, c., Austl.	243a	33.50S	151.17E
South Hempstead, N.Y., U.S.	228	40.41N	73.37W
South Hill, Va., U.S.	115	36.44N	78.08W
South Hills, neigh., S. Afr.	244b	26.15S	28.05E
South Holston Lake, res., U.S.	115	36.35N	82.00W
South Indian Lake, Can.	89	56.50N	99.00W
Southington, Ct., U.S. (sŭdh′ĭng-tŭn)	99	41.35N	72.55W
South Island, i., N.Z.	203a	42.40S	169.00E
South Loup, r., Ne., U.S. (lo͞op)	102	41.21N	100.08W
South Lynnfield, Ma., U.S.	227a	42.31N	71.00W
South Magnetic Pole, pt. of i.	219	65.18S	139.30E
South Media, Pa., U.S.	229b	39.54N	75.23W
South Melbourne, Austl.	243b	37.50S	144.57E
South Merrimack, N.H., U.S. (mĕr′ĭ-măk)	93a	42.47N	71.36W
South Milwaukee, Wi., U.S. (mĭl-wô′kė)	101a	42.55N	87.52W
South Mimms, Eng., U.K.	235	51.42N	0.14W
South Moose Lake, l., Can.	89	53.51N	100.20W
South Nation, r., Can.	91	45.00N	75.25W
South Negril Point, c., Jam. (nà-grĕl′)	122	18.15N	78.25W
South Ockendon, Eng., U.K.	235	51.32N	0.18E
South Ogden, Ut., U.S. (ŏg′dĕn)	107b	41.12N	111.58W
South Orange, N.J., U.S.	228	40.45N	74.15W
South Orkney Islands, is., Ant.	128	57.00S	45.00W
South Ossetia, hist. reg., Geor.	168	42.20N	44.00E
South Oxhey, Eng., U.K.	235	51.38N	0.23W
South Paris, Me., U.S. (păr′ĭs)	92	44.13N	70.32W
South Park, Ky., U.S. (pärk)	101h	38.06N	85.43W
South Pasadena, Ca., U.S. (păs-à-dē′nȧ)	107a	34.06N	118.08W
South Pease, r., Tx., U.S. (pēz)	110	33.54N	100.45W
South Pender, i., Can. (pĕn′dĕr)	106d	48.45N	123.09W
South Philadelphia, neigh., Pa., U.S.	229b	39.56N	75.10W
South Pittsburg, Tn., U.S. (pĭs′bûrg)	114	35.00N	85.42W
South Platte, r., U.S. (plăt)	96	40.40N	102.40W
South Point, c., Barb.	121b	13.00N	59.43W
South Point, c., Mi., U.S.	98	44.50N	83.20W
South Pole, pt. of i., Ant.	219	90.00S	0.00
South Porcupine, Can.	90	48.28N	81.13W
Southport, Austl. (south′pōrt)	203	27.57S	153.27E
Southport, Eng., U.K. (south′pôrt)	150	53.38N	3.00W
Southport, In., U.S.	101g	39.40N	86.07W
Southport, N.C., U.S.	115	35.55N	78.02W
South Portland, Me., U.S. (pōrt-lănd)	92	43.37N	70.15W
South Prairie, Wa., U.S. (prā′rĭ)	106a	47.08N	122.06W
South Range, Wi., U.S. (rānj)	107h	46.37N	91.59W
South River, N.J., U.S. (rĭv′ẽr)	100a	40.27N	74.23W
South Ronaldsay, i., Scot., U.K. (rŏn′ȧld-s′ā)	150a	58.48N	2.55W
South Saint Paul, Mn., U.S.	107g	44.54N	93.02W
South Salt Lake, Ut., U.S. (sôlt lāk)	107b	40.44N	111.53W
South Sandwich Islands, is., S. Geor. (sănd′wĭch)	128	58.00S	27.00W
South Sandwich Trench, deep	128	55.00S	27.00W
South San Francisco, Ca., U.S. (săn frăn-sĭs′kō)	106b	37.39N	122.24W
South San Jose Hills, Ca., U.S.	232	34.01N	117.55W
South Saskatchewan, r., Can. (sàs-kach′ē-wän)	84	50.30N	110.30W
South Shetland Islands, is., Ant.	128	62.00S	70.00W
South Shields, Eng., U.K. (shēldz)	146	55.00N	1.22W
South Shore, neigh., Il., U.S.	231a	41.46N	87.35W
South Side, neigh., Pa., U.S.	230b	40.26N	79.58W
South Sioux City, Ne., U.S. (so͞o sĭt′ė)	102	42.48N	96.26W
South Taranaki Bight, bt., N.Z. (tä-rä-nä′kė)	203a	39.35S	173.50E
South Thompson, r., Can. (tŏmp′sŭn)	87	50.41N	120.21W
Southton, Tx., U.S. (south′tŭn)	107d	29.18N	98.26W
South Uist, i., Scot., U.K. (û′ĭst)	150	57.15N	7.24W
South Umpqua, r., Or., U.S. (ŭmp′kwȧ)	104	43.00N	122.54W
South Walpole, Ma., U.S.	227a	42.06N	71.16W
South Waltham, Ma., U.S.	227a	42.22N	71.15W
Southwark, neigh., Eng., U.K.	235	51.30N	0.06W
South Weald, Eng., U.K.	235	51.37N	0.16E
Southwell, Eng., U.K. (south′wĕl)	144a	53.04N	0.56W
South West Africa see Namibia, nation, Afr.	212	19.30S	16.13E
South Westbury, N.Y., U.S.	228	40.45N	73.35W
Southwest Miramichi, r., Can. (mĭr ȧ-mė′shē)	92	46.35N	66.17W
Southwest Point, c., Bah.	122	25.50N	77.10W
Southwest Point, c., Bah.	123	23.55N	74.30W
South Weymouth, Ma., U.S.	227a	42.10N	70.57W
South Whittier, Ca., U.S.	232	33.56N	118.03W
South Yorkshire, co., Eng., U.K.	144a	53.29N	1.35W
Sovetsk, Russia (sô-vyĕtsk′)	166	55.04N	21.54E
Sovetskaya Gavan′, Russia (sŭ-vyĕt′skĭ-u gä′vŭn′)	165	48.59N	140.14E
Sow, r., Eng., U.K. (sou)	144a	52.45N	2.12W
Soweto, neigh., S. Afr.	244b	26.14S	27.54E
Soya Kaikyō, strt., Asia	194	45.45N	141.38E
Sōya Misaki, c., Japan (sō′yȧ mė′sä-kē)	194	45.35N	141.25E
Soyo, Ang.	212	6.10S	12.25E
Sozh, r., Eur. (sôzh)	167	52.50N	31.00E
Sozopol, Bul. (sôz′ô-pôl′)	161	42.18N	27.50E
Spa, Bel. (spä)	151	50.30N	5.50E
Spain, nation, Eur. (spān)	142	40.15N	4.30W
Spalding, Ne., U.S. (spôl′dĭng)	102	41.43N	98.23W
Spanaway, Wa., U.S. (spăn′ȧ-wā)	106a	47.06N	122.26W
Spandau, neigh., Ger.	238a	52.32N	13.12E
Spangler, Pa., U.S. (spăng′lẽr)	99	40.40N	78.50W
Spanish Fork, Ut., U.S. (spăn′ĭsh fôrk)	109	40.10N	111.40W
Spanish Town, Jam.	117	18.00N	76.55W
Sparks, Nv., U.S. (spärks)	108	39.34N	119.45W
Sparrows Point, Md., U.S. (spăr′ōz)	100e	39.13N	76.29W
Sparta see Spárti, Grc.	149	37.07N	22.28E
Sparta, Ga., U.S. (spär′tȧ)	115	33.16N	82.59W
Sparta, Il., U.S.	111	38.07N	89.42W
Sparta, Mi., U.S.	98	43.10N	85.45W
Sparta, Tn., U.S.	114	35.54N	85.26W
Sparta, Wi., U.S.	103	43.56N	90.50W
Sparta Mountains, mts., N.J., U.S.	100a	41.00N	74.38W
Spartanburg, S.C., U.S. (spär′tăn-bûrg)	97	34.57N	82.13W
Spartel, Cap, c., Mor. (spär-tĕl′)	158	35.48N	5.50W
Spárti (Sparta), Grc.	149	37.07N	22.28E
Spartivento, Cape, c., Italy	142	38.54N	8.52E
Spartivento, Cape, c., Italy (spär-tė-vĕn′tô)	160	37.55N	16.09E
Spas-Demensk, Russia (spàs dyĕ-mĕnsk′)	162	54.24N	34.02E
Spas-Klepiki, Russia (spàs klĕp′ĕ-kė)	162	55.09N	40.11E
Spassk-Ryazanskiy, Russia (ryä-zän′skĭ)	162	54.24N	40.21E
Spassk-Dal′niy, Russia (spŭsk′däl′nyē)	165	44.30N	133.00E
Spátha, Ákra, c., Grc.	160a	35.42N	23.45E
Spaulding, Al., U.S. (spôl′dĭng)	100h	33.27N	86.50W
Spear, Cape, c., Can. (spēr)	93	47.32N	52.32W
Spearfish, S.D., U.S. (spēr′fĭsh)	102	44.28N	103.52W
Speed, In., U.S. (spēd)	101h	38.25N	85.45W
Speedway, In., U.S. (spēd′wā)	101g	39.47N	86.14W
Speichersee, l., Ger.	145d	48.12N	11.47E
Speke, neigh., Eng., U.K.	237a	53.21N	2.51W
Speldorf, neigh., Ger.	236	51.25N	6.52E
Spellen, Ger.	236	51.37N	6.37E
Spencer, In., U.S. (spĕn′sẽr)	98	39.15N	86.45W
Spencer, Ia., U.S.	102	43.09N	95.08W
Spencer, N.C., U.S.	115	35.43N	80.25W
Spencer, W.V., U.S.	98	38.55N	81.20W
Spencer Gulf, b., Austl. (spĕn′sẽr)	202	34.20S	136.55E
Sperenberg, Ger. (shpĕ′rĕn-bĕrgh)	145b	52.09N	13.22E
Sperkhiós, r., Grc.	161	38.54N	22.02E
Spey, l., Scot., U.K. (spā)	150	57.25N	3.29W
Speyer, Ger. (shpī′ĕr)	154	49.18N	8.26E
Sphinx, hist., Egypt (sfĭnks)	218b	29.57N	31.08E
Spijkenisse, Neth.	145a	51.51N	4.18E
Spinazzola, Italy (spė-nät′zô-lä)	160	40.58N	16.05E
Spirit Lake, Id., U.S. (spĭr′ĭt)	104	47.58N	116.51W
Spirit Lake, Ia., U.S. (lāk)	102	43.25N	95.08W
Spišská Nová Ves, Slvk. (spēsh′skä nō′vä vĕs)	147	48.56N	20.35E
Spitsbergen see Svalbard, dep., Nor.	164	77.00N	20.00E
Split, Cro. (splėt)	142	43.30N	16.28E
Split Lake, l., Can.	89	56.08N	96.15W
Spokane, Wa., U.S. (spōkăn′)	96	47.39N	117.25W
Spokane, r., Wa., U.S.	104	47.47N	118.00W
Spokane Indian Reservation, I.R., Wa., U.S.	104	47.55N	118.00W
Spoleto, Italy (spô-lā′tō)	160	42.44N	12.44E
Spoon, r., Il., U.S. (spo͞on)	111	40.36N	90.22W
Spooner, Wi., U.S. (spo͞on′ẽr)	103	45.50N	91.53W
Sportswood, Austl.	243b	37.50S	144.53E
Spotswood, N.J., U.S. (spŏtz′wo͝od)	100a	40.23N	74.22W
Sprague, r., Or., U.S. (sprāg)	104	42.30N	121.42W
Spratly, i., Asia (sprăt′lė)	196	8.38N	11.54E
Spray, N.C., U.S. (sprā)	115	36.30N	79.44W
Spree, r., Ger. (shprā)	154	51.53N	14.08E
Spremberg, Ger. (shprĕm′bĕrgh)	154	51.35N	14.23E
Spring, r., Ar., U.S.	111	36.25N	91.35W
Springbok, S. Afr. (sprĭng′bŏk)	212	29.35S	17.55E
Spring Creek, r., Nv., U.S. (sprĭng)	108	40.18N	117.45W
Spring Creek, r., Tx., U.S.	112	31.08N	100.50W
Spring Creek, r., Tx., U.S.	113	30.03N	95.43W
Springdale, Can.	93	49.30N	56.05W
Springdale, Ar., U.S. (sprĭng′dāl)	111	36.10N	94.07W
Springdale, Pa., U.S.	101e	40.33N	79.46W
Springer, N.M., U.S. (sprĭng′ẽr)	110	36.21N	104.37W
Springerville, Az., U.S.	109	34.08N	109.17W
Springfield, Co., U.S. (sprĭng′fēld)	110	37.24N	102.04W
Springfield, Il., U.S.	97	39.46N	89.37W
Springfield, Ky., U.S.	98	37.35N	85.10W
Springfield, Ma., U.S.	97	42.05N	72.35W
Springfield, Mn., U.S.	103	44.14N	94.59W
Springfield, Mo., U.S.	97	37.13N	93.17W
Springfield, Oh., U.S.	97	39.55N	83.50W
Springfield, Or., U.S.	104	44.01N	123.02W
Springfield, Pa., U.S.	229b	39.55N	75.24W
Springfield, Tn., U.S.	114	36.30N	86.53W
Springfield, Vt., U.S.	99	43.20N	72.35W
Springfield, Va., U.S.	229d	38.45N	77.13W
Springfontein, S. Afr. (sprĭng′fôn-tīn)	212	30.16S	25.45E
Springhill, Can. (sprĭng-hĭl′)	85	45.39N	64.03W
Spring Mill, Pa., U.S.	229b	40.04N	75.17W
Spring Mountains, mts., Nv., U.S.	108	36.18N	115.49W
Springs, S. Afr. (sprĭngs)	218d	26.16S	28.27E
Springstein, Can. (sprĭng′stīn)	83f	49.49N	97.29W
Springton Reservoir, res., Pa., U.S. (sprĭng-tŭn)	100f	39.57N	75.26W
Springvale, Austl.	201a	37.57N	145.09E
Springvale South, Austl.	243b	37.58S	145.09E
Spring Valley, Ca., U.S.	108a	32.46N	117.01W
Springvalley, Il., U.S. (sprĭng-văl′ĭ)	98	41.20N	89.15W
Spring Valley, Mn., U.S.	103	43.41N	92.26W
Spring Valley, N.Y., U.S.	100a	41.07N	74.03W
Springville, Ut., U.S. (sprĭng-vĭl)	109	40.10N	111.40W
Springwood, Austl.	201b	33.42S	150.34E
Sprockhövel, Ger.	236	51.22N	7.15E
Spruce Grove, Can. (spro͞os grōv)	83g	53.32N	113.55W
Spur, Tx., U.S. (spûr)	110	33.29N	100.51W
Squam, l., N.H., U.S. (skwôm)	99	43.45N	71.30W
Squamish, Can. (skwŏ′mĭsh)	86	49.42N	123.09W
Squamish, r., Can.	86	50.10N	123.30W
Squillace, Golfo di, b., Italy (go͞o′l-fô-dē skwē-lä′chä)	160	38.44N	16.47E
Squirrel Hill, neigh., Pa., U.S.	230b	40.26N	79.55W
Squirrel's Heath, neigh., Eng., U.K.	235	51.35N	0.13E
Srbija (Serbia), hist. reg., Yugo. (sr bė-yä) (sĕr′bė-ä)	161	44.05N	20.35E
Srbobran, Yugo. (s′r′bô-brän′)	161	45.32N	19.50E
Sredne-Kolymsk, Russia (s′rĕd′nyĕ kô-lėmsk′)	165	67.49N	154.55E
Sredne Rogatka, Russia (s′red′nȧ-ya) (rô gär′tkȧ)	172c	59.49N	30.20E
Sredniy Ik, r., Russia (srĕd′nĭ ĭk)	172a	55.46N	58.50E
Sredniy Ural, mts., Russia (ó′ràl)	172a	57.47N	59.00E
Śrem, Pol. (shrĕm)	155	52.06N	17.01E
Sremska Karlovci, Yugo. (srĕm′skė kär′lov-tsė)	161	45.10N	19.57E
Sremska Mitrovica, Yugo. (srĕm′skä mė′trô-vė-tsä′)	161	44.59N	19.39E
Sretensk, Russia (s′rĕ′tĕnsk)	165	52.13N	117.39E
Sri Lanka, nation, Asia	183b	8.45N	82.30E
Srīnagar, India (srē-nŭg′ŭr)	183	34.11N	74.49E
Środa, Pol. (shrō′dȧ)	155	52.14N	17.17E
Staaken, neigh., Ger.	238a	52.32N	13.08E
Stabroek, Bel.	145a	51.20N	4.21E
Stade, Ger. (shtä′dė)	154	53.36N	9.28E
Städjan, mtn., Swe. (stĕd′yän)	152	61.53N	12.50E
Stadlau, neigh., Aus.	239e	48.14N	16.28E
Stafford, Eng., U.K. (stăf′fẽrd)	150	52.48N	2.06W
Stafford, Ks., U.S.	110	37.58N	98.37W
Staffordshire, co., Eng., U.K.	144a	52.45N	2.00W
Stahnsdorf, Ger. (shtäns′dôrf)	145b	52.22N	13.10E
Staines, Eng., U.K.	144b	51.26N	0.13W
Stains, Fr.	237c	48.57N	2.23E
Stakhanov, Ukr.	167	48.34N	38.37E
Stalingrad see Volgograd, Russia	164	48.40N	42.20E
Stalybridge, Eng., U.K.	144a	53.29N	2.03W
Stambaugh, Mi., U.S. (stăm′bô)	103	46.03N	88.38W
Stamford, Eng., U.K.	144a	52.39N	0.28W
Stamford, Ct., U.S. (stăm′fẽrd)	100a	41.03N	73.32W
Stamford, Tx., U.S.	110	32.57N	99.48W
Stammersdorf, Aus. (shtäm′ĕrs-dôrf)	145e	48.19N	16.25E
Stamps, Ar., U.S. (stămps)	111	33.22N	93.31W
Stanberry, Mo., U.S. (stan′bĕr-ė)	111	40.12N	94.34W
Standerton, S. Afr. (stăn′dẽr-tŭn)	212	26.57S	29.17E
Standing Rock Indian Reservation, I.R., N.D., U.S. (stănd′ĭng rŏk)	102	47.07N	101.05W
Standish, Eng., U.K. (stăn′dĭsh)	144a	53.36N	2.39W
Stanford, Ky., U.S. (stăn′fẽrd)	114	37.29N	84.40W
Stanford le Hope, Eng., U.K.	235	51.31N	0.26E
Stanford Rivers, Eng., U.K.	235	51.41N	0.13E
Stanger, S. Afr. (stăŋ-ger)	213c	29.22S	31.18E
Staniard Creek, Bah.	122	24.50N	77.55W
Stanislaus, r., Ca., U.S. (stăn′ĭs-lô)	108	38.10N	120.16W
Stanley, Can. (stăn′lė)	92	46.17N	66.44W
Stanley, Falk. Is.	132	51.46S	57.59W
Stanley, H.K.	241c	22.13N	114.12E
Stanley, N.D., U.S.	102	48.20N	102.25W
Stanley, Wi., U.S.	103	44.56N	90.56W
Stanley Mound, hill, H.K.	241c	22.14N	114.12E
Stanley Pool, l., Afr.	212	4.07S	15.40E
Stanley Reservoir, res., India (stăn′lė)	187	12.07N	77.27E
Stanleyville see Kisangani, Zaire	211	0.30S	25.12E
Stanlow, Eng., U.K.	237a	53.17N	2.52W
Stanmore, neigh., Eng., U.K.	235	51.37N	0.19W
Stann Creek, Belize (stăn krēk)	120a	17.01N	88.14W
Stanovoy Khrebet, mts., Russia (stŭn-ȧ-voi′)	165	56.12N	127.12E
Stansted, Eng., U.K.	235	51.20N	0.18E
Stanton, Ca., U.S. (stăn′tŭn)	107a	33.48N	118.00W
Stanton, Ne., U.S.	102	41.57N	97.15W
Stanton, Tx., U.S.	112	32.08N	101.46W
Stanwell, Eng., U.K.	235	51.27N	0.29W
Stanwell Moor, Eng., U.K.	235	51.28N	0.30W
Stanwood, Wa., U.S. (stăn′wŏd)	106a	48.14N	122.23W
Stapleford Abbots, Eng., U.K.	235	51.38N	0.10E
Stapleford Tawney, Eng., U.K.	235	51.40N	0.11E
Staples, Mn., U.S. (stā′p′lz)	103	46.21N	94.48W
Stapleton, Al., U.S.	114	30.45N	87.48W
Stara Planina, mts., Bul.	142	42.50N	24.45E
Staraya Kupavna, Russia (stä′rȧ-yȧ kû-päf′nȧ)	172b	55.48N	38.10E
Staraya Russa, Russia (stä′rȧ-yȧ ro͞os′sȧ)	166	57.58N	31.21E
Stara Zagora, Bul. (zä′gô-rȧ)	149	42.26N	25.37E
Starbuck, Can. (stär′bŭk)	83f	49.46N	97.36W
Stargard Szczeciński, Pol. (shtär′gärt shchĕ-chyn′skē)	146	53.19N	15.03E
Staritsa, Russia (stä′rē-tsȧ)	162	56.29N	34.58E
Starke, Fl., U.S. (stärk)	115	29.55N	82.07W
Starkville, Co., U.S. (stärk′vĭl)	110	37.06N	104.34W
Starkville, Ms., U.S.	114	33.27N	88.47W
Starnberg, Ger. (shtärn-bĕrgh)	145d	47.59N	11.20E
Starnberger See, l., Ger.	154	47.58N	11.30E
Starobil's′k, Ukr.	167	49.19N	38.57E
Starodub, Russia (stä-rô-drŏp′)	162	52.25N	32.49E
Starograd Gdański, Pol. (stä′rō-grad gdĕn′skē)	146	53.58N	18.33E
Starokostyantyniv, Ukr.	167	49.45N	27.12E
Staro-Minskaya, Russia (stä′rô mĭn′skȧ-yȧ)	167	46.19N	38.51E
Staro-Shcherbinovskaya, Russia	163	46.38N	38.38E
Staro-Subkhangulovo, Russia (stȧro-so͞ob-kan-go͞o′lôvō)	172a	53.08N	57.24E
Staroutkinsk, Russia (stȧ-rô-o͞ot′kĭnsk)	172a	57.14N	59.21E
Starovirivka, Ukr.	163	49.31N	35.48E
Start Point, c., Eng., U.K. (stärt)	147	50.14N	3.34W

ng-sing; ŋ-baŋk; ɴ-nasalized n; nŏd; cŏmmit; ōld; ôbey; ôrder; oi-boil; fo͞od; ŏ-as oo in foot; ou-out; s-soft; sh-dish; th-thin; pūre; ůnite; ûrn; stŭd; circŭs; ü-as in French tu; ′-indeterminate vowel.

352 Stary Sącz-Sullana

PLACE (Pronunciation)	PAGE	Lat. °'	Long. °'
Stary Sącz, Pol. (stä-rē sônch')	155	49.32N	20.36E
Staryy Oskol, Russia (stä'rē ôs-kôl')	167	51.18N	37.51E
Staryy Ostropil', Ukr.	163	49.48N	27.32E
Stassfurt, Ger. (shtäs'fo͞ort)	154	51.52N	11.35E
Staszów, Pol. (stä'shōf)	155	50.32N	21.13E
State College, Pa., U.S. (stāt kŏl'ĕj)	99	40.50N	77.55W
State Line, Mn., U.S. (līn)	107h	46.36N	92.18W
Staten Island, i., N.Y., U.S. (stăt'ĕn)	100a	40.35N	74.10W
Statesboro, Ga., U.S. (stāts'bŭr-ō)	115	32.26N	81.47W
Statesville, N.C., U.S. (stās'vĭl)	115	34.45N	80.54W
Statue of Liberty National Monument, rec., N.Y., U.S.	228	40.41N	74.03W
Staunton, Il., U.S. (stôn'tŭn)	107e	39.01N	89.47W
Staunton, Va., U.S.	99	38.10N	79.05W
Stavanger, Nor. (stä'väng'ĕr)	142	58.59N	5.44E
Stave, r., Can. (stāv)	106d	49.12N	122.24W
Staveley, Eng., U.K. (stāv'lē)	144a	53.17N	1.21W
Stavenisse, Neth.	145a	51.35N	3.59E
Stavropol', Russia	164	45.05N	41.50E
Steamboat Springs, Co., U.S. (stēm'bōt')	110	40.30N	106.48W
Stebliv, Ukr.	163	49.23N	31.03E
Steel, r., Can. (stēl)	90	49.08N	86.55W
Steelton, Pa., U.S. (stēl'tŭn)	99	40.15N	76.45W
Steenbergen, Neth.	145a	51.35N	4.18E
Steens Mountain, mts., Or., U.S. (stēnz)	104	42.15N	118.52W
Steep Point, c., Austl. (stēp)	202	26.15N	112.05E
Stefanie, Lake *see* Chew Bahir, l., Afr.	211	4.46N	37.31E
Steglitz, neigh., Ger.	238a	52.28N	13.19E
Steiermark (Styria), prov., Aus. (shtī'ĕr-märk)	154	47.22N	14.40E
Steinbach, Can.	84	49.32N	96.41W
Steinkjer, Nor. (stĕĭn-kyĕr)	146	64.00N	11.19E
Steinstücken, neigh., Ger.	238a	52.23N	13.08E
Stella, Wa., U.S. (stĕl'ȧ)	106c	46.11N	123.12W
Stellarton, Can. (stĕl'ȧr-tŭn)	85	45.34N	62.40W
Stendal, Ger. (shtĕn'däl)	154	52.37N	11.51E
Stepanakert *see* Xankändi, Azer.	166	39.50N	46.40E
Stephens, Port, b., Austl. (stē'fĕns)	204	32.43N	152.55E
Stephenville, Can. (stē'vĕn-vĭl)	85a	48.33N	58.35W
Stepn'ak, Kaz.	169	52.50N	70.50E
Stepney, neigh., Eng., U.K.	235	51.31N	0.02W
Sterkrade, Ger. (shtĕr'krädĕ)	157c	51.31N	6.51E
Sterkstroom, S. Afr.	213c	31.33S	26.36E
Sterling, Co., U.S. (stûr'lĭng)	96	40.38N	103.14W
Sterling, Il., U.S.	98	41.48N	89.42W
Sterling, Ks., U.S.	110	38.11N	98.11W
Sterling, Ma., U.S.	93a	42.26N	71.41W
Sterling, Tx., U.S.	112	31.53N	100.58W
Sterling Park, Ca., U.S.	231b	37.41N	122.26W
Sterlitamak, Russia (styĕr'lē-ta-mȧk')	164	53.38N	55.56E
Šternberk, Czech Rep. (shtĕrn'bĕrk)	155	49.44N	17.18E
Stettin *see* Szczecin, Pol.	142	53.25N	14.35E
Stettler, Can.	84	52.19N	112.43W
Steubenville, Oh., U.S. (stū'bĕn-vĭl)	98	40.20N	80.40W
Stevens, l., Wa., U.S. (stē'vĕnz)	106a	47.59N	122.06W
Stevens Point, Wi., U.S.	103	44.30N	89.35W
Stevensville, Mt., U.S. (stē'vĕnz-vĭl)	105	46.31N	114.03E
Stewart, r., Can. (stū'ērt)	84	63.27N	138.48W
Stewart Island, i., N.Z.	203a	46.56S	167.40E
Stewart Manor, N.Y., U.S.	228	40.43N	73.41W
Stewiacke, Can. (stū'wē-ăk)	92	45.08N	63.21W
Steynsrus, S. Afr. (stīns'ro͞os)	218d	27.58S	27.33E
Steyr, Aus. (shtīr)	147	48.03N	14.24E
Stickney, Il., U.S.	231a	41.49N	87.47W
Stiepel, neigh., Ger.	236	51.25N	7.15E
Stif, Alg.	210	36.18N	5.21E
Stikine, r., Can. (stĭ-kēn')	84	58.17N	130.10W
Stikine Ranges, Can.	84	59.05N	130.00W
Stillaguamish, r., Wa., U.S.	106a	48.11N	122.18W
Stillaguamish, South Fork, r., Wa., U.S. (stĭl-ȧ-gwä'mĭsh)	106a	48.05N	121.59W
Stillwater, Mn., U.S. (stĭl'wô-tēr)	107g	45.04N	92.48W
Stillwater, Mt., U.S.	105	45.23N	109.45W
Stillwater, Ok., U.S.	111	36.06N	97.03W
Stillwater, r., Mt., U.S.	105	48.47N	114.40W
Stillwater Range, mts., Nv., U.S.	108	39.43N	118.11W
Stintonville, S. Afr.	244b	26.14S	28.13E
Štip, Mac. (shtĭp)	161	41.43N	22.07E
Stirling, Scot., U.K. (stûr'lĭng)	150	56.05N	3.59W
Stittsville, Can. (stĭts'vĭl)	83c	45.15N	75.54W
Stizef, Alg. (mĕr-syä' lȧ-kôɴb)	159	35.18N	0.11W
Stjördalshalsen, Nor. (styûr-däls-hälsĕn)	152	63.26N	11.00E
Stockbridge Munsee Indian Reservation, I.R., Wi., U.S. (stŏk'brĭdj mŭn-sē)	103	44.49N	89.00W
Stockerau, Aus. (shtô'kĕ-rou)	154	48.24N	16.13E
Stockholm, Swe. (stôk'hôlm)	142	59.23N	18.00E
Stockholm, Me., U.S. (stŏk'hōlm)	92	47.05N	68.08W
Stockport, Eng., U.K. (stŏk'pôrt)	150	53.24N	2.09W
Stockton, Eng., U.K.	150	54.35N	1.25W
Stockton, Ca., U.S. (stŏk'tŭn)	96	37.56N	121.16W
Stockton, Ks., U.S.	110	39.26N	99.16W
Stockton, i., Wi., U.S.	103	46.56N	90.25W
Stockton Plateau, plat., Tx., U.S.	96	30.34N	102.35W
Stockton Reservoir, res., Mo., U.S.	111	37.40N	93.45W
Stockum, neigh., Ger.	236	51.28N	7.22E
Stöde, Swe. (stû'dĕ)	152	62.26N	16.35E
Stoeng Trêng, Camb. (stông'trĕng')	196	13.36N	106.00E
Stoke d'Abernon, Eng., U.K.	235	51.19N	0.23W
Stoke Newington, neigh., Eng., U.K.	235	51.34N	0.05W
Stoke-on-Trent, Eng., U.K. (stōk-ŏn-trĕnt)	146	53.01N	2.12W
Stoke Poges, Eng., U.K.	235	51.33N	0.35W
Stokhid, r., Ukr.	155	51.24N	25.20E
Stolac, Bos. (stô'läts)	161	43.03N	17.59E
Stolbovoy, is., Russia (stôl-bô-voi')	171	74.05N	136.00E
Stolin, Bela. (stô'lēn)	155	51.54N	26.52E
Stolpe, Ger.	238a	52.40N	13.16E
Stömstad, Swe.	152	58.58N	11.09E
Stondon Massey, Eng., U.K.	235	51.41N	0.18E
Stone, Eng., U.K.	144a	52.54N	2.09W
Stone, Eng., U.K.	235	51.27N	0.16E
Stoneham, Can. (stōn'ăm)	83b	46.59N	71.22W
Stoneham, Ma., U.S.	93a	42.30N	71.05W
Stonehaven, Scot., U.K. (stōn'hā-v'n)	150	56.57N	2.09W
Stone Mountain, Ga., U.S. (stōn)	100c	33.49N	84.10W
Stone Park, Il., U.S.	231a	41.45N	87.53W
Stonewall, Can. (stōn'wôl)	83f	50.09N	97.21W
Stonewall, Ms., U.S.	114	32.08N	88.44W
Stoney Creek, Can. (stō'nē)	83d	43.13N	79.45W
Stonington, Ct., U.S. (stōn'ĭng-tŭn)	99	41.20N	71.55W
Stony Indian Reserve, I.R., Can.	83e	51.10N	114.45W
Stony Mountain, Can.	83f	50.05N	97.13W
Stony Plain, Can. (stō'nē plān)	83g	53.32N	114.00W
Stony Plain Indian Reserve, I.R., Can.	83g	53.29N	113.48W
Stony Point, N.Y., U.S.	100a	41.13N	73.58W
Stony Run, Md., U.S.	229c	39.11N	76.42W
Stora Sotra, i., Nor.	152	60.24N	4.35E
Stord, i., Nor. (stôrd)	152	59.54N	5.15E
Store Baelt, strt., Den.	152	55.25N	10.50E
Storeton, Eng., U.K.	237a	53.21N	3.03W
Storfjorden, fj., Nor.	152	62.17N	6.19E
Stormberg, mts., S. Afr. (stôrm'bûrg)	213c	31.28S	26.35E
Storm Lake, Ia., U.S.	102	42.39N	95.12W
Stormy Point, c., V.I.U.S. (stôr'mē)	117c	18.22N	65.01W
Stornoway, Scot., U.K. (stôr'nō-wā)	146	58.13N	6.21W
Storozhynets', Ukr.	155	48.10N	25.44E
Störsjo, Swe. (stôr'shû)	152	62.49N	13.08E
Störsjoen, l., Nor. (stôr-syûĕn)	152	61.32N	11.30E
Störsjon, l., Swe.	146	63.06N	14.00E
Storvik, Swe.	152	60.37N	16.31E
Stoughton, Wi., U.S.	103	42.54N	89.15W
Stour, r., Eng., U.K. (stour)	151	52.09N	0.29E
Stourbridge, Eng., U.K. (stour'brĭj)	144a	52.27N	2.08W
Stow, Ma., U.S. (stō)	93a	42.56N	71.31W
Stow, Oh., U.S.	101d	41.09N	81.26W
Stowe Township, Pa., U.S.	230b	40.29N	80.04W
Straatsdrif, S. Afr.	218d	25.19S	26.22E
Strabane, N. Ire., U.K. (stră-băn')	150	54.59N	7.27W
Straelen, Ger. (shtră'lĕn)	157c	51.26N	6.16E
Strahan, Austl. (strā'ăn)	203	42.08S	145.28E
Strakonice, Czech Rep. (strä'kô-nyē-tsĕ)	154	49.18N	13.52E
Straldzha, Bul. (sträl'dzhȧ)	161	42.37N	26.44E
Stralsund, Ger. (shräl'sŏont)	146	54.18N	13.04E
Strangford Lough, l., N. Ire., U.K.	150	54.30N	5.34W
Strängnäs, Swe. (strĕng'nĕs)	152	59.23N	16.59E
Stranraer, Scot., U.K. (străn-rär')	150	54.55N	5.05W
Strasbourg, Fr. (strȧs-bo͞or')	142	48.36N	7.49E
Stratford, Can. (străt'fērd)	90	43.20N	81.05W
Stratford, Ct., U.S.	99	41.10N	73.05W
Stratford, Wi., U.S.	103	44.16N	90.02W
Stratford-upon-Avon, Eng., U.K.	150	52.13N	1.41W
Strathfield, Austl.	243a	33.52S	151.06E
Strathmoor, neigh., Mi., U.S.	230c	42.23N	83.11W
Straubing, Ger. (strou'bĭng)	154	48.52N	12.36E
Strauch, Ger.	236	51.09N	6.56E
Strausberg, Ger. (strous'bĕrgh)	154	52.35N	13.50E
Strawberry, r., Ut., U.S.	109	40.05N	110.55W
Strawberry Point, Ca., U.S.	231b	37.54N	122.31W
Strawn, Tx., U.S. (strôn)	112	32.38N	98.28W
Streatham, neigh., Eng., U.K.	235	51.26N	0.08W
Streator, Il., U.S. (strē'tēr)	98	41.05N	88.50W
Streeter, N.D., U.S.	102	46.40N	99.22W
Streetsville, Can. (strētz'vĭl)	83d	43.34N	79.43W
Strehaia, Rom. (strĕ-kä'yȧ)	161	44.37N	23.13E
Strel'na, Russia (strĕl'nȧ)	172c	59.52N	30.01E
Stretford, Eng., U.K. (strĕt'fērd)	144a	53.25N	2.19W
Strickland, r., Pap. N. Gui. (strĭk'lănd)	197	6.15S	142.00E
Strijen, Neth.	145a	51.44N	4.32E
Stromboli, Italy (strôm'bô-lē)	149	38.46N	15.16E
Stromyn, Russia (strô'mĭn)	172b	56.02N	38.29E
Strong, r., Ms., U.S. (strông)	114	32.03N	89.42W
Strongsville, Oh., U.S. (strôngz'vĭl)	101d	41.19N	81.50W
Stronsay, i., Scot., U.K. (strŏn'sā)	150a	59.09N	2.35W
Stroudsburg, Pa., U.S. (stroudz'bûrg)	99	41.00N	75.15W
Strubenvale, S. Afr.	244b	26.16S	28.28E
Struer, Den.	152	56.29N	8.34E
Strugi Krasnyye, Russia (stro͞o'gĭ krä's-ny'yĕ)	162	58.14N	29.10E
Struisbelt, S. Afr.	244b	26.19S	28.29E
Struma, r., Eur. (stro͞o'mȧ)	161	41.55N	23.05E
Strumica, Mac. (stro͞o'mĭ-tsȧ)	161	41.26N	22.38E
Strümp, Ger.	236	51.17N	6.40E
Strunino, Russia	172b	56.23N	38.34E
Struthers, Oh., U.S. (strŭdh'ērz)	98	41.00N	80.35W
Struvenhütten, Ger. (shtro͞o'vĕn-hü-tĕn)	145c	53.52N	10.04E
Strydpoortberge, mts., S. Afr.	218d	24.08N	29.18E
Stryy, Ukr. (strē')	155	49.16N	23.51E
Strzelce Opolskie, Pol. (stzhĕl'tsĕ ō-pŏl'skyĕ)	155	50.31N	18.20E
Strzelin, Pol. (stzhĕ-lĭn)	155	50.48N	17.06E
Strzelno, Pol. (stzhäl'nō)	155	52.37N	18.10E
Stuart, Fl., U.S. (stū'ērt)	115a	27.10N	80.14W
Stuart, Ia., U.S.	103	41.31N	94.20W
Stuart, i., Ak., U.S.	95	63.25N	162.45W
Stuart, i., Wa., U.S.	106d	48.42N	123.10W
Stuart Lake, l., Can.	86	54.32N	124.35W
Stuart Range, mts., Austl.	202	29.00S	134.30E
Sturgeon, r., Can.	83g	53.41N	113.46W
Sturgeon, r., Mi., U.S.	103	46.43N	88.43W
Sturgeon Bay, Wi., U.S.	103	44.50N	87.22W
Sturgeon Bay, b., Can.	89	52.00N	98.00W
Sturgeon Falls, Can.	85	46.19N	79.49W
Sturgis, Ky., U.S.	98	37.35N	88.00W
Sturgis, Mi., U.S.	98	41.45N	85.25W
Sturgis, S.D., U.S.	102	44.25N	103.31W
Sturt Creek, r., Austl.	202	19.40S	127.40E
Sturtevant, Wi., U.S. (stŭr'tē-vănt)	101a	42.42N	87.54W
Stutterheim, S. Afr. (stŭrt'ēr-hīm)	213c	32.34S	27.27E
Stuttgart, Ger. (shto͞ot'gärt)	142	48.48N	9.15E
Stuttgart, Ar., U.S. (stŭt'gärt)	111	34.30N	91.33W
Styal, Eng., U.K.	237b	53.21N	2.15W
Stykkishólmur, Ice.	146	65.00N	21.48W
Styr', r., Eur. (stēr)	155	51.44N	26.07E
Styria *see* Steiermark, prov., Aus.	154	47.22N	14.40E
Styrum, neigh., Ger.	236	51.27N	6.51E
Suao, Tai. (so͞oŏu)	193	24.35N	121.45E
Subarnarekha, r., India	186	22.38N	86.26E
Subata, Lat. (sŏ'bȧ-tȧ)	153	56.02N	25.54E
Subic, Phil. (so͞o'bĭk)	197a	14.52N	120.15E
Subic Bay, b., Phil.	197a	14.41N	120.11E
Subotica, Yugo. (so͞o'bô'tē-tsȧ)	142	46.06N	19.41E
Subugo, mtn., Kenya	217	1.40S	35.49E
Succasunna, N.J., U.S. (sŭk'kȧ-sŭn'nȧ)	100a	40.52N	74.37W
Suceava, Rom. (so͞o-chȧ-ä'vȧ)	155	47.39N	26.17E
Suceava, r., Rom.	155	47.45N	26.10E
Sucha, Pol. (so͞o'ĸȧ)	155	49.44N	19.40E
Suchiapa, Mex. (so͞o-chē-ä'pä)	119	16.38N	93.08W
Suchiapa, r., Mex.	119	16.27N	93.26W
Suchitoto, El Sal. (so͞o-chē-tō'tō)	120	13.58N	89.03W
Sucio, r., Col. (so͞o'syō)	130a	6.55N	76.15W
Suck, r., Ire. (sŭk)	150	53.34N	8.16W
Sucre, Bol. (so͞o'krā)	130	19.06S	65.16W
Sucre, dept., Ven. (so͞o'krĕ)	131b	10.18N	64.12W
Sucy-en-Brie, Fr.	237c	48.46N	2.32E
Sud, Canal du, strt., Haiti	123	18.40N	73.15W
Sud, Rivière du, r., Can. (rē-vyâr'dü süd')	83b	46.56N	70.35W
Suda, Russia (sŏ'dȧ)	172a	56.58N	56.45E
Suda, r., Russia (sŏ'dȧ)	162	59.24N	36.40E
Sudair, Sau. Ar. (sŭ-dä'ēr)	182	25.48N	46.28E
Sudalsvatnet, l., Nor.	152	59.35N	6.59E
Sudan, nation, Afr.	211	14.00N	28.00E
Sudan, reg., Afr. (so͞o-dän')	210	15.00N	7.00E
Sudberg, neigh., Ger.	236	51.11N	7.08E
Sudbury, Can. (sŭd'bĕr-ē)	85	46.28N	81.00W
Sudbury, Ma., U.S.	93a	42.23N	71.25W
Suderwich, neigh., Ger.	236	51.37N	7.15E
Sudetes, mts., Eur.	142	50.41N	15.37E
Sudogda, Russia (sŏ'dôk-dȧ)	162	55.57N	40.29E
Sudost', r., Eur. (sŏ-dôst')	162	52.43N	33.13E
Sudzha, Russia (sŏd'zhȧ)	163	51.14N	35.11E
Sueca, Spain (swā'kä)	159	39.12N	0.18W
Suez, Egypt	211	29.58N	32.34E
Suez, Gulf of, b., Egypt (so͞o-ĕz')	211	29.53N	32.33E
Suez Canal, can., Egypt	211	30.53N	32.21E
Suffern, N.Y., U.S. (sŭf'fērn)	100a	41.07N	74.09W
Suffolk, Va., U.S. (sŭf'ŭk)	100g	36.43N	76.35W
Sugandha, India	240a	22.54N	88.20E
Sugar City, Co., U.S.	110	38.12N	103.42W
Sugar Creek, Mo., U.S.	107f	39.07N	94.27W
Sugar Creek, r., Il., U.S. (shŏg'ēr)	111	40.14N	89.28W
Sugar Creek, r., In., U.S.	98	39.55N	87.10W
Sugar Island, i., Mi., U.S.	107k	46.31N	84.12W
Sugarloaf Point, c., Austl. (sŏgẽr'lōf)	204	32.19S	153.04E
Suggi Lake, l., Can.	89	54.22N	102.47W
Suginami, neigh., Japan	242a	35.42N	139.38E
Sühbaatar, Mong.	188	50.18N	106.31E
Suhl, Ger. (zo͞ol)	154	50.37N	10.41E
Suichuan, mtn., China	193	26.25N	114.10E
Suide, China (swā-dŭ)	192	37.32N	110.12E
Suifenhe, China (swā-fŭn-hŭ)	189	44.47N	131.13E
Suihua, China	189	46.38N	126.50E
Suining, China (so͞o'ē-nĭng')	190	33.54N	117.57E
Suipacha, Arg. (swē-pä'chä)	129c	34.45S	59.43W
Suiping, China (swā-pĭŋ)	190	33.09N	113.58E
Suir, r., Ire. (sūr)	150	52.20N	7.32W
Suisun Bay, b., Ca., U.S. (so͞oē-so͞on')	106b	38.07N	122.02W
Suita, Japan (sŏ'ē-tä)	195b	34.45N	135.32E
Suitland, Md., U.S. (sŏt'lănd)	100e	38.51N	76.57W
Suixian, China (swā shyĕn)	193	31.42N	113.20E
Suiyüan, hist. reg., China (swā-yüĕn)	188	41.31N	107.04E
Suizhong, China (swā-jôŋ)	192	40.22N	120.20E
Sukabumi, Indon.	196	6.52S	106.56E
Sukadana, Indon.	196	1.15S	110.30E
Sukagawa, Japan (so͞o'kä-gä'wä)	195	37.08N	140.07E
Sukhinichi, Russia (so͞o'kē'nē-chē)	166	54.07N	35.18E
Sukhona, r., Russia (sŏ-kô'nȧ)	166	59.30N	42.20E
Sukhoy Log, Russia (so͞o'kôy lôg)	172a	56.55N	62.03E
Sukhumi, Geor. (sŏ-kŏm')	167	43.00N	41.00E
Sukkur, Pak. (sŭk'ŭr)	183	27.49N	68.50E
Sukkwan Island, i., Ak., U.S.	86	55.05N	132.45W
Suksun, Russia (sŏk'sŏn)	172a	57.08N	57.22E
Sukumo, Japan (so͞o'kō-mō)	195	32.58N	132.45E
Sukunka, r., Can.	87	55.00N	121.50W
Sula, r., Ukr. (so͞o-lä')	163	50.36N	33.13E
Sula, Kepulauan, is., Indon.	197	2.20S	125.20E
Sulaco, r., Hond. (so͞o-lä'kō)	120	14.55N	87.31W
Sulaimān Range, mts., Pak. (sŏ-lä-ē-män')	183	29.47N	69.10E
Sulak, r., Russia (so͞o-läk')	167	43.30N	47.00E
Sulfeld, Ger. (zo͞o'fĕld)	145c	53.48N	10.13E
Sulina, Rom. (so͞o-lē'nȧ)	149	45.08N	29.38E
Sulitelma, mtn., Eur. (so͞o-lē-tyĕl'mȧ)	146	67.03N	16.35E
Sullana, Peru (so͞o-lyä'nä)	130	4.57S	80.47W

ăt; finăl; rāte; senāte; ärm; ȧsk; sofȧ; fâre; ch-choose; dh-as th in other; bē; ēvent; bĕt; recĕnt; cratẽr; g-gō; gh-guttural g; bĭt; ĭ-short neutral; rīde; ĸ-guttural k as ch in German ich;

PRONOUNCING INDEX

Sulligent–Taboão da Serra 353

PLACE (Pronunciation)	PAGE	Lat. °′	Long. °′
Sulligent, Al., U.S. (sŭl′ĭ-jĕnt)	114	33.52N	88.06W
Sullivan, Il., U.S. (sŭl′ĭ-văn)	98	41.35N	88.35W
Sullivan, In., U.S.	98	39.05N	87.20W
Sullivan, Mo., U.S.	111	38.13N	91.09W
Sulmona, Italy (so͞ol-mō′nä)	160	42.02N	13.58E
Sulphur, Ok., U.S. (sŭl′fŭr)	111	34.31N	96.58W
Sulphur, r., Tx., U.S.	111	33.26N	95.06W
Sulphur Springs, Tx., U.S. (sprĭngz)	111	33.09N	95.36W
Sultan, Wa., U.S. (sŭl′tăn)	106a	47.52N	121.49W
Sultan, r., Wa., U.S.	106a	47.55N	121.49W
Sultepec, Mex. (so͞ol-tå-pĕk′)	118	18.50N	99.51W
Sulu Archipelago, is., Phil. (so͞o′lo͞o)	196	5.52N	122.00E
Suluntah, Libya	149	32.39N	21.49E
Sulūq, Libya	211	31.39N	20.15E
Sulu Sea, sea, Asia	196	8.25N	119.00E
Suma, Japan (so͞o′mä)	195b	34.39N	135.08E
Sumas, Wa., U.S. (sū′măs)	106d	49.00N	122.16W
Sumatera, i., Indon. (sò-mä-trå)	196	2.06N	99.40E
Sumatra *see* Sumatera, i., Indon.	196	2.06N	99.40E
Sumba, i., Indon. (sŭm′bå)	196	9.52S	119.00E
Sumba, Île, i., Zaire	216	1.44N	19.32E
Sumbawa, i., Indon. (sòm-bä′wä)	196	9.00S	118.18E
Sumbawa-Besar, Indon.	196	8.32S	117.20E
Sumbawanga, Tan.	217	7.58S	31.37E
Sumbe, Ang.	212	11.13S	13.50E
Sümeg, Hung. (shü′mĕg)	155	46.59N	17.19E
Sumida, r., Japan (so͞o′mė-dä)	195	36.01N	139.24E
Sumidouro, Braz. (so͞o-mė-dō′rò)	129a	22.04S	42.41W
Sumiyoshi, Japan (so͞o′mė-yō′shė)	195b	34.43N	135.16E
Sumiyoshi, neigh., Japan	242b	34.36N	135.31E
Summer Lake, l., Or., U.S. (sŭm′ẽr)	104	42.50N	120.35W
Summerland, Can. (sŭ′mẽr-lănd)	87	49.39N	119.40W
Summerseat, Eng., U.K.	237b	53.38N	2.19W
Summerside, Can. (sŭm′ẽr-sīd)	85	46.25N	63.47W
Summerton, S.C., U.S. (sŭm′ẽr-tŭn)	115	33.37N	80.22W
Summerville, S.C., U.S. (sŭm′ẽr-vĭl)	115	33.00N	80.10W
Summit, Il., U.S. (sŭm′mĭt)	101a	41.47N	87.48W
Summit, N.J., U.S.	100a	40.43N	74.21W
Summit Lake Indian Reservation, I.R., Nv., U.S.	104	41.35N	119.30W
Summit Park, Md., U.S.	229c	39.23N	76.41W
Summit Peak, mtn., Co., U.S.	109	37.20N	106.40W
Sumner, Wa., U.S. (sŭm′nẽr)	106a	47.12N	122.14W
Šumperk, Czech Rep. (shòm′pĕrk)	155	49.57N	17.02E
Sumqayıt, Azer.	168	40.36N	49.38E
Sumrall, Ms., U.S. (sŭm′rôl)	114	31.25N	89.34W
Sumter, S.C., U.S. (sŭm′tẽr)	115	33.55N	80.21W
Sumy, Ukr. (so͞o′mĭ)	164	50.54N	34.47E
Sumy, prov., Ukr.	163	51.02N	34.05E
Sun, r., Mt., U.S. (sŭn)	105	47.34N	111.53W
Sunburst, Mt., U.S.	105	48.53N	111.55W
Sunbury, Eng., U.K.	235	51.25N	0.26W
Sunda, Selat, strt., Indon.	196	5.45S	106.15E
Sundance, Wy., U.S. (sŭn′dăns)	105	44.24N	104.27W
Sundarbans, sw., Asia (sòn′dẽr-bŭns)	183	21.50N	89.00E
Sunday Strait, strt., Austl. (sŭn′dā)	202	15.50S	122.45E
Sundbyberg, Swe. (sòn′bü-bĕrgh)	152	59.24N	17.56E
Sunderland, Eng., U.K. (sŭn′dẽr-lănd)	146	54.55N	1.25W
Sunderland, Md., U.S.	100e	38.41N	76.36W
Sundridge, Eng., U.K.	235	51.17N	0.08E
Sundsvall, Swe. (sònds′väl)	142	62.24N	19.19E
Sungari (Songhua), r., China	189	46.09N	127.53E
Sungari Reservoir, res., China	192	42.55N	127.50E
Sungurlu, Tur. (soōn′gòr-lò′)	149	40.08N	34.20E
Sun Kosi, r., Nepal	186	27.13N	85.52E
Sunland, Ca., U.S. (sŭn-lănd)	107a	34.16N	118.18W
Sunne, Swe. (so͞on′ĕ)	152	59.51N	13.07E
Sunninghill, Eng., U.K. (sŭnĭng′hĭl)	144b	51.23N	0.40W
Sunnymead, Ca., U.S. (sŭn′ĭ-mēd)	107a	33.56N	117.15W
Sunnyside, Ut., U.S.	109	39.35N	110.20W
Sunnyside, Wa., U.S.	104	46.19N	120.00W
Sunnyvale, Ca., U.S. (sŭn-nė-vāl)	106b	37.23N	122.02W
Sunol, Ca., U.S. (so͞o′nŭl)	106b	37.36N	122.53W
Sunset, Ut., U.S. (sŭn-sĕt)	107b	41.08N	112.02W
Sunset Beach, Ca., U.S.	232	33.43N	118.04W
Sunset Crater National Monument, rec., Az., U.S. (krā′tẽr)	109	35.20N	111.30W
Sunshine, Austl.	201a	37.47S	144.50E
Suntar, Russia (sòn-tår′)	165	62.14N	117.49E
Sunyani, Ghana	214	7.20N	2.20W
Suoyarvi, Russia (so͞o′ô-yĕr′vė)	166	62.12N	32.29E
Superior, Az., U.S. (su-pē′rĭ-ẽr)	109	33.15N	111.10W
Superior, Ne., U.S.	110	40.04N	98.05W
Superior, Wi., U.S.	97	46.44N	92.06W
Superior, Wy., U.S.	105	41.45N	108.57W
Superior, Laguna, l., Mex. (lä-go͞o′nå so͞o-pā-rė-ōr′)	119	16.20N	94.55W
Superior, Lake, l., N.A.	97	47.38N	89.20W
Superior Village, Wi., U.S.	107h	46.38N	92.07W
Sup′ung Reservoir, res., Asia (so͞o′po͞ong)	194	40.35N	126.00E
Suqian, China (so͞o-chyĕn)	190	33.57N	118.17E
Suquamish, Wa., U.S. (so͞o-gwä′mĭsh)	106a	47.44N	122.34W
Suquṭrā (Socotra), i., Yemen (sô-kō′trå)	182	13.00N	52.30E
Şūr, Leb. (so͞or) (tīr)	181a	33.16N	35.13E
Şūr, Oman	182	22.23N	59.28E
Šura, neigh., India	240a	22.33N	88.25E
Surabaya, Indon.	196	7.23S	112.45E
Surakarta, Indon.	196	7.35S	110.45E
Šurany, Slvk. (sho͞o′rå-nû′)	155	48.05N	18.11E
Surat, Austl. (sū-rāt)	204	27.18S	149.00E
Surat, India (sò′rŭt)	183	21.08N	73.22E
Surat Thani, Thai.	196	8.59N	99.14E
Surazh, Bela.	162	55.24N	30.46E
Surazh, Russia (so͞o-råzh′)	162	53.02N	32.27E

PLACE (Pronunciation)	PAGE	Lat. °′	Long. °′
Surbiton, neigh., Eng., U.K.	235	51.24N	0.18W
Surco, Peru	233c	12.09S	77.01W
Suresnes, Fr.	237c	48.52N	2.14E
Surgères, Fr. (sür-zhâr′)	156	46.06N	0.51W
Surgut, Russia (sòr-gòt′)	164	61.18N	73.38E
Suriname, nation, S.A. (so͞o-rė-näm′)	131	4.00N	56.00W
Sūrmaq, Iran	185	31.03N	52.48E
Surquillo, Peru	233c	12.07S	77.02W
Surt, Libya	211	31.14N	16.37E
Surt, Khalīj, b., Libya	211	31.30N	18.28E
Suruga-Wan, b., Japan (so͞o′ro͞o-gä wän)	194	34.52N	138.36E
Suru-Lere, neigh., Nig.	244d	6.31N	3.22E
Susa, Japan	195	34.40N	131.39E
Sušak, i., Yugo.	160	42.45N	16.30E
Susak, Otok, i., Yugo.	160	44.31N	14.15E
Susaki, Japan (so͞o′sä-kė)	195	33.23N	133.16E
Sušice, Czech Rep.	154	49.14N	13.31E
Susitna, Ak., U.S. (so͞o-sĭt′nȧ)	95	61.28N	150.28W
Susitna, r., Ak., U.S.	95	62.00N	150.28W
Susong, China (so͞o-sôŋ)	193	30.18N	116.08E
Susquehanna, Pa., U.S. (sŭs′kwė-hăn′ȧ)	99	41.55N	73.55W
Susquehanna, r., U.S.	99	39.50N	76.20W
Sussex, Can. (sŭs′ĕks)	85	45.43N	65.31W
Sussex, N.J., U.S.	100a	41.12N	74.36W
Sussex, Wi., U.S.	101a	43.08N	88.12W
Sutherland, Austl. (sŭdh′ẽr-lănd)	201b	34.02S	151.04E
Sutherland, S. Afr. (sŭ′thẽr-lănd)	212	32.25S	20.40E
Sutlej, r., Asia (sŭt′lĕj)	183	30.15N	73.00E
Sutton, Eng., U.K. (sut″n)	144b	51.21N	0.12W
Sutton, Ma., U.S.	93a	42.09N	71.46W
Sutton-at-Hone, Eng., U.K.	235	51.25N	0.14E
Sutton Coldfield, Eng., U.K. (kōld′fēld)	144a	52.34N	1.49W
Sutton-in-Ashfield, Eng., U.K. (ĭn-ăsh′fēld)	144a	53.07N	1.15W
Suurbekom, S. Afr.	244b	26.19S	27.44E
Suurberge, mts., S. Afr.	213c	33.15S	25.32E
Suva, Fiji	198g	18.08S	178.25E
Suwa, Japan (so͞o′wä)	195	36.03N	138.08E
Suwałki, Pol. (sò-vou′kė)	155	54.05N	22.58E
Suwanee Lake, l., Can.	89	56.08N	100.10W
Suwannee, r., U.S. (sò-wô′nė)	97	29.42N	83.00W
Suways al Ḩulwah, Tur‛ at as, can., Egypt	218c	30.15N	32.20E
Suxian, China (so͞o shyĕn)	192	33.29N	117.51E
Suzdal′, Russia (so͞oz′dål)	162	56.26N	40.29E
Suzhou, China (so͞o-jō)	189	31.19N	120.37E
Suzuki-shinden, Japan	242a	35.43N	139.31E
Suzu Misaki, c., Japan (so͞o′zo͞o mė′sä-kė)	194	37.30N	137.35E
Svalbard (Spitsbergen), dep., Nor. (sväl′bärt) (spĭts′bûr-gĕn)	164	77.00N	20.00E
Svaneke, Den. (svä′nĕ-kĕ)	152	55.08N	15.07E
Svatove, Ukr.	167	49.23N	38.10E
Svedala, Swe. (svĕ′dä-lä)	152	55.29N	13.11E
Sveg, Swe.	152	62.03N	14.22E
Svelvik, Nor. (svĕl′vėk)	152	59.37N	10.18E
Svenčionys, Lith.	153	55.09N	26.09E
Svendborg, Den. (svĕn-bôrgh)	152	55.05N	10.35E
Svensen, Or., U.S. (svĕn′sĕn)	106c	46.10N	123.39W
Sverdlovsk *see* Yekaterinburg, Russia	164	56.51N	60.36E
Svetlaya, Russia (svyĕt′lå-yå)	194	46.09N	137.53E
Svicha, r., Ukr.	155	49.09N	24.10E
Svilajnac, Yugo. (svė′lå-ė-nåts)	161	44.12N	21.14E
Svilengrad, Bul. (svėl′ĕn-gråt)	161	41.44N	26.11E
Svir′, r., Russia	166	60.55N	33.40E
Svir Kanal, can., Russia (kå-näl′)	153	60.10N	32.40E
Svishtov, Bul. (svēsh′tôf)	149	43.36N	25.21E
Svisloch′, r., Bela. (svēs′lôĸ)	162	53.38N	28.10E
Svitavy, Czech Rep.	154	49.46N	16.28E
Svobodnyy, Russia (svô-bôd′nĭ)	165	51.28N	128.28E
Svolvaer, Nor. (svôl′vĕr)	146	68.15N	14.29E
Svyatoy Nos, Mys, c., Russia (svyŭ′toi nôs)	165	72.18N	139.28E
Swadlincote, Eng., U.K. (swŏd′lĭn-kôt)	144a	52.46N	1.33W
Swain Reefs, rf., Austl. (swān)	203	22.12S	152.08E
Swainsboro, Ga., U.S. (swānz′bŭr-ô)	115	32.37N	82.21W
Swakopmund, Nmb. (svä′kôp-mònt) (swå′kôp-mònd)	212	22.40S	14.30E
Swallowfield, Eng., U.K. (swŏl′ô-fēld)	144b	51.21N	0.58W
Swampscott, Ma., U.S. (swômp′skŏt)	93a	42.28N	70.55W
Swan, r., Austl.	202	31.30S	116.30E
Swan, r., Can.	89	51.58N	101.45W
Swan, r., Mt., U.S.	105	47.50N	113.40W
Swan Acres, Pa., U.S.	230b	40.33N	80.02W
Swan Hill, Austl.	203	35.20S	143.30E
Swan Hills, Can. (hĭlz)	84	54.52N	115.45W
Swan Island, i., Austl. (swŏn)	201a	38.15S	144.41E
Swan Lake, l., Can.	89	52.30N	100.45W
Swanland, reg., Austl. (swŏn′lănd)	202	31.45S	119.15E
Swanley, Eng., U.K.	235	51.24N	0.12E
Swan Range, mts., Mt., U.S.	105	47.50N	113.40W
Swan River, Can. (swŏn rĭv′ẽr)	84	52.06N	101.16W
Swanscombe, Eng., U.K.	235	51.26N	0.18E
Swansea, Wales, U.K.	147	51.37N	3.59W
Swansea, Il., U.S. (swŏn′sē)	107e	38.32N	89.59W
Swansea, Ma., U.S.	100b	41.45N	71.09W
Swansea, neigh., Can.	227c	43.38N	79.28W
Swanson Reservoir, res., Ne., U.S. (swŏn′sŭn)	110	40.13N	101.30W
Swartberg, mtn., Afr.	213c	30.08S	29.34E
Swarthmore, Pa., U.S.	229b	39.54N	75.21W
Swartkop, mtn., S. Afr.	212a	34.13S	18.27E
Swartruggens, S. Afr.	218d	25.40S	26.40E
Swartspruit, S. Afr.	213b	25.44S	28.01E
Swatow *see* Shantou, China	189	23.20N	116.40E

PLACE (Pronunciation)	PAGE	Lat. °′	Long. °′
Swaziland, nation, Afr. (Swä′zė-lănd)	212	26.45S	31.30E
Sweden, nation, Eur. (swē′dĕn)	142	60.10N	14.10E
Swedesboro, N.J., U.S. (swēdz′bẽ-rô)	100f	39.45N	75.22W
Sweetwater, Tn., U.S. (swēt′wô-tẽr)	114	35.36N	84.29W
Sweetwater, Tx., U.S.	96	32.28N	100.25W
Sweetwater, l., N.D., U.S.	102	48.15N	98.35W
Sweetwater, r., Wy., U.S.	105	42.19N	108.35W
Sweetwater Reservoir, res., Ca., U.S.	108a	32.42N	116.54W
Świdnica, Pol. (shvĭd-nē′tså)	154	50.50N	16.30E
Świdwin, Pol. (shvĭd′vĭn)	154	53.46N	15.48E
Świebodzice, Pol.	154	50.51N	16.17E
Świebodzin, Pol. (shvyĕɴ-bo′jĕts)	154	52.16N	15.36E
Świecie, Pol. (shvyäɴ′tsyĕ)	155	53.23N	18.26E
Świętokrzyskie, Góry, mts., Pol. (shvyĕɴ-tō-kzhĭ′skyĕ go͞o′rĭ)	155	50.57N	21.02E
Swift, r., Eng., U.K.	144a	52.26N	1.08W
Swift, r., Me., U.S. (swĭft)	93	44.42N	70.40E
Swift Creek Reservoir, res., Wa., U.S.	104	46.03N	122.10W
Swift Current, Can. (swĭft kûr′ĕnt)	84	50.17N	107.50W
Swindle Island, i., Can.	86	52.32N	128.35W
Swindon, Eng., U.K. (swĭn′dŭn)	150	51.35N	1.55W
Swinomish Indian Reservation, I.R., Wa., U.S. (swĭ-nō′mĭsh)	106a	48.25N	122.27W
Świnoujście, Pol. (shvĭ-nĭ-ô-wēsh′chyĕ)	154	53.56N	14.14E
Swinton, Eng., U.K. (swĭn′tŭn)	144a	53.30N	1.19W
Swinton, Eng., U.K.	237b	53.31N	2.20W
Swissvale, Pa., U.S. (swĭs′vāl)	101e	40.25N	79.53W
Switzerland, nation, Eur. (swĭt′zẽr-lănd)	142	46.30N	7.43E
Syas′, r., Russia (syäs)	162	59.28N	33.24E
Sycamore, Il., U.S. (sĭk′ȧ-mōr)	103	42.00N	88.42W
Sycan, r., Or., U.S.	104	42.45N	121.00W
Sychëvka, Russia (sē-chôf′kå)	162	55.52N	34.18E
Sydenham, Austl.	243b	37.42S	144.46E
Sydenham, neigh., S. Afr.	244b	26.09S	28.06E
Sydenham, neigh., Eng., U.K.	235	51.26N	0.03W
Sydney, Austl. (sĭd′nė)	203	33.55S	151.17E
Sydney, Can.	85	46.09N	60.11W
Sydney Mines, Can.	85	46.14N	60.14W
Syktyvkar, Russia (sük-tüf′kär)	164	61.35N	50.40E
Sylacauga, Al., U.S. (sĭl-ȧ-kô′gȧ)	114	33.10N	86.15W
Sylarna, mtn., Eur.	152	63.00N	12.10E
Sylt, i., Ger. (sĭlt)	154	54.55N	8.30E
Sylvania, Austl.	243a	34.01S	151.07E
Sylvania, Ga., U.S. (sĭl-vā′nĭ-å)	115	32.44N	81.40W
Sylvania Heights, Austl.	243a	34.02S	151.06E
Sylvester, Ga., U.S. (sĭl-vĕs′tẽr)	114	31.32N	83.50W
Syndal, Austl.	243b	37.53S	145.09E
Synel′nykove, Ukr.	167	48.19N	35.33E
Syosset, N.Y., U.S.	228	40.50N	73.30W
Syracuse, Ks., U.S. (sĭr′ȧ-kūs)	110	37.59N	101.44W
Syracuse, N.Y., U.S.	97	43.05N	76.10W
Syracuse, Ut., U.S.	107b	41.06N	112.04W
Syr Darya, r., Asia	164	44.15N	65.45E
Syria, nation, Asia (sĭr′ĭ-å)	182	35.00N	37.15E
Syrian Desert, des., Asia	182	32.00N	40.00E
Sysert′, Russia (sĕ′sĕrt)	172a	56.30N	60.48E
Sysola, r., Russia	166	60.50N	50.40E
Syukunosho, Japan	242b	34.50N	135.32E
Syvash, zatoka, b., Ukr.	163	45.55N	34.42E
Syzran′, Russia (sĕz-rän′)	164	53.09N	48.27E
Szamotuły, Pol. (shå-mô-to͞o′wė)	154	52.36N	16.34E
Szarvas, Hung. (sôr′vôsh)	155	46.51N	20.36E
Szczebrzeszyn, Pol. (shchĕ-bzhā′shėn)	155	50.41N	22.58E
Szczecin, Pol. (shchĕ′tsĭn)	142	53.25N	14.35E
Szczecinek, Pol. (shchĕ′tsĭ-nĕk)	146	53.41N	16.42E
Szczuczyn, Pol. (shcho͞o′chēn)	155	53.32N	22.17E
Szczytno, Pol. (shchĭt′nô)	155	53.33N	21.00E
Szechwan Basin, basin, China	188	30.45N	104.40E
Szeged, Hung. (sĕ′gĕd)	142	46.15N	20.12E
Székesfehérvár, Hung. (sā′kĕsh-fĕ′hār-vär)	149	47.12N	18.26E
Szekszárd, Hung. (sĕk′särd)	149	46.19N	18.42E
Szentendre, Hung. (sĕnt′ĕn-drĕ)	155	47.40N	19.07E
Szentes, Hung. (sĕn′tĕsh)	155	46.38N	20.18E
Szigetvar, Hung. (sė′gĕt-vär)	155	46.05N	17.50E
Szolnok, Hung.	155	47.11N	20.12E
Szombathely, Hung. (sôm′bôt-hĕl′)	149	47.13N	16.35E
Szprotawa, Pol. (shprō-tä′vä)	154	51.34N	15.29E
Szydłowiec, Pol. (shid-wô′vyets)	155	51.13N	20.53E

T

PLACE (Pronunciation)	PAGE	Lat. °′	Long. °′
Taal, l., Phil. (tä-äl′)	197a	13.58N	121.06E
Tabaco, Phil. (tä-bä′kō)	197a	13.27N	123.40E
Tabankulu, S. Afr. (tā-bān-ko͞o′la)	213c	30.56S	29.19E
Tabasará, Serranía de, mts., Pan.	121	8.29N	81.22W
Tabasco, Mex. (tä-bäs′kô)	118	21.47N	103.04W
Tabasco, state, Mex.	116	18.10N	93.00W
Taber, Can.	84	49.47N	112.08W
Tablas, i., Phil. (tä′bläs)	197a	12.26N	122.00E
Tablas Strait, strt., Phil.	197a	12.17N	121.41E
Table Bay, b., S. Afr. (tā′b′l)	212a	33.41S	18.27E
Table Mountain, mtn., S. Afr.	212a	33.58S	18.26E
Table Rock Lake, Mo., U.S.	111	36.37N	93.29W
Tabligbo, Togo	214	6.35N	1.30E
Taboão da Serra, Braz.	234d	23.38S	46.46W

354 Taboga–Tarare

PLACE (Pronunciation)	PAGE	Lat. °'	Long. °'
Taboga, i., Pan. (tä-bō'gä)	116a	8.48N	79.35W
Taboguilla, i., Pan. (tä-bô-gē'l-yä)	116a	8.48N	79.31W
Tábor, Czech Rep. (tä'bôr)	154	49.25N	14.40E
Tabora, Tan. (tä-bō'rä)	212	5.01S	32.48E
Tabou, C. Iv. (tȧ-bōō')	210	4.25N	7.21W
Tabrīz, Iran (tȧ-brēz')	182	38.00N	46.13E
Tabuaeran, i., Kir.	2	3.52N	159.20W
Tabwémasana, Mont, mtn., Vanuatu	198f	15.20S	166.44E
Tacámbaro, r., Mex. (tä-käm'bä-rō)	118	18.55N	101.25W
Tacámbaro de Codallos, Mex.	118	19.12N	101.28W
Tacarigua, Laguna de la, l., Ven.	131b	10.18N	65.43W
Tacheng, China (tä-chŭŋ)	188	46.50N	83.24E
Tachie, r., Can.	86	54.30N	125.00W
Tachikawa, Japan	242a	35.42N	139.25E
Tacloban, Phil. (tä-klō'bän)	197	11.06N	124.58E
Tacna, Peru (täk'nä)	130	18.34S	70.16W
Tacoma, Wa., U.S. (tȧ-kō'mȧ)	96	47.14N	122.27W
Taconic Range, mts., N.Y., U.S. (tȧ-kŏn'ĭk)	99	41.55N	73.40W
Tacony, neigh., Pa., U.S.	229b	40.02N	75.03W
Tacotalpa, Mex. (tä-kō-täl'pä)	119	17.37N	92.51W
Tacotalpa, r., Mex.	119	17.24N	92.38W
Tacuba, neigh., Mex.	233a	19.28N	99.12W
Tacubaya, neigh., Mex.	233a	19.25N	99.12W
Tademaït, Plateau du, plat., Alg. (tä-dē-mä'ēt)	210	28.00N	2.15E
Tadio, Lagune, b., C. Iv.	214	5.20N	5.25W
Tadjoura, Dji. (tȧd-zhōō'rȧ)	218a	11.48N	42.54E
Tadley, Eng., U.K. (tăd'lē)	144b	51.19N	1.08W
Tadotsu, Japan (tä'dō-tsō)	195	34.14N	133.43E
Tadoussac, Can. (tȧ-dōō-sȧk')	91	48.09N	69.43W
Tadworth, Eng., U.K.	235	51.17N	0.14W
Tadzhikistan *see* Tajikistan, nation, Asia	164	39.22N	69.30E
Taebaek Sanmaek, mts., Asia (tī-bīk' sän-mīk')	194	37.20N	128.50E
Taedong, r., N. Kor. (tī-dŏng)	194	38.38N	124.32E
Taegu, S. Kor. (tī'gōō')	189	35.49N	128.41E
Taejŏn, S. Kor.	194	36.20N	127.26E
Tafalla, Spain (tä-fäl'yä)	158	42.30N	1.42W
Tafna, r., Alg. (täf'nä)	158	35.28N	1.00W
Taft, Ca., U.S. (tȧft)	108	35.09N	119.27W
Tagama, reg., Niger	215	15.50N	6.30E
Taganrog, Russia (tȧ-gȧn-rôk')	167	47.12N	38.56E
Taganrogskiy Zaliv, b., Eur. (tȧ-gȧn-rôk'skĭ zä'lĭf)	167	46.55N	38.17E
Tagula, i., Pap. N. Gui. (tä'gōō-lȧ)	203	11.45S	153.46E
Tagus (Tajo), r., Eur. (tā'gŭs)	142	39.40N	5.07W
Tahan, Gunong, mtn., Malay.	196	4.33N	101.52E
Tahat, mtn., Alg. (tä-hät')	210	23.22N	5.21E
Tahiti, i., Fr. Poly. (tä-hē'tē) (tä'ē-tē')	2	17.30S	149.30W
Tahkuna Nina, c., Est. (tȧh-kōō'nȧ nē'nȧ)	153	59.08N	22.03E
Tahlequah, Ok., U.S. (tă-lĕ-kwä')	111	35.54N	94.58W
Tahoe, l., U.S. (tä'hō)	96	39.09N	120.18W
Tahoua, Niger (tä'ōō-ä)	210	14.54N	5.16E
Tahtsa Lake, l., Can.	86	53.33N	127.47W
Tahuya, Wa., U.S. (tȧ-hū-yä')	106a	47.23N	123.03W
Tahuya, r., Wa., U.S.	106a	47.28N	122.55W
Tai'an, China (tī-än)	192	36.13N	117.08E
Taibai Shan, mtn., China (tī-bī shän)	192	33.42N	107.25E
Taibus Qi, China (tī-bōō-sz chyē)	192	41.52N	115.25E
Taicang, China (tī-tsäŋ)	190	31.26N	121.06E
T'aichung, Tai. (tī'chŏng)	189	24.10N	120.42E
Tai'erzhuang, China (tī-är-jůäŋ)	190	34.34N	117.44E
Taigu, China (tī-gōō)	192	37.25N	112.35E
Taihang Shan, mts., China (tī-häŋ shän)	192	35.45N	112.00E
Taihe, China (tī-hŭ)	190	33.10N	115.38E
Tai Hu, l., China (tī hōō)	189	31.13N	120.00E
Tailagoin, reg., Mong. (tī'lȧ-gän' kä'rä)	188	43.39N	105.54E
Tailai, China (tī-lī)	192	46.20N	123.10E
Tailem Bend, Austl. (tā-lĕm)	204	35.15S	139.30E
T'ainan, Tai. (tī'nan')	189	23.08N	120.18E
Tainaron, Ákra, c., Grc.	142	37.45N	22.00E
Taining, China (tī'nĭng')	193	26.58N	117.15E
T'aipei, Tai. (tī'pā')	189	25.02N	121.38E
Taipei Institute of Technology, educ., Tai.	241d	25.02N	121.32E
Taiping, pt. of i., Malay.	196	4.56N	100.39E
Taiping Ling, mtn., China	192	47.03N	120.30E
Tai Po Tsai, H.K.	241c	22.21N	114.15E
Taisha, Japan (tī'shä)	195	35.23N	132.40E
Taishan, China (tī-shän)	193	22.15N	112.50E
Tai Shan, mts., China (tī shän)	192	36.16N	117.05E
Taitao, Península de, pen., Chile	132	46.20S	77.15W
Taitō, neigh., Japan	242a	35.43N	139.47E
T'aitung, Tai. (tī'tōōng')	193	22.45N	121.02E
Taiwan, nation, Asia (tī-wän) (fŏr-mō'sȧ)	189	23.30N	122.20E
Taiwan Normal University, educ., Tai.	241d	25.02N	121.31E
Taiwan Strait, strt., Asia	189	24.30N	120.00E
Tai Wan Tau, H.K.	241c	22.18N	114.17E
Tai Wan Tsun, H.K.	241c	22.19N	114.12E
Taixian, China (tī shyĕn)	190	32.31N	119.54E
Taixing, China (tī-shyĭŋ)	190	32.12N	119.58E
Taiyanggong, China	240b	39.58N	116.25E
Taiyuan, China (tī-yůän)	189	37.32N	112.38E
Taizhou, China (tī-jō)	190	32.23N	119.41E
Ta'izz, Yemen	185	13.38N	44.04E
Tajano de Morais, Braz. (tĕ-zhä'nō-dĕ-mō-rä'ēs)	129a	22.05S	42.04W
Tajikistan, nation, Asia	164	39.22N	69.30E
Tajninka, Russia	239b	55.54N	37.45E
Tajumulco, vol., Guat. (tä-hōō-mōōl'kō)	120	15.03N	91.53W
Tajuña, r., Spain (tä-kōō'n-yä)	158	40.23N	2.36W
Tājūrā', Libya	148	32.56N	13.24W
Tak, Thai.	196	16.57N	99.12E

PLACE (Pronunciation)	PAGE	Lat. °'	Long. °'
Taka, i., Japan (tä'kä)	195	30.47N	130.23E
Takada, Japan (tä'kȧ-dä)	194	37.08N	138.30E
Takahashi, Japan (tä'kä'hä-shĭ)	195	34.47N	133.35E
Takaishi, Japan	195b	34.32N	135.27E
Takamatsu, Japan (tä'kä'mä-tsōō')	189	34.20N	134.02E
Takamori, Japan (tä'kä'mō-rē')	195	32.50N	131.08E
Takaoka, Japan (ta'kä'ō-kä')	194	36.45N	136.59E
Takapuna, N.Z.	205	36.48S	174.47E
Takarazuka, Japan (tä'kä-rä-zōō'kä)	195b	34.48N	135.22E
Takasaki, Japan (tä'kät'sōō-kē')	194	36.20N	139.00E
Takatsu, Japan (tä-kät'sōō) (mĕ'zō-nō-kō'chē)	195a	35.36N	139.37E
Takatsuki, Japan (tä'kät'sōō-kē')	195b	34.51N	135.38E
Takayama, Japan (tä'kä'yä'mä)	195	36.11N	137.16E
Takefu, Japan (tä'kĕ-fōō)	194	35.57N	136.09E
Takenotsuka, neigh., Japan	242a	35.48N	139.48E
Takla Lake, l., Can.	84	55.25N	125.53W
Takla Makan, des., China (mä-kȧn')	188	39.22N	82.34E
Takoma Park, Md., U.S. (tă'kōmȧ pärk)	100e	38.59N	77.00W
Takum, Nig.	215	7.17N	9.59E
Tala, Mex. (tä'lä)	118	20.39N	103.42W
Talagante, Chile (tä-lä-gȧ'n-tĕ)	129b	33.39S	70.54W
Talamanca, Cordillera de, mts., C.R.	121	9.37N	83.55W
Talanga, Hond. (tä-lä'n-gä)	120	14.21N	87.09W
Talara, Peru (tä-lä'rä)	130	4.32S	81.17W
Talasea, Pap. N. Gui. (tä-lä-sā'ä)	197	5.20S	150.00E
Talata Mafara, Nig.	215	12.35N	6.04E
Talaud, Kepulauan, is., Indon. (tä-lout')	197	4.17N	127.30E
Talavera de la Reina, Spain	148	39.58N	4.51W
Talca, Chile (täl'kä)	132	35.25S	71.39W
Talca, prov., Chile	129b	35.23S	71.15W
Talca, Punta, c., Chile (pōō'n-tä-täl'kä)	129b	33.25S	71.42W
Talcahuano, Chile (täl-kä-wä'nō)	132	36.41S	73.05W
Taldom, Russia (täl-dŏm)	162	56.44N	37.33E
Taldyqorghan, Kaz.	169	45.03N	77.18E
Talea de Castro, Mex. (tä'lå-ä dä käs'trō)	119	17.22N	96.14W
Talibu, Pulau, i., Indon.	197	1.30S	125.00E
Talim, i., Phil. (tä-lēm')	197a	14.21N	121.14E
Talisay, Phil. (tä-lē'sī)	197a	14.08N	122.56E
Talkeetna, Ak., U.S. (tȧl-kēt'nȧ)	95	62.18N	150.02W
Talladega, Al., U.S. (tăl-ȧ-dē'gȧ)	114	33.25N	86.06W
Tallahassee, Fl., U.S. (tăl-ȧ-hăs'ē)	97	30.25N	84.17W
Tallahatchie, r., Ms., U.S. (tal-ȧ hăch'ē)	114	34.21N	90.03W
Tallapoosa, Ga., U.S. (tăl-ȧ-pōō'sȧ)	114	33.44N	85.15W
Tallapoosa, r., Al., U.S.	114	32.22N	86.08W
Tallassee, Al., U.S. (tăl'ȧ-sē)	114	32.30N	85.54W
Tallinn, Est. (tȧl'lĕn) (rä'väl)	164	59.26N	24.44E
Tallmadge, Oh., U.S. (tăl'mĭj)	101d	41.06N	81.26W
Tallulah, La., U.S. (tă-lōō'lȧ)	113	32.25N	91.13W
Tally Ho, Austl.	243b	37.52S	145.09E
Tal'ne, Ukr.	163	48.52N	30.43E
Talo, mtn., Eth.	211	10.45N	37.55E
Taloje Budrukh, India	187b	19.05N	73.05E
Talpa de Allende, Mex. (täl'pä dä äl-yĕn'då)	118	20.25N	104.48W
Talquin, Lake, res., Fl., U.S.	114	30.26N	84.33W
Talsi, Lat. (tal'sĭ)	153	57.16N	22.35E
Taltal, Chile (täl-täl')	132	25.26S	70.32W
Taly, Russia (täl'ĭ)	163	49.51N	40.07E
Tama, Ia., U.S. (tā'mä)	103	41.57N	92.36W
Tama, r., Japan	195a	35.38N	139.35E
Tamagawa, neigh., Japan	242a	35.37N	139.39E
Tama-kyūryō, mts., Japan	242a	35.35N	139.30E
Tamale, Ghana (tä-mä'lā)	210	9.25N	0.50W
Taman', Russia (tȧ-män'')	163	45.13N	36.46E
Tamanaco, r., Ven. (tä-mä-nä'kō)	131b	9.32N	66.00W
Tamaqua, Pa., U.S. (tȧ-mô'kwȧ)	99	40.45N	75.50W
Tamar, r., Eng., U.K. (tā'mär)	150	50.35N	4.15W
Tamarite de Litera, Spain (tä-mä-rē'tā)	159	41.52N	0.24E
Tamaulipas, state, Mex. (tä-mä-ōō-lē'päs')	116	23.45N	98.30W
Tamazula de Gordiano, Mex.	118	19.44N	103.09W
Tamazulapan del Progreso, Mex.	119	17.41N	97.34W
Tamazunchale, Mex. (tä-mä-zōn-chä'lå)	118	21.16N	98.46W
Tambacounda, Sen. (täm-bä-kōōn'dä)	210	13.47N	13.40W
Tambador, Serra do, mts., Braz. (sĕ'r-rä-dō-täm'bä-dōr)	131	10.33S	41.16W
Tambelan, Kepulauan, is., Indon. (täm-bå-län')	196	0.38N	107.38E
Tambo, Austl. (tăm'bō)	203	24.50S	146.15E
Tambov, Russia (tȧm-bôf')	164	52.45N	41.10E
Tambov, prov., Russia	162	52.50N	40.42E
Tambre, r., Spain (täm'brā)	158	42.59N	8.33W
Tambura, Sudan (täm-bōō'rä)	211	5.34N	27.30E
Tame, r., Eng., U.K. (tām)	144a	52.41N	1.42W
Tâmega, r., Port. (tȧ-mā'gȧ)	158	41.30N	7.45W
Tamenghest, Alg.	210	22.34N	5.34E
Tamenghest, Oued, r., Alg.	210	22.15N	2.51E
Tamgak, Monts, mtn., Niger (tam-gäk')	210	18.40N	8.40E
Tamgué, Massif du, mtn., Gui.	210	12.15N	12.35W
Tamiahua, Mex. (tä-myä-wä)	119	21.17N	97.26W
Tamiahua, Laguna, l., Mex. (lä-gō'nä-tä-myä-wä)	119	21.38N	97.33W
Tamiami Canal, can., Fl., U.S. (tă-mī-ăm'ĭ)	115a	25.52N	80.08W
Tamil Nadu, state, India	183	11.30N	78.00E
Tampa, Fl., U.S. (tăm'pȧ)	97	27.57N	82.25W
Tampa Bay, b., Fl., U.S.	97	27.35N	82.38W
Tampere, Fin. (tȧm'pĕ-rĕ)	146	61.21N	23.39E
Tampico, Mex. (täm-pē'kō)	116	22.14N	97.51W
Tampico Alto, Mex. (täm-pē'kō äl'tō)	119	22.07N	97.48W
Tampin, Malay.	181b	2.28N	102.15E
Tam Quan, Viet.	193	14.20N	109.10E
Tamuín, Mex. (tä-mōō-ē'n)	118	22.04N	98.47W

PLACE (Pronunciation)	PAGE	Lat. °'	Long. °'
Tamworth, Austl. (tăm'wûrth)	203	31.01S	151.00E
Tamworth, Eng., U.K.	144a	52.38N	1.41W
Tana, i., Vanuatu	203	19.32S	169.27E
Tana, r., Kenya (tä'nä)	213	0.30S	39.30E
Tanabe, Japan (tä-nä'bā)	194	33.45N	135.21E
Tanabe, Japan	195b	34.49N	135.46E
Tanacross, Ak., U.S. (tă'nȧ-crŏs)	95	63.20N	143.30W
Tanaga, i., Ak., U.S. (tä-nä'gä)	95a	51.28N	178.10W
Tanahbala, Pulau, i., Indon. (tȧ-nä-bä'lä)	196	0.30S	98.22E
Tanahmasa, Pulau, i., Indon. (tȧ-nä-mä'sä)	196	0.03S	97.30E
Tanakpur, India (tŭn'ăk-pŏr)	186	29.10N	80.07E
Tana Lake, l., Eth.	211	12.09N	36.41E
Tanami, Austl. (tä-nä'mē)	202	19.45S	129.50E
Tanana, Ak., U.S. (tă'nȧ-nô)	95	65.18N	152.20W
Tanana, r., Ak., U.S.	95	64.26N	148.40W
Tanaro, r., Italy (tä-nä'rô)	160	44.45N	8.02E
Tanashi, Japan	195a	35.44N	139.34E
Tan-binh, Viet.	241j	10.48N	106.40E
Tanbu, China (tän-bōō)	191a	23.20N	113.06E
Tancheng, China (tän-chŭŋ)	192	34.37N	118.22E
Tanchŏn, N. Kor. (tän'chŭn)	194	40.29N	128.50E
Tancítaro, Mex. (tän-sē'tä-rō)	118	19.16N	102.24W
Tancítaro, Cerro de, mtn., Mex. (sĕ'r-rô-dĕ)	118	19.24N	102.19W
Tancoco, Mex. (tän-kō'kō)	119	21.16N	97.45W
Tandil, Arg. (tän-dēl')	132	36.16S	59.01W
Tandil, Sierra del, mts., Arg.	132	38.40S	59.40W
Tanega, i., Japan (tä'nå-gä')	189	30.36N	131.11E
Tanezrouft, reg., Alg. (tä'nĕz-rōft)	210	24.17N	0.30W
Tang, r., China (täŋ)	190	33.38N	117.29E
Tang, r., China	190	39.13N	114.45E
Tanga, Tan. (täŋ'gȧ)	213	5.04S	39.06E
Tangancícuaro, Mex. (täŋ-gän-sē'kwa-rō)	118	19.52N	102.13W
Tanganyika, Lake, l., Afr.	212	5.15S	29.40E
Tanger, Mor. (tän-jĕr')	210	35.52N	5.55W
Tangermünde, Ger. (täŋ'ĕr-mün'de)	154	52.33N	11.58E
Tanggu, China (täŋ-gōō)	190	39.04N	117.41E
Tanggula Shan, mts., China (täŋ-gōō-lä shän)	188	33.15N	89.07E
Tanghe, China	192	32.40N	112.50E
Tangier *see* Tanger, Mor.	210	35.52N	5.55W
Tangipahoa, r., La., U.S. (tăn'jē-pȧ-hō'ȧ)	113	30.48N	90.28W
Tangra Yumco, l., China (täŋ-rä yōōm-tswo)	186	30.50N	85.40E
T'angshan, China	192	39.38N	118.11E
Tangxian, China (täŋ shyĕn)	190	38.49N	115.00E
Tangzha, China (täŋ-jä)	190	32.06N	120.48E
Tanimbar, Kepulauan, is., Indon.	197	8.00S	132.00E
Tanjong Piai, c., Malay.	181b	1.16N	103.11E
Tanjong Ramunia, c., Malay.	181b	1.27N	104.44E
Tanjungbalai, Indon. (tän'jông-bä'lå)	181b	1.00N	103.26E
Tanjungkarang-Telukbetung, Indon.	196	5.16S	105.06E
Tanjungpandan, Indon.	196	2.47S	107.51E
Tanjungpinang, Indon. (tän'jŏng-pē'näng)	181b	0.55N	104.29E
Tanjungpriok, neigh., Indon.	241i	6.06S	106.53E
Tannu-Ola, mts., Asia	165	51.00N	94.00E
Tannūrah, Ra's at, c., Sau. Ar.	182	26.45N	49.59E
Tano, r., Afr.	214	5.40N	2.30W
Tan-qui-dong, Viet.	241j	10.44N	106.43E
Tanquijo, Arrecife, i., Mex. (är-rĕ-sē'fĕ-tän-kē'kô)	119	21.07N	97.16W
Tanshui Ho, r., Tai.	241d	25.08N	121.27E
Tan Son Nhut Airport, arpt., Viet.	241j	10.49N	106.40E
Ţanţā, Egypt	211	30.47N	31.00E
Tan-thuan-dong, Viet.	241j	10.45N	106.44E
Tantoyuca, Mex. (tän-tō-yōō'kä)	118	21.22N	98.13W
Tanyang, S. Kor.	194	36.53N	128.20E
Tanzania, nation, Afr.	212	6.48S	33.58E
Tao, r., China (tou)	192	35.30N	103.40E
Tao'an, China (tou-än)	189	45.15N	122.45E
Tao'er, r., China (tou-är)	189	45.40N	122.00E
Taormina, Italy (tä-ôr-mē'nä)	160	37.53N	15.18E
Taos, N.M., U.S. (tä'ōs)	109	36.25N	105.35W
Taoudenni, Mali (tä'ōō-dē-nē')	210	22.57N	3.37W
Taoussa, Mali	214	16.55N	0.35W
Taoyuan, China (tou-yůän)	193	29.00N	111.15E
Tapa, Est. (tä'pȧ)	153	59.16N	25.56E
Tapachula, Mex.	120	14.55N	92.20W
Tapajós, r., Braz. (tä-pä-zhô's)	131	3.27S	55.33W
Tapalque, Arg. (tä-päl-kĕ')	129c	36.22S	60.05W
Tapanatepec, Mex. (tä-pä-nä-tĕ-pĕk)	119	16.22N	94.19W
Tāpi, r., India	183	21.00N	76.30E
Tapiales, Arg.	233d	34.42S	58.30W
Tappi Saki, c., Japan (täp'pē sä'kē)	194	41.05N	139.40E
Tapps, l., Wa., U.S. (tăpz)	106a	47.20N	122.12W
Taquara, neigh., Braz.	234c	22.55S	43.21W
Taquara, Serra de, mts., Braz. (sĕ'r-rä-dĕ-tä-kwä'rä)	131	15.28S	54.33W
Taquari, r., Braz. (tä-kwä'rĭ)	131	18.35S	56.50W
Tar, r., N.C., U.S. (tär)	115	35.58N	78.06W
Tara, Russia (tä'rȧ)	164	56.58N	74.13E
Tara, i., Phil. (tä'rä)	197a	12.18N	120.28E
Tara, r., Russia (tä'rȧ)	170	56.32N	76.13E
Ţarābulus, Leb. (tȧ-rä'bō-lōōs)	182	34.25N	35.50E
Ţarābulus (Tripolitania), hist. reg., Libya	210	31.00N	12.26E
Tarakan, Indon.	196	3.17N	118.04E
Taranaki, Mount, vol., N.Z.	205	39.18S	174.04E
Tarancón, Spain (tä-rän-kōn')	158	40.01N	3.00W
Taranto, Italy (tä'rän-tô)	149	40.30N	17.15E
Taranto, Golfo di, b., Italy (gôl-fô-dē tä'rän-tô)	142	40.03N	17.10E
Tarapoto, Peru (tä-rä-pō'tō)	130	6.29S	76.26W
Tarare, Fr. (tȧ-rär')	156	45.55N	4.23E

PRONOUNCING INDEX

Tarascon–Términos 355

PLACE (Pronunciation)	PAGE	Lat. °′	Long. °′
Tarascon, Fr. (tá-rás-kôN′)	156	42.53N	1.35E
Tarascon, Fr. (tä-räs-kôN)	156	43.47N	4.41E
Tarashcha, Ukr. (tä′rásh-chá)	163	49.34N	30.52E
Tarasht, Iran	241h	35.42N	51.21E
Tarata, Bol. (tä-rä′tä)	130	17.43S	66.00W
Taravo, r., Fr.	160	41.54N	8.58E
Tarazit, Massif de, mts., Niger	215	20.05N	7.35E
Tarazona, Spain (tä-rä-thō′nä)	158	41.54N	1.45W
Tarazona de la Mancha, Spain (tä-rä-zō′nä-dĕ-lä-mä′n-chä)	158	39.13N	1.50W
Tarbes, Fr. (tárb)	147	43.04N	0.05E
Tarbock Green, Eng., U.K.	237a	53.23N	2.49W
Tarboro, N.C., U.S. (tär′bŭr-ō)	115	35.53N	77.34W
Taredo, neigh., India	240e	19.58N	72.49E
Taree, Austl. (tä-rē′)	204	31.52S	152.21E
Tarentum, Pa., U.S. (tá-rĕn′tŭm)	101e	40.36N	79.44W
Tarfa, Wādī at, val., Egypt	218b	28.14N	31.00E
Târgoviște, Rom.	149	44.54N	25.29E
Târgu Jiu, Rom.	149	45.02N	23.17E
Târgu Mureș, Rom.	149	46.33N	24.33E
Târgu Neamț, Rom.	155	47.14N	26.23E
Târgu Ocna, Rom.	155	46.18N	26.38E
Târgu Secuiesc, Rom.	155	46.04N	26.06E
Tarhūnah, Libya	184	32.26N	13.38E
Tarija, Bol. (tär-rē′hä)	130	21.42S	64.52W
Tarīm, Yemen (tá-rīm′)	182	16.13N	49.08E
Tarim, r., China (tá-rīm′)	188	40.45N	85.39E
Tarim Basin, basin, China (tá-rīm′)	188	39.52N	82.34E
Tarka, r., S. Afr. (tä′ká)	213c	32.15S	26.00E
Tarkastad, S. Afr.	213c	32.01S	26.18E
Tarkhankut, Mys, c., Ukr. (mĭs tár-kän′kŏt)	167	45.21N	32.30E
Tarkio, Mo., U.S. (tär′kĭ-ō)	111	40.27N	95.22W
Tarkwa, Ghana (tärk′wä)	210	5.19N	1.59W
Tarlac, Phil. (tär′läk)	196	15.29N	120.36E
Tarlton, S. Afr. (tärl′tŭn)	213b	26.05S	27.38E
Tarma, Peru (tär′mä)	130	11.26S	75.40W
Tarn, r., Fr. (tärn)	147	43.45N	2.00E
Târnăveni, Rom.	155	46.19N	24.18E
Tarnów, Pol. (tär′nŏf)	147	50.02N	21.00E
Taro, r., Italy (tä′rō)	160	44.41N	10.03E
Taroudant, Mor. (tá-rōō-dänt′)	210	30.39N	8.52W
Tarpon Springs, Fl., U.S. (tär′pŏn)	115a	28.07N	82.44W
Tarporley, Eng., U.K. (tär′pēr-lė)	144a	53.09N	2.40W
Tarpum Bay, b., Bah. (tär′pŭm)	122	25.05N	76.20W
Tarquinia, Italy (tär-kwē′nė-ä)	160	42.16N	11.46E
Tarragona, Spain (tär-rä-gō′nä)	142	41.05N	1.15E
Tarrant, Al., U.S. (tăr′ănt)	100h	33.35N	86.46W
Tarrasa, Spain (tär-rä′sä)	159	41.34N	2.01E
Tárrega, Spain (tä rā-gä)	159	41.40N	1.09E
Tarrejón de Ardoz, Spain (tär-rĕ-kô′n-dĕ-är-dôz)	159a	40.28N	3.29W
Tarrytown, N.Y., U.S. (tăr′ĭ-toun)	100a	41.04N	73.52W
Tarsus, Tur. (tár′sŏs) (tär′sŭs)	182	37.00N	34.50E
Tartagal, Arg. (tär-tä-gà′l)	132	23.31S	63.47W
Tartu, Est. (tär′tōō) (dôr′pät)	164	58.23N	26.44E
Ţarţūs, Syria	184	34.54N	35.59E
Tarumi, Japan (tä′rōō-mė)	195b	34.38N	135.04E
Tarusa, Russia (tä-rōōs′á)	162	54.43N	37.11E
Tarzana, Ca., U.S. (tär-ză′á)	107a	34.10N	118.32W
Tashauz, Turk. (tŭ-shŭ-ōōs′)	169	41.20N	59.45E
Tashkent, Uzb. (tásh′kĕnt)	169	41.23N	69.04E
Tasman Bay, b., N.Z. (tăz′măn)	203a	40.50S	173.20E
Tasmania, state, Austl.	203	41.28S	142.30E
Tasman Peninsula, pen., Austl.	204	43.00S	148.30E
Tasman Sea, sea, Oc.	225	29.30S	155.00E
Tasquillo, Mex. (täs-kē′lyō)	118	20.34N	99.21W
Tatarsk, Russia (tá-tärsk′)	164	55.13N	75.58E
Tatarstan, state, Russia	166	55.00N	51.00E
Tatar Strait, strt., Russia	165	51.00N	141.45E
Tate Gallery, pt. of i., Eng., U.K.	235	51.29N	0.08W
Tater Hill, mtn., Or., U.S. (tāt′ēr hĭl)	106c	45.47N	123.02W
Tateyama, Japan (tä′tė-yä′mä)	195	35.04N	139.52E
Tathong Channel, strt., H.K.	241c	22.15N	114.15E
Tatlow, Mount, mtn., Can.	86	51.23N	123.52W
Tatsfield, Eng., U.K.	235	51.18N	0.02E
Tau, Nor.	152	59.05N	5.59E
Tauern Tunnel, trans., Aus.	154	47.12N	13.17E
Taung, S. Afr. (tä′ông)	212	27.25S	24.47E
Taunton, Ma., U.S. (tän′tŭn)	99	41.54N	71.03W
Taunton, r., R.I., U.S.	100b	41.50N	71.02W
Taupo, Lake, l., N.Z. (tä′ōō-pō)	203a	38.42S	175.55E
Taurage, Lith. (tou′rá-gā)	153	55.15N	22.18E
Taurus Mountains *see* Toros Dağlari, mts., Tur.	182	37.00N	32.40E
Tauste, Spain (tä-ōōs′tå)	158	41.55N	1.15W
Tavda, Russia (táv-dá′)	164	58.00N	64.44E
Tavda, r., Russia	170	58.30N	64.15E
Taverny, Fr. (tá-vĕr-nē′)	157b	49.02N	2.13E
Taviche, Mex. (tä-vē′chĕ)	119	16.43N	96.35W
Tavira, Port. (tä-vē′rá)	158	37.09N	7.42W
Tavistock, N.J., U.S.	229b	39.53N	75.02W
Tavşanlı, Tur. (táv′shän-lĭ)	167	39.30N	29.30E
Tawakoni, l., Tx., U.S.	113	32.51N	95.59W
Tawaramoto, Japan (tä′wä-rä-mō-tō)	195b	34.33N	135.48E
Tawas City, Mi., U.S.	98	44.15N	83.30W
Tawas Point, c., Mi., U.S. (tô′wás)	98	44.15N	83.25W
Tawitawi Group, is., Phil. (tä′wė-tä′wė)	196	4.52N	120.35E
Tawkar, Sudan	211	18.28N	37.46E
Taxco de Alarcón, Mex. (täs′kō dĕ ä-lär-kō′n)	118	18.34N	99.37W
Tay, r., Scot., U.K.	150	56.35N	3.37W
Tay, Loch, l., Scot., U.K.	150	56.25N	4.07W
Tayabas Bay, b., Phil. (tä-yä′bäs)	197a	13.44N	121.40E
Tayga, Russia (tī′gä)	170	56.12N	85.47E

PLACE (Pronunciation)	PAGE	Lat. °′	Long. °′
Taygonos, Mys, c., Russia	165	60.37N	160.17E
Taylor, Mi., U.S.	230c	42.13N	83.16W
Taylor, Tx., U.S.	113	30.35N	97.25W
Taylor, Mount, mtn., N.M., U.S.	96	35.20N	107.40W
Taylorville, Il., U.S. (tā′lēr-vĭl)	98	39.30N	89.20W
Taymyr, l., Russia (tī-mĭr′)	165	74.13N	100.45E
Taymyr, Poluostrov, pen., Russia	165	75.15N	95.00E
Táyros, Grc.	239d	37.58N	23.42E
Tayshet, Russia (tī-shĕt′)	165	56.09N	97.49E
Taytay, Phil.	241g	14.34N	121.08E
Tayug, Phil.	197a	16.01N	120.45E
Taz, r., Russia (táz)	170	67.15N	80.45E
Taza, Mor. (tä′zä)	210	34.08N	4.00W
Tazovskoye, Russia	164	66.58N	78.28E
Tbessa, Alg.	210	35.27N	8.13E
Tbilisi, Geor. (′tbĭl-yē′sē)	167	41.40N	44.45E
Tchentlo Lake, l., Can.	86	55.11N	125.00W
Tchibanga, Gabon (chė-bäŋ′gä)	212	2.51S	11.02E
Tchien, Lib.	214	6.04N	8.08W
Tchigai, Plateau du, plat., Afr.	215	21.20N	14.50E
Tczew, Pol. (t′chĕf′)	146	54.06N	18.48E
Teabo, Mex. (tĕ-ä′bô)	120a	20.25N	89.14W
Teague, Tx., U.S.	113	31.39N	96.16W
Teaneck, N.J., U.S.	228	40.53N	74.01W
Teapa, Mex. (tā-ä′pä)	119	17.35N	92.56W
Tebing Tinggi, i., Indon. (teb′ĭng-tĭng′gä)	181b	0.54N	102.39E
Tecalitlán, Mex. (tä-kä-lē-tlän′)	118	19.28N	103.17W
Techiman, Ghana	214	7.35N	1.56W
Tecoanapa, Mex. (tāk-wä-nä-pä′)	118	16.33N	98.46W
Tecoh, Mex. (tĕ-kô)	120a	20.46N	89.27W
Tecolotlán, Mex. (tā-kô-lô-tlän′)	118	20.13N	103.57W
Tecolutla, Mex. (tā-kô-lōō′tlä)	119	20.33N	97.00W
Tecolutla, r., Mex.	119	20.16N	97.14W
Tecomán, Mex. (tā-kô-män′)	118	18.53N	103.53W
Tecómitl, Mex. (tĕ-kŏ′mētl)	119a	19.13N	98.59W
Tecozautla, Mex. (tā′kō-zä-ōō′tlä)	118	20.33N	99.38W
Tecpan de Galeana, Mex. (tĕk-pän′ dā gä-lā-ä′nä)	118	17.13N	100.41W
Tecpatán, Mex. (tĕk-pä-tá′n)	119	17.08N	93.18W
Tecuala, Mex. (tĕ-kwä-lä)	118	22.24N	105.29W
Tecuci, Rom. (tá-kōch′)	149	45.51N	27.30E
Tecumseh, Can. (tė-kŭm′sĕ)	101b	42.19N	82.53W
Tecumseh, Mi., U.S.	98	42.00N	84.00W
Tecumseh, Ne., U.S.	111	40.21N	96.09W
Tecumseh, Ok., U.S.	111	35.18N	96.55W
Teddington, neigh., Eng., U.K.	235	51.25N	0.20W
Tees, r., Eng., U.K. (tēz)	150	54.40N	2.10W
Teganuna, l., Japan (tā′gä-nōō′nä)	195a	35.50N	140.02E
Tegel, neigh., Ger.	238a	52.35N	13.17E
Tegeler See, l., Ger.	238a	52.35N	13.15E
Tegucigalpa, Hond. (tå-gōō-sė-gäl′pä)	116	14.08N	87.15W
Tehachapi Mountains, mts., Ca., U.S. (tė-hă-shă′pĭ)	108	34.50N	118.55W
Tehar, neigh., India	240d	28.38N	77.07E
Tehrān, Iran (tĕ-hrän′)	182	35.45N	51.30E
Tehuacan, Mex. (tā-wä-kän′)	116	18.27N	97.23W
Tehuantepec, Mex.	116	16.20N	95.14W
Tehuantepec, r., Mex.	119	16.30N	95.23W
Tehuantepec, Golfo de, b., Mex. (gôl-fô dĕ)	116	15.45N	95.00W
Tehuantepec, Istmo de, isth., Mex. (ē′st-mô dĕ)	119	17.55N	94.35W
Tehuehuetla, Arroyo, r., Mex. (tĕ-wĕ-wĕ′tlä ár-rō-yō)	118	17.54N	100.26W
Tehuitzingo, Mex. (tā-wė-tzĭŋ′gō)	118	18.21N	98.16W
Tejeda, Sierra de, mts., Spain (sē-ĕ′r-rä dĕ tĕ-kĕ′dä)	158	36.55N	4.00W
Tejúpan, Mex. (tĕ-kōō-pä′n) (sän-tyä′gô)	119	17.39N	97.34W
Tejúpan, Punta, c., Mex.	118	18.19N	103.30W
Tejupilco de Hidalgo, Mex. (tá-hōō-pēl′kō dā ē-dhäl′gō)	118	18.52N	100.07W
Tekamah, Ne., U.S. (tė-kā′má)	102	41.46N	96.13W
Tekax de Alvaro Obregon, Mex.	120a	20.12N	89.11W
Tekeze, r., Afr.	211	13.38N	38.00E
Tekit, Mex. (tĕ-kē′t)	120a	20.35N	89.18W
Tekoa, Wa., U.S. (tė-kō′á)	104	47.15N	117.03W
Tekstil′ščiki, neigh., Russia	239b	55.42N	37.44E
Tela, Hond. (tā′lä)	116	15.45N	87.25W
Tela, India	240d	28.44N	77.20E
Tela, Bahía de, b., Hond.	120	15.53N	87.29W
Telapa Burok, Gunong, mtn., Malay.	181b	2.51N	102.04E
Telavi, Geor.	167	42.00N	45.20E
Tel Aviv-Yafo, Isr. (tĕl-ä-vēv′já′fá)	182	32.03N	34.46E
Telegraph Creek, Can. (tĕl′ē-gráf)	84	57.59N	131.22W
Teleneşti, Mol.	163	47.31N	28.22E
Telescope Peak, mtn., Ca., U.S. (tĕl′ė skōp)	96	36.12N	117.05W
Telesung, Indon.	181b	1.07N	102.53E
Telica, vol., Nic. (tå-lē′kä)	120	12.38N	86.52W
Tell City, In., U.S. (tĕl)	98	38.00N	86.45W
Teller, Ak., U.S. (tĕl′ēr)	95	65.17N	166.28W
Tello, Col. (tĕ′l-yō)	130a	3.05N	75.08W
Telluride, Co., U.S. (tĕl′ū-rīd)	109	37.55N	107.50W
Telok Datok, Malay.	181b	2.51N	101.33E
Teloloapan, Mex. (tā′lō-lō-ä′pän)	118	18.19N	99.54W
Tel′pos-Iz, Gora, mtn., Russia (tyĕl′pŏs-ēz′)	164	63.50N	59.20E
Telšiai, Lith. (tĕl′sha′ė)	153	55.59N	22.17E
Teltow, Ger. (tĕl′tō)	145b	52.24N	13.12E
Teltower Hochfläche, reg., Ger.	238a	52.22N	13.20E
Teluklecak, Indon.	181b	1.53N	101.45E
Tema, Ghana	214	5.38N	0.01E
Temascalcingo, Mex. (tā′mäs-käl-sĭŋ′gō)	118	19.55N	100.00W
Temascaltepec, Mex. (tā′mäs-käl-tå pĕk)	118	19.00N	100.03W
Temax, Mex. (tĕ′mäx)	116	21.10N	88.51W

PLACE (Pronunciation)	PAGE	Lat. °′	Long. °′
Temir, Kaz.	169	49.10N	57.15E
Temirtau, Kaz.	169	50.08N	73.13E
Temiscouata, l., Can. (tĕ′mĭs-kō-ä′tä)	92	47.40N	68.50W
Témiskaming, Can. (tė-mĭs′ká-mĭng)	85	46.41N	79.01W
Temoaya, Mex. (tĕ-mô-a-um-yä)	119a	19.28N	99.36W
Tempe, Az., U.S.	109	33.24N	111.54W
Tempelhof, neigh., Ger.	238a	52.28N	13.23E
Temperley, Arg. (tĕ′m-pĕr-lā)	132a	34.47S	58.24W
Tempio Pausania, Italy (tĕm′pė-ō pou-sä′nė-ä)	160	40.55N	9.05E
Temple, Tx., U.S. (tĕm′p′l)	113	31.06N	97.20W
Temple City, Ca., U.S.	107a	34.07N	118.02W
Temple Hills, Md., U.S.	229d	38.49N	76.57W
Temple of Heaven, rel., China	240b	39.53N	116.25E
Templestowe, Austl.	243b	37.45S	145.07E
Templeton, Can. (tĕm′p′l-tŭn)	83c	45.29N	75.37W
Temple University, pt. of i., Pa., U.S.	229b	39.59N	75.09W
Templin, Ger. (tĕm-plēn′)	154	53.08N	13.30E
Tempoal, r., Mex. (tĕm-pô-ä′l)	118	21.38N	98.23W
Temryuk, Russia (tyĕm-ryŏk′)	167	45.17N	37.21E
Temuco, Chile (tā-mōō′kō)	132	38.46S	72.38W
Temyasovo, Russia (tĕm-yä′sô-vô)	172a	53.00N	58.06E
Tenafly, N.J., U.S.	228	40.56N	73.58W
Tenāli, India	187	16.10N	80.32E
Tenamaxtlán, Mex. (tā′nä-mäs-tlän′)	118	20.13N	104.06W
Tenancingo, Mex. (tå-nän-sēŋ′gō)	118	18.54N	99.36W
Tenango, Mex. (tā-näŋ′gō)	119a	19.09N	98.51W
Tenasserim, Myanmar (tĕn-ăs′ēr-ĭm)	196	12.09N	99.01E
Tendrivs′ka Kosa, ostriv, i., Ukr.	163	46.12N	31.17E
Tenerife Island, i., Spain (tå-nå-rē′fā) (tĕn-ēr-ĭf′)	210	28.41N	17.02W
Tènès, Alg. (tā-nĕs′)	147	36.28N	1.22E
Tengiz kölï, l., Kaz.	169	50.45N	68.39E
Tengxian, China (tŭŋ shyĕn)	192	35.07N	117.08E
Tenjin, Japan (tĕn′jĕn)	195b	34.54N	135.04E
Tenke, Zaire (tĕŋ′kå)	212	11.26S	26.45E
Tenkiller Ferry Reservoir, res., Ok., U.S. (tĕn-kĭl′ēr)	111	35.42N	94.47W
Tenkodogo, Burkina (tĕŋ-kō-dō′gō)	210	11.47N	0.22W
Tenmile, r., Wa., U.S. (tĕn mīl)	106d	48.52N	122.32W
Tennant Creek, Austl. (tĕn′ănt)	202	19.45S	134.00E
Tennessee, state, U.S. (tĕn-ĕ-sē′)	97	35.50N	88.00W
Tennessee, r., U.S.	97	35.35N	88.20W
Tennille, Ga., U.S. (tĕn′ĭl)	114	32.55N	86.50W
Tennōji, neigh., Japan	242b	34.39N	135.31E
Teno, r., Chile (tĕ′nô)	129b	34.55S	71.00W
Tenora, Austl. (tĕn-ôrá)	204	34.23S	147.33E
Tenosique, Mex. (tā-nō-sē′kå)	119	17.27N	91.25W
Tenri, Japan	195b	34.36N	135.50E
Tenryū-Gawa, r., Japan (tĕn′ryōō′gä′wä)	195	35.16N	137.54E
Tensas, r., La., U.S. (tĕn′sô)	113	31.54N	91.30W
Tensaw, r., Al., U.S. (tĕn′sô)	114	30.45N	87.52W
Tenterfield, Austl. (tĕn′tĕr-fēld)	203	29.00S	152.06E
Ten Thousand, Islands, is., Fl., U.S. (tĕn thou′zănd)	115a	25.45N	81.35W
Teocaltiche, Mex. (tā′ō-käl-tē′chä)	118	21.27N	102.38W
Teocelo, Mex. (tā-ō-sä′lō)	119	19.22N	96.57W
Teocuitatlán de Corona, Mex.	118	20.06N	103.22W
Teófilo Otoni, Braz. (tē-ō′fē-lō-tō′nė)	131	17.49S	41.18W
Teoloyucan, Mex. (tā′ō-lō-yōō′kän)	118	19.43N	99.12W
Teopisca, Mex. (tā-ō-pēs′kä)	119	16.30N	92.33W
Teotihuacán, Mex. (tĕ-ô-tē-wá-ká′n)	119a	19.40N	98.52W
Teotitlán del Camino, Mex. (tā-ō-tė-tlän′ dĕl kä-mē′nō)	119	18.07N	97.04W
Tepalcatepec, Mex. (tā′päl-kä-tä′pĕk)	118	19.11N	102.51W
Tepalcatepec, r., Mex.	118	18.54N	102.25W
Tepalcates, Mex.	233a	19.23N	99.04W
Tepalcingo, Mex. (tä-päl-sēŋ′gō)	118	18.34N	98.49W
Tepatitlán de Morelos, Mex. (tā-pä-tė-tlän′ dā mō-rā′los)	116	20.55N	102.47W
Tepeaca, Mex. (tā-pā-ä′kä)	119	18.57N	97.54W
Tepecoacuilco de Trujano, Mex.	118	18.15N	99.29W
Tepeji del Río, Mex. (tā-på-ĸe′ dĕl rē′ō)	118	19.55N	99.22W
Tepelmeme, Mex. (tā′pĕl-mā′må)	119	17.51N	97.23W
Tepepan, Mex.	233a	19.16N	99.08W
Tepetlaoxtoc, Mex. (tā′pā-tlä′ōs-tōk′)	118	19.34N	98.49W
Tepezala, Mex. (tā-på-zä-lä′)	118	22.12N	102.12W
Tepic, Mex. (tā-pēk′)	116	21.32N	104.53W
Tëplaya Gora, Russia (tyôp′lá-yá gô-rá)	172a	58.32N	59.08E
Teplice, Czech Rep.	147	50.39N	13.50E
Teposcolula, Mex.	119	17.33N	97.29W
Tequendama, Salto de, wtfl., Col. (sä′l-tō dĕ tĕ-kĕn-dä′mä)	130	4.34N	74.18W
Tequila, Mex. (tå-kē′lä)	118	20.53N	103.48W
Tequisistlán, r., Mex. (tĕ-kē-sės-tlä′n)	119	16.20N	95.40W
Tequisquiapan, Mex. (tå-kēs-kė-ä′pän)	118	20.33N	99.57W
Ter, r., Spain (tĕr)	159	42.04N	2.52E
Téra, Niger	214	14.01N	0.45E
Tera, r., Spain (tā′rä)	158	42.05N	6.24W
Teramo, Italy (tā′rä-mô)	160	42.40N	13.41E
Terborg, Neth. (tĕr-bōrg)	157c	51.55N	6.23E
Tercan, Tur. (tĕr′jän)	167	39.40N	40.12E
Terceira Island, i., Port. (tĕr-sā′rä)	210a	38.49N	26.36W
Terebovlya, Ukr. (tĕ-rä′bôv-lyá)	155	49.18N	25.43E
Terek, r., Russia	167	43.30N	45.10E
Terenkul′, Russia (tĕ-rĕn′kŏl)	172a	55.38N	62.18E
Teresina, Braz. (tĕr-å-sē′ná)	131	5.04S	42.42W
Teresópolis, Braz. (tĕr-ā-sō′pō-lēzh)	129a	22.25S	42.59W
Teriberka, Russia (tyĕr-ė-byôr′ká)	166	69.00N	35.15E
Terme, Tur. (tĕr′mĕ)	167	41.05N	37.00E
Termez, Uzb. (tyĕr′mĕz)	170	37.19N	67.20E
Terminal, Ca., U.S.	232	33.45N	118.15W
Termini, Italy (tĕr′mė-nė)	160	37.58N	13.39E
Términos, Laguna de, l., Mex. (lä-gō′nä dĕ ĕ′r-mē-nōs)	116	18.37N	91.32W

356 Termoli–Tinguiririca

PLACE (Pronunciation)	PAGE	Lat. °′	Long. °′
Termoli, Italy (tĕr′mô-lẻ)	160	42.00N	15.01E
Tern, r., Eng., U.K. (tûrn)	144a	52.49N	2.31W
Ternate, Indon. (tĕr-nä′tā)	197	0.52N	127.25E
Terni, Italy (tĕr′nẻ)	148	42.38N	12.41E
Ternopil', Ukr.	167	49.32N	25.36E
Terpeniya, Mys, c., Russia	165	48.44N	144.42E
Terpeniya, Zaliv, b., Russia (zä′lĭf tĕr-pă′nĭ-yȧ)	194	49.10N	143.05E
Terrace, Can. (tĕr′ĭs)	84	54.31N	128.35W
Terracina, Italy (tĕr-rä-chē′nä)	148	41.18N	13.14E
Terra Nova National Park, rec., Can.	85a	48.37N	54.15W
Terrebonne, Can. (tĕr-bŏn′)	99	45.42N	73.38W
Terrebonne Bay, b., La., U.S.	113	28.55N	90.30W
Terre Haute, In., U.S. (tĕr-ẻ hōt′)	97	39.25N	87.25W
Terrell, Tx., U.S. (tĕr′ĕl)	113	32.44N	96.15W
Terrell, Wa., U.S.	106d	48.53N	122.44W
Terrell Hills, Tx., U.S. (tĕr′ĕl hĭlz)	107d	29.28N	98.27W
Terschelling, i., Neth. (tĕr-sĸĕl′ĭng)	151	53.25N	5.12E
Teruel, Spain (tȧ-rōō-ĕl′)	148	40.20N	1.05W
Tešanj, Bos. (tĕ′shän')	161	44.36N	17.59E
Teschendorf, Ger. (tĕ′shĕn-dōrf)	145b	52.51N	13.10E
Tesecheacan, Mex. (tĕ-sĕ-chĕ-ä-kȧ′n)	119	18.10N	95.41W
Teshekpuk, l., Ak., U.S. (tē-shĕk′pŭk)	95	70.18N	152.36W
Teshio Dake, mtn., Japan (tĕsh′ẻ-ō-dä′kā)	194	44.00N	142.50E
Teshio Gawa, r., Japan (tĕsh′ẻ-ȯ gä′wä)	194	44.53N	144.55E
Tesiyn, r., Asia	188	49.45N	96.00E
Teslin, Can. (tĕs-lĭn)	95	60.10N	132.30W
Teslin, l., Can.	84	60.12N	132.08W
Teslin, r., Can.	84	61.18N	134.14W
Tessaoua, Niger (tĕs-sä′ȯ-ä)	210	13.53N	7.53E
Tessenderlo, Bel.	145a	51.04N	5.08E
Test, r., Eng., U.K. (tĕst)	150	51.10N	1.30W
Testa del Gargano, c., Italy (tās′tä dĕl gär-gä′nō)	160	41.48N	16.13E
Tetachuck Lake, l., Can.	86	53.20N	125.50W
Tete, Moz. (tā′tĕ)	212	16.13S	33.35E
Tête Jaune Cache, Can. (tĕt′zhŏn-kăsh)	87	52.57N	119.26W
Teterboro, N.J., U.S.	228	40.52N	74.03W
Teteriv, r., Ukr.	167	51.05N	29.30E
Teterow, Ger. (tā′tĕ-rō)	154	53.46N	12.33E
Teteven, Bul. (tĕt′ĕ-ven')	161	42.57N	24.15E
Teton, r., Mt., U.S. (tē′tŏn)	105	47.54N	111.37W
Tétouan, Mor.	210	35.42N	5.34W
Tetovo, Mac. (tā′tȯ-vȯ)	161	42.01N	21.00E
Tetyukhe-Pristan, Russia (tĕt-yōō′ĸĕ prĭ-stän′)	194	44.21N	135.44E
Tetyushi, Russia (tÿt-yȯ′shĭ)	166	54.57N	48.50E
Teupitz, Ger. (toi′pētz)	145b	42.08N	13.37E
Tevere, r., Italy	148	42.30N	12.14E
Teverya, Isr.	181a	32.48N	35.32E
Tewksbury, Ma., U.S. (tūks′bẽr-ĭ)	93a	42.37N	71.14W
Texada Island, i., Can.	86	49.40N	124.24W
Texarkana, Ar., U.S. (tĕk-sär-kän′ȧ)	97	33.26N	94.02W
Texarkana, Tx., U.S.	97	33.26N	94.04W
Texas, state, U.S.	96	31.00N	101.00W
Texas City, Tx., U.S.	113	29.23N	94.54W
Texcaltitlán, Mex. (tās-käl′tẻ-tlän′)	118	18.54N	99.51W
Texcoco, Mex. (tās-kō′kō)	118	19.31N	98.53W
Texcoco, Lago de, l., Mex.	119a	19.30N	99.00W
Texel, i., Neth. (tĕk′sĕl)	151	53.10N	4.45E
Texistepec, Mex. (tĕk-sēs-tā-pĕk′)	119	17.51N	94.46W
Texmelucan, Mex.	118	19.17N	98.26W
Texoma, Lake, res., U.S. (tĕk′ō-mă)	96	34.03N	96.28W
Texontepec, Mex. (tȧ-zōn-tȧ-pĕk′)	118	19.52N	98.48W
Texontepec de Aldama, Mex. (dā äl-dä′mä)	118	20.19N	99.19W
Teyateyaneng, Leso.	213c	29.11S	27.43E
Teykovo, Russia (tĕy-kô-vȯ)	166	56.52N	40.34E
Teziutlán, Mex. (tȧ-zẻ-ōō-tlän′)	119	19.48N	97.21W
Tezpur, India	186	26.42N	92.52E
Tha-anne, r., Can.	84	60.50N	96.56W
Thabana Ntlenyana, mtn., Leso.	213c	29.28S	29.17E
Thabazimbi, S. Afr.	218d	24.36S	27.22E
Thailand, nation, Asia	196	16.30N	101.00E
Thailand, Gulf of, b., Asia	196	11.37N	100.46E
Thākurpukur, India	240a	22.28N	88.19E
Thale Luang, l., Thai.	196	7.51N	99.39E
Thame, Eng., U.K. (tām)	144b	51.43N	0.59W
Thames, r., Can. (tĕmz)	90	42.40N	81.45W
Thames, r., Eng., U.K.	142	51.30N	1.30W
Thames Ditton, Eng., U.K.	235	51.23N	0.21W
Thāmit, Wadi, r., Libya	149	30.39N	16.23E
Thāna, India (thä′nŭ)	186	19.13N	72.58E
Thāna Creek, r., India	187b	19.03N	72.58E
Thanh Hoa, Viet. (tän′hō′ȧ)	196	19.46N	105.42E
Thanjāvūr, India	183	10.51N	79.11E
Thann, Fr. (tän)	157	47.49N	7.05E
Thaon-les-Vosges, Fr. (tä-ŏɴ-lā-vōzh′)	157	48.16N	6.24E
Thargomindah, Austl. (thȧr′gō-mĭn′dȧ)	203	27.58S	143.57E
Thásos, i., Grc. (thă′sȯs)	149	40.41N	24.53E
Thatch Cay, i., V.I.U.S. (thăch)	117c	18.22N	64.53W
Thatto Heath, Eng., U.K.	237a	53.26N	2.45W
Thaya, r., Eur. (tä′yȧ)	154	48.48N	15.40E
Thayer, Mo., U.S. (thâ′ẽr)	111	36.30N	91.34W
The Basin, Austl.	243b	37.51S	145.19E
Thebes *see* Thívai, Grc.	149	38.20N	23.18E
Thebes, hist., Egypt (thēbz)	211	25.47N	32.39E
The Brothers, mtn., Wa., U.S.	106a	47.39N	123.08W
The Capital, pt. of i., D.C., U.S.	229d	38.53N	77.00W
The Coorong, l., Austl. (kȯ′rŏng)	204	36.07S	139.45E
The Coteau, hills, Can.	88	51.10N	107.30W
The Dalles, Or., U.S. (dălz)	96	45.36N	121.10W
The Father, mtn., Pap. N. Gui.	197	5.05S	151.30E
The Hague ('s-Gravenhage), Neth.	142	52.05N	4.16E
The Narrows, strt., N.Y., U.S.	228	40.37N	74.03W
The Oaks, Austl.	201b	34.04S	150.36E
Theodore, Austl. (thēō′dôr)	204	24.51S	150.09E
Theodore Roosevelt Dam, dam, Az., U.S. (thẻ-ȯ-doř rōō-sȧ-vĕlt)	109	33.46N	111.25W
Theodore Roosevelt Lake, res., Az., U.S.	109	33.45N	111.00W
Theodore Roosevelt National Park, N.D., U.S.	102	47.20N	103.42W
Theológos, Grc.	161	40.37N	24.41E
The Oval, pt. of i., Eng., U.K.	235	51.29N	0.07W
The Pas, Can. (pä)	84	53.50N	101.15W
Thermopolis, Wy., U.S. (thẽr-mŏp′ȯ-lĭs)	105	43.38N	108.11W
The Round Mountain, mtn., Austl.	204	30.17S	152.19E
The Sound, strt., Austl.	243a	33.49S	151.17E
Thessalía, hist. reg., Grc.	161	39.50N	22.09E
Thessalon, Can.	85	46.11N	83.37W
Thessaloníki, Grc. (thĕs-sȧ-lȯ-nē′kẻ)	142	40.38N	22.59E
Thetford Mines, Can. (thĕt′fẽrd mīns)	91	46.05N	71.20W
The Twins, mtn., Afr. (twĭnz)	213c	30.09S	28.29E
Theunissen, S. Afr.	218d	28.25S	26.44E
Theydon Bois, Eng., U.K.	235	51.40N	0.06E
Thiais, Fr.	237c	48.46N	2.23E
Thibaudeau, Can. (tĭ′bŏ-dō′)	89	57.05N	94.08W
Thibodaux, La., U.S. (tẻ-bȯ-dō′)	113	29.48N	90.48W
Thief, l., Mn., U.S. (thēf)	102	48.32N	95.46W
Thief, r., Mn., U.S.	103	48.18N	96.07E
Thief Rivers Falls, Mn., U.S. (thēf rĭv′ẽr fôlz)	102	48.07N	96.11W
Thiers, Fr. (tyâr)	156	45.51N	3.32E
Thiès, Sen. (tẻ-ĕs′)	210	14.48N	16.56W
Thika, Kenya	217	1.03S	37.05E
Thimphu, Bhu.	183	27.33N	89.42E
Thingvallavatn, l., Ice.	146	64.12N	20.22W
Thio, N. Cal.	198f	21.37S	166.14E
Thionville, Fr. (tyôɴ-vēl′)	147	49.23N	6.31E
Third Cataract, wtfl., Sudan	211	19.53N	30.11E
Thisted, Den. (tēs′tĕdh)	152	56.57N	8.38E
Thistilfjördur, b., Ice.	146	66.29N	14.59W
Thistle, i., Austl. (thĭs″l)	204	34.55S	136.11E
Thistletown, neigh., Can.	227c	43.44N	79.33W
Thjörsá, r., Ice. (tyûr′sȧ)	146	64.23N	19.18W
Thohoyandou, S. Afr.	212	23.00S	30.29E
Tholen, Neth.	145a	51.32N	4.11E
Thomas, Ok., U.S. (tŏm′ăs)	110	35.44N	98.43W
Thomas, W.V., U.S.	99	39.15N	79.30W
Thomaston, Ga., U.S. (tŏm′ăs-tŭn)	114	32.51N	84.17W
Thomaston, N.Y., U.S.	228	40.47N	73.43W
Thomastown, Austl.	243b	37.41S	145.01E
Thomasville, Al., U.S. (tŏm′ăs-vĭl)	114	31.55N	87.43W
Thomasville, N.C., U.S.	115	35.52N	80.05W
Thomlinson, Mount, mtn., Can.	86	55.33N	127.29W
Thompson, Can.	84	55.48N	97.59W
Thompson, r., Can.	87	50.15N	121.20W
Thompson, r., Mo., U.S.	111	40.32N	93.49W
Thompson Falls, Mt., U.S.	104	47.35N	115.20W
Thomson, r., Austl. (tŏm-sŏn)	203	24.30S	143.07E
Thomson's Falls, Kenya	217	0.02N	36.22E
Thon Buri, neigh., Thai.	241f	13.43N	100.29E
Thong, Eng., U.K.	235	51.24N	0.24E
Thong Hoe, Sing.	240c	1.25N	103.42E
Thong-tay-hoi, Viet.	241j	10.50N	106.39E
Thonon-les-Bains, Fr. (tȯ-nôɴ′lȧ-băɴ′)	157	46.22N	6.27E
Thorigny-sur-Marne, Fr.	237c	48.53N	2.42E
Thornbury, Austl.	243b	37.45S	145.00E
Thorne, Eng., U.K. (thôrn)	144a	53.37N	0.58W
Thornhill, S. Afr.	244b	26.07S	28.09E
Thornleigh, Austl.	243a	33.44S	151.05E
Thornton, Eng., U.K.	237a	53.30N	3.00W
Thornton Hough, Eng., U.K.	237a	53.19N	3.03W
Thornton-le-Moors, Eng., U.K.	237a	53.16N	2.50W
Thorntown, In., U.S. (thôrn′tŭn)	98	40.05N	86.35W
Thornwood Common, Eng., U.K.	235	51.43N	0.08E
Thorold, Can. (thō′rōld)	91	43.13N	79.12W
Thouars, Fr. (tōō-är′)	156	47.00N	0.17W
Thousand Islands, is., N.Y., U.S. (thou′zănd)	99	44.15N	76.10W
Thrace, hist. reg. (thrās)	161	41.20N	26.07E
Thrapston, Eng., U.K. (thrăp′stŭn)	144a	52.23N	0.32W
Three Forks, Mt., U.S. (thrē fôrks)	105	45.56N	111.35W
Three Oaks, Mi., U.S. (thrē ōks)	98	41.50N	86.40W
Three Points, Cape, c., Ghana	210	4.45N	2.06W
Three Rivers, Mi., U.S.	98	42.00N	83.40W
Thule, Grnld.	82	76.34N	68.47W
Thun, Switz. (tōōn)	154	46.46N	7.34E
Thunder Bay, Can.	90	48.28N	89.12W
Thunder Bay, b., Can. (thŭn′dẽr)	90	48.29N	88.52W
Thunder Hills, hills, Can.	88	54.30N	106.00W
Thunersee, l., Switz.	154	46.40N	7.30E
Thurber, Tx., U.S. (thûr′bẽr)	112	32.30N	98.23W
Thüringen (Thuringia), hist. reg., Ger. (tü′rĭng-ĕn)	154	51.07N	10.45E
Thurles, Ire. (thûrlz)	150	52.44N	7.45W
Thursday, i., Austl. (thûrz-dā)	203	10.17S	142.23E
Thurso, Can. (thŭn′sȯ)	83c	45.36N	75.15W
Thurso, Scot., U.K.	150	58.35N	3.40W
Thurston Island, i., Ant. (thûrs′tŭn)	219	71.20S	98.00W
Tiananmen, hist., China	240b	39.55N	116.23E
Tiandong, China (tĭĕn-dȯŋ)	193	23.32N	107.10E
Tianjin, China	189	39.08N	117.14E
Tianjin Shi, China (tĭĕn-jyĭn shr)	192	39.30N	117.13E
Tianmen, China (tĭĕn-mŭn)	193	30.40N	113.10E
Tianshui, China (tĭĕn-shwā)	192	34.25N	105.40E
Tibagi, Braz. (tē′bȧ-zhē)	131	24.40S	50.35W
Tibasti, Sarir, des., Libya	211	24.00N	16.30E
Tibati, Cam.	215	6.27N	12.38E
Tiber *see* Tevere, r., Italy	148	42.30N	12.14E
Tibesti, mts., Chad	211	20.40N	17.48E
Tibet *see* Xizang, prov., China (tĭ-bĕt′)	188	32.22N	83.30E
Tibnīn, Leb.	181a	33.12N	35.23E
Tiburon, Haiti	123	18.35N	74.25W
Tiburon, Ca., U.S. (tē-bōō-rōn′)	106b	37.53N	122.27W
Tiburon, Ca., U.S.	231b	36.04N	119.19W
Tiburón, i., Mex.	116	28.45N	113.10W
Tiburón, Cabo, c. (kȧ′bȯ)	121	8.42N	77.19W
Tiburon Island, i., Ca., U.S.	106b	37.52N	122.26W
Ticao Island, i., Phil. (tẻ-kä′ō)	197a	12.40N	123.30E
Tickhill, Eng., U.K. (tĭk′ĭl)	144a	53.26N	1.06W
Ticonderoga, N.Y., U.S. (tī-kŏn-dẽr-ō′gȧ)	99	43.50N	73.30W
Ticul, Mex. (tē-kōō′l)	120a	20.22N	89.32W
Tidaholm, Swe. (tē′dȧ-hōlm)	152	58.11N	13.53E
Tideswell, Eng., U.K. (tīdz′wĕl)	144a	53.17N	1.47W
Tidikelt, reg., Alg. (tē-dẻ-kĕlt′)	210	25.53N	2.11E
Tidjikdja, Maur. (tẻ-jĭk′jä)	210	18.33N	11.25W
Tidra, Île, i., Maur.	214	19.50N	16.45W
Tiefenbroich, Ger.	236	51.18N	6.49E
Tieling, China (tĭĕ-liŋ)	189	42.18N	123.50E
Tielmes, Spain (tyâl-màs′)	159a	40.15N	3.20W
Tienen, Bel.	145a	50.49N	4.58E
Tien Shan, mts., Asia	188	42.00N	78.46E
Tientsin *see* Tianjin, China	189	39.08N	117.14E
Tiergarten, neigh., Ger.	238a	52.31N	13.21E
Tierp, Swe. (tyĕrp)	152	60.21N	17.28E
Tierpoort, S. Afr.	213b	25.53N	28.26E
Tierra Blanca, Mex. (tyĕ′r-rä-blä′n-kä)	119	18.28N	96.19W
Tierra del Fuego, i., S.A. (tyĕr′rä dĕl fwā′gȯ)	132	53.50S	68.45W
Tiétar, r., Spain (tẻ-ā′tär)	158	39.56N	5.44W
Tiffin, Oh., U.S. (tĭf′ĭn)	98	41.10N	83.15W
Tifton, Ga., U.S. (tĭf′tŭn)	114	31.25N	83.34W
Tigard, Or., U.S. (tī′gärd)	106c	45.25N	122.46W
Tighina, Mol.	167	46.49N	29.29E
Tignish, Can. (tĭg′nĭsh)	92	46.57N	64.02W
Tigoda, r., Russia (tē′gô-dȧ)	172c	59.29N	31.15E
Tigre, r., Peru	130	2.20S	75.41W
Tigres, Península dos, pen., Ang. (pĕ-nẻ′ŋ-sōō-lä-dȯs-tẻ′grĕs)	212	16.30S	11.45E
Tigris, r., Asia	182	34.45N	44.10E
Tīh, Jabal at, mts., Egypt	181a	29.23N	34.05E
Tihert, Alg.	210	35.28N	1.15E
Tihuatlán, Mex. (tẻ-wä-tlän′)	119	20.43N	97.34W
Tijuana, Mex. (tẻ-hwä′nä)	116	32.32N	117.02W
Tijuca, Pico da, mtn., Braz. (pē′kō-dä-tẻ-zhōō′kȧ)	132b	22.56S	43.17W
Tikal, hist., Guat. (tẻ-käl′)	120a	17.16N	89.49W
Tikhoretsk, Russia (tẻ-ĸȯr-yĕtsk′)	167	45.55N	40.05E
Tikhvin, Russia (tẻĸ-vēn′)	164	59.36N	33.38E
Tikrīt, Iraq	182	34.36N	43.31E
Tiksi, Russia (tẻk-sē′)	165	71.42N	128.32E
Tilburg, Neth. (tĭl′bûrg)	147	51.33N	5.05E
Tilbury, Eng., U.K.	144b	51.28N	0.23E
Tilemsi, Vallée du, val., Mali	214	17.50N	0.25E
Tilichiki, Russia (tyĭ-le-chĭ-kẻ)	165	60.49N	166.14E
Tilimsen, Alg.	210	34.53N	1.21W
Tillabéry, Niger (tē-yȧ-bā-rē′)	210	14.14N	1.30E
Tillamook, Or., U.S. (tĭl′ȧ-mȯk)	104	45.27N	123.50W
Tillamook Bay, b., Or., U.S.	104	45.32N	124.26W
Tillberga, Swe. (tēl-bĕr′ghȧ)	152	59.40N	16.34E
Tillsonburg, Can. (tĭl′sŭn-bûrg)	91	42.50N	80.50W
Tim, Russia (tẻm)	163	51.39N	37.07E
Timaru, N.Z. (tĭm′ȧ-rōō)	203a	44.26S	171.17E
Timashevskaya, Russia (tēmă-shĕfs-kă′yă)	167	45.47N	38.57E
Timbalier Bay, b., La., U.S. (tĭm′bȧ-lĕr)	113	28.55N	90.14W
Timber, Or., U.S. (tĭm′bẽr)	106c	45.43N	123.17W
Timberview, Md., U.S.	229c	39.13N	76.45W
Timbo, Gui. (tĭm′bō)	210	10.41N	11.51W
Timbuktu *see* Tombouctou, Mali	210	16.46N	3.01W
Times Square, pt. of i., N.Y., U.S.	228	40.45N874.00	W
Timétrine Monts, mts., Mali	214	19.50N	0.30W
Timimoun, Alg. (tē-mẻ-mōōn′)	210	29.14N	0.22E
Timiris, Cap, c., Maur.	210	19.23N	16.32W
Timiş, r., Eur.	161	45.28N	21.06E
Timişoara, Rom.	149	45.44N	21.21E
Timmins, Can. (tĭm′ĭnz)	85	48.25N	81.22W
Timmonsville, S.C., U.S. (tĭm′ŭnz-vĭl)	115	34.09N	79.55W
Timok, r., Eur.	161	43.35N	22.13E
Timor, i., Indon. (tẻ-mōr′)	197	10.08S	125.00E
Timor Sea, sea	202	12.40S	125.00E
Timpanogos Cave National Monument, rec., Ut., U.S. (tĭ-măn′ō-gŏz)	109	40.25N	111.45W
Timperley, Eng., U.K.	237b	53.24N	2.19W
Timpson, Tx., U.S. (tĭmp′sŭn)	113	31.55N	94.24W
Timsāh, l., Egypt (tĭm′sä)	218b	30.34N	32.22E
Tina, r., S. Afr. (tē′nȧ)	213c	30.50S	28.44E
Tina, Monte, mtn., Dom. Rep. (mȯ′n-tĕ-tē′nȧ)	123	18.50N	70.40W
Tinaguillo, Ven. (tẻ-nä-gē′l-yȯ)	131b	9.55N	68.18W
Tīnah, Khalīj at, b., Egypt	181a	31.06N	32.42E
Tindouf, Alg. (tẻn-dōōf′)	210	27.43N	7.44W
Tinggi, i., Malay.	181b	2.16N	104.16E
Tinghert, Plateau du, plat., Alg.	210	27.30N	7.30E
Tingi Mountains, mts., S.L.	214	9.00N	10.50W
Ting Kau, H.K.	241c	22.23N	114.04E
Tinglin, China	191b	30.53N	121.18E
Tingo María, Peru (tē′ngȯ-mä-rẻ′ä)	130	9.15S	76.04W
Tingréla, C. Iv.	214	10.29N	6.24W
Tingsryd, Swe. (tĭngs′rüd)	152	56.32N	14.58E
Tinguindio, Mex.	118	19.38N	102.02W
Tinguiririca, r., Chile (tē′n-gē-rē-rẻ′kä)	129b	34.48S	70.45W

ăt; finăl; rāte; senåte; ärm; åsk; sofȧ; fâre; ch-choose; dh-as th in other; bē; ėvent; bĕt; recĕnt; cratẽr; g-gō; gh-guttural g; bĭt; ĭ-short neutral; rīde; ĸ-guttural k as ch in German ich;

PRONOUNCING INDEX Tinley Park–Tostado 357

PLACE (Pronunciation)	PAGE	Lat. °′	Long. °′
Tinley Park, Il., U.S. (tĭn'lē)	101a	41.34N	87.47W
Tinnoset, Nor. (tĭn'nōs'sĕt)	152	59.44N	9.00E
Tinogasta, Arg. (tē-nō-gäs'tä)	132	28.07S	67.30W
Tínos, i., Grc.	149	37.45N	25.12E
Tinsukia, India (tin-soo'kĭ-ȧ)	182	27.18N	95.29W
Tintic, Ut., U.S. (tĭn'tĭk)	109	39.55N	112.15W
Tio, Pic de, mtn., Gui.	214	8.55N	8.55W
Tioga, neigh., Pa., U.S.	229b	40.00N	75.10W
Tioman, i., Malay.	181b	2.50N	104.15E
Tipitapa, Nic. (tē-pē-tä'pä)	120	12.14N	86.05W
Tipitapa, r., Nic.	120	12.13N	85.57W
Tippah Creek, r., Ms., U.S. (tĭp'pȧ)	114	34.43N	88.15W
Tippecanoe, r., In., U.S. (tĭp-ē-kȧ-noo')	98	40.55N	86.45W
Tipperary, Ire. (tĭ-pē-râ'rē)	147	52.28N	8.13W
Tippo Bay, Ms., U.S. (tĭp'ō bīoo')	111	33.35N	90.06W
Tipton, In., U.S.	98	40.15N	86.00W
Tipton, Ia., U.S.	103	41.46N	91.10W
Tiranë, Alb. (tē-rä'nä)	142	41.48N	19.50E
Tirano, Italy (tē-rä'nō)	160	46.12N	10.09E
Tiraspol, Mol.	167	46.52N	29.38E
Tire, Tur. (tē'rĕ)	149	38.05N	27.48E
Tiree, i., Scot., U.K. (tī-rē')	146	56.34N	6.30W
Tires, Port.	238d	38.43N	9.21W
Tirlyanskiy, Russia (tĭr-lyän'skĭ)	172a	54.13N	58.37E
Tírnavos, Grc.	161	39.50N	22.14E
Tirol, prov., Aus. (tē-rōl')	154	47.13N	11.10E
Tiruchchirāppalli, India (tĭr'ō-chĭ-rä'pȧ-lĭ)	183	10.49N	78.48E
Tirunelveli, India	183b	8.53N	77.43E
Tiruppur, India	187	11.11N	77.08E
Tisdale, Can. (tĭz'dāl)	84	52.51N	104.04W
Tista, r., Asia	186	26.00N	89.30E
Tisza, r., Eur. (tē'sä)	142	47.30N	21.00E
Titāgarh, India	186a	22.44N	88.23E
Titicaca, Lago, l., S.A. (lä'gō-tē-tē-kä'kä)	130	16.12S	70.33W
Titiribi, Col. (tē-tē-rē-bē')	130a	6.05N	75.47W
Tito, Lagh, r., Kenya	217	2.25N	39.05E
Titov Veles, Mac. (tē'tôv vĕ'lĕs)	161	41.42N	21.50E
Titterstone Clee Hill, hill, Eng., U.K. (klē)	144a	52.24N	2.37W
Titule, Zaire	217	3.17N	25.32E
Titusville, Fl., U.S. (tĭ'tŭs-vĭl)	115a	28.37N	80.44W
Titusville, Pa., U.S.	99	40.40N	79.40W
Titz, Ger. (tētz)	157c	51.00N	6.26E
Tiu Keng Wan, H.K.	241c	22.18N	114.15E
Tiverton, R.I., U.S. (tĭv'ĕr-tun)	100b	41.38N	71.11W
Tivoli, Italy (tē'vô-lē)	148	41.38N	12.48E
Tixkokob, Mex. (tēx-kō-kō'b)	120a	21.01N	89.23W
Tixtla de Guerrero, Mex. (tē'x-tlä-dĕ-gĕr-rĕ'rô)	118	17.36N	99.24W
Tizapán, Mex.	233a	19.20N	99.13W
Tizard Bank and Reef, rf., Asia (tĭz'ȧrd)	196	10.51N	113.20E
Tizimín, Mex. (tē-zē-mē'n)	120a	21.08N	88.10W
Tizi-Ouzou, Alg. (tē'zē-oo-zoo')	210	36.44N	4.04E
Tiznados, r., Ven. (tēz-nä'dōs)	131b	9.53N	67.49W
Tiznit, Mor. (tēz-nēt)	210	29.52N	9.39W
Tkvarcheli, Geor.	168	42.15N	41.41E
Tlacolula de Matamoros, Mex.	119	16.56N	96.29W
Tlacotálpan, Mex. (tlä-kō-täl'pän)	119	18.39N	95.40W
Tlacotepec, Mex. (tlä-kō-tà-pĕ'k)	118	17.46N	99.57W
Tlacotepec, Mex.	118	19.11N	99.41W
Tlacotepec, Mex.	119	18.41N	97.40W
Tláhuac, Mex. (tlä-wäk')	119a	19.16N	99.00W
Tlajomulco de Zúñiga, Mex. (tlä-hô-moo'l-ko-dĕ-zoo'n-yē-gä)	118	20.30N	103.27W
Tlalchapa, Mex. (tläl-chä'pä)	118	18.26N	100.29W
Tlalixcoyan, Mex. (tlä-lēs'kō-yän')	119	18.53N	96.04W
Tlalmanalco, Mex. (tläl-mä-nä'l-kō)	119a	19.12N	98.48W
Tlalnepantla, Mex.	119a	19.32N	99.13W
Tlalnepantla, Mex. (tläl-nå-pån'tlä)	119a	18.59N	99.01W
Tlalpan, Mex. (tläl-pä'n)	118	19.17N	99.10W
Tlalpujahua, Mex. (tläl-poo-ĸä'wä)	118	19.50N	100.10W
Tlaltenco, Mex.	233a	19.17N	99.01W
Tlapa, Mex. (tlä'pä)	118	17.30N	98.30W
Tlapacoyan, Mex. (tlä-pä-kō-yä'n)	119	19.57N	97.11W
Tlapehuala, Mex. (tlä-på-wä'lä)	118	18.17N	100.30W
Tlaquepaque, Mex. (tlä-kĕ-pä'kĕ)	118	20.39N	103.17W
Tlatlaya, Mex. (tlä-tlä'yä)	118	18.36N	100.14W
Tlaxcala, Mex. (tläs-kä'lä)	116	19.16N	98.14W
Tlaxcala, state, Mex.	118	19.30N	98.15W
Tlaxco, Mex. (tläs'kō)	118	19.37N	98.06W
Tlaxiaco Santa María Asunción, Mex.	119	17.16N	97.41W
Tlayacapan, Mex. (tlä-yä-kä-pä'n)	119a	18.57N	99.00W
Tlevak Strait, strt., Ak., U.S.	86	53.03N	132.58W
Tlumach, Ukr. (t'lû-mäch')	155	48.47N	25.00E
Toa, r., Cuba (tō'ä)	123	20.25N	74.35W
Toamasina, Madag.	213	18.14S	49.25E
Toar, Cuchillas de, mts., Cuba (koo-chē'l-lyäs-dĕ-tô-ä'r)	123	20.20N	74.50W
Tobago, i., Trin. (tô-bā'gō)	117	11.15N	60.30W
Toba Inlet, b., Can.	86	50.20N	124.50W
Tobarra, Spain (tô-bär'rä)	158	38.37N	1.42W
Tobol'sk, Russia (tô-bôlsk')	170	58.09N	68.28E
Tobyl, r., Asia	164	52.00N	62.00E
Tocaima, Col. (tô-kä'y-mä)	130a	4.28N	74.38W
Tocantinópolis, Braz. (tō-kän-tē-nŏ'pō-lēs)	131	6.27S	47.18W
Tocantins, state, Braz.	131	10.00S	48.00W
Tocantins, r., Braz. (tō-kän-tēɴs')	131	3.28S	49.22W
Toccoa, Ga., U.S. (tŏk'ō-ȧ)	114	34.35N	83.20W
Toccoa, r., Ga., U.S.	114	34.53N	84.24W
Tochigi, Japan (tō'chē-gĭ)	195	36.25N	139.45E
Tocoa, Hond. (tō-kō'ä)	120	15.37N	86.01W
Tocopilla, Chile (tō-kō-pēl'yä)	132	22.03S	70.08W
Tocuyo de la Costa, Ven. (tō-koo'yō-dĕ-lä-kŏs'tä)	131b	11.03N	68.24W
Toda, Japan	195a	35.48N	139.42E

PLACE (Pronunciation)	PAGE	Lat. °′	Long. °′
Todmorden, Eng., U.K. (tŏd'môr-dĕn)	144a	53.43N	2.05W
Tofino, Can. (tō-fē'nō)	86	49.09N	125.54W
Töfsingdalens National Park, rec., Swe.	152	62.09N	13.05E
Tōgane, Japan (tō'gä-nä)	195	35.29N	140.16E
Togian, Kepulauan, is., Indon.	196	0.20S	122.00E
Togo, nation, Afr. (tō'gō)	210	8.00N	0.52E
Toguzak, r., Russia (tô'gò-zák)	172a	53.40N	61.42E
Tohopekaliga, Lake, l., Fl., U.S. (tō'hō-pē'kà-lī'gȧ)	115a	28.16N	81.09W
Tohor, Tanjong, c., Malay.	181b	1.53N	102.29E
Toijala, Fin. (toi'yȧ-lȧ)	153	61.11N	23.46E
Toi-Misaki, c., Japan (toi mē'sä-kē)	194	31.20N	131.20E
Toiyabe, Nv., U.S. (toi'yä-bē)	108	38.59N	117.22W
Tokachi Gawa, r., Japan (tō-kä'chē gä'wä)	194	43.10N	142.30E
Tokaj, Hung. (tô'kô-ē)	155	48.06N	21.24E
Tokat, Tur. (tō-kät')	182	40.20N	36.30E
Tokelau, dep., Oc. (tō-kē-lä'ō)	2	8.00S	176.00W
Tokmak, Kyrg. (tôk'mȧk)	169	42.44N	75.41E
Tokmak, Ukr.	163	47.17N	35.48E
Tokorozawa, Japan (tō'kō-rō-zä'wä)	195a	35.47N	139.29E
Toksu Palace, bldg., S. Kor.	241b	37.35N	126.58E
Tokuno, i., Japan (tō-koo'nō)	189	27.42N	129.25E
Tokushima, Japan (tō'kō'shē-mä)	189	34.06N	134.31E
Tokuyama, Japan (tō'kō'yä-mä)	195	34.04N	131.49E
Tōkyō, Japan	189	35.42N	139.46E
Tōkyō-Wan, b., Japan (tō'kyō wän)	195	35.56N	139.56E
Tolcayuca, Mex. (tōl-kä-yoo'kä)	118	19.55N	98.54W
Toledo, Spain (tô-lĕ'dō)	148	39.53N	4.02W
Toledo, Ia., U.S. (tō-lē'dō)	103	41.59N	92.35W
Toledo, Oh., U.S.	97	41.40N	83.35W
Toledo, Or., U.S.	104	44.37N	123.58W
Toledo, Montes de, mts., Spain (mō'n-tĕs-dĕ-tō-lĕ'dō)	158	39.33N	4.40W
Toledo Bend Reservoir, res., U.S.	97	31.30N	93.30W
Toliara, Madag.	213	23.16S	43.44E
Tolima, dept., Col. (tō-lē'mä)	130a	4.07N	75.20W
Tolima, Nevado del, mtn., Col. (nĕ-vä-dô-dĕl-tō-lē'mä)	130a	4.40N	75.20W
Tolimán, Mex. (tō-lē-män')	118	20.54N	99.54W
Tollesbury, Eng., U.K. (tōl'z-bĕrĭ)	144b	51.46N	0.49E
Tollygunge, neigh., India	240a	22.30N	88.21E
Tolmezzo, Italy (tōl-mĕt'zô)	160	46.25N	13.03E
Tolmin, Slvn. (tōl'mēn)	160	46.12N	13.45E
Tolna, Hung. (tôl'nō)	155	46.25N	18.47E
Tolo, Teluk, b., Indon. (tō'lō)	196	2.00S	122.06E
Tolosa, Spain (tō-lō'sä)	148	43.10N	2.05W
Tolt, r., Wa., U.S. (tōlt)	106a	47.13N	121.49W
Toluca, Mex. (tō-loo'kä)	116	19.17N	99.40W
Toluca, Il., U.S. (tō-loo'kȧ)	98	41.00N	89.10W
Toluca, Nevado de, mtn., Mex. (nĕ-vä-dô-dĕ-tō-loo'kä)	116	19.09N	99.42W
Tolworth, neigh., Eng., U.K.	235	51.23N	0.17W
Tolyatti, Russia	166	53.30N	49.10E
Tom', r., Russia	170	55.33N	85.00E
Tomah, Wi., U.S. (tō'mȧ)	103	43.58N	90.31W
Tomahawk, Wi., U.S. (tŏm'ȧ-hôk)	103	45.27N	89.44W
Tomakivka, Ukr.	163	47.49N	34.43E
Tomanivi, mtn., Fiji	198g	17.37S	178.01E
Tomar, Port. (tō-mär')	158	39.36N	8.26W
Tomashevka, Bela. (tō-mà'shĕf-kȧ)	155	51.34N	23.37E
Tomaszów Lubelski, Pol. (tō-mä'shōf loo-bĕl'skĭ)	155	50.20N	23.27E
Tomaszów Mazowiecki, Pol. (tō-mä'shōf mä-zō'vyĕt-skĭ)	155	51.33N	20.00E
Tomatlán, Mex. (tō-mä-tlä'n)	118	19.54N	105.14W
Tombadonkéa, Gui.	214	11.00N	14.23W
Tombador, Serra do, mts., Braz. (sĕr'rȧ dō tōm-bä-dôr')	131	11.31S	57.33W
Tombigbee, r., U.S. (tŏm-bĭg'bē)	97	33.00N	88.30W
Tombos, Braz. (tô'm-bōs)	129a	20.53S	42.00W
Tombouctou, Mali	210	16.46N	3.01W
Tombs of the Caliphs, pt. of i., Egypt	244a	30.03N	31.17E
Tombstone, Az., U.S. (toom'stōn)	109	31.40N	110.00W
Tombua, Ang. (ȧ-lĕ-zhän'drĕ)	212	15.49S	11.53E
Tomelilla, Swe. (tô'mĕ-lēl-lä)	152	55.34N	13.55E
Tomelloso, Spain (tō-mål-lyō'sō)	158	39.09N	3.02W
Tommot, Russia (tŏm-mōt')	165	59.13N	126.22E
Tomsk, Russia (tŏmsk)	164	56.29N	84.57E
Tonala, Mex.	118	20.38N	103.14W
Tonalá, r., Mex.	119	18.05N	94.08W
Tonawanda, N.Y., U.S. (tôn-ȧ-wŏn'dȧ)	101c	43.01N	78.53W
Tonawanda, Town of, N.Y., U.S.	230a	42.59N	78.52W
Tonawanda Creek, r., N.Y., U.S.	101c	43.05N	78.43W
Tonbridge, Eng., U.K. (tŭn-brij)	144b	51.11N	0.17E
Tonda, Japan (tôn'dä)	195b	34.51N	135.38E
Tondabayashi, Japan (tôn-dä-bä'yä-shē)	195b	34.29N	135.36E
Tondano, Indon. (tôn-dä'nō)	197	1.15N	124.50E
Tønder, Den. (tûn'nĕr)	152	54.47N	8.49E
Tone-Gawa, r., Japan (tō'nē gä'wa)	195	36.12N	139.19E
Tonga, nation, Oc. (tŏŋ'gȧ)	224	18.50S	175.20W
Tong'an, China (tôŋ-än)	193	24.48N	118.02E
Tonga Trench, deep	224	23.00S	172.30W
Tongbei, China (tôŋ-bā)	189	48.00N	126.48E
Tongguan, China (tôŋ-gūän)	189	34.48N	110.25E
Tonghe, China (tôŋ-hŭ)	192	45.58N	128.40E
Tonghua, China (tôŋ-hwä)	189	41.43N	125.50E
Tongjiang, China (tôŋ-jyäŋ)	189	47.38N	132.54E
Tongliao, China (tôŋ-lĭou)	192	43.30N	122.15E
Tongo, Cam.	215	5.11N	14.00E
Tongoy, Chile (tōn-goi')	132	30.16S	71.29W
Tongren, China (tôŋ-rŭn)	188	27.45N	109.12E
Tongshan, China (tôŋ-shän)	190	34.27N	116.27E
Tongtian, r., China (tôŋ-tĭĕn)	188	33.00N	97.00E
Tongue, r., Mt., U.S. (tŭng)	105	45.08N	106.40W

PLACE (Pronunciation)	PAGE	Lat. °′	Long. °′
Tongxian, China (tôŋ shyĕn)	190	39.55N	116.40E
Tonj, r., Sudan (tônj)	211	6.18N	28.33E
Tonk, India (Tōŋk)	183	26.13N	75.45E
Tonkawa, Ok., U.S. (tŏŋ kȧ-wô)	111	36.42N	97.19W
Tonkin, Gulf of, b., Asia (tôn-kăn')	196	20.30N	108.10E
Tonle Sap, l., Camb. (tôn'lā säp')	196	13.03N	102.49E
Tonneins, Fr. (tō-năɴ')	156	44.24N	0.18E
Tönning, Ger. (tû'nēng)	154	54.20N	8.55E
Tonopah, Nv., U.S. (tō-nō-pä')	96	38.04N	117.15W
Tönsberg, Nor. (tûns'bĕrgh)	146	59.19N	10.25E
Tönsholt, Ger.	236	51.38N	6.58E
Tonto, r., Mex. (tōn'tō)	119	18.15N	96.13W
Tonto Creek, r., Az., U.S.	109	34.05N	111.15W
Tonto National Monument, rec., Az., U.S. (tôn'tō)	109	33.33N	111.08W
Tooele, Ut., U.S. (tō-ĕl ē)	107b	40.33N	112.17W
Toongabbie, Austl.	243a	33.47S	150.57E
Toot Hill, Eng., U.K.	235	51.42N	0.12E
Toowoomba, Austl. (tō woom'bȧ)	203	27.32S	152.10E
Topanga, Ca., U.S. (tō'păn-gȧ)	107a	34.05N	118.36W
Topeka, Ks., U.S. (tō-pē'kȧ)	97	39.02N	95.41W
Topilejo, Mex. (tô-pē-lĕ'hô)	119a	19.12N	99.09W
Topkapi, neigh., Tur.	239f	41.02N	28.54E
Topkapi Müzesi, bldg., Tur.	239f	41.00N	28.59E
T'oplyj Stan, neigh., Russia	239b	55.37N	37.30E
Topock, Az., U.S.	109	34.40N	114.20W
Top of Hebers, Eng., U.K.	237b	53.34N	2.12W
Topol'čany, Slvk. (tō-pōl'chä-nü)	155	48.38N	18.10E
Topolobampo, Mex. (tō-pō-lō-bä'm-pō)	116	25.45N	109.00W
Topolovgrad, Bul.	161	42.05N	26.19E
Toppenish, Wa., U.S. (tôp'ĕn-ĭsh)	104	46.22N	120.00W
Toppings, Eng., U.K.	237b	53.37N	2.25W
Torbat-e Ḥeydarīyeh, Iran	185	35.16N	59.13E
Torbat-e Jām, Iran	185	35.14N	60.36E
Torbay, Can. (tôr-bā')	93	47.40N	52.43W
Torbay *see* Torquay, Eng., U.K.	150	50.30N	3.26W
Torbreck, Mount, mtn., Austl. (tôr-brĕk)	204	37.05S	146.55E
Torch, l., Mi., U.S. (tôrch)	98	45.00N	85.30W
Torcy, Fr.	237c	48.51N	2.39E
Tor di Quinto, neigh., Italy	239c	41.56N	12.28E
Töreboda, Swe. (tû'rē-bō'dä)	152	58.44N	14.04E
Torhout, Bel.	151	51.01N	3.04E
Toribío, Col. (tō-rē-bē'ō)	130a	2.58N	76.14W
Toride, Japan (tō'rē-dā)	195a	35.54N	104.04E
Torino *see* Turin, Italy	142	45.05N	7.44E
Tormes, r., Spain (tōr'mās)	158	41.12N	6.15W
Torneälven, r., Eur.	142	67.00N	22.30E
Torneträsk, l., Swe. (tōr'nē trĕsk)	146	68.10N	20.36E
Torngat Mountains, mts., Can.	85	59.18N	64.35W
Tornio, Fin. (tôr'nĭ-ō)	142	65.55N	24.09E
Toro, Lac, l., Can.	91	46.53N	73.46W
Toronto, Can. (tō-rŏn'tō)	85	43.40N	79.23W
Toronto, Oh., U.S.	98	40.30N	80.35W
Toronto, res., Mex.	112	27.35N	105.37W
Toropets, Russia (tô'rō-pyĕts)	166	56.31N	31.37E
Toros Dağlari, Tur. (tô'rŭs)	182	37.00N	32.40E
Torote, r., Spain (tō-rō'tā)	159a	40.36N	3.24W
Tor Pignatara, neigh., Italy	239c	41.52N	12.32E
Torquay, Eng., U.K. (tôr-kē')	150	50.30N	3.26W
Torra, Cerro, mtn., Col. (sĕ'r-rō-tō'r-rä)	130a	4.41N	76.22W
Torrance, Ca., U.S. (tŏr'rănc)	107a	33.50N	118.20W
Torre Annunziata, Italy (tôr'rā ä-noon-tsē-ä'tä)	159c	40.31N	14.27E
Torreblanca, Spain	159	40.18N	0.12E
Torre del Greco, Italy (tôr'rā dĕl grā'kô)	160	40.32N	14.23E
Torrejoncillo, Spain (tôr'rā-hōn-thē'lyō)	158	39.54N	6.26W
Torrelavega, Spain (tôr-rā'lä-vā'gä)	158	43.22N	4.02W
Torrellas de Llobregat, Spain	238e	41.21N	1.59E
Torre Maggiore, Italy (tôr'rā mäd-jō'rā)	160	41.41N	15.18E
Torrens, Lake, l., Austl. (tŏr-ĕns)	202	30.07S	137.40E
Torrente, Spain (tôr-rĕn'tā)	159	39.25N	0.28W
Torreón, Mex. (tôr-rā-ōn')	116	25.32N	103.26W
Torres Islands, is., Vanuatu (tôr'rĕs) (tŏr'ĕz)	203	13.18N	165.59E
Torres Martinez Indian Reservation, I.R., Ca., U.S. (tôr'ĕz mär-tē'nĕz)	108	33.33N	116.21W
Torres Novas, Port. (tôr'rĕzh nō'väzh)	158	39.28N	8.37W
Torres Strait, strt., Austl. (tôr'rĕs)	203	10.30S	141.30E
Torres Vedras, Port. (tôr'rĕsh vä'dräzh)	158	39.08N	9.18W
Torrevieja, Spain (tôr-rā-vyā'hä)	159	37.58N	0.40W
Torrijos, Phil. (tôr-rē'hōs)	197a	13.19N	122.06E
Torrington, Ct., U.S. (tŏr'ĭng-tŭn)	99	41.50N	73.10W
Torrington, Wy., U.S.	102	42.04N	104.11W
Torro, Spain (tô'r-rō)	158	41.27N	5.23W
Tor Sapienza, neigh., Italy	239c	41.54N	12.35E
Torsby, Swe. (tôrs'bü)	152	60.07N	12.56E
Torshälla, Swe. (tôrs'hĕl-ä)	152	59.26N	16.21E
Tórshavn, Faer. Is. (tôrs-houn')	142	62.00N	6.55W
Tortola, i., V.I., Br. (tôr-tō'lä)	117b	18.34N	64.40W
Tortona, Italy (tôr-tō'nä)	160	44.52N	8.52W
Tortosa, Spain (tôr-tō'sä)	142	40.59N	0.33E
Tortosa, Cabo de, c., Spain (kà'bō-dĕ-tôr-tō-sä)	159	40.42N	0.55E
Tortue, Canal de la, strt., Haiti (tôr-tü')	123	20.05N	73.20W
Tortue, Île de la, i., Haiti	123	20.10N	73.00W
Tortue, Rivière de la, r., Can. (lä tōr-tü')	83a	45.12N	73.32W
Tortuguitas, Arg.	233d	34.28S	58.45W
Toruń, Pol.	142	53.02N	18.35E
Tõrva, Est. (t'r'vá)	153	58.02N	25.56E
Torzhok, Russia (tôr'zhôk)	166	57.03N	34.53E
Toscana, hist. reg., Italy (tôs-kä'nä)	160	43.23N	11.08E
Toshima, neigh., Japan	242a	35.44N	139.43E
Tosna, r., Russia	172c	59.28N	30.53E
Tosno, Russia (tôs'nō)	162	59.32N	30.52E
Tostado, Arg. (tôs-tà'dô)	132	29.10S	61.43W

ng-sing; ŋ-baŋk; ɴ-nasalized n; nŏd; cŏmmit; ōld; ōbey; ôrder; oi-boil; fo͞od; ŏo-as oo in foot; ou-out; s-soft; sh-dish; th-thin; pūre; ûnite; ûrn; stŭd; circŭs; ü-as in French tu; '-indeterminate vowel.

358 Tosya–Tula

PLACE (Pronunciation)	PAGE	Lat. °′	Long. °′
Tosya, Tur. (tôz′yà)	149	41.00N	34.00E
Totana, Spain (tô-tä-nä)	158	37.45N	1.28W
Tot′ma, Russia (tôt′mà)	166	60.00N	42.20E
Totness, Sur.	131	5.51N	56.17W
Totonicapán, Guat. (tô-tō-nē-kä′pän)	116	14.55N	91.20W
Totoras, Arg. (tô-tô′räs)	129c	32.33S	61.13W
Totowa, N.J., U.S.	228	40.54N	74.13W
Totsuka, Japan (tōt′sōō-kä)	195a	35.24N	139.32E
Tottenham, Eng., U.K. (tŏt′ĕn-ăm)	144b	51.35N	0.06W
Tottenville, neigh., N.Y., U.S.	228	40.31N	74.15W
Totteridge, neigh., Eng., U.K.	235	51.38N	0.12W
Tottington, Eng., U.K.	237b	53.37N	2.20W
Tottori, Japan (tô′tô-rē)	189	35.30N	134.15E
Touba, C. Iv.	214	8.17N	7.41W
Touba, Sen.	214	14.51N	15.53W
Toubkal, Jebel, mtn., Mor.	210	31.15N	7.46W
Tougan, Burkina	214	13.04N	3.04W
Touggourt, Alg. (tō-gōōrt′) (tōō-gōōr′)	210	33.09N	6.07E
Touil, Oued, r., Alg. (tōō-ēl′)	148	34.42N	2.16E
Toul, Fr. (tōōl)	147	48.39N	5.51E
Toulon, Fr. (tōō-lôn′)	142	43.09N	5.54E
Toulouse, Fr. (tōō-lōōz′)	142	43.37N	1.27E
Toungoo, Myanmar (tō-ŏŋ-gōō′)	196	19.00N	96.29E
Tourcoing, Fr. (tōr-kwăn′)	147	50.44N	3.06E
Tournan-en-Brie, Fr. (tōōr-nän-ĕn-brē′)	157b	48.45N	2.47E
Tours, Fr. (tōōr)	142	47.23N	0.39E
Touside, Pic, mtn., Chad (tōō-sē-dā′)	211	21.10N	16.30E
Toussus-le-Noble, Fr.	237c	48.45N	2.07E
Tovdalselva, r., Nor. (tôv-däls-ĕlvà)	152	58.23N	8.16E
Towaco, N.J., U.S.	228	40.56N	74.21W
Towanda, Pa., U.S. (tô-wän′dȧ)	99	41.45N	76.30W
Tower Hamlets, neigh., Eng., U.K.	235	51.32N	0.03W
Tower of London, pt. of i., Eng., U.K.	235	51.30N	0.05W
Towers of Silence, rel., India	240e	18.58N	72.48E
Town Bluff Lake, l., Tx., U.S.	113	30.52N	94.30W
Towner, N.D., U.S. (tou′nẽr)	102	48.21N	100.24W
Town Reach, strt., Asia	240c	1.28N	103.44E
Townsend, Ma., U.S. (toun′zĕnd)	93a	42.41N	71.42W
Townsend, Mt., U.S.	105	46.19N	111.35W
Townsend, Mount, mtn., Wa., U.S.	106a	47.52N	123.03W
Townsville, Austl. (tounz′vĭl)	203	19.18S	146.50E
Towson, Md., U.S. (tou′sŭn)	100e	39.24N	76.36W
Towuti, Danau, l., Indon. (tô-wōō′tē)	196	3.00S	121.45E
Toxkan, r., China	188	40.34N	77.15E
Toyah, Tx., U.S. (tô′yȧ)	112	31.19N	103.46W
Toyama, Japan (tō′yä-mä)	189	36.42N	137.14E
Toyama-Wan, b., Japan	195	36.58N	137.16E
Toyoda, Japan	242a	35.39N	139.23E
Toyohashi, Japan (tō′yô-hä′shē)	194	34.44N	137.21E
Toyonaka, Japan (tō′yô-nä′kȧ)	195b	34.47N	135.28E
Tozeur, Tun. (tô-zûr′)	148	33.59N	8.11E
Traar, neigh., Ger.	236	51.23N	6.36E
Trabzon, Tur. (tràb′zôn)	182	41.00N	39.45E
Tracy, Can.	91	46.00N	73.13W
Tracy, Ca., U.S. (trā′sē)	108	37.45N	121.27W
Tracy, Mn., U.S.	102	44.13N	95.37W
Tracy City, Tn., U.S.	114	35.15N	85.44W
Trafalgar, Cabo, c., Spain (kȧ′bô-trä-fäl-gä′r)	158	36.10N	6.02W
Trafaria, Port.	238d	38.40N	9.14W
Trafford Park, Eng., U.K.	237b	53.28N	2.20W
Trafonomby, mtn., Madag.	213	24.32S	46.35E
Trail, Can. (trāl)	84	49.06N	117.42W
Traisen, r., Aus.	145e	48.15N	15.55E
Traiskirchen, Aus.	145e	48.01N	16.18E
Trakai, Lith. (trá-káy)	153	54.38N	24.59E
Trakiszki, Pol. (trá-kē′-sh-kē)	155	54.16N	23.07E
Tralee, Ire. (trȧ-lē′)	147	52.16N	9.20W
Tranås, Swe. (trän′ôs)	152	58.03N	14.56E
Trancoso, Port. (träŋ-kō′sò)	158	40.46N	7.23W
Trangan, Pulau, i., Indon. (träŋ′gän)	197	6.52S	133.30E
Trani, Italy (trä′nē)	160	41.15N	16.25E
Tranmere, Eng., U.K.	237a	53.23N	3.01W
Transylvania, hist. reg., Rom. (trăn-sĭl-vā′nĭ-ȧ)	155	46.30N	22.35E
Trapani, Italy	148	38.01N	12.31E
Trappes, Fr. (tràp)	157b	48.47N	2.01E
Traralgon, Austl. (tră′răl-gŏn)	204	38.15S	146.33E
Trarza, reg., Maur.	214	17.35N	15.15W
Trasimeno, Lago, l., Italy (lä′gō trä-sē-mā′nō)	160	43.00N	12.12E
Trás-os-Montes, hist. reg., Port. (träzh′ōzh mōn′tāzh)	148	41.33N	7.13W
Traun, r., Aus. (troun)	154	48.10N	14.15E
Traunstein, Ger. (troun′stīn)	154	47.52N	12.38E
Traverse, Lake, l., Mn., U.S. (trăv′ẽrs)	102	45.46N	96.53W
Traverse City, Mi., U.S.	98	44.45N	85.40W
Travnik, Bos. (träv′nēk)	161	44.13N	17.43E
Treasure Island, i., Ca., U.S. (trĕzh′ẽr)	106b	37.49N	122.22W
Trebbin, Ger. (trĕ′bēn)	145b	52.13N	13.13E
Trebinje, Bos. (trå′bēn-yĕ)	161	42.43N	18.21E
Trebišov, Slvk. (trĕ′bē-shôf)	155	48.36N	21.32E
Tregrosse Islands, is., Austl. (trē-grōs′)	203	18.08S	150.53E
Treinta y Tres, Ur. (trå-ēn′tä ē träs′)	132	33.14S	54.17W
Trelew, Arg. (trē′lū)	132	43.15S	65.25W
Trelleborg, Swe.	152	55.24N	13.07E
Tremblay-lès-Gonnesse, Fr.	237c	48.59N	2.34E
Tremiti, Isole, is., Italy (ē′sō-lĕ trā-mē′tē)	160	42.07N	16.33E
Tremont, neigh., N.Y., U.S.	228	40.51N	73.55W
Trenčín, Czech Rep. (trĕn′chēn)	147	48.52N	18.02E
Trenque Lauquén, Arg. (trĕn′kĕ-lâ′ô-kĕ′n)	132	35.50S	62.44W
Trent, r., Can. (trĕnt)	91	44.15N	77.55W
Trent, r., Eng., U.K.	144a	53.25N	0.45W

PLACE (Pronunciation)	PAGE	Lat. °′	Long. °′
Trent and Mersey Canal, can., Eng., U.K. (trĕnt) (mûr zē)	144a	53.11N	2.24W
Trentino-Alto Adige, hist. reg., Italy	160	46.16N	10.47E
Trento, Italy (trĕn′tô)	148	46.04N	11.07E
Trenton, Can. (trĕn′tŭn)	85	44.05N	77.35W
Trenton, Can.	93	45.37N	62.38W
Trenton, Mi., U.S.	101b	42.08N	83.12W
Trenton, Mo., U.S.	111	40.05N	93.36W
Trenton, N.J., U.S.	97	40.13N	74.46W
Trenton, Tn., U.S.	114	35.57N	88.55W
Trepassey, Can. (trê-păs′ê)	93	46.44N	53.22W
Trepassey Bay, b., Can.	93	46.40N	53.20W
Treptow, neigh., Ger.	238a	52.29N	13.29E
Tres Arroyos, Arg. (träs′är-rō′yōs)	132	38.18S	60.16W
Três Corações, Braz. (trĕ′s kō-rä-zô′ĕs)	129a	21.41S	45.14W
Tres Cumbres, Mex. (trĕ′s kōō′m-brĕs)	119a	19.03N	99.14W
Três Lagoas, Braz. (trĕ′s lä-gô′äs)	131	20.48S	51.42W
Três Marias, Reprêsa, res., Braz.	131	18.15S	45.30W
Tres Morros, Alto de, mtn., Col. (á′l-tō dĕ trĕ′s mô′r-rôs)	130a	7.08N	76.10W
Três Pontas, Braz. (trĕ′pô′n-täs)	129a	21.22S	45.30W
Três Pontas, Cabo das, c., Ang.	216	10.23S	13.32E
Três Rios, Braz. (trĕ′s rē′ōs)	129a	22.07S	43.13W
Très-Saint Rédempteur, Can. (săn rā-dänp-tûr′)	83a	45.26N	74.23W
Tressancourt, Fr.	237c	48.55N	2.00E
Treuenbrietzen, Ger. (troi′ĕn-brē-tzĕn)	145b	52.06N	12.52E
Treviglio, Italy (trā-vē′lyô)	160	45.30N	9.34E
Treviso, Italy (trĕ-vē′sō)	148	45.39N	12.15E
Trichardt, S. Afr. (trĭ-kärt′)	218d	26.32N	29.16E
Triel-sur-Seine, Fr.	237c	48.59N	2.00E
Trier, Ger.	147	49.45N	6.38E
Trieste, Italy (trē-ĕs′tā)	142	45.39N	13.48E
Triglav, mtn., Slvn.	160	46.23N	13.50E
Trigueros, Spain (trē-gā′rōs)	158	37.23N	6.50W
Tríkala, Grc.	149	39.33N	21.49E
Trikora, Puncak, mtn., Indon.	197	4.15S	138.45E
Trim Creek, r., Il., U.S. (trĭm)	101a	41.19N	87.39W
Trincomalee, Sri L. (trĭŋ-kô-mȧ-lē′)	183b	8.39N	81.12E
Tring, Eng., U.K. (trĭng)	144b	51.46N	0.40W
Trinidad, Bol. (trē-nē-dhädh′)	130	14.48S	64.43W
Trinidad, Cuba (trē-nē-dhädh′)	117	21.50N	80.00W
Trinidad, Co., U.S. (trĭn′ĭdăd)	96	37.11N	104.31W
Trinidad, Ur.	132	33.29S	56.55W
Trinidad, i., Trin. (trĭn′ĭ-dăd)	131	10.00N	61.00W
Trinidad, r., Pan.	116a	8.55N	80.01W
Trinidad, Sierra de, mts., Cuba (sē-ĕ′r-rà dĕ trē-nē-dä′d)	122	21.50N	79.55W
Trinidad and Tobago, nation, N.A. (trĭn′ĭ-dăd) (tô-bā′gō)	117	11.00N	61.00W
Trinitaria, Mex. (trē-nē-tä′ryä)	119	16.09N	92.04W
Trinity, Can. (trĭn′ĭ-tē)	93	48.59N	53.55W
Trinity, Tx., U.S.	113	30.52N	95.27W
Trinity, is., Ak., U.S.	95	56.25N	153.15W
Trinity, r., Ca., U.S.	104	40.50N	123.20W
Trinity, r., Tx., U.S.	97	30.50N	95.09W
Trinity, East Fork, r., Tx., U.S.	111	33.24N	96.42W
Trinity, West Fork, r., Tx., U.S.	110	33.22N	98.26W
Trinity Bay, b., Can.	85	48.00N	53.40W
Trino, Italy (trē′nô)	160	45.11N	8.16E
Trion, Ga., U.S. (trī′ŏn)	114	34.32N	85.18W
Tripoli (Tarābulus), Libya	211	32.50N	13.13E
Trípolis, Grc. (trĭ′pô-lĭs)	149	37.32N	22.32E
Tripolitania *see* Tarābulus, hist. reg., Libya	210	31.00N	12.26E
Tripura, state, India	183	24.00N	92.00E
Tristan da Cunha Islands, is., St. Hel. (três-tän′dä kōō′nyà)	2	35.30S	12.15W
Triste, Golfo, b., Ven. (gôl-fô trē′s-tē)	131b	10.40N	68.05W
Triticus Reservoir, res., N.Y., U.S. (trī tĭ-cŭs)	100a	41.20N	73.36W
Trivandrum, India (trē-vŭn′drŭm)	183b	8.34N	76.58E
Trnava, Slvk. (t′r′nȧ-và)	155	48.22N	17.34E
Trobriand Islands, is., Pap. N. Gui. (trō-brē-ănd′)	197	8.25S	151.45E
Trogir, Cro. (trô′gēr)	160	43.32N	16.17E
Troice-Lykovo, neigh., Russia	239b	55.47N	37.24E
Trois Fourches, Cap des, c., Mor.	158	35.28N	2.58W
Trois-Rivières, Can. (trwä′rē-vyâ′)	85	46.21N	72.35W
Troitsk, Russia (trô′ĭtsk)	170	54.06N	61.35E
Troitsko-Pechorsk, Russia (trô′ĭtsk-ô-pyĕ-chôrsk′)	164	62.18N	56.07E
Trollhättan, Swe. (trôl′hĕt-ĕn)	146	58.17N	12.17E
Trollheimen, mts., Nor. (trôll-hĕĭm)	152	62.48N	9.05E
Trombay, neigh., India	240e	19.02N	72.57E
Trona, Ca., U.S. (trō′nȧ)	108	35.49N	117.20W
Tronador, Cerro, mtn., S.A. (sĕ′r-rô trō-nä′dôr)	132	41.17S	71.56W
Troncoso, Mex. (trôn-kô′sō)	118	22.43N	102.22W
Trondheim, Nor. (trôn′hâm)	142	63.25N	11.35E
Tropar′ovo, neigh., Russia	239b	55.39N	37.29E
Trosa, Swe. (trô′sä)	152	58.54N	17.25E
Trottiscliffe, Eng., U.K.	235	51.19N	0.21E
Trout, l., Can.	84	61.10N	121.30W
Trout, l., Can.	85	51.16N	92.46W
Trout Creek, r., Or., U.S.	104	42.18N	118.31W
Troutdale, Or., U.S. (trout′dāl)	106c	45.32N	122.23W
Trout Lake, Mi., U.S.	103	46.20N	85.02W
Trouville, Fr. (trōō-vēl′)	156	49.23N	0.05E
Troy, Al., U.S. (troi)	114	31.47N	85.46W
Troy, Il., U.S.	107e	38.44N	89.53W
Troy, Ks., U.S.	111	39.46N	95.07W
Troy, Mo., U.S.	110	38.56N	99.57W
Troy, Mt., U.S.	104	48.28N	115.56W
Troy, N.Y., U.S.	97	42.45N	73.45W

PLACE (Pronunciation)	PAGE	Lat. °′	Long. °′
Troy, N.C., U.S.	115	35.21N	79.58W
Troy, Oh., U.S.	98	40.00N	84.10W
Troy, hist., Tur.	182	39.59N	26.14E
Troyes, Fr. (trwä)	147	48.18N	4.03E
Troyits′ke, Ukr.	163	47.39N	30.16E
Trstenik, Yugo. (t′r′stĕ-nēk)	149	43.36N	21.00E
Trubchëvsk, Russia (trōp′chĕfsk)	167	52.36N	33.46E
Trucial States *see* United Arab Emirates, nation, Asia	182	24.00N	54.00E
Truckee, Ca., U.S. (trŭk′ē)	108	39.20N	120.12W
Truckee, r., Ca., U.S.	108	39.25N	120.07W
Truganina, Austl.	201a	37.49N	144.44E
Trujillo, Col. (trō-кē′l-yō)	130a	4.10N	76.20W
Trujillo, Peru	130	8.08S	79.00W
Trujillo, Spain (trōō-кē′l-yô)	148	39.27N	5.50W
Trujillo, Ven.	130	9.15N	70.28W
Trujillo, r., Mex.	118	23.12N	103.10W
Trujin, Lago, l., Dom. Rep. (trōō-кēn′)	123	17.45N	71.25W
Truk Islands, is., Micron.	198c	7.25N	151.47E
Trumann, Ar., U.S. (trōō′măn)	111	35.41N	90.31W
Trŭn, Bul. (trŭn)	161	42.49N	22.39E
Truro, Can. (trōō′rō)	85	45.22N	63.16W
Truro, Eng., U.K.	150	50.17N	5.05W
Trussville, Al., U.S. (trŭs′vĭl)	100h	33.37N	86.37W
Truth or Consequences, N.M., U.S. (trōōth ŏr kŏn′sē-kwĕn-sĭs)	109	33.10N	107.20W
Trutnov, Czech Rep. (trŏt′nôf)	154	50.36N	15.36E
Trzcianka, Pol. (tchyän′kȧ)	154	53.02N	16.27E
Trzebiatów, Pol. (tchĕ-byä′tō-v)	154	54.03N	15.16E
Tsaidam Basin, basin, China (tsī-dām)	188	37.19N	94.08E
Tsala Apopka Lake, r., Fl., U.S. (tsä′lȧ ă-pŏp′kȧ)	115	28.57N	82.11W
Tsast Bogd, mtn., Mong.	188	46.44N	92.34E
Tsavo National Park, rec., Kenya	217	2.35S	38.45E
Tsawwassen Indian Reserve, I.R., Can.	106d	49.03N	123.11W
Tsentral′nyy-Kospashskiy, Russia (tsĕn-träl′nyĭ-kôs-pash′skĭ)	172a	59.03N	57.48E
Tshela, Zaire (tshā′là)	212	4.59S	12.56E
Tshikapa, Zaire (tshē-kä′pä)	212	6.25S	20.48E
Tshofa, Zaire	217	5.14S	25.15E
Tshuapa, r., Zaire	212	0.30S	22.00E
Tsiafajovona, mtn., Madag.	213	19.17S	47.27E
Tsing Island, i., H.K.	241c	22.21N	114.05E
Tsin Shui Wan, b., H.K.	241c	22.13N	114.10E
Tsiribihina, r., Madag. (tsē′rē-bē-hē-nä′)	213	19.45S	43.30E
Tsitsa, r., S. Afr. (tsē′tsȧ)	213c	31.28S	28.53E
Tskhinvali, Geor.	168	42.13N	43.56E
Tsolo, S. Afr. (tsō′lō)	213c	31.19S	28.47E
Tsomo, S. Afr.	213c	32.03S	27.49E
Tsomo, r., S. Afr.	213c	31.53S	27.48E
Tsu, Japan (tsōō)	194	34.42N	136.31E
Tsuchiura, Japan (tsōō′chē-ōō-rä)	195	36.04N	140.09E
Tsuda, Japan (tsōō′dä)	195b	34.48N	135.43E
Tsugaru Kaikyō, strt., Japan	189	41.25N	140.20E
Tsukumono, neigh., Japan	242b	34.50N	135.11E
Tsumeb, Nmb. (tsōō′mĕb)	212	19.10S	17.45E
Tsunashima, Japan (tsōō′nä-shē′mä)	195a	35.32N	139.37E
Tsuruga, Japan (tsōō′rô-gä)	194	35.39N	136.04E
Tsurugi San, mtn., Japan (tsōō′rô-gē sän)	194	33.52N	134.07E
Tsurumi, r., Japan	242a	35.29N	139.41E
Tsuruoka, Japan (tsōō′rô-ō′kä)	194	38.43N	139.51E
Tsurusaki, Japan (tsōō′rô-sä′kē)	195	33.15N	131.42E
Tsu Shima, is., Japan (tsōō shē′mä)	189	34.28N	129.30E
Tsushima Strait, strt., Asia	189	34.00N	129.00E
Tsu Wan (Quanwan), H.K.	241c	22.22N	114.07E
Tsuwano, Japan (tsōō′wá-nō′)	195	34.28N	131.47E
Tsuyama, Japan (tsōō′yä-mä′)	194	35.05N	134.00E
Tua, r., Port. (tōō′ä)	158	41.23N	7.18W
Tualatin, r., Or., U.S. (tōō′á-lä-tĭn)	106c	45.25N	122.54W
Tuamoto, Îles, Fr. Poly. (tōō-ä-mō′tōō)	225	19.00S	141.20W
Tuapse, Russia (tô′áp-sĕ)	167	44.00N	39.10E
Tuareg, hist. reg., Alg.	210	21.26N	2.51E
Tubarão, Braz. (tōō-bä-roun′)	132	28.23N	48.56W
Tübingen, Ger. (tü′bĭng-ĕn)	154	48.33N	9.05E
Tubinskiy, Russia (tû bĭn′skĭ)	172a	52.53N	58.15E
Tubruq, Libya	211	32.03N	24.04E
Tucacas, Ven. (tōō-kä′käs)	130	10.48N	68.20W
Tuckahoe, N.Y., U.S.	228	40.57N	73.50W
Tucker, Ga., U.S. (tŭk′ẽr)	100c	33.51N	84.13W
Tucson, Az., U.S. (tōō-sŏn′)	96	32.15N	111.00W
Tucumán, Arg. (tōō-kōō-män′)	132	26.52S	65.08W
Tucumán, prov., Arg.	132	26.30S	65.30W
Tucumcari, N.M., U.S. (tōō′kŭm-kâr-ē)	110	35.11N	103.43W
Tucupita, Ven. (tōō-kōō-pē′tä)	130	9.00N	62.09W
Tudela, Spain (tōō-dhā′lä)	148	42.03N	1.37W
Tugaloo, r., Ga., U.S. (tŭg′ȧ-lōō)	114	34.35N	83.05W
Tugela, r., S. Afr. (tōō-gel′ȧ)	213c	28.50S	30.52E
Tugela Ferry, S. Afr.	213c	28.44S	30.27E
Tug Fork, r., U.S. (tŭg)	98	37.50N	82.30W
Tuguegarao, Phil. (tōō-gā-gá-rä′ō)	196	17.37N	121.44E
Tuhai, r., China (tōō-hī)	190	37.05N	116.56E
Tuinplaas, S. Afr.	218d	24.54S	28.46E
Tujunga, Ca., U.S. (tōō-jŭŋ′gá)	107a	34.15N	118.16W
Tukan, Russia (tōō′kȧn)	172a	53.52N	57.25E
Tukangbesi, Kepulauan, is., Indon.	197	6.00S	124.15E
Tūkrah, Libya	211	32.34N	20.47E
Tuktoyaktuk, Can.	84	69.32N	132.37W
Tukums, Lat. (tò′kòms)	166	56.57N	23.09E
Tukuyu, Tan. (tōō-kōō′yá)	212	9.13S	33.43E
Tukwila, Wa., U.S. (tŭk′wĭ-lȧ)	106a	47.28N	122.16W
Tula, Mex. (tōō′lä)	118	20.04N	99.22W
Tula, Russia (tōō′là)	166	54.12N	37.37E
Tula, prov., Russia	162	53.45N	37.19E
Tula, r., Mex. (tōō′lä)	118	20.40N	99.27W

PRONOUNCING INDEX

Tulagai–Uman' 359

PLACE (Pronunciation)	PAGE	Lat. °′	Long. °′
Tulagai, i., Sol.Is. (to͞o-lä'gē)	203	9.15S	160.17E
Tulaghi, Sol.Is.	198e	9.06S	160.09E
Tulalip, Wa., U.S. (tū-lā'lĭp)	106a	48.04N	122.18W
Tulalip Indian Reservation, I.R., Wa., U.S.	106a	48.06N	122.16W
Tulancingo, Mex. (to͞o-län-sĭŋ'gō)	116	20.04N	98.24W
Tulangbawang, r., Indon.	196	4.17S	105.00E
Tulare, Ca., U.S. (to͞o-lä'rå) (tul-âr')	108	36.12N	119.22W
Tulare Lake Bed, l., Ca., U.S.	108	35.57N	120.18W
Tularosa, N.M., U.S. (to͞o-lȧ-rō'zȧ)	109	33.05N	106.05W
Tulcán, Ec. (to͞ol-kän')	130	0.44N	77.52W
Tulcea, Rom. (tòl'chå)	149	45.10N	28.47E
Tul'chyn, Ukr.	167	48.42N	28.53E
Tulcingo, Mex. (to͞ol-sĭŋ'gō)	118	18.03N	98.27W
Tule, r., Ca., U.S. (to͞ol'lå)	108	36.08N	118.50W
Tule River Indian Reservation, I.R., Ca., U.S. (to͞o'lå)	108	36.05N	118.35W
Tuli, Zimb. (to͞o'lē)	212	20.58S	29.12E
Tulia, Tx., U.S. (to͞o'lĭ-ȧ)	110	34.32N	101.46W
Tulik Volcano, vol., Ak., U.S. (tò'lĭk)	95a	53.28N	168.10W
Tūlkarm, W. Bank (to͞ol kärm)	181a	32.19N	35.02E
Tullahoma, Tn., U.S. (tŭl-ȧ-hō'mȧ)	114	35.21N	86.12W
Tullamarine, Austl.	243b	37.41S	144.52E
Tullamore, Ire. (tŭl-ȧ-mōr')	150	53.15N	7.29W
Tulle, Fr. (tül)	156	45.15N	1.45E
Tulln, Aus. (tòln)	154	48.21N	16.04E
Tullner Feld, reg., Aus.	145e	48.20N	15.59E
Tulpetlac, Mex. (to͞ol-på-tlåk')	119a	19.33N	99.04W
Tulsa, Ok., U.S. (tŭl'sȧ)	97	36.08N	95.58W
Tulum, Mex. (to͞o-lò'm)	120a	20.17N	87.26W
Tulun, Russia (tò-lo͞on')	165	54.29N	100.43E
Tuma, r., Nic. (to͞o'mä)	120	13.07N	85.32W
Tumba, Lac, l., Zaire (tòm'bä)	212	0.50S	17.45E
Tumbes, Peru (to͞o'm-bĕs)	130	3.39S	80.27W
Tumbiscatío, Mex. (to͞om-bē-skä-tē'ō)	118	18.32N	102.23W
Tumbo, i., Can.	106d	48.49N	123.04W
Tumen, China (to͞o-mŭn)	192	43.00N	129.50E
Tumen, r., Asia	194	42.08N	128.40E
Tumeremo, Ven. (to͞o-må-rā'mō)	131	7.15N	61.28W
Tumkūr, India	187	13.22N	77.05E
Tumuacacori National Monument, rec., Az., U.S. (to͞o-mä-kä'kå-rē)	109	31.36N	110.20W
Tumuc-Humac Mountains, mts., S.A. (to͞o-mòk'o͞o-mäk')	131	2.15N	54.50W
Tunas de Zaza, Cuba (to͞o'näs dā zä'zä)	122	21.40N	79.35W
Tunbridge Wells, Eng., U.K. (tŭn'brĭj welz')	151	51.05N	0.09E
Tunduru, Tan.	217	11.07S	37.21E
Tungabhadra Reservoir, res., India	187	15.26N	75.57E
Tuni, India	187	17.29N	82.38E
Tunica, Ms., U.S. (tū'nĭ-kȧ)	114	34.41N	90.23W
Tunis, Tun. (tū'nĭs)	210	36.59N	10.06E
Tunis, Golfe de, b., Tun.	148	37.06N	10.43E
Tunisia, nation, Afr. (tu-nĭzh'ē-ȧ)	210	35.00N	10.11E
Tunja, Col. (to͞o'n-hä)	130	5.32N	73.19W
Tunkhannock, Pa., U.S. (tŭnk-hăn'ŭk)	99	41.35N	75.55W
Tunnel, r., Wa., U.S. (tŭn'ĕl)	106a	47.48N	123.04W
Tuoji Dao, i., China (twô-jyē dou)	190	38.11N	120.45E
Tuolumne, r., Ca., U.S. (twô-lŭm'nē)	108	37.35N	120.37W
Tuostakh, r., Russia	171	67.09N	137.30E
Tupelo, Ms., U.S. (tū'pĕ-lō)	114	34.14N	88.43W
Tupinambaranas, Ilha, i., Braz.	131	3.04S	58.09W
Tupiza, Bol. (to͞o-pē'zä)	130	21.26S	65.43W
Tupper Lake, N.Y., U.S. (tŭp'ēr)	99	44.15N	74.25W
Tupqaraghan tübek, pen., Kaz.	170	44.30N	50.40E
Tupungato, Cerro, vol., S.A.	132	33.30S	69.52W
Tuquerres, Col. (to͞o-kĕ'r-rĕs)	130	1.12N	77.44W
Tura, Russia (tòr'ȧ)	165	64.08N	99.58E
Turbio, r., Mex. (to͞or-byô)	118	20.28N	101.40W
Turbo, Col. (to͞o'bō)	130	8.02N	76.43W
Turda, Rom. (tòr'dä)	155	46.35N	23.47E
Turfan Depression, depr., China	188	42.16N	90.00E
Turffontein, neigh., S. Afr.	213b	26.15S	28.02E
Tŭrgovishte, Bul.	161	43.14N	26.36E
Turgutlu, Tur.	167	38.30N	27.20E
Türi, Est. (tü'rĭ)	153	58.49N	25.29E
Turia, r., Spain (to͞o'ryä)	158	40.12N	1.18W
Turicato, Mex. (to͞o-rē-kä'tō)	118	19.03N	101.24W
Turiguano, i., Cuba (to͞o-rē-gwä'nō)	122	22.20N	78.35W
Turin, Italy	142	45.05N	7.44E
Turiya, r., Ukr.	155	51.18N	24.55E
Turka, Ukr. (tòr'kȧ)	155	49.10N	23.02E
Turkey, nation, Asia	143	38.45N	32.00E
Turkey, r., Ia., U.S. (tûrk'ē)	103	43.20N	92.16W
Türkistan, Kaz.	169	44.00N	68.00E
Turkmenistan, nation, Asia	164	40.46N	56.01E
Turks, is., T./C. Is. (tûrks)	117	21.40N	71.45W
Turks Island Passage, strt., T./C. Is.	123	21.15N	71.25W
Turku, Fin. (tòrgokō)	142	60.28N	22.12E
Turlock, Ca., U.S. (tûr'lŏk)	108	37.30N	120.51W
Turneffe, i., Belize	116	17.25N	87.43W
Turner, Ks., U.S. (tûr'nēr)	107f	39.05N	94.42W
Turner Sound, strt., Bah.	122	24.20N	78.05W
Turners Peninsula, pen., S.L.	214	7.20N	12.40W
Turnhout, Bel. (tŭrn-hout')	151	51.19N	4.58E
Turnov, Czech Rep. (tòr'nôf)	154	50.36N	15.12E
Turnu Măgurele, Rom.	149	43.54N	24.49E
Turpan, China (to͞o-är-pän)	188	43.06N	88.41E
Turquino, Pico, mtn., Cuba (pē'kō dä to͞or-kē'nō)	122	20.00N	76.50W
Turramurra, Austl.	243a	33.44S	151.08E
Turrialba, C.R. (to͞or-ryä'l-bä)	121	9.54N	83.41W
Turtkul', Uzb. (tòrt-kòl')	169	41.28N	61.02E
Turtle, r., Can.	89	49.20N	92.30W
Turtle Bay, b., Tx., U.S.	113a	29.48N	94.38W
Turtle Creek, Pa., U.S.	230b	40.25N	79.49W
Turtle Creek, r., S.D., U.S.	102	44.40N	98.53W
Turtle Mountain Indian Reservation, I.R., N.D., U.S.	102	48.45N	99.57W
Turtle Mountains, mts., N.D., U.S.	102	48.57N	100.11W
Turukhansk, Russia (to͞o-ro͞o-känsk')	164	66.03N	88.39E
Tuscaloosa, Al., U.S. (tŭs-kȧ-lo͞o'sȧ)	97	33.10N	87.35W
Tuscarora, Nv., U.S. (tŭs-kȧ-rō'rȧ)	104	41.18N	116.15W
Tuscarora Indian Reservation, I.R., N.Y., U.S.	101c	43.10N	78.51W
Tuscola, Il., U.S. (tŭs-kō-lȧ)	98	39.50N	88.20W
Tuscumbia, Al., U.S. (tŭs-kŭm'bĭ-ȧ)	114	34.41N	87.42W
Tushino, Russia (to͞o'shĭ-nô)	172b	55.51N	37.24E
Tuskegee, Al., U.S. (tŭs-kē'gē)	114	32.25N	85.40W
Tustin, Ca., U.S. (tŭs'tĭn)	107a	33.44N	117.49W
Tutayev, Russia (to͞o-tȧ-yĕf')	166	57.53N	39.34E
Tutbury, Eng., U.K. (tŭt'bēr-ē)	144a	52.52N	1.51W
Tuticorin, India (to͞o-tē-kō-rĭn')	183b	8.51N	78.09E
Tutitlan, Mex. (to͞o-tē-tlä'n)	119a	19.38N	99.10W
Tutóia, Braz. (to͞o-tō'yȧ)	131	2.42S	42.21W
Tutrakan, Bul.	149	44.02N	26.36E
Tuttle Creek Reservoir, res., Ks., U.S.	111	39.30N	96.38W
Tuttlingen, Ger. (tòt'lĭng-ĕn)	154	47.58N	8.50E
Tutuila, i., Am. Sam.	198a	14.18S	170.42W
Tutwiler, Ms., U.S. (tŭt'wĭ-lēr)	114	34.01N	90.25W
Tuva, state, Russia	170	51.15N	90.45E
Tuvalu, nation, Oc.	3	5.20S	174.00E
Tuwayq, Jabal, mts., Sau. Ar.	182	20.45N	46.30E
Tuxedo, Md., U.S.	229d	38.55N	76.55W
Tuxedo Park, N.Y., U.S. (tŭk-sē'dō pärk)	100a	41.11N	74.11W
Tuxford, Eng., U.K. (tŭks'fērd)	144a	53.14N	0.54W
Túxpan, Mex.	116	20.57N	97.26W
Tuxpan, Mex. (to͞os'pän)	118	19.34N	103.22W
Túxpan, r., Mex. (to͞os'pän)	119	20.55N	97.52W
Túxpan, Arrecife, i., Mex. (är-rē-sē'fē-to͞o'x-pä'n)	119	21.01N	97.12W
Tuxtepec, Mex. (tòs-tå-pĕk')	119	18.06N	96.09W
Tuxtla Gutiérrez, Mex. (tòs'tlä go͞o-tyår'rĕs)	116	16.44N	93.08W
Tuy, r., Ven. (to͞o'ē)	131b	10.15N	66.03W
Tuyra, r., Pan. (to͞o-ē'rȧ)	121	7.55N	77.37W
Tuz Gölü, l., Tur.	166	38.45N	33.25E
Tuzigoot National Monument, rec., Az., U.S.	109	34.40N	111.52W
Tuzla, Bos. (tòz'lȧ)	149	44.33N	18.46E
Tvedestrand, Nor. (tvĭ'dhĕ-stränd)	152	58.39N	8.54E
Tveitsund, Nor. (tvåt'sònd)	152	59.03N	8.29E
Tver', Russia	164	56.52N	35.57E
Tver', prov., Russia	162	56.50N	33.08E
Tvertsa, r., Russia (tvĕr'tsȧ)	162	56.58N	35.22E
Tweed, r., U.K. (twēd)	150	55.32N	2.35W
Tweeling, S. Afr. (twē'lĭng)	218d	27.34S	28.31E
Twenty Mile Creek, r., Can. (twĕn'tĭ mīl)	83d	43.09N	79.49W
Twickenham, Eng., U.K. (twĭk''n-ăm)	144b	51.26N	0.20W
Twillingate, Can. (twĭl'ĭn-gāt)	85a	49.39N	54.46W
Twin Bridges, Mt., U.S. (twĭn brĭ-jĕz)	105	45.34N	112.17W
Twin Falls, Id., U.S. (fôls)	96	42.33N	114.29W
Twinsburg, Oh., U.S. (twĭnz'bûrg)	101d	41.19N	81.26W
Twitchell Reservoir, res., Ca., U.S.	108	34.50N	120.10W
Two Butte Creek, r., Co., U.S. (to͞o būt)	110	37.39N	102.45W
Two Harbors, Mn., U.S.	103	47.00N	91.42W
Two Prairie Bay, Ar., U.S. (prâ'rĭ bī o͞o')	111	34.48N	92.07W
Two Rivers, Wi., U.S. (rĭv'ērz)	103	44.09N	87.36W
Tyabb, Austl.	201a	38.16S	145.11E
Tyachiv, Ukr.	155	48.01N	23.42E
Tyasmin, r., Ukr. (tyȧs-mĭn')	163	49.14N	32.23E
Tylden, S. Afr. (tĭl-dĕn)	213c	32.08S	27.06E
Tyldesley, Eng., U.K. (tĭldz'lē)	144a	53.32N	2.28W
Tyler, Mn., U.S. (tī'lēr)	102	44.18N	96.08W
Tyler, Tx., U.S.	97	32.21N	95.19W
Tyler Park, Va., U.S.	229d	38.52N	77.12W
Tylertown, Ms., U.S. (tī'lēr-toun)	114	31.08N	90.06W
Tylihul, r., Ukr.	163	47.25N	30.27E
Tyndall, S.D., U.S. (tĭn'dȧl)	102	42.58N	97.52W
Tyndinskiy, Russia	165	55.22N	124.45E
Tyne, r., Eng., U.K. (tīn)	150	54.59N	1.56W
Tynemouth, Eng., U.K. (tīn'mŭth)	146	55.04N	1.39W
Tyngsboro, Ma., U.S. (tĭnj-bûr'ō)	93a	42.40N	71.27W
Tynset, Nor. (tün'sĕt)	146	62.17N	10.45E
Tyre *see* Şūr, Leb.	181a	33.16N	35.13E
Tyrifjorden, l., Nor.	152	60.03N	10.25E
Tyrone, Pa., U.S.	99	40.40N	78.15W
Tyrrell, Lake, l., Austl. (tĭr'ĕll)	204	35.12S	143.00E
Tyrrhenian Sea, sea, Italy (tĭr-rē'nĭ-ȧn)	142	40.10N	12.15E
Tysons Corner, Va., U.S.	229d	38.55N	77.14W
Tyukalinsk, Russia (tyò-kȧ-lĭnsk')	164	56.03N	71.43E
Tyukyan, r., Russia (tyò'kyȧn)	171	65.42N	116.09E
Tyuleniy, i., Russia	167	44.30N	48.00E
Tyumen', Russia (tyo͞o-mĕn')	164	57.02N	65.28E
Tzucacab, Mex. (tzo͞o-kä-kä'b)	120a	20.06N	89.03W

U

PLACE (Pronunciation)	PAGE	Lat. °′	Long. °′
Uaupés, Braz. (wä-o͞o'pās)	130	0.02S	67.03W
Ubangi, r., Afr. (o͞o-bäŋ'gē)	211	3.00N	18.00E
Ubatuba, Braz. (o͞o-bȧ-to͞o'bȧ)	129a	23.25S	45.06W
Ubeda, Spain (o͞o'bå-dä)	158	38.01N	3.23W
Uberaba, Braz. (o͞o-bå-rä'bȧ)	131	19.47S	47.47W
Uberlândia, Braz. (o͞o-bĕr-lá'n-dyä)	131	18.54S	48.11W
Ubombo, S. Afr. (o͞o-bôm'bō)	212	27.33S	32.13E
Ubon Ratchathani, Thai. (o͞o'bŭn rä'chätá-nē)	196	15.15N	104.52E
Ubort', r., Eur. (o͞o-bôrt')	163	51.18N	27.43E
Ubrique, Spain (o͞o-brē'kå)	158	36.43N	5.36W
Ubundu, Zaire	212	0.21S	25.29E
Ucayali, r., Peru (o͞o'kä-yä'lē)	130	8.58S	74.13W
Uccle, Bel. (ü'kl')	145a	50.48N	4.17E
Uchaly, Russia (û-chä'lĭ)	172a	54.22N	59.28E
Uchiko, Japan (o͞o'chē-kō)	195	33.30N	132.39E
Uchinoura, Japan (o͞o'chē-nō-o͞o'rȧ)	195	31.16N	131.03E
Uchinskoye Vodokhranilishche, res., Russia	172b	56.08N	37.44E
Uchiura-Wan, b., Japan (o͞o'chē-o͞o'rä wän)	194	42.20N	140.44E
Uchur, r., Russia (ò-chòr')	171	57.25N	130.35E
Ückendorf, neigh., Ger.	236	51.30N	7.07E
Uda, r., Russia (ò'dȧ)	171	52.28N	110.51E
Uda, r., Russia	171	53.54N	131.29E
Udaipur, India (ò-dŭ'ē-po͞or)	186	24.41N	73.41E
Uday, r., Ukr. (ò-dī')	163	50.45N	32.13E
Uddevalla, Swe. (o͞od'dĕ-väl-ȧ)	146	58.21N	11.55E
Udine, Italy (o͞o'dē-nå)	148	46.05N	13.14E
Udmurtia, state, Russia	166	57.00N	53.00E
Udon Thani, Thai.	196	17.31N	102.51E
Udskaya Guba, b., Russia	165	55.00N	136.30E
Ueckermünde, Ger.	154	53.43N	14.01E
Ueda, Japan (wä'dä)	194	36.26N	138.16E
Uedesheim, neigh., Ger.	236	51.10N	6.48E
Uele, r., Zaire (wā'lå)	211	3.55N	23.30E
Uelzen, Ger. (ült'sĕn)	154	52.58N	10.34E
Uerdingen, neigh., Ger.	236	51.21N	6.39E
Ufa, Russia (ò'fa)	164	54.45N	55.57E
Ufa, r., Russia	166	56.00N	57.05E
Ugab, r., Nmb. (o͞o'gäb)	212	21.10S	14.00E
Ugalla, r., Tan. (o͞o-gä'lä)	212	6.15S	32.30E
Uganda, nation, Afr. (o͞o-gän'dä) (û-găn'dȧ)	211	2.00N	32.28E
Ugashik Lake, l., Ak., U.S. (o͞o'gá-shĕk)	95	57.36N	157.10W
Ugie, S. Afr. (ò'jē)	213c	31.13S	28.14E
Uglegorsk, Russia (o͞o-glĕ-gôrsk)	165	49.00N	142.31E
Ugleural'sk, Russia (òg-lĕ-ò-rálsk')	172a	58.58N	57.35E
Uglich, Russia (o͞og-lĕch')	162	57.33N	38.19E
Uglitskiy, Russia (òg-lĭt'skĭ)	172a	53.50N	60.18E
Uglovka, Russia (o͞og-lôf'kȧ)	162	58.14N	33.24E
Ugra, r., Russia (o͞og'rȧ)	166	54.43N	34.20E
Ugŭrchin, Bul.	161	43.06N	24.23E
Uhrichsville, Oh., U.S. (ū'rĭks-vĭl)	98	40.25N	81.20W
Uíge, Ang.	212	7.37S	15.03E
Uiju, N. Kor. (ò'ējo͞o)	189	40.09N	124.33E
Uinkaret Plateau, plat., Az., U.S. (ū-ĭn'kâr-ĕt)	109	36.43N	113.15W
Uinskoye, Russia (ò-ĭn'skô-yĕ)	172a	56.53N	56.25E
Uinta, r., Ut., U.S. (ū-ĭn'tȧ)	109	40.25N	109.55W
Uintah and Ouray Indian Reservation, I.R., Ut., U.S.	109	40.20N	110.20W
Uinta Mountains, mts., Ut., U.S.	96	40.35N	111.00W
Uitenhage, S. Afr.	212	33.46S	25.26E
Uithoorn, Neth.	145a	52.13N	4.49E
Uji, Japan (o͞o'jē)	195b	34.53N	135.49E
Ujiji, Tan. (o͞o-jē'jē)	212	4.55S	29.41E
Ujjain, India (o͞o-jŭēn)	183	23.18N	75.37E
Ujungpandang, Indon.	196	5.08S	119.28E
Ukerewe Island, i., Tan.	217	2.00S	32.40E
Ukhta, Russia (o͞ok'tȧ)	166	65.22N	31.30E
Ukhta, Russia	166	63.08N	53.42E
Ukiah, Ca., U.S. (ū-kī'ȧ)	108	39.09N	122.12W
Ukita, neigh., Japan	242a	35.40N	139.52E
Ukmerge, Lith. (òk'mĕr-ghå)	166	55.16N	24.45E
Ukraine, nation, Eur.	164	49.15N	30.15E
Uku, i., Japan (o͞ok'o͞o)	195	33.18N	129.02E
Ulaangom, Mong.	188	50.23N	92.14E
Ulan Bator (Ulaanbaatar), Mong.	188	47.56N	107.00E
Ulan-Ude, Russia (o͞o'län o͞o'dä)	165	51.59N	107.41E
Ulchin, S. Kor. (o͞ol'chĕn')	194	36.57N	129.26E
Ulcinj, Yugo. (o͞ol'tsĕn')	149	41.56N	19.15E
Ulhās, r., India	187b	19.13N	73.03E
Ulhāsnagar, India	186	19.10N	73.07E
Uliastay, Mong.	188	47.49N	97.00E
Ulindi, r., Zaire (o͞o-lĭn'dē)	212	1.55S	26.17E
Ülkenözen, r.	167	49.50N	49.35E
Ulla, Bela. (òl'á)	162	55.14N	29.15E
Ulla, r., Bela.	162	54.58N	29.03E
Ulla, r., Spain (o͞ol'lä)	158	42.45N	8.33W
Ullŭng, i., S. Kor. (o͞ol'lòng')	194	37.29N	130.50E
Ulm, Ger. (òlm)	147	48.24N	9.59E
Ulmer, Mount, mtn., Ant. (ŭl'mûr')	219	77.30S	86.00W
Ulricehamn, Swe. (òl-rē'sĕ-häm)	152	57.49N	13.23E
Ulsan, S. Kor. (o͞ol'sän')	194	35.35N	129.22E
Ulster, hist. reg., Eur. (ŭl'stēr)	150	54.41N	7.10W
Ulua, r., Hond. (o͞o-lo͞o'á)	120	15.49N	87.45W
Ulubāria, India	186a	22.27N	88.09E
Ulukişla, Tur. (o͞o-lo͞o-kēsh'lȧ)	149	36.40N	34.30E
Ulunga, Russia (ò-lo͞on'gȧ)	194	46.16N	136.29E
Ulungur, r., China (o͞o-lo͞on-gûr)	188	46.31N	88.00E
Ulu-Telyak, Russia (o͞o lò'tĕlyák)	172a	54.54N	57.01E
Ulverstone, Austl. (ŭl'vēr-stŭn)	203	41.20S	146.22E
Ul'yanovka, Russia	172c	59.38N	30.47E
Ul'yanovsk, Russia (o͞o-lyä'nôfsk)	164	54.20N	48.24E
Ulysses, Ks., U.S. (ū-lĭs'ēz)	110	37.34N	101.25W
Umán, Mex. (o͞o-män')	120a	20.52N	89.44W
Uman', Ukr. (ò-mán')	167	48.44N	30.13E

360 Umatilla Indian Reservation–Valldoreix

PLACE (Pronunciation)	PAGE	Lat. °′	Long. °′
Umatilla Indian Reservation, I.R., Or., U.S. (ū-mȧ-tĭl′ȧ)	104	45.38N	118.35W
Umberpāda, India	187b	19.28N	73.04E
Umbria, hist. reg., Italy (ŭm′brĭ-ȧ)	160	42.53N	12.22E
Umeälven, r., Swe.	142	64.57N	18.51E
Umhlatuzi, r., S. Afr. (ŏŏm′hlȧ-tōō′zĭ)	213c	28.47S	31.17E
Umiat, Ak., U.S. (ōō′mĭ-ăt)	96a	69.20N	152.28W
Umkomaas, S. Afr. (ŏŏm-kō′mäs)	213c	30.12S	30.48E
Umnak, i., Ak., U.S. (ōōm′năk)	96b	53.10N	169.08W
Umnak Pass, Ak., U.S.	95a	53.10N	168.04W
Umniati, r., Zimb.	212	17.08S	29.11E
Umpqua, r., Or., U.S. (ŭmp′kwȧ)	104	43.42N	123.50W
Umtata, S. Afr. (ŏŏm-tä′tä)	212	31.36S	28.47E
Umtentweni, S. Afr.	213c	30.41S	30.29E
Umzimkulu, S. Afr. (ŏŏm-zēm-kōō′lōō)	213c	30.12S	29.53E
Umzinto, S. Afr. (ŏŏm-zĭn′tō)	213c	30.19S	30.41E
Una, r., Yugo. (ōō′nȧ)	160	44.38N	16.10E
Unalakleet, Ak., U.S. (ū-nȧ-lăk′lēt)	95	63.50N	160.42W
Unalaska, Ak., U.S. (ū-nȧ-lăs′kȧ)	95a	53.30N	166.20W
Unare, r., Ven.	131b	9.45N	65.12W
Unare, Laguna de, l., Ven. (lä-gō′nä-de-ōō-nȧ′rē)	131b	10.07N	65.23W
Unayzah, Sau. Ar.	182	25.50N	44.02E
Uncas, Can. (ŭŋ′kȧs)	83g	53.30N	113.02W
Uncia, Bol. (ōōn′sē-ä)	130	18.28S	66.32W
Uncompahgre, r., Co., U.S.	109	38.20N	107.45W
Uncompahgre Peak, mtn., Co., U.S. (ŭn-kŭm-pä′grē)	109	38.00N	107.30W
Uncompahgre Plateau, plat., Co., U.S.	109	38.40N	108.40W
Underberg, S. Afr. (ŭn′dẽr-bûrg)	213c	29.51S	29.32E
Unecha, Russia (ö-nĕ′chȧ)	162	52.51N	32.44E
Ungava, Péninsule d', pen., Can.	85	59.55N	74.00W
Ungava Bay, b., Can. (ŭŋ-gā′vȧ)	85	59.46N	67.18W
União da Vitória, Braz. (ōō-nē-ouN′ dä vē-tô′ryä)	132	26.17S	51.13W
Unidad Sante Fe, Mex.	233a	19.23N	99.15W
Unije, i., Yugo. (ōō′nē-yĕ)	160	44.39N	14.10E
Unimak, i., Ak., U.S. (ōō-nē-măk′)	95	54.30N	163.35W
Unimak Pass, Ak., U.S.	95a	54.22N	165.22W
Union, Ms., U.S. (ūn′yŭn)	114	32.35N	89.07W
Union, Mo., U.S.	111	38.28N	90.59W
Union, N.J., U.S.	228	40.42N	74.16W
Union, N.C., U.S.	115	34.42N	81.40W
Union, Or., U.S.	104	45.13N	117.52W
Union City, Ca., U.S.	106b	37.36N	122.01W
Union City, In., U.S.	98	40.10N	85.00W
Union City, Mi., U.S.	98	42.00N	85.10W
Union City, N.J., U.S.	228	40.46N	74.02W
Union City, Pa., U.S.	99	41.50N	79.50W
Union City, Tn., U.S.	114	36.25N	89.04W
Uniondale, N.Y., U.S.	228	40.43N	73.36W
Unión de Reyes, Cuba	122	22.45N	81.30W
Unión de San Antonio, Mex.	118	21.07N	101.56W
Unión de Tula, Mex.	118	19.57N	104.14W
Union Grove, Wi., U.S. (ūn-yŭn grōv)	101a	42.41N	88.03W
Unión Hidalgo, Mex. (ē-dä′lgō)	119	16.29N	94.51W
Union Point, Ga., U.S.	114	33.37N	83.08W
Union Springs, Al., U.S. (sprĭngz)	114	32.08N	85.43W
Uniontown, Al., U.S. (ūn′yŭn-toun)	114	32.26N	87.30W
Uniontown, Oh., U.S.	101d	40.58N	81.25W
Uniontown, Pa., U.S.	99	39.55N	79.45W
Unionville, Mo., U.S. (ūn′yŭn-vĭl)	111	40.28N	92.58W
Unisan, Phil. (ōō-nē′sän)	197a	13.50N	121.59E
United Arab Emirates, nation, Asia	182	24.00N	54.00E
United Kingdom, nation, Eur.	142	56.30N	1.40W
United Nations Headquarters, pt. of i., N.Y., U.S.	228	40.45N	73.58W
United States, nation, N.A.	96	38.00N	110.00W
Unity, Can.	88	52.27N	109.10W
Universal, In., U.S. (ū-nĭ-vûr′sȧl)	98	39.35N	87.30W
University City, Mo., U.S. (ū′nĭ-vûr′sĭ-tĭ)	107e	38.40N	90.19W
University Heights, Oh., U.S.	229a	41.30N	81.32W
University Park, Md., U.S.	229d	38.58N	76.57W
University Park, Tx., U.S.	107c	32.51N	96.48W
Unna, Ger. (ōō′nä)	157c	51.32N	7.41E
Uno, Canal Numero, can., Arg.	129c	36.43S	58.14W
Unterhaching, Ger. (ōōn′tĕr-hä-kĕng)	145d	48.03N	11.38E
Untermauerbach, Aus.	239e	48.14N	16.12E
Ünye, Tur. (ün′yĕ)	149	41.00N	37.10E
Unzha, r., Russia (ŏŏn′zhȧ)	166	57.45N	44.10E
Upa, r., Russia (ŏŏ′pȧ)	162	53.54N	36.48E
Upata, Ven. (ōō-pä′tä)	130	7.58N	62.27W
Upemba, Parc National de l', rec., Zaire	217	9.10S	26.15E
Up Holland, Eng., U.K.	237a	53.33N	2.44W
Upington, S. Afr. (ŭp′ĭng-tŭn)	212	28.25S	21.15E
Upland, Ca., U.S. (ŭp′lȧnd)	107a	34.06N	117.38W
Upland, Pa., U.S.	229b	39.51N	75.23W
Upolu, i., W. Sam.	198a	13.55S	171.45W
Upolu Point, c., Hi., U.S. (ōō-pō′lōō)	94a	20.15N	155.48W
Upper Arrow Lake, l., Can. (ăr′ō)	87	50.30N	117.55W
Upper Brookville, N.Y., U.S.	228	40.51N	73.34W
Upper Darby, Pa., U.S. (där′bĭ)	100f	39.58N	75.16W
Upper des Lacs, l., N.A. (dē läk)	102	48.58N	101.55W
Upper Ferntree Gully, Austl.	243b	37.54S	145.19E
Upper Kapuas Mountains, mts., Asia	196	1.45N	112.06E
Upper Klamath Lake, l., Or., U.S.	104	42.23N	122.55W
Upper Lake, l., Nv., U.S. (ŭp′ẽr)	104	41.42N	119.59W
Upper Marlboro, Md., U.S. (ûpẽr märl′bōrō)	100e	38.49N	76.46W
Upper Mill, Wa., U.S. (mĭl)	106a	47.11N	121.55W
Upper New York Bay, b., N.Y., U.S.	228	40.41N	74.03W
Upper Red Lake, l., Mn., U.S. (rĕd)	103	48.14N	94.53W
Upper Saint Clair, Pa., U.S.	230b	40.21N	80.05W
Upper Sandusky, Oh., U.S. (săn-dŭs′kē)	98	40.50N	83.20W
Upper San Leandro Reservoir, res., Ca., U.S. (ŭp′ẽr săn lē-ăn′drō)	106b	37.47N	122.04W
Upper Tooting, neigh., Eng., U.K.	235	51.26N	0.10W
Upper Volta *see* Burkina Faso, nation, Afr.	210	13.00N	2.00W
Uppingham, Eng., U.K. (ŭp′ĭng-ăm)	144a	52.35N	0.43W
Uppsala, Swe. (ōōp′sȧ-lä)	142	59.53N	17.39E
Upton, Eng., U.K.	235	51.30N	0.35W
Uptown, Ma., U.S. (ŭp′toun)	93a	42.10N	71.36W
Uptown, neigh., Il., U.S.	231a	41.58N	87.40W
Upwey, Austl.	243b	37.54S	145.20E
Uraga, Japan (ōō′rȧ-gä′)	195a	35.15N	139.43E
Ural, r. (ö-räl′′) (ū-rôl)	164	48.00N	51.00E
Urals, mts., Russia	164	56.28N	58.13E
Uran, India (ōō-rän′)	187b	18.53N	72.46E
Uranium City, Can.	84	59.34N	108.59W
Urawa, Japan (ōō′rä-wä′)	194	35.52N	139.39E
Urayasu, Japan (ōō′rä-yä′sōō)	195a	35.40N	139.54W
Urazovo, Russia (ö-rȧ′zō-vō)	163	50.08N	38.03E
Urbana, Il., U.S. (ûr-băn′ȧ)	98	40.10N	88.15W
Urbana, Oh., U.S.	98	40.05N	83.50W
Urbino, Italy (ōōr-bē′nō)	160	43.43N	12.37E
Urda, Kaz. (ör′dȧ)	170	48.50N	47.30E
Urdaneta, Phil. (ōōr-dä-nä′tä)	197a	15.59N	120.34E
Urdinarrain, Arg. (ōōr-dē-när-rȧē′n)	129c	32.43S	58.53W
Uritsk, Russia (ōō′rĭtsk)	172c	59.50N	30.11E
Urla, Tur. (ör′lȧ)	161	38.20N	26.44E
Urman, Russia (ör′män)	172a	54.53N	56.52E
Urmi, r., Russia (ör′mē)	194	48.50N	134.00E
Urmston, Eng., U.K.	237b	53.27N	2.21W
Uromi, Nig.	215	6.44N	6.18E
Urrao, Col. (ōōr-rȧ′ō)	130	6.19N	76.11W
Urshel'skiy, Russia (ōōr-shĕl′skēē)	162	55.50N	40.11E
Ursus, Pol.	155	52.12N	20.53E
Urubamba, r., Peru (ōō-rōō-bäm′bä)	130	11.48S	72.34W
Uruguaiana, Braz.	132	29.45S	57.00W
Uruguay, nation, S.A. (ōō-rōō-gwī′) (ū′rōō-gwā)	132	32.45S	56.00W
Uruguay, Río, r., S.A. (rē′ō-ō-rōō-gwī)	132	27.05S	55.15W
Ürümqi, China (ü-rüm-chyē)	188	43.49N	87.43E
Urup, i., Russia (ö′röp′)	189	46.00N	150.00E
Uryupinsk, Russia (ör′yö-pēn-sk′)	167	50.50N	42.00E
Ürzhar, Kaz.	169	47.28N	82.00E
Urziceni, Rom. (ö-zē-chĕn′′)	161	44.45N	26.42E
Usa, Japan	194	33.31N	131.22E
Usa, r., Russia (ōō′sȧ)	166	66.00N	58.20E
Uşak, Tur. (ōō′shȧk)	149	38.45N	29.15E
Usakos, Nmb. (ōō-sä′kōs)	212	22.00S	15.40E
Usambara Mountains, mts., Tan.	217	4.40S	38.25E
Usangu Flats, sw., Tan.	217	8.10S	34.00E
Ushaki, Russia (ōō′shȧ-kĭ)	172c	59.28N	31.00E
Ushakovskoye, Russia (ö-shȧ-kôv′skô-yĕ)	172a	56.18N	62.23E
Usharal, Kaz.	169	46.14N	80.58E
Ushashi, Tan.	217	2.00S	33.57E
Ushiku, Japan (ōō′shē-kōō)	195a	35.24N	140.09E
Ushimado, Japan (ōō′shē-mä′dō)	195	34.37N	134.09E
Ushuaia, Arg. (ōō-shōō-ī′ä)	132	54.46S	68.24W
Usman', Russia (ōōs-män′)	167	52.03N	39.40E
Usmānpur, neigh., India	240d	28.41N	77.15E
Usol'ye, Russia (ö-sō′lyĕ)	172a	59.24N	56.40E
Usol'ye-Sibirskoye, Russia (ö-sô′lyĕsĭ′ bēr′skô-yĕ)	170	52.44N	103.46E
Uspallata Pass, p., S.A. (ōōs-pä-lyä′tä)	132	32.47S	70.08W
Uspanapa, r., Mex. (ōōs-pä-nä′pä)	119	17.43N	94.14W
Ussel, Fr. (üs′ĕl)	156	45.33N	2.17E
Ussuri, r., Asia (ōō-sōō′rē)	171	47.30N	134.00E
Ussuriysk, Russia	165	43.48N	132.09E
Ust'-Bol'sheretsk, Russia	165	52.41N	157.00E
Ustica, Isola di, i., Italy	160	38.43N	12.11E
Ústí nad Labem, Czech Rep.	154	50.40N	14.02E
Ust'-Izhora, Russia (öst-ēz′hô-rȧ)	172c	59.49N	30.35E
Ustka, Pol. (ōōst′kȧ)	154	54.34N	16.52E
Ust'-Kamchatsk, Russia	165	56.13N	162.18E
Ust'-Katav, Russia (öst kȧ′tȧf)	172a	54.55N	58.12E
Ust'-Kishert', Russia (öst kē′shĕrt)	172a	57.21N	57.13E
Ust'-Kulom, Russia (kö′lŭm)	164	61.38N	54.00E
Ust'-Maya, Russia (mȧ′yȧ)	165	60.33N	134.43E
Ust'-Olenëk, Russia	165	72.52N	120.15E
Ust-Ordynskiy, Russia (öst-ôr-dyĕnsk′ĭ)	170	52.47N	104.39E
Ust' Penzhino, Russia	171	63.00N	165.10E
Ust' Port, Russia (öst′pôrt′)	164	69.20N	83.41E
Ust'-Tsil'ma, Russia (tsĭl′mȧ)	164	65.25N	52.10E
Ust'-Tyrma, Russia (tur′mȧ)	165	50.27N	131.17E
Ust' Uls, Russia	172a	60.35N	58.32E
Ust'-Urt, Plato, plat., Asia	164	44.03N	54.58E
Ustynivka, Ukr.	163	47.59N	32.31E
Ustyuzhna, Russia (yōōzh′nȧ)	166	58.49N	36.19E
Usu, China (ü-sōō)	188	44.28N	84.07E
Usuki, Japan (ōō′sōō-kē′)	195	33.06N	131.47E
Usulutan, El Sal. (ōō-sōō-lä-tän′)	120	13.22N	88.25W
Usumacinta, r., N.A. (ōō′sōō-mä-sēn′tō)	119	18.24N	92.30W
Us'va, Russia (ōōs′vȧ)	172a	58.41N	57.38E
Utah, state, U.S. (ū′tô)	96	39.25N	112.40W
Utah Lake, l., Ut., U.S.	109	40.10N	111.55W
Utan, India	187b	19.17N	72.43E
Ute Mountain Indian Reservation, I.R., N.M., U.S.	109	36.57N	108.34W
Utena, Lith. (ōō′tā-nä)	153	55.32N	25.40E
Utete, Tan. (ōō-tā′tȧ)	213	8.05S	38.47E
Utfort, Ger.	236	51.28N	6.38E
Utica, In., U.S. (ū′tĭ-kȧ)	101h	38.20N	85.39W
Utica, N.Y., U.S.	97	43.05N	75.10W
Utiel, Spain (ōō-tyâl′)	158	39.34N	1.13W
Utika, Mi., U.S. (ū′tĭ-kȧ)	101b	42.37N	83.02W
Utik Lake, l., Can.	89	55.16N	96.00W
Utikuma Lake, l., Can.	87	55.50N	115.25W
Utila, i., Hond. (ōō-tē′lä)	120	16.07N	87.05W
Utinga, Braz.	234d	23.38S	46.32W
Uto, Japan (ōō′tō′)	194	32.43N	130.39E
Utrecht, Neth. (ü′trĕKt) (ū′trĕkt)	147	52.05N	5.06E
Utrera, Spain (ōō-trā′rä)	148	37.12N	5.48W
Utsunomiya, Japan (ōōt′sö-nō-mē-yȧ′)	189	36.35N	139.52E
Uttaradit, Thai.	196	17.47N	100.10E
Uttarpara-Kotrung, India	186a	22.40N	88.21E
Uttar Pradesh, state, India (öt-tär-prä-dēsh)	183	27.00N	80.00E
Uttoxeter, Eng., U.K. (ŭt-tôk′sē-tẽr)	144a	52.54N	1.52W
Utuado, P.R. (ōō-tōō-ä′dhō)	117b	18.16N	66.40W
Uusikaupunki, Fin.	153	60.48N	21.24E
Uvalde, Tx., U.S. (ū-văl′dē)	112	29.14N	99.47W
Uvel'skiy, Russia (ö-vyĕl′skĭ)	172a	54.27N	61.22E
Uvinza, Tan.	217	5.06S	30.22E
Uvira, Zaire (ōō-vē′rä)	212	3.28S	29.03E
Uvod', r., Russia (ö-vôd′)	162	56.40N	41.10E
Uvongo Beach, S. Afr.	213c	30.49S	30.23E
Uvs Nuur, l., Asia	188	50.29N	93.32E
Uwajima, Japan (ōō-wä′jē-mä)	194	33.12N	132.35E
Uxbridge, Ma., U.S. (ŭks′brĭj)	93a	42.05N	71.38W
Uxbridge, neigh., Eng., U.K.	235	51.33N	0.29W
Uxmal, hist., Mex. (ōō′x-mä′l)	120a	20.22N	89.44W
Uy, r., Russia (ōōy)	172a	54.05N	62.11E
Uyama, Japan	242b	34.50N	135.41E
Uyskoye, Russia (ûy′skô-yĕ)	172a	54.22N	60.01E
Uyuni, Bol. (ōō-yōō′nē)	130	20.28S	66.45W
Uyuni, Salar de, pl., Bol. (sä-lär-dē)	130	20.58S	67.09W
Uzbekistan, nation, Asia	164	42.42N	60.00E
Uzh, r., Ukr. (özh)	163	51.07N	29.05E
Uzhhorod, Ukr.	155	48.38N	22.18E
Užice, Yugo. ōō′zhē-tsĕ	161	43.51N	19.53E
Uzunköprü, Tur.	161	41.17N	26.42E

V

PLACE (Pronunciation)	PAGE	Lat. °′	Long. °′
Vaal, r., S. Afr. (väl)	212	28.15S	24.30E
Vaaldam, res., S. Afr.	218d	26.58S	28.37E
Vaalplaas, S. Afr.	218d	25.39S	28.56E
Vaalwater, S. Afr.	218d	24.17S	28.08E
Vaasa, Fin. (vä′sȧ)	142	63.06N	21.39E
Vác, Hung. (väts)	155	47.46N	19.10E
Vache, Île à, i., Haiti	123	18.05N	73.40W
Vadstena, Swe. (väd′stĭ′nȧ)	152	58.27N	14.53E
Vaduz, Liech. (vä′dōts)	154	47.10N	9.32E
Vaga, r., Russia (va′gȧ)	166	61.55N	42.30E
Vah, r., Slvk. (väK)	147	48.07N	17.52E
Vaigai, r., India	187	10.20N	78.13E
Vaires-sur-Marne, Fr.	237c	48.52N	2.39E
Vakh, r., Russia (väK)	170	61.30N	81.33E
Valachia, hist. reg., Rom.	161	44.45N	24.17E
Valcanuta, neigh., Italy	239c	41.53N	12.25E
Valcartier-Village, Can. (väl-kärt-yĕ′vē-läzh′)	83b	46.56N	71.28W
Valdai Hills, hills, Russia (vȧl-dī′ gô′rĭ)	166	57.50N	32.35E
Valday, Russia (vȧl-dī′)	166	57.58N	33.13E
Valdecañas, Embalse de, res., Spain	158	39.45N	5.30W
Valdemārpils, Lat.	153	57.22N	22.34E
Valdemorillo, Spain (väl-då-mō-rēl′yō)	159a	40.30N	4.04W
Valdepeñas, Spain (väl-då-pān′yäs)	148	38.46N	3.22W
Valderaduey, r., Spain (väl-dĕ-rä-dwĕ′y)	158	41.39N	5.35W
Valdés, Península, pen., Arg. (väl-dĕ′s)	132	42.15S	63.15W
Valdez, Ak., U.S. (văl′dēz)	95	61.10N	146.18W
Valdilecha, Spain (väl-dē-lā′chä)	159a	40.17N	3.19W
Valdivia, Chile (väl-dē′vä)	132	39.47S	73.13W
Valdivia, Col. (väl-dē′vēä)	130a	7.10N	75.26W
Val-d'Or, Can.	85	48.03N	77.50W
Valdosta, Ga., U.S. (văl-dŏs′tȧ)	97	30.50N	83.18W
Valdoviño, Spain (väl-dō-vē′nō)	158	43.36N	8.05W
Vale, Or., U.S. (vāl)	104	43.59N	117.14W
Valença, Braz. (vä-lĕN′sȧ)	131	13.43S	38.58W
Valença, Port.	158	42.03N	8.36W
Valence, Fr. (vä-lĕnns)	147	44.56N	4.54E
Valencia, Spain (vä-lĕn′thē-ä)	142	39.26N	0.23W
Valencia, Ven. (vä-lĕn′syä)	130	10.11N	68.00W
Valencia, hist. reg., Spain (vä-lĕn′thē-ä)	159	39.08N	0.43W
Valencia, Golfo de, b., Spain	159	39.50N	0.30E
Valencia, Lago de, l., Ven.	131b	10.11N	67.45W
Valencia de Alcántara, Spain	158	39.34N	7.13W
Valenciennes, Fr. (vȧ-läN-syĕn′)	156	50.24N	3.36E
Valentín Alsina, neigh., Arg.	233d	34.40S	58.25W
Valentine, Ne., U.S. (vȧ lăN-tē-nyē′)	96	42.52N	100.34W
Valera, Ven. (vä-lĕ′rä)	130	9.12N	70.45W
Valerianovsk, Russia (vȧ-lĕ-rĭ-ȧ′nôvsk)	172a	58.47N	59.34E
Valérien, Mont, hill, Fr.	237c	48.53N	2.13E
Valga, Est. (väl′gȧ)	166	57.47N	26.03E
Valhalla, S. Afr. (vȧl-hăl-ȧ)	213b	25.49S	28.09E
Valier, Mt., U.S. (vă-lēr′)	105	48.17N	112.14W
Valjevo, Yugo. (väl′yȧ-vō)	161	44.17N	19.57E
Valky, Ukr.	163	49.49N	35.40E
Valladolid, Mex. (väl-yä-dhō-lēdh′)	116	20.39N	88.13W
Valladolid, Spain (väl-yä-dhō-lēdh′)	142	41.41N	4.41W
Valldoreix, Spain	238e	41.28N	2.04E

ăt; finȧl; rāte; senāte; ärm; ȧsk; sofȧ; fâre; ch-choose; dh-as th in other; bē; ēvent; bĕt; recĕnt; cratẽr; g-gō; gh-guttural g; bĭt; ĭ-short neutral; rīde; K-guttural k as ch in German ich;

PLACE (Pronunciation)	PAGE	Lat. °′	Long. °′
Valle, Arroyo del, Ca., U.S. (ä-rō'yō dĕl väl'yå)	108	37.36N	121.43W
Vallecas, Spain (väl-yä'käs)	159a	40.23N	3.37W
Valle de Allende, Mex. (väl'yā dā äl-yĕn'då)	112	26.55N	105.25W
Valle de Bravo, Mex. (brä'vỏ)	118	19.12N	100.07W
Valle de Guanape, Ven. (vä'l-yĕ-dĕ-gwä-nä'pĕ)	131b	9.54N	65.41W
Valle de la Pascua, Ven. (lä-pä's-kōōä)	130	9.12N	65.08W
Valle del Cauca, dept., Col. (vä'l-yĕ dĕl kou'kä)	130a	4.03N	76.13W
Valle de Santiago, Mex. (sän-tē-ä'gỏ)	118	20.23N	101.11W
Valledupar, Col. (dōō-pär')	130	10.13N	73.39W
Valle Grande, Bol. (grän'dā)	130	18.27S	64.03W
Vallejo, Ca., U.S. (vă-yā'hō) (vă-lā'hō)	96	38.06N	122.15W
Vallejo, Sierra de, mts., Mex. (sē-ĕ'r-rä-dĕ-väl-yĕ'kō)	118	21.00N	105.10W
Vallenar, Chile (väl-yå-när')	132	28.39S	70.52W
Valles, Mex.	116	21.59N	99.02W
Valletta, Malta (väl-lĕt'ä)	148	35.50N	14.29E
Valle Vista, Ca., U.S. (văl'yā vĭs'tȧ)	107a	33.45N	116.53W
Valley City, N.D., U.S.	96	46.55N	97.59W
Valley City, Oh., U.S. (văl'ĭ)	101d	41.14N	81.56W
Valleydale, Ca., U.S.	232	34.06N	117.56W
Valley Falls, Ks., U.S.	111	39.25N	95.26W
Valleyfield, Can. (văl'ē-fēld)	85	45.16N	74.09W
Valley Mede, Md., U.S.	229c	39.17N	76.50W
Valley Park, Mo., U.S. (văl'ē pärk)	107e	38.33N	90.30W
Valley Stream, N.Y., U.S. (văl'ĭ strēm)	100a	40.39N	73.42W
Valli di Comácchio, l., Italy (vä'lē-dē-kō-mä'chyō)	160	44.38N	12.15E
Vallière, Haiti (väl-yâr')	123	19.30N	71.55W
Vallimanca, r., Arg. (väl-yē-mä'n-kä)	129c	36.21S	60.55W
Valls, Spain (väls)	148	41.15N	1.15E
Valmiera, Lat. (vål'myĕ-rå)	166	57.34N	25.54E
Valognes, Fr. (vå-lôn'y')	156	49.32N	1.30W
Valona *see* Vlorë, Alb.	149	40.28N	19.31E
Valparaíso, Chile (väl'pä-rä-ē'sỏ)	132	33.02S	71.32W
Valparaíso, Mex.	118	22.49N	103.33W
Valparaiso, In., U.S. (văl-pȧ-rā'zō)	98	41.25N	87.05W
Valpariso, prov., Chile	129b	32.58S	71.23W
Valréas, Fr. (väl-rå-ä')	156	44.25N	4.56E
Vals, r., S. Afr.	218d	27.32S	26.51E
Vals, Tanjung, c., Indon.	197	8.30S	137.15E
Valsbaai, b., S. Afr.	212a	34.14S	18.35E
Valuyevo, Russia (vå-lōō'yĕ-vô)	172b	55.34N	37.21E
Valuyki, Russia (vå-lò-ē'kē)	167	50.14N	38.04E
Valverde del Camino, Spain (väl-vĕr-dĕ-dĕl-kä-mē'nō)	158	37.34N	6.44W
Vammala, Fin.	153	61.19N	22.51E
Van, Tur. (vån)	182	38.04N	43.10E
Van Buren, Ar., U.S. (văn bū'rĕn)	111	35.26N	94.20W
Van Buren, Me., U.S.	92	47.09N	67.58W
Vanceburg, Ky., U.S. (văns'bûrg)	98	38.35N	83.20W
Vancouver, Can. (văn-kōō'vĕr)	84	49.16N	123.06W
Vancouver, Wa., U.S.	96	45.37N	122.40W
Vancouver Island, i., Can.	84	49.50N	125.05W
Vancouver Island Ranges, mts., Can.	86	49.25N	125.25W
Vandalia, Il., U.S. (văn-dā'lĭ-ȧ)	98	39.00N	89.00W
Vandalia, Mo., U.S.	111	39.19N	91.30W
Vanderbijlpark, S. Afr.	218d	26.43S	27.50E
Vanderhoof, Can.	84	54.01N	124.01W
Van Diemen, Cape, c., Austl. (văndē'mĕn)	202	11.05S	130.15E
Van Diemen Gulf, b., Austl.	202	11.50S	131.30E
Vanegas, Mex. (vä-nĕ'gäs)	116	23.54N	100.54W
Vänern, l., Swe.	142	58.52N	13.17E
Vänersborg, Swe. (vĕ'nĕrs-bôr')	146	58.24N	12.15E
Vanga, Kenya (väŋ'gä)	213	4.38S	39.10E
Vangani, India	187b	19.07N	73.15E
Van Gölü, l., Tur.	166	38.33N	42.46E
Van Horn, Tx., U.S.	112	31.03N	104.50W
Vanier, Can.	83c	45.27N	75.39W
Vaniköy, neigh., Tur.	239f	41.04N	29.04E
Van Lear, Ky., U.S. (văn lēr')	98	37.45N	82.50W
Vannes, Fr. (vån)	147	47.42N	2.46W
Van Nuys, Ca., U.S. (văn nīz')	107a	34.11N	118.27W
Van Rees, Pegunungan, mts., Indon.	197	2.30S	138.45E
Vantaan, r., Fin.	153	60.25N	24.43E
Vanua Levu, i., Fiji	198g	16.33S	179.15E
Vanuatu, nation, Oc.	203	16.02S	169.15E
Vanves, Fr.	237c	48.50N	2.18E
Van Wert, Oh., U.S. (văn wûrt')	98	40.50N	84.35W
Vanzago, Italy	238c	45.32N	9.00E
Vara, Swe. (vä'rä)	152	58.17N	12.55E
Varaklāni, Lat.	153	56.38N	26.46E
Varallo, Italy (vä-räl'lō)	160	45.44N	8.14E
Vārānasi (Benares), India	183	25.25N	83.00E
Varangerfjorden, b., Nor.	143	70.05N	30.20E
Varano, Lago di, l., Italy (lä'gō-dē-vä-rä'nō)	160	41.52N	15.55E
Varaždin, Cro. (vä'räzh'dēn)	149	46.17N	16.20E
Varazze, Italy (vä-rät'sā)	160	44.23N	8.34E
Varberg, Swe. (vär'bĕrg)	152	57.06N	12.16E
Vardar, r., Yugo. (vär'där)	161	41.40N	21.50E
Varėna, Lith. (vä-rā'nå)	153	54.16N	24.35E
Varennes, Can. (vå-rĕn')	83a	45.41N	73.27W
Vareš, Bos. (vä'rĕsh)	161	44.10N	18.20E
Varese, Italy (vä-rā'så)	160	45.45N	8.49E
Vargem Grande, neigh., Braz.	234c	22.59S	43.29W
Varginha, Braz. (vär-zhē'n-yä)	131	21.33S	45.25W
Varkaus, Fin. (vär'kous)	153	62.19N	27.51E
Varlamovo, Russia (vár-lá'mô-vô)	172a	54.37N	60.41E
Varna, Bul. (vär'nȧ)	142	43.14N	27.58E
Varna, Russia	172a	53.22N	60.59E
Värnamo, Swe. (vĕr'ná-mô)	152	57.11N	13.45E
Varnsdorf, Czech Rep. (värns'dôrf)	154	50.54N	14.36E
Varnville, S.C., U.S. (värn'vĭl)	115	32.49N	81.05W
Várpalota, pt. of i., Hung.	239g	47.30N	19.02E
Vasa, India	187b	19.20N	72.47E
Vascongadas, hist. reg., Spain (väs-kôn-gä'däs)	158	43.00N	2.46W
Vashka, r., Russia	166	64.00N	48.00E
Vashon, Wa., U.S. (văsh'ŭn)	106a	47.27N	122.28W
Vashon Heights, Wa., U.S. (hītz)	106a	47.30N	122.28W
Vashon Island, i., Wa., U.S.	106a	47.27N	122.27W
Vasiljevskij, Ostrov, i., Russia	239a	59.56N	30.15E
Vaslui, Rom. (vás-lōō'ē)	155	46.39N	27.49E
Vassar, Mi., U.S. (văs'ēr)	98	43.25N	83.35W
Vassouras, Braz. (väs-sō'räzh)	129a	22.25S	43.40W
Västerås, Swe. (vĕs'tĕr-ôs)	146	59.39N	16.30E
Västerdalälven, r., Swe.	146	61.06N	13.10E
Västervik, Swe. (vĕs'tĕr-vēk)	146	57.45N	16.35E
Vasto, Italy (väs'tô)	148	42.06N	12.42E
Vasyl'kiv, Ukr.	167	50.10N	30.22E
Vasyugan, r., Russia (vás-yōō-gȧn')	170	58.52N	77.30E
Vatican City, nation, Eur.	160	41.54N	12.22E
Vaticano, Cape, c., Italy (vä-tē-kä'nô)	160	38.38N	15.52E
Vatnajökull, ice., Ice. (vät'nȧ-yû-kôl)	146	64.34N	16.41W
Vatomandry, Madag.	213	18.53S	48.13E
Vatra Dornei, Rom. (vät'rȧ dôr'nȧ')	155	47.22N	25.20E
Vättern, l., Swe.	142	58.15N	14.24E
Vattholma, Swe.	152	60.01N	17.40E
Vaucluse, Austl.	243a	33.51S	151.17E
Vaudreuil, Can. (vô-drû'y')	83a	45.24N	74.02W
Vaugh, Wa., U.S. (vôn)	106a	47.21N	122.47W
Vaughan, Can.	83d	43.47N	79.36W
Vaughn, N.M., U.S.	110	34.37N	105.13W
Vauhallan, Fr.	237c	48.44N	2.12E
Vaujours, Fr.	237c	48.56N	2.35E
Vaupés, r., S.A. (vá'ōō-pĕ's)	130	1.18N	71.14W
Vaxholm, Swe. (väks'hôlm)	152	59.26N	18.19E
Växjo, Swe. (vĕks'shû)	146	56.53N	14.46E
Vaygach, i., Russia (vī-gách')	164	70.00N	59.00E
Veadeiros, Chapadas dos, hills, Braz. (shä-pä'däs-dôs-vĕ-á-dā'rōs)	131	14.00S	47.00W
Vedea, r., Rom. (vá'dyȧ)	161	44.25N	24.45E
Vedia, Arg. (vĕ'dyä)	129c	34.29S	61.30W
Veedersburg, In., U.S. (vē'dĕrz-bûrg)	98	40.05N	87.15W
Vega, i., Nor.	146	65.38N	10.51E
Vega de Alatorre, Mex. (vā'gä dā ä-lä-tōr'rå)	119	20.02N	96.39W
Vega Real, reg., Dom. Rep. (vĕ'gä-rĕ-ä'l)	123	19.30N	71.05W
Vegreville, Can.	84	53.30N	112.03W
Vehār Lake, l., India	187b	19.11N	72.52E
Veinticinco de Mayo, Arg.	129c	35.26S	60.09W
Vejer de la Frontera, Spain	158	36.15N	5.58W
Vejle, Den. (vī'lĕ)	146	55.41N	9.29E
Velbert, Ger. (fĕl'bĕrt)	157c	51.20N	7.03E
Velebit, mts., Yugo. (vā'lĕ-bēt)	149	44.25N	15.23E
Velen, Ger. (fĕ'lĕn)	157c	51.54N	7.00E
Vélez-Málaga, Spain (vā'lāth-mä'lä-gä)	158	36.48N	4.05W
Vélez-Rubio, Spain (rōō'bē-ō)	158	37.38N	2.05W
Velika Kapela, mts., Yugo. (vĕ'lē-kä kä-pĕ'lä)	149	45.03N	15.20E
Velika Morava, r., Yugo. (mô'rä-vä)	149	44.00N	21.30E
Velikaya, r., Russia (vå-lē'kȧ-yȧ)	162	57.25N	28.07E
Velikiye Luki, Russia (vyē-lē'-kyē lōō'ke)	164	56.19N	30.32E
Velikiy Ustyug, Russia (vå-lē'kĭ ōōs-tyôg')	164	60.45N	46.38E
Veliko Tŭrnovo, Bul.	149	43.06N	25.38E
Velikoye, Russia (vå-lē'kô-yĕ)	162	57.21N	39.45E
Velikoye, l., Russia	162	57.00N	36.53E
Veli Lošinj, Cro. (lỏ'shēn')	160	44.30N	14.29E
Velizh, Russia (vā'lēzh)	166	55.37N	31.11E
Vella Lavella, i., Sol.Is.	203	8.00S	156.42E
Velletri, Italy (vĕl-lā'trē)	160	41.42N	12.48E
Vellore, India (vĕl-lōr')	183	12.57N	79.09E
Vels, Russia (vĕls)	172a	60.35N	58.47E
Vel'sk, Russia (vĕlsk)	164	61.00N	42.18E
Velten, Ger. (fel'tĕn)	145b	52.41N	13.11E
Velya, r., Russia (vĕl'yȧ)	172b	56.23N	37.54E
Velyka Lepetykha, Ukr.	163	47.11N	33.58E
Velyka Vradyyivka, Ukr.	163	47.51N	30.38E
Velykyy Bychkiv, Ukr.	155	47.59N	24.01E
Venadillo, Col. (vĕ-nä-dē'l-yō)	130a	4.43N	74.55W
Venado, Mex. (vå-mä'dō)	118	22.54N	101.07W
Venado Tuerto, Arg. (vĕ-nä'dô-tōōĕ'r-tô)	132	33.28S	61.47W
Vendôme, Fr. (väɴ-dōm')	156	47.46N	1.05E
Veneto, hist. reg., Italy (vĕ-nĕ'tỏ)	160	45.58N	11.24E
Venëv, Russia (vĕn-ĕf')	166	54.19N	38.14E
Venezia *see* Venice, Italy	142	45.25N	12.18E
Venezuela, nation, S.A. (vĕn-ē-zwē'lȧ)	130	8.00N	65.00W
Venezuela, Golfo de, b., S.A. (gôl-fô-dĕ)	130	11.34N	71.02W
Veniaminof, Mount, mtn., Ak., U.S.	95	56.12N	159.20W
Venice, Italy	142	45.25N	12.18E
Venice, Ca., U.S. (vĕn'ĭs)	107a	33.59N	118.28W
Venice, Il., U.S.	107e	38.40N	90.10W
Venice, neigh., Ca., U.S.	232	34.00N	118.29W
Venice, Gulf of, b., Italy	148	45.23N	13.00E
Venlo, Neth.	157c	51.22N	6.11E
Vennhausen, neigh., Ger.	236	51.13N	6.51E
Venta, r., Eur. (vĕn'tá)	153	57.05N	21.45E
Ventana, Sierra de la, mts., Arg. (sē-ĕ-rä-dĕ-lä-vĕn-tá'nä)	132	38.00S	63.00W
Ventersburg, S. Afr. (vĕn-tĕrs'bûrg)	218d	28.06S	27.10E
Ventersdorp, S. Afr. (vĕn-tĕrs'dôrp)	218d	26.20S	26.48E
Ventimiglia, Italy (vĕn-tē-mēl'yä)	160	43.46N	7.37E
Ventnor, N.J., U.S. (vĕnt'nĕr)	99	39.20N	74.25W
Ventspils, Lat. (vĕnt'spĕls)	166	57.24N	21.41E
Ventuari, r., Ven. (vĕn-tōōá'rē)	130	4.47N	65.56W
Ventura, Ca., U.S. (vĕn-tōō'rȧ)	108	34.18N	119.18W
Venukovsky, Russia (vĕ-nōō'kôv-skĭ)	172b	55.10N	37.26E
Venustiano Carranza, Mex. (vĕ-nōōs-tyä'nō-kär-rä'n-zä)	118	19.44N	103.48W
Venustiano Carranzo, Mex. (kär-rä'n-zỏ)	119	16.21N	92.36W
Vera, Arg. (vĕ-rä)	132	29.22S	60.09W
Vera, Spain (vā'rä)	158	37.18N	1.53W
Veracruz, Mex.	116	19.13N	96.07W
Vera Cruz, state, Mex. (vā-rä-krōōz')	116	20.30N	97.15W
Verāval, India (vĕr'vŭ-väl)	183	20.59N	70.49E
Verberg, neigh., Ger.	236	51.22N	6.36E
Vercelli, Italy (vĕr-chĕl'lē)	160	45.18N	8.27E
Verchères, Can. (vĕr-shâr')	83a	45.46N	73.21W
Verde, i., Phil. (vĕr'då)	197a	13.34N	121.11E
Verde, r., Mex.	118	21.48N	99.50W
Verde, r., Mex.	118	20.50N	103.00W
Verde, r., Mex.	119	16.05N	97.44W
Verde, r., Az., U.S. (vûrd)	109	34.04N	111.40W
Verde, Cap, c., Bah.	123	22.50N	75.00W
Verde, Cay, i., Bah.	123	22.00N	75.05W
Verde Island Passage, strt., Phil. (vĕr'dē)	197a	13.36N	120.39E
Verdemont, Ca., U.S. (vûr'dē-mŏnt)	107a	34.12N	117.22W
Verden, Ger. (fĕr'dĕn)	154	52.55N	9.15E
Verdigris, r., Ok., U.S. (vûr'dē-grēs)	111	36.50N	95.29W
Verdun, Can. (vĕr'dŭɴ')	91	45.27N	73.34W
Verdun, Fr. (vâr-dûɴ')	147	49.09N	5.21E
Verdun, Fr.	157	43.48N	1.10E
Vereeniging, S. Afr. (vĕ-rä'nĭ-gĭng)	218d	26.40S	27.56E
Verena, S. Afr. (vĕr-ĕn ȧ)	218d	25.30S	29.02E
Vereya, Russia (vĕ-rā'yȧ)	162	55.21N	36.08E
Verga, N.J., U.S.	229b	39.52N	75.10W
Vergara, Spain (vĕr-gä'rä)	158	43.08N	2.23W
Verin, Spain (vå-rēn')	158	41.56N	7.26W
Verkhne-Kamchatsk, Russia (vyĕrk'nyĕ kȧm-chatsk')	165	54.42N	158.41E
Verkhne Neyvinskiy, Russia (nā-vĭn'skĭ)	172a	57.17N	60.10E
Verkhne Ural'sk, Russia (ỏ-ralsk')	164	53.53N	59.13E
Verkhniy Avzyan, Russia (vyĕrk'nyĕ áv-zyán')	172a	53.32N	57.30E
Verkhniye Kigi, Russia (vyĕrk'nĭ-yĕ kĭ'gĭ)	172a	55.23N	58.37E
Verkhniy Ufaley, Russia (ô-fá'lā)	172a	56.04N	60.15E
Verkhnyaya Pyshma, Russia (vyĕrk'nyä-yä pōōsh'má)	172a	56.57N	60.37E
Verkhnyaya Salda, Russia (säl'dá)	172a	58.03N	60.33E
Verkhnyaya Tunguska (Angara), r., Russia (tòn-gòs'ká)	170	58.13N	97.00E
Verkhnyaya Tura, Russia (tò'rá)	172a	58.22N	59.51E
Verkhnyaya Yayva, Russia (yäy'vá)	172a	59.28N	57.38E
Verkhnye, Ukr.	163	48.53N	38.29E
Verkhotur'ye, Russia (vyĕr-kô-tōōr'yĕ)	172a	58.52N	60.47E
Verkhoyansk, Russia (vyĕr-kô-yänsk')	165	67.43N	133.33E
Verkhoyanskiy Khrebet, mts., Russia (vyĕr-kô-yänskĭ)	165	67.45N	128.00E
Vermilion, Can. (vĕr-mĭl'yŭn)	84	53.22N	110.51W
Vermilion, l., Mn., U.S.	103	47.49N	92.35W
Vermilion, r., Can.	88	53.30N	111.00W
Vermilion, r., Can.	91	47.30N	73.15W
Vermilion, r., Il., U.S.	98	41.05N	89.00W
Vermilion, r., Mn., U.S.	103	48.09N	92.31W
Vermilion Hills, hills, Can.	88	50.43N	106.50W
Vermilion Range, mts., Mn., U.S.	103	47.55N	91.59W
Vermillion, S.D., U.S.	102	42.46N	96.56W
Vermillion, r., S.D., U.S.	102	43.54N	97.14W
Vermillion Bay, b., La., U.S.	113	29.47N	92.00W
Vermont, Austl.	243b	37.50S	145.12E
Vermont, state, U.S. (vĕr-mŏnt')	97	43.50N	72.50W
Vernal, Ut., U.S. (vûr'nȧl)	105	40.29N	109.40W
Verneuk Pan, pl., S. Afr. (vĕr-nŭk')	212	30.10S	21.46E
Vernon, Can.	83c	45.10N	75.27W
Vernon, Can. (vĕr-nôɴ')	84	50.18N	119.15W
Vernon, Ca., U.S. (vŭr'nŭn)	107a	34.01N	118.12W
Vernon, In., U.S. (vûr'nŭn)	98	39.00N	85.40W
Vernon, N.J., U.S.	100a	39.00N	85.40W
Vernon, Tx., U.S.	110	34.09N	99.16W
Vernonia, Or., U.S. (vûr-nō'nyȧ)	106c	45.52N	123.12W
Vero Beach, Fl., U.S. (vē'rỏ)	115a	27.36N	80.25W
Véroia, Grc.	161	40.30N	22.13E
Verona, Italy (vā-rō'nä)	148	45.28N	11.02E
Verona, N.J., U.S.	228	40.50N	74.12W
Verona, Pa., U.S.	230b	40.30N	79.50W
Verrières-le-Buisson, Fr.	237c	48.45N	2.16E
Versailles, Fr. (vĕr-sī'y')	147	48.48N	2.07E
Versailles, Ky., U.S. (vēr-sālz')	98	38.05N	84.45W
Versailles, Mo., U.S.	111	38.27N	92.52W
Versailles, Pa., U.S.	230b	40.21N	79.51W
Versailles, neigh., Arg.	233d	34.38S	58.31W
Versailles, Château de, hist., Fr.	237c	48.48N	2.07E
Vert, Cap, c., Sen.	210	14.43N	17.30W
Verulam, S. Afr. (vĕ-rōō-lăm)	213c	29.39S	31.08E
Verulamium, pt. of i., Eng., U.K.	235	51.45N	0.22W
Verviers, Bel. (vĕr-vyā')	151	50.35N	5.57E
Vesijärvi, l., Fin.	153	61.09N	25.10E
Vesle, Ukr.	163	46.59N	34.56E
Vešn'aki, neigh., Russia	239b	55.44N	37.49E
Vesoul, Fr. (vĕ-sōōl')	157	47.38N	6.11E
Vestavia Hills, Al., U.S.	100h	33.26N	86.46W
Vesterålen, is., Nor. (vĕs'tĕr ô'lĕn)	146	68.54N	14.03E
Vestfjord, fj., Nor.	142	67.33N	12.59E
Vestmannaeyjar, Ice. (vĕst'män-ä-ā'yär)	146	63.12N	20.17W
Vesuvio, vol., Italy (vĕ-sōō'vyä)	142	40.35N	14.26E
Ves'yegonsk, Russia (vĕ-syĕ-gônsk')	162	58.42N	37.09E
Veszprem, Hung. (vĕs'prām)	155	47.05N	17.53E
Vészto, Hung. (vĕs'tû)	155	46.55N	21.18E
Vet, r., S. Afr. (vĕt)	218d	28.25S	26.37E

ng-sing; ŋ-baŋk; ɴ-nasalized n; nŏd; cŏmmit; ōld; ôbey; ôrder; oi-boil; fōōd; ŏŏ-as oo in foot; ou-out; s-soft; sh-dish; th-thin; pūre; ûnite; ûrn; stŭd; circŭs; ü-as in French tu; ′-indeterminate vowel.

362 Vetka–Viskan

PLACE (Pronunciation)	PAGE	Lat. °′	Long. °′
Vetka, Bela. (vyĕt′kȧ)	162	52.36N	31.05E
Vetlanda, Swe. (vĕt-län′dä)	152	57.26N	15.05E
Vetluga, Russia (vyĕt-lo͞o′gȧ)	166	57.50N	45.42E
Vetluga, r., Russia	166	56.50N	45.50E
Vetovo, Bul. (vā′tȯ-vȯ)	161	43.42N	26.18E
Vetren, Bul. (vĕt′rĕn′)	161	42.16N	24.04E
Vevay, In., U.S. (vē′vā)	98	38.45N	85.05W
Veynes, Fr. (vān″)	157	44.31N	5.47E
Vézère, r., Fr. (vā-zer′)	156	45.01N	1.00E
Viacha, Bol. (vēȧ′chȧ)	130	16.43S	68.16W
Viadana, Italy (vė-ä-dä′nä)	160	44.55N	10.30E
Vian, Ok., U.S. (vī′ăn)	111	35.30N	95.00W
Viana, Braz. (vē-ä′nä)	131	3.09S	44.44W
Viana del Bollo, Spain (vė-ä′nä dĕl bȯl′yȯ)	158	42.10N	7.07W
Viana do Alentejo, Port. (vė-ä′nȧ dȯ ä-lĕɴ-tā′hȯ)	158	38.20N	8.02W
Viana do Castelo, Port. (dȯ käs-tā′lȯ)	148	41.41N	8.45W
Viangchan, Laos	196	18.07N	102.33E
Viar, r., Spain (vė-ä′rä)	158	38.15N	6.08W
Viareggio, Italy (vė-ä-rĕd′jô)	160	43.52N	10.14E
Viborg, Den. (vē′bôr)	152	56.27N	9.22E
Vibo Valentia, Italy (vė′bȯ-vä-lĕ′n-tyä)	160	38.47N	16.06E
Vicálvaro, Spain	159a	40.25N	3.37W
Vicente López, Arg. (vē-sĕ′n-tĕ-lŏ′pĕz)	132a	34.31S	58.29W
Vicenza, Italy (vė-chĕnt′sä)	148	45.33N	11.33E
Vich, Spain (vēch)	159	41.55N	2.14E
Vichuga, Russia (vē-cho͞o′gȧ)	166	57.13N	41.58E
Vichy, Fr. (vė-shē′)	147	46.06N	3.28E
Vickersund, Nor.	152	60.00N	9.59E
Vicksburg, Mi., U.S. (vĭks′bûrg)	98	42.10N	85.30W
Vicksburg, Ms., U.S.	97	32.20N	90.50W
Viçosa, Braz. (vē-sô′sä)	129a	20.46S	42.51W
Victoria, Arg. (vēk-tô′rėä)	132	32.36S	60.09W
Victoria, Can. (vĭk-tō′rĭ-ȧ)	84	48.26N	123.23W
Victoria, Chile (vēk-tô-rėä)	132	38.15S	72.16W
Victoria, Col. (vēk-tô′rėä)	130a	5.19N	74.54W
Victoria, H.K.	241c	22.17N	114.08E
Victoria, Phil. (vėk-tȯ-ryä)	197a	15.34N	120.41E
Victoria, Tx., U.S. (vĭk-tō′rĭ-ȧ)	113	28.48N	97.00W
Victoria, Va., U.S.	115	36.57N	78.13W
Victoria, state, Austl.	203	36.46S	143.15E
Victoria, neigh., Arg.	233d	34.28S	58.31W
Victoria, l., Afr.	212	0.50S	32.50E
Victoria, r., Austl.	202	17.25S	130.50E
Victoria, Mount, mtn., Myanmar	183	21.26N	93.59E
Victoria, Mount, mtn., Pap. N. Gui.	197	9.35S	147.45E
Victoria de las Tunas, Cuba (vėk-tō′rė-ä dā läs to͞o′näs)	122	20.55N	77.05W
Victoria Falls, wtfl., Afr.	212	17.55S	25.51E
Victoria Island, i., Can.	82	70.13N	107.45W
Victoria Island, i., Nig.	244d	6.26N	3.26E
Victoria Lake, l., Can.	93	48.20N	57.40W
Victoria Land, reg., Ant.	219	75.00S	160.00E
Victoria Nile, r., Ug.	217	2.20N	31.35E
Victoria Peak, mtn., Belize (vėk-tōrĭ′ȧ)	120a	16.47N	88.40W
Victoria Peak, mtn., Can.	86	50.03N	126.06W
Victoria Peak, mtn., H.K.	241c	22.17N	114.08E
Victoria River Downs, Austl. (vĭc-tȯr′ĭȧ)	202	16.30S	131.10E
Victoria Station, pt. of i., Eng., U.K.	237b	53.29N	2.15W
Victoria Strait, strt., Can. (vĭk-tō′rĭ-ȧ)	84	69.10N	100.58W
Victoriaville, Can. (vĭk-tō′rĭ-ȧ-vĭl)	85	46.04N	71.59W
Victoria West, S. Afr. (wĕst)	212	31.25S	23.10E
Vidalia, Ga., U.S. (vĭ-dā′lĭ-ȧ)	115	32.10N	82.26W
Vidalia, La., U.S.	113	31.33N	91.28W
Vidin, Bul. (vĭ′dėn)	149	44.00N	22.53E
Vidnoye, Russia	172b	55.33N	37.41E
Vidzy, Bela. (vė′dzĭ)	162	55.23N	26.46E
Viedma, Arg. (vyād′mä)	132	40.55S	63.03W
Viedma, l., Arg.	132	49.40S	72.35W
Viejo, r., Nic. (vyā′hō)	120	12.45N	86.19W
Vienna (Wien), Aus.	142	48.13N	16.22E
Vienna, Ga., U.S. (vė-ĕn′ȧ)	114	32.03N	83.50W
Vienna, Il., U.S.	111	37.24N	88.50W
Vienna, Va., U.S.	100e	38.54N	77.16W
Vienne, Fr. (vyĕn′)	147	45.31N	4.54E
Vienne, r., Fr.	156	47.06N	0.20E
Vientiane *see* Viangchan, Laos	196	18.07N	102.33E
Vieques, P.R. (vyā′kås)	117b	18.09N	65.27W
Vieques, i., P.R. (vyā′kås)	117b	18.05N	65.28W
Vierfontein, S. Afr. (vēr′fȯn-tān)	218d	27.06S	26.45E
Vieringhausen, neigh., Ger.	236	51.11N	7.10E
Viersen, Ger. (fēr′zĕn)	157c	51.15N	6.24E
Vierwaldstätter See, l., Switz.	154	46.54N	8.36E
Vierzon, Fr. (vyâr-zôɴ′)	147	47.14N	2.04E
Viesca, Mex. (vė-ās′kä)	112	25.21N	102.47W
Viesca, Laguna de, l., Mex. (lä-ó′nä-dĕ)	112	25.30N	102.40W
Vieste, Italy (vyĕs′tå)	160	41.52N	16.10E
Vietnam, nation, Asia (vyĕt′näm′)	196	18.00N	107.00E
View Park, Ca., U.S.	232	34.00N	118.21W
Vigan, Phil. (vēgän)	196	17.36N	120.22E
Vigentino, neigh., Italy	238c	45.25N	9.11E
Vigevano, Italy (vė-jȧ-vä′nô)	160	45.18N	8.52E
Vigny, Fr. (vėn-y′ē′)	157b	49.05N	1.54E
Vigo, Spain (vē′gō)	142	42.18N	8.42W
Vihti, Fin. (vē′tĭ)	153	60.27N	24.18E
Vijayawāda, India	183	16.31N	80.37E
Viksøyri, Nor.	152	61.06N	6.35E
Vila Augusta, Braz.	234d	23.28S	46.32W
Vila Boacaya, neigh., Braz.	234d	23.29S	46.44W
Vila Caldas Xavier, Moz.	217	15.59S	34.12E
Vila de Manica, Moz. (vē′lä dā mä-nē′kȧ)	212	18.48S	32.49E
Vila de Rei, Port. (vē′lȧ dā rā′ĭ)	158	39.42N	8.03W
Vila do Conde, Port. (vē′lȧ dȯ kȯn′dĕ)	158	41.21N	8.44W
Vilafranca de Xira, Port. (fräŋ′kȧ dā shē′rȧ)	158	38.58N	8.59W
Vila Guilherme, neigh., Braz.	234d	23.30S	46.36W
Vilaine, r., Fr. (vē-lȧn′)	156	47.34N	2.15W
Vila Isabel, neigh., Braz.	234c	22.55S	43.15W
Vila Jaguára, neigh., Braz.	234d	23.31S	46.45W
Vila Madalena, neigh., Braz.	234d	23.33S	46.42W
Vila Mariana, neigh., Braz.	234d	23.35S	46.38W
Vilanculos, Moz. (vė-län-ko͞o′lȯs)	212	22.03S	35.13E
Vilāni, Lat. (vē′lȧ-nĭ)	153	56.31N	27.00E
Vila Nova de Foz Côa, Port. (nō′vȧ dā fȯz-kō′ȧ)	158	41.08N	7.11W
Vila Nova de Gaia, Port. (vē′lȧ nō′vȧ dā gä′yä)	158	41.08N	8.40W
Vila Nova de Milfontes, Port. (nō′vȧ dā mėl-fȯn′tāzh)	158	37.44N	8.48W
Vila Progresso, Braz.	234c	22.55S	43.03W
Vila Prudente, neigh., Braz.	234d	23.35S	46.33W
Vila Real, Port. (rā-äl′)	148	41.18N	7.48W
Vila Real de Santo Antonio, Port.	158	37.14N	7.25W
Vila Viçosa, Port. (vė-sō′zȧ)	158	38.47N	7.24W
Vileyka, Bela. (vė-lā′ė-kȧ)	162	54.19N	26.58E
Vilhelmina, Swe.	146	64.37N	16.30E
Viljandi, Est. (vēl′yän-dė)	166	58.24N	25.34E
Viljoenskroon, S. Afr.	218d	27.13S	26.58E
Vilkaviškis, Lith. (vėl-kȧ-vēsh′kės)	153	54.40N	23.08E
Vil′kitskogo, i., Russia (vyl-kēts-kōgō)	170	73.25N	76.00E
Villa Acuña, Mex. (vėl′yä-ko͞o′n-yä)	112	29.20N	100.56W
Villa Adelina, neigh., Arg.	233d	34.31S	58.32W
Villa Ahumada, Mex. (ä-o͞o-mä′dä)	112	30.43N	106.30W
Villa Alta, Mex. (äl′tä)(sän ēl-dȧ-fōn′sō)	119	17.20N	96.08W
Villa Angela, Arg. (vė′l-yä ȧ′n-ĸĕ-lä)	132	27.31S	60.42W
Villa Ballester, Arg. (vė′l-yä-bȧl-yĕs-tĕr)	132a	34.33S	58.33W
Villa Bella, Bol. (bĕ′l-yä)	130	10.25S	65.22W
Villablino, Spain (vėl-yä-blē′nȯ)	158	42.58N	6.18W
Villa Borghese, pt. of i., Italy	239c	41.55N	12.29E
Villa Bosch, neigh., Arg.	233d	34.36S	58.34W
Villacañas, Spain (vėl-yä-kän′yäs)	158	39.39N	3.20W
Villacarrillo, Spain (vėl-yä-kä-rēl′yȯ)	158	38.09N	3.07W
Villach, Aus. (fė′läĸ)	147	46.38N	13.50E
Villacidro, Italy (vē-lä-chē′drȯ)	160	39.28N	8.41E
Villa Ciudadela, neigh., Arg.	233d	34.38S	58.34W
Villa Clara, prov., Cuba	122	22.40N	80.10W
Villa Constitución, Arg. (kōn-stė-to͞o-syōn′)	129c	33.15S	60.19W
Villa Coronado, Mex. (kō-rō-nä′dhȯ)	112	26.45N	105.10W
Villa Cuauhtémoc, Mex. (vėl′yä-ko͞o-äȯ-tĕ′mȯk)	119	22.11N	97.50W
Villa de Allende, Mex. (vēl′yä′dā äl-yĕn′dȧ)	112	25.18N	100.01W
Villa de Alvarez, Mex. (vėl′yä-dĕ-ä′l-vä-rĕz)	118	19.17N	103.44W
Villa de Cura, Ven. (dĕ-ko͞o′rä)	131b	10.03N	67.29W
Villa de Guadalupe, Mex. (dĕ-gwä-dhä-lo͞o′pȧ)	118	23.22N	100.44W
Villa de Mayo, Arg.	132a	34.31S	58.41W
Villa Devoto, neigh., Arg.	233d	34.36S	58.31W
Villa Diamante, neigh., Arg.	233d	34.41S	58.26W
Villa Dolores, Arg. (vēl′yä dȯ-lō′rās)	132	31.50S	65.05W
Villa Domínico, neigh., Arg.	233d	34.41S	58.20W
Villa Escalante, Mex. (vėl′yä-ĕs-kä-lȧn′tĕ)	118	19.24N	101.36W
Villa Flores, Mex. (vėl′yä-flō′rās)	119	16.13N	93.17W
Villafranca, Italy (vēl-lä-fräŋ′kä)	160	45.22N	10.53E
Villafranca del Bierzo, Spain	158	42.37N	6.49W
Villafranca de los Barros, Spain	158	38.34N	6.22W
Villafranca del Panadés, Spain	159	41.20N	1.40E
Villafranche-de-Rouergue, Fr. (dē-ro͞o-ĕrg′)	156	44.21N	2.02E
Villa García, Mex. (gär-sē′ä)	118	22.07N	101.55W
Villagarcia, Spain (vēl′yä-gär-thē′ä)	158	42.38N	8.43W
Villagrán, Mex.	112	24.28N	99.30W
Villa Grove, Il., U.S. (vĭl′ȧ grōv′)	98	39.55N	88.15W
Villaguay, Arg. (vė′l-yä-gwī)	132	31.47S	58.53W
Villa Hayes, Para. (vēl′yä äyȧs)(hāz)	132	25.07S	57.31W
Villahermosa, Mex. (vēl′yä-ĕr-mō′sä)	116	17.59N	92.56W
Villa Hidalgo, Mex. (vēl′yäē-däl′gō)	118	21.39N	102.41W
Villa José L. Suárez, neigh., Arg.	233d	34.32S	58.34W
Villajoyosa, Spain (vēl′yä-hȯ-yō′sä)	159	38.30N	0.14W
Villalba, Spain	158	43.18N	7.43W
Villaldama, Mex. (vēl-yäl-dä′mä)	116	26.30N	100.26W
Villa Lopez, Mex. (vēl′yä lō′pĕz)	112	27.00N	105.02W
Villalpando, Spain (vēl-yäl-pän′dō)	158	41.54N	5.24W
Villa Lugano, neigh., Arg.	233d	34.41S	58.28W
Villa Lynch, neigh., Arg.	233d	34.36S	58.32W
Villa Madero, Arg.	233d	34.41S	58.30W
Villa María, Arg. (vė′l-yä-mä-rē′ä)	132	32.17S	63.08W
Villamatín, Spain (vēl-yä-mä-tė′n)	158	36.50N	5.38W
Villa Mercedes, Arg. (mĕr-sā′dås)	132	33.38S	65.16W
Villa Montes, Bol. (vė′l-yä-mô′n-tĕs)	130	21.13S	63.26W
Villa Morelos, Mex. (mȯ-rĕ′lomcs)	118	20.01N	101.24W
Villa Nova, Md., U.S.	229c	39.21N	76.44W
Villanova, Pa., U.S.	229b	40.02N	75.21W
Villanueva, Col. (vė′l-yä-nȯĕ′vä)	130	10.44N	73.08W
Villanueva, Hond. (vēl′yä-nwā′vä)	120	15.19N	88.02W
Villanueva, Mex. (vėl′yä-nȯĕ′vä)	118	22.25N	102.53W
Villanueva de Córdoba, Spain (vėl-yä-nwĕ′vä-dā kȯr′dȯ-bä)	158	38.18N	4.38W
Villanueva de la Serena, Spain (lä sā-rā′nä)	158	38.59N	5.56W
Villa Obregón, Mex. (vē′l-yä-ô-brĕ-gô′n)	119a	19.21N	99.11W
Villa Ocampo, Mex. (ȯ-käm′pō)	112	26.26N	105.30W
Villa Pedro Montoya, Mex. (vėl′yä-pĕ′drȯ-mȯn-tô′yȧ)	118	21.38N	99.51W
Villard-Bonnot, Fr. (vēl-yär′bȯn-nȯ′)	157	45.15N	5.53E
Villa Real, neigh., Arg.	233d	34.37S	58.31W
Villarreal, Spain (vėl-yär-rĕ-äl)	159	39.55N	0.07W
Villarrica, Para. (vēl-yä-rē′kä)	132	25.55S	56.23W
Villarrobledo, Spain (vēl-yär-rȯ-blā′dhō)	148	39.15N	2.37W
Villa Sáenz Peña, neigh., Arg.	233d	34.36S	58.31W
Villa San Andrés, neigh., Arg.	233d	34.33S	58.32W
Villa Santos Lugares, neigh., Arg.	233d	34.36S	58.32W
Villa Unión, Mex. (vėl′yä-o͞o-nyōn′)	118	23.10N	106.14W
Villaverde, neigh., Spain	238b	40.21N	3.42W
Villavicencio, Col. (vė′l-yä-vē-sĕ′n-syō)	130	4.09N	73.38W
Villaviciosa de Odón, Spain	159a	40.22N	3.38W
Villavieja, Col. (vė′l-yä-vē-ĕ′ĸȧ)	130a	3.13N	75.13W
Villazón, Bol. (vė′l-yä-zô′n)	130	22.02S	65.42W
Villecresnes, Fr.	237c	48.43N	2.32E
Ville-d'Avray, Fr.	237c	48.50N	2.11E
Villefranche, Fr.	147	45.59N	4.43E
Villejuif, Fr. (vēl′zhüst′)	157b	48.48N	2.22E
Ville-Maríe, Can.	85	47.18N	79.22W
Villemomble, Fr.	237c	48.53N	2.31E
Villena, Spain (vē-lyā′nȧ)	148	38.37N	0.52W
Villenbon-sur-Yvette, Fr.	237c	48.42N	2.15E
Villeneuve, Can. (vēl′nûv′)	83g	53.40N	113.49W
Villeneuve-le-Roi, Fr.	237c	48.44N	2.25E
Villeneuve-Saint Georges, Fr. (săɴ-zhôrzh′)	157b	48.43N	2.27E
Villeneuve-sur-Lot, Fr. (sür-lō′)	156	44.25N	0.41E
Villeparisis, Fr.	237c	48.56N	2.37E
Ville Platte, La., U.S. (vēl plȧt′)	113	30.41N	92.17W
Villers Cotterêts, Fr. (vē-âr′kȯ-trā′)	157b	49.15N	3.05E
Villers-sur-Marne, Fr.	237c	48.50N	2.33E
Villerupt, Fr. (vēl′rüp′)	157	49.28N	6.16E
Ville-Saint Georges, Can. (vĭl-sĕɴ-zhôrzh′)	91	46.07N	70.40W
Villeta, Col. (vē′l-yĕ′tȧ)	130a	5.02N	74.29W
Villeurbanne, Fr. (vēl-ûr-bän′)	147	45.43N	4.55E
Villiers, S. Afr. (vĭl′ĭ-ẽrs)	218d	27.03S	28.38E
Villiers-le-Bâcle, Fr.	237c	48.44N	2.08E
Villiers-le-Bel, Fr.	237c	49.00N	2.23E
Villingen-Schwenningen, Ger.	154	48.04N	8.33E
Villisca, Ia., U.S. (vĭ′lĭs′kȧ)	103	40.56N	94.56W
Villupuram, India	187	11.59N	79.33E
Vilnius, Lith. (vĭl′nė-ȯs)	164	54.40N	25.26E
Vilppula, Fin. (vĭl′pŭ-lȧ)	153	62.01N	24.24E
Vil′shanka, Ukr.	163	48.14N	30.52E
Vil′shany, Ukr.	163	50.02N	35.54E
Vilvoorde, Bel.	145a	50.56N	4.25E
Vilyuy, r., Russia (vēl′yĭ)	165	63.00N	121.00E
Vilyuysk, Russia (vė-lyo͞o′ĭsk′)	165	63.41N	121.47E
Vimmerby, Swe. (vĭm′ĕr-bü)	152	57.41N	15.51E
Vimperk, Czech Rep. (vĭm-pĕrk′)	154	49.04N	13.41E
Viña del Mar, Chile (vē′nyä dĕl mär′)	132	33.00S	71.33W
Vinalhaven, Me., U.S. (vī-năl-hā′vĕn)	92	44.03N	68.49W
Vinaroz, Spain (vē-nä′rōth)	159	40.29N	0.27E
Vincennes, Fr. (văɴ-sĕn′)	157b	48.51N	2.27E
Vincennes, In., U.S. (vĭn-zĕnz′)	97	38.40N	87.30W
Vincennes, Château de, hist., Fr.	237c	48.51N	2.26E
Vincent, Al., U.S. (vĭn′sĕnt)	114	33.21N	86.25W
Vindelälven, r., Swe.	146	65.02N	18.30E
Vindeln, Swe. (vĭn′dĕln)	146	64.10N	19.52E
Vindhya Range, mts., India (vĭnd′yä)	183	22.30N	75.50E
Vineland, N.J., U.S. (vīn′lănd)	99	39.30N	75.00W
Vinh, Viet. (vėn′y′)	196	18.38N	105.42E
Vinhais, Port. (vėn-yä′ēzh)	158	41.51N	7.00W
Vinings, Ga., U.S. (vī′nĭngz)	100c	33.52N	84.28W
Vinita, Ok., U.S. (vĭ-nē′tȧ)	111	36.38N	95.09W
Vinkovci, Cro. (vēn′kȯv-tsė)	161	45.17N	18.47E
Vinnytsya, Ukr.	164	49.13N	28.31E
Vinnytsya, prov., Ukr.	163	48.45N	28.01E
Vinogradovo, Russia (vĭ-nȯ-grä′do-vô)	172b	55.25N	38.33E
Vinson Massif, mtn., Ant.	219	77.40S	87.00W
Vinton, Ia., U.S. (vĭn′tŭn)	103	42.08N	92.01W
Vinton, La., U.S.	113	30.12N	93.35W
Violet, La., U.S. (vī′ȯ-lĕt)	100d	29.54N	89.54W
Virac, Phil. (vė-räk′)	193	13.38N	124.20E
Virbalis, Lith. (vėr′bȧ-lės)	153	54.38N	22.55E
Virden, Can. (vûr′dĕn)	84	49.51N	101.55W
Virden, Il., U.S.	111	39.28N	89.46W
Vírgen del San Cristóbal, rel., Chile	234b	33.26S	70.39W
Virgin, r., U.S.	109	36.51N	113.50W
Virginia, S. Afr.	218d	28.07S	26.54E
Virginia, Mn., U.S. (vẽr-jĭn′yȧ)	97	47.32N	92.36W
Virginia, state, U.S.	97	37.00N	80.45W
Virginia Beach, Va., U.S.	99	36.50N	75.58W
Virginia City, Nv., U.S.	108	39.18N	119.40W
Virginia Hills, Va., U.S.	229d	38.47N	77.06W
Virginia Water, Eng., U.K.	235	51.24N	0.34W
Virgin Islands, is., N.A. (vûr′jĭn)	117	18.15N	64.00W
Viroflay, Fr.	237c	48.48N	2.10E
Víron, Grc.	239d	37.57N	23.45E
Viroqua, Wi., U.S. (vĭ-rō′kwȧ)	103	43.33N	90.54W
Virovitica, Cro. (vė-rȯ-vē′tė-tsȧ)	161	45.50N	17.24E
Virpazar, Yugo. (vėr′pä-zär′)	161	42.16N	19.06E
Virrat, Fin. (vĭr′ät)	153	62.15N	23.45E
Virserum, Swe. (vĭr′sĕ-rȯm)	152	57.22N	15.35E
Vis, Cro. (vės)	160	43.03N	16.11E
Vis, i., Yugo.	149	43.00N	16.10E
Visalia, Ca., U.S. (vĭ-sā′lĭ-ȧ)	108	36.20N	119.18W
Visby, Swe. (vĭs′bü)	142	57.39N	18.19E
Viscount Melville Sound, strt., Can.	82	74.00N	110.00W
Višegrad, Bos. (vē′shĕ-gräd)	161	43.48N	19.17E
Vishākhapatnam, India	183	17.48N	83.21E
Vishera, r., Russia (vĭ′shĕ-rȧ)	172a	60.40N	58.46E
Vishnyakovo, Russia	172b	55.44N	38.10E
Vishoek, S. Afr.	212a	34.13S	18.26E
Visim, Russia (vē′sĭm)	172a	57.38N	59.32E
Viskan, r., Swe.	152	57.20N	12.25E

ăt; finăl; rāte; senȧte; ärm; ȧsk; sofȧ; fâre; ch-choose; dh-as th in other; bē; ėvent; bĕt; recĕnt; cratẽr; g-gō; gh-guttural g; bĭt; ĭ-short neutral; rīde; ĸ-guttural k as ch in German ich;

PLACE (Pronunciation)	PAGE	Lat. °′	Long. °′
Viški, Lat. (vēs′kĭ)	153	56.02N	26.47E
Visoko, Bos. (vē′sô-kô)	161	43.59N	18.10E
Vistula *see* Wisła, r., Pol.	142	52.30N	20.00E
Vitarte, Peru	233c	12.02S	76.54W
Vitebsk, Bela. (vē′tyĕpsk)	164	55.12N	30.16E
Vitebsk, prov., Bela.	162	55.05N	29.18E
Viterbo, Italy (vē-tĕr′bō)	148	42.24N	12.08E
Viti Levu, i., Fiji	198g	18.00S	178.00E
Vitim, Russia (vē′têm)	165	59.22N	112.43E
Vitim, r., Russia (vē′têm)	165	54.00N	115.00E
Vitino, Russia (vē′tĭ-nô)	172c	59.40N	29.51E
Vitória, Braz. (vê-tō′rê-ä)	131	20.09S	40.17W
Vitoria, Spain (vē-tô-ryä)	148	42.43N	2.43W
Vitória de Conquista, Braz. (vê-tō′rê-ä-dä-kōn-kwē′s-tä)	131	14.51S	40.44W
Vitry-le-François, Fr. (vē-trē′lē-fräN-swä′)	156	48.44N	4.34E
Vitry-sur-Seine, Fr.	237c	48.48N	2.24E
Vittorio, Italy (vē-tô′rē-ô)	160	45.59N	12.17E
Vivero, Spain (vê-vā′rō)	158	43.39N	7.37W
Vivian, La., U.S. (vĭv′ĭ-*ă*n)	113	32.51N	93.59W
Vizianagaram, India	183	18.10N	83.29E
Vlaardingen, Neth. (vlär′dĭng-*ĕ*n)	151	51.54N	4.20E
Vladikavkaz, Russia	167	43.05N	44.35E
Vladimir, Russia (vlá-dyē′mēr)	164	56.08N	40.24E
Vladimir, prov., Russia (vlä-dyē′mēr)	162	56.08N	39.53E
Vladimiro-Aleksandrovskoye, Russia	194	42.50N	133.00E
Vladivostok, Russia (vlá-dê-vôs-tŏk′)	165	43.06N	131.47E
Vladykino, neigh., Russia	239b	55.52N	37.36E
Vlasenica, Bos. (vlä′sĕ-nēt′sá)	161	44.11N	18.58E
Vlasotince, Yugo. (vlä′sô-tēn-tsĕ)	161	42.58N	22.08E
Vlieland, i., Neth. (vlē′länt)	151	53.19N	4.55E
Vlissingen, Neth. (vlĭs′sĭng-*ĕ*n)	151	51.30N	3.34E
Vlorë, Alb.	149	40.27N	19.30E
Vltava, r., Czech Rep.	154	49.24N	14.18E
Vodl, l., Russia (vôd″l)	166	62.20N	37.20E
Voerde, Ger.	157c	51.35N	6.41E
Vogelheim, neigh., Ger.	236	51.29N	6.59E
Voghera, Italy (vô-gā′rä)	160	44.58N	9.02E
Vohwinkel, neigh., Ger.	236	51.14N	7.09E
Voight, r., Wa., U.S.	106a	47.03N	122.08W
Voinjama, Lib.	214	8.25N	9.45W
Voiron, Fr. (vwá-rôN′)	157	45.23N	5.48E
Voisin, Lac, l., Can. (vwŏ′-zĭn)	88	54.13N	107.15W
Volchansk, Ukr. (vôl-chänsk′)	167	50.18N	36.56E
Volchonka-Zil, neigh., Russia	239b	55.40N	37.37E
Volga, r., Russia (vôl′gä)	164	47.30N	46.20E
Volga, Mouths of the, mth.	167	46.00N	49.10E
Volgograd, Russia (vŏl-gō-grä′t)	164	48.40N	42.20E
Volgogradskoye, res., Russia (vôl-gô-grad′skô-yĕ)	164	51.10N	45.10E
Volkhov, Russia (vôl′kôf)	153	59.54N	32.21E
Volkhov, r., Russia	166	58.45N	31.40E
Volkovysk, Bela. (vôl-kô-vêsk′)	155	53.11N	24.29E
Vollme, Ger.	236	51.10N	7.36E
Volmarstein, Ger.	236	51.22N	7.23E
Volmerswerth, neigh., Ger.	236	51.11N	6.46E
Volodarskiy, Russia (vô-lô-där′skĭ)	172c	59.49N	30.06E
Volodymyr-Volyns′kyy, Ukr.	155	50.50N	24.20E
Vologda, Russia (vô′lôg-dá)	164	59.12N	39.52E
Vologda, prov., Russia	162	59.00N	37.26E
Volokolamsk, Russia (vô-lô-kôlámsk)	162	56.02N	35.58E
Volokonovka, Russia (vô-lô-kô′nôf-ká)	163	50.28N	37.52E
Volozhin, Bela. (vô′lô-shēn)	162	54.04N	26.38E
Vol′sk, Russia (vôl′sk)	167	52.02N	47.23E
Volta, r., Ghana	214	6.05N	0.30E
Volta, Lake, res., Ghana (vôl′tá)	210	7.10N	0.30W
Volta Blanche (White Volta), r., Afr.	214	11.30N	0.40W
Volta Noire *see* Black Volta, r., Afr.	210	11.30N	4.00W
Volta Redonda, Braz. (vōl′tä-rā-dōn′dä)	131	22.32S	44.05W
Volterra, Italy (vôl-tĕr′rä)	160	43.22N	10.51E
Voltri, Italy (vōl′trē)	160	44.25N	8.45E
Volturno, r., Italy (vôl-tōōr′nô)	160	41.12N	14.20E
Vólvi, Límni, l., Grc.	161	40.41N	23.23E
Volzhskoye, l., Russia (vôl′sh-skô-yĕ)	162	56.43N	36.18E
Von Ormy, Tx., U.S. (vŏn ôr′mē)	107d	29.18N	98.36W
Võõpsu, Est. (vōōp′sô)	153	58.06N	27.30E
Voorburg, Neth.	145a	52.04N	4.21E
Voortrekkerhoogte, S. Afr.	213b	25.48S	28.10E
Vop′, r., Russia (vôp)	162	55.20N	32.55E
Vopnafjördur, Ice.	146	65.43N	14.58W
Vorarlberg, prov., Aus.	154	47.20N	9.55E
Vordingborg, Den. (vôr′dĭng-bôr)	152	55.10N	11.55E
Vorhalle, neigh., Ger.	236	51.23N	7.28E
Voríai Sporádhes, is., Grc.	161	38.55N	24.05E
Vorkuta, Russia (vôr-kōō′tá)	164	67.28N	63.40E
Vormholz, Ger.	236	51.24N	7.18E
Vormsi, i., Est. (vôrm′sĭ)	153	59.06N	23.05E
Vórois Evvoïkós Kólpos, b., Grc.	161	38.48N	23.02E
Vorona, r., Russia (vô-rô′na)	167	51.50N	42.00E
Voronezh, Russia (vô-rô′nyĕzh)	164	51.39N	39.11E
Voronezh, prov., Russia	163	51.10N	39.13E
Voronezh, r., Russia	167	52.17N	39.32E
Voronovo, Bela. (vô′rô-nô-vô)	155	54.07N	25.16E
Vorontsovka, Russia (vô-rônt′sôv-ká)	172a	59.40N	60.14E
Voron′ya, r., Russia (vô-rônyá)	166	68.20N	35.20E
Võrts-Järv, l., Est. (vôrts yärv)	153	58.15N	26.12E
Võru, Est. (vô′rû)	166	57.50N	26.58E
Vorya, r., Russia (vôr′yá)	172b	55.55N	38.15E
Vosges, mts., Fr. (vōzh)	147	48.09N	6.57E
Voskresensk, Russia (vôs-krĕ-sĕnsk′)	172b	55.20N	38.42E
Voss, Nor. (vôs)	146	60.40N	6.24E
Vostryakovo, Russia	172b	55.23N	37.49E
Votkinsk, Russia (vôt-kēnsk′)	166	57.00N	54.00E
Votkinskoye Vodokhranilishche, res., Russia	166	57.30N	55.00E

PLACE (Pronunciation)	PAGE	Lat. °′	Long. °′
Vouga, r., Port. (vō′gá)	158	40.43N	7.51W
Vouziers, Fr. (vōō-zyā′)	156	49.25N	4.40E
Voxnan, r., Swe.	152	61.30N	15.24E
Voyageurs National Park, Mn., U.S.	103	48.30N	92.40W
Vozhe, l., Russia (vôzh′yĕ)	166	60.40N	39.00E
Voznesens′k, Ukr.	167	47.34N	31.22E
Vrangelya (Wrangel), i., Russia	164	71.25N	178.30W
Vranje, Yugo. (vrän′yĕ)	161	42.33N	21.55E
Vratsa, Bul. (vrät′tsá)	149	43.12N	23.31E
Vrbas, Yugo. (v′r′bäs)	161	45.34N	19.43E
Vrbas, r., Yugo.	161	44.25N	17.17E
Vrchlabí, Czech Rep. (v′r′chlä-bê)	154	50.32N	15.51E
Vrede, S. Afr. (vrĭ′dĕ)(vrēd)	218d	27.25S	29.11E
Vredefort, S. Afr. (vrĭ′dĕ-fôrt)(vrēd′fôrt)	218d	27.00S	27.21E
Vreeswijk, Neth.	145a	52.00N	5.06E
Vršac, Yugo. (v′r′shàts)	149	45.08N	21.18E
Vrutky, Slvk. (vrōōt′kê)	155	49.09N	18.55E
Vryburg, S. Afr. (vrī′bûrg)	212	26.55S	24.45E
Vryheid, S. Afr. (vrī′hīt)	212	27.43S	30.58E
Vsetín, Czech Rep. (fsĕt′yēn)	155	49.21N	18.01E
Vsevolozhskiy, Russia (vsyĕ′vôlô′zh-skēê)	172c	60.01N	30.41E
Vuelta Abajo, reg., Cuba (vwĕl′tä ä-bä′hō)	122	22.20N	83.45W
Vught, Neth.	145a	51.38N	5.18E
Vukovar, Cro. (vô′kô-vär)	161	45.20N	19.00E
Vulcan, Mi., U.S. (vŭl′k*ă*n)	98	45.45N	87.50W
Vulcano, i., Italy (vōōl-kä′nô)	160	38.23N	15.00E
Vûlchedrŭma, Bul.	161	43.43N	23.29E
Vyartsilya, Russia (vyár-tsē′lyá)	153	62.10N	30.40E
Vyatka, r., Russia (vyát′ká)	166	59.20N	51.25E
Vyazemskiy, Russia (vyá-zĕm′skĭ)	194	47.29N	134.39E
Vyaz′ma, Russia (vyáz′má)	166	55.12N	34.17E
Vyazniki, Russia (vyáz′nê-kê)	166	56.10N	42.10E
Vyborg, Russia (vwē′bôrk)	164	60.43N	28.46E
Vychegda, r., Russia (vē′chĕg-d*ă*)	166	61.40N	48.00E
Vylkove, Ukr.	167	45.24N	29.36E
Vym, r., Russia (vwĕm)	166	63.15N	51.20E
Vyritsa, Russia (vē′rĭ-tsá)	172c	59.24N	30.20E
Vyshnevolotskoye, l., Russia (vŭy′sh-ŋĕ′vôlôt′s-kô′yĕ)	162	57.30N	34.27E
Vyshniy Volochëk, Russia (vêsh′nyĭ vôl-ô-chĕk′)	164	57.34N	34.35E
Vyškov, Czech Rep. (vêsh′kôf)	154	49.17N	16.58E
Vysoké Mýto, Czech Rep. (vû′sô-kä mû′tô)	154	49.58N	16.07E
Vysokovsk, Russia (vĭ-sô′kôfsk)	162	56.16N	36.32E
Vytegra, Russia (vû′tĕg-rá)	164	61.00N	36.20E

W

PLACE (Pronunciation)	PAGE	Lat. °′	Long. °′
W, Parcs Nationaux du, rec., Niger	215	12.20N	2.40E
Waal, r., Neth. (väl)	151	51.46N	5.00E
Waalwijk, Neth.	145a	51.41N	5.05E
Wabamun, Grc.	149	39.23N	22.56E
Wabamuno, Can. (wŏ′bă-mŭn)	87	53.33N	114.28W
Wabasca, Can. (wŏ-bás′kă)	87	56.00N	113.53W
Wabash, In., U.S. (wô′băsh)	98	40.45N	85.50W
Wabash, r., U.S.	97	38.00N	88.00W
Wabasha, Mn., U.S. (wä′b*ă*-shô)	103	44.24N	92.04W
Wabe Gestro, r., Eth.	211	6.25N	41.21E
Wabowden, Can. (wä-bō′d′n)	89	54.55N	98.38W
Wąbrzeźno, Pol. (vôŋ-bzĕzh′nô)	155	53.17N	18.59E
Wabu Hu, l., China (wä-bōō hōō)	190	32.25N	116.35E
W. A. C. Bennett Dam, dam, Can.	87	56.01N	122.10W
Waccamaw, r., S.C., U.S. (wăk′*ă*-mô)	115	33.47N	78.55W
Waccasassa Bay, b., Fl., U.S. (wă-k*ă*-să′s*ă*)	114	29.02N	83.10W
Wachow, Ger. (vä′kōv)	145b	53.32N	12.46E
Waco, Tx., U.S. (wā′kō)	96	31.35N	97.06W
Waconda Lake, res., Ks., U.S.	110	39.45N	98.15W
Wadayama, Japan (wä′dä′yä-mä)	195	35.19N	134.49E
Waddenzee, sea, Neth.	151	53.00N	4.50E
Waddington, Mount, mtn., Can. (wŏd′dĭng-t*ŭ*n)	84	51.23N	125.15W
Wadena, Can.	88	51.57N	103.50W
Wadena, Mn., U.S. (wŏ-dē′n*ă*)	102	46.26N	95.09W
Wadesboro, N.C., U.S. (wādz′bŭr-ô)	115	34.57N	80.05W
Wadeville, S. Afr.	244b	26.16S	28.11E
Wadley, Ga., U.S. (wŭd′lê)	115	32.54N	82.25W
Wad Madani, Sudan (wäd mē-dä′nē)	211	14.27N	33.31E
Wadowice, Pol. (vá-dô′vēt-sĕ)	155	49.53N	19.31E
Wadsworth, Oh., U.S. (wŏdz′wûrth)	101d	41.01N	81.44W
Wager Bay, b., Can. (wā′jĕr)	85	65.48N	88.19W
Wagga Wagga, Austl. (wôg′*ă* wôg′*ă*)	203	35.10S	147.30E
Wagoner, Ok., U.S. (wăg′*ŭ*n-ĕr)	111	35.58N	95.22W
Wagon Mound, N.M., U.S. (wăg′*ŭ*n mound)	110	35.59N	104.45W
Wągrowiec, Pol. (vôŋ-grô′vyĕts)	155	52.47N	17.14E
Waha, Libya	184	28.16N	19.54E
Wahiawa, Hi., U.S.	96d	21.30N	158.03W
Wahoo, Ne., U.S. (wä-hōō′)	102	41.14N	96.39W
Wahpeton, N.D., U.S. (wô′pê-t*ŭ*n)	102	46.17N	96.38W
Währing, neigh., Aus.	239e	48.14N	16.21E
Wahroonga, Austl.	243a	33.43S	150.07E
Waialua, Hi., U.S. (wä′ê-ä-lōō′ä)	94a	21.33N	158.08W

PLACE (Pronunciation)	PAGE	Lat. °′	Long. °′
Waianae, Hi., U.S. (wä′ê-á-nä′ä)	94a	21.25N	158.11W
Waidhofen, Aus. (vīd′hôf-ĕn)	154	47.58N	14.46E
Waidmannslust, neigh., Ger.	238a	52.36N	13.20E
Waigeo, Pulau, i., Indon. (wä-ê-gä′ô)	197	0.07N	131.00E
Waikato, r., N.Z. (wä′ê-kä′to)	203a	38.10S	175.35E
Waikerie, Austl. (wā′kĕr-ē)	204	34.15S	140.00E
Wailuku, Hi., U.S. (wä′ê-lōō′kōō)	96c	20.55N	156.30W
Waimanalo, Hi., U.S. (wä-ê-mä′nä-lo)	94a	21.19N	157.53W
Waimea, Hi., U.S. (wä-ê-mā′ä)	94a	21.56N	159.38W
Wainganga, r., India (wä-ēn-g*ŭ*ŋ′gä)	183	20.30N	80.15E
Waingapu, Indon.	196	9.32S	120.00E
Wainwright, Can.	84	52.49N	110.52W
Wainwright, Ak., U.S. (wān-rīt)	95	74.40N	159.00W
Waipahu, Hi., U.S. (wä′ê-pä′hōō)	96d	21.20N	158.02W
Waiska, r., Mi., U.S. (w*ă*-ĭz-k*ă*)	107k	46.20N	84.38W
Waitara, Austl.	243a	33.43S	150.06E
Waitsburg, Wa., U.S. (wāts′bûrg)	104	46.17N	118.08W
Wajima, Japan (wä′jê-má)	195	37.23N	136.56E
Wajir, Kenya	217	1.45N	40.04E
Wakami, r., Can.	90	47.43N	82.22W
Wakasa-Wan, b., Japan (wä′kä-sä wän)	194	35.43N	135.39E
Wakatipu, l., N.Z. (wä-kä-tē′pōō)	203a	45.04S	168.30E
Wakayama, Japan (wä-kä′yä-mä)	189	34.14N	135.11E
Wake, i., Oc. (wāk)	3	19.25N	167.00E
Wa Keeney, Ks., U.S. (wô-kē′nê)	110	39.01N	99.53W
Wakefield, Can. (wāk-fēld)	83c	45.39N	75.55W
Wakefield, Eng., U.K.	150	53.41N	1.25W
Wakefield, Ma., U.S.	93a	42.31N	71.05W
Wakefield, Mi., U.S.	103	46.28N	89.55W
Wakefield, Ne., U.S.	102	42.15N	96.52W
Wakefield, R.I., U.S.	100b	41.26N	71.30W
Wake Forest, N.C., U.S. (wāk fŏr′ĕst)	115	35.58N	78.31W
Waki, Japan (wä′kê)	195	34.05N	134.10E
Wakkanai, Japan (wä′kä-nä′ê)	189	45.19N	141.43E
Wakkerstroom, S. Afr. (vák′ĕr-strōm)(wăk′ĕr-strōōm)	212	27.19S	30.04E
Wakonassin, r., Can.	90	46.35N	82.10W
Waku Kundo, Ang.	212	11.25S	15.07E
Wałbrzych, Pol. (väl′bzhûk)	154	50.46N	16.16E
Walcott, Lake, res., Id., U.S.	105	42.40N	113.23W
Wałcz, Pol. (välch)	154	53.11N	16.30E
Waldbauer, neigh., Ger.	236	51.18N	7.28E
Waldoboro, Me., U.S. (wôl′dô-bŭr-ô)	92	44.06N	69.22W
Waldo Lake, l., Or., U.S. (wôl′dō)	104	43.46N	122.10W
Waldorf, Md., U.S. (wăl′dôrf)	100e	38.37N	76.57W
Waldron, Mo., U.S.	107f	39.14N	94.47W
Waldron, i., Wa., U.S.	106d	48.42N	123.02W
Wales, Ak., U.S. (wālz)	95	65.35N	168.14W
Wales, , U.K.	142	52.12N	3.40W
Walewale, Ghana	214	10.21N	0.48W
Walgett, Austl. (wôl′gĕt)	203	30.00S	148.10E
Walhalla, S.C., U.S. (wŭl-hăl′*ă*)	114	34.45N	83.04W
Walikale, Zaire	217	1.25S	28.03E
Walkden, Eng., U.K.	144a	53.32N	2.24W
Walker, Mn., U.S. (wôk′ĕr)	103	47.06N	94.37W
Walker, r., Nv., U.S.	108	39.07N	119.10W
Walker, Mount, mtn., Wa., U.S.	106a	47.47N	122.54W
Walker Lake, l., Can.	89	54.42N	96.57W
Walker Lake, l., Nv., U.S.	108	38.46N	118.30W
Walker River Indian Reservation, I.R., Nv., U.S.	108	39.06N	118.20W
Walkerville, Mt., U.S. (wôk′ĕr-vĭl)	105	46.20N	112.32W
Wallace, Id., U.S. (wŏl′ås)	104	47.27N	115.55W
Wallaceburg, Can.	90	42.39N	82.25W
Wallach, Ger.	236	51.35N	6.34E
Wallacia, Austl.	201b	33.52S	150.40E
Wallaroo, Austl. (wŏl-*ă*-rōō)	202	33.52S	137.45E
Wallasey, Eng., U.K. (wŏl′*ă*-sê)	144a	53.25N	3.03W
Walla Walla, Wa., U.S. (wŏl′á wŏl′á)	96	46.03N	118.20W
Walled Lake, Mi., U.S. (wôl′d lāk)	101b	42.32N	83.29W
Wallel, Tulu, mtn., Eth.	211	9.00N	34.52E
Wallgrove, Austl.	243a	33.47S	150.51E
Wallingford, Eng., U.K. (wŏl′ĭng-fērd)	144b	51.34N	1.08W
Wallingford, Pa., U.S.	229b	39.54N	75.22W
Wallingford, Vt., U.S.	99	43.30N	72.55W
Wallington, N.J., U.S.	228	40.51N	74.07W
Wallington, neigh., Eng., U.K.	235	51.21N	0.09W
Wallis and Futuna Islands, dep., Oc.	225	13.00S	176.10E
Wallisville, Tx., U.S. (wŏl′ĭs-vĭl)	113a	29.50N	94.44W
Wallowa, Or., U.S. (wôl′ô-w*ă*)	104	45.34N	117.32W
Wallowa, r., Or., U.S.	104	45.28N	117.28W
Wallowa Mountains, mts., Or., U.S.	104	45.10N	117.22W
Wallula, Wa., U.S.	104	46.08N	118.55W
Walmersley, Eng., U.K.	237b	53.37N	2.18W
Walnut, Ca., U.S. (wôl′nŭt)	107a	34.00N	117.51W
Walnut, r., Ks., U.S.	111	37.28N	97.06W
Walnut Canyon National Mon, rec., Az., U.S.	109	35.10N	111.30W
Walnut Creek, Ca., U.S.	106b	37.54N	122.04W
Walnut Creek, r., Tx., U.S.	107c	32.37N	97.03W
Walnut Ridge, Ar., U.S. (rĭj)	111	36.04N	90.56W
Walpole, Ma., U.S. (wôl′pōl)	93a	42.09N	71.15W
Walpole, N.H., U.S.	99	43.05N	72.25W
Walsall, Eng., U.K. (wôl-sôl)	150	52.35N	1.58W
Walsenburg, Co., U.S. (wôl′sĕn-bûrg)	110	37.38N	104.46W
Walsum, Ger.	157c	51.32N	6.41E
Walter F. George Reservoir, res., U.S.	114	32.00N	85.00W
Walter Reed Army Medical Center, pt. of i., D.C., U.S.	229d	38.58N	77.02W
Walters, Ok., U.S. (wôl′tĕrz)	110	34.21N	98.19W
Waltersdorf, Ger.	238a	52.22N	13.35E
Waltham, Ma., U.S. (wôl′th*ă*m)	93a	42.22N	71.14W
Waltham Forest, neigh., Eng., U.K.	235	51.35N	0.01W
Walthamstow, Eng., U.K. (wôl′t*ă*m-stō)	144b	51.34N	0.01W
Walton, Eng., U.K.	235	51.24N	0.25W

ng-sing; ŋ-baŋk; N-nasalized n; nŏd; c*ŏ*mmit; ōld; ôbey; ôrder; oi-boil; fōōd; ô-as oo in foot; ou-out; s-soft; sh-dish; th-thin; pūre; ûnite; ûrn; stŭd; circ*ŭ*s; ü-as in French tu; ′-indeterminate vowel.

364 Walton–Weleetka

PLACE (Pronunciation)	PAGE	Lat. °′	Long. °′
Walton, N.Y., U.S.	99	42.10N	75.05W
Walton-le-Dale, Eng., U.K. (lē-dāl')	144a	53.44N	2.40W
Walton on the Hill, Eng., U.K.	235	51.17N	0.15W
Waltrop, Ger.	236	51.37N	7.23E
Walt Whitman Homes, N.J., U.S.	229b	39.52N	75.11W
Walvis Bay, Nmb. (wôl'vĭs)	212	22.50S	14.30E
Walworth, Wi., U.S. (wôl'wŭrth)	103	42.33N	88.39W
Walze, Ger.	236	51.16N	7.31E
Wama, Ang.	216	12.14S	15.33E
Wamba, r., Zaire	212	7.00S	18.00E
Wambel, neigh., Ger.	236	51.32N	7.32E
Wamego, Ks., U.S. (wŏ-mē'gō)	111	39.13N	96.17W
Wami, r., Tan. (wä'mē)	213	6.31S	37.17E
Wanapitei Lake, l., Can.	91	46.45N	80.45W
Wanaque, N.J., U.S. (wŏn'ȧ-kū)	100a	41.03N	74.16W
Wanaque Reservoir, res., N.J., U.S.	100a	41.06N	74.20W
Wanda Shan, mts., China (wän-dä shän)	189	45.54N	131.45E
Wandhofen, Ger.	236	51.26N	7.33E
Wandoan, Austl.	204	26.09S	149.51E
Wandsbek, Ger. (vänds'bĕk)	145c	53.34N	10.07E
Wandsworth, Eng., U.K. (wôndz'wûrth)	144b	51.26N	0.12W
Wanganui, N.Z. (wôŋ'gȧ-nōō'ē)	203a	39.53N	175.01E
Wangaratta, Austl. (wŏŋ'gȧ-răt'ȧ)	204	36.23N	146.18E
Wangeroog, i., Ger. (vän'gĕ-rōg)	154	53.49N	7.57E
Wangqingtuo, China (wäŋ-chyĭŋ-twô)	190	39.14N	116.56E
Wangsi, China (wäŋ-sē)	190	37.59N	116.57E
Wangsim-ni, neigh., S. Kor.	241b	37.36N	127.03E
Wanheimerort, neigh., Ger.	236	51.24N	6.46E
Wanne-Eickel, Ger.	236	51.32N	7.09E
Wannsee, neigh., Ger.	238a	52.25N	13.09E
Wansdorf, Ger.	238a	52.38N	13.05E
Wanstead, neigh., Eng., U.K.	235	51.34N	0.02E
Wantage, Eng., U.K. (wŏn'tȧj)	144b	51.33N	1.26W
Wantagh, N.Y., U.S.	100a	40.41N	73.30W
Wantirna, Austl.	243b	37.51S	145.14E
Wantirna South, Austl.	243b	37.52S	145.14E
Wanxian, China (wän-shyĕn)	188	30.48N	108.22E
Wanxian, China (wän shyĕn)	190	38.51N	115.10E
Wanzai, China (wän-dzī)	193	28.05N	114.25E
Wanzhi, China (wän-jr)	190	31.11N	118.31E
Wapakoneta, Oh., U.S. (wä'pȧ-kô-nĕt'ȧ)	98	40.35N	84.10W
Wapawekka Hills, hills, Can. (wŏ'pă-wē'kă-hĭlz)	88	54.45N	104.20W
Wapawekka Lake, l., Can.	88	54.55N	104.40W
Wapello, Ia., U.S. (wŏ-pĕl'ō)	103	41.10N	91.11W
Wappapello Reservoir, res., Mo., U.S. (wă'pȧ-pĕl-lō)	97	37.07N	90.10W
Wappingers Falls, N.Y., U.S. (wŏp'ĭn-jẽrz)	99	41.35N	73.55W
Wapsipinicon, r., Ia., U.S. (wŏp'sĭ-pĭn'ĭ-kŏn)	103	42.16N	91.35W
Warabi, Japan (wä'rä-bē)	195a	35.50N	139.41E
Warangal, India (wŭ'răŋ-gȧl)	183	18.03N	79.45E
Warburton, The, r., Austl. (wŏr'bûr-tŭn)	202	27.30S	138.45E
Wardān, Wādī, r., Egypt	181a	29.22N	33.00E
Ward Cove, Ak., U.S.	86	55.24N	131.43W
Warden, S. Afr. (wôr'dĕn)	218d	27.52N	28.59E
Wardha, India (wŭr'dä)	183	20.46N	78.42E
Wardle, Eng., U.K.	237b	53.39N	2.08W
War Eagle, W.V., U.S. (wôr ē'g'l)	98	37.30N	81.50W
Waren, Ger. (vä'rĕn)	154	53.32N	12.43E
Warendorf, Ger. (vä'rĕn-dŏrf)	157c	51.57N	7.59E
Wargla, Alg.	210	32.00N	5.18E
Warialda, Austl.	204	29.32S	150.34E
Warlingham, Eng., U.K.	235	51.19N	0.04W
Warmbad, Nmb. (värm'băd) (wôrm'băd)	212	28.25S	18.45E
Warmbad, S. Afr.	218d	24.52S	28.18E
Warm Beach, Wa., U.S. (wôrm)	106a	48.10N	122.22W
War Memorial Stadium, pt. of i., N.Y., U.S.	230a	42.54N	78.52W
Warm Springs Indian Reservation, I.R., Or., U.S. (wôrm sprĭnz)	104	44.55N	121.30W
Warm Springs Reservoir, res., Or., U.S.	104	43.42N	118.40W
Warner Mountains, mts., Ca., U.S.	96	41.30N	120.17W
Warner Robins, Ga., U.S.	114	32.37N	83.36W
Warnow, r., Ger. (vär'nō)	154	53.51N	11.55E
Warracknabeal, Austl.	204	36.20S	142.28E
Warragamba Reservoir, res., Austl.	204	33.40S	150.00E
Warrandyte, Austl.	243b	37.45S	145.13E
Warrandyte South, Austl.	243b	37.46S	145.14E
Warrāq al-ʻArab, Egypt	244a	30.06N	31.12E
Warrāq al-Hadar, Egypt	244a	30.06N	31.13E
Warrawee, Austl.	243a	33.44S	151.07E
Warrego, r., Austl. (wôr'ē-gô)	203	27.13S	145.58E
Warren, Can.	83f	50.08N	97.32W
Warren, Ar., U.S. (wŏr'ĕn)	111	33.37N	92.03W
Warren, In., U.S.	98	40.40N	85.25W
Warren, Mi., U.S.	101b	42.33N	83.03W
Warren, Mn., U.S.	102	48.11N	96.44W
Warren, Oh., U.S.	98	41.15N	80.50W
Warren, Or., U.S.	106c	45.49N	122.51W
Warren, Pa., U.S.	99	41.50N	79.10W
Warren, R.I., U.S.	100b	41.44N	71.14W
Warrendale, Pa., U.S. (wŏr'ĕn-dāl)	101e	40.39N	80.04W
Warrensburg, Mo., U.S. (wŏr'ĕnz-bûrg)	111	38.45N	93.42W
Warrensville Heights, Oh., U.S.	229a	41.26N	81.29W
Warrenton, Ga., U.S. (wŏr'ĕn-tŭn)	115	33.26N	82.37W
Warrenton, Or., U.S.	106c	46.10N	123.56W
Warrenton, Va., U.S.	99	38.45N	77.50W
Warri, Nig. (wär'ē)	210	5.33N	5.43E
Warrington, Eng., U.K.	144a	53.22N	2.30W
Warrington, Fl., U.S. (wŏ'ĭng-tŭn)	114	30.21N	87.15W
Warrnambool, Austl. (wôr'năm-bōōl)	203	38.20S	142.28E
Warroad, Mn., U.S. (wôr'rōd)	102	48.55N	95.20W
Warrumbungle Range, mts., Austl. (wôr'ŭm-bŭŋ-g'l)	203	31.18S	150.00E
Warsaw, Pol.	142	52.15N	21.05E
Warsaw, Il., U.S. (wôr'sô)	111	40.21N	91.26W
Warsaw, In., U.S.	98	41.15N	85.50W
Warsaw, N.Y., U.S.	99	42.45N	78.10W
Warsaw, NC, N.C., U.S.	115	35.00N	78.07W
Warsop, Eng., U.K. (wôr'sŭp)	144a	53.13N	1.05W
Warszawa *see* Warsaw, Pol.	142	52.15N	21.05E
Warta, r., Pol. (vär'tȧ)	147	52.30N	16.00E
Wartburg, S. Afr.	213c	29.26S	30.39E
Wartenberg, neigh., Ger.	238a	52.34N	13.31E
Warwick, Austl. (wŏr'ĭk)	203	28.05S	152.10E
Warwick, Can.	91	45.58N	71.57W
Warwick, Eng., U.K.	150	52.19N	1.46W
Warwick, N.Y., U.S.	100a	41.15N	74.22W
Warwick, R.I., U.S.	99	41.42N	71.27W
Warwickshire, co., Eng., U.K.	144a	52.30N	1.35W
Wasatch Mountains, mts., Ut., U.S. (wô'săch)	107b	40.45N	111.46W
Wasatch Plateau, plat., Ut., U.S.	109	38.55N	111.40W
Wasatch Range, mts., U.S.	96	39.10N	111.30W
Wasbank, S. Afr.	213c	28.27S	30.09E
Wasco, Or., U.S. (wäs'kō)	104	45.36N	120.42W
Waseca, Mn., U.S. (wô-sē'kȧ)	103	44.04N	93.31W
Waseda University, educ., Japan	242a	35.42N	139.43E
Wash, The, Eng., U.K. (wŏsh)	146	53.00N	0.20E
Washburn, Me., U.S. (wŏsh'bŭrn)	92	46.46N	68.10W
Washburn, Wi., U.S.	103	46.41N	90.55W
Washburn, Mount, mtn., Wy., U.S.	105	44.55N	110.10W
Washington, D.C., U.S. (wŏsh'ĭng-tŭn)	97	38.50N	77.00W
Washington, Ga., U.S.	115	33.43N	82.46W
Washington, In., U.S.	98	38.40N	87.10W
Washington, Ia., U.S.	103	41.17N	91.42W
Washington, Ks., U.S.	111	39.48N	97.04W
Washington, Mo., U.S.	111	38.33N	91.00W
Washington, N.C., U.S.	115	35.32N	77.01W
Washington, Pa., U.S.	98	40.10N	80.14W
Washington, state, U.S.	96	47.30N	121.10W
Washington, i., Wi., U.S.	103	45.18N	86.42W
Washington, Lake, l., Wa., U.S.	106a	47.34N	122.12W
Washington, Mount, mtn., N.H., U.S.	97	44.15N	71.15W
Washington Court House, Oh., U.S.	98	39.30N	83.25W
Washington Monument, pt. of i., D.C., U.S.	229d	38.53N	77.03W
Washington National Airport, arpt., Va., U.S.	229d	38.51N	77.02W
Washington Park, Il., U.S.	107e	38.38N	90.06W
Washita, r., Ok., U.S. (wŏsh'ĭ-tô)	110	35.33N	99.16W
Washougal, Wa., U.S. (wŏ-shōō'gȧl)	106c	45.35N	122.21W
Washougal, r., Wa., U.S.	106c	45.38N	122.17W
Wasilków, Pol. (vȧ-sēl'kôf)	155	53.12N	23.13E
Waskaiowaka Lake, l., Can. (wŏs'kă-yō'wŏ-kă)	89	56.30N	96.20W
Wassenberg, Ger. (vä'sĕn-bĕrgh)	157c	51.06N	6.07E
Wassmannsdorf, Ger.	238a	52.22N	13.28E
Wassuk Range, mts., Nv., U.S. (wås'sŭk)	108	38.58N	119.00W
Waswanipi, Lac, l., Can.	91	49.35N	76.15W
Water, i., V.I.U.S. (wô'tẽr)	117c	18.20N	64.57W
Waterberge, mts., S. Afr. (wôrtẽr'bûrg)	218d	24.25S	27.53E
Waterboro, S.C., U.S. (wô'tẽr-bûr-ō)	115	32.50N	80.40W
Waterbury, Ct., U.S. (wô'tẽr-bĕr-ē)	99	41.30N	73.00W
Water Cay, i., Bah.	123	22.55N	75.50W
Waterdown, Can. (wô'tẽr-doun)	83d	43.20N	79.54W
Wateree Lake, res., S.C., U.S. (wô'tẽr-ē)	115	34.40N	80.48W
Waterford, Ire. (wô'tẽr-fẽrd)	147	52.20N	7.03W
Waterford, Wi., U.S.	101a	42.46N	88.13W
Waterloo, Bel.	145a	50.44N	4.24E
Waterloo, Can. (wô-tẽr-lōō')	91	43.30N	80.40W
Waterloo, Can.	91	45.25N	72.30W
Waterloo, Eng., U.K.	237a	53.28N	3.02W
Waterloo, Il., U.S.	111	38.19N	90.08W
Waterloo, Ia., U.S.	97	42.30N	92.22W
Waterloo, Md., U.S.	100e	39.11N	76.50W
Waterloo, N.Y., U.S.	99	42.55N	76.50W
Waterton-Glacier International Peace Park, rec., N.A. (wô'ter-tŭn-glā'shûr)	96	48.55N	114.10W
Waterton Lakes National Park, rec., Can.	87	49.05N	113.50W
Watertown, Ma., U.S. (wô'tẽr-toun)	93a	42.22N	71.11W
Watertown, N.Y., U.S.	97	44.00N	75.55W
Watertown, S.D., U.S.	96	44.53N	97.07W
Watertown, Wi., U.S.	103	43.13N	88.40W
Water Valley, Ms., U.S. (văl'ē)	114	34.08N	89.38W
Waterville, Me., U.S.	92	44.34N	69.37W
Waterville, Mn., U.S.	103	44.10N	93.35W
Waterville, Wa., U.S.	104	47.38N	120.04W
Watervliet, N.Y., U.S. (wô'tẽr-vlēt')	99	42.45N	73.54W
Watford, Eng., U.K. (wŏt'fŏrd)	150	51.38N	0.24W
Wathaman Lake, l., Can.	88	56.55N	103.43W
Watlington, Eng., U.K.	144b	51.37N	1.01W
Watonga, Ok., U.S. (wŏ-tôŋ'gȧ)	111	35.50N	98.26W
Watsa, Zaire (wät'sä)	211	3.03N	29.32E
Watseka, Il., U.S. (wŏt-sē'kȧ)	98	40.45N	87.45W
Watson, In., U.S. (wŏt'sŭn)	101h	38.21N	85.42W
Watsonia, Austl.	243b	37.43S	145.05E
Watson Lake, Can.	84	60.18N	128.50W
Watsons Bay, Austl.	243a	33.51S	151.17E
Watsonville, Ca., U.S. (wŏt'sŭn-vĭl)	108	36.55N	121.46W
Wattenscheid, Ger. (vä'tĕn-shīd)	157c	51.30N	7.07E
Watts, Ca., U.S. (wŏts)	107a	33.56N	118.15W
Watts Bar Lake, res., Tn., U.S. (bär)	114	35.45N	84.49W
Wattville, S. Afr.	244b	26.13S	28.18E
Waubay, S.D., U.S. (wô'bā)	102	45.19N	97.18W
Wauchula, Fl., U.S. (wô-chōō'lȧ)	115a	27.32N	81.48W
Wauconda, Il., U.S. (wô-kŏn'dȧ)	101a	42.15N	88.08W
Waukegan, Il., U.S. (wŏ-kē'gȧn)	97	42.22N	87.51W
Waukesha, Wi., U.S. (wô'kē-shô)	101a	43.01N	88.13W
Waukon, Ia., U.S. (wô kŏn)	103	43.15N	91.30W
Waupaca, Wi., U.S. (wô-păk'ȧ)	103	44.22N	89.06W
Waupun, Wi., U.S. (wô-pŭn')	103	43.37N	88.45W
Waurika, Ok., U.S. (wô-rē'kȧ)	111	34.09N	97.59W
Wausau, Wi., U.S. (wô'sô)	97	44.58N	89.40W
Wausaukee, Wi., U.S. (wô-sô'kē)	103	45.22N	87.58W
Wauseon, Oh., U.S. (wô'sē-ŏn)	98	41.30N	84.10W
Wautoma, Wi., U.S. (wô-tō'mȧ)	103	44.04N	89.11W
Wauwatosa, Wi., U.S. (wô-wȧ-t'ō'sȧ)	101a	43.03N	88.00W
Waveland, Ma., U.S.	227a	42.17N	70.53W
Waveney, r., Eng., U.K. (wāv'nē)	151	52.27N	1.17E
Waverley, Austl.	243a	33.54S	151.16E
Waverly, S. Afr.	213c	31.54S	26.29E
Waverly, Ia., U.S. (wā'vẽr-lē)	103	42.43N	92.29W
Waverly, Ma., U.S.	227a	42.23N	71.11W
Waverly, Tn., U.S.	114	36.04N	87.46W
Wāw, Sudan	211	7.41N	28.00E
Wawa, Can.	90	47.59N	84.47W
Wāw al-Kabīr, Libya	211	25.23N	16.52E
Wawanesa, Can. (wŏ'wŏ-nē'sä)	89	49.36N	99.41W
Wawasee, l., In., U.S. (wô-wô-sē')	98	41.25N	85.45W
Waxahachie, Tx., U.S. (wăk-sȧ-hăch'ē)	113	32.23N	96.50W
Wayland, Ky., U.S. (wā'lănd)	115	37.25N	82.47W
Wayland, Ma., U.S.	93a	42.23N	71.22W
Wayne, Mi., U.S.	101b	42.17N	83.23W
Wayne, Ne., U.S.	102	42.13N	97.03W
Wayne, N.J., U.S.	100a	40.56N	74.16W
Wayne, Pa., U.S.	100f	40.03N	75.22W
Waynesboro, Ga., U.S. (wānz'bŭr-ô)	115	33.05N	82.02W
Waynesboro, Pa., U.S.	99	39.45N	77.35W
Waynesboro, Va., U.S.	99	38.05N	78.50W
Waynesburg, Pa., U.S. (wānz'bûrg)	98	39.55N	80.10W
Waynesville, N.C., U.S. (wānz'vĭl)	115	35.28N	82.58W
Waynoka, Ok., U.S. (wā-nō'kȧ)	110	36.34N	98.52W
Wayzata, Mn., U.S. (wā-zä-tȧ)	107g	44.58N	93.31W
Wazīrābād, neigh., India	240d	28.43N	77.14E
Wazīrbad, Pak.	186	32.39N	74.11E
Wāzirpur, neigh., India	240d	28.41N	77.10E
Weagamow Lake, l., Can. (wē'ăg-ă-mou)	89	52.53N	91.22W
Weald, The, reg., Eng., U.K. (wēld)	150	50.58N	0.15W
Wealdstone, neigh., Eng., U.K.	235	51.36N	0.20W
Weatherford, Ok., U.S. (wĕ-dhẽr-fẽrd)	110	85.32N	98.41W
Weatherford, Tx., U.S.	113	32.45N	97.46W
Weaver, r., Eng., U.K. (wē'vẽr)	144a	53.09N	2.31W
Weaverville, Ca., U.S. (wē'vẽr-vĭl)	104	40.44N	122.55W
Webb City, Mo., U.S.	111	37.10N	94.26W
Weber, r., Ut., U.S.	107b	41.13N	112.07W
Webster, Ma., U.S.	93a	42.04N	71.52W
Webster, S.D., U.S.	102	45.19N	97.30W
Webster City, Ia., U.S.	103	42.28N	93.49W
Webster Groves, Mo., U.S. (grōvz)	107e	38.36N	90.22W
Webster Springs, W.V., U.S. (sprĭngz)	98	38.30N	80.20W
Wedau, neigh., Ger.	236	51.24N	6.48E
Weddell Sea, sea, Ant. (wĕd'ĕl)	219	73.00S	45.00W
Wedding, neigh., Ger.	238a	52.33N	13.22E
Weddinghofen, Ger.	236	51.36N	7.37E
Wedel, Ger. (vā'dĕl)	145c	53.35N	9.42E
Wedge Mountain, mtn., Can. (wĕj)	87	50.10N	122.50W
Wedgeport, Can. (wĕj'pōrt)	92	43.44N	65.59W
Wednesfield, Eng., U.K. (wĕd''nz-fēld)	144a	52.36N	2.04W
Weed, Ca., U.S. (wēd)	104	41.35N	122.21W
Weehawken, N.J., U.S.	228	40.46N	74.01W
Weenen, S. Afr. (vā'nĕn)	213c	28.52S	30.05E
Weert, Neth.	151	51.16N	5.39E
Weesow, Ger.	238a	52.39N	13.43E
Weesp, Neth.	145a	52.18N	5.01E
Wegendorf, Ger.	238a	52.36N	13.45E
Węgorzewo, Pol. (vôŋ-gô'zhĕ-vô)	155	54.14N	21.46E
Węgrow, Pol. (vôŋ'grôf)	155	52.23N	22.02E
Wehofen, neigh., Ger.	236	51.32N	6.46E
Wehringhausen, neigh., Ger.	236	51.21N	7.27E
Wei, r., China (wā)	188	34.00N	108.10E
Wei, r., China (wā)	190	35.47N	114.27E
Weichang, China (wā-chäŋ)	189	41.50N	118.00E
Weiden, Ger.	154	49.41N	12.09E
Weidling, Aus.	239e	48.17N	16.19E
Weidlingau, neigh., Aus.	239e	48.13N	16.13E
Weidlingbach, Aus.	239e	48.16N	16.15E
Weifang, China	189	36.43N	119.08E
Weihai, China (wā'hăī')	189	37.30N	122.05E
Weilheim, Ger. (vīl'hīm')	154	47.50N	11.06E
Weimar, Ger. (vī'mär)	147	50.59N	11.20E
Weinan, China	192	34.32N	109.40E
Weipa, Austl.	203	12.25S	141.54E
Weir, r., Can. (wēr-rīv-ẽr)	89	56.49N	94.04W
Weirton, W.V., U.S.	98	40.25N	80.35W
Weiser, Id., U.S. (wē'zẽr)	104	44.15N	116.58W
Weiser, r., Id., U.S.	104	44.26N	116.40W
Weishi, China (wā-shr)	192	34.23N	114.12E
Weissenburg, Ger.	154	49.04N	11.20E
Weissenfels, Ger. (vī'sĕn-fĕlz)	154	51.13N	11.58E
Weiss Lake, res., Al., U.S.	114	34.15N	85.35W
Weitmar, neigh., Ger.	236	51.27N	7.12E
Weixi, China (wā-shyē)	188	27.27N	99.30E
Weixian, China (wā shyĕn)	190	36.59N	115.17E
Wejherowo, Pol. (vā-hĕ-rō'vô)	155	54.36N	18.15E
Welch, W.V., U.S. (wĕlch)	115	37.24N	81.28W
Welcome Monument, hist., Indon.	241i	6.11S	106.49E
Weldon, N.C., U.S. (wĕl'dŭn)	115	36.24N	77.36W
Weldon, r., Mo., U.S.	111	40.22N	93.39W
Weleetka, Ok., U.S. (wē-lēt'kȧ)	111	35.19N	96.08W

ăt; finăl; rāte; senåte; ärm; åsk; sofȧ; fâre; ch-choose; dh-as th in other; bē; ėvent; bĕt; recĕnt; cratẽr; g-gō; gh-guttural g; bĭt; ĭ-short neutral; rīde; ĸ-guttural k as ch in German ich;

PLACE (Pronunciation)	PAGE	Lat. °′	Long. °′
Welford, Austl. (wĕl′fĕrd)	204	25.08S	144.43E
Welhamgreen, Eng., U.K.	235	51.44N	0.13W
Welheim, neigh., Ger.	236	51.32N	6.59E
Welkom, S. Afr. (wĕl′kŏm)	212	27.57S	26.45E
Welland, Can. (wĕl′ănd)	91	42.59N	79.13W
Wellesley, Ma., U.S. (wĕlz′lē)	93a	42.18N	71.17W
Wellesley Hills, Ma., U.S.	227a	42.19N	71.17W
Wellesley Islands, is., Austl.	202	16.15S	139.25E
Well Hill, Eng., U.K.	235	51.21N	0.09E
Wellinghofen, neigh., Ger.	236	51.28N	7.29E
Wellington, Austl. (wĕl′lĭng-tŭn)	204	32.40S	148.50E
Wellington, N.Z.	203a	41.15S	174.45E
Wellington, Eng., U.K.	144a	52.42N	2.30W
Wellington, Ks., U.S.	111	37.16N	97.24W
Wellington, Oh., U.S.	98	41.10N	82.10W
Wellington, Tx., U.S.	110	34.51N	100.12W
Wellington, i., Chile (ŏĕ′lĕng-tŏn)	132	49.30S	76.30W
Wells, Can.	84	53.06N	121.34W
Wells, Mi., U.S.	98	45.50N	87.00W
Wells, Mn., U.S.	103	43.44N	93.43W
Wells, Nv., U.S.	104	41.07N	115.04W
Wells, l., Austl. (wĕlz)	202	26.35S	123.40E
Wellsboro, Pa., U.S. (wĕlz′bŭ-rô)	99	41.45N	77.15W
Wellsburg, W.V., U.S. (wĕlz′bûrg)	98	40.10N	80.40W
Wells Dam, dam, Wa., U.S.	104	48.00N	119.39W
Wellston, Oh., U.S. (wĕlz′tŭn)	98	39.05N	82.30W
Wellsville, Mo., U.S. (wĕlz′vĭl)	111	39.04N	91.33W
Wellsville, N.Y., U.S.	99	42.10N	78.00W
Wellsville, Oh., U.S.	98	40.35N	80.40W
Wellsville, Ut., U.S.	105	41.38N	111.57W
Welper, Ger.	236	51.25N	7.12E
Wels, Aus. (vĕls)	147	48.10N	14.01E
Welshpool, Wales, U.K. (wĕlsh′po͞ol)	150	52.44N	3.10W
Welverdiend, S. Afr. (vĕl-vĕr-dĕnd′)	218d	26.23S	27.16E
Welwyn Garden City, Eng., U.K. (wĕlĭn)	144b	51.46N	0.17W
Wem, Eng., U.K. (wĕm)	144a	52.51N	2.44W
Wembere, r., Tan.	217	4.35S	33.55E
Wembley, neigh., Eng., U.K.	235	51.33N	0.18W
Wen, r., China (wŭn)	190	36.24N	119.00E
Wenan Wa, sw., China (wĕn′ăn′ wä)	190	38.56N	116.29E
Wenatchee, Wa., U.S. (wē-năch′ē)	104	47.24N	120.18W
Wenatchee Mountains, mts., Wa., U.S.	104	47.28N	121.10W
Wenchang, China (wŭn-chäŋ)	193	19.32N	110.42E
Wenchi, Ghana	214	7.42N	2.07W
Wendelville, N.Y., U.S.	230a	43.04N	78.47W
Wendeng, China (wŭn-dŭŋ)	190	37.14N	122.03E
Wendo, Eth.	211	6.37N	38.29E
Wendorer, Ut., U.S.	105	40.47N	114.01W
Wendover, Can. (wĕn-dōv′ĕr)	83c	45.34N	75.07W
Wendover, Eng., U.K.	144b	51.44N	0.45W
Wengern, Ger.	236	51.24N	7.21E
Wenham, Ma., U.S. (wĕn′ăm)	93a	42.36N	70.53W
Wennington, neigh., Eng., U.K.	235	51.30N	0.13E
Wenquan, China (wŭn-chyüän)	189	47.10N	120.00E
Wenshan, China	188	23.20N	104.15E
Wenshang, China (wĕn′shäng)	190	35.43N	116.31E
Wensu, China (wĕn-sò)	188	41.45N	80.30E
Wentworth, Austl. (wĕnt′wûrth)	203	34.03S	141.53E
Wentworthville, Austl.	243a	33.49S	150.58E
Wenzhou, China (wŭn-jō)	189	28.00N	120.40E
Wepener, S. Afr. (wē′pĕn-ĕr) (vā′pĕn-ĕr)	212	29.43S	27.04E
Werden, neigh., Ger.	236	51.23N	7.00E
Werder, Ger. (vĕr′dĕr)	145b	52.23N	12.56E
Were Ilu, Eth.	211	10.39N	39.21E
Werl, Ger. (vĕrl)	157c	51.33N	7.55E
Wermelskirchen, Ger.	157c	51.08N	7.13E
Werne, neigh., Ger.	236	51.29N	7.18E
Werneuchen, Ger. (vĕr′hoi-kĕn)	145b	52.38N	13.44E
Wernsdorf, Ger.	238a	52.22N	13.43E
Werra, r., Ger. (vĕr′ä)	154	51.16N	9.54E
Werribee, Austl.	201a	37.54S	144.40E
Werribee, r., Austl.	201a	37.40S	144.37E
Wersten, neigh., Ger.	236	51.11N	6.49E
Wertach, r., Ger. (vĕr′täk)	154	48.12N	10.40E
Weseke, Ger. (vĕ′zĕ-kĕ)	157c	51.54N	6.51E
Wesel, Ger. (vā′zĕl)	157c	51.39N	6.37E
Weser, r., Ger. (vā′zĕr)	142	51.00N	10.30E
Weslaco, Tx., U.S. (wĕs-lā′kō)	113	26.10N	97.59W
Weslemkoon, l., Can.	91	45.02N	77.25W
Wesleyville, Can. (wĕs′lē-vĭl)	93	49.09N	53.34W
Wessel Islands, is., Austl. (wĕs′ĕl)	202	11.45S	136.25E
Wesselsbron, S. Afr. (wĕs′ĕl-brŏn)	218d	27.51S	26.22E
Wessington Springs, S.D., U.S. (wĕs′ĭng-tŭn)	102	44.06N	98.35W
West, Mount, mtn., Pan.	116a	9.10N	79.52W
West Abington, Ma., U.S.	227a	42.08N	70.59W
West Allis, Wi., U.S. (wĕst-ăl′ĭs)	101a	43.01N	88.01W
West Alton, Mo., U.S. (ôl′tŭn)	107e	38.52N	90.13W
West Athens, Ca., U.S.	232	33.55N	118.18W
West Bay, b., Fl., U.S.	114	30.20N	85.45W
West Bay, b., Tx., U.S.	113a	29.11N	95.03W
West Bend, Wi., U.S. (wĕst bĕnd)	103	43.25N	88.13W
West Bengal, state, India (bĕn-gôl′)	183	23.30N	87.30E
West Blocton, Al., U.S. (blŏk′tŭn)	114	33.05N	87.05W
Westborough, Ma., U.S. (wĕst′bŭr-ô)	93a	42.17N	71.37W
West Boylston, Ma., U.S. (boil′stŭn)	93a	42.22N	71.46W
West Branch, Mi., U.S. (wĕst brânch)	98	44.15N	84.10W
West Bridgford, Eng., U.K. (brĭj′fĕrd)	144a	52.55N	1.08W
West Bromwich, Eng., U.K. (wĕst brŭm′ĭj)	144a	52.32N	1.59W
Westbrook, Me., U.S. (wĕst′bro͝ok)	92	43.41N	70.23W
Westbury, N.Y., U.S.	228	40.45N	73.35W
Westby, Wi., U.S. (wĕst′bē)	103	43.40N	90.52W
West Caicos, i., T./C. Is. (käē′kō) (kī′kōs)	123	21.40N	72.30W
West Caldwell, N.J., U.S.	228	40.51N	74.17W
West Cape Howe, c., Austl.	202	35.15S	117.30E
West Carson, Ca., U.S.	232	33.50N	118.18W
Westchester, Il., U.S.	231a	41.51N	87.53W
West Chester, Oh., U.S. (chĕs′tĕr)	101f	39.20N	84.24W
West Chester, Pa., U.S.	100f	39.57N	75.36W
Westchester, neigh., Ca., U.S.	232	33.55N	118.25W
Westchester, neigh., N.Y., U.S.	228	40.51N	73.52W
West Chicago, Il., U.S. (chĭ-kä′gō)	101a	41.53N	88.12W
West Collingswood, N.J., U.S.	229b	39.54N	75.06W
West Columbia, S.C., U.S. (cŏl′ŭm-bē-ȧ)	115	33.58N	81.05W
West Columbia, Tx., U.S.	113	29.08N	95.39W
West Conshohocken, N.J., U.S.	229b	40.04N	75.19W
West Cote Blanche Bay, b., La., U.S.	113	29.30N	92.17W
West Covina, Ca., U.S. (wĕst kō-vē′nȧ)	107a	34.04N	117.55W
Westdale, Il., U.S.	231a	41.56N	87.55W
West Derby, neigh., Eng., U.K.	237a	53.26N	2.54W
West Des Moines, Ia., U.S. (dē moin′)	103	41.35N	93.42W
West Des Moines, r., Ia., U.S.	103	42.52N	94.32W
West Drayton, neigh., Eng., U.K.	235	51.30N	0.29W
West Elizabeth, Pa., U.S.	230b	40.17N	79.54W
West End, Bah.	122	26.40N	78.55W
West End, Eng., U.K.	235	51.44N	0.04W
West End, neigh., Eng., U.K.	235	51.32N	0.24W
West End, neigh., Pa., U.S.	230b	40.27N	80.02W
Westende, Ger.	236	51.25N	7.24E
Westenfeld, neigh., Ger.	236	51.28N	7.09E
Westerbauer, neigh., Ger.	236	51.20N	7.23E
Westerham, Eng., U.K. (wĕ′stĕr′ŭm)	144b	51.15N	0.05E
Westerholt, Ger.	236	51.36N	7.05E
Westerhörn, Ger. (vĕs′tĕr-hōrn)	145c	53.52N	9.41E
Westerlo, Bel.	145a	51.05N	4.57E
Westerly, R.I., U.S. (wĕs′tĕr-lē)	99	41.25N	71.50W
Western Australia, state, Austl. (ôs-trā′lĭ-ȧ)	202	24.15S	121.30E
Western Dvina see Zapadnaya Dvina, r., Eur.	153	55.30N	28.27E
Western Ghāts, mts., India	183	17.35N	74.00E
Western Port, Md., U.S. (wĕs′tĕrn pōrt)	99	39.30N	79.00W
Western Sahara, dep., Afr. (sȧ-hä′rȧ)	210	23.05N	15.33W
Western Samoa, nation, Oc.	2	14.30S	172.00W
Western Siberian Lowland, depr., Russia	164	63.37N	72.45E
Western Springs, Il., U.S.	231a	41.47N	87.53W
Westerville, Oh., U.S. (wĕs′tĕr-vĭl)	98	40.10N	83.00W
Westerwald, for., Ger. (vĕs′tĕr-väld)	154	50.35N	7.45E
Westfalenhalle, pt. of i., Ger.	236	51.30N	7.27E
Westfield, Ma., U.S. (wĕst′fēld)	99	42.05N	72.45W
Westfield, N.J., U.S.	100a	40.39N	74.21W
Westfield, N.Y., U.S. (wĕst′fēld)	100a	42.20N	79.40W
Westford, Ma., U.S. (wĕst′fĕrd)	93a	42.35N	71.26W
West Frankfort, Il., U.S. (frăŋk′fŭrt)	98	37.55N	88.55W
West Ham, Eng., U.K.	144b	51.30N	0.00W
West Hanover, Ma., U.S.	227a	42.07N	70.53W
West Hartford, Ct., U.S. (härt′fĕrd)	99	41.45N	72.45W
Westhead, Eng., U.K.	237a	53.34N	2.51W
West Heidelberg, Austl.	243b	37.45S	145.02E
West Helena, Ar., U.S. (hĕl′ĕn-ȧ)	111	34.32N	90.39W
West Hempstead, N.Y., U.S.	228	40.42N	73.39W
Westhofen, Ger.	236	51.25N	7.31E
West Hollywood, Ca., U.S.	232	34.05N	118.24W
West Homestead, Pa., U.S.	230b	40.24N	79.55W
West Horndon, Eng., U.K.	235	51.34N	0.21E
West Hoxton, Austl.	243a	33.55S	150.50E
West Hyde, Eng., U.K.	235	51.37N	0.30W
Westick, Ger.	236	51.35N	7.38E
West Indies, is. (ĭn′dēz)	117	19.00N	78.30W
West Jordon, Ut., U.S. (jôr′dăn)	107b	40.37N	111.56W
West Kirby, Eng., U.K. (kûr′bē)	144a	53.22N	3.11W
West Lafayette, In., U.S. (lä-fā-yĕt′)	98	40.25N	86.55W
Westlake, Oh., U.S.	101d	41.27N	81.55W
Westland, Mi., U.S.	230c	42.19N	83.23W
West Lawn, Va., U.S.	229d	38.52N	77.11W
Westleigh, S. Afr. (wĕst-lē)	218d	27.39S	27.18E
West Liberty, Ia., U.S. (wĕst lĭb′ĕr-tĭ)	103	41.34N	91.15W
West Liberty, neigh., Pa., U.S.	230b	40.24N	80.01W
West Linn, Or., U.S. (lĭn)	106c	45.22N	122.37W
Westlock, Can. (wĕst′lŏk)	87	54.09N	113.52W
West Los Angeles, neigh., Ca., U.S.	232	34.03N	118.28W
West Malling, Eng., U.K.	235	51.18N	0.25E
West Manayunk, Pa., U.S.	229b	40.01N	75.14W
West Memphis, Ar., U.S.	111	35.08N	90.11W
West Midlands, co., Eng., U.K.	144a	52.26N	1.50W
West Mifflin, Pa., U.S.	230b	40.22N	79.52W
Westminster, Ca., U.S. (wĕst′mĭn-stĕr)	107a	33.45N	117.59W
Westminster, Md., U.S.	99	39.40N	76.55W
Westminster, S.C., U.S.	114	34.38N	83.10W
Westminster Abbey, pt. of i., Eng., U.K.	235	51.30N	0.07W
Westmont, Ca., U.S.	232	33.56N	118.18W
Westmount, Can. (wĕst′mount)	83a	45.29N	73.36W
West Newbury, Ma., U.S. (nū′bĕr-ē)	93a	42.47N	70.57W
West Newton, Ma., U.S.	227a	42.21N	71.14W
West Newton, Pa., U.S. (nū′tŭn)	101e	40.12N	79.45W
West New York, N.J., U.S. (nů yŏrk)	100a	40.47N	74.01W
West Nishnabotna, r., Ia., U.S. (nĭsh-nȧ-bŏt′nȧ)	102	40.56N	95.37W
West Norwood, neigh., Eng., U.K.	235	51.26N	0.06W
Weston, Ma., U.S. (wĕs′tŭn)	93a	42.22N	71.18W
Weston, W.V., U.S.	98	39.00N	80.30W
Westonaria, S. Afr.	218d	26.19S	27.38E
Weston-super-Mare, Eng., U.K. (wĕs′tŭn sū′pĕr-mā′rē)	150	51.23N	3.00W
West Orange, N.J., U.S. (wĕst ŏr′ĕnj)	100a	40.46N	74.14W
West Palm Beach, Fl., U.S. (päm bēch)	97	26.44N	80.04W
West Peabody, Ma., U.S.	227a	42.30N	70.57W
West Pensacola, Fl., U.S. (pĕn-sȧ-kō′lȧ)	114	30.24N	87.18W
West Pittsburg, Ca., U.S. (pĭts′bûrg)	106b	38.02N	121.56W
Westplains, Mo., U.S. (wĕst-plānz′)	111	36.42N	91.51W
West Point, Ga., U.S.	114	32.52N	85.10W
West Point, Ms., U.S.	114	33.36N	88.39W
Westpoint, Ne., U.S.	102	41.50N	96.00W
West Point, N.Y., U.S.	100a	41.23N	73.58W
West Point, Ut., U.S.	107b	41.07N	112.05W
West Point, Va., U.S.	99	37.25N	76.50W
West Point Lake, res., U.S.	114	33.00N	85.10W
Westport, Ire.	150	53.44N	9.36W
Westport, Ct., U.S. (wĕst′pōrt)	100a	41.07N	73.22W
Westport, Or., U.S. (wĕst′pôrt)	106c	46.08N	123.22W
West Puente Valley, Ca., U.S.	232	34.04N	117.59W
West Pymble, Austl.	243a	33.46S	151.08E
Westray, i., Scot., U.K. (wĕs′trå)	150a	59.19N	3.05W
West Road, r., Can. (rōd)	86	53.00N	124.00W
West Ryde, Austl.	243a	33.48S	151.05E
West Saint Paul, Mn., U.S. (sånt pôl′)	107g	44.55N	93.05W
West Sand Spit, i., T./C. Is.	123	21.25N	72.10W
West Seneca, N.Y., U.S.	230a	42.50N	78.45W
West Slope, Or., U.S.	106c	45.30N	122.46W
West Somerville, Ma., U.S.	227a	42.24N	71.07W
West Tavaputs Plateau, plat., Ut., U.S. (wĕst tăv′å-po͝ots)	109	39.45N	110.35W
West Terre Haute, In., U.S. (tĕr-ē hōt′)	98	39.30N	87.30W
West Thurrock, Eng., U.K.	235	51.29N	0.16E
West Tilbury, Eng., U.K.	235	51.29N	0.24E
West Turffontein, neigh., S. Afr.	244b	26.16S	28.02E
West Union, Ia., U.S. (ūn′yŭn)	103	42.58N	91.48W
West University Place, Tx., U.S.	113a	29.43N	95.26W
Westview, Oh., U.S. (wĕst′vū)	101d	41.21N	81.54W
West View, Pa., U.S.	101e	40.31N	80.02W
Westville, Can. (wĕst′vĭl)	93	45.35N	62.43W
Westville, Il., U.S.	98	40.00N	87.40W
Westville, N.J., U.S.	229b	39.52N	75.08W
Westville Grove, N.J., U.S.	229b	39.51N	75.07W
West Virginia, state, U.S. (wĕst vĕr-jĭn′ĭ-ȧ)	97	39.00N	80.50W
West Walker, r., Ca., U.S. (wôk′ĕr)	108	38.25N	119.25W
West Warwick, R.I., U.S. (wŏr′ĭk)	100b	41.42N	71.31W
Westwego, La., U.S. (wĕst-wē′gō)	100d	29.55N	90.09W
West Whittier, Ca., U.S.	232	33.59N	118.04W
West Wickham, neigh., Eng., U.K.	235	51.22N	0.01W
Westwood, Ca., U.S. (wĕst′wo͝od)	108	40.18N	121.00W
Westwood, Ks., U.S.	107f	39.03N	94.37W
Westwood, Ma., U.S.	93a	42.13N	71.14W
Westwood, N.J., U.S.	100a	40.59N	74.02W
Westwood, neigh., Ca., U.S.	232	34.04N	118.27W
West Wyalong, Austl. (wīălông)	203	34.00S	147.20E
West Yorkshire, co., Eng., U.K.	144a	53.37N	1.48W
Wetar, Pulau, i., Indon. (wĕt′ár)	197	7.34S	126.00E
Wetaskiwin, Can. (wĕ-tăs′kē-wŏn)	84	52.58N	113.22W
Wetherill Park, Austl.	243a	33.51S	150.54E
Wethmar, Ger.	236	51.37N	7.33E
Wetmore, Tx., U.S. (wĕt′mōr)	107d	29.34N	98.25W
Wetter, Ger.	157c	51.23N	7.23E
Wetumpka, Al., U.S. (wē-tŭmp′kȧ)	114	32.33N	86.12W
Wetzlar, Ger. (vĕts′lär)	154	50.35N	8.30E
Wewak, Pap. N. Gui. (wā-wăk′)	197	3.19S	143.30E
Wewoka, Ok., U.S. (wē-wō′kȧ)	111	35.09N	96.30W
Wexford, Ire. (wĕks′fĕrd)	147	52.20N	6.30W
Weybridge, Eng., U.K. (wā′brĭj)	144b	51.20N	0.26W
Weyburn, Can. (wā′bûrn)	84	49.41N	103.52W
Weyer, neigh., Ger.	236	51.10N	7.01E
Weymouth, Eng., U.K. (wā′mŭth)	150	50.37N	2.34W
Weymouth, Ma., U.S.	93a	42.44N	70.57W
Weymouth, Oh., U.S.	101d	41.11N	81.48W
Whalan, Austl.	243a	33.45S	150.49E
Whale Cay, i., Bah.	122	25.20N	77.45W
Whale Cay Channels, strt., Bah.	122	26.45N	77.10W
Wharton, N.J., U.S. (hwôr′tŭn)	100a	40.54N	74.35W
Wharton, Tx., U.S.	113	29.19N	96.06W
What Cheer, Ia., U.S. (hwŏt chēr)	103	41.23N	92.24W
Whatcom, Lake, l., Wa., U.S. (hwăt′kŭm)	106c	48.44N	123.34W
Whatshan Lake, l., Can. (wŏt′shăn)	87	50.00N	118.03W
Wheatland, Wy., U.S. (hwēt′lănd)	105	42.04N	104.52W
Wheatland Reservoir Number 2, res., Wy., U.S.	105	41.52N	105.36W
Wheaton, Il., U.S. (hwē′tŭn)	101a	41.52N	88.06W
Wheaton, Md., U.S.	100e	39.05N	77.05W
Wheaton, Mn., U.S.	102	45.48N	96.29W
Wheeler Peak, mtn., Nv., U.S.	96	38.58N	114.15W
Wheeler Peak, mtn., N.M., U.S.	110	36.34N	105.25W
Wheeling, Il., U.S. (hwēl′ĭng)	101a	42.08N	87.54W
Wheeling, W.V., U.S.	98	40.05N	80.45W
Wheelwright, Arg. (ŏĕ′l-rē′gt)	129c	33.46S	61.14W
Whelpleyhill, Eng., U.K.	235	51.44N	0.33W
Whidbey Island, i., Wa., U.S. (hwĭd′bē)	106a	48.13N	122.50W
Whippany, N.J., U.S. (hwĭp′á-nē)	100a	40.49N	74.25W
Whiston, Eng., U.K.	237a	53.25N	2.50W
Whitaker, Pa., U.S.	230b	40.24N	79.53W
Whitby, Can. (hwĭt′bē)	85	43.50N	79.00W
Whitby, Eng., U.K.	237a	53.17N	2.54W
Whitchurch, Eng., U.K. (hwĭt′chûrch)	144a	52.58N	2.49W
White, l., Can.	90	48.47N	85.50W
White, l., Can.	91	45.15N	76.35W
White, r., Can.	90	48.34N	85.46W
White, r., U.S.	97	35.30N	92.00W
White, r., U.S.	102	43.41N	99.48W
White, r., U.S.	109	40.10N	108.55W
White, r., In., U.S.	98	39.15N	86.45W
White, r., S.D., U.S.	102	43.13N	101.04W
White, r., Tx., U.S.	110	36.25N	102.20W

ng-sing; ŋ-baŋk; N-nasalized n; nŏd; cŏmmit; ōld; ôbey; ôrder; oi-boil; fo͞od; ŏ-as oo in foot; ou-out; s-soft; sh-dish; th-thin; pūre; ůnite; ûrn; stŭd; circŭs; ü-as in French tu; ′-indeterminate vowel.

366 White–Winter Garden

PLACE (Pronunciation)	PAGE	Lat. °'	Long. °'
White, r., Vt., U.S.	99	43.45N	72.35W
White, r., Wa., U.S.	104	47.07N	121.48W
White, East Fork, r., In., U.S.	98	38.45N	86.20W
White Bay, b., Can.	85a	50.00N	56.30W
White Bear Indian Reserve, I.R., Can.	89	49.50N	102.15W
White Bear Lake, l., Mn., U.S.	107g	45.04N	92.58W
White Castle, La., U.S.	113	30.10N	91.09W
White Center, Wa., U.S.	106a	47.31N	122.21W
White Cloud, Mi., U.S.	98	43.35N	85.45W
Whitecourt, Can. (wīt'côrt)	84	54.09N	115.41W
White Earth, r., N.D., U.S.	102	48.30N	102.44W
White Earth Indian Reservation, I.R., Mn., U.S.	102	47.18N	95.42W
Whiteface, r., Mn., U.S. (whīt'fās)	103	47.12N	92.13W
Whitefield, Eng., U.K.	237b	53.33N	2.18W
Whitefield, N.H., U.S. (hwĭt'fēld)	99	44.20N	71.35W
Whitefish Bay, Wi., U.S.	101a	43.07N	77.54W
Whitefish Bay, b., Can.	89	49.26N	94.14W
Whitefish Bay, b., N.A.	103	46.36N	84.50W
White Hall, Il., U.S.	111	39.26N	90.23W
Whitehall, Mi., U.S. (hwīt'hôl)	98	43.20N	86.20W
Whitehall, N.Y., U.S.	99	43.30N	73.25W
Whitehall, Pa., U.S.	230b	40.22N	79.59W
Whitehaven, Eng., U.K. (hwīt'hā-vĕn)	150	54.35N	3.30W
Whitehead, Ma., U.S.	227a	42.17N	70.52W
Whitehorn, Point, c., Wa., U.S. (hwīt'hôrn)	106d	48.54N	122.48W
Whitehorse, Can. (whīt'hôrs)	84	60.39N	135.01W
White House, pt. of i., D.C., U.S.	229d	38.54N	77.02W
White Lake, l., La., U.S.	113	29.40N	92.35W
Whiteley Village, Eng., U.K.	235	51.21N	0.26W
Whiteman, Ma., U.S.	227a	42.05N	70.56W
Whitemarsh, Pa., U.S.	229b	40.07N	75.13W
White Mountain Peak, mtn., Ca., U.S.	108	37.38N	118.13W
White Mountains, mts., Me., U.S.	92	44.22N	71.15W
White Mountains, mts., N.H., U.S.	99	42.20N	71.05W
Whitemouth, l., Can.	89	49.14N	95.40W
White Nile (Al Bahr al Abyad), r., Sudan	211	12.30N	32.30E
White Oak, Pa., U.S.	230b	40.21N	79.48W
White Otter, l., Can.	90	49.15N	91.48W
White Pass, p., N.A.	95	59.35N	135.03W
White Plains, N.Y., U.S.	100a	41.02N	73.47W
White River, Can.	90	48.38N	85.23W
White Rock, Can.	87	49.01N	122.49W
Whiterock Reservoir, res., Tx., U.S. (hwīt'rŏk)	107c	32.51N	96.40W
White Russia, *see* Belarus, nation, Eur.	164	53.30N	25.33E
Whitesail Lake, l., Can. (whīt'sāl)	86	53.30N	127.00W
White Sands National Monument, rec., N.M., U.S.	109	32.50N	106.20W
White Sea, sea, Russia	164	66.00N	40.00E
White Settlement, Tx., U.S.	107c	32.45N	97.28W
Whitestone, neigh., N.Y., U.S.	228	40.47N	73.49W
White Sulphur Springs, Mt., U.S.	105	46.32N	110.49W
White Umfolzi, r., S. Afr. (ŭm-fô-lō'zē)	213c	28.12S	30.55E
Whiteville, N.C., U.S. (hwīt'vĭl)	115	34.18N	78.45W
White Volta (Volta Blanche), r., Afr.	214	9.40N	1.10W
Whitewater, Wi., U.S. (whīt-wŏt'ĕr)	103	42.49N	88.40W
Whitewater, l., Can.	89	49.14N	100.39W
Whitewater, r., In., U.S.	101f	39.19N	84.55W
Whitewater Bay, b., Fl., U.S.	115a	25.16N	80.21W
Whitewater Creek, r., Mt., U.S.	105	48.50N	107.50W
Whitewell, Tn., U.S. (hwĭt'wĕl)	114	35.11N	85.31W
Whitewright, Tx., U.S. (hwīt'rīt)	111	33.33N	96.25W
Whitham, r., Eng., U.K. (wĭth'ŭm)	144a	53.08N	0.15W
Whiting, In., U.S. (hwīt'ĭng)	101a	41.41N	87.30W
Whitinsville, Ma., U.S. (hwīt'ĕns-vĭl)	93a	42.06N	71.40W
Whitman, Ma., U.S. (hwĭt'măn)	93a	42.05N	70.57W
Whitmire, S.C., U.S. (hwĭt'mīr)	115	34.30N	81.40W
Whitney, Mount, mtn., Ca., U.S.	96	36.34N	118.18W
Whitney Lake, l., Tx., U.S. (hwĭt'nē)	113	32.02N	97.36W
Whitstable, Eng., U.K. (wĭt'stăb'l)	144b	51.22N	1.03E
Whitsunday, i., Austl. (hwĭt's'n-dā)	203	20.16S	149.00E
Whittier, Ca., U.S. (hwĭt'ĭ-ēr)	107a	33.58N	118.02W
Whittier South, Ca., U.S.	232	33.57N	118.01W
Whittlesea, S. Afr. (wĭt'l'sē)	213c	32.11S	26.51E
Whitworth, Eng., U.K. (hwĭt'wŭrth)	144a	53.40N	2.10W
Whyalla, Austl. (hwī-ăl'ă)	202	33.00S	137.32E
Whymper, Mount, mtn., Can. (wĭm'pēr)	86	48.57N	124.10W
Wiarton, Can. (wī'ăr-tŭn)	85	44.45N	80.45W
Wichita, Ks., U.S. (wĭch'ĭ-tô)	96	37.42N	97.21W
Wichita, r., Tx., U.S.	110	33.50N	99.38W
Wichita Falls, Tx., U.S. (fôls)	96	33.54N	98.29W
Wichita Mountains, mts., Ok., U.S.	96	34.48N	98.43W
Wichlinghofen, neigh., Ger.	236	51.27N	7.30E
Wick, Scot., U.K. (wĭk)	146	58.25N	3.05W
Wickatunk, N.J., U.S. (wĭk'â-tŭnk)	100a	40.21N	74.15W
Wickede, neigh., Ger.	236	51.32N	7.37E
Wickenburg, Az., U.S.	109	33.58N	112.44W
Wickiup Reservoir, res., Or., U.S.	104	43.40N	121.43W
Wickliffe, Oh., U.S. (wĭk'klĭf)	101d	41.37N	81.29W
Wicklow, Ire.	150	52.59N	6.06W
Wicklow Mountains, mts., Ire. (wĭk'lō)	150	52.49N	6.20W
Wickup Mountain, mtn., Or., U.S. (wĭk'ŭp)	106c	46.06N	123.35W
Wiconisco, Pa., U.S. (wĭ-kon'ĭs-kō)	99	43.35N	76.45W
Widen, W.V., U.S. (wī'dĕn)	98	38.25N	80.55W
Widnes, Eng., U.K. (wĭd'nĕs)	144a	53.21N	2.44W
Wieliczka, Pol. (vyĕ-lēch'kȧ)	155	49.58N	20.06E
Wiemelhausen, neigh., Ger.	236	51.28N	7.13E
Wien *see* Vienna, Aus.	142	48.13N	16.22E
Wien, prov., Aus.	145e	48.11N	16.23E
Wiener Berg, Aus.	239e	48.10N	16.22E
Wiener Neustadt, Aus. (vē'nēr noi'shtät)	147	47.48N	16.15E
Wiener Wald, for., Aus.	145e	48.09N	16.05E
Wieprz, r., Pol. (vyĕpzh)	155	51.25N	22.45E
Wiergate, Tx., U.S. (wēr'gāt)	113	31.00N	93.42W
Wiesbaden, Ger. (vēs'bä-dĕn)	147	50.05N	8.15E
Wigan, Eng., U.K. (wĭg'ăn)	150	53.33N	2.37W
Wiggins, Ms., U.S. (wĭg'ĭnz)	114	30.51N	89.05W
Wight, Isle of, i., Eng., U.K. (wīt)	150	50.44N	1.17W
Wilber, Ne., U.S. (wĭl'bēr)	111	40.29N	96.57W
Wilburton, Ok., U.S. (wĭl'bēr-tŭn)	111	34.54N	95.18W
Wilcannia, Austl. (wĭl-căn-ĭȧ)	203	31.30S	143.30E
Wildau, Ger. (vēl'dou)	145b	52.20N	13.39E
Wildberg, Ger. (vēl'bĕrgh)	145b	52.52N	12.39E
Wildcat Hill, hill, Can. (wīld'kăt)	89	53.17N	102.30W
Wildercroft, Md., U.S.	229d	38.58N	76.53W
Wildhay, r., Can. (wīld'hā)	87	53.15N	117.20W
Wildomar, Ca., U.S. (wĭl'dô-mär)	107a	33.35N	117.17W
Wild Rice, r., Mn., U.S.	102	47.10N	96.40W
Wild Rice, r., N.D., U.S.	102	46.10N	97.12W
Wild Rice Lake, l., Mn., U.S.	107h	46.54N	92.10W
Wildspitze, mtn., Aus.	154	46.55N	10.50E
Wildwood, N.J., U.S.	99	39.00N	74.50W
Wildwood Manor, Md., U.S.	229d	39.01N	77.07W
Wiley, Co., U.S. (wī'lē)	110	38.08N	102.41W
Wilge, r., S. Afr. (wĭl'jē)	218d	25.38S	29.09E
Wilge, r., S. Afr.	218d	27.27S	28.46E
Wilhelm, Mount, mtn., Pap. N. Gui.	197	5.58S	144.58E
Wilhelmina Gebergte, mts., Sur.	131	4.30N	57.00W
Wilhelmina Kanaal, can., Neth.	145a	51.37N	4.55E
Wilhelmshaven, Ger. (vėl-hĕlms-hä'fĕn)	146	53.30N	8.10E
Wilhelmstadt, neigh., Ger.	238a	52.31N	13.11E
Wilkes-Barre, Pa., U.S. (wĭlks'băr-ė)	97	41.15N	75.50W
Wilkes Land, reg., Ant.	219	71.00S	126.00E
Wilkeson, Wa., U.S. (wĭl-kē'sŭn)	106a	47.06N	122.03W
Wilkie, Can. (wĭlk'ē)	84	52.25N	108.43W
Wilkinsburg, Pa., U.S. (wĭl'kĭnz-bûrg)	101e	40.26N	79.53W
Wilkins Township, Pa., U.S.	230b	40.25N	79.50W
Willamette, r., Or., U.S.	96	45.00N	123.00W
Willapa Bay, b., Wa., U.S.	104	46.37N	124.00W
Willard, Oh., U.S. (wĭl'ărd)	98	41.00N	82.50W
Willard, Ut., U.S.	107b	41.24N	112.02W
Willaston, Eng., U.K.	237a	53.18N	3.00W
Willcox, Az., U.S. (wĭl'kŏks)	109	32.15N	109.50W
Willcox Playa, l., Az., U.S.	109	32.08N	109.51W
Willemstad, Neth. Ant.	130	12.12N	68.58W
Willesden, Eng., U.K. (wĭlz'dĕn)	144b	51.31N	0.17W
William Bill Dannelly Reservoir, res., Al., U.S.	114	32.10N	87.15W
William Creek, Austl. (wĭl'yăm)	202	28.45S	136.20E
Williams, Az., U.S. (wĭl'yămz)	109	35.15N	112.15W
Williams, i., Bah.	122	24.30N	78.30W
Williamsburg, Ky., U.S. (wĭl'yămz-bûrg)	114	36.42N	84.09W
Williamsburg, Oh., U.S.	101f	39.04N	84.02W
Williamsburg, Va., U.S.	115	37.15N	76.41W
Williamsburg, neigh., N.Y., U.S.	228	40.42N	73.57W
Williams Lake, Can.	87	52.08N	122.09W
Williamson, W.V., U.S. (wĭl'yăm-sŭn)	98	37.40N	82.15W
Williamsport, Md., U.S.	99	39.35N	77.45W
Williamsport, Pa., U.S.	99	41.15N	77.05W
Williamston, N.C., U.S. (wĭl'yămz-tŭn)	115	35.50N	77.04W
Williamston, S.C., U.S.	115	34.36N	82.30W
Williamstown, Austl.	201a	37.52S	144.54E
Williamstown, W.V., U.S. (wĭl'yămz-toun)	98	39.20N	81.30W
Williamsville, N.Y., U.S. (wĭl'yăm-vĭl)	101c	42.58N	78.46W
Willich, Ger.	236	51.16N	6.33E
Willimantic, Ct., U.S. (wĭl-ĭ-măn'tĭk)	99	41.40N	72.10W
Willingale, Eng., U.K.	235	51.44N	0.19E
Willis, Tx., U.S. (wĭl'ĭs)	113	30.24N	95.29W
Willis Islands, is., Austl.	203	16.15S	150.30E
Williston, N.D., U.S. (wĭl'ĭs-tŭn)	96	48.08N	103.38W
Williston, Lake, l., Can.	84	55.40N	123.40W
Williston Park, N.Y., U.S.	228	40.45N	73.39W
Willmar, Mn., U.S. (wĭl'mär)	102	45.07N	95.05W
Willmersdorf, Ger.	238a	52.40N	13.41E
Willoughby, Austl.	243a	33.48S	151.12E
Willoughby, Oh., U.S. (wĭl'ô-bė)	101d	41.39N	81.25W
Willow, Ak., U.S. (wĭl'ō)	95	61.50N	150.00W
Willow Brook, Ca., U.S.	232	33.55N	118.14W
Willow Creek, r., Or., U.S.	104	44.21N	117.34W
Willow Grove, Pa., U.S.	100f	40.07N	75.07W
Willowick, Oh., U.S. (wĭl'ō-wĭk)	101d	41.39N	81.28W
Willowmore, S. Afr. (wĭl'ô-môr)	212	33.15S	23.37E
Willow Run, Mi., U.S. (wĭl'ō rŭn)	101b	42.16N	83.34W
Willow Run, Va., U.S.	229d	38.49N	77.10W
Willows, Ca., U.S. (wĭl'ōz)	108	39.32N	122.11W
Willow Springs, Il., U.S.	231a	41.44N	87.52W
Willow Springs, Mo., U.S. (sprĭngz)	111	36.59N	91.56W
Willowvale, S. Afr. (wĭ-lô'vāl)	213c	32.17S	28.32E
Wills Point, Tx., U.S. (wĭlz point)	113	32.42N	96.02W
Wilmer, Tx., U.S. (wĭl'mēr)	107c	32.35N	96.40W
Wilmette, Il., U.S. (wĭl-mĕt')	101a	42.04N	87.42W
Wilmington, Austl.	204	32.39S	138.07E
Wilmington, Eng., U.K.	235	51.26N	0.12E
Wilmington, Ca., U.S. (wĭl'mĭng-tŭn)	107a	33.46N	118.16W
Wilmington, De., U.S.	97	39.45N	75.33W
Wilmington, Il., U.S.	101a	41.19N	88.09W
Wilmington, Ma., U.S.	93a	42.34N	71.10W
Wilmington, N.C., U.S.	97	34.12N	77.56W
Wilmington, Oh., U.S.	98	39.20N	83.50W
Wilmore, Ky., U.S. (wĭl'mōr)	98	37.50N	84.35W
Wilmslow, Eng., U.K. (wĭlmz'lō)	144a	53.19N	2.14W
Wilno *see* Vilnius, Lith.	164	54.40N	25.26E
Wilpoort, S. Afr.	218d	26.57S	26.17E
Wilson, Ar., U.S. (wĭl'sŭn)	111	35.35N	90.02W
Wilson, N.C., U.S.	115	35.42N	77.55W
Wilson, Ok., U.S.	111	34.09N	97.27W
Wilson, r., Al., U.S.	114	34.53N	87.28W
Wilson, Mount, mtn., Ca., U.S.	107a	34.15N	118.06W
Wilson, Point, c., Austl.	201a	38.05S	144.31E
Wilson Lake, res., Al., U.S.	97	34.45N	87.30W
Wilson's Promontory, pen., Austl. (wĭl'sŭnz)	203	39.05S	146.50E
Wilsonville, Il., U.S. (wĭl'sŭn-vĭl)	107e	39.04N	89.52W
Wilstedt, Ger. (vēl'shtĕt)	145c	53.45N	10.04E
Wilster, Ger. (vēl'stĕr)	145c	53.55N	9.23E
Wilton, Ct., U.S. (wĭl'tŭn)	100a	41.11N	73.25W
Wilton, N.D., U.S.	102	47.09N	100.47W
Wilton Woods, Va., U.S.	229d	38.47N	77.06W
Wiluna, Austl. (wĭ-lōō'nȧ)	202	26.35S	120.25E
Wimbledon, neigh., Eng., U.K.	235	51.25N	0.12W
Wimbledon Common, pt. of i., Eng., U.K.	235	51.26N	0.14W
Winamac, In., U.S. (wĭn'ȧ măk)	98	41.05N	86.40W
Winburg, S. Afr. (wĭm-bûrg)	218d	28.31S	27.02E
Winchester, Eng., U.K.	150	51.04N	1.20W
Winchester, Ca., U.S. (wĭn'chĕs-tĕr)	107a	33.41N	117.06W
Winchester, Id., U.S.	104	46.14N	116.39W
Winchester, In., U.S.	98	40.10N	84.50W
Winchester, Ky., U.S.	98	38.00N	84.15W
Winchester, Ma., U.S.	93a	42.28N	71.09W
Winchester, N.H., U.S.	99	42.45N	72.25W
Winchester, Tn., U.S.	114	35.11N	86.06W
Winchester, Va., U.S.	99	39.10N	78.10W
Wind, r., Wy., U.S.	105	43.17N	109.02W
Windber, Pa., U.S. (wĭnd'bēr)	99	40.15N	78.45W
Wind Cave National Park, rec., S.D., U.S.	102	43.36N	103.53W
Winder, Ga., U.S. (wīn'dēr)	114	33.58N	83.43W
Windermere, Eng., U.K. (wĭn'dēr-mēr)	150	54.25N	2.59W
Windham, Ct., U.S. (wĭnd'ăm)	99	41.45N	72.05W
Windham, N.H., U.S.	93a	42.49N	71.21W
Windhoek, Nmb. (vĭnt'hŏk)	212	22.05S	17.10E
Wind Lake, l., Wi., U.S.	101a	42.49N	88.06W
Wind Mountain, mtn., N.M., U.S.	112	32.02N	105.30W
Windom, Mn., U.S. (wĭn'dŭm)	102	43.50N	95.04W
Windora, Austl. (wĭn-dō'rȧ)	203	25.15S	142.50E
Wind River Indian Reservation, I.R., Wy., U.S.	105	43.07N	109.08W
Wind River Indian Reservation, I.R., Wy., U.S.	105	43.26N	109.00W
Wind River Range, mts., Wy., U.S.	96	43.19N	109.47W
Windsor, Austl. (wĭn'zēr)	201b	33.37S	150.49E
Windsor, Can.	85	42.19N	83.00W
Windsor, Can.	85	44.59N	64.08W
Windsor, Can.	85a	48.57N	55.40W
Windsor, Eng., U.K.	150	51.27N	0.37W
Windsor, Co., U.S.	110	40.27N	104.51W
Windsor, Mo., U.S.	111	38.32N	93.31W
Windsor, N.C., U.S.	115	35.58N	76.57W
Windsor, Vt., U.S.	99	43.30N	72.25W
Windsor, University of, educ., Can.	230c	42.18N	83.04W
Windsor Airport, arpt., Can.	230c	42.17N	82.58W
Windsor Castle, hist., Eng., U.K.	235	51.29N	0.36W
Windsor Hills, Ca., U.S.	232	33.59N	118.21W
Windward Islands, is., N.A. (wĭnd'wērd)	117	12.45N	61.40W
Windward Passage, strt., N.A.	117	19.30N	74.20W
Winefred Lake, l., Can.	88	55.30N	110.35W
Winfield, Ks., U.S.	111	37.14N	97.00W
Wing Lake Shores, Mi., U.S.	230c	42.33N	83.17W
Winifred, Mt., U.S. (wĭn ĭ frĕd)	105	47.35N	109.20W
Winisk, r., Can.	85	54.30N	86.30W
Wink, Tx., U.S. (wĭŋk)	112	31.48N	103.06W
Winkler, Can. (wĭnk'lēr)	89	49.11N	97.56W
Winneba, Ghana (wĭn'ē-bȧ)	214	5.25N	0.36W
Winnebago, Mn., U.S. (wĭn'ē-bā'gō)	103	43.45N	94.08W
Winnebago, Lake, l., Wi., U.S.	103	44.09N	88.10W
Winnebago Indian Reservation, I.R., Ne., U.S.	102	42.15N	96.06W
Winnemucca, Nv., U.S. (wĭn-ē-mŭk'ȧ)	96	40.59N	117.43W
Winnemucca, l., Nv., U.S.	108	40.06N	119.07W
Winner, S.D., U.S. (wĭn'ēr)	102	43.22N	99.50W
Winnetka, Il., U.S. (wĭ-nĕt'kȧ)	101a	42.07N	87.44W
Winnett, Mt., U.S. (wĭn'ĕt)	105	47.01N	108.20W
Winnfield, La., U.S. (wĭn'fēld)	113	31.56N	92.39W
Winnibigoshish, l., Mn., U.S. (wĭn'ĭ-bĭ-gō'shĭsh)	103	47.30N	93.45W
Winnipeg, Can. (wĭn'ĭ-pĕg)	84	49.53N	97.09W
Winnipeg, r., Can.	84	50.30N	95.00W
Winnipeg, Lake, l., Can.	84	52.00N	97.00W
Winnipegosis, Can. (wĭn'ĭ-pē-gō'sĭs)	84	51.39N	99.56W
Winnipegosis, l., Can.	84	52.30N	100.00W
Winnipesaukee, l., N.H., U.S. (wĭn'ē-pē-sô'kē)	99	43.40N	71.20W
Winnsboro, La., U.S. (wĭnz'bŭr'ō)	113	32.09N	91.42W
Winnsboro, S.C., U.S.	115	34.29N	81.05W
Winnsboro, Tx., U.S.	111	32.56N	95.15W
Winona, Can. (wĭ-nō'nȧ)	83d	43.13N	79.39W
Winona, Mn., U.S.	97	44.03N	91.40W
Winona, Ms., U.S.	114	33.29N	89.43W
Winooski, Vt., U.S. (wĭ-nōōs-kē)	99	44.30N	73.10W
Winsen, Ger. (vĕn'zĕn)	145c	53.22N	10.13E
Winsford, Eng., U.K. (wĭnz'fērd)	144a	53.11N	2.30W
Winslow, Az., U.S. (wĭnz'lō)	109	35.00N	110.45W
Winslow, Wa., U.S.	106a	47.38N	122.31W
Winsted, Ct., U.S. (wĭn'stĕd)	99	41.55N	73.05W
Winster, Eng., U.K. (wĭn'stēr)	144a	53.08N	1.38W
Winston-Salem, N.C., U.S. (wĭn stŭn-sā'lĕm)	97	36.05N	80.15W
Winterberg, Ger.	236	51.17N	7.18E
Winterberge, mts., Afr.	213c	32.18S	26.25E
Winter Garden, Fl., U.S. (wĭn'tēr gär'd'n)	115a	28.32N	81.35W

ăt; finăl; rāte; senāte; ärm; ȧsk; sofȧ; fâre; ch-choose; dh-as th in other; bē; ėvent; bĕt; recĕnt; cratēr; g-gō; gh-guttural g; bĭt; ĭ-short neutral; rīde; κ-guttural k as ch in German ich;

PRONOUNCING INDEX Winter Haven-Xinhuai 367

PLACE (Pronunciation)	PAGE	Lat. °′	Long. °′
Winter Haven, Fl., U.S. (hā'vĕn)	115a	28.01N	81.38W
Winter Park, Fl., U.S. (pärk)	115a	28.35N	81.21W
Winters, Tx., U.S. (wĭn'tẽrz)	112	31.59N	99.58W
Winterset, Ia., U.S. (wĭn'tẽr-sĕt)	103	41.19N	94.03W
Winterswijk, Neth.	157c	51.58N	6.44E
Winterthur, Switz. (vĭn'tĕr-tōōr)	154	47.30N	8.32E
Winterton, S. Afr.	213c	28.51S	29.33E
Winthrop, Me., U.S. (wĭn'thrŭp)	92	44.19N	70.00W
Winthrop, Ma., U.S.	93a	42.23N	70.59W
Winthrop, Mn., U.S.	103	44.31N	94.20W
Winton, Austl. (wĭn-tŭn)	203	22.17S	143.08E
Winz, Ger.	236	51.23N	7.09E
Wipperfürth, Ger. (vē'pĕr-fürt)	157c	51.07N	7.23E
Wirksworth, Eng., U.K. (wûrks'wûrth)	144a	53.05N	1.35W
Wisconsin, state, U.S. (wĭs-kŏn'sĭn)	97	44.30N	91.00W
Wisconsin, r., Wi., U.S.	97	43.14N	90.34W
Wisconsin Dells, Wi., U.S.	103	43.38N	89.46W
Wisconsin Rapids, Wi., U.S.	103	44.24N	89.50W
Wishek, N.D., U.S. (wĭsh'ĕk)	102	46.15N	99.34W
Wisła, r., Pol. (vĕs'wȧ)	142	52.30N	20.00E
Wisłoka, r., Pol. (vĕs-wō'kȧ)	155	49.55N	21.26E
Wismar, Ger. (vĭs'mär)	146	53.53N	11.28E
Wismar, Guy. (wĭs'mȧr)	131	5.58N	58.15W
Wisner, Ne., U.S. (wĭz'nẽr)	102	42.00N	96.55W
Wissembourg, Fr. (vē-säN-bōōr')	157	49.03N	7.58E
Wissinoming, neigh., Pa., U.S.	229b	40.01N	75.04W
Wissous, Fr.	237c	48.44N	2.20E
Wister, Lake, l., Ok., U.S. (vĭs'tẽr)	111	35.02N	94.52W
Witbank, S. Afr. (wĭt-băŋk)	218d	25.53S	29.14E
Witberg, mtn., Afr.	213c	30.32S	27.18E
Witfield, S. Afr.	244b	26.11S	28.12E
Witham, Eng., U.K. (wĭdh'ăm)	144b	51.48N	0.37E
Witham, r., Eng., U.K.	144a	53.11N	0.20W
Withamsville, Oh., U.S. (wĭdh'ămz-vĭl)	101f	39.04N	84.16W
Withington, neigh., Eng., U.K.	237b	53.26N	2.14W
Withlacoochee, r., Fl., U.S. (wĭth-lȧ-kōō'chē)	115a	28.58N	82.30W
Withlacoochee, r., Ga., U.S.	114	31.15N	83.30W
Withrow, Mn., U.S. (wĭdh'rō)	107g	45.08N	92.54W
Witney, Eng., U.K. (wĭt'nē)	144b	51.45N	1.30W
Witpoortje, S. Afr.	244b	26.08S	27.50E
Witt, Il., U.S. (vĭt)	98	39.10N	89.15W
Witten, Ger. (vē'tĕn)	157c	51.26N	7.19E
Wittenau, neigh., Ger.	238a	52.35N	13.20E
Wittenberg, Ger. (vē'tĕn-bĕrgh)	154	51.53N	12.40E
Wittenberge, Ger. (vĭt-ĕn-bĕr'gē)	154	52.59N	11.45E
Wittlaer, Ger.	236	51.19N	6.44E
Wittlich, Ger. (vĭt'lĭk)	154	49.58N	6.54E
Witu, Kenya (wē'tōō)	213	2.18S	40.28E
Witu Islands, is., Pap. N. Gui.	197	4.45S	149.50E
Witwatersberg, mts., S. Afr. (wĭt-wôr-tẽrz-bûrg)	213b	25.58S	27.53E
Witwatersrand, mtn., S. Afr. (wĭt-wôr'tẽrs-rănd)	218d	25.55S	26.27E
Witwatersrand, University of, educ., S. Afr.	244b	26.12S	28.02E
Witwatersrand Gold Mines, quarry, S. Afr.	244b	26.12S	28.10E
Wkra, r., Pol. (f'krȧ)	155	52.40N	20.35E
Włocławek, Pol. (vwô-tswä'vĕk)	155	52.38N	19.08E
Włodawa, Pol. (vwô-dä'vä)	155	51.33N	23.33E
Włoszczowa, Pol. (vwôsh-chô'vä)	155	50.51N	19.58E
Woburn, Ma., U.S. (wō'bŭrn) (wō'bŭrn)	93a	42.29N	71.10W
Woburn, neigh., Can.	227c	43.46N	79.13W
Woerden, Neth.	145a	52.05N	4.52E
Woking, Eng., U.K.	144b	51.18N	0.33W
Wokingham, Eng., U.K. (wō'kĭng-hăm)	144b	51.23N	0.50W
Wolcott, Ks., U.S. (wōl'kŏt)	107f	39.12N	94.47W
Woldingham, Eng., U.K.	235	51.17N	0.02W
Wolf, i., Can. (wȯlf)	91	44.10N	76.25W
Wolf, r., Ms., U.S.	114	30.45N	89.36W
Wolf, r., Wi., U.S.	103	45.14N	88.45W
Wolfenbüttel, Ger. (vȯl'fĕn-büt-ĕl)	154	52.10N	10.32E
Wolf Lake, l., Il., U.S.	101a	41.39N	87.33W
Wolf Point, Mt., U.S. (wȯlf point)	105	48.07N	105.40W
Wolfratshausen, Ger. (vōlf'räts-hou-zĕn)	145d	47.55N	11.25E
Wolfsburg, Ger. (vōlfs'bōōrgh)	154	52.30N	10.37E
Wolfville, Can. (wȯlf'vĭl)	92	45.05N	64.22W
Wolgast, Ger. (vōl'găst)	154	54.04N	13.46E
Wolhuterskop, S. Afr.	213b	25.41S	27.40E
Wolkersdorf, Aus.	145e	48.24N	16.31E
Wollaston, Ma., U.S.	227a	42.16N	71.01W
Wollaston, l., Can. (wȯl'ȧs-tŭn)	84	58.15N	103.20W
Wollaston Peninsula, pen., Can.	84	70.00N	115.00W
Wollongong, Austl. (wȯl'ŭn-gŏng)	203	34.26S	151.05E
Wołomin, Pol. (vō-wō'mēn)	155	52.19N	21.17E
Wolseley, Can.	88	50.25N	103.15W
Woltersdorf, Ger. (vōl'tĕs-dōrf)	145b	52.07N	13.13E
Woltersdorf, Ger.	238a	52.26N	13.45E
Wolverhampton, Eng., U.K. (wȯl'vẽr-hămp-tŭn)	147	52.35N	2.07W
Wolverine, Mi., U.S.	230c	42.33N	83.29W
Wolwehoek, S. Afr.	218d	26.55S	27.50E
Wonga Park, Austl.	243b	37.44S	145.16E
Wŏnsan, N. Kor. (wŭn'sän')	189	39.08N	127.24E
Wonthaggi, Austl. (wōnt-hăg'ē)	203	38.45S	145.42E
Wood, S.D., U.S. (wȯd)	102	43.26N	100.25W
Woodbine, Ia., U.S. (wȯd'bīn)	102	41.44N	95.42W
Woodbridge, N.J., U.S. (wȯd'brĭj')	100a	40.33N	74.18W
Woodbrook, Md., U.S.	229c	39.23N	76.37W
Wood Buffalo National Park, rec., Can.	84	59.50N	118.53W
Woodburn, Il., U.S. (wȯd'bûrn)	107e	39.03N	90.01W
Woodburn, Or., U.S.	104	45.10N	122.51W
Woodbury, N.J., U.S. (wȯd'bĕr-ē)	100f	39.50N	75.14W
Woodbury, N.Y., U.S.	228	40.49N	73.28W
Woodbury Terrace, N.J., U.S.	229b	39.51N	75.08W
Woodcrest, Ca., U.S. (wȯd'krĕst)	107a	33.53N	117.18W
Woodford, Eng., U.K.	237b	53.21N	2.10W
Woodford Bridge, neigh., Eng., U.K.	235	51.36N	0.04E
Wood Green, neigh., Eng., U.K.	235	51.36N	0.07W
Woodhaven, neigh., N.Y., U.S.	228	40.41N	73.51W
Woodinville, Wa., U.S. (wȯd'ĭn-vĭl)	106a	47.46N	122.09W
Woodland, Ca., U.S. (wȯd'lănd)	108	38.41N	121.47W
Woodland, Wa., U.S.	106c	45.54N	122.45W
Woodland Hills, Ca., U.S.	107a	34.10N	118.36W
Woodlands, Sing.	240c	1.27N	103.46E
Woodlark Island, i., Pap. N. Gui. (wȯd'lärk)	197	9.07S	152.00E
Woodlawn, Md., U.S.	229c	39.19N	76.43W
Woodlawn, Md., U.S.	229d	38.57N	76.53W
Woodlawn, neigh., Il., U.S.	231a	41.47N	87.36W
Woodlawn Beach, N.Y., U.S. (wȯd'lôn bēch)	101c	42.48N	78.51W
Woodlawn Heights, Md., U.S.	229c	39.11N	76.39W
Woodlyn, Pa., U.S.	229b	39.52N	75.21W
Woodlynne, N.J., U.S.	229b	39.55N	75.05W
Woodmansterne, Eng., U.K.	235	51.19N	0.10W
Woodmere, N.Y., U.S.	228	40.38N	73.43W
Woodmoor, Md., U.S.	229c	39.20N	76.44W
Wood Mountain, mtn., Can.	88	49.14N	106.20W
Wood Ridge, N.J., U.S.	228	40.51N	74.05W
Wood River, Il., U.S.	107e	38.52N	90.06W
Woodroffe, Mount, mtn., Austl. (wȯd'rŭf)	202	26.05S	132.00E
Woodruff, S.C., U.S. (wȯd'rŭf)	115	34.43N	82.03W
Woods, l., Austl. (wȯdz)	202	18.00S	133.18E
Woods, Lake of the, l., N.A.	85	49.25N	93.25W
Woodsburgh, N.Y., U.S.	228	40.37N	73.42W
Woods Cross, Ut., U.S. (krôs)	107b	40.53N	111.54W
Woodsfield, Oh., U.S. (wȯdz-fēld)	98	39.45N	81.10W
Woodside, neigh., N.Y., U.S.	228	40.45N	73.55W
Woodson, Or., U.S. (wȯdsŭn)	106c	46.07N	123.20W
Woodstock, Can.	85	46.09N	67.34W
Woodstock, Can. (wȯd'stŏk)	91	43.10N	80.50W
Woodstock, Eng., U.K.	144b	51.48N	1.22W
Woodstock, Il., U.S.	103	42.20N	88.29W
Woodstock, Va., U.S.	99	38.55N	78.25W
Woodsville, N.H., U.S. (wȯdz'vĭl)	99	44.10N	72.00W
Woodville, Ms., U.S. (wȯd'vĭl)	114	31.06N	91.11W
Woodville, Tx., U.S.	113	30.48N	94.25W
Woodward, Ok., U.S. (wȯd'wôrd)	110	36.25N	99.24W
Woollahra, Austl.	243a	33.53S	151.15E
Woolton, neigh., Eng., U.K.	237a	53.23N	2.52W
Woolwich, Eng., U.K. (wȯl'ĭj)	144b	51.28N	0.05E
Woomera, Austl. (wōōm'ẽrȧ)	202	31.15S	136.43E
Woonsocket, R.I., U.S. (wōōn-sŏk'ĕt)	100b	42.00N	71.30W
Woonsocket, S.D., U.S.	102	44.03N	98.17W
Wooster, Oh., U.S. (wȯs'tẽr)	98	40.50N	81.55W
Worcester, S. Afr. (wōōs'tẽr)	212	33.35S	19.31E
Worcester, Eng., U.K. (wȯ'stẽr)	147	52.09N	2.14W
Worcester, Ma., U.S. (wȯs'tẽr)	97	42.16N	71.49W
Worden, Il., U.S. (wôr'dĕn)	107e	38.56N	89.50W
Workington, Eng., U.K. (wûr'kĭng-tŭn)	150	54.40N	3.30W
Worksop, Eng., U.K. (wûrk'sŏp) (wûr'sŭp)	144a	53.18N	1.07W
Worland, Wy., U.S. (wûr'lănd)	105	44.02N	107.56W
Wormley, Eng., U.K.	235	51.44N	0.01W
Worms, Ger. (vōrms)	147	49.37N	8.22E
Worona Reservoir, res., Austl.	201b	34.12S	150.55E
Woronora, Austl.	243a	34.01S	151.03E
Worsley, Eng., U.K.	237b	53.30N	2.23W
Worth, Il., U.S. (wûrth)	101a	41.42N	87.47W
Wortham, Tx., U.S. (wûr'dhăm)	113	31.46N	96.22W
Worthing, Eng., U.K. (wûr'dhĭng)	150	50.48N	0.29W
Worthington, In., U.S. (wûr'dhĭng-tŭn)	98	39.05N	87.00W
Worthington, Md., U.S.	229c	39.14N	76.47W
Worthington, Mn., U.S.	102	43.38N	95.36W
Worth Lake, l., Tx., U.S.	107c	32.48N	97.32W
Wowoni, Pulau, i., Indon. (wō-wō'nē)	197	4.05S	123.45E
Wragby, Eng., U.K. (răg'bē)	144a	53.17N	0.19W
Wrangell, Ak., U.S. (răn'gĕl)	96a	56.28N	132.25W
Wrangell, Mount, mtn., Ak., U.S.	95	61.58N	143.50W
Wrangell Mountains, mts., Ak., U.S.	95	62.28N	142.40W
Wrangell-Saint Elias National Park, rec., Ak., U.S.	95	61.00N	142.00W
Wrath, Cape, c., Scot., U.K. (răth)	150	58.34N	5.01W
Wray, Co., U.S. (rā)	110	40.06N	102.14W
Wraysbury, Eng., U.K.	235	51.27N	0.33W
Wreak, r., Eng., U.K. (rēk)	144a	52.45N	0.59W
Wreck Reefs, rf., Austl. (rĕk)	203	22.00S	155.52E
Wrekin, The, mtn., Eng., U.K. (rĕk'ĭn)	144a	52.40N	2.33W
Wrens, Ga., U.S. (rĕnz)	115	33.15N	82.25W
Wrentham, Ma., U.S.	93a	42.04N	71.20W
Wrexham, Wales, U.K. (rĕk'săm)	150	53.03N	3.00W
Wrights Corners, N.Y., U.S. (rītz kôr'nẽrz)	101c	43.14N	78.42W
Wrightsville, Ga., U.S. (rīts'vĭl)	115	32.44N	82.44W
Writtle, Eng., U.K.	235	51.44N	0.26E
Wrocław, Pol. (vrôtsläv) (brĕs'lou)	155	51.07N	17.10E
Wrotham, Eng., U.K. (rōōt'ŭm)	144b	51.18N	0.19E
Wrotham Heath, Eng., U.K.	235	51.18N	0.21E
Września, Pol. (vzhăsh'nyȧ)	155	52.19N	17.33E
Wu, r., China (wōō')	188	27.30N	107.00E
Wuchang, China (wōō-chäŋ)	189	30.32N	114.25E
Wuchang, China	192	44.59N	127.00E
Wucheng, China (wōō-chŭŋ)	190	37.14N	116.03E
Wuhan, China	189	30.30N	114.15E
Wuhu, China (wōō'hōō)	193	31.22N	118.22E
Wuji, China (wōō-jyē)	190	38.12N	114.57E
Wujiang, China (wōō-jyäŋ)	190	31.10N	120.38E
Wuleidao Wan, b., China (wōō-lā-dou wän)	190	36.55N	122.00E
Wülfrath, Ger.	236	51.17N	7.02E
Wulidian, China (wōō-lē-dĭĕn)	190	32.09N	114.17E
Wünsdorf, Ger. (vüns'dorf)	145b	52.10N	13.29E
Wupatki National Monument, rec., Az., U.S.	109	35.35N	111.45W
Wuping, China (wōō-pĭŋ)	193	25.05N	116.01E
Wupper, r., Ger.	236	51.14N	7.06E
Wuppertal, Ger. (vȯp'ẽr-täl)	147	51.16N	7.14E
Wuqiao, China (wōō-chyou)	190	37.37N	116.29E
Würm, r., Ger. (vürm)	145d	48.07N	11.20E
Würselen, Ger. (vür'zē-lĕn)	157c	50.49N	6.09E
Würzburg, Ger. (vürts'bȯorgh)	147	49.48N	9.57E
Wurzen, Ger. (vȯrt'sĕn)	147	51.22N	12.45E
Wushi, China (wōō-shr)	188	41.13N	79.08E
Wusong, China (wōō-sôŋ)	190	31.23N	121.29E
Wustermark, Ger. (vōōs'tĕr-märk)	145b	52.33N	12.57E
Wustrau, Ger. (vōost'rou)	145b	52.40N	12.51E
Wuustwezel, Bel.	145a	51.23N	4.36E
Wuwei, China (wōō'wā')	193	31.19N	117.53E
Wuxi, China (wōō-shyē)	189	31.36N	120.17E
Wuxing, China (wōō-shyĭŋ)	189	30.38N	120.10E
Wuyi Shan, mts., China (wōō-yē shän)	193	26.38N	116.35E
Wuyou, China (wōō-yō)	190	33.18N	120.15E
Wuzhi Shan, mtn., China (wōō-jr shän)	193	18.48N	109.30E
Wuzhou, China (wōō-jō)	189	23.32N	111.25E
Wyandotte, Mi., U.S. (wī'ăn-dŏt)	101b	42.12N	83.10W
Wye, Eng., U.K. (wī)	144b	51.12N	0.57E
Wye, r., Eng., U.K.	144a	53.14N	1.46W
Wylie, Lake, res., S.C., U.S.	115	35.02N	81.21W
Wymore, Ne., U.S. (wī'mōr)	111	40.09N	96.41W
Wynberg, S. Afr. (wĭn'bĕrg)	212a	34.00S	18.28E
Wyncote, Pa., U.S.	229b	40.05N	75.09W
Wyndham, Austl. (wĭnd'ăm)	202	15.30S	128.15E
Wyndmoor, Pa., U.S.	229b	40.05N	75.12W
Wynne, Ar., U.S. (wĭn)	111	35.12N	90.46W
Wynnewood, Ok., U.S. (wĭn'wȯd)	111	34.39N	97.10W
Wynnewood, Pa., U.S.	229b	40.01N	75.17W
Wynona, Ok., U.S. (wī-nō'nȧ)	111	36.33N	96.19W
Wynyard, Can. (wĭn'yẽrd)	84	51.47N	104.10W
Wyoming, Oh., U.S. (wī-ō'mĭng)	101f	39.14N	84.28W
Wyoming, state, U.S.	96	42.50N	108.30W
Wyoming Range, mts., Wy., U.S.	96	42.43N	110.35W
Wyre Forest, for., Eng., U.K. (wīr)	144a	52.24N	2.24W
Wysokie Mazowieckie, Pol. (vē-sô'kyĕ mä-zô-vyĕts'kyĕ)	155	52.55N	22.42E
Wyszków, Pol. (vēsh'kȯf)	155	52.35N	21.29E
Wythenshawe, neigh., Eng., U.K.	237b	53.24N	2.17W
Wytheville, Va., U.S. (wĭth'vĭl)	115	36.55N	81.06W

X

PLACE (Pronunciation)	PAGE	Lat. °′	Long. °′
Xabregas, neigh., Port.	238d	38.44N	9.07W
Xagua, Banco, bk., Cuba (bä'n-kō-sä'gwä)	122	21.35N	80.50W
Xai Xai, Moz.	212	25.00S	33.45E
Xalapa, Mex.	116	19.32N	96.53W
Xangongo, Ang.	212	16.50S	15.05E
Xankändi (Stepanakert), Azer. (styĕ'pän-ȧ-kĕrt)	167	39.50N	46.40E
Xanten, Ger. (ksän'tĕn)	157c	51.40N	6.28E
Xánthi, Grc.	149	41.08N	24.53E
Xau, Lake, l., Bots.	212	21.15S	24.38E
Xcalak, Mex. (sä-lä'k)	120a	18.15N	87.50W
Xenia, Oh., U.S. (zē'nĭ-ȧ)	98	39.40N	83.55W
Xi, r., China (shyē)	193	23.15N	112.10E
Xiajin, China (shyä-jyĭn)	192	36.58N	115.59E
Xiamen, China	189	24.30N	118.10E
Xiamen, i., Tai. (shyä-mŭn)	193	24.28N	118.20E
Xi'an, China (shyē-än)	188	34.20N	109.00E
Xiang, r., China (shyäŋ)	189	27.30N	112.30E
Xianghe, China (shyäŋ-hŭ)	190	39.46N	116.59E
Xiangtan, China (shyäŋ-tän)	189	27.55N	112.45E
Xianyang, China (shyĕn-yäŋ)	192	34.20N	108.40E
Xiaoxingkai Hu, l., China (shyou-shyĭŋ-kī hōō)	194	42.25N	132.45E
Xiaoxintian, China	240b	39.58N	116.22E
Xiapu, China (shyä-pōō)	189	27.00N	120.00E
Xiayi, China (shyä-yē)	190	34.15N	116.07E
Xicotencatl, Mex. (sē-kō-tĕn-kät''l)	118	23.00N	98.58W
Xifeng, China (shyē-fŭŋ)	192	42.40N	124.40E
Xiheying, China (shyē-hŭ-yĭŋ)	190	39.58N	114.50E
Xiliao, r., China (shyē-lĭou)	192	41.40N	122.40E
Xiliao, r., China	192	43.23N	121.40E
Xilitla, Mex. (sē-lē'tlä)	118	21.24N	98.59W
Xinchang, China (shyĭn-chäŋ)	191b	31.02N	121.38E
Xing'an, China (shyĭŋ-än)	193	25.44N	110.32E
Xingcheng, China (shyĭŋ-chŭŋ)	190	40.38N	120.41E
Xinghua, China (shyĭŋ-hwä)	190	32.58N	119.48E
Xingjiawan, China (shyĭŋ-jyä-wän)	190	37.16N	114.54E
Xingtai, China (shyĭŋ-tī)	192	37.04N	114.33E
Xingu, r., Braz. (zhĕŋ-gōō')	131	6.20S	52.34W
Xinhai, China (shyĭn-hī)	190	36.59N	117.33E
Xinhua, China (shyĭn-hwä)	193	27.45N	111.20E
Xinhuai, r., China (shyĭn-hwī)	190	33.48N	119.39E

ng-sing; ŋ-baŋk; N-nasalized n; nŏd; cŏmmit; ōld; ôbey; ôrder; oi-boil; fōōd; ȯ-as oo in foot; ou-out; s-soft; sh-dish; th-thin; pūre; ûnite; ûrn; stŭd; circŭs; ü-as in French tu; '-indeterminate vowel.

368 Xinhui–York

PLACE (Pronunciation)	PAGE	Lat. °′	Long. °′
Xinhui, China (shyn-hwā)	193	22.40N	113.08E
Xining, China (shyē-nĭŋ)	188	36.52N	101.36E
Xinjiang Uygur (Sinkiang), prov., China (shyĭn-jyäŋ)	188	40.15N	82.15E
Xinjin, China (shyĭn-jyĭn)	192	39.23N	121.57E
Xinmin, China (shyĭn-mĭn)	192	42.00N	122.42E
Xintai, China (shyĭn-tī)	190	35.55N	117.44E
Xintang, China (shyĭn-täŋ)	191a	23.08N	113.36E
Xinxian, China (shyĭn shyĕn)	190	31.47N	114.50E
Xinxian, China	192	38.20N	112.45E
Xinxiang, China (shyĭn-shyäŋ)	192	35.17N	113.49E
Xinyang, China (shyĭn-yäŋ)	189	32.08N	114.04E
Xinye, China (shyĭn-yŭ)	192	32.40N	112.20E
Xinzao, China (shyĭn-dzou)	191a	23.01N	113.25E
Xinzheng, China (shyĭn-jŭŋ)	190	34.24N	113.43E
Xinzhuang, China	240b	39.56N	116.31E
Xiongyuecheng, China (shyôŋ-yŭĕ-chŭŋ)	190	40.10N	122.08E
Xiping, China (shyē-pĭŋ)	190	33.21N	114.01E
Xishui, China (shyē-shwā)	193	30.30N	115.10E
Xixian, China (shyē shyĕn)	190	32.20N	114.42E
Xiyang, China (shyē-yäŋ)	190	37.37N	113.42E
Xiyou, China (shyē-yō)	190	37.21N	119.59E
Xizang (Tibet), prov., China (shyē-dzäŋ)	188	31.15N	87.30E
Xizhong Dao, i., China (shyē-jôŋ dou)	190	39.27N	121.06E
Xochihuehuetlán, Mex. (sō-chē-wē-wĕ-tlä'n)	119	17.53N	98.29E
Xochimilco, Mex. (sō-chē-mēl'kō)	119a	19.15N	99.06W
Xochimilco, Lago de, l., Mex.	233a	19.16N	99.06W
Xuancheng, China (shyůän-chŭŋ)	193	30.52N	118.48E
Xuanhua, China (shyůän-hwä)	192	40.35N	115.05E
Xuanhuadian, China (shyůän-hwä-dĭĕn)	190	31.42N	114.29E
Xuchang, China (shyōō-chäŋ)	192	34.02N	113.49E
Xudat, Azer.	168	41.38N	48.42E
Xuddur, Som.	218a	3.55N	43.45E
Xun, r., China (shyòn)	193	23.28N	110.30E
Xuzhou, China	189	34.17N	117.10E

Y

PLACE (Pronunciation)	PAGE	Lat. °′	Long. °′
Ya'an, China (yä-än)	188	30.00N	103.20E
Yablonovyy Khrebet, mts., Russia (yá-blô-nô-vē')	165	51.15N	111.30E
Yablunivs'kyy, Pereval, p., Ukr.	155	48.20N	24.25E
Yacheng, China (yä-chŭŋ)	193	18.20N	109.10E
Yachiyo, Japan	195a	35.43N	140.07E
Yacolt, Wa., U.S. (yă'kôlt)	106c	45.52N	122.24W
Yacolt Mountain, mtn., Wa., U.S.	106c	45.52N	122.27W
Yacona, r., Ms., U.S. (yá'cō nä)	114	34.13N	89.30W
Yacuiba, Bol. (yá-kōō-ē'bá)	130	22.02S	63.44W
Yadkin, r., N.C., U.S. (yăd'kĭn)	115	36.12N	80.40W
Yafran, Libya	210	31.57N	12.04E
Yaguajay, Cuba (yä-guä-hä'ē)	122	22.20N	79.20W
Yahagi-Gawa, r., Japan (yä'hä-gē gä'wä)	195	35.16N	137.22E
Yaho, Japan	242a	35.41N	139.27E
Yahongqiao, China (yä-hôŋ-chyou)	190	39.45N	117.52E
Yahotyn, Ukr.	163	50.18N	31.46E
Yahualica, Mex. (yä-wä-lē'kä)	118	21.08N	102.53W
Yajalón, Mex. (yä-hä-lōn')	119	17.16N	92.20W
Yakhroma, Russia (yäl'rô-ma)	172b	56.17N	37.30E
Yakhroma, r., Russia	172b	56.15N	37.38E
Yakima, Wa., U.S. (yăk'ĭm*á*)	96	46.35N	120.30W
Yakima, r., Wa., U.S. (yăk'ĭ-m*á*)	104	46.48N	120.22W
Yakima Indian Reservation, I.R., Wa., U.S.	104	46.16N	121.03W
Yakō, neigh., Japan	242a	35.32N	139.41E
Yakoma, Zaire	216	4.05N	22.27E
Yaku, i., Japan (yä'kōō)	189	30.15N	130.41E
Yakutat, Ak., U.S. (yăk'ô-tàt)	95	59.32N	139.35W
Yakutsk, Russia (yà-kòtsk')	165	62.13N	129.49E
Yale, Mi., U.S.	98	43.05N	82.45W
Yale, Ok., U.S.	111	36.07N	96.42W
Yale Lake, res., Wa., U.S.	104	46.00N	122.20W
Yalinga, Cen. Afr. Rep. (yá-lĭŋ'gá)	211	6.56N	23.22E
Yalobusha, r., Ms., U.S. (yá-lō-bŏsh'*á*)	114	33.48N	90.02W
Yalong, r., China (yä-lôŋ)	188	32.29N	98.41E
Yalta, Ukr. (yäl'tá)	167	44.29N	34.12E
Yalu, r., Asia	189	41.20N	126.35E
Yalutorovsk, Russia (yä-lōō-tô'rôfsk)	164	56.42N	66.32E
Yamada, Japan (yä'má-dá)	195	33.37N	133.39E
Yamagata, Japan (yä-má'gä-tá)	189	38.12N	140.24E
Yamaguchi, Japan (yä-má'gōō-chē)	194	34.10N	131.30E
Yamaguchi, Japan	242b	34.50N	135.15E
Yamal, Poluostrov, pen., Russia (yä-mäl')	164	71.15N	70.00E
Yamal-Nenets, state, Russia	170	67.00N	75.00E
Yamantau, Gora, mtn., Russia (gá-rä' yä'man-táw)	172a	54.16N	58.08E
Yamasaki, Japan (yä'má'sä-kē)	195	35.01N	134.33E
Yamasaki, Japan	195b	34.53N	135.41E
Yamashina, Japan (yä'mä-shē'nä)	195b	34.59N	135.50E
Yamashita, Japan (yä'mä-shē'tä)	195b	34.53N	135.25E
Yamato, Japan	195a	35.28N	139.28E
Yamato, Japan	242a	35.44N	139.26E
Yamato, Japan	242a	35.47N	139.37E
Yamato, r., Japan	242b	34.36N	135.26E
Yamato-Kōriyama, Japan	195b	34.39N	135.48E
Yamato-takada, Japan (yä'mä-tô tä'kä-dä)	195b	34.31N	135.45E
Yambi, Mesa de, mtn., Col. (mĕ'sä-dĕ-yá'm-bē)	130	1.55N	71.45W
Yambol, Bul. (yám'bôl)	149	42.28N	26.31E
Yamdena, i., Indon.	197	7.23S	130.30E
Yamenkou, China	240b	39.53N	116.12E
Yamethin, Myanmar (yŭ-mē'thĕn)	183	20.14N	96.27E
Yamhill, Or., U.S. (yăm'hĭl)	106c	45.20N	123.11W
Yamkino, Russia (yäm'kĭ-nô)	172b	55.56N	38.25E
Yamma Yamma, Lake, l., Austl. (yăm'á yăm'á)	203	26.15S	141.30E
Yamoussoukro, C. Iv.	210	6.49N	5.17W
Yamsk, Russia (yämsk)	165	59.41N	154.09E
Yamuna, r., India	183	25.30N	80.30E
Yamzho Yumco, l., China (yäm-jwo yōōm-tswo)	188	29.11N	91.26E
Yana, r., Russia (yä'ná)	165	71.00N	136.00E
Yanac, Austl. (yăn'*ăk*)	203	36.10S	141.30E
Yanagawa, Japan (yä-nä'gä-wä)	195	33.11N	130.24E
Yanam, India (yŭnŭm')	183	16.48N	82.15E
Yan'an, China (yän-än)	188	36.46N	109.15E
Yanbu', Sau. Ar.	182	23.57N	38.02E
Yancheng, China (yän-chŭŋ)	192	33.23N	120.11E
Yancheng, China	192	33.38N	113.59E
Yandongi, Zaire	216	2.51N	22.16E
Yangcheng Hu, l., China (yäŋ-chŭŋ hōō)	190	31.30N	120.31E
Yangchun, China (yäŋ-chòn)	193	22.08N	111.48E
Yang'erzhuang, China (yäŋ-är-jůäŋ)	190	38.18N	117.31E
Yanggezhuang, China (yäŋ-gŭ-jůäŋ)	192a	40.10N	116.48E
Yanggu, China (yäŋ-gōō)	190	36.06N	115.46E
Yanghe, China (yäŋ-hŭ)	190	33.48N	118.23E
Yangjiang, China (yäŋ-jyäŋ)	193	21.52N	111.58E
Yangjiaogou, China (yäŋ-jyou-gō)	190	37.17N	118.53E
Yangon *see* Rangoon, Myanmar	183	16.46N	96.09E
Yangquan, China (yäŋ-chyůän)	190	37.52N	113.36E
Yangtze (Chang), r., China (yăng'tse) (chäŋ)	189	30.30N	117.25E
Yangxin, China (yäŋ-shyĭn)	190	37.39N	117.34E
Yangyang, S. Kor. (yäng'yäng')	194	38.02N	128.38E
Yangzhou, China (yäŋ-jō)	189	32.24N	119.24E
Yanji, China (yän-jyē)	189	42.55N	129.35E
Yanjiahe, China (yän-jyä-hŭ)	190	31.55N	114.47E
Yanjin, China (yän-jyĭn)	190	35.09N	114.13E
Yankton, S.D., U.S. (yănk'tŭn)	96	42.51N	97.24W
Yanling, China (yän-lĭŋ)	190	34.07N	114.12E
Yanshan, China (yän-shän)	192	38.05N	117.15E
Yanshou, China (yän-shō)	192	45.25N	128.43E
Yantai, China	189	37.32N	121.22E
Yanychi, Russia (yä'nĭ-chĭ)	172a	57.42N	56.24E
Yanzhou, China (yän-jō)	189	35.35N	116.50E
Yanzhuang, China (yän-jůäŋ)	190	36.08N	117.47E
Yao, Chad (yä'ō)	202	13.00N	17.38E
Yao, Japan	195b	34.37N	135.37E
Yaoundé, Cam.	210	3.52N	11.31E
Yap, i., Micron. (yăp)	3	11.00N	138.00E
Yapen, Pulau, i., Indon.	197	1.30S	136.15E
Yaque del Norte, r., Dom. Rep. (yä'kå dĕl nôr'tā)	117	19.40N	71.25W
Yaque del Sur, r., Dom. Rep. (yä-kē-dĕl-sōō'r)	123	18.35N	71.05W
Yaqui, r., Mex. (yä'kē)	116	28.15N	109.40W
Yaracuy, dept., Ven. (yä-rä-kōō'ē)	131b	10.10N	68.31W
Yaraka, Austl. (yá-răk'*á*)	203	24.50S	144.08E
Yaransk, Russia (yä-ränsk')	164	57.18N	48.05E
Yarda, oasis, Chad (yär'd*á*)	211	18.29N	19.13E
Yare, r., Eng., U.K.	151	52.40N	1.32E
Yarkand *see* Shache, China (yär'mŭth)	188	38.15N	77.15E
Yarkand *see* Shache, China	188	38.15N	77.15E
Yaroslavka, Russia (yá-rô-släv'ká)	172a	55.52N	57.59E
Yaroslavl', Russia (yá-rô-släv''l)	164	57.37N	39.54E
Yaroslavl', prov., Russia	162	58.05N	38.05E
Yarra, r., Austl.	201a	37.51S	144.54E
Yarra Canal, can., Austl.	243b	37.49S	144.55E
Yarraville, Austl.	243b	37.49S	144.53E
Yarro-to, I., Russia (yá'rô-tô')	166	67.55N	71.35E
Yartsevo, Russia	165	60.13N	89.52E
Yartsevo, Russia (yär'tsyĕ-vô)	166	55.04N	32.38E
Yarumal, Col. (yä-rōō-mäl')	130	6.57N	75.24W
Yasawa Group, is., Fiji	198g	17.00S	177.23E
Yasel'da, r., Bela. (yä-syŭl'dá)	155	52.13N	25.53E
Yasinya, Ukr.	155	48.17N	24.21E
Yateras, Cuba (yä-tā'räs)	123	20.00N	75.00W
Yates Center, Ks., U.S. (yāts)	111	37.53N	95.44W
Yathkyed, l., Can. (yàth-kī-ĕd')	84	62.41N	98.00W
Yatsuga-take, mtn., Japan (yät'sōō-gä dä'kä)	195	36.01N	138.21W
Yatsushiro, Japan (yät'sōō'shē-rō)	195	32.30N	130.35E
Yatta Plateau, plat., Kenya	217	1.55S	38.10E
Yautepec, Mex. (yä-ōō-tà-pĕk')	118	18.53N	99.04W
Yavoriv, Ukr.	155	49.56N	23.24E
Yawata, Japan (yä'wä-tä)	195	34.52N	135.43E
Yawatahama, Japan (yä'wä'tä'hä-mä)	195	33.24N	132.25E
Yaxian, China (yä shyĕn)	193	18.10N	109.32E
Yayama, Zaire	216	1.16S	23.07E
Yayao, China (yä-you)	191a	23.10N	113.40E
Yazd, Iran	182	31.59N	54.03E
Yazoo, r., Ms., U.S. (yă'zōō)	97	32.32N	90.40W
Yazoo City, Ms., U.S.	114	32.50N	90.18W
Ye, Myanmar (yā)	196	15.13N	97.52E
Yeading, neigh., Eng., U.K.	235	51.32N	0.24W
Yeadon, Pa., U.S. (yē'd*ŭ*n)	100f	39.56N	75.16W
Yecla, Spain (yā'klä)	158	38.35N	1.09W
Yedikule, neigh., Tur.	239f	40.59N	28.55E
Yefremov, Russia (yĕ-frä'môf)	162	53.08N	38.04E
Yegor'yevsk, Russia (yĕ-gôr'yĕfsk)	166	55.23N	38.59E
Yeji, China (yŭ-jyē)	190	31.52N	115.57E
Yekaterinburg, Russia	164	56.51N	60.36E
Yelabuga, Russia (yĕ-lä'bò-gá)	166	55.50N	52.18E
Yelan, Russia	167	50.50N	44.00E
Yelek, r.	167	51.20N	53.10E
Yelets, Russia (yĕ-lyĕts')	164	52.35N	38.28E
Yelizavetpol'skiy, Russia (yĕ'lĭ-za-vĕt-pôl-skĭ)	172a	52.51N	60.38E
Yelizavety, Mys, c., Russia (yĕ-lyĕ-sá-vyĕ'tĭ)	165	54.28N	142.59E
Yell, i., Scot., U.K. (yĕl)	150a	60.35N	1.27W
Yellow *see* Huang, r., China	189	35.06N	113.39E
Yellow, r., Fl., U.S. (yĕl'ô)	114	30.33N	86.53W
Yellowhead Pass, p., Can. (yĕl'ô-hĕd)	87	52.52N	118.35W
Yellowknife, Can. (yĕl'ô-nīf)	84	62.29N	114.38W
Yellow Sea, sea, Asia	189	35.20N	122.15E
Yellowstone, r., U.S.	96	46.00N	108.00W
Yellowstone, Clarks Fork, r., U.S.	105	44.55N	109.05W
Yellowstone Lake, l., Wy., U.S.	96	44.27N	110.03W
Yellowstone National Park, rec., U.S. (yĕl'ô-stōn)	96	44.45N	110.35W
Yel'nya, Russia (yĕl'nyá)	162	54.34N	33.12E
Yemanzhelinsk, Russia (yĕ-mán-zhâ'lĭnsk)	172a	54.47N	61.24E
Yemen, nation, Asia (yĕm'ĕn)	182	15.00N	47.00E
Yemetsk, Russia	166	63.28N	41.28E
Yenakiyeve, Ukr.	163	48.14N	38.12E
Yenangyaung, Myanmar (yā'nän-d oung)	183	20.27N	94.59E
Yencheng, China	188	37.30N	79.26E
Yendi, Ghana (yĕn'dē)	210	9.26N	0.01W
Yengisar, China (yŭn-gē-sär)	188	39.01N	75.29E
Yenice, r., Tur.	167	41.10N	33.00E
Yenikapi, neigh., Tur.	239f	41.00N	28.57E
Yenisey, r., Russia (yĕ-nē-sĕ'ē)	164	71.00N	82.00E
Yeniseysk, Russia (yĕ-nĭĕsā'ĭsk)	165	58.27N	90.28E
Yeo, l., Austl. (yō)	202	28.15S	124.00E
Yerevan, Arm. (yĕ-rĕ-vän')	167	40.10N	44.30E
Yerington, Nv., U.S. (yĕ'rĭng-t*ŭ*n)	108	38.59N	119.10W
Yermak, i., Russia	166	66.45N	71.30E
Yeste, Spain (yĕs'tå)	158	38.23N	2.19W
Yeu, Île d', i., Fr. (ēl dyû)	147	46.43N	2.45W
Yevlax, Azer.	168	40.36N	47.09E
Yevpatoriya, Ukr. (yĕf-pä'tô-rĭ-yá)	167	45.13N	33.22E
Yexian, China (yŭ-shyĕn)	190	37.09N	119.57E
Yeya, r., Russia (yĕ'yá)	163	46.25N	39.17E
Yeysk, Russia (yĕysk)	167	46.41N	38.13E
Yi, r., China	190	34.38N	118.07E
Yiannitsá, Grc.	161	40.47N	22.26E
Yiaros, i., Grc.	161	37.52N	24.42E
Yibin, China (yē-bĭn)	188	28.50N	104.40E
Yichang, China (yē-chäŋ)	189	30.38N	111.22E
Yidu, China (yē-dōō)	192	36.42N	118.30E
Yiewsley, neigh., Eng., U.K.	235	51.31N	0.28W
Yilan, China (yē-län)	189	46.10N	129.40E
Yinchuan, China (yĭn-chůän)	188	38.22N	106.22E
Yingkou, China (yĭŋ-kō)	189	40.35N	122.10E
Yining, China (yē-nĭŋ)	188	43.58N	80.40E
Yin Shan, mts., China (yĭng'shän')	192	40.50N	110.30E
Yio Chu Kang, Sing.	240c	1.23N	103.51E
Yishan, China (yē-shän)	188	24.32N	108.42E
Yishui, China (yē-shwā)	190	35.49N	118.40E
Yíthion, Grc.	161	36.50N	22.37E
Yitong, China (yē-tôŋ)	189	43.15N	125.10E
Yixian, China (yē shyĕn)	192	41.30N	121.15E
Yixing, China	190	31.26N	119.57E
Yiyang, China (yē-yäŋ)	193	28.52N	112.12E
Yoakum, Tx., U.S. (yō'k*ŭ*m)	113	29.18N	97.09W
Yockanookany, r., Ms., U.S. (yŏk'á-nōō-kä-nĭ)	114	32.47N	89.38W
Yodo-Gawa, strt., Japan (yō'dō'gä-wä)	195b	34.46N	135.35E
Yog Point, c., Phil. (yōg)	193	14.00N	124.30E
Yogyakarta, Indon. (yŏg-yá-kär'tá)	196	7.50S	110.20E
Yoho National Park, Can. (yō'hō)	84	51.26N	116.30W
Yojoa, Lago de, l., Hond. (lä'gô dĕ yô-hō'ä)	120	14.49N	87.53W
Yokkaichi, Japan (yō'kä'ē-chē)	194	34.58N	136.35E
Yokohama, Japan (yō'kô-hä'mạ)	189	35.37N	139.40E
Yokosuka, Japan (yô-kō'sò-kä)	194	35.17N	139.40E
Yokota, Japan (yō-kō'tä)	195a	35.23N	140.02E
Yola, Nig. (yō'lä)	210	9.13N	12.27E
Yolaina, Cordillera de, mts., Nic.	121	11.34N	84.34W
Yomou, Gui.	214	7.34N	9.16W
Yonago, Japan (yō'nä-gō)	194	35.27N	133.19E
Yŏnch'on, neigh., S. Kor.	241b	37.38N	127.04E
Yonezawa, Japan (yō'nĕ'zá-wä)	194	37.50N	140.07E
Yong'an, China (yôŋ-än)	193	26.00N	117.22E
Yongding, r., China (yôŋ-dĭŋ)	192	40.25N	115.00E
Yŏngdŏk, S. Kor. (yŭng'dŭk')	194	36.28N	129.25E
Yongdŭngp'o, neigh., S. Kor.	241b	37.32N	126.54E
Yŏnghŭng, N. Kor. (yŭng'hông')	194	39.31N	127.11E
Yonghŭng Man, b., N. Kor.	194	39.10N	128.00E
Yongnian, China (yôŋ-nĭĕn)	192	36.47N	114.32E
Yongqing, China (yôŋ-chyĭŋ)	192a	39.18N	116.27E
Yongshun, China (yôŋ-shòn)	188	29.05N	109.58E
Yonkers, N.Y., U.S. (yŏŋ'kĕrz)	100a	40.57N	73.54W
Yonne, r., Fr. (yòn)	156	48.18N	3.15E
Yono, Japan (yō'nō)	195a	35.53N	139.36E
Yorba Linda, Ca., U.S. (yôr'bá lĭn'dá)	107a	33.55N	117.51W
York, Austl.	202	32.00S	117.00E
York, Can.	83d	43.41N	79.29W
York, Eng., U.K.	146	53.58N	1.10W
York, Al., U.S. (yôrk)	114	32.33N	88.16W
York, Ne., U.S.	111	40.52N	97.36W
York, Pa., U.S.	97	40.00N	76.40W

PLACE (Pronunciation)	PAGE	Lat. °′	Long. °′
York, S.C., U.S.	115	34.59N	81.14W
York, Cape, c., Austl.	203	10.45S	142.35E
York, Kap, c., Grnld.	82	75.30N	73.00W
Yorke Peninsula, pen., Austl.	204	34.24S	137.20E
Yorketown, Austl.	204	35.00S	137.28E
York Factory, Can.	89	57.05N	92.18W
Yorkfield, Il., U.S.	231a	41.52N	87.56W
Yorkshire Wolds, Eng., U.K. (yôrk′shĭr)	150	54.00N	0.35W
Yorkton, Can. (yôrk′tŭn)	84	51.13N	102.28W
Yorktown, Tx., U.S. (yôrk′toun)	113	28.57N	97.30W
Yorktown, Va., U.S.	115	37.12N	76.31W
Yorkville, neigh., Can.	227c	43.40N	79.24W
Yoro, Hond. (yō′rō)	120	15.09N	87.05W
Yoron, i., Japan	194	26.48N	128.40E
Yosemite National Park, rec., Ca., U.S. (yō-sĕm′ĭ-tē)	96	38.03N	119.36W
Yoshida, Japan (yō′shē-dá)	195	34.39N	132.41E
Yoshikawa, Japan (yō-shē′kä′wä′)	195a	35.53N	139.51E
Yoshino, r., Japan (yō′shē-nō)	195	34.04N	133.57E
Yoshkar-Ola, Russia (yôsh-kär′ô-lä′)	166	56.35N	48.05E
Yos Sudarsa, Pulau, i., Indon.	197	7.20S	138.30E
Yŏsu, S. Kor. (yŭ′sōō′)	194	34.42N	127.42W
You, r., China (yō)	193	23.55N	106.50E
Youghal, Ire. (yōō′ôl) (yôl)	151	51.58N	7.57E
Youghal Bay, b., Ire.	150	51.52N	7.46W
Young, Austl. (yŭng)	204	34.15S	148.18E
Young, Ur. (yô-ōō′ng)	129c	32.42S	57.38W
Youngs, l., Wa., U.S. (yŭngz)	106a	47.25N	122.08W
Youngstown, N.Y., U.S.	101c	43.15N	79.02W
Youngstown, Oh., U.S.	98	41.05N	80.40W
Yozgat, Tur. (yôz′gȧd)	182	39.50N	34.50E
Ypsilanti, Mi., U.S. (ĭp-sĭ-lăn′tĭ)	101b	42.15N	83.37W
Yreka, Ca., U.S. (wī-rē′kȧ)	104	41.43N	122.36W
Yrghyz, Kaz.	169	48.30N	61.17E
Yrghyz, r., Kaz.	169	49.30N	60.32E
Ysleta, Tx., U.S. (ĕz-lē′tȧ)	112	31.42N	106.18W
Yssingeaux, Fr. (ē-säN-zhō)	156	45.09N	4.08E
Ystad, Swe.	146	55.25N	13.49E
Yu'alliq, Jabal, mts., Egypt	181a	30.12N	33.42E
Yuan, r., China (yůän)	189	28.50N	110.50E
Yuan'an, China (yůän-än)	193	31.08N	111.28E
Yuan Huan, pt. of i., Tai.	241d	25.03N	121.31E
Yuanling, China (yůän-lĭŋ)	193	28.30N	110.18E
Yuanshi, China (yůän-shr)	192	37.45N	114.32E
Yuasa, Japan	195	34.02N	135.10E
Yuba City, Ca., U.S. (yōō′bȧ)	108	39.08N	121.38W
Yucaipa, Ca., U.S. (yŭ-kȧ-ē′pȧ)	107a	34.02N	117.02W
Yucatán, state, Mex. (yōō-kä-tän′)	116	20.45N	89.00W
Yucatan Channel, strt., N.A.	116	22.30N	87.00W
Yucatan Peninsula, pen., N.A.	120	19.30N	89.00W
Yucheng, China (yōō-chŭŋ)	190	34.31N	115.54E
Yucheng, China	192	36.55N	116.39E
Yuci, China (yōō-tsz)	192	37.32N	112.40E
Yudoma, r., Russia (yōō-dō′mȧ)	171	59.13N	137.00E
Yueqing, China (yůĕ-chyĭn)	193	28.02N	120.40E
Yueyang, China (yůĕ-yäŋ)	189	29.25N	113.05E
Yuezhuang, China (yůĕ-jůäŋ)	190	36.13N	118.17E
Yug, r., Russia (yôg)	166	59.50N	45.55E
Yugoslavia, nation, Eur. (yōō-gō-slä-vĭ-ȧ)	142	44.00N	21.00E
Yukhnov, Russia (yôk′nof)	162	54.44N	35.15E
Yukon, , Can. (yōō′kŏn)	84	63.16N	135.30W
Yukon, r., N.A.	96a	64.00N	159.30W
Yukutat Bay, b., Ak., U.S. (yōō-kū tăt′)	95	59.34N	140.50W
Yuldybayevo, Russia (yōld′bä′yĕ-vô)	172a	52.20N	57.52E
Yulin, China	188	38.18N	109.45E
Yulin, China (yōō-lĭn)	193	22.38N	110.10E
Yuma, Az., U.S. (yōō′mä)	96	32.40N	114.40W
Yuma, Co., U.S.	110	40.08N	102.50W
Yuma, r., Dom. Rep.	123	19.05N	70.05W
Yumbi, Zaire	217	1.14S	26.14E
Yumen, China (yōō-mŭn)	188	40.14N	96.56E
Yuncheng, China (yòn-chŭŋ)	192	35.00N	110.40E
Yungho, Tai.	241d	25.01N	121.31E
Yung Shu Wan, H.K.	241c	22.14N	114.06E
Yunnan, prov., China (yun′nän′)	188	24.23N	101.03E
Yunnan Plat, plat., China (yò-nän)	188	26.03N	101.26E
Yunxian, China (yòn shyĕn)	189	32.50N	110.55E
Yunxiao, China (yòn-shyou)	193	24.00N	117.20E
Yura, Japan (yōō′rä)	195	34.18N	134.54E
Yurécuaro, Mex. (yōō-rā′kwä-rô)	118	20.21N	102.16W
Yurimaguas, Peru (yōō-rē-mä′gwäs)	130	5.59S	76.12W
Yuriria, Mex. (yōō′rē-rē′ä)	118	20.11N	101.08W
Yurovo, Russia	172b	55.30N	38.24E
Yur'yevets, Russia	166	57.15N	43.08E
Yuscarán, Hond. (yōōs-kä-rän′)	120	13.57N	86.48W
Yushan, China (yōō-shän)	193	28.42N	118.20E
Yushu, China (yōō-shōō)	192	44.58N	126.32E
Yutian, China (yōō-tĭĕn) (kū-r-yä)	188	36.55N	81.39E
Yutian, China (yōō-tĭĕn)	192	39.54N	117.45E
Yuty, Para. (yōō-tē′)	132	26.45S	56.13W
Yuwangcheng, China (yü′wäng′chĕng)	190	31.32N	114.26E
Yuxian, China (yōō shyĕn)	192	39.40N	114.38E
Yuzha, Russia (yōō′zhȧ)	166	56.38N	42.20E
Yuzhno-Sakhalinsk, Russia (yōōzh′nô-sä-kä-lĭnsk′)	165	47.11N	143.04E
Yuzhnoural'skiy, Russia (yōōzh-nô-ô-räl′skĭ)	172a	54.26N	61.17E
Yuzhnyy Ural, mts., Russia (yōō′zhnĭ ô-räl′)	172a	52.51N	57.48E
Yverdon, Switz. (ē-vĕr-dôn)	154	46.46N	6.35E
Yvetot, Fr. (ēv-tō′)	156	49.39N	0.45E

Z

PLACE (Pronunciation)	PAGE	Lat. °′	Long. °′
Za, r., Mor.	148	34.19N	2.23W
Zaachila, Mex. (sä-ä-chē′lȧ)	119	16.56N	96.45W
Zaandam, Neth. (zän′dȧm)	151	52.25N	4.49E
Ząbkowice Śląskie, Pol.	154	50.35N	16.48E
Zabrze, Pol. (zäb′zhĕ)	147	50.18N	18.48E
Zacapa, Guat. (sä-kä′pä)	120	14.56N	89.30W
Zacapoaxtla, Mex. (sä-kä-pō-äs′tlä)	119	19.51N	97.34W
Zacatecas, Mex. (sä-kä-tā′käs)	116	22.44N	102.32W
Zacatecas, state, Mex.	116	24.00N	102.45W
Zacatecoluca, El Sal. (sä-kä-tȧ-kô-lōō′kä)	120	13.31N	88.50W
Zacatelco, Mex.	118	19.12N	98.12W
Zacatepec, Mex. (sä-kä-tȧ-pĕk′) (sän-tē-ä′gô)	119	17.10N	95.53W
Zacatlán, Mex. (sä-kä-tlän′)	119	19.55N	97.57W
Zacoalco de Torres, Mex. (sä-kô-äl′kô dā tōr′rĕs)	118	20.12N	103.33W
Zacualpan, Mex. (sä-kô-äl-pän′)	118	18.43N	99.46W
Zacualtipan, Mex. (sä-kô-äl-tē-pän′)	118	20.38N	98.39W
Zadar, Cro. (zä′där)	142	44.08N	15.16E
Zadonsk, Russia (zä-dônsk′)	162	52.22N	38.55E
Žagare, Lat. (zhȧgärĕ)	153	56.21N	23.14E
Zagarolo, Italy (tzä-gä-rô′lô)	159d	41.51N	12.53E
Zaghouan, Tun. (zȧ-gwäN′)	210	36.30N	10.04E
Zagreb, Cro. (zä′grĕb)	142	45.50N	15.58E
Zagros Mountains, mts., Iran	182	33.30N	46.30E
Zāhedān, Iran (zä′hȧ-dän)	182	29.37N	60.31E
Zahlah, Leb. (zä′lä′)	181a	33.50N	35.54E
Zaire, nation, Afr.	212	1.00S	22.15E
Zaječar, Yugo. (zä′yĕ-chär′)	161	43.54N	22.16E
Zakhidnyy Buh (Bug), r., Eur.	154	52.29N	21.20E
Zákinthos, Grc.	161	37.48N	20.55E
Zákinthos, i., Grc.	149	37.45N	20.32E
Zakopane, Pol. (zȧ-kô-pä′nĕ)	155	49.18N	19.57E
Zakouma, Parc National de, rec., Chad	215	10.50N	19.20E
Zalaegerszeg, Hung. (zŏ′lô-ĕ′gĕr-sĕg)	154	46.50N	16.50E
Zalău, Rom. (zȧ-lŭ′ŏ)	155	47.11N	23.06E
Zalṭan, Libya	211	28.20N	19.40E
Zaltbommel, Neth.	145a	51.48N	5.15E
Zama, Japan	242a	35.29N	139.24E
Zambezi, r., Afr. (zȧm-bā′zē)	212	16.00S	29.45E
Zambia, nation, Afr. (zăm′bē-ȧ)	212	14.23S	24.15E
Zamboanga, Phil. (säm-bô-aŋ′gä)	196	6.58N	122.02E
Zambrów, Pol. (zäm′brôf)	155	52.29N	22.17E
Zamora, Mex. (sä-mō′rä)	116	19.59N	102.16W
Zamora, Spain (thä-mō′rä)	148	41.32N	5.43W
Zanatepec, Mex.	119	16.30N	94.22W
Zandvoort, Neth.	145a	52.22N	4.30E
Zanesville, Oh., U.S. (zānz′vĭl)	98	39.55N	82.00W
Zangasso, Mali	214	12.09N	5.37W
Zanjān, Iran	182	36.26N	48.24E
Zanzibar, Tan. (zăn′zĭ-bär)	213	6.10S	39.11E
Zanzibar, i., Tan.	213	6.20S	39.37E
Zanzibar Channel, strt., Tan.	217	6.05S	39.00E
Zaozhuang, China (dzou-jůäŋ)	190	34.51N	117.34E
Zapadnaya Dvina, r., Eur. (zä′pȧd-nȧ-yȧ dvē′nȧ)	153	55.30N	28.27E
Zapala, Arg. (zä-pä′lä)	132	38.53S	70.02W
Zapata, Tx., U.S. (sä-pä′tä)	112	26.52N	99.18W
Zapata, Ciénaga de, sw., Cuba (syĕ′nä-gä-dĕ-zä-pá′tä)	122	22.30N	81.20W
Zapata, Península de, pen., Cuba (pĕ-nē′n-sōō-lä-dĕ-zä-pá′tä)	122	22.20N	81.30W
Zapatera, Isla, i., Nic. (ē′s-lä-sä-pä-tā′rō)	120	11.45N	85.45W
Zapopan, Mex. (sä-pō′pän)	118	20.42N	103.23W
Zaporizhzhya, Ukr.	164	47.50N	35.10E
Zaporizhzhya, prov., Ukr.	163	47.20N	35.05E
Zaporoshskoye, Russia (zȧ-pô-rôsh′skô-yĕ)	153	60.36N	30.31E
Zapotiltic, Mex. (sä-pô-tēl-tēk′)	118	19.37N	103.25W
Zapotitlán, Mex. (sä-pô-tē-tlän′)	118	17.13N	98.58W
Zapotitlán, Mex.	233a	19.18N	99.02W
Zapotitlán, Punta, c., Mex.	119	18.34N	94.48W
Zapotlanejo, Mex. (sä-pô-tlä-nä′hô)	118	20.38N	103.05W
Zaragoza, Mex. (sä-rä-gō′sä)	118	23.59N	99.45W
Zaragoza, Mex.	118	22.02N	100.45W
Zaragoza, Spain (thä-rä-gō′thä)	142	41.39N	0.53W
Zarand, Munṭii, mts., Rom.	155	46.07N	22.21E
Zaranda Hill, mtn., Nig.	215	10.15N	9.35E
Zaranj, Afg.	185	31.06N	61.53E
Zarasai, Lith. (zä-rä-sī′)	153	55.45N	26.18E
Zárate, Arg. (zä-rä′tä)	132	34.05S	59.05W
Zaraysk, Russia (zä-rä′ēsk)	166	54.46N	38.53E
Zarečje, Russia	239b	55.41N	37.23E
Zaria, Nig. (zä′rē-ä)	210	11.07N	7.44E
Zarqā', r., Jord.	181a	32.13N	35.43E
Zarzal, Col. (zär-zá′l)	130a	4.23N	76.04W
Zashiversk, Russia (zá′shĭ-vĕrsk′)	165	67.08N	144.02E
Zastavna, Ukr. (zás-täf′nȧ)	155	48.32N	25.50E
Zastron, S. Afr. (zás′trŭn)	213c	30.19S	27.07E
Žatec, Czech Rep. (zhä′tĕts)	154	50.19N	13.32E
Zavitinsk, Russia	171	50.12N	129.44E
Zawiercie, Pol. (zá-vyĕr′tsyĕ)	155	50.28N	19.25E
Zāwiyat al-Baydā', Libya	211	32.49N	21.46E
Zāwiyat Nābit, Egypt	244a	30.07N	31.09E
Zāyandeh, r., Iran	182	32.15N	51.00E
Zaysan, Kaz. (zī′sȧn)	169	47.43N	84.44E
Zaysan, l., Kaz.	169	48.16N	84.05E
Zaza, r., Cuba (zá′zá)	122	21.40N	79.25W
Zbarazh, Ukr. (zbä-räzh′)	155	49.39N	25.48E
Zbruch, r., Ukr. (zbrôch)	155	48.56N	26.18E
Zdolbuniv, Ukr.	155	50.31N	26.17E
Zduńska Wola, Pol. (zdōōn′′skä vō′lä)	155	51.36N	18.27E
Zebediela, S. Afr.	218d	24.19S	29.21E
Zeeland, Mi., U.S. (zē′lănd)	98	42.50N	86.00W
Ẓefat, Isr.	181a	32.58N	35.30E
Zehdenick, Ger. (tsā′dē-nēk)	154	52.59N	13.20E
Zehlendorf, Ger. (tsā′lĕn-dôrf)	145b	52.47N	13.23E
Zehlendorf, neigh., Ger.	238a	52.26N	13.15E
Zeist, Neth.	145a	52.05N	5.14E
Zelenogorsk, Russia (zĕ-lă′nô-gôrsk)	153	60.13N	29.39E
Zella-Mehlis, Ger. (tsâl′á-mā′lēs)	154	50.40N	10.38E
Zémio, Cen. Afr. Rep. (za-myō′)	211	5.03N	25.11E
Zemlya Frantsa-Iosifa (Franz Josef Land), is., Russia	164	81.32N	40.00E
Zempoala, Punta, c., Mex. (pōō′n-tä-sĕm-pô-ä′lä)	119	19.30N	96.18W
Zempoatlépetl, mtn., Mex. (sĕm-pô-ä-tlā′pĕt′l)	119	17.13N	95.59W
Zemun, Yugo. (zĕ′mōōn) (sĕm′lĭn)	149	44.50N	20.25E
Zengcheng, China (dzŭŋ-chŭŋ)	191a	23.18N	113.49E
Zenica, Bos. (zĕ′nēt-sä)	161	44.10N	17.54E
Zeni-Su, is., Japan (zĕ′nē sōō)	195	33.55N	138.55E
Žepče, Bos. (zhĕp′chĕ)	163	44.26N	18.01E
Zepernick, Ger. (tsĕ′pĕr-nēk)	145b	52.39N	13.32E
Zerbst, Ger. (tsĕrbst)	154	51.58N	12.03E
Zerpenschleuse, Ger. (tsĕr′pĕn-shloi-zĕ)	145b	52.51N	13.30E
Zeuthen, Ger. (tsoi′tĕn)	145b	52.21N	13.38E
Zevenaar, Neth.	157c	51.56N	6.06E
Zevenbergen, Neth.	145a	51.38N	4.36E
Zeya, Russia (zâ′yȧ)	165	53.43N	127.29E
Zeya, r., Russia	171	52.31N	128.30E
Zeytinburnu, neigh., Tur.	239f	40.59N	28.54E
Zeytun, Tur. (zā-tōōn′)	167	38.00N	36.40E
Zezere, r., Port. (zĕ′zȧ-rĕ)	158	39.54N	8.12W
Zgierz, Pol. (zgyĕzh)	155	51.51N	19.26E
Zhambyl, Kaz.	169	42.51N	71.29E
Zhangaqazaly, Kaz.	169	45.47N	62.00E
Zhangbei, China (jäŋ-bā)	189	41.12N	114.50E
Zhanggezhuang, China (jäŋ-gŭ-jůäŋ)	190	40.09N	116.56E
Zhangguangcai Ling, mts., China (jäŋ-gůäŋ-tsī lĭŋ)	192	43.50N	127.55E
Zhangjiakou, China	189	40.45N	114.58E
Zhangqiu, China (jäŋ-chyô)	190	36.50N	117.29E
Zhangye, China (jäŋ-yu)	188	38.46N	101.00E
Zhangzhou, China (jäŋ-jō)	189	24.35N	117.45E
Zhangzi Dao, i., China (jäŋ-dz dou)	190	39.02N	122.44E
Zhanhua, China (jän-hwä)	190	37.42N	117.49E
Zhanjiang, China (jän-jyäŋ)	189	21.20N	110.28E
Zhanyu, China (jän-yōō)	192	44.30N	122.30E
Zhao'an, China (jou-än)	193	23.48N	117.10E
Zhaodong, China (jou-dôŋ)	192	45.58N	126.00E
Zhaotong, China (jou-tôŋ)	188	27.18N	103.50E
Zhaoxian, China (jou shyĕn)	190	37.46N	114.48E
Zhaoyuan, China (jou-yůän)	190	37.22N	120.23E
Zhecheng, China (jŭ-chŭŋ)	192	34.05N	115.19E
Zhegao, China (jŭ-gou)	190	31.47N	117.44E
Zhejiang, prov., China (jŭ-jyäŋ)	189	29.30N	120.00E
Zhelaniya, Mys, c., Russia (zhĕ′lä-nĭ-yȧ)	164	75.43N	69.10E
Zhem, r., Kaz.	170	46.50N	54.10E
Zhengding, China (jŭŋ-dĭŋ)	192	38.10N	114.35E
Zhen'guosi, China	240b	39.51N	116.21E
Zhengyang, China (jŭŋ-yäŋ)	190	32.34N	114.22E
Zhengzhou, China (jŭŋ-jō)	189	34.46N	113.42E
Zhenjiang, China (jŭn-jyäŋ)	189	32.13N	119.24E
Zhenru, China	241a	31.15N	121.24E
Zhenyuan, China (jŭn-yůän)	193	27.08N	108.30E
Zhetiqara, Kaz.	169	52.12N	61.18E
Zhigalovo, Russia (zhē-gä′lô-vô)	165	54.52N	105.05E
Zhigansk, Russia (zhē-gȧnsk′)	165	66.45N	123.20E
Zhijiang, China (jr-jyäŋ)	193	27.25N	109.45E
Zhizdra, Russia (zhēz′drȧ)	162	53.47N	34.41E
Zhizhitskoye, l., Russia (zhē-zhēt′skô-yĕ)	162	56.08N	31.34E
Zhmerynka, Ukr.	167	49.02N	28.09E
Zhongshan Park, rec., China	241a	31.13N	121.25E
Zhongwei, China (jôŋ-wā)	188	37.32N	105.10E
Zhongxian, China (jôŋ shyĕn)	188	30.20N	108.00E
Zhongxin, China (jôŋ-shyĭn)	191a	23.16N	113.38E
Zhoucun, China (jō-tsōōn)	192	36.49N	117.52E
Zhoukouzhen, China (jō-kō-jŭn)	190	33.39N	114.40E
Zhoupu, China (jō-pōō)	190	31.07N	121.33E
Zhoushan Qundao, is., China (jō-shän-chyòn-dou)	189	30.00N	123.00E
Zhouxian, China (jō shyĕn)	192	39.30N	115.59E
Zhovkva, Ukr.	155	50.03N	23.58E
Zhu, r., China (jōō)	191a	22.48N	113.36E
Zhuanghe, China (jůäŋ-hŭ)	192	39.40N	123.00E
Zhuanqiao, China (jůän-chyou)	191b	31.02N	121.24E
Zhucheng, China (jōō-chŭŋ)	192	36.01N	119.24E
Zhuji, China (jōō-jyē)	193	29.58N	120.10E
Zhujiang Kou, b., Asia (jōō-jyäŋ kō)	193	22.00N	114.00E
Zhukovskiy, Russia (zhò-kôf′skĭ)	172b	55.33N	38.09E
Zhurivka, Ukr.	163	50.31N	31.43E
Zhytomyr, Ukr.	164	50.15N	28.40E
Zhytomyr, prov., Ukr.	163	50.40N	28.07E
Zi, r., China (dzē)	193	26.50N	111.00E
Zia Indian Reservation, I.R., N.M., U.S.	109	35.30N	106.43W
Zibo, China (dzē-bwo)	190	36.48N	118.04E

ng-sing; ŋ-baŋk; N-nasalized n; nŏd; cŏmmit; ōld; ōbey; ôrder; oi-boil; fōōd; ò-as oo in foot; ou-out; s-soft; sh-dish; th-thin; pūre; ůnite; ûrn; stŭd; circŭs; ü-as in French tu; ′-indeterminate vowel.

ăt; fĭnăl; rāte; senâte; ärm; ȧsk; sofȧ; fâre;   ch-choose;   dh-as th in other;   bē; ĕvent; bĕt; recĕnt; cratĕr;   g-gŏ; gh-guttural g;   bĭt; ĭ-short neutral; rīde;   κ-guttural k as ch in German ich;

SUBJECT INDEX

Listed below are major topics covered by the thematic maps, graphs and/or statistics.
Page citations are for world, continent and country maps and for world tables.

SOURCES

The sources listed below have been consulted during the process of creating and updating the thematic maps and statistics for the 18th edition.

AAMA Motor Vehicle Facts and Figures, American Automobile Manufacturers Association
Agricultural Atlas of the United States, U.S. Dept. of Commerce, Bureau of the Census
Agricultural Statistics, U.S. Dept. of Agriculture
Air Carrier Traffic and Canadian Airports, Statistics Canada, Minister of Industry, Science and Technology
Annual Report series (various titles), U.S. Dept. of the Interior, Bureau of Mines
Anuario Estatistico do Brasil, Fundacao Instituto Brasileiro de Geografia e Estatistica
Atlas of African Agriculture, United Nations, Food and Agriculture Organization
Atlas of Economic Mineral Deposits, Cornell University Press
Atlas of India, TT Maps and Publications\Government of India
Atlas of the Middle East, U.S. Central Intelligence Agency
Canada Year Book, Statistics Canada, Minister of Industry, Science and Technology
Catalog of Significant Earthquakes, National Oceanic and Atmospheric Administration, National Geophysical Data Center
Census of Agriculture, Dept. of Commerce, Bureau of the Census
Census of Population Characteristics: United States, U.S. Dept. of Commerce, Economics and Statistics Administration
China Statistical Yearbook, State Statistical Bureau of the People's Republic of China
City and County Data Book, U.S. Dept of Commerce, Bureau of the Census
Coal Fields of the United States, U.S. Dept. of the Interior, Geological Survey
Coal Production U.S., U.S. Dept. of Energy, Energy Information Administration
Commercial Nuclear Power Plants around the World, Nuclear News
Commercial Nuclear Power Plants in the United States, Nuclear News
Compendium of Social Statistics and Indicators, United Nations, Department of International Economic and Social Affairs
The Copper Industry of the U.S.S.R., U.S. Dept. of the Interior, Bureau of Mines
Demographic Yearbook, United Nations, Dept. of Economic and Social Development
Earthquakes and Volcanoes, U.S. Dept. of the Interior, U.S. Geological Survey
Eastern Europe Coal Infrastructure, U.S. Central Intelligence Agency
Ecoregions of the Continents, U.S. Dept. of Agriculture, Forest Service
Energy in the Newly Independent States of Eurasia, U.S. Central Intelligence Agency
Energy Map of Central Asia, Petroleum Economist
Energy Map of the World, Petroleum Economist
Energy Statistics Yearbook, United Nations, Dept. of Economic and Social Information and Policy Analysis
FAA Statistical Handbook of Aviation, U.S. Dept. of Transportation, Federal Aviation Administration
FAO Atlas of the Living Resources of the Seas, United Nations, Food and Agriculture Organization
FAO Fertilizer Yearbook, United Nations, Food and Agriculture Organization
FAO Production Yearbook, United Nations, Food and Agriculture Organization
FAO Trade Yearbook, United Nations, Food and Agriculture Organization
FAO Yearbook of Fishery Statistics, United Nations, Food and Agriculture Organization
FAO Yearbook of Forest Products, United Nations, Food and Agriculture Organization
Fiber Organon, Fiber Economics Bureau, Inc.
Geothermal Energy in the Western United States and Hawaii, U.S. Dept. of Energy/Energy Information Administration
Geothermal Resources Council, unpublished data
A Guide to Your National Forests, U.S. Dept. of Agriculture, Forest Service
Handbook of International Economic Statistics, U.S. Central Intelligence Agency
Handbook of International Trade and Development Statistics, United Nations, Conference on Trade and Development
International Data Base, U.S. Bureau of the Census, Center for International Research
International Energy Annual, U.S. Dept. of Energy, Energy Information Administration
International Energy Outlook, Dept. of Energy, Energy Information Administration
International Petroleum Encyclopedia, PennWell Publishing Co.
International Trade Statistics Yearbook, United Nations, Dept. of Economic and Social Development
International Water Power and Dam Construction Yearbook, Reed Business Publishing
Largest U.S. Oil and Gas Fields, U.S. Dept. of Energy, Energy Information Administration
Major Coalfields of the World, International Energy Agency Coal Research
Maritime Transport, Organization for Economic Co-operation and Development
Merchant Fleets of the World, U.S. Dept. of Transportation, Maritime Administration
Mineral Industries of Africa, U.S. Dept. of the Interior, Bureau of Mines
Mineral Industries of Asia and the Pacific, U.S. Dept. of the Interior, Bureau of Mines
Mineral Industries of Europe and Central Eurasia, U.S. Dept. of the Interior, Bureau of Mines
Mineral Industries of Latin America and Canada, U.S. Dept. of the Interior, Bureau of Mines
Mineral Industries of the Middle East, U.S. Dept. of the Interior, Bureau of Mines
Minerals Yearbook, U.S. Dept. of the Interior, Bureau of Mines
Monthly Bulletin of Statistics, United Nations, Dept. of Economic and Social Development
National Atlas - Canada, Dept. of Energy, Mines, and Resources
National Atlas - Chile, Instituto Geografico Militar
National Atlas - China, Cartographic Publishing House
National Atlas - Japan, Geographical Survey Institute
National Atlas - United States, U.S. Dept. of the Interior, Geological Survey
National Atlas - U.S.S.R., Central Administration of Geodesy and Cartography
National Priorities List, U.S. Environmental Protection Agency
Natural Gas Annual, U.S. Dept. of Energy, Energy Information Administration
Non-Ferrous Metal Data, American Bureau of Metal Statistics
Nuclear Power Reactors in the World, International Atomic Energy Agency
Oxford Economic Atlas of the World, Oxford University Press
The People's Republic of China - A New Industrial Power, U.S. Dept. of the Interior, Bureau of Mines
Petroleum Supply Annual, U.S. Dept. of Energy, Energy Information Administration
Population and Dwelling Counts: A National Overview, Minister of Industry, Science and Technology, Statistics Canada
Population and Vital Statistics Reports, United Nations, Dept. for Economic and social Information and Policy Analysis
Post-Soviet Geography, V.H. Winston and Son, Inc.
Primary Aluminum Plants Worldwide, U.S. Dept. of the Interior, Bureau of Mines
Public Land Surveys, U.S. Dept. of the Interior, Geological Survey
Rail in Canada, Statistics Canada, Transportation Section
Rand McNally Road Atlas, Rand McNally
Refugees, United Nations High Commissioner for Refugees
Refugee Survey Quarterly, United Nations, Centre for Documentation on Refugees
The State of the World's Refugees, United Nations High Commissioner for Refugees
The States of the Former Soviet Union: An Updated Overview, U.S. Central Intelligence Agency, Directorate of Intelligence
Statistical Abstract of India, Central Statistical Organisation
Statistical Abstract of the United States, U.S. Dept. of Commerce, Bureau of the Census
Statistical Pocket-Book of Yugoslavia, Federal Statistical Office
Statistical Yearbook, United National Educational, Scientific and Cultural Organization (UNESCO)
Sugar Yearbook, International Sugar Organization
Survey of Energy Resources, World Energy Council
This Dynamic Planet: World Map of Volcanoes, Earthquakes and Plate Tectonics, Smithsonian Institution/U.S. Geological Survey
Tin Ore Resources of Asia and Australia, United Nations, Economic Commission for Asia and the Far East
Uranium Resources, Production and Demand, Organization for Economic Co-operation and Development/International Atomic Energy Agency
U.S.S.R. Energy Atlas, U.S. Central Intelligence Agency
World Atlas of Agriculture, Isituto Geografico De Agostini
World Atlas of Geology and Mineral Deposits, Mining Journal Books, Ltd.
World Coal Resources and Major Trade Routes, Miller Freeman Publications, Inc.
World Development Report, The World Bank
The World Factbook, U.S. Central Intelligence Agency
World Gas Map, Petroleum Economist
World Mineral Statistics, British Geological Survey
World Mining Porphyry Copper, Miller Freeman Publications, Inc.
World Oil, Gulf Publishing Company
World Population Prospects, United Nations, Dept. for Economic and Social Information and Policy Analysis
World Refugee Report, U.S. Dept. of Stats, Bureau for Refugee Programs
World Transport Data, International Road Transport Union
World Urbanization Prospects, United Nations, Dept. of Economic and Social Information and Policy Analysis
Year Book Australia, Australian Bureau of Statistics
Year Book of Labour Statistics, International Labour Organization